FILM
REVIEW
ANNUAL

2001

Films of 2000

FILM

REVIEW

ANNUAL

2001

Films of 2000

Film Review Publications
JEROME S. OZER, PUBLISHER

Editor: Jerome S. Ozer
Associate Editor: Richard Zlotowitz

ISBN 0-89198-155-1
ISSN 0737-9080

Manufactured in the United States of America

Jerome S. Ozer, Publisher
340 Tenafly Road
Englewood, NJ 07631

TABLE OF CONTENTS

PREFACE

FILM REVIEWS

ADDENDUM 1588

AWARDS 1603

INDEX 1613

PREFACE

The FILM REVIEW ANNUAL provides, in a convenient format, a single reference volume covering important reviews—*in their entirety*—of full-length films released in major markets in the United States during the course of the year.

The format of the FILM REVIEW ANNUAL has been kept as clear and simple as possible. Films are reviewed in alphabetical order by title. Following each film title, we provide production information, cast and crew listings, the running time, and the MPAA rating. The reviews for each film are arranged alphabetically by publication. Each review is identified by the name of the publication, the date of the review, the page number, and the name of the reviewer. After the last review of a film, there is an *Also reviewed* section which lists other publications in which the film was reviewed. Because of restrictions in obtaining permission, we were unable to include reviews from certain publications. However, we felt that users of the FILM REVIEW ANNUAL should have help in gaining access to those reviews. Therefore, we included the *Also reviewed* section.

At the end of the FILM REVIEW ANNUAL, we provided full listings of the major film awards, including the nominees as well as the winners.

There are eight Indexes in the FILM REVIEW ANNUAL: Cast, Producers, Directors, Screenwriters, Cinematographers, Editors, Music, and Production Crew.

We have not attempted to force a single editorial style upon the reviews for the sake of achieving consistency. The reader will readily recognize that some reviews were written under deadline pressure and that others were prepared in a more leisurely and reflective style. Some reviews were written to help the moviegoer determine whether or not to see the film. Other reviews assumed the reader had already seen the film and was interested in getting another point of view. We believe this diversity of purposes and styles is one of the major strengths of the FILM REVIEW ANNUAL.

Because of our respect for the integrity of the writers' styles, we made changes from the original only where absolutely necessary. These changes were confined to typographical errors in the original review and errors in the spelling of names. When the reviewer made a reference to another film, we inserted the name of that film. Otherwise the reviews remain as written. British spelling used in English publications has been kept.

We have tried to make the FILM REVIEW ANNUAL pleasurable to read as well as useful for scholars and students of film, communications, social and cultural history, sociology, and also for film enthusiasts. We, the editors, would appreciate your suggestions about how we might make subsequent editions of the FILM REVIEW ANNUAL even more useful.

FILM REVIEWS

ADRENALINE DRIVE

A Shooting Gallery Films release of an Adrenaline Drive Committee/Kindai Eiga Kyokai Co./Gaga Communications/There's Enterprise/Nippon Shuppan Hanbai production. *Producer:* Kiyoshi Mizokami, Kenichi Itaya, and Tomohiro Kobayashi. *Director:* Shinobu Yaguchi. *Screenplay (Japanese with English subtitles):* Shinobu Yaguchi. *Director of Photography:* Takashi Hamada. *Editor:* Shinobu Yaguchi. *Music:* Seiichi Yamamoto and Rashinban. *Sound:* Masatoshi Yokomizo. *Production Designer:* Isao Hagiwara. *Art Director:* Yoshio Yamada. *Running time:* 111 minutes. *MPAA Rating:* Not Rated.

WITH: Hikari Ishida (Shizuko Sato); Masanobu Ando (Satoru Suzuki); Yutaka Matsushige (Kuroiwa); Kazue Tsunogae (Head Nurse); Yu Tokui (Chinpira); Jovi Jova (Kuroiwa's Hooligans); Kirina Mano; Koichi Ueda.

LOS ANGELES TIMES, 5/5/00, Calendar/p. 6, Kevin Thomas

The Shooting Gallery Film Club's outstanding first series comes to a slam-bang conclusion with Shinobu Yaguchi's "Adrenaline Drive," a rip-roaring romantic comedy that's as funny as it is light on its feet.

Yaguchi rigorously maintains a deliciously deadpan take on escalating absurdities as one inspired, zany moment leads to the next with unflagging zest and imagination. Yaguchi is like an impossibly audacious juggler who never drops a plate or slackens his pace. (You have to wonder whether Shooting Gallery has considered an English-language remake.)

In a sizable, unidentified Japanese city, a tall young man, Satoru (Masanobu Ando) is driving a car with his boss from hell, a jerk in charge of a car rental agency who is constantly baiting him. The older guy keeps placing his hand over Satoru's eyes, and sure enough, the car crashes into a black Jaguar—belonging, wouldn't you know, to the steely, unamused yakuza, Kuroiwa (Yutaka Matushige).

Of course, Satoru's boss, who's not about to report the incident to the company, leaves the shy youth holding the bag, wondering how on earth he will ever pay for the damages. But the bag Satoru soon ends up with contains a fortune in yakuza loot.

Satoru doesn't need to worry for long, because a terrific explosion at yakuza headquarters wipes out virtually the entire gang, sending Kuroiwa to the hospital with near-fatal injuries.

Meanwhile, there's a young nurse, Shizuko (Hikari Ishida), whose glasses hide her good looks and who despite being bashful doesn't flinch when opportunity knocks. Satoru and that ton of ill-gotten cash come Shizuko's way, and she and Satoru are off and running to a luxe mountain resort, where they register as husband and wife and plunge into the high life.

A made-over, contact-lensed Shizuko wouldn't mind having both the man and the money, but before Satoru can overcome his shyness, mayhem breaks loose, mainly in the form of half a dozen of Kuroiwa's youngest, dumbest, most brutal hooligans, the gang's apparent sole survivors. They're on order from their boss to retrieve that loot immediately. (They're played by the performance comedy troupe Jovi Jova.)

It is amazing how Yaguchi is able to come up with so many fresh, off-the-wall variations on the lovers-on-the-run plot. Good English subtitles reveal Yaguchi to have a way with witty dialogue, but his key strength is that he has a flair for knockabout physical comedy of the silent-era masters, whose humor had to rely on visual power.

This gives "Adrenaline Drive" terrific, vigorous grace—cinematographer Takashi Hamada is a virtuoso—and also detachment, letting us ponder, should we care to, about the power of money to transform lives. No matter whether Shizuko and Satoru end up with or without the money—or with or without each other—they've become assertive and free of their humdrum existences, if only temporarily.

Ishida and Ando are most appealing and adept young actors, and they are as beguiling as their movie.

NEW YORK POST, 5/5/00, p. 52, Jonathan Foreman

A witty and quietly charming road comedy, "Adrenaline Drive" is about a shy nurse and an even shyer rental-car driver in possession of a suitcase full of bloodied money and on the run from Yakuza gangsters.

The production values are not impressive, and the plot's not terribly original, but director Shinobu Yaguchi makes effective comic use of both his main characters and of members of the Jovi Jova comedy troupe, who play the Yakuza heavies.

NEWSDAY, 5/5/00, p. B7, Jan Stuart

He's a nerdy car-rental clerk. She's a plain-Jane nurse. But put them together in the same room with a bag of hot cash and bingo! They turn into Cary Grant and Grace Kelly in "To Catch a Thief."

That is the nutshell version of "Adrenaline Drive," a genial cat-and-mouse crime comedy from Japan that works up a sweat trying to be fast, kooky and clever while the audience maintains an effortless pace two steps ahead.

Kicking in with a promisingly eccentric prelude, "Adrenaline Drive" soon takes a turn down a very familiar road. After a lowly clerk named Saturo (Masanobu Ando) rear-ends a gangster's car, he is whisked off to a lair where a busy hive of bookies is raking in a load of illegal cash. When a gas explosion levels the joint, only Saturo and the head yakuza are left alive. First on the scene is Shizuko (Hikari Ishida), a seriously shy nurse who spirits the injured parties away in an ambulance, but not before Saturo has bagged up as much of the cash as he can grab.

Quickly sizing up the situation, the clerk and the nurse take the money and run, setting off on a spending spree that is a bit depressing in its utter lack of originality: expensive hotel suites, first-class restaurants, high-fashion makeovers. While they are busy turning themselves from bedraggled back-packers into Vogue models, they are pursued on separate fronts by the battered yakuza and a flaky pack of goons.

For all its air of wacky amorality, "Adrenaline Drive" wags a schoolmarm's finger over the corrupting effects of filthy lucre. Serving triple duties as writer, director and editor, Shinobu Yaguchi keeps it all moving with a light hand. But "Adrenaline Drive" stretches on too long for its modest genre intentions. Well before the two hapless heroes floor the pedal for the final chase, "Adrenaline Drive" leaves the audience behind in that old dust cloud of "Do we care?"

VILLAGE VOICE, 5/9/00, p. 134, Amy Taubin

Shinobu Yaguchi's *Adrenaline Drive* is more sluggish and contrived than his mordant debut feature, *Down the Drain,* although its premise is strikingly similar. In both films, a seemingly casual incident places the unprepossessing protagonist outside the law and transforms her or his life in ways not previously imaginable. In *Down the Drain,* the unintentional misuse of a subway pass sends a young girl on a hellish downward spiral. In *Adrenaline Drive,* a young man takes the blame when his boss's car rear-ends a yakuza's Jaguar. Forced to accompany the gangster to his headquarters, he expects the worst. Instead, he finds himself in possession of a bag full of cash when a bomb goes off, killing almost everyone else. He flees the scene with a bedraggled nurse who heard the explosion and came by to help. But the pair barely have time to enjoy their windfall when the surviving yakuza and his pickup band of thugs come after them.

Yaguchi is onto something interesting here in relation to how money transforms people's lives. Rather than feeling guilty, these two kids, formerly scapegoated at their jobs, become so confident and creative that they're able to out-maneuver their yakuza enemy. But unlike *Down the Drain,* where the surreal humor was rooted in realistic detail, the slapstick *Adrenaline Drive* is little more than a cartoon, and not a funny one at that.

Also reviewed in:
CHICAGO TRIBUNE, 5/5/00, Friday/p. H, John Petrakis
NEW YORK TIMES, 5/5/00, p. E16, Elvis Mitchell
VARIETY, 3/15-21/99, p. 43, Derek Elley

WASHINGTON POST, 5/5/00, p. C12, Stephen Hunter
WASHINGTON POST, 5/5/00, Weekend/p. 47, Desson Howe

ADVENTURES OF ROCKY AND BULLWINKLE, THE

A Universal Pictures release in association with Capella/KC Medien of a Tribeca production. *Executive Producer:* Tiffany Ward and David Nicksay. *Producer:* Jane Rosenthal and Robert De Niro. *Director:* Des McAnuff. *Screenplay:* Kenneth Lonergan. *Based on characters developed by:* Jay Ward. *Director of Photography:* Thomas Ackerman. *Editor:* Dennis Virkler. *Music:* Mark Mothersbaugh. *Music Editor:* Laura Perlman. *Sound:* Willie Burton and (music): John Kurlander. *Sound Editor:* Bruce Stambler. *Casting:* Mary Margiotta and Karen Margiotta. *Production Designer:* Gavin Bocquet. *Art Director:* Bill Rea. *Set Designer:* Mariko Braswell, Sean Haworth, Joshua Lusby, Sloane U'Ren, and Dean Wolcott. *Set Decorator:* Hilton Rosemarin. *Set Dresser:* Richard D. Wright, Geno Ghiselli, Michael P. Hunter, Paul Bortoli, and Mark Brown. *Special Effects:* Kenneth D. Pepiot. *Costumes:* Marlene Stewart. *Make-up:* John M. Elliott, Jr. *Make-up (Robert De Niro):* Ilona Herman. *Make-up (Rene Russo):* Shane Paish. *Animation Supervisor:* David Andrews. *Stunt Coordinator:* Doug Coleman. *Running time:* 88 minutes. *MPAA Rating:* PG.

CAST: Rene Russo (Natasha); Jason Alexander (Boris); Piper Perabo (Karen Sympathy); Randy Quaid (Cappy Von Trapment); Robert De Niro (Fearless Leader); June Foray (Rocky); Keith Scott (Bullwinkle); Keith Scott (Narrator); Janeane Garofalo (Minnie the Mogul); Carl Reiner (P.G. Biggershot); Jonathan Winters (Whoppa Chopper Pilot); John Goodman (Oklahoma Cop); Kenan Thompson (Lewis); Kel Mitchell (Martin); Jonathan Winters (Ohio Cop with Bullhorn); James Rebhorn (President Signoff); David Alan Grier (Measures); Norman Lloyd (Wossamotta U. President); Jonathan Winters (Jeb); Jon Polito (Schoentell); Rod Biermann (Ole); Don Novello (Fruit Vendor Twins); John Brandon (General Consternation); Harrison Young (General Foods); Nigel Gibbs (General Store); Ed Gale (The Mole); Phil Proctor (RBTV Floor Director); Dian Bachar (RBTV Studio Technician); Drena De Niro (RBTV Lackey); Mark Holton (FBI Agent "Potato"); Doug Jones (FBI Agent "Carrot"); Jane Edith Wilson (FBI Agent "Radish"); Lily Nicksay (Sydney); Julia McAnuff (Little Karen); Adam Miller (Little Ole); Steve Rankin (Arrest Cop); Philip Caruso (Rance); Brian T. Finney (Bailiff); Wesley Mann (Clerk); Jeffrey Ross (District Attorney); Arvie Lowe, Jr. (Sharp-Eyed Student); Taraji Henson (Left-Wing Student); T.J. Thyne (Right-Wing Student); Jeremy Maxwell (Angry French Student); Chip Chinery and Ellis E. Williams (Security Guards); David Brisbin (Average Dad); Kristen Lowman (Average Mom); Myrna Niles (Average Grandma); Jack Donner (Average Grandpa); Amanda Brookshire and Patric Brillhart (Average Kids); Jared Doud (Average Teen); Paget Brewster (Jenny Spy); Victor Raider-Wexler (Igor); Robert Bundy and John Campion (Dr. Spies); Max Grodenchik and Eugene Alper (Horse Spies); Alexis Thorpe (Supermodel); Billy Crystal (Traveling Mattress Seller); Whoopi Goldberg (Judge Cameo).

LOS ANGELES TIMES, 6/30/00, Calendar/p. 2, Kenneth Turan

The best thing about "The Adventures of Rocky and Bullwinkle" is that Rocky and Bullwinkle are the best thing about it. Despite the presence of name actors like Robert De Niro, Rene Russo and Jason Alexander, all eyes are on a chatty animated squirrel and a 6-foot, 7-inch animated talking moose.

Which, as the many admirers of the much-loved Jay Ward-Bill Scott TV series will attest, is as it should be. Possibly the most gleefully sophisticated cartoon show in TV history, "Rocky and his Friends" and "The Bullwinkle Show" ran for a combined 326 episodes between 1959 and 1964, combining arcane cultural references, all manner of wicked wordplay and endless battles with the evil Eastern European trio of Boris Badanov, Natasha Fatale and Fearless Leader.

Given how ineptly another Ward-Scott character, Dudley Do-Right, was transferred to film, moose and squirrel fans had reason to worry about this half live-action, half computer-animated adaptation, but in the great cartoon tradition, things have turned out fine in the end.

A film of modest aims, pleasing moments and genuine smiles, "The Adventures of Rocky and Bullwinkle" is completely in the spirit of its progenitor. Though it suffers from having to have a plot willing and able to be dragged out to feature-length (88 minutes versus 3½ for the original adventures), this attempt is closer than you might imagine to sharing the qualities that made the original such a long-lived success.

It's fortunate that director Des McAnuff, who seems to do his best big-screen work with cartoons (he produced Brad Bird's "The Iron Giant"), understands the sensibility that animated the original show and is able to meld the work of real and imaginary actors to replicate it.

But if this film has a secret weapon (aside from the return of voice-over legend June Foray, who originated Rocky on TV), it's screenwriter Kenneth Lonergan, whose soon-to-be-released "You Can Count on Me" was easily the best-written film at the last Sundance festival.

Lonergan has practically channeled the spirit of Ward and Scott, knowing just which modern phrases the guys would have leaped on ("let the healing begin," Bullwinkle says at one point) and smartly capturing the self-referential nature of the dialogue. After a tepid exchange between our heroes early on, the narrator (the excellent Keith Scott, who also does Bullwinkle) tartly comments, "even their wordplay had become hackneyed and cheap."

These particular adventures start with Rocky and Bullwinkle living in shabby-genteel two-dimensional retirement in Frostbite Falls, Minn., trying to stretch ever-diminishing residual checks (one comes in for 3½ cents) and lamenting the fact that "the world doesn't need us." Rocky, if the truth be known, has even forgotten how to fly.

Halfway across the world, in the sovereign state of Pottsylvania, Boris, Natasha and Fearless Leader, also still in animated form, are occupied doggedly tunneling to Hollywood. There they sign the rights to their story over to studio development executive Minnie Mogul (Janeane Garofalo) and are promptly transformed into real people Alexander, Russo and De Niro because, Fearless Leader explains, "we are attached to the project."

That is the first of many inside Hollywood references in Lonergan's script, including an amusing visit to the Green Light House, the top-secret nautical structure where films literally get the green light. There are also several references to specific films, the funniest being De Niro doing the Fearless Leader version of his famous "You talkin' to me" speech from "Taxi Driver."

Now that he is flesh and blood, Fearless Leader hatches a plan to become America's president. The idea is to unite all of this country's cable stations into the RBTV (as in Really Bad TV) network, with programs that turn citizens into mindless zombies who could be hypnotized into voting for Fearless for president.

Working with Rocky and Bullwinkle to stop this menace is quasi-intrepid FBI agent Karen Sympathy. Nicely played by ingenue-of-the-moment Piper Perabo (who will be operating in quite a different ambience—the raunchy New York bar scene—in the forthcoming "Coyote Ugly"), Karen remains the sweetest, most cheerful operative in the history of the bureau despite encounters with scene-stealing cameo players Carl Reiner, John Goodman, Whoopi Goldberg and Jonathan Winters.

Though it has the virtue of not taking itself too seriously, "Rocky and Bullwinkle" does go on too long, leading to inevitable dead spots. And though Alexander, Russo and De Niro are acceptable, their cartoonishness goes only so far. It's Rocky and Bullwinkle, even in their fleshed-out, computer-generated form, we want to be hanging out with. It feels good to see the boys out of reruns and in the spotlight where they belong.

NEW YORK POST, 6/30/01, p. 47, Lou Lumenick

"The Adventures of Rocky and Bullwinkle" takes the opposite tack of most movies based on old TV series, which "update" them so much, they're barely recognizable.

The sophisticated but silly sensibility that informed this early '60s animated ancestor of "The Simpsons" is surprisingly intact in this moderately clever family movie, directed by Des McAnuff ("Cousin Bette") from a screenplay by Kenneth Lonergan ("Analyze This").

Rocky the Flying Squirrel and Bullwinkle the Moose have been stuck in reruns with ever-diminishing residual checks since their series was canceled in 1964.

Meanwhile, their old enemies from Pottsylvania—Boris (Jason Alexander), Natasha (Rene Russo) and Fearless Leader (Robert De Niro) have crossed over from the cartoon world as flesh-and-blood characters, thanks to a deal with craven movie producer Minnie Mogul (Janeane Garofalo).

FBI supervisor Cappy von Trapment (Randy Quaid) assigns bumbling young agent Karen Sympathy (Piper Perabo) to bring Rocky and Bullwinkle back—to save the world from Fearless Leader's plot to turn Americans into zombies with broadcasts from his Really Bad Television Network.

"The Adventures of Rocky and Bullwinkle" works because they really are the focus—and they're excellently voiced by June Foray (who's been doing the ridiculously optimistic Rocky since 1959) and Keith Scott (who took over dimwitted Bullwinkle from the late and unrelated Bill Scott, the series co-creator, back in the '70s).

There's lots of corny wordplay—"Allow me to be frank with you," one character says to Bullwinkle, with the inevitable reply, "Oh hullo, Frank, I'm Bullwinkle"—and visual jokes, most notably the process by which Phony Pictures "green-lights" (gives a go-ahead for) a Rocky and Bullwinkle movie.

Thankfully, the filmmakers have wisely resisted the temptation to build up the supporting characters, as was done in the deservedly forgotten 1988 live-action "Boris and Natasha," which starred Dave Thomas and Sally Kellerman.

De Niro (who co-produced) doesn't have a lot to do as Fearless Leader, but he does it extremely well—a takeoff on his "You Talkin' to Me" speech from "Taxi Driver" and leading a chorus of the Pottsylvania national anthem.

Perabo—a knockout who looks like a cross between Angelina Jolie and Ashley Judd—will go a long way to making this a painless experience for dads accompanying their kids. There are also amusing celebrity cameos, most notably Jonathan Winters (in three roles) and Whoopi Goldberg as the aptly named Judge Cameo.

This movie doesn't take itself terribly seriously, making fun of its own plot twists, dialogue and special effects.

"The Adventures of Rocky and Bullwinkle" is no "Who Framed Roger Rabbit," but it has it's own goofy charms.

NEWSDAY, 6/30/00, Part II/p. B2, Jan Stuart

If the two stars accorded "The Adventures of Rocky and Bullwinkle" above could be converted into sighs, they would be for each of those the film elicits from its middle-aged audience members. The first comes almost immediately, when our seats are barely warm: the luxuriant coo of nostalgic pleasure upon hearing the unmistakable tin-circus fanfare of Fred Steiner's "Rocky Show Theme" over the opening credits.

The second sigh emerges sometime in the first half hour, as it gradually dawns upon us that this lovingly wrought resurrection of the characters introduced on "Rocky and His Friends" and "The Bullwinkle Show" is just not working. It is the sigh of dismay at watching a vanguard cartoon inflated like a Macy's parade balloon, then sent floating off listlessly like every other screen attempt at milking the vaunted television yesteryear of baby boomers.

Debuting on ABC in 1959, "Rocky and His Friends" was a cheeky antidote to the Captain Kangaroos and Howdy Doodys that had lulled kids and their parents during the Eisenhower years. Its pricelessly inept moose and squirrel, whose collective IQ could barely rival the ditz quotient of TV comedienne Gracie Allen, were merely a pretext for a very adult vaudeville of wry topical jokes, knowingly bad puns and middle-brow slapstick. Owing more to Ernie Kovacs than Looney Tunes, the "Rocky and Bullwinkle" cartoons were giddy with self-awareness, sharpening the cutting edge for animation decades before "The Simpsons" and "South Park."

Invoking Lyndon Baines Johnson and Velcro within the opening minutes of this state-of-the-art new film version, the filmmakers clearly were eager to reproduce the sophisticated tone established by the TV shows late originator, Jay Ward. Smarty pants stage-and- screenwriter Kenneth Lonergan (hotter than coals with "Analyze This" and recent Sundance winner "You Can Count on Me" under his belt) quickly reasserts the shows wired narrator's voice with a blithe return visit to Frostbite Falls and Pottsylvania, homes, respectively, to the eponymous heroes and their Cold War-inspired archvillains, Boris Badanov and Natasha Fatale.

It is not Boris and Natasha who will defeat Moose and Squirrel, however, but that dubious interloper into animated features known as live action. When Boris and Natasha burrow out of cartoon Pottsylvania early in the movie and surface in real-world Hollywood, they turn into live actors Jason Alexander and Rene Russo. Once the picture goes live, "Rocky and Bullwinkle" morph into three-dimensional figures via computer-generated animation, which has the odd effect of making Bullwinkle look like Mr. Peanut with antlers.

Warren Beatty found the perfect pitch of high style and caricature in his live-action "Dick Tracy" with which to emulate its comic-strip origins. But director Des McAnuff, who sank Balzac's "Cousin Bette" with ham-fisted farce, hasn't landed upon a similarly congenial way to translate "Rocky and Bullwinkle's" weird balance of pith and prankishness for living, breathing actors. Alexander and Russo are forced to shimmy and scurry like monkeys, and the effect is embarrassing at best.

Robert De Niro has a better time of it as the Nazi-burlesque Fearless Leader, making hilarious self-reference to his most famous line from "Taxi Driver." With De Niro as co-producer, the movie has lured a bevy of top comic talent in cameo appearances, the best of which belong to John Goodman and Whoopi Goldberg. Less fortunate are Janeanne Garofolo and Jonathan Winters, who make multiple appearances and ar just as unfunny each time. The ungainliness of much of the humor in "The Adventures of Rocky and Bullwinkle" is underscored by an angular-faced young actress with dreadful comic instincts named Piper Perabo, who plays an FBI agent assigned to protect the two heroes.

Lonergan has some wonderfully daffy jokes up his sleeve that honor the spirit of the original (a running gag about strip malls has a cunning payoff), but he is hampered by his own plot machinations, which have Boris and Natasha conspiring to turn the TV-viewing public into vegetables with bad programming. By the last half hour, you may feel zombied out yourself.

SIGHT AND SOUND, 2/01, p. 34, Leslie Felperin

US, 1964. The beloved animated television cartoon series *The Bullwinkle Show* is cancelled. Its stars, Rocky J. Squirrel and Bullwinkle J. Moose, retire to their home, Frostbite Falls.

US, the present. Film executive Minnie Mogul accidentally brings Rocky and Bullwinkle's long-time adversaries Boris Badenov, Natasha Fatale and their boss Fearless Leader—into the three-dimensional world. They launch RBTV (Really Bad Television), a station whose dull yet hypnotic broadcast will force people to elect Fearless Leader president, thus enabling him to take over the world. The FBI enlists agent Karen Sympathy to get Rocky and Bullwinkle out of retirement to thwart Fearless Leader's plan.

At a Hollywood studio Karen manages to bring the cartoon squirrel and moose into the real world by greenlighting a fantasy-adventure road movie. They set off by car to find Fearless Leader, who in turn sends Boris and Natasha after them with a device which will send them to the one place from which no one will ever hear from them again: the internet. But Boris and Natasha's efforts are repeatedly thwarted. Karen, meanwhile, is falsely imprisoned and escapes with the help of a handsome but dim security guard who falls in love with her. Rocky and Bullwinkle stop off at Bullwinkle's old alma mater, Wossamotta U, where they quell a student riot. All three meet up in New York at Fearless Leader's studio. Bullwinkle's antlers disrupt the RBTV signal, helping the gang to incapacitate Boris, Natasha al Fearless Leader. Bullwinkle enjoins the audience to vote for whomsoever they want. Incumbent president Signoff thanks them and RBTV becomes Rocky and Bullwinkle Television.

Given how abysmal some of Hollywood's regurgitations of much loved television shows have been of late *(Sgt. Bilko, My Favourite Martian,* to name but a few), fans of Rocky and Bullwinkle, the cartoon squirrel-and-moose double act who made their small-screen debut in the 50s, should be grateful their cinematic outing is only lame rather than truly atrocious. Despite an embarrassing subplot about an FBI agent discovering her inner child (played excruciatingly straight) and too many wasted cameos, *The Adventures of Rocky & Bullwinkle* manages to be vaguely amusing in places. Ultimately, though, it's little more than a dim echo of the anarchic spirit of the original cartoons. No other children's show succeeded in being so disrespectful of fourth-wall conventions (the characters would often quibble with the garrulous narrator), so openly satirical (Cold War politics were the butt of many jokes) or so nimble in its dual address to both young viewers and adults as Rocky and Bullwinkle's. That is, until *Pee-Wee's Playhouse* in the late 80s.

The "moose und sqvirell", as their nemeses Boris and Natasha would call them, were the creations of producers Jay Ward and Alex Anderson, who introduced them on *Crusader Rabbit*, a landmark cartoon series of the early 50s. Rocky and Bullwinkle and the other denizens of Frostbite Falls were mere supporting players then, and it wasn't until 1959 that they got their own show, which aired in various formats and with different titles on US television until 1964. Fans inclined towards conspiracy theory argue the show was cancelled because of network cowardice rather than bad ratings; as the film cannily acknowledges, reruns have been the lifeblood sustaining the pair's fame, if only in the US.

Gamely trying to ape the cheek of the original show, *The Adventures of Rocky & Bullwinkle* is full of self-deprecating, self-referential gags about its own tawdriness. When the otherwise flat cartoon characters Boris, Natasha and Fearless Leader are pulled into our world and turn into Jason Alexander, Rene Russo and Robert De Niro, the narrator comments, "And so the expensive animated characters were converted into even more expensive motion picture stars." The stars, at least, seem to enjoy sending themselves up—the film's best shtick is to have De Niro recite his "Are you talking to me?" speech from *Taxi Driver* (1976) in Fearless Leader's cod-mittel-European accent, but with such completely different inflection it takes a beat or two before you realise what he's saying. Unfortunately, the rest of the film and television allusions come thin and none too fast: there's a *Wizard of Oz* joke ("I don't think we're on television anymore," observes Rocky); a dance to the theme tune from *Danger Man*, for no apparent reason; and, most wittily, a reference to *Who Framed Roger Rabbit* ("Shut up! This is totally different!" insists Fearless Leader when the Robert Zemeckis film is invoked.)

But director Des McAnuff (a playwright who made his debut with the Balzac adaptation *Cousin Bette)* is no Robert Zemeckis; nor is he at all similar to Jay Ward, who regularly bit the network and sponsors' hands that fed him. McAnuff and his screenwriter accomplices haven't the stomach for a real fight. Their soft targets here are television, the internet and the political process—as easy to hit as a moose asleep on a road.

TIME, 7/10/00, p. 102, Richard Schickel

It's never easy for actors when their TV series is canceled—especially if they're a moose and a flying squirrel, which doesn't leave a lot of room to stretch beyond type. We learn in the opening moments of *The Adventures of Rocky and Bullwinkle* that the eponymous heroes of Jay Ward's beloved (and weirdly iconic) '60s television series have retreated to their home turf, Frostbite Falls; that their typical residual check has dwindled to 3.5¢; that the pretty forest where they once romped has been reduced to stumps.

Bullwinkle J. Moose, in his amiable, lunkhead way, remains perversely optimistic about the future. But Rocky has developed a psychosomatic inability to fly. Luckily for them, in far-off Hollywood a development girl (Janeane Garofalo) dreams of a feature film that will restore their fortunes. Carl Reiner's studio boss is dim on that—"I hate moose movies," he snarls, in one of the film's many self-referential lines, a tradition that was one of the hip glories of the original TV show. But by this time an actual movie, directed by Des McAnuff and written by Kenneth Lonergan, is off and running.

Or, should one say, limping. For the decision to make Bullwinkle and Rocky's old nemeses—Boris, Natasha and Fearless Leader, the scourges of Pottsylvania—into live-action characters was unwise. Jason Alexander, Rene Russo and Robert De Niro, respectively, do their best to act cartoonishly, but the Russian-accented villains were funnier when they were drawn. And when they were satirizing cold war paranoia.

This time Fearless Leader's plan is to hypnotize the American citizenry via "Really Bad Television" and then command it to elect him President. It doesn't quite wash—though Bullwinkle, naturally, thinks TV is as excellent as it was when he was a star. It suffices only to get the pair off on a cross-country odyssey aimed at thwarting the bad guys. Conducted by a naive FBI agent (Piper Perabo), they do encounter some fitfully funny comic actors (John Goodman, Jonathan Winters, Whoopi Goldberg), but neither the guest stars nor the sublimely numb

Bullwinkle manages to rescue the picture from its too comfortable reliance on retro charm. It's great to have the Moose back, but it would be greater still to see him in a humorous context fully worth of him.

VILLAGE VOICE, 7/11/00, p. 124, Michael Atkinson

Such are the secrets movie stars harbor: In the world as it should be, you couldn't get Robert De Niro to play an animated Jay Ward character-made-flesh for all the calzones in Tribeca, but here he is, Tatar-barking as the Dr. Evil-ish Fearless Leader in a witless big-screen live cartoon he coproduced. All those years of Scorsese movies and Methoding, and to where did the tenacious Inner Bobby long to return? Frostbite Falls.

Obviously cobbled together piecemeal in the dumb hope of producing yuks by happenstance—in some ways resembling the half-assed card-house USSR the movie helplessly references—*The Adventures of Rocky and Bullwinkle* takes the fondly remembered, pen-sketched characters into "the real world," which is of course Hollywood's punishingly unfunny, in-joke-ridden notion of itself. (*An Alan Smithee Movie* is an evocative corollary.) The original cartoons came in crudely designed seven-minute splats for a reason; here, the computer-generated self-mockery suggests not self-knowledge but desperation, squeezed in between cheap stunts, utterly undecipherable transitions, and pointless cameos (Don Novello, for one shot, as twin fruit-cart vendors?). Outside of the dry, fast, deadpan context of Ward's flat universe, the puns and tangents are dead in the water, no matter how often The Narrator points out that very fact.

The results are hatefully unentertaining, particularly when focused on R & B's human escort through the morass of story, an FBI agent played by newly discovered lip-and-hair teen dervish Piper Perabo. Perabo, soon to be made the new Jennifer Beals in Jerry Bruckheimer's forthcoming *Flashdance* redux, *Coyote Ugly*, has a face as fresh as unkneaded dough and a whining delivery that suggests the voice inside Britney Spears's head when the service table forgets to stock the cherry Fruit Roll-Ups.

Taking the assignment to save the earth from Fearless Leader's zombifying cable TV shows (bad Soviet sitcoms, the only good joke, squandered), Perabo's Agent Sympathy claims to have grown up with R & B, but she's too young even to have been fazed by reruns—it's De Niro who was 16 when the show debuted in 1959. Though the credits list one writer (playwright and *Analyze This* scribe Kenneth Lonergan), you get visions of the story meetings: too long, too numerous, too crowded, too many pencils in the ceiling. (For the voice of Rocky, June Foray is just one of four actors credited.) As Boris and Natasha, Jason Alexander and Rene Russo seem mortally embarrassed, as well they might: So much more than Ward's Ernie Kovacs-influenced ditties, the movie is hardly a project worthy of grown men and women. But the same could be said for loads of movies, even if few seem as ferociously pointless. The question might be, in the end: How does it honor the Americans happily imprinted with the original show's beautiful chaos to have it turned into bastard nonsense? If no one cares to say, who cares about the movie?

ALSO REVIEWED IN:
NEW YORK TIMES, 6/30/00, p. E13, A. O. Scott
NEW YORKER, 7/17/00, p. 87, David Denby
VARIETY, 7/10-16/00, p. 20, Joe Leydon

AFFAIR OF LOVE, AN

A Fine Line Features release in association with Patrick Quinet and Artemis Productions in co-production with Les Productions Lazennec/ARP/Samsa Film/Fama Films/RTBF/SRG/SFDRS, with the the participation of Canal Plus. *Producer:* Patrick Quinet. *Director:* Frédéric Fonteyne. *Screenplay (French with English subtitles):* Philippe Blasband. *Director of Photography:* Virginie Saint-Martin. *Editor:* Chantal Hymans. *Music:* Jeannot Sanavia, André Dziezuk, and Marc

Mergen. *Sound:* Carlo Thoss. *Production Designer:* Véronique Sacrez. *Costumes:* Anne Schotte. *Running time:* 80 minutes. *MPAA Rating:* Not Rated.

CAST: Nathalie Baye (Elle); Sergi Lopez (Lui).

LOS ANGELES TIMES, 8/11/00, Calendar/p. 6, Kevin Thomas

What could be more radiant than the image of a beautiful woman, smiling as she strides down a Paris boulevard? It's a secret kind of smile, and no one is better at those than lovely and accomplished Nathalie Baye, who has one of the best of her many fine roles in Frederic Fonteyne's "An Affair of Love," a film as romantic as its title. It's more appropriate to the spirit of the film, written by Philippe Blasband, than the more provocative French original, "Une Liaison Pornographique."

That title comes from Baye's unnamed heroine as she speaks to an unseen interrogator, presumably a therapist. "It was a pornographic affair: It was sex, nothing but sex, only sex," she begins, saying how she made contact with a man via the Internet. As she begins her story we cut to the man (Sergi Lopez), who is also speaking to someone who remains off screen, to whom he starts telling the story from his perspective.

Neither the man nor the woman has ever done this before, and when they meet, in a Paris cafe, they exchange neither names, phone numbers nor addresses and never disclose anything about their lives to each other—or to us. She is poised and elegant; he is a stocky teddy bear of a man, a dark-haired Spaniard, boyish-looking but, as the woman observes, handsome when he smiles.

They are an attractive couple and sufficiently mutually attracted to head for the nearby hotel room that the woman has reserved in advance. The woman is the more confident and forward of the two, but the man, who has a sweet shyness, responds rapidly enough.

Soon they are having weekly or sometimes twice-weekly trysts in the same hotel, a small, well-maintained establishment not far from the Eiffel Tower with plushy blood-red hallways and a well-upholstered boudoir, done with flocked wallpaper in intense turquoise. The decor spells sin boldly, and the couple are swiftly engaged in a torrid affair, the most intense either has ever experienced.

In time we do see them together in bed, but from a discreet perspective; neither is prepared to discuss their affair clinically with their unseen interrogator. The inevitable question is: How long will they be able to pursue such an intense passion without falling in love? And if love should flower, how will they deal with it?

The film is much concerned with the whole notion of the unknown, of how little we can know of ourselves and of each other. The question then becomes the leap of faith love requires, but which not everyone is prepared to make.

Baye, whose luminous performance took the best actress prize at Venice last year, and Lopez, so memorable as the wistful traveling salesman of Manuel Poirier's "Western" and seen in the current "The New Eve," give portrayals that attest to the power of understatement. You could imagine, for example, Julia Roberts and Richard Gere in a Hollywood remake, but there's a hitch: "An Affair of Love" is truly adult, straight to the finish. It's hard to imagine an American version that would go the distance without compromise.

NEW YORK POST, 8/11/00, p. 46, Lou Lumenick

"An Affair of Love" was originally titled "Une Liaison Pornographique" in its native France—but it's more like "Last Tango in Paris" minus most of the sex.

What Belgian filmmaker Frederic Fonteyne delivers is a beautifully acted and paced, often fascinating two-character chamber piece about a couple who meet strictly for sex—then find themselves confronting their emotions.

Except for one brief sequence, the sex is talked about rather than depicted, as an unnamed middle-aged man and woman (Sergi Lopez and Nathalie Baye) recount their somewhat differing stories to an unseen interviewer.

They agree that he answered her newspaper ad, looking for a partner to act out a specific "pornographic" sexual fantasy that is never identified, much less depicted.

By mutual consent, they don't disclose their names or anything about their backgrounds.

But things get tricky when, after several sessions in a run-down Paris hotel, they decide to have more conventional sex.

The experience proves unnerving for both, and they contemplate ending the affair before getting further involved. In some ways, "An Affair of Love" is a stunt by Fonteyne and his screenwriter Philippe Blasband—whether they can sustain audience interest, even for a scant 80 minutes, in such a minimalist story.

Thanks to the terrific Baye's nuanced performance as the aging female protagonist, this turns into a sophisticated entertainment of the less-is-more school.

NEWSDAY, 8/11/00, Part II/p. B10, John Anderson

[*An Affair of Love* was reviewed jointly with *Aimee & Jaguar*; see Anderson's review of that film.]

VILLAGE VOICE, 8/15/00, p. 124, Michael Atkinson

Whereas *Coyote Ugly* is distinguished by its irony vacuum, Frédéric Fonteyne's *An Affair of Love* comes double-dipped, at least in terms of its title: Originally called *Une Liaison Pornographique*, this sweet, pensive gabfest is neither conventionally romantic nor pornographic. Framed as a talking-heads mock doc and structured like an introverted *Last Tango, Affair* tracks the sex-only spree between an unpretentious Him (*Western*'s Sergi Lopez, resembling a lost French Baldwin bro) and an older, outspoken Her (Nathalie Baye, willowy and sharp), progressing inevitably from specific episodes of kink that are never revealed (the narrative contrivance cloys only mildly) to a more emotional bond that soon enough begins to fracture with great expectations and unvoiced desires. Too often fond of slo-mo subjectivity and joke cuts, Fonteyne makes sure the sex/love talk is concise and comprehensible—a relief—and there are some blessed interludes: The first "normal" sex scene is a hold-your-breath beaut, and a bathtub chat is stunningly intimate. A winner at Venice, Baye glows like an iron in the fire; if it's inevitable, give the remake to Streep but not to Mike Nichols.

Also reviewed in:
CHICAGO TRIBUNE, 11/3/00, Friday/p. N, John Petrakis
NEW REPUBLIC, 8/28 & 9/4/00, p. 28, Stanley Kauffmann
NEW YORK TIMES, 8/11/00, p. E25, A.O. Scott
VARIETY, 9/20-26/99, p. 89, David Rooney
WASHINGTON POST, 10/6/00, p. C12, Rita Kempley
WASHINGTON POST, 10/6/00, Weekend/p. 47, Desson Howe

AIMÉE & JAGUAR

A Zeitgeist Films release of a Günter Rohrbach/Senator Filmproduktion production. *Executive Producer:* Stefan Schieder. *Producer:* Günter Rohrbach and Hanno Huth. *Director:* Max Färberböck. *Screenplay (German with English subtitles):* Max Färberböck and Rona Munro. Based on the book by: Erica Fischer. *Director of Photography:* Tony Imi. *Editor:* Barbara Hennings and Ann Sophie Schweizer. *Music:* Jan A. P. Kaczmarek. *Music Editor:* Christopher Kennedy. *Choreographer:* Olimpia Scardi and Stefan Thalhaus. *Sound:* Michael Kranz and (music) Rafalel Paczkowski. *Casting:* Risa Kes. *Production Designer:* Mathias Schwerbrock. *Art Director:* Katja Schmidt. *Set Designer:* Albrecht Konrad. *Set Decorator:* Klaus Eckmann and Dagmar Wessel. *Special Effects:* Harry Wiessenhaan. *Costumes:* Barbara Baum Make-up: Gerlinde Kunz, Gerhard Nemetz and Horst Allert. *Stunt Coordinator:* Gerd Grzesczak. *Running time:* 125 minutes. *MPAA Rating:* Not Rated.

CAST: Maria Schrader (Felice Schragenheim "Jaguar"); Juliane Köhler (Lilly Wust "Aimée"); Johanna Wokalek (Ilse); Heike Makatsch (Klärchen); Elisabeth Degen (Lotte); Detlev Buck

(Günther Wust); Inge Keller (Lilly, 1997); Kyra Mladeck (Ilse, 1997); Margit Bendokat (Mrs. Jäger); Jochen Stern (Werner Lause); Peter Weck (Editor in Chief Keller); H.C. Blumenberg (Stefan Schmidt); Klaus Manchen (Father Kappler); Sarah Camp (Mother Kappler); Desirée Nick (Erika); Patrizia Moresco (Maria); Karin Friesecke (Marlene); Dani Levy (Fritz Borchert); Lya Dulitzkaya (Grandma Hulda); Klaus Koennecke (Mr. Ude); Barbara Focke (Mrs. Ude); Dorkas Kiefer (Tanja);   Werner Rehm (Conductor); Rüdiger Hacker (Ernst Biermösel); Peer Jäger (Mr. Pohl);   Anette Felber (Mrs. Pohl); Bastian Trost (Lieutenant); Rosel Zech (Blonde Woman); Carl Heinz Choynski (Brummer); Ulrich Matthes (Eckert); Felix Bold (Bernd Wust); Jake Steinfels (Eberhard Wust);   Yannik Richter (Reinhard Wust);   Henrik Meng (Albrecht Wust); Gabriele Schulze (Tenant); Falk Baumhauer (Tenant's Son); Ludwig Boettger (Broker); Wolfgang Woytt (Old Man);   Marc Bischoff (Sepp, the Chauffeur); Karolina Siwinska (Girl with Cap); Jerzy Milton (Aaron); Marta Lachova (Ruth); Rebekka Fleming (Frau Blockwart); Peer Jäger (Herr Pohl); Helmut Ehmig (Waiter); Klaus Schindler and Christoph Jacobi (Civil Servants); Margitta Heyn (Woman with Glasses); Klaus Hoser (Man at Concert); Heinz Trixner (Kleinert); Dorothea Moritz (Red Cross Nurse).

LOS ANGELES TIMES, 8/11/00, Calendar/p. 12, Kenneth Turan

"Aimee & Jaguar" is about falling in love, the power of love, what it gives us and the price that can be attached to its joys. It's the most familiar story in the lexicon of cinema, but watching it in this emotionally powerful film makes you feel like you've never quite seen it before.

As acted by Maria Schrader and Juliane Kohler, both of whom won Silver Bears at the Berlin Film Festival, "Aimee & Jaguar" shows individuals who are drawn to each other with such intensity we can actually feel the attraction ourselves. With key scenes so vivid they barely feel scripted, this is more than a same-sex success, it's a most affecting, most sensual on-screen love affair, period.

Based on a true story that became a bestseller in Germany in 1994, "Aimee & Jaguar" details a completely unlikely wartime romance. Not unlikely because it involved two women, but because one of them was a conventional German wife, the mother of four children with a husband at the front, while the other was a Jewish woman hiding in Berlin from an increasingly rapacious Nazi search-and-destroy machinery.

The latter would be Felice Schragenheim (Schrader), who called herself Jaguar in the erotic love poetry she wrote as a hobby. Though she lived clandestinely in the apartment of her lover Ilse (Johanna Wokalek), describing Felice as hiding, while accurate enough, gives a completely misleading impression.

A daredevil with a highly developed sense of bravado, Felice thrived on recklessness and danger. So adept at passing as an Aryan that she worked at a Nazi newspaper, Felice hung out at the best Berlin hotels yet passed information to the underground. Believing in the value of "living your life now," she was so innately duplicitous that, Ilse said, "as soon as you got hold of one Felice, another one betrayed you."

Lilly Wust (Kohler), whom Felice dubbed Aimee, was a different sort of woman. A flighty but vulnerable and unsophisticated romantic, Lilly compensated for a philandering husband away at the front by having numerous affairs with men who were worthier in her imagination than they proved to be in life.

It's through Ilse, who works as Lilly's maid, that the two women meet, and though "Aimee & Jaguar" is bookended by scenes in the present, it mostly deals with the wartime years, from 1943 on, when the relationship began. It was a peculiar time for Berlin, when the city was both physically and psychologically unraveling due to constant Allied bombing. But "Aimee & Jaguar" is apparently a departure for German film in the way it uses that period simply as a dramatic backdrop.

Though the intensity of feeling the two women almost immediately experience unnerves them both, it's the flirtatious Felice, who knows what's going on but is terrified by the onset of real emotion, who's affected first. For Lilly, who has never had a non-heterosexual thought, the emotional distance that has to be covered is if anything greater and more treacherous.

It's through acknowledging and keeping faith with these considerable difficulties that "Aimee & Jaguar" does its best work. Because Felice and Lilly are always complex, always themselves, the barriers to their having a relationship are not easy to surmount. And things like the parallel jealousies of Felice's distrustful friends and Lilly's disbelieving husband only make things harder.

NEW YORK POST, 8/11/00, p. 46, Hannah Brown

"Aimee & Jaguar," an entertaining, extravagantly emotional lesbian romance set in Berlin during World War II, has a kind of split personality.

On the one hand, it's a schmaltzy throwback to old Hollywood love stories, if you can imagine a film from the '30s or '40s about a lesbian couple.

At moments, especially during the montages of the couple's idyllic (and chaste) romps in the woods, it's possible to picture Marlene Dietrich as Lilly (Juliane Kohler), the upstanding German housewife and mother of four, nicknamed Aimee by her Jewish lover, Felice (Maria Schrader).

The shrewd but passionate Felice, who called herself Jaguar in the love poems she wrote to Lilly, could have been played by a young Bette Davis.

But there's another level to this film, and that's the wartime Jew-in-hiding story.

Felice, who reveals her religion to Lilly only late in the film; works for the Resistance and holds down a job at a Nazi newspaper. However, director Max Farberbock's heart is not in this espionage storyline.

Instead, he concentrates on Felice and her friends, a group of Jewish lesbians who are precariously passing for gentiles, and their non-Jewish protectors.

While Lilly's husband, a Nazi officer, is at the front, these women, costumed like the cast of "Cabaret," take over Lilly's apartment and turn it into a salon, a nightclub—and a hideout.

In an odd role reversal, the clueless Lilly, who is very deeply in love with Felice, is exposed to the risk of death for unknowingly harboring Jews.

The movie, based on a true story (the real-life Lilly Wust is still alive), is deftly introduced by a framing device, as the elderly Lilly (Inge Keller), meets one of Felice's other former lovers when she is admitted to a nursing home.

While it may disturb some viewers to see Nazis portrayed on screen as fully rounded characters, Lilly's intertwined sexual, romantic and political awakening makes for a touching story.

Farberbock's previous directing experience has all been for television, and some of the love scenes have the awkwardness of a TV movie.

However, the wonderful performances of the entire cast, particularly the remarkable Schrader as Felice and Keller as the present-day Lilly, make up for any cliches in the script.

NEWSDAY, 8/11/00, Part II/p. B10, John Anderson

Movie romance, especially desperate romance, is the world's greatest salesman: It gets us to swallow things we wouldn't otherwise buy in a million years. Letters of transit signed by General DeGaulle? The decades-long pursuit of Ashley Wilkes? The irresistible attraction of Freddie Prinze Jr.? We might hate ourselves in the morning, but we believe because we want to.

Which is a good thing for Max Farberbrock's "Aimee & Jaguar," because if it weren't based in fact, it's the kind of story that wouldn't get anyone through Screenwriting 101. In 1943 Berlin, as the Nazis are losing the war and stepping up the final solution, a circle of liberated Jewish lesbians led by Felice Schragenheim (Maria Schrader) avoid the Holocaust and hold orgies. Felice's slinky smile not only keeps her out of the camps but beguiles her newspaper editor boss (Peter Weck) to the point that she can feed information to the resistance. Her relationship to the Nazis is like Buffy to the vampires.

Making things more peculiar—but providing the point of the story—is the love affair that erupts between Felice and Lilly Wust (Juliane Kohler), the philandering wife of a philandering Nazi soldier (Detlev Buck). Lilly, who becomes the "Aimee" to Felice's "Jaguar," is referred to by one of Felice's pals as a "silly cow"; she could, in fact, be the star of a Bavarian "I Love Lucy." (It was the elderly Wust who provided the story for Erica Fischer's 1994 German best-selling book.) Vows of love are made, as tragedy circles the airfield.

It's a different but far more plausible weirdness that infects "An Affair of Love," which once went by the more ironically accurate "A Pornographic Affair." Meeting through a personal ad that specifies a very specific (and never-revealed) sex act, a woman (a wonderful Nathalie Baye) and a man (a laconic Sergi Lopez) meet regularly to indulge their very particular appetite. It's when they decide that perhaps regular sex might be interesting that the affair germinates, blooms and winds up rotting on the vine, because the two can't accept what everyone else can, which is that they're made for each other.

Why can't they see it? Well, that's the part that's hard to accept—Baye is magnetic, the erotic atmosphere of the film is genuinely steamy at times, but the sales pitch relies on our weakness

SIGHT AND SOUND, 5/01, p. 38, Nick Roddick

Berlin, 1943, at the height of the allied bombing. Lilly Wust is a good mother to her four children, despite the affairs she has while her husband Günther is away on the eastern front. Felice Schragenheim is a Jewish member of the underground resistance who, under the pseudonym of Schrader, has a job as assistant to the editor of the Nazi Party newspaper. Lilly and Felice meet one night through Ilse, Felice's lover and Lilly's maid. Felice begins to arrange meetings with Lilly, culminating in a drunken party where she kisses her on the mouth. Lilly is at first horrified, then runs after her. An affair begins, with Felice christening herself Jaguar and Lilly Aimée.

As Felice's underground activities demand more of her time, Lilly becomes jealous, suspecting another woman and prompting Felice to admit her Jewishness. The relationship deepens, to the point where Lilly divorces Günther and sets up house with Felice and her children. But the Gestapo are gradually closing in on Felice's network, and she is finally arrested as she and Lilly return from an idyllic day's swimming in August 1944. They never see one another. Felice is officially pronounced dead in 1948. Lilly, however, is 87 years old and still lives in Berlin.

Arriving in the UK over two years after opening the 1999 Berlin Film Festival, *Aimée & Jaguar* must have looked the perfect crossover title for the then-buoyant German industry: epic enough to be a mainstream success at home; sufficiently edgy to have arthouse appeal abroad. But uninspired direction (by German television veteran Max Färberböck, making his feature debut) and a crucial lack of focus look like thwarting both aims. The German release fizzled, and the film's best hope of a foreign audience looks like the gay circuit, where the combination of an unusual setting and some tastefully shot love scenes should have limited appeal. Sad, really, because the (true) story—about the wartime affair between Berlin housewife Lilly and a Jewish resistance fighter Felice—is fascinating and the film has some wonderful things in it, notably the central performance by Maria Schrader as the tormented Felice (aka Jaguar). Schrader treads the borderline between reckless hedonism ("I don't want 'forever'," she says at one stage. "I want now and now and now") and tragic resignation with considerable aplomb. Equally good is comic actor Detlev Buck in an uncharacteristically serious role, managing to create something memorable from the unpromising character of Lilly's husband Günther.

Flaunting its mainstream ambitions with considerable chutzpah, the film also creates a beguiling war-time Berlin, where bourgeois life maintains the façade (concerts at the Philharmonic, evenings at the Hotel am Zoo) while the city crumbles and burns. Indeed, the images of the city, shot in muddy browns, greens and greys by veteran British cinematographer Tony Imi, give the film added fascination for UK viewers, since they are so different from what we are used to in home-grown war movies.

But they are never entirely convincing. The ease with which Felice and her fellow Jewish underground comrades move in all the right circles occasionally beggars belief. Also irksome is Färberböck's television-acquired habit of cutting from scenes of happiness to moments of tragedy. The shooting of one of her fellow underground members in the street while Felice has to control her emotions and keep walking is immediately preceded by a comic sequence in which the girls pose for soft-porn photographs to be sent to the lads at the front. The first love scene between Felice and Lilly is intercut with a Gestapo raid on the former's grandmother. And the final idyll leads almost inevitably to the scene where the women return to Lilly's apartment and find the Gestapo waiting for them.

In the end, *Aimée & Jaguar* presses all the right keys but never really comes up with the tune. And the book-ending scenes showing the octogenarian Lilly leaving her flat for a retirement home, while poignant, paled into total insignificance at the Berlin premiere when the real Lilly came on stage. Hers, one feels, is the real story: a woman who gave up everything for six months of passion, followed by 50 years of emptiness. That Färberböck's film never really engages with this is a near-fatal shortcoming, since it's not so much the affair as its repercussions which make the Aimée-and-Jaguar story worth telling.

VILLAGE VOICE, 8/15/00, p. 124, Leslie Camhi

In 1943, Felice Schragenheim, a young Jewish woman circulating undercover in wartime Berlin, flirted with and then fell for Lilly Wust, mother of four sons and wife of a Wehrmacht officer. Some 50 years later, she told the story of their unlikely passion to journalist Erica Fischer, and the book, *Aimée and Jaguar*, became a bestseller in Germany.

Max Farberböck's adaptation relies on the hefty talents of its two leading ladies. Juliane Köhler portrays Lilly as a limited, silly woman, in over her head and transformed by love and suffering. Maria Schrader's Felice is the more fascinating character, at once exuberant and withholding. Elegantly turned out, she picks her way through the city's rubble to rendezvous with secretly Jewish girlfriends at the Hotel Adlon; like the real-life Felice, she seems to find the danger piquant, to consider joie de vivre and personal style as acts of defiance. Of her work in the Resistance, we learn little—a smuggled list here, a forged passport there. In the film, her political engagement is subsumed by the love which begins as a game and soon consumes her.

Aimée and Jaguar is one of a slew of recent German and East European features devoted to Jewish themes (István Szabós *Sunshine* is the latest), all variously absorbing and disturbing. Here, the story seems subtly skewed to Lilly's perspective: There's a heavy emphasis on German wartime suffering, and beyond Gestapo officers, hardly anyone appears to be a Nazi sympathizer. Perhaps Lilly's parents really did come to embrace their Jewish lesbian daughter-in-law (though it seems highly improbable that, as the film hints, the editor of the Nazi newspaper where Felice worked under an assumed name may have suspected her secret and protected her). It's possible, too, that in life Felice might have agreed to trade a few moments of perfect love for death's eternity. But the dead can't tell us about their own mixed feelings.

Also reviewed in:
CHICAGO TRIBUNE, 8/18/00, Friday/p. F, John Petrakis
NEW REPUBLIC, 9/11/00, p. 28, Stanley Kauffmann
NEW YORK TIMES, 8/11/00, p. E14, Dave Kehr
VARIETY, 2/15-21/99, p. 61, Derek Elley
WASHINGTON POST, 10/6/00, p. C12, Stephen Hunter

ALICE AND MARTIN

A USA Films release of a Les Films Alain Sarde/Vertigo Films/France 2 Cinéma/France 3 Cinéma co-production with the participation of Canal+/Studio Images 4. *Producer:* Alain Sarde. *Director:* André Téchiné. *Screenplay (French with English subtitles):* André Téchiné and Gilles Taurand with the collaboration of Olivier Assayas. *Director of Photography:* Caroline Champetier. *Editor:* Martine Giordano. *Music:* Philippe Sarde. *Choreographer:* Jorge Rodriguez. *Sound:* Jean-Paul Mugel, Jean-Pierre Laforce, Michel Klochendler, and (music) Nat Peck. *Casting:* Michel Nasri, Stéphane Foenkinos, Jacques Grant, and Benedicte Guiho. *Production Designer:* Ze Branco. *Costumes:* Elisabeth Tavernier. *Make-up:* Thi-Loan Nguyen. *Special Make-up Effects:* Dominique Colladant and Kuno Schlegelmilch. *Stunt Coordinator:* Patrick Steltzer. *Running time:* 123 minutes. *MPAA Rating:* R.

CAST: Juliette Binoche (Alice); Alexis Loret (Martin Sauvagnac); Mathieu Amalric (Benjamin Sauvagnac); Carmen Maura (Jeanine Sauvagnac); Jean-Pierre Lorit (Frédéric Sauvagnac); Marthe Villalonga (Lucie); Roschdy Zem (Robert); Pierre Maguelon (Victor Sauvagnac); Eric Kreikenmayer (François Sauvagnac); Jeremy Kreikenmayer (Martin as a Child); Kevin Goffette (Christophe); Christiane Ludot (Laurence); Véronique Rioux, Corinne Hache, Mauricio Angarita, Lilite Guegamian, and Thierry Barone (Musicians); Ruth Malka-Viellet (Tania); Jocelyn Henriot (Tania's Assistant); Patrick Goavec (The Doctor); Emmanuel Marcandier (The

Young Groom);   Thomas Vallegeas (The Neighbor);   Eric Hewson-Schmit (The Photographer); Nathalie Vignes (The Nurse);   Franck de la Personne (The Examining Magistrate).

LOS ANGELES TIMES, 8/4/00, Calendar/p. 14, Kevin Thomas

"Alice and Martin" is another of director Andre Techine's quietly shattering depth charges probing complex relationships within families and between friends and lovers. It continues a remarkable Techine cycle that includes "Wild Reeds" and "Ma Saison Preferee."

Boldly structured, intensely focused and briskly paced, "Alice and Martin" has a tremendous emotional density that places the utmost demands upon its actors—and asks a lot of audiences, too. The result is a film as provocative as it is gratifying.

It begins with a deceptive sunny casualness, sketching a warm relationship between a single mother, Jeanine (Carmen Maura), and her 10-year-old son Martin (Jeremy Kreikenmayer). Unfortunately for Martin, she has decided that it's best to send her son, born out of wedlock, to live with his father, Victor (Pierre Maguelon). He's a stern patriarch, a provincial upper bourgeois in his 60s whose home is a fine old manor house in the country.

Victor proves formidable, but his wife Lucie (Marthe Villalonga) accepts Martin in a matter-of-fact and not unkind way; he is not her husband's only offspring outside marriage, but only Martin's mother has been determined enough to see that Victor gives her son his name and makes Martin part of his family. Jeanine has sacrificed her son for what she believes will be in his own good, but Martin and Victor are at odds from the start.

These developments unfold with unsettling dispatch, capped by the announcement that 10 years have gone by. Preceded by some disturbing fragmented images and snatches of dialogue, we then see the 20-year-old Martin (Alexis Loret) running out of the house, eventually making his way to Paris, where he crashes with his closest half-brother, Benjamin (Mathieu Amalric), a struggling actor who shares a tiny apartment with Alice (Juliette Binoche), a dedicated violinist.

It is clear Martin has undergone some profoundly traumatic experience, but he responds to Benjamin's loving concern and experiences a rush of attraction for the beautiful, poised Alice, somewhat older than he and infinitely more mature.

The good-looking Martin quickly breaks into high-fashion modeling. Caught up in the swirl of workaday Paris, Martin is on the verge of being happy. Alice resists Martin's awkward overtures; she tells him she's not attracted to "cute boys," and besides, she has a warm, sustaining relationship with Benjamin, who is gay. She and Benjamin enjoy casual sex outside their relationship. Martin nevertheless persists, and Alice eventually succumbs.

All of this is essentially prologue, for when Martin's troubled emotional past catches up with him the film shifts focus to Alice and her commitment to saving him, which means overcoming the hostility of his relatives, all of whom have their reasons for feeling about Martin as they do.

What emerges from all this highly charged interaction is a sense of paradox about how people with emotional or blood ties or both can be so sustaining of one another yet also so destructive. Alice exemplifies love at its most selfless, yet in Binoche's exquisite portrayal she comes across, not as a noble martyr, but as a strong adult, clear-eyed and practical, who understands the commitment and responsibility that love entails.

Villalonga's Lucie proves to be as staunch and forthright in her way as Alice. These two formidable actresses—Villalonga will be remembered as Catherine Deneuve and Daniel Auteuil's doughty mother in "Ma Saison"—are well-complemented by Maura and by Loret, whose Martin remains sympathetic even when taxing, and Amalric, whose Benjamin is consistently the film's most likable and buoyant presence.

Caroline Champetier's camera work could scarcely be more expressive or supportive, flowing easily between scenes of intimacy and longer shots that convey a larger perspective. Techine's "Alice and Martin" is at all times supple and assured, alternately bravura and understated in its movements and images. It is the work of a master filmmaker at the height of his powers.

NEW YORK, 7/31/00, P. 52, Peter Rainer

André Téchiné the director and a co-writer of *Alice and Martin*, has one of the most rapturously lyrical film techniques around. His early works, such as *French Provincial* and *Barocco*, or, more recently, *Wild Reeds,* are pure bliss-outs. *Alice and Martin* ought to be one, too, since it's essentially a depiction of *amour fou:* Martin (Alexis Loret), running away from his damaged past, is swept up by Alice (Juliette Binoche), a violinist who lives in Paris. Though Alice initially seems closed off, Martin's extensive turmoils turn her on. Their love is meant to be a grand folly, but both Alice and Martin are too opaque to raise temperatures. It makes sense that Martin becomes a male model in Paris: He's all surface. When he's pained, it's as if he were *advertising* anguish. Juliette Binoche is a much more resonant performer, but in a way she's an advertisement, too: She might be pitching a new *parfum*, Despair. Despite some glorious passages, *Alice and Martin* is play-act passion.

NEW YORK POST, 7/21/00, p. 51, Jonathan Foreman

"Alice and Martin" is best watched while doing a crossword or reading the paper.

It starts promisingly, but after the first hour, the only things that really hold your attention are some attractive locations in Spain and southern France.

Certainly the two main characters are too thinly sketched, and their relationship too opaque to be very interesting. It's hard to believe that Andre Techine, the director of 1995's superb "Wild Reeds" could also have made such a banal, confused, and, in the end, unsatisfying melodrama.

It starts with Martin (Jeremy Kreikenmayer) as a 10-year-old being raised by his mother (Carmen Maura) in a small French town. Suddenly she decides that he would be better off living with Victor (Pierre Maguelon) the wealthy father he has never met and sends him away.

Abruptly flash forward to Martin 12 years later (Alexis Loret). He's now some kind of unshaven runaway hiding out in the countryside, stealing eggs from farms until getting caught and arrested.

Then, just as suddenly, we see Martin arriving in Paris to stay with his gay half-brother Benjamin (Mathieu Amalric) and Benjamin's best friend Alice (Juliette Binoche). Benjamin is a struggling actor who works as a security guard, Alice is a violinist.

Even though Martin is a sullen, uncommunicative youth beloved by artsy filmmakers, Benjamin and Alice take him in.

And within a few days Martin finds work as a fashion model. He also hooks up with Alice. But thanks to some tiresome mood swings it quickly becomes apparent even to Alice that Martin is burdened by some kind of dark TV-movie-style secret.

Unfortunately, when you find out through a combination of flashbacks and Alice's investigations, just what that secret is, it's kind of a letdown. For an actress with Binoche's powerful arsenal, this kind of suffering, devoted role isn't difficult and she does her best to give you something to watch even when there's no dialogue. Loret's part—the silent, brooding pretty boy—is more thankless and less interesting.

NEWSDAY, 7/21/00, Part II/p. B12, Jan Stuart

"Alice and Martin" is one of those petulant French movies in which you feel the itch to slap each of the characters at least once before it's over. Directed by Andre Techine, who gave us the petulant but poetic "Wild Reeds," it reinforces the filmmaker's sensitivity to youthful alienation but without the dynamism that made that earlier film such a turn-on.

The disaffection of the 19-year-old Martin, (Alexis Loret) is steeped in mystery. Having been dispatched by his mother (Carmen Maura) at an early age to be raised by his punitive father, Victor (Pierre Maguelon), and his wife, Lucie (Marthe Villalonga), Martin abruptly flees from home upon the death of his father. After living like a wild child in the woods, he takes up residence in the Parisian flat of his half-brother Benjamin (Mathieu Amalric) and Benjamin's musician roommate Alice (Juliette Binoche).

Martin keeps mum about his recent strange behavior as fortune smiles and he effortlessly becomes one of Paris' hottest fashion models. Willful and untouched by the glamour of his new milieu, he seduces the older, reluctant Alice, This is not an issue for Benjamin, who is gay and seems more irked by his half-brother's flash success in view of his own protracted struggle to make it as an actor.

That's pretty much it. Techine stretches these basic plot elements every which way for two hours, as Martin's moodiness and evasiveness hang like a cloud over his relationships with Alice (who becomes pregnant) and Benjamin (who mangles Broadway show tunes at the piano). Another half-brother surfaces and disappears just as suddenly, ostensibly to underscore the impact of Victor's reign of terror over his sons. Arguably more detestable is the mousy Lucie, who turns a blind eye to her husband's abuses.

Techine revels in broad narrative jumps that leave the audience in a perpetual state of "Huh?" Every 't' will be crossed and 'i' dotted before the final frame, but you may be too drained by the sheer heaviness of "Alice and Martin" to care.

NEWSWEEK, 8/7/00, p. 72, David Ansen

No brief plot synopsis can adequately summarize André Téchiné's gripping "Alice and Martin." It unfolds in time-hopping, elliptical style, dropping its psychological clues like bread crumbs in a dense forest of narrative. Téchiné, who has become, late in his career, one of the masters of French film ("Wild Reeds," "My Favorite Season"), never wastes time with the formulaic: it's the complexities and ambiguities of relationships that inspire his charged, lyrical cinema.

The mystery here is Martin (Alexis Loret), a troubled young man from the provinces who flees to Paris to live with his gay half brother, Benjamin (Mathieu Amalric). Sharing Benjamin's dumpy apartment and his life is violinist Alice (Juliette Binoche). Martin finds sudden, unexpected success as a model—a career that accentuates the blankness that seems to be at his core. Obsessed with Alice, who separates her feelings from her sexuality, Martin eventually wins her love—only to push her away and retreat into madness when she becomes pregnant. There's a guilty secret in his past he must purge before he can come back to life.

Shot and edited with crisp flair, "Alice and Martin" keeps flying off in unexpected directions, anchored by Binoche's dark, obstinate passion. Loret doesn't have her weight on screen, and his inexperience keeps the movie from achieving its full potential. But Téchiné's filmmaking dances circles around most current directors: next to the novelistic richness of this fascinating, flawed movie, most of this summer's fare looks like kid stuff.

SIGHT AND SOUND, 12/99, p. 36, Chris Darke

Ten-year-old Martin Sauvagnac's mother encourages him to visit his father Victor whom he's never met before. Although illegitimate, Martin stays and grows up with his half-brothers: François, Frédéric and Benjamin. Ten years pass. Martin flees the family house after the death of his father. After living rough he turns up at Benjamin's Paris flat which he shares with his friend Alice. Martin moves in and becomes a model. He and Alice become a couple.

While visiting Spain, Alice tells Martin she's pregnant. He collapses and is hospitalised. They move into a small cottage by the sea where he recovers. Terrified by fatherhood, Martin reveals to Alice the cause of his father's death. When François committed suicide, Martin planned to leave, unable to participate in the family's grief. In a struggle with Victor, Martin accidentally pushed him down the stairs.

Convinced he's guilty of murder, Martin has himself committed to a psychiatric clinic. Alice tries to deliver a letter from him to his stepmother Lucie but encounters obstruction from Frédéric. Martin decides to hand himself over to the police and asks Lucie to testify as a witness. Benjamin tells Alice that, because of Frédéric's political ambitions, the family is obliged to testify and Martin will be tried. Alice returns to Paris and Martin is discharged from the clinic. He turns himself over to the police and is detained. Alice waits for the birth of their child.

With his thirteenth feature, André Téchiné conducts a masterly dissection of male hysteria. From the outset Martin, the illegitimate son of a wealthy provincial bourgeois family, is damaged goods. The short opening sequence sketching his childhood has Martin attempting to persuade his father he's ill. Victor Sauvagnac, the cold, business-like patriarch who sired Martin on a local hairdresser and then denied his existence for ten years, refuses to believe him. From here on in the film charts first the symptoms and then the causes of Martin's frail psychological state.

In fact, most of the major characters are scarred by family histories. After his father's death—shown in a lengthy flashback—Martin flees into the countryside where he hides like a hunted animal, eventually making his way to Paris where he meets his half-brother Benjamin's flatmate Alice. An initially brittle and impatient presence, she describes the curious interloper as "an extra-terrestrial hobo". Alice herself is psychologically delicate; her sister died young, leaving her to negotiate warring feelings of residual grief and filial jealousy. But her life with Benjamin, a struggling gay actor played by Mathieu Amalric as the livewire black sheep of the Sauvagnac family, has allowed them both to find an asexual equilibrium. "We take turns at being each other's child," is Benjamin's analysis of their relationship. Nonetheless, this quasi-parental affection transmutes into barely repressed anger and bitterness when Alice and Martin become a couple and the causes of his distress emerge. Téchiné has been here before, most recently in *Les Voleurs*, where he explored the internal dynamics of a crime dynasty. It was the generic element of that film which felt a little forced but its family resemblance to *Alice et Martin* is clear. There's the same concern with an oppressive family inheritance, but here the issues of law and the 'family business' are more subtly interrelated.

Téchiné explicitly treats the film as a case study. When Alice asks Martin to tell her about his 'flight' from the family, she uses the French word *fugue*. The word carries a psychoanalytic connotation, describing the state in which a subject loses awareness of his identity and flees his usual environment. Indeed, the film is another French examination of a young man's growth, via crisis, to responsibility and maturity. Martin's anxieties are triggered by Alice's pregnancy, which unleashes a double-barrelled stock of guilt relating to his half-brother François' suicide and Martin's 'parricide'. Téchiné structurally underscores this by having the explanatory flashback begin the moment Martin touches Alice's growing belly.

Dense and powerful in its emotional force, *Alice et Martin*'s melodrama is tempered by superb performances. Newcomer Alexis Loret is shifty, pale and sympathetic as Martin, while Juliette Binoche (whom Téchiné directed once before in *Rendez-vous*, 1985, early in her career) develops Alice with a charged finesse, undertaking her quest with the full realisation that she too has a path to adult love before her, via Martin's self-realisation. If this is literary film-making it is the best kind, from the richness of its characterisation to the acuity of its structure. Both a cold melodrama and a psyched-up Bressonian case study, *Alice et Martin* is a masterly opening-up of classical French *intimiste* themes.

VILLAGE VOICE, 7/25/00, p. 128, Dennis Lim

For at least an hour, Andre Téchiné's latest psychological melodrama, *Alice and Martin,* gains momentum through disorientation. The film opens with 10-year-old Martin being dispatched by his hairdresser mother (Carmen Maura) to live with his wealthy, despotic father. The boy's unhappiness in his new environment instantly established, Téchiné makes an abrupt 10-year leap to the grown Martin (Alexis Loret) fleeing the family compound, and follows this with a wordless passage of the young fugitive staggering across the countryside in a daze (he tries to drown himself, devours raw eggs stolen from a chicken coop, stares transfixed as birds rip into a rotting deer carcass). And then, just as suddenly, Martin shows up in Paris, at the doorstep of his gay half-brother Benjamin (Mathieu Amalric) and his neurotic violinist roommate Alice (Juliette Binoche).

Alice and Martin do eventually get together, and Téchiné sketches the arc of their courtship in restless, anxious ellipses—and with no small measure of dry humor. The absurdly beautiful Martin finds work as a fashion model and takes to stalking Alice, who's perplexed by his clumsy, puppyish attentions—and by his recent elevation to public sex object. (In one droll scene, the "face of Lancôme" looks up in wonder at a series of Martin's cologne ads flashing by her on the Metro.) The lurching narrative generates an unsettling rhythm, forcing a closer examination of the obscure motivations and complex desires at work. Needless to say, Martin's dark secret, the trauma that so discombobulated him in the first place, returns to haunt him, and the film. Téchiné provides an extended flashback to the circumstances surrounding the death of Martin's father, then shifts the focus to Alice's attempts to comprehend and finally come to terms with her lover's consuming guilt and self-hatred.

The clunkily inserted flashback is a questionable strategy, but *Alice and Martin,* like much recent Téchiné thrives on vivid incidentals and telling details. Even as the plot crescendos to a soap-operatic pitch, the turbulence never feels less than organic or spontaneous—not least because of Téchiné's tropistic attraction to big, messy emotions and because his characters are so fully and compassionately drawn. Here it's not just the titular relationship but also the one between Alice and Benjamin that resonates—a believable symbiotic friendship between a straight woman and a gay man, rendered not as sitcom premise or *Vanity Fair* cover story, without recourse to stereotypes and with a good deal of affection.

Téchiné, who gave Binoche her first leading role in *Rendez-Vous,* could eventually do for the star what he's done for the middle-aged Catherine Deneuve—a liberating glamour bypass. Loret gives his freak-outs an agonized opacity, and the quicksilver Amalric turns the most random acts into comic grace notes—manically sucking face on a dance floor, executing a petulant dive into shallow waters after a poolside squabble (neatly echoing Bill Murray's lugubrious plunge in *Rushmore*). *Alice and Martin*'s outsize proportions can seem daunting or corny, but the shiny melodramatic surface is misleading. Téchiné, typically honest and generous, always allows the churning emotional undercurrents to take over.

Also reviewed in:
CHICAGO TRIBUNE, 9/1/00, Friday/p. A, Michael Wilmington
NEW YORK TIMES, 7/21/00, p. E10, A.O. Scott
NEW YORKER, 7/31/00, p. 84, Anthony Lane
VARIETY, 11/9-15/98, p. 34, Jonathan Holland
WASHINGTON POST, 8/4/00, p. C1, Stephen Hunter
WASHINGTON POST, 8/4/00, Weekend/p. 39, Desson Howe

ALL I WANNA DO

A Redeemable Features release of an Alliance Communications presentation of a Redeemable Features production. *Executive Producer:* Andras Hamori, Robert Lantos and Nora Ephron. *Producer:* Ira Deutchman and Peter Newman. *Director:* Sarah Kernochan. *Screenplay:* Sarah Kernochan. *Director of Photography:* Anthony C. Jannelli. *Editor:* Peter Frank. *Music:* Graeme Revell. *Music Editor:* Ashley Revell. *Sound:* Brian Avery. *Sound Editor:* Jane Tattersall. *Casting:* Ali Farrell and Laura Rosenthal. *Production Designer:* John Kasarda. *Art Director:* Kim Karon. *Special Effects:* Frank C. Carere. *Costumes:* Julie Ganton and Ann Hould-Ward. *Make-up:* Marie Nardella. *Running time:* 94 minutes. *MPAA Rating:* PG-13.

CAST: Kirsten Dunst (Verena Von Stefan); Gaby Hoffmann (Odette Sinclair); Lynn Redgrave (Miss McVane); Rachael Leigh Cook (Abby Sawyer); Thomas Guiry (Frosty Frost); Vincent Kartheiser (Snake); Monica Keena (Tinka Parker); Matthew Lawrence (Dennis); Heather Matarazzo (Tweety Goldberg); Merritt Wever (Momo Haines); Robert Bockstael (Mr. Dewey); Brenda Devine (Miss Phipps); Rosemary Dunsmore (Page Sawyer); Nigel Bennett (Harvey Sawyer); Jenny Parsons (Mrs. Dewey); Dorothy Gordon (Mrs. O'Boyle); Michael Reynolds (Mr. Armstrong); Caterina Scorsone (Susie); Michael Barry (Possum); Zachary Bennett (Skunk); Aaron Poole (Beagle); Danny Smith (Groundhog); Noah Shebib (Conrad Bateman); Paul Nolan (Schumacher); Hayden Christensen (Tinka's Date); Christopher Redmond (Danforth); Shawn Ashmore (Photographer); Jack Duffy (School Guard); Richard McMillan (Bert Chubb); Les Porter (Choirmaster); Antonia de Portago (Mlle. Mercier); Nicu Branzea (Tomas); Barbara Radecki (Tinka's Mother); Paula Barrett (Odie's Mother); Robert Bidaman (Verena's Father); Phoebe Lapine (Tinka's Sister); Margaret E. Chieffo (Student Monitor); Simone Rosenberg (Herald Tribune Girl); Tania Harbick (Girl at Dance); Ray Doucette (Trustee); Tino Monte (TV Reporter); Gayle Redshaw (Hockey Mistress); Roger Dunn (Police Captain); Holly Sedgwick and Vickie Pays (Mothers); Trevor Bain and Michael Eric Kramer (Fathers); Robin Dunne (Todd Winslow).

NEW YORK POST, 3/24/00, p. 50, Jonathan Foreman

"All I Wanna Do" was originally titled "Strike!" and later "The Hairy Bird."
Why they changed the name during the two years the film has sat on the shelf isn't clear, but the movie should be subtitled: "The half-remembered education of an upper-class '60s feminist, disguised as a slow, insipid comedy and shot through with politically correct anachronisms."

Essentially a consciousness-raising lecture aimed at 13-year-old girls—a group the film assumes are too dumb and undiscriminating not to love its creaky, hokey jokes—it often feels like it was actually written by a precocious but humorless teen.

Preachy and mostly joyless, it all-too-quickly becomes clear why this movie had its release delayed. And then you have to sit through 90 minutes that feel like three hours.

A strong cast that includes Kirsten Dunst and Lynn Redgrave is wasted.

VILLAGE VOICE, 3/28/00, p. 120, Amy Taubin

A smart, sweet, and altogether smashing evocation of teenage girlhood, *All I Wanna Do* is based on writer-director Sarah Kernochan's early-'60s experiences at Rosemary Hall, an upper-class all-girls boarding school that succumbed to economic pressures and went coed several years after she graduated. Kernochan has used the conflicts that arose from this proposed change of identity to focus her plot, but the liberties she takes with the '60s time line will be evident only to those whose memories are as vivid as her own. Given the post-pill but pre-Beatles and definitely pre-counterculture moment, Kernochan's young women exhibit extraordinary prescience when they occupy a building to protest their exclusion from the decision about the school's future.

This quibble aside, *All I Wanna Do* is a teen movie that mothers might enjoy as much as their daughters. It combines the most inspirational aspects of sisterhood with recklessly abandoned, hormonally propelled behavior and a barfing scene that's funnier than anything in, well, name your own favorite teen-boy movie. Here too, it's the boys that barf, but it's the girls that bring this embarrassment upon them by spiking their punch with ipecac. Not that these girls aren't interested in the opposite sex; they just don't want "to live in the shadow of the hairy bird." The film's original title was, in fact, *The Hairy Bird*, and the euphemism perfectly captures the pungent put-down style of its heroines; the generic *All I Wanna Do*, on the other hand, is indistinguishable from a hundred other recent titles and may doom this unique picture to a quick video release. The echoes of *The Prime of Miss Jean Brodie* and *The Belles of St Trinians* notwithstanding, *All I Wanna Do*'s combination of privileged upbringing and proto-feminist insight is almost without precedent. Its closest ally is the more broadly satiric *Clueless*.

A screenwriter often called upon to flesh out women's roles (her cowriting credits include *9 ½ Weeks* and *Sommersby*), Kernochan uses her first stint at the helm to protect the subtlety and toughness of her script rather than to show off a distinct directorial style. I'll remember a dozen lines from *All I Wanna Do*, but probably not a single image. That said, she maintains a lively pace and gets vivid performances from her young cast. The opening credit, "This is a film by everyone who worked on it," is not only a deft swipe at the inflated egos of indie auteurs—a vast preponderance of them male—but also a setup for the creative interplay that animates the narrative.

Gaby Hoffmann, the real-life daughter of two '60s superstars, Viva and Abbie, Hoffmann, plays Odette (a/k/a Odious), the unusually sophisticated and brilliant new girl in school. Odette's confidence and her collections of r&b records and Pappagallo shoes qualify her for membership in the DAR (Daughters of the American Ravioli). The name derives from the attic supply room where this subversive group holds its meetings. The leader of the DAR is Verena (Kirsten Dunst), whose talent for exposing hypocrisy is taxed to its limit by the school board's secret scheme to go coed. Verena's similarly blonde but otherwise opposite number is Tinka (Monica Keena), whose ambition is to become a famous artist/folksinger/slut. As the headmistress, Lynn Redgrave mixes propriety with an admiration for freethinking. The girls of the DAR are more to her liking than the officious campus monitor (Rachael Leigh Cook) whose mission in life is to get them expelled. Jealousy, anger, confusion about sex, and the desire for revenge are not absent from *All I Wanna Do*, but sisterhood wins hands down.

Also reviewed in:
NEW YORK TIMES, 3/24/00, p. E14, A.O. Scott
VARIETY, 8/31-9/6/98, p. 96, Ken Eisner

ALL THE PRETTY HORSES

A Miramax Films and Columbia Pictures release. *Executive Producer:* Sally Menke and Jonathan Gordon. *Producer:* Billy Bob Thornton and Robert Salerno. *Director:* Billy Bob Thornton. *Screenplay:* Ted Tally. *Based on the novel by:* Cormac McCarthy. *Director of Photography:* Barry Markowitz. *Editor:* Sally Menke. *Music:* Marty Stuart. *Music Editor:* Jay B. Richardson and Daniel Gaber. *Sound:* Paul Ledford and (music): Jim Mitchell. *Sound Editor:* Stephen Hunter Flick and Peter A. Brown. *Casting:* Mary Vernieu and Anne McCarthy. *Production Designer:* Clark Hunter. *Art Director:* Richard Johnson and Max Biscoe. *Set Designer:* Thomas Minton. *Set Decorator:* Traci Kirshbaum. *Set Dresser:* Rhonda Paynter. *Special Effects:* Margaret Johnson. *Costumes:* Doug Hall. *Make-up:* Lynne Eagan. *Stunt Coordinator:* Buddy Van Horn. *Running time:* 112 minutes. *MPAA Rating:* PG-13.

CAST: Matt Damon (John Grady Cole);   Henry Thomas (Lacey Rawlins);   Angelina Torres (Luisa);   J.D. Young (Grandfather);   Laura Poe (Mother);   Sam Shepard (J. C. Franklin); Robert Patrick (Cole);   Lucas Black (Jimmy Blevins);   Yvette Diaz (Girl);   Imelda Colindres (Girl's Mom);   Augustin Solis (Manuel);   Penélope Cruz (Alejandra);   Rubén Blades (Rocha); Elizabeth Ibarra (Maria);   Miriam Colon (Alfonsa);   Lonnie Rodriguez (Esteban);   Daniel Lanois and Raul Malo (Singers);   Fredrik Lopez (Lieutenant);   Ferron Lucero, Jr. and Manuel Sanchez (Lieutenant's Men);   Denes Lujan (Orlando);   Julio Oscar Mechoso (Captain);   Edwin Figueroa (Charro);   Matthew E. Montoya (Indian);   Julian Prada (Prison Singer);   Roberto Enrique Pineda (Doctor);   Vincente Ramos (Commandante);   George R. Lopez (Clapping Man); J.D. Garfield (Carlos);   Julio Cedillo (Campesino);   Marc Miles (Deputy Smith);   Brian Orr (Man at Car); Bruce Dern (Judge).

LOS ANGELES TIMES, 12/25/00, Calendar/p. 1, Kenneth Turan

While in general the key to value in real estate is location, location, location, the value in the specific West Texas real estate created by novelist Cormac McCarthy in "All The Pretty Horses" is a bit different: language, language, language.

McCarthy's award-winning book is one of the most beautifully written of the last 10 years, an intoxicating example of words at play. Billy Bob Thornton's respectful version of the novel stars Matt Damon and Penelope Cruz and tries, with some success, to do right by an author the director clearly admires. The film is handsomely mounted, with no end of heroic vistas shot by Barry Markowitz. But the demands of drama on the screen are different than that on the page. More simply, what makes for a great novel does not necessarily make for a great film.

The problem is that even with the benefit of a careful Ted Tally adaptation that leans heavily on the dialogue of the book, this film inevitably has to do without the glow the original language provides. With that gone, even though "Pretty Horses' " much-publicized two-hour running time plays exactly right, what's left at any length is by definition stripped down, a reduction of the book to its acceptable but not necessarily thrilling core plot and themes.

Pared down this way, "Pretty Horses" turns out to be a tribute/mash note to the mythic West, to the time when horses were horses and men, given to cauterizing wounds with red-hot pistols, were very much men. Even though one of the points here is that this era is ending before our eyes, there is still enough guys-doing-what-guys-have-to-do material to make "Pretty Horses" play like a sacred journey through the venerated traditions of the Cowboy Way.

Aside from being insistently masculine, "Pretty Horses" is too deliberate and magisterial to fully involve us. Though its characters are in the habit of losing their heads to passion, the film itself is too restrained to follow their lead. In an odd way "Pretty Horses" has been too faithful to the spirit of this somber, fatalistic, melancholy romance, too much a stubborn ode to stoicism, to light any emotional fires.

It all begins in the West Texas town of San Angelo in 1949. Young John Grady Cole (Damon) has to face the reality that with his grandfather dead, his mother is determined to sell the ranch he's grown up on, the place he considers heaven on earth, and there's nothing he can do to stop her.

Both John Grady and his best friend Lacey Rawlins (a very steady Henry Thomas) decide to act on their impulsive dream of crossing the border and going to Mexico. There are ranches down there, or so they've been told, so big you can't ride from end to end in a week. Surely, the Spanish-speaking John Grady figures, there would be situations down there for two top hands.

Before they get out of Texas, however, the boys find themselves followed by the even younger more-hat-than-cowboy Jimmy Blevins (Lucas Black, the star of Thornton's "Sling Blade"). Irascible and hot-tempered with a mysterious past, Blevins wants to join up with them. But though you'd have to be a fool not to agree with Lacey when he says he gets a "uneasy feeling" about Blevins, John Grady lets him tag along.

After some trouble inevitably involving Blevins, the two friends manage to get jobs at La Purisima, an enormous, 27,000-acre establishment that's been in the family of owner Rocha (Ruben Blades) for 170 years. With his equine skill and knowledge, John Grady soon becomes a protege of Rocha's and also finds himself desperately attracted to his young daughter Alejandra (Cruz).

How could he not be? Dark and capricious to John Grady's even-tempered blondness, Alejandra is not only everything the boy is not but also a major flirt and powerfully attractive. An innocent (the book pegs him at 16) who knows more about horses than life, John Grady is fated to ignore Lacey's sensible analysis ("I don't see you holding no aces, bud") and plunge headlong into the abyss.

Damon is well-cast and does solid work as the straight-arrow John Grady, and the same is true for the gorgeous Cruz. There is even measurable on-screen chemistry between them, but, true to the book and despite what the ads indicate, their relationship, however crucial, does not occupy a large amount of screen time. And when John Grady is alone or with male acquaintances, being brave, laconic, archetypal, whatever, his virtues may be heroic but our emotional involvement with him is not on a similarly epic scale.

NEW YORK, 1/8/01, p. 48, Peter Rainer

Most movies take a while to slip you into a stupor. *All the Pretty Horses* makes you groggy right away. Set in 1949, it's a lackadaisical series of vignettes apparently culled from a much longer movie that never made it to the screen. Be thankful for that. Perhaps it should not be held against Billy Bob Thornton, who directed from a script by Ted Tally, that the film never approximates the fragranced, laconic tone of the Cormac McCarthy novel on which it's based. Such an achievement is likely beyond the reach of any filmmaker, and probably should remain that way: Westerns, after all, are generally best when they're not so highfalutin. But small-scale does not have to mean, as it does here, small-time. The film works only fitfully as a coming-of-age ramble, starring Matt Damon as John Grady Cole, who rides out from Texas to Mexico with his buddy Lacey (Henry Thomas) and keeps getting hit upside the head with life lessons. Like the mustangs he breaks while working on a sprawling Mexican ranch, Cole yearns to run wild. (Mustangs haven't been saddled with this much metaphor in the movies since *The Misfits.*) As embodied by Penélope Cruz, the daughter of the wealthy ranch owner is the most prized of animals in Cole's line of sight, but her shared passion for him, which is supposed to be torrid, is tepid. We keep seeing what was intended in this film: the contrasts between untamed wilderness and civilization, the elegiac valedictory to the passing of the West, the crucibles of courage that make you a better man, and so on. None of it sinks in, because the landscapes have not been chosen with a painter's eye—they're rather blurry and ill-framed—and because the performances are far from grand. (There is one remarkable piece of acting, from Lucas Black as a troublesome, crack-voiced runaway.) To make a movie eulogizing the past, and its passing, it would be helpful to have a stronger sense of the present. *All the Pretty Horses* seems to be taking place in a hazy, remembered movieland of the mind.

NEW YORK POST, 12/22/00, p. 54, Lou Lumenick

"All the Pretty Horses" never really gets out of the starting gate.

Not the disaster its troubled history might suggest, this picturesque western drama has some admirable elements. But overall it's likely to leave all but the most ardent fans of Matt Damon and novelist Cormac McCarthy shaking their heads in puzzlement—if they don't nod off first.

In some ways, Billy Bob Thornton's latest as a director is this year's "Snow Falling on Cedars"—a beautiful if narratively foggy coffee-table book of a movie based on a popular novel about forbidden love and betrayal, set in the middle of the 20th century.

This time the setting is mainly Mexico, where John Grady Cole (Damon) has ridden on horseback with his buddy Lacey Rawlins (Henry Thomas) after John gets thrown off the family ranch in Texas in an inheritance dispute.

After many beautifully photographed vignettes that add up to little, they end up as hands on a massive hacienda presided over by Rocha (Ruben Blades). John falls for Rocha's beautiful daughter Alejandra (Penelope Cruz), much to the annoyance of her grandmother Alfonsa (Miriam Colon).

For reasons that may be clearer to audience members who have read McCarthy's novel than those who are struggling with the huge story gaps, John and Lacey end up in a Mexican prison, where they are reunited with Jimmy Blevins (Lucas Black), a teenage horse thief they met up with on the way to Mexico.

"All the Pretty Horses" is 116 minutes long, reportedly cut from an original running time of nearly four hours.

What's left are some pretty pictures, some nice dialogue (courtesy of McCarthy and screenwriter Ted Tally) and some very decent performances. Damon seems more comfortable, and is more convincing, as a cowhand than he was as a golfer his most recent period epic, "The Legend of Bagger Vance."

Henry Thomas does some of his best work since "E.T.," but unfortunately disappears for long stretches. But the most entertaining acting is by Black, the phenomenon from Thornton's debut film, "Sling Blade."

"All the Pretty Horses" is being sold as a romance, and on that level it disappoints immensely. There are no sparks whatsoever between Damon and Cruz, who has little to do but look beautiful in her very brief screen time.

NEWSDAY, 12/22/00, Part II/p. B8, Jan Stuart

You don't have to be old to feel out of sync with your day, to yearn for a time when houses had porches and men wore hats and seldom was heard a discouraging word. There are millions of young people who feel as if they were born decades too late. And they should be able to hook right into Matt Damon's dilemma in "All the Pretty Horses."

Damon plays John Grady Cole, a scion of generations of Texas ranchers, who realizes he is already an anachronism in 1949, when his parents divorce and the family spread is sold off to oil interests. It's an end-of-an-era scenario worthy of Chekhov: Indeed, it would be fitting if John's mother (who "wants to be in the live thee-ay-ter") wound up in some San Antonio community production of "The Cherry Orchard."

Determined to live out the cowboy's life as his granddaddy knew it, Cole sets out on horseback for Mexico with his buddy Rawlins (Henry Thomas) in search of unspoiled open spaces and some honest work. Their idealistic intentions are challenged when they are joined by an impulsive teenager (Lucas Black) who implicates them in a horse theft before they are barely over the Rio Grande border.

So begins Billy Bob Thornton's visually bountiful and lushly plotted screen adaptation of Cormac McCarthy's novel, which follows the two friends as they find employment with a wealthy Mexican rancher (Ruben Blades). Ted Tally's screenplay gets the off-the-cuff poetry and shuffling cowpoke-speak of McCarthy's protagonist, who unwisely pursues a clandestine romance with his employer's beautiful daughter, Maria, played by international traffic-stopper, Penelope Cruz.

Thornton is a first-rate storyteller who knows how to key up our anxieties over things about to spill ("One False Move" and the upcoming "Gift"). We sense he identifies with Cole, whose easy heart gets him and his friend into trouble more than once. In contrast to his languorous directing debut, "Sling Blade," Thornton seems almost too eager to move things along here. McCarthy's winding tale contains enough turbulence to power three movies—the second half kicks into a "Shawshank Redemption" gear—and the result can feel crowded and choppy at times.

But the film's swift, page-turning gait carries us with it, and it's nice to see Matt Damon in confident form after the ill-fitting demands of "The Talented Mr. Ripley." It's also refreshing to see him play off someone besides the overhyped Mr. Affleck. Henry Thomas gives an admirable performance. The former "E.T." kid has grown into a handsome critter; he wears the petulant mask well and doesn't hog the camera. But we could have lived without the coda in which kindly judge Bruce Dern offers succor to the dispirited Damon. It smacks of a therapy session, leaving us with the unfortunate final impression that Freud is to blame for the end of cowboy days.

NEWSWEEK, 12/25/00-1/1/00, p. 74, David Ansen

It's always dangerous turning a beloved novel into a film; its fans are likely to resent anyone's hijacking their own private images of the tale. In the case of a book as writerly as Cormac McCarthys "All the Pretty Horses," there's no way a filmmaker can find a visual correlative for such serpentine sentences, for rhetoric that can soar as high as a hawk over the Mexican landscapes where two young Texas boys go riding in search of adventure.

What you're left with is the story, and how well you tell it. In Billy Bob Thornton's handsome, morosely romantic, but ultimately disjointed Western, Matt Damon is John Grady Cole and Henry Thomas is his best friend, Lacey, the two lads who, displaced from their Texas ranch in 1949, wend their way to the vast estate of a rich Mexican (Rubén Blades). There, Cole is hired to break the landowner's wild horses. There, though he's warned not to, he falls in love with the man's beautiful daughter (Penélope Cruz), a dangerous move that will lead to his violent coming of age.

Thornton had bitter fights over the editing of his movie, which shrank from its first cut of four hours to its final two-hour shape. The result is a movie of arresting pieces that don't harmonize into a satisfying whole. The dialogue captures McCarthy's tangy, laconic tongue (Ted Tally did the adaptation), and the landscapes dazzle. But "All the Pretty Horses" comes fully alive only when young Lucas Black is on the scene. He plays the volatile teenager Blevins, who tags along with Cole and Lacey, bringing them bad luck at every turn. This skinny, scruffy, quicksilver young actor sneakily steals the show.

SIGHT AND SOUND, 3/01, p. 38, Edward Buscombe

West Texas, 1949. Homeless after his estranged mother has sold the ranch on which he lived with his late grandfather, John Grady Cole decides to seek adventure in Mexico with his friend Lacey Rawlins. They ride across the Rio Grande, and soon meet Blevins, a youth who has run away from home. Blevins loses his horse and pistol; attempting to retrieve it from a Mexican he is chased off into the darkness.

Cole and Rawlins ride on and find work on a Mexican ranch. Cole's expertise with horses wins him the trust of the owner, but his secret affair with the rancher's daughter, Alejandra, puts them at risk. When the rancher leaves for Mexico City, Cole and Rawlins are arrested; in jail they are reunited with Blevins, who has been caught and beaten after killing one of his pursuers. After interrogation all three are driven into the countryside, where Blevins is executed by a police captain.

Cole and Rawlins are sent to prison, and Rawlins is nearly killed in a knife fight. Later Cole is set upon, but he has secured a knife and kills his opponents. Eventually they are released from prison on the orders of the rancher. Alejandra has promised never to speak to Cole again. Cole returns alone to the ranch and persuades the girl's great aunt to give him her phone number. They meet, but Alejandra cannot bring herself to break her promise to renounce him. Cole takes the police captain hostage, and though shot in the leg gets back the three horses the Americans had ridden into Mexico. Near exhaustion, he is aided by an old man whom he had befriended in jail, whose companions take the captain away to extract revenge for the old man's treatment. Cole rides back to the US, where he has to explain his possession of the horses to a kindly judge. He is reunited with Rawlins, whom he finds feeding chickens on a lonely farm.

Until now, perhaps the nearest equivalent in film to Cormac McCarthy's powerful, sometimes brutal 'Border Trilogy' (All the Pretty Horses, The Crossing and Cities of the Plain) was Sam Peckinpah's excoriating Bring Me the Head of Alfredo Garcia (1974). Peckinpah is also the only director whom one can remotely imagine tackling McCarthy's nightmarish earlier masterpiece of the Texas border country, Blood Meridian, or The Evening Redness in the West. But this liminal theme has been a fruitful one in the Western. Two notable examples, less extreme, more nuanced, are Robert Parrish's *The Wonderful Country* (1959) and Fred Schepisi's *Barbarosa* (1982). In both, a youthful American is marked for ever by crossing the Rio Grande.

"This is another country," Mexican matriarch Dona Alfonsa says to Cole, the young Texan who has come to work on her family ranch. Mexico has always been the Western's dark unconscious. South of the border and below the belt, it is a place where unwonted emotions and unbridled desires assault the innocent American, bringing danger and sometimes death. For Cole and his friend Rawlins it holds all the fear and fascination of the unknown. They have come down to Mexico because "it ain't all fenced in", but the apparent freedom is an illusion. There are fences all around Alejandra, the ranch owner's daughter, and Cole's passion for her leads to violence and murder.

Five years after his debut with the unusual and accomplished *Sling Blade*, Billy Bob Thornton's second outing as a director is a faithful adaptation of *All the Pretty Horses*. It tells the tale in a straightforward, sincere manner, and much of McCarthy's spare, taut dialogue has survived intact. It looks good, too—landscape and people photographed in a strong, clear light. There's some excellent acting, most notably Lucas Black as the feckless, luckless Blevins, a performance that captures all the gut-wrenching anguish of the novel.

Inevitably the film has shed some detail from the book. It lacks the story of Dona Alfonsa's life, a narrative which gives Cole an insight into the position of women in Mexico, and thus makes Alejandra's later conduct more understandable, if no more welcome. The absence of this contextual material places greater weight on the personality rather than the social position of Alejandra. As a result, her behaviour is not easily explicable; having agreed to meet Cole despite her promise not to, she then tearfully announces in a protracted sequence that she will not, after all, continue the affair. Penélope Cruz's performance is charming enough, but somewhat lightweight; at this crucial moment, deprived of any real motivation for her actions, she is unable to muster a compensating gravitas that would turn pathos into tragedy.

The other weakness in the film is Matt Damon as Cole. Dogged, earnest, he manages to convey the sense of innate goodness which the role demands, but little of the depth which might convince us why he fights battles against impossible odds. It comes as a surprise at the end when he confesses to the judge that he is troubled by the killing of a man in prison, and by his failure to save Blevins. Nothing as profound as guilt seems to have vexed the smooth surface of his young face.

McCarthy's novel ought to be perfect material for a film. There are no descriptions of the characters' interior thoughts, just dialogue and action, yet the emotional effect is profound. To reproduce it on the screen is a trick that Thornton has not quite pulled off, but it's an honourable attempt.

TIME, 12/25/00-1/I/01, p. 146, Richard Schickel

In 1940s Texas, young John Grady Cole (Damon) loses the ranch he loves in a battle, rounds up a buddy (Thomas) and heads for Mexico, looking for work, looking for adventure; looking for the sort of experience that will make men in full of them.

That, stripped of the fancy writing that rendered Cormac McCarthy's novel unreadable to some of us, is the narrative essence of *All the Pretty Horses*, and it's not a bad one. The lads almost immediately encounter a funny, violent, nutsy kid (Black), and you know right away that his heedlessness is going to cause them a lot of bother. Among other things, his wild—indeed, murderous—ways will eventually mess up Grady's soulful romance with Alejandra (the lovely Cruz), daughter of the rich rancher the boys sign on with.

All in all, it is, to borrow the old bunkhouse cliché, a rattling good yarn, even if it is all surface, no subtext. Whether there was some larger meaning in director Thornton's original cut—said to have been close to four hours long—is impossible to say, at least until the DVD comes out. For the moment, we have a perfectly coherent, handsomely rendered couple of hours, animated in particular by Damon's good performance—shrewd, innocent, angry, wistful, and, above all, likable. Maybe this movie might have been more. But it could easily have been a lot less.

VILLAGE VOICE, 12/26/00, p. 142, Amy Taubin

All the Pretty Horses, Cormac McCarthy's elegiac novel about the loss of the West and the end of youth, has been adapted with respect and even some fervor by director Billy Bob Thornton and screenwriter Ted Tally. They have kept McCarthy's narrative progression and large chunks of his laconic dialogue intact, but the film is too eager to please and falls short of the novel's tragic dimension. (McCarthy's final passage is the literary equivalent of John Wayne walking alone onto the prairie at the end of *The Searchers.)* As a boy's action-adventure saga, however, it's intermittently satisfying, especially if you love looking at horses and the raw rock sweep of the Southwest desert.

Dispossessed by his own mother of the East Texas ranch where he grew up, John Grady Cole (Matt Damon), with his best friend, Lacey Rawlins (Henry Thomas), rides down to Mexico in the hopes of finding work and freedom. The year is 1949 and, in the U.S., the cowboy life is already a victim of big oil. Like the novel, the film is a classic coming-of-age tale. Lying out under the stars, the teenage Cole and Rawlins speculate about what it's like to die. They begin their journey in innocence, but once they cross the Rio Grande, they find themselves facing death for real, and their belief in themselves and their friendship is put to the test. Hired as cowhands by a wealthy Mexican rancher (Rubén Blades), they prove their worth by breaking 16 wild mustangs in a four-day marathon. The sequence, which is shot largely at night and in close-up, captures the spare but visceral quality of McCarthy's prose as nothing else in the film does.

Having earned a place in what he imagines could be his new home, Cole puts himself and Rawlins in jeopardy by becoming romantically involved with the rancher's beautiful, headstrong daughter (Penélope Cruz). Almost before they know what hit them, the two friends find themselves in a Mexican prison. It's a journey into hell which leaves them scarred in body and spirit.

There's no getting around the fact that Damon is too old to pass for a teenager. Still, he has the robust physicality and emotional honesty that the role demands. As the more retiring Rawlins, Thomas displays similar conviction. But both are upstaged by Lucas Black as Jimmy Blevins, a horse thief and fledgling psycho killer. Blevins is the cowboy version of Robert De Niro's Johnny Boy in *Mean Streets*. Moved by his vulnerability, Cole and Rawlins can't bring themselves to brush him off, but they are also powerless to save him.

Running just over two hours, *All the Pretty Horses* is a choppy ride. (It's reported to have been two hours longer in earlier versions.) What's missing from the adaptation is the sense of history that gives the novel its scope and depth. An even more crucial problem is the absence, in Thornton's direction, of a specific perspective on the land itself. Compared to films like *Thelma and Louise* or *My Own Private Idaho*, which filter familiar landscapes through the eyes of unique and profoundly alienated characters, *All the Pretty Horses* is merely picturesque.

Also reviewed in:
NEW YORK TIMES, 12/25/00, p. E1, A.O. Scott
VARIETY, 12/18-31/00, p. 26, Todd McCarthy
WASHINGTON POST, 12/22/00, Weekend/p. 41, Desson Howe
WASHINGTON POST, 12/25/00, p. C1, Rita Kempley

ALMA

An Anthology Film Archives and Life Size Releasing release of a Ruthless Films production. *Executive Producer:* Peter Wentworth.   *Producer:* Ruth Leitman, Nancy Segler, and Margie Thorpe. *Director:* Ruth Leitman.   *Director of Photography:* Ruth Letiman, Mark Petersen, and Nancy Segler.   *Editor:* Darcy Bowman, Ann Husaini, and Ruth Leitman.   *Music:* Steve Dixon and Connie Hanes.   *Running time:* 94 minutes.   *MPAA Rating:* Not Rated.

CAST: RuPaul, Alma Thorpe, James Thorpe, and Margie Thorpe (Themselves).

NEW YORK POST, 9/22/00, p. 50, Jonathan Foreman

The documentary equivalent of a Southern Gothic novel, "Alma" is about an ultra-dysfunctional Georgia family: the alcoholic, abusive father, James; the crazy and sexually abusive mother, Alma; and their (surprisingly) well-adjusted grown-up daughter, Margie.

Revelations about rape, incest and madness come up in an odd calm way, accompanied by home movies, old letters and director Ruth Leitman's unnecessarily fancy (black-and-white, bleached-out) footage of the places where the family grew up.

VILLAGE VOICE, 9/26/00, p. 152, Amy Taubin

By any standards, Alma is nightmare of a mother. A pathological narcissist who experiences frequent psychotic episodes, she has problems with boundaries, and her capacity for denial is limitless. (She refers to the uncle who raped her at age seven as her "first boyfriend.") Since she sees her daughter, Margie, as nothing more than an extension of herself, she has abused her since infancy—and we're not just talking about sexual abuse. The relationship between Margie and Alma is the subject of Ruth Leitman's low-key but compelling documentary *Alma*, which is never exploitative, prurient, or judgmental. Unlike the mother and daughter in the Maysles brothers' much lauded *Grey Gardens*, Alma and Margie never seem like sideshow attractions.

And, in fact, it was Margie, an Atlanta bartender and country singer, who approached Leitman with the idea of making a film about her mother. Leitman, whose first documentary, *Wildwood, New Jersey*, revealed the vulnerabilities and tender hearts beneath the heavy metal masquerade of a crew of adolescent girls, was intrigued by the stories Margie told about her crazy mother, who hears voices in the ceiling and spends her days douching with herbs so that her sexual organ "will smell sweet in God's nostrils." After leaving home, Margie tried to distance herself from Alma and from her passive-aggressive alcoholic father, but she talked to them on the phone every day.

Leitman filmed Alma and Margie over a period of three years. Alma, who still saw herself as the Marilyn Monroe-styled beauty she was in her youth, welcomed the attention. Her husband, clearly less enchanted with the filmmaking process, is glimpsed only in the background. Margie says he used to beat her mother's head in every Friday night, but age and alcohol seem to have worn him down.

The film threads first-person anecdotes, old home movies, and photographs through the drama of Alma's deteriorating mental and physical health and Margie's attempts to do the right thing without being suffocated by her mother's needs. The camera's presence draws Alma's competitiveness with her daughter into the open, but it also allows Margie to get the truth of her own experience on the record. "You only remember what you want," Margie says accusingly to Alma, who is lounging in the backseat of Margie's car, swathed in a coat and turban that make her look like a cross between the Easter Bunny and a more corpulent version of Gloria Swanson in *Sunset Boulevard*. To which Alma, with impeccable logic, replies, "Of course."

If the filmmaker identifies with Margie, Alma emerges less as a monster than the victim of childhood abuse, religious fundamentalism, sexual repression, misogyny, and whacked-out brain chemistry. And while participating in the film seems to have a therapeutic effect on Margie and Alma, this is in no way an Oprah-like confessional. As fragmented and unresolved as the experiences of mother and daughter, *Alma* bears witness to a situation for which there are no easy answers.

Also reviewed in:
NEW YORK TIMES, 9/22/00, p. E16, Lawrence Van Gelder

ALMOST FAMOUS

A DreamWorks Pictures and Columbia Pictures release of a Vinyl Films production. *Producer:* Cameron Crowe and Ian Bryce. *Director:* Cameron Crowe. *Screenplay:* Cameron Crowe. *Director of Photography:* John Toll. *Editor:* Joe Hutshing and Saar Klein. *Music:* Nancy

Wilson. *Music Editor:* Carlton Kaller. *Sound:* Jeff Wexler and (music) Greg Townley. *Sound Editor:* Mike Wilhoit. *Casting:* Gail Levin. *Art Director:* Clay A. Griffith, Clayton R. Hartley, and Virgina Randolph-Weaver. *Set Designer:* Charisse Cardenas, Mindi R. Toback, and Conny Boettger-Marinos. *Set Decorator:* Robert Greenfield. *Set Dresser:* John H. Maxwell, Rod Gregory, Jennine Fenton, Chris Peterson, Joe Viau, and Peter Gikas. *Special Effects:* John Frazier. *Visual Effects:* Ed Jones. *Costumes:* Betsy Heimann. *Make-up:* Lois Burwell. *Running time:* 122 minutes. *MPAA Rating:* R.

CAST: Billy Crudup (Russell Hammond); Frances McDormand (Elaine Miller); Kate Hudson (Penny Lane); Jason Lee (Jeff Bebe); Patrick Fugit (William Miller); Zooey Deschanel (Anita Miller); Michael Angarano (Young William); Noah Taylor (Dick Roswell); John Fedevich (Ed Vallencourt); Mark Kozelek (Larry Fellows); Fairuza Balk (Sapphire); Anna Paquin (Polexia Aphrodisia); Olivia Rosewood (Beth from Denver); Jimmy Fallon (Dennis Hope); Philip Seymour Hoffman (Lester Bangs); Liz Stauber (Leslie); Bijou Phillips (Estrella Starr); Alice Marie Crowe (Mrs. Deegan); J.J. Cohen (Roadie Scully); Gary Douglas Kohn (Roadie Gregg); Ray Porter (Roadie Mick); Mark Pellington (Freddy); Eion Bailey (Jann Wenner); Terry Chen (Ben Fong-Torres); Rainn Wilson (David Felton); Erin Foley (Alison the Fact Checker); Jesse Caron (Darryl); Charles Walker (Principal); Jay Baruchel (Vic Munoz); Pauley Perrette (Alice Wisdom); Peter Frampton (Reg); Zack Ward (The Legendary Red Dog); Mitch Hedberg (Eagles Road Manager); Devin Corey (The Who Road Manager); Pete Droge and Elaine Summers (Hyatt Singers); Eric Stonestreet (Sheldon the Desk Clerk); Marc Maron (Angry Promoter); Shane Willard (Ticket Scalper); Chris McElprang (Aaron Amedori); John Patrick Amedori (Himself); Kate Peckham (Quiet Girl); Julia Schuler (Waving Girl); Brian Vaughan (Real Topeka Kid); Anthony Martelli (Poolside Provocateur); Zach Clairville (Acid Kid); Ian Ridgeway, Isaac Curtiss, and Chris Lennon Davis (Topeka Partiers); Scott N. Stevens (Co-pilot); Kevin Sussman (Lenny); Reathel Bean (Warwick Hotel Clerk); Tom Riis Farrell (Plaza Doctor); Laura Bastianelli (Nurse); Daniel Wilson (Journalism Teacher); William Barillaro (Bus Driver); Holly Maples (Flight Attendant); Matt Griesser (PSA Co-pilot); Susan Yeagley (Have a Nice Day Stewardess); Nicole Spector (Hippie Girl at Airport); Patrick Irmen (Wanna Get High Guy); Nick Swardson (Insane Bowie Fan); Samer Sourakli (Mustache Boy); Michelle Moretti (Swingo's Desk Clerk); Ana Maria Quintana and Lisa Buchignani (Arizona Housekeepers).

CHRISTIAN SCIENCE MONITOR, 9/15/00, p. 15, David Sterritt

"Almost Famous" is a perfect title for the Cameron Crowe film that premiered at the Toronto festival, since the main characters are exactly that. One hero (Patrick Fugit) is a rock-music journalist still in high school. The other heroes (Billy Crudup, Jason Lee) are members of a band that has some momentum but still needs an expert manager and a little more talent.

And then there's Penny Lane, a teenage groupie (Kate Hudson) who thinks she's not a groupie but a muse, inspiring the band. She's the least likely to become actually famous because she's never dreamed she might be worthy of the honor. Her lack of self-esteem makes her the movie's saddest character.

With its imaginative screenplay and silky-smooth style, "Almost Famous" is the latest in a string of first-rate rock movies that have been shaking up screens since the 1950s. Director Crowe has done almost everything right, from discovering an excellent new star (Fugit) to filling the soundtrack with rock classics from Jimi Hendrix and David Bowie to, no kidding, David Seville and the Chipmunks. Realizing that social attitudes have changed a lot since 1973, when the movie is set, Crowe's provided an on-screen mother to worry and warn about rock-scene decadence. She's played by Frances McDormand with the wry matronliness of her great "Fargo" performance. Acting honors also go to Philip Seymour Hoffman as legendary rock critic Lester Bangs.

Veterans of the 1960s and 70s will find that "Almost Famous" captures both the raging excesses of that era and the keen-eyed alertness that allowed some savvy youngsters to survive and even profit from the scene. Everyone will find that Crudup and Fugit are qualified to drop the "almost" in their own quests for celebrity. They're among the reasons "Almost Famous" should be a full-fledged hit.

CINEASTE, Vol. XXVI, No. 1, 2000, p. 50, Thomas Doherty

From the alarm-bell jolt of "Rock Around the Clock" in *The Blackboard Jungle* (1955), rock and roll music has energized the motion picture screen as soundtrack, performance, and ritual, shaking up a remarkable range of film genres—kick-starting the traditional Hollywood musical in *Jailhouse Rock* (1957) and *A Hard Day's Night* (1964), granting a backstage pass to *cinéma-vérité* in *Don't Look Back* (1967) and *Gimme Shelter* (1970), and donating a backlog of colorful life stories for the Hollywood biopic in *The Buddy Holly Story* (1978) and *La Bamba* (1987). By the time of *U2: Rattle and Hum* (1988) and *Truth or Dare* (1991), a vanity concert film, not a platinum album, served as a confirmed ticket to the rock pantheon.

Today, of course, rock and roll proliferates on screens large and small at a rate too frenzied to track. Even the one-hit wonders and second-tier contenders get a respectful hearing in the addictive VH-1 series "Behind the Music," a weekly chronicle whose dramatic arc follows a curve of mathematical precision—hardscrabble hustling, abrupt liftoff to fame and fortune, bitter ego clashes and drug-addled acrimony, precipitous plunge into the where-are-they-now?-file, and, as coda, the economically motivated reunion for the purposes of the present episode of "Behind the Music."

In the rock-soaked realm of American cinema, one of the more intriguing variations on the theme is the rock and roll fan film, a rock-centric subgenre whose narrative spine is not the charismatic players but the obsessive fans who live lives of really loud desperation. Subordinating rock performances to rock compulsions, the rock fan film celebrates rock qua rock as a felt, almost spiritual force. Alan Parker's *The Commitments* wittily captures that target fixation of rock fandom in a confessional scene where a priest corrects a lovelorn penitent by pointing out that it was Percy Sledge, not Marvin Gaye, who sang "When a Man Loves a Woman."

The landmark entry in the rock fan film catalog is *American Graffiti* (1972), George Lucas's headlight-lit homage to a motorized California youth spent cruising to a wall to-wall soundtrack spilling out from car radios. The first filmmaker to honor rock-as-ritual by coughing up the bucks for the costly license fees for the original recordings, Lucas knew that only the authentic golden oldies would trigger private memories and tug at the heartstrings of his baby-boomer audience. Unfortunately, in the intervening decades, the gimmick has become so tedious a cliché that, like the sound men of the old studio system, who kept monkey screeches and coyote howls ready to unwind for a jungle safari or Western campfire, the vintage tunes that once struck a deep emotional chord are now liable to make auditors of all ages cringe—the intro pling/pling/pling of the guitar in the Buffalo Springfield's "For What It's Worth" (for the street fightin' turbulence of the 1960s), the spooky sitar heralding the Stones' "Paint it Black" (for the subterranean horror of Vietnam), the crashing wall of feedback in Jimi Hendrix's "Purple Haze" (for acid freak-outs, and bad craziness), and so on and on. The sure sign of a real rock and roll heart in the director's chair is access to a personal juke box, the chops to reach back deep in the charts, beyond the Top Forty chestnuts, for the choice rarity or album cut, knowledge of which separates the hardcore fan from the great pretender—for example, Martin Scorsese dredging up Mick Jagger's woozy "Memo from Turner" in *Goodfellas* (1990) or Wes Anderson opting for the original Cat Stevens version of "Here Comes My Baby" in *Rushmore* (1998).

With rock and roll currently stuck in a fallow period, two rock fan films have arisen to explore the meanings of rock culture for purposes besides a soundtrack tie-in. Both *High Fidelity* and *Almost Famous* harken back to a pre CD, pre-MTV epoch, the former symbolically, the latter literally, as if the fan base is pining for a time before digital formats and video playlets corrupted a lily-pure art form. Both luxuriate in a kind of vinyl fetishism, where fans caress stacks of records and touch the faces of album covers like the prize works of art they often were. Antique collectibles, the disks are handled with care, almost reverently, the thumb balanced on the album edge, middle finger in the center hole, the devotee careful not to scuff or scratch the surface of the icon.

A 45 single's worth of hooks in an LP format, *Almost Famous* is the autobiographical flashback of writer-director Cameron Crowe, the *wunderkind* rock journalist for *Rolling Stone* in the early

1970s, a fifteen-year-old rock savant with the most coveted byline in the New Journalism. The conceit would be laughable were it not true. The rush of early success, the smooth transition from critic to creator, and the fantasy fulfillment of marrying a certifiable rock star babe (Nancy Wilson of Heart, who composed the film's score) has not left Crowe with a tragic sense of life. No wonder his memories of post-sixties, pre-disco rock and roll are rose-colored and misty-eyed, clouded not by recreational drug use but by the bent perspective of a charmed life. Though Crowe's affinity for the revivifying power of Deep Purple, Jethro Tull, and Elton John seems eccentric, rock aficionados will appreciate his dedication to the music and his depiction of a scene that is a long time gone.

Precocious Crowe surrogate Billy Miller (Patrick Fugit) is a budding, baby-faced journalist with a doting, piece-of-work mother, Elaine (Frances McDormand). When Billy's rebellious big sister wisely flees Mom's apron strings for the faux-feminism of a stewardess's miniskirt, she leaves behind a potent legacy for Billy: her record collection. "It will set you free," she whispers like a siren. Billy flips through the touchstones of rock's high renaissance *Highway 61 Revisited, Pet Sounds, Bookends*—and realizes he has hit the motherlode.

Soon, against her better judgment, Mom is driving Billy to the arena for his first assignment for *Rolling Stone,* humiliating him with her parting warning not to take drugs. Billy is no Eve Harrington: he doesn't want to understudy for the lead guitar; he just wants to watch the action from the wings, midway up from the festival seats in the stadium, among the roadies, groupies, journalists, and record-industry creeps. Well remembering an apprenticeship as a kid dependent on the kindness of adult strangers, Crowe captures the naked yearning of standing bereft outside the stage door and the giddy thrill of admittance to the sacred realm of the elect (cf. Wayne and Garth gleefully waving their backstage passes aloft at the Alice Cooper concert in *Wayne's World.*

The pickup band—a concoction called Stillwater, a kind of Allman Brother-ish, post-Peter Frampton Humble Pie only, uh, American, and not related—is strictly bottom of the bill. Setting out self-consciously to imitate the Richards/Jagger, Page/Plant, Townsend/Daltry line-up of moody lead guitarist and sexy singer, Stillwater fronts Jeff Babe (Jason Lee) on vocals and Russell (Billy Crudup) on lead. Alas, like so many of the acts in prefab rock and roll films, Stillwater musters no power chords or topnotch tunes of its own. For all of Hollywood's rock-centricity, relatively few films have inspired memorable rock and roll songs, as opposed to feeding parasitically off them.

Offstage, Billy's object of desire is Penny Lane (Kate Hudson), the proverbial groupie with the heart of gold. No mere plaster caster or bj artist, Penny fancies herself a "band aid," a muse for the music. Glimpsed in the parking lot from afar through Billy's smitten gaze, she is meant to be a transcendent vision of loveliness amidst the grunge, yet actress Hudson, for all her publicity buildup as this year's girl, is not the luminous blue-jeaned baby Crowe craves. One suspects that the failure of *Almost Famous* to strike box-office gold—Dreamworks executives are still puzzling over the pallid response to the critically-esteemed, widely-hyped film—is partly due to Hudson's failure to deliver the screen-magic goods. (A sidebar: Crowe made an estimable contribution to film history this year with his marvelous book *Conversations with Wilder,* a dialog which finds director Billy Wilder returning more than once to the miscasting of the aged Gary Cooper opposite the blithe Audrey Hepburn in *Love in the Afternoon* (1957). Wilder is still burned by the memory of the star he couldn't land for the part, Cary Grant. In his own dotage, director Crowe may find himself lamenting the might-have-been of the actress Sarah Polley, who was originally contemplated for the part of Penny Lane.)

Once Billy, like Penny, is "with the band," *Almost Famous* settles into the familiar, vignette-friendly environs of the on-the-road rock movie—an acid-drenched descent among the common folk by lead guitarist Russell, a Capraesque singalong on the tour bus to Elton John's "Tiny Dancer," and a very bumpy ride during a thunderstorm that recalls the bad karma between rock hands and small engine aircraft. Calling in advice from the sidelines is legendary rock critic Lester Bangs (Philip Seymour Hoffman, stealing the show as usual), who takes the boy under his wing and warns him not to make friends with the band ("the enemy") and to remember that, as critics, not players, they are by definition "uncool."

Like the protagonist, and despite its unaccountable R-rating, the spirit of *Almost Famous* is pure PG-13. All the obligatory doses of sex, drugs, and rock and roll are safe and sweet: marijuana wafts through the air, but an acid trip is played for laughs and an overdose means a stomach pump not a morgue trip. The sex, too, is gauzy, dreamy, and modest. No nasty needles or ritual humiliation of groupies makes it in to the edited copy of Billy's, or Crowe's, behind-the-scenes profile. In the end, the female-dominated lad is not searching for a girl, or a rock god, but a father figure, which explains why Billy's emotional bond to Lester Bangs and Russell is more freighted than his puppy-dog crush on Penny.

High Fidelity is a smarter rock fan film—better written, better acted, and dead-on in its rendering of rock's arrogant "professional appreciators." Based on the British novel by Nick Hornby and directed by Stephen Frears, the film transports the scene to Chicago and a Wax Trax-like record store stocked with stall upon stall of precious vinyl, back issues, imports, and out-of-print classics. In tune with the refined eclecticism of the fans, the rock and roll soundtrack spurns a greatest-hits compilation for a mesh of under the radar nuggets. Best of all, record-store proprietor and sometime nightclub DJ Rob Gordon is played by the engaging John Cusack, who performs double duty as protagonist and direct-address narrator. Breaking the frame and then moving fluidly back into the tabula, Cusack delivers the kind of deft, seemingly effortless star turn that the Academy of Motion Picture Arts and Sciences always overlooks because it doesn't involve a foreign accent or a severe disability.

As *High Fidelity* opens, Rob is at low ebb, huddled morosely under his headphones as his girlfriend Laura (Iben Hjeje) walks out on him. Rob's apartment is stuffed with shelves of neatly filed records, an ironic motif: the utter mastery of rock minutia and the card catalog order of his record collection (whether alphabetically, chronologically, or autobiographically) stands in telling contrast to his messed-up personal life. Rob measures out that life not in coffee spoons but in terms of the *Billboard* charts. His all-time Top Five most memorable break-ups, do not, he insists, include the woman who has just dumped him. "Maybe you'd sneak into the Top Ten!," Rob shrieks after her. In truth, Laura is Number One with a bullet through his heart.

At the record store, Rob copes with two extreme versions of rock fandom: the nebbish Dick (Todd Louiso) and the gonzo Barry (Jack Black) "I hired these guys for three days and they started showing up every day," he says with a helpless shrug. "That was four years ago." While Rob licks his wounds, Dick prattles on about his new import acquisition, and Barry bops ecstatically to the high decibel "Walking on Sunshine." Rock snobs all, they thrust and parry with all comers, shoppers and shoplifters alike. When a square, middle-aged guy makes the mistake of asking for "I Just Called to Say I Love You" by Stevie Wonder, Barry treats him with the contempt of a maitre d' confronted by a rube who has just requested a bottle of ketchup for his *foie gras.* "Go to the mall," he sneers. For his part, Rob puts the new Beta Band EP on the store turntable with the serene confidence that he will sell five copies by subliminal suggestion. If *Almost Famous* celebrates the communal unifying power of rock and roll, *High Fidelity* delights in the ruthless one-upmanship practiced by rock's elite tastemasters.

Desperate to end his emotional gridlock, Rob decides to go back through his Top Five list and confront the women from his past—a childhood crush, a high-school girlfriend (Joelle Carter), a beautiful coed named Charlie (Catherine Zeta Jones), and the broken sparrow (Lili Taylor) picked up on the rebound during Rob's Bruce Springstein phase (with the Boss himself making a gravel-voiced cameo in a fantasy sequence). The trite device—it's at least as old as *Old Boyfriends* (1979)—hasn't aged well, especially given the present-day material sailing up the charts, in the form of the dread-locked, irresistible folksinger Marie de Salle (Lisa Bonet). Marie is aptly described by the tongue-tied but still articulate Dick as "Sheryl Crow-ish, crossed with a post-*Partridge Family*, pre-*LA Law* Susan Dey, only, you know, um, black." So hypnotic is the sight of Marie on stage covering a tune by the wimp rocker Rob dubs "Peter Fucking Frampton" that the songbird makes the boys relinquish their hatred of "Baby I Love Your Way."

The most disillusioning blast from the past is the beautiful dreamgirl Charlie. Up close, in reality, the nymph of dappled memory, the goddess that haunts his psyche, is an abrasive, vain harpie. "How did I edit all this out?," he asks, on the verge of an epiphany. Of course, the selective editing came courtesy of that endless montage of rock songs, the lachrymose pop and blistering punk alike, with their stupid girls, little queerness and pictures of lily. Rob comes to understand that he has been sold a bill of jukebox goods. The sirens of his past, and of the present, like Marie De Salle and that hot new rock-journalist chick he may or may not make a compilation tape for, are pop confections. Ultimately, they do not "deliver," as he says in a very un-pop-song-like marriage proposal to the flesh-and-blood woman whose chemical makeup, he comes to realize, feels "like home."

Against expectations, Rob finds his groove not in the long-live-rock ethos but in the rhythms of a quite sentimental love story about a guy growing up, making commitments, getting married, and taking on a real job. In a way not so unlike *Almost Famous*, *High Fidelity* melts before the healing power of rock and roll. For all the stiff-backed resistance to what Barry calls "tacky sentimental crap," all the hardrock boys end up swaying to a soulful love song: a tasty cover of Marvin Gaye's "Let's Get It On."

For the record, the all-time, Top Five fan-centered rock and roll films are:

1) *American Graffiti*
2) *The Commitments*
3) *High Fidelity*
4) *Wayne's World*
5) *I Wanna Hold Your Hand*

Almost Famous might sneak into the Top Ten.

LOS ANGELES TIMES, 9/13/00, Calendar/p. 1, Kenneth Turan

"Almost Famous" is not almost anything, it's all there. It's the latest project from writer-director Cameron Crowe, who's used the free ride he earned with "Jerry Maguire's" success to create something to cherish and enjoy, an intimate yet universal film that will delight you and involve your heart.

Almost alone among makers of personal movies, a genre frequently characterized by moping and inordinate special pleading, Crowe has used irresistible performances and fine writing to turn a dramatized version of his own past as America's youngest 1970s rock journalist into an intoxicating mixture of Hollywood and reality.

William Miller, Crowe's 15-year-old protagonist, is a young person in a very old tradition, wanting to find out about himself and the real world and hoping that the price of experience doesn't come too high. Crowe has laid hands on what's essential in his own sentimental education, has in effect made his life yours and your life his for the time this story is on the screen.

Like Jim Brooks, who's been an influence on him, Crowe has a gift for blending things that don't usually coexist. With innate fairness, he's made "Almost Famous" as pointed as it is loving, able to cast a sympathetic but always clear and unblinking eye on the foibles of human nature and the humor implicit in them.

Crowe also joins a keen sense of the richness of ordinary experience to an ability to catch humanity on the fly. His feeling for his characters is so exact, his affinity for personal frailty so touching, that, when matched with a cast in sync with his intentions, what results is a naturalness that films often forget how to convey.

Above all, "Almost Famous" knows how to deal with sentimental material—the joys and embarrassments, victories and disappointments of growing up—without pushing too hard. By resisting the temptation to jam emotions down our throats, it allows them the space to be authentically moving.

Essential to this was Crowe's decision to cast the unknown but enormously likable Patrick Fugit as William Miller.

Fugit is a kid we warm to at once, someone whose emotions are always accessible. Fugit easily conveys the levelheadedness William will need to survive in his heady environment as well as the all-encompassing sense of yearning, the drive to be what you not yet are and fear you may never be, that could well be the defining emotion of adolescence.

For William Miller is not coming of age somewhere in the Corn Belt; it's all happening to him in the middle of a full-fledged 1970s rock 'n' roll tour. With Crowe as guide, "Almost Famous" captures the rush, the buzz, the glamour of rock while giving meaning to the period's heady ambience of hysteria, decadence and unlikely innocence for those who remember it as well as for those who do not.

Though it's set in 1973, "Almost Famous" starts with a prelude four years earlier that introduces the family dynamic that shaped William (played as a young boy by Michael Angarano).

After his father's death, he's been raised in San Diego by his eccentric, fiercely protective mother Elaine (a completely wonderful Frances McDormand), a strong-minded college professor who thinks "adolescence is a marketing tool" and bans rock 'n' roll as a direct link to promiscuous sex and dangerous drugs.

This doesn't sit well with William's older sister Anita (a fine Zooey Deschanel), who loves rock and hates living in "a house of lies." One of those lies, it turns out, is William's age. Though he thinks he's 13, like his classmates, it turns out he's only 11. "This," he says woefully, "explains so much."

When Anita leaves home to become a stewardess, she whispers to William, "Look under your bed, it'll set you free." Waiting for him is Anita's clandestine stash of rock records, and as he carefully handles the albums by Dylan, Hendrix, the Rolling Stones and the Who, you can see what will become the defining passion of William's life start to stir.

By 1973, though he's only 15, William is precociously hooked on writing about rock and when his idol, Lester Bangs, one of rock criticism's seminal wild men and the editor of Creem magazine, comes to town, the kid journalist wangles a face-to-face meeting that changes his life.

Superbly played by Philip Seymour Hoffman, more and more the most gifted and inspired character actor working in film, what could have been the cliched portrait of an older mentor who speaks the straight truth blossoms into a marvelous personality. (The real-life hard-living Bangs died in 1982 at age 33.)

Write about what you know, Bangs tells him. Make your reputation on being honest and unmerciful and, most important, do not get close to the rock stars. "These people," he says with a hint of foresight, "are not your friends."

Bangs also gives William his first assignment, to cover a Black Sabbath concert at the San Diego Sports Arena. There he is befriended by the next generation of groupies, young women including Polexia (Anna Paquin) and Sapphire (Fairuza Balk) who call themselves "band aids" and are there because they truly love the music.

Leader of this particular pack is the self-invented Penny Lane, whose combination of beauty, affability, savoir-faire and determined fragility completely overwhelms William even after he realizes, in a very amusing scene, that she is barely older than he is.

Penny is played by Kate Hudson (it's her face behind the sunglasses in the film's poster), and her work is so delicate, authentic and accomplished that this is probably the last film for which anyone will feel the impulse to identify her as Goldie Hawn's daughter.

Penny Lane helps William get access to Stillwater, the concert's opening act, and to the group's charismatic, sexually charged lead guitar, Russell Hammond (a role Billy Crudup absolutely nails). Almost before he can believe it, Rolling Stone is calling William (the magazine's editor Jann Wenner has a tiny cameo as a cab passenger) to offer an assignment.

So, much to his mother's increasing horror, this pipsqueak reporter ends up hanging out with Stillwater (apparently an amalgam of the Allman Brothers, Led Zeppelin, Lynyrd Skynyrd and other bands) on their Almost Famous bus tour of America.

Protectively looked out for by the girls and benignly neglected by the band's manager ("Shine's" Noah Taylor), William thinks his toughest problem is going to be lining up quality interview time with Hammond and tendentious lead singer Jeff Bebe (an effective Jason Lee), but that proves not to be it.

Instead, all unawares, William has to face some major life issues: being a responsible journalist in an irresponsible milieu, determining who your friends are and who they're not and giving those who are on your side what they deserve. Throw in being 15 years old and you've got an exceptional dramatic scenario.

Crowe may have been over his head emotionally when he traveled with rock bands before he was out of high school, but as a director he's got the wisdom of an old soul. "I'll quote you warmly and honestly," William promises Stillwater when they ask about his journalistic style, and the qualities he guarantees the band are identical to the ones Crowe lavishes on his film. See it and it'll stay with you as your own memories do: funny, poignant, bittersweet and irreplaceable.

NEW YORK, 9/18/00, p. 66, Peter Rainer

Cameron Crowe's *Almost Famous*, set mostly in 1973, is a blissfully sweet coming-of-age movie in which everyone, young and less young, comes of age. William Miller (Patrick Fugit), the 15-year-old budding rock journalist, is the film's centerpiece, and he's a wide-eyed munchkin savant, a cherub in the Dionysian circus of rock and roll. He's so virginal he's comic; roving groupies take one look at him and can't wait to deflower him en masse, for the sport of it. On assignment to cover the touring up-and-coming Led Zeppelin-ish band Stillwater for *Rolling Stone*, William becomes its unofficial mascot. Russell Hammond (Billy Crudup), the lead guitarist, has the requisite hippie Jesus look, and he sees in William not only an acolyte but, as the relationship deepens, a musical soul mate as well. What unites these two is the ecstasy of knowing just how deep-down good rock music can make you feel. A teenage rock journalist in the seventies before writing the book *Fast Times at Ridgemont High* and getting into movies, Crowe still feels this ecstasy in his bones, which is why his movie looks vibrantly alive instead of shimmering with that phony nostalgic haze common to period films set in that era. But Crowe is also honest enough to recognize how intricately bound our feelings for rock are to our zig-zag attitudes about sex and pomp and rebellion and cool. Its the rock lifestyle as much as rock itself that is being celebrated here.

Crowe sprinkles a pinch of powdered sugar on that lifestyle, but this approach is preferable to being subjected to the usual litany of overdoses and whoring. He does indeed bring some of this material into the movie, just enough to make us feel its sting, but he's not trying for an exposé. (What's left to expose, anyway?) His movie is like a souvenir of personal memories that have been candied by time. Crowe's films, especially his first two as a writer-director, *Say Anything ... and Singles,* have always displayed an unyielding affection and longing for family, and what he finds in the rock world of *Almost Famous* is the greatest of extended families, an orgy of companionship. William's single mom, Elaine (Frances McDormand), who thinks rock and roll is a doomy siren's call, is the Mother Courage of the piece. She's already driven away William's sister Anita (Zooey Deschanel), who bequeaths her record collection to her brother. Then, for the first time in his life, William also leaves home, to follow Stillwater. Elaine is a monster but a very human one; in her own Gorgon-like way she cares deeply about her son, and she's certainly not wrong to worry about the drugs and the sex. But her defiance, which exhibits a comically overheated, rock-stars-have-kidnapped-my-son paranoia, is partly what eggs him on, and she knows it. William may be a cherub, but he's also a chip off the old block. His errantry is a backhanded tribute to his mom's mettle.

Early on, William acquires a mentor, the rock critic Lester Bangs (Philip Seymour Hoffman, who may be the best character actor in America). It is Bangs, with his gonzo's radar, who immediately perceives what lies ahead for the boy. "You cannot make friends with the rock stars," he tells him. "Friendship is the booze they feed you." And yet friendship is what William craves even more than reputation, even more than music. Crowe doesn't take a hard-line attitude toward all this: The movie is saying that some things are more important than journalism, at least to the journalist. The puff and glitz that some writers churn out may be murderous to their profession, but castigating those writers is not what this movie is about. Who can fault William for "getting too close" to his subject? *Almost Famous* isn't about the making of a great rock scribe (which Lester Bangs emphatically was). It's about how rock and roll messes you up and brings you into a new relation with yourself. Besides, William manages to deliver the goods: His story on Stillwater for *Rolling Stone,* which both he and the band at first regard as a betrayal, is an uncensored tribute to their shared spree.

Crowe brings out the emotional levels in William's odyssey. The boy's almost palpable need for a father figure is fulfilled by the yin and yang of Lester and Russell. Somehow William manages to reconcile himself to both. Usually in movies it's the rock stars who are mythologized, but here it is Lester the critic who gets the Yoda treatment, dispensing sage, scurrilous *pensées* over the phone from his platter-clogged apartment. Crowe, who recently published a book of his affectionate, wide-eyed interviews with his directing hero Billy Wilder, has an affinity for tenderizing deep-dish cynics and outlaws: the Lester Bangs of this movie is a cautionary guru who understands the rot and corruption of rock but still loves it for its charge and its disposability;

Russell Hammond assumes, uneasily, the role of rock satyr. A gifted guitarist, he seems slightly baffled by the writhings of his audience.

Russell may possess the onstage swagger of a star, but he looks to the uplifted gaze of William to validate his cool. And he really loves music. In the most serenely satisfying moment in the movie, Russell threatens to leave the band after repeated clashes with the thin-skinned lead singer (Jason Lee). He's brought back into the fold when the group, aboard their touring bus, joins in singing Elton John's "Tiny Dancer," tentatively at first and finally at full throttle. Suddenly all is right with the world. It's both a fantasy and a validation of how music can banish every bit of badness from your life.

Crowe knows how to bring out the youthful ardor in his actors. Patrick Fugit has the most difficult role, because William is essentially an observer, a peacemaker. (As a writer-director, Crowe is a peacemaker, too; he likes to bring people together.) William is the still center, or off-center, of every scene in which he appears, but his recessiveness is intensely inquiring and likeable. Kate Hudson, playing Russell's chief groupie, Penny Lane, is a swirl of concupiscence in faux-fur-collared coats and lace tank tops. Hudson brings out the preternatural womanliness and pathos in this girl, who can't be much older than William; she's wised-up already, and her baby fat is becoming hard-edged. Billy Crudup has been dubbed a star-in-waiting for so long that this film, which will surely make him one, seems almost like a coronation. His performance may resemble a loose-limbed frolic, but it's also feral and intuitive and carries within it the remembered essence of every celebrated and not-so-celebrated rocker from that pivotal era. Crudup understands Russell's complicated position in William's life, which is why the final reconciliation between the two is such a beautifully conceived finale. It's just a simple grace note of a scene, but, like the entire movie, it has the soft emotional resonance of a long-held chord.

NEW YORK POST, 9/13/00, p. 47, Lou Lumenick

Summer still has eight days to go on the calendar, but the fall movie season arrives in style with the first must-see picture, one that will surely figure prominently when Oscar nominations are announced a few months from now.

Based loosely on his experiences as a teenage writer for Rolling Stone, writer-director Cameron Crowe's "Almost Famous" is the rare movie that lives up to, and even exceeds, its advance hype.

An utter delight from the first frame to fade-out, it's a love letter to the 1970s, as seen through the eyes of William Miller, played by a wonderful young newcomer named Patrick Fugit (who greatly resembles Tobey Maguire, but is a more interesting actor).

William, a wide-eyed 15-year-old from San Diego, worships rock music and his sheer enthusiasm eventually lands him a dream gig: writing about a semi-obscure band called Stillwater for Rolling Stone.

His mentor, legendary Creem editor Lester Bangs (Philip Seymour Hoffman), warns William to keep a critical distance from his subjects. He knows William stands a real danger of being seduced by their glamorous lifestyle.

William's protective mother, Elaine (Frances McDormand), is concerned, too, about his exposure to sex, drugs and rock 'n' roll—not necessarily in that order.

William struggles to maintain his objectivity, but his very presence exacerbates the tensions between Stillwater's flamboyant lead guitarist, Russell (Billy Crudup), and the overshadowed lead singer, Jeff (Jason Lee). The teen also falls hard for Penny Lane (Kate Hudson), the band's worldy-wise lead groupie, who befriends him.

Penny loves Russell, who has an off-the-road girlfriend, and William's suffering as he watches her exploitation forms the crux of one of his two moral dilemmas. The other, of course, is the difficulty remaining a tough journalist covering people you become friends with and who share confidences with you (a dilemma shared by folks who cover politicians, among others).

This a movie of wonderful set pieces, the best of which comes during a near plane crash that prompts a hilarious (and heartbreaking) series of confessions and confrontations. As anyone who's seen the excellent trailer knows, there is also a transcendent moment on the band bus (a sign proclaims the Almost Famous—Tour 73) when the cast is united in a rendition of Elton John's "Tiny Dancer."

Less flashy but even more affecting is a sequence where William rescues Penny from a drug overdose.

In a movie with an across-the-board excellent ensemble (including Anna Paquin and Fairuza Balk as groupies and Zooey Deschanel as the sister who turns William on to rock), two players really hit it out of the park.

Kate Hudson, heretofore known as Goldie Hawn's daughter, gives a nuanced, star-making performance as the nurturing but deeply vulnerable Penny. The other breakthrough is Jason Lee (of "Chasing Amy" and other Kevin Smith movies), whose witty underplaying effectively upstages Crudup's fine Russell, who has far more screen time.

Photographed by John Toll ("The Thin Red Line") in glowing hues, "Almost Famous" boasts an almost flawless depiction of its era, from William's sexual initiation to a party where an LSD-addled Russell is goaded by a crowd to dive from the roof of a building into a swimming pool.

Hollywood history is full of writer-directors who were given carte blanche after one big hit, with disastrous results—Michael Cimino, for instance, followed "The Deer Hunter" with "Heaven's Gate."

Crowe, who had free reign after "Jerry Maguire," decided to do a very personal movie about a subject he knows well. The result is an unqualified triumph, the year's best movie so far.

NEWSDAY, 9/13/00, Part II/p. B9, John Anderson

It's 1973 and rock is dead—or so says critic Lester Bangs, who certainly is dead but comes back as a dyspeptic Obi Wan Kenobi in Cameron Crowe's Billy Wilder-esque "Almost Famous." Inhabiting the temporal vessel of Philip Seymour Hoffman, Bangs is the Force on the phone line, dispensing sage advice to 15-year-old fledgling rock journalist William Miller (Patrick Fugit) about ethics and seduction and the nature of art. Somebody should have listened to him.

If rock was dead, what killed it? Probably the same thing that damaged motion pictures, that moment in the '70s when every hack decided he was an artist. To Crowe's credit, "Almost Famous" is an almost totally unpretentious picture—rock excess has seldom seemed so innocently innocent, sexual license (pre-AIDS, of course) has seldom seemed so inconsequential.

Consequently, of course, the entire movie is as consequential as the Raspberries' greatest hits. That a movie about rock and roll should be totally dependent on music for its emotional impact makes a certain amount of sense. That the music is supplied by Elton John, the Beach Boys and Cat Stevens validates the existence of Lite FM.

Anyway. After our summer of sludge, "Almost Famous" isn't the most unwelcome of movies, although it does seem to indicate that if you make something as successful as "Jerry Maguire" you can then make a movie about yourself. When he was 15, Crowe, like his young character William, was a feature writer for Rolling Stone—although the magazine story upon which Crowe bases much of "Almost Famous" was written not by him but by Grover Lewis, a no-holds-barred profile of the Allman Brothers Band written just before they broke into the big time and published just about the time guitar god Duane Allman had his fatal motorcycle accident in the autumn of 1971. In the film, the band is called Stillwater, the Duane Allman character is called Russell Hammond (Billy Crudup) and their music is more generic hard rock than purist blues.

But the drug use, the groupies and the intra-band tensions—particularly the Allmans-Led Zeppelin-Jeff Beck-inspired domination of guitarist over frontman, here played by Jason Lee—is lifted right out of Lewis' piece.

Into the Stillwater mess parachutes young William, whose precocious rock writing has allowed the teenager to bluff his way into an assignment for Rolling Stone, going on the road to profile a "band on the brink of success" and leaving behind his fretful mother, played by Frances McDonnand (ill-used and given to reciting the famous last words of Allen Ginsberg's mother: "Don't take drugs."). Along the way, he violates every piece of wisdom his mentor Bangs has given him.

But in addition to its inherent musical contradictions (the hard rock it champions being exactly what it never uses) "Almost Famous" is a good-natured but basically dishonest movie. William is given not one but two escape hatches from his moral dilemma about writing truthfully about the band: They prove themselves louses by bartering the sweetly devoted groupie Penny Lane (Kate Hudson) to another band during a card game, and then Russell tells William, "Write what you want."

The kid never needed absolution from his subject to write an honest story, of course, but Crowe apparently feels that the basics of press integrity are too oblique or distasteful for an audience he panders to shamelessly. From the misty closeups of Penny to a singalong of "Tiny Dancer" aboard the band's tour bus, "Almost Famous" is a case study in the decline of music and movies. Both want to keep the fun in profundity. But neither has figured out how to have it both ways.

SIGHT AND SOUND, 1/01, p. 40, John Wrathall

San Diego,1973. Visiting a local radio station, rock journalist Lester Bangs is accosted by 15-year-old fan William Miller. Bangs commissions William to interview the rock band Black Sabbath for his magazine *Creem*. At the gig William meets Penny Lane, a devoted follower of the support act Stillwater who refers to herself as a "band aid" rather than a groupie. William befriends the members of Stillwater and gains backstage access to the gig. Later, William gets a call from the music editor of rock magazine *Rolling Stone* who has read his articles but doesn't realise how young he is. Commissioned to write a profile of Stillwater, William follows the band on tour, promising his mother he will be back in time for high-school graduation.

William crosses the west from gig to gig on the tour bus, but his attempts to interview Stillwater's charismatic guitarist Russell Hammond are constantly frustrated, not least by Russell's ongoing affair with Penny. When the tour reaches New York, Russell is rejoined by his girlfriend Leslie and abandons Penny. Penny takes an overdose but is saved by William; while she's unconscious, he declares his love for her. William misses his graduation.

Still trying to interview Russell, William accompanies the band on a plane trip. When the plane looks like it's going to crash, everyone confesses their secrets: Leslie learns of Russell's affair with Penny, while the lead singer Jeff Bebe admits to a fling with Leslie. William, meanwhile, blames Russell for throwing Penny away. The plane doesn't crash after all. Following Bangs' advice to be honest and unmerciful, William delivers a truthful but unflattering piece about the band to *Rolling Stone*. The band say they have been misquoted; the piece is spiked. Russell rings Penny and tells her he wants to come and see her in San Diego. Penny gives him William's address instead. When Russell unexpectedly shows up, William finally gets to interview him. Russell tells him that he's phoned *Rolling Stone* and vouched for the accuracy of William's piece; the article makes the cover of the magazine after all.

It's been four years since Cameron Crowe's last—and best—film *Jerry Maguire*. But during that period he hasn't been idle: returning to his journalistic roots, he found time to put together a 370-page book of interviews with Billy Wilder. Like Truffaut's famous book on Hitchcock, *Conversations with Wilder* (1999) offers the curious spectacle of an almost painfully sensitive and humane fan bowing down before a film-maker with a much darker, more bitter sensibility. Perhaps critics who become film-makers are destined to admire the qualities which they themselves lack. For one can't help noticing that Wilder's key virtues—cynicism, satirical bite, economy—are precisely those missing from Crowe's new film *Almost Famous*.

However, Crowe's worship of Wilder is still very relevant to a film that both addresses and embodies the idea of fandom. Loosely based on Crowe's own precocious teenage years—he was a contributor to rock magazine *Rolling Stone* at 16—*Almost Famous* follows 15-year-old journalist William Miller (Patrick Fugit) on tour with the fictional band Stillwater. Just as William is thrilled to fraternise with Stillwater's cool lead guitarist Russell Hammond (Billy Crudup), so for Crowe the film provided an opportunity to hang out with his idols. At 16, Crowe wrote the sleevenotes for Peter Frampton's hit album *Frampton Comes Alive!* A quarter of a century later, Frampton returned the favour: credited as a technical consultant, he was responsible for training Crudup and his fellow band members and also has a cameo as the manager of one of his own bands, Humble Pie. It's tempting to imagine a sequel to *Almost Famous* in which the grown-up, successful William is able to throw some gainful employment the way of the now rather overlooked Russell.

Like Crowe himself, William feels the need for a mentor. (One of the more interesting revelations in *Conversations with Wilder* is that Crowe first approached his idol to ask him to appear in *Jerry Maguire* as veteran sports agent Dicky Fox, whose aphorisms inspire Jerry. Wilder turned down the role, but their meeting led to the interview project.) In *Almost Famous*, the mentor figure is the legendary, real-life rock journalist Lester Bangs, impersonated here by the unstoppably versatile Philip Seymour Hoffman. Bangs' crucial advice to William, delivered at two separate turning points in the film, is that his writing must be "honest and unmerciful". But this ideal is hard to live up to in the real world. just as Jerry Maguire lost his job for displaying too much integrity in his mission statement, so William finds his warts-and-all profile of Stillwater spiked by *Rolling Stone* when the band refuses to confirm his unflatteringly truthful reporting.

I haven't read Crowe's music journalism, but on the strength of *Almost Famous* (and *Conversations with Wilder*, for that matter), "unmerciful" isn't the first word that springs to mind. And his view of the rock scene circa 1973 seems a lot stronger on nostalgia than on honesty. Certainly, anyone who's seen Robert Frank's suppressed documentary *Cocksucker Blues*, which followed the Rolling Stones on a 1972 US tour, will be surprised by the comparative benignity of Crowe's version. Apart from one scene straight out of *This is Spinal Tap*, where Russell and Stillwater's jealous lead singer Jeff Bebe (Jason Lee) argue about their relative positions on the band's new t-shirt, these rock stars are remarkably unegotistical and well behaved. The sex is all safely behind closed doors—with William waiting patiently outside in the hotel corridor. Russell does drop acid at a party, but the scene is played for laughs. Otherwise the drug references are limited to a tiresome running joke in which William's mother (Frances McDormand who is paranoid that he's taking drugs overhears people talking about pot every time she rings him up.

Of course, launching a 15 year-old protagonist into a full-on orgy of sex and drugs would inevitably court controversy (not to mention an 18 certificate), and controversy isn't Crowe's bag. From his days as a boy journalist Crowe certainly has plenty of first-hand experience of the world he depicts; maybe he really is trying to tell us that the truth was much less extreme than the legend. But that's hardly a thrilling premise for a rock 'n' roll movie. Besides, even in purely narrative terms, Crowe has a tendency to fudge the issues. On the road William shares his hotel room with the "band-aids", a group of teenage camp followers who class themselves a cut above mere groupies. One day they announce they're going to deflower him: cue a dreamy, slow-motion montage in which three of the band-aids undress him while Penny Lane (Kate Hudson)—the girl with whom he's actually in love—looks on with amused detachment. It's a highly charged moment—until Crowe fades to black. Next morning the band-aids' dialogue indicates that William is still a virgin; later, in New York, an enigmatic look between William and Russell suggests that he may not be after all. In the era of *American Pie*, it's bewildering to find a coming-of-age movie that's so coy about the physical part of the process.

This isn't the only issue Crowe raises, only to shy away from. At the start of the film Bangs warns William that rock 'n' roll is over, and the subsequent arrival of a corporate smoothie who takes over Stillwater's management (and nearly gets them killed when he makes them give up their trusty tour bus for a plane) seems to confirm his doom-laden predictions. But in the film's closing montage we see Stillwater (still together, despite the rifts of the previous tour) setting off on their 1973 tour, which makes you think 1973 wasn't the end of an era after all.

Always a fluent writer of dialogue, Crowe puts some rip-roaring tirades in Bangs' mouth, delivered with verve by Hoffman. When, near the end of the film, William is stuck writing his Stillwater profile, Bangs reproaches him for getting too close to the musicians, letting them make him feel cool. The point, Bangs insists, is that people like him and William aren't cool; great art, he continues, is not made by cool people—"great art is about guilt and longing." An interesting idea, but once again Crowe saddles himself with a manifesto he can't live up to.

Despite personable performances from Billy Crudup, Kate Hudson and newcomer Patrick Fugit, these characters have none of the passion and incipient mania that made Jerry Maguire—or John Cusack's Lloyd Dobler in Crowe's debut *Say Anything*—so engaging. At one point William gets angry when Penny describes him as "sweet". But all the characters here are sweet, not least the self-destructive Penny. Crowe's refusal to call a groupie a groupie (the distinction is that band-aids only give blow-jobs) is symptomatic of a very unBangsian excess of mercy towards his characters. Even Crowe's most overtly ironic, Wilderesque touch—setting the scene in which Penny has her stomach pumped after an overdose to Stevie Wonder's sickly-sweet 'My Cherie Amour'—backfires, making a traumatic event seem inconsequential. And sure enough, Penny is last seen heading for Morocco, happy, smiling and unscarred by her ordeal. In this rock 'n' roll circus there are, it seems, no casualties.

TIME, 9/18/00, p. 82, Richard Corliss

Does each generation of kids get the music it deserves? No, but it gets the music that defines it. It's in the generational blood. Every joy or pang of growing up has an accompanying sound track. And decades later, car-radio playings of specific songs, good or bad, can be as acute a prod to sweet or rueful memory as Proust's tea cake. For Cameron Crowe, the pastry was named Led Zeppelin, the Allman Brothers, Poco. And Crowe didn't just listen to them. He interviewed them. The '70s were when the machinery of rock-starmaking was perfected. The poet-satyrs onstage and the poet-flacks of the rock press fed off one another voraciously. The artists preened; the authors postured—all to make the cover of *Rolling Stone*.

What gives Crowe's story poignance is his background as a teenage working journalist. At the age when kids are supposed to be feeling those gonadal guitar jolts, for the first time, he was standing backstage during a concert, riding the band bus, eliciting sexual confessions from rock Rimbauds. This was a kid's dream. But to live it—to survive it—Crowe had to be a premature grownup.

Almost Famous has a lot of smart lines, but the best are in Patrick Fugit's face. Fugit, who plays the teen Crowe character, William Miller, has a baby face, creased with dimples and given to grins, but it is stuck on a tall, gawky body. Then he speaks, and he sounds so much older than he looks it's as if his voice had been dubbed by the adult he would become—the adult who became Crowe. Watchful and open, skeptical but not cynical, Fugit manages to embody both the child and the man, the boy who went on the trip and the writer who would remember it and shape it into comic drama.

William lucks into his on-the-road adventure with the rock quartet Stillwater, and is adopted as their chronicler and mascot. At 15 he could be the poster child for a dark odyssey of sexual and pharmacological abuse; his mother could be right when she blurts out, "Rock stars have kidnapped my son." But William and the film are too savvy for that. People use one another here, but genially, and in small doses. On this cross-country trek, everyone is, benignly, lost in poppyland. It's Oz without the wizard.

The typical boy-to-man fable is one of groping in the dark, a child beset by demons, on a road with no signposts. But William isn't clueless; he has too many clues. He is swamped in advice: from his musical mentor, the rebel critic Lester Bangs (another off-kilter, on-target tour de force by Philip Seymour Hoffman); from his muse, the knowing groupie Penny Lane (Kate Hudson, with the soft, curly haired charisma of a Woodstock Botticelli); from Stillwater's lead guitarist, Russell Hammond (Billy Crudup, who has finally found the movie role to fit his questing intelligence and almost-too-hunky features); and from his protective mom (fierce, nattering Frances McDormand). William's task is to sift all this good, or at least plausible, advice and make his own choices. On the fly, on the road, he's forced into maturity.

Most memory movies (and novels and plays) have a score to settle. When parents are depicted as idiots, teachers as tyrants and classmates as sadists, you can bet the writer feels so much better for taking revenge on the people who made his teen years miserable.

Crowe carries no such grudge. He has warm feelings for all the characters (except the *Rolling Stone* staff; they come off as naive and capricious, first deciding that an unseen article from an unknown writer should be a cover story, then killing it briefly when the band disputes a few quotes). Crowe likes the rockers, the groupies, the exasperated desk clerk at a rowdy hotel. And dammit, he *loves* his mom.

That's nice. Better yet, it is good screenwriting: giving each character his reasons, making everyone in the emotional debate charming and compelling, creating fictional people who breathe in a story with an organic life.

One associates this equipoise, this generosity of spirit, with Crowe's mentor, the writer-director James L. Brooks (*Terms of Endearment, Broadcast News*), who produced Crowe's *Say Anything...*and *Jerry Maguire*. Those early Crowe films, for all their nifty moments, reduced minor figures to stereotypes, skirted believability, settled for easy answers. The new one is a big step up. By recalling (and subtly rouging) the inner adult of his childhood, the Brooks protégé becomes his own man.

So *Almost Famous* is almost fabulous. Oh, all right. The movie's so clever and endearing, you can forget the almost.

VILLAGE VOICE, 9/19/00, p. 115, J. Hoberman

A historical marker in more ways than one, *American Graffiti* perfected a near Pavlovian formula for manufacturing the myth of a generation out of dated pop music and period ephemera. Cameron Crowe's quasi-autobiographical *Almost Famous*, which is set mainly in the spring of 1973 (a few months before *American Graffiti*'s epochal release), seems to be working to similar effect—although in a more fashionably star-struck context. *American Graffiti*'s implanted memory aspired to the generic; *Almost Famous* shows its hero inventing that memory. The scenario demonstrates its creator's preordained success.

As *Almost Famous* is dedicated to the demographic defined by its sense of having missed the big party of the '60s, Crowe begins by projecting self-righteous counterculture anticommercialism back onto his mother. His alter ego, William, is introduced as the son of a wildly controlling widow (played, with charmless aggression, by Frances McDormand). Supposedly some sort of lefty college professor and professional protest monger, Mom is sufficiently clueless to imagine Simon and Garfunkel as dangerous apostles of "drugs and sex." Mom's moralizing drives William's big sister out of the house, but before she leaves she bequeaths her LPs to the 11-year-old with the promise that "one day you'll be cool." Cut from 1969 to 1973 when precocious William (Patrick Fugit), a would-be rock critic, wangles his first assignment from *Creem* editor Lester Bangs (embodied by Philip Seymour Hoffman as a living legend).

No less than Mom, Bangs is an anticommercial loud mouth—albeit of a different type. Thus, the aspiring writer has a crazed, overprotective mother and a distant, wacky mentor who, in preparing to cede the oedipal struggle, wearily informs him that rock is over: "You got here just in time for the death rattle." In fact, rock will provide William with a surrogate family, an education, a few cheap thrills, and a clear career path. The kid can't get backstage to interview Black Sabbath, but thanks to the sympathetic groupie—"band-aid" is her preferred term—who calls herself Penny Lane (Kate Hudson), he manages to attach himself to the up-and-coming Stillwater, a sort of amalgam of Led Zeppelin and Bad Company, led by Russell Hammond (Billy Crudup) and Jeff Bebe (Jason Lee). "I'm the front man and you're the guitarist with mystique," Jeff tells Russell in an amusing contretemps over their respective placements on a promotional T-shirt.

Despite blathering Jeff's classification of the diminutive, enthusiastic William as "the enemy," Russell realizes that Stillwater (or at least he) can make use of the kid reporter and invites him to join their tour. *Almost Famous* has been described as a movie about the heroic era of rock criticism, but it has far more to do with establishing the coolness of celebrity journalism. The power of pop is seen from a backstage perspective rather than out front with the fans. William has nothing intelligible to say about Stillwater's music but everything to learn about their lifestyle. It's mere moments before the kid is called by the self-important Ben Fong-Torres and gets upgraded from *Creem* to *Rolling Stone*.

Panoramic yet cozy, enthusiastically glib, *Almost Famous* suggests a universe of interlocking sitcoms. (It might almost be a special two-hour version of *The Wonder Years.*) In one running gag, Mom keeps calling William's various hotels and compulsively tells her students that "rock stars have kidnapped my son." In another, William seeks midnight advice from the incorruptible Bangs. "I'm always home—I'm uncool," his guru frankly admits. (Hoffman and his character should have been the movie.) Warned by Bangs against imagining that he has become friends with the band, William pursues the elusive interview with rueful Russell as though it were his white whale even as Penny shacks up with the star. William is more wide-eyed than usual when he is ravished by three lesser band-aids while Penny looks on in amusement, favoring us with her trademark nose-wrinkle and pretending she possesses the wisdom of the ages.

William enjoys a few other rowdy adventures, tagging along with Russell to a teenage party in Topeka in which the star drops acid and begins proclaiming himself a "golden god." (Another sign of the times—the Orgy has penetrated deepest Kansas.) Russell jumps off the roof into the pool; I fell off the bus in the next scene, designed to provide the designated moment of communion, with the band and band-aids all singing an Elton John anthem. (It's a generational taste—like flat soda pop.) The partying and careerism get more intense as William pursues his story to Cleveland and finally all the way to New York—at which point he receives a phone call from Jann Wenner himself. (The real Wenner has a cameo here just as he did in *Jerry Maguire*.

What does it say about Crowe's directorial personality that his trademark is the presence of a powerful erstwhile employer?)

"It's not about money, it's about playing music and turning people on," the members of Stillwater keep telling each other en route to the cover of *Rolling Stone. Almost Famous* is a movie that defuses its own bad conscience. As suggested by *Jerry Maguire,* Crowe's specialty is the principled sellout. *Almost Famous* experiments with a variety of potential endings, most of them involving some sort of betrayal, before settling on the most positive alternative. You keep waiting for William to become disillusioned and he never is.

Also reviewed in:
CHICAGO TRIBUNE, 9/15/00, Friday/p. A, Michael Wilmington
NATION, 9/18/00, p. 42, Stuart Klawans
NEW REPUBLIC, 9/25/00, p. 30, Stanley Kauffmann
NEW YORK TIMES, 9/13/00, p. E1, A.O. Scott
NEW YORKER, 9/18/00, p. 153, David Denby
VARIETY, 9/11-17/00, p. 21, Todd McCarthy
WASHINGTON POST, 9/22/00, p. C1, Stephen Hunter
WASHINGTON POST, 9/22/00, Weekend/p. 45, Desson Howe

ALONE

A New Yorker Films release.   *Director:* Erick Zonca.   *Screenplay (French with English subtitles):* Erick Zonca.   *Director of Photography:* Pascal Poucet.   *Editor:* Jean Robert Thomann.   *Sound:* Jean Luc Audy. *Running time:* 34 minutes. *MPAA Rating:* Not Rated.

CAST: Florence Loiret (Amélie);   Veronique Octon (Sophie).

VILLAGE VOICE, 3/7/00, p. 128, Amy Taubin

[*Alone* was reviewed jointly with *The Little Thief*; see Taubin's review of that film.]

Also reviewed in:
NATION, 3/27/00, p. 34, Stuart Klawans
NEW YORK TIMES, 3/1/00, p. E5, Lawrence Van Gelder
NEW YORKER, 3/6/00, p. 99, Anthony Lane

AMERICAN GYPSY: A STRANGER IN EVERYBODY'S LAND

A Little Dust production. *Producer:* Jasmine Dellal, Michal Conford, Herb Bennett, and Herb Ferrette.   *Director:* Jasmine Dellal. *Screenplay (English and Romani with English subtitles):* Jasmine Dellal. *Director of Photography:* Michele Zaccheo and Jasmine Dellal. *Editor:* Joseph De Francesco and Jasmine Dellal. *Music:* John Filcich. *Running time:* 79 minutes. *MPAA Rating:* Not Rated.

WITH: Grover Marks;   Lippie Marks;   Jane Marks;   Jimmie Marks;   Ian Hancock;   William Duna.

VILLAGE VOICE, 4/25/00, p. 144, Nico Baumbach

First-time filmmaker Jasmine Dellal knows that it can be hard to dispel myths without in some way reinforcing them, especially when approaching a culture from the outside. Her documentary,

American Gypsy, focuses on what Edward Said has called the only ethnic group about which anything can be said "without challenge or demurral." The Rom (the proper term for Gypsies) are dispersed yet insular and lack a written language, leaving them open to either unabashed racism or romantic mystification. The film presents a chilling history of persecution, slavery, and genocide; the Rom generally regard gadje (as they call all non-Rom) with suspicion. Dellal focuses on Jimmy Marks of Spokane, Washington, one of the only Rom who will return her phone calls. Embroiled in a civil suit against the city over an unlawful search of his house, Marks is something of a local celebrity. Though the police clearly proceeded illegally and offended Romany beliefs about privacy, his obsession with the spotlight sometimes undermines the narrative of injustice. Dellal avoids sensationalism and editorializing, but her portrait lacks intimacy and a knack for finding productive contradictions. The most fascinating character is Jimmy's mother, Lippie. When Dellal calls her on a fib, Lippie proclaims, with a twinkle in her eye, "There is no truth." The meaning is clear—not that truth doesn't exist, or is relative, but only that the full truth can never be communicated to Dellal or us. As a Rom proverb says: "The deer in the forest is under no obligation to justify his existence to the hunter."

Also reviewed in:
NEW YORK TIMES, 4/21/00, p. E28, A.O. Scott
VARIETY, 5/8-14/00, p. 72, Dennis Harvey

AMERICAN PIMP

A Seventh Art Releasing release of an Underworld Entertainment presentation. *Producer:* Allen Hughes, Albert Hughes, and Kevin Messick. *Director:* Allen Hughes and Albert Hughes. *Director of Photography:* Albert Hughes. *Editor:* Doug Pray. *Music:* Sean Sarasov. *Music Editor:* Jonathan Karp. *Sound:* Allen Hughes. *Sound Editor:* Gregory King and Steven D. Williams. *Running time:* 97 minutes. *MPAA Rating:* R.

CAST: Rosebudd, Schauntte, Bradley, C-Note, Ken Ivy, Charm, R.P., Fillmore Slim, Sir Captain, Payroll, Gorgeous Dre, Bishop Don Magic Juan, Mel Taylor, Kenny Red, Danny Brown, Dennos Hof (Pimps); Jade, Samantha, Monica , Latrice, Spicy (Prostitutes).

LOS ANGELES TIMES, 6/9/00, Calendar/p. 14, Kevin Thomas

"American Pimp" is as effective for what it doesn't say as for what it does, inviting the audience to draw its own conclusions. The Hughes brothers, Allan and Albert, makers of the hits "Menace II Society" and "Dead Presidents," spent two years traveling to 15 cities and interviewing 30 pimps—only one of them white—and have come up with a documentary as revealing as it is disturbing, one that engrosses as it at times repulses, a film that shifts from one moment to the next from the outrageously funny to the just plain outrageous.

Wisely, the Hughes brothers don't judge—they inspire trust in their subjects and get these men and some of their women to open up about their lives and their profession. They set up their stories with a prologue composed of man- and woman-on-the-street opinions of pimps gathered mainly from white people, whose reactions are, not surprisingly, profoundly negative. As we meet one pimp after the next the Hughes brothers adroitly intersperse clips from such early '70s blaxploitation pictures as "The Mack" (which stars Max Julien) and "Willie Dynamite" and stills from the landmark book "Gentlemen of Leisure" and bridge the sequences with music of the era.

In his unforgettable memoir "Pimp" the late Iceberg Slim said if you grew up poor in Chicago's black ghetto, pimping was one of the few ways for an enterprising young man to make money. Virtually all the pimps the Hughes brothers talk to are entrepreneurs to the core, and that they chose pimping as their avenue to financial success reflects the limited options they believe society offers them. Indeed, Danny Brown, a handsome middle-aged Angeleno who has forsaken pimping for a career as a blues singer, theorizes that black pimping began when female ex-slaves were encouraged by their men to charge their former masters for what they had previously enjoyed by droit du seigneur. Slavery also fomented the enduring "Mandingo Mystique" of black males as supermen, sustained to this day in the world of sports and entertainment, other long-standing arenas of opportunity for African American men.

The pimps all say they started early, often in their teens, and that pimping was something that they fell into naturally, following in the footsteps of male relatives and neighbors. (One of the reasons the Hughes brothers were inspired to make their documentary was because a member of their family "dabbled in the pimporial arts.

There's an intriguing difference between the older men, now mainly retired, and their younger counterparts: The older generation tend to be better-looking and sharper dressers, some of them carrying on to this day stereotypical exaggerated gaudy attire and flashy jewelry and fancy cars. Whether extroverted or understated in personality and style, these men all project a strong, forceful presence necessary to attract and hold on to a stable of women.

Which brings us to the real heart of the matter and how the Hughes brothers have trusted in the power of implication. These pimps are hardheaded businessmen and take pride in being men of their word, but what this inevitably means is that they come to regard the women they control as, as one man bluntly puts it, "products." What is most devastating about the film is how the pimp-whore relationship has warped these men's view of women.

They all talk about how much they do for their women, how well they take care of them, how they are there for them, but they might as well be talking about workhorses. The dehumanizing aspect of pimping is what's scariest about the Hughes brothers' investigation—so powerful the filmmakers realize they need only to record it. As for the much-vaunted protection a pimp offers, it is limited at best, and a number of the men admit to having at least one prostitute in their stable who has been murdered by a john.

We don't meet many of the women, but most seem to be white, not all that pretty and not very intelligent. The film's two black prostitutes, however, are attractive, smart and without illusions. One has opted for the greater security of a legal Nevada brothel, operated by the film's sole white pimp. This man makes a solid case for legalized prostitution, yet on a personal level lacks the dignity, however cruel, of his black counterparts working the big-city streets.

NEW YORK POST, 6/9/00, p. 50, Jonathan Foreman

Some of the pimps interviewed in "American Pimp," the amusingly flippant foray into documentary filmmaking by brothers Albert and Allen Hughes, are so absurdly stereotypical, with their over-the-top clothes and cars and spicy speechifying about how to treat "bitches," that you wouldn't believe them in a work of fiction.

But what's really intriguing—and engaging—about this film is the glimpse it offers into how prostitutes not only become emotionally dependent on their pimps, but actually come to love them.

Apparently, a master pimp needs a powerful combination of psychological insight, ruthlessness and personal charm to "break" or "turn" a girl. (And all the pimps interviewed here are unusually charismatic, articulate, bright and often very funny.)

But once you're in the game, "it's the greatest job in the world"—for the pimps.

While playing down the violence and drug abuse that are so prevalent in the relationships between street hookers and their pimps, the film confirms many of the disturbing, deeply politically incorrect observations about men and women in Iceberg Slim's classic cult memoir, "Pimp"—a book several of the Hughes' subjects actually cite.

Unfortunately, you really only hear about prostitution from the side of the pimp.

What makes this film much more than just another episode of HBO's "Real Sex" series is the way the Hughes brothers cleverly use '70s music and scenes from blaxploitation films like "The Mack."

It reminds you that the whole hypnotic spectacle is as much a dark, amoral joke about stock figures in urban African-American culture as a serious investigation of a criminal underworld.

NEWSDAY, 6/9/00, Part II/p. B11, John Anderson

The snake-hatted, mink-coated, ingot-size-ring-wearing, Cadillac-cruising pimp of the late '70s blaxploitation movie seems to have inspired the writing-directing Hughes brothers to make a full-length documentary about men who sell women.

But really, did they need a reason? There certainly aren't enough statistics about domestic violence or the life expectancy of prostitutes or AIDS rates or the popular backlash against whatever strides women have made over the past 30 years. We needed a movie that shows the sensitive side of the men who exploit them.

In "American Pimp," Allen and Albert Hughes ("Menace II Society," "Dead Presidents") employ a mostly hands-off technique, allowing the pimps—Payroll, Charm, Fillmore Slim, Bishop Don Magic Juan—to talk and talk and talk until they establish themselves to be as morally bankrupt as we suspect they are.

And then you hear either Albert or Allen Hughes giggling along with their more outrageous assertions. And wonder again about their inspiration.

The pimps posturing, to say nothing of their language, is too self-conscious and camera-directed to be entirely believable, and you'd like to think the Hugheses—whose "Menace" was one of the great directing debuts of the '90s—were out to make a parody. But by never challenging anything their pimps say—about the techniques of "turning" women, or about what women really want, or how sex for a hooker is the same as flipping Filet-O-Fish sandwiches at McDonald's—they allow the inference that they believe it all. They allow the pimps, (or purported pimps) to vent the venomous misogyny that infects their pathetic souls. And the Hugheses seem to find it amusing.

Appropriating a common technique of the "issue" documentary, the brothers open the film with a series of brief man/woman-on-the-street interviews in which people state their presumably uninformed opinions about pimps. The movie is then poised to refute them. But the movie never refutes a thing. And the fact that all those initial interviewees are white or Hispanic implies that blacks, in toto, are in sympathy with the men of "American Pimp." And that's something for which the Hughes brothers should apologize immediately.

VILLAGE VOICE, 6/13/00, p. 155, J. Hoberman

American Pimp, the documentary by the twins Allen and Albert Hughes *(Dead Presidents, Menace II Society)*, may not be the most garrulous exploitation film ever made, but—James Toback, eat your heart out—it surely sets the modern record for the use of the word *bitch* in an 86-minute film.

Alternately mind-expanding and brain-numbing, *American Pimp* splices together interviews with a dozen or more macks, players, and perpetually wired gentlemen of leisure who—smooth, persuasive, and hyper-verbal—seize every opportunity, and more, to run their riffs. The pimp who compares his mouth to an Uzi has it exactly right. These guys talk so damn much and with such relentless self-justification they might be trying to drill a hole in your head.

An opening montage of assorted honkies dissing pimp morality immediately establishes mackdom as a race thing. Offering some history lite, the Hugheses identify their subjects with the trickster figures of West African folklore and make a vague connection to the material conditions that followed slavery. Surely more could have been done with this, but then *American Pimp is* not an educational film. (The distinctions between "macks" and "players" or "real pimps" and "perpetrator pimps" are left hanging.) The mode is strictly subcultural show-and-tell.

American Pimp is most concerned with the spell cast by an image. As more than a few rap artists have been, the Hughes brothers were captivated by Iceberg Slim's perennial best-seller *Pimp, The Story of My Life* and inspired by blaxploitation cult classics like *The Mack* and *Willie Dynamite*. The peacocks who strut through these movies so strongly resemble their real-life models that, given this rare example of Hollywood verisimilitude, one naturally wonders who was the model for whom. The Hughes brothers quote scenes from the movies while their pimps paraphrase the dialogue.

Moving from Honolulu to Vegas to San Francisco to New Orleans to Washington, D.C. (where a pimp posed in front of the Capitol laughs that he's "making more money than the president"), *American Pimp* has a tawdry jet-set ambience. If prostitution is understood as a version of interactive showbiz, the pimps are a movie in themselves—and not a silent one. "The name is internationally known: Bishop Don Magic Juan," says one by way of an introduction. Global reputation or not, the pimp in question has a collection of pictures in which, resplendently turned out in matching gator shoes, suit, and sombrero, he's posed with such kindred hustlers as Ike Turner, Marion Barry, and Donald Trump. (Later, the good Bishop reveals that "one of the greatest pimps who ever lived is called ... God.")

As with all small entrepreneurs, the pimps' commitment to the work ethic is total—so long as you're working for them. They constantly return to the bottom line, and whether or not it's true that, as one mack boasts, "anyone can be turned out," they can recognize their prey getting off the bus in any big city. One mack is as proud as Rudy Giuliani to have taken some bitch off welfare. To a man, they disdain the idea of violence or abuse. Dripping with rings that could double as brass knuckles, they promote pimping as a head trip: "I don't steal nothing but a bitch's mind." A successful pimp is the street-smart equivalent of a chess grandmaster; explaining "pimpology" to a square would be like "talking astrophysics to a muthafuckin' wino."

The plenitude of snapshots and group portraits of pimps'n'hos suggests a sort of perverse family structure. Human sentiment is not completely absent. "She was the first 'ho to pay me," one pimp recalls with a tenderness somewhat more convincing than his subsequent bid for sympathy in recounting the story of a hooker killed in action. This movie is the celluloid equivalent of a term at the Citadel. Could there possibly be a female point of view? (A paper could be written on the sociology of American Pimp as a dating flick.) The filmmakers interview only a handful of 'hos, and the most articulate is a legal sex worker employed by a sanctimonious white businessman at Nevada's Bunny Ranch. The few minutes that the Hugheses spent soaking up the circus maximus atmosphere of the Players Ball is virtually the only time in the movie we get to see the pimps together with their employees.

Not unlike the 'hos, American Pimp feels more than a little cowed by its subjects. The pimps are as hungry for stardom as Andy Warhol's drag queens, but the Hugheses are almost always outmanipulated. There's no going beneath the surface with the pimps themselves—although several reveal ambitions going back to childhood. A more creative psychologist than the filmmakers, Iceberg Slim—briefly heard incanting a poem from his 70s LP *Reflections*—posited an Orestes complex. Suggesting that pimps were taking vengeance on their rejecting mothers, he claimed to have personally known "several dozen" who were "dumped into trash bins" as infants. Of course, for some, the privilege of golfing with white business swells on the spectacular overlook of some Honolulu country club would be justification enough. Or, as another pimp snarls: "I'm not going to wipe your toilets. Fuck you."

For all its gaga repetition, American Pimp manages a few suggestive narrative shards. The saga of Fillmore Slim and the L.A. track is a Tarantino flick waiting to be made. (And just how did Bishop Don Magic Juan get religion?) I appreciated as downbeat Americana the case of the retired pimp who turned blues singer so he could keep his wardrobe. And melancholy as a twilight western is the tale of the pimp called Rosebudd. Down to one last 'ho, he married her and turned square, working to support his family as a telemarketer.

Also reviewed in:
CHICAGO TRIBUNE, 7/14/00, Friday/p. A, Mark Caro
NEW YORK TIMES, 6/9/00, p. E17, Stephen Holden
VARIETY, 2/1-7/99, p. 60, Emanuel Levy

AMERICAN PSYCHO

A Lions Gate Films release of an Edward R. Pressman production in association with MUSE Productions and Christian Halsey Solomon. *Executive Producer:* Michael Paseornek, Jeff Sackman, and Joseph Drake. *Producer:* Edward R. Pressman, Chris Hanley, and Christian Halsey Solomon. *Director:* Mary Harron. *Screenplay:* Mary Harron and Guinevere Turner. *Based on the novel by:* Bret Easton Ellis. *Director of Photography:* Andrzej Sekula. *Editor:* Andrew Marcus. *Music:* John Cale. *Music Editor:* Jeff Wolpert. *Sound:* Henry Embry and (music) William Garrett.   *Sound Editor:* Jane Tattersall.   *Casting:* Kerry Barden, Suzanne Smith, and Billy Hopkins.   *Production Designer:* Gideon Ponte.   *Art Director:* Andrew Stearn. *Set Decorator:* Jeanne Develle.   *Special Effects:* Conrad V. Brink, Jr. *Costumes:* Isis Mussenden. *Make-up:* Sandra Wheatle.   *Stunt Coordinator:* Matt Birman.   *Running time:* 104 minutes. *MPAA Rating:* R.

CAST: Christian Bale (Patrick Bateman); Willem Dafoe (Donald Kimball); Jared Leto (Paul Allen); Josh Lucas (Craig McDermott); Samantha Mathis (Courtney Rawlinson); Matt Ross (Luis Carruthers); Bill Sage (David Van Patten); Chloë Sevigny (Jean); Cara Seymour (Christie); Justin Theroux (Timothy Bryce); Guinevere Turner (Elizabeth); Reese Witherspoon (Evelyn Williams); Stephen Bogaert (Harold Carnes); Monika Meier (Daisy); Reg E. Cathey (Homeless Man); Blair Williams (Waiter 1); Marie Dame (Victoria); Kelley Harron (Bargirl); Patricia Gage (Mrs. Wolfe); Krista Sutton (Sabrina); Landy Cannon (Man at Pierce & Pierce); Park Bench (Stash); Catherine Black (Vanden); Margaret Ma (Dry Cleaner Woman); Tufford Kennedy (Hamilton);   Mark Pawson (Humphrey Rhineback); Jessica Lau (Facialist); Lilette Wiens (Maitre d'); Glen Marc Silot (Waiter); Charlotte Hunter (Libby); Kiki Buttingnol (Caron); Joyce Korbin (Woman at ATM; Reuben Thompson (Waiter 2); Bryan Renfro (Night Watchman);   Ross Gibby (Man Outside Store); Christina McKay (Young Woman);   Allan McCullough (Man in Stall); Anthony Lemke (Marcus Halberstram); Connie Chen (Gwendolyn Ichiban).

CINEASTE, Vol. XXV, No. 3, 2000 p. 43, Richard Porton

During the 1980s, *Not the New York Times,* an astute parody of our newspaper of record, christened the weekly Living section the "Having" section. Given the fact that Eighties acquisitiveness seems a bit tame compared to the lust for lucre which permeates our own 'dot-com' age, the release of Mary Harron's *American Psycho* could not be more timely. Even intellectuals look back at Sixties idealism as something of a pipe dream; the most radical sociologists are resigned to conceding that freedom is now commonly defined as 'consumer choice.' Harron and Guinevere Turner's adaptation of Bret Easton Ellis's highly controversial novel acidly dissects the warped imagination of a man who is more of a walking demographic profile than a full-bodied human being.

At the time of its publication, Ellis's book (which was unceremoniously dropped by its original publisher, Simon and Schuster) was condemned by a chorus of critics who were repulsed by its stomach-churning violence. Yet many readers were even more alienated by the prospect of spending 399 pages inside the head of a terminal bore determined to recount the brand name of every consumer item he either owned or coveted. The bore, and antihero, in question, Wall Street hot-shot Patrick Bateman, is probably the most passionless serial killer in either literary or cinematic history. Unlike Dostoyevsky's Raskolnikov or Hitchcock's Norman Bates, Bateman's personal history is thoroughly irrelevant. Bereft of both a tangible past (except a Harvard degree, which functions as another brand-name allegiance) and any conception of the future, he lives in an eternal present where introspection is impossible and altruism is a joke. Within this air-tight universe (to quote J.G. Ballard, a media-saturated world where "any free or original response to experience" has been preempted), traditional notions of character development are, inevitably, impossible. And Ellis's bland, almost mechanical prose, while providing a precise simulation of the protagonist's inner void, lacks the verbal frisson that traditionally accompanies 'great fiction.'

For most audience members, viewing Harron's streamlined adaptation will prove a considerably less onerous task than plowing through Ellis's opus. While every satirical nugget in the film is directly appropriated from the novel, Bateman's monomaniacal narcissism is tempered by Harron's occasional willingness to give us access to other characters' points of view. In addition, the monotonous drone of Bateman's self-regard is at least partially alleviated by the witty visual flourishes brought to the film by Gideon Ponte's inventive production design and Andrzej Sekula's handsome cinematography. Ponte's conception of Bateman's apartment is especially clever in evoking an era where surface took precedence over substance—pristine white interior unadorned by a single book or newspaper perfectly expresses the minimalist esthetic of the Eighties (an austerity so extreme that it becomes excessive). The film opens with one of Harron's most ingenious visual flourishes—droplets of blood superimposed on the credits are transformed into an order of squid ravioli ready to be devoured by yuppie hordes. The peculiarly anal-retentive nature of nouvelle cuisine—food which is almost too dainty to be eaten and meted out in portions too small to satisfy a healthy appetite—meshes well with Bateman's own obsession with ultracleanliness. For the more slovenly members of the audience, his morning ablutions, during which he applies a dizzying array of creams, gels, and facial masks, will seem like some alien tribe's strangely masochistic ritual. Harron manages to depict this regimen with a facetious elan that never congeals into campiness (Bateman's voice-over tribute to his favorite toiletries combined with a closeup of him showering resembles a warped parody of television advertising.)

Despite some critics' jibes, it is completely appropriate for Harron to follow Ellis's lead and focus on Bateman's hedonistic preoccupations with television programs, recreational drugs, fashion, pop music, and restaurants. The corporate ideology of the Eighties dispensed with the moralistic bromides disseminated during the Eisenhower era, as well as (despite a thin gloss of Reaganite rhetoric) the 'family values' embraced by prototypical 'organization men' of the Fifties. In fact, the Eighties were useful for demonstrating that capitalism can thrive without a puritanical veneer; Bateman and his fellow Wall Streeters are as addled with drugs as Sixties counterculturalists (once denounced by conservatives as 'unproductive') while paying obeisance to a work ethic purged of phony moralism. Like Patrick's musical hero, Huey Lewis, the Wall Street crowd believes that it's "hip to be square," and the pleasure-seeking money men of the Eighties succeeded in erasing previous distinctions between hipness and squareness. The self-abnegation once advocated by Ben Franklin is superseded by absurd forms of status seeking. *American Psycho's* most amusing example of hollow one-upmanship (culled lovingly from the novel) is a scene where Bateman proudly produces his new business card, printed on "eggshell" stock and featuring a stylish typeface, only to be trumped by associates who brandish even more impressively tasteful cards. Another running gag involves Patrick's attempt to convince rivals that he has instantaneously obtained reservations at a hot new restaurant named Dorsia where tables must be booked weeks in advance.

Of course, when Bateman isn't savoring arugula or kiwi and watching porn videos, his real business is killing innocent men and women. His first quarry is a terrified homeless man whose ability to consume either rarefied cuisine or fine fashions is obviously limited. Patrick snarls that he has "nothing in common" with this frightened African-American, and it's difficult not to compare this cavalier attitude with Mayor Giuliani's ongoing war against the poor. Subsequently, when Bateman murders an associate, Paul Allen, the film moves into territory that could be labeled urban magical realism. All of Bateman's colleagues come off as fairly interchangeable specimens—preppy guys with slicked-backed hair and a taste for Cerruti suits and Oliver Peoples glasses. But Allen enrages Patrick by committing the cardinal sin of renting a posher apartment, a commodious pad with a great view of Central Park.

Harron's insistence that none of the film's events are intended to appear 'hallucinatory' seems slightly disingenuous. She obviously eschews naturalism by ignoring Bateman's actual workday (even the most amoral investment bankers put in grueling hours). Once inured to the film's not quite seamless mixture of black humor and restrained Grand Guignol, it is no surprise that a young female acquaintance misconstrues Patrick's boast of specializing in "murders and executions" as a mundane reference to mergers and acquisitions. The film's tendency to abjure realism, however, becomes slightly compromised near its conclusion as the protagonist, never anything more than a virtual automaton in Ellis's novel, briefly emerges—however inadvertently—as an object of pathos. Confused and hysterical, the American psycho himself loses his hauteur and begins to behave like a garden-variety maniac. Tempting us to view Bateman as a conventional psychotic, not a symptom of deeply rooted political and social psychosis, the narrative's satirical thrust is temporarily derailed.

Ultimately, the major chasm between the book and the Harron/Turner adaptation resides in the contrast between Ellis's graphic, detailed accounts of Bateman's murderous rampage and the film version's relatively delicate treatment of the same events. While some disgruntled readers believed that Ellis's nauseating descriptions of victims (mostly women) being stabbed, mutilated, or chainsawed to death were written with a suspect relish, no one could accuse Harron of a prurient approach to bloodletting. The book's gory killing of Paul Allen (called Owen by Ellis) is transformed into stylized slaughter; the ever-fastidious Bateman dons a slicker to deflect blood that lands like Jackson Pollock paint drippings on his well-scrubbed face.

More importantly, Harron's conception of the film as a feminist project nurtures tangible empathy for the movie's female prey. Close-ups are compassionately deployed to indicate the queasiness a hard-working prostitute feels as she crosses the threshold of Bateman's apartment. Additionally, in a climactic scene that has no parallel in the book, Patrick's secretary, Jean—a woman with a palpable crush on her boss—recoils in horror as she surveys his date book's misogynistic doodles.

One of the book's most intriguing paradoxes was the fact that an author marinated in pop culture ended up skewering its banalities with deadpan aplomb. Entire chapters are devoted to Bateman's paeans to some of the most insipid songs in the history of pop music.   Whitney Huston's "The Greatest Love of All," to take a particularly on-target example, is one of Patrick's favorite anthems. Houston's signature song echoes the platitudes of innumerable self-help books; Bateman's pumped-up arrogance illustrates the affinities between self-help and self-delusion. In the film, the comic brio of these passages is intensified, since Bateman recites these mock homages to future victims, who, logically enough, are completely bewildered by his in-depth dissection of crooners like Phil Collins and Huey Lewis.

A movie striving for a precarious equilibrium between satire and genuine horror requires virtuosic performances, and Christian Bale's chilling impersonation of Patrick Bateman certainly fills the bill. A key factor in Bale's effectiveness is his realization that the character's vapidity could not be conveyed with the usual recourse to psychological clichés favored by most American actors. Bale instead concentrates on Patrick's buffed exterior, casual smirk, and haughty Ivy League speech patterns. As he told *Interview*, "Bateman is constantly performing. He really has no sense of self except for a complete lack of self." The key female performances, on the other hand, especially the gifted stage actress Cara Seymour's turn as a haunted prostitute and Chloë Sevigny's depiction of the ingenuous Jean, are nuanced portraits of women who cannot comprehend Bateman's homicidal brand of cynicism.

Towards the end of *American Psycho*, the avuncular figure of Ronald Reagan, lying through his teeth about the consequences of the Iran/Contra debacle, appears on a television screen. For some naysayers, a film that confirms, however elegantly, the Reagan era's longstanding reputation for greed and narcissism is merely reiterating stale arguments. Nevertheless, the film's critique transcends the peculiarities of the Eighties. Harron's bleak comedy has its pulse on the ideological residue of the Reagan era that remains with us today—what the sociologist Zygmunt Bauman terms the propensity "to treat the whole of life as one protracted shopping spree... casting the world as a warehouse overflowing with consumer commodities." Audaciously linking shopping sprees and murder sprees, Harron's film is a mordantly funny death knell for a despicable decade and a cautionary tale tailor-made for the uncertain present.

FILM QUARTERLY, Winter 2000-01, p. 41, Linda S. Kauffman

What a difference a decade makes! When Bret Easton Ellis published *American Psycho* in 1991, he was universally reviled for his portrait of Patrick Bateman, a stockbroker/serial killer with yuppie-and cannibalistic-tastes. Simon and Schuster was originally slated to publish the novel, but reneged on the contract just a month before the book was scheduled to arrive in bookstores. Sonny Mehta finally published it in Random House's Vintage Contemporary series, and sold 250,000 copies. Mehta and Ellis both received anonymous death threats, including photos of Ellis with an axe drawn in his forehead, eyes gouged out. The National Organization of Women organized boycotts not just of the novel, but also of products that appear in the novel; they eventually extended the boycott to all Random House and Vintage titles. De facto censorship set in after publication: numerous bookstores refused even to carry the book.

In retrospect, it is clear that Ellis's novel was a casualty of corporate clashes, not conscience, for the real reason Simon and Schuster dropped it is that Martin Davis, CEO of Paramount Communications, ordered Dick Snyder, Simon and Schuster's CEO, to kill it, despite the objections of senior editors, who urged Snyder not to bow to corporate authority. What was Martin Davis's claim to fame before this fiasco? He produced movies, including all the *Friday the 13th* films. As other publishing houses continue to be gobbled up by entertainment conglomerates, corporate interference like this has not only become increasingly common in the last decade, it has become the norm. (André Schiffrin cites numerous examples of market censorship and self-censorship in his recent *The Business of Books: How International Conglomerates Took Over Publishing and Changed the Way We Read* [2000].

What books did Simon and Schuster publish in the spring of 1991 when they breached the contract with Bret Easton Ellis? One title on their list was *Women Who Love Men Who Kill*, about women who fall in love with serial killers. By 1994, when they published Howard Stern's *Private Parts*, they had apparently shucked all conscience and fastidiousness. Other publishers promoted such novels as Susanna Moore's *In the Cut* (1995), an edgy portrait of a sex-seeking woman and a murderer, and Caleb Carr's *Alienist* (1994), with its focus on a monster-cannibal. The protagonist of Joyce Carol Oates's *Zombie* (1995) is a sex maniac; A.M. Homes's *The End of Alice* (1996) is a *Lolita*-inspired novel about a nymphet killed by a psychopath. Dennis Cooper and Will Self made their reputations with darkly satiric, often savagely nihilistic fiction: recent works include Cooper's *Guide* (1997) and *Period* (2000), and Self's *Sweet Smell of Psychosis* (1999) and *How the Dead Live* (2000). Many of these books are serious fiction, and share *American Psycho*'s motifs: the craven addiction to sex and commodities, the convergence of consumerism and psychosis in alienating urban environments.

The critical reception of Ellis's novel can only be labeled a media tirade. No book since Salman Rushdie's *The Satanic Verses* had been so poorly read. No one noticed Ellis's debt to *The Great Gatsby*, another tale about self-fashioning in a gilded age of greed. Reviewers also ignored the fact that cannibalism was a metaphor for the conspicuous consumption of Ronald Reagan's America in the 1980s.

If the novel is as simplistic as reviewers claimed, how could they overlook the satire? Ellis's parody of *New York Magazine* skewers the food and music reviews. Ironically, reviews of the novel duplicated the satire of reviewing in the novel, for most critics exhibited the herd mentality epitomized by Roger Rosenblatt, who wanted to "snuff this book." Rosenblatt assumed that Ellis and Patrick Bateman were interchangeable, despite the fact that the novel's repellent, emotionless prose marks the distance between novelist and narrator. In fact, not one word in the novel suggests that Ellis shares his narrator's sentiments. Instead, he depicts a society that fills every minute of the day with self-promotion in the tabloids and on the talk shows. Ellis invented an impressionable copycat killer specifically to skewer those critics who regard readers as mere dupes, incapable of distinguishing representation from reality, words from deeds. That is why his portrait I of robotic consumption is so exaggerated, and why so many name-brand products are amassed in such tedious detail.

David Cronenberg, another Canadian who contemplated adapting the novel to the screen, told me in 1997,

> I was amazed at how good the book was. I felt it was an existentialist epic.... You invent a world where clothes and money and brand names are the value system and you are in the mind of someone who is locked into that. But inside that mind there is an awareness that it all is meaningless and artificial, completely invented. And the murders, the hideousness, are an attempt to break out of that, to try to shatter it and to connect with something real.

It's an interesting moment in our culture when filmmakers are better readers than book reviewers.

Now, in the gold-rush atmosphere of dot-com billionaires and television game shows like "Greed," "How to Marry a Multi-Millionaire," and "Survivor," Canadian filmmaker Mary Harron *(I Shot Andy Warhol)* has audaciously brought Ellis's allegorical tale to the screen. Christian Bale *(The Portrait of a Lady)* stars as Patrick Bateman; his costars are Chloë Sevigny, Willem Dafoe, Jared Leto, Cara Seymour, Reese Witherspoon, and Krista Sutton. Cinematographer Andrzej Sekula gives the film a look as stylish as that in his earlier work, *Pulp Fiction:* all polished surfaces, sometimes tinged with glossy surrealism. The relentlessly upbeat soundtrack features 1980s groups like Huey Lewis and the News, which provide a satiric counterpoint to Bateman's grisly deeds. While preparing to off his first victim with an axe, Bateman maniacally delivers an exegesis of "Hip 2 Be Square." The victim, an uppity yuppie rival, must die because he trumped Bateman's taste. (Bateman's idols are Oliver North and Donald Trump.)

I spoke with Harron by telephone a month before the film's 2000 premiere. In terms of the controversy surrounding *American Psycho*, I ask her if she thinks it makes a difference that it was she who made this film, rather than a man. "Yes, I think it will make a difference. In some ways, people will look at it more *critically* because I'm a woman. But it feels like it's safer to people in some ways for a woman to do it. I think we (co-writer Guinevere Turner) had a more cold, detached view of the male character. We also tried to build up the female characters."

The film transforms each woman into a full-dimensional character. Bateman's shy, sensitive secretary, Jeanne (Chloë Sevigny), is devoted to him. "Have you ever just wanted to make someone happy?" she asks. The prostitute Christie (Cara Seymour) has a deer-in-the-headlights passivity, but she can barely conceal her loathing for Bateman and his rich friends when asked, "Did you go to Dalton? Did we meet in Southampton?" (Since Harron is Canadian, I ask whether she feels that affected her perception of the United States. She responds, "It does give me an outsider's perspective. I grew up in Canada and Britain and I think I definitely have a detached perspective on America.")

The film translates Ellis's minute attention to social forms and surfaces into an extravagant visual banquet. In the first scene, waiters serve exquisite dishes in an expensive restaurant. Presentation is all-important. "Consumption" is a portmanteau pun; it signals the excesses of crass materialism and simultaneously transforms "good taste" literally into a matter of life or death. Bateman has taste, but no gusto whatsoever. He is completely anesthetized by sex, drugs, and violence. "I don't feel one emotion except greed and disgust," he confesses. He only becomes animated when a rival's taste bests his own. Harron stages the scene where stockbrokers compare their handsomely engraved business cards like a duel straight out of Sergio Leone's spaghetti Westerns, complete with parodic close-ups. "I like Leone. I wanted the scene to look like a poker game," she explains.

Harron cleverly captures the atavistic narcissism and tedious repetitiveness of Bateman's world: obsessive-compulsive about his facials, his muscles, his music, his videos, and his food, he is a control freak who is losing control. Deftly played by a buff Christian Bale, he cares more for products than people. "Don't touch the watch! Or that robe! Or put that glass on that table!" he shrieks at various women who come to his apartment. Light bounces off his mirrored sunglasses and brass suspenders. His cardinal virtue is his "hard body"; exercise is one of his many autistic occupations. He favors activities that do not entail relating to anybody else. When he has sex, he makes love to his own image in mirrors; he wears a Walkman at work and with his fiancée. His passions are never aroused, even in the sex scenes, and when he dumps his fiancée, he tells her brutally, "We have no past. I have nothing in common with you." Like the Prince of Darkness, he is all polish, devoid of authenticity.

In another cautionary tale about inauthenticity and self-invention, Nick Caraway describes listening to Jay Gatsby's story about the sad thing that happened to him in his youth as being like "skimming hastily through a dozen magazines." Ellis updates Fitzgerald's fable of extravagant self-fashioning, for reading it is like skimming *GQ, Rolling Stone, Interview, Playboy, Hustler, Spy*. Just as Gatsby invents a Platonic ideal of himself, Bateman confesses (while peeling off a facial mask), "There is an idea of a Bateman, but I am simply not there. "Since all his cronies imitate what they see in ads, they all look almost like clones, and even the posh Manhattan pads become interchangeable as Bateman's sanity slips. In the wickedly deadpan scenes with the detective (Willem Dafoe), Harron evokes Ionesco's Theater of the Absurd and Luis Buñuel's *The Discreet Charm of the Bourgeoisie*. Harron explains, "Bateman is so bored and has so little personality or center that he doesn't know how to act, so he watches and imitates in order to get ideas about how to behave."

In this regard, Bateman is the dark double of Chauncey Gardiner in *Being There:* he parrots whatever he sees in popular culture. Ironically, censorship is based on that same monkey-see-monkey-do premise—the assumption that spectators will enact whatever behavior is depicted onscreen. Harron protests, "There's a strange assumption now that if you show bad actions, it is somehow an endorsement of those actions. If you really take that attitude to its logical conclusion, then you simply can't make any serious films at all. It's amazing how prevalent that's become—it's the current new hypocrisy."

Brian De Palma once defended his films by saying that violence is part of the creative palette of cinema; violence is specifically cinematic. When I ask Harron whether she agrees, she ventures, "I think if you refuse to have violence in the cinema, then you will be leaving out many of the greatest American movies: *The Godfather 1* and *2; Taxi Driver; Raging Bull*; even *Saving Private Ryan*—it isn't one of the greatest movies ever made, but it's a very interesting film. Violence is prevalent in the culture, and De Palma is right: it's an element in the filmmakers' repertoire, whether they choose to use it or not. To say that someone *can't* use it is incredible. Even worse is when someone says, "Oh, it's a good film, but I'm not sure it should have been made." I don't understand that, because if it's a good film, it *should* be made!"

Harron adds, "There is a complete frenzy over violence in entertainment, post-Columbine and various other high school shootings. The rumbles in Washington about cracking down on Hollywood have made everyone jumpy. There's not just more censorship, there's more self-censorship, and I think there will be more and more self-censoring. A few years ago, the studios all wanted another *Pulp Fiction,* and now they're very scared. But their reactions aren't particularly consistent. Instead, they are somewhat illogical, because at the same time, they're looking for the next blockbuster like *The Matrix.* "

Harron's own work does seem to have an internal logic, for her 1996 bio-flick, *I Shot Andy Warhol,* is about Valerie Solanas, author of the SCUM (Society for Cutting Up Men) Manifesto. Harron laughs when I suggest that she has progressed nicely from focussing on a female Man-hater (Solanas) to a male Man-hater (Bateman). Like *American Psycho, Warhol* focuses on an obsessive character who is fixated on the totemic power of celebrity. When I compare Valerie Solanas, a lesbian-marxist-feminist, to Andrea Dworkin, Harron replies, "I am actually kind of a fan of Dworkin's, even though I don't agree with her views on censorship. She's a great writer and polemicist, and a brave figure in what she was trying to do. I guess I have a lot of affection for the angry outsider."

Dworkin's novel *Mercy,* published a year before *American Psycho,* similarly depicts the predatory struggle between rich and poor. The protagonists in both novels go mad and end by murdering homeless people. Both novels, moreover, were targets of censorship. But if two novelists at opposite ends of the ideological spectrum concerning free speech can both be targets of censorship, shouldn't that perhaps make us more wary of censorship in general? Moreover, anyone can take a stand against censorship when the book is a masterpiece. But Americans suffer from a pervasive historical amnesia, forgetting that most major American writers were unheralded in their day until critics helped to rescue them from being forgotten or misunderstood, as was the case with, for instance, William Faulkner (his work was not only ridiculed, but prosecuted for obscenity; it was not until 1948 that the first thoughtful judicial opinion was written about the complexities of literary value, when Judge Curtis Bok freed *Sanctuary* and *The Wild Palms*).

Harron's film slyly alludes to the historical amnesia of American society. Who now remembers the Savings and Loan scandal, which costs U.S. taxpayers $500 billion while lining the pockets of Wall Street financiers like Charles Keating and Ivan Boesky? (Boesky is another one of Patrick Bateman's idols.) Who remembers that Ellis wrote his novel in the wake of the stock market crash of 1987? The closest Bateman will ever come to poverty is his bathroom poster of the Broadway show *Les Miz.* In a restaurant, he makes a vapid speech to his zoned-out friends: "Do massacres affect us? Apartheid, hunger, racial discrimination, civil rights, women's rights... we have to promote these things."

I mention novelist J. G. Ballard to Harron, because Ballard long ago predicted that a kind of fin-de-millennium panic would result in a harsh new Puritanism. Harron ventures, "The new hypocrisy is such that you're almost *required* to show positive images, as if that will make everything alright. It's as if you must portray all nineteenth-century women as suffragettes. I find it particularly disturbing when the historical record is distorted that way. Women weren't free; they were domestic slaves completely oppressed. There's also this notion in Hollywood that if you present these kinds of saccharine, positive images, then that makes the world alright—but it's not all right! There's an unwillingness to look at reality."

Perhaps that unwillingness was the real reason for Ellis's negative reception a decade ago. As British novelist and satirist Fay Weldon remarked, "This man Bret Easton Ellis is a very, very good writer. He gets us to a 'T.' And we can't stand it. It's our problem, not his. *American Psycho* is a beautifully controlled, careful, important novel that revolves about its own nasty bits. Brilliant."

Bateman is the conspicuous consumer run amok, more predatory than Bruce the Shark. In the film, all those who service the rich (waiters, limo drivers, masseuses, dry cleaners) are minorities—black, Asian, Hispanic. Bateman's humiliation about his inferior business card prompts him to assault a homeless black man while parroting the platitudes of Reagan's social policy: "Just say no to drugs! Why don't you get a job? You have a negative attitude. You are a loser. I have nothing in common with you."

The film's final scene marks Bateman's total disintegration. He can no longer distinguish between fantasy and reality, but no one seems to notice. Framed in front of a sign that says, "This is not an exit," Bateman wonders, "Will I get away with it this time?" He suddenly sees Ronald Reagan on CNN. Instead of accounting for the bloodshed, murder, and corruption of Iran Contra, Reagan feigns complete ignorance. "How can one lie like that?" Bateman's stockbroker cronies ask incredulously. "Everybody's in denial," says one. Bateman has the last word: "I'm not harmless, but inside doesn't matter. All that remains is viciousness, mayhem, pain. I don't hope for a better world. There is no catharsis, no new knowledge. My confession has meant nothing."

When I ask Harron what initially attracted her to Ellis's novel, she explains, "The satire of the 1980s and Wall Street culture. But when we started writing the script in 1996, even four years ago, we viewed the phenomenon of massive consumption as well over. I saw the book as a period piece that had relevance today, but I thought of it as a bygone time—a kind of weird madness that was long over. It's odd how much has returned; the culture of spending that has come back is amazing. Society just seems to be awash in money."

To appreciate *American Psycho*'s satire, maybe we had to wait for the dot-com billionaires. We must have compassion for their struggles: A front-page story in the *New York Times* in March 2000 reports on "Teaching Johnny Values Where Money Is King"—about 13-year-olds playing the stock market. Another *Times* headline the same week, "Nothing Left to Buy: Pondering the Indiscreet Charm of the Superrich," echoes Harron's homage to Buñuel. Tabloid reality-based television shows now display a level of crassness devoid of parody.

Mary Harron braced herself for a controversial reaction to her film, but she was nevertheless astonished when a lawyer in Florida threatened a lawsuit while admitting that he had not read the book or the script, and had not even seen the film. Eleanor Smeal, the president of the Feminist Majority Foundation, announced: "There are no redeeming qualities to a misogynist product like this"—without having seen it. Patrick Bateman is the nightmare America created. In retrospect, it seems clear that the initial reception of Ellis's novel was a matter of "slaying the messenger." Sadly, Mary Harron's sly, fiendishly funny film has met the same fate.

LOS ANGELES TIMES, 4/14/00, Calendar/p. 1, Kenneth Turan

Suppose, just suppose, we take "American Psycho" at its word and agree that this little number is, in the words of director and co-writer Mary Harron, "a comedy, a satire on the late 1980s." The question becomes: a) How sharp and penetrating a satire is it?, and b) Are the pungency of its barbs worth what must be endured to receive them? The answers: not very and definitely not.

Even for argument's sake, it's tough to imagine a hypothetical viewer coming out of this Harron-Guinevere Turner adaptation of the Bret Easton Ellis novel, smacking a forehead with the palm of one hand and exclaiming: "The 1980s! A decade of excess! Who knew! People consumed by possessions and status and making a mockery of conventional morality and enduring human values! I had no idea!"

Could such a cave-dweller be found, who would want to subject him (or her) to "American Psycho's" particular brand of enlightenment? Promotional blather about its satiric thrusts notwithstanding, the bottom line is that this film is 100 minutes spent with an unpleasant, unmotivated, disconnected psychopath named Patrick Bateman (Christian Bale), who enjoys hacking folks into pieces and storing body parts in a freezer. Which is pretty much 100 minutes too many.

Perhaps knowing what it was up against, "American Psycho" has taken considerable pains to look its best. Coolly photographed by Andrzej Sekula ("Pulp Fiction") with production design by Gideon Ponte, this has to be one of the most elegant films ever made about someone who relishes chopping people up. Its characters live in a world of designer labels and chic restaurants and clubs and the film has certainly got that part right.

Also, to be fair, "American Psycho" is not as violent as it could be; director Harron, content to be up to her ankles in bloody doings rather than hip-deep, often forgoes the most gruesome shots. Still, even with this forbearance, there's so much carnage here that only an organization as penny-wise and pound-foolish as the MPAA could have horse-traded it down from an NC-17 (and that for sex, not violence) to its current R.

As played by Bale (a young British actor who looks a bit like Ellis' current author photo), the 27-year-old Bateman is the ultimate product of a society obsessed with consuming. Faultlessly groomed but empty of all feeling, he may say "I believe in taking care of myself," but in truth there's no self to take care of. Bateman is simply a healthy corpse who is accurate when he says, "There is no real me. I simply am not there."

While Bateman's grasping girlfriend, Evelyn Williams (Reese Witherspoon), is determined to get married, Bateman is more interested in cheating on her with her comatose best friend, Courtney Rawlinson (Samantha Mathis). Bateman has barely disguised contempt for his contemporaries, including rival Paul Allen (Jared Leto), uncomplicated secretary Jean (Chloe Sevigny) and co-workers who produce silver cases to compare expensive business cards the way the Sharks and the Jets pulled out switchblade knives once upon a time.

Unfortunately for us, the only way Bateman can feel alive is to kill and kill again. He starts with a few men, but soon enough women become his victims of choice, so much so that he breaks out the chain saw when they're around. While Ellis' novel was criticized for being misogynistic, Bateman and his pals are so uniformly hateful and heartless (more like the Ripley of the Patricia Highsmith novel than the recent film) that "American Psycho" feels equally guilty of the opposite sentiment, man-hating misandry.

Judging by the hilarity with which they spoke about it at its Sundance Film Festival debut, Harron and her collaborators had a high old time playing around with "American Psycho's" blood and body parts, but this kind of carnage is not nearly as much fun to experience on the screen and most audiences will likely feel left out of the joke.

Similarly, the games the film plays as to whether these murders are real (Willem Dafoe plays an investigator) or simply Bateman's fantasies come off as seriously beside the point. We have to experience these uncomfortable events as if they were flesh-and-blood happenings, and that is what matters. The difficult truth is that the more viewers can model themselves after protagonist Bateman, the more they can distance themselves from the human reality of the slick violence that fills the screen and take it all as some kind of a cool joke, the more they are likely to enjoy this stillborn, pointless piece of work.

NEW STATESMAN, 4/24/00, p. 46, Jonathan Romney

Suppose you want to film one of the most extreme and scandalous novels of recent years, one that genuinely deserves the description "unfilmable". You could play down the extremity—both the graphic brutality and the asperities of the writing itself. Or you could dare to make a film that is unwatchable in the same way that the book is, unreadable. A nice thought, but one that flies in the face of commercial sense. Truly extreme books rarely become truly extreme films—a rule proved first by David Cronenberg's somnolent version of *Crash,* and now by Mary Harron's, adaptation of *American Psycho.* Harron's version is in many ways a much better work than Bret Easton Ellis's original: but it fails precisely because it doesn't take on the crazier and more perplexing of the book's failings.

American Psycho was published in 1991, to much protest at the gloatingly forensic tone of its descriptions of violence towards women. Its narrator and anti-hero is Patrick Bateman, a spoiled Wall Street broker (the story takes place at the height of the 1980s finance boom) and a consumer *par excellence*—notably, of disparate parts of women's bodies. Behind his urbane surface is a serial killer and cannibal: Ellis's satirical point, at its simplest, is that yuppie and psycho are much the same, that a culture which values perfect exteriors must surely harbour diseased innards. But what made the book compellingly freakish was the texture of the writing: a droning litany of restaurants and designer labels, interspersed with long, hideously precise passages of slaughter, offset at key points (perhaps the most ghoulish touch) with poker-faced tributes to Phil Collins and Whitney Houston. Ellis's novel wildly overstates its case. Yet the overstatement makes it something else—a genuinely cacophonous text, airport novel and intransigent avantgardism wrapped up between the same covers.

The film's director, again Harron, made the witty, acute *I Shot Andy Warhol*; her co-writer is Guinevere Turner, best known as writer and star of the no-budget lesbian hit *Go Fish*. That two women have taken on a novel attacked for vicious misogyny already establishes a crucial element of distance from the book. Another is that, whereas Ellis in 1991 was writing about the very recent past, the film is a historical piece, as retro as *Boogie Nights*. Effectively a costume drama, it wryly evokes those bygone braces and shoulder pads.

You could argue that, even if hairstyles go out of fashion overnight, social attitudes don't, and that *American Psycho* is nonetheless a story about today. But the film is so laden with precise references that it feels like social archaeology: the (inadvertent) subtext is that, if we; now know better in terms of taste, then we surely know better morally, too. A potential victim (played by co-writer Turner) asks Bateman, "You actually *own* a Whitney Houston CD?" and we immediately hear a knowing contemporary voice mocking Bateman's outmoded naffness.

The film always lets us know where we stand, starting with the credit sequence, set to John Cale's playful "pizzicati", as a drip of blood turns into the coulis of a *nouvelle cuisine* dish. (*American Psycho* refers less to a state of mind than to a style of restaurant, along the lines of "classic Californian" or "Mexican-Korean fusion".) This is a playful black comedy, then; we can rest easy that we're not going to be immersed in the book's repetitive textures of madness. Harron and Turner artfully fillet the book's chaos: we get the key sequences in a manageable order; fewer characters, less interchangeable than the book's; and, mercifully, murders played for concise, grim humour. One killing is a farcical dance routine with conscious echoes of *Reservoir Dogs,* as Bateman enthuses about the Eighties soft-rocker Huey Lewis: the song is "Hip To Be Square". The only genuinely nightmarish scene, with Bateman brandishing a chain saw, is strictly genre pastiche, reminding us that the film is a conflation of two key strands of Eighties cinema—slasher thriller and yuppie comedy.

You can see why Harron insisted on casting Christian Bale—his Bateman seems at once smooth, crazed, menacingly clever and somehow stupid; he's a man who knows it all, yet still doesn't get the point. His butch *basso* delivery gives the character some heft, but loses the sexual indeterminacy: where Ellis's Bateman seems like a drag act, a queeny impersonation of heterosexuality, Harron's is close to being a grotesque medallion man.

It comes as a relief that Harron restores some humanity to the women. There's something quite touching in the way that Bateman's mistress, Courtney (Samantha Mathis), seems trapped and infantilised by luxury. And there's a black irony to Patrick's date with his secretary Jean (Chloe Sevigny, spot-on as ever). "I don't want to be bruised," she says (emotionally, she means, although we know she'll be worse than bruised if she sticks around).

Filmed with cool precision by Andrej Sekula, *American Psycho* is perfect as a study of glazed surfaces. A deft touch, heightening the unreality, is the New York skyline outside Patrick's window, just a little skewed, not *too* obviously a *trompe l'oeil* backdrop. The elegance and streamlining are what make *American Psycho* so effective as a film, but they are also the reason it is finally so slight. Harron has created something cool, precise and intelligent, but you miss the authentic babble of nightmare: even the nightclubs seem quieter.

NEW YORK, 4/24/00, p. 130, Peter Rainer

Bret Easton Ellis's 1991 novel *American Psycho* is about a Wall Street hotshot and serial killer whose life is a fetish of conspicuous consumption. Patrick Bateman—note the reference to Norman Bates of *Psycho*—is all roiling surface, and Ellis expends reams of prose cataloguing the man's designer preferences for everything from gazelle-skin wallets to crocodile loafers. The conceit is that Bateman the trendoid couture lunatic is a metaphor for the self-aggrandizing yuppie creep made possible by the Reagan eighties. He's the Frankenstein monster the Gipper hath wrought. Ellis may have intended the book as Swiftian satire, but his metaphor is none too swift. Extending the thrill of investment upswings to include the thrill of murder, he misses out on the biggest joke of all—that a killing on Wall Street would make actual killing redundant for a guy like Bateman. The book, despite its wry mordancy, is opportunistic in a flashy, high-concept way, an excuse to buy off blood-bucket porno pulp by toning up its social pedigree.

American Psycho, the movie that director and co-screenwriter Mary Harron has made from the novel, pares down Ellis's numbing, voluminous cataloguing—and, mercifully, also tamps down his goriest passages. (The film is still pretty icky.) Clearly, Harron is sold on the Bateman-as-metaphor bit, and, like Ellis, she overconceptualizes everything: Bateman, played by Christian Bale, is all of a piece with his off-white Upper West Side apartment and his deep-cleansing face mask. He's a buff hologram inside a product-placement universe (although, for obvious reasons, the actual products being placed are, by current movie standards, relatively few—a great inadvertent joke). Bale is a good choice to play Bateman, because his florid, sharply cut handsomeness already has a jolt of the sinister about it. When Willem Dafoe turns up playing a private investigator, he looks so much like Bateman that the film begins to resemble a convention of gargoyles. Haven't we already been here with David Cronenberg?

The time to have made this movie was back in the early nineties, when master-of-the-universe misogyny and murderous manners were at their peak. Since then, the money culture has changed. The market is no longer the near-exclusive province of gentrified yups and alpha males; it's more like the national pastime—who wants to be a millionaire?—and even small-timers can get into the game. The snob-appeal acquisitiveness that is so hilariously nightmarish in both the book and the movie doesn't look so threatening anymore (although the rise over the past decade in obnoxious cell-phone usage could easily justify for me an *American Psycho II*). All this may change, of course: Boom times come and go. But for better or for worse, it's the wrong cultural moment to be demonizing Wall Street, or, for that matter, New York, which is portrayed as the den of perdition from which all this horror bubbles up. Without this demonization working for it, *American Psycho is* left to fall back on the blood lust of its monster. And because the monster is deliberately depicted without psychological depth, the movie, for all its fussy pretensions, resembles nothing so much as a classy slasher flick.

NEW YORK POST, 4/14/00, p. 56, Jonathan Foreman

Both trite and heavy-handed, "American Psycho" is satire for the sanctimonious: a misfiring black comedy oddly reminiscent of all those bad 1990s movies about strippers getting killed at bachelor parties.

Of course, it's better made than the ultra-dark comedies that followed Quentin Tarantino's ascent—it's beautifully shot, boasts a starmaking performance by Christian Bale and features some witty jokes about restaurant culture in the '80s—but unlike them it's burdened by colossal pretensions to social significance.

Like the notorious 1991 novel on which it's based, "American Psycho" offers a cheap and hypocritical critique of American consumerism and vanity—diseases that presumably don't afflict celebrity novelists and Hollywood filmmakers—that actually tells you more about its creators' smugness and vanity than about the culture they claim to satirize.

Sure, the movie isn't quite as cynical or as repulsive as the book: Writer-director Mary Harron has the good sense to drop most of the fantasies of misogynistic sadism that author Bret Easton Ellis hoped (rightly) would cause a scandal and revive

Bale, a British actor with an uncanny ability to channel Tom Cruise, plays Patrick Bateman, an investment banker with a perfect apartment, a perfect body and perfect skin—thanks to the lotions and potions he applies during and after his morning shower. He and his obnoxious, bigoted banker friends are all obsessed by clothes, business cards and restaurant reservations.

One evening, Bateman puts Phil Collins on the stereo, delivers the first of several (increasingly tedious) lectures about his love for bland middle-of-the-road rock bands, and kills one of his colleagues (Jared Leto) with an ax.

He then embarks on an odyssey of killing that becomes increasingly surreal, until you wonder if the whole thing isn't taking place in his head. There's a particularly strange and over-the-top slasher sequence during which a naked Bateman carrying a chainsaw (now a symbol for female fears of violent men?) chases a screaming, bloodied hooker through the corridors of a tony apartment building.

The always superb Chloe Sevigny makes the most of a small role as Bateman's mousy, vulnerable secretary. Reese Witherspoon plays Bateman's obnoxious fiancée. And Willem Dafoe is the detective investigating Bateman's first murder. But the real stars of the movie are the impressively stylish sets.

NEWSDAY, 4/14/00, Part II/p. B3, John Anderson

Some books cry out to be made into movies. Other books simply cry out. "No! Stop! Not Thaaaat! EEEAAAHHHRRRGGGHHH! "

"American Psycho"? The latter category, for sure. When the novel, a fictional memoir of a go-go stockbroking, bloodlusting, dismembering serial killer, was published by Bret Easton Ellis in the early '90s, it got some of the worst reviews of the then-young decade. And it seemed, particularly to those who hadn't read it, to be a rather sophomoric exercise in shock and gore—even if its theme of money-bred soullessness was as apt an editorial on the Reagan '80s as had yet come along, albeit stumbling and bleeding.

Who knew that the book's secondary metaphor—the tedium of sensationalism—would have such currency now, the era of "Cops," Internet necrophilia and the New York Post? Or that the seemingly unstoppable economic SUV now hurtling along with real estate, gas prices and the population in its luggage rack would have unrefined avarice back on the "in" list for the year 2000?

There were certainly whys surrounding Mary Harron's making of "American Psycho," but they should already become why nots by the time you see the movie—at which point, the logic of bringing Ellis' novel to the screen not only should make eminent sense, it should seem inevitable. Harron ("I Shot Andy Warhol") does many things right in this film, but preeminent is the sense that the movie had to be made. And that the movie she made is the definitive realization of Ellis' moral fable.

Our hero, so to speak, is Patrick Bateman (revelatory, eye- popping Christian Bale), a Harvard-educated Wall Street peer whose mind is marinating in murder—of a homeless bum, of various girlfriends, of a business rival named Paul Allen (Jared Leto), whom Bateman gets drunk, positions atop dozens of New York Times Styles sections (nice touch) and executes with a highly polished, chrome-headed designer ax—while Patrick, in a transparent plastic raincoat lest his Valentino suit get splattered, regales Paul with a career overview of Huey Lewis and the News.

What separates Harron's film from the rank depths of exploitation is that "American Psycho" refuses to let the audience off the hook to judge Bateman's indulgent insanity as something entirely Other. The sumptuousness of Gideon Ponte's production design and Andrzej Sekula's cinematography makes us covetous—whether of Bateman's job, his clothes, his white-on-white apartment or Christian Bale's body. One may stop short of the free-range rabbit with plum coulis or whatever myriad dishes, structured like orchids, are preferred by the platoon of waiters who move and mutter their way through the film. But from the droplets of red that introduce the opening titles (could it be... raspberry compote?) to the nouvelle starvation promoted by Manhattan restaurants in the '80s, one suspects that if Bateman ate real food his bloodlust might be sated.

But fetishizing Bateman, with his gleaming teeth and runway strut, is nothing compared with Bateman's fetishizing of himself. His morning toilette—complete with 1,000 stomach crunches and the application of "an herbal mint facial mask"—is bound to be parodied on the cable comedy shows. What it says about the narcissism of plenty is pointed and funny. "There is no real me," Bateman recognizes. And he never does a thing about it.

Why should he? He does no discernible work, has a fiancee (Reese Witherspoon), a mistress (Samantha Mathis) and an adoring secretary (Chloe Sevingy) who meekly tolerate the rampaging misogyny that defines their relationships. He answers to no one. And because of his position and money and color—hell, because of his clothes—he can walk through Manhattan without being stopped, frisked or shot. "This confession has meant nothing," he says at the end. Neither does Patrick Bateman. But "American Psycho" means something, even if it's not a pretty picture.

SIGHT AND SOUND, 5/00, p. 42, Tony Rayns

Manhattan, 1987. Patrick Bateman, a 27-year-old Wall Street broker, spends most of his time and substantial income on clothes, dining and clubbing. Notionally engaged to Evelyn Williams, he is having an affair with Courtney Rawlinson, the fiancée of his colleague Luis Carruthers. An avid consumer of drugs, pornography and prostitutes, Bateman fantasises murdering friends, rivals and strangers.

Upstaged at a board-room meeting by his colleague Paul Allen, Bateman works off his frustration by knifing a street sleeper and later contrives to murder Allen with an axe. He lets himself into Allen's apartment and re-records the answering-machine message to say that Allen has gone to London. But when private investigator Donald Kimball begins enquiring into Allen's disappearance, Bateman grows nervous.

Events spiral out of control, at least in his mind. An attempt on the life of Carruthers (who is gay) is misinterpreted as an expression of closeted affection. He is deflected from murdering his secretary Jean when Evelyn calls at the crucial moment. A threesome in Allen's apartment with his friend Elizabeth and prostitute Christie turns into a chaotic bloodbath in which both women die. The shooting of an interfering old woman leads to a police chase through the night streets; Bateman kills a cop and at least two others before hiding in his office and calling his lawyer to confess everything. But when he next visits Allen's apartment he finds it being redecorated and up for sale. In Bateman's absence, Jean checks his private diary and finds doodled evidence of his psychosis. Bateman runs into his lawyer (who takes him for someone else) and learns that Paul Allen is indeed in London.

Psycho killer, qu'est-ce que c'est? The widely shared intuition that lousy books make good movies and vice versa finds a partial corroboration in Mary Harron's long-coming adaptation of *American Psycho*. Bret Easton Ellis' stream-of-unconsciousness novel maps its narrator's befuddled stasis in a miasma of designer labels, hard-to get bookings in fashionable restaurants and psychotic fantasies. Resting on the thin conceit that an 80s Manhattan consumerist lifestyle would be the perfect cover for random serial killing and on a series of overplayed gags (identikit personalities lead to recurrent cases of mistaken identity, intense emotional crises are triggered only by fears of losing status in the food chain), the book runs out of shtick around the halfway mark but dances on the spot for another 200 pages. As a satire of a social phenomenon, it's no more cutting than the caricature of a braying, depraved yuppie in *Naked*.

Against the odds, Mary Harron and Guinevere Turner have succeeded in extracting a viable narrative screenplay from this plotless blank. Almost everything in their film comes from the book, but they have sensibly junked a huge amount: the recitations of designer brands, the taunting of beggars with banknotes, the obsession with a morning television talkshow, the 'ironic' ubiquity of *Les Misérables* in the background, the starved rat and most of the sex, violence and sadism. What's left is a brittle and stylised satire of Me-generation values rather conventionally structured as an escalation into madness.

The opening scenes sketch the norms and parameters of Bateman's life: platinum AmEx cards, the workless office, the Robert Longo painting, exfoliating skin creams, that kind of thing. Unsubtle pointers to his psychosis are dropped in sparingly at first but gradually allowed to take over the film until they climax in the night-time shoot-out with the cops on Wall Street, complete with exploding cars and circling helicopters like something out of a Jean-Claude Van Damme movie. The film presents its psychotic episodes as fantasies from the get-go (Bateman leaves trails of blood on his sheets, his walls a across the lobby of his W. 81st Street building without arousing suspicions), which turns Willem Dafoe's scenes as an investigating gumshoe into dramatisations of Bateman's paranoia and makes the closing scenes—in which Bateman is forced to confront the unreality of his dreams—more interesting than they otherwise would have been.

Thanks to excellent art direction and a set of self-effacing performances from those playing the yuppies, Harron captures late 80s vacuity better than she captured late-60s vacuity in *I Shot Andy Warhol*. She flatters the book by playing up its humour: the decision to turn into dialogue three of the book's interpolated critiques of MOR rock-pop stars (on Phil Collins, Huey Lewis and Whitney Houston, all spoken while preparing people for the slaughter) was sort of inspired, and the sex scene in which Bateman never stops admiring his own prowess in a mirror is genuinely funny. Christian Bale makes a fine co-conspirator in all this, presenting Bateman as a man on the cusp between braggadocio and a barely suppressed awareness of his own insignificance.

And yet the film doesn't work. Late in the game Harron brings in Ronald Reagan (seen defending the Iran-Contra scandal to provide an objective correlative gap between surface and substance found in the yuppie milieu generally and in Bateman in particular. But Bateman has insisted from the moment he started intoning voiceovers that he exists only as a cipher ("I simply am *not there*"), and so it's hardly a knockout conceptual punch to close the film with a threatening closeup of his eyes and a threatening assertion on the soundtrack that he has gained no insight into himself or catharsis from his experiences. The problem, again, is the book, an insurmountable obstacle. If Harron and Turner had set out to make a real movie on these themes, they would never have started from a script like this. As it is, they've come up an ingenious adaptation, minimising the book's shortcomings and maximising its intermittent panache. But they remain prisoners of the smug and self-satisfied Bret Easton Ellis.

TIME, 4/17/00, p. 78, Richard Corliss

How to capture the soul of an age that has no soul? That was the task facing Bret Easton Ellis at the end of the '80s. For Ellis, the death of feeling among hip young urbanites was a criminal act. And so, in his black-comic tour de force novel *American Psycho*, Ellis pushed past parody into nightmare farce. He created, in his antihero Patrick Bateman, a moneyman with a true killer instinct: mergers and acquisitions become murders and executions. "I have all the characteristics of a human being," Patrick (Christian Bale) says in Mary Harron's handsome, icily funny film version, "but not a single identifiable human emotion, except for greed and disgust."

Ellis didn't lack for formal audacity. He Cuisinarted a bunch of cultural influences, with Dostoyevsky, the '80s preppie-murder case and the original *Psycho* (Norman Bates=Patrick Bateman) sliced and spliced into an inversion of *The Bonfire of the Vanities*. In Tom Wolfe's novel, Wall Streeter Sherman McCoy accidentally kills someone and gets hounded by an entire city. Patrick, who works at the same fictional firm as McCoy (Pierce and Pierce, if you get the joke's knife point), slaughters half a dozen people, or maybe 20 or 40; and not only does he get away with the crimes, but he can't get anyone to believe him when he confesses. This is partly because his friends are as vacant as he is; they talk but don't listen. And also because Patrick, for all his brutal truth telling, is an unreliable narrator. You see, he is mad—so mad, he probably committed the murders only in his head. Which still makes him one sick yuppie.

The novel confused as many readers as it outraged. They simply didn't get Ellis' thesis: that the young millionaires who pushed paper all day and gazed glazedly at violent porn all night, and who got seizures of envy when a rival sported a smarter suit or business card, were in danger of being set fatally adrift from their moral moorings. The critics couldn't see past the fulsome descriptions of Patrick's killings—which were no more exhaustively itemized than the contents of his wardrobe or CD rack. (Guys love to make lists; cf. *High Fidelity*.)

Harron and co-screenwriter Guinevere Turner do understand the book, and they want their film to be understood as a period comedy of manners. Patrick and his non-friends care only about their abs and their and social lives. ("I'm not really hungry," one of them says, "but I'd like to have reservations someplace.") Some of the wit may sound insidey—Ed Gein, the real-life inspiration for Norman Bates, is ID'd as the "maitre d' at Canal Bar"—but it makes a point. To Patrick serial killers and café staffers are interchangeable celebrities.

Yes, this is also a comedy of murders. There are chain saws and nail guns, and a severed head cellophaned in the fridge. But the carnage, like the sex scenes, is shot so pristinely that it becomes a nouvelle-cuisine feast; this is a splatter film Martha Stewart could love. The acting is similarly fastidious. A trio of beguiling actresses (Reese Witherspoon, Chloë Sevigny, Samantha Mathis) sing backup as Patrick's favorite victims.

The film rests on the shoulders and taut torso of Bale, who as a child starred in Steven Spielberg's *Empire of the Sun* and played Jesus in a recent TV movie. His Patrick is stylish and creepy—Jack the Ripper in an Armani outfit. Bale's dishy anonymity (he stares at himself and says, "I simply am not there") makes him the ideal black hole at the center of this movie. It needs to be seen and appreciated, like a serpent in a glass cage.

VILLAGE VOICE, 4/18/00, p. 153, J. Hoberman

"His normality is more terrifying than all atrocities together." So hyperbolized Hannah Arendt of Adolf Eichmann, the unprepossessing Nazi bureaucrat who organized the transport of several million European Jews to death camps, on the occasion of Eichmann's 1961 trial in Israel.

Arendt's key formulation—"the banality of evil"—became a mid-20th-century catchphrase, reaching its ultimate banalization with Bret Easton Ellis's quasi-pornographic 1991 novel, *American Psycho*. After a decade of Clinton, Springer, and gangsta rap, this deadpan, extremely detailed, and programmatically un-p.c. portrait of a young Wall Street broker as misogynist serial killer is about to embark upon a second career.

Director Mary Harron, who sympathetically depicted a would-be assassin (and polemical pornographer) in her estimable *I Shot Andy Warhol*, has a healthier sense of humor than Ellis. Adapting his novel with sometime actress Guinevere Turner, she treats the whole notion of a status-obsessed, fashion-enslaved yuppie engaged in Ed Gein-type ritual sex-killings as a joke—on the author.

Harron opens wittily by equating bodily fluids with nouvelle cuisine, although nothing that follows is nearly so Swiftian. She effectively burlesques Ellis's affectless carnage amid a mannequin-parade of product endorsements—itself a provocatively tedious riff on the high Reagan world of *Wall Street* and *Bonfire of the Vanities*—but the edge has already been blunted by the funnier, more disturbing *Fight Club*. (Indeed, *Fight Club* may soften up some critics for *American Psycho* as *Happiness* did for the far less daring *American Beauty*.)

"I have all the characteristics of a human being," Patrick Bateman explains, by which he means greed and disgust. With his newsreader voice and immaculate coif, the sleek, well-toned, Armani-ized Christian Bale is more than serviceable in the title role, a part once briefly coveted by Leonardo DiCaprio. Bale is the better actor, but the baby-faced icon would have been far more discomfiting. (Given the movie's pervasive '80s nostalgia, the template is the young Tom Cruise.) If anything, Bale is too knowing. He eagerly works within the constraints of the quotation marks Harron puts around his performance—taking an ax to a colleague while Huey Lewis sings "Hip to Be Square."

American Psycho is basically a succession of escalating atrocities. There's a feeble attempt at suspense. As Bateman realizes his fantasies, he's investigated by Willem Dafoe's suspiciously amiable detective. The private eye is another textual effect; like everyone else, he constantly confuses the psycho with various peers. (Our hero is the one who works out to *The Texas Chainsaw Massacre*, watches himself on TV as he cavorts with two hookers—stunned beyond submission by his passionate explication of Phil Collins—and keeps a human head in the fridge.)

While *American Psycho* is filled with visual references to the painting and photography of the '80s, it lacks the visual élan and period pathos of *I Shot Andy Warhol*. Acting as a kind of responsible parent, Harron strictly minimizes the on-screen violence against women—this despite the presence of the prime potential victims played by Reese Witherspoon and Chloe Sevigny. Any one of Ellis's countless descriptions of torture and mutilation is more disgusting than the movie in toto. Harron has deftly transformed the naughty-boy original into the anti-masculinist satire Ellis claims it always was. (The writer resembles his creation in that no one believes his admissions.)

The novel was Ellis's risky, not unambitious attempt at Dostoyevsky lite. The movie is certainly less offensive—for which many might well be grateful—but, lacking any equivalent to the Sadean excess of Ellis's prose, it is also further evacuated of purpose. As the antihero himself sneers at the bloody finale, "This confession has meant nothing." It's a form of poetic justice that *American Psycho* would be impaled on its own point.

Also reviewed in:
CHICAGO TRIBUNE, 4/14/00, Friday/p. A, Michael Wilmington
NEW YORK TIMES, 4/14/00, p. E1, Stephen Holden
NEW YORKER, 4/17/00, p. 124, Anthony Lane
VARIETY, 1/31-2/6/00, p. 34, Dennis Harvey
WASHINGTON POST, 4/14/00, p. C5, Stephen Hunter
WASHINGTON POST, 4/14/00, Weekend/p. 45, Desson Howe

ANGEL'S LADIES

A Cowboy Booking International release of a FilmKitchen.com production in association with Marquee Productions. *Executive Producer:* Ron Habakus and Gil Donaldson. *Producer:* Doug Lindeman and Straw Weisman. *Director:* Doug Lindeman. *Screenplay*: Doug Lindeman.

Director of Photography: Brad Laven, Doug Lindeman, and Rick Lunn.   *Editor:* Rick Lunn. *Running time:* 80 minutes.   *MPAA Rating:* Not Rated.

WITH: Mack Moore; Angel Moore; Kevin Moore; Linda Moore; Melody Moore.

NEW YORK POST, 11/10/00, p. 58, Jonathan Foreman

It's been a good year for documentaries about swingers, hookers, strippers, etc. So it's a shame that "Angel's Ladies"—a film about a small, downmarket Nevada brothel owned by a former cemetery operator and his wife, Angel—should turn out to be so tedious, and so amateurishly made.

After all, prostitution is a fascinating subject, and the wider society is becoming increasingly aware that sex workers are too often stereotyped as pathetic junkies or the helpless victims of patriarchy.

But this woefully underedited film spends far too much time interviewing the weird, sad owners of the joint and not enough talking to the "girls, who work there.

VILLAGE VOICE, 11/14/00, p. 136, Amy Taubin

When Mack Moore, a 70-year-old cemetery honcho, and Angel, his second wife, got tired of carrying the weight of their past lives, they relocated from rainy Oregon to sunny Nevada. There, they bought Fran's Star Ranch, a small brothel located between Death Valley and the Nuclear Weapons Testing Range, and renamed it Angel's Ladies. Religious fundamentalists, the Moores viewed their new business as not very different from their old one: Both enabled them "to service human needs."

With their Christian rationales, Mack and Angel seem a bit delusional. Not so the three prostitutes who work for them: ranch hand and nature girl Kevin, middle-class career woman Linda, and Melody, the most politically sophisticated, who's saving her money so she won't be "one man away from homelessness." There's more tell than show in the documentary, which eventually takes the form of an argument between labor and management. The prostitutes fault Mack for trying to "date" his own girls ("I didn't want to give the money to my competitors," he counters) and Angel for starting to turn tricks at age 55. But Angel believes she's merely "giving comfort" to the elderly and disabled who would otherwise be turned away by choosy "independent contractors."

Crosscutting between the two sides, Lindeman gives everyone equal time. But according to the head of the local health clinic, Angel's Ladies is doomed any way you look at it. With prostitution legalized, big corporations are eating the small-time operations alive.

Also reviewed in:
NEW YORK TIMES, 11/10/00, p. E25, Lawrence Van Gelder

ANIMAL FACTORY

A Silver Nitrate Releasing and New City Releasing presentation of a Franchise Pictures/Phoenician Entertainment/Artists Production Group production. *Executive Producer:* Allan Cohen and Barry Cohen. *Producer:* Julie Yorn, Elie Samaha, Andrew Stevens, and Steve Buscemi. *Director:* Steve Buscemi. *Screenplay:* Edward Bunker and John Steppling. *Based on the novel by:* Edward Bunker. *Director of Photography:* Phil Parmet. *Editor:* Kate Williams. *Music:* John Lurie. *Sound:* Ye Zhang and (music) Jaime Scott. *Sound Editor:* Warren Shaw. *Casting:* Sheila Jaffe.   *Production Designer:* Steven Rosenzweig.   *Art Director:* Roswell Hamrick. *Set Decorator:* Christine Wick.   *Set Dresser:* Sharon Potts.   *Costumes:* Lisa Parmet. *Running time:* 95 minutes.   *MPAA Rating:* R.

CAST: Willem Dafoe (Earl Copen);   Edward Furlong (Ron Decker);   Seymour Cassel (Lt. Seeman);   Mickey Rourke (Jan, the Actress);   Tom Arnold (Buck Rowan);   Steve Buscemi

(A.R. Hosspack);   John Heard (James Decker);   Edward Bunker (Buzzard);   Danny Trejo (Vito);   Jake La Botz (Jesse);   Afemo Omilami (Captain Midnight);   Mark Boone, Jr. (Paul Adams);   Mark Engelhardt (T.J.);   Christopher Bauer (Bad Eye);   Michael Buscemi (Mr. Herrell);   Victor Pagan (Psycho Mike);   Larry Fessenden (Inmate);   Ernest Harden, Jr. (Richland);   James Martin Kelly (Sgt. Armstron);   Brian Anthony Wilson (Ponchie);   J.C. Quinn (Ivan McGhee);   Freddie Ganno (Prison Guard);   Sal Mazzotta (Florizzi);   Patrick McDade (DA McDonald);   Paul L. Nolan (Sheriff);   Wendee Pratt (Prosecutor);   Jonny Spanish (Billy).

LOS ANGELES TIMES, 11/10/00, Calendar/p. 8, Gene Seymour

[The following review by Gene Seymour appeared in a slightly different form in **NEWSDAY, 10/20/00, Part II/p. B7.]**

Actors who direct movies tend, naturally, to be labor-intensive on the performance front, and it's no surprise that Steve Buscemi's "Animal Factory" is distinguished from top to bottom with actors as intensely committed as he is. (Mickey Rourke and Tom Arnold, for instance, play sweet and savage deviants with consummate bravado.)

But this adaptation of a novel by Edward Bunker (whose "No Beast So Fierce" was made into the 1978 Dustin Hoffman prison film, "Straight Time") is also noteworthy for being one of the least sensationalistic—and therefore, more unsettlingly plausible—visions of prison life ever transfigured into big-screen drama.

Buscemi's movie doesn't bleach away the grit, dung and fear associated with life "in stir." But maintained throughout is an almost eerie atmosphere of tension barely contained by stoicism, even a kind of grace. The locus for this mood—and the anchor for the film—is Willem Dafoe's lizard-cool portrayal of Earl Copen, whose unofficial reign as Eastern State Penitentiary's 800-pound gorilla is undisputed even by the black and Latino convicts who have sullenly detached themselves from the prison mainstream.

Dafoe is a proven commodity playing hard guys whose savvy is leavened by tenderness. But neither sentiment nor crassness is allowed to penetrate the thick layers of Earl's contradictions. When the movie begins, a new inmate named Ron Decker (Edward Furlong) is deposited in Eastern's narrow, crowded yard. Ron's a rich kid given hard time for selling pot. The "new fish" looks ripe for gutting, but Earl takes him under his wing and guides him through several safety zones within the prison's perilous infrastructure.

Even the guards wonder if Earl and Ron's relationship is unhealthy. But the bond between them is far less sordid and far deeper than one expects from stories like this. In many ways, Earl seems a better father to Ron than the latter's real father (John Heard), who seems frantic and clueless by comparison.

Dafoe and Furlong play off each other's emotions like skilled session musicians, and their characters' relationship is one of the many subtle ways "Animal Factory" transcends the narrow confines of its genre to say, as the very best prison movies have, how life behind those forbidding walls isn't too far removed from the life that cruises and wobbles along on the outside.

NEW YORK POST. 10/20/00, p. 52, Jonathan Foreman

"Animal Factory" is a wonderfully acted, strangely low-key prison movie, the very opposite of the gothic horror show that is HBO's brilliant "Oz" (even though "Animal" director Steve Buscemi has been a director on that show).

Buscemi, who as an actor has been one of the glories of American independent film (he was Mr. Pink in "Reservoir Dogs," for example), has directed one previous movie, "Trees Lounge" (1996), a classic little indie about an alcoholic and the Long Island bar where he hangs out.

With "Animal Factory," Buscemi widens his canvas, but he shows the same intelligence, the same restrained touch, the same skill with actors.

Ron Decker (Edward Furlong) is a 25-year-old from the middle class sentenced to 10 years in Eastern State Penitentiary.

Small and good-looking, he's an extremely vulnerable "fish." But he's fortunate enough to be taken under the wing of Earl Copen (Willem Dafoe), a longtime inmate who's essentially the king of the prison yard.

Although Decker fears that Copen's protectiveness is merely the older man's means to an end—making Decker his "punk"—Copen's motives are actually more complicated.

"I probably wouldn't help you so much if you were ugly," he says. "But that's my problem."

Both men have an incentive to stay out of trouble with the prison authorities: Copen is up for parole and Decker has a chance to get his sentence reduced.

But Decker's youth and attractiveness mean trouble is coming their way. One form it takes is a particularly vicious redneck rapist played by, of all people, Tom Arnold.

It's one of several superb performances that Buscemi draws from his fine cast, which includes Seymour Cassel and John Heard.

Dafoe, one of our best actors, is as intense, yet believable, as ever. Furlong shows that he's more than a pretty face. But the biggest surprise comes from Mickey Rourke, unrecognizable and completely convincing as Decker's drag-queen cellmate.

Buscemi builds tension with great skill, without resorting to graphic brutality.

But the film ends abruptly, and there are times during "Animal Factory" when the story feels like it's been taken from another era, the era of "Shawshank Redemption."

VILLAGE VOICE, 10/24/00, p. 146, Amy Taubin

Months after it was sent down to cable, Steve Buscemi's *Animal Factory* has been granted a much deserved theatrical release. A performance driven prison drama with a riot scene that allows the actor-turned-director to show his action chops, the film is richer than Buscemi's Cassavetes-influenced debut feature, *Trees Lounge*. The ensemble of underground all-stars features an almost unrecognizable Mickey Rourke as a motor-mouthed transvestite, but it's the relationship between Willem Dafoe, as Earl, the hard-time veteran, and Edward Furlong, as Ron, the new boy he takes under his wing, that makes the film so compelling. With his head shaved and a simian gait held over from his epic-scale star turn in the Wooster Group's adaptation of O'Neill's *The Hairy Ape*, Dafoe doesn't soft-pedal the brutality that ensures Earl's survival. But he also lets us see the interior contradictions of a man whose need for power and control is part of what turns him into a near saint. "I probably wouldn't help you so much if you were ugly, but that's my problem," he says to Ron, who's worried that his mentor wants to get into his pants. Deserted by his own father when he needed him most, Ron craves Earl's attention but also insists on preserving as much independence as he can within the stratified prison society. Too proud to risk rejection and aware that his feelings for Ron extend beyond sexual desire, Earl settles for becoming his savior. Tender, poignant, and homoerotically charged, this complicated father-son relationship is brought to life by two brilliant actors and a director who's canny enough to give them all the room they need.

Also reviewed in:
NEW YORK TIMES, 10/20/00, p. 21, Elvis Mitchell]
VARIETY, 1/31-2/6/00, p. 35, Dennis Harvey

ART OF AMÁLIA, THE

An Avatar Films and Quad Films release of Arco Films/Valentim de Carvalho Televisão production.   *Producer:* Manuel Falcão. *Director:* Bruno de Almeida.   *Screenplay:* Frank Coelho, Vitor Pavão dos Santos, Artur Ribeiro, and Bruno de Almeida.   *Director of Photography:* Mustapha Barat. *Editor:* João Ascencio. *Running time:* 90 minutes. *MPAA Rating:* Not Rated.

CAST: Amália Rodrigues (Herself);   John Ventimiglia, Joaquim de Almeida, and Maria de Medeiros (Narrators); David Byrne.

NEW YORK POST, 12/8/00, p. 54, Jonathan Foreman

Amalia Rodrigues, the Portuguese-diva who died in 1999, had one of the great voices of the 20th century, but she remains surprisingly little known here.

This film, introduced by David Byrne, should remedy that, with its extraordinarily extensive collection of footage from her 50-year career.

Amalia first achieved renown as a singer of "Fado," the melancholy Portuguese musical form, heavily influenced by Arabic traditions, that is famous for its deep melancholy (the word "fado" means "fate").

Mostly the film is just a record of her various concert tours, her film roles, and her experimentation with other musical traditions as she steadily became more and more famous—interspersed with excerpts from an interview she gave in her last decade.

It's hardly a dramatic story. You learn absolutely nothing about her personal life—except that she considered suicide in New York in the 1980s. But there is plenty of drama in that amazing, soulful voice and the songs she sang.

NEWSDAY, 12/8/00, Part II/p. B9, Gene Seymour

Amalia Rodrigues' stirring, all-embracing voice is as inimitable and as vital to the 20th Century as those of Maria Callas, Billie Holiday, Edith Piaf and Hank Williams. That she managed to outlast all of those star-crossed legends may explain, in part, why she isn't as well known in this country as she should be. A woman who was able to sing Portuguese "fado" songs with such passion, energy and a consummate sense of tragedy appropriate for this indigo-colored musical idiom seemed destined for the kind of premature martyrdom that the world can't get enough of.

But Rodrigues died just last year at 79 after a long, prodigious career of mythic dimensions, especially in her native Portugal. And if you've never heard her before, "The Art of Amalia" offers you an opportunity to fall helplessly in love with an irresistible force. You will watch the film wondering where she's been all your life. You will leave it wondering where you can get more of her. "Amalia" Rodrigues is a controlled substance whose effects can only make you a better person.

Bruno de Almeida's documentary makes no effort to be anything other than a labor of love—which is why it gives you little more than the basic facts of her life as well as extensive clips of her performances, some dating as far back as the late 1930s. (Love that clip from a 1953 Eddie Fisher show!) It is the "art" more than the life that the movie promises to deliver. Given the dimensions of her career and the grandeur of her art, that's more than enough.

Maybe you'd like to know more of the specifics behind her bout with suicidal depression in the early 1980s beyond what she tells you in the movie. But the omission of such details, for whatever reason, challenges you to wonder how necessary it is to know any artist's pain in order to love the sound she or he makes.

VILLAGE VOICE, 12/12/00, p. 182, Richard Gehr

Having so far devoted four projects to singer Amália Rodrigues, ranging from a 1990 concert film to a five-part television documentary, director Bruno de Almeida might be expected to have lost perspective on the woman whose 50-year career is synonymous with the dark, bluesy Portuguese song form known as fado, meaning fate. And that expectation would be correct. De Almeida's latest hagiographic effort diminishes Amália's legend by purifying it.

The Art of Amália opens with David Byrne twitchily acknowledging Amália's knack for expressing the "sadness of the universe." Having established her contemporary street creed, de Almeida skips back to her 1920 birth and plods dutifully through her major professional achievements via a dry voice-over, an impressive array of archival footage, and dispassionate affirmations of her celebrity by a bored eightysomething Amália herself ("All I needed were two guitarists, a dress, and a black curtain," she says).

Take the title seriously. With a single exception, de Almeida edits out every nonartistic aspect of Amália's life once she stops selling fruit by Lisbon's docks and takes to the stage. No mention is made of any husband, lover, or family—although her music overflows with the romance of absence—nor of the decades of dictatorship in Portugal and what that might have meant to her

("I'm embracing all of Portugal!" exclaims a smitten Caetano Veloso in the film's most spontaneous scene). We only learn that Amália traveled around the world recording slapdash (yet immensely successful) albums of tarantellas in Italy, of rancheras in Mexico. Real life intruded in the mid '80s, however. Amália recounts how a cancer scare nearly drove her to suicide while she was living in a New York hotel. But she did survive and sing again, for the largest and most adoring audiences of her career as heads of state showered her with awards. Amália Rodrigues died last year, and de Almeida has entombed her accordingly.

Also reviewed in:
CHICAGO TRIBUNE, 2/16/00, Friday/p. L, John Petrakis
NEW YORK TIMES, 12/8/00, p. E20, Stephen Holden

ART OF WAR, THE

A Warner Bros. release of a Morgan Creek Productions, Inc. and Franchise Pictures and Amen Ra Films presentation of a Filmline International production. *Executive Producer:* Elie Samaha, Dan Halsted, and Wesley Snipes. *Producer:* Nicolas Clermont. *Director:* Christian Duguay. *Screenplay:* Wayne Beach and Simon Davis Barry. *Story:* Based on the "The Art of War" by: Sun Tzu. *Director of Photography:* Pierre Gill. *Editor:* Michel Arcand. *Music:* Normand Corbeil. *Music Editor:* Craig Pettigrew. *Fight Choreographer:* Jeff Ward. *Sound:* Donald Cohen and (music) Sylvain Lefebvre and Steve Smith. *Sound Editor:* Michel B. Bordeleau. *Casting:* Rosina Bucci, Vera Miller, and Nadia Rona. *Production Designer:* Anne Pritchard. *Art Director:* Pierre Perrault and Jean Morin. *Set Decorator:* Ginette Robitaille and Paul Hotte. *Special Effects:* Louis Craig. *Costumes:* Odette Gadoury. *Make-up:* Melissa Purino. *Stunt Coordinator:* Michael Sherer and Jeff Ward. *Running time:* 105 minutes. *MPAA Rating:* R.

CAST: Wesley Snipes (Neil Shaw);   Anne Archer (Eleanor Hooks);   Maury Chaykin (Cappella); Marie Matiko (Julia Fang); Cary-Hiroyuki Tagawa (David Chan); Michael Biehn (Bly); Donald Sutherland (Douglas Thomas);   Liliana Komorowska (Novak);   James Hong (Ambassador Wu);   Paul Hopkins (Ray);   Glen Chin Ying-Ming (Ochai);   Ron Yuan (Ming); Bonnie Mak (Anna); Uni Park (Tina Chan); Erin Selby (Hong Kong Reporter);   Fernando Chien (Zeng Zi);   Paul Wu (Shades);   Noel Burton (Alex Wingate);   Andrew Peplowski and Andrew Nichols (TNN Reporters);   Mike Tsarouchas (NYPD Lieutenant);   Steve Park (Tatoo); Yardly Kavanagh (Reporter at Chan's Hotel);   Frank Schorpion (TWN News Anchorman); Fred Bessa and Terry Simpson (NY Cops); Tony Calabretta (Detective 2);   Fred Lee (Doctor Chin); Tang Weifeng and Huy Phong Doan (Triad Hoods);   Phil Chiu (Triad Hood, Driver);   Jeniene Phillips (TWN Reporter);   Frank Cavallaro (Reporter 6);   Michelle Sweeney (Diner Waitress); Richard Jutras (Larry, Hook's Secretary);   Jeff Ward (FBI Agent, Times Square);   Ken Tran (Triad Bruiser);   Marlon Sterling Long (FBI Agent 1, Athletic Club);   Han Zhenhu (Athletic Club Shopkeeper);   Danny Blanco-Hall (NY Cop 2, Athletic Club Kitchen);   Paul Stewart (American Ambassador);   Jason Cavalier (Security Guard);   Tracey McKee (Times Square Reporter);   Toula Bassanoff (FBI Agent, Elderly Chinese Hobo).

LOS ANGELES TIMES, 8/25/00, Calendar/p. 1, Kenneth Turan

It seems an odd question to propose about a gifted actor whose name is above the title in a major studio release, but seeing "The Art of War" makes you want to raise your hand and ask: "Whatever happened to Wesley Snipes?"

It's not that Snipes hasn't been busy or successful. His "Blade," the publicity boasts, has grossed more than $150 million worldwide, and before that there have been films like "U.S. Marshals," "Money Train," "Drop Zone," "Demolition Man" and "Passenger 57."

But like "The Art of War," where Snipes plays a covert operations type working for the U.N., those are largely the modern equivalents of B-pictures, relatively inexpensive genre items in which the action is brisk and reliable but the dramatic moments are close to nonexistent.

Snipes no doubt has his reasons for sticking closely to those types of roles, but audience members who remember his exceptional work in more substantial films like "The Waterdance" and "White Men Can't Jump," not to mention his involvement as a producer on "Down in the Delta" and the thoughtful documentary "John Henrik Clarke: A Great and Mighty Walk," can't help but miss his appearance in more emotionally resonant material.

For, even in as insubstantial a film as "The Art of War," Snipes' charisma and skill are much in evidence. Even if action is his genre of choice, there have to be more involving scripts than this, just as there are more involving off-genre vehicles than his choices of "The Fan," "One Night Stand" and "To Wong Foo, Thanks for Everything, Julie Newmar."

Named for Sun Tzu's famous book of military strategy, "The Art of War" is typical of what Snipes has been doing lately. Written by Wayne Beach and Simon Davis Barry and directed by Canadian Christian Duguay, it's very much a standard brand, alternating acceptable action sequences with unconvincing plotting and characterization that pretty much just mark time until the chases and shooting start up again.

"The Art of War" begins with a faux-James Bond set piece where agent Neil Shaw (Snipes) crashes a glitzy Hong Kong New Year's Eve party given by international businessman Chan (Cary-Hiroyuki Tagawa) in the top floor of a skyscraper high above the busy city.

After subtly blackmailing a North Korean general into returning to the peace table, Shaw beats up on a number of martial arts foes before making a most dramatic exit with mission accomplished. "How," asks grateful U.N. Secretary-General Douglas Thomas (Donald Sutherland on automatic pilot), "do you give a medal to someone who doesn't exist for something that didn't happen?"

Shaw, it turns out, has other skills as well. He can pick handcuffs with stray pieces of metal, snap evildoers' necks if the situation demands and even read the auras of crime scenes to figure out what happened before he got there. But because he takes beaucoup physical risks without so much as a health plan, Shaw is thinking of retiring after that exhausting Hong Kong escapade.

His immediate superior, U.N. head of covert operations Eleanor Hooks (Anne Archer), wants him for one more job, planting a wire on Ambassador Wu (James Hong), a Chinese diplomat visiting the United States to sign a major free trade pact. It should be a walk in the park, but, true story, it's not.

Soon enough Shaw finds himself a suspect in a major crime, with crotchety FBI Agent Capella (Maury Chaykin) eager to arrest him and no one on his side but suspicious (albeit gorgeous) U.N. translator Julia Fang (Marie Matiko). Not even better health insurance would make up for a fix like that.

Duguay, a cinematographer for a decade before turning to directing, has put the most passion and craft into the action parts of "The Art of War," relegating everything else to second place. Overly plotted and too coincidence-ridden for a story that's basically about nothing, this is a film that almost is not there. It is hardly the worst project Snipes has been in, but wouldn't it be nice to come out of a theater and say it's his best? Everyone, the actor most of all, deserves as much.

NEW YORK POST, 8/25/00, p. 45, Lou Lumenick

As one character aptly describes this story, it's "reality mixed with fiction, mixed with illusion—mixed with guys in dire need of psychiatric care."

At its best, this slickly produced conspiracy thriller is also a 21st-century equivalent of the early James Bond flicks—a grade-A popcorn movie form—fitted to the star persona of Wesley Snipes, who kicks some very serious butt.

Nowhere is this more apparent than in the bravura opening sequence, set in a lavish Hong Kong hotel during a millennium eve celebration.

A shadowy agent named Shaw (Snipes) scales the outside walls so he can embarrass a North Korean defense minister by broadcasting his sexual shenanigans live to the crowd on a giant video screen— and blackmail him by intercepting defense secrets.

"I want you back at the negotiating table with the South Koreans tomorrow morning! " orders Shaw before all hell breaks loose—and he matches kung-fu kicks with a platoon of bad guys.

It turns out Shaw is working covertly for the U.N. secretary general, played with his tongue firmly in his cheek by Donald Sutherland.

Six months later, Shaw wants to retire and buy a McDonald's franchise.

But the equivalent of M (Anne Archer, who fiercely seizes the opportunity in a drastic change-of-pace role) asks Shaw to bug the Chinese ambassador to the United Nations (James Hong), whom they suspect may be working with a shady Chinese businessman (Cary-Hiroyuki Tagawa) to derail a pending U.S.-Chinese trade agreement.

After another terrific sequence, Shaw ends up accused of the ambassador's assassination and is forced to go on the lam with a Chinese translator (newcomer Marie Matiko, who is not only gorgeous but also no slouch as an actress), who can't stand him. But he's forced out in the open to protect the United Nations.

This maze of double-crosses and plot twists may not bear close scrutiny, but director Christian Dugay (the superb "The Assignment") keeps things moving so swiftly it barely matters. The man knows how to knock your socks off, whether it's an attack on a police van in Central Park or a raid on an Asian sex club that amusingly shares quarters with a garment sweatshop.

Unlike this month's two other visually elegant thrillers ("The Cell" and "Hollow Man"), "The Art of War" involves the audience with a hugely enjoyable central performance. Snipes' Shaw is so ultra-cool and so lithe that I'll bet the producers of "Shaft" are kicking themselves they didn't go with him instead Samuel L. Jackson, a great actor who is 15 years older.

Snipes also gets solid support from the likes of Maury Chakin, as a comic-relief FBI agent, and Michael Biehn, as a fellow U.N. operative who likes to quote from the ancient book by Chinese general Sun Tzu that gives the movie its title (Sample quote: "Appearances are everything—in politics and deception.")

Though notably more violent and gory than "Mission: Impossible 2," the PG-13 spy epic that opened the summer season, the taut, R-rated "The Art of War" is even more fun than that John Woo action film.

NEWSDAY, 8/25/00, Part II/p. B3, John Anderson

"On contentious ground," Chinese military strategist Sun Tzu wrote in his "Art of War," some 2,400 years ago, "I would hurry up my rear." Timeless advice. Regarding Christian Duguay's "The Art of War," we suggest you do the same, in the direction of another movie.

Save for a passing reference, Duguay's alleged thriller, starring the eminently watchable Wesley Snipes as a UN operative, has nothing to do with Sun Tzu's treatise on tactics, which has inspired followers everywhere, from Wall Street to the NBA (Pat Riley being just one celebrated acolyte). But while Sun Tzu's text is ancient, its namesake movie just seems old: Structured around a plot to undo a trade agreement with China—or some such trade agreement—the film was obviously intended for release well before the measure was passed by the House in June. As a result, its politics may be less urgent.

And if anyone on the conservative right is looking for evidence of a leftist Hollywood cabal, "The Art of War" presents itself as exhibit A—although it's so confused, it could possibly be the other way around. When a pile of dead Vietnamese refugees is found in the hold of a Chinese ship—explain that, please, someone—passage of the troubled Chinese treaty is imperiled, something exacerbated by the assassination of the Chinese ambassador (James Hong) and wounding of a dubious, Trumpish Hong Kong businessman (Cary-Hiroyuki Tagawa). Snipes' UN agent, Shaw, is framed for the crimes and has to crack the case with the assembled manpower of the city, the state, the feds and Maury Chaykin on his back, while certain authority types inveigh against illegal Chinese campaign contributions and possible leaks of nuclear secrets—and they're the bad guys.

What's going on? We don't have a clue, not about the plot. What seems clear about the movie's motives, however, is that with post-Cold War Hollywood desperate for a nation to villainize, China fits the bill perfectly—except for the small obstacle of 2 billion consumers. So we get this kind of hash, wherein audiences can more or less find what they want. You think the Sino-Clinton scandals are a disgrace? "The "Art of War" is with you! You think such criticism is all part of a right-wing conspiracy? "The Art of War" is with you.

Of course, the callowness, illogic and political naivete of the storyline, even the galloping disregard of rudimentary physics, would be forgivable, if "The Art of War" weren't such an incompetently made movie. Snipes can be a terrific action star, but Duguay & Co. don't know how to make an action film. The fights are hapless, the computer-generated stuff is lame. Overall, the movie lacks integrity, because it lacks respect for space.

But all this is getting us nowhere. What "The Art of War," ultimately tells us is that a "chaotic" movie is not the same as a movie made in chaos. And that a film intended as mindless fun has to be something more than mindless.

SIGHT AND SOUND, 1/01, p. 40, Kim Newman

Hong Kong, New Year's Eve, 1999. Neil Shaw, a covert agent for the United Nations, infiltrates a millennium party thrown by Chinese tycoon David Chan. Backed up by his superior Eleanor Hooks and partner Bly, Shaw is there to blackmail a North Korean general into returning to the negotiating table.

Six months later, at the behest of Canadian secretary-general Douglas Thomas, Hooks has Shaw attend a function in New York at which the Chinese UN ambassador Wu is due to speak in favour of a treaty that will open China up to trade with the west. Wu is assassinated. After pursuing the killer, Shaw is picked up by the FBI, though agent Cappella realises—thanks to the testimony of translator Julia Fang—he is not the assassin.

Shaw is kidnapped from custody by Triads, who try to murder him. He escapes and tries to contact another agent, Novak, who is also murdered recording of a brief conversation between Chan and Wu before the latter's assassination. Shaw contacts Julia, ostensibly for help in translating the tape but also because the conspirators are after her too. Shaw reasons that Chan was in on Wu's assassination because the treaty Wu supported would break his monopoly on Chinese trade. Before he can talk, Chan is killed by Bly, who has been working for Hooks to subvert the UN in order to pursue her right-wing, pro-US agenda. Shaw defeats Bly in one-on-one conflict and exposes Hooks, who is murdered by the Triads. Shaw's own death is faked and he joins Julia in the south of France.

In setting its prologue against the pre-millennial celebrations that also provided a backdrop for the Sean Connery heist movie *Entrapment, The Art of War* establishes the feeling that we've been here before. A vital difference, though, is that *Entrapment,* while nothing special, was released in 1999, before we knew the millennium bug would be such a damp squib. This film trails along a full year later and though it contains such topical material as a scene in which a container-load of dead refugees from China turns up in the west, it still feels curiously behind the times, if only because Hollywood tends to set its political-action thrillers in a not-too-distant future, presumably to avoid touching on potentially controversial present-day realities.

The film offers nothing that hasn't been seen elsewhere. Check off: the partner thought dead early on who reappears as a nemesis *(GoldenEye),* the Far-Eastern manipulator-cum-patsy played by Cary-Hiroyuki Tagawa *(Rising Sun),* the UN backdrop *(North by Northwest),* endless downloading and logging-on for clues *(Mission Impossible, Eraser* and dozens of other high-tech thrillers), hero Shaw's habit of experiencing deductive flashbacks at site of crimes (the television show *Millennium),* lengthy chases through rainy cityscapes *(Seven),* slo-mo bulletry and martial arts (John Woo films and *The Matrix),* the innocent heroine caught up in spy shenanigans (most episodes of *The Man From U.N.C.L.E.* and every other Bond film) and Wesley Snipes as a disavowed spy hunted by his own corrupt agency *(U.S. Marshals).* Even the ridiculously on-the-cheap epilogue, which hauls a 2CV on to an obvious set to represent UN translator Julia's escapist fantasy of sitting in a French café tabac, is bizarrely familiar, being a parallel to the punchline of *Nurse Betty.*

At the heart of the film is a potentially interesting subject, the long-standing friction between UN and US interests. Though it plays like typical sub-par Hollywood, *The Art of War* was directed and written by Canadians (director Christian Duguay made two straight-to-video sequels to David Cronenberg's *Scanners)* and uses several prominent north-of-the-border character actors, even imagining Donald Sutherland as a fictional Canadian UN secretary-general. The recent attempts of successive US governments to usurp UN authority and to use NATO as an instrument of American military might make a fascinating backdrop for a John Le Carré-style tale of cynical espionage. Instead, this cooks up a Fu Manchu-level bit of business in which everyone except the hero seems to have an interest in the death of Ambassador Wu, China's representative to the UN, and a few mumbled quotes from Sun Tzu to justify the title if little else.

Snipes' Shaw is yet another emotionless, characterless hero ("How can I give a medal to someone who doesn't officially exist?" asks Sutherland's UN chief of him). It comes as a tacked-on surprise that his bullying of whiny heroine Marie Matiko has turned into a romantic relationship, though it may be that Snipes the executive producer has noticed how rarely Snipes the star gets the girl in action outings. Otherwise, the film offers Michael Biehn doing smiling psycho again, Anne Archer in a sneery change of pace after a run of stay-at-home imperiled wives and Maury Chaykin providing welcome humour as the FBI agent under threat of suspension because of his weight. Duguay has paid attention to his Hong Kong actioners and tries hard with a blue-grey look and a lot of fast cutting, though this tends to render the action scenes less exciting since it's often hard to tell who has been hit and whether we should be pleased or worried by the current state of play.

VILLAGE VOICE, 9/5/00, P. 118, Michael Atkinson

After years of strip-mining headlines, the Hollywood action movie appears to be running red-alert low on raw materials. In Christian Duguay's anonymous, muddled pileup *The Art of War*, a U.S.-China trade agreement is the macguffin of choice, a matter so crucial ("1.5 billion new customers!" the characters proclaim) that bodies on all sides drop like autumn apples. Neither cash nor power is at stake, precisely, just market share, and if this is the management-meeting-dull tenor of the new World Economy, I'll take Dr. Evil's "One Million Dollars!" straight up, to go. Wesley Snipes is a virtually indestructible covert agent (Energizer-bunny-like, he jumps from third-story windows onto concrete and keeps going, many times) working for the United Nations (!), a job that has Snipes first blackmailing Korean officials into returning to the treaty table by secretly videotaping their New Year's blow jobs and then instantly plastering them across a Jumbotron before thousands of revelers.

If only it were amusing: Duguay's grotesque excess of visual and aural noise squelches thought as it's designed to; the movie's sub-Tony Scott distraction strategy is even complemented by a Chomsky-esque political scenario that's climactically conjured from nothing to assuage our notice of all those cold-blooded Asian killers. That is, if we're not already razzled by the predictable arsenal of techno-gadgets, which leaves us with the impression that if Snipes wanted to jack into a top-secret mainframe by way of satellite-dialing your colon on his Devil Dog-sized cell phone, he could. On the run as an identity-free spy who can't come in from the corpse-stacked cold, Snipes does a lot of bolting across rooftops and moping in parked cars when he isn't snapping the necks of thugs he knows nothing about. After a while he picks up a petulant Chinese operative (Marie Matiko) for a requisite testy-respectful fugitive relationship as he evades the cops who want him for the few killings in the movie he didn't commit. Far more preposterous in its details than the average blam-quip-kerplow, *The Art of War* isn't helped by the performances; watching Anne Archer, as covert ops leader, read expository dialogue is like watching milk curdle in time-lapse.

Also reviewed in:
NEW YORK TIMES, 8/25/00, p. E25, Stephen Holden
VARIETY, 8/21-27/00, p. 15, Emanuel Levy

AUTUMN IN NEW YORK

A Metro-Goldwyn-Mayer Pictures release in association with Lakeshore Entertainment of a Lakeshore Entertainment Gary Lucchesi/Amy Robinson production. *Executive Producer:* Ted Tannenbaum and Ron Bozman. *Producer:* Amy Robinson, Gary Lucchesi, and Tom Rosenberg. *Director:* Joan Chen. *Screenplay:* Allison Burnett. *Director of Photography:* Changwei Gu. *Editor:* Ruby Yang. *Music:* Gabriel Yared. *Music Editor:* Andrew Dorfman. *Choreographer:* Paul Pellicoro. *Sound:* Christopher Newman and (music) Paul Golding. *Sound Editor:* Pat Jackson. *Casting:* Sheila Jaffe and Georgianne Walken. *Production Designer:* Mark Friedberg. *Art Director:* Jess Gonchor. *Set Decorator:* Catherine Davis. *Set Dresser:* Joann Atwood and Zach Jasie. *Special Effects:* Mark Bero. *Costumes:* Carol Oditz. *Make-up:* Linda Grimes.

Make-up (Richard Gere): Hallie D'Amore.   *Make-up (Winona Ryder):* Kathrine James. *Stunt Coordinator:* Jodi Michelle Pynn.   *Running time:* 105 minutes.   *MPAA Rating:* PG-13.

CAST: Richard Gere (Will Keane);   Winona Ryder (Charlotte Fielding);   Anthony LaPaglia (John);   Elaine Stritch (Dolly);   Vera Farmiga (Lisa); Sherry Stringfield (Sarah);   Jill Hennessy (Lynn);   J.K. Simmons (Dr. Grandy);   Sam Trammell (Simon);   Mary Beth Hurt (Dr. Sibley); Kali Rocha (Shannon);   Steven Randazzo (Alberto);   Toby Poser (Autumn Woman #1);   George Spielvogel III (Netto); Ranjit Chowdhry (Fakir);   Audrey Quock (Eriko);   Tawny Cypress (Melissa); Gabriel Portuondo, Laurent Schwaar, and Patrick Price (458 Waiters);   Ted Koch and Alvin Einbender (458 Bartenders);   Daniella Van Graas and Rachel Nichols (Models at Bar); Paige Handler and Liza Lapira (Charlotte's Birthday Friends);   Sarah Burns (Little Girl at Playground); Bill Raymond (Michael, Doorman); Earl Carroll (Will's Driver);   David Filippi (Taxi Driver); Becca Lee (Michelle);   Estelle Robinson (Old Frail Lady);   Brittney Bunkis (Little Girl at Museum);   Delores Mitchell (Librarian); Hatsumi Yoshida (Clown at Halloween Party);   Kristi Lee Guinness (50's Girl at Halloween Party);   Luca Waldman (Vampire at Halloween Party); Daniella Cantermen and Deanna Cantermen (Twins);   Harry Burney (Choirmaster);   Cheyne M. Hansen (Boy at Rockefeller);   Pamela Twyble (Nurse at Cleveland Heart Institute);   Iris Flick (Nurse at New Haven Hospital);   Kathleen Goldpaugh (St. Vincent's Nurse);   Robert Plunket (Grubby Man).

LOS ANGELES TIMES, 8/14/00, Calendar/p. 3, Kevin Thomas

Richard Gere has protested MGM opening his latest, "Autumn in New York," without press previews, and rightly so, for it contains one of his most unsparing, far-ranging performances.

Yet you can see why MGM chose its course—not because it is a bad movie, which is the customary reason for avoiding opening day reviews, but because it is so vulnerable. In an era of easy irony, "Autumn" dares to wear its heart on its sleeve, and it also has a plot that not only shouldn't be given away, but may sound like a cliche when it is. In any event, this unpredictable, even rigorous film deserves a chance to find its audience.

It is entirely respectable to admire those sweeping screen romances of Hollywood's golden era, but they daunt today's filmmakers, who are afraid of seeming corny and self-conscious. Not so director Joan Chen and writer Allison Burnett, who go for an all-stops-out love story, but do so with uncommon intelligence and honesty. Ultimately, however, the love story serves as a frame for a portrait of a man in the process of a painful, long delayed self-discovery. Silver-haired and durably handsome, Gere's Will Keane has managed to do whatever he pleased with tremendous success in both his personal and professional lives throughout his entire 48 years, but now, is unexpectedly overcome with genuine emotion and all the responsibility that it can entail.

We meet Will as he has attained a pinnacle: his picture on the cover of New York magazine. He is the proprietor of one of the trendiest restaurants in Manhattan. His business, his home and his wardrobe are a triumph of elegance. His every move, his every word, his every gesture ooze a smooth, easy self-confidence. Can it be a surprise that Will is a legendary lady-killer?

Drawn to his restaurant for her birthday party on the basis of that cover story, Winona Ryder's Charlotte Fielding is just the kind of well-bred radiant beauty who would attract Will, who is conscious of, but hardly daunted by, the quarter of a century differences in their ages. He has no trouble in sweeping Charlotte off her feet, but in doing so is about to discover what kind of man he is—and what sort of man he might become.

"Autumn in New York" begins in a lyrical mood as Will and Charlotte meet and begin an affair in a New York at its most romantic and inviting. The film's burnished glow remains even as it plumbs unanticipated emotional depths. Chen unerringly guides Gere in a role that taps his reserves and skills fully, for Will is ultimately driven to bare his soul. When we meet him he's a man who lives for sexual conquest, but when we leave him he has discovered an entire new meaning and scope in his life. Ryder's role is scarcely less challenging, for she's playing the woman who has the potential for stopping this Don Juan in his tracks as no other woman ever has—not even her late mother, who had been smitten with Will herself.

Indeed, Charlotte's grandmother Dolly (Elaine Stritch) is not so happy about history repeating itself with her granddaughter, but she's a sophisticated, salty aristocrat who might talk plain to Will but is by breeding too reticent to reach out to Charlotte to guide her in matters of the heart.

Stritch is a marvel of subtle nuances, playing a woman who has lost much but soldiers on, fortified by a stiff drink in hand. Anthony LaPaglia is Will's down-to-earth bartender and business partner in whom Will glimpses what he might be missing in life, and Vera Farmiga is a lovely woman whose interest in Will proves most unromantic.

At first glance the director of the bleak but exquisite "Xiu Xiu: The Sent Down Girl," a prize-winning account of a young girl and her fate during the Cultural Revolution, might seem an unlikely choice for "Autumn in New York," but Chen, in only her second feature, proves ideal. She's as skilled at making the film worth taking seriously as she is in directing actors. Having played "The Last Emperor's" consort, she understands well how poignant beauty combined with vulnerability can be. Stylish and finely crafted, "Autumn in New York" inevitably will strike some as a sleek soap opera. What it really is a classic woman's picture that is also a depiction of a man transformed by love beyond his imagining.

NEW YORK, 8/28/00, p. 133, Peter Rainer

Early in *Autumn in New York* Winona Ryder, in a romantic mood outdoors with Richard Gere, tells him she can smell the rain. If she had inhaled deeply, she might have smelled something a bit more pungent. The aroma of fetid formulas wafts about her in this movie, which blurs May-December love (albeit mostly in the fall) with disease-of-the-week weepies. Ryder's irrepressibly winning Charlotte—she says "Wow!" a lot—suffers from some kind of inoperable life-threatening condition. Gere's Will Keane is the celebrity restaurateur and rake who, to his own dismay, finds himself misty-eyed in her presence. Everyone says he's too old for her, but why kid yourself? This is, after all, Richard Gere, who periodically turns his silvered mane to catch the light as if he were a newly minted commemorative medallion. Still, one gets the feeling that the filmmakers weren't entirely happy with the political incorrectness of this pairing, which is why Charlotte, who is literally heartsick, exists in a state of continual near-expiration while Will is made to lament her impending loss. The message here is, if you guys are going to romance women half your age, be prepared to suffer for it. (This should serve as a wake-up call for half the honchos in Hollywood.)

The director of *Autumn in New York* is Joan Chen, who made an auspicious debut last year with *Xiu Xiu, the Sent-Down Girl*; this is her first Hollywood feature. She has a lovely sense of film rhythm and a sophisticated eye for luxe effects, but she fell into this vat of goo and there's no climbing out of it. My guess is that she knew she was taking on a script that resembled a four-hankie version of *The Blob* and decided to go with it anyway in order to press her credentials as an auteur. *Autumn in New York* is terrible, but the real scandal here is that Chen, a spirited, original performer who speaks perfect, unaccented English and is one of the screen's great beauties, finds it necessary to direct such tripe because, as she has admitted in interviews, Hollywood has so little to offer her as an actress except the usual exotica. At a time when even Madison Avenue and the boob tube have moved beyond the lotus-blossom syndrome, it's maddening to see such attitudes still perpetuated onscreen.

NEW YORK POST, 8/12/00, p. 21, Lou Lumenick

"You've got to look on the bright side," a dying Winona Ryder tells much-older boyfriend Richard Gere. "In a year or so, I'll be this sob story you can use to bag more chicks."

Love means never having to say you're sorry—and despite MGM's decision to sneak "Autumn in New York" out without advance critics' screenings, it's not exactly something requiring profuse apologies.

Sure, this May-September spin on "Love Story" has no shortage of howlers and telegraphs its plot twists a mile away—but this ultra-glossy weepie turns out to be something of a guilty pleasure almost because of its extreme predictability.

Gere is Will, a 48-year-old womanizing celebrity restaurateur with his picture on the cover of New York magazine. Winona is Charlotte, a 22-year-old Emily Dickinson-quoting hat designer with a novel-sounding medical condition—a tumor that's slowly destroying her heart.

The two stars actually have surprisingly plausible chemistry together—and the acting is fairly decent, considering this is the sort of movie whose four-hankie emotions are expressed almost exclusively through overripe dialogue.

Will: "We have no future. All I have to offer you is this, until it's over."
Charlotte: "Love is not a race."
Will: "Our love is."
In another scene: Will's best friend (Anthony LaPaglia) observes: "She's the perfect woman—young, beautiful and on her way out... maybe [your romance] makes a sad girl happy and a desperate guy think."
Then there's the movie's big mushy moment.
Charlotte: "What should we do with this moment we're in?"
Their first kiss, cut to a shot of doves, then the two of them in bed together.
The only thing they ever seem to talk about besides her health are their respective ages.
In fact, Will used to date Charlotte's late mother—her grandmother (Elaine Strich) assures her they never slept together—and he has an illegitimate daughter (Vera Farmiga) Charlotte's age.
Will's never even met the daughter—but she jumps at the chance to help him find a heart surgeon who might be able to save Charlotte's life!
If you can figure that one out, maybe you could tell me why St. Vincent's Medical Center would want such prominent product placement in a movie about a dying heroine.
Actress Joan Chen, who directed the terrific "Xiu Xiu: The Sent-Down Girl," couldn't have chosen more different material for her second film—but she admirably underplays the movie's more mawkish aspects of Allison Burnett's heavy-handed screenplay.
Chen and cinematographer Changwei Gu lavish such elegance on the visuals that you're almost willing to buy such clichés as falling leaves, rain-swept breakups and ice-skating in Rockefeller Center.
Too bad the movie has to keep reminding us that Will is so attractive and that Charlotte is, as Will puts it, "completely unprecedented and therefore, utterly unpredictable."
"Autumn in New York" certainly isn't—and that may be precisely why it charms many people.

NEWSDAY, 8/14/00, Part II/p. B2, Jan Stuart

In a stratagem that gives a new lease on life to the term "eleventh hour," the producers of "Autumn in New York" decided to make their new film available to the press all of 30 minutes prior to its first public 11 a.m. showing on Friday. At the time, one could only have imagined that they were attempting to sequester overzealous critics, who might get it in their heads to storm the theater lobbies and physically prevent early-bird moviegoers from walking through the door.
One wonders what they were antsy about. "Autumn in New York," will neither tarnish the venerable MGM name nor change the course of filmmaking forever and a day. It's a perfectly respectable weeper, a glossy, star-powered throwback to the sorts of four-hanky pictures MGM and Warner Bros. churned out in the days when Bette Davis was more than just a cherished memory.
Instead of Bette Davis, we now have Winona Ryder as a dying swan debutante, chirpy and slightly eccentric in the way that only heiresses can afford to be. Through the magic of expensive makeup, insouciant temper and fortunate genes, the pushing-30 Ryder gets to play the 21-year-old Charlotte Fielding, a free-spirited creature with an aortic tumor that spells doom in just a year's time.
Celebrated Manhattan restaurateur and veteran lothario Will Keene (Richard Gere) isn't hip to Charlotte's ticking clock when he decides to put the moves on her. He does know that she is the grown daughter of a woman he tried to seduce decades back, and that he is a little too old to be chasing after women who are young enough to be his daughter. Yet even after she tells him of her condition, Will and Charlotte decide to go for broke. How do you say no to Winona Ryder, even a terminal Winona Ryder? How do you say no to Richard Gere, even a Richard Gere nearing eligibility requirements for the AARP?
Romances like these are constructed entirely around the assumption that no one in their right mind would say no to Winona Ryder and Richard Gere, especially amid an autumnal splendor that bathes Central Park in the unnatural orangy oranges and lemon yellows of Trix cereal. Director Joan Chen seems to understand this, allowing her leads ample time to make idealized love from behind beveled glass and gaze moony-eyed at one another along riverside promenades that are improbably free of other pedestrians.

To their credit, neither the stars nor screenwriter Allison Burnett take the film's assumptions for granted. If Burnett's script goes by the book, it does so with an intelligence that gives its actors a little something to chew on as they make their way toward its foreseeable final page. Burnett garnishes the suds generously with a mysterious woman from Will's past (Vera Farmiga), a boozing Fielding family matriarch (Elaine Stritch, who else?) and a confidant for Will (appealingly played by Anthony LaPaglia) who makes ouch-inducing comments such as "She's the perfect woman: young, beautiful and on her way out."

Ryder and Gere do whatever it is they do as well as they do it: Gere winces at the sky charmingly whenever Will is caught in the act of being a jerk, while Winona glistens winsomely from beneath funny, Calder-like hats that Charlotte designs. But Will is right when he advises Charlotte that she is a little too long in the tooth to be saying "wow" so much. Ryder better start acting her age or she'll someday find herself the only octogenarian star in a 2050 remake of "Heathers."

SIGHT AND SOUND, 7/01, p. 40, Kay Dickinson

Manhattan, the present. Twenty-one-year-old milliner Charlotte is celebrating her birthday in a restaurant with friends and her grandmother, Dolly At the bar Dolly bumps into Will, a celebrity chef who owns the restaurant. A former friend of Dolly's dead daughter and now a middle-aged playboy, Will is introduced to Charlotte's party. Later that week, Will phones Charlotte to commission a hat for his partner to wear at a charity ball. It soon transpires that this is a ruse for him to invite Charlotte instead. At the ball, Charlotte is approached by Lisa who turns out to be Will's estranged child by a friend of Charlotte's mother. That evening, Will and Charlotte sleep together, but Will is reluctant to commit to more. Charlotte reveals that she suffers from a terminal heart condition; spurred on by their limited time together, they embark on a relationship.

Some time later, Will has sex with Lynn, a former lover. Charlotte then calls the relationship off, but Will wins her back. Charlotte's health declines; Will persuades her to agree to a controversial surgical procedure which may save her life. She collapses on Christmas Day and finally dies in the operating theatre.

Autumn in New York probes a May-to December relationship between Will, a philandering celebrity chef, and Charlotte, a feisty just-come-of-age hobo. It's a potentially interesting premise; Hollywood films often pair middle-aged actors with far younger actresses, but they rarely comment on the disparity in age as this film does. The casting as Will of 51-year-old Richard Gere, no stranger to having much younger actresses play his love interest, therefore seems astute. Unfortunately Gere's limited acting style has a way of short-circuiting the effusive emotionalism aspired to by Allison Burnett's script. Not known for performing with passion, Gere seems ill at ease with such lines as "Can't you let me love you? Please, please, please, please." This isn't to refute the nimble work done in the past with Gere's slender range (his aloofness is essential to *American Gigolo*, his slight charm an asset to *Pretty Woman*). But in this case, the script asks more than he can deliver.

To make matters worse, Will's backstory insufficiently accounts for his flightiness. His behaviour often seems to spring from insouciant shallowness which stifles any empathy for his growing anguish as Charlotte's heart disorder takes hold. Admittedly Gere is running up hill with the material on offer here—even the more plausible Winona Ryder, who plays Charlotte, struggles with such lines as "What about love?" (delivered after her *beau* has a dalliance with an old flame). We're clearly meant to believe that Will's character deepens with every moment he spends with spontaneous, Emily Dickinson-spouting Charlotte, but his risible line in half-baked aphorisms ("Food is the only beautiful thing which truly nourishes") stretches our credulity.

Despite acknowledging the age-difference between Will and Charlotte, the film conveniently condemns Charlotte to a terminal illness, which means her romance with Will is conducted with brief intensity. This expedient plot device excuses the filmmakers from having to explore the complex public repercussions—of the kind featured in such fine films as *The Graduate* (1967) and *American Beauty* (1999)—of Charlotte and Will's cross-generational relationship. Charlotte's illness also means she doesn't have to consider the long-term anxieties of her involvement with a much older man: not for her any later mid-life urge to scarper from Will's approaching senility and weak bladder.

Also reviewed in:
CHICAGO TRIBUNE, 7/28/00, Friday/p. G, John Petrakis
NEW YORK TIMES, 8/12/00, p. B14, Stephen Holden
VARIETY, 8/21-27/00, p. 21, Emanuel Levy
WASHINGTON POST, 8/12/00, p. C1, Rita Kempley

BABYMOTHER

An Independent Pictures and Fine Line Features release of a FilmFour presentation in association with The Arts Council of England of a Formation Films Production. *Executive Producer:* Margaret Matheson. *Producer:* Parminder Vir. *Director:* Julian Henriques. *Screenplay:* Julian Henriques and Vivienne Howard. *Director of Photography:* Ron Fortunato. *Editor:* Jason Canovas. *Music:* John Lunn. *Music Editor:* Richard Todman. *Choreographer:* L'Antoinette "Osun Ide" Stines. *Sound:* Tim Fraser. *Sound Editor:* Nick Adams. *Casting:* Carol Dudley. *Production Designer:* Choi Ho Man. *Art Director:* Niall Moroney. *Set Decorator:* Rebecca Gillies. *Costumes:* Anne Curtis Jones. *Make-up:* Sue Wyburgh. *Stunt Coordinator:* Rod Woodruff. *Running time:* 80 minutes. *MPAA Rating:* R.

CAST: Anjela Lauren Smith (Anita);   Wil Johnson (Byron);   Caroline Chikezie (Sharon); Jocelyn Esien (Yvette);   Don Warrington (Luther);   Tameka Empson (Dionne);   Diane Bailey (Bee);   Vas Blackwood (Caesar);   Andrea Francis (Yvette's Sister);   Anton Rice (Anton);   Saffron Lashley (Saffron);   Corrine Skinner Carter (Mistress Edith);   Suzette Llewellyn (Rose);   Clive Buckley (Matt);   Bushman (DJ on Radio);   Badi Uzzaman (Shopkeeper);   Tippa Irie (MC); Governor Tiggy (Bee's Act);   Peter Hunnigale (Matt's Act);   Barbara Lawrence, Stella Pilaya, and Tanitia (Dionne's Posse);   Dujhan Dennis Planter (Blues Party Performer);   Superflex, Bubbler Ranks, and Richie Dan (Performers at Sound System);   General Levy, Lorna G, and Caibo (Recording Artists in Studio).

NEW YORK POST, 3/17/00, p. 48, Lou Lumenick

Imagine "Flashdance" set to reggae music and reset in a London slum with a single mother as the heroine—and you've got a rough idea of "Babymother."

Anita (Anjela Lauren Smith) wants to be queen of the dance hall—but her main competitor is Byron (Wil Johnson), a reggae star who's also the father of her two children.

Writer-director Julian Henriques does a great job staging the lively musical numbers. He is on less solid ground in dramatic sequences.

SIGHT AND SOUND, 9/98, p. 38, Melanie McGrath

Anita is a 'babymother', raising two children with the help of her mother Edith on a rundown estate in north-west London. Byron, her baby's father and a local reggae star, casually invites her to perform in his show, but doesn't follow up the offer. Frustrated, Anita sets up her own act with friends Sharon and Yvette. When Byron turns up to apologise, she rebuffs him. Anita's first performance at a party goes well until Byron arrives with Anita's rival Dionne, who fights with Anita.

When Edith suddenly dies, Anita guesses correctly that her 'sister' Rose is her real mother. Still hoping to be a reggae star, Anita asks Rose for money to cut a record but Rose refuses. Anita then reluctantly agrees to a 'date' with Sharon's boyfriend Caesar in return for free studio time, but he reneges on the agreement. Later, Anita takes Byron's money while he's sleeping and heads for the studio.

Promoter Bee offers Anita and her friends a spot in a competition against Byron's promoter Luther. To thwart Anita's ambitions, Byron—furious after finding out about Anita and Caesar—agrees to perform on Bee's side at the competition and Anita and her friends are dropped. Anita persuades Luther to let her perform on his side, and they beat Byron.

Babymother marks a refreshing departure from the tradition of black film-making which seeks to contextualise black experience against the backdrop of a hostile system. Few British film-makers have dared to produce a film without a single significant white character, and that in itself makes *Babymother* an original. The sheer credibility of such an all-black world says much—seemingly without intending to—about the separation of people in Britain.

Billed as a reggae musical, *Babymother* might have been a black *Strictly Ballroom* if director Julian Henriques had pushed the grammar of the musical a little further. But he allows his previous experience as a documentarist to intervene and the result is an unfortunate hybrid caught somewhere between the loose, lush strains of a Baz Luhrmann production and the more spartan (and very British) realist tradition of Ken Loach. That said, Henriques extracts flexible, thoughtful performances from his cast and directs a classy-looking production with careful intelligence. Anjela Lauren Smith is luminous as Anita, making a relaxed witty ensemble with Caroline Chikezie and Jocelyn Esien, though these two are let down by thin characterisations.

Babymother's musical sequences are so beautifully choreographed and the music itself so vital that it's hard to care much about the trite linking narrative. This wouldn't matter much if Henriques had stuck firmly to the musical genre. As it is, however, plot devices such as Edith's death bump the narrative unevenly towards the next musical sequences while at the same time asking the viewer to stop and take note. And more could, and should, have been made of the relationship between Anita and Rose (the latter serenely played by Suzette Llewellyn). A few charming moments between the musical sequences such as when Anita, Sharon and Yvette are caught shoplifting hint at the rigorous pacing, characterisation and visual scripting that could have made *Babymother* really sing.

Also reviewed in:
NEW YORK TIMES, 3/17/00, p. E27, Stephen Holden
VARIETY, 9/28-10/4/98, p. 38, Derek Elley

BACKSTAGE

A Dimension Films release in association with Roc-A-Fella Records and The Island Def Jam Music Group. *Executive Producer:* Bob Weinstein, Harvey Weinstein, Cary Granat, and Lyor Cohen. *Producer:* Damon Dash. *Director:* Chris Fiore. *Director of Photography:* Elena "EZ" Sorre, Mark Petersson, and Lenny Santiago. *Editor:* Chris Fiore and Richard Calderon. *Sound:* Griffin Richardson. *Sound Editor:* Jeff Sullivan and Aaron Graves. *Running time:* 99 minutes. *MPAA Rating:* R.

WITH: Jay-Z.; DMX; Method Man; Redman; Beanie Sigel; Memphis Bleek; DJ Clue; Amil; Ja Rule; Damon Dash.

LOS ANGELES TIMES, 9/6/00, Calendar/p. 2, Steve Hochman

What did it take to be backstage on last year's Hard Knock Life tour—touted as the most successful and problem-free major rap concert tour up to the time? Well, unless you were a rapper worthy of being in the company of Jay-Z, DMX, Method Man and the other Hard Knock performers or a member of their retinues or families, apparently the only way to get behind the scenes was to be a pot dealer or a young woman willing to expose body parts (or more).

Or be a documentary filmmaker.

At the behest of the tour's organizers, director Chris Fiore took a crew on the trek to chronicle the backstage life. And from his perspective, as shown in "Backstage," it seems that there were three primary activities: doing business, smoking dope and ogling and/or fondling women.

On the first front, Fiore makes good use of his access. While the boasts about the tour's success aren't really explored, the dynamics of such a venture and the personalities behind it unfold through what prove to be the most entertaining sequences.

The highlights may well be a couple of displays of entrepreneurial muscle by Damon Dash, co-founder and CEO of Roc-A-Fella Records and a key partner in the tour. He's also the producer of the film, so it's not surprising that he gets a generous (and flattering) amount of screen time.

But a scene where he, while getting a hair trim, goes head to head with a co-sponsoring record company's executive, berating him for what he sees as trying to steal the tour's limelight, rivals any of the concert performance clips that thread through the film. Jay-Z and DMX may be better with a rhyme, but Dash's verbal dances stand as business freestyling at its best.

On the second matter, it's amusing and informative to watch as, one by one, the performers are profiled as smart (street-smart and/or otherwise), talented and ambitious, and then one by one melt into stoned stupor. It may not have been Fiore's intent to transmit an anti-pot message, and in fact the audience may well find the rap heroes' habits amusing or even a romantic part of that existence. But the footage speaks for itself.

Ditto for the groupies sequences, in which these street-toughened men turn into silly little boys. Very much lacking is any perspective on this from the women involved in the tour, especially performers Eve and Amil. The former, who emerged from the tour a big star, is hardly seen and barely heard at all. Amil is given screen time, but the focus is much more on her supermodel looks than on her rapping talents.

Frankly, not many issues surrounding the tour are addressed in any depth. This didn't need to be a state-of-rap film exploring the plethora of controversies out there, but it would be nice to get some sense of what made this an unprecedented tour package. And it would be very valuable to have some examination of the reasons earlier rap tours had been either financial failures or plagued by violence and how Hard Knock managed to transcend that.

And most lacking, perhaps, is the music itself. Onstage clips are generally excerpts rather than whole songs, and while there's enough to show charming Jay-Z's gifts as a crowd-pleaser, DMX's strong street poetry and the likable Beanie Sigel's versatile rhyming skills, hard-core fans (and who else will be in the audience?) may feel shortchanged. Of course, the film is titled "Backstage," not "On Stage," and it delivers the stars in unguarded moments that should give fans—if not everyone—some kicks.

NEW YORK POST, 9/6/00, p. 52, Jonathan Foreman

There are times in this concert documentary—when the performers wave at the camera on their way out to the stage or tell boastful stories about themselves to an interviewer who drinks it all up—when "Backstage" comes perilously close to "Spinal Tap"-like satire.

There are also times when the urban dialect is so thick, you wish the film came with subtitles, and times when you've been so battered by the "n" word, it feels like you've staggered out of a KKK "konvention."

But if the film brims with familiar music industry and hip-hop clichés—is it possible for a rapper not to go on about how his lyrics merely describe his violent, gangsta life back in the hood?"—it's still essential viewing for dedicated fans of Jay-Z, DMX, Method Man and the other rappers who headlined the 1999 multi-artist tour called "Hard Knock Life."

And it's fascinating to see—even though the performers rarely mention it—how very white the vast national hip-hop audience has become. As one female fan announces in her best faux Brooklyn, "I've come all the way from Montana to see Jay-Z!"

The promotional materials make much of the "uncensored" character of the movie, and you do indeed get to witness a lot of pot smoking and watch a furious Damon Dash, head of Rock-A-Fella records, tear a long, obscenity-laden strip off Def-Jam President Kevin Liles, (about an apparent attempt by Def-Jam to "hijack" the tour by giving out tour jackets with the Def-Jam logo) while getting his head shaved.

There are also several scenes of female fans—their faces blurred—stripping or fooling around with the talent.

But for the most part you get to enjoy watching the mostly rather charming performers—including the female rapper Amil, who bears a striking resemblance to Juliette Lewis—bond, argue and horse around in buses and hotels.

NEWSDAY, 9/6/00, Part II/p. B2, Gene Seymour

At one point in "Backstage," a behind-the-scenes documentary about an all-star rap tour, one of the performers mutters something to the effect that the "only way out" for "brothers" like him is either being able to rap or have a jump shot.

"Really?" you want to answer back. Now just who or what told you that? Voices coming out of the television set? Or is this the cumulative wisdom of street folklore, under-funded schools and racism-induced self-loathing? If this sounds like "old-school" churlishness, so be it. Hip-hop may well be the revitalizing force in our culture that its devotees say it is. And as last year's "Hard Knock Life Tour" chronicled in "Backstage" proved, it is eminently capable of breaching racial, cultural and geographic boundaries. But if the horizons of its practitioners are as narrow as those articulated above, then one can only wonder just how "fresh" the air on Planet Hip-Hop really is.

Neither "Backstage" nor "Turn It Up"—a standard-issue shoot-em-up starring Fugees founder Pras as a drug courier striving for rap stardom—spends a whole lot of time examining the breadth of hip-hop dreams. (Or lack thereof.) Perhaps that's too much to ask of both films since their task is to connect with the faithful and reinforce their expectations.

In the case of Chris Fiore's documentary, that means squeezing in as much of the myriad sensations of a high-profile pop tour as possible. Thus, "Backstage" comes across as a hypersonic collage of discordant, inchoate images. One second, you're on the buses watching rap stars, managers, family members and hangers-on laugh or grouse at each other. The next second, you get a voyeur's view of the rappers "living large" with the groupies (faces wittily obscured, the rest of them not). Interspersed with all this action are samples of, among others, Beanie Sigel or Ja Rule or "femme fatale" Amil firing verbal fragment bombs from a generic stage to a generic audience.

You notice lots of white faces in the front row of these shows. Is it because they can afford the seats? No time to answer. No time, really, to breathe. Fiore speed-dials everything in this movie to the point where you don't have time to absorb even the performances of Hard Knock Life headliners Jay-Z and DMX, both of whom clearly have the dynamism and chops to carry the whole package by themselves. But even their personalities become sucked up in the movie's clatter and din.

If "Backstage" is hobbled by excess, "Turn It Up" is bum-rushed by its limitations. Writer-director Robert Adetuyi shows a yeoman's skill with the elements of the "Saturday-night thriller." But there isn't a whole lot in the movie that its target audience hasn't seen before, from the chest-exploding violence to the show-biz dreams of Pras' Diamond, who comes across as a sullen stiff compared with his short-fused buddy Gage, played with ingratiating menace by the aforementioned Ja Rule.

VILLAGE VOICE, 9/12/00, p. 156, Nick Rutigliano

High-concept cinema this ain't: As any moron could tell ya, a product selling out some large-ass stadiums is one begging for a post-performance second take. Mo' money mo' problems? Run that one by Hollywood folk and see what kinda response you get. Show 'em a massive consortium of platinum-tongued hip-hop stars, and you might just snag yourself a chance to represent on the silver screen. Thus *Backstage:* Produced by Rock-A-Fella Records CEO Damon Dash with aid from the Weinsteins, Chris Fiore's chronicle of 1999's Hard Knock Life Tour (concocted by Dash; featuring Jay-Z, DMX, and others) hasn't a nun's chance in hell of masking its intentions.

Thankfully—the odd preachy interlude aside—it doesn't bother trying, and at its best *Backstage* plays as an amiably profane fish-outta-water romp.

While we're treated to the usual groupie groping and tour-bus bitching, the sight of DMX calmly restraining his baying pit bull from shredding a posh hotel lobby beats all manner of rock star histrionics. Marveling at their staggering success while exploiting its perks, the tour's wayward personnel cut capers as sharp as anything in gangsta mockumentaries *CB4* and *Fear of a Black Hat.* Boom operators are tormented, snooty camerawomen schooled, and the antics of Method Man and Redman (double-vision analogues of Marlon Wayans's blunted *Scary Movie* joker) include calling a time-out for the purpose of "hearing what [their] nuts are saying," then snorting with disbelief when the film crew dutifully lends an ear.

Likewise, footage of their dangling-from-the-rafters set neatly hyperbolizes the degree to which these cats are walking on sunshine—or at least on brilliantly hyped bravado. That they frequently don't seem to give a shit is what propels *Backstage,* even if keepin' it real is really part 'n' parcel of the mega-MC game. As Beanie Sigel quips when told how ill he is, "I ain't that sick—I got a cold."

Also reviewed in:
CHICAGO TRIBUNE, 9/6/00, Tempo, p. 2, John Petrakis
NEW YORK TIMES, 9/6/00, p. E5, Elvis Mitchell
VARIETY, 9/11-17/00, p. 23, Scott Foundas

BAIT

A Warner Bros. release of a Castle Rock Entertainment presentation. *Executive Producer:* Tony Gilroy and Jaime Rucker King. *Producer:* Sean Reyerson. *Director:* Antoine Fuqua. *Screenplay:* Andrew Scheinman, Adam Scheinman, and Tony Gilroy. *Director of Photography:* Tobias Schliessler. *Editor:* Alan Edward Bell. *Music:* Mark Mancina. *Music Editor:* Craig Pettigrew. *Sound:* Bruce Carwardine and (music) Steve Kempster. *Sound Editor:* Per Hallberg and Karen M. Baker. *Casting:* Leanna Sheldon and Susan Forrest. *Production Designer:* Delphine White. *Art Director:* Peter Grundy. *Set Decorator:* Jaro Dick. *Set Dresser:* David Orin Charles. *Special Effects:* Michael Kavanagh. *Costumes:* Delphine White. *Make-up:* Liz Gruska. *Make-up (Jamie Fox):* LaLette Littlejohn; *Make-up (Kimberly Elise):* LaLette Littlejohn. *Stunt Coordinator:* John Stoneham, Jr. *Running time:* 120 minutes. *MPAA Rating:* R.

CAST: Jamie Foxx (Alvin Sanders); David Morse (Edgar Clenteen); Doug Hutchison (Bristol); Robert Pastorelli (John Jaster); Kimberly Elise (Lisa Hill); David Paymer (Agent Wooly); Mike Epps (Stevie Sanders); Jamie Kennedy (Agent Blum); Nestor Serrano (Agent Boyle); Kirk Acevedo (Ramundo); Jeffrey Donovan (Julio); Megan Dodds (Agent Walsh); Tia Texada (Tika); Neil Crone (Supervisor); Matthew Witherly and Jason Jones (Guards); Bill Lynn (Night Watchman); Glyn Thomas (Chem-Tech Agent); Victor A. Young and Don Allison (Senators); Paul Miller (Dr. Harris); Grouchy Boy, Arnold Pinnock, Cle Bennet, and Desmond Campbell (Convicts); Shawn Lawrence (Warden Clay); Lee Rumohr and Norm Spencer (Bound Guards); Tom Cappadona (Cab Driver); Jonathan Hadary (Cafe Owner); Ritchie Coster (Buyer); Stan Coles (General); Larry Block (Customer); Billy Otis (Odd Inmate); Navaco Bernice Downey (Girl in Club); John Berger (Medical Examiner); Joe Pingue and Martin Roach (Cops); John Harper (Running Man); Dylan Bierk (Police Photographer); Bruce Beaton (Agent with Coffee); Ron Kennell and Conrad Bergschneider (Mobile Agents); Nick Pjoternicky (Agent); Ron Bell (Trucker); Joanna Polley (Rhonda Glimsher's Voice); Lorraine McNeil (Woman Looking in Car Window); Al Cerullo, William Richards, and Dave Tomassini (Helicopter Pilots).

LOS ANGELES TIMES, 9/15/00, Calendar/p. 11, Gene Seymour

[The following review by Gene Seymour appeared in a slightly different form in **NEWSDAY, 9/15/00, Part II/p. B2.]**

The techno-sleek veneer of "Bait" isn't thick enough to hide the hand-me-downs littered over it's landscape. Those who cobbled together this star vehicle for Jamie Foxx—who's earned the chance, after all, by running away with last year's Oliver Stone pro-football epic, "Any Given Sunday"—don't seem bothered that they've lifted slabs of "Enemy of the State" and meshed them unevenly with slivers of every chase comedy-thriller ever made: good, bad and (mostly) indifferent.

Foxx deserved better, and watching him make his way through this muddle, one gets the feeling that maybe he thought so too. His brand of sidelong spritzing and off-the-cuff commentary on the action generally come across in a lower key and with a sneakier edge than those of other comics upgrading their movie profile. Here, he seems bored with his own riffing, grappling for a breadth and poignancy in his character, the hapless thief Alvin Sanders. In doing so, the story keeps out of reach.

But the movie has no more respect for Foxx's Sanders than the U.S. Treasury agents, led by a dour hardhead with the curious name of Clenteen (David Morse). The Feds bend, fold and mutilate Sanders into an unknowing search engine for a homicidal hacker (Doug Hutchison), who stole $42 million in gold from the U.S. Federal Reserve.

Antoine Fuqua, who directed 1998's equally slick and numbingly derivative "The Replacement Killers," smears this ostensibly comic narrative with flashy crosscuts, claustrophobia-inducing close-ups and digitalized effects intended to show the dimensions to which the Feds are keeping track of him. It would have been nice if the script had teased funnier possibilities than the inexplicable sums of money literally dropping into Sanders' hands to keep him on the streets, where the hacker can get to him. But what little humor there is in the movie becomes subservient to the grisly violence, gratuitous cruelty and ugly car chases.

You have the theater carrying what feels like a low-grade fever with unwanted tremors and mild delirium. Maybe it's that fever talking, but I imagine that it will all turn out for the best, ultimately. Foxx will get another, better property—perhaps one from hard-boiled novelist-screenwriter John Ridley, who came up with the story for "Three Kings" and writes novels whose titles alone ("Everybody Smokes in Hell") are a lot funnier than anything in this movie. Fuqua, meanwhile, will get the chance to be Michael Bay when, and if, he grows up. And "Bait" will be remembered, if at all, as a bad patch in both of their careers.

NEW YORK POST, 9/15/00, p. 55, Jonathan Foreman

Unfortunately for Jamie Foxx and "The Green Mile's" David Morse, both of whom deserve better, "Bait" is one of those thriller-comedy combos that never get the balance quite right.

It doesn't help matters that two of the more important action scenes—including the climactic race-track sequence—simply don't work.

Thanks to Antoine Fuqua's ("The Replacement Killers") feverish and self-indulgent MTV-inspired direction, with its desperate overreliance on close-ups, you just can't tell what's going on.

Foxx plays hapless but good-natured small-time thief Alvin Sanders. We first see him stealing prawns from a restaurant warehouse with his brother Steve (Mike Epps).

Unknown to the brothers, there's a major heist going on at the other end of town: Two far more professional criminals are pulling off the impossible by lifting $42 million in gold from the Federal Reserve.

Caught with his fishy loot, Alvin is sent to Rikers Island, where he finds himself rooming with Jaster (Robert Pastorelli from "Murphy Brown"), one of the Federal Reserve crooks who has been picked up on a DWI charge.

Jaster had a last-minute falling-out with his partner and has hidden the entire $42 million somewhere in New York.

A team of crack federal agents, led by the ruthless, humorless Clenteen (David Morse), fingers Jaster for his part in the heist, but the ailing robber dies before he can give away the location of the gold—or, more important to the agents, the identity and whereabouts of Bristol (Doug Hutchison), his computer-genius partner.

Clenteen comes up with a clever plan to catch Bristol, using Alvin as bait.

His agents secretly implant a tiny bug-cum-homing device in Alvin's jaw and then, knowing that Bristol can hack into their computers, send internal Treasury e-mails implying that Alvin is actually an undercover agent who had been planted in Jaster's cell to find clues to the whereabouts of the stolen gold.

Unfortunately for Clenteen's plan, Alvin is constantly getting into trouble, partly thanks to his brother's involvement with an incompetent gang led by Julio (Jeffrey Donovan) and Ramundo (Kirk Acevedo), and the Feds have to turn cartwheels to keep him out of jail. And in any case, Bristol is one step ahead of them.

There are some cute moments when the increasingly concerned Federal team (including David Paymer and Megan Dodds) overhears Alvin's attempts to resist criminal temptation and to reunite with his girlfriend (Kimberly Elise).

But Fuqua seems to be trying to imitate "Enemy of the State" more than he's recycling "Blue Streak," and the film's darker elements coexist uneasily with its comic ones.

Hutchison, who played the psychotic prison guard in "The Green Mile," here does an almost perfect imitation of John Malkovich in villain mode.

Tia Texada, so bright in "Nurse Betty," has a small and depressingly stereotypical role as Steve Sanders' Puerto Rican paramour.

Morse, a fine actor who deserves a decent major role after so many good performances, is wasted as the brutal Clenteen.

Nor is the movie likely to do much for the reputation of Foxx, who proved his comic charm on his TV show and his mettle as an actor in Oliver Stone's underrated "Any Given Sunday."

Also reviewed in:
CHICAGO TRIBUNE, 9/15/00, Friday/p. A, Michael Wilmington
NEW YORK TIMES, 9/15/00, p. E23, Stephen Holden
VARIETY, 9/4-10/00, p. 23, Dennis Harvey
WASHINGTON POST, 9/15/00, p. C5, Rita Kempley
WASHINGTON POST, 9/15/00, Weekend/p. 47, Desson Howe

BALLAD OF RAMBLIN' JACK, THE

A Lot 47 Films release of a Crawford Communications/Journeyman Pictures/Plaintain Films production. *Executive Producer:* Hunter Gray, Tyler Brodie, and Jesse Crawford. *Producer:* Aiyana Elliott, Paul Mezey, and Dan Partland. *Director:* Aiyana Elliott. *Screenplay:* Aiyana Elliott and Dick Dahl. *Director of Photography:* Aiyana Elliott. *Editor:* David Baum and Susan Littenberg. *Music:* Ramblin' Jack Elliott. *Sound:* Greg Crawford. *Running time:* 105 minutes. *MPAA Rating:* Not Rated.

WITH: Ramblin' Jack Elliott; Arlo Guthrie; Nora Guthrie; Pete Seeger; Odetta; Dave Van Ronk; Kris Kristofferson; Alan Lomax; D.A. Pennebaker; June Shelley.

CHRISTIAN SCIENCE MONITOR, 8/18/00, p. 15, David Sterritt

Ramblin' Jack Elliott may not be a familiar name to young music listeners, and the rustic overtones of his moniker—the folksy adjective, the dropped consonant, the jaunty apostrophe—may seem affected nowadays.

But Elliott was a quintessential hero of the great folk-music revival that swept American youth in the 1960s. Some critics have made his contribution sound more indispensable than it really was, but it's fair to describe his performances as a key link between the undiluted traditionalism of pioneers like Woody Guthrie, on one hand, and the folk-inflected innovations of Bob Dylan's generation, on the other.

Ironically, the very authenticity of his ramblin' persona helped cultivate the semi-obscurity he now endures—or enjoys, to judge from his good-humored appearances in "The Ballad of Ramblin' Jack," the new documentary about his life. He really was a ramblin' man, often showing up late for concerts and recording dates, or missing them altogether.

He neglected to master the fine art of dealing with record companies, as well, collecting only a fraction of the royalties that should have made him a financial success as well as an artistic one. And he was a rambler in another sense, too, as fellow singer Kris Kristofferson points out in an on-screen interview: a rambling talker, who sometimes gabbed so much during his shows that fans heard far less music than they'd expected for their money.

There's much archetypal appeal in this portrait of the artist as an unmercenary minstrel—part cowboy, part hobo, part folkloric researcher, part barroom raconteur—forever wandering America's highways and byways in search of the nation's elusive soul. But as "The Ballad of Ramblin' Jack" makes clear, Elliott has been a bundle of contradictions, and these lend the movie much of its fascination. While he lived the life of a genuine rambler, he was born the opposite, entering the world as Elliott Adnopoz, the son of a Jewish doctor who wanted his child to stay in Brooklyn and follow in his medical footsteps.

Elliott claimed he changed his name because rodeo announcers couldn't pronounce it—he could hardly pronounce it himself, he amusingly adds—but he saw his wandering-cowpoke fantasies as a route to public adulation and private gratification. In short, he invented the character of Ramblin' Jack Elliott from a mixture of personal and professional motives, and then played his self-devised role in an all-embracing performance that defined his life and work.

Adding another layer of interest to "The Ballad of Ramblin' Jack" is the fact that his daughter, Aiyana Elliott, directed it. Maintaining a stable domestic environment was never high on the singer's list, and he didn't spend much quality time with his children (two) or wives (four) during his peripatetic career. He appears to have settled down in recent years—he's in his late 60s now—but some of the movie's poignant moments occur when his director-daughter enters the picture to grab some fatherly attention she didn't get while growing up.

"The Ballad of Ramblin' Jack" will appeal to just about anyone interested in music, Americana, or family dynamics. But it will have extra appeal for folk fans who remember the glory days of the 1950s and '60s, when legendary giants like Lead Belly were recent memories, Guthrie was still a living inspiration, and gifted newcomers like Elliott could tap into a community of young talents in urban and rural centers around the country.

The movie is simplistic in some respects; it returns so often to Manhattan's fabled Washington Square Park, for instance, that you might think this was the singular hub of the folk universe. But its affectionate heart makes up for its sometimes offhanded historical sense. And its superb archival and interview footage—of towering figures like Pete Seeger and Dave Van Ronk—is priceless.

LOS ANGELES TIMES, 8/25/00, Calendar/p. 4, Kenneth Turan

Elliott Charles Adnopoz, the oldest son of Flossie and Dr. Abraham Adnopoz of Brooklyn, N.Y., dreamed the most powerful dream.

Living on prosaic Linden Boulevard, young Elliott didn't merely wish he was a riding, roping, don't-fence-me-in cowboy, he convinced himself he actually was. With a vision that uncompromising, it was only a matter of time until reality caught up and made the dream flesh.

In one of the great confirmations of America's receptivity to personality remakes, Elliott Adnopoz reinvented himself into Ramblin' Jack Elliott, the folk-music legend, cowboy icon and recipient of the National Medal of Arts whom Sam Shepard called "a wandering true American minstrel." Added Johnny Cash, "Nobody I know, and I mean nobody, has covered more ground, made more friends and sung more songs than Jack Elliott."

There's material enough in that transformation, and in Elliott's place as a kind of missing link in American music, to make "The Ballad of Ramblin' Jack" an excellent documentary, but filmmaker Aiyana Elliott, who directed, co-wrote and co-produced, adds another, more poignant level. She's not just an NYU film school graduate with a great subject, she's also the subject's daughter.

If Jack Elliott was king of the hard travelers, he was also the most evasive dad ever; it's no accident that this film's first shot of him is hazy and unclear. A man with a gift for making strangers feel like friends, Elliott simultaneously kept those closest to him at arm's length, both physically and psychologically.

As a result, "Ballad" is part of what Aiyana calls "a lifelong struggle to get time with my dad," to understand and accept him and overcome the frustration of "having the world's greatest rambler" for a father. Rather than clashing, the film's professional and personal aspects reinforce each other, creating, with the help of generous doses of Elliott's captivating music, a warm and feisty documentary that is as much inquiry as it is tribute.

The singer always resented the indignity of being born in Brooklyn ("My parents," he says, "did it to me out of spite"), and as soon as he could, when he was 14, he ran away and joined the Col. Jim Eskew Ranch Rodeo and learned to sing and play some of the songs he'd heard on late-night radio visits to the Grand Ole Opry.

Eventually tracked down by his parents, Elliott returned to New York and fell under the spell of the raw, unadorned honesty of Woody Guthrie. The Oklahoma troubadour was living in Coney Island at the time, and Elliott not only became Guthrie's protege, he moved in with the family.

Guthrie could be touchy about his music ("You can steal whatever you like, but I'm not giving it away," he told Elliott), but interviews with children Arlo and Nora Guthrie make it clear that the singer, stricken with Huntington's chorea, was grateful for someone to pass his legacy on to.

Elliott traveled around America and made an extended visit to Will Geer in Topanga Canyon in the mid-1950s. There he met first wife June Shelley, who joined him in what turned into six years of performing in Europe. His return to the United States in 1961, as the folk-music revival was hitting its stride, created a sensation.

It wasn't just Elliott's abilities as a yodeler, flat picker and world-class storyteller that earned him fans, it was his rascally persona as well. With dark good looks, a wry sense of humor and perpetual cat-eating-the-canary half-grin, Elliott fit the "rake and a rambling boy" mold as if it'd been made for him.

The singer also came back to the United States in time to meet a very young Bob Dylan at Woody Guthrie's bedside. As much of a devoted protege as Elliott had been to Guthrie, so Dylan became to Elliott, so much so that when the young man had his first gig at New York's Gerde's Folk City, the sign read "The Son of Jack Elliott."

What Dylan had, and Elliott did not, was burning ambition, but that was only one of the reasons the older man never progressed far past cult. Someone who thrived on disorganization and irresponsibility, Elliott could not focus enough, let alone plan enough, to have a major career. No, he tells the camera, he never had a manager: "I just had wives, and I wore out four of them."

The daughter of Elliott's last marriage, filmmaker Aiyana Elliott tries to capture her father by following him to favorite haunts like the Cowboy Poetry Gathering in Elko, Nev., and interviewing ex-wives and girlfriends as well as fellow travelers like Kris Kristofferson, Pete Seeger, Dave Van Ronk and Odetta.

If "Ballad" shows us exactly why Aiyana Elliott is so frustrated, it lets us in on some of her father's disappointments as well, like an eventual chilly aloofness on the part of Dylan even though, as Arlo Guthrie puts it, "there wouldn't be any Bob Dylan without Ramblin' Jack Elliott."

That National Medal of Arts as well as winning a Grammy for best traditional folk album for 1995's "South Coast" have apparently helped soothe Elliott's generic irritations with the music business. It would be something if this fine documentary helped more in restoring Elliott's luster, and better still if it created the kind of closeness with his talented daughter she is yearning for and deserves.

NEW YORK, 8/28/00, p. 133, Peter Rainer

The legendary Ramblin' Jack Elliott, epitome of the folkie singing cowboy and compadre of Woody Guthrie, was born Elliott Adnopoz, the son of a Jewish doctor in Brooklyn. Elliott's screwy digression of a life is lovingly, skeptically documented by his daughter Aiyana Elliott in *The Ballad of Ramblin' Jack*, and as Kris Kristofferson makes clear in an interview here, that ramblin' refers as much to Jack's jabber as it does to his itinerancy. The reinvention of Elliott Adnopoz into Jack Elliott comes across as the most American of makeovers: His inauthenticity is the most authentic thing about him.

NEW YORK POST, 8/16/00, p. 64, Hannah Brown

"Ramblin'" Jack Elliott, a legendary folk singer who emulated Woody Guthrie and influenced Bob Dylan, has faded from the limelight over the last 20 years.

He emerges from this bittersweet and often funny but overlong documentary by his daughter Aiyana as charming but not really likable.

He seems like someone you might enjoy having a beer with, but not the kind of friend you can count on when the chips are down.

Still, Jack Elliott, now 69, is a difficult but interesting man, who created the "Ramblin' Jack" persona from scratch.

Born Elliott Adnopoz, the son of a Jewish doctor and teacher, he was raised in Brooklyn. Always attracted by cowboy music, he ran away to join a rodeo when he was in his teens.

After returning home, he met Woody Guthrie, who was living in Queens and suffering from Huntington's Chorea. Guthrie befriended the 15-year-old Elliott, by then an aspiring guitar player, and taught the boy everything he knew.

The two played together in private and in public, and Jack Elliott the folk singer was launched.

Friends knew Elliott for years, sometimes decades, without knowing of his origins. To this day, he affects a down-home drawl.

As his daughter tries to probe his feelings about his transformation, his early success and later failures, his falling out with Bob Dylan (who once worshipped him), his four failed marriages and other matters, he continually rebuffs her.

He prefers to tell long stories or chat with anyone who passes by than answer any of his daughter's questions.

It soon becomes clear, as Kris Kristofferson says in an interview, that he became known as "Ramblin' Jack" not because of his traveling, but because "he doesn't shut up" and doesn't focus.

Finally, at a concert, he admits, "I haven't been a very good father" and dedicates a song to all the bad fathers in the audience, adding, "I know I attract them."

It's a touching moment, but it comes too late in the film, which is overloaded with interviews with Elliott's contemporaries—including Arlo Guthrie, Dave Van Ronk and Pete Seeger—and rare film clips of Woody Guthrie and Bob Dylan.

All of this material is interesting, but there's too much of it. There are also too many interviews with Elliott's friends, ex-wives and ex-lovers.

While his talent distinguishes him from the many other irresponsible charismatic ramblers we've all met or heard about, Elliott the husband and father is a familiar figure.

It's only natural that Aiyana Elliott had a hard time getting some distance on her subject, but it's also a shame.

NEWSDAY, 8/16/00, Part II/p. B9, Gene Seymour

How did that line from Shakespeare's "King Lear" go? You know. The one in which the old, bitter, put-upon monarch rails against what he perceives to be an "ungrateful child" and says that such ingratitude is "sharper than a serpent's tooth"?

Well, "The Ballad of Ramblin' Jack," Aiyana Elliott's documentary about her own mercurial, 69-year-old living legend of a papa, is hardly steeped in ingratitude. But her ambivalence toward—and struggle to come to terms with—both the myths and the reality surrounding Ramblin' Jack Elliott provide a serrated counterpoint to this otherwise laid-back, odd-duck hybrid of cultural history, concert movie and cathartic memoir.

The history part is put together well, with archival footage and interviews with the likes of Pete Seeger, Arlo Guthrie, Dave Van Ronk and others, combining to chronicle one of the soon-to-be-completed century's more remarkable stories of cultural transformation.

The first-born son of a Jewish doctor living in Brooklyn, Elliott Charles Adnopoz would come to transform his boyhood fantasies about the Wild West and the Grand Ole Opry into a persona that made him an internationally renowned progenitor of the great folk-music revival of the 1950s and 1960s.

Inspired and schooled by Woody Guthrie, Ramblin' Jack adopted an artistic vision steeped in plain, honest, vital expression while staying just out of reach of the star-making machinery. Though Bob Dylan and many others were inspired by Elliott's example, he seemed perpetually stuck to the mainstream's fringes, to the point of adopting a two-decade-long boycott of the recording industry.

Elliott's resilient integrity is clearly a source of pride to his daughter, who nonetheless frames this story with her bittersweet recollections of a father who often strayed, literally and figuratively, from her mother, Martha, Elliott's fourth wife and one of a couple of ex-spouses who testify to the man's exasperating emotional distance.

Even while "bonding" on a recent road tour, both father and daughter are shown having a rough time communicating with each other, even when seated in adjoining seats on a van. Clearly, the distance separating the two is wider than a seat and to her credit, Aiyana Elliott, who is heard more often than seen throughout, spares the audience little in the way of her own smoldering resentment and her father's woozy attempts to soothe her scars.

VILLAGE VOICE, 8/22/00, p. 129, J. Hoberman

An unusually rich music doc, *The Ballad of Ramblin' Jack* has three concerns. The first is the tradition created on behalf of the folk during the middle third of the 20th century; the second is the process by which doctor's son Elliott Adnopoz, born in Brooklyn 69 years ago, ran off to join the rodeo, and returned as Ramblin' Jack Elliott; the third is the attempt by filmmaker Aiyana Elliott to make contact with this elusive figure, her father.

Some people are born authentic, others achieve authenticity. Ramblin' Jack never made the big time. (The film suggests a 1969 appearance on Johnny Cash's TV show as his career high point.) But, true to his invented persona, he's still doing the same thing that, back in 1961, made him the heartthrob of Gerde's Folk City, picking and yodeling his "cowboy music"—a hipster in a battered Stetson, peering through wire-rimmed glasses with the quizzical air of a wizened yeshiva student.

A bit meandering itself, *Ramblin' Jack* has a home-movie quality—and not just because of the amazing amount of old footage the filmmaker has excavated. There's plenty of family stuff to ponder. Ancient relatives dis Jack's overbearing parents—citing a nasty streak that one can see has been passed on. Young Elliott was expected to be a doctor, but he found himself a new father. Astonished to discover Woody Guthrie living in Coney Island, Elliott all but moved into the Guthrie household. As the ailing singer-songwriter's last and most adoring sidekick, he would subsequently channel Woody for a younger generation of performers—including Bob Dylan, another curly-haired Jewish cowboy, who began his career by parroting Ramblin' Jack's nasal, faux-Okie bawl.

The filmmaker, meanwhile, is stuck with the father she barely knew. "The thing is, I can't remember having an actual conversation with my dad," she recalls. The sagelike advice she receives from Arlo Guthrie—another, if differently abandoned child—is that she never will. Aiyana is still trying to get her father's attention even as he receives the ultimate Ozark recognition—a National Medal of the Arts presented by the ultimate '60s rambling man, Bill Clinton.

Also reviewed in:
CHICAGO TRIBUNE, 9/8/00, Friday/p. H, John Petrakis
NEW YORK TIMES, 8/16/00, p. E5, Stephen Holden
VARIETY, 2/14-20/00, p. 45, Dennis Harvey
WASHINGTON POST, 9/15/00, p. C5, Stephen Hunter
WASHINGTON POST, 9/15/00, Weekend/p. 48, Richard Harrington

BAMBOOZLED

A New Line Cinema release of a 40 Acres and a Mule Filmworks production. *Producer:* Jon Kilik and Spike Lee. *Director:* Spike Lee. *Screenplay:* Spike Lee. *Director of Photography:* Ellen Kuras. *Editor:* Sam Pollard. *Music:* Terence Blanchard. *Choreographer:* Savion Glover. *Sound:* Rolf Pardula and (music) Geoff Foster and James Anderson. *Sound Editor:* Philip Stockton. *Casting:* Aisha Coley. *Production Designer:* Victor Kempster. *Art Director:* Harry Darrow. *Set Decorator:* Ford Wheeler. *Set Dresser:* Jeff Butcher, Robert A. de Mar, James W. Callahan, Donald Grant, Bill Kolpin, Jeff Naparstek, and Mark Simon. *Special Effects:* Neal Martz. *Costumes:* Ruth Carter. *Make-up:* Eleanora Winslow. *Stunt Coordinator:* Manny Siverio. *Animator:* Joel Sevilla. *Running time:* 135 minutes. *MPAA Rating:* R.

CAST: Damon Wayans (Pierre Delacroix); Savion Glover (Manray/Mantan); Jada Pinkett-Smith (Sloan Hopkins); Tommy Davidson (Womack/Sleep 'N Eat); Michael Rapaport (Dunwitty); Thomas Jefferson Byrd (Honeycutt); Paul Mooney (Junebug); Sarah Jones (Dot); Gillian Iliana Waters (Verna); Susan Batson (Orchid Dothan); Mos Def (Big Black); M.C. Serch (1/16th Black); Gano Grills (Double Black); Canibus (Mo Black); DJ Scratch (Jo Black); Charli

Baltimore (Smooth Black);   Mums (Hard Black);   Dormeshia Sumbry-Edwards (Topsy);
Tyheesha Collins (Aunt Jemima);   Cartier Williams (Lil' nigger Jim);   Jason Bernard (Jungle
Bunny);   Baakari Wilder (Sambo);   Sekou Torbet (Rastus);   Ahmir "?uestlove" Thompson (The
Roots);   Christopher Wynkoop (Massa Charlie);   Jani Blom (Jukka Laks);   Dina Pearlman (Myrna
Goldfarb);   Imhotep Gary Byrd (Himself);   Johnnie L. Cochran, Jr. (Himself);   Al Sharpton
(Himself);   Mira Sorvino (Herself);   Matthew Modine (Himself);   Arthur Nascarella (Police
Chief);   Liza Jessie Peterson (Ruth, Casting Director);   Don Ezzard Peavy II (Auditioning
Dancer);   Tony Arnaud (Auditioning "Digeroo-Doo Player");   Tuffy Questell (Auditioning
"Singer");   David Wain (Bunning);   Ron Lawrence (Mau Mau's Engineer);   Al Palagonia
(Bobby);   Mildred Clinton (Louise);   Ephraim Benton (Tre);   Tanesha Marie Gary (Stacy);
Shannon Walker Williams (Young Black Woman);   Matthew Cole Weiss (Young White Man);
Coati Mundi (Papo);   La Bruja (Cuca);   Rodney "Bear" Jackson and Rafael Osorio (Stage
Security Guards);   Anna Hsieh (Joan);   Kris Park (Fish);   Cheryl Lynn Bowers (Mona);   Julie
Dretzin (Beth);   Steven McElroy (Seth);   Stephen Kunken (David);   Katie MacNichol (Anna);
Joshua Weinstein (Kirk);   A.D. Miles (Aaron);   Daniel Milder (Peter);   Jason Winther (Jeff);
Ed Blunt and Renton Kirk (CNS Security Guards);   Kim Director and Connie Freestone (Starlets);
Rayietta Hill (Hottie);   John Wallace and Arthur Thomas (Dawgs);   Danny Hoch (Timmi
Hillnigger);   James 'Kamal' Gray and Leonard 'Leo' Hubbard (Alabama Porch Monkeys);   Kyle
'Scratch' Jones (The Roots);   Tariq Trotter (Levi, Musical Director of The Roots).

CHRISTIAN SCIENCE MONITOR, 10/6/00, p. 15, David Sterritt

A friend of mine once likened a Spike Lee movie to an over-loaded truck.

It's piled too high, it's going too fast, it tilts precariously as it speeds around the bends, and
sometimes it hops the curb and sends pedestrians running for their lives. But it's exciting to
watch, your eyes are riveted to its every move and you have to admit you've never seen anything
like it.

Lee outdoes himself in his new picture, "Bamboozled," which is like several of those
overloaded trucks piled on top of one another. By any conventional standard, it's an overstuffed,
overambitious jumble. Yet it has more pungent themes, and takes more cinematic risks, than any
other movie on the current scene.

It's a vintage Lee production: sometimes brilliant, frequently infuriating, never dull, and so
jammed with provocative ideas that you're uncertain whether to yell "Right on" or throw your
popcorn at the screen.

Damon Wayans plays Pierre Delacroix, an African-American writer who's determined to turn
his creative talent and Ivy League education into a successful media career. He's taken a job at
a cable TV network with perilously low ratings. A bold new concept is needed in a hurry to
reverse its slide.

Pierre decides he has two options: present his bosses with the wildest idea he can dream up—on
the theory that only an aggressive gamble can save this rapidly sinking ship—or make the ship
sink even faster, but save his own skin, by getting fired before it goes down for good.

He puts both plans into operation by designing a show so outrageously awful that the network
will self-destruct, and he'll watch the disaster from the safety of his next job.

It's the idea Pierre pitches that makes "Bamboozled" such an audacious satire. The
entertainment industry has made a fortune by exploiting African-Americans through demeaning
images, he reasons. So he'll reach directly into that long, disheartening heritage and steal its most
shameless tricks.

Hiring a couple of gifted black performers, he makes them conspicuously blacker—with large
dollops of burnt-cork makeup—and christens their act "The New Millennium Minstrel Show,"
surrounding them with every humiliating cliché he can find.

Surely this travesty will crash in the ratings, the offending network will zoom into oblivion, and
Pierre will move on to more meaningful projects? Just the opposite: The show is a smash, racist
images and epithets become the hottest thing in entertainment, and Pierre finds himself the most
controversial guy in town.

Lee says "Bamboozled" was inspired by' "Network" (1976) and "A Face in the Crowd" (1957),
two classics, of media-minded cinema. He must also have thought of Mel Brooks's farce "The

Producers" (1968), about two Jewish con artists who stage an outlandish show ("Springtime for Hitler") that foils their swindle by becoming a box-office hit.

What sets "Bamboozled" apart from these precedents is Lee's willingness to push his satire beyond ordinary limits of taste. Scene after scene mixes in-your-face comedy with over-the-top plot twists and outspoken social commentary and Lee backs it all up with a barrage of film clips and other artifacts with blatantly racist messages—that makes the movie as impossible to dismiss as it is disturbing to watch.

"Bamboozled" is a unique blend of history and hysteria. Is it entertaining, or educational, or both, or neither? How willing are you to engage with a filmmaker who insists on following his convictions to extreme conclusions?

The picture's box-office prospects may benefit from its raucous humor and first-rate cast: Wayans as the protagonist, Jada Pinkett-Smith as his assistant, Savion Glover as the minstrel-show star, and Michael Rapaport as the network chief.

But its long-run significance rests on the dead-serious themes beneath its flamboyant surface.

Whatever you think of Lee's provocations, remember that the title comes from his hero Malcolm X, in a speech we hear within the movie. "You've been hoodwinked," the black leader tells his listeners about their treatment by mainstream society. "You've been had. You've been took. You've been led astray, led amok. You've been bamboozled."

Are the shock tactics of "Bamboozled" bamboozling us in turn? Or is Lee opening our eyes in ways no commercial filmmaker has ever tried before?

That's for every viewer to decide—and if enough spectators take up the challenge, the coming debate will be as invigorating as anything on the screen itself.

LOS ANGELES TIMES, 10/6/00, Calendar/p. 1, Kenneth Turan

"Bamboozled" is a defining film for Spike Lee. Not because it's necessarily his best work as a writer-director—though it is up there—but because it feels like his most characteristic, shedding a powerful light on the core drives of an always controversial career.

Savage, abrasive, audacious and confrontational, "Bamboozled" is the work of a master provocateur, someone who insists audiences think about issues of race and racism we'd rather not face, especially when we go to the movies. It's the angriest film an unfailingly angry filmmaker has yet made, skewering almost everyone in it, both black and white. Taking comfort in its own fury, it doesn't necessarily care if you agree with its points, just as long as you take the time to listen.

Like most polemical films, "Bamboozled" offers little in terms of drama and character; it's a satire that's abandoned everything in the service of its rage. Yet that single emotion brings so much passion with it that this has to be counted as Lee's most involving film in some time. The points it's trying to make couldn't be clearer, and the ways he's chosen to say them couldn't be more painful and discomforting.

"Bamboozled's" African American protagonist is Pierre Delacroix (Damon Wayans), a sophisticated Harvard-educated writer with a ridiculous, contrived accent. He works for the struggling Continental Network System and is so out of touch with black popular culture he can't identify the star athletes on his boss Dunwitty's (Michael Rapaport) office walls.

Dunwitty, by contrast, is a crude, posturing white guy, even more of a poseur than Delacroix, who worships hip-hop slang and feels free to use the N-word in casual conversation. "I don't," he says, "give a damn what Spike Lee says." He tells Delacroix he's blacker than he is and dares the writer to "dig deep into your pain" and create a show that will make headlines.

Helped by his loyal but conflicted assistant Sloan Hopkins (Jada Pinkett Smith) and with a homeless street performer named Manray (brilliant tapper Savion Glover) and his pal Womack (Tommy Davidson) in mind, Delacroix does just that. He changes Manray's name to Mantan (in tribute to 1940s black actor Mantan Moreland), Womack's to Sleep 'N Eat, and casts them as "ignorant, lazy and unlucky" characters in his "Mantan: The New Millennium Minstrel Show."

It's a program that glories in every hideous, stridently offensive racial stereotype imaginable, from rolling eyes and shuffling feet to the extensive use of burnt cork blackface and bright red lipstick to artificially accentuate grinning mouths.

Hard as it is to read about "The New Millennium Minstrel Show," it's even more upsetting, almost horrifying to experience, to see, for instance, the show's all-black house band called the Alabama Porch Monkeys dressed in convict stripes and balls and chains.

Lee doesn't care if you're offended; in fact, he seems to hope you will be. His thesis is that what's truly disturbing is what he sees as the reality behind those awful images, that from the 19th century to the 21st, American society has only wanted to see black people as buffoons. "It's always been our job to amuse white people," he told The Times' Patrick Goldstein. "You have to ask the question: 'Is the audience laughing with you or are they laughing at you?'"

"Bamboozled" is merciless toward white people for finding this kind of hurtful, demeaning behavior entertaining and toward blacks for being willing to provide it. He mocks almost anything that moves, from the stereotype of the "grateful Negro" to a rap singer (played by Mos Def) who changed his name from Julius to Big Black African and heads a self-proclaimed revolutionary rap crew called the Mau Maus, which spends most of its time getting high.

The only character in "Bamboozled" who escapes the film's scorched-earth policy is a gifted stand-up comic named Junebug (Paul Mooney), who had too much dignity and integrity to make it in Hollywood. Junebug mocks the current rage among white people like Dunwitty to act black, as does Chris Rock, heard in a clip from his HBO show saying that his white writing staff "wanted to really know the black experience, so I fired them."

One of Delacroix's rationalizations for putting a minstrel show on TV is to wake up America, to move the nation to change, to give the stereotypes visibility in order to destroy them. Naturally, it doesn't happen. "The New Millennium Minstrel Show" becomes a huge hit, a World Wrestling Federation-type success that creates all kinds of unforeseen agony for everyone.

Though Lee of course mocks Delacroix for his pretensions and delusions, he seems to have made "Bamboozled" with something of the same aims in mind. Some of the most haunting, affecting footage in the film (shot by independent film stalwart Ellen Kuras) consists of slow, lingering pans over a large selection of racist toys and other black collectibles (some of which come from the director's collection). Also unsettling is the film's closing montage of film clips, showing well-loved stars like Judy Garland and Mickey Rooney happily performing in blackface.

While critics and audiences will argue bitterly if Lee has overstated his case, or if bringing these kinds of images to theatrical screens under any guise does more harm than good, after viewing this footage it will be difficult to claim the filmmaker has made things up out of whole cloth.

"Race has always been a sensitive issue in this country," one character says, and Lee is unwilling to let anyone forget that. "By Any Means Necessary," the motto at the end of all his films, has never seemed more to the point than it does here.

NEW YORK, 10/9/00, p. 88, Peter Rainer

Bamboozled, the latest cri de coeur from Spike Lee, is about a frustrated black television writer, Pierre Delacroix (Damon Wayans), who ends up creating a new program for his network—a variety-act minstrel show set on a plantation and featuring black performers in blackface. Despite protests, the show—featuring Manray (Savion Glover), a formerly homeless tap dancer who is dubbed Mantan after the pop-eyed black comic Mantan Moreland, and titled *Mantan: The New Millennium Minstrel Show*—is a winner. Blackface, worn by all races, becomes the new national rage. Delacroix's boss, Dunwitty (Michael Rapaport), a vice-president of the lagging Continental Network System, is ecstatic. Even President Clinton is shown watching the show and chortling.

Lee loads up his movie with so many hot buttons that the film resembles a compendium of all his previous provocations. It's the Compleat Spike Lee. If dunning and baiting and chastising and lecturing were all it took to create a powerful experience in the movies, then *Bamboozled* would be a masterpiece. It's far from that, although clearly the intention here was to be more than a movie anyway. Lee wants *Bamboozled* to be a call to action: Stop the minstrelsy in our popular culture.

The new minstrelsy, as alluded to in the film, shows up most readily on television, which is where Delacroix, the sole black writer on his network's staff, has been toiling without success. Delacroix believes the black middle class has not been given a chance to sample anything more than race-demeaning monkeyshines. His own shot-down ideas, which include a show about a black headmaster in an eastern boarding school, don't sound so great, either, which may or may not be intentional. The implication here is that Delacroix, Harvard-educated and with a phony, pseudo-cultured accent, is a man out of touch with his blackness. And yet in the beginning, he remains angry enough to stick it to his white bosses. His pitch for the televised minstrel show describes it as satire; he talks about digging deep into his own pain, but what he really aims to prove is that the networks don't want to see blacks on TV unless they are buffoons.

This motive is blended in with another: Delacroix believes that by viewing something so offensive and racist, the country will wake up and move on to a better place. Of course, things don't work out that way, and he becomes an official advocate of the show's success and a self-hating sellout. His assistant, Sloan (Jada Pinkett-Smith), goes along for the ride for a while but is aghast at what her boss has wrought; her brother Big Black Africa (Mos Def), who heads the rap group Mau Maus, is outraged enough to take up arms. (The group's final ambush by the police is meant to conjure the most notorious NYPD shootings of African-Americans.)

Lee shot *Bamboozled* in digital video using multiple cameras, and it has the hepped-up quality of an exposé. Some of its tactics are lifted directly from *Network,* which also slammed viewers with self-righteousness and berated us for the soullessness of our appetites. Lee is a great hater. His distaste for Delacroix is so pronounced that the man never comes across as a tragic figure or much of anything else except a puppet. Even his education is held against him. (Maybe while he was at Harvard he should have taken a class with Henry Louis Gates Jr., who has written admiringly of Lee's movies.)

The real hero of the film is Delacroix's father, Junebug (Paul Mooney), a racy comic reduced to playing ghetto dives because, as he explains it, he had too much integrity to allow himself to be neutered by Hollywood. No sellout he. Lee sees this neutering specifically in racial terms, but of course television is an equal-opportunity ball-buster. It is also, on occasion, a place for great comics, including black comics, to shine. Lee isn't terribly specific about what current shows, or movie stars, he believes are causing all the problems. He exhibits a more generalized anger, and in a climate where black movie stars and comics, despite ongoing injustices, have never been more popular with a wider range of audiences, that anger has its hollow side. The excitement and the craziness in pop culture right now have a lot to do with the ways in which racial categories in entertainment, which used to be pretty clear-cut, are now so jumbled. The racial divide is no longer Grand Canyonesque, but Lee wants us to know it's all a sham. At times, it appears that what's really riling him is not that black culture has, in his view, been minstrelized for public consumption but that so many whites are mixing it up with that culture.

A less punitive filmmaker might see something liberating or flattering or even comic in this state of affairs: Movies and TV and hip-hop have turned a vast swatch of white kids into a nation of White Negroes. Lee shows us white people in *Bamboozled,* most pointedly Dunwitty, who think they're real soul brothers or sisters, and we're supposed to regard most of them with utter scorn. And Lee makes it easy for us to do so, since more often than not their hypocrisies are right on the surface. The Amos 'n' Andy-loving Dunwitty, whose office is plastered with photos of black sports greats and who has a black wife, tells Delacroix, "I'm more of a nigger than you are." His media consultant, a Yale Ph.D. in African-American studies whose parents marched with Dr. King in Selma, proffers slick advice about how to buy the NAACP's complaisance regarding the minstrel show. The consultant's name is Myrna Goldfarb, and Dunwitty, who says mazel tov and jokes about the size of his nose, is clearly also meant to be a member of the tribe. What is this scapegoating doing in a movie that claims to promote healing?

The film never makes it believable to us that blackface could become a national craze, or that critics would champion the minstrel show as groundbreaking. Does the show's runaway success mean that it's being interpreted by audiences and commentators as subversive satire designed to wake America up? Or does it mean, as Delacroix's disapproving mother laments to her prodigal son, that "a coon is a coon"? The latter, I think. The pickets against the show are led by the Reverend Al Sharpton and Johnnie Cochran, and they are not deluded men. The notion of a craze for blackface serves the film's hysteria about populism run amok in the liberal atmosphere of the new millennium. The film's model is not only *Network* but *A Face in the Crowd* (1957), in which a guitar-picking corn-pone con man, Andy Griffith's Lonesome Rhodes, becomes a television celebrity and bamboozles the nation with his homespun charm. (Lee's movie is dedicated to Budd Schulberg, that film's screenwriter.) Savion Glover's Mantan is like a more innocent version of Lonesome—innocent, that is, until Sloan and his minstrel partner, Womack (Tommy Davidson), wise him up about how demeaning his success is. Sloan offers up little mini-tutorials in the history of minstrelsy; she confronts Delacroix with a videotape compilation of atrocious racial stereotypes from the history of film and television and shouts, "Look at what you contributed to!"

As awful as many of these images are, there is another side to this tragedy that *Bamboozled* is unconcerned with: the ways in which black entertainers, even in the most cruelly stereotypical of roles, often managed to steal the show anyway with their wiles and timing and spirit and beauty. Who could not have eyes for Bill "Bojangles" Robinson, even if he was hoofing with Shirley Temple? Poor Mantan Moreland and Hattie McDaniel and all the rest are made to take the rap in this movie for contributing to a legacy of racist degradation. One would think, given what they were up against, that a bit more sympathy might be shown to these people. But sympathy doesn't have much truck in *Bamboozled,* where rancor takes the place of argument and outrage is palmed off as art.

NEW YORK POST, 10/6/00, p. 45 , Lou Lumenick

George S. Kaufman famously defined satire as "something that closes on a Saturday night." "Bamboozled" opens with a more technical definition—but even that seems utterly inadequate to describe the ferocious comic style of Spike Lee's incendiary and brilliant new film.

Put simply, it's an utterly devastating commentary on contemporary "black" show business—and how people of all races respond to it.

Harvard-educated Pierre Delacroix (a dead-perfect Damon Wayans), the sole black writer for a struggling UPN-style network, is so determinedly assimilationist, he's changed his accent and his name. His proposal for a gentle, "Cosby"-style sitcom is rejected and he's ordered to come up with something more "edgy."

Dela, as he's called, channels his anger into a proposal for a variety program modeled directly on the minstrel shows that were a staple of American culture for a century, until about 50 years ago.

Stereotypically depicting blacks as stupid and lazy will be acceptable to people of color, he facetiously argues, because they will be played not by whites—but by blacks wearing burnt-cork blackface makeup.

Dela expects to be fired, but to his amazement, he's put in charge of producing the show.

He recruits two penniless street performers who are so desperate for work, they eagerly debase themselves, allowing Dela to rename them Mantan (Savion Glover) and Sleep N Eat (Tommy Davidson), after two black Hollywood actors of the '30s notorious for their eyeballing-rolling, shuffling portrayals.

"Mantan: The New Millennium Minstrel Show" depicts its characters (among them Topsy and Aunt Jemima) in the crudest possible situations, with no offensive archetype, watermelon patch or chicken coop left unturned. Of course, it becomes a huge ratings hit, inspiring a blackface revival among white viewers, as well as people of color.

The nonplused Dela is soon under pressure to make the show even more outrageous, even as his black secretary, Sloan (Jada Pinkett-Smith), tries to prick his conscience and the Rev. Al Sharpton (playing himself) marches on the network to protest.

"Bamboozled," which takes its title from a Malcolm X speech, doesn't pull punches and is likely to make audiences of every pigment very, very uncomfortable.

At a screening I attended, a scene depicting white audience members nervously watching their black counterparts' reactions at a "Mantan" taping was being played out in the real audience—by whites who seemed barely less shocked at what they were seeing than the blacks did.

Lee has found many targets for his blowtorch style, which fits the material perfectly.

When Dela wins an Emmy, he gives it to his presenter (Matthew Modine, playing himself) and executes a moonwalk to pander to his mostly white audience, simultaneously parodying real-life acceptance stunts by Ving Rhames and Cuba Gooding Jr.

Lee spares neither "In Living Color" (on which Wayans and Davidson made their reputations), suggesting it is not all that far removed from "Amos and Andy," nor black Hollywood superstars like Will Smith, his leading lady's husband.

My main quibble with "Bamboozled"(which Lee, acknowledges was inspired by "Network" and "A Face in the Crowd") is the ending, which seems more predictable than the rest of the movie.

Still, it's hard not to be awfully impressed as Lee, never more in control of the medium, juggles as many characters, and a whole lot more issues, than any Robert Altman film.

An entire movie could be devoted to Dela's relationship with Sloan (with its Clarence Thomas-Anita Hill overtones), Sloan's defiantly illiterate rapper brother (Mos Def) or Dela's patronizing white boss (the hilarious Michael Rapaport), who gleefully boasts he's blacker than Dela is.

Lee's most powerful movie since "Do the Right Thing" will confuse people, make them angry and, most important, make them think. It pushes the envelope to raise the bar—unlike, say, "Scary Movie," which merely lowers it.

"Bamboozled" may not be the year's best movie, but it's undoubtedly the most important.

NEWSDAY, 10/06/00, Part II/p. B3, John Anderson

It's intriguing, and sad, to imagine what Spike Lee might have been had he not insisted on the appellation "writer-director" and settled instead for being merely a director. His body of work likely would have been stronger, less full of unguided anger. Other writers might have provided less logic-abusing vehicles for Lee's often limpid visual imagery. He might still be taken seriously.

Instead, we get "Bamboozled," a movie-as-provocation, the kind of film made by someone who sets six houses on fire and then complains about the rising rate of arson.

It's not that his story isn't on to something. The United States is racist. The television-watching public is an undiscriminating, pestilential mob. The culture abuses blacks (often, as Lee points out repeatedly, with their own compliance). But a smash-hit blackfaced minstrel show starring "a coupla real coons!"? Subtlety, thy name is not Spike Lee.

"Mantan: The New Millennium Minstrel Show" is the creation of the film's Pierre Delacroix (Damon Wayans), a Harvard-educated dandy with a torturously cultivated accent, who opens the movie by reciting the Webster's definition of "satire"—which usually implies humor, something "Bamboozled" is painfully without. Pierre is Lee's Faustian malefactor. Or is he?

Dressing better, speaking better and apparently thinking better than anyone else at the Continental Network System, Pierre is under pressure from his boss Dunwitty (Michael Rapaport), a black-talking (and Jewish) white exec who thinks he has his finger on the pulse of the African-American public. Pierre wants out. But he has a contract. So he enlists a couple of street performers, Manray and Womack (Savion Glover and Tommy Davidson) to star in the most virulently, offensively racist TV revue he can devise. The show, of course, is a smash.

And the movie's a mess. Instead of slinking off, Pierre becomes the show's champion. Why? Because he's a sellout and a moral bankrupt. Like everyone else. When Pierre and his long-suffering assistant, Sloan (Jada Pinkett-Smith), hold auditions, they're swamped—the message being, black performers can't get work. And yet, almost every one is awful. They include Sloan's brother, Big Black Africa (Mos Def) and his black-nationalist group the Mau Maus, portrayed as a band of malt-liquor-swilling morons.

"I don't want to be involved with anything black for a week," Pierre sighs. And, as villain, he gets away with it.

The much-honored Pierre is used by Lee to smear a raft of so-called collaborators—Cuba Gooding Jr. (his Oscar acceptance speech), Ving Rhames (for giving his Golden Globe to Jack Lemmon). A clip of Bill Clinton is dropped in to suggest the president is watching the show. Black audience members laugh gleefully along with Womack and Manray—renamed Sleep 'N' Eat and Mantan—whose studio audience starts showing up in blackface, too. Let's not even get started on the Jews (including a character named Myrna Goldfarb, hired by CNS to smooth-talk the NAACP).

The culture's traditionally racist depiction of blacks is much better illustrated by Lee's use of old film clips of the pop-eyed '40s actor Mantan Moreland, Stepin Fetchit, Burt Williams and Shirley Temple, and by the racist black collectibles that populate the background of the movie. You have to wonder, though, about his abuse of Savion Glover, generally regarded as a genius of tap dancing and whose art is portrayed in "Bamboozled" as one more instrument of racial degradation. If he really can't separate dancing from racism, Lee has problems deeper than his scriptwriting.

SIGHT AND SOUND, 5/01, p. 42, Xan Brooks

New York City, the present. The only black executive at television network CNS, Pierre Delacroix is pressurised by his white boss Dunwitty to devise a new hard-hitting, trend-setting series. Aided by his sceptical secretary Sloan, Delacroix dreams up a satirical spoof of the old black-face minstrel shows, which he hopes will backfire on the network in general and Dunwitty in particular. Delacroix recruits two street buskers, Manray and Womack, as the stars of his show, renames them Mantan and Sleep 'N' Eat and has them black their faces with cork.

Delacroix is taken aback when the series, entitled *Mantan—The New Millennium Minstrel Show*, becomes a critical and commercial success. Sloan begins an affair with Manray, while Delacroix is lavished with awards. But the minstrel show has its critics, notably New York's black activists and the militant gangster-rap group Mau Mau. Riddled with self-disgust, Manray breaks down before the live studio audience and is thrown off the set by Dunwitty's henchmen. Outside Manray is abducted by Mau Mau who later execute him live on the internet. Grief-stricken, Sloan storms Delacroix's office and shoots him dead.

Spike Lee's *Bamboozled* takes its title from a Malcolm X speech ("You've bee led astray, led amok, you've been bamboozled"). It arrives dedicated to Budd Schulberg, writer of Elia Kazan's 1957 media satire *A Face in the Crowd* (apparently one of Lee's favourite films). A kamikaze assault on racial stereotyping, the picture polarised opinion in the US, where the internet journal *Salon* called *Bamboozled* "a near masterpiece" while prominent film critic Roger Ebert concluded that "Spike Lee has misjudged his material... The power of the racist image tramples over the material and asserts only itself" In a sense, both judgements are valid. Yes, *Bamboozled* is a picture of genuine importance. Yes, it is also crude, unstable and hazardous. In teasing and taunting the audience, it often ends up bamboozling itself.

On the face of it, Lee's intentions are clear enough. Shot on fuzzy-edged digit video, *Bamboozled* repackages 100 years of media stereotyping and rams it back down our throats. Significantly, the film bows out with an extended montage from Hollywood's hall of shame (archive footage from *Birth of a Nation*, 1915; the glimpse of a corked-up Judy Garland; a black-face Bugs Bunny). But its present-day setting drives home the point that little has changed. Lee's broadsides at "Timmi Hillnigger", a pale-faced clothing mogul, and white television network bigwig Dunwitty, the wannabe home-boy who's "keeping it real", hint at an Afro-American culture that's been co-opted and corrupted by the white establishment. More crucially, his *Mantan—The New Millennium Minstrel Show*, a ghastly exercise in retro-racism—commissioned by black executive Delacroix in which black-face clowns gambol around a watermelon patch, can only be intended as a one-step-removed satire on mainstream media as a whole. (In recent months Lee has lambasted the depiction of Afro-Americans on primetime television and in such Hollywood pictures as *The Patriot, The Family Man* and *The Legend of Bagger Vance.)*

But there is danger here too. For while Lee is intelligent enough to realise that the situation is more complex than a simple them-against-us showdown, he's not quite rigorous enough to force this line of reasoning towards a satisfactory dramatic conclusion, One of the film's key points, for instance, is the way in which black America is at least part-way complicit in its ruin. The first person to applaud the *Minstrel Show* is a black audience member, while the militant rap act Mau Mau turn against the show only after they've failed an audition to appear on it, Meantime Delacroix, played by Damon Wayans, is revealed to have run from his roots and affected an over-formal diction that annoys his father, an old-style Harlem comedian ("Nigga, where the fuck did you get that accent?"). And yet Wayans' protagonist is left frustratingly vague: a plot pawn, a random mouthpiece. Is he motivated by greed, naivety or a desire to sabotage the system from within? It's never made clear. In acknowledging black culpability, Lee so dazzles himself that his film subsequently loses its bearings.

Judged on sheer voltage and ambition, *Bamboozled* ranks among the director's finest pictures *(Malcolm X, Do the Right Thing)*, while its best spells evoke the pitch and panache of Ralph Ellison's landmark novel *Invisible Man*—a broad and bawdy call to arms. But the tale finishes up as a fascinating, unresolved tumult. In one key scene, Delacroix is spooked by his "Jolly Nigger Bank", a racist antique which begins feeding itself of its own accord. *Bamboozled* is a lot like that itself. What we have here is a mischievous cinematic play-thing; at once mocked and mocking, and more than a little out of control. Undeniably it is Lee who lets it out of the box and first sets it moving. But by the end you can't help but wonder whether it is still him who's working the controls.

TIME, 10/9/00, p. 108, Richard Corliss

The blackface charade is on the air! A troupe of darkies in their field-workers' clothes and prison garb are singin' and dancin' and funnin' away, in a skewed, bitter, made-for-TV version of the old minstrel show. The feet flash, the banjos are pummeled; the energy level ascends in megavolts, moving beyond satire into irresistible entertainment. And suddenly a weird thought creases the moviegoer's skull: TV could use a comedy-variety show with a self-lacerating edge; and *Mantan: The New Millennium Minstrel Show*—the defiantly offensive TV parody that is at the heart of Spike Lee's *Bamboozled*—might just be the one. This show could be a hit.

Bamboozled is Lee's latest and most telling outrage—a spurning fulmination on the racial stereotypes that Americans, black and white, endure and perpetuate. A political parody of media venality, it's *The Producers* crossed with *In Living Color,* or *Network* meets *Bulworth.* And despite its sternest intentions and laudably high squirm content, the movie is often fun. just as Mel Brooks had to turn the *Springtime for Hitler* production number into a giddy riot of goose steps, the polemicist in Lee occasionally surrenders to the entertainer in him and allows his sour minstrel travesty to effervesce. He points fingers but can't help snapping them.

At *Bamboozled*'s fictional TV network, Harvard-educated Pierre Delacroix (Damon Wayans) is the token black executive. His abrasive boss (Michael Rapaport) charges him to devise a hot, edgy new series. Angry and desperate, Pierre proposes a minstrel show—a format "so negative, so offensive and racist" that it will prove his point about the lack of ethical or aesthetic standards on TV. Aided by his skeptical, ambitious assistant (Jada Pinkett-Smith), he hires as his stars a homeless tap dancer (Savion Glover) and his pal (Tommy Davidson). Renamed Mantan and Sleep 'n Eat they are given a supporting cast of Topsy, Rastus, Sambo and Aunt Jemima—enough reminders of racism to spur protests from an enraged citizenry. Guess what? The show is a smash. Audience members show up in blackface. The unknowns become stars. America loves *Mantan.*

Bamboozled puts fashionable technology (the movie was shot with digital video cameras and transferred to film) in the service of a backstage tale as familiar as *42nd Street.* It's Lee's usual mix of slapdash dramaturgy and sharp performances; note especially Paul Mooney, cogent and sexy as Pierre's dad, and Thomas Jefferson Byrd as the *Mantan* show's announcer. It has big third-act problems, when the caricatures are meant to morph into poignant humans. Then everyone pulls guns out. Insanity!

But say this for Lee: he is an equal-opportunity annoyer. He condemns whites for manufacturing the old image of the shiftless, larcenous Negro and for still seeing blacks through that warped prism. He also chastises blacks for inhabiting restrictive new and polar-opposite categories: the gangsta and the Buppie. Satire typically proceeds from two impulses: rage at the powerful and contempt for the masses. Lee has both.

Social and cinema history back him up. The first great movie epic *(The Birth of a Nation)* and the first talkie sensation *(The Jazz Singer)* wallowed in racial derision, personified by white actors in blackface. Mickey Rooney and Judy Garland, Fred Astaire and Bugs Bunny defaced themselves in minstrel cork. Egregious stereotyping can still be heard, most mornings, on Don Imus' and Howard Stern's radio shows—aural blackface. Somebody had to shout "Enough," and, whaddaya know, it was Spike Lee.

In hindsight we scorn the whites who loved minstrel shows and pity the blacks who had to play in them. But there are shades of culpability. Astaire, donning blackface for his *Bojangles of Harlem* number, probably thought (from ignorance, not malice) that he was paying sincere tribute to the great dancer Bill Robinson. As for Mantan Moreland, the black comic whose bug-eyed mugging in Charlie Chan films earns Lee's particular ire, he also was the star of films made for, and presumably appreciated by, the black audience. Perhaps we all have 20/20 vision of the past; it's the present that blurs. Today most whites are ashamed of the degrading racist stereotypes. Years from now, blacks may be chagrined to recall that their young men addressed one another familiarly as "Nigger" and chose hoodlums as their cultural gods.

Satire at its sharpest leaves the stain of guilt in all who are exposed to it. With his panoramic rage, Lee shows how every generation, of every color, runs the risk of being bamboozled.

VILLAGE VOICE, 10/10/00, p. 130, Amy Taubin

What better title than *Bamboozled* for a film in which the most electrifying dance numbers since the days of Vincente Minnelli occur within an updated minstrel show and feature a tap-dancing shaman with dreadlocks flying around his corked-up black face, a fast-talking sidekick (also a black actor in minstrel makeup), and a chorus line of coons, mammies, and pickaninnies? The sequence is so deliriously transgressive, and its ironies so tricky to unpack, that it puts the preachy satiric narrative in which it's framed to shame.

Bamboozled may prove to be Lee's most controversial, least commercial film. It's also a seriously schizophrenic work made up of two incompatible movies. One—a terrifying nightmare in which the confusion between identity and stereotype leads to martyrdom and murder—is affecting but underdeveloped, its potential undercut by the more dominant film, a justified but overly reductive attack on the television industry for its degrading representations of African Americans and on the audience that swallows the racist brew and begs for more.

Lee has never made a secret of his anger toward *In Living Color*. In part, *Bamboozled* is an act of revenge on the show and on one of its creators and stars, Damon Wayans, who's made to pay for his success in more ways than one. Lee has done Wayans no favors by casting him as *Bamboozled*'s snobbish, confused, and cowardly protagonist, Pierre Delacroix, a Harvard-educated television writer. Pressured by his white boss (Michael Rapaport), whose blacked-up pose he despises, to write a cutting-edge series, Delacroix finds his inspiration in *Amos 'n' Andy* and *The Jeffersons* . His program, *Mantan: The New Millennium Minstrel Show,* set in a watermelon patch and starring "two real coons," Mantan and Sleep 'N Eat, is so tauntingly racist that he expects to be fired for insubordination. Instead, the show is a huge hit. Delacroix pockets his check, but his repressed rage and guilt drive him over the edge.

Wayans hasn't a clue how to play a character as cerebral and alienated from himself as Delacroix, and Lee gives him no help. Wayans's performance is so one-dimensional, stiff, and monotonous that it could hurt his career. It also nearly destroys the movie. As his assistant, Jada Pinkett-Smith is burdened with an unlikely character arc; she begins as the voice of moderation and ends as a combination of Cassandra and Antigone. It's a punishing role, though not as humiliating as that of Verna (Gillian Iliana Waters), the Jewish publicist (a female version of the music promoters in *Mo' Better Blues)* who only exists so Lee can take some anti-Semitic potshots.

If *Bamboozled*'s primary story line is clumsy and badly acted, the subplot involving Manray (Savion Glover) and Womack (Tommy Davidson), homeless street performers who become overnight sensations when Delacroix casts them as Mantan and Sleep 'N Eat, is extremely moving and filled with possibilities. The movie comes to life in the backstage scenes, where they look at themselves in the mirror as they coat their faces with cork, paint their lips fire-engine red, and try to swallow their dismay at what they have to do to earn a living. Mantan's stardom enrages the Mau Maus, gangsta rappers with stereotypes of their own to account for. Eventually, the Mau Maus (whose members include Mos Def and Canibus) hijack the movie and turn it into a tragedy in cyberspace or maybe inside someone's psyche. Narrative consistency is not Lee's strong suit.

On the other hand, iconography is. Lee is unparalleled among American directors in his talent for seizing upon hot, subversive images and having the guts to put them on the screen. The black collectibles that line Delacroix's shelves, the montage of Hollywood classics in which racist stereotypes were taken for granted, and, most of all, the minstrel show itself make *Bamboozled* a scary movie indeed. For the performers—Manray, Womack, Junebug (Paul Mooney), and Honeycutt (Thomas Jefferson Byrd), whose "niggers is a beautiful thing" routine boggles the mind—the minstrel show is an exorcism, and their discovery that the studio audience views it as mere entertainment is the first step in their coming to consciousness.

Also reviewed in:
CHICAGO TRIBUNE, 10/6/00, Friday/p. A, Michael Wilmington
NATION, 11/6/00, p. 34, Stuart Klawans

NEW REPUBLIC, 10/30/00, p. 32, Stanley Kauffmann
NEW YORK TIMES, 10/6/00, p. E14, Stephen Holden
NEW YORKER, 10/9/00, p. 100, Anthony Lane
VARIETY, 10/2-8/00, p. 20, Emanuel Levy
WASHINGTON POST, 10/20/00, p. C1, Stephen Hunter
WASHINGTON POST, 10/20/00, Weekend/p. 43, Desson Howe

BARENAKED IN AMERICA

A Shooting Gallery release of a Netfilms production. *Executive Producer:* Pierre Tremblay. *Producer:* Cheryl Teetzel and Susanne Tabata. *Director:* Jason Priestley. *Director of Photography:* Danny Nowak. *Editor:* Al Flett. *Music:* Barenaked Ladies. *Sound:* Bill Sheppard. *Running time:* 90 minutes. *MPAA Rating:* Not Rated.

CAST: Ed Robertson, Steven Page, Jim Creeggan, Kevin Hearn, and Tyler Stewart (Barenaked Ladies).

LOS ANGELES TIMES, 9/29/00, Calendar/p. 12, Steve Hochman

[*Barenaked in America* was reviewed jointly with *Bittersweet Motel*; see Hochman's review of that film.]

NEW YORK POST, 9/29/00, p. 55, Jonathan Foreman

"Barenaked in America" couldn't be further from the kind of rockumentary spoofed in the recently re-released "This Is Spinal Tap."
There's no groupie action here, no overdoses, no vicious arguments, no manipulative girlfriend who breaks up the band. But then, "Barenaked Ladies" is a band without any rock 'n' roll pretensions, whose songs represent a very Generation X, very collegiate sensibility: ironic, referential and daffy. And even by Canadian standards, these guys lack edge.
As a result the first half of Jason Priestley's behind-the-scenes look at the Barenaked Ladies on tour is genial, if not very compelling, footage of the band's members, all pleasant, well-spoken, thirtysomething Canadian guys, talking about their touring as work.
Occasionally, they make stereotypically Canadian chip-on-the shoulder complaints about "Canadian" being a pejorative word in the United States.
But as you get to know the Barenaked Ladies and see the band in concert, if s hard not to be won over. They're genuinely funny, smart guys. And when keyboardist Kevin Hearn is diagnosed with advanced leukemia just as the band is about to go on tour, you get to see what decent people they are, too.
In the second half, Jason Priestley, former "Beverly Hills, 90210" star turned director, includes among the concert footage—and the slightly awkward interviews with Jeff Goldblum, Conan O'Brien and Jon Stewart (the funniest)—some cool, surprising moments, like when the band members sing the U.S. national anthem at a hockey game in Philadelphia, and when they tell the director of one of their videos that his efforts look "boring and flat."
There's something oddly endearing about the Barenaked Ladies. And by the end of the movie, you begin to see just what it is that inspires such intense fan loyalty. It's likely to grow stronger when they see this film.

NEWSDAY, 9/29/00, Part II/p. B7, John Anderson

With music that's a mix of retro-harmonic pop, guitar jangle, Pop 'n' Fresh hip-hop and a frat-house worldview, "Barenaked" Ladies have risen like yeast to the top of the charts, despite the awesome handicap of being Canadian. (Never mind Joni Mitchell, Neil Young, Crash Test Dummies, Bryan Adams, Alanis Morrisette, Sarah McLaughlin and, of course, Paul Anka.) This has stirred the actor-turned-director Jason Priestley, compatriot and fan, to make a documentary about the group.

There are documentaries, and there are documentaries—the ultra-objective POV of a Fred Wiseman or Maysles brothers; the ultra-personal ruminations of Ross McElwee. Priestley, originally from Vancouver, comes down somewhere else entirely, never imposing himself on the film (he's only in camera range once or twice), but making no pretense either about being the least bit objective. He loves the band, loves the fact that they're Canadian and even includes footage of guitarist Steven Page directing a concert audience to give him "reaction" shots for the film.

When we finally get a few people voicing unfavorable views of the band's music ("They --.") you know these people are token cranks, their misguided assessments used by Priestley as tongue-in-cheek gestures to evenhandedness.

But could it have been any other way? "Barenaked" Ladies—led, like the Beatles or Squeeze, by two members, Page and fellow singer-guitarist Ed Robertson—are a user-friendly group, comfortable enough with their audience to fashion spontaneous raps onstage (not always successfully) or exhorting fans to drop their drawers. In turn, the band is regularly flashed by devoted Ladies-ites and pelted with Kraft macaroni and cheese (inspired by the song "If I Had a Million Dollars").

Priestley does a good job of fashioning a narrative arc out of the Ladies' story, which began in Toronto in 1988 and culminates in burgeoning U.S. popularity (85,000 at a Boston record promotion), the all-arena Stunt Tour '98 (from which Priestley gleans most of the performances in the film) and a No. 1 U.S. chart hit ("One Week"). Bookending the movie is the battle fought by keyboardist Kevin Hearn, who developed leukemia just as the band was hitting its stride. Hearn's battle isn't a matter of suspense, just gravity—something Barenaked Ladies generally go without.

VILLAGE VOICE, 10/3/00, p. 238, Jessica Winter

Valiant *90210* parolee Jason Priestley set out to document dogged cult band and fellow Canadians Barenaked Ladies on their tour of the States in 1998 and found himself filming a breakout success with a love-or-loathe No. 1 U.S. single ("One Week"). *Barenaked in America* is a pleasant if overlong road show starring five witty, sweet, humble guys, who know fans by name and improvise songs on the spot for tickled audiences (much of the concert footage was shot in longtime Barenaked stronghold Buffalo). It's unabashed niche-market programming (with a lousy sound mix), but it seems as much a valentine to Barenaked fans as to the Ladies themselves—not least because the band members are such generous old-school showmen.

Also reviewed in:
CHICAGO TRIBUNE, 9/29/00, Friday/p. G, John Petrakis
NEW YORK TIMES, 9/29/00, p. E16, Lawrence Van Gelder
VARIETY, 9/20-26/99, p. 87, Brendan Kelly

BASKET, THE

A Privileged Communications release of a North By Northwest Entertainment production. *Executive Producer:* Marc Dahlstrom, Dave Holcomb, Greg Rathvon, and Dave Tanner. *Producer:* Rich Cowan. *Director:* Rich Cowan. *Screenplay:* Don Caron, Rich Cowan, Frank Swoboda, and Tessa Swoboda. *Director of Photography:* Dan Heigh. *Editor:* Rich Cowan. *Music:* Don Caron. *Sound:* Nigel Elliot. *Casting:* Michael Greer and Robin Nassif. *Production Designer:* Vincent DeFelice. *Set Decorator:* Jana Treadwell. *Costumes:* Nanette M. Acosta. *Make-up:* Julie Farley. *Stunt Coordinator:* Mark De Alessander and Ron Otis. *Running time:* 104 minutes. *MPAA Rating:* PG.

CAST: Peter Coyote (Martin Conlon); Karen Allen (Bessie Emery); Robert Karl Burke (Helmut Brink); Amber Willenborg (Brigitta Brink); Jock MacDonald (Nicholas Emery); Eric Dane (Tom Emery); Brian Skala (Nathan Emery); Casey Cowan (Samuel Emery); Tony Lincoln (Reverend Simms); Patrick Treadway (Frederick Treadway); Ellen Travolta (Agnes); Jack Bannon (Marcus); Elwon Bakly (Ben Emery); Joey Travolta (Charlie Cohn); Paul Hostetler (Old Helmut Brink); Kelly B. Eviston (Nancy Danielson); Cole Gamble (Erik Danielson); Jeff Waggoner (George Haines); Michael Van Gelder (Lewis Tinsley); MacKenzie Koppa (Katie Danielson); Heidi Nelson (Sara Barnes); Jamie Flanery (David Tinsley); John Rustan (George Ranson); Michael Ferguson (Daniel Haines); Ron Vavela (Mel Hester); Sara Edli (Immigration Officer); Gordon Grove (Referee); Terry Sticka (Kal Brink); Mark Forman (Bartender); Tami Grady (Mrs. Haines); Lindsey Kiehn (Sara Barnes); Jerry Fleming and Tim Sanger (American Soldiers); Cecil Ellsworth (Janitor); Stan Calder (Train Conductor); Henry Swobada (Basketball Timekeeper).

LOS ANGELES TIMES, 5/5/00, Calendar/p. 14, Robin Rauzi

"The Basket" holds a jumble of things. There's the Great War. There's opera. There's forbidden love. And then there's this strange new game called basketball.

It's a lot, yes, but by and large, "The Basket" carries it off.

Three newcomers disrupt a small town in eastern Washington. It's 1918, and Helmut (Robert Karl Burke) and Brigitta (Amber Willenborg), German siblings orphaned by the war, come to live with the local doctor. Then a new teacher, Martin Conlon (Peter Coyote), arrives at the one-room schoolhouse with his opera records and round leather ball.

No one's quite sure what to make of these new folk, least of all the Emery family, whose oldest son has just returned from the war missing half his leg. Patriarch Nicholas Emery (Jock MacDonald) wants those German kids sent back to an internment camp, and he doesn't like that teacher and his German music, neither.

First-time director Rich Cowan (who also produced, edited and co-wrote) tosses a lot of balls into the air, including a budding romance between another Emery boy and Brigitta, a fancy crop harvester the town can't afford, and a $500 prize for any basketball team that can beat the team from Spokane. Cowan has a lot of ground to cover, so he doesn't dig too deep into any of it. The war, for instance, is greatly simplified: It's the U.S. vs. Germany.

This is an old-fashioned movie, a bit slow by most kids' entertainment standards. It maybe a hard sell to the Gameboy generation, but "The Basket" has charms that may be more evident to adults.

Cowan and co-writers Frank and Tessa Swoboda try to make basketball-loving preteen Helmut the central character (starting with a pointless voice-over), apparently to hook youngsters. But the film doggedly remains an ensemble piece. There are a lot of people to keep track of, including four Emery sons and their mother, Bessie (Karen Allen). Allen's part is small, but her naturalness and intensity seem to elevate the inexperienced cast surrounding her. The amiable Coyote excepted, the actors mostly have only TV guest appearances or commercials to their credit. A few are novices. The questionable German accents indicate that a dialogue coach wasn't in the $3-million budget.

The production values belie that budget, however. Cinematographer Dan Heigh takes advantage of the lingering golden hours around sunset, and in a few shots, works magic. Production designer Vincent De Felice keeps the sets spartan but nails the details. And unlike "Legends of the Fall," set in Montana in the same period, the costumes don't look like they came from the Gap.

The score, by Don Caron, is mostly the opera music from the fictional "Der Karb" (The Basket). Caron's themes feel authentic, but attentive ears will tire of the same riff over and over.

NEW YORK POST, 5/5/00, p. 52, Lou Lumenick

Give director Rich Cowan points for ambition—"The Basket" combines basketball, opera and anti-German prejudice in 1918 America, all on a shoestring budget.

It's good to see the underrated Peter Coyote, lately reduced to a bit part in "Erin Brockovich" and announcing duties at the Oscars, in a starring role as a schoolteacher who arrives in a small farming community in Washington state.

He's not the only newcomer. A teenage brother and sister (Robert Karl Burke and Amber Willenborg) who are German refugees from World War I have arrived in town and inspired nasty hatred—something Coyote's character, Martin Conlon, tries to alleviate by using a German anti-war opera as a teaching tool.

Conlon also instructs his students in basketball, a then new sport he learned directly from its inventor, Dr. James Naismith. Before long, he's fielding a team against a Seattle squad to win a $500 prize—money the farmers need to make the down payment on a new harvesting machine.

The nicely understated acting keeps the overplotted story (written by Frank Swodoba) from lapsing into melodrama.

And Dan Heigh's cinematography is exemplary, whether he's shooting landscapes or the still heart-stoppingly gorgeous Karen Allen ("Raiders of the Lost Ark"), who has a small but key role as the wife of a bigoted farmer.

"The Basket" would be solid family entertainment if it weren't for the funereal pacing, which may kill its appeal among young audiences.

NEWSDAY, 5/5/00, Part II/p. B6, Jan Stuart

The timeless nature of athletic prowess to unite people is at the heart of "The Basket," a movie that reminds us simultaneously how far basketball and the culture of prejudice have evolved in America. Dulled by a doggedly formulaic mind-set, however, it also reminds us that the art of making movies has not budged an inch in certain quarters.

Set on the wheat farms outside Spokane, Wash., during World War I, "The Basket" follows the travails of Helmut and Brigitta (Robert Karl Burke and Amber Willenborg), two German orphans who have been transferred from an internment camp to the care of a local pastor. Barely recovered from the devastation of losing their parents, they now must put up with the derision of the local community.

Coming to their rescue is the enlightened new schoolteacher from Boston, Martin Conlon (Peter Coyote), who attempts to becalm the aliens' antagonists by introducing opera and basketball into the classroom. While some parents are addled (the opera he is teaching is in German), it is not long before the local boys are slam-dunking rugby balls into peach baskets and all the townfolk are relating details from the opera's libretto as if it were local gossip. Soon, Conlon has enlisted the wife (Karen Allen) of the town's most strident bigot to make uniforms for a playoff between the farm boys and the tough runts from the city.

Corny? You betcha. Not only does Helmut get his chance to shine at the big game, he also gets a shot at resurrecting the bigot's dead tractor and saving his epileptic son from a near-fatal fall.

Could anything save "The Basket" from such a terminal case of the hokums? They try. Conlon turns out to have a shady past, but the four screenwriters are so bent on virtuousness that he uses it to positive advantage at the eleventh hour. The big game does have a charming period energy to it, like an old college gymnasium photograph come to life. If director Rich Cowan had simply panned and scanned some of those old photos in Ken Burns-documentary fashion instead of opting for a live-action story, "The Basket" might have been more than the sum of its good intentions.

VILLAGE VOICE, 5/9/00, p. 138, Emily Bobrow

A weak-kneed feel-good film about overcoming prejudice in the wake of World War I, The Basket is a moralistic history lesson designed to charm parents. But it's hard to imagine kids will be amused by the film's pedagogical stock characters. The story is set in a small town in the Pacific Northwest, amidst acres of billowing wheat, rusty tractors, and endless sky. A new and somewhat mysterious teacher (Peter Coyote) takes over the one-room schoolhouse, and his unorthodox methods for engaging students—opera lessons (in German, no less) and a strange new game called basketball—raise eyebrows among the locals. The community's already strained nerves—pulled taut by hard economic times and the ongoing war—are further tweaked by the arrival of two young German orphans (how they manage to come to this town in 1918 is never explained). The concept of basketball as a metaphor for life is what nudges this film toward its triumphant lesson: Teamwork conquers all. Bigotry melts away once the town discovers how well young Helmut shoots baskets. Everything plays out with the insipid drama of the preordained—with halfhearted dialogue accompanied by soundtrack crescendo. A throwback in the family-entertainment genre, *The Basket* combines the wholesomeness of *Old Yeller* with the moral and physical claustrophobia of *The Waltons*.

Also reviewed in:
CHICAGO TRIBUNE, 5/5/00, Friday/p. L, John Petrakis
NEW YORK TIMES, 5/5/00, p. E29, Stephen Holden
VARIETY, 5/31-6/6/99, p. 37, Deborah Young

BATTLEFIELD EARTH

A Warner Bros. release of a Morgan Creek Productions, Inc. and Franchise Pictures presentation of a Franchise Pictures/Jonathan D. Krane/JTP Films production. *Executive Producer:* Andrew Stevens, Ashok Amritraj, and Don Carmody. *Producer:* Elie Samaha, Jonathan D. Krane, and John Travolta. *Director:* Roger Christian. *Screenplay:* Corey Mandell and J.D. Shapiro. *Based on the novel by:* L. Ron Hubbard. *Director of Photography:* Giles Nuttgens. *Editor:* Robin Russell. *Music:* Eliz Cmiral. *Music Editor:* Mike Flicker. *Sound:* Patrick Rousseau and (music) John Whynot. *Sound Editor:* Christopher Aud. *Casting:* Lynn Stalmaster. *Production Designer:* Patrick Tatopoulos. *Art Director:* Claude Paré. *Set Designer:* Lev Bereznycky, Joseph Browns, Simon Guillault, Claude Lafrance, Russell Moore, Richard Shean, and Lucie Tremblay. *Set Decorator:* Anne Galéa. *Visual Effects:* Erik Henry. *Costumes:* Patrick Tatopoulos. *Make-up:* Jocelyne Bellemare. *Special Effects Make-up:* Adrien Morot. *Stunt Coordinator:* Mark Riccardi and J.P. Romano. *Running time:* 117 minutes. *MPAA Rating:* PG-13.

CAST: John Travolta (Terl); Barry Pepper (Jonnie Goodboy Tyler); Forest Whitaker (Ker); Kim Coates (Carlo); Richard Tyson (Robert the Fox); Sabine Karsenti (Chrissy); Michael MacRae (District Manager Zeta); Michael Byrne (Parson Staffer); Sean Hewitt (Heywood); Michel Perron (Rock); Shaun Austin-Olsen (Planetship); Christian Tessier (Mickey); Sylvain Landry (Sammy); Christopher Freeman and John Topor (Processing Clerks); Tim Post (Assistant Planetship/Psychlo Guard); Earl Pastko (Bartender); Todd McDougall (Psychlo Wrangler); Derrick Damon Reeve (Psychlo Hoser); Jason Cavalier (Floyd); Andrew Albert (Labor Supervisor); Alan Legros (Heavy Set Guard); John Topor (One-eyed Guard/Teleportation Supervisor); Andy Bradshaw (Mason); Jim Meskimen (Blythe); Robert Higden (Supply Clerk); Rejean Denoncourt (Communication Officer); Tait Ruppert (Rodman); Mulumba Tshikuka (Human Pilot); Kelly Preston (Chirk); Marie-Josée Croze (Mara); Nadine Corde (Psychlo Babe); Russell Yuen (Speaking Bandit); Andrew Campbell (Leering Grin Bandit); Noel Burton (Clinko).

LOS ANGELES TIMES, 5/12/00, Calendar/p. 1, Robin Rauzi

"Battlefield Earth" is set in the year 3000, but stuck in the 1970s—and not in any hip, retro way.

As taken from L. Ron Hubbard's 1982 novel, in the year 2000 aliens called the Psychlos conquered Earth. The Psychlos are a species/corporation whose guiding moral principle is profitability. By 3000, the only humans left are slaves or Neanderthals hiding in the hills. Both groups have the intellect of baboons, but that doesn't prevent them from staging a revolution with perfectly preserved 1,000-year-old American military weapons.

Sure, science fiction gets some leeway in the reality department, but "Battlefield Earth" doesn't even make sense on its own terms. Compounded by a dated visual style, patched-together special effects and ludicrous dialogue, "Battlefield Earth" is a wholly miserable experience.

At ground zero of this disaster sits John Travolta, producer and star. (Travolta is a longtime follower of the Church of Scientology, which Hubbard founded, and was instrumental in getting the film made.) He plays Terl, the Psychlos' chief of security who thinks he's above his station. "Groomed from birth to conquer galaxies" is how he describes himself.

He looks like he hasn't been groomed, period. His head is covered with this falling-apart dreadlocked beehive hairdo. He's stumbling around in platform boots that are supposed to make him appear 7 feet tall, but instead just make him clumsy. (At least when he was in platforms before, in the disco' classic "Saturday Night Fever," he moved better.)

Travolta's played pure-evil villains before, notably in John Woo's "Face/Off." But there's something new—a campy, fey style—to his turn as Terl. Is that a bit of Bette Davis as he cackles, "As a friend, I could forget to file the report. But unfortunately I'm not your friend!"? His dialogue throughout is punctuated with a wicked laugh that recalls Vincent Price—but again, more campy than eerie.

It's an embarrassing performance that begs the question, "What was he thinking?" But that at least gives the audience something to ponder while this scenario—it can hardly be called a plot—rumbles on.

Barry Pepper plays Jonnie, a restless young human captured by the Psychlos and used for experiments by Terl. In a nonsensical development, Terl decides to mine gold in an area too radioactive for Psychlo health. So he tries to smarten up one of these man-animals to see if he can learn to operate mining equipment.

Jonnie gets strapped into a learning machine and knowledge—from world history to Euclidean geometry—gets pumped into his brain. The Psychlos apparently don't believe in doling out information on a need-to-know basis. Pepper's performance alternates between a startled expression and a snarl. The most intriguing thing about him is his hairdo; apparently even in the primitive cave-man-like world he inhabited, there was time for braiding. Forest Whitaker is the only recognizable face, though in his Psychlo get-up he resembles Bert Lahr's cowardly lion.

The script by Corey Mandell and J.D. Shapiro may be laughable, but the film itself is grim. It's not just the violence—much of which remains distractingly off-screen—but the whole tenor of the movie. When Terl starts shooting the legs off cows, science fiction hits a new low.

Director Roger Christian got his start as a set decorator on "Star Wars" and has—though it's hard to believe—made films before("Underworld" and "Masterminds"). His sole visual device is framing shots at a 15-degree angle. Maybe that's so no one will notice how unbalanced the Psychlos are in those ridiculous boots.

The aesthetic in "Battlefield Earth" seems deliberately 1970s sci-fi. (Why someone would choose that is another question.) Cuts between scenes are done with wipes across the screen. The weapons could be leftovers from the "Star Trek" TV series. Christian makes some lines of dialogue resonate—literally—with echoes.

The visual effects come from nine production houses, and the patchwork shows. Some of the computer-generated imagery looks fine, but others—the Psychlos' home planet, for one—would be comical on "Star Trek: Voyager." The rains of American cities have a distinct "Logan's Run" quality to them. But it's the non-computer stuff that's really bad. Shots don't match. The climactic battle of "Battlefield Earth" is nothing but a loud chaotic assault on the audience.

This film aspires to the simple rah-rah good vs. evil frenzy that fueled blockbusters from "Star Wars" to "Independence Day," but it doesn't come anywhere close. In the post-apocalyptic adventure genre, "Battlefield Earth" makes "Waterworld" look like a masterpiece.

Swaggering about in his platforms and padded leather outfit, Travolta (and much of the movie) is almost over-the-top enough to be bad in a good way. But it's too lame even for that. Maybe he needed higher platforms.

NEW YORK POST, 5/12/00, p. 49, Lou Lumenick

Earth to John Travolta—you've got a Y3K problem! It's called "Battlefield Earth," a truly dire and silly rehash of "Planet of the Apes," derived from a novel by Scientology founder L. Ron Hubbard.

It's the year 3000 and, as the titles announce, "mankind is an endangered species." Those who have not been enslaved for a thousand years since an invasion from the planet Psychlos have become cave-dwelling, spear-carrying hunters.

Earth is being overseen by Chief of Security Terl—a big-domed 7-foot Psychlo with breathing tubes, spectacularly bad teeth, dreadlocks and a drinking problem. Terl is played by Travolta, who happens to be a famous Scientology follower and proudly co-produced this mess.

Passed over for a promotion and stuck on Earth, Terl schemes to skim some gold from the Psychlos' mining operation.

For this job he trains a rebellious "man animal" named Jonnie Goodboy Tyler (Barry Pepper, who vaguely resembles that other well-known Scientologist, Tom Cruise).

But Jonnie, who's apparently the last person on Earth with access to a good dentist, has other ideas.

Inspired by reading the Declaration of Independence during a visit to the ruins of the Denver public library—quite an accomplishment, since his illiterate species has spent centuries in caves—he schemes to outwit Terl and lead a revolt against the Psychlos.

It's at this point where the film goes from being tediously terrible to downright gigglesome. Especially ludicrous is the scene where Jonnie and his fellow cavemen, after a pit stop in Washington D.C., quickly locate the remains of Fort Knox—and quite literally walk into the gold-filled vaults.

What really set a preview audience howling with laughter was the idea that these spear-carriers could operate fighter jets, thousand-year-old fighter jets, with great precision, after minimal training—and deploy high explosives to destroy a massive dome that looks distressingly like the Javits Center over the ruins of Denver.

Did I mention they also nuke Terl's home planet?

Nobody expects great acting in this kind of movie, but Travolta seems to be enjoying his ultra-campy turn—he laughs maniacally at every opportunity—a lot more than audiences will. His wife, Kelly Preston, turns up as Terl's secretary just long enough to unfurl a 3-foot-long tongue.

Pepper, one of the angelic prison guards in "The Green Mile," will no doubt someday try to live this down the same way Cruise tries to forget his failed supernatural epic "Legend." Forest Whitaker seems utterly miserable as Terl's sidekick, as he should be.

For a movie directed by the art director of "Star Wars"—Roger Christian also helmed the second unit for "The Phantom Menace"—"Battlefield Earth" looks surprisingly crummy.

The depiction of ruined cities doesn't markedly improve upon the 32-year-old "Planet of the Apes," and many of the effects shots look downright cheesy.

Warner Bros. is trying to lure audiences for "Battlefield Earth" with a "Take Back the Planet" contest, offering a grand prize of $ 100,000.

It ain't enough.

NEWSDAY, 5/12/00, Part II/p. B3, Gene Seymour

Because L. Ron Hubbard is the founder of Scientology and because John Travolta is a Scientologist, there have been those who have already forged a prejudicial syllogism about "Battlefield Earth," an adaptation of a Hubbard science-fiction novel starring and co-produced by Travolta.

The logic of these skeptics has stigmatized the movie in advance as some sort of solemn religious tract. There are even some hysterical types who believe the film carries subliminal messages intended to convert the masses who will supposedly flock to this picture the way seagulls gather at Jones Beach at sunset in July.

But it's hard to imagine any message, subliminal or otherwise, piercing through the swampy goo of this post-apocalyptic war story. The words "so bad it's good" strain to make themselves heard through the film's coarse bluster and grimy din. But there are times, especially toward the end, that one feels hard-pressed to even use the catchall catcall of, "camp" to justify the movie excesses, especially its unformed, altogether bewildering climax.

Whatever else there is to say about the movie, one couldn't exactly call it a vanity project on Travolta's part, since he's playing the vilest of the vile creatures, called Psychlos, who, by the year 3000, exert iron-fisted rule over Earth's dwindling population of humans.

Travolta's revolting character is named Terl, who, with his dreadlocks, pale complexion, dark teeth and tubes coming out of his nose, looks like a giant albino Rastafarian with bad hygiene and a bronchial disorder. Terl has been serving as a kind of Earthbound regional supervisor for his home planet's strip-mining operation.

But Terl's no happy camper, feeling just as enslaved as his human laborers. "I hate this world," Terl hisses to his subordinate (Forest Whitaker). "The gravity is so ... so ... different!" But the Psychlo elders back home keep Terl lashed to his post, apparently because they hate him even more than the earthlings who suffer under his cruel lash.

One of these earthlings is Jonnie Goodboy Tyler (Barry Pepper), a nomadic hunter caught in the Psychlos' slave net. Terl thinks the kid is feisty enough to be trained to mine a secret vein of gold somewhere in the Rockies. What he doesn't count on is Jonnie putting his little bit of knowledge to use in organizing a human insurrection against the big, bad aliens.

Director Roger Christian infuses each scene with a dank, unrelenting smudginess and keeps the camera tilted at odd angles, giving his audience the rough movie equivalent of reading ham-fisted pulp romance. For the first half-hour or so, the film makes such a headlong dive into the story's pulp and cheesiness that it's almost disarming.

The same could be said for Travolta!s gusto for playing Terl. Yet his thin voice, even at those times when it's electronically enhanced and garbled, never quite convinces you of his character's supreme malevolence. (He really needs John Woo to show him how to be bad.)

SIGHT AND SOUND, 7/00, p. 40, Kim Newman

A thousand years hence. The Earth has long since been occupied by the Psychlos, an aggressively capitalist species of giant humanoid aliens. Humans live either in servitude to the invaders or in small tribes. Jonnie Goodboy Tyler, a young tribesman, leaves his homestead and falls in with Carlo, a hunter. They are soon captured by a Psychlo raiding party rounding up slaves.

Terl, Psychlo Security Chief on Earth, is condemned by his superiors to stay indefinitely at his post. Assisted by his deputy Ker, Terl plots to make a fortune by secretly training humans to mine in radioactive areas. Terl trains Jonnie for the job, subjecting him to a machine that fills him with Psychlo knowledge. Jonnie counterplots against Terl, using his acquired skills to scavenge gold from Fort Knox and fighter jets and nuclear weapons from a US military base. In a mass uprising against the Psychlos, Carlo sacrifices himself to destroy the dome over Denver, letting in air fatal to the Psychlos. Jonnie uses a teleport link with the Psychlos' home planet to send the aliens a suicide raider with a nuclear device, which ignites the atmosphere of the planet. Ker sides with the humans; Terl is imprisoned as insurance against reprisal from other Psychlo colonies.

The 1066 page novel *Battlefield Earth* was L. Ron Hubbard's first published science fiction after a prolonged break from the genre spent inventing Dianetics, the peculiar system of DIY psychic self-improvement that forms the basis of the Church of Scientology. At the time of publication, it was remarked that Hubbard had retrofitted his belief system into pulp plotting by setting out a story—young man overcomes initial ignorance to achieve mastery of Earth—which could easily be read as an allegory of an initiate's progress through Scientology. It was also clear that Hubbard had take little notice of how the genre had changed since his days in the late 30s writing at a penny a word for such magazines as *Astounding Science Fiction*. Full of gosh-wow devices that had long since become clichés, *Battlefield Earth*'s juvenile tone was more in tune with the post-Star Wars science-fiction films of the late 70s than the literary field which had nurtured Philip K. Dick, Harlan Ellison and Alfred Bester.

For this reason, *Battlefield Earth* is likely to go down better with Scientology devotees—for whom Hubbard is an almost sacred figure—than with serious science-fiction fans. The path to enlightenment taken by the film's pouting, callow hero Jonnie is as fuzzy as any other post-Skywalker attempt to yoke in teachings from Joseph W. Campbell to add mythic muscle to an action scenario. It doesn't help that the film's premise, which sees stone-age cavemen turn into ace fighter pilots with only a week's training, is as naive as that of the 1939 serial *Buck Rogers,* where Buck mastered futuristic flying machines in as ludicrously short a period.

Roger Christian presumably won this big-budget science-fiction gig on the basis of his second-unit work on the *The Phantom Menace.* Unfortunately, star and co-producer John Travolta seems to have failed to notice that among Christian's mixed, often interesting directorial credits *(The Sender, Nostradamus)* was a previous science-fiction action film *Lorca and the Outlaws* that managed with far fewer resources to be exactly as muddy, silly and tedious as this effort. *Battlefield Earth* has the added misfortune to arrive as the latest in a line of similar exercises

(Waterworld, The Postman) that have become standing jokes in the genre, failing entirely to match the hairy mix of satire and spectacle found in the first *Planet of the Apes* films or the *Mad Max* series. With sub-Gene Roddenberry bathos, villain Terl's big mistake is not filling Jonnie's head with science (basic algebra, the ability to fly a spaceship) but encouraging him to examine a dusty copy of the Declaration of Independence that inspires his rebellion.

Though he originally intended to play the hero, Travolta presumably switched to the role of alien villain because he recognised that the scheming baddie is a far meatier part. Scientology at least notionally stands as a reaction to the grey flannel-suit excesses of early-50s US corporate culture, and the most deeply felt aspect of the novel that transfers to the film is its depiction of the Psychlos as members of a corrupt corporation where every executive is out to maximise his own personal profit. it's panto-level satire, but one that allows for welcome moments of camp—notably Travolta and Forest Whitaker's blustering, back-stabbing double act—that break up the pompous rebel-rousing. An ending which leaves them both alive while wiping out their homeworld (a blithe genocide prompting the *Clerks* cry of "What about the builders?") raises the possibility of a sequel, drawn from the second half of the novel. Since the plot hinges on the aeronautical prowess of stoneage-like tribesmen, it's futile to complain about lesser demands on suspension of disbelief such as the Psychlo homeworld's possession of an atmosphere that can fortuitously combust after the detonation of a simple atom bomb.

VILLAGE VOICE, 5/23/00, p. 141, J. Hoberman

Battlefield Earth, the big-time Warner Bros. summer sci-fi extravaganza, got nearly as many laughs as *Small Time Crooks*—at least at the all-media screening I attended. Set a thousand years in the future, the movie posits a world conquered by extraterrestrial Psychlos who, operating out of their Human Processing Center in the sooty rubble of suburban Denver, have enslaved most of humanity and reduced the rest to a pathetic pagan tepee-and-buckskin lifestyle. The Psychlos, led by John Travolta and a Wookie-like Forest Whitaker, are big fellas with green eyes, dreadlocks, formidable paws, and mossy teeth. They are much given to evil chortling, and, when they're not sadistically zapping the "man-animals," their idea of fun is to hang around a windowless bar swilling tumblers of a chartreuse liquor with the baleful glow of radioactive urine.

The movie's mode is brutal and excremental. Such narrative as there is pivots on Travolta Psychlo's scheme to strip-mine the Rockies for gold using man-animal labor. To facilitate this, Jonnie Goodboy Tyler (Barry Pepper), the most belligerent of the man-animals, is treated to an educational light show so he might be taught the Psychlo language. But the human learning curve is steeper than Psychlos imagine. Jonnie quickly picks up Euclidean geometry and the skill to operate a remote control. Before long, he reads the Declaration of Independence, flies a plane to the Library of Congress, and discovers Fort Knox. Under his tutelage, man-animals need barely 45 minutes to climb from the caves to the stars, egging themselves on with the primitive chant "Piece o' cake."

Remarkable mainly for rendering the prospect of human extinction inconsequential, *Battlefield Earth* was adapted from the 1982 mega magnum opus by L. Ron Hubbard, the Golden Age sci-fi writer who parlayed a pop positivist version of Freud into the Church of Scientology and composed this novel at a moment when his church was beset by lawsuits, federal indictments, and charges of criminal conduct. Since the movie's star and coproducer Travolta is also a longtime Scientologist (reported in The Washington Post to be an Operating Thetan who can control "matter, energy, space, time, form, and life"), there has been much cyberspeculation that B.E would bristle with subliminal messages and overt propaganda to advance the Scientology agenda.

No such luck. Though *Battlefield Earth* may have some relation to the church's more arcane theories of alien control, its most disappointing aspect is the absence of subtext. No less than that of the industry that spawned it, the movie's main purpose appears to be making money from the suspension of disbelief. Its one moment of truth is Travolta's sneering reference to "stupid humans."

Also reviewed in:
CHICAGO TRIBUNE, 5/12/00, Friday/p. A, Michael Wilmington
NEW YORK TIMES, 5/12/00, p. E10, Elvis Mitchell

NEW YORKER, 5/22/00, p. 98, Anthony Lane
VARIETY, 5/15-21/00, p. 26, Dennis Harvey
WASHINGTON POST, 5/12/00, p. C1, Rita Kempley
WASHINGTON POST, 5/12/00, Weekend/p. 51, Desson Howe

BEACH, THE

A Twentieth Century Fox release of a Figment film. *Producer:* Andrew Macdonald. *Director:* Danny Boyle. *Screenplay:* John Hodge. *Based on the book by:* Alex Garland. *Director of Photography:* Darius Khondji. *Editor:* Masahiro Hirakubo. *Music:* Angelo Badalamenti. *Music Editor:* Gerald McCann. *Sound:* Peter Lindsay and (music) Geoff Foster. *Sound Editor:* Glenn Freemantle. *Casting:* Gail Stevens and Kate Dowd. *Production Designer:* Andrew McAlpine. *Art Director:* Kuladee Suchatanun. *Set Decorator:* Anna Pinnock. *Special Effects:* Clive Beard. *Costumes:* Rachael Fleming. *Make-up:* Sallie Jaye. *Make-up (Leonardo DiCaprio):* Sian Grigg. *Stunt Coordinator:* Marc Boyle. *Running time:* 120 minutes. *MPAA Rating:* R.

CAST: Leonardo DiCaprio (Richard);   Daniel York (Hustler);   Patcharawan Patarakijjanon (Hotel Receptionist); Virginie Ledoyen (Francoise); Guillaume Canet (Etienne); Robert Carlyle (Daffy);   Samboon Phutaroth (Cleaning Woman);   Weeratham "Norman" Wichairaksakul (Detective); Jak Boon (Travel Agent);   Peter Youngblood Hills (Zeph);   Jerry Swindall (Sammy);   Krongthong Thampradith (Woman with Key);   Abhijati "Muek" Jusakul (Senior Farmer);   Paterson Joseph (Keaty);   Zelda Tinska (Sonja);   Victoria Smurfit (Weathergirl); Daniel Caltagirone (Unhygenix); Peter Gevisser (Gregorio);   Lars Arentz Hansen (Bugs);   Tilda Swinton (Sal);   Lidija Zovkic (Mirjana);   Samuel Gough (Guitarman);   Staffan Kihlbom (Christo);   Jukka Hiltunen (Karl);   Magus Lindgren (Sten); Saskia Mulder (Hilda);   Simone Huber (Eva);   Raweeporn "Non" Srimonju (Sumet).

CHRISTIAN SCIENCE MONITOR, 2/11/00, p. 17, David Sterritt

Leonardo DiCaprio became a superstar in "Titanic," which became a superhit largely because of his uncanny appeal to moviegoers in general and teenage girls in particular. His fans have been wondering what he'd do for an encore, and today the answer arrives in "The Beach," an action drama so dark that "Titanic" fans may choose to swim away from it fast.

DiCaprio plays an American drifter who wanders into faraway Thailand, where he hopes to find experiences more daring and different than the usual tourist excursions. His wish comes true when a mysterious stranger tells him about a secluded island paradise that's known only to the fortunate few who have the courage and stamina to get there.

He promptly enlists a young French couple as his traveling companions, and a reel or two later they arrive at their destination, sparking a series of daunting adventures.

The best things about "The Beach" are its magnificent Thai scenery, Darius Khondji's shimmering camera work, and yes, DiCaprio's vigorous acting. Tilda Swinton shows her usual talent as the matriarch who keeps the paradise running smoothly, and Robert Carlyle makes a suitably creepy impression during his brief appearance as the map-drawing weirdo who gets the story going.

The worst things about "The Beach" are its undercurrents of xenophobia and racism, its surprisingly sour attitude—as peevish and pessimistic as "Titanic" was ripe and romantic—and its limitless penchant for borrowing from other movies.

It begins like a rehash of "Return to Paradise," evolves into a hippie version of "Lord of the Flies," and knocks off everything from "Jaws" to "The Blair Witch Project" along the way.

When all else fails, director Danny Boyle turns the whole picture into a wide-screen video game, which may earn a few laughs but does little for the picture's shaky logic and sketchy character development.

DiCaprio's charm may be enough to turn "The Beach" into a box-office winner, especially with all those waving palm trees and splashing waterfalls to set off his sparkling eyes. But its driving force is less his performance than Boyle's dour vision of the world, which he's developed in pictures like "Trainspotting" and "Shallow Grave" over the past few years.

"The Beach" gives us a hero who craves romance and novelty, then spends the next two hours whisking both out of his reach—and doing the same, regrettably, to its audience.

LOS ANGELES TIMES, 2/11/00, Calendar/p. 1, Kenneth Turan

The crippling search for perfection can affect anyone, a traveler looking for a dreamy retreat from modern life or an actor searching for exactly the right role. In "The Beach," it afflicts both at the same time

For Leonardo DiCaprio, as for Richard, the American vagabond in Thailand he plays, dealing with paradise is a tricky dilemma. Think about being both a gifted performer as well as, after "Titanic," perhaps the hottest acting commodity in the world, and you can see how the role of a young man who doesn't know how to react when confronted by the perfect leisure opportunity spoke to DiCaprio's personal dilemma of not knowing what choice to make when literally everything is open to him.

Making "The Beach" even more enticing for an actor who perhaps feels all this success has come out of nowhere is that Richard (like the protagonist in "American Psycho" whom DiCaprio also considered playing) is not exactly a role model. Naive, self-involved, pretentious, he is a character who gets into situations over his head and has the ability to drag everyone else down with him.

But even if starring in "The Beach" was a life lesson for DiCaprio, there's little in this tedious and unsatisfying film for anyone else. Made by the same British team (director Danny Boyle, screenwriter John Hodge, producer Andrew Macdonald) that succeeded with "Trainspotting" and sank with "A Life Less Ordinary," "The Beach," like its hero, is nowhere near as wise and accomplished at it would like to pretend.

Adapted from Alex Garland's successful novel, "The Beach" connects with its protagonist as a new arrival in Bangkok, a good-time city where "the hungry come to feed." He's a traveler searching for "experience" and, like many disaffected young people, desperate to be different.

"My name is Richard, so what else do you need to know?" his fake-breezy, self-important voice-over tells us. In Thailand "looking for something more beautiful, more exciting, more dangerous," Richard wants his motto to be "Keep your mind open. Suck in the experience. If it hurts, it's probably a good thing." We'll see about that.

Because this is a movie, the people who are going to change Richard's life just happen to be in the rooms next to him in his bare-bones Bangkok hotel. On one side are Francoise (Virginie Ledoyen, one of France's top young actresses) and Etienne (Guillaume Canet), a photogenic pair of lovebirds, and on the other side, well, on the other side is Daffy.

Played with his trademark (and at this point a bit threadbare) manic energy by Robert Carlyle, Daffy has been there, done that and, witness his name, fried his brain in the process. In between psychotic rages, he tells Richard about an ultimate paradise, a perfect Thai beach undiscovered by tourists and unspoiled by the ravages of encroaching civilization. Even better, he gives Richard a rough map (we're not talking Michelin here) indicating how to get there.

Richard first convinces the French pair to make the trip with him, and then, in an act of unconvincing stupidity the film never recovers from, gives a copy of the map to two of the biggest party animal idiots in all of Southeast Asia. As my mother used to say, no good will come of this.

It turns out that Daffy wasn't lying—a self-sufficient community of dropouts and slackers, "a beach resort for people who don't like beach resorts," does in fact exist on a remote Thai island. A true lost world, it's run by no-nonsense matriarch Sal (Tilda Swinton), whose manner is half den mother, half Captain Bligh.

Part of "The Beach's" problem is that, Richard's insistent "this is paradise" voice-over notwithstanding, the island's community seems slightly weird and sinister almost immediately. Gun-toting marijuana farmers share the island and the settlement resembles the village in "Apocalypse Now" crossed with a rave site.

Making things worse is the air of sexual tension Richard brings with him. "Desire is desire wherever you go," he puts it with typical pomposity. "The sun will not bleach it, nor the tide wash it away." Richard is attracted to the seductive Francoise and other people are attracted to him. It's bad karma all the way around.

Director Boyle's quartet of films ("Shallow Grave" was his debut) show him to be a glib and facile filmmaker, but injecting significance into this wearisome story is beyond this crew. Caring about what happens to Richard and his cohorts is not to be, and neither is investing yourself emotionally in any aspect of the proceedings.

As for DiCaprio, his great likability makes him an unrewarding choice to play the murky, ambivalent Richard. (Ewan MacGregor, the star of Boyle's previous films and under consideration here, would have been better.) As his character heads for "The Beach's" predictable heart of darkness denouement, only die-hard fans will have the heart to tag along.

NEW YORK, 2/21/00, p. 99, Peter Rainer

The Beach isn't just the new Leonardo DiCaprio movie. Following the ensemble dud *The Man in the Iron Mask* and a cameo in *Celebrity*, it's his first big post-*Titanic* movie. His *Titanic* co-star Kate Winslet was praised last year for not going the cash-in route; it's not every day, after all, that one follows Hollywood's biggest blockbuster with the likes of *Hideous Kinky* and *Holy Smoke*. DiCaprio's latest choice, as it turns out, is in some ways just as shaggy as Winslet's. (The films share a certain hippie-dippy mind-set.) But just because DiCaprio's new movie isn't a crass piece of megafroth doesn't mean it's good. You come away from it almost wishing he *had* done a flat-out commercial job. At least that might have been more invigorating.

DiCaprio plays an American backpacker who shows up in Bangkok itching for something dangerous and unfamiliar. He's a kid without much of a past. "My name is Richard," he tells us in a voice-over at the beginning. "What else do you need to know?" The tone is portentous, juvenile, and a bit film noir-ish, and the rest of his narration is in the same vein: He's one florid flower child. Bunking alone in a cheap hotel, he connects with a bonkers traveler named Daffy (Robert Carlyle), who turns Richard on to a hand-drawn map describing the location of a secret island, a paradise-on-earth. A young French couple in the flophouse, Etienne (Guillaume Canet) and Françoise (Virginie Ledoyen), accompany him by train and boat and, finally, by swimming across an open sea, until they reach an island of dope fields protected by armed guards.

Jumping from the top of a steep waterfall, they escape to what appears to be a coven of multinational dropouts. Setting up their own back-to-nature encampment, secreted from the world except for the occasional run to Bangkok for supplies, they swim with the sharks and play cricket and teach each other languages; this crowd does everything but sing "Kum-ba-ya" around the campfire. The paradise of a beach that we keep hearing so much about turns out to be a pretty patch of white sand and a lagoon walled in by tall cliffs—alluring, certainly, but no more so than your garden-variety Club Med spread, and without those all-you-can-eat buffets.

The Beach is intended as some kind of Conradian cautionary tale: Richard seeks paradise and ends up in purgatory. Mess with nature at your peril; human beings can't abide freedom—you know the script by now. Director Danny Boyle and his screenwriter, John Hodge, adapting the novel by Alex Garland, work up a heavy-duty tone of *Apocalypse Now*-style jungle fever. (A clip from Coppola's film is shown.) Richard starts out in the Willard role and ends up more like Kurtz, babbling epiphanies and peeking through the dark leaves at the blood sport of mortals. Since Richard is pretty much a cipher all the way through, his descents and ascents don't pack much emotional oomph. The only real suspense in the movie is when he will break down the supercilious French reserve of Françoise and do the nasty. Their coupling finally commences in a lagoony fizz of glowing plankton.

There's a terrific, if underexplored, idea here: How might paradise look to the digital-age generation? The answer in *The Beach* is that every generation pretty much has the same secret-island fantasy, but that isn't much of a response. What is intended as a universal truth comes across instead as just laziness on the part of the filmmakers. Notwithstanding Richard's flights of fancy transforming the island into his own private video arcade, Boyle and Hodge come up with few new-style wrinkles on a utopian theme. We're even handed that ultimate cop-out: Richard informs us that paradise isn't a place, it's how you feel inside—which is particularly unhelpful since he doesn't seem to have much going on inside, either. DiCaprio can be a marvelous actor, and he goes all-out here, but his performance is all blank visionary stares and tantrums. He holds the screen long after we in the audience have let go.

NEW YORK POST, 2/11/00, p. 49, Jonathan Foreman

Leo is surprisingly masculine, charming and effective in this stylish, gorgeous, but clumsily structured Nintendo-generation update of "Lord of the Flies." Despite an excess of plot and skimpy characters, the film still works. Virginie Ledoyen has very French sex-appeal, and Tilda Swinton is strong as a hippie tyrant.

Filled to bursting with gorgeous landscapes, photography and people, "The Beach" is the kind of stylish, ambitious film you would expect from the makers of "Trainspotting" and "Shallow Grave."

Clearly aimed at a cyber-hip Generation Y audience, it radiates a sexy, Euro-coolness.

It is also the Leonardo DiCaprio movie for people—like myself—for whom his appeal was a mystery explicable only by pubescent girls, or who just couldn't stand the world's hottest young star.

Not only does DiCaprio now look more like a handsome young man rather than an androgynous 14-year-old, he also takes the risk of playing a self-deprecatingly charming but in some ways unattractive hero. And it pays off.

But despite its visual beauty, "The Beach" is a flawed affair, mainly because it sticks so close to Alex Garland's somewhat overpraised 1997 novel of the same name.

Writer John Hodge and director Danny Boyle try to cram a miniseries worth of plot into the movie's 120 minutes, while at the same time sacrificing background information necessary for the story to make complete sense. The characters are too sketchy to really work.

Still, this update of "Lord of the Flies" crossed with "Apocalypse Now" catches you quickly. It should strike a particular chord with anyone who's spent time traveling through Asia on a budget.

Richard (DiCaprio) is a young American backpacker hanging out in Bangkok, obsessed with the Vietnam War—though it ended before he was born—and desperate to experience a life more intense and dangerous and "real" than his own.

In an authentic-looking fleabag hotel, a suicidal Scottish junkie named Daffy (Robert Carlyle) gives Richard a map to a place of legend: the last unspoiled beach in Thailand, the secret home of a community of hard-core travelers.

Enlisting the help of Etienne (Guillaume Canet) and Francoise (Virginie Ledoyen), the good-looking French couple in the room next door, Richard goes in search of the beach.

It turns out to be in a lagoon on an island that is forbidden to foreigners, both as a national park and as the domain of armed marijuana farmers. But Richard, Etienne and the delectable Francoise (on whom Richard has a major crush) manage to find it all the same.

It's every bit as stunning as they hoped, but it gradually becomes clear that there is something ever so slightly sinister about the well-established community of young people they find there.

It turns out to take hard work to keep paradise perfect, not to mention the rule of Sal (the terrific Tilda Swinton) a charismatic but ruthless unofficial leader of the commune. Nor is a twentysomething's paradise necessarily a good place for the unhealthy or imperfect.

When Sal realizes that Richard may have compromised the secrecy of the community by giving a copy of his map to some party hearty Americans he met before coming to the beach, she exiles him to the other side of the island as a lookout. There, as he watches the sea for the arrival of strangers and keeps out of the way of the Thai drug farmers, Richard's Vietnam War fantasies start to take over his conscious mind.

By the time the guys with the map turn up on the island, the stage is set for things to go horribly, bloodily wrong.

Cinematographer Darius Khondji does a superb job of conveying both the sensual beauty (there's a spectacular moonlight-on-the-water sex scene with Leo and the lovely Ledoyen), and the darkness of Richard's paradise lost.

NEWSDAY, 2/11/00, Part II/p. B2, John Anderson

One of the tenets of western lit says that if a story involves Paradise Found, it will certainly involve Paradise Lost; the only interesting thing is how you get from point A to point B.

The other rule is: If you pay $20 million for something, you want to get your money's worth. Both issues apply to "The Beach," which, as every schoolgirl knows, is the test of both Leonardo DiCaprio's post-"Titanic" charisma (his cameo in Woody Allen's "Celebrity" doesn't count) and whether he's really worth Jim Carrey-size paychecks. Since the financial aspect of motion pictures has become far more interesting than the artistic one, let's first address Leo's value: Although "What's Eating Gilbert Grape?" "This Boy's Life" and "Marvin's Room" all proved that DiCaprio was one of, if not the, best actor of his generation, what "The Beach" proves is that he needs a director.

In fact, "The Beach" needed a director, because it's a little tough to tell what Danny Boyle was doing all those months in Thailand, having monkeyed around with the actual Phi Phi Le island (so "perfect" the filmmakers had to change its topography), enraging Thai environmentalists (scandalously dismissed in a current Premiere puff piece) and making statements that made him, producer Andrew Macdonald and writer John Hodge (the "Trainspotting" posse) sound a lot like the entitled brats at the center of their movie. Maybe that was it: Boyle was inventing Method Directing.

Or, he just didn't have a clue. Or much of a script either, for that matter. DiCaprio's Richard is a footloose American adrift in Bangkok who meets up with Francoise and Etienne (Virginie Ledoyen and Guillaume Canet) in a low-rent hotel that's also home to Daffy (Robert Carlyle), an older beach bum who's clearly off his rocker. Through a cloud of pot smoke, Daffy tells Richard about an idyllic beach that's free of tourists and full of marijuana; before he cuts his wrists, Daffy pins a map to Richard's door. And before Richard heads for that beach with Francoise and Etienne, he makes a copy for some fellow Americans—the fatal mistake that makes "The Beach" the tragedy it is.

Other than the size and cultishness of the hippie community the three find on the island—which is run by Sal (Tilda Swinton) and which they share with some gun-toting Thai pot farmers—not much happens in "The Beach" that you don't know will happen long before it happens. What is surprising is how DiCaprio is allowed to chew the leafy green scenery so furiously. And frequently. When Richard isn't talking to himself—or, in one fit of pique, dissing Etienne as "French boy!"—he's putting on displays of machismo that are pretty close to laughable. Boyle doesn't exactly give the movie gravitas with his incessant camera manipulation, inexplicable intrusions of slo-mo, or the sequence in which a delusional Richard turns into a video game.

Of course, he had to do something to kill time between the arrival at Eden and the inevitable fall. What he fails to do along the way is make us care about anyone—Etienne turns out to be the one moral person on the island, but the others are self-indulgent to point of pain. Maybe that's why Boyle poses them, like so many mannequins, all over his beach and allows them to act like the road company of "Melrose Place." Pictorially, he's made a better-than-average Club Med ad. Emotionally, it's more like "Jacqueline Susann's Lord of the Flies."

Far more troubling than the film's dramatic incompetence, though, is the portrait it paints of Thailand, a country the filmmakers more or less abused and have now portrayed as a nation of thugs and hustlers. Going back soon, boys? I wouldn't.

NEWSWEEK, 2/21/00, p. 57, David Ansen

A friend who'd seen a trailer for "The Beach" described it, only half joking, as a cross between "The Blue Lagoon" and "Lord of the Flies. " It's easy enough to see why Danny Boyle's movie would evoke such analogies. Here are nubile young Westerners in pursuit of endless pleasure cavorting on a lush Thai tropical island. And here, of course, is paradise lost—the inevitable moment when the dreams of these young utopians turn into nightmares, and violence supersedes peace, sex and pot-laced pipe dreams.

"The Beach" is a much less silly film than "The Blue Lagoon'" that "tasteful" 1980 exploitation film designed to showcase Brooke Shields's kiddie-porn chic. But I have a hunch that "Lagoon" will be remembered longer than Boyle's gorgeous but curiously weightless fable—in spite of the fact that it is Leonardo DiCaprio's eagerly awaited follow-up film to You Know What.

DiCaprio, to his credit, has never courted matinee-idol status. The character he plays here, Richard, a young backpacker in search of extreme experience, is no sane person's dream date, cute as he may be. A callow American kid with no moral bearings and little common sense, Richard arrives in Bangkok, where he encounters a mad, suicidal Brit (Robert Carlyle) who gives him a map showing the location of an island that, legend has it, is as close as it gets to paradise on earth. Richard's travelling companions are a pretty French girl he covets (Virginie Ledoyen) and her boyfriend (Guillaume Canet), whom Richard is happy to betray.

This eye-popping isle, they discover, has already been colonized. Half of the island is run by machine-gun-toting dope growers. The other is a secret community of half-clad fellow travelers led by a commanding Englishwoman named Sal (Tilda Swinton). Can these lotus eaters create their own Eden? One guess. Unfortunately, as screenwriter John Hodge (working from Alex Garland's novel) tells it, the crackup of this would-be utopia is a banal, unsurprising event. No tragic resonance here. Richard, acting out his "Apocalypse Now" fantasies, goes temporarily (and unconvincingly) bonkers in the jungle; the other characters are so sketchy ifs impossible to care about any of them. Boyle and Hodge ("Trainspotting) rely heavily on Richard's narration to spell out the meaning of what we are watching; it's as if they knew they had failed to dramatize the story correctly.

"The Beach" is nothing to write home about, though the landscapes are ravishing. The movie itself is neither fish nor fowl—the first half is not nearly as sexy as it should be, and the decline and fall is about as harrowing as an expulsion from summer camp. "The Blue Lagoon" meets "Lord of the Flies"? We wish.

SIGHT AND SOUND, 3/00, p. 39, Xan Brooks

Richard, an American backpacker in Thailand, alights at a fleabit Bangkok hotel where he meets Daffy, a drug-addled Scotsman. Daffy gives Richard a map to an Edenic island and then kills himself. Richard and a French couple, Françoise and Etienne, set off to find the island. En route, Richard leaves a copy of the map with two fellow-Americans, Zeph and Sammy. Richard, Françoise and Etienne swim to the island, navigate an illegal marijuana plantation policed by armed guards and discover an idyllic stretch of beach inhabited by a commune of western travellers.

The three visitors are inducted into the commune. Later, Françoise dumps Etienne for Richard. On a supply-buying trip with the commune's leader Sal, Richard learns Zeph and Sammy are coming to the island. Sal blackmails Richard into having sex with her. Back on the island, one backpacker is killed by a shark, and another, Christo, fatally injured in the attack. Richard is posted to the jungle to watch out for the arrival of Zeph and Sammy. Rejected by Françoise and ostracised from the group, he spies on the plantation guards and is visited by the ghost of Daffy. Zeph and Sammy arrive with two German girls in tow; all four are shot dead by the guards. The guards raid the commune; Sal must either kill Richard or everyone must leave. The gun they give her turns out to have no bullets. Everyone but Sal leaves the island.

"My name is Richard. So what else do you need to know?" runs The Beach's opening voiceover. It's like Moby Dick's opening "Call me Ismael" gambit farmed through Trainspotting's blasted "Choose life" mantra, and effectively sets the film's tone from the start. In adapting Alex Garland's best-selling novel, the filmmaking troika of director Danny Boyle, producer Andrew Macdonald and writer John Hodge look to be going back to basics. Stung by the poor critical and commercial response to their magic-realist folly A Life Less Ordinary, the team appear to be beating a retreat to the misanthropic, twentysomething kicks peddled by the likes of Shallow Grave and Trainspotting. Strange to report, then, that The Beach winds up an oddly wayward and uncertain effort, its tailor-made ingredients only fitfully hanging together.

On the face of it, Garland's source novel is ideally suited to the cinema. First published in 1994, The Beach boasted a roster of young, western characters, a glamorous foreign backdrop, a zeitgeisty flavour (tapping into the 90s rise in eco-tourism) and a high-concept narrative. Its young author has admitted to feeling more affinity with comic books than traditional literature (its father is Daily Telegraph cartoonist Nicholas Garland). Accordingly, Garland writes the sort of zesty, dialogue-driven prose that converts easily into a screenplay format.

But in the event, the film version of *The Beach* has been plagued by problems. First, its original star choice Ewan McGregor was dropped in favour of the more bankable Leonardo DiCaprio. Later, the production itself was disrupted by protests that the film-makers had damaged their location. Moreover, the makers have tweaked the original storyline, shoe-horning in two romantic encounters for the previously celibate Richard (reportedly on the direct orders of DiCaprio) and downplaying the book's communal spirit in favour of a loving focus on its hero. So rising French actress Virginie Ledoyen makes do with a pallid support slot as Richard's love interest, while a steely, tranquil Tilda Swinton struggles to make an impact as the demagogic Sal. Most disconcerting of all is the sight of Robert Carlyle reduced to bug-eyed histrionics in a shamefully underwritten role as the spectral Daffy. In this way, DiCaprio spreads his towel all over *The Beach* It's a classic example of Hollywood muscle run riot.

It says a lot for the inherent momentum of Garland's story that *The Beach* maintains its trajectory well into the second half. The set-up is efficiently handled, the trip to the island tightly plotted and the multi-cultural commune sketched out with a minimum of fuss. However, when *The Beach* should be gearing up for a grand finale, instead it nosedives into weary hallucinogenics. With Richard exiled to the jungle and cracking up fast, Boyle substitutes empty pyrotechnics for stringent psychological examination. His direction cannibalises *Apocalypse Now*'s mix of hard light with deep shadow, while a flashy arcade-game interlude (in which a digitised DiCaprio zaps tigers as he runs through the jungle) is a show-off flourish which hints, perhaps, at an underlying desperation.

These moments reveal *The Beach*'s true colours. Compare it to *Trainspotting* and the difference is striking. *Trainspotting* was a low-budget, organic product—properly cinematic yet generally faithful to the spirit of its source novel. It was, significantly, a film that broke out from its indie niche to find a mainstream audience. By contrast, *The Beach* seems to have sold its soul too early. In pitching for the mass market, Boyle's film has allowed itself to be rebranded as a Hollywood star vehicle, a cynical assemblage that is never more than the sum of its market-researched parts. *The Beach* is set on a tropical beach. It has killer sharks in it. It stars Leonardo DiCaprio. So what else do you need to know?

VILLAGE VOICE, 2/22/00, p. 135, Amy Taubin

Explaining what drove him to get rich quick, Seth [The reference is to *Boiler Room*] cites the example of the former child actor whose price is now $20 million a picture. *The Beach* is barely a movie, but it does prove that Leonardo DiCaprio suffers the elements in some small way for his money and his art. Why else would he leave the comforts of the Mercer Hotel to run around the jungles of Thailand for six months? But however you look at it, this is an ill-chosen project. Adapted from Alex Garland's beach-read of a novel, the film plays like a combination of *The Blue Lagoon* and a video game. In fact, it literally turns into a video game three-quarters through when DiCaprio, all alone in the jungle, must elude a band of dope farmers armed with AK-47s and machetes. The star has a flair for action, but the wrong skin for a beach bunny. Perhaps it was the sunblock in his makeup that causes his face to look so curdled.

The Beach was directed, written, and produced respectively by Danny Boyle, John Hodge, and Andrew Macdonald, the team that gave us the overrated *Shallow Grave* and *Trainspotting*. Caught between a star and an anxious studio, they opted for making as bland a film as possible. Still, the bummer tone of the novel comes through right up until the last shot, which undermines any meaning the film might have had. *The Beach* is not a total waste of time thanks to Tilda Swinton's performance as the mad, power-driven den mother to an international colony of twentysomething travelers. Swinton looks like a scary but gorgeous praying mantis. When she seduces DiCaprio, she really seems to eat him alive.

Also reviewed in:
CHICAGO TRIBUNE, 2/11/00, Friday/p. A, Michael Wilmington
NEW YORK TIMES, 2/11/00, p. E1, Elvis Mitchell
NEW YORKER, 2/14/00, p. 84, Anthony Lane
VARIETY, 2/7-13/00, p. 48, Todd McCarthy

WASHINGTON POST, 2/11/00, p. C1, Stephen Hunter
WASHINGTON POST, 2/11/00, Weekend/p. 41, Desson Howe

BEAU TRAVAIL

A New Yorker Films release of a la Sept Arte/Tanais Com/SM Films/Pathe Television co-production with the participation of Centre National de la Cinématographiè. *Producer:* Jérôme Minet and Patrick Grandperret. *Director:* Claire Denis. *Screenplay (French with English subtitles):* Jean-Pol Fargeau and Claire Denis. *Director of Photography:* Agnès Godard. *Editor:* Nelly Quettier. *Music:* Eran Tzur. *Choreographer:* Bernardo Montet. *Sound:* Jean-Paul Mugel and Dominique Gaborieau. *Sound Editor:* Christophe Winding. *Casting:* Nicolas Lublin. *Art Director:* Arnaud de Moléron. *Costumes:* Judy Shrewsbury. *Make-up:* Danièle Vuarin. *Running time:* 90 minutes. *MPAA Rating:* Not Rated.

CAST: Denis Lavant (Galoup); Michel Subor (Commandant Bruno Forestier); Grégoire Colin (Gilles Sentain); Marta Tafesse Kassa (Young Woman).

CINEASTE, Vol. XXV, No. 4, 2000, p. 40, George Rafael

Claire Denis is one of the best-kept secrets of the French cinema—which is a pity, as she deserves to be better known. You might remember her impressive debut film, *Chocolat* (1988), an oblique, semiautobiographical portrait of a young girl growing up in Cameroon at the end of French colonial rule. A richly textured, ambiguous work seething with racial and sexual tension, *Chocolat* was the intelligent, mature distillation of a seemingly complete filmmakers—a born artist. In actuality, Denis was already something of an old hand, having learned her craft as an assistant to Wim Wenders, Costa Gavras, Jacques Rivette, and Jim Jarmusch, and, before that, acting on screen and stage. More importantly, this self-described 'fille d'Afrique'—her parents were progressive civil servants who taught her that Africa was not their birthright—cast a clear but not cold eye on the marginals of French society—the African guest workers, West Indian immigrants, displaced *pieds noirs,* disaffected youth, the druggies, sharpies, and hustlers who pass away their lives in the neglected *banlieues* of Paris and Marseille. Unfortunately, as in the case of so many gifted foreign directors in recent years, her films have had limited release in this country, only one other of her seven works prior to this one, the well-received *Nénette et Boni* (1996), appearing here since *Chocolat.* One hopes that *Beau Travail,* one of the two or three best films of the year—in my opinion, the best—will change all that.

In *Beau Travail* Denis has relocated the late eighteenth-century Royal Navy setting of the Melville classic, *Billy Budd, Sailor,* to a present-day French Foreign Legion outpost in Djibouti on the Gulf of Aden. For Billy Budd, the saintly swabbie who's admired unto love by everyone, we have a brave young recruit, Sentain (Grégoire Colin), whose humane instincts nearly cost him his life; for the wicked petty officer Claggart, who destroys him in a pique of jealousy, we have a pitbull of a sergeant, Galoup (Denis Lavant), who is not so much wicked as, in an affecting way, naive and unformed; and for the fatherly commanding officer figure, Captain Vere, who is powerless to prevent a tragedy he can foresee, an accident waiting to happen, we have the magnetic, mysterious presence of Bruno Forestier (Michel Subor), Godard's *Petit Soldat* forty years on, 'disappeared completely' from his OAS days. The understated, intuitive performances of this trinity are riveting.

The story of *Billy Budd/Beau Travail* is a deceptively simple one, a Homeric ode disguised as a morality tale for Melville, a relentless exploration into human nature for Denis. In Marseille, Galoup remembers his time in the Legion in his diary entries, which are unwittingly melancholy; he is 'unfit for civilian life' but, as he admits, he 'screwed up'; he does not pity himself. The regimented life which he enjoyed with his men, sculpted young fighting machines, was the life for him—days spent playing war games, doing road repairs. This rough idyll—and his almost girlish pash for his tough superior, Forestier—is disrupted when a new recruit, Sentain, attracts the notice of his CO and upsets the balance of power. Sentain is noble, innocent, and adored by his comrades for his kindness and his courage. Galoup is beside himself, his world, the only one he knows, is threatened; he can't bear or fathom the attention and respect that Sentain inspires.

Driven to murderous rage, Galoup plots to put Sentain out of action but needs an excuse, which he finds—Sentain, out of the goodness of his heart, disobeys an order (he gives water to an African recruit who's been unjustly punished) and is himself punished by being forced to find his way back to the outpost from the deadly salt flats with only the aid of a compass. Galoup's plan—which nearly results in Sentain's death—is found out, and he is drummed out of the Legion, returning to Marseille where so many ex-Legionnaires wind up, exiles and misfits.

A simple story, then, but what Denis does with it is mesmerizing. The sum of *Beau Travail*'s parts make up an overwhelming, powerfully moving whole. It's difficult to know where to begin, so striking, so deeply evocative are Denis's many touches and details, all suggestion and ellipses, that it almost defies analysis. Adapting *Billy Budd* is no easy task but here she succeeds with grandeur in terms of the totality of her achievement, to borrow that Wagnerian term—because there's nothing else—*Beau Travail* is a *Gesamtkunstwerk*.

Denis has not altered the essence of Melville's story much, which is about envy and the evil men do, though she has reduced the novella's sublimated homoeroticism to merely another facet of the film, neither greater nor lesser than any other facet, a point most reviewers have missed (probably because most of them aren't really familiar with the source; more on this later). She reinterprets the biblical cadences of Melville's language in the dreamlike imagery and rhythm of the film. Like Antonioni and Bresson, her other acknowledged influences in addition to Godard, Denis is masterful at allowing her stationary camera to soak up the atmosphere and minutiae of a given time or place. She lingers over objects, whether it's a skull found on the salt flats of the desert interior or the iconic face of Forestier/Subor, seen through a blue haze of cigarette smoke; she becomes absorbed in abstract beauty, draws out the tears in things, the lacrimae rerun, weighs the moment.

But unlike Antonioni (but not Bresson, of whom she is the other side of his minted coin, she being austerely sensual, he sensually austere), Denis's longueurs never seem precious; they do not become self-indulgent. Her formality is never just for form's sake, but is a means of advancing the 'story.' While *Beau Travail*'s narrative might seem random, with a minimum of authorial intrusion and absence of obvious 'plot arcs,' its form and content mesh seamlessly, one tableau giving way to another imperceptibly. It breathes.

Likewise the terse quality of the dialog, built on the sad back of Galoup's diary entries, has the resonance of poetry; each word and intonation tells. So do the physical gestures of the actors, calculated with the precision and meaning of Racine, or Godard at his most nonchalant and ironic. Witness the blow Sentain delivers to Galoup's mug (a nod to Godard), or the balletic rigor of the military drills, performed under a merciless sun, a ritual at once purifying and ecstatic. The music—ranging from choruses of Britten's opera to East African blues, French military songs and chants, and the wild disco hit "The Rhythm of the Night"—is never inappropriate or obtrusive; the latter jolts us out of our senses and seats as a cathartic release.

With the Djibouti setting, Denis also gets to address her pet concerns about identity, belonging or not belonging, relations between the races and the sexes. In this case, however, the women of *Beau Travail,* lovely town girls wanting fun at the local discotheque, and Galoup's girlfriend, are peripheral—they will never mean as much to the Legionnaires as the regiment and their fellow Legionnaires. But Denis is not a political filmmaker in the sense that Ken Loach or Oliver Stone is; she doesn't thunder or rail; she doesn't even insinuate; the very nature of her work makes its social or political statement by indirection or seepage; we feel it. For Denis, as for the early Godard, politics is personal; it is not by chance that Forestier/Subor is in *Beau Travail*. Denis adheres to Godard's famous dictum, that "every movement of the camera, every cut in the film, is a moral act" (sic). She is, quite consciously, and in a very Gallic fashion, in the direct line of the great humanist tradition of filmmaking that begins with Vigo and Renoir.

Finally, anyone who has read of *Beau Travail* will note that I have not dwelled on the element of homoeroticism. That aspect of *Beau Travail* has been stressed to such a degree by desperate-to-be-with-it, hip reviewers that one might think the film is merely a blown-up Calvin Klein ad with subtitles attached. What none of these reviewers note is that the gaze is female—it is the gaze of the director. Denis has admitted in interviews that she likes writing about men, usually fighting or working or even sleeping, because she likes to observe and imagine them. Activity, physical engagement with one's environment, not talking, grabs her—which is in stark contrast to much of mainstream French cinema. And though there is a sexual undertone to *Beau Travail,* it has less to do with perceived desires than with something more subtle and enduring: the wish to dominate, the will to power, which can be expressed—and is, in *Beau Travail*—violently. That is a universal. Put another way, to say that *Beau Travail* is just a story about repressed sexuality is like saying that *Moby Dick* is just a story about a whale.

LOS ANGELES TIMES, 6/2/00, Calendar/p. 14, Kevin Thomas

With "Beau Travail" (Good Work) Claire Denis transposes, with her customary finesse, Herman Melville's "Billy Budd" to present-day Djibouti, a small East African nation on the Gulf of Aden. Formerly French Somaliland, it still hosts a small French Foreign Legion outpost. A ruggedly beautiful landscape of desert and sea provides a dramatic setting for a psychological drama told with the utmost rigor—and unabashed eroticism.

Life at the outpost is ritualized in the extreme. A contingent of 15 young men spend their days in calisthenics, on maneuvers or in training, or in preparing meals and washing and ironing their uniforms. At nights they head for a local disco. The men are put through their paces by the resolute, perfectionist Chief Master Sgt. Galoup (Denis Lavant), a dedicated careerist although not much older than his men.

Galoup has a girlfriend, the most beautiful in the disco, Rahel (Marta Tafesse Kassa), and a commandant, the mature and worldly Bruno Forestier (Michel Subor), he admires. (Significantly, Subor played a character of the same name in Godard's controversial 1963 Algerian War commentary, "Le Petit Soldat.")

"Beau Travail" unfolds as a flashback, a story told by Galoup, a man who had found the ideal world for himself but who in retrospect decides he is also a man who stayed away from France too long.

That world starts unraveling with the arrival of Gilles Sentain (Gregoire Colin), a tall, self-possessed 22-year-old. Gilles fits in immediately with the other young men, but Galoup feels Gilles does not belong—that he will be a source of trouble. The trouble, however, lies entirely within Galoup, who senses that Gilles, for all his impeccable conduct, is not submissive in nature.

Gilles is tall, with a striking profile whereas Galoup is short and has a gnomish countenance that is not unattractive. There is both strength and a distinctive beauty to Gilles that Galoup clearly finds profoundly threatening. Galoup is most likely a repressed homosexual in the throes of denial, but Gilles' serene presence would intimidate a brooding loner like Galoup in any event. Understatement and subtlety key all the performances, and Denis' actors suggest much complexity with minimal dialogue.

All sorts of meanings could be read into "Beau Travail," but the one thing Denis, whose childhood was in French Colonial Africa, makes clear is that there doesn't seem much point to the legionnaires' sweaty regimen, a source of amusement to the locals. There's not an ounce of body fat among the entirety of the young legionnaires, and Denis does celebrate the physical perfection of the young men as they exercise. (They do their ironing with the same precision, to amusing effect.) "Beau Travail" is a work of deliberate and subversive sensuality that suggests a hollowness to all this furious activity. You sense that it's being performed in the name of an imperial grandeur that has passed.

Denis most effectively draws upon the images of cinematographer Agnes Godard and Eran Tzur's original score, which incorporates passages from Benjamin Britten's "Billy Budd" and even "Rhythm of the Night." "Beau Travail," which unfolds like a ballet, represents the most stylized and venturesome film to date from the masterful director of "Chocolat," "I Can't Sleep" and "Nenette and Boni."

NEW STATESMAN, 7/17/00, p. 46, Jonathan Romney

It's not unusual to see a film and to find that one, especially resonant image stays with you. But with Claire Denis's *Beau Travail,* it feels as if you could isolate any one of its shots or sequences and it could encapsulate the entire film. When a group of legionnaires run a practice assault on the skeletal framework of a building, it could stand for the way Denis strips the army film to its bare bones; rows of fatigues drying on lines evoke the soldiers themselves, reduced to interchangeable figures staked out in a landscape. But often the images can't be milked for simple meanings: they just have a hard, irreducible presence that transcends the film's narrative or its metaphoric drift. They have the same stark autonomy as the film's desert setting; more than that, they have the elusive ring of absolute necessity.

This is the eighth feature by the French director, but it is her first to be released in Britain since her 1988 debut *Chocolat*, a relatively straight vignette about growing up in colonial Africa. Since then, Denis's work has been increasingly terse and telegraphic, and *Beau Travail* takes her penchant for ellipsis to a dazzling new level. She's the kind of director you can imagine reshaping a film entirely at the editing stage, refitting its narrative into a free-form mosaic. Not that *Beau Travail* is designed to perplex, but its sinuous discontinuity engages the viewer's imagination to the maximum; it feels like a particularly austere dream that you can't shake off.

Denis's anecdote of jealousy and vengeance in the French Foreign Legion is inspired by Herman Melville's story *Billy Budd*, about an innocent sailor martyred for the jealousy he inspires in his superior officer, the malevolent Claggart. Denis's story belongs to Claggart, here renamed Galoup; it begins with him exiled in Marseille, recounting the events that led to his being drummed out of the legion. His tragedy really is a fall from Eden; bleak as the Djibouti camp is, it's where he belongs. Acting as a fondly fierce watchdog to his men, he serves a distant, fatigued commander, Forestier (played by Michel Subor), who was a character of the same name—conceivably a younger version of the same character—in Jean-Luc Godard's 1960 film *Le Petit Soldat*.

On one level, Galoup's lost idyll is straightfowardly homoerotic—a Spartan utopia in which muscular, shaven-headed young men leap walls, walk wires and execute elegantly brutal manoeuvres like animated statues under the sun. In these sequences, the narrative fractures into abstract dance; Denis worked closely with a choreographer, Bernardo Montet. Regarded by the locals with wry amusement, the soldiers seem to have no real function in Djibouti, other than to practise their bizarrely arduous form of performance art.

On another level, the legionnaires' world is aggressively heterosexual; in a nightclub, they engage in wary flirtation with African women dancing to Islamic-themed disco. But they are as much separated from the women by their maleness as they are from Africa by their colonial authority. Arguably, the film's predominant theme is military authority and the mixture of solitude, disempowerment and even servitude that it entails. Galoup's post estranges him from his men, and he's often seen in a servant's role, rather than a commander's, washing up or laying out the places for the troops at table.

But it seems almost reductive to discuss *Beau Travail*'s meaning, rather than the way it works. Denis was inspired by Melville's poems as well as his story, and *Beau Travail* is poetic in the sense that its discrete, highly plastic images—a salt-bleached ram's skull, a burst of blood in green water—form something like a succession of lines for the viewer to connect into an overall pattern. The photographer Agnès Godard has a flawless eye for the placement of bodies in the desert landscape, and Denis matches her images with an always unexpected use of music—choruses from Benjamin Britten's opera *Billy Budd* for the dance-like rituals; a hypnotic Neil Young song for a desert march.

The actors, too, are used for their sculptural physical being: Grégoire Colin's recruit isolated against a blue sky; Subor's languid basilisk features seemingly calcified by legion life. Galoup is played by Denis Lavant, the commandingly weather-beaten lead of Leos Carax's first three films; here older and craggier, with the tortured troglodyte physique of an Egon Schiele portrait, Lavant has a galvanising energy. He stores up his tensions as if in an emotional battery, then releases them in the final scene, dancing a convulsive solo as if shaking the demons out of his body; set to a rivetingly brainless piece of Euro-disco, this is a marvel of recent cinema.

Beau Travail feels endlessly watchable—I've seen it three times and I know I'll see it again. You can tell it was a tough film to make, and not just by the way the actors are sweating. Cast and film-makers alike seem physically and imaginatively pushed to the limit, and the result is a sense of place and action that is so specific to it that *Beau Travail* resembles no other film I know. It's mesmerising, like a season in hell.

NEW YORK POST, 3/31/00 p. 54, Jonathan Foreman

"Beau Travail" is another visually gorgeous film by French director Claire Denis ("Chocolat").

It brims with beautiful images of desolate African landscapes, the sun glimmering on the Red Sea, and half-naked young men exercising silently in the heat.

But this contemporary adaptation of Melville's "Billy Budd" (transposed to a French Foreign Legion outpost in Djibouti) is so minimalist in characterization and dialogue that the plot all but evaporates—and so does any dramatic power.

The story is narrated—if you can call his sparse, brief ruminations a narration—by Sgt. Galoup (Denis Lavant).

Now living in Marseille, he used to run a small training detail for the Legion. His troops included men from all over the world, but the arrival at the outpost of Sentain (Gregoire Colin), a young fellow who turns out to be the perfect recruit, angers Galoup and causes him to destroy the young man and his own career.

Director Denis, who co-wrote the screenplay with Jean-Pol Fargeau, seems to be above the task of mere storytelling.

You are told that Galoup hates Sentain—and that the other soldiers, including the commanding officer, Forestier (Michel Subor), like him—but you don't get to see much evidence of these feelings.

The result is that, despite the presence of strong actors like Lavant and Subor, the whole tale ends up no more emotionally involving than the superior travelogue it resembles.

SIGHT AND SOUND, 8/00, p. 38, Charlotte O'Sullivan

An ex-soldier, Galoup, looks back on his days in the Foreign Legion. Stationed in Africa, he enjoys a relationship with a local prostitute and relishes his role as second-in-command to handsome commandant Bruno Forestier. A young soldier, Gilles Sentain, arrives. Fearing his captain will be tempted by this beautiful boy, Galoup tries to tarnish Sentain's reputation. But when the youth rescues a drowning man, his popularity increases.

Galoup decides to take a group of the men, including Sentain, on a series of exercises away from the commandant. After a few days, he provokes Sentain by picking on one of the men. Sentain slaps him. Galoup now has grounds to dismiss him; Sentain goes off into the desert. On return to camp, Galoup faces a court martial and is expelled from the army. Sentain is later found by nomads. Galoup makes peace with himself.

Claire Denis is good with bodies and in this most spectacularly somnambulant of narratives they do a lot of work. As soon as we see the soldiers Sentain and Galoup, we know they are two forces which can only cancel each other out. Where Denis Lavant's Galoup has a face as rough as a lion's, Grégoire Colin's Sentain's is as smooth as a stone. Sentain's body tells us nothing about what he's thinking, while Galoup's blares out his sexual secrets. As a result, while we can empathise with Sentain, we never identify with him.

We first see Galoup's beloved captain Forestier in a black-and-white photograph. When this is replaced by the 'real' image of him smoking it's difficult to tell the difference—he still looks as mysterious as any *noir* hero. The same is true, too, of the men in the army and the prostitutes who service them: they're all gorgeous, iconic and remote.

What you realise, slowly, is that this is because they're all creatures of Galoup's memory. When, as a bitter civilian, Galoup presses an iron into his clothes, he looks stiff and ludicrous—a man doing a woman's job. But when the soldiers iron their clothes, they look fluid and complete. As they do their exercises, the camera crawls up their arms and thighs, asking us to breathe in their perfection. Like Galoup, we can't escape these visions of loveliness and begin to feel almost as oppressed by them. Are we and Galoup the aberrations, or are they? As the glowing landscape—yellow sand, green water, white rocks—pulsates behind the men's bodies, we enter into Galoup's masochistic, waking dream in which the answer, over again, seems to be that it's only the beautiful who belong.

Framing her essay on sexual identity like a thriller—"one stays and two are expelled," says Galoup of the trio he forms with Sentain and Forestier, prompting the question, which two?—Denis hooks our attention. Having allowed us to meet Forestier, she then has the screen fade to black, creating a sense of narrative expectation. The commandant's behaviour reveals flickers of nerves (unlike Sentain, he's self-conscious, given to gazing at himself in the mirror) which makes us wary of how he might treat the possessive Galoup. It's important that we don't sympathise with Galoup (or Sentain) too soon; looking for weak spots or the seeds of triumph in all three men, we see both, everywhere. Unable to judge these characters, we just have to stay with them.

The obvious dramatic models for *Beau Travail*'s jealousy-fuelled narrative are *Othello*, Herman Melville's *Billy Budd* (Benjamin Britten's music for the opera based on Melville's novella dashes gloomy panic into our ears) and Greek tragedy. Denis clearly enjoys paying homage to other texts: Michel Subor's commandant is called Forestier, the name of the character the actor played in Jean-Luc Godard's *Le Petit Soldat* (1960). Like the soldiers who never engage in 'real' fighting, but merely prepare themselves, endlessly, the film feels like a dress rehearsal, full of props over-eager to simulate life.

The language in the film is excessively formal. Galoup's diary entries are entirely elegant (unlike the man). And it's as if he's supplying the words for everyone else, too. Thus a languid Forestier tells his men, "If it weren't for fornication and blood we wouldn't be here [in Africa]", while they themselves make clunky reference to the fact that Forestier is the "father" of their family unit. The language here is unnatural, stylised, but that's why it works. Galoup's jealousies are all about the body, but like a puppet master—or even a precious screenwriter—he seeks to control any jerky, commonplace impulses. The dialogue continually alerts us to this controlling desire, and its limitations.

What makes *Beau Travail* so special—and confounding—is that after all these clotted, self-defeating demonstrations of control, Galoup does find release. Early on, he tells himself that there's "freedom in remorse". It seems like just another sonorous try-out for genuine feeling, but towards the end we suddenly discover a new side to Galoup. He's in a disco, the anthemic club track "The Rhythm of the Night" is playing and suddenly all the elements we've seen up to now—caged beast, clockwork toy, villain—blaze manically into life. With movements that are almost spasms, Lavant turns Galoup's body into something that takes up space rather than watches others encroach.

It's quite right that Sentain, Forestier and the prostitute should remain loose ends, untouched by reality. Perfect, saintly young boys may not really exist; prostitutes may not lead sleepy, ecstatic lives; captains may not stretch and tease in *noir* bubbles; but everyone except Galoup already knew that. It's also right that his sexuality should remain an unknown quantity—repression can't be undone in a day. What's important is that, while he may still be invisible to others (the disco is empty), Galoup can at last see himself and like what he sees—a glorious moment for him and for us.

VILLAGE VOICE, 4/3/00, p. 121, J. Hoberman

Claire Denis is a sensational filmmaker—with all that implies. Her *Beau Travail*, opening after its well-received local premiere at the New York Film Festival, is a movie so tactile in its cinematography, inventive in its camera placement, and sensuous in its editing that the purposefully oblique and languid narrative is all but eclipsed.

"I've found an idea for a novel," a Godard character once announced. "Not to write the life of a man, but only life, life itself. What there is between people, space ... sound and colors." His words might serve as Denis's manifesto. Her transposition of Herman Melville's novella *Billy Budd* to a French Foreign Legion post on the Horn of Africa is a mosaic of pulverized shards. Every cut in *Beau Travail* is a small, gorgeously explosive shock.

Denis's main principle is kinesthetic immersion. A former French colonial who spent part of her childhood in Djibouti, she introduces her material with a pan along a crumbling wall mural, accompanied by the legionnaire anthem; this is followed by close-ups of the soldiers dancing with their sultry African dream girls—a vision of sexual glory accentuated by the flashing Christmas lights that constitute the minimalist disco decor—and then by images of the shirtless recruits exercising in the heat of the day to excerpts from Benjamin Britten's *Billy Budd* oratorio.

The filmmakers style is naturally hieroglyphic. There is little dialogue, and although *Beau Travail* feels present-tense, it is actually an extended first-person flashback. Denis puts her version of the Melville tale of the "handsome sailor" martyred by an evil superior in the villain's mouth.

The movie is narrated by the ex-sergeant Galoup (Denis Lavant), after he has been expelled from the Legion for his mistreatment of the popular and gung-ho recruit Sentain (Grégorie Colin).

Short and bandy-legged, with odd aquatic features and a face like a Tom Waits song, Lavant's Galoup is a figure of pathos. The Legion, if not the legionnaire, he loved is lost to him.

Time drifts, memories flicker. *Beau Travail* is the recollection of elemental pleasure. The recruits drill under the sun or scramble around the empty fort, when they are not skin diving or performing tai chi. The heat, the disco, the golden beaches, and the turquoise sea suggest a weird sort of Club Med. Apparently crucial to their basic training is the ability to iron a perfect uniform crease. Forestier (Michel Subor), the commanding officer, is fond of chewing the local narcotic, qat. "if it wasn't for fornication and blood we wouldn't be here," he tells someone.

Sentain rescues a downed helicopter pilot and Forestier takes a liking to him, further feeding Galoup's jealousy. The sergeant orchestrates a situation to destroy Sentain, bringing the recruits to a barren strip of the coast for some character-building convict work, digging a purposeless road or doing their exercises at high noon. (The locals impassively watch these peculiar antics, modernistic hug-fests that might have been choreographed by Martha Graham.) The movie turns wildly homoerotic. Egged on by Galoup, and Britten's incantatory music, these legionnaires are exalted in their minds. Finally, but without overt cause, Galoup and Sentain stage a one-on-one bare-chested face-off, circling each other on a rocky coast with Britten's oratorio soaring.

In its hypnotic ritual, *Beau Travail* suggests a John Ford cavalry western interpreted by Marguerite Duras—Galoup always has time to scribble his obsessions in a diary. As in *Billy Budd,* the sergeant suckers the enlisted man into the fatal mistake of slugging him. (Typically, the filmmaker handles this crucial incident in four quick shots.) But, unlike Melville, Denis has no particular interest in Christian allegory. She distills Melville's story to its existential essence. A final visit to the disco finds Galoup flailing out against the prison of self, dancing alone to the Europop rhythm of the night.

Like Denis's previous films, *I Can't Sleep* and *Nénette and Boni*, her latest is a mysterious mix of artful deliberation and documentary spontaneity. To watch it is to wonder about the process. Are her often elaborate shots generated by the scenes she's set up? Does she find her structure in the editing room? One thing's for sure, along with her regular cinematographer, Agnes Godard, Denis always opts for beauty. *Beau Travail* indeed.

Also reviewed in:
CHICAGO TRIBUNE, 5/26/00, Friday/p. C, Michael Wilmington
NATION, 4/17/00, p. 34, Stuart Klawans
NEW YORK TIMES, 3/31/00, p. E27, Stephen Holden
VARIETY, 10/4-10/99, p. 89, Deborah Young

BEAUTIFUL

A Destination Films release in association with Flashpoint Limited and Prosperity Pictures of a 2 Drivers/Fogwood Films Ltd. production. *Executive Producer:* Richard Vane, Kate Driver, Wendy Japhet, Barry London, Brent Baum, Steve Stabler, Marty Fink, David Forrest, and Beau Rogers. *Producer:* John Bertolli and B.J. Rack. *Director:* Sally Field. *Screenplay:* Jon Bernstein. *Director of Photography:* Robert Yeoman. *Editor:* Debra Neil-Fischer. *Music:* John Frizzell. *Music Editor:* Bruno Coon. *Sound:* Pawel Wdowczak. *Sound Editor:* Gregory M. Gerlich. *Casting:* Amanda Mackey Johnson and Cathy Sandrich. *Production Designer:* Charles Breen. *Art Director:* Leslie Thomas. *Set Decorator:* Jeffrey Kushon. *Special Effects:* Matt Falletta. *Costumes:* Chrisi Karvonides-Dushenko. *Make-up:* Anthony C. Ferrante. *Running time:* 112 minutes. *MPAA Rating:* PG-13.

CAST: Minnie Driver (Mona Hubbard); Joey Lauren Adams (Ruby); Hallie Kate Eisenberg (Vanessa); Kathleen Turner (Verna Chickle); Leslie Stefanson (Joyce Parkins); Bridgette Wilson (Lorna, Miss Texas); Kathleen Robertson (Wanda Love, Miss Tennessee); Antonia Katsopolis (Hayden); Michael McKean (Lance De Salvo); Gary Collins (Miss American Miss

Host);   Linda Hart (Nedra);   Brent Briscoe (Lurdy);   Colleen Rennison (Mona at 12);
Jacqueline Steiger (Ruby at 12);   Sylvia Short (Alberta); Herta Ware (Clara);   Ali Landry
(Belindy Lindbrook);   Robin Renee (Miss Alabama);   Chuti Tiu (Miss Hawaii);   Samantha
Harris (Miss Minnesota);   Dawn Heusser (Miss West Virginia);   Julie Condra (Miss Iowa);
Jessica Collins (Miss Lawrenceville);   Deborah Kellner (Reigning Miss Illinois);   Brent Huff
(Miss Illinois Local Pageant Host);   Charles Dougherty (Director);   Shawn Christian (Wink
Hendricks);   Margaret Emery (Pageant P.A.);   Irene Roseen (Woman Official);   Mark
Christensen (Production Assistant); William Forward (Orthodontist); Elizabeth Lang (Dental
Nurse);   Alexander Folk (Tom the Grocer);   Lu Elrod (Neighbor Woman);   Adilah Barnes
(Home Economics Teacher);   Cindy Montoya-Picker (Dance Teacher);   Landry Allbright
(Summer);   Lorna Scott (Mother in Diner); Earl Schuman (Elderly Man in Restaurant);   Mary
E. Thompson (Elderly Woman in Restaurant); Rosine 'Ace' Hatem (Theresa);   Claire Benedek
and Dale Raoul (Shoppers);   Robert Phelps (Mr. Willoughby);   Jordan Lund (Detective);
Warren Munson (Judge);   Keli Daniels and Susan Segal (Fitness Club Ladies);   Annabella Price
(Mother at Slumber Party);   Sydney Berry (Little Girl at Slumber Party); Ken Baldwin (E.I.
Crew Member);   Spice Williams (Female Prisoner);   Timothy Anderson and Zachary Woodlee
(Dancers);   Brittany Crutchfield (Autumn Meadowbrook);   Daniel Dehring (Joey);   Phil Hawn
(Man with Newspaper);   Kimberly Lyon (Miss New York).

LOS ANGELES TIMES, 9/29/00, Calendar/p. 2, Kevin Thomas

Minnie Driver easily lives up to the title of the film "Beautiful," in which she stars so
impressively under Sally Field's aptly nuanced direction. Yet Driver's angular features are just
distinctive enough to make it credible that her small-town Illinois beauty contestant might find it
a struggle to come out a winner.

Written perceptively by Jon Bernstein, "Beautiful" is not yet another easy satire on a target that
is by now overly familiar. Field and Bernstein understand that beauty contests can be so
inherently silly and demeaning that they satirize themselves without undue extra nudging. This
film's wise and compassionate view is that, for many young women of limited opportunities,
winning a beauty contest represents their best hope, realistic or not, for a better life. This is
certainly the case for Mona, who starts dreaming of beauty contest stardom in childhood—and
with good reason.

Played by Colleen Rennison, in a great matchup with Driver, the 12-year-old Mona has a
flashy, unimaginative and indifferent mother (Linda Hart) and a slob of a stepfather (Brent
Briscoe). They are a booze-cigarettes-and-TV couple who see no point in trying to make
something of one's life.

Beauty contests mesmerize Mona, and she starts seeing them as a way of escape. She swiftly
realizes that she'll get no help or support in achieving her goal from her mother. Determination
spurs enterprise, and soon Mona is taking on enough after-school jobs to get herself—all on the
installment plan—braces, entry fees for contests like the Pretty Little Princess Pageant, and
singing, dancing and modeling lessons from the formidable, husky-voiced Verna Chickle (an
amusing Kathleen Turner), who seems to see herself as a Lauren Bacall stranded in the heartland.

Mona has become a breathtakingly self-sufficient outsider totally focused on a goal regarded as
misguided by everyone who knows about it. It is entirely possible, even likely, that Mona would
eventually refocus her energies had she not come across a pair of world-class enablers. Little
Ruby (Jacqueline Steiger) is a fellow social outcast, apparently because she wears glasses and is
of modest background. Ruby is a quiet, selfless type who not only buys into Mona's dream, but
also takes her home to meet her loving grandmother Alberta (Sylvia Short), a nurse who is also
a fabulous seamstress only too glad to whip up Mona's contest costumes. The loving support she
receives from Ruby and Alberta allows Mona to become all the more self-absorbed and not just
a little ruthless.

The pattern of Mona's life is now firmly established. We flash forward to the adult Ruby (Joey
Lauren Adams) and Mona (Driver) not only sharing an apartment, but Ruby also pretending to
be the mother of 8-year-old Vanessa (Hallie Kate Eisenberg, another great match-up with Driver),
whom Mona bore out of wedlock.

All of this is essentially an absorbing and expertly told prologue to the main event, which occurs
when, against all odds, Mona beats out all those conventionally pretty, perky blonds to become

Miss Illinois, which places her in the hallowed Miss American Miss competition. A somewhat contrived, but forgivably so, incident places Ruby out of action, leaving Mona to head off to Long Beach for the finals without her.

In her loneliness she urges the feisty Vanessa, a veritable carbon copy of herself in temperament as well as looks, to come along with her. Mona inadvertently has brought about a confrontation with herself even more important than whether or not she becomes Miss American Miss.

Driver has that invaluable gift of taking us into the imagination of the young women she plays so compellingly—this ability is in full force here as it was, for example in "The Governess." We understand and empathize with Mona and her ardent dreams so well that we never lose sympathy for her no matter how selfish and calculating she becomes.

In a film of strong performances—Leslie Stefanson's vengeful Joyce and Herta Ware's blissfully suicidal Clara among them—Adams deserves special credit in making Ruby seem selfless without becoming a wimp. (Still, you would like to know whether or not she ever makes time for boyfriends or, indeed, whether she has a job that allows her to support Mona so that she can be a full-time beauty contestant.)

In a feature directorial debut that never feels like one, Field is as effortless behind a camera as she is in front of one. Bernstein, a gifted writer of women's roles, even allows Kathleen Robertson and Bridgette L. Wilson dimension as two of Mona's top competitors. It is Robertson's Miss Tennessee who has the film's key line: "We're just white trash girls trying to break the code."

NEW YORK POST, 9/29/00, p. 54, Lou Lumenick

Sally Field's directing debut is the kind of movie that connoisseurs of bad cinema will really, really like. Rarely does a movie go so thoroughly wrong in so many ways.

It's the sort of comedy about female empowerment and inner beauty that presents most of its women as shallow, manipulative imbeciles.

The usually charming Minnie Driver is miscast—and thoroughly grating—as Mona, a vain, self-centered young Illinois woman who has devoted her entire life since the age of 8 to entering beauty contests.

This is understandable, Jon Bernstein's utterly illogical screenplay argues in an interminable prologue set in 1986, because her white-trash parents ignored her, or worse.

So driven is Mona in pursuit of a crown that she's passed off her roommate Ruby (Joey Lauren Adams) as the mother of Mona's young, illegitimate daughter, Vanessa (Hallie Kate Eisenberg, the little girl in all those Pepsi TV spots).

We're still trying get a handle on the exact nature of the relationship between Mona and Ruby—neither of whom seem to have any men in their lives—when Ruby gets thrown into jail in the most contrived plot twist I've seen in years.

Mona is thus forced to act as surrogate mother to Vanessa—who doesn't realize that Mona is her real mother. Actually, they act as if they've barely been introduced, though they've apparently been living together for years. But they dislike each other intensely.

And, oh, did I mention Mona is finally a finalist in the National Miss Junior Miss Championship—and will be disqualified if her secret is exposed by a TV reporter (Leslie Stefanson) whose own beauty-contest ambitions Mona painfully sabotaged years earlier by putting industrial-strength adhesive on her rival's flaming baton?

"Beautiful" has its comic moments—Mona's increasingly desperate attempts to explain her strong resemblance to Vanessa are good for a few chuckles, as is a memorable Gilbert and Sullivan rendition by Miss Texas (Bridgette Wilson), via her ventriloquist's dummy.

But just when the movie threatens to rise to the level of a second-rate rehash of the classic beauty-contest satire, "Smile" (complete with Gary Collins sending himself up as the host), it nose dives into a two-handkerchief, everyone-is-beautiful climax.

Besides being a disjointed mess, "Beautiful" is a rare exception to the rule that movies directed by actors are at the very least well-acted.

Probably the worst offender here is Kathleen Turner, frighteningly over the top—even by her extravagant, standards—as Mona's beauty pageant mentor.

NEWSDAY, 9/29/00, Part II/p. B3, John Anderson

The best thing that can be said about Sally Field's "Beautiful" is that it isn't "Drop Dead Gorgeous." Which, of course, isn't saying much.

In that earlier travesty, the beauty pageant and its ilk were sent up as the maladjusted spawn of a culture in which people will do virtually anything to win virtually nothing. "Beautiful" doesn't give the hard rap to the pageant phenomenon per se. It saves the big hammer for the participants, particularly the thoroughly unsympathetic Mona Hibbard (Minnie Driver), a love-starved child who grows up to be a pageant-obsessed and, more important, unlovable megalomaniac.

Sound appetizing? A story in which the chief protagonist is so distinctly unsympathetic more or less demands a compensatory level of humor. But Jon Bernstein's screenplay for "Beautiful" comes up decidedly short—unless the offhand emotional abuse of a child by cartoonishly insensitive parents is someone's idea of fun. The main idea of the story is plain enough: Mona, from the time she's a little girl, is obsessed with becoming the nation's reigning beauty queen (Miss America, obviously, although the filmmakers couldn't use the name), to compensate for a childhood devoid of affection. How she gets there—by exploiting her best friend, Ruby (Joey Lauren Adams), by pretending her own daughter, Vanessa (Hallie Kate Eisenberg), is Ruby's and by generally making everything and everyone subordinate to her pathetic dream—is not so pretty.

Exacerbating the problem, although it's clearly a question of personal taste, is Minnie Driver. Under the best conditions, my Driver threshhold is about three minutes—so "Beautiful" has the needles in the red from Act 1, Scene 2. Field, making her feature directorial debut after a couple of TV projects, conceivably wanted an actress guaranteed to irritate the life out of her audience or the audience out of the theater. But it was actually Driver and her sister Kate who brought the project to Field, apparently on the presumption that the part was perfect for Driver. They may have been right and, considering the real politik of star power in Hollywood, are also at fault.

Field actually stages a convincing pageant of her own during the culminating moments of "Beautiful," wherein Mona and Vanessa have their reconciliation and Mona realizes the error of her ways—the error of her life, more to the point. Kathleen Robertson and Bridgette Wilson, playing Miss Tennessee and Texas, respectively, actually perform during the talent portion of the program—Robertson with a fiddle and Wilson with a ventriloquist's dummy. At this point, "Beautiful" wanders into the cross-fertilized realm of the bizarre and the emotionally calculated, and the boundaries between real pageant and fictional pageant meld into a sticky goo.

VILLAGE VOICE, 10/10/00, p. 134, Jessica Winter

Surpassing Dan Aykroyd's *Nothing but Trouble* as the most astoundingly atrocious walrus-flop of a directorial debut by a languishing actor ever contrived, Sally Field's *Beautiful* attempts to satirize beauty pageants through grotesque white-trash stereotypes, sickening incest allusions (did you know that young girls, if they're as savvy as our heroine, can choose whether or not their stepdads molest them?), and a bizarre moral scale by which sociopathy is arbitrarily rewarded and punished. Minnie Driver, most likely cast as the lead toothy shrew due to her shivery resemblance to the satanic Pepsi girl who plays her daughter, stomps through the film in ill-fitting Wonder Woman gear; her eye-gouging performance improves if you imagine her as the star of *The Sally Field Story.*

Also reviewed in:
CHICAGO TRIBUNE, 9/29/00, Friday/p. A, Mark Caro
NEW YORK TIMES, 9/29/00, p. E23, Stephen Holden
VARIETY, 9/18-24/00, p. 33, Emanuel Levy
WASHINGTON POST, 9/29/00, p. C12, Stephen Hunter
WASHINGTON POST, 9/29/00, Weekend/p. 45, Desson Howe

BEAUTIFUL PEOPLE

A Trimark Pictures/British Film Institute/Channel Four release of a Tall Stories production in association with The Arts Council of England and the Merseyside Film Production Fund with the participation of BSKYB and British Screen. *Executive Producer:* Roger Shannon. *Producer:* Ben Woolford. *Director:* Jasmin Dizdar. *Screenplay:* Jasmin Dizdar. *Director of Photography:* Barry Ackroyd. *Editor:* Justin Krish. *Music:* Garry Bell. *Sound:* Simmy Claire. *Sound Editor:* Stephen Griffiths, Phil Barnes, Kallis Shamaris and Kevin Brazier. *Casting:* Suzanne Crowley and Gilly Poole. *Production Designer:* Jon Henson. *Art Director:* Cristina Casali. *Costumes:* Louise Page. *Make-up:* Penny Smith. *Stunt Coordinator:* Roderick P. Woodruff. *Running time:* 107 minutes. *MPAA Rating:* R.

CAST: Charlotte Coleman (Portia Thornton);   Charles Kay (George Thornton);   Rosalind Ayres (Nora Thornton);   Roger Sloman (Roger Midge);   Heather Tobias (Felicity Midge); Danny Nussbaum (Griffin Midge);   Siobhan Redmond (Kate Higgins);   Gilbert Martin (Jerry Higgins);   Steve Sweeney (Jim);   Linda Bassett (Sister);   Nicholas Farrell (Dr. Mouldy);   Edin Dzandzanovic (Pero Guzina);   Julian Firth (Edward Thornton);   Walentine Giorgiewa (Dzemila Hadzibegovic);   Dado Jehan (Serb);   Faruk Pruti (Croat);   Edward Jewesbury (Joseph Thornton);   Nicholas McGaughey (Welshman);   Jay Simpson (Bigsy);   Radoslav Youroukov (Ismet Hadzibegovic);   Thomas Goodridge (Youth with Mobile Phone);   Tony Peters (Bus Driver);   Bobby Williams (Tim Mouldy);   Joseph Williams (Tom Mouldy);   Elizabeth Isiorho (African Woman);   Dev Sagoo (DSS Clerk);   Vera Jakob (Waitress);   Melee Hutton (Mrs. Mouldy);   Louise Breckon-Richards (Policewoman);   Sharon D. Clarke (Nurse Tina);   Jessica Brandon (Chloe Higgins);   Martin Alderdice (BBC Camera Man);   Niall Ivers   (Hashim); Raules Davies (UN Soldier);   Alan Cowan (Immigration Official);   Jonny Phillips (Brian North); Craig Stokes (Hospital Security Guard);   Kenan Hudaverdi (Railway Worker);   Annette Badland (Psychologist);   Peter Harding (Detective);   Andrew Logan (Hypnotherapist);   Anthony Carrick (Retired Tory MP).

CINEASTE, Vol. XXV, No. 3, 2000, p. 45, Andrew Horton

A British doctor who has just delivered a baby to a refugee Bosnian Muslim couple in a London hospital in 1993 asks what they will name the child. "Chaos," they say almost joyfully. This is just one moment among many in a carnival of seven intertwined stories that unfold in first-time director/writer Jasmin Dizdar's London-based film, *Beautiful People,* which won the 1999 Cannes Prix Un Certain Regard. But "chaos" embraces much of the spirit of the whole work. Indeed, this British-financed film rides a surprisingly successful line between Bosnian chaos and British order, resulting in waves of laughter and some tears as well. Having left Bosnia before the war that destroyed so much of his native country, Dizdar became a naturalized British citizen in 1993, while war was still raging in the Balkans. In *Beautiful People,* he wryly captures a feisty tapestry of many 'fish out of water' tales which weave in and out of contemporary London, with one key scene set in the midst of the Bosnian war.

"Chaos" is an appropriate name for the new child, neither Bosnian nor British, born as the result of a Serbian gang rape during the war in Bosnia. The mother, Dzemila (Walentine Giorgiewa), pleads unsuccessfully for an abortion, yet once the child is born, she becomes a happy parent with her accepting husband (Radoslav Youroukov). The doctor (Nicholas Farrell), whose own marriage has collapsed, finds inspiration in their joy as he invites this fragile new family to live in his own home. By film's end, he is dancing with them, reexperiencing pleasures that he has obviously long forgotten.

Dizdar has made it clear in interviews that *Beautiful People* is not a polemical war story such as, for instance, Goran Paskaljevic's darkly etched comedy-drama *Cabaret Balkan* (1999) or Emir Kusturica's *Underground* (1997). "Physical war is boringly simple," says the thirty-eight-year-old writer/director. "Urban London family drama is far more interesting to me." Dizdar graduated from the famed FAMU film school in Prague that was also the formative training ground for many of the former Yugoslav directors including Emir Kusturica, Goran Paskaljevic, Srdjan

Karanovic, and Rajko Grlic, to name but a few. What Dizdar appears to have taken to heart—even in such a comment about "physical war" and "family drama"—is the gift for finely tuned social comedy that Prague has produced, known as the 'Czech touch,' and seen in the works of Milos Forman, Jiri Menzel, and others. Dizdar has, in fact, penned a study of the Czech touch in *Milos Forman: King of Satire*, and much of *Beautiful People* explores the same human absurdity and humor-through-pain we have seen recently in Czech films such as *Kolya* (1997).

Yet this is not to say Dizdar's film is derivative. It is not. Rather, the film unfolds as a roller coaster of personal relationships that do suggest the world of 'London' as a gumbo of nationalities, refugees and 'natives' who can also feel like aliens in their own land. The film is framed by two comically ragtag middle-aged Bosnians, one Croatian (Faruk Pruti) and the other Serb (Dado Jehan), who had lived in a village next to each other before the war. Now they have carried the war to London, as they chase each other through the streets in the shadow of a Winston Churchill statue and Big Ben, pounding each other so badly that they wind up in a hospital room shared with a Welsh terrorist.

More than half the characters, however, are British. Thus we track, in true British fashion, both the 'Upstairs' and 'Downstairs' divisions of social class that British comedy has always played with so well. There is even a sparkling performance by Charlotte Coleman who appeared in *Four Weddings and a Funeral*. Coleman, here the daughter of a stuffy upper-class Parliamentarian, is in love with a handsome Bosnian basketball star, Pero (Edin Dzandzanovic), whose skimpy English leads him proudly to proclaim, "Thank you for your hostility!" (in place of "hospitality"), when he dines for the first time with Coleman's disapproving, stuck-up aristocratic parents and boring brother.

On the 'Downstairs' end of the social spectrum, Dizdar follows a drug addicted, skinhead soccer fan, Griffin (Danny Nussbaum), whose middle-class parents have not a clue as to the world he inhabits with his pub-and-soccer-loving mates. In the most surrealistic sequence of the film, Griffin, in a drug haze, is accidentally dropped into Bosnia by a NATO-UN food plane. Yes! We track Griffin failing asleep at the Amsterdam airport on his way back to London, choosing a pile of UN food packages as accidental bedding. Once a fork lift loads the goods, we are treated to a montage, both hilarious and dismal, of the plane reaching Bosnia and dropping our hapless young Brit into the middle of the Balkan war. That Dizdar works such an unlikely strand to the point that it actually pays off as something that *could* happen, is a measure of his comic talent, arising delightfully from such surprising incongruities. This extended Bosnian scene helps anchor the rest of the film in a sense of the 'other' world, as we follow the stories unfolding in London with their unusual but engaging mix of strong emotion and humor.

There is even a Scottish television journalist (Gilbert Martin), also involved in a troubled marriage, who succumbs to "Bosnia Syndrome." What's that? Late in the film, as the journalist begs to have his leg amputated just like the poor Bosnian he observed in a UN field hospital, a nurse explains that with Bosnia Syndrome, "You become obsessed with doing good. You identify with the victims. You become the victim and the victim becomes you."

Put another way, Dizdar has managed to pull off what award-winning Belgrade director Srdjan Karanovic has explained all good films share: a sense of cinema as "documentary fairytale." That is, each of the seven tales is anchored in a 'documentary' reality we can recognize as true to life. There are failed marriages, new romances, friendships fractured by ethnic conflict, misunderstandings and simple pleasures that make up 'real life' as we know it. Yet Dizdar infuses a sense of surprise and wonder in the midst of all this so that every one of the seven tales has a 'happy ending' that we take more as the stuff of fairy tales. It is a tribute to Dizdar's talent that we willingly participate in these tales, realizing how unlikely such festive, embracing endings are in most lives. The closing credit sequence returns us to Bosnia in the form of a home video. We watch the mother of the baby Chaos—dancing in her wedding dress on a Bosnian slope—before the chaos of war was let loose. The dramatic gap between this image of a happy bride 'over there' and the same woman in London, as mother of a child of war, is gripping. Yet Dizdar does not let that gap turn to despair or easy cynicism. Rather the chaos and chance of each relationship explored suggest the birth of new, potentially positive possibilities.

On one hand, *Beautiful People* joins the shelf of post-*Short Cuts* and *Pulp Fiction* films that mix violence and humor in intertwined narratives, that include recent additions such as *Run Lola Run* and *Magnolia*. But more specifically, we can almost begin to trace a subgenre of Balkan refugee films that have emerged as Yugoslavia collapsed and ethnic tensions have turned to murder throughout the region. In all cases, these films—which include *Broken English* (1996, Gregor Nicholas, New Zealand), about Croatians in New Zealand, and Goran Paskaljevic's *Someone Else's America* (1996) about Serbs and Hispanics in Brooklyn—speak both about the 'old' country, but more importantly, about paths of renewal and change within other cultures. I am careful not to use the word 'assimilation,' for we never feel that any of Dizdar's Bosnians become 'British' in the British sense. Yet we end the film feeling that Britain itself has changed as it embraces—willingly or not—those who have taken up residence within her land. Take the fate of the two ragtag Bosnians pounding each other in the opening frames. By film's end, they have won over the portly nurse in the hospital as they all join in a festive game of cards, along with the wounded Welsh terrorist sharing their room. The carnival of good cheer suddenly dissolves all concerns for nationalities, either British or foreign.

Another important film in this emerging subgenre that Dizdar almost certainly references yet has definitely transcended, is Milcho Manchevski's Oscar nominated *Before the Rain* (1994). Set in his native former Yugoslav republic of Macedonia and in London just after the Bosnian war, Manchevski's film traces three interconnected stories in a jumbled time sequence. Dizdar has managed to deliver what Manchevski attempted but did not succeed in capturing within his London sequence: a multilayered foreground/background sense of confusion between British culture and an ongoing Balkan conflict. Dizdar clearly has learned the lesson of not trying to capture the Balkan war per se in London; instead, he traces the effects of Bosnians trying to settle into their new homeland, while old memories continue to haunt them.

Finally, Dizdar has gathered a splendid cast of actors to populate this Brueghelesque canvas and has directed them with verve and an eye for telling detail. One will not easily forget, for instance, the spunky nurse (Sharon Clark) who manages with high spirits to squash the anger of the Serb and Croat in the hospital as she holds up their shoes, noting that their feet are the same size, no matter their differences in politics and beliefs. And whenever Dizdar's camera travels through the streets of London, faces of all nationalities appear, each suggesting multiple stories that could be told, lives that could be followed with similar results.

Like early Milos Forman and others of the Czech school, Dizdar enlightens without preaching, while making us laugh at the human condition. In a season of lame social comedies within our own culture, ranging from *Drowning Mona* and *The Next Best Thing* to *Hanging Up*, we definitely can salute a comedy suggesting that our humanity itself has much to do with what makes us all beautiful—much like the delayed appearance of the word "Beautiful" after the letters forming "People" have already landed on screen in the title sequence. If we are able to step back from the struggles surrounding us, Dizdar suggests, there is beauty to be found.

LOS ANGELES TIMES, 3/3/00, Calendar/p. 16, Kevin Thomas

Bosnian-born filmmaker Jasmin Dizdar sets the tone for his bravura allegory "Beautiful People" right at the start, as two men, one a shaggy Croat (Faruk Pruti), the other a swarthy Serb (Dado Jehan), recognize each other on a crowded London bus. Neighbors-turned-enemies back in their native village, they are swiftly at each other's throats. Dizdar brings a caustically comic point of view toward this violent encounter that will run through his corrosive yet ultimately tender vision of a vast multicultural contemporary metropolis. It is from the perspective of London that Dizdar, in turn, drives home to an all-too-indifferent West the agony of Bosnia.

With the confidence born of a bristling, passionate conviction and imagination, coupled with a scabrous absurdist sense of humor, Dizdar, in his feature debut, swiftly introduces us to several groups of highly disparate Londoners whose lives will intersect randomly yet dramatically by the time the picture reaches its stunning, sweeping climax. There are echoes of "MASH" in one key and unexpected sequence, and Dizdar perceives the possibilities in chaos, as did Lina Wertmuller in "Seven Beauties."

Among the families we follow are the Thorntons, a snobbish aristocratic family, verging on caricature and headed by a veteran calcified Member of Parliament. Their medical student daughter Portia (Charlotte Coleman) will end up treating and falling in love with a brand-new Bosnian emigre, Pero (Edin Dzandzanovic), struck by a car as he runs through busy streets, the result of a paranoid misunderstanding.

Meanwhile, Griffin Midge (Danny Nussbaum), slacker son of a schoolteacher (Roger Sloman), who has given up on him, and his dithery wife (Heather Tobias), has taken up hard drugs with his really rotten pals Jim (Steve Sweeney) and Bigsy (Jay Simpson), who think nothing of beating and robbing a youth to get enough money to take off to Rotterdam for a soccer match.

Down the street from the Midges' comfortable row house is the home of Dr. Mouldy (Nicholas Farrell), a sweet-natured, attractively rumpled National Health Service doctor so overworked and bleary his wife leaves him. As heartbroken as he is, he nevertheless acts kindly to a Bosnian refugee (Walentine Giorgiewa), pregnant through rape and therefore not wanting the baby fathered by an enemy. Dr. Mouldy's sons go to the same school attended by the young daughter of an artist (Siobhan Redmond) of more flamboyance than talent and a celebrated BBC-TV war correspondent from Glasgow (Gilbert Martin) determined to plunge into the thick of battle in Bosnia.

Dizdar, who has lived in London since 1989, is unflaggingly inventive in where he takes his large cast. He hits hard in his depiction of both the horrors of war and the perils and hardships of immigrants in London struggling to survive in the face of language barriers, poverty, prejudice and injustice, and above all, a collective obtuseness and indifference directed not just at Bosnians but all refugees. Obviously, "Beautiful People," with little adjustment, could just as easily be set in Paris, New York or Los Angeles.

A film that lives up to its ambitiousness in all its aspects, "Beautiful People" is suffused in an anger that gradually gives way to an aura of affectionate reconciliation, a tone that rightly smacks of just enough wishful thinking to stave off accusations of sentimentality yet raise the possibility of hope. The timeless point that Dizdar makes with so much zest—and no less feeling—is simply that it can be hard to hate those so seemingly different from you once you get to know them.

NEW YORK POST, 2/18/00, p. 54, Jonathan Foreman

Inside "Beautiful People," a film by London-based Bosnian director Jasmin Dizdar, there's a terrific film trying to get out.

Unfortunately, it's smothered by an excess of plot lines, an abundance of clichéd English social types and some clunkily obvious political messages.

Still, "Beautiful People" is playful, unpredictable and astonishingly optimistic, given that it's a movie about Bosnian refugees in Britain and the effect they have on locals from different social and ethnic groups.

In style, it's yet another "Magnolia"/"Short Cuts" type of movie that features several slightly soap-operatic stories joined by coincidences.

Two Bosnian refugees (Faruk Pruti and Dado Jehan) from the same village, one Serb, one Croat, see each other on a London bus and immediately start fighting—to the astonishment of the other passengers.

They end up sharing a hospital ward with a Welsh nationalist arsonist (Nicholas McGaughey), who tells them his pathetic tale of oppression before realizing where they come from.

In the same hospital, an exhausted Dr. Mouldy (Nicholas Farrell, in a one-note role) tries to cope with the departure of his wife while dealing with a Bosnian couple who insist that he terminate the wife's 9-month-old pregnancy.

In one of the film's more infuriating scenes, it becomes obvious that the wife has been raped, but the Bosnians don't speak English and the doctor is too dim to figure it out or get an interpreter.

In Dizdar's apparently newspaperless England, locals are all clueless about the former Yugoslavia, despite the presence of British peacekeepers there.

In other plots, a young junkie skinhead (Danny Nussbaum) finds himself in Bosnia by accident, after a drunken hooligan outing to Rotterdam, and becomes an unlikely hero.

You also have a Scots war correspondent driven mad by his experience of the conflict, and a rebellious, upper-class medical student (Charlotte Coleman from "Four Weddings and a Funeral") falling in love with Pero (Edin Dzandzanovic), a Bosnian refugee basketball player.

NEWSDAY, 2/18/00, Part II/p. B6, Jan Stuart

A Serb and a Croat from the same village lie in adjacent beds in a London hospital, where they furtively try to pull out each other's life-support tubes. A trio of smack-addicted white punks assault a black teenager to get money to go to a ball game in Rotterdam. A guileless Bosnian immigrant attempts to return a handbag to an Englishwoman who has left it behind on a cafe table, and she tries to have him arrested.

Throughout the fractious opening reels of "Beautiful People," we can only conclude that writer-director Jasmin Dizdar was pushing irony to unsubtle heights when he titled his rambunctiously original debut feature. His densely populated melting pot of characters bubbles over the top with such discordancy that we are prompted to talk back to it, Rodney King-style: Can't we all just get along?

Then slowly, almost when we are not looking, something unexpected occurs. Belligerent neighbors are coaxed into gestures of goodwill. Contentious souls find common ground. Selfish lugs commit acts of heroism, almost in spite of themselves. Grace happens.

"Beautiful People" is a comedy, if you will, about traumatized Bosnians who have been displaced by war to another country. In this instance, their new home is England, a formerly sedate and self-contained civilization whose rapidly changing complexion is further challenged by the spillover from the recent conflicts in Yugoslavia. And like so many European countries whose national pride was fostered on cultural sameness and an imperial reach that has long since faded, its wealthiest and poorest are united in a common resentment of the foreigners they perceive to be spoiling their party.

The 38-year-old Dizdar, himself born in Bosnia and resettled in England, reflects these tensions through an intricately aligned constellation of Londoners whose lives bump up against one another with a sly happenstance that makes us smile even as we wince. If this chaotic assemblage could be said to have a center, it is the romantic relationship that brews between a hapless, poor Bosnian emigre named Pero (Edin Dzandzanovic, a winning non-actor) and the rebellious upper-middle-class Portia Thornton (the excellent Charlotte Coleman), whom he encounters in her rounds as a hospital intern.

Among the lives swirling and colliding around them are a thuggish middle-class ne'er-do-well named Griffin Mudge (an amusingly bewildered Danny Nussbaum); a BBC reporter from Glasgow (Gilbert Martin), who is pushed over the edge by his latest assignment in Bosnia; an expectant Bosnian mother (Walentine Giorgiewa) who contemplates murdering her baby as soon as she gives birth and the marriage-embattled family doctor (Nicholas Farrell) who tries to talk her out of it.

In other hands, this raw material would be insufferably dour. But Dizdar weaves his strands together with the sort of waggish pleasure in coincidence that informed Paul Thomas Anderson's "Magnolia," minus that film's self-importance. The script exudes a playful, slightly malevolent sense of humor ("Thank you for your hostility" says Pero, stumbling over his English before his condescending, upper-crust hosts) and an abiding compassion for all its characters. It's a miracle, really: a deeply humane film that ennobles the most ordinary people without romanticizing or trivializing them.

SIGHT AND SOUND, 9/99, p. 41, Stella Bruzzi

London. The lives of numerous characters intersect. Two Bosnian men—one Serb, the other Croat—fight and end up in adjacent hospital beds. Griffin prepares to go to Rotterdam for the England-Holland 1994 World Cup qualifier. Doctor Mouldy is left by his wife. Jerry, a BBC correspondent, is leaving for Bosnia. Pero, another Bosnian refugee, is run over and put on the same ward as the Croat, the Serb and a Welsh nationalist. There he meets Portia, a doctor and daughter of a Tory MP. Elsewhere in the hospital, a Bosnian woman begs Mouldy to abort her child, the result of her being raped by soldiers. After the birth, she and her husband bond with their daughter and name her Chaos. After England loses (2-0), Griffin and his two junkie mates shoot up in a Rotterdam pub toilet. At the airport they become separated. Griffin collapses on a UN military aircraft pallet and is parachuted into Bosnia, where he is caught in a mortar attack. At a UN field hospital he provides heroin for a leg amputation which Jerry is filming.

In London, a reformed Griffin returns home with a Bosnian boy blinded during the attack. Jerry also returns, shot in the leg and suffering from 'Bosnia syndrome'. Mouldy, now without his two sons, invites baby Chaos' parents to stay with him. Jerry wants his leg amputated; a sanitised version of his Bosnian report is broadcast and Griffin, now a hero, is reconciled with his parents. Griffin takes the blind boy to a pub where another England match is on and meets his old friends. The police arrest Pero's African neighbour. Pero marries Portia.

Beautiful People's broad intention is to marry romance and politics both literally and metaphorically, if one considers its concluding wedding. The political contextualisation of its characters within the ethnic conflicts of the former Yugoslavia saves *Beautiful People* from seeming too whimsical, although Jasmin Dizdar's film remains idiosyncratically devoid of cynicism (as its title suggests), but also of real bite. Partly this stems from the film's schematic take on ethnic conflict, and partly from its breathlessly optimistic denouement during which Mouldy says, "It doesn't take much to make life beautiful," and one is led (almost) to believe him. A nurse tells her turbulent ward that they have come to hospital to heal, and *Beautiful People* seems to want to effect a similar cure on its audience.

The film is, however, ambivalent. On the one hand its conclusion offers hope and closure with the birth of baby Chaos and the marriage between a Bosnian who repents his past war crimes and the idealistically liberal offspring of a blanketed, old-school Tory. On the other, it signals instability and the continuation of nationalist conflict: as the Serb, Croat and Welsh zealots play a hand of cards with the Ward Sister, the previous tensions—represented by the recurrent fights between the Serb and the Croat that have punctured the film's superficial optimism throughout—are barely disguised. So *Beautiful People* is a film of unusual potency, a romantic comedy predicated upon coincidence which isn't undercut by the bleakness of its politics.

The problems with *Beautiful People* stem from Dizdar cramming in too many narrative ramifications in his eagerness to dramatise the issue of nationalism and to force a tenuous parallel between Bosnia and Britain. As a traditional morality tale, *Beautiful People* bears more than a passing resemblance to Shakespeare's *Romeo and Juliet* with its opening Capulet-versus-Montague fight between two sworn enemies from the same Bosnian town. The peripatetic slugging match that ensues is just one of many such accidental encounters that drive the action, as they do in classic tragedy. But for contemporary cinema the film's use of implausible coincidences such as the Serb and the Croat adversaries finding themselves on the same ward, or Doctor Mouldy treating the pregnant Bosnian woman in the same hospital, falsifies the film's dominant realism.

Counteracting this formulaic structuring, however, is a pervasive playfulness, a tone that situates *Beautiful People* within a distinctly European tradition of surrealism, irreverence and anarchic political commentary. Particularly inspired is the sporadic sequence of scenes featuring actual or potential leg amputations. Like an absurd game of consequences (and indeed one of the surrealist automatic writing games was a version of this), a potentially arbitrary link is forged between Jerry's daughter watching the scene in *The Railway Children* (1970) in which the schoolboy almost gets his leg severed by an oncoming locomotive, the amputation in a Bosnian field hospital and Jerry's attempt to lose his injured leg via *The Railway Children* method. There is a liberation about this style, in contrast with some of the film's more leaden aspects, such as its clunky parallel editing and rather obvious flagging of Britain as multi-ethnic not unlike Yugoslavia. Dizdar is careful not to impose his politics, which means that the film could be accused of being uncommitted.

Within its plotting frenzy, *Beautiful People* leaves little time to explore the many issues it touches on, such as the diagnosis of Jerry's malaise as 'Bosnia syndrome'—a total identification with the victim—or Pero confessing to a violent past almost as the credits roll. In all the freneticism, there is no time to think, which makes its status as a political allegory a bit of a problem.

VILLAGE VOICE, 2/22/00, p. 135, Amy Taubin

A husband and wife, refugees from the former Yugoslavia, visit a London obstetrician. The husband wants the wife to abort the baby she's carrying because it was conceived during a rape by a band of enemy soldiers. The doctor avoids taking action; when the baby is born, the adoring couple names her Chaos. A teenage junkie, on his way to a soccer match abroad, nods off in an airport baggage bin and winds up in Bosnia, where he uses his heroin stash to anesthetize a man who's about to have his leg amputated. The junkie is feted as a war hero and becomes the caretaker of a blind child. The rebellious daughter of a Conservative member of Parliament falls in love with a refugee from the former Yugoslavia and brings him home to dinner. He presents his hostess with flowers and says, "I want to thank you for your hostility."

Jasmin Dizdar's generous, low-budget British feature was one of the best films at last year's Cannes Film Festival. Nine months later, it seems like a more witty, wise, and succinct *Magnolia*. Dizdar employs the same woven-tapestry approach as Paul Thomas Anderson, but to diametrically opposite ends. For Dizdar, it's political and cultural conflict, rather than narcissism, that shapes the human comedy.

Also reviewed in:
CHICAGO TRIBUNE, 3/3/00, Friday/p. O, Michael Wilmington
NEW YORK TIMES, 2/18/00, p. E12, A.O. Scott
VARIETY, 6/7-13/99, p. 32, Derek Elley
WASHINGTON POST, 3/17/00, Weekend/p. 47, Desson Howe

BEDAZZLED

A Twentieth Century Fox and Regency enterprises release of a Trevor Albert production. *Executive Producer:* Neil Machlis. *Producer:* Harold Ramis and Trevor Albert. *Director:* Harold Ramis. *Screenplay:* Harold Ramis, Peter Tolan, and Larry Gelbart. *Director of Photography:* Bill Pope. *Editor:* Craig P. Herring. *Music:* David Newman. *Music Editor:* Tom Villano and Curt Sobel. *Sound:* Steve Cantamessa and (music) John Kurlander. *Sound Editor:* Sandy Berman. *Casting:* Julia Kim. *Production Designer:* Rick Heinrichs. *Art Director:* John Dexter. *Set Designer:* Jann Engel, Kevin Ishioka, and Darrell Wight. *Set Decorator:* Garrett Lewis. *Set Dresser:* James Meehan and James Malley. *Special Effects:* Alan E. Lorimer. *Visual Effects:* Kim Doyle. *Costumes:* Deena Appel. *Make-up:* Cheri Minns. *Make-up (Brendan Fraser):* Ben Nye, Jr. *Make-up (Elizabeth Hurley):* Tracey Lee. *Stunt Coordinator:* John Moio. *Running time:* 93 minutes. *MPAA Rating:* PG-13.

CAST: Brendan Fraser (Elliot Richards); Elizabeth Hurley (The Devil); Francis O'Connor (Alison Gardner/Nicole); Orlando Jones (Dan/Esteban/Beach Jock/Sportscaster/African Party Guest); Miriam Shor (Carol/Penthouse Hostess); Paul Adelstein (Bob/Roberto/Beach Joch/Sportscaster/Lincoln Aide); Toby Huss (Jerry/Alejandro/Beach Jock/Sportscaster/Lance); Gabriel Casseus (Elliot's Cellmate); Brian Doyle-Murray (Priest); Jeff Doucette (Desk Sargeant); Aaron Lustig (Synedyne Supervisor); Rudolf Martin (Raoul); Julian Firth (John Wilkes-Booth); Bonnie Somerville and Sadie Kratzig (Girls at Beer Garden); David Bain (McDonald's Employee); William Salyers (Elegant Devil); Tom Woodruff, Jr. (Biggest Devil); William Marquez (Eduardo); Ilya Morelle (Russian Drug Dealer); Paul Simon (Police Officer); R. M. Haley (Mover); Ray Haratian (Pablito); Mickey Victor (Drug Factory Foreman); Stephan A. McKenzie (DV8 Bouncer); Christine Cameron (DV8 Waitress).

LOS ANGELES TIMES, 10/20/00, Calendar/p. 11, Kenneth Turan

Selling your soul to the devil is not just a figure of speech, it happens in the movie business all the time. In fact, it seems to have happened with "Bedazzled," a film about just such a transaction.

Inspired by the original "Bedazzled," a modern-day Faust story starring Peter Cook and Dudley Moore, directed by Stanley Donen and one of the wittiest films of the 1960s, the new version does have its virtues: After all, when you barter your soul, you definitely get something in return. But the trade-off, as per usual, is awfully steep.

The best thing about the current "Bedazzled" is its perfectly cast stars: Elizabeth Hurley as the tart-tongued devil and especially Brendan Fraser as the kind of "lovesick, lonely, desperate" guy who would seriously consider such a trade. These roles are the equivalent of a fat pitch across the heart of the plate, and neither actor has any difficulty connecting.

But as written by Larry Gelbart, director Harold Ramis and Peter Tolan, this "Bedazzled," though amusing from moment to moment, is erratic, unfocused and uncertain where it's going. And whenever it gets too insecure about itself, the film falls back, in classic the-devil-made-me-do-it Hollywood fashion, on explosions, gunfights, helicopter stunts, car crashes and computer-generated effects. What should be a drawing-room comedy ends with moments best left to "Gone in 60 Seconds."

"Bedazzled" is strong in its setup, with a witty introduction of Fraser's Elliot Richards and his meeting with the Queen of Darkness. Elliot works as a technical support person for computer manufacturer Synedyne, and he has no visible competition for the role of company pariah, the man everyone is desperate to avoid.

A pathetic irritant who bores people way past tears, Elliot's only sympathetic trait is his crush on beautiful co-worker Alison (Frances O'Connor of "Mansfield Park" and the delightful "Love and Other Catastrophes"), who is of course barely aware of his existence. "Dear God," Elliot says passionately, "I would give anything to have that girl in my life."

This is all the devil (energetically played by Hurley), who almost always wears something red and provocative, needs to hear. A very modern malefactor who has a license plate reading "Bad 1," runs an after-hours club called DV8 and has "offices in Purgatory, Hell and Los Angeles," the devil offers Elliot the chance to reinvent himself and advises him the soul is "like your appendix: You'll never miss it."

Naturally, he agrees to the trade: seven wishes in exchange for his spiritual essence.

After this diverting setup, "Bedazzled" turns into a series of skits, with Elliot thinking up identities he would like to try on (all involving a relationship with Alison) and the devil, being deviousness incarnate, amusing herself by finding loopholes that turn his fantasies into awful nightmares.

One of those actors who thrives on throwing himself into goofy scenarios, Fraser turns "Bedazzled" into a successful one-man comedy review, relishing his opportunity to play everything from a Colombian drug lord to the dominant player in the National Basketball Assn. It is a treat to see the actor in this series of bizarre characterizations, and if the picture were only about how consistently amusing his different impersonations are, it would be a lot easier to endorse.

But funny as Fraser is, he can't eliminate those extraneous stunts and special effects, he can't turn a series of scenes into a coherent whole, and he can't steer the film away from its sappy, programmatic ending. If those were the concessions the devil extracted for Fraser's enjoyable performance, the evil one is a tougher bargainer than anyone imagined.

NEW YORK POST, 10/20/00, p. 53, Lou Lumenick

"Souls are overrated," coos the devil, as impersonated by supermodel Elizabeth Hurley in a series of form-fitting, eye-popping outfits. "It's like your appendix—you'll never even miss it."

The Princess of Darkness ("with offices in purgatory, hell and Los Angeles") is trying to get Elliot (Brendan Fraser), a socially challenged San Francisco computer geek, to sign away eternity on the dotted line in return for seven wishes.

I can make the whole world love you," the devil promises, sounding like a particularly high-priced public relations consultant in this dumbed-down remake of "Bedazzled," the 1968 cult classic.

So Elliot signs, and wishes to be rich, powerful and married to Alison (Frances O'Connor), a beautiful co-worker he worships from afar.

He gets his wish. Unfortunately, he's now a Colombia drug lord whose wife is cheating on him.

After 15 minutes of subtitled hilarity, Elliot exercises his option for his next wish, and the devil warns him to be more specific.

He figures he'll win Alison's heart by becoming the most sensitive man in the world—but ends up crying at sunsets and getting sand kicked in his face by bullies.

Thanks to the prank-loving devil, Elliot's subsequent stints as a star basketball player, a Pulitzer Prize-winning author and the president of the United States, are equally disastrous.

"Bedazzled" has some great quips and clever situations, but it's involving—as an OK date movie—primarily because of a tour de force as Elliot's multiple selves by Brendan Fraser, who's developed into one of the most dependable light comedians of his generation.

Fraser, who's been equally deft in big-budget blockbusters ("The Mummy") and intimate dramas ("Gods and Monsters"), combines a skill for slapstick pratfalls with leading-man looks in a manner seldom seen since Cary Grant's heyday.

Though he and Hurley have genuine chemistry together and she gets most of the best lines (especially when dispensing M&Ms instead of drugs to patients at a nursing home), Hurley isn't nearly as hilarious as she could be.

Unlike the hunky Fraser, Hurley is too self-conscious of her stunning looks—and reads her dialogue like a road-company Joan Collins.

And what exactly is the point of making the devil a sexpot if she isn't going to make more than a perfunctory attempt to seduce Elliot?

In the original version, the devil was drolly played by Peter Cook, who co-wrote the script with Dudley Moore, who had Fraser's role (they share screenwriting credit for this version with Larry Gelbart, Michael Tolin and the new director, Harold Ramis).

As directed by Stanley Donen, the original was a hip, smart updating of Faust set in mod London that still plays extremely well on video.

This remake, which is much more elaborate, but directed without much flair by Ramis ("Analyze This"), is fun but instantly forgettable.

NEWSDAY, 10/20/00, Part II/p. B6, John Anderson

It would probably be in bad taste to say "Thank God" for "Bedazzled," but coming as it does at the end of a purgatorial year for movies, it's more than welcome. And more than funny. And despite the subtle accents of brimstone and sulphur, a breath of fresh air.

We can't say anyone expected it, frankly. In 1967, Stanley Donen directed the "Beyond the Fringe" stars Dudley Moore and Peter Cook in a loose retelling of the Faust legend: The lordly Cook was Satan, Moore the hapless, lovesick diner cook who makes the ultimate deal of selling his soul. It's not as if anyone was clamoring for a remake of that dryly stylish film.

But as directed by Harold Ramis, the new "Bedazzled" arrives much as "Analyze This" did a couple of years ago, just in time to restore one's faith in the possibility of a funny movie. Not coincidentally, "Analyze This" was written by Ramis and Peter Tolan, who scripted "Bedazzled" with help from Larry Gelbart ("M*A*S*H"). In addition to their smart jokes, the new film is possessed of two strokes of brilliance: casting Elizabeth Hurley as the Prince(ss) of Darkness, and, in lieu of any respect for the original, adopting an attitude of freewheeling giddiness.

Our soul-bargaining hero, Elliot Richards (Brendan Fraser), is insufferably geeky, a cross between Rick Moranis in "Ghostbusters" and Rob Schneider's copy geek on "Saturday Night Live." He tucks in his sweater. He wears his employee name tag to the local bar—where his co-workers literally hide from him. His attempts to make small talk with Alison (Frances O'Connor), the object of his affection, are almost too excruciating. So when the Devil shows up and offers him seven wishes in return for his mortal soul, Elliot is too lovesick to resist.

He's also too thickheaded to realize that this leggy Lucifer with the red wardrobe and black Lamborghini has 6,000 years of experience bilking gullible humans out of their afterlife.

Each time he makes a wish, Elliott's words are used by She-Devil to turn his expectations upside down. To give away the various scenarios would spoil the fun, but Fraser makes the most of them, giving a virtuosic comic performance that's sometimes like a cross between Jim Carrey and John Barrymore.

For her part, Hurley has the best role she's ever had—or probably ever will. As the ultimate Bad Girl, she plays the Devil with full-throttled slinkiness, every gesture overdone and oversexed. She also knows how to deliver an irreverent laugh line, and the script for "Bedazzled" is full of them.

Its comedy is a little inconsistent, but "Bedazzled" is fast-paced and full of small comic details, including the multiple roles played by the trio of Orlando Jones, Toby Huss and Paul Adelstein, the last of whom perpetrates a parody of Bob Costas that's worth the price of admission. Especially if you watched the Olympics.

SIGHT AND SOUND, 12/00, p. 40, Andrew O'Hehir

San Francisco, the present. Elliot Richards nurses an unrequited passion for his co-worker Alison. The Devil appears to him as a beautiful woman and offers him seven wishes in exchange for his soul. He first wishes to be rich and married to Alison. The Devil makes him a Colombian drug lord whose wife detests him. He then wishes to become a sensitive man but his pathetic blubbering drives Alison into the arms of a macho creep. Next he wishes to become a basketball superstar, but both his brain and his sexual equipment are diminutive. Wishing to be a brilliant, handsome man with ample genitalia with whom Alison falls madly in love, he turns out to be a gay writer. Then, wishing to be president of the United States, he becomes Lincoln on the night of his assassination.

Learning the Devil has duped him out of one of his wishes, he uses his last wish to demand a happy life for Alison. This selfless act voids the contract. Restored to his old life, Elliot asks Alison out. She rejects him, but he gets on well with his new neighbour, a dead ringer for Alison.

Lacking most of the wit and style that made Stanley Donen's 1967 original a classic of its Swinging London era, Harold Ramis' *Bedazzled* remake settles for Elizabeth Hurley in a series of slinky designer outfits and an agreeable everyman performance from Brendan Fraser. Not that there's anything wrong with Ramis' central gambit: that of making the Devil a seductive female. Hurley is well suited for *Bedazzled*'s genial gags and attacks them with gusto. "I think you're hot," gulps Elliot, the lovesick chump who exchanges his soul for seven wishes, after she corners him. "Baby, you have no idea," Hurley purrs.

Of course the first *Bedazzled* was crucially a satire of its time, matching Dudley Moore's trod-upon bourgeois bedsitter-dweller with Peter Cook's laconic rock-star Satan. When Moore asks for an ice lolly and Cook makes him buy it (thus wasting one of his wishes), we see his Devil as a prankster skewering middle-class expectations. Hurley carries no such social significance, and the transcultural translation of the ice-lolly scene—Fraser and Hurley ride the bus to a San Francisco McDonald's—only seems peculiar, as she's next seen giving him a lift in her Lamborghini.

Not that Ramis and his co-writers (Larry Gelbart and Peter Tolan) had any aspirations to satirise contemporary US mores. Instead their film creates a series of elaborate set pieces for Fraser's good-natured goofballing. Hurley and Fraser actually have few scenes together after their promising initial encounter so the enjoyable sexual tension between them is frittered away. By the end of the film they seem like best pals rather than erotically charged adversaries. An able physical comedian, Fraser is at his best in the earlier, pre-Lucifer scenes, playing Elliot as a loser whose desperate desire to be liked only makes him intolerable. The character has a close kinship to Jim Carrey's information driven nerd in *The Cable Guy*, when Alison, the girl he dotes on, can't remember having spoken to him before, Elliot clarifies matters: "It was the first week of June, three years ago. I said it was really wet out."

As Elliot's various wish scenarios play out, *Bedazzled* labours ever harder for diminishing returns. The drug-lord sketch is modestly amusing, but the scenes in which Fraser plays a weepy beach poet in natural fabrics and an oversized NBA superstar with a mini-manhood are no better than second-rate television sketch material. His turn as a suave gay writer is depressingly obvious, and the scene's attempt to lampoon a Manhattan literary party is embarrassing, especially for writers with Ramis and Gelbart's connections. The Lincoln gag is a one-liner, but at least it's a gag; it would work better if it were as brief as the convent scene in Donen's film.

This *Bedazzled* won't show us Elliot and his love object as lesbian nuns, nor does it depict the memorable confrontation between Satan and God seen in the original. Indeed, Hurley doesn't seem much like the genuine Devil to me; perhaps Elliot has gotten tangled up with a saucy, slightly wayward angel who's trying out some of her uncle Lucifer's tricks. She seems positively chipper when Elliot frees himself from her clutches and sends him on his way with a nugget of New Age wisdom that serves as this simple-minded remake's coda: "You don't have to look hard for heaven and hell. They're right here on earth."

TIME, 10/30/00, p. 82, Richard Corliss

When the devil offers you seven wishes, you'd better have Henry Kissinger or Johnnie Cochran nearby to read the small print. For a start, you'll probably get only six; for another, Beelzebub has an impish sense of foul play that turns any wish into a curse. Ask to be rich, powerful and married to your dream girl and—*poof!*—youll become a cuckolded drug lord. Say you want to be a star athlete, and you'll be missing some important jock equipment. Request a smart Satanic comedy, and you'll get this bag of old tricks.

Bedazzled, a Faust farce directed by Harold Ramis, is quite close in silhouette to the Peter Cook-Dudley Moore *Bedazzled* of 1967—with the petty distinction that the old film was funny, the new one mostly not. A lonely dweeb (Brendan Fraser) is so desperate to win the affections of a co-worker (Frances O'Connor) that he signs a pact with the Horned One (Elizabeth Hurley) that offers him seven shots at ecstasy for his puny little soul. Alas, the skitcom format soon becomes tiresome; comic inventiveness should have been Ramis' first wish.

Can't fault the stars. Fraser is that lovely commodity, a big man with physical grace and an underdog charm. He's drollest in his early scenes as the consummate loser with a coprophagous grin—a character perilously close to Rob Schneider's needy-nerdy copy-machine guy on *Saturday Night Live* years ago. (Similarly, O'Connor looks so much like the younger Kathie Lee Gifford that she could be accused of face-lifting.) Hurley slinks through her role with the purr and swagger of a dominatrix in the Profumo years. Her lithe body has the sexy lines that are often missing from the script of this underachieving immorality play.

VILLAGE VOICE, 10/31/00, p. 174, Michael Atkinson

Harold Ramis used to be an actor (one of the funniest riffers on the old *SCTV*), but as an A-list sitcom maven, he seems to respond to scenarios *(Groundhog Day, Multiplicity)* in which a troubled mensch endures a high-concept, reality-mutilating ordeal that offers him a variety of ways to self-realize, all of which fail in favor of being a good Christian. Not nearly as subversive as Peter Cook's original, *Bedazzled* has its comedy-pro moments, though Elizabeth Hurley, as the Devil granting wishes to un-geek Brendan Fraser, burbles her lines as if she's reading lottery ping-pong balls. It might be worth enduring the Limburger to see Fraser morph from freckled-faced Rod McKuen dweeb to seven-foot albino ball star and never miss a beat.

Also reviewed in:
CHICAGO TRIBUNE, 10/20/00, Friday/p. A, Michael Wilmington
NATION, 11/13/00, p. 34, Stuart Klawans
NEW YORK TIMES, 10/20/00, p. E25, A. O. Scott
VARIETY, 10/16-22/00, p. 21, Joe Leydon
WASHINGTON POST, 10/20/00, p. C5, Rita Kempley
WASHINGTON POST, 10/20/00, Weekend/p. 41, Desson Howe

BEFORE NIGHT FALLS

A Fine Line Features release of a Grandview Pictures/El Mar Pictures production. *Executive Producer:* Julian Schnabel and Olatz López Garmendia. *Producer:* Jon Kilik. *Director:* Julian Schnabel. *Screenplay:* Cunningham O'Keefe, Lázaro Gómez Carriles, and Julian Schnabel. *Based on the documentary "Havana" by:* Jana Bokova. *Director of Photography:* Xavier Perez Grobet and Guillermo Rosas. *Editor:* Michael Berenbaum. *Music:* Carter Burwell. *Music Editor:* Todd Kasow. *Choreographer:* Caridad Martínez Menocal. *Sound:* Christian Wangler and (music) Michael Farrow). *Sound Editor:* Bob Hein. *Casting:* Monica Nordhaus. *Production Designer:* Salvador Parra. *Art Director:* Antonio Muñohierro. *Set Designer:* Juan Pablo García Tames. *Set Decorator:* Sandra Cabriada and Paula Caso Serran. *Special Effects:* Alejandro Vázquez Effeccine. *Costumes:* Mariestela Fernandez. *Make-up:* Ana Lozano. *Running time:* 125 minutes. *MPAA Rating:* Not Rated.

CAST: Javier Bardem (Reinaldo);   Johnny Depp (Bon Bon/Lieutenant Victor);   Sean Penn (Cuco Sánchez);   John Ortiz (Juan Abrau); Santiago Magill (Tomas Diego);   Michael Wincott (Heberto Zorilla Ochoa);   Najwa Nimri (Fina Zorilla Correa);   Alfredo Villa (Armando García); Rene Rivera (Recruit Driver);   Maurice Compte (Nicolas Abrau);   Vincent Laresca (José Abrau);   Manuel E. González (José Lezama Lima);   Hector Babenco (Virgilio Piñera); Olatz López Garmendia (Reinaldo's Mother);   Vito Maria Schnabel (Teenage Reinaldo);   Patricia Reyes Spíndola (María Teresa Freye de Andrade);   Pedro Armendáriz (Reinaldo's Grandfather); Ofelia Medina (Landlady);   Giovani Florido (Young Reinaldo);   Loló Navarro (Reinaldo's Grandmother);   Sebastián Silva (Reinaldo's Father);   Carmen Beato (Teacher);   Cy Schnabel and Olmo Schnabel (Smallest School Children);   Diego Luna (Carlos);   Liz Chapman (Lolin); Jerzy Skolimowski (Professor);   Aquiles Benites (Translator);   Eva Piaskowska (Pretty Blonde Student);   Andrea Di Stefano (Pepé Malas);   Marlene Díaz and Olga Borayo (Women in Car); Manolo García (Faustino);   Lola Schnabel (Girl with Keys);   Lois Barragan (Woman, UNEAC); Eduardo Antonio (Nightclub Singer);   Stella Schnabel (Valeria);   Olivier Martinez (Lázaro Gómez Carriles);   Claudette Maille (María Luisa Lima);   Chanel Puertas (Blonde on the Beach); Manuel Rivero (Royal Gay);   Nemo (Pedro, the Bus Driver);   Andrea Fassler (French Tourist); Magda (Santería Dancer);   Julian Bucio (Violent Soldier);   Jorge Zaráte (Prosecutor);   Francisco Gatorno (Jorge Camacho);   Marisol Padilla Sánchez (Margarita Camacho);   Jorge Zamora (Kid with Kite);   Noel Medina (Policeman on Beach);   Jorge Zepeda (State Security on Beach); Julyan Díaz and Eduardo Arroyuedo (Teenagers);   Antonio Zavala (Stranger in Lenin Park); Eloy Ganuza (State Security in Lenin Park);   Khotan (Young Man with Bird);   René Pereira (Antonio);   Abel Woolrich (Hungry Inmate);   Mario Oliver (Gay Inmate);   Robertico Valdez (Singing Prisoner);   Claudio Osoria (Guard at El Morro);   Diahnne Dèa (Blanca Romero); Caridad Martínez (Dancer in the Convent);   Zulema Cruz (Zulema);   Annie Gil (Blanca's Teenage Daughter);   Filiberto Estrella (Dwarf);   Juan Cristobal Murillo (Immigration Officer); Filiberto Hebra (Man at Mariel Harbor);   Matthias Ehrenberg (Officer at Mariel Harbor);   Jack Schnabel (Jack);   Esther Schnabel (Mrs. Greenberg); Xavier Domingo (Death);   Eric Springer (Orderly);   Jimmy Nugent (Taxi Driver).

LOS ANGELES TIMES, 12/22/00, Calendar/p. 2, Kenneth Turan

Redolent of atmosphere and rapturously cinematic, "Before Night Falls" has a gift for creating visual mood that's so strong you'd swear it couldn't last—but you'd be wrong. Anchored by a charismatic and accessible performance by Javier Bardem as star-crossed Cuban writer Reinaldo Arenas, this florid examination of an artist's coming of age, of cultures in collusion and conflict, is difficult to resist.

Stronger on images than on dialogue and with a tendency to embrace excess for its own sake, "Before Night Falls" is not without its shortcomings. But ultimately this powerful, beguiling film about a poet whose homosexuality put him at odds with the state seduces us just as it seduced Bardem (who resisted the part but ended up winning best actor at the Venice Film Festival) and director Julian Schnabel, who has made a much better film than anyone might have expected.

Hardly the modest artisan, Schnabel is a famously successful artist whose feature debut, "Basquiat," was more on the order of a self-indulgent dabble in another form. There are similar indulgent elements here, like the stunt casting of his friends Sean Penn and Johnny Depp in cameo roles and putting his wife, his five children and his parents in the picture, but what's remarkable about "Before Night Falls" is how much Schnabel has surmounted this gimmickry and turned out a deservedly confident and artistic piece of work.

It all starts with that intoxicating look. Collaborating with cinematographers Xavier Perez Grobet and Guillermo Rosas and production designer Salvador Parra, and with Mexico standing in for Cuba, Schnabel has turned out an exceptional re-creation of several exotic worlds. The Edenic rural Cuba of Arenas' childhood, the hothouse sensuality of Havana just after the old regime's fall and the nightmarish prisons that are the revolution's darker side combine to create visual poetry of a high order.

Ironically for a film about a poet, it's the scenes without words, or rather the scenes where excerpts from Arenas' wonderful poetry and prose are read by Bardem in the original Spanish over magical images and Carter Burwell's hypnotic music that are the most successful. The script by Cunningham O'Keefe, Arenas confidant Lazaro Gomez Carriles and the director is at its weakest when it resorts to dialogue, both because its take on emotions is more operatic than realistic and because Bardem's uncertain command of English frequently makes him hard to understand.

On the other hand, that heavy accent is a price easily worth paying for the actor's exceptional performance. A major star in his native Spain but little-known here, Bardem brings grace, empathy and sensitivity to his portrait of the poet who makes the journey from innocence to experience without losing his freshness and his receptivity to new sensation. Though Bardem is on the screen in almost every scene, his is a presence that never wears out its welcome.

It's Arenas' childhood we experience first, growing up in rural Oriente "a child of absolute poverty, absolute freedom." Raised by his mother (Olatz Lopez Garmendia, Schnabel's wife) and a supportive matriarchy, young Reinaldo experiences the first stirrings of what will be the twin passions of his life, poetry and men.

Captivated by Fidel Castro and his revolution, Arenas ends up in Havana in 1964, a shy, modest, would-be poet and novelist. His early work catches the eye of some well-known writers, and his physical gifts attract the notice of Pepe Malas (Andrea Di Stefano), who guides the young author (and us) through the city's quasi-clandestine gay subculture.

Those early days of the revolution are portrayed as a pansexual fever dream when everything was tolerated. Gradually, however, the Castro regime gets increasingly rigid and views Arenas, both as a gay man and as a writer, as the kind of threat it doesn't want to tolerate. "Artists are escapists, counterrevolutionaries," someone tells the poet. "People who make art are dangerous to any revolution."

"Before Night Falls" presents an especially damning look at the Cuban revolution's attitudes toward homosexuals, and, in a wider sense, at the way increasingly repressive regimes try to marginalize anyone who bucks the imperative to conform. Though the last parts of Schnabel's film are not up to its best segments, its wholehearted embracing of what the poet believed in and its ability to unfold like a veritable dreamscape, to use the camera to expand our world, are virtues in short supply. "Before Night Falls" commands our involvement and our respect.

NEW STATESMAN, 6/25/01, p. 45, Charlotte Raven

When *Before Night Falls* was shown at the Human Rights Watch festival in London earlier this year, the Cuba Solidarity Campaign picketed the screening. The least sustainable of the campaigners' objections was that the director, the painter Julian Schnabel, had failed to reveal his subject as the slag he clearly was. By his own account, the Cuban writer Reinaldo Arenas had sex with more than 5,000 men. In the romantic terms of a film that sees shagging as dissident activity, this (under the circumstances) reckless commitment to the act is presented as both daring and heroic. Far from underplaying the extent of Arenas's promiscuity, Schnabel boasts about it in an effort to convince the audience that radicalism—real radicalism, as opposed to the phoney sort that lay behind the Cuban revolution—is a matter not of what you say or think, but of what you essentially are. To this end, Schnabel portrays Arenas (Javier Bardem) as someone who never chose to write. Rather, he was chosen by the same deity that bestowed on this director his own burning desire to create, to be one of those people charged with expressing the truths of all humanity. We know Arenas is one of Them because, as a young boy at the start of the film, he is compelled to write gnomic messages on trees. The public reception of this early 'work'—his teacher hails him as a poet and his father beats him—is a foretaste of what the Artist can expect from a world that will adore and revile him in equal measure. As his mentor tells him later: 'The people that make art are dangerous.' Whether they are painting watercolours or writing polemical tracts, the very fact of their existence is an affront to any system that relies for its success on colonising the souls of its subjects. Thus, when Arenas is spending what appear to be idle hours entwined with 'the youth of the time', we know that what he's really engaged in is the battle to save us all from stiffs in shirts who haven't tuned in to their own poetic rhythms.

This noble calling occupies him for the first five years of the post-revolutionary period. At a time when you might have thought a writer would be rather busy making sense of these historic events, Arenas is down on the beach, making eyes at sun-kissed Habaneros. Incredibly, we never get the slightest hint of what he thinks about Castro's government. His opposition, such as it is, is presented as aesthetic and poetic. It's bare chests versus starched collars, naked arses versus buttoned lips, life versus death. Not having read the memoir on which the film is based, I don't know whether this is a grotesque misrepresentation of Arenas or a pretty accurate portrayal of a man who shared Schnabel's belief that the purpose of art is to transcend, rather than illuminate, material reality. In choosing to feature only those bits of his work that deal with a Brodie's Notes idea of Universal Human Themes, Schnabel confines himself to filming an A-level essay about an artistic archetype as quaint and outmoded as his belief that Castro's Cuba is a straightforward dictatorship. No one thinks that any more. And only children and hippies still believe in the vagabond poet whose special status gives him the right to exist outside the main arenas of human life.

'I live on the margins of every society,' says Arenas, just before discovering that the US health-care system has the same arbitrary notion as the Cuban militia of whose life is worth saving. Dying of Aids in a hovel because no hospital will take him in, he sees no irony in the fact that the American doctors have managed what a period in a god forsaken Cuban jail could not. Fading as he was at this point, I just wanted him to rouse himself to tell me how he felt about the situation. Was he dying a cynical man whose faith in human beings had been tested beyond endurance, or was he an idealist who never lost that conviction for a minute? Did he wish things had been different? Had his outlook been much altered by the transition from dissidence to exile?

I know it all sounds a bit Paxmanish, but nothing at the end of this film redeemed Arenas from the appearance of being a man to whom nothing of note had ever happened. Insulated from experience and detached from his physical context, this Arenas was praised for ending his life the same way as he had started it—as the enigmatic poet-outsider, for whom art was a means of escaping hard-to-connect-with things such as mothers and revolutions. As innocent of everything as he was the moment he appeared on the screen, Arenas fumbled towards oblivion with the same stoic indifference that he had betrayed in the face of every other momentous event.

NEW YORK, 1/8/01, p. 49, Peter Rainer

Reinaldo Arenas, the dissident Cuban writer who died of aids in exile in New York in 1990 at the age of 47, is portrayed in Julian Schnabel's *Before Night Falls* by the Spanish actor Javier Bardem in a performance that never, thankfully, locks into any single mode. Emotionally, it's all over the place, and so, deliberately, is the movie: Scenes of camp frippery alternate in a blink with ravishingly lush evocations of nature and sequences that are almost giddy with a sense of dread. Bardem has a heroic presence that allows him to express a crazy quilt of emotional colorations and still seem whole, but he doesn't give a great-man performance. Arenas—whose autobiographical memoir *Before Night Falls,* along with other writings and poems, forms the basis for much of the movie—can be regarded as a suffering martyr under the Castro regime; but Arenas, in the film, is too randy and freewheeling, too much in love with the sensual possibilities in life, to ever be regarded as a sacrificial icon. As a young man, he believed in the Cuban revolution, but as an artist and homosexual, he soon found himself cast out, imprisoned. Arenas has a cheeky, fractured sense of the world; he knows he is not wanted in Castro's Cuba, he knows the revolution was not meant for him, and yet he cannot suffer silently. His taunting is a provocation; he writes, he tells a friend at one point, for revenge.

Still, it would be a mistake to characterize the Arenas of this film as a freedom fighter; his agenda, such as it is, is essentially amoral—he writes to stir his own juices. Bardem doesn't sentimentalize Arenas's anguish, which is often as lush as his elation. When the writer, leaving Cuba in the Mariel Harbor boatlift, makes it to New York, his life is not renewed by happiness. Although Schnabel, working from a screenplay by himself and Cunningham O'Keefe and Lázaro Gómez Carriles, is severely critical of Castro, it's also clear that Arenas's unsettled soul is not utterly dependent for its welfare on any one system, communist or capitalist. Ultimately, the movie is not really about an artist deranged by the politics of his homeland. It's about an artist deranged, and rejuvenated, by his own temperament.

NEW YORK POST, 12/22/00, p. 56, Lou Lumenick

"Before Night Falls" traces the life of Reinaldo Arenas, a noted Cuban poet who joined in Castro's revolution only to end up in jail because he was gay.

But anyone expecting a hard-hitting biography will be disappointed by Julian Schnabel's soft-edged, dreamy and relatively nonpolitical film, derived from the writings of Arenas, who died of AIDS in New York City in 1990.

It's a sumptuously photographed, very loosely strung series of vignettes, going all the way back to Arenas' birth in rural poverty in 1943. As a teenager, he eagerly joins with the guerrillas who overthrow dictator Fulgencio Battista and, as a young man, gladly accepts a job as a librarian.

But he falls afoul of Castro's increasingly intolerant regime after publishing his first book; all of his subsequent writings are printed abroad and banned in his homeland.

Arenas is ultimately jailed for two years for defying Castro, finally allowed to leave for Miami as part of the Mariel boatlift in 1980, along with other homosexuals and "undesirables." The film treats his decade in the U.S. as a brief coda.

Schnabel, an artist whose debut film "Basquiat" was nowhere near as seductive as this one, seems more interested in Arenas' sexuality (complete with full frontal male nudity) than the turbulent historical canvas.

Arenas is a triumph for Javier Bardem, a Spanish actor best known for Pedro Almodovar's "Live Flesh." He has an inner fire that illuminates the film even in the early sequences, when the middle-aged actor is somewhat uncomfortably playing a 20-year-old.

Olivier Martinez is very good as Arenas' shifty bisexual lover, but the real scene-stealer is Johnny Depp, who plays two separate roles. He's an officer who tries to seduce' Arenas into signing a confession in a very funny seduction sequence, as well as a drag queen who smuggles one of Arenas' manuscripts out of prison in a very private place.

Sean Penn fares less well in a cameo as a gold-toothed farmer who speaks in the Spanish-accented English that alternates with Spanish dialogue throughout the film, seemingly without rhyme or reason.

NEWSDAY, 12/22/00, Part II/p. B8, Jan Stuart

If the Motion Picture Academy is of sound mind these days, the folks who award those little gold men in April will be cozying up to Javier Bardem. Hitherto known here for his work in Pedro Almodovar's "Live Flesh," the Spanish-born Bardem performs one of those triumphs of total immersion in "Before Night Falls" that make us marvel at the occasional heroism of screen actors.

Bardem is the charismatic center of "Before Night Falls," a spellbinding treatment of the life of the late Cuban writer Reinaldo Arenas that also confirms painter Julian Schnabel as a director of the first rank. Schnabel proved himself a shrewd observer of the downtown art scene with "Basquiat," but there he was operating on home turf. While his new film also pits a renegade artist against a hostile system, the status quo under scrutiny here is nothing less than Fidel Castro's revolutionary Cuba, a state of mind that Schnabel tastes and breathes with the love-hate passions of a refugee.

The Cuba that one experiences in "Before Night Falls" is filtered through the writings and biases of its subject, an out gay poet who was forced to go underground as Castro's regime hit its full repressive stride. The complexity of that regime's evolution can be measured through Arenas, whose life is charted from the mud-carpeted playpens of his impoverished infancy to the dank holding pens of Castro's concentration camps, and finally to the emergency-room purgatory of an uninsured New York immigrant with AIDS.

It is Castro's revolutionary fervor that initially inspires the sensitive adolescent Arenas to flee his farm family in his teens. And Arenas is the beneficiary of Castro's educational-program largesse, winning writing prizes at the University of Havana even as established artists are beginning to be banned.

Bardem effects an elastic transformation of his own, growing from the Chico Marx-like waggishness of Arenas' student days to the reckless daring of a liberated gay man, emboldened by a sexual revolution in high gear in the mid-'60s, When Castro comes down on artists and homosexuals with a harsh Stalinist force, Arenas falls victim to the cruelties of labor camps. In a witty strike at the sexual polarization of Castro's ideal Cuba, Schnabel double-casts Johnny Depp as a flamboyant drag-queen prisoner and a camp guard with a terminal case of machismo.

"Before Night Falls" shifts into escape drama in its second half, but it transcends its epic-biography conventions through the high-stakes performance of its star and the metaphoric eye of its director. Schnabel honors his subject's verbal lyricism with visual grace notes of his own, locating pregnant meaning in the crashing of a red kite or the romantic tension of two synchronized swimmers. There is even an oblique reference to "The Wizard of Oz" before Arenas escapes to New York and discovers, after a fashion, that he is not in Kansas anymore. In Schnabel's jaundiced portrait of a vanquished paradise, it is bitterly clear that he was never in Kansas to begin with.

NEWSWEEK, 12/25/00-1/1/01, p. 75, David Ansen

The life of Reinaldo Arenas, the prize-winning Cuban exile writer who died in New York in 1990, was lived at a level of fever-pitch intensity. A prolific writer from a peasant background who produced more than 20 books, only one of which was allowed to be published in Cuba, a sensualist of pagan proportions whose homosexuality put him on a collision course with the hysterical homophobia of the Castro regime, Arenas crammed several lifetimes of pleasure and horror into his 47 years. This is not a life that can be contained in a conventional biopic, and Julian Schnabel, painter and filmmaker, lets Arenas's passionate, idiosyncratic personality set his tone. This powerful, lyrical meditation on Arenas's life achieves a kind of hallucinatory urgency as it leaps and twists from his childhood to his disillusionment with the Castro regime, his brutal persecution and imprisonment, his escape to New York in the 1980 Mariel boatlift and his bitter final days struggling with AIDS. It is not a shapely movie (it wasn't a shapely life), but it's a devastating one.

Javier Bardem, who usually plays macho heartthrobs, miraculously transforms himself into the defiantly gay author. It's an astounding performance that honors Arenas's courage, wit and hunger for freedom at any cost. Schnabel, in his second film after "Basquiat" is a master of milieu, transporting us to a revolutionary Cuba that feels utterly authentic. His painterly eye is alert to the jarring contradictions of a sensual culture in the grips of a puritanical ideology. Schnabel's moving film is a passionate but clear-eyed memorial to a brilliant man caught in a lethal maelstrom of art, eroticism and politics.

SIGHT AND SOUND, 6/01, p. 39, Peter Matthews

Oriente Province, Cuba, 1943. Deserted by her lover, a young woman gives birth to the future poet and novelist, Reinaldo Arenas. From childhood, Reinaldo shows an aptitude for writing, much to the displeasure of his grandfather. Shortly after the family moves to the town of Holguín in 1958, Reinaldo joins the communist rebels hoping to overthrow the dictator Fulgencio Batista. Fidel Castro's revolution is victorious and Reinaldo lands a job at the National Library in Havana.

Reinaldo's literary talent attracts the attention of the well-known Cuban writers José Lezama Lima and Virgilio Piñera, who assist in publishing his first novel Singing from the Well (1963). He also discovers Havana's gay subculture and takes up with a variety of lovers, including the fickle bisexual Pepé Malas.

In the late 60s, the government begins to crack down on the alleged subversive activities of artists and homosexuals. A Parisian couple agree to smuggle the manuscript of Reinaldo's second novel Hallucinations out of Cuba. Its subsequent publication in France antagonises the Castro regime. After an argument with two youths on a beach in October 1974 Reinaldo is arrested on a false charge of sexual molestation. He escapes from jail and makes an unsuccessful attempt to float to the US in an inner tube. Rearrested, Reinaldo is sent to El Morro prison where he serves two years. Branded a CIA agent, he continues to write secretly. The authorities uncover his plan to have a new novel spirited out of the prison, and Reinaldo is punished by a stint in solitary confinement. He is released after being forced to confess his counter-revolutionary crimes and moves into an artists' colony. Here he meets Lázaro Gómez Carriles, who becomes his best friend. A scheme to flee the island in a hot-air balloon is foiled when Pepé shows up and steals the balloon.

In 1980 Castro initiates a policy of dumping criminals, homosexuals and other undesirables on the shores of Florida. A strategic alteration to Reinaldo's passport allows him and Lázaro to leave Cuba undetected. Settling in New York, Reinaldo achieves minor celebrity as a writer-in-exile. A few years later, he contracts Aids. Terminally ill, he commits suicide with the help of Lázaro in 1990.

The biopics the old studios used to churn out were necessarily episodic, but they adhered to a neat formula. The intrepid writer, composer, scientist or whoever endures a period of bitter struggle, then makes the startling breakthrough that certifies his or her genius. But the world scoffs at so fantastic a notion, and the movie comes down to a pivotal sequence where, say, Paul Muni as Louis Pasteur triumphantly proves the existence of microbes before the assembled forces of reaction. Hilariously reductive though the great man-of-history template now appears, it had the advantage of clarity. The script followed a tight narrative logic and conferred an unmistakable meaning upon the life's work. It's understandable that contemporary screen biographers might wish to avoid this square approach and the romantic ideology that goes with it. But the danger of a more open dramaturgy is that the subject's career will devolve into a picaresque collage of events signifying nothing in particular. That's what happens in *Before Night Falls*, which tells the story of Cuban author Reinaldo Arenas from his serene childhood in the rural outback through political persecution, exile and death.

The director Julian Schnabel seems to be specialising in a new mini-genre—the brief lives of artists. His 1996 debut feature *Basquiat* charted the meteoric rise and fall of the titular Afro-American painter, seen as an otherworldly cherub unable to cope with the realpolitik of the New York art scene and succumbing to a heroin overdose at 24. While Arenas (played by the sensual, heavy-lidded Javier Bardem) survived until the relatively ripe age of 47, he too was an exemplary sufferer—first brutalised by Castro's henchmen, then battling the depredations of Aids. Indeed, Schnabel's morbid fixation on the male body in torment would raise a speculative eyebrow if either film invited the least emotional participation. But together with Robert Longo, John Maybury, David Lynch and the late Derek Jarman, Schnabel belongs to that small club of artists-turned-film-makers and labours under its chief occupational vice. That is, he thinks almost entirely with his optic nerve. The images in *Before Night Falls*—a river flooding its banks during the rainy season or a joy-ride on a snowy Manhattan evening—are often lushly beautiful. Yet pried loose from the gravitational field of story structure, they just float affectlessly in their own aestheticised twilight zone. After a scant two movies, Schnabel is already developing recognisable tics. He likes to switch the dialogue off and then lay down a contrapuntal soundtrack (a wildly gyrating party, for instance, will be scored with a mournful operatic aria). It's your classical MTV style rarefied for the arthouse, and it produces the same effect of mood liberated from content.

Basquiat was riddled with similar gaps and aporias, but one could argue that it thereby preserved the enigma of its aloof, quicksilver protagonist. The straightforwardly heroic Arenas isn't nearly as intriguing a figure, so the fractured ambiguity of *Before Night Falls* feels imposed from outside. Schnabel would probably claim to seek a higher truth than literal chronology, his darting, associative method giving Arenas' own brand of magic realism a run for its money. The shifting shapes, patterns and tones suggest a kaleidoscope—here a grainy newsreel showing post-revolutionary jubilation, there a snatch from the writer's verse or a nature documentary on the secret life of the forest. You need clairvoyance to fathom portions of the movie, especially as Schnabel and his co-screenwriters Cunningham O'Keefe and Lázaro Gómez Carriles include several scenes that playfully withhold their ontological status. (The most amusing features Johnny Depp as a military martinet who rubs his crotch energetically while grilling Arenas in what may or may not be a gay disciplinarian fantasy.) This confusion in registers is presumably meant to exhibit the poetic sensibility at work the elastic artist doesn't distinguish between the subjective and objective levels of reality. *Basquiat* kept circling back to a mysterious surfer in the sky as a short-hand for creative inspiration, and *Before Night Falls* has its comparable primal image—the lost mother endlessly beckoning from the past. In the movie's high-flown conception, the artist's uncensored receptiveness to beauty puts him instinctively at odds with authority. Arenas' body is tortured by the state, but his soul remains at liberty. Despite the postmodern trappings, that's the traditional Hollywood corn served up *virgo intacta*. The glamourised childhood scenes offer the dubious conceit that only in abject poverty was Reinaldo truly free. Free to starve, one might retort, though the photogenic squalour of pre-Castro Cuba should go down well with the new Bush administration.

VILLAGE VOICE, 12/26/00, p. 148, Dennis Lim

Swapping the wanton excesses of the 1980s New York art world for the puritanical confines of the Castro regime, Julian Schnabel continues to tread the myth-rich, landmine-ridden terrain of the martyred-artist biopic. It's beside the point to compare the febrile Rabelaisian phantasmagoria of Reinaldo Arenas, the late gay Cuban poet and novelist who is the subject of Schnabel's *Before Night Falls,* with the snazzy neo-expressionism of Jean-Michel Basquiat (Arenas, for that matter, experienced neither meteoric ascent nor backlash flameout), but the filmmaker's basic attraction to these two all-too-brief lives warrants scrutiny. Both movies cleave to an unabashedly romanticized notion of art as a tool of self-preservation; both bitterly lament the tragedy of a singular talent worn down by an inhospitable environment—first seduced then cruelly betrayed.

As with *Basquiat,* there's a certain dreamy opacity to *Before Night Falls.* Schnabel is an empathic, often admiring biographer, but he's uninclined to pause for analysis, as if any lasting residue of insight would irredeemably mire the reverie. By way of compensation, though, the winking insider's perspective of the earlier film has relaxed into the unguarded stance of a newly enraptured observer. Named for Arenas's posthumously published memoir (though drawing equally from his scabrous *pentagonia* of loosely autobiographical novels), *Before Night Falls* glides, perhaps a little too serenely, through the writer's life, its anecdotal obviousness leavened by some memorable grace notes. After an impoverished, absent-father rural childhood (given a lush magic-realist gloss), Reinaldo runs away to join the revolution and discovers sexual rather than political fulfillment. (He's played from young adulthood on by the Spanish actor Javier Bardem.) Schnabel dampens Arenas's fabled promiscuity, a misstep given the writer's tireless emphasis on sex-as-emancipation. Still, helped by cinematographers Xavier Perez Grobet and Guillermo Rosas's warmly saturated colors and Carter Burwell's voluptuous score, he has a blast recreating the Caribbean Babylon of '50s Havana (in Mexico), a heady, eroticized idyll of azure sky and sea (and cute boys in Speedos).

The new regime soon brought with it further disillusionment, persistent persecution, and eventual incarceration. This horrific chapter (during which Schnabel incongruously retains his buoyant touch) ends with Arenas's flight from Cuba in the 1980 Mariel boatlift. Bypassing Miami entirely, Schnabel transports his subject, in one breathtaking cut, from the Straits of Florida to the wintry canyons of Manhattan; what follows, essentially a postscript, is a direct, moving account of Arenas's battle with AIDS, which led to his suicide in 1990.

Schnabel's refusal to psychoanalyze his subject can be taken as a wary nod to the pitfalls of biopic convention, even if this respectful approach precludes any discussion of Arenas's complex sexuality. A more immediate problem is the filmmaker's failure to convey a substantial sense of Arenas as a writer, save for a couple of key sequences (a montage of newsreel footage of the revolution, a taxicab contemplation that cross-cuts between New York and Havana) in which Bardem recites Arenas's poetry in voice-over (in Spanish; much of the film requires the actors to speak in accented English). The director's weakness for flashy cameos is balanced by his good sense to enlist only professional scene stealers: Sean Penn as a smirking gold-toothed cart driver, and Johnny Depp, who appears as transvestite bombshell Bon Bon, then, disorientingly, a few minutes later as a macho, crotch-grabbing lieutenant. *Before Night Falls* is really a one-man show, though, anchored by a performance of impressive magnitude and nuance. The film's ephemeral, semi-evasive lyricism ultimately works as a modest frame for Bardem's tender, deft portrait, which is in turn suitably expansive and rooted in the most concrete details—Arenas's pride and anger, his unsentimental wit and defiant vitality.

Also reviewed in:
CHICAGO TRIBUNE, 2/2/01, Friday/p. A, Mark Caro
NEW YORK TIMES, 12/22/00, p. E30, Stephen Holden
NEW YORKER, 1/8/01, p. 90, David Denby
VARIETY, 9/11-17/00, p. 21, David Rooney
WASHINGTON POST, 2/2/01, p. C1, Rita Kempley
WASHINGTON POST, 2/2/01, Weekend/p. 41, Michael O'Sullivan

BELFAST, MAINE

A Zipporah Films release of a Belfast, Inc. production. *Producer:* Frederick Wiseman. *Director:* Frederick Wiseman. *Director of Photography:* John Davey. *Editor:* Frederick Wiseman. *Running time:* 248 minutes. *MPAA Rating:* Not Rated.

CHRISTIAN SCIENCE MONITOR, 1/28/00, p. 15, David Sterritt

Of all Wiseman's movies, none is more probing or intelligent than "Belfast, Maine," a four-hour-plus film that ranks with his greatest work. On its most obvious level, it's a portrait of a small New England city on the Atlantic coast, complete with eye-catching shots of fishermen on the swelling sea, homes nestled at the forest's edge, and some of the most sky-filling sunsets you ever saw.

On a deeper level, it's a study of "a community in flux," as Wiseman describes it. A notably scenic area with many poor residents, Belfast is making a complicated transition from blue-collar hinterland to service-economy center.

Still deeper below the surface, "Belfast, Maine" takes on meanings even more fascinating. To detect these, it's necessary to consider two major threads. One is a series of assembly-line scenes that show raw materials being processed by sophisticated machines and meticulous workers into packaged foods and other consumer goods. The other is a series of person-to-person scenes presenting heartfelt conversations between troubled individuals and others—social workers, health-care authorities, and the like—who sincerely want to help.

These two categories seem unrelated, but connections become apparent as the film proceeds. Wiseman has always been interested in systems and organizations that help people face daily challenges.

As many of his movies demonstrate, the best of these institutions are invaluable places where earnest, compassionate folks come together to support those less privileged than themselves. Yet people on both sides of this arrangement—those helping and those being helped—pay a price for their participation, since such interactions can only take place in bounded, structured circumstances where the full range of human possibility is limited by rules and conventions. Our physical and psychological well-being may benefit, but our deepest selves may suffer from being squeezed into socially approved molds—symbolized by Wiseman's shots of the "processing" that living plants and animals go through when smoothly running factories get hold of them.

This idea is crystallized late in the movie when we visit a Belfast high-school teacher, who sounds like French philosopher Michel Foucault as he articulately lectures his students on Herman Melville's pessimistic attitude toward social and cultural organizations. A similar message is conveyed when we visit a church at the end of the film. It's a wonderful church with a loving pastor who obviously cares about every member of her congregation. Yet the church is far from crowded—younger folks seem especially unenthusiastic about the place—and the people listening to the sermon don't seem much livelier than the stones in the "Our Town"-type cemetery just outside the door.

At these moments, both strands of Wiseman's filmmaking philosophy come to the fore. We see the Wiseman who untiringly seeks out admirable institutions (the school, the church) so he can celebrate their contributions. And we see the Wiseman who finds institutions falling sadly short of their aspirations when they fail to touch the deepest needs of the people they want to serve.

Interweaving these threads with a glowing artistry that suggests compassionate ideas without ever manipulating his audience, Wiseman reaches the peak of his powers in "Belfast, Maine," a modestly titled masterpiece that deserves to be seen by the widest possible audience.

Also reviewed in:
NATION, 2/14/00, p. 34, Stuart Klawans
NEW YORK TIMES, 1/28/00, p. E17, Stephen Holden
VARIETY, 9/20-26/99, p. 92, Eddie Cockrell

BELOVED/FRIEND

A Cowboy Booking International release of an Els Films de la Rambla, S.A. production with the collaboration of Television Espanola/Televisio de Catalunya and Canal +. *Producer:* Ventura Pons. *Director:* Ventura Pons. *Screenplay (Spanish with English subtitles, based on his play "Testament"):* Josep M. Benet I Jornet. *Director of Photography:* Jesús Escosa. *Editor:* Pere Abadal. *Music:* Carles Cases. *Sound:* Boris Zapata. *Art Director:* Bello Torras. *Running time:* 90 minutes. *MPAA Rating:* Not Rated.

CAST: Josep Maria Pou (Jaume Clara); Rosa Maria Sardà (Fanny); Mario Gas (Pere Roure); David Selvas (David Vila); Irene Montala (Albà).

NEW YORK POST, 2/4/00, p. 054, Hannah Brown

"Beloved/Friend" is a talky, pretentious soap opera about Spanish intellectuals.

A dying middle-aged professor, Jaume (Josep Maria Pou), becomes infatuated with one of his students, the cruel, handsome David (David Selvas), who supports himself by working as a male prostitute.

When Jaume learns by chance that David has impregnated the daughter of his best friend, Pere (Mario Gas), he becomes obsessed with the idea of making the child his heir.

During a long day and night, Jaume talks over the matter with Pere and confesses his unrequited love to his old friend, and then gets involved in twisted, sadistic games with David.

The intelligent script takes on some big questions (the nature of life, death, love, sex) and is occasionally insightful. But the characters are walking cliches, and—in spite of the film's short running time—often repetitive.

Pou gives a masterful performance in the central role, but he's not enough to make the movie worth watching.

NEWSDAY, 2/4/00, Part II/p. B11, Jan Stuart

The Ghost of Lola Lola, Marlene Dietrich's iconic femme fatale from "The Blue Angel," hovers over "Beloved/Friend." In the updated guise of this new drama from Spain, the object of a professor's self-destructive obsession is not a sultry nightclub singer but rather a bruising, callous hustler.

In this wildly contrived Barcelona tale, ailing academic Jaume Clara (Josep Maria Pou) is head over heels for his model student David (David Selvas), a bisexual hustler who only has eyes for himself. When the dying professor learns that David has impregnated the daughter of his best friend and colleague Pere Roure (Mario Gas), he sees an opportunity to achieve both a legacy—and a connection to his beloved but indifferent David—through the yet-unborn child.

Directed with artful earnestness by Ventura Pons, "Beloved/Friend" relies upon such a shameless pileup of coincidences, one would be led to conclude that Barcelona has a population of five. In addition to the improbable one degree of separation that links the two academics in a tug-of-wills with the hedonistic David, guess who happens to show up at Jaume Clara's door when he phones an escort service for a little paid recreation?

Adapted by Josep M. Benet I Jornet from his own play, "Beloved/Friend" fancies itself a profound meditation on the nature of desire, friendship, fulfillment and redemption. But it's little more than a pretentious soap opera goosed up with a cheap thrill or two. It is difficult to work up much sympathy for either the masochistic professor or his sullen protege, who radiates his lost-cause status with every self-absorbed breath.

"Beloved/Friend" benefits from a fetching score by Carles Cases and the refreshing presence of Rosa Maria Sardà as Pere Roure's wise and open-minded wife, Fanny. We would much prefer to hang out with Sardà, but she's tethered off-screen for most of the way, presumably marking time in a makeup trailer where life is less complicated.

VILLAGE VOICE, 2/8/00, p. 146, Dennis Lim

Taking the opposite tack—minimal production values, messy and overwrought ideas [The reference is to *Santitos*; see Lim's review of that film.]—Catalan director Ventura Pons's *Beloved/Friend* is an improbably absorbing study of intergenerational conflict. A gay, fiftyish medieval-lit professor (Josep Maria Pou) discovers he has a terminal illness and decides to tie up loose ends: This involves confessing to his colleague and best friend that he was in love with him for years and entrusting his mysterious final essay to the brilliant bad-boy student and part-time hustler whom he now adores. Through a web of unconvincingly rendered coincidences, psychosexual turmoil mounts: It turns out that the student has impregnated the best friend's daughter.

There's much hand-wringing over notions of testaments and legacies, a good deal of it pompous, but Pons (adapting a play by Josep M. Benet I Jornet, who also wrote the screenplay) digs into them with such fervor and his actors respond with such anguished intensity that the result is compelling, sometimes even electrifying. The recent recipient of a Walter Reade retro (whose previous film, *Caresses*—a smart, thorny *La Ronde,* also based on a play—is newly available on video), Pons is a provocateur who works without a net; the scenes that feel most unmoored are often the most revelatory. There's a regrettable lack of surface attention here (conspicuously bad art direction, drab cinematography, and a sappy score), but when *Beloved/Friend* palpitates into life, it's more exciting and truthful than most better-looking films dare to be.

Also reviewed in:
NEW YORK TIMES, 2/4/00, p. E16, Elvis Mitchell
VARIETY, 2/1-7/99, p. 56, Jonathan Holland

BENJAMIN SMOKE

A Cowboy Booking International and a C-Hundred Film Corp release of a Gravity Hill Films and Pumpernickel coproduction. *Executive Producer:* Noah Cowan. *Director:* Jem Cohen and Peter Sillen. *Director of Photography:* Jem Cohen and Peter Sillen. *Editor:* Nancy Roach. *Music:* Benjamin Smoke. *Sound:* Jem Cohen and Peter Sillen. *Running time:* 80 minutes. *MPAA Rating:* Not Rated.

WITH: Robert Dickerson/Benjamin; and members of Smoke: Patti Smith, Tim Campion, Brian Halloran, Coleman Lewis, and Bill Taft.

LOS ANGELES TIMES, 8/11/00, Calendar/p. 14, Kevin Thomas

You don't have to know anything about music, you do not even have to have heard of the man whose name and band provide the title for "Benjamin Smoke," a haunting portrait of a lyricist-singer who is the very embodiment of Edna St. Vincent Millay's famous observation that burning the candle at both ends produces "such a lovely light."

Born in Jonesboro, Ga., in 1960 and known as Robert Dickerson, after one of his numerous stepfathers, the man who would eventually call himself Benjamin and his band Smoke was a smiling, towheaded boy who discovered that he liked to dress up in his mother's clothes and that he was gay.

He was living in rural Waco, Ga., on a dirt road in a house without plumbing when he first heard Patti Smith on the radio. Up till then he had no particular interest in music but then realized that it "could be different. I never felt that before." Pretty soon Benjamin was wholeheartedly throwing himself into a life of sex, drugs and rock 'n' roll, becoming a fixture in the underground music scene of Athens, Ga., as well as Atlanta.

It was in Athens, in 1989, that Jem Cohen, who made this film with Peter Sillen, first saw Smoke at the urging of Michael Stipe of R.E.M., whom Cohen was filming at the time. Back then, Benjamin was performing in drag as Opal Foxx, who led a band in a riveting and eclectic set of songs.

When we first hear Benjamin singing at the opening of the film, he sounds a lot like Tom Waits, and when we meet him, sitting on an Atlanta apartment building rooftop, he is a ravaged-looking, rail-thin man, once handsome, who looks a lot older than someone in his late 30s, (You inevitably think of Chet Baker in his last days.)

Benjamin speaks without self-pity and often with humor of having lived hard and poor, relentlessly on the margins, and of his drug use and his struggle with AIDS. There is so much passion and eloquence in everything he says that he brings to mind the poets—from Keats and Shelley to Sylvia Plath—who seem unable to create without consuming themselves in the process. A chain-smoker and pot lover, Benjamin also used speed and barbiturates, which he gave up to improve his health as much as possible.

Before cleaning up his act and moving into that Atlanta apartment, Benjamin is seen in his cottage in Atlanta's Cabbagetown, a picturesque, ramshackle and dangerous area surrounding an abandoned mill about to be overtaken by gentrification. In rooms decorated with thrift shop finery, he recalls another gay underground artist, New York filmmaker Jack Smith, also a man who looked fragile but lived his life fearlessly.

Benjamin speaks of his derelict neighborhood affectionately as a place he had been drawn to in his youth because of its hustlers and glue sniffers. He recalls a short period in Manhattan in the late '70s, in which he got a job sweeping up broken glass on the floor of the legendary Bowery punk club CBGB—and where he met his idol, Patti Smith, briefly.

Despite his painfully obvious ill health, Benjamin keeps on performing with his group Smoke, composed of a group of young men as talented as they are ordinary-looking and who seem to be in robust health. Benjamin's big moment occurs when Patti Smith asks them to open for her in Atlanta. He says he can't believe she had their two CDs, "Another Reason to Fast" and "Heaven on a Popsicle Stick," and could quote from them.

The filmmakers, whose spare, spontaneous yet poetic style echoes that of their subject, keep the focus firmly on Benjamin, recording his observations and performances over a period of time. There's no conventional biographical background provided or interviews with friends and colleagues, nor is there any need for them.

There's such a rawness, purity and even mystical force to everything Benjamin says or sings, that anything else would seem extraneous and detracting from the impact of a man who has lived his life with absolutely no holds barred. In his most substantial personal allusion he notes that there's nothing like AIDS to reunite a son and his mother.

There is a coda to "Benjamin Smoke" in which Patti Smith speaks of Benjamin and his impact on her and her work, and of the bravery and determination with which he continued to perform despite his declining health. A quote from a poem by Smith in honor of Benjamin opens the film, capturing the essence of his spirit: "With a throat smooth as a lamb yet dry as a branch not snapping/He throws back his head yet he does not sing a thing mournful."

NEW YORK POST, 7/21/00, p. 51, Lou Lumenick

The subject of this documentary is a Georgia rock musician, drag queen and amphetamine addict who died of AIDS the day after his 39th birthday.

He went only by the name Benjamin—and Smoke was the last of several bands he sang with. Benjamin's admirers included REM's Michael Stipe, who co-produced this film.

Filmmakers Jem Cohen and Peter Sillen offer only the briefest snippets of Benjamin's performances. Mostly he's seen—or heard, superimposed over photographs—as a ravaged waif talking about his life as drug addict.

Benjamin was undeniably some kind of presence, but "Benjamin Smoke" is a rather morbid celebration of his excesses.

NEWSDAY, 7/21/00, Part II/p. B7, John Anderson

"Benjamin", the single-named subject of "Benjamin Smoke," remembers his first gig in an Atlanta club. The power was cut. The cops were called. Benjamin in a tutu, was trying desperately to find the five Nembutol he had in his purse, to augment the five he'd already taken "All I could think of," he says, "was that I was going to jail with one shoe on and one shoe off."

It probably doesn't need to be said, but the key to making a successful documentary portrait is finding a character worth watching. Benjamin is certainly that. And co-director Jem Cohen certainly knew it: He'd been introduced to the rock-poet drag queen in 1989 by R.E.M.'s Michael Stipe (whose C-Hundred Film Corp. is "presenting" the film) and almost immediately started collecting the footage for what would be "Benjamin Smoke." Along with Peter Sillen—director of the splendid documentary "Speed Racer," about paraplegic singer-songwriter Vic Chesnutt—Cohen has created an impressionistic/pointillist portrait of Benjamin, a man so purely determined to live his own life he seems both archaic and angelic.

His voice a Tom Waits-inspired croak, Benjamin sings songs whose lyrics are punkishly nihilistic, but whose orchestration includes cello, trumpet, banjo and, according to one story, once included a pistol used as percussion. That Benjamin performs in a sapphire evening gown may distract a bit from the music, but what's there is original and moving.

Cohen and Sillen chronicle Benjamin's public life and private pain from his days as Opal Foxx, fronting the Opal Foxx Quartet, through his battle with HIV and his association with his hero, rock poet-singer Patti Smith. What's left after "Benjamin Smoke" is the feeling that you've had an encounter with a singular human and, in an era when everyone considers him—or herself a creative entity, someone with a genuine vision. You may not like his music, you may not like him, but his life is a work of art.

VILLAGE VOICE, 7/25/00, p. 124, Amy Taubin

A delicate, raunchy drag-queen heartbreaker, Benjamin—the focus of the documentary *Benjamin Smoke*—had the face of Tom Verlaine and the voice of Tom Waits. An Atlanta singer-songwriter and an underground music legend, he died of AIDS in 1999. Off and on for 10 years, Jem Cohen filmed him performing in clubs with his bands, the Opal Foxx Quartet and Smoke, and in his Cabbagetown house, where he shared his insights into music, drugs, and sexuality; modeled his treasured blue taffeta cocktail dress; and proved himself in every way a mensch.

With Peter Sillen, Cohen shaped the footage into *Benjamin Smoke,* a film as ethereal, moving, and uncompromising as its subject. Cohen captures the intensity of Benjamin's music and his performing persona. Like its frail but resilient protagonist, the film cherishes the poverty of its materials (it's shot in both black-and-white and color on scraps of 16mm and Super 8) and uses them to expressive effect. The filmmakers, however, make a misstep when they bring in Patti Smith to read a poem in Benjamin's honor. Benjamin, who started wearing dresses when he was nine, didn't realize that he could be a musician until he heard *Horses* as a teenager. And since the high point of his last years seems to have been opening for Smith when her band played Atlanta, he would have been thrilled that Smith is in the movie. But Smith has a celebrity and a marquee value that Benjamin did not, and to put her center screen at the climax of the film undermines the celebration of its main figure. This quibble aside, *Benjamin Smoke* is a bittersweet pleasure.

Also reviewed in:
NEW YORK TIMES, 7/21/00, p. E20, A. O. Scott
VARIETY, 3/13-19/00, p. 26, Eddie Cockrell

BEST IN SHOW

A Castle Rock Entertainment/Warner Brothers release.   *Executive Producer:* Gordon Mark. *Producer:* Karen Murphy.   *Director:* Christopher Guest.   *Screenplay:* Christopher Guest and Eugene Levy. *Director of Photography:* Roberto Schaefer.   *Editor:* Robert Leighton. *Music:* Jeffrey C.J. Vanston. *Music Editor:* Fernand Bos.   *Sound:* Mark Weingarten and (music) David Cole. *Sound Editor:* Hamilton Sterling. *Casting:* Stuart Atkins. *Production Designer:* Joseph T. Garrity.   *Art Director:* Gary Myers.   *Set Designer:* Kelvin Humenny.   *Set Decorator:*

Dominique Fauquet-Lemaitre. *Special Effects:* Gord Davis. *Costumes:* Monique Prudhomme. *Make-up:* Kate Shorter. *Stunt Coordinator:* David Alexander. *Running time:* 89m minutes. *MPAA Rating:* PG-13.

CAST: Parker Posey (Meg Swan); Michael Hitchcock (Hamilton Swan); Catherine O'Hara (Cookie Fleck); Eugene Levy (Gerry Fleck); Bob Balaban (Dr. Theodore W. Millbank III); Christopher Guest (Harlan Pepper); Michael McKean (Stefan Vanderhoof); John Michael Higgins (Scott Donlan); Patrick Cranshaw (Leslie Ward Cabot); Jennifer Coolidge (Sherri Ann Ward Cabot); Don Lake (Graham Chissolm); Jane Lynch (Christy Cummings); Fred Willard (Buck Laughlin); Jim Piddock (Trevor Beckwith); Jay Brazeau (Dr. Chuck Nelken); Carrie Aizley and Lewis Arquette (Fern City Show Spectators); Dany Canino (Fern City Show Judge); Will Sasso and Stephen E. Miller (Fishin' Hole Guys); Colin Cunningham (New York Butcher); Jehshua Barnes (Scott's Wild Date); Scott Williamson, Deborah Theaker, and Rachael Harris (Winky's Party Guests); Fulvio Cecere (Airport Passerby); Linda Kash (Fay Berman); Larry Miller (Max Berman); Ed Begley, Jr. (Mark Shaffer, Hotel Manager); Cody Gregg (Zach Berman); Teryl Rothery (Philly AM Host); Tony Alcantar (Philly AM Chef); Camille Sullivan (Philly AM Assistant); Dave Cameron (Philly AM Host); Lynda Boyd, Madeleine Kipling, Merrilyn Gann, and Andrew Johnston (Cabot Party Guests); Malcolm Stewart (Malcolm); Jay-Lyn Green (Leslie's Nurse); Earlene Luke (Mayflower Hound Judge); Carmen Aquirre (Taft Hotel Maid); Harold Pybus (Mayflower Toy Judge); Hiro Kanagawa (Pet Shop Owner); Cleo A. Laxton (Mayflower Terrier Judge); Corrine Koslo (Mayflower Sporting Judge); Andrew Wheeler (Mayflower Ring Steward); Don Emslie (Mayflower Non-sporting Judge); Don S. Davis (Everett Bainbridge, Mayflower Best in Show Judge); Steven Porter (Bulge); Melanie Angel (American Bitch Photo Editor); Doane Gregory (Terry the Photographer).

LOS ANGELES TIMES, 9/27/00, Calendar/p. 1, Kenneth Turan

"Best in Show" has both bark and bite. The latest comic mockumentary to be masterminded by director Christopher Guest, its low-key but sharp and amusing sense of humor is a nice fit with the frenetic world of competitive dog shows.

"Best in Show" lists Guest and co-star Eugene Levy as co-writers, but this film, like Guest's previous "Waiting for Guffman" and the even-earlier "This Is Spinal Tap" (directed by Rob Reiner) are in reality tributes to the art of improvisation. Working within a general outline, cast members play out elaborate riffs that live and die by the amount of inspired byplay the actors can come up with.

Though "Best in Show" is a little more hit-or-miss than its predecessors, it benefits from the energy generated by an actual dog show competition and has enough raucous moments to carry you over the rough spots. And when Fred Willard as TV dog-show commentator Buck Laughlin gets into the act midway through the picture, "Best in Show" really catches fire.

The dog show world is a more obvious target, as well as one with broader popular appeal, than the amateur theatricals of "Guffman" or even the heavy-metal universe of "Tap," but the philosophy behind these films remains the same.

Once again, Guest and company focus on accentuating the eccentricities of their characters, in this case the owners of five dogs all intent on taking their animals all the way to the top. That would be winning best of show in Philadelphia's prestigious Mayflower Dog Show (modeled on the Westminster show in New York), the Mt. Olympus of canine events.

The happy and not so happy owners and their charges cut a wide swath through the human condition. They include:

Gerry and Cookie Fleck (SCTV alumni Levy and Catherine O'Hara) of Fern City, Fla., who so love their Norwich terrier, Winkie, they've written the song "God Loves a Terrier" in his honor. Gerry has two left feet, literally, while Cookie has so many panting ex-beaus that, in a comical running joke, she can't go anywhere without colliding with one of them.

Midwesterners Meg and Hamilton Swain (Parker Posey and Michael Hitchcock), whose dysfunctional marriage isn't helped by their dysfunctional Weimaraner Bernice. Though the Swains' brand-name lifestyle is a dead-on satire on consumerism, the couple's incessant bickering is one of the film's least successful stratagems.

Wealthy socialite Sherri Ann Cabot ("American Pie's" Jennifer Coolidge) and her much older husband, Leslie Ward Cabot (Patrick Cranshaw). We share a lot of interests, coos Sherri, "we love soup and the outdoors." Looking after their dog, two-time best-in-show standard poodle Rhapsody in White, is fanatical handler Christy Cummings (Jane Lynch), who doesn't quite share Sherri Ann's passion for makeup as an art form.

Hair salon owner Stefan Vanderhoof and his flamboyant partner Scott Donlan (John Michael Higgins) are equally committed to their Manhattan lifestyle and their Shih Tzu, Miss Agnes. Vanderhoof is played by longtime Guest collaborator Michael McKean, a long way from his David St. Hubbins character in "Spinal Tap."

Even further away from his role as "Tap's" hard-driving Nigel Tufnel is Guest himself, deeply unrecognizable as slow-talking Harlan Pepper of Pine Nut, N.C., owner of both "The Fishin' Hole" and a noble bloodhound named Hubert. It's an inspired, juicy part, aided by lines like one thrown at him by a pal as he heads off to Philadelphia: "If you get hungry, eat something."

Best in this particular show is not any of the owners but the irrepressibly buffoonish play-by-play man, the red-bow-tied Laughlin. Created by Willard, a veteran of both "Tap" and "Waiting for Guffman," Buck has a breezy bravado that consistently poleaxes his partner, the quite proper Trevor Beckwith (Jim Piddock). "How do they miniaturize dogs, anyway" is one of Buck's many irresistibly inane ripostes. When this man is on his game, "Best in Show" is being all it can be.

NEW YORK, 10/2/00, p. 84 Peter Rainer

Several years ago, I stopped off at a motel in Massachusetts and discovered that about half of the other guests had checked in for the night with their prize canines. Exotic, fluffy breeds were paraded behind the motel in preparation for a regional dog show the following day. None of the owners, or handlers, showed the slightest regard for anybody else, least of all the other entrants; they had the sniffy disdain that royalty exhibits for pretenders to the crown. The dogs, even after being enclosed in cages for the night, shared in this hauteur. They wouldn't even deign to bark, and they probably were better-fed than most of the motel staff.

The bizarreness of this episode came back to me as I watched *Best in Show*, which is about contestants vying for the top prize at a major dog show in Philadelphia. The film, which was directed by Christopher Guest—who also stars in it and was co-writer with Eugene Levy— captures the preening and the deep-down silliness (though not to its participants) of the world-within-a-world of dog contests. Guest actually staged his own show with his cast members mixed in with real handlers and judges, and the verisimilitude makes everything seem even funnier. We've entered a specialized universe that nonetheless seems instantly recognizable; the procession of egos on display during the Mayflower Dog Show is flabbergasting in the same way that, say, the Oscars or the Tonys are. The perfectly coiffed dogs trotted out for our delectation are almost comically beautiful, and so, in their loopy narcissism, are their owners. It's not just that many of them look like their dogs. Maneuvering their canines through their motions, they are their dogs.

Guest uses the same kind of improvisational, mock-documentary structure as in his last film, *Waiting For Guffman*, which was about the staging of a small-town musical and featured Guest as Off-Off Broadway director-in-exile Corky St. Clair, with his flamer's flamboyance and gumption. Guest plays Harlan Pepper in *Best in Show*, a fly-fishing-shop owner from Pine Nut, North Carolina, who has high hopes for his bloodhound, Hubert. He's absolutely convincing, right down to the slow, syrupy drawl and heavy-lidded peepers. There's a touch of the grandee about Harlan. Guest isn't just a revue-sketch comic; he's a real actor, perhaps a great one. Most comic actors start with a character and then fine-tune it to caricature. Guest reverses the process. He gives you someone you think you can size up at a glance, then proceeds to add layer upon layer. Guest allows his performers a great deal of latitude in this film, and many of them are pungent, peerless jokesters, but he gives himself over to his own role with a steel-willed commitment that's unlike anything I've ever seen in a comic actor of his generation. Guest's Harlan believes he exists on a spiritual plane with his pet. When he shows Hubert off before the judges, he lopes beside him in a contrapuntal prance. Hubert and Harlan have the same red hair and the same big-limbed grace and winsome dogginess; they might be different swatches of the same species.

Guest shot the film in super 16-mm., mostly with hand-held cameras, and the technique allows the performers to work up their characters right in front of us. Much more footage was shot than made it into the movie, but the cut-and-paste randomness is part of the fun; the tantrums and the silliness on display don't have that prepared-for feeling common to so many movie comedies. Lots of comics from the *SCTV* and *Saturday Night Live* generation have made it into the movies, but most of their films feel straitjacketed by stale dramatic ploys derived from Broadway and sitcoms. Guest is one of the few filmmakers who recognize that if you want to capture some of that original improvisational freshness, you need to carry over the impromptu spirit into the act of filmmaking itself.

Guest has a relish for eccentricity that seems more deeply British than American. He's not interested in normalcy. The cast of characters in *Best in Show* are a gaggle of silly gooses and dolts and dauphins, and Guest lavishes his sincerest sympathies on them. (The nuttier they are, the more affection he shows.) The yuppie lawyers Meg and Hamilton Swan (Parker Posey and Michael Hitchcock) fear their own relationship problems are turning their sleek, imperially mopey weimaraner, Beatrice, into a head case. Their almost psychotic indulgence of Beatrice is all of a piece with the way they shop by mail-order catalogue only; in both cases, the less contact with people, the better. Gerry and Cookie Fleck (Eugene Levy and Catherine O'Hara), with their Norwich terrier, Winky, are so mismatched that they seem perfectly harmonious together, like the fittings in a Cubist painting. A menswear salesman, Gerry is owlish and bucktoothed and always a beat behind the scattered sensuality of his wife, who keeps encountering old boyfriends on the trek from their home in Florida to Philadelphia. The guys from her checkered past have such disdain for Gerry that they practically drool on her in his presence. Cookie has chosen the sedate life, and yet she's piqued by their attentions; she enjoys being in heat again.

There's also professional handier Scott Donlan (John Michael Higgins) and his longtime partner, hair-salon owner Stefan Vanderhoof (Michael McKean), and their Shih Tzu, Miss Agnes. These two turn their Philly hotel room into a casbah of kimonos and silk, and treat the Mayflower procession as a fashion show. In the most touchingly deranged moment in the movie, Stefan sings a lullaby, "Barbara Allen," to Miss Agnes's partner, Tyrone (named after Tyrone Power), over the phone. I could have done with a bit less of the butch-bimbo combo (Jane Lynch and Jennifer Coolidge) and their poodle, but providing the Mayflower Dog Shows play-by-play is Fred Willard as broadcast announcer Buck Laughlin, and he steals the movie whenever his motormouth is running, which is most of the time. (In this elite company, stealing the movie is grand theft indeed.) Laughlin's Joe Garagiola-ish bonhomie can't disguise the fact that he doesn't begin to know what he's talking about, though he's blithely unfazed by his own cluelessness. In his own blockhead way, Laughlin gets right to the down-and-dirty point: The stream of idiocies he spouts are like the thoughts we might have while watching the dog show if we let our id run wild. (He has fun wrapping his mouth around *Shih Tzu.*)

Most contemporary comedies are so timorous when it comes to being politically incorrect, or else so in-your-face about it, that *Best in Show,* with its deadpan incivilities, is practically a comedy of manners by comparison. It indulges our worst suspicions about the way people behave, but it's also a tribute to how screw-loose we can be. The real prize specimens in this movie parade about on two legs, not four.

NEW YORK POST, 9/27/00, p. 52, Lou Lumenick

Christopher Guest's long-anticipated follow-up to "Waiting for Guffman" turns out to be well worth the four-year wait: I was laughing so hard, tears were streaming down my cheeks.

"Best in Show" does for dog shows what "Guffman" did for amateur theatrics, and that's enough to re-invigorate the overworked mockumentary genre that Guest pioneered as one of the stars and co-writer of the seminal rock spoof "This Is Spinal Tap."

As affectionate about its subject as it is devastating, "Best in Show" focuses on the fictional Mayflower Dog Show in Philadelphia, where a muttley, er, motley group of humans—largely played by veterans of the "Guffman" cast—have entered canines competing to be top dog.

There's a Norwich terrier named Winky whose owners are long-suffering menswear salesman Gerry Fleck (Eugene Levy) of Fern City, Fla., and his wife, Cookie (Catherine O'Hara, Levy's old "SCTV" cast-mate), a former waitress whose former romantic conquests they constantly encounter.

A Shih Tzu is being fielded by New York hair salon owner Stefan Vanderhoff (Michael McKean) and his longtime partner, flamboyant professional handler Scott Donlan (John Michael Higgins).

Meanwhile, there are sapphic sparks between handler Christy Cummings (Jane Lynch, who manages a dead-on parody of both Ellen and Anne) and the voluptuous Sherri Ann Cabot (Jennifer Coolidge spoofing Anna Nicole Smith), who, along with her doddering, oblivious husband, is entering a standard poodle. There is nothing but tension between yuppie lawyers Meg Swan (Parker Posey) and her husband Hamilton (Michael Hitchcock), who bicker constantly over care of their neurotic Weimaraner, who they've sent to a psychiatrist after he saw them having sex.

Guest himself plays Harlan Pepper, a seriously weird fly-fishing shop owner and aspiring ventriloquist from Pine Nut, N.C. with high hopes for his bloodhound.

While each of the cast has priceless moments, the blue-ribbon goes to Fred Willard as a dog-show commentator whose inane remarks ("In some countries these dogs are eaten") drive his colleague, brilliantly played by British actor Jim Piddock, to quiet desperation.

Most of "Best in Show" was improvised around a story line devised by Guest and Levy, and the ad-libs are as impressive as the mock dog show that Guest has staged, complete with two major backstage crises.

The Swans go to pieces when their dog loses his favorite toy; and Gerry, who literally has two left feet, is forced to show his animal in his ailing wife's place.

You don't have to know anything about purebreds or dog shows to appreciate that this is far and away the year's funniest movie. Guest and company should take a bow-wow.

NEWSDAY, 9/27/00, Part II/p. B2, John Anderson

Call it suicidal. Hollywood, already on very thin ice with most right-leaning factions of the American electorate and viewed with a jaundiced eye by the liberal left, now takes a bite out of the fiercest, most uncompromising special-interest group in the country:

Dog owners.

Pretty? No. Funny? Yes—with some reservations. "Best in Show," Christopher Guest's mock-doc, set in and around a big-stakes dog show (the fictional Mayflower Kennel Club, not to be confused with you-know-what), is a bit like shooting fish in a barrel, not to mix pet metaphors. Combining the doc style of "This Is Spinal Tap" (in which Guest played lead guitarist Nigel Tufnel) and the middle-American, middlebrow ilk of his brilliant "Waiting for Guffman," Guest lampoons the neurotic, obsessive, compulsive and megalomaniacal behavior of people who are funny just because the objects of their devotion are, if you'll pardon the expression, dogs.

And that's not quite right either: They're really funny because the dogs serve as such a distraction from their wildly dysfunctional selves. To that end, Guest and co-writer Eugene Levy have set up a rather predictable array of targets for their pet-and-sex potshots—for instance, the yuppie-lawyer couple (Parker Posey and Michael Hitchcock) with the high-strung weimaraner, whose craziness is just a mask for the fact that their marriage is DOA.

Likewise, the others are funny because of who they are—the gay owners of the pampered shih tzu (Michael McKean and John Michael Higgins); the rubes from Florida (Levy and Catherine O'Hara) with the scruffy Norwich terrier, and the professional dog handler, Christy Cummings (Jane Lynch), who is having a torrid affair with her dog's owner, the dopey-yet-buxom Sherri Ann (Jennifer Coolidge).

The sexual orientation of his characters, repressed or otherwise, is of paramount comic interest to Guest, whose own role—Harlan Pepper, fishing-store and bloodhound owner out of Pine Nut, N.C.—seems like a classic southern closet case. It's a hackneyed device, but the actors' attitudes make it work well enough.

The only thing we have to say about dog owners is they're not as smart as cat owners; what Guest has to say about them would curl a Chihuahua's hair. So it's perhaps no surprise that the funniest person in "Best in Show" isn't an owner at all, but Fred Willard as Buck Laughlin, the clueless color commentator who wouldn't know a Bouvier des Flandres from Jackie Kennedy. Anyone who's ever listened to Joe Garagiola do the Westminster Kennel Club broadcast will know where Willard's inspiration comes from—the impersonation is hilariously dead on, as is Jim Piddock's English-accented dog expert, Trevor Beckwith, Buck's bemused on-air partner.

Balancing out the piano-wire personalities of Guest's dog owners, Buck makes the movie, a sports broadcaster who is not as smart as his subjects.

NEWSWEEK, 10/2/00, p. 72, David Ansen

This is "Spinal Tap" and "Waiting for Guffman"—the pitch-perfect pinnacles of the "mockumentary" form—have inspired one too many bad imitations like "Drop Dead Gorgeous." But just when you thought the genre had lost its sparkle, along comes Christopher Guest to remind us how good it can be. Guest, who played in "Spinal Tap" and directed and starred in "Guffman" gathers his best improvisational-team players for "Best in Show," a sharp-eyed satire of the arcane world of dog shows. While it may not be as flat-out hilarious as its predecessors, it's as smart, quiveringly alert and fleet of foot as a purebred pointer on the scent of fresh game.

The scenario is simple: we follow the owners and handlers of five dogs (a Weimaraner, Norwich terrier, bloodhound, Shih Tsu and standard poodle) headed for the prestigious Mayflower Dog Show in Philadelphia. The cast, which includes Parker Posey, co-writer Eugene Levy (as a man with two left feet), Catherine O'Hara, John Michael Higgins and Guest as a Southern bloodhound owner and aspiring ventriloquist, is uniformly wonderful. But best in show may have to go to Fred Willard as the dog show's boisterously inappropriate announcer Buck Laughlin. Guest seems to know just how far he can stretch reality without losing the crucial texture of verisimilitude. This is a comedy even cat lovers might adore.

SIGHT AND SOUND, 3/01, p. 39, Andy Richards

US, the present. A disparate group of dog owners gather for the Mayflower Dog Show in Philadelphia. Yuppies Meg and Hamilton Swan are concerned their Weimaraner Beatrice is traumatised from seeing them having sex. Gerry and Cookie Fleck own Winky, a Norwich terrier. Much to Gerry's discomfort, Cookie is recognised by ex-lovers everywhere they go. Couple Stefan and Scott are submitting Miss Agnes, one of their shih-tzus. Fishing-shop owner, backwoods hunter and amateur ventriloquist Harlan Pepper is the proud owner of a bloodhound. Favourite to win is two-time champion poodle Rhapsody in White, owned by Sherri Ann Ward Cabot and her elderly millionaire husband. Sherri Ann has hired lesbian dog trainer Christy Cummings to ensure a third win for Rhapsody.

On the day of the show, the Swans realise that they have forgotten Beatrice's bumblebee toy. They argue violently. The show's commentary is conducted by ignorant Buck Laughlin and his British counterpart, Trevor Beckwith. Beatrice misbehaves during the competition and is dismissed by the judges. Winky is declared the overall winner. The Flecks become local celebrities and record a CD tribute to their dog. Sherri Ann and Christy start a magazine, *American Bitch*, for lesbian dog owners. The Swans get a new dog, less "negative" than Beatrice, who enjoys watching them have sex.

Christopher Guest's latest film confirms him to be one of the sharpest of contemporary film satirists. His loose, heavily improvised brand of ensemble comedy, which features precisely drawn characters within a realistically observed milieu, is a rare treat in an era of increasingly tired mainstream comedy. After the rock histrionics of Rob Reiner's 1983 *This Is Spinal Tap*, co-written by and starring Guest, and the community-theatre antics of *Waiting for Guffman* (1996), Guest and his collaborators skewer the world of the pure-breed dog shows with this, their latest mockumentary.

As with the earlier films, the satire is aimed at a community afflicted with a disproportionate sense of self-importance. Unlike, say, the recent *Drop Dead Gorgeous*, which took swipes at the easy target of small-town beauty pageants, *Best in Show* treads a fine line between mocking its earnest competitors and extending sympathy towards them. There is no film-maker character (like *Spinal Tap*'s Marty DiBergi) to guide us through this strange, obsessive world, but one of Guest's most astute narrative devices is Fred Willard's character Buck Laughlin, a novice dog-show commentator whose crass observations on proceedings—he wonders aloud if a bribe would influence the judges' decisions and speculates that the bloodhound's chances might improve if he were to wear a deerstalker—compels his mortified British colleague to explain the different competition classes and the judges' criteria, providing the viewer with a thorough education in the process. As with *Spinal Tap*, the wealth and authenticity of the film's incidental detail are impressive; by avoiding cartoonish excess, Guest's film permits its likeable characters to engage our sympathies.

The pathos derives, of course, from the fact that the dogs function as surrogate children for characters who, for the most part, are lonely or isolated. The film's married couples are all, to some degree, estranged from each other: Gerry's perplexed expressions as man after man whom he encounters travelling from Florida to Philadelphia recalls having sex with his wife Cookie are pricelessly painful; the siliconed Sherri Ann says of her wealthy geriatric husband: "We could not talk or talk forever and still find things to not talk about." The Swans, meanwhile, have acquired their Weimaraner as an accessory in their designer-aspirational lifestyle, and turn on each other with crazed vehemence when the dog becomes "disturbed" after witnessing them essaying the 'Congress of the Cow' pose from the *Kama Sutra*. Given that Guest's character Harlan Pepper is a backwoods loner, the only happy couple are the film loving gay shih-tzu owners Stefan and Scott (the former played by *Spinal Tap*'s Michael McKean), whose dogs are named after Agnes Moorehead and Tyrone Power. The film calendar photos they pose for in the coda are a cherishable comic highlight in a beautifully turned out film of real pedigree.

VILLAGE VOICE, 10/10/00, p. 138, Mark Holcomb

In 1996's snarky *Waiting for Guffman* and now in *Best in Show*, actor-director-screenwriter Christopher Guest takes a scattershot approach to satire, putting so many freakishly absurd characters on the screen that you scarcely notice how little regard he has for them. This time, the targets of his faux-doc ridicule are pixilated dog-show rivals who converge on a national competition in Philadelphia. There's a pair of suburban status slaves (Parker Posey and Michael Hitchcock) with a neurotic weimaraner; a trés tawdry, shih tzu-pampering gay couple (Michael McKean and John Michael Higgins); a low-rent, mismatched slut 'n' nerd duo with a terrier obsession (Catherine O'Hara and cowriter Eugene Levy, in cuckolded Elmer Fudd mode); and a lonely backwoods bloodhound owner with a yen for ventriloquism (Guest). The plot is trivial and meandering, and the only humor mined from the dog show itself comes courtesy of Fred Willard's gleefully moronic commentator. For Guest, the self-absorbed folly of the human mutts matters most. He and Levy do exhibit more affection for this ensemble than *Guffman's*, but *Best in Show* succeeds only insofar as you're willing to laugh at a bunch of sad freaks.

Also reviewed in:
CHICAGO TRIBUNE, 10/13/00, Friday/p. I, Michael Wilmington
NEW YORK TIMES, 9/27/00, p. E1, Stephen Holden
VARIETY, 9/25-10/1/00, p. 63, Eddie Cockrell
WASHINGTON POST, 10/13/00, p. C5, Rita Kempley
WASHINGTON POST, 10/13/00, Weekend/p. 43, Desson Howe

BETTER LIVING

A Cowboy Booking International release of a Goldheart Pictures production. *Producer:* Ron Kastner, Lemore Syvan, and Max Mayer. *Director:* Max Mayer. *Screenplay:* Max Mayer and George F. Walker. *Director of Photography:* Kurt Lennig. *Editor:* Steve Silkenson. *Music:* John M. Davis. *Sound:* Skeeter Jarvis and (music) Yvonne Yedibalian. *Sound Editor:* David Paterson. *Casting:* Sheila Jaffe and Georgianne Walken. *Production Designer:* Mark Ricker. *Art Director:* Shawn Carroll. *Set Dresser:* Heather Gray, Michael N. Horan, and Ed Ricker. *Costumes:* Laura Cunningham. *Make-up:* Kyra Panchenko. *Stunt Coordinator:* Manny Siverio. *Running time:* 95 minutes. *MPAA Rating:* Not Rated.

CAST: Olympia Dukakis (Nora); Roy Scheider (Tom); Edward Herrmann (Jack); Deborah Hedwall (Elizabeth); Catherine Corpeny (Maryann); Wendy Hoopes (Gail); James Villemaire (Junior); Phyllis Somerville (Nellie); Scott Cohen (Larry); Jamie Gonzalez (Pock); Dan

Moran (Dan);   Brian Tarantina (Danny);   Myra Lucretia Taylor (Waitress);   Jessy Terrero and
Gary Azaulka (Bikers).

CHRISTIAN SCIENCE MONITOR, 8/4/00, p. 15, David Sterrit

Better Living reminds us that impressive names in the cast don't guarantee pleasing results on
the screen.

Olympia Dukakis plays the *de facto* head of an eccentric household that's been more troubled
than usual since her nasty policeman husband (Roy Scheider) abruptly vanished. The troubles
don't end when he abruptly reappears, seizes control of the family, and drags them into a
cockamamie plan to improve their fortunes. Other key characters include the clans three grown
daughters and a clergyman (Edward Herrmann) with unorthodox ideas.

Dukakis and Scheider both have long strings of commendable credits, but neither is brilliant
enough to surmount the artificial dialogue, arbitrary plot twists, and wan humor of this limp
comedy-drama. They're too talented to be doing time in this forgettable offering.

NEW YORK POST, 8/4/00, p. 52, Lou Lumenick

Director Max Mayer and his cast are appearing in person at this weekend's showings of this
excruciating vanity production at the Screening Room—so watch out for rotten tomatoes.

"Better Living" takes place in an unidentified suburb, where dear demented dad (Roy Scheider),
a retired NYPD detective, returns after a 15-year-absence.

He rallies dotty Mom (Olympia Dukakis) and his three almost equally disturbed grown
daughters (Deborah Hedwall, Catherine Corpeny, Wendy Hoopes) into excavating their back yard
to build a survival shelter.

This stagy adaptation of George Walker's play is not only boring and incomprehensible, it also
boasts scenery-chewing performances by the normally reliable Scheider, Dukakis and Edward
Herrmann as mom's brother, an alcoholic priest.

NEWSDAY, 8/4/00, Part II/p. B10, Jan Stuart

What's all the ruckus? Could it be Mom down in the cellar, blasting a big hole into the yard
with a jackhammer? Or Dad, playing fisticuffs with daughter Elizabeth on the kitchen floor?
Perhaps daughter Maryann is up in the bedroom, having noisy sex with boyfriend Junior? Again.
Or is it Uncle Jack in the front yard, advising his niece Gail to seriously consider suicide? (Uncle
Jack, not incidentally, is a priest).

Welcome to "Better Living," where the house is alive with the sound of wacky family doings.
Adapted from a dark stage comedy by George F. Walker, "Better Living" extorts laughs with an
air of desperate whimsy as it charts the sea change that occurs in a suburban New York family
when its once-homicidal patriarch (Roy Scheider) returns after a long absence.

Olympia Dukakis flirts with self-caricature as dotty mom Nora, holding seances and declaring
with pride how "all of my daughters have been encouraged to copulate for the good of our
general health." As Uncle Jack, Edward Hermann mopes and sighs like an aging Charlie Brown
who has been drummed into the clergy at gunpoint. The only ray of hope in a house fit to explode
with overacting is the excellent Deborah Hedwall, a vinegary delight as the sole family member
with her feet planted firmly on the ground.

Despite the mediation of cameras and lighting, "Better Living" makes you feel as if you're
being held hostage in a purgatory of every bad wacky family play you've ever seen. It could well
be The Last American Wacky Family Play but for the fact that dramatist George F. Walker is
from Canada. Known to be a sharp political observer, he is ill-served by director-screenwriter
Max Mayer, who slides from cutesy to shrill in short shrift. By the final scene, in which Dukakis'
Nora ponders the giant trench she has dug in her yard, we are as battle-fatigued as her family.
For the good of our general health, we encourage her daughters to toss the script into the hole,
throw a flag over it and play "Taps."

VILLAGE VOICE, 8/8/00, p. 144, Jessica Winter

Is *Better Living* the most pointlessly vile movie of the year? It's hard to imagine what foul wind could topple this suburban charnel house of poisonous dichotomies. At once man-hating and misogynist, obstreperously offensive and pitifully idiotic, Max Mayer's parable of evil patriarchs (namely Roy Scheider, looking heavily sedated) and the cattle-brained women who love them (among others, Olympia Dukakis, raiding the same pharmaceutical cabinet) is a no-budget vomit launch that can raise your ire like usually only a fascistic Hollywood blockbuster can.

Also reviewed in:
NEW YORK TIMES, 8/4/00, p. E16, Elvis Mitchell
VARIETY, 11/16-22/98, p. 37, Oliver Jones

BETTER LIVNG THROUGH CIRCUITRY

A Seventh Art Releasing release of a Cleopatra Pictures production. *Executive Producer:* Brian Perera. *Producer:* Brian McNelis and Stuart Swezey. *Director:* Jon Reiss. *Screenplay:* Jon Reiss, Stuart Swezey, and Brian McNelis. *Director of Photography:* Jon Reiss, Steve Janas, Byron Shah, Michael Bartowski, Lee Abbot, Joe Plonsky, John Preibe, and Stacey Tisdall. *Editor:* Eric Zimmerman. *Music:* Cary Berger. *Sound Editor:* Ben Wilkins. *Running time:* 92 minutes. *MPAA Rating:* Not Rated.

WITH: The Crystal Method; Roni Size and Reprazent; DJ Spooky; Electric Skychurch; Jason Bentley; Wolfgang Flür of Kraftwerk; Superstar DJ Keoki; Meat Beat Manifesto; Carl Cox; Frankie Bones; Moby; Genesis P-Orridge/Psychic TV Scanner; Lords of Acid; Medicine Drum; Juno Reactor; Atomic Babies; Loop Guru; Heather Heart; System 7; Philip Blaine; Mike Szabo; Simply Jeff.

LOS ANGELES TIMES, 5/26/00, Calendar/p. 6, Eric Harrison

With all their talk of positive energy, peaceful coexistence and drugs, you'd think the blissed-out dervishes in the documentary "Better Living Through Circuitry" had just drifted in from the '60s. But the throbbing, wordless sound they're whirling to isn't the Beatles. It isn't even Crosby, Stills & Nash.

Youth cultures come and go, and it probably is a given that each generation thinks their's is the only one that matters. So you'll excuse this baby boomer his air of condescension as he circles the phenomenon known as raving. What, after all, could be so special about dancing till you drop?

Apparently plenty judging by all the folks who find their way to those underground tribal gatherings. Some of the people director Jon Reiss interviews in "Better Living" drive up to 10 hours to attend them, trekking out to the countryside or to spooky abandoned warehouses. And they do it week in and week out.

What motivates them? What reward at journey's end could possibly make it all worth while? The movie seems to have been designed to answer such questions for viewers not yet familiar with the rave scene. Though they doubtless will be entertained, the movie probably plays better to audiences who don't need to ask questions to begin with.

This is one of a small wave of new films—"Human Traffic" and the upcoming "Groove" are others—that focus on this influential subculture that often is viewed by outsiders with suspicion. Raves, after all, to the consternation of partisans, usually attract mainstream attention only in connection with drugs.

"Better Living" takes us deeper, possibly deeper than you'll want to go unless you're already in love with electronic dance music and other elements of the rave phenomenon.

Filled with interviews with people whose lives intersect with rave culture—deejays, graphic artists, promoters and folks who just like to dance—the movie also is pretty much wall-to-wall music and dancing.

A movie about raves could never fully capture the sense of exhilaration that attends these events, filled as they are with movement, spectacle and the frisson of human contact. So unless you attend it with a reservoir of easily accessible memories to supply the missing thrills, "Better Living," at one hour and 25 minutes, might get a tad wearying.

Until then, though, what Reiss shows us is intriguing—yes, and thrilling. This is true in part because of the energy of the raves themselves and the behind-the-scenes look at how the music is created and how it continues to evolve along with the technology.

The movie is a good introduction to the work of artists like Moby, Crystal Method, Electric Skychurch and DJ Spooky as well as a couple of dozen other musicians, many of whom also are interviewed.

Although there is no formal connection between this documentary and "Modulations," a 1998 film about electronic music, they may be viewed as companion pieces. In much the same way that that movie traced the music's development, this one lays out the whys and hows of raves, at which people seem to get high by dancing.

The movie doesn't try to hide that quite a few revelers reach elevated states with the aid of pharmaceuticals, but it also makes it clear that there is more to raves than drugs.

One reason why the film is so intriguing is that some of the interview subjects Reiss and his producers have chosen are eloquent, thoughtful adherents of the subculture.

When one deejay discusses the excitement of mixing music and sampling "live" before an audience, he sounds less like a pop performer than a French lit. major discussing the application of existentialist principles to daily life. Later he says he learned to love music because of the record collection he inherited from his father, who died when he was 3.

"To me, sampling is like ancestor worship," he says, and though he's discussing his own life, the statement also seems to encapsulate a philosophical rationale for styles of music and performance—perhaps even of being—that to many of us probably seemed like mere thievery.

Several of those interviewed speak candidly about the use of drugs during raves, particularly ecstasy. At one point Reiss interviews paramedics who are on hand at a rave in case of emergencies.

Much electronic music comes from recording and manipulating everyday sounds. When one artist interviewed speaks of "the malleability of reality," we see how the talk of drug-induced altered states of consciousness connects in a fundamental way with the music itself.

Such talk provides interesting fodder for thought, but Reiss interviews enough people who speak as if by rote of how they're drawn to raves because of the "family atmosphere," good times and easy acceptance of diversity that the audience is never able to forget for long that the events are really nothing but big parties.

As musician Moby says about raves at one point, the best thing about them is "the naive sense of celebration." Plenty of that is on display in the movie.

NEW YORK POST, 5/26/00, p. 50, Hannah Brown

It's lots of fun to go to a rave—an all-night dance party with pounding electronic music, mellow twentysomethings and moderate drug use.

At least that's what participants, musicians, promoters and various talking heads have to say in the documentary "Better Living Through Circuitry," which opens today.

However, it's not much fun to watch people go to raves. And it's even less fun to listen to people talk about how much fun it is to go to raves.

Still, "Circuitry," which focuses on the rave phenomenon in the United States, is a well-crafted film.

Director Jon Reiss skillfully shows the contradictory sides of the rave culture by interviewing an articulate group of enthusiasts.

On the one hand, the raves create an overwhelming sense of abandon. "It's about creating this oblivion, where nothing outside this room matters," says Joel Jordan, a graphic designer.

But the other side of the story is that the ravers, who all seem to be yuppies or aspiring yuppies, are rather tame in spite of all their gyrating—at least according to their portrayal in this film.

They carry cartoon-character backpacks, gulp designer water and seem oddly asexual.

The most interesting side of the raves is the rejection of the traditional club scene, where bouncers turn away people who aren't dressed right.

No one dresses up for raves and everyone gets in.

And anyone with a computer and the right software can create the electronic music popular at raves, an ethos known as "DIY"—"Do-It-Yourself."

One aspect of rave culture that's downplayed is the ravers' frequent consumption of the drug Ecstasy, as well as other drugs.

The talking heads are not especially illuminating. Genesis P'Orridge is particularly ponderous, saying things like, "[Rave culture] is a potential breeding ground for an alternative way of being."

Still, rave-goers will enjoy seeing their scene portrayed so lovingly on film, especially with energetic performances by some rave favorites, including Moby.

Others will just find "Circuitry" makes them feel old and/or out of it.

NEWSWEEK, 6/5/00, p. 69, David Ansen

Every generation needs its ecstatic rituals, and today's kids have raves, chemically friendly overnight bliss-outs presided over by electronic shamans with names like DJ Spooky or Scanner or Moby. Manning the control boards like captains of a psychedelic ship, they guide the dancers on a throbbing techno tide, lifting the crowd's communal spirit up, up and away on a sweat-drenched transcendental joyride. This underground techno-rave culture is the subject of two current movies, the documentary "Better Living Through Circuitry" and the indie feature "Groove'—a sure sign that the phenomenon has not only reached sea level, but probably peaked.

Though the musical terminology—jungle, acid house, trance—may be new, the idealistic rhetoric we hear in interview after interview in director Jon Reiss's documentary will ring a bell for any veteran of a 60s be-in. "The age of Aquarius, it's here," says DJ Keoki, but without the optimism of the "Hair" years: he's seen the deep alienation that drives some kids to seek oblivion in drugs. These idealistic electronic rituals belong to an era of diminished expectations; the political grandiosity of the '60s (and its accompanying sense of privilege) has been replaced with a more circumscribed notion of bliss—nirvana as a night on the town. Like the musical notion of sampling—which the eloquent DJ Spooky compares to "ancestor worship"—the ravers are more mix-and-match revisionists than revolutionaries.

Fascinating but repetitious, "Better Living Through Circuitry" does a good job describing the scene. Writer-director Greg Harrison's Sundance hit "Groove," which follows its clutter of characters through a rave in an abandoned San Francisco warehouse, comes closer to capturing what it feels like. Lively, likable and refreshingly unsensationalistic about the drugs and sex that come with the territory, this techno-propelled mash note to the rave spirit sticks to the surface, but it burrows just far enough inside its young, confused, pleasure-seeking characters to make us care how they greet the dawn. Like any good musical, it makes you want to leap to your feet and dance.

VILLAGE VOICE, 5/30/00, p. 132, Simon Reynolds

By far the most exciting part of the recent U.K. club-culture movie *Human Traffic* is the opening documentary-footage montage of illegal street parties, joyous protests against the British government's anti-rave legislation. Jon Reiss's documentary about the American rave scene, *Better Living Through Circuitry: A Digital Odyssey Into the Electronic Dance Underground*, similarly thrills with its tableaux of overexcited crowds doing the swirly Mandelbrot-limbed dance known as "liquid." But when it comes to making you understand the culture rather than just feel the vibe, *Better Living* is less successful, featuring platitudes about "positive energy" from a middlebrow selection of DJs, producers, and bands (Atomic Babies? Electric Skychurch?!). Still, its dance floor orientation makes it a useful complement to Iara Lee's *Modulations*, which focused on home-oriented electronica and lofty auteurs rather than having-it crowds.

Highlights here include an amusing appearance by ex-Kraftwerk percussionist Wolfgang Flur and producer BT discoursing fascinatingly on "photic and auditory driving" (tribal techniques of inducing an alpha-wave trance through flicker patterns, unwittingly reinvented by ravers with strobes and oscillating keyboard vamps). Rave DJ stalwarts Frankie Bones and Keoki are charming, and a couple of paramedics outside a rave confess that they've started getting into the music despite themselves. On the minus side, Genesis P. Orridge repeats the self-serving myth that Psychic TV catalyzed the U.K.'s acid-house revolution and drops his well-worn rave-as-nouveau-tribalism insights like they're mind bombs.

Better Living's cursory segment on drugs is something of a whitewash (possibly out of a forgivable desire not to give the Enemy any ammunition, what with the major crackdown on raves from Toronto to Florida). The film comes through in its home stretch with interesting stuff on rave's utopian spirituality and "implicit politics"-kids who "make for themselves some of the things that are missing from their lives," according to one talking head. By the end, I was even feeling a little teary-eyed.

Also reviewed in:
NEW YORK TIMES, 5/26/00, p. E12, Stephen Holden
VARIETY, 5/17-23/99, p. 58, Charles Lyons

BEYOND THE MAT

A Lions Gate Films release in association with Imagine Entertainment. *Producer:* Brian Grazer, Ron Howard, Michael Rosenberg, Barry Bloom, and Barry W. Blaustein. *Director:* Barry W. Blaustein. *Screenplay:* Barry W. Blaustein. *Director of Photography:* Michael Grady. *Editor:* Jeff Werner. *Music:* Nathan Barr. *Music Editor:* Brian Richards. *Sound:* Shawn Holden and Peter Verrando. *Running time:* 102 minutes. *MPAA Rating:* R.

WITH: Vince McMahon; Darren Drozdov; Roland Alexander; Tony Jones; Mike Modest; Terry Funk; Vicki Funk; Stacey Funk; Brandee Funk; Paul Heyman; Jake Roberts; Brandy Smith; Chyna; Matt Hyson; Coco Bware; Jesse Ventura; New Jack; Dennis Stamp; Mick Foley; Collette Foley; Dewey Foley; Noelle Foley; Steve Austin, Barry W. Blaustein, Mark Calloway, Duane Johnson, Jerry Lawler, Michael Paul Levesque, Shane McMahon, and Jim Ross.

CHRISTIAN SCIENCE MONITOR, 3/3/00, p. 15, David Sterritt

Hollywood is so hooked on happy endings and feel-good stories that other types of movies, brought to the screen by independent and international filmmakers, often do a better job of providing serious looks at the darker sides of life. Two new documentaries provide sober views of material that's frequently unpleasant to watch but has much to reveal about disquieting aspects of our world.

The more contemporary of the two films is "Beyond the Mat," a rambunctious study of professional wrestling. Mature moviegoers might normally steer away from this so-called sport, but there's no denying that its shenanigans have gathered a large and varied audience in recent years. This qualifies it as a legitimate subject for serious commentators who want to understand its inner workings and illuminate them for the rest of us.

That's what director Barry Blaustein does in his remarkable study. He begins the movie by admitting his longtime fascination with the knockabout antics of the World Wrestling Federation, the outfit that controls American pro wrestling. He then delivers a behind-the-scenes examination that focuses to some extent on the sport's well-known fakery and foolery, but puts most of its emphasis on the real-life personalities of the men who bash one another around in the ring.

They turn out to be an interesting group, full of surprising character traits—such as the eagerness of Mick Foley, who wrestles under the name Mankind, to be known as the sport's most polite and courteous figure. They're also challenged by a complex array of personal problems that their unconventional occupation often intensifies, despite the fame and fortune its most successful members accumulate.

Blaustein is a veteran screenwriter whose credits include "The Nutty Professor" with Eddie Murphy, and his experience at building comic and dramatic moods is fully evident in this riveting nonfiction film. See it if you want an eye-opening scoop on one of today's biggest pop-culture attractions—but stay far, far away unless you can handle the copious amounts of blood (some of it phony) and sometimes agonizing psychological problems (all of them real) that its participants face on what seems like a daily basis.

"Homo Sapiens 1900" turns to recent history for its disturbing subject: the rise and fall of the eugenics movement, a pseudoscientific effort to "improve" the human race by making procreation a matter of political policy rather than personal choice.

The film traces this intermittently successful crusade through several countries including Germany, where the Third Reich used it to cultivate physical beauty; the Soviet Union, where communists hoped to breed intellectual titans; and the United States, where it influenced various health-improvement and family-values campaigns.

The thoughtful narration clarifies the two main branches of the movement—one taking a "negative" approach that discouraged "inferior" births, the other a "positive" approach that encouraged "superior" people to pass along their genes—while painting a vivid portrait of its insidious influence on its adherents.

Directed by Peter Cohen, whose 1989 documentary, "The Architecture of Doom," was a memorable study of Nazi aesthetics, "Homo Sapiens 1900" avoids the temptation to liven up its topic with fast-paced editing and fancy visual effects. Instead, it moves at a leisurely pace, giving us plenty of time to study its images and ideas, and to draw our own conclusions about them. Anyone interested in the troubled history of the 20th century should seek it out.

LOS ANGELES TIMES, 10/22/99, Calendar/p. 9, Kevin Thomas

Barry W. Blaustein's "Beyond the Mat" connects the antics of professional wrestlers with their lives out of the ring with such compassion, humor and perception that the result is utterly captivating. By the time this unique and touching documentary is over, you may be surprised how involved you have become with individuals who are full of contradictions and surprises.

With brisk humor, Blaustein—a Hollywood comedy screenwriter who made his mark with "Saturday Night Live" and whose off-screen narration is warm and candid—introduces us to the carnival world of wrestling, acquainting us with the glitzy aspirations of wrestlers on the way up and wrestlers on the way down.

He emphasizes spectacle over sport and doesn't dwell on the way bouts may be "choreographed" but makes clear that, regardless, it's a brutal, dangerous profession. He lets promoters, the wrestlers themselves and all others involved speak for themselves and has the patience to stick with people until they've moved past the point of mere self-promotion.

Deftly woven into Blaustein's overview of the world of wrestling are portraits of three men who have captured his interest. There's Terry Funk, a renowned Texas-based champ who at 53 has been wrestling for 32 years. He's still a rugged guy, but arthritis is wrecking his knees.

However, Funk, who insists wrestling is fun, is having a hard time letting go despite his bad knees. His devoted wife, Vicki, is resigned to telling herself that he'll know when to retire, but he could wind up making more farewell appearances than Sarah Bernhardt. That goes for Jake the Snake Roberts, too. A wrestler now on the skids and admitting to crack cocaine addiction, Jake is a ruggedly handsome middle-aged man who's grown paunchy and balding. The effects of a horrendous childhood, of being an absent husband and father, and of indulging in a fast life on the road have caught up with him big time, leaving him lonely yet wary.

Funk has frequently teamed with Mick Foley, a.k.a. Mankind, a bearded, beefy giant of a man 20 years Funk's junior. Like Funk, Foley is a devoted family man, with a beautiful wife and adorable young children; it's as if he and Funk work out so much aggression in the ring that they make the most tender of husbands and fathers. Foley is highly articulate and reflective, a man of such clear intelligence it becomes all the more difficult to accept that he specializes in the most extreme forms of wrestling.

Foley swears he's going to quit in a year or two, but you can see he will have trouble letting go—he also admits he hasn't been able to figure out what else he might do with his life. As Blaustein bids farewell to these men and others, he comes up with a concluding remark that couldn't be improved upon: "They're just like you and me—except they're really different."

NEW YORK, 3/27/00, p. 102, Peter Rainer

The professional wrestlers in Barry Blaustein's documentary *Beyond the Mat* are a race of men who speak louder than the rest of us. It's as if they all carry around in their larynxes their own built-in amplification system. Even though the film is billed as a look into the wrestlers' lives outside the ring, it's often difficult to separate out the real person from the act. The best of the camera subjects, such as aging vet Terry Funk, or Jake the Snake Roberts, have a carny charisma that works on both sides of the ropes. Blaustein, who was a supervising producer for *Saturday Night Live* and has co-written a bunch of Eddie Murphy movies, is drawn not only to the wrestling circuit's circus-like nuttiness but also to its sob-story undercurrents. Watching the once-stellar Jake the Snake down on his luck in some fourth-rate venue, we're prompted to recall *Requiem for a Heavyweight*, and when he recounts his sordid family past, or is shown failing to connect with his estranged daughter, he's the living embodiment of every country-western lament you've ever listened to. The wrestlers are cannier than Blaustein probably gives them credit for; they seem to be offering up their backstage lives to him in ways that mimic the soppiest of melodramas, and he falls for it. Mick "Mankind" Foley, for example, who wears a Hannibal Lecter-ish mask in the ring and seems to lack a central nervous system, troops out his adoring wife and two giggly children for the cameras at every opportunity. The most disturbing moment in the film comes when his family is shown at ringside, his two children cringing, as he gets smashed up by The Rock. Some of the blood may be fake, but the pain on his kids' faces is entirely real, and even though Foley himself later cringes at the sight of their terror as he watches their reactions on a video playback, the question is left unanswered: Why did he allow them ringside in the first place? In moments like these, *Beyond the Mat* is beyond the pale.

NEW YORK POST, 3/17/00, p. 49, Lou Lumenick

"Politics is way more cutthroat than wrestling is," observes Minnesota Gov. Jesse Ventura in "Beyond the Mat"—a documentary that body slams his former occupation.

Writer-director Barry Blaustein, a self-described wrestling fan, spent five years putting together a fascinating collection of matches and interviews.

While he includes brief upbeat segments—including World Wrestling Foundation President Vince McMahon's comparing the development of new wrestling characters to Muppets—Blaustein is mostly drawn to the dark side of this entertainment form, which he half-heartedly argues is also a sport.

"Three years ago you were teaching third grade, Blaustein, who wrote the remake of "The Nutty Professor," cheerfully observes to one bloodstained young hopeful. "Now you're mutilating yourself every night."

Even WWF superstar Mick Foley, who wrestles under the name "Mankind," is shown risking serious injuries in his bouts, much to the horror of his family.

"Maybe it would be better if Dad did something else," one of his young daughters says.

Two decades in the ring have caught up with aging star Terry Funk, who is forced to hang it up at the age of 53 because of severe arthritis—but who pushes himself into the ring for one last bout.

Funk is in much better shape than Jake "The Snake" Roberts, a once-major name who's been reduced to wrestling in makeshift venues for little or no money.

Blaustein catches up with him at a bowling alley in North Platte, Neb., where Roberts talks candidly about the drugs he took to maintain a grueling schedule—and the camera captures his wary reunion with his estranged daughter.

When McMahon describes wrestling as "all about giving the audience what they want," he could be talking about this film, which contains several sequences that seem to be staged by Blaustein, who doesn't hesitate to arrange a WWF tryout for a young wrestler.

"Beyond the Mat," may not be strictly objective—and it's far from the no-holds-barred exposé implied in the ads. But it's the most entertaining look at its world since "Pumping Iron" took on body-building.

NEWSDAY, 3/17/00, Part II/p. B13, Jan Stuart

There are essentially two audiences for "Beyond the Mat," a new documentary that burrows into the strange world of championship wrestling. There are the folks who will be happy when the guys stop bashing each other and start talking, and the folks who will be happy when the guys stop talking and start bashing each other.

What may surprise both audiences is that the talk director Barry W. Blaustein has cajoled from some of wrestling's biggest stars is frequently engaging and occasionally quite stirring. Blaustein chooses subjects you feel you can cozy up to, not what one expects from latter-day Alley Oops whose day jobs amounts to gladiator labor, gussied up with torchlight processions, "Carmina Burana" and costumes that suggest a particularly bad acid trip.

Blaustein is a self-described sucker for the sport's grandiose pretensions, which he succumbs to when he opines "Extreme Championship Wrestling is the Ellis Island of wrestling, where old wrestlers go to be reborn and young wrestlers go to be discovered." (Say what?)

A screenwriter best known for Eddie Murphy's "The Nutty Professor," Blaustein injects himself as a tour guide into the offices and motel rooms of wrestling's top cats. The most abrasive are the backroom movers and shakers. At the top is Vince McMahon, the garrulous head of the World Wrestling Federation, seen here cheering on a new recruit whose unique talent is vomiting on cue. For all his wealth and power, McMahon is easily as wormy as Roland Alexander, an exploitive wrestling-school entrepreneur with a hawk-eye trained on tuition fees.

By contrast, the wrestlers garner the filmmaker's sympathy, no more so than the ones who have missed the gravy train altogether or reached the pinnacle only to fritter it away on women and drugs. Blaustein, who grew up in Westbury, is not the most probing of journalists: We meet a wrestler who is a former United Nations scholar and another who can quote "Henry IV, Part III" without fully understanding why former seekers of truth are driven to a lifetime of put-on. And relatively little screen time is devoted to chronicling the sport's notorious artifice, the rehearsals and backstage huddles that go into setting up a routine.

The link between wrestling, violence and the American family emerges as one of the film's unstated themes. The most compelling character is Jake (The Snake) Roberts, a crack user who has survived a chilling family legacy of rape and murder only to raise a daughter he does not see for years at a time. The camera captures a remarkable reunion between father and daughter that could have been scripted for a Lifetime movie of the week, except that it is sadly authentic.

Paternal disconnect of another order characterizes Mick Foley as he subjects his wife and two small children to witnessing a match in which his head is beaten to a bloody pulp. A lovable lug from East Setauket who clearly adores his kids, Foley is obviously prompted by some sincere notion of fatherly pride and family cohesion. While Blaustein goes as far as to point up his own problems with Foley's actions, he leaves the armchair analysis to the viewer, which sometimes makes "Beyond the Mat" feel as superficial as the sport it is tracking.

SIGHT AND SOUND, 9/00, p. 38, Fiona Morrow

A longterm fan of the sport, Barry W. Blaustein sets off to make a documentary about wrestling. He meets Vince McMahon, head of the World Wrestling Federation (WWF), who's about to start a marketing campaign for a new wrestler, Darren Drozdov. He visits Roland Alexander, an amateur promoter, and meets his most promising competitors, Tony Jones and Mike Modest, before arranging a try-out at the WWF for them.

Blaustein meets veteran wrestler Terry Funk. He accompanies Terry to the first pay-per-view event of the Extreme Championship Wrestling (ECW). The organisation is run from the basement of founder Paul Heyman and prides itself on its violent approach. Funk wrestles; his family look on in tears as he becomes bloodied. Blaustein meets the wrestler, Mick Foley, and we see home-movie footage of him as a teenager throwing himself from the roof of the family home. Blaustein then meets Jake Roberts, a famous wrestler whose career has been destroyed by his various addictions. Terry Funk retires. When shown footage of his wife and children upset at his violent bout with Rocky Maivia, Foley questions his actions. Blaustein meets New Jack, a wrestler with convictions for four justifiable homicides, who would like to become an actor. Blaustein arranges for him to meet with a casting agent. We learn that Funk is fighting again, Roberts has been taken to court for non-payment of child support and neither Jones or Modest were taken on by the WWF We also learn that Drozdov was paralysed during his debut match.

Better known as the scriptwriter of the Eddie Murphy vehicle *The Nutty Professor*, Barry W Blaustein makes his directorial debut with this documentary on wrestling, a sport which has entranced him since childhood. Luckily for him, he makes contact with a number of complex, intriguing men, happy to talk about their lives on camera. Lucky, because Blaustein hasn't an idea how to structure a narrative, seemingly believing that documentary film-making means presenting events in the order in which they were filmed. Consequently, we are left with a thematic jumble as Blaustein drives between various states visiting people apparently at random. He also directly intervenes in the lives of those he is filming: he sets up a try-out for two amateur wrestlers with the World Wrestling Federation, arranges a casting session for a wrestler with ambitions to act and shows Mike Foley the footage he has shot of the wrestler's family deeply distressed while watching him fight.

But despite breaking some of the unwritten (and admittedly malleable) laws of documentary here, Blaustein's film is less a provocative engagement with established forms of non-fiction film as a home movie, albeit one that's been bankrolled by Universal Studios. You're left with the impression Blaustein wanted to make personal connections with the wrestlers as much as he wanted to direct a documentary. His scene with Foley owes less to the sequence in the Maysles brothers' record of the Altamont pop festival *Gimme Shelter,* (1970) where Mick Jagger was filmed watching the footage of the fatal stabbing that occurred during the concert, than it does to Blaustein's need to be seen to care.

Blaustein was clearly surprised at what he found and struggles to adapt to the reality of physical injury, addiction and exploitation in the world of professional wrestling. At least he has the good sense to keep his camera running, for amid the structural mayhem there is something moving, challenging and surprising about these men's lives. During the scenes where Jake Roberts meets his estranged daughter, then talks about his abusive upbringing and the lonely, soulless life of a showman in decline, we find ourselves in the heart of something cruel and compelling.

Unfortunately Blaustein isn't an experienced enough film-maker to make much of such material. A more insightful approach to the subject can be found in Kim Longinotto's forthcoming television documentary *Gaea Girls,* a film about women wrestlers in Japan.

VILLAGE VOICE, 3/21/00, p. 144, Michael Atkinson

Just as fraught with phallic angst, if a good deal less conscious of it, [The reference is to *Treasure Island*; see Atkinson's review.], Barry Blaustein's *Beyond the Mat* focuses a fan's unquestioning eye on the wide, wide world of pro wrestling, from Vince McMahon's WWF empire (which has its own costume designers and scriptwriters, big surprise) to the dregs of wannabe training camps and amateur nights at the local gym. An ex-*SNL* writer, Blaustein suggests wrestling's appeal—as a kind of primal spectacle closer to parades and pageants than any accepted form of sport—without wondering at all why he finds it compelling. In fact, after he demonstrates that wrestling and its attendant damage is real albeit rehearsed, Blaustein prefers to focus only on the not-so-private lives involved: the autumnal trials of fading star Terry Funk, the fascinating menopausal crucifixions of star-turned-crackhead Jake the Snake Roberts, and the traumas endured by Mick "Mankind" Foley's family as they watch him get beat to a bloody pulp, over and over, again.

Also reviewed in:
CHICAGO TRIBUNE, 3/17/00, Friday/p. H, John Petrakis
NEW YORK TIMES, 3/17/0, p. E14, Elvin Mitchell
VARIETY , 10/25-31/99, p. 38, Robert Koehler
WASHINGTON POST, 3/17/00, p. C1, Rita Kempley
WASHINGTON POST, 3/17/00, Weekend/p. 47, Desson Howe

BIG KAHUNA, THE

A Lions Gate Films release of a Franchise Pictures presentation of a Trigger Street production. *Producer:* Elie Samaha, Kevin Spacey, and Andrew Stevens. *Director:* John Swanbeck. *Screenplay (Based on his play "Hospitality Suite")* by: Roger Rueff. *Director of Photography:* Anastas Michos. *Editor:* Peggy Davis. *Music:* Christopher Young. *Production Designer:* Kalina Ivanov. *Running time:* 91 minutes. *MPAA Rating:* R.

CAST: Kevin Spacey (Larry); Danny DeVito (Phil); Peter Facinelli (Bob).

LOS ANGELES TIMES, 4/28/00, Calendar/p. 23, Kevin Thomas

For Kevin Spacey, "The Big Kahuna" is far from an ideal commercial follow-up to "American Beauty" in reaffirming his new star status. It's a small picture, its stage roots all too evident, and the role Spacey plays is superficially so similar to the one that won him an Oscar it invites comparisons between the two films unfavorable to "The Big Kahuna."

But as an actor and co-producer, it's understandable that Spacey and theater director John Swanbeck, in his film debut, would be eager to bring Roger Rueff's prizewinning 1992 play "Hospitality Suite" to the screen. If you're prepared to accept an inherent staginess that gradually fades as the film progresses, you can become caught up in a drama of extraordinary power and insight with dazzling performances from not only Spacey but also Danny DeVito (who may well be at his best ever) and from newcomer Peter Facinelli.

"The Big Kahuna" was shot over 16 days in New York (plus some establishing shots filmed in Wichita). It's unlikely to be anything near a big hit but clearly was so comparatively inexpensive to make that it doesn't have to set box-office records to have been well worth making.

"The Big Kahuna" takes place almost entirely in a 16th-floor hospitality suite in a Wichita hotel. It has been rented by DeVito's Phil, a 52-year-old marketing rep for a manufacturer of industrial lubricants. The occasion is the annual convention of the Midwest Manufacturers' Assn., and Phil and his soon-to-arrive fellow rep and colleague of 12 years, Larry (Spacey), are out to catch "the big kahuna," the president of a manufacturing company, that could result in the biggest contract of their careers.

Phil has summoned a young man from his employer's research division to supply technical information just in case it's needed, but as far as Phil is initially concerned, Bob (Facinelli) is little more than requisite window dressing.

Larry arrives in full bombast, criticizing everything in high dudgeon. In his vociferous view the suite's too small and drab and the hors d'oeuvres woefully inadequate. He gives the stunned Bob, who's been with the company only six months, the third degree and then some. Gradually, we realize that Larry is working through a feeling of desperation and also wants to make sure that Bob will do absolutely nothing to louse up the deal.

Beneath a crust of corrosive cynicism, Larry is actually a dedicated professional, a decent man of principle who has never cheated on his wife of 15 years. He's a man with whom Phil would trust with his life. At the moment, however, Phil, who is going through a divorce, doesn't think much of his life. He speaks of making changes and has developed a craving for spirituality—he's thinking a lot about God.

Phil and especially Larry are none too thrilled with Bob. He's bright and personable but religious in a pious, narrow way. No small amount of humor develops, however, when a series of clever plot developments force Larry and Phil to realize that they are going to have to depend upon Bob to deliver the account.

When Rueff attended a manufacturer's convention (in Wichita yet) as a chemical engineer at Amoco's research center in Illinois, he was inspired to write this play, not based on any actual salesman or himself, but rather a situation that lent itself to exploring issues of honesty, integrity, loyalty and spirituality in regard to the relationship between one's work and one's life. The film's key exchange occurs when Phil, a man of wisdom and character, tries to open up the mind and heart of Bob and free him of his self-righteous, judgmental ways without casting any aspersion on his—or anyone else's—religion.

DeVito has moments of mesmerizing calm as Phil, which allows him to draw upon resources that prove as formidable in supplying seriousness as in his more familiar comic mode. Spacey is just as savagely dyspeptic as he was in "American Beauty," but here Larry's torrent of scabrously cynical remarks proves to be surprisingly at odds with the admirable man lurking just below the surface. Larry affords Spacey terrific range and virtuosity, but ultimately the essential gravity of DeVito's resigned Phil anchors the film. Facinelli brings to Bob a fine mix of diffidence and pride, topped with just enough ambiguity to keep us wondering just how sincere this priggish fellow really is. Could Bob actually be a slick operator beyond Larry and Phil's imagining?

Production designer Kalina Ivanov has got that hospitality suite just right. It's done in shades of safe, dull browns. It's not truly small yet is not quite spacious. It has the look of having been decorated by a conservative professional but is totally impersonal. It's entirely acceptable but is exactly the environment calculated to depress Phil and Larry, who could use a real lift to their spirits.

NEW YORK, 5/8/00, p. 72, Peter Rainer

Kevin Spacey, Danny DeVito, and Peter Facinelli play industrial-lubricant salesmen holed up in a dingy hospitality suite in Wichita in *The Big Kahuna*, directed by John Swanbeck and based on a play by Roger Rueff. In the beginning, their jabber is about life, but soon the subject is Life. I realize we live in a free-market economy, but maybe it's time for American playwrights to give the salesman metaphor a rest.

NEW YORK POST, 4/28/00, p. 54, Lou Lumenick

Anything from Kevin Spacey immediately after "American Beauty" was bound to disappoint—so he was probably smart to opt for "The Big Kahuna," a low-stakes adaptation of a three-man stage play.

Spacey (who produced this $1.8 million movie, shot in 16 days) may be the Big Kahuna in Hollywood these days, but he's not the title character here—a briefly glimpsed, Godot-like CEO whose arrival is nervously awaited by three industrial-lubricant salesmen in their Wichita, Kan., hotel suite.

In what's less a movie than a Mamet and Rabe-tinged acting exercise (based on a play by Roger Rueff, which, understandably, never got any closer to Broadway than Pasadena, Calif.), the trio pass the time by contemplating the meaning of life.

Falling into the same trap as theater-turned-movie directors Matthew Warchus ("Simpatico") and Julie Taymor ("Titus"), first-timer John Swanbeck has chosen second-rate material and encouraged his cast to let 'er rip, capturing the interaction with an overabundance of close-ups that saps their vitality.

That said, Spacey is such an exciting actor he's probably worth watching even if he's reading the telephone book. He has the least challenging role here, a sarcastic, bullying cynic whose exterior hides deep compassion—a part he could probably play in his sleep.

Danny DeVito, cast against type and giving a beautifully nuanced performance, has never been better. He's deeply moving as Spacey's burned-out longtime colleague, who yearns for meaning in life after his wife leaves him.

It doesn't hurt that he has most of the best lines and his monologue at the end is an exciting moment in a film that could use more of them.

Newcomer Peter Facinelli more than holds his own as the third salesman, a pious newlywed who's scandalized by the salty older salesmen—but is gradually revealed to be just as big a hustler, and a hypocrite to boot.

"The Big Kahuna" is a flawed labor of love that's definitely worth a look.

NEWSDAY, 4/28/00, Part II/p. B3, John Anderson

It's been said that if you want to appreciate the full measure of your cosmic insignificance, travel. And, as per "The Big Kahuna," if you're a salesman for a manufacturer of industrial lubricants, travel to Wichita.

That's where three conventioneers find themselves in John Swanbeck's debut feature, "The Big Kahuna," based on Roger Rueff's play "Hospitality Suite," and poised to roll out as one of those men-being-men movies—the type in which morals, manners and possibly hygiene suffer terrible indignities. But while "The Big Kahuna" may be a minor movie—based on a play, it feels like a play—it's also a film of fairly potent ideas. Trust. Wisdom. Duty. None of them dealt with casually. And it has Kevin Spacey in a role that seems to be custom fit.

In a hotel room catered with cheap eats and a small ocean of booze, Larry (Spacey), Phil (Danny DeVito) and their young initiate Bob (Peter Facinelli) await an onslaught of would-be customers, hoping to land the big fish, a faceless manufacturer named Dick Fuller, aka "the kahuna grande"—the man with the money, the power and the promise of financial redemption for both the lubricants company and its longtime sales grunts, Larry and Phil. The Kahuna—like Godot, Lefty, Guffman or whomever desperate characters are ever waiting for—assumes in his absence a mythic significance, sparking a dark night of the soul for three wary men.

Not too dark, though. Spacey's Larry is an entertaining cynic who's audaciously blunt, harbors a deep loyalty to the all-but-exhausted Phil and can't resist poking at Bob's thick cushion of sanctimonious Christianity; not entirely unlike Lester Burnham, who won Spacey his Best Actor Oscar for "American Beauty." Larry is considerably more complex, his satiric spiel rooted in pain and his near-loathing of Bob—who is loathsome—being the byproduct of middle-age regret.

Spacey, who consistently massages the script for laughs and totally dominates the screen, might have let Larry simply run amok. But outside of that slo-mo intro at the beginning of the film (pure star fodder), he gives a deceptively controlled performance, providing Rueff's dialogue its full breadth and intent.

DeVito, conversely, explores the silence, playing counterpoint to Spacey's mania as a man examining his life and work and finding them wanting. Bob? Bob, the pious evangelist and enthusiastic newlywed, thinks it's appropriate to discuss with potential customers his personal relationship with Christ. "It's very important to me that they know about Jesus," he says, and Larry's demolition of Bob's logic, his very angry and reasoned explanation of why it's Bob who's the phony, is the highlight of Rueff's very effective script.

It's certainly no revelation, but "The Big Kahuna" can easily be interpreted as the story of one character at three stages of his life, a kind of Willie Loman triptych with Bob at one end, Phil at the other and Larry—scornful of one and fearing the other—occupying the middle ground. It's also a line graph of masculinity, the three actors representing both physically and spiritually the mutually exclusive rise and fall of naivete and character, energy and wisdom, passion and knowledge. Not a lot of room for optimism in "The Big Kahuna." So thank God it's a funny film.

VILLAGE VOICE, 5/2/00, p. 130, Brian Parks

In director John Swanabeck's tedious feature, three guys from Lodestr Industries rent a hospitality suite at a major manufactureres' convention. Their goal is to land a fat account with an important but elusive buyer—the titular big kahuna. The movie's goal, though, is to explore what it means to be a man, through that jalopy of a metaphor, the salesman. Kevin Spacey is slick-talking Larry, Danny DeVito his world-weary colleague Phil, and Peter Facinelli their initiate Bob, a young researcher being introduced to the rituals of the business conference. As the men argue strategy in their drab hotel room, they begin to peel back layers of their personalities, offering up middlebrow analyses of their sorta aching Midwestern souls.

Echoing both *American Buffalo* and *The Iceman Cometh*, *The Big Kahuna* joins that vast Rotary Club of art about American business, though as an extremely junior member. The predictable homoerotic overtones abound: three men in a hotel room professing love for each other, all in search of a guy named Dick Fuller ("The last thing I need to do is grease another asshole for the lubricant industry," says Spacey at one point.) Spacey spends the movie performing his usual snake act, though DeVito manages a few touching moments of regret. Facinelli is so baby-faced he looks like he was pulled from the womb and hosed down only minutes before shooting.

Kahuna deserves credit for trying to examine male identity without resorting to firearms, but its good intentions get suffocated by its visual and emotional claustrophobia. "How does a person attain character?" young Bob asks. Perhaps by choosing better scripts.

Also reviewed in:
CHICAGO TRIBUNE, 5/12/00, Friday/p. A, Michael Wilmington
NEW REPUBLIC, 5/1/00, p. 24, Stanley Kauffmann
NEW YORK TIMES, 4/28/00, p. E14, Elvis Mitchell
VARIETY, 9/27-10/3/99, p. 40, Emanuel Levy
WASHINGTON POST, 5/12/00, p. C1, Stephen Hunter
WASHINGTON POST, 5/12/00, Weekend/p. 51, Desson Howe

BIG MOMMA'S HOUSE

A Twentieth Century Fox and Regency Enterprises release of a David D. Friendly/Runteldat Entertainment production. *Executive Producer:* Martin Lawrence, Jeffrey Kwatinetz, Rodney Liber, and Arnon Milchan. *Producer:* David T. Friendly and Michael Green. *Director:* Raja Gosnell. *Screenplay:* Darryl Quarles and Don Rhymer. *Story:* Darryl Quarles. *Director of Photography:* Michael D. O'Shea. *Editor:* Bruce Green and Kent Beyda. *Music:* Richard Gibbs. *Sound:* Thomas Causey. *Sound Editor:* Bob Grieve and Jan Del Puch. *Casting:* Nancy Klopper. *Production Designer:* Craig Stearns. *Art Director:* Randy Moore. *Set Designer:* Mariko Braswell and Charisse Cardenas. *Set Decorator:* Ellen Totleben. *Set Dresser:* Josh Warner, Neil Bowman, William D. DeBiasio, Jeff Halvorsen, Peter Joseph Lakoff, and Robert "Patrick" McGee. *Costumes:* Francine Jamison-Tanchuck. *Special Make-up Effects:* Greg Cannom. *Make-up:* Beverly Jo Pryor. *Make-up (Martin Lawrence):* Debra Denson. *Stunt Coordinator:* Ernie Orsatti. *Running time:* 97 minutes. *MPAA Rating:* PG-13.

CAST: Martin Lawrence (Malcolm Turner); Nia Long (Sherry); Paul Giamatti (John); Jascha Washington (Trent); Terrence Howard (Lester); Anthony Anderson (Nolan); Ella Mitchell (Big Momma); Carl Wright (Ben); Phyllis Applegate (Sadie); Starletta DuPois (Miss Patterson); Nicole Prescott (Lena); Octavia L. Spencer (Twila); Tichina Arnold (Ritha); Cedric "The Entertainwr" (Reverend); Philip Tan (Kang); Edwin Hodge and Aldis Hodge (Basketball Teens); Brian Palermo (Cazwell); Brian Paul Stuart (Prison Doctor); Sarah Zinsser (Receptionist); Sean Thibodeau (Jud); Ramsey Luke (FBI Agent); Rosi Rosi, Minnie O. Burton, and Rita (Peggy) Fagan-Lewis (Nolan's Volunteers); John Eddins (Police Officer); Louis Archie Shackles (Choir #1); Tameka Holmes (Choir #2); Ellis Hall (Organist); Jesse Mae Holmes (Miss Other Patterson); Sean Lampkin (Cab Driver); Tony McEwing (Anchorperson).

LOS ANGELES TIMES, 6/2/00, Calendar/p. 4, Robin Rauzi

Let us all now give praise to the individual who designed the poster for "Big Momma's House," currently on prominent display on buses throughout Los Angeles County. He or she has done a tremendous service to filmgoers—neatly summarizing all we need to know about this new comedy.

The image is this: a corpulent female figure in a red flower-print dress, holding an FBI identification card picturing Martin Lawrence.

So there you go. If you think that Martin Lawrence dressed up as a hefty grandmother is funny, be gone with you. Off to the cineplex. Be assured that Lawrence, in disguise, will behave quite un-grandmotherly—and expect humor no more sophisticated than that. For the rest of you, you'd be better off just taking a ride on the bus.

In the movie, there is some sort of situation that demands that master-of-disguise FBI agent Malcolm Turner (Lawrence) dress up as Big Momma—besides the fact that without this gag there'd be no movie. It has something to do with staking out Sherry (Nia Long) to catch her ex-boyfriend, an escaped murderous bank robber, Lester (Terrence Howard).

That said, forget about Lester. The filmmakers did. (Howard gets about 2½ minutes of screen time skulking around in the dark.)

Meanwhile, the faux Big Momma is busy with episodic segments: playing basketball, taking a self-defense class, delivering a baby. Oh, yes, and getting the hots for—er, uh, investigating—Sherry.

"Big Momma's House" might seem at least novel if we hadn't seen these makeup tricks before, notably in "The Nutty Professor." Lawrence has spent too much of his career already being compared to Eddie Murphy, and donning this fat suit isn't going to help.

Lawrence's abilities as a physical comedian break through the layers of silicone—his dancing Big Momma can really bust a move—but not much else does. The whole project works so hard at creating funny situations that Lawrence gets no chance to be funny as himself. His handful of scenes as Malcolm are oddly tame—no doubt to secure that PG-13 rating and the teen audience it ensures. Who else besides teens are going to laugh hysterically at a septuagenarian using the toilet?

Long handles her scenes with charm—but everything is so secondary to the Gag that there's no getting invested in her, or any, character. Likewise for John (Paul Giamatti), the partner with no personality.

Director Raja Gosnell, whose previous credits include "Home Alone 3" and "Never Been Kissed," walks this crooked line between sweet-natured characters and bitterly gross humor. A former editor, he's made odd choices in putting together his own film. Scenes just trail off. And after two full scenes, 10 minutes into the film, more opening credits start rolling, as if the movie wants to start over.

But it's too late. The script by Darryl Quarles and Don Rhymer is off and stumbling over unfunny one-liners. In the first scene, Malcolm's mask disguising him as an Asian man gets pulled off his face. "What?" he says. "You never heard of Seoul, Korea?" Soul, Seoul, get it? They try to spread some emotional icing over this rotten confection, mostly having to do with Sherry's inability to trust people after her last boyfriend turned out to be a sociopathic criminal.

So Malcolm/Big Momma spends the awkward scenes between random antics trying to find out something—we're never sure exactly what—from Sherry. The explanation goes something like: "Malcolm, you gotta get her to confess everything before we catch Lester, or she's going down with him." That may be the most hilarious part of all.

Unless, that is, if you think Martin Lawrence is just funny in a dress.

NEW YORK POST, 6/2/00, p. 47, Jonathan Foreman

"Big Momma's House" is clearly meant to be that winning combination of "Beverly Hills Cop" and "The Nutty Professor" that will make Martin Lawrence the successor to Eddie Murphy.

Unfortunately, it's not only inferior to all Murphy's movies (even "Coming to America"), it's a lot less funny than most of Lawrence's own film work. And not just "Bad Boys" and "Nothing to Lose"; "Blue Streak" had many, many more laughs than this.

Lawrence plays FBI agent Malcolm Turner, who's not just streetwise and tough, but a master of disguise.

When Sherry (Nia Long), an escaped convict's old flame and apparent partner in crime, suddenly flees L.A. for her grandmother's house in Georgia, Malcolm and his partner, John (Paul Giamatti), are sent to stake out the house, in the hope they will catch the convict.

The two agents arrive before the young woman. And when they see the 300-pound matriarch, known as "Big Momma" (Ella Mitchell), unexpectedly leaving town, Malcolm decides to take her place.

The disguise is just good enough to fool Sherry, who duly turns up with her preteen son, Trent (Jascha Washington), but as Malcolm begins to fall for the attractive young mother—who may be innocent, after all—it gets harder and harder to keep the charade going.

It's all very predictable stuff, and director Raja Gosnell (who made the superior "Never Been Kissed") lets everything take a little too long, so you notice the gags that don't work and the lack of chemistry between Long and Lawrence.

On the other hand, along with some disgusting toilet jokes, there are some genuinely funny set pieces: Lawrence as Big Momma playing basketball, Lawrence as Big Momma taking a self-defense class from a bullying instructor.

But whenever Lawrence is out of costume and trying to play a romantic lead, the movie sags.

The script, by Darryl Quarles and Don Rhymer, gives neither Paul Giamatti, so delightful in "Man on the Moon" and Howard Stern's "Private Parts," nor Long ("The Best Man," "Boiler Room" and "Boyz N the Hood") much opportunity to shine.

It also revels in stereotypes about Southern black life: from lard-laden cooking to comically depicted "testifying" in church.

Anthony Anderson, who was one of the better things in "Romeo Must Die," also contributes needed energy to this film, as Nolan, a security guard desperate to be a cop.

NEWSDAY, 6/2/00, Part II/p. B3, John Anderson

Big Momma is fat. Not phat, FAT. How fat is she? When she sits around the house (everybody!) she sits around the house. When she puts on a belt, she has to use a boomerang. Her clothes come in three sizes: Large, Extra-Large and oh, my God, it's coming toward us! Each of her thighs has its own congressman.

None of these hoary old gags gets repeated in "Big Momma's House," because they would have actually freshened the air over what is a real recycling plant of a movie. Starring Martin Lawrence as an FBI agent impersonating a generously proportioned southern grandma just writing that down makes it seem all the more ridiculous), the film is a perhaps inadvertent but certainly undernourished overture to "Nutty Professor II: The Klumps, " which will star Lawrence's "Life" partner and comic superior, Eddie Murphy, trussed up in his own rubber implants and upholstery. One suspects that Fox got this one out quickly, before unpleasant comparisons could be made.

FBI agent and master-of-disguise Malcolm Turner (Lawrence), pursuing an escaped killer (Terrence Howard), tracks the killer's old girlfriend Sherry (Nia Long) to her "Big Momma's" house in Georgia. When Grandma abruptly leaves town, it opens the door for Malcolm and his partner, John (Paul Giamatti), to do the logical thing: Dress Malcolm up like grandma and get Sherry to spill the beans.

It's a good thing Sherry hasn't seen Big Momma in a while, because she doesn't look well: Her face is kind of leprous; her breasts keep moving around like the 49ers' backfield. What's really overstuffed, though, is the script, an amalgam of "Mrs. Doubtfire," "Tootsie" (the temporarily transvestite Malcolm falling for the oblivious Sherry) and, most larcenously, "Kindergarten Cop," although the ending is no way near as ultra-violent as that Schwartza-Wagnerian masterpiece.

Lawrence's career has lived by the sitcom ("Martin") and seems poised to die by the sitcom: "Big Momma's House" is little but a sitcom, exploring to the nth degree every possible embarrassing or ridiculous situation one can think of involving a young man dressed up as an old woman. excuse me, an old fat woman. The rest of the film is just limp. Although the lovely Nia Long does as good a job as anyone could standing around looking radiant, that's about all she's required to do. Sherry's son Trent (Jascha Washington) suffers from Screenwriter Attention Deficit Disorder by Proxy. The usually serviceable Giamatti is more or less hamstrung by the standard-issue shlemiel role he's given, playing the hapless foil to Malcolm's reckless inanity.

Given that the film's director, Raja Gosnell ("Home Alone 3," "Never Been Kissed"), is a longtime former film editor, it seems strange that the movie should suffer from a lack of both fluid or forward motion. But the more irritating aspect of "Big Momma's House" is the feeling of inevitability attached to each and every assembly-line joke (we're not thinking Lucy Ricardo), as well as the Shermanesque tour of cultural stereotypes we get of the South: Big Momma cooks with too much Crisco; Big Momma goes to self-defense class and beats up the instructor; Big Momma goes to church and revs up the gospel choir (Cedric the Entertainer, as the reverend, is a short breath of fresh air); Big Momma tells off the gentleman caller, himself the embodiment of the oversexed and apparently over-Viagra'd southern black male. Big Momma does a Pearl Harbor on the toilet bowl. Wait: That really is Big Momma (Ella Mitchell). Will the real Big Momma please stand up? On second thought, never mind.

SIGHT AND SOUND, 8/00, p. 39, Ken Hollings

USA, the present. Violent bank robber Lester breaks out of jail to look for his former girlfriend Sherry, who is suspected of being his accomplice in a $2 million bank robbery. FBI agent Malcolm Turner and his partner keep Sherry's grandmother's house in a small southern town under surveillance, suspecting she might flee there and lead them to the missing money.

When the grandmother, known as Big Momma, is unexpectedly called away, Turner decides to use his talent for disguise to impersonate the old woman. Sherry turns up with her young son; having been out of touch with Momma for some years, she is taken in by Turner's disguise. He eventually wins her confidence and finds out that she was not involved in the theft and wants nothing more to do with Lester. Lester shows up at a surprise party thrown in Momma's honour. The real Momma appears too. Exposed as an FBI agent, Turner arrests Lester. Having fallen in love with Sherry, Turner wins her forgiveness for his deception.

Considering past revelations of one-time FBI director J. Edgar Hoover's secret passion for cross dressing and his hounding of civil-rights campaigner Martin Luther King, the prospect of a black male FBI agent, played by Martin Lawrence, dragging himself up as a southern momma has distinct comic, if not satiric potential. Clogged up by tired routines and befuddled scripting, *Big Momma's House* comes across instead as an updated version of the 1890s cross-dressing farce *Charley's Aunt* rewritten by comedian and blaxploitation star Rudy Ray Moore, but lacking the subtle sophistication of either. There is little in Martin Lawrence' simpering parody of Momma's behaviour to suggest that he, or the character he's playing, has given any thought to his new identity. Other character details are similarly sketchy: miss a fleeting reference to Armani and you might never know that FBI agent Turner is supposed to be a hip urbanite unused to living in the Deep South. The evocation of southern culture is just as flat: a gospel choir in the local church, for instance, signal their fervour by singing 'Oh Happy Day' not just once but twice.

A comedy that revolves around deception must concern itself with the characters involved, their respective blind spots and prejudices if it is to be plausibly entertaining. But here we learn next to nothing about them and so care even less. The female roles are particularly undeveloped: Sherry, Momma's granddaughter, is never allowed to be more than a bundle of curves for Turner to roll his eyes at; a scene that features a woman's pain during labour, meanwhile, is played for the broadest of laughs. The attentions of the randy old stud pursuing Turner in the mistaken belief that he's a woman are quickly forgotten about once the FBI agent reveals his true identity. In a blithe endorsement of Joe E. Brown's observation in *Some Like It Hot* (1959) that "nobody's perfect", *Big Momma's House* doesn't trouble itself with Turner's erstwhile admirer's response to the discovery that he's allowed himself to become aroused by a man in drag.

Ella Mitchell, however, brings a wild, dirty energy to her portrayal of the 'real' Big Momma. Bad-tempered, with a bludgeoning tongue and a sulphurous bowel disorder, she dominates the small community of old ladies grouped around her. It's hard to figure out why the film isn't centred on Momma and her friends rather than Lawrence's tiresome mugging. But the pets, peeves and gossiping of these women are unfortunately never allowed to intrude on Lawrence's one-joke performance; you're left wondering what a director like John Waters, who exploited the titanic comic talents of Jean Hill in *Desperate Living* and *Polyester* with real verve, would have made of such material.

VILLAGE VOICE, 6/13/00, p. 158, Jessica Winter

The first half of Martin Lawrence's foray into prosthetic calisthenics, *Big Momma's House,* travels in nasty, scatological, *Martin*-sitcom territory: a big fat lady with biblical diarrhea, said big fat lady naked in supercloseup, and a birth scene involving dirty salad tongs and Crisco that ups the ante on *Big Daddy*'s pioneering studies in the comic possibilities of child endangerment. (We should prepare ourselves, perhaps, for *Big Brother's Fist* and *Big Auntie's Rancid Ham.*) But *Big Momma's House* ends up waddling its way toward gentler, mistier climes, stopping just shy of *Doubtfire* country. It doesn't run out of smelly steam so much as downshift and become a different movie.

Lawrence plays an FBI agent and master of disguises who goes to small-town Georgia to stake out the home of the titular massive, muumuu'd matron (Ella Mitchell) in anticipation of a visit from her granddaughter (hardest-working woman in show business Nia Long), who may or may not be a bank robber's accomplice. When Big Momma leaves town, Lawrence assumes her identity just in time for Long's arrival. Cue the increasingly heartwarming set pieces: Lawrence as Big Momma kicks ass at self-defense class; Lawrence as Big Momma helps Long's son (Jascha Washington) beat some bullies on the basketball court; Lawrence as Lawrence romances Little Momma with a fishing trip and tender attentions paid to her boy. The screenwriters, thankfully, leave out the usual scene where the double-dealer has to be two different people in two places at once, but countless other comic possibilities are left hanging pendulous, Long has little to do but look sweet and quizzical, and the star-executive producer seems bored and distracted under and out of his makeup. Still, Lawrence is enough of a gentleman to let Ella Mitchell, the movie's biological Momma, completely upstage him in her handful of scenes. She's an avalanche force of nature, groceries, and good sportsmanship.

Also reviewed in:
NEW YORK TIMES, 6/2/00, p. E16, Elvis Mitchell
VARIETY, 6/5-11/00, p. 17, Todd McCarthy
WASHINGTON POST, 6/2/00, p. C1, Stephen Hunter
WASHINGTON POST, 6/2/00, Weekend/p. 54, Desson Howe

BIG TEASE, THE

A Warner Bros. release of a Crawford P. Inc. production in association with I Should Coco Films. *Executive Producer:* Sacha Gervasi, Craig Ferguson, and Kevin Allen. *Producer:* Philip Rose. *Director:* Kevin Allen. *Screenplay:* Sacha Gervasi and Craig Ferguson. *Director of Photography:* Seamus McGarvey. *Editor:* Chris Peppe. *Music:* Mark Thomas. *Sound:* Kenneth G. McLaughlin and (music) Paul Golding and James Collins. *Sound Editor:* Stephen Hunter Flick. *Casting:* Kris Nicolau. *Production Designer:* Joseph Hodges. *Art Director:* Mark A. Thomson. *Set Decorator:* Cloudia. *Set Dresser:* Mike Malone. *Special Effects:* Ken Estes. *Costumes:* Julie Miller-Bennett. *Make-up:* Roxy D'Alonzo. *Running time:* 88 minutes. *MPAA Rating:* R.

CAST: Craig Ferguson (Crawford Mackenzie);   Chris Langham (Martin Samuels, BBC Interviewer);   David Rasche (Stig Ludwiggssen);   Frances Fisher (Candy Harper);   Mary McCormack (Monique Geingold);   Donal Logue (Eamonn);   Isabella Aitken (Mrs. Beasie Mackenzie);   Kevin Allen (Gareth Trundle);   Angela McCluskey (Senga Magoogan);   Francine York (Elegant Woman);   David Hasselhoff, Drew Carey, Cathy Lee Crosby, Bruce Jenner, Veronica Webb, and Jose Eber (Themselves);   Nina Siemaszko (Betty Fuego);   Melissa Rosenberg (Dianne Abbott);   Norm Compton (Cop Driver); Loren Lazerine (Bear Suit Person); Robert Fisher (Bunny Suit Person); Steven Porter (Chicken Suit Person);   Evie Peck (Reindeer Suit Person);   Michael Paul Chan (Clarence);   Robert Sherman (Constance);   Charles Napier (Senator Warren Crockett);   Lawrence Young (Dave London);   Justin Pierce (Skateboard Kid); Marcia Wright (Monique's Receptionist);   Koji Toyoda (Dick Miyake);   Larry Miller (Dunston Cactus);   Ted McGinley (Johnny Darjerling);   Kyle Kraska (Bob Flaps);   Richard Callen (Frank Wad);   Sara Gilbert (Gretle Dickens); William Fisher (TV Reporter);   Vicki Liddelle (Margaret Sim);   Padam Singh (Mr. Patel); Robert Maffia (Police Officer);   Evelyn Iocolano (Hotel Receptionist);   Sam Rubin (TV Anchor);   John Paul Dejoria (John Paul Mitchell);   Elois Dejoria, Giuseppe Franco, Sascha Ferguson, and Millie Gervasi (Judges);   Kylie Bax (Stig's Hair Model);   Kimora Lee (Dick Miyake's Hair Model); Contrelle Pinkney (Dave London't Hair Model);   Emily Proctor (Young Valhenna Woman);   Bobbie Bluebell (Angry Hedge Man); Sergio Brie (Ronnie the "Beefeater").

LOS ANGELES TIMES, 1/28/00, Calendar/p. 22, Kenneth Turan

"The Big Tease" is "Strictly Ballroom" with scissors. And not just any pair of shears, thank you very much. These are the coveted Platinum Scissors, "their origins shrouded in mystery," presented to the winner of the World Freestyle Hairdressing Championship, L.A.'s annual hair extravaganza. "One hairdo, one stylist, one model," the emcee breathlessly explains, "one shot at the big prize."

Wanting that shot is Scottish hairdresser Crawford Mackenzie, ready for the major leagues after "years of dominating the Glasgow hair scene." Known in his salon as the trouble-shooting "Red

Adair of hair" (although, he confides, "we never use explosives"), Crawford understands that the challenges of international competition will be stiff. But, as he tells the BBC documentary crew shadowing his every snip, "this was something I had to do, not for me, for Scotland."

A breezy look at what befalls Crawford once he lands in L.A., "The Big Tease" is a cheerful and smart mock documentary about hairdressing and Hollywood that knows enough not to take itself too seriously. Loose and lively, it was exactly tailored to the specifications of star Craig Ferguson, who not only plays Crawford, but co-executive-produced the film and co-wrote the cleverly tongue-in-cheek script with Sacha Gervasi.

Best known as Drew Carey's boss, Mr. Wick, on the TV show bearing the comedian's name, Ferguson is energetic and effervescent as the Scottish hair artiste. A cheerful enthusiast with an expansive grin and the willingness to party in clothes he describes as "Braveheart meets Liberace," Crawford has so much fun living his life that it's hard not to enjoy being along for the ride. Crawford's opposite number is Martin Samuels (Chris Langham), the dour, nervous director putting together a "fly-on-the-wall documentary" about our hero. Nothing comes easily to Martin, whether it's evading an obstreperous neighbor to interview Crawford's mother (who remembers the boy putting costumes on chess pieces for a performance of "South Pacific") or talking to Crawford's acquaintances, who more or less wish him well "being amongst his own kind in Los Angeles."

Once on the ground in L.A., Crawford makes a fast friend in a limo driver and entrepreneur, and feels immediately at home, looking at freeway signs from the car window and fondly remembering, "I knew a drag queen named Marina del Rey." He especially likes his lodgings in the posh Century Plaza Hotel, but that's where his problems begin.

A dispute about his bill leads Crawford to Monique Geingold (Mary McCormack), head of WIHF, the World International Hairdressing Federation. It turns out there's been "a wee misunderstanding." Crawford has not been invited to actually compete with international clipping stars like the pompous Beverly Hills Norwegian Stig Ludwiggssen (David Rasche); he's been invited to be part of the audience.

Determined not to have flown 7,000 miles without getting a chance to demonstrate his art, Crawford won't be denied his shot, even if it means facing daunting odds to get his official membership card in the all-powerful Hairdressers of America Guild, HAG for short.

In fact, it's remarkable how many amusing obstacles "The Big Tease" places in Crawford's way. He not only has to learn to schmooze, he has to figure out what the word means. Fortunately, Crawford is not only a genius with hair, he also ends up with the help of Candy Harper (Frances Fisher), one of the most powerful publicists in Hollywood. And anyone who really knows the business knows it's the publicists who truly manage everything.

Like "Strictly Ballroom," "The Big Tease" takes a real competition (believe it or not, hairdressing contests like the Platinum Scissors do exist) and runs with it. The film also knows its Hollywood territory, from people in animal suits who insist on being called actors to a hotel manager proud of not having had a drink "in over five days."

Directed by Briton Kevin Allen ("Twin Town") with just the right light touch, this unpretentious film strikes a blow for "the little people," who, as Crawford well knows, "usually get squashed by the big people." This time around, they've got a fighting chance.

NEWSDAY, 1/28/00, Part II/p. B3, Gene Seymour

Anyone who's ever gotten a withering look from an officious receptionist while waiting all day in a plush office suite can find something in "The Big Tease" to identity with. This mock-heroic quest, which lazily mixes bits of "Rocky," "Shampoo" and "This Is Spinal Tap" into a kitschy, low-flying blend of "Candide" and Pedro Almodóvar, pushes the buttons of those who chase big dreams and keep tripping over airheads along the way.

But then, the hero of "The Big Tease" is something of a dreamy airhead himself. Crawford Mackenzie (Craig Ferguson) is Glasgow's nonpareil hairdresser who decides to follow up on what he believes to be an invitation to compete in the "World Freestyle Hairdressing Competition" in Los Angeles.

Accompanying him on this 6,000-mile trek to almost certain stardom is a BBC documentary crew helmed by a fellow named Martin (Chris Langham), whose dour personality conceals a naivete of no less grand dimensions than that of his subject.

On arriving in Lotus Land, Crawford and Martin are in for a cruel surprise. The "invitation" to Crawford was to be a guest, not a competitor. (Mary McCormack, playing the officious program director, is impeccably smarmy.) Crawford has no intentions to be a spectator at a game he feels qualified enough to win. So he wanders all over Beverly Hills and Hollywood in search of the necessary certification and "buzz" to get him into the duel for the coveted Platinum Scissors.

During his odyssey of embarrassment and blundering, Crawford runs into the defending champion, Stig Ludwiggssen (David Rasche), a smug hunk of Euro-Trash who humiliates Crawford at every opportunity. Easing both Crawford's pain and his path to the competition is ace publicist Candy Harper (Frances Fisher), whose own makeover at Crawford's hands makes her his biggest fan.

There's an amiable, pokey sweetness to "Big Tease" that, when compared with the crass, gratuitous outrageousness of most Hollywood doofus comedies, makes it seem almost radical. Emphasize the "almost," because there's nothing at all radical about the film's pseudo-documentary style, the jokes, the plot or the souffle-fluffy targets of derision. The buildup to the all-but-inevitable ending is labored and about as extraneous as a third layer of lacquer.

Still, there are glimpses of the psychic terrain "Big Tease" could have opened if it had the nerve. When Crawford wanders L.A. hair salons in search of a job that would qualify him for the contest, his face registers deep hurt over what he terms the "racism" of one such salon that ridicules his accent, his homeland, his very being.

This seems a good place to mention that Ferguson, who co-wrote the script, has a jittery big-screen presence that gives you the jitters at first, but starts to grow on you deeper into the movie. Whether it's enough to get him out from under his TV persona of Mr. Wick on "The Drew Carey Show" is an open question. Still, he's smart enough about the situation to give Carey a cameo and a line. Yep, only one line. But it's one of the best in the movie.

SIGHT AND SOUND, 1/00, p. 43, Edward Lawrenson

Glasgow, the present. Hairdresser Crawford Mackenzie—the subject of filmmaker Martin Samuels' latest fly on-the-wall documentary—receives an invitation to the World Freestyle Hairdressing Championship in Los Angeles. Assuming he has been invited to compete, he flies over only to discover he's only been invited as a spectator.

Still determined to compete in the tournament, Crawford must become a member of the Hairdressers of America Guild in order to qualify. Crawford fails to get a job in hair-stylist Stig Ludwiggssen's Beverly Hills salon. However, Hollywood agent Candy Harper—whose dowdy haircut is given a stylish makeover by Crawford—helps him get guild membership by finding him work experience. She then raises Crawford's profile in Los Angeles by introducing him to a raft of celebrities. Yet again refused a place in the championship, Crawford sets up a meeting with the competition's chief sponsor Senator Warren Crockett who allows Crawford to compete. His entry, an outrageous hairstyle entitled 'Flower of Scotland', wins the first prize. Triumphant, Crawford returns to Glasgow.

Back in 1988 The Big Tease's director Kevin Allen had a bit part in The Strike, a very funny television spoof about a big US studio's attempt to turn the 1984 miners' strike into multiplex fodder. Peter Richardson played Al Pacino playing Arthur Scargill (a kind of industrial action hero), supported by Jennifer Saunders as Meryl Streep as Scargill's wife, making the film within the film a delicious send-up of the very worst that can happen when film-makers fly to foreign shores and make movies in countries they know very little about.

You can't help thinking there was a lesson here for Allen. Unravelling as a mockumentary which follows Glaswegian hairdresser Crawford Mackenzie's attempts to make it big in LA, The Big Tease turn out to be just as crass in its observation of life in California as The Strike's fictionalised producers were of UK labour relations. Admittedly, the stakes aren't as high: what was so funny about The Strike was seeing such a sensitive topic as pit closures turned into shameless schmaltz and thundering cliché. With its hoard of tired and distinctly second-hand jokes about such things as the impossibility of getting appointments in exclusive Beverly Hills salons and the haughtiness of waiters, The Big Tease simply comes across as insipid, lazy satire. Los Angelenos are safe from its biting wit.

Where Allen's film comes into its own is in giving free rein to former stand-up Craig Ferguson's comic talents. Ferguson—who co-wrote the script with Sacha Gervasi—hasn't given himself great material to work with (Crawford's stumbling attempt to define his sexuality, "I prefer women with penises", is one of the film's few funny lines) but his performance is ebullient and likeable. Describing himself as a cross between Liberace and Braveheart, Crawford also encapsulates the film's fond attitude towards a characteristically Scottish brand of kitsch which culminates in his championship entry, a thistle-shaped beehive. Following *Twin Town,* Allen seems to be making a career for himself playing with and ironising the traditional trappings of Celtic identity—and exploring issues of nationality is no bad thing, of course, even in a light-hearted fish out of-water comedy such as this.

But what's so grating here is that it's irony without self-deprecation. Too often the film comes across as smug and self-congratulatory. Crawford's winning haircut, for instance, might be kitsch, but it's meant to be prize-winning, world-beating kitsch. Even a joke about Scottish tight-fistedness allows him to gain the upper hand on Californian avarice.

This builds to a genuinely curious and triumphanlist climax. Crawford is driven through LA in a limo, brandishing a saltire flag which flaps in the wind, the on-looking pedestrians greeting his procession with a roar of approval. 'Like, who cares,' would be a more typical Los Angeleno response, a reaction many UK viewers might have to this unremarkable film.

VILLAGE VOICE, 2/1/00, p. 118, Amy Taubin

If *Stella Does Tricks* [see Taubin's review] comes out of the strongest tradition of British TV realist drama and documentary, *The Big Tease* is strictly boob tube. (To be specific, the film is Scottish, but I doubt many Scots would welcome the connection.) A sub-sitcom stretched to an interminable 85 minutes, *The Big Tease* follows the adventures of Crawford Mackenzie (Craig Ferguson), a dim-witted but determined Scottish hairdresser who flies to L.A. under the misapprehension that he's been invited, all expenses paid, to participate in an international hairstyling competition when, in fact, he's merely been sent a form letter inviting him, at his own expense, to be part of an informed audience. With a documentary filmmaker (Chris Langham) following his every move, Mackenzie mounts a frantic campaign to gain his rightful place in the competition and finds an unlikely champion in Candy Harper (Frances Fisher), publicist to the stars, who never again will have to suffer a bad hair day.

Ferguson, a well-known Scottish comedian, who lives in L.A. and is one of the regulars on *The Drew Carey Show,* is the moving force behind *The Big Tease.* He's the cowriter, coproducer, and star. In the press notes, he claims to have wanted to make a film that deals with a gentler side of Scotland than did *Braveheart* or *Trainspotting.* He also claims to have come up with the story over lunch. I don't doubt him for an instant.

Also reviewed in:
CHICAGO TRIBUNE, 2/11/00, Friday/p. D, Michael Wilmington
NEW YORK TIMES, 1/28/00, p. E25, Stephen Holden
VARIETY, 8/30-9/5/99, p. 56, Derek Elley
WASHINGTON POST, 2/11/00, p. C5, Rita Kempley
WASHINGTON POST, 2/11/00, Weekend/p. 43, Desson Howe

BILLY ELLIOT

A Universal Pictures release of a Working Title Films and BBC Films presentation in association with The Arts Council of England of a Tiger Aspect Pictures production in association with WT². *Executive Producer:* Natascha Wharton, Charles Brand, Tessa Ross, and David M. Thompson. *Producer:* Greg Brenman and Jon Finn.   *Director:* Stephen Daldry.   *Screenplay:* Lee Hall. *Director of Photography:* Brian Tufano.   *Editor:* John Wilson.   *Music:* Stephen Warbeck. *Choreographer:* Peter Darling.   *Sound:* Mark Holding and (music) Chris Dibble.   *Sound Editor:* Zane Hayward.   *Casting:* Jina Jay.   *Production Designer:* Maria Djurkovic.   *Art Director:*

Adam O'Neill. *Set Decorator:* Tatiana Lund. *Special Effects:* Stuart Murdoch. *Costumes:* Stewart Meachem. *Make-up:* Ivana Primorac. *Stunt Coordinator:* Lee Sheward. *Running time:* 90 minutes. *MPAA Rating:* R.

CAST: Jamie Bell (Billy); Jean Heywood (Grandma); Jamie Draven (Tony); Gary Lewis (Dad); Stuart Wells (Michael); Mike Elliot (George Watson); Billy Fane (Mr. Braithwaite); Nicola Blackwell (Debbie); Julie Walters (Mrs. Wilkinson); Carol McGuigan (Librarian); Joe Renton (Gary Poulson); Colin MacLachlan (Mr. Wilkinson); Janine Birkett (Billy's Mum); Trevor Fox (PC Jeff Peverly); Charlie Hardwick (Sheila Briggs); Denny Ferguson (Miner); Dennis Lingard (NCB Official); Matthew Thomas (Simon); Steve Mangan (Ballet Doctor); Paul Ridley (Tutor in Medical); Patrick Malahide (Principal); Barbara Leigh-Hunt (Vice-Principal); Imogen Claire, Diana Kent, Neil North, and Lee Williams (Tutors); Merelina Kendall (Secretary); Zoe Bell (Sandra); Tracey Wilkinson (Geography Teacher); Merryn Owen (Michael, Age 25); Adam Cooper (Billy, Age 25).

LOS ANGELES TIMES, 10/13/00, Calendar/p. 6, Kenneth Turan

It's not enough, Willy Loman famously tells his sons in Arthur Miller's "Death of a Salesman," to be merely liked. You have to be well-liked. But focusing too much on being well-liked, the Lomans find to their eventual despair, can be a trap, and it's a trap that "Billy Elliot" falls into.

For there are things to genuinely like about this crowd-pleasing story of 11-year-old Billy, growing up in the coal-mining North of England during the 1984 miners' strike, who resolves against obvious odds to be a ballet dancer. But in its determination to overdo sure-fire material, "Billy Elliot" becomes as impossible to wholeheartedly embrace as it is to completely reject.

The best aspects of "Billy" all involve Jamie Bell, the young actor who plays him. A natural talent with an open smile and an eagerness for experience stamped on his face, Bell portrays Billy as a real boy's boy, a good lad whose defining trait is a constitutional inability to simply stand still.

Even before he takes a liking to ballet, Billy feels the music in his life, running and jumping when everyone else is marking time. The best scenes in "Billy Elliot" are invariably the dialogue-less ones in which the boy, briskly choreographed by Peter Darling, tears down the streets of his hometown, often with the vintage music of T. Rex on the soundtrack. Unlike its contrived dramatic aspects, this film's sense of the joy inherent in pure physical movement never lets it down.

"Billy Elliot" begins with a kind of reverse twist on "Girlfight," about a girl attracted to the world of boxing. Billy is busy taking boxing lessons when Mrs. Wilkinson's ballet class, displaced by the soup kitchen used to feed the striking miners, arrives to share the gym space. Almost viscerally, Billy is drawn toward this gaggle of baby ballerinas in white tutus and the strange but graceful movements they are learning.

The boy is rather more ambivalent about Mrs. Wilkinson herself, a tart-tongued woman of middle years (the perennially overripe Julie Walters) much given to dramatic gestures with a cigarette and a tough love approach to teaching. It's a shock to both of them to realize that Billy has a true gift for dance and that Mrs. Wilkinson has the ability to encourage and motivate him.

Certainly there is little in Billy's background that would make this talent predictable. His older brother Tony (Jamie Draven) would as soon smack him as look at him; his widower father ("My Name Is Joe's" Gary Lewis) goes off as regularly as Old Faithful; and neither man has had his disposition improved by participation in a strike that grows increasingly bitter and partisan as the film progresses.

The biggest hurdle for Billy to overcome, it turns out, is the familiar one of sexual stereotyping and family disapproval. "It's not for lads," his perplexed dad says of the boy's passion, and Billy finds himself continually educating the louts in town who think male ballet dancers are invariably gay.

There's of course a lot of potential in a story like this and no compelling need to push it as hard as possible, but the concept of leaving well enough alone is clearly alien to screenwriter Lee Hall and debut director Stephen Daldry. Not trusting the audience to have any reaction that has not been completely stage-managed, they lay on the sentimentality and the cliches as thick as they can, which is pretty thick. What results is a prime example of major studio emotional heavy-handedness seeping into even small independent films.

The situation gets even worse when Mrs. Wilkinson mentions that Billy might just qualify for acceptance in London's prestigious Royal Ballet School. No sooner is the goal presented than the filmmakers throw more obstacles in the boy's way than a Grand National Steeplechase, milking the situation almost beyond endurance. If "Billy Elliot's" plot had even a fraction of the grace and control its dancing does, we'd all be a lot better off.

NEW STATESMAN, 10/2/00, p. 45, Jonathan Romney

Stephen Daldry's debut feature was screened in cannes this year under the title *Dancer*. The name has now been changed to *Billy Elliot*, so there's no chance of confusing it with Lars von Trier's Cannes hit *Dancer in the Dark*. Not that you could confuse von Trier's chaotic deconstructionist take on the musical genre with the absolute bangon brio of Daldry's hoofing routines. However, what the films have in common is using dance as a means of attaining emotional immediacy—in von Trier's case, a sort of melodramatic hysteria; and, in Daldry's, a cosy, uncomplicated sentimentalism that is very English.

Daldry—a former artistic director of London's Royal Court Theatre, and best known for his tricksy, design—heavy production of *An Inspector Calls*—has made a film that has remarkably little theatrical artifice. Not so much a musical as a realist drama with dance interludes, *Billy Elliot* pushes our emotional buttons in a way that is entirely mechanical and yet altogether uncynical. Daldry takes the project seriously as an exercise in genuinely populist cinema, which is why it can hardly fail at the box office. The script is by the playwright Lee Hall, the author of the award-winning tearjerker *Spoonface Steinberg*, and the story has all the heartwarming potential that is his stock-in-trade. In a County Durham colliery town, 11-year-old Billy (Jamie Bell) bunks off the boxing classes that his wiry old tyrant of a dad (the impressively sour Gary Lewis) sends him to, and learns ballet instead, under the auspices of the abrasive but tender Mrs Wilkinson (who else, but the ever-twinkling Julie Walters?). Ballet school beckons, if only Dad can be shaken in his conviction that dance is strictly a nelly business.

This is a schematic conflict, with a no less schematic outcome—but there's a political angle to make things slightly more complex. The action takes place in 1984, during the miners' strike. Conditions are tough, the police are moving in, and Billy's militant brother knows that this is no time to be prancing around in tights: ballet is surely not only unmanly, but a form of class treason. But Billy has his own needs, even if they are the needs of high art. This dilemma yields one genuinely disturbing scene, when Billy's father sacrifices all for his lad's happiness, and goes against this own political faith. But this seems less a dramatic crisis than an unresolved shock that begs too many questions. Should we read it as a triumph for paternal love, or as art's triumph over contingent world events? Maybe the lesson is only that, while unions and governments may come and go, somewhere there will always be a production of *Swan Lake*.

Daldry and Hall may have their hearts in the right place, but the film's political content fails to convince. You can't help feeling that the mining conflict is included only to thicken the dramatic soup, and it can be read all too easily as just another layer of period set dressing, on a level with Billy's beloved TRex songs and a brief glimpse of that Seventies playroom fetish, the *Spacehopper*. Present-day politics rarely feature in British cinema: but step a couple of decades back, and such themes can be handled as reassuringly as on *The Rock 'n' Roll Years*.

The film's politics of sexual identity also seem half-hearted and confused. This is a very anti-macho film, the miners' hardened masculinity finally making them seem like dinosaurs, fated to be replaced by a sensitive generation of arty lads in tights. Yet the film scrupulously plays down any sexual ambivalence that may be too much for the mainstream, even as it flirts not inconsiderably with camp. After all, Billy dances to Marc Bolan, skips around the streets in shorts and white socks, and has a friend called Michael who likes to wear his mum's lipstick. But Michael's budding gayness seems designed purely to get Billy off the sexual hook.

When Billy's dad is at last won over by his son's display of defiant hoofing, there is a sense that this show of rebellious anger vindicates his son's maleness. Thus the film is cautiously de-queered: the poster could have borne the tag line "Billy Elliot—he's norra poof, mind".

Let's not be churlish. *Billy Elliott* will bring many viewers a great deal of pleasure. It goes about its business honestly and with unflashy art; and its young star, Jamie Bell, is terrific—he can act, he can hoof like a good'un, he'll go far. But *Billy Elliot* is so much a British film of the moment: one that plays down complexity, addresses the heart, rather than the mind, and uses stereotypes just because they are there, even if it does attempt to undermine them just a little. It asks no real questions about the tensions between art (especially art that might be perceived as elitist) and class politics, and finally offers a simplistic solution—you've got to be true to yourself and dance those blues away.

I doubt that a theatre director like Daldry would settle for such dewy-eyed simplicity on stage; but often, when theatre people turn to the supposedly more innocent realm of cinema, they leave their sharper critical perceptions at home. In *Billy Elliot*, a very intelligent, accomplished stage director is letting his hair down and opting for Hovis-ad dopiness.

NEW STATESMAN, 11/27/00, p. 28, Sean French

Once a new art form is invented and established, an infrastructure develops to maintain it: a college to train people to do it, buildings dedicated to it, professional guilds, awards, grants. But, like anything else, art forms can become defunct. This is especially true of forms that depend on performance: masques, mystery plays. W H Auden's first published work, *Paid on Both Sides*, is a "charade", written to be performed in a country house. "The country house charade is among the most living drama of today," he wrote, ludicrously.

Sometimes a form can be dead, but won't lie down, remaining propped up by its infrastructure. Even while working as the jazz critic for the Daily Telegraph, Philip Larkin believed that jazz was dead, "dead as the Gregorian chant". He believed that it had moved so far away from anything that could be described as jazz that it had become something entirely different (and he hated it). He may have been right, or maybe he was just growing old. And there can be another problem with experience, or growing old, or however you describe it. When Clive James gave up his TV column in the Observer, it was, he wrote, partly because he was tired of old ideas coming round again and being greeted as new ideas.

I went to see *Billy Elliot* this week at my local multiplex. Stephen Daldry's debut film has been acclaimed by some people as the greatest British film ever made. It has been a huge financial success, and looks as if it will win a sackful of Oscars. I choose this example because it is a film I liked. It is beautifully made, superbly acted, cleverly written and I sobbed throughout. But the truth is that this film is entirely constructed out of other films. Now, I know all the arguments about how Shakespeare borrowed virtually all his plots from other people, about homages, or rather hommages (it sounds so much more acceptable in French), but still...

Let me give some examples. I assume that everybody knows the very simple plot: a boy in a mining community during the 1984 miners' strike develops a passion for ballet. Will he win over his father and brother? Will he get into the Royal Ballet School? The story is *Kes* remade in the affirmative style of *The Full Monty* (the borrowing of the boy's older brother from *Kes* is breathtaking, as is the imitation of the final freeze-frame from *The Full Monty*). *The Full Monty*—ex-miners redeemed by stripping—was itself almost identical to the slightly tougher *Brassed Off*— ex-miners redeemed by brass band. I would love to have been at the pitching sessions in which somebody told the story to a movie executive and the executive said: "Oh, that's a good idea."

Then there is the genre of the middle-aged teacher running a class in some dusty hall or schoolroom, clinging on to lost ideals, possibly redeemed by the student or students. Julie Walters, who plays Billy's ballet teacher, has been in a couple of such films: *Educating Rita* (English literature) and *Stepping Out* (ballroom dancing). Through his theatrical career, Daldry must be most acquainted with the tough political version of the story in Trevor Griffiths's *Comedians*.

Then there is the sub-genre of the audition scene, in which the stuffy professors are startled by the unconventional performance of the young genius. Obvious examples are the opening sequence of *Fame* and the closing sequence of *Flashdance* (also about a working-class young person with dreams of becoming a dancer). In the case of *Billy Elliot*, more subtly, the professors are impressed not so much by Billy's dancing as by his touching description of why he dances (which struck me as reminiscent of Eric Liddell's lines in *Chariots of Fire* about why he runs). And I could go on and on.

I am torn by my reactions to this film. In many ways, I thought it was lovely and humane. If it is sentimental and soft-edged, then it's in a good cause. I can imagine it educating a generation of boys out of their attitudes of conformity, philistinism, homophobia—or at least it might if they weren't banned from seeing it by its ludicrous 15 certificate. Thank God for videos.

But isn't there a problem here? What happened to real life? It reminds me of the introduction given to Dennis Wheatley, the author of books about the occult such as *The Devil Rides Out*, when he once came to give a speech at the Oxford Union. The chairman declared himself a great fan: "Not only have I read all Mr Wheatley's books; I have also seen the films on which they're based."

NEW YORK, 10/23/00 p. 92, Peter Rainer

It's Northern England in 1984, and the miners are on strike. What's the poor son of a striker to do except—dance? *Billy Elliot* is the latest in a line or ersatz feel-good movies from Britain set against a backdrop of grime and joblessness. *The Full Monty* to be the most baleful of influences on English cinema; not that such movies have much to do with England. They are aimed far more at Americans, specifically American tourists, than at Brits: Squalor is transformed into quaintness; book your plane reservations early.

In *Billy Elliot*, our eponymous young hero (Jamie Bell) opts out of the family boxing tradition to become, clandestinely at first, a ballet dancer. His hard-nosed father (Gary Lewis) is, of course, worried that the boy is a poof, and the director, Stephen Daldry, seems a bit worried we'll think so, too. So he has young Billy practically bouncing off the ballet-school walls. Manly dancing, this. What finally brings Dad around is his realization the ballet will keep Billy out of the mines (it takes him an awfully long time to come up with this revelation). *Billy Elliot* is such a prodigious feat of four-hankie engineering that Julie Walters fierce performance as the boy's dance instructor may get lost in the suds. That would be a far greater injustice than anything Billy endures.

NEW YORK POST, 10/13/00, p. 52, Jonathan Foreman

"Girlfight" inverted and then crossed with "Flashdance," "Billy Elliot" is an uplifting, crowd-pleasing film in the tradition of "The Full Monty" that could easily win Oscar nominations for both its 11-year-old star, Jamie Bell, and first-time director, Stephen Daldry.

Like his fellow English theater director Sam Mendes, Daldry has transferred his talents from stage to screen with striking results.

Set in a working-class English town convulsed by the bitter miners' strike of the mid-1980s, (when the Thatcher government ordered the closing of uneconomic collieries), "Billy Elliot" tells a story that is entirely conventional and predictable, but it does so with great charm.

Billy (Bell), an 11-year-old filled with energy, is the younger son of a striking miner (Gary Lewis from "My Name is Joe").

His father makes him go to the local gym to learn boxing. But the boy is attracted to a ballet class taught by the chain-smoking Mrs. Williamson (Julie Walters of "Educating Rita").

The only boy in a room full of tutu-wearing little girls, Billy tries his hand—or rather, his feet—at the barre and finds he likes it.

Despite the assumption of everyone he knows—especially his macho father and brother—that ballet is for "poofs" (homosexuals), Billy becomes obsessed with dance, and the no-nonsense Mrs. Williamson realizes that the boy is so talented, he really should try for a scholarship at the Royal Ballet School in faraway London.

Unfortunately, after a year of preparation, as Mrs. Williamson is about to take Billy to an audition for such a scholarship, his horrified father discovers his secret passion.

Supported by wonderfully nuanced performances by Waters, Lewis and the rest of the cast, Bell is terrific as Billy, and his dancing is both good enough and rough-hewn enough for us to believe that the boy really is an untrained prodigy.

The screenplay by Lee Hall includes deftly drawn, agreeably restrained side plots involving Bill's best friend (Stuart Wells) and Billy's older brother (Jamie Draven).

People who know northeast England well may cavil at inaccuracies and inconsistencies in the characters' accents and culture (where's the soccer so important to northeast culture?) and its treatment of the miners' strike.

But the same people have helped make "Billy Elliott" a huge hit in Britain (after delighting audiences at Cannes and other film festivals).

The film's "R" rating is yet another travesty by the Motion Picture Association of America; the censors should be ashamed of tarring this sweet little film (with its odd four-letter word) with the same label they accorded nasty, explicit stuff like "The Cell" and "8mm."

NEWSDAY, 10/13/00, Part II/p. B6, Gene Seymour

There's no denying that "Billy Elliot" has "crossover hit" written all over its gritty surface. Even its basic concept packs what used to be called a "boffo" punch. Mix spoonfuls of "The Karate Kid," "Chariots of Fire," "Rocky" (the first one, anyway), "The Red Shoes" and some Gene Kelly-esque razzle-dazzle with some forbidding backwater British scenery and you can just see the dollar signs materializing in the eyes of art-house managers nationwide.

The movie proves worthy of any good fortune that comes its way. Working from an intelligent, tightly written script by Lee Hall, director Stephen Daldry resists the temptation to go hard for the audience's guts and tells his story with short, contained strokes. The movie doesn't altogether avoid stepping in mush and treacle. But its dry humor, earthy performances and distinctive take on the clash between art and life help it earn every tear and cheer.

Set in a small northern England town during the 1984 coal miners' strike that all but paralyzed the nation, "Billy Elliot's" eponymous hero is a 14-year-old son of a recently widowed miner (Gary Lewis), whose truculence is made worse by the fact that both he and his eldest son (Jamie Draven), also a miner, have been living on strike-fund money for many months.

Billy, played with simmering intensity by Jamie Bell, seems headed for the same dead-end life as his dad, who encourages the boy to take boxing as a way out of the mines. Billy's a dud in the ring, but he's entranced by the ballet class being conducted at another corner of the local gym by Mrs. Wilkinson (Julie Waters), a dour, chain-smoking teacher from the not-so-poor side of the tracks. She tells him to either stop staring or join in. So he does. And he continues to study with her in secret so as not to attract attention from any male he knows, especially his dad.

Eventually, his dad finds out where the 50 pence he's been scraping each week for Billy's boxing lessons has been going and yanks him away from Mrs. Wilkinson. But not before both she and Billy are convinced that he's got enough talent and drive to audition for classes at London's Royal Ballet School. No way, says his dad. Dancing is for "poofs." It takes him some time to believe otherwise, but when he does...

Well, knowing where this all leads won't ruin the overall impact of this film, which is unusually observant about how dreams in forbidding environments can be waylaid by prejudice and redeemed by love.

NEWSWEEK, 10/16/00, p. 68, David Ansen

Billy Elliot is an 11-year-old English coal miner's son with an unexpected gift, and passion, for ballet. It's a name you will remember, and not just because the movie "Billy Elliot" bears his moniker. As played by a wonderful 13-year-old newcomer named Jamie Bell, he may be the most endearing prepubescent hero since the disarming Swedish waif in "My Life as a Dog" 15 years ago. And this delightful film, with its surprising depth charges of emotion, has the feel of a movie that's going to lodge itself in the public's affections for a long time to come.

To say that "Billy Elliot" is a crowd pleaser is a no-brainer, but it doesn't do the movie justice, and it doesn't convey just how passionately audiences take this small English film to heart. In Britain, where it was No. 1 its opening weekend, it surpassed the opening numbers for "Four Weddings and a Funeral" and almost equaled those for "The Full Monty"—the two most successful British films to date. The London critics have been raving, and even the hippest moviegoers have been spotted dabbing their eyes with hankies as they emerge from Billy's excellent adventure.

Set in northeast England in 1984, "Billy Elliot" unfolds in the midst of the miner's strike that pitted Margaret Thatcher against the unions. Billy's widowed father (Gary Lewis) and his older brother (Jamie Draven) are out on strike, but though the family is hurting badly there's still a little money set aside for Billy's boxing lessons. In the same gym where he's putting on his gloves to fight, the town's chain-smoking dance instructor, Mrs. Wilkinson (Julie Walters), is teaching the tutu-clad local girls to plié. Embarrassed but intrigued, Billy slips into line with the girls and gets his first inkling that he was meant to express himself through his feet, not his fists. This is a dangerous enthusiasm in a beer-swigging working-class town. Subterfuge is required. Billy knows he can't be seen checking out that ballet book at the mobile library, so he swipes it. And God forbid his angry father, who would naturally assume any boy who liked to dance had to be a poofter, ever found out where his boxing money was really going.

This is the first film of celebrated London stage director Stephen Daldry, and he fleshes out Lee Hall's fine screenplay with theatrical flair and a keen understanding of what it takes to be a performer. Like Sam Mendes's "American Beauty," it's a debut that will guarantee his future in movies. Eschewing the gritty realism that is de rigueur in tales of the British working class, Daldry and cinematographer Brian Tufano produce rich, colorful images; Daldry can drape the gym in pools of light as stylized as the vistas in his acclaimed stage production of "An Inspector Calls." When the leaping, tap-dancing Billy, a pint-size Gene Kelly, furiously careers down the narrow streets of his mining town, the movie gives off the joyful exuberance of an old Hollywood musical. The characters—like Lewis's macho, angry father—may start as stereotypes, but they take you by surprise. Lewis's performance as a man struggling with his own prejudices is one of the movie's many treassures, as is Walter's portrait of a tough old teacher shaken from her routine by the boy's heart-stopping potential.

Daldry isn't afraid of going for the emotional jugular, but he deftly sidesteps the mawkish. Yes, "Billy Elliot" follows a well-trod formula, and it hits one or two false notes (the "big" scene in which Billy reads aloud a letter from his dead mum to Mrs. Wilkinson is too calculated for its own good). But in the face of a movie so artfully made, so deeply charming, so heartfelt, it's not only pointless to resist, it's damn near impossible.

The key to the film's success was finding the right boy to play Billy. "It was a tall order," recalls Daldry. "You've got to find a kid who can hold the whole film down, who has the gift of dance." And he had to have the proper northern accent. Two thousand boys were auditioned before Bell was chosen. He was found in the working-class town of Billingham, but he comes from a long line of dancers—his sister, mother, aunt and grandmother had all at one time danced seriously. "I always wanted to be a hockey player," says Bell, now 14, taller and more of a handsome young man than the cute boy on screen. "I used to play all the time—until I saw a game. It wasn't very nice," he deadpans. "Then when I was 6 I got dragged to this one dance competition and saw this girl dancing on the stage. And she wasn't doin' it properly. I said to my mum, 'I can do better than that.' So she bought me a pair of tap shoes."

Like Billy, Jamie kept quiet about his extracurricular activities. When it got out, he was hassled. "All the stuff that's in the movie happened—people call me a poof, 'Get your tutu on, Jamie.' It gave me more determination to prove it wasn't just for girls." Daldry was amazed by Bell's abilities as an actor. "There are two sorts of child actors" he explains. "There's the child actor who basically plays himself, and then there's the transforming actor. The great advantage of Jamie is that I could work with him exacily as I would work with an adult and he would be able to understand and play and change."

Bell just finished shooting a six-part series for British TV, but he says that's it for a while for his acting career. "I'm actually looking forward to going back to school." But what if the movie's a big hit, and he's flooded with lucrative offers? "Well," he says, "I'll just have to turn them down."

SIGHT AND SOUND, 10/00, p. 40, Claire Monk

County Durham, 1984. Eleven-year-old Billy endures the hardship of the year-long miners' strike, living with his striking father, brother Tony and grandma. During a boxing lesson, Billy becomes fascinated with a ballet class being conducted in the same hall. Dared to join the session by the teacher, Mrs Wilkinson, he shows talent and secretly drops boxing for her class. When his father finds out, he bans Billy from further lessons. Convinced of Billy's potential, Mrs Wilkinson trains him for free, preparing him for a regional audition for the Royal Ballet School.

Tony is beaten up by the police and arrested, causing Billy to miss the audition. Mrs Wilkinson urges Billy's dad to support him, but a row ensues.

At Christmas, Billy breaks into the village hall with his friend Michael and dances. His father sees him and recognises his son's talents. Now determined Billy should audition for the ballet school, his dad plans to return to work to pay for the trip to the audition, but is dissuaded from doing so by his fellow strikers, who help him raise the fare. Following an audition, Billy is offered a place at the school. Later, Dad and Tony travel to London to see Billy in *Swan Lake*.

Hailed as the next likely feelgood British hit, *Billy Elliot* like *Brassed Off* and *The Full Monty* before it, revisits the formerly industrial north of England—here, a colliery town during the miners' strike of the mid 80s. The feature debut of theatre director Stephen Daldry, it also replicates the earlier two films, curious, but very Blairite, narratives where post-industrial despair and masculine crisis are resolved through an engagement with the entertainment or cultural industries. (Here, Billy's dreams of becoming a ballet dancer create tensions between the 11-year-old and his striking dad.) But *Billy Elliot* reconfigures these ingredients rather than simply reheating them. While it lacks the dreamlike ambiguity of Lynne Ramsay's *Ratcatcher*, its quirky focus on the transitional zone between childhood and adulthood recalls that film as much as its more commercial precursors.

Daldry and screenwriter Lee Hall's film also feels a lot truer to authentic experience than *The Full Monty* or *Brassed Off* perhaps because it's less fraudulently upbeat. Major credit must go to Jamie Bell as Billy: gangly and sandy-haired, he's a knockout dancer who also perfectly conveys an adult-child mix of mouthy defiance and sensitive introspection. Billy's circumstances are signalled with quiet economy. When his dad smashes his late mother's piano with an axe, we assume this is yet another act of aggression. But then we see the piano hammers burning as firewood. The gulf of class and culture which Billy will have to cross if he is accepted at the Royal Ballet School is never discussed; yet we only have to see Billy and his father cowed by the school's neoclassical interior to feel (wrongly) that Billy will never join this world.

Where *Brassed Off* and *The Full Monty*'s trips to declining industrial heartlands proved to be excuses for emotive male bonding, *Billy Elliot*'s boy-doing-ballet premise leads to a more equivocal relationship to dominant masculinity. At times, the film seems embarrassed by the burden of sexual/gender politics attached to its theme. The script, and Billy's robust dancing (which owes more to Michael Flatley than Frederick Ashton) work overtime to assure us that it's "not just poofs" who do ballet. Unfortunately for Billy, the example he cites to his dad here is Wayne Sleep, a dancer as camp as they come. But the film's notion of acceptable male identities is more polymorphous than this joke suggests. When unveiled as a cross-dresser, Billy's best friend Michael claims to have picked up the habit from his dad. Later, it becomes clear Michael is attracted to Billy. Billy doesn't reciprocate, but this doesn't provoke a crisis in their friendship, either. Billy's own sexuality remains undefined. He may not fancy Michael, but he is equally uninterested in his teacher Mrs Wilkinson's daughter Debbie.

Billy Elliot's story could plausibly belong to the present, raising the question of why it's set in 1984. Given the emotions surrounding the miners' strike, the film is politically circumspect to an extent which seems evasive. In narrative terms, the striking miners (represented by Billy's aggressive father and brother Tony) function as little more than a sign of the masculine class culture which initially thwarts Billy's ambitions. But *Billy Elliot* is equally mistrustful of those who opposed the strike, and its avoidance of politics only serves to underline the difficulty of neatly tying up the conflicts underlying the dispute. The 15-year ellipsis before the films rapturous ending leaves much unanswered. We see Billy leave for ballet school but never learn how happily he fitted in, or at what cost. We only know that he can dance.

TIME, 10/16/00, p. 110, Richard Corliss

A confession is in order: There are movies whose feel-good sentiments and slick craft annoy me so deeply that I know they will become box-office successes or top prizewinners. I call this internal mechanism my Built-In Hit Detector. I squirm through these masterpieces of emotional pornography, jotting down derisive notes. Oh, if the contrivance is blatant enough, I may get a bit teary; it is, after all, no more difficult for filmmakers to make an audience cry by depicting, say, a child in jeopardy than it is for a lap dancer to evoke an erection in her client. At the end

I have the gloomy certitude that moviegoers will love *Ghost* or *Cinema Paradiso* or *The Full Monty* every bit as much as I disliked it. There—I've said it. Is everyone alienated?

Billy Elliot, the new British film about an 11-year-old from a coal-mining town who wants to be a ballet dancer, is a prime example of elevated kitsch. Written by playwright Lee Hall, *Billy* echoes most of the manipulative inspirational films of the past 20 years. The movie could be called *Chariots of Flashdance, Strictly Ballet, Smile—Life Is Beautiful!* Audience members, already primed to love a losers-win story about a poor boy with big dreams, don't have to bring anything to the film, because director Stephen Daldry does all the work for them. Sentimental movies need subtlety; this one goes after every sweet little effect with a sledgehammer so large that the film could have been produced by Jerry Bruckheimer.

We're in the drab northeastern town of Easington in 1984, the year of a crippling coal strike, and Billy (Jamie Bell) is taking boxing lessons at the insistence of his gruff widower dad (Gary Lewis). But the boy really wants to dance. He's got happy feet that can drive him into a dervish fury. He finds a crabby, loving teacher Julie Walters), who is impressed enough by his skill and spirit that she prods him to apply to the Royal Ballet school. Thus ensue the inevitable domestic disputes, softening of hard hearts and pirouettes in heroic slow motion.

This is the first feature for stage director Daldry *(An Inspector Calls),* yet he displays an awesome instinct for cinematic manipulation. He loads every image with emotive propaganda (this character noble, this one morally myopic) and lards it with music that cues you to weeping or cheering. *Billy Elliot* is about as open to unforced feeling as Leni Riefenstahl's *Triumph of the Will.*

The Truth in Criticizing Law demands that I tell you what's good about the movie. The cast is mostly fine, especially the kids: Stuart Wells as Billy's effeminate friend (at home he dresses up in women's clothes—just like his dad!); Nicola Blackwell as the teacher's precocious daughter (she has a near sex experience with Billy); Jamie Draven as Billy's tough brother (star quality could be blooming there); and Bell, a comely lad whose unaffected poise carries the film and brings charm to its excesses. It's a victory for Bell to be so natural in a movie so calculating. And victorious they both may be, perhaps even at Oscar time. At a Manhattan screening last week, one Academy member effused, "I'm marking it off in all categories!"

So bank on my Hit Detector. The better class of moviegoers will love *Billy Elliot.* And I loved hating it.

VILLAGE VOICE, 10/17/00, p. 140, Leslie Camhi

Durham County, England, in 1984, is a land of dreary brick houses and circumscribed horizons. *Billy Elliot,* British director Stephen Daldry's intensely moving first feature, takes place during a miners' strike that paralyzed the region. Eleven-year-old Billy looks after his senile grandmother, while his widowed father and older brother walk the picket line. He's a sensitive child, who registers violence like a Geiger counter—his father's barking, his brother's rage, and the screaming strikers who face off every morning against scabs and bobbies.

It's the kind of place where boys risk growing into drunken men who urinate on their children's snowmen. Billy's father wants him to learn boxing, but when a dance class begins practicing at his gym, he eyes their tutus with blatant curiosity. Soon his pliés and sashays have captured the attention of his hard-bitten, chain-smoking ballet teacher.

Gary Lewis, as Billy's father, embodies paternal stupidity, brutality, and tenderness; Julie Walters makes Billy's grizzled teacher world-weary and just a bit unsympathetic. Jamie Bell's Billy is luminous and wounded; he almost pulls off some spontaneous dance numbers à la Gene Kelly, though they might have worked better in a theatrical setting.

But in small, deft strokes, Daldry subtly renders the presence of Billy's dead mother in his imagination, as a mark of his difference from other children, a source of grief and inspiration. His emerging sexuality is also handled with great delicacy—he's friends with a boy who likes to wear dresses and declines a little girl's offer to show him her "fanny," but his coming out as an artist takes pride of place over all other declarations of identity. The deepest issues here concern the sense of family betrayal that often haunts working-class children who embrace artistic vocations. By setting this intimate conflict against a wider social drama, Daldry makes his portrait of a dancer all the more compelling.

Also reviewed in:
CHICAGO TRIBUNE, 10/13/00, Friday/p. D, Mark Caro
NATION, 11/6/00, p. 34, Stuart Klawans
NEW REPUBLIC, 11/6/00, p. 30, Stanley Kauffmann
NEW YORK TIMES, 10/13/00, p. E29, A.O. Scott
NEW YORKER, 10/30/00, p. 115, Anthony Lane
VARIETY, 5/29-6/4/00, p. 20, David Rooney
WASHINGTON POST, 10/20/00, p. C4, Stephen Hunter
WASHINGTON POST, 10/20/00, Weekend/p. 43, Michael O'Sullivan

BITTERSWEET MOTEL

A Stranger Than Fiction Films release of an Aviva Entertainment/Little Villa Features/Bittersweet Films production. *Executive Producer:* Joshua Plank. *Producer:* Todd Phillips. *Director:* Todd Phillips. *Director of Photography:* Elia Lyssy. *Editor:* Alan Oxman. *Music:* Phish. *Sound:* Paul Languedoc. *Sound Editor:* Dave Ellingwood. *Running time:* 80 minutes. *MPAA Rating:* Not Rated.

WITH: Phish: Page McConnell; Trey Anastasio; Jon Fishman; Mike Gordon.

LOS ANGELES TIMES, 9/29/00, Calendar/p. 12, Steve Hochman

"I figure if you're going to be a dork, be a dork. The world would be better if there were more dorks."

That comment by a fan of the rock band Phish seen in "Bittersweet Motel," a documentary of the group's 1997 concert tour, inadvertently provides the more or less linking aesthetic between this film and "Barenaked in America," a documentary of a 1998 tour by the band Barenaked Ladies.

The members of the two bands are, well, dorks. Really nice dorks. Even talented dorks. But dorks. And the music each makes is dork-rock.

At least that's the impression likely to be taken away from each film by viewers who aren't already rabid fans themselves. It's a common problem with rockumentaries made by True Believers, which seem to be more about trying to show the world what's so special about their fave raves than really digging deep inside a group's dynamic or surrounding pop culture phenomenon.

"Bittersweet Motel" director Todd Phillips ("Road Trip") was not a fan when recruited by Phish, a band that came out of Vermont in the early '90s to build a loyal, neo-hippie following akin to that associated with the Grateful Dead. But he became one, and it seems that he wants nothing more for this film than to show the world the joy of following Phish and to share the wisdom and insights of its members—charming, thoughtful guys who really care about what they do and never take their fans for granted.

Phillips follows the band from rehearsals in snowy Vermont to a series of U.S. "dates and then to Europe for club shows (the fan base there isn't as big) and then back to the U.S. for the Big Went, an annual festival in which the band plays five or six sets over the course of two long days. It makes for some interesting bits, but nothing we haven't seen in countless rock films or MTV shows. Singer-guitarist Trey Anastasio comes off as unaffected and down-to-earth, but Phillips spends so much time with him addressing the band's critics that he ultimately comes across as whiny.

The director-fan for "Barenaked Ladies" is none other than former "Beverly Hills, 90210" actor Jason Priestley, who seems on a double mission here. One goal is to show what makes the band special to him and other followers. The other is to promote a Canadian mind-set, something he shares with the Toronto-based group.

What it all seems to come down to is incessantly jokey, if clever repartee, which is also the essence of the Ladies' songs. As the lyrics to one tune put it, "Our life is just one big pun." This is the kind of band you'd expect to have formed from a friendship of two camp counselors, which is exactly the case with frontmen Ed Robertson and Steven Page. There's cleverness in their sing-along songs, but not a lot of depth. (Unfortunately, Priestley felt it necessary to get into the joke-slinging himself in one sequence of banter, which though distracting, proves that he too is a dork.)

One element isn't so pun-able: Shortly before the tour started, keyboardist Kevin Hearn was diagnosed with leukemia. But Priestley fails to give that side story much weight—it would have been fascinating to intertwine the sunny tales of the band, on the road in the U.S. as it rises from cult status to having a No. 1 hit with the pun-filled "One Week," with the dark shadow of Hearn having to stay behind, his future uncertain. It's addressed here and there, but not in a way that adds up to much.

Just as Priestley doesn't exploit the dramatic devices that fell into his lap, Phillips fails to find anything surrounding Phish to give his film dramatic momentum, even though the raw material is staring him in the face. While the time he spent with Phish didn't feature anything as strong as a rise to No. 1 on the charts or a serious illness—it was just one of the band's many tours—there were two things that could have provided that focus. The European trip, with the band playing small clubs rather than the large venues it fills in North America, offered possibilities for an interesting study, rather than just a segment.

More meaty fodder, though, would have been the Great Went, the '97 edition of the band's own annual Woodstock with 70,000 fans camping out. A film devoted entirely to this endeavor, from planning sessions through the end, would probably have been much more involving. Instead, we have a film without a framework, without a skeleton—a Phish philet, if you will.

You have to wonder if these directors have even seen the truly great rockumentaries: "Woodstock," the terrifying "Gimme Shelter" account of Altamont, "The Last Waltz" in which Martin Scorsese chronicles the Band and its final concert event, not to mention the archetypal tour film, "This Is Spinal Tap." Drawing on those models could have made these films better services for all dorkdom.

NEW YORK POST, 8/25/00, p. 59, Dan Aquilante

This little movie will take Phish-heads behind the scenes of the rock group, one of the most important rock bands of the '90s.

How important? Without a radio hit or a video, these guys have sold 5 million albums, and last year they grossed more than $40 million just from concerts.

Between nicely shot (but flat) concert footage, the four rockers speak frankly about their craft and their personal lives in this cinéma vérité.

Fans will love this quick flick by director Todd Phillips, but it better serves as an introduction for the uninitiated.

NEWSDAY, 9/15/00, Part II/p. B3, Glenn Gamboa

Unless you're a fan of the musical-heroes-in-question, most rock documentaries are only baby-steps of attractiveness above the Aruba honeymoon home movies of perfect strangers.

Rockumentaries appeal intensely to small audiences, who are usually the only ones who know these movies even exist. The fact that movie muckety-mucks think a broader audience would be interested in "Bittersweet Motel," a behind-the-scenes look at jam band Phish, is a tribute to the quartet's massive, dedicated fanbase.

Unfortunately, that doesn't make it a good movie.

"Bittersweet Motel" will be a hit with Phishheads. The concert snippets will help relive the magic, as well as serving as a primer to anyone considering trailing the Vermont band around the country like Generation Next Deadheads.

Newcomers can save considerable time and energy by seeing the movie before piling into that beaten-up VW bus.

Everyone else, though, will wonder about Phish's appeal.

Director Todd Phillips splices together interviews and concert footage designed to unravel "the Phish mystique" for the 85-minute rockumentary, but it doesn't quite work.

The songs are Phishy enough—mostly midtempo, rock weighed down by Trey Anastasio's often-thin voice and often-rambling guitar solos. Those who have seen the band live know how the quartet effortlessly switches tempos and genres at the drop of a high-hat. Yet, aside from a stunning cover of "2001," a beautifully shot, smoke-machine-heavy extravaganza that ends in a dramatic fireworks display, most of the mystique is missing.

Backstage antics don't help much either.

We see band members pose for pictures and purposefully point the camera down so fans will not get a snapshot with them. We see how they aren't really into nailing all the chord changes, man, but way into the energy of the show. We see amazingly successful regular guys in jeans and T-shirts who hang out, drink, make music and, oh, happen to be millionaires. We don't, however, see why.

Anastasio does much of the talking, as the rest of the band—drummer Jon Fishman, bassist Mike Gordon and keyboard player Page McConnell—fades into the background. Actually, Anastasio does much of the defending, since Phish is a big target for musicians and critics.

"The suburban white kid is part of American music history," he says in one lengthy rant to explain the band's roots. "We are. Take it or leave it."

Such railing makes Tom Green, who starred in director Phillips' teen romp "Road Trip" earlier this summer, look like an affable Rhodes scholar in comparison.

"Bittersweet Motel" would be better if it followed the Phishheads around more. Brief introductions to the duo who biked 1,400 miles from Charlottesville, Va., to get to a concert or the girl-crazy, pot-smoking teenage dudes who make the Phish guys seem even duller.

Sometimes, the movie even seemed to confuse the band.

"I lost the point," says Fishman, during one of his few interviews. "Why would I want to make a movie about myself again?"

Good question. A better one is: "Who would want to watch it?"

VILLAGE VOICE, 8/29/00 p. 146, Michael Atkinson

Just the kind of rectal self-massage that only pop icons habitually allow themselves—albeit of a kinder, gentler nature, given Phish's high-but-low profile and relaxed lack of hit-making ambition—Todd Phillips's *Bittersweet Motel* is as homey as old sweats. For rock docs, though, something historic or anarchic is usually required. It's Phish's film, literally—like Sting, Madonna, and U2 before them, Phish decided they wanted a film made about themselves and actively sought out the right filmmaker to follow them on the road. By all lights they seem to enjoy the attention. Still, that Trey Anastasio and his bandmates don't exhibit Sting-like vanity doesn't mean there's much else on view, or that the reasons for their phenomenal popularity become crystal clear.

In any case, Phish-heads will forgive a great deal, which is of course what makes them what they are. Defined in the press that notices them by their Dead-like following, and likewise the honor of a Ben & Jerry flavor namesake, this aw-shucks group of middle-road musicians manages to be nearly as dull as the Dead. (A certain frumpy, Rorschach-like blandness might be an essential specification for the building of a full-on band cult.) Following the band on its 1997 tour from Europe to Limestone, Maine, Phillips (who went on to make *Road Trip)* buttresses the concert footage with de rigueur interviews and backstage shenanigans, and even the fans seem like recycled Deadheads. Anastasio spends a good deal of time responding to magazine reviews, and the claims for Phish concerts being explosive, anything-can-happen free-for-alls turn out to mean they simply don't follow a playlist.

Also reviewed in:
NEW YORK TIMES, 8/25/00, p. E25, Stephen Holden
VARIETY, 8/28-9/3/00, p. 28, Dennis Harvey

BLACK AND WHITE

A Screen Gems release in association with Palm Pictures. *Executive Producer:* Hooman Majd, Edward R. Pressman, Mark Burg, and Oren Koules. *Producer:* Michael Mailer, Daniel Bigel, and Ron Rotholz. *Director:* James Toback. *Screenplay:* James Toback. *Director of Photography:* David Ferrara. *Editor:* Myron Kerstein. *Music:* Oli "Power" Grant and American Cream Team. *Sound:* Antonio L. Arroyo. *Sound Editor:* Byron Wilson. *Casting:* Louis DiGgaimo and Stephanie Corsalini. *Production Designer:* Anne Ross. *Art Director:* Alisa Grifo. *Set Decorator:* Maureen Osborne. *Special Effects:* Drew Jiritano. *Costumes:* Jacki Roach. *Make-up:* Nuria Sitja. *Running time:* 100 minutes. *MPAA Rating:* R.

CAST: Scott Caan (Scotty); Robert Downey, Jr. (Terry); Stacy Edwards (Sheila King); Gaby Hoffmann (Raven); Allan Houston (Dean); Kidada Jones (Jesse); Jared Leto (Casey); Marla Maples (Muffy); Kim Matulova (Kim); Joe Pantoliano (Bill King); Bijou Phillips (Charlie); Power (Rich Bower); Raekwon (Cigar); Claudia Schiffer (Greta); William Lee Scott (Will King); Brooke Shields (Sam Donager); Ben Stiller (Mark Clear); Eddie Kaye Thomas (Marty King); Elijah Wood (Wren); Method Man, Mike Tyson, George Wayne, Brett Ratner, Fredro Starr, Inspector Deck, Ghostface, and Master Killer (Themselves); James Toback (Arnie Tishman); Scott Epstein (Scott); Thaddaeus Birkett (Twin); Chip Banks (Nicky); Hassan Iniko Johnson (Iniko); Larry Shaw (Duke); Superb (Pap); Tyrone Walker (Tye); Richard Akiva (Richie); Shawn Regruto (Victor); Justin Ske (Jus Ske); Richard Voll (Richie V.); Steven Beer (Attorney); Sabine Lamy and Michelle Dent (Girls in Bed); Frank Pesce (Joey); Richard Rose (Newscaster); Chuck Zito (Chuck); Robert B. Alexander (Darren); Sheila Ball (Sheila); John Bolger (Peter); Joseph Bongiorno (John); Frank Adonis (Frank); Jodi Cohen (Jodi); John Mailer (John); Tina Nguyen (Tina); Gary Pastore (Benny); Richard Elms (Driver); Keith Grayson (Kayalay); Janine Green (Janine); Cara Hamill (Cara); Katie Hamill (Katie); Michael Jordan, Duane McLaughlin, and Jade Yorker (Teens); David Alastair King (King); Kristin Klosterman (Charlotte); Eric Keith McNeil (Combo); Lauren Pratt (Sandy); Shari Raghunath (Shari); Katie Sagona (Katie); Melvin James Shaad (Doorman); Tyree Simpson (Club Security); Patrick Watt (Thomas).

LOS ANGELES TIMES, 4/5/00, Calendar/p. 4, John Anderson

[*The following review by John Anderson appeared in a slightly different form in* NEWSDAY, 4/5/00, Part II/p. B2.]

Having written "Bugsy" (1991) and "The Gambler" (1975) and having directed what some feel was among the great debuts in American film—"Fingers" (1977)—James Toback carries around a credibility that's belied by almost every movie he's subsequently made (most recently, 1998's "Two Girls and a Guy").

Add to this his much-publicized private life and views thereof—the basis, presumably, for his overrated "The Pick-Up Artist" of 1987—and you can't help but view every Toback project as the Freudian projection of a fevered libido.

In "Black and White," Toback explores the fascination among white teenagers—Manhattanites in this case—for hip-hop culture and, by Toback's extension, the lure of black sexuality. Think "Kids" meets "Jungle Fever" meets Norman Mailer's hipster opus "The White Negro."

Add to this the stunt casting of people such as model-actress Claudia Schiffer, boxer Mike Tyson, New York Knick Allan Houston and Toback regular Robert Downey Jr. as the weird, gay (and funny) husband of filmmaker Brooke Shields and "Black and White" starts to resemble such star-crusted movies as 1992's "Where the Day Takes You," in which a mob of fashionable faces (Will Smith, Ricki Lake, Lara Flynn Boyle, Alyssa Milano, David Arquette, etc.) pooled their resources to make a statement about the homeless in Hollywood. It was this short of laughable.

Likewise, "Black and White" features a herd of emerging talent—Bijou Phillips, Gaby Hoffmann, Elijah Wood, Jared Leto, Scott Caan—and is laughable in its way.

But it's also hard, excuse me, impossible, to watch "Black and White" and not imagine that what you're watching are the voyeuristic indulgences of a middle-aged filmmaker playing out his most deep-seated and unresolved sexual fantasies and anxieties.

The three-way interracial al fresco sex scene that begins the movie is indeed a startling way to open a picture, and more startling when we realize what buttons Toback thinks he's pushing. The exploitation and sexual commodification of black men is a valid point for Toback to make—in a movie that does its share of exploiting black men.

Easily the weirdest scene in a weirdly disjointed movie is one in which Mike Tyson, playing Mike Tyson, urges Harlem rapper Rich Bower (Power of Wu Tang Clan) to commit murder. You wonder if Tyson had his parole officer vet the script, and doubt Toback ever thought to suggest it.

NEW YORK, 4/17/00, p. 79, Peter Rainer

Most of the proliferating teen pix crowding the mini-malls don't acknowledge the way hip-hop has become the sanctuary of upstart white kids looking for an alternative lifestyle to cross over into. The recent *Boiler Room*, about mostly white chop-shop brokers who come on like rap masters, touched on the subject, and *Black and White*, the new James Toback film, mainlines it. It's a free-form, new-style movie, with music by American Cream Team, worked around a lot of old-style plot devices: It features delinquent kids bucking their staid, well-to-do parents; turf wars involving black gangs and the Mafia; two childhood friends who went their separate ways, one into crime, one into sports (and then crime); and many other roasted chestnuts. It also features a performance by Robert Downey Jr., as the gay husband of a documentary filmmaker played by Brooke Shields, that's one of the funniest pieces of acting I've ever seen. When Downey, coming on to Mike Tyson, playing himself, is bitch-slapped for his troubles, the screen is abuzz with a million incongruities.

Toback is no Johnny-come-lately to the racial-cultural wars. Back in 1971, he wrote a Maileresque, hero-worshippy book about Jim Brown, and he featured Brown in his directorial debut, *Fingers*, which was thick with the musk of black-white sex. The aliveness that Toback brings to *Black and White* owes at least as much to his continuing racial obsessions as it does to the cultural moment. Lucky for him right now, the two are joined.

NEW YORK POST, 4/5/00, p. 51, Lou Lumenick

"Black and White" may be the first fictional film in which the best scene features two real-life convicted felons—Oscar winner Robert Downey Jr. and ex-heavyweight champ Mike Tyson.

Downey's character, who's married but unmistakably gay, tries to pick up Iron Mike at a party—"I had a dream about you," he coos—and Tyson's apparently improvised reaction and the resulting mayhem is the high point in a movie that could use more of them.

Writer-director James Toback frantically tries to be edgy, but this exceedingly talky take on race relations has far less to say—and says it with far less panache—than Toback buddy Warren Beatty's "Bulworth." (Toback wrote another Beatty film, "Bugsy.")

For all its gangsta trappings and rap score, "Black and White" is at heart a cliché-strewn melodrama about a bunch of white, upper-class Manhattan kids who aspire to ghetto culture.

It's a provocative theme, and it holds your interest for maybe half an hour. But Toback's overwrought attempt to ape Robert Altman with overlapping stories ends up a tedious mess.

Ben Stiller is extremely funny in a small role as a sleazy, manic NYPD detective who traps a star college basketball player (Allan Houston of the Knicks, who shouldn't give up his day job) into accepting a bribe to throw a game—triggering an uninteresting series of manipulations by their devious mutual girlfriend (Claudia Schiffer).

Bijou Phillips is awfully one-note as a gold-toothed gangsta-wannabe prep-school student who's seen in the eye-opening first scene having three-way sex with Schiffer and a tough rapper (Oli "Power" Grant of Wu-Tang Clan) in the middle of Central Park.

There are especially cringe-worthy turns by a dreadlocked Brooke Shields as Downey's clueless wife—who claims to be shooting a documentary on these racial pretenders with her camcorder—and Marla Maples as Phillips' quail-loving WASP mother.

It's heavy-handed satire that trades too heavily on the stereotypes it's supposedly trying to send up—all blacks are thugs, athletes or both.

Toback fails to deliver any sort of dramatic climax—an assassination carried out by the son (William Lee Scott) of the Manhattan DA is inexcusably clumsy and dull—and sort of lets the movie limp to the end.

NEWSWEEK, 4/10/00, p. 79, Jack Kroll

Maverick moviemaker James Toback ("Two Girls and a Guy" has latched on to the most fascinating cultural phenomenon the American moment in his film "Black and White"—the interaction, culturally, musically, sexually, between young whites and blacks. In 1957, when Norman Mailer wrote his essay on "The White Negro," it was elitist hipsters who identified with black culture; today 70 percent of hip-hop record sales go to whites. "I want to be black," says a teenager. "I can do whatever I want; I'm a kid in America."

Toback captures the problematic, syncopated dynamics of this crossover with his story involving a creepy white cop who bribes a pro basketball player throw a game, then uses the player to nail a rapper-gangbanger. Swept up in this tale is a multicultural slew of characters played by a fascinatingly variegated cast, including teen diva Bijou Phillips, members of Wu-Tang Clan, supermodel Claudia Schiffer, New York Knicks star Allan Houston and ex-champ Mike Tyson. These icons hold their own with the pro actors, among them a nose-ringed Brooke Shields as a documentary filmmaker, Robert Downey Jr. as her gay husband and Ben Stiller as the creepy cop. Many scenes are improvised, notably one in which Downey makes a pass at Tyson (playing himself), who wasn't told what was going to happen. The astounded Tyson promptly uncorks a sea shot to the face. It may be the realest punch in movie history.

SIGHT AND SOUND, 12/00, p. 41, Xan Brooks

New York City, the present. Black hoodlum Rich Bower decides to ditch crime in favour of a new career as a rap artist. In doing so, he finds himself surrounded by white businessmen and a crop of wealthy white Manhattan teens in thrall to African-American culture: among them Charlie, whose father is an investment banker, and Will, the estranged son of the district attorney. These youngsters become the subject of a documentary by eccentric married film makers Sam and Terry.

Meanwhile, Rich's childhood friend Dean, now a successful college basketball player, is offered $50,000 by a white gambler, Mark, to throw a game. Dean complies but the arrangement is a sting: Mark is an undercover cop intent on using Dean as a way to prosecute Rich. Dean confides in his anthropologist girlfriend Greta, who promptly betrays him to Rich, with whom she has sex. After consulting with boxer Mike Tyson, Rich decides to have Dean killed and orders Will to shoot him in the gym. Will completes the job but is photographed leaving the building by Mark.

Mark presents the evidence to Will's DA father and the pair hatch a deal. The DA will throw a case out of court that may otherwise damage Mark's career in return Mark will destroy the evidence in order to shield Will from justice.

A film about racial politics in modern-day New York, *Black and White* hurls itself at the screen with such abandon that it's in danger of breaking up on impact. What we have here is a picture of its time; a study in cultural blurring; a tale of the disintegration that follows integration. If *Black and White* sometimes comes over as too undigested to be fully successful, that may be because its subject matter is itself too confused and volatile to be ordered into a neat dramatic framework.

As a result, writer-director James Toback's flawed, fascinating rhapsody gives the impression of discovering itself as it goes along. Largely improvised by an ensemble cast, the film starts out as a social portrait of a crop of wealthy uptown white adolescents who "wanna be black" (aping the dress code, accents and mannerisms of the ghetto) before switching guises into a *noir* thriller full of stings and double-crosses and eventual murder. The transformation is initially jarring, but there is a method to it too. In involving us in the tale of a black basketball player Dean who is forced to shop his gangster friend Rich (played by Power, of rap act Wu Tang Clan fame) to a white NYPD cop Mark, Toback provides the film with its cautionary pay-off. The end result of white meddling with black culture, he implies, is the death of a young African-American. The venal, shifty whites (represented here by Ben Stiller's unstable cop and William Lee Scott's rich-kid killer) get off scot-free. Push this doctrine to its logical conclusions and it verges on separatism. Except that *Black and White* is never that blunt. Instead, as with Toback's other notable works *(Fingers,* 1977; *Two Girls and a Guy,* 1977), the film is a study in greys: a *vérité* whirl that's too close to the meat of its subject to draw any lofty analytical conclusions. Its dynamic is an indistinct jumble of the real and the fake, of improvised stylings and subtle plotting. Toback casts his actors against type (Brooke Shields as a dreadlocked documentary film-maker, model Claudia Schiffer as a graduate student). He ropes in celebrities (Mike Tyson, *Rush Hour* director Brett Ratner) to play what one assumes to be themselves and lands his characters with non-gender-specific names (married couple Sam and Terry). It all adds to the sense of pose and artifice, of people who are not what they seem. This ploy reaches its giddy climax in a scene in which Robert Downey Jr's bisexual film-maker comes on to Mike Tyson at a New York party. Toback has said that he had deliberately left Tyson with no idea as to which direction the conversation would take. Judging from the man's reaction, Toback might just as well have detonated a bomb beside him.

Black and White is full of such explosions, such moments of rough-hewn ingenuity. By the same token, it also has scenes where it ambles or hits flat notes. A study in multiculturalism, Toback's film is something of a melting-pot itself: mixed-up, messy and teeming with vitality.

VILLAGE VOICE, 4/11/00, p. 153, J. Hoberman

A steamier view of New York's oral history [The reference is to *Joe Gould's Secret*] James Toback's *Black and White* peaks with its opening scene—a lip-smackingly posed two-girls-and-a-guy teenage interracial orgy-cum-after-school special in the middle of Central Park. The money shot, so to speak, has participant Charlie (Bijou Phillips) sauntering home to her parents' Park Avenue apartment for dinner. "I can do whatever I want—I'm a kid in America," she later tells her high school class.

Free to be you and me: As embodied by Phillips's kewpie-doll homegirl delivery and digital documentary filmmaker Brooke Shields's orange dreadlocks, *Black and White* has something to do with rich white wannabes hanging with soon-to-be-rich rappers, mainly Wu-Tang associates Power and Raekwon. More self-sufficient than Joe Gould, the rap artists wonder what these white people really want, and—not unreasonably, given the nature of Toback's movie—assume it is a parasitic attempt on the black-planet life force.

Toback, a firsthand observer of Norman Mailer's late-'60s celluloid debacle, *Maidstone,* has a similar sense of movie as mad cocktail party. Lampshade on head, *Black and White* pirouettes in and out of self-parody. At the same time, the mosaic structure and channel-surfer attention-span suggests an impacted *Nashville*—at one point, all the characters, hip or clueless, including Charlie's history teacher (Jared Leto) and her mother (Marla Maples), meet up at the same club. Toback, who appears uncredited as an oily music producer, casts hapless Shields in the Geraldine Chaplin role and saddles her with a madly cruising husband (Robert Downey Jr.) reckless enough to hit on Mike Tyson. "I'm on parole, brother, please..." the ex-champ pleads before he snaps and begins throttling his persistent admirer.

Elsewhere on the celebrity-romance front, Knick star Allan Houston plays a college basketball prospect while, as his grad-student girlfriend, Claudia Schiffer sucks cheek with brisk hauteur. Toback knows it's unfair to ask her to act. When she betrays the Houston character with his best friend, he thoughtfully dubs in "if You Want This Pussy (You Can Have It)." An exaggerated faith in music notwithstanding, *Black and White* is characterized mainly by its fabulous lack of conviction. The crucial murder is completely without consequence.

This hodgepodge only intermittently rises to the laughable (the bizarrely extended riff about undercover cop Ben Stiller delivering a payoff in the Time Café toilet), but, given the cast, it always has the potential to deliver some outlandish cameo—most often Tyson. I'm not sure I want to know the unconscious *Black and White* purports to channel. Suffice to say that Iron Mike emerges as the movie's most articulate and sensitive presence.

Also reviewed in:
NATION, 5/15/00, p. 34, Stuart Klawans

NEW REPUBLIC, 5/8/00, p. 24, Stanley Kauffmann
NEW YORK TIMES, 4/5/00, p. E1, Elvis Mitchell
NEW YORKER, 4/10/00, p. 99, David Denby
VARIETY, 9/20-26/99, p. 88, Todd McCarthy
WASHINGTON POST, 4/5/00, p. C10, Rita Kempley

BLESS THE CHILD

A Paramount Pictures and Icon Productions release of a Mace Neufeld production. *Executive Producer:* Bruce Davey, Robert Rehme, and Lis Kern. *Producer:* Mace Neufeld. *Director:* Chuck Russell. *Screenplay:* Tom Rickman, Clifford Green, and Ellen Green. *Based on the novel by:* Cathy Cash Spellman. *Director of Photography:* Peter Menzies, Jr. *Editor:* Alan Heim. *Music:* Christopher Young. *Music Editor:* Tanya Noel Hill. *Sound:* Owen Langevin and (music) Robert Fernandez and Dick Lewzey. *Sound Editor:* Stephen Hunter Flick and Beth Sterner. *Casting:* Deborah Aquila and Sarah Halley Finn. *Production Designer:* Carol Spier. *Art Director:* Elinor Rose Galbraith. *Set Designer:* Michael Madden and Elis Lam. *Set Decorator:* Peter P. Nicolakakos. *Special Effects:* Michael Kavanagh, John MacGillivary, and Danny White. *Costumes:* Denise Cronenberg. *Make-up:* Shonagh R.B. Jabour. *Make-up (Creature Effects):* Greg Cannom. *Stunt Coordinator:* Matt Birman. *Running time:* 115 minutes. *MPAA Rating:* R.

CAST: Kim Basinger (Maggie O'Connor); Jimmy Smits (John Travis); Rufus Sewell (Eric Stark); Ian Holm (Reverend Grissom); Angela Bettis (Jenna); Holliston Coleman (Cody); Christina Ricci (Cheri); Lumi Cavazos (Sister Rosa); Michael Gaston (Bugatti); Eugene Lipinski (Stuart); Dimitra Arlys (Dahnya); Anne Betancourt (Maria); Helen Stenborg (Sister Joseph); Matthew Lemche (New Dawn Kid at Van); Vincent Corazza (Reverend's Assistant); David Eisner (Doctor Ben); Gary Hudson (Maggie's Date); Samantha O'Dwyer (Cody, 3 Years Old); Nicolas Marti Salgado (Martin Casillas); Marcia Bennett (Head Nurse); Peter Mensah (Good Samaritan Janitor); Yan Birch (Good Samaritan on Bridge); Alexa Gilmour (Good Samaritan in Subway); Wanda Lee Evans (Woman on Bus); Cedric Smith (Pediatric Doctor); Dwayne McLean (Homeless Man); Brenda Devine (Woman with Sick Daughter); Lauren Spring (Daughter); Christopher Redman (New Dawn Intern); Jovanni Sy (Code Blue Doctor); Trevor Bain (Task Force Investigator); Brian Heighton (Techie); Chris Marren and Todd William Schroeder (Diner State Troopers); John Healy (Diner Local Policeman); Dylan Harman (Boy in Playground); David Sparrow (Crawford); Michael Copeman (Police Lieutenant); Richard Carmichael (Task Force Detective); Roman Podhora (Desk Sargeant); Dean Gabourie and Arnold Pinnock (Alley Officers); Teresa Pavlinek (Dentist's Receptionist); Jeffrey Caudle (Boy in Dentist's Chair); Catherine Fitch (Sister Helena); Neville Edwards (Pier Cop); John Shepherd (Mr. Czernik); Norma Edwards (Mrs. Czernik); Leeza Gibbons (Herself); Dan Duran and Sandi Stahlbrand (Reporters); Mia Lee (Newscaster); Matt Birman (Upstate Cop); Meredith McGeachie (Nurse); Henry Alessandroni (Hospital Cop); Austin Reed, Corrina Reed, and Brianna Reed (Baby Cody).

LOS ANGELES TIMES, 8/11/00, Calendar/p. 8, Kevin Thomas

[*The following review by Kevin Thomas appeared in a slightly different form in* NEWSDAY, 8/12/00, Part II/p. B9.]

"Bless the Child" opens strongly, as a nurse in a New York hospital (Kim Basinger), on a Christmas Eve, suddenly finds herself with her drug-addicted sister's newborn abandoned child. But from that point its credibility as a thriller of the supernatural starts eroding quickly, to the point that it lapses into an exercise in foolishness.

Nurse Maggie O'Connor's niece Cody (Holliston Coleman) is mildly autistic and also blessed with "special powers" coveted by a Satanist, Eric Stark (Rufus Sewell). Eric is a onetime child

TV star who hit the skids and now operates a nationwide network of outreach centers for troubled, substance-abusing youths ripe for recruitment for the devil's work.

Stark has his minions slay five New York children all born on the same day—and all left branded with an ominous crooked pitchfork design—until he comes across Cody, who has both the right birth date and the right supernatural gifts in healing, telekinesis, etc., to exploit for his evil purposes.

Conveniently, Maggie's sister Jenna (Angela Bettis) has fallen into Eric's thrall, and after an absence of six years, she turns up with Eric at Maggie's apartment to claim Cody, whom they swiftly kidnap despite her aunt's valiant struggle to stop them.

Meanwhile, FBI agent John Travis (Jimmy Smits), an expert in ritual murder, has taken charge of the investigation into the killings. He comes to the aid of Maggie, when he learns Cody shares the same birth date with the slain children. Travis, a brilliant onetime seminarian and devoutly religious, exudes an almost saintly aura along with his strong, reliable presence.

Yet Maggie, armed with the address of Eric's secret headquarters given her by a would-be defector (Christina Ricci), heads there all by herself without telling Travis—a dumb move if ever there was one but clearly undertaken in the name of projecting Maggie as a fearlessly independent, take-charge modern heroine. When she barely escapes Eric's lair, where he keeps Jenna enslaved with drugs, Maggie, by golly, tries to snatch the kid all over again on her own.

Directed in blunt, straight-ahead fashion by Chuck Russell, whose credits include "The Mask" and "Eraser," "Bless the Child" was written by Tom Rickman and Clifford & Ellen Green in a hopelessly contrived fashion.

The film means to give way to a larger commentary on the lack of spirituality in contemporary life and also to assert that the lack of faith in God leads to the belief that true evil does not exist. But for the film to emerge as the potent contemporary parable that it so earnestly wants to be, its plot would have to grow out of the character and conflicts of its people rather than just manipulating them.

Basinger gives it her considerable all, playing with a conviction the film sorely lacks and repeatedly undercuts. Smits has an easy natural authority, but his role allows him little range. Newcomer Coleman makes a fine impression, and there's solid support from Bettis as the ravaged, distraught Jenna and from Ricci as the brave Cheri. Sewell and Ian Holm (as a renegade priest) ham it up, the only way to go with their parts; if you didn't know otherwise, you might not suspect that both are actors of formidable range, versatility and subtlety.

"Bless the Child" has the suitably Satanic special effects you would expect of such a film and the all-around sleek production values typical of a major studio release. For all its aborted attempt at allegory as well as suspense and action, it is ultimately most disturbing that Basinger is still unable to find roles that are worthy follow-ups to her Oscar-winning performance in "L.A. Confidential."

NEW YORK POST, 8/11/00, p. 47, Jonathan Foreman

A movie at times so bad it feels like a Leslie Nielsen joke, "Bless the Child" is trying to be an update of supernatural thrillers like "The Exorcist" and "The Omen."

After a slow start, it becomes enjoyably creepy, only to decline sharply into a morass of ever more inane ridiculousness. Soon the unintentionally funny lines are coming thick and fast. During the last 40 minutes, you wonder if the screenplay (credited to Tom Rickman, Clifford Green and Ellen Green) wasn't finished off by distracted studio execs.

One Christmas night, divorced New York nurse Maggie (Kim Basinger) finds Jenna, her heroin-addicted sister (Angela Bettis), on her doorstep. Jenna leaves her week-old daughter Cody with Maggie and disappears. Maggie treats Cody as the child she has always wanted, despite her apparent autism—a real turnoff to Maggie's suitors.

When Cody (Holliston Coleman) is 6, she begins to manifest special powers, including the ability to bring dead birds back to life. Maggie doesn't really notice.

But a self-help cult, secretly run by satanists led by Eric Stark (British theater actor Rufus Sewell, "Dark City," "Dangerous Beauty") is looking for a child with just such potential. You can spot Stark's young cohorts a mile off because of their East Village wardrobe: They wear black clothes, combat boots and sport facial piercings as well as the cult's tattoo.

Maggie begins to realize that Cody is in danger, thanks to visions of her house being invaded by nasty, rubbery rats with glowing red eyes, and a warning from Christina Ricci in a brief cameo. But the forces of evil get hold of the little girl and Maggie must find some way of getting Cody back before she can be seduced to Satan's side by Stark.

Maggie is all alone in her quest to rescue Cody, except for a seminary student-turned FBI agent (Jimmy Smits). Of course, you know that at some point Maggie will have to seek the advice of a renegade cleric who has been disavowed by the Vatican for his warnings about the satanic plan, and here comes Ian Holm, doing a bad Irish accent.

Smits is simply awful, and even though Basinger, beautiful as ever, has a talent for portraying bruised innocence, there are times you wonder if she should confine her future career to playing mutes.

There are plenty of things in the film to irritate sharp-eyed New Yorkers. Seconds after the little girl is taken from her house in what looks like a suburban section of Queens, Maggie is talking to cops at a precinct house in TriBeCa. And the movie treats as perfectly ordinary Maggie's miraculous ability to snag taxicabs in the pouring rain.

Unlike many satanic thrillers—the execrable "End of Days" comes to mind—"Bless the Child" does at least believe in God and Goodness as well as Satan and Evil.

In fact, the only interesting and unusual thing about "Bless the Child" is the way it takes Christian theology completely seriously—something rare in today's ultrasecular Hollywood.

In fact, if its theology weren't so Catholic, this could be a big-budget version of one of those apocalyptic thrillers popular among Protestant fundamentalists. But in the end, orthodoxy deserves better.

SIGHT AND SOUND, 2/01, p. 36, Kim Newman

New York. In December, with the Star of Bethlehem again in the sky, psychiatric nurse Maggie O'Connor is visited by her sister Jenna who leaves her new-born daughter Cody with her and disappears. Maggie raises Cody, who is diagnosed as near-autistic but displays miraculous powers of telekinesis and healing.

Seven years on, a serial killer is at work in the city, murdering children born on the same date as Cody. FBI agent John Travis, a former seminary student, is called in to consult on the case. Jenna reappears, married to wealthy self-help guru Eric Stark, who has Cody kidnapped. When Maggie reports the abduction to the police, Travis assumes a link between the case and Stark, who heads a Satanic cult. Cheri, an escapee from the cult, approaches Maggie and tells her where Cody is being held, but is then murdered by Stark's minions.

Stark tries to tempt Cody, who has divine potential, to worship Satan, but the child resists. Maggie snatches Cody from the cult and Travis establishes that Stark was involved in the murders of the children. The cultists recapture Cody and take her to a deconsecrated church upstate for a Black Easter ceremony, at which she will either convert to Satanism or be sacrificed to the devil. As Cody is imperilled, she summons angelic intervention, which thwarts Stark, who is killed in a fire. Maggie rescues Cody.

Comically serious, with a streak of the devoutly ridiculous, *Bless the Child* is a fundamentalist horror movie which can conceive of good and evil only in the simplest of terms and uses the power of faith as an expedient plot device to justify absurd story turns. Telling of a Satanic cult's attempts to turn a divinely gifted child, Cody, over to the devil and of her foster mother Maggie's attempt to get her to safety, the film feels like a curiously dated throwback to the religious themed horror movies of the 70s, borrowing not only from the generic dead end of William Friedkin's overrated *The Exorcist* (1973) and the biblical footnotery of *The Omen* (1976) but also from the rash of television movies that proliferated around that time, which discovered robed devil-worshippers in suburbia (*The Devil's Daughter*, 1973; *Good against Evil*, 1977) or in various educational establishments (*Satan's School for Girls*, 1973; *The Initiation of Sarah* 1978).

Aside from ominous gargoyles under the opening credits and, implausibly, just opposite Cody's bedroom window (which find an echo in the robed CGI demons Maggie sees after she's been bashed on the head), *Bless the Child* has few visual frills, which means that the divine or demonic interventions come from nowhere and provoke giggles rather than awe or terror. Chuck Russell, a shaky A-list director on the strength of *The Mask* (1994) and *Eraser* (1996), rattles through the film on auto-pilot, (opting as in 1999's *End of Days*, which saw Arnold Schwarzenegger do battle with Satan) for action over atmosphere and hoping against all sense that the theology will take care of itself.

Based on a novel by Cathy Cash Spellman, the script is credited to Tom Rickman, and to Clifford and Ellen Green, who have taken this route before with the equally devout and unlikely *The Seventh Sign* (1988). Don Roos reportedly provided a polish to their script, and it was perhaps his involvement in the project which persuaded Christina Ricci, who starred in his 1998 debut *The Opposite of Sex*, to take the tiny but hilarious role of cult runaway Cheri. But it's Holliston Coleman as Cody who emerges better from this farrago than any of the more experienced players, working hard at innocent ambiguity with a side order of messianic glower, raising doves from the dead and demonstrating telekinetic power over plates and snow globes. Cody, we are told, is destined "to lead a lot of people to God", though the script doesn't go quite so far as to say that she is Jesus reborn, avoiding the need to tackle any of the problems established Christian churches might have with a female messiah.

The devil's representative on Earth, meanwhile, is given the form of cult leader Eric Stark. Rufus Sewell has to make do with thin material in the role, despite his elaborate backstory (he's a former child star turned addict turned rehab guru turned devil's acolyte). And in the end, Stark loses not only because God is against him but because he makes the elementary mistake of blundering against unsteady burning braziers while wearing inflammable robes.

Unusually for a horror movie, *Bless the Child* allows the good guys to call on God for help, which often comes in the form of polite strangers who offer advice ("A good man is never alone," a lowly janitor informs FBI agent Travis) or direct assistance (Maggie is hauled out of a car just as it's about to go over a bridge and escapes from pursuers because a woman holds open a subway train door). Trouble is, this reduces the film's characters to little more than chess pieces, moved about by God's mysterious agency, which leaves you querying the logic behind His interventions: why, for instance, was Maggie trusted to escape from the subway train but not the teetering car?

VILLAGE VOICE, 8/22/00, p. 134, Mark Holcomb

As jaw-droppingly close to Christian propaganda as Hollywood is likely to get, *Bless the Child* makes *Godzilla 2000* look like a model of ingenuity. Psychiatric nurse Maggie O'Connor (Kim Basinger), forced to raise her sister's abandoned daughter, goes on the lam when her junkie sis (Angela Bettis) and Satan-worshiping hubby (Rufus Sewell channeling John Cassavetes in *The Fury*) return to abduct little Cody (Holliston Coleman), who may be the second Christ. (The first one makes an appearance on a Toronto stand-in for the Queensboro Bridge.) FBI agent Jimmy Smits investigates, while ex-satanist Christina Ricci and Ian Holm's anesthetized cleric turn up to offer advice on how to beat the devil. Combining Sunday-school scare tactics and heavy-handed piety, *Bless the Child* plays like *Rosemary's Baby* reinterpreted for the PTL set. Yet beneath its boorish symbolism and groaning stereotypes (the movie's African American and Latino characters are inevitably its most "spiritual"), this is a callous piece of work that exploits images of children in pain or jeopardy. If you're so inclined, pray that the responsible parties crawl back into whatever hole they emerged from.

Also reviewed in:
CHICAGO TRIBUNE, 8/11/00, Friday/p. A, Vicky Edwards
NEW YORK TIMES, 8/11/00, p. E7, Elvis Mitchell
VARIETY, 8/14-20/00, p. 18, Robert Koehler
WASHINGTON POST, 8/11/00, p. C12, Rita Kempley
WASHINGTON POST, 8/11/00, Weekend/p. 32, Michael O'Sullivan

BLOOD SIMPLE

A USA Films release of the Director's Cut of a 1984 film, see *Film Review Annual 1984*. *Executive Producer:* Daniel F. Bacaner. *Producer:* Ethan Coen. *Director:* Joel Coen. *Screenplay:* Joel Coen and Ethan Coen. *Director of Photography:* Barry Sonnenfeld. *Editor:* Roderick Jaynes and Don Wiegmann. *Music:* Carter Burwell. *Music Editor:* Todd Kasow. *Sound:* Lee Orloff. *Sound Editor:* Skip Lievsay and Michael R. Miller. *Casting:* Julie Hughes and Barry Moss. *Production Designer:* Jane Musky. *Set Dresser:* Nancy Griffith. *Costumes:* Sara Medina-Pape. *Make-up:* Jean Ann Black. *Special Make-up Effects/Prosthetics:* Paul R. Smith. *Running time:* 96 minutes. *MPAA Rating:* Not Rated.

CAST: John Getz (Ray); Frances McDormand (Abby); Dan Hedaya (Julian Marty); Samm-Art Williams (Meurice); M. Emmet Walsh (Visser); Deborah Neumann (Debra); Raquel Gavia (Landlady); Van Brooks (Man from Lubbock); Señor Marco (Mr. Garcia); William Creamer (Old Cracker); Loren Bivens (Strip Bar Exhorter); Bob McAdams (Strip Bar Senator); Shannon Sedwick (Stripper); Nancy Ginger (Girl on Overlook); William Preston Robertson (Radio Evangelist).

NEW YORK POST, 7/7/00, p. 52, Hannah Brown

The director's cut of the Coen brothers' "Blood Simple" is exactly that—a shorter version.

In an interview released to critics to promote what's being billed as a "newly restored and re-edited" version of their 1984 neo-noir thriller, writer/producer Ethan Coen says of their debut film, "We've just taken out some of the boring parts."

But these cuts are so smooth, only a Coen brothers' scholar could notice them.

More jarring is the addition of a prologue, with an uncredited actor playing egghead "film preservationist" Mortimer Young, who goes on about the Coens' contribution to independent film.

As funny as this is, the old opening needed no tweaking. It was nice and, well, simple: the camera shows a deserted stretch of highway, with M. Emmet Walsh's Texas twang in a voice-over intoning the words, "The world is full of complainers."

Walsh's performance as the ironic, unscrupulous private detective who plays both sides of the game still delights, as does Frances McDormand (writer/director Joel's wife), perfect as the dewy-eyed babe with a heart of steel who outsmarts everyone.

McDormand, of course, went on to star in and win an Oscar for her role as the pregnant state trooper in the Coen brothers' "Fargo," for which they also collected an Original Screenplay award.

Dan Hedaya, now familiar from dozens of other character roles in films that include "The Usual Suspects," "Clueless," and "Dick," simmers with dangerous rage as the betrayed husband.

Although the performances of this trio are flawless and the twisty script constantly keeps the audience guessing (and laughing, often at the oddest moments), "Blood Simple" keeps its characters at arms' length , which is the one real flaw in the otherwise dazzlingly elegant design.

In later Coen brothers' movies, they learned to love their characters, especially McDormand's Marge in "Fargo" and Jeff Bridges' Dude in "The Big Lebowski."

But 16 years ago, they held themselves aloof from their own creations. You don't really root for McDormand or her lover (John Getz) to break free in "Blood Simple," so much as you wait to see who'll double-cross whom next. It's like watching Alfred Hitchcock try to solve a Rubik's cube in a roadside diner.

As Ethan Coen says of this new version, "We said it was restored, we didn't say it was any good."

VILLAGE VOICE, 7/11/00, p. 119, J. Hoberman

Appearing amid the same NYU-fueled mid-'80s indie boom that introduced Spike Lee, Jim Jarmusch, and Susan Seidelman, Joel and Ethan Coen's boldly facetious and monstrously clever *Blood Simple* was immediately heralded as something new. This was an independent movie unburdened by political or cultural aspirations—a signal that indies might just want to be fun.

Blood Simple, which reopened in a remixed and slightly reedited version the Coen brothers are calling the "director's cut," gave further notice that the material that had once been the province of Hollywood B movies was now up for grabs. Taking its title from Dashiell Hammett and borrowing a situation from James M. Cain, the Coen's 1984 debut was arguably the most influential noir since *Chinatown* (and until *Reservoir Dogs*). More specifically, *Blood Simple* gave an already highly aestheticized mode an ironic honky-tonk spin—or, rather, twang—while creating a precedent for indies like *One False Move, Red Rock West*, and *Bound*, as well as everything ever adapted from Jim Thompson.

Thus the movie became a cultural landmark after all. Nothing if not self-aware, the Coens are fully cognizant of this fact. Their rereleased *Blood Simple* may be the first so-called director's cut to be shorter than the original-release version, but that's only so they can include another joke. Actually, the new version is exactly the same length as the original because the filmmakers have added an introduction in which a distributor identified as Mortimer Young credits *Blood Simple* with "ushering in the era of independent cinema" and claims that now that the movie has been "digitally enhanced and tastefully restored" (with the "boring parts" excised and the unmistakable voice of Holly Hunter revealed on a telephone answering machine), it will be "forever young."

This epithet has a double meaning. *Blood Simple* is not exactly in the *Strike-Citizen Kane-Breathless* league, but if there ever was a movie-brat debut, it's the Coens' aggressively stylish mixture of showboat formalism and insouciant nose-thumbing. The movie's Texas landscape is as deliberate as its low-budget economy is ostentatious. This motel-room, two-lane-blacktop love triangle gone sour is a movie of suspicious minds and cartoonish performances. Glowering cuckold Dan Hedaya can hold the screen and nominal heroine Frances McDormand is scarcely less focused here than she would be in *Fargo*, while M. Emmett Walsh's good-old-boy affability is allowed to develop a suitably psychotic edge. Fall guy John Getz is the weak link-monotonously dry-mouthed and angst-ridden, he seems to be the one participant not in on the joke.

From the initial storyboard to the final sound design, *Blood Simple* is a supremely calculated intellectual exercise. The super-studied, neon-color compositions are stippled by perfectly arranged shadows. In addition to its cast *Blood Simple* boasts some distinguished credits—it was the first feature shot cinematographer-turned-director Barry Sonnenfeld and the first scored by the prolific composer Carter Burwell. There are some classic attention-grabbers, and the movie builds to a stunning denouement—including the horrendous image of an impaled hand—that owes a bit to the Coens' erstwhile mentor, Sam *"Evil Dead"* Raimi. (A dozen years later, Raimi would return the compliment with his succès d'estime *A Simple Plan.*)

Unextended to their characters, the Coens' generosity is expressed mainly in the movie's trove of sight gags, visual surprises, and little knickknacks to keep the frame busy. There is the sense that the Coens are examining life under a microscope or putting rats through mazes for their own amusement. *Blood Simple* features a hero so stupid that he manages to frame himself, even as he squanders whatever audience sympathy he might have earlier enjoyed. From first shot to last, the Coens seldom miss an opportunity to suggest that theirs is a movie made by evolutionarily advanced life-forms touring a primitive planet.

When I reviewed *Blood Simple* 15 years ago, I wrote that the film had "the heart of a Bloomingdale's window and the soul of a résumé." Though I still feel that way, the Coens eventually grew up—or, rather, brought themselves down. With *Fargo* and *The Big Lebowski*, the brothers subsumed their own egos into those of their stars—which is to say they finally managed to place their precocious virtuosity in the service of something approaching human warmth.

Also reviewed in:
CHICAGO TRIBUNE, 7/14/00, Friday/p. D, Michael Wilmington
WASHINGTON POST, 7/14/00, p. C1, Stephen Hunter
WASHINGTON POST, 7/14/00, Weekend/p. 34, Desson Howe

BLUE MOON

A Castle Hill Productions release of a Paradise Pictures film. *Executive Producer:* Norman Chanes. *Producer:* Ronnie Shapiro and Sylvia Caminer. *Director:* John Gallagher. *Screenplay:* John Gallagher. *Story:* Stephen Carducci. *Director of Photography:* Craig DiBona. *Editor:* Craig McKay and Naomi Geraghty. *Music:* Stephen Endelman. *Casting:* Bonnie Timmerman and Judy Henderson. *Production Designer:* Wing Lee. *Costumes:* Catherine Thomas. *Running time:* 90 minutes. *MPAA Rating:* PG-13.

CAST: Ben Gazzara (Frank); Rita Moreno (Maggie); Alanna Ubach (Peggy); Brian Vincent (Mac); Burt Young (Bobby); Vincent Pastore (Joey); Heather Matarazzo (Donna); Victor Argo (Tony); David Thornton (Frank's Father); Lillo Brancato, Jr. (Pete); Shawn Elliott (Ambassador).

LOS ANGELES TIMES, 11/17/00, Calendar/p. 22, Kevin Thomas

"Blue Moon" is a warm and pleasant romantic fantasy that shows Ben Gazzara and Rita Moreno to advantage but is better suited to the tube or the stage.

Adapted by its director, John Gallagher, from Stephen Carducci's story, this Castle Hill release simply isn't distinctive or substantial enough to warrant theatrical presentation, especially when screens are crowded with much stronger fare at this time of year.

Gazzara and Moreno play an attractive, wealthy couple who have been happily married for 40 years. Gazzara's Frank Cavallo, a hard-working, self-made man, has just retired from his textiles business and is at loose ends. The christening of his grandchild, coupled with a new lack of purpose, has left him depressed and discontent—and feeling hopelessly old and useless.

At the party after the christening, he drinks too much, and in their envy, he and some pals are unwittingly rude to the very young new wife of one of their friends, treating her as if she were a bimbo instead of the erudite archeologist she is.

All the while Moreno's Maggie keeps a wary eye on her clearly miserable husband, trying to curb his drinking and maneuver him into going home. Chic, vibrant and lovely, Maggie is a wise and special lady, handling Frank with a light touch.

When the closemouthed Frank refuses to open up to her, Maggie at last insists they take off for their vacation home in the Catskills. Alone with her husband, Maggie isn't so restrained, raising hell when he insists on listening to his beloved game on their car radio instead of the easy music she prefers.

Once at their place, it's clear that Maggie has her work cut out for her in getting Frank to talk about what's bothering him. Frank responds so thoroughly to Maggie's efforts to cheer him up that he becomes amorous, and while he heads for the bedroom she slips into a slinky nightgown—only to find him fast asleep.

But the night is not going to be like any other, for the moon has turned blue. Frank and Maggie are startled to be awakened by a young couple (Alanna Ubach and Brian Vincent) entering their cabin. The couple insist that they've rented the place, and as everyone starts calming down and trying to straighten out the seeming misunderstanding, Maggie gradually realizes that she and Frank are having a magical encounter with their 40-years-younger selves.

Their younger selves are encouraged to discover what a happy and successful future lies ahead for them, once they've overcome the obstacle of their very different backgrounds—he's blue-collar Italian American, she's the daughter of super-rich, super-snobbish Spanish nobility—during their courtship. Frank, it's hoped, will discover a sense of renewal in realizing anew what a good life and marriage he really has had.

Not surprisingly, Gazzara and Moreno are most effective, and Ubach and Vincent are appealing counterparts, even if their physical resemblance to the older Frank and Maggie is not all that strong.

"Blue Moon" has charm and wisdom, but its glow is too modest to expect it to attract crowds to theaters.

NEW YORK POST, 11/3/00, p. 51, Jonathan Foreman

If you care at all about independent film, then the fact that "Blue Moon" not only got made but found distribution and exhibition (in three Manhattan cinemas no less), represents an outrage—a cultural crime whose victims include all the genuinely talented people whose work hasn't made it to the screen.

Not to mention those of us forced by reviewers' ethics to endure every cringingly awful minute.

A hideously cloying, stunningly unimaginative, glacially slow fable about an irritable long-married couple who magically encounter their younger selves on a weekend trip to the Catskills, it unaccountably stars Ben Gazzara and Rita Moreno.

Gazzara plays grumpy, sulky Frank, a sixty-something Brooklyn businessman and new grandfather, now on the verge of retirement. Moreno is Maggie, his still vivacious wife. Frank's hopeful younger self—who we discover, delayed getting married to Maggie because he was still traumatized by his own father's violent abuse—is impersonated by Brian Vincent. Alanna Ubach does Maggie when she was still the spoiled daughter of the Spanish ambassador.

Neither Gazzara and Moreno nor anyone else in the cast are able to breathe life into writer-director John Gallagher's amateurish dialogue. This is a screenplay that would not pass muster for the lowest grade of hokey TV sitcom: Every joke falls flat, every labored attempt to be charming comes across as cutesy rather than cute, every moment of melodrama is irredeemably trite.

And these days, you would be hard pressed to find on TV ethnic stereotypes as crude as Gallagher's goombah Italian-Americans.

NEWSDAY, 11/3/00, Part II/p. B7, Gene Seymour

Most of us would gladly watch Ben Gazzara and/or Rita Moreno make funny faces at the audience for an hour and a half. That's how suggestive and magnetic they are as screen presences. Decades of experience have given these wonderful actors the seemingly magical ability to extract truth from a character or a phrase without strain.

And they try—oh, how they try!—to bring enough magic to wash away the clumps of bathos clinging to "Blue Moon," in which they are cast as Frank and Maggie, a prosperous, 60-ish couple who should be enjoying their sunset years together if it weren't for a smoldering, unresolved ache in Frank's soul.

Maggie thinks what Frank needs is a weekend in their Catskills cabin to rekindle their lost spark—or whatever cliche fits the situation. (There are plenty in the script to choose from.) But it's just like home. All Frank wants to do is watch sports and mope by the lake. While he sleeps, Maggie makes a wish on the "blue moon" outside.

Which comes true in the form of a young couple named Mac (Brian Vincent) and Peg (Alanna Ubach), who arrive at the same cabin, dressed and coiffed as if it's the 1950s. To them, it is the '50s, and they're about to bunk down for the night when they find Frank and Maggie in their bed. As the older couple hear the younger couple bicker between themselves, they get a strange feeling they've heard—and had—this same argument before. About 40 years before...

At this point, Rod Serling needs to step from the shadows. In fact, writer-director John Gallagher's script would have sounded a lot less labored and gaseous if it had been sliced to roughly the length of a 1960s "Twilight Zone" episode. As it is, the movie, far from transporting you into mystic romance, feels as if it's choking your senses in overcooked, underimagined dialogue and situations.

VILLAGE VOICE, 11/7/00, p. 138, Michael Atkinson

A significantly less plagued middle-aged couple [The reference is to *Boesman & Lena*; see Atkinson's review.] stands at the center of John Gallagher's *Blue Moon*—vaguely dissatisfied New Yawkas Frank and Maggie (Ben Gazzara and Rita Moreno), who attempt to rekindle their marriage at their Catskills vacation villa. Thanks to Gallagher's ludicrously coy script, the lucky pair wish (on the moon) for their younger selves and get them, literally: 25 years old, oblivious and randy. The four have a big chat, with flashbacks. Retarded magical-realist heartwarmth that demands a gross of Zantac in its own big way, Gallagher's movie never climbs out of its tuna can, despite the favors granted from the local paisano talent pool (Victor Argo, Vincent Pastore, Lillo Brancato Jr., Burt Young, etc.). A real midlife crisis might be more enjoyable.

Also reviewed in:
NEW YORK TIMES, 11/3/00, E16, Stephen Holden
VARIETY, 2/7-13/00, p. 57, Robert Koehler

BOESMAN & LENA

A Kino International release of a Pathé Image/Primedia Pictures production with the participation of Canal +/La Sept Arte.   *Producer:* François Ivernel and Pierre Rissient.   *Director:* John Berry.   *Screenplay:* John Berry.   *Based on the play by:* Athol Fugard.   *Director of Photography:* Alain Choquart.   *Editor:* Claudine Bouché and Jeanne Moutard. *Music:* Wally Badarou. *Sound:* Brigitte Taillandier and Emmanuel Augeard and (music) Jean-Paul Loublier. *Choreograper:* Alvon Collison.   *Sound:* Brigitte Taillandier and Emmanuel Augeard. *Casting:* Leo Davis and Jackie Mayou. *Production Designer:* Max Berto. *Art Director:* Mike Berg. *Set Decorator:* Fred Du Prez.   *Special Effects:* Mickey Kirsten. *Costumes:* Diana Cilliers. *Make-up:* Diana Hammond.   *Stunt Coordinator:* Mo Marais.   *Running time:* 88 minutes. *MPAA Rating:* Not Rated.

CAST: Danny Glover (Boesman); Angela Bassett (Lena); Willie Jonah (Old Man); Graham Weir (Recycle Man); Anton Stoltz (Farmer).

CHRISTIAN SCIENCE MONITOR, 11/3/00, p. 15, David Sterritt

"Boesman & Lena," a French-South African coproduction, takes place in the bad old days of South Africa's apartheid system. Its two main characters are a mixed-race man and woman wandering the roads outside Capetown in search of a place to hunker down after being driven from their meager home by white authorities.

Boesman is angry, bitter, and ready for violence at the slightest provocation, while Lena is more thoughtful, philosophical, and willing to take comfort from her memories of better times. Their emotionally complex relationship meets a new challenge when a down-and-out black tribesman strays across their path, desperate for a bit of food and a hint of human kindness.

He's with them for a short time, but it's long enough to catalyze a new phase in their lives as they struggle for meaningful interaction in a social situation based on oppressions that dehumanize everyone they touch.

Danny Glover and Angela Bassett play the title characters with great energy, and the late director John Berry has invested the movie as a whole with the moral conscience that underpinned his entire career. Athol Fugard's dialogue seems written for the stage rather than the screen, however—it has a larger-than-life quality that comes across too strongly when magnified in the movie theater—and the stars are so eager to be interesting that they don't always manage to be convincing as well. "Boesman & Lena" is a constructive film and in some ways an important one. But its impact doesn't live up to its ambitions.

LOS ANGELES TIMES, 11/17/00, Calendar/p. 14, Kevin Thomas

"Boesman & Lena" begins with a flurry of black-and-white images that first show people fleeing from their shantytown community, then cut to a mudflat alongside a river somewhere in the countryside outside Cape Town, South Africa, where a ragged-looking couple, among those driven from their makeshift shelters, have taken refuge. That's how the late John Berry begins his film of Athol Fugard's 1969 play, with Danny Glover and Angela Bassett triumphing in the title roles.

Be prepared to allow yourself to get used to this film. Berry decided, wisely it turns out, not to tone down the inherent theatricality of the material. Consequently, that it is shot on location at first seems merely to accentuate the feeling that we're looking at a filmed play.

But, gradually, the power of the material and the stars takes hold, flashbacks begin to flesh out the characters' lives, and "Boesman & Lena" comes alive—achingly and passionately, for time and circumstance have truly caught up with this couple, who have come to a dead end.

The beautiful but worn Lena still has flashes of her former allure and vitality, but grinding tragedy and hardship are dimming her eyesight and confusing her mind. The strong, strapping Boesman, somewhat older than Lena, is verging on a silver-bearded, bitter old age. In time we discover that the couple's life as farmers living in a modest but pleasant home started unraveling with the death of their only child at 6 months. Their downward spiral is barely glimpsed, but their all-consuming loss has left them vulnerable to apartheid's harshest realities.

They are reduced to a life of impermanence, eking out a living collecting bottles—some of which they've clearly emptied themselves—and redeeming them for a pittance. Home is whatever they've been able to cobble together from salvage. And it's because they've been forced to pull up stakes so often that Lena, desperate to give her hard experiences some sort of coherence, struggles to retrace their steps in her mind.

She's not about to get help from the sullen Boesman, who like many profoundly frustrated men through all time, takes out his rage on his wife. What is all too evident is that Boesman and Lena only have each other, but that's precisely what they need to acknowledge if they're to survive.

Out of nowhere emerges a weary, aging Xhosa tribesman (Willie Jonah), whose presence proves pivotal. That he cannot understand a word of English swiftly becomes beside the point to Lena, who's verging on hysteria.

This old man is to bear witness to all her ills, all her perplexities over the human condition and, above all, her grievances against Boesman, who is stunned that she would be willing to give up a bottle of wine simply to sit by the fire with the elderly stranger.

Lena is the showier role, and Bassett certainly catches all of the woman's mercurial mood swings: her sultriness, despair, courage, confusion and pride, drawing us into the sheer pain and injustice of her existence. Glover, in turn, shows us a man made brute, and who first must crumble before rediscovering his humanity.

Bassett and Glover rise to the challenge of these larger-than-life roles, just as you would expect. The strength of "Boesman & Lena" is that it is not merely an indictment of apartheid, but also a depiction of a marriage in which love has waned, regardless of who or what is to blame, and what must happen if there is to be even a possibility of its renewal.

In the end, the simplicity and directness of Berry's approach pay off. Berry, a survivor of the Hollywood blacklist, began his career in the theater and assumed the direction both in New York and on the road for the 1940 stage version of Richard Wright's "Native Son."

Throughout his career, Berry illuminated the lives of blacks in America and in South Africa, and directed Fugard plays in London and New York.

In a very real sense, therefore, his career came full circle with "Boesman & Lena," which he directed onstage in New York in 1970. He died in Paris last November at 82, a few days before completing post-production work on this film, the first version of which was made in 1976, with Fugard himself playing Boesman.

NEW YORK, 11/13/00, p. 77, Peter Rainer

Athol Fugard's play *Boesman & Lena* has been given a respectable presentation in the late director John Berry's adaptation, starring Danny Glover and Angela Bassett (particularly fine) as an itinerant, furiously divided mixed-race couple for whom the South African Cape Flats have become a landscape out of Beckett. Despite the staginess and stentorian line deliveries, there's an easeful naturalism to the racial and emotional horrors on view that makes them seem even more horrible.

NEW YORK POST, 11/3/00, p. 51, Lou Lumenick

Some might argue that "Boesman and Lena" deserves 3½ stars, purely on the basis of its good intentions. But this labor of love from Athol Fugard's 1970 play is awfully poky, even for an art film.

Major Hollywood stars like Danny Glover and Angela Bassett certainly deserve credit for participating in this low-budget filming of what's basically a two-person, one-set, very talky if worthwhile play.

The director is John Berry, a victim of Hollywood's 1950s blacklist who died during post-production.

Berry, who worked in Europe before returning to the U.S. in the late '70s to helm pictures like "Claudine," was a close friend of Fugard, who played Boesman himself in a forgotten 1976 film version of the play.

Boesman and Lena are a mixed-raced South African couple who have been driven from their shanty by the white minority during the apartheid era. They seek refuge in a makeshift campsite outside Cape Town.

Lena wants to talk about their flight, recalling happier times, which are depicted in brief flashbacks. But the embittered Boesman turns to booze to soothe his pain, and the couple battles verbally and physically.

As night falls, they encounter a Xhosa tribesman (Willie Jonah). Though he speaks a different language, Lena befriends the old man.

Boesman wants nothing to do with him and mocks Lena for her sympathy. When the man dies, Boesman worries he will be charged with murder.

This Beckett-like scenario is difficult enough to produce for the stage, and the movie (beautifully shot on location in South Africa by Alain Choquart) works only in fits and starts.

Though he has his moments, Glover is too one-note and seems uncomfortable leaving behind his good-guy persona to play his first really disagreeable character since "The Color Purple."

While too young and too pretty for the part, Bassett is more successful than Glover: Her proud Lena has enough shadings and sparks that it might conceivably get her an Oscar nomination in a lean year.

NEWSDAY, 11/3/00, Part II/p. B7, Jan Stuart

Late into "Boesman and Lena," a beautiful young woman dances before a strapping young man at an outdoor party. Her dance is ebullient and seductive, a prelude to what should be an enduring relationship. But instead of joy, we experience sadness and a crashing sense of irony, knowing that we are seeing a flashback to a distant moment that would be impossible to re-create.

For most of this soul-stirring adaptation of a play by Athol Fugard, we observe the couple years after the music has died. We can still make out traces of their youthful beauty beneath the exhausted eyes and graying hair, but their spirit has been broken by now, their joy spent. They are freshly homeless, wandering the mudflats of South Africa in search of scrap metal with which to build a shelter, as well as answers to the mystery of how they got to this junction in their lives.

When we first meet the couple, Boesman (Danny Glover) and Lena (Angela Bassett), they are plodding along a country road, the sum total of their belongings on their heads and backs. That morning, a government plow has leveled the lean-to home of this mixed-race couple (black and Colored, respectively), and they are returning to a nomadic place they have been many times before.

Rather than take comfort in each other's company, they vent their despair on one another. They goad, they needle, they fire invective with the instinctual aim of a marksman who can plug an Achilles heel in the pitch dark. Lena is starved for some sense of meaning to their Sisyphean existence, but Boesman refuses to grant her the satisfaction of a response. And when an old Xhosa tribesman (Willie Jonah) stumbles into their encampment, he becomes a lightning rod for their frustrations and a target for the hate that Boesman has internalized from the white elite.

Fugard wrote "Boesman and Lena" at the crest of apartheid, in 1969. While the psychological traumas felt by his couple still resonate, there is an italicized lyricism to Fugard's language (his characters often refer to themselves in the third person, among other mannerisms) that reminds us why his plays defy screen adaptations.

But before his death, John Berry did a creditable job of finding the blood in the piece, inspiring a staggering performance from Bassett that is punch-drunk with agony and ecstasy. The score by Wally Badarou is spare and haunting, just like the mudflats where "Boesman and Lena" find their way.

SIGHT AND SOUND, 5/01, p. 43, David Jays

Apartheid-era South Africa. Coloured couple Boesman and Lena arrive at the Swartkops river estuary. Their home was bulldozed earlier that day, and Lena is bruised where Boesman beat her. An old black man appears, and Lena invites him to join them, despite Boesman's hostility. She tries to confide in the visitor, but he speaks only Xhosa. She gives Boesman her bottle of wine in return for allowing the old man to spend the night with them. She reveals their history—how she and Boesman had a child who died as a baby, her subsequent miscarriages, their mutual estrangement. That night, Boesman threatens Lena. The old man dies. Boesman panics and tries to beat the corpse into life. Lena defies her husband, but at dawn they leave together.

With its combative itinerant protagonists, *Boesman & Lena* may be playwright Athol Fugard's *Waiting for Godot*, requiring only "an empty stage". Filmed on location in Cape Town, this second big-screen version (there was a 1973 Zimbabwean production directed by Ross Devenish) contains the action in a temporary camp on the mud flats near Port Elizabeth, South Africa. It begins in strong light, the sun etching stark shadows, the unforgiving landscape echoed by Lena's rust-coloured headcloth and Boesman's blue shirt.

Director John Berry's screenplay is a severely pruned affair. He chooses not to accompany the characters when they collect water or firewood. His camera moves between close-up and middle distance, shifting angle to reinforce the sense of an arena, or framing the actors in alienating compositions. Boesman's monologue about rubbish, for instance, is delivered from one side of the image, as if the character is being edged out.

Berry uses various registers for the flashbacks prompted by Lena's reminiscences to an old black man they meet, which begin with the bulldozing of the coloured couple's corrugated iron shack earlier that day. He shuffles hostile environments—urban, agrarian, elemental—to intensify our sense of their alienation. Glimpses of their early marriage present a prelapsarian world of lush greenery. The couple look young and trim, and Lena is pregnant. We construct a chronology through fading smiles, battered clothes, physical distance. The film creates a sense of a past gone wrong, paying increased attention to the couple's dead children. We see a baby's coffin, and then the next shot is a cardboard box used for a subsequent miscarriage. The dog that briefly hounded them also features—Lena smiling at the shadow of its profile. For her the dog was "another pair of eyes" giving credence to her life; so too does the old man and, by extension, the camera.

A scavenging aesthetic informs the layered costumes and ramshackle shelters. "We're white man's rubbish," asserts Boesman. "We've been thrown away". The tall, weathered old man is even more battered than his hosts. Whites are notably absent, except in fleeting flashback, and the marginalised coloured and black characters are placed in uneasy opposition, despising each other and their own economic dependence.

Angela Bassett's battered survivor sustained by riffs of song recalls her Tina Turner in *Tina What's Love Got To Do with It?* Vivacious in adversity, she shimmies in the face of Boesman's indifference, but seems weary when she makes her great gesture: retaining humanity in such conditions is arduous. Her final defiance is etched in burnished close-up by the fire, while Boesman flusters in the blurry background.

If Bassett is occasionally melodramatic, Danny Glover softens Boesman's bullying. Yet his monolithic presence is powerful, spitefully grinding bread underfoot and raging with self-hatred. Again, flashbacks provide resonant backstory—Berry shows him pondering the burning shanty town, enjoying his moment of release and rushing forwards until he arrives at the edge of a half-built freeway. Then the picture swoops back to a tangle of bare branches. The visual metaphors for stalled progress may not be subtle, but they are effective.

VILLAGE VOICE, 11/7/00, p. 138, Michael Atkinson

That John Berry's adaptation of Athol Fugard's apartheid melodrama *Boesman & Lena* was graced with an indulgent slot in the latest New York Film Festival is a testament to the harrying grip HUAC still exercises over the consciences of American movie culture. With paradise once lost to careerist skulduggery, attempts at regaining Hollywood's squandered princess crown and hymen persist, even as the witnesses all face the business end of their *Biography* specials. The unpopular Oscar canonization of Elia Kazan, and the accompanying amnesia about the late Abraham Polonsky notwithstanding, Berry was one of the McCarthy gauntlet's last men standing, exiled to decades of European obscurity by the blacklist. Long a race-relations flag-waver (he acted in a 1940 stage version of *Native Son)*, Berry died last year while *Boesman & Lena* was in postproduction, and there will be those for whom the film's blunt-cudgel obviousness will seem a fitting coda. I haven't suffered such overcooked caterwauling since my first Rangers game.

A personal disclaimer seems called for: In general, the leaden, loud indulgences and speechifying Tinker Toy-ness of filmed theater give me gas. Whereas *Boesman & Lena* might not have been a return to the fold for Berry, it's no challenge to middlebrow sanctimony, either. Fugard's sermon on racism boils down to two voices and a junk heap; it's Beckett if Beckett were John Singleton, and *Waiting for Godot* were *Higher Learning*. Boesman (Danny Glover) and Lena (Angela Bassett) are an aging, half-crazy homeless couple carving out a night's shelter on the barren but lovely Cape Flats, after being bulldozed from their shantytown. Their relentless, overenunciated bickering—shut up, no you shut up—focuses on their ingrown love-hate while picking over the pair's recent series of flop-stops, Boesman's fondness for violence, and an elderly tribesman (Willie Jonah) who wanders into their riverside power struggle.

Stilted as a beach house, the movie crawls from one harangue to another, and the passionate tirades against the "white man" are duly overshadowed by the passion for actorly Excess. You have to appreciate the effort—Bassett in particular works up a ferocious aerobic spritz—but the effect resembles seals begging for fish, not incisive social drama. Berry, in the end, could be gracelessly literal, but *Boesman & Lena* is simply served stagecraft, which is the most and least that can be said for it. The flat, frighteningly empty South African cape lands, on the other hand, wait on the outskirts of society for a filmmaker to exploit their metaphoric torque.

Also reviewed in:
CHICAGO TRIBUNE, 2/2/01, Friday/p. I, John Petrakis
NEW REPUBLIC, 11/13/00, p. 26, Stanley Kauffmann
NEW YORK TIMES, 9/23/00, p. B17, A.O. Scott
VARIETY, 5/15-21/00, p. 30, Todd McCarthy

BOILER ROOM

A New Line Cinema release of a Team Todd production. *Executive Producer:* Claire Rudnick Polstein and Richard Brener. *Producer:* Suzanne Todd and Jennifer Todd. *Director:* Ben Younger. *Screenplay:* Ben Younger. *Director of Photography:* Enrique Chediak. *Editor:* Chris Peppe. *Music:* The Angel. *Music Editor:* Lisé Richardson. *Sound:* Peter Schneider. *Sound Editor:* Frank Gaeta. *Casting:* John Papsidera. *Production Designer:* Anne Stuhler. *Art Director:* Roswell Hamrick and Mark White. *Set Decorator:* Jennifer Alex. *Set Dresser:* Henry Kaplan, Dana Neuwirth, and Jeffrey S. Rollins. *Costumes:* Julia Caston. *Make-up:* Caryn Brostoff. *Make-up (Nia Long):* Kyra Panchenko. *Stunt Coordinator:* Mike Russo. *Running time:* 110 minutes. *MPAA Rating:* R.

CAST: Giovanni Ribisi (Seth Davis); Vin Diesel (Chris); Nia Long (Abby Halperin); Nicky Katt (Greg Feinstein); Scott Caan (Richie); Ron Rifkin (Seth's Father); Jamie Kennedy (Adam); Taylor Nichols (Harry Reynard); Bill Sage (Agent Drew); Tom Everett Scott (Michael); Ben Affleck (Jim Young); John Griesemer (Concierge); David Younger (Marc); Russell Harper, Mark Webber, and Christopher Fitzgerald (Kids), Donna Mitchell (Seth's Mother); André Vippolis (Neil); Jon Abrahams (Jeff); Will McCormack (Mike the Casino Patron); Jared Ryan (Casino Steve); Anson Mount, Kirk Acevedo, Seth Ullian, and Eddie Malavarca (Brokers); Carlo Vogel (Rude Kid); Matthew Saldivar (Series Seven Kid); Serge Skliarenko (Croatian Broker); Lisa Gerstein (Sheryl); Ross Ryman (Isaac); Marjorie Johnson (Abby's Mother); Peter Rini, Raymond Pirkle, and Joe Pretlow (JP Brokers); Peter Maloney (Dr. Jacobs); Lori Yoffe (Secretary); Alex Webb (FBI Director); Gillian Sacco (Waitress at Mickey's); Don J. Hewitt (Local); Mark Moshe Bellows (John Fineman); Daniel Serafini-Sauli (Broker Steve); Lucinda Faraldo (Trendy Hostess); Neal Lerner (Gay Man); Taylor Patterson

(Sara Reynard); Michael McCarthy (Max Reynard); Marsha Dietlein (Susan Reynard); Joseph Tudisco (Janitor); Judy Del Guidice (Office Woman); Siobhan Fallon (Harry's Supervisor).

LOS ANGELES TIMES, 2/18/00, Calendar/p. 10, Eric Harrison

Every generation, or so it would seem, needs its own bleak tale about the manly world of business. One would have thought Arthur Miller had made the definitive statement with "Death of a Salesman" in 1949, but then came David Mamet with "Glengarry Glen Ross" to show that there was plenty of wear left in those old shoes.

Oliver Stone added a very-'80s twist with "Wall Street," dressing up his ruminations on fathers, sons and money in thousand-dollar suits and situating them in the high-pressure world of stock trading.

Now comes "Boiler Room," and like a coat of many colors stitched from secondhand cloth, the movie draws from the works that preceded it, then takes to the street with a too-cool hip-hop strut. The result isn't pretty—some colors clash and the design could use some work. From a distance, though, it's fly.

The search for life's meaning in a world that measures success only through money is a perennial and always timely theme. And first-time writer-director Ben Younger's depiction of an amoral Wall Street subculture where young blue-collar men become millionaires overnight is often quite intriguing.

Giovanni Ribisi plays Seth, a college dropout driven to get rich quick by greed and a misguided desire to please his dad. His stern, demanding father is a judge, which makes you wonder why Seth thinks breaking the law will win his love. But after first running an illegal casino out of his home, he follows the smell of money to the testosterone-fueled war zone of a sleazy brokerage firm.

"The white boy's way of slinging crack rock" is how he describes it in voice-over. The film paints the traders as a sort of upwardly mobile street gang. They're hoodlums in tailored suits, snorting coke, starting fights, getting rich on other people's misery. They talk unsuspecting investors into putting their money into bogus stocks. Then, in a complicated scam, they leave the buyers high and dry.

When it's introducing us to this world and its coldhearted characters, the movie is nothing less than compelling. But as soon as Younger tries to spin all of this into a story, he goes astray. There are too many subplots, for one thing, and they nearly all are peopled by ciphers.

Then there's Seth's budding love affair with Abby, the firm's good-hearted but compromised black secretary. With a white actress as Abby, the role would've floated away—it's that negligible. But casting Nia Long adds layers of implication and shading.

This workplace is rife with animosity and name-calling. Jews bait Italians. Italians slander Jews. And everyone slurs black people who, with the exception of pretty Abby, can't even get through the door. Before meeting Seth, she was sleeping with one of the bigoted senior brokers. Her race is only touched upon lightly, but because she's African American, her interactions with all the other characters are electric.

Ribisi carries the film quite nicely. He is an intense, brooding presence. With his sad, droopy eyes and pale skin, and hair slicked back like Gordon Gekko's, he comes to resemble a vampire over the course of the movie. He's playing a man who sucks others dry, but Ribisi makes us care about Seth's struggles with his conscience.

The way this movie deliberately evokes memories of "Wall Street" and "Glengarry Glen Ross" invites the audience to make comparisons. Ben Affleck plays a small role that is clearly modeled on the tough, arrogant Alex Baldwin character in "Glengarry." And "Boiler Room" tips its hat to "Wall Street" with a funny scene in which the brokers watch the older film on TV, speaking the lines along with the characters. This doesn't work in its favor. Mamet's play and the 1992 movie made from it are perhaps the most trenchant handling of these themes since "Salesman."

And "Wall Street," a schematic and overly didactic movie, nevertheless operates on several levels in a way that is beyond Younger's reach. In a scene in "Wall Street," for example, Charlie Sheen's broker challenges his father on a Manhattan sidewalk. They talk about the fate of an airline where the father works. But the fight also registers both as a turning point in their relationship and a philosophical debate about values and the American economy.

"Boiler Room" never achieves that sort of synthesis. It tries to make larger points, but it trips over itself just trying to make the small ones.

Its corresponding scene strains mightily to be significant on just a father-son level, and it falters. Ribisi gets whipped into such a lather that he lapses into a bad Marlon Brando imitation—he all but sobs, "I cudda been a contenduh."

It is perhaps a sign of changing times that in Miller's play, Willy Loman is grappling with the meaninglessness of his life and the lies he's had to tell himself to make it through the day. In "Boiler Room," the stakes aren't that high. Ribisi's Seth Davis just wants his dad to love him. He's a scared little boy in fancy clothes. A simple pat on the head and none of this sturm und drang would've been necessary.

NEW YORK, 2/28/00, p. 54, Peter Rainer

The unofficial motto of the chopshop brokerage firm J.T. Marlin, with its twentysomething trainees and Gen-X millionaire mentors, is "Honor is in the dollar." Part Rat Pack, part Hitler Youth, these all-male brokers are part of the boiler-room subculture that hard-sells dubious stocks to unwitting customers, gets rich on outrageous commissions, and always tries to stay half a step ahead of a federal investigation. In *Boiler Room*, the 29-year-old first-time writer-director Ben Younger captures the adrenaline-pumped rush of this world, which seems initially like a fantasy land but is probably only slightly exaggerated. Younger was a stand-up comic and worked in New York State politics as a campaign manager and policy analyst before starting out in the movie business as a video cameraman. Researching the sock-it-to-me telemarketing and brokerage-firm underground for this film, he probably figured he hit the high-concept jackpot; and, at least for the film's first hour or so, he does hit it, repeatedly.

What makes the film such a giddy ride is that Younger doesn't really separate himself out from the sharkiness on the screen; it's not an outsider's view of an insular tribe. Instead, we have the tang of an insider's take—Younger is caught up in the chase, too. Even toward the end, when the film gets moralistic and remorseful and heavy on the Freud, the dullness doesn't entirely becloud the glitzy corruption that came before. Younger may want to rack up points for being a humanitarian, but his real juices are elsewhere: in the scrape and bounce of the swindle in all its fine fettle.

Seth Davis (Giovanni Ribisi) is our tour guide through the underbrush: A college dropout who runs his own casino out of his Queens apartment, he is motivated by a fierce desire to win the respect of his unyielding father (Ron Rifkin), a New York judge who sees his son as a flop and a crook. Seth's entrance into J.T Marlin is, in a sense, a continuation of his casino operation, a way to score big and be a success in his father's eyes. Younger sets up this father-son stuff as if he were really saying something, but it reeks of Screenwriting 101: Lock in Your Motivation. What is glaringly obvious is that Seth is drawn to the game because it makes him feel like a player. Seth is in his element when he's cold-calling a dupe on the phone, scamming the poor soul with stock options for a company that may not even exist. Closing the deal isn't just an adrenaline rush, it's testosterone heaven.

Younger plays not only on our avidity for becoming instant millionaires but also on our resentments toward the dot-com culture, with its slicksters spinning around in Ferraris when they seem barely old enough to drive. In one of his periodic somnolent voice-overs, Seth says of his roving pack of brokers, "They had all the money in the world and not a clue what to do with it," and it's hilariously true. (The crackerjack crew includes Scott Caan, Vin Diesel, and Jamie Kennedy.) The mansion of one of his mentors is like a garish mausoleum; cooling out after a hard day bilking investors, his cohorts sit around in the TV room watching Oliver Stone's *Wall Street* on video and gleefully reciting the dialogue right alongside Michael Douglas's Gordon Gekko. Younger gets at the ways in which these guys, not just the chop-shoppers but also, by implication, the big-time brokerage boys, model themselves after their pop-culture stand-ins.

Younger draws a lot from David Mamet in his depictions of this seller's hothouse, but he does it with a twist: The salesmen here are fully conscious of being Mamet-y; their bible is Alec Baldwin's big, win-at-all-costs speech from the movie of *Glengary Glen Ross*. J.T. Marlin's head recruiter, played by Ben Affleck, does a series of riffs on Baldwin's aria, and each one is funnier and crueler than the last. (One ironclad rule is "Don't pitch the bitch"—don't sell stock to women.) Stock-selling as it's practiced here is a contact sport, and the stock jocks, clumped together in bars or on the streets, are as itchy to rumble as any gang. Shimmying before his boiler-room buds, Seth's nemesis Greg (Nicky Katt) crows, "I am a Jew, I have the mind of a champion," and it's both a taunt and a celebration: This guy, like the other chop-shop superstars, does his greatest selling job on himself.

"Do you know how good it is to close someone?" Seth says to us after a particularly spectacular play, and we realize it's a high he can never really come down from. Once he gets religion, he's *on* all the time; even when he receives a call at home from a *Daily News* subscription telemarketer, he can't resist teaching the bumbler how to improve his pitch. As the film streaks along, Seth grows increasingly pale, vampirish almost, as if his swindles had drained all his blood away. By the end, he looks positively cadaverous, and yet, in this cutthroat milieu, the look fits. His bone-whiteness is chic evidence of a job well done. He's chosen the right profession. So has Ben Younger.

NEW YORK POST, 2/18/00, p. 55, Lou Lumenick

Who wants to be a millionaire?

Seth Davis (Giovanni Ribisi), the morally challenged hero of "Boiler Room," writer-director Ben Younger's exciting debut feature, certainly does.

Overly eager to win the respect of his disapproving father (Ron Rifkin), college dropout Seth hopes to do better than his current occupation—running an illegal casino catering to students in the basement of his Kew Gardens home.

So he signs up with J.T. Marlin, an obscure, high-pressure stock brokerage on Long Island.

Promised he'll become a millionaire in months, trainee broker Seth quickly learns from more seasoned colleagues as they bully unwitting strangers they "cold call" into buying dubious stocks that will earn the brokers huge commissions.

Seth easily slides into this high-testosterone world of amoral Goldman Sachs-wannabes who can recite dialogue from Oliver Stone's "Wall Street" by heart and who gleefully model themselves on the real-estate sharks of David Mamet's "Glengarry Glen Ross."

But Seth has a fatal flaw for this kind of work—a gnawing curiosity and conscience that will have terrible consequences for himself and his father, an emotionally frigid federal judge straight out of Steinbeck's "East of Eden."

For a film so indebted to other works—which Younger, to his credit, fully acknowledges—"Boiler Room" has energy and wit to bum. The blue-lit boiler-room scenes have the knowing vitality of observed life.

Younger, whose background is in music videos, begins the movie with flashy jump cuts that don't really suit the material, but quickly switches to a more traditional style of storytelling.

That approach rarely falters over the course of two riveting hours, except for an overly melodramatic depiction of how one of Seth's scams unravels the life of a Wisconsin caterer (Taylor Nichols).

Pasty-faced Ribisi—who was in "Saving Private Ryan"—is terrific as Seth, whipsawed between his greed and his rigidly moral upbringing, as exemplified in another razor-sharp performance by Rifkin.

Vin Diesel and Nicky Katt are outstanding as ruthless senior brokers who compete for Seth's loyalty, and Nia Long ("The Best Man") is touching as a secretary who becomes romantically involved with Seth.

Ben Affleck does the best acting of his career in the small but very showy part of the brokerage's pile-driving recruiter, who exhorts his trainees to—in Mamet's words—"always be closing."

"Boiler Room" pays off with emotional dividends well worth the time investment.

NEWSDAY, 2/18/00, Part II/p. B7, John Anderson

The people behind the thoroughly derivative but fascinatingly current "Boiler Room" might want to give thanks—maybe even co-producer credit—to Bill Clinton, Alan Greenspan and whomever else they think has been behind our ongoing economic growth/orgy of avarice. Theirs is such a movie, of its moment that any serious dip in the fiscal zeitgeist might have rendered "Boiler Room" an immediate antique. As it is, the timing's just about perfect.

And while that's more than you can say for the movie, it's still a fast-clipped, tightly drawn drama and the kind of entertaining morality tale that manages to have things both ways—we're drawn in by the easy-moneymakers, consoled by their comeuppance. Set amid the "stock-jocks" of a Long Island-based brokerage ("Exit 53 on the LIE... a half-hour from Wall Street"? Right-by helicopter), it's about a world of cold callers where fortunes can be made, fortunes can be lost, but the rules of the Securities and Exchange Commission are always made to be broken.

The testosterone at J.T. Marlin—where Seth Davis (Giovanni Ribisi) comes to make his fast buck and make his jurist father (Ron Rifkin) love him—is thick enough to cut with a Peter Luger steak knife; its mysogyny is only slightly less severe than "In the Company of Men." (Marlin's rule one: "Don't pitch the --- and, yes, it rhymes.) The greed is, appropriately enough, comparable to that of "Wall Street," which the brokers rent for inspiration.

But the movie most responsible for "Boiler Room" is "GoodFellas": From Seth's rueful narration (and its retrospective perspective) to the almost inevitable outcome, debuting writer-director Ben Younger is tapping Scorsese like untaxed revenue.

And like Ray Liotta's Henry Hill, Seth is a born hustler; having dropped out of college, unbeknownst to Dad, he's running a lucrative casino in his rented Queens living room. When Greg (Nicky Katt), one of J.T. Marlin's Ferrari-driving slicksters, gets cleaned out by Seth, he sees a possible candidate for his firm. But can Seth cut it?

Of course he can, but not until after a predictably rocky start that begins with an anti-pep talk by the head recruiter (Ben Affleck, phoning it in), some inspired phone-seduction by the firm's leading con man, Chris (a solid Vin Diesel) and an ill-advised romance with receptionist Abby (Nia Long, who's great). The last incident incurs the jealous wrath of Greg, who gets even more unhappy when Seth becomes a star.

Then the feds arrive, as the feds do, and Seth is faced with losing it all, including his compromised father. What "Boiler Room" could have used is Joe Pesci being homicidal. What it has is its roots in a music-video sensibility and the accompanying philosophy of letting soundtrack dictate visuals. Ben Younger shows a lot of promise in "Boiler Room," but next time out he should maybe make a movie that's entirely his own.

SIGHT AND SOUND, 6/00, p. 36, John Wrathall

New York, the present. To the disgust of his father, a judge, 19-year-old Seth Davis has dropped out of college. On the commendation of a friend, he goes for a job at J. T. Marlin, a fly-by-night brokerage firm run by the charismatic Michael. Seth is soon hooked on the thrill of the fast buck and impressed by his millionaire colleagues. He passes his stockbroker's exams and wins his father grudging respect.

Seth starts to date the receptionist Abby, thereby earning the enmity of his team leader Greg, who's Abby's ex-boyfriend. When Seth discovers one of the medical companies whose stock he has been selling is just a shell, he realises that the whole operation is fraudulent and illegal.

When one of his clients, Harry Reynard, loses his life savings on stock Seth sold him, Seth appeals to his father for help, which he refuses to give. Arrested by the FBI, Seth is played a tape phone call in which he discussed a deal with his father. Rather than see his father's career ruined, Seth agrees to testify against J. T. Marlin. Just before the office is raided, Seth uses his sly sales skills to trick Michael into compensating Harry Reynard for the money he lost.

The writing and directing debut of 27-year-old Ben Younger, *Boiler Room* wears its influences very much on its sleeve. When Seth first goes for a job at J. T. Marlin, he and the other applicants are treated to an inspirational harangue from a recruiter who promises them they'll be millionaires in three years if they can stay the course. Moments later, as if atoning for the extent of his lift from a similar scene with Alec Baldwin in *Glengarry Glen Ross*, Younger has one of his characters namecheck that film and its author, David Mamet. And before we can say *Wall Street*, Younger shows us the guys from J. T Marlin sitting around at home watching a video of Oliver Stone's 1987 film, parroting Gordon Gekko's "Lunch is for Wimps" speech word for word. Younger seems to be trying to convince us that it's his characters, rather than himself, who are imitating these films.

However great his debt to Mamet and Stone, Younger certainly succeeds in adding a few phrases of his own to the lexicon of macho sales talk, notably "Don't pitch the bitch," (a J. T Marlin house rule forbids employees to sell stock to women because supposedly they'll always be calling back and making a fuss). But despite its wealth of relishable dialogue, Younger's script has problems in other departments. Whenever he strays away from self-contained set-piece scenes—Ben Affleck's harangues as the recruiter; a classic moment when Seth gets a call from a salesman flogging newspaper subscriptions and coaches him on his pitch—Younger falls back on cliché. Seth's paper-thin relationship with the receptionist Abby is just an excuse to whip up some rivalry with his boss Greg, while his yearning to win his father's respect depends on an astonishingly clunky piece of backstory involving the ten-year-old Seth and his new bike.

The awkward structure—opening at a not particularly significant moment half way through the story, then flashing back "three months earlier"—and a rambling voiceover don't help. Both devices seem like last-ditch attempts to inject momentum into the narrative and explain the bewildering financial small print of J. T. Marlin's scam. Or perhaps Younger just wanted to pay Scorsese homage while he was at it.

As director, Younger throws in a couple of montages of people driving around, ostentatiously edited to the hip hop score, but otherwise relies on fuzzily photographed dialogue scenes. He does extract some boisterous performances from his young cast, notably Vin Diesel as Seth's mentor Chris. But Giovanni Ribisi, such a promising supporting actor in *Saving Private Ryan* as a medic and *Friends* as Phoebe's dopey brother, doesn't seem a big enough presence for a starring role yet. His emotional breakdown in front of his father is plain embarrassing, and even his sales patter never seems quite slick enough. To convince us that Seth really is the dynamite salesman we need to believe he is, Younger has to fall back on another woeful cliché: the FBI agent listening in to Seth's phone calls and commenting, to no one in particular, "This kid is really good."

TIME, 2/28/00, p. 96, Richard Schickel

Seth Davis (Giovanni Ribisi) makes money the old-fashioned way: he has turned his college-dropout pad into a mini-casino, where he deals blackjack. It's a nice living, but not a lifestyle that offers much in the way of parental bragging rights. This is a matter of some moment to Seth's sour father (Ron Rifkin), a federal judge who has sentenced his son to life in the doghouse for his slacker ways.

What Seth needs in a hurry—that is, before he turns 30—is a Ferrari, a closetful of Armanis, a couple of mil—and, oh yes, respectability. That's where J.T. Marlin, the brokerage firm, comes in. O.K., it isn't exactly J.P. Morgan. It is, in fact, as the title of writer-director Ben Younger's morally earnest yet very lively first feature has it, a *Boiler Room*.

That is to say, it's a large, open, blue-lit space where dozens of young men, operating at the top of their lungs, sell disreputable stocks to people who mostly can't afford them. Phony pharmaceuticals are particular favorites, which compounds the moral squalor of the operation. In their off-hours the young hustlers watch *Glengarry Glen Ross* to learn the tricks of their trade and *Wall Street* to justify it. But they don't really need audio-visual education. Not when they have Jim Young so close at hand. He's their recruiter, mentor, goad and ideal. He's played by Ben Affleck, and the role may be the best thing Affleck has ever done—so abusive, yet so coldly glamorous in his amorality.

Seth gets good at the game under Jim's tutelage. By which we mean, of course, bad. But not irredeemable. Can that be a hint of remorse we see lurking in his eyes as he devastates the life savings and the marriage of an innocent wholesale grocer? Can that be a hint of relief we sense in him when the feds close in with their offer of immunity if he rats the whole place out? Yes, and yes again.

Director Younger is only 27, and possibly just a tad retro. If he were really on cynicism's cutting edge, wouldn't Seth have a dotcom and be frantically kiting an ipo? Maybe not. Maybe that's the sequel. In the meantime, we have this curiously intense, alertly principled, refreshingly uncynical movie to savor.

VILLAGE VOICE, 2/22/00, p. 135, Amy Taubin

Goodfellas meets *Wall Street* indie-style. *Boiler Room* takes us inside a stock-trading chop shop where 22-year-old guys earn millions by conning people into investing in nonexistent companies. It's a seemingly no-holds-barred depiction of an ugly milieu that's a decade overdue for exposure on the big screen; and I suspect its biggest fans are going to be young men from legitimate Wall Street firms, who will think themselves honest and virtuous by comparison. But writer-director Ben Younger has set his sights wider. *Boiler Room* picks away at the money-ruled mentality of the moment, which makes anyone who didn't seize the opportunity to make big bucks in the '90s now feel like a fool.

Our guide to this mind-set is Seth Davis (Giovanni Ribisi), a Queens College dropout and talented entrepreneur. Seth is running a casino in his Kew Gardens basement when he's recruited by J.T. Marlin, a small brokerage house located in a Long Island strip mall. Believing that this is a serious career opportunity, one that will legitimize him in the eyes of his disapproving father (Ron Rifkin), Seth plunges in and discovers that he enjoys peddling stocks over the phone, that he gets an adrenaline rush from seducing customers by preying on their fear of missing out and from fulfilling the boiler room's guiding principle, "Always be closing" (borrowed from *Glengarry Glen Ross*, a film which, along with *Wall Street*, is these hotshots' bible). But unlike his fellow workers, who either don't want to know or know and don't care what they're selling, Seth is curious. He's also troubled by the pangs of an underdeveloped but active conscience. Still, he's too preoccupied to notice the feds closing in.

Restless and driven, *Boiler Room* distributes its energy differently than do the high-testosterone, Scorsese-influenced indies of the past decade. While cinematographer Enrique Chediak doesn't eschew handheld and Steadicam moves, he doesn't call attention to them either. Although visually rather static, the film is still quite beautiful in its high-contrast, dark-toned use of color. More cerebral than kinetic, Younger keeps his focus on the actors and on his own punchy, revealing dialogue.

Like *Mean Streets* and *Goodfellas*, *Boiler Room* takes us inside the consciousness and the coded masculine world of a single character. Younger gives Ribisi a star-making role and he more than delivers. Ribisi has a feline body and pale-skinned face that's at once soft and angular. His most notable feature is a Cupid's-bow mouth, held slightly agape as if it were sucking in information. He can resemble either Gary Oldman or Christopher Walken, but he has a shy, sly sexuality that's all his own.

His greatest asset here may be his voice, which makes it seem as if he's confiding secrets. "The Notorious B.I.G. said it best," Seth tells us in his opening voice-over. "Either you've got a wicked jump shot or you're slinging crack rock." His way of slinging crack rock, Seth continues, is to become a stockbroker. There's a lot at stake in this deceptively casual self-analysis. One of the most interesting aspects of the film is the mix of envy and fear in the relationship of the boiler-room white guys to gangsta rap, a relationship that's never again openly stated but is implied through a terrific wall-to-wall score by The Angel.

The ensemble cast behind Ribisi never makes a misstep, but there are particularly strong performances by Rifkin, Vin Diesel as a senior partner who's making millions but still lives with his mother, and Nia Long as J.T. Marlin's executive secretary and only African American employee, who falls for Seth as much as he falls for her.

Although the plotting gets a bit predictable toward the end, the script is intelligent and boldly written throughout. Seth's colleagues like to put *Wall Street* on the VCR and parrot the dialogue; their real-life counterparts as well as those who sanctimoniously look down on them may find similarly choice lines in *Boiler Room*. When Seth makes junior partner, some of the senior partners take him into Manhattan to celebrate. They wind up at the Odeon, Seth's suggestion no doubt. The gay art-world types at the next table object to the boys' dick-slinging jokes and loutish behavior, inquiring if it's their way of making themselves attractive to the bridge-and-tunnel crowd. "They should take all of you and throw you on a fucking island somewhere," yells one of the boiler-room boys. "Well, I've got news," counters one of the art-world types. "You're on it."

Also reviewed in:
CHICAGO TRIBUNE, 2/18/00, Friday/p. A, Mark Caro
NATION, 3/20/00, p. 52, Stuart Klawans
NEW REPUBLIC, 3/13/00, p. 35, Stanley Kauffmann
NEW YORK TIMES, 2/18/00, p. E30, A. O. Scott
NEW YORKER, 3/13/00, p. 100, David Denby

VARIETY, 2/7-13/00, p. 52, Emanuel Levy
WASHINGTON POST, 2/18/00, p. C1, Stephen Hunter
WASHINGTON POST, 2/18/00, Weekend/p. 45, Desson Howe

BOOK OF SHADOWS: BLAIR WITCH 2

An Artisan Entertainment release of a Joe Berlinger/Haxan Films production. *Executive Producer:* Daniel Myrick and Eduardo Sanchez. *Producer:* Bill Carraro. *Director:* Joe Berlinger. *Screenplay:* Dick Beebe and Joe Berlinger. *Director of Photography:* Nancy Schreiber. *Editor:* Sarah Flack. *Music:* Carter Burwell. *Music Editor:* Todd Kasow. *Sound:* Jay Meagher and (music) Michael Farrow. *Sound Editor:* Paul P. Soucek and Warren Shaw. *Casting:* Bernard Telsey, Will Cantler, and David Vaccari. *Production Designer:* Vince Peranio. *Art Director:* Rob Simons. *Set Decorator:* Susan Kessel. *Special Effects:* Steve Kirshoff and Will Caban. *Costumes:* Melissa Toth. *Make-Up:* Gina W. Bateman. *Special Make-up Effects:* John Caglione, Jr. *Stunt Coordinator:* George Aguilar and Peter Buccossi. *Running time:* 90 minutes. *MPAA Rating:* R.

CAST: Kim Director (Kim); Jeffrey Donovan (Jeff); Erica Leerhsen (Erica); Tristen Skyler (Tristen); Stephen Barker Turner (Stephen); Kurt Loder (Himself); Chuck Scarborough (Himself); Bruce Reed, Lynda Millard, Deb Burgoyne, and Andrea Cox (Burkittsville Residents); Joe Berlinger and Sara Phillips (Burkittsville Tourists); Lann Flaherty (Ronald Cravens, Burkittsville Sheriff); Pete Burris, Ed Sala, and Robert M. Kelly (MBI Men); Briton Green and Erik Jensen (Stoners); Peggy K Chang, Tony Tsang, and Anja Baron (Foreigners); Kevin Murray (Doctor); Keira Naughton (Nurse); Lauren Hulsey (Eileen Treacle); Tyler Zeisloft, Richard Kirkwood, and Justin Fair (Teenagers); Raynor Scheine (Rustin Parr); Brilane Bowman (Ham Lady); Kennen Sisco (Peggy); Dina Napoli (WBAL Reporter); Landra Booker (Fox 45 Reporter); Jacqui Allen (Reporter); Sloane Brown (WJZ 13 Reporter).

LOS ANGELES TIMES, 10/27/00, Calendar/p. 1, Kenneth Turan

A fake spawned by a bigger, more successful fake, "Book of Shadows: Blair Witch 2" was doomed to be inconsequential and forgettable, and it is.

Despite grossing $250 million worldwide on a $30,000 budget, the original "Blair Witch Project" was no more than a mildly spooky charade powered by a brilliant marketing campaign. The sequel is here only because of that success: The dynamics of the marketplace (follow-ups to successful films earn at least half of what their predecessor did) insisted it exist, and so it does.

Aware of the vulnerable position he's in, "Book of Shadows" director Joe Berlinger (who also co-wrote with Dick Beebe) has provided journalists with a three-page, single-spaced "Director's Statement" that talks about what he did and why. It's a fascinating document, much more interesting than the film, though its chances of persuading anyone that what we've got here is "a meditation on violence in the media, and how the media shapes an event" are not great.

Berlinger was an interesting choice to make "Book of Shadows." He's been primarily a documentary director up to now, which fits with the fake-doc aspects of the original "Blair." And his best-known works, "Brother's Keeper" and "Paradise Lost," were filmed in milieus similar to the rural environs of Burkittsville, Md., population 200, where both "Blairs" are set.

Berlinger's sequel, in fact, does come up with a plausible premise, one that plays with the fact that the original's Web site fooled many viewers into thinking that its tall tale of three young people who disappeared tracking a legendary witch was true. It doesn't continue the first film's story but concentrates on another youthful group whose members, like many of their peers, saw the film and can't decide if it was real or not.

"Book of Shadows" opens in this playful mode, with a mini-mockumentary about the effect "Blair Witch" had on Burkittsville, which was invaded by true believers (Berlinger gives himself an amusing cameo as one of them) intent on buying authentic Blair stones and sacks of bona fide Black Hills dirt.

But as if suddenly remembering what kind of film it's supposed to be, "Book of Shadows" gets down to the formulaic and mostly unfunny business of putting together what becomes a piece of standard scare fare, full of people screaming, vanishing and saying, "I think something really bad has happened."

First comes the introduction of the victims, led by Burkittsville native Jeff (Jeffrey Donovan), who missed the "Blair" opening due to an enforced visit to a mental hospital but made up for that by seeing the film 17 times once he got out. A "Blair" entrepreneur, he's begun a new business called "Blair Witch Hunt—Tours by Appointment," and we get to go along on his maiden minibus voyage. "We provide the amenities," he feebly jokes; "you risk certain death and dismemberment."

Along for the ride are Tristen (Tristen Skyler) and Stephen (Stephen Barker Turner), a couple working on a book to be called "Blair Witch: Hysteria or History" that looks to combine his rationalism and her belief. Also on the bus are Kim (Kim Director), a Morticia look-alike who has some ill-defined psychic powers, and Erica (Erica Leerhsen), a Wiccan or modern-day witch who is irate that "'Blair Witch' set us back 300 years, ruined our image."

Out this group troops to some picturesque Black Hills ruins, the very spot where the original "Blair Witch" videotapes were allegedly found. Erica hopes to contact the actual 18th century witch, Elly Kedward, and use her as her mentor, and indications are she may have succeeded too well.

The one night the group spends in the woods, not to mention the succeeding time they hang out in Jeff s dilapidated residence, an abandoned broom factory (brooms, get it?), is filled with all kinds of strange and inexplicable doings that seem like witch-inspired mayhem. Or do they? That's the gimmick in a nutshell.

Despite some visual tricks and persistent flash-forwards, "Book of Shadows" is very conventional at heart with something of a Roger Corman horror-film feeling about it. Attempting to do things differently than the original "Blair," it allows blood on screen and shows knives poking around where you wouldn't want them to be, but by the standards of the genre doesn't qualify as excessive.

Audiences who show up for the reason Kim gives for signing up for the tour—"I thought the movie was cool"—may not be so taken with the witch this time around.

NEW STATESMAN, 10/30/00, p. 45, Jonathan Romney

The Blair Witch Project may not rank among the very greatest horror films, but it was one hell of a marketing opportunity. The "mockumentary" premise was that the film comprised footage made by three students who had wandered into the deep, dark woods, never to return. Part HP Lovecraft, part Hansel and Gretel, the film was shot on camcorders by the actors themselves, and its greatest asset was the power of suggestion, the creeping presence of whatever you thought you saw looming in the juddery, lowresolution darkness.

With excitement cranked up by an ingenious website, the film took more than $140m in the US alone, making it a miracle of cost-effectiveness. It also created a brand, which is now shamelessly exploited in Book of Shadows: Blair Witch 2. The original film-makers, Daniel Myrick and Eduardo Sanchez, neither directed nor wrote it, but are credited as executive producers. They know a milch cow when they see one; the question is whether the poor beast is being milked or ritually slaughtered.

The premise sounded interesting at first—the sequel would not feature the same actors or characters, nor even be in the same style as the original. While the first film masqueraded as documentary—all the better to avoid the cliches of contemporary horror—Book of Shadows was entrusted to a real documentarist, Joe Berlinger, best known for a film about child murders. Yet, perversely, he has turned out a standard teen horror flick, jammed with all the cliches. Book of Shadows does, however, claim to be something else: the first caption announces "a fictionalised re-enactment of events after the release of "The Blair Witch Project". We are on well-mapped territory, then—like the Scream franchise, this is another self-conscious horror film about horror.

Book of Shadows begins in the world we know, in which The Blair Witch Project has been a huge hit. In Burkittsville, Maryland—the scene of the original—the locals are heartily sick of visiting fans trekking through the woods. The souvenir trade, however, is doing nicely, and local boy Jeff is running a Blair Witch Tour. His clients include a nervy, colourless academic couple, a wry Goth and a latter-day New Age witch. Needless to say, they should have stayed home and rented *Blair Witch #1* on video.

Like all sequels, this one promises to be a little different and a little the same. Like Myrick and Sanchez, Berlinger uses video footage supposedly shot by the characters, and also has the characters and cast share the same names, in the interest of that elusive blurring of reality and fiction. But unlike Myrick and Sanchez, Berlinger pulls every catchpenny trick in the book: a soupcon of vaguely raunchy sex, loads of tricksy MTV effects and swathes of thrash metal soundtrack. Call me old-fashioned, but loud electric guitars and the uncanny somehow don't go together—Marilyn Manson just doesn't chill my marrow. There's a nice comic moment at the start, when the group meets a rival tour and the two leaders face off with their camcorders. Then it descends into an idiot abyss: hell-hounds with digitally whitened fangs; ghostly 1890s urchins; a bridge that collapses, then doesn't; and, most gratuitously of all, what looks like a cameo from *The Exorcist*'s demon child.

Let's give Berlinger and his co-writer, Dick Beebe, the benefit of the doubt, and accept that, as Berlinger claims, the object is "a meditation on violence in the media". The argument is that the characters are suffering from collective hysteria: they have taken the whole Blair Witch phenomenon a bit too seriously. Let's accept also that Berlinger wanted to extend the original film's exploration of camcorder phenomenology—hence, some nutty business about videotapes that show bizarre midnight orgies, but only when played backwards. A very generous interpretation, then, would be that the film's ludicrous excesses are really the excesses of a hypothetical sensationalist "re-enactment" of what might have happened to Jeff and co. Berlinger is actually parodying a very bad *Blair Witch* sequel that someone else might have made.

Do we buy this? I hope not. Berlinger wants to have it both ways. In the film, much talk is devoted to demystifying witchcraft—or Wicca, as devotees prefer to call it. Erica, its representative here, is a healthy New Age lass who simply likes to get her kit off outdoors. Yet the film's message is clear, and in keeping with the most conservative horror: don't mess with what you don't understand, because it will destroy you. And, more unpleasantly, if you must go into the dark woods, avoid the locals—ugly, intolerant hicks who will happily throw rocks at anyone under 20. This is horror designed to appeal to embittered teenage Limp Bizkit fans.

Book of Shadows claims to be interested in the moral panic over screen violence, ending with a TV newsreader tuttutting that "violent art has inspired real-life violence". Yet the film finally seems to endorse that condemnation. The message seems to be that, if a horror film doesn't make you violent, it will drive you mad—or perhaps just bore you stupid. Berlinger's film is either witless or too clever for its own good—which, in horror, is as good as being witless. The audience that loved the original film will feel horribly shortchanged by this mess. *Blair Witch 3* is already in the works: perhaps its subject matter will be the sinister curse that made the second film bomb.

NEW YORK, 11/6/00, p. 84, Peter Rainer

When *The Blair Witch Project* turned out to be a smash hit, it was inevitable in this franchise-obsessed world of ours that we would soon be hearing about sequels and prequels. Made for $30,000, the film had been bought at Sundance for a cool million by Artisan Entertainment, a figure that, at the time, prompted the joke that the scariest thing about the movie was the amount of money Artisan paid for it. But the pooh-poohers were wrong: The film grossed $141 million in the summer of '99 and made the cover of *Time*. On the other hand, they turned out to be right: If a cheapo scam like *The Blair Witch Project* can command those numbers, then look out. In the high-stakes world of Hollywood hucksterism, there is nothing scarier for the movie studios than being beaten at their own game.

Artisan's much-admired and envied marketing campaign for the film, involving extensive use of the Internet and a cable documentary chronicling the movie's supposed real-life happenings, was much more original than the film itself, which, while occasionally terrifying, was undone by its motion-sickness-inducing cinematography and its screaming-meemies heroine. One wishes the witch, or whatever it was, had gotten to her a lot sooner.

Book of Shadows: Blair Witch 2 acknowledges the bogus nature of its predecessor while creating its own bogus mind warp. Five obsessed fans of the first film, led by a local (Jeffrey Donovan) recently released from a lunatic asylum, participate in a guided tour of the same Black Hills location where the first film was shot; the quintet includes a perky Wiccan (Erica Leerhsen), a mime-white-faced Goth (Kim Director), and a grad-student couple (Tristen Skyler and Stephen Barker Turner) researching the Blair Witch phenomenon—is it truth or mass hysteria? All come to a bad end, but since the next film in the franchise is supposedly the prequel, their fate is presumably of lesser importance.

Book of Shadows does not require Dramamine to sit through, and for that it has my most grateful thanks. But why sit through it at all? The first film was marketed for the willfully gullible; even after the supposedly slaughtered protagonists turned up on *David Letterman,* there were still those who thought the whole thing was real.

For *Book of Shadows,* the target audience, besides the first film's fans, is all those pointy-headed cynics who place themselves above the fray. This selling technique is known as expanding your franchise base. Joe Berlinger, a respected documentarian making his dramatic-feature-film debut, offers up a Director's Statement in the press notes that explains, "I thought it was important to examine and comment upon the impact of the general conflation of fiction and reality that has occurred over the last decade or so." There's a sucker born every minute. (In this case, the director could be his own best sucker.) I don't think this approach will work as well as the old one, not because cynics are any less gullible than the booboisie but because this sort of thing has already been done to death by the likes of Wes Craven and David Cronenberg. The cheapo horror films from many decades past didn't have to carry all this academic baggage. Nowadays even something as crassly commercial as the sequel to *Blair Witch* palms itself off in postmodern doublespeak. Now, *that's* scary.

NEW YORK POST, 10/27/00, p. 49, Lou Lumenick

This execrable follow-up to the surprise smash "The Blair Witch Project" is considerably less scary than watching Joan Rivers on Oscar night.

What *is* frightening, though, is imagining the fury of legions of fans of the first movie who not only discover they've been rooked out of $9.50 to be bored witless—but that this sequel gleefully ridicules their enthusiasm for "Blair Witch."

Without the "Blair Witch" name attached, this grade-Z mishmash would be lucky to go straight to video, much less open on 3,000-plus screens.

As if being handed Joe Berlinger's "director's statement" defending his unseen work on the way into the screening wasn't a bad enough omen, the movie opens with the announcement that what we're going to see is a "fictionalized" re-enactment of events following the opening of the first movie.

That's right. The first "Blair Witch" was, duh, just a movie (a device used with rapidly diminishing returns by two other horror sequels this year, "Scream 3" and "Urban Legends 2: Final Cut"). The phenomenon is commented upon by the likes of Kurt Loder and Roger Ebert and the residents of Burkittsville, Md., in a none-too-sharp mini-mockumentary.

It gets worse, Much worse.

It's the fall of 1999, and Jeff (Jeffrey Donovan), a recently released mental patient, is cashing in on the "Blair Witch" craze, selling stickmen on the Internet and conducting a "Blair Witch Hunt" tour in the woods of Maryland's Black Hills section.

His first (and last) tour group includes Erica (Erica Leerhsen), a Wiccan; Kim (Kim Director), a Goth chick; and Tristen (Tristen Skyler) and Stephen (Stephen Barker Turner), a pair of grad students who are writing a book called "The Blair Witch: Hysteria or History."

After a night at the site where the student filmmakers supposedly disappeared during the first movie (which was really just a movie), Tristen suffers a miscarriage and the five discover they can't account for five hours they spent there—much less the slaughter of five people in another tourist-group nearby.

The slaughter is shown in brief, grainy clips that are played over and over again. Most of the film takes place in the abandoned brewery where Jeff lives, where they argue incessantly and endlessly watch video footage shot during their visit.

In his statement, Berlinger, who didn't direct the first movie, claims to be seizing on "a unique opportunity to break new ground." But he's merely replaced the refreshing shaky-cam minimalism of the first "Blair Witch" by recycling every hoary slasher-flick cliché of the last 30 years—precisely the stuff its predecessor, which I liked a lot, studiously avoided.

Berlinger halfheartedly tries to disguise the dumbness of the story line and the groan-inducing dialogue (which he devised with Dick Bebee, who was behind last year's "House on Haunted Hill" remake) by throwing in flashbacks, flash forwards and fantasy sequences.

But "Book of Shadows: Blair Witch 2" isn't funny, frightening or even engaging—even by contemporary horror-movie standards.

The acting wouldn't pass muster in an elementary-school Halloween skit, the editing and lighting are hopeless and even the copious use of thundering heavy-metal numbers may fail to keep audiences awake.

Berlinger, a respected director of documentaries, writes that he wanted to make "a different kind of sequel—one that defies expectations."

What he's done is repeatedly thumb his nose at the elaborate mythology constructed by the creators of the first film, not to mention audience members he apparently thinks were stupid to suspend disbelief.

Berlinger wasn't content to kill the golden goose, he also had to dismember it. "Blair Witch," R.I.P.

NEWSDAY, 10/27/00, Part II/p. B3, John Anderson

Have no fear "Book of Shadows: Blair Witch 2" is enough of a radical deviation from the hugely popular and profitable "Blair Witch Project" to make both fans and non-fans happy. The grand mal camera techniques are all but gone, so it won't induce either seasickness or cries of "ripoff!" It doesn't masquerade as a documentary. The production values are high. And there are some real ideas—mostly about the skewed perceptions of a world that could create a "Blair Witch Project" in the first place.

And as a horror movie? Like we said, have no fear.

The original "Blair Witch" was based on the recovered "lost footage" of a trio of witch hunters who disappeared into the Maryland woods—and which was marketed via a Web site that implied the story was real. This ticked off a lot of people when (and if) they finally figured it out. But the movie's directors also understood the essence of real screen horror: It isn't what you see that makes you scared. It's the opposite. And thanks to the obscured, tremulous perspectives of "The Blair Witch Project," there was a lot of room for runaway imagination.

The horror genre—or the teen horror genre, because that's how it's evolved—has now come full circle via Joe Berlinger's "Book of Shadows." What the talented documentarian ("Brother's Keeper," "Paradise Lost") did was fashion his sequel not around the story of the first film, but the phenomenon it created. So in "Blair Witch 2," he has five curiosity seekers of various stripes—a former mental case, a Wiccan witch, a Goth girl and two romantically involved researchers—go into the Black Hills near Burkittsville, Md., where they drink, smoke, black out and then awake with mayhem on their hands.

But this is not much of a leap from the farmhouse-campsite-dorm room scenaria of the classic slasher/horror movies of Tobe Hooper, John Carpenter or especially Wes Craven (it's no accident Berlinger's local sheriff is named Craven), whose "Scream" movies have taken the horror genre one way—into a postmodern parody of itself. "Blair Witch," faced with an exhausted and special-effects sodden genre, went the other way-beyond back-to-basics, to a kind of bleached-bone approach.

Ironically, Berlinger's ideas about reality programming and mass hysteria are topical and pointed, but he's constructed around his and Dick Beebe's script a pretty traditionalist fright film. Put together a group of people, some of whom you wouldn't mind seeing mass-murdered (Erica Leerhsen's strident Wiccan is one of the more annoying characters ever) and have chaos ensue. Had he, in fact, played his hand more straightforwardly, "Book of Shadows" might have worked better, because to create chaos you need a certain amount of clarity. And the movie's various subplots, flashbacks and hallucinations are tripping all over each other.

In setting up what he calls his "anti-sequel," Berlinger opens with a little faux-doc of his own, a series of talking heads with Burkittsville "residents" and tourists (Berlinger himself is one of them) who talk abut the town being overrun by people who still think "The Blair Witch Project" was real. This is preceded by bits of footage from the programs of Jay Leno, Conan O'Brien, Roger Ebert and Chuck Scarborough, all talking about "BWP." Leno, and O'Brien are entertainers, and exempt. But Ebert and Scarborough are supposed to be journalists. And that they appear in a movie ostensibly protesting the vanishing point between reality and entertainment means that Berlinger got in at least one good joke: The inmates really are running the asylum.

NEWSWEEK, 11/6/00, p. 78, David Ansen

All the best stuff in "Book of Shadows: Blair Witch 2" happens before the credits—and the credits aren't at the end. This sequel is set after the release of the original "Blair Witch Project" and in the faux-documentary spirit of the original the townsfolk of Burkittsville are interviewed about the havoc the blockbuster movie has wreaked on their lives. Joe Berlinger, a documentary filmmaker himself ("Brother's Keeper" and the HBO hit "Paradise Lost: The Child Murders at Robin Hood Hills"), gets these snippets of duplicitous "reality" just right. It's a clever, funny start, and, for a moment, you may think there actually was a good reason to make a sequel to last year's one-of-a-kind phenomenon.

And then the movie proper begins, in slick 35mm color, and it is just another dreadful teen horror flick—albeit one gussied up with self-conscious notions about the thin line between perception and reality. Once more we set out into the Black Hills of Maryland, but the characters have changed. They are four amazingly unappealing twentysomethings who have paid to go on a "Blair Witch Hunt: a grad-student couple researching mass hysteria (Stephen Barker Turner and Tristen Skyler), a comely Wiccan (Erica Leerhsen) who believes in Nature, not Evil, and the psychic Kim (Kim Director), whose pancake-white Elvira makeup never seems to smudge, even when the orgiastic blood rituals begin. Their tour guide is former mental-institution inmate and Blair Witch entrepreneur Jeff (Jeffrey Donovan), Burkittsville's black sheep. When a competing gaggle of tourists is found slaughtered in the nearby woods, this motley crew become the likely suspects.

Berlinger was an intriguing choice—his documentaries reveled in dark, outré subject matter—but he seems to have no idea how to work with actors. The entire cast should sue him for malpractice: not since the death of B movies has there been so much cheesy overacting. The writing is on a similar level. With each new gory development, someone delivers a variation on the line "What the f--k is going on?" What indeed. "The Blair Witch Project" was no masterwork, but in its no-budget way it gave the audience something it hadn't seen before. There was no way its success could be duplicated. But why would anyone think *this* was the way to carry on the name? If you harbor any fond feelings for the original, stay far away from this mess.

SIGHT AND SOUND, 12/00, p. 42, Kim Newman

It's a year after the release of *The Blair Witch Project*, a film consisting of footage shot by three students who were making a documentary about a witch in the woods near Burkittsville, Maryland. The town is overrun by sensation-seeking tourists. Jeff, a local youth, hosts a *Blair Witch*-themed tour of the area. His first customers are graduate students Stephen, who is writing a book on the *Blair Witch* phenomenon, and Tristen, his pregnant girlfriend; Wiccan Erica, who argues that the film maligned her religion and is seeking communion with martyred witch Elly Kedward; and Kim, a goth girl who claims to have psychic powers.

The group venture to the ruined house where the original *Blair Witch* footage was found and run into a rival tour, whom they misdirect to another witch-related site Coffin Rock. While camping overnight, the group black out for several hours and wake to find Stephen's manuscript in tatters and Jeff's camera equipment smashed. Tristen has a miscarriage. The group retreat to a nearby disused factory to examine the tapes shot during their blackout. Erica disappears and is discovered stabbed to death. The local sheriff calls to tell them the rival group has been found murdered at Coffin Rock. Later, ghost children cause Kim to crash a van.

The tapes apparently reveal that the group, possessed by the spirit of Elly Kedward or her tormentors, destroyed the equipment. Tristen, transformed into the Blair witch, taunts Stephen into killing her. The survivors are taken into custody and the tapes prove them collectively guilty of murdering the rival group and individually of separate killings—Kim of a grocery-store clerk, Jeff of Erica, Stephen of Tristen.

Although no one involved in the making of *Book of Shadows* is a household name, there's a lot of classy talent behind the follow-up to a film which derived much of its potency from its apparent emergence out of nowhere. Director-writer Joe Berlinger comes from the documentary tradition *The Blair Witch Project* so cunningly imitated, having won plaudits for *Brother's Keeper* and *Paradise Lost The Child Murders of Robin Hood Hills*. To build on the improvised dialogue, thrown-together artefacts and minimal soundtrack of the first film, the sequel calls in co-writer Dick Beebe (who wrote the remake of *House on Haunted Hill,* art director Vince Peranio (who does wonders with the witch's new lair, an abandoned broom factory), composer Carter Burwell (a Coen brothers regular) and musician Marilyn Manson (who assembles a selection of goth-rock tracks). The film may not have a blockbuster budget, but it's clearly well-funded in an independent sort of way, with the money saved from hiring an unfamiliar cast used to haul in behind-the-camera expertise.

The Blair Witch Project could only ever have been a one-off, but in the year that's followed its release there's been a flurry of spoofs (*The Bogus Witch Project*), disreputable footnotes *(The Erotic Witch Project),* blatant rip-offs *(The St. Francisville Experiment)* and the first of what one dreads will be a slew of shaky camcorder killer in-the-woods quickies (*Camp Blood*). Artisan the US distributor who hit big with *Blair Witch,* and Haxan, the production company, put the sequel project out to tender and went with one of several suggested continuations (the film follows a small group of *Blair Witch* fans on a tour of sites connected with the original movie). Probably wisely, Berlinger breaks from the *faux*-documentary framework of the first film; although we see a lot of video footage apparently shot by the characters (or even by the unseen witch), most of the movie sticks to the formal rules of mainstream film-making. Though there are no on-screen monsters, there are some gruesome special effects in flashes or close-ups and the dialogue is solidly competent (lacking the improvisary feel of the original).

There are interesting ideas throughout: by replaying certain characters' actions on videotapes that show radically different versions of incidents we saw earlier (in a conventionally shot sequence *Blair Witch* fan Kim has an argument with a grocery clerk; a security camera later shows the same scene, although this time she stabs the woman to death), the film unsettles some of the assumptions underlying *The Blair Witch Project*. After all, if the witch can manipulate video and film footage, then what status can the material that made up the original have? The sloppy but amusing opening of *Book of Shadows,* with Burkittsville residents who live near the witch's stomping ground jeering at a flood of *Blair Witch* fans or trying to hawk them souvenirs, already blurs the films status as a fiction— in the narrative universe of *Book of Shadows,* is *The Blair Witch Project* a film by Heather Donahue, one of that movie's characters, or by credited directors Daniel Myrick and Eduardo Sanchez? Tellingly, the local sheriff complains about the unethical use of the word documentary. Given this confusion, even what seems like a plain lapse (the tapes contain footage of the tapes being buried) might be another manifestation of the witch's influence, like the witch marks that sprout like poison ivy on the characters' bodies.

Like Berlinger's *Paradise Lost, Book of Shadows* is about the search for scapegoats. Each of the characters is set up to take the blame for the murders: Kim, the goth girl, claims that in her home town she is treated like a mad killer because she wears black clothes and make-up; Erica, a real witch, insists on arguing with the media's misrepresentation of her beliefs and shares the pain of Elly Kedward, the witch from the original film, during her protracted execution; Jeff is a released mental patient and net-nerd; and Stephen is consumed by his research on a book entitled *Blair Witch: Hysteria or History?* As the film comes to a close, after the bodies have inevitably piled up, a news commentator claims "sadly, as so often in this country, violent art has inspired real-life violence". The moment comes too late, after too much ordinary or uninspired business, but again the *Blair Witch* franchise is asking its audience to think again about its definitions of "violent art" and "real life".

TIME, 11/6/00, p. 113, Richard Corliss

The original movie was a cool joke America decided to play on itself. *The Blair Witch Project,* which last year earned a huge $140 million on a teeny $30,000 budget, was not by any stretch a great film. It was a clever prank, brilliantly peddled, that played on primal fears. And everyone had to be a part of it. Let's be scared by a horror movie with no visible monster. Let's convince ourselves it's real. Like kids in the dark, let's pretend.

But who would want to play the same joke twice, or be the butt of it? *Book of Shadows: Blair Witch 2* arms a new bunch of young people with video cameras, throws them into the Maryland woods and lets hysteria ensue. The notion of director Joe Berlinger and writer Dick Beebe is that the five new recruits (Jeffrey Donovan, Tristen Skyler, Stephen Barker Turner, Erica Leerhsen and Kim Director) know the first film was fake and are cynical of the industry built around it, yet get sucked into the legend. Then everyone goes nuts—this time with flash cuts and gross-out special effects. An all-in-the-mind thriller degenerates into the *Linda Blair Witch Project*.

Berlinger, who has co-directed true-crime documentaries in rural settings *(Brother's Keeper, Paradise Lost)*, juxtaposes the real with the surreal, whatever those words mean in a fictional spin-off of a pseudo documentary. *BW2* ends in a delirious ambiguity, which can be solved by the maxim "Films lie; video tells the truth." But few movies have spread their fibs or facts as clumsily as this one. There's not an emotionally plausible moment in the picture. If Berlinger thinks he's commenting on media sensation—and not trying to exploit it—then the joke's on him.

VILLAGE VOICE, 11/7/00, p. 130, J. Hoberman

Book of Shadows, documentary filmmaker Joe Berlinger's sequel to *The Blair Witch Project*, announces itself as a "fictionalized reenactment" of something that actually happened after the movie *The Blair Witch Project* opened. By this, *Book of Shadows* means to reflect on its precursor's phenomenal success. The hype continues.   The hype continues. *Book of Shadows*, which is set in the summer of 1999, features actual TV news items about *Blair Witch* along with some broadly staged satire of tourists and crazies descending on the Maryland backwater where the movie was supposedly set.

The basic premise, not too dissimilar from the self-parodic *Scream* and its sequels, sends a group of cute kids—including a Goth psychic, a Wiccan hottie, and an unhappy couple who are collaborating on a book with a title like *Blair Witch: Modern Myth or Collective Delusion?*—on a magical mystery tour organized by the enterprising Jeff, a graduate of the local mental hospital. Their first night in the woods starts like a dorm-room bull session. Berlinger misses an opportunity here in not making this a discussion of possible sequels to the movie with which these happy campers are obsessed. Still, he shows a flair for drama by contriving to have this first bunch run into a rival tour group. It's a good joke that, unfortunately, turns out to be the movie's last. Suffice to say that something weird happens that night and the gang winds up at Jeff's isolated, bunker-like souvenir emporium-cum-mixing studio.

Where the original *Blair Witch* was based totally on the power of suggestion, *Book of Shadows* is filled with all manner of tawdry tricks—dreams, hallucinations, flashbacks, flash-forwards, bloody inserts, raucous Satan rock, and inane run-ins with hysterical locals, most appallingly the local sheriff who seems to believe that he's Slim Pickens back from the grave. *Blair Witch* was conceptually rigorous; *Book of Shadows* is elaborately self-referential. The kids are trapped chez Jeff and so are we—although the creepiest echo in this hall of mirrors is that of Berlinger and Bruce Sinofsky's 1996 *Paradise Lost*, a two-and-a-half-hour documentary about the murder of three Arkansas boys allegedly by a teenage trio of devil-worshipers.

Blair Witch's Dogme-like camerawork assaulted the eyes; *Book of Shadows* attacks the ears. The only thing in this noisy bore that's more clamorous than the various poltergeist visitations is the self-reflexive quips—mainly the characters screaming at each other that nothing makes any sense.

Also reviewed in:
CHICAGO TRIBUNE, 10/27/00, Friday/p. A, Mark Caro
NEW YORK TIMES, 10/27/00, p. E13, Stephen Holden
VARIETY, 10/30-11/5/00, p. 21, Dennis Harvey
WASHINGTON POST, 10/27/00, p. C1, Stephen Hunter
WASHINGTON POST, 10/27/00, Weekend/p. 38, Desson Howe

BOOKWARS

An Avatar Films release of a Camerado production. *Producer:* Jason Rosette. *Director:* Jason Rosette. *Screenplay:* Jason Rosette. *Director of Photography:* Jason Rosette. *Editor:* Jason Rosette. *Music:* Rich Goldstein, Little Muddy, and Jack McDuff. *Sound:* John Travis. *Special Effects:* Eric Schira. *Running time:* 79 minutes. *MPAA Rating:* Not Rated.

CAST: Peter Whitney (Street Bookseller, Toadlover, Artist); Rick Sherman (Street Bookseller, Magician, Wiseguy); Marvin (Street Bookseller, Angel, Recovering Alcoholic); Paul (Street Bookseller); Everett Shapiro (Street Bookseller, End-of-the-Night Journeyman); Polish Joe (Street Bookseller, Smoker of 100 Cigarettes); Al Mappo (Street Bookseller, Seller of Maps); Margueritte (Street Bookseller, Strong Woman); Ron Harris (Street Bookseller, DAMN-that guy); Jason Rosette (Street Bookseller, Media Maker).

CHRISTIAN SCIENCE MONITOR, 6/9/00, p. 15, David Sterritt

High-tech filmmaking grabs the headlines, especially when epics like "Gladiator" and "Mission: Impossible 2" hit the screen. But low-tech filmmaking remains alive and well, allowing directors to take more personal approaches to more idiosyncratic subjects.

Take the new "BookWars," by Jason Rosette, a proudly independent filmmaker. Its topic has never received feature-length treatment before, even though it's familiar to anyone who's strolled down a city sidewalk: the street-side booksellers who peddle their wares like urban nomads, braving all kinds of weather and occasional raids by police.

Staying true to his subject, Rosette has filmed "BookWars" not in glossy 35mm film, but in a range of inexpensive formats including Super-8 film, Super VHS, digital video, and two kinds of 8mm video. This lends an appropriate feeling of intimacy without hampering the director's ability to tap a few of the special effects so popular today—slow-motion has been added and Rosette has even concocted a brief dream sequence.

What the movie presents through these unassuming means is a smart and funny depiction of the book-selling scene in New York's art-conscious Greenwich Village, portraying its participants and showing what happens when the forces of law and order—embodied by a local university and a city-sponsored campaign to unclutter the sidewalks—decide to expel them from their turf.

It's a small-scale film in every way, made by a former member of the book-peddling trade who respects the privacy of his "characters."

At a time when many young directors aspire to be the next Steven Spielberg, it's refreshing to find one who names Walt Whitman and old westerns among his influences. "BookWars" is as winning as it is modest.

NEW YORK POST, 6/9/00, p. 50, Lou Lumenick

The title promises rather more conflict than is delivered in this soporific documentary about the city's sidewalk book vendors, which only fleetingly covers the Giuliani administration's attempt to limit them.

Director Jason Rosette, a former street bookseller who teaches digital video production at NYU, lovingly depicts his struggles and those of his eccentric colleagues.

In monotonous narration, Rosette rants that the vendors' right to free speech should allow them to obstruct sidewalks, but the portrait of his subculture is so vaguely rendered, it will likely put audiences to sleep rather than change minds.

VILLAGE VOICE, 6/13/00, p. 160, Michael Atkinson

Jason Rosette's *BookWars* is a pungent example of what Wintonick's old-timers are talking about: an artless but seductive piece of DIY sociology, made by a West 4th Street bookseller about other West 4th Street booksellers, with whatever format camera he could find. Hardly profound or penetrating (it's no *Salesman*, on which Maysles in Wintonick's film muses, "There's the selling, and the Bible: In a way, what else is there to indicate what America is all about?"), Rosette's film suffers from cheap-hipster narration and transitional muddiness. But the street vendors, operating on the disorderly edge of commerce (truly, what is less valuable to capitalist culture than a used paperback?), are entertainingly eccentric travelers, with an ersatz knowledge of Camus and Heidegger and an animus for Giuliani's Quality of Life cleanup. It's vérité, but after all, isn't everything?

Also reviewed in:
NEW YORK TIMES, 6/9/00, p. E18, Elvis Mitchell

BOOTMEN

A Fox Searchlight Pictures release in association with the Australian Film Finance Corporation a Hilary Linstead/Dein Perry production. *Executive Producer:* Dein Perry. *Producer:* Hilary Linstead. *Director:* Dein Perry. *Screenplay:* Steve Worland. *Story:* Steve Worland, Hilary Linstead, and Dein Perry. *Director of Photography:* Steve Mason. *Editor:* Jane Moran. *Music:* Cezary Skubiszewski. *Music Editor:* Laurence Maddy. *Sound:* Andy Baldwin, Laurence Maddy and (music) Andy Baldwin and Robin Gray. *Sound Editor:* Andrew Plain. *Casting:* Christine King. *Production Designer:* Murray Picknett. *Art Director:* John Rohde. *Set Decorator:* Lea Worth. *Special Effects:* David Trethewey. *Costumes:* Tess Schofield. *Running time:* 93 minutes. *MPAA Rating:* R.

CAST: Vaughan Sheffield (Young Sean); Christian Patterson (Young Mitchell); Lisa Perry (Sean and Mitchell's Mother); Adam Garcia (Sean); Bruce Venables (Williams); Sam Worthington (Mitchell); William Zappa (Walter); Christopher Horsey (Angus); Matt Lee (Johnno); Sophie Lee (Linda); Justine Clarke (Kim); Andrew Doyle (Gerard Ball); Anthony Hayes, Craig Anderson, and Jonno Zissler (Huey's Mates); Richard Carter (Gary); Harry Dakanalis (Footy Player); Lee McDonald (Derrick); Andrew Kaluski (Colin); Susie Porter (Sara); Dein Perry (Anthony Ford); Kelly Aykers (Anthony Ford's Girlfriend); Reid Perry (Mitch, Junior).

LOS ANGELES TIMES, 10/6/00, Calendar/p. 14, Kevin Thomas

For the past four years, the Australian dance troupe Tap Dogs has become a sensation the world over with its stageful of men in work shirts and cleated work boots stamping out rugged routines to rock tunes. Their infectious Aussie high spirits and striking contrast to the traditional tie-and-tails sophistication associated with tap virtuosity has assured their popularity. It's as if Crocodile Dundee had taken over from Fred Astaire.

"Bootmen" was inspired by director—and Tap Dogs founder—Dein Perry's experiences growing up in the Australian industrial city of Newcastle. This vital, engaging drama with dance, written by Steve Worland from a story he wrote with Perry and Hilary Linstead, is more mythological than autobiographical. Yet you can imagine that on a creative level Perry must have gone through much of what the film's hero, Sean (Adam Garcia), experiences in discovering the need not merely to dance in the traditional style but also to create dances that grow out of his own environment. Indeed, Perry used as a key setting the steel mill in which he had actually worked.

In "Bootmen" you hear the incessant clang of steel, a glorious sound all but vanished in America and fading from Australia as well, which sets the beat for Perry's stage productions as well as the vigorous numbers of his film. In his first directorial effort in film, Perry displays enviable ease in allowing dance to flow naturally from his story.

With their late mother's encouragement, Sean and his older brother Mitchell performed a tap-dance act as small boys, but now they've grown up. Mitchell (Sam Worthington) is more interested in affording the truck of his dreams than in dancing and has turned into a car thief to finance it.

Sean works in the mills along with his father (Richard Carter) but has not lost his passion for dancing. He's a cocky guy whose unwillingness to take directions all but blows his audition for a revue in Sydney, where he's fired from the chorus, almost as swiftly as he was hired, for upstaging the star.

A hairdresser, Linda (Sophie Lee), he met at the audition falls prey to the manipulation of Mitchell, who convinces her that Sean won't be returning. Consequently, as Sean discovers his path in dance while returning to his old job at the factory, his slowly emerging dream is complicated by his conflicted feelings over Linda and by Mitchell's continuing criminal activity.

Although the audition that took Sean ever so briefly to Sydney revealed that Newcastle had plenty of young people eager to dance professionally, he faces considerable obstacles to forming the kind of dance troupe he envisions. First of all, he has no money. Second, no matter how rugged his Bootmen troupers are, they are not surprisingly often accused of being gay in their macho, blue-collar world. One of Sean's dancers, a local dance teacher, in fact turns out to be gay but is just as prepared as anyone else to use his fists if called for.

"Bootmen's" stars (Garcia, Worthington and Lee) are great-looking, talented and charismatic—particularly Garcia, who also performed in the opening ceremonies of the Olympics in Sydney. "Bootmen," which proves to be a real heart-tugger, is in fact accomplished in all its aspects.

Once it's out of first runs—hopefully, that will not be for some time—it will inevitably be paired with "Strictly Ballroom," which celebrates a far different kind of dance, in repertory theaters.

NEW YORK POST, 10/6/00, p. 57, Lou Lumenick

This latest and lamest attempt to clone "Full Monty" is directed by Australia's Dein Perry, creator of the phenomenally popular Tap Dogs dance troupe, which performs its numbers in faux-industrial settings.

The bland Adam Garcia plays Sean, who blows his break at a tap-dancing career and returns to his old job as a steel worker, where he proceeds to organize a fund-raising dance show with his mates.

Sean also has to deal with his disapproving father (William Zappa) and his brother (Sam Worthington), a small-time crook who's gotten Sean's hairdresser girlfriend (Sophie Lee) pregnant.

There's 80 minutes of mawkish, overacted melodrama—laced with gratuitous violence and profanity—before we get to anything more than the briefest snippet of a dance number.

Perry may know how to stage rousing tap routines on steel beams, but he's got two left feet when it comes about how to photograph and edit them so they don't come out looking like a third-rate music video.

NEWSDAY, 10/6/00, Part II/p. B6, Jan Stuart

The male dancer as jackhammer was the image left behind by "Tap Dogs," the percussive, hyper-masculine dance show that blew into New York from Australia in 1997. Conceived by a former factory mechanic from Newcastle named Dein Perry, this small troupe of work-booted fellas was a blue-collar fantasy, pushing a Fred Astaire conceit (the environment as one's dance partner) into an industrial landscape. The show was noisy, sexy and fun, as far as it went.

With an inventive cinematographer, "Tap Dogs" could have been turned into an exhilarating filmed concert. But no, Perry had to make a movie.

He got the cameraman (Steve Mason, who is quite good), but he leashed him and four of the original "Tap Dogs" to a flea-bitten screenplay having to do with a tap-crazy steelworker named Sean (Adam Garcia) who leaves his factory goggles behind to make it as a hoofer in Sydney. When he returns home to discover his girlfriend Linda (Sophie Lee, off the Olivia Newton-John assembly line) has been sleeping with his car-thief brother, Mitchell (Sam Worthington), Sean does what anyone in his situation would do: He starts an all-guy tap troupe with all his buddies.

As in the old Mickey and Judy musicals, there is a big show in store for the climax that the guys must raise lots of money to produce and rehearse for amid evil antagonism (Mitchell's nasty car-thief rival). No obstacle they face, however, is quite as terrifying as Steve Worland's dialogue, which sets off a sweaty competition of fidgeting and squirming among the audience that is at least as athletic as any of the recent Olympic events in Sydney.

Compared with Perry's original tappers, who exhibit a suggestion of libidinous charisma, Perry's leads (Christopher Horsey, Andrew Kaluski, Matt Lee and Lee McDonald) project the soft-core blandness one might expect from a down-under "Baywatch." While "Bootmen" is not the last in this season's parade of plain-folks musicals ("Dancer in the Dark," "Billy Elliott" and "Songcatcher"), we can only pray it will be the least.

VILLAGE VOICE, 10/10/00, p. 138, Edward Crouse

Working-class lives get the steel-and-leather treatment in *Bootmen*. The hardheaded creators of *Tap Dogs* trade rinky-dink tapping for a more martial clomp (or *Stomp)*, ditching loafers for work boots. Lead dancer Sean (Adam Garcia, crossing tufts of Rupert Graves with Tom Cruise-oid showboating) is fired from a trad tap show in Sydney and returns to Newcastle to knit his own *Full Monty* troupe of reluctant working stiffs. The Big Show, which could be a great Dickies ad, is affably clunky, its music a Vegas take on early-'90s grunge. The best sequences—auditions in a strip bar and a public bathroom—still can't compete with that industrial musical called *Pola X*.

Also reviewed in:
CHICAGO TRIBUNE, 12/1/00, Friday/p. F, John Petrakis
NEW YORK TIMES, 10/6/00, p. E22, Lawrence Van Gelder
VARIETY, 9/25-10/1/00, p. 68, David Stratton

BORICUA'S BOND

A USA Films release of an October Films presentation of a Rogue Picture production in association with MIA. *Executive Producer:* Alan Novich. *Producer:* Greg Scheinman, Robyn Kark, Val Lik, Alex Bartkow, Rip Robinson, Darryl Simmons, and David Turner. *Director:* Val Lik. *Screenplay:* Val Lik. *Director of Photography:* Brendan Flynt. *Editor:* Doug Abel. *Music:* Marti Cuevas. *Sound:* Evan Messares. *Sound Editor:* John Salk. *Casting:* David Turner. *Production Designer:* Luis DeJesus. *Art Director:* Lisa Cruz. *Set Decorator:* Jasmine P. Martinez and Eileen Yaghoobian. *Costumes:* Carolina Martinez. *Make-up:* Sanna Riley. *Running time:* 105 minutes. *MPAA Rating:* R.

CAST: Frankie Negron (Tommy); Val Lik (Allen); Ramses Ignacio (Axel); Jorge Gautier (Wilson); Jesglar Cabral (Antonio); Geovanny Pineda (Avery); Erica Torrres (Christine); Kaleena Justiniano (Rose); Robyn Karp (Susan Miller); Marco Sorisio (Officer Highlander); Jeff Asencio (Paco); Michael Demitro (Sammy); Pietro González (Diner Owner); Manuel Cabral (Tommy's Father); Elsa Canals (Tommy's Mother); Maurice Phillips (Santa); Edison Torres (Priest); Vanessa Del Sol (Princess); Jack "JDS" Da Silva (Blinky); Footprintz (Seta); Paul Manion (Detective Chroney); Freddie Lopez (Singer on the Street); Luis Torres (Christine's Father); Lissette Montolio (Christine's Mother); Olga Lebron (Christine's Aunt); Gerson Munoz (Christine's Trick); Yanira Canals (Hazel); Ileana Rodriguez (Lady in Window); Daniel Ruiz and Carlos Ruiz (Bouncers); Austin Stark (Willie); Jeffrey Karp (Diner Customer).

NEW YORK POST, 6/21/00, p. 50, Lou Lumenick

As made-on-a-shoestring movies made in the South Bronx go, this coming-of-age effort is neither the best nor the worst.

Val Lik, a 21-year-old émigré, has overextended himself by not only writing and directing, but also starring as Allen, a white teenager who moves into a depressed Puerto Rican neighborhood with his mother.

Orson Welles he's not.

While trying to fit into an alien environment, Allen forms a friendship with Tommy (Latin pop star Frankie Negron), a *boricua* (Puerto Rican) from the neighborhood who rescues Allen from an attacking street gang.

Like many first films, "Boricua's Bond" is wildly uneven.

A few street gang scenes are so real, they have a gritty, fly-on-the-wall feel.

At other points, it's painfully obvious you're watching untrained actors (including the especially awkward Lik) going through their paces.

This is particularly noticeable when the street kids act out in a restaurant where Lik's struggling character is working as a busboy. The scene founders badly.

Predictably, racial prejudice drives a wedge between Allen and Tommy, an aspiring artist who's framed by a bad cop.

There's nothing really new in this movie. Its biggest selling points, beside Negron, are cameo appearances by rappers DMX, Method Man, KRS-One, Stickyfingaz and the late Big Punisher.

NEWSDAY, 6/21/00, Part II/p. B11, Jan Stuart

Loyalty is one of the buzzwords uttered with great reverence in "Boricua's Bond" by a circle of South Bronx teenagers who otherwise seem too morally depleted to pay it more than lip service. Buddies trading friendly banter in a card game one second are holding pistols to each other's heads the next. After a young woman witnesses her girlfriend being sexually assaulted by a policeman, she withholds testimony from another cop who intervenes, mumbling simply, "I have nothing to say."

By contrast, Val Lik, the striking neophyte star, writer, director and co-producer of "Boricua's Bond," has so much to say that we're not always sure what it is. All of 20 years young when he assembled this grungy urban kaleidoscope, the Russian-born, East New York-reared Lik puts across a conflicting range of messages, which probably boil down to one: It's not the streets that are mean, it's the people who walk them.

The dark-haired and diminutive Lik plays Allen Miller, a burger-shop waiter who stands out as the only white kid in the neighborhood when he moves to the South Bronx with his widowed mother (Robyn Karp). After being roughed about, he wins the confidence of Tommy Rivera (singer Frankie Negron), an artist with a combustible cadre of friends. Soon, Allen gains entree into a predatory world of corrupt cops, hair-trigger violence and blithe disrespect for women that makes the gang assaults in Central Park earlier this month seem like another day in the life.

"Boricua's Bond" gains in authenticity from Lik's assertively casual neo-realist style—don't expect to hear every line of dialogue—and from a supporting cast of Latino and black hip-hop veterans. Lik is less successful as a screenwriter; he hasn't yet gotten the hang of building a dramatic arc within scenes, which rise and crash with jarring abruptness. There is little in the way of surprise and variety among the succession of unpleasant encounters, and even less compassion: Lik's people are remarkable only for their tireless ability to let each other, not to say themselves, down. He chokes us in grim truths, leaving us gasping for poetry and hope.

VILLAGE VOICE, 7/4/00, p. 124, Amy Taubin

What could have possessed USA Films to release *Boricua's Bond* at all, let alone a week after the Puerto Rican Day Parade incident? Made by Val Lik, a 21-year-old Russian immigrant, the film suggests that moon 'n' maul is the standard sexual approach of Latino men to any and every woman. (Lik has a weird way of paying tribute to the Puerto Rican community in which he grew up.) *Boricua's Bond* begins with some not unpromising scenes of guys hanging out (connected by flashy zip pans and propelled by a wall-to-wall rap track), but even those made me nervous about what would happen when the plot finally kicked in. And kick in it does. Despite its incoherence and inaudible dialogue, this slice-of-life film manages to be simultaneously thuggish and platitudinous. Since Lik shows a glimmer of talent, the best thing that could happen is for *Boricua's Bond* to disappear before too many people take notice.

Also reviewed in:
NEW YORK TIMES, 6/21/00, p. E5, A.O. Scott
VARIETY, 6/26-7/9/00, p. 22, Robert Koehler

BOSSA NOVA

A Sony Pictures Classics release of a Lucy & Luiz Carlos Barreto and Filmes do Equador production in association with Globo Films. *Executive Producer:* Bruno Barreto. *Producer:* Lucy Barreto and Luiz Carlos Barreto. *Director:* Bruno Barreto. *Screenplay (English and Portugese with English subtitles):* Alexandre Machado and Fernanda Young. *Adapted from the novel "Miss Simpson" by:* Sérgio Sant'Anna. *Director of Photography:* Pascal Rabaud. *Editor:* Ray Hubley. *Music:* Eumir Deodato. *Casting:* Fernanda Ribas, Marcela Altberg, Sheila Jaffe, and Georgianne Walken. *Art Director:* Cassio Amarante and Carla Caff. *Costumes:* Emília Duncan. *Running time:* 95 minutes. *MPAA Rating:* R.

CAST: Amy Irving (Mary Ann);   Antônio Fagundes (Pedro Paulo);   Alexandre Borges (Acácio);   Débora Bloch (Tania);   Drica Moraes (Nadine);   Giovanna Antonelli (Sharon); Rogério Cardoso (Vermont);   Sérgio Loroza (Gordo);   Flávio Sao Thiago (Peçanha); Alberto de Mendoza (Juan);   Pedro Cardoso (Roberto);   Stephen Tobolowsky (Trevor);   Kazuo Matsui (Wan-Kim-Lau);   Cássia Linhares (Reporter);   Kate Lyra (English School Receptionist);   Mara Carvalho (Tailor Shop Receptionist).

LOS ANGELES TIMES, 5/12/00, Calendar/p. 10, Kevin Thomas

Bruno Barreto's "Bossa Nova" is too much of a good thing. It has the irresistible music of the film's title to set its seductive mood and pace, a Rio that glows with sensuality—and too many people and too many complications threatening to obscure the romantic comedy's main attraction: Amy Irving and major Brazilian star Antonio Fagundes.

The chemistry is so right between these two charmers that we want to spend more time with them and less with some tedious types that clutter up the plot. The result is a film that tilts toward the slight and merely pleasant when it could have had much more emotional impact. We need more of a chance to get involved with Irving's widowed Mary Ann and Fagundes' attorney Pedro Paulo, whose frivolous wife (Debora Bloch) has just left him for a sexy young tai chi instructor (Kazuo Matsui).

Since Pedro Paulo's master-tailor father has his business in the same Art Deco building where Mary Ann teaches English in a language school, it's not surprising that their paths eventually cross. Pedro Paulo signs up for a class with Mary Ann, more to get to know her than to put an extra polish on his English pronunciation.

When Mary Ann, a lovely and poised former flight attendant from the U.S., lost her husband in a drowning accident two years earlier, she figured she had lost the love of her life.

Then along comes Pedro Paulo, silver-haired and handsome in that fleshy way of sleek, well-fed lawyers and businessmen who look born to wear double-breasted suits. Pedro Paulo's impact is not lost on Mary Ann, but it's forever getting short-circuited.

First there's one of her pupils, obnoxious soccer star Acacio (Alexandre Borges), as eager to score with Mary Ann as on the playing field. Then there's another student, Nadine (Drica Moraes), in need of constant advice on her Internet romance with a New Yorker (Stephen Tobolowsky). Then there's Pedro Paulo's obnoxious new intern (Giovanna Antonelli), who attracts Pedro Paulo's quiet younger brother (Pedro Cardoso) as well as Acacio. Meanwhile, Pedro Paulo is representing his dapper father, Juan (Alberto de Mendoza), whose fourth and much younger wife is suing him for divorce.

It's as if writers Alexandre Machado and Fernanda Young, in freely adapting Sergio Sant'Anna's novel "Miss Simpson," didn't think Mary Ann and Pedro Paulo's budding romance could be interesting enough in its own right—and, in fact, there seem to be no real obstacles between them to prevent its full flowering—so they keep cutting to sidebar characters as a source of distraction and misunderstanding.

Barreto has directed with his usual skill, but "Bossa Nova" winds up a minor item from the director of the classic "Dona Flor and Her Two Husbands," "Four Days in November" and numerous other notable films.

NEW YORK POST, 4/28/00, p. 53, Lou Lumenick

Movies about middle-age romance are so scarce that you can't easily dismiss something as slight as "Bossa Nova," which offers the added fillip of gorgeous Rio de Janeiro.

"Bossa Nova" isn't great. But I had fun watching Brazilian writer-director Bruno Barretto return to the same theme—widowhood—that he explored far more entertainingly in his best-known work, "Donna Flor and Her Two Husbands."

This new effort stars the director's wife, the too-seldom-seen Amy Irving, in what may be her most rewarding role since "Crossing Delancey."

Irving plays Mary Ann, a retired stewardess whose husband drowned two years earlier. She's teaching English at a Rio adult school, where she catches the eye of Pedro Paulo (Brazilian star Antonio Fagundes), a burned-out lawyer whose wife (Debora Bloch) has just left him for her tai-chi instructor (Kazuo Matsui).

Bruno sets up a romantic roundelay of romantic confusions and mistaken identities, involving a soccer player (Alexandre Borges), a soccer-mad intern (Giovanna Antonelli), an American (Stephen Tobolowsky) and a host of other characters.

It's more than a little predictable, but it has its share of laughs and there are several achingly romantic moments.

NEWSDAY, 4/28/00, Part II/p. B7, Jan Stuart

That loud whooshing sound you hear escaping from the theater where "Bossa Nova" is playing is the contented sigh of baby-boomer women having a bonding moment with Amy Irving. On screen, a glowingly middle-aged Irving is staggering along the sands of Rio's shores, merrily pie-eyed from caipirinhas, the heady Brazilian cocktail. An adoring, smoothly masculine Brazilian attorney is at her heels. The warm Ipanema breeze blows, caressing her gold blouse. The bossa nova music is chicka-chick-ing. She trips, he catches her in his arms.

To find a romantic comedy about people of a certain age amid the haystack of teen date movies is such a rarity, one is inclined to herald its arrival with ticker tape. If Bruno Barreto's "Bossa Nova" makes its audience feel like kids again, however, it is because it demonstrates that midlife romance flicks can be as infantile in their effects as the ones targeted for the Jennifer Love Hewitt generation.

You couldn't find a more appealing poster girl for midlife yearning than Irving, whose radiant self-awareness helped make "Crossing Delancey" one of the happier screen romances of the 1980s. She looks great as Mary Ann, a widowed ex-flight attendant living a pleasant enough existence teaching English in Rio when she catches the eye of Pedro Paulo (Antonio Fagundes), a successful attorney who has just been dumped by his wife for a Chinese tai chi instructor.

Pedro's pursuit of Mary Ann is but one of multiple romantic crosscurrents in "Bossa Nova" that also include Pedro's beautiful, brainy intern, his sad-eyed tailor brother, a randy soccer star and a dorky American businessman pursuing one of Mary Ann's friends over the Internet. One admires Barreto for keeping so many balls in the air and allowing them to land with some measure of unpredictability. But the farcical humor is numbingly broad and occasionally crude (the scene in which Mary Ann teaches the soccer player English curse words had a few in stitches), and a fantasy ballroom dance between Irving and Fagundes is strictly amateur hour.

For some, that magical Brazilian synergy of bossa nova, beaches and stirring hormones will be enough. The rest would be advised to buy the soundtrack and wait it out till "Bossa Nova" arrives at its inevitable place of honor, on the Romance Classics channel.

VILLAGE VOICE, 5/2/00, p. 136, Jessica Winter

Brazilian director Bruno Barreto calls his 14th film a gift to his wife and leading lady, Amy Irving, and if *Bossa Nova* avoids tripping a single booby trap of the cinematic-valentine variety, it's in making Irving's character—ostensibly the magnetic pole for Barreto's ensemble of limpwit dating misfits—so wan and humor-challenged. Irving plays an American widow who gives English lessons out of her Rio apartment—a set piece allowing for a few halfhearted attempts at sexual hijinks and, in consideration of the U.S. audience for which *Bossa Nova* is blatantly designed, ample opportunity to laugh at the funny foreigners with their funny accents. Barreto elsewhere courts the Yanks by retreading *You've Got Mail* with an Internet-romance subplot and rendering the Brazilian coastline as Miami brochure. The opening credits dedicate the film to François Truffaut, and Barreto's allegorical reliance on translation mishaps, not to mention clumsy lunging toward a certain self-consciously naive romanticism, are surely meant to summon *Domicile Conjugal*. Truffaut may have dipped more than a toe in the bourgie reflecting pool with his light comedies, but *Bossa Nova* dives in headlong and never comes up for air.

Also reviewed in:
CHICAGO TRIBUNE, 5/26/00, Friday/p. A, Michael Wilmington
NEW YORK TIMES, 4/28/00, p. E30, Elvis Mitchell
VARIETY, 2/28-3/5/00, p. 46, Joe Leydon

BOUNCE

A Miramax Films release of a Steve Golin and Michael Besman production.   *Executive Producer:* Bob Weinstein, Harvey Weinstein, Bob Osher, and Meryl Poster. *Producer:* Steve Golin and Michael Besman.   *Director:* Don Roos.   *Screenplay:* Don Roos. *Director of Photography:* Robert Elswit.   *Editor:* David Codron.   *Music:* Mychael Danna. *Music Editor:* Tom Milano and Mike Baber.   *Sound:* Willie D. Burton and (music) Brad Haehnel.   *Sound Editor:* John Leveque.   *Casting:* Patrick J. Rush and Sharon Klein.   *Production Designer:* David Wasco.   *Art Director:* Daniel Bradford.   *Set Designer:* Natalie Richards.   *Set Decorator:* Sandy Reynolds Wasco.   *Set Dresser:* Todd Morris, Sean Langdon, James Malley, and Gyula Toth. *Special Effects:* Ron Bolanowski.   *Costumes:* Peter Mitchell.   *Make-up:* David Craig Forrest. *Make-up (Gwyneth Paltrow and Ben Affleck):* Tina Earnshaw.   *Running time:* 102 minutes. *MPAA Rating:* PG13.

CAST: Ben Affleck (Buddy Amaral); Gwyneth Paltrow (Abby Janello); Edward Edwards (Ron Wachter);   Jennifer Grey (Janice Guerrero);   Tony Goldwyn (Greg Janello);   Natasha Henstridge (Mimi);   Lisa Carpenter Prewitt (Carol Wilson);   Lisa Joyner (TV Announcer); Richard Saxton (CNN Reporter);   Caroline Aaron (Donna Heisen);   David Dorfman (Joey Janello); Alex D. Linz (Scott Janello); Juan Garcia (Kevin Walters); Mary Ellen Lyon (Ellen Seitz);   Joe Morton (Jim Weller);   Thea Mann (Karen); Matthew Frauman (Luke);   Sam Robards (Todd Exner);   Ty Murphy (Josh);   Dave McCharen (Narrator, Infinity Air Commercial); Julianne Christie (Zola);   Jeff Garlin (Emcee);   Johnny Galecki (Seth);   Nicole Tocantins (Dionne);   Ashley Montgomery (Prom Girl);   Eric Aude (Prom Boy);   Scott Alan Smith (Jack);   Mark Ankeny (Tom),   Julia Campbell (Sue);   Michael Laskin (Frank Steadman);   Michael Ayala (Court TV Reporter);   David St. James (Judge);   Don Amendolia (Infinity Attorney);   John Levin (Janice's Attorney);   Chris Harrison (Chicago Anchor);   David Paymer (Prosecuting Attorney Mandel).

LOS ANGELES TIMES, 11/17/00, Calendar/p. 2, Kenneth Turan

Aside from its contrived and listless tear-jerker narrative, which is about as moving as a month-old Kleenex, there are several other things about "Bounce" you would find difficult to believe if you didn't already know them:

* that leads Ben Affleck and Gwyneth Paltrow are considered two of the industry's best young actors;

* that they had a relationship with each other in real life;

* that cinematographer Robert Elswit is the same man who shot the wild and crazy "Magnolia";

* that filmmaker Don Roos is the same writer-director who made the snarky and self-consciously bitchy "The Opposite of Sex." Clearly there is such a thing as going too far to escape typecasting.

In fact, though they all try very hard, none of the principals in this failed romantic weepie has much of an affinity for the genre. As two people brought together by a tragedy that only one of them knows is a factor in their relationship, Affleck and Paltrow, who've been excellent elsewhere, display less chemistry than they've shown in magazine photo shoots. Even Woody and Bo Peep had more going on between them in "Toy Story" than these two manage here.

To be fair, both stars are more than a little straitjacketed by the standard, cliched nature of a script about a cold-hearted advertising guy working through tragedy to learn the meaning of life. Plus there's that calamitous plot gimmick, simultaneously solemn, smarmy and squeamish, which makes the Buddy Amaral-Abby Janello relationship one we'd rather not watch developing.

It's Buddy (Affleck) we meet first. He's gloating in a limo, about closing a major deal with Infinity Airlines and acting, as he later accurately describes himself in a more somber, reflective mood, like "one of those people who thought they were hot stuff."

But that's getting ahead of the story, such as it is. For now, ever so full of himself, Buddy is trapped by weather in a Chicago airport. He meets earnest young playwright and family man Greg Janello (the versatile Tony Goldwyn), decency itself down to his tweedy jacket and cable-knit sweater (Buddy wears Armani, of course). Eager to seduce a comely fellow strandee (Natasha Henstridge), Buddy gives Greg his ticket back to L.A. Which might have passed for a good deed except that the plane crashes, and there are no survivors. Zero. Nada. Not even one.

Because Buddy needs to change from a shallow jerk into someone we have a shot at caring about, the next chunk of "Bounce" deals with his survivor guilt, which puts him into a deep funk for the better part of a year. He turns into an alcoholic, he goes into rehab, he resists and then embraces AA, but, unfortunately, Buddy is no more interesting, no more palatable after he's chastened by experience than before.

Meanwhile, Greg's widow, Abby (Paltrow, with dyed brown hair that was thought better-suited than blond to a role as a Valley housewife and mother), is coping as well as she can with her two button-cute sons and a new job in real estate. When Buddy looks her up, apparently to set the record straight about why her husband was on that plane, she lies and says she's divorced, which provides him with a convenient rationale to pretend his meeting with her is completely random.

Buddy feels ill at ease not leveling with Abby even as he's falling in love with her; Abby feels ill at ease dating so soon after her husband's death, even as she's falling in love with him. The result is wall-to-wall awkwardness, and awkwardness is one of the many things that "Bounce" does not do well. Add in an over-complicated plot and a ridiculously contrived final act, and the result is a movie that's all but impossible to involve yourself in.

There are several precedents, both dramatic and romantic, for situations similar to this one, from Cornell Woolrich's (writing as William Irish) pulpy "I Married a Dead Man" to the deliriously melodramatic 1942 "Random Harvest," in which an amnesiac Ronald Colman coldly hires Greer Garson to be his assistant, not remembering that she's the love of his life. "Bounce," named for a quality of resilience it hasn't a prayer of mustering, doesn't bare its heart nearly as effectively.

NEW YORK POST, 11/17/00, p. 57, Lou Lumenick

"Bounce" is the most depressing date movie since "Random Hearts," which also suggested a plane crash was the ideal way for relatives of dead victims to meet cute.

Why Hollywood executives find this a romantic notion is beyond me.

This time out, the guilt-ridden meet-cutes are played by Gwyneth Paltrow and Ben Affleck, who may or may not be a couple in real life, but certainly exhibit zero chemistry together on screen.

He's Buddy, a wisecracking advertising executive who gives up his seat on the last plane out of Chicago to a TV writer who needs to get home to help his son sell Christmas trees. The plane crashes, killing everyone and throwing Buddy into an alcoholic tailspin.

When he gets out of rehab, Buddy decides to check up on the dead man's widow, Abby (Paltrow), who has two young sons (who barely figure in the story) and works as a realtor. Without telling her who he is, Buddy throws her a lucrative commission and starts dating her.

What will happen when Abby discovers the truth? What will happen when she discovers that Buddy knows *she's* been lying by claiming to be a divorcee?

The script by director Don Roos (who did the wonderful "The Opposite of Sex") constantly telegraphs the answers.

You know what's going to happen a half-hour before it happens—even in a ridiculous courtroom scene where Buddy, for reasons that are too complicated and silly to explain, testifies against the airline in the crash, which happens to be his agency's biggest client.

The general ennui is enhanced by another lazy performance by Affleck, whose small part in "Boiler Room" showed he is capable of much better than his half-hearted drunk scenes here.

Paltrow, a brunette this time out, tries harder, but she's defeated by a cringe-worthy script that requires her, among other things, to tell Ben she bought a Rottweiler for her sons "as a consolation prize for their father."

Roos wastes an impressive supporting cast—among them Joe Morton, Natasha Henstridge, Tony Goldwyn, Caroline Aaron, Jennifer Grey and David Paymer—in one-note and/or one-scene roles. The only survivor is Johnny Galecki, who steals all his scenes as Buddy's bitchy gay assistant. It's petty larceny.

"Bounce" exists on a level of heightened unreality that's impressive even by Hollywood's rarefied standards. At one point, Buddy's agency produces a TV commercial for the airline celebrating the victims of the crash.

Yeah, right.

After winning an award for the spot, a drunken Ben cracks: "Kind of makes you wish you crashed more often."

Audiences will harbor no such wishes. Two dud romances centering on plane crashes in a year are two too many. A pity the script didn't go down with the plane.

NEWSDAY, 11/17/00, Part II/p. B7, John Anderson

Although it goes against every law of God, man and Miramax, "Bounce" is an American movie crying out for a European remake. Someone like Eric Rohmer, just as a for instance, might have brought forth the humanity and humor in the bones of its story. And he would have found the mature, seasoned actors appropriate to inhabit its atmosphere of love and loss.

Instead, "Bounce" stars Ben Affleck and Gwyneth Paltrow, who are very attractive people but don't give the impression they've ever lost anything other than their way to an Oscar after-party. Skimming blithely over the surface of actual passion, emotion and pain, they make brief stops at grief, a side trip to introspection and recklessly negotiate the drive-thru window of redemption.

We apologize for the car metaphors because this is, after all, a plane movie (not that you'll ever see it on a plane). Buddy Amaral (Affleck) is a hot-shot exec for a small but growing ad firm, who finds himself getting snowed in at O'Hare. In the airport lounge, he meets the very friendly but not very discriminating Mimi (Natasha Henstridge) and family man Greg (Tony Goldwyn). In order to stay and sleep with Mimi, he gives Greg his own first-class ticket. And the plane goes down.

Meanwhile, back at the ranch house, Greg's wife, Abby (Paltrow), is trying to piece together what happened, because the passenger list has been altered by Buddy's old flame, ticket agent Janice Guerrero (Jennifer Grey), so no one's sure who's lived or died. The whole thing gets straightened out, so to speak. And it's nice to see Grey. But the amount of time spent on establishing that 1) Greg is dead, 2) Abby is heartbroken and 3) Buddy feels guilty might have been done with two bits of cross-cutting and a fadeout. In other words, "Bounce" takes a lot of time telling us things that, as humans, we already suspect.

It's too bad that writer-director Don Roos, of the justly admired "The Opposite of Sex," has segued from that spunky little movie into what constitutes a rare animal, the situation tragedy. Buddy, having completed a tour of rehab after a year-long, alcohol-greased skid into career suicide (this, at least, is treated somewhat economically), goes looking for the family of the man he feels he killed. She is valiantly trying to make ends meet with two kids and no talent for real estate. Romance, as is its wont in these kinds of movies, blooms. But not, of course, without the requisite detour to recrimination and anguish—without which, there would be no movie, just a fairly believable happy ending.

SIGHT AND SOUND, 2/01, p. 37, Geoffrey Macnab

Chicago, Christmas Eve. As he waits for his flight to LA, ad-agency hotshot Buddy flirts with Mimi, a businesswoman he's just met. They're joined by playwright Greg Janello, on his way back for a family Christmas. They drink together and play around with a video camera. Buddy gives up his seat on the plane to Greg in order to be next to Mimi.

The flight to LA crashes. Greg is among the many passengers killed; Buddy feels responsible for his death. Back in LA, he drinks heavily and is disgusted by the ad campaign his company wages on behalf of the airline whose plane crashed. After being discharged from rehab, he tracks down Greg's wife Abby and her kids. On discovering that she is working as an estate agent, Buddy makes sure Abby is hired to supervise his firm's relocation. They begin dating (although Abby pretends she is divorced from her husband). Returning from a weekend away together, Buddy warns Abby he has something important to tell her, but won't reveal what in front of the kids.

By chance, Mimi passes through town. She looks up Abby, whom she has never met, and gives her the video she shot that night in the airport. Abby watches it and realises that Buddy knew her husband. She breaks off the relationship. Buddy testifies at the inquiry into the plane crash, where his testimony proves that the airline had not been following safety procedures and allows the victims' relatives to win a massive lawsuit. Abby sees Buddy on television and is moved by his honesty. Buddy resigns from his job. Abby turns up at his beachside house and the couple are reconciled.

Bounce is a film out of time. Its characters seem to have stumbled, rheumy-eyed, out of some 50s tearjerker. You could easily imagine Gwyneth Paltrow's Abby a clumsy, nervous suburban mom—played by Doris Day, and Ben Affleck's obnoxious ad-agency man Buddy by Cary Grant. The storyline about a romance between a widow and the man who switched plane tickets with her husband on the night he died—is straight from the Nora Ephron school of early-90s schmaltz.

But it is not so much the sentimentality of the film which surprises as its conservatism—for one thing, you don't usually associate Miramax, which produced *Bounce,* with wholesome romantic melodramas. In his earlier work, writer-director Don Roos was much more adventurous: his screenplay for Jonathan Kaplan's *Love Field* about a Jackie Kennedy-obsessed housewife making an epic trek to JFK's funeral, may have had its moments of mawkishness, but it dealt with racism and class, and provided Michelle Pfeiffer with probably her best role; Roos' directorial debut *The Opposite of Sex,* meanwhile, boasted a memorable, Lolita-like teenage temptress and dialogue steeped in wicked irony. But with *Bounce,* Roos uses every cornball cliché imaginable, undercutting moments of high emotion with lachrymose music and throwing in cutesy, heart-tugging scenes with Abby's two doe eyed kids.

The film's underlying 'message' is glib and moralistic. As in Brett Ratner's *The Family Man,* this film features an arrogant yuppie who learns the usual hoary old lessons about love, loyalty and good citizenship after spending time in the suburbs. (It's just a pity that a plane has to crash to give him his stab at redemption.) Unfortunately, Buddy was a much more interesting character before he went into rehab than after. The film's occasional flickers of life come when Buddy is in conflict with his ad agency, which makes a series of tasteless commercials on behalf of the airline responsible for the crash. There's also an intriguing subplot which casts him as 'the insider' dishing the dirt on corporate America, but it's dealt with only in passing.

Despite its title, *Bounce* is curiously flat and listless. The actors are amiable, if a little bland. Roos still knows how to write barbed one-liners, but the director shies away from tackling the subjects the film purports to be about—guilt, grief, betrayal—in any depth. The best weepies are fuelled by risk and doubt, but nothing much seems at stake here.

VILLAGE VOICE, 11/28/00, p. 138, Dennis Lim

A close encounter with death provides the narrative motor in *Bounce*. Raising the bar for morbid high-concept romance, Don Roos's second feature compounds *Random Hearts'* aviation-disaster matchmaking with *Return to Me's* why-do-you-remind-me-of-my-dead-spouse quandaries. Ad exec Ben Affleck, opting to spend the night with Natasha Henstridge in an airport hotel, donates his ticket to amiable stranger Tony Goldwyn. The plane crashes; Ben guzzles whiskey and thinks about fate—which naturally plummets him into rehab, his guilt all the while exacerbated by the fact that he was on his way home from securing a lucrative deal with the airline in question. A year on, Ben tracks down widow Gwyneth Paltrow and finds her tragic aura irresistible.

The least sympathetic performers in the Miramax clan, Affleck and Paltrow generally fail to convince when required to project love in any direction other than inward, though the pairing flatters her—if only because crumple-faced emoting is somewhat more tolerable than smirky preening. The script calls for Affleck's cocky swagger to redemptively evaporate, but it simply morphs into dubious fratboy sensitivity. A calculated departure from the lockjawed wisecracks of Roos's *The Opposite of Sex*, *Bounce* suggests a grown-up (or is that ingrown?) *Dawson's Creek:* syncopated glibness, discreet sentimentality, wall-to-wall Sarah McLachlan-and-friends soundtrack. It's been smoothed over plenty, but this is one creaky, rigged contraption. (An early giveaway: Affleck and Goldwyn's fleeting airport interaction is videotaped, earmarked as a subsequent bombshell.) Roos works hard at flattering his audience as urbane and intelligent: a repeated Whitman reference, a bitchy gay assistant for Ben, numerous smug assertions that advertising is heinous (also a convenient way to justify his lead's helpless smarminess). The real subject of the film is the alleviation of guilt—not just Ben's and Gwyneth's, but that of viewers who might normally have reservations about succumbing to this kind of schmaltz.

Also reviewed in:
CHICAGO TRIBUNE, 11/17/00, Friday, p. A, Mark Caro
NEW REPUBLIC, 12/11/00, p. 24, Stanley Kauffmann
NEW YORK TIMES, 11/17/00, p. E20, Stephen Holden
NEW YORKER, 12/4/00, p. 115, David Denby
VARIETY, 11/20-26/00, p. 14, Todd McCarthy

BOYS AND GIRLS

A Dimension Films release of a Punch 21 production. *Executive Producer:* Bob Weinstein, Harvey Weinstein, Jeremy Kramer, and Jill Sobel Messick. *Producer:* Jay Cohen, Lee Gottsegen, and Murray Schisgal. *Director:* Robert Iscove. *Screenplay (as the Drews):* Andrew Lowery and Andrew Miller. *Director of Photography:* Ralf Bode. *Editor:* Casey O. Rohrs. *Music:* Stewart Copeland. *Music Editor:* Michael Dittrick. *Choreographer:* Jerry Evans. *Sound:* Steve Nelson, Mark Weingarten, and (music) Joseph Magee. *Sound Editor:* Paul Timothy Carden. *Casting:* Joseph Middleton and Lesa Lotito. *Production Designer:* Marcia Hinds-Johnson. *Art Director:* Bo Johnson. *Set Designer:* Scott Herbertson. *Set Decorator:* Suzette Sheets. *Costumes:* April Ferry. *Make-up:* Scott H. Eddo. *Running time:* 90 minutes. *MPAA Rating:* PG-13.

CAST: Freddie Prinze, Jr. (Ryan); Claire Forlani (Jennifer); Jason Biggs (Hunter); Amanda Detmer (Amy); Heather Donahue (Megan); Alyson Hannigan (Betty); Raquel Beaudine (Young Jennifer); Brendon Ryan Barrett (Young Ryan); Lisa Eichhorn (Shuttle Passenger); Monica Arnold (Katie); Gay Thomas (N.Y. Flight Attendant); David Smigelski (Homecoming King); Blake Shields (Homecoming Knight); Sean Maysonet (Michael); John X (DJ);

Tsianina Joelson (Girl in Bar);   Kristofer Mickelson (Big Guy);   Matt Carmody (Kirt); Richard Hillman (Frat Guy); Tim Griffith (Timmy); Timi Prulhiere (Andie); Eric Rutherford (Noah); Matt Schulze (Paul);   Angela Oh (Waitress); Brian Poth (Guy in Diner); Mimi Rose (Girl in Diner); David Correia (Shuttle Driver); Lee Garlington (L. A. Flight Attendant); John Henry Redwood (Businessman);   Barbara Spiegel (Saleswoman);   Susan Kellerman (Therapist); Damon Williams (Prince).

LOS ANGELES TIMES, 6/16/00, Calendar/p. 12, Kevin Thomas

"Boys and Girls," a likably thoughtful romantic comedy, suggests that as we enter the new millennium the dating game is getting tougher by the second, especially among the best and the brightest. So self-conscious and ultimately just plain scared are Freddie Prinze Jr.'s Ryan and Claire Forlani's Jennifer that they are in danger of succumbing to total paralysis.

Jennifer and Ryan did not get off to the best of starts, when, as kids, they happen to be seated next to each other on a plane. Ryan and Jennifer are both smart and opinionated and quickly clash with her telling the boy he's ugly as her parting shot. They later cross paths in a large L.A. high school, where Jennifer ends up dismissing Ryan as dumb. Wouldn't you know that the first person Ryan, whose goal is to become a structural engineer, runs into at UC Berkeley's Sather Gate is Jennifer, a Latin major.

This time things are different. It's as if Jennifer looked at Ryan for the first time, not for his looks (which are just fine) but for his intelligence. She's involved with a rock musician, and Ryan has a girlfriend but she's off on a distant campus. They spar a bit, but when the rocker dumps Jennifer, she looks to Ryan's shoulder to cry on.

A friendship of opposites blossoms: Jennifer is spontaneous, direct and hasn't a clue as to what she'll do with her Latin beyond a post-grad sojourn in Italy (and even there, Latin isn't of much use nowadays). Ryan, ever the engineer, believes his life can be as carefully designed as the Golden Gate Bridge; it seems significant that Ryan is unaware that its building did not proceed without snags or loss of life. Even so, he becomes a sympathetic and concerned friend to Jennifer.

Romantic involvements come and go in Jennifer's life, and Ryan even manages a desultory relationship with a forthright electrical engineer ("The Blair Witch Project's "Heather Donahue). As time goes on, Jennifer values Ryan increasingly as her key source of stability and security. He becomes, as she puts it, her very best friend in the entire world. As a risk-taker in romance, she's been hurt so often she would never let anything jeopardize her hard-won friendship with Ryan. But what to do if they at last fall in love? Andrew Lowery and Andrew Miller, the screenwriting team who call themselves the Drews, have brought more depth and complexity to romantic comedy than is usually the case. It pays off in Forlani and Prinze's luminous portrayals under the well-paced and perceptive direction of Robert Iscove, who recently directed Prinze in the teen comedy hit "She's All That."

While Forlani shows us the bedrock honesty that underpins Jennifer's quicksilver temperament, Prinze manages to reveal the warmth and charm within Ryan's button-down, often-clenched personality. Amanda Detmer is Jennifer's sweetly neurotic roommate, and Jason Biggs, whose career skyrocketed with "American Pie," is Ryan's even more neurotic roomie, who hasn't a clue to his own identity as he tries desperately to score with girls. Biggs' shenanigans are often credibility-defying outlandishness, but he's so skilled a comedian that he provides sharp, lively relief to Ryan's resolute seriousness.

"Boys and Girls" makes good use of the Berkeley campus and environs but no more than a tourist's view of San Francisco; still, we have to be grateful that Vancouver isn't being passed off as the Bay Area (as it was in "Romeo Must Die," among other examples). "Boys and Girls," a sure-fire date night movie, proves to be more than that and represents a career boost to all its young people on both sides of the camera, especially Forlani, a real dazzler.

NEW YORK POST, 6/16/00, p. 53, Lou Lumenick

Will somebody please—*please*—create a TV series for Freddie Prinze Jr.?

Anything that will keep this cute-but-hopeless leading man from ripping off paying customers with the likes of "Boys and Girls," which manages the near-impossible feat of being even lamer than his last romantic comedy, "Down to You."

Just how lame? Lame enough to make "Road Trip" look like "Some Like it Hot" by comparison.

Consider this scintillating exchange:

He (quoting her): "I'm... stupid... and uptight and ugly."

She: "I said all of that before I was on Prozac."

He (astonished): "You're... on... Prozac?"

She (laughing): "I wish!"

I can't recall a more cluelessly written and more tedious version of the old story about burned-by-love, commitment-phobic male-female best friends who resist falling in love—until the inevitable happens.

In this case, they're students at UC Berkeley (he's major in engineering, she in Latin)—which means nothing more than a few San Francisco locations, which are used less well than in your average Rice-A-Roni commercial.

Prinze, whose idea of characterization begins and ends with wearing a pair of glasses that he mysteriously discards halfway through the movie, is allowed by director Robert Iscove (who directed Freddie in the feeble "She's All That") to drag out the simplest scenes so endlessly that 90 minutes feel like nine hours.

Claire Forlani ("Meet Joe Black"), who is way too sophisticated to be playing his friend, wears two expressions—one more than Prinze, who resembles a deer caught in the headlights so often that the Humane Society should be called in.

One of Forlani's is boredom (and who could blame her); the other is the exasperation of an actress trying to carry scene after scene with an actor who has nothing to give except taking off his shirt.

Nobody else in the movie—a newly buff (and seemingly lobotomized) Jason Biggs ("American Pie"), Amanda Detmer ("Final Destination") and Heather Donahue ("The Blair Witch Project")—is asked to do anything except briefly act stupid.

At the screening I attended, the audience members who didn't flee in disgust remained to hoot at Prinze's big romantic speeches in this otherwise laugh-free exercise, credited to screenwriters Andrew Lowery and Andrew Miller (the hapless Dennis Rodman vehicle "Simon Sez").

Everyone involved with "Boys and Girls" should be ashamed of themselves—from Dustin Hoffman's company, which produced it, if that's the word, to the Miramax marketing geniuses who are foisting this pathetic excuse for a movie on an unsuspecting public.

Calling "Boys and Girls" the year's worst movie makes it sound more entertaining than it actually is. At least we won't have to suffer through another Prinze movie until February.

NEWSDAY, 6/16/00, Part II/p. B6, Gene Seymour

I'd like to take this opportunity to explain why there has not been and probably should never be romantic comedies about film critics. See, we—geez, how do I put this?—expect too much from ourselves and from others. You know? And, like, well, we can't give in to our own desires without wondering if they're—I don't know— earned? Genuine? You know?

If you can follow all that nonsense, then you should have no trouble whatsoever accepting Ryan (Freddie Prinze Jr.) and Jennifer (Claire Forlani), two whip-smart California kids who have been accidentally bumping into each other all their lives and have somehow managed to contrive reasons to push away from each other.

Fate eventually places them both in the relatively controlled environment of UCal-Berkeley, where they ease up on their defenses and become each other's closest confidants. Just about everyone within spitting distance, including Ryan's pathological liar roommate Hunter—or is it Steve? (Jason Biggs)—and Jennifer's neurotic gal pal Amy (Amanda Detmer), can see that R and J are Meant To Be. But if logical Ryan and impulsive Jennifer agree on anything, it's that they're too close to be intimate.

Yeah, right. You've been at this rest stop so many times before that you can see the end of "Boys and Girls" coming after 7 minutes. The same can be said for all romantic comedies. What matters is how much charm and energy can be summoned in such a movie to deliver the inevitable conclusion.

It's a close call, but chalk it up as a loss. Screenwriters Andrew Lowery and Andrew Miller write banter that's as cute, ingratiating and ultimately annoying as their professional nickname, "The Drews." The direction by Robert Iscove, coming off the inexplicable cult hit "She's All That," is brisk, sharp and uncluttered. Their combined talents keep things humming along agreeably enough to fit the date-movie profile. But the film coarsens so disagreeably toward the climax that everything that comes before it is blighted.

Still, it's a pleasant movie to stare at, partly because cinematographer Ralf Bode gives such a golden glow to the Bay Area and mostly because of the attractive cast. Biggs is well on his way to establishing himself as the Geek of the Moment, while Prinze and, especially, Forlani are sexy and resourceful enough to carry their characters through their intended and unintended embarrassments.

VILLAGE VOICE, 6/27/00, p. 154, Nick Rutigliano

Unwaveringly arbitrary in nature, Robert Iscove's teenflick *Boys and Girls* approaches such niceties as construction and character motivation with a decidedly wanton shrug. Reunited with his *She's All That* star Freddie Prinze Jr. and emboldened by screenwriters Andrew Lowery and Andrew Miller (simperingly billed as "the Drews"), Iscove concocts a cat-and-dog romantic squabbler so garbled you'd need a centrifuge to sort things out. Prinze plays anal geekboy Ryan, whose friendship/romance with twitchy Ally McBeal knockoff Jennifer (Claire Forlani) is stretched over a decade and laced with vile faux-*Seinfeld* chatter. Iscove, however, ups the ante on the Drews' soulless word salad through blithely disjunctive editing and composition—"romantic chemistry," we assume, occurs when the leads actually occupy the same shot. Undaunted by the movie fraying around him, Freddie discovers L.O.V.E. with lumbering gravity, even as Forlani devotes all her lid-fluttering, lip-scrunching attention to the horde of invisible bats that she seems to detect flitting about Prinze's head.

Potentially diverting costars are squandered: *Blair Witch* nostril-flarer Heather Donahue bitch-slaps unfaithful steady Prinze and skedaddles, *Buffy*'s affable near-witch Alyson Hannigan has a less-than-cameo, and during one pointless interlude, yammering Amanda Detmer finds the kibosh immediately placed on her lust for roomie Forlani. Only Jason Biggs, renowned for making the dessert with two backs in *American Pie*, has any fun as Prinze's prevaricating roommate, snarkily disregarding any expression of the brothers-in-arms spirit they're supposed to share. Biggs ends up an audience surrogate, exclaiming, "I don't know what you want from me... I don't know what anybody wants from me!" with the exasperation of one hopelessly adrift. Such thoughts occur long before *Boys and Girls* arrives at its (literally) flatulent denouement.

Also reviewed in:
CHICAGO TRIBUNE, 6/16/00, Friday/p. F, Monica Eng
NEW YORK TIMES, 6/16/00, p. E12, A.O. Scott
VARIETY, 6/19-25/00, p. 26, Robert Koehler

BOYS LIFE 3

A Strand Releasing release. *Running Time:* 79 minutes. *MPAA:* Not Rated

MAJORETTES IN SPACE: *Director:* David Fourier. *Screenplay:* David Fourier. *Director of Photography:* Pierre Stoeber. *Editor:* Fabrice Rouaud. *Sound:* Renaud Michel. *Running Time:* 6:13 minutes.

WITH: Cleo Delacruz; Aurelien Bianco; Jean-Marc Delacruz; Elise Laurent; Olivier Laville; Philippe Bianco.

HITCH: *Director:* Bradley Rust Gray.   *Screenplay:* Bradley Rust Gray.   *Director of Photography:* Sarah Levy and Bradley Rust Gray.   *Editor:* Bradley Rust Gray.   *Music:* Mike Rechner.   *Sound:* Sage Vanden Heuvel, Mariana Yarovskaya, Sunil Vernekar, and Addison Teague.   *Running Time:* 18:21 minutes.

CAST: Drew Wood (Jason); Jason Herman (Porp).

INSIDE OUT: *Producer:* Thom Fennessey and Jason Gould.   *Director:* Jason Gould. *Screenplay:* Jason Gould.   *Director of Photography:* Sharone Meir.   *Editor:* Christopher Holmes.   *Music:* Michael Skloff.   *Running Time:* 27 minutes.

CAST: Alexis Arquette (Adam); Katie Asner (Susan); Charlie Brill (Winkler); Christina Crawford (Herself); Anne DeSalvo (Phyllis); Steve Flynn (Michael); Elliot Gould (Aaron's Father); Jason Gould (Aaron); Sam Gould (Simon); Tara Karsian (Woman at Group); Jordan Ladd (Summer); Ken Lerner (Judge Levin); Jon Polito (Paparazzi); Luis Raul (Autograph Seeker); Judy Toll (Rochelle).

JUST ONE TIME: *Producer:* Exile Ramirez and Lane Janger.   *Director:* Lane Janger. *Screenplay:* Lane Janger.   *Director of Photography:* Tim Naylor.   *Editor:* Francois Keraudren. *Music:* Gerry Gershman and David Frank.   *Production Designer:* Heather Mosher.   *Costumes:* Karen Bermudez.   *Running Time:* 7:28 minutes.

CAST: Joelle Carter (Amy); Guillermo Diaz (Victor); Jennifer Esposito (Michelle); Lane Janger (Anthony).

$30:   *Producer:* Line Postmyr, Gregory Cooke, and Christopher Landon.   *Director:* Gregory Cooke.   *Screenplay:* Christopher Landon.   *Director of Photography:* Dermott Downs.   *Editor:* Lorne Morris.   *Music:* Peter Rafelson.   *Casting:* Eleanor Cooke.   *Running time:* 19:10 minutes.

CAST: Sara Gilbert (Emily); Erik MacArthur (Scott); Greg Itzin (Scott's Father).

LOS ANGELES TIMES, 12/8/00, Calendar/p. 8, Kevin Thomas

Strand Releasing is promoting "Boys Life 3," its third collection of gay-themed short films, with the slogan, "Third time's a charm." It proves an apt description of this lively, amusing collection of five films that take a wry look at being gay. Previous collections, in 1994 and 1998, launched several filmmakers into features, and this could happen for some of those represented in this offering.

The most idiosyncratic of the narratives is Bradley Rust Gray's "hitch," which is notable for the inventive ways in which Gray uses a camera to express the claustrophobic, intimate atmosphere inside a van in which two twentysomething men are crossing the country. Jason (Drew Wood) is a sturdy gay guy who sets off his macho cowboy look with blue glitter nail polish. He has the itch, and it's Porp (Jason Herman), a looker with dirty blond locks, who's the hitch—the guy to whom Jason has given a lift.

Confident and persistent, Jason makes his moves on Porp shrewdly, realizing that Porp is at once in the throes of sexual frustration and upset by a call he has placed to his girlfriend. "hitch" is as psychologically persuasive as it is remarkably economical and announces the arrival of a fresh talent.

Jason Gould's "Inside Out" and Gregory Cooke's "$ 30" are notable as assured, fully realized examples of skillful, mature screen storytelling. Gould casts himself as the gay son of celebrities—and Barbra Streisand and Elliott Gould are in fact his parents. Gould's Aaron is a likable young man determined to establish his own identity. That Aaron, automatically the constant target of paparazzi on account of his famous parents, is gay makes his life especially challenging; luckily, he has a good sense of humor with a highly developed sense of absurdity.

While his lifelong pal (Alexis Arquette) is helping him find Mr. Right, he's confronted at a market checkout line with a tabloid headline shrieking, "Superstar's Son Marries Male Model."

Aaron tries for a "I should be so lucky" shrug yet finds himself, at the urging of his father (played by Elliott Gould) to try Scientology, whose hard-sell pitch is amusingly satirized, and he even attends a children-of-celebrities support group, run by Christina Crawford, "Inside Out" builds gracefully in a relaxed manner to a warm note of reconciliation with the world.

Written by Christopher Landon, Cooke's "$ 30" is as crisply made as it is tender in tone. As a 16th birthday present, a macho-seeming father (Greg Itzin) delivers his ill-at-ease son (Erik MacArthur) to an apartment house where he is to lose his virginity with a prostitute (Sara Gilbert), who swiftly senses that MacArthur's Scott is gay.

Gilbert's attractive and intelligent Emily is seriously selling herself short for 30 bucks, for she has the wisdom and kindness with which to help Scott take a step toward self-acceptance while not embarrassing him in front of his father. The result is a poignant moment in which strangers manage to reach out to each other in friendship. Landon, the son of the late Michael Landon, wrote the script for Larry Clark's adventurous "Another Day in Paradise."

Much shorter than either "Inside Out" or "$ 30," Lane Janger's funny "Just One Time" finds a pretty girl (Joelle Carter) turning the tables on her boyfriend (Janger) when he keeps pressing her to accept another woman in their sexual encounters.

"Boys Life 3" opens with French filmmaker David Fourier's zany, experimental "Majorettes in Space," which makes a deadly serious point about the Roman Catholic Church's abhorrence of abhorrence of condom's, even amid the continuing spread of AIDS.

NEW YORK POST, 12/8/00, p. 54, Lou Lumenick

"Boys Life 3," the latest collection of gay-themed shorts, is worthwhile mainly because of "Inside Out," a 28-minute autobiographical film written, directed and starring Jason Gould, who not-so-incidentally is Barbra Streisand's son.

Gould's subject is irresistible: the misery of life as the son of two famous parents (his real-life dad, Elliott Gould, appears as his on-screen dad; mom doesn't) who happens to be gay. That includes coping with a tabloid report he's married a male model, fighting off paparazzi and trying to find a lover who isn't intimidated by his lineage.

Gould is a very appealing performer and his writing and direction are fresh and funny as he takes on Scientology and his father's drug use, among other targets. A high point is Gould's visit to a meeting for "survivors of celebrity parents," presided over by Christina Crawford, daughter of Joan and the author of "Mommy Dearest" (who plays herself).

"Wire hangers are no longer an issue," she tells the group.

NEWSDAY, 12/8/00, Part II/p. B10, Jan Stuart

The ongoing omnibus of gay-themed films known as "Boys Life" continues to demonstrate how uniquely gratifying the short form can be when the subject is in harmony with the scale. Alternately saucy, steamy and disarming, the five films that constitute "Boys Life 3" show the series at its rogue best.

The most original offering of the lot is also the first, a smart-alecky French import that answers the pressing question, what do drum majorettes, Russian cosmonauts and Pope Paul have in common? With deadpan narration, David Fourier's "Majorettes in Space" also manages to throw cows, Polish vodka and gay pride marches into a mordantly funny miniature that comes down hard on the lethal dangers of moral prudishness.

Sex and the single boy are the subjects of "hITCH" and "$30," two engaging close encounters that go at the gay closet from strikingly different angles. In Bradley Rust Gray's sultry "hITCH," two straight-seeming dudes who share a Volkswagen van across the country mask their mutual attraction under a veil of Playboy foldouts and homophobic epithets. Gray's hidden-between-the-lines script and cinematographer Sarah Levy's telling closeups turn a porn-film set-up into a crackling study of sexual tension.

Convention is also subverted with smart dialogue and keen performances in a sweet-souled "$30," written by Christopher Landon (son of the late actor Michael) and directed by Gregory Cooke. Eighteen-year-old Scott (Erik MacArthur) reluctantly visits a prostitute, a rite-of-passage birthday present courtesy of his father. As dad hovers in the motel lot below, the prostitute,

Emily (Sara Gilbert), uncovers the root of Scott's shyness. It's no big surprise, but Gilbert's warmly non-flashy performance makes it click.

A celebrity scion also powers the series' centerpiece, "Inside Out," a hilarious lament on living in the shadow of fame from Jason Gould, doing a writing, directing and starring turn that honors his hands-on mom, Barbra Streisand. Playing a fictional variant on himself, Gould pays through the nose for Scientology classes and attends a Survivors of Celebrity Parents support group in order to stabilize a lifestyle fraught with tabloid paparazzi and short-term boyfriends who are intimidated by his family background.

Connections obviously didn't hurt filmmaker Gould in casting his movie, with a slick ensemble that includes Alexis Arquette, Joe Polito and his good-sport father, Elliott Gould. But the younger Gould earns his stripes as he gently satirizes that which he knows best. There is also, admittedly, a fanzine fascination in the echoes of his mother's comic mannerisms and the homage to mom's roller-skating bit in "Funny Girl."

"Boys Life 3" is rounded out by Lane Janger's "Just One Time," a decent blackout joke, which was regrettably blown up into a full-length film released the other month. It's worth seeing, if only as a textbook example for neophyte artistes on When to Put Down the Brush.

VILLAGE VOICE, 12/12/00, p. 178, Dennis Lim

The gay shorts profitably anthologized by Strand every few years have largely avoided formal and thematic risks in favor of quippy, frothy uplift. That the directors featured in the first two collections have gone on to inflict more widespread damage with *54, I Think I Do, Speedway Junky,* and *Psycho Beach Party* can only bode ill for *Boys Life 3,* but this third installment, though far from painless, is comparatively substantial, and thoughtfully front-loaded to boot (feel free to evacuate the theater after the first 25 minutes).

First, shortest, and best, French director David Fourier's six-minute mock-instructional free association, *Majorettes in Space,* is alone almost worth the price of admission. A flashcard series of Python-esque non sequiturs traces arcane connections between safe sex, space sex, Gay Pride marches, marching-band bootees, cattle, and the pope, hurtling headfirst from nihilist rage to ineffable sorrow. Bradley Rust Gray's *hITCH* (previously screened, like *Majorettes,* in the New York Film Festival) is a slyly minimal road movie. There's not much to it besides barely repressed lust—which turns out to be exactly the point. Every look and gesture, however oblique, glistens with erotic meaning.

Stay on at your own risk. Rubber neckers may not be able to resist Jason Gould's autobiographical *Inside Out,* which, true enough, opens with tremendous train-wreck potential. Post tabloid outing, the son of Elliott and Babs—essentially playing himself—joins a Christina Crawford-run support group for celebrity offspring. Gould Sr contributes a bewildered cameo; Mommie Dearest is conspicuously unacknowledged. By the time the film ends, with a rollerblade striptease-cum-paparazzo fingerwag, it's clear that beyond so-bad-it's-good camp lies an altogether scarier dimension of ineptitude. More possibly true Hollywood stories: Mysterious *Little House on the Prairie* connections abound in Gregory Cooke's platitudinous *$30,* written by Christopher Landon (son of Michael) with Sara Gilbert unconvincingly playing a hooker who becomes confidante to a confused teen. In its original seven-minute incarnation, Lane Janger's *Just One Time* (which has since inexplicably spawned a feature) has the advantage of brevity, but its morbid narcissism and tragic witlessness shine through regardless.

Also reviewed in:
NEW YORK TIMES, 12/8/00, p. E20, Elvis Mitchell
VARIETY, 12/11-17/00, p. 26, Dennis Harvey

BRIDGE, THE

A Phaedra Cinema release of a DD Productions/TFI Films/Roissy Films/Compagnie Cinematographique Prima co-production with the participation of Canal+ and the CNC.

Executive Producer: Jacques Bar.   *Director:* Gérard Depardieu and Frederic Auburtin. *Screenplay (French with English subtitles):* François Dupeyron. *Story:* Alain Leblanc. *Director of Photography:* Pascal Ridao. *Editor:* Noelle Boisson. *Music:* Frederic Auburtin. *Sound:* Pierre Gamet, Gerard Lamps, and Christophe Winding. *Art Director:* Michele Abbe. *Costumes:* Tom Rand. *Running time:* 92 minutes. *MPAA Rating:* Not Rated.

CAST: Carole Bouquet (Mina);   Gerard Depardieu (Georges);   Charles Berling (Matthias); Stanislas Crevillen (Tommy);   Dominique Reymond (Claire Daboval);   Melanie Laurent (Lisbeth).

LOS ANGELES TIMES, 12/8/00, Calendar/p. 18, Kevin Thomas

"The Bridge," starring Carole Bouquet and Gerard Depardieu, who was co-director with the film's composer, Frederic Aubertin, is a quiet, powerful tale of adultery.

You cannot watch this sophisticated, understated film without thinking of all the people who are unaware that the bloated buffoon Depardieu plays in "102 Dalmatians" also is the greatest male star of his generation in the French cinema. This film and the Disney holiday film were made close together, but Depardieu not only seems many pounds lighter here but also slimmer than he has in years.

The setting is a picture-postcard town in Normandy in 1962, a charming place but the epitome of provincial propriety. Depardieu's Georges has been a successful enough masonry contractor to afford a sunny, spacious home on the edge of town. But he's lost his small business and hangs out a lot in a local cafe while his beautiful wife, Mina (Bouquet), and their 15-year-old son Tommy (Stanislas Crevillen), a serious, reflective youth, go to the movies.

One evening they're watching "West Side Story," and when the lights go up Mina realizes that the clean-cut man (Charles Berling) sitting next to her has been reduced to tears, as she has. Their common emotional reaction is enough to start a conversation going and then to prompt an invitation to mother and son from Berling's suave Matthias to join him in a drink at a nightclub, where he and Mina dance up a storm.

Once home, Mina assures her son of the innocence of the evening and in fact has no plans ever to see Matthias again. But when she does, she plunges headlong into a grand, all-consuming passion and places her son in the uncomfortable position of having to cover for her. Meanwhile, Mina has taken a job as a maid in the home of her friend, Claire Daboval (Dominique Reymond), an aristocrat whose family lives in an ancient manor house nearby.

Shortly thereafter, Georges lands a job as head of a construction crew working on an immense bridge project that will take three years to complete. One evening, while preparing to serve an elaborate meal at the manor house, Mina discovers not only that Matthias is Claire's cousin but is also the chief engineer on the bridge—and in effect, her husband's new boss, who will be staying at the manor house for the duration. At the same time, Claire's anti-establishment daughter Lisbeth (Melanie Laurent) is pursuing Tommy.

What's of primary interest here is that Mina, once romance has made her realize how suffocating her existence has become, unhesitatingly follows her heart. She wants to avoid hurting her son and husband as much as possible, but she experiences no deep conflict in embracing the promise Matthias holds in opening up a whole new world for her—of wealth and privilege as well as torrid lovemaking. (There's no talk of marriage, though, for Matthias has a wife who prefers to stay in Nice while the bridge is being built.) Georges is loving and intelligent, and as profoundly hurt as he inevitably will be, this strong man will not express his pain in violence.

Thus, "The Bridge" becomes a confrontation between a woman whose resolve will not be weakened by the excruciating emotional wound she has inflicted and the man who must cope with this painful wound as best he can. Mina's forthrightness gradually earns our respect.

Bouquet's Mina doesn't ask for sympathy from us or from anyone else; she has the courage of her passion. Depardieu's terrible calm as Georges offers an equally strong counterpoint that gives the film tension and balance; both stars could not be better, which is saying a lot for the always-estimable Bouquet as well as Depardieu.

This elegant and beautiful film suggests that while love can be cruelly selfish in its impact on the innocent, it does not judge Mina for pursuing it at the expense of others. "The Bridge" is as compassionate as it is unsentimental.

NEW YORK POST, 10/27/00, p. 47, V.A. Musetto

It isn't often we get to see Gerard Depardieu cry on screen. He does in this French drama, and with good reason—his wife (Carole Bouquet) is having an affair with his boss (Charles Berling) on a bridge-construction project.

Co-directed by Depardieu and Fred Auburtin, "The Bridge" is set in 1962 Normandy. Depardieu and Bouquet are a seemingly average blue-collar, small-town couple with a teenage son.

But after 15 years of marriage, Bouquet is growing increasingly bored. She escapes by going to movies such as "Jules et Jim" and "West Side Story." It is at one screening that she, meets Berling. Soon, the two are sharing a bed.

"The Bridge" features convincing performances all around. And it avoids the theatrics and clichés found in Hollywood movies about cheating spouses. The manner in which the conflict resolves itself should come as a pleasant surprise.

VILLAGE VOICE, 10/31/00, p. 174, Michael Atkinson

Anything can happen when actors direct—from Robert Montgomery's sojourns into subjective weirdness to Robert Redford's flatulent mythopoeia—but we could hardly have expected the modesty and sober gentility of Gérard Depardieu's debut, *Un Pont Entre Deux Rives*, prosaically retitled *The Bridge* and seemingly destined to be underseen. Co-directed with Frédéric Auburtin, another actor trying on the breeches, *The Bridge* visits a familiar happening—the slow, accidental dissolution of a marriage—but the mood is Renoir without the twist of lemon: quiet, mature, sensible, accepting. Depardieu is Georges, a small-town laborer out of work in 1961; Mina (Carole Bouquet), his serenely beautiful, relaxed wife, reveals her secret dissatisfaction only through her elated repeat viewings of *West Side Story*. As Georges finally finds employment on a distant bridge site that requires him to bunk away every week, Mina and her teenage son, Tommy (Stanislas Crevillen), meet the suave-doughy Matthias (Charles Berling) at the theater; it's not long after Matthias reveals that he's an engineer on the bridge that he and Mina begin a barely perceptible co-seduction, leading to a remarkably guiltless affair.

Bouquet, one of France's preeminent movie stealers (*Grosse Fatigue* no longer belonged to Michel Blanc after she showed up), makes *The Bridge* seem active and joyful even when the scenario lays low; her soulful intelligence never stops humming. But she's never given a scene in which the liaison's euphoria becomes clear—in fact, the love scenes seem strangely, purposefully bloodless. The impression is that the characters are harboring deeper secrets, or, eventually, that the first-time directors were at a loss. Once Georges discovers the affair, we're not shocked that the movie resists melodrama, but his tortured, responsible compliance is odd and moving coming from Depardieu, just as his movie is mysteriously haunted by civility under extreme pressure. Scarcely profound, *The Bridge* might be too restrained for its own good—with subtitles, cataclysm sells better.

Also reviewed in:
NEW REPUBLIC, 11/20/00, p. 24, Stanley Kauffmann
NEW YORK TIMES, 10/27/00, p. E16, Stephen Holden
VARIETY, 4/26-5/2/99, p. 45, Lisa Nesselson

BRING IT ON

A Universal Pictures and Beacon Pictures release.   *Executive Producer:* Armyan Bernstein, Max Wong, Caitlin Scanlon, and Paddy Cullen.   *Producer:* Marc Abraham, Thomas A. Bliss, and John Ketcham.   *Director:* Peyton Reed.   *Screenplay:* Jessica Bendinger. *Director of Photography:* Shawn Maurer.   *Editor:* Larry Bock.   *Music:* Christophe Beck.   *Music Editor:* Fernand Bos. *Choreographer:* Anne Fletcher.   *Sound:* Robert Trevor Black and (music) Casey Stone.   *Sound Editor:* Cormac Funge.   *Casting:* Josephine Middletown.   *Production Designer:* Sharon Lomofsky. *Art Director:* Timothy Whidbee. *Set Decorator:* Jill McGraw. *Set Dresser:* David Brownell, Christopher L. Marsteller, Robert Naefke, Glen Marc Shearer, and Robb Abramson.   *Costumes:* Mary Jane Fort.   *Make-up:* Selina Jayne.   *Make-up (Kirsten Dunst):* Jo-Anne Smith.   *Running time:* 110 minutes.   *MPAA Rating:* PG-13.

CAST: Kirsten Dunst (Torrance Shipman);   Eliza Dushku (Missy Pantone);   Jesse Bradford (Cliff Pantone);   Gabrielle Union (Isis); Clare Kramer (Courtney);   Nicole Bilderback (Whitney); Tsianina Joelson (Darcy); Rini Bell (Kasey); Nathan West (Jan); Huntley Ritter (Les);   Shamari Fears (Lava);   Natina Reed (Jenelope);   Brandi Williams (Lafred);   Richard Hillman (Aaron);   Lindsay Sloane (Big Red);   Bianca Kajlich (Carver);   Holmes Osborne (Bruce Shipman); Sherry Hursey (Christine Shipman); Cody McMains (Justin Shipman); Ian Roberts (Sparky Polastri);   David Edwards (Toros Tight End);   Ashley Howard (Toros Quarterback); Nikole Lee Amateau and Clementine Ford (New Pope Cheerleaders); Grant Thompson (Costa Mesa Quarterback);   Leonard Clifton (Costa Mesa Linebacker);   Marie Wise (Argumentative Girl);   Dru Mouser (Been-Crying-For-Hours Girl);   Tracy Pacheco (Rappin' White Girl);   Alicia Michelle Sassano (Be Aggressive Girl);   Natasha Soll (Star-Over Girl); Ryan Drummond (Theatre Boy);   Paullin Wolfe (Tiny Tot Cheerleader);   David E. Willis and Beth LaMure (Emcees);   Anne Fletcher (Event Coordinator);   Doug Waldo (UCA Official); Annie Hinton (High-Stung Mom);   Louise Gallagher (Class Monitor);   Edmond Clay (Football Announcer);   Daniella Kuhn (T.V. Reporter);   Aloma Wright (Pauletta);   Paul Bloom (T.V. Commentator);   Melanie Atmadja (Jamie);   Silencio Por Favor (Mime);   Jodi Harris (Cheer Coach);   Nectar Rose (Nervous Cheerleader);   Hilary Salvatore (Toothless Cheerleader); Elizabeth Johnson (Confident Cheerleader);   Riley Smith (Guy Cheerleader);   Carla Mackauf (Aaron's Lover);   Anna Lisa Mendiola (Clover Cheerleader).

LOS ANGELES TIMES, 8/25/00, Calendar/p. 2, Kevin Thomas

"Bring It On," a smart and sassy high school movie that's fun for all ages, opens with Kirsten Dunst's cheerleader having a dream in which she suddenly realizes that she's been going through her routines—wearing not a stitch. Actually, a real-life nightmare awaits her.

Her joy at being elected team captain at her high school in a posh San Diego area evaporates when she learns she'll be leading her team, the Toros, national champ for five years running, into the regionals with a hip-hop routine her predecessor lifted move for move from a Compton high school with which they'll eventually be competing.

Dunst's Torrance learns the bad news from Missy (Eliza Dushku), who's just moved from L.A. and has reluctantly joined the Toros since the school does not offer the gymnastics in which she excels. Missy recognizes the hip-hop routine from the time her former L.A. area high school played football with the Compton team.

The cheerleaders see no recourse but to brazen it out at the regionals, but for the finals Torrance turns to a professional choreographer (Ian Roberts) recommended to her by her ultra-glib boyfriend (Richard Hillman), now at college. Roberts' Sparky Polastri is a hilarious martinet who takes his moves and look from Bob Fosse, but there's a hitch with him, too.

"It's only cheerleading," Missy reminds the distraught Torrance as the troubles start piling up. "I am only cheerleading," replies Torrance honestly. This exchange goes to the heart of Jessica Bendinger's crackling good script, sharply directed by Peyton Reed.

This sun-filled, lively Universal presentation has a light satirical touch, works up lots of laughter, but is not heavy-handed about Torrance and her squad taking cheerleading so seriously. Rather than lament how winning a cheerleading trophy seems vastly more important to the squad members than getting the grades that will get them into college, Bendinger and Reed instead show us the likable Torrance and her pals receiving some unexpected life lessons.

The way the film plays out undercuts suspense as to who's going to win the nationals trophy, but then the picture subversively suggests that sometimes there are more important values in life than winning. It even dares to suggest that one of the Toros cheerleaders is gay (Huntley Ritter) and comfortable about it.

The filmmakers take the trouble to make that hip-hop squad, the Clovers, integral to their story. Having endured their dynamic routines being ripped off repeatedly, the Clovers this time will be competing in the regionals and are determined to raise the funds that will take them to the finals for which they almost certainly will qualify.

The Clovers' team leader, Isis (Gabrielle Union), is as proud as she is smart and tough, and her strong presence and character provokes Torrance into unaccustomed reflection about such matters as fair play, social inequities and respect for yourself and others. "Bring It On" can get away with comic exaggeration all the more effectively because of such ballast.

No teen film would be without romance, and as it happens Missy has a brother, Cliff (Jesse Bradford), just as smart as she is and quickly smitten with Torrance but fearing he can't compete with Hillman's slick and shallow Aaron.

On target in all aspects, "Bring It On" is a summer tonic arriving in time for Labor Day weekend and just as kids are preparing to head back to school for the fall semester. The timing of the release of "Bring It On," like everything else about it, seems just right.

NEW YORK POST, 8/25/00, p. 51, Jonathan Foreman

Essentially a feature-length commercial for both the growing sport of competitive cheerleading and ESPN2—the network that carries the principal cheerleading competitions—"Bring It On" is yet another film that goes as far as it can within the constraints of a PG-13 rating to exploit the Britney Spears/Christina Aguilera sex appeal of a nubile cast.

An exhilarating, very funny opening sequence suggests that you're about to see a teen pic of "Clueless" quality.

Unfortunately, "Bring It On" does not live up to such promise. But it does, somehow, overcome a number of grave faults—a stale plot, cringe-inspiring dialogue and several ineptly staged scenes—to be much more enjoyable than it should be.

Fortunately the movie boasts Kirsten Dunst with all her likability and skill, a fresh co-star in Eliza Dushku (Faith in TV's "Buffy the Vampire Slayer"), some good jokes, and some exuberant cheerleading sequences that make the most of the sport's often spectacular combination of gymnastics, dance and sex appeal.

(And it is as much a sport, at least as much, as synchronized swimming or floor gymnastics.)

Torrance (Dunst) is the perky, devoted new captain of the cheerleading squad of Rancho Carne High School in San Diego. The team has won the national championship five years in a row, in marked contrast to the school's dreadful football team.

When Torrance recruits transfer student Missy (Dushku), a tough gymnast with a cute brother (Jesse Bradford), she's confident she can lead the squad to victory. But Missy reveals that the team's routines were in fact stolen by the ruthless former captain from an inner-city school in East Compton.

A visit to the Compton school not only confirms the theft, it also introduces Torrance to Isis (Gabrielle Union from "She's All That," "10 Things I Hate About You"), the determined and very angry captain of the predominantly African-American team there. (All the African-American roles in "Bring It On" are particularly one-dimensional.)

It turns out that for the first time ever the Compton Clovers will be taking part in national cheerleading competitions and the Rancho Carne Toros better not use the stolen routines.

There are a few moments when you wonder if a dentist didn't exert a strong influence on the production.

The lead players have strangely fake-looking teeth—they look like they've been painted with Wite-Out—and there's an admittedly original flirtation scene that centers on brushing and rinsing.

NEWSDAY, 8/25/00, Part II/p. B7, Jan Stuart

Proponents of sexual abstinence for high schoolers will be interested to learn of a new development in creative intimate relations known as "cheer sex." If one of the characters in "Bring it On" is correctly understood, cheer sex is when a cheerleader goes all the way with a sports fan, purely by eye contact. In such a manner, Kevin Spacey was able to defile his daughter's best friend in "American Beauty" without budging from the basketball stands.

Cheer sex is but one of the bizarre social rituals touched upon in "Bring It On," an endlessly genial comedy about a San Diego cheerleading team that delivers the clinical fascinations of an anthropological study with its tongue firmly in cheek.

Writer Jessica Bendinger has obviously studied her Brian De Palma in tandem with her cheerleading moves, as "Bring It On" opens with a dream-sequence curve ball that reminds us just how much damage "Carrie" has inflicted upon popular culture. The beautiful dreamer is Torrance Shipman (Kirsten Dunst), a tenacious head-cheerleader aspirant who will soon be faced with the task of leading her squad, the Toros, to their fifth consecutive victory at the national cheerleading championships.

Such problems, such pressures, they could drive a person of lesser integrity to nefarious means. That is exactly what Torrance learns when she discovers that her predecessor has been ripping off routines from the Clovers, a largely African-American squad from East Los Angeles. In addition to hiring a drill-sergeant choreographer to fashion an original routine for the championships, Torrance must balance her devotion to her college-frosh boyfriend Aaron (Richard Hillman, a younger, smarmier Marlon Brando) with her burgeoning affection for an untidy acolyte of The Clash named Cliff (an appealing Jesse Bradford).

"Bring It On," walks a fine line between admiring the commitment and gymnastic prowess of cheerleaders and sending it up, leaning ultimately toward the former. These girls clearly mean business ("Remember, they give extra points for alacrity and effulgence," says one Toro to another), taking their mission with a dead earnestness that seems to escape their male co-squad members, who seem more concerned with defending their sexuality from attack.

As high-stakes, high school travesties go, "Bring It On" is not quite this year's "Election." Dunst's Torrance lacks the malevolent charisma of Reese Witherspoon's student council president wannabe, and unlike that film, this one doesn't purport to be about anything but winning the big cheer-off. Like the Toros, however, it has an unbending vitality that gets to you even when the jokes flag, which they inevitably do.

The biggest disappointment is the photography and editing, much too MTV-restless during the competition sequences to give the cheerleaders their due. As a result, the Toros' routines have a sameness about them that robs from the frisson of watching them in action. Compared to the ramshackle "The Replacements," however, "Bring It On" flies like the "Citizen Kane" of the sports comedy genre.

SIGHT AND SOUND, 11/00, p. 45, Stephanie Zacharack

San Diego, the present. Under the leadership of Torrance, five-times national high-school cheerleading champs the Rancho Carne Toros start the school year certain they're on their way to their sixth victory. When a member of the team is injured, she's replaced by tough school newcomer Missy. Although championed by Torrance, who has a crush on her brother Cliff, Missy is the target of the other cheerleaders' scorn. They like her even less when she reveals that their potentially award winning cheers have been stolen, by the Toros' previous captain, from the squad of an East Compton high school that's considered "invisible" because it's in a black neighbourhood.

The Toros try to get a new routine into shape by hiring a choreographer which only results in their humiliation at the regional competition when another squad shows up with the same act. They then devise and perfect their own routine, which leads them to win second place in the nationals. The East Compton team, competing for the first time, takes first prize.

Conscious perhaps that the world doesn't need a biting satire of cheerleading, *Bring It On*'s director Peyton Reed (who has worked largely in US television) gives us a pointedly funny and good-natured picture, one that takes the silliness of its subject as a given and moves on with intelligence and verve. *Bring It On* opens with a neat dream sequence featuring the Toros, a prize-winning school cheerleading team, which spells out everything that cheerleaders are thought to be—stuck-up, catty, super-popular, aggressively attractive, shallow—and then wallows gloriously in it. Before long, you're so revved up you can't wait to see their next routine.

The East Compton squad the Clovers, from a predominantly black neighbourhood, are particularly thrilling to watch. Led by the take no-prisoners class act Isis (Gabrielle Union) and including members of the real-life R&B group Blaque, their sassy routines raise the cool quotient of a traditionally maligned sport. It's no wonder an all-white cheerleading squad would want to steal from them. But embedded in this particular theft is a bitter truth: the former cheerleading captain who stole from the Clovers clearly assumed it was OK to appropriate their material. Without being sticky sweet or sanctimonious, *Bring It On* makes you consider that injustice seriously. What begins as a theft ends up being a spur to both sides to do more daring work—a wry comment, perhaps, on the positive effects of cross-cultural pollination?

Bring It On spins off one sly little joke after another, and the smart ensemble makes every one of them work. Eliza Dushku (who plays Faith in *Buffy the Vampire Slayer*) is likeable as the tough girl Missy who is really a serious gymnast but gradually becomes seduced by miniature uniforms and opposing-team taunts such as "That's all right, that's OK, you're gonna pump our gas someday!" Kirsten Dunst looks like every American high-school boy's dream date, and she plays captain Torrance's shallow suburban cluelessness with such a light touch that it's more endearing than wearying. When new kid Cliff Pantone ambles into the classroom wearing a Clash t-shirt, she asks with a shiver of girlish enthusiasm, "So, is that your band or something?" Later, when Torrance spends the night at Missy's house, she and Cliff find themselves sharing the bathroom mirror as they brush their teeth; their embarrassment at having to spit in front of one another makes for a beautifully staged comic flirtation. Given the movie's off-kilter *savoir faire,* it makes sense that their courtship should begin with starry eyes and foamy mouths.

VILLAGE VOICE, 9/5/00, p. 122, Jessica Winter

Those culture consumers who've never really understood the old adage that life is like high school will be further flummoxed by *Bring It On*, which frames high school cheerleading as a microcosm of the real world (or perhaps—judging from the use of MTV staples like strobe-speed editing, garish set design, anonymous power-pop soundtrack, and hordes of stylist-retaining young irritants—*The Real World)* in all its racial and sexual tensions and cutthroat bitch-eat-bitch corporate-style competition. All the girls are 16 going on 29, and all of them fire off misanthropic quips like they're at a Friars Club roast scripted by the Heathers.

Most recognizably human among them is maniacally perky senior Torrance (Kirsten Dunst), recently elected cheer captain of the national-champ Toros squad in a tony, lily-white San Diego suburb. Bored with her condescending boyfriend (he'll soon be replaced by a dark horse who—get this—listens to this crazy punk band called the Clash) and disheartened by her loathsome crew of poisonous snapdragons, Torrance discovers that her predecessor stole their routines from a mostly black squad, the Clovers, who cheer for a financially strapped East Compton school. This twist means that *Bring It On* puts a new leaping spin on the old rock'n'roll tradition of, um, appropriating black ideas for white(bread) audiences, and the movie gets you thinking despite itself. The Clovers, led by the regal anti-Torrance, Isis (Gabrielle Union, not in the movie nearly enough), have the more interesting story (albeit one tailor-made for an inspirational morning-show segment), but their existence is just a device for nudging Torrance's race anxieties. Brandishing white privilege in the form of white guilt, her do-gooder exhibitionism reaches its apex when she shows up at a Clover practice waving a Daddy-signed check to fund their trip to Nationals.

Screenwriter Jessica Bendinger exhibits a numbing fixation on the sadism of teenage girls (she misses that chestnut of wisdom found in *Welcome to the Dollhouse*: High schoolers; do continue with the nasty badinage of junior high, "only not so much to your face"). Bendinger and leering director Peyton Reed (who, equipped with fantastic gymnasts among his extras, can't once fit an entire stacking formation in the frame) richly deserve each other: She'll pen a locker-room scene in which one skinny cheerleader tells another, "You put the ass in massive," and he'll shoot the girls tottering about in their undies and bending over on cue, in sync. At least reigning jailbait Dunst, who's been infusing wise young blood into movies for going on a decade, delivers a performance as sprightly and knowingly daft as her turn in *Dick*. She provides the only major element of *Bring It On* that plays as tweaking parody rather than slick, strident, body-slam churlishness.

Also reviewed in:
CHICAGO TRIBUNE, 8/25/00, Friday/p. A, Vicky Edwards
NEW YORK TIMES, 8/25/00, p. E8, A.O. Scott
VARIETY, 8/28-9/3/00, p. 25, Robert Koehler
WASHINGTON POST, 8/25/00, p. C1, Rita Kempley
WASHINGTON POST, 8/25/00, Weekend/p. 36, Michael O'Sullivan

BROKEN HEARTS CLUB, THE: A ROMANTIC COMEDY

A Sony Pictures Classics release of a Banner Entertainment production. *Producer:* Mickey Liddell and Joseph Middleton. *Director:* Greg Berlanti. *Screenplay:* Greg Berlanti. *Director of Photography:* Paul Elliott. *Editor:* Todd Busch. *Music:* Julianne Kelley. *Sound:* David Chornow. *Casting:* Joseph Middleton. *Production Designer:* Charlie Daboub. *Set Dresser:* Mark Macauley. *Costumes:* Mas Kondo. *Make-up:* Saundra Jordan. *Running time:* 94 minutes. *MPAA Rating:* R.

CAST: Zach Braff (Benji); Dean Cain (Cole); Andrew Keegan (Kevin); Nia Long (Leslie); John Mahoney (Jack);   Mary McCormack (Anne);   Matt McGrath (Howie);   Timothy Olyphant (Dennis); Billy Porter (Taylor); Justin Theroux (Marshall); Ben Weber (Patrick); Robert Arce (Purple Guy); Michael Bergin (Kip Rogers); Chris Payne Gilbert (Larry); Nora Burns (Female Shopper); John Brandon (Mickey); Diane McBain (Josephine); Robert Peters (Cop); Leeza Vinnichenko (Russian Woman); Chris Wiehl (J. Crew Guy); Jennifer Coolidge (Betty); Kerr Smith (Catcher); Ken Kerman (Umpire); Brian Gaskill (Brian); Chris Kane (Idaho Guy); David Youse (Barry); Chris Weitz (Director).

CHRISTIAN SCIENCE MONITOR, 9/29/00, p. 15, David Sterritt

"The Broken Hearts Club: A Romantic Comedy", follows the frequent indie practice of niche marketing—in this case, the sizable audience for gay-oriented stories made in a mainstream style.

In many respects, the movie is as old-fashioned as its subtitle, spinning the interwoven yarns of several lovelorn Los Angeles characters. The only twist is that its heroes are primarily gay men, played with varying degrees of charm by a mostly young cast presided over by the more seasoned John Mahoney, of TVs popular "Frasier" show.

As much as they'd like to attract general audiences, director Greg Berlanti and the other makers of "The Broken Hearts Club" will surely be content if they can dominate their chosen niche—unlike the "Girlfight" producers, who clearly hope for a demographic sweep.

LOS ANGELES TIMES, 9/29/00, Calendar/p. 15, Kevin Thomas

Greg Berlanti's lively and engaging "The Broken Hearts Club" is subtitle "a romantic comedy" but is much more than that: a sharply observed yet affectionate and humorous critique of the values of the gay world of West Hollywood, where one's circle of friends can be as unintentionally destructive as it is warmly supportive.

A co-executive producer of TV's "Dawson's Creek," Berlanti brings a smart, witty, mainstream style to his well-crafted picture, which surely enhances its crossover appeal. Tart dialogue, deft characterizations and finely tuned ensemble performances from a hunky cast should further guarantee that this Sony Pictures Classics release will be one of the most popular gay-themed films to date.

The pivotal figure among six gay friends is Timothy Olyphant's Dennis, an aspiring photographer approaching 30, an age of inevitable stock-taking. Dennis is nice-looking, quick with a comeback and beginning to see that he's not getting anywhere professionally or personally. His romantic life adds up to little more than a series of one-night stands with men as attractive as himself, while he's still working at a restaurant run by a paternal and kindly retired actor, Jack (John Mahoney).

Dennis shares a tasteful, well-appointed home—you would hardly expect otherwise—with a shameless love-'em-and-leave'em type, a great-looking aspiring actor, Cole (Dean Cain). They take in their co-worker Taylor (Billy Porter) when his longtime lover dumps him.

Also in their group are Zach Braff's Benji, a sweet-natured youth with spiky blond hair and leather pants who dulls his vulnerability with drugs; Andrew Keegan's Kevin, a guy so young he's not actually out yet and a co-worker of the smitten Benji; Matt McGrath's Howie, who's such a chronic complainer and pessimist that he can't accept that his handsome, long-suffering companion Marshall (Justin Theroux) really does care for him; and Ben Weber's self-pitying Patrick, a perfectly nice-looking man who nevertheless feels that he fails miserably to meet community standards for looks.

"Gay men in L.A. are a bunch of 10s looking for 11s," says Patrick, hitting the nail squarely on the head in regard to the value placed on appearances in his world. Not surprisingly, these guys are caught up in a constant pursuit of sex and romance, confusing the two and getting hurt in the process.

In the course of everyday life, none of these men end up in the same place they're in when we first meet them. Kevin's growing discontent and his increasing resolve to make drastic changes in his life give the film its key focus and development. Everyone in the cast makes a strong impression, especially the rugged Cain, who is completely at ease in playing a far-from-sympathetic gay man (who, you can be sure, gets his comeuppance).

Berlanti's script crystallizes how the constant pursuit of sexual partners and partying can deflect some gay men from making something of their lives, that friends are great when chips are down but they can also be a powerfully negative force—especially when it's so easy for minorities to unconsciously absorb the majority's often hostile and oppressive views of them.

Berlanti even touches upon the plight of aging gays: In one scene, Jack, who is in a happy and long-term relationship, states in a fatherly fashion to Dennis that he loves him, giving him an affectionate rather than romantic kiss. Yet this trim, still-attractive man feels compelled to assure Dennis that senior gays don't expect to be kissed back. Jack not only has made his restaurant a hangout—and for some, a source of employment—for Dennis and his pals, but he also serves as coach for the group's softball team, the Broken Hearts.

"The Broken Hearts Club" is a very knowing film, in its perceptions and in the way it is made. It has the professional sheen of a Hollywood production without undue glitz, a deft balance between the hilarious and the heart-tugging. It's specific in sexual orientation and locale, yet Berlanti's observations surely apply in general to young urban straights and their friends as they try to get on with their personal and professional lives.

Indeed, the key achievement of the film is that there's nothing marginal—or marginalizing—about the way it was made or in the lives of the men it depicts. To describe "The Broken Hearts Club" as commercial is to pay it a compliment.

NEW YORK POST, 9/29/00, p. 54, Jonathan Foreman

Notwithstanding the fact that the filmmakers were so scared of people getting the wrong idea that they included the words "romantic comedy" in the title, "The Broken Hearts Club" represents a kind of breakthrough.

Not only is it a mainstream Hollywood movie about young gay men, its also a movie about gays that features no queer-bashing, no hysterical breakdowns, no tearful comings--out, and no heartrending of scenes people dying of AIDS.

The only "issue" touched on by the film—and lightly—is the occasional harshness of a subculture obsessed with physical beauty. (And, of course, even the guy who's supposed to be ugly has better-than-average looks.)

Indeed, this film even presents a relatively plausible (yet comic) portrayal of gay life—or as least as lived by a group of good-looking twentysomethings in West Hollywood, Calif, whose lives and conversations are almost entirely informed by their sexuality.

But despite some funny and charming scenes, "Broken Hearts Club" turns out to be a choppily written, unevenly acted exercise, no less shlocky and predictable than any of Hollywood's average second-string heterosexual comedies. (This one also gives away its best scenes in the trailer.)

Dennis (Timothy Olyphant from "Go") is a 28-year-old photographer who together with friends Benji (Zach Braff), Cole (Dean Cain), Kevin (Andrew Keegan), Howie (Matt Mcgrath) Patrick (Ben Weber) and Taylor (Billy Porter) works and hangs out in a West Hollywood restaurant.

The restaurant is owned by the group's genial father figure, Jack ("Frasier's" John Mahoney) who also coaches their softball team, the Broken Hearts Club.

Everyone talks all the time about being gay. Everyone except Jack has relationship problems of one kind or another, though most of them mistakenly think that they would be happy if only they had the dazzling looks of Cole. One character gets into a dangerously druggy social scene. Another cannot commit to the man he loves because he's convinced he could do better.

There's an underdeveloped subplot in which Patrick is asked to donate sperm to the partner (the fine Nia Long) of his lesbian sister (Mary McCarthy).

Olyphant and Cain give strong, convincing performances, but several scenes have the unconvincing feel of a filmed rehearsal.

NEWSDAY, 9/29/00, Part II/p. B7, Jan Stuart

From the evidence at hand in "The Broken Hearts Club"—A Romantic Comedy," gay men have made giant strides in some areas in the three decades since "The Boys in the Band" and continue to run in place in others. Gone is the self-loathing of Mart Crowley's poisonous birthday gathering. Gone is the obsession with mortality that accompanied AIDS in the '80s and early '90s. What lingers—impertinently defiant of any social strides or medical innovations—is that persistent malady known as intimacy issues.

When it comes to matters of the heart, clogged emotions are a guy thing, not a gay thing. Or at least a young guy thing. How else are we to interpret the case made by Greg Berlanti's endearingly funny comedy, in which the only settled characters among a galaxy of self-dramatizing homosexuals are lesbian and older male couples?

A birthday party also provides a centerpiece for this contemporary look at gay male camaraderie. The honoree is Dennis (Timothy Olyphant), an attractive West Hollywood photographer who wakes up at the wizened age of 28 to realize that he has had it with meaningless casual relationships. A birthday party pick-up who can't share in his joy for Karen Carpenter records is quickly sent packing. Nor does Dennis have it in his heart to take advantage of an impressionable teenager named Kevin (Andrew Keegan) who seems begging for someone to help him out of the closet.

You can't tell the tears from the broth for all of Dennis' pals' crying into their soup. Taylor (Billy Porter) is reeling from a recent break-up, Howie (Matt McGrath) is over-analyzing his relationship to death, Patrick (Ben Weber) bemoans being an ugly duckling in a pond of buffed bodies, Benji (Zach Braff) yearns to be on the arm of a buffed body. Everyone envies Cole (Dean Cain), the actor friend who goes through men like a navy recruitment center, and everyone aspires to be Jack (John Mahoney), the older friend whose wisdom and long-term relationship provides these boys at sea with an anchor.

Many pictures have attempted to dramatize the secondary families created by gay men seeking a level of support denied by the straight world. And most of them sink in a mire of artificial dialogue and forced camp. "The Broken Hearts Club" is the rare bird that gets it right, from the tense and tenuous borders of friendship between support and competitiveness to the cruisy, improvisational banter over gourmet coffee. It's a smart-talking honey of a movie.

VILLAGE VOICE, 10/3/00, p. 232, Dennis Lim

The mating habits of gay men come under scrutiny yet again in *The Broken Hearts Club*, a Sundance favorite that, for release, has been helpfully subtitled *A Romantic Comedy*. Indistinguishable from any number of morbidly solipsistic rom-coms to tackle the deathless subject of being gay and lovelorn, *BHC* throws the by now customary hissy fit, feigning an aggrieved disavowal of gay-scene frivolity and superficiality, before instinctively backpedaling into a cozy affirmation of those very attributes.

Writer-director Greg Berlanti has assigned each member of his *Broken Hearts* ensemble—a group of West Hollywood gay friends who happen to almost all be white and gym-toned (not to mention callow, petty, and judgmental)—a personal-growth project to complete before the end of the movie. Aspiring photographer Dennis (Timothy Olyphant) has arrived at a crushing conclusion: "All I'm good at is being gay." His actor roommate, Cole (Dean Cain), is a dim, callous slut. One friend has an inferiority complex. Another is involved in a misguided breakup. Yet another, ignoring uniformly knee-jerk warnings, falls for a gym rat, and suffers the consequences. The token black character is also the token flaming queen, called upon to expectorate strenuously catty put-downs and flap his arms during softball.

The outsider's perspective is provided by a vulnerable young man (Andrew Keegan) who flip-flops between Dennis and Cole, and sees his new acquaintances as a bunch of "bitter, jaded" narcissists. This perceptiveness is, however, ascribed to closetdom, and he's eventually inducted into the feel-good club. The film has better actors than it deserves: Olyphant is charismatic enough for his worst lines not to stick; Matt McGrath, as the insecure Howie, provides a sorely needed note of psychological credibility when the script allows; John Mahoney does his affable best with a pitiful mother-hen role. Berlanti is a producer on *Dawson's Creek,* which may account for the bloated loquaciousness, damp self-absorption, and defensive reflexiveness on display here. In one typical conversation, someone bemoans the lack of true-to-life gay characters in movies, then squeals, "Can you imagine if they made a film about us?" Actually, yes, and so can anyone who's seen *Jeffrey, Trick, Love! Valour! Compassion!,* or *Billy's Hollywood Screen Kiss.*

Also reviewed in:
CHICAGO TRIBUNE, 11/10/00, Friday/p. D, Loren King
NEW YORK TIMES, 9/29/00, p. E6, Dave Kehr
VARIETY, 2/28-3/5/00, p. 52, Dennis Harvey

BUDDY BOY

An Independent Picture release of a Woods Entertainment and IP production.   *Executive Producer:* Eliot Lewis Rosenblatt.   *Producer:* Cary Woods and Gina Mingacci.   *Director:* Mark Hanlon.   *Screenplay:* Mark Hanlon.   *Director of Photography:* Hubert Taczanowski.   *Editor:* Hughes Winborne.   *Music:* Michael Brook, Brian Eno and Graeme Revell.   *Music Editor:* Fernand Bos.   *Sound:* Aletha Rodgers and Paul Marshall.   *Casting:* Dan Shana and Michael Testa.   *Production Designer:* Robert Morris.   *Set Decorator:* Alice Baker.   *Special Effects Make-up:* Howard Berger.   *Running time:* 103 minutes.   *MPAA Rating:* R.

CAST: Aidan Gillen (Francis);   Emmanuelle Seigner (Gloria);   Susan Tyrrell (Sal);   Mark Boone, Jr. (Vic);   Harry Groener (Father Gillespie);   Hector Elias (Mr. Salcedo);   Jon Huertas (Omar);   Richard Assad (Haroonian);   Jessica Gaona (Love Pendant Girl;   Ray Miceli (Arguing Man).

LOS ANGELES TIMES, 3/31/00, p. 10, Kevin Thomas

Production notes for Mark Hanlon's "Buddy Boy" describe it as "a dark and twisted exploration of faith, alienation and madness"—and is it ever! Aidan Gillen's Francis is an introverted stutterer who lives in an extravagantly decrepit inner-city apartment with his disabled stepmother, Sal (Susan Tyrrell), a hard-drinking, chain-smoking, cackling old harpy in a fright wig who's forever warning Francis of God's wrath hailing down upon him. Francis' priest, noting his infrequent confessions, reminds him that "we are all soldiers in the struggle for redeeming ourselves."

Devout in his faith, tormented by sexual longings, Francis cringes his way through life, processing photos at a local sundries shop and secretly spying on the beautiful young woman (Emmanuelle Seigner) who lives in a fine old apartment building across the street. One day he rescues her from muggers, and his life begins to change. Grateful to him, she extends her friendship and in time they become lovers. He is as perplexed as we are that she should be attracted to so clenched a man.

Were not Francis so damaged maybe Seigner's Gloria could liberate him with her love. Instead, the passion she evokes in him unleashes what seem clearly to be paranoid delusions. Meanwhile, Francis realizes that a pretty little girl in a photo he processed is a kidnap victim the police are seeking—and that the lazy plumber (Mark Boone Jr.) who's supposed to be fixing a bathtub pipe has virtually moved in, spending the day boozing and joking with Sal.

All these developments, especially the unexpected love of Gloria, are more than a man as withdrawn as Francis can handle. He has real trouble distinguishing between fantasy and reality, and all his inner conflicts are eroding his faith. It's as if his world is crumbling around him.

In his feature debut Hanlon has put a lot on his plate, but his psychological insights are quite compelling: Francis may be going crazy, but we certainly can understand why. But "Buddy Boy" is an example of the right idea expressed in the wrong key. Instead of going for a gritty, low-key approach that might be all the more chilling as a result, Hanlon indulges in bursts of theatricality so intense you can all but see the proscenium looming overhead. Gillen and Tyrrell are directed to act up a storm, an approach that might in fact play well on the stage but seems mainly artificial on the screen. (Seigner, who's also in "The Ninth Gate," fares better, but it's impossible to understand how Francis could win and hold the love of so beautiful and urbane a woman.) The grandiose quality of the film is heightened by a slow pace, forays into the surreal and an ominous Graeme Revell score.

Hanlon dives into his picture so deeply he takes himself as seriously as his material. A more detached, underplayed tack might have made a crucial difference. You respect Hanlon's passion and fervor and his willingness to come to grips with the question of faith amid a tangle of Catholic guilt, sexual frustration and loneliness. But less Grand Guignol and more Robert Bresson would be welcome.

NEW YORK POST, 3/24/00, p. 50, Lou Lumenick

Motherhood, vegetarianism and the Catholic Church take it on the chin in "Buddy Boy"—but first-time writer-director Mark Hanlon lands only glancing blows in this grim black comedy.

Francis (the bland Aiden Gillen), a photo-processing technician who lives in a squalid walkup with his shut-in mom, has his faith severely tested by mom's drunken taunts and his romance with a gorgeous vegetarian neighbor who he's spying on through a hole in the wall.

One-time Oscar nominee Susan Tyrell ("Fat City"), as the mom, doesn't chew the scenery—she devours it whole and spits it out. She vies for overacting honors with Emmanuelle Seigner (the neighbor), who demonstrates her atrocious line readings in hubby Roman Polanski's movies (most recently "The Ninth Gate") aren't his fault.

NEWSDAY, 3/24/00, Part II/p. B12, Jan Stuart

Vegan bashing is the newest wrinkle on trendy sectarian persecution in "Buddy Boy," a nutcase of a psychological thriller. Spaghetti squashes take on very sinister possibilities in Mark Hanlon's directing debut, which manages to find its own quirky voice as it filches from the paranoid fantasies of Roman Polanski, Michelangelo Antonioni and Alfred Hitchcock.

Voyeurism and spiritual devotion oil the dreary day-to-day of Hanlon's protagonist, Francis (Aiden Gillen), a lowly film processor who scopes out the girl next door through his binoculars when he isn't attending to the needs of his infirm, God-fearing stepmother. Cowed by this harridan matriarch (Susan Tyrell, chewing the scenery with a blowsy, Baby Jane abandon), he slowly begins to emerge from his shell after a chance encounter with the beautiful neighbor (Emmanuelle Seigner) ignites his first-ever relationship.

But love exacts a price. When confronted with the militant vegetarianism of his new girlfriend and the moral laxity of his stepmother's personal life (she's carrying on with the plumber), something in Francis begins to crack. His binocular escapades become increasingly surreal, while the world he encounters through his film developing takes on a terrible reality.

Gillen's appealingly odd-duck presence, sly turns of dialogue and atmospheric interior cinematography rescue the film from its occasional heavy hand. Catholics who have felt on the defensive recently may be dismayed to find that "Buddy Boy" harbors a certain degree of suspicion toward church dogma. But they also may be relieved to see that it saves its unkindest cuts for people who fill their fridge to bursting with okra.

VILLAGE VOICE, 3/28/00, p. 120, Amy Taubin

Graeme Revell, who provided the sprightly score for *All I Wanna Do,* is credited with the grating, tone-deaf horror music that washes over *Buddy Boy,* Mark Hanlon's ridiculous and repellent hash of *Repulsion* and *Psycho,* with scenic elements of *Seven* thrown in for good measure. How two such attractive and talented actors as Aidan Gillen and Emmanuelle Seigner became involved in such a project is unimaginable. But given Hanlon's evident infatuation with *Repulsion,* obtaining the services of Roman Polanski's wife and long-reigning cinematic muse—and getting her to bare her exquisite, very French breasts—was a coup. Perhaps he has a talent for persuasion that doesn't translate to the screen.

Also reviewed in:
NEW YORK TIMES, 3/24/00, p. E22, Dave Kehr
VARIETY, 10/4-10/99, p. 89, David Stratton

BULLS' NIGHT OUT, THE

A Cobra Communications release.   *Producer:* Arun Vir.   *Director:* Lindley Farley. *Screenplay:* Lindley Farley. *Based on a story by:* Lindley Farley and Pasquale Gaeta. *Director of Photography:* Cornelius Shultz-Kraft. *Editor:* Elizabeth Bouiss, Lindley Farley, and Diphu Mehta. *Music:* Frank Foster. *Running time:* 82 minutes. *MPAA Rating:* Not Rated.

CAST: Jack Marnell (George Wall); Steve Kasprzak (Louie Esposito); A.J. Johnson (J.J. Clark); J J. Flash (Paul "Zap" Zachry); Jayne A. Larson (Ruby Wall); Steve Roberts (Wachter the Baker); Russ Romano (Bill Wilson); David Harman (Capt. Ralph Abruzzi); Shane Barbanel (Jeremy).

NEW YORK POST, 9/6/00, p. 52, V.A. Musetto

This seems to be the season for geezer movies—take "The Crew" and "Space Cowboys," for example.

The latest entry in this category is "The Bulls' Night Out," a shoestring-budget street drama marking the feature directorial debut of Lindley Farley.

The geezers are four ex-cops who hang out at a Brooklyn bar owned by one of them, a beefy, white-haired chap named George Wall (Jack Marnell).

With drug dealers slowly taking over the neighborhood, the four drinking buddies band together to "take the streets back."

When a robber invades the bar, they easily disarm him, break his left hand with a baseball bat and toss him out the back door.

Adrenalin flowing, the boys go after street dealers—with disastrous results. They shoot and kill a "dealer" who turns out to be an undercover federal agent.

According to the production notes, "Bulls" cost just $37,000 to make. Farley certainly got his money's worth—strong performances from a cast of unknown actors as well as gritty street scenes by cinematographer Cornelius Shultz-Kraft.

A subplot involving the love life of Wall's daughter is never fleshed out and only distracts from the otherwise effective script. That aside, "The Bulls' Night Out" is an impressive screen debut.

VILLAGE VOICE, 9/19/00, p. 119, Mark Holcomb

The messy emotional confrontations missing from *The Watcher* [see Holcomb's review] are everywhere in *The Bulls' Night Out.* Shot in 1995 on a meager budget, Lindley Farley's urban thriller follows a group of retired cops who fuck up badly when they try to police their

Greenpoint neighborhood the old-fashioned way: through intimidation and murder. *Bulls' Night Out* is awkwardly overplayed—a domestic subplot involving the lead cop's daughter is particularly punishing—and Farley helps himself to every Scorsese trick in the book. Nevertheless, it's a likable, earnest character study with a rare sense of purpose and not a serial killer in sight.

Also reviewed in:
NEW YORK TIMES, 9/7/00, p. E3, Elvis Mitchell

BURLESK KING

A Strand Releasing release of a Seiko Films production. *Producer:* Robbie Tan. *Director:* Mel Chionglo. *Screenplay (Tagalog with English subtitles):* Ricardo Lee. *Director of Photography:* George Tutanes. *Editor:* Jess Navarro. *Music:* Nonong Buencamino. *Sound:* Leody Maralit. *Production Designer:* Edgar Martin Littaua. *Running time:* 109 minutes. *MPAA Rating:* Not Rated.

CAST: Rodel Velayo (Harry); Nini Jacinto (Brenda); Leonardo Litton (James); Raymond Bagatsing (Mario); Elizabeth Oropesa (Betty); Cherrie Pie Picache (Aileen); Gino Ilustre (Michael); Joonee Gamboa (Miong); Tonio Ortigas (Leo); Joel Lamangan (Odette).

NEW YORK POST, 6/30/00, p. 47, Hannah Brown

If you see only one movie about male strippers in Manila this year, you won't want it to be "Burlesk King," a muddled, overlong melodrama that will appeal mainly to child molesters who have lost their Internet access.

The rambling plot concerns Harry (Rodel Velayo), a spunky teen who returns to Manila from a rural area in the Philippines, where he had lived since escaping from his abusive American father who beat and prostituted both him and his mother.

In a plot that plays like a week's worth of "Jerry Springer" shows, Harry finds shelter with a friendly lesbian; hooks up with an old pal who works as a gay hustler; falls for Brenda (Nini Jacinto), a teen whore with a heart of gold who sees herself as a Mother Teresa figure for the local street kids; reunites with his mother (Elizabeth Oropesa), now a streetwalker; and abandons his plan to take revenge on his father, who is dying of AIDS.

Of course, he also triumphs in his new career as a stripper, and wins the honor that is the film's title.

The film features lots of soft-core sex scenes, mostly between Harry and Brenda, who seems to spend every spare minute in bed with him.

Velayo has a flat, jaded sneer that makes him all-too-convincing as a child-abuse victim.

Although "Burlesk King" is apparently intended as a morality play, it uses the very outrages it purports to expose to titillate viewers. Still, the film is so sloppily made it's hard to know whether this is entirely cynical or mostly accidental.

Other than its young actors' toned bodies, there's nothing attractive about "Burlesk King."

VILLAGE VOICE, 7/4/00, p. 128, Dennis Lim

Not even passable as a waxy-beefcake oglefest, Mel Chionglo's *Burlesk King* fully consigns the Filipino go-go-boy melodrama (a blueprint drawn by the late Lino Brocka with 1989's *Macho Dancer*, sloppily xeroxed by Chionglo, Brocka's assistant, in 1995's *Midnight Dancers)* to the realm of exploitation movie. Prowling once more the Manila gay bars populated by generously oiled dancer/hustlers, Chionglo sets his gaze on buff, blank-eyed Harry, a young man traumatized by childhood memories of his American father—a monster who abused and pimped Harry and his mother before accidentally killing her. With an amnesiac's disregard for continuity, *Burlesk King* staggers punch-drunk from one stodgily hysterical episode to another. Chionglo relies on a tsunami's worth of exaggerated pelvic undulations—coyly choreographed macho-dancer routines featuring the strategic use of stripper props (feathers, soap suds, popping balloons). The casually polymorphous sexual landscape seems to be economically determined: Harry, his friend James, and the other hustlers, who identify as straight (more to the point, are required to do so by the job description), have no qualms about selling sex to both men and women; Harry falls for a hooker, the self-proclaimed Mother Teresa of the city's red-light district, and the lovers repackage their relationship as a two-for-one special. (Fucking is rendered Cinemax style: more discreet grinding.) *Macho Dancer* (and to a lesser degree *Midnight Dancers*) had a messy vitality and, within the parameters of shrill melodrama and softcore titillation, a way of haphazardly lapsing into sociopolitical critique. *Burlesk King*, so titled because Harry is eventually crowned champion gyrator, is not only too inept to be lurid; it's almost aggressively disinterested in any semblance of social reality.

Also reviewed in:
NEW YORK TIMES, 6/30/00, p. E30, A.O. Scott
VARIETY, 2/7-13/00, p. 60, Emanuel Levy

BUT FOREVER IN MY MIND

An Intra Films release of a Fandango/Mikado/Rai Cinemafiction production. *Executive Producer:* Gianluca Arcopinto. *Producer:* Domenico Procacci. *Director:* Gabriele Muccino. *Screenplay (Italian with English subtitles):* Gabriele Muccino with the collaboration of Silvio Muccino and Adele Tulli. *Based on an idea by:* Marco Valerio Fusco. *Director of Photography:* Arnaldo Catinari. *Editor:* Claudio Di Mauro. *Music:* Paolo Buonvino. *Sound:* Bruno Pupparo. *Production Designer:* Eugenia F. di Napoli. *Set Decorator:* Marco Tripaldi. *Costumes:* Roberta Bocca, Donato Citro, and Gianna Jacobelli. *Make-up:* Clara Hopf. *Running time:* 88 minutes. *MPAA Rating:* Not Rated.

CAST: Silvio Muccino (Silvio Ristuccia); Giuseppe Sanfelice di Monteforte (Ponzi); Giulia Steigerwalt (Claudia); Giulia Carmignani (Valentina); Simone Pagani (Martino); Luca de Filippo (Silvio's Father); Anna Galiena (Silvio's Mother); Enrico Silvestrin (Alberto Ristuccia); Giulia Ciccone (Chiara Rustuccia); Caterina Silva (Giulia); Sara Pelagalli (Marta); Saverio Micheli (Filippo); Cristiano Juliano (Lorenzo); Nicola Campiotti (Gustavo); Alessandro Palombo (Leon); Adele Tulli (Veronica); Valeria D'Obici (Giulia's Mother); Mauro Marino (Leon's Father); Luis Molteni (School Headmaster); Antonio Luigi Grimaldi (Head of Police); Alfonso Favino (Boccia); Diane Fleri (Arianna); Veronica Gentili (Francesca); Gregorio Paolini (Gregorio); Giorgio Pasotti (Matteo); Francesco Rotoli (Cagnetti).

NEW YORK POST, 12/20/00, p. 48, V.A. Musetto

It's a time of turmoil in Italy. Student radicals protesting "the privatization of education and the standardization of the individual" have occupied scores of schools.

They include the one in Rome attended by a 16-year-old virgin named Silvio in "But Forever in My Mind," a charming teen romance from Italy.

Silvio is not especially interested in politics. But taking part in the occupation will give him a chance to be around a sexy schoolmate, Valentina.

So he joins in, despite the misgivings of his parents, who were agitators themselves in the 1960s but have since sold out to a comfortable, middle-class life. ("We had real issues back then," his dad fumes.)

When Silvio and Valentina share an innocent kiss, the entire school finds out, enraging her steady boyfriend. Soon, fists are flying.

There's more discord when Silvio's parents try to get him to see a shrink.

Thirty-three-year-old Gabriele Muccino, here directing his second feature, has assembled a cast of fresh-faced non-professional teenagers.

They include his cute brother Silvio as the boy with the same name; Giulia Carmignani as Valentina; Giulia Steigerwalt as Claudia, a schoolmate with a crush on Silvio; and Giuseppe Sanfelice di Monteforte as Silvio's indiscreet best pal, Ponzi.

They're personable and attractive, show an amazing knack for acting, and give the film, a youthful zest.

No one will mistake "But Forever in My Mind" ("Come te Nessuno Mai") for something by Fellini or Visconti. But it is, in its own way, skillful and most entertaining.

VILLAGE VOICE, 12/26/00, p. 148, Dennis Lim

For a quality horny-Italian-teen frolic, you need look no further than Film Forum, which has shrewdly counterprogrammed Gabriele Muccino's spry, affectionate *But Forever in My Mind*. The backdrop is a high-school student occupation involving a passionate if hopelessly vague fight against "privatization and standardization," but the real tumult—not least for wide-eyed Silvio (Silvio Muccino, the director's brother)—is hormonal (an excuse for a sleepover!). The director collaborated on the script with his brother and another real-life high-schooler, Adele Tulli, and the result is a credible, sardonic snapshot that, for all its infectious energy, captures the very real frustrations of inchoate adolescent rebellion ("At least my sister had the Cold War," one student moans), compounded in many cases by generational conflict with ex-counterculturalist parents. Unmistakably related to *Show Me Love* and *New Waterford Girl*, *But Forever* bears the hallmark of a serious-minded teen comedy—it gently mocks but never condescends.

Also reviewed in:
NEW YORK TIMES, 12/20/00, p. E5, A.O. Scott
VARIETY, 6/12/99, p. 65, David Rooney

BUT I'M A CHEERLEADER

A Lions Gate Films release of an Ignite Entertainment production. *Executive Producer:* Michael Burns, Marc Butan, Peter Locke, and Donald Kushner. *Producer:* Andrea Sperling and Leanna Creel. *Director:* Jamie Babbit. *Screenplay:* Brian Wayne Peterson. *Story:* Jamie Babbit. *Director of Photography:* Jules Labarthe. *Editor:* Cecily Rhett. *Music:* Pat Irwin. *Music Editor:* Greg Vossberg. *Choreographer, Cheerleaders:* Candice Hinds and Heather Jones. *Sound:* Shawn Holden and (music) William Garrett. *Sound Editor:* Trip Brock. *Casting:* Sheila Jaffe, Georgianne Walken, and Julia Kim. *Production Designer:* Rachel Kamerman. *Digital Effects:* Tony Venezia. *Art Director:* Macie Vener. *Costumes:* Alix Friedberg. *Make-up:* Rosemary Lawrence. *Running time:* 84 minutes. *MPAA Rating:* R.

CAST: Natasha Lyonne (Megan Bloomfield); Clea DuVall (Graham Eaton); Dante Basco (Dolph); RuPaul Charles (Mike); Eddie Cibrian (Rock); Bud Cort (Peter Bloomfield); Melanie Lynskey (Hilary); Wesley Mann (Lloyd); Joel Michaely (Joel); Richard Moll (Larry); Kip Pardue (Clayton); Katrina Phillips (Jan); Douglas Spain (Andre); Mink Stole (Nancy Bloomfield); Katherine Towne (Sinead); Brandt Wille (Jared); Cathy Moriarty (Mary J. Brown); Ione Skye (Kelly); Michelle Williams (Kimberly); Katie Donahue (Cheerleader 1); Danielle Reneau (Cheerleader 2); Kyle Thatcher (Joel's Father); Robert Pine (Mr. Eaton, Grahams's Father); Rachelle Carson (Graham's Stepmom); Julie Delpy (Lipstick Lesbian); Charles Braden (Bruce).

LOS ANGELES TIMES, 7/21/00, Calendar/p. 4, Kevin Thomas

"But I'm a Cheerleader" is the result of the kind of good intentions with which the road to hell is paved.

Director Jamie Babbit and co-writer Brian Wayne Petersen set out to send up the cruel absurdity of aversion therapy designed to turn gays into straights, but the task proves way beyond their abilities. Their jaunty, superficial humor tends more to confirm homosexual stereotypes for easy laughter than to skewer the horror of trying to change an individual's sexual orientation against his or her will.

This picture is too puny and square to accomplish such a task; what is needed is satire at its most corrosive, humor at its most outrageous—a challenge better suited to someone like Todd Solondz ("Welcome to the Doll House," "Happiness") or Miguel Arteta and Mike White ("Chuck & Buck").

Natasha Lyonne stars as Megan, a pretty, peppy high school cheerleader whose burgeoning attraction to her own sex is noticed by everybody but herself. Megan is an innocent, the daughter of a pious, purse-lipped couple (Bud Cort, and John Waters regular Mink Stole) who finally decide they have no recourse but to pack her off to the countryside. There, in a Victorian mansion painted candy colors inside and out, Cathy Moriarty's Mary Brown presides over her True Directions institution.

This Nurse Ratched of aversion therapy administers her five-step program to heterosexuality to a bunch of gay kids with the help of ex-gay assistant Mike (RuPaul Charles, out of drag). The hapless teens are browbeaten into admitting to being homosexual—something Megan doesn't realize she is till she falls into Mrs. Brown's clutches—and then submitted to a barrage of crude behavior modification: For example, girls are taught how to look and behave in a more traditionally feminine manner; boys, more masculine.

The process boils down to bullying the kids into dissembling and struggling to exercise willpower over what stimulates them sexually. Mrs. Brown, who doesn't seem to notice that her hunky gardener son (Eddie Cibrian) is gay, has a simple technique: Anyone who disagrees with her views is told that he or she is in a state of denial. As Mrs. Brown, Moriarty carries on in a near-constant state of shrill hysteria, but the filmmakers merely make fun of her rather than challenge her assumptions.

Graham (Clea DuVall, who looks like a teenage Glenda Jackson) refuses to kid herself, and eventually she and Megan are drawn to each other as the program wears on. But it's a risky business, because Babbit and Peterson, to their credit, do make clear that if Mrs. Brown's charges flunk her course, they risk being disowned by their parents.

RuPaul is as funny out of drag as he is in it, and one wishes he, Stole and Cort were in a far better movie; Lyonne and DuVall are appealing and convincing. In an era in which gay men and lesbians continue to face prejudice that results in assaults both political and physical, it's hard to find anything very funny about "But I'm a Cheerleader."

NEW YORK POST, 7/7/00, p. 52, Lou Lumenick

There is probably an amusing movie to be made about camps that try to "rehabilitate" homosexuals—but this thuddingly stupid satire isn't it.

"But I'm a Cheerleader" starts brightly enough, with Megan (the appealing Natasha Lyonne) secretly ogling her fellow cheerleaders while enduring clumsy kisses from her boyfriend.

Megan, who's blissfully unaware of her sexual confusion, is confronted by parents (Bud Cort and Mink Stole) and friends with "evidence" of her lesbian leanings, including vegetarianism and an Alanis Morissette poster.

She's shipped off to True Directions, a candy-colored rehabilitation camp populated by gay stereotypes—mincing boys and tomboyish girls, including Graham (the striking Clea DuVall), whom Megan promptly falls for.

A macho ex-gay counselor named Mike who wears an "It's Great to Be Straight" T-shirt (an out-of-drag RuPaul), teaches the boys to fix cars, while his boss, Mary (Cathy Moriarity), instructs the girls on the fine points of diaper changing.

First-time director Jamie Babbitt offers a singularly toothless and heavy-handed satire of fundamentalist Christians—fifth-rate John Waters.

Except for the two leads, the acting is terrible—especially Moriarity's, who delivers a frightening cross between Kathleen Turner in "Serial Mom" and Faye Dunaway in "Mommie Dearest."

Though directed by an avowed lesbian, "But I'm a Cheerleader" draws such an offensive portrait of gays, it would draw howls of protest coming from a straight director.

NEWSDAY, 7/7/00, Part II/p. B6, John Anderson

Borrowing heavily from the John Waters school of naughty-but-nice social outrage, "But I'm a Cheerleader" gives us Megan (Natasha Lyonne), a high school cheerleader who eats tofu and, as far as we know, not much else. She keeps a picture of a female bathing beauty on her locker door, has a penchant for Georgia O'Keefe-inspired decor and doesn't like it that her boyfriend tries to give her a tonsillectomy every time they kiss. So her family and friends decide she's a lesbian and send her off to be deprogramed.

Places and people such as the hot-pink True Directions and its homophobic dragon lady, Mary Brown (Cathy Moriarty), really exist (in less of a Liberace-esque incarnation, we're sure) and that gives "But I'm a Cheerleader" a dash of social credibility; the idea that people should be proud of who and what they are is a point made early and often. And we mean often.

But the movie kind of shoots itself in the foot by milking most of its humor out of outrageous gay stereotypes. There's Mike (an out-of-drag RuPaul), the True Directions camp counselor who wears a "Straight Is Great" T-shirt and certainly isn't. Mary's son, Rock (Eddie Cibrian), gads about in short-shorts, does improper things with garden tools and keeps his mother's homophobia at a fever pitch. The bare-legged male inmates wear modified English schoolboy suits, mince, lisp, try hopelessly to chop wood and live in fear of having to watch sports on TV.

The girls? One practices sexual aversion therapy with a stun gun. Others are more honest, such as Graham (Clea Duvall), who doesn't fool herself about her sexual preferences but is under the thumb of her domineering father and, increasingly, under the sway of Megan. Their gradual, shall we say, understanding, is the emotional high point of the movie, a kind of thing that was done much more intelligently in the recent "Show Me Love" and, of course, with much more ardor during the Charlton Heston-Stephen Boyd scenes in "Ben-Hur."

SIGHT AND SOUND, 3/01, p. 41, Matthew Leyland

US, the present. Megan, a 17-year-old cheerleader with a boyfriend of two years, is confronted by her family and friends who believe she is a lesbian. She is sent away to True Directions, a camp run by the draconian Mary who pledges to turn gay teenagers into heterosexuals. Megan embarks on the camp's five-step orientation programme. She admits she is gay and begins to learn how to be straight by performing supposedly traditional female activities. In a group activity, Megan is partnered with Graham, a rebellious rich girl.

During family therapy, Mary concludes that Megan is gay because she witnessed a reversal of traditional gender roles when her father lost his job and her mother became the family breadwinner. One night, the students sneak off to a gay bar where Megan and Graham kiss. The pair begin a relationship, which Mary later finds out about. Megan is removed from the programme and seeks sanctuary at a gay safe house run by two ex-True Directions counsellors. There, she hooks up with Dolph, a former fellow resident at True Directions, who was thrown off the course for having a fling with Clayton, another student. Megan and Dolph gatecrash the camp's graduation ceremony. Megan declares her love for Graham, who flees with her. Later, Megan's parents publicly proclaim their daughter's homosexuality.

Intended as a rejoinder to the canon of lesbian movies that privilege the butch viewpoint (*Go Fish*, 1994; *The Incredibly True Adventures of Two Girls in Love*, 1995), But *I'm a Cheerleader* offers, in the words of debut director Jamie Babbit, "a unique feminization of the camp aesthetic". What this amounts to is a sub John Waters satire which takes place at a camp intended to inculcate teenage gays and lesbians into a straight lifestyle with the most eye-popping candy pink production design since *Ma vie en rose*. Though likeable enough—thanks largely to the warm performances of Natasha Lyonne and Clea DuVall as students Megan and Graham—and pleasingly brisk, the film isn't consistently funny, nor is it especially trenchant.

The notion of a homosexual 'rehabilitation' camp—of which there are more than 200 across the US, according to the production notes is so absurd it barely needs satirising. However, Babbit and scriptwriter Brian Wayne Peterson attempt to do so by creating a 50s style cartoon world where young lesbians and gays undergo "treatment" by practising hyper conventional heterosexual behaviour. While the girls (dressed in hot pink) learn to hoover and change nappies, the boys (attired in baby blue) chop logs and do car maintenance.

But the scenes here are repetitious, and ultimately made to seem trite by the excessive use of slapstick; they gaudily parade Babbit's stated fascination with stereotypes without really exploring how insidious such stereotypes can be. Moreover, the film scarcely hints at the physical and psychological trauma such camps would visit on their inmates: a scene where a girl zaps herself with an electroshock device in order to stymie her lesbian urges is played purely for laughs, while the camp's final test—in which male and female students must simulate straight sex seems little more than an excuse to stage some handsomely stylised kitsch tableaux.

The surprisingly tame treatment of Cathy Moriarty's homophobic camp-leader Mary exemplifies the film's failure to nail its targets satisfactorily. Played by Moriarty as if auditioning for the Faye Dunaway role in a remake of *Mommie Dearest* (1981), Mary never receives the comeuppance she deserves, perhaps because, by the end of the film, Babbit seems more interested in the sweetly affecting love story between Megan and Graham. Aside from the chemistry between Lyonne and DuVall, the film's other pleasures include a *mise en scène* that, at times, evokes 50s teen romance comics so strongly, you half expect speech bubbles to hover above the characters' heads; and the chance to see pop diva RuPaul, not only out of drag but in a "Straight Is Great" T shirt.

VILLAGE VOICE, 7/11/00, p. 124, Amy Taubin

A teenage lesbian comedy with the insouciance of *Buffy the Vampire Slayer, But I'm a Cheerleader* is the debut feature of Jamie Babbit, a director with terrific potential who's still at an awkward stage of development. Set in an adolescent homosexual-rehab camp, the film, on its most obvious level, is a satire of the ex-gay movement. But more subversively, it's a send-up of gender stereotyping in all its inescapability. *Cheerleader* is not as skillful, subtle, or hilarious as *Some Like It Hot,* but its anti-essentialism vis-à-vis gender roles is just as sharp and exhilarating. The fortune-cookie version of Babbit's message: Never play a role that doesn't please you and never pretend to have a desire you don't feel is your own.

Megan (Natasha Lyonne), the eponymous cheerleader, is sent to gay rehab by her straitlaced parents, who've figured out something she's yet to understand. They're sure that their daughter's vegetarianism, her fondness for Melissa Etheridge, and her lack of responsiveness to her boyfriend's demands to suck face add up to a lesbianism which must be nipped in the bud. Megan, who just wants to be normal (and has never considered that visions of creamy-thighed cheerleaders might not dance in every girl's head), goes along with the program until she falls in love with Graham (Clea DuVall), the baddest girl in the camp. It's a case of the irresistible attraction of opposites. Graham knows she's gay (and she likes it), but she's determined to put on enough of an act to graduate from rehab and claim her car, her college tuition, and her trust fund.

The girls' dormitory (decorated in a Home Shopping Network version of brothel chic, all orange and hot pink plastic and lace) is the scene of whatever minimal expressions of desire got past the sexist and homophobic eyes of the MPAA ratings board. Babbit escaped the dreaded NC-17 only by excising the word *muff-diving* and a shot of a girl's hand touching another girl's belly. But Babbit seems also to have applied a form of self-censorship. The R-rated *Cheerleader* is too PG-13 for its own good and too juvenile for its target audience: lesbians in search of a romantic comedy. The raunchy edge that cuts through the fairy-tale syrup in Babbit's short *Sleeping Beauties* (an embryonic version of *Cheerleader)* is missing here, making the film more one-note than it should be.

The performances are a mixed bag. Cathy Moriarty is over-the-top as the camp's prurient headmistress, but Eddie Cibrian as Rock, her butch-queen son and groundskeeper, who delights in flaunting his tree cutter—and his package—and an out-of-drag RuPaul Charles, as the ex-gay boys' group leader who can't keep his eyes off Rock, have a suitably light touch. Lyonne makes Megan's initial confusion quite moving, but too often she substitutes petulance for the curiosity and determination the role requires. DuVall, however, is fabulous as the film's object of desire. At once sullen and sweet, with a sassy mouth, eyes that see through everyone's bullshit including her own, and the hiked-shoulder stance of a hockey player, she seems both aloof and available. Unlike most of her fellow actors, DuVall knows that comedy is more than mugging and that giving her character an interior life doesn't weigh her down.

Also reviewed in:
CHICAGO TRIBUNE, 7/14/00, Friday/p. A, Monica Eng
NEW YORK TIMES, 7/7/00, p. E10, Elvis Mitchell
VARIETY 9/27-10/3/99, p. 42, Emanuel Levy
WASHINGTON POST, 7/14/00, p. C12, Rita Kempley
WASHINGTON POST, 7/14/00, Weekend/p. 33, Michael O'Sullivan

BUTTERFLY

A Miramax Films release of a Sogetel/Las Producciones del Escorpion/Grupo Voz production with the collaboration of Canal+Spain, TVE, and TVG. *Executive Producer:* Fernando Bovaira and José Luis Cuerda. *Producer:* José María Besteiro. *Director:* José Luis Cuerda. *Screenplay (Spanish with English subtitles):* Rafael Azcona. *Based on the short story collection "Qué Me Quieres, Amor?" by:* Manuel Rivas. *Director of Photography:* Javier Salmones. *Editor:* Nacho Ruiz Capillas. *Music:* Alejandro Amenábar. *Sound:* Goldstein & Steinberg. *Art Director:* Josep Rosell. *Set Decorator:* Balter Gallart. *Costumes:* Sonia Grande. *Make-up:* Ana L. Puigcerver. *Running time:* 96 minutes. *MPAA Rating:* R.

CAST: Fernando Fernán Gomez (Don Gregorio); Manuel Lozano (Moncho); Uxia Blanco (Rosa); Gonzalo Uriarte (Ramón); Alexis de los Santos (Andrés); Jesús Castejón (D. Avelino); Guillermo Toledo (Otis); Elena Fernández (Carmiña); Tamar Novas (Roque); Tatán (Roque Padre); Roberto Vidal (Boal); Celso Parada (Marcías); Celso Bugallo (Cura); Tucho Lagares (Alcalde); Milagros Jiménez (Nena); Lara López (Aurora); Alberto Castro (Jose Maria); Diego Vidal (Romualdo); Xosé Manuel Olveira (Accordeon); Manuel Piñeiro (Trumpet); Alfonso Cid and Manuel Seara (Sax Players); José Ramón Vieira (String Bass); Antonio Pérez (Singer); Eduardo Gómez (Wise Man); Eva Maria Fernández (Neighbor #1); Feli Manzano (Neighbor #2); José F. Expolio (Tight Rope Walker); Golfo (Tarzán).

LOS ANGELES TIMES, 6/16/00, Calendar/p. 18, Kevin Thomas

"Butterfly" takes us back in time to a picturesque Spanish village in Galicia where life seems idyllic. People have their differences and their inevitable losses and disappointments, yet harmony reigns, and in the town's daily routines you sense life going through its eternal cycles.

The town's dominant personality is one of its teachers, Don Gregorio (Fernando Fernan Gomez), a tall, commanding man of much warmth and wisdom who is nearing retirement.

Moncho (Manuel Lozano), the tailor's son, has been prevented from starting school until his asthma attacks can be brought under control. He arrives at school for his first day filled with terror because he knows full well that his older brother Andres (Alexis de los Santos) regularly comes home beaten by his teacher for no good reason.

Moncho's mother, Rosa (Uxia Blanco), unwittingly has gotten her younger son off to a bad start when she is overheard by the other schoolboys describing him to Don Gregorio as "like a sparrow leaving its nest."

Immediately, dubbed "Sparrow" by his new classmates, Moncho runs away. The delicacy, shrewdness and kind humor with which Don Gregorio resolves this situation, getting Moncho back in class and accepted by the other boys, is impressive. In short order Don Gregorio assumes a grandfatherly role in Moncho's life, introducing him to the joys and wonders of nature, eager to show him that even butterflies have tongues.

In the meantime director Jose Luis Cuerda also tells us of Andres' aspirations as a saxophonist. He joins a local dance band and experiences his first onrush of romantic feelings for a young woman. There's also a comical subplot involving Carmina (Elena Fernandez), the community's good-time girl, whose unusual turn-on is to bite her men as they make love to her.

Cuerda gets us so caught up in the lives of the townspeople that we tend to forget that the time is the mid-1930s, at the tail end of Spain's five-year experience as a republic, which is about to be overthrown in the brutal civil war that brought General Franco to power for the next four decades. Many citizens freely declare their support of the republic that has brought unprecedented freedom and liberty, but you just know that there are dark forces lying low in the community, including the church, waiting for the opportunity to bring Spain under right-wing military rule.

An enlightened man who does not subscribe to the traditional hellfire-and-damnation views of the local priest, Don Gregorio, at the time of his retirement ceremonies, declares courageously: "If we allow just one generation to grow up in freedom, they will never allow liberty to be taken from us."

We know that the Spanish Civil War will at last arrive here, but we are not prepared for how chillingly and how convincingly ordinary people can be consumed and transformed monstrously by fear.

Drawing from Rafael Azcona's deft adaptation of three stories from a prize-winning 1997 collection by Manuel Rivas, Cuerda does not judge the townspeople but takes the tragic view of events that a broad perspective allows.

"Butterfly" is a beautiful, harrowing film of understated power and perception that affords Fernando Fernan Gomez, the Spanish cinema's great, weathered veteran, yet another of his unforgettable performances. He was last seen in the 1998 Academy Award-nominated "The Grandfather," which won him a Goya, Spain's Oscar.

NEW YORK POST, 6/16/00, p. 53, Lou Lumenick

Not to be confused with the 1978 Pia Zadora stinker of the same name, "Butterfly" is a tender coming-of-age story told against the background of the Spanish Civil War.

The conflict between the left-leaning Republicans and the fascist Nationalists doesn't come to the forefront until the final, shattering scenes of Jose Luis Cuerda's film, which he and screenwriter Rafael Aconza adapted from short stories by Manuel Rivas.

But it's never very far from this tender story of Moncho, a shy, asthmatic 7-year-old played by Manuel Lonzano in the best screen performance by a child since Haley Joel Osment of "The Sixth Sense."

It's 1936 in a small village in Galicia. Moncho is taken under the wing of Don Gregorio (the great Spanish actor Fernando Fernan Gomez, most recently seen in "The Grandfather"), a crusty but kind old teacher.

So scared in his first day at school that he wets his pants, Moncho is brought out of his shell by Don Gregorio, who introduces him to literature and the wonders of nature (the movie's more appropriate original title in Spanish is "La Lengua de las Mariposas"—"The language of the butterflies" in English).

The liberal Don Gregorio is an atheist who shares a political outlook with Moncho's father (Gonzalo Uriarte), a tailor with a guilty secret who comes to deal with the rise of Franco's fascists in a radically different manner than the teacher. Eventually, Don Gregorio is led off by the army with other "radicals" as the tearful Moncho is forced to shout epithets.

The film's other major character is Moncho's older brother (Alexis de los Santos), an aspiring musician who gets a chance to mime trumpet-playing with a local band.

This is a film full of beautiful touches and subtle yet effective metaphors for the dangers of fascism.

"Butterfly" doesn't require much knowledge of history to appreciate, but it really isn't suitable for very young audiences either. At one point, Moncho witnesses a fairly graphic sex act that earns this movie its R rating.

NEWSDAY, 6/16/00, Part II/p. B10, Gene Seymour

Everything about "Butterfly" appeals to the humanist in all of us. It views animals and insects with as much tenderness and solicitude as it deals with people. It is a tale told through the eyes of a skittish, painfully introverted young Spanish boy (Manuel Lozano), who has the dismal luck to emerge from asthma-enforced isolation shortly before his country is engulfed in brutal civil war. Love, religion and politics, all of them subjects that inflame passions, are engaged with gentle equanimity.

All of which makes "Butterfly" worth seeing to the many who embraced such foreign films as 1994's "The Postman" or 1988's "Cinema Paradiso." Each of them, like "Butterfly," gently guides the audiences to higher aesthetic values or flatters the collective intellect of those who find communion in such enlightenment.

But formula is formula, no matter how exalted or elevated the project. And despite a smart script, sensual interludes and its shrewd perspective on what history's jackboots can do to everyday people, "Butterfly" subverts its own aggressively pluralistic perspective with a strategy that is both overwrought and calculated.

The movie would lack a sense of gravity if it weren't for the austere and magnetic presence of Fernando Fernan Gomez as a crusty-on-the-outside, toasty-on-the-inside schoolteacher who demands clear heads and open minds from his young charges. In Lozano's Moncho, Fernan-Gomez' Don Gregorio sees a helpless captive of fear and superstition. He makes Moncho his special project, taking the boy on nature walks, lending him books, lighting up his teeming brain with insight and wonder.

As Moncho's consciousness expands, life goes on in its mundane, halting way in his town, which, as with everywhere else in the country in 1936, is caught between cheerleading the reforms of the nascent republic and keeping a wary eye on those seeking to "restore order." In the meantime, Moncho, away from his teacher, picks up a few life lessons in matters of lust and longing—mostly from his older brother's thwarted yearnings for an unhappily married woman. The republic's fall leads to a heartbreaking end to both Moncho's education and the movie itself.

Jose Luis Cuerda directs with an expansive eye and a heavy hand. For every moment that's handled with delicacy there are many more that are too blunt and off-rhythm. Still, it's hard to be too angry at a movie that dares teach its audience, as Don Gregorio does Moncho, that hell doesn't exist except in the hurtful things we do to one another.

VILLAGE VOICE, 6/20/00, p. 156, Michael Atkinson

A sunset painted on black velvet by comparison, José Luis Cuerda's *Butterfly* bears no relation to the 1981 Pia Zadora landmark, though like me you may pine for a Pia-in-the-tub scene not long in. Rather, it's boilerplate Miramax: a sentimental import with lovingly photographed Euro locales, an adorable kid (Manuel Lozano) learning about life (and watching a randy couple rut in a haystack!), a crusty old man (Fernando Fernán Gómez) dispensing wisdom, a tsk-tsk-ready historical trauma (the ascent of the fascists in 1936 Spain). Originally titled *The Tongue of the Butterfly* (a title that belongs in Pia's oeuvre), Cuerda's unconvincing mush could warm the innards of only the truly desperate, or those for whom seeing *Cinema Paradiso* was a transcendental moment.

Also reviewed in:
CHICAGO TRIBUNE, 6/23/00, Friday/p. D, John Petrakis
NEW YORK TIMES, 6/16/00, p. E18, A.O. Scott
VARIETY, 10/18-24/99, p. 44, Jonathan Holland
WASHINGTON POST, 6/23/00, Weekend/p. 38, Michael O'Sullivan
WASHINGTON POST, 6/24/00, p. C3, Stephen Hunter

CALLE 54

A Miramax Films release of a Fernando Trueba PC/Cinétévé/SGAE/ARTE France Cinema co-production in association with Canal+/TVE/VIA Digital. *Executive Producer:* Laurence Miller. *Producer:* Cristina Huete and Fabienne Servan Schreiber. *Director:* Fernando Trueba. *Director of Photography:* Jose Luis López-Linares. *Editor:* Carmen Frías. *Music:* Julio Martí. *Sound:* Pierre Gamet, Martin Gamet and (music) Thom Cadley. *Running time:* 105 minutes. *MPAA Rating:* G.

CAST: Paquito D'Rivera (Alto Sax/Clarinet);   Eliane Elías (Piano);   Chano Domínguez (Piano);   Jerry González (Flugelhorn/Congas); Michel Camilo (Piano);   Gato Barbieri (Tenor

Saxophone); Tito Puente (Timbales/Vibraphone); Chucho Valdés (Piano); Chico O'Farrill (Conductor); Israel "Cachao" López (Double Bass); Orlando "Puntilla" Ríos (Congas/Vocals); Y Carlos "Patato Valdés (Congas); Bebo Valdés (Piano).

LOS ANGELES TIMES, 11/22/00, Calendar/p. 7, Kevin Thomas

Fernando Trueba, Oscar-winning Spanish director (for "La Belle Epoque"), describes his new film, "Calle 54," as a "musical banquet" to which he invited his favorite Latin jazz musicians to perform at a Sony recording studio on Manhattan's 54th Street. For some, the distance from their homes was a matter of blocks, but others came from as far away as Stockholm, Havana, and Cadiz, Spain, as well as Miami. Trueba in turn filmed all of them in their own cities. His tribute to these musicians and their music adds up to a joyous occasion.

Trueba explains he got hooked on Latin jazz when a friend gave him an album back in the '80s, and he has drawn upon his considerable skill as a director to present a dozen major artists and their bands in an inviting, gracefully cinematic fashion.

In almost every instance we are introduced to the musicians on their home ground; later in the studio, Trueba and his cameraman, Jose Luis Lopez-Linares, film them and their bands with maximum flexibility, with an eye to simplicity and superb lighting and recording. As a result, "Calle 54" is visually as pleasing as it sounds.

You don't have to be a certified aficionado or expert to enjoy "Calle 54" thoroughly, and you come away with more appreciation of how inclusive Latin jazz, with its roots in Africa, really is. One of the highlights of the film is having the late Tito Puente, "the godfather of Latino music," showing off the large mural that covers an entire wall of his City Island restaurant. The ebullient, silver-haired maestro, who died June 1 at 77, points out Dizzy Gillespie—his love of Afro-Cuban music was well-known—Cal Tjader and Miles Davis alongside such Latin jazz greats as Machito and Israel "Cachao" Lopez, the latter performing in the film, as does Puente.

Cachao—"still the king of the bass," says Puente—performs in a remarkable reunion with pianist Bebo Valdes, who fled Cuba in 1960 for Sweden. The two old friends join forces for "Lagrimas Negras" (Black Tears), and then Valdes, once the orchestra leader of Havana's famed Tropicana nightclub, performs "La Comparsa" at twin Steinways with his son Chucho, a Havana celebrity in his own right; father and son had not seen each other in five years. (Earlier, Chucho plays solo the haunting "Caridad Amaro.")

Seated in a Central Park horse-drawn carriage, tenor saxophonist Gato Barbieri, a stocky man of considerable mystique who turned his back on recording from 1982 to 1996, speaks of a time when for him film and music were close: "Godard, Pasolini, Glauber—'Antonio des Mortes,'" he mutters emotionally. "It is not possible to live without Rossellini." The Argentine-born Barbieri composed the scores for Bertolucci's "Before the Revolution" and "Last Tango in Paris."

Described by Trueba as "the architect of Latin jazz worldwide," the Cuban-Irish Chico O'Farrill, who came to New York in 1948, emerges from a Manhattan building a frail old man who walks slowly; at the studio, conducting a big band of the size he has always advocated, he becomes a dapper bundle of energy, generating a resounding rendition of Afro-Cuban jazz. His sequence is filmed in sepia, evoking the way big bands looked as well as sounded in '40s movies.

Each man—and one woman, beautiful Brazilian piano virtuoso Eliane Elias, who plays sambas barefoot—are presented as the distinctive presences they are. "Calle 54" opens with Paquito D'Rivera, heir to Gillespie's orchestra, getting the film off to an appropriate start with "Panamericana." Other artists highlighted are Chano Dominguez, Jerry Gonzalez and his Fort Apache Band, dazzling pianist Michel Camilo and, performing together, Orlando "Puntilla" Rios and Carlos "Patato" Valdes.

NEW YORK, 10/30/00, p. 93, Peter Rainer

Fernando Trueba's *Calle 54* is a staged concert documentary featuring twelve separate Latin-jazz performances, and for each one it's difficult to resist rising out of your seat and moving to the music. Many world-class artists play their hearts out in this film, including the late, great Tito Puente; the ravishing pianist Eliane Elias, who plays barefooted; Chucho Valdés and his father

Bebo; and Gato Barbieri, who explains that playing music makes him feel free. He didn't have to tell us.

NEW YORK POST, 10/20/00, p. 50, Lou Lumenick

This rousing musical documentary is especially worthwhile for the appearance of Tito Puente, the Latin jazz legend who died this spring.

Interviewed at his restaurant on City Island, Puente delivers a short lecture on the history of the art form. Then he performs "New Arrival" on the timbales and vibraphone, and his sheer exuberance is electrifying.

There are 11 other beautifully-shot numbers in this documentary filmed by Fernando Trueba, the Spanish director of the Oscar-winning "Belle Epoque."

While not up to last year's "Buena Vista Social Club," this is a film that fans of Latin jazz won't want to miss.

NEWSDAY, 10/20/00, Part II/p. B6, Gene Seymour

It's little wonder that so many people these days find jazz music so boring. Whenever a jazz performance is captured on film or video, the tendency is to let the camera do little more or less than just sit and stare at the musicians. Such distance is easily transferred to the audience, which takes the hint that engagement with the music is suggested, never implored.

The glory of "Calle 54," Fernando Trueba's thrilling valentine to Latin jazz, is the way in which its cameras give in to rapture. By the time the movie ends, so will you surrender.

Showcasing the finest Latin instrumentalists in studio performances lit and framed in juicy colors, "Calle [street] 54" isn't content to be presentational. It moves giddily with the music, jumping and gliding all over place with the controlled exuberance of competitive swing dancers.

Thus, in watching Brazilian pianist Eliane Elias playing "Samba Trieste" with her trio, we don't get only the tight close-ups of her striking the keyboard. We leap back and forth from her bassist's hands, to her bare feet on the pedal, to the drummer's face, lost in the beat. At that relatively early point in the film, you can barely imagine the potential of high-speed virtuosity. Watching pianists Michel Camilo and Chucho Valdes do their thing will render the "eye-popping" platitude obsolete.

There's so much to look at here: Saxophonist Gato Barbieri, caustic and world-weary in his mid-60s, but still able to summon the keening electricity of his youth; Valdes and his father, Bebo, engaged in brightly bursting colloquy for the first time in decades. And, not least, a sustained glimpse of the late Tito Puente, garbed in white like one of heaven's citizen-legislators, leading his Latin All Stars with gleeful abandon. And for heaven's sake, why are you reading this? Go see this movie, pronto!

VILLAGE VOICE, 10/24/00, p. 150, Ed Morales

Since 1999's fabled Latin pop explosion, our understanding of la música has been framed by media gatekeeping: Ricky Martin becomes the emblem of ambiguous vida-loca sexuality; the late Tito Puente, the father of all possible Nuyorican beats; the Buena Vista Social Club, the poster boys of embargo-busting. But many crucial figures of the genre, having struggled to endow Latin music with the artistic merit of North American jazz, remain obscured by hype. Fernando Trueba's documentary Calle 54 clarifies matters—it is a dazzling, long-overdue tribute to the true stars of Latin music.

Trueba got the idea for the film when he was shooting the Latin jazz-jam finale for Two Much, a rather vacant mid-'90s Antonio Banderas romantic comedy designed to break the director out of his native Spain. In Calle 54, he indulges his passion for the music, capturing exhilarating, once-in-a-lifetime performances. Although Trueba is fond of Wim Wenders-style floating-p.o.v. slow pans, don't expect Buena Vista Social Club's intimate narrative here. When Gato Barbieri reminisces about old filmmaking friends like Glauber Rocha, Rossellini, and Godard, it's one of the few times the musicians reveal anything personal. For the most part Trueba lets them speak only through their performances, often bathed in primary colors in neutral studio settings. The technique works best when Jerry González of the overlooked Fort Apache Band seems to burst into red flames during a flügelhorn solo and Tito Puente's all-star configuration shimmers in spiritual white outfits. Trueba uses a dark blue tint, reminiscent of Bertrand Tavernier's smoky jazz café opus, *'Round Midnight,* when the father and son Bebo and Chucho Valdés engage in a piano duet that serves as an emotional reunion.

Also reviewed in:
NATION, 6/4/01, p. 36, Gene Santoro
NEW YORK TIMES, 10/20/00, p. E12, Elvis Mitchell
VARIETY, 11/6-12/00, p. 20, David Stratton

CARRIERS ARE WAITING, THE

A Samuel Goldwyn Films release of a K-Star production with the participation of Canal+. K2, RTBF, and CAB Productions. *Producer:* Dominique Janne. *Director:* Benoît Mariage. *Screenplay (French with English subtitles):* Benoît Mariage, Emmanuele Bada, and Jean-Luc Seigle. *Director of Photography:* Philippe Guilbert. *Editor:* Philippe Bourgueil. *Music:* Stéphane Huguenin and Yves Sanna. *Sound:* Olivier Hespel. *Sound Editor:* Anne Frey. *Casting:* Patrick Hella. *Production Designer:* François Hoste. *Art Director:* Chris Cornil. *Special Effects:* Olivier de Laveleye. *Costumes:* Anne Fournier. *Make-up:* Michèle Constantinides and François Joset. *Running time:* 94 minutes. *MPAA Rating:* Not Rated.

CAST: Benoît Poelvoorde (Roger);   Morgane Simon (Luise);   Bouli Lanners (Coach); Dominique Baeyens (Mother); Philippe Grand-Henry (Felix); Jean-François Devigne (Michel); Lisa Lacroix (Jocelyne);   Philippe Nahon (Overseer);   Edith Lemerdy (Edith, Jocelyne's Mother);   Patrick Audin (Patrick, Joselyne's Father);   Claude Caudron (Schoolteacher); Simone Tasiaux (Radio Announcer); Renaud Rutten (Pushy Pigeon Raiser); Benjamin Minne (Pupil);   Georges Taminiaux (Station Master);   Francine Taminiaux (Station Master's Wife); Jean-Marie Hubot (Policeman);   Henri Bruwier and Francine Bruwier (Cheese Sellers);   Boris Humblet (Boris, Popcorn Pupil); Sabrina de Baets (Lead Drum Majorette); Philippe Resimont (MC);   Rene van Loo (Bailiff);   Raymond Laverdisse (Farmer);   Germaine Puillon (Burgomaster);   Mike Steven (Elvis);   Isabel Sánchez (Nurse);   Joel Gilles (Postman);   Jean Remotte (Ringer);   Jean-Claude Jassogne (Mister Walloon);   Jeanne Mencaccini (Mister Walloon's Mother);   Benoît Bertuzzo (Driver of the Lada);   Claude Goederd (Policeman at Accident); Jacques Verrees (Policeman at Accident); Roger de Looz (Driver of Pick-up);   Marc Rase (Assistant Overseer);   Frederic Coppens (Watchman);   Kashmira Wojewoda (Pigeon Raiser's Secretary);   Pol Lombeau (Photographer).

NEW YORK POST, 3/15/00, p. 57, Lou Lumenick

Roger (Benoit Poelvoorde), who mans a police scanner for the ironically named Daily Hope newspaper, is a major control freak. He compulsively and artfully rearranges the miseries (car wrecks, hail storms) he records and checks his daughter's stockings for runs.

He's exasperated by his Elvis Presley-worshiping teenage son Michele (Jean-Francois Devigne), who aspires to nothing more than doing weekly segments on movie bloopers for the local radio station. Roger decides that Michele should break the world's door-opening record and win a sedan in the process.

As the reluctant Michele half-heartedly trains on a doorframe in his backyard with an exasperated, American-influenced coach, his neglected little sister, Luise (the hauntingly sad-eyed Morgane Simon), is developing an innocent friendship with an eccentric neighbor (Philippe Grand-Henry) who trains the carrier pigeons that give the movie its title.

"The Carriers Are Waiting" takes its sweet time delivering its message about misguided parental aspirations at the millennium, but this gentle mixture of comedy and tragedy is worth the wait.

VILLAGE VOICE, 3/21/00, p. 140, Dennis Lim

In *The Carriers Are Waiting* Benoit Poelvoorde, the charismatic killer in *Man Bites Dog*, plays an altogether different and perhaps more problematic monster. Well-meaning but far from harmless, Roger Closset is a chronic dreamer whose outsize fantasies have a way of seeming touching one moment and terrifying the next. A tabloid photographer in a small Belgian industrial town, Roger is also a hotheaded boor, who gets his irrational schemes off the ground by browbeating his family—an exasperated wife, a morose teenage son, a watchful younger daughter. All worked up about a local competition offering a new car to anyone who breaks a world record, Roger decides that his visibly torpid son Michel should train to become a champion ... door-opener.

Shot in luminous black and white, *The Carriers Are Waiting* is mainly pitched in a mournful deadpan, though first-time director Benoit Mariage, a former photojournalist, is equally comfortable puncturing the glumness with bursts of hilarity or pushing it to the brink of full-scale tragedy. He has a flair for offhand, outlandishly absurd detail (Michel hosts a radio show devoted to continuity errors in movies) and an acute feel for the comedy of embarrassment—the particularly mortifying form that only parents can inflict on their children. Mariage takes his time and allows the film to drift in an almost ostentatiously casual manner; that the result is neither flimsy nor indulgent has much to do with the young daughter, Luise, played by Morgane Simon (the title, incidentally, refers to the shy, slow pigeon breeder next door whom Luise befriends, a subplot left mercifully underdeveloped). Surrounded by pushovers and nutjobs yet improbably serene and resilient, Luise is the movie's center of gravity, its Lisa Simpson. Riding on the back of her dad's motorbike as he rushes from one ambulance-chasing gig to another, her steady but perceptibly sad gaze provides the film with its most enduring image.

Also reviewed in:
NATION, 4/10/00, p. 32, Stuart Klawans
NEW YORK TIMES, 3/15/00, p. E5, Janet Maslin
VARIETY, 5/17-23/99, p. 62, Brendan Kelly

CAST AWAY

A Twentieth Century Fox and Dream Works Pictures presentation of an Imagemovers/Playtone Production. *Executive Producer:* Joan Bradshaw. *Producer:* Steve Starkey, Tom Hanks, Robert Zemeckis, and Jack Rapke. *Director:* Robert Zemeckis. *Screenplay:* William Broyles, Jr. *Director of Photography:* Don Burgess. *Editor:* Arthur Schmidt. *Music:* Alan Silvestri. *Music Editor:* Ken Karman. *Sound:* William B. Kaplan and (music) Dennis Sands. *Sound Editor:* Dennis Leonard. *Casting:* Victoria Burrows. *Production Designer:* Rick Carter. *Art Director:* Jim Teegarden, Stefan Dechant, and Elizabeth Lapp. *Set Designer:* Alicia Maccarone and Patte Strong-Lord. *Set Decorator:* Rosemary Brandenburg and Karen O'Hara. *Set Dresser:* Kristin Jones, Mark B. Palmer, Steve O. Ladish, Glenn Roberts, Edward J. Protiva, William Acedo, Gregory N. Rocco, and Richard Wester. *Special Effects:* John Frazier and Kenneth D. Pepiot. *Visual Effects:* Ken Ralston. *Costumes:* Joanna Johnston. *Make-up:* Daniel C. Striepeke. *Make-up (Tom Hanks):* Daniel C. Striepeke. *Make-up (Helen Hunt):* Ronnie Specter. *Stunt Coordinator:* Bud Davis and Doug Coleman. *Running time:* 143 minutes. *MPAA Rating:* PG-13.

CAST: Paul Sanchez (Ramon); Lari White (Bettina Peterson); Leonid Citer (Fyodor); David Allen Brooks (Dick Peterson); Yelena Papovic (Beautiful Russian Woman); Valentina Ananyina (Russian Babushka); Semion Sudarikov (Nicolai); Tom Hanks (Chuck Noland); Peter Von Berg (Yuri); Dmitri S. Boudrine (Lev); François Duhamel (French FedEx Loader); Michael Forest (Pilot Jack); Viveka Davis (Pilot Gwen); Nick Searcy (Stan); Jennifer Choe (Memphis State Student); Helen Hunt (Kelly Frears); Nan Martin (Kelly's Mother); Anne Bellamy (Anne Larson); Dennis Letts (Dennis Larson); Wendy Worthington (Wendy Larson);

Skye McKenzie (Skye Larson);   Valerie Wildman (Virginia Larson);   John Duerler (John Larson);   Steve Monroe (Steve Larson);   Ashley Trefger and Lindsey Trefger (Lindsey Larson);   Alyssa Gainer, Kaitlyn Gainer, and Lauren Gainer (Katie Larson);   Albert Pugliese and Gregory Pugliese (Gregory Larson); Brandon Reinhart and Matthew Reinhart (Matt Larson); Lisa Long (Lisa Madden);   Lauren Birkell (Lauren Madden);   Elden Henson (Elden Madden); Timothy Stack (Morgan Stockton);   Alice Vaughn (Alice Stockton);   Chase Bebak (Chase Stockton);   Gage Bebak (Gage Stockton); Amanda Cagney and Andrea Cagney (Amanda Stockton);   Fred Semmer and Peter Semmer (Fred Stockton);   Joe Conley (Joe Wally);   Aaron Rapke (Ralph Wally);   Vin Martin (Pilot Al);   Garret Davis (Pilot Blaine);   Jay Acovone (Pilot Peter); Christopher Kriesa (Pilot Kevin); Chris Noth (Jerry Lovett);   Fred Smith (Himself); Michelle Robinson and Tommy Cresswell (FedEx Anchors);   Jenifer Lewis (Becca Twig); Geoffrey Blake (Maynard Graham);   Rich Sickler (FedEx Manager);   Derick Alexander (Taxi Driver).

LOS ANGELES TIMES, 12/21/00, Calendar/p. 1, Kenneth Turan

Just a single space separates "Cast Away" from "Castaway," but there is a universe of difference in the implications of those words.   In truth, that gap summarizes the disparity between the film director Robert Zemeckis, writer William Broyles Jr. and star Tom Hanks think they've made and what is actually on the screen.

"Cast Away" is the film's actual title, and it implies philosophical questions about what's thrown aside and what's retained, what's important in life and what isn't. It's the right title for a film that Zemeckis describes in the press notes as being about "the survival of the human spirit and an illustration of the idea that surviving is easy, it's living that's difficult."

That high-minded picture, however, is only sporadically in front of us. Something unfortunate happened on the way to making it: The filmakers got waylaid by what feels like a boyish enthusiasm for the survivalist aspects of a Robinson Crusoe tale of a man shipwrecked on an island, an enthusiasm that does not translate to the viewer.

As a result, so much time is spent on a handsomely made, instructive but finally tedious blow-by-blow training film on island survival that it throws the entire venture out of balance, capsizing the enterprise and making it difficult to keep any kind of message afloat. Which is how "Cast Away" became "Castaway" in fact if not in name.

The film's basic idea of a guy isolated on a speck of land originated with Hanks, and it's not difficult to see why it intrigued him as a change of pace and why its self-imposed challenges of shooting on a remote Fiji locale over 16 months—including an unprecedented one-year hiatus for the actor to lose enough weight and grow enough hair to make his long island sojourn believable—appealed to Hanks' "Forrest Gump" director Zemeckis.

As we've come to expect from Zemeckis, "Cast Away's" level of filmmaking is top of the line. Sweeping camera movements and masterful visuals (courtesy of cinematographer Don Burgess) are plentiful, sound virtuoso Randy Thom's work is especially in evidence, and so much prodigious care has been taken with details across the board that even the dirty snow of Moscow visible in early scenes has been rendered with complete authenticity. All this expertise, however, one has to ask, is in service of what?

For despite all these good things, "Cast Away" comes off as convincing but never compelling. There's a ponderous quality to it, as if it's forever clearing its throat to say something of value that doesn't quite get articulated. In truth, the film doesn't even begin to get emotionally involving until its final 30 minutes, at which point it's been running for nearly two hours, which is very late in the game indeed.

One of "Cast Away's" odder aspects is that it plays like an extensive advertorial for the Federal Express shipping service. Hanks plays Chuck Noland, a FedEx systems engineer first glimpsed giving new employees in Moscow a spirited pep talk.

Chuck, it turns out, is the ultimate can-do company man who lives and dies by the clock. "We can never allow ourselves the sin of losing track of time," he roars at befuddled Muscovites. No problem is unsolvable for a man who does whatever it takes to get a package delivered.

Back home in Memphis, Tenn., Chuck has a loving girlfriend named Kelly Frears (Helen Hunt), who knows enough about her man not to be surprised when yet another emergency takes him away on Christmas Eve. The couple exchange presents in a Jeep Cherokee at the airport (she gives him a family heirloom watch with her picture in it) and he vows, "I'll be here New Year's Eve, I promise." Not quite.

For the FedEx cargo plane Chuck is hitching a ride on goes down (in an unnervingly realistic storm and crash) over the Pacific, and Chuck washes up on a deserted island as pristine as the tropical locale Jodie Foster ended up in Zemeckis' "Contact." And, for at least an hour, "Cast Away," which has already put a lot of minutes into marking time, comes to a halt.

Though it feels heretical to say so, given how much expense and trouble went into creating it, Chuck's stretch on that spot comes off as boring and anticlimactic. The possibilities for a man alone on an island are not infinite, quite the opposite. Any situation Chuck might conceivably face has already been endlessly explored in other movies, so the conditions for surprise and interest are close to nonexistent. What we're left with is a home movie of a trip we're glad we weren't on, a visual version of the current best-selling "The Worst Case Scenario Handbook."

In theory, having Hanks, an excellent and well-loved performer, as our surrogate on the island should compensate for this, and it does, just not enough. He is an actor whose partisan we become without having to think about it, but because his character is alone he can't resist overdoing the inevitable actorish touches until we're watching a one-man stage show more than a movie performance.

Just when we're ready to write "Cast Away" off, however, the locale shifts off the island and, almost immediately, like the flipping of a switch, things get more intriguing. The scenario goes from predictable to involving and the change from monologue to dialogue leads to Broyles' best, most emotional writing. But by then the film is about 80% over, and this, its most interesting section, comes off as severely truncated an shortchanged. What "Cast Away" itself has squandered and cast aside in its pursuit of Boys' Life heroics is its own potential for success.

NEW YORK, 12/18-25/00, p.168, Peter Rainer

Tom Hanks plays Federal Express systems engineer Chuck Noland in *Cast Away*, and his job takes him all over the world with very little advance notice. He's such a manic, time-is-money company man that it comes as something of a relief to us when he ends up stranded, after a plane crash, on a remote and uninhabited island in the South Pacific. Only the memory of his girlfriend Kelly (Helen Hunt), whom he intended to propose to on New Year's Eve, keeps hope alive—her Christmas gift to him, a family-heirloom timepiece with her picture inside, becomes his talisman.

At its most basic level, *Cast Away* is a graceful and powerfully rendered survivalist saga. Hanks's Everyman quality has never been more aptly utilized: He's the perfect stand-in for all of us who never made it to Eagle Scout. Robert Zemeckis, who directed from a script by William Broyles Jr., doesn't overdo the Robinson Crusoe stuff: we get just enough information to show us how Chuck makes it through. With virtually no dialogue for long stretches of the movie, Hanks brings us very close to the man's utter terror and loneliness.

And yet there's something generic about Chuck's plight. Zemeckis has said that his movie is "not so much about the survival of a human being but rather the survival of the human spirit," and this tone of uplift sits heavily on the story. *Cast Away* turns out to be a movie about what is important in life—about what all that surviving is for. We're supposed to divine, along with Chuck, life's higher purpose. The filmmakers don't opt for the usual happy-face Hollywood ending, but even the half-smile they provide smacks of inspirationalism. Hanks, who conceived this project years ago and clearly has an emotional investment in it, wants us to be carried away by the power of faith and redemption. But he's too good, too honest an actor to fully buy into his own agenda. He brings a bleakness to Chuck that extends right through to the end of the movie, and it's too unsettling for this instructional fable of hope. What I took away from *Cast Away* was not its mite of message but instead the image of Chuck shrouded in seclusion, with no companion but a washed-up volleyball from the plane crash, onto which he has painted, in his own blood, a human face.

NEW YORK POST, 12/22/00, p. 49, Lou Lumenick

A blockbuster with the soul of an art film, "Cast Away" is an enormously gratifying surprise ending to a generally disappointing year at the movies. Tom Hanks gives one of the towering screen performances of all time as a modern-day Robinson Crusoe who's stranded for four years on a South Pacific island.

I can think of no other actor working today who has the combination of star power and sheer craft needed to hold the screen by himself for nearly 90 minutes, enthralling audiences every second.

But "Cast Away" is so much more than an acting tour de force. Hanks (who lost 50 pounds for the role) and his "Forrest Gump" director, Robert Zemeckis, use their Oscar-winning clout to bend the rules of Hollywood filmmaking, paying huge artistic and emotional dividends.

The film's first section brilliantly and concisely sketches Hanks' character, Chuck Noland, a time-obsessed troubleshooter for Federal Express who's first seen supervising a frantic package-shortage operation in Red Square.

Chuck loves his girlfriend Kelly (a very fine Helen Hunt) back home in Memphis, even if he treats her as another item to squeeze into his frantic schedule.

En route to Tahiti on yet another emergency mission during the holiday season, Chuck's plane goes down in a storm. This is the scariest plane-crash sequence you've ever seen in a movie, and it alone is probably worth your $9.50.

Chuck is the sole survivor who washes up on an unpopulated tropical island. He must fend for himself, using the native plant life and items from a handful of packages that have washed ashore.

He learns, for instance, that a seemingly useless pair of ice skates can open coconuts and be used to perform impromptu dental work.

A volleyball he nicknames "Wilson" (after its corporate logo) becomes, after he paints a face on it with his own blood, the virtual Man Friday to whom he addresses sarcastic quips.

He even finds a way to use videotape in the packages in one of his two exciting, and very scary, attempts to brave huge waves to leave the island.

Chuck sets aside one package, with a pair of wings painted on, that will come to symbolize his determination to eventually return to civilization—and at least symbolically fulfill his obligations as a FedEx manager.

Most movies would cut away from Hanks's solo scenes for glimpses of the rescue search and his anxious loved ones back home. "Cast Away," daringly does not and the movie is better for it because tension is maintained.

Even more unusually, "Cast Away" mostly does away with a musical score. Zemeckis trusts his ability to move the audience through Hanks' funny and touching performance and the elegant, inventive camerawork supervised by Don Burgess, without the kind of manipulative music that so many filmmakers rely on as a crutch.

That's partly a tribute to William Broyles' uncommonly intelligent script, which makes the specifics of Chuck's stay on the island so specific and credible that you may forget you're watching a movie—especially when, after four years on the island, the once-pudgy Chuck is an emaciated wraith with a scraggly beard.

Broyles and Zemeckis have also devised an ending that is much more clever and touching than the one you may think you're getting from the much-criticized coming attractions trailer.

"Cast Away" flirts with many of the same philosophical issues that were in the foreground of "Forrest Gump," but basically this is a really classic adventure yarn with one of Hollywood's great actors hitting one out of the ballpark.

If you're seeing only one movie this season, this is the obvious choice.

NEWSDAY, 12/22/00, Part II/p. B3, John Anderson

Since he's marooned on his atoll in 1995, you have to assume that Chuck Noland, the systems analyst-turned-Robinson Crusoe of Robert Zemeckis' "Cast Away," never got a chance to see "Scream" (1996). If he had, of course, he'd know better than to say, "I'll be right back.

"Cast Away" may be a horror movie only in a very metaphysical sense, but a horror movie it is. Anyone who has ever given it any thought, as director Robert Zemeckis and his star, Tom Hanks, obviously have, realizes that the dream of an escape to a deserted island is pure chimera. No, there would be no cell phones or SUVs or Fox News. But there would also be no dentists. No antibiotics. No coffee. The sun would be your enemy. So would the water. The sound of rainfall would be a nightmare. Any sound, in fact, would be sheer terror.

When Chuck says he'll be back, he thinks he's heading off to troubleshoot for the well-known overnight courier company for which he works so diligently, browbeating his worldwide employees (the Muscovites seem eager for the return of Communism) and regularly leaving his fiancee, Kelly (Helen Hunt), home alone. No five minutes of screen time elapse without the courier company's logo somehow floating across our field of vision, but, as product placement, it's a mixed blessing: Zemeckis' most harrowing sequence is of Chuck's cargo plane going down, somewhere in the Asian Pacific, where the pilots already have strayed well off course and where Chuck, very much alone, washes up on what is basically a coral reef with pretensions.

Still: A South Pacific island? With a moderate climate? Plenty of coconuts and fish? No people? Yes, in other words, hell: The island also has almost no fresh water, nothing to eat but coconuts and fish, and no people. In addition to the physical hardships endured by Chuck Noland—and they are at times gruesome—there's a sadness that infects the entire movie, a sadness born of the very spiritual vacuum this kind of film is supposed to fill.

"Cast Away" is, for very large portions of its more than two-hour length, a silent movie. Hanks and Zemeckis could have pooled their considerable clout to make "Gump II: This Time It's Personal" but instead have made a very thoughtful if emotionally uneven movie that shows how fragile, both physically and emotionally, we are.

Chuck manages to avoid sunburn, sepsis and sharks, but he does have to extract a rotten tooth; he laps up water from muddy puddles and dribbles water from stingy coconuts. He also goes through a kind of one-man evolutionary process, learning to fashion tools out of rocks and sticks and the few items that wash ashore from his demolished plane—including the shoes of a sea-bleached fellow passenger and a pair of ice skates being overnighted somewhere, presumably, much farther north. When he smears blood on a volleyball that's come ashore, he paints a face on it, calls the ball Wilson (the most shameless product plug in the movie) and makes it his best friend.

He also has a picture of Kelly, inside a watch that doesn't work (one of the rather heavy-handed symbols punctuating Chuck's sentence). When he isn't busy just surviving, this keeps him afloat. And, like Wilson, it's the flimsiest of lifelines. To Zemeckis' credit, nothing really develops the way it's expected to. And neither does Chuck. Some audiences will read what they want into the character's ordeal, finding predictably uplifting aspects or some kind of optimistic learning experience in "Cast Away," but the lesson is really an existential one, the portrait of a man with no foundation to his life besides corporate loyalty.

Which, of course, won't feed the soul when no one knows you're alive. "Cast Away" can be marketed any way they like, but feel-good it's certainly not.

NEWSWEEK, 12/25/00-1/1/01, p. 75, David Ansen

There are shots and sequences in Robert Zemeckis's audacious new movie as dazzling as any you'll see this year. After about 40 minutes, Zemeckis stages a plane crash in the midst of a storm over the Pacific that is breathtaking in its horror: it may be the greatest plane crash on film. This is the disaster that hurls Tom Hanks out of his orderly life and onto a desert island where he will struggle to survive, utterly alone, for more than four years. Hanks plays a revved-up, type-A FedEx efficiency expert whose whole life is measured in seconds and minutes. Rushing around the world from Moscow to Memphis, he's had little time for the woman (Helen Hunt) he intends to marry. It's the overriding irony of William Broyles's screenplay that this globe-trotting, always-hurried hero should find himself trapped on an island where time comes to a stop and the horizon never changes.

Hanks, who can make the smallest gesture speak volumes, has no trouble holding the screen by himself for close to 70 minutes. (Nor does he have the help of a musical score: the whole time he is on the island we hear only natural sounds.) To survive, he must start from scratch, inventing tools for eating, rediscovering fire, employing the contents of the FedEx packages that have washed ashore. In one is a volleyball to which he gives a face, names Wilson and begins to talk to.

Up to the point when Hanks is finally rescued from his ordeal, "Cast Away" is a triumph. But once he returns to the world, the movie takes one wrong turn after another. What would that first re-entry feel like, for a man driven to the brink of madness by solitude? That's just what the filmmakers *don't* show us. (Instead, we get a maddening title card, FOUR WEEKS LATER, and a hero halfway recovered from culture shock.) Worse, "Cast Away" tries to twist itself into some kind of love story, assuming that the audience gives a fig whether he gets back together with Hunt. It's sad to see such stunning work self-destruct. You leave haunted by the movie that might have been.

SIGHT AND SOUND, 2/01, p. 37, Danny Leigh

US, 1990. FedEX worker Chuck Noland delivers a package to a Midwestern location before travelling to Moscow to help establish the company there. Returning home to Memphis just before Christmas, he is reunited with his girlfriend Kelly Frears, but has to leave again for a FedEx training session in South America. En route, his flight crashes in the Pacific, marooning him on an uninhabited island.

After attempting to escape on an inflatable raft, Noland realises the tides make the journey impossible and awaits rescue, crafting rudimentary tools and subsisting on crabs and coconuts. Four years later, he escapes on a raft constructed from a corrugated sheet of plastic which was washed up on shore. He is picked up at sea by a freighter. Four weeks later, Noland returns to Memphis, only to learn that Kelly—having presumed him dead—is now married with children. That night, Noland visits Kelly's home. The two kiss, but decide Kelly must stay with her family. Noland delivers another package to the Midwestern drop-off he visited before the plane crash.

For those who shudder at the memory of Robert Zemeckis' insidious 1994 homily *Forrest Gump*, the prospect of this portentously saccharine director reunited with his leading man from that project, Tom Hanks, will induce despair and despondency. Yet notwithstanding *Cast Away*'s heavy-handed closing sequence, which sees Hanks' FedEx delivery man return to his job after four years of seclusion marooned on an otherwise uninhabited island as if nothing had happened, Zemeckis' fable of loneliness and salvation avoids the glutinous excesses of his previous work. Set against the kind of purposefully emotive storytelling in which understatement is at a premium, there is even room for some subtlety. Rather than hammer home the irony of Hanks' obsessively punctual Chuck Noland being stranded on an island where time has no meaning, Zemeckis lets the audience get the joke for itself, before engineering a sly plot point: that, thanks to the currents surrounding him, Noland's belated departure must be carried out to a strict schedule.

It's hardly a coincidence that such verve shows itself while Hanks' clock-watching everyman is stuck twiddling his thumbs on his remote island. Within his classical three-act narrative—charting descent, despair and redemption—Zemeckis is at his most convincing detailing his hero's troubled adjustment to desert-island life. The rest, ultimately, feels like so much bookending: a hurried opening stuffed with exposition and signposting ("I'll be right back," Hanks tells his sweetheart prior to his ill-fated flight) and an unsatisfying 30-minute coda that struggles to say anything insightful about the nature of change.

Which leaves us with the compelling central portrait of Noland, alone and increasingly hopeless somewhere west of Tahiti. Despite Zemeckis'" darkly existential" aspirations, the film isn't as stark and austere as its Beckettian premise might suggest. All the same, one would be hard pressed to find another example of such a definitively mainstream enterprise so boldly defying convention, not least in leaving its star in silence for an hour of screen time. By the time the chronically cloistered Noland eventually starts talking to a volleyball (a potentially disastrous motif executed with remarkable assurance), you wonder if this device was intended for the character's benefit or ours, such is the disorientating effect on us of his solitude.

Cast Away doesn't romanticise Noland's desolation. Despite the expedient ellipsis of four years on the island, it's made clear that much of that time was devoted to finding workable methods of suicide. And while Zemeckis allows Noland the brief exultation of lighting his first fire, boys'-own heroism is absent. Instead, director and leading man settle into a hypnotic pattern of near absurdist vignettes, typified by a sequence where Noland reluctantly breaks his FedEx code of honour and opens an array of washed-up parcels, including video tapes, a pair of ice skates and a sheaf of divorce papers otherwise ordinary objects which seem surreal given the extraordinary circumstances.

TIME, 12/25/00-1/1/01, p. 146, Richard Corliss

Tom Hanks is back on a killer beach, this time alone. The soldiers hitting the Normandy sands in *Saving Private Ryan* faced grim death, but it might come in the arms of a buddy. Chuck Noland, the FedEx manager stranded on a Pacific island after a plane crash, has no one to talk to, to bray at, as he did to his harried underlings at work—no one to shore up his resolve or share his desperation. Well, all right. Chuck is a doer. So he will fashion tools, clothing, shelter; find food, draw cave paintings, make fire. He will replicate the ascent of man, all by his lonesome. He'll be Robinson Crusoe without Friday, Gilligan without the crew, *Survivor* without all those annoying other survivors.

Hanks has often played a decent man isolated—in his mind *(Forrest Gump)*, his disease *(Philadelphia)*, his bereavement *(Sleepless in Seattle)* or outer space *(Apollo 13)*. As Chuck, he finds his best, most resourceful self in isolation. So does William Broyles Jr.'s script; the 80 minutes it spends on the atoll alone with Hanks make for engrossing storytelling. The film is less surefooted back in civilization, with the girl Chuck left behind (Hunt). For its soul is on the beach, in its gradually unfolding secrets, its new perils and triumphs. The film has loved inhabiting the real estate of a restless, splendid solitude. So, perhaps, has Chuck; he's Adam in a more daunting Eden.

VILLAGE VOICE, 12/26/00 p. 137, J. Hoberman

It's perversely appropriate that the holiday season would be marked by not one but two evocations of overwhelming solitude. Robert Zemeckis's *Cast Away* is an updated *Robinson Crusoe* in which Tom Hanks plays an excitable Federal Express manager who has just become engaged to America's sweetheart Helen Hunt when he is stranded alone on an uninhabited South Pacific atoll after his company cargo plane goes down in a Christmas Day storm.

Zemeckis's facility at F/X management is a given and the plane's crack-up is impressively visceral—the climax of *Titanic* compressed into 10 harrowing minutes of plunging vessels and flaming seas. Nor does the pummeling stop once Hanks is washed up on the white-sand beach of his personal Club Med. Island life is a baffling, bloody ordeal complicated by unsmashable coconuts and the bad tooth throbbing in the survivor's head like a time bomb. While *Robinson Crusoe* was a paean to the practical middle-class virtues that allowed its industrious hero (and the nation he represents) to re-create civilization out of nothingness, *Cast Away* is a far less triumphalist peek into the nothingness at the heart of civilization.

Fortunately, a few indestructible FedEx boxes wash ashore—one containing an apparently useless volleyball that, as soon as Hanks paints a face on its surface, becomes his combined pal, pet, and pagan idol. In another bit of product placement, Hanks calls the ball by its trade name: Wilson. Although *Cast Away* is very much Hanks's extreme everyman solo, his inanimate Man Friday deserves recognition as one of the year's best supporting actors. At the very least, Wilson gives the star a pretext for the movie's most emotionally wrenching scene. Alone with this absurd self-projection, Hanks spends four years on his island before building a getaway raft. The shot in which he looks back at his verdant prison, having arduously paddled free into the open ocean, is pure science fiction: He's blasted out into space, accompanied by his sidekick, Wilson.

The raft sequence has intimations of *2001* that don't stop even after Hanks returns to civilization (on a plane of total solitude) to hear how the "FedEx family" lost five of its "sons" and endures a bad-beyond-belief meeting with his dentist. I was amazed at the depth of alienation with which Zemeckis infused these scenes. But as if frightened at having conjured up the least compromising, bleakest vision of the human condition in any Hollywood A-picture since Douglas Sirk's *Imitation of Life* , Zemeckis casts it away with pumped-up affirmation. God moves in mysterious ways. It's a wonderful life after all.

Also reviewed in:
CHICAGO TRIBUNE, 12/22/00, Movies/p. 7, Michael Wilmington
NEW REPUBLIC, 1/1 & 8/01, p. 22, Stanley Kauffmann
NEW YORK TIMES, 12/22/00, p. E1, Stephen Holden
NEW YORKER, 12/18/00, p. 108, David Denby

VARIETY, 12/11-17/00, p. 21, Emanuel Levy
WASHINGTON POST, 12/22/00, p. C1, Rita Kempley
WASHINGTON POST, 12/22/0, Weekend/p. 40, Desson Howe

CATFISH IN BLACK BEAN SAUCE

A Hill Pictures and Black Hawk Entertainment release of a Black Hawk Entertainment production. *Producer:* Chi Muoi Lo. *Director:* Chi Muoi Lo. *Screenplay (Vietnamese and English with English subtitles):* Chi Muoi Lo. *Director of Photography:* Dean Lent. *Editor:* Dawn Hoggat. *Music:* Stanley A. Smith. *Casting:* Eileen Mack Knight. *Production Designer:* Skyler J.D. Adler. *Costumes:* Maral Kalinian. *Running time:* 110 minutes. *MPAA Rating:* PG-13.

CAST: Paul Winfield (Harold Williams); Mary Alice (Dolores Williams); Chi Muoi Lo (Dwayne Williams/Sap); Lauren Tom (Mai); Kieu Chinh (Thanh); Sanaa Lathan (Nina); Tyler Christopher (Michael); Tzi Ma (Vinh); George Wallace (James); Wing Chen (Samantha); Amy Tran (Young Mai); Kevin Lo (Young Dwayne); Kevin D'Arcy and Andre Rosey Brown (Guards); Ron Galbraith (Doctor); Calvin Nguyen (Teacher); Richard Whiten (Motorcycle Cop); Lalanya Masters (Bank Teller); Mark Daniel Cade (Assistant Bank Manager); Jedda Jones (Agnes); Roxanne Reese (Nadine); Saachiko Magwili (Mother); William Thomas (Douglas); April Tran (Interpreter); Tom Ryan (Lt. Davis); Carol Kiernan (Nurse); Thu Hong (Opera Singer); Ho Lo (Man at Airport); Vien Hong (Transvestite); Pamela Gordon (Voice of Jasmine); Christal L. House (Voice of Lang).

LOS ANGELES TIMES, 6/9/00, Calendar/p. 16, Kevin Thomas

"Catfish in Black Bean Sauce" marks the ambitious feature debut of Vietnamese-born Chi Muoi Lo, who wrote, produced and directed this film as well as acted, in a leading role. Chi has spread himself too thin, resulting in an uneven picture but one that has plenty of substance and emotion.

Chi has been singularly fortunate in his stars, Mary Alice and Paul Winfield, veterans of such resources and presence that they make the entire film worth watching. What they can accomplish with a glance and a shrug is a pleasure to behold.

Alice and Winfield play a kindly middle-aged, middle-class African American couple, Dolores and Harold Williams, who were unable to have children of their own. While serving in Vietnam, Harold came to the rescue of a 10-year-old Vietnamese girl and her little brother, who were put up for adoption by their desperate mother. Dolores, a woman with a considerable sense of propriety, and the laid-back Harold have been outstanding parents, with their daughter Mai (Lauren Tom) married to another Vietnamese refugee (Tzi Ma) and their son Dwayne (Chi) a bank manager on the verge of presenting an engagement ring to Nina (Sanaa Lathan), a beautiful young African American who puts in long hours at a medical clinic.

In an instant this image of cross-cultural solidarity and contentment is shattered when Mai joyfully announces that she has finally located her birth mother, due to arrive in a week. Dolores and Harold were under the impression that Mai had given up her search long ago, and her thoughtlessness in not preparing them leaves Dolores stunned and hurt yet determined to rise to the occasion with dignity. Their birth mother, Thanh (Kieu Chinh), while having been through a terrible ordeal and ecstatic at being reunited with her children, proves to be a haughty, critical woman.

The plan had been that Thanh should live with Mai and her husband, but Thanh insists on moving in with Dwayne and his roommate Michael (Tyler Christopher), although Dwayne barely remembers her and harbors deep resentment toward her for abandoning him.

In short, Chi has created a volatile situation ripe for both humor and pathos, and he discovers plenty of both. He should have quit while he was ahead. Instead he throws in a murky and contrived subplot in which Dwayne finds himself in a curiously passionless relationship with Nina while becoming mightily upset that his hunky roomie has become involved with a pre-op Chinese transsexual, Samantha (Wing Chen). You're given the impression that Dwayne is struggling to deny his attraction to Michael, but Chi raises this possibility only to back away from it. That Thanh seems a latent racist, not at all pleased that Dwayne is engaged to Nina and eager to line up a Vietnamese girl for him, is quite enough of a complication; Michael and Samantha are a whole other movie.

Chi is on far surer ground as a writer-director in the film's more serious moments or at those times when the humor seems to arise naturally from a complicated predicament. He is a good director of actors, though a bit of a showoff himself, too eager to hog the spotlight. Yet in its theatrical way "Catfish in Black Bean Sauce" does end on a note of hard-earned wisdom and reconciliation.

NEW YORK POST, 8/25/00, p. 59, Lou Lumenick

Chi Muoi Lo, a Vietnamese actor who's had small roles in a handful of Hollywood films, turns writer-director-producer as well as star of this intriguing indie effort.

Drawing on his own experiences as a war refugee, he plays Dwayne, a confused young banker who was adopted as a child by an African-American couple (Paul Winfield and Mary Alice).

Dwayne's cultural dislocation increases when his sister (Lauren Tom) brings their long-lost birth mother (Kieu Chinh) to America, causing him to question his engagement to a black businesswoman (Sanaa Lathan).

Like many first films made on a shoestring budget, this one improves dramatically from its tedious, awkwardly staged opening scenes to its stylishly slapstickish climax.

"Catfish in Black Bean Soup" ranges from exquisitely sensitive (the conflict between Dwayne's black and Asian mothers) to crass (a homophobic subplot about a buddy's affair with a transvestite), but overall, it's an interesting effort.

NEWSDAY, 8/25/00, Part II/p. B7, Gene Seymour

There are good movies, bad movies, good-bad movies and bad-good movies. And then, there are the ones that really make you crazy: The ones that aim so far above pop-cultural conventions that their failure to match their intentions with their achievements seems more grievous than something that's merely atrocious.

Such a film is "Catfish in Black Bean Sauce," Chi Muoi Lo's comedy-drama about two Vietnam War orphans raised by an African-American couple (Paul Winfield, Mary Alice) and coming of age with markedly different attitudes about their adoptive country.

Dwayne (Lo), for instance, is a prototypical 20-something L.A. yuppie, who runs a bank branch in his working-class neighborhood. He speaks fluent hip-hop and is engaged to a pretty young buppie named Nina (Sanaa Lathan from "Love and Basketball"), who loves him despite his low-grade commitment phobia.

Dwayne's older sister Mai (Lauren Tom) is, to say the least, far more ambivalent about her American-ness and has become obsessed with finding their biological mother. She succeeds, and when she brings Thanh (Kieu Chinh) from Vietnam to the United States a culture clash ensues, as does a smoldering war between the two moms that escalates into a gratuitous, hair-pulling catfight.

Which should give you some idea of how heavily Lo's script leans on the hackneyed contrivances of the sitcom and the soap opera. He throws all kinds of subplots into his stew, including a running gag about whether the Asian woman dated by Dwayne's white roommate (Tyler Christopher) is really a woman, that are neither fresh nor particularly funny.

In fact, most of the truly interesting transactions in "Catfish," especially those involving Mai and her two moms, are overwhelmed by the script's awkward clutter of Big Moments (yes, gentle people, I'm afraid there is...a life-threatening illness) that contribute nothing to one's understanding of the characters or their motives.

Lo, an undervalued character actor in movies and TV, gives Dwayne a slack-jawed bewilderment that makes him watchable for a while. But it isn't long before his confusion is transferred to the audience. If, for instance, he wants so much to settle down, why is he skittish about marrying Nina? (And why, for that matter, does Nina still bother with him?) The movie tries hard, but, like Dwayne, it seems scared of its own yearnings.

VILLAGE VOICE, 8/29/00, p. 135, Amy Taubin

The family in *Catfish in Black Bean Sauce* is also multicultural, but that's where comparison with *Chalk* [see Taubin's review] ends. Chi Muoi Lo wrote, directed, and also stars in this social satire about a Vietnamese brother and sister, Dwayne (played by the filmmaker) and Mai (Lauren Tom), who came to California as refugees and were adopted by an African American couple (Paul Winfield and Mary Alice). Twenty-five years later, Mai locates their birth mother and brings her to America, throwing the entire family into a crisis of identity. Particularly confused is Dwayne, who is African American-identified and about to marry a beautiful young black woman (Sanaa Lathan).

Catfish in Black Bean Sauce (the title refers to a Vietnamese dish that originated in China, cooked by Dwayne's adoptive mom at the family reunion to unanimous dissatisfaction) is a progressive but not very funny comedy of manners. Lo is too limited a director to handle the most touchy aspect of social satire—that it derives humor from the very stereotypes it critiques. He also puts the film at a disadvantage by casting himself in the lead. Despite the autobiographical elements in the script, Lo's performance is broad and impersonal, and his lack of chemistry with Lathan adds to the sense that the film is all concept and no flesh and blood.

Also reviewed in:
CHICAGO TRIBUNE, 7/28/00, Friday/p. I, Monica Eng
NEW YORK TIMES, 8/25/00, p. E10, Elvis Mitchell
VARIETY, 6/14-20/99, p. 39, Joe Leydon

CECIL B. DeMENTED

An Artisan Entertainment release in association with Le Studio Canal Plus of a Polar Entertainment production. *Executive Producer:* Anthony DeLorenzo and Fred Bernstein. *Producer:* Joe Caracciolo, Jr., John Fiedler, and Mark Tarlov. *Director:* John Waters. *Screenplay:* John Waters. *Director of Photography:* Robert Stevens. *Editor:* Jeffrey Wolf. *Music:* Zoë Poledouris and Basil Poledouris. *Music Editor:* Robb Boyd. *Sound:* Rick Angelella. *Sound Editor:* John Nutt. *Casting:* Pat Moran, Billy Hopkins, Suzanne Smith, and Kerry Barden. *Production Designer:* Vincent Peranio. *Art Director:* Rob Simons. *Set Decorator:* Barbara Haberecht. *Special Effects:* David Blitstein. *Costumes:* Van Smith. *Make-up:* Cheryl "Pickles" Kinion. *Stunt Coordinator:* Steve Davison. *Running time:* 88 minutes. *MPAA Rating:* R.

CAST: Melanie Griffith (Honey Whitlock); Stephen Dorff (Cecil B. Demented); Alicia Witt (Cherish); Adrian Grenier (Lyle); Larry Gilliard, Jr. (Lewis); Maggie Gyllenhaal (Raven); Jack Noseworthy (Rodney); Mink Stole (Mrs. Sylvia Mallory); Ricki Lake (Libby); Patricia Hearst (Fidget's Mom); Mike Shannon (Petie); Kevin Nealon (Himself); Eric M. Barry (Fidget); Zenzele Uzoma (Chardonnay); Erika Lynn Rupli (Pam); Harriet Dodge (Dinah); Roseanne (Herself); Eric Roberts (Honey's Ex); Ray Felton (Roy Stillings); John Michaelson (Charles); Jewel Orem (Maid); Bill Grimmett (Mayor Adam Fenwick); Jeffrey Wei (William, Boy in Wheelchair); Sloane Brown (Newscaster); Billy Green, Mia Walker and James Klingenberg (Children); Ginger Tipton (Box Office Lady); Nathan Stolpman (Ticket Taker); Melanie Gorombol (Candy Counter Girl); Gary Wheeler (Theatre Manager); Joyce Flick Wendl (Puker); Tyler Mason Buckalew (Teen Boy); Tar Garwood (Charles Theater Girl); Marty Lodge (Film Commissioner); James Byrne Reed (Producer); Mark Bernier (Studio Executive); Patsy Grady Abrams, Rhea Felken, and Shana Gelbard (Family Women); Susan Lowe and Mary Vivian Pearce (Family Ladies); Michael Gabel (Film Delivery Driver); Mark Joy (Fidget's Dad); Alan J. Wendl (Security Teamster); Peter Gil (Director); Eric

Richardson (Director of Photography);   Marybeth Wise (Assistant Director);   Cyntha
Webb-Manley (Large Lady);   Channing Wilroy (Shop Steward);   O. Lee Fleming (Sniffles);
Scott Morgan (Groupie);   Tim Caggiano (Porno Fan);   Judith Knight Young (Ticket Seller);
Tyler Miller (Fan A);   Geoffrey I. Grissett (Boy Fan);   Brook Houghton (Girl Fan);   Joshua
Billings (Drive-in Manager);   Jeff Perryson and Terry McCrea (Jocks);   Conrad Karlson
(Psychiatrist);   Rosemary Knower (Cecil's Mom);   Doug Roberts (Cecil's Dad);   Nat Benchley
and Dave Trovato (SWAT Cops);   Billy Tolzman (Petie's Trick);   Jonathan Fiorucci (Raven's
Groupie);   John Waters (Reporter in Honey's Hotel Room).

LOS ANGELES TIMES, 8/11/00, Calendar/p. 2, Kevin Thomas

What better place to launch a broadside at mindless mainstream movies than from within a
mainstream movie? John Waters, Baltimore's master of subversive cinema, knows this better than
anyone as he takes aim at big-deal, big-screen bores and all other manner of Hollywood excesses
in "Cecil B. DeMented," a fast, furious and funny fusillade of a movie.

Yes, it celebrates guerrilla-style filmmaking, but it's also an uproarious, smartly crafted, hard
action flick with a certified Hollywood star, Melanie Griffith. You don't need to know film
history to kick back with "Cecil," but it can't be denied that catching a glimpse of a marquee
proclaiming "Les Enfants du Paradis—The First Time in English" offers a special jokey horror.

Griffith plays Honey Whitlock, a spoiled, bitchy show-biz veteran who has come to Baltimore,
"a dump of a town" in her view, for the benefit premiere of her latest movie, "Some Kind of
Happiness." Honey gets her kicks from making everybody jump through hoops, but she's right
on when she has an ominous premonition as a white limo pulls up to her luxury hotel to take her
to the premiere.

"White limos are for Liberace's lover," she declares haughtily, pointing out that a black limo
is in her contract.

In any event, Honey has barely started on her sugary onstage speech when she is seized by a
pack of "cinema terrorists," one Cecil B. DeMented (Stephen Dorff) and his crew, the Sprocket
Holes, and whisked off to the city's vast old derelict Hippodrome, where Cecil is making his
movie and simultaneously plotting a revolution against mainstream pictures, which he will film
as part of his own movie. Honey, now in punker gear, is to star as the beleaguered proprietor
of an art theater that's threatened with extinction.

Honey, targeted not only because she has conveniently come to town but also because she
represents all that Cecil hates about Hollywood, is none too happy to become a kidnap victim.
The Sprocket Holes, a grungy collection of punkers, dopers, radical gays, a porn actress and a
Satanist, are intimidating to say the least, each one sporting the tattooed name of a favorite
Waters director, from schlockmeister Herschell Gordon Lewis to such auteurs as Almodovar,
Fassbinder and Preminger. (A large-format book on David Lean, however, serves as a target for
sharpshooter practice.)

The Hippodrome interior has been transformed by Waters' long-time production designer
Vincent Peranio into an intricate and intriguing work space, set and living quarters created from
junk and thrift shop treasures. Other Waters veterans turn up on screen: Ricki Lake as Honey's
hapless assistant, Mink Stole as the premiere chairman and Patricia Hearst as the concerned
mother of one of the Sprocket Holes.

DeMented more than lives up to his name, and Honey, no fool and a pro after all, starts giving
her best performance in years. She's further egged on by a Time magazine review of "Some
Kind of Happiness" that finds her past her prime to be carrying such a picture, a sure-fire $30-
million loser. Honey begins to start seeing things from DeMented's point of view, crazed as he
is by pointless sequels, video game adaptations, Hollywood remakes of foreign films and old TV
series. Wouldn't you know that the Maryland Film Commission, Waters' long-ago nemesis, is
making a big fuss over a Baltimore-made sequel to "Forrest Gump"?

Waters pokes fun at DeMented et al, too, but with affection. As hilariously zany as "Cecil" is,
it is charged with a passion and energy beyond most of Waters' ventures into mainstream
production; all that Waters protests in such scabrous fashion is clearly a matter of conviction for
him.

Cecil B. DeMented, played to the hilt by Dorff, really is ready to die for his beliefs and to get
his movie made. And this film is Waters' tip of the hat to the outlaw cinema from which he

emerged. He's managed to stay true to it arguably better than anyone else who emerged from American underground cinema.

NEW YORK, 8/21/00, p. 57, Peter Rainer

John Waters, in his public appearances, does such a good job being "John Waters" that his movies often seem superfluous. He's his own best creation. With his pencil-line mustache and pomade and campy non sequiturs, the lewd outrager from Baltimore has become the darling of college cinema societies and the film-festival circuit. Waters began his career as a pioneer in the now-burgeoning field of the gross-out movie, and some of that grossness, viewed again in films like *Pink Flamingos,* is still impressively icky. But you no longer go to Waters's movies to be outraged or revolted. You go for the enjoyable spectacle of seeing the zero-budget *yeccch-meister* fit his frissons into the woozier reaches of mainstream moviemaking. It's not as if Waters has sold out; the dream factory's sobby soap-opera side, after all, has always been his clarion call. His new movie, *Cecil B. DeMented,* is ostensibly an attack on Hollywood, but Waters also wants it to be his version of that archetypal love/hate Hollywood movie *Sunset Boulevard.* For Waters, his "going Hollywood" is the ultimate joke, the ultimate subversion.

Waters is bothered by the fact that the studios turn out garbage—and that the garbage is machine-tooled. He likes his schlock to have some aroma. In *Cecil B. DeMented,* the eponymous Cecil (Stephen Dorff) is the manager of a restored Art Deco movie palace in Baltimore who, together with his clan of renegades calling themselves the Sprocket Holes, kidnaps Honey Whitlock (Melanie Griffith), a movie queen with a diva-size ego who is in town for a benefit premiere of her new film. Cecil terrorizes her into service as the star of his guerrilla movie production *Raving Beauty.* The gonzo crew, including a sweet-tempered occultist (Maggie Gyllenhaal), a self-hating heterosexual hairdresser (Jack Noseworthy), and a porn star (Alicia Witt) who performs onscreen with a gerbil, take their cue from Cecil and shout slogans like "Power to the people who punish bad cinema!" They tattoo the names of outlaw directors on their arms: Spike Lee, Sam Peckinpah, David Lynch, Sam Fuller, William Castle. (Cecil's choice is Otto Preminger, whose martinet ways would seem to be the prime reason for the adulation.) They disrupt the stuffed-shirt proceedings of the Maryland Film Commission, which is hosting lunch for a bunch of oyster-slurping dolts, and they wreck the filming of the sequel to *Forrest Gump,* starring Kevin Nealon in the title role. Eventually, Honey Whitlock comes around to the idea that her kidnapping is a good career move.

The plot device of a kidnappee falling in with her kidnappers is an old one, but Melanie Griffith, who is the Norma Desmond in this crackbrained *Sunset Boulevard,* gives it a fresh spin. Part gorgon, part den mother, Griffith accentuates her tinkly-voiced fogginess, her way of speaking her lines as if she had just been put into a dainty trance. Periodically she roars through the film's mild mood with a movie-star snit. The film needs Griffith's dippy modulations, because without her it's mostly a brassy rant. Waters wants *Cecil B. DeMented* to be a goof, but even more than that, he wants to sock it to Hollywood. He really means it when he has his cultists revolutionizing to end bad cinema, but his own filmmaking skills are fairly skimpy, and so the satiric idea never explodes into something wonderful. (If the early Godard or De Palma had seized upon this idea, the resulting movie would have been a wingding.) Like Andy Warhol when he made movies, Waters preempts negative criticism by laying out his ineptitude in plain view. The amateurishness of the production isn't just an antidote to Hollywood's slickness; it's also supposed to be more heartfelt, more real. In *Cecil B. DeMented,* Waters the camp hipster tries to finish off one kind of bad cinema and ends up replacing it with another kind. His.

NEW YORK POST, 8/11/00, p. 47, Jonathan Foreman

It's sad to report that the only remotely shocking thing about the latest movie by provocative "Pink Flamingos" auteur John Waters is the heavy-handedness of its humor and the blunt ineffectiveness of its diatribes against the excesses of Hollywood.

There are some decent jokes (how could there not be in a Waters movie?), but they are too few and far between and some of the most obvious ones are dragged on for so long or so many times that they die of exhaustion.

Somehow the movie's contemporary setting (Waters is so much better in the '50s—viz "Cry Baby" and "Hairspray") and close-to-the-bone subject matter—filmmaking and radical activism—seems to have blunted Waters' justly famous wit.

Cecil B. Demented (Stephen Dorff) is both guerrilla filmmaker and a filmmaking guerrilla: He'd kill to make a film—one with the integrity of art.

As part of his ruthless do-or-die campaign against Hollywood awfulness, he kidnaps spoiled movie star Honey Whitlock (Melanie Griffith) from a Baltimore premiere.

Cecil wants her to star in the no-budget film he's making of various gun-and-grenade terrorist attacks he and his cult-like gang, "the Sprocket Holes," commit in Baltimore against such targets as a shopping mall theater and a party given by the Maryland Film Commission.

All of the gang members, including the former porno star Cherish (Alicia Witt) and the drug-obsessed Lyle (Adrien Grenier), are tattooed with the names of cineaste heroes like Fassbinder, Sam Fuller, Warhol (and, more surprisingly, Almodovar) and have taken a vow of chastity until the film is completed.

At first Honey resists, but after the media make mean remarks about her appearance, Honey begins to do a Patty Hearst (who has a cameo in the movie) and to buy into Cecil's beliefs.

The action scenes are appallingly choreographed and shot. The acting often goes over the top—partly because all the characters, if you can call them that, seem to be just mouthpieces for Waters himself.

NEWSDAY, 8/11/00, Part II/p. B2, John Anderson

Herschell Gordon Lewis directed more than 40 films between 1960 and '72, from "Prime Time" to "The Gore-Gore Girls," leaving the cultural landscape littered with such midnight mayhem as "Blood Feast" (1963), "Two Thousand Maniacs" (1964) and "Monster a Go Go" (1965). By the '70s, however, changing tastes and mores—the fact that "Deep Throat" could be booked into mainstream movie houses—sent the slasher-nudie-exploitation director into forced retirement.

That Lewis' name is evoked twice in John Waters' less-than-a-screamfest "Cecil B. Demented," is both ironic and purposely weird. Obviously, Waters is familiar with Lewis' story; surely Waters also knows that his own particular brand of outrageous bad taste, once so pungent in "Pink Flamingos" and "Female Trouble," now has the biting social relevance and satirical content of your elderly aunt throwing her skirt over her head. Waters does know all this. Which makes "Ceeil B.Demented" all the more puzzling and sad.

Following his usual pattern of campy stunt-casting, Waters has Melanie Griffith play Honey Whitlock, a haughty Hollywood witch on wheels who's in Baltimore (where else in a Waters film?) to open her new movie, "Some Kind of Happiness." The much-publicized event prompts a band of militant cinema guerrillas, led by self-proclaimed "ultimate auteur" "Cecil B. Demented" (Stephen Dorff), to kidnap Honey, launch a reign of terror on mainstream movie houses and film it all in the hopes of having a hit.

The ironies are rich, if not deep. At one point (one of the better scenes), Waters sends a literally flaming film director off a roof in a wheelchair screaming, "I have a vision!"—a somewhat gratifying moment for anyone remotely fatigued by the quasi-rapturous, Sundance-cultivated concept of indie cinema as secular religion. But Waters is self-immolating, too. The kidnapers are a debauched, delusional and, in one case, satanically possessed crew of incompetents and drug addicts, whose banal sloganeering ("Outlaw cinema has no limits!") is just one tiresome aspect of a tiresome script. If "Cecil's" gang-indies, like Waters—are just self-delusional misfits, does that make their screed against Hollywood invalid? Who knows? The jokes are stacked like plague victims, mute and untouchable.

Although postmodern aesthetics proclaim otherwise, Griffith was precisely the wrong choice for Honey Whitlock, whose story parallels that of Waters friend and frequent featured player Patricia Hearst (who shows up here, too). Unlike Hearst, Honey isn't coerced into cooperating with her captors, despite a grueling hair-dye scene where they take Honey "off the deep end of the Clairol color chart." To make the most of the character's comic possibilities, however, Waters needed an actress who could swing from Honey's public face to private bitchiness to bad screen acting to good screen acting. With Griffith, it's hard to tell where we are.

No one in the cast is particularly well-used. Alicia Witt is debased in the role of Cherish, the porn star who wants to finish the movie so she can get down with "Cecil." (The idea of porn being indie cinema is made several times by Waters.) Dorff gives a lackluster reading of a lackluster script, not even attempting to infuse it with irony or distance. Maggie Gyllenhaal's devil-worshipping Raven is played for laughs, but the reappearance of Waters regulars like Mink Stole, Ricki Lake and Hearst emphasizes the feeling of movie-as-retread.

Over the years, Waters has made for some hilarious cinema, but it's almost impossible to swing a big satiric stick at the cultural hypocrisy or upright standards of a movie-going public that makes a "Scary Movie" the biggest hit of the summer. "Pecker," the director's last film, was weak but charming. "Cecil," however, is far from demented enough.

SIGHT AND SOUND, 1/01, p. 42, Peter Matthews

Hollywood star Honey Whitlock agrees to attend the premiere of her new film *Some Kind of Happiness* in Baltimore, Maryland, the movie's location. The gala's venue, the Senate Theatre, is infiltrated by the Sprocket Holes, a cadre of cinematic terrorists led by guerrilla film-maker Cecil B. Demented, otherwise known as Sinclair Stevens, the Senate's manager. The Sprockets kidnap Honey and tell her of their plan to force her to star in a subversive epic called *Raving Beauty*. Initially scornful, she is soon converted and joins the gang in a series of assaults on mainstream cinema locales: first, they disrupt a showing of *Patch Adams: the Directors Cut* while Cecil films the mayhem; then they invade an outdoor reception held by the Maryland Film Commission. Make-up artist Rodney is killed when police fire on the Sprockets. Pursued by a mob of conservative filmgoers, the outlaws take refuge in a cinema screening a karate marathon and rouse the action fans to protect them.

Back at the hide-out, Cecil tells of his plan to stage a *coup d'etat* at the location where the sequel to *Forrest Gump, Gump Again* is being filmed. This time, Honey's co-star Lyle is gunned down by a technician and angry Teamsters chase the terrorists into a cinema showing the works of ex-porn star Cherish. Again, the Sprockets are defended, this time by exploitation fans. Cecil's final location is a drive-in cinema playing a Honey Whitlock triple bill. When the police arrive, more Sprockets are killed, Cecil immolates himself and Honey is escorted into a police van, while adoring fans look on.

Of all the directors who have made names for themselves over the past 30 years, John Waters is possibly the most critic-proof. It would be a stretch to call the perpetrator of such midnight-movie classics as *Female Trouble* (1974) and *Polyester* (1981) an artist, but he's undoubtedly some kind of auteur. Even with the modest commercial budgets vouchsafed to him nowadays, Waters has stayed true to his own brand of flaky amateurism: the flat, ugly staging, the frowzy cinematography and the cheesily outré set design one finds in his films supply an authorial signature as patent as Orson Welles' use of deep focus. There's a conscious ironic sensibility in Waters' movies that lifts them out of the barrel-scraping Ed Wood class. His amiable grotesques find a paradoxical grace in their abjection (as in the competition to be the "filthiest person alive" in *Pink Flamingos,* 1972). Indeed, one could argue an interesting case for Waters' mystical Catholic leanings if that weren't too pompous a way of addressing a filmmaker whose charm lies in his utter lack of pretension. Attacking a Waters movie on aesthetic grounds seems as redundant an activity as lamenting the culinary deficiencies of tinned spaghetti. His films are so blissfully aware of their own tackiness that they're just about impossible to resist.

Despite its high quotient of masturbation gags, *Cecil B. Demented* is as pleasantly anodyne as all Waters' recent productions. Just as Hollywood has cottoned on to the lucrative possibilities of gross-out comedies, Waters has started making pictures you could show to your Aunt Eileen. No doubt the mainstream invasion of his underground turf obliged him to move on, but there was always a touch of Capra about Waters' films. The sick-making coda to *Pink Flamingos* (Divine cheekily munches on a dog turd) doesn't carry the transgressive force it would in, say, Buñuel—it's more in the nature of a schoolboy dare.

The oddly wholesome quality of Waters' obscenity is probably a function of how he relates to his characters. For Waters never presents a mere freak show á la Todd Solondz; far from laughing up his sleeve at the human dregs he portrays, Waters bows to their lumpen integrity.

The shoddiness of his cinema should consequently be recognised for the principled moral gesture it is—even on the level of style, Waters is determined not to pull rank.

If *Cecil B. Demented* represents a technical advance over its predecessors, that isn't saying much. Waters displays a new penchant for mock-pretty effects (as in the rim lighting of the gala sequence) and proves he can handle action scenes skilfully enough. Otherwise, it's the same dog's breakfast as before, only this time the rough aesthetic bears a quasi-political import. Ever since he took the mickey out of the race-relations message movie in *Hairspray*, Waters has been developing the semblance of a social conscience: here he attacks our soulless multiplex era, bloated by formulaic high-concept drivel. In a witty conflation of Patty Hearst's escapades with the Symbionese Liberation Army and the Dogme group's drive for cinematic purity, *Cecil B. Demented* tells how screen diva Honey Whitlock gets brainwashed by a clan of movie-mad terrorists, the Sprocket Holes. Waters' native Baltimore serves as the benchmark of authenticity—its nameless genre fans offer sanctuary to the Sprocket Holes whenever the forces of reaction threaten—and the premise allows for plenty of swipes at corporate Hollywood. But story structure not being Waters' strong card, the film dawdles and repeats itself to the point of exhaustion. And hard as the professional actors try they lack the spark of genuine dementia Waters formerly elicited from personal 'discoveries' such as Mink Stole (who makes a brief appearance). Stephen Dorff in particular is strangely flat as the eponymous messianic Sprockets leader. But Melanie Grfffith throws herself into the part of Honey as if clutching at last straws. What used to be said of Walt Disney seems true of Waters: he gets them on the way up (Johnny Depp in *Cry-Baby)* and also on the way down.

TIME, 8/14/00, p. 70, Richard Corliss

In the land of no taste, the man with bad taste is king. John Waters has been lobbing turd grenades at American culture since *Pink Flamingos* in 1972. These days, with unimaginative grossness prevailing in popular art, Waters seems a throwback, an Edwardian dandy forced to babysit the *South Park* kids. How to offend, he must wonder, without being an old fart?

Here's one way: make a comedy about a radical group that kidnaps a rich young woman and brainwashes her into joining their cause. And, in a piquant move, cast the real Patty Hearst in a small role. But since this is a movie about movies—spoiled film fatale Honey Whitlock (Melanie Griffith) is taken hostage by a cinematic liberation army led by a dreamy buff who calls himself Cecil B. DeMented (Stephen Dorff)—an air of fantasy permeates the entire jape, detoxifying it. There's a geniality to gags about ratings ("Hey, hey, M.P.A.A., how many movies did you censor today?") and Robin Williams weepies ("*Patch Adams* does not deserve a director's cut; the original was long enough"). Waters wants everyone to have a good laugh, targets and audience included.

The two stars give their roles a dizzy spin. Dorff's Cecil sports a manic gleam that could be dementia or star quality (if there's a difference), and Griffith is aces as the Hollywood harridan; when she sees her super-stretch limo, in white, she snarls, "Do I *look* like a coke dealer?" Maybe Waters is ironizing his anger at the movie brats who have stolen his attitude but don't understand his spirit. If so, the master is giving the kids a lesson here. *Cecil B.* proves how a dose of *smart* bad taste can be jolly good fun.

VILLAGE VOICE, 8/22/00, p. 129, J. Hoberman

John Waters began his career as a quasi-underground director whose shoestring productions satirized hippie tolerance even as they exploited it. Thus, *Cecil B. DeMented* is both a parody of and a tribute to the '60s that proclaims, "Power to the people—perish bad cinema." Would that it were so.

A cult of Baltimore-based guerrilla filmmakers led by the eponymous tousle-haired punk (Stephen Dorff) infiltrates a charity benefit premiere and kidnaps the guest of honor, overripe Hollywood diva Honey Whitlock (Melanie Griffith). Honey is held captive in their secret movie set and forced to act in DeMented's "outlaw sinema"—a movie that will destroy the mainstream. The contradiction between the cult's high-minded anticommercialism ("We believe technique to be nothing more than failed style") and low-minded taste for gossip and innuendo (asking Honey about "Mel Gibson's dick and balls") is resolved with the invocation of Andy Warhol.

Less grandiose than his alter ego, Waters is content to take potshots at the current system. The DeMented gang desecrates a biography of David Lean, shoots up a theater showing the "director's cut" of *Patch Adams*, battles Teamsters to disrupt the filming of *Gump Again* with Kevin Nealon in the title role, and takes refuge in a friendly porn theater. Honey, ultimately made up to resemble Waters's first diva, Divine, is tricked into launching a terrorist attack on the Maryland Film Commission luncheon and consequently considered to have joined the gang. Although the cult has a Yippie-like appreciation of the media and uses a few Manson Family formulations, this is Waters's version of the '60s-ending Patty Hearst story. (Indeed, Patty herself has a celebrity cameo.)

The movie is disappointingly flat, but at least it's not mawkish. Where *Steal This Movie!* delivers a final insult by ending with a sappy blast of Crosby, Stills, and Nash ("Rejoice, rejoice, we have no choice"), *Cecil B. DeMented* has the grace to send the audience out with a piece of Waters-written rap that brags, "We ain't got no budget. Fuck keeping it clean. Ain't nobody putting us in turnaround. We ain't recouping shit."

Also reviewed in:
CHICAGO TRIBUNE, 8/18/00, Friday/p. B, Michael Wilmington
NEW YORK TIMES, 8/11/00, p. E14, Stephen Holden
NEW YORKER, 8/21 & 28/00, p. 170, Anthony Lane
VARIETY, 5/22-28/00, p. 23, David Rooney
WASHINGTON POST, 8/11/00, p. C1, Rita Kempley
WASHINGTON POST, 8/11/00, Weekend/p. 33, Michael O'Sullivan

CELL, THE

A New Line Cinema release of a Caro-McLeod/Radical Media production. *Executive Producer:* Donna Langley and Carolyn Manetti. *Producer:* Julio Caro and Eric McLeod. *Director:* Tarsem Singh. *Screenplay:* Mark Protosevich. *Director of Photography:* Paul Laufer. *Editor:* Paul Rubell and Robert Duffy. *Music:* Howard Shore. *Music Editor:* Suzana Peric. *Sound:* James Thornton and (music) Simon Rhodes. *Sound Editor:* J. Paul Huntsman. *Casting:* Ronna Kress. *Production Designer:* Tom Foden. *Art Director:* Geoff Hubbard *Set Designer:* Dean Wolcott, Joshua Lusby, and Luke Freeborn. *Set Decorator:* Tessa Posnansky. *Set Dresser:* Bart Barbuscia, Skip Crank, Kris Fuller, Louis Terry, and Martin Milligan. *Special Effects:* Clay Pinney. *Costumes:* Eiko Ishioka and April Napier. *Make-up:* Michèle Burke. *Make-up (Vincent D'Onofrio):* James Ryder. *Stunt Coordinator:* Jack Gill. *Running time:* 110 minutes. *MPAA Rating:* R.

CAST: Jennifer Lopez (Catherine Deane); Colton James (Edward Baines); Dylan Baker (Henry West); Marianne Jean-Baptiste (Dr. Miriam Kent); Gerry Becker (Dr. Cooperman); Musetta Vander (Ella Baines); Patrick Bauchau (Lucien Baines); Vincent D'Onofrio (Carl Stargher); Catherine Sutherland (Anne Marie Vicksey); Vince Vaughn (Peter Novak); James Gammon (Teddy Lee); Jake Weber (Gordon Ramsey); Dean Norris (Cole); Tara Subkoff (Julia Hickson); Lauri Johnson (Mrs. Hickson); John Cothran, Jr. (Agent Stockwell); Jack Conley (Agent Brock); Kamar de las Reyes (Officer Alexander); Christopher Janney (Swat Team Member); Nicholas Cascone (FBI Technician); Joe La Piana (FBI K-9 Agent); Pruitt Taylor Vince (Dr. Reid); Jake Thomas (Young Carl Stargher); Gareth Williams (Stargher's Father); Glenda Chism (Woman in Tub); Monica Lacy, Joy Creel Liefeld and Leanna Creel (Mothers); Alan Purwin (Helicopter Pilot).

LOS ANGELES TIMES, 8/18/00, Calendar/p. 1, Kenneth Turan

Some movies make you sorry you've seen them, and "The Cell" is one of those. Creepy and horrific, it's a torture chamber film about a man who tortures women that puts viewers through as much misery as the people on the screen. In the year 2000, that's entertainment.

The debut film for both trendy commercial director Tarsem Singh and screenwriter Mark Protosevich, "The Cell" crystallizes many of the excessive obsessions of modern popular culture: blood, violence, bondage, expanded states of consciousness and bizarre sex. But mostly what it's about is torture.

Though the film stars Jennifer Lopez as Catherine Deane, an empathetic psychologist able to use sci-fi techniques to enter other people's minds, its central figure is a twitchy, demented serial killer (do the movies admit to any other kind?) named Carl Stargher (Vincent D'Onofrio), whose M.O. is re-created in nauseating detail.

First Stargher stalks and kidnaps women. Then he imprisons the victims in a water-tight cell and batters them with high-pressure jets of water: Repellent videos of these women whimpering and suffering are given lots and lots of play. Eventually the sufferers drown, but for the audience the film is just beginning.

Stargher, who has somehow found the time to embed 14 steel rings in the flesh of his back, attaches these rings to dangling hooks and, horrifically suspended by his stretched skin alone, apparently (thankfully, one can't be sure) has sex with the corpse, which he then drowns in bleach until it resembles a doll. Which probably explains why this film is rated R instead of NC-17, a rating the MPAA seems to have forgotten in is its repertoire.

"The Cell's" central plot contrivance is that Stargher turns comatose just before his capture, meaning that the only way to save his latest victim, imprisoned in a secret location, is for Deane to enter his "Welcome to My Nightmare" mind and find out where the young woman is.

That schizophrenic psyche would seem to be a don't-go-there location if ever there was one. But, encouraged by handsome FBI agent Peter Novak (Vince Vaughn), the plucky femme takes the plunge. It's not a happy decision.

For not only does Deane encounter women in still more painful and demeaning situations, she gets embroiled with Stargher himself, "a king in a very twisted kingdom." No kidding. Soon "The Cell" is smoothly cutting back and forth between Deane being tormented in the madman's mind and his latest victim being brutalized in that watery chamber. All torture, all the time, all photographed (by Paul Laufer) and production designed (by Tom Foden) as if it were a TV spot for Chanel.

From the film's opening dream sequence (Lopez, relishing playing the diva in a pure white Eiko Ishioka dress, riding a jet-black horse over spotless sands against a cloudless blue sky), it's obvious that director Tarsem has the kind of slick but overripe visual facility that characterizes top-of-the-line European-style commercials.

Even moderate praise for any aspect of "The Cell," however, soon tastes like ashes because it's enervating to see cinematic skill put to such meretricious uses. This is a film where no opportunity for grotesqueness is lost, no possible nightmare scenario ignored, up to and including seeing someone's entrails extracted and twisted on a spit like so much link sausage. Just wait until the Gore-Lieberman forces get their hands on clips of that.

At its hollow core, "The Cell" is, regrettably, only the latest example of the push-the-envelope school of filmmaking that lives, like its largely male, largely teenage potential audience, only to go where others haven't been before. While it can be argued that putting women in jeopardy has been a film staple since the movies began, that even Dorothy ran into some trouble on the way to Oz, "The Cell" is graphic proof that we're not in Kansas anymore. Not even close.

NEW YORK POST, 8/18/00, p. 49, Lou Lumenick

If looks could kill, this would be the best movie of the summer. But beneath the considerable eye candy—including Jennifer Lopez as the world's most glamorous child therapist—"The Cell" is an awfully generic variation on the overworked serial-killer genre.

Vincent D'Onofrio plays Carl Stargher, a killer who ends up in a coma—immediately after installing his latest female victim (Tara Subkoff) in a glass cell that will automatically fill with water in a few hours.

This is obviously the wrong movie for anyone who asks why a sadistic killer would want to automate a process that he would obviously enjoy doing personally.

But then again, it's so slow, you have plenty of time to wonder, say, who installed the hooks on Carl's back by which he suspends himself from the ceiling before lapsing into a coma.

The only way the FBI can find the victim and save her is to employ a high-tech technique—developed at great expense, for equally murky reasons, by a multinational company—that allows Lopez's character, Catherine, to enter Carl's mind.

Tarsem Singh, the music-video director making his feature debut, doesn't seem to have a whole lot of interest in the perfunctory scenes that set up the story, such as they are.

The performances are so flat, there isn't a huge difference between D'Onofrio, who's in a coma for most of the picture, and the rest of the cast, including Vince Vaughn and Jake Weber as intrepid FBI agents, and Dylan Baker and Marianne Jean-Baptiste as scientists supervising the experiment.

With stone faces, they deliver such by-the-numbers dialogue as: "There's one thing I know for certain: If we can't stop him, he ain't going to stop himself."

Unlike "The Silence of the Lambs" and "Seven," both of which "The Cell" weakly echoes—along with everything from "Hellraiser" to "2001: A Space Odyssey"—there are no characters you care the least bit about in Mark Protosevich's screenplay.

What "The Cell" is really about—and what aficionados will cut straight to on DVD—are the lengthy sequences inside Carl's brain, in which Catherine appears as everything from an S&M pinup to the Virgin Mary.

Lopez isn't really required to do much more than look great—and, boy, does she.

The production design, effects and costumes are so dazzlingly executed that it's almost possible to overlook the hackneyed view of Carl's psyche, which was twisted by his (yawn) sadistic father.

Will Catherine bond with Carl's inner child? Or will she be trapped in his twisted mind?

We've seen it all before, and better—including such stomach-churning sights as intestines being pulled out of someone's navel.

"The Cell" is definitely a movie where there's less than meets the eye.

NEWSDAY, 8/18/00, Part II/p. B3, Jan Stuart

The title of "The Cell" refers to a stark, glass-and-tile-encased chamber in which a deranged man locks up women, containing them for 40 hours until he fills it with water and drowns them. Like another serial killer of fictional notoriety, Hannibal Lecter, he is a sadist of unfathomable proportions. Unlike Lecter, he is not conscious and incapable of doing any more harm for the better part of the film.

Instead of a battle of wits, we witness a duel of painterly visions. Closer in spirit to the psychedelic fantasias of "Altered States" than the ghoulish psycho-suspense of "The Silence of the Lambs," "The Cell" offers up an extravaganza of fabulous dreamscapes and disturbingly surreal nightmares. Seekers of cheap thrills might want to go elsewhere: The goose bumps delivered by this film are of a more aesthetic sort, and look to have been obtained at considerable expense.

Vincent D'Onofrio plays the film's resident sicko, Carl Stargher, who lures his victims with a sweet albino German Shepherd and gradually transforms them into big, lifeless dolls. It's a very elaborate operation—movie serial killers have come such a long way since Jack the Ripper—made even more demented by the steel rings piercing Carl's back, which enable him to indulge kinky impulses that you probably don't want to read about over your scrambled eggs and coffee.

Once Carl is nabbed by the police after sinking into a catatonic state, however, his grotesque pathology takes a back seat to the dreamlike detective work employed to track down the next victim he has squirreled away. Enter FBI agent Peter Novak (Vince Vaughan) and therapist Catherine Deane (Jennifer Lopez), who uses a futuristic technology to enter the subconscious minds of her patients and manipulate their fears in healing ways.

Directed by video and commercial director Tarsem Singh, "The Cell" is dominated by a series of extravagantly intense, dreamlike canvases that realize the subconscious meanderings of its villains and heroes in floridly symbolic terms. This high art/sci-fi twist goes a long way toward upgrading it from crass exploitation flick into a realm of visual experimentation that links the movie to the earliest surreal visions of silent film pioneer Georges Melies.

Interesting as all of its leads are, the real stars of "The Cell" are cinematographer Paul Laufer and designers Tom Fodden, Eiko Ishioka and April Napier, who crib from a legacy of 20th-

Century artists that references everything from the glass-encased animal sectionings of Damien Hirst to the body-engulfing capes of Martha Graham dancers. With these inspirations, the dark-dungeon thoughts of Carl are contrasted with the brightly colored Madonna and Child fantasies of Catherine, fashioned after Mexican religious icons. And a desert landscape dappled with snow and cherry blossoms hearkens back to Kurosawa's anthology film, "Dreams."

The imagery is so lush that, once it goes away, we are reminded of the banal damsel-in-distress machinery that is propelling the picture. Taken on its own boldly visual terms, "The Cell" can be enjoyed as a stroll through a contemporary museum of your purplest imaginings. How far we've come since Salvador Dali mined the dreams of Alfred Hitchcock.

SIGHT AND SOUND, 11/00, p. 46, Ken Hollings

California, the present. Catherine Deane is a psychotherapist employed by the Campbell Center to experiment with a new treatment that permits her to enter the minds of catatonic patients. The technique, involving drugs and an advanced cybernetic bodysuit, is being used on a comatose boy who fails to show any signs of recovery. Meanwhile psychotic serial killer Carl Stargher suffers an irreversible neural breakdown following his arrest by the FBI and falls into a coma.

With Stargher's last female victim still imprisoned in his secret cell, which is slowly filling with water, the FBI ask Deane to search Stargher's mind for information about the girl's whereabouts. However, when Deane becomes trapped within Stargher's sadistic inner fantasies, believing them to be real, FBI agent Peter Novak enters the killer's mind to rescue her. Novak also uncovers a clue to the cell's location, and while he rushes to free the trapped girl, Deane invites Stargher into her own mind, where she overcomes his murderous nature, allowing him to die in peace. Equipped with this new therapeutic method of bringing subjects into her own consciousness, Deane returns to treating her young patient.

The latest sign of Hollywood's unconsummated digital affair with virtual reality, Tarsem Singh's directorial debut occupies the hinterland between the deep sensory immersion experiments of the 90s and a 60s LSD head trip. "According to the FBI," agent Novak remarks to his travelling companion, psychotherapist Deane, after his journey through the inner world of a comatose serial killer, "you put me through a drug-fuelled mind-bender". There's little evidence to say he's wrong. The film vibrates with references to psychedelic mental overload, from Howard Shore's resonant score featuring the Master Musicians of Jajouka and dissonant orchestral references to Ligeti and the Beatle's, "A Day in the Life" to the similarity between the vertiginous hallucinatory lightshow that greets Novak's entry into killer Stargher's consciousness and that experienced by astronaut Bowman at the end of *2001: A Space Odyssey* (1968).

The Cell establishes an intriguing correlation between Deane's pad and the serial killer's workshop; the ingenious paraphernalia assembled by Stargher for his sexualised murders finds a direct counterpart in the lush contents of Deane's apartment, where she is shown sitting at her iMac smoking a joint, listening to dub reggae. This attention to detail is typical of Tarsem (he tends to be known only by his first name): a prize-winning director of television commercials and music videos, he loads the screen with a dizzying display of gimcracks and references to such eclectic cultural artefacts as Piranesi's *Carceri* engravings, Oscar Schlemmer's Bauhaus costume designs and Damien Hirst's artworks. There's plenty here to keep the eye busy, but this kind of visual chewing-gum can't completely divert attention from the fact that Mark Protosevich's patchy script—which at times resembles *The Silence of the Lambs* rewritten by Carlos Castaneda—doesn't have much else going for it. With little room for either narrative detail or character development, Tarsem's exploration of a deranged mind soon loses momentum. By the time Deane gets in touch with Stargher's inner child, still tortured by memories of his abusive father, the dense fetishism of the original imagery has given way to camp metaphysical banalities and sketchy plot resolutions.

There's also something vaguely trite about characters having to remind each other of what is real and what is fantasy in a film where the FBI can assemble scores of heavily armed police at a moment's notice and on the flimsiest of circumstantial evidence. However, Tarsem's consummate ability to create small glossy fantasies out of inanimate consumer durables provides *The Cell* with its greatest and most hallucinatory irony. The material world that exists outside the main protagonists' minds has been captured with such close and loving attention to surface detail that every car, helicopter, building facade and interior threaten to take on a life of their own and overwhelm the poorly defined humans that move among them. Beyond computer-generated space, hallucinogenic drugs and violently aberrant psychologies, it seems that television commercials still constitute the ultimate virtual reality.

VILLAGE VOICE, 8/29/00, p. 135, Amy Taubin

The summer's silliest cinematic experience has to be *The Cell*, ostensibly a slightly futuristic serial killer movie but, subtextually, a commercial for the Saatchi collection. Carrying to extremes the postmodern notion that art is never original, director Tarsem Singh not only uses *The Silence of the Lambs, Se7en*, and *Strange Days* as ur-texts but scavenges from 20 years of music videos (including his own for R.E.M.'s "Losing My Religion") and 35 years of art references—which are amusing enough but absurd as a hook for a mass-market movie.

This hook is made physical in the form of metal rings screwed into the back of a serial killer (Vincent D'Onofrio) who hangs himself from them à la performance artist Ron Athey. Other prominent sources are Joseph Beuys, Joan Jonas, Lisa Yuskavage, Matthew Barney, the Chapman brothers, Damien Hirst—the sliced horse is hilarious even if you see the joke coming long in advance. Singh seems hell-bent on including every piece from the "Sensation" show. What with the Master Musicians of Jajouka on the soundtrack and Eiko Ishioka's gorgeous, kabuki-like costumes, *The Cell* is a bit of a multiculti experience as well.

If you aren't intent on keeping an art checklist, I don't know how you'll get through *The Cell* without falling asleep. Singh isn't big on suspense or shock. The ludicrous plot devolves into a triangle formed by the killer, a psychotherapist (Jennifer Lopez) who enters his unconscious via some top-secret electro-chemical device, and an FBI agent (Vince Vaughn) whose mission is to locate the killer's final victim before it's too late.

In lieu of acting, Lopez, Vaughn, and D'Onofrio engage in some kind of pouting competition the rules of which only they are aware. (Lopez's most memorable moment comes when Singh catches her casually examining the interior of her fridge, the curving line of her buttocks approximating the sinuous shape of the Sahara sand dunes where we first encounter her.) The scene where the gold-dusted D'Onofrio plaintively sings "Mairzy Doats" as he disembowels a prone, struggling Vaughn takes digitized wet dreams to a new level (warning: this is not a pull quote), but, overall, *The Cell* is not nearly the mindfuck it wants to be.

Also reviewed in:
CHICAGO TRIBUNE, 8/18/00, Friday/p. A, Mark Caro
NEW YORK TIMES, 8/18/00, p. E7, Elvis Mitchell
VARIETY, 8/14-20/00, p. 17, Emanuel Levy
WASHINGTON POST, 8/18/00, p. C1, Stephen Hunter
WASHINGTON POST, 8/18/00, Weekend/p. 36, Michael O'Sullivan

CENTER STAGE

A Columbia Pictures release of a Laurence Mark production. *Producer:* Laurence Mark. *Director:* Nicholas Hytner. *Screenplay:* Carol Heikkinen. *Director of Photography:* Geoffrey Simpson. *Editor:* Tariq Anwar. *Music:* George Fenton. *Music Editor:* Graham Sutton and Stephanie Lowry. *Choreographer:* Susan Stroman, (Jonathan's Ballet) Christopher Wheeldon, (Swan Lake) Lev Ivanov, (Romeo and Juliet) Kenneth MacMillan, and (Stars and Stripes) George Balanchine. *Sound:* Michael Barosky and (music) John Richards. *Sound Editor:* Tim Hands. *Casting:* Daniel Swee. *Production Designer:* David Gropman. *Art Director:* Peter Rogness. *Set Decorator:* Susan Bode. *Costumes:* Ruth Myers. *Make-up:* Naomi Donne. *Running time:* 113 minutes. *MPAA Rating:* PG-13.

CAST: Amanda Schull (Jody); Christine Dunham (Audition Teacher); Stephen Stout (Mr. Sawyer); Maryann Plunkett (Mrs. Sawyer); Laura Hicks (Nervous Mother); Barbara Caruso and Jeffrey Hayenga (ABA Scouts); Zoë Saldana (Eva); Victor Anthony (Thomas); Karen

Shallo (Mother at Audition);   Carlo Alban and Giselle Daly (Eva's Friends);   Ethan Stiefel
(Cooper);   Susan May Pratt (Maureen);   Shakiem Evans (Erik);   Ilia Kulik (Sergei);   Sascha
Radetsky (Charlie);   Peter Gallagher (Jonathan);   Donna Murphy (Juliette);   Lisa Leguillo
(ABA Girl's Class Teacher);   Robert Montano (ABA Pas De Deux Class Teacher);   Megan
Pepin (Anna);   Victoria Born (Emily);   Kirk Peterson (ABA Boys' Class Teacher);   Julie Kent
(Kathleen);   Debra Monk (Nancy);   Sandra Brown, Elizabeth Gaither, Oksana Konobeyeva,
and Ekaterina Shelkanova, (Swan Lake Soloists);   Elizabeth Hubbard (Joan Miller);   Eion
Bailey (Jim);   Nancy McDoniel and Sandy Hamilton (Gala Patrons);   Olga Merediz (ABA
Receptionist);   Elvis Crespo and Giselle Tcherniak (Salsa Singers);   Jamie Bonelli and Micki
Paley (Girls at Salsa Club);   Randy Pearlstein (Jim's Friend);   Nancy Hess (Sergei's Salsa
Partner);   Lovette George (Jazz Class Receptionist);   Priscilla Lopez (Jazz Class Teacher);
Brenda Thomas Denmark (Jonathan's Secretary);   Warren Carlyle (Cooper's Assistant);   Marcia
Jean Kurtz (Emily's Mother);   Aesha Ash and Sean Stewart (Jonathan's Ballet Soloists).

LOS ANGELES TIMES, 5/12/00, Calendar/p. 16, Jan Stuart

[The following review by Jan Stuart appeared in a slightly different form in
NEWSDAY, 5/12/00, Part II/p. B3.]

From "The Red Shoes" to "The Turning Point," dramatic films about the ballet world have
begged the question: How is it that such a serious and disciplined performing art attracts such
silly and chaotic people?

The callow young dance aspirants in "Center Stage" weren't even born when Mikhail
Baryshnikov flaunted his famous leaps in "The Turning Point" (1977). But the tensions and
obstacles are as unchanging as the Lincoln Center plaza where his co-stars Shirley MacLaine and
Anne Bancroft ripped each other's hair out: sex, family, competition and making choices.

"Center Stage" is a quintessential backstage-movie cocktail, about four parts hooey to one part
reality, chased by a big swig of high-stepping razzle-dazzle. Written with transparent ink by
Carol Heikkinen, it follows the tribulations of a sextet of ballet students as they train at the
ultra-competitive American Ballet Academy (helmed by that swan prince of arrogance, Peter
Gallagher).

All of the neophytes have been cast with professional dancers, which makes for some wobbly
toed performances. There is the naive but determined Jody (Amanda Schull); the rebellious,
smart-mouthed Eva (Zoe Saldana); the bulimic diva-in-training, Maureen (a convincing Susan
May Pratt); the All-American hunk from Seattle, Charlie (Sascha Radetsky); the Russian roue,
Sergei (Ilia Kulik); and the token black homosexual with no personal life, Erik (Shakiem Evans).

Typically, "Center Stage" hyperventilates in an effort to show that all male dancers are not
pansies, so Heikkinen unambiguously asserts the sexual orientation of every guy in their first
lines of dialogue. Within minutes, Erik is cruising Charlie, Charlie is swooning for Jody, Jody
is falling for international star Cooper (American Ballet Theater headliner Ethan Stiefel, a rather
terrible actor), Maureen is succumbing to the advances of a premed student, and Sergei is
striking out at every turn.

We don't really care about any of this, because "Center Stage" only really kicks in when it is
dancing, which is about half the time. Susan Stroman, the reigning Miss Thing of Broadway
hoofing, makes her film choreography debut with mixed results. Predictably, her best work is
the "Flashdance"-like stuff at a disco or in a Broadway dance class. The more ambitious
crossover piece at the big closing performance, weaving urban iconography into classical ballet
language, might seem clever and even electric in live performance but seems a bit dumb as
captured on film.

It's rarely boring, because director Nicholas Hytner ("The Crucible," "The Madness of King
George") knows how to energize theater-oriented work. But he's used to far better material, and
it feels like he's slumming here. He has recruited a dandy group of New York actors to play the
grown-ups, so we can revel in Debra Monk as an overbearing stage mother and the wonderful
Donna Murphy, who penetrates the artifice with genuine feeling as the most sympathetic of the
dance instructors.

"A Chorus Line's" charismatic Priscilla Lopez makes an exuberant impression as a jazz dance teacher, an all-too-brief cameo that leaves us with the sobering suggestion of what awaits those who are lucky enough to grab their 15 minutes of dance fame.

NEW YORK POST, 5/12/00, p. 51, Lou Lumenick

Let's get right to the bottom line: "Center Stage" is the best dance movie since "Flashdance. "It's not surprising to read that Columbia Pictures Chairman Amy Pascal—whose mentor, the late Dawn Steel, produced "Flashdance"—personally commissioned this patchwork of characters, situations and clichés that draws on practically every dance movie ever made.

What is surprising is that what results is rousing pop entertainment—largely thanks to spectacular dance numbers by red-hot Broadway choreographer Susan Stroman ("Contact" and "The Music Man"), as well as the sure-footed direction that Nicholas Hytner ("The Objection of My Affection") has given the large cast of unknowns.

Made with the cooperation of the American Ballet Theater, "Center Stage" follows a group of students at the American Ballet Academy—a barely fictionalized stand-in for the ABT's School of American Ballet—through months of grueling preparations for a recital that will either land them jobs—or end their lifetime dreams of dancing careers.

There's the girl (Amanda Schull) determined to make the cut despite bad feet and the wrong body type; another (Susan May Pratt) with anorexia and an overbearing stage mother (Debra Monk); the wisecracking gay black male dancer (Shakiem Evans)—and the gifted Latina (Zoe Saldana) whose 'tude puts her on a collision course with an imperious teacher (Donna Murphy).

In short, no cliché has been left unturned by screenwriter Carol Heikkinen, who actually has people say things like, "I'm not dancing for them anymore—I'm dancing for me!"

The movie makes a half-hearted attempt to appeal beyond its target demographic by cooking up conflict between the company's artistic director (Peter Gallagher in a riff on Zack of "A Chorus Line") and a rakish star dancer (real-life ABT superstar Ethan Stiefel) who's choreographing a number for a student workshop that prankishly spoofs his rival—when he isn't wooing one of the dancers.

Movie buffs will recognize bits of "The Turning Point," "Dirty Dancing," "Saturday Night Fever," and other films stretching back as far as "42nd Street. "

But in the end, it's the young performers and the dances—especially the rousing, high-energy finale, which has Stiefel arriving in black leather on a motorcycle amid high-kicking ballerinas in swan drag—that put "Center Stage" en point.

SIGHT AND SOUND, 11/00, p. 47, David Jays

New York, the present. Jody auditions for the exclusive American Ballet Academy, which is attached to a leading dance company, and is offered a place. She shares a room with students Eva and Maureen. In class, Jody struggles to hone her technique, while Eva resists the teachers' discipline. Maureen's vigilant weight-watching is turning into a serious eating disorder, as the medical student she dates realises. Warned by Jonathan, the academy's artistic director, that she may not last the course, Jody explores less inhibited forms of dance, at a salsa club and a class in jazz dance, where she meets Cooper Nielsen, the star of the adult company. Cooper and Jody have a fling. Although he includes Jody in a piece he is choreographing for the end-of-year show, Cooper ends the relationship.

As the show approaches, Eva practises with greater determination, and Jody is encouraged by her fellow student Charlie. At the last moment, Maureen pulls out of her classical show-piece, allowing Eva to take her place, and Jody scores a triumph in Cooper's work. Jonathan offers her a place in the adult company, but she decides to join Cooper's new company instead.

As in a classic school story, the ballet students in *Center Stage* are released from parental control from the start. After the opening audition, they join the alternative family of an exacting dance academy. Jody's parents are frumpy fuss-budgets who really don't get the lure of dance—they want her to study in Indiana, after all—and only Maureen's scheming mother, who works at the school, remains, a cold-blooded blood relative. Wolfish Peter Gallagher leads a faculty of near-parody adults, the men seductive cads, the women steely ("Eyes off the mirror, please") and glamorous—the prima ballerina swans around in a huge brimmed hat like a Gatsbyesque vision.

Nicholas Hytner's previous films, like his stage work, are polished but disengaged, as if they can't bear too much reality. The adolescent passions of *Center Stage*, nurtured in the academy's hothouse, suit him perfectly. Everyone is self-obsessed, intense and silly: dance an teen television both value a pubescent sheen, and this is *Dawson's Creek* in toe shoes. Fluffy bunny Jody bumbles through classes, flinching when the teachers demand, "Jody—flutter!" She is all soft pliancy, white swan to Maureens' brutally svelte black, and the film traces the loss of her emotional puppy fat.

Hytner has an eye for the process of theatre—the most moving scene in his debut film *The Madness of King George* shows the monarch fumbling for his wit while reading *King Lear*. The relentless grind that shapes the students' lives is not shirked—there are fascinating sequences of tenderising pointe shoes and bandaging vulnerable toes. Close up, the pointes are seen to be scuffed, the tendons raw. The spectre of eating disorders also haunts the film—this is a world where incaustious snacking can push you out of the competition: a glistening spread of pizzas and fries tempts Maureen to go to the bad much as a case of jewels might have lured her Victorian counterpart.

Like *Stage Door* (1937), *Center Stage* presents a dream of New York, the school's vast windows giving on to gleaming skyscrapers, a backdrop of sunny aspiration. Attractively open, the studios also invite ceaseless scrutiny. Their wide vistas alternate with the gossipy clusters of dorm and bathroom novices crammed in windowless cells. The school seems a panopticon of surveillance and mortification.

Ballet's rigours are counterpointed with the salsa club, rippling with Latin glitz, and the chat and tumble of the public class in jazz dance, where people munch muffins and hug. Hytner and screenwriter Carol Heikkinen register resistance to ballet's conventions and containment. Rebellious student Eva chews gum and talks sass, but dance is her every movement—she even grinds out a cigarette with a perfectly pointed toe. Cooper, the adult company's arrogant star, also has his iconoclasm painfully signalled—open shirt, Harley storming through the sunset, choreographing appalling modern dance and urging everyone to keep it "real". His routine for the end-of-year show is the film's only big embarrassment: featuring leather trousers, a motorbike and scanty black underwear, it feels like a pelvis-pushing Pirelli calendar.

Non-naturalistic changes of costume and weaving camera nonetheless pay homage to Gene Kelly's choreographic fantasy sequences, and *Center Stage* also provides a cheerfully hackneyed compilation of iconic moments from backstage movies: wishful neophytes sneak on to the empty stage for a premonition of stardom; *two* girls who start out as nobodies end up as stars. Eva gets to swan in tulle against a starlit backdrop, and to vow, magnificently, "I'm not doing it for them—I'm doing it for me!" while Jody gets to bump and grind, a child no more.

VILLAGE VOICE, 5/16/00, p. 140, Elizabeth Zimmer

People who succeed at ballet are good at following directions; they take thousands of lessons over a decade and then get jobs before their peers head off to college. The great majority of them are white.

So the most encouraging thing about *Center Stage* is its multiracial cast. Of six students chosen from the entire graduating class of the top New York ballet school to join its affiliated company, two are black. One (Shakiem Evans) has his leg in a cast, and the other (Zoë Saldana), a girl from a rough part of Boston who's always late for class, has just defied school policy to secretly replace a friend in the school's prestigious workshop performance. In real life the former person would be deferred, at best, and the latter thrown out, but this is a fantasy in which everybody's dreams come true. The shy kids develop confidence, the arrogant ones grow centered and wise, the girl with the "wrong body" (Amanda Schull) emerges as a star in a new fusion jazz troupe and gains the courage to blow off a bad guy.

Nicholas Hytner's movie might be subtitled *Beverly Hills 90210 Goes to Juilliard*. The young performers, many of them trained dancers making their screen debuts, are operating in sitcom country (albeit on the Upper West Side), while the adults (Peter Gallagher convincingly impersonating NYCB director Peter Martins, Debra Monk as a manipulative stage mother, and

Donna Murphy as a teacher who spots the professional inside the brat) give strong performances. Straddling their worlds is Ethan Stiefel, in real life a motorcycle-riding star at American Ballet Theatre, and here a jilted dancer who gets into pissing contests (they take the form of multiple pirouettes) with rivals; his ex-girlfriend, now attached to the company chief, is given genuine warmth by ABT principal Julie Kent.

There's a lot of choreography (by Susan Stroman and Christopher Wheeldon, as well as chunks of Ivanov, MacMillan, and Balanchine), but it remains in the background; the camera often cuts away from the stage to follow confrontations in the lobby. *Center Stage* pays lip service to the seriousness of craft but won't let us watch the dancing.

Also reviewed in:
CHICAGO TRIBUNE, 5/12/00, Friday/p. E, Monica Eng
NEW REPUBLIC, 6/5/00, p. 27, Stanley Kauffmann
NEW YORK TIMES, 5/12/00, p. E10, A.O. Scott
NEW YORKER, 5/29/00, p. 142, David Denby
VARIETY, 5/8-14/00, p. 49, Emanuel Levy
WASHINGTON POST, 5/12/00, p. C5, Rita Kempley
WASHINGTON POST, 5/12/00, Weekend/p. 53, Desson Howe

CHALK

A Tenderloin Action Group/Pacific Rim Media presentation. *Producer:* Rand Crook and Ethan Sing. *Director:* Rob Nilsson. *Screenplay:* Don Bajema and Rob Nilsson. *Director of Photography:* Mickey Freeman. *Editor:* David Schickele. *Music:* Tim Alexander. *Sound:* Jeff Roth. *Production Designer:* Lee Patzer. *Running time:* 135 minutes. *MPAA Rating:* Not Rated.

WITH: Kelvin Han Yee; Don Bajema; Denise Concetta Cavaliere; Johnnie Reese; Edwin Johnson; Destiny Costa; John Tidwell; Chris McDonald.

NEW YORK POST, 8/25/00, p. 50, V.A. Musetto

Rob Nilsson's low-budget drama "Chalk" is unremittingly dark, both in its murky, nearly lightless cinematography and in its raw, edgy subject matter.

Things start off leisurely, with Nilsson introducing the misfits who inhabit a rundown pool hall in Richmond, Calif, where the entire movie unfolds.

But the momentum builds, and a crucial pool match provides an exciting, if somewhat gory, finale.

The cast is made up mostly of homeless people from the streets of San Francisco. They give such realistic performances that at times "Chalk" has the feel of a documentary.

Special note should be made of Kelvin Han Yee as the central character, a pool shark who finds himself in the most important game of his life, and Denise Concetta Cavaliere as his sexy, white-trash girlfriend.

Nilsson is an outsider himself Although his first flick, "Northern Lights," won the Palm d'Or at Cannes in 1978, he has had trouble getting financing for nearly every film he has made since then.

The director thus can identify with his characters and with his actors. And it shows in each frame of this difficult but rewarding film.

VILLAGE VOICE, 8/29/00, p. 135, Amy Taubin

Just in time to put Lars von Trier and his hype-happy Dogma spawn in perspective, Rob Nilsson's 1996 *Chalk*—an Oedipal drama so raw it feels like falling facedown onto a pile of bricks—is finally getting a New York opening. Nilsson, whose first movie, *Northern Lights,* won the Cannes Camera d'Or in 1979, has been shooting features on video and transferring them to 35mm for release since the mid '80s. *Signal 7* (1985) exposed the world of nighttime San Francisco cabbies. *Heat and Sunlight* (1988), a Sundance Grand Prize winner, plunged into the obsessions attendant on the end of a love affair.

For the past 10 years, Nilsson has been the creative force behind the Tenderloin Action Group, an acting workshop mostly for street people from San Francisco's skid row. *Chalk* grew out of Nilsson's involvement with the group, where video is used as a teaching tool, but in no way does it seem like a workshop film.

A slow starter, *Chalk* is at least 30 minutes under way before the plot kicks in and we get a glimmer of how much is at stake for Watson (Edwin Johnson) and his two sons, T.C. (Kelvin Han Yee) and Jones (Johnnie Reese). Watson, the 60-year-old black proprietor of the Crabtree, a vast, rundown pool hall, is dying of lung cancer. Jones, the son he fathered with a Korean woman, is jealous of Watson's love for his adopted son T.C., a Chinese American pool prodigy. He pushes T.C. into a big-money match with Dorian (Don Bajema), a ranking pro, knowing that T.C. lacks the confidence to win.

Chalk's finale is a 40-minute match that will have you holding your breath whether or not you know or care anything about pool. As adroit as Nilsson is in depicting the game and its rituals, it's the underlying crisis of masculine identity that mesmerizes. Like Watson, a star who choked during a big match and turned to heroin to forget, T.C. is terrified of failure. But so is the older, crazed Dorian, who prepares for the battle by having his girlfriend stick a pool cue up his ass.

Bajema, a Nilsson regular, sufficiently resembles Tom Cruise to suggest what the fledgling pool shark of Scorsese's *The Color of Money* would have looked like if he stayed in the game long enough for his dazzling smile to turn to a rictus grin. He and the smoldering, volatile Yee are the only professionals in the large cast, most of whom were drawn from the Tenderloin Action Group. Nilsson gets convincing performances from almost everyone, but what gives the film extra weight is the sense that these are not just actors trying to enhance their careers but real people seizing a chance for immortality.

Nilsson combines a performance-oriented, Cassavetes-like realism with a painterly, expressionist sense of color and composition. At first, *Chalk* seems like a slice of life, but by the end it has the heightened quality of a pool-hall legend. Collaborating with cameraman Mickey Freeman, Nilsson exploits the mobility, intimacy, and low-light capability of the video camera. There are long sequences where every shot is a surprise without being flashy or gratuitous. With an electronic palette made up of a dozen shades of brown punctuated with hits of acid greens and iridescent violet, *Chalk* is in every sense a dark film. Its beauty is the result of pushing the unique qualities of video to their limit rather than trying to approximate the look of shooting on celluloid. Nilsson's long-standing commitment to video production would place him smack in the middle of Indiewood's digital revolution, if his vision weren't so bleakly existential and unsparing.

Also reviewed in:
CHICAGO TRIBUNE, 10/27/00, Friday/p. Q, John Petrakis
NEW YORK TIMES, 8/25/00, p. E18, Dave Kehr
VARIETY, 4/29-5/5/96, p. 134, Dennis Harvey

CHARLIE'S ANGELS

A Columbia Pictures release of a Leonard Goldberg/Flower Films/Tall Trees production. *Executive Producer:* Betty Thomas, Jenno Topping, and Joseph M. Caracciolo. *Producer:* Leonard Goldberg, Drew Barrymore, and Nancy Juvonen. *Director:* McG (Joseph McGinty Nichol). *Screenplay:* Ryan Rowe, Ed Solomon, and John August. *Based on the television series created by:* Ivan Goff and Ben Roberts. *Director of Photography:* Russell Carpenter. *Editor:* Wayne Wahrman and Peter Teschner. *Music:* Edward Shearmur. *Music Editor:* Michael T. Ryan and Daryl K. Kell. *Choreographer:* Marguerite Derricks. *Sound:* Willie Burton and (music) Chris Fogel and Dan Wallin. *Sound Editor:* Michael J. Benavente. *Casting:* Justine

Baddeley and Kim Davis-Wagner. *Production Designer:* J. Michael Riva. *Art Director:* David F. Klassen and Richard F. Mays. *Set Designer:* Clare Scarpulla, Dawn Brown Manser, and Noelle King. *Set Decorator:* Lauri Gaffin. *Special Effects:* Paul Lombardi. *Special Effects (Martial Arts):* Yuen Cheung-Yan. *Costumes:* Joseph G. Aulisi. *Make-up:* Kimberly Greene. *Special Make-up Effects:* Rob Bottin. *Stunt Coordinator:* Vic Armstrong. *Running time:* 92 minutes. *MPAA Rating:* PG-13.

CAST: Cameron Diaz (Natalie); Drew Barrymore (Dylan); Lucy Liu (Alex); Bill Murray (Bosley); Sam Rockwell (Eric Knox); Tim Curry (Roger Corwin); Kelly Lynch (Vivian Wood); Crispin Glover (Thin Man); John Forsythe (Voice of Charlie Townsend); Matt Le Blanc (Jason); LL Cool J (Mr. Jones); Tom Green (Chad); Luke Wilson (Pete); Sean Whalen (Pasqual); Tim Dunaway (Flight Attendant); Alex Trebek (Himself); Raleigh Wilson (Reform Officer); Mark Ryan (Fencing Opponent); Bobby Ore (Driving Instructor); Guy Oseary (DJ); Joe Duer (UPS Delivery Guy); Matthew Frauman and Reggie Hayes (Red Star Systems Techies); Melissa McCarthy (Doris); Bob Stephenson and Ned Bellamy (Red Star Systems Directors); Raymond Patterson (Director's Buddy); Bjorn Flor (Red Star Systems Security Guard); Gaven E. Lucas and Michael Barryte (Boys); Andrew Wilson (Corwin's Driver); Branden Williams (Assistant Director); Michiko Nishiwaki (Stuntwoman); Frank Marocco (Accordionist); Darrell Pfingsten (Partygoer); Jimmy Calloway and Kevin Grevioux (Bouncers); Michael Papajohn (Bathroom Thug); Jim Palmer and Shawn Woods (Shooters); Kenny Endoso and Tom Garner (Getaway Drivers); Isaac C. Singleton, Jr. (Kidnapper).

LOS ANGELES TIMES, 11/3/00, Calendar/p. 1, Kenneth Turan

"Charlie's Angels" is a potato chip of a movie. Tasty and lightweight, it's fine for a cinematic snack, if that's what you're looking for. Making it an entire meal, however, really isn't advisable.

Starring Cameron Diaz, Drew Barrymore and Lucy Liu as "an elite crime-fighting unit backed by an anonymous millionaire" and based on a 1970s TV series that no one ever confused with "Masterpiece Theater," "Charlie's Angels" has morphed into a more entertaining movie than you might expect, especially compared with the fiasco that was "The Mod Squad."

For one thing, the film's writers, those who got credit (Ryan Rowe and Ed Solomon, and John August) plus the horde that apparently did not, have en masse studied the series' episodes with the zeal of PhD candidates in popular culture, peppering the script with tough questions like "Does he have any enemies?" and generic comments on the order of "This is where you come in, Angels," and "Angels, break it down."

This "Charlie's Angels" also has a definite sense of humor about what it's doing, practically a necessity for a venture of this type. Any picture having an opening sequence highlighting an in-flight film called "T.J. Hooker: The Movie" is not in any danger of taking itself too seriously.

"Angels," moreover, is the latest studio venture (is a kung fu remake of "Gilligan's Island" next?) to wholeheartedly embrace the glories of Hong Kong-style martial arts action. With James Bond stunts and fight scenes choreographed by Cheung-Yan Yuen (whose brother did the honors for "The Matrix"), "Charlie's Angels" understands that it's incumbent on films like this to really move.

Yet though all this is fun and engaging in short bursts (it does not come as a surprise that debuting director McG's previous work is in commercials and music videos), it wears thin and strains our patience when stretched to cover even this film's brief 92-minute length.

Part of the problem is that the insistent freneticism of this style of filmmaking flirts with overkill. Squeezing all that deadly kicking as well as some 40 songs ("Push the tempo" shouts one especially apt lyric) into so short a space is exhausting, a gimmicky letdown on a par with the director's three-letter name.

As in the TV show, the Angels never get to meet Charlie (voiced, as he was decades ago, by John Forsythe) and instead take their marching orders from the suave Bosley. Bill Murray, an actor who can make anything funny, has the role, and though action has never been counted as his forte, he is amusing as always.

The Angels are hired this time around by Vivian Wood (a convincing Kelly Lynch), whose boss, soft-wear entrepreneur Eric Knox (Sam Rockwell) has been brazenly kidnapped. The suspicion naturally falls on media kingpin Roger Corwin (Tim Curry) and a possible henchperson known only as Thin Man (Crispin Glover).

In addition to trying to sort out the implications of the crime—"you can imagine how dangerous it would be," someone says with a straight face, "if this got into the wrong hands"—the Angels have their love lives to deal with. Liu's Alex is involved with action star Jason (Matt LeBlanc), Diaz's Natalie is eyeing bartender Pete (Luke Wilson), while Barrymore's Dylan is embroiled with a forlorn sea captain named Chad (Tom Green), her real-life beau).

Some of these situations, as movie situations will, involve dialogue, but though adroit visually, McG has no gift for the spoken word and whenever characters talk for a minute or two, the film rolls over and plays dead. There are, after all, only so many times you can cut to tongue-in-cheek shots of one of the Angels rapturously tossing her hair.

The film also reaches into the past for its sexual politics, with mildly risque language (example: "My hands aren't going anywhere near your staff") going hand in hand, so to speak, with low-cut, tight-fighting costumes and more loving shots of well-built rear ends than a month of Dodge Truck commercials. No doubt this is what original executive producer Leonard Goldberg means when he says his show "may have been the beginning of the empowerment of women within popular culture."

Certainly empowered in terms of today's Hollywood (co-star Barrymore is a producer and one of the driving forces in getting the film made), the three actresses who play the Angels all seem to be having fun on screen. How well that translates depends on how much of an empty-calories mood you happen to be in.

NEW YORK, 11/13/00, p. 77, Peter Rainer

Unlike *Bagger Vance* [see Rainer's review], *Charlie's Angels* is about as unserious as you can get. Drew Barrymore, Cameron Diaz, and Lucy Liu play the modern-day Angels, spun off from the seventies TV series that, according to its executive producer Leonard Goldberg, "may have been the beginning of the empowerment of women within popular culture." (Goldberg is also one of the movie's producers.) What I remember most about the TV series is perfect teeth, big hair, and cleavage-in-motion.

What I recall most about the movie, which was directed by a music-video maven whose name, McG, sounds like a specialty burger, is the sight of three rowdy, kung fu-giddy chicks in stretch-fabric actionwear kicking butt. Their targets, a prize assortment of male crazies, include Tim Curry, whom I can never get enough of, and Crispin Glover, who is never quite all there. (He's turned neurasthenia into an acting style.) Bill Murray plays Bosley, the Angels' sidekick, or whatever he's supposed to be, and he's in prime crazy mode, too. The cast members seem to be having a high old time, and with sharper dialogue, an even higher time might have been had by all. Seventeen writers worked on the movie, only three for credit. No matter. Spandex and high spirits are a potent combo. The empowerment of women continues.

NEW YORK POST, 11/3/00, p. 47, Jonathan Foreman

This campy feature remake of the cheesy 1970s TV series is not only much more enjoyable than you might expect, it turns out to be a kind of Bond movie (with an action style based on Hong Kong kung fu flicks) updated for the post-feminist era, so that some fiercely liberated babes get to kick butt—and to shake it teasingly at the camera

The film's tongue is so firmly in cheek that, without being a spoof like "Dragnet" or "The Brady Bunch Movie," it has more in common with the "Austin Powers" films than with feature remakes of old TV series like "Mission: Impossible."

While the plot could hardly be less substantial (and you're unlikely to remember much of anything a minute or so after the end credits), "Charlie's Angels" is utterly good-hearted, mildly naughty fun that moves along at a cracking pace to the tune of a trendy pop score.

If you're one of the few people in America who somehow missed the original series, it was a shlocky but ostensibly serious crime show whose subtexts were the glory of bralessness and designer jeans.

The "Angels" were three cops-turned-private investigators who worked for a secretive millionaire named Charlie who communicated with them only by speakerphone and through a cuddly intermediary named Bosley (Bill Murray). (The cast changed over time, but there were always two sexy angels with lots of hair, and a cerebral one with a more sensible cut.)

The movie breaks from the original program by making Natalie (Cameron Diaz), Dylan (Drew Barrymore) and Alex (Lucy Liu) far less bimbonic as well as more athletic than their predecessors. They talk to each other in Japanese when they want to be discreet, and they have pasts and hobbies.

Alex, for example, is a former astronaut who tells her actor boyfriend Jason (Matt LeBlanc) she's a bikini-waxer in order not to intimidate him, and struggles without success to cook him edible meals.

Dylan is a tough, former bad girl with a soft spot for doofus guys that lands her and everyone else in trouble.

And Natalie is a klutzy, socially graceless former "Jeopardy" winner, hopeless with men, whose great wish is to be a dancer on "Soul Train."

The Angels' mission is to solve the kidnapping of Eric Knox (Sam Rockwell), the founder of a high-tech company. The suspects include Knox's partner Vivian Wood (slinky Kelly Lynch) and his chief rival Roger Corwin (the always fun Tim Curry), who runs the world's largest satellite network.

But the only thing the Angels and Bosley know for sure is that the kidnapping was carried out by a sinister-looking, chain-smoking "thin man" (Crispin Glover).

Recovering Knox and bringing the perpetrators to justice requires the Angels to go undercover as geishas, race-car drivers, waitresses, young men, belly dancers and, in the case of Alex, as a leather-clad corporate efficiency expert with dominatrix tendencies.

It also puts them and Bosley in mortal danger.

Director McG (yes, that's his name), a veteran of many commercials and videos, makes the most of the considerable sex appeal and comic talent of his three female stars, though he's clearly more comfortable speeding up or slowing down the action sequences than in scenes featuring dialogue.

Barrymore is as charming and sweetly seductive as ever, Liu more than holds her own in her second comic role (after "Shanghai Noon"), but it's Diaz who dominates the show as a lovable geek.

Murray gets surprisingly little to do as Bosley and Luke Wilson is wasted as a potential boyfriend for Natalie.

The weakest link in the movie is comic Tom Green, (now Mr. Drew Barrymore) as a half-witted fisherman and love interest called "The Chud."

NEWSDAY, 11/3/00, Part II/p. B3, Gene Seymour

Practically from its inception, "Charlie's Angels," the movie, has been one of those unavoidable facts of daily life. All your questions about its casting, its day-to-day production, its on-set squabbling could be answered on- and off-line throughout the past year or so.

The only question that couldn't—and didn't seem worth asking by the hype machinery—is why it needed to be made in the first place.

Let's not waste oxygen talking about the "iconography" of Farrah Fawcett, Jaclyn Smith, Kate Jackson, Cheryl Ladd or any of the other beauties cast as leads throughout the mid- to late-1970s run of that airhead detective show. Besides the buffed-up, bright-eyed, fluffy-haired appeal of those women, there's very little that I or anyone else I know can remember about the show besides its insipid scripts and implausible behavior.

The only way such an enterprise could possibly justify its existence would be for it to turn the original series' debits into assets. And that's just what this flaky, sugar-frosted souffle of a movie does. Brazenly vapid and aggressively silly, this big-screen "Charlie's Angels" flaunts its campy pedigree and earns for itself a wobbly but affecting status as postmodern (maybe post-postmodern) ironic spoof.

The movie's run-and-gun self-mockery asserts itself from the start with a passenger jet teaser staged and written as if it were a Mad magazine parody of its "Mission: Impossible 2" counterpart. ("Another movie made out of a TV series," growls one passenger upon seeing that

"T.J. Hooker: The Movie" is the in-flight entertainment.) The pace never lets up, juiced by martial arts sequences staged by stunt-master Cheung-Yan Yuen ("The Matrix") and a brash, busy visual flow orchestrated by first-time feature director and video whiz kid McG.

The angelic trio is drawn in the same thinly sketched lines as the original. Natalie (Cameron Diaz) is the fizzy blond klutz-savant in the Farrah-Jill mold, while Alex (Lucy Liu) is the steely technician in the Kate-Sabrina-um-"tradition." This leaves Dylan (co-producer Drew Barrymore), by default, as the worldly seductress in the same general neighborhood as Jaclyn-Kelly. Personally, I think they're all closer to the Cartoon Network's "Powerpuff Girls" than to the original "Angels." And I mean that as very high praise indeed.

All of them, of course, have their not-so-discreet charms. Liu leans somewhat on her "Ally McBeal" dour hellcat persona, but the softer edges applied here can only increase her market value. Barrymore looks both puppyish and mildly hangdog, but she's, like, so into being a street-smart superhero that it's infectious. (That so-called moonwalk's got to go, though.) Of the three, it's Diaz who has the most juice, courtesy of her luminous physical attributes and limber comedic energy.

What plot there is in this "Angels" movie is appropriately anorexic. There's this boyish high-tech tycoon Eric Knox (Sam Rockwell) who'd been kidnaped by a rival company owned by Roger Corwin (Tim Curry, once again, having fun), presumably in order to achieve global domination through cell phones. It turns out that what it'd really all about is a plot to kill the Angel's beloved Charlie (John Forsythe, once again, heard, never seen). Also involved are such trademark side villains as a leather-clad dominatrix (Kelly Lynch) and a thin, hawk-like man in black (Crispin Glover, most effective here for being seen, never heard.)

If what results from this pastiche is an elongated trailer, then at least it's a trailer with a sense of humor that never winks too broadly. (Having Bill Murray around as Charlie's man Friday, Bosley, helps maintain the movie's ironic edge.) The gauzy clatter of genre sight gags may remind some oldsters of such 1960s Euro-trash sex-and-spandex romps as "Modesty Blaise" and "Barbarella." It took almost 40 years, but someone finally made one of these things right.

Forty years from now, academics may want to deconstruct this movie into semiotic sushi. (Suggested topic: Why do all the male love interests, Rockwell, Luke Wilson and Matt LeBlanc, look alike? Discuss.) For now, it's best that you turn off your brain and dip into the meringue.

SIGHT AND SOUND, 1/01, p. 43, Andy Medhurst

California, the present. Natalie, Dylan and Alex, three crime-fighters known as Charlie's Angels because they work for the mysterious unseen millionaire Charlie, are given a new assignment. Computer genius Eric Knox has been kidnapped, and the prime suspect is Roger Corwin, a rival magnate who wishes to obtain Knox's revolutionary new voice-decoding technology. Knox's business partner Vivian Wood hires the Angels and their sidekick Bosley to rescue Knox.

After infiltrating Corwin's headquarters, they manage to free Knox. Corwin is later killed, however, and it becomes apparent that the Angels have been the victims of Knox and Wood's trickery. Knox has used them to gain access to Charlie, whom he blames for the death of his father in Vietnam. He plans to use his voice decoder to locate the reclusive Charlie's whereabouts by tracing one of his regular calls to the Angels. Discovering this, the Angels pursue Knox, Wood and their henchmen to a remote coastal hideout where they save Charlie and kill Knox with his own bomb.

Given the pre-release rumours of script rewrites, warring star egos, and the risk of using a novice director on such a big-budget project, it's a pleasant surprise to find that *Charlie's Angels,* the big-screen version of the 70s television series about a trio of female crime busters, is actually rather entertaining. The entertainment it offers is primarily that of the brain-free, spectacle-overload variety, but within those parameters it flourishes, shrewdly choosing to celebrate its own absurdities through strategic self-mockery. It embraces its own foolishness and encourages its audience to join in the party.

Its success pivots, inevitably, on the three central performances, and here we must borrow the words of that noted philosopher Meat Loaf and conclude that two out of three ain't bad. Cameron Diaz is fantastic, wittily playing on her beauty in several scenes which have no plausible function other than to set her admirers drooling (her early-morning underwear dance is already the subject of numerous sticky tributes on the internet). She has an old-style star power which lights up the screen the second she smiles, and the plot capitalises on this when she uses her appearance to exploit besotted men.

Drew Barrymore is wry and funny, snaring most of the good lines in her role as reformed rock chick Dylan, and she and Diaz have a real affinity in their comic exchanges. Lucy Liu, however, disappoints. Saddled with the most thankless role—rich, brainy, techno-wizard Alex—she is largely excluded from the film's comic discourse, smiling only in the goof-off out-takes that play before the final credits. Given little to do she does it glumly and grimly, which makes the triangular relationship between the Angels seem like two best friends having a great time while an interloper glares in from the sidelines.

First time director McG cut his teeth on television commercials and music videos, and this background serves him well here. The film's storyline is a mere peg on which to hang a series of showy action sequences and a succession of stardom-enhancement moments for the leads. The opening scene is a flagrantly flashy calling card, a mid-air hijack that bears no relation to the rest of the film other than to initiate the audience into its visual world of outlandish stunts and female flesh. The debt to the *Bond* series here is evident, much as the special-effects martial-arts devices used later tip their hat to *The Matrix*. Even in these, however, the need to frame the Angels in iconic poses takes precedence over any credibility of combat. The Angels bookend all their high-kicking assaults with static tableaux where they flex limbs and try to look menacing—throwing much the same shapes as Po does when she wants to impress the other Teletubbies.

What sets the film apart from its generic peers, of course, is its gender emphasis. Does placing women at the centre of an action picture lead to an interesting spin on conventional sexual politics? Those who recall the television series may be forgiven for doubting this, given that the series used an infinitesimal veneer of designer feminism to excuse its tendency to stuff its heroines into bikinis at every available opportunity. The film is more ambivalent: the Angels disrobe, display and jiggle wherever they can, and the central plot's nakedly Oedipal obsession with father-figures lends an undeniably patriarchal tone to the proceedings. Nonetheless, the sight of Diaz and Barrymore mowing down ranks of goons does carry a certain charge. It would be rash to call the film feminist, but its delight in the powerfulness of femininity does mark it out from all those action pictures where machismo is the governing religion.

TIME, 11/13/00, p. 112, Richard Schickel

What *Charlie's Angels* has going for it is a good joke about bikini waxing, another about blueberry muffins as lethal weapons, and a third about the difficulties of finding viable male companionship in Los Angeles. You would think any movie employing 17 writers (according to the Los Angeles *Times*) would have, let's say, 14 more funny lines—one per desperate scrivener.

Charlie's Angels also offers us cute, peppy Cameron Diaz as the most adorable of the Angels, Drew Barrymore as the most vulnerable of them (she seems actually to be acting now and then, which is probably a mistake in this context) and Lucy Liu as the most ferocious, albeit in an interesting, crabby way. Under the guidance of a music-video director who is known simply as McG, they all manage to not quite fall out of their costumes numerous times.

But that's about it for suspense. Mostly, this movie is a succession of knock-offs. Of the old TV show, naturally, but also of the lesser James Bond entries, of *The Matrix*'s visual effects in the fight scenes and of the penetration of a technologically well-defended vault, à la the first *Mission: Impossible*

The plot—something about computer geeks double-crossing one another—is of no consequence. The film is essentially about displaying the Angels in ways that are titillating to adolescent males, yet give their dates the impression that something inspiring is being said about female empowerment. It is, on both counts, just a tease. The best you can say for this version of *Charlie's Angels* is that it retains a sort of chipper, eerie good nature as it wastes the studio's money and our time.

VILLAGE VOICE, 11/14/00, p. 131, J. Hoberman

The Karate Boogaloo of the 1970s lives: *Charlie's Angels*, the first feature directed by the music-video ace known as McG is about as subtle as a boombox. But this amiably idiotic $90 million inflation of the haute-'70s TV show is immeasurably helped by Yuen Cheung-yan's martial arts leap-kick-chop choreography. Thus, when they're not wrapped in bikinis, wet suits, and towels (and sometimes when they are), Drew Barrymore, Cameron Diaz, and Lucy Liu complement their flirty butt-thrusts with a ferocious assortment of midair spins and ninja gyrations.

A small army of writers was reportedly required to produce this episodic televisual narrative in which the indestructible Angels, disguised variously as Middle Eastern belly dancers, Japanese hostesses, and even Bavarian barmaids, fight the good fight against "the end of privacy as we know it." Not only does *Charlie's Angels* take a courageous stand against corporate, computer-driven, Big Brother chicanery, it deserves an award from the Dairy Farmers of America: The cheesy disco action scenes are topped only by the movie's ripe double entendres and continual cheesecake.

The lanky, grinning Diaz gets the most opportunity to exercise her considerable talent for physical comedy—it's almost worth the price of admission to see her booty-shaking appearance on *Soul Train*. The movie is basically a girlfight, although Bill Murray, Crispin Glover, and Tim Curry are on hand to add to the clownshow antics. Even John Forsythe is exhumed to provide the voice of the godlike Charlie—although in the unavoidable sequel I hope to see his part taken by that other '70s retread, Tim Meadows's Ladies Man.

Also reviewed in:
CHICAGO TRIBUNE, 11/3/00, Friday/p. A, Michael Wilmington
NEW YORK TIMES, 11/3/00, p. E16, A.O. Scott
NEW YORKER, 11/13/00, p. 183, Anthony Lane
VARIETY, 10/30-11/5/00, p. 21, Todd McCarthy
WASHINGTON POST, 11/3/00, p. C1, Rita Kempley
WASHINGTON POST, 11/3/00, Weekend/p. 41, Desson Howe

CHICKEN RUN

A DreamWorks Pictures release in association with Pathé of an Aardman production. *Executive Producer:* Jake Eberts, Jeffrey Katzenberg, and Michael Rose. *Producer:* Peter Lord, David Sproxton, and Nick Park. *Director:* Peter Lord and Nick Park. *Screenplay:* Karey Kirkpatrick. *Based on an original story by:* Peter Lord and Nick Park. *Director of Photography:* Dave Alex Riddett. *Editor:* Mark Solomon. *Supervising Animator:* Lloyd Price. *Music:* John Powell and Harry Gregson-Williams. *Music Editor:* Richard Whitfield. *Sound:* Adrian Rhodes and (music) Nick Wollage. *Sound Editor:* Graham Headicar and James Mather. *Casting:* Patsy Pollack. *Production Designer:* Phil Lewis. *Art Director:* Tim Farrington. *Set Designer:* Alastair Green. *Set Dresser:* Maria Hopkinson, Lizzy New Bones, Manon Roberts, Justeen Bailey, Rachel Bowen, Kitty Clay, Anita Clipston, and Melanie Ford. *Costumes:* Shane Dalmedo, Nicola O'Toole, and Jane Whittaker. *Animator:* Loyd Price. *Running time:* 86 minutes. *MPAA Rating:* G.

VOICE: Phil Daniels (Fletcher);   Lynn Ferguson (Mac);   Mel Gibson (Rocky);   Tony Haygarth (Mr. Tweedy);   Jane Horrocks (Babs);   Miranda Richardson (Mrs. Tweedy);   Julia Sawalha (Ginger);   Timothy Spall (Nick);   Imelda Staunton (Bunty);   Benjamin Whitrow (Fowler);   John Sharian (Circus Man);   Jo Allen, Lisa Kay, and Laura Strachan (Additional Chickens).

LOS ANGELES TIMES, 6/21/00, Calendar/p. 1, Kenneth Turan

As the owner and eminence grise of Tweedy's Egg Farm, the autocratic Mrs. Tweedy thinks she knows chickens. "They don't plot, they don't scheme, they are not organized," she tells her (inevitably) hen-pecked husband. "Apart from you, they are the stupidest creatures on the planet." Or so she, and the rest of us, believe.

Along with its virtues as a delightful example of clay animation, "Chicken Run" also exposes a previously hidden world of poultry behavior. Before our disbelieving eyes, a pageant of jeopardy, romance and rescue unfolds. Chickens yelling, " She's gonna blow," chickens jitter-bugging to the classic "Flip Flop and Fly," chickens creating the kind of rousing action finale John Woo would relish. It's enough to make you swear off fricassee for life.

If anyone could provide this service, it would have to be Britain's foremost animator, Nick Park. The winner of three short-film Oscars ("The highest Oscar-to-output ratio," one minute-counting journalist has calculated, "in the history of motion pictures"), this is a man who knows his animals.

Park won his first Oscar for "Creature Comforts," deadpan interviews with hyper-articulate zoo animals. Then came the Wallace and Gromit films about a dog smarter than most men. One such adventure, "The Wrong Trousers," even has a chicken in a key role. (He's not really a chicken, as it turns out, but rather a penguin deviously pretending to be a chicken—but it's the thought that counts.)

Now Park and his Aardman Animation partner and co-director Peter Lord have put chickens front and center where they belong with this gleeful parody of prison and escape movies. No one who remembers "Stalag 17" will have to guess at the number that's on the front of the hen house, and no veteran of "The Great Escape" will fail to recognize the contours of the farm, complete with barbed wire fencing, barking dogs, and a suspicious Mr. Tweedy checking the locks and muttering about what the chickens are up to.

Hens and roosters may be unlikely heroes for an action adventure film, but Park, Lord and writer Karey Kirkpatrick have given "Chicken Run" the unmistakable hallmarks of the charming and clever style that turned Wallace and Gromit into great favorites over here as well as in Britain.

Simultaneously understated and hang-loose, the humor in "Chicken Run" is genial and playful, able to treat the wildest concepts with total seriousness. This film is also much the funnier for being site-specific: Though no one, not even the smallest child, will have any trouble following the plot, the use of Britishisms like "you old sausage" and "give it over" add unmistakably to the comic flavor.

The reason Mr. Tweedy (voiced by Tony Haygarth) is assiduously checking those locks is that one of his hens is addicted to escape attempts. That would be Ginger (Julie Sawalha of "Absolutely Fabulous"), jaunty as the neck scarf she wears. Believing that "there's a better place out there," Ginger is determined not only to break herself out, but also to free all the hens who live under the gloomy threat of death (as the pigs do in "Babe") if they don't produce.

Ginger's accomplices include Mac (Lynn Ferguson), the mechanical genius, as well as Nick (Timothy Spall) and Fletcher (Phil Daniels), a completely funny pair of conniving black marketeer rats, always aghast at the hens' attempt to pay them in, yes, chicken feed. Even less focused is Babs ("Little Voice's" Jane Horrocks), who treats Ginger's confinements in solitary as the equivalent of a holiday. "It's nice," she says vacantly, "to get a bit of time by yourself."

Dropping in, literally, on this self-described "group of rather desperate chickens" is the American rooster Rocky Roads (wonderfully done by Mel Gibson), a confident Rhode Island Red who's done "that whole barnyard thing" and now considers himself something of a "Lone Free Ranger."

Much to the disgust of resident rooster Fowler (Benjamin Whitrow), an RAF veteran who mutters the classic World War II British jibe at Yanks ("overpaid, oversexed, over here"), Rocky, who claims to have had considerable experience in the area, agrees to teach the hens to fly.

Though he and Ginger don't get along (he insists on calling her "Dollface" and considers her so tough, she's "the first chick I ever met with the shell still on"), they have to cooperate because the devious Mrs. Tweedy (the letter-perfect Miranda Richardson) has come up with a scheme so evil it makes everyone in the barnyard quake.

Making what Park and company have accomplished here even more impressive is how labor-intensive clay animation's stop-motion technique is. The Plasticine models have to be changed frame by frame, with 24 frames making up but a single second of on-screen time.

But though hundreds of people were employed creating "Chicken Run," with as many as 30 different sets operating at the same time, the film never loses its priceless stamp of individuality.

Reduced to its essence, this is a joke told by a person, not a corporation—and that makes all the difference.

NEW YORK, 7/10/00, p. 50, Peter Rainer

A much better movie about U.S.-British relations is *Chicken Run*, which also features a jauntier performance by Mel Gibson, as the voice of the rooster Rocky "the lone free-ranger" Roads [The reference is to *The Patriot*; see Rainer's review.]. This first feature-length claymation marvel from the Bristol, England-based Aardman studios—which brought us, among other delicacies, the *Wallace and Gromit* shorts—is a prison-break movie starring chickens. The idea itself is funny—an egg-layer *Stalag 17*—but that's just where the fun begins. The hens dreamed up by co-directors Nick Park and Peter Lord embody all the biddiness and eccentricity of English spinsterhood. When Rocky, an American interloper into their barbed-wire-enclosed egg farm, struts his roosteriness, he's both caricature and exemplar, the Yank in all his high-flying pluckiness. His inamorata, Ginger, voiced by *Absolutely Fabulous*'s Julia Sawalha, is so considerate and matronly that she can support a prison break only if all the hens are saved. Most recent animated features, such as *Dinosaur* and *Titan A. E*, are fine as long as you're looking and not listening. *Chicken Run*, with a script by Karey Kirkpatrick, is fun even with your eyes closed; the jokes and Britishisms and sound effects work all by themselves. It's a good thing the jokes *are* worthy: These chickens have crack comic timing and deserve the best.

NEW YORK POST, 6/21/00, p. 49, Jonathan Foreman

With its clever references to the great POW movies, and excellent voicing by the likes of Mel Gibson and Miranda Richardson, this triumph of claymation about hens escaping from a farm is as hilarious for adults as it is for kids.

"Chicken Run" is the first full-length feature by Peter Lord and Nick Park, the Oscar-winning Aardman team of "claymation" masters, and the creators of the great Wallace and Gromit films, and it's a triumph: as charming as "Babe" and at least as smart as "Toy Story."

Filled with clever, jokey references to World War II POW movies and the occasional visual homage to scenes in "Alien" and the "Indiana Jones" flicks, it is not only an amazing technical accomplishment, it's also the wittiest and best-voiced animated movie to come along in years.

Written by Karey Fitzpatrick, the film has an understated humor reminiscent of the Ealing comedies of the '40s and '50s—though it deals with some of the same dark themes of oppression and lethal machinery that run through Park's "The Wrong Trousers" and "A Close Shave."

Set sometime in the '50s, the story starts on the Tweedy Egg Farm, a dreary place where chicken coops are arranged in rows not unlike the huts in World War II movies like "Stalag 17" and "The Great Escape."

The farm is run by the ruthless Mrs. Tweedy (voiced by Miranda Richardson) and her easily dominated husband (Tony Haygarth). Hens that don't produce enough eggs are likely to end up on a plate.

Most of the birds are resigned to short, miserable lives, but not Ginger (Julie Sawalha, so good as Saffy in "Absolutely Fabulous"), who leads one failed escape attempt after another.

After one bid to dig a tunnel underneath the barbed wire, Ginger is punished by solitary confinement in a trash can in a scene reminiscent of the sweatbox sequence in "Bridge Over the River Kwai."

There, she passes the time by throwing a Brussels sprout against the wall, like Steve McQueen threw a baseball in "The Great Escape."

Ginger is beginning to give up on her dream of freedom when she sees Rocky (Mel Gibson), a brash, show-offy American rooster, fall out of the sky.

Thinking that she has at last found a way off the farm, Ginger hides Rocky from farmer Tweed, on the condition he teach her and the rest of the hens how to fly.

In the meantime, Mrs. Tweed has decided that the profits from the egg business are too small.

So she has invested in a vast infernal processing machine that takes a whole live chicken at one end and produces a chicken pie at the other.

As soon as the machine is ready, and the hens have been fattened up by double rations, all the feathered inhabitants of the farm will get the chop. Finding a way out, with or without Rocky's help, becomes a race against time.

You're pretty sure that Ginger and her friends are going to make it somehow, but their journey takes some unexpected turns.

And although the movie rattles along at a cracking pace, there's still time for dances, fights, pranks and even some romance.

The "acting" in "Chicken Run" is simply outstanding, especially compared with the voicing in recent animated features like "Titan A.E."

Gibson deftly plays off his cocky screen image, Richardson is wonderfully evil as Mrs. Tweedy, and Jane Horrocks (from "Ab Fab" and "Little Voice") is the voice of complacency and resignation as the overweight Babs.

But the film really belongs to Sawalha.

The chickens don't particularly resemble real fowl: Not only are they cuter, rounder and less dumb-looking, they also have teeth and three-fingered Simpsonesque hands, rather than wings.

But what's really remarkable about them is their range of facial expression—especially given that the painstaking claymation technique requires the animators to change the Plasticine faces of the chicken for each of the 24 frames that runs through a camera every second.

NEWSDAY, 6/21/00, Part II/p. B2, John Anderson

Singing, dancing, flapping and clucking its winged way into a world of special interests and speciesism, "Chicken Run" stands on its drumsticks, ready to unite peoples and chickens of all socio-political dispositions. To say nothing of bedtimes.

The most sophisticated, smartly amusing G-rated film since...ever, "Chicken Run" relies heavily, and cheekily, on World War II-style bravado (WWII movie-style bravado, at any rate), its plucky Claymation characters displaying an understated and distinctly English-accented gallantry of the type that won the war and inspired books by Tom Brokaw. At the other end of the cultural spectrum (and CBS-TV demographic), PETA members protesting rat atrocities on "Survivor" should be overjoyed by the film's portrayal of Tweedy's Farm—a chicken ranch-cum-POW camp inspired by "The Great Escape."

Children? We're all children in the glow of "Chicken Run." The first feature-length film from the U.K.'s Aardman Animation and "Wallace and Gromit" creator Nick Park, this stop-action animation adventure is not quite as tightly wound or consistently witty as Park's "W&G" Oscar-winners, "The Wrong Trousers" and "A Close Shave" (his co-director, Aardman co-founder Peter Lord, has two Oscar nominations of his own, but the flavor is pure Park). What we lose in consistency, however, we gain in character (of chicken) development.

Ginger (voice of "AbFab's" Julia Sawalha) is our egg-laying Steve McQueen, courageously executing one failed escape attempt after another; when she bounces a cabbage baseball-like against the wall of her cell/coal bin, the McQueen homage is complete. Her fellow prisoners are a birdbrained lot, especially Babs (Jane Horrocks), who knits and frets and doesn't really see the point of all this escaping, don'tcha-know, even when Ginger implies that their fate inevitably includes being "plucked, stuffed and roasted." "It's a living," bubbles Babs.

Two momentous developments change the psychological landscape of Tweedy's Farm: the arrival of American "flying ace" Rocky (Mel Gibson), the "lone free ranger" who arrives wounded but bombastic, and whom Ginger mistakenly assumes will (to quote Gibson in "Lethal Weapon") get the flock outta here—by going over the barbed wire. Adding urgency to the big escape is the new piece of farm equipment purchased by the evil Mrs. Tweedy (Miranda Richardson): a chicken-pie-making machine. Chickens go in, but they don't come out. Except in a crust.

Much of the charm of "Chicken Run," which is, in fact, defused a bit by the Gibson character and a couple of refugee Disney rats named Nick and Fetcher (Timothy Spall and Phil Daniels), is Park-Lord's aversion to/suspicion of modern technology (a hallmark of "Wallace & Gromit"). Also, an affection for lumpen middle-class Englishness (of which Wallace was a prime example). The hens of "Chicken Run," seem to be modeled after the old Monty Python housewives-in-drag with the "penguin on the telly," housecoated and a bit thick-witted but endearing in their lack of perspective. Ginger is a revolutionary among these tea-sipping jailbirds, but even she has a sense of propriety, which makes "Chicken Run" resemble "The Lavender Hill Mob" a lot more than it does "Stalag 17."

The Aardman method itself, especially in this age of runaway computerized technique, seems as much a throwback as Babs and the girls. At a film speed of 24 frames a second and manipulating their moldable cast by hand, Park and Lord have a possible 24 shots a second to shoot—and they never make it feel as if a frame is wasted. Each shot, whether of a lifted eyebrow or flash of chicken teeth, seems to be used to flesh out these chickens, whose characters are far better developed than most of the humans in most movies. Take Fowler (Benjamin Whitrow), the harrumphing Royal Air Force vet who is called upon by Ginger to take over the inmates' handmade plane. "They never let me fly a plane," Fowler says of the RAF. "I'm a chicken!" Sometimes, during "Chicken Run," you need to be reminded.

NEWSWEEK, 6/26/00, p. 59, David Ansen

There is something wonderfully improbable, anachronistic and quixotic about "Chicken Run." Squatting down in the midst of Hollywood's high-tech, computer-generated summer, this delightfully handmade 80-minute Claymation feature about a veddy British flock of hens plotting to escape from a grim chicken farm is (to mix a menagerie of metaphors) the tortoise to "Dinosaur's" thoroughbred hare.

Where nothing in computer animation is real, in stop-motion animation the animators film actual plasticine figures moving across miniature sets—one frame at a time. Each second of film comprises 24 shots, and the creators must make minuscule adjustments to their characters after each click of the shutter to create the illusion of continuous motion.

The masters of this mad, painstaking form are the blokes at Aardman animation studios in Bristol, England. And their star creator—who codirected "Chicken Run" with Aardman founder Peter Lord—is the nearly legendary Nick Park, the 40-year-old adolescent who created the Oscar-winning "Wallace & Gromit" shorts, 30-minute marvels of sophisticated wackiness featuring a soft-spoken suburban inventor and his silent but highly resourceful dog. The first of these, the 23-minute "A Grand Day Out," Park made entirely by himself. It took him six years to finish it. The $40 million "Chicken Run," part of a five-picture deal with Dream Works, employed some 300 people, and still took more than two years to shoot. "It was an entirely different ballgame," says the thin, soft-spoken, achingly polite Park. "It felt like 20 times, 30 times more work."

In 1995 Park and Lord were sitting in a café drinking coffee and doodling "when somehow this drawing just formed. It was a chicken digging its way out of a coop," Park says. For both men, having been fans of World War II prison movies "The Great Escape" and "Stalag 17," the notion for Aardman's first feature film began to form. "In a way, they were the worst creatures we could have chosen. Chickens have large, round bodies which make them very top-heavy. And they have thin legs, so it's hard for them to stand up. But it wouldn't have worked if it was 'The Great Escape' with beavers."

It's not just the technique that separates "Chicken Run" from its animated competitors. From its quirkily understated British sense of humor to its dark, concentration camp-inflected imagery, "Chicken Run" doesn't play by the usual colorful cartoon rules. The prisoners of Tweedy's Egg Farm have been trying, and failing, to escape for years, led by the indomitable Ginger (the voice of Julia Sawalha, who played the level-headed daughter in "Absolutely Fabulous"). But their efforts take on a new urgency when the pinched, greedy Mrs. Tweedy (Miranda Richardson), hoping to increase her profits, installs a terrifying chicken-pie-making machine in her farmhouse. Our dotty, baffled-looking heroines now face mass extinction—and in the most astonishing sequence in the film, in which Ginger, clamped upside down by her ankles, is fed to the infernal Rube Goldbergish machine and narrowly escapes baking—the comedy gives us the charred suggestion of hen holocaust.

Hope arrives in the form of Rocky the Flying Rooster (Mel Gibson), a cocky Yank ("I'm the lone free-ranger") on the lam from a traveling circus. It's his mission impossible to teach these imperiled chicks to fly. "Chicken Run" is in no hurry to wow us. It starts quietly, introducing its splendid gallery of fowl, rats and humans, then builds and builds until it achieves full comic liftoff.

Can this funky chicken tale compete against its sleek CGI rivals? Isn't clay a dinosaur form? "It is" acknowledges Park, "but I think that's where we score. We've got novelty on our side. I'm a great admirer of Pixar and 'Toy Story.' And also of 'Dinosaur.' But I think already people know you can do anything with computer animation. But its just a tool, like clay is a tool. It can only ever be as good as the ideas. The worst thing is if people came out of the theater and said, 'Nice animation; shame about the movie.'"

No danger there. The shame would be to miss this smart, handcrafted charmer.

SIGHT AND SOUND, 8/00, p. 41, Kim Newman

Tweedy's Chicken Farm, somewhere in England, the 50s. Ginger, a hen, plans a series of escape attempts. Despite foiling all of these planned breakouts, the farmer Mr Tweedy is unable to convince his wife that the chickens are organised. Rocky, a rooster who has escaped from a circus, seems to fly into the farm. Ginger enlists his reluctant aid in teaching the chickens how to fly. Mrs Tweedy, tired of low-profit egg farming, orders a new machine which kills chickens to produce ready-made pies. After installing it in the barn, Mr Tweedy singles out Ginger to test the machine. During his rescue attempt, Rocky unwittingly joins Ginger inside the contraption. Before sabotaging the device and breaking free of it, Ginger and Rocky realise that all the farm's chickens are slated for slaughter.

Despite winning the admiration of the chickens, Rocky slips away at night, leaving behind proof he was only able to fly when shot out of a cannon. Ginger calls on Fowler, an aged cockerel who is always reminiscing about his wartime experience, to supervise the construction of an ornithopter out of odds and ends scavenged by rats Fetcher and Nick. Having fixed the pie machine, the Tweedys chance upon the chickens as they prepare for their escape bid; the chickens take to the ornithopter. With the help of Rocky—who unexpectedly returns to the farm—the chickens fly over the farm's fence, dropping Mrs Tweedy, who has been hanging on since the machine took off, and settle in a bird sanctuary.

The high concept behind *Chicken Run* is that it is a prisoner-of-war film featuring grimacing plasticine chickens in place of Richard Attenborough, John Mills or any other persistent screen escapee from Colditz or Stalag 17. To underline this, there are enormously pleasurable quotes from John Sturges' *The Great Escape* (1962), the only POW film liable to be familiar to an international audience. After each failed escape attempt, Ginger, the mastermind behind the chicken's plans, is confined to a coal bunker where she bounces a Brussels sprout just as "cooler king" Steve McQueen did a baseball in solitary confinement. The finale of the film also sees a tricycling Rocky, a rooster, pull off (albeit in reverse) the wire jumping motorcycle stunt that was McQueen's finest moment in *The Great Escape*.

From the hoary but still-fresh experiences of World War II which the cockerel Fowler recounts to the snatches of early rock 'n' roll ('Flip, Flop and Fly') on the wireless, *Chicken Run* would seem to be set sometime in the 50s. Not only does this make for some lovely period touches (a Toblerone carton is used for a "chocs away" gag), but the setting allows directors Nick Park and Peter Lord—both leading figures in Aardman, the Bristol-based animation company behind *Chicken Run*—to play on the fact that an oppressive farm from that time, with its barbed chicken wire and neat rows of wooden huts, bears some resemblance to a movie stalag. Thankfully, they avoid any direct references to modern battery farms, which if transplanted to Aardman-land might seem more like extermination camps than rough-and-ready POW enclosures. This said, the film isn't without its darker moments, notably a post-*Babe* touch of cruelty when Mrs Tweedy uses a chopper to dispose of an unproductive hen.

The chickens' construction of a homemade flying machine has a precedent in an episode of the 70s television series *Colditz* where prisoners cobbled together a glider from found materials (which itself echoes a true historical incident). In *Chicken Run* the aircraft knocked together by the inmates is a delightful combination of slave galley and airliner with lazily flapping wings. It's tempting here to detect the influence of such film fantasists as Karel Zeman or Terry Gilliam. But the flying machine has a more immediate stylistic predecessor in the elaborate contraptions which featured in co-director Park's award-winning Wallace and Gromit short films. Though the characters in *Chicken Run* are well defined and have their share of memorable moments, no cast members quite match up to Wallace and Gromit's inspired inventor-dog double-act. The added length of a feature doesn't help: some of the minor players—wartime bore Fowler, aggressive hen Bunty—are one-joke creations who repeat their shtick two or three times with little development and diminishing effect.

Pitched almost as a UK answer to *Toy Story*, *Chicken Run* offers a specific British setting (albeit with an American guest star) and employs animation techniques which are (ostensibly) fashioned and hand-crafted as *Toy Story*'s CGI imagery is high-tech and virtual. Like *Toy Story*, the tale hinges on bickering between two characters, replacing the past/future opposition of Woody and Buzz with the Brit/Yank opposition of Ginger and Rocky. Ginger, voiced with spirit by Julia Sawalha, is a British escape-film officer incarnate, not satisfied unless the whole prison population can head for freedom, while Rocky, drawled to near-creepy perfection by Mel Gibson, is the hollow blowhard hero who pulls through in the end.

The voice casting—including instantly recognisable turns from Jane Horrocks as the chicken with an obsession with holidays and Timothy Spall and Phil Daniels as wide-boy rats who object to being paid "chicken-feed"—is spot-on. But it's the model work and animation that make these creatures so vivid. With wide eyes and broad grins (hen's teeth are not rare hereabouts) the poultry cast are capable of an extraordinary range of expression, especially during the sad or mildly scary scenes.

Taking a sequence almost at random and breaking it down to its components, you realise just how much physical and emotional texture Park and Lord have worked into crafting their film's seemingly effortless charm. (As with the best children's movies, which are likely to be viewed over again on video by their young audiences, *Chicken Run* rewards repeated viewings.) The scene in which Ginger discovers the truth about Rocky, for instance, features an inspired narrative device as she joins together two halves of a poster that reveal the rooster can only fly by being shot from a cannon. It's a small masterpiece of cinematic storytelling: as tear-like animated raindrops fall all around, a thunderclap in the distance, acting as a literal burst of understanding and an imagined, mocking echo of Rocky's impression of flight.

VILLAGE VOICE, 6/27/00, p.151, J. Hoberman

If you plan to catch *Chicken Run* best to do so before seeing *Me, Myself & Irene* [see Hoberman's review]. The latter's designated outrage—a cop buggered with a chicken—might place the bouncy claymation poultry of Aardman Studio's first feature animation in an unexpected and unwholesome light.

Chicken Run envisions a poultry farm as a concentration camp from which the biddies, led by the indomitable hen Ginger, attempt repeated breakouts. Located on a bleak north English moor, the place is surrounded by vicious dogs and administered by cruel, stupid humans. To add to the terror, the script (by Karey Kirkpatrick, who adapted *James and the Giant Peach* for Disney) allows for actual, if offscreen, butchering. With their wide, glassy eyes and clenched-teeth grimaces, the chickens project pure anxiety, if not a recent experience with electroshock therapy. Still, this up-market production is jollier than its premise. If the Aardman menagerie strikes you as funny, the movie will too. Other characters include a pompous old fowl who identifies with the Royal Air Force, an American rooster named Rocky (voiced by Mel Gibson), and a pair of cockney rats who sometimes disguise themselves as garden gnomes.

Nick Park is a bit of a slowpoke director, and *Chicken Run* only comes alive with the big swing number, where Rocky teaches the barnyard to shake a tail feather—a prelude to the superb set piece that has Ginger and Rocky trapped inside an extravagantly jerry-built machine for the mass production of chicken pot pie. I can't say that *Chicken Run* is as successful as the Wallace and Gromit shorts that have made Aardman a perennial Oscar winner, but at least the movie is boldly inappropriate. The mixture of the grim, the ridiculous, and the inspirational—not to mention the promised-land finale—suggests that, in seeking a screenplay suitable for their patron, DreamWorks, Aardman came up with a combination of *Barnyard Follies* and *Schindler's List*.

Also reviewed in:
NATION, 7/17/00, p. 35, Stuart Klawans
NEW YORK TIMES, 6/21/00, p. E1, Elvis Mitchell
NEW YORKER, 7/10/00, p. 78, Anthony Lane

VARIETY, 5/12-18/00. p. 14, Todd McCarthy
WASHINGTON POST, 6/23/00, p. C1, Rita Kempley
WASHINGTON POST, 6/23/00, Weekend/p. 37, Desson Howe

CHILDREN OF CHABANNES, THE

A Castle Hill Productions and HBO Signature Double Exposure release of a Perennial Pictures/Wetherell & Associates production. *Producer:* Lisa Gossels and Dean Wetherell. *Director (French and English with English subtitles):* Lisa Gossels and Dean Wetherell. *Director of Photography:* Mustapha Barat and Philippe Bonnier. *Editor:* Lisa Gossels and Dean Wetherell. *Music:* Joel Goodman. *Sound:* Fred Gremeaux, Gerard Vicot, and Tony Volante. *Sound Editor:* Doug Roberts. *Running time:* 91 minutes. *MPAA Rating:* Not Rated.

WITH: Georges Loinger, Reine and Renée Paillassou and Rachel Pludermacher (Teachers); Peter Gossels, Werner Gossels, Norbert Bikales, Wolfgang Blumenreich, Jerry Gerard, Ruth Keller and Ernest Rosner (Children of Chabannes); Serge Klarsfeld (Historian).

NEW YORK POST, 6/9/00, p. 50, Hannah Brown

The documentary "The Children of Chabannes" uncovers a fascinating and obscure story from the Holocaust.

It's a moving look at a French village, Chabannes, that took in and sheltered 400 Jewish children during World War II. What sets this story apart is that the whole community—and not just a brave few—pitched in to help these refugee children.

The effort was led by the cantankerous head of a local organization, Felix Chevrier.

The film, co-directed by Lisa Gossels, the daughter of one of the Chabannes children, and Dean Wetherell, mixes interviews with photos and, most effectively, a journal kept by Chevrier and the staff of the school.

VILLAGE VOICE, 6/13/00, p. 158, Amy Taubin

The Children of Chabannes is a more modest but also more informative and moving film about the situation of European Jews during the Nazi period. [The reference is to *Sunshine*; see Taubin's review of that film.] Lisa Gossels and Dean Wetherell's documentary uses extensive interview and archival material to depict how the people of Chabannes, a small, relatively isolated agricultural village, resisted the Vichy government, sheltering 400 Jewish children during the war and keeping all but six of them from being deported to the camps. (Among the saved children was Peter Gossels, Lisa's father.)

While most of the French communities credited with saving Jews were strongly religious (either Catholic or Protestant), Chabannes was not. Its citizens viewed themselves as "true Republicans," believers in freedom and the brotherhood of men, inheritors of the spirit of the French Revolution. In the face of massive evidence of French collaboration and anti-Semitism, *The Children of Chabannes*, among other things, restores the belief that the romance of a France still committed to its revolutionary ideals does in fact exist.

Gossels conceived the film when she accompanied her father to the 1996 reunion of the villagers with the children they had saved. In Chabannes, a remarkable cast of characters presented itself, including many of the teachers whose ingenuity, dedication, and courage insured the survival of the refugees, who were integrated into the village school until the Vichy government started rounding up children for deportation in 1942. George Loinger, a Jewish engineer turned gym teacher, trained the children's bodies so that they could endure the possible hard times ahead; the Paillassou sisters demanded that their German—and Polish—speaking students learn perfect French so they'd be easier to hide. Both teachers and pupils pay tribute to Felix Chevrier, the principal of the school, who defied the authorities on many occasions, risking his own life. Chevrier, who was already in his late fifties during the war, died in 1962, but he left an archive of the children's drawings and compositions in addition to his own journals.

Chevrier and the Paillassou sisters managed to find sympathizers in the police and the Vichy government who would warn them when there was going to be a roundup. The police would arrive, find no one in the school, and accuse Chevrier of hiding the children. His response: I don't know where they are. They can go wherever they want. They're free."

Also reviewed in:
NEW YORK TIMES, 6/9/00 p. E12, A.O. Scott
VARIETY, 7/26-8/1/99, p. 36, Lisa Nesselson

CHOCOLAT

A Miramax Films presentation of a David Brown production. *Executive Producer:* Bob Weinstein, Harvey Weinstein, Meryl Poster, and Alan C. Blomquist. *Producer:* David Brown, Kit Golden, and Leslie Holleran. *Director:* Lasse Hallström. *Screenplay:* Robert Nelson Jacobs. *Based on the novel by:* Joanne Harris. *Director of Photography:* Roger Pratt. *Editor:* Andrew Mondshein. *Music:* Rachel Portman. *Music Editor:* David Carbonara. *Choreographer:* Scarlett Mackmin. *Sound:* Chris Munro and (music) Chris Dibble. *Sound Editor:* Michael Kirchberger. *Casting:* Billy Hopkins, Suzanne Smith, and Kerry Barden. *Production Designer:* David Gropman. *Art Director:* John Frankish. *Set Decorator:* Stephanie McMillan. *Set Dresser:* Joe Dipple and Peter Wallis. *Special Effects:* Stuart Brisdon. *Costumes:* Renée Ehrlich Kalfus. *Make-up:* Naomi Donne. *Make-up (Johnny Depp):* Patty York. *Running time:* 121 minutes. *MPAA Rating:* PG-13.

CAST: Juliette Binoche (Vianne Rocher);   Lena Olin (Josephine Muscat);   Ron Cook (Alphonse Marceau);   Johnny Depp (Roux); Elisabeth Commelin (Yvette Marceau);   Judi Dench (Armande);   Alfred Molina (Comte de Reynaud);   Leslie Caron (Madame Audel); Peter Stormare (Serge);   Antonio Gil-Martinez (Jean-Marc Drou);   Carrie-Anne Moss (Caroline Clairmont);   Hélène Cardona (Françoise Drou);   Harrison Pratt (Dedou Drou);   John Wood (Guillaume Blerot);   Gaelan Connell (Didi Drou);   Hugh O'Conor (Pere Henri);   Guillaume Tardieu (Baptiste Marceau);   Victoire Thivisol (Anouk Rocher);   Michèle Gleizer (Madame Rivet);   Aurèlien Parent Koenig (Luc Clairmont); Dominique MacAvoy (Madame Fouget); Arnaud Adam (George Rocher);   Christianne Gadd (Chitza);   Marion Hauducoeur (Gati); Esteban Antonio (Thin Grizzled Man);   Sally Taylor-Isherwood (Re-voicing);   Tatyana Yassukovich (Storyteller).

LOS ANGELES TIMES, 12/15/00, Calendar/p. 2, Kevin Thomas

"Chocolat" is as delectable as its title, but for all its sensuality it is ultimately concerned with the spirit. A fable of deceptive simplicity, adapted for the screen with mature skill and wisdom by a young American screenwriter, Robert Nelson Jacobs, from Joanne Harris' novel, it emerges as a splendid work in the grand humanist tradition of the classic cinema of France, where it takes place.

It was filmed in English (by superb British cinematographer Roger Pratt) with a multinational cast under the exquisitely subtle and shaded direction of Swedish-born Lasse Hallstrom, who has Jean Renoir's gift of embracing people in all their follies and strengths. It seems as French to the core as it seems very much the work of Hallstrom, whose gift in bringing outsiders in from the cold has shone in such cherished landmark films as "My Life as a Dog," "What's Eating Gilbert Grape" and "The Cider House Rules."

On a wintry day in 1959—it could just as easily be 1859 in this unchanging French town—a beautiful woman, Vianne Rocher (Juliette Binoche at her most ravishing) and her small daughter, Anouk (Victoire Thivisol), come upon an ancient stone village perched high on a promontory over a river, bordered on its other side by vast, spectacular fields. You feel as if you have entered a Dutch or Flemish Old Master landscape.

Vianne rents a dusty, long-unused pastry shop from cranky old Armande Voizin (Judi Dench) and with breathtaking dispatch transforms it into an enchanting chocolaterie. The townspeople are entranced, but the town's grand seigneur, Comte de Reynaud (Alfred Molina), is not amused that Vianne should open her doors with the advent of Lent.

The count rules the town as did his ancestors, setting an example of piety. He quickly views Vianne as the enemy, especially because her chocolates seem to possess unusual properties, capable of curing or easing various ailments and restoring passion to stale marriages.

Vianne is a woman of mystery, and just as we're beginning to wonder whether there's something sinister about her or her chocolates, the film's perspective widens and deepens. We realize the mysteries that concern the filmmakers are those of the human heart.

The village is inviting, yet it is actually a somber place in the grip of a puritanical religiosity. Vianne does not hide that she is an unwed mother and refuses to attend church. There is something downright pagan about the subversive power of her chocolate; there's got to be a story about her that she does not care to reveal, but when all is told, she is a free spirit prepared to stand her ground against the count, who would like to send her on her way—just as his ancestors did with the Huguenots.

Despite having been declared an undesirable by the count, Vianne attracts admirers. Her hot cocoa has eased the pains of her landlady, an independent soul long at odds with the community. While remaining feisty in her heart, Armande has mellowed and become Vianne's friend.

On a far more controversial note, Vianne has given shelter and work to the long-abused wife (Lena Olin) of the local tavern keeper (Peter Stormare). Terrified to the point of incoherence, Olin's Josephine goes on to blossom in her new circumstances; indeed, so haggard and ragged is the woman that we at first don't realize it is Olin, an enduring beauty of the international screen. Ever so gradually, Josephine is reborn as a woman and regains her looks in the process. But when the handsome river rat Roux (Johnny Depp) drops anchor, you know there's going to be big trouble ahead. .

What concerns the filmmakers is religious practice that condemns rather than forgives, that excludes rather than includes. On one level, "Chocolat" is quite serious; on another it is equally droll, and its sterling cast easily handles its shifting moods. "Chocolat" is the human comedy in the form of a fairy tale, and as such, it takes formidable skill and judgment to pull off; the slightest misstep, and the whole thing collapses.

Thus, "Chocolat" represents an inspired collaboration between director, writer and cast to bring dimension and depth to its people, resulting in a raft of some of the year's most glowing performances. Binoche not only presents Vianne as a dazzling enigma but also illuminates the brave and lonely woman behind it; Molina's count is a maddeningly pious prig, but his basic impulses are actually well-meaning, and he too is basically a lonely man.

Dench and Olin have been given richly evolving roles to play, and neither could be better. Sporting what sounds like a hazy Irish accent, Depp, who was Hallstrom's memorable Gilbert Grape, easily fills the bill as bold romantic rebel.

There's also splendid work from little Thivisol, whose Anouk bears the brunt of her mother's nonconformity; from Aurelien Parent Koenig as Armande's clenched little grandson, intimidated by his zealously proper and repressed mother (Carrie-Anne Moss); and from Stormare as Olin's brutal and pathetic alcoholic husband. Leslie Caron lends a radiant presence as a widow worshiped too long from afar by shy neighbor John Wood. And finally there's Hugh O'Conor's wistful priest, a secret Elvis fan.

"Chocolat" is a work of artistry and craftsmanship at the highest level, sophisticated in its conception and execution, yet possessed of wide appeal. It's that rarity, a movie that opens at Christmas that reflects the true (as opposed to commercial) spirit of the season.

NEW YORK POST, 12/15/00, p. 58, Lou Lumenick

"Chocolat" is a bittersweet confection that few holiday filmgoers will be able to resist, thanks to melt-in-your-mouth performances by Juliette Binoche, Alfred Molina and Judi Dench.

Less saccharine and cloying than director Lasse Hallstrom's "The Cider House Rules," it's not exactly cutting-edge filmmaking, but rather the soothing cinematic equivalent of a warm cup of decadently rich cocoa.

This comic fairy tale takes place in a fictional hamlet so deep in the French countryside that virtually the only contemporary reference (the time is 1959) is the young town priest's adoration of Elvis. The real threat to the village's centuries of tradition and routine comes with the arrival of Vianne (Juliette Binoche) and her young daughter, Anouk (Victoire Thivisol).

Vianne quickly sets tongues wagging: Not only is she a proud unwed mother, but she favors cleavage-baring couture and red spike heels (this is the wrong movie for those hard-hearted realists who might wonder exactly where Vianne is getting her endless high-fashion changes).

Even worse, she opens a shop offering hugely tempting chocolates just as the Lenten fast season is beginning in a village populated by devout Roman Catholics (all of whom, incidentally, speak English). That provokes a McCarthyish crusade against Vianne by the uptight Comte de Reynaud (Alfred Molina), the town's mayor and self-appointed protector of its morals.

But Vianne's mother (who figures in the season's second funeral-urn-spilling scene, after "Meet the Parents") was a South American witch, so her sinfully rich chocolates work magical spells over the townspeople. They include an abused wife (a nice turn by Lena Olin, the director's wife) and an elderly couple desperate for a late-in-life romance (John Wood and the still lovely Leslie Caron).

Binoche is absolutely delicious as the big-hearted Vianne, whose other good work is engineering a four-hankie reunion between a diabetic who eagerly chooses death by chocolate (Judi Dench in a shameless Oscar bid) and her estranged daughter (Carrie-Anne Moss) and grandson (Aurelien Parent Koenig).

By far the juiciest performance is by Molina, a terrific actor who's often wasted in nothing supporting roles. His massively repressed Comte is an inventive comic masterpiece, and his eventual comeuppance in the window of Vianen's shop is one of the year's funniest scenes.

Hallstrom's biggest misstep is casting Johnny Depp, who is ridiculous (and boasts an indescribable accent) as a "river rat" who romances Vianne and provokes a manipulative arson subplot. Fortunately for the movie his participation is much briefer than Miramax's ads suggest.

The screenplay, attributed to Robert Nelson Jacobs, downplays the priestly villainy of Joanne Harris' novel and instead gives the cleric a stunningly anachronistic speech about inclusiveness that wouldn't seem out of place at next year's Oscar ceremonies.

Where, come to think of it, I wouldn't be surprised to see "Chocolat" turn up.

NEWSDAY, 12/15/00, Part II/p. B6, John Anderson

Chocolate is dark, dangerous and, as any self-respecting restaurant menu will tell you—while selling you 500 gratuitous calories—decadent. "Chocolat," on the other hand, is buoyant, guileless and as righteous as a decaffeinated coffee.

This doesn't mean "Chocolat" is bad. It just means it isn't chocolate.

What it is, however, represents what can most conveniently be called the Miramax Aesthetic. Once upon a time, the New York-based film company bought and distributed such audience-friendly imports as "Cinema Paradiso," "Like Water for Chocolate" and "Life Is Beautiful." Now it makes films like "Chocolat." Either way, the result is a co-opting of the exotic and/or intellectual cachet of Other Language movies, creating a kind of Foreign Film Lite—the type of movie that makes audiences feel both sated and intelligent, the way a diner does after three eclairs and a coffee with Sweet'n Low.

Lasse Hallström, who is apparently now devoting his career to adapting best-selling novels ("The Cider House Rules" was his last; "The Shipping News" is his next), has also made Joanne Harris' "Chocolat" a movie novel of beautiful faces. Juliet Binoche, never more conventionally glamorous, is Vianne, the mysterious chocolatier who arrives in the sleepy village of Lansquenet with her daughter, Anouk ("Poinette's" Victoire Thivisol), in a pair of Jacobin cloaks and carrying the seeds (or beans) of revolution. Her seductive chocolates and cocoa (anointed with ground chili, for one thing) turn Lansquenet, a seemingly tranquil town seething with dysfunction, into a hotbed of lust and liberal thinking.

Vianne is something of a missionary, which makes the dynamic between her and the despotic, highly Catholic town father, the Comte de Reynaud (Alfred Molina), a little nonsensical, and certainly not a victim/perpetrator situation. Vianne is too intelligent and worldly not to realize that the arrival of a non-churchgoing, unwed mother and chocolate-making femme fatale (the time is about 1960) will turn a town like Lansquenet upside down. Still, she actively seeks out the nutty Josephine Muscat (Lena Olin), abused wife of the local tavern keeper (Peter Stormare), urging her to leave her husband. She defies the repressed Caroline (Carrie-Ann Moss) by letting her estranged mother, Armande (Judi Dench), and son, Luc (Aurelien Parent Koenig), meet under her roof. She purposely befriends the "river rats," led by Roux (Johnny Depp), just to tweak the Comte's nose. And then she acts surprised when someone retaliates.

Like the other major food movies of recent years—"Like Water for Chocolate," "Babette's Feast," "Eat, Drink, Man, Woman"—"Chocolat" is a feminist fable, more simplistic than most, perhaps, but well-meaning enough.

It's pretty, picturesque and peopled, as we said, by beautiful faces. Why it was shot on location in France and England is a mystery; an aerial of Lansquenet reveals one of the cheesiest toy towns ever photographed. And no narrative thread is pursued long or hard enough to create what you'd call an emotional fabric. Still, "Chocolat" is a reasonably uplifting Christmas cookie.

Even if it takes place during Lent.

NEWSWEEK, 12/15/00, p. 77, David Ansen

Once upon a time in 1959, in the pious, picturesque and puritanical French town of Lansquenet, a mysterious woman and her daughter, cloaked in red, blew into town on the wake of a north wind. The woman, Vianne (Juliette Binoche), opens a *chocolaterie*, and her rich, sweet confections, containing magical aphrodisiacal qualities, unlock the pent-up desires and appetites of the townsfolk, pitting the forces of liberation against the forces of repression, and bringing down the wrath of the rigid, powerful Comte de Reynaud (Alfred Molina), upholder of the town's stuffy traditional values.

The ingredients of "Chocolat" director Lasse Hallstrom's fanciful and stylish fable, could have been mixed in 1959, when artists declared open season on uptight conformists and the world began to let down its hair in preparation for the oncoming '60s. Amazingly, decades after the sexual revolution, these old battles seem to have acquired a new resonance. *Plus ça change, plus c'est la même chose.* Like the edgier "Quills" (also set in the land Americans have always associated with sexual liberty), "Chocolat" is a seriocomic plea for tolerance, gift-wrapped in the baby blue colors of a fairy tale and served up with a sybaritic smile.

The moral argument may be pat and predictable, but the movie disarms you with its charm and its solid craftsmanship. In more vulgar hands, "Chocolat" could have been insufferably precious, or smug, or sentimental. But Hallstrom ("My Life as a Dog'" "The Cider House Rules") has always had a delicate touch, not to mention the old-fashioned virtue of good taste. He also has an extraordinary cast at his disposal, including Judi Dench as a crusty 70-year-old lotus eater, Lena Olin as a terrorized wife who finds refuge at the chocolaterie, Peter Stormare as her alcoholic fool of a husband, Leslie Caron as a widow who's been in mourning for 40 years and Johnny Depp as a dashing Irish vagabond with as big a case of wanderlust as Vianne. Screenwriter Robert Nelson Jacobs, adapting a 1999 novel by Joanne Harris, keeps the whimsy rooted in real emotions, and wisely allows even the control-freak Comte his humanity. There's a touch of "Babette's Feast" here, a soupçon of "Like Water for Chocolate" and some old spices that might remind you of the plays of Jean Anouilh and Jean Giraudoux. However familiar, the taste is still sweet, the texture light as a soufflé, the sentiments pleasantly high caloric.

SIGHT AND SOUND, 3/01, p. 42, John Mount

France, the 50s. Vianne Rocher and her daughter Anouk arrive with the north wind in the village of Lansquenet. The pious Comte de Reynaud is outraged when he discovers that Vianne, a single mother who doesn't go to church, is opening a *chocolaterie* during Lent. Reynaud, who can't admit his wife has left him, rewrites the sermons of the priest, Père Henri, in order to turn the villagers against Vianne. But Vianne's kindness—and her chocolates—win them over; her business catches on. When Josephine Muscat leaves her abusive husband, café-owner Serge, she starts works for Vianne. Reynaud responds by trying to reform Serge; when Josephine refuses to return home, Serge attacks her. Vianne reunites her landlady Armande with her grandson Luc, much to the annoyance of Armande's estranged daughter Caroline, who works for Reynaud. Caroline reveals that Armande is diabetic and should be in care.

A group of travellers arrive and camp on the river; Reynaud orchestrates the villagers' protests against them. When Vianne befriends Roux, one of the travellers, she risks being further ostracised. On the point of accepting defeat, Vianne is asked by Armande to organise her birthday party. A big success, the party culminates in a dance on Roux's boat; Armande dies happy later that night. Vianne and Roux, meanwhile, slip away for a romantic encounter. They are woken by a fire started by Serge on Roux's boat. Reynaud is horrified and orders Serge to leave town; the count finally snaps and one night gorges himself on Vianne's window display. She finds him the next morning and cleans him up. An emboldened Père Henri preaches in praise of tolerance. Vianne holds a chocolate festival. The north wind blows; Vianne scatters her grandmother's ashes in the breeze and resolves to stay in Lansquenet. Some time later Roux returns.

Wry, heart warming ensemble pieces that celebrate the diversity of human experience are director Lasse Hallström's stock-in-trade. When the underlying story has some substance, he can create memorable films, such as *My Life as a Dog* or *What's Eating Gilbert Grape*, when his material isn't so strong, he still makes charming, soft-centred entertainments with marvellous acting. *Chocolat* falls into the latter category: it might seem an obvious choice for Hallström's bittersweet humour, but the film proves disappointingly slight—although it is lifted by a radiant central performance from Juliette Binoche and appealing supporting turns from Judi Dench and Johnny Depp.

Based on Joanne Harris' popular novel, *Chocolat* is set in 50s rural France but played in English and in a comic vein reminiscent of the BBC's adaptation of Gabriel Chevalier's novel about French village life *Clochemerle,* first broadcast in the early 70s. But the sight of so many English actors speaking in heavy Gallic accents—alongside French performers such as Binoche and Leslie Caron—also raises the spectre of the British television sitcom *'Allo' Allo!*, most notably in Alfred Molina's otherwise engaging portrayal of the local repressed killjoy. Fortunately this doesn't prove too intrusive; Johnny Depp's solution to the language problem, for instance, is to deliver all his lines in an Irish accent.

The moral of the tale—which sees Binoche's kind-hearted Vianne open a chocolate shop and free up the stuffy locals—is disarmingly simple: a little of what you fancy does you good. But there's enough here to create an amusing battle of wills in which, quite reasonably, self-indulgence wins out against self-denial. All of which is artfully double-dipped in a quasi-mystical discourse on the invigorating properties of chocolate and the secret spicy recipes of the Mayans. It is also a tribute to Binoche that she is able to create such a captivating portrayal of a character who, for all her restless, liberating nature, is really only a slightly racy version of Mary Poppins; Johnny Depp, meanwhile, provides a strong romantic foil as the raffish gypsy guitarist Roux.

Along with the hearts and flowers, Hallström adds a shot of bitter reality in the various personal crises that the villagers must overcome. Most notable here is the transformation of Josephine, played with some intensity by Hallström's wife Lena Olin, from a neurotic battered wife into an independent woman. In all cases, Vianne is the catalyst to help the villagers liberate themselves—all except the wife beating café-owner Serge whose bruising libidinal desires force him into exile; his removal from the film is perhaps a tacit admission of the limits of the salving power of chocolate—and signals the film's reluctance to let darker, more unpalatable undercurrents disturb its sweetly smooth surface.

As one takes for granted with Hallström, the film is beautifully shot, by British director of photography Roger Pratt, and boasts terrific period production design by David Gropman *(Cider House Rules).* But by the end the myriad metaphors involving chocolate as a panacea for all ills have been wildly overextended and leave a cloying aftertaste. *Chocolat* is pleasantly digestible eye candy, but an insightful moral fable? I should cocoa.

TIME, 12/25/00-1/1/01, p. 148, Richard Schickel

One snowy day, a woman names Vianne Rocher (Binoche) and her daughter Anouk (Victoire Thivisol) arrive in the staid if picturesque French village of Lansquenet. Their intent is to open a chocolate shop, the sensual products of which are bound to remind the locals that life has more to offer than churchgoing and spousal abuse. Their goodies place them in conflict with the rectitudinous mayor (Alfred Molina) but warm the chilled souls of various inhabitants (Judi

Dench, Lena Olin, John Wood). Vianne eventually makes common romantic cause with a riverboat wanderer (Depp), who also scandalizes the town with his unsettled and unsettling ways. The chocolatier will perhaps evoke for sardonic viewers the old dope peddler of Tom Lehrer's song, "spreading joy wherever [s]he goes." Indeed, some of the desserts apparently contain aphrodisiacs. The movie itself may suggest to those who find themselves unsusceptible to its fabulistic charms how easy it has become to travesty the manner of what used to be thought of as "art movies." This one has something of their air—an attractive, slightly exotic setting; characters who appear to have some substance and some curious quirks. But everything is spun toward sugary sentimentality.

And relentless predictability. Vianne always knows, and we always know, what effect her concoctions will have on her customers. They always shake off their repressions and troubles at precisely the right inspirational moment. Dench's character even manages to die just when she should, with her life's work neatly completed. Made with a sort of tasteful vulgarity, this movie never disappoints the slack-minded audience's anticipation of the humanistically healing banality, the life-crushing behavioral cliché.

VILLAGE VOICE, 12/19/00, p. 150, Dennis Lim

Lasse Hallström's *Chocolat* shares with the director's previous Miramax Oscar cause—the sheepish, unwittingly contradictory pro-choice homily *The Cider House Rules*—an assumed demographic, and panders accordingly. A condescending, self-congratulatory attack on provincial sanctimony, *Chocolat* (sadly unrelated to Claire Denis's terrific first feature of the same name) positions a kind, wise, modern woman against the twin evils of organized religion and institutional patriarchy. Though bludgeoningly metaphoric, this cloying fable on the dangers of appetite suppression is at bottom too literal-minded to accommodate any potentially helpful magic-realist flourishes. Worse, its broad farcical pratfalls are grossly incompatible with its zealous lunges for moral significance.

Accounting for the missing *e* in the title, the setting is *une petite ville tranquille* in the 50s, where the inhabitants speak numerous versions of a lightly French-accented English. Vianne Rocher (Juliette Binoche) and her daughter (*Ponette* heartbreaker Victoire Thivisol) blow into town in matching red capes, and the locals are promptly scandalized when the sexy, soulful single mother opens a chocolaterie (during Lent, no less). But the establishment, with its bold turquoise walls and yummy calorific treats, becomes a serene oasis of enlightenment in this drab, self-denying bourg. Vianne divines her customers' favorite candies, matchmakes, engineers reconciliations, revives sex lives, and raises feminist consciousness. Her witchy traits are later ascribed to her Mayan mother, from whom she inherited the therapeutic secrets of the cocoa bean and the mission of rampaging through the French countryside leaving a trail of truffles-induced epiphanies in her wake. Vianne's contagious heathenism provokes Alfred Molina's apoplectic mayor to declare a jihad, soon accelerated by the arrival of a band of Irish "river rats" led by Johnny Depp (who plays an almost identical part in Sally Potter's upcoming, inadvertently riotous *The Man Who Cried*).

Airy, pseudo-folkloric gibberish at best, *Chocolat* affects shrill agnosticism in the service of a disingenuous pro-tolerance rallying cry. Reduced to pawns, the charismatic cast—battered kleptomaniac Lena Olin, sweet-toothed diabetic Judi Dench, priggish control freak Carrie-Anne Moss—goes to waste, as does the blessedly swoony coupling of Binoche and Depp. More troubling, it's now clear that the limpid, unforced melancholy of Hallström's early films has Miramaxed into industrial strength sweetener—the chief ingredient in this confection is corn syrup.

Also reviewed in:
NEW REPUBLIC, 1/15/01, p. 20, Stanley Kauffmann
NEW YORK TIMES, 12/15/00, p. E1, Elvis Mitchell
VARIETY, 12/11-17/00, p. 22, Lael Loewenstein
WASHINGTON POST, 12/22/00, p. C5, Rita Kempley
WASHINGTON POST, 12/22/00, Weekend/p. 41, Desson Howe

CHUCK & BUCK

An Artisan Entertainment and Blow Up Pictures release of a Flan de Coco production. *Executive Producer:* Jason Kliot and Joana Vicente. *Producer:* Matthew Greenfield. *Director:* Miguel Arteta. *Screenplay:* Mike White. *Director of Photography:* Chuy Chávez. *Editor:* Jeff Betancourt. *Music:* Joey Waronker, Tony Maxwell, and Smokey Hormel. *Sound:* Yehuda Maayan. *Sound Editor:* Andrew DeCristofaro. *Casting:* Meredith Tucker and Miranda Thompson. *Production Designer:* Renée Davenport. *Set Decorator:* Isabelle Stamper. *Costumes:* Elaine Montalvo. *Make-up:* Jane Nan Kelly. *Running time:* 95 minutes. *MPAA Rating:* R.

CAST: Mike White (Buck O'Brien);   Chris Weitz (Charlie "Chuck" Sitter);   Lupe Ontiveros (Beverly);   Beth Colt (Carlyn);   Paul Weitz (Sam);   Maya Rudolph (Jamila);   Mary Wigmore (Diane);   Paul Sand (Barry);   Gino Buccola (Tommy);   Arnette Murphy (Tommy's Mom); Glory Simon (Witch);   Doug Kieffer (Mark);   Jonathan Brown (Jake);   Ruthie Bram (Dorothy);   Giovanni Gieco (Scarecrow);   Linda Lichter (Bank Teller);   Meredith Tucker (Jolie);   Zak Penn (Josh Weintraub);   Tony Maxwell and Vince Duffy (Themselves);   Dana Baratta (Melissa Booth);   Pamela Gordon (Buck's Mom);   Josephina J. Rocha (Pilar);   Jesse Lee Thomas (Young Chuck, photos);   Caleb Wilson (Young Chuck, film);   Nathaniel Olderman (Young Buck);   Miranda Thompson (Cocktail Waitress);   Ron Yerxa (Minister);   Yehuda Maayan (Man at Wedding).

LOS ANGELES TIMES, 7/14/00, Calendar/p. 12, Kevin Thomas

Watching "Chuck & Buck" is like watching a tightrope walker: One slip-up and the film would surely plummet into incredibility or sheer tastelessness.

Yet writer Mike White, who plays Buck, and director Miguel Arteta never stumble as they traverse a very high wire. Not everyone will be willing or able to go the distance with them, but those who do are giving themselves a chance to experience a fresh, original sensibility in White—both as a writer and as an actor. Arteta, whose debut film was the offbeat "Star Maps," has a sensitivity equaled by his daring. It is ever the case: The riskier the film, the richer the payoff—provided that everything works.

When we first meet the 20-something Buck, a boyish, nerdy redhead with a dying mother, he is so childlike as to seem mentally disabled. When she does die, in their splendid vintage Spanish colonial estate in the Montecito-Santa Barbara area, all Chuck has to cling to are his toys. So it's not surprising that he swiftly embraces his boyhood best friend, Chuck (Chris Weitz), whom he has invited to the funeral.

They haven't seen each other in more than 15 years, since Chuck moved away with his family. Chuck is now at the acme of L.A. upward mobility: He's a handsome music executive with an elegant home and a beautiful live-in fiancee, Carlyn (Beth Colt), he is about to marry. Chuck is startled, to say the least, that when Buck does embrace him he also gropes him, prompting Buck's quick departure—but not before Carlyn, unaware of the incident, thoughtfully invites Buck to come visit sometime.

She might as well have shot Buck out of a cannon. In no time, he withdraws $10,000 from the bank and heads for Los Angeles, settling in a modest motel room and swiftly making himself a pest in Chuck's life, at his office as well as his home. Chuck, who now calls himself Charlie, and Carlyn are decent, well-mannered people who do not want to be unkind to Buck yet are soon fervently eager to discourage him. Buck, however, is not one to fold his tent easily, and one day while hanging around Chuck's office, which looks to be in a posh Sunset Strip office building, he is drawn to the children's theater across the street. He's suddenly inspired to write a play, with which he intends to impress Chuck and once again be in his good graces.

Buck approaches the theater's house manager, Beverly (Lupe Ontiveros), and offers her enough money so that she can't say no. Beverly is under the impression that as an adult Buck surely must realize that the play, which is to be staged only once, is, in her words, a "homoerotic, misogynistic love story"—not exactly children's theater. It's to be called "Hank & Frank"—and Hank's wife is an evil witch out to destroy Hank and Frank's friendship.

Long before this point, you'll be asking yourself what's going on with Buck. The film surely has all the makings of a "Fatal Attraction," only to take off in an unexpected direction. White gradually peels away layer by layer to reveal Buck as a case of arrested development—the product of a dysfunctional family whose world stopped expanding when Chuck moved away, then shattered completely with Buck's mother's death. Buck is single-minded: He is in love with Chuck. But just how dangerous is Buck to himself or to Chuck—or even Carlyn—and how will Chuck deal with so obsessive an individual?

Let's just say that "Chuck & Buck" flies in the face of contemporary paranoia and celebrates life's possibilities without losing touch with reality or slipping into sentimentality. Maybe people, even men, can actually grow up. Maybe lives can take new directions. "Chuck & Buck" asks us to question assumptions, to look at people, situations and ourselves in new ways that will inspire us to take risks.

White and Arteta stir this all up amid a mix of wild humor and genuine sentiment, and their film demands the utmost of their actors in sustaining that all-important suspension of disbelief. White's Buck comes on as pathetic bad news, and just when he's at his scariest he starts seeming to be more than that. Weitz has the tricky business of embodying archetypal L.A. cool and success without slipping into caricature. Ontiveros, a great character actress in one of her best parts, must seem caring of Buck without seeming dumb not to regard him as outright crazy. And far from being his enemy, Colt's intelligent Carlyn is the person who understands Buck the best. Paul Weitz's Sam, a New Jersey carpet layer cast by Buck as Hank despite the fact he has scant discernible acting ability, provides the film with some of its funniest moments. (Brothers Chris and Paul Weitz produced and directed "American Pie," and Chris appeared in "Star Maps.")

"Chuck & Buck's" other equally inspired elements—cinematography, music, production design and editing, etc.—blend in seamlessly with a film that is all of piece, to a degree that is as essential as it is impressive. "Chuck & Buck" succeeds because it turns out not to be the movie it might so easily have been.

NEW YORK, 7/24/00, p. 57, Peter Rainer

The Buck of *Chuck & Buck* is a 27-year-old man-child (Mike White) who sucks lollipops and speaks in a slow drawl that sounds as if he's readying the sentences in his head before mouthing them. At times, he looks like a young Stan Laurel, and at first glance, you might think he has Laurel's aloof innocence. When his mother dies, leaving him alone in her house with his old records and kid-stuff memorabilia, he attempts to reconnect with chuck (Chris Weitz, a childhood friend who has moved away and whom he hasn't seen in many years. Chuck was Charles back then; now he's a slick record executive with a gorgeous house in the Hollywood Hills and a fiancée (Beth Colt) to match. At the wake for his mother, Buck comes on to Chuck. Gently but forcibly rebuffed, Buck becomes a species of stalker, moving down the coast to be close to Chuck and insinuating himself into the man's life.

If you think this all sounds like a demento erotic thriller, you're half right. The other half—the message portion of the movie—is what we're supposed to take home with us and mull over. Buck, you see, represents the childhood we must relinquish if we are to become responsible adults. Chuck, on the other hand, who is indeed responsible and adult, is portrayed as a kind of fraud, a reconstructed man who has become a "player"at the expense of his lost innocence. Chuck is the hotshot phony we misguidedly aspire to be, but Buck represents who we really are. Despite the air of menace in his goggle-eyed goofiness, Buck is the hero of the piece because he is still in touch with his inner child. To stay in touch, he doesn't have to go very far.

The best sequences in *Chuck & Buck,* which was directed by Miguel Arteta, are the tense, creepy ones in which Buck preys on his friend. He has a nut-brain aplomb when he's carrying out his schemes, and both as actor and as the film's screenwriter, Mike White knows how to bring the audience into Buck's confidences. Chris Weitz, on the other hand, makes Chuck so bland that you can't figure out if he's commenting on the guy or just being a bland actor. Because of this imbalance, Buck has practically all the movie's best bits. (The rest of the best are stolen by Lupe Ontiveros as a local theater manager who sees through Buck with a maternal clarity.)

Buck remains, I think, a lot more disturbing than the filmmakers realize; their touchy-feely folderol prevents them from giving full dramatic license to their own best creation. How can we accept Buck as a poster child for reconciliation and forgiveness when, for example, he peers at night into Chuck's window as Chuck makes love to his fiancée, or neglectfully allows a boy actor he has befriended to injure himself with firecrackers? This odd, uneven movie, with its trumped-up ending that makes zero emotional sense given what came before, is perplexing in the extreme. Experiencing it is a bit like being asked to accept dear old Norman Bates as Huck Finn.

NEW YORK POST, 7/14/00, p. 47, Jonathan Foreman

Almost too creepy to be poignant, and generally funny only in an uncomfortable, squirm-in-your seat way, the indie dark comedy "Chuck & Buck" is still a remarkable and original achievement, especially given its low budget and use of non-professionals in major roles.

Unlike Hollywood movies that center on adults who are still children in their mental and emotional lives, this one has the courage not to shy away from acknowledging a slightly scary, almost predatory pubescent sexuality in such people.

But then director Miguel Arteta ("Star Maps") and screenwriter Michael White (who also stars as Buck) seem determined to avoid stereotypes. And the end result is a film that is both audacious and troubling. Which makes it more of a shame that "Chuck & Buck" ends in a way that's less than entirely satisfying.

Buck is 27 and has never held a job or gone to college. At the beginning of the movie he's living at home with his ailing mother, in a bedroom filled with a 12-year-old's toys.

His childhood friend, Chuck (Chris Weitz) on the other hand, has grown up. He's now a successful if shallow record producer in Hollywood, engaged to be married to the beautiful Carlyn (Beth Colt).

When Buck's mother dies, he gets in contact with his old friend who comes to the funeral with Carlyn. Buck hopes to pick up their friendship just as it was 16 years before—including its element of sexual experimentation—but Chuck, who's now called Charlie, has no intention of doing so.

Buck isn't to be deterred however. He moves to L.A. and stakes out Chuck's home and office. When Chuck won't take his calls anymore, Buck unfairly blames his unfriendliness on Carlyn, who's actually preternaturally tolerant.

He's also inspired to write a play about their relationship titled "Hank & Frank," which he puts on at the children's theater opposite Chuck's workplace, with the help of theater manager Beverly (the excellent Lupe Ontiveros). He hopes that if his obsession sees the play, he'll come to his senses.

Buck, the socially maladroit 12-year-old in a 27-year-old's body, is played with remarkable skill and pathos (reminiscent of Philip Seymour Hoffman's character in "Boogie Nights") by Mike White, who also wrote the screenplay.

The filmmaking team of Chris and Paul Weitz ("American Pie") both give effective naturalistic performances. The latter is particularly good as a hopelessly untalented tough actor, Sam, who wins the lead role in Buck's play because of his resemblance to Chuck.

Shot on video, it's not an elegantly photographed film.

But the movie's main weakness is a cop-out failure to explain just what happened in childhood to make Buck—and Chuck—the way they are.

NEWSDAY, 7/14/00, Part II/p. B7, John Anderson

For all the Toys "R" Us aesthetic and Roches-evoking music (actually Gwendolyn Sanford), "Chuck & Buck" is close to being a nightmare—although it's tough to say whose: the 27-year-old 11-year-old, or the other 27-year-old and object of the 11-year-old's affection?

One of the better films to come out of Sundance this year, "Chuck & Buck" is the work of director Miguel Arteta ("Star Maps") and writer Mike White (early "Dawson's Creek," and "Freaks and Geeks"), who has written and stars in this year's most exhilaratingly weird movie.

Buck (White) has nursed his ailing mother for years, and, when she dies, he gets in touch with Chuck (Chris Weitz), who was his best friend when they were 11. Chuck, who has matured normally (for a record producer, at least) arrives for the funeral with his fiancee, Carlyn (Beth Colt), and finds Buck virtually unchanged from the kid he last saw 16 years before.

Things get sexually strange, and Chuck bolts back to Los Angeles, but Buck takes the couple's offhand invitation literally, packs his bags, empties his bank account and moves into a low-rent L.A. motel so he can be near Chuck.

This may make Buck sound like the spawn of Satan, but he is easily the most sympathetic figure in the film, odd but honest, and so totally smitten with Chuck it's hard to fault him. Chuck, on the other hand, is so uptight about his adolescent adventures with Buck that he seems unworthy of Buck's affections. Besides, he looks like a big kid himself.

White and Arteta create, via Buck's longing, a complex prism through which the film takes on far grander and disturbing perspectives than its sitcom setup suggests. Buck is, for all intents and purposes, really a kid—when he's mocked or ignored or his affections aren't returned, it's as if a child is being abused. This is due in large part to White's ever-grinning portrayal of Buck, which makes him more child than man. But, at the same time, he's still a man. Besides, the so-called adults he meets—Chuck, or Sam (Paul Weitz), the untalented actor Buck casts in the play he writes ("Hank & Frank")—are children, too, albeit in more subtle and damaging ways.

White is primarily a writer and the other principals are also nonactors—the Weitz brothers are writers-directors ("American Pie"); Colt is a producer and talent manager. All are good, but the actor who steals the movie is Lupe Ontiveros, as kind-if-caustic theater manager Beverly. "it's a homoerotic, misogynistic love story," she says of "Hank & Frank." Although that doesn't quite describe "Chuck & Buck," it's nice having Beverly act as our proxy, startled but definitely amused.

SIGHT AND SOUND, 12/00, p. 44, Edward Lawrensen

Buck lives in California with his mother. When she dies, Buck's estranged boyhood friend Chuck arrives at the funeral with his fiancée Carlyn. When Buck grabs Chuck's crotch, Chuck leaves. Buck moves to Los Angeles and begins stalking Chuck. He writes a play, called *Hank and Frank* based on their friendship, to be staged in the theatre near Chuck's office. Visiting Chuck's house, Buck suggests he and Chuck indulge in the sex games they used to play when they were kids. Chuck refuses and tells Buck to leave him alone.

Buck befriends Sam, the actor performing Hank (the play's equivalent of Chuck). After drinking in his place, Buck makes a move on Sam, who rejects him. Chuck reluctantly accompanies Carlyn to the only performance of *Hank and Frank* after watching the play, Carlyn storms off. Buck tells Chuck that he will leave him alone if they have sex one last time. Chuck acquiesces. Buck moves in opposite Sam, who has forgiven him. Later, he is invited to Chuck and Carlyn's wedding.

In this, Miguel Arteta's second feature, the title character Buck writes a play, a thinly veiled autobiographical account of his childhood friendship with Chuck, now a bigshot in the music industry. Beverly, the theatre manager hired to direct the play, doesn't quite know what to make of it. "It's like a homoerotic misogynistic love story," she hazards.

Watching *Chuck & Buck* you recognise her bewilderment. Buck, played by the film's writer Mike White, is an oddball, a 27-year-old man-child who sucks on lollipops, still plays with toy cars and blunders into situations, blithely unaware of the adult tensions underlying them. In one sense, Buck's childlike take on things cuts through the frippery of Chuck's LA life: at a party Chuck is having for his record-industry colleagues, Buck shoots dead any attempt at smalltalk; later he admires Buck's place "I like your house... it's kind of old personey." The use of a child or childlike protagonist to puncture the pretensions of adulthood is common enough in contemporary Hollywood (from *Big* to *Forrest Gump),* but what makes *Chuck & Buck* so fresh is that it pushes the logic of this device to absurd degrees. Buck's attempts to reignite his friendship with Chuck are funny (like Mike Leigh, Arteta, whose first film *Star Maps* was unreleased in the UK, knows how to turn embarrassment into laughs) but there's also something sad, if not dysfunctional about Buck's refusal to let go of his childish ways.

The film takes on a darker, more unsettling edge when it becomes clear that Buck's attachment to Chuck stems from the sex games they used to play when they were 11 years old—"Suck and fuck" as Buck remembers one of them. At first, you're not sure whether to trust Buck's recollections: shot, like the rest of the film, on digital video, his flashbacks have a desaturated, over-exposed quality to them, like memories half imagined, as insubstantial as the misty wisps that billow from Buck's humidifier. But once Chuck, in a brilliantly played, disquieting scene, confirms what happened between them as boys, the film is on difficult uncertain ground: in questioning the standard notion that children of that age are wholly desexualised, Arteta does a spot of taboo-breaking which iconoclastic philosopher Michel Foucault could be proud of—and it's certainly a long way from the saccharine depictions of childhood Hollywood tends to favour. But in making light comedy out of the premise, Arteta soft pedals the way these two men might have been affected by participating in such precocious sexual experiments; worse still, in poking fun at the idea that Buck still fancies Chuck, the director seems to connect Buck's homosexuality—he is also taken with macho-man Mike, who acts (ineptly) in his play—to his arrested development, as if his gay crushes were a further sign of emotional immaturity But just as Beverly's damning description of Buck's play doesn't quite do the beguilingly amateurish performance justice, the sour note struck here by the film is sugared by Arteta's many graceful and delicate touches. For all its rebarbative moments, *Chuck & Buck* is a film which you can't quite get a fix on: it's a movie about child sex which is also as airy and sweetly likeable as anything you'll see this year. What makes it such strange viewing is that it's hard to tell whether this is a sign of Arteta's achievement as a film-maker or his failing.

TIME, 7/17/00, p. 72, Richard Schickel

Chuck & Buck is amateurishly acted and glacially directed, and its story line is blithely blind to its most offensive implications. In short, you're going to be hearing a lot about this movie in the next few weeks. So what you're about to read constitutes fair warning: Don't believe the fuzzy buzz already surrounding it. Any movie that sentimentalizes stalking ought to be shunned.

The film's prime mover is Buck, played by its writer, Mike White, who was also a producer on the flop-d'estime TV show *Freaks and Geeks*. Buck is in his late 20s, but his development was arrested in preadolescence. Jobless, he lives with his mother, who dies in the opening sequence. He invites his old pal Chuck (Chris Weitz) to the funeral.

Chuck, who now prefers to be called Charlie, has not seen Buck in 15 years, has a fast-track job in the Los Angeles music industry and a seemingly strong relationship with his fiancé Carlyn (Beth Colt), and has long since put aside childish things, especially his boyhood fling with Buck, who gropes him at the funeral. Undeterred by Chuck's resistance, Buck moves to Los Angeles, where Chuck becomes his occupation. Make that preoccupation. He intrudes on him at his home and his office; he peers through the window when Chuck and Carlyn make love; he mistakes their puzzled politeness for encouragement. Like any nice bourgeois couple, they are reluctant to make a scene, especially with such a pathetic case. They keep hoping he will go away.

If we develop sympathy for anyone in director Miguel Arteta's film, it is for this put-upon couple. We have all been driven crazy, sometime or other, by the peculiar persistence of the unshakable nerd who refuses to take the hint of our indifference, even when it escalates to rudeness. This nerd, though, is in a class by himself. He writes and produces what seems to be an expressionistic but childlike play about their former relationship. When it's over, he offers Chuck a deal: one night of grown-up love and then he will leave him alone.

By this time, the deal looks like the only way out for Chuck and we are given to understand that they both emerge from the experience better men. Chuck and Carlyn get married, and Buck is seen at their wedding sidling up to a more appropriate object for his affections. We, however, are left in a somewhat larger emotional limbo.

It is not Buck's homosexuality that disturbs us. (Who, outside the Christian right, cares anymore about anyone's sexual orientation?) What's upsetting about the movie is its refusal to judge Buck's intrusiveness. Sometimes it seems to think it's funny; all the time it begs us to sympathize with it. But obsession, no less than the cell phone or the unerasability of our Internet wanderings, is a threat to our privacy, possibly our lives. Any movie, especially one as crude and inept as this one, that refuses to acknowledge that fact is dishonest—sort of a *Scream IV* without that series' exemplary scariness.

VILLAGE VOICE, 7/18/00, p. 117, J. Hoberman

A script-driven tale of tormented love, *Chuck & Buck is* a low-budget indie that manages to be not only consistently droll but cumulatively poignant and even scary.

Buck (Mike White) is 27 and still living in the suburban bedroom where he first played Star Wars. When his mother dies, Buck's first thought is that her funeral might serve as bait to lure back his long-moved-away boyhood best friend, Chuck *(American Pie* coproducer Chris Weitz). Chuck's magical reappearance—he's now grown into an L.A. music executive with a fiancée named Carlyn (Beth Colt)—leaves Buck with an unquenchable desire to resume their friendship at the point where it ended, on the confused cusp of adolescence. He relocates to L.A., along with his toy collection, and, re-creating his room in a motel, begins his pursuit.

Chuck & Buck was directed by Miguel Arteta and written by TV producer White (among the perpetrators of *Dawson's Creek),* whose comic performance is the movie's central creation. Sucking on lollipops and drawling his lines with a hopeful little smile, Buck is a fascinating doppelganger for a Hollywood success like White—precisely the sort of mush-mouthed village idiot Taylor Mead used to play in the underground movies of the early '60s. His scenes with Chuck's smooth and insincere Tom Cruise type have the quality of a protracted phony phone call. "It's weird you have this office," Buck remarks, having inserted himself into Chuck's workday afternoon. Ignoring the fact that this nudnick lacks the social skills of even a backward 10-year-old, Carlyn invites him to Chuck's promotion party. "I notice there are no pictures of me" is Buck's first observation of Chuck's "old person-y" dream pad.

Shot on digital video, *Chuck & Buck* has an engagingly slapdash quality—there's some occasional scan-line wiggle and the lighting is uneven. Surprisingly, though, the filmmakers know where to take this nightmare. *Chuck & Buck* compounds White's psychodrama as Buck writes his own autobiographical play, *Hank and Frank,* which he manages to get staged (once) at a community theater rented for the occasion. "It's like a homoerotic misogynistic love story," the practical house manager Buck's hired to direct tells him—not unkindly. Lupe Ontiveros's down-to-earth, smoky-voiced performance adds another dimension of humor, especially since the playwright doesn't know what she means. The proceedings begin to darken as Buck gets involved with his actors—one of them 10 years old, the other an adult with a mental age of perhaps even less.

Chuck & Buck has the same sense of mounting hysteria as Arteta's *Star Maps,* although the narrative is better held in check. The deadpan attitude, if not the filmmaking, has some resemblance to *Rushmore* and *Happiness.* (The main theme is a perky pop madrigal with an idiotic refrain: "Ooodly ooodly ooodly—fun fun fun!") A knowing little movie about the end of innocence and its dogged persistence, *Chuck & Buck* has one joke but the riff is sustained.

Also reviewed in:
CHICAGO TRIBUNE, 7/21/00, Friday/p. A, Mark Caro
NEW YORK TIMES, 7/14/00, p. E10, A.O. Scott
NEW YORKER, 7/24/00, p. 87, David Denby
VARIETY, 2/7-13/00, p. 54, Dennis Harvey
WASHINGTON POST, 7/21/00, p. C12, Stephen Hunter
WASHINGTON POST, 7/21/00, Weekend/p. 35, Michael O'Sullivan

CHUTNEY POPCORN

A Mata Films release of a Mata production.   *Executive Producer:* Trina Wyatt.   *Producer:* Susan Carnival, Nisha Ganatra, Sarah Vogel, Rober E. Kass, and Kelley Forsyth.   *Director:* Nisha Ganatra.   *Screenplay:* Nisha Ganatra and Susan Carnival.   *Director of Photography:* Erin King.   *Editor:* Jane Pia Abramowitz.   *Music:* Karsh Kale.   *Sound:* Missy Cohen.   *Casting:* Judy Henderson.   *Production Designer:* Jody Kipper.   *Costumes:* Robin Shane.   *Make-up:* Gabriella Voight.   *Running time:* 92 minutes.   *MPAA Rating:* Not Rated.

CAST: Jill Hennessy (Lisa); Nisha Ganatra (Reena); Nick Chinlund (Mitch); Madhur Jaffrey (Meenu); Sakina Jaffrey (Sarita); Ajay Naidu (Raju); Cara Buono (Janis); Daniella Rich (Tiffany); Eliza Foss (Dr. Brendel); Priscilla Lopez (Loretta); Alisa Mast (Becca); Amy Veltman (Jet).

NEW YORK POST, 9/22/00, p. 50, Jonathan Foreman

Nisha Ganatra's big-hearted romantic comedy is about a young Indian-American lesbian named Reena (played by Ganatra), who lives with her girlfriend, Lisa ("Law & Order's"Jillian Hennessy), in the East Village.

Reena surprises everyone when she offers to have a baby for her sister, Sarita (Sakina Jaffrey)—not least, her traditionalist mother (Madhur Jaffrey), who hopes that the experience might cure her "disability."

There's some lumpy writing and uneasy acting, but it's easy to see why this charming, inventive film won prizes at festivals in San Francisco and Newport, R.I.

NEWSDAY, 9/22/00, Part II/p. B10, John Anderson

A tartly funny movie is one thing. A tartly funny movie that discovers there are taboos left to break—and then breaks them—is another. "Chutney Popcorn," the feature debut of director Nisha Ganatra, is a movie with lesbian themes, set within an immigrant Indian milieu. Presumably, it was the combination of elements that kept the film on the shelf so long. It certainly wasn't the movie.

With a fresh, unpredictable screenplay co-written by Ganatra and Susan Carnival, "Chutney Popcorn" is consistently amusing, because it's constantly surprising. Ganatra's themes—family, loyalty, honesty, sacrifice—are nothing new, but her approach is. She consistently takes left turns, finding unlikely parallels between her gay characters' ad hoc community and the world of expatriated Indians, from the henna tattooing practiced by Reena (Ganatra herself) that punctuates so many sequences, to the outsider status felt by those on both sides of the film.

Reena, whose lesbianism is barely acknowledged by her mother (the veteran Indian actress—cookbook author Madhur Jaffrey), is given an opportunity to "redeem" herself in her family's eyes: Act as surrogate mother for her childless sister, Sarita (Sakina Jaffrey). Nothing quite works out as expected, of course. Reena's girlfriend Lisa (Jill Hennessy, formerly of TV's "Law & Order") feels cut out of the loop; Reena's sister has an 11th-hour change of heart and Mom sees the whole pregnancy thing as a way of "curing" her wayward daughter. En route to a virtual orgy of self-reassessment, "Chutney Popcorn" remains witty and droll.

It's the kind of movie that gives indie filmmaking a good name. The actors are terrific—particularly Hennessy and Cara Buono ("Next Stop, Wonderland"), who plays a particularly ascerbic member of Reena's troupe. Ganatra has received a number of awards from a number of festivals for a film that couldn't have been easy to make (if any, in fact, are). Personally, we can't wait for her to get back to work.

VILLAGE VOICE, 9/26/00, p. 147, Jessica Winter

Nisha Ganatra writes, directs, and stars in *Chutney Popcorn*, and while her feature debut is low-key and affectionate, it's also hobbled by wish fulfillment and identity posturing. Ganatra plays Reena, an Indian American henna artist who bears a child for her infertile sister, Sarita, and brother-in-law against the immediate wishes of her white girlfriend, traditional Indian mom, and—as it turns out—Sarita herself. The director has a fitfully deployed gift for droll humor, but *Chutney Popcorn* mostly provides evidence that the ins and outs of the improvised multiparent family can be as prosaic as the nuclear Eisenhower model.

Also reviewed in:
NEW REPUBLIC, 10/9/00, p. 30, Stanley Kauffmann
NEW YORK TIMES, 9/22/00, p. E14, Stephen Holden
VARIETY, 5/3-9/99, p. 85, Lael Loewenstein

CINEMA VERITE: DEFINING THE MOMENT

A National Film Board of Canada release with support from Telefilm Canada.   *Executive Producer:* Sally Bochner, Doris Girard, and Adrienne Bournevill.   *Producer:* Eric Michel and Adam Symansky.   *Director:* Peter Wintonick.   *Screenplay:* Kirwan Cox.   *Director of Photography:* Francis Miquet.   *Editor:* Marlo Miazga and Peter Wintonick.   *Music:* Jimmy James.   *Sound:* Peter Wintonick. *Running time:* 102 minutes.   *MPAA Rating:* Not Rated.

WITH: D.A. Pennebaker; Richard Leacock; Wolf Koenig; Albert Maysles; Hope Ryden; Richard Ballentine; Jean Rouch; Doug Leiterman; Jean-Pierre Beauviala; Michel Brault; Gillian Caldwell; Robin Cowie; Robert Drew; Jennifer Fox; William Greaves; Gregg Hale; Roman Kroitor; Barbara Kopple; Terrence McCartney Filgate; Pierre Perrault; Karel Reisz; Jean Rouch; Floria Sigismondi; Frederick Wiseman; David Bowie, Marcel Carrièr, Henri Cartier-Bresson, Fred Davis, Anne Drew, Bob Dylan, Jane Fonda, John Grierson, John F. Kennedy, Robert F. Kennedy, and Peter Wintonick.

NEW YORK POST, 6/9/00, p. 50, Lou Lumenick

"Cinema Verite: Defining the Moment" ought to be required viewing for today's documentary filmmakers, many of whom have forgotten how their predecessors liberated the form from preachiness by simply recording their subjects.

It's worth sitting through self-consciously shot interviews with pioneers like Karel Reisz and director Peter Wintonick's corny framing devices in this somewhat self-promotional National Film Board of Canada production.

Eventually, you get to excerpts from some classics.

There are all-too-brief extracts from Richard Leacock's electrifying "Jazz Dance"; William Greaves' gripping "Emergency Room," shot at Montreal General Hospital; Reisz's "We Are the Lambeth Boys"; Robert Drew's "Primary," which follows John F. Kennedy's 1960 presidential campaign; and Barbara Kopple's Oscar-winning documentary about mining families, "Harlan County USA."

VILLAGE VOICE, 6/13/00, p. 160, Michael Atkinson

Unlike many of the midcentury's cinematic "movements," cinema vérité has faded from view not because it is dated but because it is now utterly ubiquitous. In fact, the label is, more than ever, "meaningless," as Frederick Wiseman says in Peter Wintonick's talking-codgers doc *Cinema Vérité: Defining the Moment*. No longer the running-with-the-devil antithesis to the documentary tradition but the tradition itself, today vérité is a way of life; anyone can, and often will, make their own high-res/digital-video doc. Wintonick eventually ends up at the brink of the vérité to come (several of the vets are experimenting with palm-corders and Web distribution), but in sketching out the glory days of old men, he misses vast opportunities to examine the nature of vérité, and therefore our experience of the world, in relation to 24-hour life-cams and global simultaneity.

Date the wave's origins however you want; being a Canadian supported by the National Film Board, Wintonick locates the roots of the sensibility in the unheralded likes of Michel Brault and Wolf Koenig loosening up the rigidities of Canadian TV news. As they articulate what defined "vérité" in the making, nearly all of the big guns—including Drew, Leacock, Wiseman, Pennebaker, Rouch, Greaves, and Reisz—climax their frontier-forging tales with the stunned realization of how damn easy making a documentary is now. But only Albert Maysles is particularly eloquent, defining his approach as a search for "uncontrolled cinema" in which a genuine respect for the subject is all, and maintaining that "if you're worried about objectivity and subjectivity, you're afraid to film." Visits with Barbara Kopple, Jennifer Fox, and Gillian Caldwell (who trains international activists to shoot footage of human rights abuses for the Witness Web site) are a welcome acknowledgment of the last quarter-century, but Wintonick (who codirected the similarly gimmicky *Manufacturing Consent*) spends far too much time involving himself in the action as he jumps from one flatbed to the next. As slight and useful as a Cliffs Notes, the film helplessly skimps on the style as a viewing experience; excerpted clips just don't have that real-time vérité juice.

Also reviewed in:
NEW YORK TIMES, 6/9/00, p. E21, A. O. Scott
VARIETY, 11/29-12/5/99, p. 57, Ken Eisner

CIRCUS

A Columbia Pictures release of a Film Development Corporation production.   *Executive Producer:* Alberto Ardissone.   *Producer:* James Gibb and Alan Latham.   *Director:* Rob Walker.   *Screenplay:* David Logan.   *Director of Photography:* Ben Seresin.   *Editor:* Oral Norrie Ottey.   *Music:* Simon Boswell.   *Sound:* Bill Dodkin and (music) Geoff Foster.   *Sound Editor:* Campbell Askew.   *Casting:* Michelle Guish.   *Production Designer:* James Merifield.   *Art Director:* Peter Wenham.   *Set Decorator:* Gina Cromwell.   *Special Effects:* Tom Harris and Paul Kelly.   *Costumes:* Anna Sheppard.   *Make-up:* Pam Haddock.   *Stunt Coordinator:* Peter Brayham.   *Running time:* 95 minutes.   *MPAA Rating:* R.

CAST: John Hannah (Leo Garfield); Famke Janssen (Lily Garfield); Peter Stormare (Julius Harvey); Brian Conley (Bruno Maitland); Tiny Lister (George "Moose" Marley); Amanda Donohoe (Gloria); Fred Ward (Elmo Somerset); Eddie Izzard (Troy Cabrera); Ian Burfield (Caspar Glit); Neil Stuke (Roscoe); Michael Attwell (Magnus); Jason Watkins (Dom); Christopher Biggins (Arnie); Lucy Akhurst (Helen); Louise Rolfe (Kelly); Hinda Hicks (Beautiful Singer); Rob Walker (Old Tramp); Marcus Heath (Paul); Christopher Tune (Boy Racer); Louis Hammond (Jeweler); Evelyn Duah (Jeweler's Assistant); Steve Toussaint (Black); Julie Saunders (Hotel Receptionist); Che Walker (Nightclub Worker).

SIGHT AND SOUND, 6/00, p. 37, Geoffrey Macnab

Brighton, the present. Gangster boss Bruno Maitland orders the killing of his double-crossing accountant. Bruno hopes to recruit con artist Leo Garfield to run his casino. Leo is reluctant to take the job. He and his wife Lily are planning their own scam: Leo has been hired to murder Gloria by her husband, businessman Julius Harvey. But Harvey has double crossed Leo: Gloria isn't his wife after all. He begins to blackmail Leo, who is already in trouble with psychopathic local bookie Troy.

It turns out that Gloria was the girlfriend of Bruno's bodyguard Moose. Distraught at her disappearance, he chases Leo into a hotel and is about to kill him when he realises Gloria is still alive. Leo staged the killing to hoodwink Harvey. Meanwhile, Lily's ex-boyfriend, Elmo Somerset, has come to Brighton to kill her. (Years before, she abandoned him mid-heist.) It turns out that Harvey is Bruno's new accountant and they are plotting against Leo together.

Everybody seems to be double-crossing one another. Leo and Harvey appear to be working in cahoots to swindle Bruno. They've managed to embezzle millions from him. There's a final shoot-out during which Leo and Harvey kill Bruno and Lily. They escape. Leo drugs Harvey and abandons him. Leo goes to the station to leave town. Waiting for him there is Lily. Her death turns out to have been faked.

"Don't trust any of these clowns," reads the tagline for *Circus*, an enjoyably awful Brighton-set crime movie which touts itself as a British answer to *The Usual Suspects*. It's a warning worth heeding. From the very first scene in which a criminal boss (rather improbably played by comedian Brian Conley) chews off a victim's ear, the film teeters on the edge of self-parody. The presence of Conley's fellow comedian Eddie Izzard (a loveable psychotic who enjoys going skinny dipping near Brighton Pier) reinforces the sense that we're not watching a proper gangster movie at all—rather one of those *Comic Strip Presents* spoofs which Peter Richardson, Keith Allen *et al* used to make in the 80s.

The film-makers blithely invoke every gangster movie cliché available. Conley may dress for much of the movie like Nehru, but he performs as if he is parodying Bob Hoskins in *The Long Good Friday*. The setting rekindles memories of the seedy Brighton written about by Patrick Hamilton and Graham Greene. There are plenty of nods in the direction of *film noir*, a few bows in the direction of *Lock, Stock and Two Smoking Barrels*, and even one or two murkily lit *Cincinnati Kid*-style gambling sequences.

One character, Conley's gigantic but simple-minded minder Moose, seems to have been taken directly from Raymond Chandler's *Farewell, My Lovely*. Lily, the double-crossing *femme fatale*, is presumably intended as a counterpart to the equally hard-boiled dames played by Barbara Stanwyck and Lauren Bacall, but she's lumbered with some woeful dialogue. ("I love you, you slinky, short-arsed Scotsman," is not a line Bacall would ever have uttered.) *Circus* is full of such bizarre juxtapositions. Fred Ward, as craggy and imposing as character actors come, is well cast as an American hoodlum, but is then lumbered with the sort of saucy scenes you used to find in Dick Emery or Benny Hill sketches. And Peter Stormare's gawky, vaguely sinister accountant is even more mannered than his John Lennon soundalike in *The Million Dollar Hotel*.

Howard Hawks famously observed that he never really understood the labyrinthine plot of *The Big Sleep*. He would have been totally baffled by *Circus*. David Logan's screenplay is so full of twists and reversals that the film-makers themselves seem bewildered by it. Certain characters, for instance Izzard's bookie or Amanda Donohoe's vamp, simply vanish. It is not clear how somebody as resourceful and cunning as Leo ever managed to get into hock to a low-life like Izzard's Troy Cabrera in the first place, nor how certain characters die in one scene and are miraculously resurrected in the next. The plotting is more tricksy than ingenious. The facile humour (pitbulls running themselves to a standstill on exercise machines and the like) undercuts any air of menace or tension. Still, the Simon Boswell soundtrack lends at least the illusion of urgency to the storytelling and the entire project is eccentric enough to qualify for cult status.

Also reviewed in:
CHICAGO TRIBUNE, 9/18/00, Tempo/p. 2, John Petrakis
NEW YORK TIMES, 9/16/00, p. B14, Lawrence Van Gelder
VARIETY, 5/8-14/00, p. 50, Derek Elley

CIRQUE DU SOLEIL: JOURNEY OF MAN

A Sony Pictures Classics release of a Cirque du Soleil/Motion International production. *Executive Producer:* Mitchell Cannold. *Producer:* Andre Picard and Peter Wagg. *Director:* Keith Melton. *Screenplay:* Peter Wagg and Steve Roberts. *Director of Photography:* Reed Smoot and John Hora. *Editor:* Harry B. Miller. *Music:* Benoît Jutras. *Music Editor:* Robb Boyd. *Sound:* Dan Gleich. *Production Designer:* John Zachary. *Visual Effects:* Peter Anderson. *Costumes:* Mark Bridges. *Make-up:* Melanie Robinett. *Running time:* 38 minutes. *MPAA Rating:* G.

CAST: Ian McKellen (Narrator); Nicky Dewhurst (Young Man); Brian Dewhurst (Old Man); Anait Karagyezyan (Vagabond Girl); Mikhail Matorin (Cube Act); Chris Van Wagenen (Youth); Kenny Raskin (Man); Cully Smoller (Infant/Child); Yves Decoste and Mario Laure Mesnage (Statues); Josette Dechene and Paul Vachon (Flounes); Jennifer Clèment (Character Statue).

LOS ANGELES TIMES, 5/19/00, Calendar/p. 10, Kevin Thomas

Imax 3-D seems an ideal medium for the Cirque du Soleil, but their first collaboration, "Journey of Man," proves to be an arty, kitschy allegory.

After a prologue featuring taiko drummers in a cave, we are plunged undersea for an aquatic ballet celebrating the birth of human life. A little boy, Infant (Cully Smoller), explodes from the briny deep into a leafy glade, where he is greeted in the forest primeval by the clown-like shamans, the Flounes (Josette Dechene, Paul Vachon), who introduce him to joy, fear, courage and wonder. The latter emotion is elicited by a fanciful Bungee act, a popular Cirque attraction, in which the performers are dressed like yellow bird-like creatures.

The boy, now a Youth (Chris Van Wagenen), is next transported to a dramatic rocky landscape—actually, Nevada's Valley of Fire State Park—where muscular Mikhail Matorin, a Cirque stalwart, is balancing and spinning a large metallic cube on a mountain parapet as a prelude to his spectacular flying routine. Having gotten an idea of how challenging life can be, the Youth becomes a Young Man (Nicky Dewhurst), whom we meet on the grounds of a vast estate with a reflecting pool, where a pair of marble statues, a man (Yves Decoste) and a woman (Marie-Laure Mesnage), come to life to perform a balancing act on an outsize lily pad.

Although the number is more gymnastic than erotic, the Young Man discovers the notion of love in contemplating them. But he apparently doesn't get the message, for when we discover him as a Mature Adult (Kenny Raskin), he is quite alone in his palatial residence—represented by the Grecian deco lobby of Severance Hall, a former Cleveland movie palace. But soon the lobby is filled by shabbily dressed acrobats (members of the Cirque's Banquine troupe). So impressed is he by the troupe that he forsakes materialism and embraces a rainbow coalition of young people, proceeding in Old Age (Brian Dewhurst) to visit Berlin's Brandenburg Gate, symbol of a new beginning.

Individual acts are thrilling in Imax 3-D, but stringing them together in so precious an allegory, as producer-writer Peter Wagg, co-writer Steve Roberts and director Keith Melton have, seems unnecessary and silly. No doubt small children and admirers of the Liberace aesthetic will be delighted.

NEW YORK POST, 5/12/00, p. 50, Hannah Brown

When you watch "Cirque du Soleil: Journey of Man," a new, 3-D IMAX movie opening today, you'll understand why clowns often make children scream with terror, not joy.

The ugly, witless pair of clowns (Josette Dechene and Paul Vachon) who flit through the movie are emblematic of everything that is wrong with this dull, monumentally pretentious mess.

Fans of the acclaimed "Cirque du Soleil" troupe will be especially disappointed.

This film attempts to present, according to the press kit, "the stages of human development from birth to maturity."

The filmmakers string together a series of circus acts in garish costumes, linked by unintentionally hilarious narration (sample: "One day, I learned joy has a friend called fear.") and an "Everyman" character—the protagonist—followed by those hideous clowns.

This could have worked if the acts were filmed imaginatively and given ample time to perform. Unfortunately, they're not.

The movie opens with the Taiko Drummers, who pound away briefly in a cave, while a little boy (Cully Smoller) in a white body stocking appears, looking as if he smells something bad.

The scene shifts underwater, where a group of synchronized swimmers go through a genteel routine.

Next, he's dressed like a character in "Waiting for Godot." The clowns give him a teddy bear and lead him through an enchanted forest.

Soon, he's a teenager (Chris Van Wagenen) who finally shakes the clowns as he follows Cube Man (Mikhail Matorin), an acrobat he watches spinning and balancing a huge cube which bursts into flame.

Eventually he grows up, discovers love, becomes cynical and gets reacquainted with his inner child.

In the finale, the adult Everyman (Kenny Raskin) leads a multiracial group of children arm in arm to the Brandenberg Gate.

Perhaps this mega-cliché was meant as parody—or maybe it's just a joke on the audience.

In any case, it's not an entertaining film. No doubt there could be an enjoyable movie showcasing the talent of Cirque du Soleil, but this isn't it.

NEWSDAY, 5/19/00, Part II/p. B6, Gene Seymour

A curious compound of wonder and languor is in store for the person staring through 3-D goggles at "Cirque du Soleil: Journey of Man." No other reaction seems possible to a film—or "filmed experience"—that so inchoately blends awesome feats of physical daring with pompous head cheese about growing up, growing old and Keeping the Inner Child Alive.

It's the kind of pageant that a Broadway impresario of 100 years ago would have mounted without irony, beginning with a set piece with scantily clad guys playing drums that (like almost all the other set pieces) seems longer than it is. Through the smoke and din, a boy named Boy (you were expecting "Norbert"?) emerges with a white bodysuit. His primordial gestation is celebrated in a captivating display of synchronized swimming.

Then these two annoying clowns, collectively dubbed "Instinct," meet Boy and take him into the next phases of life—or Life—where layers of innocence are shed and marked by dozens of acrobats performing rigorous, complex and seemingly impossible routines with what can properly be characterized as the greatest of ease.

For those who have never beheld the fabled "Cirque du Soleil" in live performance, this IMAX "experience" represents a worthy introduction to both the troupe's wonders and its pretensions. One wonders, however, why anyone went to the trouble of wrapping these acts in such thick, amorphous gloss. Children may be dazzled, but don't be surprised if your own Inner Child gets itchy and cranky before this "Journey of Man" completes its 38-minute run.

VILLAGE VOICE, 5/23/00, p. 146, Jessica Winter

Cirque du Soleil's campy, crackbrained, and in no way unenjoyable 3-D IMAX pageant *Journey of Man* might be the oddest movie offering of the year so far. Guided by hilariously solemn voice-over (Man is an old English guy), the voyage begins in the midst of dry ice and bare-chested Fabio look-alikes banging on drums; a child in a hooded white bodysuit emerges from the smoke and, eventually, ends up in a forest dressed in Dickensian-scamp raiment and led about by two clowns babbling in Teletubbese. Later, another shirtless hunk of beefcake spins a cube on his head (narrator: "My childhood dreams were behind me"); at a pool deck some Greek statues perform gravity-defying yoga ("I had found love, and had to own its secret"); back home in Man's mansion-cum-museum-cum-seraglio, dozens of cute boys leap out from behind red velvet curtains and do gymnastics ("Occasionally, doubts and troubles invaded my seclusion"). Kitschy theme-park kid stuff or agreeably deranged coming-out tale? With that 3-D headset, can you go wrong either way?

Also reviewed in:
NEW YORK TIMES, 5/10/00, p. E10, Stephen Holden
VARIETY, 5/22-28/00, p. 21, Lael Lowewenstein

CLAIRE DOLAN

A Film Sociaty of Lincoln Center and the Independent Feature Project release of an Ann Ruark production in association with Time Warner Cable and the Sundance Channel. *Producer:* Ann Ruark. *Director:* Lodge Kerrigan. *Screenplay:* Lodge Kerigan. *Director of Photography:* Teodoro Maniaci. *Editor:* Kristina Boden. *Music:* Ahrin Mishan and Simon Fisher Turner. *Music Editor:* Daniel Evans Farkas. *Sound:* Peter Schneider, Kelly Neese, and (music) Tony Volante. *Casting:* Avy Kaufman. *Production Designer:* Sharon Lomofsky. *Set Decorator:* Susan Ogu. *Costumes:* Laura Jean Shannon. *Make-up:* Jorge Nelson. *Stunt Coordinator:* Blaise Corrigan and Douglas Crosby. *Running time:* 95 minutes. *MPAA Rating:* Not Rated.

CAST: Katrin Cartlidge (Claire Dolan);   Vincent D'Onofrio (Elston Garrett);   Colm Meaney (Roland Cain);   John Doman (Cain's Friend);   Maryann Plunkett (Mary Egan);   Miranda Stuart Rhyne (Angela, Elton's Daughter);   Kate Skinner (Madeleine Garrett); David Little (Man in Chicago Cafe);   Lola Pashalinski and Candy Buckley (Salon Clients);   Jim Frangione (Man in Bar);   Ed Hodson (Driver);   Tom Gilroy ($1000 Trick);   John Ventimiglia (Newark Cab Driver);   Patrick Husted (George);   Muriel Maida (Claire's Mum);   Lizabeth Mackay (Administrator);   Svetlana Jovanivich (Eva);   Madison Arnold (Priest);   Brenda Thomas Denmark (Woman at Book Stand);   Sean Powers (Driver's Friend);   Sally Stark (Waitress at Newark Diner);   Sarah Rose Hendrickson (Siobhan, Mary's Daughter);   Babo Harrison (Salon Owner);   Marian Quinn (Woman in Park);   Missy Yager (Cathy);   Henry Morales-Ballet and Gary Warner (Tricks);   Alan Davidson (Man in Diner);   Dominic Marcus (Newark Cab Driver);   Adrianna Sevan (Woman at Cab Stand); Michael Laurence (Elton's Fare);   Blaise Corrigan (Gunman);   Bruce MacVittie (Obstetrician).

NEW YORK POST, 2/25/00, p. 57, Hannah Brown

"Claire Dolan," which opened at the Walter Reade Theater and kicked off the American Independent Visions film series there, is a chilly, intelligent tale of an alienated prostitute trying to start a new life.

Watching it is a frustrating experience, because, although it has moments of emotional intensity, it leaves, so many questions about its heroine unanswered.

The central mystery about Claire (Katrin Cartlidge) is why such a poised, striking young woman would choose to work as a call girl. She says she got into it because she needed the money, but it seems odd that there are no alternatives for someone who feels as degraded by the daily humiliations of her life as the poker-faced Claire.

She seems especially pained when trying to sweet-talk the crude, wealthy businessmen who are her clients.

Much of the film takes place in a Manhattan made up entirely of steel-and-glass skyscrapers and beige, tastefully underfurnished hotel suites. Writer/director Lodge Kerrigan paints a meticulous portrait of New York as a spotless, almost empty metropolis.

Claire, an Irish immigrant, is in debt to a sinister pimp (Colm Meaney) who takes the lion's share of her earnings and murmurs the kind of world-weary, philosophical ramblings that are frequently spouted by celluloid pimps. But when Claire's mother, who is in a nursing home (presumably supported by the pimp) dies, Claire takes the opportunity to change her life and flees to Newark. There, she gets a job in a hairdressing salon and starts dating a divorced, sad-sack cab driver, Elton (Vincent D'Onofrio).

But the pimp tracks her down and orders her back to New York. Meekly, she obeys.

Elton won't give up, either, and he finds her. When she is finally able to pay off the pimp, she convinces Elton that they should have a child together.

Every frame in this bleak film, however, indicates that there will be no happy ending for anyone.

The actors deliver their dialogue in uninflected tones of voice, reminiscent of the films of Hal Hartley. The effect is powerful, although sometimes grating.

"Claire Dolan" occasionally evokes Jean-Luc Godard's "My Life to Live" and Neil Jordan's "Mona Lisa," both stories of women who tried to sell their bodies and hold onto their souls.

But, unfortunately, "Claire Dolan" is too studied and remote to have the impact of these other dramas.

In spite of Cartlidge's impressive performance in the lead, the film is simply not as involving or moving as it should be.

SIGHT AND SOUND, 5/00, p. 45, Ken Hollings

New York, the present. Calling herself Lucy, Claire Dolan works the hotels as a call girl but gives most of her money to Roland Cain, an old family friend to whom she owes money and who acts as her pimp. When Claire's mother dies in a nursing home, she doesn't inform Cain (although he is paying for the old woman's treatment) and flees to Newark, New Jersey, shortly after the funeral.

Finding work as a beautician, she meets Elton, a divorced cab driver, and they embark on an affair. Cain shows up in Newark and forces Claire back to New York, where he supplies her to his friends for free. Elton follows her and learns the truth about her existence. He gives Claire money to help settle the debt to Cain, but knowing she is a prostitute unsettles him. Elton agrees to her having their baby, but the relationship collapses. Claire, now pregnant, pays off Cain and leaves for Chicago to have the baby and start anew. Several months later, Cain meets Elton on the street, accompanied by his new wife who is happily expecting their first child. They talk as if they were old friends but neither mentions Claire.

Throughout this stylishly austere follow-up to writer/director Lodge Kerrigan's 1993 debut *Clean, Shaven* the Manhattan skyline dominates the action with an intrusive, enigmatic presence. Never have its towers and facades looked sexier or more forbidding. From the cool formalism of the title sequence, in which grids of concrete and reflective glass fill the screen, through to the last sidewalk confrontation framed against blocks of impassive concrete, the architecture of New York organises and isolates the human protagonists, arranging them as if they were on display in the panels of some joyless adult comic strip.

The first time we see call girl Claire (played with twitchy wariness by Katrin Cartlidge) she is encased in a rectangular glass phone booth, trading fake intimacies with her clients as she arranges her schedule. Immediately afterwards, she contemplates her image in the interior of a mirror-lined hotel elevator on her way up to an assignation. In the ensuing sex scene, DP Teodoro Maniaci brings echoes of the lush erotic fantasies Helmut Newton created in the late 70s but without their mock-heroic celebration of power and passion. The room's ceiling is oppressively low, while the skyscrapers outside form mute voyeuristic panoramas.

Although Cartlidge manages to signal a great deal from behind Claire's hunted exterior, everything around her is featureless and numb. Sometimes she seems as detached from the film as she is from her nameless succession of partners. Adept at swallowing her fear and facing men down when the need arises, Claire remains visibly intimidated by her pimp Cain, who seems disturbingly aware of everything happening inside her. With the nature of her debt to him and his connection to her family left unexplained, Cain becomes an external manifestation of Claire's inner loathing. That both their names are near anagrams of each other indicates some unspoken link, especially since *Clean, Shaven* featured a protagonist who heard voices.

Colm Meaney's performance lends a bluff, pinched quality to the mysterious Cain, suggesting a man uninclined to waste his energy on violence when a little gentle persuasion will do. "I've known Claire since she was 12 years old," he hisses at Elton after punching him in the gut, "and I knew then what I know now, that deep inside she's a whore. She was born a whore and she'll die a whore." If the fumbling, unfortunate Elton has little to counter this assertion with, it's because the film's sparse dialogue, fleeting visual clues and Claire's displays of counterfeit emotion for strangers hardly give much more away.

As the curious outsider, Elton acts as a cipher for both the director and the audience, prying into cupboards, flicking through photographs and watching from a distance. Vincent D'Onofrio has less of a character than a series of reactions to work with. This gives the film one voyeur too many, resulting in a loss of narrative focus towards the end. However, it's the lean and eloquent camerawork, capturing a blow job reflected in a television screen or the dark swirl of lights in a road tunnel at night, from which *Claire Dolan* ultimately derives its taut inner life. With a carefully sculpted soundtrack that blends a haunting, minimalist score with the raw sounds of high-rise city life, Kerrigan's second feature maintains an impressively restrained assault upon the senses.

VILLAGE VOICE, 2/29/00, p. 107, J. Hoberman

A bit precious, ultimately wearisome, *Judy Berlin* [see Hoberman's review] deserves to alternate reels with Lodge Kerrigan's even more pretentious Amerindie, *Claire Dolan*. Indeed, in a more perfect universe, *Claire Dolan* would be the feature in which Judy got her break.

Like Kerrigan's first feature, the genuinely disturbing *Clean, Shaven* (1933), *Claire Dolan*, released by New Yorker Films, is a character study about an ostentatiously opaque character. The film is impeccably shot and utterly absurd. Superstudied telephoto compositions map a cold urban geometry of steel furniture and rippling reflections. Katrin Cartlidge, most familiar for her garrulous roles in Mike Leigh's *Naked* and *Career Girls*, has here been silenced, playing a high-class hooker who operates out of an East Side apartment with the charm of a dentist's waiting room.

Claire Dolan is hardly a slice of life. Once you buy into the idea of a call girl without a cell phone or even a beeper—when first seen, Claire is working a grimy midtown pay phone—anything is possible. Clients don't call her, she calls them, professing her desire and promising unimaginable pleasures in a flat monotone. Embodied by Cartlidge as dourly antierotic, she's gawky and severe, squinting balefully at her tricks as she's metaphorically nailed on the grid of a heartless city. In short, Claire (who owes money to her unctuously solicitous pimp until suddenly she doesn't) is an abstract entity.

Kerrigan's dialogue is as purposefully stilted as his mise-en-scène is aggressively antiseptic. This supremely alienated movie can't decide if it's *Crash* or *Working Girls* or maybe *Jeanne Dielmann* in reverse. Every interaction is tortuous—Claire's numerous sexual encounters not the least. At one point, she escapes to Newark, gets a new job, and picks up a sensitive cabbie named Elton (played by a smirking Vincent D'Onofrio as if without direction). Then, operating by some mysterious radar, her bluff, hearty pimp (Colm Meaney) comes to fetch her home, reinforcing his ruthlessness by casually tossing a pet kitty out the window.

Clean, Shaven demonstrated Kerrigan's intermittent brilliance. (Here, the movie jumps to life when Elton, in a scarily intense burst of adrenaline, is robbed in his cab.) But, even more than his heroine, the filmmaker seems boxed in by his own schemata. Less awful than inert, Claire Dolan comes across as a willfully bad movie. The moment of maximum stupefaction arrives when Claire affectlessly announces her desire. "I want to have a child," she abruptly informs Elton, adding without inflection, "we can make it work." Her conviction is underwhelming.

Also reviewed in:
CHICAGO TRIBUNE, 6/2/00, Friday/p. B, Michael Wilmington
NEW YORK TIMES, 2/25/00, p. E20, Stephen Holden
VARIETY, 5/25-31/98, p. 60, Todd McCarthy

CLEOPATRA'S SECOND HUSBAND

An Indican Pictures release of a Cucoloris Films/Flying Cow Productions presentation. *Executive Producer:* Claire Best, Peter Getty, and Linda Stewart.   *Producer:* Jill Goldman, David Scott Rubin, Jacqui de la Fontaine, and Jon Reiss. *Director:* Jon Reiss. *Screenplay:* Jon Reiss. *Director of Photography:* Matt Faw.   *Editor:* Toby Yates.   *Music:* Cary Berger. *Sound:* B.J. Lehn. *Casting:* Lindsay Chag. *Production Designer:* John Di Minico and Thomas Thurnauer.   *Costumes:* Scott Freeman.   *Running time:* 92 minutes.   *MPAA Rating:* R.

CAST: Paul Hipp (Robert Marrs);   Boyd Kestner (Zack Taylor);   Bitty Schram (Hallie Marrs); Radha Mitchell (Sophie);   Alexis Arquette (Alex);   Jonathan Penner (Jon);   Nancye Ferguson (Asti).

LOS ANGELES TIMES, 12/1/00, Calendar/p. 8, Kevin Thomas

"Cleopatra!s Second Husband," a diabolically clever psychological suspense movie, arrives today, just now getting an L.A. theatrical release after scattered bookings elsewhere. It marks an assured and daring dramatic feature debut for writer-director Jon Reiss, whose documentary on the rave scene, "Better Living Through Circuitry," received wide acclaim. (Reiss worked on both movies at the same time, and he finished work on this 1998 L.A. Independent Film Festival entry a few weeks ahead of completing photography on "Circuitry.")

Robert Marrs (Paul Hipp) and his wife, Hallie (Bitty Schram), are hardly an atypical L.A. yuppie couple. Robert is an aspiring photographer who, through shrewd investments, is able to afford a pleasant lifestyle that includes a spacious, tastefully decorated, vintage Spanish-style house. Prone to sinus problems, migraine headaches and similar chronic health problems, Robert is a slight, nice-looking young man whose passive nature allows Hallie to dominate him easily, perhaps even unconsciously. Self-absorbed to the extent that she is oblivious to his needs and desires, she is intent on becoming pregnant but rebuffs his sexual overtures unless the timing is right for her to conceive.

She nonetheless has worked out a plan for a vacation in the country that she thinks will provide a calm atmosphere that will increase her chances of becoming pregnant and has lined up a young couple, Zack (Boyd Kestner) and Sophie (Radha Mitchell), who are friends of friends, to house-sit. The Marrs have barely started their rather edgy vacation when Robert gets an offer from an important photo magazine to publish his work, an unexpected windfall of such significance that he uncharacteristically asserts himself, and he and Hallie return home.

Robert is outraged to find their fish dead in the aquarium and suggests Zack and Sophie leave, but they ask to stay on a few days to find an apartment, which it's obvious they have no intention of trying to locate. Hallie, out of sorts at her husband for cutting short their getaway, insists that the couple be allowed to remain a full week—more than enough time for these guests to wreak havoc. Zack is rugged, sexy and as assertive as Robert is meek, and Sophie is quite a dish. They make love frequently and loudly. And when Sophie comes on to Robert, he succumbs swiftly. The fun and games now begin in earnest.

Were Robert and Hallie bound by love rather than convenience and convention, they would not be so vulnerable to such manipulative, amoral opportunists. Not incapable of kindness, Sophie's just along for the ride, but Zack is an all-out sociopath.

Robert and even Zack might both have passed their lives more or less uneventfully, but having met, they bring out in each other aspects of themselves that are confounding in their extremity.

Joseph Losey's "The Servant, " with Dirk Bogarde and James Fox, as master and servant who reverse roles as their ambiguous relationship develops, comes immediately to mind, but Reiss takes this similar situation to lengths that are deeply disturbing in their implications for human nature, and even the creation of art. Reiss illustrates clearly how disturbing a disassociation between a work of art and its inspiration can be, and he goes on to turn upside down the conventional notions of what can destroy or liberate an individual.

"Cleopatra's Second Husband," which finds in Hallie and Robert's relationship a parallel to that of Cleopatra and Marc Antony, is so consistently inventive and compelling that it sustains a seemingly downward trajectory that would be an increasingly morbid turn-off in lesser hands.

Robert and Zack truly, are not what they at first seem, and they reflect in each other human impulses at their darkest. What Reiss is able to pull out of Hipp and Kestner is amazing, and the uncanny rightness of their casting is echoed in the presence of Schram and Mitchell as well.

In the more demanding of the two women's roles, Schram really nails down Hallie, a woman who isn't such a bad sort but is simply shallow and obtuse, which, ironically, makes her resilient rather than vulnerable. Provocative, well-shot (by Matt Faw), brisk and unpretentious, "Cleopatra's Second Husband" works up a considerable chill.

NEW YORK POST, 10/20/00, p. 50, Lou Lumenick

This is one of those potentially interesting movies that takes its sweet time getting to the point—by which time many audience members will likely have bailed out or dozed off.

It starts out as a not terribly interesting black comedy of manners. Robert (Paul Hipp), a milquetoastish photographer, is bullied by his wife, Hallie (Bittie Schramm), into subletting their handsome house in California while they go on vacation.

When they return, Robert discovers that not only have his precious fish died, but the tenants are in no hurry to leave.

But all of this is so much foreplay. The last section of the inexplicably named "Cleopatra's Second Husband" (including a male rape) is a lot more involving and twisty than what came before—a real pity.

VILLAGE VOICE, 10/24/00, p. 150, Mark Holcomb

Cinema's assault on the middle class continues with *Cleopatra's Second Husband*, an engagingly grim psychological thriller from 1998. Unlike its Hollywood kin, however, this scene from the class gurgle has the courage of its convictions—which are misanthropic enough to make Neil LaBute wince.

Treading in early Polanski territory, *Cleopatra* charts the disruptive influence of a pair of freewheeling intruders on the lives of a bored L.A. couple. Shy photographer Robert Marrs (Paul Hipp, who has something of Kid in the Hall Kevin McDonald's deadpan charm) and his shrill missus, Hallie (Bitty Schram), leave their house in the care of sexy friends-of-friends Zach and Sophie (Boyd Kestner and Radha Mitchell) while on vacation. The house sitters stay on after the Marrses return home and use Robert to his full doormat potential, eventually causing Hallie to split. Zach then catches Sophie in bed with Robert and possibly rapes him as payback. She leaves and the two men set up house, with Zach dominating Robert into a crippling depression, but he ultimately rebounds from his funk to exact an excruciatingly prolonged revenge.

Cleopatra's Second Husband doesn't go much deeper than *American Beauty*'s lesson that angst and repression make unimpressive suburban men irresistible to hot young blonds and homicidal psychopaths alike. But unlike that odious specimen of yuppie self-loathing, it neither telegraphs its plot twists nor lets its protagonist off the hook. Robert's masochistic passivity becomes at least as pathological and threatening as Zach's casual sadism. Reiss maintains a wry tone up to the queasy finale, and while his unflinching view of human relationships may be insupportable, his understated style and wit have kinky rewards all their own.

Also reviewed in:
CHICAGO TRIBUNE, 11/17/00, Friday/p. Q, John Petrakis
NEW YORK TIMES, 10/20/00, p. E22, Stephen Holden
VARIETY, 5/11-17/98, p. 22, Todd McCarthy

CLOSER YOU GET, THE

A Fox Searchlight Pictures release of a Redwave production.   *Producer:* Uberto Pasolini. *Director:* Aileen Ritchie.   *Screenplay:* William Ivory.   *Story:* Herbie Wave.   *Director of Photography:* Robert Alazraki.   *Editor:* Sue Wyatt.   *Music:* Rachel Portman.   *Choreographer:* Sian Williams.   *Sound:* Peter Lindsay and (music) Chris Dibble..   *Sound Editor:* Zane Hayward.   *Casting:* Maureen Hughes.   *Production Designer:* Tom McCullagh.   *Art Director:* Shane Bunting and Jean Kerr.   *Special Effects:* Martin Neill.   *Costumes:* Kathy Strachan. *Make-up:* Pamela Smyth.   *Stunt Coordinator:* Donal O'Farrell.   *Running time:* 92 minutes. *MPAA Rating:* PG-13.

CAST: Niamh Cusack (Kate); Sean McGinley (Ian); Ian Hart (Kieran); Ewan Stewart (Pat); Sean McDonagh (Sean); Cathleen Bradley (Siobhan); Pat Shortt (Ollie); Deborah Barnett (Ella); Risteard Cooper (Father Hubert Mallone); Ruth McCabe (Mary); Maureen O'Brien (Dollie); Pat Laffan (Giovanni); Frank Laverty (Brian); Britta Smith (Mrs. Duncannon); Patricia Martin (Mrs. Lock); Doreen Keough (Mrs. Giovanni); Pauline Hutton (Deirdra); Nuala O'Neill (Molly); Dessie Gallagher (Mickey); Michael McDougall (Liam); Nora Keneghan (Mrs. Campbell); Brian Cannon (Bus Driver); Nikki Fox, Karen Noble, and Regina Ford (American Girls); Jackie Quinn (Jackie Fitzpatrick).

LOS ANGELES TIMES, 2/25/00, Calendar/p. 8, Kevin Thomas

[*The following review by Kevin Thomas appeared in a slightly different form in* **NEWSDAY, 2/25/00, Part II/p. B7.**]

"The Closer You Get" is a droll, hearty Irish comedy with a serious undertow all the more effective for its unexpected candor and depth. It was adapted by William Ivory from Herbie Wave's story and has a wonderfully bemused, compassionate understanding of the woes that can beset the ordinary bloke. Significantly, it was produced by Uberto Pasolini, who produced the mega-hit British comedy "The Full Monty."

The earlier film was famously concerned with a bunch of laid-off English factory workers driven by desperation to become strippers; in this film, directed by Aileen Ritchie with an astringent sense of humor, Ivory takes a look at the lack of romance in the lives of five men living in a gloriously picturesque village on Ireland's Donegal coast. That a woman is directing such a male-oriented story gives the film added tension and sharpness; "Closer" marks strong feature debuts for both Ritchie and Ivory.

One night at the local pub, the young butcher Kieran O'Donnagh (Ian Hart), who fancies himself more sophisticated than his peers, persuades his pals to advertise in the Miami Herald—yes, that's right—inviting eligible young beauties to attend the annual St. Martha's Day Dance, making it clear that he and his friends are all eligible bachelors—and solvent to boot. Besides Kieran, there's his older brother Ian (Sean McGinley), a sheepherder; the burly Ollie (Pat Shortt), a 36-year-old virgin still living with his mother; and Sean (Sean McDonagh), the youngest of the group, possibly still in his teens. The pub is owned by former soccer star Pat (Ewan Stewart) and his wife, Kate (Niamh Cusack), ostensibly happily married. Still Pat, the one handsome man in the entire community, not only spruces up his bar but starts working out to get back into top shape.

There's a hitch in the form of the town's formidable grocer-postmistress, Mary (Ruth McCabe), who sees nothing wrong in steaming open other people's mail when it arrives or before she sends it on its way. From the get-go, therefore, Mary sees to it that the women of the village know what Kieran et al are up to. While there's not a super-abundance of eligible women in the community, there's not such a drastic shortage that the men have to advertise for companionship. But one of the women observes that sometimes "the closer you get" the more likely you are to overlook what's right under your nose. In that regard Kieran is completely oblivious to Siobhan (Cathleen Bradley), his pretty but severe assistant, who in turn is put off by his crude ways.

Like many astute comedies with more than just laughs on, its mind, "The Closer You Get" gets more serious as it progresses, even amid a series of amusing situations set off by the men's plan and the women's awareness of it. "The Full Monty" made clear—beneath the laughter generated by its unlikely male strippers—that being laid off with little prospect of new employment can be demoralizing. And "Closer" makes clear the soul-withering prospect of a loveless existence.

If politics and economics are the villains of the "Monty" plot, "Closer" implies unmistakably that Roman Catholicism's puritanical tradition, which tends to set the flesh and the spirit at war, plays a pivotal part in keeping many of the villagers emotionally crippled, as well as sexually frustrated. Indeed, by the end of the film the village's young priest (Risteard Cooper), though not exactly a radical, is nudging his flock in directions that surely would not sit well with the Vatican. The film is not necessarily singling out Catholicism for criticism; it's just that it's the local faith and, therefore, influences everyone in the community.

Ritchie and Ivory never lose sight, however, that their film is a comedy, and they take pains to earn the amusing yet touching finale. In a fine ensemble cast, Hart stands out. His Kieran is homely, boorish and abrasive, yet his laughable pretensions to sophistication reveal an intelligent yearning for connection with the larger world and a determined unwillingness to accept the status quo.

While "The Closer You Get" may not become the box-office phenomenon that "The Full Monty" was—few foreign films do—Pasolini and Fox Searchlight look to have another hit on their hands.

NEW YORK POST, 2/25/00, p. 57, Lou Lumenick

St. Patrick's Day arrives early this year in the form of "The Closer You Get," an engaging bit of blarney set in a small fishing village on Ireland's west coast.

Less gritty than the Ireland of "Angela's Ashes" or "Agnes Brown," it combines lovely scenery and likable performers with a whimsical conceit along the lines of "The Full Monty" and "Waking Ned Devine."

When "10" is accidentally shown at the town church—the priest had actually ordered "The Ten Commandments" but there was a mixup—the village's horny bachelors, fired up by the sight of Bo Derek, decide to import some American beauties.

The men advertise for "fit and healthy" brides in the Miami Herald, much to the consternation of the village's unattached female population, none of whom had shown much interest previously in the pub-dwelling bachelors.

No women from America actually come for the village church festival, but the village lasses show up their men by luring in some Spanish sailors to dance with.

This has the effect of bringing together the sexes—particularly Kieran (Ian Hart), the local butcher, and his adoring assistant Siobhan (Cathleen Bradley), whom he faintly praises as "acceptable" if unsophisticated.

Hart (who provided much-needed life to "The End of the Affair" as the bumbling detective, and who resembles the young Sean Penn here) is very amusing as Kieran, who dyes his hair blond because he thinks it makes him more enticing.

Bradley is charming as the spirited Siobhan.

Other standouts in the excellent cast include Ruth McCabe as the nosy village postmistress, who steams every letter open; Sean McGinley as Kieran's older brother, who pursues his own romantic fantasies; and Pat Shortt, hilarious as a frustrated 36-year-old virgin.

Aileen Ritchie, an Irish stage director making her feature debut, handles the whimsy with an agreeably light hand.

"The Closer You Get" offers no stunningly original observations on men's tendency to ignore attractive women in their midst, but it goes down as smoothly is a pint of Irish ale.

SIGHT AND SOUND, 7/00, p. 41, Kevin Maher

A small village on the coast of Donegal, Ireland, the present. Local bachelors led by Kieran O'Donnagh, the village butcher, write a personal ad in the *Miami Herald* asking for available young American women to join them for the upcoming St Martin's Day celebrations. Mary the postmistress steams open the ad before sending it and tells the local women about the men's plan. At work, Kieran is excited, much to the annoyance of his doting assistant Siobhan. Kieran, his brother Ian, friends Ollie and Sean and bar owner Pat prepare for the St Martin's Day dance. Meanwhile, the womenfolk, led by Siobhan and Pat's unhappy wife Kate, invite a group of Spanish sailors to the dance.

The American girls fail to appear at the dance. Ian and Kate have an impromptu midnight stroll and Kieran fights one of the sailors over Siobhan. Furious with Kieran, Siobhan kisses the sailor. The next day Ian has a fight with Pat over Kate. Ollie, nervous about his sexual inexperience, purchases pornographic magazines from Amsterdam. Pat leaves Kate. Kate decides she must leave the village also, but Ian wins her back. Kieran asks Siobhan out on a date and she agrees. Mary, excited by Ollie's interest in pornography, has sex with him. Sean leaves town, just as the American girls arrive.

Three years later and the aftershocks from *The Full Monty*'s success story continue to reverberate. Following *Saving Grace, House!* and *The Match, The Closer You Get* is yet another innocuous provincial comedy radiating feel good insincerity and cleanly packaged for an international audience. But here producer Uberto Pasolini *(The Full Monty, Palookaville)* and debut director Aileen Ritchie have gone one further, borrowing Mont's central premise—a group of marginalised male characters negotiate their collective crisis of masculinity by embarking on a harebrained scheme—and wrapping it up in a haze of Celtic whimsy.

Set in a rural idyll in the west of Ireland, *The Closer You Get*'s compulsion to embrace tiresome national stereotypes overrides even the slightest interest in lived reality Hence Kieran and his mob are perpetually surrounded by pints of Guinness; they actually say "sláinte" when they drink (a toast used only by visiting US tourists); and Ollie needs to write to Amsterdam to get access to pornography. The last detail is particularly telling: bypassing common sense—Ollie could just as easily have gone online to procure such material just as Kieran could have e-mailed the *Miami Herald* with his ad—William Ivory's script depends for important plot points on a vision of Ireland as backward. Even when it occasionally lurches beyond the familiar, the film tests the limits of credibility. The central location, a village in Donegal, is underpopulated yet manages to be fantastically affluent, supporting an independent butcher's, a post office, a barber's and a brothel. There's a similar lack of narrative cohesion to the script, which relies on a voiceover from a character who makes a few perfunctory appearances at the film's beginning and end, but is otherwise absent from the story.

Working from such frivolous material, it's an accomplishment that Ian Hart's energetic burlesque remains generally engaging. French director of photography Robert Alazraki *(La Belle Verte, This Year's Love)* shoots the village and its surrounding countryside proficiently, but the deadly familiar visual iconography of this quaint Irish town has a license of its own. Its verdant

CLOSER YOU GET, THE   315

pastures, rocky coastlines and snugly nestled houses are gaudy signifiers of a jaded sensibility. And no amount of coldly calculated *Full Monty* feeling can change it.

VILLAGE VOICE, 2/29/00, p. 114, Amy Taubin

Just as clichéd and condescending to its audience (in this case, the American viewers who flocked to *The Full Monty* and *Waking Ned Devine*), *The Closer You Get* is set in a tiny Irish seaside town whose male inhabitants, blind to the attractive women in their midst, advertise for mates in a Florida newspaper. The most deluded among them is played by Ian Hart, who gives this wretched vehicle his all—going so far as to peroxide his hair and strut around in mail-order Carnaby Street attire. I can't fault Hart for trying; I just wish someone would give him the great role he deserves.

Also reviewed in:
NEW YORK TIMES, 2/25/00, p. E28, Elvis Mitchell
VARIETY, 2/28-3/5/00, p. 40, Todd McCarthy

CLOUDS

An In Pictures release in association with NextPix and Pacific Grove Productions. *Executive Producer:* Wayne Moore. *Producer:* Don Thompson and Gary Lindsay. *Director:* Don Thompson. *Screenplay:* Don Thompson. *Director of Photography:* Gary Lindsay. *Editor:* Gary Lindsay. *Music:* Nawang Khechog. *Sound:* Jay Patterson and Thomas Pinney. *Production Designer:* Gordon Halloran. *Art Director:* Kristin Poulin. *Set Decorator:* Laura Doyle. *Costumes:* Kristin Poulin. *Make-up:* Troy Showerman. *Running time:* 95 minutes. *MPAA Rating:* Not Rated.

CAST: Michael Patrick Gaffney (Robert St. John); Jennifer Jordan Day (Beatrice); Richard Barrows (Tab); Rob Nilsson (Frank); Patricia Ann Rubens (Mrs. Martin); Ryan Mickels (St. John as Child); Amy Leonard (Little Girl); Sandy Rouge Anderson (Juanita); Dick Kellogg (Professor Steiner); Christine Stafford (Vera); Hans Larson (Vera's Boyfriend); Jamuna Llewellyn (Woman St. John Meets in Restaurant); Bill Lindsay Lindsay (Man in Restaurant); Marilyn Lindsay (Woman in Restaurant); Tim Furness and Jaz Halloran (Boys at Video Arcade); Rex Gardiner (Man in Park); Rita Gardiner (Woman in Park); Amy Champ (Fellini Woman in Park/Woman at Bar/Woman in Riverwalk); Chloe West (Cinderella Girl); Caitlin Hicks (Cinderella Mom); Linda Bennett and Cora Gwynn (Women at Bar); Jewel Sandoval (Mouth Harp Player); Zeke Wheeler (Man in Riverwalk); Sashalai Stanger (Young Girl at Accident); Lori Halloran (Newscaster).

NEW YORK POST, 9/8/00, p. 46, V. A. Musetto

Robert St. John (Michael Patrick Gaffney) is a physics professor who gives up teaching "to work on my theory."

He checks into a seaside apartment, where he's befriended by an artist (Richard Barrows) who hasn't painted since he left the SoHo art world a year earlier.

They spend their days at a bar managed by yet another loser, an actor (Rob Nilsson) who says he's appeared in "30 of the s---tiest movies ever." Like "Invasion of the Giant Worm."

Enter a mysterious woman who goes by the one-letter name B (Jennifer Jordan Day). She insists she and St. John have met before. He doesn't remember her.

So goes "Clouds," playwright Don Thompson's first time out directing a feature film.

He says his movie was influenced by Antonioni and Bergman. It probably was. And that's the problem.

Thompson is too intent on giving "Clouds" an "arty" European look. The black-and-white images, repeated shots of the sky and the ocean, and cryptic flashbacks to St. John's childhood are greatly overdone. Add dumb dialogue ("What do you think the purpose of life is?" B wonders at one point) and wooden acting, and you have an amateurish, pointless exercise in filmmaking.

VILLAGE VOICE, 9/12/00, p.156, Michael Atkinson

Let's reserve outrage enough for Don Thompson's *Clouds*, which is like getting a tooth drilled and all you can see is ceiling. A clotted, student-filmish death march that appears to have been acted and directed under a particularly portentous lake, *Clouds* follows around a gloomy physics teacher (Michael Patrick Gaffney) who goes on a moody sabbatical to a moody seaside resort to moodily work on his "theory," and thereby learn that life is more than high math. At least he seems to learn something; Gaffney has the demeanor of a mud puddle, and Thompson's script should have biohazard warnings on it. (Typical exchange: "What do you mean?" "I mean exactly what I said." "What exactly did you say?" "Maybe I didn't say anything, exactly...") A Jarmusch movie if Jarmusch had been born with a skull full of liquid and nerve bundles instead of a brain, *Clouds* has nice, pearly, black-and-white cinematography, but it also has the shocking temerity to run over 100 minutes. Sweet air is required.

Also reviewed in:
NEW YORK TIMES, 9/8/00, p. E23, A. O. Scott

COLLECTORS

Director: Julian P. Hobbs. *Running time:* 80 minutes. *MPAA Rating:* Not Rated.

WITH: Rick Staton; Tobias Allen.

NEW YORK POST, 10/27/00 p. 47, V.A. Musetto

Some people collect stamps. Others prefer baseball cards. And then there are two gentlemen who collect art work by mass murderers such as Charles Manson and John Wayne Gacy.

They're Rick Staton, a funeral director by profession, and his pal, Tobias Allen. And they're the subjects of this documentary, directed by Julian P. Hobbs.

The film follows the two on their journey from Baton Rouge, La., to Houston, Texas, where a gallery is showing works by one of their favorite jailhouse Rembrandts—Elmer Wayne Henley, who is serving six life sentences for the murder of 27 children in the early '70s.

Hobbs is careful not to be judgmental, and he allows everybody—shrinks, killers, victims' rights advocates and victims' relatives—to have their say. It's all very fascinating, but one thing is missing—Hobbs never attempts to probe the minds of Staton—who went so far as to have Gacy paint a portrait of his young son—and Allen to find out what is behind their morbid obsession. Too bad.

NEWSDAY, 10/27/00, Part II/p. B6, John Anderson

Is there anything sicker than somebody who'd deal in the artwork of imprisoned mass murderers? How about the people who buy the artwork? How about someone who'd make a movie about it? How about a critic who'd review such a movie? How about a newspaper that would run the review?

How about a reader who'd read the review? You now have only a few words more before you become complicit, too... OK, you're in. We're all officially guilty. May the review commence.

"Collectors," an agonizingly impartial documentary by Julian P. Hobbs, focuses on two of the more unusual and blithely bizarre art dealers in the country. One is Rick Staton, an embalmer-mortician from Baton Rouge, La., whose fascination with serial murder led to his friendship and professional association with Illinois child-sex murderer John Wayne Gacy, Houston child-sex murderer Elmer Wayne Henley (whose art "career" began at Staton's suggestion) and a collection of the "works" of Richard Ramirez and Charles Manson.

The other is Tobias Allen, whose board game "Serial Killer" was banned in Canada and who helps Staton mount "Death Row Art Shows" throughout the country. Other characters—and we mean it—include Joe Coleman, a Brooklyn-based death connoisseur, holder of a Christ relic, a lock of Manson's hair and the opinion that "the act of stabbing is an act of communication."

Freak show? Yeah, but Hobbs, shooting in pristine images that reinforce his icy reserve, lets everyone have his say. The effect is coolly appalling. The one drawback is that the impassioned protests of victims' advocates and victims' relatives sound shrill up against the hobbyist-style enthusiasms of people such as Allen and Staton. How can you blame two guys for indulging a minor obsession? Turns out it's easy enough.

VILLAGE VOICE, 10/31/00 p. 170, Nick Rutigliano

"This is the happiest day of my life!" gushes Baton Rouge funeral director Rick Staton in a home video edited into Julian P. Hobbs's documentary *Collectors*. His glee accompanies his long-dreamt-of admittance to the Sharon Tate mansion shortly before demolition. Such are the thrills of serial-killer aficionados Staton and best bud Tobias Allen—when they're not surveying notorious murder sites or bartering for shrunken heads, the duo write to the killers themselves, encouraging them to take up painting and make a few bucks off their notoriety. Staton hit upon the idea after becoming the "exclusive dealer" of John Wayne Gacy's garish acrylics—further knotting the snarled system of exploitation and ritual at the core of Hobbs's film, albeit in clumsily managed and trivialized form. The titular packrats may be forthright about their obsession, but *Collectors* remains maddeningly blasé about its own position in the serial-killer mythos.

That we're never quite convinced the two men aren't creepy assholes seems integral to the film's concerns, but all the truly eye-rolling sound bites come from inarticulate victims'-rights advocates. Similarly, sobering counterpoints to Staton and Allen's fun are marred by crass overkill, as when horrific stills of mutilated children (slain by the collectors' client/pen pal Elmer Wayne Henley) are bombastically scored and presented in fetishistic close-up. Hobbs (a Court TV alumnus) has his own ritualistic agenda—part of which is keeping mum on his degree of collusion with his subjects. When Staton shows off a Gacy painting of his young son (based on photos Staton lent the killer), we wonder how the collector's unseen wife feels about such tribute. *Collectors* never even thinks to ask.

Also reviewed in:
NEW YORK TIMES, 10/27/00, p. E28, Stephen Holden

COLOR OF PARADISE, THE

A Sony Pictures Classics release of a Varahonar Company production. *Executive Producer:* Ali Kalij and Mehdi Karimi. *Producer:* Mehdi Karimi, Ali Ghaem Maghami, and Mohsen Sarab. *Director:* Majid Majidi. *Screenplay (Iranian with English subtitles):* Majid Majidi. *Director of Photography:* Mohammad Davoodi and Hashem Attar. *Editor:* Hassan Hassandoost. *Music:* Alireza Kohandairi. *Sound:* Yadollah Najafi and Mohammad Reza Delpak. *Production Designer:* Masood Madadi. *Set Designer:* Asghar Nezhadeimani. *Special Effects:* Mohssen Rouzbahani, Majid Soleimani, and Reza Torkaman. *Costumes:* Asghar Nezhadeimani. *Make-up:* Seyyed Mohsen Musavi. *Running time:* 90 minutes. *MPAA Rating:* Not Rated.

CAST: Mohsen Ramezani (Mohammad); Hossein Mahjub (Hashem, Mohammad's Father); Salime Feizi (Granny); Elham Sharim (Hanyeh, Mohammad's Sister); Farahnaz Safari (Bahareh, Mohammad's Sister); Mohammad Rahmaney and Zahra Mizani (Blind Center Teachers); Kamal Mirkarimi (Blind Center Dean); Morteza Fatemi (Carpenter); Masoomeh Zeinati (Young Woman); Ahmad Aminian (Young Woman's Father); Moghadam Behbahani (Village School Dean); Behzad Rafeiey (Village Teacher); Johnali Khorami (Villager).

LOS ANGELES TIMES, 3/31/00, Calendar/p. 12, Kevin Thomas

As in his Oscar-nominated "The Children of Heaven," Iran's Majid Majidi once again deals with a youngster coping with adversity in "The Color of Paradise." There is no question Majidi has a way with children, and his rapport with little Mohsen Ramezani is remarkable. Ramezani, who appears to be actually blind or nearly so, plays Mohammad, who fears that he has been left stranded when the special school he attends in Tehran closes for the summer.

While waiting for his father to pick him up, Mohammad reveals an acute hearing that connects him to a universe that fills him with awe. In the wooded area around the school the boy hears the chirp of a baby bird that has fallen from its nest; so in touch with his environment is Mohammad that not only is he able to locate and rescue the tiny creature but climb a tree and return it safely to its nest.

That is a fate Mohammad craves for himself, but it soon becomes clear that there is a part of his tardy father, Hashem (Hossein Mahjub), who wishes that his son would have fallen to his death from that tree. Pleading hardship, Hashem begs the school officials to keep his son over the summer. They refuse and reprimand him for trying to shirk his responsibility as a father.

We learn that Hashem has come, albeit reluctantly, a great distance, for he lives in a forested area in Northern Iran. A coal worker, he does some farming and takes on odd jobs to support his mother (Salime Feizi) and two little daughters, Hanyeh (Elham Sharim) and Bahareh (Farahnaz Safari). Widowed five years, Hashem is about to make an advantageous marriage to an attractive young woman, whose fiance has died and whose father sees Hashem as his only hope for a husband for his daughter. In his loneliness and desperation, Hashem does not want any obstacles in his path to matrimony and clearly sees Mohammad as a potential problem.

Hashem is not unsympathetic, for he is a man in a constant state of guilt and anguish and certainly has a hard life. By contrast, the boy's sisters and their grandmother embrace Mohammad joyously. Hashem does see a way out in apprenticing the boy to a blind carpenter who lives far enough away to require boarding a bus to visit him. This might actually be a solution, or a part of it, if Hashem had the wisdom, patience and skill to work it out.

But Hashem, who cannot see that his son has been truly touched by the hand of God in his extraordinary rapport with nature and his clear intelligence, wants to be free of Mohammad immediately.

It's no small irony that "The Color of Paradise" is set in what certainly looks to be an earthly paradise, alive with green fields and thickets of trees, mountains and nearby sea, all bespeaking an unspoiled natural grandeur that Mohammad perceives a great deal more sharply than his father. Majidi is not above resorting to melodramatics reminiscent of D.W. Griffith's "Way Down East" to bring Hashem to a shattering moment of truth, and the director concludes on a note that also seems straight out of the silent era.

As worthy and moving as "The Color of Paradise" is, it is not entirely free of the manipulative, the arbitrary and the downright punitive. Majidi has talent and skill but lacks the breadth of vision and sophistication of Iran's greatest directors, such as Abbas Kiorastami or Darius Mehrjui. Yet there's no denying that in its baldly heart-tugging way, "The Color of Paradise" is a powerful experience.

NEW YORK POST, 3/31/00, p. 54, Jonathan Foreman

"Color of Paradise" is the latest film by Majid Majidi, the celebrated Iranian director of last year's wonderful "Children of Paradise."

His new work is set in the lush countryside of Northern Iran and tells a less conventional, more religiously symbolic story than the previous film.

It doesn't have the overwhelming emotional punch, political subtext or satisfying structure of "Children," but its just as visually lovely, and it, too, affords a fascinating window into a society closed to Americans.

The movie opens at a school for blind children in Tehran on the eve of the summer vacation. In the morning, all the parents come to pick up their kids, but 8-year-old Mohammad (Mohsen Ramezani) finds himself alone in the schoolyard waiting for his widowed father, Hashem, (Hossein Mahjub).

When Hashem finally turns up, he asks the teachers to take his son permanently. Shocked, they refuse, and Hashem brings Mohammad back to the verdant mountains of Northern Iran.

Hashem is consumed with bitterness at the hand dealt him by life, and when it seems there's a chance he could marry a young woman from a strict religious family, he schemes to get rid of his son by apprenticing him to a blind carpenter.

Mohammad begins to adjust to a new life with the carpenter. But his father's selfishness and self-pity brings about disaster.

Director Majidi is less fashionable with critics than some of his more academic and experimental Iranian contemporaries, because of the accessibility and what some would call the sentimentality of his films.

But he uses children to great effect, and in young, blind Mohsen Ramezani, Majidi has found another child actor with extraordinary screen presence.

He also does such a terrific job with a sequence on a whitewater river that you can't help wondering if he wouldn't make a fine director of action flicks if he were to come to the United States.

NEWSDAY, 3/31/00, Part II/p. B6, Jan Stuart

The colors that surround young Mohammad when he visits his grandmother in the country are certainly worthy of paradise: lush forest greens, poppy reds, tulip yellows. But Mohammad cannot see them. He is blind. Instead, he finds his paradise in the conversation of woodpeckers, or in the bumpy surfaces of alfalfa or pebbles, from which he is able to pick out words as if he were reading pages of his Braille homework.

If this sounds like a sentimental tribute to the blind, it is. "The Color of Paradise," a visually seductive poem of a movie from Iran, wallows in a cultural tendency to idealize the seeing-impaired at the expense of the seeing. But director Majid Majidi manages to keep its more maudlin impulses in check for much of the way, providing a rigorously felt glimpse into places of the heart that transcend geography.

When we first meet Mohammad (Mohsen Ramezani, a remarkable nonprofessional), he is toiling away at a dictation lesson at a Tehran school for the blind. He pokes away at his work sheet with amazing dexterity, an industry he soon brings to the rescuing of a fledgling bird that has fallen from its nest. The metaphor washes over us in its simplicity. Mohammad, his mother dead and his father hoping to abandon him for good at the school, has been tossed rudely from his own family nest.

Inquisitive and soulful, Mohammad is less a prisoner of his blindness than he is of his father's galling irresponsibility. His widowed father (Hossein Mahjub) is a dull-headed coal worker who wants nothing more than to be rid of his blind son and marry a country girl he is promised to. Lacking even a trace of his son's spiritual appreciation for life, he dwells in a constant torpor of "Why me?" Whenever the boy seems to be finding love and reinforcement, be it from his adoring grandmother (a radiant Salmei Fehzi) or a tiny rural schoolhouse where he is the big man on campus, the father can be counted on to drag the boy off against his will.

But for Mohammad, always a compelling figure thanks to the full-hearted performance of the young Ramezani, most of the film's main characters lean toward the archetypal. The filmmaker labors to impose symbolic weight on his simple story with an overemphatic deployment of bird imagery. His slow-building narrative weaves its spell quietly, however, and Majidi conveys a bewitching grace in the faces of his country peasants. It makes one sad to realize that this Mideast Shangri-la and its inhabitants are so far out of reach, held in check by the chicanery of adversarial heads of state propelled by all the bullish instincts of Mohammad's father.

SIGHT AND SOUND, 9/00, p. 40, Jonathan Romney

Eight-year-old Mohammad stays at an institute for blind children in Tehran. At the end of term, his widowed father Hashem asks Mohammad's teachers to keep the boy over the holidays. They refuse and Hashem reluctantly takes Mohammad back to their village in northern Iran. There, the boy is reunited with his grandmother and his young sisters Hanyeh and Bahareh.

Hashem starts courting a young woman; her family agrees a marriage date and Hashem works hard to pay for the gifts. Hashem takes Mohammad away to be apprenticed to a carpenter.

Mohammad's grandmother argues with Hashem over his selfishness; when she dies, Hashem's prospective in-laws cancel the wedding, believing he brings bad luck. Hashem collects Mohammad from the carpenter's and takes him home through a wood. A bridge collapses under them and Mohammad is carried down river through rapids. Swimming after him, Hashem wakes on a shore is grief-stricken on finding Mohammad apparently dead, but the boy's hand responds to a ray of sunlight.

While casting for his previous film *Children of Heaven,* director Majid Majidi visited a school for blind children, and was intrigued enough to explore the theme of blindness further in *The Colour of Paradise.* Not surprisingly, *The Colour of Paradise*'s early scenes, which explore the relationship between the blind children at Mohammad's school and their environment, contain the film's real substance. There's an appealing quasi-documentary quality here, one that's shared by the development of the film's most engaging relationship, between young Mohammad and his jovial teacher. At one point, the teacher keeps Mohammad amused by joking about the boy's mobile phone—in reality, a soap dish. These early sequences concisely and inventively demonstrate how a blind child eager for knowledge can not only explore the known universe but also recreate it as an imaginative playground. Guided by touch and sound, Mohammad rescues a fallen chick and returns it to its nest: the images of the boy poking his fingers at the chick's open beak, or of his legs scrabbling against a tree trunk, demonstrate Majidi's acute sense of tactility and detail.

But once Mohammad's moody, embittered father Hashem turns up, the film takes a banal melodramatic turn. The point is quickly made that while Mohammad truly sees the world, his sighted father is really the blind one: a redemption is clearly in the offing. Majidi's *mise en scène* underscores the different ways man and boy see life: while Hashem toils away in a hard, grey world of coal, Mohammad is heir to a environment of vivid colour, best evoked by an almost abstract sequence in which the screen is filled with flowers and the natural dyes they produce. Majidi may be emphasising the intensity of the boy's inner sight in such idyllic-looking sequences, but this tactic takes the film into the realm of kitsch. The boy's grandmother is flawlessly smiling and sweet-natured, his sisters perfect bucolic little angels, and even the reds, yellows and pink of the flowers in the landscape seem to belong more to nursery wallpaper than the natural world. Perhaps the landscape of northern Iran really is this florid, but it might have been more aesthetically effective had Majidi chosen a valley a little less like the Tyrol of *The Sound of Music* (1965).

While it comes as a relief that Hashem is ultimately redeemed by last-minute celestial intervention rather than the innocent teaching of his life-loving child, the ending is clumsy and manipulative. The finale, involving a perilous tumble down river, is awkwardly edited and les than thrilling, and the glimmer of sunlight on Mohammad's hand, betokening God's redemptive touch, is rather anti-climactic after the more menacing divine presence experienced by Hashem as an ominous boom in the woods. (The original title actually means *The Colour of God,* which would seem to emphasise the film's pantheistic message rather than themes of mortality and earthly idyll.)

The film comes alive in a few sequences, but these stand out incongruously from the whole: the otherwise two-dimensional lost soul Hashem, for instance, has some nice moments, courting his bride-to-be like a nervous youth. As Mohammad, Mohsen Ramezani is an enthusiastic, vivacious presence, although you rather wish for some of the abrasive matter of-factness of the children in Abbas Kiarostami's films (for instance, *Where is My Friend's House,* (1989). You can see why Majidi's work has been distributed in the US by Miramax—this is very much the marketable face of Iran's cinema of childhood, a pastoral symphony that pales beside the hard simplicity of, say, Samira Makhmalbaf's *The Apple* or Jafar Panahi's *The White Balloon.* And it might have helped if some of the subtitles ("Beautiful Granny! I am over here!"; "Dear Bahareh! Go and gather alfalfa!") hadn't read quite so much like parodies of international art house ruralism.

VILLAGE VOICE, 4/3/00, p. 126, Michael Atkinson

To make a film about and with a blind child is to court the fates of hand-wringing bathos and overscored pluck, and Majid Majidi, whose preciously titled *The Color of Paradise* focuses on a blind eight-year-old agog in the soundscapes of north Iran, is no rookie at hitting below the belt. (His last movie, *The Children of Heaven,* was a whorish spectacle of teary kids and unlikely triumphs.) But *Paradise* has a measure of realist grandeur that can be surprising. We'd be foolish to assume that Iranian filmmakers aren't eyeing the American marketplace and trying their best to become Kiarostamian, and here Majidi does something of a grand-slam job balancing the two desires. The opening sequence watches Mohammad (Mohsen Ramezani) carefully as he finishes up his last day at his Tehrani school for the blind (Majidi knows to leave the stupefying effect of a roomful of whispering children frantically taking Braille dictation unpunctuated), and immediately it's clear that Ramezani, with his back-flipping eyeballs, toddler's run, and tentative hands, is an awesomely authentic presence no amount of filmmaking misjudgments can dilute.

But unlike his more famous, though doubtless less popular, contemporaries, Majidi is tempted by Spielbergian swellings, and Mohammad's tribulations—taken by his fed-up father to his grandmother's farm, where the boy both sucks up nature with every orifice and turns out to be an obstacle for the fathers remarriage—are soon awash with slo-mo epiphanies and tiring portents. An upside-down turtle even gets its own cutaway, and every bird noise triggers a power-dolly up to the boy's listening puss. Like a Hollywood dolt, Majidi strives to overwhelm us with emphasis, but it's the reality he was savvy to load his movie with that's touching.

Also reviewed in:
CHICAGO TRIBUNE, 6/2/00, Friday/p. A, Michael Wilmington
NEW YORK TIMES, 3/31/00, p. E25, Stephen Holden
WASHINGTON POST, 5/5/00, Weekend/p. 45, Desson Howe

COMING SOON

A Unapix Films/A-Pix Entertainment release of a Key Entertainment production in association with Bandeira Entertainment. *Executive Producer:* Thomas Augsberger and Matthias Emcke. *Producer:* Beau Flynn, Stefan Simchowitz, and Keven Duffy. *Director:* Colette Burson. *Screenplay:* Colette Burson and Kate Robin. *Director of Photography:* Joaquin Baca-Asay. *Editor:* Norman Buckley. *Music:* Barklie Griggs. *Music Editor:* Fernand Bos. *Sound:* Alex Wolfe. *Casting:* Marcia Shulman. *Production Designer:* Anne Stubler. *Art Director:* Mark White. *Set Decorator:* Susan Ogu. *Costumes:* Melissa Toth. *Make-up:* Nicki Ledermann. *Running time:* 91 minutes. *MPAA Rating:* R.

CAST: Tricia Vessey (Nell Kellner);   Gaby Hoffman (Jenny Simon);   Bonnie Root (Stream Hodsell);   James Roday (Chad);   Mia Farrow (Judy Hodsell);   Spalding Gray (Mr. Jennings); Ryan Reynolds (Henry Rockefeller/Lipschitz);   Ryan O'Neal (Dick);   Peter Bogdanovich (Bartholomew);   Kevin Corrigan (Sid);   Bridget Barkan (Polly);   Ramsey Faragallah (Wahid); Ellen Pompeo (Upset Girl);   Dmitry Lipkin (Young Teacher);   Jared Ryan (Petrus);   Leslie Lyles (Vivien Simon);   Candy Buckley (Madame Aurevoir);   Abigail Revasch (Renee);   Ranjit Chowdhry (Afshin);   Sarah Trelease (Stash);   Ashton Kutcher (Louie);   Tim Cunningham (Dr. Frank);   Rhasaan Orange (Sincere Boy);   Victor Argo (Mr. Neipris);   Timothy Stickney (Suave Man);   Merrit Nelson (Ms. Metcalf); Jessica Munch (Very Young Model);   Ruthanna Hopper (Intense Woman);   Yasmine Bleeth (Mimi);   Elzbieta Czyzewska (Dr. Luft);   James McCaffrey (Dante),   Colette Burson (Art Nun);   Ivan Martin (Indie VJ);   Xenia Buravsky (Liza);   Mary Diveny and Irma St. Paule (Blind Ladies);   David Eigenberg (Andy);   Anna Heins (Volunteer);   Kerry Lea (Stream's Friend);   Seth Michael May (Freckled Kid).

LOS ANGELES TIMES, 6/16/00, Calendar/p. 15, Kevin Thomas

"Coming Soon" might well be subtitled "Going Fast," because it will be. Debuting director and co-writer (with Kate Robin) Colette Burson has created three attractive high school seniors with some personality but no individuality. They attend a posh New York private school and express concern with being accepted into Ivy League schools, but in keeping with movie tradition they never seem to crack a book.

Similarly, they have no discernible interest in the world in which they live, for their self-absorption borders on the total. All they have on their minds—you already guessed—is sex. And more sex. It's amazing how boring endless talk about more and better orgasms can become. The title, in fact, is a crude pun.

Our heroine, Stream Hodsell (Bonnie Root), is fairly new to Manhattan, having been raised in New England by her now-divorced parents (Mia Farrow, Ryan O'Neal), who were partners in a Tom of Maine-like natural products business successful enough to afford the mother and daughter a spacious Manhattan apartment with a luxe address.

When we meet Stream she has just submitted to deflowering by an exceedingly popular fellow student, Chad (James Roday), who is concerned solely with his own gratification. Gradually, Stream's best pals, super-rich Jenny (Gaby Hoffmann) and the exquisite Nell (Tricia Vessey), realize that not only has Stream never experienced orgasm but has no idea of what it is. A horrified Jenny and Nell, who are not without vulnerabilities for all their sexual experience, set about correcting the situation.

Stream carries naivete and inexperience to just plain dimness—and this is a girl trying to get into Harvard? She resists noticing that Chad is a jerk in every way, and not till the end of the picture does a young man who's been trying to get her attention from the outset register with her. His name is Henry Rockefeller (Ryan Reynolds) but insists on going by his mother's maiden name, Lipschitz. Henry is tall, handsome, witty, intelligent, literate, and he even has his own rock band. He holds the radical notion that it's nice to get to know a girl before he even kisses her, let alone have sex with her.

However, our Stream (of No Evident Consciousness) reacts as if he were Attila the Hun.

With such a numb-skull heroine, we are all the more grateful that Farrow is on hand, in the film's only role with any dimension, as Stream's '60s dippy-hippie mother, all but hidden in cascades of curly auburn hair. She may have been a flower child but discovers she's a traditional mother underneath, shocked that her high school senior daughter is experimenting with sex.

She herself has a new boyfriend (Peter Bogdanovich), a South African artist who goes on about how hard it is to express human suffering in ceramics. O'Neal has but a cameo appearance, and Spalding Gray is on hand as a guidance counselor hawking his own guide to sure-fire entry into the college of your choice.

The script manages a deft phrase now and then, and Burson's not bad with actors, all whom have what it takes to move on to more rewarding projects. Her point may be that privileged Manhattan prep schoolers can be just as unsure of themselves as kids in less sophisticated locales, but there's not enough to most of her characters to make us care.

Credit where credit is due: "Coming Soon" is a good-looking New York picture that seems to have actually been shot there and not Toronto.

NEW YORK POST, 5/12/00, p. 50, Lou Lumenick

Too crude for serious audiences and too serious to be good exploitation, "Coming Soon" is a teen sex comedy that's predictably getting a token theatrical release prior to its imminent debut on home video.

Writer-director Colette Burson's slick and impressively cast debut feature has been around long enough that it contains references to "Sen. D'Amato" and "it's the '90s"—but was reportedly dumped by its original U.S. distributor, Twentieth Century Fox, after getting slapped with an NC-17 rating because of its gaminess.

Set in a world of rich Manhattan prep-school students that Burson seems to know well, "Coming Soon" focuses on the difficulty that Stream (Bonnie Root) and her friends Jenny (Gaby Hoffmann) and Nell (Tricia Vesey) are having, achieving, well, orgasm.

Even in the edited, R-rated version that's turning up at the Village East, there is much very explicit talk. There's no nudity, but it's hard not to be embarrassed for Root, a promising young actress, when she mimes finally reaching sexual fulfillment—in a whirlpool and with a punk-rocking Rockefeller (Ryan Reynolds)—as if she were a third-rate porn star.

Root, Hoffman and Vesey hold their own with such comic heavyweights as Spalding Gray (as a fatuous guidance counselor), Mia Farrow (hilarious as Stream's hippie mom) and Peter Bogdonavich (wry as mom's new boyfriend).

But when one of the girls turns out to be a lesbian, it's completely out of left field. And while "Coming Soon" is knowing enough to cast Ryan O'Neal as Farrow's ex-husband, it's clueless (or perverse) enough not to give us a single scene reuniting the "Peyton Place" stars, TV's hottest couple of 1966.

VILLAGE VOICE, 5/16/00, p. 140, Amy Taubin

A high school girl comedy with a slightly didactic edge, Colette Burson's *Coming Soon* is located in an exclusive New York prep school, where our three heroines worry about their college prospects and fear that sex is not what it's cracked up to be. The film is refreshingly direct and even courageous in its confrontation of female pleasure—specifically orgasms and masturbation, the staple of teen-boy comedies, but hitherto off-limits for girls.

Stream (Bonnie Root) is never more than a cell-phone call away from her best friends, Jenny (Gaby Hoffman) and Nell (Tricia Vesey). More sexually precocious than Stream, Jenny and Nell are rooting for Stream to lose her virginity to rich, spoiled Chad (James Roday), who's hardly the great lover he imagines he is. Chad almost convinces Stream that she's had an orgasm with him on the floor of his family's stretch limo; Stream discovers the truth when she finds herself pressed up against a Jacuzzi spout. Her newfound ecstasy provokes her friends to question their own experiences.

Made on a limited budget, *Coming Soon* is too sketchy to be a satisfying comedy of manners. Burson shows intelligence and promise as a filmmaker, but she adopts an arch, relentlessly bright tone in an effort to keep up the pace. Everyone in the large cast, which includes Mia Farrow, Peter Bogdanovich, and Spalding Gray in thankless adult roles, works much too hard. The ideas behind *Coming Soon* evoke more sympathy than the film itself.

Also reviewed in:
NEW YORK TIMES, 5/12/00, p. E8, A. O. Scott
VARIETY, 7/19-25/99, p. 30, Lael Loewenstein

COMMITTED

A Miramax Films release of a Dean Silvers/Marlen Hecht production. *Executive Producer:* Bob Weinstein, Harvey Weinstein, Jonathan Gordon, and Amy Slotnick. *Producer:* Dean Silvers and Marlen Hecht. *Director:* Lisa Krueger. *Screenplay:* Lisa Krueger. *Director of Photography:* Tom Krueger. *Editor:* Curtiss Clayto and Colleen Sharp. *Music:* Calexico. *Music Editor:* Mark Wlodarkiewicz and Nicolas Ratner. *Sound:* Robert Eber and (music) Craig Schumacher. *Sound Editor:* Tony Martinez. *Casting:* Billy Hopkins, Suzanne Smith, and Kerry Barden. *Production Designer:* Sharon Lomofsky. *Art Director:* Timothy Whidbee. *Set Decorator:* Lisa Kent. *Set Dresser:* Carol Ann Napier. *Costumes:* Beth Pasternak. *Make-up:* Steve Artmont. *Stunt Coordinator:* Mike Gunther. *Running time:* 97 minutes. *MPAA Rating:* R.

CAST: Heather Graham (Joline);   Casey Affleck (Jay);   Luke Wilson (Carl);   Goran Visnjic (Neil);   Patricia Velasquez (Carmen); Alfonso Arau (Grampy);   Mark Ruffalo (T-Bo);   Art Alexakis (Car Thief);   Kim Dickens (Jenny);   Clea Du Vall (Mimi);   Summer Phoenix (Meg); Mary Kay Place (Psychiatrist);   Dylan Baker (Carl's Editor);   Wood Harris (Chicky);   Laurel Holloman (Adelle); Robert Acoto (Pierced Man);   Davina Lane (Pierced Woman);   William Marsh (Hyundai Man);   Kyme McMahan (Hyundai Woman); Robert Holguin (El Paso Times Photographer);   Chairez Brothers (Mexican Seranaders);   Benjamin Jacob Lewis (Toby); Javier Renteria (Cop #1);   Rafael Anaya (Cop #2);   Forrest Silvers and Tyler Silvers (Wedding Guests).

LOS ANGELES TIMES, 4/28/00, Calendar/p. 8, Kenneth Turan

"Some people are born with a knack for faith. They're not afraid of permanence, they're at home with it. When it comes to bonding with another human soul, they're going to consider that bond sacred." That's Joline (Heather Graham) speaking, and given that she's tattooed her wedding ring on her finger, there's little doubt she's one of them.

What happens in "Committed," Lisa Krueger's wry comic fable about love and yes, commitment, is going to test Joline's belief system something fierce. A person who keeps her word no matter what, who insists "for better or for worse" is a sacred trust, Joline is going to take her faith to extremes few people could imagine, let alone attempt.

Writer-director Krueger, whose debut was the wonderfully eccentric "Manny and Lo," has the kind of distinctive voice and quirky sense of humor that fits this kind of scenario. Like "Manny and Lo," "Committed" accompanies slightly unhinged people trying to get along in a so-called rational world, constructing their own particular kinds of family as they go. Their luck is mixed, and so finally is this film's.

After glimpsing her the day of her marriage to handsome Carl (Luke Wilson), "Committed" catches up to Joline (an on-screen title tells us) 597 days later. The manager of a Manhattan rock club who has to deal with crises like the Love Army band being reduced to just one guy, Joline is unfailingly supportive of Carl, a newspaper photographer who keeps getting sent out to shoot food when he'd rather have a taste of hard news.

One day, Carl goes out to immortalize a pancake breakfast in New Jersey and never comes back. He leaves a confused message about his need for "space to get out of the fog," which forces Joline to fall back for emotional support on her extremely unreliable brother Jay (a loopy Casey Affleck), who can't even imagine what a committed relationship would be like.

Undaunted, Joline decides to seek out Carl to assure him of her support in his crisis of faith. Determining that she has enough money to cover "two regular-sized states or one big one," and liking the sound of Texas as "one of those states where lost people go to get more lost," Joline focuses on the massive Lone Star state as the likely refuge of her guy.

Naturally, this being the movies, Joline has little difficulty locating Carl hanging out in El Paso and environs. Ever solicitous of his problem and not wanting to reveal herself until she senses that he's ready, Joline follows a policy she defines as "keeping a protective eye" on her husband, as opposed to what less charitable souls might call spying or even stalking.

Keeping Joline company on her quest are a variety of genial eccentrics. There's Carl's baffled boss ("Happiness'" Dylan Baker), not to mention her husband's confused new girlfriend, Carmen (Patricia Velasquez), an ex-boyfriend (Mark Ruffalo) who wants to tear Carl's New York guts out, and Carmen's bemused medicine-man grandfather (Mexican director Alfonso Arau). There's even room for "Manny and Lo" co-star Mary Kay Place as a psychiatrist who does not believe in the easy way out, not one little bit.

It's in dealing with these shambling, off-center, peripheral characters that filmmaker Krueger and "Committed" are at their best. With its capacity to surprise, the film comes to life when you don't expect it to, in tiny but wonderfully off-center moments, like Joline's encounter with both desert bandits and serenading Mexican musicians.

Where "Committed" runs into more trouble is in making these exceptional moments coalesce enough to have a cumulative impact. Part of the problem is with Joline herself. Although Graham has exactly the kind of zoned-out, true-believer rigidity the part calls for, it is a delicate thing making people who flirt with sanity appealing, and by the film's end Joline's welcome is looking a bit worn. Ditto for Neil ("ER's" Goran Visnjic), a folk artist whose passion for Joline is increasingly off-putting. Still, with all the endearing people Krueger and her cast do create, we can be as forgiving of her as Joline is of Carl. At any rate, this film makes us want to try.

NEW YORK POST, 4/28/00, p. 54, Jonathan Foreman

A hit at the Sundance Film Festival, where it won an award for its cinematography, "Committed" is a cute and light romantic comedy about a young hipster chick who takes her marital vows so seriously that she has her wedding band tattooed on her ring finger.

But the real test for club-owner Joline (Heather Graham) comes two years after her wedding when her husband, Carl (Luke Wilson), a frustrated food photographer, ups and leaves for somewhere out West.

Joline calmly rents a car, drives to Texas and starts searching for him. She figures that she's on a quest, "Like Joan of Arc or Billy Jack."

She locates Carl in El Paso, where he's working for a newspaper. There, living in her rental car, she stakes out his new life.

Taking care not to let him know she's around, Joline does her best to help and protect Carl, even though he's taken up with a Mexican waitress (model Patricia Velasquez), and she herself is increasingly charmed by the flirtatious attentions of a handsome young artist (Goran Visnjic).

Graham, a 1960s-style beauty with huge round eyes, has mostly had supporting roles in ensemble films. In "Committed" she finally gets the chance to carry a movie, and she does so admirably, with her blend of vulnerability, quiet strength and half-acknowledged sexual appeal.

Still, much of the movie's pleasures come from the supporting cast, including Velasquez in her film debut and Mark Ruffalo as her violent truck-driver suitor.

The always terrific Casey Affleck is especially funny as Joline's deadpan, amoral brother Jay, an unlikely Lothario who seduces at least one of his lesbian roommates (Clea Du Vall and Kim Dickens).

There's a remarkably erotic scene between the handsome Goran Visnjic (from "ER") and Graham that's all the more effective for the fact that it involves no physical contact at all.

Although "Committed" is about the value of commitment in general—whether to your goals, your art or your partner—writer-director Lisa Krueger ("Manny and Lo") clearly takes issue with '60s/baby-boomer orthodoxies about love and relationships.

NEWSDAY, 4/18/00, Part II/p. B6, Jan Stuart

Lisa Krueger's "Manny and Lo" was one of the unexpected delights of the 1996 movie year. An irresistibly poker-faced comedy about two adolescent sisters who turn outlaw when the older of them becomes pregnant, it earned Krueger a place at the front ranks of a new wave of American women film directors that also included Alison Anders ("Gas Food Lodging") and Rose Troche ("Go Fish").

Her latest comedy, "Committed," reaffirms a predilection for renegade heroines and an eye for off-center characters who are never as eccentric as they initially appear. If the whole doesn't add up to the sum of its intelligent parts, we still emerge with the palpable sense that we are in the presence of an American original with a great movie somewhere up her sleeve.

Krueger's new protagonist shares with Manny and Lo a single-minded resolve that gets her into trouble, albeit in the service of another. A downtown New Yorker surrounded by transitory relationships, Joline (Heather Graham) takes her marital vows very seriously. So much so that when her husband, Carl (a charmingly clueless Luke Wilson), absconds to Texas to find himself, she tracks him down and sets up camp across the road in an effort to keep him and their marriage on a steady path.

Like the peasant who went after the golden goose, Joline pulls along a diversified trail of followers in pursuit of her man. Among them are her sexually frustrated brother Jay (Casey Affleck, an annoying actor who seems to be in a perpetual stoned haze), a waitress named Carmen with an impulse toward married men (Patricia Velazquez, a kinder, gentler Mercedes Ruehl), a Mexican medicine man (Alfonso Arau) and a seductive artist (Goran Visnjic of "ER"), who makes constructions out of paper towels.

Despite the colorful dramatis personae and some genuinely quirky touches, the film plods along with a self-consciously literary narrative voice. It takes a while for Joline's persona to come into focus; while Heather Graham projects an independent spirit, she's neither off-center nor witty enough to give the character the sort of odd-duck charisma the part demands. "Committed" labors to be unpredictable, but there is never a moment's doubt as to where it is taking us.

VILLAGE VOICE, 5/2/00, p. 130, Amy Taubin

With its richly saturated, high-contrast cinematography, Lisa Krueger's *Committed* looks like a 3-D postcard, but as romantic comedy, it falls flat. Heather Graham plays a dynamo of the

Downtown club scene who believes that commitment means forever. When her wimpy husband of less than two years packs up and moves to Texas, she follows him, stakes out his trailer, befriends his new sweetheart, and even enlists the help of a grizzled Mexican mystic to teach her how to cast spells.

Many jilted lovers indulge in a bit of stalking, even if it's only phoning the beloved at inappropriate times and hanging up. But when the stalker goes to the extremes that Graham does here, it's very creepy to watch. *Committed* is a less glossy version of *Addicted to Love*, in which Meg Ryan and Matthew Broderick got together while spying on their respective exes. Krueger is attempting to use a light touch to illuminate a difficult aspect of relationships: how to distinguish between healthy commitment and obsession. And were it not for its central performance, the film might have had a chance. But Graham is so wrapped up in her own kookiness, it's impossible to believe she notices anyone else's existence, let alone that she could be in love. With Graham center screen in almost every scene, *Committed* becomes a film about a pathologically narcissistic woman, which I don't think is Krueger's intent. Committing to an actor is every bit as perilous as choosing a mate.

Also reviewed in:
CHICAGO TRIBUNE, 5/5/00, Friday/p. B, Michael Wilmington
NEW YORK TIMES, 4/28/00, p. E14, A. O. Scott
VARIETY, 2/14-20/00, p. 44, Emanuel Levy
WASHINGTON POST, 5/5/00, p. C12, Rita Kempley

CONDO PAINTING

A USA/October Films release of a Pod Squad Productions film. *Producer:* Dana Giacchetto. *Director:* John McNaughton. *Screenplay:* George Condo and John McNaughton. *Director of Photography:* John McNaughton. *Editor:* Elena Maganini and Tom Keefe. *Music:* Jim Sampas. *Music Editor:* Ronald Ivan Staley and Brian Ohlsen. *Sound:* Ken Hale. *Special Effects:* Tim Kitz and Tom Trucco. *Animation:* Gary Leib. *Running time:* 87 minutes. *MPAA Rating:* Not Rated.

WITH: Patrick Achdjian; George Condo; William S. Burroughs; Anna Condo; Eleonore Condo; Raphaelle Condo; Allen Ginsberg; Dana Sunshine; Eric Barnes; John Sampas; Pasquale Condo; Muriel Condo; Jim Sampas; Karin Weiner; Bernard Picasso.

LOS ANGELES TIMES, 3/17/00, Calendar/p. 6, Kevin Thomas

John McNaughton's documentary "Condo Painting" sounds like a put-on, and in a way it is, even though that title refers not to an apartment house getting a face lift but to a witty study of artist George Condo at work. A boyish-looking man in his 40s with a shock of thick, black hair, Condo is an important figure in the Manhattan art scene.

Condo, who has a quiet though intense demeanor, explains that the fantasy creatures in his imagination, which he calls "antipodes," demand that he express them on canvas. It sounds like a fancy way of saying he's been inspired by cartoon and comic-book characters he fell in love with in childhood.

While he doesn't delve into the subject of animation and animators, he goes on about the cherished TV series of his youth. At one point we see him affixing head shots of Lucille Ball, Irene Ryan as Granny in "The Beverly Hillbillies" and others onto the classic portraits of the Old Masters in a lavish coffee-table-type history of art.

Surely, he asks, is not "Granny" as important as the "Mona Lisa"? It's a surprising question, really, when you consider how long popular culture has been taken seriously, especially since Andy Warhol taught us it was OK to admit what we already secretly liked much of in the first place—movie star publicity shots and the familiar images of commercial art specifically.

The focal point of the documentary, which was shot over several years beginning in 1996, is Condo's concentrated painting—and painting over and over again—an image of a Mickey Mouse-like creature on a gigantic canvas. In the course of its evolution, Condo visits William S. Burroughs, and they chat about Abstract Expressionism and collaborate on an action painting (made with a plumber's plunger and human excrement). Allen Ginsberg visits Condo, who paints a white skeleton on his black sweater and pants.

Condo visits his parents in Massachusetts, not far from the hometown of his other Beat hero, Jack Kerouac, who is heard reciting his "Sea Is My Brother." There is no question that Condo is an intellectual deeply influenced in his thinking by the Beat writers, and the deaths of Burroughs and Ginsberg, whom he calls his best friends.

Indeed, Condo paints over his fanciful Mickey-like image with its pink sky and turns to an increasingly somber, simpler style until he arrives at a wistful, dark red mouse peering out from a gray background.

Shot in High-8 video later transferred to 35-millimeter film, "Condo Painting" has an edgy feel and a knockout soundtrack featuring music and original songs by Danny Elfman, Tom Waits, Philip Glass, Beck and many others. "Condo Painting" exudes East Coast hipness and chic, and McNaughton's approach to Condo is sharp enough to keep us intrigued if not exactly rewarded.

Eventually, Condo signs his painting and it's time for him to step back and let us appraise it. One film critic described it as looking like a Disney cartoon cel, and that's on the money. In this instant you realize, if you had not already done so, that the finished picture makes much of Condo's remarks seem silly and pretentious. Condo has an imagination that can amuse and delight, and maybe he really ought to let his work speak for itself.

NEW YORK POST, 3/10/00, p. 56, Lou Lumenick

"Condo Painting" is a documentary that has nothing to do with condominiums or wall coverings—but it's still about as exciting as watching paint dry.

George Condo is a Manhattan painter specializing in fantasy images that somewhat resemble an unholy cross between mice, cats, clowns and Smurfs.

Jim Nabors is heard singing "You'll Never Walk Alone" over the opening credits, and Condo explains the major influences on his work include not only "Gomer Pyle," but also Granny of "The Beverly Hillbillies," whom he compares to the Mona Lisa.

"Condo Painting" might have made a tolerable five-minute "mockumentary," but it's apparently meant seriously.

NEWSDAY, 3/10/00, Part II/p. B7, Gene Seymour

To slightly paraphrase a famous maxim, life is short and art is long. Movies about the artistic life can sometimes seem longer than they should, simply because creative processes, especially those that involve a single imagination's will, can be a lot more boring to behold than the results. (Put it another way: Do you want to spend even a minute watching somebody else write a poem? Or me write this review?

Nevertheless, director John McNaughton, whose filmography ranges from such grisly independent dares as "Henry: Portrait of a Serial Killer" (1986) to off-kilter genre pieces such as "Wild Things" (1998), takes a mighty swing at this ball with "Condo Painting," a documentary that follows painter George Condo as he tries, fails and tries again to make a picture that satisfies his rococo imagination.

Even a few minutes in Condo's company makes one understand why McNaughton believed him worthy of a feature-length film. He's a pretty funny guy. Anybody who can talk one minute about abstract expressionism and move seamlessly the next minute to a loving deconstruction of "The Beverly Hillbillies" would be an asset at any cocktail party.

And if you're at all nostalgic for the "Beat" sensibility of spontaneous invention and mischievous abandon, then you start out at least accepting the seemingly haphazard collision of images and narrative angles taken by McNaughton in following Condo as he romps all over his studio, in the streets and at his boyhood home of Lowell, Mass. which is also Jack Kerouac's birthplace, one of many opportunities taken by Condo to display his close identification with the Beats. (Cameo appearances by Allen Ginsberg and William S. Burroughs, both of whom are now dead and gone, cast a ghostly pallor over the antic proceedings, especially when Condo paints a skeleton on Ginsberg's black-clad frame.)

In its often-disorienting shift of visual motifs (colors go negative, sounds are crunched), "Condo Painting" makes the same demands of the audience that modern or postmodern art sometimes compels from museum goers. In other words, you're given little easy access to McNaughton's subject and must take it from whatever perspective you can muster.

This makes the enterprise an intriguing artifact, but not a terribly satisfying movie if you're not willing to accept either Condo's personality and his vision of "artificial realism." McNaughton's own gamble to make Condo's reality artificial is a worthy one. But none of the pyrotechnics he displays in this effort are, finally, as provocative as the one very real sequence where we're allowed to see a small breach in Condo's buoyant aura after a painting goes sour.

VILLAGE VOICE, 3/14/00, p. 130, Jessica Winter

Those hoping to apply a little cultural-studies eugenics to the miscegenation of high art and low pop would no doubt have their knickers in a knot after a little time spent with artist George Condo. A post-postmodern absurdist equally comfortable discussing Gorky as portal to abstract expressionism or the merits of King Crimson ("I'd say they're worthy of animation but not a play"), he paints colorful, vaguely menacing imaginary beasts; with their outsize features—Dumbo ears, cathedral-door eyes, cystlike cheeks—they're cartoons of cartoons. In his spare time, he'll blow off steam action-painting with a toilet plunger (his late friend William Burroughs shows up for these forays), or talk about the mysterious "antipodal beings" who act as his muses, or glue cutouts of television characters onto reproductions of Dutch old master paintings. The *Beverly Hillbillies* fan asks, deadpan, "Was Granny as important as the Mona Lisa? And if so, why didn't the Mona Lisa ever have her own TV series?"

This is more than self-amused irony; this is kitsch as religion, and John McNaughton's *Condo Painting* is an ode to whimsical devotion that tries to approximate *Fast, Cheap & Out of Control.* McNaughton evokes Condo's collage paintings (one turns Bill Gates into a Renaissance grandee) by stacking his lysergically colored documentary with tricks (film run backward, use of negatives) and trippy non sequiturs: Bubbles float across the screen with Condo inside them—blowing bubbles. Condo's creations might strike you as another kind of infinite regression, but for a while you're trapped in a Flaming Lips video with Condo and happy to be there, not least for his quixotic sense of dedication; the one constant thread is footage of him obsessively painting and repainting the same canvas. But then, oddly, McNaughton puts Condo in a car to his hometown of Lowell, Massachusetts, to visit the family and Jack Kerouac's grave, and the film stops dead (the amazing soundtrack—including DJ Spooky, Beck, Tom Waits, and lots of Residents—notwithstanding). It briefly revives only at the end, when Condo and a friend (who wears an old-man mask and huge red gloves) stake out a garbage dump hunting down an "antipodal being" known as "Big Red." It's like an episode of *Cops* staged by Spike Jonze.

Also reviewed in:
NEW YORK TIMES, 5/10/00, p. E20, A. O. Scott
VARIETY, 8/23-29/99, p. 111, Derek Elley

CONTENDER, THE

A DreamWorks Pictures and Cinerenta/Cinecontender release of a Battleground production. *Executive Producer:* Rainer Bienger, Gary Oldman, and Maurice Leblond. *Producer:* Marc Prydman, Douglas Urbanski, Willi Baer, and James Spies. *Director:* Rod Lurie. *Screenplay:* Rod Lurie. *Director of Photography:* Denis Maloney. *Editor:* Michael Jablow. *Music:* Larry Groupé. *Music Editor:* Richard Harrison. *Sound:* Jay Meagher and (music) Armin Steiner. *Sound Editor:* Stephen Hunter Flick. *Casting:* Mary Jo Slater. *Production Designer:* Alexander Hammond. *Art Director:* Halina Gebarowicz. *Set Decorator:* Eloise Stammerjohn. *Special Effects:* Robert Vasquez. *Costumes:* Matthew Jacobsen. *Make-up:* Fabrizio Sforza and

Alessandra Sampaolo.   *Stunt Coordinator:* Loyd Catlett.   *Running time:* 132 minutes.   *MPAA Rating:* R.

CAST: Gary Oldman (Shelly Runyon);   Joan Allen (Laine Billings Hanson);   Jeff Bridges (President Jackson Evans);   Christian Slater (Reginald Webster);   Sam Elliott (Kermit Newman);   William Petersen (Jack Hathaway);   Saul Rubinek (Jerry Toliver);   Philip Baker Hall (Oscar Billings);   Mike Binder (Lewis Hollis);   Robin Thomas (William Hanson);   Mariel Hemingway (Cynthia Lee);   Kathryn Morris (Paige Willomina);   Kristen Shaw (Fiona Hathaway);   Douglas Urbanski (Makerowitz);   Noah Fryrear (Timmy);   Angelica Torn (Dierdra);   Joe Taylor (Paul Smith);   Kevin Geer (Congressman Skakle);   Doug Roberts (Congressman Harding);   Bev Appleton (Congresssman Marshall);   Sandra Register (Glenda); Tony Booth (Peter Crenshaw);   Andrew Boothby (Steve Poullet);   Irene Ziegler (Maggie Runyon);   Del Driver (Director Friend);   Sean Pratt (Wilke);   Bill Bevins (Anchorman);   Ed Sala (Show Producer); Kirk Penberthy (Stevenson); Justin Dray (Stagehand); Jackie Laubacher (Reporter 4);   David Bridgewater (Aide);   Kevin Grantz (Secret Service Chief);   Michael Kennedy (Congressman Fletcher);   David Londoner (Congressman Jones);   Billy Dye (Waiter); Larry King (Himself);   Amit Mehta (Abu Hunter);   Greg Cooper (Ted Edwards);   J. Scott Shonka (Cappy);   Scoot Powell (Attorney); Catharine Schaffner (Patricia Lavameer);   Stan Kelly (Alan);   William L. Chandler (Personal Waiter);   Liz Marks (Sheila);   Robert Harvey and Steve Hurwitz (Lobbyists);   Heather Rosbeck (Elaine Bidwell);   Roderick Jimenez (Trevor);   Donald Campen (Sergeant at Arms);   Justin Lewis (Producer);   Fred Iacovo (Joe Smith);   Dawn Westbrook (Secretary);   Jolene Carroll (Maid).

CHRISTIAN SCIENCE MONITOR, 10/13/00, p. 15, David Sterritt

"The Contender" is being touted as a timely release, on the assumption that moviegoers are riveted by the real-life presidential sweepstakes. It's far from certain that audiences are eager to increase their autumn political intake with a movie about a down-and-dirty Washington power struggle. But at least Rod Lurie's melodrama only lasts about two hours, which gives it one big advantage over the real thing.

The story begins when the chief executive is called on to replace the vice president, who unexpectedly dies. His choice is a female senator who has all the right qualities, plus a regrettably wrong one: an alleged sex scandal that surfaces from her distant past.

Will the president stick to his convictions and help her refurbish her reputation? Will opposition leaders succeed in besmirching them both? And what will follow from the explosive event that opens the movie, a jolting accident that boosts yet another politician to prominence?

This is fascinating material, and a well-chosen cast gives it extra oomph: Jeff Bridges as the president, Gary Oldman and Christian Slater as congressional players, and Joan Allen as the vice-presidential hopeful, in one of the rare opportunities she's had to play a three-dimensional character.

"The Contender" is more consistent and coherent than Lurie's previous political thriller, "Deterrence," also about a presidential crisis. But its story is so calculated and its outcome so rigged that it ultimately bears little relation to the real world. Calling this a substantial political allegory would be like calling the average presidential debate a gripping entertainment—a judgment that isn't likely to sweep the nation.

LOS ANGELES TIMES, 10/13/00, Calendar/p. 2, Kenneth Turan

An unlikely combination of "West Wing" and the National Enquirer, "The Contender" is the type of trashy but watchable political melodrama we don't get much of anymore.

Ripped from today's headlines with a veneer of social consciousness thrown in free of charge, it's bombastic, pulpy and way contrived. But it does move right along and it's enlivened by stronger, more enjoyable acting than this kind of picture usually provides.

"The Contender" can also be seen as, drumroll please, the first post-Monica Lewinsky potboiler. It's hard to imagine the seamier aspects of the film's plot being even as marginally credible as they are now without those endless discussions of foreplay in the Oval Office. As it is, "The Contender" dreams up a really nasty sexual/political scandal, makes the most of it, and then after the titillation is over finds time to wave the flag and be patriotic. Which is why, though political leaders come and go, there'll always be a Hollywood.

It's not President Jackson Evans (Jeff Bridges) who's in trouble this time; he's too preoccupied dreaming up dishes for the White House kitchen to prepare ("the perk of the century") to do anything naughty. But his vice president has inconveniently died and a fierce battle to be a heartbeat away from the power to order shark sandwiches a la carte is underway.

Gov. Jack Hathaway (William Petersen) is thought to be a top contender, especially after an act of personal heroism that opens the film, but the president, as presidents will, has other ideas. He wants Laine Hanson (Joan Allen), a senator from Ohio who's a recent convert to the president's party.

Attractive, well-spoken, the daughter of a governor and married with a small son, Hanson would seem to be a trouble-free candidate. But then testimony and even photographic evidence surfaces insisting that as a freshman in college she engaged in the kind of sexual practices we usually don't have photographs of vice presidents engaging in.

Actually, this stuff doesn't just surface. Its appearance is orchestrated by an old enemy of the president's and friend of Hathaway's, the man coincidentally in charge of the confirmation hearings, Congressman Shelly Runyon. Rumpled, twitchy and nervous, with thinning curly hair and a noticeable bald spot, Runyon resembles a younger Arthur Miller and not at all like the man who's playing him, Gary Oldman.

Having the English-born actor, better known for overtly villainous, at times over-the-top performances, take on the role of a shambling, opportunistic Midwestern congressman may sound like something of a stunt. In fact, Oldman does a remarkable job with the role, channeling his considerable energy and skill into hiding the person we're used to seeing and creating this brand-new and convincing individual.

Writer-director Lurie has said that he wrote not only the starring role but this entire picture with Joan Allen in mind, and it's everyone's great good fortune that she ended up playing Laine Hanson. The senator is the heart of the picture, and Allen, without doubt as fine an actress as is working today, makes the difficult role of a woman who cannot reveal her increasingly intense feelings in public look natural, seamless and completely convincing.

"The Contender" does touch on some serious issues (the double standard in public life for men and women, whether a politician's personal life is anyone's business but his or her own) but its heart lies with the luridness of its plotting. The film's lively twists are not too difficult to see coming down the road, but the proceedings still hold our attention and keep us wanting to know how it's going to turn out. Which is more than you can say about real political events in this day and age.

NEW YORK, 10/23/00, p. 90, Peter Rainer

The timing of the release of the new political drama *The Contender* can be viewed as either impeccable or a redundancy. The film keys into the current election season, of course, and for political junkies who can't get a big enough fix from the real thing, it presents a reasonable facsimile of headline-making subterfuges and skulduggery and speechifying. And yet for all its superficial topicality, *The Contender*, which was written and directed by Rod Lurie and stars Joan Allen and Jeff Bridges, is a political film of the old school: not the smarty-pants satires we've become used to, such as *Wag the Dog*, but rather the low-down, high-minded message movies of the *Advise & Consent* ilk, complete with music-swelling sentiment. It's a movie that wallows in the muckiness of the political process as it's played out in Washington while at the same time celebrating with a Founding Fathers righteousness the guiding principles of that process. (Lurie doesn't seem to be aware of how that kind of pushy righteousness can itself seem mucky.) The timing of *The Contender* may be up-to-date, but its ringing, upstanding tone deliberately links it to an earlier era when political movies were still consumed by audiences supposedly unjaded by terminally hip cynicism.

Is it such a bad thing that we can't take our political dramas straight anymore? And isn't it the height of sentimentality to assume that we once, unequivocally, could? (Did people swallow even Frank Capra movies like *Mr. Smith Goes to Washington* whole, or do we just like to think they did?) The politically oriented movies that have always meant the most to me are not films like

Advise & Consent or even *The Best Man* but *The Manchurian Candidate* and *Dr. Strangelove*—movies that put our own nutso disbelief in the political process right onto the screen. Playing it straight in the political-movie realm has always yielded a few big, square pleasures, but the political circus in this country is too baroque and vehement, too much of a self-satire already, to be adequately expressed by traditionalists. One reason political movies are so rarely even attempted anymore is because the real-life shenanigans are so much more compelling, even cinematic. Washington may be working itself into one of its periodic election-eve high dudgeons about the depravities of Hollywood, but the ways in which the elections and the issues are covered on television and the rest of the media, as well as the ways in which politicians and their handlers spin themselves, owe a tremendous debt to Hollywood.

Lurie's saving grace as a filmmaker is that, although he's prone to pontification, he has a melodramatist's flair and a talent for summoning the cured, Grade A porker in his performers. When the cast, which also includes Gary Oldman as a scurvy Republican congressman, Sam Elliott as chief of staff, and William Petersen as a dismayed governor, is as accomplished as this one, that hamminess can be immensely enjoyable. Joan Allen, whose hamminess here takes the form of an almost ascetic under-emoting, plays Democratic senator Laine Hanson, who is proffered by president Jackson Evans (Bridges) as his new vice-presidential appointee after his sitting VP suddenly dies in office. Well into his second term, Evans wants to claim the legacy of having the first female veep. Bridges plays the president without stuffiness; Evans is a human being who also happens to be commander-in-chief, and his craftiness and double-dealing are just politicized versions of what he might be up to if he were a corporate CEO or just about anything else. He enjoys the blood sport of politics, while Hanson values principle above power. For Lurie, principles are a liability in Washington, which is why, when a sex scandal from Hanson's sorority days threatens her confirmation, he turns her into a feminist standard-bearer for the right to privacy and sets practically everyone on both sides of the aisle against her. She refuses to confirm or deny the scandal, and she refuses to sling mud in her defense even when her allies heap mudballs in her hands.

Lurie is making a movie about sexual McCarthyism in Washington, but he does so with a woman, and not a Clintonesque president, as its focus. His point seems to be that men in Washington enjoy a double standard, although Gary Hart, not to mention Bill Clinton, might have a somewhat different take on the matter. He rigs the game by dressing Hanson in that typically starched and sexless armor that female politicians use to gird themselves for life on Capitol Hill. The film would have been more daring, and earned its righteousness more, if she had been less patrician and more rowdy. But Hanson, who doesn't budge in her beliefs even with the president and who defends herself before the jackals in the confirmation committee with a resoluteness that would give Patrick Henry pause, is Lurie's kind of heroine. Like the president here, he's interested in laying down a legacy, too. (The films dedication reads, "For all our daughters.") Here's hoping big bad Hollywood will bleach the do-goodnik out of him so he can realize his much more juicy talent for portraying the unprincipled.

NEW YORK POST, 10/13/00, p. 53, Lou Lumenick

Clearly inspired by President Clinton's impeachment, "The Contender," an extremely well-acted if predictable movie, asks whether a politician's sex life is the public's business.

What's presented, though, is a scenario very different from Clinton's Oval Office hanky-panky, a subject we all wearied of many moons ago.

Sen. Laine Hanson, a second-term liberal Democrat who's the fictional protagonist of "The Contender," is alleged to have participated in an orgy way back in college.

She has been nominated to fill out the term of a recently deceased vice president, but the stories about her supposedly wild youth are a dream come true for Shelly Runyon, a Republican congressman whose committee is holding confirmation proceedings on Hanson's appointment.

Runyon has a few scores to settle with liberal President Jackson Evans. And the congressman would also prefer Jack Hathaway, a senator and Vietnam war hero whom the president passed over, to Hanson, who deserted the Republican party.

Runyon vows to "gut the bitch in the belly" by leaking incriminating photos of Hanson to a Web site. But Evans stands by his nominee, even when she refuses, as a matter of principle, to confirm or deny the allegations.

And the president isn't above a few dirty tricks of his own. Even if all its twists and turns don't always stand up to close scrutiny, "The Contender" has crackling dialogue—and it's always watchable for its power-house cast.

The underrated Joan Allen is superb as the sometimes impossibly high-minded Hanson, who decides not to use the information that, years ago, the wife of the "pro-life" Runyon had an abortion, at his request.

(The scene where Runyon's wife tells this to the Christie Whitmanesque Hanson is probably the most unbelievable in a major movie this year.)

The men have more fun than Allen—especially Jeff Bridges as the slick, Clintonesque president. He gets a big, Oscar-nomination-worthy speech at the end, but his classic scene here comes during a visit from a freshman Democratic congressman (Christian Slater) who is flirting with the anti-Hanson forces.

Writer-director Rod Lurie, who used to be a film critic in Los Angeles, provides plenty of good material for his well-chosen cast, including Sam Elliott, cast against type as a gruff presidential advisor, and William Petersen as the John McCainish Hathaway, who, the opening sequence hints, may have a Chappaquiddick-style skeleton in his closet.

The most flamboyant turn is by a nearly unrecognizable Gary Oldman, in glasses and with a receding hairline, as the obsessed Runyon, who is presented as a man of his principles, of the Henry Hyde-Newt Gingrich school, as misguide as Lurie thinks they might be.

Lurie made his directing debut with one of my favorite little movies this year, "Deterrence," which revolved around an American president in a nuclear showdown with Iraq.

That movie quickly disappeared without a trace, but, overall, it was better constructed (if less slick) than "The Contender," whose ending seems more predicated on pleasing the audience than reflecting any kind of political reality.

Lurie also lingers a bit too leeringly over Hanson's sex life. In a movie that takes the position that pols' sex lives are none of our business, that borders on being as hypocritical as the villains of "The Contender."

NEWSDAY, 10/13/00, Part II/p. B2, John Anderson

You used to be able to find former radio broadcaster/celebrity suppliant Rod Lurie's name in the quote ads for really stupid movies. Now he's in the credits of a really stupid movie. Who says the American Dream is dead?

Not us. But Lurie's second directorial effort, "The Contender," seems to suggest that our political system is imperiled by shady, underhanded, unscrupulous people. That the nation is obsessed by sex. That women are held to a different standard than men. Who knew?

A movie out of the "Advise and Consent" school, "The Contender" is timed for maximum election-season synergy but fails to provide the basic elements of a good political thriller: verisimilitude. A reality quotient. A biting sense of sophisticated intrigue. A feeling among its audience that, yes, this could really happen. Maybe it can in the mind of Rod Lurie. In fact, if you're completely obtuse, "The Contender" is probably a pretty good time. Otherwise, the naivete and illogic of the thing are too distracting even to induce a good laugh.

Where to begin? How about the storyline: When a woman senator named Laine Hanson (Joan Allen) is named to fill the term of a deceased vice president, it's discovered that not only did she spend an early college evening as frat-house sex toy, but that photographs exist—photos that have never surfaced previously, photos that neither the president (Jeff Bridges) nor his chief of staff (Sam Elliott) was aware of when they made the appointment and photos that materialize mere moments after the congressional opposition leader, Shelly Runyon (Gary Oldman), decides to destroy Hanson's career.

That's one large load of political incompetence.

Then there's the nature of Hanson's "offense." A past sex life is one thing. Having submitted oneself to the assembled occupants of "Animal House" is another. The incident seems to raise at least some question about Hanson's psychology. But the various characters don't.

Then, of course, there's the first scene of the movie (skip the rest of this paragraph if you want to remain in the dark). Sen. Jack Hathaway—William Petersen, looking more than a bit like John McCain—is the odds-on favorite to get the nomination that ultimately goes to Hanson. He's fishing with a Washington Post reporter when a car goes off the overpass above. Hathaway dives in, but can't save the girl at the wheel. And his failure—with its echoes of Chappaquiddick—is the explanation given for why he doesn't get the nod. Anything smell fishy to you?

Thusly, "The Contender" hinges on an 11th-hour revelation that's no revelation at all. It's also clumsily shot but well-acted: Allen is a likely Oscar-contender, because everyone likes her and she never gets to dominate a movie. Oldman also is good, almost unrecognizable as the ravaged-looking Runyon. And although he seems to be in another movie, Bridges makes President Jackson Evans a good ol' boy with the capacity for lethal politics: His subtle intimidation of Christian Slater's callow congressman, Reginald Webster, is the best thing in the film. And a symbol of its unrealized potential.

Perhaps the worst aspect of "The Contender"—dedicated "to our daughters"—is the way Lurie appropriates the issue of privacy, sets Hanson up as a virtuous candidate who refuses to discuss her sexuality—and then totally cops out at the end. It's cheap, it's vulgar, it's a sellout. And we're sure some of Lurie's old quote-hound buddies will be calling "Contender" the movie of the year.

NEWSWEEK, 10/16/00, p.70, David Ansen

The vice president of the United States has died, and the president (Jeff Bridges) startles the nation by naming a woman—Sen. Laine Hanson (Joan Allen)—as the new No. 2. Unfortunately for Senator Hanson, Shelly Runyon (Gary Oldman), the right-wing Republican who will preside over the confirmation hearings, is determined to dig up all the dirt he can find to stop her. He comes up with a lulu: nude photos of the 19-year-old Laine at a collegiate orgy. Her response? Principled silence. Her private life is her own business, and it is beneath her dignity to reply. If she were a man, nobody would give a fig about her youthful romps.

So begins, promisingly, "The Contender," written and directed by former movie critic Rod Lurie. His movie, which aspires to be a kind of feminist Capraesque morality play, surfs on the ripples of recent events. The moral dilemma it explores—does one respond to dirty tricks in kind, or preserve one's soul and risk one's political career by taking the high road—is the same one both Gore Vidal's "The Best Man" and "Primary Colors" examined.

"The Contender" is not in their class. Lurie can write tasty dialogue, but his tale is so riddled with implausibilities and plot holes that it collapses into hokum long before its rousingly phony conclusion. (That none of the ghosts from Laine's past have ever come up before is just the first of many puzzlements.) Silly as it is, "The Contender" has a lurid zest that keeps you hooked, and a rambunctiously good cast. Bridges revels in his role as the wily, profane president; an unrecognizable Oldman makes a hissable villain. It's great to see the terrific Joan Allen at the center of a movie; too bad her enigmatic role is underwritten. Lurie is more interested in Laine as a principle than as a person. "The Contender" may qualify as a guilty pleasure, but it could have been much more. It could have been a contender.

SIGHT AND SOUND, 4/01, p. 41, Richard Kelly

Democrat senator Laine Hanson is chosen by US president Jackson Evans to replace his recently deceased vice-president. Republican congressman Shelly Runyon, chairman of Hanson's confirmation hearings, prefers governor Jack Hathaway, ruled out by Evans after a freak accident in which he tried but failed to save a drowning woman. Runyon uncovers photographs seemingly showing Hanson in a college gang-bang, leaks them on to the internet, and questions Hanson's moral character in the hearings; she insists on her right to privacy. Runyon's wife tells Hanson she had terminated a pregnancy years earlier, but Hanson refuses to exploit the information.

After Hanson's husband's ex-wife testifies that he and Hanson began their affair adulterously, Evans urges Hanson to confess to the college indiscretion, but she refuses. Over dinner Evans indicates to Runyon that he is willing to dump Hanson for Hathaway. However, the president fails to tell Runyon that he is aware Hathaway—under investigation by the FBI—staged the 'accident' hoping to display heroism. Having publicly declared his preference for Hathaway, Runyon is humiliated when the president has the governor arrested for setting up the accident. Thinking that she is no longer in the running for V-P, Hanson tells Evans that she is not the woman in the photos. The following day, Evans refuses to let her withdraw from the V-P nomination.

In early 1992, presidential wannabe Bill Clinton went on to Phil Donahue's television talk show, hoping to duck allegations about his adulterous affair with Gennifer Flowers. When this hope crashed, Clinton threatened to sit through the interview in silence, protesting that no 'decent human being' should suffer such prurient questioning. Remarkably, the ruse worked. Six years later, under the cosh again, Clinton tested a variation of the same defence ("Even presidents have private lives") on independent counsel Kenneth Starr. But by then, rather fewer Americans felt that Clinton was wholly deserving of "decent human being" status.

Like ex-president Bill, Rod Lurie's *The Contender* argues that the sexual peccadilloes of politicians are small beer next to the great business of delivering government to the people. Unlike Clinton, Lurie's protagonist Laine Hanson is not actually guilty of sexual misdeeds (or acts of perjury and corruption stemming from the same). Rather, she can claim to be a stoic victim of "sexual McCarthyism" practised by a cabal of pro-lifers gathered around Gary Oldman's Shelly Runyon. One is reminded of Hillary Clinton's panicky claim (ventured after the Lewinsky affair first made news) that a "vast right-wing conspiracy" was plotting against her husband. *The Contender* swallows whole this Clintonoid sophism, and regurgitates it with additional and rather more defensible quasi-feminist overtones. Through Laine Hanson's spotless demeanour, Lurie seems to be trying to expiate Clinton's failings, restoring to a fictional Democrat White House the aura of "honesty and decency" that might, in real life, have saved the US (and indeed all of us) from George W Bush.

Initially, though, Lurie achieves a fairly convincing portrait of today's Washington as a barrel of scrapping vermin, essentially bipartisan on most issues other than that of who gets to be king rat. So when Hanson raises some footling moral objection to Runyon's tactics, she's slapped down by tough as-boots chief of staff 'Kermit' Newman. President Evans' backing of Hanson is merely a cynical wager that the promotion of a woman to the Executive will embellish his "legacy". Hanson herself is not hugely sympathetic: a Republican who crossed the floor, her motives seem fairly inscrutable. But she's introduced to us while humping her husband atop her work desk, and Lurie strains to suggest that, beneath Joan Allen's impassive mien, Hanson is hot stuff. When Christian Slater's sophomoric congressman Webster upbraids her over the photographs that allegedly show her participating in a college gang-bang, she dismisses him with a rueful sigh ("You're young...") that had this viewer hoping Hanson was about to step out of the closet as an unrepentant 60s Child.

Instead, despite ambush by tabloid television and relentless browbeating by Evans and Kermit, Hanson sticks to her privacy defence and concludes the hearings with a pious speech outlining her liberal credentials. (Lurie has admitted that he accepted Steven Spielberg's advice that "ennobling music" be added here.) Affirmative action and a woman's right to abortion are Hanson's main interests, and since Runyon has branded the former as "a cancer" and the latter as "a holocaust of the unborn", she easily claims the moral high ground. Still, the shades of Clintonian pragmatism enveloping Evans suggest Hanson will be sacraficed: her name recalls the luckless Lani Guinier, Clinton's old Yale classmate, whom he nominated for the justice department in 1993 and then cravenly ditched after attacks from the right. But instead, Evans rumbles Runyon's protégé Jack Hathaway's failed publicity stunt, and this silly twist sinks the film, which gets much worse. Over more treacly music, Evans forgets his cynicism and tells congress that Hanson's confirmation will ensure the triumph of "greatness" over "misogyny". Finally the movie is dedicated "For Our Daughters", so encapsulating the crass sanctimony of the last few reels.

For all this nonsense, *The Contender* still has its moments. Lurie covers an inordinate amount of the action with Steadicam, allowing the scenes to breathe and encouraging his skilful cast. But rather than Jeff Bridges, who plays Evans, and Oldman munching the scenery around Allen's serene centre, one would have liked to see more of the excellent Saul Rubinek as communications chief Toliver, Kathryn Morris as diligent FBI agent Willomina, and Kristen Shaw as foul-mouthed Fiona Hathaway.

TIME, 10/16/00, p. 110, Richard Corliss

Another confession: Liberal movie critics tend to be critical of liberal movies. We're more susceptible to the red meat of an old Clint Eastwood actioner than to the good intentions of a warm-'n'-fuzzy plea for brother- and sisterhood. It's not the politics that rankles so much as the piety. That's where *The Contender*, Rod Lurie's new Washington drama, stumbles. It has surface smarts but a soft head. *Billy Elliot* appeals to liberal emotions, *The Contender* to liberal righteousness.

The Vice President has suddenly died, and President Jackson Evans (Jeff Bridges) needs a replacement. Surprise: he wants a woman, Senator Laine Hanson (Joan Allen). She's flinty, principled and perhaps fatally compromised by allegations that she participated in an orgy in her college days. If she is ratified, it will be over the sternest objections of Representative Shelly Runyon (Gary Oldman, sporting a cornpone accent and the most preposterously wayward Capitol Hill hairdo since Everett Dirksen's). "We're both sticking to our guns," Runyon warns Evans. "The difference is, mine are loaded." He is determined to corner Hanson with the question she refuses to answer: Are you now, or have you ever been, a slut?

The writer-director, son of political cartoonist Ranan Lurie, lets his large, attractive cast display varieties of charisma and chicanery for an hour or so. Then he has everyone make speeches; it's as though a TV remote control had switched from *The West Wing* to the Lieberman-Cheney debate. All drama, not to mention insider dish, gets lost in the wind tunnel. By the end, *The Contender* is as edifying and stultifying as what would the real-life equivalent be?—a Ralph Nader presidency.

VILLAGE VOICE, 10/17/00, p. 131, J. Hoberman

The Contender will be no one's idea of an October surprise, although, barring some late-breaking revelation of George Bush fratboy shenanigans, Rod Lurie's meditation on the American political process is about as enjoyably lurid as the current campaign is likely to get.

It's amply evident in this kiss-and-tell (Oprah) political season that eight years of Bill Clinton brought the politics of entertainment to a new stage. Hollywood got the message early, responding to the Clinton administration with a cycle of soft-issue presidential movies even more extensive, if considerably less apocalyptic, than those of the early '60s. *The Contender* may be considered the culminating example of cine Clinton—not because it's any better than its precursors or because it corrals and crams together a host of Billious (and Gorey) themes just in time for the election, but because it's the closest the political film has come to merging with daytime TV.

Graceless writing and shameless plot contrivance are part of the fun. Lurie, a former entertainment reporter, has designated *All the President's Men* as his favorite movie. But while *The Contender* takes as a given the post-Watergate notion of Washington as a sewer of slimy ambition, the movie more closely resembles the senatorial drama of *Advise and Consent* and backstage skullduggery of *The Best Man*—both movies about ambitious pols with guilty secrets. Adding to the magpie construction are bits of business swiped from *Blow Out*, *The Candidate*, and *Air Force One*, not to mention the Clarence Thomas confirmation hearings and, above all, the Clinton impeachment.

For all the hot air expended on prescription drug benefits and mandatory school testing, the theatrics of the first Bush-Gore debate were all about projecting alpha maleness and strategic empathy. Lurie similarly understands American politics as more a matter of power and demographics than democracy. His first feature, the low-budget and widely derided *Deterrence*, featured the nation's first unelected Jewish president trapped by a blizzard in a Colorado diner as he ponders the possibility of nuking Iraq. *The Contender* revolves around a second-term president's look to his legacy in attempting to replace his deceased running mate with America's first unelected female vice president.

This historic feat is rendered all the more problematic by the insatiable thirst for tabloid trash that the media has induced in the American public. As in some nightmare episode of *The Jerry Springer Show*, the vice president designate is confronted with the revelation of a nasty, supposedly deposed and documented bacchanal in her teenaged past. It's not a crime, but to the relief of audiences everywhere, it insures that the confirmation hearings can be all about sex. As a resident media-savvy wise man puts it, "The one thing that the American people cannot stomach is a vice president with a mouth full of cock."

I'm sure Joe Lieberman and Dick Cheney will be pleased to know that. *The Contender* is a movie where you are what you eat and politicians are all creatures of appetite. President Jackson

Evans (Jeff Bridges in prize hambone mode) is a cigarette-smoking, glad-handing Clintonesque blowhard whose main psychological quirk seems to be that he's always hungry—for food, that is. His vice president designate, Senator Laine Hanson (a tailored and determined Joan Allen, for whom Lurie wrote the role), is introduced having sex atop her office desk—albeit with her husband. Their nemesis is Republican congressman Shelly Runyon (Gary Oldman, hilariously tricked out in fake hair-plugs), a poky Henry Hyde type whose unhealthy if not murderous instincts are several times suggested by the gusto with which he tucks into a big slab of bloody steak.

Because the lusty Laine is identified with liberalism, abortion, and affirmative action, she becomes the object of a vast right-wing conspiracy. She will be hillary'd. "We have to gut the bitch in the belly," a member of the instant cabal smirks moments before the story of her long ago frat-house indiscretion breaks on the Internet. (Not for nothing did Allen play the bride of Nixon.) Reading the situation clearly, the president warns his candidate that "the whole world [is] thinking you're something out of a crazed soap opera." He advises her to take a leaf from the Bill Clinton playbook and make a public confession.

But that's not exactly Lurie's game plan. As the president tells his nominee to go beyond embarrassment, so Lurie himself ventures beyond cynicism. *The Contender* is an attack on itself—or maybe a defense. Having created a situation in which his heroine can self-righteously invoke the House Committee on Un-American Activities, sexual McCarthyism, and the "ideological rape of all women," Lurie decries the existence of a double standard—the better to demonstrate its dramaturgical necessity.

Bizarrely pugilistic, *The Contender*'s title refers mainly to Joan Allen's Oscar prospects, and why not? Cheesy as the movie is, it allows the actress to play Bill to her own Monica and emerge from the Washington cesspool satisfyingly unbesmirched.

Also reviewed in:
CHICAGO TRIBUNE, 10/13/00, Friday/p. A, Michael Wilmington
NATION, 10/30/00, p. 36, Stuart Klawans
NEW REPUBLIC, 10/23/00, p. 28, Stanley Kauffmann
NEW YORK TIMES, 10/13/00, p. E12, Stephen Holden
NEW YORKER, 10/16 & 23/00, p. 256, David Denby
VARIETY, 9/11-17/00, p. 25, Emanuel Levy
WASHINGTON POST, 10/13/00, p. C1, Stephen Hunter
WASHINGTON POST, 10/13/00, Weekend/p. 43, Desson Howe

COTTON MARY

A Merchant Ivory Productions and Universal Pictures release. *Executive Producer:* Paul Bradley. *Producer:* Nayeem Hafizka, Richard Hawley, Producer: Gil Donaldson and Ismail Merchant. *Director:* Ismael Merchant. *Screenplay:* Alexandra Viets. *Director of Photography:* Pierre Lhomme. *Editor:* John David Allen, Giorgio DeVincenzo, Roberto Silvi, and Jack Tucker. *Music:* Richard Robbins. *Sound:* Giovanni Di Simone and (music) Kirsty Whalley. *Sound Editor:* Nigel Mills. *Casting:* Celestia Fox. *Production Designer:* Alison Riva. *Art Director:* Charmian Adams. *Costumes:* Sheena Napier. *Make-up:* Marina Köhl. *Running time:* 125 minutes. *MPAA Rating:* Not Rated.

CAST: Greta Scacchi (Lily MacIntosh); Madhur Jaffrey (Mary); James Wilby (John MacIntosh); Nina Gupta (Blossom); Sarah Badel (Mrs. Evans); Joanna David (Mrs. Smythe); Gemma Jones (Mrs. Freda Davids); Nadira (Mattie); Surekha Sikri (Gwen); Laura Lumley (Theresa MacIntosh); Riju Bajaj (Mugs); Gerson da Cunha (Doctor Correa); Sakina Jaffrey (Rosie, Mary's Niece); Firdausi Jussawalla (Mr. Panamal); Mahabanoo Mody-Kotwal (Wellington Hospital Matron); Prayag Raaj (Abraham, Lily's Manservant); Captain Raju (Inspector Ramiji Ray); Shobha Vijay (Ayah 2); Matteo Piero Mantegazza and Olivia Caesar ('Baba' MacIntosh); Cuckoo Parameswaran, Beena Manoj, and Maggie Arthasery

(Wellington Hospital Nurses);   Harshiya Rafiq (Mira);   Vinnie D'Souza (Guitar Player); Chinappa and Ashok Koshy (Tea Workers); Shirly Somasundaram (Ayah 1);   Jaya George (Ayah 3);   Philip Tabor (Jack); Luke Jones (Charlie);   Susan Malick (Bunny Rogers); Hamza (Fisherman);   Virendra Saxena (Joseph); Poornima Mohan (Receptionist);   Caroline Charlety, Ranjini Haridas, and Gayatri Krishnan (Stylists);   Txuku Iriarte Solana (Sylvie D'Costa).

LOS ANGELES TIMES, 3/17/00, Calendar/p. 12, Kevin Thomas

"Cotton Mary," which takes us to the Malabar Coast in South India in 1954, is the third feature in the last seven years to be directed by Ismail Merchant, the producing half of the distinguished filmmaking team he formed with director James Ivory nearly 40 years ago. Not only is it Merchant's best directorial effort to date but also is among the finest films the Merchant Ivory company has ever made.

It is a splendid and subtle evocation of India in the post-colonial era, when the British influence lingered treacherously in some quarters, and it offers the formidable, internationally renowned Madhur Jaffrey, who also received co-director credit, the role of a lifetime and the most complex part Greta Scacchi has ever played on the screen. Engrossing from the first frame and written with admirable skill and insight by Alexandra Viets, "Cotton Mary" is a milestone for Merchant Ivory and a pleasure for the company's admirers.

For about 500 years, Anglo Indians, those individuals born of mixed British and Indian parentage, have had an equivocal status in Indian society, often enjoying greater privileges in colonial society than full-blooded natives but nothing like equality with the full-blooded Brits. Whatever standing the Anglo Indians had was severely undermined with the coming of independence, for their clinging to British ways invited widespread hostility and rejection.

No one could possibly have a stronger identity with the British—or a stronger denial of her partial Indian heritage—than the woman with the curious name of Cotton Mary (Jaffrey). When Scacchi's Lily MacIntosh arrives at the hospital where Mary works as a nurse, the middle-aged Mary seizes the opportunity to consolidate her sense of British identity.

Lily has just gone through the ordeal of the premature birth of her second daughter, and Mary devotes all of her attention to caring for Lily and her baby, for whom she finds a wet nurse when Lily is unable to nurse her baby herself. So swiftly does Mary ingratiate herself with Lily that, of course, Lily wants her to stay on with her at a fine old cliffside estate that Lily has inherited from her parents.

Lily's husband, John (James Wilby), is an often-absent, self-absorbed correspondent for the BBC who, on the rare occasions when he is home, has a bad habit of not listening to his wife.

John makes Lily feel chronically ineffectual, and since she does not enjoy the company of the snobby, racist and gossipy British wives, preferring to spend hours working in her garden, she is vulnerable to Mary's implacable determination to take over the household. So needy is Mary of seeming British in her own eyes, to make real her fantasy that she is the true lady of the house, that she maliciously starts undermining Lily's longtime servant Abraham (Prayag Raaj), who has been with Lily's family since her childhood and is like a loving grandfather to Lily's 7-year-old daughter, Theresa (Laura Lumley).

While Mary is every bit as calculating as "Rebecca's" infamous Mrs. Danvers, we see her as a pathetic, even potentially tragic figure rather than a villainess.

Yet Mary has a natural intelligence and a force of personality that make her a much stronger woman than Lily, who suffers from her husband's neglect and her sense of not fitting in to society any more than Mary. Scacchi has long played well-bred wantons but rises to the challenge of creating a woman who needs to get in touch with herself as much as her servant does.

A sense of time and place, with evocative, precisely detailed settings and costumes, is a Merchant Ivory hallmark, but the beauty of the Malabar Coast and the elegant interiors of this film throw into relief rather than blunt Merchant's bitter sense of injustice at the plight of Anglo Indians, caught so cruelly between two of the most class-conscious peoples on Earth, the British and the Indians. It's a sense of injustice that extends to the generally inferior status of women everywhere in the '50s.

Merchant never loses sight of the mitigating opportunities for humor and sensuality in telling the story of two women whose lives become more interlocked than they could ever imagine. Ironically, Jaffrey had one of her best screen roles as an Indian princess living in London and reminiscing about lost splendor with her late father's tutor (James Mason) in Ivory's exquisite 1975 "The Autobiography of a Princess." What a contrast to her Mary, who so unwittingly betrays her lowly origins in her earthier moments, for the father she insists was an officer of the regiment was apparently only a lackey who polished the officers' boots.

It is ironic too to realize that in the very year that this film takes place, audiences around the world were seeing a well-cast Merle Oberon as Empress Josephine to Marlon Brando's Napoleon in a now-largely forgotten film, "Desiree." To see "Cotton Mary" is to understand why Oberon strove her entire life to hide the fact that she was born in Bombay—not Tasmania, as she claimed—to a British father and a Ceylonese mother.

NEW YORK POST, 3/15/00, p. 57, Lou Lumenick

"Cotton Mary" is an infrequent directorial outing by Ismail Merchant, who usually produces movies directed by his longtime partner, James Ivory.

Part travelogue and part vehicle for the great Indian actress and Merchant-Ivory regular Madhur Jaffrey ("Shakespeare Wallah") it's very much in line with Ivory's movies, particularly "Heat and Dust."

The Australian actress Greta Scacchi, who starred in that arid 1982 drama, returns to post-colonial India for the seriocomic "Cotton Mary," though her role, as a wealthy Briton named Lily, is very much subsidiary to that of Jaffrey, who receives an unusual credit as co-director.

Jaffrey has a field day in the title role, an Anglo-Indian nurse who moves in with Lily after the birth of Lily's second daughter.

Lily is unable to nurse, so Mary enlists her wheelchair-bound sister (Neena Gupta) as a wet nurse.

Mary quickly takes over the household, pushing aside the longtime family major-domo (Prayag Raaj) and unwittingly manipulating Lily's distracted reporter husband (James Wilby) into a relationship with her beautiful niece (Sakina Jaffrey).

Jaffrey has several great scenes, notably a beauty-shop confrontation with Lily's pals, who have become alarmed about Mary's increasingly strident manner.

Working from an intelligent screenplay by Alexandra Viets, Merchant makes witty and subtle points about discrimination and class, albeit in the leisurely and somewhat bloodless style so typical of the Merchant-Ivory canon.

"Cotton Mary" is uncommonly well-acted and beautifully shot on location in southern India, but it's not exactly riveting.

NEWSDAY, 3/15/00, Part II/p. B9, Gene Seymour

Racism's insidious, often painful impact on those born between disparate cultures is a subject few movies have bothered to approach. Partly it's because the trope of the "half-caste" person or "tragic mulatto" fixtures of such late-1940s "problem pictures" as "Lost Boundaries" and "Pinky" has long since become as hidebound and patronizingly racist as the problems those movies were supposed to be attacking.

There remain, however, many opportunities to probe the wounds of mixed-race peoples. Given its impressive Merchant-Ivory production pedigree, "Cotton Mary" offered at least a faint promise of insightful, well-wrought exploration into such issues. Instead, it's a flat, turgid botch.

Set in 1954, seven years after India's independence from Great Britain, "Cotton Mary" takes its title from the name of an Anglo-Indian nurse (Madhur Jaffrey) given to extravagant fantasies in which she somehow claims what she believes to be her birthright to the lifestyle of the British who remain in their one-time colony.

She sees her chance when one of her patients, Lily MacIntosh (Greta Scacchi), the wife of a BBC correspondent (James Wilby), panics because she can't feed her newborn infant. Lily's desperate plea that Mary come home with her to help with the baby is the first in a series of delusional contrivances on the part of both mother and nurse. Mired in what must be the thickest post-partum funk in medical history, Lily seems incapable of noticing that her husband's blithe diffidence masks his cold-blooded philandering or that Mary has been pilfering goods and clothing from the household and blaming it on the family's faithful servant, Abraham (Prayag Raaj).

With the exception of poor Abraham and Lily's observant older daughter (Laura Lumley), neither of whom is fully developed in Alexandra Viets' script, everybody in "Cotton Mary" is, in some way, emotionally deformed or spiritually debased. Mary, being both, is made to seem especially pathetic in light of the racism, blatant or otherwise, of the white characters, especially a trio of blimpish hens who roll their eyes whenever Mary comes into their circle.

Altogether, the movie isn't a pleasant experience—which may not be the point, since it's not supposed to be a pleasant story. But what makes "Cotton Mary" so excruciating isn't its theme, but its leaden pace, its mawkish acting and startlingly inept staging. That Ismail Merchant, who usually produces the movies that James Ivory directs, is at the wheel of this project suggests he's better off staying in the background.

SIGHT AND SOUND, 1/00, p. 46, Claire Monk

Kerala, India, the 50s. Lily MacIntosh, wife of BBC correspondent John MacIntosh, gives premature birth to their second child during one of John's many absences. Lily cannot produce milk, so 'Cotton' Mary, one of many Anglo-Indian (mixed race) nurses at the hospital, hints at a solution. Mary starts secretly taking the ailing baby (named 'Baba') to her sister Blossom, a wheelchair-bound wet-nurse, for feeding. Identifying as British, both sisters yearn for the colonial past and are thrilled to have a white child to care for once more.

Credited with saving Baba's life, Mary joins the MacIntosh household as an *ayah* (nurse) and, with Lily depressed and withdrawn, works her way into a position of increasing power. She supplants Joseph, a loyal servant, and harbours delusions of replacing Lily as the lady of the house, unaware her niece Rosie has become John's lover. Blossom, still feeding Baba, becomes resentful at receiving no white recognition. Mary promises a visit from Lily and Blossom makes elaborate preparations, but the guest who arrives is Mary dressed in Lily's clothes. Furious, Blossom denounces Mary's delusions and tells her of Rosie and John's affair. Rosie tells John how his baby is being fed and, disgusted, he rejects her. Distraught, Mary taunts Lily about John's infidelity and is dismissed. With John also gone, Lily can breastfeed at last and returns to England with her children. Mary, half mad, is cared for by Blossom and the other Anglo-Indians.

Cotton Mary continues the interest in cultural identity shown in director Ismail Merchant's previous film *The Proprietor*. Mercifully, *Cotton Mary* is an enormous improvement on its predecessor. It also marks an absorbing (although not uncontentious) return to India and that country's entangled cultural relations, the trademark setting and subject of the bulk of Merchant Ivory's films before the 80s. (Merchant is the producing half of the Merchant Ivory partnership with James Ivory.) Although doubtful directorial choices are still evident—such as the swelling score that swamps the narrative—*Cotton Mary* has strengths which outweigh such eccentricities. Most crucially, it has a scrupulously intelligent script by first-timer Alexandra Viets and a striking central performance from Madhur Jaffrey.

"You're not a white man—you're neither fish nor fowl," El Hadji, the anti-hero of Ousmane Sembéne's *Xala* (1974) was told by his astute mother-in-law in that classic satire on postcolonial identity crisis. *Cotton Mary* is essentially an extended essay on the same theme, but set in India in the 50s, a moment when (in the resonant words of one character), "Mr Gandhi has been and gone." Its subject is the complex and troubled identity of the mixed-race Anglo-Indian community, a minority whose status and self-image have been damagingly dependent on fluctuations in British colonial policy and attitudes over the centuries. Favoured in the early stages of colonisation, many Anglo-Indians identified so strongly with the British they regarded themselves as such, only to find themselves rejected as fears about racial purity and native uprisings began to surface.

The damaging psychic effects of this history are powerfully and minutely conveyed in the film via Jaffrey's Cotton Mary. She embodies a contradictory internalisation of 'English' values in which snobbery and terror of being 'mistaken' for an Indian conceal frustrated ambition and suppressed loathing, all pathologically mingled. An anachronism, Mary is forever bolstering a white-over-brown racial hierarchy which other characters are discarding. Her distorted perspective is conveyed via an ironic use of subjective shots and soundtrack: arriving as the MacIntoshes' live-in nanny, she sees herself being greeted by a butler at an English country house to the strains of 'God Save the Queen'. However, her self-delusion turns sinister as she gradually assumes Lily's identity as the white 'Madam'. In the film's climactic moment of cultural cross-dressing, she promenades around town in an outfit stolen from Lily with Lily's baby in the pram, dropping in for a coiffure at the English Club. But her 'true' cultural identity is unmasked when the pram starts to smell and the source is revealed as a tongue which Mary has bought from a street stall en route.

As these examples suggest, the humanist, 'quality' tradition of film making to which *Cotton Mary* belongs places limitations on its strategies for dealing with its subject. While its makers clearly understand that the problematic Anglo-Indian identity represented by Mary has historical causes, the film can only show effects; in place of a collective problem of cultural identity, it explores an individual character. This approach risks inviting a reactionary reading by audiences. There is little to prevent us from responding to Mary as mad or evil rather than understanding her malaise as the product of a larger social problem. Nor does the film—structurally, a cuckoo in-the-nest or nanny-from hell narrative—prevent a snobbish, or even racist, reading of her behaviour.

However, *Cotton Mary* counteracts such reductiveness by offering a rich multiplicity of meanings. Structurally, it can be seen as Lily's story as much as Mary's. If the surface problem motivating (and resolved in) the narrative is Lily's inability to breastfeed, the underlying problem is that both women are trapped within a dying colonial, patriarchal system which they do not know how to reject. As Mary's mental state declines, a whole history of embedded racial, sexual and class fears and aspirations surface in her ramblings. The film ends eerily with her teaching a young girl the Lord's Prayer and instructing her: "Keep your mind on the job, or you'll never get out of here." The camera pans away to frame the Anglican church, the cornerstone of Anglo-Indian values in the film, but the music we hear is from a sitar a parting shot which seems to apportion both blame for Mary's values and reject them.

VILLAGE VOICE, 3/21/00, p. 144, Leslie Camhi

Umbrellas in the sun protect the Anglo-Indian characters in *Cotton Mary* from "unsightly" darkening. Ismail Merchant (one half of Merchant-Ivory Productions) has gone solo for this tale set in India a few years after independence and focusing on the lingering ghosts of colonial rule. Lily (Greta Scacchi), a British woman living on her family's estate in southern India, gives birth prematurely in a former British hospital while her journalist husband (James Wilby) is away on assignment. Distraught and unable to breast-feed, she turns to Cotton Mary (Madhur Jaffrey), an Anglo-Indian nurse who promises that "God will feed the child."

"God," as it turns out, is Mary's crippled sister, Blossom, a wet nurse who lives in a nearby alms-house. Mary brings her the baby for secret feedings, and introduces her beautiful niece (Sakina Jaffrey) into Lily's household. Meanwhile, Mary's obsession with whiteness and the lives of her masters threatens to spin out of control.

Merchant's filmmaking is at times wooden and conventional, but *Cotton Mary* is brought to life by the weirdness of its subject matter and the risks Madhur Jaffrey takes in her brilliant performance. Almost all the characters, from Mary to Lily to Blossom, are disoriented by the new social relations of an independent India; each lives in a dreamworld where she builds a shrine to Englishness. Lily withdraws from her children and philandering husband, cultivating her garden with roses and delphiniums; Blossom yearns for recognition from the madam, which never comes to her. Mary emerges as a tragic figure of racial longing, by turns servile, wild, and terrifyingly knowing—maniacally preoccupied with a social hierarchy that is failing to pieces, and where her place was never really secure or comfortable. And at the center of all this turmoil is that most complex and yet most simple relation, when one body takes nourishment from another.

Also reviewed in:
CHICAGO TRIBUNE, 3/31/00, Friday/p. J, John Petrakis
NEW YORK TIMES, 3/15/00, p. E5, Elvis Mitchell
VARIETY, 11/22-28/99, p. 87, Derek Elley

COYOTE UGLY

A Touchstone Pictures and Jerry Bruckheimer Films release. *Executive Producer:* Mike Stenson and Scott Gardenhour. *Producer:* Jerry Bruckheimer and Chad Oman. *Director:* David McNally. *Screenplay:* Gina Wendkos. *Director of Photography:* Amir Mokri. *Editor:* William Goldenberg. *Music:* Trevor Horn. *Music Editor:* Shannon Erbe and Tami R. Goldman. *Choreographer:* Travis Payne. *Sound:* Petur Hliddal, Bob Eber, and (music) Tim Weidner and Steve Macmillan. *Casting:* Bonnie Timmerman. *Production Designer:* Jon Hutman. *Art Director:* Gae Buckley and Bruce Alan Miller. *Set Designer:* John Warnke and John Perry Goldsmith. *Set Decorator:* Rosemary Brandenburg. *Special Effects:* Robert J. Scupp. *Costumes:* Marlene Stewart. *Make-up:* Darla Albright. *Stunt Coordinator:* Buddy Joe Hooker and Danny Aiello III. *Running time:* 94 minutes. *MPAA Rating:* PG-13.

CAST: Piper Perabo (Violet Sanford); Adam Garcia (Kevin O'Donnell); Maria Bello (Lil); Melanie Lynskey (Gloria); Izabella Miko (Cammie); Bridget Moynahan (Rachel); Tyra Banks (Zoe); Del Pentecost (Lou); Michael Weston (Danny); John Goodman (Bill); LeAnn Rimes (Herself); Jeremy Rowley (William Morris Receptionist); Ellen Cleghorne (Music Publishing Receptionist); John Fugelsang (Richie the Booker); Bud Cort (Romero); Freeze Luv (Fiji Mermaid Club Bouncer); Greg Pitts (Fiji Mermaid Waiter); Whitney Dylan (Fiji Mermaid Worker); Marvin Krueger (Surgeon); Victor Argo (Pete); Peter Appel and John Mondin (Pizza Customers); Frank Medrano (Walt); Elizabeth Beckwith (Management Office Receptionist); Diane Hudock (Open Mic Woman); Tara McLean (Open Mic Singer); Eric Ritter and Thomas R. Martin (Arlene's Grocery Audience Members); Ken Campbell (Biker); Jorgen De Mey (Coyote Ugly Customer); Jimmy Shubert and Greg Ginther (Coyote Ugly Drunks); Jeff Michalski (Fire Marshall); Jack McGee (Pitcher); Paul Davis-Miller (Sam Ash Salesman); Johnny Zander (Roy, the Busboy); Wali Collins (Critch); Nicole Ghastin (Lyndsay Morgan); Jonathan Klein (Manager); Alexandra Balahoutis (Hostess); Johnny Knoxville and Chris Wylde (College Guys); Michael Bay (Photographer); Chip Chinery and Nick Vallelonga (Cops); Joseph Patrick Kelly and Greg Collins (Coyote Ugly Bar Patrons); Stephen Snedden (Customer, Fancy Drinks); Chris Soldevilla (Man Ordering Shots); Joseph Bucaro III and James T. Sale (Finale Club Drunks); Heather Shannon Ryan (Sorority Girl); Biljana Filipovic (Bar Fight Girlfriend).

LOS ANGELES TIMES, 8/4/00, Calendar/p. 1, Kenneth Turan

Let's be honest here. "Coyote Ugly" may be a bad movie—in fact it is a bad movie—but it's not one of those fiascoes that leave you in a foul mood. Rather, like some odoriferous cheese that drives epicures wild but baffles ordinary folk, it's a bad movie for connoisseurs of the genre, a shameless but very watchable piece of youthful romantic fantasy that will have the cognoscenti shaking their heads in wonder.

The story of a small-town innocent who moves to New York to, yes, follow her dream, "Coyote Ugly" has a combination of sentimental romance and carefully sanitized raunch that is "Flashdance" all over again. It's a PG-13 date-night movie precisely designed for teens of both sexes: Guys get to admire peekaboo shots of attractive women in breath-constricting clothing, while girls safely swoon over a fairy-tale romance that looks hot and contemporary, but in reality is about as steamy as "National Velvet."

So wall-to-wall with cliches that practically jostle each other in a rush to get on the screen, "Coyote Ugly" is saved by its complete faith in its gee-whiz situations. An unintentionally preposterous film that encourages chuckles while its heroine is in tears, it defeats all skeptics with its tireless good humor and Energizer Bunny energy level.

Peppily written (Odyssey Theater veteran Gina Wendkos gets the credit), "Coyote Ugly" is directed by first-timer David McNally, who brings the brisk pacing and perpetually sunny outlook of television commercials (he's directed lots, including one for Budweiser that Entertainment Weekly voted the Top Super Bowl Spot of 1999) to the material at hand. Like a shark, this movie threatens to die whenever it stops moving, but reflective moments (this is a Jerry Bruckheimer-produced film after all) are thankfully rare.

Critical to the film is its choice, made after the de rigueur nationwide talent search ("We left no stone unturned, " the director insists) for the right actress to play Violet Sanford, a 21-year-old pizzeria waitress in South Amboy, N.J., who, not surprisingly, dreams of life beyond sausage and pepperoni.

Getting the role was Piper Perabo, also seen as straight-arrow FBI agent Karen Sympathy in "The Adventures of Rocky and Bullwinkle," and her guileless, trusting face does make her the obvious choice. Part snubbed urchin, part well-scrubbed kewpie doll, all wide-eyed innocence, Perabo brings so much earnestness to the part she wouldn't have been out of place as one of the gang who helped Judy Garland and Mickey Rooney put on shows in the Andy Hardy movies of long ago.

Did anyone mention that Violet has a dream? Though her father Bill (the always reliable John Goodman), a hefty toll-taker on the New Jersey Turnpike, doesn't understand, his daughter is compelled to move the 42 miles to the city to see if she can make it as a songwriter. After all, if you can make it there, you can ... well, you get the idea.

So, though she deserves to have rose petals strewn before her, Violet moves to Chinatown, where they throw fish heads instead, to a fifth-floor walk-up grungy enough to disconcert Limp Bizkit. The only place she can work on her music is the building's beautifully lit roof, where she gets inspired by the sounds of the city. Yes, she really does. All Violet wants is for someone like Whitney or Mariah to sing her songs, but bad-tempered music business receptionists—the fools—barely acknowledge her presence.

Violet does have a cute-meet with the cutest guy in Manhattan, Kevin O'Donnell (Adam Garcia), an Australian short-order cook who, like all fairy-tale princes, has a soft and pleasing accent. They don't get on at first—big surprise—but Kevin really believes in her music and, through an obligatory series of bogus crises, tries to help her overcome her crippling stage fright and get out there and sing her stuff herself.

Meanwhile, Violet's kindergarten-teacher looks and pizzeria-honed people skills get her a job at the hottest bar in Manhattan, Coyote Ugly. Owned by tough-talking, no-guff-taking Lil ("ER's" Maria Bello in the film's best performance), Coyote is one of those post-feminism establishments that announces it's OK for women to act like sex toys if they do it with attitude and sass.

So Coyote's female bartenders (played by Izabella Miko, Bridget Moynahan and, very briefly, Tyra Banks, whose character is soon off to law school) dish out hostility with the alcohol, whipping the tired businessmen and sailors on shore leave in the audience into the kind of carefully staged bacchanalian frenzy that makes AA meetings look awfully appealing.

When they're not taunting men, the women dance on Coyote Ugly's bar. Not just simple clog dances, thank you very much, but tightly choreographed Las Vegas-style routines through flames that are so elaborate that the film employs not only dance doubles, body doubles and leg doubles but, in what might be a Hollywood first, a fire leg double as well. (Sad to say, Perabo doesn't sing her own Dianne Warren-written songs either; the honor goes to LeAnn Rimes. And that's not a working photographer taking pictures at the bar, it's veteran Bruckheimer director Michael Bay.)

Naturally Violet, whom Lil cleverly nicknames "Jersey," makes all the first-timer mistakes possible, but gosh dam it if her spunky determination doesn't count for a lot even here. Wouldn't it be a kick if the self-assurance she gets from entertaining inebriated New Yorkers could translate into a loving relationship with Kevin and the confidence she needs to belt out those songs all by herself? Thank goodness the creators of "Coyote Ugly" can take those predicaments seriously; that way, no one else has to.

NEW YORK, 8/14/00, p. 65, Peter Rainer

The dreadful *Coyote Ugly* seems to have been made for prepubescent dirty old men. Piper Perabo plays an aspiring songwriter who moves from Jersey to New York to Make It and ends up, as one might expect in a Jerry Bruckheimer movie, wriggling on a bar top with a bevy of other Barbies while unshaven guys slaver and whoop. Somehow this is all meant to be empowering for the women. I'm not saying one goes to a film like this for intellectual stimulation, but be forewarned: It makes *Flashdance* seem like *Copenhagen*.

NEW YORK POST, 8/4/00, p. 53, Jonathan Foreman

"Coyote Ugly" is the kind of excrescence that makes you wonder if the Taliban, the French and all the other foreigners who whine about the awfulness of Hollywood "product" might actually have a point.

Large chunks of this movie are so laughably cheesy that at first the whole thing seems like a high-concept spoof: "Cocktail" meets "Showgirls." Then it becomes horribly clear that none of it is intended as a joke.

There's no limit to "Coyote Ugly's" crass shamelessness: Producer Jerry Bruckheimer genuinely expects you to buy this glossily soulless, ultraformulaic tripe, reeking as it does with contempt for the audience.

Presumably he doesn't care that the dreadful script—blamed by the credits on Gina Wendkos—epitomizes the leering sensibility of some, middle-aged strip-club addict, and is so ignorant of the story's New York setting that it makes jokes about parking validation.

Nor does he seem to mind that it's directed like a third-rate beer commercial by newcomer David McNally.

"Coyote Ugly" is really just an excuse to get some hot actresses together and have them do sexy dances in skimpy clothes.

And there's nothing wrong with that. But instead of giving you a steady stream of eye-candy, Bruckheimer & Co. try to justify the dance sequences with a tedious "plot"—really just a soiled string of ancient movieland cliches—about Violet the songwriter (Piper Perabo) who comes to New York to make it, but suffers from stage fright.

Violet hails from South Amboy, N.J., which the filmmakers conceive of as a desert island without TV, movies, libraries or magazines.

Because, while not exactly a moron, Violet could hardly be more clueless about the music industry she's supposed to be so keen to join.

She gets a job at a rowdy Meat District bar called "Coyote Ugly," inspired by a real-life bar in the East Village.

Run by tough Lil (Maria Bello, so watchable in "ER" and "Permanent Midnight" but wasted here), this watering hole is a frat boy's fantasy where bartenders played by Tyra Banks, Izabella Miko and Bridget Moynahan keep jumping on the counter to perform Stringfellows-style dance routines.

Working there helps Violet deal with her shyness, but jeopardizes her relationships with her toll-taker dad (John Goodman in a terrible hairpiece) and Kevin, (Adam Garcia) her Australian love interest, who of course has a hilariously lame Painful Secret of his own.

At least there's genuine chemistry between the attractive young stars.

Garcia, a star of the West End stage, does his creditable best to bring alive a skimpily drawn character, and Perabo has the looks and presence of a young Julia Roberts.

You can tell that the bar-dance sequences are mostly performed by substitutes, but watching the undulating figures is certainly less tedious than the agonizing dialogue.

NEWSDAY, 8/4/00, Part II/p. B3, John Anderson

As the most critic-proof of this summer's critic-proof movies, "Coyote Ugly" has the simplest concept—sumptuous bartenders shaking their collective booty—and, presumably, the easiest marketing job of any movie out there. And yet, it's hard to imagine a more egregious example of false advertising: Who expected the thing to have a story?

And what a story it is. Proving that he really is a sadist—how else do you explain "Top Gun," "Con Air" and, most appropriately, "Flashdance"—producer Jerry Bruckheimer waits a full half hour before giving his audience what he's promised, which is a long, sexy MTV video, had MTV been around in the 70s. (In the movie, there's not a song nor a hairstyle that wasn't an oldie when Ronald Reagan hit the White House.)

Instead, Bruckheimer—director David McNally is really just an accomplice—makes them sit through the totally insipid, not-quite-rags-to-riches tale of Violet Sanford, played by the Julia

Roberts lookalike-laughalike Piper Perabo. Violet's a Perth Amboy-bred would-be songwriter who moves to Manhattan, where every other beautiful young woman, of course, is trying desperately to make it in show business. And she gets very, very upset when the William Morris Agency won't accept her demo tapes. So, instead, she winds up working at the Coyote Ugly Saloon, where the only water allowed is what's soaking down the T-shirts and the owner (Maria Bello) practices a managerial style not seen since Victor MacLaglen in "She Wore a Yellow Ribbon."

The Coyote girls don't wear much more than that, but in keeping with Bruckheimer's portrayal of New York as a big nasty place, the saloon is a strip joint where nobody strips. Sorry, young fella. This is a certified chick flick, especially for chicks with a Spice Girls view of the world. Violet will make it big with very little effort, the bar babes will make the men grovel like the worms they are and the only male, outside of Violet's love interest Kevin (played by Hugh Grant clone Adam Garcia), is John Goodman as Violet's father, who looks like he's about to explode.

You have to give Goodman credit. No, not for his acting; his acting, like everyone else's, is atrocious. Rather, for appearing in a movie with so much otherwise fabulous flesh, and not a brain in its lovely little head.

SIGHT AND SOUND, 11/00, p. 49, Mark Olsen

Leaving behind the security of life at home with her widowed father in suburban New Jersey, Violet Sanford moves to Manhattan to pursue her dream of becoming a songwriter. Mistaking him for a music booker, she gives grill cook Kevin a tape of her songs; the two soon begin dating.

After her apartment is robbed, Violet nears the end of her tether, emotionally and financially. She learns that there might be a job opening in a bar called Coyote Ugly. Dropping by, Violet is offered a position by the owner Lil. When she returns at night, Coyote Ugly is swarming. The bartenders get up to dance on the bar but Violet refuses to join in; Lil sends her home. Seeing Violet break up a fight on her way out, Lil gives her a second chance.

Soon Violet gets used to the demands of her new job. She continues to attempt to realise her song-writing ambitions although she is plagued by stage fright when she has to sing for people. When her father drops in at the bar on a rowdy night, they have a falling out. Soon after she loses Kevin and her job. Later, Violet finally overcomes her stage fright, wins a song-writing competition and reconciles with her dad and Kevin. In the end, Violet and country-music star LeAnn Rimes perform their hit song in Coyote Ugly.

Pity the young director who works for producer Jerry Bruckheimer. The man behind such films as *Con Air, Enemy of the State* and *Gone in Sixty Seconds*, Bruckheimer creates movies with such a distinctive style one imagines it must be difficult for a director to exert creative influence. Typically, the producer plucks his directors from the world of commercials and music videos, and his films tend to show the kind of quick-cutting, high-sheen aesthetic characteristic of television advertising and MTV.

In *Coyote Ugly* it is at once startling and no surprise at all that Bruckheimer and debut director David McNally tell the relatively small story of young Violet Sanford moving to the big city to pursue a career as a songwriter in a high-impact manner. Essentially treating the story like an action picture, they map the big-fisted, hyperbolic dynamics of the action set-piece on to *Coyote Ugly*'s bar-room sequences (where the glamorous bartenders dance for their spirited customers). Instead of blowing up cars or buildings, Bruckheimer and McNally create a film in which the girls themselves are oversized, larger than life—and it's their over-the-top antics which sustain the film rather than the scant character and plot development.

It's hard then to see *Coyote Ugly* as a back-to basics exercise for Bruckheimer, although the film ostensibly revisits the smaller scale of such works as *Flashdance* (which he made with fellow producer Don Simpson in 1983). The characterisation is kept at an elemental level so as to keep the story moving, and in an effort to prove it has a healthy attitude towards the modest degeneracy it features, the screenplay (by Gina Wendkos, based on a magazine article by Elizabeth Gilbert) repeatedly falls back on the so-called empowerment of contemporary shake-that-thing feminism to the point of a certain guarded defensiveness in a number of the dialogue exchanges. Throughout, *Coyote Ugly* tries hard to maintain its appeal to both male and female audiences, just as it strives to veer between winsomely light-hearted and inspiringly dramatic tones.

Relative newcomer Piper Perabo in the central role of Violet exudes a certain charm but is ultimately sunk by the schematic nature of her character's rise. Her fellow bartenders (Izabella Miko, Bridget Moynahan and Tyra Banks) are ridiculously underdeveloped, with only Maria Bello's tough/tender bar owner making any sort of lasting impression. John Goodman tries hard in the role of Violet's overprotective father, but he can't overcome the material at hand. Stalwart character actors such as Victor Argo and Bud Cort are similarly underused in small roles, though Bruckheimer collaborator Michael Bay (director of *Armageddon* and the upcoming Pearl *Harbor)* pops up amusingly as a newspaper photographer.

More laughably misguided than outright offensive, *Coyote Ugly* ultimately has such an odd good-naturedness about it that it is difficult to take it seriously, let alone grow angry at it. Some sort of achievement in the ongoing oeuvre of Jerry Bruckheimer, *Coyote Ugly* is distastefully irresistible, a product that delivers more or less what it promises.

VILLAGE VOICE, 8/15/00, p. 124, Michael Atkinson

Clearly Jerry Bruckheimer thinks it is, but is this the inevitable moment for a *Flashdance* redux, a shake-your-money-maker urban Cinderella fable that this time centers on a not-quite-notorious East Village dive where fully clothed barmaids pull stripper moves on the bar to Don Henley songs and spray the crowd with club soda? All I know is, that new Harry Potter book is super-duper. All that stuff, the Ragworts or whatever, just terrific.

Look, focusing your equipment on the happy horseshit of *Coyote Ugly* is like remembering a very bad burn—your body will do what it can to keep you from it. I'd rather eat ball bearings. Not that this Jersey-girl-comes-to-NYC-to-make-it-big-as-a-songwriter mendacity doesn't know how to fondle your medulla, if that's what you like in movies. Of course, the bar sequences' boozy montages and circular jolt-pans are edited into an Eisensteinian throttle, but the dialectic here says: You're a Barbary ape with a drinking problem, and we have your money. The movie's Odessa Steps is a stompin', Charlie Daniels-scored riverdance that could drive a dog to suicide.

While in, say, *Rocky & Bullwinkle* (to index thoroughly the Piper Perabo oeuvre) you are led to ponder why it is that Robert De Niro seems to have as much respect for his craft as a Grand Central Station toilet scrubber has for his, in *Coyote Ugly* everyone has found their level, except perhaps for tough-talking bar owner Maria Bello, who is too snappy and clear-eyed by half; she stands out like a seagull among slow-moving crabs. (Tyra Banks is one of the crabs.) At her best, Perabo is little more than the affliction of a wistfully crooked grin upon the sanity of the civilized world, whining through what drama there is in the stunning realization that your father (John Goodman) and new boyfriend (Adam Garcia) aren't delighted when you pour bourbon on your shirt in front of a gaggle of power-drunk sailors. You don't want to know more.

Also reviewed in:
CHICAGO TRIBUNE, 8/4/00, Friday/p. F, Mark Caro
NEW YORK TIMES, 8/4/00, p. E22, Elvis Mitchell
VARIETY, 8/7-13/00, p. 15, Robert Koehler
WASHINGTON POST, 8/4/00, p. C1, Stephen Hunter
WASHINGTON POST, 8/4/00, Weekend/p. 34, Michael O'Sullivan

CRANE WORLD

A Cowboy Booking International release of a Stantic-Univ. del Cine production. *Producer:* Lita Stantic and Pablo Trapero. *Director:* Pablo Trapero. *Screenplay (Spanish with English subtitles):* Pablo Trapero. *Director of Photography:* Cobi Migliora. *Editor:* Nicholás Goldbart. *Music:* Francisco Canaro. *Sound:* Catriel Vildosola. *Production Designer:* Andrés Tambornino. *Running time:* 90 minutes. *MPAA Rating:* Not Rated.

CAST: Luis Margani (Rulo);   Adriana Aizemberg (Adriana);   Daniel Valenzuela (Torres); Roly Serrano (Walter); Federico Esquerro (Claudio);   Graciana Chironi (Rulo's Mother); Alfonso Rementeria (Sartori).

NEW YORK POST, 4/7/00, p. 57, Hannah Brown

"Crane World" is an artless, slice-of-life story about a Buenos Aires construction worker that will either charm viewers or bore them silly.

Shot in black and white, the film opens with sharp, clean shots of the crane that Rulo (Luis Margani) hopes to get a job operating, like a holy grail.

Now in his 50s, the unemployed, divorced Rulo is a one-hit-wonder rock musician who hasn't played in 15 years.

As he trains for the job, the pot-bellied Rulo suddenly gets the confidence to start courting a woman who runs a sandwich shop and get tough with his lazy son.

But when the construction company learns from his insurance physical that he has some medical problems, he's quickly fired.

Blacklisted at all the construction sites in Buenos Aires, Rulo heads off to Patagonia. In this desolate setting, he winds up living in poverty and sadness.

This straightforward story often lacks momentum, but at least partly makes up for this by the grace and conviction of its acting and the elegant simplicity of the script, by director Pablo Trapero.

VILLAGE VOICE, 4/10/00, p. 158, Amy Taubin

Rulo is a middle-aged Argentinean with a potbelly and a heavy nicotine habit. As played by Luis Margani, who's like a Latin Jean Gabin, he's generous, sloppy, and resourceful—an all-around good guy. In his youth, Rulo tasted fame as the bass player with a group that had a hit single. Today, he works at a construction site; it's heavy, dangerous work, but the pay is decent, and Rulo has a mother and a grown son to support. That he could never afford to live in the high-rises he builds doesn't lessen his enthusiasm for the job.

Pablo Trapero's *Crane World* is, largely, a character study of Rulo, shot in episodic, vérité style. We follow him around Buenos Aires as he drives his failing car to and from work. We hang out in his grimy, cluttered apartment, where he makes indoor barbecue for his friends, works on his car motor, argues with his son, and on most nights, falls asleep alone in front of the TV. Rulo is also dating the proprietor of the local sandwich shop, who remembers him as a star from his club days.

An oral personality, he organizes his social interactions around food and he's never without a cigarette dangling from his lips. Rulo's pleasures have a downside. A physical exam reveals enough health problems to make him an insurance risk and he's laid off the very day that he's scheduled to take over the operation of a 300-meter crane. Unable to get another construction job in Buenos Aires, he's forced to travel a thousand miles south to Patagonia, where he's been promised work on a site in the desert. *Crane World* depicts two faces of Argentina: the burgeoning city, where the benefits of economic expansion barely trickle down to most of its population, and the daunting countryside, where development is as sporadic as in the Third World. When Rulo's friends drive down for a visit, they wind up at the local recreation spot: a barren, dusty slope at the edge of a dried-up lake.

From the worn-out sedans on the street to the old movies on Rulo's cable-free television set (he couldn't get his MTV even if he wanted), this is a country where modernization seems barely to have progressed since the end of World War II. In keeping with that, Trapero shot *Crane World* on black-and-white stock that looks as if it had been light-struck and gone brownish with age. To call it sepia would imply a glamour that's conspicuously absent. *Crane World* isn't a beautiful film, but it's remarkable for the tenderness and tenacity it shares with its memorable protagonist.

Also reviewed in:
NEW YORK TIMES, 4/3/00, p. E5, Stephen Holden
VARIETY, 10/18-24/99, p. 45, David Stratton

CREW, THE

A Touchstone Pictures release of a George Litto Pictures and a Sonnenfeld/Josephson Worldwide Entertainment production. *Executive Producer:* George Litto and Michael S. Glick. *Producer:* Barry Sonnenfeld and Barry Josephson. *Director:* Michael Dinner. *Screenplay:* Barry Fanaro. *Director of Photography:* Juan Ruiz-Anchia. *Editor:* Nicholas C. Smith. *Music:* Steve Bartek. *Music Editor:* Tom Drescher. *Sound:* Joe Foglia and (music) Robert Fernandez. *Sound Editor:* Dave Hankins. *Casting:* June Lowry Johnson. *Production Designer:* Peter Larkin. *Art Director:* J. Mark Harrington. *Set Designer:* Stephanie Girard. *Set Decorator:* Barbara Peterson. *Special Effects:* Richard Lee Jones. *Costumes:* Betsy Cox. *Make-up:* Jay S. Cannistraci. *Stunt Coordinatro:* Artie Malesci. *Running time:* 88 minutes. *MPAA Rating:* PG-13.

CAST: Richard Dreyfuss (Bobby Bartellemeo); Burt Reynolds (Joey "Bats" Pistella); Dan Hedaya (Mike "The Brick" Donatelli); Seymour Cassel (Tony "Mouth" Donato); Carrie-Anne Moss (Detective Olivia Neal); Jennifer Tilly (Ferris "aka Maureen" Lowenstein); Lainie Kazan (Pepper Lowenstein); Miguel Sandoval (Raul Ventana); Jeremy Piven (Detective Steve Menteer); Casey Siemaszko (Young Bobby Bartellemeo); Matt Borlenghi (Young Joey "Bats" Pistella); Billy Jayne (Young Tony "Mouth" Donato); Jeremy Ratchford (Young Mike "The Brick" Donatelli); Mike Moroff (Jorge); Jose Zuniga (Escobar); Carlos Gomez (Miguel); Louis Guss (Jerry "The Hammer" Fungo); Joe Rigano (Frankie "Rash" Decuello); Ron Karabatsos (Fat Pauly); Frank Vincent (Marty); Manuel Estanillo (Louis Ventana); Marc Macaulay (Driver); Cullen Douglas (Young Man); Jim Coleman (Paramedic); Louis Lombardi (Jimmy Whistles); Aaron Elbaz (Young Joey); Vince Cecere and Allan Nicholls (Wiseguys) Dana Daurey (Model Girl); Jeremy Shore (Model Guy); Hope Pomerance (Realtor); Penelope Alexitch, Christy Tummond, and Elizabeth Powers (Girls); Evelyn Brooks (Grandmother); Don Williams (Elderly Husband); Jill Beach (Newscaster); Lorri Bagley (Sofa Girl); Antoni Cornacchione (Officer); Ian Marioles (Security Guard); Fyvush Finkel (Sol Lowenstein); Mal Jones (Dr. Ward); Ru Flynn (Mommy); Ginger Southall (Reporter); Gino Salvano (Raul Guy); Jay Cannistraci (Tommy "Shakes"); John Archie (Doctor); Christa Campbell (Nurse); Adam Cronan (Burger King Manager); Judith Delgado (Judge); April Engel (Ferris Dancer); Patrick Fox (Jet Ski Kid); Daniel A. Leone (Barber Shop Guy); Yoset Rosenberg (Rabbi); Fabian Hernandez (Bus Boy); David H. Steel (Coach); Susie Park (Asian Masseuse); Carlo Perez Allen (Latino Mobster); George Fisher (Tony the Torch); Harry Boykoff (Louie the Lip).

LOS ANGELES TIMES, 8/25/00, Calendar/p. 6, John Anderson

[The following review by John Anderson appeared in a slightly different form in **NEWSDAY, 8/25/00, Part II/p. B6]**

A shaggy-dog story in support hose, "The Crew" should effect a marked upswing in the opening of IRAs, Keoughs and contributions to 401(k)s. After all, who wants to end up like its four hotel-dwelling wheeze-guys, standing in the rain for early-bird specials, driving cars with fins and watching the EMS bring out the old while the real estate agents bring in the new?

Fortunes change, as they must, in this feature by Emmy-winning director Michael Dinner, which must have made for an exciting pitch meeting and certainly couldn't have been made without its fab four—Burt Reynolds, Richard Dreyfuss, Dan Hodaya and Seymour Cassel. None of them can possibly be this old. But the end result shows how easily movies based on good ideas get made without scripts. The movie is so mild, so benign, its humiliation-to-vindication arc so predictable and its old-folks jokes so feeble that you want them to start shooting the remake immediately.

Doesn't it seem like only yesterday that Reynolds was ventilating sodomites in "Deliverance"? As Joey (Bats) Pistella, he's terrorizing mothers at Burger King. And threatening to exercise his own brand of squeeze play on male underwear models with apartment envy.

His buddies, friends since their New York mob apprenticeships, are more mellow, but no better off. Bobby Bartellemeo (Dreyfuss) is in Miami because he's looking for his long-lost daughter;

Mike the Brick Donatelli (Hedaya) is just as thick as he was in the '60s, when he had the brainstorm of a labor union for mob soldiers; and Tony the Mouth Donato (Cassel) is as closemouthed as ever—except with a certain member of the "leisure profession" named Ferris (Jennifer Tilly). This becomes a problem after the already deceased John Doe the boys use to feign a yuppie-scattering mob hit at their hotel turns out to be the father of a paranoid South American drug lord (Miguel Sandoval).

Investigating the crimes both real and fabricated are detectives Olivia Neal (Carrie-Anne Moss of "The Matrix") and her ex-wannabe boyfriend Steve (Jeremy Piven), who should know better than to date a woman who can perform DNA tests on the rogue blond hairs that turn up on his clothing. Like the yearning of Bobby for his daughter, the young couple's romantic wrangling merely distracts from Dinner's better bits: an arson-abetting rat that sets fire to the drug lord's house or the quasi-fantasy sequence involving the drug lord's dead father (Manuel Estanillo) and his last day on the beach. Lainie Kazan is at her blaring best as Ferris' deli-owning stepmother.

But best of all is the wise guy reunion at movie's end, which seems to feature every Scorsese extra in existence as well as the four horsemen of the mob apocalypse—Frank Vincent, Louis Guss, Ron Karabatsos and Joe Rigano, who offer a wise lesson: If you fire a shotgun from a wheelchair, you have to watch out for the recoil.

NEW YORK POST, 8/25/00, p. 51, Jonathan Foreman

With "The Crew"—"Space Cowboys" crossed with "Tough Guys" (the Burt Lancaster, Kirk Douglas vehicle of 1986)—the mob-comedy and grumpy-old-guy genres may have reached the end of their natural lives.

Most of the jokes work well but too many of them have the ritual, predictable feel of sitcom humor.

Still, there are moments in "The Crew" when the comedy rises above the level of network TV, particularly in a hilarious scene involving a rat and a Molotov cocktail, and in a sequence that involves entering a restaurant through the kitchen in a spoof of "Goodfellas."

If it's harder than it should be to get into the spirit of "The Crew," it's because the crew's members simply look and sound too young to be believable alter-kocker gangsters living in impoverished retirement in Florida.

Burt Reynolds is 64, Seymour Cassel is 65, Dan Hedaya is 60 and Richard Dreyfuss is a mere 52. With the exception of Dreyfuss, they're all obviously in great shape, and Reynolds' features now have an eerie Bride of Wildenstein tautness.

Bobby Bartellemeo, Joey "Bats" Pistella, Mike "The Brick" Donatelli and Tony "Mouth" Donato are wise guys who have known each other since childhood.

Back when they were a successful young crew in the '60s, they made the most of the good life, as you see in a flashback recalled by narrator Bobby (Dreyfuss).

Life was so good they used to make fun of Mike The Brick's (Hedaya) idea that they form a wise-guy labor union.

Now they wish they had provided better for a tedious old age spent sitting on the hotel balcony waiting for the early-bird special.

Facing eviction by a hotel management anxious to bring in the younger, more upscale clientele taking over the South Beach neighborhood, they come up with a plan.

They steal a fresh corpse from the mortuary where Mike The Brick works as a makeup artist, shoot it and leave it outside the hotel in such a manner as to suggest a mob murder.

The gambit works: The young newcomers move out and the crew's rent goes down. But it turns out that the body they picked belonged to the aged, senile father of Miami drug kingpin Raul Ventana (Miguel Sandoval). And the apparent killing sparks a gang war, as Ventana seeks vengeance on anyone who could have had anything to do with the murder.

To make matters worse, Tony "Mouth" Donato (Cassel) tells the truth to stripper/hooker Ferris (Jennifer Tilly—always so good as a bimbo). She blackmails the crew, threatening to give their names to Ventana unless they kill her wealthy stepmother Pepper Lowenstein (Lainie Kazan).

Meanwhile, there are a couple of police detectives sniffing around: Jeremy Piven's sleazy Steve and Carrie-Anne Moss's Olivia—who unbeknownst to her is Dreyfuss' long-lost daughter

Sandoval and Kazan are particularly funny, even though the ethnic characters they portray are so stereotypical they verge on the offensive.

VILLAGE VOICE, 9/5/00, p. 122, Nico Baumbach

By now, even Scorsese might have difficulty mining fresh absurdist material out of a premise that confronts mobsters with the quotidian. Nonetheless, we have *The Crew*, a film as generic as its title, about four grumpy old retired gangsters getting their grooves back. Threatened by gentrification in South Beach, Miami, they conspire to keep rents down by faking a mob hit in their apartment building. Their return to a life of crime begins as a stunt but quickly goes awry, leaving them pursued by both cops and robbers. None of the details make much sense, but *The Crew* glibly coasts on the assumption that we won't notice or care.

Leading the grade-B *Space Cowboys* cast, Richard Dreyfuss, as the one character not intended as a caricature, is the pivot for the requisite maudlin subplot, in which he's looking for his long-lost daughter (Carrie-Ann Moss), who just happens to be the detective on their tracks. Moss is as grimly affectless as she was in *The Matrix*, but here it feels more motivated by the material than the character. The other crew members are each summed up by a tic and known by corresponding nicknames, lest we forget who's who and why we're meant to be laughing. For example, Dan Hedaya's character is called "Brick" because he's stupid.

In other words, the humor is even more geriatric than the cast. The day-to-day tedium of the men's lives is meant to contrast with the carefree bravado that we expect from mobsters and they expect from themselves. But whatever life might be eked out of this setup is forfeited by cartoonish treatment. If (and it's a big if) there's a laugh in the awakening of Seymour Cassel's long-dormant libido after a kiss from a beach bunny, it's not to be found, as director Michael Dinner gambles, in the interior of Cassel's mouth. Though typical, *The Crew* stays clear of topical (i.e., no wince-inducing Viagra jokes), but really, could that have hurt? Perhaps the hope is audiences have the same lackluster attitude toward comedy that we're told senior citizens have toward life; we just want the comfort of the familiar.

Also reviewed in:
CHICAGO TRIBUNE, 8/25/00, Friday/p. A, Michael Wilmington
NEW YORK TIMES, 8/25/00, p. E23, A. O. Scott
VARIETY, 8/28-9/3/00, p. 25, Joe Leydon
WASHINGTON POST, 8/25/00, p. C1, Stephen Hunter
WASHINGTON POST, 8/25/00, Weekend/p. 36, Michael O'Sullivan

CRIME + PUNISHMENT IN SUBURBIA

A United Artists release of a Killer Films production. *Producer:* Pamela Koffler, Larry Gross, and Christine Vachon. *Director:* Rob Schmidt. *Screenplay:* Larry Gross. *Director of Photography:* Bobby Bukowski. *Editor:* Gabriel Wrye. *Music:* Michael Brook. *Music Editor:* Gabriel Wrye. *Sound:* Craig Woods. *Sound Editors:* Roland N. Thai, Catherine Speakman, and Ann Scibelli. *Casting:* Susan Shopmaker and Matthew Barry. *Production Designer:* Ruth Ammon. *Set Decorator:* Amy Botefuhr Vuckovich. *Special Effects:* Frank Ceglia. *Costumes:* Sophie de Rakoff Carbonell. *Make-up:* Amanda Carroll. *Stunt Coordinator:* Al Jones. *Running time:* 98 minutes. *MPAA Rating:* R.

CAST: Monica Keena (Roscanne Skolnik); Vincent Kartheiser (Vincent); Jeffrey Wright (Chris); James DeBello (Jimmy); Michael Ironside (Fred Skolnik); Christian Payne (Dean); Conchata Ferrell (Bella); Marshall Teague (Coach); Nicki Aycox (Cecil); Brad Greenquist (Calvin Berry); Ellen Barkin (Maggie Skolnik); Lucinda Jenney (Vincent's Mom); Black C. Shields (Moznick); Anthony C. Chow (Teacher); Bonnie Somerville (Stuck Up Girl); Jim Boyce (Mr. Dwyer); Matt Champagne (Counsellor Lord); Jim Swanson (Rat Fink Neighbor); Tommy Perna (Officer Lambert); Tommy Bush (Chief Judson); Susan Davis (Grandmother); Dennis Liss (Bailiff); Jeff Lawrence (Judge Jack); Valerie Wildman (Prosecutor); Jack Angel (Russ).

LOS ANGELES TIMES, 9/15/00, Calendar/p. 14, Kevin Thomas

Those who manage to make it through to the end of "Crime + Punishment in Suburbia" may well feel that the "crime" was that it was made in the first place and the "punishment" is having to watch it.

Jonathan Kaplan's unsettling 1979 "Over the Edge" was a groundbreaker in the depiction of alienated kids at loose in an arid new tract-house community, and when it comes to dissecting the dysfunctional suburban family, "American Beauty" would be hard to top.

Director Rob Schmidt and writer Larry Gross inevitably bring to mind those two films without coming even remotely within shouting distance of them.

Monica Keena plays the stolid, bosomy Roseanne, who lives in a luxurious, outsized tract house with her sullen mother, Maggie (Ellen Barkin), and Maggie's husband, Fred (Michael Ironside, at his least subtle), a crude, drunken, tyrant forever reminding Maggie and Roseanne that they would be in the gutter if it were not for him. (We know nothing of Roseanne's actual father or his fate.)

Although her personality verges on blankness, Roseanne is supposedly the most popular girl in school, and she has the requisite football-player boyfriend (James DeBello), whose clumsy, aggressive advances she is fighting off all the time.

She is constantly being watched by a skinny kid with a camera (Vincent Kartheiser), whose weirdness gives way to the not entirely convincingly beatific.

You wouldn't want to give any of these people the time of day in real life. They are blah or worse, and they are headed for some violent confrontations that seem pointless because they are so unworthy of our attention in the first place.

At first you think the filmmakers are attempting dark comedy, but you can't say for certain and soon you don't care one way or another. "Crime + Punishment" offers the worst case scenario: It's trashy without being fun.

What the filmmakers do have in mind is redemption for some of these people, but they have given us no reason to care about any of them. (Only DeBello and Wright manage to work up any humor or personality.)

Cinematographer Bobby Bukowski's gorgeous, stylized images and Michael Brook's score, plus music supervisor Liza Richardson's selection of songs are so strong they overwhelm the film, serving only to underline its pretentiousness.

NEW YORK POST, 9/15/00, p. 54, Jonathan Foreman

It's perfectly understandable that "Crime + Punishment in Suburbia" is less an updated version of the Dostoevsky novel than an unusually somber Hollywood teen love story. Guilt—especially guilt tinged with religious fear—is a notion that has little resonance in today's popular culture.

It would presumably take some persuading to convince an audience weaned on "Pulp Fiction" that a young person could kill someone (in this story, with some justification) and then feel so bad about the crime that it destroyed him or her.

And screenwriter Larry Gross, who co-wrote "48 Hours" and "Streets of Fire," only makes vague gestures in that direction, before returning to a more conventional movie narrative about adversity prompting a hot cheerleader to fall for the school rebel.

The story takes place in an unnamed, wealthy California suburb and is narrated by Vincent (Vincent Kartheiser), one of those lank-haired, black-clad high school loner/losers so often played as nonconformist heroes in post-"Heathers" Hollywood.

Shutterbug Vincent is obsessed by gorgeous Roseanne Skolnick (her name is the film's primary tribute to the novel, whose protagonist was named Raskolnikov), played by Monica Keena.

Roseanne, the most popular girl in school, is going out with Jimmy, the football player (James de Bello); she thinks Vincent is a creep, but feels slightly drawn to him.

But things aren't great for Roseanne at home: Her deeply unhappy mother, Maggie (Ellen Barkin), is cheating on her bitter, boozy stepfather, Fred (Michael Ironside), with handsome bartender Chris (Jeffrey Wright).

When Fred finds out about the affair, Maggie moves out of the house and Fred gets drunker and meaner until he finally, inevitably, attacks Roseanne.

Roseanne then plans to kill Fred with Jimmy's help.

Keena looks and acts just like a brunette Alicia Silverstone. Barkin is as compelling and lopsidedly attractive as ever, and the always wonderful Jeffrey Wright brings surprising life to a small role.

Director Rob Schmidt photographs the action in that visually clichéd, MTV-influenced manner now de rigeur in much of independent cinema: time-lapse shots, fake still photographs, etc.

In one typically self-conscious and overheated scene, a high school pep rally is made to look like Woodstock '99 crossed with a Nuremberg rally.

NEWSDAY, 9/15/00, Part II/p. B6, Jan Stuart

"Crime and Punishment in Suburbia" is the faux-literary title for 98 minutes of pulp fiction that aspires to be "Son of American Beauty."

You couldn't make a more earnest parody of the new suburbia-hell-genre if you marketed a line of Kevin Spacey and Annette Bening dress-up dolls. All the elements are there: the embittered, boozing dad, his unloved, cheating wife, their baronial slice of American real estate, their pouty, Playboy foldout of a teenage daughter, the creepy loner who stalks her with a camera.

Indeed, all that's missing is the happy gay couple next door, whom one can only assume have moved to a more original neighborhood.

The new wrinkle in Rob Schmidt's film is that it is told from the point of view of the nerdy shutterbug and the nubile object of his affections. Vincent, the film's central narrator (Vincent Kartheiser), is a nihilistic, pale phantom of a teenager who furtively photographs his classmates while they are pledging allegiance and invents fatuous fortune-cookie sentiments such as "Guilt is this secret inside of you that destroys the fabric of everything, then everything is unreal."

Vincent freaks everyone out with his paparazzi moves and self-styled alienation. Infatuated with Roseanne Skolnick (Monica Keena), the most popular babe in school, he shadows her and her lust-puppy jock boyfriend Jimmy (James DeBello). He also keeps tabs on Roseanne's troubled upper-middle-class household: her nasty, alcoholic dad Fred (Michael Ironside), his malcontent wife, Maggie (Ellen Barkin), and the bartender she is keeping company with (Jeffrey Wright).

After asserting Vincent's primacy in the scenario, screenwriter Larry Gross clumsily contrives to move him into the background so that the melodrama of the Skolnick family can take over. The only thing sillier than Vincent's philosophic musings is the spectacle of Michael Ironside as bad dad Fred, snorting feverishly, a la Jack Nicholson in "The Shining," and repeating "your mother's a whore" like some blithering soap star in denial over having had his part cut from "Ryan's Hope." Fred clearly has to go. Roseanne takes matters in hand, and things get really messy.

Despite the thoughtful efforts of Barkin and Wright, a more unsympathetic constellation of characters could not be found if David Mamet updated "Titus Andronicus" to chart the rise and fall of the Khmer Rouge. There is a lot of arty photography and snarling rock music that panders to a disaffected college-age crowd and is calculated to make everyone else feel like the source of society's ills. "Crime and Punishment in Suburbia" is said to be loosely adapted from a novel by Dostoevsky, but it's just another dumb movie about the geek who gets the girl.

SIGHT AND SOUND, 2/01, p. 38, Kim Newman

Suburban US, the present. Vincent, a teenage misfit, is obsessed with his popular classmate Roseanne Skolnik, who is dating football player Jimmy. Roseanne lives with her mother Maggie and stepfather Fred. Jimmy warns Vincent off, but Roseanne lets him take photographs of her. Maggie starts seeing barman Chris, and soon leaves Fred and Roseanne to be with him. Fred drinks more and more heavily and, one night, forces himself on Roseanne.

Roseanne persuades Jimmy to help her kill her stepfather. Maggie and Chris tussle with the gun-waving Fred, and a neighbour overhears Maggie tell of her intention to kill him. Later that night, Roseanne and Jimmy slip away from a school party and corner Fred at home. Roseanne kills Fred with an electric carving knife, while Jimmy stands by in shock. Maggie discovers the body, incriminating herself by leaving fingerprints on the weapon. As Maggie goes up for trial, Roseanne breaks up with Jimmy. She spends more time with Vincent, who knows what she has done. Suspecting she is guilty, Chris confronts Roseanne; drunk, Jimmy turns up and attacks

Chris. Chris then shoots Jimmy, injuring him, and flees town. Roseanne confesses her crime and receives a light sentence. Vincent visits her in prison.

Fyodor Dostoevsky's classic novel *Crime and Punishment* has already been adapted several times to modern settings: George Lampin's 1956 version shifts the action from 19th-century St Petersburg to 50s Left Bank, and sees Robert Hossein take the role of Raskolnikov, the novel's brooding anti-hero whose 'perfect murder' is slowly unpicked by a persistent investigator, while Denis Sanders' *Crime and Punishment U.S.A.* (1959) featured George Hamilton as the chillingly amoral murderer in contemporary America. Here screenwriter Larry Gross takes a more difficult road, leaving the original plot behind (for one thing, Raskolnikov switches sex, changing into high-school pupil Roseanne Skolnik) while attempting to develop a modern-day equivalent of Dostoevsky's fatal vision.

The whole story is filtered through the teenage misfit Vincent and broken into scratchily titled chapters, emphasising a Dostoevskian insistence on a possibly futile search for meaning and order in chaos. As the title suggests, the film is as much an exploration of suburban existence as it is of crime or punishment. Although director Rob Schmidt (whose debut feature was the 1999 thriller *Saturn*) spends very little time in typically suburban domestic spaces—the Skolniks' house has dark gothic interiors and is situated on a byway that might as well be called Elm Street—he observes characters lost in sparsely graffitied schoolyards, anonymous locker rooms, stretches of concrete wilderness and coldly functional courtrooms. It's a world that might have driven Dostoevsky further into despair, yet the inquisitive, clear-eyed Vincent is on hand to provide a wry commentary on the surroundings although his conclusion ("What a strange path it took to find your heart") sounds more like a David Lynch cast-off than true depth.

Early on, as Vincent obsessively photographs Roseanne and we observe the sexual tensions and dissonances swirling around Roseanne's middle-aged mother and stepfather Maggie and Fred, the film inevitably evokes Sam Mendes' study of suburban ennui *American Beauty*. If anything the comparison shows up how neat and tidy the Oscar-winning hit was: *American Beauty* humanised its weirdos, so everyone was ultimately understandable and sympathetic; here, all the characters are strangled by mixed motives, so that even the drunken, violent Fred—Michael Ironside, establishing his character's hollowness by failing to understand why some people think the old black-and-white version of the television show *The Outer Limits* is superior to the colour revival—is more like a messy, flawed human being than the straightforward bogeyman of the piece. Nothing works out as it is supposed to: the late-in-the-day sleuthing by Maggie's boyfriend Chris, for instance, lands him in prison and forces Roseanne to confess to murder, just as her mother is about to be convicted of the crime.

Schmidt adopts a striking (and risky) visual design, with patches of the screen in sharp focus while others are blurred as if seen through rain or tears. He also stages some of the night scenes with hallucinatory blobs of bright colour piercing the darkness—the soundtrack uses well chosen snatches of grunge music to the same effect. In contrast with so many teen movies, the high school is decidedly unglamorous—it looks less inviting than the prison Roseanne winds up in— and the kids are actually seen doing class work and homework between dating and killing. The young leads are photogenic without seeming blandly air-brushed: Roseanne's jock boyfriend Jimmy is handsome but awkward in posture as if expecting to be body-slammed at any moment (the one time he relaxes on the football field, that's exactly what happens to him) while Vincent's geek cool, which extends to a sober speech about an ex-girlfriend who taught him to smoke crack, is also spikily disturbing. Ultimately, *Crime + Punishment in Suburbia* falters at the end, with a narrated wrap-up and a few weak lines, but it is, for the most part, a remarkable, haunting work.

VILLAGE VOICE, 9/19/00, p. 126, Jessica Winter

Borrowing its unwieldy title if little else from Dostoyevsky, *Crime and Punishment in Suburbia* eschews the novel's labyrinthine intersections of reason and evil for a straightforward avenging-angel plot, yet it does manage an intriguing gloss on the unique logic of vengeance.

Raskolnikov becomes Roseanne Skolnik (Monica Keena), a well-off high-schooler with an adoring lunkhead football boyfriend, Jimmy (James DeBello). After her bitter mom (Ellen Barkin) finally breaks off her miserable marriage, Roseanne's alcoholic, grotesquely self-pitying stepfather (Michael Ironside) transforms into a full-bore monster, raping Roseanne and terrorizing his estranged wife and her new beau (Jeffrey Wright) until the girl takes drastic action. Much of the ongoing horror is viewed through Roseanne's eyes, but her perspective is tempered by co-narrator Vincent (Vincent Kartheiser), a pallid Goth wraith whose obsession with Roseanne is mostly healthy and potentially redemptive.

The movie often succumbs to the craven hysteria perhaps inherent in its hoary premise—Ironside's heavy-hoofed expositional rants amount to "Fee, fi, fo, fum"—and tends to smother itself with music-video tics. But director Rob Schmidt and screenwriter Larry Gross cast sharp, generous eyes on the ways teenagers speak and interact—conveying, for instance, Roseanne and Jimmy's sex-driven rapport with neither judgment nor tongue-lolling titillation. Schmidt's *2001*-like spatial sense is impeccably alienated, and the director guides Keena to a poignant performance that's like the flip side of Sheryl Lee's astounding immolation in the otherwise pointless *Twin Peaks* movie. A dead ringer for Kate Winslet with a hint of Corin Tucker from Sleater-Kinney, Keena quietly signals the implications of what an S-K lyric calls being "born to accommodate"—watch how she attempts affectionate banter with her simmering stepdad as they plow through a greasy take-out dinner, or how she soothes a drunken, jabbering Jimmy as she would a petulant child. Roseanne's lamentably expert coping mechanisms explain why she never seems capable of any of the crime and punishment going down in this Californian suburbia, but the inconsistency doesn't derail the film. Her shy, trauma-induced movements away from her dick-swingin' goofball Jimmy and toward the sweet, fucked-up, vaguely androgynous outsider Vincent feel blisteringly true; the film's instantly dated stylizations begin to appear as a welcome distancing device from the pain of being young, trapped, and hatefully vulnerable.

Also reviewed in:
CHICAGO TRIBUNE, 9/22/00, Friday/p. K, Mark Caro
NEW YORK TIMES, 9/15/00, p. E10, A. O. Scott
VARIETY, 2/21-27/00, p. 43, Todd McCarthy

CRIMINAL LOVERS

A Strand Releasing release of a Fidélité Productions/EuroSpace/Studio Canal+/La Sept/ARTE co-production with the participation of Canal +.   *Producer:* Marc Missonnier and Olivier Delbosc. *Director:* François Ozon.   *Screenplay (French with English subtitles):* François Ozon. *Director of Photography:* Pierre Stoeber.   *Editor:* Dominique Petrot.   *Music:* Philippe Rombi. *Sound:* François Guillaume.   *Production Designer:* Arnaud de Moleron.   *Running time:* 90 minutes. *MPAA Rating:* Not Rated.

CAST: Natacha Régnier (Alice); Jérémie Rénier (Luc); Miki Manojlovic (The Woodsman); Salim Kechiouche (Saïd); Yasmine Belmadi (Karim).

NEW YORK POST, 7/21/00, p. 50, Jonathan Foreman

Though a bit slow by U.S. standards, this French homoerotic thriller puts an intriguing twist on the Hansel and Gretel fairy tale, not to mention at least a dozen American movies.

The beautiful Alice (Natacha Regnier of "The Dreamlife of Angels") is a teenage seductress who cajoles her naive and impotent admirer, Luc (Jérémie Renier), into murder. Things go awry and they end up in the clutches of a sadistic hunter (Miki Manojlovic) who locks them in his rat-infested cellar with the corpse.

The hunter puts a leather collar on Luc and turns him into his sex slave and, by golly, Luc's impotence is cured. Luc is so grateful he passes up a chance to kill the hunter when the two finally do escape.

Francois Ozon, perhaps France's hottest director of the moment, is often better creating stylish visuals than dramatically credible situations, but "Criminal Lovers" is never boring.

NEWSDAY, 7/21/00, Part II/p. B6, John Anderson

"Badlands" meets "Hansel and Gretel" in "Criminal Lovers," a deliciously nasty and misogynistic parable of love and death, which further establishes the young François Ozon as one of the leading Marx-and Coca-Cola-bred provocateurs of current French cinema. It also sets him up as the heir apparent to Germany's Werner Rainer Fassbinder: Ozon's mission is mining the homoerotic impulse; his gift is convincing you it was your own idea.

With the current "Water Drops on Burning Rocks" (his adaptation of an early Fassbinder script) and now "Criminal Lovers," Ozon builds on the promise of his deeply disturbing "See the Sea" (1997), in which sex, solitude and bodily functions were slowly stirred into a murderous cocktail. In "Criminal Lovers" the murder comes first: Said (Salim Kechiouche), a student and boxer, is viciously stabbed to death by Luc (Jeremie Renier) while in a naked clinch with Alice (Natacha Regnier, of "Dreamlife of Angels") on the floor of their high school locker room.

Alice has lured Said to his death; she's orchestrated the murder as well: Having driven Luc to distraction with a tale of gang rape and dirty pictures, she gets him to eliminate her object of sexual fascination—Said—while keeping Luc at arm's distance. As the director of the film's action, Alice is, on one hand, Ozon's surrogate. On the other, she's a vapid string-puller with a paucity of self-awareness. Having proposed cold-blooded murder to Luc, she says, "We'll discuss it later; I've got class." Soon, with Said's body in the trunk, she sheds tears for a road-killed rabbit.

We seem headed for "Natural Born Killers"-ville, but when the two young fugitives are taken captive by a strange woodsman (Miki Manojlovic, the hardest-working Yugoslav in show business), "Criminal Lovers" takes a Hitchcockian left turn: imprisonment, starvation, sodomy, cannibalism. In one of Ozon's foreshadowing, flip-flopping flashbacks, Alice reads from Rimbaud: "If I think I'm in hell, I am." She does. They are.

Ozon has a seemingly effortless way of finding emblems in his architecture, from the forward prow of the couple's getaway boat to the jagged ruins of the woodsman's hut. He also has a wicked sense of humor, as evidenced by themes of burial, disinterment and the tongue-in-cheek romantic music that accompanies the big consummation scene. For Luc, everything has been building up to... this? He'd like to go back to the hut. As in most fairy tales—and "Criminal Lovers" is a fairy tale—the real perversity is never getting what you really want. Or even knowing what it is.

VILLAGE VOICE, 7/25/00, p. 119, J. Hoberman

Like *Rififi*'s central scene, François Ozon's *Criminal Lovers* is a smoothly calculated piece of work—and a nasty one too.

This may be Ozon's moment, in lower Manhattan at least. His third feature—*Water Drops on Burning Rocks*, reviewed here last week—is installed at the Film Forum. His second opens Friday at the Quad. The 32-year-old former Super-8 filmmaker is a cool customer with a taste for kinky provocation, and, true to form, *Criminal Lovers* opens creepy with teenage Alice performing a mock striptease for her blindfolded admirer and classmate Luc.

Initially, *Criminal Lovers* seems like a Gallic *Natural Born Killers*, as Alice and Luc butcher a fellow student who has provoked Alice's interest. The gradual disclosure of the couple's sexual pathology makes their act less irrational but also weirder. As these remorseless thrill killers drive off into the countryside to dispose of their victim's corpse, Alice becomes upset when Luc runs over a rabbit: "We have to bury it." It's not long before the quarrelsome children are lost in the forest and stumble across a version of the witch's gingerbread house. In *Water Drops*, Ozon donned the mantle of R.W. Fassbinder. Here, he does something at least as tricky in creating a contemporary, tabloid Hansel and Gretel.

Criminal Lovers may be as gimmicky as Ozon's other features, but it's also more resonant and even haunting. Natacha Regnier, last seen here in *The Dreamlife of Angels*, is bizarrely confident and mercurial as the disturbed Alice. Her nerdy accomplice, as hypnotized by her bare legs as he is repulsed by her sexual bravado, is played by Jeremie Renier, the boy in *La Promesse*. (Both are Belgian; that Renier is about a decade Regnier's junior provides additional subtext.) The ogre in the woods is embodied by the terrific, and here terrifying, Yugoslav actor Miki Manojlovic.

The pair's fairy-tale captivity is interspersed with flashbacks so that the initial murder is replayed mid-film to even more disturbing effect. Some of the revelations are overdetermined, as in Alice's enthusiasm for Rimbaud and the visual references to *Psycho* that introduce Luc. If the most Hitchcockian aspect of the movie is the way Ozon exploits and confounds spectator sympathies, the most Ozonian is its movement from claustrophobic nightmare to pure dream state. Down to Luc's dog collar, the climactic love scene might have been swiped from an X-rated *Bambi*.

Also reviewed in:
NEW YORK TIMES, 7/21/00, p. E18, Elvis Mitchell
VARIETY, 8/23-29/99, p. 108, Lisa Nesselson

CROUCHING TIGER, HIDDEN DRAGON

A Sony Pictures Classics and Columbia Pictures Film Production Asia release in association with Good Machine International of an Edko Films, Zoom Hunt International production in collaboration with China Film Co-Production Corp. and Asian Union Film & Entertainment Ltd. *Executive Producer:* James Schamus and David Linde. *Producer:* Bill Kong, Hsu Li Kong, and Ang Lee. *Director:* Ang Lee. *Screenplay:* James Schamus, Wang Hui Ling, and Tsai Kuo Jung. *Based on the novel by:* Wang Du Lu. *Director of Photography:* Peter Pau. *Editor:* Tim Squyres. *Music:* Tan Dun. *Action Choreographer:* Yuen Wo-Ping. *Sound:* Andrew Paul Kunin and (music) Richard King. *Sound Editor:* Eugene Gearty. *Production Designer:* Tim Yip. *Art Director:* Eddy Wong, Yang Xin Zhan, and Yang Zhan Jia. *Costumes:* Tim Yip. *Make-up:* Man Yun Ling. *Martial Arts Coordinator:* Ku Huen Chiu and Wong Kim Wai. *Running time:* 120 minutes. *MPAA Rating:* Not Rated.

CAST: Chow Yun Fat (Li Mu Bai); Michelle Yeoh (Yu Shu Lien); Zhang Ziyi (Jen Yu); Chang Chen (Lo); Lung Sihung (Sir Te); Cheng Pei Pei (Jade Fox); Li Fa Zeng (Governor Yu); Gao Xian (Bo); Hai Yan (Madam Yu); Wang Deming (Tsai); Li Li (May); Huang Su Ying (Auntie Wu); Zhang Jin Ting (De Lu); Yang Rui (Maid); Li Kai (Gou Jun Pei); Feng Jian Hua (Gou Jun Sinung); Du Zhen Xi (Shop Owner); Xu Cheng Lin and Lin Feng (Captains); Wang Wen Sheng (Gangster A); Song Dong (Gangster B); Ma Zhong Xuan (Mi Biao); Li Bao Cheng (Fung Machete Chang); Yang Yong De (Monk Jing); Zhang Shao Jun (Male Performer); Ma Ning (Female Performer); Zhu Jian Min (Waiter); Don Chang Sheng (Homeless Man); Shih Yi (Waitress); Chen Bin (Servant); Chang Sao Chen (Nightman).

CHRISTIAN SCIENCE MONITOR, 12/15/00, p. 15, David Sterritt

[*Crouching Tiger, Hidden Dragon* was reviewed jointly with *Vertical Limit;* see Sterritt's review of that film.]

CINEASTE, Vol. XXVI, No. 4, p. 71, Pauline Chen

While Ang Lee's *Crouching Tiger, Hidden Dragon* is often hailed as a great leap forward from the swordplay films mass produced in Hong Kong in the Sixties and Seventies, in one respect it closely resembles its low-budget predecessors: its slipshod subtitles, which leave out or mistranslate significant portions of the Mandarin dialog. This lapse is surprising in a film otherwise so exquisitely attentive to esthetic detail. It is also unfortunate in that it further blunts the film's already murky and convoluted exploration of philosophical and psychological themes, allowing martial arts pyrotechnics to largely overshadow emotional impact.

The film depicts the intertwined romances of two pairs of lovers. Old friends Yu Shu Lien (Michelle Yeoh), the head of a security company, and famous swordsman Li Mu Bai (Chow Yun Fat) have long shared an unspoken love, while the pampered aristocrat Yu Jiaolong (Zhang Ziyi), whose name means 'Winsome Dragon,' pines for the bandit chief Luo Xiaohu (Chang Chen), whose name is 'Little Tiger.' (That these Chinese names, which help to illuminate the significance of the film's title, are rendered uninformatively as "Jen" and "Lo," respectively, is but one minor example of the numerous infelicities committed by the subtitlers.) Li wishes to give away his sword, with its burden of death and enmities, and to retire to a peaceful life with Shu Lien. However, when the sword is stolen by Jiao-long, a.k.a. Jen, and when Li's old nemesis Jade Fox (Cheng Pei Pei) resurfaces as Jen's mentor and ally, Li is drawn irrevocably back into his old existence of violence and intrigue.

The film seems primarily concerned with suggesting the tragic impossibility of individual freedom, as epitomized by the characters' inability to achieve happiness through the fulfillment of romantic love. On the surface it seems that the external constraints of competing social obligations and bonds hamper the characters from pursuing their love. The film depicts a complicated social world in which political savvy and respect for hierarchy and convention are necessary for survival, and in which personal desires have little place. For example, Jen's father, newly transferred from a remote provincial posting to serve as a high official in Beijing, seeks to consolidate his position in the capital by betrothing Jen to the scion of a powerful political family, regardless of her wishes.

Such implacable social codes and hierarchies govern not only the political and cultural elite to which Jen belongs, but also the marginal, disreputable world of *jianghu* to which Li, Lo, and Shu Lien are linked. *Jianghu*, literally 'rivers and lakes,' is a term for the Robin Hood-esque underworld of chivalrous, wandering outlaws, which typically forms the backdrop for swordplay novels and films. While Jen wistfully imagines that *jianghu* offers freedom from constraints, the other three characters, for all their swashbuckling adventures, are portrayed as rigidly bound by traditional Confucian ideals of filiality, fidelity, chastity, and respect for teachers and elders. In a manner that may seem alien to Western audiences, each of these characters denies him or herself romantic fulfillment out of deference to such Confucian values. Shu Lien represses her love for Li out of fidelity to her dead fiancé, while Lo encourages Jen to leave his desert lair to return to her parents out of empathy for their distress at her disappearance. Li Mu Bai puts off his romance with Shu Lien in order to fulfill his duty to his late teacher by avenging his death and to attempt to detach Jen from Jade Fox to become his own pupil.

Moreover, *jianghu,* while perhaps easy to enter, proves difficult to escape. Li finds it impossible to leave old scores unsettled and to relinquish his sense of mission as defender and transmitter of the teachings of his school of fighting, while Lo, determined to earn a place in legitimate society in order to win Jen, is dogged by his disreputable past. The film demystifies *jianghu* and paints it as tragically trapping its members in its insistent undertow, in contrast to the more idealized depictions of many earlier swordplay novels and films.

In addition to the external constraints imposed by the Confucian social code, the film poses another, perhaps ultimately more powerful, obstacle to the characters' realization of happiness through love: repressed or conflicting inner desires—or the "crouching tigers, hidden dragons" of the human psyche. The significance of the film's title, which is a Chinese idiom referring to hidden or unsuspected forces or powers, is glossed in a key line spoken by Li to Shu Lien as they pause at a teahouse in their pursuit of Jen and the stolen sword. "In *jianghu* there are crouching tigers and hidden dragons, just as there are in men's hearts. Blades and swords conceal evil, just as men's emotions do," he reflects, as he explains his failure to renounce his life of violence and intrigue as he had originally intended. This line is translated in the subtitles simply as, "Giang Hu *[sic]* is a world of dragons full of corruption," which inadequately conveys the original insight on how internal conflicts, unacknowledged desires, and impulses for destruction and betrayal hamstring the characters' pursuit of the love and happiness they purport to want. Thus, even when social constraints are thrown off—as when Jen runs away from her bridegroom and parents, or when Li finally dares to clasp Shu Lien's hand—the happy union of the pairs of lovers fails to materialize.

The petulant and capricious Jen, who began to withhold secret martial arts techniques and her mastery of them from her teacher at age eight, is the character most obviously dogged by inner demons. After escaping from her nuptial chamber to the countryside, she uses her newfound freedom not to join her lover Lo, but instead to roam about picking fights and bad-mouthing Li, apparently victim to a poisonous combination of resentment and secret desire for him. Similarly,

Li, apparently serene and transcendent in contrast to the impulsive and tempestuous Jen, is equally torn by internal conflicts. At the beginning of the film, Li has just abandoned his protracted quest for enlightenment in the midst of a key phase of meditation, thwarted by a matter of the heart which he leaves unspoken, presumably his love for Shu Lien. Soon after, however, he fails to fulfill his avowed intention of leaving *jianghu* to settle down with Shu Lien. Derailed from enlightenment by earthly love for Shu Lien, and again balked from love by the temptations of vengeance and mastering Jen, Li seems paralyzed by the conflicting impulses for spiritual transcendence, love, social responsibility, and carnal pleasure.

Providing a counterpoint to Jen's and Li's inner struggles is Lo's story of a young man whose wish that his ailing parents be cured is granted when he shows his sincerity by leaping off a cliff; Lo explains this miraculous occurrence by invoking the Chinese saying, "A true heart makes wishes come true." The story and saying may be understood as shedding a little light on the film's otherwise rather baffling tragic denouement. Incapable of fixing on a single wish whole-heartedly, Jen and Li bring misery on themselves and others.

Crouching Tiger, Hidden Dragon's most basic problem may be its choice of the action genre to examine this fascinating but abstruse problem of the vagaries of the human heart. Essentially plot-driven, as most action films are, *Crouching Tiger* might have been aided by consistent characters with clear-cut motivations to provide momentum and coherence across the twists and leaps of its various narrative strands. Instead, the characters, especially Jen and Li, seem exasperatingly muddled. Nor do the performances generate much insight or sympathy for the characters' inner struggles. Chow is charismatic, but his air of serene nobility gives little indication of the internal turmoil from which he apparently suffers: Zhang's lightning fluctuations between childish vulnerability and waspish aggression suggest the throwing of a switch. Yeoh's performance, by contrast, more convincingly suggests the passion and inner conflict that may lurk behind a reserved exterior.

Even more problematic is the role of the fight scenes in the film's existential meditations. As dynamically as these scenes are choreographed, performed, and shot, they seem curiously static and without suspense. Frankly, one often doesn't know exactly why the characters are fighting (over a comb? over a sword?) and worse yet, may not even care who wins. Certainly the sense of urgency, of righteous fury, that fuels the best films of the action genre—whether a Hollywood Western or a Hong Kong martial-arts film—is notably absent. Rather, the film's fight sequences resemble the song and dance numbers in musical theater, as if harking back to the martial-arts films' roots in Chinese opera; they are expressive and enjoyable, but essentially unmotivated. By showing characters seizing weapons as readily as if they were merely bursting into song, *Crouching Tiger* fails to answer the question fundamentally posed by the action film: When and under what compulsion do good characters resort to violence? Treating fighting as an esthetic divertissement rather than confronting its import for death and chaos, *Crouching Tiger* is an action movie that packs no punch.

LOS ANGELES TIMES, 12/15/00, Calendar/p. 1, Kenneth Turan

Films we can categorize, that's what we're used to. Good or bad, fiascoes or masterpieces, we put them in their place, every one. What we're not used to, what we haven't had much of at all, are films that transcend categorization, that remind us—simply, powerfully, indelibly—what we go to the movies for. Ang Lee's "Crouching Tiger, Hidden Dragon" is that kind of a picture.

A delightful one-of-a-kind martial arts romance where astounding fight sequences alternate with passionate yet idealistic love duets, "Crouching Tiger" is a fusion film from top to bottom. By joining emotional sophistication to the most thrilling kind of Hong Kong-style acrobatic action, by having classical cellist Yo-Yo Ma and preeminent fight choreographer Yuen Wo-Ping in the same film, "Crouching Tiger" brings a specific national cinema fully into the world spotlight. It can do all this so successfully because Lee reconciles these opposites in his own life and work.

Lee, who at varying times has called this film "'Sense and Sensibility' with martial arts" and "Bruce Lee meets Jane Austen," was born in Taiwan and moved to the U.S. when he was 24. He followed his first three Taiwanese features (the "Father Knows Best" trilogy of "Pushing Hands," "The Wedding Banquet" and " Eat Drink Man Woman") with the English-language trio of "Sense and Sensibility," "The Ice Storm" and "Ride With the Devil."

But Lee, now 46, had a childhood dream of making a film based on the wuxia novels and films he grew up with, where the rules of behavior are strict but the laws of gravity do not apply. It's a Chinese genre about the adventures of Confucian-era wandering warriors described by co-screenwriter and frequent Lee collaborator James Schamus as "knights-errant skilled in martial arts and Taoist spiritual practices who fight on behalf of their principles as well as against their own desires."

It's a world of hidden identities and mystical situations, of legendary swords and stolen secret manuals that "Crouching Tiger" takes us into, a maelstrom of forbidden loves, bitter rivalries and indomitably heroic looks. With impeccable production and costume design by Tim Yip and sweeping cinematography by Peter Pau (who also did John Woo's "The Killer"), it's also a strikingly beautiful world, featuring elaborate costumes and picturesque vistas selected from all across mainland China.

It was director Lee who found the 70-year-old Wang Du Lu novel that Schamus, Wang Hui Ling and Tsai Kuo Jung adapted. He was also the person who insisted on a thrilling but almost impossible-to-shoot battle at the tops of bamboo trees and who opted to film "Crouching Tiger" not in the more commercially viable English or the Cantonese of most of his cast but his more lyrical native Mandarin. "Otherwise," he has said, "it would be like watching John Wayne speak Chinese in a Western."

The director of "Sense and Sensibility," concerned in many of his films with women and their options for freedom, was not surprisingly drawn to a story that focuses on women not as objects of romance (though there is that, too) but as fierce and relentless fighters, resourceful and defiant. Three indomitable women are the centerpiece of "Crouching Tiger," and it would be a mistake to anger any one of them.

Though Lee has admitted to going further with romanticism here than ever before, his natural reserve and discretion as a filmmaker are equally important to "Crouching Tiger's" success. Rather than start the film with a major action sequence, Lee, sure of what's in store, has the confidence to carefully set his stage. "Crouching Tiger" gradually widens and expands its vistas, both physical and emotional, continually surprising us by increasing our involvement.

Equally confident is the film's top-of-the-line cast, though each had a reason not to be. Asian superstar Chow Yun Fat was not only not the director's first choice (he got the part after action master Jet Li dropped out), he'd also never handled a sword before. Co-star Michelle Yeoh, a martial arts veteran, was hampered for a time by a knee injury and had to do one of her key dramatic scenes with her leg stretched out on an off-camera apple box. And newcomer Zhang Ziyi, recommended to Lee by director Zhang Yimou, was a 19-year-old drama student when she got her part, and needed the permission of her school to accept it.

"Crouching Tiger" starts with a reunion between Yu Shu Lien (Yeoh), the head of a security service, and Li Mu Bai (Chow), the great martial artist of his day, a couple we sense might have more than friendship between them if codes of behavior permitted.

Despite his skill, Li has returned from a meditation retreat determined, like Alan Ladd's Shane, to put his profession behind him. As a token of this, he asks Yu to deliver his legendary, 400-year-old sword, the Green Dynasty, to a court official named Sir Te in Beijing. Though he regrets not being able to avenge the death of his master at the hands of the sinister Jade Fox (Cheng Pei Pei, a star of 1960s martial arts films), Li feels he has no choice.

When Yu hands over the sword, she meets a beautiful and well-born bride-to-be named Jen (Zhang Ziyi), a prim porcelain doll who says she envies the freedom of the martial arts life women such as Yu enjoy. Yu tries to tell Jen there are obligations as well as adventures to this life, a truth that all the film's characters get to experience for themselves when the Green Dynasty is mysteriously stolen and the connections between what has happened in the past and what the future might bring come into focus in the battle for its recovery.

Setting "Crouching Tiger" apart from the standard martial arts film is the care both the screenwriters and the actors have taken with the dialogue. Lee fought for this even though he understood it was "almost against nature" because paying attention to language and character might distract an actor and cause an injury during the action sequences.

It is that action everyone will remember most about "Crouching Tiger." Choreographed by the masterful Yuen Wo-Ping, who brought his decades of expertise to bear on "The Matrix," the fights feature intricate hand-to-hand combat with a variety of weapons as well as bare hands. Best in show, however, are the airborne battles that particularly characterize the genre.

For it's one of the givens of these films that great fighters, through a combination of secret manuals and mind control, can literally fly at will. Even when you know this flying effect is created by attaching the actors to steel cables a la Peter Pan and then optically removing the wires, that in no way lessens the breathtaking effect.

Actors move with reality-defying speed and lightness, floating over rooftops and tiptoeing across lakes with unimaginable grace. With its gift for showing things that can't be described, "Crouching Tiger's" blend of the magical, the mythical and the romantic fills a need in us we might not even realize we had.

NEW STATESMAN, 1/8/01, p. 33, Jonathan Romney

Over the past decade, the Taiwanese director Ang Lee has offered a teasing challenge to students of auteur consistency. An analyst of editing technique, shot lengths and deep-structure subtexts could probably tell you immediately what kind of signature unites Lee's disparate films. However, for most of us, it's simply a question of being dazzled by his accomplished genre-hopping. He has made domestic comedies in both America and Taiwan (*The Wedding Banquet, Eat Drink Man Woman*), a trenchant study of mid-1970s suburban America (*The Ice Storm*), a Jane Austen adaptation (*Sense and Sensibility*) and, rather less successfully, an American civil war drama (*Ride With the Devil*).

But Lee is clearly not one of those try-anything directors who simply bob along with whatever chance offers them. For all his reluctance to plaster an immediately apparent self over his work, he is anything but anonymous; rather, his reserve comes across as a sort of masterly tact. His latest film, *Crouching Tiger, Hidden Dragon*, takes on yet another genre, the Asian martial arts adventure, and one metaphor in it offers a rather elegant key to his work. The film's young heroine leads a double life, following a clandestine career as a swordfighter as well as dutifully studying the traditional female arts such as calligraphy. But, it is pointed out in one scene, "Calligraphy is so similar to fencing." So, too, with Lee's art as director: we are used to characterising directorial flourishes as a kind of macho swordsmanship but, even in a film specifically about combat, Lee's style cultivates the virtues of elegance and control. The thrill here, as in his other films (notably *Eat Drink*, his treatise on families and cuisine), lies in invention, expertise and intelligence.

Set during the Qing dynasty, in the early 19th century, *Crouching Tiger* is something that western cinema rarely produces convincingly, *Charlie's Angels* notwithstanding—a really rattling girl's adventure story. One of its heroines, the young Jen Yu (Zhang Ziyi), is destined to be married, but leads a fighter's existence by night, having once shared a romantic idyll with the dashing brigand Lo (Chang Chen). Its other heroine, Yu Shu Lien (Michelle Yeoh), runs a company that is rather comically referred to in the subtitles as "Sun Security" (no satin bomber jackets here), and herself entertains an unspoken passion for the august, heroic swordsman Li Mu Bai (Chow Yun-Fat). The plot involves the theft of an antique sword and, whether or not the Chinese dialogue makes it clear, the subtitles certainly play on its phallic nature, given that it is fated to fall into the hands of so many swashbuckling women. "Two foot nine inches long, seven-tenths of an inch thick," comments a greybeard, appraising it ruefully. "It only comes alive through skilful manipulation."

The sexuality is not just a matter of innuendo: erotic tensions are close to the surface, especially in the rapturous extended flashback of Jen's meeting with Lo. It begins as a chase through imposing desert scenery (shot by Peter Pau, this is, among other things, a dazzling landscape film), becomes a hand-to-hand conflict and culminates in a subterranean lovers' rhapsody. The echoes here of Rudolph Valentino's Sheik are surely no accident—Lee and his regular American writer-producer, James Schamus (who collaborated with the Taiwanese screenwriters Wang Hui-Ling and Tsai Kuo Jung), are pretty knowing in their cross-cultural references. Although it can be facile to map one set of cultural references on to another, you can't help hearing playful genre echoes here: *Crouching Tiger* feels very much like an Asian western, as it were, with Yeoh as a trail boss, a tough Barbara Stanwyck sort of dame, and Chow Yun-Fat as a lone Alan Ladd gunman. Asian and American cinemas were reworking each other's myths well before *Seven Samurai* was remade as *The Magnificent Seven*, but these days the two-way traffic is more complex than ever, with Yeoh and Chow Yun-Fat among several Asian stars to cultivate Hollywood careers. *Crouching Tiger* itself reworks the martial arts movie for an international market accustomed to the quickfire special-effects action of sci-fi movies such as *The Matrix*, which borrowed its best combat riffs from the east; indeed, it shares that film's "action choreographer", Yuen Woo-Ping.

"Choreography" is the word. Few action films are as joyously musical, as dance-like, as this one. Here, a fight is never just a fight, but can come in several different registers—from the comic chaos of Jen's saloon brawl with an army of plug-uglies to the balletic weightlessness of an airborne battle above a bamboo grove, the opponents pacing each other like elegant phantoms. It is a scene that genuinely gives battle the feathery elegance of calligraphy.

Crouching Tiger is not only a stunningly accomplished entertainment, but also something of a test case, if not an open attempt to redraw the map of international cinema. A Chinese/Taiwanese/American co-production, it was the most prominent of the several Asian films that dominated last summer's Cannes Film Festival. It has done extremely well in Asia, where it was received as a mainstream blockbuster. However, in the west, it will be marketed as a foreign-language "art-house" release. The "art-house" tag is meaningless, given that the film delivers all the pleasures traditionally expected of (and all too rarely delivered by) big-budget Hollywood action films. The film opened in the United States in December, and American critics were dazzled by its artistic swagger. Several Asian action directors have found their own place in the Hollywood mainstream, to largely unsatisfying effect—witness John Woo's dreary *Mission: Impossible 2*. But the decidedly un-mainstream Ang Lee has rewritten the rules, and is offering the international market a film that is Chinese to the core. I'd be amazed if it doesn't clean up in the west.

NEW YORK, 12/11/00, p. 76, Peter Rainer

Ang Lee has called his new film, *Crouching Tiger, Hidden Dragon*, "a kind of dream of China," and that's exactly what it feels like. Set in the early nineteenth century, and starring the great Chow Yun Fat and Michelle Yeoh, it's a martial-arts fantasia that combines the pop impulse of Hong Kong fighting films with the delicacy and classicism of an earlier, more spiritual style of storytelling. The effect is paradoxical: a muted extravaganza.

The Taiwanese-born Lee is best known as the director of such films as *The Ice Storm* and *Sense and Sensibility*, and perhaps too much can be made of the parallels between those films and this one; conflicts between loyalty and desire are, after all, ever present in drama. But Lee's approach to the rigors of his material—grace and heroism as expressed in the traditional *wuxia* mythology of knightly chivalry dating from the ninth century—is supremely heartfelt. (The script, derived from a pre-World War II Chinese novel, is by Wang Hui Ling, Tsai Kuo Jung, and Lee's regular writing-producing collaborator, James Schamus.) Lee emphasizes not only the startling, high-flying mechanics of swordplay and martial artistry but also warfare's deeply human dimension, in which lives are truly lost. The battles between the main antagonists, including three women warriors, are like conversations carried out almost entirely in movement. The athleticism is as eloquent as any speech; the fighters' gestures, nuanced and distinctive, are human calligraphy. The spiritual possibilities of these people are most profoundly realized when they're battling. Sitting or standing apart from one another in normal workaday situations, they relate with a formalized repressiveness, but in combat their full fury comes through. Some of the most vehement clashes are between people who love each other, or want to. Their features, their souls, seem rent in these moments, and the rending has a tragic weight.

Lee is working here with Hong Kong action choreographer (and sometime director) Yuen Wo-Ping, who was responsible for the fight wizardry in *The Matrix* and in many of the best Jackie Chan and Jet Li films. Yuen's incomparable acrobatic forays fused with Lee's graceful sensibility result in a series of yin-yang battles that are probably the best ever seen in the martial-arts genre. What's beautiful about them is not just their roiling poetry but also the lyricism of the emotion behind them. The great silent comics, especially Buster Keaton, had this gift for lyricized athleticism; Keaton put his soul into his body movements, which is why his flips and clambers and pratfalls are at once hilarious and intensely, mysteriously *moving*. This mysteriousness of motion in which the soul is laid bare is what Lee and Yuen and their actors achieve in *Crouching Tiger, Hidden Dragon*. The film's protagonists are both forceful archetypes and highly particularized personalities. They may choose to sink into the Tao of selflessness, yet they remain almost shockingly vivid.

Chow Yun Fat plays Li Mu Bai, a legendary warrior who wishes to renounce his warring ways along with his 400-year-old sword, Green Destiny. "Too many men have died at its edge," he says, and he passes it along for safekeeping to his longtime ally and friend Yu Shu Lien (Yeoh), who is en route to Beijing. Li and Shu Lien have a deep, unspoken ardor for each other, but complications from the past have kept them apart. In Beijing, the sword is stolen as another key character is introduced, Jen (the marvelous newcomer Zhang Ziyi), a politician's daughter whose seeming primness doesn't jibe with the feral gleam in her eye. The film's first major confrontation is a night fight between Shu Lien and a masked intruder, and even though we (and Shu Lien) can guess who that intruder might be, it doesn't diminish the sheer leaping grandeur of the scene, with both women soaring in the darkness. If anything, the grandeur for us is increased, since we feel we have been brought intimately into a secret. The hushed, spectral quality of this combat is balletic in the best sense; it's like a reverie of weightlessness. (The wire work that makes such leaping possible is rendered invisible.) You watch the swirling battles in this film, their freestyle precision, with the same rapture as you would watch Astaire and Rogers, or Donald O'Connor bouncing off the walls in *Singin' in the Rain*. Throughout the movie, Lee mounts increasingly elaborate set pieces for our delectation, and because the emotional stakes are higher each time, the sequences deepen as they accumulate.

The story winds through many levels. Li returns to rescue his sword and avenge the long-ago murder of his master, killed by the notorious female bandit Jade Fox (the veteran Hong Kong star Cheng Pei Pei). He tries to enlist the unruly Jen, in whom he recognizes a kindred spirit, as his disciple. The fight between them, as they cling to the tops of swaying bamboo in a dark forest, is one of the most magical passages in the history of movies. A martial-arts film that is also, in the deepest sense, a romance, *Crouching Tiger, Hidden Dragon* has the potential to harmonize audiences usually thought to be poles apart: the action crowd and the art-house crowd. Its distributor, Sony Pictures Classics, is giving it a cautious, initially small-scale release. Yet even with its subtitles—the language spoken is Mandarin—the film is, I would think, extraordinarily accessible. It's rare to find a film that satisfies our craving for pop while giving us the transcendence of poetry. But isn't this what the promise of popular art in the movies has always been about? Ang Lee may have begun this project with the idea of re-creating the warrior tales of his boyhood, but, like his soaring romancers here, he's taken a great leap into the beyond.

NEWSDAY, 12/18/00, Part II/p. B8, Jan Stuart

Midway into "Crouching Tiger, Hidden Dragon," a small army of hulking warriors approaches a delicate-looking swordsman who is seated on the balcony of a two-floor restaurant, trying to have a meal in quiet. The thugs swagger up the steps with don't-mess-with-me vibes that let you know they are angling for a brawl. Within moments, the swordsman flattens the first challenger with one arm while still seated in his chair. He then somersaults backward down the stairs, spins back up to the balcony like a flying top and picks off the rest of the gang in a dizzying swoosh of movement that sends the staircase crashing to the floor, almost as an afterthought.

There are a number of improbabilities here, the least of which is the gravity-shrugging leaps the swordsman is able to make without so much as a superhero's cape or a fortifying bowl of Wheaties. The swordsman, to begin with, is a diminutive teenage woman. Second, this martial-arts carnival of a movie was filmed by Ang Lee, an upper-middlebrow director known for his razor-fine comedies of manners ("Sense and Sensibility"), contemporary American satire ("The Ice Storm") and double-edged domestic dramas ("The Wedding Banquet," "Eat, Drink, Man, Woman"). Most incongruously, perhaps, is that this unabashed burst of cartoon violence informs one of the year's most soul-stirring entertainments.

It is fitting that Ang Lee should find his populist groove at a time when everything from Marvel Comics to "Charlie's Angels" is being reformatted to indulge the inner child in grown-up moviegoers and the sophisticate in growing kids. The source for Lee's spectacular is a five-part novel written before the Second World War that delves into the Guang Hi world of fictional

Chinese pop culture, a floating population of super-skilled fighters who exist beyond the borders of everyday society.

One of the greatest of these fighters, Li Mu Bai (Chow Yun-Fat), is longing to leave this world behind for a life of inner tranquillity. In accordance with the unwritten rules that govern aging pop warriors, however, Li must wage one more blowout battle before hanging up his sword. And he has formidable opponents in the malevolent Jade Fox (Cheng Pei Pei), an embittered hag who long ago poisoned Li's master, and her disciple, Jen Yu (Zhang Ziyi), an aristocratic young woman who is going to extraordinary lengths to avoid a marriage of family convenience.

This potboiler of a myth, propelled by a grail-like sword known as the Green Destiny, is given a potently human dimension by two romantic subplots.

The benign woman warrior Yu Shu Lien (the radiant Michelle Yeoh, who exudes an effortless grace and magnetism throughout) pines in silence for her old friend Li, while the bellicose Jen yearns for her secret lover, the bandit chief Lo (a jauntily charismatic Chang Chen).

The melancholic undertow of these parallel amours is given poignant emphasis by Tan Dun's ravishing cello themes (played by Yo-Yo Ma). The love stories also provide an emotional center of gravity for a light-footed parade of martial-arts extravaganzas (staged by "The Matrix'' fight whiz Yuen Wo Ping) that have characters ping- ponging between walls and moonwalking over rooftops like reindeer buzzing on Ecstasy.

Anyone expecting much in the way of character development has wandered into the wrong theater. If you become restless with Yuen's blinding fight ballets, as I did on occasion, gaze upon Tim Yip's treasure trove of costumes or any one of the majestic vistas captured by Peter Pau's wide-screen lens. There is a Zen-like peace to be found in Lee's panoply of mountains, forests and rooftops.

And you don't have to sacrifice your Green Destiny, whatever that may be, to achieve it.

NEWSWEEK, 12/4/00, p. 62, David Ansen

At once elegant and sublimely silly, contemplative and gung-ho, balletic and bubble-gum, a rousing action film and an epic love story, "Crouching Tiger, Hidden Dragon" is one bursting-at-the-seams holiday gift, beautifully wrapped by the ever-surprising Ang Lee.

Lee, sly fox that he is, starts slow. Like a poker player artfully hiding the full house in his hand, he gives us 10 minutes of stately, nearly immobile exposition. Then, in a nocturnal showdown of martial-arts finesse, all heavenly hell breaks loose. Two female warriors circle each other warily; then, with the gravity-defying logic of a dream, they leap into the air and literally fly to the top of a building. At the breathless end of this lyrically choreographed battle, audiences around the world have been known to burst into applause. And there is more, and even better, yet to come.

For many American viewers, "Hidden Dragon" may be the first Chinese-language film they've ever seen. And they will no doubt feel that (comparisons to "The Matrix's" fight scenes aside) they have never seen anything like it before. But in fact Lee's film comes out of a time-tested tradition. It's an artful pastiche of many Hong Kong movies before it, from King Hu's 1971 historical martial-arts epic "A Touch of Zen" to the wild, gender-bending acrobatics of the Tsui Hark production "Swordsman II" (1991), next to which this looks positively sedate.

"Crouching Tiger" doesn't so much break new ground as reconfigure the genre with the pomp and ceremony of Western production values and the psychological nuance that only the director of "Sense and Sensibility" and "The Ice Storm" can add to the brew. Lee grounds the high-kicking mayhem in poetic gravity, which gives it a flavor all its own, as plangent and lovely as the cello strains of Tan Dun's memorable score.

There are two delectably different love stories inside this tale of revenge, honor and swordsmanship. Chow Yun Fat and Michelle Yeoh, two of Hong Kong's greatest stars, play the seasoned veteran warriors whose code of honor has prevented them from expressing the love they have felt for each other for most of their lives. Zhang Ziyi and Chang Chen are the younger, more dangerous and impetuous lovers—she's a demure aristocrat by day, a masked warrior by night out to steal Chow's ancient sword, while Chang plays the desert bandit who steals her heart.

The plot is far too byzantine to untangle here. But the well-crafted screenplay (by James Schamus, Wang Hui Ling and Tsai Kuo Jung) unfolds the twisted tale elegantly, maintaining a delicate balance between stillness and freneticism, between fairy-tale deeds and down-to-earth emotions. Lee's movie ends, hauntingly, in free fall: an apt image for an entertainment that has the power to sweep us magically off our feet.

SIGHT AND SOUND, 1/01, p. 45, Tony Rayns

Qing Dynasty China. Disturbed by dark thoughts during a meditative retreat, Wudan-school swordsman Li Mu Bai decides to retire without having avenged his murdered master. He asks his friend Shu Lien (who has long adored him from afar) to pass his antique sword Green Destiny to Sir Te in the capital. No sooner has she done so than the sword is stolen.

Li joins her to investigate the theft; they cross paths with the constable Tsai and his daughter who are on the trail of Jade Fox, the "witch" who poisoned Li's master. They learn that Jade Fox is working in the household of Governor Yu—and secretly training his daughter Jen in martial arts with the aid of a stolen Wudan manual.

Jen (who stole Green Destiny) has also learned to hate the patriarchal Wudan traditions. Forced by her father into a politically opportune marriage, she absconds and (posing as male) becomes a roving swordsman. But despite herself she pines for her first true lover, the Xinjiang bandit Lo, not knowing that Li Mu Bai has drafted him for training in Wudan skills. Shu Lien and Li catch and challenge her, but she is saved by Jade Fox. They trace her to jade Fox's secret lair, where the witch fatally poisons Li before being overcome. Remorse-stricken, Jen rushes to fetch an antidote but arrives back too late. At Mt. Wudan she is reunited with Lo—but her skills already far surpass his.

Almost all Chinese directors feel they have a *wuxia pian*—martial chivalry film—in them; even Hou Hsiao-Hsien speaks of wanting to make one. Ang Lee's *Crouching Tiger, Hidden Dragon* is at once the fulfilment of a boyhood dream and a sophisticated attempt to reconcile his wish to stay in touch with his Chinese roots with his current need to produce work for a global audience. The last classical *wuxia pian* launched on the world stage was King Hu's A *Touch of Zen (Xia Nü*, 1969), screened in the Cannes competition in 1975, which was widely enough admired but never went beyond a niche audience in western markets. Lee, his regular screenwriter James Schamus and their financiers in the US and East Asia (not to mention their distinguished composer Tan Dun, who contributes a very original percussive score) are calculating that John Woo, Tsui Hark and Hong Kong action movies in general have now paved the way for large international audiences to accept a Chinese-language revival of the old genre. Early indications are that they're right.

The most surprising thing about *Crouching Tiger, Hidden Dragon* is that in most respects it's so resolutely generic. Rather than follow the revisionist tracks of such films as Wong Kar-Wai's *Ashes of Time* and Tsui Hark's *The Blade*, this looks back directly to the genre peaks of the 60s—hence the casting of Cheng Pei-Pei, nowadays a dancer-choreographer based in New York, who starred in both King Hu's *Come Drink with Me (Da Zui Xia*, 1965) and its notional sequel *Golden Swallow (Jin Yanzi*, 1968), directed by Zhang Che. Hardly any of the film's themes, motifs or settings would have been out of place in those movies: everything from the stolen manual of secret martial-arts techniques to the young woman posing as a swordsman is routine for the genre.

Crouching Tiger, Hidden Dragon is based on a novel (the fourth in a sequence of five) by the early-20th-century writer Wang Du-Lu, not one of the giants in *wuxia* fiction. The storyline contrasts two couples. The middle-aged Li Mu Bai and Shu Lien would have been lovers had they not been archetypal Han Chinese denizens of the *jianghu*—literally, 'rivers and lakes'; figuratively, the world in that martial-arts fiction is conventionally set—a fate that dooms them to lives of stoic loneliness and selfless moral probity. Jen and her sometime kidnapper/lover Lo, who are explicitly not Han Chinese (she is Manchu; he is from one of Xinjiang's Muslim minorities), are both rebels against this orthodoxy; they are, respectively, the dragon and the tiger of the title, she the demure, filial daughter secretly seething with inner protest, he the dangerously unpredictable, selfish outlaw. (One of the film's small mysteries is why the rather amateurish subtitles should obscure their eponymous status by dubbing them "Jen" and "Lo", names nowhere used in Chinese. But then, the subtitles also render *jianghu* as "Giang Hu".) The emphasis on youthful rebellion against a Confucian moral order brings the film into line with

Lee's earlier Chinese films The *Wedding Banquet* and *Eat Drink Man Woman* both of which centred on offspring chafing at constraints imposed by their parents.

Partly because of Zhang Ziyi's stellar performance, vastly more substantial and impressive than her debut in Zhang Yimou's *The Road Home,* the character of Jen dominates the film. It's quite startling to see stars of the calibre of Chow Yun-Fat and Michelle Yeoh sidelined by a relative newcomer, but they and their director sensibly give the girl her head. Jen animates all of the set-piece fight scenes, from the airborne clash-by-night with Shu Lien during the theft of the sword to the climactic treetop duel with Li Mu Bai, the latter more a swooning seduction than a fight as such; she also performs the film's show-stopper, the comic eradication of a group of armed heavies in a small-town inn. By comparison, her foil Chang Chen (so haunting in Edward Yang's *A Brighter Summer Day)* is used as little more than local colour.

Always entertaining and exhilarating as a genre piece, *Crouching Tiger, Hidden Dragon* is most notable for going beyond genre norms in two striking ways. One is its post-*Matrix* action choreography, which takes weightless aerial combat literally to new heights; Yuen Wo-Ping has definitively left his days of directing knockabout Jackie Chan farces far behind. The other is its overtly feminist thrust. Jade Fox and her protégée Jen start from the assumption that men are to be hated and despised and see all their actions as anti-patriarchal. The euphoric final shot suggests that sisters can, indeed, do it for themselves.

TIME, 12/4/00, p. 166, Richard Corliss

From the beginning, the film seemed cursed. "We started shooting in the Gobi Desert," recalls director Ang Lee, dimpled but unsmiling. "That night the crew got lost in the desert until 7 a.m. We finally got going, and after the second shot, a sandstorm came in." Could things get worse? Ask producer Bill Kong. "The Gobi is the hottest, dryest place on earth," he says. "So each morning we lit incense for good luck. Well, we had dreadful luck—it rained sheets, nonstop, ruining our schedule. After a while one of the local people came around and said the gods must be smiling on us. We asked why. 'Because you burned the incense,' he said. We burn the incense when we want it to rain.'"

With good or bad luck *Crouching Tiger, Hidden Dragon* would have provided a stern challenge. Consider these factors: a $15 million action movie that was also to be a poignant, tragic romance; a fight choreographer, Yuen Wo-ping, who had won international acclaim for his work on *The Matrix* and was bound to tangle with the soft-spoken, hard-to-budge Lee; a top-flight all-Asian cast featuring Chow Yun Fat (Hong Kong), Michelle Yeoh (Malaysia), Zhang Ziyi (Beijing) and Chang Chen (Taiwan). Only one of the stars—Zhang, then a 19-year-old ingenue—spoke anything like the classical mainland Mandarin that Lee demanded.

At least these difficulties were built into the scenario. What no one expected was that Yeoh would injure her knee and need a month's rehab in the U.S., or that the whole ordeal would be so damned exhausting. "We shot around the clock with two teams," says Lee, 46. "I didn't take one break in eight months, not even for half a day. I was miserable—I just didn't have the extra energy to be happy. Near the end, I could hardly breathe. I thought I was about to have a stroke."

As the sage said, dying is easy, filmmaking is hard. But everyone was so serious on *Crouching Tiger* because Lee, who made his reputation with adult dramas of manners like *The Wedding Banquet* and *Sense and Sensibility,* had a child inside screaming to get out. He wanted to pay homage to his lifelong ardor for martial-arts novels and pictures. He had made beautiful films; now he would bend his considerable artistry to make, dammit, a movie. The sad story has a happy ending. All that agony has produced exactly what Lee hoped to create—a blending of Eastern physical dexterity and Western intensity of performance. High art meets high spirits on the trampoline of an elaborate plot. *Crouching Tiger* is contemplative, and it kicks ass. Or put it this way: it's a powerful film and a terrific movie.

Based on part of a Wang Du Lu novel from the 1930s, the script by James Schamus, Wang Huiling and Tsai Kuojung concerns the theft of a sword, the Green Destiny. This is the holy weapon of Li Mubai (Chow), a legendary warrior looking for peace in his later days. He entrusts the sword to Yu Shulien (Yeoh), a gifted martial artist with whom he shares an unspoken love. Then Jen (Zhang), daughter of a political bigwig, arrives, and everything tips off-balance. The wiser, more cautious adults sense Jen's avidity for rare and dangerous toys like the Green Destiny. They are also suspicious of her governess (Cheng Peipei), who bears a resemblance to the ruthless killer jade Fox. Then one night the sword disappears. And everyone springs into frantic, purposeful motion.

In *Crouching Tiger,* that motion has its own poetry, for these semi-gods and demi-devils possess a buoyancy to match their gravity. The film's first action scene, with Shulien chasing the sword's thief (who, we soon learn, is Jen), sets the tone and the rules. The two fight hand-to-hand and foot-to-foot. Jen suddenly floats up, as if on the helium of her young arrogance, and canters up and down the courtyard walls as if they were velvet carpets, with Shulien in urgent pursuit.

Everywhere in the world—in Asia, during the film's original commercial run, and at the Cannes, Toronto and New York City film festivals—audiences have had the same response to *Crouching Tiger*—rapture. They gasped with glee as Jen and Jade Fox soar into the night. They misted up at the friendship of Mubai and Shulien, two brave warriors who haven't quite the courage to say I love you. They happily took the film's 20-minute detour to the Gobi, where Jen meets her bandit beau Lo (Chang). At the end, they sobbed farewell to an old warrior who gives a lovely valediction.

The movie has its roots in Asian action movies of around 30 years ago. It quotes famous fight scenes from two films by the action master King Hu: *Come Drink with Me,* in which the young, fierce Cheng Peipei defeats an inn full of martial studs, and *A Touch of Zen,* with two knights doing battle in a grove of bamboo trees. Lee had the inspired—or crackpot—idea of staging the fight between Mubai and Jen on the trees' branches, 60 ft. in the air. "I'd fantasized about this since boyhood," Lee says, "but a lot of my ideas weren't feasible or didn't look good. Nobody, including Yuen, wanted to do the tree scene, for a simple reason: it's almost impossible. The first three days of shooting were a complete waste. There were 20 or 30 guys below the actors trying to make them float. It was just chaotic." Finally it worked—a scene so buoyant that the audience soars along with the stars.

Lee is a visionary and a perfectionist; he demands more than his colleagues can freely give. For the dapper, amiable Chow—Hong Kong cinema's top tough guy before he became Jodie Foster's regal pupil in *Anna and the* King—the experience was often "awful. The first day I had to do 28 takes just because of the language. That's never happened before in my life." Lee drove Yeoh, whose family's language is English, nearly to tears with his insistence on precise speech. But the beautiful action star thinks it was worth the trouble. "I've been waiting 15 years to work with this guy," she says. "He's gentle and very emotional. During a sad scene at the end of the film, he kept telling me to do different things, and when he'd come over I'd see he was red-eyed, teary. He gets so completely involved. And when he says, 'Good take' after a shot, he really means it."

For all its pan-Asian star power, *Crouching Tiger* depends on Jen—on Zhang, in only her second film. The actress says she labored under "a pressure not to disappoint the director. I felt I was a mouse and Ang Lee a lion." When first seen, Jen seems lovely but unformed, a dreamy adventuress, a spoiled rich girl with a skill to match her will. Gradually, though, Jen (or, rather, Zhang) reveals a more toxic, intoxicating beauty. Will she become a fearless heroine or a ferocious killer? Zhang, surely, is guilty of one crime: she steals the film. "She allows the audience to pour themselves into her imagination," Lee says. "It's not really her in the movie, it's you. That's beyond acting. It's cinematic charisma."

Before shooting, Zhang and her young screen lover Chang worked with an acting coach. Chow and Yeoh crammed to speak Mandarin. And throughout, Lee was learning the limitations in the laws of stunt physics from the martial master Yuen. Movies are an education on the fly, with pop quizzes every moment. How apt, then, that the theme of *Crouching Tiger* should be teaching. In this war of the generations, the adults are as eager to instruct the young as the kids are to rebel against authority. In life as in martial arts, knowledge is power. And only the most powerful, like Chow's Mubai, can share it. He hopes to share it with Jen. Teaching this bright, willful girl is as close as he will come to fatherhood—even if the job carries fatal risks.

A film director is the ultimate father figure, doling out responsibility, praise and censure. On *Crouching Tiger,* Lee, who secured his early fame with the so-called *Father Knows Best* trilogy (*Pushing Hands, The Wedding Banquet, Eat Drink Man Woman*), was a father-teacher to Zhang the budding actress, to Yeoh the tentative Mandarin student, to Chow the man on the flying bamboo, And behind Lee was another family figure—the young Ang, mesmerized by tales of great fighters and images of impossible physical grace.

However much the middle-aged Ang Lee suffered in making this exquisite film, he should take a little pleasure in knowing that he helped realize the young Ang Lee's dream.

VILLAGE VOICE, 12/12/00, p. 173, Amy Taubin

Although hardly a connoisseur of Chinese martial arts movies, I count among my most delirious cinematic experiences a Berlin Film Festival midnight screening of Tsui Hark's *Peking Opera Blues* in 1986. Halfway through the picture, the entire audience was on its feet, clapping and cheering as if at a rock concert. "It could be the next *Raiders of the Lost Ark*, but with women," I enthused to an industry friend. "Forget it," he replied. "It has subtitles!"

Fifteen years later, Sony Pictures Classics plans to have Ang Lee's *Crouching Tiger, Hidden Dragon* (in Mandarin with English titles) in at least 300 theaters by January 12 and is mounting a campaign for a Best Picture Oscar nomination. With its sumptuous sets and costumes, magisterial pacing, and expensive digitally enhanced aerial effects, *Crouching Tiger* was constructed to cross over—and not only from Asia to the West. It's the Masterpiece Theater version of a *wu xia* (martial chivalry) movie; instead of punchy pop poetry, it gives us smoothly flowing prose—so smooth it borders on the soporific. The defining element of martial arts movies—what makes them kinetic and poetic—is their ellipticality. In great fight scenes, the cuts often coincide with the moments of impact. You feel the blows in your own body precisely because you don't see them land on the screen. It's the editing that sends you reeling. A rare blend of low and high art, Wong Kar-wai's *Ashes of Time* radicalizes the genre's visual and narrative disjunction to the point of abstraction.

Studiously middlebrow, *Crouching Tiger, Hidden Dragon* takes the opposite tack. Rather than leaping about in time, the story meanders along a linear route, plugging up gaps with character psychology and set decoration. But even on its own terms (writer and executive producer James Schamus pitches it as *"Sense and Sensibility* with sword fights"), the film is unsuccessful. *Crouching Tiger*'s dramatic line is so blurry that the central character is only a bystander to the climactic fight between forces of good and evil.

Basically a female coming-of-age tale, the film revolves around Jen (Zhang Ziyi), an aristocratic young woman who longs to escape the confines of an impending marriage by becoming a freelance swordfighter. Jen has a gift that almost excuses her irritating narcissism. She can fly, as we soon see in a bravura extended fight scene that brings together four of the five leading characters. With the help of her teacher, the evil Jade Fox (Cheng Pei-Pei, the great female action star of King Hu's early films), Jen steals the Green Destiny sword, bringing her into conflict with its guardians, the peerless veteran Wudan warrior, Li Mu Bai (Chow Yun Fat), and his comrade Yu Shu Lien (Michelle Yeoh). Li and Yu are on the verge of admitting their love and walking arm and arm into the sunset when the theft of the Green Destiny (the Wudan clan's version of the Arthurian Excalibur) gives Li unfinished business to settle. He needs to dispose of Jade Fox and set the talented but misguided Jen on the path of righteousness.

The fifth wheel in the plot is Lo, a dreadlocked desert bandit with whom Jen has a couple of one-night stands. Played by Chang Chen (*Happy Together*'s young heartthrob), he's easily the most electrifying figure on the screen. Lo is madly in love with Jen, who's torn between her attraction to him and her feminist desire for freedom. Or at least that's what the film would have us believe. I saw it slightly differently. Jen treats Lo as carelessly as she does everyone else. Her sense of entitlement is so great that she treats all relationships as a form of slumming. By the final fade, Jen hasn't even achieved the self-awareness of the Alicia Silverstone character in *Clueless*.

This isn't the fault of the actress, but of the script and the direction. Despite scrupulous attention to expository detail, Lee fails to dramatize the conflict within Jen, or any of the characters. The other disappointment is Chow, who is more stolid than stalwart. Yeoh, however, is incredibly moving. She brings a host of subtexts into play with a single movement of her eyes. Veteran martial arts choreographer Yuen Woo-Ping, who achieved long overdue recognition in the U.S. for making Keanu fly in *The Matrix, is* responsible for the fight scenes. The opening four-way and the gorgeous treetop match between Li and Jen are intermittently breathtaking. If you snooze a bit in the hour or so that elapses between them, you won't miss much at all.

Also reviewed in:
NEW REPUBLIC, 12/25/00, p. 22, Stanley Kauffmann
NEW YORK TIMES, 10/9/00, p. E1, Elvis Mitchell
NEW YORKER, 12/11/00, p. 129, Anthony Lane
VARIETY , 5/22-28/00, p. 20, Todd McCarthy
WASHINGTON POST, 12/22/00, p. C1, Stephen Hunter
WASHINGTON POST, 12/22/00, Weekend/p. 40, Desson Howe

CROUPIER

A Shooting Gallery release of a Channel Four Films presentation in association with Filmstiftung NRW, WDR and La Sept Cinema and ARTE of a Little Bird and Tatfilm production in association with Compagnie Des Phares & Balises. *Executive Producer:* James Mitchell. *Producer:* Jonathan Cavendish.   *Director:* Mike Hodges.   *Screenplay:* Paul Mayersberg. *Director of Photography:* Mike Garfath.   *Editor:* Les Healey.   *Music:* Simon Fisher Turner. *Sound:* Ivan Sharrock and (music) Richard Preston. *Sound Editor:* Colin Miller. *Casting:* Leo Davis. *Production Designer:* Jon Bunker. *Art Director:* Ian Reade Hill. *Set Decorator:* Gillie Delap. *Costumes:* Caroline Harris.   *Make-up:* Horst Allert and Delia Mundelein.   *Stunt Coordinator:* Graeme Crowther. *Running time:* 89 minutes. *MPAA Rating:* Not Rated.

CAST: Clive Owen (Jack Manfred); Gina McKee (Marion Neil); Kate Hardie (Bella); Alex Kingston (Jani de Villiers);   Alexander Morton (David Reynolds);   Nick Reding (Giles Cremorne); Nicholas Ball (Jack Sr.); Ozzi Yue (Mr. Tchai); Tom Mannion (Ross); James Clyde (Gordon); Emma Lewis (Fiona); Kate Fenwick (Chloe); Ciro De Chiara (Arabic Man); Barnaby Kay (Car Dealer); Sheila Whitfield (Manicurist); John Radcliffe (Barber); Eddie Osei (West Indian Punter); Doremy Vernon and Claudine Carter (Women); George Khan (Medical Man); David Campbell (Casino Supervisor); Carol Davis (Table Supervisor); Joanna E. Drummond (Agnes);   Rhona Mitra (Girl with Joint);   John Baker and Vidan Garman (Couple in Toilet); George Khan (Coughing Man); Christine Niemöller (Pat); Claudia Barth (Waitress);   Tom Mannion (Detective Inspector Ross);   Arnold Zarom (Habib the Terrorist); Rosemarie Dunham (Jewish Woman); Magnus Hastings (Gigolo); John Surman (Loser); Mark Long and Michail Golzarandi (Gangsters); Karl-Heinz Ciba (Accusing Punter); Loretta Parnell (Lucy);   Simon Fisher Turner (Ironic Punter).

LOS ANGELES TIMES, 4/21/00, Calendar/p. 14, Kenneth Turan

Intense, hypnotic, assured, "The Croupier" mesmerizes from its opening image of a roulette ball on the move. A taut journey inside the world of professional gambling, this enigmatic, beautifully made film crosses the traditions of film noir with a distinctly modern anomie with results as ice cold and potent as the vodka its protagonist keeps in his freezer.

It's been nearly 20 years since "Croupier's" director Mike Hodges made "Get Carter," arguably the most influential of British gangster movies, described by one disapproving critic as "a bottle of neat gin swallowed before breakfast." And it's been almost 25 since writer Paul Mayersberg wrote the haunting, David Bowie-starring "The Man Who Fell to Earth." Collaborating for the first time, Hodges and Mayersberg have fashioned an elegant jewel, hard and bright, where the austerity of Robert Bresson meets the laconic toughness of Raymond Chandler.

Our guide is Jack, a tyro writer with dyed blond hair compellingly played by Clive Owen. Jack's detached habit of referring to himself in the third person in "Croupier's" extensive voice-over gives him a distant, uninvolved air, but don't confuse his coldness with complete amorality.

For Jack's lack of surface emotion masks passions he's had to bury because in his world, no moment of humanity or warmth goes unpunished.

Jack is no more than half in love with Marion ("Notting Hill's" Gina McKee), the London policewoman turned store detective he lives with. "You're an enigma, you are," she says fondly, to which Jack accurately responds, in the voice-over only the audience hears, "Not an enigma, a contradiction," someone whose unspoken credo is "Hang on tightly, let go lightly."

Jack is trying to be a writer, but the only editor he knows is not exactly encouraging: "Celebrity is what sells books," the man tells him. "We can always find someone to do the writing." So when Jack's estranged, amoral father calls and says he's lined up a job for his boy at London's Golden Lion casino, he's more receptive to the offer than he might have been.

For Jack, as it turns out, has had enough casino experience in South Africa to make him wary of returning to the pit. But the lure of regular income persuades him to take his hair back to its original, more sepulchral, jet black and accept a job as croupier, the person who rakes in the chips and pays the winners on games of chance from roulette to blackjack.

Though we never learn exactly why, Jack categorically refuses to gamble and has near-contempt for those who do. Still, when he enters the mirror-walled Golden Lion for the first time, his needling voice-over insists, "Welcome back, Jack, to the house of addiction." Later, Jack elaborates in the usual third person: "A wave of elation came over him. He was hooked again, watching people lose."

Photographed by Mike Garfath and edited by Les Healey, "Croupier" beautifully captures the tactile quality of the gaming world: the inviting spin of the roulette wheel, the click of the chips, the whoosh of cards turning over on felt. The film, smartly acted across the board, also allows audiences to feel how and why all this becomes addictive, to experience the rush inside that airless world rather than simply have it described.

Being a croupier demands the nerves and skill of a close-up magician, and though Jack likes to behave like a detached voyeur, much given to ironic comments, in fact the pressure is so unbearable he literally shakes for hours after his shift. Ever the writer, Jack quotes Hemingway from "A Farewell to Arms" about his own situation: "The world breaks everyone and afterward many are strong at the broken places. But those that will not break it kills."

Despite his attachment to Marion, Jack is drawn to two very different women he meets through the casino. One, Bella (Kate Hardie), is a mousy fellow dealer he glances at and concludes, "She looks like trouble." The other, Jani de Villiers ("ER's" Alex Kingston), is a glamorous gambler who's also spent time in South Africa. Mayersberg's intricate, carefully structured plot involves them all as they try their best to survive in a "bent world" where no one can be trusted, yourself least of all.

NEW STATESMAN, 6/18/01, p. 44, Charlotte Raven

There's a certain male version of cool that consists of refusing to smile when amused and never answering questions directly. The purpose of this strategy is to distance the self-styled hipster from all of the bothersome trivia that passes in polite society for meaningful conversation. Enigmatic to everyone who can't read his peculiar manner, this fellow is just too damned honest to burble on about stuff that doesn't relate to the Ultimate Truth of his being. He is happy for the rest of us to do it, as long as he can make us feel stupid by drawing attention to how facile our flailing attempts at interaction really are. Anyone who remembers D A Pennebaker's film of Bob Dylan's 1965 solo tour will know how this tactic looks if the practitioner is a master who can thwart all attempts to draw him into "normal" conversation with glittering, surreal ripostes. The legacy of this, unfortunately, was the conviction of succeeding generations that being cool meant giving silly answers to straight questions. Thus, if you are at a party and someone asks you how you know the host, it's cooler to say that you used to share works when you both lived underneath Waterloo Bridge than the truth, that he was in your year at school.

It's funny that the lead character of *Croupier* tells us that he went to Bedales, the famously liberal private school that specialises in producing facetious toffs who think they are Dylanesque wits, because if I hadn't known, that is just where I would have placed him. Within ten minutes of his appearance on the screen, I wanted to ask him to get me a drink so I could run away before he came back. Although he didn't look anything like him, he reminded me, rather uncannily, of Will Self. You know that way he has of saying everything slowly and overemphatically, in order to distinguish it from common chatter? That's what this hero does. It would not be so bad if it was ever anything worth waiting for, but Jack Manfred, played by Clive Owen, is basically a hip square who strikes conversational poses—"the cynical lover", "the cynical writer/observer of the human condition", "the morally disenchanted voyeur"—along lines that will be familiar to anyone who hasn't grown out of Camus and Satire. It is hard to say how far it was the intention of the director, Mike Hodges, to make his hero as alienating as he is alienated, but I suspect he quite likes Jack and sees something admirable in what, for me, is the acme of pseudocoolness—the fetishisation of authenticity. When Jack becomes a croupier in order to earn the money to write his novel, he boasts of his immunity to that environment ("I never gamble"). It can't touch him, he thinks, because he is on a higher plane to the losers who frequent the Golden Lion. His smug conviction that he could never be like them is founded on an understanding that he would never put himself in situations where he wasn't in control. As all this unfolded, I hoped the film would disabuse him of his rather outmoded belief in his inviolable self. I wanted love to penetrate through all the layers of nonsense, or failing that, for someone to tell him that the way he talked to people made him look like a complete prat. If there had been any justice, the hairdresser who asked him if he lived locally would have smacked him when he answered facetiously: "My business is in Shanghai." Then, his poor girlfriend would have been spared his infidelity with another croupier, not to mention the unenviable task of having to read the first draft of his novel.

At first she doesn't like it. Jack's hero Jake is an amoral "I want to fuck the whole world over" type, and she thinks he's not very nice. Jack knows, but finds himself identifying with him anyway. He starts to see the business as Jake would, and, for a while, you think that is going to be the end of his "not for me, thanks" incarnation. Sadly, this proves not to be the case. Although he does become an accessory to a robbery in the casino—an act that supposedly embraces his Jake side—it plays as nothing more significant than a tiny shift of ethical emphasis. Jack himself is unaffected by it and, again, I couldn't work out what tone Hodges was trying to strike. At just the point where it looks as if Jack would have to ditch the poses and begin to accept his humanity, Hodges rewards him instead. God knows why. I can only assume that he has a stronger stomach than I do for Bedales boys taking what the Sex Pistols once referred to as "cheap holidays in other people's misery" and erecting plate glass between them and the "losers" they have come to watch.

NEW YORK, 5/1/00, p. 57, Peter Rainer

Clive Owen gives a witty, superbly clenched performance in *Croupier*, directed by the underrated Mike Hodges *(Get Carter, Pulp)* and scripted by the overrated Paul Mayersberg *(The Man Who Fell to Earth, Eureka)*, who fortunately tones down his flossier excesses this time around. Movies about gambling often devolve into existential quagmires, but the best of them, Jacques Demy's *Bay of Angels* and Robert Altman's *California Split*, are intoxicated by the vagaries of chance. *Croupier* isn't on their level, but it's a small-scale triumph of sharp storytelling and dry-ice urbanity. Owen's Jack Manfred is a would-be novelist making a living as a croupier in a posh London casino. Sometimes speaking directly to us, he scatters bright-boy aphorisms as if they were blackjack chips (sample: "Gambling is about not facing reality, about ignoring the odds"). He doesn't gamble himself, and he enjoys watching others lose. Jack may think he's in control of his life, but of course he's not. His comeuppance is, for us, almost as delicious as his ascent. I'm not sure why this 1998 film went unreleased in this country for so long. Too smart, maybe?

NEWSDAY, 4/21/00, Part II/p. B7, Gene Seymour

Few, if any, movies exist these days whose words follow you home in the dark the way "Croupier's" does. It may not be the kind of movie that radically alters the global landscape or makes you want to dress formally in its presence. But "Croupier's" seemingly effortless display of high style, smooth craft and an intelligence that generously respects the audience's is so rare and so evocative of a lost era of genre moviemaking that one can't help but get excited about its very existence.

There are many layers to peel off "Croupier's" sleek surface. At its core is a gimlet-eyed enigma named Jack Manfred (Clive Owen), a London-based writer who for reasons that escape him is being pressed by his agent to write a soccer novel. Just as he's making yet another futile swipe at a title for this book, Jack embraces an offer to return to his onetime profession as a casino dealer.

Though he's a startlingly proficient croupier, Jack hates the sordidness of the gambling profession, even in the posh casino that takes him on. Nonetheless, he comes to revel in the subtle, implacable autonomy he holds over the so-called "punters" crowding the table. He is offended, yet fascinated by the shades of gray that creep into his job's ethical code. Soon a whole other book takes shape in his imagination, borrowing freely from his night job.

While his detective girlfriend (Gina McKee) wishes he could find something else to write about, Jack finds more interesting things to put into his book. He also strikes up a chaste, yet professionally risky, friendship with, a sultry South African (Alex Kingston from "ER"), who needs his help in a scheme to rob the casino.

The plot is tricky enough to engage the most demanding crime story aficionado. Yet the screenplay by Paul Mayersberg also works as a sly-witted meditation on the nature of telling stories and the attraction of taking chances.

For all its virtues, "Croupier," released in England two years ago, may be a hard sell to American audiences because of its complexity and also because Kingston's the only widely known name on these shores. She's first-rate, but so is the rest of the cast. Owen especially is a magnetic central presence, reminiscent of Michael Caine's steely, principled hit man in the 1971 cult classic "Get Carter."

Both that film and "Croupier" are directed by Mike Hodges, and this latest movie feels so ripe and fresh that it comes across as a first feature rather than the accomplished work of a veteran. You find yourself, for many reasons, welcoming "Croupier" by wondering what took it so long to get here.

NEWSWEEK, 5/29/00, p. 68, David Ansen

Coolly hypnotic, the lean British sleeper "Croupier" is a reminder that movies don't have to wave their arms and scream to hold our attention. Stillness can be as riveting as frantic activity, and there is a chilly stillness in the eyes of Jack Manfred (Clive Owen), an aspiring novelist who finds his subject matter in the airless casinos of London, where he deals blackjack, spins the roulette wheel and becomes "hooked on watching people lose."

Tautly directed by Mike Hodges, who made the classic 1971 noir "Get Carter," and cunningly written by Paul Mayersberg, "Croupier" is a thriller whose thrills derive less from the suspense of a heist Jack is lured into joining than from the mysteries of identity. People are not quite who they appear to be in this slippery tale, including our unnervingly detached protagonist, who splits himself into two people—Jack the novelist and "Jake" the hero of the gambling novel he's writing. Equally ambiguous are the three women in his life—his girlfriend Marion (Gina McKee), a department-store detective; his lover Bella (Kate Hardie), an ex-hooker turned dealer, and the vibrant, enigmatic South African high roller Jani ("ER's" Alex Kingston). The last card "Croupier" deals is wild: it forces you to reshuffle the movie's meaning in your mind.

SIGHT AND SOUND, 7/99, p. 39, Philip Strick

Would-be novelist Jack Manfred lives in London with Marion, a store detective. Jack is prompted by his father to become a dealer at the Golden Lion Casino. Trained in South Africa, where his father still works, Jack is a skilful croupier but despises the job. However, he is soon fascinated again by the environment, although the new routine strains his relationship with Marion, who prefers him as a struggling writer.

After Jack gets in a fight with a cheating punter, fellow dealer Bella tends his bruises and they make love. Another casino employee, Matt, also cheats; Jack threatens to expose him and eventually does. Jani, a South African girl, befriends Jack and turns to him when in trouble. Inspired by these events, Jack makes headway with his writing.

Disastrously in debt, Jani passes him £10,000 to create a diversion while her creditors rob the casino. But Marion finds the money and intercepts Jani's phoned signal. Unprepared, Jack is beaten up as the robbery fails. Marion threatens to expose him unless he leaves his job, but is killed suddenly in a road accident. Jack dedicates his finished novel to her. Published anonymously, *I, Croupier* is a success but Jack accepts he's a one-book writer. Setting up house with Bella, he returns to the casino. Following a phone call from Jani, now in SA, he realises his father was behind the robbery scheme.

To see *Croupier* as more writer Paul Mayersberg's work than director Mike Hodges' is a powerful temptation. But as *Get Carter* reminds us (looking on reissue like a cross between *Alfie*, 1966, and *Bande à part* (1964), Hodges is unfailingly professional in matching style to story. He sets up the context for his players with a discretion verging on anonymity and then, on a whim, takes time out for a striking detail (for example, in 1974's *The Terminal Man* the silent invasion of white floor-tiles by bloodied water). Even so, given his special fluency with long shots, the confines of *Croupier* have cramped Hodges considerably: this is a basement-flat London, briefly glimpsed between forests of mirrors.

Reflections are integral to Mayersberg's scenario, as might be expected after the emphatic self-regarding theme of his Eureka script. Hodges' contribution is to fashion the casino as a glass cage of distortions, the eye constantly deceived by misshapen figures and rippled furniture, as unreliable as the occupants. Otherwise, he captures with a merciless accuracy the bedsit decor, the cramped kitchens and sparse sitting rooms, tiny arenas of emotional combat. Even when the scene shifts to a country mansion, the sense of entrapment is maintained, and the camera lingers on a copy of Géricault's painting *The Raft of the Medusa* in recognition of a similar predicament: despair, madness and an intolerable intimacy unite the drifting group of the near-dead. Where Hodges and Mayersberg also seem well attuned is in the isolation of their wheel-spinner, a recognisable fusion of the two jacks—Carter and McCann from *Eureka* —who fell to earth in their separate ways. The croupier particularly resembles *Eureka*'s lost plutocrat in finding his plot of gold, a best-seller, and freezing into satisfied inaction. In fact, Mayersberg's reported starting point for *Croupier* was Kurosawa's *The Hidden Fortress* (1958), in which two peasants share a befuddled panic on the edges of a tumultuous history far beyond their comprehension.

In *Get Carter* the ruthless hitman uncovers a malevolent network for whom his personal vendetta is insignificant. Similarly in *Croupier* the dealer is not so much crushed as anaesthetised when he learns he's simply been a card in somebody else's winning hand all along. His compensation, apart from a slightly dodgy new girlfriend, is the daily opportunity to indulge in the joyful exercise of numbers, a hobby lifted directly from the father-daughter relationship in *Eureka*. His mission accomplished, he hails himself master of the game with the power "to make you lose". This dubious accomplishment is neatly celebrated by sweeping the camera (us), along with a pile of gambling chips, down a conclusive black hole.

Part of the intricacy of *Croupier* (very Mayersbergian) lies in the intermingling of 'fiction' and 'reality', portions of the story being disguised as the croupier's novel. Since all the characters are living their own fictions anyway, the flatly rendered dialogue, spoken as if quoting a text, adds to the sense of a writer shuffling phrases and episodes until he finds the most suitable. At one point the on-screen Jack even corrects the off-screen Jake, who has been chipping in throughout the film with information and opinion. Such ironies aside, and despite earnest performances by all concerned, *Croupier* is an absorbing rather than an appealing exercise. As the croupier's partner observes on first reading: "There's no hope in it." But the misanthropist is dismissive: "It's the truth," he says.

VILLAGE VOICE, 4/25/00, p. 142, Michael Atkinson

Another blast from the past: Brit has-been Mike Hodges—legendary in some circles for *Get Carter* and overlooked for *The Terminal Man* —brings us *Croupier,* an existential hard-boil about the lowlife, in which an inscrutable writer (Clive Owen) takes a job dealing in a London casino and wades into the human pit despite (or because of) his ex-cop girlfriend (the exquisitely sad Gina McKee) and his distaste for gambling. A heist eventually gives him something to worry about, brought to his attention by sultry grifter Alex Kingston. Polished and adroit ado about next to nothing, Hodges's film owes everything to Owen, who nails the vaguely unsavory, unreadable, half-lidded hunks that inhabit every profitable entertainment-industry outpost.

Also reviewed in:
CHICAGO TRIBUNE, 4/21/00, Friday/p. H, John Petrakis
NEW REPUBLIC, 8/7/00, p. 30, Stanley Kauffmann
NEW YORK TIMES, 4/21/00, p. E18, Stephen Holden
VARIETY, 4/13-19/98, p. 31, Derek Elley
WASHINGTON POST, 4/21/00, p. C12, Stephen Hunter
WASHINGTON POST, 4/21/00, Weekend/p. 47, Desson Howe

CUP, THE

A Fine Line Features release of a Palm Pictures presentation of a Coffee Stain Productions film. *Executive Producer:* Hooman Majd and Jeremy Thomas.   *Producer:* Malcom Watson and Raymond Steiner.   *Director:* Khyentse Norbu.   *Screenplay (Bhutanese with English subtitles):* Khyentse Norbu.   *Director of Photography:* Paul Warren.   *Editor:* John Scott.   *Music:* Douglas Mills.   *Sound:* Bronwyn Murphy and (music) Phillip Beazley.   *Sound Editor:* Mark Blackwell.   *Casting:* Mo.   *Production Designer:* Raymond Steiner.   *Running time:* 94 minutes. *MPAA Rating:* G.

CAST: Orgyen Tobgyal (Geko);   Neten Chokling (Lodo);   Jamyang Lodro (Orgyen);   Lama Chonjor (Abbot);   Godu Lama (Old Lama);   Thinley Nudi (Tibetan Layman);   Kunsang (Cook Monk);   Kunsang Nyima (Palden);   Pema Tshundup (Nyima);   Dzigar Kongtrul (Vajra Master);   Dhan Pat Singh (TV Shop Owner);   Oga (Abbot's Attendant);   Raj Baboon (Taxi Driver);   Jamyang Nyima (Sleeping Monk);   Pema Wangchen and Namgyal Wangchuk (Storytelling Monks);   Dundrup Gyamtso (Tea Monk);   Orgyen Tsering (Foootball Can Monk);   Rigzin Wangchuk (TV Watch Monk);   Palden Gyatso and Ngawang Gelek (Satellite Dish Monks);   Kelsang (Magazine Monk);   Tupten Loday, Drapka Tenzin, and Gaday Tsering (Lights Out Monks);   Cheying Pading (Leather Sandal Monk);   Tracy Mann (Newsreader); Shanti Steiner (Aerobics Instructor);   Dickey Wangmo (Tibetan Woman Voice);   Pema Yonten (Tibetan TV Bouncer).

CHRISTIAN SCIENCE MONITOR, 1/28/00, p. 15, David Sterrit

People certainly don't think of Bhutan when they think of the Academy Awards race. But the first feature-length production ever made in that small Asian country has been entered in the running for best foreign-language film, and it's as worthy as any contender around.

"The Cup" takes place in an Indian monastery, where exiled Tibetan Buddhists await the hoped-for day when China will relinquish their homeland and allow them to return in freedom. They're a devout group, but that doesn't mean they have no interest in entertainment.

Some of the younger folks have developed a taste for soccer, and the World Cup match is coming soon. They'd give anything if they could watch it on TV—only first they'd have to get a TV, and figure out how it works, and convince the elder monks it's good clean fun. Can they accomplish all this in the days before the big event? They're determined to try, and the suspense is building.

Directed by Khyentse Norbu in his filmmaking debut, "The Cup" tells this lighthearted tale through smart performances, eye-catching images, and unfailing good humor. It's coming to American theaters this week, and its bid for an Oscar nomination may help it reach more screens. Anyone who likes high-spirited storytelling should try to see it.

LOS ANGELES TIMES, 1/28/00, Calendar/p. 2, Kenneth Turan

What could be more surprising than "The Cup"? Not only is its country of origin unexpected (the East Asian kingdom of Bhutan not being previously known as a filmmaking center), so was its becoming the object of a mini-bidding war among independent distributors after its successful debut at the Directors Fortnight in Cannes.

Set in a Tibetan exile monastery, starring Tibetan monks and written and directed by a man described as "one of the most important incarnate lamas in the Tibetan Buddhist tradition," "The Cup," in fact the first feature ever made in Bhutan, is also surprising in its subject matter. Charming, slyly comic and far from conventionally religious, it shows what happens when, of all things, an intense case of World Cup fever infects a holy sanctuary.

Make no mistake, the monks in "The Cup" (filmed in Bhutan's Chokling Monastery) are the real deal, genuine prayer-chanting, horn-blowing, gong-sounding, big hat-wearing, butter tea-drinking individuals who have made a decision to "take refuge in the Buddha."

Based on a true story and written and directed at a leisurely pace by Khyentse Norbu, "The Cup" takes its time immersing viewers in the monastery's world, allowing us to experience the slow rhythms of the place's daily life.

Everything that happens, down to the way the monks wear their robes ("It's a 2,500-year-old fashion," one of them cracks), is steeped in the most ancient custom. But there is a place for playfulness as well as ritual, because even monks engage in food fights and general horsing around when young.

Just being a monk is different in this modern age, especially in a country in which the modernizing influence of India is very strong. Young monks are more worldly than their elders were at their time of life, and that creates the kind of push-pull between tradition and modernity that is at the center of "The Cup's" appeal.

Making the monastery an especially intriguing place is filmmaker Norbu's genial and unforced feeling for character. Everyone in the institution, from Geko the tireless disciplinarian to a deranged soothsayer who never washes his hair to the wry old abbot who longs to return to Tibet but fears it will never happen, is well defined in a way that helps fuel the story and is appealing in its own right.

Shot in a straightforward style by Paul Warren, "The Cup" has a neo-documentary feel that was enhanced by the way it was made. Having written his script in English for a non-English-speaking nonprofessional cast, Norbu briefed the actors on what they should be doing before each scene. "Dialogue was prompted and memorized on the spot," the press notes inform, "and most scenes were completed within three takes or less—a testament to the actors' monastic discipline and concentration."

Lama Chonjor, the real-life abbot of Chokling Monastery, plays himself as an other-worldy type who is especially worried about a pair of young Tibetans who, a letter from a family member informs him, are attempting to sneak across the border and join his religious order.

The abbot confides his worries to his major-domo, the monastery's hard-line Geko (played by Orgyen Tobgyal, a major lama in his own right), but this stern upholder of tradition has other things on his mind. It's 1998, the World Cup is going on and the young monks have little else on their minds.

Most soccer-mad of all is 14-year-old Orgyen (Jamyang Lodro, Tobgyal's real-life son). A relentless live-wire, Orgyen lives and breathes the World Cup, but with a Tibetan twist. His favorite player is Reynaldo (whose No. 9 jersey he wears under his robes), in part because the Brazilian's head is shaved like a monk's, and his favorite country is France because it's the only nation to have spoken out for Tibetan rights.

A miniature hustler always looking for an angle, Orgyen will let nothing stand in the way of his watching the Cup games, while Geko is equally determined to uphold the monastery's discipline. What happens when this miniature unstoppable force meets an apparently immovable object over the Cup final is the film's charming centerpiece.

"The Cup" is not in a hurry to tell its story, but it wouldn't be effective if it was. When the incongruity of World Cup soccer ("Two civilized nations fighting over a ball" is how Geko bemusedly describes it to the abbot) is joined to the incongruity of sports-crazed monks, the slow buildup creates wonders all its own.

NEW YORK, 2/7/00, p. 54, Peter Rainer

The Cup is set in a Tibetan monastery—in exile in the foothills of the Himalayas, and the spaciousness and calm is lulling. But this is also a movie about the vagaries of the monastic life, centering on young monks obsessed with World Cup soccer. The Bhutanese director, Khyentse Norbu, is an incarnate lama and throne-holder of a monastery in eastern Tibet, but his touch is playful, not lordly. The movie, which is slight but resonant, both mystifies and demystifies. We get a sense of the disciplinarian order but also of how that order is changing: The abbot (Lama Chonjor) who longs to return to Tibet and who keeps his bags packed understands that the tradition he has devoted his life to is slipping away. Will these young monks ever know what Tibet is like? Their fascination with soccer gives them a way to create a community of their own, and their avidity, far from impious, is a sign of life.

NEW YORK POST, 1/28/00, p. 51, Hannah Brown

"The Cup," the story of Tibetan monks living in Bhutan who become obsessed with World Cup soccer, is so joyous it can actually shake viewers out of a bad mood.

But what saves it from being just another feel-good flick—"Rocky" in orange robes—is that it also takes a profound look at the plight of Tibetans exiled from their Chinese-occupied homeland and the struggle to keep their culture alive.

"The Cup" was directed by Khyentse Norbu, a Tibetan believed to be the reincarnation of a 19th-century Buddhist lama. Norbu was introduced to filmmaking when he became an adviser to Bernardo Bertolucci on "Little Buddha."

With "The Cup," his debut feature, he achieves the difficult task of giving Western audiences a sense of what Buddhism and Tibet mean to exiled Tibetans.

In this he succeeds where both his mentor Bertolucci and Martin Scorsese, in "Kundun," failed.

While Scorsese focused on the pageantry of Buddhist ceremonies, Norbu gets beyond the exotic trappings.

For the Tibetans in "The Cup," Buddhism is simply a way of life.

They honor the memory of their parents by living a monastic life, but it doesn't make the modern world—including professional sports—any less alluring.

The fast-talking, 14-year-old monk Orgyen (Jamyang Lodro) studies soccer magazines the way the other monks treasure trinkets from their parents.

He leads a group of monks who sneak out of the monastery at night to watch World Cup soccer matches on a grainy black-and-white TV in a local store.

When they are caught by the monastery's disciplinarian, Geko (Orgyen Tobgyal), the teenage soccer nut asks that the monks be allowed to watch the World Cup final at the monastery.

The abbot (Lama Chonjor) displays the kind of flexibility that has allowed this community to survive in exile for so many years when he grants the request.

The final third of the film, in which Orgyen and his cronies collect money, rent a satellite dish and try to hook it up so they can watch the final, are a remarkable achievement in bittersweet comedy.

The actors are gifted non-professionals. The film is beautifully photographed by cinematographer Paul Warren.

The freshness and intensity of the film, which pokes fun at the monks' humanity while treating their plight with respect, recalls such classics as Vittorio de Sica's "The Bicycle Thief."

The film's most serious flaw is its lack of suspense. It's simply hard to imagine an obstacle that Orgyen won't overcome. But the film. is unpredictable enough that it's never dull.

So much more than a rah-rah sports film or noble "free Tibet" movie, "The Cup" is simply an amazingly original, exhilarating film.

NEWSDAY, 1/28/00, Part II/p. B7, John Anderson

Today's quiz question: What's the difference between Hayley Mills and a Tibetan Buddhist monk?

Not as much as you might think. Back in 1966, Mills starred in "The Trouble With Angels" (director: Ida Lupino!) a somewhat cloying but ultimately touching Catholic comedy in which she and June Harding drove Mother Superior Rosalind Russell to the point of conversion. In "The Cup," Jamyang Lodro and Neten Chokling play two spunky young monks who make life less than contemplative for their superior, Geko (Orgyen Tobgyal). Sex, religion, language and locale may have changed, but the basic thrust is the same.

Of course, Mills never cared much about soccer, which is the compulsive obsession of Orgyen (Lodro) and Lodo (Chokling), the movie's high-spirited reincarnates who spend much of their time scheming to watch the 1998 World Cup finals. Nor did Mills have China breathing down her neck, and the subtle political shadow cast over "The Cup" keeps matters from getting overly gleeful.

It's a fairly delicate balancing act performed by Khyentse Norbu (himself a high-ranking incarnate lama), who gives us a solid sense of life among the monks as well as the political realities of their life. The benevolent abbot, for instance (Lama Chonjor, the real-life head of the film's Chokling Monastery), is in exile from Tibet. Two refugee monks from Tibet arrive early in the film, bringing tales of Chinese atrocities. Meanwhile, Orgyen, who wears a hand-inked jersey with the name and number of Brazilian star Ronaldo ("His head's shaved, but he's not a monk"), has been warned by Geko about staying out late to watch matches. He gets kicked out of a local club for being too loud. And—to help finance the rental of a satellite dish—coerces a cherished watch out of the youngest refugee. "Buddhists aren't supposed to be attached," Orgyen says, matter-of-factly.

Director Norbu—who set "The Cup" in India, but shot it in his native Bhutan—makes the most of his story's inherent comic contradictions and demolishes any popular conception of monks being quiet, selfless or oblivious to worldly matters. The World Cup matters, especially the final, between Brazil and Orgyen's favorite, France—"The only nation that fully supports Tibet." Norbu doesn't overdo the politics, but neither does he let us forget about Beijing, which for almost a half century has been trying to wipe out Tibetan culture and religion and, as far as any future World Cups are concerned, should be condemned to bad seats and bad reception.

SIGHT AND SOUND, 12/99, p. 41, Geoffrey Mcnab

1998. Two young Tibetan boys, Palden and Nyima, arrive at a Tibetan monastery-in-exile in the foothills of the Himalayas where they are ordained into monastic life. Orgyen, a 14-year-old monk, is obsessed with the World Cup. He sneaks out of the monastery at nights to watch soccer matches. He takes Palden on one of his missions to see a World Cup semi-final in a local shop, but is caught by Geko, a strict disciplinarian. The boys face expulsion, but the abbot, although he doesn't understand their obsession with soccer, decides to be lenient. The monks are given permission to watch the final. To pay for a satellite dish, Orgyen goes on a relentless fund-raising drive and eventually gathers enough cash. He and the other monks collect a huge satellite dish from a television dealer and take it back to the monastery where they install it on the roof After much fiddling, they get their black-and-white set to work. The monks watch, absorbed, as France beats Brazil in the final.

The Cup, the directorial debut of Bhutanese writer/director Khyentse Norbu, is set in a monastery in the foothills of the Himalayas. Its actors are real monks studying at a college of Buddhist philosophy. None had any professional experience. As the producers note, "Dialogue was prompted and memorised on the spot, and most scenes were completed within three takes or less—a testament to the actors' monastic discipline and concentration."

To outsiders who imagine Tibetan monks live an impossibly austere life, the film can't help but come as a surprise. The youngsters under the control of their strict taskmaster Geko are mischievous and playful. At times, as they tease the straggly-bearded yogi or head out on illicit trips to watch football on television, *The Cup* seems like a Buddhist variation on the 'schooldays' movie. Although set in the same corner of the world recreated in Powell and Pressburger's *Black Narcissus* (1947), it has little of that film's artifice or flamboyance. Norbu's shooting style is relatively restrained. There are no explosions of colour as in Scorsese's *Kundun*. Norbu (who worked on Bertolucci's *Little Buddha)* elicits remarkably relaxed and natural performances from his untrained cast. He knows the monastic world from the inside. A lama himself (he is recognised as the reincarnation of Jamyang Khyentse Wangpo, a religious reformer and saint who is revered for his part in protecting Buddhism in Tibet in the late nineteenth century), he shows the day-to-day workings of the monastery and demystifies it in the process.

The narrative is deceptively simple. On the face of it, this is a charming but rather whimsical tale about the monks' battle to watch the World Cup final. As they haggle with a shop owner, pawn belongings, search for cash and battle with unwieldy satellite equipment, we can't help becoming caught up in their quest. By the end, when the entire monastery sits down to watch,

The Cup has begun to seem like an Ealing comedy in which a community draws together to achieve a shared objective.

However, in its own oblique way the film touches on some deeper issues than which team is going to win. We're left in little doubt about the unhappiness and resentment the monks-in-exile feel. Thanks to the Chinese, they have had to leave Tibet to pursue their education. Norbu avoids polemics. Rather than have characters make angry speeches about Red Army imperialism, he hints at their anger and unhappiness simply by having them grumble about the tastelessness of Chinese rice. The boys' homesickness is not just for their families but for their homeland too. Without a team of their own to support, the monks rally behind France (which has consistently supported Tibetan independence). They watch the football with wide-eyed awe. Two civilised nations fighting over a football in the hope of winning a cup—could there be anything more bizarre? To outsiders, the codes of monastic life may seem strange, but they're nothing compared to the absurdity of the rituals that surround the World Cup.

VILLAGE VOICE, 2/1/00, p. 115, J. Hoberman

The most crowd-pleasing attraction at the last Toronto Film Festival, *The Cup* represents a new development in the merger of Western and Tibetan pop culture. Khyentse Norbu's first feature—the first by a Bhutanese-born director and perhaps the first made by an incarnate lama since Irving Thalberg—is an exceedingly gentle comedy set in an exiled Tibetan monastery in northern India (ribbed several times for its "underdevelopment").

The lovability quotient is as high as the altitude. The kids play kick the (Coca-Cola) can and the smallest and spunkiest of the gang is a total soccer fanatic—a uniform beneath his saffron robe, a pinup shrine in his room—who is obsessed with the World Cup matches, sneaking into town at night to follow its televised progress and ultimately convincing the abbot to allow him to rent a TV so that the entire monastery can watch the final game between Brazil and France. *The Cup* is small but conventionally well-made. It's officially an Australian production and the mode is far closer to Anglo-Euro art cinema than to Asian pop—shot on location with natural lighting and no zooms. Nor is the cuteness raised to the miramax. Despite a natural spot for Hot Chocolate's "I believe in miracles" refrain, the sparse background music is provided by authentic Mongolian overtone singers. Indeed, *The Cup* is a sort of psychodrama in that the nonprofessional cast is drawn mainly from the monastery where the movie was shot and play versions of themselves.

It's also a new kind of sports inspirational. No movie has ever celebrated TV more joyously. The satellite is connected and suddenly the world arrives! The monks can only thank Buddha that the big game wasn't preempted by a visual kali-yuga like *Any Given Sunday*.

Also reviewed in:
CHICAGO TRIBUNE, 2/11/00, Friday/p. F, Mark Caro
NEW YORK TIMES, 1/28/00, p. E25, A. O. Scott
VARIETY, 5/23-30/99, p. 70, Derek Elley
WASHINGTON POST, 2/25/00, Weekend/p. 47, Desson Howe

CYBERWORLD

An Imax Film Distribution release of an Imax Sandde Animation/Spin Entertainment presentation. *Producer:* Steve Hoban and Hugh Murray. *Director:* Colin Davies and Elaine Despins. *Segment Director:* Jerzy Kular, Satoshi Kitahara, Howard Greenhalgh, Paul Sidlo, Peter Spans, Eric Darnell, Tim Johnson, and Bob Anderson. *Screenplay:* Charlie Rubin, Steve Hoban, and Hugh Murray. *Story:* Hugh Murray. *Music:* Hummie Mann. *Music Editor:* Chris Ledesma. *Sound:* Mark Wright and Tom Wood. *Animators:* ExMachina, Kitahara Kaneko, Noriaki Kaneko, Ian Bird, John Wake, Paul Sidlo, Sabine Lang, Ismail Acar, Rex Grignon, and Bob Anderson. Running time: 55 minutes. *MPAA Rating:* G.

VOICES: Jenna Elfman (Phig); Matt Frewer (Frazzled); Robert Smith (Buzzed/Wired); Dave Foley (Hank the Technician); Woody Allen (Z-4195); Hank Azaria (Police Chief Clancy Wiggum/Professor Frink); Nancy Cartwright (Bartholomew "Bart" Wilson); Dan Castellaneta (Homer Simpson/Abraham "Abe/Gramps" Simpson); Julie Kavner (Marjorie "Marge" Bouvier Simpson/Patty Bouvier/Selma Bouvier/Terwilliger Hutz McClure); Cara Pifko (Computer Voice); Harry Shearer (Dr. Julius Hibbert/Rev. Timothy "Tim" Lovejoy); Yeardley Smith (Lisa Simpson); Sylvester Stallone (Weaver); Sharon Stone (Pricess Bala).

LOS ANGELES TIMES, 10/6/00, Calendar/p. 18, Charles Solomon

"CyberWorld 3D" is a state-of-the-technology collection of computer-animated clips, rendered for the three-dimensional Imax format, that stubbornly remains less than the sum of its parts.

Much of the program consists of rock videos, excerpts and portfolio pieces from the last several years, many of which reveal just how quickly the art of computer graphics is evolving. "The Prince of Egypt," "The Iron Giant" and "El Dorado" all boasted more convincing computer-generated water than the endless cascades falling among the towers in "Flipbook/Waterfall City" by Satoshi Kitahara (Japan).

Expanding the barroom scene from DreamWorks' "Antz" to fit the Imax screen doesn't really add anything to it. Hearing the voices of Woody Allen and Sylvester Stallone coming out of insect bodies is still nicely incongruous, but the increased size only makes the limits of the animation more apparent than they were on regular screens.

After years of special effects, commercials, network logos and station IDs, it's hardly news that computer animation can produce realistic views to infinity, intricately detailed patterns and reflecting surfaces of metal and glass. But CG is far less effective at conveying a convincing sense of weight or organic motion. The flying creatures in the Pet Shop Boys' "Liberation" (Eye Animation, England) simply wave their wings up and down: There's no feeling of propulsion or power. Similarly, the sea monsters in "KraKKen" (Exmachina, France) fail to communicate a believable sense of muscles propelling bulky bodies through the water.

Tying the segments together is Phig (voice by Jenna Elfman), a computer-generated hostess with an attitude, who guides the viewers around a sort of cybermall. The animation of Phig displays all the weaknesses of CG and motion-capture techniques: She seems utterly weightless; her movements have an odd, staccato quality; and her gestures lack individuality.

As "CyberWorld" progresses, Phig battles three software bugs, Buzzed, Wired and Frazzled. The artists are clearly trying to capture the feel of classic cartoons with these characters, but the timing is flaccid and humor forced. The lame jokes, combined with endless movements and turns in depth, make these sequences feel like a rejected introduction for the Star Tours ride in Disneyland.

The most entertaining segment in "CyberWorld" is the "Homer Cubed" sequence from "Treehouse of Horrors VI," an episode of "The Simpsons" that aired in 1995. Trying to escape a visit from his sisters-in-law Patty and Selma, Homer stumbles into another dimension that reminds him of "that twilighty show about that zone."

"The crew at Pacific Data Images did an excellent job of translating Homer's two-dimensional form into three dimensions, and the backgrounds spoof the look of other pieces in the program. As he surveys this high-tech world of glowing grids and geometric shapes, Homer observes, "This place looks expensive. I feel like I'm wasting a fortune just standing here."

"CyberWorld 3D" will delight video game fans in search of over-scaled eye candy, but as "Homer Cubed" demonstrates, clever writing and finely honed vocal performances can make limited animation far more engaging than lavish but empty visual effects.

NEW YORK POST, 10/6/00, p. 57, Jonathan Foreman

There are some stunning images in "CyberWorld, images that actually take advantage of the opportunities offered by the gigantic IMAX format and modern 3-D technology.

Sometimes you really do think you could just reach out and touch the movie's narrator, "Phig," a typically slim but buxom cartoon woman voiced by Jenna Elfman.

Unfortunately, the movements of Phig's lips seem unconnected with Elfman's voice, and all too often there's something strangely lifeless about many of the computer generated characters in the film's live interlinked mini-stories. (The sampled bits from "Antz" and "The Simpsons"' "Tron" episode are an exception.)

And, as is generally the case with films using the IMAX format, "CyberWorld" is crippled by lame storytelling.

The basic plot—which seems to reflect the influence of Intel, the corporation "presenting" the film—involves three talking, critter-like "bugs" who start eating away at the computer-generated worlds within a futuristic cybernetic "gallery."

Phig must get into the system and stop the bugs or somehow get the whole program rebooted.

NEWSDAY, 10/6/00, Part II/p. B6, Gene Seymour

Maybe it's a little unfair to ask the family audience targeted by "CyberWorld 3-D" to mediate the vast space between "Oh, wow" and "Ho-Hum." So it doesn't. Those extremes, folks, are your only choices here. Whichever way you fall depends on how novel you find the whole digital animation thing and whether you appreciate having shiny objects waved in your face for an hour.

As anyone who's seen—and loved—both "Toy Story" movies can tell you, there's a whole lot of lively, groundbreaking stories being told through digital animation. But you'd never know it from this first-ever 3-D IMAX animated film's contrived, resolutely unfunny wraparound segments in which a fetching animated humanoid named Phig (voiced gamely by Jenna Elfman) acts as your "guide" through a towering gallery of special effects, illuminated numbers and film clips goosed into three dimensions.

Some of this stuff, notably Jerzy Kular's futuristic fish story, "KraKKen" (who thinks of these titles?) and Satoshi Kitahara's exotic air show "Flipbook/Waterfall City," is meant for gaping. Others, like the 1994 Pet Shop Boys video, "Liberation," aim higher and deeper, but miss the target because of heavy hands and thick brains.

"Liberation's" ponderousness is relieved somewhat by Peter Spans' "Joe Fly & Sanchez-Mostly Sports," a knockdash 1995 slice of gelatinous slapstick about recreational violence among vividly rendered insects. Speaking of which, the disco dance sequence from 1998's "Antz" is reprised for "CyberWorld." It's clever and fun, but then again, the movie was clever and fun in two dimensions. Adding a third neither detracts from nor enhances the original. So what's the point of including it here?

"Homer3," a segment from the 1995 edition of "The Simpsons'" annual Halloween bash, carries a similar archival whiff. But it's the only time when "CyberWorld" really seems as fresh and vital as it tries to be. Maybe it's because it's not enough that Homer and Bart enter the "black hole" of thicker skins and spatial displacement. They remain, throughout, Homer and Bart. Which means they talk and act as funny and as clever as always. A pity, though, that they left out the part where "Homer3" drops into the real, but no less terrifying, world back-alley Los Angeles.

VILLAGE VOICE, 10/17/00, p. 144, Nick Rutigliano

Suggestion to Sony: Since never-say-die metal gawd Rob Halford recently penned a riotous tune called "Cyber World," and since he'll be gigging in NYC soon anyway, why not finagle a live accompaniment from him for IMAX's new animation spectacular *CyberWorld 3-D* ? Touring on lyrics like "At speed of lies I will connect/I search and surf as I infect/Computerized catastrophe," Halford and company would fit right dandy into the slapdash jumbo-screen phreak-out, in which a ray-traced Jenna Elfman battles narsty flesh 'n' exoskeleton bugs who munch on strangely alphanumeric source code. And that's just the glue binding a bunch of randomly accessed cartoon memories—a bit from *Antz*, a truncated *Simpsons* segment (Homer's z-axis excursion, natch), various latter-day *Beyond the Mind's Eye* wannabes—together into the Epcot ride from e-Hell. Like Rob sez: "Your information's what I steal/I scan you till you are unreal."

Now, don't get me wrong. While Halford, if they could get 'im, would certainly up *CyberWorld*'s humor quotient *(Simpsons* aside), nothing's lacking in the execution. See, the technology's way beyond head-movie par-everything from PC-smashing gorillas (don't ask) to deep-sea plunges roaring at ya in full-on eight-story 3-D overkill. An under-60-minute run time nearly negates the faulty construction, and hell, what's not to love in the sequence depicting a musty circus stationed aboard a zeppelin being pulled by airborne whales? All in all, it kinda follows Rob's lead, "spreading there inside your brain/a Trojan Horse that eats your mind," a techno-happy bumrush screaming the joy of never thinking twice about repeating things ad nauseam, and as loud as possible.

Also reviewed in:
CHICAGO TRIBUNE, 10/6/00, Friday/p. F, Robert K. Elder
NEW YORK TIMES, 10/6/00, p. E27, A. O. Scott
VARIETY, 10/9-15/00, p. 23, Dennis Harvey

DANCER IN THE DARK

A Fine Line Features and Zentropa Entertainments 4/Trust Film Svenska/Film i Vast/Liberator Productions presentation of a Zentropa production. *Executive Producer:* Peter Aalbaek Jensen. *Producer:* Vibeke Windelov. *Director:* Lars von Trier. *Screenplay:* Lars von Trier. *Director of Photography:* Robby Müller. *Editor:* Molly Malene Stensgaard and François Gédigier. *Music:* Björk. *Music Editor:* Valgeir Sigurdsson. *Choreographer:* Vincent Paterson. *Sound:* Per Streit, Ad Stoop, and (music) Valgeir Sigurdsson. *Sound Editor:* Kristian Eidnes Andersen. *Casting:* Avy Kaufman. *Production Designer:* Karl Juliusson. *Art Director:* Peter Grant. *Costumes:* Manon Rasmussen. *Make-up:* Sanne Gravfort. *Special Effects Make-up:* Morten Jacobsen. *Stunt Coordinator:* Stig Günther. *Running time:* 134 minutes. *MPAA Rating:* Not Rated.

CAST: Björk (Selma Jezková); Catherine Deneuve (Kathy); David Morse (Bill); Peter Stormare (Jeff); Joel Grey (Oldrich Novy); Vincent Paterson (Samuel, the Director); Cara Seymour (Linda); Jean-Marc Barr (Norman, Shop Foreman); Vladica Kostic (Gene, Selma's Son); Siobhan Fallon (Brenda, Prison Warder); Zeljko Ivanek (D.A.); Udo Kier (Dr. Pokorny); Jens Albinus (Morty); Reathel Bean (Judge); Metter Berggren (Recptionist); Lars Michael Dinesen (Defense Attorney); Katrine Falkenberg (Suzan); Michael Flessas (Angry Man); John Randolph Jones (Detective); Noah Lazarus (Officer of the Court); Sheldon Litt (Visitor); Andrew Lucre (Clerk of the Court); John Martinus (Chairman); Luke Reilly (New Defense Council); T.J. Rizzo (Boris); Stellan Skarsgard (Doctor); Sean Michael Smith (Person in Doorway); Paprika Steen (Woman on Night Shift); Eric Voge (Officer); Nick Wolf (Man with Hood); Timm Zimmermann (Guard).

CHRISTIAN SCIENCE MONITOR, 9/22/00, p. 16, David Sterritt

Say what you will about Danish director Lars von Trier, but you have to admit he's full of surprises.

His latest film, "Dancer in the Dark," is a genre-bending extravaganza that can only be described as a musical tragedy.

It stars the pop-music icon named Björk, who's never appeared in a major movie before. Its premier at last spring's Cannes filmfest elicited boos and catcalls as well as applause and cheers—yet it went on to win the festival's highest prize, plus an acting award for Björk.

It remains to be seen how prerelease reactions to the picture—complicated mixtures of enthusiasm, puzzlement, discomfort, and ridicule—will affect its US box-office prospects. Adventurous movie buffs will be lining up out of sheer curiosity, though, and even multiplex crowds might find it to their liking if they open their eyes, ears, and minds to the eccentric, but often compelling experience it offers.

Björk plays a single mother who supports herself and her little boy by working in a factory. She brightens her leisure time by rehearsing with her best friend (Catherine Deneuve) for an amateur production of "The Sound of Music," which contains plenty of the Hollywood-style songs that are her greatest pleasure in life. But her days are darkened by a realization that she's gradually going blind, and that her son will also lose his sight if she can't pay for an expensive surgical procedure.

The plot takes a startling turn when a trusted neighbor tries to snatch her savings away from her, leading to an eruption of violence and a series of increasingly grim events.

This isn't the sort of subject matter that movie musicals usually deal with. It would be perfectly at home in a melodrama or an opera, though, and Von Trier's larger-than-life style aims in precisely those directions. He blends over-the-top emotions with deliberately artificial techniques in ways that are difficult to describe but take on vibrant, passionate life when they're actually spilling across the screen.

Björk's beguiling performance deserves much of the credit for the movie's effectiveness, pointing to a potentially dazzling film career for this multitalented Icelandic star, who also composed the picture's score. Deneuve and David Morse are also effective in the generally good supporting cast.

Another key contribution is Robby Müller's explosive cinematography. It's especially powerful in the highly unconventional song-and-dance numbers—shot with an army of 100 cameras, in a radical departure from the minimalist Dogma 95 style that Von Trier pioneered in works like "Breaking the Waves" and "The Kingdom," his offbeat TV series.

The ultimate surprise of "Dancer in the Dark" is how richly it celebrates the joy of living even as it moves toward one of the bleakest climaxes in memory.

It's not for everyone, but those who take a chance on it are likely to agree it's one of a kind, for better or for worse.

LOS ANGELES TIMES, 10/6/00, Calendar/p. 2, Kenneth Turan

Lars von Trier's "Dancer in the Dark," that most morose of musicals, is so exasperating in its contradictions, so frustrating in its fakery, so deeply irritating in its pretensions, it's frankly hard to know where to begin to dissect it.

This is truly a through-the-looking-glass movie, where pervasive inauthenticity is meant to be taken as a mark of transcendent genuineness, where every shameless contrivance, every cynical manipulation, every frame of carefully calculated clumsiness—awkward writing, bungled acting, intentionally ugly cinematography, co-star Catherine Deneuve dressed in the kind of threadbare shmates my old aunts used to wear—is intended as further proof of an honesty and profundity that is supposed to make us grateful instead of aggravated beyond measure.

If further complications are needed, ponder the following: This movie, which worships preposterousness and considers the false to be true, nevertheless contains a remarkable performance by Icelandic pop diva Bjork. Playing a factory worker with more woes than Job, she is, against all reason and expectation, honest and genuine. Go figure that one out.

Easier to figure is where "Dancer's" artistic point of view comes from. Like the keep-it-real philosophy of Denmark's Dogma 95 group, of which Von Trier is a founding member, it stems from an almost visceral disgust at the visual slickness, the callow professionalism, the glossy craft skill of the kind of Hollywood cinema that is relentlessly taking over the world. Although not technically a Dogma film, "Dancer's" delight in the crude and the ugly for their own sake clearly has its roots there.

But, again paradoxically, "Dancer" may be abandoning Hollywood techniques but not the venerable, so-old-they're-new dramatic forms that have been studio staples for forever. Not only is "Dancer" a musical, it is entirely composed of the rankest, most blatant melodramatic elements, plot contrivances so excessive they make the unsubtle output of producer Jerry Bruckheimer look like the work of austere French director Robert Bresson. In fact, based on this film's reception, Bruckheimer may be justified in feeling that the only thing that separates his pictures from a Palme d'Or at Cannes and the prestigious opening-night slot at the New York Film Festival is grainy cinematography, a tragic ending and a von in the middle of his name.

In terms of story line, "Dancer's" tale of a poor little match girl of a Czech immigrant who suffers, suffers, suffers (oh, how she suffers) in rural Washington in 1964 has links to his earlier "Breaking the Waves." Both are stories of saintly women, too good, too pure, too innocent for this sinful world, women who are abused, tortured and finally destroyed by men. Why do you make films, a female journalist asked the director at Cannes, that could have the collective title of "Breaking the Wives." Von Trier said he didn't know.

The simple-minded sufferer this time around is Selma Jezkova (Bjork), an industrious young mother who works a machine at the John Anderson Tool Co. Everyone in town, including her considerate neighbors Bill, the town policeman (David Morse), and his wife, Linda (Cara Seymour), knows Selma's sight is bad, but no one knows that she's in the grip of a dread but nameless disease that's going to blind her in a New York minute. This dread but nameless disease (DBND for short) is also hereditary, but Selma is determined it's not going to ruin the sight of her 10-year-old son, Gene. It turns out, by the merest chance, that not only is there an operation that can cure the DBND, but it's regularly performed at a hospital close to Selma's humble trailer home.

The worse Selma's eyes get (and yes, they do get worse), the harder she works, taking on a second shift at the plant, ignoring Jeff (Peter Stormare), the hapless geek who is in love with her, even taking on the piece-work job of arranging bobby pins on strips of cardboard. Every penny—it comes to a heart-tugging total of $2,056.10 at last count—must be saved for Gene's operation. That's close to enough, but anyone who thinks our young heroine is going to achieve her goals without the most painful, agonizing and bogus experiences Von Trier can imagine hasn't been paying attention.

The only diversion Selma allows herself are musicals. She watches them with best friend Kathy (Deneuve), shows up at rehearsals for the most pathetic amateur production of "The Sound of Music" in American theatrical history, and even uses her imagination to turn her factory daydreams and reveries into musical production numbers.

Though they may appear unusual to domestic audiences, songs and dances set amid machines were, as detailed in the wonderful documentary "East Side Story," a staple of musicals made behind the Iron Curtain. What's different here is the deadly lugubriousness of the dancing, the thudding nature of routines that are notable only for their glumness and zombie-like lack of joy.

Cut from the same cloth is the listlessness of most of the acting, a state encouraged by Von Trier, who has never been to this country and clearly couldn't care less if the line readings sound recognizably American or not. Just to make sure everyone gets his message, the director operated the camera himself (veteran Robby Muller was the cinematographer) and imposed a jittery, intrusive visual style that pushes the image right in the viewer's face, the better to milk the already overdone emotions.

The only actor to survive 2 hours and 20 minutes of this tedium is Bjork. Called on to carry a misery-laden picture without any acting training to fall back on, Bjork, by all reports, had to more or less live Selma's tortured life to get it on film. "Bjork was not acting anything, she was feeling everything," is how Von Trier explained the process in Cannes, "and that made it extremely hard on herself and everyone else."

In her case, at least, this process was worthwhile, as the intensity with which Bjork threw herself into the role and the degree to which she believed in her preposterous character lend an undeniable integrity and authenticity to Selma and made Bjork's best actress prize at Cannes more universally popular than the film's Palme d'Or. With her whimsical half smile, indescribable accent and overall impish quality, Bjork's Selma has something wonderfully alive and genuine about her that even the waves of surrounding dross can't completely tarnish.

"In a musical, nothing dreadful ever happens," says Selma during a break between the tortures of the damned. "When I worked in the factory, I used to dream of being in a musical." After all she's been through, who has the heart to tell her she couldn't possibly stand the one's she's in.

NEW STATESMAN, 9/18/00, p. 44, Jonathan Romney

Relations were so strained between Lars von Trier and his star Bjork while shooting *Dancer in the Dark* that, at one particularly stressful moment, the Icelandic singer apparently "ate her blouse". When the film was premiered in Cannes this year—winning the Palmed' Or and the Best Actress prize for Bjork—many critics ate theirs, too. *Dancer in the Dark* has divided audiences like no other film in ages. Some people have emerged in tears at the film's heart-tugging simplicity. Personally, I'm with the critic who announced that it was the worst musical he had ever seen, "and that includes *Springtime for Hitler*".

Some people tell me that older, hardened hearts simply don't get the film. It may indeed be a matter of age, because *Dancer in the Dark* strikes me as a genuinely infantile work. The story is sketched in the broadest melodramatic strokes, invoking only elemental emotions—the joy of rhythm, the pleasures of nature, mother love. The heroine Selma (Bjork) is a rosy cheeked innocent, so zestful that she makes Maria in *The Sound of Music*—Selma's favourite musical—look like a sulking Goth chick. But, coming from the seasoned provocateur von Trier, the gaucheness is more than suspect: it looks like a celluloid sophisticate's jaded nostalgia for the thrill of the pure and direct.

Selma—"Silly Selma", as she calls herself in song—is a single mother, a Czech immigrant working in a factory in small-town America, in what seems to be a fantasy version of the 1950s or 1960s. She loves musicals almost as much as she loves her ten-year-old boy, Gene, but both mother and son are losing their sight, and she keeps the money for his eventual operation tucked away in a biscuit tin. Her neighbour, the local cop Bill (David Morse, the most substantial performance here), seems like a nice guy, but he has his own troubles; before long, they are raining on Selma, too.

Blindness, troublesome neighbours and the heavy hand of justice notwithstanding, it's not such a bad world. *Dancer in the Dark* adheres to the moral pattern of melodrama, in which individual aspects of life can be unspeakably awful, in which infants must turn chimney sweeps and wicked landlords cast mothers into the snow, without the overall order of things being anything but reassuring. So, while fate is stacked against Selma, most of the characters go out of their way to make her lot a little gentler. Her best friend (played by Catherine Deneuve) signs on to the night shift specially to give Selma a hand, and the director of an amateur production of *The Sound of Music* is obliging enough to employ a drummer purely on rhythm-crazy Selma's whim, even though she is playing only a second-string nun. Everything is so sweet and tender that, when nastiness intrudes, it is all the more distressing. You may find yourself reaching for the sick bag, rather than the Kleenex.

Selma is a spiritual sister to the heroine of von Trier's 1996 film, *Breaking the Waves*, a powerful but contentious story about a woman who martyrs herself sexually in order to save her husband. Von Trier's obsession with virtuous female suffering—his "Patient Griselda" complex—makes sense if you think of his films not as conventional dramas, but as cinematic operas. In its grand emotional gestures, *Dancer in the Dark* is as close to opera as modern cinema gets, but, as a bona fide musical, it leaves much to be desired—not least because Bjork's songs are grating, melodically unmemorable and lyrically banal ("Remember what I have said/Remember about the bread/Do this do that, make your bed").

Almost any cue will turn Selma's daily grind into a full blown song-and-dance routine. The clanking of machinery sends the whole shop floor swinging and hoofing; a walk along railway tracks takes on the heroic pastoral sweep of a Sixties eastern bloc musical. Von Trier seems to have another sort of musical in mind—those made in the Sixties by the late Jacques Demy, who, in *Les Parapluies de Cherbourg* and *Les Demoiselles de Rochefort*, proved that the most unpromising provincial settings could become a stage for rapturous fiestas more than the equal of MGM's finest.

The Demy connection in *Dancer in the Dark* is his regular star Deneuve, who seems an unnecessarily opulent casting choice. In overalls and headscarf, French cinema's most regal diva becomes less a character than a gracious fairy godmother guest star. As for the song sequences, they don't work by any conventional standards. Von Trier's grand formal gesture is the fussy cutting between no fewer than 100 digital cameras which, throughout the film, are stuck anywhere that von Trier and the photographer Robby Muller damn well please—up walls, in a river, on a bicycle wheel. Vincent Paterson's all-jumping, all-tapping, all spanner-wielding choreography looks as though it might be galvanising, but the editing works so epileptically against any sense of space and rhythm that it feels like an act of wilful self-sabotage.

The bottom line is, can you accept Bjork as a tragic heroine? Festival juries adore her: a non-actor playing with ingratiating naturalness to the camera, too infatuated with her own disorderly realness to play the game of mere plausibility. This wildly mannered turn, half ten-year-old, half granny gnome, isn't helped by a distractingly weird accent—not so much Czech as Martian Cockney.

I can buy Julie Andrews as an Austrian novice nun, at a pinch, but you have to draw the line somewhere, and I think it should be drawn at this ugly, self-indulgent folly. Silly Selma, indeed.

NEW YORK, 10/9/00, p. 90, Peter Rainer

Lars von Trier's *Dancer in the Dark* stars the Icelandic singer and composer Björk as Selma, a Czech immigrant and single mother living in a trailer in a working-class town in Washington State in 1963. Going blind, Selma stashes her meager paycheck from a local factory job in order to pay for an operation that will spare her son a similar fate. Her passion is musicals, and periodically she fantasizes her own life as a big production number. The results of these imaginings, with music and singing by Björk, rank with *At Long Last Love* and *Everyone Says I Love You* as examples of the worst musical scenes ever. Von Trier placed some 100 stationary video cameras around the set—that's 100 too many. It's not just that the numbers are berserkly bad; they also don't seem to have any emotional connection to this bedraggled, Dickensian waif. Von Trier puts Selma through so many motions of sorrow and cruelty that the film turns into a masochist's orgy. Björk won the Best Actress prize at Cannes for her performance, but I found her elfin intensity more creepy than moving. Von Trier piles on the extreme close-ups of her tremulous pathos, just in case we missed the intensity.

NEW YORK POST, 9/22/00, p. 47, Jonathan Foreman

Lars von Trier's controversial musical tragedy is manipulative schlock decked out in the trappings of art. If it weren't for a terrific central performance by the Icelandic pop singer Bjork, "Dancer in the Dark" would be all but unwatchable. As it is, the controversial winner of the Palme D'Or at this year's Cannes Film Festival is as meretricious a piece of fakery as ever beguiled an audience.

Kitschy schlock gussied up with the trappings of artsiness and buttressed with canned anti-American politics, it shares nothing with Lars von Trier's powerful "Breaking the Waves"—except another dim child-woman heroine who destroys herself in an avoidable act of self-sacrifice.

It's so unrelenting in its manipulative sentimentality that, if it had been made by an American and shot in a more conventional manner, it would be seen as a bad joke.

Its musical and dance sequences are so poorly performed and shot, they work neither as homage to the genre nor as an ironical deconstruction of it.

Worse still, the whole story groans with cheap irony and is laced with a superficial, reflexive anti-Americanism: If the story makes any sense at all, it's as a heavy-handed indictment of America's failure to provide free health care and legal services—not to mention its use of the death penalty, its fascination with guns, its crass anti-communism, etc.

The place is the American Northwest; the time, the early '60s. Selma (Bjork) is an immigrant from Czechoslovakia who works in an East European-looking factory that churns out tin trays 24 hours a day. Though she tries to hide it, she is gradually going blind, thanks to a hereditary condition, and only the help of her best friend, Kathy (Catherine Deneuve), prevents her from losing her job.

Unknown to anyone, Selma is secretly saving her wages from the factory to pay for an operation that will ensure her 12-year-old son, Gene, who doesn't know he has inherited the condition, keeps his sight. As her vision fails, she starts to work double shifts at the factory, while continuing to rehearse for her role as Maria in the local production of "The Sound of Music."

Exhausted, she daydreams constantly, and in those dreams, people around her behave just like the people in her beloved musicals, suddenly bursting into song and dance.

"In a musical, nothing dreadful ever happens," says Selma—who presumably never saw "West Side Story." As if to underline the point that the traditional musical is a kind of cultural opiate designed to distract people from dreadful reality, Selma's real life is shot in dreary video; the dream sequences are shot in luxurious color.

Then things really start going wrong. Her seemingly nice landlord (David Morse) turns out to be a monster, or at least a man driven by financial pressures and a wife's boundless consumerism to commit a terrible crime. (That's capitalism for you.) His act prompts Selma to make a series of disastrous and increasingly ridiculous choices that land her on death row.

In "Breaking the Waves," you understood why Emily Watson's character behaved the way she did. Here, the female victim-martyr suffers mainly to serve the requirements of an absurd plot that could come straight out of a particularly sentimental Victorian novel (think the death of Dickens' "Little Nell").

With the exception of Bjork's extraordinary turn as Selma and Deneuve's raw performance as Kathy, the acting is of extremely variable quality. And von Trier's use of 100 cameras in the dance sequences fails to produce imagery of any particular beauty or interest.

NEWSDAY, 9/22/00, Part II/p. B2, Jan Stuart

Scandinavia, an earnest gathering of countries generally not known for their fashion consciousness, has exported a veritable fall line of emperor's new clothes. The tailor is Danish film maverick Lars von Trier, who has stitched together a jaw-dropping shmata called "Dancer in the Dark" that sucker-punched the Cannes Film Festival and aimed its next snow job on the opening-night crowd at the New York Film Festival.

Von Trier, whose Dogma '95 collective espouses simplicity in filmmaking, has pushed that militantly articulated ethos to the limits in movies calculated to provoke, from the transcendent "Breaking the Waves" to the fidget-inducing "Idiots."

"Dancer in the Dark" provokes as well, but not for pressing the usual hot buttons of sex, politics or religion. A postmodern antimusical composed by and starring Icelandic pop sensation Björk, it plays like a loud, gut-venting belch, at least for fans of the moribund movie musical who hoped the form's redemption might lie in just the sort of cutting-edge artists showcased here. It revels in its audacity, but it's merely inept, derivative and dreary.

Björk wears thick, class-wallflower glasses to play Selma, a sight-impaired Czech immigrant in America who lives in a trailer, working double shifts at a tool-and-die factory in the Northwest to buy her son an operation that will rescue him from the congenital disease that is making her blind. She brightens her austere days attending Busby Berkeley movies and rehearsing to play Maria in a community staging of "The Sound of Music" with her friend Kathy (Catherine Deneuve).

Selma's exasperating martyrdom (she keeps the operation a secret) is soon enhanced by her friends Bill (David Morse) and Linda (Cara Seymour). Bill is in dire financial straits and has his eye trained on Selma's nest egg, while Linda mistakenly thinks Selma has her failing eyes on Bill. Tears fall. Accusations fly. Cries. Whispers. Betrayals. Gunshots. Blood. Police. Lawyers. Trials. Hope. Despair. Oy. Vey.

This is breast-beating melodrama of a level that would have been hooted off the desks of Lillian Gish and D.W. Griffith had it been sent to them 85 years ago. No fool he, von Trier intends to undermine both the sentimental conventions of his story and those of the movie musicals he references. But juxtaposing the grim realities of Selma's existence with the schnitzel-with-noodle cheer of "My Favorite Things" exemplifies the sheer triteness of von Trier's strategy of subversion, down to a dark conclusion that rips off Dennis Potter's infinitely superior "Pennies From Heaven."

Beginning with a Wagnerian-heavy preamble that sounds like the lost Ring Cycle overture, Björk has composed a series of giggle- making numbers that take their rhythmic cue from the clacking of trains on tracks or the drone of factory machines, a la "Stomp" or Fred Astaire's "Slap That Bass" number. There are high-kicking factory workers and hobos on trains, but von Trier hasn't the first clue how to film a musical number. His jittery handheld camera suddenly gives way to fancy ceiling shots and MTV-style cuts that sabotage the choreography and lend an unintended new meaning to the film's title.

Much of your tolerance for all of this will hinge on your feelings for Björk, a small, feline creature whose vocal style vaults between a cat's whimper and the noise that same animal might make if twirled by the tail and flung off a cliff. She may be an actress, but to judge from her 140-minute film debut, a long Björk goes a little way.

SIGHT AND SOUND, 10/00, p. 41, Peter Matthews

Washington State, 1964. Selma, a Czech immigrant, lives with her son Gene on the property of policeman Bill and his wife Linda. Despite poor eyesight, Selma operates a machine press at a tool company. A fan of musicals, Selma attends drama class, where she is rehearsing for a production of *The Sound of Music*. One day, Bill confesses to her that the bank will soon repossess his house; Selma reveals she is going blind from a hereditary condition and saving for an operation to rescue Gene's sight. After Selma refuses to loan him money, Bill discovers where she hides her savings.

Helped by her friend Kathy, Selma begins working the night shift, but gets sacked when she breaks the machinery. Selma discovers she has been robbed. Bill admits the crime, only to tell Linda that Selma was attempting to steal *his* money. When Selma tries to take back her savings, Bill pulls a gun and is mortally wounded in the ensuing struggle; he begs Selma to finish the job, and she batters him to death with a strong box. Selma then visits the doctor to pay for Gene's operation. Soon after, the police arrest her. On trial, Selma claims to have sent the money to her father Oldrich Novy, a musical star in Czechoslovakia. Novy arrives and refutes this. Selma is found guilty and sentenced to death. Her friend Jeff finds out about Gene's operation and gets the case reopened. But Selma refuses to use the money to pay for the lawyer. In the execution room, Selma sings a song and is hanged.

Björk gives an astonishing performance in *Dancer in the Dark* one which deserves all the praise that has been lavished upon it. Let's admit, however, that the role is an easy one, almost guaranteed to reduce us to blubber. In her pop-star incarnation, Björk plays the ethereal sprite whose plaintive voice can break your heart, and it's a down-market version of this persona she embodies here. Dreaming of Hollywood musicals as she works at the tool factory, Selma cuts a poignant figure with her glaring spectacles and frumpy cardigans. Our lumpen heroine, moreover, is going blind while saving for an operation that will rescue her son Gene from the same fate. The situations that writer-director Lars von Trier serves up here might be embarrassingly florid, but the coupling of his manipulative skills and Björk's showy intensity results in a movie with the force of an emotional bulldozer.

From the catcalls the film has received in some quarters, one gathers it's possible to dismiss the whole exercise as meretricious tosh. It's true that set beside a certifiable masterpiece such as Robert Bresson's *Mouchette* (1966), another tale of an abject waif who goes from bad to worse, *Dancer* reveals itself as a gleeful tear-jerker. Unlike Bresson, who refuses to enlist facile sympathy for his protagonist, von Trier practically hog-ties us into accepting Selma as the most adorable Raggedy Ann we have seen. Yet there are undeniable pleasures to be gained from submitting to luxurious emotions you suspect are fake. Even more patently than von Trier's *Breaking the Waves*, *Dancer* recalls such weepies as *Stella Dallas* (1937) or *Camille* (1936)—pictures where misunderstood women suffered and performed acts of saintly masochism. But those classic melodramas were motivated by a belief in the beauty of distilled pathos. Here, von Trier appears to be up to something more duplicitous.

Indeed, the main difficulty presented by the movie is determining how far it can be taken straight. It's ultimately undecidable whether *Dancer* is a transcendental experience or just the newest confidence trick from the reigning mountebank of European art cinema. Following *Breaking the Waves* and *The Idiots,* the director undergoes mystical self-abnegation with his familiar hair-shirt style, and once again, his film comes across as the most arrant form of self-promotion. The studied home-movie technique (the film was shot, largely handheld, on digital video camcorders) consorts rather weirdly with the kitschy flamboyance of the plot; but instead of naturalising the artifice, it only throws it into bolder relief. The film flicks between endorsing its delirious excess and ironically disavowing it, a double-jointed manoeuvre that puts one in mind of 50s soap king Douglas Sirk. But where Sirk deployed reflexivity for a political critique, von Trier seems interested in flaunting his own conceptual cleverness.

You get the sense that von Trier is using popular culture as so much grist for his mill, especially during the movie's musical sequences. in the very first scene, Selma quavers through a rendition of 'My Favourite Things' while executing a few klutzy dance steps; but her touching ineptitude is transmogrified for periodic fantasy interludes when she and the other characters writhe callisthenically in tight formation, During these sequences, in which Selma's vision is restored and a murdered man comes alive, you can't fail to grasp the idea that musicals comprise a utopian space where suffering is abolished. As an organising conceit, it sounds promising. But, as José Arroyo suggested (S&S, September), the trouble is von Trier seems staggeringly insensitive to the values of film musicals. The director has copped much publicity for marshalling 100 stationary cameras to film the dancers as they charge about, but the stunt makes a hash of Vincent Paterson's choreography. Von Trier also spitefully denies us the joy of watching troupers strut their stuff, notably *Cabaret* star Joel Grey. Catherine Deneuve, as Selma's friend Kathy, is called upon to tweak our memories of *Les Parapluies de Cherbourg* (1964), but thereafter looks baffled at being given so little to do. Yet despite everything, the musical numbers fulfil their brief and raise the viewer to a pitch of exaltation. The credit must go largely to Björk's plangent score, which adds the precise quality of yearning for release that the movie needs to work. And *Dancer* does work, for all that's sly about it. The gruesome finale is obscene in the way it rapes the audience's sensibilities but it's also devastating. Von Trier treads a very thin line where fraud can no longer be distinguished from genius.

VILLAGE VOICE, 9/26/00, p. 139, J. Hoberman

The title *Dancer in the Dark* promises a stunt performance, and the film, which opened at the New York Film Festival doesn't disappoint. Lars von Trier's latest curiosity is too calculated to seem like a folly but too clumsily executed to exert much mind control. At the very least, this deliriously downbeat vehicle for the postpunk diva Björk has generated the controversy the Danish dogmatist has relentlessly courted. Is *Dancer in the Dark* a feel-bad, anti-American parody of Hollywood musicals or a quasi-documentary exploitation of its unusual leading lady? The answer, of course, is both.

The movie announces its pretensions with a three-minute road-show overture, then plunges immediately into a disorienting amateur rehearsal of *The Sound of Music*. Peering through outsize, horn-rimmed glasses, the frumpy-looking, childlike Björk is playing the part of Maria, with her friend, a wanly chic Catherine Deneuve, as who knows what. The scene is infectiously humorous in an unavoidably snide way—not to mention fascinating. As an actress, Björk is purely behavioral, and if Deneuve—playing a character with the un-Deneuve-like diminutive "Cathy"—seems a bit put out, it may be because she's unsure just how long von Trier is prepared to let this creature perform.

For the most part, *Dancer in the Dark* is shot vérité style, on video, with jump cuts, broken pans, and English dialogue that might have been improvised on the spot. Björk is cast as a fey yet feisty waif, a pathetic Iron Curtain refugee who is losing her sight even as her imagination is nourished by old movie musicals—she's twice shown watching *42nd Street*. The numbers she envisions are filmed in full color with studio lighting, although, as befits the movie's stark, tear-jerking plot, their context is aggressively drab. To add to the distanciation, the characters are apt to discuss musicals and their relationship to life. Meanwhile, Björk—who is not only in every scene but sings every solo—is an automatic alienation-effect who always seems to be speaking phonetic English and dancing with herself.

To call *Dancer in the Dark* melodramatic is to say the least. The plot would shame D.W. Griffith: Single mother Björk is working two factory shifts and saving her pennies to get her son an operation before he goes blind as well. The same day that she's fired for inadvertently breaking a machine, a kindly neighbor steals her money. The circumstances that drive Björk to murder turn the movie from the merely hopeless to the actively unpleasant. Once she's busted, *Dancer in the Dark* moves into its Joan of Arc phase, complete with Björk caterwauling "My Favorite Things" a cappella on death row.

Von Trier's press statements have made much of his "communist" parents' disapproval of Hollywood musicals. To judge from *Dancer in the Dark*'s blatant Cold War signposting, they must have immersed young Lars in Soviet kitsch. An elfin immigrant from People's Czechoslovakia, Björk's character lives in an imaginary America that, despite its *Twin Peaks* patina, is far closer to the invented U.S.A. of Soviet propaganda films like *Silver Dust*. (The foreman has a picture of Dwight Eisenhower in his office.) Her machine-music-scored dances of industrial production suggest the Stalinist Cinderella story *The Shining Path*, while her eventual plight even has echoes of Ethel Rosenberg.

The crazy thing is that, sarcastic as *Dancer* is, it actually works as an anti-capital-punishment tract—an appropriately Pyrrhic victory for a movie far too mannered to be much more than an elaborate prelude to an abrupt punchline.

Also reviewed in:
CHICAGO TRIBUNE, 10/20/00, Friday/p. H, Michael Wilmington

NATION, 10/23/00, p. 34, Stuart Klawans
NEW YORK TIMES, 9/22/00, p. E1, A.O. Scott
NEW YORKER, 9/25/00, p. 100, Anthony Lane
VARIETY, 5/22-28/00, p. 22, Derek Elley
WASHINGTON POST, 10/6/00, Weekend/p. 45, Desson Howe

DARK DAYS

A Palm Pictures and Wide Angle Pictures release of a Picture Farm production in association with the Sundance Channel. *Executive Producer:* Paolo Seganti, Randall Mesdon, Morton Swinsky, and Gordon Paul. *Producer:* Marc Singer and Ben Freedman. *Director:* Marc Singer. *Director of Photography:* Marc Singer. *Editor:* Melissa Neidich. *Music:* DJ Shadow. *Sound Editor:* Barbara Parks, Peter Levin, and Timothy Anderson. *Running time:* 84 minutes. *MPAA Rating:* Not Rated.

CAST: Rick Rubell (Amtrak Community Relations Officer); Mike Harris (Representative from Coalition for the Homeless) and with Tommy, Tito, Ralph, Greg, Henry, Ronnie, Clarence, Dee, Julio, Lee, Brian, Bernard, José, Marayah, Cathy, S. Henry, Esteban, Atoulio, Joe, The Twins, Ozzie, Maria, Jasmine.

LOS ANGELES TIMES, 10/27/00, Calendar/p. 6, Kenneth Turan

"When I first came into the tunnel, I was scared," the man says. "It was dark, even in the daytime. It looked dangerous." That day is now years in the past; the tunnel is now home. "You'd be surprised," the man says, "what the human body, the human mind can adjust to."

"Dark Days," Marc Singer's exceptional documentary on the people who live in train tunnels beneath Manhattan, won three awards at the Sundance Film Festival and may have deserved more. It's remarkable for where it takes us, how it takes us there, and the quiet way it changes our view of the world by giving a voice to people no one has much listened to before.

Producer-director Singer was so far from being a filmmaker when he started "Dark Days," he had to be shown how to load a camera. More an advocate for the homeless, he had as his aim not to win prizes but to somehow earn money to get these people above ground. He ended up not only living in the tunnels himself for extended periods of time, but he also used his subjects as his entire film crew. Rarely has the typical closing dedication to those "who put their hearts and souls into making this project against all the odds" meant as much as it does here.

This kind of personal involvement makes "Dark Days" all the more powerful for being nonjudgmental. Told from deep inside by people who trusted Singer enough to be open and candid, the film treats its subjects straight-on, without the kinds of patronizing or romanticizing that often mar generically well-meaning documentaries on the dispossessed.

Inspired in part by "Hoop Dreams," Singer ended up investing nearly six years, all told, in "Dark Days." And as happened with the landmark basketball documentary, the director discovered that spending that much time with a subject allows reality to come up with unexpected twists that fiction would have a hard time matching.

"Dark Days" begins in daylight, with a man walking down a flight of stairs. Then, like Alice, he continues his journey through a hole in the ground. While he doesn't end up in a wonderland, the destination is not a complete nightmare either.

In fact, it's one of the ironies of "Dark Days," and a bleak comment on the kind of society we've created, that the tunnel's residents almost uniformly feel far safer and more secure down there than anywhere up on the surface. "Ain't nobody in their right mind coming down here," a man named Greg says. "They're not going to mess with you."

The tunnel community turns out to be—and why should this surprise us?—a very human place, a kind of parallel universe where young and old, black and white, male and female try to survive and even get a little bit ahead. Though the percentage of crack addicts is considerable, many tunnel dwellers are eager, as Greg says, "to make that almighty dollar," even if it means collecting cans and bottles and selling things scavenged from the trash.

Ignoring as best they can the omnipresent rats and horrific noise of Amtrak trains hurtling past, tunnel residents plug into available electricity and use scavenged material to build and furnish wood-walled shacks so sturdy that when some say they don't consider themselves homeless, you know what they mean.

In addition to the talkative Greg, "Dark Days" introduces us to a tunnel cross-section including former crack addict Ralph, energetic and motivated dog fancier Tommy and a woman named Dee who unburdens herself of a life story that is heart-rending. None of them are archetypes, or even types, but rather people more like us than we really want to acknowledge.

Like regular citizens, many of the characters in "Dark Days" have a great desire to be busy, to be productive, to be doing something. And like homeowners everywhere, they are forever tinkering with their roofs, their walls, even their makeshift security systems. So when a crisis arises and armed Amtrak police give them 30 days to evacuate, it's an action that's both profoundly shocking all the way around and the catalyst for a powerful ending.

Despite filmmaker Singer's lack of previous experience, "Dark Days" is smartly shot on black-and-white film and makes excellent use of a moody, evocative soundtrack by DJ Shadow. Like a Dante back from the deepest circles of despair, Singer has personalized his friends and neighbors and made it as hard as it should be to look on homeless people as no more than a shapeless, formless mass.

NEW YORK, 9/4/00, p. 55, Peter Rainer

For two years, the filmmaker Marc Singer lived inside the Amtrak tunnels beneath midtown Manhattan in order to document its homeless population in their makeshift huts of plywood and plastic. *Dark Days* which was filmed—remarkably well—by a crew of people from the tunnel, captures the livid squalor of the scene but also its fierce, lower-depths sense of community. (The extraordinary editing is by Melissa Neidich.)

Many of the denizens are black, most are crackheads or former crackheads, and they exhibit a mixture of pride (in having survived) and self-loathing (for the miseries that brought them low). What comes through most is their need to sustain a sense of personal integrity. One man, using power tapped from the city's electrical sources, mixes up some corn bread with a gourmet's panache; another shows off his hovel's jerry-built décor as if he were a real-estate agent on Sutton Place. What comes through also is humor: Two grinning, emaciated guys, probably high on something or other, go into a fractured discourse about pets, and one of them reveals his amazement at how gerbils eat their young. But he adds, "Then how come there are so fucking many of them?"

Misery pours out, too: A man who spent all but two months of his past ten years in prison recounts the horrors visited upon his young daughter, for which he holds himself responsible by his absence. His underground life is, for him, a penance and a punishment. The woman he lives with, whom he has been trying to get off crack, breaks into utter, stark-faced anguish at the thought of her own abandoned motherhood. The people in this movie don't have that primed-for-the-camera look that so many interviewees have now in documentaries; their lives don't appear to be shaped by the culture of television, and so their feelings come through in all their rawness and transparency. It's a near-great film, reminiscent of the early Frederick Wiseman movies like *Welfare* and *Hospital* that left you both aghast and exhilarated at what human beings are capable of.

NEW YORK POST, 8/30/00, p. 57, Jonathan Foreman

Marc Singer's "Dark Days" is a fascinating, beautifully photographed portrait of a vanished community: a group of homeless people who built a shanty town in the train tunnels beneath Penn Station.

Given that Singer, a Londoner in his 20s who moved into the tunnels for two years to make the movie, was a first time filmmaker and used tunnel residents as his crew, "Dark Days" is a remarkable achievement, worthy of the three prizes it won at the Sundance Film Festival.

Of course, it may not be a truly representative or accurate portrait. Singer generally avoids the more degrading aspects of homeless life. His black-and-white photography tends to diminish the visceral impact of rats, trash and graffiti.

And his universally charming, sympathetic and often very funny subjects often seem to be playing to the camera. But all the same, it is a provocative and surprisingly entertaining picture that deserves to be seen by a wide audience.

As Singer paints it, life near the tracks is surprisingly normal, thanks to stolen electricity and skillful scavenging of cooking utensils, food, TVs, even refrigerators. As one of his subjects—who doubled as a crew member—says, "I get so comfortable down here... the only thing we don't have here is running water."

But in 1997, Amtrak officials, declaring the tunnels were too dangerous and unsanitary for human habitation, threatened to evict what seems to have been—assuming that Singer isn't selectively prettifying it (we only meet a dozen of the 75 or so residents)—a real community in the tunnels.

Before the eviction went ahead, a threatened lawsuit by the Coalition for the Homeless prompted public officials to utilize a forgotten batch of Section 8 federal housing vouchers. The tunnel residents then knocked down their shacks and moved into subsidized apartments.

Singer's tendency to make heroes of the Coalition for the Homeless—a highly politicized advocacy group which fought for reform of New York's shelter system and notoriously misled the public as to the role drug abuse and mental illness play in homelessness—makes it all the more troubling that he fails to follow up on his fascinating, likable subjects, and to let us know what happened to them once ensconced in their new apartments.

It's as if he no longer found these people interesting or worthy of notice once out of the tunnels—or if he expects you to believe their addictions and problems were magically cured by the provision of regular housing.

SIGHT AND SOUND, 3/01, p. 45, Danny Leigh

A documentary which portrays one group among the estimated hundreds of homeless people living in the subway tunnels beneath Manhattan in the late 90s. Interviews are intercut with footage of the tunnel-dwellers' daily lives. The subway's owners Amtrak announce their forced eviction. After the intervention of New York's Coalition for the Homeless, many are found homes in low-cost housing projects.

While the subject matter of Marc Singer's study of New York's subterranean homeless during the late 90s may be familiar to those acquainted with Jennifer Toth's 1993 non-fiction best-seller *The Mole People*, the dazzling physicality of his film-making debut almost certainly won't be. Shot in high contrast black and white on 16mm (a relatively arduous method of filming, recommended to Singer, bizarrely, by a friend), the stark monochrome and filmic grain of *Dark Days* looks less like the majority of contemporary, video-dependent documentary, more like an inspired homage to vintage photo journalism.

Indeed, comparisons already made to the likes of Lewis Hine and Robert Frank are not far off the mark—but, as glimpsed in an early shot of an anonymous body lying prone in a tunnel, the influence of Weegee seems just as valid a reference point. That said, Singer's project amounts to far more than an exercise in visual aesthetics. In his grasp of structure, for instance, punctuating interviews with footage of rattling, oblivious Amtrak trains and scuttling, omnipresent rats, Singer displays a sharp sense of cinematic grammar.

Aside from its visual appeal and structural conviction, the gulf between Singer and his ostensible peer group is also evident in the intimacy he and his cumbersome 16mm camera achieve with the inhabitants of Manhattan's labyrinthine subway system. The empathy the director strikes with his protagonists is, perhaps, no surprise: after sinking all his funds into the film over a period of six years, British émigré Singer briefly became homeless himself.

As well as recording the filth of the subway tunnels and a colony of ramshackle, *favela*-like shacks, Singer films a series of vignettes and interviews. The material he garners here is often heartbreakingly unguarded: the youthful Tommy, with his gaggle of puppies kept on his rooftop; Ralph, the recovering addict whose painting of "No Crack" on his front door marries his two best defined traits (a fiercely houseproud streak and the desire to stay off crack cocaine); and, most strikingly, subway veteran Greg, who makes "top dollar" selling discarded porn and electrical goods. The image of an individual living off the detritus of the consumer frenzy going on above ground is arresting, but what's more potent is Singer's ability to coax from Greg the admission that he sees himself as a *bona fide* entrepreneur. In attempting to salvage some pride from a situation too desperate for most of us to imagine, he has recast himself as an honest, hard-working American in an America that has rendered him invisible.

What the interviewees' openness reveals is rarely less than compelling. When the affable, community-minded Ralph, say, finally talks about the terrible disintegration of his life after his first taste of crack, or the film's one female protagonist Dee weeps in remembrance of her failed motherhood, the effect is devastating. Yet rather than give his film a vicarious, zoo-like quality, Singer's evident affinity with his subjects humanises them. With material that could induce gawping, Singer forces us to engage with his subjects as *people*.

Which is due, at least in part, to Singer's reluctance to exploit the shock value of their plight. Regret, tragedy and paranoia are constants, of course, but the bulk of the film is concerned with the almost inconsequential minutiae of life underground (putting lye down for the rats, showering in leaking, freezing water pipes, swapping recipes for meatballs). It's almost as if the sundry horrors of the tunnels don't need articulating—explicitly acknowledged or not, they remain inescapable in this remarkable documentary.

VILLAGE VOICE, 9/5/00, p. 113, Amy Taubin

"We have TV down here," says one of the tunnel dwellers in Marc Singer's *Dark Days*. For five years, Singer documented the men and women who forged a precarious community deep in the Amtrak tunnels beneath Manhattan. *Dark Days* concludes in the late '90s, just after Amtrak evicted the squatters and the Coalition for the Homeless found them housing aboveground. Thus, we'll never know how Dee (the crack addict who wept for her two children, killed in a fire while she was in jail) or Tommy (the runaway who kept a family of dogs and had managed to equip his shack with a shower) or Lee (who showed off photos of his deceased cats, gerbils, and birds, and who committed suicide before the film was completed) would have responded to the concept of survival as game show. I suspect they'd prefer that other Nielsen winner, *Who Wants to Be a Millionaire*.

Dark Days is right on the millennial zeitgeist, where every experience—from cancer to a Prada sale—is fed into an all-encompassing narrative of survival while the planet careens toward destruction. That, in part, accounts for the film's out-of-the-blue success (three big prizes at Sundance alone). The survivalist tale that we see on the screen has its counterpart in the film's actual production. Singer devoted six years to the project, racking up a huge debt and briefly becoming homeless in the process. And—although we only discover this in the end credits—the film depended on the cooperation of the tunnel people, not only for its cast but also its crew. They had the know-how to tap into power lines for juice, they built and pushed dollies, they carried and hung the minimal lights. Singer doesn't inscribe these behind-the-scenes details in the film itself; the spirit of collaboration, however, informs every frame.

With no firsthand knowledge of filmmaking, Singer took the impractical advice of an acquaintance and shot in 16mm black-and-white rather than in user-friendly video, which for a decade has been the documentarian's basic tool. The high-contrast, grainy celluloid look is not only beautiful, it connects *Dark Days* to a history of film and photography that takes life on the margins of America as its subject and includes such epic image-makers as Lewis Hine and Robert Frank.

The economics of film production (film stock is more costly than videotape) forced Singer to plan what he was going to shoot, rather than just running camera for hundreds of hours, as is now customary. *Dark Days* has an elliptical, stripped-down structure that doesn't squelch the spontaneous behavior on the screen. Organized around the rituals of daily life, the film shows the tunnel people cooking, cleaning, socializing, and tending to the shacks they've ingeniously constructed from scavenged materials, and which they must constantly secure from marauding humans and rodents. Singer achieves remarkable intimacy with his subjects, who share their experiences and joke around with the man behind the camera as freely as they do with their peers.

The film shows us the underground shantytown through the eyes of those who've taken refuge there, and who, despite the inconveniences, squalor, and bad air, find it a less threatening place than the streets, subways, and homeless shelters where they lived before. The film neither pumps up the drama of their situation nor cosmeticizes it (although a bucket of shit is easier to look at in black and white than it would be in living color). Acclimated to life underground, they manage to block out its nightmare aspects until they return to the surface and, thanks to the Coalition for the Homeless, real apartments. At this point, the film turns unexpectedly mushy, ignoring the fact that, for most of the tunnel people, addiction, poverty, and lack of education predated their sojourns underground. There are too many shots of the tunnel dwellers gleefully wrecking their shacks (Amtrak insisted that the "tenants" return the property to the condition in which they found it) and of their happy faces and glib pronouncements as they take possession of their new dwellings. On a human level, it's hard to fault Singer for being supportive, but *Dark Days* suffers from a lack of rigor at the very end.

Also reviewed in:
CHICAGO TRIBUNE, 10/20/00, Friday/p. F, John Petrakis
NEW YORK TIMES, 8/30/00, p. E1, Stephen Holden
VARIETY, 2/7-13/00, p. 56, Dennis Harvey

DAY SILENCE DIED, THE

A First Run Features release of a Pegaso Producciones production. *Executive Producer:* Ute Gumz. *Producer:* Martin Proctor. *Director:* Paolo Agazzi. *Screenplay (Spanish with English Subtitles):* Paolo Agazzi and Guillermo Aguirre. *Director of Photography:* Livio Delgado and Guillermo Medrano. *Editor:* Paolo Agazzi and Nelson Rodriguez. *Music:* Cergio Prudencio. *Sound:* Ramiro Fierro. *Casting:* Wendy Alcazar. *Production Designer:* Marta Méndez Iturriaga. *Costumes:* Reny Galleguillos. *Running time:* 108 minutes. *MPAA Rating:* Not Rated.

CAST: Dario Grandinetti (Abelardo); Gustavo Angarita (Oscar); Maria Laura Garcia (Celeste); Elias Serrano (Ruperto); Norma Merlo (Amelia); Jorge Ortiz Sánchez (Padro Isidoro); Guillermo Granda (Jose); Blanca Morisson (Celina); Edgar Vargas (Gumercindo); David Mondaca (Gaston).

NEW YORK POST, 12/8/00, p. 54, V. A. Musetto

Howard Stern has nothing on Abelardo, the mysterious, mustachioed gentleman who sets up a radio station in an isolated Bolivian village.

Actually, it's not exactly a radio station. Since the town lack electricity, radios are useless. So Abelardo (Dario Grandinetti) broadcasts over loudspeakers set up around town.

He charges the locals a few pesos to broadcast musical requests (Elvis' "Jailhouse Rock" causes a sensation), or to go on the air live with messages and/or insults.

Abelardo's little venture does well until he becomes obsessed with a luscious teenager, Celeste (Maria Laura Garcia). She has been kept chained up at home by her crazed dad ever since the night his wife ran off with a traveling actor after the entire town caught the two having sex.

It's all downhill from there for Abelardo.

Paolo Agazzi directs this, Bolivian comedy with a light-hearted flair. The cast is charming, and Garcia is especially easy on the eye. If you're looking for a pleasant way to escape the madness of the holiday season, this is your answer.

NEWSDAY, 12/8/00, Part II/p. B10, John Anderson

In an atmosphere that usually exists only in novels by Gabriel Garcia Marquez, a mysterious stranger, looking like Lee Van Cleef in a Sergio Leone western, rides into town, carrying an implement of destruction: mass communication. Abandon all hope, etc., etc. The 20th Century has arrived in the Andes.

The Bolivian Paolo Agazzi, who hasn't made a movie since the mid-80s, makes a winsome, ironic return with "The Day Silence Died," a cumbersome title for a buoyant, wryly funny movie. In his remote Bolivian village, circa 1960—a magic realism—infected, unwired backwater—the aging author Oscar (Gustavo Angarita) writes to the tune of a gourd-based sprinkler system that creates the sound of rain outside his windows. The once-cuckolded, shotgun-wielding convulsive Ruperto (Elias Serrano), keeps his Botticellian daughter Celeste (Maria Laura Garcia) chained by the ankle. And people nurse grudges as they would sickly livestock.

When the stranger Abelardo (Dario Grandinetti) arrives, with an electric generator and a microphone, the placid days of Villaserena are over. Although more public-address system than radio station, "Radio Nobleza" sells time to the locals, who request songs, air messages (one peso) and hurl insults (two pesos). With the town ringing with the news of bad loans, adultery and missing chickens, the writing is on the wall for Abelardo, a combination doomed prophet and Prof. Harold Hill.

Abelardo will become enchanted by the imprisoned Celeste; so will Jose (Guillermo Granda), a laborer mistaken by Celeste for the silken voice she hears wafting over her walls. "The Day Silence Died" is a sun-dappled romance, but the reactions of its characters are more than eccentric. Old secrets are revealed; workers become disgruntled. An old man hears radio and rises from his deathbed. And one old woman, hearing her name broadcast to everyone she knows, runs inside and locks the door.

VILLAGE VOICE, 12/12/00, p. 178, Michael Atkinson

Displaying a good deal less respect for marginalized average-guyness, Paolo Agazzi's sumptuously shot but stodgily staged Bolivian trifle *The Day Silence Died* sets up a near Buñuelian premise and then bags out. A mustachioed con man (Dario Grandinetti) arrives at a dusty, pre-electric hamlet and installs his own radio station, complete with loudspeakers and pay rates for villagers who want to dedicate songs, make public announcements, and, eventually, roast each other for sins real and imagined. Little fallout, comic or otherwise, results; instead, the stranger becomes besotted with a deranged cuckold's imprisoned daughter (who's forever bathing or doing laundry). Though an eccentric writer (Gustavo Angarita) may or may not have created the whole shebang on the page (at one point, he complains, "My characters are getting boring," and he's not wrong), Agazzi's movie rather provincially hints at sexiness, humor, and satire without actually manifesting them.

Also reviewed in:
NEW YORK TIMES, 12/8/00, p. E20, A. O. Scott
VARIETY, 2/7-13/00, p. 58, Robert Koehler

DECLINE OF WESTERN CIVILIZATION, PART III, THE

An Abbey Entertainment release of a Spheeris Films, Inc. production. *Producer:* Scott Wilder. *Director:* Penelope Spheeris.   *Director of Photography:* Jamie Thompson.   *Editor:* Ann Trulove.   *Music:* Phil Suchomel.   *Music Editor:* Steve McCroskey.   *Sound:* Mike Chock. *Running time:* 88 minutes.   *MPAA Rating:* Not Rated.

WITH: Why-me; Keith Morris; Ezzat Soliman; Final Conflict; Litmus Green; Naked Aggression ;   Resistance, The; Flea.

LOS ANGELES TIMES, 11/13/98, Calendar/p. 4, Kenneth Turan

It's a tradition for documentaries to explore inaccessible, even dangerous locales, mounting voyages of discovery to places few people have been. "The Decline of Western Civilization Part III" fits that definition, but instead of going to the headwaters of the Orinoco or the far reaches of the Kalahari, it unveils a disturbing world that's just down the street.

Shot on and around Hollywood Boulevard over a span of 11 months, "Decline" focuses on the subculture of gutter punks, the elaborately pierced and tattooed young people with kaleidoscope hair shaped into skyscraper mohawks. They're a familiar local sight, but until this intelligent, provocative and sympathetic film by Penelope Spheeris, it's unlikely that most people have given them much thought.

"Decline" is the 12th feature on Spheeris' wildly divergent filmography. She's made both Hollywood ephemera like "Wayne's World," "The Beverly Hillbillies" and "The Little Rascals" and a series of honest, groundbreaking documentaries on rock 'n' roll themes of which this is the third.

The first "Decline," which focused on the early L.A. punk scene, was made in 1979 before most of the punks in "Part III" were even born, and Spheeris uses interviews with some of the old-timers to try to put the new kids into perspective.

Rick Wilder of the Mau-Maus, now a sepulchral presence with long flaming red hair, calls punk "a shrieking siren" conveying "anger at everything." And today, says Keith Morris, formerly with Black Flag and the Circle Jerks, "there's more people, more crime, more corruption, more reasons to be angry and upset."

"Decline" features performance footage of current punk bands with names like Final Conflict, the Resistance and Naked Aggression, as well as interviews with the members of that last group, who turn out to be politically aware individuals with musical backgrounds in classical guitar, piano and French horn.

The heart of the film, and equally surprising, are the extended talking-head interviews Spheeris does with the kids on Hollywood Boulevard, who've taken street names like Squid, Troll, Hamburger and Why-me.

To see these gutter punks is not to love all aspects of them. They brag about drinking every night until they black out, talk openly about thievery, and at times display typical teenage sullenness and bravado.

But Spheeris has deftly captured another side of these people, which makes the sight of wasted lives sadder than it would otherwise be. Along with their baby-faced nihilism, the gutter punks also display a poignant idealism about the decency they'd like to see in the world, a wistful sense of being let down by forces beyond their control and by a society that is often judgmental, violent and uncaring.

Surprisingly bright and articulate, many of these kids turn out to be victims of adult abuse who turned angry and anarchistic because they felt no hope of fitting in. Their toughness ("We're the cockroaches, we're the ones that can live through anything"), as it turns out, does not always run deep. "We get our feelings hurt," one girl says, "and we cover it up with spikes and color." Adds another punk, speaking for them all: "It's not really fun to be in reality."

With her unblinking but nonjudgmental eye, Spheeris doesn't shy away from the horrifying, at times violent messes these kids make of their lives, but she is always sensitive to the pain behind everything, to the unhappy futility of squandered potential.

Spheeris plans to donate any profits from this self-financed venture to charities for homeless young people and abused children. In her introduction to this film when it debuted at Sundance (where it won the Freedom of Expression award), the director said that of all her films "this one is closest to my heart, the one that I feel, if I die tomorrow, I've done something." She certainly has.

NEW YORK POST, 7/7/00, p. 52, Hannah Brown

Penelope Spheeris'"The Decline of Western Civilization, Part III" is a powerful, upsetting look at the homeless teens who follow the punk music scene in Los Angeles.

Her two earlier entries in the "Decline of Western Civilization" trilogy, made in 1981 and 1988, focused more on the music and musicians than on the audiences.

"Part III," although it has clips of bands with names like Naked Aggression and Final Conflict in concert, keeps its focus squarely on the bobbing heads in the mosh pits.

These fans are so young that they weren't even born when punk rock started, although they sport the spiky hair, body piercings and dog collars that are straight out of '70s fashion fads.

At 15 or 16, they aren't just mouthing lyrics about nihilism and desperation. They've run away or been kicked out of their families, and they live on the streets or in abandoned buildings.

Their fascination with punk music and culture isn't just a lark before they start UCLA Business School. It's their way of expressing themselves, just as the runaways of the '60s spouted a hippie ethos.

In fact, Spheeris' probing questions to the teens, as well as her blessed lack of preachiness, invite comparisons to Joan Didion's 1967 essay on street culture in San Francisco, "Slouching Towards Bethlehem."

Many of Spheeris' subjects are the children of Didion's runaways. One boy who calls himself Squid tells Spheeris that his ambition is to start "an alcoholic commune."

Spheeris, who has such mainstream hits as "Wayne's World" to her credit, manages to draw out these kids, even getting them to laugh at themselves a little.

You begin to notice their eyes more than their piercings, and the movie becomes unexpectedly moving.

The squeamish should be warned, though. The gross-out factor in the movie is high. Not since "Trainspotting" has the camera lingered so long on drug addicts' bodily fluids and mutilated bodies. The difference here is that, since this is a documentary, everything on view is infinitely more disturbing.

Still, those with the stomach to sit through "Decline" will be rewarded with a lively, masterful documentary.

NEWSDAY, 7/7/00, Part II/p. B10, John Anderson

That she has directed "Wayne's World," "The Beverly Hillbillies," "Black Sheep" and "The Little Rascals" suggests Penelope Spheeris has contributed enough to the decline of Western civilization. But in between the Hollywood comedies, the filmmaker has devoted more than two decades to her documentary trilogy on the punk rock scene, the finale of which—"The Decline of Western Civilization Part III"—concludes one of the most remarkable achievements in contemporary independent cinema.

If Spheeris seems like a contradiction, she's nothing compared with the subjects of her new film, the spikey-haired, near-angelic derelict teenagers of Hollywood's underbelly—the homeless, usually alcoholic, frequently drug-addicted byproducts of modern life, who exhibit such a passionate devotion to the proposition that life offers nothing to get passionate about.

Spheeris' subjects—individuals like Squid, Why-Me? and Filth; bands such as Naked Aggression and Litmus Green—may embrace an outlaw lifestyle and a squalid poverty, but their political positions are utopian. Racial, ethnic and religious tolerance are their principal ideals (followed closely by beer); their chief enemies are the so-called Nazi skinheads, whose pastime is hate-mongering and violence, and the police, who believe—often quite rightly, judging by Spheeris' interviews—that punk rockers are an unstable lot.

Spheeris doesn't endorse; neither does she judge. It's clear without her telling us that what the punk rockers represent—in their nihilistic self-loathing, self-abuse and sad longing—should keep the rest of America awake at night. The content of the film would make it impossible, of course, but in an ideal world "The "Decline of Western Civilization" would be shown in schools.

VILLAGE VOICE, 7/11/00, p. 128, Jessica Winter

Having toiled for the last decade in big-screen TV treatments and David Spade vehicles, Penelope Spheeris returns to her old moshing grounds with *The Decline of Western Civilization Part III*. If the first *Decline* (1981) contextualized L.A. punk as cause and effect of sociopolitical upheaval (its sequel, 1988's *The Metal Years*, was a deadpan joke on big hair and rocker hubris), then itemizes the failures of that revolt and marks punk as a refuge from a city that's only gotten nastier and more economically bipolar. Spheeris gives every indication of having gotten too close to her material, but her film's overall air of discombobulation is poignant in itself.

Her opening gambit—asking some fans queued up for a show about the first *Decline*—might seem needlessly self-reflexive, but Spheeris uses the original as an instant-cred all-access pass, and the responses she elicits set a gallows-humor tone that the movie only fitfully maintains (one boy says that in 1981, "I was an abortion that couldn't get paid for"). At first, frenetic concert footage and offstage patter (notably from Resistance lead singer Eyeball, who provides the closest the film comes to a Darby Crash star turn) alternate with fan interviews, but the kids in the pit soon consume all of Spheeris's attention.

L.A.'s current punk fans are teenagers who've been kicked out and kicked around. Kids like Troll, Filth, Why Me?, and Little Tommy the Queer get by on panhandling; many share a mordant wit and alcoholism in common, and most have been abused or neglected—which adds a frisson of black humor to one cop's dubious claim that the LAPD is "trying to get these kids back in touch with their parents." (The ghastly bracelet of self-inflicted cigarette burns on one girl's arm suggests innumerable unspoken horrors.)

Spheeris doesn't trust the immediate power of her raw material, so she throws all manner of sucker punches: keeping the camera tight on one boy, then pulling back abruptly to reveal his wheelchair; waiting until the last possible second to reveal the murder of another. She can't stop asking the kids if they feel sad—the answer, almost invariably, is No, which implies that numbness is a fail-safe survival technique. ("It's not really fun to be in reality," one glassy-eyed girl says.) Spheeris's approach sometimes smacks of tsk-tsk tourist pity, which might explain why *Decline III* never gets around to linking the euphoria of a good punk show with the oblivion sought after the lights go up.

Also reviewed in:
NEW YORK TIMES, 7/7/00, p. E10, Elvis Mitchell

DETERRENCE

A Paramount Classics and TFI International release of a Battleplan production.   *Executive Producer:* Maurice LeBlond and Steve Loglisci.   *Producer:* Marc Frydman and James Spies. *Director:* Rod Lurie.   *Screenplay:* Rod Lurie.   *Director of Photography:* Frank Perl.   *Editor:* Alan Roberts.   *Music:* Lawrence Nash Groupe.   *Sound:* Peter Meiselmann.   *Production Designer:* W. Brook Wheeler.   *Costumes:* Matt Jacobsen.   *Running time:* 101 minutes.   *MPAA Rating:* R.

CAST: Kevin Pollack (Walter Emerson); Timothy Hutton (Marshall Thompson); Sheryl Lee Ralph (Gayle Redford); Sean Astin (Ralph); Bajda Djola (Harvey); Clotilde Courau (Katie); Michael Mantell (Taylor Woods); Kathryn Morris (Lizzie Woods); Mark Thompson (Gerald Irving); Ryan Cutrona (Agent Dexter); J. Scott Shonka (Capt. Coddington); Rigg Kennedy (Howard); Joe McCrackin (Agent Williams); Scoot Powell (Noah); James Handy (Lancaster/President Buchanan); Graham Galloway (George Carvelli/Jeter); John Cirigliano (Martin Keller); Amit Mehta (Abu Hussein); Steve Loglisci (Nick Macario); Kristen Shaw (Alexandra); Robert Harvey (Agent Hunter); June Lockhard (Secretary of State Clift); Sayed Badreya (Omari); Roger Steffans (Daniel Golan); Leslie Harter (Sylvia Charles); Rod Lurie (John Desimio); Marc Frydman (Gestaing); Edward James Gage (Riley); Jack Angel (Secretary of Defense); Rosemary Lord (Female Translator); Buckley Norris (Isaacson); Fred Ornstein (Rubenstein); James Spies (Mark Stone); Uzi Gal (Iraqi Ambassador).

CHRISTIAN SCIENCE MONITOR, 3/10/00, p. 15, David Sterritt

Politics is in the air, and at the movies, too. "Deterrence" takes on volatile issues in the folksy setting of a snow-bound Colorado diner.

That's where Walter Emerson, fighting to remain president of the United States in the 2008 election, is stranded during a campaign trip. A few hours of downtime might seem like a relaxing prospect, but problems soon arrive. Asia is in a state of crisis. and now Iraq has invaded Kuwait, touching off an emergency recalling the Persian Gulf war of 1990—only this time the Iraqi dictator has lethal missiles aimed directly at American allies, and there's every chance he'll fire them if provoked.

Emerson has only moments to make his decision: Should he unleash his nuclear arsenal or rely on conventional weapons and diplomacy? Situations don't come more suspenseful, and writer-director Rod Lurie piles on more complications for good measure. Emerson became president only four months before when his predecessor died; he's Jewish, which causes some—including the Iraqi leader—to question his objectivity In dealing with an Arab antagonist.

The movie's isolated setting allows Lurie to explore international conflict from a high-tech perspective, as Emerson communicates with far-flung advisers, and a just-folks perspective, as everyday people watch these explosive circumstances unfold in the eatery. "Deterrence" has gripping ingredients, but several flaws. I'll let the largest of these pass without comment, since disclosing it—a gaping hole in the plot's logic—would give away the ending. The others are bad enough. For one, the setting is so conspicuously cramped that it makes the story feel contrived.

More important, the movie's political views are confused. Emerson "stands tall" in ways that sharply divide the people around him. The film presents this in a manner suggesting that he's a hero—yet in a public statement about the picture, director Lurie calls him a villain scarred by hypocrisy and racism. As a former film critic, Lurie presumably knows how to communicate ideas, but there's an unbridgeable gap between the movie he thinks he's made and the movie he's actually made.

Audiences are likely to ignore this film, on the reasonable ground that international affairs are complicated enough without movies adding to the perplexity.

LOS ANGELES TIMES, 3/10/00, Calendar/p. 14, Jan Stuart

[*The following review by Jan Stuart appeared in a slightly different form in* **NEWSDAY, 3/10/00, Part II/p. B6.**]

The doomsday thriller gets an old lease on life in "Deterrence." First-time writer-director Rod Lurie invokes the courtroom classic "12 Angry Men" as the inspiration for his one-set drama, but it's really a throwback to "The Petrified Forest," that 1936 chestnut in which gangster Humphrey Bogart holds a cafe's patrons hostage.

Simultaneously quaint and au courant, "Deterrence" is a crackling exercise in international gamesmanship whose high-stakes political circus is perpetually subdued by the bozos tossing peanuts from the gallery.

There are no gangsters in the snowbound Colorado diner in which President Walter Emerson wanders with an entourage of advisors and bodyguards, although there are many who would consider Emerson's responses to an exploding Mideast crisis to be of a grossly criminal bent.

Set in 2008, "Deterrence" reconfigures several White House scenarios from the last 20 years to produce a very plausible political imbroglio. Former Vice President Emerson (Kevin Pollak) has inherited his chief executive post midterm from the recently deceased president and appears to be the clear favorite to be nominated in the current primaries.

That he is also the first Jewish president does not become clear until an Iraqi leader invades Kuwait, heating up old tensions that had been simmering since the days of President Bush and Operation Desert Storm.

Within minutes of a TV news bulletin, the diner turns into a mini-Pentagon and broadcast station from which Emerson must decide the fate of Baghdad: to bomb or not to bomb. Pulling his decision in varying directions are advisors Marshall Thompson (Timothy Hutton) and Gayle Redford (Sheryl Lee Ralph), as well as a chorus of locals who have camped out for the duration of the winter snow and have very strong opinions of their own.

Despite its one-set locale, there are actually two dramas percolating in "Deterrence." A former film critic and investigative reporter, director-writer Lurie displays impressive political savvy with the ins and outs of split-second political decision-making. The spitfire exchanges between Emerson and his advisors have a nerve-tugging authenticity, raising some troubling questions about executive responsibility, America's stigmatizing of Arabs and the loaded perceptions that feed into a Jewish president making red-button decisions concerning the Mideast. Lurie leaves his own position somewhat ambiguous, although a devastating phone exchange between Emerson and a French minister leaves a slyly Francophobic aftertaste.

All good stuff. But Lurie undermines his high-wire act with the melodramatic carryings-on of the diner patrons: an obnoxious redneck, a visiting New York couple, a French Canadian waitress and the diner's disapproving owner. Everyone acts out; everyone has a hissy fit. The supporting cast is wildly uneven. The leads, thankfully, send sparks flying. Hutton is marvelously alert as Emerson's right-hand man, while Pollak grows more presidential—and more disturbing—with every passing scene.

NEW YORK POST, 3/10/00, p. 56, Lou Lumenick

"Deterrence" is a nuclear-war thriller with a difference: The bad guy—or is he the good guy?—is the president of the United States.

It's primary season, the year 2008.

Walter Emerson (Kevin Pollak), an appointed vice president who took over for a dead president, is campaigning in Colorado when he's stranded in a remote diner by a freak snowstorm.

The short, uncharismatic Emerson suddenly gets a chance to be very presidential.

Most of America's troop strength is tied up in a confrontation with China. Saddam Hussein's son takes advantage of the situation, and Iraq invades Kuwait again.

American soldiers are killed, and Emerson decides to go George Bush one better. Rather than launching another Gulf war, he gives Iraq 90 minutes to begin pulling back its troops—or he's going to nuke Baghdad!

That's the rather riveting premise of "Deterrence," a very effective updating of the underrated Cold War thriller "Fail-Safe."

Rod Lurie, a movie critic for Los Angeles magazine making an impressive debut as a writer-director, wrings a great deal of suspense from the plot's many twists and turns.

Cast wildly against type, Pollak virtually defines the banality of evil—a totally unassuming guy willing to throw the world into chaos to put himself on the map.

Or is there a method behind his madness?

Timothy Hutton gives his best performance in years as Emerson's chief of staff, who is quietly appalled with the president's unilateral decision to make the threat.

Sheryl Lee Ralph is equally effective as the president's national-security adviser, who argues strenuously against Emerson's ploy, and Sean Astin has a neat turn as a civilian who supports the president.

With all the action confined to a single set (with outside action depicted on TV sets), "Deterrence" is a triumph of low-budget filmmaking.

VILLAGE VOICE, 3/14/00, p. 130, Jessica Winter

The United States as world's policeman gets a stern once-over from the oafish *Deterrence,* in which a newly unelected president (think Gerald Ford) gets snowed in at a Colorado diner that fatuously doubles as a cross-section of America (dumb immigrant, dumb redneck, angry black guy) and, faced with a scenario similar to the Gulf War, decides to drop a nuclear bomb on Baghdad. The film begins and ends with footage of FDR intoning "I hate war," something the film takes two interminable hours to say.

Also reviewed in:
CHICAGO TRIBUNE, 3/17/00, Friday/p. A, Michael Wilmington
NEW YORK TIMES, 3/10/00, p. E27, Stephen Holden
VARIETY, 5/24-30/99, p. 71, David Stratton
WASHINGTON POST, 3/17/00, p. C1, Stephen Hunter
WASHINGTON POST, 3/17/00, Weekend/p. 46, Desson Howe

DIGIMON: THE MOVIE

A 20th Century Fox release of a Fox Kids presentation of a Saban Entertainment/Toei Animation Company production. *Executive Producer:* Tan Takaiwa, Teruo Tamamura, Tsutomu Tomari, Yasushi Mitsui, Makoto Shibazaki, Makoto Yamashina, and Makoto Toriyama. *Producer:* Terry-Lei O'Malley. *Director:* Mamoru Hosoda and Shigeyasu Yamauchi. *Screenplay:* Reiko Yoshida. *From an original concept and character design by:* Akiyoshi Hongo. *Director of Photography:* Shigeru Ando. *Editor:* Douglas Purgason and Gary A. Friedman. *Music:* Udi Harpaz and Amotz Plessner. *Music Editor:* Jim Wheeler, Liz Magro, Mark Ryan, and Mark Rubino. *Sound:* Mark Ettel and (music) Israel David and Eitan Shamy. *Sound Editor:* Johnnie Valentino. *Casting:* Paul Di Franco. *Animator:* Takaaki Yamashita, Hisashi Nakayama, and Masahiro Aizawa. *Running time:* 89 minutes. *MPAA Rating:* PG.

VOICES: Lara Jill Miller (Karir/Young Kari); Joshua Seth (Young Tai/Tai); Colleen O'Shaughnessy (Sora/Male Student); Philece Sampler (Mimi/Cody/Matt's Grandma); Bob Papenbrook (Red Greymon); Mona Marshall (Izzy/Terriermon); Michael Lindsay (Joe/Greymon); Michael Reisz (Matt); Wendee Lee (Young Tk/Little Girl 1/Party Girl 1/Little Kokomon); Dorothy Elias-Fahn (Tai's Mom); Doug Ehrholtz (Tk); Michael Sorich (Mik/Big Agumon/Gargomon); David Lodge (Parrotmon); Peggy O'Neal (Botamon); Brianne Sidall (Koromon/Kuramon); Jeff Nimoy (Tentomon/Phone Voice 1/Truck Driver 1/Kabuterimon/Floyd the Barber/Barney/Megakabuterimon/Cabbie/Kids); Bob Bucholz (Truck Driver 2/male Customer/Phone Voice 2/Voice Mail Operator/Uncle Al/Andy/Squad Leader); Elizabeth Rice (Boy 1/Sora's Mom/Operator/Kid 2); Anna Garduno (Boy 2/Palmon/Aunt Bea/Truck Driver/Kid 1); Neil Kaplan (Twin Boy 1/computer Voice 2/Hawkmon/Halsemon); Tifanie Christun (Birthday Girl/Grocery Girl/Biyomon/Yolei); Ralph Garman (Newsman); Paul St. Peter (Keramon/Infermon/Diaboromon/Kokomon); Tom Fahn (Agumon/Digmon); Michael Reynolds (Gennai); Kirk Thornton (Gabumon/Metalgarurumon/Omnimon); Laura Summer (Patamon); R. Martin Klein (Gomamon); Edie Mirman (Gatomon/Recorded Operator/Angewomon/Magnadramon); Steven Jay Blum (Computer Voice 1/Poromon/Flamedramon/Raidramon/Magnamon); Joseph Pilato (Metalgreymon); Lex Lang (Wargreymon/Omnimon/Rapidmon); David Greenlee (Professor); Bob Glouberman (Young Willis/Willis); Brian Donovan (Davis); Dave Mallow (Upamon/Angemonn/Seraphymon); Derek Stephen Prince (Veemon/Demiveemon/Pizza Guy); Robert Axelrod (Armadillomon).

LOS ANGELES TIMES, 10/6/00, Calendar/p. 8, John Anderson

[The following review by John Anderson appeared in a slightly different form in **NEWSDAY, 16/6/00, Part II/p. B7.]**

Like goblins in the forest or the Man in the Moon, the TV-generated phenomenon of "Digimon"—a.k.a. Digital Monsters—makes a certain amount of sense. The mythologizing of the unknown is a timeless human impulse, whether the content involves sea monsters, Martians or, now, cuddly bomb-breathing creatures spawned by the Internet.

If a fairy tale, however high-tech or improbable, can help kids wrap their heads around the vastness of cyberspace, it hardly seems either insidious or particularly novel.

On the other hand, it seems unlikely that Homer, the Grimm brothers or Jules Verne had a line of action figures to promote. "Digimon: The Movie," of course, does. And the only unknown that seems of any concern to 20th Century Fox is how many millions can be tempted out of its 5-to-10-year-old audience before this particular fad expires.

A few, we expect. Add what they saved on the lackluster animation and it should amount to a tidy profit. Granted, "Digimon: The Movie" is, and should be, of interest only to those who love the show; rather than watch, parents might want to take up smoking, so they'll have an excuse to wait outside. At any rate, the filmmakers could have made it look a little better than this.

The story begins by flashing back eight years, to the virtual infancy of both the World Wide Web and Tai, the leader of the "DigiDestined," the group of kids including Sora, Matt, Izzy and

Joe who are attuned to the evil potential of the DigiWorld. "Sometimes," one says, "you've got to save the world." (If you smell a little "Paradise Lost" in all this, you're not far off.)

The gist of the story line is the birth on the Internet of a new, dangerous digimon, which consumes computer data at an alarming rate and even manages to launch U.S. nuclear warheads and aim them at Japan. (The fact that this is a mostly Japanese production shouldn't be lost on anyone.) Viruses are involved. So are Tai's mother's health-food concoctions (liver sticks, beefjerky shakes, potato juice).

Do justice and virtue prevail? Duh. It's an awfully confusing journey, unless you're of pro-Digi-ous intelligence. Or a digimaniac. Or just 6.

A word of caution: The "prelude" that runs before "Digimon: The Movie"—in essence, a commercial for the movie you've already paid to see—is thoroughly obnoxious, promoting elitist, consumerist and anti-intellectual behavior among children who, considering all of their other influences, don't need any help. In other words, if you're late for the show, don't sweat it.

NEW YORK POST, 10/6/00, p. 21, Lou Lumenick

"Digimon: The Movie," the feature version of the popular animated TV series (a knockoff of you-know-what), is the second Japanese production this year featuring a monster that cripples Tokyo by eating computer data.

Brightly colored and pleasingly drawn, "Digimon" has more fun with this idea than "Godzilla 2000" did and, in its first half at least, refreshingly refuses to take itself as seriously as Fox's last foray into animation, the deadly "Titan AE."

The villain is a rapidly multiplying digital monster corrupted by a computer virus—and the only force that can stop them are good digital monsters and their human kid friends, the DigiDestined.

The kid voices, by a non-star cast, are lively, and as much footage is devoted to domestic complications as the children's struggle to save the world.

"Digimon" is surprisingly tolerable, at least for the first 45 minutes, which include a five-minute prologue featuring characters from another cartoon series, "Angela Anaconda," poking gentle fun at the whole Digimon phenomenon.

But after the monster is subdued, then there's a much less humorous, and more mindlessly violent second half. The kids, and an endless array of other digital' monsters, battle another villainous mutant amid dialogue loaded with techno-babble.

Kids may like it, but adults will be among the DigiBored.

SIGHT AND SOUND, 3/01, p. 45, Kate Stables

Tokyo, the present. Toddler Kari finds a digital egg emerging out of her father's computer screen. She and elder brother Tai hide and tend the creature that hatches from the egg; known as a "digimon", or digital monster, it undergoes a series of transformations, or "digivolutions", to emerge as a vast fire-breathing dinosaur. The digimon breaks out of Kari and Tai's apartment to engage in a streetfight with an evil digimon, which it kills with help from Kari.

Four years later, Kari and Tai are part of a network of "DigiDestined"—children who are secret keepers of online digital monsters. One day Tai and his computer boffin friend Izzy spot a baby digimon merging online with a computer virus. The digimon turns into the powerful and evil Diaboromon and begins to consume data at a vast rate, blocking worldwide communication channels and launching a nuclear missile against Tokyo. Tai, Izzy and the DigiDestined conduct an online battle with their digimons, defeating Diaboromon with a blizzard of e-mail.

Four years later, on holiday in New York, the DigiDestined find themselves menaced by a giant rogue digimon, Kokomon. After much persuading, his American keeper Wallace reveals Kokomon's secret—he was infected by the Diaboromon virus during the previous battle. Forming a team, the children conduct a digimon assault which defeats the virus and reinstates Kokomon as a good digimon.

Digimon Digital Monsters The Movie is the kind of frenetic, cacophonous and brightly coloured kids' cartoon offering which adults wearily condemn as a videogame thinly masquerading as a film. But to dismiss the movie, which features a host of shape-shifting creatures called digimon which can switch between cyberspace and the real world, along these lines would be a wicked calumny against most videogames, which can boast far more considered content than the insipid assembly-line animation and repetitive narrative on offer here. The proper grounds for condemning *Digimon* is that it is, in fact, three Japanese *anime* shorts thinly masquerading as a feature film (the filmmakers have attempted to weld together *Digimon Adventure, Our War Game* and *The Golden Digimentals* into a convincing whole by judicious use of voiceover). Armed with this information, the viewer can make some sense of the film's structural shortcomings, notably its relentlessly episodic nature and the several bizarre points of closure that fall mid-narrative. What knowledge of the film's unusual provenance fails to explain away, though, is the cookie-cutter characterisation of the child characters most of whom are computer buffs, charged with responsibility for the various digimon—and the frantic edits that render the battle and transformation scenes impenetrable to all but the keenest Digienthusiast.

The other great black mark against the Digimon movie—that it's a blatant rip-off of the *Pokémon* franchise frankly counts for very little. As in its televisual incarnation, *Digimon* is significantly sassier and funnier than anything *Pokémon* has fielded to date. Though it shares with the *Pokémon* cartoons a propensity for heavy-handed moralising about teamwork and character-building, here you'll find a pop-culture spoof occasionally digivolving out of the main plot. Monster battles in Tokyo streets are staged as a sly homage to *Godzilla* movies, and when one kid solemnly informs another that "There are actually two worlds. Our world and the digital world," we are momentarily in *Matrix* territory. Its web-conscious themes also throw up the odd neat narrative conceit, such as the decision by two of the film's young heroes to slow down the fast-replicating evil digimon Diaboromon online by bombarding it with innumerable e-mails.

But neither these knowing eruptions, nor a surprisingly hip soundtrack (including tracks from the Barenaked Ladies and Fatboy Slim, at nose-bleed volume) can propel this frantic merchandising fest into the category of movies that one would watch willingly. Adults pressurised into viewing it by the twin imperatives of half term holidays and pester power can comfort themselves with this: it is a mere 89 minutes long.

Also reviewed in:
CHICAGO TRIBUNE, 10/9/00, Tempo/p. 2, Vicky Edwards
NEW YORK TIMES, 10/6/00, p. E20, Lawrence Van Gelder
VARIETY, 10/9-15/00, p. 22, Robert Koehler
WASHINGTON POST, 10/6/00, p. C12, Stephen Hunter

DINOSAUR

A Walt Disney Pictures release. *Producer:* Pam Marsden. *Director:* Ralph Zondag and Eric Leighton. *Screenplay:* John Harrison and Robert Nelson Jacobs. *Based on an original Screenplay by:* Walon Green. *Story:* Thom Enriquez. *Music:* James Newton Howard. *Music Editor:* Jim Weidman and David Olson. *Sound:* Christopher Boyes and (music) Shawn Murphy. *Sound Editor:* Frank Eulner. *Casting:* Ruth Lambert and Mary Hidalgo. *Production Designer:* Walter P. Martishius. *Art Director:* Cristy Maltese. *Visual Effects:* Neil Krepela. *Digital Effects:* Neil Eskuri. *Character Animation:* Mark Anthony Austin (Aladar): Trey Thomas (Plio); Tom Roth (Yar); Bill Fletcher (Zini); Larry White (Suri); Eamonn Butler (Kron); Joel Fletcher (Neera and Juvenile Dinosaurs); Dick Zondag (Bruton); Michael Belzer (Baylene & Url); Gregory William Griffith (Eema); Atsushi Sato (Carnotaurs & the Herd). *Running time:* 90 minutes. *MPAA Rating:* PG.

VOICES: Alfre Woodard (Plio); Ossie Davis (Yar); Max Casella (Zini); Hayden Panettiere (Suri); D.B. Sweeney (Aladar); Samuel E. Wright (Kron); Peter Siragusa (Bruton); Julianna Margulies (Neera); Joan Plowright (Baylene); Della Reese (Eema).

LOS ANGELES TIMES, 5/19/00, Calendar/p. 1, Kenneth Turan

"Dinosaur" astonishes and disheartens, as only the most elaborate, most ambitious Hollywood products can. A technical amazement that points computer-generated animation toward the brightest of futures, it's also cartoonish in the worst way, the prisoner of pedestrian plot points and childish, too-cute dialogue. A look at our planet during the late Cretaceous period, 65 million years ago, "Dinosaur" also cost the earth and involved an almost incalculable amount of work supervised by co-directors Ralph Zondag and Eric Leighton: 1,300 individual effects shots created during 3.2 million processing hours and encompassing 100 million individual computer files on 70,000 CD-ROMs. The aim was to blend computer-generated characters with live-action backgrounds, and, on the visual level at least, it works beautifully.

A good example, and in many ways the film's most effective sequence, is its bravura opening, which follows a dinosaur egg on a quite incredible journey. Fought over or eyeballed by so many different dino species that only a brainy 10-year-old could name them all, the egg ends up in the mouth of a flying pteranodon as the camera dives in and out of grand scenery shot in Florida, Venezuela, Hawaii and the coast of Australia before depositing the egg with a family of Lemur monkeys on a remote island.

This kind of privileged, dazzling glimpse into a time that is no more is part of what we go to the movies for. Dinosaurs have always attracted animators (Winsor McCay's 1914 Gertie remains charming to this day) and though these beasts have apparently been slightly modified for dramatic purposes, to see the great panoply of extinct creatures lumber across the screen in their computer-generated physicality is to watch the best circus parade of all time.

But then, in a moment paralleling the unnerving one in " Singin' in the Rain" when Jean Hagen's silent star Lena Lamont opens her mouth and everyone cringes, these dinosaurs start to talk and we would give anything to put that particular genie back into the bottle.

It's not that the idea of speech per se is verboten for dinosaurs, though it should be noted that the vicious, villainous carnotaurs ("a mouthful of teeth with a bad attitude" is how they're described) are the film's most effective creations partly because they do not talk. And it's not that speech makes the film's Lemurs resemble puppets more than they need to, though it does. The problem is what the dinosaurs are given to say.

Initially the monkeys talk just to get the film's plot moving. Despite the fears of grandfather Yar (Ossie Davis, muttering, "We'll turn our backs and it'll be picking us out of its teeth"), mother Plio (Alfre Woodard), who must have seen "Tarzan," decides to raise the baby iguanodon to be the interspecies brother of her own children Zini (Max Casella) and Suri (Hayden Panettiere).

The baby grows into the full-sized Aladar (D.B. Sweeney), who feels kind of awkward when monkey mating season takes place. He'll have a lot of company in that, because the cloying adolescent dialogue around monkey love is one of the first indications of how lacking in anything worth hearing the "Dinosaur" dialogue (credited to John Harrison and Robert Nelson Jones, based on a screenplay by Walon Green) turns out to be.

It's not that lines like "I've got blisters on my blisters" are wearying in and of themselves, it's that "Dinosaur" has to be compared to its predecessors in computer-generated features, the Pixar-produced "Toy Story," "Toy Story 2" and "A Bug's Life." Nothing demonstrates the value of Pixar guru's John Lasseter's sharp story sense and ear for dialogue more than the difficulty of sitting through a CGI film that lacks them.

One of the odder things about "Dinosaur" is that while its talk is childish, it has a dark and somber core. Monkey mating season is barely over when, in a terrifying visualization of one theory of dinosaur extinction, a fiery asteroid collides with Earth, sending up an ominous mushroom cloud that blocks out the sun and blights the landscape.

Aladar and his monkey pals join up with a mixed herd of all kinds of surviving dinosaurs as they head for the traditional nesting grounds. On the way, Aladar makes friends with the 70-ton, 70-foot-high Baylene (Joan Plowright), an aging brachiosaur, and Eema (Della Reese), a cranky old styracosaur.

Aladar also meets up with the fetching fellow iguanodon Neera (Julianna Margulies). "You know how to catch a girl's eye, Stud," the regrettably irrepressible Zini tells him, but Neera has the last word: "That," she says in his direction, "is what's known as a jerkasaurus."

Neera's brother Kron (Samuel E. Wright) runs this herd, but he is guilty of thinking, well, like a dinosaur. Aladar, by contrast, has learned the virtues of teamwork and cooperation, perhaps from his monkey peers, perhaps from watching other Disney movies, and he clearly is the most modern guy on four legs, a trait even dinosaurs come to value.

Because of its theme of potential extinction and the scariness of the carnotaur, "Dinosaur" is the first Disney cartoon in awhile to be rated PG, but even with that the film's emotional level in no way matches its visual one or, for that matter, the emotional level of those Pixar films.

President Abraham Lincoln, or so the story goes, wanted to find out what the victorious Gen. U.S. Grant was drinking and send it to the rest of his commanders. In the same way, it's too bad they can't bottle what John Lasseter is drinking and send it to the gang at Disney. Despite their peerless visual magic, they need it, they really do.

NEW YORK, 5/29/00, p. 103, Peter Rainer

Disney's *Dinosaur* is the first animated feature spawned by the studio's new $80 million digital-production studio, and the film's budget has been estimated at about $140 million. I'm confused: Aren't animated movies supposed to be *cheaper* than live-action films? At this rate, actors like Mel Gibson and Harrison Ford may soon decide there's more money to be made as digitally enhanced 'toons than as flesh-and-blood performers. In *Dinosaur,* the digital beasties, often combined with digitized live-action backdrops, are so expertly rendered that you don't really miss actors on the screen. The musculature and overall expressiveness of the iguanodons and carnotaurs and brachiosaurs and all the rest compensate for what is otherwise standard Disney whimsy: A meteor shower forces a family of lemurs and its adopted dino into a trek with a multitude of other dinos across predators' terrain to the promised land. The moral is that survival goes not to the fittest but to the chummiest. You have to stay together to make it. All this may sound ripe for musicalization, but thankfully we're spared; the only score is James Newton Howard's *Lion King*-ish throbbings on the soundtrack, which take a backseat to the plummy voicings of the creatures by the likes of Ossie Davis, Joan Plowright, Della Reese, and Alfre Woodard. With few exceptions, such as the *Toy Story* movies, feature animation has reached the point now where technical wizardry has far outstripped story values and dialogue. *Dinosaur* is no different. If studios are going to be paying out hundreds of millions of dollars for these films, shouldn't some of that money go to writers whose imaginations match the visuals?

NEW YORK POST, 5/19/00, p. 43, Lou Lumenick

The opening scenes of Disney's $200 million "Dinosaur" will take your breath away—an iguanodon is killed by a rampaging carnotaur, and her egg is launched on an epic journey through the primeval forest.

The state-of-the-art digital graphics deployed here make the monsters in "Jurassic Park" look positively prehistoric—and Disney probably has a monster hit on its hands, despite a storyline patched together from other animated films.

In fairness, any narrative would probably seem mundane compared to the eye-popping visuals, which bring lavishly detailed dinosaurs to life amid live-action backgrounds photographed around the world.

It's so ultra-realistic that you come to accept such cartoonish conceits as dinosaurs who talk—and who are presented as smarter than mammals (who didn't exist at the same time, anyway).

Our hero is Aladar (voice by D.B. Sweeney), orphaned in the opening attack (shades of "Bambi") and raised by a family of lemurs (a la "Tarzan") after his egg hatches on a remote island.

When he grows to adulthood, massive meteor showers devastate much of the world—a spectacle that will thrill most audiences.

Aladar and his pals join up with a herd of dinosaurs led by the hard-driving but stubborn Kron (Samuel E. Wright)—setting up a romance with Kron's sister (Julianna Margulies) and a conflict with Kron straight out of the John Wayne cattle-drive classic "Red River."

Unfortunately, none of the characters is as involving as those in, say, "The Lion King," especially the self-righteous and humorless Aladar. His lemur surrogate parents (Ossie Davis and Alfre Woodard) seem like third-generation carbons from "The Lion King,"

There isn't more than a half-hearted attempt at comic relief—by a lovesick lemur (Max Casella)—and this is the first Disney animation in years without any songs. (Elton John, where are you when we really need you?)

But it does offer heavy doses of political correctness—Darwin be damned, it actually argues against survival of the fittest and goes as far as to feature what appears to be film's first elderly, inter-species dinosaur couple (Joan Plowright and Della Reese).

None of which is likely to matter much to the target audience —even if, after the first half-hour, the film may not delight adults as much as the two digitally animated "Toy Story" films and "A Bug's Life," which were distributed by Disney but produced by the more story-savvy Pixar.

"Dinosaur" is an expensive demonstration that all the spectacular effects in the world aren't enough to make a great film—but it's worth seeing for that stunning half-hour alone.

NEWSDAY, 5/19/00, Part II/p. B3, Gene Seymour

Engineers and accountants may be better equipped to review "Dinosaur," than we humble professional spectators. Every other word used to write about this movie so far has been a number, especially ones preceded by a dollar sign. As with the behemoths being depicted, Disney's digitally animated project overwhelms at the outset with both the density and enormity of its production.

As the studio is more than happy to tell you, it took roughly 12 years for computer technicians working at more than 500 work stations for more than 3.2 million processing hours to put together a film that occupies more than 45 terabytes of disk space. (Trust me. That's a lot of disk space. The equivalent of oh, let's say, more than 72,000 CD-ROMs.)

The cost for all this technological wizardry has been estimated from $150 million to $350 million, prompting muted snickers throughout the show-biz press peanut gallery, whose cheekier skeptics cling to the belief that anything that costs that much must have attracted flies in the process. One of the directors has publicly responded to such cheap shots by maintaining that, whatever the cost, audiences will see every penny represented on the screen.

No doubt about that. From its opening sequence, "Dinosaur" overpowers your field of vision with scenery so thick with grit and greenery that you'll swear you can reach out and grab a fistful of dirt. The team of animators, led by Ralph Zondag and Eric Leighton, has, at the very least, succeeded in pushing open doors to new ways of mounting animated characters upon real-life backdrops.

That opening sequence, by the way, is a wonder: An abandoned iguanodon egg—which, you assume from the start, contains our hero—undergoes a breathtaking, perilous voyage over land and sea before landing in a tree of talking lemurs, whose crusty old leader Yar (voice by Ossie Davis) is, of course, skeptical at best about keeping the egg's content alive. ("Things like that eat things like us," he says.) But—also of course—he's talked out of it by a soft-spoken member of the species named Plio (voice by Alfre Woodard), who decides that all God's creatures need to be cared for. Especially when they're as cute as this.

Sound familiar? It should. It's the narrative template for just about every Disney feature made since the Dawn of Time. Aladar (voice by D.B. Sweeney), the egg matter now grown up, is very much in the tradition of "The Jungle Book's" Mowgli, "The Lion King's" Simba and "Dumbo's" Dumbo-sweet-natured orphans separated from their own kind, misunderstood by the world and blessed with raw courage that comes to the fore at the right moment.

Aladar's challenge comes after a devastating meteor shower forces him and his adoptive family to join a massive caravan of refugee dinosaurs in search of water and greenery. Kron (voice by Samuel E. Wright) is the nasty, brutish leader of the pack, who—yes, of course—takes an instant dislike to the youngster, especially when he's making eyes at his sister (voice by Julianna Margulies). Anthropomorphic soap operatics aside, kids who are sticklers for authenticity in their prehistoric creatures will be pleased with the movie's depiction of every wattle, crevice and lesion decorating the characters' thick hides.

No, there are not as many flies on "Dinosaur," as pundits anticipated, But if it's so amazing, why isn't it great? Part of the problem is that, after a while, the visual innovations overpower the viewer like the unending tread of big-footed beasts. Also, it wouldn't have hurt to spend some of that money to tell a story as original as the movie's design—though I'm sure I speak for millions in thanking Disney for not including any stupid songs. By staying close to the corporate formula, "Dinosaur" comes across, for all its bluster and power, as the meekest of breakthroughs.

SIGHT AND SOUND, 11/00, p. 50, Leslie Felperin

An earthly land mass, the late Cretaceous period. Aladar, an iguanodon, is separated from his family and raised by kindly lemurs. One evening, a meteorite shower wipes out their island habitat and kills most of the tribe, but Aladar escapes to the safety of the mainland with his adopted lemur family. While wandering in the desert, Aladar and friends join up with a mixed herd of dinosaurs migrating to a new nesting ground. The leader of the herd, iguanodon Kron, enforces a brutal timetable for the march and has little sympathy for the weaker dinosaurs such as Eema, a styrachosaur, and Baylene, a brachiosaur. Ferocious carnotaurs and velociraptors plague the herd, picking off the weak.

Kron's sister Neera finds herself attracted to Aladar and his gentler, co-operative strategies for survival. At a desiccated lake bed, Aladar helps save the herd by encouraging Baylene to stamp up water to the surface. This, and Aladar's altruistic salvation of Kron's lieutenant Bruton from a carnosaur attack, threatens Kron's leadership. Near the nesting ground, Aladar and his friends are separated from the other dinosaurs. They find a short cut to the nesting ground through a tunnel, but when they go to find the others to help them through, tensions escalate between Aladar and Kron. A fight ensues from which Aladar emerges victorious. The herd makes it to the nesting ground and Aladar and Neera look set to mate while the herd settles r his leadership.

Even before such hugely successful pop-science entertainments as *Jurassic Park* and the BBC documentary series *Walking with Dinosaurs*, it was a truism in children's publishing and programme-making that you could never go wrong with dinosaurs. These long-extinct creatures have fascinated the imaginations of *Homo sapiens*, particularly the young of the species, ever since the discovery of the first 'dragon' skeletons in the early 17th century. This makes it all the more surprising that the Disney company, usually so canny about tapping into children's desires, have been so slow cash in on prehistoric subject matter. There were dinosaurs in *Fantasia*s 'Rite of Spring' section, but in very little else. Rivals Universal made a fair stab at the subject with their 1988 film *The Land before Time* (produced by Steven Spielberg), but this film wasn't as successful an animated feature as it deserved to be.

Whether planned or not Disney's tardiness in producing an all-dinosaur movie has reaped them the benefits of computer technology. The CGI that directors Ralph Zondag and Eric Leighton used for *Dinosaur* is undoubtedly magnificent, capable of rendering exquisitely detailed skin textures and impeccably realistic backgrounds, garnered by extensive 'research' trips abroad (at a cost of around $200 million, this is one of the five most expensive films ever made). Sadly, there is little sign of the benefits of evolution in the storytelling itself, which sticks too closely to a narrative template seemingly dating back to the Mesolithic era. Here, an orphaned creature (*Bambi*, 1942, *Dumbo*, 1941 *et al*) ends up saving his adoptive family (*Tarzan*, 1999) through disingenuous goodness and a luckily placed cliff ledge (*cf Snow White*, 1937, and others).

Those interested in modern theories of evolution will be intrigued, however, by the way the film revives amateur scientist and anarchist Prince Peter Kropotkin's once discredited but now fashionable theories about the utility of altruism in the development of the species, as propounded in his 1902 book *Mutual Aid: A Factor of Evolution*. Protagonist iguanodon Aladar (even his name has an altruistic echo) is put in conflict with the fiercely Darwinian herd leader Kron, who preaches that only the strong will survive. Kron's defeat could be read as either a triumph of Kropotkinism, or perhaps as Disney's attempt to play to the Middle-American creationist lobby, a constituency the company has recently alienated with its recognition of the rights of gay employees and other liberal temperings in its corporate policies. Nonetheless, this doesn't help the film-makers escape the melancholy historical irony known to every schoolchild over the age of eight: regardless of whatever evolutionary strategy the dinosaurs here 'adopt', they, somewhat like the Native Americans who triumph at the end of *Pocahontas*, still face a bleak future.

VILLAGE VOICE, 5/23/00, p. 146, Jessica Winter

Twelve years and $200 million in the making, the debut feature from Disney's digital studio finally lumbers into view, clutching in its jaws a *Newsweek* cover story promising that "the hearts of millions of little boys and girls are going to race at this bone-crunching spectacle." The wee bairns certainly deserve more blood and entrails floating in their ciné-soup, but inappropriate gushing notwithstanding, *Dinosaur* cuts a bland, compliant figure, its narrative and characterizations subservient to splashy feats of CGI legerdemain. Aladar (voiced by D.B. Sweeney), an orphaned dinosaur raised by lemurs, is the Moses/Tarzan figure who battles Darwinian tyrant Kron (Samuel E. Wright) for command over a massive group of refugees searching for water and grazing land; thus *Dinosaur* amounts to 80 minutes of discouraged Cretaceous trudging, punctuated by the occasional fight or stampede and one pyrotechnic coup: a truly thrilling meteor shower. Aladar and the rest move robotically, their facial movements apparently patterned after Teddy Ruxpin's, but their skin and musculature have the every-nook-and-cranny resolution of a really boss video game, as do the deft meldings of real landscapes with computerized imagery. *Dinosaur* takes one more earth-shaking step toward a movie world computer-generated by George Lucas clones, in which technology is not the handmaiden of storytelling but the domineering bride. Where are those humanist wizards at Pixar when you need them?

Also reviewed in:
CHICAGO TRIBUNE, 5/19/00, Friday/p. A, Mark Caro
NEW YORK TIMES, 5/19/00, p. E10, A. O. Scott
NEW YORKER, 5/29/00, p. 142, David Denby
VARIETY, 5/15-21/00, p. 25, Todd McCarthy
WASHINGTON POST, 5/19/00, p. C1, Stephen Hunter
WASHINGTON POST, 5/19/00, Weekend/p. 45, Desson Howe

DISAPPEARANCE OF FINBAR, THE

A Film 4 International release of a Channel Four Films/Pandora Cinema presentation of a First City Features/Samson Films/Victoria Film production. *Executive Producer:* Jonathan Olsberg, Ole Sondberg, and Rod Stoneman. *Producer:* Bertil Ohlsson and Martin Bruce-Clayton. *Director:* Sue Clayton. *Screenplay:* Sue Clayton and Dermot Bolger. *Based on the novel "The Disappearance of Rory Brophy" by:* Carl Lombard. *Director of Photography:* Eduardo Serra. *Editor:* J. Patrick Duffner. *Music:* Davy Spillane. *Choreographer (Tango):* Jan Aström and Rosario Rojas. *Choreographer (Irish):* Cindy Cummins *Sound:* Ron Bailey and (music) Colin Boland. *Casting:* Nuala Moiselle and Louise Thuren. *Art Director:* Ned McLoughlin, Conor Devlin, and Bengt Fröderberg. *Special Effects:* Maurice Foley. *Costumes:* Marie Tierney and Kersti Vitali. *Make-up:* Morna Ferguson and Maria Strid. *Running time:* 103 minutes. *MPAA Rating:* Not Rated.

CAST: Luke Griffin (Danny Quinn); Jonathan Rhys Meyers (Finbar Flynn); Sean Lawlor (Michael Flynn); Jake Williams (Young Finbar Flynn); Robert Hickey (Young Danny Quinn); Eleanor Methven (Pat Flynn); Marie Mullen (Ellen Quinn); Don Foley (Grandpa Quinn); Conor Fitzgerald (Fergal Flynn); Aoife Doyle (Jodie Flynn); Lorraine Pilkington (Katie Dunnigan); Laura Brennan (Sinead); Tina Kellegher (Ms. Byrne, School Teacher); Sean McGinley (Detective Roche); Barry McGovern (Action Committee Chairman); Clara Wong (Girl in Chip Shop); Derry Power (Seamus, Barman); Larry Murphy (Bouncer); Joe Savino (Luke, Talent Scout); Rob Brown (Pop Singer); Louise Loughman and Pamela Flood (Pop Video Dancers); Jan Mybrand (Immigration Officer); Per Mattsson (Karl); Lina Englund (Girl in Bar); Li Wen (Chinese Man); Zheng Wei (Chinese Woman); Juhani Haapala (Man in Store); Lille-Mor Falk (Woman in Store); Mikael Töyrä (Big Finnish Driver); Kent Sturk (Man in Kiosk); Kurt Johannsson and Olof Mukka (Singing Miners); Sten Ljunggren (Finn Bar Barman); Antti Reini (Antti); Thomas Hedengran (Matti); Lennart Johansson (Pauli); Thomas Laustiola (Jukka); Fanny Risberg (Abbi); Sif Ruud (Johanna, Abbi's Grandmother); Erkki Junkkarinen and Markus Allan (Tango Singers).

NEW YORK POST, 3/17/00, p. 48, Jonathan Foreman

"The Disappearance of Finbar" is supposed to be saying deep symbolic things about the glories of European unification, but the story can't bear the weight of all this meaning.

Part of the problem is that the Finbar character is both underdeveloped and unattractive—you don't get a sense of why anyone would miss him, let alone go searching for him in the snow.

Jonathan Rhys-Meyers, so good as a pretty-boy psychopath in "Ride With the Devil," here looks like Angelina Jolie's twin brother.

But it's his impressive Irish co-star Luke Griffin who gets the most screen time and does the most with his (also underwritten) role.

He's also the one who gets the sexy Swedish babe, played by Fanny Risberg.

SIGHT AND SOUND, 11/98, p. 46, Rob White

Fourteen-year-old Finbar Flynn leaves his Irish home town for a trial with Swiss football team AC Grasshoppers. A month later, he returns: he couldn't take the pressure. He slips back into an aimless life, arguing with his father, his schoolteacher and his best friend Danny Quinn. One night he climbs up an unfinished flyover and disappears. The community is rocked by the incident. Finbar's parents are distraught; an action committee is set up. Detective Roche shadows Danny, convinced he knows Finbar's whereabouts. Years pass. The action committee has become part of the town's social life. Danny is woken up one night by Finbar leaving a drunken message on Danny's ansaphone: he explains that he's in Stockholm, having fallen into a truck of sugar beets headed for Gothenburg.

Danny travels to Stockholm. He makes enquiries at the town hall, and tracks down a flat where Finbar lived. He's told that Finbar has gone to the far north. Up north, he is misdirected by some miners to the Finn Bar, a tango bar populated by suicidal Finns. At the bar he meets Abbi, with whom he sleeps. The following night he returns to the Finn Bar; Finbar appears. The reunion is spoiled when Danny realises that Abbi is Finbar's girlfriend. At a reindeer corral, Abbi appears to reject Finbar in favour of Danny. Finbar disappears again while Danny stays on in Sweden.

The Disappearance of Finbar, is, according to the film's producers, the first-ever co-production between the UK, Ireland, Sweden and France. Set in the infamous Tallaght housing estate in Dublin, and then in Stockholm and Lapland, it's an ill-conceived, pointless amalgam of various European and US-independent idioms (reminiscent of the work of Jim Jarmusch, Aki Kaurismäki, Mike Leigh, and Gus Van Sant). As part of the "epic" production, director Sue Clayton, whose first feature this is (she's made numerous documentaries and a short, *Heart Songs*), had a motorway flyover partly constructed in Dublin.   The flyover is meant to symbolise what the producers call "a community divorced from Dublin and the promised future Europe." However, if the structure still exists, it must be a reminder only of the film-makers' hubris.

That this film is technically accomplished only points up its creative flaws. Strong performances by the young leads (Luke Griffin from BBC's *Ballykissangel* as Danny; the impressive Jonathan Rhys Meyers from *Velvet Goldmine* as Finbar) and some beautiful photography by Eduardo Serra (*The Wings of a Dove*) cannot disguise the underlying weakness of the script.

One can see how the film's premises—it's based on a novel by Carl Lombard and adapted by the admired Irish novelist Dermot Bolger—might have seemed promising.   When Finbar disappears from his housing-estate home, he leaves behind distraught friends and family. Some years later his best friend Danny discovers Finbar went to Sweden and pitches up in Lapland, surrounded by mad, drunken, tango-obsessed Finnish immigrant workers. A kind of inversion and revision of Kaurismäki's *Leningrad Cowboys Go America*—Irish teenagers go Sweden—*The Disappearance of Finbar* is populated by eccentric outsiders united by a taste for strange music that is occasionally effective. It is surely no accident that Danny sports a Leningrad Cowboy-like quiff, though without the exaggerated style of the Cowboys. Finbar's father plays kitsch country music with the Roscommon Cowboys, while a sub-Leonard Cohen Europop song is written about Finbar's vanishing. And the Finns tango in a vodka-fuelled haze.

All this has 'quirky' written all over it, as if a sheaf of peculiar songs, locations and demented characters were enough to make a successful independent-minded movie or, more to the point, as if including these characteristics were enough to repay the debt to Jarmusch or Kaurismäki which the film-makers so obviously owe. (One of the film's producers, Martin Bruce-Clayton, worked on Kaurismäki's *I Hired a Contract Killer.*) But things are much more important to Kaurismäki and Jarmusch's work: ensemble acting, a sense of place rather than location, absurd humour mixed with melancholy, the threat of crime and violence, the pathos of unfulfilled lives. These elements are traceable here, but they hardly ever become vivid, and you're left instead with the impression of an assemblage of borrowed styles.

VILLAGE VOICE, 3/21/00, p. 144, Jessica Winter

One of the few discernible emotions evinced by Finbar Flynn, as played by Jonathan Rhys Meyers in *The Disappearance of Finbar*, is contempt—for his family, his best pal Danny, and his desolate concrete slab of a nothing Irish hometown. One day he jumps off a building and doesn't leave behind a corpse. He remains trapped in an enervating road movie-shelved so long that Rhys Meyers still appears to have baby fat—summed up when Finbar, who turns up in Finland (natch), asks whey-faced Danny, "You couldn't find anything better to do than to come find me?!"

Also reviewed in:
NEW YORK TIMES, 3/17/00, p. E18, Lawrence Van Gelder
VARIETY, 12/23/96-1/5/97, p. 43, David Rooney

DISNEY'S THE KID

A Walt Disney Pictures release. *Executive Producer:* Arnold Rifkin and David Willis. *Producer:* Jon Turteltaub, Christina Steinberg, and Hunt Lowry. *Director:* Jon Turteltaub. *Screenplay:* Audrey Wells. *Director of Photography:* Peter Menzies, Jr. *Editor:* Peter Honess and David Rennie. *Music:* Marc Shaiman. *Music Editor:* Stephanie Lowry. *Sound:* Peter J. Devlin and (music) Tim Boyle and Rick Norman. *Sound Editor:* Mark Mangini. *Casting:* Marcia Ross, Donna Morong, and Gail Goldberg. *Production Designer:* Garreth Stover. *Art Director:* David S. Lazan. *Set Designer:* Charisse Cardenas, Gary A. Lee, Beck Taylor, and Sloane U'Ren. *Set Decorator:* Larry Dias. *Set Dresser:* Carolyn Lassek. *Special Effects:* David Blitstein. *Costumes:* Gloria Gresham. *Make-up:* Melanie Hughes. *Make-up (Bruce Willis):* Gerald Quist. *Make-up Effects:* Gerald Quist and Julie Hewett. *Stunt Coordinator:* Jack Gill. *Running time:* 101 minutes. *MPAA Rating:* PG.

CAST: Bruce Willis (Russ Duritz); Spencer Breslin (Rusty Duritz); Emily Mortimer (Amy); Lily Tomlin (Janet); Jean Smart (Deirdre Lafever); Chi McBride (Kenny); Daniel Von Bargen (Sam Duritz); Dana Ivey (Dr. Alexander); Susan Dalian (Giselle); Stanley Anderson (Bob Riley); Juanita Moore (Kenny's Grandmother); Esther Scott (Clarissa); Deborah May (Governor); Vernee Watson Johnson (Newstand Cashier); Jan Hoag (Newsstand Tourist); Melissa McCarthy (Sky King Waitress); Elizabeth Arlen (Gloria Duritz); Alexandra Barreto (Flight Attendant); John Apicella (Hot Dog Vendor); Brian McLaughlin (George); Steve Tom (Lawyer Bruce); Marc Copage (Lawyer Jim); Rod McLachlan (Lawyer Seamus); Scott Mosenson (Wedding Guest); Brian Fenwick (Governor's Aide); Dusan Fager (Governor's Other Aide); Toshiya Agata (Sushi Chef); Joshua Finkel (Josh); Lou Beatty, Jr. (General Manager); E. J. Callahan (Principal); Daryl Anderson (Janet's Husband); Darrell Foster (Best Man); Michael Wajacs (Security Guard); John Travis (Chef Mike); Larry King (Himself); Stuart Scott, Rich Eisen, and Harold Greene (Themselves); Kevon Edmonds (Wedding Singer); Jeri Ryan and Nick Chinlund (Larry King's Guests); Reiley McClendon (Mark); Brian Tibbetts (Herbert).

CHRISTIAN SCIENCE MONITOR, 7/7/00, p. 15, David Sterritt

Not long ago, when Bruce Willis needed a hit he'd fall back on a "Die Hard" picture. Now he's found another formula: Make a movie with a little boy, and hope for the same box-office rejuvenation that "The Sixth Sense" brought last year.

Fortunately for audiences, his latest kid-centered offering—called "The Kid," appropriately enough—is fine summer fun. Willis plays an image consultant named Russ, who gets other people's acts together while letting his own life become an antisocial mess. He needs a major dose of self-knowledge, and he gets it when an unlikely visitor arrives on the eve of his 40th birthday: Russ himself as a nine-year-old, equally mystified by their time-warping encounter but loaded with clues as to how he became the creep he is today.

"The Kid" gets much of Its humor from the frustration Russ and his younger self, Rusty, feel toward each other's faults. What a klutzy kid I was, thinks Russ, flooded with memories he's spent 30 years trying to erase instead of understand. What a loser I'm destined to become, thinks Rusty distressed that his future self is an unmarried workaholic who doesn't even have a dog. But both dimly realize there are lessons to be learned here, and eventually they try to fathom each other in ways that might weave their personalities into a better-than-ever whole.

Willis has a solid gift for comedy and director Jon Turteltaub makes the most of it, rarely forcing laughs but letting them emerge from situations in their own good time. (One shudders to think what a cloying farce this might have been with Robin Williams in the spotlight.) Spencer Breslin is even better as the title character, cleverly blending crabbiness and congeniality. Together they make "The Kid" the standout comedy so far this season.

NEW YORK, 7/17/00, p. 82, Peter Rainer

Disney's The Kid is the official title of the new Bruce Willis movie, in order to distinguish it, I suppose, from Charlie Chaplin's *The Kid*. Disney should be so lucky. It's the latest in a burgeoning lineup of Hollywood movies portraying bighearted, yearning, family-minded men, including films as disparate as *Frequency, The Patriot, Gladiator*, and *Big Daddy*. Willis plays Russ Duritz, a smirky, caustic image consultant who makes a highly lucrative living bossing important people around; single and childless, he's on the verge of turning 40 when he starts to catch fleeting glimpses of a plump 8-year-old and thinks he's hallucinating. It turns out that Rusty (Spencer Breslin) is Russ's very own 8-year-old self magically transported to the here and now. Once over the shock, the two compare disappointments: Rusty is annoyed that his older self doesn't have a dog, that he isn't a pilot; Russ is mortified to be reminded of the cowardly loser he thinks he was. Guess which one of these two gets a total makeover?

Despite the two-ton whimsy, the basic premise is promising: Who wouldn't, on some level, want to reconnect with the kid he or she once was? The problem here is that the director, Jon Turteltaub, and his screenwriter, Audrey Wells, play things out almost entirely as a life lesson. Russ is ashamed of who he was, and so, naturally, he must be made to realize that he wasn't so bad after all and that the walled-in creep he has become isn't the real him. Russ turns out to be a sensitive kind of guy, with a soft spot for puppies and his (sort-of) girlfriend Amy (Emily Mortimer). She sees in the outer adult the inner child. Or maybe it's the other way around.

Turteltaub is aiming for a *Christmas Carol*-style classic. Russ the Scrooge looks back on who he was and reforms not only his present but his future. (Did I already mention that there's a pooch in that future?) The point seems to be that you have to accept, and love, who you are, but the point is smudged since Russ, through a bit of time-travel trickery, gets to rework his own childhood-defining moment and punch out some grade-school bullies. Interlarded with all this inspirational twinkliness is some standard Psych 101: The traumatized kid's inability to defend himself has resulted in gross overcompensation. The bullied has become the bully. In order to be a caring individual now, Russ needs to go back in time and fight.

The Kid operates on the assumption that the children we once were are the essence of who we are, and that, by not coming to terms with our inner dweeb, we're just making ourselves miserable no matter how successful we may become. I wish the filmmakers had taken a less gaga route: What's infuriating about people isn't the ways they've changed but the ways they haven't.

The Kid might have been a lot funnier, and less homiletic, if it had shown Rusty to be a pint-size jerk instead of a chubby-cheeked charmer.

Although Russ and Rusty are technically the same person, the relationship comes across essentially as father and son. Rusty's unruliness is squarely in the standard precocious-tyke mode; Russ's exasperations with him have a sitcom familiarity. (In those sitcoms, the kid is always wiser than the parent.) Russ's actual father is shown to have been a closed-off man himself, and Russ's mother died when he was young; in that curious logic by which Hollywood operates, Russ implicitly forgives his estranged father by accepting the boy he, Russ, once was. His conflicts are cured. Love makes him whole.

The Kid offers up a drippier variation of the latest movie cliché: the tough guy who, in loving his progeny, reveals a tender heart. In *The Patriot*, it is Mel Gibson's love for his family, for his children, that sets him off on the bloody road to righteousness; in *Gladiator*, we are subjected to the numerous meltingly delicate family reveries of Russell Crowe; in *Frequency*, a cop reunites with his long-dead fire-fighter father across time and ends up reconstituting his own life and saving his dad. Fatherhood is being used as a tenderizer in movies about manly men. The bonding ritual in *The Kid*, despite its sitcom trappings, is carried out with great solemnity, and Bruce Willis wears a long face throughout, as if he were trying to channel his performance from *The Sixth Sense*.

All this heavy-duty gooeyness about tough-tender guys is basically old-style Hollywood sentimentality in a new context. What these films are perhaps symptomatic of is the male-achiever version of having it all: The macho commanders of the corporate era have figured out that there may be more to life than raking it in and bossing people around, so now they want to be thought of as caregivers, husbands—homebodies. Except the gladiators, both old and new, in these movies rarely have a fulfilling connection with any woman, at least not until the fade-out. Women don't have much to do in these films except react to the guys with appropriately dewy sympathy; after all, they're *women*. The primal relationship is generally between man and boy, father and son, or else some domestic arrangement that is more of a faded memory than a reality. Even in a familial setting, the men are essentially loners, and that's also a part of the films' ersatz romanticism. These guys most likely are too damaged to be successful fathers and husbands, but at least they are made to know what they're missing, and what to reach for.

It's too bad that Bruce Willis isn't playing a movie producer in *The Kid* instead of an image consultant; if he were, the film's self-serving sentimentality might really have rocked. We're still left with a lulu of a high-concept weepie: A man searching for his inner child literally finds him. But I'm not all that impressed. After all, Hollywood has never had much of a problem locating its inner child. It's the inner adult who's always been awol.

NEW YORK POST, 7/7/00, p. 49, Lou Lumenick

Anyone who still doubts that Bruce Willis is one of the best actors working in films today should check out how he punches up this fluffy fantasy about a mid-life crisis.

Willis has a field day as Russ Duritz, a hard-driving image consultant—a sarcastic, overbearing jerk who barks orders at his father, a psychiatrist and total strangers with equal glee.

As his 40th birthday approaches, Russ suffers what appears to be a nervous breakdown—and experiences several hallucinations, including a close encounter with a red biplane that figures heavily in the proceedings.

Finally, he meets up with his 8-year-old self (played by a very funny newcomer named Spencer Breslin).

Whether it's real or not, both are horrified by the encounter.

Russ, because he's embarrassed by the pre-adolescent Rusty, a whiny, chubby loser who picks his nose and keeps getting beaten up by bullies.

Rusty isn't thrilled, either, to learn he's going to grow up to be a humorless drone who disdains French fries and has neither a dog nor a family.

Even worse, his grown-up self is not doing something fun like working as a pilot—but rather, as he puts it, helping other people lie about who they are for a living.

Willis and Spencer—who couldn't be more different in temperament or physique than the actor's last kid co-star, the eerie Haley Joel Osment in "The Sixth Sense"—have great chemistry together and their arguments are consistently amusing.

In the movie's funniest scene, a furious Russ discovers Rusty is doing his bidding by proposing marriage to an employee who's long had a crush on him.

This is basically a very modest journey of self-discovery in the "Big" genre—at least until screenwriter Audrey Wells (who wrote and directed last year's delightful "Guinevere") tries to pull a three-hankie finale out of left field.

Then it turns into a minor-league "Frequency," as Rusty and Russ are transported back to 1968, so that Russ can relive a traumatic childhood event he's blocked from his memory.

Any reasonably alert adult will have figured out Russ' problem at least a half an hour earlier—interestingly, it's exactly the same thing that caused Demi Moore to develop a split personality in her recent mid-life crisis movie, "Passion of Mind."

Its dime-store psychology aside, Willis' movie is fortunately much more enjoyable than his estranged wife's new-agey soap opera.

Lily Tomlin has a couple of priceless scenes as Russ' long-suffering but sharp-tongued personal assistant, and Jean Smart is very well deployed as a TV anchorwoman who helps Russ find his inner child.

But it's Willis who delivers the goods in scene after scene, triumphing over a thin script, often bland direction by Jon Turtletaub ("Phenomenon")—and so many over-lit close-ups that you can practically count the hairs on his toupee.

NEWSDAY, 7/7/00, Part II/p. B3, Gene Seymour

I can't think of any nation on the planet whose adult citizens need less inducement to "find the inner child" than these United States of America. The whole mass culture of bread and circuses and computer games and Sharper Image catalogs practically demands that its consumers be 8- to 13-year-olds in perpetuity. Some would even say it's what makes our country great and, on those days when I'm flipping through my collection of 1950s Little Lulu comic books or shooting marbles in the ophthalmologist's waiting room, I can't disagree.

So omnipresent is this "I don't wanna grow up" mentality that one wonders why movies like "Disney's The Kid" are needed to reinforce it. But then, the fact that this feel-good fantasy is entitled "Disney's The Kid" instead of just "The Kid" gives away its tactics. The movie is not even bothering to draw out your "inner child." It's slapping your inner grown-up upside its receding hairline, keeping it contrite enough to let the not-so-inner child continue to patch into the corporate mass entertainment Leviathan for more toys, games and rides.

Does this sound grumpy? Hey, I'm a giggling prankster compared with the movie's protagonist, Russ Duritz (Bruce Willis), whose veins channel liquid nitrogen instead of red blood. He's an image consultant, pulling down thousands of dollars a day to spin-dry personas of the rich and famous. Such lucrative feats of dubious magic have left Russ about to turn into a crabbed, lonely (if impeccably dressed) 40-year-old. Not even the combined warmth of a crackerjack secretary (Lily Tomlin at her crispest) or an adoring assistant (Emily Mortimer at her soggiest) can melt the ice cavern of Russ' soul.

Then a chubby kid (Spencer Breslin) materializes in Russ' duplex, flying a toy airplane. A quick check of each other's physical scars confirms that this intruder is Russ' awkward, dreamy 8-year-old self, who prefers being called Rusty. It's not a happy reunion. The adult is mortified to see what a klutz he was as a kid, while the kid is stunned to see that he's grown up to be a "loser" in a suit instead of a man with his own airplane, a family and, most especially, a dog.

Now the notion of a stunted grown-up finding completion in his (or her) younger being doesn't have to come across as hackneyed as it sounds. And because screenwriter Audrey Wells flashed gimlet wit in 1996's "The Truth About Cats and Dogs," one wants to give her the benefit of the doubt when she conceived this script.

But all traces of subtlety and intelligence are stomped by the in-your-face, crowd-pleasing mechanics of director Jon Turteltaub ("Instinct," "Phenomenon"), who guns the sentimental cues as if they were tanks pile-driving over your own emotional resistance. This movie doesn't just want to win your heart. It wants to beat the mortal stuffing out of it until it begs for mercy. If people cry at the end, it'll probably be from the pain of all that pummeling.

Somewhat surprisingly, Willis' easy-does-it star power provides what grace the movie has to offer and his interplay with newcomer Breslin (who comes across as a smoother, gentler Mason Reese) is ingratiating and neatly wrought. There's also an appealing turn by Jean Smart in her southern belle mode as a news anchor getting an on-the-spot makeover from a reluctant Russ.

NEWSWEEK, 7/10/00, p. 64, David Ansen

Image consultant Russ Duritz (Bruce Willis) is rich, mean, selfish and incapable of commitment. On the brink of 40, he has a mysterious run-in with, you should pardon the expression, his "inner child." Except that pudgy 8-year-old Rusty (Spencer Breslin) is no metaphor but a flesh-and-blood kid who is downright appalled by the man he's become—a guy with a twitch who lives without a dog or a woman and has a job teaching people to pretend to be what they're not. The grown-up is no more delighted to meet his former self—a pathetic dweeb who's the butt of schoolyard bullies. Both Russes, in each other's eyes, are losers.

One doesn't need to be much more than 8 to predict where "Disney's The Kid" is headed. The presence of Disney in the title ensures that eye-misting life lessons will be learned. But if the endpoint is a homiletic given, the journey itself is more charming, and less sentimental, than you might suspect. Screenwriter Audrey Wells ("The Truth About Cats and Dogs;" "Guinevere") fleshes out this potentially gloppy premise with real flashes of wit and well-earned warmth, and director Jon Turteltaub ("While You Were Sleeping") mostly keeps a close rein on the whimsy.

Willis proves again his deft comic touch—he knows better than most the adage that acting is reacting. Breslin is mulishly funny, his abrasiveness matching up nicely with the boorishness his older self has cultivated. British actress Emily Mortimer plays the woman Russ doesn't want to fall for. It's a generic part, but she gives it charm. The icing on the cake is Lily Tomlin as Russ's much-abused assistant: wry doesn't get any wryer. This is one both your inner child and your child can enjoy.

SIGHT AND SOUND, 12/00, p. 44, Rob White

US, the present. Russ Duritz is an image consultant about to turn 40. He bullies his secretary Janet, provokes his girlfriend Amy and dismisses his father's attempts at bonding. One day he finds a boy in his house: by an act of time-travel it's his eight-year old self, Rusty. Russ thinks Rusty is a wimp; Rusty thinks Russ should be married and own a dog. Rusty is being bullied. Russ takes him to a client, a boxer, to learn to fight. At the boxer's wedding Rusty proposes to Amy, Russ laughs it off. Russ tells Rusty how his life will turn out and works out that if he can remember his childhood the time-travel will be reversed. As they talk in his car, Russ remembers a fight with a school bully.

Suddenly he and Rusty are in Rusty's time, just before the fight. Using his new boxing skills, Rusty beats the bully. His father is furious at Rusty because the fight is stressful for Rusty's dying mother. Russ takes the tearful Rusty to a diner at an airport. There they meet 70-year old Russ who's a pilot, is married to Amy and is accompanied by a dog. Back in his own time, Russ buys Janet a holiday, is reconciled with his father and goes to Amy's house with a puppy.

In *Disney's The Kid* a crease in time allows Russ Duritz, a successful image consultant, to be visited, on the eve of his fortieth birthday, by Rusty, his eight-year old younger self. Hollywood time-travel comedies—notably the *Back to the Future* series and *Peggy Sue Got Married*—do various kinds of work: they are science-fiction spin-offs more or less enchanted by their paradoxical premise, baby-boomer nostalgia exercises that rosily illuminate the 50s and 60s and morality plays where family suffering is smoothed out in the impossible collision of the worlds of childhood and adulthood. *The Kid*, unlike *Back to the Future*, spends little time on the intricacies of time-travel. Director Jon Turteltaub (*Instinct*) and screenwriter Audrey Wells (*The Truth about Cats & Dogs*) take no delight in probing the paradox of how time looping back on itself might change the future. Their film doesn't even bother to include a humdrum device that supposedly engineers the travel. Instead a red plane careens above Russ' car, signalling the crease out of which Rusty will emerge. *The Kid* lacks the basic invention that in similar films tends to distract from the pathos of the premise.

Russ has to confront the dreams that he had when he was Rusty. Rusty's view of life, of course, wins out in the end, but not before the story has forked in two directions. First Russ travels back to Rusty's schooldays, when he was bullied and when his mother was terminally ill. Trained to box by one of Russ' clients, Rusty wins the schoolyard fight that Russ had originally lost. But this moment of victory leads only to Rusty's father being called to the school. Russ watches the ugly scene between father and son unfold and his adult eyes see the complexity of the situation. Rusty returns to childhood, Russ to his present where he's reconciled with his father and girlfriend. Before Russ and Rusty separate there's the second forking in which they encounter their older self at a radiant 70: Russ at 39 is thus only an aberration in Rusty's realised dream of life. This final contrivance literalises the film's underlying pattern of wish-fulfilment so there's no room for ambiguity, no sense of an unpredictable future. The fact that lives aren't like this is less important than the fact that the film shuts out any psychological interest in order to handcuff itself to the most banal interpretation of the idea that the child is father of the man.

The Kid works only intermittently because it tries to speak to children in the adult voice of nostalgic fantasy. It is sunny and antiseptic, which means it avoids at all cost reflecting on what life will have in store for both Russ and Rusty now the know their own future.

TIME, 7/10/00, p. 102, Richard Schickel

Bruce Willis has been lucky, lately, with mysterious little boys. In *The Sixth Sense*, he rescued Haley Joel Osment from his uncomfortable relationships with the undead. In the altogether more benign—but still rather charming—*The Kid,* it is the child (chubby, good-natured Spencer Breslin) who saves Willis.

The star plays an image consultant named Russell Duritz whose clients are scumbags and whose life consists mainly of barking into cell phones, snapping at his assistant (played by Lily Tomlin, who is nobody's doormat) and avoiding a meaningful relationship with a morally centered woman named Amy (Emily Mortimer). Into his rich, empty life the title character drops, and it takes Russell a little time to realize that Rusty, as the child is known, is himself when he was eight years old. It takes him a bit longer to understand that Rusty—whom he at first believes to be a hallucination—is the means by which he can begin to understand why he has, at age 40, become such a cold and driven creep, the Scrooge of sterility.

As Rusty scornfully discovers, he doesn't even have a dog. Or the highly developed taste for junk food he once enjoyed. Eventually the kid conducts Russell back to his past to find out what ails him, what makes him so angry with the world.

What he learns is not exactly earth-shattering. But perhaps the ordinariness of his troubles is one of the movie's points. It doesn't take much to turn a life sour. It can take quite a bit of effort to sweeten it after the bad, vengeful habits have set in. What's good about this movie, written with witty restraint by Audrey Wells, is that it doesn't try to explain how Rusty arrived in the year 2000 from 1968. He is not an angel from heaven; he's just a kid lost in a time warp, as puzzled as anybody else about the trip he's on, and often hungry. Nor does the director, Jon Turteltaub, make a big mawkish deal out of this strange voyage of discovery. It just unfolds, making no particular effort to loosen our tear ducts.

It's nicely played too—particularly by Willis, who neatly nails both his character's funny nastiness and his unsentimental reform once he begins to recover from his emotional amnesia. One doesn't want to oversell *The Kid*. It's a modest little fantasy. But it's also well made, unpretentious and refreshing—like a cool and fizzy bottle of soda pop on a hot summer's day.

VILLAGE VOICE, 7/18/00, p. 126, Jessica Winter

Supernatural child-bonding having paid off so handsomely last summer, Bruce Willis in *The Kid* (or *Disney's The Kid*, like *Jesus' Son*) once again plays a dead-inside workaholic who, with the help of a disturbed youngster, stumbles toward the enlightened path. Willis's snide, selfish image consultant has a phone headset grafted to his skull and a moony, masochistic girlfriend (Emily Mortimer) who puts up with his bullshit only because, she explains, "Once in a while I get a glimpse of the kid in you." Cue the titular scamp—a screeching, supremely irritating eight-year-old (Spencer Breslin) who turns out to be Bruce as a child—and much odd-couple downtime as our hero(es) slowly discovers that the child is the father of the man.

The Kid's pedigree stretches all over the pop-cult map, from *A Christmas Carol* (or rather, Richard Donner's *Scrooged)* to spousal counterpart *Passion of Mind* to Jean-Claude Van

Damme's *Timecop, which* meditated on the grave consequences of material meddling with the space-time continuum—concerns eschewed by Audrey Wells's sub-Fox Family Channel script in lieu of Freud 101 set pieces, including a boxing match between Big Bruce and Little Bruce. Director Jon Turteltaub, culpable for *Phenomenon* and *Instinct,* seems skittishly averse to framing more than one actors' face at a time, which means clumsy reaction shots and general inertia. Willis, whose limited range was touchingly deployed in *The Sixth Sense,* pulls his upper lip and delivers his lines with perhaps more fatuous smarm than necessary (though he and Breslin do share a cathartic weepfest late in the going that, as tear-jerking ambushes go, rivals the mute moppet in *The Patriot* crying for "Papa!").

The final scenes, involving Marc Shaiman's shameless orchestral nudging (which, given his *South Park* triumph last year, evokes an evil genius grinning maniacally over a baby grand) and multiple Bruces assembling on an *airstrip,* is nonsensical in a way that's insulting even for a mawkish time-travel film. Referencing *La Jetée* in the service of yuppie self-affirmation, *The Kid*'s denouement resembles the nightmare that would have transpired had execs foisted a toupee and a happy ending on *12 Monkeys.*

Also reviewed in:
CHICAGO TRIBUNE, 7/7/00, Friday/p. A, Michael Wilmington
NEW YORK TIMES, 7/7/00, p. E10, A.O. Scott
NEW YORKER, 7/17/00, p. 88, David Denby
VARIETY, 7/10-16/00, p. 19, Todd McCarthy
WASHINGTON POST, 7/7/00, p. C1, Rita Kempley
WASHINGTON POST, 7/7/00, Weekend/p. 34, Michael O'Sullivan

DIVINE TRASH

A Winstar Cinema release of a Divine Trash production. *Executive Producer:* Caroline Kaplan, Jonathan Sehring, Tim Kahoe, Brooks Moore, and Thomas W. Yeager. *Producer:* Cindy Miller and Steve Yeager. *Director:* Steve Yeager. *Director of Photography:* Jeff Atkinson, Jim Harris, and Steve Yeager. *Editor:* Terry Campbell, Tim Kahoe, and Steve Yeager. *Music:* Don Barto. *Sound:* Don Barto, Ted Ayd, Terry Campbell, Jim Harris, Bill Kaplan, and Bill Porter. *Running time:* 97 minutes. *MPAA Rating:* Not Rated.

WITH: John Waters; Jeanine Basinger; Steve Buscemi; Patricia Hearst; Ken Jacobs; Jim Jarmusch; George Kuchar; Mike Kuchar; Herschell Gordon Lewis; Jonas Mekas; Paul Morrissey; Mary Vivian Pearce; Robert Shaye; Mink Stole; John Waters Sr.; Patricia Waters.

VILLAGE VOICE, 4/3/00, p. 132, Amy Taubin

As suave today as his films were once gross, John Waters is an almost foolproof documentary subject. In *Divine Trash,* director Steve Yeager traces the career of Baltimore's most notorious filmmaker from his high school 8mm days through his collaborations with his great star, Divine. As always, Divine steals the show. Claiming that *The Howdy Doody Show* inspired his own career, Waters describes Divine as "Clarabell the Clown and Jayne Mansfield put together, the Godzilla of drag queens." Yeager uses behind-the-scenes footage of Divine eating the dog shit in *Pink Flamingos* as the climax of *Divine Trash.* "There's no law against it," says Waters, "because who was ever going to do that again?" While Waters is an amusing and articulate spokesman for his work, Yeager gets additional perspective from his parents ("He became entranced with the wicked witch in *Snow White,* Captain Hook in *Peter Pan,* and he went on from there"), the minister of the Episcopal church where Waters premiered his first film, Roman Candles, and various underground and indie authorities. Waters acknowledges his debt to Warhol, Kenneth Anger, and the Kuchar brothers, but when asked in a late-'60s television interview about his idols, the director responds, "My idols? The Manson girls and Russ Meyers, but I don't really pray to them."

Also reviewed in:
CHICAGO TRIBUNE, 5/26/00, Friday/p. J, John Petrakis
NEW YORK TIMES, 3/31/00, p. E15, Stephen Holden
VARIETY, 3/30-4/5/98, p. 44, Emanuel Levy

DR. SEUSS' HOW THE GRINCH STOLE CHRISTMAS

A Universal Pictures and Imagine Entertainment release of a Brian Grazer production. *Executive Producer:* Todd Hallowell. *Producer:* Brian Grazer and Ron Howard. *Director:* Ron Howard. *Screenplay:* Jeffrey Price and Peter S. Seaman. *Based on the book by:* Dr. Seuss. *Director of Photography:* Don Peterman. *Editor:* Dan Hanley and Mike Hill. *Music:* James Horner. *Music Editor:* Joe E. Rand, Jim Henrikson, and John LaSalandra. *Choreographer:* Daniel Ezralow. *Sound:* David Macmillan, and (music) Simon Rhodes. *Sound Editor:* Scott Hecker. *Casting:* Jane Jenkins and Janet Hirshenson. *Production Designer:* Michael Corenblith. *Art Director:* Dan Webster and Lauren Polizzi *Set Designer:* Kevin Cross, Al Hobbs, Andrea Dopaso, Suzan Wexler, and Will Hawkins. *Set Decorator:* Merideth Boswell. *Set Dresser:* Charles T. Gray, Ryan Mennealy, Gregori Renta, Mark Palmer. *Special Effects:* Allen Hall. *Visual Effects:* Kevin Mack. *Costumes:* Rita Ryack. *Make-up:* Toni G.. *Make-up Effects:* Rick Baker. *Make-up (Grinch):* Kazuhiro Tsuji. *Stunt Coordinator:* Charles Croughwell. *Running time:* 102 minutes. *MPAA Rating:* PG.

CAST: Jim Carrey (Grinch); Taylor Momsen (Cindy Lou Who); Kelley (Max); Jeffrey Tambor (May Who); Christine Baranski (Martha May Whovier); Bill Irwin (Lou Lou Who); Molly Shannon (Betty Lou Who); Jeremy Howard (Drew Lou Who); T.J. Thyne (Stu Lou Who); Lacey Kohl (Christina Whoterberry); Nadja Pionilla (Junie); Jim Meskimen (Officer Wholihan); Clint Howard (Whobris); Michael Dahlen (Customer); Rance Howard (Elderly Timekeeper); David Costabile (Biker Who); Mary Stein (Miss Rue Who); James Ritz (Crazy Mose); Deep Roy (Post Office Clerk); Jessica Sara (Sophie); Mason Lucero (Who Boy); Ben Bookbinder (8-year Old May Who); Michaela Gallo (School Girl); Landry Allbright (8-Year Old Martha); Reid Kirchenbauer (8-Year Old Whobris); Josh Ryan Evans (8-Year Old Grinch); Kevin Isola (Tree Trimmer); Rachel Winfree (Rose); Mindy Sterling (Clarnella); Gavin Grazer (Yodeler); Walter Franks (Clerk); Verne J. Troyer (Band Member); Clay Martinez (Cook); Q'Orianka Kilcher (Little Choir Member); Reid Kirchenbauer (Kid); Caroline Williams (Tiny Who Woman); John Short (Tiny Who Man); Grainger Esch (Near Miss Who); Eva Burkley (Pudding Chef); Bryce Howard (Surprised Who); Charles Croughwell (Balloon Who); Frank Welker (Voice of Max the Dog); Anthony Hopkins (Narrator).

CHRISTIAN SCIENCE MONITOR, 11/17/00, p. 17, David Sterritt

There are two schools of thought about how to decorate a Christmas tree. One believes in enhancing the tree with a tasteful smattering of ornaments so its natural beauty remains visible. The other finds the ornaments more fun than the tree itself, hanging every branch with as many baubles and bangles as it can hold. Neither school is "correct," and each finds plenty of members as the holiday season rolls around.

If it were a tree instead of a movie, "How the Grinch Stole Christmas" would represent the second category. This year's first bona-fide Yuletide entertainment is big, brash, colorful, and laden with so many gimmicks that you can hardly detect the old-fashioned message it carries in its heart.

The message is there, to be sure, along with marvelous flashes of the crazy-quilt wit that makes Dr. Seuss books the family-fun classics they are. But you cant help feeling there's a quieter, more natural kind of cheer that the movie doesn't quite reach, because its makers cared more about dazzling our senses than celebrating the Christmas spirit in itself.

Jim Carrey plays the title character, a mountain-dwelling monster whose grouchy disposition becomes even more so when the residents of nearby Whoville get ready for their annual dose of Yuletide merriment. Visiting the town to make some mischief, he meets Cindy Lou Who, a little girl who wonders why her neighbors greet the season with more hustle and bustle than generosity and joy. Her quest for an answer brings her closer to the green-skinned Grinch, who's hatching a nefarious plot to steal Whoville's holiday goodies.

Carrey is the movie's best asset, making the most of his prodigious comic gifts. Also fun is the eye-spinning color scheme dreamed, up by director Ron Howard, and the nonstop sense of movement.

Less appealing are the film's occasional touches of vulgarity, smacking more of Hollywood childishness than Dr. Seuss' heartily clean-cut visions. Also disappointing is the absence of any first-rate comic talent to provide a foil for Carrey's manic acting. It's not hard to name Christmas movie classics with more riches to offer, such as the Alastair Sim version of "A Christmas Carol" or Jean Shepherd's hilarious "A Christmas Story."

It's likely that "How the Grinch Stole Christmas" will stand with this year's most popular movies. But deep down, this big-budget holiday blockbuster seems as materialistic as the gift-obsessed Whovillians it pokes fun at. And that's a letdown at this special time of year.

LOS ANGELES TIMES, 11/17/00, Calendar/p. 1, Kenneth Turan

"Dr. Seuss' How the. Grinch Stole Christmas" is one overstuffed movie, but it's by no means a turkey. Yes, it's odd to see a $ 100-million-plus extravaganza that mocks materialism and extols simplicity. Yes, the film's frenetic attempts to create a full-length feature film out of a slender, albeit beloved, children's book can be exhausting. Finally, however, the lively and amiable spirit of the endeavor converts our inner curmudgeon just as the spirit of Christmas eventually overpowered that larcenous Grinch.

A major holiday presence since it was published in 1957, so popular it's even sold 24,000 copies in Latin (under the title "Quomodo Invividosulus nomine Grinchus Christi natalem abrogaverit"), "Grinch" has also been successful as a 1966 Boris Karloff-narrated Chuck Jones animated featurette.

But that made-for-TV item lasted less than 30 minutes, and achieving good results at close to two hours seemed an almost impossible task. Making that stretch possible was what turned out to be a delicate balancing act between four powerful forces that could have clashed but ended up in harmony: Ron Howard's balanced direction, a cheerful and inviting look guided by production designer Michael Corenblith and visual effects supervisor Kevin Mack, Jeffrey Price & Peter S. Seaman's clever script ideas and, the sine qua non, Jim Carrey as the Grinch.

In a part he seems almost predestined to play, Carrey uses his unequaled physicality and a face so mobile it seems computer-generated to turn the grumpy green monster into an antic combination of Chewbacca and Jerry Lewis. Holed up in a lair on Mt. Crumpit that's part Bat Cave, part an especially messy teenager's room, this character comes alive not as a person but as a creature, someone capable of treating his dog Max as an equal and, in a voice that's part Karloff, part W.C. Fields and part Sean Connery, arguing violently with a sassy echo.

Though Carrey has called the 92 days he spent in the hand-dyed, yak-fur Grinch suit designed by Rick Baker "like being buried alive on a daily basis," the remarkable thing about his performance is that you'd never know it. No amount of makeup can mask or hinder the actor's ability to make crazy faces, and if he seems too much in overdrive from time to time, that's just the way it has to be.

Just as arresting visually is the village of Whoville, which, despite verging on being over-designed, manages to come off as a playful, old-fashioned toyshop of a town whose almost but not quite human residents say "what the hey" and where everyone really, really, really loves Christmas.

Think of Mayberry on an insulin drip, think of a Disneyland that makes the Anaheim one look restrained, and you'll have an idea of what 52,000 Christmas lights, 8,200 ornaments, 1,938 candy canes and more than five miles of electrical wire can accomplish when joined to a wacky architectural spirit that production designer Corenblith says was inspired by the personal design interests of Seuss' alter ego, Theodor Geisel.

Without insider knowledge, it's hard to say whether the production team or the scriptwriters came up with some of the niftiest features of Whoville, like a "Dumpit to Crumpit" garbage chute that the Grinch uses as an expressway to town, and the stamp the Whoville post office puts on packages that need to be expedited: "Heckuvarush."

These touches indicate the cleverness with which writers Price and Seaman (who both also worked on "Who Framed Roger Rabbit") approached the task of fleshing out the original Seuss narrative, which now takes up roughly the second half of the film. They've expanded the roles of characters already in the book, like Max the dog and Cindy Lou, the curious little girl, and they've come up with an amusing back story detailing why, in addition to having a heart two sizes too small, the Grinch has such an animus toward Christmas.

Doing her research, Cindy Lou discovers that the Grinch, Whoville mayor May Who (Jeffrey Tambor) and town heartthrob Martha May Whovier (Christine Baranski) were once classmates involved in a romantic triangle that did not end well. Can the Grinch, who still keeps a mailbox in town despite his Mt. Crumpit residence, be reintegrated into Whoville society? One thing for sure, it won't be easy.

Riding herd on all this commotion is director Howard, whose innate earnestness as a director not only matches Cindy Lou's but also turns out to be the perfect attitude when paired with the script's wackiness and Carrey's mania. With anyone less sane in charge, this "Grinch" might have tilted too much in unfortunate directions.

Still, even this "Grinch" can wear on you from time to time, as it either runs out of things to do or stops dead to listen to one of its several underwhelming songs. And there are moments when Seuss' philosophy ("Maybe Christmas doesn't come from a store. Maybe Christmas ... perhaps ... means a little bit more!") threatens to get buried under all those visual gimcracks.

But on the other hand, "Grinch" wears its virtues lightly, and its dearth of gross-out material is remarkable both for a Carrey vehicle and for young-skewed films in general. "That 'American Pie' stuff," Audrey Geisel, the author's widow, who had script approval, told Entertainment Weekly, "has no place in Seuss." That counts for a lot, especially at this time of year.

NEW YORK POST, 11/17/00, p. 53, Jonathan Foreman

By far the best and cutest thing about "How the Grinch Stole Christmas" is the dog Max, played with astonishing expressiveness by one Kelley, a soulful terrier mutt trained by Roger Schumacher, who also trained the dog in "As Good as It Gets."

That doesn't mean the movie is awful—it's actually pretty entertaining, even for grown-ups, once you get through the first 10 minutes—just that it's no kids' classic like "The Wizard of Oz."

Jim Carrey brings his usual manic energy to the title role, but little or no charm.

The costumes and sets, though vaguely reminiscent of the drawings in the Dr. Seuss book, are remarkably ugly.

And perhaps because the film is directed by Ron Howard—rather than an anti-sentimentalist like Tim Burton—stretches of it give off the sickly-sweet reek of studied whimsy.

Though most small children won't get the grown-up jokes scattered here and there, there is one moment of startling grossness, involving the dog's butt.

Still, the original story by Dr. Seuss (real name, Theodor S. Geisel)—lines from which are read by a subdued Anthony Hopkins—and some funny dialogue by screenwriters Jeffrey Price and Peter S. Seaman ensure that "Grinch" is never less than enjoyable, despite its flaws.

If you've never read Dr. Seuss' slim classic or the 22-minute cartoon narrated by Boris Karloff, the Grinch is a curmudgeonly creature who lives on a mountain outside the village of Whoville.

In the book, he doesn't look all that different from the inhabitants of Whoville. Here, he's not just green, he's also hairy as a "Star Wars" wookie.

And the early part of the film fleshes out the original tale by making that physical difference the source of the Grinch's grumpiness.

In this stretched-out version of the Seuss story, the Grinch sneaks into town and, in the post office, encounters little Cindy Lou Who (Taylor Momsen), an angelic blond child with enormous fake eyelashes.

She happens to be the only person in town who harbors reservations about Christmas, and who doesn't have a strange, disfiguring nose.

Without thinking, the Grinch saves her life from a postal machine, and when he disappears again, Cindy starts interviewing the townsfolk about the Grinch and his childhood.

Predictably, she finds out the Grinch hates Christmas because he was laughed at for his ugliness as a child—especially by a boy who grew up to be the present mayor of Whoville (Jeffrey Tambor)—and that he and the town's middle-aged vamp, Martha May Whovier (Christine Baranski), once shared a mutual crush.

Cindy Lou is determined to reintegrate the Grinch into town life, and at the same turn its communal Christmas into something less commercial and more open-hearted.

But her plan involving the Grinch doesn't go quite as planned, and, indeed, prompts him to "steal Christmas" before things can be resolved.

Carrey, Momsen and Baranski share screen time with Bill Irwin and Molly Shannon, but the latter are underused and almost unrecognizable under their makeup.

NEWSDAY, 11/17/00, Part II/p. 3, John Anderson

As the horror of Whoville, the mean/green one with the heart two sizes too small, the bad banana with the greasy black peel, Jim Carrey's "Grinch" suggests what the cast of "Cats" would have looked like after another 20 million performances: Paunchy, mangy and in need of remedial hygiene.

As a portrait of humbuggery poised for holiday redemption, Carrey is perfect—which is a lot more than can be said for "Dr. Seuss' How the Grinch Stole Christmas," the $100-million-plus version of the late Theodor (Dr. Seuss) Geisel's small story about the homey Whos and the misanthropic gnome who tries to ruin their holiday.

It's evident that no expense has been spared to turn the Seuss story into a live-action extravaganza—and Whoville into a cross between Munchkinland and a Kathie Lee Gifford Christmas special. Everyone there bears a passing resemblance to Wallace Shawn, the holidays have been grossly overcommercialized and the townsfolk are neurotic, social climbers or harried civil servants such as Bill Irwin's Lou Lou Who. Only his daughter, Little Cindy Lou Who (the muffin- faced Taylor Momsen), suspects the true meaning of Christmas—and that maybe the Grinch himself holds the key.

The Grinch hated Christmas! The whole Christmas season!

Now, please don't ask why. No one quite knows the reason.

We do now. The Grinch, it seems, was the product of an abusive childhood: The squat, bristle-coated, lime-complected fellow was picked on at Who school, laughed at by his fellow man (or Who, or What) and frustrated at love: His all-but-requited romance with Martha May Whovier (rhymes with Bouvier)—played as a youth by Landry Allbright and as an adult by Christine Baranski—was written off as Who-bris. After a particularly cruel Christmas episode, Grinch retreats to Mt. Crumpit to dwell alone.

The newfangled Grinch is no longer an uncomplicated, hateful, vaguely lovable personification of evil. He's just a big green cynic. And his climactic transformation ("Help me, I'm feeeeeling...") is pure nonsense. Obviously, he's been feeling things all along.

In addition to giving us "Dr. Freud's How the Grinch Stole Christmas," director Ron Howard and his Imagine Entertainment partner Brian Grazer have remained blissfully unaware of the law of diminishing returns. The original Dr. Seuss work runs only 212 lines of very economical verse, less than 1,400 words, and takes about seven minutes to read. The Chuck Jones cartoon—"How the Grinch Stole Christmas!" narrated by Boris Karloff—was only half an hour, less with commercial interruptions, and even then the producers had to pad the story out with songs and that break-neck sleigh ride. Multiply that running time by 3½ and you have the length of the Howard-Grazer version, in which you feel every prolonged moment.

The press materials proudly catalog the number of props, ornaments, outfits and makeup created, as if this somehow should validate the movie. It doesn't. What they forgot to budget for was heart. What was simple and uplifting in Seuss has been complicated and set designed into joylessness. Granted, Carrey is a manic, sarcastic Grinch, prancing, dancing and blitzing around his diseased-looking lair on Mt. Crumpit, a squalid den that suggests the interior design of Oscar the Grouch's garbage can. He'll make children laugh—I'm sure I heard a couple—because he really hates the Whos. The thing is, who can blame him?

SIGHT AND SOUND, 1/01, p. 49, Leslie Felperin

Inside a snowflake: the town of Whoville, populated by creatures called Whovians, prepares for Christmas. In a mountain eyrie lives the Grinch, a hairy creature who is inured to Christmas cheer because his heart is too small. The Grinch became a hermit when his schoolmates mocked his attempts at shaving, although town beauty Martha May Whovier still harbours memories of her attraction to him. Five-year old Cindy Lou Who has begun to doubt what Christmas is for. After meeting the Grinch during one of his visits to Whoville, Cindy Lou perceives there is good in him.

She nominates him to be Holiday Cheermaster for the town, a post he accepts, to the resentment of Mayor Augustus May Who, who taunted the Grinch when they were children and is now courting Martha May. The Grinch's investiture as Cheermaster goes wrong when he is enraged by the gift of an electric shaver and runs amok.

Bent on revenge, on Christmas night the Grinch steals every present and decoration from the homes of the Whovians. In the morning, May Who blames Cindy for inviting the Grinch to the town. Cindy's father Lou Lou Who defends her, insisting she has shown the true spirit of Christmas. The town sings a Christmas song, the sound of which reaches the Grinch on the mountain. His heart suddenly grows three sizes. After saving Cindy, who's come to visit him, from falling over a precipice, the Grinch returns all the presents to the Whovians, thus winning the heart of Martha May.

Theodor S. Geisel, aka Dr Seuss, was prompted to write the children's book *The Cat in the Hat* by his publisher's challenge to compose a story that would use some 250 words easy enough for a first-grader to absorb. After seeing *The Grinch*, the new live-action film adaptation of Seuss' 1957 classic *How the Grinch Stole Christmas*—about a Scrooge-like grump who steals all the presents from a town of snout-faced Crimble lovers—smart first graders paying particular attention to the dialogue might be able to expand their vocabulary with such words as "avarice", "recycle" and "garbage", the last a fairly good description of the film itself.

Seuss resisted for many years efforts by Hollywood to adapt his books, perhaps aware of the compromises the industry was prey to, having had an unhappy time writing the 1952 film *The 5,000 Fingers of Dr. T* before he co-created the UPA cartoon character Gerald McBoing Boing. This said, he sanctioned a few adaptations, the standout of which is the 1966 version of *Grinch* directed by Warner Bros cartoon auteur Chuck Jones, which gave life to Seuss' charming curvilinear and primary hued characters and backgrounds with minimum fuss.

Faithful to the book, the Jones cartoon runs a mere 26 minutes, even with the song 'You're a Mean One, Mr Grinch' which the makers of *The Grinch* have incorporated into this film. In order to pad out the plot sufficiently to fill up a feature, director Ron Howard and screenwriters Jeffrey Price and Peter S. Seaman have dumped all sorts of junk into the stew here, including flashbacks to the Grinch's childhood, a love interest played by Christine Baranski (one of the best things in the film) and the young Cindy, a moppet so impossibly sweet she could induce a diabetic shock. These interventions muddy the clarity of the original tale, while the critique of consumerism reeks of bad faith considering how heavily merchandised the film has been in the US.

Vaguely redeeming features include Jim Carrey's lead turn, a hairy echo of his exercise in latex and green face paint for *The Mask*. Rick Baker's make-up allows Carrey enough freedom to gum and grimace as we expect of him and to reproduce reasonably well the exaggerated postures and poses of Seuss' and Jones' versions of the character. Sadly, the ruthless impishness that marks his usual style seems watered down here for young audiences. There are a few genuinely funny moments: one where the Grinch reviews his diary for the day ("Four o'clock: wallow in self-pity. Five o'clock: stare into the abyss") and one where, finding himself uncontrollably beginning to speak in Seussian rhymes, he corrects his end-rhyme "but how?" to "but in what way?"

VILLAGE VOICE, 11/28/00, p. 133, J. Hoberman

Is the Grinch, that nasty creature who steals Christmas from the Who people in the celebrated Dr. Seuss book, a sadist? He rejects prevailing religious dogma, suffers a sort of solitary imprisonment, abuses his pet dog, appears to take pleasure in self-abnegation, and—especially in the current movie version—captivates a fearless and innocent young girl.

Expensively expanded from Seuss (and the half-hour Chuck Jones animation that has been a TV staple for three decades), *How the Grinch Stole Christmas* would seem to be director Ron Howard's bid for immortality. The movie is intended to be a perennial that will flower at the box office every holiday season. Considerable effort has gone into the production: Whoville is a regular Emerald City whose inhabitants are tricked out with adorable prosthetic snouts—except for the little girl, who has a towering hairdo and oversize front teeth. The art design is suitably Seussian and impressively total—although, more dutiful than inventive, it's no *Nightmare Before Christmas*. The movie is perhaps 20 minutes too long and subject to torpor.

As the Grinch, Jim Carrey is, initially at least, unrecognizably green and hairy, with his entire face masked and a mouth full of mismatched teeth. (This hellish costume would surely be sufficient to turn anyone into a grinch—or worse.) It requires some concentration to even find Carrey beneath his makeup, but he's there, albeit too often restricted to do much more than merely strike poses. The movie rises to another level whenever its star has a chance to cut loose—leading the ensemble in a conga line, winning a sack race in slow motion, torching the Whos' Christmas tree while screaming, "Burn baby burn," and otherwise directing the inmates of Whoville in a diabolical drama of his own devising.

Also reviewed in:
CHICAGO TRIBUNE, 11/17/00, Friday/p. A, Michael Wilmington
NEW YORK TIMES, 11/17/00, p. E20, Stephen Holden
NEW YORKER, 11/27/00, p. 183, Anthony Lane
VARIETY, 11/20-26/00, p. 13, Todd McCarthy

DR. T & THE WOMEN

An Artisan Entertainment release of a Sandcastle 5 production. *Executive Producer:* Cindy Cowan. *Producer:* Robert Altman and James McLindon. *Director:* Robert Altman. *Screenplay:* Anne Rapp. *Director of Photography:* Jan Kiesser. *Editor:* Geraldine Peroni. *Music:* Lyle Lovett. *Music Editor:* Helena Lea. *Sound:* John Patrick Prichett and (music) Nathaniel Kunkel. *Sound Editor:* Frederick Howard. *Casting:* Pam Dixon Mickelson. *Production Designer:* Stephen Altman. *Art Director:* John E. Bucklin. *Set Designer:* Pamela Klamer *Set Decorator:* Chris Spellman. *Costumes:* Dona Granata. *Make-up:* Micheline Trépanier. *Running time:* 122 minutes. *MPAA Rating:* R.

CAST: Richard Gere (Dr. Sullivan "Dr. T" Travis); Helen Hunt (Bree Davis); Farrah Fawcett (Kate Travis); Laura Dern (Peggy); Shelley Long (Carolyn); Tara Reid (Connie Travis); Kate Hudson (Dee Dee); Liv Tyler (Marilyn); Robert Hays (Harlan); Matt Malloy (Bill); Andy Richter (Eli); Lee Grant (Dr. Harper); Janine Turner (Dorothy Chambliss); Holly Pellham-Davis (Joanne); Jeanne Evans (First Exam Patient); Dorothy Deavers (Patient with Cane); Ramsey Williams (Menopausal Patient); Ellen Locy (Tiffany, Tiffany & Co. Saleswoman); Cameron Cobb and Mike Scot (Golf Pro Shop Boys); Irene Cortez (Maria); Clara Peretz (Lacey); MacKenzie Fitzgerald (Amber); Juliette Loraine Gauntt (Kristin); Susan McLaughlin (Hospital Receptionist); Oliver Tull (Psychiatric Ward Nurse); Kelli Finglass (Cheerleader Director); Judy Trammell (Cheerleader Choreographer); Eric Ryan (Birth Baby).

LOS ANGELES TIMES, 10/13/00, Calendar, p. 2, Kevin Thomas

Talk about perfect casting! Who better to play the most popular gynecologist in Dallas than Richard Gere in Robert Altman's sparkling and wise romantic comedy "Dr. T & the Women"?

As dashing as ever, Gere is still young enough to appeal to all the generations of women who crowd his office like Grand Central Station at rush hour. What's more, Gere's Dr. Sully Travis is not just a guy who's all looks and charm but a man who truly loves and respects women—he considers them downright sacred.

Indeed, the perils of placing a woman on a pedestal are at the heart of this beguiling film that re-teams Altman with screenwriter Anne Rapp, with whom he collaborated so successfully on "Cookie's Fortune." Rapp is clearly in sync with Altman's peerless sense of rhythm and knows how to write incisively and economically for Altman's cherished large ensemble casts. What's especially good here is that while everyone is well-defined, there is a core group that stands out sharply, giving the film focus and guaranteeing swift involvement.

Dr. T, when we meet him, is riding high, his hectic workday cushioned by his exceedingly solicitous—and, truth to tell, nosy—head nurse Carolyn (Shelley Long), who clearly worships him. He breaks his routine regularly by playing golf at his country club and by hunting with his buddies (Robert Hays, Matt Malloy and Andy Richter, Conan O'Brien's former sidekick). It's true that things are a bit hectic at home, as his beloved wife Kate (Farrah Fawcett) prepares for the wedding of their older daughter Dee Dee (Kate Hudson) and his divorcing sister-in-law Peggy (Laura Dern) has moved in temporarily with her three small children.

Then one day at a ritzy shopping mall, Kate starts zoning out, gradually stripping off her clothes for a romp in a fountain. Her psychiatrist (Lee Grant) explains that Kate is regressing to her childhood because her life has become so perfect it has no meaning or purpose. Sully has provided her with everything for so long and so devotedly that there are no challenges left for her.

But just as Kate is seemingly fading away from his life, Sully is swiftly consoled by his country club's new assistant golf pro, Bree (Helen Hunt), a lovely, open young woman whose naturalness in personality and style offers quite a contrast to the fluffy, overdressed wealthy women who make up the bulk of his patients. Naturally, Sully is not really out of the woods, and the film's greatest pleasures come in not being able to guess where Altman and Rapp are taking us.

The way in which they wrap up "Dr. T & the Women" is inspired, and it leaves Sully Travis with a renewed sense of purpose in a way he could not possibly have guessed. Gere moves through all these developments with a warm responsiveness that makes Sully one of the most appealing characters he has ever played.

And is he ever surrounded by lovely, impressive actresses. Hunt's Bree is just too good to be true because she proves to be lots more casual about relationships than Sully, who hasn't listened closely enough, realizes. Looking ravishing, Fawcett is completely credible as a wife in retreat, certainly a disconcerting figure but one played lightly enough to avoid an unwanted tragic effect.

Dern's Peggy is the most overdressed of the ladies, a classic desperate Southern belle who keeps up her spirits with spirits, hitting party champagne and slugging the harder stuff in secret. Long's Carolyn all but walks off with the picture with her sheer expressiveness, allowing the nurse to emerge as more amusing than martyred.

On one level "Dr. T & the Women" is an affectionate satire on nouveau riche Dallas mores—the expensive but rather bland and tasteless homes, the fancy clothing and hairdos. Costume designer Dona Granata and production designer Stephen Altman and their staffs are on the money, and Lyle Lovett (who does not appear) has contributed a breezy, good-natured score.

NEW YORK, 10/16/00. p. 88. Peter Rainer

Richard Gere plays a gynecologist in Robert Altman's *Dr. T & the Women*, and it's such a funny high-low concept that at the outset you wonder if the film will be able to do it justice. Gere has been playing self-infatuated studs in such a self-infatuated way for so long that I came prepared for a star turn of truly embarrassing proportions. It's to his credit, and most certainly to Altman's, as well as to his screenwriter Anne Rapp's *(Cookie's Fortune)*, that what comes through is something no one could have predicted: As Dr. Sullivan ("Sully") Travis, who ministers to Dallas's high-society ladies of leisure, Gere is the most relaxed and self-deprecating he's ever been. It's as if he had suddenly been made moonstruck. Dr. T, who is married with two daughters, believes that women are saints. "They're sacred and should be treated that way," he says, and he truly means it. The joke here is that Dr. T is a bona fide innocent, while the women who buzz about him and crowd his office all have designs on him. He's like a pampered prince presiding over a planet of screwball females. But it's a benevolent dictatorship. All he wants is for everybody to be happy.

Virtually all of the women in the movie are blonde (with one significant exception: a wedding wrecker played by Liv Tyler), and they have a tinseled glow. These ladies are haloed by their own privileges. Altman uses Dr. T's waiting room as a kind of command post from which to reveal a cross section of Dallas damselry. The jabber level is high, and the overlapping dialogue creates a wall of sound of gossip and backbiting. Altman seems to take an almost anthropological delight in situating himself inside this colony, and no doubt there will be those who object to the airheadedness of it all. I suppose you could argue that this is an old man's movie (Altman is 75) and therefore he should be excused for portraying society women as kooks for whom feminism never happened; but I doubt Altman, who has always had his subversively mischievous side, would have made a much different film if he had shot it 30 years ago.

There's no malice in this film's depiction of the country-club set; it's more like a wide-eyed awe at the pageantry of gender. The movie is not only about the extravagances of women but also about the ways in which men are flummoxed by those extravagances. No excuses need be made for Altman. Dr. T & the Women isn't just a comic escapade; it's a comic vision that, in its own frothy way, harks back to Altman's more emotionally complex movies such as McCabe & Mrs. Miller. Dr. T is a bit like Warren Beatty's McCabe, who also had a core of innocence and was ultimately demolished by it. (In this, he also resembles the hairdresser Beatty played in Shampoo.) The Mrs. Miller of this movie, the one woman who sees things without sentimentality, is Helen Hunt's Bree, the new golf pro in town who sizes up the doctor's unhappy marriage in a flash and moves in on him with practiced ease. She's not enthralled by his pure heart, and her coolness toward him, the ways in which the traditional sex roles appear to be reversed between them, turns him into a kind of soap-opera Job.

The men in Dr. T & the Women, when we see them at all, are just as gender-typed as the ladies. Dr. T's hunting buddies (Robert Hays, Andy Richter, Matt Malloy) are flush with male chumminess. It is a point of pride that these guys do not understand the women in their orbit. Dr. T doesn't understand them, either, except in a gynecological sense, but his reverence counts for him as a higher understanding. That's why he can't fathom the breakup of his marriage, when his wife (Farrah Fawcett), at the outset of the movie, suddenly takes leave of her senses and retreats into childhood. Her condition is clinically diagnosed as Hestia complex, which apparently affects only upper-class women who are loved too much and have everything they need. (The complex is satiric, but it's not so far-fetched.) He also can't fathom the waywardness of his eldest daughter, Kate Hudson's Dee Dee, on the eve of her wedding; Dee Dee is a cheerleader who turns out to be rallying a different game altogether. (Hudson gives the role a precocious confidence.) Dr. T's frazzled, predatory chief nurse, Carolyn (Shelley Long), and his boozy sister-in-law, Peggy (Laura Dern), who seems to like hearing the echo of her voice from the bottom of a wineglass, are among the other luminaries put on earth to test Dr. T's contention that all women are in a state of grace.

Most movies about men who love women focus on the hypocrisy behind the love. The men end up exposed as cads. Altman and Anne Rapp are after something gentler. Behind Dr. T's ministrations isn't ill will but rather a kind of deluded tenderness. In the end, he is undone by his own sweet sympathies for how things should be. This is not a man you can hate, and Altman gives him a hearty, cosmic send-off that ranks as one of the director's most lyrically loony passages. The gale force of women is rendered quite literally, and it gusts our hero right into a grand epiphany.

NEW YORK POST, 10/13/00, p. 49, Lou Lumenick

The biggest surprise in this delightful comedy isn't the "surprise" ending, which I've been asked not to divulge—though director Robert Altman's fans will see it coming a Texas mile away.

No, it's Richard Gere's charming, Cary Grant-caliber performance as Dr. Sullivan Travis, gynecologist to Houston's smart set.

Altman and screenwriter Anne Rapp (who collaborated on last year's little-seen gem "Cookie's Fortune") have playfully turned upside down any expectations raised by Gere's normally aloof star persona.

And the actor, never one of my favorites, has responded with his most engaging, least narcissistic work since "An Officer and a Gentleman," two decades ago.

Dr. T, you see, is a genuinely nice guy who worships women—from his stiletto and Prada-wearing patients to the ditzy women in varying shades of blond who make up his extended professional and personal family. He's helpless and clueless as an estrogen-driven storm develops around him. It begins with his pampered wife (Farrah Fawcett), who's committed to an institution after she takes a nude dip in a shopping-mall fountain. Diagnosed as suffering from too much love from her spouse, she wants out of their marriage.

Dr. T is vulnerable to an approach from his club's new golf pro, who seems to be more interested in a fling than a serious relationship (Helen Hunt, devastatingly funny as a female version of the character Gere usually plays).

Meanwhile, Dr. T's champagne-swilling sister-in-law (a hilarious Laura Dern) has moved in with her three pre-schoolers and proceeds to wreak havoc.

And his daughter Marilyn (Tara Reid), who works for a museum devoted to conspiracy theories about the Kennedy assassination, is raising disturbing questions about his other daughter, who is about to be married.

Specifically, she wonders about the relationship between her sister, Dee Dee (Kate Hudson, confirming her star-making role in "Almost Famous"), and Dee Dee's bridesmaid (Liv Tyler, who stands out in the ensemble as the only major brunette character).

It's all too much for poor Dr. T, who also has to fend off a hilarious advance from his chief nurse (Shelley Long, in her first good movie role since 1984's "Night Shift"). This comes amidst a slowly building day from hell at the office that's the movie's comic high point.

Though Altman's trademark overlapping dialogue will take a little getting used to for those unfamiliar with his films, it's well worth the effort.

Overall, this may well be Altman's most accessible and crowd-pleasing work since "M*A*S*H."

My only complaint is with the less than completely satisfying "surprise" ending, which needlessly prolongs the movie to the two-hour mark.

Altman and Rapp skirt the fine line between satire and caricature, stopping just short of ridiculing the women who pack Dr. T's office because, as one of them puts it, "The man knows his way around a speculum."

Gere may not be the one in the stirrups, but he's definitely the one who rides "Dr. T & the Women" into the winner's circle.

NEWSDAY, 10/13/00, Part II/p. B3, John Anderson

The degradation of Hot Lips Houlihan, the bottomless quartet of "Short Cuts," the fact that his best female character, Mrs. Miller, was a trollop—there seems to be a question pending about Robert Altman's problem with women. And as his new movie proves, there's no question at all.

"Dr. T and the Women," which might have been titled "Dr. T and the Miserable Hos," is set in Dallas, a city that even Altman has admitted has no reason to exist (no river, no harbor, none of the usual provocations). Likewise his movie—which makes it, if not actually coherent, at least curious.

Dallas, capital of conspicuous consumption and down-home opulence, possesses an ethos you might call Altmanesque—a kind of gluttony, exemplified in the films by a Babel-ish torrent of colliding dialogue, star-glutted casts, overreaching storylines. The director also has proved himself a sponge—he not only absorbs, digests and interprets his material, he apparently believes it. And in recent years, this has resulted in the star-worship of "The Player," the biliousness of "Short Cuts," the vacuity of "Pret a Porter" and the southern silliness of "Cookie's Fortune."

This last was written by Anne Rapp, who also contributes the screenplay of "Dr. T and the Women." A seemingly frothy, inconsequential tale, "Dr. T" has at its center a rather provocative thesis: Men can't win. No matter what they do, or how kind they are, there's no hope. By extension, why not be a louse?

Why not? Dr. Sullivan Travis (Richard Gere) is the most popular gynecologist in Dallas, inspector of the upper crust and a wizard with a speculum (as one of his more candid patients puts it). Travis' bedside manner is sexily avuncular; Gere plays T soft to the point of pliancy. But his patients can't seem to stay away from his office. At home, however, things are a shambles.

T's wife, Kate (Farrah Fawcett), has lost her mind, waded into the fountain at the mall, regressed to an infantile state. The diagnosis? Travis has been such a nurturing, understanding, sensitive husband that, deprived of anything to worry about, Kate's mind has been forced to create its own crisis.

Again, you just can't win.

Altman has always delighted in casting to type, but the use of Fawcett as a mental case, given her notorious late-night-TV meltdown on David Letterman's show, seems unnecessarily cruel. Less cruel is the casting of ubiquitous starlet Kate Hudson as Travis' self-absorbed daughter Dee Dee, a ditz who takes cell phone calls during her initial rehearsal with the Dallas Cowboy Cheerleaders and whose upcoming wedding is imperiled by her love for Marilyn (Liv Tyler). Travis' other daughter, Connie (Tara Reid), is a JFK conspiracy theorist; his sister Peggy (Laura Dern) is a lush; his secretary Carolyn (Shelley Long) is in love with him, and the women in his waiting room (including, for some reason, Janine Turner) are clamoring to climb into the stirrups.

Amid the chaos, Travis decides to blemish his record of marital fidelity with a golf pro named Bree (Helen Hunt) (beware of golf pros named Bree), who sleeps with him but won't follow when he finally decides he's had enough of Dallas. What a witch.

In case anyone is missing his point, Altman gives us an ending that's both phantasmagorical and a rhapsody to the birth of boy children, punctuating the message of "Dr. T and the Women"—most of whom are in the movie for no reason anyway. The story is about Travis and Bree and the rest is filler, in a movie made by a guy who seems to have watched too many Robert Altman films. Some may think he's picking on Dallas. I think Dallas got its revenge.

SIGHT AND SOUND, 7/01, p. 41, Philip Kemp

Dallas, Texas, the present. Dr Sullivan Travis is the city's most popular gynaecologist; his schedule is overbooked and his waiting room, presided over by chief nurse Carolyn, is crowded with well-to-do women. Dr T (as he's generally called) is also beset by family pressures. His wife Kate is slipping into madness; his sister-in-law Peggy has moved in along with her three small daughters; his younger daughter Dee Dee is about to get married. Dr T occasionally relaxes on hunting trips with his friends Harlan, Bill and Eli.

Kate strips off at a downtown mall and is committed to a home. At his golf club Dr T meets the new pro, Bree Davis, and starts an affair with her. Marilyn, a friend of Dee Dee's from college, arrives to act as maid of honour for Dr T's elder daughter Connie, a conspiracy theorist who shows tourists around the Kennedy Assassination trail, seems to dislike her.

With the wedding imminent and Bree away in New Orleans, Dr T hears that Kate wants a divorce. Connie tells him that Dee Dee and Marilyn are ex lovers. Carolyn makes an unsuccessful pass at him. The wedding takes place as a storm approaches; at the last minute Dee Dee rejects her groom and elopes with Marilyn. Rushing to Bree, Dr T begs her to run off with him, but she turns him down. He concludes she's having an affair with Harlan and drives off on to the freeway. His car is sucked up by a twister that deposits him in the desert near a Mexican pueblo, where he helps a young woman give birth to a son.

Robert Altman has always been a gambler—he claims he once lost $60,000 on a single bet and there's something of a what-the-hell, gambler's-luck attitude to the way he makes films. Like John Huston (another lifelong devotee of gaming) Altman is a prolific, wildly uneven film-maker, seemingly hoping that if this movie proves a turkey, the next one will hit the spot. Which may explain why a filmography that includes *McCabe & Mrs. Miller*, *Nashville* and *Short Cuts* also takes in *O.C and Stiggs*, *Beyond Therapy* and *Pret-a-Porter*. *Dr T & the Women*, alas, falls thuddingly into the latter camp.

The film's central joke, for what it's worth, is that Dr Travis, a gynaecologist who lives his life surrounded by (indeed swamped by) women, proves utterly incapable of dealing with them unless they've got their legs apart and their feet up in stirrups. "The man knows how to handle a speculum," observes one adoring patient, but that's about all he does know. "By nature," he observes woozily "women are saints, they're sacred," which evidently absolves him from seeing them as people. This might be OK as a premise, were it not that Altman seems to endorse his lead character's reversed-out misogyny. "Every single woman," states Travis at another point, "has something special about her." Not in this life, she doesn't. The patients at Dr T's surgery, his all-female staff, the members of his family (all female bar him), the guests at his daughter's wedding (90 per cent female), are virtually interchangeable: over-privileged, over-dressed, self-obsessed feather-brained chatterers, constantly talking across each other 19 to the dozen. (Altman's trademark overlapping dialogue is in this film wholly monosexual.) Even the Mexican peasants who drag Dr T into their pueblo in the final sequence are, economic status apart, cut from the same cloth, yattering ceaselessly while he, sole man as ever, gets on with the serious business of facilitating, not merely new life, but—glory be!—the birth of a boy. The one exception to this stereotyping, Helen Hunt's down-to earth golf pro, seems to have strayed in from another movie, possibly one directed by Howard Hawks.

Since this kind of marshmallow social satire can't provide much in the way of narrative momentum, *Dr T & the Women* keeps itself going by glueing together plot fragments from other, better Altman movies—notably *A Wedding* (1978) and *Health* (1980—and bolts on a final peripeteia shamelessly lifted from Paul T. Anderson's *Magnolia*. As Travis, Richard Gere reprises his all-purpose lost puppy dog grin, while several fine actresses are misused. Given the level of talent involved, *Dr T* inevitably includes a few diverting scenes, but at over two hours, the lack of substance and patronising treatment of the characters become dispiriting. Let's hope that his forthcoming English country house movie *Gosford Park* finds Altman lucking into a better roll of the dice.

VILLAGE VOICE, 10/17/00, p. 136, Dennis Lim

Robert Altman calls his latest film a "love letter to the women of Dallas," but it's hard to detect anything resembling affection in *Dr. T and the Women*—at best, a snickering empathy for Richard Gere, cast effectively enough as the squintingly perplexed, emasculated center of a raging estrogen tempest. Gere's well-groomed smoothy, Travis Sullivan, is the gynecologist of choice for the dowagers and debutantes of Dallas high society. The opening credit sequence, a trademark tracking-camera grandstander, fluidly details the fur-flying chaos that seems to erupt daily in his waiting room—a horde of disgruntled harridans descending on beleaguered nurse Shelley Long.

The home front is no less treacherous. After Dr. T's wife, Kate (Farrah Fawcett), disrobes in a shopping mall and leaps into a fountain, she's diagnosed with Hestia syndrome—a childlike regression that afflicts those who are "loved too much." (Altman keeps her institutionalized and blank-eyed for most of the film, though—like Letterman last week—he can't resist wheeling her out for an encore flip-out.) Kate's permanently sloshed, soon-to-be-divorced sister (Laura Dern) moves into the opulent Sullivan residence, little girls in tow. And as Travis's cheerleading eldest daughter (Kate Hudson) prepares for her wedding, her scheming sibling, a JFK-conspiracy buff and tour guide (Tara Reid), runs to Daddy with some interesting news about her sister and the maid of honor (Liv Tyler). Everywhere the good doctor turns, women bustle and swarm and teem—spoiled, irrational creatures who demand constant, unwavering attention. The one slacks-wearing exception, golf pro Bree (a sporty-spiced Helen Hunt), offers Travis down-to-earth consolation, but soon proves to be as great a source of confusion.

A flabby farce in which everyone seems to be making it up as they go along (Lyle Lovett's score cannily mirrors the quasi-improvisatory scatter), *Dr. T* is not exactly uninvolving—mainly because it's such a curiously bumpy ride. The movie ambles along with a semi-agreeable absent-mindedness, stirring randomly from its distracted daze for some stale nudge-wink humor and bouts of casual mockery and contempt. Written by Anne Rapp (who also scripted *Cookie's Fortune*), *Dr. T* is garbled enough to encourage rampant projection: Is this a sitting-duck attack on sodden Southern privilege? An old-fashioned what's-a-guy-to-do lament? A snide critique thereof? A restless expression of Freudian male paranoia? A snide critique thereof? For what it's worth, there's more than a hint of gynophobia in the twist ending, which, if nothing else, explodes the movie's self-satisfied dottiness into full-bore insanity.

Also reviewed in:
CHICAGO TRIBUNE, 10/13/00, Friday/p. A, Michael Wilmington

NEW YORK TIMES, 10/13/00, p. E12, A. O. Scott
NEW YORKER, 10/16 & 23/00, p. 260, David Denby
VARIETY, 9/4-10/00, p. 19, Todd McCarthy
WASHINGTON POST, 10/13/00, p. C1, Rita Kempley
WASHINGTON POST, 10/13/00, Weekend/p. 45, Desson Howe

DON'T LET ME DIE ON A SUNDAY

A First Run Features release of a Program 33 production with the participation of Canal Plus. *Director:* Didier le Pêcheur.   *Screenplay (French with English subtitles):* Didier le Pêcheur. *Director of Photography:* Denis Rouden.   *Editor:* Sylvie Landra.   *Music:* Philippe Cohen-Solal. *Sound:* Pascal Armant.   *Running time:* 86 minutes.   *MPAA Rating:* Not Rated.

CAST: Elodie Bouchez (Teresa);   Jean-Marc Barr (Ben);   Martin Petitguyot (Ducon);   Patrick Catalifo (Boris);   Gérard Loussine (Abel);   Jean Michel Fête (Nico);   Zazie (Jeane/Helene); Jeanne Casilas (Marie).

NEW YORK POST, 4/21/00, p. 50, Jonathan Foreman

Even the participation (including some nude scenes) of Elodie Bouchez, charming star of "The Dreamlife of Angels," isn't, enough to make "Don't Let Me Die on a Sunday" watchable.

Sure, it's hard to believe that a film about S&M sex—that begins with an apparently dead club girl reviving as a mortuary attendant rapes her corpse—could be deeply dull, but French director Didier Le Pecheur pulls it off with this aridly pretentious, ultra-talky, absurdly self-conscious exploration of sexual extremism.

It's almost plotless and visually uninteresting. Much of the acting is way over the top and characters are always saying Gallic, pseudo-profound things like: "Pain is better than love because you cannot forget the other person."

VILLAGE VOICE, 4/25/00, p. 138, Leslie Camhi

After you've tried necrophilia on the first date, what do you do for an encore? That's the dilemma facing the characters in *Don't, Let Me Die on a Sunday*, director Didier le Pêcheur's morose Foucauldian drama. Ben (Jean-Marc Barr) kills time on his job at the morgue by talking to coworkers about sex and watching porn. Early one Sunday morning, a new body rolls in, a girl who overdosed at last night's rave. The corpse, formerly known as Teresa and played by Elodie Bouchez (from *The Dreamlife of Angels)*, proves irresistible. But when his impulsive act brings her back to life, Ben doesn't know how to handle her. So, because he has trouble showing affection, they traipse around Paris to various sadomasochistic clubs and orgies. They also abduct a friend with AIDS from the hospital and take him to a remote island where he can die with dignity. The film is meant as a serious meditation on sex, death, and fin de siècle nihilism. But it manages to be both ponderous and silly.

Also reviewed in:
CHICAGO TRIBUNE, 8/11/00, Friday/p. M, John Petrakis
NEW YORK TIMES, 4/21/00, p. E34, A. O. Scott
VARIETY, 1/4-10/99, p. 103, Derek Elley

DOUBLE PARKED

A Castle Hill Productions release of a 44th Street Films production. *Executive Producer:* Mark Montgomery.   *Producer:* Stephen Kinsella and Matthew Meyers.   *Director:* Stephen Kinsella.

Screenplay: Stephen Kinsella and Paul Solberg. *Director of Photography:* Jim Denault. *Editor:* Seth E. Anderson. *Music:* Craig Hazen and David Wolfert. *Sound:* Thomas Varga and (music) Matt Anthony. *Sound Editor:* Stephen Altobello. *Casting:* Adrienne Stern. *Production Designer:* Anthony Gasparro. *Art Director:* Elizabeth Sarkisian. *Costumes:* Monica Willis. *Make-up:* Dana Elder. *Running time:* 98 minutes. *MPAA Rating:* Not Rated.

CAST: Callie Thorne (Rita Ronaldi); Noah Fleiss (Brett); Rufus Reed (Matt); P. J. Brown (Warren); William Sage (Karl Severson); Eileen Galindro (Dolores Gonzalez); Anthony De Sando (Angel Gonzalez).

NEW YORK POST, 9/22/00, p. 50, Jonathan foreman

Set in Jersey City, "Double Parked" is essentially a downscale TV movie about spousal and child abuse—except that such films usually feature more likeable protagonists than abrasive single mom Rita Ronaldi ("Homicide's" Callie Thorne) who become's a meter maid to support her teenage son Matt (Rufus Reed). The boy, who suffers with bullies and cystic fibrosis, is befriended by a criminally inclined classmate, Brett (Noah Fleiss), who turns out to be his half-brother.

All performances are strong, particularly Thorne's.

NEWSDAY, 9/22/00, Part II/p. B7, Jan Stuart

Meter maids everywhere who have been waiting for their moment on the silver screen might find some solace in Stephen Kinsella's "Double Parked." Its heroine, Rita Ronaldi (do we hear a Beatles song coming on?) could be a poster girl for traffic enforcement. She looks great, she takes lip with the best of them, and best of all, she won't stoop to over-ticketing to meet a quota.

As played with a brash mouth and a Bronx twang by "Homicide's" Callie Thorne, Rita also is vaguely evocative of Fran Drescher, giving this contrived but eager-to-please comedy/drama a sitcom tickle when a gritty urban punch is wanted.

Rita falls into that currently popular movie demographic of feisty single moms whose love for their precocious pre-teen is commensurate with their chutzpah. And she needs all the brass she can get. She has no employable skills to speak of, her son Brett (Noah Fleiss) is hamstrung by cystic fibrosis, her estranged, abusive ex-husband and Brett's father Warren (P.J. Brown) has re-entered her life, and his juvenile-delinquent son by another mother, Matt (Rufus Read), is working overtime in an effort to bring good half-brother Brett down into the gutter with him.

As in a more clever variation on the vervy single mom drama, "Tumbleweeds," Rita is rescued in the nick of time from smarmy men and an insecure existence by honest labor and an intellectually upscale white knight, in this instance Brett's teacher Karl Severson (William Sage). Since director-writer-producer Kinsella has himself faced the humiliations of an unemployed actor, the most truthful parts of "Double Parked" reflect the absurdity of job interviews in which one is compelled to justify one's enthusiasm for employment that shouldn't happen to a robot.

Too much of the film, however, has the taint of artifice about it. Moreover, the workaday travails of city traffic enforcers are glossed over in a montage of angry motorists that suggests the writer did the most cursory research on these beleaguered workers. Meter maids, and movie audiences, deserve more.

VILLAGE VOICE, 9/26/00, p. 152, Leslie Camhi

Nuance is not a strong point of *Double Parked,* Stephen Kinsella's feature about a down-and-out single mother in Jersey City. Callie Thorne plays Rita Ronaldi, who walks out on her abusive, alcoholic husband. A decade later, recently fired, she learns that her ex has moved back to town. Landing a job as a meter maid cheers her, but then her son, Matt (Rufus Read), now a nerdy adolescent suffering from cystic fibrosis, befriends Brett (Noah Fleiss), the class delinquent. They don't know it, but they're half brothers. Matt gives Brett his homework; in return, Brett teaches him to spit and steal from parking meters. Luckily, a cute science teacher gets involved and becomes all flustered when he meets Rita. Thorne's perennial feistiness becomes wearisome; the kids do their best with lines like "The teacher is playing hide-the-salami with your mom." Child abuse, domestic violence ' and the struggles of single mothers deserve better treatment than this.

Also reviewed in:
NEW YORK TIMES, 9/22/00, p. E16, Lawrence Van Gelder
VARIETY, 3/27-4/2/00, p. 25, Todd McCarthy

DOWN TO YOU

A Miramax Films release of an Open City Films production. *Executive Producer:* Bobby Cohen, Bob Weinstein, Harvey Weinstein, and Jeremy Kramer.   *Producer:* Jason Kliot and Joana Vicente. *Director:* Kris Isacsson. *Screenplay:* Kris Isacsson. *Director of Photography:* Robert Yeoman. *Editor:* Stephen A. Rotter. *Music:* Edmund Choi. *Music Editor:* Chuck Martin. *Choreographer:* Lance MacDonald. *Sound:* Gary Alper. *Sound Editor:* Eliza Paley. *Casting:* Douglas Aibel. *Production Designer:* Kevin Thompson. *Art Director:* Tracey Gallacher and Marc Dabe. *Set Decorator:* Ford Wheeler. *Set Dresser:* Anthony Baldasare, James Callahan, William Kolpin, Mark Simon, and Victoria Vanasco. *Special Effects:* Drew Jiritano. *Costumes:* Michael Clancy. *Make-up:* Nicki Lederman. *Stunt Coordinator:* Douglas Crosby. *Running time:* 89 minutes. *MPAA Rating:* PG-13.

CAST: Freddie Prinze, Jr. (Al Connelly); Julia Stiles (Imogen); Selma Blair (Cyrus); Shawn Hatosy (Eddie Hicks); Zak Orth (Monk Jablonski); Ashton Kutcher (Jim Morrison); Rosario Dawson (Lana); Henry Winkler (Chef Ray); Lucie Arnaz (Judy Connelly); Lauren German (Lovestruck Woman);   Zay Harding (Lovestruck Man); Amanda Barfield (Faith Keenan); Chloe Hunter (Megan Brodski); Granger Gren (Haley Heller); Jed Rhein (Gabe Stiano); Joseff Stevenson (Ted McGurran); Elizabeth Levin (Carbs Girl); Lola Glaudini (Parolee); Robin Nance (Daddy's Girl);   Mary Wigmore (Pearly Whites);   Caroline Ambrose (Kissing Babe/Woman); Adam Carolla and Jimmy Kimmel ("The Man Show" Hosts); Jason Bailey (Angry Audience Member); Jennifer Albano (Emma); Chris Desmond (Man with Emma); Susan J. Blommaert (Psychologist); Julian Caiazzo (Young Al, age 5); Jerry Carreccio (Young Al, age 12); Chloe Beardman (Young Imogen, age 11); Frank Wood (Doctor); Joanna P. Adler (Piercing Woman); Mimi Langeland (Leather Woman); Elizabeth Page (Stage Manager); Mark Blum (The Interviewer); David Logan (Suburban Husband); Joanna Myers (Suburban Wife); Richard Galella and Michael J. Conti (SWAT Team).

LOS ANGELES TIMES, 1/22/00, Calendar/p. 2, Kevin Thomas

[The following review by Kevin Thomas appeared in a slightly different form in
NEWSDAY, 1/25/00, Part II/p. B20.]

Freddie Prinze Jr. and Julia Stiles are as appealing a pair of young lovers as you could wish for. And as long as first-time writer-director Kris Isacsson focuses squarely on them, "Down to You" plays well as a story of how two intelligent, privileged people meet in college, then fall passionately in love lots faster than they were prepared for.

Once they get used to each other, they start realizing that they are in no way ready for a major commitment, let alone marriage, yet their deep bond remains. Perhaps they will find the emotional maturity to start over—or move on separately. The way in which their relationship develops, and the ways in which they deal with it and each other is engaging.

But while "Down to You" shows its young stars, who have a potent chemistry between them, to fine advantage, the film itself is mediocre at best. Isacsson unfortunately weighs down his highly romantic movie with an over-abundance of narration and asides to the camera from Prinze's Al and Stiles' Imogen.

Isacsson, furthermore, does himself no favors by casting Al's and Imogen's observations and confidences ahead of the action, which makes the film in effect unfold as a flashback. This needlessly gives the film a feeling of taking place in the past tense just when it's most in need of forward momentum. As a result, "Down to You" plays as if it's at least a two-hour movie when it's actually only 89 minutes.

Clearly, Isacsson cares deeply for his lovers and takes pains to make them persuasive and worth caring about. But it would seem, however, that his commitment to telling their story has used up all his imagination and falls back on shtick to characterize the supporting roles. Shawn Hatosy, who has been making a terrific impression in one film after another, is stuck playing a numskull. Zak Orth fares better, cast as an aspiring actor who seems to be envisioning himself as another Orson Welles.

"Down to You" summons too many images of too many other movies just when you should be feeling that Al and Imogen's love story is happening in the real world. (Typical for student love stories, you are given the impression that nobody studies and everybody parties all the time.) Henry Winkler plays Al's loving father, a durably popular TV chef, and Lucie Arnaz, as Al's DJ mother, has so little screen time that it's all she can do to register vivaciousness.

"Down to You" takes place in a glossy Manhattan, accompanied by a throbbing rock score too reminiscent of the tracks of a zillion other pictures. Isacsson, however, has poured so much feeling into Al and Imogen and directed Prinze and Stiles to play them so effectively that the picture does them more good than harm. In the meantime, the best the makers of "Down to You" can hope for is that girls in their early teens—clearly the film's target audience—will be so carried away by its charismatic stars that they'll overlook the film's various flaws.

NEW YORK POST, 1/21/00, p. 50, Lou Lumenick

So where are the reviews of "Down to You," the romantic comedy starring Freddie Prinze Jr. that opened at a theater near you?

You will find them here and in other newspapers—because the movie wasn't shown in advance to critics.

The same thing happened last week with MGM's sci-fi epic "Supernova," and is not uncommon when a studio finds it has a stinker and wants to slip it into theaters before it gets hammered by reviewers.

There were several releases from last year that opened without advance screenings and quickly disappeared. New Line's "Dog Park," with Janeane Garofalo, was a dog, and Sony's "Virtual Sexuality" was dead on arrival.

Independent Artists' "Simon Sez" quickly went on its way to home video, and Universal's "Virus" was a box-office plague, and Artisan didn't exactly look smart when the studio hid "Foolish" from critics.

It might seem incredible that a movie studio would forgo opening-day reviews, which amount to millions of dollars in free publicity, and settle for notices in small-circulation Saturday papers.

But clearly Hollywood suits don't always believe the old adage that the only bad press is no press.

I've never gotten a publicist to admit it except in private, but, there's only one reason why a studio chooses not to show a movie to critics: They expect it to be trashed.

Instead, they speak of "problems finding a print" (for a film that's opening in 2,000 theaters) or "letting the movie find its audience"—meaning they don't want interference from us nasty critics.

This is how a spokesman for Miramax—which initially claimed that technical problems were to blame for scuttled screenings of "Down to You"—spun its no-show policy to The Post's Page Six:

"After a strong teen response at junket screenings and at the premiere, a marketing decision was made not to have critics' screenings."

Now, "Down to You" may turn out to be one of my favorite movies of the year. I'll be delighted if it is. But double talk like this doesn't exactly make me optimistic.

In the studios' defense, withholding movies from critics is occasionally a sound business decision. Particularly on a movie with a grabby-sounding premise, the tactic can maximize box-office returns before the bad word gets out.

This strategy paid off handsomely for the terrible "House on Haunted Hill," which wasn't screened and took in a whopping $15.1 million—roughly what it cost—over the Halloween weekend, making it the No. 1 movie.

But usually, hiding a movie from critics isn't going to turn a bomb into a hit.

NEW YORK POST, 1/22/00, p. 21, Lou Lumenick

Stinko movies often unwittingly critique themselves—and the brain-dead romantic comedy "Down to You" (which Miramax understandably didn't screen in advance for critics) is no exception.

Wearing a hang-dog expression (which he alternates throughout with a deer-caught-in-headlights look), Freddie Prinze Jr. observes: "You watch people go through this stuff on TV, and it always seems fake. When it happens to you, there's nothing fake about it."

"This stuff"—which bears no resemblance to half-decent TV, let alone reality—is the on-again, off-again romance between Al (Prinze) and Imogen (Julia Stiles, who deserves better), two students at a New York City college that probably would sue if it were identified.

To call "Down to You" trite would be complimenting director Kris Isacsson's screenplay, the dramatic high point of which involves Al trying to kill himself by consuming a bottle of shampoo.

Even when Isacsson has a semi-clever idea—Al's dad (an embarrassed-looking Henry Winkler), a TV chef, fantasizes about a cooking-show version of "Cops"—the director hasn't a clue how to stage it.

Some scenes are so dimly lit they make this film look like a bargain-basement Troma production—minus the smut and the entertainment.

"Down to You" seems destined for a quick trip to a video store near you—where I'd recommend you rent Steve Martin's "The Lonely Guy" instead.

SIGHT AND SOUND, 6/00, p. 40, Jamie Graham

New York City, the late 90s. Sophomore college student Al meets freshman Imogen at a bar. They begin a relationship. The honeymoon period is cut short by Imogen's annual family trip to France for the summer. After her return, the pair continue where they left off, but the chemistry has waned. Their sex life is now intermittent and both find themselves tempted by others. Imogen's fears are compounded by a false pregnancy scare. Attending a party with Al that night, the duo argue bitterly and go their separate ways. The next morning, Imogen calls for Al and confesses she cheated on him the night before. They split up, and Imogen moves to San Francisco while Al, after graduation, becomes a chef. Unable to get over Imogen, he swallows a bottle of her shampoo. Al recuperates and attends a party thrown by his parents. Imogen surprises him by turning up. The pair are reconciled and move west together.

Like Rob Reiner's *The Story of Us* and Stephen Frears' upcoming *High Fidelity*, both of which scrutinise the highs and lows of modem relationships, *Down to You* initially seems better than it actually is by pressing the right buttons. If *The Story of Us* looks at early fortysomethings and *High Fidelity* mid thirtysomethings, *Down to You* is the late teen version, set amid college students living in a romantically photographed New York City. Hence the topic is not just love but *first* love, with all its extra freight of emotion and impact. The opening stages of the film are full of energy as Al and Imogen's relationship accelerates, with flashbacks, flashbacks within-flashbacks, split screens, pop irises and straight to-camera-addresses lifting the proceedings.

Debut director Kris Isacsson, who comes to *Down to You* off a series of short films, is at pains to keep things snappy and imaginative, but his head of steam disperses when it's time to deal with the souring of his duo's relationship. He tries to bring a little enterprise to the inevitable scenes of bickering and moody silence, but by now the vitalising tactics seem out of place. One device is particularly misjudged as Al, having just had his sexual advances batted off by Imogen, switches on the television to see himself being mocked on an imaginary talk show for his wet personality. Considering Al is so square you could cut yourself on his corners, it only serves to reinforce the viewer's wonder as to just what Imogen sees in him in the first place. Certainly Julia Stiles' previous incarnation, the spiky Katarina in *10 Things I Hate about You*, wouldn't have given him a second glance. *Down to You* is irreparably crippled, however, when Imogen moves to San Francisco. Becoming the filmic equivalent of a wailing Bon Jovi ballad, it leaves us to chew our fists as Al sits drunk and forlorn in his empty apartment, conversing with a spider. But not even that plumbs the embarrassing depths of a perplexing sub plot in which Al's closest friend becomes the star of a string of pornographic epics.

Also reviewed in:
NEW YORK TIMES, 1/22/00, p. B14, A. O. Scott
VARIETY, 1/24-30/00, p. 57, Brendan Kelly
WASHINGTON POST, 1/22/00, p. C1, Stephen Hunter

DREAM CATCHER, THE

A Redeemable Features release of a Transparent Films production. *Producer:* Julia Reichert, Steven Bognar, and Ed Radtke. *Director:* Ed Radtke. *Screenplay:* Ed Radtke and M. S. Nieson. *Director of Photography:* Terry Stacey. *Editor:* James Klein. *Music:* Georgiana Gomez. *Sound:* Scott Stoltz. *Production Designer:* Sally Petersen. *Running time:* 99 minutes. *MPAA Rating:* Not Rated.

CAST: Maurice Compte (Freddy); Paddy Connor (Albert); Jeanne Heaton (Katherine); Larry John Meyers (Freddy's Uncle); Joseph F. Arthur (Freddy's Father); Patrick Shining Elk (Church Caretaker); David Reece (Deer Hunter); Lesie Orr (Woman at ATM); Amanda Lanier (Rhea); Danny Morris (Jerry); Buck Truitt (Cashier); Sean Wolf Hill (Threatening Driver); Michael Conn (Pisser); Tom Wamsley (Trucker in Bathroom); Robin Thomas (Raymond); Melanie Johnson (Brenda); Fred Gloor (Fisherman); Kim Tuvin (Nursing Home Nurse); Temba Nggakayi (Irate Driver); Christopher Edward Miller (Marine); Jim Brooks (Justin); Lonna D. Kingsbury (Cafeteria Worker); Jeff Carter (Principal); Frank R. Lewis (Garage Attendant); Robin Mullins (Albert's Mom); Richard E. Corey (Carny); Howard Shook (Lead Thug); Kevin Rotramel and Dan Kiger (Thugs); Zuella Murray (Caretaker's Wife); Andrew John and Dallas James Naljahih (Caretaker's Kids); Miya Cerno (Infant); Les Paul (Man in Pick-up Truck); Patricia Martinez (Young Woman in Truck); Gary Zweig (Store Manager); Robert Grant Elkins (Old Cop) Stephen M. Francia, Jr. (Young Cop); Matt Miller (Lieutenant); Tony Darnell-Davis (Carl); Roger Winkler, James Taylor and Val Worbman (Diner Regulars): Dalton Bybee and Dylan Bybee (Kids in Van); Henley Green and Stuart Klorfine (Parents in Van).

NEW YORK POST, 9/15/00, p. 66, Lou Lumenick

The world may need another gloomy indie movie about two delinquent teenagers on the Middle-American road, about as much as it needs another "Highlander" sequel, but Ed Radtke's film-fest favorite does at least boast some fine acting, excellent photography and an authentic feel for life on the highway.

Freddy (Maurice Compte), a handsome but silent and irritatingly self-pitying youth, flees Philadelphia and his pregnant girlfriend, hopping a train with a vague notion of visiting his uncle, or even finding the jailbird father who abandoned him long ago.

In a truck stop rest room Freddy meets glib, hyperactive young thief Albert (Paddy Connor), who has just escaped from juvenile detention and has a notion of locating his long lost mother in Reno.

To begin with, the two boys have little in common besides a lack of cash and a willingness to steal things, but they travel together all the way to Nevada, and it eventually becomes obvious that both of them are desperate for family.

The boys and their world feet more real than Keanu Reeves and River Phoenix in "My Own Private Idaho" but their realistic unlikability makes it harder to care about them, especially during the long, silent scenes of travel through the bleak expanses of the West.

VILLAGE VOICE, 9/19/00, p.120, Amy Taubin

A distinctly American vision of the fragile ties among men, Ed Radtke's *The Dream Catcher* provides a fresh perspective on that old standby, two boys on the road. Freddy (Maurice Compte) and Albert (Paddy Conner) meet while hitchhiking west. Although they claim to be looking for family members (Albert for his mother; Freddy for, first, his uncle, then his ex-con father), they both know deep down that the adults who abandoned them are not waiting with open arms. They're not so much moving toward someone or somewhere as fleeing situations that are too painful to bear. Albert, who's about 15, has escaped from some kind of juvenile detention; Freddy, who's about five years older, has a pregnant girlfriend and is terrified of becoming a father when he's still hungering for the dad he hardly knew.

Compte and Conner may resemble Keanu Reeves and River Phoenix in *My Own Private Idaho*, but they are less glamorous and less easy to love. Compte's Freddy is locked up inside himself, but he can lash out violently when he's angered or trapped. Conner's Albert, the more fragile of the two, is part bereft child clowning for attention and part budding sociopath, who steals from anyone and everyone. Albert isn't capable of bonding, but Freddy is, and through his attempts to protect Albert, he finds the father in himself.

A highly talented filmmaker, Radtke draws intense, focused performances from these two inexperienced young actors. The supporting cast, however, is less credible. Radtke brings to the film a firsthand knowledge of life on the road, infusing it with small surprises from beginning to end. He also has a great feel for the look of the land, although occasionally he strains for effect. Not even John Wayne and Jimmy Stewart could have gone *mano a mano* against the vast expanse of the Utah salt flats without looking slightly silly.

Also reviewed in:
NEW YORK TIMES, 9/15/00, p. E20, Stephen Holden
VARIETY, 5/3-9/99, p. 85, David Finnigan

DREAM OF LIGHT

This film was first reviewed in *FILM REVIEW ANNUAL*, 1993. A re-release led to additional reviews, which are included here. *Executive Producer:* María Moreno. *Director:* Victor Erice. *Screenplay (Spanish with English subtitles):* Victor Erice and Antonio López. *Director of Photography:* Javier Aguirresarobe and Angel Luis Fernández. *Editor:* Juan Ignacio San Mateo. *Music:* Pascal Gaigne. *Sound:* Ricardo Steimberg and Daniel Goldstein. *Running time:* 139 minutes. *MPAA Rating:* Not Rated.

WITH: Antonio López; María Moreno; Enrique Gran; José Carrtero; Maria López; Carmen López; Elisa Ruíz; Amalia Avia; Lucio Muñoz; Esperanaz Parada; Julio López Fernández; Janusz Pietrziak; Marek Domagala; Grzegorz Ponikwia; Fan Xiao Ming; Yan Shen Dong.

NEW YORK POST, 5/3/00, p. 52, Hannah Brown

"Dream of Light," an austere documentary about a painter working on a single painting, is anything but dreamlike.

To paraphrase that old quip about slow-paced art films, it literally is watching paint dry.

Director Victor Erice, best known for his 1973 film "Spirit of the Beehive," films Spanish artist Antonio Lopez Garcia as he plans, sketches and paints a still life of a quince tree.

Lopez Garcia is the antithesis of the tortured, passionate artist, just as this film is the polar opposite of the Hollywood version of the creative process as seen in films like "Lust for Life."

The director provides no biographical information on Lopez Garcia. The artist does not address the camera, and no art experts discuss the significance of his work.

Instead, he simply appears one day in late September, cleans up his studio, readies a canvas, mixes paint and makes some mysterious white marks on the tree's trunk and leaves.

Then, and only then, does he begin to paint.

There is almost no dialogue. Friends and relatives come and go. Workmen renovate the house, occasionally listening to the radio while they work.

The radio brings news of events outside the garden: traffic accidents, wars, etc.

But Lopez Garcia's focus remains firmly on the tree and, especially, the sunlight that he wants to capture in a particular way.

Eventually, he abandons the canvas, simply because winter is approaching and there is not enough light each day for him to continue.

In two conversations with other artists, one a Chinese woman and the other a Spanish colleague, Lopez Garcia discusses his technique.

"The best part is being close to the tree," he insists.

This is the closest he comes to revealing anything about himself.

"Dream of Light" is not like Martin Scorsese's "Life Lessons" segment of "New York Stories" in which a single canvas becomes a means of telling a story about the artist.

"Dream" is only about art. Watching it demands a tremendous amount of patience and concentration. It could be fascinating for those with a serious interest in painting, but the technical detail will be lost on most others.

VILLAGE VOICE, 5/9/00, p. 129, J. Hoberman

From the Dream that was Rome to a *Dream of Light:* Nearly as long as *Gladiator* and almost as extravagantly praised, Victor Erice's 1992 feature is another sort of Mediterranean epic. This is a movie about the making of a static image, an unscripted (if staged) documentary in which artist Antonio López Garcia tries to paint the quince tree in his backyard—and fails.

Recently voted the best film of the past decade by the Cinematheque Ontario's international panel of 60 programmers and archivists, *Dream of Light* is an autumnal tale that marks the passing of a single season. It begins in Madrid on September 29, 1990, with López's preparations—making a frame, stretching his canvas, setting up an easel, studying and sniffing around the quince tree. Whether or not the artist is acting, this fastidious method seems appropriate to a filmmaker like Erice, who has made but three features in as many decades.

Nothing rushes the wonderfully alert and capable López. He creates precise spatial coordinates, first in the yard and then on his canvas. He uses white paint-marks to place the tree and its fruit. Other work goes on around him—some Polish laborers are renovating the apartment building. (At one point, they help the artist construct a shelter around his setup.) A colleague, the loquacious Enrique Gran, drops by to reminisce with López about their art-school days. The weather changes. Occasionally, Erice's camera tilts up to reveal a larger world. Meanwhile, the radio reveals historic doings in the Soviet Union and Persian Gulf. Throughout, López (a sort of painterly postimpressionist) keeps his eyes on the tree, working until he abruptly switches medium. He can no longer paint the tree but only draw it. The October light has become too erratic.

Sketching now in a chilly wind, López tells some foreign visitors that "the best part is being close to the tree." Whatever the artist's motivations, Erice is illustrating the notion articulated in André Bazin's "Ontology of the Photographic Image" that the visual arts are an atavistic desire to arrest nature's flux. Hence the film's many references to copies. The old painters keep returning to the subject of a snapshot taken of them 40 years before; López has a room full of busts and life masks; his studio is dominated by a model of the Venus de Milo.

By December, the quinces have begun to fall. In the movie's supreme gesture, López picks one and then another. Time has prevailed. He disassembles his easel, brings his drawing inside, and dismantles the shelter. Erice doesn't end here, though. He provides a coda in which the artist's wife, Maria Moreno—credited as the movie's producer—poses him on a cot for her painting. (Although he might be on his deathbed, she's painting him as a young man.) López falls asleep and Erice provides him with a dream as the camera, seemingly alone in the garden, continues to film the tree and its decomposing fruit.

More analytical than contemplative, never less than straightforward, *Dream of Light* makes no showy bid for the sublime. This philosophical film blots out vain pomp in suggesting that art is the imitation of nature. Marcus Aurelius would have approved.

Also reviewed in:
NEW YORK TIMES, 5/3/00, p. E9, Janet Maslin

DROWNING MONA

A Destination Films release of a Neverland Films/Jersey Shore production. *Executive Producer:* Danny DeVito, Michael Shamberg, Stacey Sher, and Jonathan Weisgal. *Producer:* Al Corley, Bart Rosenblatt, and Eugene Musso. *Director:* Nick Gomez. *Screenplay:* Peter Steinfeld. *Director of Photography:* Bruce Douglas Johnson. *Editor:* Richard Pearson. *Music:* Michael Tavera. *Sound:* Mark Weingarten and (music) Scott Cochran. *Sound Editor:* Jeff Kushner. *Casting:* Monika Mikkelsen. *Production Designer:* Richard Toyon. *Art Director:* Jim Donahue. *Set Designer:* Betty Krul. *Set Decorator:* Karen Agresti. *Set Dresser:* Freddy Waff. *Costumes:* Terry Dresbach. *Make-up:* Carol Strong. *Running time:* 90 minutes. *MPAA Rating:* PG-13.

CAST: Danny De Vito (Chief Wyatt Rash); Bette Midle (Mona Dearly); Neve Campbell (Ellen Rash); Jamie Lee Curtis (Rona Mace); Casey Affleck (Bobby Calzone); William Fichtner (Phil Dearly); Marcus Thomas (Jeff Dearly); Peter Dobson (Feege); Kathleen Wilhoite (Lucinda); Tracey Walter (Clarence); Paul Ben-Victor (Tony Carlucci); Paul Schulze (Jimmy D); Mark Pellegrino (Murph); Raymond O'Connor (Father Tom); Will Ferrell (Cubby); Lisa Rieffel (Valerie); Robert Arce (Doctor Schwartz); Brittany Peterson (Marla Lasala); Philip Perlman (Charm Motel Cashier); Melissa McCarthy (Shirley); Jason Monkarsh (Benny); Brian Doyle-Murray (Two Truck Drive); Yul Vazquez (French Instructor); Linda Carol and Adam Vernier (Townsfolk).

LOS ANGELES TIMES, 3/3/00, Calendar, p. 2, Kevin Thomas

[The following review by Kevin Thomas appeared in a slightly different form in NEWSDAY, 3/3/00, Part II/p. B7.]

"Drowning Mona" takes a fresh and funny spin on the classic mystery plot in which someone is so universally loathed that practically everyone is a credible suspect.

With an inspired and frequently hilarious script by newcomer Peter Steinfeld, director Nick Gomez, in his fourth feature, has done his best work since his knockout 1991 first feature, "Laws of Gravity," a gritty take on a pair of feckless Brooklyn thieves.

The sure feel Gomez had for blue-collar life in that film carries over to "Drowning Mona," but this time he plays it for comic effect, alternately tart and affectionate. The setting is a little lower-middle-class village in Upstate New York overlooking the Hudson River—which is where Bette Midler's dreadful Mona Dearly winds up when the brakes on her car mysteriously fail, causing it to sail over a cliff into waters far below. A blowzy, embittered middle-aged woman with a cowed yet unfaithful husband, Phil (William Fichtner), and a thick-headed son Jeff (Marcus Thomas) who somehow lost his right hand, Mona is one of those ferocious types stuck in a perpetual state of rage.

A lot of her anger is directed at the sweet-natured but timid Bobby (Casey Affleck), who has unwisely started up a gardening business with the klutzy, loutish Jeff. The business is not really making it, but Mona is not about to let Bobby, at whom she lunges like an attack dog, out of the deal. She is as quick to defend Jeff like a mother bear her cubs as she is to turn on him like she does everyone else.

Poor Bobby is always struggling for money, especially as he has an impending marriage to his live-in girlfriend, Ellen (Neve Campbell), daughter of the local chief of police, Wyatt Rash (Danny DeVito). Wyatt's a warm, capable man with a sharp mind whose references to Broadway musicals, his grand passion, are lost on one and all. He's quick to sniff something fishy about Mona's death.

Mona's demise, swiftly followed by Rash's probings, throws the town into jangling conflicting emotions. Everyone is ecstatic over being freed from Mona!s baleful presence but fears that a too-candid expression of relief might make them suspects. No one is more nervous about this prospect than diner waitress Rona (Jamie Lee Curtis), who's slouching toward middle age while carrying on what has been up to now a futureless, mechanical affair with the rather dim Phil, who she fears will end up taking the rap for killing his wife, even if he didn't.

Steinfeld is endlessly clever at keeping us guessing as well as laughing. He tantalizes us with letting us think we know who did it early on, which gets us wondering as to how he will manage to work everything out, only to throw us yet another curve. Along the way, the film works up a shrewd, amused view of the myriad workings of human nature, and in flashbacks allows Mona a key scene that goes a long way to illuminating her frustration as a once-attractive woman too intelligent for the dummies—i.e., her husband and son—who surround her.

Steinfeld's clever script with its zingy dialogue enables Gomez to draw comically yet delicately nuanced portrayals from his delightful ensemble. Affleck is a wonder at suggesting that his chin will start quivering in fear at any second. Midler, DeVito, Campbell and Curtis are as skilled and amusing as we would expect, but Gomez gets the same level of accomplished portrayals right down the line as he does from his stars.

Fichtner made an impression as the rugged cop in "Go" who proves to be a surprisingly insinuating swinger in one of that film's funniest scenes, and as the randy but slow-witted Phil, he's once again a standout. Similarly, Kathleen Wilhoite is very funny as the ultra-competent, ultra-focused local auto mechanic who whips out her guitar as she performs her comically folk-style "Ode to Mona Dearly"; what's more, the film handles a pass she makes at Ellen with good-natured, even-handed humor.

NEW YORK POST, 3/3/00, p. 52, Lou Lumenick

How you respond to "Drowning Mona" may depend on whether you're amused by the sight of a one-armed man strumming a guitar with his stump.

My wife wasn't. She hated the picture, as did a sizable minority of people at the screening I attended, judging from the number who walked out.

The movie made me laugh quite a bit, though nowhere near as often as I had hoped, based on the hilarious trailer.

Essentially a white-trash variation of Hitchcock's "The Trouble With Harry" set in a small hamlet in northern Westchester about a decade ago, "Drowning Mona" opens with the title character (Bette Midler) and her yellow Yugo hurtling through a guard rail into the Hudson River.

Wyatt Rash (Danny DeVito), Verplanck's mild-mannered, show-tune-loving police chief, discovers most of the population had ample reasons to kill Mona, a person so vile that Wyatt's own deputy proclaims "Ding Dong, the Witch Is Dead" when he learns of the accident.

Chief among suspects are her unemployed widower, Jeff (William Fichtner), who proclaims himself a victim of spousal abuse and repairs to a room at the Charm Motel with his mistress Rona (Jamie Lee Curtis), a waitress at the local bar.

He is soon joined by Mona's cretinous, one-armed son, Jeff (Swedish actor Marcus Thomas, who is excellent), who also enjoys Mona's lewd imitations of Vanna White.

Bobby Calzone (Casey Affleck), Jeff's dim-bulb partner in a struggling landscape business, doesn't have much love for Mona either. Nor did his fiancée, Rash's daughter Ellen (Neve Campbell), who is struggling to organize a wedding at the diner before she gives birth to Bobby's child.

Directing his first feature since the grim "Iltown" four years ago, Nick Gomez (who's been helming episodes of "The Sopranos" and other TV shows) is less interested in the mystery than deploying his great cast in crude antics that, at their best, recall "There's Something About Mary."

Appearing together for the first time since "Ruthless People," Midler—hamming it up to great effect in a series of pointed flashbacks—and DeVito disappointingly have only one scene together, where the chief attempts to calm down the foul-mouthed Mona after she loses a knife-throwing competition.

Mona's skill (or lack thereof with a knife also figures in the last of a hilarious series of "Rashomon"-like accounts of how her son came to lose his arm because of his fondness for beer.

"Drowning Mona" has its lulls and is certainly not for all tastes. But I find it hard to dislike a movie where all the characters drive Yugos—probably the cheapest and worst imported car of all time, even if they did come from the land of my ancestors.

TIME, 3/6/00, p. 72, Richard Schickel

Irony is a mode unknown to Peter Steinfeld and Nick Gomez, respectively the writer and director of *Drowning Mona*. They take the citizens of Verplanck, N.Y., as they find them, which is to say none too bright. All you need to know about this small town is that it was once a test market for the Yugo, and most of the citizenry still happily get about in decrepit versions of that universally unloved car.

They are equally delighted when Bette Midler's title character is murdered in the film's first scene, for she was, as flashbacks reveal, crazy mean. Almost everyone—including Jamie Lee Curtis, Neve Campbell and Casey Affleck—has a motive for offing her, but mostly what police chief Danny DeVito's investigation reveals is a city-wide pattern of irredeemable obtuseness.

Gomez and Steinfeld aren't superior to this stupidity—nothing smug about them, partly because as virtual unknowns, they're eager to please. On the other hand, there's a definite limit to the number of moron jokes we can absorb in 100 minutes, and their movie exceeds it. These guys have a nice gift for sly, side-long comic glances. One appreciates the Coke machine that stands, uncommented upon, in the middle of the funeral parlor. One would not entirely mind seeing the dinner-theater production of *Oh! Calcutta!* they casually mention. But they need to be as smart as they can be instead of as dumb as the dominant (or *Austin Powers: The Spy Who Shagged Me*) comedy market will surely encourage them to be.

VILLAGE VOICE, 3/7/00, p. 128, Amy Taubin

Reindeer Games [see Taubin's review] seems like trash with panache compared to *Drowning Mona*, which looks like a New Jersey version of *Li'l Abner* without tits or biceps. The more relevant inspiration is probably *The Sopranos*, where middle-aged Mafia worker bees turn out to have as many neurotic personal relationships as everyone who gets HBO. *Drowning Mona* is probably only the first of many movies coming down the pike in which people with bad 70s haircuts, living in small towns and letting their homicidal impulses run amuck, expect us to find them cute. Bette Midler and Danny De Vito mug more shamelessly than usual; it's better for the careers of the other actors that they remain nameless. Nick Gomez, one of the most promising filmmakers of the last decade, was chosen for this gig on the basis of his direction of some episodes of *The Sopranos*. Either they had something on him or he needed the money.

Also reviewed in:
CHICAGO TRIBUNE, 3/3/00, Friday/p. G, Michael Wilmington
NEW YORK TIMES, 3/3/00, p. E26, Elvis Mitchell
NEW YORKER, 3/6/00, p. 98, Anthony Lane
VARIETY, 2/28-3/5/00, p. 39, Todd McCarthy
WASHINGTON POST, 3/3/00, p. C5, Stephen Hunter

DUDE, WHERE'S MY CAR?

A Twentieth Centur Fox release of a Wayne Rice/Gil Netter production. *Producer:* Wayne Rice, Gil Netter, Broderick Johnson, and Andrew Kosove. *Director:* Danny Leiner. *Screenplay:* Philip Stark. *Director of Photography:* Robert Stevens. *Editor:* Kimberly Ray *Music:* David Kitay. *Music Editor:* Terry Wilson. *Choreogapher:* Marguerite Derricks. *Sound:* Jose Antonio Garcia and (music) Damon Tedesco. *Sound Editor:* Bruce Fortune. *Casting:* Ronnie Yeskel and Richard Hicks. *Production Designer:* Charles Breen. *Art Director:* Charles Butcher. *Set Designer:* Bruce West. *Set Decorator:* Jeffrey Kushon. *Set Dresser:* Kurt Hulett. *Special Effects:* Dave Kelsey. *Visual Effects:* Heather Ignarro. *Costumes:* Pamela Withers. *Make-up:* Lydia Milars. *Stunt Coordinator:* Monty Cox. *Running time:* 90 minutes. *MPAA Rating:* PG-13.

CAST: Ashton Kutcher (Jesse);   Seann William Scott (Chester);   Jennifer Garner (Wanda); Marla Sokoloff (Wilma);   David Herman (Nelson);   Christian Middelthon (Nordic Dude #1); David W. Bannick (Nordic Dude #2);   Charlie O'Connell (Tommy); Kristy Swanson (Christie Boner);   Teressa Tunney (Tania);   Mitzi Martin (Jumpsuit Chick #1);   Nichole M. Hiltz (Jumpsuit Chick #2);   Linda Kim (Jumpsuit Chick #3);   Mia Trudeau (Jumpsuit Chick #4); Kim Marie Johnson (Jumpsuit Chick #5);   Bill Chott (Big Cult Guy #1);   Michael Ray Bower (Big Cult Guy #2);   Turtle (Jeff);   Kevin Christy (Zellner);   Kristoffer Winters (Zilbor);   Mary Lynn Rajskub (Zelmina);   Robert Clendenin (Zarnoff);   Hal Sparks (Zoltan);   Linda Porter (Mrs. Crabbleman);   "Stuttering" John Melendez (Gene);   Joanna Bacalso (Redheaded Bartender);   Katherine Baker (Stripper);   Keone Young (Chinese Tailor);   Marc Lynn (Ray Cop);   Christopher Darga (Anderson Cop);   Pat Finn (Rick Cop);   Dwight Armstrong (Fun O'Rama Employee);   Cinco Paul (Counselor);   Brendan Ian Hill (Stuart);   Jona Kai Jacobsen (Anthony);   Cleo King (Penny);   Big Johnson (Birthday Father);   Galvin Chapman (Birthday Son);   John Toles-Bey (Mr. Pizzacoli);   Jod Ann Paterson (Super Chick);   Freda Foh Shen (Chinese Food Lady); Fabio (Fabio);   Claudine Barros (Patty);   Dominic Capone (Mr. Pizzacoli, Jr.);   Sydney (Jackal).

NEW YORK POST, 12/16/00, p. 23, Jonathan Foreman

The talented folk who cut the trailer for "Dude, Where's My Car?" deserve congratulations for their skill—and blame for perpetrating a fraud on the movie-going public.

The trailer made the film look as if it could be funny in the tradition of dumb youth comedies about pot-smoking slackers (the Cheech & Chong films, "Fast Times at Ridgemont High," etc.)

But the sad truth is that Fox didn't screen "Dude, Where's My Car?" for critics for very good reason: This movie is an almost chuckle-free mess, so amateurish and lame that the cast often has that embarrassed look you see on dogs given ridiculous haircuts.

The idea is that two stoner dudes, Jesse (Ashton Kutcher) and Chester (Seann William Scott), wake up one morning with absolutely no memory of their party the night before.

They therefore have no idea where their car is, why their fridge is filled with chocolate pudding, how their twin girlfriends' house got trashed or how they apparently scored with a bevy of strippers and local babe Christie Boner (Kristy Swanson).

They go out searching for answers in their supposedly lovable, knuckle-headed way, and find themselves caught in a three-way contest between two groups of space aliens and some earthling science nerds seeking a device that could save the universe.

One group of aliens looks like sexy brunettes in jumpsuits, while the other takes the form of Germanic, muscular gay guys in leather vests. Like so much else in "Dude," the alien jokes are just half-baked borrowings from a funnier film—in this case, "Galaxy Quest."

The scene set in a day camp for blind kids is, of course, a bad, lazy imitation of the disabled day-camp sequence in "There's Something About Mary." (The script is credited, if that's the word, to Philip Stark.)

To make the rip-off complete, you never really do find out what happened the, night before.

SIGHT AND SOUND, 3/01, p. 46, Kay Dickinson

Suburban America, the present. Jesse and Chester, avid party-goers, wake up to find they've forgotten where they parked their car the previous night. It's also the first anniversary of their relationship with their girlfriends, twins Wilma and Wanda. Having left their girlfriends' anniversary presents in the boot, Jesse and Chester go in search of the missing vehicle.

On their odyssey to recover the car, they also realise that they've mislaid the "continuum transfunctioner", a mysterious instrument capable of saving the universe. Also on the hunt for this gadget and desperately trying to thwart each other are the cult of Zoltan, a strange sect, and two sets of aliens: the jumpsuit Chicks and the Nordic Dudes. Although the boys aren't able to track down their car, they get hold of a key which unlocks a locker which opens on to an amusement arcade. There, they find a bundle of game tickets which they use to win a toy they believe to be the continuum transfunctioner. The Jumpsuit Chicks, the Nordic Dudes and the cult arrive; the three groups begin to barter for a Rubiks cube Jesse and Chester have been carrying with them, in the mistaken belief that it is the continuum transfunctioner. The jumpsuit Chicks then turn out to be the embodiment of a malevolent force and transmogrify into a giant alien which Jesse and Chester destroy. Having eventually obtained the continuum transfunctioner, the Nordic Dudes erase the boys' memories. Jesse and Chester awake the next morning, oblivious to their past adventures, find their car and deliver the presents to the twins.

It's no great revelation to say that Hollywood often pampers to the sensibilities of straight adolescent boys, but few movies in recent memory can have targeted this demographic so brazenly as *Dude, Where's My Car?* Charting the attempt by two spaced out slackers to find their car, the film plays like a check list of the teen movie's most basic component parts, all of which have been successfully road tested by earlier films; consequently expect to encounter extra-terrestrials, a fusillade of wannabe catch-phrases, a cloud of soft-drugs references, and—most predictably of all—a preoccupation with large breasts. Indeed, breasts abound in *Dude,* from the slack-jawed lead duo Jesse and Chester's grabbing of the regrettably named Christie Boner's assets to the parting gift they receive from the aliens—a pair of necklaces which induce mammarial swelling. Although it's more amiable in its frolicking, the film is essentially a *Porky's* for today's generation of teenage boys, who have flocked to the equally derivative *American Pie.* This is a world where seeing girls' underwear is at the top of everyone's wish-list, a desire the slavering camera is all too willing to indulge.

Despite its hunger for exposed flesh, the most naked thing in *Dude* is perhaps the pubescent male psyche. The movie is so attentive to the anxieties of teenage boys, with its unremitting and nervous joshing about testicular damage, transgendered people and homosexuality, that beneath its jokey bravura, the picture it paints of that age group is inadvertently raw and touchingly vulnerable.

With this tension so palpable, it comes as no surprise that Dude's screenwriter, Philip Stark, also worked on televisions *South Park.* But whereas *South Park* sparkles with wit, *Dude* merely flickers—a failing that can probably be traced to its focus on adult rather than child protagonists. Jesse and Chester's regressive cluelessness doesn't tally with their rent paying, car driving grown-up existences. The goofy charm of the leads in such films as *Bill & Ted's Excellent Adventure* is part and parcel of their school age ingenuousness; here, when Jesse and Chester utter such lines as "I've got three words for you. Anger. Manage. Ment" as fully fledged adults, they come across as untenably immature. No doubt these flaccid jokes spring from a desire to tap some of the success Jim Carrey has had with his dumbed-down *shtick,* but Carrey is arguably at his best projecting a man child persona, disconnected from such grown-up preoccupations as long-term relationships. In contrast, *Dude's* two boneheads have inexplicably snagged perfect girlfriends. Then again, this character detail is perhaps not so surprising given that the movie seems to be aimed at boys with no points of comparison save their fantasies.

VILLAGE VOICE, 1/2/01, p. 106, Jessica Winter

There is simply no good reason why 20th Century Fox refused to screen the radiantly stoopid *Dude, Where's My Car?* for critics—it's a welcome whiff of potsmoke in an especially fetid Oscar-baiting season, an absurdist Homeric epic to show the Coen brothers what for Young weed—whackers Jesse (Ashton Kutcher) and Cheste (Sean William Scott) wake up in their studiously filthy apartment one morning to cabalistic pudding cups spilling out of their refrigerator and, devastatingly, an empty parking spot out front. The ensuing quest for Jesse's auto entails menacing fratjocks, deep-throated space-alien babes, stampeding ostriches (or llamas—this is subject to some debate), a Heaven's Gate-ish cult, a benevolent pair of "totally gay Nordic dudes," and a historically precise non sequitur recreation of an early-'90s poolside hip-hop video.

Director Danny Leiner, who has helmed episodes of *Strangers Mth Candy* and Freaks and Geeks, has a keen for comic grace notes and, propitiously, doesn't know when to say when: The jokes rely strongly upon fearless repetition and protraction, creating the impression of Abbott and Costello as directed by the Farrellys (that DUDE/SWEET tattoo joke, milked mercilessly in the TV ads, doesn't age a second). Screenwriter Philip Stark demonstrates impeccable taste in thievings that run the gamut from *Half-Baked* to *Being John Malkovich,* and t movie's lineage descends from the best nobrainer teen comedies of the mid '80s, notably *Revenge of the Nerds* though the absurdly beautiful Kutcher doesn't try too hard to approximate a sex-starved stoner dork. But Scott, nearly as pretty, does, yanking and crumpling his rubbery face into a Carreyesque repertoire of idiot grins, thrusting his jaw into a friendly Beavis underbite.

Indeed, Butt-head and his better half would seem the worthy models for these indeterminately financed, apparently parentless boys: Jesse is the droll, essentially functional leader, while Chester is the pliant tagalong who, while hazardously dim-witted most of the time, is also capable of sublime flights of insight But it's also worth pointing out that Jesse and Chester, who haven't slept with their twin girlfriends after a year's courtship, spend scarcely a moment apart (at one point Chester correctly guesses that Jesse needs to take a dump, and squeals triumphantly, "I know your body!"), bicker like an old married couple, keep waking up next to each other in various mysterious locations, and enjoy a tender, Fabio-instigated (if you have to ask ...) make-out session, are, like those sweet Nordic dudes, totally gay. Daft and lovable and even kinda daring, Dude deserves its truly clueless studio's belabored support. My friend even supplied a blurbable quote: "The best dumbass-buddy comedy I've seen since *Wayne's World*!"

Also reviewed in:
NEW YORK TIMES, 12/16/00, p. B20, Stephen Holden
VARIETY, 12/18-31/00, p. 24, Joe Leydon

DUETS

A Hollywood Pictures release in association with Seven Arts Pictures and Beacon Pictures of a Kevin Jones production. *Executive Producer:* Lee R. Mayes, Neil Canton, Tony Ludwig, and Alan Riche. *Producer:* Kevin Jones, Bruce Paltrow, and John Byrum. *Director:* Bruce Paltrow. *Screenplay:* John Byrum. *Director of Photography:* Paul Sarossy. *Editor:* Jerry Greenberg. *Music:* David Newman. *Music Editor:* Carl Kaller. *Sound:* Eric Batut and (music) John Kurlander. *Sound Editor:* Donald J. Malouf and Todd Toon. *Casting:* Francine Maisler and Kathleen Driscoll-Mohler. *Production Designer:* Sharon Seymour. *Art Director:* William Heslup. *Set Designer:* Bill McMahon. *Set Decorator:* Lesley Beale. *Set Dresser:* Patrick Kearns, Audra Neil, J.P. Bagshaw, Steve Roland, and Paula R. Montgomery. *Special Effects:* Darryn Marcoux. *Costumes:* Mary Claire Hannan. *Make-up:* Tina Earnshaw and Jo Ann Fowler. *Stunt Coordinator:* Ernie Jackson. *Running time:* 113 minutes. *MPAA Rating:* R.

CAST: Lochlyn Munro (Ronny Jackson);   Carol Alexander (Beth the Hostess);   Michael Rogers (Tulsa Bartender);   Huey Lewis (Ricky Dean);   Amanda Kravat (Redhead);   Paul Giamatti (Todd Woods);   Ian Robison, Roger Haskett, and John Payne (Sales Guys);   Scott Speedman (Billy);   Tom Bougers (Desk Sergeant);   Marian Seldes (Harriet Gahagan);   Angie Phillips (Arlene);   Steve Oatway (Ralph Beckerman);   Erika Von Tagen (Julie);   Kiersten Warren (Candy Woods);   Laura Murdoch (Dead Showgirl);   Gwyneth Paltrow (Liv);   Angie Dickinson (Blair);   Roman Danylo (Albuquerque Desk Clerk);   Keegan Tracy (Sheila);   Ann Warn Pegg (Taffy);   Mario Bello (Suzi Loomis);   Ron Small (Old Homeless Man);   Tony Marr (Japanese Business Man);   Brian Jensen (Cincinnati Bartender);   Tom Heaton (Charlie);   Andre Braugher (Reggie Kane);   Andrew Johnston (Shop Manager);   Wyley Vlahovic (Desert Joint Man);   Beverly Elliott (Desert Joint Woman);   Diane Brown (Desert Joint Hostess);   Warren Takeuchi (Texas Trooper);   Aaron Pearl (Buddy);   J. B. Bivens (Clark);   Candus Churchill (Karaoke Woman);   Brent Butt (Kansas Motel Clerk); David Neale (Desk Manager);   Mike "Mitch" Mitchell (K. C. Gas Station Attendant); Iris Quinn (K. C. Hostess);   Brenda Crichlow (Omaha Clerk);   Maya Rudolph (Omaha Karaoke Hostess);   Anita Dutton (Tonia Kasper);   Larry Dutton (Hobie Kasper);   Gary Hetherington (Omaha Police Captain);   John Pinette (John);   Susan Campbell (Airline Representative).

LOS ANGELES TIMES, 9/15/00, Calendar/p. 2, Kenneth Turan

[The following review by Kenneth Turan appeared in a slightly different form in
NEWSDAY, 9/15/00, Part II/p. B3.]

"Duets" is six characters in search of a movie. Any movie will do, and a lot are tried: a tedious road picture, a joyless comedy, a toothless social satire, to name a few. The only aspect of "Duets" that is successful is its singing, which not only sounds good, but keeps all that other nonsense off the screen.

Directed by successful TV producer Bruce Paltrow ("St. Elsewhere," "The White Shadow") and co-starring his daughter Gwyneth, along with Maria Bello, Andre Braugher, Paul Giamatti, Huey Lewis and Scott Speedman, "Duets" is set in the world of karaoke, where the music is famous but you're not. At least not yet. "You get to be the star for three minutes," one devotee says. "It's a rush like you wouldn't believe."

Having six people simultaneously trying to find themselves and win the $5,000 Grand Prize Karaoke Contest in Omaha is a legitimate concept for a film, but as written by John Byrum, whose credits include underachievers like "Mahogany" and "Sphinx," it ends up a lifeless screwball comedy that is neither screwy nor funny.

In addition to its other shortcomings, "Duets" is awfully slow in getting going, and it seems like forever before all six characters—quasi-losers and lovable misfits every one—are introduced and tidily matched off into nonromantic pairs.

Glimpsed first is Ricky Dean (Lewis), a practiced karaoke hustler (admit it, you didn't know the profession existed) and habitual rolling stone. Eventually he hooks up with Liv (Paltrow), a long-limbed Las Vegas showgirl who is noticeably short on family connections.

Billy Hannon ("Felicity's" Scott Speedman) is a saintly underachiever who wanted to be a priest but ended up driving a cab. Naturally, he is matched with Suzi Loomis, young, attractive and willing to trade any sexual favor you can think of to advance her singing career. Suzi is played by the always-involving Bello, and it's a mark of how soporific this production is that even her usual high energy can't successfully shake things up.

The third pairing is the most problematic. Reggie Kane (Braugher) is an armed and dangerous ex-con who's never found an outlet for his fine voice. He gets connected with Todd Woods (Giamatti), a traveling salesman so wired he's never sure what state he's in.

Ignored by his family on the rare occasions he's home, Todd goes on an extended walkabout and turns into a childish, self-indulgent troublemaker whose sour and violent rants about the American dream not working anymore sound suspiciously like writer Byrum wants us to take them seriously.

In addition to continually saying "I'm supposed to be out buying a pack of cigarettes" like it was funny, Todd is also involved in the film's two violent sequences, set pieces that, according to trade reports, delayed "Duets' " release. The scenes have been greatly trimmed, but they still feel like they belong in a different movie. If ever a film miscalculated its effects, it's this one.

The only bright light in "Duets" is that the singing its stars do is quite pleasant. It's no surprise that Lewis, front man for Huey Lewis & the News, can handle songs like "Feeling Alright" and "Lonely Teardrops," but hearing Paltrow singing "Bette Davis Eyes," Bello doing "Sweet Dreams (Are Made of This)" and Giamatti and Braugher (with some help from Arnold McCuller) belt out "Try a Little Tenderness" are almost the only pleasures this film has to offer.

Though "Duets" characters are forever saying karaoke is a way of life, we never really feel that or see it on screen. In fact, the film's attitude becomes so who-cares it neglects to wrap up its biggest plot point. But the truth is, by the time "Duets" faces the music, hardly anyone is going to care.

NEW YORK, 9/25/00, p. 61, Peter Rainer

Do we really need a movie that uses the karaoke-bar scene as a metaphor for life? *Duets* interweaves the disparate stories of three couples chasing the American Dream, and its woozy with its own windy philosophizing. Todd Woods (Paul Giamatti) is the bedraggled corporate salesman who spends so much time in look-alike hotel rooms and airports that he often can't remember what city he's in; when we first see him, he's pitching an eco-disaster of a theme park to some gents in Houston while thinking he's in Orlando. Todd is the hurt-puppy centerpiece of *Duets*. His wife and children barely acknowledge him when he makes it back to his nondescript suburban tract home, so he cracks and hits the road, sporting an earring and stopping in at hotels along the way. When he reluctantly enters a karaoke contest and lets loose his inner Sinatra, Todd is hooked.

Giamatti is best known for playing Pig Vomit in Howard Stern's *Private Parts*, and he has a gift for playing wheedling small-timers (a great gift, I would say, having also seen him on Broadway as one of the barflies in *The Iceman Cometh*). In *Duets*, Giamatti plays Todd as someone whose life force is dangerously out of control, which may be more than director Bruce Paltrow and his screenwriter, John Byrum, bargained for. The filmmakers are life-affirming types—why else would they make this sludgy piece of serial inspirationalism?—and Giamatti is too rancid and frazzled for the hopeful send-off they give him. His performance is a prime example of how actors striving to maintain their dignity in subpar situations can turn their roles around with a denunciatory force.

Another specialist in this sort of thing is Andre Braugher, playing Reggie Kane, an ex-con, or maybe he's an escaped con, who is picked up hitchhiking by Todd and becomes a soul mate. Braugher has such seething energy that he's like a human time bomb; given almost nothing to work with, he creates a character whose instincts are with the underworld. We can believe that Reggie spent a good chunk of his life in jail because he looks around him as if through an escape hatch. He's visored by fear. It's the film's conceit that Reggie has a voice to die for and a heart as big as Kmart. He coaxes Todd into returning to his family and sacrifices himself in the process. There's a whiff of *Touched by an Angel* in all this, and it undercuts Braugher's power.

The other duets don't have much power to undercut. Scott Speedman plays a cabdriver trying to achieve some kind of inner harmony, although there doesn't seem to be enough in him to harmonize with; he's paired with Maria Bello, playing an ambitious crooner who, in a tasteless running gag, screws her way into all kinds of freebies on the road to redemption. Bello played the owner of the hooters club in *Coyote Ugly*, it's time she quit the bar scene. Gwyneth Paltrow is a Vegas showgirl who meets up with the father she never knew, played by Huey Lewis, and ends up, like the other principals in the cast, journeying to Omaha for a karaoke contest. Paltrow does her own singing, and she has a pleasing voice that goes well with Lewis's mellifluous rasp, but she's playing a character of such bemused innocence that she seems stunted. She's insufferably dewy. (Have we gone back to that silent-movie notion that virginal maidens are the only pure-in-heart?) Paltrow is always best playing slutty, edgy types, as in *Flesh and Bone* and *Hard Eight* and moments in *The Talented Mr. Ripley*, but her weeping-willow goldenness, which has its heavily bland side, is what attracts most filmmakers (her father is her director here).

Karaoke bars allow real people in boozy public gatherings to do things best left for the privacy of their own shower. This sentiment is not, however, endorsed by the film, which pushes the cant that karaoke allows us to throw off society's shackles and all be stars, if only for a brief, shining hour. For a movie bursting with so much blather about the virtues of small-time selfhood, *Duets* has an unseemly tendency to be goggle-eyed about celebrity.

NEW YORK POST, 9/15/00, p. 51, Lou Lumenick

I say we take the country back from the McDonalds, the Pizza Huts and the Wendys," one character actually exclaims in "Duets," a bizarrely dated drama about karaoke aficionados. "We should tear down the strip malls and get in touch with our inner core."

Though it takes place in the present, the ill-starred "Duets," as this bit of dialogue beautifully illustrates, has a sensibility firmly rooted in the 1980s.

It begins with a shot of a mechanical bull that seems an homage to "Urban Cowboy," a vastly superior movie from that bygone era.

Small wonder: The screenwriter, John Byrum, was most prominent in that decade, when he wrote and directed such quintessentially misbegotten works as "Inserts," an ancestor of "Boogie Nights" that almost destroyed Richard Dreyfuss's career, and the jaw-droppingly dreadful remake of W. Somerset Maugham's "The Razor's Edge" with Bill Murray.

Director Bruce Paltrow is also firmly identified with the 1980s, creating two landmark TV series of the era, "The White Shadow" and "St. Elsewhere." This is only his second feature film; the other was "A Little Sex," a negligible 1984 comedy with Tim Matheson and Kate Capshaw.

As all Page Six readers know, Paltrow (along with his buddy Byrum) is back in the feature business, thanks to Oscar-winning daughter Gwyneth, part of an ensemble cast that at one point was to include her ex-boyfriend, Brad Pitt.

Now, after a much-reported dispute between Paltrow senior and the studio over editing of the movie's violence that delayed the film's planned May release, "Duets" is here. And it is, not to put too fine a point on it, pretty awful.

Gwyneth plays Liv, the world's most flat-chested Las Vegas showgirl, who meets up with her long-missing dad, Ricky (singer Huey Lewis, who can kindly be described as a minimalist screen presence), at her mother's wake.

They are introduced by her grandmother (Angie Dickinson), who recalls that "when Mr. Sinatra got me my job at the Dunes, my roots began to sprout." Ouch.

At Grandma's insistence, Ricky, who makes his living as a karaoke hustler, takes Liv to the national championship in Omaha, where he'll compete for a $5,000 prize.

Also Omaha-bound are a couple of other odd couples. Todd (Paul Giamatti), a burned-out businessman obsessed with redeeming his 800,000 frequent-flyer miles who finds God behind a karaoke microphone, hooks up with Reggie (Andre Braugher), an escaped convict.

The less-than-scintillating septet is completed by Billy (Scott Speedman of "Felicity"), a cuckolded cab driver who teams up with Suzi (Mario Bello of "Coyote Ugly"), an aspiring singer who isn't adverse to trading oral sex for a paint job for Billy's cab.

A virtual compendium of mercifully forgotten movies of the 1980s—most particularly, John Schlesinger's road comedy, "Honky-Tonk Freeway"—"Duets" lurches its way from bar to bar through Middle America (actually, Vancouver), climaxing in the second of two clumsily staged shootout sequences.

The talented cast doesn't stand much of a chance in this rambling, pointless narrative, reeling off such howlers as:

"I've waited all my life to spend time with you."

"When someone real comes into your life, you just can't deal with it."

"Live in the moment."

"It's a rush like you wouldn't believe—you get to be a star for three minutes."

Yes, all of the stars (save Speedman) sing—and, except for Lewis, their warbling is pretty excruciating.

Lewis nearly carries Gwyneth through a duet of Smokey Robinson's "Cruisin'," but listening to her off-key solo rendition of "Bette Davis Eyes" comes dangerously close to cruel and unusual punishment.

Next year, couldn't Gwyneth give her dad a necktie for Father's Day?

SIGHT AND SOUND, 12/00, p. 45, John Wrathall

Middle America, the present. In Las Vegas for the funeral of a former lover, Ricky Dean, who makes a living by hustling for cash at karaoke competitions, meets his long-lost daughter Liv who decides to follow him on the road. Cab-driver Billy Hannon discovers his girlfriend is cheating on him. Drunk in a bar, he is picked up by singer Suzi Loomis who persuades him to drive her to California for a karaoke contest. Todd Woods, a real-estate executive in the grip of a mid-life crisis, walks out on his wife and wanders into a bar where he discovers the liberating power of karaoke singing. Hitting the road, he gives a lift to ex-con Reggie Kane, who's on the run after sticking up (and apparently killing) a truck driver. In a bar, Todd introduces Reggie to karaoke. Finding Reggie's gun, Todd uses it to stick up a service station. Reggie tries to stop him. In the ensuing shootout the garage attendant is killed.

The three couples converge on a hotel in Omaha, Nebraska, for a karaoke competition. In the foyer, Billy meets Liv; they instantly fall for each other. Meanwhile the police are closing in on Reggie, who decides to take the blame for the shooting at the service station. While Reggie is on stage, police enter the auditorium. Reggie pulls out a gun and is shot dead.

Todd is reunited with his wife, who has been summoned to Omaha by Reggie. Billy and Suzi offer Ricky and Liv a lift to another karaoke competition in Nevada.

The idea of Gwyneth Paltrow and Huey Lewis duetting with Smokey Robinson's "Cruisin" might not seem like an immediate selling point for a movie. But Duets, set in the karaoke bars of the Midwest, actually works best in its musical moments: like the best musicals, it makes us care about the characters' state of mind whenever they open their mouths to sing. It's when they put the mikes down that Duets runs into problems.

Screenwriter John Byrum introduces his characters effectively in a series of wry vignettes. Todd, the travelling salesman on the verge of a breakdown, stumbles into a meeting room and is half way through his sales pitch before realising he's in the wrong hotel in the wrong town in the wrong state. Cabdriver Billy is summoned to drive a fare home from the police cells, only to discover it's his old teacher. Washed-up hustler Ricky, in Las Vegas to pay his last respects to his dead ex, gets chatting to a spaced-out showgirl at the funeral parlour before realising she's his long-lost daughter Liv. Thereafter the film settles down into a loose road-movie format, tracking its three mismatched duos from bar to bar across the Midwest.(Writer director of the 1979 Jack Kerouac/Neal Cassady biopic *Heart Beat,* Byrum clearly knows his genre.)

Unfortunately, as with so many of the current crop of multi-strand movies (including the top-of-the-range *Magnolia),* you can't help wishing the writer had concentrated on the most interesting story of the bunch—in this case Todd's odd-couple friendship with fugitive hitchhiker Reggie. While the Todd/Reggie strand provides the film's dramatic and comic highlights, it also seems underdeveloped. A fugitive killer who decides to play guardian angel to a complete stranger (and turns out to sing like a dream), Reggie is a barely credible creation, despite André Braugher's charismatic performance. As if aware of the flaws here, director Bruce Paltrow cuts away at the two crucial moments when Reggie is about to shoot someone presumably it's easier for the audience to love a killer if we don't actually see him killing. A bolder film-maker would have shown the murders full on and found a way to embrace the contradiction in Reggie's character.

Paltrow is an experienced television director, best known for his work on hospital soap *St. Elsewhere, Duets,* however, is his first feature film in 18 years, following his long-forgotten debut *A Little Sex.* One can only assume that his daughter Gwyneth's willingness to appear in a comparatively minor role helped get the project greenlit. Paltrow senior succeeds in extracting solid performances (and decent singing) from an interesting cast, not least Huey Lewis, who brings a craggy, worldly authority to Ricky, and the pop-eyed Paul Giamatti as Todd, finally getting a juicy lead after a string of nerdy supporting roles. But a younger, hipper director might have given this the edge it sorely lacks.

VILLAGE VOICE, 9/26/00, p. 147, Dennis Lim

Karaoke represents liberation in *Duets*—far more than a train-wreck by-product of oblivious drunkenness, it's a transformative escape for the wounded souls here, who stumble upon true meaning in the act of belting out some moldy oldie that we haven't heard nearly often enough. A more interesting movie would have positioned karaoke, with its sad, cruel sense of repetition and predestination, not as a cure but a metaphor for the deadening treadmill routineness of modern life. As it is, *Duets* merely confirms that, in all karaoke-related matters, intoxicants help—a truism the film half-heartedly acknowledges by having one character ingest a handful of beta-blockers before bursting into song.

Duets is, broadly speaking, a road movie, though there's a decided lack of forward motion in the way it ushers together three odd couples for a climactic amateur night in Omaha. Bitch-on-wheels Maria Bello finds a savior in sappy-doormat cab driver Scott Speedman. Glazed Vegas showgirl/naïf Gwyneth Paltrow (who doesn't embarrass herself with her singing; her concussed acting is another matter) demonstrates clingy, creepy affection for her recently discovered father, a crumpled karaoke hustler played by Huey Lewis (a subplot made doubly icky by the presence of Gwyneth's dad, Bruce, behind the camera). Angry white man Paul Giammati, a new convert to the joys of karaoke, turns into Kevin Spacey in *American Beauty* (though unfortunately not Edward Norton in *Fight Club)* and, mid-rampage, picks up a hitchhiker, escaped convict and designated font of wisdom Andre Braugher. Bruce Paltrow adopts a milder variation of a manipulation technique Lars von Trier hones to evil perfection in *Dancer in the Dark:* numbing the audience, with an onslaught of sustained miserableness, into helplessly anticipating the musical numbers. This works up until about "Islands in the Stream."

Also reviewed in:
CHICAGO TRIBUNE, 9/15/00, Friday/p. A, Mark Caro
NEW YORK TIMES, 9/15/00, p. E8, A. O. Scott
VARIETY, 9/18-24/00, p. 31, Todd McCarthy

WASHINGTON POST, 9/15/00, p. C5, Megan Rosenfeld
WASHINGTON POST, 9/15/00, Weekend/p. 46, Desson Howe

DUNGEONS & DRAGONS

A New Line Cinema presentation of a Sweetpea Entertainment production. *Executive Producer:* Joel Silver, Allan Zeman, and Nelson Leong. *Producer:* Courtney Solomon, Kia Jam, and Tom Hammel. *Director:* Courtney Solomon. *Screenplay (Based on the Dungeons & Dragons property owned by Wizards of the Coast, Inc.):* Topper Lilien and Carroll Cartwright. *Director of Photography:* Doug Milsome. *Editor:* Caroline Ross. *Music:* Justin Caine Burnett. *Music Editor:* Tod Holcomb. *Sound:* Mark Holding and (music) Malcolm Luker. *Sound Editor:* Stephen Barden. *Casting:* Elisa Goodman, Abra Edelman, and Jeremy Zimmerman. *Production Designer:* Bryce Perrin. *Art Director:* Ricardo Spinace. *Set Designer:* Stuart Kearns. *Set Decorator:* Tomas Hais. *Set Dresser:* Vladimir Jezek and Josef Vecerek. *Special Mechanical Effects:* George Gibbs. *Costumes:* Barbara Lane. *Make-up:* Tara Smith. *Make-up (Jeremy Irons):* Linda De Vetta. *Special Make-up Effects:* Martin Astles. *Stunt Coordinator:* Graeme Crowther and Petr Drozda. *Running time:* 108 minutes. *MPAA Rating:* PG-13.

CAST: Jeremy Irons (Profion); Bruce Payne (Damodar); Justin Whalin (Ridley Freeborn); Marlon Wayans (Snails); Robert Miano (Azmath); Tomas Havrlik (Mage); Thora Birch (Empress Savina); Edward Jewesbury (Vildan Vildir); Zoe McLellan (Marina Pretensa); Lee Arenberg (Elwood Gutworthy); Kristen Wilson (Norda); Martin Astles (Orc #1); Matthew O'Toole (Orc #2); David O'Kelly (Three Eyes); Richard O'Brien (Xilus); Kia Jam (Thief #1); Nicolas Rochette (Thief #2); David Mandis (Thief #3); Robert Henny (Crimson Brigade); Stanislav Ondricek (Another Mage); Roman Hemala (Council Mage); Tom Baker (Halvarth); Andrew Blau and Marta Urbanova (Elves); Jiri Machacek (Loyalist General).

LOS ANGELES TIMES, 12/8/00, Calendar/p. 17, John Anderson

[The following review by John Anderson appeared in a slightly different form in
NEWSDAY, 12/8/00, Part II/p. B8.]

Dragons, despots, dwarfs, elves. Interspecies political infighting. Marx-less proletariat uprisings. Bald guys with blue lips. Yod know: the usual. Not too many dungeons, though. But once you've weathered "Dungeons & Dragons," you might want to go stretch out in one.

For 25 years, the role-playing game Dungeons & Dragons has been keeping otherwise productive people occupied and, if you believe some court testimony, inspiring more psychotic behavior than "The Catcher in the Rye." This, we're sure, is slander; those people were time bombs anyway.

But we've seen the movie, which apparently requires a more intimate knowledge of D&D than is possessed by the normal—I mean, average—moviegoer, or which can be explained during the brief prelude that begins the picture. Either that or it's just confusing.

In brief, the commoners and the Mages (the ruling class) are at odds, as are Empress Savina, (Thora Birch) and the power-mad Profion (Jeremy Irons) who wants to thwart her dreams of democracy by getting his hands on the precious Dragon's Eye and the scarlet scepter that controls the Red Dragon. Ridley and Snails (Justin Whalin and Marlon Wayans), a kind of medieval Crosby-Hope road team, begin as mere thieves but through their dealings with Marina of the Magic School (Zoe McLellan), Norda the elf (Kristen Wilson) and Elwood the dwarf (Lee Arenberg) become major players in the salvation of their people (or, you know, whatever).

Some of the effects are quite interesting, particularly the dragons, and something that looked like a many-tentacled gum wad. A sequence in which Ridley conquers a lethal maze in order to get to the Dragon's Eye is good too. But Courtney Solomon, whose chief qualification for directing this movie seems to have been his ownership of the film rights, has neither the capacity to make us care about any of his characters nor a cast (with the exception of Wayans) to help him out. Whalin is awful, Birch is saddled with lines that would make a silent film star blanch and

Irons devours huge chunks of scenery with the ferocity of one of those dog-fighting dragons, which scream through the computer-generated skies with the greatest of ease.

NEW YORK POST, 12/8/00, p. 53, Lou Lumenick

If I had actually paid to see "Dungeons & Dragons," I would not only ask for my money back, but I would demand triple reparations.

Inspired less by the '70s board game than a desire to rip off as many other fantasy movies as possible, this tacky-looking, incoherent, badly acted and hopelessly directed disaster is easily the dullest adventure film of 2000.

Debuting director Courtney Solomon boasted in an interview that his experience was limited to high school theatricals. That's most painfully obvious in the immensely bored performance of Thora Birch ("American Beauty") who looks like a thrift-shop version of a "Star Wars"-style empress and seems to be delivering her lines from a teleprompter, one... word... at... a... time.

She doesn't have a lot of screen time; nor does Jeremy Irons, who apparently desperately needed a paycheck. He wears lot of eye shadow and hams relentlessly to no avail as a wizard who plots against her.

The actual plot—so incomprehensibly edited that even D & D devotees may wonder if the projectionists showed the reels in the wrong order—revolves around magic scepters, rods, scrolls, dungeons and dragons.

Joining together to save the empress' empire are a pair of "Dawson's Creek" rejects (Justin Whalin and Zoe McLellan), a jive-talking black (Marlon Wayans, a long way from "Requiem From a Dream"), a sexy but sullen elf (Kristen Wilson) and a dwarf (Lee Arenberg) with atrocious table manners and a red beard that looks like it came from a dollar store.

Trust me, they're not a bunch even die-hard gamers will want to spend 107 endless minutes with. Better you should track down a rental copy of the 1982 made-for-TV "D & D" knockoff "Mazes and Monsters," which is no great shakes but stars, no kidding, Tom Hanks.

Employing crummy-looking sets and cheesy special effects, "Dungeons & Dragons" makes a half-hearted attempt at copying the Cantina scene from the original "Star Wars," but it's no more likely to keep audiences awake than a silly variation on a scene from "Raiders of the Lost Ark."

As adaptations of games go, "D & D" is right down there with "Super Mario Bros." and "Mortal Kombat."

SIGHT AND SOUND, 4/01, p. 44, Kim Newman

A pseudo-medieval fantasy world. Savina, empress of Izmer, plans to break the rule of the mages over the common people. The wicked wizard Profion sends his chief henchman Damodar to fetch the Rod of Savrille, a magical staff which will give him power over the flock of red dragons he needs to defeat Savina and usurp her empire. Ridley Freeborn, a mage-hating thief, and his sidekick Snails break into the house of wizard Vildan Vildir just as he and his assistant Marina Pretensa are poring over a scroll that might lead to the staff. Damodar also turns up and kills Vildir. Ridley, Marina and Snails escape with the scroll, but Damodar frames them for the killing.

Norda, the empress' elf tracker, sets out in search of the adventurers, who have been joined by dwarf warrior Elwood Gutworthy. Profion, meanwhile, infects Damodar with a demon parasite to motivate him to obtain the rod. Despite squabbling, Ridley and Marina form a team, coping with a succession of perils. Snails is killed by Damodar and Ridley is wounded, only to be revived by elf magic. Ridley gets the rod, only for Damodar to obtain it from him by threatening Marina. After killing Damodar, Profion goes to war with Savina. As dragons fight over the capital city, a newly heroic Ridley, potentially a powerful magic ruler, intervenes to retrieve the rod and commands a dragon to eat Profion.

The role-playing game Dungeons & Dragons was introduced in 1974, and became a craze in the late 70s and early 80s, spinning off into a range of best-selling books to which this limp fantasy effort bears little resemblance. The original devisors of D&D set out to create a backdrop which serves fantasy adventure much as the often-reused western town sets of old Hollywood served their genre. Decorated with pillagings from the works of J. R. R. Tolkien, Robert E. Howard, Fritz Leiber and Michael Moorcock, there was nothing distinctive about the narrative world of D&D, but then that was never the point: adopting fantasy identities and reacting to ever-changing scenarios, D players drove the game by providing it with characters and stories. Twenty-five years on, this pick-and-mix approach fatally scuppers the long-in-development movie version, which would presumably like to aspire to compete with Peter Jackson's forthcoming *Lord of the Rings*, but instead feels more like an out-of-time knock-off of such 80s blockbusters as *Conan the Barbarian* and *Willow*, settling right in the rut of the justly forgotten likes of *Krull* and *Red Sonja*.

A fatally cheap-looking epic shot in the Czech Republic, *Dungeons & Dragons* is doomed to be remembered mostly for the extreme shoddiness of its performances. The ever-grinning Justin Whalin, whose career highlight to date is the dead-loss role of Jimmy Olsen, the sidekick from television's *Lois & Clark The New Adventures of Superman* makes a feeble attempt at nimble heroism, while his teaming with the uncontrollable, irritating Marlon Wayans oddly keys into the underlying appeal of the original game: that contemporary American losers could project themselves into a fantasy European otherworld. The same is true of Thora Birch, who is stuck with the most ungainly dialogue imaginable as the democratically inclined teenage American empress in a role which simultaneously rips off Queen Amidala from *The Phantom Menace* and Joan of Arc. The biggest losers of all, though, come from the British contingent: Tom Baker and Richard O'Brien are in for a scene apiece as an elf ("You mages use magic, we are a part of it") and a master crook ("Honour among thieves, what a romantic notion") that fail even as camp. Bruce Payne, still the poor man's—or desperate producer's—Julian Sands, has a throbbing bald head, blue lipstick, a demon parasite that extrudes tentacles from his ears and an unwieldy leather fascist outfit to cope with, while Jeremy Irons, screaming and gurning as evil wizard Profion, has no excuse at all for villainous work that could give John Travolta's *Battlefield Earth* baddie unexpected competition in the Raspberry Awards this year.

VILLAGE VOICE, 12/19/00, p. 150, Dennis Lim

Bypassing the overripe goofiness of kindred quasi-medieval crock like *Labyrinth* and *Willow*, the film version of '80s role-playing thingy *Dungeons & Dragons* instead attempts an earnest, tacky synthesis of *Phantom Menace*, *Mortal Kombat*, and *Xena: Warrior Princess*. At once laboriously expository and defiantly incomprehensible, the movie seems to involve the hunt for an enchanted "rod," a threat to the prevailing "fabric of magic," the fight for democracy in the kingdom of Izmer, and the ritual humiliation of actors. In ascending order of ignominy: haughty apprentice mage Zoe McLellan; Skywalkerish commoner Justin Whalin (the new Sean Patrick Flanery or the new Robert Sean Leonard? Discuss); his bumbling sidekick Marlon Wayans (in a role with more suspect racial overtones than Jar Jar Binks); squawking, Glenn Close-channeling Jeremy Irons; and fair-minded empress Thora Birch, who models a series of headpieces cribbed from 70s disco album sleeves and throughout sustains the impression of having learned her lines phonetically.

Also reviewed in:
NEW YORK TIMES, 12/8/00, p. E16, A. O. Scott
VARIETY, 12/11-17/00, p. 26, Scott Foundas
WASHINGTON POST, 12/8/00, p. C1, Rita Kempley
WASHINGTON POST, 12/8/00, Weekend/p. 55, Michael O'Sullivan

EAST IS EAST

A Miramax Films release of a Film Four presentation of an Assassin Films production. *Executive Producer:* Alan J. Wands. *Producer:* Leslee Udwin. *Director:* Damien O'Donnell. *Screenplay (based on his play):* Ayub Khan-Din. *Director of Photography:* Brian Tufano. *Editor:* Michael Parker. *Music:* Deborah Mollison. *Choreographer:* Sue Lefton. *Sound:* Christian Wangler and (music) Steve Price. *Sound Editor:* John Downer. *Casting:* Joan McCann and Toby Whale. *Production Designer:* Tom Conroy. *Art Director:* Henry Harris. *Set Decorator:* Eliza

Solesbury. *Set Dresser:* Fiona Greaves, Zoe Harvey, Ros Ward, and Tina Kalivas. *Costumes:* Lorna Marie Mugan. *Make-up:* Penny Smith. *Stunt Coordinator:* Tom Delmar. *Running time:* 96 minutes. *MPAA Rating:* R.

CAST: Om Puri (George Khan); Linda Bassett (Ella Khan); Jordan Routledge (Sajid Khan); Archie Panjabi (Meenah Khan); Emil Marwa (Maneer Khan); Chris Bisson (Saleem Khan); Jimi Mistry (Tariq Khan); Raji James (Abdul Khan); Ian Aspinall (Nazir Khan); Lesley Nicol (Auntie Annie); Emma Rydal (Stella Moorhouse); Ruth Jones (Peggy); Ben Keaton (Priest); Kriss Dosanjh (Poppa Khalid); John Bardon (Mr. Moorhouse); Gary Damer (Earnest Moorhouse); Albert Moses (Abdul Karim); Jimmi Harkishin (Iyaaz Ali Khan); Rosalind March (Helen Karim); Kaleem Janjua (Mullah); Gary Lewis (Mark); Ralph Birtwell (Doctor); Madhav Sharma (Mr. Shah); Saikat Ahamed (Zaid); Bruce McGregor (Bouncer); Margaret Blakemore (Trisha); Thierry Harcourt (Etienne Francois); Leena Dhingra (Mrs. Shah); Tallat Nawaz (Nigget Shah); Shireen Kareem (Nushaaba Shah).

LOS ANGELES TIMES, 4/14/00, Calendar/p. 20, Kevin Thomas

In the last two decades Om Puri has become one of India's major screen actors and now he's emerging as an international star as well. In the acclaimed British comedy "My Son the Fanatic" he was a nonreligious taxi driver whose life is turned upside down when his son becomes an Islamist. Now, in "East Is East," he's the traditionalist, the Pakistani proprietor of a Manchester fish and chips shop, married 25 years to an Englishwoman (Linda Bassett), who has borne him seven children.

The couple live in Salford, a red brick row-house working-class neighborhood; the time is 1971. If Puri's George Khan is a bit bombastic, Bassett's Ella, an earthy, chain-smoking redhead, has the spunk to talk back to him. George is a loving, hard-working responsible man but his by and large happy household is about to be plunged into crisis.

The cultural give-and-take in the Khan family has been reasonably workable—never mind that George left a first wife back in Pakistan when he emigrated in 1937 or that he married an Englishwoman—but now that his eldest sons are reaching adulthood, George reverts to a passionate adherence to custom. Without consulting anyone, he has arranged the marriage of his eldest son, Nazir (Ian Aspinall), to a Pakistani girl. Just as Nazir is about to say "I do" to a woman he has never before seen—she proves to be a beauty, however—he panics and announces he can't go through with the ceremony. He runs off and is instantly considered dead by his father.

Scant time passes before George is arranging the marriages of his next eldest sons, Tariq (Jimi Mistry), a handsome disco king, and the seemingly dutiful Abdul (Raji James), to two homely but well-off sisters. It's at this point "East Is East," adapted by Ayub Khan-Din from his semi-autobiographical play, begins moving from raucous comedy to volatile drama. George's stubbornness brings to the surface his family's deep resentment that he's never really listened to any of them. "East Is East" is above all a man's confrontation with self in middle-age and his need to accept the fact that his children, beyond their mixed ancestry, are after all native-born English citizens.

It is, therefore, natural they will rebel against arranged marriages, a custom from a distant land that they have never seen and that goes completely against the grain of the free society in which they've been raised. George truly believes that he's doing what is best for his sons while forgetting that he defied tradition himself in marrying their mother.

For a film that is essentially a comedy, and one with some very broad strokes at that, "East Is East" nonetheless allows the craggy, forceful Puri to discover some Lear-like dimensions in George, who is as capable of violence as he is of affection, and is a man torn apart by his refusal to comprehend the reality of his family's life or his own chauvinist nature. Similarly, Ella is forced to accept that her spunkiness is superficial—that she is either going to have to give in completely to her husband or to stand up to him bravely and without fear of consequences. Like Puri, Bassett is more than up to the challenges of playing this sensible, loving woman.

Khan-Din and director Damien O'Donnell do a masterful job in making this stage adaptation seem completely cinematic, and amid much rowdy humor and emotional fireworks, "East Is East" never loses sight of what's going on in the world outside of the Khan home. George responds with anguished concern to India's aggression in East Pakistan, and the film takes note of an

English politician's repatriation—i.e., back to Pakistan (and India) scheme, indicative of a persistent racism that confronts the Khans—indeed, an old man who lives across the street from them refers to Pakistanis as "pickaninnies." The American-flavored pop culture so embraced by the Khan children is also noted, with the affection that permeates the entire picture, embracing as best as it can, even George, understanding that he means well, even in the throes of his worst behavior.

NEW YORK, 4/24/00, p. 130, Peter Rainer

The great Indian actor Om Puri has made nearly 40 films in his country, but very few have been shown here. Wouldn't it be great if some enterprising local film programmer staged a Puri festival? (It could start with Satyajit Ray's *Sadgati*). Best known here for his role in *My Son The Fanatic*, where he played a sweet-souled Pakistani cabdriver in England whose son becomes an Islamic fundamentalist, Puri makes another resplendent appearance in *East Is East*, where he once again plays a Pakistani in England; only this time, it is he, and not his family, who is locked vise-like into tradition. As George Khan, a fish-and-chips-store owner who came over as an immigrant in 1937 and married an Englishwoman (Linda Bassett), Puri transforms what might have been a mixed-race *Life With Father* into a jagged comedy bristling with emotional contradictions.

George arranges marriages for his uncooperative sons with Pakistani girls, and yet his own marriage, maddening as it often is, sustains him. He's torn between believing he's a bad Muslim or just a thwarted one, and as his frustrations mount, he seems throttled by his own ferocity. The film, set in the seventies and directed by Damien O'Donnell from a script by Ayub Khan-Din based on his play, offers Puri a wide dramatic range, which the actor extends even further. George is no mere monster; although his rages are truly frightening, he can also light up like a cherub when he has a treat to share. Giving his indulgent, uncomprehending wife the present of a barber chair, he carries on as if it were the queen's throne. Puri shows us a man who is riven not only by his own religious conflicts but also by an England that cannot accept his differentness. He's proud of that differentness, and yet, in a way he may not be able to admit to himself, he's also contrite. He's caught up in a racist culture calling for his repatriation, and on some level, he's ready to comply and chuck it all. George is both a success story and a horror story of the immigrant experience; Puri gives him his full measure of complexity.

NEW YORK POST, 4/14/00, p. 57, Jonathan Foreman

A huge hit in Europe—and winner of a British Academy best-picture award—"East Is East" is "The Full Monty" of 2000, a fresh, funny and poignant film filled with sparkling performances.

Adapted by Ayub Khan-Din from his autobiographical hit play of the same name, "East Is East" shuns the whining, sentimental clichés so common in plays and movies that deal with the experience of children growing up in South Asian immigrant or mixed-race families.

Instead, you get a subtle, multilayered depiction of love, pain and generational conflict among superbly written, utterly believable characters.

Set in the poor but amiable working-class town of Salford in 1971, the film depicts the havoc caused by a Pakistani father's attempt to marry off his sons to good Muslim girls even though his wife is English and his sons are mostly very assimilated and secularized—and one of them is gay.

George Khan (the celebrated Indian actor Om Puri, in a wonderful performance), has long forced his six sons and one daughter to learn Urdu and attend the mosque, but they live in—and prefer—their world of discos and soccer and sexual experimentation with neighboring kids.

George's English wife, Ella (the terrific Linda Bassett), tries to keep the peace between the irritable husband she adores and her beloved but rebellious kids. Unfortunately, George's desperate need for respect from the Pakistani community, and his refusal to accept the free and easy morality of this place and time, makes him capable of cruelty that could undermine even her devotion and loyalty.

First-time helmer Damien O'Donnell directs this film with the dexterity and eye for detail of a bold master surgeon. He elicits uniformly excellent performances from his fine cast, but (along with Bassett and Puri) Jimi Mistry stands out as Tariq Khan, heartthrob of the Salford disco scene and the most rebellious of the Khan clan.

NEWSDAY, 4/14/00, Part II/p. B6, John Anderson

Based on the play by screenwriter Ayub Khan-Din, "East Is East" is a masala dramedy in which the father in question is both a fool and a beast; if anyone dared ask them, his own family would want him sent back where he came from. And while this may be a novel way to approach the political questions of cultural assimilation, it's a little jarring dramatically.

In fact, George Khan (the esteemed Indian actor Om Puri), owner of a fish-and-chips shop and a firm believer in a "traditional" Pakistani upbringing for his seven half-English children—the same upbringing he presumably fled Pakistan to escape—is less father and more occupying army. His wife, Ella (Linda Bassett), is loyal and loving, but after his third or fourth abusive tirade you kind of wonder why. He already has exiled one of the sons, Nazir (Ian Aspinall), after the latter fled his arranged marriage before the vows were taken; having learned nothing from that, George has made similar recruitments for Tariq (Jimi Mistry) and Abdul (Raji James), who aren't having any. When Ella objects, she gets George's mouth, and then his fists.

The comedy—very broad and episodic—of "East Is East" is shadowed by the question of what George and Ella are all about. They don't communicate very well—Puri, who was so great in last year's "My Son the Fanatic," speaks in some impenetrable pidgin English, and they're poles apart on the happiness of their children. There's no detectable chemistry between them, no apparent explanation for why they ever married. Was George a hot catch in his day? Maybe, but whatever made him attractive once has become elusive—maybe not to Ella, but definitely to us.

SIGHT AND SOUND, 11/99, p. 43, Liese Spencer

Salford, 1971. Proud Pakistani chip-shop owner George Khan lives in a terraced house with his white wife Ella and their seven children. Determined to raise them as traditional Muslims, George sends sons Nazir, Abdul, Tariq, Saleem, Maneer and Sajid to the mosque and makes daughter Meenah dress in saris, but the kids rebel.

When George arranges a marriage for eldest son Nazir, he flees mid-ceremony. Undeterred, George plots to bring Tariq and Abdul into line by marrying them to the daughters of Bradford butcher Mr Shah. When Tariq discovers the plan, he smashes the gold watches George has bought as wedding gifts. Maneer refuses to tell George who was responsible; as Ella tries to stop George beating him, George turns on her. Nazir returns home but a bruised Ella tells him to leave before George gets back. The next day the Shahs pay a patronising visit with their daughters. Art student Saleem arrives with his latest artwork—a lifesize, latex pudenda—which accidentally falls into Mrs Shah's lap. As the Shahs leave in disgust, George turns on Ella, who tells him that if he can't accept his family as they are he should leave. He does. Ella finds a tearful George sitting alone in the chip shop. They drink a cup of tea together.

"You can both fuck off if you think I'm getting married to a fucking Paki," Tariq (Jimi Mistry) tells his parents in *East Is East*. Coming from a mixed-race Mancunian that could sound a little like self-denial, but while Tariq and his six siblings may be Pakis to their racist neighbour Mr Moorhouse (John Bardon) and Muslims to their proudly Pakistani father George 'Genghis' Khan (Om Puri) they know they're English and they're not standing for any of that arranged-marriage stuff.

Set among the back-to back red-brick terraces of 70s Salford, this funny, feel-good film from first time director Damien O'Donnell looks set to do for race relations what *The Full Monty* did for unemployment. Just as *Monty* made light of its post-industrial gender politics, so *East is East* is unashamedly entertaining in its exploration of the Anglo-Asian culture clash, approaching its sensitive subject with a good-natured gusto that's hard to resist.

East Is East first appeared at the Royal court in 1997. Since then screenwriter Ayub Khan-Din has worked hard to open up his semi-autobiographical stage play for the screen with cinematic set pieces such as the family trip to Bradford (or Bradistan as the city's graffitied sign reads) and a jolly Bollywood pastiche set in the backyard of the family fish-and-chip shop. New characters have been added (such as Tariq's peroxide blonde girlfriend Stella and her chubby mate Peggy) and Khan-Din's trenchant verbal wit has been translated into more slapstick visual gags: when tomboy Meenah (Archie Panjabi) kicks a football through Mr Moorhouse's window, his angry face is framed, end-of-the-pier fashion, by what remains of his Enoch Powell poster.

Introducing a wide cast of characters with broad, comic strokes and moving the action along at a swift pace, O'Donnell still finds time for pleasing visual flourishes. In one scene the permanently parka-clad Sajid (Jordan Routledge) and his friend Earnest (Gary Damer) appear upside down, through Meenah's legs, as she plays ball on the street. In a point of-view shot for Sajid we see the world framed by the fluffy periscope of his parka hood. But for all its visual verve, the film doesn't wholly escape its theatre origins.

With its low-budget, sitcom-style set-up—one street, two or three interiors, neighbours who pop in and out of each other's houses—this BBC/FilmFour co-production feels instead like virtuoso small-screen drama. Watching it, what strikes you is how far England has moved on since such television series as *Love Thy Neighbour*. Broadcast at the time *East Is East* is set (the spin-off film came out in 1973), that now notorious sitcom saw the east-west culture clash through the eyes of a white racist, while his West Indian neighbours were never anything more than smiling, stoic strangers.

In *East Is East* Anglo-Asian relations are examined from within the Khans' household, where the gap between first- and second-generation immigrants offers a more interesting microcosm. While the tyrannical George struggles to maintain his identity as traditional Pakistani patriarch, his kids explore the Swinging 60s counterculture that has at last reached Salford. Ladies' man Tariq (or Tony as he's known at the disco) is more interested in snogging blondes than in attending Arabic lessons at the mosque; Nazir (Ian Aspinall) leaves his bride at the altar to make fancy hats with his friend Mr François; Meenah would rather brawl in a pair of bell-bottoms than sit demurely in a sari.

As civil war rages in the Khans' house (when Powell appears on television ranting about repatriation the kids wryly suggest a whip-round to send Genghis back home), it's the white neighbours who remain peripheral and, literally, colourless. Mr Moorhouse's silent hostility is comically undermined by friendly overtures of his son Earnest, who longs to be part of the Khans' gang. And when his daughter Stella attempts to play Juliet to Tariq's Romeo—"I'll never let your father's colour come between us"—she is unceremoniously cast aside in the real-life revelations of the Khans' own family Mahabharata. Only Annie (Lesley Nicol) best friend to George's long-suffering Ella (Linda Bassett), has a real role to play, and then only as Salford's answer to a Greek chorus: arms folded, fag jammed in the corner of her mouth.

Conceived back in the 80s, when Khan-Din was still at drama school, *East Is East* grew from frustration at being offered only clichéd Asian acting roles. The result is a crowd-pleasing romp which manages to be honest without succumbing to the po-faced perils of issue drama. That the characters are real rather than emblematic is partly down to Khan-Din's ear for slangy dialogue and partly to the energetic, well-nuanced performances. Linda Bassett is superb as the salt-of-the-earth Lancastrian mum who must choose between her marriage and her children; the soulful Om Puri brings real humanity and pathos to his role as chip-shop despot.

Of course some of the humour comes from incongruity—from hearing a young man gilded from head to toe in Muslim wedding finery open his mouth and speak broad Salford—but beneath the easy laughs a stealthy intelligence is at work. Acute observations are often disguised as throwaway gags. Saleem (Chris Bisson), a hippie art student, is supposed to be studying engineering—a Pakistani father's vocational dream. And when the uncircumcised Sajid is finally divested of his tickle tackle, George presents him with a gold watch from the market that tells the time in Arabic—a symbol at once tacky, touching and proprietorial.

As the story darkens the film seems to sacrifice such quirky naturalism for brute farce in the form of a rutting Great Dane, a fat girl in boots and a flying pudenda. If such scenes don't match the subtlety of what has gone before, they do point up the breezy iconoclasm of Khan-Din's writing. Eschewing the racist gags of the 70s and the politically correct stand-up of the 80s, his kitchen-sink comedy is stamped with the same self-mocking confidence as such recent sketch series as *Goodness Gracious Me*. Like the characters in *East Is East* English culture-clash comedy looks like it's come of age.

TIME, 4/17/00, p. 78, Richard Schickel

Sometimes he's choleric. Sometimes he's obsequious. Always he's a man lost and trying desperately to find his way through a strange country in which the natives can barely see him through their veils of contempt.

He's a wonderful actor named Om Puri—a pockmarked, middle-age Pakistani. A year ago, in *My Son, the Fanatic,* he was a taxi driver in a grim industrial town in the north of England. Now he's back in a similar hardscrabble environment, this time as George, the proprietor of a fish-and-chips shop in a working-class London suburb in the '70s. He long ago married an Englishwoman (Linda Bassett, in a splendidly grounded performance). But he is determined that his numerous progeny embrace tradition—especially when it comes to love. As *East Is East* opens, one of his sons is bolting an arranged marriage, bringing shame on George, who did not happen to notice that the boy was gay. George's attempt to marry two more of his kids to a pair of plug-ugly sisters comes to similar grief.

The film, based on a play by actor Ayub Khan Din, is the first feature by director Damien O'Donnell. It is billed as a comedy, and George's frustrations with his elusive, secretive family are surely funny. But Puri makes him more touching than a crude family tyrant. There is something lonely in his bustling blindness, something right about his resistance to sleazy modernism. He's both wrongheaded and goodhearted, and the actor and the film make something fine, winning and memorable of that conflict.

VILLAGE VOICE, 4/18/00, p. 158, Amy Taubin

The conflicts of assimilation and intermarriage are treated more seriously and more raucously in *East Is East* [the reference is to *Keeping the Faith*], social satire about a Pakistani shopkeeper in the throes of an identity crisis. George (Om Puri) emigrated to the north of England just before WWII, married an English woman, and had seven children. Now middle-aged, George feels less than a man in the eyes of his white neighbors, who at this moment in the early 70s are supporting the racist Enoch Powell for Parliament. But he feels even more ashamed in relation to the Pakistani community, which disapproves of his wife and of his children's liberal ways. In an effort to return his family to the fold, he tries to force three of his sons into arranged marriages. When they refuse, he turns into a tyrant; frustrated by his lack of power, he becomes physically abusive to them and to his wife.

Puri, who was so affecting as a man caught between cultures in *My Son the Fanatic,* gives an even more explosive and anguished performance here. Without sentimentalizing George, Puri makes us aware of the terrible sense of loss and failure that pushes him over the edge. An ethnically specific character, George is also a kind of displaced patriarchal everyman. More than any character in *Keeping the Faith,* he reminded me of my first-generation Jewish-American dad.

You don't have to be Pakistani to empathize with George's problems. But that doesn't justify Miramax's use of a young white actress who's barely onscreen for 10 minutes as the focus of the *East Is East* poster. Similarly, George's misogyny doesn't justify using women as the butt of the cheapest jokes in the film. Like far too many British comedies about the lower middle class, *East Is East* frequently slips across the line from satire to ridicule. Making his directorial debut, Damien O'Donnell shows more affinity with *Muriel's Wedding* than *My Beautiful Laundrette.*

With the exception of George and his wife, Ella (Linda Bassett), the film gives us cartoons rather than complicated human beings. *East Is East* is best when it lets us see the bewilderment beneath George's rage or the way Ella walks a tightrope to defend her children without undermining her husband's shaky self-esteem. Bassett has a quiet authority and an appealing sense of humor, but *East Is East* is largely a showcase for Puri, and he rises to the occasion with a performance that bursts from the screen and tears into your heart.

Also reviewed in:
CHICAGO TRIBUNE, 4/21/00, Friday/p. B, Michael Wilmington
NATION, 5/15/00, p. 34, Stuart Klawans
NEW YORK TIMES, 4/14/00, p. E16, A. O. Scott
NEW YORKER, 4/24 & 5/1/00, p. 223, David Denby
VARIETY, 5/31-6/6/99, p. 29, Derek Elley
WASHINGTON POST, 4/21/00, p. C12, Rita Kempley
WASHINGTON POST, 4/21/00, Weekend/p. 45, Desson Howe

EAST-WEST

A Sony Pictures Classics release of a UGC YM presentation of a UGC YM/NTV Profit/Mate Productions/Gala Film/France 3 Cinema co-production. *Executive Producer:* Alexandre Rodniansky, Galina Toneva, Stephan Kyrilov, Patrick Sandrin, and Evgueni Guindilis. *Producer:* Yves Marmion. *Director:* Regis Wargnier. *Screenplay (French and Russian with English subtitles):* Roustam Ibraguimbek, Serguei Bodrov, Louis Gardel, and Regis Wargnier. *Director of Photography:* Laurent Dailland. *Editor:* Herve Schneid, Isabelle Proust, and Eric Dardill. *Music:* Patrick Doyle. *Music Editor:* Roy Prendergast. *Sound:* Dominique Dalmasso, Guillaume Sciama, Gérard Hardy, Olivier Burgaud, and (music) Nick Wollage. *Sound Editor:* Alexandre Widmer and Marilena Cavola. *Casting:* Gerard Moulevrier. *Production Designer:* Vladimir Svetozarov and Alexei Levtchenko. *Art Director:* Rossitsa Bakeva, Jean-Philippe Reverdot, Svetlana Filakhtova, Mikhail Levtchenko, Yvetta Kotcheva, Tsvetana Yankova, and Garabed Garabedian. *Set Decorator:* Jean-Philippe Reverdot. *Costumes:* Pierre-Yves Gayraud. *Make-up:* Jocelyne Lemery, Marie-France Taulere, and Mina Matsumura. *Running time:* 115 minutes. *MPAA Rating:* PG-13.

CAST: Sandrine Bonnaire (Marie);   Oleg Menchikov (Alexei);   Catherine Deneuve (Gabrielle); Serguei Bodrov, Jr. (Sacha);   Ruben Tapiero (Sérioja at 7 years);   Erwan Baynaud (Sérioja at 14 years);   Grigori Manoukov (Pirogov);   Tatiana Doguileva (Olga);   Bogdan Stupka (Colonel Boiko);   Meglena Karalambova (Nina Fiodorovna);   Atanass Atanassov (Viktor);   Tania Massalitinova (Alexandrovna);   Valentin Ganev (Volodia Petrov);   Nikolaï Binev (Serguei Koslov);   René Feret (French Ambassador);   Daniel Martin (Turkish Captain);   Hubert Saint-Macary (Embassy Advisor);   Jauris Casanova (Fabiani);   Joel Chapron (Theatre Interpreter); Maria Verdi (Dresser);   Yvan Savov (Middle Petrov);   Alexandre Stoliartchouk (Younger Petrov);   Tania Lioutzkanova (Invalid's Wife);   Youri Yakovlev (Old Man at Commune);   Malin Krastev (Drunk);   Ivan Petrov (Invalid);   Stefan Mladenov, Evguenia Anguelova, and Mac Marinov (Children in Apartment);   Viara Tabakova (Drunk's Wife); Dimitar Nikolov (Truck Driver);   Alexei Vertinski (Policeman);   Petro Panchouk (Father Guerorgui);   Kalin Lavorov (Leonid Kozlov);   Mikhail Ganev (Dimitri);   Banko Bankov (Interrogating Officer);   Robin Kafaliev and Plamen Manassiev (Wharf Officers);   Maxim Guentchev (Mayor of Kiev); Krassimir Rankov (Androv);   Emil Marcov (Caucasian);   Nicolina Beletskaia (Irina);   Igor Karalenko (Acrobat);   Oleg Lissigor (Anatoly);   Tamara Alexandrova (Selector);   Jordan Gospodinov (Sofia Taxi Driver);   Valentin Tanev (Bulgarian Police Controller); Alexandre Stoyanov (KGB Policeman);   Tsvetana Mirtcheva (Inhalations Worker).

LOS ANGELES TIMES, 4/7/00, Calendar/p. 12, Kevin Thomas

Regis Wargnier's Oscar-nominated "East-West," a superb follow-up to his 1993 Oscar-winning "Indochine," takes the most somber of predicaments, and makes it involving, romantic and ultimately intensely suspenseful.

In doing so, it brings to light the dire fate of some 120,000 forgotten people and their descendants—Russians who after the 1917 revolution fled to France, Bulgaria and Yugoslavia. After World War II, they were warmly invited home by Josef Stalin to help rebuild the devastated country. The USSR needed them, but with the dawning of the Cold War, Stalin feared them even more, regarding them as "imperialist spies." (The Soviets also wanted to reduce the size of the expatriate communities in case they at some point tried to claim that they represented the legitimate Russian government.)

Wargnier and his co-writers, which include "Prisoner of the Mountains" writer-director Sergei Bodrov—and inspired by real-life experiences—tell of a young, Russian-born French doctor, Alexei (Oleg Menchikov), who in June 1946 returns to the Soviet Union with his French wife, Marie (Sandrine Bonnaire), and their little son. Upon arrival, the three are separated. Officials tell Alexei to divorce Marie, who at that moment is being brutally beaten as a spy, her French passport torn to shreds, but Alexei stands by his wife.

In short order, Alexei, reunited with Marie and their son, is sent off to Kiev to become a factory medical officer, where he and his family are housed in an old mansion-turned-tenement. Marie and Alexei are trapped in a harsh, paranoid totalitarian state, and their predicament exacts its toll on the marriage. Alexei does well in his job, but Marie, in her bitterness and frustration, does not fully acknowledge how vulnerable her husband is and how concerned he is in protecting her and their son.

Their relationship has deteriorated badly when several years later Marie sees her first opportunity to regain her freedom with the arrival of a celebrated French actress, Gabrielle (Catherine Deneuve), and her acting troupe. Watching Gabrielle in a production of "Mary Tudor," Marie can't help but respond to the queen's observation that "we poor women truly never know what a man's heart holds." But even if Marie is able to speak with Gabrielle of her plight, how and when will the French actress be able to help her?

It's at this point that, after depicting the cruel realities of Alexei and Marie's existence with the utmost persuasiveness, the film shifts gears and gathers momentum, gradually but consistently building suspense as Marie becomes increasingly determined to escape the Soviet Union. As with "Indochine," Wargnier displays his mastery in blending epic scale with the highly personal, and "East-West," filmed on location in Russia and elsewhere has sweep, grandeur, an aura of authenticity and an eye for the telling detail.

Artistry and craftsmanship abound in this period-perfect film, which was photographed stunningly in appropriately muted hues by Laurent Dailland. The film's performances are equally glowing. Bonnaire has the angular beauty and strength of character to portray to perfection a woman whose proudly defiant spirit proves unquenchable. Menchikov expresses quietly the agony of a man put in a terrible position, a man who quietly continues to love his wife even after she believes he has forsaken her.

For all its fervent protest, sweeping romanticism and gathering suspense, "East-West" is anchored by a strong sense of everyday life—of people making the best of grim circumstances. Playing an activist-actress modeled after Simone Signoret and Maria Casares, Deneuve has the film's pivotal role even though she does not appear until halfway through. When she does, you must believe in her Gabrielle instantly, both as a great star and a woman of courage and determination. With her authority and beauty, Deneuve is ideal casting, and it is her radiant presence and absolute conviction that makes the film work.

Sergei Bodrov Jr. has the film's other key role as Sacha, a handsome young neighbor whose once-wealthy family owned the grand townhouse in which he, Marie and Alexei live in such crowded conditions. Another outstanding collaboration from Wargnier and Deneuve, who first teamed on "Indochine," "East-West" may have lost the best foreign language film Oscar to "All About My Mother," but it's still a winner.

NEW YORK, 4/10/00, p. 88, Peter Rainer

The spirit of the cold war lives on in the hokey, enjoyably florid *East-West*, which begins in June 1946 with a band of emigrants from the West arriving in Stalin's Russia expecting amnesty and good will only to be executed or sent to forced-labor camps. For propaganda purposes, a Russian-émigré physician (Oleg Menchikov) and his French wife (Sandrine Bonnaire) are spared, but he is boxed in by his "model-returnee" status, and she aches for Paris. Catherine Deneuve turns up as a celebrated French actress who aids the cause of freedom, and the West has never looked so glamorous. Who would have believed that eyeliner and lip gloss and great cheekbones could be this political?

NEW YORK POST, 4/7/00, p. 56, Jonathan Foreman

"East-West" is the movie that deserved to win the Oscar for foreign-language film, and one of the best movies ever made about life behind the Iron Curtain.

Based on several true stories, it's a tight, compelling, intelligent drama that never descends to the level of propaganda, but instead makes the struggle for human liberty real and intimate.

The film follows the fortunes of a white Russian Dr. Alexei Golovine (Oleg Menchikov), his French wife, Marie (Sandrine Bonnaire), and their young son, who accept Stalin's invitation to return to the Motherland after World War II.

When the boatload of formerly exiled Russians arrives in Odessa in 1946, they get a very different welcome than the one promised by Soviet diplomats back in Paris.

The doctor's family is billeted in a communal apartment, and Alexei is appointed the medical supervisor for a factory complex.

The couple grow apart: Alexei begins an affair with the woman who runs the communal apartment, and Marie, disgusted as much by Alexei's submissiveness to the system as by his infidelity, develops an increasingly intimate friendship with Sacha (Serguei Bodrov Jr.), her handsome 17-year-old neighbor.

The arrival in Kiev of a French theater troupe headed by famous actress Gabrielle Develay (Catherine Deneuve) and Sacha's chance to take part in an international swimming competition in Vienna offer them chances to escape.

But getting out turns out to be a much more difficult and dangerous process than Marie could imagine.

All the performances are uniformly excellent, but Bonnaire's is superb.

NEWSDAY, 4/7/00, Part II/p. B12, Gene Seymour

If nothing else, "East-West" will give you another reason not to miss the 20th Century. Its setup is one of history's more sadistic practical jokes. This one was pulled on those who left their native Russia after the 1917 Bolshevik revolution, but were offered a chance to return home after World War II. But as soon as they set foot on Soviet soil, these returnees are roughly herded into separate groups, splitting up families. Those with complaints are either shot on sight or compelled to perform a fierce tango with the KGB—who always lead.

Alexei Golovine (Oleg Menchikov) is luckier than the other returnees. He gets to stay with his French wife, Marie (Sandrine Bonnaire), and young son because Alexei's reputation as a doctor makes him "useful." They must live in Kiev, squeezing themselves and their belongings into an apartment already inhabited by several characters, including a slatternly informer and a young swimming champ (Serguei Bodrov Jr.), whose grandmother is detained for no good reason by the government.

Marie, who's been slapped around by secret police who suspect her of spying, is understandably eager to go back to France. But her husband seems to be doing everything in his power to keep them in the USSR, and she becomes emotionally involved with the swimmer, who shares her dreams of westward flight. Both, in different ways, literally place their hopes in the hands of an internationally renowned French actress (Catherine Deneuve), who agrees to help Marie escape.

Director Regis Wargnier, whose previous films "Une Femme Francaise" (1994) and the Academy Award-winning "Indochine" (1992), has an affinity for decorous historic epics in the David Lean tradition. "East-West," which was nominated this year for Best Foreign Film, aims for a sweeping, romantic grandeur frequently at odds with the mundane grimness of life in Stalinist Russia. These motifs clash to such an extent that both the narrative pace and emotional life hit dead spots, especially in the plodding dialogue. (The guy who leads the Red Army chorus gets the best lines. And that's not saying much.)

Bonnaire and Menchikov are so adroit at enacting the tension and duplicity between their characters that it's almost impossible to imagine that they were ever in love with each other. That's not necessarily a bad thing in general. But it makes the stakes in this romantic thriller seem smaller than they should,

It's also true that Deneuve's star power gives the movie an electric charge every time she's onscreen. There are several sequences in "East-West" that grip and, in the case of the climactic chase scene, even inspire. But having seen "Khroustalov, My Car!" a Russian epic chronicling the same sad era with more grit, daring and mordant humor, I have to say that even an earnest effort like "East-West" seems reined in and compromised by comparison.

SIGHT AND SOUND, 12/00, p. 46, Michael Witt

The USSR, 1946. Responding to Stalin's attempts to lure back Russian emigrants to their homeland, young doctor Alexei Golovin, his French wife Marie and their son Sérioja arrive in Odessa from France. Many of their fellow returnees are tortured, executed or deported to forced labour camps. Alexeï is allocated a room in a communal apartment in Kiev and made responsible for the health of the workforce in a local factory. He considers any form of resistance dangerous, while Marie remains fixated on escape. At a performance given by a visiting French theatre troupe, Alexel is paraded by the authorities as a returnee from the west who has turned into a model Soviet citizen. Marie tells celebrated actress Gabrielle Develay of her unhappiness.

The family drifts apart: Alexeï embarks on an affair and Marie takes a lover, teenager Sacha. Implicated in Sacha's escape to the west, Marie is sent to the Gulag. After Stalin's death six years later, she is released. A further two years on, Alexei and Gabrielle orchestrate Marie and Sérioja's escape to the west via the French embassy in Bulgaria. Alexei is sent to a labour camp to work as a doctor. He has to wait until the dawn of the Gorbachev era 30 years later before rejoining his family in France.

Following the only modest success of 1994 study of an army marriage *Une femme française*, director Régis Wargnier returns in *East-West* to the slick wide-angle historical melodrama of his earlier hugely popular *Indochine* (1991). In *East-West* he sets himself the daunting task of grappling with four decades of Soviet history and east-west relations through the vehicle of a simple love story. At the heart of the film is the relationship between Oleg Menchikov's Russian doctor Alexei, who settles in the USSR just after World War II, and his French wife Marie, the superb Sandrine Bonnaire here making a rare but welcome foray into mainstream cinema.

Wargnier is at his most comfortable exploring marital love in its various guises: young passion, physical desire, the onset of antagonism and a mature sense of mutual support and self sacrifice. The pent up energy and erotic charge of the human body (in particular, the muscular physique of Sacha, the young swimming champion with whom Marie has an affair) provide a counterpoint to the monotony of the Soviet regime, conveyed by the blue-grey hue that pervades the imagery. Wargnier uses water motifs in a similar way: a constant reminder of loss and separation (Marie and Alexei arrive in the USSR by boat from France), the swimming scenes at the pool and lake offer visual relief from the drab Kiev backdrop and cumulative sense of claustrophobia and surveillance in the couple's cramped apartment. This symbolic treatment of water and of the human body culminates in the beautifully shot and edited central escape sequence in which Sacha braves the dangerous seas in his bid for freedom.

East-West is pitched unashamedly as a broad brushstroke historical melodrama. But the historical part of the equation is underdeveloped. Wargnier pays lip service to key dates and introduces a sprinkling of stock figures from Cold War mythology, but these aren't enough to provide any credible sense of the reality of daily life in the USSR in the late 40s. The Russian, Ukrainian and Bulgarian cast members lend a superficial air of authenticity to the film's unabashedly cartoonish sensibility (Alexei doesn't work in any old factory; he works in one which produces red flags!). But it doesn't help that Wargnier recycles familiar images of heel clicking leather-coated KGB baddies shouting "don't let them escape".

Wargnier's attempt to portray this relatively uncharted slice of recent history is, of course, inherently presumptuous; but faced with the task, his film is low on humility. It deploys stylistic grandiosity—as in the irritating recurrent use of unmotivated slow camera tracks—that speaks more of an aimless and distasteful display of manufactured gravitas than of a sensitive approach to historical realities.

VILLAGE VOICE, 4/1/00, p. 162, Leslie Camhi

In 1946, Stalin issued a proclamation offering Russians in exile Soviet citizenship if they would return to help rebuild their ravaged homeland. Thousands heeded the call, only to fall through the cracks between warring ideologies, face xenophobic accusations of espionage by Soviet authorities, and be imprisoned or executed. Only a master could resist the temptations of melodrama in rendering this tragic chapter of Cold War history. Régis Wargnier *(Indochine)* is not that director. For *East-West*, he's assembled a stellar French and Russian cast, but all that talent can't overcome his heavy-handed screenplay.

As the film opens, Alexei, a Russian doctor (Oleg Menchikov), is returning by ship to the motherland with his French wife, Marie (Sandrine Bonnaire), and their young son. Any utopian ideals they may harbor are shed on the loading dock in Odessa, where one of their fellow passengers is executed. Roughed up and sent to Kiev, the family is issued a room in a cramped communal apartment. Marie dreams of fleeing; Alexei knows they're trapped. The gap between them grows wider, as Marie enlists the aid of their teenage neighbor (Sergei Bodrov Jr.), a talented swimmer, in her plans for escape, while Alexei becomes, at least in appearance, a model apparatchik. Enter Catherine Deneuve, playing (of all things) a famous French actress who meets Marie while on tour and resolves to help her. Yet many years and twists of fate will intervene.

Wargnier is best at depicting the corrosive atmosphere of petty surveillance and suspicion that pervaded daily life in Stalin's Soviet Union. Still, his KGB bigwigs are stock villains in dark hats and coats; if they had mustaches, they'd twirl them. In a fine performance, Bonnaire provides a key note of understatement. (Deneuve's role leaves little room for development.) Menchikov, an actor of feline grace, is wonderful to look at, but until the film's final moments, we never know what he's really thinking.

Also reviewed in:
CHICAGO TRIBUNE, 4/28/00, Friday/p. P, Michael Wilmington
NEW REPUBLIC, 4/17 & 24/00, p. 63, Stanley Kauffmann
NEW YORK TIMES, 4/7/00, p. E1, A. O. Scott
VARIETY, 8/9-15/99, p. 41, Derek Elley
WASHINGTON POST, 4/28/00, p. C5, Stephen Hunter
WASHINGTON POST, 4/28/00, Weekend/p. 53, Michael O'Sullivan

EDGE OF THE WORLD, THE

A Milestone Film and Video release.   *Producer:* Joe Rock.   *Director:* Michael Powell. *Screenplay:* Michael Powell.   *Director of Photography:* Monty Berman, Skeets Kelly, and Ernest Palmer.   *Editor:* Derek Twist.   *Music:* Cyril Ray.   *Running time:* 81 minutes. *MPAA Rating:* Not Rated.

CAST: Eric Berry (Robbie Manson);   Belle Chrystal (Ruth Manson);   Finlay Currie (James Gray);   Margaret Grieg (Baby); Kitty Kirwan (Jean Manson);   John Laurie (Peter Manson); Niall McGinnis (Andrew Gray); Michael Powell (Yachtsman);   Campbell Robson (Laird); George Summers (Skipper);   Grant Sutherland (Catechist).

NEWSDAY, 1/14/00, Part II/p. B7, John Anderson

Rarely seen and rarefied, Michael Powell's "The Edge of the World" so impressed producer Alexander Korda in 1937 that he introduced Powell to screenwriter Emeric Pressburger, helping to found one of the movies' great collaborations, the Archers. Powell-Pressburger were responsible for one of the strongest filmographies in the history of the cinema, including "I Know Where I'm Going," "The Life and Death of Colonel Blimp," "The 49th Parallel," "A Matter of Life and Death" (aka "Stairway to Heaven"), "The Red Shoes" and "Black Narcissus." That last film, set among the nosebleed—and psychosis—inducing Himalayas, may be the most obviously influenced by "The Edge of the World," which takes place atop, below and beside the daunting cliffs of a remote Scottish island called Hirta (or "death"). But "The Edge of the World" is full of other Powell trademarks, from an ethereal sense that gravity has been suspended, to the majesty of Powell's declarative imagery to the sheer joy of living possessed by his characters (a very "Blimp"-ish quality), even when faced with tragedy and need.

The people of Hirta are struggling to support themselves on an island where the waters are over-fished and the soil is played out, and at least one islander—Robbie Manson (Eric Berry)—has decided not to bring his wife-to-be back, but to move to the mainland himself. Andrew Gray (Niall MacGinnis), who's in love with Robbie's sister, Ruth (Belle Chrystall), quarrels with Robbie about his decision, and they decide to settle things according to island tradition a race up the impossible cliffs of Hirta.

Robbie falls to his death, Ruth's father (John Laurie) blames Andrew, Andrew leaves the island and Ruth turns out to be pregnant. Crises ensue.

Parable-like in its simplicity/profundity, "The Edge of the World" opens with Andrew returning to the now-evacuated island and relating its story to his shipmates. Not till later, of course, does the impact of Andrew's return make itself fully felt. But when it does, don't be surprised if it's accompanied by an urge to visit Hirta one more time.

Also reviewed in:
CHICAGO TRIBUNE, 6/9/00, Friday/p. C, Michael Wilmington
NATION, 1/31/00, p. 36, Stuart Klawans
NEW YORK TIMES, 1/14/00, p. E16, Stephen Holden

8½ WOMEN

A Lions Gate Films release of a Woodline Productions Ltd./Movie Masters B.V./Delux Productions s.a./Continent Film GmbH presentation of a Kees Kasander production. *Executive Producer:* Terry Glinwood, Bob Hubar, and Denis Wigman. *Producer:* Kees Kasander. *Director:* Peter Greenaway. *Screenplay:* Peter Greenaway. *Director of Photography:* Sacha Vierny. *Editor:* Elmer Leupen. *Kabuki Choreographer:* Kanyo Fujima and Toyonosuke Fujima. *Sound:* Garth Marshall. *Sound Editor:* Luuk Poels. *Casting:* Danielle Roffe, Aimi O., and Carrie O'Brien. *Production Designer:* Wilbert van Dorp. *Set Dresser:* Elise Menghine-Hill. *Special Effects:* Osamu Kume. *Running time:* 120 minutes. *MPAA Rating:* Not Rated.

CAST: John Standing (Philip Emmenthal); Matthew Delamere (Storey Emmenthal); Vivian Wu (Kito); Shizuka Inoh (Simato); Barbara Sarafian (Clothilde); Kirina Mano (Mio); Toni Collette (Griselda); Amanda Plummer (Beryl); Natacha Amal (Giaconda); Manna Fujiwara (Giulietta/Half Woman); Polly Walker (Palmira); Elizabeth Berrington (Celeste); Myriam Muller (Marianne); Don Warrington (Simon); Claire Johnston (Philip's Wife); Paul Hoffmann, Tony Kaye and Ann Overstall (Mourners); Malcolm Turner (Undertaker); Patrick Hastert (Man in Street); Julian Vincent, Claran Mulhern and John Overstall (Men in Cinema); Derek Kueter and Jules Werner (Debt Collectors); Sophie Langevin (Debt Collector Woman); Denise Grégoire (Sister Nun); Dean Harrington (American Businessman); Noriyuki Konishi (Korean Businessman); Jean-Gabriel Dupuy and Stéphane Prevot (French Businessmen); Katsuya Kobayashi (Simato's Father); Ryota Tsuchiya (Simato's Brother); Takumi Matsui (Simato's Fiancé); Kiyoshi Ishiguro (Brother's Fiancé). Hairi Katagiri (Half Women Companion); Yurika Sano (Half Woman, 8 Years Old); Satomi Ando (Half Woman, 10 Years Old); Sachiko Meguro, Hisayuki Yoshioka, and Hanji Mishima (Mio's Companions); Toyonosuke Fujima (Kabuki Father); Kanyo Fujima (Kabuki Son); Senyoichi Nishikawa (Kabuki Onnagata).

LOS ANGELES TIMES, 5/26/00, p. 14, Kevin Thomas

Peter Greenaway's "8½ Women" is a nod to Fellini—and that "half" turns out to be a typically dark Greenaway twist. No artistic temperaments could be more different than those of Greenaway and Fellini. Greenaway is the detached, pitiless intellectual whose magistral experimental flourishes can be recondite in the extreme, whereas "Fellini is the lyrical, compassionate sensualist who celebrates the beauty of the women in his all-encompassing embrace.

Even the most stunning woman will have her pores revealed in close-up by Greenaway, for whom lust seems invariably dry as dust. (You have to wonder what Greenaway and fellow Brit, painter Lucian Freud, with their common preoccupation with less than perfect flesh, think about each other's work.)

Yet this film, one of Greenaway's most amusing and accessible, actually arrives at moments of tenderness, even love, fleeting though they may be. "8½ Women" finds Greenaway in a contemplative mood, musing about the interplay of sex and love and mortality, and the bonds between father and son—within the context of mordant absurdist humor, to be sure. It's not that

Greenaway has gone soft and sentimental but rather that he's dared to allow a rare drop of humanity to emerge in his characters' relationships with one another.

In jaunty, elliptical fashion Greenaway introduces Philip Emmenthal (John Standing), a Geneva-based financier and banker, in the midst of driving so hard a bargain in acquiring a Kyoto pachinko parlor for his business associate and architect son Storey (Matthew Delamere) that he gets his nose bloodied.

Not long after Storey agrees to accept as a payment of indebtedness the sexual favors of pretty, fiery Simato (Shizuka Inoh), as urged by her father—and her fiance—he has to return to Geneva when his mother dies. Philip is bereft, overcome with the loss of his wife, more a companion than a lover, and Storey suggests that to cheer himself up his father turn his immense period palace into a virtual harem. From Japan (depicted here as constantly rattled by earthquakes) Storey brings Simato; the exquisite Mio (Kirina Mano), whose goal is to be more female than the Kabuki's female impersonators; and his father's relentlessly efficient representative Kito (Vivian Wu).

Additions to the harem present themselves rapidly. Toni Collette's Griselda satisfies Philip's fantasies involving naked nuns only to discover she might really like to be a nun and even start her own order. Amanda Plummer's highly theatrical Beryl has a passion for horses and horse-riding and for her immense pig Hortense, and lands in one of Philip's many guest suites to recuperate from an injury.

Within an increasingly rich and diverse assortment of fine ladies, the most captivating is Polly Walker's Palmira, a sophisticated adventuress who failed to lasso Philip some three years earlier and is taking a leave of absence from her ardent affair with an opera singer (Don Warrington) to snare him this time.

To be sure, Philip's harem-building is not without pitfalls, virtually all of them funny. These women are not in Philip's thrall; rather it is he who is in theirs. If there is a moral to the film—and there may be many—it is that in amour, women are always the winners, and that men toy with them at their peril.

"8½ Women" has the superb production design and glorious cinematography (by the veteran Sacha Vierny) typical of Greenaway works, plus a raft of scintillating portrayals. Standing has lent staunch support in many a film, and it is a pleasure to find him in the central role as a man of formidable savoir-faire.

Philip and Storey are wits rarely at a loss for words—even at the movies watching "8½" or at the opera for a performance of "La Giaconda." They're engaging, if astringent, personalities, but you wouldn't want to sit behind them in a theater.

NEW YORK POST, 5/26/00, p. 51, Jonathan Foreman

For years, painter-turned-filmmaker Peter Greenaway has made films that are the last word in boring, self-righteous pretension.

They are inaccessible because they are incompetent, not because they have ambitious, complex artistic goals.

The best thing that can be said about "8 ½ Women," his ludicrous, pseudo-daring "tribute" to Fellini, is that it's not quite as stab-yourself-in-the-eyes boring as films like "In the Belly of an Architect" or as crude in its elitist politics as "The Cook, The Thief, His Wife & Her Lover."

Storey Emmenthal (Matthew Delamere) is a wealthy young man who lives in Kyoto, Japan, where he owns a *pachinko* (slot machine) parlor.

His father, Philip (John Standing), lives in a vast mansion outside of Geneva. When Philip's wife dies, Storey returns to Europe.

To comfort his father, who fears that no one will want him anymore, Storey has sex with him. Then the two of them watch Fellini's "8½" and resolve to start a collection of women who will service them in return for financial help.

The idea is that the collection includes various fantasy archetypes.

The 8½ women include a nun, naked under her habit (Toni Collette), a hooker with a heart of gold (Polly Walker), a woman obsessed with horses (Amanda Plummer) who spends most of the film in a transparent plastic bodycast, a shoe-obsessed Japanese girl who wants to be a female impersonator (Kirina Mano), and, of course, a double amputee—the half woman (Manna Fujiwara).

As in all of Greenaway's films, each shot is composed with painterly skill, and there is a dominant color that runs throughout (in this case, a rusty red).

But Greenaway is, as usual, unwilling or unable to tell a story, and as it rambles on, his incompetent script has a distinctly amateurish, undergraduate feel.

One horribly contrived line follows another, stunning much of the cast—but especially Matthew Delamere—into performances of embarrassing badness.

The movie contains a great deal of full frontal nudity, both male and female, but despite the presence of a beauty like Walker ("Patriot Games," "Sliver") most of it is not especially erotic.

At one point, the Storey character says, "All this narcissism is rather boring isn't it?" It's a statement that applies all too aptly to the whole film.

NEWSDAY, 5/26/00, Part II/p. B6, Gene Seymour

Peter Greenaway never claimed to be a crowd-pleaser, and anyone whose filmography includes such dark, astringent slices of perversity as "The Draughtsman's Contract" (1983), "The Belly of an Architect" (1987) and "The Cook, the Thief, His Wife & Her Lover" (1989) deserves credit for sticking to his overall vision. If said vision is colder than a Himalayan temple with paper walls in the dead of winter, it's still provocative enough to keep audiences on their toes in an era when filmmakers everywhere seem compelled to cover their rear flanks.

Hardly anyone's flank is covered in Greenaway's "8½ Women." But that still isn't enough to keep you interested in it. This ostensible homage to Fellini's epic advertisement for himself feels like a weekend in a locked room in which one is left only with one's own sexual obsessions. And, no matter how extravagant the imagination, such a weekend gets pretty boring after only a day.

About the only aspect of the film that lightens the mood is the insouciantly arch interaction between a wealthy, recently widowed banker (John Standing) and his indolent, narcissistic son (Matthew Delarnere). It's the son's notion to relieve his father's grief by bringing several women from Europe and Japan into their Swiss mansion for various degrees of kinky fun.

The high-lit wit of father and son is pleasurable. But whether you enjoy everything else depends on whether watching Amanda Plummer naked atop a horse or Toni Collette wearing nothing except a nun's wimple or Polly Walker in or out of plumage is enough to get you aroused, especially since there's nothing else about them that's given any significance. Personally, I thought the soul kiss laid on Delamere by earth mother Natacha Amal was the hottest thing in the movie. But, then, I'm weird.

SIGHT AND SOUND, 1/00, p. 48, Richard Falcon

Tokyo, the present. Businessman Philip Emmenthal acquires eight and a half pachinko parlours. He puts his son Storey in charge. During an earthquake, Storey learns his mother has died. He returns to the family chateau in Geneva to nurse Philip through his grief. There he sleeps with Philip, introduces him to Fellini films and persuades him to convert the chateau into a private bordello. In Japan, aided by Storey's female interpreter Kito, Storey first recruits Simato, a pachinko addict. At a kabuki-theatre performance, they persuade Mio, a woman who aspires to the femininity epitomised by kabuki transvestites, to join the harem along with Kito. Storey and Philip have a *ménage á trois* with Simato.

Back in Geneva, Philip blackmails bank teller Griselda into becoming the lascivious nun of his fantasies. After injuring horse thief and pig-lover Beryl in a road accident, he and Storey coerce her into joining the bordello. They also acquire Giaconda, a fecund Italian. Clothilde, a female servant at the chateau, plots revenge, while con-artist Palmira lays down her terms for becoming one of the eight and a half women, a number completed by a "half-woman" named Giulietta. The bordello soon begins to unravel. Simato financially exploits the other women. Mio commits suicide. Giaconda is dispatched to South America. Clothilde attempts to poison Philip but only kills Beryl's pig. Beryl rides off. Griselda becomes a real nun and Kito is killed in an earthquake. Philip dies happy in bed with Palmira who then rejects Storey and leaves him alone with Giulietta. A final earthquake rocks Geneva.

8½ Women sets out its organising principles in the title while the director Peter Greenaway offers in the press notes his customary auto-exegesis for baffled critics, explaining that the film is constructed around an intentionally comic parade of eight and a half archetypes of male sexual fantasy, as represented in western art practice down the ages. For each figure, a list of artists could be matched. Griselda's chaste nun in starched linen? Try Rembrandt, Diderot and de Sade. The *Madame Butterfly* syndrome of the oriental female used and abandoned by a western male? How about Delacroix, Ingres, Flaubert and Matisse? It is also intended as a comic (a word not readily associated with Greenaway) homage to both Fellini and Godard. But at the same time it is his conceptually thinnest and visually least ravishing film.

As a comic meditation on cinema's contribution to the topography of male fantasy, *8½ Women* begins—in very Godardian fashion—with money as Philip signs a contract transferring ownership of some pachinko parlours to him. The pachinko parlours with their little silver balls are the first comic link between money and sex in the chain of financial exchanges that transforms Philip's Geneva chateau into a brothel. Philip, unlike the earlier hubristic Greenaway technocrats (draughtsmen, natural historians, architects and so on), is a grieving businessman. But as in a *Zed & Two Noughts,* this grief instigates a deviation towards taboo rather than condolence and reassurance, which Greenaway has always disliked in "dominant cinema". The Vermeer-like composition of Philip next to his wife's deathbed and the misogyny of Philip's comment that she was asleep when their son Storey was conceived are chilly moments leading to the film's most perverse and effective sequence when father and son sleep together. It's an act which recommends itself to Greenaway because, unlike sons sleeping with their mothers, it's something which supposedly "has no name".

Philip's views on conventional cinema seem very close to Greenaway's: "I hate the cinema," he confides to Storey. "Everybody feeling the same thing at the same time. It's too intimate." Video, however, allows Storey to talk Philip into sexual experimentation: lying together on a bed like teenagers, watching a tape of Fellini's *8½*, Philip is curious about the number of film-makers who make films to satisfy their sexual fantasies. "All of them," replies Storey. (His bedroom in Japan, in contrast with Philip's book-lined chateau, is full of television monitors; the relative absence of the written word here along with the film's frequent close-ups also set this apart from recent Greenaway films.) When the pair's private bordello is up and running, Philip explicitly links it to what used to be termed the 'plenitude' offered by the cinematic apparatus: "Most films are about what people haven't got: sex and happiness. We have them both." Unfortunately, given the film's lack of eroticism, a more resonant moment for many will be the one when father and son compare bodies in front of a mirror and Storey wonders whether "all this narcissism is really boring."

The invocation of Fellini is deeply ironic. *8½*—centred on Fellini's alter ego Marcello Mastrioanni's search for an actress to embody the ideal woman—pre-empted the allusive richness of Greenaway's cinema. Fellini's vitality and profound scepticism towards intellectualism as a solution to the creative impasse there seem worlds apart from Greenaway's aloof taxonomy. The fetishistic perspex corset worn by pig-loving Beryl after her fall from her horse and the wheelchair-bound "half-woman" Giulietta (seemingly named after Fellini's wife Guiletta Masina) seem a curiously insulting form of homage, closer to Cronenberg's *Crash* than Fellini. The final chapter of this saga—the destruction of the bordello—is intended to invoke Godard's recent deconstruction of cinema: the reason why, for Greenaway, we cannot return to the art cinema of Fellini. This is territory many will feel Greenaway has investigated more successfully outside cinema, for example in his grandiose installation *In the Dark* for the Spellbound exhibition at London's Hayward Gallery which broke filmmaking down into its constituent parts in Godardian fashion.

Perhaps to counter inevitable charges of misogyny, the women in climax take charge again. However, the terms of this female revenge smack also of male self pity ("Men love women love children, children love hamsters—it's a one-way street," Palmira tells the other women). Maybe the strongest impression left by *8½ Women* is that the constraints of the feature film against which Greenaway has always chafed have led him to paint himself into the kind of misanthropic self-referential corner his other films always avoided. Ultimately, these men behaving badly are comically indulged: Philip dies in bed with his dream woman, and Storey, left alone with the half-woman of the narcissistic, male, erotic-cinematic imagination, has the earth move for him.

VILLAGE VOICE, 5/30/00, p. 130, Dennis Lim

The deeply ridiculous *8½ Women* could have been made only by a cranky dotard. Peter Greenaway's new film is, needless to say, a compulsively referential work, pedantically obsessed with words, numbers, form, and high art. But it marks a minor departure in terms of visual style (intercutting the trademark fastidious wide-angle tableaux with uncharacteristic extreme close-ups) and tone—Greenaway's distinctive brand of cerebral, gross-out, body-horrific humor has never been so shrill or so unfunny. A British father and son (John Standing and Dave Foley look-alike Matthew Delamere) shuttle between Kyoto, where they own a chain of pachinko parlors, and Geneva, where they are converting the family estate into a private harem. The 8½ concubines (the half woman, if you must know, is an amputee) include Toni Collette as a faux-nun and Amanda Plummer as a horseback-riding goth who ends up in an unflattering plastic neck brace. It's safe to say that Fellini, to whom this film pays dubious homage (the amputee is named Giulietta, presumably after Signora Fellini), would have abhorred any association with this dismal mortuary slab of a movie.

Also reviewed in:
CHICAGO TRIBUNE, 6/9/00, Friday/p. A, Michael Wilmington
NEW YORK TIMES, 5/26/00, p. E10, Stephen Holden
VARIETY, 5/31-6/6/99, p. 32, Godfrey Cheshire
WASHINGTON POST, 5/25/00, Weekend/p. 52, Desson Howe

EMPEROR'S NEW GROOVE, THE

A Walt Disney Pictures release. *Executive Producer:* Don Hahn. *Producer:* Randy Fullmer. *Director:* Mark Dindal. *Screenplay:* David Reynolds. *Story:* Chris Williams and Mark Dindal. *Based on an original story by:* Roger Allers and Matthew Jacobs. *Editor:* Pamela Ziegenhagen-Shefland. *Music:* Sting and David Hartley. *Music Editor:* Paul Silver. *Sound:* Tim Chau and (music) Shawn Murphy. *Sound Editor:* Donald Sylvester, David Kern, Albert Gasser, and Nils C. Jensen. *Casting:* Ruth Lambert and Mary Hidalgo. *Production Designer:* Paul Felix. *Art Director:* Colin Stimpson. *Visual Effects Animators:* Dorse A. Lampher and David (Joey) Mildenberg. *Animator Kuzco/Kuzco Llama:* Nik Ranieri. *Animators: Pacha*: Bruce W. Smith; *Yzma*: Dale Baer; *Kronk*: Tony Bancroft; *Chicha*: Doug Frankel; *Tipo*: James Lopez; *Chaca/Bucky*: Brian Ferguson; *Guy/Waitress/Old Man/Official/Maidens*: Sandra Lucio Cleuzo. *Animation Editor:* James Melton and Hermann H. Schmidt. *Running time:* 78 minutes. *MPAA Rating:* G.

VOICE CAST: David Spade (Kuzco/Kuzco Llama); John Goodman (Pacha); Eartha Kitt (Yzma); Patrick Warburton (Kronk); Wendie Malick (Chicha); Eli Russell Linnetz (Tipo); Kellyann Kelso (Chaca); Robert Bergen (Bucky); Tom Jones (Theme Song Guy); Patti Deutsch (Waitress); John Fiedler (Old Man); Joe Whyte (Official).

LOS ANGELES TIMES, 12/15/00, Calendar/p. 8, Kevin Thomas

"The Emperor's New Groove" is a delightful, effervescent morality tale for children conveyed with such wit and sophistication that adults are likely to be enchanted as well. In short, Disney's fabled animation division has done it again, coming up with a treat that arrives just in time for Christmas. Director Mark Dindal, his story co-writer Chris Williams and screenwriter David Reynolds pack an awful lot of holiday cheer in just 81 minutes.

It's narrated by the emperor (voice of David Spade) himself, who tells us how it happened that he, an Incan-like ruler of limitless power, got turned into a llama; he muses about how someone could ever want to ruin the life of the "nicest guy in the world."

Not surprisingly, this self-appraisal by Emperor Kuzco might not be shared by everyone. He talks like a Hollywood whiz kid, the kind who tucked out big time, and has become an object of such fawning attention that he has lost all perspective on himself. He could scarcely be more obnoxious yet of course considers himself the coolest dude in the universe.

As it happens, Kuzco has decided to construct a summer villa high on a pinnacle above a deep gorge. It is the site of the cottage home of the good-hearted peasant Pacha (voice of John Goodman) and his sharp-witted wife, Chica (voice of Wendie Malick, a co-star with Spade on the TV sitcom "Just Shoot Me"). When, in an audience with the emperor, Pacha asks him what is to become of him and his family, Kuzco is nonchalantly dismissive: "Don't know, don't care."

In the meantime Kuzco has decided it's time to get rid of the venerable imperial advisor Yzma (voice of Eartha Kitt), who he senses is encroaching on his absolute power. Chic, cadaverously thin, Yzma is in fact an evil schemer. Yet so out of touch is Kuzco with his true spoiled, petulant self that he can't imagine Yzma has foolishly entrusted the concoction of a poison to off the emperor to her sweet-natured but thick-headed muscle stud, Kronk (voice of Patrick Warburton, Puddy of "Seinfeld" fame). The result: Instead of being assassinated, Kuzco is turned into a llama. While he's stranded in the jungle, who should come to his aid but Pacha, who insists on seeing the good in everyone.

Thus are launched the cliffhanging adventures of the llama and Pacha, as Kuzco in animal form attempts to return to his vast city-state, transform himself back to human form with Yzma's antidotes and resume his throne. Along the way, as arrogant as Kuzco remains—even as a llama—he's for sure going to learn some humility from Pacha. Yzma and Kronk are swiftly on the llama's trail, determined not to let Kuzco get back into his old groove.

Art director Colin Stimpson and his staff traveled to Peru's Incan ruins of Machu Picchu, but thankfully such a seeming concern for authenticity didn't keep them from coming up with a domain for Kuzco that would appear to owe more to the heady look and atmosphere of movie palaces of the '20s—the Mayan in downtown L.A. comes to mind. Indeed, Yzma, invested with witty hauteur by Kitt, resembles a silent-movie vamp who has lived to a scrawny but indomitable ancient age. The voices and the personalities of the actors fit their animated characters perfectly.

Vast mountain ranges and lush jungles are drawn with the same exotic flair as monumental settings in the Incan manner, and John Debney's score contributes both to the film's sense of adventure and its tropical mood. Sting has written some special songs for the film, most notably its catchy theme tune, "My Funny Friend and Me." Tom Jones sings "Perfect World," and the filmmakers also incorporate Antonio Carlos Jobim's "The Girl From Ipanema." "The Emperor's New Groove" stays as light as a souffle. It has the giddy panache of a '30s screwball comedy.

NEW YORK POST, 12/15/00, p. 59, Lou Lumenick

"The Emperor's New Groove" is a lively, if only partly successful, attempt by Disney animators to find a, well, new groove to escape the studio's over reliance on tried-and-true story formulas.

Originally conceived as a much more serious epic called "The Empire of the Sun," this latest effort has evolved into something lighter and more simple than the ponderous "Dinosaur," Disney's umpteenth story about a young animal separated from his mother.

The movie's bumpy production history is most noticeable in the wall-to-wall narration, a crutch live-action filmmakers often employ to paper over narrative gaps, but rarely used in animation.

This take on the uncredited "The Emperor's New Clothes" opens with Kuzco (voiced by David Spade), a young king in 15th-century South America, recalling how he was turned into a llama by his scheming adviser, Yzma (Eartha Kitt).

Sting composed a full musical score for the would-be-epic, but the only surviving major number is a show stopper called "Perfect World," belted out by Tom Jones, depicting Kuzco's imperious rule.

When the king informs Yzma, " We're not picking up your option," she plots to kill him with poison. But her bumbling assistant, Kronk (Patrick Warburton), mixes things up and Kuzco is instead turned into an endlessly braying llama.

Only one person can help Kuzco, an earthy shepherd named Pacha (John Goodman), who wants to keep Kuzco from razing Pacha's hillside village to make room for the king's summer residence.

Kuzco learns a little humility from Pacha in a story that's notably more slapsticky and less preachy than standard Disney fare.

"Emperor" also refreshingly flirts with a very un-Disney political incorrectness, openly mocking Yzma's advanced age, giving Kuzco near-homophobic lines and literally making the only other female character (Pacha's wife, voiced by the under-used Wendy Malick) barefoot and pregnant.

"Emperor" has some of the most effective voice work in a recent cartoon, and Warburton (forever known as Elaine's fiance, Puddy, from "Seinfeld") is especially funny as Kronk, whose scheming against the heroes keeps getting sidetracked by his passion for cooking.

The big problem is that, even at 78 minutes "Emperor" often feels long, like a half-hour cartoon stretched to feature length. The endless bickering between Yzma and Kronk, and especially between Kuzco and Pacha, starts to wear on the nerves. (Spade's obnoxious character is especially grating).

As a consequence, "The Emperor's New Groove" is overall less fun than the underrated "The Road to Eldorado," another beautifully drawn film that shares a very similar historical setting.

But as family entertainment, "Emperor" is still a demonstrably superior choice to that hideous bore known as "Dr. Seuss' the Grinch That Stole Christmas."

NEWSDAY, 12/15/00, Part II/p. B3, Gene Seymour

"The Emperor's New Groove" is the best Warner Bros. cartoon ever created by the Walt Disney Studios. Neither Warner nor Disney will relish the comparison, even though it is intended as the highest possible praise. They'll just have to deal with it.

Especially Disney, which hasn't released a conventionally animated film this rudely energetic in decades. In fact, the narrative anarchy, knockabout drollery and savagely enacted sight gags are, like, so not Disney—made from spare parts of the aborted musical "Kingdom of the Sun"—that the whole film could be the product of an outlaw alternate-universe Disney. If so, one question: Are there any more where this came from? The opening scene, a llama weeping in a heavy forest downpour, makes you think that this "Groove" will fall into the same sentimental pattern of other Disney full-length 'toons of recent vintage. You're still waiting for sap to rise as the opening credits roll and Tom Jones' vocalizing of Sting's music kicks in.

The llama, as it doesn't take long to figure out, used to be Kuzco (voice by David Spade), swaggering boy emperor of a culturally indeterminate fantasyland. Calling Kuzco self-centered is like saying Shakespeare had a way with words. What he wants, he gets. What he doesn't want, he literally throws away.

Which he does with both Pacha (voice by John Goodman), a kindly peasant whose family home is about to be displaced by Kuzco's summer palace and Yzma (voice of Ertha Kitt), Kuzco's wicked old adviser whom he downsizes away, in part because he vaguely suspects she wants his throne.

He's not wrong. With help (sort of) from dim-bulb palace guard and gourmet chef Kronk (voice by Patrick Warburton, "Seinfeld's" Puddy), Yzma arranges one literal last supper for Kuzco. The poison they deposit in his drink turns out to be a potion that turns him into the llama you remember from the beginning.

As you hear Kronk hum his own background music while he sneaks the transformed Kuzco out of the palace, you're now certain that the sap isn't going to rise as it usually does in Disney movies. Oh, sure, a warm-and-fuzzy "reluctant friendship" emerges between Pacha and Kuzco. But the movie can't keep itself from cracking wise, keeping the mushiness in check. For instance, there's this oh-so-cutesy squirrel that carries out one of the oldest, cruelest tricks on Kuzco to sublime perfection.

The voices are likewise sublime. Kuzco is Spade's best big-screen role yet—which may not be saying much, but give Mr. Smarmy-Pants his due. Kitt is also a hoot without having to camp it up too much. But it's Warburton's Kronk, with his conflicted ethics, goofy inflections and spinach puffs, who all but runs away with the whole kaboodle.

NEWSWEEK, 12/15/00, p. 77, David Ansen

For a Disney animated movie, "The Emperor's New Groove" arrives on the Christmas scene as quietly as a mouse in padded slippers. Where's the usual brass band, the tie-in merchandise, the Emperor's New King-Size Burger? The lack of hype is refreshing, but will it help or hurt this larkish comic fable? The animation may not have the whirling computer-enhanced movement of a "Tarzan," the rich hues of a "Lion King;" the intricate detail work of a "Beauty and the Beast": it's drawn in broad, bold outlines. But the unfussy, tossed-off quality actually helps give this original story zippy irreverence some of Disney's plusher cartoons lack.

The antihero of "The Emperor's New Groove" is a thoroughly obnoxious teenage monarch named Kuzco, a ruler so accustomed to having his every whim catered to that he has no concept of compassion. David Spade does his voice, with a callow petulance that nails the brat perfectly. Unfortunately for Kuzco, his ambitious witch of an adviser, Yzma (Eartha Kitt), hoping to supplant him on the throne, transforms the young emperor into a llama. And a homely llama at that. Cast out in the jungle, where he has zero survival skills, the four-legged Kuzco teams up with Pacha (John Goodman), a good-natured peasant, hoping he can dupe the bumpkin into leading him home. The evil Yzma—a scene-stealing harridan in the grand if somewhat misogynistic Disney tradition—has other ideas. This vain, rail-thin, tropical Cruella De Vil and her musclebound manservant Kronk (Patrick Warburton) want to make sure he never makes it back alive.

Directed by Mark Dindal, with songs by Sting and David Hartley, this is a fleet, funny family entertainment that should tickle parents as well as tykes. Think of it as a palate cleanser after that overstuffed, soporific Thanksgiving family blockbuster that has little else but hype going for it.

SIGHT AND SOUND, 3/01, p. 47, Kim Newman

Pre-Columbian Meso-America. Just before his eighteenth birthday, Emperor Kuzco fires his long-term advisor Yzma, a power-seeking witch, and informs summoned peasant Pacha that he intends to demolish his village in order to build a swimming pool there. Yzma and her soft-hearted henchman Kronk plot to poison Kuzco, but accidentally use a transforming potion, which turns the Emperor into a talking llama. Kronk is ordered to murder Kuzco, but the llama winds up in a sack on Pacha's cart and is taken to his mountain top village.

Kuzco sets off for the palace despite Pacha's warnings of the dangers of the jungle. An encounter with jaguars convinces him to pledge he won't destroy the village if Pacha guides him home. Yzma discovers that Kuzco is still alive, and searches for the llama to kill him. Crossing a bridge to the palace, Pacha falls through rotten boards and is imperilled, whereupon Kuzco sneers that he never intended to honour his promise. But when Kuzco also falls through boards, the pair must cooperate to stay alive. Back at the palace, Kuzco and Pacha discover Yzma's collection of identical-seeming potions. In a round of drinking during a chase, Kuzco is transformed into many animals and Yzma becomes a cat before the Emperor is restored to human form. Kuzco decides to build his pool on the mountain next to Pacha's village.

One of the singular humanitarian achievements of Disney's current chief Peter Schneider is that by approving the mid-development rethink of this project—the tale of an arrogant South American ruler, Kuzco, forced to mend his ways, which began as a 'traditional' take on Hans Christian Andersen's *The Emperor's New Clothes*—he spared us no fewer than six songs from Sting. The two survivors are a raucous imperial theme voiced by Tom Jones and a glutinous end-credits effort few audiences will stay to hear.

Like the increasingly tiresome cartoon monoliths the company has been crafting annually ever since 1989's *The Little Mermaid*, *The Emperor's New Groove* mines the themes and images of classic Disney: the obnoxious central character who becomes humanised by suffering and the scenes of human animal shapeshifting are obviously from *Pinocchio* (1940), while villainous henchman Kronk's abandonment rather than murder of the usurped heir is a plot lick from *Snow White and the Seven Dwarfs* (1937). Chief baddie Yzma, a power hungry witch, meanwhile follows in the tradition of scrawny villainesses that ranges from *Snow White*'s Wicked Stepmother to Cruella De Vil from *One Hundred and One Dalmatians* (1960). But whereas *The Little Mermaid* or even Walt's own *Sleeping Beauty* (1958) feel like attempts to get back to the garden, this film admits it's part of a tradition, then zigzags its own way, revising rather than repackaging the studio's past—and even blows raspberries at sacred cash cows.

Mark Dindal's film distances itself from the big-budget summer pictures produced under former Disney chairman Jeffrey Katzenberg by using jungle swinging gags and overwhelmingly hostile fauna (jaguars, crocodiles, vampire bats—none at all cute) to parody or subvert the likes of *The Lion King* and *Tarzan*. The Meso-American setting is a logical development of *Mulan*'s venture to China, but it's also a smart-mouthed one-upping of the indifferent *Road to El Dorado,* the most recent animated product from Katzenberg's rival DreamWorks set-up. David Spade's voice work as Kuzco delivers a stream of mean-spirited but hilarious put-downs (with many anachronisms) only momentarily interrupted by his metamorphosis into a llama (at one point, he stops the action to insist the audience sympathise with his plight rather than his peasant companion Pacha's).

The Emperor's relishable rottenness, epitomised by his defenestration of a palace official who has thrown off his "groove", is leavened by the John Goodman-voiced Pacha, whose bulky good-heartedness with underlying smarts and calm provides the heart of the bickering-buddy partnership. Eartha Kitt huskily provides tones that equally suit the angular Yzma and the round fluffy kitten body she winds up trapped in, while Patrick Warburton makes a meal of the surprisingly complex and appealing toy boy/henchman/bumbler/chefwannabe Kronk (liable to be the break out children's favourite character).

The setting and the approach allow for imaginative incorporation of Inca design aspects into the backgrounds, though the film does evoke *The Flintstones* by presenting an alien world as a caricature version of America, complete with a jungle diner that serves up rain-forest specials such as giant lice. This may well be the least 'Disney' of the studio's recent animated efforts, informed as it is by knockabout and fast-talking comedy in the manner of Chuck Jones' take on Warner Bros. favourites Bugs Bunny and Daffy Duck or Friz Freleng's Pink Panther cartoons. But it may well be that Walt himself, who greenlit such colourful and flip South American ventures as *Saludos Amigos* (1942) and *The Three Caballeros* (1944), made under the State Department's 'Good Neighbor' initiative which was intended to foster warm relations between the US and South America, would have enjoyed this a lot more than, say, *Pocahontas* or *The Hunchback of Notre Dame.*

TIME, 12/25/00-1/1/01, p. 147, Richard Corliss

This feature-length cartoon writhed for four years in development hell (or as they say at Disney, Development Heck) before its title was changed from *Kingdom of the Sun,* its scope narrowed from spectacle to intimacy, its tone altered from the brashly comic and all but one of its songs scrapped. There were other ominous signs: Disney didn't blanket the TV air with commercials; and Spade, in a recent visit with Jay Leno, was loath to mention his new movie. All of which meant, in the end, nothing; the film is a funny, breezy romp.

Emperor Kuzco (very much like the sarcastic brat Spade plays on *Just Shoot Me* and everywhere else) is turned into a llama by his in-house sorceress (Kitt) and her dull aide (Warburton). Kuzco has only one ally, the gentle shepherd Pacha (Goodman). Despite their mutual hatred, they are just the pair to retrieve the remedy for his curse and restore the llama Kuzco to emperor status.

So here's the story of a thinks-he's-hip fellow amusingly vexed at losing his identity. It could be called *Dude, Where's My Karma?* The cast, especially Spade (we keep wanting to call him David Snide) and Warburton, give bounce and sass to a script full of clever ideas. You won't find the emotional grandeur of *The Lion King* here, but that's O.K. *Emperor* doesn't aim too high or strain too hard; it is at ease inhabiting its pretty, miniature realm.

Also reviewed in:
CHICAGO TRIBUNE, 12/15/00, Friday/p. A, Michael Wilmington
NEW YORK TIMES, 12/15/00, p. E26, Stephen Holden
VARIETY, 12/11-17/00, p. 25, Robert Koehler
WASHINGTON POST, 12/15/00, p. C12, Rita Kempley

ERIN BROCKOVICH

A Universal Pictures and Columbia Pictures release of a Jersey Films production. *Executive Producer:* John Hardy and Carla Santos Shamberg.   *Producer:* Danny DeVito, Michael Shamberg, and Stacey Sher.   *Director:* Steven Soderbergh.   *Screenplay:* Susannah Grant.

Director of Photography: Ed Lachman. *Editor:* Anne V. Coates. *Music:* Thomas Newman. *Music Editor:* Bill Bernstein. *Sound:* Thomas Causey and (music) Dennis S. Sands. *Sound Editor:* Larry Blake. *Casting:* Margery Simkin. *Production Designer:* Philip Messina. *Art Director:* Christa Munro. *Set Designer:* Masako Masuda and Patricia Klawonn. *Set Decorator:* Kristen Toscano Messina. *Set Dresser:* Dale E. Anderson, Bart Barbuscia, Brent Blom, Gary Brewer, Glenn M. Carrere, Cheryl Gould, and Jennifer Lagura. *Special Effects:* Kevin Hannigan. *Costumes:* Jeffrey Kurland. *Make-up:* Susan Cabral-Ebert. *Make-up (Julia Roberts):* Richard Dean. *Stunt Coordinator:* John Robotham. *Running time:* 127 minutes. *MPAA Rating:* R.

CAST: Julia Roberts (Erin Brockovich); David Brisbin (Dr. Jaffe); Dawn Didawick (Rosalind); Albert Finney (Ed Masry); Valente Rodriguez (Donald); Conchata Ferrell (Brenda); George Rocky Sullivan (Los Angeles Judge); Pat Skipper (Defending Lawyer); Jack Gill (Defendant); Irene Olga López (Mrs. Morales); Emily Marks and Julie Marks (Beth, 8 months)); Scotty Leavenworth (Matthew); Gemmenne De La Peña (Katie); Erin Brockovich-Ellis (Waitress); Adilah Barnes (Anna); Irinia V. Passmoore (Babystitter); Aaron Eckhart (George); Ron Altomare and Charles John Bukey (Biker Friends); Marg Helgenberger (Donna Jensen); Randy Lowell (Brian Frankel); Jamie Harrold (Scott); Sarah Ashley (Ashley Jensen); Scarlett Pomers (Shanna Jensen); T. J. Thyne (David Foil); Joe Chrest (Tom Robinson); Meredith Zinner (Mandy Robinson); Michael Harney (Pete Jensen); William Lucking (Bob Linwood); Mimi Kennedy (Laura Ambrosino); Scott Sowers (Mike Ambrosino); Cherry Jones (Pamela Duncan); Kristina Malota (Annabelle Daniels); Wade Andrew Williams (Ted Daniels); Cordelia Richards (Rita Daniels); Ashley Pimental and Brittany Pimental (Beth, 18 months); Tracey Walter (Charles Embry); Larry Martinez (Nelson Perez); Judge LeRoy A. Simmons (Himself); Don Snell and Michael Shamberg (PG & E Lawyers); Gina Gallego (Ms. Sanchez); Peter Coyote (Kurt Potter); Ronald E. Hairston (Car Messenger); Veanne Cox (Theresa Dallavale); Scott Allen (Town Meeting Plaintiff); Sheila Shaw (Ruth Linwood); Matthew Kimbrough (Bartender); Jason Cervantes (Check Messenger).

CHRISTIAN SCIENCE MONITOR, 3/15/00, p. 15, David Sterritt

Lawsuits make good entertainment, in the multiplex if not in real life. "Erin Brockovich," the new fact-based comedy-drama by Steven Soderbergh, picks up themes treated in recent movies as different as "A Civil Action," which didn't win its case with audiences, and "The Insider," now contending in the Oscar race.

Soderbergh's entry in the legal-eagle category isn't great cinema, but it has enough engaging moments—and enough of Julia Roberts's photogenic face—to expect sure-fire success at the box office.

Roberts plays the title character, a single mother whose streetwise sensibility—accompanied by notably short skirts and four-letter language—hinders her quest for middle-class stability. This changes when she wangles a job in a law office and gets interested in a case her boss has hardly noticed: a real-estate transaction involving a utility company and a family dogged by a surprising amount of illness.

Why have the family's medical records been placed in the same file as their business papers? Does the corporation know something about hidden health hazards—pollution, contamination—surrounding the little home it suddenly wants to buy? Erin is on the case, riffling through utility files and interviewing everyone in sight.

What she discovers is a conspiracy to cover up an environmental debacle caused by sloppy disposal of dangerous chemical waste. The next step is to organize the community affected by this horror, helping ordinary folks band together and fight for compensation.

Erin has to learn the legal skills—and people skills—she'll need if she and her new acquaintances are to succeed.

"Erin Brockovich" is Roberts's movie, focusing on her feisty performance even when other impressive talents—such as Albert Finney as the attorney—are sharing the screen with her. This will please her zillions of fans, who can be expected to line up early and often at the ticket window.

A major beneficiary of this commercial outlook could be director Soderbergh, who has been trying desperately for a second hit ever since he scored in 1989 with "sex, lies, and videotape," the offbeat comedy that placed him—and the whole phenomenon of American independent film—on the cultural map. Nothing has done the trick so far, even when recent efforts like "The Limey" and "Out of Sight" racked up favorable reviews.

If it clicks as well as expected, "Erin Brockovich" could be Soderbergh's ticket back to the big time. Ironically, though, some of his admirers may feel his victory isn't entirely sweet. "Erin Brockovich" proves he can deliver pleasing mass-audience package, but it lacks the special artistic touches that made his most interesting films (like "The Underneath" and "King of the Hill," both badly underrated) great fun to watch even as they bombed at the box office.

"Erin Brockovich" is smooth, efficient—if you don't find its 131-minute running time too long—and calculated, right down to the split-second timing of its surprisingly off-color punch line. But it's neither as personal nor as imaginative as Soderbergh's best work.

That said, there's plenty to praise in Thomas Newman's laid-back music score and Ed Lachman's unflashy cinematography.

The cast includes a performance for every taste, from Roberts's cheerfully earthbound acting to Aaron Eckhart's brawny biker with a talent for baby-sitting—a character who'd make a stronger impression if his subplot (a bit of love interest) didn't seem tacked onto the movie as a half-hearted afterthought.

If you'd like to see a community-centered legal tale with a truly philosophical edge, rent Atom Egoyan's superb "The Sweet Hereafter," one of the greatest films of the past decade.

But if a mischievous retelling of the David and Goliath story strikes your fancy, "Erin Brockovich" is definitely the movie to check out

CINEASTE, Vol. XXV, No. 3, p. 40, Thomas Doherty

"Here they are—Jayne Mansfield!," snickered Jack Paar on the old *Tonight Show*, an introduction that, adjusted for inflation, might herald Julia Roberts as the titular protagonist of *Erin Brockovich*, a buoyant tribute to American mammary-centricity stuffed into a legal payback melodrama. Whether sculpted by cosmetic surgery or cushioned by high-lift suspension, the new augmentations fix the gaze not on the florescent smile, the shimmering hair, or the limber gams, but on heretofore unexplored regions of Hollywood's brightest star. Fore and aft, in close-up or long shot, you can't take your eyes off her.

The motion-picture phenomenon that is Julia Roberts surely warrants a critical once-over, albeit from a level perspective. In the age of rampant *auteurism* and CGI FX, she is a timely reminder of the absolute magnetism certain humans exert from the motion-picture screen. Blessed with the elusive "gene for the screen," as director Robert Wise dubbed it, she nourishes audiences by animated visage and magnetic personality alone.

An accurate measurement of Roberts's star magnitude may well echo the tones of press-agent puffery. Though a bankable commodity since *Pretty Woman* (1990), she has lately rocketed to that airy, iconic realm reserved for true screen immortals. The career arc traced by *My Best Friend's Wedding* (1997), *Stepmom* (1998), and the double-barrel blockbusters *Notting Hill* (1999) and *Runaway Bride* (1999), soars ever upward with *Erin Brockovich*, a total star vehicle, sans gentleman caller. How far back must one reach for an actress this illustrious and beloved? Mary Pickford? In the post-classical era, only Barbra Streisand challenges her preeminence, and Streisand's fan base comprises a niche market compared to Roberts's all embracing multitudes. More than any performer on screen today, Roberts attracts gushy good feeling, and not just from the usual chick-flick demo of high-school girls, blue-haired matrons, and reluctant men dragooned by insistent dates. The back to back success of last summer's *Notting Hill-Runaway Bride* twinpack—same genre, same star, interchangeable male lead—awed Hollywood moneymen: the appetite for Roberts was insatiable.

Defining the appeal of a motion-picture star is bound to get fuzzy around the penumbra, but any vessel for imaginative projection needs to be well-defined enough to inspire adoration and open-ended enough to provide space to fill in the blank spots. At once glamorous (celestial) and tangible (down to earth), Roberts satisfies the eye of all beholders. Men want her; women want to be like her; men are at ease with her; women do not resent her. In an already beautiful package, the keen sense of comic timing and the willingness to take a pratfall are unexpected bonuses. *Notting Hill* slyly exploited the double reaction of awe and aw-shucks: the worshipful male spectator (British beta male Hugh Grant) stares spellbound at superstar-actress Anna Scott on the motion-picture screen, but when she alights into his bookstore or breaks bread with his wacky friends, she is not a goddess deigning to sup among puny mortals, but a cozy intimate. Unlike the regal Garbo or the centerfold Monroe, guys really can imagine taking her to a baseball game (as in *My Best Friend's Wedding*), and girls really can imagine dishing the dirt with a sister (as in *Runaway Bride*). No wonder the signature Julia Roberts moment is the Dress Up Metamorphosis, when the gawky girl in down-market duds dolls up to the nines and knocks the smitten male suitor purblind. Unique among contemporary screen sirens, too, Roberts entices by keeping her clothes on—notice how both *Notting Hill* and *Runaway Bride* tantalize spectators with the off-screen existence of nude photographs.

Inevitably, the star persona that sustains the actress and soothes her fans also limits her range. Roberts has yet to stretch her chops too far beyond romantic comedy. When the script is lame or the male star limp, not even she can save the confection from going sour. Her pairing with Nick Nolte in *I Love Trouble* (1994) never clicked. Her pairing with Woody Allen in *Everyone Says I Love You* (1996) was just plain creepy. Likewise, Roberts's mousey turn in the somber *Mary Reilly* (1996) and her standby role in the reverent *Michael Collins* (1996) seemed to dull her her reflexes, as if the light behind her eyes had been switched off by a bad generic match-up. Being an ambitious professional, she seems poised for a regimen of Serious Acting, perhaps something with a severe disability or a foreign accent.

Of course, *Erin Brockovich* is serious acting in the classical American style, without affectation or tics, where the star seems to be cruising on automatic while energizing every nanosecond of screen time. Plotwise, the film is a dressed-down, distaff version of *A Civil Action*. Working-class single mother Erin begs her way into a temp job at the two-shingle law firm of crusty attorney Ed Masry (Albert Finney). Soon, she is rifling through old files that link the Pacific Gas and Electric Company to the contamination of ground water beneath the hamlet of Hinckley, California. Painstakingly gathering evidence and interviewing hundreds of victims, she spearheads a direct-action lawsuit that nails PG&E for a record judgment of $333 million.

At home Erin juggles the demands of three children and the affections of helpmate George (Aaron Eckhart), the most sensitive ponytail biker guy in the history of the Harley Davidson company. Playing Erin's exceedingly low maintenance boyfriend, Eckhart is very appealing in the kind of role that June Allyson might have been saddled with in the 1950s (and suitable penance it is for being such a despicable bastard in *In the Company of Men*). As sweet-tempered and conciliatory as Erin is tempestuous and foul-mouthed, George is great with the kids, handy around the house, and warmly nurturing, except for some whining about Erin's workaholic neglect of his feelings, damn it.

Former indie *wunderkind* Steven Soderbergh directs with studio-system efficiency, but the moody discontent of films like *sex, lies, and videotape* and *The Limey* surfaces only occasionally, mainly in the bleak desert vistas of godforsaken Hinckley, a burg that looks like it was a toxic waste site long before PG&E hit town. Like Garbo's directors, Soderbergh knows he is on the payroll to showcase the actress to maximum effect. Julia talking, Julia driving, Julia walking, Julia crying, Julia pissed off, Julia collecting dead frogs. In an instructive two-shot, Roberts sits screen right beside the old pro Finney, a crack shot with any line reading. No matter. As he speaks, Roberts looks intently off-screen. Your eyes lock on her face. Finney could set himself on fire and you would not look away.

Without inquiring overmuch into how a woman this savvy wound up with three kids, two ex-husbands, and no marketable professional skills, the screenplay by Susannah Grant works hard to locate Erin amidst the *déclassé* clutter of paycheck-to-paycheck single motherhood. Interior decoration by Kmart, a kitchen of cockroaches and canned goods, and a banged-up jalopy measure out the home life of the family Brockovich. But if the furnishings are dull and impoverishing, Erin's closet is a vibrant factory outlet for low-couture fashion. With each new entrance, Julia struts down the celluloid catwalk poured into another trashy outfit, with the model form-fitted into tight miniskirts and falling out of her blouses. Advised by Ed that she might want to "rethink" her wardrobe, she pinpoints a rival site for spectatorial attention and pledges to showcase her ass while she still has one, not two.

As with so many female-centered narratives, the interclass, intragender tension in *Erin Brockovich* is fiercer than the boy-girl face-offs. Outgunned by what she packs in her holsters, men are infinitely pliable, mainly pitiable creatures. Before her primal female power, the opposite sex can do naught but wilt. The advertising tagline puts it succinctly: "She brought a small town to its feet and a huge company to its knees." After their meet-cute spat, hunky, tattooed George collapses face first on her lawn, knocked flat, in mock swoon. When she sashays into the county records office and leans her cleavage over the counter, the dork at the desk is stupefied, bewitched, and obedient.

Erin's out-front femaleness also shames and subdues the desexed, mannish ladies from the big law firms, women who have hidden their curves and hearts in frumpy clothes and frigid demeanor, repressing what Erin flaunts. As in *Pretty Woman,* the sexual hierarchy overturns the class structure: the dried-up yuppies and the fertile working class, the dressed-for-success and the dressed-for-excess, the prim and proper and the trim and randy. Even among her peers in the law office, Erin is the snippy siren not the serene secretary. "Bite my ass, Krispy Kreme," she snaps at an overweight office worker.

Erin can, in fact, be a real pain in the ass, but the sharp-tongued vixen of the workplace goes all squishy among the folksy plaintiffs downwater from PG&E. To a man, woman, and child, they bond instinctively with their cultural kith and kin. For all her transcendent luster, Roberts never seems to be slumming in blue-collar quarters. "Stay for a fucking cup of coffee, Ed," Erin orders her nominal boss, knowing that the hard-scrabble culture of Hinckley has manners and rituals, too, that good breeding demands a polite chat over bundt cake.

Ideologically, the film pivots both ways on the American legal system: lawsuits are the only democratic weapon with which to hobble the titans of industry, but the lawyers who wield the writs and take the depositions are scum. For all the legal maneuvering, the action hardly ever moves into court. Just as well. Too many John Grisham and Scott Turow melodramas have taken the shine off the mahogany banister of courtroom set design. Perhaps, too, in a post-O. J. America, the native faith in the jury system is not quite boundless. A lone judge, not a jury of one's peers, hammers down the gavel of justice, and this off-camera. The drama revs down quietly, not triumphantly. For the victims, the $333 million judgment against PG&E is not a lottery payoff, but a grim acknowledgment of culpability.

Wisely too, save for a brief glimpse of the company's lawyers, PG&E is never personified; it looms ominously, institutionally, on the Hinckley horizon. In telling contrast, however, the flesh and blood victims are finely drawn, never just case studies. A young girl with cancer, bald and shrunken, robbed of puberty and soon life, peeks up at Erin, who joshes about her being a future heartbreaker, though they both know better. As a housewife realizing that PG&E has stolen her health and jeopardized her children, Marg Helgenberger strongly registers a seesaw of confusion, anger, and pain. Ravaged by cancer, she wonders to Erin whether a woman without breasts and a uterus is "still technically a woman." Although Erin reassures her, the question hangs in the air. After all, Erin Brockovich has very strict ideas of what makes a woman, technically and biologically.

However environmentally sound the surface politics, Julia Roberts's astonishing star vehicle is propelled by the oldest of fossil fuels. The ecological mindset is nothing if not traditional. PG&E's crime is not a violation of civil law but a sin against nature, a rape of the land. Male, scientific rationality has poisoned the nurturing soil, defiling Mother Nature and deforming her offspring. The tokens of Erin's fecundity ("They're called boobs, Ed") are the breastplate of an avenging angel, the earthy mother come to banish the despoilers and nurse her children back to health.

LOS ANGELES TIMES, 3/17/00, Calendar/p. 1, Kenneth Turan

Underqualified, underdressed and increasingly desperate, Erin Brockovich opens the film with her name on it pleading for a skilled job she can sense is not going to be hers.

No, she says, she has no actual medical training, but she does have three kids. She's great with people, and a fast learner, too. And she's always been interested in science, to the point of once being "madly in love with geology." Doesn't all that count for anything?

Not yet it doesn't, but before "Erin Brockovich" is over those qualities will surface as major players in this irresistible, hugely satisfying feminist fairy tale that turns "Norma Rae" into the protagonist of "A Civil Action" and makes us believe it.

Based on the true story of a woman the world didn't take seriously who empowered herself by helping others gain justice, "Erin Brockovich" does more than chronicle the rebirth of a downtrodden individual. It serves as a career milestone for director Steven Soderbergh, writer Susannah Grant and, most of all, star Julia Roberts.

With films collectively hitting a worldwide gross of $2 billion, Roberts is arguably the most successful—and certainly most highly paid—of contemporary actresses. Yet there is the sense about "Erin Brockovich" that this is the part Roberts has long been looking for. It's a role that allows the actress, like her character, to use her allure for a good cause, to put her undeniable star qualities, her great gift for humor, empathy, romance and vulnerability, at the service of a character with real texture.

Make no mistake, this is very much of an old-fashioned crowd-pleasing diva part, allowing Roberts to laugh and bawl, be sensitive and take no prisoners, but it also makes points about corporate malfeasance, self-esteem and the place of women in society that fluffier scenarios want no part of. Long determined to be taken seriously as an actress, Roberts has kissed a lot of frogs (wouldn't everyone like to forget "Mary Reilly"?) on the way to this satisfying triumph.

As to director Soderbergh, who started with the justly celebrated "sex, lies, and videotape" and then went all over the place, his career has been no one-way rocket either. But two years ago, with the exceptional George Clooney-Jennifer Lopez vehicle "Out of Sight," he revealed an unlooked-for talent that's on display here as well.

What Soderbergh can do as well as anyone is bring restraint, intelligence and subtlety to mainstream material, and what a difference that makes. To infuse an essential sense of unforced reality into stories that sound formulaic is to walk quite a fine line, and Soderbergh's gift for that, combined with Roberts' stardom, should finally supply the major box-office success that eluded him with "Out of Sight."

Uniting that film and this one (and what hampered the clumsily written but well-directed one that came between them, "The Limey") is the presence of a strong and beautifully structured script.

Writer Grant (helped by an uncredited polish from Richard LaGravenese) has presented strong women before in "Pocahontas" and "Ever After." But this script has more of a sense of life and it's especially adroit in placing believable and well-timed obstacles in the path of its inevitable resolution. In fact, given that the film's ad line ("She brought a small town to its feet and a huge company to its knees") effectively gives away the entire plot, it's amazing how much drama and pins-and-needles worry the film manages to wring from a foregone conclusion.

Helping Soderbergh realize this script's potential are top-of-the-line people on both sides of the camera, including veteran independent film cinematographer Ed Lachman, five-time Oscar-nominated editor Anne V. Coates and costume designer Jeffrey Kurland, who has had enormous fun creating clothes for a character who is not afraid of a little exposure.

For though her moral fiber couldn't be more spotless if she were played by Julie Andrews, Erin Brockovich does not dress like a saint. In fact, with her big hair, tiny miniskirts, 3-inch heels and an encyclopedic knowledge of the uses of cleavage, she looks more like a hooker than the character Roberts played in "Pretty Woman."

Erin is also in the habit of speaking truth to power, of saying whatever comes into her mind to whoever's in her line of fire. "Two things aggravate me," she claims in something of an understatement, "being ignored and being lied to." Roberts is especially adept at taking advantage of Erin's gift for devastating one-liners, none of which can be repeated in a family newspaper.

One of the themes of "Erin Brockovich" is that appearances can be deceiving, so we know at once that Erin is a woman of sterling qualities. Yes, she's twice-divorced, $17,000 in debt with $74 in the bank, but Roberts' presence makes us implicitly believe it's only a matter of time until the world understands that under those skimpy clothes is a smart, hard-working, self-reliant woman just waiting to be gainfully employed.

That employment was looking chancy until Erin came into contact with the majesty of the law as personified by Los Angeles attorney Ed Masry (Albert Finney). He represents her in a personal injury lawsuit that doesn't turn out well, and because Ed's the only potential employer she knows, Erin lays siege to his office until a barely entry-level job is forthcoming.

Finney's role is largely that of Roberts' straight man, reacting with looks of horror at her unpredictable shenanigans. Still, the importance of Finney to the film's success shouldn't be underestimated. A well-schooled veteran, he brings integrity, stature and a sense of humor to the role of audience surrogate, never too blase to be flummoxed by what Erin is up to.

The other man in Erin's life is George ("In the Company of Men's" effective Aaron Eckhart), a motorcycle hunk with enough skin art to necessitate a credited Tattoo Designer. George not only lives next door to Erin, he's her masculine don't-trust-your-eyes mirror image, someone who under all that leather has the temperament of a caring nanny eager to watch her children while she attempts to save the world.

Early on in her filing work at Ed Masry's office, Erin comes across some pro bono work he's doing involving residents of the Mojave Desert town of Hinkley. They're all getting sick and the mammoth PG&E corporation; the place's biggest employer, suspiciously claims to have nothing to do with it. Intrigued, Erin convinces Ed to let her look into the situation, and soon enough she is using her people skills and interest in science, not to mention her world-class flirting ability, to get at the heart of the problem and convince the townsfolk to let her and the lawyers do something about it.

"Erin Brockovich" is helped, as was "Out of Sight," by excellent acting down to its smallest roles. Finely cast by Margery Simkin, the script was strong enough to attract talents like Cherry Jones and Marg Helgenberger to supporting but pivotal roles as townspeople and is obviously much the stronger for it. There are also a pair of amusing cameos, one by the real Erin Brockovich as a waitress who waits, in effect, on herself, and the other by producer Michael Shamberg, convincing as an untrustworthy corporate attorney.

Though the publicity material huffs and puffs about Erin being a role model for the new millennium, in fact what's most exciting about this film is how old-fashioned it is at its core. It uses standard Hollywood building blocks like big stars and a Cinderella story line laced with laughter and tears and reminds us why they became standard in the first place. More than anything, it reminds us how much intelligent entertainment value there can be in traditional material, if only someone has the wit to realize it and the skill to get it out.

NEW YORK, 3/27/00, p. 101, Peter Rainer

In *Erin Brockovich*, directed by Steven Soderbergh and written by Susannah Grant, Julia Roberts plays a sparsely educated, twice-divorced mother of three who favors spike heels and cleavage-enhancing tops and blunt talk. She also happens to be a real-life crusader who spearheads an investigation leading up to the largest pay-off ever made in a direct-action lawsuit. In other words, it's the perfect all-in-one part for an actress, a real gimme-an-Oscar role. It's not a particularly subtle or incisive acting job, but Roberts isn't the actress you go to for a full-scale emotional tour de force anyway; she's too spry and quicksilver and fun-loving. She's always at her best playing someone for whom life is a spree, and the legal maneuverings and skullduggery in *Erin Brockovich* occasionally reflect that freewheeling spirit. If, say, Meryl Streep had played Erin instead—and, in a sense, she already did, in *Silkwood*—she would have brought out the whorls and shadows of contradiction in her personality. She would have made us gasp at what ordinary people are capable of. With Roberts, Erin is the ordinary made triumphant, and her victory is meant to be a win for all the beauty-queen, trailer-trashy types who ever had to suffer the indignities of the effete, educated elite in this country.

The early sequences featuring Erin juggling her kids while trying to land a job have a warmly observant, off-the-cuff quality, plangent and uncondescending. They hold out the promise that we'll be treated to something rare in American movies, an embracing and clearheaded view of class. (It's what Jonathan Demme's *Melvin and Howard* had.) Steven Soderbergh is a marvelously adept filmmaker with a dubious penchant for artiness—*The Limey*, most recently—but here he sticks to the story and brings out its grace notes, its little human bits of business. When Erin is banged up in a car accident in the San Fernando Valley and fails to win a settlement, she browbeats her lawyer, Ed Masry (Albert Finney) into giving her a job in his firm as payback. The relationship is set up as an odd-couple running gag: He's kindly and exasperated; she's always mouthing off. It's hokey all right, but it's also charming, because the performers seem to genuinely enjoy playing off each other. They're very good at conveying the needling and frolics that can go on between co-workers. This sort of thing, of course, has already been done to a fare-thee-well in any number of sitcoms, but the tone here isn't as clipped or propulsive as you often get in the TV shows. It's gentler; initially even Erin's rowdiness is made to seem moonstruck.

When Erin pokes around in a pro bono case that leads her to a small California desert town and its Pacific Gas & Electric plant, the film begins to lose its jaunty specialness and settle into something more rallying and conventional. With no legal training but lots of smarts and empathy, Erin discovers that the water surrounding the facility is toxic and responsible for hundreds of grievous maladies among the townspeople.

Because she is depicted as manifestly just-folks, Erin, unlike the big-shot lawyers, has a privileged way with these small-timers; when she interviews the sick and the worried, they pour out their fears to her, and the testimonies open the way for a massive lawsuit against PG&E that consumes Erin's life and also reinvents it. She has less time for her children, who resent her for it, and she skimps on her relationship with the kindly local biker George (Aaron Eckhart), who loves taking care of the kids but feels jilted by their mother. George is the male version of all those movie wives and girlfriends who loiter on the edge of the action, simpering, while their men have the audacity to go out and conquer the world. Either way, this role's a drag.

It's a cheat for this film to turn so self-righteous as it moves along. As the high dudgeon gets higher and higher, the charm seeps out of Julia Roberts's performance. Erin becomes a feminist heroine, a role model, a champion, and her nostrils flare accordingly. While all this Oscar-preening is going on, our attention shifts to Albert Finney, whose rumpliness here is a state of grace. He keeps the tone light whenever he's around, and that's a blessing: More than anybody else connected with this movie, he seems to understand that the cause of seriousness isn't necessarily undercut by an actor's being deft and a bit silly. Clarion-call movies about the righting of real-life wrongs are on the rise in Hollywood, as in, most recently, *A Civil Action* and *The Hurricane,* and they all share an oppressive do-goodism. The trick is to make us care without turning it all into waxworks. *Erin Brockovich* has some real shine but succumbs to waxy build-up.

NEW YORK POST, 3/17/00, p. 47, Lou Lumenick

Julia Roberts got a reported $20 million—the record for a female star—for "Erin Brockovich," and boy, she earns every penny of it.

Playing an uneducated, trash-talking secretary who spearheads a legal assault on a utility she links to a cancer cluster, Roberts gives a hugely entertaining, Oscar-worthy movie-star performance—her best ever.

I'm notoriously resistant to movie stars playing blue-collar types—the memory of Meryl Streep getting down-and-dirty in "Silkwood" still makes my skin crawl—but Roberts inhabits the skin of the real-life Erin Brockovich while letting her 5,000-watt smile shine through.

A single mom with three kids, Erin is injured in an auto accident and loses a suit against the other driver.

Desperate for a job, she bullies her attorney, Ed Masry (Albert Finney) into taking her on as a secretary—though her tight, sexy clothing draws derision from her colleagues.

While she's filing, a seemingly routine real-estate case piques her interest—and her investigation gradually mushrooms into the largest direct settlement in U.S. history ($333 million), as Pacific Gas & Electric is accused of knowingly polluting the water supply of a small California desert town with deadly hexavalent chromium.

"Erin Brockovich" is less a courtroom drama than a journey of self-discovery. Erin, a former Miss Wichita, gets people to respect her for the first time in her life—strictly on her terms—as she prods the victims and attorneys to pursue the case in the face of attempts by PG&E to buy them off.

Swearing up a storm and showing off a terrifically toned body in her most revealing outfits since "Pretty Woman," Roberts brings Erin to life so vividly that you forget the story is basically a fairy tale with great punchlines.

Roberts is greatly abetted by old-vet Finney, whose sly performance as the rumpled Ed—basically Lou Grant to Roberts Mary Richards—makes her star shine all the brighter.

Just watch his reactions to see a great supporting actor at work—not stealing his scenes but handing them to Roberts on a silver platter.

Aaron Eckhardt has the less interesting role of Erin's long-suffering, sexy, angelic biker boyfriend—think Sam Elliott in "Mask."

He takes care of her kids while she's off nailing PG&E to the wall—the scene in which she learns from him via cell phone of her youngest child's first words may in itself win her the Oscar.

Other roles are well cast, particularly Marg Helgenberger and Cherry Jones as two women who suffer at PG&E's hands.

Eschewing his usual flashy style in favor of something more straightforward and old-fashioned, director Steven Soderbergh delivers an unabashed crowd-pleaser.

"Erin Brockovich" is the kind of stand-up-and-cheer movie Hollywood is supposed to have forgotten how to make—"Norma Rae" with T & A.

NEWSDAY, 3/17/00, Part II/p. B3, John Anderson

Flame-haired, sun-buffed, legs up to her shoulder blades—the Julia Roberts of "Erin Brockovich" is the most unlikely looking blue-collar archangel ever to rescue the downtrodden from the perfidy of corporate America. But then, "Brockovich" (or "Erin Go Brockovich," for St. Patrick's Day) is really several movies at once: social drama and runway show, pinup calendar and consumer manifesto, a feminist tract in Frederick's of Hollywood clothing.

That it works as well as it does—and it does—is testimony to both Roberts' pure screen presence and the particular genius of Steven Soderbergh. In his career trajectory from "sex, lies, and videotape," "Kafka" and "King of the Hill" to the more recent "Out of Sight" and "The Limey," the director has established himself as probably the most successful underachiever currently making movies. The story of the real-life Erin Brockovich—single mother and untrained legal secretary, who was instrumental in winning a $333-million pollution settlement from the $30-billion Pacific Gas & Electric—sounds like something he might have done in his sleep.

But this doesn't mean Soderbergh doesn't have a distinct sense of style. Or a sense of humor, either. In fact, the way he pushes Roberts and her distracting physique in our face (for some reason, I kept thinking of the Sea of Tranquility) eventually becomes kind of funny, although it's definitely an example of directorial ingenuity. Any movie that announces itself as "based on a true story" immediately abdicates suspense; when was the last time anyone made a movie about a working-class, single mother who lost a multimillion-dollar lawsuit against a major utility? The answer is never. So Soderbergh has to look elsewhere for tension, finding it in the edge-of-your-seat question of whether Roberts is going to fall off those nosebleed-inducing spiked heels.

If "Brockovich" is Roberts' bid for credibility, it's a pretty solid bid. Unlike her colleagues in the sex-symbol-cum-social-conscience sorority (think of the long-suffering Sharon Stone in "Last Dance," or Susan Sarandon in any number of noble endeavors), Roberts never makes Erin sentimental or weighty or, frankly, boring. Her limitations as an actress are obvious enough—when she smiles the world smiles with her; when Erin occasionally snaps nasty, the movie takes a left and we take a right. She can't make Erin's charmlessness charming, and the woman's flaws—her trash taste in clothes, her inappropriate mouth—have to be portrayed as virtues, because Roberts can't walk that wire. But when she's playing sunny, it's convincing, and she's sunny most of the time.

She's also surrounded by fine actors. Albert Finney, who gets better all the time, plays the rumpled, grumpy lawyer Ed Masry, who as Erin's lawyer blows her car-crash case and as a result gets her as an employee. It's one of those oil-and-water relationships that might have been cloying but remains honestly abrasive (with the exception of the movie's all-too-obvious epilogue). Aaron Eckhart, who made people hate him in "In the Company of Men," plays Erin's biker-next-door George, and how can you dislike an actor who can deliver a line like "You're a special lady" without making us reach for the air-sickness bag?

Marg Helgenberger and Cherry Jones are solid, too, playing a couple of the more prominent PE&G victims, many of whom developed cancer from the company's use of a certain strain of chromium in its Hinckley, Calif., water-supply plant. Erin can relate to these hard-luck cases because she's a hard-luck case herself; in orchestrating that car crash early in the film, Soderbergh makes it clear Erin was never going to stop, even if the light hadn't changed in her favor. Slightly self-destructive, moderately desperate, Erin pursues a case that's all but hopeless (the real Brockovich has a cameo in the film, as a waitress) and in saving others, she saves herself. "When I walk into a room," Erin says, explaining her die-hard dedication, "people shut up to hear if I have something to say." They probably always shut up, you'll think. The sentiment, nonetheless, is irresistible.

SIGHT AND SOUND, 5/00, p. 47, Andrew O'Hehir

Los Angeles, the 90s. Erin Brockovich, an unemployed, ex-beauty queen with three children, is sideswiped in a car accident. Her abrasive behaviour in court sabotages her case, but she insists her lawyer Ed Masry give her a job. Erin also begins an affair with her neighbour, a biker named George who babysits her children. Erin investigates a case in the desert town of Hinkley, Ca., where Pacific Gas & Electric has contaminated the water with toxic chromium and is trying to buy the townspeople's silence by buying their homes.

By interviewing hundreds of Hinkley residents, many of whom have cancer or other diseases, and studying the local water board's records, Erin builds a class action lawsuit against PG&E. Her children grow resentful at her frequent absences and George leaves her. When Ed brings in Kurt Potter, a high-powered lawyer, Erin feels undermined, but agrees to convince the Hinkley residents to accept binding arbitration instead of a court case that could drag on for years. The townspeople are awarded $333 million (the largest such payment in US history). Ed pays Erin $2 million, and she and George reconcile.

Much has been made of Julia Roberts' purported sexiness in *Erin Brockovich* and there's no doubt the star is an eyeful in her endless array of cleavage-exposing blouses and minuscule skirts (the question of where a nearly destitute woman gets all these clothes is not answered). But the real brilliance of Roberts' performance lies in the edgy, defensive quality beneath Erin's aggressive hotness. It's as if Erin accepts the world's judgement that her sex appeal is her most valuable attribute, but isn't sure it's ever brought her anything worth having. Still, the former Miss Wichita has no compunctions about employing her assets when necessary. When her lawyer boss, the rumpled, beefy Ed asks her how she's so sure she can extract the necessary records from the water board's offices, she replies: "They're called boobs, Ed." Erin may be a hero, but she's definitely no angel. She's hot-headed, short-tempered, insecure and vain. She can be gratuitously cruel to her co-workers and has little interest in female solidarity. She addresses one overweight female employee as "Krispy Kreme" (a popular doughnut chain) and scorns the suggestion her revealing attire makes other women uncomfortable. "As long as I have one ass instead of two, I'll wear what I want," she says.

It's difficult not to sympathise with her easy-going biker boyfriend George, who feels he's bearing the brunt of all Erin's pent up resentment against men. But Roberts is completely convincing as a woman who feels she can't afford anything like George's laissez-faire attitude toward love and life. There's a magnificent moment when Erin senses herself falling for him despite her better judgement, and her mouth twists into a grimace of temptation and regret, like someone biting into a delicacy she has sworn off.

If Roberts' delightful performance, shaded with a depth and complexity unprecedented in her career, is the centrepiece of *Erin Brockovich,* considerable praise is also due to Steven Soderbergh's restrained, respectful direction. Armed with a fine screenplay by Susannah Grant (based on the real PG&E/Hinkley case), Soderbergh never sentimentalises his David-and-Goliath story (in the vein of *Norma Rae* and *Silkwood)* or tricks it up with unnecessary cinematic gamesmanship. Edward Lachman's camerawork is fluid but never intrusive. He and the director are content to allow the actors and the crystalline light of California's high desert enough space to do the work.

Perhaps Soderbergh's idiosyncratic pattern of bouncing from star-driven Hollywood vehicles *(Out of Sight)* to zero budget independent productions *(Schizopolis)* has lent him the confidence and perspective for *Erin Brockovich.* Many mainstream film makers would have focused almost entirely on Erin's search for love and validation and boiled the lawsuit down to one or two scenes of heroic courtroom drama. Soderbergh's leisurely pace yields all sorts of unforced moments that heighten the film's naturalism, from Erin's first angry meeting with George tuning up his Harley-Davidson outside at night, to the scene in which she convinces cancer stricken Donna Jensen PG&E has poisoned her water and lied to her about it. Horror spreading slowly across her face, Donna abruptly runs outside to drag her kids from the swimming pool.

There's also room in *Erin Brockovich* for fine acting in minor roles, including Marg Helgenberger and Cherry Jones as Hinkley women with whom Erin bonds and Tracey Walter as a slightly creepy local man who seems to be stalking her (but who, of course, holds a valuable secret). Albert Finney's Ed is another of the actor's familiar cantankerous types, mannerisms and accent apparently borrowed from W C. Fields. Jamie Harrold offers an amusing shtick as a water-board clerk smitten by Erin; Peter Coyote is less fortunate with the generic role of a hotshot lawyer, one of the script's few weak links. Perhaps the best thing about this relaxed and supremely engaging film (for my money the best work either the director or his star has ever done) is that even its near-fairytale resolution doesn't offer a magical transformation. When we leave Erin, she is far richer and more successful than when we found her, but she's just as highly-strung and nearly as neurotic. Like the people of Hinkley, she isn't free from the consequences of American life, but she has done what she can to take control of her little piece of it.

VILLAGE VOICE, 3/21/00, p. 40, Amy Taubin

In the thoroughly winning *Erin Brockovich*, Julia Roberts plays a single mother who, without any legal training, uncovers the evidence and marshals the people power to win the largest settlement ever paid in a direct-action lawsuit in the U.S.: $333 million. How does she bring Pacific Gas and Electric (the guilty party) to its knees? Through daring and determination born of a well-developed underdog outrage and the shameless, strategic deployment of t&a.

The fabulously knowing joke at the center of *Erin Brockovich* is that Julia Roberts's breasts (pushed up and nearly jiggling free of tiny halters and tank tops) and her perfectly molded ass, which practically salutes the camera whenever she turns her back, have the same effect on audiences as they do on the characters in the film. Just as the eponymous heroine flaunts her body to win over the men whose help she needs, *Erin Brockovich* —essentially a women's picture—uses Roberts as eye candy for boyfriends and husbands. She's not a cocktease; there's never a suggestion that she's going to put out. It's more like she makes you want to be on her team because that way you'll have a chance to took at her a lot.

What's pretty original about the picture is that it focuses an investigative drama based on a true story around a comic performance. Without Roberts's combination of exuberance and irony, *Erin Brockovich* would have been a replay of the earnest *A Civil Action*, in which John Travolta brings suit against a big corporation that's been dumping toxic waste in a town's water supply. *Erin Brockovich* has an almost identical plot, but it's closer in tone, and even politics, to *Thelma and Louise*. Outlaw humor is its survival tool.

Erin Brockovich is a former Miss Kansas with two bad marriages in her past and three kids to support. Having bullied her way into a job for a tired, ambulance-chasing lawyer (Albert Finney), she starts a little investigation on her own when she finds a strange medical record in a real estate case file. Director Steven Soderbergh employs more mainstream gloss than in previous films, but his knack for getting career-defining turns from actors is intact. This is the Julia Roberts performance her fans have been waiting for since *Pretty Woman*.

Soderbergh underlines the contradictions that make Roberts a star. Her Erin Brockovich is impulsive and a bit scattered, but she swears like a stevedore and has the endurance of an ox. There's a conscious makeover here that goes beyond three colors of eye shadow and frosted big hair. Roberts still has that mouth and those legs—which have been imprinted on our retinas at the expense of everything else about her—but there's a more grown-up quality to her body, mind, and spirit. And unlike her legs or her lips, her breasts seem neither unique nor perfect—just nice and real.

Finney huffs and puffs perhaps a bit too much as Erin's initially unwilling mentor, but Aaron Eckhart, as the biker next door turned househusband, is sexy and endearing (qualities undisclosed in his previous films for director Neil LaBute). The scenes between him and Roberts generate a sweet heat.

Also reviewed in:
CHICAGO TRIBUNE, 3/17/00, Friday/p. A, Michael Wilmington
NATION, 4/10/00, p. 32, Stuart Klawans
NEW REPUBLIC, 4/3/00, p. 24, Stanley Kauffmann

NEW YORK TIMES, 3/17/00, p. E1, A. O. Scott
NEW YORKER, 3/27/00, p. 135, David Denby
VARIETY, 3/6-12/00, p. 32, Todd McCarthy
WASHINGTON POST, 3/17/00, p. C1, Stephen Hunter
WASHINGTON POST, 3/17/00, Weekend/p. 45, Michael O'Sullivan

EVERLASTING PIECE, AN

A DreamWorks Pictures and Columbia Pictures release of a Bayahibe Films production in association with Baltimore/Spring Creek Pictures Productions. *Executive Producer:* Patrick McCormick. *Producer:* Mark Johnson, Louis DiGiaimo, Jerome O'Connor, Barry Levinson, and Paula Weinstein. *Director:* Barry Levinson. *Screenplay:* Barry McEvoy. *Director of Photography:* Seamus Deasy. *Editor:* Stu Linder. *Music:* Hans Zimmer. *Music Editor:* Vicki Hiatt and Mark Jan Wlodarkiewicz. *Sound:* Kieran Horgan and (music) Slamm Andrews and Alan Meyerson. *Casting:* John Hubbard and Ros Hubbard. *Production Designer:* Nathan Crowley. *Art Director:* Padraig O'Neill and Mark Lowry. *Set Decorator:* Laura Bowe. *Costumes:* Joan Bergin. *Make-up:* Lynn Johnston. *Running time:* 109 minutes. *MPAA Rating:* R.

CAST: Barry McEvoy (Colm); Brian F. O'Byrne (George); Anna Friel (Bronagh); Pauline McLynn (Gerty); Ruth McCabe (Mrs. O'Neill); Laurence Kinlan (Mickey); Billy Connolly (Scalper); Des McAleer (Mr. Black); Colum Convey (I.R.A. Man); Ian Cregg (Milker); David Pearse (Comrade); Enda Oates (Detective); Des Braiden (Vicar); Seamus Ball (Mr. Duggan); George Shane (Billy King); Brendan Costelloe (English Patient); Simon Delaney (Orderly); Olivia Nash (Eileen McGivern); Kathleen Bradley (Bronagh's Cousin); Maclean Stewart (Masked Man #1); A. J. Kennedy (Masked Man #2). Darren Lawlesss (Smok Mullen); Peter Quinn (Que McKeever); David Howarth (British Officer); Mark Carruthers (TV Anchor); Nevan Finnegan (Dixieland Man); Samuel Bright (Wee Messer); Philip Young (Man in Cinema); Conor Bradford (News Reporter); Martin Nicholl (Hard Man); Michael Fieldhouse (Barrister); Bryan McCaugherty (Creeped Youth); Jack Quinn (Bronagh's Dad); Frank O'Keefe (Professor); Paul Clancy (Butcher); Little John Nee and Jonathan Shankey (Toupee Men); Paula McFetridge (IRA Man's Wife).

LOS ANGELES TIMES, 12/25/00, Calendar/p. 11, Kevin Thomas

"An Everlasting Piece" is that rarity: a film that opens on Christmas Day that actually is in the spirit of the season. Set in Belfast in the '80s, it's a comedy of high and zany spirits that effortlessly touches on matters of moral choice, reconciliation and forgiveness and the value of the generous gesture.

The teaming of the film's young star and writer, Barry McEvoy, and its veteran director, Barry Levinson, is as fortuitous as the teaming of Levinson and Warren Beatty on "Bugsy." (It probably helps that Belfast-born McEvoy has lived in Levinson's beloved Maryland since he was 15, and that the port cities of Belfast and Baltimore have such a similar look and feel.) This late-in-the-year gem glows with Levinson's characteristically warm embrace of a wide range of people and his superlative sense of time and place.

McEvoy's highly original tale is set in motion when Bronagh (Anna Friel), the smart and sultry girlfriend of McEvoy's Colin, gets him a job as a barber in the mental institution where she is a nurse. Right away, the brash Cohn hits it off with his equally young fellow barber, the timid George (Brian F. O'Byrne).

Not only do their temperaments complement each other, but they also share a gift of gab, a way with rhyme—George in fact has a passion for poetry. Friendship swiftly transcends the reality that Colin is a Catholic and George a Protestant. When they learn that one of the patients (Billy Connolly) was running a toupee business when he flipped his wig, so to speak, and scalped four of his customers, Colin and George seize the chance to buy him out and try to corner the hairpiece market in Northern Ireland.

They hadn't reckoned with their well-financed rival, Toupee or Not Toupee, but that just adds to the fun. Armed with the scalper's prospective client list, they swiftly find out that selling hairpieces to hardheaded working-class Irishmen is not so easy but frequently amusing. From its beginning, the film makes clear that tensions are running high in Belfast, but they don't intrude on the film's good humor.

As devised by McEvoy and directed by Levinson, Colm and George's inevitable entanglement with the grim political and military realities that surround them is a small miracle of comic imagination, handled deftly with the lightest of touches, a splendid example of putting comedy in the service of deadly serious issues.

One of the film's most confoundingly funny moments occurs when the boys pitch a rug to a vicar, who is amenable—provided the hair came from the head of a Protestant! This note of preposterousness rings so true to human foibles that you have to wonder whether it was drawn from an actual experience of McEvoy's father, a barber and sometime hairpiece salesman whose stories provided a source of inspiration for his son. In short, we come to see, through Colm and George's humorous adventures, both the tragedy and the absurdity in the seemingly endless conflict that holds Northern Ireland in its ancient thrall.

"An Everlasting Piece" is a film rich in picturesque settings and varying moods, all of which is beautifully enhanced by Seamus Deasy's camera work, with its play of light and shadow, and Hans Zimmer's lively yet poignant score. It is also a film of some notably sharp supporting performances, most notably by Colum Convey as an IRA man in need of a toupee and Des McAleer, who wants a rug but doesn't want to pay for it. "An Everlasting Piece" is a tad long and a bit rambling, but you're not likely to mind too much.

NEW YORK, 1/1/01, p. 81, Peter Rainer

Catholic Colm (Barry McEvoy) and Protestant George (Brian F. O'Byrne) work together in a hospital barbershop in Belfast; you could say that hair brings them together. They cook up a plan to corner the Northern Ireland market in hairpieces, billing themselves as the Piece People. Their competition: a company known as Toupee or Not Toupee. This is the backdrop for Barry Levinson's comedy *An Everlasting Piece*, set sometime in the eighties, which was written by McEvoy. (His father is a barber who used to sell hairpieces.) It's a truism that the unlikeliest comic situations sometimes result in the most likable of comedies, and this one, at its best, is a real original—as lyrically nutty as a vintage Bill Forsyth picture. It's filled with marvelous little folkloric throwaways, like the bit with Colm's mother wearing a hair net so the smoke from her cigarette won't stain her locks.

Movies about Ireland tend to be bloated with blarney, but Levinson doesn't press the whimsy; coming from outside the culture probably helped him to see things with a fresh eye. His approach to the Troubles is so oblique you may forget that the blood-and-bullets backdrop is real. And yet, by giving us a cockeyed spin on the factionalism, *An Everlasting Piece is* probably a stronger political experience than many a more somber movie. Maybe comedy is the *only* way to present this material anymore. The joke here is that vanity is the great unifier: Catholics and Protestants, the IRA and the British, all value the plumage of a good hairpiece. Colm and George are like a great comedy team; they have an avidity for rhyming each other's sentences, and when they have a falling-out, they're miserable—they need to get their lives back into sync. McEvoy is a crackerjack performer who knows how to play off O'Byrne's moonstruck timing, and Anna Friel, as Colm's powerhouse girlfriend, keeps juicing the comedy; she's the only performer I've ever seen who can make nagging seem sexy. The one letdown is that there isn't nearly enough of Billy Connolly, playing a crazed hospital patient known as the Scalper, who first gives the boys the idea to take over the toupee market. Connolly has a scene behind bars, where he gulps down a buzzing fly and then dithers on about Saint Paul and the hermaphrodites, that is such a loony jag that you want him along for the whole movie and not just in dribs and drabs. The filmmakers have scalped the Scalper, but just about everyone else in this small-scale classic gets the full treatment.

NEW YORK POST, 12/22/00, p. 52, Lou Lumenick

Director Barry Levinson abandons Baltimore for Belfast in "An Everlasting Piece," a laugh-filled comedy that might be described as "The Full Monty" meets the Three Stooges.

This shaggy hair story, much given to puns like its title, follows the exploits of two wig salesmen—one Catholic, one Protestant—at the height of Northern Ireland's partisan conflict in the '80s.

Colm (Barry McEvoy, who also wrote the script) is the cocky Catholic and George (Brian F. O'Byrne) is the more restrained Protestant. They work together as barbers at a mental institution when a business opportunity presents itself in the person of a newly admitted patient nicknamed the Scalper (Billy O'Connolly).

The Scalper was the sole wig salesman in North Ireland before he flipped his wig, so Colm and George set about securing his lucrative franchise with the help of Colm's nurse girlfriend Bronagh (Anna Friel), who is a lot brighter than either of them.

Their efforts as salesman are laughably inept. When they finally sell a hairpiece, the customer refuses to pay or return the wig.

Worse still, the wig manufacturer in England has set a Christmas Eve deadline for awarding the sole franchise; Colm and George are competing with a much savvier outfit called To Be or Not Toupee.

Just when things look hairiest, our heroes—who shave their heads in one particularly ridiculous sales ploy—have a scary encounter with the IRA (led by a vain terrorist very well played by Colum Convey) that yields a very large order, a moral dilemma and a surprising solution.

McEvoy and O'Byrne, whose characters are continually at odds, play beautifully off each other.

Levinson, who surprisingly seems almost at home here as in his famous Baltimore films like "Diner," constructs several highly entertaining comic episodes. When the women in Colm's family start to undress a drunken man, watch out for what may be the year's funniest scene.

To best appreciate this light-weight comedy, which sometimes teeters on the brink of silliness, it helps to have a high tolerance for wig jokes, schmaltzy endings and a determinedly lighthearted approach to a grim political situation.

NEWSDAY, 12/22/00, Part II/p. B14, Jan Stuart

Set in and around Belfast in the 1980s, "An Everlasting Piece" is a period film. After a fashion. The ethnic tensions surrounding its enterprising heroes are, sadly enough, still very much alive. But the hair panic that drives this buoyant surprise from director Barry Levinson seems more and more a quaint artifact of the 20th Century.

Sinead O'Connor's message had yet to reach Belfast when Colm and George meet while cutting the hair of patients at a mental institution. The pair become fast friends through a mutual passion for poetry, despite the fact that Colm (Barry McEvoy) is a Catholic and George (Brian F. O'Byrne) is a Protestant. And like anyone else who might not appreciate having their ear chomped into by a client in the middle of a job, they are looking to better their situation.

The answer arrives via one of the hospital's scarier residents, an unkempt bundle of raw nerve-endings nicknamed The Scalper (Billy Connolly), who bends Scripture in perverse ways and has cultivated a wig business through nefarious means. Within days, Colm and George are knocking on doors, soliciting clients from the follicly challenged of Belfast.

Anyone concerned that this sounds like a daffy setup for a latter-day Hope and Crosby in "The Road to Belfast" can relax. Any movie about a Catholic and Protestant trying to sell hairpieces in Northern Ireland is never merely about hairpieces, male-role insecurities or even the art of salesmanship.

Screenwriter-actor McEvoy obviously knows the territory, and he adroitly spills his pacifist protagonists into the fray of warring factions. As they bump up against both the Irish Republican Army and the British military, Colm and George are forced to consider how they can compromise their neutrality, and camaraderie, to profit from an untenable civil war. It's a shrewd and wondrously clever piece of writing: McEvoy knows how to get a big laugh, but he's more interested in the small daily absurdities of living in a society in which even selling a wig becomes fraught with political choices, especially when the sales team is

Director Barry Levinson has found two captivating and charismatic team players in McEvoy and O'Byrne, who connect naturally from their first scene together. Levinson is a fascinating choice to direct this material. While he certainly understands cultural tensions from a personal vantage point (the Baltimore blacks and Jews of "Liberty Heights"), he melts into this foreign woodwork with a self-effacing gift and respect for the author's voice we used to see in John Huston. Belfast is one of those places where it looks like it just rained a minute ago, and Levinson gets that dank, stressed-out atmosphere just right. At once humane and miraculously even-handed, "An Everlasting Piece" hangs tall as one of Levinson's best films.

SIGHT AND SOUND, 4/01, p. 47, Richard Kelly

Belfast, the 1980s. Colm O'Neill, a young Catholic, finds work as a barber in the psychiatric hospital where his girlfriend Bronagh is a nurse. He befriends his Protestant colleague George. When they learn that one inmate, nicknamed 'The Scalper', was a toupee salesman, they persuade him to part with his list of leads, form a company called Piece People, and try to win business by making house calls on bald men. Challenged one night by an IRA patrol, they sell a wig to its commander.

Their supplier Wigs of Wimbledon decrees that they enter a sales contest with rival company Toupee or Not Toupee, the winner earning exclusive distributorship. The IRA commander loses his wig during an operation, and Colm and George are interrogated by police. Colm receives an order from the IRA for 30 wigs, the ethics of which Bronagh disputes. Instead she arranges a big sale to the British army, whose soldiers are suffering from anxiety-related hair-loss. Colm consents to this deal as "a gesture", thus winning the contest.

Since the prospect of lasting peace broke out in Northern Ireland, both inward investment and cultural production have flourished amid the Six Counties. Suggestive of these trends is Barry Levinson's new comedy, funded by DreamWorks SKG and written by actor Barry McEvoy (who also stars, most appealingly, as Colm O'Neill). In his teens McEvoy quit Belfast for the US, but his father's tales of barbershop life inspired him to write this script, in which Catholic Colm and his Protestant partner George struggle to make a profitable (and ecumenical) business out of hawking hairpieces. Eventually McEvoy's project secured the patronage of Steven Spielberg, though this may have been a mixed blessing.

It's a measure of McEvoy's material that director Barry Levinson seems quite comfortable in handling scenes replete with what poet Tom Paulin calls "the crack and buzz of Ulster speech". Belfast's down-at-heel loveliness is also well drawn: even the city's murals acquire a new splendour thanks to DoP Seamus Deasey. Elsewhere deft touches abound. To convey the quandary of the O'Neill family in living on the 'peace line', Levinson simply doodles helpful arrows and tags on to the screen. Then again, levity in these matters isn't everyone's cup of tea, not least while sectarian pipe-bomb attacks remain depressingly frequent in the 'peace line' vicinity.

Still, there's something affirmatively cheeky about this film, recalling the great comedian James Young who once entertained all parties in the North with such characters as 'Orange Lil' and Mrs O'Condriac (who had "trouble with her veins"). The best moments are funny not least because they ring true. On his first day at work Colm meets a succession of big, bluff men, all called Billy. The name Colm and George select for their business, Piece People, puns on that of a well-meaning cross-community movement of the 70s. The IRA's representatives are grim-visaged connoisseurs of fried chicken. And McEvoy has a sly grasp of the local preoccupation with "indecency", so Pauline McLynn fits right in as Colm's easily shocked auntie.

More unnerving moments suggest the awful, stifling conformity of sectarianism. A night at the pictures for Colm and girlfriend Bronagh (a lively Anna Friel) turns sour when bullet-headed youths coerce them into standing dutifully face-front for the closing rendition of 'God Save the Queen'. But then Levinson and McEvoy are sufficiently astute to appreciate aspects of oft-maligned 'Protestant culture.' Van Morrison, alumnus of Orangefield High School, graces the soundtrack with his lovely ballad 'On Hyndford Street'. And George, whose liking for poetry is merely a joke in the first reel, is later seen reciting passionately on stage at Queens University.

Spielberg has been charged with "burying" this film so as to curry favour with the Labour government that lately knighted him. Levinson has suggested that DreamWorks slashed the release pattern following disagreements between himself and Jeffrey Katzenberg over issues of political context. But then what is the film actually saying? There's a useful moment after Colm's efforts to reclaim a wig from a defaulting customer are undercut when George panics and flees. Later, George forlornly concedes to his furious partner, "Punch me if you want. I'm a coward." Colm weighs this up, and arrives at a thoughtful conclusion. "Fuck it. You're alright. I'm a dick." This quality of self-abnegation is reprised in the film's climax, as Colm spurns one order from the IRA yet accepts another from Her Majesty's armed forces. But Colm claims to be making "a gesture", one that is his and not George's to make; and only on the proviso that the Brits are charged double rate.

Maybe this is just a gag about the entrepreneurial instinct; one that won't be to all tastes. Still, it's worth noting that gestures of all kinds have enabled some improbable reconciliation in the North of recent years. Such is the spirit evoked in Michael Longley's 1994 poem 'Ceasefire', wherein the defeated Trojan king Priam makes the ultimate abnegation ("I get down on my knees and do what must be done/and kiss Achilles' hand, the killer of my son"). Naturally there's nothing of comparable gravity here, but Levinson may have been mindful of the words he gave to Paul Reiser's character Modell in his debut feature *Diner*. "Gesture is a good word. At least you know where you stand with gesture."

VILLAGE VOICE, 12/26/00, p. 154, Michael Atkinson

The homilies are late in coming in Barry Levinson's pleasant but trifling Belfast pratfall, *An Everlasting Piece*, but they come all the same: As in, friendship is more important than civil war, which is arguable on a few levels at least. Written by Irish nobody Barry McEvoy, Levinson's singsong farce starts with Colm (McEvoy) and George (Brian F. O'Byrne) as two hospital barbers—one Catholic, one Protestant—who decide to get rich by appropriating the North Irish monopoly on toupees after its owner, nicknamed the Scalper (Billy Connolly), goes certifiable. It's a sprightly, low-fiber comedy while the comedy lasts. Levinson knows how to make the minor characters matter, but the heroes are bland and the not-quite-screwball-enough tale becomes bogged in issues of loyalty, heading toward a face-down with the IRA and the Brit Army that is neither ponderous nor memorable.

Also reviewed in:
NEW REPUBLIC, 1/1 & 8/01, p. 22, Stanley Kauffmann
NEW YORK TIMES, 12/25/00, p. E5, A. O. Scott
VARIETY, 12/18-31/00, p. 28, Todd McCarthy
WASHINGTON POST, 12/22/00, Weekend/p. 41, Desson Howe
WASHINGTON POST, 12/25/00, p. C4, Rita Kempley

EYE OF THE BEHOLDER

A Destination Films and Behaviour Worldwide release in association with Village Roadshow-Ambridge Film Partnership presentation of a Hit & Run/Filmline International production. *Executive Producer:* Hilary Shor and Mark Damon. *Producer:* Tony Smith and Nicolas Clermont. *Director:* Stephan Elliott. *Screenplay:* Stephan Elliott. *Based on the novel by:* Marc Behm. *Director of Photography:* Guy Dufaux. *Editor:* Sue Blainey. *Music:* Marius De Vries. *Music Editor:* Dina Eaton. *Sound:* Claude La Haye, Viateur Paiement, Hans Peter Stuhl, and (music) Geoff Foster and Mike Nielsen. *Sound Editor:* Sofie Essiembre. *Casting:* Vera Miller and Nadia Rona. *Production Designer:* Jean-Baptiste Tard. *Art Director:* Real Prouix. *Set Decorator:* Michèle Forest, Suzanne Cloutier, and Sonia Venne. *Special Effects:* Jacques Langlois. *Costumes:* Lizzy Gardiner. *Make-up:* Francine Gagnon. *Stunt Coordinator:* Stéphane Lefebvre. *Running time:* 102 minutes. *MPAA Rating:* R.

CAST: Ewan McGregor (Eye); Ashley Judd (Joann Eris); Patrick Bergin (Alex); k.d. lang (Hilary); Jason Priestley (Gary); Geveviève Bujold (Doctor Brault); Anne-Marie Brown and Kaitlin Brown (Lucy); David Nerman (Mike); Steven McCarthy (Paul); Vlasta Vrana (Hugo);

Janine Thériault (Nathy); Don Jordan (Toohey); Maria Revelins (Ms. Keenan); Lisa Forget (Nurse); Gayle Garfinkle (Head Waitress); Russell Yuen (Federal Agent 1); Stephane Levasseur (Federal Agent 2); Al Vandecruys (Alaskan Federal Agent 1); Sam Stone (Alaskan Federal Agent 2); Mauro Venditelli (Boss); Josa Maule (Receptionist); Carole Collin (Secretary); Stephanie Sbrega (Sandra); Philip Le Maistre (Gas Attendant); Michel Perron (Fat Businessman); Maria Bircher (Waitress); Howard Bilerman (Waiter); Cara Reynolds (Young Joanna); Leonard Farlinger (Young Joanna's Father); Jason Baerg (Gay Man); Michelle Sweeney (Salvo); Donovan Reiter (Local 1); Amanda Davis (Girl); Carl Crevier (Chauffeur); Erwin Goldberg (Doctor); Garth Gilker (Airport Guard); James Hieminga (Wade); Bob Brewster (Cop); Charles Powell (Prisoner); Thomas Karle (Fat Man); Louis Negin (Bartender); Al Clark (Redneck); Una Kay (Hilary's Mother); Merlee Shapiro (Reva Desk Clerk); Vera Miller and Nadia Rona (Tea Trolley Ladies); Erik Johnson (Local 2).

LOS ANGELES TIMES, 1/28/00, Calendar/p. 12, Eric Harrison

Mr. Adams, my old elementary school principal, frowned on negativity. "Try to find something good to say about everyone," he told us one day in assembly. "If you see a dead dog lying in a ditch, say something nice, even if it's only that it has nice, white teeth."

It is "Eye of the Beholder," the new Ashley Judd movie, that brings Mr. Adams' teachings to mind. Having seen it, I am pleased to report that not only are Judd's teeth white, but that her co-star Ewan McGregor's are as well. Their teeth are so white and they both are so attractive and talented that I predict many fine movies lie in their future.

Furthermore, let me hasten to add that "Eye" isn't the abomination you might expect, considering the way its distributors kept it under wraps, slipping it into theaters with only one last-minute screening for reviewers. It isn't well-made by any means (sorry, Mr. Adams), but nobody has anything to be ashamed of here. It isn't insultingly bad; it's just incompetent.

The central conceit is an interesting one: McGregor plays a surveillance expert so disengaged from life that he is hardly a physical entity anymore, a professional voyeur hiding behind a wall of gadgetry. We never even learn his name. Someone calls him "Lucky Legs" at one point; the production notes identify him simply as Eye.

He has suffered an unbearable loss. But he is pulled back into the world when he becomes obsessed with a serial killer (Judd) whom he'd been assigned to spy on. She, too, has a void in her soul. He senses a connection.

Eye follows her bloody trail across the country, listening to her conversations, spying on her in her bedroom, watching her kill. He protects her from harm and from capture by the police, biding his time until he can make his presence known.

Adapted from a novel by Marc Behm, "Eye of the Beholder" is a psychologiccal thriller, or at least it should be. As so often happens, the filmmakers are more interested in thrills than psychology, in sensation over credibility and depth.

And so, to make us empathize with Judd's identity-shifting killer, we're given a couple of ridiculously pat rationales for her turning out bad. And when Eye reenters the physical world, creeping awkwardly out of his high-tech cocoon, this disembodied geek becomes suddenly quite handy with guns and with his fists.

Writer-director Stephan Elliott, best known for the comedy "The Adventures of Priscilla, Queen of the Desert," also employs several dubious narrative devices. In one case, he turns a character from Eye's past, basically a figment of his imagination, into a physical presence who talks to him and moves in and out of scenes. It's intriguing at first, in a "Sixth Sense" sort of way, until we figure out what's going on. Then it becomes annoying.

But before too long, Elliott abruptly and clumsily drops the gambit, which merely underscores how contrived and unnecessary it was to begin with.

Perhaps because he doesn't care to spend time creating credible characters and developing his themes through their interactions (that's called drama in some circles), Elliott compensates by being literal and heavy-handed.

An example: He wants us to know that the Eye has become a guardian angel to the character Judd plays, so Elliott plants angel statuary and the word "angel" all over the place. Then, in case we still don't get it, he has Judd spell it out in dialogue.

He also likes to use songs to tell the audience what to think. Several times he sticks a pop song on the soundtrack to tell us exactly what the scene playing out on screen has just shown us.

And then there's the way Elliott continually undercuts the themes he ostensibly wants to express: McGregor's character has lost a daughter, Judd's has lost a father. This is the tie that binds them. This may be the one Hollywood movie in which the male lead really ought to be old enough to be the female lead's father.

Oh, but you say that might've skewed the movie toward a different demographic. Silly me. I thought there was a point to making movies beyond marketing.

Be that as it may, though, there's no doubt about it: Everyone involved has sure got white teeth.

NEW YORK POST, 1/28/00, p. 45, Lou Lumenick

Long on style but perilously short on logic and coherence, "Eye of the Beholder" is watchable even when what's going on makes no sense whatsoever.

Stephan Elliott, the Australian writer-director responsible for the drag-fest "Adventures of Priscilla, Queen of the Desert," has stitched together elements from a dozen films, most notably "Vertigo" and "Blowup," as well as their respective Brian De Palma knockoffs, "Obsession" and "Blow Out."

Ewan McGregor ("Star Wars: Episode 1—The Phantom Menace") plays a Washington-based British secret-service agent nicknamed "The Eye" who—for reasons that are totally unclear—gets assigned to keep tabs on glamorous serial killer Joanna (Ashley Judd, sporting an impressive selection of wigs and accents).

The Eye has been wiggy ever since his wife bolted years earlier with his young daughter (with whom he regularly has fantasy conversations). Now he's become obsessed with Joanna. In his deranged mind, he's convinced that she's somehow connected with the missing daughter.

When the Eye isn't watching Joanna with high-tech surveillance devices, he's following her on a colorful cross-country chase, punctuated by several gruesome murders. Anyone who's wondering just how she drowns one victim in a water-filled railroad-car bathroom has obviously wandered into the wrong movie.

When a pregnant Joanna moves to San Francisco and settles down with a winery owner (Patrick Bergin), the Eye comes up with a novel way to stop her from killing her new beau: He does the job himself, with a telescopic rifle trained from the bell tower where he's taken up residence.

Others who figure in the increasingly silly proceedings include Genevieve Bujold (from "Obsession") as a psychologist with a hilariously overdecorated apartment; k.d. lang, the only recognizable human on view, as the Eye's exasperated supervisor; and Jason Priestly as a sleazy drifter.

"Eye of the Beholder" doesn't offer much in the way of suspense until its final, mind-boggling half hour, when the equally crazy Eye and Joanna finally bond in an Alaskan diner.

But it's quite an eyeful.

NEWSDAY, 1/28/00, Part II/p. B7, Gene Seymour

Witless in almost every sense of the word, "Eye of the Beholder" transforms a devilishly clever premise into a fashion spread with corpses.

Which wouldn't be so bad if the movie had been more liberally spiked with the kind of dry, mordant outrageousness found in Marc Behm's 1980 neo-noir thriller about a detective, known only as "the Eye," who trails a woman who kills several men from sea to shining sea. The joke is that he can't bring himself to even approach her, much less arrest her, because she represents, in some oblique way, his own long-lost daughter.

One imagined the Eye, in Behm's original conception, as an older man, easy to lose in a crowd. Gene Hackman, who's played that kind of role several times before, would have been perfect. Clint Eastwood, his chiseled visage weather-beaten into a haunted mask, would have been an interesting choice. Even slightly younger, but no less world-weary guys, such as Jeff Bridges or John Travolta, would have been up to the task.

But writer-director Stephan Elliott, whose "The Adventures of Priscilla, Queen of the Desert" (1994), offered a different, but no less surrealistic road trip, chose to make the Eye an owlish, reserved young British secret agent, played by Ewan McGregor. He's a good actor, but he's in the wrong role at the wrong time. No matter how much he may lay on the pathos, McGregor never quite convinces you that he's earned his character's angst. He seems to be struggling throughout the movie to fit himself into the Eye's cosmic blankness.

Such miscasting throws the whole movie out of whack, though it begins promisingly with some nifty red herrings, a clever way of bringing the Eye's chimerical daughter into the mix and, best of all, k.d. lang as McGregor's saucy colleague. If only everyone else in the movie lightened up as much as lang, then the second half of the movie in which the Eye dives deeper into his obsession with serial killer Joanna Eris (Ashley Judd) wouldn't feel so loaded down with explanation, rationalization and stylized sludge. Jason Priestley provides some relief from the prevailing solemnity as a desert rat who wants to do very bad things to Joanna.

As the enigmatic object of the Eye's quixotic pursuit, Judd is poised to be just out of reach of his own comprehension throughout the film. Her Joanna materializes in various wigs and equally varied states of dress and undress. His confusion and fascination with her becomes our own. It's a potentially rich metaphor for voyeurism in general and movie-going in particular. But as with just about everything else in this vein, Hitchcock did it better. (For proof, you're strongly advised to check out the master's "Rear Window.")

Besides, as wonderful as Judd is to behold in her sundry transformations, she's not someone we want to see in sections. Her sloe-eyed intelligence and cat-like agility have made her a box-office draw, and "Eye of the Beholder" offers only a few frustrating glimpses of these attributes. Still, she has just enough fine moments of emotional power to allow her potential for big-time stardom to wriggle through the movie unscathed. It's the niftiest escape act the movie offers.

SIGHT AND SOUND, 7/00, p. 42, Ken Hollings

Washington DC, the present. While using his surveillance techniques to investigate a possible diplomatic scandal, an anonymous British intelligence agent witnesses a premeditated murder committed by a mysterious young woman named Joanna Eris. Obsessed with memories of his lost daughter, whose ghostly image appears in a photograph he has taken of Joanna inside a museum, the agent continues to spy on her as she travels across America committing further murders.

Digging into Joanna's past he discovers that she was abandoned by her father as a child and has subsequently attempted suicide several times. Starting to involve himself more actively in Joanna's life, the agent kills a blind San Francisco millionaire whom she was intending to marry. After beating up a young junkie who was threatening Joanna's life, he loses track of her, only to discover that she has checked into a Boston hospital suffering a miscarriage. The two meet in Alaska where the agent helps her to evade capture by the FBI. Joanna dies during their escape but not before admitting that she recognises the agent as the man who photographed her the museum.

The true dandy, poet Charles Baudelaire once observed, reveals himself through his attention to detail. Stephan Elliott, responsible for the flamboyant cross-dressing road movie *The Adventures of Priscilla Queen of the Desert*, has dispensed with the sequins and glitter this time around, as he packs his central characters off on another trans-continental journey of discovery. Sporting a bedraggled red nylon anorak and lugging a battered suitcase crammed with complex surveillance devices, Ewan McGregor's British intelligence agent would appear to be the antithesis of the ironic, preening self-involvement displayed by *Priscilla*'s very dandified drag queens. But the agent's bruised professionalism and sense of weary detachment as he leads his shadowy existence in Washington's bustling diplomatic community are reflections of an equally mannered and complex sensibility.

The grim satisfaction with which he posts compromising video evidence of a grubby after-hours sexual liaison on the internet during the opening sequence betrays the mark of a true artist. He's a technological aesthete, beyond human society, and the homicidal Joanna, played with mercurial hauteur by Ashley Judd, is right out there with him. While the agent carries out distracted conversations with a fondly imagined memory of his missing daughter, Joanna has been indoctrinated by her parole officer Dr Brault never to reveal herself to any man who does not need to know. Both are so determined to conceal their true feelings, maintaining a distance between voyeur and subject that is as much emotional as it is physical, that details are all that remain to bring them together.

This finds neat expression in *Eye of the Beholder*'s richly detailed *mise en scène* which is full of obsessive strophes and allusions, ranging from astrological symbols and depictions of angels to the agent's gradual acquiring of Joanna's drinking and smoking habits. Joanna's change of name and appearance, together with the agent's growing collection of forlorn snow globes as the pursuit takes them from one city to the next, suggest just how deep Elliott's passion for formal precision runs. The film's design and camerawork also hint at very deliberate shifts in both time and place. New York is filled with sophisticated echoes from 40s Hitchcock thrillers; San Francisco is a golden 60s bohemian paradise; Alaska has been transformed into a 50s wilderness of chrome dinettes and trailer parks.

McGregor's and Judd's attentive, focused performances never allow their characters to become lost in Elliott's fractured, virtual America. The sense of pain and despair seep through: "The last time I blinked," the agent confesses to a vision he has of his daughter when Joanna flees outside the range of his electronic sensors, "I lost you, I lost my wife and I nearly lost my mind. She's all I've got left." Considering how few scenes they share together, Joanna's dying moment of recognition in the agent's arms has a true breadth to it. A solid supporting cast fleshes out the film's intricate fascinations. Geneviève Bujold's pointedly brusque performance as Dr Brault endows her with a presence extending far beyond her limited screen time, while singer k.d.lang brings remarkable warmth to the part of Hilary, the agent's Washington handler who interacts solely with McGregor's voice and scanned image on a computer terminal. Jason Priestley puts a mean, predatory shimmer into his portrayal of the sleazy cowboy smackhead who tries to kill Joanna. His unwashed and peroxide tangle of hair lets just enough of the dark roots show through to remind us how important attention to detail can be.

VILLAGE VOICE, 2/8/00, p. 144, Jessica Winter

High-buffed, low-rack pulp, *Eye of the Beholder* is lovable in its own addled, literal-minded way. Its neo-noir, psych-thriller signifiers—Hitchcock fixation, shlumpy voyeur, femme fatale going "incognito" in fright wig and mink stole—don't just provide goofy flash via flashback but service a grief-concerned narrative in which time and space collapse into a surrealist black hole.

Said narrative is rather gimpy, aided along by Ewan McGregor—whose stoic, sorrowing British intelligence agent enjoys uncanny luck in tracking suspects who have sex and/or kill people in front of uncurtained windows—and by Ashley Judd, whose murderous vixen is considerate enough to off her first victim in a well-lit glass house. McGregor can't bust her, though, because the specter of his missing daughter, Lucy—an accusatory phantom menace straight out of *The Sixth Sense*—implores him not to. McGregor gradually gleans Judd's sad backstory—abandoned by Dad as a child, traumatic stint in juvie—and the Lucy, figure fades out as he begins stalking his surrogate lost child across the country, watching from afar as Judd kills, marries, and wanders into bad straits with a bleached drifter (Jason Priestley, whooping it up). What started out as *Rear Window* redux becomes *Vertigo* with a twist of *Limey*. Judd's ability to make a bloodthirsty nutbag sympathetic and still maintain a spiked camp edge is thrilling; she even manages to turn a dopey astrology motif into a humanizing character quirk. When hunter and hunted finally meet in an Alaskan diner, Judd and McGregor achieve Mulder-and-Scully chemistry; two consummate pros haven't slummed so grandly in a genre piece since Pacino and De Niro went mano a mano over Formica in *Heat*.

Also reviewed in:
CHICAGO TRIBUNE, 1/28/00, Friday/p. A, Michael Wilmington
NEW YORK TIMES, 1/28/00, p. E21, Stephen Holden
VARIETY, 10/4-10/99, p. 89, Deborah Young
WASHINGTON POST, 1/28/00, p. C5, Stephen Holden
WASHINGTON POST, 1/28/00, Weekend/p. 38, Desson Howe

EYES OF TAMMY FAYE, THE

A Lions Gate Films release of a World of Wonder Productions, Inc. in association with Channel Four & Cinemax Reel Life. *Executive Producer:* Sheila Nevins. *Producer:* John Hoffman, Randy Barbato and Fenton Bailey. *Director:* Fenton Bailey and Randy Barbato. *Director of Photography:* Sandra Chandler. *Editor:* Paul Wiesepape. *Music:* Jim Harry. *Narrator:* RuPaul Charles. *Running time:* 79 minutes. *MPAA Rating:* Not Rated.

CAST: Tammy Faye Messner (Televangelist);   Roe Messner (Church Contractor);   Jim Bakker (Televangelist);   Jamie Bakker (Minister);   Mel White (Author and Minister);   Pat Boone (Christian Entertainer);   Tammmy Sue Bakker Chapman (Tammy Faye's Daughter);   Steven Chao (President of USA Cable);   Jim J. Bullock (Gay Comedian);   Roseanne (Entertainer);   Greg Gorman (Celebrity Photographer);   Charles Sheperd (Author);   James Albert (Law Professor at Drake University/Author).

LOS ANGELES TIMES, 7/28/00, Calendar/p. 2, Kenneth Turan

"The Eyes of Tamny Faye" not only gives us the skinny on the most celebrated eyelashes of our time (they're permanent albeit augmented by generous dollops of L'Oreal mascara), it very much sees the world through the eyes of that particular beholder.

It may seem odd to treat the former Tammy Faye Bakker, the erstwhile first lady of Christian broadcasting, with the kind of empathetic reverence usually reserved for Nobel Peace Prize winner Aung San Suu Kyi, but having celebrated drag star RuPaul Charles and not Walter Cronkite as your narrator is a tip-off that this is not a "just the facts, ma'am" type of documentary.

Half serious, half campy, "The Eyes of Tammy Faye" takes an amusingly sob sister approach to the woman who, along with former husband Jim Bakker, helped found no less than three televangelism networks as well as Heritage USA, at one time this country's most popular theme park if those with Disney in their name were bumped from the list.

Taking Tammy Faye at face value, so to speak, does mean that filmmakers Fenton Bailey and Randy Barbato display a weakness for overwrought voice-over lines like "Twelve long years after her fall from grace, Tammy Faye lives in virtual exile in Palm Desert, California" and "She returned to the desert, alone with her dolls, her dogs and her faith."

But if the film's devotion to its subject means that its analysis of the factors that led to the demise of the Bakkers' PTL (for Praise the Lord) network shouldn't necessarily be taken as gospel, that doesn't mean that their film can't be thoroughly enjoyed as a privileged look at one of the loopiest of late 20th century lives. "She's a survivor," explains Jim J. Bullock, who once co-hosted a TV show with her. "After the holocaust, there will be roaches, Tammy Faye and Cher."

A naturally theatrical personality quite comfortable living her private life in public, the remarried Tammy Faye Messner is always close to emotion and tears. Adroit at using her vulnerability as a strength and a shield, Tammy Faye may not be quite as guileless as the film makes her out, but anyone who can read a poem beginning "Loneliness clings to me like a second skin" and follow it with the comment "It's a little dramatic, I guess" is a heck of a lot of fun to be around.

Born Tammy Faye LaValley in International Falls, Minn., the eldest child of a sternly religious household, this outgoing young woman met Jim Bakker at Minneapolis' North Central Bible College when she was 17 and married him at 19. Soon they were involved in the fledgling field of televangelism, but, though successful, they could not find a home.

Their children's show with hand puppets Susie Muppet and Allie Alligator helped launch Pat Robertson's Christian Broadcasting Network, but the Bakkers left after Robertson took over "The 700 Club" talk show that Jim had started. Internecine battles forced them out of their next start-up, Trinity Broadcasting, but they hit pay dirt with PTL, one of the first four satellite networks in the world, with Jim dramatically promising to broadcast "24 hours a day until the second coming of Christ."

While "The Eyes of Tammy Faye" is more interesting in exploring Tammy Faye's openness, including her early embracing of AIDS patients, than wondering if the huge sums televangelism raises might not be the greatest thing in the world, it does gleefully explore the very public problems Jim and Tammy Faye did have to deal with. First came his liaison with Jessica Hahn, followed by her addiction to painkillers that ended with an accidental overdose and a stay in the Betty Ford clinic.

Painted as the Judas behind the Bakkers' ultimate demise is the Moral Majority's Jerry Falwell, who, the film asserts, posed as the PTL's savior while secretly scheming to take over the ministry and then destroy it. While Tammy Faye is obviously sincere in these beliefs, that doesn't ensure their complete accuracy, and having divergent points of view wouldn't have hurt.

But filmmakers Bailey and Barbato are clearly not concerned with making anything like a conventional documentary, and while their adventurousness doesn't always work (breaking the film into sections and using hand puppets to read the titles aloud comes off as way too cutesy) it succeeds more often than not. Of course, having a subject who is not only willing to say, "You cannot go forward looking into the rearview mirror of life," but actually believes it doesn't hurt one little bit.

NEW YORK POST, 7/21/00, p. 50, Lou Lumenick

This is less a, uh, straight documentary than a campy tribute to the mascara-addicted wife of the fallen evangelist, complete with hand-puppet intros and fawning narration by RuPaul.

Which is to say it's highly entertaining, even if it's almost entirely one-sided.

Tammy Faye Bakker Messner is a heroine in gay circles, as much for her worship of makeup and big hair as her big heart—she and her ex-hubby Jim embraced AIDS sufferers and homosexuals who were considered pariahs by other fundamentalist Christian televangelists.

And Lord, were they entertainers!—some will consider "The Eyes of Tammy Faye" worth a look just for its priceless collection of TV clips featuring the Bakkers in a dazzling array of 70s and early '80s fashions and hairstyles, beginning with a program showcasing them and puppets Tammy Faye fashioned from the caps of shampoo containers.

Squeezed out of Pat Robertson's Christian Broadcasting Network (now the Fox Family Channel) and the Trinity Broadcasting Network after putting them on the map, the Bakkers founded the PTL (Praise the Lord) cable network, Where Tammy Faye improvised on the air for hours a day, at the same time recording 40 albums and raising two troubled children (who are barely heard from here).

As the documentary has it, their empire toppled and their marriage collapsed because Jim devoted so much energy to Heritage USA, a vast Christian theme park in Charlotte, N.C., whose attendance was claimed to trail only Disney World and Disneyland.

British filmmakers Randy Barbato and Fenton Bailey accept at face value Tammy Faye's assertion that Moral Majority leader Jerry Falwell's scheming was more to blame than her husband's well-publicized affair with Jessica Hahn and subsequent conviction for massive financial fraud.

Addicted to anti-anxiety medication as well as mascara, Tammy Faye flipped out (on the air, as we see here) and landed in the Betty Ford Clinic around the same time Jim landed in prison.

She remarried, to Roe Messner the builder of Heritage USA, but he too ended up behind bars for fraud.

But she's a survivor, even if she long ago became a national joke.

Among her varied defenders are the gay comic Jim J. Bullock (with whom she hosted a short-lived syndicated show) and Pat Boone, who pointedly remarks that Christian fundamentalists are "one army that kills our wounded."

In the end, even the Charlotte Observer reporter who exposed the Bakkers financial excesses is reduced to asking for her autograph.

Though the Bakkers' saga was dramatized in a lurid TV movie, Tammy Faye is such an oversized character that only she can play herself—in many ways she's the ultimate drag queen.

VILLAGE VOICE, 7/25/00, p. 128, Michael Atkinson

The horror, the horror: What lies beneath the painted rictus of Tammy Faye Bakker, televangelical gargoyle, tabloid cuckoldette, rehab princess, gay-cult jester? Nothing much, according to filmmakers Randy Barbato and Fenton Bailey, whose *The Eyes of Tammy Faye* is an über-kitschy, RuPaul-narrated gloss over the disastrous life and times of America's favorite mascara smashup. It is a horror film, in every sense: Each shot is simultaneously dedicated to reglorifying Tammy Faye's public image (the PTL song-and-dance flashbacks are as chilling a vision of Yankee foolishness as you'll ever see), and contemptuously pissing on her for it.

Mocked by sock-puppet intros, E!-doc faux dramatics, and pitiless close-ups of makeup carnage, our heroine seems only glad for the attention. Overt camp culture is a matter of bullies and victims, and though Tammy Faye emerges standing—she seems, in fact, to walk the real Christian walk, unlike Falwell and other ministry gold brickers—her cinebiographers come off as smirking buffoons. In fact, the movie cannot help but be merely another debacle that Tammy Faye will survive, eyelashes and integrity intact.

Also reviewed in:
CHICAGO TRIBUNE, 8/4/00, Friday/p. I, John Petrakis
NEW YORK TIMES, 7/21/00, p. E20, Elvis Mitchell
VARIETY , 2/14-20/00, p. 46, Dennis Harvey
WASHINGTON POST, 8/4/00, p. C14, Rita Kempley

FAMILY MAN, THE

A Universal Pictures and Beacon Pictures release of a Riche/Ludwig-Zvi Howard Rosenman-Saturn production. *Executive Producer:* Armyan Bernstein, Thomas A. Bliss, and Andrew Z. Davis. *Producer:* Marc Abraham, Zvi Howard Rosenman, Tony Ludwig, and Alan Riche. *Director:* Brett Ratner. *Screenplay:* David Diamond and David Weissman. *Director of Photography:* Dante Spinotti. *Editor:* Mark Helfrich. *Music:* Danny Elfman. *Music Editor:* Ellen Segal. *Sound:* Kim Ornitz and (music) Dennis Sands. *Sound Editor:* Gregory King and Darren King. *Casting:* Matthew Barry and Nancy Green-Keyes. *Production Designer:* Kristi Zea. *Art Director:* Steve Saklad. *Set Designer:* Lori Rowbotham. *Set Decorator:* Leslie Pope. *Set Dresser:* Amanda Serino. *Visual Effects:* Mat Beck. *Costumes:* Betsy Heimann. *Make-up:* Felicity Bowring, Carrie Angland, and Valli O'Reily. *Make-up (Nicolas Cage):* Allen Weisinger. *Stunt Coordinator:* Pete Bucossi and Conrad Palmisano. *Running time:* 120 minutes. *MPAA Rating:* PG-13.

CAST: Nicolas Cage (Jack Campbell); Téa Leoni (Kate); Don Cheadle (Cash); Jeremy Piven (Arnie); Saul Rubinek (Alan Mintz); Josef Sommer (Lassiter); Makenzie Vega (Annie); Jake Milkovich and Ryan Milkovich (Josh); Lisa Thornhill (Evelyn); Harve Presnell (Big Ed); Mary Beth Hurt (Adelle); Amber Valletta (Paula); Francine York (Lorraine); Ruth Williamson (Mrs. Peterson); John O'Donahue (Tony the Doorman); Daniel Whitner (Frank the Security Man); Lucy Lin and Lisa Lo Cicero (Executives); Wass Stevens (Trader); Thomas James Foster (Joe the Valet); Irene Roseen (Mintz's Assistant); Ken Leung (Deli Clerk); Mak Fai (Grandfather at Deli); Maggi-Meg Reed (Lady in Deli); Kate Walsh (Jeannie); Ray Valentine (Evelyn's Husband); Gianni Russo (Nick); Tom McGowan (Bill); Joel McKinnon Miller (Tommy); Tanya Newbould (Nick's Wife); Hilary Adahms (Party Guest); Troy Hall (Kenny); Kathleen Doyle (Big Ed's PA Voice); Mary Civiello (CNBC Reporter); Paul Keith (Suit Salesman); Elisabeth Sjoli (Hostess); Philippe Bergeron (Waiter); Christopher Breslin (Restaurant Patron); Si Picker (Tire Customer); Lisa Guzman (Girl at Market); Robert Downey Sr. (Man in House); P.J. Barry (Limo Driver); Nina Barry (Kate's Assistant).

LOS ANGELES TIMES, 12/22/00, Calendar/p. 1, Kevin Thomas

"The Family Man" is an ambitious, carefully crafted Christmas movie that tries to be "It's a Wonderful Life" for the new millennium but lacks the honesty to pull it off. Not even a sincere and heroic effort by Nicolas Cage can redeem the film's essential phoniness. Still, Cage's charisma and a lot of shameless heart tugging will surely prove a potent lure with many moviegoers.

Cage's Jack Campbell, the hard-driving president of a major Wall Street corporation, is on the brink of closing a $130-billion merger deal. Deciding to stay home on Christmas Eve, he stops by a convenience store, where he defuses a rapidly escalating and dangerous racial clash between its Asian proprietor and an African American customer.

The customer named Cash (Don Cheadle) proves to be an angel in street punk disguise. In a brief exchange with Cash, which brings out Jack's rusty humanitarian impulses, Campbell assures him that "I have everything I've ever wanted."

Stretched out on his bed in his sleek, high-rise apartment, Jack falls asleep, only to awaken in a suburban New Jersey bedroom. Writers David Diamond, David Weissman and director Brett Ratner are going to give Jack a glimpse of what his life might have been had he not, 13 years earlier, disregarded his college sweetheart's dark premonition of disaster and flown off to London for a year's internship at a bank. He assures Tea Leoni's Kate, who's off to law school herself, that their love will survive the one-year separation, but clearly their relationship did not.

Jack awakens to discover that he's married to Kate and is a tire salesman, working for his highly successful father-in-law (Harve Presnell), that Kate is a bono attorney, that they have a 6-year-old daughter and a baby son and a big mortgage on a comfortably cluttered house. Since this is a Hollywood movie, it is more gorgeous than ever and their marriage is intensely passionate. Nobody takes much notice that Jack is acting mighty peculiar, as if he didn't quite know his neighbors or what was going on, except for his precocious daughter, Annie (Makenzie Vega), who decides he's an alien and keeps him clued in.

Now, Jack does find himself warming to the idea of a wife and children, and that's certainly understandable, but everybody and everything else seems pretty boring—perhaps more boring than the filmmakers intended. Just when the film begins to cloy in earnest, it takes off in an unexpected and encouraging direction when fate gives Jack the opportunity to hold on to his newly acquired family life while earning back his old corporate job.

Kate lays on a massive guilt trip about him wanting to move back to Manhattan as part of the deal—just as she had done 13 years earlier about him going to London. Haven't these people heard about commuting? (For that matter, she and Jack could have surely managed some budget flights between London and New York back in 1987.)

It all makes you wonder: What is going on here? Kate is presented as the perfect wife, but if so, why can't she understand that a man of Jack's obvious brilliance might not be fulfilled selling tires? For that matter, what if it had been Kate who had wanted to go off to London? If Jack had tried to stop her, he would have been labeled a male chauvinist pig.

"The Family Man" is trying to make a grand statement about the value of family over career, and in doing so, paints Jack, before the "what if?" fantasy overtakes him, as a ruthless materialist. Everyone knows that striking a balance between career and family nowadays requires the skill of a master juggler, but there are plenty of hugely successful men who are also dedicated husbands and fathers—and some of them are plenty ruthless in the boardroom.

There's a false dichotomy running through this film, making career and family an either-or choice, and Kate, for all Leoni's radiance, is more killjoy than dream girl. Cage is a protean actor of wide range and authority, and the film's cast is large and substantial, including Saul Rubinek, Josef Sommer and Mary Beth Hurt as Jack's business associates and Jeremy Piven as Jack's New Jersey neighbor and best pal, and Francine York as his mother-in-law. But in terms corporate Jack would understand, it's still no deal.

NEW YORK POST 12/22/00, p. 54, Lou Lumenick

"The Family Man" is a coal lump of a Christmas present from Universal, which gave us the charmless "Dr. Seuss' How the Grinch Stole Christmas"—and laughed all the way to the bank, critics be damned.

This distasteful riff on "It's a Wonderful Life" and "A Christmas Carol" isn't quite as depressing, thanks to performances by Nicholas Cage and Tea Leoni that are much better than the material deserves.

But mostly it's a reminder of better movies in this genre, most notably Cage's previous entry in the what-if sweepstakes, Francis Ford Coppola's sweet and funny "Peggy Sue Got Married."

"The Family Man" on the other hand, invites comparisons with more dire yuletide misfires like Bill Murray's "Scrooged" and the still all-time-worst in category, "Mr. Destiny."

Credited to TV writers David Diamond and David Weissman, and directed without a shed of subtlety or wit by Brett Ratner ("Rush Hour"), this is high-concept comedy at its most synthetic—so predictable that you'll figure out the ending long, long before an inexcusable 125 minutes have elapsed.

Nicolas Cage plays Jack, a high-rolling Master of the Universe who's visited by a streetwise angel (Don Cheadle, reduced to stereotype) on Christmas Eve and given a glimpse into what would have happened if he hadn't dumped his sweet fiancee, Kate (Leoni), 13 years earlier.

In his alternative existence, they're living deep in the Jersey 'burbs with an infant and a 6-year-old named Annie (the charming Mackenzie Vega), who gives the clueless Jack some quickie child-rearing tips. He long ago abandoned Wall Street for a career as a tire salesman, and, worst of all, goes bowling regularly with his best pal (Jeremy Piven).

Beyond the cliched diaper-changing scenes and the oh-so-predictable romantic complications, the film inadvertently insults its presumed target audience by suggesting that the only reason anyone in their right minds would want to live in the 'burbs is for the sake of the children.

Not that its Hollywood hack's nightmare fantasy of suburbia is any more convincing, even on a comic level, than its portrayal of high-level finance, which seems to be derived from a long-ago viewing of "Wall Street."

Here's hoping you find a tape of "Peggy Sue Got Married" in your Christmas stocking.

NEWSDAY, 12/22/00, Part II/p. B9, Jan Stuart

Single-living investment brokers everywhere will snigger at "The Family Man," a Christmas heartwarmer that takes elaborate measures to point up just how barren and empty their fast-track lifestyle is when compared with the average married tire salesman in New Jersey.

This is more or less the lesson gleaned by Nicolas Cage as Jack Campbell, a high-rolling Wall Street power broker who is magically spirited into the cozy domestic nest he might have built had he not drop-kicked his college sweetheart back in 1988. With the unsolicited help of a wise African-American angel who appears out of nowhere (Don Cheadle, doing the Bagger Vance role), Jack suddenly wakes up to find himself flogging Goodyear tires and married 13 years to his former love (Ta Leoni), a low-earning public defense attorney. Together, they share a modest suburban home (that has been interior-decorated within an inch of its Martha Stewart life) and raise two kids—a 4-year-old daughter with bizarre speech patterns and a baby boy who spritzes his wastes like a Yellowstone Park geyser.

Jack stumbles into this world kicking and screaming—you would, too, if your little girl talked like Elmer Fudd—but it is only a matter of time before he will come to appreciate the unalloyed pleasures of mall shopping and kissing your spouse with chocolate cake smeared all over your face.

The few moments that do not seem as factory constructed as the tires in Jack's shop belong mostly to Leoni, all crooked Tom Cruise smiles and milk-fresh warmth. She goes a long way toward camouflaging the utter illogic of her character, whose unresponsiveness to her husband's abrupt and flamboyant disorientation is dumbfounding to behold. Cage is as sincere and unself-conscious as an actor can be who seems to have a clause in his contract requiring him to appear only in his underpants at least three times before the closing credits.

NEWSWEEK, 12/25/00-1/1/01, p. 76, David Ansen

While you're watching this fable about a rich, single, hedonistic Wall Street "master of the universe" who wakes up one morning to find himself living the life of a suburban dad married to his college sweetheart, countless other movies may come to mind: "It's a Wonderful Life" "Big" "Regarding Henry," "Sliding Doors." "The Family Man" borrows bits and pieces from the large library of Hollywood fantasies about alternative lives and magical transformations. Originality is not exactly its strongest suit.

What gives Brett Ratner's sentimental comedy its own distinctive flavor is the casting: Nicolas Cage plays the Ferrari-driving stock trader transformed into a tire salesman, and Téa Leoni plays his beguiling wife, a pro bono lawyer. Cage has never been an actor to take the straight and narrow road to a characterization; he's drolly discombobulated as a father so unprepared for his familial duties that he expects a receipt when he drops his daughter off at day care. Leoni's smart, effervescent sexiness makes it easy to understand why Cage might stick around to change diapers.

As the supernatural, agent of our hero's journey, Don Cheadle is wasted in a poorly conceived role that manages to combine two offensive stereotypes for the price of one: the mystical black man as the white man's savior and the black man as urban thug. The movie's predictable pro-family, anti-corporate-greed philosophy is the usual Hollywood knee-jerk bow to middle-class values it likes to pretend to believe in. Still, one doesn't have to take "The Family Man's" messages too seriously to enjoy the elegance of Dante Spinotti's camerawork, or the palpable chemistry between its stars. What charm, quirkiness and warmth the movie possesses is due largely to them.

SIGHT AND SOUND, 2/01, p. 41, Geoffrey Macnab

Wall Street, Christmas Eve. Banker Jack Campbell is working late on a big deal. On his way home, he stumbles on a hold up in a convenience store. A street punk called Cash claims he has a winning lottery ticket, but the store owner doesn't believe him. Jack intervenes; he leaves the store with Cash who then offers him "a glimpse" of another life.

Next morning, Jack wakes up to discover that he is living in New Jersey with his wife Kate, the college sweetheart whom he abandoned 13 years earlier to pursue his career. He has two children and works selling tyres. Back in New York nobody knows him; Cash explains that he has been given the chance to see what his life would have been like had he never left Kate. Jack warms to his new role as a family man. He thinks about getting a job on Wall Street, but decides against it. Cash appears and returns an unwilling Jack to his former life.

Waking up on Christmas Day in his Manhattan apartment, he vows to change his life and goes to find Kate. A successful businesswoman, she's about to fly to Paris to start a new job. They go for coffee and Jack describes the family life they still could have together.

A shamelessly derivative Christmas movie, *The Family Man* is a deft blend of Charles Dickens and Frank Capra—with a pinch of *National Lampoon*-style humour thrown into the mix. Instead of Scrooge, we're offered Wall Street banker Jack, the kind of driven yuppie ("a credit to capitalism") who might have been held up as a role model in the 80s, but is now frowned upon by Hollywood; and instead of Clarence, the unlikely angel from *It's a Wonderful Life*, Capra's 1947 loose reworking of *A Christmas Carol*, a street punk called Cash gives Jack an opportunity to experience the family life—in suburban New Jersey—which he turned down as a young man. Thankfully, director Brett Ratner has a knack for making even the most hackneyed storylines seem fresh, as he showed with the Jackie Chan/Chris Tucker buddy movie *Rush Hour*.

The premise is also similar to that of the recent Australian comedy *Me Myself I*, in which a single journalist was given a chance to live out the life of a suburban housewife. There are even many of the same jokes: Jack has to get used to his wife, Kate, to whom he has supposedly been married for 13 years, as well as his newly acquired friends and children. The best gags hinge on his initial disgust at the family man he is turning into: used to wearing sleek designer suits, for instance, he's appalled by his drab line in clothes. Instead of playing things for easy laughs, Nicolas Cage brings a sense of gravitas and moose-like melancholy to the role; like an amnesiac in some modernist novel, he's forced to piece his own identity together by observing what is going on around him.

Just as James Stewart's suffering George Bailey learned that "No man is a failure who has friends" in *It's a Wonderful Life*, here Jack comes to realise that no man is a failure who has family. And yet there's something perverse about the way the film celebrates family values: in his New Jersey incarnation, Cage drinks too much, is strapped for cash and has a dead-end job selling auto supplies—but this is presented as infinitely preferable to life as a successful Wall Street executive.

Other elements in the screenplay don't add up: we know that Jack is college-educated and that he was already a banker when he left Kate, but once he's whisked off to the suburbs, he stumbles several rungs down the social ladder, and it's never explained why he can't do better than selling car tyres for a living. The opposition between New Jersey and New York seems overly simplistic, too: at the outset, his life in Manhattan is glamorous and cosmopolitan, but after the clutter of his suburban home, it comes to look oppressively empty. In case we've missed the point, Ratner throws in some harsh lighting and looming camera angles.

Thankfully, there's enough irony in David Diamond and David Weissman's screenplay to undercut the mawkishness. The well-observed comic turns from Saul Rubinek as one of Jack's Wall Street colleagues and Jeremy Piven, who plays his best friend in New Jersey, also help. Handsomely shot by Dante Spinotti, *The Family Man* manages to transcend its own inconsistencies. Despite—or perhaps because of—its sanctimony and sentimentality, it's the kind of movie you can imagine being revived every Christmas for years to come.

TIME, 12/25/00-1/1/01, p. 47, Richard Corliss

Scrooge never dressed so smartly. Wall Street wolf Jack Campbell (Cage) looks cool and talks cruel: there's a big merger brewing, so everyone in his mergers and acquisitions firm *will* work on Christmas Day. But Scrooges have to sleep on Christmas Eve; that's when revelations and atonement come. Jack nods off on satin sheets and wakes in another bed—his own, in a parallel universe, where for years he's been married to Kate (Leoni), the sweetheart he left behind to be a zillionaire. In this nightmare world he has two squalling kids, a cruddy job selling tires in his father-in-law's store, a bunch of bowling buddies, an old van and—can it get worse for this chic Manhattanite?—he lives in New Jersey.

These days the only way Hollywood can tell a story of ordinary people struggling with the awesome challenges and compromises of family life is to reduce them to sugarific fantasy. And further, to view life's choices as Manichean, Jack is either a rich creep or a humanized husband and father. Kate sees it that way: when Jack talks his way into a job with the firm he used to run, she all but refuses the move to Manhattan. Who'd want to leave misery in the 'burbs?

Family Man is a film that's fun to argue with. But at the end you may surrender to its *Wonderful Life* portrait of middle-class coping, and to Cage's poignant anguish. His features crumble, his shoulders sink under the burden of a strong man's perplexity.

VILLAGE VOICE, 12/26/00, p. 154, Michael Atkinson

Another midlife-crisis seizure courtesy of the spawning tribe of teary-eyed, silk-suited daddies who occupy the hills of Santa Monica, Brett Ratner's *The Family Man* plays like fallout from the stock market downturn—once the portfolios begin correcting, you'd better have a house full of kids to sulk back to. The rigged debate between single, affluent workaholism and breeder-burb orthodoxy centers on smug Manhattan megabroker Jack Campbell (Nicolas Cage), who, once he's beset by Don Cheadle's vaguely defined, Capraesque Ghost of Christmas Other, wakes up in Jersey married to a woman (Téa Leoni) he left 13 years earlier, plus two kids, a dog, and a lousy job selling tires. Ripped off wholesale from this year's Rachel Griffiths import *Me Myself I*, Ratner's movie inexorably bulldozes toward the moment when Jack, after the requisite struggle with diapers, dog walking, middle-class income, and toddler communication, realizes rapture as the titular mensch.

Trolling singles should therefore beware, however useful the movie might be as a Bromo-Seltzer in answer to *American Beauty*'s still beloved antisuburban bean gas. The screenplay helplessly writes itself into a corner, but there are a surprising number of mitigating tonic-shots amid the treacle: The Wall Street-bazooka lifestyle is derided largely for its glib materialism, not its unreproductive freedoms; the filmmakers know a potent parental jolt (stroking a sleeping child's hair, etc.) when they see one. Cage returns halfheartedly to form: Jack's transition to Mr. Minivan has its raving *Vampire's Kiss*-ish moments. A single shot of Cage, sitting in the dark fending off sleep because he knows he'll wake up in that barren apartment alone, is haunting enough to make the whole movie feel chilling when it means to be warm. It's an easier movie to tolerate than it should be if, like me, you're in love with Téa Leoni, who, as a lithe, lusty, strangely patient firecracker Superwife in a shag, rescues the movie from the tar pit of irrelevance. With some decent lines, she could be the new Myrna Loy.

Also reviewed in:
NEW YORK TIMES, 12/22/00, p. E17, Elvis Mitchell
VARIETY, 12/11-17/00, p. 24, Joe Leydon
WASHINGTON POST, 12/22/00, p. C1, Stephen Hunter
WASHINGTON POST, 12/22/00, Weekend/p. 42, Desson Howe

FAMILY TREE

A WarnerVision Films release in association with Curb Entertainment of a Curb Entertainmant production. *Executive Producer:* Quinn Coleman and Clifford Werber. *Producer:* Mike Curb and Carole Curb Nemoy. *Director:* Duane Clark. *Screenplay:* Paul Canterna. *Director of Photography:* John Peters. *Editor:* Matthew Booth. *Music:* Mike Curb, Randy Miller, and Joey Lawrence. *Sound:* Jeff Vaughn. *Production Designer:* Katherine G. Vallin. *Art Director:* Gay Perello. *Costumes:* Dorothy Amos. *Make-up:* Heidi Grotsky. *Running time:* 90 minutes. *MPAA Rating:* G.

CAST: Naomi Judd (Sarah Musser); Andrew Lawrence (Mitch Musser); Robert Forster (Henry Musser); Matthew Lawrence (Mark Musser); Cliff Robertson (Larry); Tyler Hoechlin (Jeff Jo); Jeffrey Pace (Shawn); Corbin Bleu (Ricky); Quinn Beswick (Duffy); George Murdock (Big Wig); Susan Gayle Watts (Mayor Margaret Jones); Gregg Binkley (Bill Belko); D. Elliot Woods (Councilman Jordan); Eddie Ebell (Luigi); Faith McDevitt (Mrs. Ferguson); Jack Donner (Joseph); Hamilton Camp (Bob); Ken Johnson (Store Owner); Leonard Termo (Vince); David Carpenter (Dirt Jo); Steve Wilde and John Mastando (Surveyors); Kate Forster (Ms. Krynock); Genevieve Butler (Diane); Alan David Gelman (Ed); Beecey Carlson (Connie); Ken Duncan (George); William Dennis Hurley (Mayor's Aide); Brendan Dawson (Truck Driver); Austin Stout (Allen); Krystal Benn (Jessica); Tony Tarantino (Dr. Stevens).

LOS ANGELES TIMES, 4/21/00, Calendar/p. 8, Kevin Thomas

"Family Tree" is decent but tedious family fare awash with fine sentiments but marred by repetitiveness. There are some solid performances under Duane Clark's workmanlike direction, but they're not enough to make the difference. This Curb Entertainment production is for those who insist in wholesomeness above all else.

"Anything worth having is worth fighting for," says erstwhile small-town developer Henry Musser (Robert Forster), encouraging his older son Mark (Matthew Lawrence) in his efforts to succeed as a high school football player. But the words are not lost on his younger son Mitch (Andrew Lawrence), who's going through that awkward stage and who finds solace in talking to an old oak near the edge of an open field.

As it happens the community's last factory closed two years earlier, leaving widespread unemployment. Henry, out of a job himself, has succeeded in convincing a plastics company to locate in the town, constructing a plant on that open field. You got it: The old oak has got to go, but 9-year-old Mitch is prepared to dig in his heels to save his beloved tree, with his neighbors gradually throwing support behind him. He gets unexpected support from a man (Cliff Robertson) who is a stranger to him, a man who has returned to his hometown after a long absence but who will have crucial impact in resolving the impasse.

From the outset it's clear that this is a send-'em-home-happy movie, which is all the more reason for writer Paul Cantera to provide more complexity. Why can't the new plant incorporate the tree into its design? Why can't the community at least explore what's involved in moving the tree, if possible? What about recycling the old factory that's now closed? These possibilities are given very short shrift indeed, as father and son keep repeating their clashing stances over and over again.

In any event Forster is quietly staunch as Henry, a community leader who has good reason to sacrifice the oak only to be confronted by a small son in whom he has instilled the virtue of standing up for what you believe. Young Andrew and Matthew Lawrence do well as Henry's sons, and country singing legend Naomi Judd makes a gracious acting debut as the boys' loving mother, the one person who is sympathetic to her son's views.

NEWSDAY, 4/21/00, Part II/p. B7, Gene Seymour

Mitch Musser (Andy Lawrence) is a 10-year-old who's such a social outcast that his nickname's "Mess." He finds his only solace chronicling his awkward-age mishaps to the noble, accessible tree known throughout the small, economically depressed community he lives in as "Old Oak."

The tree proves more attentive to Mitch's problems than are either his superjock big brother (Andy's real brother Matthew) or his developer dad (Robert Forster), who's preoccupied with convincing a plastics company to build its plant in town and bring a fresh influx of jobs. He succeeds, but there's a catch: Old Oak's in the way of the new factory and may have to be cut down.

Mitch is alarmed but can't argue with anyone, especially his father, on the tree's behalf by himself. He gets help from an unexpected source: an old farmer (Cliff Robertson) who enjoys exalted status for his exploits as a Korean War hero and NFL star. He and Mitch stage their own nonviolent siege against the company's chain saws and bulldozers. To Dad's consternation, the protest begins to draw support even from some who are anxious to get work at the prospective plant.

Directed by Duane Clark (son of Dick), the movie strains to get big ideas across while managing to get a lot of little things right, such as the subtler aspects of sibling rivalry and peer-group dynamics among kids and grown-ups.

But the thick, goopy overlay of sugary pop songs and thinly developed relationships between characters betray both a sloppiness in conception and a refusal to trust the audience, especially the kids, to find their own emotional connection to the story.

Also reviewed in:
NEW YORK TIMES, 4/21/00, p. E16, Lawrence Van Gelder
VARIETY, 4/24-30/00, p. 31, Scott Foundas

FANTASTICKS, THE

A United Artists Films release of a Michael Richie Productions/Radmin Company/Sullivan Street Productions film. *Executive Producer:* Art Schaefer. *Producer:* Michael Ritchie and Linne Radmin. *Director:* Michael Ritchie. *Screenplay (based on their play):* Tom Jones and Harvey Schmidt. *Director of Photography:* Fred Murphy. *Editor:* William Scharf and Francis Ford Coppola. *Music:* Harvey Schmidt and Tom Jones. *Choreographer:* Michael Smith. *Sound:* Kim Harris Ornitz and (music) Tim Boot. *Sound Editor:* Richard E. Yawn and Gordon Ecker. *Casting:* Rick Pagano. *Production Designer:* Douglas W. Schmidt. *Art Director:* Edward L. Rubin. *Set Decorator:* Alan Hicks. *Set Dresser:* Andrea Guy and Richard Hansen. *Special Effects:* Cliff Wenger. *Costumes:* Luke Reichle. *Stunt Coordinator:* Robin Navlyt. *Running time:* 86 minutes. *MPAA Rating:* PG.

CAST: Joel Grey (Bellomy); Barnard Hughes (Henry); Jean Louisa Kelly (Luisa); Joseph McIntyre (Matt); Jonathon Morris (El Gallo); Brad Sullivan (Ben Hucklebee); Arturo Gil (The Bavarian Baby); Tony Cox (His Assistant); Victoria Stevens (Jo Jo, the Chicken Lady); Trayne Thomas (Tattooed); Shaunery Stevens and Dyrk Ashton (Roustabouts); Teller (Mortimer).

LOS ANGELES TIMES, 9/22/00, Calendar/p. 14, Kevin Thomas

"The Fantasticks," the beguiling musical in which reality collides with romance, has become America's longest-running theatrical production, an off-Broadway stalwart for more than four decades. Half a decade ago, director Michael Ritchie completed a film, but it lingered on the shelf until Francis Ford Coppola stepped in to oversee some crucial cutting.

The delay was worth it, because the result is pure enchantment that emerges as an inspired transposition of a musical to the screen—one that manages to honor the theatricality of the source yet becomes a fully cinematic experience.

It's always a tricky business to flesh out that which so successfully has left so much to the imagination. On stage, "The Fantasticks," in which a dreamy young woman falls under the spell of a bandit, is performed with minimal props and settings. However, Ritchie had the splendid notion of setting the story in the U.S. heartland of the 1920s. This choice pays off handsomely in several ways.

It is a time and place in which the innocence of the heroine and her boy-next-door beau are wholly credible.

It also invokes a grand theme of silent movies: the city and its denizens as a dangerous temptation to naively virtuous rurals. Thus, "The Fantasticks" in this aspect recalls F.W. Murnau's "Sunrise" and a slew of D.W. Griffith films and keys the film's visual grandeur, made possible by those endless stretches of wheat fields.

Indeed, it is in the midst of a seeming nowhere that a colorful traveling carnival pitches its tent in the film's opening scene. It's a striking image, at once preserving the play's intense theatricality as it unfolds against shifting, sweeping panoramas possible only on a big screen—and shot in rich Panavision to boot. In one stroke, the camera's capacity for creating an aura of realism and the human capacity for conjuring up delirious romantic fantasy, provoked by the carnival performer's practiced artifices, are boldly contrasted.

Luisa (Jean Louisa Kelly) is a lovely young woman living in a neat-as-a-pin farmhouse with her devoted widower father, Bellomy (Joel Grey), separated by a fence from their next-door neighbors, Hucklebee (Brad Sullivan), who lives in a ramshackle farmhouse with his son Matt (Joe McIntyre). The fathers, it turns out, have conspired to stage a mock feud between them, thus guaranteeing that in defiance, the young people will swiftly bond.

As the carnival sets up for business, Luisa is drawn to the dashing El Gallo (Jonathon Morris), portrayed here as a traveling magician, who casts a spell of grand romance upon the couple. When humdrum everyday existence returns, Luisa and Matt experience such a letdown that she all but throws herself at El Gallo.

As mesmerizing as all this is for us—a pleasure that embraces a clutch of evocative and unforgettable Tom Jones-Harvey Schmidt songs, including such standards as "Try to Remember" and "Soon It's Gonna Rain"—"The Fantasticks," for all its seductive strategies, takes some getting used to. That's simply because we've grown so unused to the unique suspension of disbelief required of classic musicals—i.e., the phenomenon of someone breaking into song and dance with the seeming spontaneity of merely walking and talking. In a few minutes, however, we begin to feel the joy of the stylish and venturesome Arthur Freed-produced musicals from the MGM of an earlier era.

Indeed, Kelly and McIntyre remind you of the effortless charm and skill of Jane Powell and Howard Keel. Veterans Grey and Sullivan draw upon those finely polished musical comedy skills—the perfect comic timing, the flawlessly executed moves, the easy shifts from the comic to the serious—that have all but vanished from the screen. Morris is as devilishly handsome as Errol Flynn, but El Gallo's mission is ultimately not to seduce but to enlighten Luisa, and there's further robust comic support from Barnard Hughes as the carnival's brave but forgetful old Shakespearean ham and his mute sidekick, appropriately played by Teller, of Penn and Teller.

"The Fantasticks" is a film in which settings and costumes play a major part in creating a unique world. Production designer Douglas W. Schmidt and his crew and costume designer Luke Reichle give us a rural 1920s as yet untouched by flapper clothes and Art Deco design, and a carnival that preserves its florid 19th century P.T. Barnum colors and baroque styling. They succeed flawlessly, with Fred Murphy's gloriously rich and fluid camera work capturing it all and expressing Ritchie's perceptive vision of what "The Fantasticks" could be on the screen.

Starting with "Downhill Racer" and "The Candidate" and on through the seriously underappreciated "Smile" and continuing on through "The Positively True Adventures of the Alleged Texas Cheerleader-Murdering Mom," Ritchie continues in "The Fantasticks" to discover—sometimes satirizing, other times celebrating—the uniquely American experience.

"The Fantasticks" is a gem, but so virtually extinct is the screen musical that the looming question remains as to whether people will care. It's one thing to pack Manhattan's small Sullivan Street Playhouse with "The Fantasticks" decade after decade, and quite another to pull crowds with gossamer, lyrical make-believe to the country's multiplexes.

NEW YORK POST, 9/22/00, p. 51, Lou Lumenick

It's not hard to see why this film version of the long-running (40 years and counting) off-Broadway classic has been gathering dust on MGM's shelf for nearly five years.

"The Fantasticks," which is finally getting a token theatrical release to fulfill contractual obligations prior to its Jan. 1 release on video, is a brave but ultimately futile attempt at adapting a piece that is so quintessentially theatrical that it defies translation to another medium.

At least it's better than the horrific 1964 TV version that starred Ricardo Montalban.

Besides a timeless score, a lot of the appeal of "The Fantasticks" is in its simplicity—it takes place in no specific time or place and it's traditionally staged on Spartan sets.

In adapting their work for the screen, Tom Jones and Harvey Schmidt (who also wrote the songs) have pinned the action down to the American Midwest of the mid-1920s—and director Michael Ritchie, in what was obviously a labor of love, shot the film on location.

The specificity and the admittedly handsome wide-screen lensing (at times somewhat reminiscent of Fred Zinnemann's film version of "Oklahoma," a musical with which "The Fantasticks" couldn't have less in common) all but overwhelm the very slight story about two widowers (Joel Grey and Brad Sullivan) who stage a mock feud to bring together their respective teenage children (Jean Louisa Kelly and Joseph McIntyre).

As part of their plot, they hire El Gallo (Jonathon Morris in the part originated by Jerry Orbach on stage, way back in 1960) to stage a mock abduction. But the girl becomes infatuated with El Gallo along the way to a happy ending.

What seems charming on stage comes off as cloying or precious on a big screen, which usually requires scenes either be strictly realistic or utterly fantastic; too many here fall into the fey in-between category.

While it's good to see Grey in his first musical since "Cabaret"—and he's the only cast member whose dancing isn't painful to watch—his and Sullivan's relentless mugging (too often captured in closeup) tend to grate on the nerves.

Morris makes a singularly narcissistic El Gallo, though his rendition of "Try to Remember"—strangely moved to the end of the film—is pretty good.

Unlike most stage productions, which feature actors in their 20s, "The Fantasticks" has actual teenagers (at least they were in 1995) playing teenagers, with dubious results.

Though a decent singer, McIntrye, an erstwhile member of New Kids on the Block, never comes close to suggesting a 1920s youth. The more classically trained Kelly is more convincing and does better with the challenging songs, but she isn't much of an actress.

Though well-meant, "The Fantasticks" ends up as another nail in the coffin of the Hollywood musical.

NEWSDAY, 9/22/00, Part II/p. B6, Gene Seymour

For a while, it seemed as if the movie version of "The Fantasticks" would end up as one of those film follies mired forever in pre-release hell. Then director Michael Ritchie showed his 1995 print of "The Fantasticks" to Francis Ford Coppola, who suggested shaving off set pieces and songs from the full text of the Off-Broadway perennial—which is still running like a Timex watch after 40 years.

And so, United Artists is letting loose this version, boiled, peeled and whipped up for audience consumption. We may never know how leaden and ponderous the original version was. But this stripped-down "Fantasticks" suffers from the opposite effect. It seems so slight that it leaves one emotionally detached from the story of young lovers Matt (ex-New Kid on the Block Joe McIntyre) and Luisa (Jean Louisa Kelly) and their manipulation by both their allegedly feuding dads (Joel Grey, Brad Sullivan) and the dashing magician El Gallo (Jonathon Morris).

Ritchie's idea to fix the play's timeless setting somewhere in the American plains, circa 1920s, wasn't a bad one. The vistas are wide, the colors are striking and the corn is as high as... sorry, wrong musical.

But while this production knows where and how to place its actors within its broad frames, it doesn't move them around very well. The dances are abysmally shot. But then, filming musical set pieces seems in general to be a lost art beyond the retrieval of even talented directors such as Woody Allen. In the end, this is an elusive dream that fades under harsh light much as Matt and Luisa's initial hopes for perfect love. It may be, at best, serviceable to those who have seen the stage production so often they sing "Soon It's Gonna Rain" or "Try to Remember" even under anesthesia.

Also reviewed in:
NEW YORK TIMES, 9/2/00, p. E14, A. O. Scott
VARIETY, 9/18-24/00, p. 30, Scott Foundas

FASTPITCH

An Artistic License Films release of a Shortstop Films production. *Executive Producer:* Catherine Stickney Steck.   *Producer:* Jeremy Spear.   *Director:* Jeremy Spear and Juliet Weber. *Screenplay:* Jeremy Spear, Juliet Weber, and Fred Kaufman. *Director of Photography:* Elia Lyssy.   *Editor:* Juliet Weber. *Music:* William "Spaceman" Patterson. *Sound:* Mike Harlow, Mariusz Glabinskkky, and Ira Spiegel. *Running time:* 90 minutes. *MPAA Rating:* Not Rated.

WITH: Jeremy Spear; Shane Hunuhunu; Nick McCurry; Peter J. Porcelli, Jr.; Darren Zack; Ken Billingley; Tony Hunhoff; Lila Leiter.

NEW YORK POST, 8/25/00, p. 50, Hannah Brown

The documentary "Fastpitch" has the charm of a well-played baseball game on a lazy Sunday afternoon, without any of the forced sentimentality that has marred so many recent sports movies (think "For Love of the Game").

It presents an affectionate portrait of the fast-fading world of professional fast-pitch softball, a game that lasts only seven innings and is played on smaller diamonds than hardball.

But what sets "Fastpitch" apart from nearly every other sports film ever made is that its director, Jeremy Spear, is also a fast-pitch player himself.

Spear, a New York City-based artist, decided in his mid-30s to give professional sports one last shot and spent a season bouncing from team to team in the fast-pitch world.

Perhaps because Spear has been a participant in and not only a fan of the sport, "Fastpitch" has an unusual intimacy and lack of condescension.

Fast-pitch is truly a fascinating world, and the film is filled with comedy and drama. The sport is very popular in New Zealand, and many of those who play it here are Maori tribesmen from that country.

They're certainly a party-hearty group, as they crush full beer cans on camera and drink out of them sideways. The biggest star in the league is Shane Hunuhunu, who can barely keep his hands off his American girlfriend and has to contend witt groupies.

Another ethnic group involved in the sport are Native Americans, who field a team called the North Americans made up entirely of recovering alcoholics and junkies.

While most teams in the tiny towns where the sport is played can barely afford to pay their players much more than enough to cover room and board, the Tampa Bay Smokers, backed by manic businessman Peter Porcelli, lure players from all over the country with lucrative contracts.

Porcelli tries to dazzle the competition by dressing his players in different color uniforms every day of the playoffs. "I have more talent than a human being really deserves," he says.

The last third of the film focuses on whether Porcelli's players will beat a more modestly paid team, in a cheerful microcosm of the kind of battle that is taking place everywhere in the sports world.

Perhaps the best compliment that anyone can pay to Spear and his movie is that he makes you want to run out and catch a fast-pitch game in person before it's too late.

NEWSDAY, 8/25/00, Part II/p. B6, John Anderson

Director Jeremy Spear's arsenal consists of more floating lobs than blistering fastballs, but he manages to get it across the plate in "Fastpitch," his documentary about the reputedly vanishing world of men's semipro softball.

Spear's debut movie may be to the summer blockbuster what the New Jersey Gators are to the New York Yankees, but because both he and Hollywood rely on the same three things—memorable characters, a solid story line and a determined point of view—he outplays the budgetary big boys at almost every turn. A New York-based artist and onetime varsity shortstop for Yale, Spear has a gift for being charmingly obtuse—in setting things up, he tells us that his years on the Manhattan art scene left him craving "the thrill of competition." Huh? Still, he knew what he had in the venerable world of men's fastpitch—where the ball travels 90 mph, but the pitcher is 15 feet closer, and the batter's reaction time a tenth of a second shorter than in regulation baseball. Pathos, bathos and the kind of personalities needed for a first-rate movie.

There's Nick McCurry, the wry, slightly crusty money-juggling manager of Spear's team, Ashland Abbott Labs of Ohio. There's Darren Zack, the Ojibway Indian and acknowledged king of the mound, whose career with the Toronto Gators is all about Native Pride. There's Peter Porcelli Jr., sultan of junk mail and owner of the Tampa Bay Smokers (their logo: a Jolly Roger-ish baseball with a cigar in its mouth), who spends half a million dollars in a $30,000-a-year sport. And Shane Hunuhunu, a New Zealand Josh Gibson whose experience in Ashland is a credit to Ohio, but who still has to work in a car wash to keep the wolf away from the door.

And then there are the North Americans, an all-American-Indian team whose anti-drug and alcohol message is as important as their playing and who, with Zack, probably could have made for a separate movie altogether. And probably should have. Rather than weave the Indian aspects smoothly into his Rust-Corn-Bible Belt travelogue, Spear felt compelled to break off in an awkward digression into Zack's family life and the North Americans' school campaign. You can sympathize with Spear's sentiments, but structurally, its a little like moving the dugout to centerfield.

Still, Spear's season-long portrait of the "vanishing" world of fastpitch is a moral fable in which everyone plays his part naturally, particularly Porcelli, an unctuous self-promoter whose high spending scares sponsors away from other teams and is seen as hastening the sport's demise. While the corruption of sport by money is hardly unexplored territory, Spear manages to give it an eloquently simple illustration, in the joylessness that accompanies a Smokers victory and the forced gaiety of Porcelli's hired guns. Even Porcelli seems less than convinced of his own happiness, having sullied what Spear calls "a purity that's hard to find in sports today" and moved men's fastpitch toward a place where survival will rely less on community fervor than on corporate logos, cable rights and $8 hot dogs.

VILLAGE VOICE, 8/29/00, p. 146, Michael Atkinson

From the artless, intriguing gist of Jeremy Spear's doc *Fastpitch,* it seems that at least the fading sandlot sport of fastpitch softball might be worth going all squirrelly about. A neglected subculture that inhabits the vast badlands between American cities, fastpitch is a rough game, with briefer-than-pro-ball pitch visibility for the batter (due to a shorter mound-to-home stretch). An ex-Yale ballplayer and conceptual artist who dropped out of the gallery scene to pursue athletic glory for the last time, Spear encounters all manner of demigods, including the Ojibway pitching megalith Darren Zack and Maori home-run icon Shane Hunuhunu. As it is with so many clear-eyed documentaries of American substrata, Spear's portrait of unpaid, passionate fastpitchers could give filmmakers of all budgets a notion of how real Americans speak. Fastpitch may be a matter of faith by this point, but the believers aren't obsessives—just working stiffs with a vocation.

Also reviewed in:
NEW YORK TIMES, 8/25/00, p. E24, Lawrence Van Gelder

FEAR OF FICTION

A Pioneer Theater presentation. *Producer:* Gerry Kagan and Charlie Ahearn. *Director:* Charlie Ahearn. *Screenplay:* Charlie Ahearn. *Director of Photography:* John Foster. *Editor:* Christina Boden. *Music:* Evan Lurie and Lee Ranaldo. *Sound:* Paul Hsu and Margaret Crimmins. *Casting:* Judy Henderson and Robyn Knoll. *Production Designer:* Debi Zelko. *Running time:* 99 minutes. *MPAA Rating:* Not Rated.

CAST: Melissa Leo (Sigrid Anderssen);   Sam Trammell (Red Hopkins/Tom Hopkins);   Penn Jillette (Albert);   Reno (Master of Ceremonies/Herself); David Wheir (Victor); Clark Johnson (Gary);   Linda Larkin (Liz);   Annie Giobbe (Debbie); Stephen Pearlman (Mr. Basketball Head); Jay Devlin (Ray); Irma St. Paule (Gertrude); Talmadge Lowe (George); Lee Bryant (Mrs. Hopkins); Augusta Dabney (Mrs. Anderssen); Patrick Brinker (Serviceman); Marion Nixon (Housekeeper); Kelly Carangelo (Café Girl).

NEW YORK POST, 7/13/00, p. 53, Hannah Brown

A lot has been written about how twins understand each other better than anyone else can, and "Fear of Fiction" explores the nature of that bond, and of love in general, by focusing on a love affair between a man and a woman, each of whom has a twin brother.

This off-beat, original film, which takes place mainly during a road trip, stars Melissa Leo (of TV's "Homicide") as Sigrid, an aspiring New York novelist in her late 30s, the daughter of a famous writer.

She can't finish the book she is writing (which she plans to call "Fear of Fiction") and decides that going to visit her family's' cabin on a lake in Washington state will help her overcome her writer's block.

Answering an ad, she hooks up with Red (Sam Trammell), a cute, mellow twentysomething guy who is heading cross country, and soon they are traveling together.

After they visit Red's parents in upstate New York, they run into Tom, Red's identical twin brother (also played by Trammell). Unlike the poised, charming Red, Tom gets upset easily and tends to rant and rave.

Tom, offended that Red and Sigrid have not asked him to join the trip, begins hitchhiking after them. And Tom has good reason to feel left out. Soon after they begin their trip, Sigrid and Red's relationship becomes sexual, then romantic.

She tells Red about her own twin brother, who committed suicide, and her angry, judgmental father, who taunted her and belittled her ambitions.

Meanwhile, Tom meets an entertaining bunch of weirdos on the road, most notably a fanatic admirer of garage bands, played by magician Penn Jillette (the one who talks in the Penn & Teller duo). Director Charlie Ahearn, whose previous film credit is the 1982 "Wild Style," an early look at the hip-hop craze, has filled the sound track with songs by Sonic Youth and the Lounge Lizards.

It's obvious from early on that the movie is heading for a showdown among the three main characters at the country house, and when it comes, there are few surprises. The script, by Ahearn, begins to fall back on clichés.

Although he sets up a beautifully original situation, he can't sustain it. To emphasize the fact that Red and Sigrid feel a bond because both are twins, for example, the script has Red say, while they are making love, "They say all twins come from one seed," and impart other genetic information while Sigrid moans in ecstasy.

Although the film isn't long, toward the end, especially, it starts to drag. The talky script is the main culprit. Still, in spite of these flaws, "Fear of Fiction" is an intense film with many touching and funny moments.

VILLAGE VOICE, 7/18/00 p. 130, Nick Rutigliano

A massive plaster gander atop a highway restroom proves the most telling image in writer-director Charlie Ahearn's addled road psychodrama, *Fear of Fiction*. In recounting the tale of two irritating strangers' memory-clotted, trans-Canadian journey, the film ends up resembling nothing so much as a wild-goose chase. Ostensibly concerned with the enigmatic bond between twins and the fluidity of personal identity, *Fear of Fiction* teems with stand-ins and doppelgängers, calculated repetitions and ponderous coincidences. Such heady concerns are glibly skirted, however, and Ahearn's maddening game of connect-the-dots is content to collapse inward with honking, preening abandon.

Knottier than warped plywood, *Fear of Fiction*'s plot recounts the intersection of vampish wannabe-author Sigrid (Melissa Leo, formerly of *Homicide)* and sketchy college kid Red (Sam Trammell) with Red's creepy twin, Tom (Trammell again), Sigrid's dead twin brother, stoned Sisters of Mercy, and Penn Jillette's garage-rock-crazed tweaker, among others. Jillette's tape-shuffling tenuously accounts for the movie's Roman-chorus sound track (tunes courtesy of Lounge Lizard Evan Lurie and Sonic Youth's Lee Ranaldo). It's a cavalier linkage, but such aggressive authorial monkeying is par for *Fear of Fiction*'s course, as low-rent aesthetics do little to streamline metaphysical grandstanding. That it all might be the contents of Sigrid's eponymous novel is the final snotty, scatterbrained wink on Ahearn's part—for Sigrid, after all, is just another grating fiction concocted by the filmmaker himself.

Also reviewed in:
NEW YORK TIMES, 7/13/00, p. E8, Elvis Mitchell

FILTH AND THE FURY, THE

A Fine Line Features release of a FilmFour Ltd. presentation in association with the Sex Pistols/Jersey Shore/Nitrate Film Productions. *Executive Producer:* Eric Gardner and Jonathan Weisgal. *Producer:* Anita Camarata and Amanda Temple. *Director:* Julien Temple. *Editor:* Niven Howie. *Music:* John Lydon. *Sound:* Dave McGrath. *Sound Editor:* Paul Davies. *Running time:* 105 minutes. *MPAA Rating:* R.

WITH: Paul Cook (Himself); Steve Jones (Himself); Glen Matlock (Himself); Johnny "Rotten" Lydon (Himself); Sid Vicious (Himself); Malcolm MacLaren (Band's Manager/Himself); Stewart Copeland (Himself); Billy Idol (Himself); Siouxsie Sioux (Herself); Nany Spungen (Herself); Sting (Himself); Andy Summers (Himself).

FILM QUARTERLY, Spring 2001, p. 57, Bryant Rhodes

You might say that a single image from *The Filth and the Fury* defines the hysteria that engulfed London's punk rock scene in 1977: Sid Vicious, on stage, spraying spit directly into the camera's eye. In the words of one British television news anchorwoman at the time, "Raw, outrageous, and crude!" For those old enough, it's not hard to recall the nightly news flashes that greeted the Sex Pistols when they made their assault on the United States in January of 1978. Since their collapse at San Francisco's Winterland on that tour, a sizable legend has grown up around the band. This delirious documentary, which Julian Temple is credited with directing, purports to tell the "truth" about their story. But the film is less an attempt to give a historical account of the band's rise and fall than it is a claim, by the band's surviving members, for credit for the Sex Pistols' powerful cultural impact. Temple serves as a facilitator for this agenda and the film is always candid about its biases.

Although the Pistols were heavily influenced by their predecessors in the New York underground rock scene—particularly the New York Dolls and Iggy and the Stooges—they, more than any other band, defined the image and attitude of punk. The combustible combination of a highly calculated campaign of provocation by the band and its representatives and a feeding frenzy among the British tabloids propelled this quartet of spiky tops to worldwide infamy. If the Sex Pistols have any legacy at all, they can claim to have changed the course of fashion and attitudes much more than music.

The subtext of *The Filth and the Fury* is the fight over the true authorship of the whole cultural phenomenon surrounding the Sex Pistols. In one corner is Malcolm McLaren, the boutique owner and erstwhile art student who managed the group. In the mid-1970s, McLaren owned a fashionable shop on the King's Road called Sex that was the incubator from which the band emerged. For years McLaren, not entirely unjustifiably, claimed—in innumerable rockumentaries, interviews, and the pages of *The New Yorker*—to be the impresario who had engineered the excitement and enormous volume of publicity that accompanied the Sex Pistols' every move. It was also his girlfriend, British punk fashion designer Vivian Westwood, who had a hand in styling the look of the band. (She shows up, without being named, in a single portrait shot in tile film.)

A few years before the Sex Pistols came together, McLaren had ventured to America and become the manager of the prototypical glam rock band the New York Dolls. During the Dolls' final throes, he used his keen eye for fashion to study the New York scene, and returned to England with some definite ideas for style and image. It was his dream to meld music and politics into situationist pranks. In 1980 he took the opportunity to tell his side of the Sex Pistols' story in *The Great Rock and Roll Swindle*—a film composed of a series of fictionalized sketches, also "directed" by Temple (he actually recycled some of the footage for *The Filth and the Fury*). But in the case of both films, Temple is more like a hired gun than an auteur. As an early follower of the band, he made himself indispensable by filming the group almost from its inception. In McLaren's words, the Pistols were a "cash for chaos" scam he perpetrated on the established record companies and authority figures of bourgeois society. In *The Filth and the Fury*, he claims—in a voiceover recording from an old interview—that "creating something called the Sex Pistols was my painting, my sculpture."

In the other corner is John Lydon, a.k.a. Johnny Rotten, the lead singer and most intelligent and articulate member of the group. He was recruited by McLaren to be the band's charismatic frontman. He auditioned in McLaren's shop, singing over the sound of Alice Cooper's "Eighteen" belting out of the jukebox. At the age of twenty, Johnny Rotten was an alienated and rebellious youth who questioned the relevance of the fashionable peace-and-love hippy philosophy in an age when every young person in England seemed to be on the dole.

Part of what made Johnny Rotten such a commanding stage presence was his refusal to be governed by the norms of popular entertainment. "This band," he asserts in the film, "was not about making people happy. It was about attack! Attack! Attack!" On stage, he appeared crazed and wild-eyed in a ripped-up jacket adorned with crucifixes, buttons, and safety pins. He shouted taunts at the audience. He embodied the complete subversion of prior conventions and expectations in concert performance. After the sudden disintegration of the whole spectacle in January of 1978, Lydon initiated a legal action against McLaren to gain control of the Sex Pistols' commercial interests. Not unsurprisingly, he disputes McLaren's claim to being the creator of the band's look and provocative political stance: "You don't create me," he sneers.

The most remarkable thing about *The Filth and the Fury* is the incredible amount of period file footage and news broadcasts the filmmakers unearthed for the project, much of it taken from Temple's archive of vintage home videotapes. The degraded color images are pitch-perfect for punk. They recapture, with a certain humor, the social pain and misery of a once proud English nation. Temple assembled long-lost Super-8 movies of the streets of London and performance videos of hip popular acts like David Bowie and Roxy Music to illustrate what youth culture was like immediately prior to the Sex Pistols. The almost exclusive use of contemporary footage effectively anchors the film in the past. Added to this are cartoon animated sequences recycled from *Swindle*, a selection of extracts from Lawrence Olivier's histrionic rendition of *Richard III*, and an assortment of clips of British slapstick comedians that lend the film a distinctive national feeling as well as a persistent undercurrent of low comedy.

The "narrative" begins with Lydon pontificating on the sociological origins of the strikes, riots, and pervasive discontent that afflicted the country in 1976. He surveys England's economic conditions and simmering class conflicts, and the failures of the Labour Party, then each of the surviving band members gives an account of his background and childhood experiences. They all came from working-class families, felt unwanted, and failed at school—models of delinquent youth resistant to authority and filled with inchoate rage.

During their early rehearsals and gigs, one can see the band defining itself as a do-it-yourself antidote to the bloated progressive rock supergroups that were dominating the airwaves. Their own music was a brutal blast of noise with a venomous attitude on the vocals—Johnny Rotten's discordant voice shouting angry words of nihilistic protest. Although the Sex Pistols were rank amateurs who could hardly play their instruments, their stripped-down, primitive style resonated with disaffected youth and created a new teenage cult with street stars like Billy Idol and Siouxsie Sioux.

The pivotal moment that catapulted the band to notoriety was their infamous December 1, 1976 appearance on the Thames TV's "Today Show" with Bill Grundy. The host and the lads showed mutual contempt, Grundy ultimately provoking a torrent of profanity from Rotten entirely unsuitable for broadcast television. It made the Sex Pistols front-page news.

From that moment on the band was public enemy number one. They were dropped from record companies anxious to preserve some semblance of respectability. They were banned from performing in numerous towns across the English countryside. The ultimate affront to propriety came on June 7, 1977, when McLaren orchestrated—in honor of the Silver Jubilee celebrating the 25th anniversary of the queen's accession to the throne—the premier performance of the band's outrageous song "God Save the Queen" aboard a boat sailing near the queen's flotilla on the River Thames. This irreverent tweaking of royalty created a national scandal. The next day, "Punk Rock Jubilee Shocker" was emblazoned on the front page of one tabloid. The Sex Pistols' record went straight to number one, but the band's shock tactics so offended public sensibilities that the song was "listed" on the British charts by a black line in the top slot. Record stores refused to sell it; the BBC refused to play it. As Lydon tells it, "We declared war on England without meaning to."

By then, external pressures had fractured the internal dynamics of the group. Rotten instigated the ouster of bassist Glen Matlock. He was replaced with Sid Vicious, an avid follower of the punk movement and an adoring fan of the Pistols. According to guitarist Steve Jones, "He was a face." In an interview that Temple conducted with Sid at the time, he says, "I just cashed in on the fact that I'm good-looking, girls like me, and I have a nice figure." A considerable amount of the lore generated by the Sex Pistols concerns Sid's toxic relationship with Nancy Spungen (Jones comments, "Everyone knows when a bird starts poking her nose into a rock-and-roll band it's fucking suicidal"). This dope-and-circus atmosphere only exacerbated tensions among the members.

Frustrated by the official response to their antics in England, the band embarked on an ill-fated tour of the American South, playing to hostile crowds in out-of-the-way cow palaces with names like Randy's Rodeo and the Longhorn Ballroom. Sid Vicious took the stage shirtless, with the words "Gimme a Fix" carved into his chest. The band was pelted with bottles and flying debris.

So, does *The Filth and the Fury* really set the record straight? As the version of events authorized by the surviving members of the band, one expects the film to take their point of view. But it goes much further than dispelling misconceptions or debunking the notion that the Sex Pistols were merely marionettes manipulated by puppetmaster Malcolm McLaren. In the film's semi-tragic third act, McLaren is squarely blamed for the acrimony and dissention that precipitated the band's sudden breakup, and denied any credit at all for the Pistols' style, image, and cultural impact. One cannot but suspect that the film's secret agenda is to exact revenge and settle old scores, rather than reveal the truth.[2] Yet, in its own playful way, *The Filth and the Fury* does manage to transport the viewer back to 1977. One of the virtues of airing the long-unseen footage is that it recreates the London street subculture for the considerable portion of the film's intended audience who weren't even born then. The film's unconventional use of collage juxtaposes a cacophony of source material into a symphony of vivid remembrances. And it doesn't try to gloss over the irony of how an anti-establishment, anti-commercial band hell-bent on fomenting anarchy was ultimately commodified and absorbed into mainstream culture.

While being candid about the band's failure to make an enduring political or cultural impact, the film fails to disclose its partisan position when it makes assertions about who can rightfully claim credit for the Sex Pistols' astonishing notoriety. The truth of the matter is that it was most likely the combination of McLaren's flair for publicity and Rotten's offensive persona that made them so infamous.

Notes
1. Malcolm McLaren, "Elements of Anti-Style," *The New Yorker*, September 22, 1997, pp. 90-102.
2. This is partly explained by the story of the film's production. See the official film Website: www. filth-and fury.com/htmlnoflash/who_production html.

LOS ANGELES TIMES, 4/14/00, Calendar/p. 12, Kenneth Turan

Though the group lasted only 26 months, produced but a single record album and broke up more than two decades ago, the Sex Pistols continue to fascinate. Maybe they're just a blip on the rock 'n' roll/popular culture landscape, but they are a significant blip, and one that just won't go away.

That's because, like a jar of snake venom, the Sex Pistols represent the concentrated essence of the rebelliousness and rage that have always been one of rock's key components. Outlandish, crude, raw but honest, the Pistols in their late-1970s prime spewed forth almost primal hostility in once-heard never-forgotten songs like "Anarchy in the UK," "Pretty Vacant," "EMI" (a savage attack on the recording giant for dropping them) and the anti-anthem "God Save the Queen."

One of the earliest of the punk bands, the Pistols managed to offend nearly all the people nearly all the time. A London politician, typical of many, called the group "the antithesis of humankind" and hypothesized that "the whole world will be better for their nonexistence."

Given that this was one of the most fed-up bands of all time, that dissolution was predictably not long in coming. Its four members, including vocalist Johnny Rotten, bass player Sid Vicious, guitarist Steve Jones and drummer Paul Cook, didn't much like anyone, least of all one another. The group's demise has the makings of a cautionary tale, but—as detailed in Julien Temple's intriguing new documentary, "The Filth and the Fury," a film as arresting and at times as frustrating as the Pistols themselves—it's hard to say what it's supposed to caution us about.

Temple, a British director with credits including "Absolute Beginners" and "Earth Girls Are Easy," is no newcomer to the Sex Pistols arena. His 1980 documentary, "The Great Rock 'n' Roll Swindle," was an earlier look at the phenomenon, told largely from the point of view of the group's former manager Malcolm McLaren.

Now Temple is back, offering not only the best of some 20 hours of early Pistols footage recently discovered in an English storage facility, but also a more balanced portrait as well, one that takes into account the point of view of the band, especially lead singer Rotten.

"The Filth and the Fury" (the title comes from a Daily Mail headline describing the reaction to one of the group's chaotic early BBC appearances) also takes pains to set the group in the context of Britain in a time of working-class discontent and disconnection, when social upheaval was a frequent answer to the rigid stratification of the British system.

No one was more angry than the Pistols, initially masterminded by hipster McLaren ("he used people like an artist," is one of the milder comments about him) but soon being driven by the anarchic anger of Rotten (real name John Lydon), whose very first lyric line for the band was "I am an anti-Christer."

As brief as the Pistols' career was, words like that and antics to match contributed to the group's frequent change of labels in a still-conservative Britain. The only section of society that secretly loved the band from beginning to end was the media: More newspapers were sold about the Pistols' antics than about the Armistice that had ended World War II.

A group whose members got truly, deeply sick of one another wasn't destined to spend decades together (Rotten and Jones in particular didn't get along). The presence of Sid Vicious, a bass player who couldn't play bass, didn't help. His thralldom to both hard drugs and Nancy Spungen, an American groupie with an unpopular personality, though it briefly united the group in distaste, ultimately hastened their demise.

Temple certainly knows this material well, perhaps too well, and the very U.K. parts of the film, like a montage of unidentified British TV and music hall comics of the Benny Hill variety, will mystify local audiences. Some of his stylistic touches, like intercutting scenes of Laurence Olivier's dazzling "Richard III," are successful, while others, like filming the band members today with their faces totally hidden (apparently so we won't see how they've aged), are continually irritating. We probably shouldn't expect a completely conventional documentary about a group this lawless, but there are moments when you wish we'd gotten one anyway.

NEW YORK POST, 3/29/00, p. 43, Jonathan Foreman

Essential viewing for anyone who loved—or loathed—punk rock. This bizarre, original and brilliantly crafted documentary about the Sex Pistols is funny and at times moving—despite all the ugliness and stupidity it depicts.

The antithesis of the old-fashioned rock-documentary spoofed by "This Is Spinal Tap," "The Filth and the Fury" is a brilliant, exuberant collage that doesn't just tell the funny, sad, bizarre story of the world's most notorious punk-rock band but also takes you back into the era that formed them.

In some sequences, music-video pioneer Julien Temple seems just to be telling a conventional rock 'n' roll story (great band is destroyed by drugs and an evil girlfriend) in a technically extraordinary way: using cartoons, newsreels, commercials, scenes from Shakespeare movies and contemporary film of the surviving band members with faces hidden.

But its soon clear that the Sex Pistols aren't really part of the history of popular music at all, but rather the history of fashion and publicity.

This film is intended as an antidote to Temple's 1980 documentary "The Great Rock 'n' Roll Swindle." That movie told the Pistols' story from the point of view of manager Malcolm McLaren.

And while its still clear that McLaren and his partner, designer Vivienne Westwood, did play an important role in nurturing the Pistols' image, you do get a sense that lead singer Johnny Rotten (aka John Lydon), was the band's true guiding spirit.

According to Rotten, now a talk-show host living in Malibu, Calif, the Pistols and their angry spitting rejection of everything that wasn't ugly expressed something significant about the state of Britain in the late '70s, when the country was paralyzed by strikes and social unrest.

But Rotten also takes pains to plant the roots of the whole Pistols shtick in music hall, traditional English comedy, and, especially in the case of his own stage act, Shakespeare's "Richard III."

When Rotten talks about the supposed oppressiveness of the England of his youth, he can seem pretty silly and self-aggrandizing.

But when he speaks of the heroin addiction and death of bassist Sid Vicious, his anger and sorrow are raw, genuine and affecting.

The alternative conformity of the punk movement, the joy its adherents took in ugliness, are all here.

And even though its pretty clear that there wasn't much more to the whole phenomenon than cheap nihilism and teenage showing off, Temple tells the story with such exuberance that he's able to make punk look like both an appropriate reaction to living in the '70s and a truly funny form of protest.

NEWSDAY, 3/29/00, Part II/p. B9, John Anderson

The Sex Pistols, a band that worked in saliva the way Francis Bacon worked in oil, were about liberation through self-debasement. So it's rather poignant that throughout "The Filth and the Fury," the surviving members appear only in shadow. Given no reason to think time hasn't ravaged them, we imagine it has—and conclude that vanity has at long last conquered the rock-and-roll anarchists who once lobbed sonic bombs at the blow-dried narcissism of '70s pop.

It's sad, but then the Sex Pistols' story was never a happy one—the final, fatal overdose of Sid Vicious (and his suspected murder of ur-goth girlfriend Nancy Spungen) is the most notorious chapter, but the entire history of the band was a desperate, anti-aesthetic reaction to the depressing state of Laborite England. (Just wait, you want to say: "Thatcher's coming!") A band that couldn't play, they were a statement with a shelf life.

"The Filth and the Fury" is director Julien Temple's rebuttal of his own 1980 film "The Great Rock 'n Roll Swindle," in which he allowed the band's onetime manager Malcolm McLaren to take credit for the entire Pistols phenomenon. Given their own voice, the surviving Pistols—singer John Lydon (Johnny Rotten), guitarist Steve Jones, original bassist Glen Matlock and drummer

Paul Cook—excoriate McLaren not just for run-of-the-mill exploitation but for actually enabling Vicious' heroin addiction, which kept him both belligerent and controllable and kept the band in bookings. One of the blackly funny aspects of the Pistols' history is that each time a record company fired them for their antisocial antics, the next record company would sign them for an even larger amount of money.

Temple begins by shaping '70s TV commercials, music and newsreels into a Richard ("Help!") Lester homage and then lets all the gritty Pistols performances, interviews and previously unseen footage (including an appalling interview with Spungen and Vicious) fester into an organic whole. But even though "The Filth and the Fury" arrives with freak-show potential, Temple keeps it—you hate to say it—respectable.

SIGHT AND SOUND, 6/00, p. 43, Mark Sinker

This documentary features interviews old and new, film footage shot between 1975 and 1979 and footage from television at that time to retell the story of the Sex Pistols, the key outfit in the emergence of UK punk. Narrated primarily in voiceover from surviving band members John Lydon/Rotten, Steve Jones, Paul Cook and Glen Matlock, the cultural and political background is sketched. A portrait emerges of the group's formation, public arrival, combined chart success and media outrage, and collapse while touring America.

A hitherto-unseen interview with bass player Sid Vicious (real name John Beverly), who died of a heroin overdose, is framed by interviews with the other band members in the present. They discuss how and why it all happened, and how much responsibility their manager Malcolm McLaren (not interviewed except in archive footage) can be allowed for the triumphs or the catastrophes of the group.

In late 1976, 20 years after Elvis Presley's worldwide arrival, the Clash presented their notorious rejectionist manifesto of punk renewal: "No Elvis, Beatles or Rolling Stones in 1977". Implied here was a self-removing, rarely honoured promise: "No Pistols or Clash in '78". This is just one reason why Julien Temple's return, two decades on, to the subject matter of *The Great Rock 'n' Roll Swindle* (1980), the movie that gave him a career in Hollywood, can only betray the material it noisily claims to be rescuing: the Sex Pistols' brief, calamitous career.

In fact, despite its much touted previously unseen footage and video material, the documentary is little more than a clumsy bid for atonement for Temple's earlier role as Malcolm McLaren's puppet on the set of *Swindle*, directing to the Pistols' manager's brief. Yet by gracelessly demonising McLaren—often by editing in fragments of *Swindle*, itself a prankishly radical essay in self demonisation—*The Filth and the Fury* panders to all the participating survivors as they retrospectively recast their stories. This time round our blithely revisionist director makes sure he's 'in' with the 'lads'.

Insofar as Temple manages a structure at all, the story is framed by two events. The first is the band's debut television appearance, shown in full. Host Bill Grundy patronises, goads and hits on this bevy of nervous kids. With Johnny Rotten cowed by the occasion, Steve Jones seizes the stage, cussing—as requested—in language both archaic and stilted: "What a fucking rotter!" The result was a notorious headline in the *Daily Mirror* (which gives the film its title), yet the most obvious point to make today is how mild this palaver seems. Mid-evening sitcoms now routinely dribble out stronger stuff.

The second event was less Bash-Street-Kids, yet its status as myth remains just as unaddressed. In 1979, in the wake of his girlfriend Nancy's murder in the Chelsea Hotel, chief suspect Sid Vicious overdosed on heroin, and this probable suicide became the instant of the movement's failure on its own terms. Haunted by the sordid debacle of his best friend's public immolation, Rotten is allowed by Temple to vomit forth slanderous contempt towards one-time co-conspirator McLaren, although the 'anti-drugs' line he takes, preeningly moralistic and evasive, simply turns him into Sting saving the Rainforest.

In an age when subconscious folk memories of 1977 are endlessly mobilised within the media industry to invoke uncritical tolerance of every new trend, this documentary needed, at a minimum, to confront its principals with the history of the last 20 years.

Unsurprisingly, gravity and the good life have thickened up even these once-skinny popstar bodies. But Temple interviews them in friendly silhouette, daylight streaming past their now somewhat Grundified outlines, in this context an act of cowardice, especially when long-noted contradictions, historical inaccuracies and rock-chat clichés are all allowed to wobble by unremarked. It's as if the same amber that Temple mummifies poor dead Sid in must necessarily gum up the living.

A director less compromised by his own wannabe-punk influences might have cut through to fresh insight at any number of opportunities during these interviews. For example, at one point we see images from the Pistols' benefit performance at a party for the children of striking firemen, when their position as media demons had them banned from most orthodox venues. The fact that a smiling Rotten handed out cake to tots had to be hidden at the time, for the sake of establishing the intransigent 'rawness' of punk. Besides, the 'humanising' effect of any such counter-demonisation would have been swiftly sentimentalised.

But sentimentalisation comes in many forms. Much of Filth's feebleness stems from its spavined attitude to class. Where the ex-Pistols continue to cast weird, lurid, revelatory light on the English working-class' mutilated sense of itself, Temple does his best to muddy everything they give him, to represent the chafing inflammation within the band of subtly distinct social layers and tensions—the root of its iconoclastic energy—as mere personality clash. Meanwhile, the banishment of McLaren to the role of deluded bourgeois parasite, effectively reduces punk to just a clichéd "kick up the bum for the music business". Actually, only within the dream-field of McLaren's titanically irresponsible improvisation and self-absorbed utopian carelessness could two such inchoately ambitious, clever and dissimilar prole sensibilities as Lydon's and Jones' have combined, let alone fused, mutated and flared.

The blizzard of marketing which followed Sid's death was a disaster rock-careerwise, but only because it flushed out Rotten's fundamental rock 'n' roll decency, at the expense of his flagellant daring as a performer. Unburdened by such pseudo-situationist game-play, the weary Sex Pistols might well have sunk their differences for a time (with each other, and with their record company). By not splitting, they could have become the next Jethro Tull-style dinosaurs, desexed, artistically 'serious'—and pathetically irrelevant.

VILLAGE VOICE, 4/3/00, p. 121, J. Hoberman

Julien Temple's The Filth and the Fury feels familiar and it is—the third feature-length documentary on the rise and fall of the Sex Pistols (in addition to Alex Cox's estimable Sid Vicious biopic Sid and Nancy) and the second by Temple. The filmmaker might be accused of preaching to the choir were the story not so compelling and the performances so strong. Twenty-three years have scarcely dulled the frisson of Johnny Rotten's "Anarchy in the U.K."

Alternating between appreciation and analysis, Temple links the advent of British punk rock to the prole confusion of the mid 70s, using urban riot footage to set the scene: "The Sex Pistols should have happened and did," the voiceover announces. Managed by the self-proclaimed Situationist Malcolm McLaren, the band inspired more public antipathy in less time than any act in pop history. The movie's title is taken from the tabloid headline the morning after their fabulously profane and insulting debut on British TV.

The Filth and the Fury has a proudly cruddy look, and it's filled with what the Situationists called détournement ("the integration of present or past artistic production into a superior construction"). Temple incorporates grainy Super-8 performance footage as well as cartoons from The Great Rock'n'Roll Swindle and American concert material from Lech Kowalski's still scary D.O.A. Repeatedly, he juxtaposes Johnny Rotten with images of Laurence Olivier's over-the-top Richard III. Suddenly, Rotten's hunchback stance and hilarious wide-eyed smirk have a classical pedigree.

Temple also places the Sex Pistols in the context of low comics like Norman Wisdom and Benny Hill. "There's a sense of comedy in the English," the present-day former Rotten muses. True enough, although more might have been made of the singer's Irish background. The gleeful glint of madness in Rotten's taunting performances goes well beyond vulgar pratfall—as does his sometimes sentimental moralizing. Indeed, he all but delivers a punk version of "Danny Boy" when, tearfully recalling the pathetic tale of Sid Vicious, he tells Temple that "only the fakes survive."

Also reviewed in:
CHICAGO TRIBUNE, 4/7/00, Friday/p. K, John Petrakis
NEW YORK TIMES, 3/29/00, p. E1, A. O. Scott
NEW YORKER, 4/3/00, p. 101, Anthony Lane
VARIETY, 2/14-20/00, p. 44, Todd McCarthy
WASHINGTON POST, 4/28/00, Weekend/p. 53, Desson Howe

FINAL DESTINATION

A New Line Cinema release of a Warren Zide/Craig Perry production. *Executive Producer:* Brian Witten and Richard Brener. *Producer:* Glen Morgan, Warren Zide, and Craig Perry. *Director:* James Wong. *Screenplay:* Glen Morgan, James Wong, and Jeffrey Reddick. *Story:* Jeffrey Reddick. *Director of Photography:* Robert McLachlan. *Editor:* James Coblentz. *Music:* Shirley Walker. *Music Editor:* Thomas Milano. *Sound:* Eric J. Batut and (music) Bobby Fernandez. *Sound Editor:* David McMoyler. *Casting:* Jori Woodman. *Production Designer:* John Willet. *Art Director:* William Heslup. *Set Designer:* Anneke Van Oort, Geoff Wallace, and John Alvarez. *Set Decorator:* Mary-Lou Storey. *Set Dresser:* Laurie E. Edmundson, Aoife O'Carroll, Kasia Dzieciolowska, Iain A. Macleod, Rick Patterson, and Doug McCord. *Special Effects:* Terry Sonderhoff. *Visual Effects:* Charlene J. Eberle. *Costumes:* Carolyn Pavelick. *Make-up:* Lisa Love. *Stunt Coordinator:* JJ Makaro. *Running time:* 110 minutes. *MPAA Rating:* R.

CAST: Devon Sawa (Alex Browning); Ali Larter (Clear Rivers); Kerr Smith (Carter Horton); Kristen Cloke (Valerie Lewton); Daniel Roebuck (Agent Weine); Roger Guenveur Smith (Agent Schreck); Chad E. Donella (Tod Waggner); Seann William Scott (Billy Hitchcock); Tony Todd (Bludworth); Amanda Detmer (Terry Chaney); Brenden Fehr (George Waggner); Forbes Angus (Larry Murnau); Lisa Marie Caruk (Christa Marsh); Christine Chatelain (Blake Dreyer); Barbara Tyson (Barbara Browning); Robert Wisden (Ken Browning); P. Lynn Johnson (Mrs. Waggner); Larry Gilman (Mr. Waggner); Guy Fauchon (Hare Krishna); Randy Stone (Flight Attendant); Mark Holden (Co-pilot); Marrett Green (TV News Anchor); Fred Keating (Howard Seigel); John Hainsworth (Minister); Pete Atherton (Student Singer); Nicole Robert (Ticket Clerk); Kristina Matisic (Reporter).

LOS ANGELES TIMES, 3/17/00, Calendar/p. 10, Kevin Thomas

"Final Destination" opens like a segment on the nightly news. Forty high school seniors from an affluent Manhattan suburb, accompanied by four teachers, take off from JFK for a 10-day Paris field trip. Their jetliner barely leaves the ground before it explodes, killing everybody aboard.

The catch in this superior thriller is that the disaster actually hasn't happened—yet. It takes place, with bone-chilling authenticity, as a premonition in the mind of one of the students, Alex (Devon Sawa), an otherwise regular though very bright guy. Never before has Alex experienced a premonition, but it occurs to him with such force and power that he tries to get everyone to leave the plane before it takes off.

In the ensuing turmoil, five others involved wind up ordered off the plane. Only one person, Clear (Ali Larter), a fellow student who has not shared in Alex's hellish vision but has experienced an overwhelming sense that he is right, joins him in disembarking of her own volition. You guessed it: When the plane finally does take off it immediately explodes.

This swift and scary New Line release marks a terrific theatrical feature debut for television veterans Glen Morgan and James Wong, executive producers of TV's "The Others" series, whose work as supervising producers of "The X-Files"—they also wrote and Wong directed one segment—won them a 1996 Golden Globe. Morgan produced "Final Destination," Wong directed it, and they collaborated with Jeffrey Reddick in turning his story into a script. Morgan and

Wong's previous big-screen credit was as co-writing Penelope Spheeris' unsettling 1985 "The Boys Next Door."

Alex's life swiftly turns hellish, even though FBI investigators soon clear him of any involvement in the explosion. Alex's dire premonition so upsets his community that he is widely regarded with fear and loathing. At one point he exclaims that he, after all, did save six other lives.

Or did he? What if the plane disaster simply signified, in mystical terms, that it was in fact everyone aboard's time to die? What if freak accidents were to start eliminating the survivors? And, if so, will they die in some sort of order, according to plan? And how can this "plan" be discerned, and beyond that, altered? Along with the fast pace and hard action genre thrillers are expected to deliver, "Final Destination" unfolds on an unusually intelligent and philosophical plane.

"Final Destination" makes us feel helpless before fate, and as Alex becomes obsessed with cheating death, Clear counters wisely: "The only way to beat death is to make something special of this life." But will they get much of a chance to do so?

When catastrophe strikes in "Final Destination," as you know it will again, these incidents, including the airplane explosion, are terrifyingly real—and therefore, too intense for youngsters. They don't have that credibility-defying exaggeration of those big, razzle-dazzle blockbusters but of the more mundane and therefore scarier combinations of fire, electricity and water; of deadly contacts between elements and items in most every household.

As a director, Wong is as adept at guiding actors as he is in communicating complex ideas and thoughts. "Final Destination," photographed by Robert McLachlan, is an intensely visual experience.

It wittily pays homage to a roster of suspense and horror masters in many of its characters' surnames, including Universal's prolific George Waggner, who directed "The Wolf Man" and many of the studio's Maria Montez Technicolor epics. "Final Destination" is a worthy tribute to them.

NEW YORK POST, 3/17/100, p. 49, Lou Lumenick

Fewer things can be more anxiety-provoking than waiting for your plane to take off—something that's captured with great skill in the opening moments of "Final Destination."

Alex (Devon Sawa), a senior at a Long Island high school who's leaving on a class trip to Paris, has no ordinary case of pre-flight jitters. He has an awesomely depicted premonition of a Flight 800-type disaster, and when he freaks out, he and five pals get thrown off the plane.

Sure enough, the plane explodes—and before long, it's not the only thing going down in flames. An OK premise—can death be cheated?— quickly deteriorates into a silly slasher movie, minus the slasher.

A mysterious force starts killing off the survivors, causing much anxiety for Alex, who quickly figures out who's next based on, duh, the plane's seating chart. But can he prevent their deaths, and with what consequences?

James Wong, responsible for several celebrated episodes of "The X-Files" and making his debut as a feature director, seems much less interested in metaphysical questions than in choreographing mayhem and explosions.

The victims' gory deaths—preceded by much teasing of the audience—involve, among other things, decapitation, high-tension wires and the dangers of dropping vodka into a computer monitor.

Even when Wong gets a good sequence going—one of the teens decides to beat death to the punch by parking his car in the path of an oncoming train—the effect is undercut by the talky and jokey script.

It's the sort of movie where someone impaled on the kitchen floor with a carving knife is seriously instructed, "Don't move!"

It doesn't help that the cast—Ali Larter and Kerr Smith among them—makes the "Scream" crew look like the Royal Shakespeare Company by comparison.

The only actor here who seems to be in on the joke is Tony Todd ("Candyman"), who turns up as an undertaker only long enough to warn that "in death, there are no accidents, no coincidences and no escapes."

"Final Destination" offers plenty of all three for those who are in the mood.

NEWSDAY, 3/17/00, Part II/p. B7, John Anderson

Conceding that the teen horror movie can seldom be genuinely scary but usually can be genuinely tedious, "Final Destination" starts with an aircraft explosion and goes downhill from there. Taking the Wes Craven "Scream" conceits to their goofiest conclusion, director James Wong makes fun of genre conventions, imbues the most innocent household item with dread (even water) and—cruel as it may be—employs the late John Denver as a harbinger of evil ("I've seen it rainin' fire in the sky ...")

But as hilarious as all of this probably sounds, Wong does it without Craven's cleverness, or much narrative originality either. Which is not to say the movie doesn't have its moments. "They died. We lived. Get over it," snaps one character, who is immediately turned into ketchup by a speeding city bus. Justice this swift is always entertaining.

In any event, "they" are the 40 or so high school students who are on JFK Flight 180 to Paris when it blows up over Long Island (sound familiar?). "We" are the handful of people who get off the plane after the otherwise normal Alex Browning (Devon Sawa) has a nerve-racking premonition that turns the preflight safety instructions into an experiment in hysteria. Having foreseen the tragedy and saved himself, Alex immediately comes under suspicion by the FBI as well as his classmates and teachers, although his girlfriend-to-be, Clear (Ali Larter), whom we first see strolling through the airport reading Henry Miller, stands by her clairvoyant man. After his best friend Tod (Chad E. Donella) manages to hang himself at home on a shower clothesline (an item we've only seen in hotels, but who knows?), Alex concludes that because they all cheated death when their time was up, their time is still up and Death wants his due. This makes him even more popular.

Whether the next to die will be Carter (Kerr Smith), Billy (Seann William Scott) or their teacher, Miss Lewton (Kristen Cloke), is something only Alex knows—although he never seems to know in time to save anyone's life.

Between the movie's faux-grandiose discussions of death, fate and the characters' wheel of misfortune, director Wong spends a lot of time demonizing people and things through lighting, music and jagged angles. But it's like putting icing on a saltine; you can't accessorize the totally insubstantial.

Cheap claps of thunder, lightning and all the Rube Goldberg-inspired domestic accidents may have teenagers in the audience clinching, but "Final Destination" doesn't give you that much reason to break a sweat—although if you're taking a flight to France, it might make you queasy about teenagers boarding your plane.

SIGHT AND SOUND, 7/00, p. 43, Kim Newman

New York, the present. Just after boarding an aeroplane for a school trip to France, teenager Alex Browning has a vision of a mid-air explosion. In a panic, he tries to warn his friends but gets into a scuffle with Carter Horton; they along with four other students (Tod, Billy, Carter's girlfriend Terry and quiet girl Clear) and teacher Valerie Lewton are ejected from the plane, which explodes after take off.

FBI agents Weine and Schreck suspect Alex of involvement but can't prove this. With the exception of Clear, Alex's fellow-survivors stay away from him, scared of his foresight. When Tod, Terry and Miss Lewton die in freak accidents, Alex figures out that by saving seven lives he has cheated death and that a malign force is out to restore its plan by killing off the survivors in the order they would have died on the plane. Alex gets together with Billy, Carter and Clear and explains his theory. Carter, next in line, drives on to a railroad track but Alex, after another premonition, is able to save him, whereupon Billy is killed. Alex holes up in the woods to protect himself, only to realise that Clear is the next target; he rescues her from a fire. Months later, the three survivors make it to Paris.

The opening sequence of *Final Destination* may not have the elaborate effects of the plane crashes that start *Alive* or *Fearless*, but it does manage to convey every white-knuckle flyer's vision of the worst aspects of air travel. Grimly silent as his friends argue among themselves, Alex observes a succession of details that convince him the flight is a death trap: the gap between boarding tunnel and plane door, miserable weather outside, patches of rust on the fuselage, alarmingly casual staff and piped John Denver music ('Didn't he die in a plane crash?"). There's a real feeling to the chaos that ensues after Alex's freak-out, and when the actual explosion finally comes, it's shatteringly done—a puff of flame appears in the distance before the blast shatters the terminal windows.

Unfortunately *Final Destination* has after its impressive set-up literally nowhere to go. It may be that debut feature director James Wong and his writing partner Glen Morgan have not been able to let go of the habits acquired in scripting many episodes of *The X Files* and *Millennium*, whose series format—where mysteries are spun out over successive shows—lessens the need for narrative closure. It doesn't help that Jeffrey Reddick's script—with its incoherent vision of life and death—falls down under close examination. Story problems really set in when its psychic protagonist begins laboriously to work out who is next in line for an *Omen*-style accident by overlaying the path of the explosion over the doomed flight's seating plan, only to realise that death is working down a differently ordered list.

As an entry in the current cycle of teenage horror films, *Final Destination* has chosen to tackle its one allotted weighty subject—dying young—with all due reverence: for a change, we see that the sudden deaths of kids affect an entire community. But in doing so, there isn't time to grapple with thornier issues such as free will and predestination. In his ominous one-scene cameo, Tony Todd (of the *Candyman* films) spiels about death's design; but he's more concerned with providing gruesome laughs by spouting his lines while calmly embalming the dead Tod, taking the film well beyond the realism it has hitherto espoused.

The film's show-stopping sequences are the accidents that kill off Alex's friends, accompanied by such supernatural effects as passing shadows and mysteriously seeping water. Director Wong stuffs rooms full of seemingly ordinary objects (a leaky toilet, a cracked vodka mug) which conspire against the unwary, and sets up the neat joke of Alex alone in a cabin putting corks over every protruding nail and taping down anything that might be a threat. However, the biggest scare in the movie is the one death that comes out of nowhere in the middle of a dialogue sequence, delivering a shock much greater than that of the foreshadowed set-pieces.

Though it falls to bits by the end, the film has quite a lot going for it: the young cast may have the usual teen-model looks but play well together, and Devon Sawa makes an acceptable everyman protagonist. Given a story that makes sense, Wong has the potential to be a major director: as in his *X Files* episodes, he works wonders with unsettlingly inappropriate music (the John Denver theme runs throughout), stray bits of decor that become ominous and deftly sketched background characters. It may well be time, however, to retire the habit of naming characters after important figures in the history of the horror film—Weine, Shreck, Murnau, George Waggner, Browning, Val Lewton, Hitchcock, Chaney—unless there's some real thematic reason for it.

VILLAGE VOICE, 3/28/00, p. 126, Justine Elias

As a group of high school students boards a transatlantic flight, one nervous boy surveys his fellow passengers (bright-eyed schoolmates, a wailing newborn, a brain-damaged man trailing an oxygen canister) and observes that only "a really fucked-up God" would let this particular flight of innocents crash. Just after takeoff, he finds out how twisted God and fate and first-time screenwriters can be: The plane explodes, and everybody on board dies. Saved from the crash, but not from the horror that follows, are one teacher (Kristen Cloke) and six students, including Alex (Devon Sawa), whose preflight freakout got the group ejected from the doomed plane.

Alex, who has the sweaty, haunted look of the undermedicated, suffered a gruesome premonition of the tragedy, and in the movie's skillfully staged, sick-funny opening scenes, it's not clear whether he's the subconscious author of his destiny or its helpless victim. But like *I Know What You Did Last Summer*, whose opening act was a delicious indulgence in adolescent fantasies of self-blame and punishment, *Final Destination* quickly descends into mahem. Death can't be cheated; like the film's intended audience, it demands a blood offering. Conveniently, Alex and his friends all live in badly wired houses filled with deadly appliances, power tools, and exposed nails. *Final Destination* is one creepy idea played out with numbing literal-mindedness. Scenes seem to have been deleted haphazardly, and the indicatively named characters (Tod, Shreck, Val Lewton—consult your German/English dictionary or your local video store) barely register. Even a lively appearance by Tony "Candyman" Todd as the town mortician feels completely random: Fate, like this movie, has a savage but brilliant casting director.

Also reviewed in:
CHICAGO TRIBUNE, 3/27/00, Friday/p. H, Barbara Shulgasser
NEW YORK TIMES, 3/17/00, p. E14, Stephen Holden
VARIETY, 3/20-26/00, p. 25, Joe Leydon

FINDING FORRESTER

A Columbia Pictures release of a Laurence Mark production in association with Fountainbridge Films. *Executive Producer:* Dany Wolf and Jonathan King. *Producer:* Laurence Mark, Sean Connery, and Rhonda Tollefson. *Director:* Gus Van Sant. *Screenplay:* Mike Rich. *Director of Photography:* Harris Savides. *Editor:* Valdis Oskarsdottir. *Music:* Hal Wilner. *Music Editor:* Ken Karman. *Sound:* Brian Miksis and (music) Dennis Sands. *Sound Editor:* Kelley Baker. *Casting:* Francine Maisler, Bernard Telsey, and David Vaccari. *Production Designer:* Jane Musky. *Art Director:* Darrell K. Keister. *Set Decorator:* Susan Tyson. *Set Dresser:* Joseph M. DeLuca. *Visual Effects:* Bob Munroe. *Costumes:* Ann Roth. *Make-up:* Michal Bigger. *Make-up (Sean Connery):* Melanie R. Hughes. *Stunt Coordinator:* George Aguilar. *Running time:* 136 minutes. *MPAA Rating:* PG-13.

CAST: Sean Connery (Forrester); Rob Brown (Jamal); F. Murray Abraham (Crawford); Anna Paquin (Claire); Busta Rhymes (Terrell); April Grace (Ms. Joyce); Michael Nouri (Dr. Spence); Richard Easton (Matthews); Glenn Fitzgerald (Massie); Zane R. Copeland, Jr. (Damon); Stephanie Berry (Janice); Fly Williams III (Fly); Damany Mathis (Kenzo); Damien Lee (Clay); Tom Kearns (Coach Garrick); Matthew Noah Word (Hartwell); Charles Bernstein (Dr. Simon); Matt Malloy (Bradley); Matt Damon (Sanderson); Jimmy Bobbitt (Rapper); Capital Jay (Opposing Player); James T. Williams II (Student); Cassandra Kubinski (Claire's Friend); Sophia Wu (Librarian); Gerry Rosenthal (Student Speaker); Tim Hall (Student Manager); Tom Mullica (Old Money Man); David Madison (Kid in the Hall); Joey Buttafuoco (Night Man); Jaime McCaig and William Modeste (Referees); Daniel Rodriguez (Hallway Boy); Samuel Tyson (Creston Player); Vince Giordano (Big Band Leader); Gregory Singer (Violinist); Dean Pratt and Kerry MacKillop (Trumpet Players); Harvey Tibbs (Trombone Player); Conal Fowkes (Piano Player); Matt Munisteri (Guitarist); John Meyers (Drummer); Ron Morgan (Mailor Priest); Alex Trebek (Himself); Michael Pitt (Coleridge); Allison Folland (Jeopardy Contestant).

LOS ANGELES TIMES, 12/19/00, Calendar/p. 1, Kenneth Turan

"Finding Forrester" is "Good Will Hunting in the Bronx," and whether that is good news or not depends on how you reacted to the original Boston-based production.

Once again we meet a gifted young person who prefers to hide his accomplishments from his peers and an experienced mentor who learns a lesson or two himself as he helps the youngster find a place in the world. Once again, Gus Van Sant is directing and, in case we miss the connection, there's even a cameo for "Good Will" star Matt Damon.

One more time, as well, we're presented with a well-oiled piece of Hollywood machinery, pat and overly familiar but tolerably entertaining until it piles on the contrivances at the close. And "Finding Forrester" does have advantages in the acting department, and not necessarily the ones you might think.

Sean Connery is the film's star as well as one of its producers, but his I'm-crankier-than-you-are performance, though glib and entertaining, feels like a reprise of a lifetime of greatest hits. More affecting, and more surprising, is the debut work done by a 16-year-old actor named Rob Brown.

A novice who never even thought of acting before he tried out for this part, Brown turns out to be something of a natural. His wary and dignified presence, nicely set off by a great smile, enables him to make working with Connery appear simple, and he has enough self- possession to look, even if unintentionally, a bit embarrassed at the shenanigans that are taking place around him.

Brown plays Jamal Wallace, a 16-year-old African American who lives in the Bronx with his mother and expends a good part of his energy keeping his braininess, and especially his interest in writing, hidden from friends who are happiest considering him nothing more than an excellent basketball player and regular guy.

Jamal and company play ball on a court that faces a venerable prewar apartment house, on whose top floor lives a mysterious binocular-wielding presence the kids call, in one of debuting screenwriter Mike Rich's nicer touches, the Window.

Lots of strange urban legends have grown up around the Window, and when Jamal, on a dare, goes up to investigate, he ends up leaving behind a knapsack containing the journals he's been surreptitiously writing. Imagine (just imagine!) Jamal's surprise when those journals get returned with pithy comments like "constipated thinking" and "this passage fantastic" written all over them in red.

His curiosity aroused, Jamal goes back and begins a tentative protege relationship with this strange old recluse (Connery, of course), prickly and prone to mind games, who spends most of his time drinking scotch in his pajamas in his Miss Havisham-type ruin of an apartment.

At just about this time, Mailor-Callow, one of Manhattan's top prep schools, shows an interest in Jamal largely because of his basketball prowess. It offers to take him out of the Bronx, which, though it looks about as dangerous as Mayberry with car fires, is conceded to be not the best place to get an education.

Mailor-Callow is so upper-crust it might as well have "Give me your rich, your bored, your over-privileged" carved in stone above the entrance. Fortunately, Jamal finds a guide who speaks the language in Claire Spence (Anna Paquin), a young woman with the kind of world-weary attitude that rarely survives high school. He also acquires a nemesis in a viperish English teacher named Crawford (F. Murray Abraham).

It's at Mailor-Callow that Jamal discovers the Window's secret identity. Believe it or not, the boy is being tough-love-tutored by the legendary William Forrester, an author who essayed a J.D. Salinger-esque withdrawal from the literary world after winning the Pulitzer Prize with his first novel 40 years earlier.

There is a smooth, practiced charm to all of this, but, even with Connery fulminating for all he's worth, it wears thin. Plot strands, like a rivalry with another Mailor-Callow athlete and even Jamal's friendship with Claire, disappear without a by-your-leave, and even the inevitably bumpy relationship between Forrester and Jamal, though amiable enough, is never completely convincing. Even fairy tales could use a bit more substance than this.

NEW YORK POST, 12/19/00, p. 59, Jonathan Foreman

"Finding Forrester" is an inoffensive and often pleasing Hollywood fantasy about a good-hearted, well-educated old white guy who helps a young black guy from the ghetto, and in doing so, is able once-again to live life to the fullest.

It starts out as a sentimental but effective combination of "Educating Rita" (crusty old teacher learns to embrace life again thanks to relationship with student) with "Good Will Hunting," then turns into "Stand By Me" (everyone assumes academically successful poor minority lads must be cheating) and climaxes in a scene lifted wholesale from "Scent of a Woman."

But it feels less predictable and derivative than it is, thanks to Gus Van Sant's deft direction and two fine central performances.

Up in the South Bronx, a bunch of black teens shooting hoops notice that they are being watched through curtains by a ghostly old white man (Sean Connery) who never leaves his apartment (his groceries are delivered once a week by a nervous lawyer).

One of the teens, Jamal (Rob Brown), breaks into the strange, book-filled apartment on a dare, is almost caught by the old man, and escapes, leaving his back pack behind.

The backpack contains Jamal's notebooks. Jamal, it turns out, is a kind of ghetto miracle, a superbly well-read kid who has been able to develop his spectacular literary talent without help from family or school.

The old man, who himself turns out to be Forrester, a J.D. Salinger-like author who has lived a secretive, hermit-like existence for decades, and who spends all day in his pajamas like a celibate Hugh Heffner, goes through the notebooks and immediately recognizes Jamal's potential.

When the backpack arrives back in his hands, Jamal's notebooks have all been "corrected" by the mysterious stranger, prompting the young man to pay the apartment another visit. Forrester quickly becomes the mentor anyone who has ever wanted to write should have, and so begins one of those relationships in which teacher learns at least as much as the pupil.

Things are complicated by Jamal's winning a scholarship to a fancy Manhattan private school impressed by his test scores—and by his basketball skills.

While Jamal does well there and begins a flirtation with an extremely cute fellow student played by Anna Paquin, one of his teachers (F. Murray Abraham) is convinced that his brilliant essays are in fact plagiarized. The only way Jamal can prove his innocence, is if he breaks his promise to Forrester to keep their friendship a secret.

Abraham's Crawford is an unbelievable cartoon villain, and the film's final act becomes more ridiculous by the minute: featuring a sentimental visit to Yankee Stadium in the middle of the night, a (televised) private-school basketball championship in Madison Square Garden, and a school assembly that doubles as a kind of trial.

Although cast very much against type—Connery gives an energetic (if not especially subtle) and mostly convincing performance, and enjoys remarkable chemistry with terrific first-time actor Rob Brown.

NEWSDAY, 12/19/00, Part II/p. B13, John Anderson

The year 2000 has been one of the greatest ever in the history of motion pictures—if you watch the first half, of movies. Unfortunately, most of us insist on staying till the end. Will we ever learn.

Maybe. "Finding Forrester" might just do it. Like a lot of recent films, Gus Van Sant's latest, in which Sean Connery plays the J.D. Salinger-like title character and young Rob Brown is his literary prodigy, starts off well enough. Although the concept—old white hermit-genius mentors young black writer-genius—is strictly racism-under-the-rug, feel-good formula, the characters are honest and the situation nearly believable.

Brown, a Queens resident and Brooklyn prep school student who plays Jamal Wallace, is particularly good, his character neither patronizing nor stereotypical. Connery may be cruising on pure personality, but Busta Rhymes is terrific as Jamal's brother and the movie moves with a seductive rhythm-aided by a Miles Davis-heavy score that puts just the right mournful edge on a mournful Bronx.

In other words, it has one of the better first halves of the holiday season.

You might say Jamal himself is a racist creation—What? No other black teenager in the Bronx can read?—except that Jamal, who doesn't want to stand out, would stand out as glaringly at a convention of Nobel prize-winning, Oxford-graduated Mensa members as he does in the lowly Bronx. And did we mention he plays basketball? When a precious white Manhattan prep school comes calling, luring him into a nest of advantage and betrayal, Jamal has to face the fact that he's brilliant.

But Jamal has a secret: Willie "Forrester," who 50 years earlier published his one and only novel (with strong suggestions of Salinger's Seymour Glass), won the Pulitzer Prize and retired from life. The Pynchonesque mystery about his writing and whereabouts haven't hurt sales any, but "Forrester" remains in his Bronx apartment, having food and liquor delivered and providing the neighborhood with its own local myth—"The Window" as he's called, said to be a crazy, a murderer, whatever. It takes Jamal to scale the fire escape, enter Forrester's home and ultimately draw him into the sunshine.

Why does Jamal decide to do it now, when Forrester's been up there for half a century? Because the movie has started, that's why. The formulaic elements of Mike Rich's script don't stop with race relations. They include the disappointed and racist teacher (F. Murray Abraham), who provides villainy by dismissing the brilliant Jamal as a basketball player; Claire (Anna Paquin), the saucy white outcast who immediately befriends Jamal and provides sexual taboo; the school itself, which provides Jamal his crisis, and Forrester, who in a scene right out of "Scent of a Woman" has to leave his comfy home and do the right thing.

The right thing, of course, is to have left an hour earlier.

SIGHT AND SOUND, 3/01, p. 50, Peter Matthews

William Forrester, author of the American classic *Avalon Landing*, has for decades been living as a recluse in the Bronx. Jamal Wallace is a 16 year old high-school student whose athletic ability disguises a brilliant writing talent. On a dare, he breaks into Forrester's flat. Surprised by Forrester, Jamal flees, leaving his bag behind. Inside are some notebooks, which the novelist corrects before tossing them out of the window to Jamal. The youth returns to ask for further guidance, and the two strike up a warm teacher-pupil relationship.

Jamal's state test-scores are impressive, and he is awarded a scholarship to Mailor-Callow, a prep school. There he meets Claire Spence, whose father is a school governor. He joins the basketball team and enrols in Robert Crawford's creative writing class. When shown an edition of *Avalon Landing*, Jamal recognises the photograph on the flap and confronts William. Demanding anonymity, the author agrees to help Jamal with his entry in the annual prose competition. Jamal reworks a supposedly unpublished piece of Forrester's and submits it. Forrester reveals that he went into seclusion after the death of his brother. One night, Jamal entices Forrester out of his flat by taking him to a baseball game. Later Jamal humiliates Crawford by besting him in a round of literary quotations. The professor then accuses Jamal of plagiarism, having dug up the published version of Forrester's original piece. Claire's father offers to forget the affair if Jamal leads his team to victory in the basketball championship. Jamal throws the game instead. William shocks everyone by showing up at the prize ceremony for the competition. After reading a new work to applause, he announces it was written by Jamal. Forrester leaves for his native Scotland and dies of cancer some time later. He leaves Jamal his flat and the manuscript of a second novel.

It's obvious why Gus Van Sant was hired to direct *Finding Forrester*—the film so strongly resembles his 1997 *Good Will Hunting* that it qualifies as a virtual remake. Since Van Sant's last picture was a carbon copy of Hitchcock's *Psycho* and this new one climaxes with a charge of plagiarism brought against the hero, it would be tempting to suppose another round of giddy post-modern poaching. But that concedes too much cleverness to a moist hunk of humanist uplift that sets a caesura on Van Sant's once-promising indie career. Before the opening credits, there's a self-reflexive bit involving a rap artist and a clapper board which might be taken as a vestigial gesture towards experiment. Otherwise, the movie plays straight to the dignified aspirations of this year's Oscar voters. *Good Will Hunting* concerns a mathematical prodigy from south Boston who learns to love through the example of nurturing father figure Robin Williams. With bold originality, *Finding Forrester* tells of a literary whiz kid from the Bronx who gains self-confidence through the mediation of nurturing father figure Sean Connery.

Both films present an idealised cartoon of the creative process rather than dramatising its sweat and frustration. In the case of *Forrester*, the Salingeresque hermit played by Connery bestows non-stop nuggets of wisdom such as "Write your first draft with your heart and your second with your head." Both films conceive of genius as something God-given that strikes the humble as well as the great—a consoling myth of class mobility, especially as neither protagonist faces serious resistance from his support network of proletarian chums. If *Good Will Hunting* has the edge, it's because its writers aren't afraid to make their proto-Einstein an arrogant little sod who holds his gift in disdain. There's nothing in *Forrester* to compare with that startling scene where Will puts a match to the recondite algebraic proof that came so easily to him, while his academic mentor scrambles to rescue it. First-time screenwriter Mike Rich avoids gumming up the works with messy inner conflicts, hatching a melodramatic nemesis for budding scribe Jamal in the shape of snooty Professor Crawford, who can't believe that a mere tenement punk could be so smiled on by the muse. But if you feel shut out from all the bookish shop talk, you can at least enjoy Jamal's deft dribbling on the basketball court. This sporting sub-plot seems to have been included in the hope of luring a crossover audience, whom it should help to reassure that the namby-pamby wordsmith is a regular guy after all.

Or maybe not. Van Sant seems to have cornered the market in a new kind of upscale male-bonding movie where the partners connect with brains instead of brawn. As in any romantic comedy, the predestined couple know their affinity through a mystical dovetailing of attributes. Here, Jamal picks up handy prose tips and reciprocally lends the cloistered novelist courage to enter the world again. Pressing the issue a step further, one could make a fair argument for *Finding Forrester*—and *Good Will Hunting*—as steamy homoerotic fantasies detailing the pedagogic relationship between an older 'bear' and his dewy acolyte. Van Sant's previous forays in the buddy genre *(Mala Noche, Drugstore Cowboy, My Own Private Idaho)* would appear to justify the innuendo—even if his own upward mobility necessitates a tad more sublimation these days. Though *Finding Forrester* isn't quite so touchy-feely as *Good Will Hunting*'s orgy of back-slapping, hugs and coy reminders to keep off each other's ass, it offers the curious spectacle of Connery spying with binoculars on the Afro-American youths who practise slam-dunking beneath his window. Almost needless to say, Jamal gets hooked up with a nice young collegiate, played by Anna Paquin, by way of lowering the testosterone level. But the damage is already done, and the movie should prove a goldmine to queer textual saboteurs for years to come.

TIME, 12/25/00-1/1/01, p. 147, Richard Schickel

Forrester (Connery) is a one-book novelist, fallen into an endless Salingeresque funk. From the window of his Bronx apartment, he watches black kids playing basketball in a vastly changed neighborhood. The best and brightest of them, Jamal (good newcomer Brown), penetrates his lair on a dare, and a mentoring relationship develops between the cranky old writer and the, very bright teenager. The film's twists and turns are as predictable as the patronizing racism at the private school that grants the boy a scholarship. Something more surprising might have been made of this odd couple, but Van Sant, emptily employing the realist manner of his early films, is goodwill hunting in all the wrong places.

VILLAGE VOICE, 12/26/00, p. 154, Michael Atkinson

Gus Van Sant's *Finding Forrester* redoes *Scent of a Woman* by way of the Iowa Writers' Workshop— *Good Will*-ish 16-year-old savant Jamal (Rob Brown), who reads Kierkegaard and Joyce, meets up with hermitted, Pynchon/Salinger-like novelist legend William Forrester (Sean Connery, looking more like bearded Bea Arthur than ever) in his Bronx neighborhood. Jamal gets writing lessons, the old coot slowly learns to embrace life again, the old coot musters crusty bon mots, Jamal snaps 'em back—Mike Rich's script can't be eaten with a fork, you need a spoon. "You write your first draft with your heart!" the old Scots giant roars in pajama bottoms. " *Punch* the keys, for God's sake!—as if Jamal were David Helfgott hammering out that Rachmaninoff concerto on his Royal standard. Read what you will into the fact that Mishima is on both characters' bookshelves, but the literary life is used as a built-in narcotic: Readers are made to feel dopily good about themselves, and meanwhile barely a word of Jamal's or Forrester's fulsomely praised prose is read or heard. The entire project, including an obligatory climactic writing competition where Forrester strides in and sets right the obligatory wrong perpetrated by an overweening hump of an English prof (F. Murray Abraham), hinges on Jamal's writing being "pungent!" but it could be brain-dead prattle for all we know. At times you can feel Van Sant trying to loosen the movie's wind pipe-folding collar, but he doesn't get far, except with Busta Rhymes, as Jamal's gone-nowhere big brother, whose moments are so full of bounce and warmth they feel like invasions from the screen next door.

Also reviewed in:
NEW YORK TIMES, 12/19/00, p. E3, Stephen Holden
VARIETY, 12/18-31/00, p. 21, Emanuel Levy
WASHINGTON POST, 12/22/00, Weekend/p. 40, Michael O'Sullivan
WASHINGTON POST, 12/25/00, p. C1, Stephen Hunter

FIVE SENSES, THE

A Fine Line Features release of an Alliance Atlantis presentation of a Five Senses production. *Executive Producer:* Charlotte Mickie, Ted East, and David R. Ginsburg. *Producer:* Camelia Frieberg and Jeremy Podeswa. *Director:* Jeremy Podeswa. *Screenplay:* Jeremy Podeswa. *Director of Photography:* Gregory Middleton. *Editor:* Wiebke Von Carolsfeld. *Music:* Alexina Louie and Alex Pauk. *Sound:* Philip Stall and (music) Jeff Wolpert. *Sound Editor:* Garrett Kerr. *Casting:* Julia Tait, John Buchan, Juliette Menager, Fabiola Banzi, and Adrienne Stern. *Production Designer:* Taavo Soodor. *Art Director:* R. James Phillips. *Set Decorator:* Darryl Dennis Deegan and Erica Milo. *Special Effects:* Tim Good. *Costumes:* Gersha Phillips. *Make-up:* Sylvain Cournoyer. *Running time:* 105 minutes. *MPAA Rating:* R.

CAST: Mary-Louise Parker (Rona); Pascale Bussières (Gail); Richard Clarkin (Raymond); Brendan Fletcher (Rupert); Marco Leonardi (Roberto); Nadia Litz (Rachel); Daniel MacIvor (Robert); Molly Parker (Anna Miller); Gabrielle Rose (Ruth Seraph); Tara Rosling (Rebecca); Philippe Volter (Dr. Richard Jacob); Elise Frances Stolk (Amy Lee Miller); Clinton Walker (Carl); Astrid Van Wieren (Richard's Patient); Paul Bettis (Richard's Doctor); James Allodi (Justin); Gavin Crawford (Airport Clerk); Sandi Stahlbrand (TV Reporter 1); Amanda Soha (Sylvie); Gisele Rousseau (Odile); Damon D'Oliveira (Todd); Sonia LaPlante (Monica); Janet Van De Graaf (Policewoman); Paul Soles (Mr. Bernstein); Clare Coulter (Clare); Roman Podhora (Policeman 1); Shaun O'Hara and Glen Peloso (Park Cruisers); Tracy Wright (Alex); Darren O'Donnell (Medic); Greg Ellwand (Policeman 2); Ola Sturik (TV Reporter 2); Daniel Taylor (Singer).

CHRISTIAN SCIENCE MONITOR, 7/14/00, p. 15, David Sterritt

"The Five Senses" comes from Canada and tells a more complicated story—or set of stories, to be precise. Its characters are loosely connected and relate in different ways to an event that sets the movie in motion: the disappearance of a little girl in a Toronto park. Filmmaker Jeremy Podeswa's interest lies in how our physical senses shape our social and psychological lives. He explores this through interwoven experiences: a music-loving eye doctor who's losing his hearing, a massage therapist who touches her clients but is losing touch with her daughter, a wedding-cake baker whose taste isn't all it should be, and so on.

Podeswa has filmed "The Five Senses" with uncommon skill. A number of today's most talented Canadian filmmakers, including such world-class talents as Atom Egoyan and Don McKellar, have a liking for fragmented stories told from multiple points of view, perhaps reflecting the ungraspable sprawl and diversity of Canada itself. "The Five Senses" is a splendid example of this increasingly impressive breed.

LOS ANGELES TIMES, 7/21/00, Calendar/p. 6, Kenneth Turan

"The Five Senses" is an elegant, deliberate film about loneliness and hope, connection and loss. What makes it intriguing is not its subject matter but the way Canadian writer-director Jeremy Podeswa approaches it.

Well-received at both the Cannes and Toronto film festivals and winner of the Genie (Canada's Oscar) for directing, Podeswa's film does more than use the senses as a convenient title.

Intent on exploring how hearing, sight, smell, taste and touch connect us to one another and the world, Podeswa uses them as entry points into his story. It may sound like a gimmick, and the film is hampered by some banal scripting, but the skill of the writer-director and his crew, especially cinematographer Gregory Middleton, largely keeps that from happening.

From its assured opening shot of a young mother named Anna Miller (Molly Parker) relaxing in a flotation tank before getting a massage, "Five Senses" is an artful, sensual film, fluidly directed and alive to feelings of all kinds. Even when the story bogs down or wanders into sterile byways, the deliberateness and beauty of its style create interest.

Podeswa's script details the loosely interconnected stories of a number of people who live or work in the same Toronto building. Ruth, the massage therapist (Gabrielle Rose, the bus driver in "The Sweet Hereafter") obviously represents touch, though it is not immediately clear that her bratty 16-year-old daughter Rachel (Nadia Litz) will come to voyeuristically represent sight.

Hearing is the concern of ophthalmologist Richard (Philippe Volter), who becomes obsessed with recording certain sounds when he learns he is going deaf. Rona (Mary-Louise Parker in her best performance to date) makes inventive and artistic cakes that don't come close to tasting good. And her bisexual best friend Robert (Daniel MacIvor) is a housecleaner with such a highly developed sense of smell that he wants to try to discover what true love does to your nose.

Robert's despair at being alone and his determination to reconnect with all his old lovers, to in effect sniff out love, is one of the crises of various sorts (Richard's loss of hearing is another) that involve the characters with one another as well as their senses.

A cute Italian guy (Marco Leonardi) Rona became involved with on vacation decides to visit Toronto and stay with her, though he speaks no English. And, most problematically, Rachel, who is supposed to be baby-sitting Anna's young daughter Amy Lee during a massage, looks away and finds that the little girl has disappeared.

Though in general these stories unfold in such a moody, delicate way that only in retrospect is the underlying skeleton visible, some of "The Five Senses'" plotting is schematic. There are improbable elements and narrative dead ends, and not all the strands are worked out with equal intelligence and insight. But misfires are inevitable with an ambitious film, and watching this one can be a sensitizing process in itself, making us more aware of our senses and the often unnoticed parts they play in our lives.

Most of all, "Five Senses" underlines the poignancy of wanting to connect, wanting to have more intense personal experiences but being blocked by our own deficiencies as well as everyone else's. People, it seems, are all we have to hook up with in this world. Imperfect creatures, to be sure, but there it is.

NEW YORK POST, 7/14/00, p. 46, Jonathan Foreman

Fake-sounding dialogue, some over-deliberate performances and five amazingly trite linked stories, ensure that "The Five Senses" a somber, underlit film from Canadian writer-director Jeremy Podeswa, is almost comically portentous. It keeps your interest in a soap-operatic way but it is slighter, less significant project than the filmmaker seemed to realize.

The film begins with Anna Miller (a fine Molly Parker) getting a massage from Ruth (Gabrielle Rose). During the session Ruth asks her difficult teenage daughter Rachel (Nadia Litz—in the film's best performance) to take Anna's 3-year-old Amy Lee out to the park. But once there, Rachel gets distracted by a couple of young lovers and loses the little girl.

The massive search for and media frenzy about the missing toddler for the next three days provides the backdrop for the film's real subject: the inner lives of five interlinked characters whose problems have something to with sight, smell, hearing, touch or taste.

It's all very programmatic and obvious. Teenage Rachel is a voyeur who loses sight of what's important. Her mother Ruth, the widowed masseuse, has fallen out of touch (get it?) with her daughter and with own feelings.

Then there's Rona (Mary-Louise Parker), the cake-maker who works upstairs. She makes great-looking cakes that taste bad. She also has an Italian lover, Roberto (Marco Leonardi), whom she doesn't trust.

Her best friend, Robert (Daniel MacIvor), is a swishy gay house cleaner with a hypersensitive sense of smell. He interviews all his former lovers, convinced that he'll be able to smell the one who really loves him.

Also working in the same building as Rona and Ruth is Richard (Philippe Volter), an eye doctor who is going deaf. He takes time off to collect a mental library of sounds—until a prostitute with a heart of gold teaches him that there are other ways to hear than through your ears.

While writer-director Jeremy Podeswa links his five characters' stories with considerable skill, so the shifts are smooth and swift, everything else about the film feels forced and unnatural.

NEWSDAY, 7/14/00, Part II/p. B6, John Anderson

This just in from the genome: We are, we humans, 99.9 percent the same. If there were a hostile attack from outer space, we'd suddenly look even more alike. Where we differ, it seems, is largely a matter of choice. And, of course, perception.

And if the brotherhood-of-(wo)man theme was the sole purpose of Jeremy Podeswa's "The Five Senses," it would all be pretty banal—as banal as the conversations on which Richard (Philippe Volter), an eye doctor going deaf, obsessively eavesdrops through the vents of his Toronto apartment." Or the catty observations made by Robert (Daniel MacIvor), a bisexual house cleaner, while dusting the apartments of his clients. Or the Bauhaus-inspired, inedible birthday cakes of Rona (Mary-Louise Parker), Robert's love-leery confidante, whose mother is driving her crazy by dying with dignity.

What's far from banal—and which ratchets everything in the film up to an emotional delirium—is the disappearance of a 3-year-old named Amy Lee (Elise Frances Stolk). While her mother Anna (Molly Parker) is being treated by Ruth the massage therapist (Gabrielle Rose), Ruth's alienated daughter Rachel (Nadia Litz) takes the baby out and loses her, while spying on a couple making love.

The schematic to the film, Podeswa's follow-up to his much admired "Eclipse," is easy enough to follow: Ruth, who can heal with her touch, can't see her daughter for who she is; Rona backpedals when Roberto, the Italian hunk she slept with in Italy, arrives for a long-term visit, even though every indication says she should take the emotional plunge; Richard, an opera lover and long-distance father, thinks his life will end when he can no longer hear Puccini or his daughter's voice; Robert—whose olfactory sense is so acute he can smell love—hasn't got a whiff of self-knowledge.

There are many character names that start with R; those who don't are heavy on the soft A. The men—particularly Richard, Roberto and Robert's client Raymond—share a very similar Mediterranean look and the women all seem to have popped out of the same gene pool. Why? To emphasize the point made throughout the film, that our similarities outweigh our differences. And to add a layer of mystery to an already inscrutable enterprise.

Cinematographer Gregory Middleton's use of light-exalted, amber and often ingeniously artificial—gives this Canadian production its own solid sensory values. But it's largely Podeswa's timing, and that of his cast (particularly Mary-Louise Parker) that makes "The Five Senses" such a delight. It was a crapshoot, of course: Not only another multicharactered, cloverleafing character study, but a highly sensual work about sensory perception. In the end, I thought I smelled art.

SIGHT AND SOUND, 1/00, p. 49, Liese Spencer

Five stories set in modern Toronto interweave. Anna gives Ruth a massage while Ruth's sulky 16-year-old daughter Rachel takes Anna's three-year-old daughter Amy out to play. In the park, Rachel leaves Amy and follows a necking couple into the woods. On Rachel's return, Amy is gone. As the police search the city, Anna allows the mortified Ruth to stay with her. Rachel, meanwhile, meets a youth in the park. Together they watch men cruising. Soon he reveals his fascination with crossdressing.

In the same apartment block, Richard, a French-speaking ophthalmologist, is losing his hearing. He makes a list of things to listen to and tries to build a "sound library" of aural memories, yet it is his friendship with a prostitute that breaks his sense of isolation. Fascinated with smell, house cleaner Robert interrogates his past lovers, both male and female, looking for the smell of love. After a *ménage à trois* with a young couple, one of whom designs perfumes, he finds the smell in a bottle. Robert's cake-making friend Rona is followed back to Canada by Roberto, her Italian lover. Although he cooks for her, she suspects him of an affair with another woman and they fall out. When Amy is found, Ruth and Rachel meet back at home and hold hands.

"The senses are elemental, and in connecting us to the world, they connect us to others," says director Jeremy Podeswa in the press notes for *The Five Senses*. It's a profound-sounding statement which on closer inspection appears self-evident. Watching his ponderous exposition of this concept is a similarly underwhelming experience. Full of sombre portent as the film opens, his deftly interwoven tales of touch, taste, smell, sight and sound are less beguiling than they at first appear.

Shot in a wintry palatte of greys and browns and set largely among the light-starved apartments of a Toronto building, Podeswa's film opens with mother Anna entrusting her young toddler Amy to the care of sulky teenager Rachel. When Rachel's neglect leads to Amy's disappearance, the subsequent police search provides the link between the characters of the five linked vignettes.

Podeswa deserves praise for not always picking the most obvious metaphor (for the 'touch' story, the masseuse must learn how to make emotional contact with her child). Yet many of his slight tales remain fraught with a suggestive symbolism they cannot support. In one scene cake decorator Rona realises her cakes should taste good as well as look beautiful. But watching her mash a failed sponge into the bin, it's unclear what this has to do with her relationships with her Italian boyfriend and her dying mother.

At first her lonely friend Robert's decision to smell his way through a list of male and female ex-lovers seems more obvious. He's sniffing out real affection, but aside from being an unconventional approach to reviving relationships what does his bizarre scheme signify? When a young couple he works for present him with a gift of perfume, he says it "smells like love" and jumps into bed with both of them.

Robert's intuitive odyssey might have been engagingly surreal were it not for the earnestness with which Podeswa presents it. Indeed, the whole film is composed of 'significant' exchanges, characters swapping gnomic greetings before going on their way. The following is typical: "Why did you leave Belgium?" asks a policeman making door-to-door enquiries about the missing girl. "I thought I would like the winters," replies one character. "Did you?" "No."

Meticulously intercut, such scenes suppress character development and encourage only the emotional build up to a sentimental knot-tying conclusion. (Even Molly Parker, so affecting as the necrophiliac in *Kissed*, makes little impression as the distraught mother.) For a film about the importance of intimacy and communication, little sense of real warmth or sensuality is conveyed here. *The Five Senses* is exquisitely made and well acted but it's still a slow dance of chilly ciphers to somnolent music in a mournful *mise en scène*.

VILLAGE VOICE, 7/18/00, p. 130, Michael Atkinson

Canadian mezzo-brow Jeremy Podeswa specializes in circle jerks, too, but of a wholly different stripe: portentous sand castles designed as structuralist Kieslowski/Egoyan rondeaux. But his ideas are trite: *Eclipse* (1995) followed a circular path of dull sexual encounters centered upon, for no meaningful reason, a solar eclipse, while his new film, *The Five Senses*, presents yet another haphazard tapestry in which individuals and their stories are, God help us, represented by the ear, the eye, the nose, et cetera. ("The senses are elemental," Podeswa is quoted in the press notes, "and in connecting us to the world, they connect us to others," a rumination so inflated and idiotic it evokes Ed Wood.) So, we get a gay house cleaner (Daniel MacIvor) who can smell true love, an optometrist (Philippe Volter) who experiences things mostly by hearing, a hesitant cake designer (Mary-Louise Parker) whose food lacks flavor, et cetera. The only thread that overshadows the lumbering conceit involves a missing child, lost by a teenage malcontent (the arresting Nadia Litz, whose secretive brooder could be the central figure in another, more attentive movie) babysitting in the park. Because the situation (dominated by the child's shattered mother, played by Molly Parker) is so painful, shrill, and chaotic, it feels real in a way Podeswa couldn't rein in. Beautifully shot and littered with disquieting character business, the film is hog-tied by its own bad Big Idea. At least Peter Greenaway used to be funny and original with his structures; grave and self-important, Podeswa thinks clichés are the path to enlightenment.

Also reviewed in:
CHICAGO TRIBUNE, 7/28/00, Friday/p. D, Michael Wilmington
NEW YORK TIMES, 7/14/00, p. E10, Elvis Mitchell
VARIETY, 5/31-6/6/99, p. 31, Brendan Kelly
WASHINGTON POST, 7/28/00, p. C12, Stephen Hunter
WASHINGTON POST, 7/28/00, Weekend/p. 38, Desson Howe

FLINTSTONES IN VIVA ROCK VEGAS, THE

A Universal Pictures release of a Hanna-Barbera/Amblin Entertainment production. *Executive Producer:* William Hanna, Joseph Barbera, and Dennis E. Jones. *Producer:* Bruce Cohen. *Director:* Brian Levant.   *Screenplay (based on the animated series by Hanna-Barbera Productions, Inc.)* Deborah Kaplan and Harry Elfont, Jim Cash, and Jack Epps, Jr.   *Director of Photography:* Jamie Anderson. *Editor:* Kent Beyda. *Music:* David Newman. *Music Editor:* Tom Villano. *Choreographer:* Corain Grusman. *Sound:* Ed Tise and (music) John Kurlander. *Sound Editor:* Mark Mangini.   *Casting:* Nancy Nayor.   *Production Designer:* Christopher Burian-Mohr.   *Art Director:* Bradford Ricker.   *Set Designer:* Andrea Dopaso, John Berger, Stephanie J. Gordon, Wil Hawkins, Bruce Hill, Gerald Sullivan, and Bruce K. West.   *Set Decorator:* Jan Pascale. *Set Dresser:* Louise Del Araujo, Jenny Baum, Craig R. Baron, Sara Jane Bos, F. Alan Burg, Dennis De Groot, Ryan Hedgecock, and Rick Pond.   *Special Effects:* Burt Dalton. *Visual Effects:* Justin Ritter.   *Costumes:* Robert Turturice.   *Make-up:* Christina Smith. *Gazoo/Alien Prosthetics:* Matthew W. Mungle.   *Stunt Coordinator:* Joel Kramer.   *Running time:* 90 minutes. *MPAA Rating:* PG.

CAST: Mark Addy (Fred Flintstone);   Stephen Baldwin (Barney Rubble);   Kristen Johnston (Wilma Slaghoople);   Jane Krakowski (Betty O'Shale);   Thomas Gibson (Chip Rockefeller); Joan Collins (Pearl Slaghoople);   Alan Cumming (Gazoo/Mick Jagged);   Harvey Korman (Colonel Slaghoople);   Alex Meneses (Roxie);   John Taylor (Keith Rockhard);   Tony Longo (Big Rocko);   Danny Woodburn (Little Rocko);   Taylor Negron (Gazaam/Gazing);   Jack McGee and David Jean-Thomas (Bronto Crane Examiners);   Gary Epp (Dean Agate); Jennifer Simard (Bride-to-Be);   Heather McClurg (Tennis Girl);   Chene Lawson (Kitty);   John Cho (Parking Valet);   Nora Burns and Mark Kubr (Party Guests);   Cheryl Holdridge-Post (Genvieve);   Buck Kartalian (Old Man at Bronto King);   Matt Griesser (Booth Worker);   Irwin Keyes (Joe Rockhead);   Mary Jo Smith (Gambler Woman);   Duane Davis (Good);   Kevin Grevioux (Associate Goon);   Steven Schirripa (Croupier);   John Wills Smith (Casino Security Guard);   Lucille M. Oliver (Hotel Worker);   Joel Virgil Vierset (Keyboard Player);   John Prosky, Rachel Winfree, Ted Rooney, and Jim Doughan (Confessors);   Jason Kravitz (Choreographer);   John Stephenson (Showroom Announcer);   Brian Mahoney (Audience Man); Ann Martel Mahoney (Audience Woman);   Walter Gertz (Wedding Minister);   Beverly Sanders (Photographer);   Phil Buckman (Stoney);   Mel Blanc (Voice of Puppy Dino);   Rosie O'Donnell (Voice of Octopus Masseuse).

LOS ANGELES TIMES, 4/28/00, Calendar/p. 12, Eric Harrison

The 1994 movie "The Flintstones" was such a dreary affair that it's hard to get excited about a new film based on that 1960s cartoon classic. The earlier movie re-created signature scenes from the television series while capturing little of the tone. But "The Flintstones in Viva Rock Vegas" is something else altogether. It's livelier, it feels more like a cartoon, and when you're dealing with modern Stone Age families, that can only be a plus.

This is a love story—the tale of how Fred and Barney (Mark Addy and Stephen Baldwin, respectively) meet and fall in love with Wilma and Betty (Kristen Johnston and Jane Krakowski). With the same studio and director in charge, the new movie technically is a prequel, but it's a brontosaurus of a different color. In addition to its lighter tone, it has all new actors in the lead roles. (John Goodman, Rick Moranis, Elizabeth Perkins, Rosie O'Donnell and Elizabeth Taylor starred in the 1994 film.) Addy's bellowing Fred is a credible younger version of Goodman's, and the normally unimpressive Baldwin may finally have found his calling—he should stick to portraying dimwitted cartoon characters.

The female characters, especially, are better developed this time out, but it's hard to imagine some of the personalities here (especially Johnston's exuberant, towering, pratfalling Wilma) maturing into the characters in the other film. This and several inconsistencies between the movies point up how little thought was given to the characters' back stories in the first film.

"Viva Rock Vegas" opens with Fred and Barney, longtime best friends from the trailer park, graduating from the Bronto Crane Academy and starting construction jobs. Wilma Slaghoople, meanwhile, lives in an opulent mansion on the hill overlooking Bedrock.

Rejecting the values of her snobbish mother (Joan Collins), who wants her to marry the dashing Chip Rockefeller (Thomas Gibson), Wilma runs away. She is taken in by Betty, a kindhearted waitress who thinks Wilma is "caveless."

Surveying Betty's modest Melrock Place digs, Wilma enthuses, "I always wondered what it would be like to live in an apartment." Her meaning is totally misunderstood.

The first film showed a dirty, threatening and rather shadowy prehistoric world, and it twisted the cartoon elements to fit into a Capra-esque plot about greed and human dignity, with a "Perils of Pauline" ending tacked on for good measure. The new movie also deals with issues of class and greed, but it doesn't let those issues weigh it down. There's no worker's revolt in the new film, for instance, and it doesn't subject audiences to jarring sights such as the near lynching of Fred and Barney for getting too close to the corporate bosses.

Filmmakers who adapt lowly TV shows or comic books tend to overload the plots, probably to keep hyperactive youngsters in their seats, and the people behind "Viva Rock Vegas" are guilty of this. For no good reason, they include a wispy subplot involving the Great Gazoo (Alan Cumming), a tiny, green-faced alien who appeared in a number of the television episodes. And a large portion of the movie takes place in Vegas, where Rockefeller, a casino owner with money problems, tries to break up Fred and Wilma so he can marry her and get his hands on the Slaghoople fortune.

English rock stars, threatening hoodlums and Harvey Korman as Wilma's daffy dad all get more screen time than they probably need.

Part of the fun of these movies is watching the inventive prehistoric versions of modern conveniences. Early in the movie, Fred drives over a bridge that really is a giant domesticated dinosaur. And picture-taking is possible because little bird-like creatures hide in cameras to peck out people's likenesses.

The movie's high point, though, may be the birth of Dino, the Flintstones' pet. A tiresome presence in the first film, as a pup the frisky beast brings a smile whenever he runs yapping across the screen.

NEW YORK POST, 4/28/00, p. 55, Lou Lumenick

"The Flintstones in Viva Rock Vegas" is actually more entertaining than its 1994 predecessor—which is not to say it's a yabba-dabba-doozy. This prequel boasts an all-new, more down-market (but better chosen) cast, more lavish sets and effects—and another plot that must have seemed dated in the Paleolithic era.

Beefy British actor Mark Addy ("The Full Monty") as the blustering Fred and Stephen Baldwin (the youngest and skinniest of the acting brothers) as the sweet but clueless Barney are improvements over John Goodman and Rick Moranis, who brought a bit too much star baggage to the last version.

Addy and Baldwin have better chemistry together, and their best scenes are a reminder that "The Flintstones" was very much inspired by "The Honeymooners."

As Wilma, Kristen Johnston, the Amazon from TV's "3rd Rock From the Sun," is much funnier than Elizabeth Perkins—she's a terrific physical comedian and plays well off Addy. Completing the quartet is Jane Krakowski ("Ally McBeal") whose wide-eyed subtlety is a welcome change from the overpowering Rosie ("Look at me, I'm funny") O'Donnell.

Kids will love the crowd-pleasing depiction of an entire prehistoric world, complete with an adorable baby Dino—and loads of great sight gags and puns.

Their parents will groan at the story, which has blue-collar Fred courting wealthy Wilma over the strenuous objections of her snobbish mother. Joan Collins, in the old Elizabeth Taylor role, looks great and attacks her first part in years as if it were Noel Coward.

Most of the machinations—briskly directed by Brian Levant, who also did the '94 film—involve Wilma's ex-boyfriend, Chip Rockefeller (Thomas Gibson of "Dharma and Greg"), who schemes to bust up the lovebirds' romance at his hotel in Rock Vegas.

The endless subplots (four writers are credited) include a tiny, sarcastic extraterrestrial named the Great Gazoo (Alan Cumming) sent to Earth to observe the mating habits of humans.

At one point, he orders Barney (who has fallen out of a hammock onto Fred's rump) and Fred to "go to it." Though they don't comply, it makes you wonder about the reference in the old "Flintstones" theme to "a gay old time."

Cumming, the British star of "Cabaret" who played the sleazy desk clerk in "Eyes Wide Shut," is less annoying in a second role, as a Neanderthal rocker named Mick Jagged (of "The Stones") who competes with Barney for Betty's affections.

"The Flintstones in Viva Rock Vegas," complete with a title song performed by Ann-Margrock, er, Ann-Margret, is more than OK family entertainment.

NEWSDAY, 3/28/00, Part II/p. B7, John Anderson

Like the first "Flintstones" movie—we hesitate to say "original"—the sequel, "The Flintstones in Viva Rock Vegas," has nowhere to go but up, just because the TV show it was based on was so unfunny. Unless the film versions are totally obnoxious, you have to consider yourself ahead of the game.

The evolutionary theory of Flintstonia begins, of course, with "The Honeymooners"—a fact acknowledged by Mark Addy, erstwhile "Full Monty" stripper and current Fred Flintstone, who may look like Rosie O'Donnell (the first film's Betty Rubble) but sounds just like Jackie Gleason.

Which at least gives you something to listen to.

What to watch? Alan Cumming, doing double duty as Gazoo, extraterrestrial pest-cum-sex researcher, and rock star Mick Jagged of (you guessed it) the Stones.

Mostly head, Gazoo flits about inflicting insults on Fred and Barney (Stephen Baldwin, doing a pretty accurate Mel Blanc) and studying the messy mating rituals of prehistoric earthlings as Fred pursues Wilma (Kristen Johnston) and Barney chases Betty (Jane Krakowski). Why little kids would be interested in this kind of a plot line is a little obscure, but the dinosaur flatulence will have them in stitches.

There is a distinct feeling of second-class citizenship inflicting this movie, which is adequately, occasionally quite manically, and always colorfully directed by Brian Levant (whose full-bore finale evokes a Stanley Donen-Gene Kelly musical).

The sight gags are as funny as they can be and the Addy-Johnston-Baldwin-Krakowski quartet is a lot more energetic than John Goodman, et al—although when someone actually gets a custard tart in the face, you'll feel like you're back in the Pleistocene Epoch.

SIGHT AND SOUND, 9/00, p. 41, Amanda Lipman

Bedrock, the Stone Age. Gazoo, an alien, is sent to earth to examine human mating rituals. He lands right by Fred Flintstone and Barney Rubble, both newly graduated from college and about to start work at the rock quarry. Wilma, dissatisfied with her vacuous, rich lifestyle, runs away from home and is taken in by Betty, a waitress at the Bronto King. The girls go out on a double date with Fred and Barney where Barney pairs off with Betty and Fred with Wilma.

Pressurised to do so by her mother, Wilma takes her friends home for her father's birthday party; there, they are ridiculed by her snobbish friends. They are invited to stay in the Rock Vegas hotel of her devious ex-boyfriend Chip Rockefeller who wants to win Wilma (and her money) back by shaming Fred. He lets Fred win a huge amount of money at the gaming tables only to make him lose it and then accuse him of stealing Wilma's jewellery. Meanwhile, Betty has spied Barney with Chip's female accomplice Roxie and goes off in a huff with the pop star Mick Jagged. Fred and Barney are arrested, but with the help of Gazoo, they escape from jail and win back Wilma and Betty.

The Flintstones in Viva Rock Vegas is the second live-action feature film based on the Hanna-Barbera produced animation series which ran on US television from 1960 to 1966. Like the first movie *The Flintstones* (also directed by Brian Levant), there is something dispiriting about live actors playing characters who were originally two dimensional cartoon figures. So it's a relief to see the addition of a new character, the alien Gazoo, providing a disdainful anthropological commentary on the human inhabitants of Bedrock at selected moments in *Viva Rock Vegas*. Played by Alan Cumming (who also plays the rock star Mick Jagged), Gazoo is a refreshing and ironic counterpoint to the film's flatly rendered cavemen heroes Fred and Barney, here seen before they settled down with wives Wilma and Betty.

This aside, it's largely business as usual. Sticking to the example set by the series and the first film, *Viva Rock Vegas* features plenty of gleeful crudity, not least in the endless rock puns—Rock Vegas, Bronto Rock, Melrock Place—most of which become tiresome pretty quickly. The Neanderthal retro chic that was the cartoon's lasting joke is made even more kitsch by the addition of designer vulgarity, provided by Joan Collins as Pearl, Wilma's mother. Draped in extravagant dresses, Collins vamps and camps her way through the film as if she were in an episode of *Dynasty*. Only her bare feet beneath the peacock dresses remind us of the stone-age setting. There is a more melancholy ring to the friendly dinosaurs, trained and tamed by people, that roam around unthreateningly, ostensibly as a sign of our symbiosis with animals, but also a perhaps unconscious reflection on our urge to subjugate.

The youthful Fred and Barney bring to mind the eponymous heroes of the *Bill & Ted* films. Affable but a little gormless, their brief moments of clarity are soon fogged by appeals to their childlike greed (Wilma's ex-boyfriend, the rich Chip Rockefeller, gets Fred into trouble by tempting him with huge winnings at the Rock Vegas gaming tables). But despite the fun the script has at their stupidity, there is a feeling that Fred and Barnie deserve to be winners. When they turn, in seconds, from dreamy adolescents to fully fledged adults desirous of marriage, we are supposed to believe in them. They are simple innocents, let loose in a corrupt world that they eventually get the better of, a world personified by the posh, too-clever-by-half Chip at one end and the ridiculously vain pop star Mick Jagged at the other. This is staple American dream stuff, where the ordinary working man triumphs, picking up a spot of good-natured ribbing on the way. It is harder, however, for contemporary audiences to understand why headstrong, intelligent Wilma, heroically turning her back on her frivolous upbringing, would opt for suburban bliss with Fred. As we all know from the television series, which caught up with Fred and Wilma in middle age, modern stone-age family life is hardly the most exciting of prospects.

Also reviewed in:
CHICAGO TRIBUNE, 4/28/00, Friday/p. F, Michael Wilmington
NEW YORK TIMES, 4/28/00, p. E30, Lawrence Van Gelder
VARIETY, 5/1-7/00, p. 32, Joe Leydon
WASHINGTON POST, 4/28/00, p. C5, Stephen Hunter
WASHINGTON POST, 4/28/00, Weekend/p. 53, Michael O'Sullivan

FOLLOWERS

A Castle Hill Productions release of a Castle Hill/Wildgoose Productions film. *Producer:* Jonathan M. Flicker, Stuart Ginsberg, Dennis Gossett, Jr., and Naiem Mohammad. *Director:* Jonathan M. Flickr. *Screenplay:* Jonathan M. Flicker. *Director of Photography:* William M. Miller. *Editor:* Jonathan M. Flicker. *Music:* Joe Kurasz. *Sound:* Molly Harris. *Sound Editor:* Peter Levin and Barbara Parks. *Casting:* Adrienne Stern. *Production Designer:* Dennis Gossett, Jr. *Art Director:* Jason Fetvedt. *Stunt Coordinator:* Neil Ruddy. *Running time:* 87 minutes. *MPAA Rating:* Not Rated.

CAST: Sam Trammell (John Dietrich); Eddie T. Robinson (Steven Trayer); Jerry Laurino (Allen Phillips); Jessica Prunell (Cynthia Gordon); Mark Dobies (Jake Tyler); Cary Phillips (Terry Graham); Crew Hoakes (T. J. O'Malley); Willie C. Carpenter (Mr. Trayer); Carol Clarke (Mrs. Trayer); Robert Flicker (Mr. Dietrich); Paul Raggio (Lawyer); Jonathan M. Flicker (Jeff Portnoy); Dave Hugas (Fredericks/KPL Brother); Marino Wecer (Frank/KPL Brother); Douglas Eldridge (Police Officer); Peter Catenacci (Police Officer/Paramedic); Brian Lubroth (Paramedic); William M. Miller (Witness); Steve Moreno (Bartender); Naiem Mohammad (Guy Walking with Steve); David Frigerio (Jerk at Party); Piper Perabo and Robin Eads (Girls at Party). Lisanne Franco (Subway Voice).

NEW YORK POST, 10/13/00, p. 65, Jonathan Foreman

The all-round amateurishness and the repellently self-satisfied and predictable way it protests against racism and fraternity culture quickly eliminates any temptation to be kind to "Followers" just because it was made for only $50,000.

Atrociously written, it's the kind of pious would-be "provocative" warning you could imagine being commissioned by college guidance counselors in coalition with student activists—the contemporary equivalent of 1950s anti-marijuana diatribes.

NEWSDAY, 10/13/00, Part II/p. B12, Gene Seymour

"Reason is the enemy" is the first sentence in "Followers" and in the taped confession of young John Dietrich (Sam Trammell), who went from college freshman to ex-convict in just two years because he took the rap for a vicious fraternity hazing that killed a friend and fellow student.

Dietrich goes on to say that if he had rejected "reasoning" in favor of his initial instincts then he wouldn't have become part of the goon squad fraternity at "prestigious" Harrington College that ended one life and ruined his own. Which suggests that two years in jail haven't taught Dietrich very much. Reason had less to do with his actions than a willful succession of instincts, all of them as crude and out-of-focus as "Followers" itself.

Dietrich recalls how he arrived at Harrington a nave farm boy (is there any other kind?) from Nebraska. He befriends two other freshmen: Allen (Jerry Laurino), a malleable dullard from Connecticut, and Steve (Eddie T. Robinson), a high-strung, upper- middle-class African-American nerd from New York.

The three form a cheerful, if tentative bond until KPL, the 800-pound gorilla of campus frats, sends out its call for new members. Dietrich and Allen are in while Steve is, in no uncertain terms, on the outs. Forced to choose between Steve's friendship and the dubious "networking benefits" of KPL camaraderie, Dietrich goes for the latter with predictably calamitous results.

Inspired by a 1993 hazing at New Jersey's Rider College (which didn't have fatal consequences, but was almost as brutal), "Followers" was made with a $50,000 budget and the bare bones of the production are harshly exposed throughout. Writer-director Jonathan M. Flicker should be commended for his initiative—and for setting off rhetorical brush fires on campuses where this movie has already been screened. But one suspects the proper venue for "Followers" is a high school auditorium, where it should be scrutinized by seniors who may feel an uncomfortable affinity with any and all of its star-crossed characters.

VILLAGE VOICE, 10/17/00, p. 136, Dennis Lim

There's a perverse integrity to the anti-hazing drama *Followers,* a movie so seamlessly and comprehensively dreadful that its very existence (let alone its appearance in theaters) beggars belief. Two freshmen buddies—one white, one black—try to join a neo-Nazi-ish fraternity, with calamitous results. The microbudget and the oblivious determination of writer-director Jonathan M. Flicker inspire a degree of underdog sympathy—though it's quickly obliterated by the hallucinogenically bad acting and script. Both are in fact well below the standards of the social-guidance movie, Flicker's apparent exemplar.

Also reviewed in:
NEW YORK TIMES, 10/13/00, p. E24, Lawrence Van Gelder

FRAGMENTS * JERUSALEM

A New Yorker Films release of a Ron and Jacqueline Havilio/Israel Film Service/Israel Broadcasting Authority/Fund for the Promotion of Israeli Quality films co-production. *Producer:* Ron Havilio and Jacqueline Havilio. *Director:* Ron Havilio. *Screenplay (English narration and English subtitles):* Ron Havilio. *Director of Photography:* Ron Havilio. *Editor:* Tor Ben Mayor and Yael Perlov. *Sound:* Jacqueline Havilio. *Running time:* 360 minutes. *MPAA Rating:* Not Rated.

CAST: Ron Havilio (narrator).

NEW YORK POST, 3/22/00, p. 53, Hannah Brown

An awkward blend of the political and the personal that doesn't quite gel, the chief problem with the film is its length. At nearly six hours, "Fragments" demands a great deal of patience and indulgence from the viewer.

Though the film is being screened in two approximately three-hour chunks, it simply goes on too long.

Havilio worked on this project for over 10 years, from 1986 to 1996, and assembled an amazing collection of rare archival material, including 19th-century engravings and photos, a Seventeen magazine article from the '50s about a typical Jerusalem teenager, newsreel footage of Independence Day parades from the '60s, film of a 1920 snowfall that blanketed Jerusalem and much more.

For those with a strong interest in the history of the city, it's worth seeing at least part of "Fragments" for this footage alone, as well as for Havilio's knowledge of and feeling for his birthplace.

But the problem comes when Havilio tries to mix his family's history with that of the city.

It is possible to make effective documentaries on personal subjects, as Alan Berliner has shown with "Nobody's Business" and "Intimate Stranger."

But when Havilio cuts moments with his wife and daughters with scenes of the destruction of the old neighborhood of Mamila, the contrast seems trivial and self-indulgent.

Later sections work better, such as one in which he looks at his father's decision to join the Haganah underground, the precursor to the Israeli army.

Havilio's musings, delivered in English, also often lapse into ponderous clichés.

Buildings in the "No Man's Land" in between Jordan and Israel in the '50s, "remain a monument to the hatred that sometimes grips mankind," he says, at one point.

"Fragments" could have been a brilliant but much shorter film. In its current form, it would work better being shown in installments on television than as a big-screen marathon.

VILLAGE VOICE, 3/28/00, p. 113, J. Hoberman

There's a strain of high modernist hubris that, predicated on the act of remembering, attempts to grasp and single-handedly transform antiquity. As personified by James Joyce, it's more evident in 20th-century literature than at the movies. But this week brings two ambitious epics working similar territory and clearing their own space on the scene: Ron Havilio's 1996 *Fragments * Jerusalem* and Krzysztof Kieslowski's 1989 *Decalogue*.

Havilio's monumental home movie, which, showing in two three-hour cycles, gets its first theatrical run after several festival screenings, and Kieslowski's 10-part telefilm, finally released here on video, both concern themselves with integrating an individual's private history into a city's (and by extension a civilization's) collective past. Indeed, as Havilio's title suggests, *Fragments * Jerusalem* is a conscious shoring up of ruins.

Twelve years in the making, at once a family photo-album and a national pageant, Havilio's magnum opus is, in some ways, comparable to the ongoing personal film diaries with which Lithuanian-born Jonas Mekas documents his displacement in America and, in others, analogous to the form of cine-archival history developed by Ken Burns in his various,PBS miniseries. Like Mekas, Havilio is a first-person filmmaker who serves as his own narrator—offering a guided tour through a self-curated museum whose ingenuity rivals that of Burns.

Exploring Jerusalem, Havilio is both a flaneur and a time traveler. Like the city he excavates, *Fragments * Jerusalem* is a film of unexpected byways. The streets are saturated with remembrance. One need't strain to make these phantoms contemporary. Jerusalem does not live in the past; its history and historical destiny exist in the present. Based on interpenetrated time strata and reveling in temporal match-cuts, the discontinuous here-and-now of Havilio's "fragments" has intimations of biblical antiquity on the one hand and the millennial future on the other.

As in Jerusalem itself, all periods coexist. Scenes typically combine past and present. *Fragments * Jerusalem* is profoundly anachronistic—among other things, it preserves the sense that motion pictures are a medium of (and not only for) preservation. Childhood memories merge with the remote past. *Fragments * Jerusalem* opens with an hour-long meditation on the filmmaker's birthplace, the no-longer-extant Mamila district—Jerusalem's commercial center during the British mandate, divided by a wall after the 1948 war of independence. When the city was reunited under Israeli rule in 1967, the shattered neighborhood was demolished, and remained a deserted construction site for nearly two decades. That Havilio filmed much of his Mamila footage during the *intifada* emphasizes the no-man's-land feel, even as the images of urban debris evoke the primal Jewish disaster—the destruction of the First Temple in 587 B.C.E.

In ways both significant and trivial, Havilio's family history is entwined with that of the city. Expelled from Spain in 1492, the Havilios arrived in Jerusalem by way of the Balkans. Some were cabalists, others vendors of sweets. Fired by messianic expectation, Havilio's maternal forebears came to Jerusalem from Vilnius three centuries later. The focus of millennial longing for nearly 2000 years, Jerusalem was again a majority Jewish city. Even before 1900, the overcrowded Jewish quarter spilled over and precipitated a wave of building outside the city walls—a geography mapped by the peregrinations of the Havilio family.

Again and again, the film recapitulates that passage through the Jaffa Gate, entering at various points between 1896 and 1996 the "dark, sloping alleys" of the labyrinthian old city with its incredible mix of Bedouins, Hasidim, Ottoman soldiers, and European tourists. The snowfall of January 1992 recalls the great winter storm of 1920 and the birth of the filmmaker's father. The *intifada* harks back to the 1921 pogrom, in which, for the first time in centuries, Muslims attacked their Jewish neighbors. Yet, for all the tumult of wars, riots, and terrorist attacks (Jewish and Arab) that the movie records, *Fragments * Jerusalem* retains a serene detachment in its chronicle of daily life.

Intercut throughout with unpretentious domestic scenes, *Fragments * Jerusalem* suggests an enchanted picture-book in which time continually folds back on itself. Havilio mixes tinted postcards with old actualités and period lithographs, incorporating both his parents' 8mm movies and archival footage from the period of Zionist idealism, reading from newspapers and period accounts, playing phonograph records (a mainly Mediterranean mix of Greek laments, Arabic, pop, Israeli tangos, Hebrew prayers, and Portuguese fados). The presence of Havilio's three young daughters also serves to mark the passage of time.

The film's last image is of an illuminated Ferris wheel set up outside the old city walls in the wasteland of Mamila. The circle is unbroken but the film itself remains unfinished. Havilio has as yet been unable to raise funds for a third cycle that would evoke the Israel he missed while living abroad in the 1950s. It would also bring home Jerusalem's most persistent issue of spatiotemporal authority by focusing on the house in Ein Karem, the once-Arab neighborhood where Havilio has lived with his family for the last quarter-century.

Also reviewed in:
CHICAGO TRIBUNE, 5/12/00, Friday/p. H, John Petrakis
NEW YORK TIMES, 3/22/00, p. E3, Anita Gates
VARIETY, 10/5-11/98, p. 71, Ken Eisner

FREQUENCY

A New Line Cinema release of a Gregory Hoblit film. *Executive Producer:* Robert Shaye and Richard Saperstein. *Producer:* Hawk Koch, Gregory Hoblit, Bill Carraro, and Toby Emmerich. *Director:* Gregory Hoblit. *Screenplay:* Toby Emmerich. *Director of Photography:* Alar Kivilo. *Editor:* David Rosenbloom. *Music:* Michael Kamen. *Music Editor:* Tom Kramer. *Sound:* Douglas Ganton and (music) Joel Iwataki. *Sound Editor:* Tom Bellfort. *Casting:* Amanda Mackey Johnson and Cathy Sandrich. *Production Designer:* Paul Eads. *Art Director:* Dennis

Davenport. *Set Designer:* Elis Lam. *Set Decorator:* Gordon Sim. *Set Dresser:* David Evans. *Special Effects:* Martin Malivoire. *Costumes:* Elisabetta Deraldo. *Make-up:* Donald J. Mowat. *Special Make-up:* John Caglione, Jr. *Stunt Coordinator:* G. A. Aguilar. *Running time:* 100 minutes. *MPAA Rating:* PG-13.

CAST: Dennis Quaid (Frank Sullivan);   Jim Caviezel (John Sullivan);   Shawn Doyle (Jack Shepard);   Elizabeth Mitchell (Julia Sullivan);   Andre Braugher (Satch DeLeon);   Noah Emmerich (Gordo Hersch);   Melissa Errico (Samantha Thomas);   Daniel Henson (Johnny Sullivan at 6 years);   Jordan Bridges (Graham Gibson);   Stephen Joffe (Gordo Hersch at 8 years);   Jack McCormack (Commander O'Connell);   Peter MacNeill (Butch Foster);   Michael Cera (Gordie Jr. at 10 years); Marin Hinkle (Sissy Clark); Richard Sali (Chuck Hayes);   Nesbitt Blaisdell (Fred Shepard);   Joan Heney (Laura Shepherd);   Jessica Meyer (Teenage Runaway); Kirsten Bishopric (Carrie Reynolds);   Rocco Sisto (Daryl Adams);   Rosemary DeAngelis (Mrs. Finelli);   Dick Cavett and Brian Greene (Themselves);   Melissa Fitzgerald (Linda Hersch); John DiBenedetto (Con Ed Supervisor);   Terry Serpico and Brian Smyj (Con Ed Workers); Nicole Brier (Stoned Teenage Girl);   Brantley Bush (Young Intern);   David Huband (Lounge Bartender); Timothy Brown (Roof Man Billy);   Chuck Margiotta (Pedestal Man Gino);   Karen Glave (Lanni DeLeon);   Frank McAnulty (Desk Sergeant);   Derek Aasland (Stoned Man); Jim McAleese (Cozy Bartender);   Catherine Burdon and Jennifer Baxter (Young Women); Desmond Campbell (Forensic Tech Hector);   Danny Johnson and Colm Magner (Uniformed Cops); Brigitte Kingsley (Bar Waitress); Tucker Robin (Frank, Jr.).

CHRISTIAN SCIENCE MONITOR, 4/28/00, p. 11, David Sterritt

Good science fiction thrives on innovation, and not every SF saga has to follow established rules.

According to an old convention of time-travel stories, for instance, even a tiny alteration in the past can affect the future in drastic ways. A writer can change this notion, but there should be a good reason, and the story should indicate why its rules are different from the ones obeyed by previous tales.

"Frequency," the new SF fantasy from director Gregory Hoblit, waters down the time-travel rules for reasons that are all too apparent.

The movie's main interests aren't the fascinating paradoxes of time travel at all, but the thrills and chills of ordinary melodrama. Although the plot has a science-fiction premise, this only sets the stage for a story oscillating between family sentimentality, on one hand, and the violence of a serial-killer manhunt, on the other. These are reliable box-office commodities, so the picture may do well financially. But science-fiction buffs won't find much here to broaden their horizons.

The main characters are Frank Sullivan, a New York City firefighter, and police officer John Sullivan, his son. Tinkering with an old ham-radio set one evening. John finds himself in contact with the last person he would have expected: his father, Frank. who died years earlier in the line of duty.

Realizing that they've entered a radio-wave time warp—the cause turns out to be a magnetic storm on the sun—they make the most of the occasion, with John telling Frank how to avoid the accident that's due to kill him.

This alters their family's past in profound ways: Frank survives the deadly fire, and John finds his mind flooded with new memories of their additional years together.

But history has changed in negative ways too, putting the life of another loved relative on a collision course with a demented murderer.

Burning up the airwaves with their radio hookup, John and Frank join forces across the years to track down the killer, and deepen their own relationship in the process.

"Frequency" builds a fair degree of suspense in its sometimes violent crime sequences, and many viewers will shed a tear over the family affection that John and Frank share during their gradual progress to a genuinely sweet finale.

But while family values are the films strongest emotional suit, a single-minded emphasis on them weakens the story's underlying logic.

Frank and John make enormous changes to the past events of their lives, and all the effects of these alterations revolve around their own domestic situation, as if the rest of New York—even the rest of the planet—were a mere backdrop to their household.

A more sophisticated yarn would pursue its time-warping possibilities in less restricted directions, tying the fate of one family to the larger world around it.

"Frequency" is warm and endearing. but it could have been a great deal more.

LOS ANGELES TIMES, 4/28/00, Calendar/p. 2, Kenneth Turan

"The past is a funny thing," John Sullivan (Jim Caviezel) says in "Frequency," an effective but finally overreaching science-fiction thriller, but even he doesn't yet appreciate just how out of the ordinary it can be.

Cleverly written by Toby Emmerich and tightly directed by the very capable Gregory Hoblit, "Frequency" takes a standard sci-fi stratagem and runs with it. No, its plot doesn't make conventional sense, but we are happy to buy into it—at least up to a point. We empower films like this because we want to, because filmmaking skill encourages us to suspend disbelief and agree, even if only for awhile, that seeing really is believing.

Links between the present, the future and the past, the ability to move people (or in this case, information) through time is a science-fiction staple with understandable appeal. Who wouldn't want to go back and correct a past mistake or embark, with the wisdom of hindsight, on a path foolishly not taken?

There is, of course, a classic hitch to this perpetual daydream. Anything you redo in the past by definition affects the future (that's in fact the plot hook of both "Terminator" epics), and often in ways that are impossible to foresee. It's a domino effect with potentially catastrophic implications, a poison pill that lies at the heart of this film's complicated structure.

"Frequency" opens with something very concrete and specific: a graphic tanker truck accident on an offramp of New York's George Washington Bridge. This bravura sequence not only sets up Frank Sullivan (Dennis Quaid) as the kind of casually heroic fireman who thinks risking his life is no big deal, it establishes the action bona fides of director Hoblit.

Working with cinematographer Alar Kivilo and editor David Rosenbloom, Hoblit knows how to ratchet up the tension and isn't afraid to do so, giving us reason to be patient through the extensive exposition that follows before the excitement starts up again.

Though it looks contemporary, that rescue scene takes place on Oct. 10, 1969. Sullivan, married to the appealing Julia (Elizabeth Mitchell) and with a 6-year-old son named Johnny, lives in Bayside, Queens, and is by all appearances the happiest family man in all five boroughs.

In whatever time he can spare from teaching Johnny to ride a bike, Sullivan is a ham radio operator, and that night turns out to be a special one. Aurora borealis, the northern lights, are visible over Queens and doing strange things to the atmosphere. "I'm picking up frequencies," Sullivan says, "from places I could never reach." No kidding.

Just like that, it's 30 years later, Oct. 10, 1999, the northern lights have returned, and little Johnny is grown up into darkly handsome John, a New York City police detective. Conveniently enough he still lives in the Bayside house he grew up in though his father is now dead and his mother moved to an apartment.

Rummaging through a closet, John comes across his dad's old shortwave set and, on a whim, sets it up again while a TV talk-show voice in the background philosophizes about "time being far more fluid than anyone could have imagined." A voice crackles through the static that sounds awfully familiar. Could it be his father, speaking to him from that same night 30 years ago? Though it astounds both men when they realize what's happening, that's exactly the case.

Suddenly, John realizes what the date is. On Oct. 11, 1969, his father died a hero's death in a warehouse fire. Desperately, the heedlessly, he gives his father some hurried advice over the radio that he hopes will save his life.

Apparently not a sci-fi fan, John doesn't realize that attempting to make changes in the past will have powerful and unforeseen consequences in the present, but the rest of "Frequency" will teach him that lesson in a big way. In fact, John starts to feel he's living in two realities at once, the one he remembers and the new one his actions have somehow created.

This is, as noted, not the most realistic of scenarios but it's the gift of "Frequency" to make us feel it's plausible. Strong acting is a key, especially by Caviezel, memorable as the AWOL soldier in "The Thin Red Line," and by Andre Braugher as the policeman friend of two generations of Sullivans.

Also critical is Hoblit's ability to add a level of realism to the proceedings. As he demonstrated in his two previous features, "Primal Fear" and "Fallen," Hoblit has the kind of driving, involving style that is capable of creating credibility for far-fetched situations. In a scenario where reality can change in an instant, that's a formidable talent to have.

Unfortunately, "Frequency," after keeping its balance over much treacherous terrain, greedily overreaches and stumbles badly at the close. Screenwriter Emmerich (brother of actor Noah Emmerich, who plays John Sullivan's pal Gordo Hersch) ends up trying for one twist too many and causing the whole delicately balanced house of cards to collapse. If only he could go back to the past and rewrite that part of the script, we'd all be grateful.

NEW YORK, 5/8/00, p. 72, Peter Rainer

In *Frequency*, Jim Caviezel is a Queens cop who ends up communicating, courtesy of an old ham radio and a rip in the space-time fabric, with his firefighter father (Dennis Quaid), who perished in a 1969 blaze. It's a good thing the radio is a ham, because all the actors are, too. So is the story. I'm all in favor of astrophysicists trying to get the lowdown on superstrings and the theory-of-everything, but I wonder if it's all worth it if the result is something like *Frequency*, which has so little faith in its *Twilight Zone*-ish yarn that it resorts to a pulpy serial-killer subplot to juice the mumbo-jumbo. Also, the film's overreliance on nostalgia for the World Champion '69 Mets seems a bit misplaced since the 2000 team is looking even better.

NEW YORK POST, 4/28/00, p. 55, Lou Lumenick

One of the reasons I love movies is that the right actor and director can make you believe passionately in the wildest storyline—and "Frequency" had me watching through misty eyes, at least for the first half.

For your consideration, as Rod Serling used to say on "The Twilight Zone," I give you NYPD Detective John Sullivan (Jim Caviezel of "The Thin Red Line"). He has a perpetually hurt look, drinks too much, and his girlfriend has walked out on him.

Before you can say "It's a Wonderful Life," he discovers a great gift in a closet of the Bayside, Queens, home where he's lived his entire life. It's an old ham radio on which, through some celestial quirk, he's able to contact his late father, Frank (Dennis Quaid).

Better still, John starts chatting with the old man, a firefighter, on the day before the defining event of the son's childhood—dad's death in an awful blaze 30 years earlier.

John is able to wise up an unbelieving Frank and save his father's life. Suddenly, pictures of a middle-aged Frank appear on the walls—and there's not likely to be a dry eye in the audience.

But messing with the past has its consequences, as any science-fiction fan knows. It's giving away a lot less than the spoiler-filled trailer to report that Frank's survival helps a serial killer—whose victims will include John's mom (Elizabeth Mitchell), unless father and son, working together, can alter the past again.

It was there that the movie started to let me down. I was buying it, largely thanks to Quaid's stellar work and the skill of the director (Gregory Hoblit of "Primal Fear") at shifting gears from nail-biting suspense to male-weepy scenes that put "Field of Dreams" to shame.

But the plot becomes ever-more complicated and credibility-defying. I started wondering: How on earth can they ever end this in a dramatically satisfying fashion?

The you-can-have-it-all ending that they settled on didn't work for me, but I'll be darned if I can think of a better one.

The movie's flawless evocation of 1969 Queens, where I grew up—the Mets' World Series' victory figures prominently in Toby Emmerich's script, which has many subtle touches and a neat joke about Yahoo—deeply resonated with me, as did the movie's theme.

Quaid, one of our most underrated actors, has rarely been better—and he has great chemistry with Caviezel.

My head says "Frequency" has a 3½-star first half and 2½-star second half, averaging out to three stars.

But my heart says: Don't miss this one.

NEWSDAY, 4/28/00, Part II/p. B6, Gene Seymour

"Better Living Through Sunspots" would have worked as a title for "Frequency," given the transformative effects of unusual astral phenomena on the lives of two honest, hard-working guys from Queens.

One is Frank Sullivan (Dennis Quaid), a swashbuckling firefighter whose reckless disregard for his own skin belies the coziness of his home life with devoted spouse Julia (Elizabeth Mitchell) and young son John. It is October, 1969, and what Frank doesn't know is that his beloved Mets are about to pull off a miracle, and he won't live to see it happen since he's about to take one chance too many.

Flash-forward 30 years to the same house, where only John Sullivan (Jim Caviezel from "The Thin Red Line") now lives. He has grown into a sullen NYPD homicide "hotshot" who carries an ache for the long-dead father he barely knew.

As a half-hearted effort to commemorate the 30th anniversary of his dad's death in a warehouse fire, John tinkers with Frank's old ham radio while solar flares dance overhead in the New York night. John is startled to hear his father's voice come through. John doesn't take too much time to understand why this is happening. He warns his dad of the latter's impending death and tells him how to avoid it.

Which Frank does. Now the only problem is that John's mom, who had been alive and well in the present time, is long dead and gone, one of several women murdered by a serial killer way back when. So, of course, father and son team up across several presidential administrations to stop him cold.

The time-spanning premise in Toby Emmerich's script has so many knots in it that one would think it could only work if played for laughs. Yet "Frequency" manages, by the skin of its teeth, to get away with playing this convoluted enchanted thriller with a straight face and surprising control.

Once again, director Gregory Hoblit ("Primal Fear") bears down on one's senses with clusters of tight close-ups, and he takes his foot off the gas when you wish he'd move things along. But not even his heavy hand can keep the audience from playing along with the complex, if improbable games played with time.

The only thing that would have made "Frequency's" crowd-pleasing finish more gratifying would be for things to have turned out as well for the Mets last year as they did in 1969. And, maybe, for Dick Cavett (sitting early in the film in what looks like Charlie Rose's chair) to still have a late-night talk show.

SIGHT AND SOUND, 8/00, p. 44, Tom Tunney

1969. Frank Sullivan, a fireman and ham radio enthusiast, lives with his wife Julia and six-year-old son John in New York.

In the same house 30 years later the adult John, a policeman, sets up his late father's long-neglected ham radio. Due to unusual climatic conditions, he is able to contact Frank, sitting in the same room with the same radio 30 years before. John tells his father that he will die the next day in a fire. Forewarned, Frank survives the blaze. But his survival has one unforeseen consequence: the unsolved 1969 case of a local serial murderer—which John is working on—now has 10 victims instead of three, one of whom is John's mother, Julia.

Briefed by John from the 1999 police files, Frank sets out to stop the mystery killer striking again. He saves one would-be victim by talking to her all night. The killer, Jack Shepard, a policeman, realises he is being followed when Frank zeroes in on his next victim. Shepard beats Frank up and steals his driving licence, which he leaves beside his victim's body. Frank becomes the police's prime suspect. John tells him to hide his wallet (which contains the killer's fingerprints) in the house. John retrieves it 30 years on and is able to identify Shepard as the killer.

Back in 1969, Frank is arrested. After being threatened by Shepard in his cell, Frank escapes, pursued by the killer. Shepard appears to drown during a fight with Frank at the waterfront.

Later, John tells Frank that Julia is still due to be killed by Shepard. As they speak, Shepard appears: as a young man in 1969, he tries to kill Frank; and as an older man in 1999, he tries to kill John. In 1999, an older version of Frank turns up and shoots Shepard dead. Back in 1969, Shepard disintegrates.

In 1999 Frank, John and their family enjoy a game of baseball.

Frequency is the story of a father, a son and a holy ghost. The spiritual dimension of director Gregory Hoblit's entertaining, if baffling film takes the form of sunspots in the night sky which allow detective John Sullivan to communicate with his father Frank 30 years ago. This intriguing idea—which sees information rather than people journey though time—sets *Frequency* apart from other time travel movies such as *Time after Time* (1979) and the *Back to the Future* series. But like these films, *Frequency* has its share of sly ironies which play on the audience's knowledge of the course of history: the adult John, for instance, gives his brother 30 years' advance notice to invest in e-commerce; while back in 1969 Frank imagines mobile phones to look like "big field radios they have in the army".

But such references to contemporary reality are rare—perhaps an indication of the inherently preposterous nature of Toby Emmerich's screenplay. Despite a commendation from physics professor Brian Greene—who appears in the film, first as a young man in 1969, then 30 years later—it's difficult not to notice certain dramatic flaws in *Frequency*'s speculative narrative logic. As the parallel realities pile up like successive drafts of a developing screenplay—John is able to tamper with the past by forewarning his father of key events—the tension drains from the film: if John is able to change the course of given event—you're left thinking—everything, including the danger posed by serial killer Shepard, is open for revision, for erasure (in his climactic fight with Frank in 1969, Shepard literally disintegrates. For the most part, Hoblit distracts us from the manifest absurdities of his plot through taut and pacey direction. Having helmed episodes of television's *NYPD Blue*, he's far better on the mechanics of police procedure than he is on the dizzying implications of his time-travel scenario. There's also an impressive attention to detail—Frank's cigarette burn on the table, for instance, appears suddenly 30 years later—which suggests *Frequency* has at least superficially been well thought out.

Ultimately, though, for all its multiplying versions of history and its chaos theory approach to narrative causality, *Frequency* is more about preserving the past than changing it. Like *Back to the Future* and *Peggy Sue Got Married, Frequency* evokes the past as an innocent, more wholesome time. The scenes with Frank might be set in 1969 but there's little indication of the turbulent social change then taking place. First glimpsed in an all-night bar, Shepard, the serial killer with designs on John's mother, is the malevolent threat to the stability of the Sullivan family unit. Having blotted Shepard from history, John recaptures the family values of his childhood in the film's final scene—an idyllic multi-generational game of baseball. This may smack of wish-fulfilment, but then the idea that the scene could be one of many alternative realities is never too far away to upset the tidy sense of closure.

VILLAGE VOICE, 5/2/00, p. 134, Dennis Lim

A movie primed to make grown men cry, the time-travel thriller *Frequency* comes on like a sensitive-jock older brother to the cutely paranormal alt-destiny reveries *Sliding Doors* and *Me Myself I*. Set in two intersecting time periods and under a cloud of moist manliness, the film uses fanciful cosmological chicanery to hatch a doleful, soft-boiled paean to absent fathers and baseball-kindled nostalgia (think *Back to the Field of Dreams)*.

John Sullivan (Jim Caviezel) is a Queens cop whose firefighter father (Dennis Quaid) died on the job in 1969. Now in his mid 30s and irreversibly scarred by this early ordeal, John discovers Dad's old ham radio, and—thanks to a meteorological fluke (an electrical storm sparking aurora-borealis-like fireworks in the night sky)—finds himself talking to his father, Frank. It's exactly 30 years ago, mere days before Frank will perish in a warehouse fire. By predicting the outcome of a World Series game, John convinces his father that his receiver is picking up signals from the future, and persuades him, at the fateful moment, to ignore the instincts that would prove fatal.

The first third of *Frequency* plays like the entirety of a generic time-travel movie. But the screenplay, by Toby Emmerich (a New Line exec), lingers stubbornly on the hazardous domino effect of rewriting history. John learns to his dismay that, in saving his father, he unwittingly paves the way for the grisly murder of his mother (Elizabeth Mitchell). Separated by three decades, father and son collaborate to catch a serial killer. Frank's preventive measures in 1969 resurrect long-dead victims in 1999; each time a new parallel universe is created, freshly minted memories compete for space with old ones in John's increasingly addled brain. The mindfuck potential—through the roof given the younger Sullivan's alarmingly mutable surroundings—goes untapped (as does the implicit surrealist comedy; the premise cries out for a Jonze/Kaufman remake). Instead, Emmerich and the reliably unsubtle director Gregory Hoblit work so hard at smoothing out any Möbius-strip complications that only the tidiest slipknots remain.

Caviezel, the dusky, serenely haunted transcendentalist of *The Thin Red Line,* is, against all odds, sympathetic and believably depressed, though neither he nor Quaid can withstand the climactic tsunami of treacle. At heart a shameless go-getting parable (the obligatory joke about time-travel prescience concerns the acquisition of Yahoo! stock), *Frequency* dispenses with the notion of time traveler as arrogant meddler. The movie's fantasy hyperspace offers amusingly absolute control. (The critical rule: Mess with history all you want, and don't even think of stopping until everything is exactly as you want it.) If nothing else, *Frequency* succeeds as a testament to the power of oblivious, tick-like tenacity and an inflated sense of entitlement.

Also reviewed in:
CHICAGO TRIBUNE, 4/28/00, Friday/p. A, Mark Caro
NEW YORK TIMES, 4/28/00, p. E9, Stephen Holden
VARIETY, 4/17-23/00, p. 26, Todd McCarthy
WASHINGTON POST, 4/28/00, p. C1, Rita Kempley
WASHINGTON POST, 4/28/00, Weekend/p. 51, Michael O'Sullivan

FROM THE EDGE OF THE CITY

A Mythos Productions release in association with Rosebud/Hot Shot Productions/Picture This! Entertainment and the Greek Film Centre. *Executive Producer:* Maria Powell. *Producer:* Dionysis Samiotis and Anastasios Vasiliou. *Director:* Constantinos Giannaris. *Screenplay (Greek and Russian with English subtitles):* Constantinos Giannaris. *Director of Photography:* George Argiroiliopoulos. *Editor:* Ioanna Spiliopoulou. *Music:* Akis Daoutis. *Sound:* Dinos Kittou. *Casting:* Spyros Charalambous. *Production Designer:* Roula Nicolaou. *Art Director:* Michalis Samiotis. *Costumes:* Sanny Alberti. *Make-up:* Eleftheria Efthymiou. *Running time:* 94 minutes. *MPAA Rating:* Not Rated.

CAST: Stathis Papouidis (Sasha); Dimitris Papadoulidis (Giorgos); Theodora Tzimou (Natasha); Costas Cotsianidis (Cotsian); Panagiotis Chartomtsidis (Panagiotis); Anestis Polychronidis (Anestis); Simela Chartomatsidi (Sasha's Sister); Emilios Chilakis (Nikos); Vasias Eleftheriadis (Father); Constantine Giannaris (Voice of Interviewer); Kostas Gogos (Pimp in Brothel); Savas Iliadis, Aristidis Ioannidis, Stavros Karasavvidis, Giannis Mavridis, Giorgos Pasalidis, and Christos Polychronidis (Children); Nikos Kamontos (Philippos); Giannis Kontraphouris and Tasos Nousias (Pimps); Giannis Kotsiphas (Dimitrakis); Tamila Koulieva-Karantinaki (Voice of Natasha); Giorgos Mavridis (Chorny); Eleni Philippa (Madam in Brothel); Nina Polychronidou (Voice of Mother); Paulina Santalova (Svetlana); Evri Sophroniadou (Mother); Katerina Takouli (Olga); Stelios Tsemboglidis (Stelios); Anastasios Vasiliou (Voice of Theodora's Father); Silvia Venizelea (Theodora); Panagiota Vlachosotirou (Elenitsa); Argyris Xafis (Taxi Driver).

LOS ANGELES TIMES, 12/15/00, Calendar/p. 12, Kevin Thomas

"From the Edge of the City" is set in today's Athens but could just as easily take place in Los Angeles or any other metropolis that attracts immigrants seeking a better life. The title of Constantinos Giannaris' raw, brutal yet lyrical film refers to Menidi, a community of Pontians, Greeks who emigrated to Russia, settling along the Black Sea, but have now returned to their ancestral homeland to face hardship and discrimination.

You won't see the Parthenon in this movie, and in fact Athens looks and feels a lot like L.A., where some people have plenty of money but more have very little. Sasha (Stathis Papadopoulos) is a rugged 17-year-old who arrived in Greece at age 10. He's frequently overcome by memories of running free with other youngsters over rural fields in Russia yet is attracted to the glittery, fast side of urban life with its treacherous lure of maximum cash for minimal effort, which has become his goal.

No student, he's fed up with the grind of working in construction and becomes part of the world of sex and drugs along with many of his pals. We learn that he's been working as a male hustler since he was 13, and now his older friend and mentor Giorgos (Dimitris Papoulidis) wants him to become a pimp.

Sasha and Giorgos are sparring partners and take pride in staying in top shape, and not just for appearances: They must be prepared to defend themselves or enforce their will at any moment. They also live hard, with a lot of partying, lots of women and late nights. Drug dealing—and using—goes hand in hand with life in the fast lane, but Sasha resists the hard drugs enslaving his friends.

The turning point arrives when he takes over prostitute Natasha (Theodora Tzimou) from, Giorgos because he feels she's become too emotionally involved with him. Natasha is apparently an illegal immigrant, which means that she's a virtual slave to be exploited sexually for maximum profit. Sasha accepts the realities of the system, but since both he and Natasha are young and beautiful the question becomes whether Sasha can keep emotion out of their relationship. Indeed, can he stave off all human feelings, which he must do if he is not to cross Giorgos, who has the eyes of a dead man and is unmistakably ruthless?

Because Sasha is as reflective as he is charismatic, it is not hard to become involved in his fate and that of Natasha. Principal among Sasha's pals are his likable neighborhood sidekick Cotsian (Costas Cotsianidis), who's beginning to be more in demand as a hustler than Sasha because he's younger and newer to the streets; and Panagiota (Panagiota Vlachosotirou), made vulnerable because he may be gay while his hustler pals revel in their machismo.

There's something of the young Robert De Niro in Papadopoulos, with his direct gaze, looking out at a harsh world with eyes that are still full of innocence and longing yet register the wounds of a brutal, hardening existence. "From the Edge of the City" bristles with an energy and passion intensified by Akis Daoutis' driving hard-rock score. Constantine Giannaris has made sharp and fresh a story both timeless and universal.

NEW YORK POST, 4/21/00, p. 51, Hannah Brown

The story of alienated teenagers from Kazakh families living in a drab suburb of Athens, "From the Edge of the City" feels like a Greek version of "My Own Private Idaho."

Director and writer Constantinos Giannaris set out to make a documentary about "Pontians," the children of ethnic Greek immigrants from Soviet Khazakstan who moved to Greece after the fall of the Berlin Wall.

Using the young people he met while researching his documentary, Giannaris decided to make a feature film instead—one infused with intensity and sensuousness.

The hero, or anti-hero, is 17-year-old Sasha (Stathis Papadopoulos). Too bored, lazy and angry to get up at 5 a.m. for his construction job, he quits, then spends his days taking drugs with his friends and his nights hanging out at discos.

To support his drug habit, he works as a male prostitute, but he doesn't consider himself gay. In fact, he has fantasies of the most conventional kind about marrying Elena (Panagiota Vlachosotirou), a cute, sexy Pontian girl with a rich boyfriend.

His cousin, Giorgos (Dimitri Papoulidis), recruits him as a junior pimp for Natasha (Theodora Tzimou).

He begins to have feelings for her, leading to problems with the brutal Giorgos.

Toward the end, the plot becomes confusing, and the film suffers, like the lives of its characters, from a certain aimlessness.

But the direction is sure-footed and energetic, and the stylish cinematography gives the film a kind of romantic glamour.

Best of all, Stathis Papadopoulos—a non-professional, like all the cast members—has a riveting screen presence as Sasha.

SIGHT AND SOUND, 3/00, p. 43, José Arroyo

Athens, Greece, the present. Sasha, a 17-year-old petty thief and rent boy, rollerskates around town with his friends Kotsian and Panagiotis, breaking into cars and stealing radios. Sasha has quit the construction job he hated but is now too old to do much business selling himself. He scrounges money by occasionally bullying younger boys like Kotsian out of their nightly takings or by servicing rich women. Even former regular customer Nikos now prefers the younger Panagiotis. When Giorgos, an older pimp, proposes Sasha take over the handling of Russian prostitute Natasha while he finds a buyer, Sasha agrees.

Sasha is in love with Elenitsa but she's finished with him because of her father's objections to him. Sasha begins to have feelings for Natasha and decides to run away with her. Meanwhile his friend Anestis dies from bad heroin and Panagiotis falls to his death while trying to escape from Nikos' apartment. Sasha brings Natasha to his parents' house but his father instantly recognises her as a prostitute and kicks them out. Sasha asks Kotsian to call him a taxi but Kotsian betrays him and brings Giorgos instead. In a fight, Sasha accidentally kills Giorgos. Natasha goes away with her new owners. The police drive Sasha away.

From the Edge of the City fits into a long and illustrious tradition of films about young no-hopers on the road to nowhere, such as William Wyler's *Dead End* (1937), Luis Buñuel's *Los olvidados* (1950) and Hector Babenco's *Pixote* (1981). But the gang depicted in *From the Edge of the City* is not just marginalised by youth, poverty and criminality but also by cultural dislocation. It depicts the flip side to (and would make a perfect double bill with) Ana Kokkinos' recent *Head On*. Both depict social, sexual and cultural conflicts within a Greek diaspora. But where Kokkinos sets her film in the context of Greek immigrants in Australia, the kids in *From the Edge* are Russian Pontians, people of Greek ancestry from the Black Sea area of Kazakhstan who returned to their ancestral homeland in 1990 only to find themselves strangers in their new country.

The great achievement of *From the Edge of the City* is the way it successfully conveys a sense of multidimensional alienation throughout. The boys are old enough to be considered sexually over the hill but not yet adults. They are not as ostracised as the Albanians they insult, but have no illusions they'll be accepted as fully Greek. Most reside in Menidi, a suburb of Athens, but make a living in Omonia, Athens' famous sex and crime district. While they sell their bodies to men, they distinguish themselves from 'faggots'. Sex is easily available, love visible but out of reach. They don't fit into their 'natural' identities (family, ethnic, national, sexual) yet have themselves formed a community with its own values.

Structurally, the film focuses on an individual, Sasha, who is allegorised as a representative of the group. The narration veers between a third-person narrator who sees everything and a first-person account by Sasha, addressed directly to the camera, in response to an unseen interrogator. Set mostly at night and grittily shot with a somewhat faded look, the film contrasts the poverty of the characters' present reality with the plenitude of their imaginary past (brilliant sunlight, sharper imagery, richly coloured straw tones). The film combines quickly edited stop-motion photography, creating the impression of a headlong rush, with freeze frames (particularly in the sex scenes) that convey a sense of dead time. Even the acting contributes to the film's depiction of diasporic alienation, of belonging to several places and nowhere at all, by combining professional actors with street kids. The latter's presence has a curious effect: their occasionally clumsy line readings (in Russian and Greek) simultaneously remind us we're seeing a movie and that they are not actors and yet the film seems more authentic *because* they're not actors.

Director Giannaris knows his film history: the opening, with the boys rollerskating through Athens, is straight out of one of Jean-Daniel Cadinot's porn movies; there are several references to *My Own Private Idaho* and Jean Genet. But Giannaris also knows how to direct. For example, there's a small scene where the gang is hanging out and Sasha and Kotsian begin to dance. Half way through, it we realise the scene is composed of one complexly choreographed, extremely long Steadicam shot, using non-professional actors; and yet dramatic value and characterisation are not sacrificed. It's this skilful but never flashy treatment which makes *From the Edge of the City* such a pleasure.

VILLAGE VOICE, 4/25/00, p. 142, Dennis Lim

A free-associative initiation to an altogether different kind of teenage wasteland [the reference is to *The Virgin Suicides*] Constantinos Giannaris's *From the Edge of the City* hurtles along with a heedless motion that, in accordance with the laws of physics if not of narrative, can only end with tragic abruptness. The city in question is Athens; 17-year-old Sasha and his friends are Kazakh refugees of Greek origin, doubly displaced youth who have fallen into a grueling routine of theft, prostitution, and drug use. The mood is despondent, the skimpy plot despondently familiar. Entrusted with the care of a hooker about to be sold by her paramour to evil provincial pimps, Sasha puts himself in danger to save her. Giannaris tries anything, everything—jump cuts, zip pans, bravura Steadicam, POV shots, to-camera asides, split-second interpolations—and scrambles the movie together in a flailing style that favors harsh juxtapositions: hand-held agitation and freeze frames, deafening techno and dead silence, dutifully squalid grit and outrageous fantasy lyricism. The viewer, though unavoidably alert, is before long too numb to care.

Also reviewed in:
NEW YORK TIMES, 4/21/00, p. E22, Stephen Holden
VARIETY, 1/25-31/99, p. 77, Philip Kemp

GENDERNAUTS

A First Run Features release of a Hyena Films production in association with WDR/Arte. *Producer:* Monika Treut. *Director:* Monika Treut. *Screenplay:* Monika Treut. *Director of Photography:* Elfi Mikesch. *Editor:* Eric Schefter. *Music:* Georg Kajanus. *Sound:* Andreas Pietsch and (music) Pierre Brandt. *Production Designer:* Madeleine Dewald. *Running time:* 86 minutes. *MPAA Rating:* Not Rated.

WITH: Sandy Stone; Texas Tomboy; Susan Stryker; Max Valerio; Jordy Jones; Stafford; Tornado; Hida Viloria; Annie Sprinkle; Joan Jett Blakk; Sister Roma; Queer David; Mo B. Dick; Uncle Louie; Willy Rider; Nicky Fingers; Lucky 7; Duke; Mark Freeman; Ray Rea; Veronica Register; Linette Martinez; Barry Zevin; Chrystal Weston; Baby Zeff; Dieta Sixt; Roland Scheikowski; Conny Champagne; Klara Lux; Eva Koenigova; Pearle Harbour; Elvis Herselvis; Veronica Klaus; Bob Davis; Juerg Roffler; Andreas Gerber; Tammy Hall.

NEW YORK POST, 2/4/00, p. 55, Hannah Brown

You can't be too rich or too thin, but you can spend too much time obsessing over gender issues, as "Gendernauts" proves.

The director of this documentary, Monika Treut, travels to San Francisco—a city one of the film's interviewees calls the "transgender mecca"—to explore the phenomenon of women who seek to become men through hormonal therapy.

The film is narrated by the extraordinarily annoying Sandy Stone, one of many jargon-spouting academics who appear.

Proclaiming herself "the goddess of cyberspace" (the film is filled with "cyber" references, although it isn't clear what computers or the Internet have to do with gender), she announces that the concept of only two genders is terribly limiting and sets off to set matters straight, so to speak, by interviewing a collection of Bay Area residents.

While there may be more than two genders in the world, apparently there are only two professions in San Francisco: professor and video artist.

The one big name in the movie is performance artist Annie Sprinkle, who displays some unambiguously feminine cleavage and contributes a profoundly unpleasant video clip showing her being intimate with the survivor of a botched female-to-male sex-change operation.

The rest of the film is merely annoying, as viewers may be tempted to yell "Get a life!" at women who undergo dangerous, untested drug therapies and multiple surgeries just so they will look and feel more macho.

SIGHT AND SOUND, 9/00, p. 42, José Arroyo

Over images of spotted hyenas in the wild, director Monika Treut tells us that nature can be more inventive than culture. The female of this species has a clitoris that looks like a penis but also serves as a birth channel; she's larger, heavier and more aggressive than her male counterpart and leads other hyenas in packs.

Treut then introduces Sandy Stone, academic and "Goddess of Cyberspace". A series of interviews with people who inhabit a variety of gender identities follows.

With cinematographer Elfi Mikesch, Monika Treut has over the years produced a series of films notably—*Seduction: The Cruel Woman (1985)*, about a Hamburg dominatrix, and *The Virgin Machine* (1988)—which consistently pushed the envelope in terms of sexual and gender representation. But her latest film *Gendernauts*, a documentary focusing on a group of transgender people, is a disappointment both as a film and as an argument about gender.

Formally, *Gendernauts* is a grubby exercise. Treut makes no attempt to create moments of poetry or beauty. What we get is stock footage of hyenas, followed by crudely shot talking-head interviews with people who are redefining traditional gender-based roles. Treut's main concern during the shooting seems to be that the subject is in the frame and the sound audible. She makes some concession to old-school vérité aesthetics by alerting the viewer to her role shaping the movie, but her occasional narration, mostly paeans to San Francisco and congratulatory appreciations of her subjects' adopted roles, has a touch of voice-of-God smugness about it.

As an argument on gender, the film is confusing and contradictory. Treut holds up hyenas as an example of how "nature can be more inventive than culture." (The female of the species has a clitoris which looks like a penis and tends to be more aggressive than the male.) But her film then shows how such medical procedures as testosterone shots and surgery are used precisely to change 'nature'. Sandy Stone, a professor at Berkeley and the film's intellectual guide, goes on to cite the figure of the cyborg as an ideal: "cyborgs are us, made up of many parts, continually in motion and in change made of human and machine, mechanic and electronic." Perhaps Treut is arguing here that both nature—as represented by the hyenas—and culture—represented by the cyborg—are proof that traditional concepts of gender don't apply in the new millennium. But while the film tells us that there are more genders than society allows for (one of the film's talking heads, Annie Sprinkle, uses the multiplicity of bird species as a model for how different types of gender might exist alongside one another) this radical message is contradicted by what *Gendernauts* shows.

Though the subjects of *Gendernauts*—mainly artists and intellectuals—speak of a diversity of sexual practices, their gender ideals tend to lean towards either side of the traditional binary. Texas Tomboy, for instance, is born with female genitalia, but she's based her look and actions on models associated with conventional forms of masculinity. Similarly, Max Valerio shows us his boxing prowess and an unnamed drag artist opens his fly and swings a big plastic dick around. Even Hida Vilario, an intersex person (what used to be known as a hermaphrodite), tells of first playing with being very feminine, and now being mistaken for a young gay man. So while the film advances the notion that gender can take every possible form, it actually shows us that traditional binaries exercise an extraordinary pull, even to subjects who consciously strive to think beyond them.

This said, these intelligent and articulate people provide *Gendernauts'* most appealing and informative moments. Despite aesthetic shortcomings and intellectual incoherence, the film's depiction of gender non-conformists attempting to forge new ways of being in the world is enough to generate a lively discussion among people interested in the issue of gender.

VILLAGE VOICE, 2/8/00, p. 144, Jessica Winter

Annie Sprinkle, is a featured player in Monika Treut's doc *Gendernauts*, which tracks a loose circle of transgender Bay Area denizens and friends. Treut sometimes loses focus, but her observational skills are manifest in the film's wealth of quotable quotes ("is that your Giuliani impression?" a New York import asks a pelvic-thrusting drag king) and the sense it leaves of both the toll and the kick of self-invention. "When people ask me if I'm a boy or a girl," says one interviewee, "I say, Yes."

Also reviewed in:
CHICAGO TRIBUNE, 9/1/00, Friday/p. K, John Petrakis
NEW YORK TIMES, 2/4/00, p. E8, A. O. Scott
VARIETY, 3/15-21/99, p. 43, Eddie Cockrell

GEORGE WASHINGTON

A Cowboy Booking International release of a Blue Moon Productions and Code Red production. *Executive Producer:* Sam Froelich.   *Producer:* David Gordon Green, Sacha W. Mueller, and Lisa Muskat.   *Director:* David Gordon Green.   *Screenplay:* David Gordon Green.   *Director of Photography:* Tim Orr.   *Editor:* Steven Gonzales and Zene Baker.   *Music:* Michael Linnen, David Wingo, Andrew Gillis, Brian McBride, and Mazinga Phaser.   *Sound:* Chrisof Gebert. *Sound Editor:* Ben Zarai.   *Art Director:* Richard Wright.   *Costumes:* Michael Tully.   *Make-up:* Michael Tully.   *Running time:* 89 minutes.   *MPAA Rating:* Not Rated.

CAST: Candace Evanofski (Nasia);   Donald Holden (George);   Curtis Cotton III (Buddy); Eddie Rouse (Damascus);   Paul Schneider (Rico Rice);   Damian Jewan Lee (Vernon);   Rachael Handy (Sonya);   Jonathan Davidson (Euless);   Janet Taylor (Ruth);   Scott Clackum (Augie); Jason Shirley (Lancaster);   Christian Gustaitis (Tyler);   Beau Nix (Rico's Father);   Joyce Mahaffey (Tyler's Mom);   Johnny "Blue" Gardner (George's Doctor);   Rudy Anderson (Sonya's Attorney);   Henry A. Harris (Baptist);   Alan Thompson (George's Father);   Stephanie Grant (Buddy's Momma);   Tabitha Bell (Interviewer);   Chris Kennedy (Strong Man);   Richard Skaggs (Uncle Sam);   Stephen Vasquez (Boy at the Wreck);   Jocelyn Bond, Kimberly Rogers, and Olivia Walker (Nasia's Friends);   Yolanda Hairston (News Woman);   Thomas Cormier (Camera Man);   Christof Gebert (The Sound Man);   Clinton Campbell, Jr. (Photographer).

NEW YORK, 11/6/00, p. 85 Peter Rainer

David Gordon Green, the 25-year-old writer-director of *George Washington*, has a feeling for children's faces, too, and a light, lyrical, impressionist touch. Set in a rural southern town, with a mostly African-American cast of preteen nonprofessionals, George *Washington* has the amble of a movie that's trying to discover itself in the process of being made. George (Donald Holden), who, because of a cranial deformity, could die if his head gets wet, is the film's standard-bearer; his tart sort-of girlfriend, Nasia (Candace Evanofski), dubs him George Washington, and there's much ardor in that appellation.

He's her savior because his shining example reminds her of what her possibilities are in life. Green, with his cinematographer, Tim Orr, captures the wayward beauty and rot of the town, with its rusted-out carcasses of machinery sitting out in the tall grass like modernist sculpture. What he isn't able to do is bring his lyric impressions to a boil; or maybe he's not interested in that—he's more the simmering sort. When one of the children dies accidentally, and the rest of them must deal with the ramifications, the playing-out of the tragedy feels lackadaisical, unbuttressed. Green is so intent on not pushing the melodrama that he goes to the other extreme, into a dreamtime dreamland. *George Washington* is a gracious sleepwalk of a movie that could have used a firmer strut.

NEW YORK POST, 10/27/00, p. 48, Lou Lumenick

Once in a great while, you find a fictional movie that looks like real life captured by hidden cameras.

Though its grim intensity is not for all tastes, "George Washington" is a very auspicious debut by 25-year-old director David Gordon Green.

Stunningly photographed in North Carolina (in Cinemascope, an unusual choice for a low-budget indie but one that pays real dividends here), it fuses poetry and neorealism to focus on a group of urban poor kids on the cusp of adolescence.

The title character (the engaging Donald Holden) is a bespectacled, introspective youth whose skull bones have never fused properly due to a medical condition. He wears a football helmet to protect his head and has been forbidden to go swimming because he would risk injury.

George and his companions—Nasia (Candace Evanofski), Sonya (Rachael Handy), Vernon (Damian Jewan Lee) and Buddy (Curtis Cotton III)—spend most of the time hanging out in an abandoned amusement park. Adult supervision is mostly either absent or of questionable value (George's uncle kills his dog).

Working in a loose-limbed style that recalls both Terrence Malick and Bruce Forsyth, Green doesn't so much tell a story as let events slowly unfold. Suffice to say that George becomes a cape-wearing hero—while some of his friends aren't quite so lucky.

Green encouraged his young actors to improvise their scenes, and the results are some of the most natural child performances I've seen in long while. (I enjoyed watching Haley Joel Osment act as much as the next person, but his work in "Pay it Forward" is about as natural as Pamela Anderson's décolletage.)

"George Washington" occasionally flirts with melodrama and some of the sound work makes the dialogue difficult to follow, a common problem with indie product.

But for those willing to work a bit at it, this is the sort of artistry many American independent movies aspire to—but rarely achieve.

NEWSDAY, 10/27/00, Part II/p. B6, Jan Stuart

Late into David Gordon Green's many-splendored "George Washington," a girl with a talent for car theft confides to a male buddy that she thinks she's basically no good. "What if it's contagious?" she worries. "What if everyone who touches me loses what they got?"

Her friend tries to allay her fears. "I ain't going to catch it," he responds, "'cause I ain't got nothing to lose."

The line captures the mopey poetry of Green's southern working-class characters, a ragtag collection of predominantly black kids whose limited opportunities do little to obscure their ability to articulate their condition. Their playing ground is an industry-battered landscape of public pools, train yards and abandoned lots so neglected you could dump a TV set or a dead body there and no one would be the wiser.

Perhaps inspired by his environment, Green has created the most off-the-beaten-track sort of coming-of-age movie you could ever imagine. Girls talk about boys and boys talk about girls, but the talk is so matter-of-fact in a dippy-lyrical way that it seems almost secondary to capturing mood and place with an all-seeing, black-and-white Cinemascope lens. William Faulkner would be thrilled, or jealous, or both.

What there is of a conventional plot revolves around a hang-out circle consisting of George (Donald Holden), a taciturn fellow with a sensitive cranial condition; Buddy (Curtis Cotton III), a soulful 11-year-old who is devastated when his 12-year-old girlfriend dumps him; Damascus (Eddie Rouse), a bruiser of a guy whose heart is as expansive as his shoulders, and Sonya (Rachel Handy), a diminutive blond girl whose quiet demeanor conceals an outlaw spirit.

"George Washington" is narrated by Nasia (Candace Evanofski), the girl who breaks Buddy's heart, with a droopy absence of inflection that recalls the youthful heroine of Terence Malick's "Days of Heaven." We don't see all that much of her, as if she's keeping tabs on the congenial rail workers (the film's running Greek chorus, dominated by a sweetly engaging Damian Jewan Lee), George's surly, destructive uncle (Paul Schneider) or a little red-headed kid named Tyler who can hold his breath under water for six minutes. Or so he claims.

Green takes his time, reveling in language and eccentricity. The pacing is so elegiac and the acting so unaffected that we are almost knocked out of our seats when one of the kids is accidentally killed and George is vaulted into the public eye for a random act of heroism. The events are fraught with irony, but as with everything else here, it falls across our shoulders gently. "George Washington" is a bona fide American original, a movie that ennobles kids with the dignity and angst of existential crises.

SIGHT AND SOUND, 10/01, p. 49, Philip Kemp

Summer in a small North Carolina industrial town. Buddy, an insecure black 10-year-old, is dismayed when his girlfriend Nasia spurns him in favour of their friend George Richardson. He asks his older friend Vernon to intercede, but Nasia won't be swayed. George lives with his uncle and aunt because his father is in jail. He adopts a stray dog, but has to keep it out of sight because uncle Damascus hates animals. Damascus' temper isn't improved when he's fired from the salvage gang in the town's railyard.

George, Vernon, Buddy and a young white girl, Sonya, go swimming in the local pool. Afterwards, while they're horsing about in the washrooms, Buddy hits his head and dies. His friends smuggle the body out and hide it in a derelict building. George, who has a soft fontanelle and isn't supposed to get his head wet, rescues a young white boy, Tyler, from drowning. When George recovers he finds himself publicly acclaimed a hero and starts dressing as a caped superhero, confiding to Nasia that he plans to become President.

George, Vernon and Sonya are questioned by police about Buddy's disappearance. They admit nothing, but Vernon is tormented by guilt. He persuades Sonya to run away with him; they steal a car but crash it, and limp off down the railroad tracks. Damascus kills George's dog; he apologises to his nephew and makes him a cap out of the skin. Nasia affirms her faith in George's glittering future.

George Washington arrives garlanded with festival awards and ardent US reviews—some perhaps pressing a touch too heavily on the rave pedal. In *The New York Press* Armond White concludes a long appreciative review with the statement, "In recent film history there has been no greater achievement." It's the kind of hype that, especially if taken out of context, could do the movie a disservice. Twenty-four-year-old David Gordon Green's first feature is fresh, poetic, tender, utterly individual and richly atmospheric, but *Citizen Kane* it's not. It does what it does superbly and with great originality, but within a narrow range. Which isn't a fault, of course, but it is a limitation.

No question, though, that *George Washington* looks stunning. Tim Orr's widescreen photography lavishes mellow softness on burnished visuals, hazy with slow summer heat. The camera lingers on scenes of industrial dereliction, finding beauty in junkyards and rusting machinery, tossing in odd disquieting images: a soft white hat on fire in the grass, a snake gasping and dying on a dusty road. Never, surely, has a dead-end, poverty-trap little Southern township been made to look so glowingly attractive.

The film, which follows the lives of a group of children in a North Carolina town, could be accused of aestheticising social deprivation, and certainly one effect of this visual opulence is to rob *George Washington* of any political dimension (perhaps ironic in a movie named after a politician). There's no sense of anger, nor the least hint that anything should be done to help people lift themselves out of this kind of economic disaster-zone. From that angle the film might be seen as politically conservative. Green and Orr themselves—fellow-students of the newly-founded North Carolina School of Arts film course—seem to have no polemical agenda, justifying their approach in purely aesthetic terms. "Most low-budget movies don't have a look," says Orr. "We wanted to try to make something where we took care to make it look and feel as good as we could."

In any case, this lush visual treatment is of a piece with the film's mesmerised, dreamlike mood. A lot of the time we watch nothing very much going on, and even when crucial events do occur—10-year-old Buddy's death, his friend George's rescue of the drowning Tyler—they're filmed in a languid, matter-of-fact style, devoid of all urgency. Buddy's fatal accident in fact happens off-screen: we hear a thud, not very loud, see the other kids reacting with mild concern, and only then does the camera pan unhurriedly rightwards to Buddy as he slides quietly down to the toilet floor, leaving a red smear on the wall. The effect is to align our reactions with those of Buddy's friends in their bemused, slowly-eroding disbelief. Surely this can't be death? Isn't it too casual, too undramatic to be anything so serious?

Green's most remarkable achievement is the spontaneous, understated performances he's drawn from his young cast—all amateurs, most of whom he recruited in and around the town (Winston-

Salem, North Carolina) where the film was shot. There's a gentleness and an honesty, and often an unselfconscious poetry about their dialogue that attests to the rapport Green established with his actors and the success of his partly-improvised approach.

This tone of naive eloquence is at its most distinctive in the voiceover commentary by the 12-year-old Nasia, musing on events around her as she tries "to find clues to all the mistakes and mysteries God had made." Green has cited Terrence Malick as a major influence, and the poised, slightly fey quality of this voiceover often recalls Malick's *Days of Heaven* (1978), which similarly used an adolescent's voiceover, precocious but marginally at odds with what we're seeing, to counterpoint his plot. There are moments when this heightened, meditative style of talking—shared by all the cast—slips into banality: "Too bad you can't see the stars on account of all the smoke," says one character. But at other times it attains an appealingly skewed comedy. At one point Euless, a member of the railyard salvage gang, launches into a heartfelt riff on the importance of eating right to achieve a good bowel movement: "When I go to the bathroom," he announces, "I like to be proud of what happens."

"I wanted it to play less like a structured Hollywood film and more like a piece of music," Green has said of his debut film. Half-heard music, at that: *George Washington* is as much about things not happening as happening, and the things that do happen often seem gratuitous or trail off unaccountably, as if their resolution takes place in some other story altogether. Rico, the white son of the salvage gang boss, embarks on an affair with a young black woman; but how or if it progresses, and whether it arouses any social tensions, we never learn. (In general, racial concerns seem to float smokily around the periphery of the action, but never coalesce into anything tangible.) Mid-way through the movie, a date—"The 1st of July"—appears on screen, but no other dates are ever shown, nor do the events of this particular day seem more significant than those of other days. But Green clearly isn't interested in conventional narrative logic, and the emotional impact of his film is cumulative, not dynamic. Seen in retrospect, *George Washington*'s lack of closure is its strength, letting it sink into the mind and linger insidiously like the restless dream of a warm summer night.

TIME, 10/30/00, p. 82, Richard Corliss

The two sit, their backs to a wall, parsing the end of their affair. "Did you think we were gonna be together forever?" Nasia says, as much in elegy as in anger. "I just can't stand you anymore." Buddy, flailing for a lifeline, asks, "Can I say I'm sorry?" Nasia says it's too late. So he asks, "Can I kiss you one last time?" But she wants a different parting gift: "Tell me that you love me." He is silent. "Do you love me?" she asks. Buddy looks away. What can a 13-year-old boy say to a 12-year-old girl who has outgrown his puppy love?

We are about to place the burden of praise on a small film, a movie no larger than its main characters—kids 9 to 13, in a rural corner of North Carolina a decade ago. But *George Washington* can carry the weight. David Gordon Green's ensemble drama reveals emotional breadth on its miniature canvas. It shows that kids share with adults more than we imagine. Anyone, regardless of age, can fall in love or be crushed by it; anyone can surrender to despair and self-loathing, or pursue a dream that others think is folly.

In this class portrait distinct personalities soon emerge: Nasia (Candace Evanofski), already aware of her gift for beguiling the opposite sex; Buddy (Curtis Cotton III), who looks ready to make a career of his heartbreak, the mismatched couple Vernon (Damian Jewan Lee), big and black and Sonya (Rachael Handy), a runty blond; and George (Donald Holden), who has a soft head—he wears a helmet to protect his skull—and a warm heart. He sees a boy floating face down in a swimming pool and dives in to save him. Already racked by an inadvertent tragedy, George assigns himself the mission of saving people. Striding through town in a bedsheet cape, sports tights and a helmet, he seems an endearingly preposterous figure. But Nasia is drawn to a man with a quest. "If I ever get in trouble," she says, "will you save my life?"

Here is a film about yearning—the ache for love—and the way wounded people express it. The coup of Green's script is to render complicated feelings in a mix of plangent clichés and vernacular poetry. Listen to Buddy, lovesick over Nasia's desertion, as he bares his soul. "I gave my all to her," he moans. "A plastic ring and a kiss. I mean, it's the thought that counts."

Movies about kids often portray adults as the enemy, clueless or villainous. This one doesn't. The children, most of them stranded in the waiting room of prepubescence, look to adults for guidance and offer unconditional love in return. George, visiting his father in jail, says, "I love you so much, sometimes I can't even breathe." Buddy's ma has trouble sleeping, so he lullabies her with favorite tunes ("She likes the theme to *Blazing Saddles*"). George's uncle Damascus (Eddie Rouse) is a violent man whose fear of dogs impels him to kill George's treasured stray. From guilt and love, he fashions a cap out of the dead mutt's pelt and gives it to the boy to protect his head. It's the thought that counts.

This first feature by Green, just 25, will evoke memories of David Lynch's *Blue Velvet* (the rapturous weirdness of small-town life) and Terrence Malick's *Days of Heaven* (a tough girl's narration, set to gorgeous cinematography). But this kid doesn't need famous parents. It stands, soars on its own. It moves to a seductive rhythm and vision. And it has, like each of the children in it, a restless beauty that haunts their lives and the viewer's heart.

VILLAGE VOICE, 10/31/00, p. 164, J. Hoberman

George Washington, the first feature by 25-year-old David Gordon Green, is the year's most fascinating American indie precisely because it's the most baffling. This haphazardly lyrical, yet heavily symbolic, account of a tragic incident involving a racially mixed group of kids on the outskirts of a small Southern city is a true anxious object—it's at once brilliant and inept.

Green's intentions are as obscure as his command of film craft is unclear—his originality is indistinguishable from his mistakes. Not surprisingly, *George Washington*'s curiouser-and-curiouser quality has been amply reflected in its reception: The movie was rejected by Sundance, the festival that logic dictates as its natural habitat, to premiere weeks later in Berlin's International Forum of Young Cinema; there it became a word-of-mouth must-see that, despite strenuous marketing, was ignored by every major American distributor. Passed on by "New Directors/New Films," another congenial showcase, *George Washington* surfaced instead at the New York Film Festival; having been dismissed by *Variety* in a perfunctory two-paragraph review, it was hailed by *The New York Times* as a movie for the ages.

Green, a native Texan, studied filmmaking in North Carolina, and that's where George, Washington was shot. The locations seem less a specific American reality than an emptied-out world, populated by the amiable survivors of some ancient cataclysm—perhaps the wreckage of regional granola cinema. *George Washington* feels sui generis because while it evokes a number of models it fails to successfully imitate any of them. Green's arty, scene-setting montage, his use of slight slow-motion underscored by a portentous drone-tone, the movie's skewed voice-over narration, its sumptuous Cinemascope compositions, and lush bucolic mood remind many people of Terrence Malick. This modest movie is draped in visual grandeur, like a kid trying on an overlarge suit—far from overweening, the effect is oddly disarming. (To add to the mystery, cinematographer Tim Orr gets an onscreen credit nearly equal to Green's, but barely a mention in the press notes.)

Similarly, *George Washington*'s teenage rat pack and derelict locations have prompted comparison to Harmony Korine's confrontational *Gummo*. (In Berlin, Green even made the Korine-like assertion that his favorite movie was *The Bad News Bears*.) For all its troubling incidents, however, what's most shocking about *GW* is its tender regard. The movie is unabashedly utopian. (Green lived communally with the cast and crew during production.) It also suggests Boaz Yakin's *Fresh* in its programmatic subtraction of all popular culture from the lives of its child protagonists. (And, as with *Fresh*, *GW* was made by a white filmmaker who has been assumed to be black.) But, unlike Yakin, Green allows his performers remarkable space before the camera to simply be, whether surprisingly good or eloquently terrible.

Green's nonprofessional cast is a lumpy blend of self-conscious kids and awkward adults—an equation that's regularly complicated by many scenes in which the actors are called upon to riff and banter across generational lines. In addition to the narration, delivered with many a casual non sequitur by 12-year-old Nasia (Candace Evanofski), the characters are prone to soliloquies. Just about everyone in the movie is some sort of philosopher—except for the 13-year-old designated hero, the silent, self-contained George Richardson (Donald Holden), whom Nasia adores.

The scenes in which these kids discuss their precocious love lives and generally get up in each other's business, with oversized Vernon (Damian Jewan Lee) aggressively wondering why Nasia dropped his pal Buddy (Curtis Cotton III) in favor of the inexplicable George, have a charming absence of profanity. The film's unusual narrative progression reinforces its attempt to capture some imagined childish innocence, as does the backstory assigned its protagonist. The plates of George's skull have not successfully melded; for much of the movie, he wears a football helmet to protect his soft head. But George is not the only vulnerable creature. Fooling around with a group of kids in an abandoned building, he gets his head bumped and inadvertently responds by hurling Buddy to the ground. The boy passes out and dies. The other children hide his body, complete with T. Rex mask, in some abandoned lot—a sort of Spielberg-meets-*Los Olvidados* maneuver.

As the town prepares to celebrate Independence Day, the kids start to freak—Vernon bonding with diminutive, stony Sonya (even younger than 12 and already a hardened car thief).

Subsequent developments have little to do with solving the mystery of Buddy's disappearance and much with a desire to somehow make things right. Rather than suspense, the movie dwells on absence. In the most astonishing ploy, George actualizes his wish fulfillment by saving another kid's life and is declared by the newspapers to be the hero that Nasia tells us he always knew he would become. (George's sense of destiny is reflected in the movie's title, although not the least of its comic enigmas is the portrait of a smiling president George Bush on his family's kitchen wall.) Solemnly directing traffic and checking smoke alarms in helmet, tights, and cape, George casts himself as the neighborhood superhero.

By any objective standard, *George Washington* is a meandering experience, filled with stilted performances and characterized by an erratic point of view. A missing poster identifies Buddy as 10, although he has earlier been referred to as 13. Scarcely an omniscient narrator, Nasia theorizes that "Buddy ran away because he still has a crush on me." A scene in which George's sullen and possibly violent uncle confesses his own childhood trauma (being sexually abused by a dog) is, like much else in the movie, simultaneously touching and ridiculous. (In a follow-up sequence, the man who has perhaps killed the mangy stray George adopted as a pet fashions the boy a sort of Davy Crockett cap from its remains.)

George Washington would not be so confounding were it less polished or more overtly fantastic—but the sense of failed magic realism is what gives the movie its pervasive sadness, which is to say, its magic. Having balanced his movie on the edge between poignance and absurdity (and worked without a net), Green provides the perfect vanishing act—leaving the audience wondering what he could possibly do for an encore.

Also reviewed in:
NATION, 11/13/00, p. 34, Stuart Klawans
NEW YORK TIMES, 9/29/00, p. E12, Elvis Mitchell
VARIETY, 4/17-23/00, p. 29, Joe Leydon

GET CARTER

A Warner Bros. release of a Morgan Creek Productions, Inc. and Franchise Pictures presentation of a Franchise Pictures and Canton Company production. *Executive Producer:* Andrew Stevens, Don Carmody, Billy Gerber, Ashok Amritraj, Steve Bing and Arthur Silver. *Producer:* Mark Canton, Elie Samaha, and Neil Canton. *Director:* Stephen Kay. *Screenplay:* David McKenna. *Based on the novel "Jack's Return Home" by:* Ted Lewis. *Director of Photography:* Mauro Fiore. *Editor:* Jerry Greenberg. *Music:* Tyler Bates. *Production Designer:* Charles J.H. Wood. *Costumes:* Julie Weiss. *Running time:* 115 minutes. *MPAA Rating:* R.

CAST: Sylvester Stallone (Jack Carter); Miranda Richardson (Gloria); Rachael Leigh Cook (Doreen); Michael Caine (Cliff Brumby); Mickey Rourke (Cyrus Paice); Alan Cumming (Jeremy Kinnear); Rhona Mitra (Geraldine); Johnny Strong (Eddie); Gretchen Mol (Audrey).

LOS ANGELES TIMES, 10/7/00, Calendar/p. 8, Kevin Thomas

What's with these Seattle people anyway? This guy, built like Superman and dressed like a high-class gangster, glares at them and speaks to them in a deep, serious voice that suggests none too subtly that he means business. But nobody takes him seriously, which makes him very, very angry.

These intense encounters run throughout the "Get Carter" remake, which was heavily promoted by Warner Bros. but opened Friday without benefit of press previews. These encounters are of course setups designed to allow Sylvester Stallone as Carter to express his rage physically.

Stallone's most stalwart fans most likely will enjoy these bravura displays of violence, but there are so many and they are so showy that they undercut a film that actually has more going for it than most Stallone vehicles. He actually is well-cast as a seasoned Las Vegas underworld enforcer who returns home to Seattle after an absence of five years or so to attend the funeral of his younger brother.

He is not welcomed with open arms by his sister-in-law (Miranda Richardson), who has a where-were-you-when-we-needed-you?attitude. He's greeted with even less enthusiasm by a raft of shady types when he starts questioning the circumstances of his brother's death in an apparent drunk-driving accident. His teenage niece (Rachael Leigh Cook), to whom he is "only a picture on the piano," nonetheless starts warming to him enough to tell him that her late father hadn't been drinking in years.

About the time Carter left town, his brother became manager of a nightclub owned by a suave, canny Brit (Michael Caine, star of the 1971 "Get Carter"). Apparently, the brother's life thereafter proceeded without incident until his death. Carter's inquiries turn up a nerdy computer zillionaire (Alan Cumming), who had turned to an old Carter henchman (Mickey Rourke) to supply him with girls. (You can be sure Stallone and Rourke display lots of swagger when they go toe to toe.) In return the computer genius has provided his pimp with some form of online service, not realizing that it would enable him to peddle porn on the Internet. Carter will have to deal with assorted other sleazeballs to get at the truth about his brother's death.

Weathered but superfit as ever, Stallone has the right world-weary look and is the right age for a professional hired gun to be made vulnerable by intimations of mortality, intimations that send him down the path of vengeance even as it sparks a yearning for redemption. Stallone skillfully expresses Carter's isolation, his awakening paternal feelings of concern for his niece, his sense that he has let his brother down in not staying around to steer him clear of the underworld. Scenes between Stallone and Cook are quite affecting under Stephen Kay's direction. The film could use more such scenes, but Kay and screenwriter David McKenna keep punching up the formula action at the expense of the reflection their hero is beginning to develop.

Although this "Get Carter" has its share of cliched, tough-talk dialogue, it is not a terrible movie, and Stallone has appeared in far worse. It's just that, although diverting, it's too routine for its own good, despite its sleek look and splendidly photographed Seattle locations—and this is what Warners must have concluded too. Once there was a time not so long ago when movies that opened without previews, thus avoiding opening-day reviews, were virtually always low-budget exploitation pictures. "Get Carter" is the second recent major studio release with a veteran star to open cold nationwide. The first was the Richard Gere-Winona Ryder starrer "Autumn in New York," unabashedly old-fashioned yet effective, if only on its own terms.

Ironically, neither version of "Get Carter," even though the stylish first interpretation enjoys cult status, is the most persuasive film made from Ted Lewis' novel, "Jack's Return Home." It's the modestly budgeted 1973 "Hit Man," written and directed by George Armitage.

Made as part of the burgeoning blaxploitation cycle of that time, it starred Bernie Casey, who investigated his brother's death, not so much out of revenge but from his lack of faith in the police. The talented, underutilized Armitage is best known for the more recent "Miami Blues" with Alec Baldwin.

NEW YORK POST, 10/7/00, p. 21, Lou Lumenick

Should you get Carter? Sure—but make it the Michael Caine classic Warner Bros. is releasing on video next week.

Avoid, at all costs, the putrid Sylvester Stallone remake, which the same studio dumped into theaters without advance screenings, stinking like a 3-week-old flounder.

Where Caine was the epitome of taciturn cool in the 1971 British original, Stallone's Jack Carter can't shut up—and his sentimental ramblings, accompanied by facial twitches that are apparently meant to approximate acting, are stupefying.

Though the action has been moved from Northern England to Seattle, the story line is similar. Carter, here a Las Vegas mob enforcer, comes home for the funeral of his brother, who was killed in a car crash Carter begins to suspect was no accident.

As soon as he begins asking questions, people start asking Carter to leave town.

This rendition is slower, much less coherent and notably less violent than Caine's version, which originally carried an "X" rating. But what beatings, shootings and car chases there are (staged by "Mod Squad" director Stephen Kay in by-the-numbers fashion) seem more offensive in the almost total absence of dramatically credible situations.

This is the sort of movie where your mind is constantly wandering as it wends its way to the oh-so-familiar conclusion.

Why is the wetness of Carter's suit so consistent, no matter how long he stays out in the movie's many rain scenes? How come, in action set over 36 hours, there are Christmas decorations on the streets in some scenes, but not in others?

There isn't much diversion in the many uninteresting supporting characters. Among them: the brother's wife (Miranda Richardson), his teenage daughter (Rachael Lee Cook), his boss (Michael Caine himself), a computer mogul (Alan Cumming) and Jack's partner (John C. McGinley)—all impersonated by able actors who seem vaguely embarrassed "acting" with Stallone.

Where the Caine original was a knowing homage to the pulp fiction of Raymond Chandler, this one seems more a tribute to the Stallone of the "Nighthawks" era. The script is attributed to David McKenna, who wrote the excellent "American History X."

Poor Sly. Caine had a memorable phone sex scene with Britt Ekland in '71; all Stallone gets is a chance to flirt with a porn mogul played by Mickey Rourke, the only cast member who needs a comeback more than he does.

Carter keeps telling people, "You don't want to know me." Truer words haven't been said in an American movie this year.

NEWSDAY, 10/09/00, Part II/p. B8, Gene Seymour

"Do you want to take this to the next level?" asks professional leg breaker Jack Carter (Sylvester Stallone) as he's about to make someone's bad luck a lot worse.

The fact that Stallone is playing the eponymous hero of "Get Carter," a remake of a classic 1971 British crime thriller, suggests that he's certainly grasping for some sort of "next level." Three years is a long time between movies, and Stallone's box-office mojo has been in deep freeze for longer than that. Taking on Michael Caine's legendary role of a hard-case criminal returning to his up-north home to track down his brother's murderers would be one way to get attention.

Caine himself has a supporting role in this updated version as the jovial owner of a Seattle watering hole where Jack's brother worked. Even if he did nothing else but show up for work, Caine by his presence alone provides gravity to a film. that often goes slack from an overabundance of flash and stylized grit.

Sporting a goatee and spiffy sharkskin, Stallone's Carter at first comes across as if he's so used to leaning on deadbeats that he's pushing the rain sideways. But as he reconnects with his sullen sister-in-law (Miranda Richardson) and his secretive niece (Rachael Leigh Cook, who's quite good), Stallone softens the edges of Carter's scowling malevolence even as he's intimidating a software tycoon (Alan Cumming) and a porn king (Mickey Rourke) somehow joined at the hip.

In defense of both director Stephen T. Kay ("The Last Time I Committed Suicide") and screenwriter David McKenna, the densely wired setup is compacted for easier consumption by the video-game crowd without mussing one's fond memories of the original. All that comes later with a messy, cacophonous series of multiple car chases, fistfights and assorted acts of truly meaningless violence.

And Stallone? He's OK. At least, he doesn't quite make a botch of this role as he did playing the sad-sack sheriff in his previous bid for Higher Things in 1997's "Cop Land." But once again, he cops out on shadows and dimension. He can't help wanting everyone to keep on loving him as always. But if he really wants to take things to another level, his characters may have to risk coming up with less cathartic victories than they're used to.

Also reviewed in:
CHICAGO TRIBUNE, 10/9/00, Tempo/p. 1, Mark Caro
NEW YORK TIMES, 10/7/00, p. B12, Elvis Mitchell
VARIETY, 10/9-15/00, p. 21, Todd McCarthy
WASHINGTON POST, 10/6/00, Weekend/p. 47, Desson Howe

GETTING TO KNOW YOU

A ShadowCatcher Entertainment and SearchParty Films release of a Gabbert/Lavoo production. *Executive Producer:* Scott Rosenfelt, Larry Estes, and David Skinner. *Producer:* George Lavoo and Laura Gabbert. *Director:* Lisanne Skyler. *Screenplay:* Lisanne Skyler and Tristine Skyler. *Based on stories from "Heat" by:* Joyce Carol Oates. *Director of Photography:* Jim Denault. *Editor:* Julie Janata and Anthony Sherin. *Music:* Michael Brook. *Music Editor:* Ron Finn. *Choreographer:* Luis Perez. *Sound:* Antonio L. Arroyo, Jose Torres, and (music) Rick Maclane. *Casting:* Jordan Beswick. *Production Designer:* Jody Asnes. *Art Director:* Katherine L. Spencer. *Set Decorator:* Brian Elwell. *Set Dresser:* Mimi Lien. *Costumes:* Astrid Brucker. *Make-up:* Susan Reilly. *Stunt Coordinator:* Brian Hite and Brian Smyj. *Running time:* 91 minutes. *MPAA Rating:* Not Rated.

CAST: Heather Matarazzo (Judith); Zach Braff (Wesley); David Aaron Baker (Dr. Clarke); Catherine Anne Hayes (Large Woman); Craig Anthony Grant (Ticket Clerk); Michael Weston (Jimmy); Richard Bright (Lotto Man); Celia Weston (Bottle Lady); Bebe Neuwirth (Trix); Mark Blum (Darrell); Bo Hopkins (Officer Caminetto); Tom Gilroy (Jimmy's Father); Tristine Skyler (Irene); Sonja Sohn (Lynn); Rich T. Alliger (Blackjack Skeptic); Chris Noth (Sonny); Kevin Black (Brady); Dilyn Cassel (Young Mother); Mary McCormack (Leila Lee); Jacob Reynolds (Lamar Pike Jr); Leo Burmester (Lamar Pike Sr); Peggy Gormley (Leila's Neighbor); Jonathan Hogan (Trix's Friend).

NEW YORK POST, 6/28/00, p. 46, Hannah Brown

Sad, strange and blessedly unpredictable, "Getting to Know You" marks the feature film debut of a remarkable new talent, writer/director Lisanne Skyler.

Based on three short stories by Joyce Carol Oates, "Getting to Know You" has the unabashedly intelligent and distinctive, slightly stilted quality of the films of Hal Hartley.

"Getting to Know You" stars Heather Matarazzo (best known for her role in "Welcome to the Dollhouse") as Judith, a teenage girl waiting with her brother, Wesley (Zach Braff), in a bus station in a small town in upstate New York.

Their mother, Trix (Bebe Neuwirth), a failed actress, is in a mental hospital and their father, Darrell (Mark Blum), refuses to take their phone calls.

Judith and her introverted, brilliant brother are headed for separate destinations; he for a college to which he has won a scholarship, she to a boarding school.

Judith wants to talk to Wesley about their parents, but all he wants to do is study.

As they wait, Jimmy (Michael Weston), a boy who says he remembers Judith from school, comes over and starts telling her stories about the odd characters in the bus station.

These stories are then dramatized. The first is a romantic but familiar tale of a woman (Tristine Skyler, the co-writer of the screenplay and the director's sister) who falls in love with a high-stakes gambler (Chris Noth) in Atlantic City.

In the second, a woman (Mary McCormack) marries an older, religious man (Leo Burmester) and finds herself caught up in a bizarre war between him and his odd teenage son (Jacob Reynolds), who is obsessed with science fiction.

As Jimmy and Judith talk, she gradually reveals the story of her own parents' marriage. Suddenly, she becomes less passive and more independent than she seemed at first.

Matarazzo, so gawky and nervous, gives a wonderful performance in the lead, although at times she seems stiff, like an actress in a school play. Braff and Weston, as her brother and friend, are also outstanding. In fact, the entire ensemble is terrific.

But the true star of the film is the brilliant, literary script by the Skylers, which takes much of its spirit from the stories on which it was based.

The film is the director's first theatrical feature (she has made some documentaries) and there is some evidence of her inexperience, particularly in a few clunky moments of exposition.

But the flaws are minor. This is an intelligent, emotionally charged film, not easily forgotten.

NEWSDAY, 6/28/00, Part II/p. B13, John Anderson

Spun out of three stories from the Joyce Carol Oates collection "Heat," "Getting to Know You" doesn't just reaffirm one's flagging faith in independent cinema. It vindicates the very process, oft-abused as it is, of adapting literature into film.

Director Lisanne Skyler and co-writer Tristine Skyler didn't need a reason to adapt Oates' work—God knows, recent film history is littered with movies of stories no one needed to see, or in some cases even read. But the Skyler sisters not only keep faith with Oates' luckless characters and tidy dramas, they use the stories in a way that translates the very act of creating fiction as a gesture of self-defense.

Heather Matarazzo (most recently of TV's "Now and Again") made a startling debut at age 13 in "Welcome to the Dollhouse" (1996) and has become an increasingly interesting and disarmingly unmannered actress. As Judith, waiting for a bus at an upstate New York station, she's the picture of adolescent bewilderment, albeit of a rather tortured variety: She's just left her mother, Trix (Bebe Neuwirth), in a mental ward, her father Darrell (Mark Blum) has cut them loose, her brother Wesley (Zach Braff) is heading to college on a different bus and Judith is adrift in guilt and confusion.

At the bus terminal, she's approached by a local kid named Jimmy (Michael Weston) and together they tell stories. Judith's are about her family, how Trix and Darrell had been dancers, reluctant parents, drinkers, cheaters and the sorrow of their children. Jimmy's stories, how he amuses himself during his many days at the station, are about the imagined histories of his fellow bus travelers. Around one visibly harried woman (Tristine Skyler), he conjures up a tale of Atlantic City (from Oates' "Craps") and a midnight tryst with a troubled gambler (Chris Noth). Around another (Mary McCormack), he constructs a tale of domestic abuse and murder (Oates' "Leila Lee"). Judith, getting with the program, starts correcting Jimmy's assumptions and observations, their mutual healing taking an artistic turn.

As a director, Lisanne Skyler maintains a discreet presence, which isn't to say that every angle, composition and color scheme isn't employed for optimal emotional clout. Hers may be a deceptively powerful movie, but powerful it is.

VILLAGE VOICE, 7/4/00, p. 124, Amy Taubin

In the rock-'em-sock-'em environment of Sundance, films that eschew an excess of violence or sentimentality are often overlooked. A delicate balance of head and heart, Lisanne Skyler's *Getting to Know You* proved too subtle for jury members and distributors alike. But here in New York, where there's still room for brainy oddballs, it registers as a pitch-perfect portrait of adolescence, a film so fragile and uncompromising that you want to throw your arms around it and protect it from the jerks who won't know how special it is.

Adapted from three Joyce Carol Oates stories, *Getting to Know You* weaves the memories and desires of three teenagers who've been forced too soon to fend for themselves. The main location is a bus depot in one of those economically stagnant upstate New York towns that make news only in an election year. Waiting for buses to take them in different directions are a sister and brother, Judith (Heather Matarazzo) and Wesley (Zach Braff). Wesley is bound for college; Judith is returning to the group home where she's lived since their mother was committed to a psychiatric institute and their father decided that his family was not his responsibility.

Also at the station is Jimmy (Michael Weston), a teller of tales, some tall, some true. While Wesley takes refuge in his math books, Jimmy strikes up a conversation with Judith. The stories he invents about their fellow transients reflect on her painful, guilt-ridden relationship with her mother and father, wannabe performers whose careers were cut short by the economic burdens of parenthood. Making up stories is Jimmy's way to avoid dealing with his own feelings of guilt. In the course of six hours, the two forge an emotional bond that gives them the courage to venture into adulthood.

Getting to Know You moves fluidly among worlds: the here and now of the bus station, the romances Jimmy invents, and Judith's recollections of familial happiness turned to grief and horror. As her memories pile up, we realize that this is a film about the cathartic effect of storytelling and that, as such, it succeeds by example. Every disclosure opens a door onto a greater mystery until a liberating level of truth can be reached.

Written by the director and her sister, Tristine, the script is exceptionally subtle, and, despite the way it leaps about in time, almost classic in its three-act structure. Jim Denault's cinematography strikingly limits its palette to the basic expressive difference between blues and reds. (The film might have been titled *Tangled Up in Blue.*) But in the end, *Getting to Know You* is driven by its ensemble cast, in particular Matarazzo and Weston.

Matarazzo still has the deer-caught-in-the-headlights quality that made her so discomfiting to watch in *Welcome to the Dollhouse,* but her emotional range has widened. She lets Judith wear her heart on her sleeve even when she retreats inside herself. Judith's desire to be loved by her beautiful, distant, and self-destructive mother (Bebe Neuwirth) won't be fulfilled; Matarazzo lets us understand Judith's pain without allowing the character to fall into self-pity. Weston has soft, slightly feline features, a live-wire energy, and eyes that lead you to wonder what he's going to do next. That he's a babe is a given; that he makes us believe Jimmy is a babe with brains and the soul of a romantic suggests he has a shot at becoming a star.

Also reviewed in:
CHICAGO TRIBUNE, 9/1/00, Friday/p. I, John Petrakis
NEW YORK TIMES, 6/28/00, p. E3, Elvis Mitchell

GHOST DOG: THE WAY OF THE SAMURAI

An Artisan Entertainment release of a JVC/Le Studio Canal+/Bac Films presentation in asociation with Pandora Film and ARD-Degeto Film of a Plywood production. *Producer:* Richard Guay and Jim Jarmusch. *Director:* Jim Jarmusch. *Screenplay:* Jim Jarmusch. *Director of Photography:* Robby Müller. *Editor:* Jay Rabinowitz. *Music:* RZA. *Music Editor:* Jay Rabinowitz. *Sound:* Drew Kunin. *Sound Editor:* Chic Ciccolini III and Daniel Pagan. *Casting:* Ellen Lewis and Laura Rosenthal. *Production Designer:* Ted Berner. *Art Director:* Mario Ventenilla. *Set Decorator:* Ronnie Von Blomberg. *Special Effects:* Drew Jiritano. *Costumes:* John Dunn. *Make-up:* Judy Chin. *Special Effects Make-up:* Neal Martz. *Stunt Coordinator:* Jeff Ward, Manny Siverio, and Norman Douglass. *Running time:* 116 minutes. *MPAA Rating:* R.

CAST: Forest Whitaker (Ghost Dog); John Tormey (Louie Bonacelli); Cliff Gorman (Sonny Valerio); Henry Silva (Ray Vargo); Isaach de Bankolé (Raymond); Tricia Vessey (Louise Vargo); Victor Argo (Vinny); Gene Ruffini (Old Consigliere); Richard Portnow (Handsome Frank); Camille Winbush (Pearline, the Little Girl); Dennis Liu (Chines Restuarnt Owner); Frank Minucci (Big Angie); Frank Adonis (Valerio's Bodyguard); Damon Whitaker (Young Ghost Dog); Kenny Guay (Boy in Window); Vince Viverito (Johnny Morini); Gano Grills, Touché Cornel and Jamie Hector (Gangstas in Red); Chuck Jeffreys (Mugger); Yan Ming Shi (Kung Fu Master); Vinnie Vella (Sammy the Snake); Joe Rigano (Joe Rags); Roberto López, Salvatore Alagna, and Jerry Todisco (Punks in Alley); Gary Farmer (Nobody); Clebert Ford (Pigeonkeeper); José Rabelo (Rooftop Boatbuilder); Jerry Sturiano (Lefty); Tony Rigo (Tony); Alfred Nittoli (Al); Angel Caban (Social Club Landlord); Luz Valentin (Girl in

Silver); Rene Bluestone and Jordan Peck (Club Couple); Jonathan Cook and Tracy Howe (Bear Hunters); Harry Shearer (Voice of Scratchy); Vanessa Hollingshead (Female Sheriff); Sharon Angela (Blonde with Jaguar); Rza, The (Samurai in Camouflage).

LOS ANGELES TIMES, 3/17/00, Calendar/p. 2, Eric Harrison

"Everything seems to be changing all around us."

This sentiment is expressed more than once in "Ghost Dog: The Way of the Samurai," and on this thematic level Jim Jarmusch's rueful, funny, deliciously off-kilter new film couldn't be clearer. You have no doubt what this movie is about when you walk out of the theater.

But as for what the movie is about—you know, in the way your pal Mikey will mean when he asks about it—that's likely to give you trouble. There's no way to tell him that makes sense.

There's this hit man, see, and his name is Ghost Dog. And he communicates with his boss by carrier pigeon.

Chances are Mikey will stop you right there. What year and country is this set in? he'll want to know. For Mikey's information, the time is now, and the place is New York City. But this is only the first of this movie's wacky anachronisms.

"Ghost Dog" is a further exploration of themes that Jarmusch handled in more solipsistic (and less entertaining) fashion in "Dead Man," his 1995 western starring Johnny Depp. Both movies are, in part, meditations on death and dying, spiritualism and ancient codes of conduct.

(Jarmusch links the two movies by having characters in "Ghost Dog" equate African Americans with American Indians. And he includes a Cayuga Indian actor from "Dead Man" in a small role here to utter a more profane version of his "stupid white man" refrain from that film.)

The filmmaker might be faulted for exchanging one brand of exoticism for another and for making a too-easy (and cliched) correlation between pre-modern societies and moral superiority. He does it so inventively, though (commingling ancient Japanese culture with black inner-city life and an antiquated Cosa Nostra moral code), that we're willing to take the ride.

Cultures collide in "Ghost Dog," old ways of being fall before the advance of progress. Jarmusch shows the Mafia as it has never been seen—a collection of aging men in a changing neighborhood who can't pay the rent on their hangout and who waste their days engrossed in vintage cartoons on television.

The movie is full of Jarmusch's trademark offbeat humor. Ghost Dog (Forest Whitaker in a gracefully minimalistic performance) is best friends with an exuberant Haitian ice cream vendor who speaks only French. Neither can understand a word the other says and yet they converse anyway, somehow comprehending all.

One of the nice things about this movie is the way it doesn't explain itself to you as it follows its unpredictable path. The watchful, bear-like Ghost Dog lives in a shack atop a tenement roof with his pigeons, and he's dedicated his life to the study and practice of the samurai code.

We never learn how he went from getting beat up on the street eight years ago (in what may or may not have been a hate crime) to becoming this inscrutable hip-hop warrior. But he has pledged himself in zen-like fashion to Louie (John Tormey), the low-level Mafiosi who saved his life.

Also, while there is indication that Ghost Dog communicates with animals—he's kind of a lord of the urban jungle—it never is explained how he manages to know all that he knows about the whereabouts and plans of the mobsters who decide early in the movie that he must die.

People of honor in this movie live by their own moral codes and respect the codes of others. Ghost Dog carries around a book that he is always reading, the 18th century Japanese warrior text "Hagakure: The Book of the Samurai." Periodically, sayings from the book are superimposed on screen. The movie is full of other texts, as well—novels, rap songs, even cartoons—that reflect directly on what is happening on screen.

The mobsters can't even absorb the wisdom of Betty Boop or Felix the Cat, the texts they consume daily. If they did, Ghost Dog wouldn't be able to catch them unawares. In one scene, for example, he spies (and kills) a hood who had been watching a cartoon character rain bullets on an enemy by firing a gun into a rain spout. Minutes later, Ghost Dog dispatches another gangster pretty much the same way.

The movie contains a big, vengeful rampage scene that might remind viewers of Steven Soderbergh's film of last year, "The Limey." Soderbergh won high praise for his chop-and-dice technique in that movie even though it had been done a dozen times better by filmmakers from John Boorman to Alain Resnais. But what Jarmusch does here is wholly original. It's a nearly pitch-perfect melding of genres, influences and modes of expression—it's the first Mafia movie for the hip-hop age. Or maybe it's a samurai western spliced with rap and humor. (The movie is evocatively scored by the rapper The RZA of the Wu-Tang Clan.)

Whatever you call it, it's so wonderfully eccentric that it cries out for a new way of discussing it. Gnomic epigrams, perhaps, scattered amid promiscuously allusive, scat-like prose. Or a hyperlinked dissertation on ancient warrior codes. (Yes, the new mode of movie review this film needs necessarily would come at you from cyberspace.)

And from the speakers while you read it, some Earth, Wind and Fire, perhaps. "That's the Way of the World"? You know it. But only for those not hip enough for the RZA.

Self-indulgent, you say? Perhaps. But as Ghost Dog tells Louie: "Everything seems to be changing all around us."

Nothing makes sense anymore.

NEW YORK, 3/20/00, p. 58, Peter Rainer

Forest Whitaker carries about him an air of gracious somnolence, but there's also a charge at the center of his sleepiness that works extremely well for his latest movie. In Jim Jarmusch's *Ghost Dog: The Way of the Samurai*, he plays a hit man who lives in a ratty rooftop apartment festooned with pigeons and pores over the precepts of an eighteenth-century warrior text. The film is by turns irritating and inviting; Jarmusch's allusive metaphysics has a sensual glide, but much of what he's doing here is also too, too hip.

NEW YORK POST, 3/3/00, p. 53, Jonathan Foreman

"Ghost Dog: The Way of the Samurai" is a freaky accomplishment. As you might expect from an excruciatingly cool filmmaker like Jim Jarmusch, this film about a black assassin who works for the Mafia but sees himself as a modern-day samurai is pretentious, self-congratulatory and filled with a white hipster's embarrassing adulation of both hip-hop culture and Eastern martial-arts mysticism.

Yet it's also a highly entertaining, often very funny movie that treats the many genres it combines with a respect all too rare among arty filmmakers.

That the movie works so well against heavy odds is largely thanks to an extraordinary and almost silent performance by Forest Whitaker.

It's the first film in which this superb actor has taken a starring role since Clint Eastwood's "Bird" in 1988, (though he's delivered any number of memorable performances in supporting roles from "Good Morning, Vietnam" to "Species.")

It also benefits from a terrific, eerie score by the RZA, founder of the Staten Island rap group Wu-Tang Clan.

Ghost Dog (Whitaker) is a contract killer for the mob in a rundown Eastern city, and, like so many recent movie assassins, he's a decent and lovable guy.

Though he dresses like any ghetto thug and uses snazzy, high-tech devices in his work, Ghost Dog is a devotee of martial arts and, just like Alain Delon in Jean Pierre Melville's 1967 film "Le Samurai," he lives by the samurai code.

(Every day he reads from Hagakure's "Book of the Samurai," and Jarmusch puts various quotations from the book, some of them ridiculously opaque, on title cards.)

Ghost Dog's "retainer"—with whom he communicates by carrier pigeon—is Mafia soldier Louie (John Tormey), who saved his life years ago. The story begins when Louie is ordered by his boss, Ray Vargo (Henry Silva), to arrange the killing of a made man who is the lover of Vargo's daughter (Tricia Vessey).

But after Ghost Dog carries out this task, Vargo decides he wants Ghost Dog dead, too.

Of course, Ghost Dog is not an easy man to kill, and soon the aging soldiers of this small-time mob family—all of whom are obsessed with cartoons—discover they're in a war they cannot win.

Jarmusch sometimes pushes the whimsy a little too far, as in the friendship between Ghost Dog and Raymond (Isaach de Bankole), an ice-cream vendor who speaks only French. And sometimes the parallels between the anachronistic, loyalty-based codes of the samurai and the Mafia are stressed too heavily.

But the film is so filled with amusing, idiosyncratic touches and unexpectedly charming characters that you mostly don't mind its excesses.

NEWSDAY, 3/3/00, Part II/p. B6, John Anderson

The muted cool of Jim Jarmusch has defined an entire school of independent film-Euro-influenced deadpan comedies afloat on irony, existential dread and an oxymoronic cocktail of alienation and tenderness. The same branding, however, has limited Jarmusch's flexibility—or, rather, that of his audience: When his masterpiece "Dead Man" appeared in 1996, it was described in various ways as "the Old West meets the Lower East Side"—an absurd assessment, even if it did provide the shorthand for linking Jarmusch to his movie.

So you have to give the Manhattan-based director credit for not giving a damn and virtually pleading for further misinterpretation. "Ghost Dog: The Way of the Samurai" stars Forest Whitaker as an African-American hit man armed with an attache case full of weapons and a copy of the Japanese "Hakure" or Book of the Samurai. Living a solitary existence on a rooftop he shares with a coop-full of pigeons, Ghost Dog has taken as his master a low-level, middle-aged mob soldier named Louie (John Tormey), who once saved his life from a racist beating. Louie isn't aware of the honor he's received, but he knows that his mystery employee is a flawlessly efficient assassin who corresponds with him by carrier pigeon and will accept payment only once a year, on the fall equinox.

To say that "Ghost Dog" is ripe with the potential for cheap irony and low-rent humor is putting it mildly.

And there is cheap irony and low-rent humor. But for all the dry jokes and odd characters, "Ghost Dog" is at heart an anti-irony movie, one that questions the very postmodern mechanics that made the early Jarmusch hits ("Stranger Than Paradise," "Mystery Train") the touchstones they were and are. Wearing its attitude on its sleeve and lofted along on the atmospheric grooves of Wu-Tang Clan, "Ghost Dog" assumes an attitude of hip—at the same time intrepidly exploring the nature of devotion, tradition and sincerity. The voice-overs by Whitaker, reciting the "Hakure's" Japanese prose poems with street inflection, or his purposeful strides through a city that doesn't see him, are exercises in pseudo-mythic cinema. Scratch the surface, though, and you hit a vein.

What is Whitaker's "Ghost Dog" about? America, for one thing, and the answering of violence with violence. Survivor guilt, for another: How does he make sense of a racist society that both beats him and saves him? overcoming what certainly appears to be a native aversion to blood, Ghost Dog pays his debt the only way his creditor can appreciate. He transcends himself—achieving, if you will, the American Dream. And loses himself in the process.

Giving one of his best performances, Whitaker uses his mournful, sleepy-eyed countenance to mirror Ghost Dog's grief for his work, all the while performing it with cold-blooded finesse. Even his fatal misstep isn't his fault: Neatly killing Handsome Frank (Richard Portnow), G.D. makes the mistake of doing it while mob princess Louise Vargo (Tricia Vessey) is in the room, thus incurring the wrath of her father Ray Vargo (Henry Silva), who then orders Ghost Dog killed.

Jarmusch overplays the humanizing elements of Ghost Dog's life—that his best friends, for instance, are a French-only speaking-ice cream man (Isaach de Bankole) and an 8-year-old bookworm (the adorable Camille Winbush). Or that the slaughter of his pigeons drives him to vengeance. But he doesn't glorify violence via Ghost Dog. The movie's various shootouts are too sad, funny or stupid to inspire mayhem, even among the weakest of mind. The recurring shots of a bird in flight is in a large sense a joke (Soar like a pigeon?). To say "Ghost Dog" operates on multiple levels is silly. All movies do. "Ghost Dog" just does so more deliberately than most, with a more profound message than most and with the very good news that Jarmusch hasn't lost his sense of humor.

SIGHT AND SOUND, 5/00, p. 49, Xan Brooks

The US, the present. Ghost Dog keeps pigeons, consults the samurai Code *Hagakure* and works as an assassin for the Mob. He has two friends: Raymond, a Haitian ice cream vendor, and Pearline, a bookish little girl he meets in the park. Ghost Dog is commissioned by Mob foot soldier Louie to kill another gangster, Handsome Frank, who is having an affair with Louise, the niece of Mafia don Vargo. But when Louise witnesses the hit, Vargo and his underboss Sonny decide Ghost Dog must be killed.

Aided by a reluctant Louie, Sonny and Vargo send their goons to Ghost Dog's home where they destroy his pigeon coop and shoot a man by mistake. Ghost Dog tracks down Louie but refuses to kill him because his samurai code forbids a retainer from killing his master. Later, he drives out to Vargo's country home where he kills his guards and shoots the don as Louise sits watching. Returning home, he also shoots two hunters who have killed a bear out of season. He then kills Sonny. Ghost Dog travels to the park and gives his *Hagakure* book to Pearline and his personal effects to Raymond. Louie arrives and Ghost Dog allows himself to be shot dead. At home, Pearline begins reading *Hagakure*.

Jim Jarmusch once remarked that his films are made up of the bits that other film-makers would cut out of their movies. His pictures have traditionally been comprised of the time between big events, the moments when the characters are either in transit or idling in a lugubrious neutral. The inhabitants of *Down by Law* are prison break-outs with no particular place to go. In *Mystery Train* the setting is the low-rent hotel where a crop of Memphis tourists cool their heels. In *Night on Earth* a series of taxi cabs ferry their respective passengers between points A and B. At its best, Jarmusch's work circles so deliberately around conventional Hollywood notions of drama as to evolve a new drama all of its own.

What is one to make, then, of *Ghost Dog The Way of the Samurai*? Face it head-on and this urban thriller signals a startling volte-face. Where Jarmusch used to score his films to avant-garde punk or white guitar music (his last picture, *The Year of the Horse*, was a documentary on old friend and collaborator Neil Young), *Ghost Dog* comes powered by a spare, trip-hop soundtrack from Wu Tang Clan frontman RZA. And where Jarmusch's previous pictures were contemplative and unimpeded by straightforward narration, *Ghost Dog* teems with action. Its lead character is a hitman hounded by the Mob. Its body count is epic. It builds to a *Scarface*-style shoot out. It is, in short, a very different breed of Jarmusch movie.

Except it's not really. Much as he did with his unloved but ambitious Western *Dead Man*, Jarmusch has taken hold of a genre template and remade it in his own image, sprinkling in some incongruous ingredients. As a result, *Ghost Dog* comes across as an eccentric salad of styles (a hip-hop Mafia samurai thriller, no less), its core pure Jarmusch. This, it turns out, is both a blessing and a curse. On the one hand, *Ghost Dog* is underpinned by the film-maker's familiar blend of warmth and cool-eyed distance, a mix as disarming as it is eccentric. It allows Jarmusch to poke gentle fun at his characters (and much of *Ghost Dog* is very funny) while simultaneously regarding them with a genuine affection. In this, he is helped by some fine performances, most notably from Henry Silva's gimlet-eyed Mob boss and Forest Whitaker's stoic, soulful hitman with a heart—stereotypes but likeable ones, with just enough kinks to keep them interesting.

But in its broader picture, *Ghost Dog* can be frustratingly lazy The transplanting of old eastern codes to the present day west is a device that's been attempted by everyone from John Sturges (*The Magnificent Seven*, (1960) to Jean-Pierre Melville (*Le Samuraï*, 1967) to John Frankenheimer (*Ronin*), but in adopting the same tack Jarmusch instigates a debate he can't quite resolve. *Ghost Dog* offers some intriguing insights on the melting-pot US, a place where Sicilian mobsters mouth Flavor Flav lyrics and the black underclass study Japanese philosophy. But it complicates matters by drawing a link between both old school Mafia codes and ancient samurai honour and (more crucially) between black urban culture and ancient samurai honour. The first link is credible; the second less so. Jarmusch offers no illumination as to why Ghost Dog feels an affinity with samurai teachings, nor why he insists on passing those teachings on to an Afro-American child. Instead, he tosses in bland Hollywood shorthand. Ghost Dog is black, *ergo* he is soulful.

Not that Jarmusch has ever been known for his rigour, and *Ghost Dog* is no exception. This is a picture by turns amusing and melancholic, sweet-centred and dark edged. Jarmusch clearly finds observations easier than analysis, and the trip more satisfying than the destination. *Ghost Dog's* shoot-out is not a climax; just another port of call in its creator's endless voyage around himself.

VILLAGE VOICE, 3/7/00, p. 121. J. Hoberman

Canon formation is typically a matter of official look-backs and critical group-think. *Raging Bull,* to take one example, was not born a masterpiece. It became one nearly 10 years after its release when, in 1990, it unexpectedly topped a number of critics' polls. Indeed, the drive for consensus was such that the editor of a film monthly where I then wrote a column hastily revamped her own '80s 10-best list to include the Scorsese opus.

Similarly, Jim Jarmusch's *Dead Man* (a movie first held back, then dumped, and finally yanked by its own distributor) has emerged as one of the most critically revered American features of the '90s—placing ahead of such relative blockbusters as *Schindler's List, JFK,* and *Pulp Fiction* in various recent surveys. It hardly seems coincidental that Jarmusch's visionary western would be chosen to open the series "Top of the World: *Film Comment* Selects the Most Important Films of the '90s" this Friday at the Walter Reade. But will *Dead Man* lend additional luster to Jarmusch's latest, *Ghost Dog: The Way of the Samurai?* I think not. *Variety* panned *Dead Man,* then used it as a stick to beat *Ghost Dog* —a film whose omission from the last New York Film Festival ended Jarmusch's record of six consecutive inclusions.

A more crowd-pleasing exercise in fathomless cool than its predecessor, *Ghost Dog* is an impeccably shot and sensationally scored deadpan parody of two current popular modes—the hit-man glorification saga and the Cosa Nostra family drama—and is predicated on the clash of at least as many behavioral codes. The hired gun known as Ghost Dog (Forest Whitaker) is introduced reading the 18th-century samurai manual *Hagakure.* His lips don't exactly move, but the text thereafter serves as the major indicator of his consciousness: "The samurai is as if dead." (It does not take long for these quotes to seem precious and then irksome.)

Ghost Dog has pledged his fealty to a somewhat baffled small-time mobster with whom he communicates by carrier pigeon. Like the Parisian hit man who is the antihero of Jean-Pierre Melville's 1967 *Le Samurai* (which, no less stylized, opens with a quote from the invented *Book of Bushido),* Ghost Dog is an ascetic loner who must ultimately wreak vengeance on the employer who betrays him. Cowled like a monk in his hooded sweatshirt, the urban samurai leaves his rooftop shack, complete with pigeon coop and Shinto altar, to glide unseen through the nighttime streets of his derelict neighborhood (a seeming mixture of Brooklyn and Jersey City).

To a large degree, Whitaker's state of grace is the movie's subject. From *The Color of Money* through *The Crying Game,* the actor has created some of the most vivid character performances of the past 15 years. *Ghost Dog* is Whitaker's first chance since *Bird* to carry an entire movie—although Jarmusch, as is his wont, uses him more as an icon than a performer, trading heavily on Whitaker's mournful yet impassive bearing. Programmatically devoid of emotion throughout, Whitaker is supported by a yapping crew of secondarios who play mobsters so deadbeat they're being dunned for their clubhouse rent—Cliff Gorman, John Tormey, Gene Ruffini, and Scorsese favorite Victor Argo. Henry Silva, a onetime Rat Pack crony and eponymous star of the seminal hit-man flick *Johnny Cool, is* the exception as the don whose brain-dead dignity mirrors Whitaker's uncanny stillness.

Ghost Dog's master commissions him to eliminate the wiseguy who has been unwise enough to romance the don's daughter Louise (Tricia Vessey). Unfortunately, when the hit man fulfills his contract, Louise herself is on the scene, wearing a red slip, reading *Rashomon,* and watching Betty Boop. This fondness for televised cartoons runs in the family—the don is subsequently shown staring with fierce incomprehension at Felix the Cat turning diamonds into jelly beans. But then, as propelled by RZA's ominous, pulsating score, *Ghost Dog* is itself something of a cartoon—well stocked with Jarmusch's absurdist running gags and populated by birds, bears, and other funny animals.

Although Jarmusch will never be mistaken for John Woo (who has similarly paid homage to *Le Samurai), Ghost Dog* is easily the most violent movie the New York independent has made to date. Perhaps that is why the action is tempered by the extended whimsy of Ghost Dog's largely telepathic friendship with two innocents—a voluble Haitian ice cream vendor (Isaach de Bankolé) who speaks and understands only French yet intuits all of Ghost Dog's lines, and the wise little girl (Camille Winbush) with whom the hit man strikes up an acquaintance based on their mutual love of reading.

A movie as laconic as its hero, *Ghost Dog* is nonetheless diminished by its most un-Zen-like attachment to this underlying sentimentality. *Ghost Dog*'s journey into the void lacks the cosmic, primal mystery of *Dead Man*'s wilderness trip. Most of the movie's pleasures are derived from Jarmusch's comic timing and minimalist mise-en-scéne. But, although a lesser film in the Jarmusch oeuvre, *Ghost Dog* demonstrates enough incidental grit and throwaway brilliance to suggest the filmmaker's capacity to rise from the *Dead*.

Also reviewed in:
CHICAGO TRIBUNE, 3/17/00, Friday/p. A, Michael Wilmington
NATION, 3/13/00, p. 34, Stuart Klawans
NEW REPUBLIC, 3/6/00, p. 26, Stanley Kauffmann
NEW YORK TIMES, 3/3/00, p. E1, A. O. Scott
VARIETY, 5/24-30/99, p. 65, Todd McCarthy
WASHINGTON POST, 3/17/00, p. C1, Stephen Hunter
WASHINGTON POST, 3/17/00, Weekend/p. 45, Desson Howe

GIRL NEXT DOOR, THE

An Indican Pictures and Blackwatch Releasing presentation of a Berns Brothers/Cafe Sisters production. *Executive Producer:* Michael Berns. *Producer:* Christine Fugate, Adam Berns, and Eren McGinnis. *Director:* Christine Fugate. *Director of Photography:* Christine Fugate nd Neal Brown. *Editor:* Christine Fugate and Kate Amend. *Music:* Denis M. Harrigan. *Costumes:* Antoinette Messam. *Running time:* 85 minutes. *MPAA Rating:* Not Rated.

WITH: Stacy Valentine (Herself).

NEW YORK POST, 4/14/00, p. 56, Jonathan Foreman

You would expect the story of an Oklahoma housewife who became a porn star, to make a fascinating documentary, and despite inadequate editing and overreliance on bad background music, "The Girl Next Door" doesn't disappoint.

It takes you on a seductive—if not very sexy—tour of the weird reality underlying the industry so amusingly fictionalized in "Boogie Nights," and it partly answers one of the big questions avoided by that film: namely what kind of personal lives do porn stars have outside of work?

For two years, filmmaker Christine Fugate followed Stacy Valentine (the oddly conventional porno name adopted by Stacy Baker)—who escaped from a bad marriage and a dull life to become an adult-video star (after her bullying then-husband made her submit nude photographs to a skin mag).

To Fugate's apparent surprise, Stacy turns out not to be a victim of childhood sexual abuse or junkie, but a sweet, rather ordinary woman who generally enjoys her work, but who suffers from loneliness and a surprisingly poor body-image. The ugliest, most disturbing scenes in the movie are her liposuction operations.

VILLAGE VOICE, 4/18/00, p. 164, Jessica Winter

Stacy Valentine, née Stacy Baker, began making movies when her bullying husband—a man reminiscent, she implies, of her bullying father—browbeat her into posing nude for an adult magazine. She soon dumped the husband and embarked on a porn-film career, two years of which are chronicled in Christine Fugate's occasionally smirky documentary *The Girl Next Door*. We watch naked Stacy sweep up after ants invade a poolside hardcore scene, graphic footage of breast-enlargement surgery and liposuction, and her boyfriend/colleague's humiliation when he can't get aroused for a filmed three-way—he has to sit and watch as Stacy performs fellatio on their costar. Fugate is patient and sympathetic with her subject—a sad, fiercely solitary woman with "Trust no one" tattooed in Japanese on her neck—but the point of this project remains oblique. As we know from *Boogie Nights* and the recent Annabel Chong doc, making porn is bad for you. Staring at the raw evidence of this conclusion, through however compassionate a frame, is either an act of useless pity or sneering voyeurism.

Also reviewed in:
CHICAGO TRIBUNE, 5/5/000, Friday/p. I, John Petrakis
NEW YORK TIMES, 4/14/00, p. E22, Stephen Holden
VARIETY, 4/24-30/00, p. 35, Joe Leydon

GIRL ON THE BRIDGE

A Paramount Classics release of a Christian Fechner presentation of a UGCF/Films Christian Fechner/France 2 Cinéma co-production with the participation of Sofica Sofinergie 5/Canal+/Centre National de la Cinématographie. *Executive Producer:* Hervé Truffaut. *Producer:* Christian Fechner. *Director:* Patrice Leconte. *Screenplay (French with English subtitles):* Serge Frydman. *Director of Photography:* Jean Marie Dreujou. *Editor:* Joëlle Hache. *Sound:* Dominique Hennequin and (music) Didier Lizé. *Sound Editor:* Paul Lainé and Jean Goudier. *Production Designer:* Daniel Baschieri. *Art Director:* Ivan Maussion. *Special Effects:* Philippe Hubin. *Costumes:* Annie Perier. *Make-up:* Joël Lavau and Christophe Danchaud. *Running time:* 92 minutes. *MPAA Rating:* R.

CAST: Daniel Auteuill (Gabor); Vanessa Paradis (Adèle); Claud Aufaure (Suicide Case); Farouk Bermouga (Young Man on Train); Bertie Cortez (Kusak); Nicola Donato (Monsieur Loyal); Enzo Etoyko (Italian Speaker); Giorgios Gatzios (Warmup Man); Demetre Georgalas (Takis); Catherine Lascault (Irène); Didier Lemoine (Train Conductor); Pierre-François Martin Laval (Fireman 1); Stéphane Metzger (Italian Boy); Franck Monsigny (Hospital Intern); Mireille Mossé (Miss Memory); Boris Napes (Barman); Luc Palun (Stage Manager); Isabelle Petit-Jacques (Bride); Jacques Philipson (Man in Swimming Trunks); Frédéric Pflüger (Contortionist); Jean-Paul Rouvray (Fireman 2); Philippe Sire (Concierge); Natascha Solignac (Nurse); Isabelle Spade (Woman at Casino); Jacques Vertan (Clown); Bruno Villien (Gambler).

LOS ANGELES TIMES, 7/28/00, Calendar/p. 10, Kevin Thomas

The French take emotions so seriously that even in the most unabashedly romantic of comedies you find yourself looking for a sobering subtext. You will search in vain for it, however, in Patrice Leconte's heady "Girl on the Bridge."

Still, it is steeped in that very French quality, characteristic of so many cherished vintage movies: an all-pervasive fatalism. No wonder Leconte had his cinematographer, Jean-Marie Dreujou, shoot in glorious black and white, for his film is inconceivable in color.

The result is a sophisticated diversion that makes no real demands beyond submitting to subtitles.

Even the name of the film's leading lady, Vanessa Paradis, evokes that of a star of an earlier, more glamorous era—Viviane Romance comes to mind.

Paradis' Adele, like many a despairing heroine before her, is preparing to jump off a Paris bridge into the Seine when she is spotted by a stranger who will become her savior—or will he? He is Gabor (Daniel Auteuil), a circus performer in need of salvation himself.

Overcome by Adele's youthful beauty and vulnerability, the middle-aged knife-thrower knows he has found his new partner. Rejuvenated, Gabor bluffs himself into a circus performing in Monte Carlo by promising he will do his act blindfolded. What he and Adele discover is that they are so much on the same wavelength as to be downright telepathic in their ability to communicate without either sight or sound. They also discover that in performing their routine they both experience a terrific rush that can only be regarded as sexual. Adele also gets the same rush as Gabor from gambling when he sends her in his place to the gaming tables; he's been banned because of his clairvoyant powers.

Athens and Istanbul beckon beyond Monte Carlo, but the tables are beginning to turn. Gabor has fallen in love so completely with Adele that he's in danger of becoming consumed by his demons. Now it's her turn to return the favor, but just how strong is that telepathic bond between them anyway? Will Gabor ever be able to declare his love to Adele—and how will she respond?

Leconte has long been fascinated with the human capacity for obsession films as "Monsieur Hire," "The Hairdresser's Husband" and "Ridicule."

He's more purely romantic here, yet both Auteuil and Paradis are so clearly committed to bringing alive what is essentially a fairy tale that they both were nominated for Cesars, with Auteuil coming up a winner.

Locale is crucial here, and Monte Carlo, Athens and Istanbul are a wonderful trio of cities for glamorous romance, intrigue and danger—and they could not seem more richly atmospheric with Dreujou's lush camerawork. This counterpoints a score assembled by Leconte entirely from existing music, ranging from selections of Marianne Faithfull, Benny Goodman, Brenda Lee—and the Istanbul Oriental Ensemble.

Leconte has acknowledged the influence of Ophuls and Fellini, but his film. recalls even more the poetic spirit of the Marcel Carne films of the '30s and '40s.

Leconte has remarked of his film that "when you're alone you're nothing. But when you're two, you can do anything. Luck exists only when you've found that other half of that torn bill," referring to a dollar bill that Gabor has symbolically ripped in two, presenting Adele with one half.

Spoken like a true Frenchman.

NEW YORK, 8/7/00, p. 67, Peter Rainer

Patrice LeConte's *Girl on the Bridge*, shot in silky black-and-white that at times turns sulphurous, has the look of a forties Hollywood film noir crossed with a French art-house classic, and that might describe its content, too: Gabor (Daniel Auteuil), a has-been knife thrower, rescues a despairing girl, Adele (Vanessa Paradis), from jumping into the icy Seine and recruits her as the new partner in his act. The two form a chaste, mystical bond; the sex is all in the throwing, as Gabor, whose eyes glower here like no one's since Bela Lugosi's, flings his blades around Adele's curvy form as she gasps deliciously. This doesn't even qualify as metaphor, does it? Renowned for his versatility, Leconte will go *anywhere* for an effect. In *Girl on the Bridge*. he throws it all in—fairy tales and occultism and Felliniesque carny melodrama and casinos on the Riviera. His mixture of moods and styles really doesn't add up, but the two leads have an intriguing Svengali-Trilby thing going on, and the knife-throwing sequences are so rattling that you leave the theater grateful you weren't nicked.

NEW YORK POST, 7/28/00, p. 48, Lou Lumenick

This is one hot summer movie! French director Patrice Leconte ("Ridicule") turns up the erotic heat in the most gorgeously photographed black-and-white film since Wim Wenders' sublime "Wings of Desire."

This romantic fable is ultimately too self-conscious to be anywhere near as intoxicating as the Wenders movie, but it has enough moments to be one of the season's most entertaining foreign films.

Daniel Auteuil (who won France's top acting award, the Cesar, for the role) is terrific as Gabor, a middle-aged, world-weary knife thrower who recruits his latest partner from a bridge near the Eiffel Tower.

That's Adele (the gorgeous Vanessa Paradis, the French singer-actress who is married to Johnny Depp), a 21-year-old who is contemplating suicide because of a series of disastrous romantic misadventures.

Gabor convinces Adele that her streak of bad luck has come to an end—and that she has psychic powers that complement his, making her ideal for this risky line of work.

After a stunning debut in Monte Carlo (where Gabor pins Adele beneath a sheet with his knives), their engagements take them to Italy and aboard a cruise ship in the Mediterranean.

Though Gabor promises their relationship will be strictly professional, he quickly succumbs to Adele's gamine charms, and the knife-throwing sessions become progressively more erotically charged.

A scene of them practicing together in a barn is perhaps the year's sexiest sequence—way steamier than Adele's couplings with a succession of romantic partners, including a contortionist.

When Serge Frydman's script, which is stronger on dialogue than on plot, has Adele temporarily leaving Gabor for a Greek newlywed, the film falters for a spell—though there's a priceless dark gag involving the old Brenda Lee song "I'm Sorry."

"Girl on the Bridge" is well worth seeing for the chemistry between the leads—and the sumptuous photography by Jean-Marie Dreujou.

NEWSDAY, 7/28/00, Part II/p. B8, Jan Stuart

Adele is one of life's all-time losers, a 21-year-old runaway who is used and trashed by men as fast as a six-pack of beer. "I'm like a vacuum cleaner, picking up all the dirt I left behind," she confesses, demonstrating a prodigious gift for simile, if not self-esteem.

Gabor is a self-styled "manic-eccentric," a poker-faced drifter with an uncanny talent for throwing knives. Because of the dangerous nature of his circus act, he must ferret out his human targets from the down and out. "Burned-out people are my stock in trade," he concedes without a hint of shame.

They are a match made, if not in heaven, then on a Paris bridge. It is there that Gabor (Daniel Auteuil) saves a suicidal Adele (French pop star Vanessa Paradis) from ending her life in the Seine. But when an emergency medic who fishes the pair from the river asks Gabor if he jumped in to rescue Adele, he answers cryptically, "It was so dark, it was hard to say who rescued whom."

Thus begins Patrice Laconte's magical, mystical "Girl on the Bridge," an ultimate love story about two people who are so symbiotically connected that it is never entirely clear who is saving whom from his or her darker nature. Attempting to explain their acute interdependency, Gabor holds up a $50 bill severed at the center, showing that one half is worthless without the other.

And indeed, once Adele agrees to be Gabor's partner, luck trails them noisily, like tin cans strung to a "just married" car. The act becomes an instant, international hit. They win like gangbusters at the raffles and roulette tables. And while they never consummate their relationship sexually, in a formal sense (Gabor frees Adele to satisfy her promiscuous tendencies), their knife-throwing sessions take on an increasingly erotic frisson that reflects their deepening need.

If "Girl on the Bridge" is a fable about the unexplainable energy shared by two people destined for each other, it is, on another level, about that elusive movie thing known as star chemistry. Alone, Auteuil projects a commanding sobriety and sex appeal. On her own, Paradis displays a quirky sensuality that can stop the heart. But together, Auteuil and Paradis are the stuff that celluloid dreams are made of, sending out a crackling charge of made-for-each-other ions that harks back to Signoret and Montand and beyond to Gable and Colbert...

Handsomely photographed with a wide-screen black-and-white canvas that takes in Athens, Istanbul, circus glare and carnival lights, "Girl on the Bridge" has already been compared to the films of Fellini. But it lacks the deeper theological undertones of "La Strada;" its metaphysical concerns are much more what-you-see-is- what-you-get. And what you see is wise, witty and unique, a romantic universe unto itself.

SIGHT AND SOUND, 6/00, p. 43, Ginette Vincendeau

France, the present. Young Adèle is interrogated by a psychologist, seemingly while in jail. She confesses to a string of sexual encounters and continuing bad luck. She is next found on a bridge in Paris, about to jump. Knife-thrower Gabor rescues her and offers her a job as a human target. In Monte Carlo, he changes her hairstyle and wardrobe. Their dangerous act (he throws knives blindfolded at Adèle) is popular and their relationship grows affectionate, although Adèle keeps having sex with other men. Gabor declares they are in luck as long as they stay together.

They win money in the casino and go to San Remo where they win a car in a lottery. They drive at night without lights and crash in a field. On a cruise ship, where Gabor throws knives while Adèle spins on the wheel of death, they meet newly married Takis and his bride. Adèle runs away with Takis. Gabor uses the bride as target but wounds her and loses his job. Meanwhile Takis' boat breaks down. He abandons Adèle, who ends up broke in Athens. Gabor turns up in Istanbul equally destitute. She finds him as he is about to jump into the Bosporus. They walk away together.

Popular French cinema usually comes to the UK in two guises: action thrillers, such as Luc Besson's, or heritage films, of which director Patrice Leconte's *Ridicule* is a good example. *La Fille sur le pont* is another kind of movie altogether, what one might call a 'popular auteur' French film. Made by a prominent director (Leconte) to a high standard of craftsmanship, featuring an ambitious contemporary script, it's nonetheless aimed at a mainstream audience. Leconte (who last November lead a controversial battle against French film critics for their alleged bias against French cinema) is now in the same class of renown as Bertrand Blier, Bertrand Tavernier and Coline Serreau, among others. However, *La Fille sur le pont* fizzled at the box office in France, despite its three-star—Leconte, Daniel Auteuil, Vanessa Paradis—status, humour and upbeat happy ending.

There's much to savour here: shot beautifully in black and white, the film features marvellous widescreen camerawork and excellent turns from Paradis and Auteuil. But these achievements, together with flamboyant dialogue *à la* Blier and pointed New Wave references (the *Les Quatre Cent Coups*-like interview with protagonist Adèle at the beginning, the *La Baie des anges*-style picture of the Côte d'Azur) cannot compensate for the script's flimsiness. Granted, as the film keeps telling us, we are watching a fairy tale: "I'm [her] good fairy," says knife-thrower Gabor of Adèle to a young man on the train; Adèle and Gabor act as good-luck charms to each other; significant objects mysteriously appear at key moments. But this tale of mutual salvation is strangely old-fashioned, despite Adèle's slangy lines and casual promiscuity. The view of the circus follows age-old cinematic clichés: circus people are basically sad, their acts disasters waiting to happen.

La Fille sur le pont lacks novelty in another, more interesting way: it uncannily fits the recurrent French father-daughter theme, now starting to look a little dog-eared. As in some of Brigitte Bardot's 50s films or those in the 80s and 90s with Charlotte Gainsbourg, Marie Gillain and indeed Vanessa Paradis, a world-weary middle-aged male enacts the fantasy of saving/loving a delinquent daughter-figure, an erotic rescue fantasy mixed with the Pygmalion myth. "I want to turn you into Cinderella," says Gabor before giving Adèle a make-over in Monte Carlo. Typically, the young woman is motherless while her father is played by a big star—here it's Auteuil, while Gérard Depardieu played Paradis' father in *Elisa*. Even more strikingly, in Leconte's *Une chance sur deux* she had two fathers, played by Alain Delon and Jean-Paul Belmondo.

Equally characteristic of this father-daughter sub genre is the way the younger men are ineffectual and quickly marginalised despite their sexual usefulness, while the relationship between ageing male and young woman is sexually sublimated. In this case though, the knife-throwing metaphor turns both farcical and nasty, as Paradis passively waits to be wounded. Just in case we hadn't figured it out, the sexual metaphor is underlined by Paradis noting that it invokes "fear and pleasure at the same time" in her. As in other examples of this genre, misogyny is cleverly occluded by the beauty of the images and the male lead's accomplished acting. We even end up feeling sorry for Gabor when he can't throw his knives any more. Auteuil's ability to evoke winsome vulnerability almost makes us forget the symmetry of his and Adèle's fate is illusory: in their particular game, he risks losing his job but she risks losing her life.

VILLAGE VOICE, 8/1/00, p. 75, J. Hoberman

Tastefully directed by French veteran Patrice Leconte, *Girl on the Bridge* is a film of fake magic and facile enchantment—a slick bit of Fellini, a hint of *Wings of Desire*, a sort of Leos Carax lite. This ardently eccentric love story is mild stuff, but the jaunty, eclectic score and choppy camera give the impression of something more—in the same spirit that the tinted black-and-white cinematography feels forever trembling on the brink of color.

Leconte's romantic fable opens with a burst of North African music and a pretty young girl named Adele (pop star Vanessa Paradis) telling the sad tale of her naive affairs. This backstory is the setup for sadly promiscuous and pertly despairing Adele to hurl herself off a Paris bridge—a fate from which she is saved by the timely appearance of an irritating middle-aged bore (Daniel Auteuil) who turns out to be the great Gabor, a professional knife thrower in need of a lissome new target. Together, Adele and Gabor plunge into the circus backstage. The knife-throwing performances are filmed as though they were sexual encounters; not only the audience but the whole sideshow is transfixed by their erotic power. (Although Gabor sublimates his sexuality in his public performances, the filmmakers take care to confirm his normality by including a wistful former lover.) Adele's fooling around with assorted train conductors and contortionists notwithstanding, the two expand their rapport to include a telepathic roulette racket.

The gap-toothed Paradis is certainly a cutie pie. So is the movie, and some people are bound to come under its somewhat shopworn spell. *Girl on the Bridge* is painless—not particularly funny and not even remotely moving. Most of the big scenes are shamelessly prompted by the soundtrack, as the couple wander along the Mediterranean, playing an Italian carnival and an Adriatic cruise ship. The latter proves critical to their relationship while providing the movie's single most satisfying joke, Which involves a badly aimed throw and the Brenda Lee chestnut "I'm Sorry."

Also reviewed in:
CHICAGO TRIBUNE, 8/4/00, Friday/p. B, Michael Wilmington
NEW YORK TIMES, 7/28/00, p. E19, A. O. Scott
VARIETY , 4/5-11/99, p. 32, Lisa Nesselson
WASHINGTON POST, 8/18/00, p. C1, Stephen Hunter

GIRLFIGHT

A Screen Gems and the Independent Film Channel Productions release of a Green/Renzi production. *Executive Producer:* John Sayles, Jonathan Sehring, and Caroline Kaplan. *Producer:* Sarah Green, Martha Griffin, and Maggie Renzi. *Director:* Karyn Kusama. *Screenplay:* Karyn Kusama. *Director of Photography:* Patrick Cady. *Editor:* Plummy Tucker. *Music:* Theodore Shapiro. *Sound:* Judy Karp and (music) Michael Tudor. *Casting:* Maria E. Nelson and Ellyn Long Marshall. *Production Designer:* Stephen Beatrice. *Art Director:* Miguel Fernandez. *Costumes:* Marco Cattoretti and Luca Mosca. *Stunt Coordinator:* Manny Siverio. *Running time:* 90 minutes. *MPAA Rating:* R.

CAST: Alicia Ashley (Ricki Stiles); Thomas Barbour (Ira); Elisa Bocanegra (Marisol); Paul Calderon (Sandro); Santiago Douglas (Adrian); Louis Gus (Don); J.P. Lipton (Mr. Price); Iris Little-Thomas (Ms. Martinez); Herb Lovelle (Cal); Jack R. Marks (Pawnbroker); Diane Martella (Gym Coach); Belqui Ortiz (Karina); Dadi Pinero (Edward); Jose Rabelo (Al); Michelle Rodriguez (Diana Guzman); Anthony Ruiz (Tino); Ray Santiago (Tiny); John Sayles (Science Teacher); Victor Sierra (Ray); Jaime Tirelli (Hector); Shannon Walker Williams (Veronica); Graciella Ortiz (Girl Student); Chuck Hickey (Gym Janitor); José Espinal (Ray's Friend); Yiyo Guzman (Ray's Corner Man); Michael Bentt (Fight Pro); Gus Santorella and Courtney Krause (Fight Pro Posse); Edgardo Claudio, Allan Gropper, and Danny Gant (Referees); Millie Tirelli (Candice); Josephine Pignataro (Wife).

CHRISTIAN SCIENCE MONITOR, 9/29/00, p. 15, David Sterritt

"Girlfight" emerged from the midwinter Sundance Film Festival—like "Sex Lies, & Videotape," which helped put Sundance on the cultural map—and gathered more advance momentum at other specialized events. Its theatrical debut was cannily delayed until autumn, allowing word-of-mouth buzz to build for months and positioning it as a "serious picture" with spirit and substance.

All of which means indie-conscious moviegoers are primed for "Girlfight." They'll find it delivers what its promotion promises: a touching plot about a teenager who uses prizefighting as an escape route from her working-class home, and a punchy performance by Michelle Rodriguez as the heroine.

They may find Karyn Kusama's filmmaking a touch on the conventional side, however, recalling other movies—even Hollywood ones—about troubled households and feisty kids. While the picture may score a knockout by attracting everyday audiences as well as indie buffs, there's a chance it will do disappointingly with both groups, appearing too traditional for the indie crowd yet too scruffy for multiplexes. Its progress will be instructive to watch.

LOS ANGELES TIMES, 9/29/00, Calendar/p. 1, Kenneth Turan

"Girlfight's" first image tells you everything, pulling you into what turns out to be a powerful and empathetic melodrama with feminist underpinnings.

Eighteen-year-old high school senior Diana Guzman (Michelle Rodriguez, in a potent debut) is leaning against her locker and giving us the Stare. Sullen, pugnacious, looking out from under half-closed lids like a terror from hell, Diana's punishing attitude is more than unnerving, it's authentic enough to add conviction to everything that follows.

That air of reality is essential because in broad outline the plot of "Girlfight" is certainly recognizable. This is, after all, a boxing story, the latest in a long line of familiar fistic tales like "Golden Boy," "Body and Soul," "Champion" and "Rocky," in which the disappointed, the disenchanted and the disenfranchised find their way into the ring and try to make things right.

"Girlfight's" writer and director, Karyn Kusama, who split the Grand Jury Prize and won the directing award at Sundance for this impressive debut feature, has been shrewd enough to see how malleable and forever young these traditional forms can be, and how they can take up new causes and sensibilities. For the difference in this film is that the person needing to become somebody through time in the ring, the underdog being empowered, turns out to be a woman.

Given that look on her face, it's no shock that Diana lives in a state of constant rage. Continually busted for fighting in school, her undisguised hostility and smart-mouthed comebacks, not to mention a chip on her shoulder the size of Bensonhurst, all combine to earn remarks from her peers like "She should be put in a cage" and the more pointed "That bitch is psycho."

Diana lives in the Red Hook section of Brooklyn, a working-class area where "you can get killed doing your laundry." Her mother died when she was young, and the family now consists of affable younger brother Tiny (Ray Santiago) and their father, Sandro (Paul Calderon), a sour layabout who spends considerable time playing cards and drinking beer.

One fateful day, Sandro deputizes Diana to go to the Brooklyn Athletic Club to pay a trainer named Hector for the boxing lessons he's giving Tiny. This turns out to be a classic run-down establishment, filled with aging characters and hand-lettered signs that say things like "Winners never quit, quitters never win." Something clicks for Diana as soon as she walks in the door. She instinctively senses a determination and purposefulness she hasn't found elsewhere—not to mention a chance to hit people.

Hector (Jaime Tirelli, in one of the film's many fine supporting performances) isn't so sure. It's not right, he says when she asks for lessons; it's dangerous, girls can't fight. Etc. But like everyone else Diana comes in contact with, he's as fascinated as taken aback by the nonstop ferocity that oozes out of this young woman. Finally, he agrees—how could he not?—with a single caveat: "You don't sweat for me, you're out of my life."

Diana, obviously, is the light of nobody's life, the polar opposite of a character audiences instinctively warm to. It's the challenge of "Girlfight" to get us on this person's side, to convincingly humanize her without either removing her edge or diluting her fury or her tendency to push every situation to an extreme. It's a challenge that's much more than met.

Though the sport turns out to be a greater test than Diana anticipated, she readily takes to boxing. It's a place where she feels the warmth of accomplishment and where she's treated with the kind of respect she's never had before. Also, because it's an activity where there's no one to depend on but yourself, it perfectly suits her worldview.

Perhaps inevitably, the gym also provides a romantic partner in the person of a promising young fighter named Adrian (a convincing Santiago Douglas). Soon, though it violates Hector's Rule No. 1 ("no personal business in the gym"), these two take tentative steps toward becoming involved. It's one of the marks of this film's authenticity that both participants approach this possibility with a believable sense of wariness.

Without Rodriguez as its lead, "Girlfight's" many accomplishments are difficult to imagine, let alone achieve. Speaking after the film's debut screening at Sundance, director Kusama said that while the actress made a strong first impression, "she had no training in any way, and casting her was too frightening to imagine." While only time and other roles will reveal the extent of Rodriguez's talent, a more promising debut is hard to imagine. "I kind of lucked out," the director added. "I told my casting director I needed Brando as a teenage girl, and I found her."

As for Kusama herself, she's a John Sayles disciple who has well learned his lessons of craft, empathy and respect. Her cast is uniformly strong; cinematographer Patrick Cady has made the film both gritty and somehow poetic; and though the plot's last section may raise a few eyebrows, the script has so carefully prepared us that we go with it and are glad we did. Watching "Girlfight," it's hard not to feel that the writer-director is her protagonist's double in terms of drive, commitment and ability. This is not a great story in the abstract for Kusama; this is something she felt, and deeply.

NEW YORK, 10/9/00, p. 90, Peter Rainer

The best reason to see Karyn Kusama's *Girlfight* is for the surly, indrawn expressiveness of its star, Michelle Rodriguez. She plays Diana Guzman, who lives in the projects in Brooklyn and can't find an outlet for her aggressions until she starts boxing lessons at a local gym. There have been other recent movies about women fighters, including *Shadow Boxers* and *On the Ropes*, but those were documentaries. Through Rodriguez's performance, *Girlfight* brings into the fictional realm some of that caught-in-the-moment documentary realism; Rodriguez had never boxed before nor acted except as an extra, and she seems to be thinking through every move she makes. Yet her acting is also sensual and instinctive. Her performance is an amateur triumph, but the same can't really be said for the film, which doesn't know what to do with Diana's unruliness except to channel it into a feminist fable of empowerment in which the girl is finally forced to square off against her boyfriend (Santiago Douglas) in a metaphorical battle of wills. Violence is meant to be her salvation, but the bruised look she sends out suggests a different, and more interesting, story. Her glare tells us that what saves her is also what immolates her.

NEW YORK POST, 9/29/00, p. 55, Jonathan Foreman

Film festival audiences are so often enraptured by undeserving or pretentious material that it's almost shocking that Karyn Kusama's terrific "Girlfight" was such a resounding triumph, not just at Sundance (where it won the best-directing award and the Grand Jury prize), but also at Cannes, Toronto and Deauville.

Although a combination of familiar genres, "Girlfight" is refreshing and surprising, the way independent movies are supposed to be.

It isn't just that, unlike so many contemporary movies, "Girlfight" is defiantly—and unpatronizingly—about urban working people (as opposed to whiny post-collegiate Gen-Xers, gorgeous teenagers or middle-age suburbanites).

Or that it's about a woman who undergoes the kind of character transformation through struggle you generally identify with men in movies about sports or the military.

"Girlfight" is also refreshing because writer-director Kusama has a talent for understatement that matches her talent for inspiring actors: She steadfastly avoids even the slightest hint of cheesiness.

Every time you think the foot is about to drop and you're going to get some after-school-special lesson about the importance of discipline or family, or opportunities for women, Kusama deftly turns the film in another direction.

Defiantly tomboyish Diana Guzman (Rodriguez) lives with her dismissive father Sandro (Paul Calderon) and younger brother Tiny (Ray Santiago) in a project in the Red Hook section of Brooklyn.

She's a sullen high school junior, as uninterested in romance and sex as she is in her studies, and so quick to fight in the hallways she's on the verge of expulsion.

Tiny on the other hand is studious and artistic, so much so that a worried Sandro is paying for boxing lessons for him at the local gym. One day, Diana is sent by Sandro to pick up Tiny from the gym, and something about the place strikes a chord in her.

She persuades Tiny's coach, Hector (the excellent Jaime Tirelli), to teach her how to box, but has to steal cash from her father in order to pay for the lessons.

At first Hector is as put off as everyone else by Diane's bad attitude, even while he's impressed by her native aggression, physical strength and sheer will power.

But as she trains and grows stronger in his care, Diana begins to change inside. And as she starts to compete in amateur bouts against both women and men, she also begins to fall for handsome featherweight Adrian (Santiago Douglas).

To be sure, "Girlfight" is not without flaws. There's some obvious dialogue, and parts of the story line feel hoarily Hollywoodesque, especially the coincidence that forces the two lovers to battle each other in the ring—and the sheer unlikeliness of what happens to their relationship after the fight.

But everything else about "Girlfight"—from its performances to its depiction of the desperate world of local boxing gym, to its evocation of combat in the ring—is marvelously real and authentic.

And then there is the extraordinary Michelle Rodriguez. This kind of story wouldn't work without a convincing, charismatic actor at its center. But Rodriguez, in a powerful, nuanced debut that has rightly been called Brandoesque, does more than make the film work—she makes it sing.

NEWSDAY, 9/29/00, Part II/p. B6, John Anderson

Set in the bowels of Brooklyn, amid lugs, mugs, ex-pugs and the pungent, steamy hiss of old "Rocky" movies, "Girlfight" has a Sundance grand jury prize in its pocket, a string of hit appearances at international festivals and perhaps the easiest-to-market plot line of any indie ever. A boxing film about a woman? Get out the purse. And we don't mean the Fendi.

But "Girlfight" also has in its corner the gloriously sullen Michelle Rodriguez, who has never acted before but brings to the screen one of the more intriguing faces in the business. In fact, as Rodriguez' pugnacious Diana Guzman tapes up her hands, climbs in the ring and shrugs off the expectations of her sex, half the tension in the film comes from worrying about that face.

Karyn Kusama, an NYU grad making her feature debut as writer-director, has made a movie as tough-minded as its right-hooking heroine, and just as intelligent. While the domestic aspects of Diana's story are visually static—she lives at home with a geeky younger brother Tiny (Ray Santiago) and a bullying father (Paul Calderon), whom she blames for her mother's death—life there is exactly that. It isn't until Diana discovers the leaky, moldy gym where her father is having her brother coached that things change. As she begins to train surreptitiously under the father-like Hector (Jaime Tirelli), the camera gets more fluid. Kusama starts to vary her visual techniques. And the film opens up and blossoms, a lot like Diana herself.

While the melodramatic elements of "Girlfight" will be its fortune, Kusama's agenda is more serious, and she's decidedly subtle about it. Diana sneers at the "girly" masquerade/intrigues of her female schoolmates and would rather throw a punch and negotiate later. But what she's seen of a woman's lot in life—beginning with the beatings her father gave her mother—offer her little reason for optimism. Kusama can be a wiseguy—she gives the name Adrian to Diana's prize-fighting love interest (Santiago Douglas), which was, of course, the name of the whiny wife in the "Rocky" movies. But elsewhere she's a stealth propagandist: Diana, watching TV, hears a news report about a husband setting his wife on fire; looking out her window, she sees a stressed-out mother dragging her child by the hand; in the ring she's introduced as the fighter "in the lovely purple shorts." Even Hector disappoints: At his house, three little girls in a picture are identified as "Hector's kids; he doesn't see them too often." That she can give her heart to Adrian is an act of blind, reckless faith.

The boxing ring has a long, hallowed history as a film set, because what happens there is edgy and brutal. "Girlfight" is edgy, but not brutal, and the climactic ring battle between Diana and Adrian is more than a bit contrived. But as a story, "Girlfight" ties you up, Kusama practices a certain kind of magic and Rodriguez, as Terry Malloy might have put it, is definitely a contendah.

SIGHT AND SOUND, 4/01, p. 48, Leslie Felperin

Brooklyn, NYC, the present. Truculent Latina high-school senior Diana Guzman often gets into fights at school. At home, she lives with her widowed father Sandro and her younger brother Tiny. Sandro insists Tiny takes boxing lessons. At the gym one day, Diana asks Tiny's trainer Hector to take her on; he scoffs initially but agrees when she shows up with the money, stolen from Sandro. Diana impresses Hector with her skill. The scholarly Tiny gives over his fee money to Diana so she can continue to train, a fact they keep secret from Sandro.

Diana meets Adrian, a promising young fighter. They begin a tentative romance, although Adrian abstains from sex. Hector signs Diana up to an amateur women's boxing league and discovers she can officially fight with male boxers her age. Diana fights another boy from the gym and wins. Her commitment to training estranges her from her best friend Marisol. After discovering her secret, Sandro forbids her to box. Diana beats him when he's drunk and confronts him about the physical abuse he meted out to her mother that ultimately drove her to suicide. Eventually, Adrian and Diana fight each other in the ring. She wins the bout, and he shuns her for a few days, although a reconciliation suggests they might have a future as a couple.

Most boxing movies—with a few noble and notable exceptions *(Raging Bull,* 1980, or *Fat City,* 1972, for example)—are ruthlessly formulaic. We could boil almost all of them down to the following tropes: working-class tough discovers a sense of self-worth through boxing, attains a sense of honour by refusing to throw a fight and wins father's or surrogate parent's respect after a big bout. *Girlfight* incorporates nearly all the above clichés, but by putting a female protagonist in the ring instead of a man manages to seem as raw as a wound. We expect the discovery-of-self-worth story arc in a boxing film much as we expect a towel will be used to mop a sweaty brow between chimes of the bell. But who would predict the throwing-the-fight scene would pivot on a love story—fighter Diana is matched with her boyfriend Adrian in the climactic bout or that the plotline concerning parental respect would be given such a dark and violent twist? The gender tweak reconfigures all the genre's lines of perspective, like seeing *Othello* with the races reversed or an all-male *Swan Lake.*

Girlfight's accomplished script and direction are the handiwork of first-time director Karyn Kusama, formerly an assistant to indie-film godfather John Sayles (credited here as an executive producer). Kusama trained as a fighter and captures with great affection the squalid, macho atmosphere of the gyms with their peeling paintwork and fetid cupboards. Her dialogue is low on frill although the exchanges between the female characters such as Diana and her friend Marisol have the voracious snap of real girl talk. The men ring a little less true, but the cast bring conviction to the proceedings, particularly Jaime Tirelli as the wry trainer Hector. Best of all, the film features an exceptionally confidant central performance by Michelle Rodriguez as our pugilist heroine Diana, whose jutting jaw and 10-mile stare hold the viewer's attention like a clamp.

Those familiar with Sayles' work *(Lone Star, Men with Guns)* might be tempted to read his hand in the script's neatness, its empathetic treatment of an underdog protagonist, light dusting of liberal values, and the film's disciplined low-budget aesthetic. The movie also draws on the talents of several other Sayles regulars including editor Plummy Tucker and producer Maggie Renzi. Certainly there's something rather Saylesian about the ambiguous and only superficially triumphant ending (cf. *Lianna* or *Limbo).* But it would be a shame if Sayles' shadow overcasts Kusama's achievement, particularly the feat of coaxing such confident performances from her young cast. Given this is a film about a young woman's empowerment (a message driven home perhaps a shade too didactically), we ought to beware of giving too much credit to the coach and not enough to the director-fighter herself.

TIME, 10/2/00, p. 88, Richard Corliss

All right, it's *Rocky* redux. A nobody rises to boxing glory—same long odds, same grizzled trainer, same love interest (called Adrian!). But was there ever a boxing movie that had the two combatants cuffing each other and, when they clinch, one saying to the other, "I love you"?

You could call *Girlfight* a new kind of corny. But this isn't the heroic treacle of the NBC Olympics. Like the better indie films, *Girlfight* dares to play sentiment straight. It makes boxing a civilizing occupation; learning to do something well turns a girl with too much attitude into a woman—almost a lady. The camera performs some fancy footwork, but the film is closer to John

Sayles than to Martin Scorsese. It gives its fine actors room to breathe and behave—and in Michelle Rodriguez's case, glow.

In an early, glowering closeup, she eyes the camera: two threats, framed in mascara. This is a face made to smolder—the young Brando womanized. She knows she can hold a movie's center just by being onscreen. And she grows with the role. A star is born? Better: an actress. Watch out, Jennifer Lopez. Rodriguez is a challenger who could be the next champ.

VILLAGE VOICE, 10/3/00, p. 227, J. Hoberman

Karyn Kusama's *Girlfight* sublimates more than a few *Taboo*-esque [see Hoberman's review of *Taboo*] notions of sex and violence in its underdog celebration of a teenage athlete's true grit. This widely heralded movie is a near-irresistible button-pusher that's agile enough to hold a mirror to its own aspirations: The Sundance prize-winning filmmaker and her prize discovery, Michelle Rodriguez, merge in the image of a self-invented amateur boxer.

Diana (Rodriguez) is a Brooklyn high school senior with a major league scowl and a monster chip on her shoulder—a tough girl, but not a sexualized one. Sent by her crudely dismissive father on an errand to the gym where her dweebish younger brother Tiny (Ray Santiago) is unwillingly being taught to defend himself, she discovers her destiny—training in secret with a soulful ex-fighter (Jaime Tirelli), whom she pays with money stolen from Dad. The emphasis is on willpower and inner direction (little brother really wants to study art), and Rodriguez, who had no previous acting experience, reeks of raw conviction. She has a fighter's slightly lopsided face, and when she narrows her eyes her whole body seems to glare. No other performance comes close—there are scenes where everyone seems to be acting in their own movie.

Diana is ambivalently attracted to the handsome boy who is the gym's most promising prospect (Santiago Douglas), who, with an amusing nod to *Rocky*, is named Adrian. Conflicts in place, the movie's second half proceeds from bout to bout pretty much by rote as Diana slugs it out with girls, boys, and her father. (The fights, mainly shown in unflashy middle-shot, are stolidly convincing.) Like *Taboo*, *Girlfight* has its inevitable climax in a battle between two lovers. Although the movie gives the so-called sweet science a new meaning, it conjures up a post-macho relationship that would take very special training to resolve.

Also reviewed in:
CHICAGO TRIBUNE, 9/29/00, Friday/p. G, Michael Wilmington
NATION, 10/30/00, p. 36, Stuart Klawans
NEW REPUBLIC, 10/23/00, p. 28, Stanley Kauffmann
NEW YORK TIMES, 9/29/00, p. E22, A. O. Scott
NEW YORKER, 10/2/00, p. 147, David Denvy
VARIETY, 1/31-2/6/00, p. 30, Emanuel Levy
WASHINGTON POST, 9/29/00, p. C1, Rita Kempley
WASHINGTON POST, 9/29/00, Weekend/p. 43, Desson Howe

GLADIATOR

A DreamWorks Pictures and Universal Pictures release of a Douglas Wick production in association with Scott Free Productions. *Executive Producer:* Walter F. Parkes and Laurie MacDonald.   *Producer:* Douglas Wick, David Franzoni, and Branko Lustig. *Director:* Ridley Scott.   *Screenplay:* David Franzoni, John Logan, and William Nicholson.   *Story:* David Franzoni. *Director of Photography:* John Mathieson. *Editor:* Pietro Scalia. *Music:* Hans Zimmer and Lisa Gerrard. *Music Editor:* Dashiell Rae. *Sound:* Ken Weston and (music) Alan Meyerson. *Sound Editor:* Per Hallberg. *Casting:* Louis DiGiaimo. *Production Designer:* Arthur Max. *Art Director:* John King, David Allday, and Benjamin Fernandez. *Set Decorator:* Crispian Sallis, Sonja Klaus, Jile Azis, and Elli Griff. *Special Effects:* Neil Corbould. *Costumes:* Janty Yates. *Make-up:* Paul Engelen. *Stunt Coordinator:* Phil Neilson. *Running time:* 150 minutes. *MPAA Rating:* R.

CAST: Russell Crowe (Maximus);   Joaquin Phoenix (Commodus);   Connie Nielsen (Lucilla);
Oliver Reed (Proximo);   Richard Harris (Marcus Aurelius);   Derek Jacobi (Gracchus);   Djimon
Hounsou (Juba);   David Schofield (Falco);   John Shrapnel (Gaius); Tomas Arana (Quintus); Ralf
Moeller (Hagen);   Spencer Treat Clark (Lucius);   David Hemmings (Cassius);   Tommy
Flanagan (Cicero);   Sven-Ole Thorsen (Tiger);   Omid Djalili (Slave Trader);   Nicholas
McGaughey (Praetorian Officer);   Chris Kell (Scribe); Tony Curran and Mark Lewis (Assassins);
John Quinn (Valerius);   Alun Raglan (Praetorian Guard 1);   David Bailie (Engineer);   Chick
Allen (German Leader);   Dave Nicholls (Giant Man);   Al Hunter Ashton (Rome Trainer 1);
Billy Dowd (Narrator);   Ray Calleja (Lucius' Attendant);   Giannina Facio (Maximus' Wife);
Giorgio Cantarini (Maximus' Son).

CHRISTIAN SCIENCE MONITOR, 5/5/00, p. 15, David Sterritt

There are at least two reasons "Gladiator" will probably conquer its competitors in box-office
combat. For one, it offers a whopping 150 minutes of non-stop spectacle and violence, and
Hollywood has a special genius for marketing those particular commodities. For the other, Russell
Crowe was an Oscar contender for his acting in "The Insider," one of last year's very best
pictures, and his presence lends a touch of class to what is otherwise, well, a whopping 150
minutes of nonstop spectacle and violence.

But none of this means "Gladiator" is a movie to rush out and see. Ridley Scott's filmmaking
is as blunt and bullying as the combat it depicts, crashing from one over-heated close-up to
another, as if we won't notice a stabbing, slicing, or bludgeoning if it isn't rubbed in our faces.

And while Crowe's acting is certainly more subtle than most of the brouhaha around him, he
has little chance to display the affecting humanity that's one of his chief assets.

He plays Maximus, an ancient Roman general who's chosen by the aging Marcus Aurelius to
assume his place on the emperor's throne. The ruler's evil son, Commodus, covets this position,
though, and it doesn't take long for him to dispatch his illustrious dad and sell Maximus into
slavery.

Maximus always thought of himself as a humble sort of guy, but this new lifestyle isn't what
he had in mind. He spends the next few reels slaying other gladiators before bellowing Roman
crowds, thinking up ways to reduce the carnage among his fellow warriors, and dreaming of
revenge against you-know-who.

Hollywood used to thrive on epics like this, especially in the 1950s, when "sword and sandal"
sagas filled the increasingly wide screens of theaters eager to compete with television's rising
popularity. The genre has since lain fallow, but advance, enthusiasm over "Gladiator" suggests
that its appeal is as unkillable as both Maximus and Commodus appear to be.

The picture's likely triumph may distress moviegoers who had hoped the studios would wait for
summer before releasing their most flamboyant fantasies. Since there's no way to stop the
juggernaut, consolation must be sought in a few intermittent virtues—the glimmering intelligence
of Crowe's performance and the chance to see a final appearance by Oliver Reed, who completed
his portrayal of a gladiator coach shortly before his death.

Younger audiences may also enjoy the occasional bouts of slow-motion mayhem, à la Oliver
Stone or John Woo, and older viewers can let their minds wander to days of yore when the likes
of Victor Mature and Debra Paget would have grappled with the one-dimensional roles. They
wouldn't have fared any better with this script than their descendants do; but their surroundings
wouldn't have been so bone-crunchingly brutal, either.

LOS ANGELES TIMES, 5/5/00, Calendar/p. 1, Kenneth Turan

"Gladiator" delivers when it counts—but then and only then. Like an aging athlete who knows
how to husband strength and camouflage weaknesses, it makes the most of what it does well and
hopes you won't notice its limitations. With someone like Russell Crowe in the starring role, it
doesn't have much to worry about.

An intensely masculine actor with the ability to be as thoroughly convincing in a tailored suit
("The Insider") as in a suit of armor here, Crowe has a patent on heroic plausibility. Whether it's
as commanding general Maximus, adored by the armed multitudes, or a friendless man fighting
for his life in a "When Bad Things Happen to Good People" plot, Crowe brings essential physical

and psychological reality to the role. Even Spartacus himself might want to echo Billy Crystal's Oscar night wail of "I am so not Spartacus" after seeing what Crowe is up to here.

If Crowe is well suited to be this film's star, the same can be said for Ridley Scott as its director. From "The Duelists," his 1977 debut, through classics like "Alien" and "Blade Runner," Scott has demonstrated a wonderful gift for ambience, for making out-of-the-ordinary worlds come alive on screen.

Initially inspired by a nifty 19th century painting of gladiators in combat by French artist Gerome, Scott and his production crew, led by cinematographer John Mathieson and production designer Arthur Max, have briskly re-created the Roman empire, circa AD 180.

"Gladiator" is supremely atmospheric, shrewdly mixing traditional Roman movie elements like neatly trimmed senators in carefully pressed togas and fighters who say, "We who are about to die salute you," with the latest computer-generated wonders. Yes, we've all seen the initials "SPQR" Maximus has tattooed on his arm, but the Goodyear blimp-type shot floating over an SRO Coliseum is something invitingly new.

The problem with "Gladiator" is that Scott is so good at creating alternate universes that he hates to leave and overstays his welcome. Too long at a full two and a half hours, "Gladiator" is not as nimble outside the arena as inside.

The film depletes its considerable resources and hampers its momentum by spending too much time on predictable plot twists and standard "The mob is Rome, who will control them?" dialogue by the screenwriting tag team of David Franzoni, John Logan and William Nicholson.

"Gladiator" opens with one of its best sequences, a "Saving Private Ryan"-type battle between the Roman legions led by Maximus and rowdy German tribes who, to paraphrase Raymond Chandler, picked the wrong empire to get tough with. Wrecking an area of Britain that had previously been scheduled for deforestation, the struggle utilized 16,000 flaming arrows and 10,000 of the non-flaming variety, not to mention fully functional catapults in a violent conflagration made a bit more palatable by the lightning editing of Pietro Scalia (who cut Oliver Stone's "JFK").

All Maximus wants after the fight is over is to go home to Spain and his wife and son, but Marcus Aurelius, the wise old owl of an emperor (Richard Harris, one of the film's detachment of British actors), has other plans. He wants to bypass his son Commodus and have Maximus succeed him at the top. "Commodus is not a moral man," the emperor says somberly. "You are the son I should have had."

A single glimpse of Commodus, played by Joaquin Phoenix, and you know that the old man is being too kind. From his first frame, the emperor's son has the look of complete dementia, combining ruthlessness, ambition and lack of decency in one sniveling body. Not even his shrewd sister Lucilla (Connie Nielsen), who apparently had a "do you think a princess and a guy like me" romance with Maximus years earlier, is a match for him in connivance.

Before you can say, "We who are about to die" etc., Maximus suffers through a complete life change. He ends up a slave chained to Juba ("Amistad's" Djimon Hounsou) and owned by Proximo, a provincial trainer of gladiators. Energetically played by Oliver Reed in the last role of his life, Proximo is a former gladiator himself who teaches Maximus the tricks of the trade and makes it possible for him to go to Rome and dream of revenge against the new emperor. That's right, it's our old friend Commodus, and he's more twisted than ever.

It's in the backstage intrigue that surrounds the emperor and his court that "Gladiator" is at its least compelling. Too much time is spent on vacillating senators, pro forma betrayals and over-familiar lines like "The beating heart of Rome is not the marble of the Senate but the sand of the Coliseum." Close your eyes and you can almost hear Victor Mature saying the same thing.

When it comes to hand-to-hand combat inside the arena, which the film treats like the professional wrestling of its day, albeit with more permanent results, "Gladiator" is more in its element. Helped by Crowe's physicality, some cooperative tigers (real and digital) and an effective score (co-written by Hans Zimmer and Dead Can Dance's Lisa Gerrard, who also worked on "The Insider"), these matches provide all the visceral excitement you could ask for.

It's interesting to note that though Maximus is an invented character, both Marcus Aurelius and Commodus are drawn from history. In fact, the real Commodus, or so one respected authority tells us, was "one of the few Roman emperors of whom nothing good can be said," a gladiator groupie who ended up being strangled by one of his wrestling partners "with the collusion of his favorite mistress."

Let's see the World Wrestling Federation touch that.

NEW YORK, 5/15/00, p. 68, Peter Rainer

Set in that most Hollywood of eras, A.D. 180, *Gladiator* is an attempt to make a lavish Roman epic on the scale of *Spartacus* or *Ben-Hur* while at the same time providing us with a hero, Russell Crowe's Maximus, who is all simmer and scowl. It's a spectacularly over-the-top production starring a monumentally indrawn protagonist. General Maximus, who begins the movie massacring Yeti-looking barbarians in the forests, doesn't suffer fools gladly. He doesn't suffer *anything* gladly, not even suffering. He's the archetypal strong, silent type, and when he speaks, his words are as blunt as his knife blade is sharp. But Crowe, unlike, say, Clint Eastwood, knows how to make all that strong-silent masculinity expressive; as he also demonstrated in *The Insider,* he can play a character in a state of near stasis and still create a force field of rage and longing and hurt. Whenever Maximus the brooder moves into action, it's as if everything coiled inside him automatically springs to life. Readiness, for him, is a state of being.

Ridley Scott, directing from a script by David Franzoni, John Logan, and William Nicholson, is a filmmaker who likes to create worlds, and the world he has created here is a coming-together of Kubrick and Sergio Leone and the World Wrestling Federation, all of it heightened by Scott's inimitably stentorian style. Scott is the movie-making equivalent of a writer who types everything uppercase. He's a hard-sell visionary, and maybe that's why parts of *Gladiator,* particularly the fighting parts, resemble nothing so much as his specialty, the ultimate Super Bowl half-time commercial.

But what is Scott selling, exactly? It's a bit much to claim, as some have, that *Gladiator* is a breakthrough example of Roman-epic revisionism. What, after all, has been revised? Many of the film's plotlines and tropes are readily familiar, not only from *Spartacus* and *Ben-Hur* but also from *The Fall of the Roman Empire* and *Barabbas* and *Cleopatra* and the whole sweaty *Hercules* ilk. Marcus Aurelius (an impressively restrained Richard Harris) is that most standard of all Caesars: the ailing philosopher-king who laments his warring years. Maximus is the loyal soldier who, having done his duty for Rome, wants only to return to his wife and young son and live a quiet country life among the poplars. But Maximus is also the son Caesar wishes he had (another well-worn Roman-movie trope). Alas, the regal coot is saddled with Joaquin Phoenix's Commodus—think commode—who smothers the old man when he discovers that Maximus, whom he subsequently dispatches for execution, has been tapped to restore the Republic.

Then there's Commodus's sister, Lucilla (Connie Nielsen), another mainstay of the toga party; her father actually says to her, "if only you would have been born a man, what a Caesar you would have made." When Maximus is made a slave, and then a gladiator, we're presented with yet more Roman-epic stalwarts, including the gladiator ringmaster Proximo, played with ripe relish by Oliver Reed in his last screen appearance, and Juba (Djimon Hounsou), the noble black man and fellow fighter whose sinews are strung tight with a yearning for freedom. He's Woody Strode redux.

Actually, I'm glad *Gladiator* is not, to my way of thinking, terribly revisionist. It's been years, after all, since the last Roman epic, and the genre has always been a personal guilty pleasure: all those chariots and amphitheaters and centurions and sandals and mincing cutthroats. In terms of sheer flamboyant nastiness, Roman epics give you more bang for your buck than just about any other kind of movie. The biggest problem with *Gladiator* is not that it's timeworn but rather that it's not old-fashioned *enough*. The genre's kitsch pleasures are overridden by Scott's periodic attempts at grandiosity. The Forum looks like something out of *Triumph of the Will,* and the battle sequences, especially the opener, suffer from tour-de-force-itis. The sheer percussiveness of it all, along with too many close-ups of flailing limbs and bits of bodies, are enough to make one break out in hives. Scott does occasionally pull off a whopper, like the first, sweeping, can't-believe-our-eyes glimpse of the Colosseum (partially re-created with computer-generated imagery), but I'd gladly sacrifice most of these moments for more like the one in which the incestuous, thin-lipped Commodus, in full eyeliner appliqué, mutters to himself, "I'm terribly vexed."

Halfway into the movie, Proximo tells his prize gladiator, Maximus, "Win the crowd and you win your freedom." Winning the crowd at all costs is also the mantra of Hollywood, and Ridley Scott places his film squarely in that tradition. He treats his audience alternately like epicures and like a vulgar, bloodthirsty mob not dissimilar to the one that crowded the Colosseum. Whatever it takes to bring down the house. Without Russell Crowe's dynamism holding it all together, *Gladiator* might have devolved into a rash of overblown pandering. Crowe plays a character with a genius for survival, and he saves the movie, too.

NEW YORK POST, 5/5/00, p. 51, Jonathan Foreman

More than just a welcome revival of the toga movie—a genre dead for more than 30 years, if you don't count Bob Guccione's gamy "Caligula"—"Gladiator" is an exhilarating, sweeping epic that begs to be seen on the largest possible screen.

At times it's surprisingly languorous for a modern actioner. But it also boasts some of the most exciting pre-gunpowder combat sequences ever: Not only are the battles in "Gladiator" superior to—and more realistic than—anything in "Braveheart," they're equal in excitement to the classic arena contests in "Ben Hur" and "Spartacus."

They're so gripping, in fact, that they're disturbing: Long before the final duel, you find yourself cheering as wildly as the bloodthirsty Colosseum crowd.

Directed by Ridley Scott ("Alien," "Blade Runner"), "Gladiator" also features breathtaking photography, sets and computer-generated images.

But the real glory of the movie is Russell Crowe, who is simply magnificent as a mythical Roman general turned gladiator. Like James Mason, he is one of those actors who can make the lamest line (and like its sword-and-sandal predecessors, "Gladiator" has some clunkers) sound like Shakespeare.

"Gladiator" opens on the empire's wintry, forested northern frontier, with Maximus (Crowe) leading his legions against the ferocious German hordes. In a stunning battle sequence, clearly influenced by "Saving Private Ryan," Maximus routs the last threat to Rome's domination of Europe, as the ailing Emperor Marcus Aurelius (Richard Harris) looks on.

The emperor offers him supreme power; Maximus says he would rather retire to his farm in Spain. But before he can make up his mind, Commodus (Joaquin Phoenix) the emperor's son, who is visiting the front with his sister Lucilla (Connie Nielsen), murders Aurelius and assumes the purple.

Commodus immediately arranges to have Maximus killed. The general escapes this fate but finds disaster at home before being captured by slave traders. Taken to North Africa, Maximus is sold to the gladiatorial impresario Proximo (the late Oliver Reed, as rascally and charming as ever in his final role).

Initially reluctant to fight, Maximus proves to be an extraordinarily deadly gladiator. Accordingly, Proximo brings him to Rome to compete in games sponsored by the sports-mad Commodus.

"Gladiator" draws heavily on its '60s ancestors, but unlike them it contains no Christian message, and, more surprisingly, no sex.

Scott fills the movie with visual allusions to his own work as well as to "Spartacus" and even "Apocalypse Now." There are also some arty indulgences, including Maximus' bleached-out visions of his own death, shots of speeded-up clouds scudding over the desert, and black-and-white parade scenes that are clearly intended to evoke both Nazi-era Berlin and "Triumph of the Will."

However, there are no silly anachronisms—apart from an attempt to give the drama a modern political dimension. Periodically the characters spout historical absurdities about "a dream that was Rome" and "giving power back to the people" as if screenwriters David Franzoni, John Logan and William Nicholson were recycling Princess Leia's lines from "Star Wars."

Ancient-history buffs might also quarrel with military details. The Romans didn't use artillery except in sieges, for example, and employed their swords for stabbing, not slashing. Nor could they engage in cavalry charges, because the stirrup hadn't yet made it to Europe.

NEWSDAY, 5/5/00, Part II/p. B3, Gene Seymour

"Gladiator," at the very least, gets the grandeur down pat. Ancient Rome looks as splendiferous as we all remembered from the dozens of toga-sandal-and-chariot epics that came in waves back in the late 1950s and early '60s, when, like now, Americans were both generally prosperous and quite nervous about it.

As you may have heard, virtual effects are responsible for much of the gloss and glory that make up the backdrop of Ridley Scott's epic. But that's to be expected of a postmodern spectacular that, unlike such predecessors as "Ben Hur" and "Spartacus," has most of the religious and sociopolitical implications sandblasted away in favor of a cagey inquiry into the very nature of the infotainment age that rules the known world as the Caesars once did.

The vehicle for this inquiry is a streamlined, grimly efficient ripsnorter that sets things off with a fiery bloodbath in the snowy Germanic corner of the Roman Empire, circa AD 180. Quarterbacking the empire against the Gothic hordes is Maximus (Russell Crowe), a heroic general whose ice-blue eyes and cool magnanimity cloaks a skilled, terrifying ferocity in combat. He could have beaten the other guys by himself, a fact not lost on either the ailing emperor, Marcus Aurelius (Richard Harris), or his sybaritic, amoral offspring, Commodus (Joaquin Phoenix), champing at the bit to sit on his daddy's throne.

Aurelius, however, would prefer that his valiant general—the "son" he'd wished he'd had—assume provisional command of the empire until the senate can "give power back to the people." Commodus responds to this plan by literally squeezing the life out of his father and ordering Maximus' execution. The warrior escapes death, but his beloved wife and son are slaughtered back at his family farm. Grieving and wounded, he is taken captive by slave traders and purchased by Proximo (Oliver Reed, who died during the filming), a one-time gladiator who leads a traveling team of indentured killers from arena to arena.

Eventually, Proximo's globetrotters are beckoned to the biggest stage of all, the Colosseum, where Commodus keeps the bread-and- circuses going to distract the public from realizing that they're being ruled by a crazed doughball who has unhealthy designs on his own beauteous sister Lucilla (Connie Nielsen), who (of course) once had a thing for Maximus. At one Colosseum contest, Maximus emerges as such a favorite of the rabble that Commodus can't follow his natural instincts and have him put to death. That, as they say, is show biz!

And what's both distressing and clever about "Gladiator" is the way it implicates its audience in the sordid dilemma being dramatized. Your buttons are being pushed along with those of the ancient spectators as the movie piles atrocity upon atrocity, cheap thrill upon cheap thrill, severed limb upon severed limb. The movie is too slick to actually raise—instead of bruise—its audience's consciousness. But you're so caught up in the whirlwind of steel, sand and torn membranes that you haven't the time to feel too guilty about it.

Crowe's brooding melancholy is matched with his riveting physical presence and a grubby intensity. But it's Phoenix' bravado turn as the saturnine weasel Commodus that delivers the biggest surprise in the cast. He gives the 9-year-old in all of us someone who deserves our hissing.

SIGHT AND SOUND, 6/00, p. 34 & 44, Leslie Felperin

Germania, 180 AD. The Roman Army, led by General Maximus, vanquishes the last barbarian hordes to resist Rome. Passing over his scheming son Commodus, the dying emperor Marcus Aurelius asks Maximus to take command of the empire in order to make it once more into a republic. Commodus kills his father immediately afterwards, and orders the execution of Maximus and his wife and son in Spain. Maximus escapes but is too late to save his family. Captured by a slave trader, he's sold to Proximo, who organises gladiatorial bouts. Maximus is forced to fight in the local arena where he wins acclaim from the crowd and the respect of his fellow gladiators, including the African Juba and the Teutonic Hagen.

Meanwhile, in Rome, Commodus revives gladiator fights in the Coliseum (where they have been banned for five years) in order to curry favour with the people of Rome. His lack of interest in administration annoys Senator Gracchus, who aspires to restore the republic, while Commodus' murderous nature and incestuous desires worry his sister Lucilla, whose son Lucius is in line for the throne.

Maximus and the other gladiators fight in Rome, where Maximus' strategic skills make them victorious. Commodus is shocked and angry to find him still alive, but hesitates to have him killed because of his popularity with the mob. Lucilla, an old flame of Maximus', secretly plots with him and Gracchus to raise his old army against Commodus and re-establish the republic. But Commodus rumbles the plot and praetorian guards kill Proximo, Hagen and other gladiators while Gracchus is arrested. To win the respect of the people, Commodus decides to fight Maximus himself in the arena, but mortally wounds him to ensure his own victory. Nonetheless, Maximus kills Commodus in combat. Before he dies, he bestows power on Gracchus and has the surviving gladiators freed. He rejoins his family in the afterlife.

The *Encyclopaedia Britannica* imperiously dismisses the Roman philosopher-emperor Marcus Aurelius as "a historically overrated figure, presiding in a bewildered way over an empire beneath the gilt of which there already lay many a decaying patch." In Ridley Scott's magnificent new action film *Gladiator* the patch has become a serious infestation of dry rot that no amount of gilt, indigo or porphyry can disguise. The damage is carved on the performers themselves, many of whom seem to have been cast for their interesting facial scars as much as for their acting ability. As we watch the story—of Maximus (Russell Crowe), a Roman general demoted to a gladiator-slave who eventually revenges himself on the emperor Commodus (Joaquin Phoenix), murderer of Maximus' family and of his own father Marcus Aurelius (Richard Harris), and the ruin of Rome—it seems fitting that most of the awesome buildings we see are computer or effects-generated. For all their seeming solidity, they're illusions standing in for ephemeral structures, projections of the melancholic Piranesian ruins they would become, as incorporeal and doomed as the neon-limned Los Angeles of Scott's *Blade Runner*. Look on ye mighty and despair.

The biblical and Roman epics of the 50s and 60s were spectacles tooled to lure back the crowds with their historically justified bloodbaths and widescreen scale after television had begun to erode cinema's audience. But they also fulfilled a more mass-psychological function. Clearly they were working out anxieties about the west's imperial role in the new world order, a west beset by barbarians on every front *(The Fall of the Roman Empire*, 1964, on which *Gladiator* is largely based); fears about growing secularism *(Ben-Hur*, 1959); and coded justifications for the growing civil rights movement *(Spartacus*, 1960). Even if the heroes lose their lives in the film's short term, we know the values they stand for—individual freedom, democracy, republicanism, monotheism—are going to win in the end.

Gladiator's subtext is as frank as a codpiece. Rome here stands in for America: corrupt at its heart, based on enslavement, dedicated to sustaining pointless wars abroad while the mob happily forgoes a more civil society for bread and circuses. One of the film's better jokes is the way we're invited to see parallels between its gladiatorial arenas and the sports arenas of today, right down to the announcer/promoter (David Hemmings) who hypes up the combatants before the bouts. While serving up dollops of exquisitely choreographed violence, *Gladiator* the movie is nonetheless implicitly critical of the present-day culture which spawns television shows like, well, *Gladiators*—the spandex-clad mock-heroic gameshow—and makes modern emperors of sportspeople and entertainers. When Commodus' sister Lucilla (Connie Nielsen) tries to persuade Maximus to help her overthrow her brother, he complains, "I have the power only to amuse the mob." To which she replies, "That is power."

Having won the war against the barbarians, Maximus is a reluctant, apolitical hero. According to one report he was tellingly named Narcissus in David Franzoni's original script, since rewritten by John Logan and William Nicholson but still an admirably expository and cerebral piece of work. Battle-weary, Maximus dreams only of husbandry (in every sense of the word) and of rejoining his family either in Hispania or the afterlife. In the subtextual schema of the film, he's Shane with a shield, the good-but-innocent sword-slinger reluctantly recruited to clean up the town or, given that he never actually gets to rule, Colin Powell, the most popular Republican president that never was. (You could have a lot of fun mapping the current US presidential race on to *Gladiator*—could spoilt, slimy Commodus be George Bush Jr.?) Thankfully, the film eschews the heavy-handed religious symbolism that weighs down the older generation of epics; human through and through, Maximus is no Jesus figure, though casting directors ought to take a look at fervid-eyed Phoenix if anyone's thinking of remaking the Passion.

An effortlessly charismatic screen actor, Crowe brings shades of his other well-known roles to the part: the ruthless violence of his neo-Nazi in *Romper Stomper*, the guileless strength of his thug cop in *L.A. Confidential,* his arrogant but righteous whistleblower in The *Insider.* Mel Gibson was apparently considered for the role (and it's easy to see how *Braveheart* was an exemplar for the story), but the choice would have been too pat, too easily crowd pleasing. More deadpan and quotidian-looking, the younger Australian (mostly keeping his native accent, as do almost all the actors here, successfully suggesting the multicultural nature of the empire) commands the movie magisterially, never more so than when hacking down opponents with a casual economy of movement, barely breaking into sweat.

Maximus' humourlessness is delicately balanced by the preening lasciviousness Phoenix brings to Commodus, managing to wriggle out of the shadow cast by Christopher Plummer's own career-making turn in the same role in *The Fall of the Roman Empire.* With practically the only speaking part for a woman, Nielsen (kitted out in a fetching array of quasi-modern primitive frocks complete with bondage ribbons and hennaed bindi dots between her brows) shows impressive range and projects a regal sexiness. Finally, adding ballast to the rest of cast is a gaggle of old-timers: Derek Jacobi, invoking memories of his title role in *I, Claudius,* plays an epicene senator; Harris' Marcus Aurelius is both ethereal and imposing; and Oliver Reed—most of whose performance seems to have survived into the film considering he died while making it—swan-songs with his best performance since the Ken Russell days (the computer-generated footage of him is barely noticeable).

For my money, it's also the best film Ridley Scott has made *(Blade Runner* and *Alien* have been overrated for too long). Less an auteur than a top-dollar *metteur en scène,* he's a self-effacing master of the action sequence. Here he's made the quintessential big-budget studio product that's smarter than it looks, a fiendish arduous logistical feat that clicks together like a well-tailored suit of armour. If there's a thematic line running through his work, maybe it's the focus on heroes—Deckard in *Blade Runner,* Ripley in *Alien,* even girl gladiator Jordan O'Neil in *G.I.Jane*—who put their necks on the line for corrupt organisations that don't deserve their loyalty (an allegory of the sacrifice film makers make for studios and the braying spectator mob suggests itself).

Maximus defends the empire to Marcus Aurelius by saying he's seen the rest of the world and it's "brutal and cruel and dark. Rome is the light." But his words seem mere idealistic rhetoric by the end: the light is dimming; the barbarians "don't know when they've been conquered"; the people don't deserve the republic he's returned to them. The promise *(Titanic* style) of recompense in the afterlife is the merest plaster over the decay that waits to spread.

TIME, 5/8/00, p. 83, Richard Corliss

It seemed a quixotic notion: "Hey, guys, let's make a movie in a genre that went out of fashion when *The Sound of Music* came in; that will cost $100 million, require arduous location shooting and elaborate computer effects; whose director hasn't made a film grossing even $50 million domestically in 20 years; whose script will be retooled by three writers turning in new pages during shooting; and whose 'star' is a gifted actor but also, by all accounts, a severe rectal itch." We can hear the moguls chorusing: *"Gladiator?* Thumbs down."

Today Douglas Wick, the movie's producer, can say, "Anyone with a little showman in his blood knew it could work." And now the rest of Hollywood knows too. Even before it opens, *Gladiator* smells like a hit. Its early glow has movie people saying "Of course!" Of course there's a magnetic pull of audiences to Roman Empire epics—stories about palace sex, political backstabbing and violent raids are as today as the Clinton Administration. Of course Ridley Scott, whose only big hit was the 1979 *Alien* but who directed influential films such as *Blade Runner* and *Thelma & Louise,* possessed the vision and stamina to bring a complex story to screen life. And you bet Russell Crowe has the thoughtful, coiled danger, the unfakable maleness to become one of Hollywood's most wanted actors. He simply needed a showcase as grand as this one.

Gladiator is quite a good movie—a big, fat, rousing, intelligent, daring, retro, many-adjective-requiring entertainment. It has lots of fighting, but with a posh accent; this may be the first culturally acceptable version of WrestleMania. Beyond the spectacle of large men grabbing and stabbing one another, *Gladiator* offers body halvings, decapitations, unhandings. A pity the slaves must die for the public's sport and a pleasure that we get to watch. Violence is an issue directors love to deplore *and* exploit.

Every movie pitch is a variation on "It's old, but it's new!" As Walter Parkes, the production boss at DreamWorks who green-lighted *Gladiator*, says, "Recently there have been very successful movies—*Titanic, The Mask of Zorro, Saving Private Ryan*—that introduced classic genres to new audiences, employing modern writing and digital techniques. The Roman epic occupies a strange, special place in the heart of moviegoers. We love the good ones like *Ben-Hur* and *Spartacus*, but even the bad ones are guilty pleasures." Scott recalls seeing these epics in his youth. "I loved the costume drama of it all and remembered that world vividly," he says. "But I also knew you can't bring that to bear today. You've got to reinvent it."

The plot, familiar from the 1964 epic *The Fall of the Roman Empire*, is this: in A.D. 180, Emperor Marcus Aurelius (Richard Harris) is ailing. He anoints his best general, Maximus (Crowe), a man whose motto is "Strength and Honor," as Protector of Rome until it can again become a republic. Before announcing his decision, Marcus informs his son Commodus (Joaquin Phoenix), who lusts to be Emperor. Commodus is displeased by the news; he smothers Marcus in his bosom, murdering him with a filial embrace, and proclaims himself Emperor. In short order, the nasty boy has swiped Maximus' job, ordered his death, killed his boss, razed his home, and had his wife and son defiled and slaughtered. The soldier has reason for revenge.

Maximus escapes the executioner's blade and is sold into a troupe of gladiators, including the African Juba (Djimon Hounsou). Their job is to fight and die, and their Vince McMahon is the wily Proximo (Oliver Reed). Act II of *Gladiator* is a backstage show-biz story, the one about the old pro who makes a comeback in a new role. Maximus' battleground is now the arena; instead of barbarians, his opponents are hungry tigers. Proximo tells Maximus he must make the crowd love him. If he does, he'll go out there as Tiger Chow but come back a star.

The gladiator revue is such a hit in the provinces that it is soon playing Rome. There, Maximus takes two wary allies: Senator Gracchus (Derek Jacobi), who needs help in restoring the republic; and Lucilla (Connie Nielsen), Commodus' sister, who loved Maximus. But it won't be easy out-foxing Commodus. His Heinous Highness loves an unfair fight.

The idea for *Gladiator* began in the '70s when screenwriter David Franzoni read Daniel P. Mannix's *Those About to Die*, a briskly lurid history of the Roman games. "It really made a connection between that era and ours," Franzoni says, "about how sports heroes are slavishly worshiped by their fans." A few years ago, while writing his script for Steven Spielberg's *Amistad*, he worked on an idea about gladiators as commercialized idols, their endorsements on frescoes, chariots and jars of olive oil." When Scott was hired, he brought in John Logan *(Any Given Sunday)* to create Maximus' life as a slave and playwright William Nicholson *(Shadowlands)* for further character shadings.

Casting the film, Scott tested Jude Law for Commodus but went with Phoenix, an odd, inspired choice: beneath the villain's sliminess is an unloved child with vivid plans for vengeance. Scott's choice of Nielsen also was resisted, but the Danish beauty brings a regal presence to the film. The boozy, exuberant Reed gave a superbly knowing performance—alas, his last. He died toward the end of shooting; one scene was accomplished with a body double and some digital legerdemain (which also added tiers to the Colosseum). Crowe, deep into his Jeffrey Wigand character in *The Insider,* was persuaded to discuss the lead role. Scott was impressed—and knew he could spend more money making the film look good if he spent less for a star name.

To judge by reports from the set, Crowe could have played Maximus or Commodus: he was all warrior, all tyrant. A hard-drinking perfectionist, he got into brawls with villagers on one location and laid such waste to his rented villa in Morocco that the caretaker protested to Scott, saying "He must leave! He is violating every tenet of the Koran!" Crowe questioned every aspect of the evolving script and strode off the set when he did not get answers. Says a DreamWorks exec: "Russell was not well behaved. He tried to rewrite the entire script on the spot. You know the big line in the trailer, 'In this life or the next, I will, have my vengeance'? At first he absolutely refused to say it. He did a lot of posturing and put the fear of God into some people. Thankfully, Ridley never yelled. He was the voice of reason dealing with many unreasonable factors, not the least of which was his lead."

Crowe could be a nicer fellow but hardly a better actor. His Maximus is a cousin to the haunted Wigand, a powerful man troubled by the things he has to do. It is a delicate, indelible portrait. To *Gladiator*, a film in need of a star and a working-class hero, Crowe brings strength and honor.

VILLAGE VOICE, 5/9/00, p. 129, J. Hoberman

There's more wind than light in the thunderous hokum that is Ridley Scott's *Gladiator*. This gusty sub-Hong Kong action flick has been as rapturously received by some reviewers as *Titanic* was three years ago ("A truly great movie" per *Talk* magazine) and the projects are not dissimilar.

Like *Titanic*, *Gladiator* is a fearfully expensive, relentlessly high-tech revival of deeply retro material—in this case, the ancient-world epics invented by Italian filmmakers before World War I. *Gladiator* also comes complete with sentimental love story and otherworldly palaver. But the presence of Russell Crowe in a loincloth does not a billion-dollar triumph make. Scott misses the boat by not contriving to have his titular hero—the general-reduced-to-slave-redeemed-as-gladiator Maximus—fight his final match in old Pompeii the day Vesuvius blew its stack.

Gladiator opens well, as Roman legions mass in Germania and the great Maximus (Crowe) sets the barbarian woods on fire with a barrage of flaming arrows. The general wins the battle but loses the war, a victim of the monstrous sibling rivalry of the emperor Marcus Aurelius's son, Commodus (Joaquin Phoenix). Thus, *Gladiator* picks up the spectacle of antiquity where the genre collapsed 35 years ago, with *The Fall of the Roman Empire,* by spinning a similar fiction around the death of the philosopher-king and the tyranny of his ignoble successor. *Gladiator* borrows from *Spartacus* as well, although the conflict here is less a matter of collective injustice than individual payback.

Marcus Aurelius, a haggard Richard Harris sounding a bit like the legendary king he played in *Camelot,* muses that "there once was a dream that was Rome." Maximus agrees, even though this stalwart son of Iberia has never actually seen the seat of the empire. Marcus (who, in reality, advocated acceptance that all is change) wants the incorruptible Max to restore power to the people, but these hopes are smothered by the rejected Commodus, who sentences the general to death and for good measure massacres his family.

Taking a leisurely two and a half hours to recount the tale of Max's betrayal, martyrdom, and vengeance, *Gladiator* is not the bore it might have been. But self-proclaimed "world-creator" Scott only intermittently obliterates the turgid narrative and mediocre dialogue. This revenge tragedy echoes Shakespeare and Sergio Leone but without their dramaturgy. Having killed six armed men and then passed out on his plantation, Max awakes on the other side of the Mediterranean (and seemingly several centuries in the future). Arab slave traders put him on the block and he is bought, along with his African pal (Djimon Hounsou), by Proximo (an irrepressibly hammy Oliver Reed, who died before the shooting was completed).

Scarcely more expressive than Charles Bronson in *Once Upon a Time in the West,* Crowe plays Max as a glowering loner. Given his uncanny ability to single-handedly dispatch half a dozen heavily armed bruisers—not to mention the odd tiger—in less than a minute without losing his breath, he might have been more entertainingly embodied by Jet Li. But then, *Gladiator* might have been more fun if Scott's screenwriters had followed Jim Jarmusch's *Ghost Dog* in making their warrior a follower of the Way, meditating on such Aurelius-isms as "blot out vain pomp" and "all is ephemeral." Max's real guru is the sly Proximo, who coaches him in showmanship: "Win the crowd, and you will win freedom." Thus the gladiator is ready for his close-up when Commodus reopens the Colosseum, that his father shut down.

The movie's secret producer, Commodus decrees that Rome will be entertained by nonstop death games. (It was Scott's idea that these be punctuated by scenes of clouds streaming across the sky toward a sunburst vortex.) Phoenix plays Commodus as a flaming neurotic looking for approval even as he slavers in tongue-wagging excitement over the historical battles he's restaging. This resident tyrant has the best lines. "My history's a little hazy, but shouldn't the barbarians lose the battle of Carthage?" he waspishly asks a flunky after Max scores yet another upset victory. Discovering just who this mock Carthaginian is, he petulantly whines, "Why is he still alive? It vexes me!" To add to his villainy, the naughty boy wants to have his sister Lucilla. As the sex interest in this least licentious of Roman spectaculars, stately Connie Nielsen looks properly agonized, wincing from an overapplication of glycerin to her eyes.

Scott imagines Rome as a place of sinister, Nazi-like pomp combined with suitably mad street life. It's easy to marvel at his multimillion-dollar computer-generated aerial pans over the digital landscape. Still, *Gladiator* wages a lunkhead struggle against the excesses of its mise-en-scène. (The golden interiors, bluish haze, and overall lack of visual definition might have seemed bold in 1960, but, in the Scott oeuvre, the movie is far closer to *1492* or *Legend* than *Blade Runner*.) The filmmaker wants to show he can do action, but repetitively predicated on a mix of slow motion and fast cutting, the big slugfests keep *Gladiator* marching in place.

Will the world buy it? Some might reasonably consider *Gladiator* an inferior *Star Wars* without the cute critters. The digital animation is far more evident here than in *The Phantom Menace*—the fights often seem lifted from a Mack Sennett two-reeler, undercranked for comic effect. At least the scenario is self-reflexive. Proximo might be speaking for James Cameron when he explains to Max that "the power to amuse a mob" is power. Although Proximo tries to excuse himself from the final uprising, protesting that he is only an entertainer, showbiz does rule—forcing Commodus into a final fatal image war.

Also reviewed in:
CHICAGO TRIBUNE, 5/5/00, Friday/p. A, Michael Wilmington
NATION, 5/22/00, p. 34, Stuart Klawans
NEW YORK TIMES, 5/5/00, p. E1, Elvis Mitchell
NEW YORKER, 5/8/00, p. 125, Anthony Lane
VARIETY, 4/24-30/00, p. 27, Todd McCarthy
WASHINGTON POST, 5/5/00, p. C1, Stephen Hunter
WASHINGTON POST, 5/5/00, Weekend/p. 45, Desson Howe

GOD'S ARMY

An Excel Entertainment presentation of a Zion Films production. *Producer:* Richard Dutcher. *Director:* Richard Dutcher. *Screenplay:* Richard Dutcher. *Director of Photography:* Ken Glassing. *Editor:* Michael Chaskes. *Music:* Miriam Cutler. *Sound:* Doug Allen. *Casting:* Jennifer Buster. *Production Designer:* Gena Downey. *Art Director:* Heath Houseman. *Running time:* 108 minutes. *MPAA Rating:* PG.

CAST: Richard Dutcher (Elder Marcus Dalton); Matthew Brown (Elder Brandon Allen); DeSean Terry (Elder Banks); Michael Buster (Elder Kinegar); Luis Robledo (Elder Sandoval); Jacque Gray (Sister Fronk); Jeff Kelly (Elder Mangum); John Pentecost (President Beecroft); Lynne Carr (Sister Beecroft); Kelli Coleman (Sister Monson); Anthony Anselmi (Elder Harmer); Peter Jackson (Elder Downey); Seamus Hurley (Elder Rex); Francine Riber (Connie); Fawn Perez (Laura); Lorena Mena (Lyla); John Kraemer (Tim); Jennifer Christopher (Karla); Erica Clare (Sindy); Todd Davis (Elder Stokes); Louie Olivos, Jr. (Laura's Father); Lance Johnson (Brother Rose); Darron Johnson (Lionel); Elaine Hill (Elaine); Doug Stewart (Benny); Malayika Singley (Jenna); Dominque Dumas and Jeremiah Dumas (Jenna's Boys); Taz Brighton Dodge, Eli Dutcher, and Kiki Kehoe (Tim's Kids); Paul Downey (Paramedic); Albert Cabrera (Ambulance Driver); Scott Sandler (Nurse); Gwen Dutcher (Sexy Mormon Lady); Ethan Dutcher and Lucas Dutcher (Beach Kids); Paul Vito Abato (Old Man); Sherri Boyza (Dragon Lady); Soledad St. Hilaire (Latina); James Thiel (Bathroom Man); Cody Rosenberg (Coroner); Larry Bagby and Richard Radstone (Cops); Lance Schmidt (Mortician); James Powell (Gene Dalton); Cade Kleven (Little Pop #1); A. J. Desveaux (Little Pop #2).

LOS ANGELES TIMES, 4/27/00, Calendar/p. 21, Kathleen Craughwell

"God's Army" is a well-made independent movie about a 19-year-old Mormon missionary from Kansas adjusting to life in Los Angeles. Although the title communicates zealotry of the most off-putting kind, the movie is actually a sensitive and thoughtful probe into questions of faith and the difficulties faced by those who are called to teach others.

Matthew Brown plays Brandon Allen, or Elder Allen as he's called by his fellow missionaries. Soon after he's picked up at LAX and introduced to his surly partner Elder Dalton (Richard Dutcher, who also wrote, directed and produced the movie), Brandon is tramping the streets of

Los Angeles, going door-to-door in working-class neighborhoods where, not surprisingly, he's met mostly with rejection, hostility and indifference.

At the end of his first exhausting day Brandon meets his roommates—a merry band of pranksters partial to playing practical jokes on the new guy. The other missionaries include Elder Banks (DeSean Terry), a young African American convert; Elder Sandoval (Luis Robledo), the ladies man of the group; and Elder Kinegar (Michael Buster), the group's doubting Thomas who studies anti-Mormon literature to better educate himself about the "enemy."

The living quarters in their low-rent Hollywood apartment are cramped and the schedule—which includes daily prayers, personal reflection and group study in addition to missionary work and chores—is exhausting.

The key relationship in the film is between Brandon, who's as green as a husk of corn, and Elder Dalton, who at age 29 is considered ancient by his young cohorts (they refer to him as "Pops"). Both men have serious personal issues: Brandon's stepfather, the one who converted him to Mormonism, has been convicted of an insidious crime; Elder Dalton is in the final stages of cancer but is determined to finish his mission.

The questions posed by the two men to each other and to themselves are universal questions of faith. What does God expect from us? What constitutes a moral life? Are miracles possible through the intercession of God? How is one to communicate a spiritual message in our largely secular world?

Although Dutcher and several of the others involved with the movie are devout Mormons, this is not a movie heavy on proselytizing. Save for a few touchy-feely moments, "God's Army" is a mostly nonsentimental look at a world of believers and issues of faith, both of which we rarely

NEW YORK POST, 8/25/00, p. 59, Lou Lumenick

More a triumph of commerce than art, this $300,000 indie film has reportedly grossed $2.3 million before its New York debut—mighty impressive for a serious movie about religion.

Writer-director Richard Dutcher, whose background is in documentaries, also effectively plays the central role, a crabby, 29-year-old mentor to a group of young Mormons who are doing their required two-year stint as missionaries on the mean streets of Los Angeles.

His mission is given special urgency because he's in the final stages of cancer and has a few months to live—and he wants badly to guide a fresh-faced but troubled teenager from Kansas (Matthew Brown) who, like the others in his prank-playing God squad, is grappling with his own faith while proselytizing door to door.

While this intelligent movie admirably doesn't quite end up preaching to the converted, its intriguing subject matter is diluted by too many bland performances, clumsily staged scenes and laggard pacing that drags out the proceedings for nearly two hours.

VILLAGE VOICE, 8/29/00, p. 146, Michael Atkinson

Bittersweet Motel may not be a vision from deep within the cult-mold hothouse [see Atkinson's review], but Richard Dutcher's *God's Army* is. One of the new "niche-marketed" Christian indies that get rolled out in a theater-by-theater, city-by-city distribution scheme, Dutcher's film lacks the conspirational creepiness of the Trinity Broadcasting Network-produced idiocy, *The Omega Code*, but—made by and for Mormons—it's no less out of this world. An earnest, professionally shot comedy-drama about a wise, seasoned Elder showing his fresh-faced, Kansas-bred "companion" the ropes of putting on black ties and shirtsleeves and knocking on strangers' doors with a backpack full of pamphlets (in L.A., yet), *God's Army* tries to show the oh-so-human side of Gospel-hawking, His Word, the Path, and so on. The preachifying and cliché wallpaper may prove a believer's point, but for the number of Mormons in New York, you wonder if it's worth the UPS bill from Utah. As for Dutcher, it's easy enough to respect his faith, as H.L. Mencken said, "only in the sense and to the extent that we respect his theory that his wife is beautiful and his children smart."

Also reviewed in:
NEW YORK TIMES, 8/25/00, p. E18, Lawrence Van Gelder
VARIETY, 5/15-21/00, p. 33, Scott Foundas

GODS OF TIMES SQUARE, THE

A Glass Eye Pix and Scorpio Dogs Productions release. *Director:* Richard Sandler. *Director of Photography:* Richard Sandler. *Editor:* Dan Brown. *Running time:* 94 minutes. *MPAA Rating:* Not Rated.

NEW YORK POST, 9/22/00, p. 50, Lou Lumenick

Having lived and worked for years in and around Times Square, I am not the slightest bit nostalgic for the days when sidewalks were crammed with self-styled preachers screeching hate-filled rants.

Documentarian Richard Sandler giver, these "religionists" the spotlight in footage he shot over a six-year period beginning in 1992—roughly parallel the area's resurgence as a Disneyfied family entertainment district—a development Sandler views with alarm.

VILLAGE VOICE, 9/26/00, p. 152, Amy Taubin

When Alma [see Taubin's review of *Alma*] has to go to court because she pulled a gun on her neighbors, she carries a piece of frozen lamb with her, explaining that "the Bible says 'to overcome by the blood of the Lamb the word of your testimony.'" Alma might find kindred souls among the soapbox preachers, spiritual seekers, and just plain mad folk who populate Richard Sandler's *The Gods of Times Square*. Sandler videotaped the Times Square scene over a period of roughly five years (from Mark Wahlberg looking down upon the lesser-endowed mortals below from his Calvin Klein billboard to Rudy Giuliani policing the millennium celebration). A collage of caught-on-the-fly interviews, *The Gods of Times Squares* so casually put together it barely counts as a movie, but in these slickster days, that's almost a relief.

Also reviewed in:
NEW YORK TIMES, 9/20/00, p. E5, Lawrence Van Gelder

GODZILLA 2000

A Toho Films/TriStar Picture release of a Toho Pictures, Inc. production. *Executive Producer:* Shogo Tomiyama. *Producer:* Toshihiro Ogawa and Michael Schlesinger. *Director:* Takao Okawara. *Screenplay (Japanese with English dubbed):* Hiroshi Kashiwabara and Wataru Mimura. *Director of Photography:* Katsuihiro Kato. *Editor:* Yoshiyuki Okuhara. *Music:* Takayuki Hattori. *Sound:* Teiichi Saito. *Sound Editor:* Darren Paskal. *Casting:* Glen Chin (voice), Michael Mahoney, and Tadao Tanaka. *Production Designer:* Takeshi Shimizu. *Art Director:* Takeshi Shimizu. *Set Decorator:* Chuichi Yanagibori. *Special Effects:* Kenji Suzuki. *Running time:* 90 minutes. *MPAA Rating:* PG.

CAST: Takehiro Murata (Yuji Shinoda, Director); Shiro Sano (Shiro Miyasaka); Hiroshi Abe (Mitsuo Katagiri, the Chief); Naomi Nishida (Yuki Ichinose); Mayu Suzuki (Io Shinoda); Tsutomu Kitagawa (Godzilla); Koichi Ueda (Military Man), Shelley Sweeney (Reporter); Tsutomu Kitagawa (Gojira); Makoto Ito (Orga).

LOS ANGELES TIMES, 8/18/00, Calendar/p. 18, Kenneth Turan

[*The following review by Kenneth Turan appeared in a slightly different form in* **NEWSDAY, 8/18/00, Part II/p. B9.**]

This wasn't supposed to happen. The king was dead, the nearly two dozen Japanese films over 40 years, after fighting off Mothra, Megalon, Hedora, Biolante and others too numerous to mention, Godzilla, the once and future King of the Monsters, died in 1995. It wasn't beauty that killed the beast. Not this time anyway. It was Hollywood.

For in anticipation of competition from the much-ballyhooed 1998 mega-expensive "Godzilla" directed by Roland Emmerich, Toho Pictures, Mr. G's longtime home, killed the trusty veteran off in "Godzilla vs. Destroyer." Or so they thought.

But Hollywood's "Godzilla" didn't do too well in the face of some truly fire-breathing reviews, and Sony, which financed it, decided that it was the better part of valor to give the big guy back to the people who know how to treat him with respect.

In Japan, under his real name of Gojira (producer Joseph E. Levine came up with his American alias), Godzilla has been a national treasure since the first film came out in 1954. Schoolchildren could probably name the different actors who've worn the Godzilla suit, prowling around Tokyo knocking down miniature buildings, and if pressed could tell you that the sounds of the monster's awful footsteps are made by beating a kettle drum with a heavy rope knotted at one end.

So it's especially satisfying to report that "Godzilla 2000" is yet another traditional Japanese production, weakly plotted, woodenly acted and indifferently dubbed. Yet, for all of that, there is something pleasant and familiar about this old-fashioned home-cooking approach, as well as something powerful about the Japanese attitude toward this particular monster. When they star you in 23 movies, there has got to be a reason

Because the 21st century is upon us, the new Godzilla has been given a make-over. He's lost some height (down from 328 feet to approximately 170), but his mouth is now wider (the better to bite you with), his skin coarser, his dorsal fins longer and spikier. And even though computer-generated imagery is no longer taboo, the Godzilla suit has been handed down to the next generation, a former stuntman for action star Sonny Chiba named Tsutomu Kitagawa, who reports, for those who had their doubts, "playing Godzilla is not for someone who's claustrophobic."

Big and destructive though he is, Godzilla can be reclusive and hard to find, which is presumably why the Godzilla Prediction Network, or GPN, came into being. It's not much of a network, really, mostly renegade scientist Yuji Shinoda (Takehiro Murata) and his precocious daughter Io (Mayu Suzuki), who do sci-fi things like "monitor density changes in the plasma" to keep track of the behemoth.

Shinoda is a renegade because he wants to study Godzilla, to find out what makes him tick, and his knowledge is already extensive. "When Godzilla attacks," the scientist somberly announces, "he advances, not retreats." Better hold the presses for that one.

On the other side, Mitsuo Katagiri (Hiroshi Abe), head of the government's powerful Crisis Control Intelligence Agency, wants to get it over with and kill Godzilla as quickly as possible. He and sidekick Shiro Miyasaka (Shiro Sano) are eager to use the army's latest armor-piercing missiles to test how strong the monster's coarse new skin really is.

One of the intriguing subtexts of "Godzilla 2000" is that even with that toothier new mouth Godzilla is such a familiar face in Japan that no one ever seems surprised to see him. Not even the man who says, "The damn teriyaki is cold again," before Godzilla flattens a pub seems at all put out as the walls crash down around him.

"Godzilla 2000's" plot is triggered by an irritable career-girl photographer named Yuki Ichinose (Naomi Nishida), who says things like "Bite me" (surely not a direct translation from the Japanese) and worries, when her plan to get Godzilla snapshots doesn't pan out, "God must be punishing me for being ambitious."

Soon enough, however, Yuki's and everyone else's concerns matter little as a vicious and gigantic alien creature named Orga, in an especially bad mood because it's been asleep for 60 million years and missed a lot of cool stuff, tries to take over the world. This, we are told in no uncertain terms, "could be the end of civilization."

But the truth is that after decades spent using Tokyo as his literal stomping grounds, Mr. G., beady eyes and radiation breath notwithstanding, has become a friend of the family. He's like a mean-tempered junkyard dog who may have differences with the human race but certainly isn't going to let another alien horn in on his territory without a fight.

It's in watching the climactic battle between Orga and Godzilla that the essence of this series' long-lived appeal comes into focus. For there is a surprising level of the nightmarishly primeval in these tussles, a sense of watching an ancient religious rite with mythic roots, that makes the made-in-Japan fights stand apart from the kinds of surfacy battles American monsters engage in.

"The American Godzilla was a target the humans had to beat, and, ultimately, they did," executive producer Shogo Tomiyama explains. "But the Japanese Godzilla is totally different—he is the star of the movie." Which may be why Japanese audiences feel, as one of the characters puts it, "Godzilla is inside each one of us."

Or maybe it's just a bad case of heartburn.

NEW YORK POST, 8/18/00, p. 53, Lou Lumenick

He's baaack! Godzilla's 24th screen outing reveals the giant amphibian is at least as durable as Clint Eastwood, that other prehistoric legend who also made his first screen appearance in 1954.

Mercifully, this latest adventure has no connection to Roland Emmerich's dreadful, special-effects-driven 1998 American version, in which Godzilla took on the Big Apple.

Instead, this is Classic Godzilla: A stunt man in a big rubber suit, trampling a scale-model Tokyo to the accompaniment of inexpertly dubbed English dialogue.

The special-effects work is so low-tech-any 5-year-old will know it's not real—that it's sort of refreshing and fun to watch after a season crammed with envelope-pushing computer-generated imagery.

The story line vaguely harkens back to the original Japanese "Gojira," which was renamed "Godzilla, King of the Monsters" when it was released in the U.S. in 1956, complete with Americanized inserts featuring Raymond Burr (who also appeared in "Godzilla 1985" and would doubtless be in this one, too, if he hadn't died in 1989).

When Godzilla leaves his underwater home and begins heading for a Japanese nuclear power plant ("Oh, great, another Chernobyl," someone remarks), the military tries to stop him with armor-piercing missiles.

"They'll go through Godzilla like s--- through a goose," predicts an evil government official (Hiroshi Abe), who opposes efforts by a sympathetic scientist (Takehiro Murata) and his young computer-whiz daughter (Mayu Suzuki) to save Godzilla for study.

There is also a spunky girl reporter (Naomi Nishida) who whines to her boss, "You promised you'd put me on hard news if I got a picture of Godzilla! "

As he's done for decades, Godzilla (Tsutomu Kitagawa is the man in the suit) handily survives all attacks to do his ritual walk-through sparking high-tension lines.

He's just in time to save Tokyo from a shape-shifting, 60-million-year-old monster from outer space, who at one point tries to eat Godzilla to absorb his mojo.

Takao Okawara, a Kurosawa disciple who directed two earlier Godzilla installments in the early '90s, knows what he's doing—the lengthy, Tokyo-smashing battle scene that climaxes the film is particularly impressive, especially when Godzilla unleashes his atomic breath.

Originally shot in Japanese, the film has been dubbed into American-accented English. The distinct lack of synchronization between lips and dialogue and many of the lines themselves—someone actually says "Great Caesar's ghost!" when Godzilla attacks—suggest someone had his tongue firmly in his cheek.

At 97 minutes, "Godzilla 2000" is about 15 minutes too long. But heck, it's great to have the big guy back.

VILLAGE VOICE, 8/22/00, p. 134, Mark Holcomb

Proving once again that a fire-spewing radioactive dinosaur can ruin your whole day, Toho Studios' *Godzilla 2000* advances the long-running series like Roland Emmerich's 1998 knockoff never happened. If this latest entry lacks the American remake's eye-popping effects, it also eschews the tiresome irony that made that budget-besotted mess so painful to endure. If nothing else *G2K* gives Godzilla a more formidable opponent than Matthew Broderick.

Specifically, an extraterrestrial being that's been disturbed from its 6000-year underwater nap by government scientists. This creature begins its unscrutable rampage in the guise of a giant flying rock before morphing into a shiny flying saucer, a metallic squid, and finally a knuckle-dragging, reptilian thingamajig that tries to swallow our hero in order to absorb his regenerative powers. Meanwhile, a compassionate scientist, his daughter, and a perky journalist clash with an obsessive government agent who wants Godzilla dead. Like us, these characters mostly wait around for the giant monsters to start knocking each other silly.

Though it lacks the antic verve of its mid-'60s predecessors, *Godzilla 2000* offers some interesting twists for connoisseurs. It all but ignores the other 20-odd sequels to *Gojira* (1953) and attempts to recapture that film's funereal tone. Moreover, what CGI there is marks an improvement over earlier entries—Godzilla's heat ray is particularly impressive—even if the principal effect is still a guy in a lizard suit. Expecting innovation from a 40-year-old franchise may be naive, but it's tempting to imagine Godzilla shedding his "savior of Tokyo" role and returning to his former glory as a city-stomping pulp metaphor for nuclear lunacy. How could that be any worse than the proposed sequel to Emmerich's film?

Also reviewed in:
CHICAGO TRIBUNE, 8/18/00, Friday/p. A, Mark Caro
NEW YORK TIMES, 8/18/00, p. E12, Stephen Holden
VARIETY, 8/21-27/00, p. 16, Joe Leydon
WASHINGTON POST, 8/18/00, p. C12, Stephen Hunter
WASHINGTON POST, 8/18/00, Weekend/p. 37, Michael O'Sullivan

GONE IN 60 SECONDS

A Touchstone Pictures and Jerry Bruckheimer Films release. *Executive Producer:* Jonathan Hensleigh, Chad Oman, Barry Waldman, Denise Shakarian Halicki, Robert Stone, and Webster Stone. *Producer:* Jerry Bruckheimer and Mike Stenson. *Director:* Dominic Sena. *Screenplay (based on the motion picture "Gone in 60 Seconds):* Scott Rosenberg. *Director of Photography:* Paul Cameron. *Editor:* Tom Muldoon and Chris Lebenzon. *Music:* Trevor Rabin. *Music Editor:* Will Kaplan. *Sound:* Peter Devlin and (music) Steve Kempster. *Sound Editor:* George Watters II. *Casting:* Victoria Thomas. *Production Designer:* Jeff Mann. *Art Director:* Stacey Litoff-Mann and Andrew Laws. *Set Designer:* Greg Hooper, Eric Sundahl, Fanée Aaron, Mariko Braswell, and Stacey Byers. *Set Decorator:* Don Diers. *Set Dressers:* Tyler Patton, Nelson Bush, Robert L. Robinson, John A. Bruno, Michael O'Donnell, Mykal Williams, and Michael Vojvoda. *Special Effects:* Mike Meinardus. *Costumes:* Marlene Stewart. *Make-up:* Julie Pearce. *Make-up (Nicholas Cage):* Allen Weisinger. *Make-up (Angelina Jolie):* Janeen Schreyer. *Make-up (Delroy Lindo):* Barbara Augustus. *Make-up Effects:* Matthew Mungle and Clinton Wayne. *Stunt Coordinator:* Chuck Picerni, Jr. *Running time:* 119 minutes. *MPAA Rating:* PG-13.

CAST: Nicolas Cage (Randall "Memphis" Raines); Angelina Jolie (Sara "Sway" Wayland); Giovanni Ribisi (Kip Raines); Delroy Lindo (Detective Roland Castlebeck); Will Patton (Atley Jackson); Christopher Eccleston (Raymond Calitri); Chi McBride (Donny Astricky); Robert Duvall (Otto Halliwell); Scott Caan (Tumbler); Timothy Olyphant (Detective Drycoff); William Lee Scott (Toby); Vinnie Jones (The Sphinx); James Duval (Freb); T J Cross (Mirror Man); Frances Fisher (Junie); Grace Zabriskie (Helen Raines); Mike Owen (Kid in Rice Burner); Jamie Bergman (Blonde in Drag Race); Holiday Hopke (Waitress); Harry van Gorkum (Forge); Grace Una (Jenny); Jesse Corti (Cop at Quality Café); Step[hen Shellen (Exotic Car Salesman); Alexandra Balahoutis (DMV Clerk); Rainbow Borden (Car Jacker 1); Victor Manni (Worker); Sanjay Pandya (Glass House Guy); Doria Anselmo (Glass House Girl); Lois Hall (Old Woman); Dean Rader Duval (Hype); C.J. Picerni (Go Cart Kid); Kevin Weismann (Intern 2); Anthony Boswell (Buddy); Billy Devlin (Detective Jurgens); Bodhi Elfman (Fuzzy Frizzel); Arye Gross (James Lakewood); Greg Collins (San Pedro Cop); Cosimo Fusco (Adjacent Mechanic); Eddie Mui (Billy Moony); Joseph Patrick Kelly (Snake G.R.A.B.); Scott Burkholdler (Rent a Cop); Margaret Kontra Palmer (Televangelist Wife); Charlene Bloom (Swimming Girl); Kevin West (Intern 1); Billy "Sly" Williams (Cop); Alex Walters (Fireman); Lombardo Boyar (Paramedic); Angela Tassoni (Accident Victim); Scott Rosenberg (Private Doctor); Steve Danton (G.R.A.B. Officer 2); Tyler Patton (Security

Guard);   Carmen Argenziano (Detective Mayhew);   Dan Hildebrand (Saul);   King Alexander (Bar Dude);   Nick Meaney (Thug);   Michael A. Pena (Ignacio); Juan Pina (Gang Banger 2); Tim Dezarn (Shotgun Guy);   John Carroll Lynch (Impound Manager);   Doug Bennett (Wreck Drive "Mel");   Bob Sattler (C.H.P.);   Trevor Goddard (Don);   Master P (Bob Trutwell); Ken Jenkins (Televangelist).

CHRISTIAN SCIENCE MONITOR, 6/9/00, p. 15, David Sterritt

The on-screen emblem of Jerry Bruckheimer Films, producer of action flicks like "Con Air" and "Armageddon," shows a zooming stretch of highway through the windshield of a speeding car. Living up to its logo, the company has now cranked out "Gone in 60 Seconds," a two-hour version of the same idea.

It's just as catchy for the eye, just as empty for the brain.

Nicolas Cage plays the protagonist, a reformed auto thief forced back into the business by an evil thug who's pledged to kill his brother if he doesn't steal 50 cars within the next three days. Helping out are a couple of old friends: a former crook who runs an auto-repair shop, and a driving instructor who finds crime less hazardous than his current profession. On their trail are two policemen who know as much about cars as they do.

True to the Bruckheimer tradition, director Dominic Sena and screenwriter Scott Rosenberg have souped up this idea—purloined from a 1974 movie of the same title—with a complete set of trendy Hollywood formulas, including perfunctory nods to women's lib (Angelina Jolie is the gang's female member) and family values (Cage's character is only doing this to rescue his brother and save their mom some grief). The result is cinema at its most mind-numbingly trite, from its car-heisting prologue to its Evel Knievel climax.

All of which may please die-hard fans of the genre, but what's really indefensible is the movie's PG-13 rating. "Some material may be inappropriate" hardly begins to cover its bone-crunching violence, barbaric language, and gratuitous sexuality—not to mention the plot, designed to have us rooting for the crooks over the cops!

Where was the rating committee on this one? Gone in 60 seconds?

LOS ANGELES TIMES, 6/9/00, Calendar/p. 1, Kenneth Turan

If "Gone in 60 Seconds" were a car, you'd say it had more muscle than finesse. Fast and flashy in spurts, it has a tendency to run ragged and spends an unhealthy amount of time idling pointlessly at intersections. It's not the car of anyone's dreams, though it might well have been.

The most regrettable thing about "Gone in 60 Seconds" is that it doesn't rise to the level of its excellent trailer. That pumped-up piece of business has focus, pacing, concision and wall-to-wall action—all the things the full-scale version does without.

Given that the logo for Jerry Bruckheimer's production company features a fast-car motif, it's natural that he would want to remake H.B. "Toby" Halicki's 1974 cult classic, the original "Gone in 60 Seconds," famous among auto wreckage aficionados for devoting its last 40 minutes to one hell of a car chase.

The new version, starring Nicolas Cage and Angelina Jolie and directed by Dominic Sena, features some fine driving of its own, (though chopping the sequences up with trendy editing makes them less effective than what John Frankenheimer and company managed in the under-appreciated "Ronin"). The problem is not what "Gone" does on the straightaways, it's how it maneuvers through those hard-to-handle character curves.

Written by Scott Rosenberg, whose credits include "Things to Do in Denver When You're Dead" and the Bruckheimer-produced "Con Air," "60" seems determined to be character driven despite having characters who hesitate over the question "What's more exciting, having sex or stealing cars?"

So while audiences may be primed for more squealing tires and revving engines, this film is inordinately interested in the tedious relationships Randall "Memphis" Raines (Cage) has with younger brother Kip (Giovanni Ribisi) and ex-girlfriend Sara "Sway" Wayland (Jolie).

There was a time, six years ago, when Memphis Raines was the king of Southern California car thieves, so good at snatching top-of-the-line vehicles that when he suddenly quit the game and moved up north, auto theft in the South Bay went down 47%.

Kip, exhibiting more nerve than sense in the film's crisp opening sequence, has the bravado to steal a Porsche right out of a Wilshire Boulevard showroom window. Unfortunately, following in his brother's footsteps gets Kip on the wrong side of the evil Raymond Calitri, a.k.a. "the devil come to Long Beach" (British actor Christopher Eccleston), who soon enough offers Memphis, the legend himself, a veritable devil's bargain.

Come out of retirement, Calitri proposes, breaking your sacred word to your mother in the process, and steal 50 unstealable cars for me in four days, or else I will place your brother in a coffin I have personally handcrafted out of wood just to show what a psycho I am. Memphis, not a legend for nothing agrees.

Step one of this car theft extravaganza is rounding up Memphis' old gang, including Otto (Robert Duvall), Atley (Will Patton), Donny (Chi McBride) and two people Memphis would just as soon avoid: the nonspeaking Sphinx (Vinnie Jones) and the beautiful Sway. Given that 50 is a lot of cars, Memphis agrees to let Kip and his kiddie gang (Scott Caan and comedian TJ Cross among them) in on the action.

Soon getting word of this potential heistathon (which is to include a 1967 Shelby Mustang GT 500, the only car Memphis has never taken) is top detective Roland Castlebeck (Delroy Lindo), who'd like nothing better than busting Memphis. Wanting to bust him in a different way is Johnny B (Master P), a rival crook who's always resented Memphis' celebrity.

Acting would only get in the way of all this frantic activity, so "60" doesn't bother to offer much, instead allowing us to watch capable performers struggling with weak material. Cage lets his sunglasses do the work for him, Jolie has little outlet for her trademark charisma, and Vinnie Jones, memorable in "Lock, Stock and Two Smoking Barrels," comes off best by having the least to say.

Except for the lamentable "Kalifornia," director Sena has spent most of his career as either a director or cameraman on videos and commercials. So it's not surprising that he has more success showing us the, nifty gizmos the thieves use to do their work than illuminating their characters.

Not that the improbable script gives us that much to illuminate. Taking time for niceties like ethnic stereotyping and a subplot involving dog manure, "60" often appears to forget completely what it's supposed to be about. Maybe if the guys had to steal more than 50 cars, they wouldn't have the time for so much extraneous foolishness.

NEW YORK POST, 6/9/00, p. 47, Lou Lumenick

"Gone in 60 Seconds" is Hollywood's latest trip back to the future. It revisits the heyday of car-chase movies—the 1970s and 1980s—as enthusiastically as "U-571" introduced young audiences to World War II submarine movies and "Gladiator" brought back the sword-and-sandal epic.

As car-chase movies go—and I haven't exactly missed them, to be honest—it isn't bad, but it isn't terrific, either.

But shame on Disney for the movie's highly misleading ads. Besides making the film look like "Mission: Impossible 3," they promise an intriguing romance between Nicolas Cage and Angelina Jolie.

Fugeddaboudit.

Her star billing notwithstanding, Jolie has perhaps the ninth-largest part in the movie (behind seven humans and a dog), playing Cage's ex-girlfriend.

Based very loosely on actor/stuntman/director Toby Halicki's obscure 1974 flick (famous for a 40-minute chase sequence) the "new," cliché-ridden story casts a peroxided Cage as Memphis Raines, a legendary car thief who's forced out of retirement.

Raines is given a list of 50 cars that he must steal within four days—or a Los Angeles automobile smuggler (Christopher Eccleston) will have Raines' younger brother, Kip (Giovanni Ribisi), killed.

"The cars are on the boat or your brother's in the coffin," the bad guy tells him.

Raines recruits a team of ex-colleagues—all of whom, incredibly, have gone straight, including his mentor, Otto (Robert Duvall)—and plots to steal everything in one night, from a 2000 Volvo Turbo Wagon to Raines' favorite, a 1967 Shelby Mustang GT 500 that he dubs "Eleanor."

Meanwhile, Raines' return to L.A. hasn't gone unnoticed by Roland Castleback (Delroy Lindo), an LAPD detective specializing in car theft, with whom he has a longtime "Smokey and the Bandit" relationship.

None of the actors (including Will Patton, Scott Caan and Frances Fisher) takes the material any more seriously than it should be taken. Neither screenwriter Scott Rosenberg nor director Dominic Sena ("Kalifornia") provides the underused Cage much room to strut his stuff in this frantically edited film.

Cage's best scene, in which he poses as a snooty Mercedes customer, lasts all of 60 seconds. Jolie's role—basically, an extended cameo—consists mostly of a few quick shots of the Oscar winner hot-wiring cars. Her one "romantic" scene with Cage is a quick tease that goes no further than a kiss.

"What do you think is more exciting—having sex or boosting cars?" Raines asks her.

"How about having sex while boosting a car?" she replies.

Not in this PG-13-rated movie (which pushes the limit for vehicular mayhem), they don't. The filmmakers clearly think boosting cars is more exciting—though, surprisingly, the cars don't get much more footage than Jolie.

"Gone in 60 Seconds" isn't going to make anyone forget the classic chases in "Bullitt" or "The French Connection."

Still, the climactic pursuit—highlighted by Raines launching Eleanor off a ramp over a score of vehicles on a bridge—is a real hoot.

NEWSDAY, 6/9/00, Part II/p. B3, John Anderson

The mark of producer Jerry Bruckheimer is not exactly the mark of Cain, but he's certainly branded his own terrifying territory in the realm of motion pictures. These include the films that have helped turn Nicolas Cage from the quirky, skinny indie star he was into the quirky, skinny blockbuster star he's trying to become ("Con Air," "The Rock"). For this, Bruckheimer should probably be sent to a place where he has to watch Penny Marshall movies for the rest of eternity.

Still, "Gone in 60 Seconds," for all its inanity and pandering, is exactly what audiences expect from a big summer movie. Good-looking people, easy emotional catharses, stuff blowing up-aka Fun. With Cage as car thief Randall (Memphis) Raines, it's among this season's heat rash of "Shane"-style dramas (master warrior/soldier/car thief is brought reluctantly out of retirement by family/friends/ offer he can't refuse). It's also a movie in which the formula is both so obvious and well packaged that it might as well be a symposium on what makes the movie masses tick.

There's a basic plot, yes: Memphis has spent the past six years away from his mother (Grace Zabriskie) and brother Kip (Giovanni Ribisi) in order to escape his past as the world's greatest booster of upscale autos. When Kip commits to stealing 50 top-end cars and can't pull it off, his villainous employer, Raymond Calitri (the too-nuanced-for-blockbusters Chris Eccleston) promises to kill Kip unless Memphis can fulfill the contract. Et cetera, et cetera, et cetera.

Thus we have, in short, that enduring audience favorite, Morally Justified Crime. But neither Bruckheimer, nor director Dominic Sena ("Kalifornia"), nor screenwriter Scott Rosenberg ("Armageddon") is naive enough to think that one story line will mollify the slavering hordes of summer. So "Gone in 60 Seconds" becomes the March of the Subplots:

Memphis' father-son relationship with his old crony Otto (Robert Duvall), whom he seduces out of a respectable auto-body business and back into theft.

His unarticulated sexual relationship with that most unlikely-looking car thief, Sway (Angelina Jolie).

His love-hate history with police Det. Roland Castlebeck (Delroy Lindo).

His much stranger history with the near-mythic '67 Shelby Mustang GT 500.

The black gang that wants to kick Memphis' butt.

The Hispanic gang that wants to kick his brother's butt.

The trunkful of heroin that Kip's buddy Freb (James Duval) discovers after his freelance heist of a Cadillac.

The dog who eats the Mercedes keys and the all-too-intimate details of their retrieval.

Calitri's fetishistic relationship with wood (he makes furniture).

The Asian woman who can't drive.

Rosenberg has written some lines that, delivered as they are with the utmost sincerity, might make you choke on your popcorn, if not your tongue. Calitri, says Memphis' confederate Atley (Will Patton), is on some "devil came down to the Bayou trip." According to Otto, Calitri is a "jackal tearing at the soft belly of our fair town." Memphis' mom says of Kip, "He's lost that ... sweetness." It's so touching you can't stop laughing.

The goofiness runs amok: Before his crew begins its night of larceny, Memphis—who dons his leather coat the way Dirty Harry holsters his Magnum—leads them in a locker-room-style inspirational moment, which consists of listening to the old War song "Low-Rider." It's hilarious, as well as the cue that all bets are off.

You certainly don't care that, despite the most horrific car crashes, no one dies, much less that when Jolie puts on lipstick in one shot it disappears in the next. Or that time becomes increasingly flexible or compressed as the movie requires. Or that Memphis, in his climactic car chase, violates every law of physics, God and man.

It's summer, baby. Let the hot cars and the good times roll.

NEWSWEEK, 6/19/00, p. 70, David Ansen

There are certain things you can depend upon in a Jerry Bruckheimer-produced summer movie. It will be slick, loud and fast moving ("Con Air," "Armageddon"). It will be lit like a TV ad. It will feature very good actors in roles for which they are overqualified. It will be a testosterone-fueled celebration of outlaw male bonding. And whatever it's about can be articulated in one punchy sentence. Take "Gone in 60 Seconds." A reformed car thief (Nicolas Cage) has to round up a crew and steal 50 cars in one night or his brother (Giovanni Ribisi) will be killed. Any further description is really unnecessary.

"Gone in 60 Seconds" is a pumped-up remake of a 1974 quickie of the same name. The original was made by actor/writer/director H. B. Halicki, who died that year in a car stunt while making a sequel. That one's claim to fame was a climactic 40-minute car chase that aficionados of the genre put right up therewith the chase in "Bullitt."

What's this one's claim to fame? Not Angelina Jolie, whose disposable role as a car mechanic/bartender/love interest gives her little to do but handle a gearshift lustily. Director Dominic Sena ("Kalifornia") whips up a respectable amount of mayhem, but we're in Evel Knievel fantasyland. Our team of good-guy bad guys (including Robert Duvall, Chi McBride and Vinnie Jones) is divided into the wise, wizened old timers and the callow computer-hip youngsters. They are a passable neo-dirty dozen, but not even as memorable as the rogues' gallery in "Armageddon." What's missing from "Gone in 60 Seconds" is anything new. There's a "been there, done that" feeling to the enterprise. The truth is, the brother Cage has to save barely seems worth saving, and the movie's fetishistic worship of Mercedeses, Lamborghinis, Ferraris and one old Mustang named Eleanor is an obsession all too easy to resist.

SIGHT AND SOUND, 8/00, p. 46, Xan Brooks

Los Angeles, the present. Reformed car thief Randall 'Memphis' Raines has been straight for six years. However, when his wild younger brother Kip bungles a job stealing cars for British crime boss Calitri, Randall agrees to fill Calitri's order by stealing 50 luxury cars in four days. To meet his target, he ropes in former cohort Otto, old flame Sway and heavy-man Sphinx. But Randall finds his progress impeded by rival car thief Donny and local detective Roland Castlebeck.

Randall's team spend three days ascertaining the whereabouts of their shopping list of 50 'ladies'. On the final night, they begin rounding them up from locations around the city. In the course of their crime spree, they deliver Donny's gang into the hands of the cops and spirit three Mercedes from the LAPD compound. But Randall leaves the most valuable car on the list, a 1967 Ford Mustang, until last. Spotted by Castlebeck stealing this Mustang, Randall evades squad vehicles and a police helicopter to drop off the car, slightly damaged in the chase, with Calitri. Calitri, though, reneges on the deal and tries to kill both Randall and Kip. Castlebeck turns up, intent on arresting Randall. In the subsequent shoot-out, Randall saves Castlebeck's life and Calitri falls to his death. The detective allows Randall to go free and retrieves all the stolen cars bar one. Randall and Sway ride off in the road-worn Ford Mustang.

Stephen King once memorably dismissed his best-selling horror novels as the literary equivalent of a Big Mac and fries. If King has a cinematic cousin, it must surely be producer Jerry Bruckheimer. Working with the late Don Simpson, Bruckheimer served us such mass-market treats as *Top Gun* and *Days of Thunder*, solo he's responsible for *The Rock, Con Air* and now this big-budget overhaul of director H. B. Halik's obscure 1974 B-movie. The title *Gone in Sixty Seconds* refers to the time it takes to 'boost' a locked vehicle—Nicholas Cage's car thief is given four days to steal 50 luxury cars—but it could just as easily apply to how long the movie sticks in the memory afterwards.

The fact that *Gone in Sixty Seconds* is junk food, then, is hardly news. What's notable is just what pallid fare it proves to be. While *The Rock* and *Con Air* moved with a certain dunderheaded intensity, *Gone in Sixty Seconds* runs on auto-pilot throughout: its direction by Dominic Sena (*Kalifornia*) offers slick ad-land emptiness, its plot rings no changes on the one-last-heist cliché and its characters are so stock as to verge on parody.

The screenplay by Scott Rosenberg (*Things to Do in Denver When You're Dead*) is at its most contrived when introducing us to lead characters: Randall 'Memphis' Raines (Cage) is "the best booster in the world, but I dunno if he's gonna make this one", while Christopher Eccleston's villainous crime lord is "bad—really bad". Old war horse Otto (Robert Duvall), meanwhile, is "all about second chances", and Raines' wayward brother Kip "met up with some bad people and he changed—he lost that sweetness." What makes such threadbare character development all the more insulting is that *Gone in Sixty Seconds* has assembled a war chest of acting talent and then let it idle. Cage and Duvall appear to be playing with one eye on their pay cheques, while Eccleston, having seized the Hollywood dollar, looks abruptly paralysed by self-revulsion.

Most disheartening is the sight of Oscar winning Angelina Jolie relegated to the dreadlocked sex-object role of Sway. "What do you think is better—having sex or boosting cars?" Sway enquires feebly, as if already anticipating the answer. Pitted against 50 fuel-injected "ladies," the film's flesh-and-blood female characters seem superfluous. Sena's camera skirts hastily over Jolie and lavishes so much love on shots of radiator grills and dashboards you half suspect television's motoring expert Jeremy Clarkson to start providing the voiceover. The car is the star in *Gone in Sixty Seconds*. Its central love affair is the romance between Randall and Eleanor, the 1967 Mustang he boosts. Its moment of consummation takes the form of a squealing cannonball run through the streets of LA. In the film's dying seconds, a blissed-out Randall takes permanent possession of Eleanor and noses her out towards the open highway. Almost as an afterthought, he lets Sway ride shotgun.

TIME, 6/19/00, p. 130, Richard Corliss

Guys love cars. Put a teen or a senior behind the wheel, set him loose on a dirt road or a freeway at 3 in the morning and he is a free man, a king in his mobile castle, a top-gunner, a strong, tireless, cunning and faithful lover.

Jerry Bruckheimer loves guys who love cars. He produces movies for them, four-on-the-floor vehicles like *Days of Thunder* (Tom Cruise in a stock car, making two hours of left turns) and *The Rock* (Nicolas Cage revving a yellow Ferrari). *Beverly Hills Cop, Bad Boys*, even *Top Gun* and *Con Air* (planes are just cars on a highway of clouds) and *Armageddon* (grease monkeys in outer space), all celebrate speed, combat and heavy machinery—three things that make every ride a macho adventure. A Bruckheimer movie without a car chase would be like a Woody Allen movie without whining.

So Bruckheimer's new one, the loud, fast and terminally conflicted *Gone in 60 Seconds*, must be his *Annie Hall*—the apotheosis of his obsessions. It's a love story about a man and his car. Actually, a man and other people's cars, for Randall ("Memphis") Raines (Cage) is a car thief, a legend among the felon class of Long Beach, Calif. Six years ago, Memphis gave up stealing cars so his young brother Kip (Giovanni Ribisi) would have a better role model. But Kip went into boosting cars anyway, and now he's in trouble. Your standard movie wacko (Christopher Eccleston) will kill the kid if Memphis doesn't come out of retirement and steal 50 cars in three days.

In this film we learn that it takes 8,000 lbs. of pressure to crush a car but only one credited screenwriter (Scott Rosenberg) to pound out such a lame script. In the Bruckheimer tradition, Memphis assembles a team to carry off the job: a father figure (Robert Duvall), the token black (Chi McBride) and a mute (Brit footballer Vinnie Jones) with a gift for setting cars on fire. Angelina Jolie is here as the nominal girl-jock love interest, but Memphis' true love is a Ford

Mustang Shelby GT 500. As he says of his early career, "I didn't do it for the money. I did it for the cars."

Dominic Sera, like many Bruckheimer directors a graduate of TV spots, gives the dialogue scenes a kinetic pizazz. But they didn't make this movie for the characters; they did it for the cars—for a Knievel-like stunt that sends the Shelby over a dozen or so autos on a bridge, and for the joy of showing young people stealing cars, then driving them recklessly around a crowded city. Why don't these kids do something less dangerous, like heroin? At least then they'd kill only themselves.

The press notes for *Gone in 60 Seconds* feature some cute bits of data: the first car owned by each prominent member of the cast and crew ("Cages first purchase was a yellow Triumph Spitfire he bought for $2,000"). These folks treasure their cars and might not think highly of a fellow who stole them. Yet the film has few quibbles about the ethics of boosting. Hey, guys in the film (and guys who made it): maybe a wage slave left his PC in the hunk of that Toyota you stole; maybe a child's first drawing is in the glove compartment of that HumVee pickup. For people who love their cars to make a movie that lionizes a person who steals them is a textbook case of sociopathic schizophrenia. We almost hope that when they leave work this evening, their Lamborghinis are gone.

VILLAGE VOICE, 6/20/00, p. 156, Dennis Lim

Producer Jerry Bruckheimer, bravely soldiering on after the death of partner-in-excess Don Simpson, lords over what is now the most emblematic of Hollywood summer styles: the demolition-derby impressionism associated with blockbuster-as-bazookas like *The Rock* and *Armageddon.* It's no surprise that Bruckheimer has, for his latest feat, resurrected the quaint yet eminently mayhem-ready auto-porn genre of the late '60s and early '70s. (He's dabbled in the past: *The Rock* was most memorable for its S.F.-chase *Bullitt* homage, and he co-engineered the Tom-Nicole racetrack meet-cute *Days of Thunder.)* The car-thief caper *Gone in 60 Seconds* puts the Bruckheimer aesthetic to its ultimate use. The movie doesn't just look and sound like a car commercial. It is a car commercial.

Too lazy to do more than pick up exactly where the genre left off, the movie remakes a 1974 cult curio by the late HB Halicki. Plot, minimal to begin with, is distilled to its Bruckheimerian essence: men bonding loudly. When his doofus brother, Giovanni Ribisi, pisses off a thug, legendary car booster Nicolas Cage comes out of retirement for one final haul, reassembling the old gang to help him steal 50 cars in one night. Director Dominic Sena, perhaps better known for Nike promos than for his only previous feature, *Kalifornia,* provides the obligatorily baleful music-video hues but unwisely jettisons the 40-minute chase sequence for which the original gained notoriety. A little more road rage might have helped. The movie proceeds with dull checklist efficiency (how many hot-wirings can you get off on?) until the condensed climactic pursuit, when Sena finally adopts the spine-rattling, cornea-scratching rapid-fire tricks that Michael Bay (for one) would shoot a funeral with, and by then is so badly in need of a jump-start that he brings on a wrecking ball.

Both stakes and body count are low by Bruckheimer standards, and the film at times seems self-conscious about the artificially inflated presentation. ("Who gives a shit about grand theft auto?" someone demands at one point.) There's some life in the supporting cast—Delroy Lindo and Timothy Olyphant as snooping detectives, Christopher Eccleston as a wild-eyed English villain—most of whom understand that acting is obviously beside the point. Angelina Jolie, as Cage's nominal love interest, kills time with a form of lip exercise that involves simultaneously sneering and pouting, but cinema's rich sex-and-cars tradition—from Anger's *Kustom Kar Kommandos* to Cronenberg's *Crash*—is otherwise ignored (or, to look at it another way, unsullied). The only sexual moment, with Nic whispering to Angie about carburetors, rivals the Liv/Ben/animal crackers horror in *Armageddon.* If there's a romance to be found here, it's the one between a boy and his stick shift.

Also reviewed in:
CHICAGO TRIBUNE, 6/29/00, Friday/p. A, Michael Wilmington
NEW YORK TIMES, 6/9/00, p. E1, Elvis Mitchell

VARIETY, 6/12-18/00, p. 14, Todd McCarthy
WASHINGTON POST, 6/9/00, p. C1, Stephen Hunter
WASHINGTON POST, 6/9/00, Weekend/p. 43, Desson Howe

GOOD BABY, A

A Curb Entertainment release of a Good Baby/Kardana Films production. *Producer:* Lianne Halfon and Tom Carouso. *Director:* Katherine Dieckmann. *Screenplay:* Katherine Dieckmann. *Based on the novel by:* Leon Rooke. *Director of Photography:* Jim Denault. *Editor:* Kristina Boden, Malcolm Jamieson and Katherine Dieckmann. *Music:* David Mansfield. *Sound:* William Kozy. *Sound Editor:* Nicholas Renbeck. *Production Designer:* Debbie DeVilla. *Costumes:* Kathryn Nixon. *Running time:* 90 minutes. *MPAA Rating:* Not Rated.

CAST: Henry Thomas (Raymond Toker); David Strathairn (Truman Lester); Cara Seymour (Josephine Priddy); Danny Nelson (Hindmarch); Jayne Morgan (Sarah); Allison Glenn (Sister); Jerry Foster (Trout); Jerry Rushing (Wallace); Emilie Jacobs (Lena); Hannah Grady (Baby); Danny Vinson (Cal); Lance Holland and Bob Post (Men Fixing Truck); Palma Kauppert (Woman Shaking Rug); April Chapman (Farm Woman); Chester Ervin and Chris Levi (Men in Passing Car); Rhoda Griffis (Mother in Shack); Caroline Hunter Wallace (Mother's Baby); Neva Howell (Woman at Mailboxes); Toby Huss (AmeriShine); Leslie Riley (Suburban Customer); Ashley Roberts (Suburban Baby); Emily Johnson-Erday (Ashley Jean); Ralph Gates (Man on Tractor); Bonnie Mackenzie (Customer in Cal's).

NEW YORK POST, 12/1/00, p. 53, V.A. Musetto

'Tis the season for Hollywood studios to flood moviehouses with high-budget, low-brainpower flicks they hope will capture an Oscar or two. But there are alternatives for discerning viewers—like "A Good Baby," an indie gem.

The setting is the hillbilly mountains of North Carolina, where a reclusive young man named Raymond Toker finds an abandoned newborn girl.

Thanks to a brief prologue, viewers already know the baby's parents and why the child was left to die.

But that doesn't lessen the movie's impact, as Toker—played with laid-back charm by Henry Thomas, the kid in "E.T."—roams his isolated town looking for the parents or anyone who will care for the child.

"That baby could cook me steak and eggs, and I still wouldn't take it," says one local, an attractive blonde (Cara Seymour) who would give herself to Toker if he were interested, which he isn't.

When their are no takers for the baby, Toker brings her to the storm cellar he calls home. Soon, he has become emotionally attached to the baby, who is forced to use a dresser drawer as a crib.

"A Good Baby" is the feature directorial debut of Katherine Dieckmann, who adapted the script from a novel by Leon Rooke. The beautiful cinematography is by Jim Denault.

Riveting performances by Thomas and Seymour (most recently seen in "Dancer in the Dark" and "American Psycho") are complemented by David Strathairn as the villain, an oily traveling salesman in a cheap brown suit and oversized Dodge; Jayne Morgan as a tough-talking but kind-hearted storeowner and Allison Glenn as the sad-faced younger sister of the baby's mom.

This is moviemaking as it should be.

NEWSDAY, 12/1/00, Part II/p. B6, Gene Seymour

Hannah Grady plays the title role in "A Good Baby" and she's so laid-back, wide-eyed and softly musical in the sounds she makes that she almost outshines everyone else in the cast. Almost.

Really, the best thing writer-director Katherine Dieckmann has going for her in this adaptation of Leon Rooke's novel is a charismatic cast, beginning with Henry Thomas, best known for his role as E.T.'s best friend. Here, Thomas is "all growed up" as Raymond Toker, seemingly the only member of his ne'er-do-well family of mountain dwellers in western North Carolina who isn't in jail or wandering the woods in a drunken stupor.

While out hunting one day (a day, one presumes from the period decor, sometime in the early 1970s), Raymond finds a newborn infant wrapped in a dirty blanket. No one is around who either claims or wants this truly sweet—and unaccountably clean—bundle of joy, whose mere sight repulses a grouchy, sultry neighbor named Josephine Priddy (Cara Seymour of "Dancer in the Dark" and "American Psycho"). None of the pitiably small handful of neighbors, including an equally grouchy, if semimystical, woman storekeeper (Jayne Morgan), seems to want the baby, either, so Raymond takes it back to his hovel. At least it's someone to talk to.

Unknown to Raymond, he and his baby, are being stalked by one Truman Lester (David Strathairn), an oily, nightmare embodiment of every traveling-salesman story ever told. While plying glass cleaners to the yokels, Truman is trying to cover up a nasty bit of business that has more than a little to do with the baby girl in Raymond's care.

Dieckmann, a one-time film critic, shows in her first feature a ravenous eye for color, shadow and rich landscapes. Her story is a rough cinematic equivalent of a distant bluegrass riff that may trail off into the void, but is no less pretty or haunting. Thomas' modulated steeliness, Seymour's prickly sensuality and Strathairn's grace notes of pathos add resonance to the melody.

VILLAGE VOICE, 12/5/00, p. 138, Amy Taubin

The best thing about *a Good Baby* is the way it maps narrative onto landscape. Katherine Dieckmann's first feature is set in a small Appalachian town where houses, scattered miles from one another, are linked by a two-lane country road that curves through the surrounding wooded hills. There's nothing dramatic about the scenery: The woods are neither thick nor sparse; the hills are neither high nor low; the colors of the sky, leaves, and earth are nondescript. This is a landscape that seems at once real and abstract, an undifferentiated terrain on which we chart the perambulations and intersections of the film's three main characters. Unlike conventional film narratives, which build from scene to scene through causal connections, *A Good Baby* takes form through solitary wanderings and intermittent fateful meetings.

The film revolves around an abandoned newborn baby girl. Left alone in the woods to die, the infant not only survives, but becomes an object of desire for almost every character in the film. She's found by Raymond Toker (Henry Thomas), a reclusive young man who blames himself for the death of his younger sister years ago. As he searches for clues to the baby's origins, he carries her everywhere in his arms. Raymond doesn't know what the audience has already concluded on the basis of the film's sinister opening scene: Just after giving birth, the baby's mother was murdered by the traveling salesman (David Strathairn) who impregnated her. Driving around and about the town, he keeps returning to the scene of his crime and becomes obsessed with getting the baby back.

Made with intelligence and formal sophistication, *A Good Baby* uses fabulist elements within a basically realist framework. The combination is not unusual in literature, but in film, it's more difficult to negotiate. Except for Thomas, as moving here as he was once upon a time in E.T., and the very assured Cara Seymour, as the woman who's sweet on Raymond but refuses to live in a small town the rest of her life, the actors seem troubled about exactly what kind of film they're in, and the dialogue, which lapses in and out of poeticized mountain-speak, doesn't help. Strathairn's religious nut job is shifty-eyed and menacing, but the performance is all twitches with nothing much underneath; lacking a center, it eventually careens over the top. Despite these flaws, *A Good Baby* is a fascinating debut by a filmmaker with a unique perspective and the courage to take big risks putting it on the screen.

Also reviewed in:
NEW YORK TIMES, 12/1/00, E10, Stephen Holden
VARIETY, 5/3-9/99, p. 85, Lael Loewenstein

GOSSIP

A Warner Bros. release in association with Village Roadshow Pictures and NPV Entertainment of an Outlaw production. *Executive Producer:* Joel Schumacher and Bruce Berman. *Producer:* Jeffrey Silver and Bobby Newmyer. *Director:* Davis Guggenheim. *Screenplay:* Gregory Poirier and Theresa Rebeck. *Story:* Gregory Poirier. *Director of Photography:* Andrzej Bartkowiak. *Editor:* Jay Cassidy. *Music:* Graeme Revell. *Music Editor:* Ashley Revell and Angie Rubin. *Choreographer:* Clarence Ford. *Sound:* Douglas Ganton and (music) John Kurlander and Mark Curry. *Sound Editor:* George Simpson. *Casting:* Lora Kennedy. *Production Designer:* David Nichols. *Art Director:* Vlasta Svoboda. *Set Decorator:* Michelle Convey and Enrico A. Campana. *Special Effects:* Martin Malivoire. *Costumes:* Louise Mingenbach. *Make-up:* Marilyn Terry. *Stunt Coordinator:* John Stoneham, Jr. *Running time:* 90 minutes. *MPAA Rating:* R.

CAST: James Marsden (Derrick); Lenda Headey (Jones); Norman Reedus (Travis); Kate Hudson (Naomi); Marisa Coughlan (Sheila); Sharon Lawrence (Detective Kelly); Eric Bogosian (Professor Goodwin); Joshua Jackson (Beau); Edward James Olmos (Detective Curtis); Kwok-Wing Leung (Chinese Man); Mif (Doorman); Poe (Female Singer); Vicky Lambert and Kenya Massey (Club Dancers); Naom Jenkins (Bartender); Stephanie Mills (Rebecca Lewis); Raven Dauda (Andrea); Kristin Booth (Diane); Novie Edwards (Ms. Waters); Shanly Trinidad (Marie); Samantha Espie (Leslie); Christopher Ralph (Bill); Kristen Holdenried (Bruce); Deborah Pollitt (Gina); Balazs Koos (Rick); Robin Brülé (Louise); Sadie LeBlanc (Erica); Elizabeth Guber (Grace); Roman Podhora (Detective Ayers); Marc Hickox (Paul); Jessica Greco (Charlene); Alexia Landeau (Sasha); Bill Lake (Lieutenant Miles); David Nichols (Professor Vindaloo); Sanjay Talwar (Taxi Driver); Timm Zemanek (High School Principal); Norma Dell'Agnese (Danbury Typist); Mairon Bennett (Vlasta); Marc Cohen (Offficer Stevens); Charles Guggenheim (Derrick's Father); Marion Guggenheim (Derrick's Mother); John Wills Martin (Stranger).

LOS ANGELES TIMES, 4/21/00, Calendar/p. 12, Kevin Thomas

Despite its title, "Gossip" won't be able to count on good word of mouth, for loose lips will surely sink this silly, shallow melodrama that turns upon the havoc wreaked by rumor. It's a total waste of time and the talent of such proven film craftsmen as cinematographer Andrzej Bartkowiak and composer Graeme Revell, who strive mightily to create mood and suspense not provided in Gregory Poirier and Theresa Rebeck's heavily contrived script and Davis Guggenheim's flashy direction.

The key setting is a vast, ultra-luxe high-tech loft in Toronto (but the filmmakers surely wouldn't mind if you took it to be Manhattan). It belongs to smirky rich college kid Derrick Webb (James Marsden), who shares his trendy digs with fellow students Cathy (Lena Headey) and Travis (Norman Reedus).

They have nothing to recommend them beyond youthful good looks. They seem to party most all the time, and neither they nor anyone else is shown to be so vulgar as to be actually cracking a book.

The only class they're seen attending is a communications course conducted by Eric Bogosian's gadfly professor, a character with possibilities—in another, hopefully better movie.

One day Derrick speaks up in defense of gossip, which is the trio's favorite pastime, and one night at a drunken party he spies a young man on a bed with a girl who has passed out.

They decide to spread the rumor that the couple have had sex—and pretty soon the girl (Kate Hudson) is screaming rape without any basis whatsoever. The plot cannot be said truly to thicken but rather merely to become increasingly farfetched and attenuated.

It's tough to get involved in a picture in which its principals are nasty or dumb or both, and this bleak film does nothing to advance its young stars while giving little opportunity for such established performers as Bogosian and Edward James Olmos (as a cop). Worst of all, the film merely exploits rather than develops its serious theme of the malicious rumor that leaps beyond the control of its perpetrator and threatens to backfire.

NEW YORK POST, 4/21/00, p. 50, Lou Lumenick

"Gossip" is a remarkably accurate title for a glossy, shallow thriller where not a single scene rings true.

Watching this loathsome concoction, I ended up feeling like the theater critic who complained that he left a musical humming the scenery.

Though I did my best to concentrate on the ever-more-ridiculous story and performances, my attention kept drifting back to the main set—a to-die-for three-story Manhattan loft that's home to three college students.

I kept wondering exactly who was paying the tab for the place, which would go for at least $2 million on the open market, not including the artfully lavish furniture and what seems like half the Williams-Sonoma catalog—so seductively photographed by Andrzej Bartkowiak, it makes the interiors in "American Psycho" look positively shabby.

Oh, yes, back to the story: Those three obnoxious college students decide, as a class project, to start a rumor—that a famously chaste coed did the nasty with her boyfriend during a party—and track its progress.

Things soon spiral out of control—the woman, who passed out at the party before anything happened, accuse the boyfriend of date rape—as quickly as the movie, which takes a potentially interesting theme and piles one unbelievable scene on top of another.

By the time one of the gossips (James Marsden) confesses ulterior motive ("spreading the rumor wasn't the nicest thing to do") to his pals (Lenda Headey and Norman Reedus), the movie has left behind any pretense of coherence.

The red-herring-filled screenplay, attributed to Gregory Poirier and Theresa Rebeck, is about as convincing as the film's (unsuccessful) attempt to pass off Toronto as the Big Apple.

Such seasoned pros as Eric Bogosian, Sharon Lawrence and Edward James Olmos are as terrible as the great-looking, beautifully dressed younger cast members.

Among the latter are Kate Hudson—Goldie Hawn's real-life daughter—as the rape "victim" and blank-faced "Dawson's Creek" hunk Joshua Jackson, whose performance as a rich college student here is indistinguishable from his turn as a poor college student in the slightly better teen thriller "The Skulls."

The inept direction—which can't begin to sell a "surprise" ending that's as predictable as it is unbelievable, as well as contradicting numerous earlier scenes—is by Davis Guggenheim, a TV helmer who's married to Elisabeth Shue.

Were it more skillfully done, the flip treatment "Gossip" gives to rape (and its cynically casual evocation of preppy rapist Alex Kelly) would make it the year's most offensive movie. Instead, it's merely the worst.

NEWSDAY, 4/21/00, Part II/p. B7, Jan Stuart

Psssst. Rumor has it that there is a secret laboratory in the San Fernando Valley where young actors are reproduced daily using cloning methods first perfected on sheep in England. They look alike, they walk alike, at times they even talk alike. You could lose your mind. Or what's left of it after a steady diet of "Beverly Hills 90210" and "Dawson's Creek."

From the evidence put forth by "Gossip," a provocative and surprisingly edgy college drama directed by Davis Guggenheim, rumors often prove to be unfounded. While one can find fault in this ultimately overheated tale about the tragic consequences of embroidering truths, one can also take heart in the very original sparks being sent out by its youthful cast, who demonstrate that all twentysomething performers are not created equal.

The chief cause for hope is Lena Headey, a striking actress who commands attention throughout and stylishly reaffirms the sensual potential of black-framed eyeglasses. Headey plays Jones, a sly university student who concocts a rumor for a journalism class abetted by her loft-mate buddies Derrick (James Marsden) and Travis (Norman Reedus). Feeding off the smallest kernel of truth, the trio spread word that fellow student Beau (Joshua Jackson) has raped his wealthy girlfriend, Naomi (Kate Hudson).

Within days, the campus gossip mill is churning overtime. Beau gets into hot water and skeletons tumble out of the closet, challenging the long-term veracity of one of the rumor-spinners.

Before descending into a preposterous finale, "Gossip" writers Gregory Poirier and Theresa Rebeck score high marks for braving the psychologically complex waters of date rape and burrowing into that dark place where truth, presumption and fabrication blur together. They also provide uncommonly gritty business for their glamorous cast of almost-neophytes to sink their teeth into.

Along with Headey, Kate Hudson intrigues us as the victimized student who may or may not be succumbing to the strong undertow of gossip. Rumored, quite reliably, to be the daughter of Goldie Hawn, Hudson projects both intelligence and heat. As Headey's accomplices in gossip, Reedus has an appealing nerd quality about him and Marsden has the sort of blandly charming smile that can turn smarmy on a dime.

It also should be noted that these students do a stunning amount of hard boozing. So many cosmopolitans and whiskeys are downed before the denouement, a wary parent may be tempted to rescind their kids' higher education plans and ship Muffy and Junior off to a monastic dairy farm.

SIGHT AND SOUND, 10/00, p. 44, Edward Lawrenson

US, the present. Students Cathy Jones, Derrick Webb and Travis share a flat. At a party, Derrick observes the arrival of Naomi Preston, daughter of a wealthy businessman, and her boyfriend Beau Edson. Spying on the two in a bedroom, Derrick watches Naomi and Beau smooch before Naomi drunkenly falls asleep. Later, Cathy, Derrick and Travis agree to spread a rumour that Beau and the reputedly chaste Naomi had sex that night, and to write up the effects of this falsehood as an assignment for one of their lecturers, Professor Goodwin.

The rumour spreads and soon reaches Naomi. With no memory of the event, she contacts the police, who charge Beau with rape. Cathy admits to the authorities that she made up the rumour, but they refuse to believe her. Later, she discovers Derrick went to the same high school as Naomi. After having sex with Derrick, she travels to his old school; looking through the past year-books, she deduces that Derrick and Naomi were a couple. When asked about this, Derrick admits to spreading the rumour because Naomi accused him—falsely, he says—of raping her. Derrick then visits Naomi and admits he, not Beau, raped her that night.

Back in the flat, Travis tells Derrick that Naomi has committed suicide. Some time later, a detective, Curtis, turns up to question Derrick about Naomi's death, which he's treating as homicide. With the net closing in, Derrick attempts to flee, but Travis pulls a gun on him. In the ensuing struggle, Cathy is accidentally shot. Derrick then angrily admits to raping Naomi, at which point Travis and Cathy—whose injuries were simulated—admit to pretending that Naomi had killed herself and faking a police inquiry in order to coax this confession, which they secretly filmed, out of Derrick.

There's a moment in *Gossip* when rich college kid Derrick tells his flatmate Cathy to stop worrying. The two are responsible for spreading a rumour—which they know to be false—about their fellow student, the glamorous Naomi Preston. Except what started out as a mischievous prank has turned nasty, landing Naomi's boyfriend Beau in jail for rape. 'This is an ugly turn,' Cathy remarks, with some understatement, but Derrick is unfazed: 'It's all just words,' he says. He's wrong, of course: as played by James Marsden, Derrick is a smoothly amoral character with a nice line in Nietzschien asides ("Naomi's weak, she's always been weak" is his chilly reaction to her apparent suicide). And it's pretty clear from early on in the film that he's the villain of the piece, for all his emollient delivery and simulated sincerity.

The screenplay by Gregory Poirier and Theresa Rebeck is thick with intrigue and elaborate attempts to wrongfoot the audience. In the film's final reel, the sky is inky black and the rain unrelenting—but while the weather is pure *noir*, *Gossip*'s characters lack the moral ambiguity for Poirier's myriad plot turns to work. Derrick is slick but untrustworthy (even his sumptuous apartment, packed with designer desirables, points an accusatory finger at him, as if he's house-sitting for *American Psycho*'s Patrick Bateman); Cathy might indulge in the odd student prank, but there's a wholesome decency about her character which is barely dented by the events of the film (she comes from Plymouth Rock, and Derrick needles her about her "pilgrimatic" sense of moral rectitude); and the last of the gossip-mongers, Travis, an art student who spends most of the film creating a rather tacky collage about the guilty consequences of the rumour he helped spread, is too much the mousy, sensitive type to be embroiled in any dark double-dealing.

Gossip's one standout moment is a montage sequence, handled with some flair by director Davis Guggenheim (who worked on episodes of *ER* and *NYPD Blue*), depicting the way the rumour about Naomi spreads across campus: accompanied by Graeme Revell's frantic orchestration, the fairly unremarkable news that the supposedly chaste Naomi and her boyfriend had sex at a college party is embellished with sordid details, whipped up into a scandal as it passes from one mouth to the other (filmed in tight close-up). As with the rest of the film, the dialogue here is smart, the one-liners zippy, the caustic asides piercing; but there's something sadly apt about all this disembodied gabbing. Predictable at every turn, glossy but stagy, and full of unengaging, underdeveloped characters, *Gossip* too is 'all just words'.

Also reviewed in:
CHICAGO TRIBUNE, 4/21/00, Friday/p. I, Monica Eng
NEW YORK TIMES, 4/21/00, p. E31, Stephen Holden
VARIETY, 4/24-30/00, p. 30, Dennis Harvey
WASHINGTON POST, 4/21/00, p. C12, Rita Kempley

GOYA IN BORDEAUX

A Sony Pictures Classics release of an Andrés Vicente Gómez production for Lolafilms in co-production with Italian International Film. *Producer:* Andrés Vicente Gómez. *Director:* Carlos Saura. *Screenplay (Spanish with English subtitles):* Carlos Saura. *Director of Photography:* Vittorio Storaro. *Editor:* Julia Juaniz. *Music:* Roque Baños. *Choreographer:* Matilde Coral. *Sound:* Carlos Faruolo and (music) José Vinader. *Production Designer:* Carmen Martínez. *Art Director:* Pierre Louis Thévenet. *Set Decorator:* Luis Ramirez. *Special Effects:* Angel Alonso. *Costumes:* Pedro Moreno. *Make-up:* José Quetglas. *Running time:* 94 minutes. *MPAA Rating:* R.

CAST: Franciso Rabal (Francisco de Goya); José Coronado (Goya as a Young Man); Maribel Verdú (Duchess of Alba); Eulalia Ramón (Leocadia); Dafné Fernández (Rosarito, Leocadia's Daughter); Emilio Gutiérrez Caba (José de la Cruz); Joaquín Climent (Moratín); Manuel de Blas (Salcedo); Carlos Hipólito (Juan Valdés); Pedro Azorín (Braulio Poe); Joan Valles (Novales); Cristina Espinosa (Pepita Tudó); Paco Catalá (Asensio); Saturnino Garcia (Priest/San Antonio); José María Pou (Godoy); Franco Di Francescantonio (Doctor in Andalucía); José Antonio (Dancer Duke de Osuna); Mario de Candia (Bayeu); La Fura dels Baus (Los Desastres de la Guerra); Concha Leza (Woman in Andalucía); Jaime Losada (Gaulon); Aihnoa Suarez (Rosarito, age 6); José Reche (Murdered Corpse); José Sainz (Guilty Gravedigger); Demetrio Julian (San Antonio's Father); Stephane Salom (Young French Man); Roberto Arcilla (Chubby French Man); Lorena Pellarini (French Woman); Azucena de la Fuente (Josefina Bayeu); Natalie Pinot (Piano Teacher); Olivier D'Belloch (Gaulon's Assistant); Borja Elgea (Goya's Friend); Vicente Moraleda (Goya Double).

LOS ANGELES TIMES, 9/15/00, Calendar/p. 17, Kevin Thomas

Carlos Saura's superb, contemplative" Goya in Bordeaux" imagines the great painter (Francisco Rabal), at 82, recalling key events in his tumultuous life to the youngest of his daughters (Daphne Fernandez), who looks to be a young teenager. So much for the conventions of film biography, for this framing narrative is but a point of entry for Saura into Goya's mind and imagination as his thoughts wander between memories and dreams.

This adds a stunning, surreal dimension to the film and a glorious free-flowing quality that allows Saura and incomparable cinematographer Vittorio Storaro to bring to life a number of

Goya's greatest paintings—most spectacularly, "The Disasters of the War, 1810-14," as the artist remembers the events and individuals that inspired them.

That ancient, oft-quoted Chinese curse, "May you live in interesting times," applies to Goya (1746-1828) with particular force. He survived the imperial decline of Spain spanning four controversial monarchies, the country's invasion by France under the leadership of Napoleon's brother Joseph Bonaparte, and Spain's struggle for independence.

Goya saw all this tumult and suffering as a struggle between the forces of light and dark—between the Age of Enlightenment and that of the Inquisition. Eventually, he and other liberals saw no recourse but exile, and Goya was part of such a group that settled in Bordeaux, where he said he missed only his Madrid villa.

Through the fragments of his memories we find the ambitious Goya (Jose Coronado, in his younger years) determined to become the portrait painter of choice in the royal court and beyond—and a lady-killer in the process. He's eventually transformed by the loss of his hearing at 46, the terrible fate of his greatest love, the beautiful and free-spirited Duchess of Alba (Maribel Verdu), and the savage and bloody chaos that overcame Spain itself.

Goya moved from painter of the richest and most powerful to chronicler of the horrendous suffering of the people. In exile he turned to engraving, determined to persist with his art despite the ravages of age.

And what ravages! If you did not know, you would never guess that the great Spanish actor Rabal, a Bunuel favorite, was once as handsome and dashing as Errol Flynn. Grown stout, his otherwise bald pate framed by an aureole of white hair, his face mottled and doughy, Rabal is perfect casting for a libertine from whom tragedy and passing time have exacted a brutal toll.

Yet the dark eyes retain their fire, the deep voice its richness and strength. Rabal has become wondrous at playing wrecks who have not lost their passion, spirit or dignity, retaining a presence that is commanding still. Surely, this film is as much a homage to Rabal as it is to Goya.

"Rembrandt, Velazquez and Imagination!" thunders Goya, citing his gods. "Goya in Bordeaux" is, itself a portrait of the artist as a Renaissance man, learned, appreciative of his predecessors in a brilliantly perceptive manner and ultimately committed to placing his boldly critical and innovative art in the service of change.

You can see the universal aging artist in the particulars of Goya's creative credo and his life and times—his impassioned outbursts, the curse of escalating infirmities, the losses and regrets painfully recalled and the spontaneous gestures of kindness and caring.

NEW YORK, 9/25/00, p. 62, Peter Rainer

Carlos Saura's *Goya in Bordeaux* is photographed by Vittorio Storaro with a florid palette that might have given even Goya hives, but at the center of it all is the venerable Spanish actor Francisco Rabal, with his jagged, knobby, bullish countenance. Rabal's Goya is such a great camera subject that one regrets the camera doesn't do him justice; Saura fancifies everything, and yet Rabal triumphs. Goya himself would have clamored to capture his gouty, lusting presence.

NEW YORK POST, 9/15/00, p. 54, V.A. Musetto

Sad to say, the latest by Carlos Saura ("Tango," "Carmen") is pretty but tedious Euro-pap at its most self-indulgent.

Amateurishly acted and written with laughable crudeness, it paints a portrait of the great Spanish artist that could hardly be more trite—or less dramatic.

Sure, "Goya in Bordeaux" boasts gorgeous lighting and lovely photography by Vittorio Storaro (Bertolucci's favorite photographer). But both are put to the service of a formal theatrical conception that is so static, you could almost be watching a slide show or a primer on set design.

The result is an achingly tedious 94 minutes—reminiscent of Peter Greenaway's duller works—that demonstrate once again that film is not simply a visual medium; it requires a modicum of storytelling skill.

NEWSDAY, 9/15/00, Part II/p. B11, Jan Stuart

The life and art of the Spanish master Francisco Jose de Goya y Lucientes is the ostensible subject of Carlos Saura's "Goya in Bordeaux." As with most films that endeavor to concretize the unfathomable workings of genius, however, it inevitably turns into a meditation on the problems of making a movie about great artists.

The Spanish-born Saura is as qualified as anyone to delve into the world of Goya. He has forged a reputation with painterly films about romantic passion, often translated through the medium of dance ("Carmen" and, most recently, "Tango"). Not surprisingly, there is a fair amount of flamenco display enlivening what is otherwise a stately pageant of a movie.

Saura has fixed upon a fairly conventional frame for his biography: The artist in his final days relates the seminal moments of his life to a captive audience (in this instance, his daughter Rosario). Somewhat stoned on the valerian he must drink to ease his infirmities, Goya (played by the redoubtable spanish actor Francesco Rabal) drifts in and out of dreamlike visions in which the specters from his great paintings come back to haunt him.

These reveries become the excuse for a series of sumptuously theatrical tableaux vivant animating iconic works that were generated before and after Goya lost his hearing at 45 from a near-fatal illness: portraits of his favorite love, the Duchess of Alba (Maribel Verdu); the dome fresco of St. Anthony's miracle; and the horrific sketches recording the tortures of Napoleon's troops in Spain.

Immaculately detailed (by costumer Pedro Moreno and art designer Pierre-Louis Thevenet) and gorgeously lit (by the great cinematographer Vittorio Storaro) to emulate the nocturnal, candlelit environment in which Goya worked, these scenes provoke the requisite ooh-and-aah response in the viewer. But Saura is more obsessed with decor than he is with conflict. Without a sufficiently potent dramatic context, these interludes lack any impact to approximate the power of seeing a finished work.

The film is as flat and occasionally hokey as it is lovely to look at. While Goya reproaches himself for not being able to achieve the serenity of Velasquez because he is too passionate a man, one can only lament that his screen biographer was unable to breathe that fire through his lens.

SIGHT AND SOUND, 11/00, p. 52, Paul Julian Smith

Bordeaux, 1828. The 82-year-old Spanish artist Francisco de Goya is living in exile. His younger lover Leocadia and her daughter Rosarito, an aspiring artist, take care of him in his final illness; Goya himself is working on lithographs and socialising with fellow radical exiles. Over the course of the last months of his life, Goya recounts his life story to Rosarito. He recalls his entrance into the glittering Madrid court of the Bourbons, the illness that led to his early deafness, his love affair with the Duchess of Alba, who dies poisoned by conspirators, the French invasion of Spain and the Peninsular War. Meanwhile his major works, including his portraits for Charles III's court, the *caprichos* series of etchings, the Black paintings, and the *Disasters of War* series, are brought to life in on-screen *tableaux*. Finally Goya dies; his body is discovered by Rosarito.

Time has not been kind to Spanish director Carlos Saura. Spain's greatest film-maker during the final years of Franco's rule and the country's transition to democracy and the auteur of such oblique and resonant psychological dramas as *Cría cuervos* (1975), Saura was laid low in the 80s by the costly fiasco of his historical epic *El Dorado*. More recently, he made *Taxi* (1996), a liberal-minded but routine thriller about neo-Nazi gangs in Madrid which showed little sign of his personal style, while his 1998 film *Tango* prompted Spaniards to ask whether he had progressed since his earlier dance tragedy *Carmen* (1983). *Goya in Bordeaux*, whose release in Spain inadvertently coincided with *Volaverunt*, Bigas Luna's lavish biopic of the artist, combines elements from *Taxi* and *Tango*. Saura, screenwriter as well as director, stresses the liberal credentials of his Enlightenment hero, who was fiercely opposed to tyranny; this political commentary is accompanied by an abstract and theatrical *mise en scène* whereby Goya's works are brought to life in startling *tableaux vivants*, a visual style familiar from the director's dance films.

It's an ambitious undertaking, especially given that the Spanish film industry is now dominated by coarse post-Almodóvar comedies, and the contrast between the naturalism of the historical drama and the stylisation of the aesthetic performance is sometimes jarring. Shot in the studio, with sliding screens on which the artist's works are projected, *Goya in Bordeaux* often evokes a fluid cinematic space analogous to the free-floating world of the artistic imagination. The expressionist lighting and colour of cinematographer Vittorio Storaro (*Taxi* and *Tango*) produce powerful graphic effects. For example, in the credit sequence the camera slowly tracks over sodden black earth and tilts up to a blood-red hanging carcass, whose entrails morph into the dying Goya's head. Images are often dense and multilayered: in one extended travelling shot the old Goya walks in front of a translucent scrim of prints from his *caprichos* series while the young Goya shadows his movements behind: it's an impressive sequence which aptly recreates the simultaneity of artistic experience.

But the problem with *Goya in Bordeaux* is that this visual dimension is more eloquent than the verbal element. Saura's dialogue is clunky, even clichéd. Such lines as "The spiral is like life," "Deafness left me isolated" and even "This will be a masterpiece" would not be out of place in a Hollywood biopic from an earlier era. Audiences, even in Spain, need to be reminded of the historical ironies of Goya's life, such as his early admiration of France which was later to invade Spain so brutally. But the presentation of these complexities is only fitfully integrated into the narrative. Moreover, the flashback format leads to longueurs and repetitions, leaving the viewer as frustrated and bewildered as the young girl to whom Goya recites his life story. The absence of narrative drive and characterisation (Maribel Verdú's Duchess of Alba, Goya's true love, is a cipher) makes the experience of watching the film akin to leafing through a deluxe volume of illustrations: these are visually sumptuous, often ravishing images but they fail to connect with each other or the spectator.

This is unfortunate because there is so much to like about *Goya in Bordeaux*. The shifting and shimmering *mise en scène*, based on montages, lighting effects and transparent panels, is an impressively realised collaboration between the director, cinematographer and art director (Pierre Louis Thévenet, best known for Almodóvar's *High Heels*). And the imagery never subsides into the clichéd Goya-esque. Catalan physical theatre group La Fura dels Baus, known for their visceral performance pieces, are ideally suited to act out the graphic sequence based on Goya's *Disasters of War* print series. José Coronado, now best known in Spain as the lead in top-rated television drama *Periodistas*, is assured as the young artist. Francisco Rabal, the fresh-faced señorito of Buñuel's *Viridiana* (1961), has long since become a grizzled veteran, his crown of white hair backlit here like a halo. Rabal performs with matchless pathos as the dying genius, even attempting some perilously dignified dance steps. But surely the hidden story of *Goya in Bordeaux* is that of Saura himself: a once brilliant and fashionable artist who is now out of favour in his own country.

VILLAGE VOICE, 9/19/00, p. 122, Michael Atkinson

Sharing more nowadays with Ken Russell than with his own, Franco-era filmmaking self, Carlos Saura seems to be turning into a middle-class formalist, manufacturing elaborate, meta-theatrical tableaux for the purposes of putting over Spanish cultural history. Movies, as such, don't seem to interest him any longer; they're a means to a duller ethnic end. By the lantern light of *Goya in Bordeaux*, a cluttered, dreamy meditation on the iconic imagemaker's autumn years in exile, Saura seems to have fallen into the midperiod Greenaway waxworks, and Goya's life plays like a Broadway musical—*Goya!*—waiting for its book. (The paintings are even reenacted on an overlit stage à la *Les Miz*.) The actors—particularly Francisco Rabal as the elderly, porcine Goya—don't interest Saura as much as the wall-shifting, scrim-lighting set design that he and DP Vittorio Storaro also used in *Tango* and *Flamenco*. What looks like Victorian wallpaper becomes suddenly translucent when Storaro turns on one of his Crayola lights.) Once he's filled a set with extras, Saura can't resist panning fruitlessly over it a few times. Bordeaux itself is largely beside the point; we don't see real sky until 90 minutes in.

It's a study for a movie rather than the real thing. There's certainly plenty of texture and color (Storaro bathes whole images in pomegranate red), but they're used only to emphasize big, stilted, biographical points, which are in turn scripted with classroom-film simplicity. What, anyway, can a movie tell us about the painter that the paintings do not? The effort has done no favors for Picasso or Rivera or Bacon. At least Saura has spared us the spectacle of Goya covering himself torturously in paint, but the pictures do occasionally morph and bleed, and his writhing subjects do leap off the canvas as paint-globbed actors and breathe down his neck. What this is supposed to literalize is far from clear; Saura, like many filmmakers before him, seems to think artists live in a constant state of psychological attack by their old images. It's hogwash, especially for someone as prolific as Goya, and visualizing it only recalls the days when Russell would try to make us see a Mahler movement.

The handful of resonant moments derive, unsurprisingly, from the paintings; Goya's brief, private collision with a Velàzquez provides the film's only insight, and because it's about the practical concerns of technique and excellence, it's fascinating. But Saura would rather rouse the belfry bats. So beautifully, preciously composed and lit that soon you're pining for a lens flare or a rogue ray of actual sunlight, Goya is almost absurdly un-Goya-esque, and naive as a schoolkid at the Met.

Also reviewed in:
CHICAGO TRIBUNE, 10/20/00, Friday/p. E, Michael Wilmington
NATION, 10/9/00, p. 50, Stuart Klawans
NEW REPUBLIC, 10/2/00, p. 30, Stanley Kauffmann
NEW YORK TIMES, 9/15/00, p. E10, Stephen Holden
VARIETY, 9/20-26/99, p. 91, Eddie Cockrell
WASHINGTON POST, 10/13/00, p. C5, Stephen Hunter

GRASS

A Unapix Films release of a Sphinx Productions production. *Executive Producer:* Keith Clarkson. *Producer:* Ron Mann. *Director:* Ron Mann. *Screenplay:* Solomon Vesta. *Editor:* Robert Kennedy. *Music:* Guido Luciani. *Sound:* Rosnick MacKinnon. *Art Director:* Paul Mavrides. *Running time:* 80 minutes. *MPAA Rating:* Not Rated.

CAST: Woody Harrelson (Narrator).

LOS ANGELES TIMES, 6/16/00, Calendar/p. 9, Kenneth Turan

Weed, blow, Mary Jane, reefer, muggles, pot, tea. Marijuana is a drug that travels under numerous aliases—nicknames that indicate how pervasive it's been in American popular culture. When director Ron Mann chose "Grass" as the title for his excellent documentary on the evil weed, he probably didn't worry that anyone would be expecting a treatise on disease-resistant Bermuda strains.

Written by Solomon Vesta and aided by jazzy and informative graphics by cartoonist Paul Mavrides, "Grass" is told with a sense of humor: "No hippies," the final credits read, "were harmed in the making of this movie." But, confounding expectations, it's definitely not the goofy celebration of the glories of smoke you might expect with pro-hemp firebrand Woody Harrelson reading the narration.

Rather, this turns out to be an informative, involving, even sobering advocacy film that not only argues that society's total war against this drug has been misguided and ruinously expensive, but also seeks to demonstrate how easily public opinion can be manipulated by tireless zealots hoping for overreactions based on misleading information. "Grass" shows how marijuana has been an ever-pliant boogeyman for several generations of alarmists, willing to take the rap for any and all difficulties caused by other forces in society.

Mann, whose fine docs include "Comic Book Confidential" and the rock-themed "Twist," has scoured numerous archives and come up with all manner of visual surprises, starting with a clip from a 1953 anti-drug educational film called "Marijuana: Threat or Menace," which has the narrator all but screaming at the audience, "Don't do it!"

Also visible are Sonny Bono's anti-drug message, soldiers in Vietnam using the barrel of a weapon to smoke the stuff and Cab Calloway and his orchestra singing "That Reefer Man" from

1933's "International House." Marijuana-related music plays a large part in the soundtrack, with tracks like "One Toke Over the Line" and Peter Tosh's "Legalize It (Don't Criticize It)."

Mann and writer Vesta have roughly structured "Grass" around an ever-changing series of official truths regarding the putative horrors caused by the drug. The first, coinciding with marijuana!s appearance in the U.S. in the early 20th century (brought in by Mexican laborers) was "If you smoke it, you will kill people."

"Alien Weed Makes Men Into Killers" read a headline in the El Paso Times, and a 1920s silent film called "High on the Range" showed an innocent cowboy turning into a homicidal maniac after just one puff of what the intertitle ominously calls "a new kind of cigarette."

If there is a villain in "Grass," it is Harry J. Anslinger, head of the Federal Bureau of Narcotics, a man who wanted to be toward drugs what J. Edgar Hoover was toward crime. Hoping to persuade states to adopt uniform anti-marijuana laws, Anslinger helped promulgate official truth No. 2, visible in exploitation films like "The Burning Question" (later renamed "Reefer Madness"): "If you smoke it, you will go insane."

Adroit at publicity management, Anslinger also successfully buried more reasoned approaches to the drug, such as 1944's La Guardia Committee Report, commissioned by the mayor of New York and reporting that "the sociological, psychological, and medical ills commonly attributed to marijuana have been found to be exaggerated."

As the times changed, the enemies of the drug were ready with new dictums, even insisting that Red China was upping production in "a Communist plot to dope up America." Successive official truths, as detailed by on-screen graphics, included "If you smoke it, you will become a heroin addict," "If you smoke it, you will become an unmotivated, dysfunctional loser," and the especially devious "If you smoke it, bad things will happen but we don't know what they are."

While, like any narcotic, marijuana has its dangers, "Grass" posits that treating it as, in President Reagan's words, "the most dangerous drug in America" has proved to be a counterproductive—not to mention extremely costly—proposition. By intensely criminalizing the substance, by pushing for laws mandating harsh minimum sentences, the anti-marijuana forces have helped create a multibillion-dollar, not terribly effective, war on drugs and a society that puts more people behind bars than almost any on Earth. Where there's smoke, there's not necessarily fire.

NEW YORK POST, 5/31/00, p. 60, Hannah Brown

Strident, unrepentantly one-sided but often entertaining, "Grass" is a detailed documentary on the history of the U.S. government's anti-marijuana crusade.

Director Ron Mann puts everything in black-and-white terms throughout the film.

His thesis is simple: Marijuana isn't bad at all; in fact, it's good—or certainly much better than alcohol—so anyone who thinks it should be illegal is a hysterical zealot.

If you agree with this premise, you may find the film's jabs at the anti-drug establishment enjoyable. Those who disagree will find the film simplistic and offensive.

But no one's opinions will be challenged by what they see here, and that's the real problem.

"Grass," which is narrated by pro-hemp activist and actor Woody Harrelson, is at its best when it presents little-known gems of anti-pot propaganda.

The most amazing is a clip from a 1929 silent film called "High on the Range" about cowboys who try marijuana, go berserk and kill each other.

There's also a series of sexy scenes from a 1966 film called "Mondo Mod/Teenage Revolution" which asks the question, "Will drugs pave the road to destruction for the 'Now Generation'?"

And, of course, there are clips from the classic "Reefer Madness."

But the movie focuses more on demonizing Harry Anslinger, the first head of the Federal Bureau of Narcotics, who created a national anti-marijuana drug policy.

Although the movie presents impressive statistics on the billions of dollars spent (and, according to the director, wasted) in the fight against the drug, these don't have the impact they would have were the film less shrill.

NEWSDAY, 5/31/00, Part II/p. B9, Gene Seymour

"Grass" is "J'accuse" that kicks like a vintage rhythm-and-blues record. To deploy a carny-barker alliteration, it is a fast, funny and ferocious polemic that advances the cause of drug law reform by simply showing the absurd extremes through which those in authority have come down hard on the humble cannabis plant and those who use it to relax.

Which, according to Ron Mann's documentary, is all that marijuana was perceived to be good for a mere century ago, when Mexican farm workers smoked it to unwind from a hard day in the fields.

Somehow, a welter of anti-immigrant prejudice, post-Prohibition fervor and unchecked righteousness transmogrified this homely little weed into Satan's prized houseplant, a treacherous substance capable of turning unsuspecting users into homicidal maniacs, heroin addicts and progressive politicians.

The chief architect of this paranoia—and the presiding dark angel of the mad, sad story of "Grass"—is Harry J. Anslinger, who in the 1930s became America's first de facto drug czar as the U.S. Federal Bureau of Narcotics' top cop. Anslinger, as shamelessly media savvy as his FBI counterpart, J. Edgar Hoover, managed through sheer force of will to convince lawmakers and plain folks from sea to shining sea that marijuana was a menace to public health.

There would be counterarguments as far back as 1944, when a medical commission appointed by New York City Mayor Fiorello La Guardia marshaled considerable evidence showing marijuana's effects to be relatively benign. But by that time, movies like 1936's "Reefer Madness" (whose now-campy outrages are lovingly excerpted here) had, with Anslinger's help, rendered any rational examination of the issue into insignificance.

Mann, whose 1991 documentary "The Twist" showed a comparably droll shrewdness toward the vagaries of pop culture, is adept at maneuvering the egregious ironies dominating the decades-long push-me pull-you debate over marijuana, which becomes a funhouse mirror reflection of the socio-political upheaval of mid-20th-Century America.

For instance, clips from 1950s educational films with wild-eyed high-school kids drinking from broken bottles because of marijuana use are placed in the wider context of Cold War politics.

It's all pretty funny except when the toll for this popularly enforced hysteria is assessed in billions of federal dollars and the jail time imposed achieves critical mass.

Beneath its jaunty satire, the film does a fairly credible job chronicling the ups and downs of anti-pot hysteria through the "Just Say No" 1980s. You wonder, though, how a film this conscientiously ironic forgot to mention the disqualification of Republican Supreme Court nominee Douglas Ginsberg over his youthful dalliances with pot. Or, for that matter, First Boomer Bill Clinton's indelibly disingenuous confession that he smoked "but did not inhale" marijuana.

But by the end "Grass" has stopped having fun and is intent on making a direct plea for reform. The film makes its points so trenchantly that you're left wondering just what could be rationally argued in rebuttal.

VILLAGE VOICE, 6/6/00, p. 139, J. Hoberman

Canadian documentary filmmaker Ron Mann (*Comic Book Confidential, Twist,* and *Poetry in Motion*) will never be mistaken for John Woo, but his latest cultural survey, *Grass,* is an unexpectedly brash and punchy affair. This pot paean is supercharged with all manner of fake headlines and jazzy graphics designed to compound the dated hysteria of vintage anti-marijuana exploitation films.

As social history, *Grass* is pat but entertaining. The film is largely a compilation of head lore and connoisseur clips, including the loco-weed freak-outs from the cautionary oater *High on the Range* (1929) and a scene from *Reefer Madness* (1936) in which a ham actor seizes his moment, as Jack Smith wrote in these pages, "to disintegrate to the point of gilded splendor." Cab Calloway sings "The Reefer Man"; Sonny Bono postscripts *Tammy's on a Bummer* with a solemn warning to the kids of stupefied suburbia; *Mondo Mod* stages an interracial pot party that's nearly as funny as anything in *Black and White.*

The film, narrated by Woody Harrelson, reminds the viewer of the surprisingly tolerant (and suppressed) 60-year-old La Guardia Commission report and the overwhelming presence of reefer in the 'Nam while reiterating two political points. The first is that, in the absence of any hard evidence of marijuana's deleterious effect, it was drafted—mainly by the original drug czar, Harry J. Anslinger—as a way to police Mexican laborers, control jazz musicians, and harass campus radicals. A weed for all seasons, it has been blamed on Chinese Communists and charged, almost simultaneously, with creating both juvenile delinquency and teenage apathy. Mann's second point is that the campaign to eradicate pot has been tremendously expensive. In its way, *Grass* is doggedly straightforward. No matter how thick the purple haze, you'll get the idea. Mann doesn't spend much time evoking a marijuana aesthetic—the movie's acme of cannabis-infused artistry is Cheech and Chong. Nor does Mann bother with epiphenomena like *High Times*—although the magazine is unlikely to forget him when it gives out its annual Dopey awards next year.

Richard Nixon is cast as the movie's most villainous cop; Ronald Reagan is used to signify the end of society's tolerance—and of mine too, I'm afraid. *Grass*'s relentless hard sell ultimately grows wearisome. Although only 80 minutes, it ends, and not a moment too soon, with a pot legalization rally that might well be reproduced outside the theater.

Also reviewed in:
CHICAGO TRIBUNE, 6/16/00, Friday/p. J, Michael Wilmington
NEW YORK TIMES, 5/31/00, p. E1, Elvis Mitchell
VARIETY, 9/27-10/3/99, p. 44, Brendan Kelly
WASHINGTON POST, 9/22/00, Weekend/p. 46, Michael O'Sullivan

GREAT DANCE, THE: A HUNTER'S STORY

A Craig Foster and Damon Foster production. *Director:* Craig Foster and Damon Foster. *Running time:* 90 minutes. *MPAA Rating:* Not Rated.

CAST: Karoha Langwane (Himself); Xlhoase Xlhokhne (Himself); !Nqate Xqamxebe (Himself).

NEW YORK POST, 9/29/00, p. 55, V.A. Musetto

When the Xo San bushmen of the central Kalahari desert in southern Africa get a hankering for meat, they have to get it the hard way: Hunting down animals, then killing them with spears and poisoned arrows.

As shown in the documentary "The Great Dance," this might involve chasing after an animal for three hours in 120-degree heat, until their prey can't run anymore.

But as one native says, "Tracking is like dancing, because your body is happy."

Or it may involve following a cheetah to a pregnant deer the big cat has killed, then feasting on what is left of the corpse—including the unborn. "Our faraway village will have meat at last," a bushman exclaims.

The Xo San are believed to be the oldest inhabitants of southern Africa, living much the same way their ancestors did. But time is running out.

"Since these scenes were filmed, the Xo people's individual hunting licenses have been revoked," the closing credits report. "Their hope is to regain rights to ancestral land, where their forefathers hunted and gathered for over 30,000 years."

"The Great Dance" is the labor of love of South African brothers Craig and Damon Foster, who directed and photographed this intriguing documentary.

Shots of dead animals being ravished by predators may not be to everybody's liking, but the film will get you thinking about how "progress" can often be a step backwards.

NEWSDAY, 9/29/00, Part II/p. B7, John Anderson

No disrespect to any Olympian in Sydney, but the greatest athletes in the world may well be !Xo San Bushmen of Africa's Kalahari Desert. After running down a kudu for three hours—while carrying spears—the !Xo hunter kills the deer-like beast, builds a fence of thorns against lions and hyenas, builds a fire, butchers the game, cures the meat and then carries it back to the tribe.

What would we call it? The meat-athlon? As illustrated by the first-rate documentary "The Great Dance: A Hunter's Story," it is just a source of food and life for a people who find themselves as endangered as any other species on the southern African plain.

Exquisitely photographed and directed over a three-year period by brothers Craig and Damon Foster, "The Great Dance" is one of those rare films that successfully captures and communicates a way of life and an aesthetic that, while part of the parched Kalahari landscape for 30,000 years, is indeed exotic—and vanishing, thanks to the pressures of cattle ranching and, ironically, wildlife parks. Still, the Bushmen pursue meat the way Bushmen have since pre-history, maintaining a spiritual link to the natural world that is precisely defined and inseparable from their temporal lives.

"Tracking is like dancing," says !Nqate Xqamxebe, whose words provide the film's story line. "Your body feels happy. It knows the hunt will be good. You feel it in the dance. It's like talking to God."

In other cultures such words would be used to describe art, which is precisely the point. The !Xo hunter's duty is an art, one learned through dedicated practice and perfected only by becoming one with his medium—in this case, the animal he intends to kill.

The "Great Dance" is not, it must be said, for the squeamish. The !Xo are nothing if not pragmatic, and if gaining food for their children means stealing game from other hunters—a cheetah, perhaps, or in rare instances a lion—then so be it. This practicality includes chasing vultures off carrion, which is consumed on the spot. "As children," relates !Nqate, "we often grew up eating rotten things. It doesn't make us sick." For audiences it may be another story.

This is a small part, of course, of a much bigger and quite stirring movie, which includes some truly astounding photography of animals big, small and dead. At one point you watch vultures scurrying around a dead springbok, the perspective being from inside the body. Carrion-cam? You won't see that at the Olympics.

VILLAGE VOICE, 10/3/00, p. 238, Edward Crouse

A grassroots refutation of Discovery Channel/*National Geographic* dispassion, *The Great Dance: A Hunter's Story* is hot and sweaty with fetching curves. From the opening shots—a series of kaleidoscopic video views that suggest a camera tunneling through either a nightscape or someone's digestive tract—the hyperfocal visuals clear out any thought that this might be PBS. Lensing in cooperation with the Working Group of Indigenous Minorities in South Africa, Craig and Damon Foster spent three years alongside the !Xo San bushmen in the central Kalahari. At times their technique implies an equal amount of time taking in extreme sports videos. For all the intensive wrangling of digital-video footage and data, it appears as if a good deal of the shoot was spent breaking the portable cameras—as evidenced by certain perilous shots, like the ones that go nose-to-nose with a lion or a lens-pecking vulture. The !Xo have never been documented from the inside out, Coke-promoting tale *The Gods Must Be Crazy* notwithstanding. *The Great Dance* mostly covers the "chasing hunt," a process in which three hunters, !Nqate, Karoha, and Xlhoase, track an animal through shimmering, sweltering heat waves, with minimal water, in an attempt to take over its mind and wear it out. The photography not only inhabits the eyes of the hunters but takes on the point of view of beetles, scorpions, cheetahs, even raindrops. The lens distortions are so intense that when the camera tracks a real-life cheetah close-up, the animal seems to house two battling dwarves. The only generic doc tic here is the jollified narration by South African actor Sella Maake Ka-Ncube, which resembles the least effort by *Annie*'s Geoffrey "Punjab" Holder.

Also reviewed in:
NEW YORK TIMES, 9/29/00, p. E16, Lawrence Van Gelder

GRIZZLY FALLS

A Providence Entertainment and Behaviour Worldwide and Norstar Filmed Entertainment Inc. release in association with Le Sabre of a Peter Simpson and Allan Scott production. *Executive Producer:* Mark Damon, Raylan Jensen, and Georges Campana. *Producer:* Peter R. Simpson and Allan Scott. *Director:* Stewart Raffill. *Screenplay:* Richard Beattie. *Story:* Stuart Margolin. *Director of Photography:* Thom Best. *Editor:* Nick Rotundo. *Music:* David Reilly and Paul J. Zaza. *Sound:* Jack Buchanan. *Sound Editor:* Tim Lewiston. *Casting:* Ron Leach. *Production Designer:* Thomas Carnegie. *Set Decorator:* Cheryl Dorsey. *Special Effects:* Ron Craig. *Costumes:* Minda Johnson. *Running time:* 94 minutes. *MPAA Rating:* PG.

CAST: Daniel Clark (Young Harry);   Bryan Brown (Tyrone Bankston);   Tom Jackson (Joshua);   Oliver Tobias (Genet);   Richard Harris (Old Harry);   Brock Simpson (Lanky); Chantal Dick (Young Jennifer);   Trevor Lowden (Joshua Jr.);   Marnie McPhail (Harry's Mother);   Ken Kramer (House Master);   Colin D. Simpson (Grits);   James Bearden (Menke); John Tench (Wes);   Hayden Simpson (Boy).

LOS ANGELES TIMES, 1/28/00, Calendar/p. 16, Robin Rauzi

[*The following review by Robin Rauzi appeared in a slightly different form in* **NEWSDAY, 1/29/00, Part II/p. B19.**]

A small sigh of relief, please, for this children's movie with no fast-food tie-ins, no toy marketing deals, no future Halloween costume in sight.

But only a small sigh.

For while "Grizzly Falls" delivers action and adventure in the great outdoors, it leaves viewers longing a bit for the creature comforts of big studio pictures. No committee of writers smoothing out the bumpy dialogue here, no computer animator compensating for the acting foibles of a 1,200-pound grizzly bear.

The story, set in 1913, concerns a 13-year-old boy, Harry (Daniel Clark). After his mother dies, his father, Tyrone (Bryan Brown of "Breaker Morant" and "Gorillas in the Mist"), decides to take his son into the Canadian Rockies to track a grizzly bear. Tyrone, a globe-trotting game hunter, doesn't want to kill this particular bear—a concession to the animal rights groups, perhaps?—but just to "capture" it so it can be "studied." But everything goes awry when the hunters wind up with two caged cubs and one very angry mama bear. Unable to free her own kin, the grizzly drags Harry—who fainted dead away at the sight of her—off into the wilderness. It is unfortunate that screenwriter Richard Beattie (working from a story by Stuart Margolin) both underestimates and overestimates grizzly bears. This one seems to manage a hostage trade negotiation, but stares helplessly at the flimsy cage that holds her cubs. Any camp counselor knows a grizzly would make kindling of that cage. Heck, so would the cubs. OK, no one really expects strict realism from a movie about a boy carried off by a bear. And here, as in most kidnapping movies, the heart of the story is the relationship between abductor and captive. The kid follows the bear, which provides safety from other wild animals, and learns how to fend for himself. They fish. They eat honeycomb. They bond.

Meanwhile Tyrone and a Native American animal tracker, Joshua, try to catch up and rescue Harry. Tyrone has some issues of his own, which have something to do with his own father and maybe another grizzly bear, but it only amounts to emotional filler. Tom Jackson plays Joshua so far against the stereotype that, for adults, the performance will seem to border on parody. Rather than stoic, he is touchy-feely, always analyzing Tyrone's emotions. What they should have been tracking was a better casting director. Here the producers seemed pleased to sign recognizable faces, and everyone suffers the consequences later. Passing reference are made to multiple residences for Tyrone and Harry—an attempt to pave over the conflicting accents of Brown (Australian), Clark (American) and Richard Harris (British), who plays Harry as an old man. Director Stewart Raffill, who most recently made a violence-marred TV version of "Swiss Family Robinson," isn't scared to push the PG rating. Genet (Oliver Tobias), a mean hunter who works for Tyrone and wants to kill the bear, gets mauled. Wolves threaten Harry and Tyrone, and there's lots of gunfire.

Cinematographer Thom Best never captures the glory of the Canadian Rockies, and the uncredited editing is jarring and unconvincing in key action sequences.

Hackneyed, too, are the scenes that bookend the film in which Harris as old Harry (he'd be 100 if he was 13 in 1913) retells the story to his grandkids.

All might be forgiven if, in the end, "Grizzly Falls" amounted to something more than a camping bedtime tale, but alas, it does not.

NEW YORK POST, 1/28/00, p. 50, Lou Lumenick

The first movie in ages that depicts someone dying of consumption, "Grizzly Falls" is a hapless family film that's too scary for little kids and too boring for everyone else.

Ali Oop, the grizzly, easily outacts the human cast in this lumbering tale of a she-bear who abducts young Harry (the inexpressive Daniel Clark) in the Canadian wilderness after his father (Bryan Brown), who's just lost his wife, captures her two cubs.

Dad, whose own father was abducted by a grizzly, grimly takes up the pursuit with an aphorism-spouting Indian ("You must find your own way") played by Tom Jackson. Harry, meanwhile, bonds with the bear and delivers anachronistic dialogue ("You ruined my whole life!").

The production notes set the action in 1913, which would make Richard Harris, who briefly appears as the elderly Harry with his grandchildren in a contemporary prologue and epilogue, around 100.

Directed without much flair by '70s Sunn Classics vet Stewart Raffill, "Grizzly Falls" is just short of being un-bear-ably ridiculous.

Also reviewed in:
CHICAGO TRIBUNE, 1/28/00, Friday/p. C, John Petrakis
NEW YORK TIMES, 1/28/00, p. E28, Lawrence Van Gelder
VARIETY, 1/31-2/6/00, p. 31, Robert Koehler

GROOVE

A Sony Pictures Classics release in association with 415 Productions. *Executive Producer:* Jeff Southard and Michael Bayne. *Producer:* Danielle Renfrew and Greg Harrison. *Director:* Greg Harrison. *Screenplay:* Greg Harrison. *Director of Photography:* Matthew Irving. *Editor:* Greg Harrison. *Music:* Wade Randolph Hampton. *Music Editor:* Greg Harrison. *Sound:* Lori Dovi. *Sound Editor:* Andrea Gard. *Casting:* Maria Ray. *Costumes:* Kei Hashinoguchi and Elizabeth Rodriguez. *Make-up:* Divi Crockett and Tonya Crooks. *Running time:* 86 minutes. *MPAA Rating:* R.

CAST: Mackenzie Firgens (Harmony Stitts); Lola Glaudini (Leyla Heydel); Denny Kirkwood (Colin Turner); Hamish Linklater (David Turner); Rachel True (Beth Anderson); Steve Van Wormer (Ernie Townsend); Bradley Ross (Aaron Lubiarz); Jeff Witzke (Neil Simonton); Ari Gold (Cliff Rafferty); Angelo Spizzirri (Todd Lowman); Nick Offerman (Sgt. Channahon); Chris Ferreira (Bill Neuman); Elizabeth Sun (Maggie McMullen); Dimitri Ponce (Guy Pritchkin); Aaron Langridge (Joe Torres); Wendy Turner-Low (Lisa Monroe); Matthew Bernson (Record Store Customer); Bing Ching (DJ Snaz); Jill Jose (Monique Adderly); Chris Stone (Geo Lafont); Lew Baldwin (Tobin Claussen); Jonathan Muller (Crew Member); Eva Christiansen and Sam Trychin (Car Passengers); Vincent Riverside (Anthony Mitchel); Pete Davison (Cigarette Guy); Karl Ackermann (Shep DeBone); Christoph Klotz (Arty Phipps); Brian Behlendord (Chill DJ 1); Polywog (Dance Floor DJ 2); Justin Baumrucker (Sticker Kid); Ed Abratowski (Green-haired Guy); Forest Green (Dance Floor DJ 3); Daniell Renfrew (Map Point Betty); No Battles (Chill DJ 2); WishFM (Dance Floor DJ 4); Monty Luke (DJ

5);   Kei Hashinoguchi and Melissa Leebove (Body Painters);   Jeffrey Crane (Scammer at Door);
Casey Landis and Rob Schroeder (Cops);   Shranny (Chill DJ 3);   John Digweed (Dance Floor
DJ 6);   Matthew Tyreman (Digweed's Roadie);   Brian Benson (Toll Booth Operator).

LOS ANGELES TIMES, 6/16/00, Calendar/p. 16, John Anderson

[The following review by John Anderson appeared in a slightly different form in
NEWSDAY, 6/9/00, Part II/p. B3.]

Before the '60s were over, the boomers had already made it clear that prefab nostalgia was a
potential gold mine. (Why else was Sha Na Na so popular at Woodstock?) Ever since, music-
saturated movies have been proving the point. "American Graffiti" (1973). "Animal House"
(1978). "Dazed and Confused" (1993). Not great cinema in every case, but cultural phenoms
whose charm was embodied in their ad hoc (and sometimes quasi-criminal) communities.

Where Greg Harrison's "Groove" strays from the fold—the only way it strays from the fold—is
in locating its community in the here and now, in present-day music and mores. Inside an
abandoned San Francisco warehouse, a crew of guerrilla promoters plots out an illicit rave—a
party/perpetual-motion machine where the engine is the DJ, the fuel is acid and Ecstasy, the
invitations are e-mailed and the barely post-adolescent sense of self-absorption leads to soul-
baring, -searching and -scorching. You've seen it before. You just might not have heard it before.

DJ-of-the-moment John Digweed is the biggest name in writer-director Harrison's debut film,
but among the things "Groove" has in common with those other youth movies (and "The
Breakfast Club," and "Fast Times at Ridgemont High" and "Empire Records," etc.) is a cast of
young unknowns so poised for discovery their performances feel like unsolicited deliveries of
bursting fruit. Ripest of all is Lola Glaudini ("NYPD Blue," "Down to You"), whose black-clad
Leyla is a New York transplant, and her urban-sexual cool masks a sad sense of non-achievement.
Drawn to her—and open about it, only because the drugs have overridden his programmed
timidity—is David (Hamish Linklater), a would-be novelist currently writing repair manuals.

Around them swirls a night's worth of characters whose problems and personalities wouldn't
be particularly exotic on your basic daytime drama. Harmony and Colin (Mackenzie Firgens and
Denny Kirkwood) are young lovers who get engaged at the beginning of the evening, but by the
end they have their romance rocked by overindulgence. (Harrison is brazenly blunt about drug
use at raves, although it would be inaccurate to call "Groove" a pro-drug movie.) Anthony (Vince
Riverside) is a kind of predator, skulking around exploitatively and instinctively, rubbing decent
people like Beth (Rachel True) the wrong way. Ernie (Steve Van Wormer), your host for the
evening, spends his time sobering up overdoses, conning cops and striving for the "nod"—the
gesture of approval he gets from the ravers he entertains.

Harrison gives us a glimpse into a subculture that thrives on an intrinsic underground-ness, but
it's only a glimpse. There's not enough sustained musical momentum to simulate the energy of
an actual rave; the characters are likable but unremarkable. The most resonant aspect of "Groove"
is the paradox of pop-music movements: how transient they are as well as critically important,
at least when it's your first time around.

NEW YORK, 6/19/00, p. 60, Peter Rainer

The underground rave culture in San Francisco is given the touchy-feely treatment in Greg
Harrison's *Groove*, a sweet, disposable concoction that at times resembles one of those sixties
American International Pictures like *The Trip*, with some Frankie and Annette thrown in, and at
other times resembles a seventies disco flick. Despite all the drugs ingested, everything going on
inside the warehouse during this all-night odyssey is a lot closer to chill-out than to freak-out.
Located somewhere inside all the techno-thump is your classic boy-meets-girl scenario. Some
things never change.

NEW YORK POST, 6/9/00, p. 51, Jonathan Foreman

With the exception of Doug Liman's "Go," which dealt with the scene mostly in passing, Greg Harrison's exuberant "Groove" is by far the most enjoyable movie to be inspired by the whole rave subculture, with its swirling mix of techno music, giant illegal parties and mass use of the drug Ecstasy. One of the hits of the Sundance Film Festival, the movie recycles plotlines, characters and dialogue from a plethora of familiar high school and dance movies. But, thanks in part to the filmmakers' skillful use of a terrific soundtrack, it also succeeds in capturing the rapturous excitement of a really great party.

The rave movement came out of the U.K. in the late 1980s, then spread around the globe. "Groove" follows a group of San Francisco twentysomething acquaintances, from the beginning to the end of a night in an abandoned warehouse that has been transformed into the perfect rave venue—replete with a quiet "chill room."

There's a chemistry grad student-cum-drug dealer (Ari Gold), his working class pal, who despises the whole finger-painting, neo-hippie scene, a squabbling gay couple who're celebrating their first anniversary together, a young deeJay from Fresno, and Ernie (Steve Van Wormer), the hard-working rave organizer who never has time to dance but who does it all just for "the nod" from the partyers whose lives he's changed.

But the most important character is David (Hamish Linklater), an uptight, rather sour writer from the Midwest, whose cooler brother Colin (Denny Kirkwood from "Never Been Kissed") invites him to a rave where Colin plans to propose to his sprite-like girlfriend Harmony (Mackenzie Firgens).

At the party, David takes Ecstasy and is helped through the experience by Leyla (Lola Glaudini), a beautiful raver increasingly burned out on hedonism.

There are times when writer/director Greg Harrison is so desperate to convey the innocent charm of the scene he has "discovered" that it's embarrassing.

This earnest evangelism prevents him from explaining aspects of the scene to outsiders, like what it is that celebrity deejay's (like the great John Digweed) do to make them the object of such worship. And who's paying for all this equipment, bottled water, etc.?

To its credit, "Groove" doesn't try to disguise the dungeons 'n' dragons dorkishness of so many ravers, the white upper-middle classness and strange sexlessness of the whole scene, its sad dependence on pharmaceutically assisted togetherness, or the corniness of its warmed-over, hippie-trippy blather.

The performances are extremely variable, with the lows provided by the mournful, flat Linklater and the highs by sensational newcomer Lola Glaudini.

NEWSWEEK, 6/5/00, p. 69, David Ansen

[*Groove* was reviewed jointly with *Better Living Through Circuity*; see Ansen's review of that film.]

SIGHT AND SOUND, 3/01, p. 51, Danny Leigh

San Francisco, the present. Ernie Townsend and a group of his friends break into an abandoned warehouse for an organised rave. As Ernie spreads word of the venue through his e-mail network, ravers arrive on the premises. Their number includes habitual clubber Leyla, young couple Harmony and Colin, and Colin's workaholic brother David, for whom tonight will be his first rave. As the rave gets under way, Colin and Harmony announce their engagement. Despite David's misgivings, all three take Ecstasy in celebration. David meets Leyla and spends the rest of the evening with her.

As the rave progresses, Colin is seen kissing another man by a distraught Harmony. A large group of refugees from another rave attempt to gatecrash the warehouse. In the resulting melee, the police arrive and close down the party In the confusion, David and Leyla are separated. An hour later, British DJ John Digweed—the star of Ernie's lineup—arrives. Ernie reconnects the electricity and the party continues. David and Leyla are reunited. The next morning, they leave in tandem, while Harmony and Colin also return home together.

Groove's status as the first relatively mainstream American rave movie—other US movies, notably *Go*, have simply flirted with club culture—is hard to evaluate without reference to its more obviously credible British counterparts (the UK having got there first, for better or worse, with both rave and its documentation). Specifically, Greg Harrison's leaden feature debut remains hugely indebted to Justin Kerrigan's cartoonish *Human Traffic*, of which it frequently resembles a more po-faced and didactic mirror image. Which isn't to say that Harrison is guilty of quite the same inanity as Kerrigan: in fleeting moments, he proves himself a visual stylist of some wit and imagination, his glitter balls on subway carriages and dreamily lit, sybaritic chill-out rooms a refreshing left turn from *Human Traffic*'s noisy film-school trickery. It's unfortunate, therefore, that *Groove* is saddled with such a stupefyingly naive and/or disingenuous approach to its subject matter. From the opening scenes of Ernie and his can do pals breaking into their San Franciscan warehouse like the cast of *Scooby Doo*, to the fond imagining of real-life DJ John Digweed performing for whatever paltry stipend Ernie's $2 entrance fee has raised, there's an unreality to Harrison's film that capsizes the various insights he's so eager to regale us with. And what adolescent insights they are: given the archetypal nature of his protagonists and their sundry monologues on just how dramatically raves have improved their quality of life, the audience is led by the nose to conclude that US raving must be a phenomenon of profound socio-cultural importance. Sadly, other than a brief sermon from Ernie as to his motives for organising raves (apparently, for "the nod" of gratitude from peers), Harrison's script is unable to articulate why or how his cast are anything more than just another generation of stoned Haight-Ashbury party hardies.

Harrison's habitually wooden characterisations don't help; the director merely wheels out a series of ciphers: the upstanding, good-hearted Ernie, the timid, work-obsessed David, the enigmatic, seductive Leyla. Sure enough, the bickering gay couple and jabbering drugs casualty aren't far behind. But beneath the hackneyed plotting and sloppy characterisation, is a deeper flaw—that Harrison never once seems clear on who *Groove* is meant for. At times, he seems intent on making a celebration designed for those already initiated into the world of raves and raving; if so, his project is short on both detail and conviction. Then again, given that we are invited to view proceedings largely through the addled eyes of token square David, perhaps we are meant to take this as a guide for the culturally curious. In which case, *Groove* is ultimately redolent of listening to someone detail their first drug experience—all very meaningful for the individual concerned, but sadly unengaging for anyone else.

VILLAGE VOICE, 6/13/00, p. 160, Dennis Lim

The first American fiction feature to embrace the rave scene as more than colorful scenery, *Groove* is less a work of subcultural ethnography than a curiously dorky act of hipster sincerity, less party movie than cheesy valentine. Writer-director Greg Harrison corrals a bunch of representative types into an all-night San Francisco warehouse rave and allows the Ecstasy-plus-techno headrush to work its magic. The result doesn't lack for affection or enthusiasm, but Harrison's attempts to convey rave's transformative euphoria are too often declared instead of simulated, and every other line of dialogue uttered in this movie begs to be drowned out by the music. Harrison's firsthand familiarity with the scene is evident in *Groove*'s attention to detail, and it's a mystery why this insider's account should assume such a drably familiar shape. The context may be fresh, but Harrison shoehorns into it a moth-eaten *American Graffiti* model—one busy night of youth-ensemble crisscrossing. In a tip-off that the most responsive audience might be nonravers (club kids are in fact least likely to be transported by these proxy thrills), the nominal protagonist and convenient viewer surrogate is a rave skeptic, David (Hamish Linklater), who's dragged by his hard-partying younger brother to—what else—the first night of the rest of his life.

A dour aspiring novelist who writes computer manuals for a living, David swallows his first tab of E and promptly runs into a soul mate, Leyla (Lola Glaudini), a seasoned raver who finds David's initial disorientation and subsequent chemical epiphanies not only endearing but somehow revelatory in terms of her own comfortably numb hedonism. "I'm alive—I haven't felt that way in a long time," he gushes. "I just want to commit to something without any fear," she confesses. Granted, they're fucked-up, but it's in moments like this, when *Groove* prioritizes intimate drama over dance-floor communion, that it runs aground. The other strands of the freewheeling yet plodding narrative are similarly thin: an oily scene-ster comes between David's brother and his ditzy girlfriend; a kid nearly ODs on GBH; the organizers good-naturedly try to outwit the cops; and in a colossally misguided attempt at a running joke, a disco-napping gay couple oversleep and get lost on their way to the rave (cue plenty of queeny bickering).

Loosely structured around a series of DJ sets, *Groove* builds to a climactic appearance by mega-DJ John Digweed (playing himself). The Digweed set itself is a blast, and Harrison has fun capturing it, but having finally come close to a visceral evocation of a transcendent rave moment, Harrison buries it under a landslide of mawkishness—he has David and Leyla lock eyes across a crowded floor and, the morning after, engineers a cringe-inducing chat between Digweed and a fanboy DJ ("Can I touch you?"). Worse, the movie hammers home the point made earlier by head promoter Earl (Steve Van Wormer), already painful the first time, that he goes to the trouble of organizing illegal raves all for the sake of "the nod" (acknowledgment from a total stranger), a cornball philosophy that the film unselfconsciously inflates into its own mission statement. *Groove* lacks the wit of *Graffiti*, not to mention the quirks and textures that Richard Linklater brought to a similar form in his early films, and there seem to be fewer obvious breakout stars among its ensemble than there were in *Graffiti* and *Dazed and Confused*—if anything, the actors (Hamish Linklater, in particular) illustrate with unfortunate clarity the pitfalls of affecting a pharmaceutical high. With its loved-up, it's-all-good pseudo-spirituality, *Groove* is even more woefully earnest than its disco ancestors like *SNF* and *Thank God It's Friday*—think of it, for better or worse, as rave's *Godspell*, with Digweed as Jesus.

Also reviewed in:
CHICAGO TRIBUNE, 6/30/00, Friday/p. L, Mark Caro
NEW YORK TIMES, 6/9/00, p. E8, Elvis Mitchell
VARIETY, 2/7-13/00, p. 55, Dennis Harvey
WASHINGTON POST, 6/30/00, p. C12, David Segal

GUN SHY

A Hollywood Pictures release of a Fortis Films production.   *Producer:* Sandra Bullock. *Director:* Eric Blakeney.   *Screenplay:* Eric Blakeney.   *Director of Photography:* Tom Richmond.   *Editor:* Pamela Martin.   *Music:* Rolfe Kent.   *Music Editor:* Nick South. *Choreographer:* Juan Llano and Karen Russell.   *Sound:* Geoffrey Patterson and (music) John Vigran.   *Sound Editor:* Dave Hankins. *Casting:* Laurel Smith.   *Production Designer:* Maher Ahmad.   *Art Director:* Seth Reed.   *Set Designer:* Domenic Silvestri.   *Set Decorator:* Maurin Scarlata.   *Set Dresser:* Todd S. Morris.   *Special Effects:* Ron Trost.   *Costumes:* Mary Claire Hannan.   *Make-up:* Pamela S. Westmore.   *Stunt Coordinator:* Doc Duhame and Mike Russo. *Running time:* 102 minutes.   *MPAA Rating:* R.

CAST: Liam Neeson (Charlie);   Oliver Platt (Fulvio Nesstra);   Jose Zuniga (Fidel Vaillar); Michael DeLorenzo (Estuvio);   Andy Lauer (Jason Cane);   Richard Schiff (Elliott);   Paul Ben-Victor (Howard);   Gregg Daniel (Jonathan);   Ben Weber (Mark);   Sandra Bullock (Judy Tipp);   Mary McCormack (Gloria Nesstra);   Michael Mantell (Dr. Bleckner);   Mitch Pileggi (Dexter Helvenshaw); Louis Giambalvo (Lonny Ward);   Rick Peters (Bennett);   Dusty Kay (Kapstein);   Jerry Stahl (Lucien);   Michael Weatherly (Dave Juniper);   Hank Stratton (Carmine Minnetti);   Frankie Ray (Joey);   Taylor Negron (Cheemo Partelle);   Joe Maruzzo (Warren Ganza); Aaron Lustig (Fulvio's Neighbor);   Tracy Zahoryin (Jason's Girlfriend);   Michelle Joyner (Elliott's Wife);   Manny Perry (Cheemo's Bodyguard);   David Carpenter (SEC Agent Cohler);   Tommy Morgan, Jr. (SEC Agent Harris);   Roy Buffington (FBI Agent Clemmens); Myndy Crist (Myrna);   Ramona Case (First Class Stewardess);   Derek Sitter (Waiter at Night Club);   Ron Reaves (Manager at Bistro).

LOS ANGELES TIMES, 2/4/00, Calendar/p. 2, Eric Harrison

T.S. Eliot was wrong about April being the cruelest month. For moviegoers, at least, that honor belongs to January, with some of the nasty stuff bleeding into February. This is when studios tend to unload the films they don't know what to do with, the ones they don't expect anyone to like.

"Gun Shy," a new movie starring Liam Neeson and featuring a now-you-see-it-now-you-don't performance by Sandra Bullock, has virtually nothing to recommend it. OK, that's an overstatement. But what use is journeyman acting, quality set design and a kicky, eclectic score in a movie that's so ineptly scripted? The effect is of polishing a car that has no engine.

The movie is part of the trend of self-aware pictures that spoof movie conventions at the same time that they exploit them. With its sensitive tough guys and psychiatric theme, "Gun Shy" belongs to the budding mob-meets-shrink genre, along with "Analyze This" and the HBO series "The Sopranos." Only here it isn't the Mafia boss who's in therapy—it's the undercover Drug Enforcement Administration agent (Neeson).

He's headed for a breakdown after a sting went bad, leaving his partner dead. It ought to be funny to watch him in group therapy with a bunch of whiny men, all of them "sharing" about problems at their white-collar jobs.

There's much about this movie that ought to be funny. Taken individually, the scenes work. Or, rather, one suspects that they would if only they were in a movie in which the characters and storytelling engaged us.

But time and again, writer-director Eric Blakeney sets up comic situations—we can see the payoff coming—but then he doesn't follow through. Instead, the first-time director strings scenes together in such a way—jumping back and forth between people and time frames—that the viewer's identification with the characters and involvement with the plot don't develop.

Bullock, who also produced this movie, plays a nurse in a gastroenterologist's office who gets smitten with Neeson's character while giving him an enema. Amazingly, that sounds funnier than it plays. Hours after they meet, they're rolling together on a bed of manure. (The movie is obsessed with all things scatological). Bullock's role is thoroughly superfluous.

The plot involves DEA infiltration of a Mafia scheme to launder Colombian drug money on the stock market. Oliver Platt plays a mobster so mean he's first seen about to chop off a neighbor's hand with an ax because he suspects him of pilfering a newspaper.

Like just about every other man in this movie, though, he's really a softie, a neurotic mess who only wants to stop living the life of a gangster movie cliche.

One of the funny ideas that works here is the way everyone is aware that they are cliches straight out of an episode of "Miami Vice." It's fun to watch the movie subvert the stereotypes. But, in addition to Blakeney's poor handling of story mechanics, the movie is marred by an overreliance on unfunny bathroom gags and by the way it tastelessly expects us to laugh at two stereotypically gay characters.

You'd think a movie like this, populated by so many self-aware stereotypes, would be aware enough to know when it was exploiting them. But then that wouldn't be this movie—or this cruelest of movie seasons.

NEW YORK POST, 2/4/00, p. 54, Lou Lumenick

"Gun Shy" is the first comedy in which the hero (Liam Neeson) meets his love (Sandra Bullock) while she is giving him a barium enema. Let's hope it's the last. Though Bullock produced this weird exercise in toilet humor, her part is comparatively brief. Playing a gastroenterologist's nurse, she first appears 30 minutes into this alleged comedy and figures in several scenes—most notably one in which a toy wheelbarrow full of dirt is playfully dumped on her by Neeson's DEA agent as she tends her huge Manhattan rooftop garden.

She then disappears until the ridiculous climax.

Did she use her clout as producer to have her scenes cut from this embarrassing mess? Or were her scenes added after the fact to salvage this grisly project?

There's plenty of time to contemplate such questions as TV producer Eric Blakeney, making an inauspicious feature writing-directing debut, lays out his flatulent story. Neeson's agent is begging for early retirement after 18 years with the DEA; after a bloody shoot-out that left his partner dead during a drug sting, his nerves and his colon are shot. The movie's opening scene, takes place in a toilet, as do many others.

But first, he has to finish one last job (there's an original idea!)—masterminding a boringly complex money-laundering sting involving a Mafia don's son-in-law (Oliver Platt, who less resembles a human being than a cartoon with each new role) and a Colombian drug lord's son (Jose Zuniga).

The former suffers from prostate problems and the latter is a closeted gay. Both are psychotic.

The movie's scatological obsessions aside, Blakeney works very familiar mob-comedy territory. In an inversion of the "Analyze This"/"Sopranos" formula that yields very mild chuckles, Neeson's cop is the one who resorts to psychiatry, horrifying fellow members of his therapy group with his own job problems.

Playing against type, Neeson is funnier than you'd expect from the star of "Schindler's List"—but he's no threat to Billy Crystal. The only notable performer is Mary McCormack, who provided much needed laughs in her brief role as Platt's sarcastic wife.

This low-caliber "Gun Shy" has singularly ugly cinematography by Tom Richmond that at one point shows off Bullock's facial hair.

NEWSDAY, 2/4/00, Part II/p. B7, John Anderson

If it's true that "Gun Shy" was one of those "troubled" productions, you have to wonder: What was the first clue? "Analyze This" was already playing catchup with "The Sopranos" a year ago, so when Sandra Bullock decided to produce this faux-gangster-in-therapy comedy, someone must have anticipated comparisons. Maybe the trouble began when the filmmakers realized they'd cast a 6-foot-4 Irish actor (Liam Neeson) as the fed who's supposed to infiltrate a mob full of Italians and Colombians? Maybe it was the antique Jeffrey Dahmer joke? The "Godfather" ripoffs? The shootout at the urinal?

It's likely that none of this would have mattered if "Gun Shy" had a script or even an idea in its feathery little head. But it doesn't. What's morbidly fascinating is watching Neeson—who's quite likable and an excellent actor and, as we all know, a hunk—being humiliated to quite this extent. Example: The first time his character, Charlie—whose near-execution atop a table full of fruit salad has apparently made him swear off roughage— meets Bullock's character, Judy, is when she's administering a barium enema to the nerve-racked DEA agent. It doesn't get any worse than that. But it doesn't get much better.

Director Eric Blakeney has a very laid-back style that meshes not at all with his story or his script, which involves the rather stale and unsavory idea that homicidal criminals are people, too. Fulvio (Oliver Platt) is a vicious hit man, but that's only because 1. his capo di tutti frutti father-in-law (Frank Vincent) hates him; 2. his harpie wife (a hilarious Mary McCormack) holds him in utter contempt, and 3. because he really wants to live in Italy and grow tomatoes. Instead, he kills people. Or, in the aforementioned urinal scene with the gay Colombian gangster Estuvio (Michael DeLorenzo), he shoots off half of Estuvio's manhood.

Laughing? I didn't think so. Getting back to "troubled": The most interesting thing about "Gun Shy"—in which Charlie finds group therapy, the group helps him defeat some evil feds and they all join Judy on a tugboat out of town—is that it got made at all. Do these projects, especially those championed by a box-office winner such as Bullock, just take on a life and momentum of their own? Do the cast and crew and studio become victims of mass hysteria? Isn't there an "off" switch? A movie like "Gun Shy" is something like an uncontrolled nuclear reaction. Without the laughs.

SIGHT AND SOUND, 12/00, p. 48, Rob White

DEA Agent Charlie's nerves are on edge following a violent drugs bust. In New York he enters group therapy to help him through his next case, undercover on a Mafia money-laundering scam. Small-time crook Fulvio has set up the deal; Colombian drug baron Fidel is financing it; Jason is the crooked dealer executing it. Charlie starts seeing Judy, a nurse who gives him an enema. Fulvio is mocked by his wife and her father, Don Carmine. The deal begins to unravel when

Fidel is insulted by Jason's suggestion that they launder the money by buying Soya beans. Charlie tries to accelerate the bust but his boss Dexter refuses to jump the gun.

After the eventual success of the first laundering deal an even bigger scam is proposed by Jason who's secretly in cahoots with corrupt Dexter. Another DEA agent finds out about this but Dexter kills him before he can tell Charlie. Everybody plans to double-cross each other; the various plotters are about to have a violent showdown in a dockside factory, but Charlie's group-therapy partners prevent this by bursting in, dressed in fake FBI uniforms, brandishing toy guns. Fulvio gets away to Italy; Fidel swims off with his bodyguard lover; Jason and Dexter are arrested by the real FBI; Charlie, Judy and his friends from therapy sail off in a tugboat.

"I'm very sensitive to this Colombian coke-dealer stereotype," says the Colombian coke dealer Fidel in debut director Eric Blakeney's *Gun Shy*. Later Fulvio, his small-time mafioso partner in a money-laundering scheme adds, "I'm sick of being a cliché." Fulvio is trying to impress his sceptical father-in-law Don Carmine by setting up the deal, but what he really wants is to cultivate the soil in Italy. His wife mocks him when he can't grow tomatoes, and as she walks off he looks desolately at his lone, sickly fruit and sprays it with fertiliser, thinking no doubt—as we do—of *The Godfather*'s Don Vito Corleone's altogether more impressive agricultural skills and the gardening implement Corleone's grandson sprays him with before he realises he's dead.

Gun Shy makes light comedy out of the premise that modern-day gangsters have all seen *The Godfather* and *Miami Vice*. As such it seems to resemble televisions *The Sopranos*. But whereas *The Sopranos* brilliantly used the comedy of this premise as a way of reinvigorating gangster mythology, *Gun Shy* simply embellishes it for the sake of mild fun.

Liam Neeson stars as Charlie, a veteran DEA agent traumatised by a bungled drugs bust. In order to make it through his next assignment—working undercover on the deal Fidel and Fulvio are putting together—he enters group therapy with several frustrated corporate executives. (Another nod to *The Sopranos*, as well as to *Analyze This*.) It seems like Charlie's participation in therapy will derail the sessions since his traumas are so disproportionate to his fellow patients' (who are bothered by lack of promotion and office politics). In fact the men easily find common ground and therapy just becomes a convenient if unlikely pretext for them to bond, a neat device which keeps the plot moving. In an even more unlikely scenario, but one that's in keeping with the light comedic tone, Charlie starts going out with Judy (played by Sandra Bullock) the nurse who, having just given him an enema, decides the root of his troubles is his inability to enjoy the small things in life. Bullock produced *Gun Shy* and her wholesome persona pervades the film. Harmless jokes about flatulence abound, the plot makes reasonable screwball sense and the protagonists who aren't truly vicious end the film with their desires fulfilled: Fulvio gets his garden, Fidel abandons his family for his one testicled bodyguard lover, Charlie and Judy sail into the sunset on board a tugboat. Occasionally harsher notes creep in as if reminding us of reality. A young DEA agent who's been shadowing Charlie is found murdered in his car and another is killed before he can warn Charlie about a double-cross. But these are less moments of serious discordance than slight misjudgements by Blakeney (whose writing credits include episodes of television series *Cagney and Lacey* and *Moonlighting*): likewise the odd flashback sequences in which drug dealers being gunned down are seen by Charlie as ballet dancers spinning in mid air.

VILLAGE VOICE, 2/15/00, p. 126, Michael Atkinson

Just when we assumed we were already chin-deep in badda-bing hardy-hars about neurotic Mafiosos, Eric Blakeney's *Gun Shy* stumbles into release following a conspicuous wave of nonhype. It's a last-ditch, Friday-night New Release waiting to happen, as even producer-star Sandra Bullock seemed to know, winnowing her girlfriend role down to its barest Bullock essentials: stray forelocks and oversized shirts. Blakeney is a TV writer whose ideas stop at the pitch—an undercover cop laundering money for Colombian drug lords and the New York families is plagued with self-doubt, panic attacks, and gastrointestinal agony. Continuing the once amusing strategy of casting non-Italian paisans, Blakeney has Oliver Platt and Mary McCormack as the lower-rung gangster couple (McCormack spits sizzling Bronx bile better than anyone since Cathy Moriarty), thus paying for a few snappy line readings with any semblance of credibility. But it's the casting of Liam Neeson as the nervous breakdown that turns the movie to asphalt—it's like watching Andre the Giant play Woody Allen.

Also reviewed in:
NEW YORK TIMES, 2/4/00, p. E17, Elvis Mitchell
VARIETY, 2/7-13/00, p. 49, Robert Koehler

HAMLET

A Miramax Films release of a Double A Films production. *Executive Producer:* Jason Blum and John Sloss. *Producer:* Andrew Fierberg and Amy Hobby. *Director:* Michael Almereyda. *Screenplay:* Michael Almereyda. *Based on the play by:* William Shakespeare. *Director of Photography:* John de Borman. *Editor:* Kristina Boden. *Music:* Carter Burwell. *Music Editor:* Todd Kasow. *Sound:* Noah Vivekanand Timan and (music) Michael Farrow. *Sound Editor:* Elmo Weber. *Production Designer:* Gideon Ponte. *Art Director:* Jeanne Develle. *Set Dresser:* Jeffrey Everett and Joshua Drew. *Special Effects:* Drew Jiritano. *Costumes:* Luca Mosca and Marco Cattoretti. *Make-up:* Kyra Panchenko. *Stunt Coordinator:* Manny Siverio. *Running time:* 112 minutes. *MPAA Rating:* R.

CAST: Ethan Hawke (Hamlet); Kyle McLachlan (Claudius); Diane Venora (Gertrude); Sam Shepard (Ghost); Bill Murray (Polonius); Liev Schreiber (Laertes); Julia Stiles (Ophelia); Karl Geary (Horatio); Paula Malcomson (Marcella); Steve Zahn (Rosencrantz); Dechen Thurman (Guildenstern); Rome Neal (Barnardo); Jeffrey Wright (Gravedigger); Paul Bartel (Osric); Casey Affleck (Fortinbras); Robert Thurman (Priest); Tim Blake Nelson (Flight Captain); John Martin (Claudius' Bodyguard); Bernadette Jurkowski (Blockbuster Clerk); Robin MacNeil (Player King); D.J. Dara, Sinead Dolan; Paul Ferriter; Larry Fessenden; Sarah Fiol; Tanya Gingerich; Paul Graham; Henry Griffin; India Reed Kotis; Ayun Halliday; Greg Kotis; Barry Manasch; Phillip McKenney; Anne Nixon; Colin Puth; Charles Renfro; Giancarlo Roma; Thomas Roma; Kelly Millicent Sebastian (Special Guest Appearances).

CINEASTE, Vol. XXV, no. 4, p. 37, Martha P. Nochimson

Tired of the same old Hamlet flailing around his medieval Danish castle, and wondering where be Yorick's gibes? Michael Almereyda's new adaptation of *Hamlet* for the screen has given the prince a makeover. Now sans Yorick, Shakespeare's much filmed drama about the difficulty of making ethical choices has been shifted from Elsinore on the coast of Jutland to the Elsinore Hotel in New York City. This Hamlet (Ethan Hawke) is impelled to flail around New York for the old, familiar reason: his mother, Gertrude (Diane Venora), has married his uncle, Claudius (Kyle MacLachlan), suspiciously soon after his father's death, and dad's Ghost (Sam Shepard) confirms that Claudius murdered him. Vengeance is the task set for Hamlet. But under what circumstances is a son supposed to take a ghost's word about his father's murder? Certainly if he is the son of a King, intended to bind the laws of heaven to earth, he should take heed when the other world calls.

Hamlet's dilemma about obeying the ghostly imperative, however, is quite another prospect in the context of the twenty-first-century Denmark Corporation set in a cityscape where royals are reduced to literal pedestrians, scattered among anonymous urban apartments and hotel rooms. Watching Hawke, Venora, and MacLachlan thread their way among the monolithic skyscrapers of New York, articulating Shakespearean cadences in flat modern tones, has the charm of innovation. Still, once the majesties of Denmark become mere New York media celebrities, no longer the representatives of the deity on earth, their "o'er hasty re-marriage" is no longer an affront to the cosmos, is it?

The urgency of Hamlet's quest, in the Shakespearean original, grows from his position in a tightly interrelated community in which his identity, his very life, depends on a complex system of universal values more important than the desires of any single person. But in the unfathomable chaos of urban sprawl, clutching his camcorder, this Hamlet is a part of an individualist society where nothing supersedes private wishes. Almereyda's audacious attempt to adapt the play to the screen for a modern culture characterized by fragmentation, alienation, and discontinuity is not just a change of scene, but a change of ethos that kicks the supports out from under all the motivations in his source of inspiration. There is nothing in this movie that helps us to understand what prevents this Hamlet from hitting Route 66, making for San Francisco, and chilling out until he can fit the Ghost's message into his personal space.

It is no coincidence that Almereyda is alone among the Shakespeare adapters of the past ten years in taking a dauntingly postmodern approach. The urban setting, saturated by the empty images of late capitalism, leaves Hamlet, his family, and his friends at loose ends in a distinctly Un-Shakespearean universe with a void at its core. So, it's not just that this approach has discarded Yorick; it's not just that most of the resonant lines that define the world of Hamlet have been eliminated by a spare script. It's the disappearance of the matrix: not the digitalized portal of illusion in the film of the same name, but the matrix in its root sense, the maternal womb of society. None of the recent Shakespeare films has hazarded a deviation from the organic, interconnected society of its original because of how essential the organic community is to Shakespearean drama. Kenneth Branagh removed his recent *Hamlet* (1996) to the nineteenth-century to intensify the claustrophobic atmosphere of the court. His adaptation renders the poison of corruption spreading through Elsinore an illness spawned by too much recirculation of twice-breathed air. (Even Baz Luhrmann's swish pans in his frenetically paced *Romeo & Juliet* (1996) are but a new way to ricochet around the close-knit social structure of Verona Beach.)

When Branagh's nineteenth-century Ophelia (Kate Winslet) goes mad and commits suicide, her plight as a daughter constrained by her father's and her society's absolute authority over her has relentlessly led to this breakdown. She has been overwhelmed by a clearly defined social conditioning that has deprived her of the means to cope with the absence of her brother, the inconsistency of her lover, and the death of her father. Almereyda's rootless twenty-first-century Ophelia (Julia Stiles) has no such constraints. Dressed in trendy, 'whatever' liberated outfits and living in grunge chic in a Lower East Side apartment, she comes and goes as she pleases. The question Almereyda needed to examine is what a father like Polonius (Bill Murray) might mean to her, and to the more conservative but still bumptious Laertes (Liev Schreiber), since the original impetus for the brother and sister to trim their passions to suit traditional rules is inoperative.

Polonius is personally a fool in the original play, but his connection to the monarchy as a loyal retainer invests him with the consequence of his place in the scheme of things. He has been stripped to less than zero in the corporate setting, as has any sense of authority he might have. This Polonius is a cipher. As a result, the famous advice scene in which the old boy tells Laertes as he departs for Paris, "This above all, to thine own self be true," is almost unplayable. Polonius is a suit, with not even the buttress of convention to support his empty clichés.

The center of gravity in this scene shifts radically to the relationship between Laertes and Ophelia and his advice to her to keep "her chaste treasure" from Hamlet, ostensibly because princes cannot choose mates on a personal basis. Although this is a statement that has no literal meaning whatsoever in this context, it gains interest from the emotional authority of the lines, murmured intimately, in a manner that trembles with incestuous implications. Julia Stiles's impressively modulated performance radiates complex suggestions of emotional abuse by her brother, making this a compelling stand-alone moment, which fleetingly translates these characters into a pair of contemporary, imploding siblings. But the scene prefigures nothing that can justify Ophelia's permitting her father to wire her body with a tape recorder so she can spy on Hamlet. There is still less to justify Stiles's later, intense (also impressive) performance of insane rage in response to her father's death.

This is not to say that there can be no such thing as a successful post-modern *Hamlet*, and Almeredya's production bristles with hints about what it might be like. Extricating the familiar figures from the Shakespearean coils of political hierarchy, authority, and the implacable Great Chain of Being, Almereyda gives them interestingly tenuous connections via fax, computer, telephone, the omnipresent video camera, and obsessive sex. Hamlet's alienation is nicely defined by his intimate relationship to his camcorder-and to no one else. General social fragmentation is evoked when Rosencrantz (Steve Zahn) and Guildenstern (Dechen Thurman), Hamlet's turncoat friends who are spying on him, report back on a speakerphone while Gertrude and Claudius abandon themselves to sexual foreplay.

There are also a number of humorous allusions to the empty images of an uncentered culture, the most successful of which is the recorded, suggestive purr of Eartha Kitt's voice in a taxi, incongruously telling Hamlet, Rosencrantz, and Guildenstern to use their seat belts. And, after Hamlet's inadvertent murder of Polonius, there is a brilliantly conceived confrontation between Hamlet and Claudius in a launderette among the whirring, stainless steel washing machines, in one of which Hamlet is washing Polonius's blood out of his clothes. This is a true twenty-first-century vision of ethics in crisis. Hamlet nervously tries to wash away the consequences of his actions in the rinse cycle. Claudius, another form of stainless steel mechanism, brutally beats Hamlet into 'coming clean' about the location of Polonius's corpse, as he hides an even greater crime.

But these are moments that can pick up no momentum because they are thwarted by Almereyda's failure to translate the teleology of tragedy, with all its implication of an ordered and just universe, for a modern setting. (Jim Jarmusch's deeply moving *Ghost Dog*, a film released at about the same time, reflects instructively on Almereyda's misfire. In a film that is in many ways more true to the original spirit of *Hamlet* than Almereyda's literal adaptation, Jarmusch creates an existential tragic hero who willingly dies to preserve the larger meaning of his faith in the thick of modern corruption, grafting justice and meaning onto the shallow chaos of modern life.) Almereyda simply ignores the problem and gives the play only half a transformation. As a result, his Hamlet and Ophelia seem gratuitously forced by the script when they attend to values of obedience and loyalty that have no place in the society around them.

More regrettably, the sublime Diane Venora, as the finest Gertrude in the history of filmed *Hamlet*s, is lost in this film as she brings to it the kind of depth, fire, and emotional commitment that are only possible in a world with moral and social underpinnings. In the last scene, when Gertrude's realization that she has been implicated in her husband's murder impels her to take the poison Claudius intended for Hamlet, her terrifying honesty returns the action to its rightful gravity. But it removes her from the film's zeitgeist, in which earlier, in the spirit of postmodern pastiche, her first husband's ghost dematerialized into a soda machine.

Can you empty a tradition and lean on it at the same time? It seems that Almereyda would like to try. In his previous full-length feature film, *Nadja* (1994), he gave us a bloodless (in all ways) modern vampire melodrama that capriciously jettisoned vampire lore while depending on interested audience familiarity with it. His film of *Hamlet* makes a similar assumption that audiences already know and credit the story, so it doesn't have to attend to the arduous task of reinterpreting the deep structure of its motivations, only to refurbishing its surfaces. His casual dismissal of the foundations of the play's meaning reaches its disastrous extreme when he portrays the Ghost making direct physical contact with Hamlet. In a first for any production of *Hamlet* on stage or screen, as far as I know, Shepard grabs and violently shakes Hawkes to make his point.

Well, there has certainly been a lot of variation in the representation of the Ghost. But the revenant of Old Hamlet is always impalpable and just out of Hamlet's reach, in keeping with its insubstantiality, the elusiveness of justice, and the difficulty of meeting standards of rational proof, especially in the case of a murder about which only the victim can speak. The mind boggles at the meaning of Sam Shepherd's visceral ectoplasm. Is this a case of being gripped by an idea? Or touched by an angel? Or is this the Billy Bigelow approach to Shakespeare? There's trouble for sure when you find yourself wondering why such a material ghost can't pick up a gun and skip the middle-man—and the movie.

CHRISTIAN SCIENCE MONITOR, 6/9/00, p. 15, David Sterritt

Some purists look down on movie adaptations of William Shakespeare's plays, as if serious artists hadn't made truly great works within the genre—think of Laurence Olivier's brooding "Richard III" or Orson Welles's explosive "Othello," for instance.

Sometimes the argument against Shakespearean cinema is more specific, centering on the scene-cutting and text-trimming that such films often indulge—as if most stage productions didn't do this too, and as if pictures like Olivier's reshuffled "Hamlet" and Welles's stitched-together "Falstaff" weren't excellent all the same.

This said, some adaptations are obviously more successful than others. The latest to arrive, a new "Hamlet" and "Love's Labour's Lost," drastically shorten the Bard's originals. They also do the kinds of chronological updating and geographical transplanting that invite charges of gimmickry and superficiality. But this is all they have in common. "Hamlet," by American experimentalist Michael Almereyda, is bold and beautiful. "Love's Labour's Lost," by British writer-director-actor Kenneth Branagh, is a mishmash.

The new "Hamlet" is the third of the past decade, following an ornate rendering by Franco Zeffirelli (with Mel Gibson as the melancholy Dane) and an equally lavish edition (with uncut text) by Branagh himself. To introduce Almereyda's version by describing its most conspicuous changes—the action is moved to modern-day Manhattan, the Ghost is spotted on a video-surveillance camera, and so on—is to make it sound tricky and artificial, when in fact it's the opposite. Metropolises like New York are the world's post-industrial power centers, after all, and if a restless ghost did show up with something to say, it's likely an alert security system would announce his arrival.

But more important than the trappings of this "Hamlet" is what Almereyda does with them. Earlier films he's directed ("Nadja," "The Eternal") have weighed down his highly inventive visual style with lackluster scripts. Even in severely shortened form, "Hamlet" provides him with transcendent dramatic material that's also ideally suited to his vision of our world as a dark, dreamlike domain where distinctions between reality and illusion are often impossible to grasp.

Add a well-chosen cast—Ethan Hawke as the tragic hero, Julia Stiles as Ophelia, the versatile Bill Murray as Polonius—and you have the most sensitive and audacious "Hamlet" since Ingmar Bergman unveiled his avant-garde stage version years ago.

Shakespeare helped put Branagh on the movie-making map when his overrated "Henry V" reached the screen in 1989. Follow-ups like "Much Ado About Nothing" and "Hamlet" have done less for his career, and "Love's Labour's Lost" isn't very memorable, either. Not that the new picture, about a King who decides to substitute philosophizing for partying, lacks color and liveliness. Moving the comedy to the 1930s era, Branagh telegraphs its basic story with "newsreels" full of background information—a useful "Shakespeare for Dummies" device—and energizes the action with quickly paced editing.

In a maneuver that makes Almereyda's innovations seem tame, he also spices the picture with frequent musical numbers. Shakespeare fans may groan, but George Gershwin and Cole Porter fans have every reason to cheer—unless they care about the context surrounding their favorite songs, in which case they'll groan, too, since Branagh has evidently thought more about the songs' rhythms than their meanings.

When he punches up the film's climax with a bouncy rendition of "There's No Business Like Show Business," one suspects he's trying to convince us we're being far more entertained than we actually are.

LOS ANGELES TIMES, 5/12/00, Calendar/p. 14, Kevin Thomas

Director Michael Almereyda imagines "Hamlet" taking place in present-day Manhattan with such vigor, insight and originality that the power and immediacy of his film makes Shakespeare accessible in an exciting and provocative manner beyond all expectations.

Best known for the stylish—though sometimes tedious—vampire picture "Najda," Almereyda has pared down the text but not changed a word of dialogue and makes it come alive in a world so fully realized visually that the play of words and fresh images against each other intensifies the tragedy, heightening meaning and emotion. And in Ethan Hawke he's found a superb Prince of Denmark: youthful, sensitive, passionate but with a mature grasp of the workings of human nature that inexorably yields tragic insight.

This "Hamlet" has the gritty look of an indie New York movie and proceeds with dispatch and economy. Denmark has become the Denmark Corp., a multimedia conglomerate, and Elsinore a luxury high-rise hotel. Hamlet is a shaggy, aspiring filmmaker in an environment in which, as Almereyda has said, "there's hardly a single scene without a camera, a photograph, a TV monitor or electronic recording device of some kind."

From all this modern technology he has created a visual language worthy of Shakespeare. And he has done so with wit: Here's Hamlet pacing the aisles of the action movies section of a Blockbuster store as he's beginning to wonder whether "to be or not to be..." The Ghost (Sam Shepard) of Hamlet's father at one point disappears into a Pepsi machine. Spectacular high-rise penthouses, the grandly spiraling interior of the Guggenheim Museum, a laundry and a diner—these are the ultra-contemporary settings in which tragedy unfolds, accompanied by Carter Burwell's dynamic score, which incorporates a string ensemble with electronic loops and references to music inspired by "Hamlet" from Tchaikovsky to Nick Cave. John de Borman's harsh, vibrant cinematography, production designer Gideon Ponte's bold sense of scale and Luca Mosca and Marco Cattoretti's apt costumes are all crucial to the film's success. Kyle MacLachlan's Claudius is every bit the modern corporate mogul: trim, well-tailored with a forceful manner underlined by the jut of his jaw. He's a man in his prime, and it's completely understandable how Diane Venora's sensual Gertrude could be overcome by him. Once the Ghost has appeared to ask his son to avenge him, this Hamlet doesn't hesitate but instead deliberates, deciding ultimately that he should not slay Claudius. Instead he confronts him with his guilt with his video, "The Mousetrap," a spot-on example of what a young filmmaker would create, incorporating reprocessed found footage, animation, etc., in an experimental style. But tragedy has been set in motion when Hamlet unwittingly kills Polonius (Bill Murray), hiding behind a sliding mirror-paneled wardrobe door.

Almereyda's stellar ensemble speaks in crisp standard American English. This helps invest meaning and emotion in the soaring poetic language that in some of its usage grows ever more distant from us. The cast succeeds admirably in this, and in creating characters at once contemporary and timeless.

Murray is a special marvel: His Polonius is a thoughtful family advisor, a concerned father to his lovely but fragile daughter Ophelia (Julia Stiles) and his son Laertes (Liev Schreiber). This Polonius is no fool, but a man who grows verbose in his nervousness at having to deliver bad news. Also on hand, impressively, are Karl Geary as Horatio and Steve Zahn as Rosencrantz and Dechen Thurman as Guildenstern.

A touch of the stentorian creeps into the line readings of the otherwise protean Schreiber, who effectively suggests a strain of incest in his loving concern for his sister. Shepard's strong, weathered features are fine for the Ghost, but he's the one person in the cast who seems a little uncomfortable with Shakespearean cadences.

Almereyda has pulled off a formidable coup: He's made Shakespeare come alive for contemporary audiences of all ages, especially young people. He's made a "Hamlet" they can connect with—but in no way pandering to them despite its present-day context.

NEW YORK, 5/22/00, p. 88, Peter Rainer

It's not every day that you encounter a *Hamlet* in which you hear the voice of Mr. Moviefone. Or hear *To be or not to be* recited as the Prince of Denmark (Ethan Hawke) wanders the Action section at Blockbuster Video. It's also not often that you catch the ghost of Hamlet's father (Sam Shepard) disappearing into a Pepsi machine. Yet these dissonances, seemingly facetious, are also weirdly apt. Michael Almereyda, who directed the film in super 16-mm. and did the stripped-down, contemporary adaptation, sets the play in a ghastly, gleaming, fortress-like New York that is all video monitors and mirrored surfaces and product logos. *Hamlet* is a play about paranoia (along with a million other things), and this latest movie incarnation—coming after the Zeffirelli-Mel Gibson drearfest and Kenneth Branagh's bigger, longer, and uncut version—readily lends itself to a high-tech consumerist culture where everyone is watching and being watched. No matter how covert their designs, everybody will be found out. Denmark here is not a country but a megaconglomerate whose CEO, Claudius (Kyle McLachlan), has the square-jawed forthrightness of a captain of industry. In other words, he's already a villain even without the added bonus of being the murderer of Hamlet's father. Hamlet is a tatty romantic who slumps his way about the city in a furiously alienated funk. He's the most grad-student-ish of all movie Hamlets, and also, I believe, the youngest: a *Reality Bites* Hamlet and a hippie Hamlet, too, with some James Dean thrown in. (Dean's image is invoked in the movie.) The more one sees of this loquacious moper, the more he resembles a refugee from the counterculture wars. Corporatism in this movie is the big bad wolf. At large in a global media culture, Hamlet is as dewy a rebel as any flower-powered precursor. A would-be digital filmmaker, he fights the enemy with its own weapons: His version of *The Mousetrap,* the play-within-the-play that captures Claudius's conscience and leaves him aghast, is rendered here as a movie-within-a-movie. If the success of any *Hamlet* ultimately rests on the quality of its lead performance, then Almereyda's version is middling. Hawke isn't terrible. His lines are delivered unaffectedly, in a way that allows the poetry to come through without seeming either too familiar or arch. Plus, as he also demonstrated in Richard Linklater's neglected *Before Sunrise,* he has a scruffy, moonstruck quality that works well all by itself. But it's difficult to find a way into Hamlet's torrential musings in a production as overstocked as this one. Hawke doesn't have the formidableness to break through the jabber of experimental-film imagery and shock cuts and surfaces reflecting back on surfaces. Maybe no actor could have broken through. But what is missing from this performance, and this production, is the sense that Hamlet is, as Mark Van Doren wrote, "trying to be more than a man can possibly be."

At times it seems as if Hamlet were a bit player in his own extravaganza, a counterpart to Rosencrantz and Guildenstern. This effect may be intentional, of course, but that doesn't make it laudable. There is a tendency to overpraise Shakespeare productions (whether for stage or film) proffering some imposing, overarching concept, as if the only way to prove his universality is to bend his drama into a Möbius strip of newfangled meanings. There are times in this new *Hamlet,* as with so many other hepped-up Shakespearean productions, when I just wanted to clear the decks of all the conceptualizing and folderol and get back to the beauty of the lines, of the emotions. Sometimes the most radical way to interpret a text is simply to serve it up unadorned.

Nevertheless, this *Hamlet* is not a movie to place beside, say, Baz Luhrmann's *Romeo + Juliet* or similar travesties. Almereyda isn't pandering to youth the way that film did. You can be less than ecstatic about what he's trying for here and still respect the attempt. By equating the garish feudalism of the play's original setting with the megalopolis of today's New York, he's at least on the right track. The problem is, it's just about his *only* track. And for New Yorkers, the equation between the two may be less than shocking anyway. So what else is new?

There are still plenty of reasons to check out this new *Hamlet.* There's a marvelous mad scene in which Ophelia (a Fiona Appleish-looking Julia Stiles) screams like a banshee within the coiled tiers of the Guggenheim. If Ethan Hawkes's performance doesn't carry the day, there are others that do, chiefly Liev Schreiber's elegantly seething Laertes, Sam Shepard's rude, startlingly present Ghost, Diane Venora's Gertrude, and (yes) Bill Murray's Polonius. Murray gives his lines a slightly skewed twist that makes them seem both eccentric and naturalistic. His Polonius is a voluble old fud who is also immensely touching; his murder is the only time in the film when one feels a life has been taken away. Diane Venora is the cast's most experienced Shakespearean performer—she once played the Melancholy Dane for Joe Papp and recently returned to Papp's New York Shakespeare Festival as Gertrude opposite Liev Schreiber's Hamlet—and she demonstrates yet again that she is one of the most gifted (and underused) actresses around. Her Gertrude is both solicitous and passionate, a queen gravely troubled by what is going on all around her and inside herself. She is a worthy counterpart to Hamlet, and her depth-charged brooding makes it clearer than ever how closely blood-linked this woman is to her son. For all of Almereyda's nouveau overconceptualizing, his *Hamlet* ultimately comes down to a story about a boy and his mother.

NEW YORK POST, 5/12/00, p. 51, Jonathan Foreman

The only tragic thing about the gorgeously photographed but embarrassingly sophomoric new "Hamlet" is the lonely spectacle of Liev Schreiber giving a deeply felt, expertly spoken performance as Laertes that deserves to seen in a top-notch production of the play. His scenes are among the few when the film and Shakespeare's language come alive.

The rest of the time this umpteenth movie version of the play is suffocated by the swollen egos of Michael Almereyda and Ethan Hawke, the movie's director and star respectively.

Almereyda, seems to have one idea: that it would be cool to do a slickly high-tech, modern, Manhattan-set "Hamlet," in which much of the dialogue comes out of speakerphones, computer screens, etc., and in which the "to be or not to be" soliloquy is delivered in a Blockbuster store.

Of course, it's perfectly OK to set Shakespeare in modern times. Baz Luhrman did it in an entertaining and powerful way with his MTV-esque "Romeo and Juliet" with Leonardo DiCaprio and Claire Danes.

But here the language is overwhelmed by a setting that really has nothing to do with the ideas and images that flow through the play—and everything to do with the director's callow theory that living in a high-tech, global media culture somehow makes us all Hamlets.

Still, an empty resetting of the play isn't enough to render "Hamlet" dull when you have a generally talented, if quirky, cast.

To really suck the life out of the play, you need a lead actor who fails to invest the ultimate role with any energy or enthusiasm: In other words, Ethan Hawke, who was good back in the days of "Dead Poets Society," once again playing his trademark whiny goateed slacker guy from "Reality Bites."

Denmark, in this version, becomes the name of a Manhattan corporation rather than a country. Hamlet's father (Sam Shepard) is its recently murdered CEO, whose wife, Gertrude (Diane Venora), has married Claudius (Kyle MacLachlan), his brother and successor.

Hamlet himself is some kind of rich-kid video artist with greasy hair under a Peruvian knit cap. His girlfriend Ophelia (a disappointingly mannered Julia Stiles,) is a truculent teen with her own downtown loft.

Besides Schreiber's Laertes, the most enjoyable and effective performances come from Steve Zahn and Dechen Thurman as Rosencrantz and Guildenstern.

NEWSDAY, 5/12/00, Part II/p. B7, John Anderson

"The King and CEO of Denmark Corporation is dead," announces Michael Almereyda's "Hamlet," via titles projected through the sunroof of a limousine. The cashmere-coated Claudius has executed a hostile takeover of the lust-besotted Gertrude. The goateed Hamlet is eyeballing the troubled landscape through the viewfinder of his digital camera. And the fragile Ophelia waits in vain for her moody ersatz Dane, in the public-access spaces of corporate Manhattan.

Any updating, modernizing or, in this case, urban renewal of Shakespeare's greatest play could easily have been undone by its own cleverness. And Almereyda has plenty of cleverness—the ghost of the King, for instance, being spotted on the closed-circuit TV of Denmark Corp., using a terraced apartment for his parapet and disappearing into a Pepsi machine when security finds him out. Or the conscience-catching "Mousetrap" being presented as a piece of video art.

But Almereyda's "Hamlet" doesn't merely put the play on film and in a modern world. It adapts the play for film—and for the modern world. Using a seriously truncated text (as most non-Branagh productions do), it features a performance by Ethan Hawke in the title role that suggests what James Dean or Johnny Depp might have made of it. But that's fine: Hamlet is the most internalized of literary monuments and Hawke's callow-bordering-on-surly Prince is everything a '00-ish Wittenberg grad student should be—a model of self-absorption whose psychological fetal position nearly makes him disappear.

Hawke's attitude also works toward a solution of the Hamlet Conundrum, the lack of a so-called "objective correlative" cited by T.S. Eliot and others, who've found in the plot a lack of justification for Hamlet's tortured soul, his inability to kill the man who killed his father, married his mother and usurped his throne (or, in this case, the comer office). But Hawke's Hamlet virtually wallows in post-adolescent suffering, flagellates in existential angst; if Almereyda's Hamlet fell down in the woods and there was no one there to hear it, he probably wouldn't make a sound.

Which is less than you can say for the rest of the cast, whom Almereyda (best known for his Pixel-visioned junkie-AIDS vampire comedy "Nadja") has directed toward a rereading of the entire text. Most entertainingly, Bill Murray, as the wise old windbag Polonius ("neither a borrower nor a lender be ... "), finds the humorous possibilities in every other line. Most poignantly, Julia Stiles ("10 Things I Hate About You"), mad scene aside, is a mostly mute Ophelia whose injuries are nonetheless eloquent and whose manipulation and grief are heartbreaking. When Polonius, her father, counsels her about Hamlet's untrue heart, and almost absentmindedly ties her sneaker, it constitutes a moment so gloriously human it's practically, well, Shakespearean.

SIGHT AND SOUND, 1/01, p. 50, Peter Matthews

New York City, 2000. A month after the King of the Denmark Corporation is found dead, his brother Claudius marries his widow Gertrude, angering her grieving son Hamlet. Hamlet's friend Horatio sights the king's ghost at the Denmark building. Keeping watch that night, Hamlet sees the ghost, which accuses Claudius of murder. Meanwhile, SoHo photographer Ophelia is unsure how to handle Hamlet's romantic advances. She shows one of his love letters to her father Polonius, an executive at Denmark; judging from the letter's tone that Hamlet has gone mad, Polonius consults Claudius and Gertrude. They hire Hamlet's acquaintances, Rosencrantz and Guildenstern, to discover the reason for his strange behaviour. Hamlet produces an art video that re-enacts his father's murder; a guilt-stricken Claudius rushes from the screening room. Confronting Gertrude in her apartment, Hamlet accidentally shoots Polonius, hiding in the closet. Flying to England attended by Rosencrantz and Guildenstern, Hamlet discovers a commission for his murder. Now insane, Ophelia drowns herself. Back for the funeral, Hamlet quarrels with her brother Laertes, who swears revenge for Polonius' death. Hamlet and Laertes square off at a fencing demonstration, where Claudius secretly poisons his nephew's wine. Discovering this, Gertrude drinks the poison and dies. Laertes pulls a gun on Hamlet; both are fatally wounded. Dying, Hamlet shoots Claudius dead.

Traditionally, adapters of Shakespeare's most garrulous play have laboured under varying degrees of bad faith, striking an uneasy bargain between respect for the text and commercial feasibility (the only screen version to run the full four hours is Kenneth Branagh's 1996 stiff—hardly the best advertisement for literary fidelity). Michael Almereyda,on the other hand, is an indie hipster who chops and changes with guilt-free abandon. At just 111 minutes, his brash modernisation must be one of the speediest *Hamlet*s of the sound era. Since it features teen heart-throb Ethan Hawke in the title role, one might be tempted to attribute his to demographics. But the film is unlikely to panic them at the multiplex, for the rat-a-tat technique is geared towards an insistently tricky piece of conceptual art.

That won't come as news to anyone who saw Almereyda's cerebral 1994 horror flick *Nadja,* where the joke was that a tale of vampires should be so torpidly aestheticised and, well, bloodless. There's something equally self-defeating about a *Hamlet* that takes a no-frills approach to the language. In the play, all the characters are spellbound by words that pour out of them, paralysing their ability to act. The playwright is as bewitched, redoubling the fanciful conceits, getting lost in his own tortuous poetry, ending up with a sprawling monster of a drama that no one has ever really licked. The inevitability of failure seems merely to have emboldened Almereyda, for he treats the great soliloquies as so many found objects to be slapped up in a loose, experimental bricolage. When the verse hasn't been blasted to smithereens, it's upstaged by the busy visuals—and that's where the director reveals his portentous drift. Set amid the steel canyons of corporate New York, the film portrays a Baudrillardesque world bombarded by mass media, one in which it's no longer possible to distinguish what's real. In this post-literate Hamlet, the quondam student prince is recast as a dissident video artist who contemplates snuffing it while cruising the action releases at Blockbuster—and, in one vertiginous moment, scans a television image of John Gielgud in the role.

That deft bit of intertextual foolery is probably meant in the nature of an apologia. Almereyda presumably doesn't claim to have nailed down *Hamlet,* only to have added another twist to the endless spiral of its interpretations. No hard feelings, then, if he offends traditionalists through such expedients as having the ghost disappear into a Pepsi machine and Ophelia strew Polaroids instead of the traditional posies. Yet in some ineffable way, the film falls victim to the same malaise it diagnoses, for the imagery hurtles by pell-mell without making a strong dent on the memory. Shooting cheap and fast, Almereyda has assembled a rough patchwork that suggests a home-movie version of the play. But while the impromptu tone is often charming, it doesn't allow the story much chance to build up a head of steam. It's just about impossible for the actors to sustain an emotional arc when the editing reduces their performances to a dissociated shambles. Almereyda seems blind to the paradox of proceeding at a jog-trot through Shakespeare's immortal study in procrastination. The existential ditherer is more a take-charge guy in this incarnation—a shift that relieves Hamlet of its whole brooding point.

VILLAGE VOICE, 5/16/00, p. 135, J. Hoberman

Obsessed with his role-playing, even as he rebels against it, Hamlet may be the most self-conscious poseur in English theater. It's a part ready-made for mannerism, which is perhaps what attracted Ethan Hawke to the material. Consequently, downtown filmmaker Michael Almereyda's slimmed-down, updated version of the Shakespeare tragedy—with Hawke in the title role—is stylish, funny, and smart ... but only up to a point.

Almereyda's revamped scenario concerns a power struggle within the Denmark Corporation, a vaguely defined multinational whose headquarters appear to be the Hotel Elsinore in Times Square. Claudius (Kyle MacLachlan) has taken over the company and married his murdered predecessor's wife, Gertrude (Diane Venora). Opposing these evil, parental suits, Hamlet is a blandly obnoxious aspiring digital videomaker who affects throughout a grungy Peruvian wool hat.

You might well wonder if Hawkes's Hamlet is the curtain-raiser for Kelsey Grammer's upcoming Macbeth. (Could it be a harbinger of George Clooney's Lear? Adam Sandler's Richard III?) But the star, who evidently used his bankability to get this 16mm movie made, is not the only behavioral performer here. Hawkes's combination of self-importance and callow cool is complemented by Julia Stiles's Ophelia, a sullen teenager with her own lower Manhattan loft. (Stiles exudes such agonized petulance one suspects Almereyda deliberately kept her waiting an hour before each take.)

Hamlet is predicated on stunt casting—which, though it may not enrich the material, at least provides a subtext. MacLachlan is an actor who never appears less (or more) than fake. Venora herself played Hamlet in a celebrated Joseph Papp production, and her Gertrude has far more physical authority than actual dialogue. Bill Murray's Polonius seems to have taken literally Hamlet's description of his character as "a foolish prating knave." As Laertes, Liev Schreiber—another recent Hamlet—is the most conventionally Shakespearean in his carefully tossed-off line readings. (Schreiber's scenes with Murray and Stiles place him uncomfortably between the facetious and the inept; those with Hawke leave the unmistakable impression of an actor who cannot help but think he should have been cast in the lead.)

Given the free-floating narcissism, *Hamlet* is appropriately image-haunted. The prince delivers his first soliloquy via Pixelvision on a laptop screen. His father's ghost is initially glimpsed in an elevator monitor. (There's another specter in a fleetingly televised James Dean, surely the Hamlet to which the mumbling Hawke might aspire.) Throughout, Almereyda layers the visual information through a panoply of computer screens, TV sets, bookcases. Hamlet's "To be or not to be" soliloquy is staged in the action aisle at Blockbuster Video, and the movie's comic high point is the video Hamlet presents to catch the king's conscience—a found-footage assemblage encompassing everything from Edison's *Electrocuting an Elephant* to a bit of Lewis Klahr cut-and-paste animation. *Hamlet* is not quite camp—although this is a movie where it always seems to be Halloween. Making much of faxes and speaker-phones, the movie has more than a casual resemblance to Aki Kaurismäki's 1987 *Hamlet Goes Business*. (The rubber duck that Ophelia returns to Hamlet is an homage—in Kaurismäki's supremely sarcastic film, Claudius is attempting to corner the world market in bath toys.) Like the Finnish director's mock grandiloquent noir, Almereyda's *Hamlet* is at least part thriller, and as diffident as he might seem, the director does imbue the proceedings with a measure of moody urgency.

From the opening low-angle traveling shot through Times Square to Hamlet's hasty trip to JFK in the company of those duplicitous dudes Rosencrantz and Guildenstern (Steve Zahn and the star's brother-in-law Dechen Thurman), *Hamlet* is a swiftly paced rhapsodic nocturne. The movie has the benefit of Carter Burwell's lush, brooding score and cinematographer John de Borman's glowing, saturated palette. Almereyda uses midtown Manhattan as evocatively as he did the East Village in *Nadja*. There's a visual poetry to the looming towers of power and the chrome and glass apartments in the sky.

But the joke only goes so far, and even at a relatively svelte 112 minutes *Hamlet* comes apart in its final third. Effectively snarky to begin with, reasonably mad throughout the middle scenes, Hawke has nothing left but attitude for the finale, particularly once the supporting cast begins dropping out around him. Can we term this a vanity project? Well before TV commentator Robert MacNeil appears to deliver the suitably glib wrap-up, it's apparent that "the rest is silence."

Also reviewed in:
CHICAGO TRIBUNE, 5/19/00, Friday/p. A, Michael Wilmington
NEW REPUBLIC, 6/5/00, p. 26, Stanely Kauffmann
NEW YORK TIMES, 5/12/00, p. E1, Elvis Mitchell
NEW YORKER, 5/15/00, p. 105, David Denby
VARIETY, 1/31-2/6/00, p. 37, Dennis Harvey
WASHINGTON POST, 5/19/00, p. C5, Stephen Hunter
WASHINGTON POST, 5/19/00, Weekend/p. 47, Desson Howe

HANGING UP

A Columbia Pictures release of a Nora Ephron and Laurence Mark production. *Executive Producer:* Delia Ephron and Bill Robinson. *Producer:* Laurence Mark and Nora Ephron. *Director:* Diane Keaton. *Screenplay:* Delia Ephron and Nora Ephron. *Based on the book by:* Delia Ephron. *Director of Photography:* Howard Atherton. *Editor:* Julie Monroe. *Music:* David Hirschfelder. *Music Editor:* Richard Whitfield. *Sound:* Charles M. Wilborn and (music) Dennis Sands. *Sound Editor:* Michael Wilhoit. *Casting:* Lisa Beach. *Production Designer:* Waldemar Kalinowski. *Art Director:* Troy Sizemore. *Set Designer:* Mick Cukurs. *Set Decorator:* Florence Fellman. *Special Effects:* J.D. Streett IV. *Costumes:* Bobbie Read. *Make-up:* Steve Artmont. *Make-up (Meg Ryan):* Karen Kawahara. *Make-up (Diane Keaton):* Kelcey Fry. *Make-up (Lisa Kudrow):* Angela Levin. *Stunt Coordinator:* Jack Gill. *Running time:* 92 minutes. *MPAA Rating:* PG-13.

CAST: Meg Ryan (Eve); Diane Keaton (Georgia); Lisa Kudrow (Maddy); Walter Matthau (Lou); Adam Arkin (Joe); Duke Moosekian (Omar Kunundar); Ann Bortolotti (Ogmed Kunundar); Cloris Leachman (Pat); Maree Cheatham (Angie); Myndy Crist (Dr. Kelly); Libby Hudson (Georgia's Assistant); Jesse James (Jesse); Edie McClurg (Esther); Tracee Ellis Ross (Kim); Celia Weston (Madge Turner); Bob Kirsh (Nixon Library Representative); Stephanie Ittleson (Victoria); Venessia Valentino (Nurse at Mesh Window); R.A. Buck and Phil Levesque (Gay Men); Paige Wolfe (Six Year Old Eve); Charles Matthau (Young Lou); Ethan Dampf (Four Year Old Jesse); Mary Beth Pape (Mother at Party); Catherine Paolone (Doctor); Carol Mansell (Woman Who Recognizes Maddy); Katie Stratton (Twelve Year Old Georgia); Talia-Lynn Prairie (Four Year Old Maddy); Kristina Dorn (Young Pat); Lucky Vanous (Montana Dude); Bill Robinson (Doctor on Soap).

CHRISTIAN SCIENCE MONITOR, 2/18/00, p. 15, David Sterritt

[*Hanging Up* was reviewed jointly with *The Whole Nine Yards*; see Sterritt's review of that film.]

LOS ANGELES TIMES, 2/18/00, Calendar/p. 1, Kevin Thomas

"Hanging Up" has all the ingredients of a success—a stellar cast, a promising premise, a strong production team—but nothing comes together in satisfying fashion.

Delia and Nora Ephron's script, adapted from Delia's novel, is underdeveloped and fails to mesh serious concerns with comedy. Director and co-star Diane Keaton is never able to achieve a mastery of shifting tones essential for the film to seem credible rather than contrived. It comes off synthetic despite the all-too-real issues it raises.

Delia and Nora are the daughters of the highly successful playwriting and screen-writing team Henry and Phoebe Ephron, and Delia has said that her novel drew from her experience of being the only one of four sisters in Los Angeles during her father's final years. She took inspiration for her book from her father's remark, "I live half my life in the real world and half on the telephone."

In "Hanging Up," Walter Matthau's irascible Lou Mozell, hospitalized and with his mind wandering, lives practically all his life on the phone to his middle daughter Eve (Meg Ryan), who in turn is constantly on the phone with her self-absorbed sisters, Georgia (Keaton), a high-powered New York-based editor in chief of her own women's magazine, and Maddy (Lisa Kudrow), a soap opera actress chronically upset that her sisters never watch her show.

The advent of the cell phone has, in fact, turned the charming but eternally frazzled Eve's life into chaos, as she struggles to be a wife and mother while working as a party planner. She's the responsible sister who lets everyone walk all over her, her often-absent and frequently exasperated husband (Adam Arkin) is wont to point out. She has yet to acknowledge that she is a martyr, in a way her own worst enemy.

Matthau can do irascibility like no one else, and he can show us the humor in it when it's pushed to outrageous extremes. Although Lou's decline triggers in Eve flashes of memories when her father was playful and loving with her when she was a small child, he has clearly been a cruel, nasty man for a very long while, his years of success long behind him. He craves attention, appeals for it shamelessly from Eve, only to turn on her savagely.

In one recent flashback we see a drunken Lou wreck his little grandson's birthday party, but we never see how the rightly enraged Eve reconnects with him. In a brief, chilling scene Eve visits her long-estranged mother (Cloris Leachman) who walked out on her family ages ago; her explanation is that she just never took to motherhood. But what of her feelings for Lou, past or present?

Furthermore, we don't get to see enough of Georgia and Maddy, who are, in effect, caricatures until the last reel demands they do 180-degree turnarounds. Actresses of the talent and skill of Keaton and Kudrow might have pulled this off if the film had any sense of irony about the situation; the sisters are only able to start bonding once their impossible father is well on his way to his reward.

In any event, the Ephrons and Keaton are unable to make a convincing serious comedy of Eve's predicament when her father and her sisters are so dreadful for so much of the time. Not helping matters is that the film takes place in the glossy universe of Hollywood mainstream movies when a grittier feel, a sharper edge, seem to have been in order. We gather that Arkin's Joe is a correspondent for National Public Radio, so unless he has inherited a fortune unbeknownst to us, we are puzzled as to how he and Eve can live in a totally fabulous 1920s Spanish-style estate, the kind favored by extravagant silent stars. (If Eve and Joe can afford to live so grandly, why doesn't Eve hire competent people to help with her staggering responsibilities?) While   Ryan, Keaton, Kudrow and Matthau certainly have their moments, there's not nearly enough of them for "Hanging Up" to add up to much. This formidable quartet may constitute enough star power to open "Hanging Up," but it's hard to imagine that it will stick around for very long.

NEW YORK, 2/28/00, p. 55, Peter Rainer

The title of the new Diane Keaton-directed film, *Hanging Up*, adapted from the Delia Ephron novel by the author and Nora Ephron, is metaphorical, but it's literal too: The main hung-up characters—the three sisters, played by Keaton, Meg Ryan, and Lisa Kudrow, and their father, played by Walter Matthau—spend a lot of time on the phone hanging up and calling up, and we're supposed to understand that this is how they best express' their rages and frustrations and love. Ryan, in a decent, sweet performance, is the middle daughter, a professional events-planner, who bears the brunt of caring for her harebrained, hospitalized father in lieu of more support from Kudrow's soap-opera actress or Keaton's magazine-editor tycoon. Recriminations fly, flashbacks ensue, there's lots of laughing through tears and crying through laughs, but none of it has much more weight than medium-grade Neil Simon. Keaton made a marvelous feature-film-directing debut with *Unstrung Heroes*, and, when she isn't trying to clonk us, she still knows how to put across a sharp, quiet moment. (Best is when Cloris Leachman, playing the women's out-of-touch mother, explains to Ryan with bloodcurdling matter-of-factness that she had no use for being motherly.) But the film is "personal" in mostly impersonal ways. It's difficult to get worked up about the gravity of this sisterly contretemps when it happily resolves itself in a funny little food fight.

NEW YORK POST, 2/18/00, p. 47, Jonathan Foreman

"Hanging Up" is the beneficiary of the most deceptive movie marketing campaign in years.

The ads make it look like a cheery if shmaltzy "First Wives Club"-style comedy about three glamorous sisters learning to deal with their philandering old father and their own sibling rivalry.

But, in fact, the jokes are few and far between, and the film is really a depressing, trite and mawkishly Hollywood story about the death of a creepy old man and its effect on his spoiled grown-up daughters.

Lou Mozell (Walter Matthau) is a retired screenwriter who's had a minor stroke. Only his responsible but frazzled middle daughter, Eve (Meg Ryan), cares enough to visit him in the hospital.

The other two children are too busy with their own lives and careers.

Georgia (Diane Keaton), the oldest, is the super-successful, cheerfully self-involved editor of a Lear-like magazine named after herself, and Maddy (Lisa Kudrow, doing her usual ditsy shtick), is a failing soap-opera actress.

In return for Eve's devotion, Lou telephones her constantly, mainly to ask about Georgia but occasionally to talk about his wife, who abandoned the family years before.

He's dying, but before he goes, Ryan's character has flashbacks to two key incidents in the family's recent past. What makes the whole dish so unappetizing is the sheer unlikability of all the characters.

This is a story about Hollywood folk by Hollywood folk—who clearly have no clue how repellent their world is. In particular, the drunken father—who is supposed to be lovable despite his many obvious faults—is so loathsome you wish he'd expire right away.

Instead you have to put up with him until the mushy, phony end.

On the plus side, the sets are terrific, Ryan has great hair (which she tugs on while upset) and Keaton shows that she still has stunning legs.

NEWSDAY, 2/18/00, Part II/p. B3, John Anderson

Like a low-grade fever, "Hanging Up" is something you wish would simply end, but you're quite sure will linger on till ... well, till it's over. The upside is, there's little danger of hallucinations. Unless you count Diane Keaton trying to pass herself off as Lisa Kudrow's sister. Nah, couldn't be.

This anemic comedy of modern ill manners was scripted by sisters Delia and Nora Ephron and adapted from Delia's novel. Although directed by Keaton, the film is more significantly part of the Ephron oeuvre. And it suggests a troubling trend.

In "You've Got Mail"—which, like "Michael," was also co-written by the sisters—the current-events ploy used to spring jokes and influence narrative was e-mail and AOL. In "Hanging Up," a semi-autobiographical tragi-comedy about a parent's mental disintegration and how it defines his children, the Ephrons use the oh-so-entertaining cell phone and its accompanying bad manners to help tell the story.

What's next? Time shares? Fur? The sport utility vehicle?

Driving one-badly-and occupying the bulk of the screentime is Eve (Meg Ryan), middle child of one-time Hollywood screenwriter Lou (Walter Matthau), a grizzled character who's increasingly demented and increasingly a burden, although judging by the overlapping, muddling flashbacks we're treated to, Dad was never much of a picnic. When he wasn't being a drunk, he was being a pain. Still is. So where's the conflict?

Keaton, who made such a nice directing debut with "Unstrung Heroes," resorts to loads of filler and a virtual catalog of romantic-comedy cliches in telling a story that's not a romance at all (unless you count the lifelong infatuation of Eve for her father). There isn't much of a story, either, for that matter, but there seldom is in an Ephron movie. Even in the most successful of Nora's features—"When Harry Met Sally ..."—the story line was an excuse for stand-up comedy, bits of shtick strung together on the flimsiest of pretenses.

The difference is, "Harry" was straight comedy. "Hanging Up" takes wild stabs at pathos, and when it does, it leaves you reeling. with the exception of Eve, the characters in "Hanging Up" generally conform to the demands of the joke at hand. And Matthau, who's often very funny, has to sporadically act like a senile madman. The effect is painful. And for none of the right reasons.

Lou makes lame cracks about John Wayne's manhood and a girl he once knew—Frieda Moo Goo Gai Pan—who was half Jewish, half Chinese. ("They called her the Orienta...") Kudrow, as the youngest actress, sister Maddy, plays a modified "Friends" riff like she's beating a drum (or a dead horse). And Keaton, as the eldest (at least she's the eldest), runs a self-titled magazine called Georgia and is clearly a spoof of the Tina Brown-Anna Wintour-Frances Lear dominating editrix. With all the other problems in "Hanging Up," the viewer might not even notice the inherent misogyny of Keaton's character, an odd creation for a pair of studio scriptwriting sisters. But not, of course, two who will do anything for a joke.

NEWSWEEK, 2/21/00, p. 57, David Ansen

In "Hanging Up," Director Diane Keaton aims for the laugh-through-your-tears mode of "Terms of Endearment." Three working sisters (Keaton, Meg Ryan and Lisa Kudrow), who communicate largely via telephone, are forced to deal with the imminent death of their father (Walter Matthau). Dad, a former Hollywood screenwriter (as was the father of Delia and Nora Ephron, who based their script on Delia's novel), is a monster who, though losing his marbles, can still fire off a mean one-liner. In flashback, we see the damage this alcoholic, selfish man has inflicted on his daughters. Ryan, the perpetually flustered middle daughter, is forced to deal with his hospitalization—she's the sister with "heart," as we're repeatedly told. Keaton, the family superstar, is a self-involved careerist too busy running a magazine she's named after herself to deal with the mess. Kudrow, the youngest, is a ditsy soap-opera actress who can't get anyone to take her seriously.

There are some raw, uncomfortable emotions bubbling deep under the surface of "Hanging Up" but Keaton is loath to deal with them. Like people who compulsively giggle whenever they tell you bad news, the movie runs for cover in lame, comic shtik. Why are we watching cute-dog jokes? Why are the actors trying to out-cute the dog? And why does this L.A.-based movie look as if it had been shot through a thick London fog? More to the point, why tell this story if you're afraid to tell it like it is? This is sugar-coating that melts in your hand, not your heart.

SIGHT AND SOUND, 5/00, p. 50, Stephanie Zacharek

Los Angeles, the present. Eve Marks realises her addled, elderly, ex-screenwriter father must go into hospital. Her two sisters, soap-opera starlet Maddy and egotistical magazine editor Georgia, are too wrapped up in their own lives to share significantly the responsibility of caring for him, despite Eve's efforts to involve them.

Eve loves her father, but their relationship has always been prickly: she frequently flashes back to difficult moments they've had in the past, and she also has difficulty dealing with her cold, distant mother, who estranged herself from the family years earlier.

Eve is also continually frustrated with the behaviour of her two sisters, despite the sometimes grudging affection the three of them share. She and Maddy become incensed when Georgia, who has flown out to LA from her home in New York to give a speech to a women's group, uses their father's illness as a tear-jerking way to win over her audience. Directly following the speech the sisters receive a call telling them that their father has slipped into a coma. They rush to his bedside and reconcile their differences as they wait, hoping for his recovery. He awakens momentarily only to utter his last words.

A few months later, the sisters, bonded in grief and getting along fabulously, throw flour at one another as they cook a Thanksgiving dinner.

Sisterhood is powerful. So why, in *Hanging Up,* does it have to smell so bad—like a cross between musty perfume and an overpowering air freshener? Co-screenwriters (and sisters) Delia and Nora Ephron (the latter directed *Sleepless in Seattle* and *You've Got Mail* bring out the worst impulses in each other, and it's frustrating: *Hanging Up* occasionally brushes up against some thorny family issues, particularly the problems inherent in dealing with a difficult, ageing parent, and sometimes it almost tricks us into believing it just might deal with them in an original and believable way But the Ephrons always end up going for the predictable jokes (it doesn't help that they've got eternally cute moppet Meg Ryan as their handmaiden), and the picture's resolution feels cowardly at best. It's laced with bittersweetness, but not nearly enough of it—as if the Ephrons needed to make sure they wouldn't scare off all the women's book groups, the *Oprah* fans, the frazzled and sensitive soccer moms out there in the audience.

In that respect, *Hanging Up* is the worst kind of 'women's' picture, the kind that sets out to give women what they supposedly want in a movie even as it seems to be painting by numbers, insulting everyone's intelligence in the process. You'd expect more from director Diane Keaton, whose *Unstrung Heroes* had so much free-wheeling warmth. There are a few lovely touches here—particularly a flashback near the end showing the girls' parents slow dancing in a slo-mo haze that gets at the subtle idea that the bond between parents, even those who end up estranged from one another, is often something that their children can't, and aren't meant to, understand.

But the most memorable images *Hanging Up* are Meg Ryan flashing that curlicue smile, absent-mindedly smashing up her vehicle and padding around her picture-perfect California home in puffy footgear that's probably supposed to make her look adorably clownish. Walter Matthau, with his leering, gummy smile, makes for one very annoying old man—a candidate for plug-pulling if ever there was one. Lisa Kudrow, predictably, plays the dizzy sister, but her sometimes appealing spaciness reads like nothing so much as shtick here. Keaton has the most amusing bits—she's got the aura of New York women's magazine editors down cold, right down to her smug, ruthless, we're-all just-girls-here crocodile smile. But no actress can redeem a movie with as many shameless greeting-card moments as *Hanging Up.* "I am just the tiniest bit jealous of your heart," Keaton tells Ryan in one of the movie's pivotal scenes, and the sisters' smiles crinkle more loudly than cellophane. There are other lessons to be learned from watching *Hanging Up:* a wise and wonderful mother figure unexpectedly enters Ryan's life and, after listening to her woes, informs her, "Sometimes it's necessary to disconnect." That's the obvious message of *Hanging Up*. It's little wonder, then, that it has all the profundity of a dial tone.

TIME, 2/28/00, p. 94, Richard Schickel

Hanging Up has the perky pace and the arch attitudes of a comedy. Everyone looks as if he or she is about to deliver a funny line. It's only after 20 expectant minutes or so that you realize you haven't laughed yet. And that the hope for humor—as opposed to frazzle, which soon gives way to frenzy—is growing dimmer.

Adapted by Delia and Nora Ephron from the former's novel, which drew from their lives, the film is scarcely a tragedy. But it is a meditation on the inconvenience of mortality, about the way a parent's final illness can intrude on his children at the worst possible moment, about how the business of conducting him out of this life with some dignity has to be improvised amid all the distractions of the day: the fender bender, the shrilling of the cell phone, the dog eager to gnaw that phone into silence.

The parent here is a difficult case. A onetime screenwriter named Leo Mozell whom Walter Matthau plays with unforgiving ferocity, he was a monster of self-absorption in his better days. Now there's almost no self to preoccupy him—just a few random shards of cranky sense that senility has unaccountably left him.

The burden of caring for him falls mainly on his middle daughter Eve (Meg Ryan), who is trying to get a business going and keep a family functioning. Her elder sister Georgia (Diane Keaton, who also directed) is a high-powered, terminally distracted Manhattan magazine editor. Her younger sibling Maddy (Lisa Kudrow) is a soap-opera actress. These ladies, needless to say, have their own messy, unresolved issues.

Which are perhaps too predictable. And they get papered over in an easy ending that would look simpy even on a comedy. Before it arrives, however, *Hanging Up* reminds us, as most movies refuse to do, that the only thing death can possibly inspire in us is dread.

VILLAGE VOICE, 2/29/00, p. 114, Amy Taubin

Imagine *King Lear* as a contemporary, more comic than tragic "woman's picture," with Meg Ryan as Cordelia, Diane Keaton and Lisa Kudrow as her evil sisters Goneril and Regan, and Walter Matthau as their dying father. This may not be what director Keaton and writers Nora and Delia Ephron had in mind when they conceived *Hanging Up*, a movie so hackneyed and so condescending to its potential audience (adult women) that even Lifetime might hesitate before running it. Still, the *Lear* parallel gives you something to think about. The film is in fact based on Delia Ephron's 1995 roman à clef, in which the author emerges as the only member of the family with recognizable human emotions. It would be stretching a point to attribute human emotion to Ryan, who has never been so cloying nor so perfectly coiffed as she is here. Kudrow and Keaton are lucky in that they have few scenes, though as director, Keaton has to answer for every last mawkish moment. While the good sister is constantly at her father's beck and call, the bad sisters are just too busy with their careers to bother with him until he's in a coma. This is the way successful professionals like Keaton and the Ephrons try to guilt-trip other women who might want to follow in their footsteps. Keaton's character, by the way, is such a blatant caricature of Grace Mirabella that she might have grounds to sue.

Also reviewed in:
CHICAGO TRIBUNE, 2/18/00, Friday/p. A, Michael Wilmington
NEW YORK TIMES, 2/18/00, p. E9, Stephen Holden
VARIETY, 2/14-20/00, p. 39, Emanuel Levy
WASHINGTON POST, 2/18/00, p. C1, Stephen Hunter
WASHINGTON POST, 2/18/00, Weekend/p. 45, Desson Howe

HELD UP

A Trimark Pictures release in association with Minds Eye Pictures. *Executive Producer:* Mark Amin and Devin Dewalt. *Producer:* Neal H. Moritz, Jonathon Komack Martin, and Stokely Chaffin. *Director:* Steve Rash. *Screenplay:* Jeff Eastin. *Story:* Jeff Eastin and Erik Fleming. *Director of Photography:* David A. Makin. *Editor:* Jonathan Chibnall. *Music:* Robert Folk. *Music Editor:* Christine Luethie. *Sound:* Craig Woods. *Sound Editor:* Jay Nierenberg. *Casting:* Mary Vernieu and Anne McCarthy. *Production Designer:* Rick Roberts. *Art Director:* Marion Pon. *Set Decorator:* Paul Healy. *Set Dresser:* Jordy Wihak, Brent Russell, Craig Lazdines, Gary Varro, and Tim House. *Special Effects:* Jim Cammaert. *Costumes:* Eduardo Castro. *Make-up:* Tracy George. *Make-up (Nia Long):* Gloria Elias-Toulakany. *Stunt Coordinator:* Kirk Jarrett. *Running time:* 91 minutes. *MPAA Rating:* PG-13.

CAST: Jamie Foxx (Michael); Nia Long (Rae); Barry Corbin (Pembry); John Cullum (Jack); Jake Busey (Beaumont); Michael Shamus Wiles (Biker); Eduardo Yanez (Rodrigo); Sarah Paulson (Mary); Diego Fuentes (Sal); Roselyn Sanchez (Trina); Julie Hagerty (Gloria); Sam Gifaldi (Rusty); Dalton James (Sonny); Sam Vlahos (Jose); Billy Morton (Delbert); Herta Ware (Alice); Harper Roisman (Howard); Natalia Cigliuti (Wilma); Gary Owen (Clute); David Deveau (Delinquent); Kimberly Karpinski (Reporter); Tim Dixon (Leon); Alvaro Gonzalo (Electrician); Grant Boulton (Cameraman); Andrew Jackson (Billy); Cabral Rock (Messenger); Kathryn Winslow (Pilot); Chris Scott (Gladys); Ian Black (Man); Ron Sauve (No Teeth); Gerry Quigley (Horace); Lane Price (Cowboy); Alex Docking (TV Newscaster).

LOS ANGELES TIMES, 5/12/00, Calendar/p. 8, Kevin Thomas

Not far from the Grand Canyon, Michael (Jamie Foxx) and Rae (Nia Long)—a vacationing couple from Chicago—are driving across the desert in a mint-condition '57 Golden Hawk Studebaker. Rae is not as thrilled with her fiance's recent purchase as he is, especially since the radio doesn't work and the only tape on hand is Tony Orlando and Dawn's "Tie a Yellow Ribbon."

Alas, for the easygoing Michael, Rae's bad mood is but the beginning of a rotten day about to go infinitely worse when they stop at a gas station-convenience store, the Sip & Zip.

Learning that Michael actually paid $13,000 for the car and not the $5,000 that he said, Rae realizes he has blown their down payment on a house and, enraged, hitches a ride to the nearest airport. When Michael discovers he's locked himself out of his treasured car, a woman appears to come to his rescue—only to drive off in the Golden Hawk. Then Michael finds himself a hostage in a stickup of the Sip & Zip.

This is just the beginning of the amiable cross-cultural comedy "Held Up," written by first-timer Jeff Eastin and directed by the veteran Steve Rash. The Sip & Zip is owned and operated by the acerbic Jack (John Cullum) and the key robber is Eduardo Yanez's Rodrigo, an inept rank amateur, who has turned desperado under dire personal circumstances.

Also on hand are pretty local housewife (Sarah Paulson); a biker (Michael Shamus Wiles), a veritable walking encyclopedia; and a little boy (Sam Gifaldi), the only person in the area who thinks that it's cool that Michael happens to be black; when the boy asks him if he's really Puff Daddy he sees no reason not to disabuse him of the notion. In no time the sheriff (Barry Corbin) and his chief deputy (Jake Busey) and his trigger-happy men have the Sip & Zip under siege. (The adults garble Michael's last name, Dawson, and conclude that he's none other than Mike Tyson—a clever jab at the they-all-look-alike syndrome experienced by all racial minorities.)

The filmmakers are good at suggesting an underlying wariness caused by racial and cultural differences that adds to the tension of the situation without seeming heavy-handed. Ironically, were these people not caught up in a hostage situation they would not otherwise get to know one another. Of course, such a standoff means a halt to conventional action, which presents a challenge to the filmmakers to sustain interest and momentum until the crisis is resolved.

The makers of "Held Up" don't do too badly, but there is a lull half way through the film, which is typical of fledgling screenwriters. (Veterans know that to keep a film's middle perking can be a greater challenge than getting a film started or winding it up.)

Foxx is so likable and funny, and he's so well-supported by a substantial cast—including Julie Hagerty as an airport waitress—that the film should probably slide by its more static moments on good will. "Held Up" is a pleasant diversion, and its makers have been smart enough to keep it unpretentious.

NEW YORK POST, 5/12/00, p. 50, Lou Lumenick

This is a cheap-looking lowbrow comedy that likely would have gone straight to home video if its star, Jamie Foxx, hadn't created a sensation in Oliver Stone's "Any Given Sunday."

"Held Up" has a couple of funny scenes, but this formulaic fish-out-of-water comedy isn't much of a vehicle for Foxx, who plays a Chicago businessman stranded at convenience store with your standard-issue yokel types on the edge of the Grand Canyon.

Dumped by his fiancee (a pre-"Best Man" Nia Long, who's off screen for most of the film), his car stolen, mistaken for Puff Daddy (an idea whose comic potential is scarcely explored), Foxx gets taken hostage when an inept Mexican (Eduardo Yanez, the funniest performer here) tries to stick up the store—just as the cops are arriving to investigate the stolen car.

It's your basic "Dog Day Afternoon" in the desert—clueless cops following an FBI hostage manual with improvisations such as substituting a skunk for tear gas, and a TV crew that mistakes Foxx for Mike Tyson. The main running gag involves a deputy sheriff who keeps fondling his crotch.

Director Steve Rash (who once helmed "The Buddy Holly Story") appears to have left Foxx, who looks glum throughout, pretty much to his own devices.

Better served are erstwhile "Northern Exposure" stars John Cullum and Barry Corbin, who are showcased as the crotchety convenience-store owner and the crotchety sheriff, respectively.

Actually filmed in Saskatchewan, Canada—look quickly for a long shot of an inept miniature of the convenience store digitally superimposed over the real Grand Canyon—this slow and talky sitcom may leave its paying customers feeling "Held Up."

NEWSDAY, 5/12/00, Part II/p. B7, Gene Seymour

Some very funny and appealing people were gathered together in the middle of nowhere to perform in "Held Up." On paper, anyway, this low-flying, backwater take on "Dog Day Afternoon" probably made these nice folks think they were making good use of their time.

But if wasting personality posed a toxic hazard, the federal government would be sealing off this movie and evacuating everyone within 50 miles of the multiplex. Investigators could begin their inquiry wondering why anyone in their right mind would split up Jamie Foxx and Nia Long, one of the most potentially charismatic romantic comedy teams in memory, just as they're getting warmed up.

Foxx is Mike Dawson, a smug, self-important Chicago guy who's traveled to Arizona to buy a classic Studebaker for a lot more money than he's told Rae (Long), his fiance. When she finds out he's blown their nest egg on the car, Rae storms off, leaving him stranded at a Sip & Zip convenience store. Soon, Mike's car also roars away with a teenage car thief behind the wheel.

So what else could go wrong? Well, besides having to endure acerbic jibes from the store's laconic owner (John Cullum), Mike and about three other desert misfits find themselves in the midst of what appears to be a holdup by three confused Mexicans, lugging a huge crate in the back of an old car. A motley, inept band of cops, led by cranky Sheriff Pembry (Barry Corbin), is called to the scene. How dumb are they? Well, they somehow mistake Mike Dawson for Mike Tyson.

No, I didn't think it was funny, either. There are points in the movie where you think you're ready to laugh, but, like the movie as a whole, they don't amount to much. As noted, everyone gives his or her best, especially Foxx, Cullum, Corbin and Eduardo Yanez as the frantic lead bandit. But all the professionalism in the world doesn't prevent "Held Up" from ending up as an amiable trifle. At best.

Also reviewed in:
CHICAGO TRIBUNE, 5/16/00, Tempo/p. 2, John Petrakis
NEW YORK TIMES, 5/12/00, p. E10, A. O. Scott
VARIETY, 5/15-21/00, p. 26, Robert Koehler

HELLHOUNDS ON MY TRAIL: THE AFTERLIFE OF ROBERT JOHNSON

A Nonfiction Films/Miramax Film/Dimensions Films and Mug-Shot Productions release of a Davis-Panzer Productions/Dimension Films and Mandalay Pictures production. *Executive Producer:* Julie R. Goldman and Michael Olivieri. *Producer:* Robert Mugge and Jeff Sanders. *Director:* Robert Mugge. *Director of Photography:* Lawrence McConkey. *Editor:* Robert Mugge. *Music:* Robert Santelli. *Sound:* William Barth and (music) Big Mo. *Running time:* 95 minutes. *MPAA Rating:* Not Rated.

INTERVIEWS WITH: Peter Guralnick, Stephen C. La Vere, and Willie Coffee.

WITH: Bob Weir; Rob Wasserman; Keb Mo'; Robert Lockwood, Jr.; Joe Louis Walker; Bill Branch; Sonny Landreth; Chris Whitley; G. Love & Special Sauce; Tracy Nelson; Marcia Ball; Irma Thomas; Alvin Youngblood Hart; Guy Davis; Government Mule; David Honeyboy Edwards; Rory Block; Roy Rogers; Henry Townsend; Billy Hector Trio; Bill Morrissey; Peter Green; Nigel Watson; Roosevelt Barnes; R.L. Burnside; Robert Johnson; David A. Stewart.

NEW YORK, 1/24/00, p. 64, Peter Rainer

The Screening Room is offering up a week-long retrospective of music documentaries by Robert Mugge, and they're well worth checking out. Each day's double bill features Mugge's latest, *Hellhounds on My Trail: The Afterlife of Robert Johnson*, paired with earlier works on blues, zydeco, Gil Scott-Heron, and Al Green. Mugge is part ethnographer, part fan, and although he doesn't get into things very deeply, he showcases communities and sounds that are a complete reason for going to his movies. *Hellhounds on My Trail* is keyed to a week-long tribute to Johnson that was staged in the fall of 1998 at the Rock and Roll Hall of Fame, and a fair amount of blather seeps into the proceedings. (We're told by the keynote speaker, Peter Guralnick, for example, that Johnson's art "defies explanation," which doesn't stop everybody from trying.) Fortunately, most of the movie features first-rate musicians, including Johnson's stepson Robert

Lockwood Jr. and Johnson's contemporaries David Honeyboy Edwards and Henry Townsend, covering the great bluesman's compositions, and their range of energy and inspiration is staggering. The movie isn't so much about Robert Johnson as it is about what was passed along, from one hellhound to another.

NEW YORK POST, 1/21/00, p. 50, Hannah Brown

Just like the best tribute CDs, in which the songs of one artist are performed by dozens of others, "Hellhounds on My Trail: The Afterlife of Robert Johnson" leaves you hungry for the music of the man who inspired the film.

Robert Johnson, a blues guitarist and singer from Mississippi who died at age 27 in 1938, made few records but developed a cult following because of his influence on such rock musicians as the Rolling Stones and Eric Clapton, who recorded his work.

In 1986, he was inducted into the Rock and Roll Hall of Fame, and in 1998, the Hall of Fame held a week-long celebration of his music and life. "Hellhounds" both records the celebration and explores the sometimes bizarre phenomenon of the Robert Johnson cult.

"Hellhounds on My Trail" is the title of one of Johnson's most haunting songs, but the hellhounds in the movie are those trying to cash in on Johnson's legend, those who are obsessed with the rumors about him (that he sold his soul to the devil in exchange for his talent, for example) and, perhaps, the academics who have made the search for the truth about him their life's work.

It's hard to know whether director Robert Mugge, who's known for his music documentaries, including "The Kingdom of Zydeco" (a look at the music of Southwest Louisiana) and "Deep Blues" (a more extensive exploration of the music of the Mississippi Delta), is poking fun at some of the deadly serious professors and music critics who speak at a college panel on Johnson.

Is "Hellhounds" meant to be a mockumentary? If so, then Mugge includes more footage than necessary to make the point. But the movie comes alive through its music, and it features performances of Johnson's songs by his stepson, Robert Lockwood Jr., as well as other blues musicians, including Henry Townsend, David "Honeyboy" Edwards, Guy Davis and others.

For both old Johnson fans and newer admirers, "Hellhounds" is a loving look at his music and the devotion it continues to inspire.

NEWSDAY, 1/21/00, Part II/p. B7, John Anderson

The enigmatic Delta bluesman Robert Johnson supposedly sold his soul to the devil; traveled the '30s South under a string of aliases; was poisoned by a jealous husband at a Mississippi roadhouse; died baying at the moon.

Most of what really happened—who Johnson really was, in other words—has evaporated into the satanic mist that seems to envelope his best recordings. What's indisputable is Johnson's status as the most influential bluesman of the prewar era, the spiritual godfather of Chicago blues, rock and roll, Mick Jagger and Hank Williams.

Throwing additional fuel on the fire of Johnson's myth is the fact that his case for greatness is based on only two sets of recording sessions—in San Antonio, November, '36; and Dallas, June, '37. That he died, probably murdered, the following year doesn't exactly temper things. Moreover, Johnson's masterpiece, the song that elevates him beyond every other blues player, survives in only one take (unlike most others), was played in a guitar tuning Johnson never used again and was not part of Johnson's standard repertoire: "Hell Hound on My Trail."

It's more than fitting, then, that Robert Mugge, whose previous films include "Deep Blues" and the Sonny Rollins documentary "Saxophone Colossus," should have titled his Johnson tribute "Hellhounds on My Trail: The Afterlife of Robert Johnson," although "afterlife" is the real clue. Not one note of Johnson's voice is heard. (If Mugge made any contractual tradeoff with Johnson's estate that provided for the appearance here of its lawyer, Stephen La Vere, Mugge got the short end of the stick.) The performances within the movie take place mostly during a Johnson tribute mounted by the Rock and Roll Hall of Fame in Cleveland and many of them—by Johnson's stepson Robert Lockwood Jr. (nee Robert Jr. Lockwood), or the Olympian blueswoman Rory Block—are first rate. The most glaring omission, however, is Johnson himself.

Author Peter Guralnick, whose small book "Searching for Robert Johnson" is the essential primer on its subject, is shown between performances addressing the Hall of Fame's Johnson seminar, and his comments are revealing and eloquent. However, in Mugge's efforts to separate truth from the many fictions about his subject—particularly about whether Johnson was murdered—he misses the boat. David (Honeyboy) Edwards, who performs alone and with Lockwood, was supposedly with Johnson the night he was poisoned. Edwards is never asked a question.

Likewise, during La Vere's patronizing interview with Johnson's childhood friend Willie Coffee, Coffee says the story told at the time (August, 1938) was that Johnson died of pneumonia—which seems a likely alibi for a family that didn't want the more shameful poison story circulated, nor the cause of death listed by the coroner: syphilis.

Mugge provides some terrific music, but doesn't seem to impose any standard on what he includes. As long as it's a Johnson song, it doesn't matter if it's sung by the authentic and impressive Alvin Youngblood Hart or by ex-Grateful Dead warbler Bob Weir. As far as a work of history, Guralnick's book is a far wiser place to begin searching for Robert Johnson than Mugge's film. The director may be a first-rate music filmmaker, but he has tackled a subject who has been a phantom for 60 years and is likely to hang on to the title.

VILLAGE VOICE, 1/25/00, p. 132, Abby McGanney Nolan

The books and movies about long-gone bluesman Robert Johnson have been coming fast and furious, hellhounds on his trail, particularly since Columbia's *Complete Recordings* box set was released in 1990. Sixty years after his death, the few existing photos of him have become fetish objects, and his idiosyncratic guitar style and otherworldly howls and murmurs have translated into over 500,000 sets sold. Now comes Robert Mugge's latest music documentary (a theatrical premiere within a week-long Mugge retrospective), and the trail doesn't extend too much beyond Cleveland and a recent Rock and Roll Hall of Fame tribute.

For fans of *Deep Blues,* Mugge's wonderful 1991 collaboration with the late critic Robert Palmer, this may come as a disappointment. The earlier film provided a sharp guided tour of the Mississippi Delta and its active blues musicians in juke joints and on back porches. This film features varied performers (including Johnson's stepson, Robert Lockwood Jr., Henry Townsend, Joe Louis Walker, Billy Branch, Sonny Landreth, Peter Green, Rory Block, Chris Whitley, and Keb' Mo') with spirited versions of Johnson's songs, but they have to share screen time with panel discussions and some self-important experts. The controversies surrounding Johnson's life and legacy—the ever appealing Faustian tale of his soul selling, his death at age 27, his much-fought-over inheritance, etc.—are mentioned in passing, rather than plumbed for their ironies. And in place of the understated observations of Palmer or keynote speaker Peter Guralnick, we get as mediator Stephen C. LaVere, the man who tracked down Johnson's half sister in 1973 and arranged for copyright protection for Johnson's work. He now controls the commercial portion of the estate; the movie could not have been made without his cooperation. (At least LaVere doesn't get to recite his liner notes for the 1990 box set, e.g., "When he was with his music, he became one with it and sang with such inspiration that his songs became fervent cries in the universal language of a broad overview.")

In one of the few and much needed forays into Johnson's stomping grounds, LaVere sits down with one of the legend's childhood friends, Willie Coffee. Warmly recalling distant details, Coffee describes the galvanizing effect Johnson had when he walked into a club and the way the floors would sometimes buckle under the dancers when Johnson played. Some of this passion is captured in the performances here, and they make up for the filler.

Mugge has made 14 music films, and the series showcases four of his best: *Deep Blues;* 1982's *Black Wax,* a reverent portrait of Gil-Scott Heron; 1984's *Gospel According to Al Green;* and 1994's *Kingdom of Zydeco,* in which the late Beau Jocque, whose accordion funk chugged along irresistibly, sparred with his onetime model Boozoo Chavis for the zydeco crown.

Also reviewed in:
NEW YORK TIMES, 1/21/00, p. E24, Stephen Holden
VARIETY, 10/18-24/99, p. 39, Dennis Harvey

HERE ON EARTH

A Fox 2000 Pictures release of a David T. Friendly production. *Executive Producer:* Jeffrey Downer. *Producer:* David T. Friendly. *Director:* Mark Piznarski. *Screenplay:* Michael Seitzman. *Director of Photography:* Michael D. O'Shea. *Editor:* Robert Frazen. *Music:* Andrea Morricone. *Music Editor:* Jim Harrison *Sound:* Robert Janiger and (music) John Kurlander. *Sound Editor:* Trevor Jolly. *Casting:* Nancy Foy. *Production Designer:* Dina Lipton. *Art Director:* James F. Truesdale. *Set Designer:* Richard Fernandez and Richard Romig. *Set Decorator:* Diana Stoughton. *Set Dresser:* Trish Herrmann. *Special Effects:* John Hartigan. *Costumes:* Isis Mussenden. *Make-up:* June Brickman. *Stunt Coordinator:* Ron Stein. *Running time:* 97 minutes. *MPAA Rating:* PG-13.

CAST: Chris Klein (Kelley); Leelee Sobieski (Samantha); Josh Hartnett (Jasper); Michael Rooker (Malcolm Arnold); Annie Corley (Betsy Arnold); Bruce Greenwood (Earl Cavanaugh); Annette O'Toole (Jo Cavanaugh); Elaine Hendrix (Jennifer Cavanaugh); Stuart Wilson (John Morse); Ronni Saxon (Robin Arnold); Maureen O'Malley (Patty); Tac Fitzgerald (Pete); Jessica Stier (Vanessa); Erik Kristofer (Charlie); Zach Fehst (Steve); Michael Piznarski (Albert); Peter Gregory Thomson (Abel Shiverson); Isabell Monk (Judge Maddick); Garth C. Schumacher (Pastor); Chris Carlson (Paramedic); Jack Walsh (Mr. Lackett); Peter Syvertsen (Vin Pemrose); Stephen Yoakam (Dr. Falco); Eden Bodnar (Amanda Fielding); Mary Woolever (Nurse); Barbara Kingsley (Hospital Nurse).

LOS ANGELES TIMES, 3/24/00, Calendar/p. 10, Kevin Thomas

Tone down a bit of already reasonably discreet sexual candor and you could believe that "Here on Earth" not only takes place in the '50s but was actually made back then. It's an old-fashioned story of young love, enlivened by an attractive cast and settings, that evolves into a shameless tear-jerker of the most manipulative sort.

This may, however, make it just the ticket for girls in their early teens, for stars Chris Klein, Leelee Sobieski and Josh Hartnett are already teen favorites. You can in fact appreciate the sincerity of their performances even if you find the picture pretty sappy.

Klein's Kelley is a young man who seems to have everything. In addition to being tall, dark and handsome, he's also smart and rich. On the eve of Kelley's graduation from a venerable New England prep school, his father presents him with a Mercedes. Kelley's not supposed to drive it until after he's delivered his speech as valedictorian of his class, but what the heck: He and some pals pile in and head for the local diner, traditionally off-limits for preppies in a community beset by unaccountably high town-and-gown tensions.

Kelley is waited on by the lovely Samantha (Sobieski), who has college and possibly medical school in the future and who shares an appreciation for poetry with the sophisticated and cocky Kelley. Their mutual attraction is instantaneous, and thereby Kelley incurs the anger of Samantha's boyfriend, Jasper (Hartnett), who's in the diner with his own pals. Pretty soon Kelley and Jasper are caught up in a chicken race that winds up with them crashing their vehicles into the diner/gas station. No one is seriously hurt, but the diner et al. is wrecked by fire.

The upshot is that even though the local judge is happy to have Kelley's father foot the bill for rebuilding the roadside establishment, she insists that Kelley and Jasper spend their summer helping in its reconstruction. The film doesn't spend much time with the guys on tho job and instead focuses on the more than ample free time that allows Kelley and Samantha to fall in love. Jasper's and Samantha's families are less than thrilled with this development, of course, but Kelley and Samantha's love flourishes.

It would have been good to see whether their relationship would stand the test of time and distance, for it is pretty clear that wherever—or whenever, for that matter—Samantha ends up for her college education, it's not likely to be Princeton, where Kelley is headed in the fall. But no, writer Michael Seitzman throws in an ancient plot device that in effect arbitrarily takes responsibility away from Kelley and Samantha in regard to working out their destinies so that the film may indulge in some sure-fire heart-tugging.

As contrived as "Here on Earth" seems, it nonetheless benefits from committed direction by TV veteran Mark Piznarski in his feature debut. Indeed, the film is sturdy enough to allow Klein and Sobieski to shine. Hartnett has the toughest role, for he has to become noble and self-sacrificing, which he manages to do without becoming either insufferable or wimpy. "Here on Earth" is a fine-looking film with much pastoral beauty and a quaint village setting, though its neatest trick is to pass off Minnesota as Massachusetts.

NEW YORK POST, 3/24/00, p. 51, Lou Lumenick

When was the last time you heard a contemporary teenager say "gosh"?
Someone under 50 named Jasper?
The retro confusion of a movie set in the present-day Berkshires where everyone acts like they're in 1959 Kansas (it was actually shot in Minnesota and practically everyone has California accents) is only one of the problems crippling "Here on Earth," a hokey and ineptly made tear-jerker.
Chris Klein, the hunky non-actor who was delightfully cast as the amiable jock who runs for class president in "Election," is in way over his head in the main role.
He strains credulity, to put it mildly, as Kelley, a wealthy, Princeton-bound prep-school valedictorian who experiences the sort of character-building summer devised by hack screenwriters (Michael Seitzman is credited here).
Kelley and a poor townie, the aforementioned Jasper (Josh Harnett) get into a drag race that ends in the destruction of Mable's Table restaurant. They're sentenced to rebuild the diner and, in a gimmicky twist, Kelley is required to live with Jasper's family.
He's a snob who wants nothing to do with his hosts or the other townies, but the sulky Kelley wins the heart of Jasper's girlfriend Samantha (Leelee Sobieski), whose mother (a nearly unrecognizable Annette O'Toole) owns the trashed diner.
This Kelley does by quoting Robert Frost, whose poetry provides "Here on Earth" with its title—and whose heirs should immediately consult their lawyers.
It isn't exactly a revelation that Samantha has cancer—the crude direction by Mark Piznarski ("The '60s" miniseries) and the ultra-schmaltzy score by Andrea Morricone start signaling her demise about 10 minutes in. In case anyone misses the hint, Michael O'Shea's deodorant-commercial-style cinematography has an alarming number of sunset scenes.
Sobieski—the nymphet of "Eyes Wide Shut" and TV's Joan of Arc—is much better than the threadbare material, surviving such howler-filled exchanges as this:
Samantha: "You could be arrested for this."
Kelley: "Do you have handcuffs?
Samantha: "Do you want handcuffs?"
That saucy exchange aside, "Here on Earth" remains firmly anchored in the '50s, with the climax taking place at the town's big Fourth of July dance.
It makes the similarly themed "Love Story" seem positively sophisticated by comparison.

NEWSDAY, 3/24/00, Part II/p. B12, Jan Stuart

Oh, to be young, to be beautiful! Oh, to be filthy rich, but miserable! To feel the pangs of true love and the sorrow of mortality! To possess a soul as deep as a well and yet only be able to recite the same lousy Robert Frost poem over and over again!
You don't have to know Frost's "Birches" to like "Here on Earth," a dopey splish-splash through the pools of teenage angst. In fact, it really helps if you know next to nothing, either about poetry or movie or why the sea is boiling hot and whether pigs have wings.
The warm, puffy clouds of deja vu hang over Putnam, the fictional Berkshire community where two guys duke it out over the girl they love. Kelley (Chris Klein) is Boston old-money: smug, arrogant, the valedictorian of his prep-school class. His rival Jasper (Josh Hartnett) is solid, humble farm stock, a bit rough around the edges but true in his love for Samantha (Leelee Sobieski), the good girl who waits tables at the local diner run by her family.
When Kelley comes on to Samantha in plain sight of Jasper, the boys floor the testosterone pedal, hot-rodding through the back roads till they end up totaling the diner. As punishment, the

boys are thrown together to rebuild the cafe over the summer, during which time Samantha discovers which of the two she really loves.

If you think you saw this in another lifetime starring Pat Boone, you're probably right. But rich-boy Kelley doesn't get to sing "April Love" from the wheel of his roadster and moony-eyed Samantha is deprived of a wistful chorus of "It Might As Well Be Spring." Instead, Kelley traces the Northeast corridor states on Samantha's belly and commiserates with the barn animals. ("Moo," says the cow.) The lovers recite "Birches" and duck out of the way of the boom mike that drops lazily from the top border of the screen. There are health complications, and everyone behaves nobly.

As we said, the less you know, the happier you'll be. If you haven't seen Klein's charming dodo-head athlete in "Election" or Sobieski's sympathetic hooker in "Eyes Wide Shut," you won't know just how ignominiously both have fallen in "Here on Earth." If they keep this up, they may never again be seen anywhere on earth. Still, there will always be camp preservationists around like John Waters who specialize in rekindling the careers of over-the-hill heartthrobs. Troy Donahue, forever!

Also reviewed in:
CHICAGO TRIBUNE, 3/24/00, Friday/p. A, Michael Wilmington
NEW YORK TIMES, 3/24/0. p. E16, Elvis Mitchell
VARIETY, 3/20-26/00, p. 26, Robert Koehler

HIGH FIDELITY

A Touchstone Pictures release of a Working Title Films production in association with Dogstar Films/New Crime Productions. *Executive Producer:* Mike Newell, Alan Greenspan, and Liza Chasin. *Producer:* Tim Bevan and Rudd Simmons. *Director:* Stephen Frears. *Screenplay:* D.V. DeVincentis, Steve Pink, John Cusack, and Scott Rosenberg. *Based on the book by:* Nick Hornby. *Director of Photography:* Seamus McGarvey. *Editor:* Mick Audsley. *Music:* Kathy Nelson. *Music Editor:* Mike Higham. *Sound:* Petur Hliddal and (music) Ed Rak and Gareth Jones. *Sound Editor:* Peter Joly. *Casting:* Victoria Thomas. *Production Designer:* David Chapman and Thérèse DePrez. *Art Director:* Nicholas Lund. *Set Decorator:* Larry P. Lundy. *Set Dresser:* Phillip Ellman. *Special Effects:* Sam Barkan. *Costumes:* Laura Cunningham Bauer. *Make-up:* Jeanne Van Phue. *Make-up (Iben Hjejle):* Naomi Donne. *Stunt Coordinator:* Rick LeFevour. *Running time:* 107 minutes. *MPAA Rating:* R.

CAST: John Cusack (Rob); Iben Hjejle (Laura); Todd Louiso (Dick); Jack Black (Barry); Lisa Bonet (Marie De Salle); Catherine Zeta-Jones (Charlie); Joan Cusack (Liz); Tim Robbins (Ian); Chris Rehmann (Vince); Ben Carr (Justin); Lili Taylor (Sarah); Joelle Carter (Penny); Natasha Gregson Wagner (Caroline); Shannon Stillo (Alison Jr. High); Drake Bell (Rob Jr. High); Laura Whyte (Laura's Mom); Sara Gilbert (Anaugh); Rich Talarico (Barry's Customer); Matt O'Neill (Beta Band Customer); Brian Powell (Middle Aged Customer); Margaret Travolta (Rob's Mom); Jill Peterson (Laura's Sister Jo); Dick Cusack (Minister); Susan Yoo (Girl, 19-year-old); Chris Bauer (Paul); K.K. Dodds (Miranda); Marily Dodds Frank (Alison's Mom); Duke Doyle (Kevin Bannister); Aaron Himelstein (Boy in Park); Jonathan Herrington (Chris Thompson); Daniel Lee Smith (Rock Guy); Leah Gale and David Darlow (Mourners); Erik Gundersen (Marco); Bruce Springsteen (Himself); Alex Desert (Louis); Alan S. Johnson (Man in Store); Liam Hayes (Piano Player); Damian Rogers (Greenday Girl); Robert A. Villanueva (Skateboarder); Joe Spaulding (Flea Market Musician); Scott A. Martin (Bartender); Heather Norris (Laura's Friend).

CHRISTIAN SCIENCE MONITOR, 3/31/00, p. 15, David Sterritt

Hopes have run high for "High Fidelity" one of the most promising Hollywood packages this year.

John Cusack plays Rob, the proprietor of a Chicago record store (yes, records—the old-fashioned vinyl kind) that might turn a profit if the staff could stop insulting the customers for a minute. Music is the second-most-important thing in Rob's life. The most important is romance, and he's doing poorly in that department since his girlfriend left him for another man.

Tired of the failure that has dogged his romantic trail, he decides to track down his past girlfriends to learn why they dumped him. This sparks a series of encounters and reunions that teach him more than he wants to know about his own personality and the demands of adult relationships. He also finds time to banter with his shop assistants and strike up a new affair with a gorgeous singer.

The movie alternates between Rob's interactions with the women in his life and his antics at the record store. This allows for a wide range of moods, from lovelorn wistfulness to lowdown farce, all accompanied by conspicuously hip music. Lending additional spice is Rob's habit of speaking to the camera, making us privileged visitors to his private world.

Add a remarkably diverse cast—Jack Black as a wannabe rock star, Joan Cusack as a trusty friend, Lisa Bonet as Rob's new flame—and you have all the elements for a surefire entertainment. Or do you?

The ingredient that lowers "High Fidelity" is its screenplay, penned by no fewer than four writers (a frequent sign of behind-the-scenes trouble) and so scattered and meandering that individual scenes rarely gather the emotional energy they need. Instead of burrowing into Rob's life, we feel like we're skimming across it, as if one of his goofy employees kept switching from one so-so record to another when we'd rather hear a good one from start to finish.

Admirers of director Stephen Frears—better known for dramas like "Dangerous Liaisons" and "My Beautiful Laundrette" than for comedies like this—might want to catch it, and Cusack fans will get their fill. But others may find its channel-surfing style too superficial for comfort.

CINEASTE, VOL. XXVI, #1, p. 50, Thomas Doherty

[*High Fidelity* was reviewed jointly with *Almost Famous;* see Doherty's review of that film.]

LOS ANGELES TIMES, 3/31/00, Calendar/p. 1, Kenneth Turan

"What came first," Rob Gordon (John Cusack) desperately wants to know, "the music or the misery?"

Over-stimulated by the sounds coming out of his outsize headphones, morose Rob is seizing the moment of his breakup with Laura (Iben Hjejle) to reflect on "the thousands of hours of heartache, rejection, pain, misery and loss" he experienced while exposing himself to wave after wave of popular music. "Did I listen because I was miserable," he wonders, "or was I miserable because I listened?"

That is saying something, because Cusack, talented as well as shrewd about what he gets himself into, doesn't go in for weak material. Rob Gordon, a part Cusack had a hand in writing, is specifically tailored to his everyman persona, to his gift for intimacy with the audience and his ability to humanize characters who are difficult and potentially off-putting.

The last time out for Cusack and writing partners D.V. DeVincentis and Steve Pink was "Grosse Point Blank," in which the actor played a hit man with a career crisis; "High Fidelity" presents them with a character who faces a less lethal kind of challenge. (Scott Rosenberg of the glib "Things to Do in Denver When You're Dead" and "Con Air" also gets a writing credit.)

The Cusack pack had the advantage of starting from Nick Hornby's fine novel, a delightful book that is very savvy about the vagaries of relationships, especially from the male point of view. It's Rob, using either voice-over or direct talk to the camera, who preserves the book's first-person quality as well as chunks of its dialogue. "High Fidelity" presents him as someone who's his own worst enemy, a tortured and grumpy eternal adolescent who doesn't have to hide his weakness for being a real jerk to gain our sympathy.

Given his opening rant about the pernicious effect of lyrics, it's not a surprise that Rob's life is pop music. He owns Championship Vinyl, a Chicago establishment (smoothly moved from the novel's London) that's a shrine to old-fashioned phonograph records and mecca to obsessive geeks who "spend a disproportionate amount of their time looking for deleted Smiths singles and 'ORIGINAL NOT RERELEASED' underlined Frank Zappa albums."

This universe's two biggest geeks, Dick and Barry, a.k.a. "the musical moron twins," just happen to work for Rob, and as played by Todd Louiso and Jack Black are the comic center of the film. Dick is the sensitive flower while Barry is rowdy, abrasive and downright hilarious. They join Rob in insulting the customers, making abstruse jokes about the Beta Band and Ryuichi Sakamoto and constructing an endless number of all-time Top 5 lists, from Top 5 dream jobs to Top 5 songs about death ("Leader of the Pack," "Dead Man's Curve," "Tell Laura I Love Her," etc).

Though the Championship Vinyl store (magnificently created for the film by a crew that includes production designers David Chapman and Therese DePrez, art director Nicholas Lund, set decorator Larry P. Lundy and property master Timothy W. Tiedje) is real enough to be a character in its own right, it's not the best place for empathy, and that's what Rob needs after his break with Laura. Initially he faces the split with bravado, yelling at her that she doesn't even make his all-time Top 5 list of memorable split-ups (yes, he has one), but that fighting spirit is not fated to last.

As the pain of Laura's absence (and her possible connection with someone else) sinks in, Rob is forced, for perhaps the first time, to think about his life and confront this difficulty with romance and commitment. "What's wrong with me? Why am I doomed to be left?" he wonders plaintively and, in an attempt to find out, thinks back on that list of all-time memorable ruptures, amusingly reconsidering liaisons with Catherine Zeta-Jones, Lili Taylor and others.

Director Frears, who is noticeably good with realistic relationships that have a touch of comedy in them ("The Snapper," "My Beautiful Laundrette"), knows his way around this scenario. Under his guidance, Cusack's painful but funny reexamination leads to a getting of wisdom that is no less welcome for coming years later than it should have.

Cusack, with his ability to project glowering desperation and a sense of aggrieved entitlement, is perfect for this role. As Laura, the woman he can't live with or without, Danish actress Hjejle (recently seen as a prostitute-turned-housekeeper in that country's "Mifune") displays both faultless English and a formidable sense of integrity that allows her to more than hold her own in fairly heady company.

For it's a tribute to how well "High Fidelity" has been written (and to the respect other performers have for Cusack and Frears) that the film employs quite a number of excellent actors in small roles. In addition to Taylor and Zeta-Jones, there are parts for Tim Robbins, Joan Cusack, Lisa Bonet, Sara Gilbert and Natasha Gregson Wagner. The film's music (more than 50 songs are listed in the credits, with artists ranging from Aretha Franklin to stereolab) is sexpertly chosen, and there's even a cameo by Bruce Springsteen, giving sage romantic advice. Of course Rob needs it, but whether he can take it is, obviously, quite another story.

NEW YORK, 4/10/00, p. 85, Peter Rainer

Rob Gordon (John Cusack), who runs the Chicago retro record store Championship Vinyl, is a maestro at creating compilation tapes, and *High Fidelity*, the movie he figures in, is something of a compilation tape, too. It's Rob's confessional—he often speaks directly to us—and its rhythms are alternately sodden, imploring, rapt, antic. Stephen Frears, directing from a script by D. V. DeVincentis, Steve Pink, John Cusack, and Scott Rosenberg based on the highly regarded London-based Nick Hornby novel, doesn't keep things on an even keel; that's not his idea of a good time. The film has the herky-jerky propulsion of an interior monologue, but there's no real rage lurking inside Rob's obsessiveness. He's too shallow for that, too juiced by his own funk. Frears has made a movie about extreme narcissism that somehow also manages to be self-effacing. The discombobulated lives on display, despite all the turmoil and regret, are essentially comical. Frears's characters see themselves as players on a stage; the drama being enacted is the battle of the sexes, and they enjoy gaping at their own spectacle. They're bemused by how screwed-up they are, and how screwed-up everybody else is, too.

When Rob's live-in girlfriend, Laura (Iben Hjejle), walks out on him because she doesn't see him moving on in his life, the rupture kicks off a long-term wallow in which he ranges back over his catalogue of Top Five Breakups. (Rob is always making top-five lists, such as Top Five Songs About Death and Top Five First Cuts on First Albums.) The flashbacks to these breakups, which begin with a spurning in middle school and move on past the college years, are like little blackout sketches, piquant and deadpan. They encompass a wide range of female partnership, from the mousy to the chaste to the glamorous (Catherine Zeta-Jones plays Charlie, the glamour-puss). The film is saying that women, in their own special ways, mess men up (and perhaps men deserve it). Later, Rob comes up with the notion of actually getting back in touch with his top five. The before-and-after contrasts are predictable: Everything has changed, nothing has changed. Laura is right. Rob hasn't really moved on in his life; he's stuck in the same vinyl groove. But she's wrong too, and maybe this is why she keeps drifting back to him even after walking out. What she senses is that their breakup is a scrambling of all the big breakups he's ever had, a compilation tape of cracked connections, and that maybe he's ready to change tracks. Still, she's clear-eyed about Rob's mopiness, and her sporadic re-entrances into his life seem to be more for his benefit than for hers. She's a *generous jilter*.

Even though *High Fidelity* is framed as a male confessional, it gives its women equal space in the confession booth. (It could stand as a companion piece to Cusack's earlier *Say Anything.*) There's no rancor in this film's view of men's waywardness and no great sentimentality either. If the Woody Allen of a few decades ago had made this movie, he might have turned it into a nutty, prickly harangue; Albert Brooks, who has already covered some of this same terrain, especially in *Modern Romance,* would have brought out the natteriness and raging ego in his lovelorn stupe. John Cusack plays Rob as a living contradiction, a restless layabout. Todd Louiso and Jack Black, who play Rob's co-workers in the record store, are bookends of guy geekiness; the latter is a stumpy, wise-ass know-it-all, and the former, with his chalky pallor and faint eyes, is so recessive that he's practically a revenant.

Cusack, who was so remarkable in Frears's *The Grifters,* seems to respond particularly well to this director, embodying his every-which-way sensibility. Cusack can go from explosive to winsome in a flash, and then on to something else entirely, and it all adds up. This quality makes him the perfect actor for a movie in which, without being highfalutin about it, he has to play a youngish Everyman. He projects, at various times, all the flavors of male privilege, and the various females he provokes all respond to different aspects of him. Except Laura, who seems to "get" him in toto. Rob gets Laura, too; he's sharp-eyed about the ways of women. He just can't do all that much, in the end, with his information.

As a man-out-of-time, Rob seems peculiarly up-to-date. In his mid-twenties he was afraid of being alone for the rest of his days, and now, a decade later, he's caught between postadolescence and a premature midlife crisis. He's a welter of wacked-out life cycles, and there's something appealingly familiar about his mishmash. He's the scraggly standard-bearer for his generation. His retroness is half of who he is; musically, he's hip to both boomer rock perennials and punk and hip-hop, and he has a snob's taste in both. It's the middle range, the soft-pop standards, he can't abide. (He can't understand how Laura can like both Art Garfunkel *and* Marvin Gaye.) Rob's musical tastes are keyed to his emotional situations; at times, he seems to live his life in either a rave or a dive. He frequents a bar with a sign saying al capone drank here often, and he points out for us the movie theater where John Dillinger—betrayed by a woman, of course—was gunned down. For Rob, Chicago indulges his hurt feelings, and it plays into his charade of being, in some small way, both gangster and gangsta. It's a city where he can keep his options open. *High Fidelity* is the rare comedy that gets inside the ways men try to make sense of themselves, and it does so without special pleading. It's a sweet, raffish entertainment, blessedly free of baloney.

NEW YORK POST, 3/31/00, p. 47, Lou Lumenick

Movie critics tend to overpraise studio movies that don't feel like the product of a marketing committee—but the quirky "High Fidelity" really deserves being called the first must-see movie of the century.

John Cusack, a gifted performer who's one of Hollywood's keenest judges of material, follows his triumph in "Being John Malkovich" with a quite different but only slightly less twisted comic tale of obsession—with love and popular music.

Cusack's Rob Gordon owns Championship Vinyl, a sparsely patronized record shop where he and his staff pass most of the day compulsively compiling Top 5 lists of songs from the '60s to the present—first cuts on first albums, songs about death, etc.

Rob's compulsiveness only escalates when his neglected live-in girlfriend, Laura (Iben Hjejle), leaves him for a ponytailed lawyer (a priceless Tim Robbins)—and thoughtfully quotes him odds on a reconciliation (9 percent). Rob places her on his list of Top 5 breakups—"No. 5 with a bullet," in other words, moving rapidly up the charts, in Billboard magazine's lexicon.

Urged on by Bruce Springsteen—yes, the film-shy Boss in a movie, however briefly—in a fantasy visit, Rob decides to look up his ex-girlfriends to see why he's been stuck in the same groove of romantic failure.

Though his recollections and re-encounters with these women—among them Lili Taylor and Catherine Zeta-Jones—are hilarious, director Stephen Frears is on to something much more interesting than a male version of the 70s chick flick "Old Boyfriends. "

"High Fidelity" is a brilliantly modulated character study revolving around its subject— how men use their obsessions (records, movies, sports) to shield them from true intimacy—like one of Rob's beloved discs.

Cusack, an expert in tortured romantics since "The Sure Thing," plays Rob as petty, jealous and self-absorbed.

He's utterly miserable and clueless about why he can't connect with the women in his life, who also include Lisa Bonet and Natasha Gregson Wagner (in knowing cameos as a Frampton-covering wannabe-diva and a rock journalist, respectively), and real-life sister Joan Cusack as his on-screen sister.

"High Fidelity," which has a fantastic 59-song soundtrack, falls short of four stars because of leading lady Hjejle, who can also be seen in "Mifune," an import from her native Denmark.

She's a beautiful and arresting presence, but she and Cusack lack chemistry together, and at times its painfully obvious she's struggling with lines in a language not her own.

The real discoveries are the hulking Jack Black and pasty-faced Todd Louïso as Rob's demented employees, a Laurel and Hardy-ish pair of music snobs who violently argue over such arcane matters as the influence of Stiff Little Fingers on Green Day.

Black, the lead singer for cult band Tenacious D, has a massive physical presence that recalls John Belushi. He expresses nothing but pity for anyone who doesn't own an original copy of "Blonde on Blonde."

Four writers (including Cusack and his screenwriter collaborators on "Grosse Point Blank") are credited with this inventive adaptation of Nick Hornby's cult novel, which was set in London.

Cusack and Frears even make the hoary device of a character directly addressing the audience seem fresh. The several fantasy sequences (particularly multiple versions of Robbins' visit to the record store) are standouts.

"High Fidelity" is on my list of Top 5 movies for the year—with a bullet.

NEWSDAY, 3/31/00, Part II/p. B3, John Anderson

"Empire Records", a movie featuring then-unknowns Renee Zellweger and Liv Tyler, was released in theaters for about 15 minutes back in 1995, which was probably more than it deserved. But it's become a huge cult hit on video, especially among young teenagers. So it seemed inevitable that someone would eventually take the formula and try to make more mon—I mean, a better movie.

Although "High Fidelity" is a better movie—and is actually based on a novel by Nick Hornby—the similarities to "Empire Records" are striking, most significantly the hip-yet-womb-like attraction of the record‚store owned by Rob (John Cusack). A romantically confused audiophile who sells original Captain Beefheart records and talks to the camera about his love life—which is in ruins, by the way—Rob is a ruminating hero with the personality profile of a serial stalker. But at Championship Vinyl, adulthood has been put on hold; guys like Dick and Barry (the very funny Todd Louiso and Jack Black), who would barely function in the outside world, flourish among the racks of rare LPs. It's a place where weirdness is a virtue. And while that's a very adolescent sentiment, it's a sentiment that knows no age limit.

"High Fidelity" is definitely a boomer movie—the better to sell soundtracks featuring Marvin Gaye, Bob Dylan and Katrina and the Waves, presumably—but being a pseudo-adult is Rob's problem. Just as he and his comical sidekicks arrange the world according to Top 5 this and Top 5 that, Rob has a list of Top 5 Breakups, which has just been adjusted to include Laura (Iben Hjejle), who has her own very valid Top 5 reasons for walking out on him. ("High Fidelity" is, quite often, one of those Makes You Proud to Be a Man movies.) Rob copes with his loss of Laura by revisiting the women who dumped him, finding ways to reason away the obsession he's had about each one, but not at the cost of his own ego.

With Cusack talking to the camera all the way through the film—and co-writing and co-producing with his "Grosse Pointe Blank" teammates D.V. DeVincentis and Steve Pink—well, that's a whole lotta Cusack. Stephen Frears is not a director without ideas, and you sense the intelligence he imposes throughout, even in a story as slight as this. But Cusack's a little old for the role, frankly. And his co-star Iben Hjejle, the lovely Danish star (currently of "Mifune"), doesn't seem all that comfortable acting in English. Throw in all the stunt casting—Rob's various girlfriends are played by the likes of Lili Taylor, Lisa Bonet and Catherine Zeta-Jones; Bruce Springsteen has a cameo inside Rob's head—and there's not much to convince you that "High Fidelity" isn't a vanity production with some good tunes.

SIGHT AND SOUND, 8/00, p. 47, Andy Medhurst

Chicago, the present. Rob, the owner of a record store, breaks up with his girlfriend Laura. While he worries about what went wrong, he and his employees Barry and Dick visit a bar to hear singer Marie De Salle. Later, she and Rob have a one-night stand. Rob decides to make contact with three previous girlfriends, to see if investigating the reasons these relationships failed might shed light on his break-up with Laura.

Rob is distraught to find Laura has moved in with former neighbour Ian. Dick, meanwhile, is dating a customer, Anaugh, while Barry starts singing in a local group. Laura's father dies unexpectedly; Laura asks Rob to join her at the funeral. Berated for his treatment of Laura by his friend Liz, Rob leaves. Laura follows him and they make love.

To celebrate their reunion, Laura organises an event in a local nightclub at which Rob will DJ. Rob flirts with a music journalist covering his gig; to seal his commitment to Laura, he proposes marriage, which she turns down. At the gig, which boasts Barry's band's debut, Laura and Rob kiss.

On the penultimate page of his novel *High Fidelity,* a story of love gone briefly wrong and a hymn of praise to second hand record shops, Nick Hornby sums up the reconciliatory conclusion thus: "The rest of the evening is like the end of a film." The cinematic version takes him at his word, staging an outrageously feel-good climax in which all tensions are dissipated in a tableau of togetherness. It's heartwarming stuff, but so shockingly old-fashioned you almost expect Mickey Rooney and Judy Garland to step out of the shadows and croon a duet, and it points to one of the most intriguing aspects of *High Fidelity* (both in print and on screen): its ability to sell a tale drenched in sentiment to an audience of supposedly world-weary cynics.

The film, just like the novel, pulls off that stunt by playing a shrewd double bluff. It knowingly catalogues the tropes and rigmaroles of heterosexual romance so as to display its cleverness, to signal its superior distance from naive texts that take those games at face value, but then reinvests in those same clichés with a wholeheartedness that might have given even the late Barbara Cartland cause to blush. It invites us to enjoy the predictabilities because we know they are predictabilities—it's a text that lets us signal our smartness through our knowing surrender to dumb romance.

All of which makes director Stephen Frears' *High Fidelity* sound icily calculating, when in fact its great strength (its supreme dissembling trick if you want to see it that way) is to come at you as warmly and eagerly as a large loping puppy. The story holds few surprises—there's never a shred of doubt that Rob's lawyer girlfriend will come back to him. The only reason she leaves at all is to open up the space for Rob to indulge in extended reflections on life, love, the magic of great music and the hopelessly adolescent fixations he carried with him into early middle age. The film's decision to render those reflections through on-screen, straight-to- camera monologues is one of its few stylistic gambles. The model aspired to, evidently, is *Alfie,* though the comparison founders on the fact that Michael Caine's serial exploiter in the 60s film was revealed as a deeply nasty piece of work, whereas *High Fidelity* must, at all costs, keep Rob sweet and adorable. If anything, John Cusack's solo musings reminded me rather more of the teenage know-all in the American television series *Clarissa Explains It All.* Clarissa's world is exactly that—Clarissa's, mediated wholly through her perspectives and sensibilities, and similarly in *High Fidelity* we see nothing that isn't filtered through Rob's eyes and mind.

Consequently, the film stands or falls on the portrayal of Rob, so it's fortunate in calling on the services of an actor as accomplished as John Cusack. He lights up the screen with the glowing assurance of a man fully aware that he's the kingpin of all he surveys. Failure would have been catastrophic—if you don't warm to Rob, there isn't any film left—but happily Cusack delivers a brilliantly weighted study in calculated helplessness. The supporting players are pretty flawless too, with Jack Black's Barry a deft exercise in John Belushi impersonation and Todd Louiso all but stealing the picture by turning the lame duck Dick into a gentle doe-eyed creature that's half Michael Stipe and half Moomintroll. Tim Robbins enjoys a brief cameo as Ian, the villain who briefly steals Laura's affections, turning him into a hilariously hateful caricature of a New Age-y New Man, all ponytail and sanctimoniousness.

Note, however, all those male names. *High Fidelity* remains a lads' game from start to finish. The Danish actress Iben Hjejle impresses as Laura, the only woman remotely allowed to approach three-dimensionality, but female space elsewhere consists of a parade of fantasy figures, meek handmaidens and victims of jokes. The film's abiding disinterest in taking women seriously is encapsulated by its decision to offer only a couple of lines to Sara Gilbert *Roseanne*'s magnificent Darlene, turning her into the kind of appendage girlfriend Darlene would have torched with righteous contempt. Making Marie (played by Lisa Bonet), the singer Rob beds during his break with Laura, black (she's white in the novel) is also a dubious touch. It makes unavoidably obvious what was only a glimpsed subtext in Hornby's writing, the use of blackness as a crass signifier of authenticity among well-meaning white liberals.

The relentless masculinity of the film will be no surprise to readers of Hornby's novel, but what might wrongfoot them is the switch in location. On the whole, the Americanisation of the story does surprisingly little damage, though Rob's involvement in managing a pair of young skate/grunge musicians strikes a slightly jarring note. It's the only subplot the film adds to the novel, and it feels gestural and tacked-on, too crudely seeking to broaden the audience demographic. Similarly, I can't imagine Hornby's English Rob tolerating a Queen song on the soundtrack, though the use of music in the bulk of the film is so apposite as to form one of its major pleasures. Hornby's original musical reference points are both updated and broadened, but with knowledgeable finesse, making this almost certainly the first Hollywood film to namecheck Stereolab, the Beta Band and Belle & Sebastian. Rob's regrettable fondness for Bruce Springsteen (this is, after all, a story about heterosexuality) is taken a stage further, with Springsteen cropping up as a one-man Greek chorus.

High Fidelity also succeeds in convincing you that working in a record shop might just be the best job in the world, at least for certain kinds of emotionally retarded men. Rob's joy in being master of his own little vinyl principality is lovingly conveyed; he's the unchallenged taste-meister, mapping out the parameters of acceptable and unacceptable music, gently shepherding customers towards records they didn't come in to buy, but he knows will enrich their lives. It's a great act, and so easy to fall for that the day after the screening I went out and bought one of the albums Rob champions, though I can't disclose which one, since that would reveal my unhipness in not having it already—and no fan of *High Fidelity* could risk such an aesthetic *faux pas*.

Transplanting Rob's tribulations from London to Chicago leaves the core of the story untroubled. Boys will be boys in both cultures, after all, and *High Fidelity* is at its best when anatomising the foibles and failings of a particular kind of underachieving, obsessional male. The analysis never shifts into real critique, preferring gently and superficially to chide Rob's immaturity and fecklessness while massively endorsing him in the process. He may be a smart-aleck and a drifter and he puts all the emotional energy into pop-music trivia that he ought to invest in adult relationships, but he just can't help it and he's really cute too. No wonder so many men (me included) loved the book, and the film is far too sly and canny to disappoint us.

VILLAGE VOICE, 4/10/00, p. 158, Amy Taubin

When Rob (John Cusack), the proprietor of a Chicago record store specializing in used and rare rock vinyl, is abandoned by his girlfriend, he tries to work off his despair by rearranging his record collection—not alphabetically or chronologically, but autobiographically. He also starts compulsively talking to the camera about his many failed romances, as if the viewer were his shrink. Shrinks, however, are well-paid to listen to the same litany of despair over and over; viewers hand over their 10 bucks because they hope for something fresh and exciting.

Or maybe not: Some viewers—dedicated Woody Allen fans, for example—want to be confirmed in what they've already figured out about their own lives. Stephen Frears's *High Fidelity*, adapted from Nick Hornby's popular novel and transposed with minimal upset from blue-collar England to blue-collar Chicago, is a Woody Allen film for youngish white males who fetishize rock music and its many memorabilia and have commitment problems when flesh-and-blood women, as opposed to women in song lyrics, are involved. It may seem perverse to fault a movie for being too accurate, but when surface accuracy is coupled with tunnel vision about self and society the result is a wee bit irritating. *High Fidelity* may be the only music film since 1990 not to acknowledge the existence of rap or hip-hop. That the characters are part of an isolationist subculture (veneration for Marvin Gaye notwithstanding) is what makes the film seem so painfully like real life. That the film doesn't put this isolationism in perspective is what makes it dismissible.

Also reviewed in:
CHICAGO TRIBUNE, 3/31/00, Friday/p. A, Mark Caro

NEW REPUBLIC, 5/1/00, p. 25, Stanley Kauffmann
NEW YORK TIMES, 3/31/00, p. E15, Stephen Holden
NEW YORKER, 4/3/00, p. 99, Anthony Lane
VARIETY, 3/20-26/00, p. 26, Joe Leydon
WASHINGTON POST, 3/31/00, p. C1, Rita Kempley
WASHINGTON POST, 3/31/00, Weekend/p. 43, Desson Howe

HIGHLANDER: ENDGAME

A Dimension Films release of a Davis/Panzer production. *Executive Producer:* Bob Weinstein, Harvey Weinstein, and Cary Granat. *Director:* Douglas Aarniokoski. *Screenplay:* Joel Soisson. *Based on a story by:* Eric Bernt, Gillian Horvath, and William Panzer. *Based on characters created by:* Gregory Widen. *Director of Photography:* Doug Milsome. *Editor:* Christopher Blunden, Michael N. Nue, Robert Feretti, Tracy Granger, Rod Dean, and Donald J. Paonessa. *Music:* Stephen Graziano. *Martial Arts Choreographer:* Donnie Yen. *Sound:* Rick Alexander, Rick Hart, and (music) Malcolm Luker. *Sound Editor:* Trevor Jolly. *Casting:* Michelle Guish. *Production Designer:* Jonathan Carlson. *Art Director:* Ben Zeller and Christian Niculescu. *Set Decorator:* Mary Beth Noble. *Special Effects:* Nick Allder, Jeff Clifford, Garth Inns, and Terry Schubert. *Visual Effects:* Michael Sagol, Alison Savitch, and Greg Nelson. *Costumes:* Wendy Partridge. *Stunt Coordinator:* Joe Dunne. *Running time:* 95 minutes. *MPAA Rating:* R.

CAST: Adrian Paul (Duncan MacLeod); Christopher Lambert (Connor MacLeod); Bruce Payne (Jacob Kell); Lisa Barbuscia (Faith/Kate); Donnie Yen (Jin Ke); Jim Byrnes (Dawson); Peter Wingfield (Methos); Damon Dash (Carlos); Beatie Edney (Heather); Sheila Gish (Rachel Ellenstein); Oris Erhuero (Winston); Ian Paul Cassidy (Cracker Bob); Adam Copeland (Lachlan).

LOS ANGELES TIMES, 9/4/00, Calendar/p. 4, Kevin Thomas

"Highlander: Endgame" brings the popular, Gothic, supernatural fantasy-adventure series to a spectacular finish—but leaving immortality with a really bad name. That's because Christopher Lambert's Connor MacLeod and his younger clansman, Duncan (Adrian Paul, who starred in the "Highlander" TV series), seem to spend most of their limitless time in bloody combat, fighting off bad guys across the centuries.

No wonder Connor remarks to Duncan in despair, "Every life I touch ends in killing without a reason," after his archenemy blows up his foster daughter in her Manhattan antique shop. In nearly 500 years, Connor in fact has slain 262 adversaries—to Duncan's mere 174. But that archenemy, Jacob Kell (Bruce Payne, a world-class scenery-chewer), has slain 661 people, and he is rapidly becoming so powerful his evil threatens to escalate beyond defeat.

Connor and Jacob, originally best friends, became enemies way back in the 16th century in the Scottish Highlands. A priest declared Connor's mother a witch and ordered her burned at the stake while her son watched behind bars. Connor breaks loose, saves his mother from incineration though not death and in revenge kills the priest, upsetting Jacob mightily. When in the ensuing melee Connor receives a wound that ought to have been fatal, he discovers that he is one of the Immortals and has been around for some 5,000 years without realizing it—and that Jacob is one of the Immortals, too.

We time-travel over the past half-millennium, checking in on the respective battles of the MacLeods and Kell and we're made to feel that we've missed none of them. At long last Connor and Duncan have a final face-off with Kell on a Manhattan rooftop—but only one of the MacLeods, by Immortal rules, can go up against Kell. (For "Highlander" trivia buffs, the only way you can kill an Immortal is by separating his head from his body.)

Filmed largely in Romania, "Highlander: Endgame" looks sensational, moves like lightning. But its script (by Joel Soisson) makes no pretense about being logical or even comprehensible, which undermines Douglas Aarniokoski's vigorous, commanding direction and Lambert's and Paul's surprisingly poignant performances. It celebrates extreme combat between men and then suggests that this can become wearying after awhile to even the most durable of warriors. Even more wearying, unless you're a rabid Highlander fan, is having to watch all this carnage.

NEW YORK POST, 9/2/00, p. 21, Jonathan Foreman

The fourth "Highlander" movie is remarkable in several regards. For one thing, much of it was shot in Romania.

For another, its story is so incompetently constructed that the long lulls between nonsensical action scenes make you wonder if it was written by a prepubescent fan.

How else to explain the comically bad dialogue, cheesy flashbacks or the confused way the plot staggers around until the final, unimpressive battle?

"Highlander: Endgame" is inferior not only to the original 1986 "Highlander" movie about warriors who stay the same age forever (and can only be killed by beheading), but also to most episodes of the spin-off '90s TV series.

Unbeknownst to 500-year-old Connor MacLeod (Christopher Lambert) a bad, but very powerful "fellow immortal" named Jacob Kell (a scenery-chewing Bruce Payne), whose father was semi-accidentally killed by MacLeod back in 1555, has been following him through the centuries, killing off his loved ones.

With the help of a multiracial, Mad Max-style immortal motorcycle gang, Kell is also trying to wipe out threats to his future world domination by killing off the other "immortals." But Kell would rather keep Connor MacLeod alive to endure the loss of his protégé Duncan MacLeod (Adrian Paul, star of the TV series). The only way Kell can be defeated is if one MacLeod kills the other, therefore absorbing his power.

Pathetically, "Highlander: Endgame" (script attributed to Joel Soisson) isn't even true to its apocalyptic title: At the end, there is still more than one "immortal" and the scene is set for more sequels, with the franchise torch passed on to the cast of the TV version.

For some reason, first-time director Douglas Aarniokoski felt it necessary to reshoot (rather than cut in) scenes from the first movie. By evoking memories of the original "Highlander," he makes his own seem all the more wretched.

Also reviewed in:
CHICAGO TRIBUNE, 9/4/00, Tempo/p. 10, Vicky Edwards
NEW YORK TIMES, 9/2/00, p. B15, Elvis Mitchell
VARIETY, 9/4-10/00, p. 20, Derek Elley

HILLBROW KIDS

A Media Luna release of a Film Forum presentation of an Open Society Institute production in Afrikaans with English subtitles. *Producer:* Mirjam Quinte. *Director:* Michael Hammon and Jacqueline Görgen. *Director of Photography:* Michael Hammon. *Editor:* Michael Hammon and Yvonne Loquens. *Music:* Harald Bernhard and Matthias Kratzenstein. *Running time:* 94 minutes. *MPAA Rating:* Not Rated.

CAST: Regina Ndlovu (Storyteller); Silas, Shadrack, Jane, Vusi, and Bheki (Street Children).

NEW YORK POST, 12/6/00, p. 56, V.A. Musetto

"Anybody who lives here must be crazy," says one of the subjects of "Hillbrow Kids," the compelling documenatary about street kids in Johannesburg, South Africa.

"You don't have a life anymore. You just suffer," complains a second.

"I want to get off the streets, but I don't know how," muses yet another of the tattered black kids who hang out on the congested streets of Hillbrow, an inner-city residential neighborhood.

As the political situation in South Africa has changed, so have the demographics of Hillbrow. A mostly white area in the 1970s, it is now overwhelmingly populated by blacks—migrants from the troubled country's townships and rural areas, and from elsewhere in Africa.

"Hillbrow Kids," a German-produced documentary by veteran directors Michael Hammon and Jacqueline Gorgen, takes a look at the young vagabonds who call the streets home.

In disturbing detail, we see these aimless kids, who often appear to be 10 years old—or younger!—as they beg for money and food, sniff glue, sleep under bridges in cardboard boxes and fight off predators.

One boy, 13, sobs as he tells of being raped. Others tell of an old man who beat them with a whip.

But there is a glimmer of hope. A boy dreams of being a fireman, "because you can earn at lot of money." Says another, with conviction: "One thing is sure—I won't die here."

You would have to be a grouch not to root for these unfortunate young people.

VILLAGE VOICE, 12/12/00, p. 178, Jessica Winter

"On the white line, no one can knock me over," says a boy panhandling in the midst of oncoming Johannesburg traffic. The scalding *Hillbrow Kids* is full of acts that mingle recklessness with confrontational self-preservation. Michael Hammon and Jacqueline Gorgen's 16mm documentary about the street children of Johannesburg etches in blood, dirt, and tears the titular neighborhood that the kids call their own, and—without the aid of a single talking head—the socioeconomic realities of postapartheid South Africa that have propelled them there.

Hillbrow is a mine-ridden playground, where malnutrition, rape, and child prostitution are everyday facts of life, and even glue-sniffing can seem pragmatic. "It's like this: Sometimes it gets very cold... and I like to change my thoughts," explains young Vusi. At one point he returns to his desolate township, where the unwired, unplumbed shacks built from plywood and corrugated iron somewhat resemble the tarpaulin sheds that Vusi and his friends fashion underground. The filmmakers quietly catalog his visit: His mum bathes him, lays out clean clothes, and casually asks for money for a new TV battery. (The youths who made up part of the massive post-1994 urban migration in South Africa were not just runaways, but also children sent away to the city to hustle cash for their families.)

Vusi's is not the only childless mother in *Hillbrow Kids:* Teenaged Jane, first seen nursing her baby on the side of a road, becomes a blank-staring wraith after she loses her son to her boyfriend's family. The film's narrator of sorts, Regina Ndlovu, tells four folk tales as allegorical counterpoint to the footage and can occasionally be spotted not far off from the street kids, watching over them like a would-be adoptive parent. This rupture of the documentary format, though miscalculated, doesn't dilute the power of the footage—which crackles with ferocious energy whenever a boy named Shadrack is on-screen. He understands both the family cycles of poverty and ignorance that apartheid left behind ("They don't know how to *think,* " he says bitterly of his unseen parents) and the bedrock of racism that will take generations to erode. As clairvoyantly aware of a world outside his dire circumstances as he is of the near-impossibility of reaching it, Shadrack's intelligence and force of will seem, in the cruelest irony of this utterly necessary film, like just another source of pain.

Also reviewed in:
NEW YORK TIMES, 12/6/00, p. E5, Elvis Mitchell

HOLLOW MAN

A Columbia Pictures release of a Douglas Wick production.   *Executive Producer:* Marion Rosenberg.   *Producer:* Douglas Wick and Alan Marshall.   *Director:* Paul Verhoeven. *Screenplay:* Andrew W. Marlowe.   *Story:* Gary Scott Thompson and Andrew W. Marlowe. *Director of Photography:* Jost Vacano.   *Editor:* Mark Goldblatt.   *Music:* Jerry Goldsmith. *Music Editor:* Kenny Hall and Darrell Hall.   *Sound:* Joseph Geisinger and (music) Bruce Botnick.   *Sound Editor:* Scott A. Hecker.   *Casting:* Howard Feuer. *Production Designer:* Allan Cameron.   *Art Director:* Dale Allan Pelton.   *Set Designer:* Daniel R. Jennings.   *Set Decorator:* John M. Dwyer.   *Set Dresser:* James F. Husbands and Mara Massey.   *Special Effects:* Stan Parks and William Aldridge.   *Visual Effects:* Scott E. Anderson.   *Supervising Puppeteer:* Alec Gillis.   *Costumes:* Ellen Mirojnick.   *Make-up:* Whitney L. James.   *Make-up (Elisabeth Shue):* Desne Holland.   *Stunt Coordinator:* Gary Combs and Gil Combs.   *Running time:* 114 minutes. *MPAA Rating:* R.

CAST: Elisabeth Shue (Linda McKay);   Kevin Bacon (Sebastian Caine);   Josh Brolin (Matthew Kensington);   Kim Dickens (Sarah Kennedy);   Greg Grunberg (Carter Abbey);   Joey Slotnick (Frank Chase);   Mary Randle (Janice Walton);   William Devane (Dr. Kramer);   Rhona Mitra (Sebastian's Neighbor);   Pablo Espinosa (Warehouse Guard);   Margot Rose (Mrs. Kramer); Jimmie F. Skaggs (Wino);   Jeffrey George Scaperotta (Boy in Car);   Sarah Bowles (Girl in Car);   Kelli Scott (Mom);   Steve Altes (Dad);   J. Patrick McCormack (General Caster);   Darius A. Sultan (Gate Guard);   Tom Woodruff, Jr. (Isabelle the Gorilla);   David Vogt (Helicopter Pilot).

LOS ANGELES TIMES, 8/4/00, Calendar/p. 9, Kenneth Turan

Like a demented salesman, invisible man Sebastian Caine (Kevin Bacon) keeps trying to convince us of the virtues of not being seen. "You have no idea how much fun this is," he says, adding later, "You have no idea what it's like, the power, the freedom." He's right about that much: We have no idea.

Maybe it's inevitable, given its name, but the most remarkable thing about "Hollow Man" is how insubstantial it is. Despite a wealth of special effects and direction by Paul Verhoeven, Mr. Over-the-Top himself, this movie is surprisingly inert, more dull than anything else, with little to recommend it on any level. Even the classic 1933 James Whale-Claude Rains "Invisible Man" manages, its great age notwithstanding, to do a more imaginative job of putting invisibility on the screen.

Not helping things is the voyeuristic bent of the film's Andrew W. Marlowe screenplay. For, despite his crowing about invisibility's limitless possibilities, all Caine can think of to do when he is out of sight is torment, harass, humiliate and in general abuse women who can't see him. As another character mildly but accurately puts it: "The whole thing gives me the creeps."

Researcher Caine is surely a familiar type: the cocky, cerebral scientist who drives a fast sports convertible, doesn't sleep much because DaVinci didn't and tells everyone who'll listen that "I am a god----genius."

Mostly the people who listen are those who have to—Caine's staff on the hush-hush Pentagon-funded project on invisibility he runs in a secret underground location in Washington, D.C.

Second in command is Linda McKay (Elisabeth Shue), Caine's former girlfriend who is now secretly involved with teammate Matthew Kensington (Josh Brolin). Quite the cozy little group.

It turns out that making living things invisible is the easy part of the process; Caine's lab features several animals, including a cranky gorilla named Isabelle, who've made the transformation and can only be seen with the aid of infrared goggles. Getting them back to where the naked eye can see them has proved to be more problematical.

Caine soon figures that one out, but he lies to his superiors at the Pentagon and says he's still working on it. He doesn't want his discovery to go through a boring testing process; he wants to try it out himself. Now. "You don't make history by following rules," he insists. "You make it by seizing the moment."

Even when people could see him, Caine was never the nicest guy in the lab: "I am not," he barks at animal-loving vet Sarah Kennedy (Kim Dickens), "running a god---- zoo." And once he's invisible, like Isabelle the gorilla, he gives in completely to his dark side, though Isabelle has the good taste not to play Peeping Tom, grope co-workers and worse.

"Hollow Man's" special-effects budget went largely to a much more detailed look at the invisibility process than we've enjoyed to date. First the flesh goes, then the muscles, then the organ's, then the blood vessels and finally the skeleton. It's a neat trick, but more off-putting than exciting to observe.

And, as noted, once Caine is invisible, "Hollow" can't figure out anything involving for him to do. Plot constraints keep the scientist in the lab, and a lot of that time is spent encased in a latex mask, so he isn't really invisible at all.

Verhoeven tries to rouse the audience from the effects of all this tedium with a murderous, gory finale, but it is more a deadening experience than anything else. The film's only horrifying moment is its first, when a lab rat is grabbed and squashed by an invisible hand, which then drips blood onto a barely visible skeletal jaw. Unpleasant though that image is, it at least gets your attention, which is more than you can say for anything that follows.

NEW YORK, 8/14/00, p. 64, Peter Rainer

Hollow Man is intended as *The Invisible Man* for the computer-generated-imagery generation, and it makes you long for the old Claude Rains film's tacky, witty pleasures, for pencils floating through space and bandages unraveled to reveal... nothing! This new version is hollow, all right: It's a cautionary tale about the dangers of soullessness that never had any soul to lose. The director, Paul Verhoeven, has been working in a Metallica mode ever since he came to Hollywood from Holland almost fifteen years ago, where he made, among other notable movies, *Soldier of Orange,* one of the best and most humane war thrillers ever filmed. Verhoeven didn't simply go Hollywood; he went RoboHollywood—not only with techno-opuses *(RoboCop, Total Recall, Starship Troopers)* that seem machine-tooled but with his real-people movies like *Basic Instinct* and *Showgirls,* to take the best and the worst, which also seem populated with audio-animatronic banshees. Base and gothic, Verhoeven's Hollywood movies look like they were hatched in a high-tech bunker, conceivably the same one on display throughout most of *Hollow Man.* Didn't it occur to the makers of this movie that turning oneself invisible might also be fun?

That bunker in *Hollow Man* is a top-secret Defense Department laboratory where Sebastian Caine is the reigning martinet conducting experiments turning animals invisible and back again. Sebastian's chief assistants, played by Elisabeth Shue and Josh Brolin, are also clandestine lovers—clandestine because Shue had once been Sebastian's squeeze and Sebastian has a temper. Sebastian is the kind of guy who jokes about how he's God, making it clear he thinks he really is. He pooh-poohs the Defense Department brass and, bypassing all protocols, volunteers himself as his own first human test subject. "You don't make history following the rules," he sneers at his cohorts. (And you don't make great movies with dialogue like this.)

Kevin Bacon, even when he's playing good guys, has a feral, skinned-rabbit look that villainizes him (the same is true for James Woods). In *Hollow Man,* he brings out the venom in Sebastian from the first frame. This is a mistake, although at least it means he's watchable, which is more than you can say for the other cast members, dullards all. But by starting out Sebastian as a livid, false messiah, Bacon has nowhere to go but sideways: When Sebastian's invisibility cannot be reversed, he simply becomes a wraithlike version of the same vengeful jerk he always was.

Secreted inside the bunker while his assistants take turns monitoring him, he goes stir-crazy and slips away, then slips back in. Most of the time he's truly invisible, but when smoke or steam or water is put in his way, his form partially reappears, and for a time he is also encased in a plasticlike substance and cowl that give him the look of a deranged Trappist monk.

What is the point of making a movie about an invisible man if you don't sink into dirty-minded voyeurism? Most of the time Sebastian never even leaves the compound; we're prisoners with him in a dank dungeon of stainless steel and plate glass, and we're never encouraged to identify with him. He's just an id in a snit. If Brian De Palma had made this movie—he already has, in a way, repeatedly—we would be out with Sebastian nightly on a Cook's tour of purgatory. Verhoeven indulges an occasional low-mindedness, having Sebastian intrude on a buxom neighbor or his rutting cohorts, and he includes a scene where the brainiac appears to be observing a female assistant on the potty. But fantasy-wise, this stuff is pretty slim pickings. Is it because the filmmakers were straining for allegory? (Sebastian's last name isn't Caine for nothing.) In the press notes, Verhoeven refers to Plato's deep musings on invisibility and morality, but his movie doesn't recall Plato's *Republic*. It recalls Republic Pictures: hollow actors in hollow sets hurling hollow dialogue. Even the scenes in which Sebastian is strapped to an operating table and rendered invisible, which should be horrifying, are cheesy. He's stripped away, layer by layer and organ by organ, but he resembles nothing so much as a giant writhing slab of prosciutto. *Hollow Man* may be a dud high and low—no Plato, no porno—but it didn't have to be that way. In a world in which cybercommunication has, in a sense, rendered many of us invisible travelers, the time was ripe for a remake of a movie about phantom identity. Virtual reality isn't so virtual anymore, and that's a great subject for a movie, scary or otherwise. If the makers of *Hollow Man* had any wit, they might have realized that, in the modern world, the invisible man is just as corporeal as his flesh-and-blood brethren.

NEW YORK POST, 8/4/00, p. 53, Lou Lumenick

Paul Verhoeven's graphic update of "The Invisible Man" boasts special effects that are really spectacular—too bad it lacks flesh-and-blood characters.

Instead, we have the most photogenic and unlikeliest group of research scientists since "Flatliners," a film whose title pretty well describes the silly narrative arc of the script by Andrew Marlowe (the abysmal "End of Days").

Kevin Bacon is encouraged to ham it up mercilessly as Sebastian Caine, a brilliant but megalomaniacal scientist who develops an invisibility formula and then, unbeknownst to his Pentagon bosses, decides to test it on himself at his top-secret lab.

Does he use his invisibility to steal America's nuclear secrets? To blackmail senior government or corporate officials?

No, Caine is more interested in fondling his female colleagues—and raping a beautiful blond neighbor (in a sequence of stunning flipness).

It's not your father's H.G. Wells, who understood his story was more interesting if the invisible protagonist became progressively more insane.

Caine is so crackers from the get-go that it's hardly surprising when—frustrated by his inability to reverse the invisibility process—he decides to bash an invisible pup to death.

The acting here is really appalling—especially by erstwhile Oscar nominee Elisabeth Shue ("Leaving Las Vegas") as Caine's research assistant and former girlfriend, who has moved on to another colleague, a hunky scientist played with boyish enthusiasm, if minimal credibility, by Josh Brolin.

The interminable, suspenseless, lady-in-peril chase sequences—complete with overripe dialogue—are not what one would expect from the director of "Basic Instinct."

That it's not a disaster on the order of Verhoeven's "Showgirls" is due entirely to the sometimes stomach-churning special effects, the best since "The Matrix."

We see Caine slowly disappear—organ by organ, bone by bone, artery by artery... you get the idea. And vice versa.

The computer-graphics staff has also devised amazing depictions of the invisible Caine moving through various types of smoke and water.

But, in the end, "Hollow Man" is just that—a hollow excuse for a movie.

NEWSDAY, 8/4/00, Part II/p. B2, John Anderson

Say what else you want about it, but this summer's movie season has been crying out for a film by Paul Verhoeven ("Showgirls," "Total Recall," "Basic Instinct"). You know, the kind of elevating entertainment that ... well, that just MAKES US BETTER PEOPLE.

"What would you do if no one could see you?" asks the cruel and unusual "Hollow Man," and the answers—as they pertain to our almost unbearably smarmy central character, Sebastian Caine (Kevin Bacon)—include rape. Murder. More murder. Various forms of sexual harassment. The gruesome, if not precisely on-camera, slaughter of a dog. And the kind of acting that makes you wish the whole cast would disappear.

As in H.G. Wells' "The Invisible Man"—or the creaky-but-droll 1933 James Whale version starring Claude Rains—invisibility carries the price tag of madness. Verhoeven's excuse? Making a sci-fi movie for hormonally intoxicated, criminally inclined 14-year-old males isn't a crime. Yet. But the film's degree of viciousness, which certainly isn't limited to Caine's nocturnal wanderings, makes one hope Verhoeven isn't taking any potions. Not this one, at least.

The director's quite obvious stand-in, the unctuous Dr. Caine, leads the kind of research team you wouldn't entrust with matches and gasoline through a multibillion-dollar military experiment into "molecular phase-shifting." Or something. Deputy Chief of Knuckleheads is Linda McKay, played by Elisabeth Shue, who seems to have been instructed by Verhoeven to play the part in a state of constant sexual arousal—which makes sense, since she is not only Caine's ex-girl, but sleeping with colleague Matthew (Josh Brolin) and not sure in whose bed she wants to be.

For their part, both Bacon and Brolin seem to have been dipped in Nair; they're hairless, as well as nuance-free. Which says as much about Verhoeven's aesthetic as it does about Linda's taste, especially as Caine begins his ascent into full-blown lunacy.

More interesting, pathologically at least, is Kim Dickens' Sarah, a veterinarian and animal rights activist who thinks it unfair that a test gorilla warped by their serum—and given a nasty appetite for rats—should be put down. As the resident party pooper, Sarah is not just foul-tempered but strangely butch. Coincidence? No, no, no. No more than the disappearance from the script of Caine's random rape victim—immediately post-rape—was an administrative accident. People are meat to Verhoeven. And used meat is discarded—unlike, unfortunately, hack directors too immature to be unprofitable.

SIGHT AND SOUND, 10/00, p. 45, David Thompson

Working in a secret underground laboratory funded by the Pentagon in Washington DC, scientist Sebastian Caine has created a serum that can make living creatures invisible. With the aid of his team, which includes his former lover Linda McKay, he experiments on animals, but so far is unable to bring them back from a state of invisibility. He finally works out a reversal formula, which he successfully tests on a gorilla. When he reports to his boss at the Pentagon, Dr Kramer, Caine lies about this breakthrough, fearing his funds will be cut off. He returns to his team, declaring they have approval to move on to Phase Three, in which he himself will be given the serum.

Caine is made invisible, but the reversal procedure proves a failure. His irresponsible nature comes to the fore, and he escapes to his apartment, and then gains access to the flat of a neighbour, whom he assaults. Tampering with a video camera to convince his team he is still in the laboratory, Caine then spies on McKay, discovering that her new lover is a senior member of his team, Matthew Kensington. McKay finds out about Caine's deception, and she and Kensington visit Dr Kramer to reveal what has happened. Caine then kills Dr Kramer before he can speak to anybody. Returning to the laboratory, Caine begins to murder his team one by one and plants a time bomb. McKay manages to avoid his traps and, believing she has killed Caine with jets of fire, escapes to the lift shaft with a wounded Kensington. Caine reappears, and just as he demands a final kiss from her, she manages to send him plunging to his death.

With *Hollow Man* director Paul Verhoeven has delivered exactly the kind of special-effects movie that Hollywood wants—violent, action-driven, but with just enough restraint in the sexual domain to please the MPAA ratings board. After the relative box-office failures of *Showgirls* and *Starship Troopers*, *Hollow Man* finds the director living up to his reputation of being a superior craftsman, while eradicating the confrontational elements of his previous films. Verhoeven has invoked Plato here in suggesting that invisibility would cause a man to abuse power, but though there are a few instances of the camera as sexual voyeur, the 'bad boy' elements of his make-up are rarely apparent. Just as the invisible scientist Caine creeps up on his half-naked neighbour, the scene cuts away, leaving us to imagine the worst. Once Verhoeven would have shown the consequences of Caine's actions, and then led us to question who is morally more questionable: the film-maker or the audience? In *Hollow Man* the issue is simply avoided.

Much of the blame for the relative blandness of *Hollow Man* must be placed on Andrew Marlowe's script. Marlowe *(End of Days)* fails to provide either characters or a plot with any shading or surprises. Caine moves from an arrogant scientist to a psychotic killer consumed with sexual jealousy without much of a gear shift. In James Whale's classic 1933 film version of H. G. Wells' *The Invisible Man* the scientist-hero becomes mad as a side effect of the drugs he's been trying out. He also has insane plans for world domination, and given *Hollow Man*'s Washington setting, Marlowe seems to be missing a trick: why doesn't Caine use his invisibility to infiltrate the Pentagon or even spy on the president, a rich territory for voyeuristic gags, surely?

Instead, the final act of *Hollow Man* becomes a claustrophobic battle between Caine's bland colleagues and a malevolent 'thing' in their midst. Caine's main adversary, McKay, comes across as little more than an enterprising head girl, while the banter between the embattled scientists is in need of some Hawksian verve, particularly given their mantra-like response to any situation: "Oh, shit."

On the positive side, *Hollow Man* demonstrates that Verhoeven remains masterful at integrating state-of-the-art special effects into a rigorous, Hitchcockian *mise en scène*. Working with his regular collaborators, the director gives the visuals a hard, metallic texture. He heightens human flesh tones to give his actors a waxy gloss, so that when their bodies are penetrated, the impact of the wounds is intensified. Verhoeven has always had a brutalist attitude to the human form, and it is the scenes of bodily transformation that have the greatest intensity here. The reduction of the body of a man to bone, muscular tissue and blood vessels as it shifts in and out of invisibility is strikingly beautiful, like a series of animated Vesalius drawings. The disappointment of *Hollow Man* is that this is the only real depth the film achieves.

TIME, 8/7/00, p. 84, Richard Schickel

For reasons known only to the kind of people who take the Star Wars missile-defense system seriously, the Pentagon thinks the capacity to make yourself invisible has huge military potential. It is underwriting Dr. Sebastian Caine's expensive experiments in dematerialization.

This is silly. Every schoolboy knows the only worthwhile reason to become invisible is so you can case the girls' locker room undetected. Caine (an utterly charmless Kevin Bacon) does use his power voyeuristically in *Hollow Man*. But this being an up-to-date—that is to say, thoroughly ugly—movie, he doesn't stop there. He becomes a rapist. And then, of course, a murderer.

Perhaps he is merely acting out the implicit logic of the 1933 film of H.G. Wells' *The Invisible Man,* of which Paul Verhoeven's new movie is an entirely unacknowledged remake. Both Caine and Claude Rains' Jack Griffin find it easier to attain the ectoplasmic state than to return from it; both become increasingly megalomaniac as a result of the scientific process they embrace. The big difference between the two pictures is attitude. James Whale, who directed the first movie, made a kind of moral comedy of the situation—lots of befuddled English country types doing dialect jokes—but with some nicely put thoughts about messing with nature. Verhoeven simply makes a mess of it.

Too many special effects, many of them stomach churning; too much pornographically arranged death. Early in the picture you wonder why Verhoeven is so obsessively interested in a perfectly ordinary elevator. Later on you see why: it's where the climactic fireball is going to explode, imperiling Elisabeth Shue's and Josh Brolin's hairdos. They deserve better than this. But so do we all.

VILLAGE VOICE, 8/15/00, p. 115, J. Hoberman

A spasm of annoyance convulsed the normally placid world of film crit last week. Yes, of course, bad boy Paul Verhoeven had released a new comedy—the provocatively titled *Hollow Man*.

Having worked with Arnold Schwarzenegger, Michael Douglas, and (more than once) Joe Eszterhas, Verhoeven is the undisputed King of the Tinseltown Creeps; in the current issue of *Film Comment*, His Nastiness even cites *Triumph of the Will* as a guilty pleasure. This 62-year-old Dutchman has replaced Brian De Palma as the splashiest misanthrope in Hollywood—a culture to which he held up a mirror in the camp classic *Showgirls*. Verhoeven's no candidate for the Jean Hersholt Humanitarian Award—sensitive people find the monstrous bugs in *Starship Troopers* more sympathetic (and less synthetic) than the film's humanoids—and *Hollow Man* will not blemish his record.

An uncredited remake of James Whale's 1934 *Invisible Man*, *Hollow Man* seems to take even more inspiration from the educational transparent plastic anatomy model known as the "Visible Man." Verhoeven, however, is interested not just in body but soul. Beneath the scientist's lab coat beats the heart of an insanely jealous and megalomaniacal power-mad rapist. Does it take one to know one? *Hollow Man* opens with a shot of a wriggling lab rat held up by its tail before the camera. The rodent is released and scampers away (still in close-up) only to be chomped to pieces by some slavering invisible thing. Never let it be said that this director declines to zap the audience to let them know where they stand.

Verhoeven is not ashamed to take his film's title personally. *Hollow Man* is gleefully confrontational in its ludicrous, pulpy tawdriness. Its mad scientist antihero, Sebastian Caine (Kevin Bacon), can drop his smirk only when it's time to lurk. Sebastian, introduced peeking through his venetian blinds to ogle the luscious babe in the neighboring apartment, heads up a government research team working on a top secret invisibility study. These geniuses have already produced an invisible gorilla—it soon gets loose, leaving Krell-like footprints all over their dungeonlike lab—but the "reversion" serum is unstable. In the movie's most memorable special effect, the injected antidote snakes through the writhing creature's bloodstream, rendering it visible biostrata by biostrata, like successive overlays in an anatomy textbook.

Set largely in a claustrophobic medical facility where facetious banter is the coin of the realm, *Hollow Man* suggests a particularly grotesque hospital drama. As Sebastian is a supremely irritating and arrogant egocentric braggart, as well as an eyesore who dresses in electric blue shirts and iridescent purple ties, his team has every reason to want him to vanish—none more than his assistant and former girlfriend Linda (Elisabeth Shue), who straddles the team's resident pretty boy, Matthew (Josh Brolin), at every opportunity. (Verhoeven has never met a bad actor he couldn't use.) Sebastian's failure to fulfill this lusty lass is one of the movie's psychological underpinnings.

If you've read H.G. Wells's *The Invisible Man* or seen the Whale movie, you know that invisibility does not improve personality. Stripped of his appearance and freed from social restraint, Sebastian wants only to spy on, and play doctor with, the girls. The first thing the invisible scientist does is expose one female associate's breast; his next experiment is to follow another into the toilet. Once Sebastian is stuck in invisibility, his team represents his emptiness by covering his face with liquid latex goop to sculpt a cadaverous Kevin Bacon mask. The "hollow man" has lost his superego. He responds with a reign of terror that lasts for the rest of the movie—pranking, raping, and killing.

Thanks to Sebastian's mischief (and the script's cynical plot twists), *Hollow Man* doesn't have too many dull patches—but neither is there much subtext. Still, the movie trades well on a certain rank symmetry. The more disembodied Sebastian gets, the bloodier the action becomes. This vengeful invisible force devotes itself to turning everybody else inside out. Trust the rat to go for the cheese.

Also reviewed in:
CHICAGO TRIBUNE, 8/4/00, Friday/p. A, Mark Caro
NEW YORK TIMES, 8/4/00, p. E13, A. O. Scott
NEW YORKER, 8/14/00, p. 88, David Denby

VARIETY, 8/7-13/00, p. 15, Robert Koehler
WASHINGTON POST, 8/4/00, p. C5, Stephen Hunter
WASHINGTON POST, 8/4/00, Weekend/p. 34, Desson Howe

HOMO SAPIENS 1900

A First Run Features release of an Arte Factum/Swedish Television production. *Producer:* Peter Cohen. *Director:* Peter Cohen. *Screenplay:* Peter Cohen. *Director of Photography:* Peter Ostlund and Mats Lund. *Editor:* Peter Cohen. *Music:* Matti Bye. *Sound:* Peter Cohen. *Running time:* 85 minutes. *MPAA Rating:* Not Rated.

WITH: Steven Rappaport (Narrator).

CHRISTIAN SCIENCE MONITOR, 3/3/00, p. 15, David Sterritt

[*Homo Sapiens 1900* was reviewed jointly with *Beyond the Mat*; see Sterritt's review of that film.]

NEW YORK POST, 3/3/00, p. 52, Jonathan Foreman

A documentary about eugenics, the supposed "science" of improving the human species through selective breeding, "Homo Sapiens 1900" is essentially a none-too-coherent, rather slow-moving illustrated lecture.

And it uses doomy music to create atmosphere and to make up for its disorganized structure.

Eugenics had a powerful influence on four countries: Germany, where it inspired nudists as well as Nazis; the Soviet Union, where it focused on the brain rather than the body; Sweden and the United States.

Although director Peter Cohen has found some remarkable film, including a clip from 1917's "The Black Stork"—in which Dr. Harry Haiselden plays himself as a doctor allowing a baby with birth defects to die—he fails to put the movement in its historical or scientific context, or to explain why notions like "degeneration" had such resonance at the beginning of the last century.

NEWSDAY, 3/3/00, Part II/p. B7, Jan Stuart

In the first of many disturbing archival films excerpted in Peter Cohen's documentary "Homo Sapiens 1900," we see a large clan gathered for a family portrait, circa early 20th Century. Amid this sprawling collection of elders, parents and toddlers, our eye is drawn to a woman seated to one side who is chattering madly and rocking in her chair, apparently the victim of a nervous disorder of some sort. Looking closely at a few of those clustered around the woman, we can sense them trying to make allowances for her manic behavior, overcompensating for the cameraman with excessive shows of dignity.

What troubles us as we stare at this woman is the knowledge that somewhere in the complex mix of our reactions to her—sadness, amusement, compassion, morbid fascination—is a vague irritation. We empathize, if only just a little, with her family members. What a handful she must be! See how she throws the group off balance! See how she throws a kink into a portrait of family harmony!

It is only a short leap from those ornery sentiments to a baser impulse that says, well, couldn't we just, you know, eliminate her? Without so much as commenting on the family gathering, the filmmaker implicates us in the history of eugenics, that dubious pseudo-scientific campaign to weed out the dross from the imperfect garden of humanity.

Filmed in black and white, "Homo Sapiens 1900" is a dispassionate look at the evolution of eugenics that is no less unsettling for its cool-headedness. Employing an eyebrow-raising collection of laboratory photographs, silent movies, documents and art plates, Swedish director Peter Cohen traces the history of eugenics back to its beginnings in 1895 as "race hygiene," a term coined by a German doctor who thought it humane and expedient to cut short the life of malformed babies with an extra dose of morphine.

Race hygiene would find its ultimate expression four decades later, when Fritz Lenz' Kaiser-Wilhelm Institute offered an academic rationale for Nazism. The mass extermination of Jews was accompanied by the sterilization of 400,000 Germans considered to be of inferior stock. But as "Homo Sapiens 1900" makes pungently clear, the practice of sterilization would find its proponents in countries as seemingly fair-minded as the United States and especially Sweden, where eugenics provided a scientific context for the welfare state.

Cohen sets out an exhaustive cast of characters, delineating with particular care the revolutionary zeal with which great Russian writers and politicos contributed to the study of eugenics until Stalin, of all people, nipped it in the bud. He misses some good opportunities, particularly in his failure to link the beauty pageant craze with the earliest eugenics fairs that gave out prizes for human pedigree. But as the next generation of biologists tinker with the possibilities of cloning, "Homo Sapiens 1900" offers up a sobering reality check.

VILLAGE VOICE, 3/7/00, p. 121, J.Hoberman

The Swedish documentary-essayist Peter Cohen uses his latest film, *Homo Sapiens 1900,* to examine the ideologies of the last century through the prism of eugenics—which is to say, in light of the notion that humanity must seize control of its own evolutionary destiny by instituting a program of selective breeding. As the current debate over biotechnology and genetic engineering suggests, the issues are far from resolved.

Cohen's two previous documentaries, *Chaim Rumkowski and the Jews of Lodz* and *The Architecture of Doom,* both dealt in various ways with the impact of Nazi ideology. But, as *Homo Sapiens* makes clear, it was not only the Nazis who believed that society was something to be cultivated like a garden. (Cohen locates the German notion of "race hygiene" in a context that also includes turn-of-the-century enthusiasms such as Jugendstil design and open-air nudism.) Actually, the two national cultures initially most impressed by eugenics were the United States, where by 1907 over 20 states had enacted compulsory sterilization laws (Cohen includes some amazing footage from the 1916 movie *The Black Stork,* made by and starring the American apostle of euthanasia, Dr. Harry Haiselden), and Sweden, which established the first government institute of race biology, effectively integrating eugenics into the social policies of the welfare state.

The Nazis were, however, the first political party to make "racial hygiene" a crucial part of their agenda. The contradiction between protecting family values and the need to breed the master race was resolved by focusing on negative eugenics—that is, by eliminating the deformed and "subhuman." Positive eugenics were restricted to the aesthetic realm. It's almost a too perfect dichotomy that where the Soviets were fascinated by brains (collecting and preserving "genius" specimens for scientific study), the Nazis were obsessed with bodies. Race-based eugenics were naturally problematic in the multicultural Soviet Union. Cohen excerpts a 1926 Soviet film that argues, against Mendelism, for the inheritance of acquired characteristics. A cameo by Minister of Enlightenment Anatoli Lunacharsky adds to the authority; the Soviets ultimately identified all genetic research with fascism.

Deliberately paced and shot in solemn black and white, *Homo Sapiens 1900* has an undeniable pathos. Cohen quotes Zola to the effect that the late 19th century's new biological sciences "belong just as much to the poet as the scientist." Self-conscious as it is, our species imagines ideals that cannot possibly be achieved.

Also Reviewed in:
CHICAGO TRIBUNE, 11/10/00, Friday/p. P, John Petrakis
NEW YORK TIMES, 3/3/00, p. E34, Stephen Holden

HOUSE OF MIRTH, THE

A Sony Pictures Classics release of a Showtime and Granada presentation of a Three Rivers production in association with the Arts Council of England/Film Four/The Scottish Arts

Council/Glasgow Film Fund. *Executive Producer:* Bob Last and Pippa Cross. *Producer:* Olivia Stewart. *Director:* Terence Davies. *Screenplay:* Terence Davies. *From the novel "The House of Mirth" by:* Edith Wharton. *Director of Photography:* Remi Adefarasin. *Editor:* Michael Parker. *Music:* Adrian Johnston. *Sound:* Louis Kramer. *Sound Editor:* Catherine Hodgson. *Casting:* Billy Hopkins, Suzanne Smith, and Kerry Barden. *Production Designer:* Don Taylor. *Art Director:* Diane Dancklefsen. *Set Decorator:* John Bush. *Special Effects:* Stuart Murdoch. *Costumes:* Monica Howe. *Make-up:* Jan Harrison Shell. *Running time:* 140 minutes. *MPAA Rating:* Not Rated.

CAST: Gillian Anderson (Lily Bart);   Dan Aykroyd (Gus Trenor);   Eleanor Bron (Mrs. Peniston);   Terry Kinney (George Dorset); Anthony LaPaglia (Sim Rosedale);   Laura Linney (Bertha Dorset);   Elizabeth McGovern (Carry Fisher);   Jodhi May (Grace Stepney); Eric Stoltz (Lawrence Selden);   Penny Downie (Judy Trenor);   Pearce Quigley (Percy Gryce);   Helen Coker (Evie Van Osburgh);   Mary MacLeod (Mrs. Haffen);   Paul Venables (Jack Stepney); Serena Gordon (Gwen Stepney);   Lorelei King (Mrs. Hatch);   Linda Marlowe (Madame Regina);   Anne Marie Timoney (Miss Haines);   Claire Higgins (Mrs. Bry);   Ralph Riach (Lord Hubert Dacy);   Brian Pettifer (Mr. Bry);   Philippe de Grossourvre (Ned Silverton);   Trevor Martin (Jennings, the Butler);   David Ashton (Lawyer);   Lesley Harcourt (Mattie Gormer); Mark Dymond (Paul Morpeth);   Pamela Dwyer (Edith Fisher);   Kate Wooldridge (Parlour Maid); Graham Crammond (Clerk);   Roy Sampson (Dorset Butler);   Alyxis Daly (Landlady).

CINEASTE, Vol. XXV1, no. 2, p. 41, Martha P. Nochimson

Gertie Farish is missing. The drab little social worker with the improbable, comic name, a crucial character in Edith Wharton's novel *The House of Mirth,* has been deleted by Terence Davies from his adaptation for the screen of the early twentieth-century classic, and his film has paid the price, although the cost may not be immediately evident. Davies has, in many other ways, faithfully reproduced Wharton's story about Lily Bart (Gillian Anderson), the beautiful socialite who struggles against her hidden passion for Lawrence Selden (Eric Stoltz), looking elsewhere for marriage because Selden has the intelligence and the breeding, but not the money and no way to get it. Like Lily, Selden is only on the periphery of good society, and Lily has been programmed to want a piece of the rock. But she is only semiperfect trophy-wife material. Stunningly attractive and elegantly mannered, she cannot compromise her emotions sufficiently to follow through on her plans to snag a suitably rich husband, the destiny she was bred to pursue.

When Lily dallies briefly with Selden during a husband-hunting weekend in the country, she loses her chance with the boring but fabulously wealthy Percy Gryce (Pearce Quigley), the match everyone assumes that she will make. From there, she slips off the glass mountain of fortune and fashion as her inability to anchor herself in a suitable marriage leads to poverty and death. Reduced to the life of a working-class woman, Lily inadvertently overdoses on the chloral she takes to make herself sleep because she has become insomniac from the pressures of such independence. Yes, this is the path of Wharton's heroine, but she has lost something in this translation to the screen and gained something distinctly unsavory. This Lily is no longer the original complex image of female yearning that points beyond social limits, but rather a *memento mori* for any woman who would dare to be her own person. And her suffering is no longer a struggle toward something better, but rather a delectable spectacle.

In Davies's film, a defenseless (unmarried) Lily is hounded to a sordid death by the women of her class, a tragic fall in which Davies regards her as somewhat complicit, and her progress tearfully and titillatingly reinforces old clichés about the masochism of women and the inevitable failure of female forays into freedom. This is not the situation in Wharton's novel, in which Lily is granted a lot more capacity for independence and a powerful emotional ally: Gertie. In the novel-reflecting Wharton's painful relationship with a glacial, socially motivated mother—Lily's most profound problem is her lack of maternal support, and the coldness of the women of her class, who either want to lead her away from her heart (Selden) toward socially desirable marriages, or viciously compete with her for Selden. Wharton created Gertie as a real point of human contact for Lily to emphasize the need women have for warm motherly and sisterly bonds.

By contrast, in the film, there is no one to take up that task. Davies has chosen the cliché that women must, above all, beware of other women and has given Lily only a false female confidant, her jealous, conniving cousin Grace Stepney (Jodhi May), whose love for Selden dries up any empathy for Lily. Grace not only fails to bond with Lily, but actually revenges herself on the despised object of Selden's affection by successfully encouraging Mrs. Peniston, Lily's aunt (Eleanor Bron), to disinherit her and relegate her to the poverty that kills her.

Davies keeps the action moving, but leaves a thematic void where Wharton's Lily found a possible alternative to upper-class dehumanization. Davies says he chose Wharton's novel to make his first attempt at linear storytelling. But it is really because Davies strips the nonlinear elements of his source, the counter forces that sustain Lily, that he arrives at the rigid linearity that drives Lily down the straight and narrow conveyor belt to ruin. In so doing, Davies has made his film a compelling Exhibit A for Michel Foucault's idea that unremittingly conventional forms necessarily reiterate unremittingly conventional clichés. The consequences of the imposed linearity begin to make themselves manifest in the story's catalytic scene in which Lily's naive trust in Gus Trenor (Dan Akroyd), the alpha patriarch in patriarchal society, is shown to be a fatal mistake. Lily, who has depended on Gus to invest her modest income, discovers that he has compromised her by investing his money for her. Adding injury to insult, Trenor tries to exact payment in kind from Lily for his services and though Lily escapes the near-rape, this is the beginning of her fall from social grace, as Gus's rage at being rejected alienates her from what meager support she once enjoyed among the elite.

In the book, after fighting Gus off, Lily receives comfort from Gertie, who literally holds her through the night, providing a safe harbor. (Fascinatingly, this is the only physical love scene for Lily in the novel, though certainly it is not sexual, as sex is generally understood, despite its blurring of main-stream parameters for women's relationships.) In the film, by contrast, Lily is a study in perpetual victimization. Returning home, she is savaged by her aunt (because of the rumors about Lily and Trenor) and betrayed by Grace (who has contrived to ensure that the rumors reached Lily's aunt). This is a chilling scene that effectively embeds the social forces arrayed against Lily in Aunt Peniston's uncomprehending conformity that passes for ethics and in Grace's self-serving conviction that her personal inferiority to Lily justifies all actions she may take in competition with her cousin.

Davies should be faulted not for the quality of this intense scene, but rather for its substitution for one that grants Wharton's Lily the warmth of a friend outside the sterile, coldly artificial house of mirth. In the book, that friendship leads Lily to do charity work for a settlement house where she meets Nettie, a working-class girl whom Lily encounters again just before she overdoses on chloral. Nettie has found love in marriage, and Lily finds it too as the witness to this possibility in Nettie's cramped apartment, especially as witness to the pleasure of Nettie's motherhood. In the novel, as Lily dies, she imagines holding Nettie's baby and thereby has the tragic moment of recognition of authentic life—too late, of course, but it is a moment that in part redeems Lily's suffering. Since Davies's narrative choices have rendered all persons outside of the golden inner social circle anonymous and irrelevant, Davies's Lily has no such moment.

Davies's Lily has only Selden, and he has little to give her aside from a series of unconsummated, clandestine raptures that replace the physically chaste psychosexual sparring between Lily and Selden in the book with closer encounters of a more sensual kind. In her first scene with Selden in the film, Lily moves into nuzzling distance of his lips and goes on, in subsequent scenes, to steal some kisses that fill her with bosom-heaving pleasure. There is a wonderful rapport between Anderson and Stoltz in their sexual interplay, and a very clever representation of these refined social rebels as redheads, standing out from the others with their heads, in a manner of speaking, on fire. (They are not redheads in the book.) Davies's decisions to omit the physical relationship between Lily and Gertie, however, and to juice up her physical relationship with Selden reflect a timidity that one would not have expected from him, considering his previous films: *The Neon Bible* and *The Long Day Closes*.

Worse, in trapping Lily in such erotically charged affliction, Davies glamorizes Lily's suffering in a way reminiscent of the women's films of the 1940s that specialized in dooming beautiful, passionate, head-strong women. These films thrilled the audience with a goddess-like heroine, and at the same time reassured its most conventional longings to see women kept in their places. The resemblance is buttressed by Davies's visual homage to Elia Kazan's *A Streetcar Named Desire,* as Davies's Lily first appears in a puff of smoke from a steam locomotive like Vivien Leigh's Blanche, evoking both the magic of the woman and the Anna Karenina-like destiny of the female nonconformist. Similarly, as with Bette Davis and Paul Henreid in *Now, Voyager,* there is a lot of cigarette shtick between the nonconsummating lovers. While these images are effective, possibly even mesmerizing in themselves, as part of this narrative they speak of the thematic loss. Davies, in connecting Lily with the repression of female desire in the manner of the old-studio woman's picture, does not even give his heroine the modicum of victory that Wharton and many a classical woman's picture allowed. True, Viv's Blanche accurately prefigures the fate of Davies's Lily. But Bette, Barbara Stanwyck, Joan Crawford, and Katharine Hepburn got to do some high flying before they got their wings clipped. Gillian Anderson's Lily is falling apart from the beginning, her body a study in nervous repression, her anxiety already peeking through her calculated airs and graces—a very regressive choice.

Another puzzlingly regressive choice on Davies's part is his representation of Sim Rosedale (Anthony LaPaglia), the Jewish outsider who is fast making himself an undeniable economic force among the mainstream, upper-class WASPS. While LaPaglia turns in a likable performance as a man who, alone among Lily's acquaintances, is honest and accurate in his assessment of her situation, again Davies recalls the worst of classical Hollywood by repressing the word 'Jew' from the dialog and attempting to substitute dated codes. He visualizes Rosedale as the stereotypical dark non-WASP, instead of the blonde, blue-eyed presence he was in Wharton's novel, as if that were all necessary to establish Rosedale's identity. The upshot is a potential confusion for millennial audiences who have become used to overt acknowledgment of ethnic identification and are no longer primed to read the shorthand promoted by the studio system, when viewers were expected to automatically equate Danny Thomas's nose with Jewishness and unquestioningly understand why Betty Grable wasn't interested. Here, Rosedale's marginality, Lily's genteel revulsion at his attempts at friendship even before he proposes marriage—despite his kindness and good intentions—may bewilder some audience members. Others may find LaPaglia, despite a good performance, set up unpleasantly as a ghost of the all-purpose ethnic of classical Hollywood.

Tonally, and apart from its social vision, Davies's film fares only a bit better. The visual and narrative rhythms of the film progress in starts and fits. We are treated to the long, deliberate, beautiful slow takes we expect from Davies. But where, in *The Neon Bible* they reflect the pace of the protagonist's life and embed his interior reality in the film's images, in *The House of Mirth* they clash tonally with the overheated melodrama in the narrative development and with the pace of elements impatiently thrown into the movie without any expository explanation. The uneasy combination creates a sense of haste and carelessness in the telling of the story that contrasts strangely with Davies's leisurely panning of rooms and waterways.

The worst of the undigested fragments thrown precipitously at the viewer is a cinematically incomprehensible moment when, at a society party, stage curtains part and Lily is displayed momentarily, costumed and posed in a tableau in which she is said to represent Summer. (This interlude is meaninglessly excerpted from a long, significant, fully-developed scene in the novel, which plays on voyeurism and sexuality and should have been a natural for the film.) The eruption of this image is so brief that it can be easily discounted by the viewer speeding ahead with Lily's story, but it lingers as part of a botched series of mood swings in the film. These are relatively negligible in the entertaining first half of the film, but become increasingly jarring in the last half when the hankies come out.

Similarly, the casting of the film is erratic. Davies boldly gambled (and won) with two television actors. Anderson, a seven-season veteran of *The X-Files,* and Stoltz, a star *of Chicago Hope,* each demonstrate that television training can be invaluable in honing an actor's skills in using the face as an instrument. Both, and especially Anderson, register character nuances through sensitive facial modulations. Dan Aykroyd's catastrophic performance as Gus Trenor, however, calls attention to itself in another way. Aykroyd demonstrates how television training can foster the success of a lightweight actor, as he threatens to turn the pivotal plot event of Trenor's abuse of Lily into a *Saturday Night Live* sketch. Another casting choice that should not go unmentioned is Laura Linney, who gives a brilliant, potentially Oscar-winning performance as Bertha Dorset, the most dangerous cat in the social jungle, a study in refined, heartless, lethal hypocrisy.

Davies made his reputation as an intensely personal director of films driven by sensibility rather than plot. His previous films have been fueled by the pain of his childhood, and his need to deal with his homosexuality, which made him the butt of school bullies and a moving target for reactionary elements in church dogma. His previous films have been unsentimental (the adjective of choice for critics speaking of his work) and resistant to the bathetic cliché of the doomed deviant. But he has fallen head first into bathos and cliché in telling Lily's story. And so have many other smart people in the audience. Gay or straight, male or female, a large number of folks in our culture seem to have a jones for female immolation. (Do the names Marilyn Monroe and Judy Garland ring a bell?) The film has garnered many enthusiastic reviews, and, in a recent private conversation with me, a thoughtful and influential colleague not only extolled the virtues of the film, but described being 'thrilled' by it in a way the book did not excite him.

It is fruitless to condemn the private experience of euphoria at the erotic spectacle of female masochism that Davies has made of Lily; it seems so deeply embedded in cultural responses. But at this point in our public debates about gender, it would have been more hopeful to have had a *House of Mirth* that, if it did not disavow its relish of the endlessly tormented woman, at least troubled that programmed response with reflexive self-awareness that Hitchcock, Welles, and Lynch have already had the grace to exhibit.

LOS ANGELES TIMES, 12/22/00, Calendar/p. 1, Kevin Thomas

Through his acclaimed autobiographical films, most notably "Distant Voices, Still Lives," England's Terence Davies has demonstrated a knack for bring the past alive to disclose pain and treachery beneath a seductively evocative surface. He proves well-suited to bring to the screen "The House of Mirth," a devastating expose of the cruelty and hypocrisy of high society a century ago. As a portrait of the vulnerability of women of meager means but social entre "The House of Mirth," an ironic title if ever there was one, recalls Oscar Wilde's "The Ideal Husband" and Henry James' "The Europeans" but takes a far harsher tone.

With Glasgow standing in for New York in the years between 1905 and 1907, this Sony Pictures Classics release re-creates the Gilded Age in all its magnificence and misery, and affords a glorious role for "The X-Files' " Gillian Anderson, whose performance as the ill-fated Lily Bart is one of the year's best.

Anderson's Lily has been raised to believe that a woman's only goal is to land a husband, the richer the better. Lily is too honest and intelligent not to go about her husband-hunting without a lot of forthright irony, a stance that conceals her actual naivete. She has captured the attention of a socialite attorney, Lawrence Selden (Eric Stoltz), who toys with Lily's emotions yet has no intention of marrying her—it would seem that while he makes enough to live comfortably as a bachelor, he cannot afford a wife and still live in acceptable style. (It would also seem that he indulges in affairs only with married women).

In an effort to conform, Lily has taken to playing card games she neither enjoys nor, much worse, can afford. With only a tiny income and handouts from rich, sour old aunt (Eleanor Bron), Lily finds herself saddled with gambling debts and turns to help from the husband (Dan Aykroyd) of her best friend (Penny Downie), only to discover that he expects her to repay him by becoming his mistress. Shocked, Lily refuses, taking her first steps toward a spiritual odyssey harrowing as the ordeals experienced by Robert Bresson's heroes and heroines.

Gossip and malicious mischief preoccupy most of the women in Lily's world, in which appearance and status are everything, and Lily finds her reputation compromised all the faster because of her actual innocence. In an atmosphere of social mobility oiled by new money, Lily emerges as a true aristocrat, a woman of unswerving character and nobility of spirit.

She also discovers the terrible truth of her uselessness—of her inability to support herself in her increasingly dire straits. "The House of Mirth" becomes bleak as any play pertaining to the House of Atreus, but it possesses such a fire-and-ice intelligence and passion that its sense of the tragic is exalted in effect as in the tragedies of Aeschylus.

Davies does a splendid job as a writer and director. Stoltz's beautifully drawn Selden, a man who has allowed his intelligence to be undermined by shallowness, recalls a character played by Gena Rowlands in Davies' 1995 "The Neon Bible," an easygoing band singer, who, like Selden, never considers the impact she has on those who come to adore her. Stoltz heads a scintillating supporting cast that includes Aykroyd; Anthony LaPaglia as a self-made man eager to make the marriage that will prove him socially acceptable; Laura Linney as the nastiest of the socialites; and Elizabeth McGovern as the nicest.

There is an aesthetic unity to "The House of Mirth" that Martin Scorsese's Wharton adaptation, the costlier and starrier "The Age of Innocence," lacked. This film avoids the jarring anachronisms in decor that marred the Scorsese film, it is fortunate to have Aykroyd to supply a certain plain-spoken earthiness, because the Glasgow milieu is too tasteful to reflect the all-American exuberance and vulgarity that characterized so much in American taste and design in early 20th century. But this is a minor quibble in the light of Davies' accomplishment, which above all else expresses the timeless impact of Lily Bart's plight.

NEW YORK, 1/11/01, p. 80, Peter Rainer

Terence Davies's *The House of Mirth* is a rigorously elegant adaptation of the Edith Wharton novel, and unlike in some other Davies movies, the rigor here doesn't turn into rigor mortis. The tragic, ambiguous note is struck from the first, when we see Lily Bart (Gillian Anderson) emerging from Grand Central Terminal and realize she is just as ethereal as the vast plume of smoke through which she appears. A socialite in *Belle Époque* New York, Lily is almost poignantly fragile; although her quest for a moneyed husband seems predatory, she is too decent in the end, too sorrowful and full of grace, to be a successful huntress. Instead, she is undone by the cruelties of the lavish world she wants to make her own. Each defeat for her carries the force of a death knell, and no man, not the financier Sim Rosedale (Anthony LaPaglia) or the lawyer Lawrence Selden (Eric Stoltz) or anyone else, can save her from a doom she has been warming to all along.

Davies shows an immense affinity for Lily's troubled soul. The viciousness and glitter of beau monde New York in 1905—scrupulously re-created here—is filtered through her frightened awe. Davies pulls off some bravura sequences—including a series of majestic camera sweeps that take us in one long glissando from a vacant mansion to the prow of a yacht cutting through the waves—but the overall effect here is one of rapt stillness. This is dourness of a degree you won't find in Wharton, but in its own shadowed terms the film is a triumph. The darkness in Davies's conception allows the bloom of Gillian Anderson's face to come through. Her close-ups have the delicacy of a silent-film maiden's—the delicacy of someone who can't survive the world's harshness and yet lights that world from within.

NEW YORK POST 12/22/00, p. 55 Lou Lumenick

Mulder, we've got a problem. "X-Files" diva Gillian Anderson, in her first major non-Scully film role, is lethally miscast in this interminable version of Edith Wharton's all-too-ironically named drama of manners, "The House of Mirth."

Sure, the titian-haired beauty looks great in corsets as long-suffering socialite Lily Bart.

But as an actress she comes off, at best, as a truck-and-bus version of Julianne Moore, who would have lent some life, not to mention a little humor, to what turns out to be the most bloodless and least involving film about turn-of-the-century society since Merchant Ivory's "The Bostonians."

The blame isn't entirely upon Anderson, whose chilly Lily is a tough sell as a guy magnet.

The overrated British director Terence Davies ("The Long Day Closes") moves things along at a positively funereal pace. In his attempt to avoid the overstuffed cliches of period films, he goes for less than obvious casting chances.

Unfortunately, except for a chilling cameo by Laura Linney as a scheming adulteress, they don't work. Dan Aykroyd, Anthony LaPaglia and Eric Stoltz tend to confuse smugness for the emotional repression of an earlier era as they play the men in Lily's life.

It's New York of 1905 and Lily is a spinster of a certain age whose inherited money is fast running out. She needs a wealthy husband to maintain her social standing, so she brushes off the love of her life, a lawyer played by Stoltz.

She also parries, until it's too late, a social-climbing lawyer (LaPaglia), instead unwisely accepting "advice" from a piggish married financier (Aykroyd), at the eventual cost of her reputation.

Lily suffers a long and severe decline, reduced to going to work as a social secretary and worse. It all seems terribly inevitable, not to mention inconsequential.

"The House of Mirth" was produced by Showtime and a British network, and its spare period settings, though elegantly photographed, make it resemble an overgrown TV movie that's getting a theatrical run only because of Anderson's notoriety.

"X-Files" fans probably won't be able to resist, but those seeking a more satisfying Wharton adaptation are hereby warned to instead patronize their nearest video store for a copy of Martin Scorsese's sublime "The Age of Innocence." It's everything that this movie is not.

NEWSDAY, 12/22/00, Part II/p. B3, Gene Seymour

She materializes as if in a fairy tale through a sheer white curtain of steam. She is dressed in the billowy, corseted style of 100 years ago. You can't quite believe your eyes, but there she is: Agent Scully herself, Gillian Anderson of "The X-Files," all frills, linen and bunting, peering from beneath the broad brim of an extravagant hat, aiming her ice-blue eyes and bemused grin at Eric Stoltz and declaring, "Mr. Selden! What good luck!"

Watching this take place at the very start of "The House of Mirth," you're inclined to say to yourself, "There's no way."

But after two hours have passed, Anderson convinces you otherwise. More than that, she has shattered your emotional reserves and made her character's heartbreak your own. She's all but blasted away your TV-fed preconceptions and made you believe that she is, in fact, Lily Bart, the enchanting, principled and doomed heroine of Edith Wharton's 1905 novel about genteel barbarism among New York's moneyed classes.

Anderson's performance is—and should be—the centerpiece of writer-director Terence Davies' adaptation of Wharton's novel. It is by no means the film's only virtue. But such an audacious and unexpected triumph as Anderson's enhances everything around it. She seems to have internalized Wharton's character from beginning to end, and Davies, one of the great pictorial artists in contemporary film, has framed her portrayal with a vision as cool and as fierce as Wharton's own.

Lily, as those familiar with the novel will tell you, probably never had a chance, because she begins this story caught between two warring impulses. She is casting about for someone to marry. Yet while her head encourages her to find a well-to-do husband no matter how dull, her heart wants someone she can love. As the opening would indicate, she's drawn to Stoltz's Selden, a dashing, circumspect attorney who is richer with connections than he is with money. But they stay just out of each other's reach.

As wealthy prospects wander away to the altar with other women, Lily finds herself entangled, against her will, in some sticky imbroglios. One of which involves the oily husband (Dan Aykroyd) of her best friend, who pretends to be helping her financially but wants her for a mistress. Her rebuff helps ignite a savage process in which her reputation is painstakingly eviscerated within the New York aristocracy.

Lily is one of the most complex heroines in literature, as much a victim of her own misplaced integrity as she is of the jealousy and cravenness of her enemies. Anderson deftly conveys Lily's stubborn pride while evoking, mostly through body language, the fault lines in her poised self-assurance. As Lily's radiance gives way to bewilderment and despair, it is the implacable intelligence of Anderson's craft that illuminates her character's dark fate.

Davies, the British filmmaker responsible for such visually resonant pictures as "Distant Voices, Still Lives" (1988) and "The Long Day Closes" (1992), presides over a richly detailed production, its sense of place as sumptuous as any so-called "corset drama." But even as the drifting camera lingers and takes in as many sun-kissed landscapes as it can devour, you're more aware of the blunt, shadowy edges of this distant era than you would be in the average art-house period piece. If the past is a "foreign country," as L.P. Hartley once declared, then Davies clearly views it as hostile territory, booby-trapped with terrors cloaked in gentility.

SIGHT AND SOUND, 11/00, p. 53, Kevin Jackson

New York, 1905-7. Lili Bart, a young lady of slender means, arrives in New York and meets her friend Lawrence Selden, a bookish bachelor, who invites her to his flat. Leaving, Lily is spotted by rich businessman Sim Rosedale. Staying at the country retreat of friends Judy and Gus Trenor, Lily woos the wealthy but boring Percy Gryce, but he rejects her advances on learning of her gambling debts. Later, she and Lawrence kiss, although they skirt the issue of marriage. When staying at the country house of her aunt, Mrs Peniston, who pays her a modest allowance, Lily purchases letters which reveal that Lawrence had an affair with married socialite Bertha. On hearing of her money difficulties, Gus Trenor offers to invest Lily's savings, and introduces her to Rosedale, whose offer of marriage she refuses. Later, after he reveals he used his own money to augment her savings, Gus makes a move on Lily, which she angrily rejects. Gus then demands she pay back the money he invested for her.

Facing mounting debts, Lily joins Bertha and her husband George on vacation in Monte Carlo, not realising that Bertha is using her as a shield for an affair. Bertha then accuses her of seducing George. Outcast by her circle, left only a small sum when her aunt dies, and unwilling to use the incriminating letters to tarnish Bertha, Lily falls down the social scale, from secretary to drudgery in a milliner's to unemployment and chloral addiction. Bertha visits Selden and throws his letters into the fire. Using a loan from Rosedale to pay off her debt to Trenor, Lily takes a lethal dose of chloral; Selden—having retrieved the letters from the fire—discovers her body.

"The world is vile," murmurs one of Lily Bart's few loyal allies, Carry Fisher, as she reflects sadly on the cruel stupidity with which their social circle has cast out and is gradually destroying her young friend. In Edith Wharton's novel, it is Lily herself who speaks the line, but writer-director Terence Davies is wise to have changed it: it resonates in his film as a grimly impartial summing up, not as the personal grievance of a lady who has run out of luck. For the world of *The House of Mirth* is indeed largely vile, one in which the unprincipled and vigorously hypocritical, like Gus Trenor and Bertha Dorset, tend to triumph while the idealistic (Lily grows braver, less venal and more magnanimous as her worldly fortunes fail) are branded as immoral and ruined, unless cushioned, like Lily's lover Selden, by enough money and the appropriate chromosomes.

This beady-eyed view of the early 20th century's *nouveaux riches* (a rather different tribe from the Old New Yorkers of *The Age of Innocence*, but no less savage at heart) was Wharton's own, and Davies has preserved its astringent spirit in bringing it to the screen. It's rare that a period film, however seriously intended, doesn't fall at least half in love with its fancy frocks and immaculate crockery, but *The House of Mirth* is quite different. Though handsomely designed (by Don Taylor) and lovingly shot (by Remi Adefarasin)—there's one dissolve, from pellets of rain lashing the surface of a cold pond to the softly glowing waters of the Mediterranean, that's almost excessively gorgeous—it never loses sight of the fact that the pretty graces of this world are also, as it were, the trophies of barbarism.

Wharton was keenly interested in the writings of her contemporary Thorstein Veblen, the first sociologist to make the insolent comparison between the leisure classes and ancient warrior hordes; Veblen, one suspects, would have appreciated the unbeglamoured eye of Davies' film. Indeed, far from diluting the remorseless quality of Wharton's social tragedy with the familiar backward glancing nostalgia of most costume pieces, Davies has, if anything, accentuated its melancholy

A modest budget no doubt played the decisive part in having Lily walk on to the screen alone at the beginning of the film, rather than weaving her way through the afternoon crush of Grand Central, but the effect is more than apt: the image of Lily emerging from a cloud of railway steam evokes *Anna Karenina*, and hints proleptically at her sticky end. And when we arrive at that sticky end, Davies certainly out-does Wharton in bleakness: where the novel's heroine drifts off into a more or less accidental drugged sleep and the soothing fantasy of nursing a child, the film terminates in unambiguous suicide.

As with Davies' trilogy of autobiographical short films, there are sequences in *The House of Mirth* (the misleading title, taken from the Old Testament, was applied by newspapers to an insurance scandal of 1905) so gloomy they border on the excruciating; as in those shorts, the redemptive qualities here are eloquence, precision and grace. If Gillian Anderson's first scenes bear the inescapable trace of her role in *The X Files*, she rapidly sheds it. Apart from her un-Lily like inability to pronounce French words appropriately, she is not merely plausible but exceptionally powerful, and she makes Lily's final self-lacerating encounter with Selden horribly real.

Anderson more than vindicates Davies' idiosyncratic casting decision (as, in a different register, does Dan Aykroyd, whose smug violence as Trenor is miles away from anything he's shown on screen before), and lends both sympathy and dignity to a character who could too easily provoke—as she sometimes appears to provoke even in Edith Wharton impatience and scorn. Fine as she is, though, the film's finest quality is its typically quiet attentiveness to tone of voice, posture, nuances of facial expression Anderson proves herself a grand mistress of that most elusive look, the crestfallen. It's a remarkable, if sometimes harrowing adaptation: beautifully intelligent, intelligently beautiful.

TIME, 12/25/00-1/1/01, p. 148, Richard Corliss

Lily Bart (Anderson) has a knack for audacity. "My genius," she says, "seems to consist in doing the wrong thing at the right time." Men want to leave their fortunes to her, or their wives for her. But in old, moneyed Manhattan, sensation was more narrowly defined, more severely censured. Lily's charm is punishable by exile.

Edith Wharton wrote subtly withering novels of privileged folks whose moral myopia appalled her; she screamed in whispers. Lily is an affront to social order—the order of financial and emotional comfort. Her luck turns to ashes when she rejects love (Stoltz) for a betrothal that promises security. She must be reduced to poverty by an upper class tired of her coquetry and unaware of her special heroism in refusing to destroy a rival (Linney).

Men too can be scorned; Sim Rosedale (La Paglia), another of Lily's suitors, earns scowls because he was crude enough to earn his money instead of inheriting it. But Lily has no wealth to cushion her fall. Her old, sure sashay down garden paths is now a scurry along tenement streets; she is afraid of being seen by those who once were pleased to say they knew her.

Anderson plays Lily, handsomely, as a rare creature trapped under glass. The air thins; her breath shortens. And the viewer watches, appreciative of her plight, all but moved. The film is under glass as well. Davies, whose *Distant Voices, Still Lives* is a muted masterpiece, here is closer to *Masterpiece Theatre*, tastefully observing the glamour of social ruin.

VILLAGE VOICE, 12/26/009 p. 137, J. Hoberman

The stylized silhouette of doomed soubrette Lily Bart emerges from the steam cloud produced by a train just about to leave the station: From its opening shot, *The House of Mirth* is marked by a sense of tragic inevitability. The perfection of Lily's form, matched by her unperturbed perambulation, underscores the sense that she has just missed her moment—identified by a title as "New York 1905."

For much of this leisurely yet streamlined film, brilliantly adapted by British filmmaker Terence Davies from Edith Wharton's most powerful novel, the unfortunate Lily (Gillian Anderson) engages in an elaborate chess game. Addicted to the lifestyle of New York's wealthy smart set but financially dependent on a disapproving aunt, Lily is constrained by social rules as severe as any corset. Halfheartedly trying to make a wealthy marriage, she dallies with a confirmed bachelor of modest means, allows herself to be "compromised" by a married man, and is finally duped by an adulterous wife. For this, she is cast out by a society more than willing to say and think the worst of her and, in effect, destroy its most sublime creation.

The novel's title is sternly Old Testament—"The heart of fools is in the house of mirth"—and Davies's sense of the material is closer to a Mizoguchi geisha drama than *Masterpiece Theatre*. His *House of Mirth* depicts a prolonged martyrdom in which the heroine is tricked, abused, or betrayed by almost every character she meets. Wharton describes Lily as breathtakingly beautiful; Anderson, although attractive, is more striking than exquisite. Davies says she was cast for her looks, which reminded him of the society women painted by John Singer Sargent. In any case, the filmmaker plays down Lily's cleverness and vanity to emphasize her intelligence, honesty, and heartbreakingly imprudent naïveté. Anderson, who is present in virtually every scene, gives an unexpectedly stunning, perhaps behavioral, performance as a woman who is simultaneously overvalued and underestimated by the creatures who surround her.

The controlled overacting creates an ongoing *Pilgrim's Progress* effect in which each of the supporting players is characterized by one or two medieval humors. Eric Stoltz's worldly bachelor, Lawrence Selden, is supercilious and cowardly. The rest are brutes: Dan Aykroyd's predatory Gus Trenor is self-congratulatory and swinish; Laura Linney's Bertha Dorset is a viper so cool and dangerous she nearly eclipses her own sympathetic performance in *You Can Count*

On Me; Eleanor Bron's Aunt Julia is fearsomely unforgiving; Anthony LaPaglia's parvenu Sim Rosedale is suavely crass. (Davies tactfully erases Rosedale's ethnicity, expunging the taint of the novel's anti-Semitism and simplifying Wharton's more complicated social scenario.)

As the performances are boldly emblazoned, so the filmmaking is remarkably subtle. *The House of Mirth* is set in the first decade of the motion pictures, and like the earliest actualities, it's a feast of small sensations—a movie of gestures in which cigarette smoke hangs voluptuously in the air and a daring hint of Borodin ("This Is My Beloved") insinuates itself into a scene in which Lily actually proposes marriage to the supremely diffident Selden. The wide-screen mise-en-scène is superbly restrained; the colors are richly muted. Making strategic use of close-ups and studio process shots, Davies resists the idealizing soft-focus glamour or nostalgic ostentatious opulence of similar period adaptations to conjure up a stark turn-of-the-century New York from the Beaux Art buildings of contemporary Glasgow. It's no fetishized lost world, but one that is fiercely, uncomfortably present.

At the same time, *The House of Mirth* offers itself as an object of contemplation. The characters materialize into their scenes—a ghostly quality is accentuated by the movie's halo lighting. Emotion is rarefied. Action is oblique. The film's showiest transition begins by tracking through rooms full of covered furniture (closer to a canvas by Magritte than Sargent) and ends with summer rain in an empty garden dissolving to the sun on the Mediterranean Sea. Struggling uselessly against her fate, Anderson's Lily is a character who seems to be lucidly conscious as she sleepwalks toward the abyss and who manages to maintain her considerable social graces even as she tumbles in. The actress holds herself in reserve for her last scenes with Rosedale and Selden to devastating effect.

Poverty is the ultimate nightmare in this grimly material order. Perhaps the most Catholic of Anglo-Saxon directors, Davies stages the culminating act of Lily's martyrdom as a religious epiphany that, having absorbed the full impact of her lonely end, freezes into the painterly image marked "New York 1907." It is Davies's unswerving allegiance to the visual that raises *The House of Mirth* from tasteful literary adaptation to a full-bodied movie to set beside *The Magnificent Ambersons* and *The Life of Oharu.*

Also reviewed in:
CHICAGO TRIBUNE, 12/22/00, Tempo/p. 11, Mark Caro
NEW REPUBLIC, 1/15/01, p. 20, Stanley Kauffmann
NEW YORK TIMES, 9/23/00, p. B16, Stephen Holden
VARIETY, 8/14-20/00, p. 20, Derek Elley
WASHINGTON POST, 1/19/01, p. C1, Rita Kempley
WASHINGTON POST, 1/19/01, Weekend/p. 41, Michael O'Sullivan

HUMAN RESOURCES

A Shooting Gallery release of a La Sept ARTE and Haut et Court co-production. *Executive Producer:* Barbara Letellier. *Producer:* Caroline Benjo and Carole Scotta. *Director:* Laurent Cantet. *Screenplay: (French with English subtitles):* Laurent Cantet. *Director of Photography:* Matthieu Poirot Delpech and Claire Caroff. *Editor:* Robin Campillo and Stéphanie Leger. *Sound:* Philippe Richard, Jonathan Acbard, Antoine Ouvrier, Didier Leclerc, and Fabrice Conesa Alcolea. *Sound Editor:* Valérie Deloot. *Casting:* Constance Demontoy and Pascal Truant. *Production Designer:* Mat Troi Day. *Art Director:* Romain Denis, Caroline Bernard, Florent Maillot, Evariste Richer, and Loic Lemoigne. *Costumes:* Marie Cesari. *Running time:* 100 minutes. *MPAA Rating:* Not Rated.

CAST: Jalil Lespert (Frank); Jean-Claude Vallod (Father); Chantal Barré (Mother); Véronique de Pandelaère (Sylvie); Michel Begnez (Olivier); Lucien Longueville (The Boss); Danielle Mélador (Madame Arnoux); Pascal Sémard (Personnel Manager); Didier Émile-Woldemard (Alain); François Boutigny (Betty); Félix Cantet (Félix); Marie Cantet (Marie); Stéphane Tauvel (Christian); Jean François Garcia (François); Gaëlle Amouret

(Frédérique);   Marie-Laure Potel (François' Friend);   Patrick Baron and Patrick Pignard (Unionists); Jean-Pierre Dolinski, Olivier Bourguet, Jean-Jacques Abadie (Foremen);   Rufin Verliefde, Claude Verdier, and Emile Louis (Managers); Stéphanie Chevret (Secretary);   Anne Lebert (Alain's Wife); Annie Duval (Customer at Restaurant); Jean-Sébastien Cerdan, Frédéric Dubois, and Paul Gomis (Nightwatchmen).

LOS ANGELES TIMES, 9/15/00, Calendar/p. 10, Kenneth Turan

Work is a defining activity, a source of self-respect, the core of many people's lives. But when it comes to movies, filmmakers in this country mostly make believe work doesn't exist. Get lucky, get rich quick, take this job and shove it—that's more our style.

In Europe, where workers are either burdened or blessed (depending on your point of view) with much greater class consciousness, that's not the case. Directors like Ken Loach in Britain and the Dardennes brothers in Belgium understand how intrinsically dramatic working-class conflicts can be. "Human Resources," an effortless dramatic first theatrical feature from French writer-director Laurent Cantet, is very much in that tradition.

Saying a film deals with class disputes doesn't sound that exciting. But "Human Resources" defies that judgment by focusing on issues without shortchanging emotional connections. Concerned with fathers and sons, expectations and dreams, ideals and reality, this completely engrossing film gets more involving as it goes on. While it's clear which side it is on, it never descends into dogmatism.

The film's star, Jalil Lespert, is its only professional actor. The rest of the cast was selected by Cantet from unemployed individuals who in flusher times held the same kinds of jobs as their characters. They also participated in a certain amount of workshopping that Cantet and Gilles Marchand (who has a "written in collaboration with" credit) made use of in constructing the film's script.

Lespert plays a young man named Frank, introduced on a train ride from Paris to his native Normandy. A student at a prestigious business school, Frank is not only going home, he's going to spend the summer as an executive trainee in the same factory whose shadow he grew up in.

Now a part of an international conglomerate called Group TGT, the factory is filled with presses that stamp out sheet metal parts that couldn't be more anonymous. Frank's father (Jean-Claude Vallod), at his press 30 years, is proud of his ability to turn out 700 of these pieces an hour.

A taciturn, undemonstrative man, Frank's father is nevertheless proud of his son's success, his quickness and his ability to get on well with the factory boss (Lucien Longueville). Frank, too, with his open, easy-to-read face, is pleased despite himself at having risen in the world.

Not that there aren't problems. It's no longer seemly for Frank to eat with his old pals in the factory, and he finds himself irritated at his pre-biz-school friends. The way his parents whisper to each other in their own house so as not to disturb him while he works at home makes him feel understandably ill at ease.

Frank has chosen a study of a potential 35-hour-week for the factory as his project, a decision that exacerbates tensions. The workers are worried the new situation will cost jobs and mean more work for less pay. Mrs. Arnoux (a wonderful Danielle Melador), the factory's passionate Communist union representative, is especially scornful of the plan and Frank's role in it.

Sure of himself and what he can accomplish, Frank doesn't realize what the film carefully and thoughtfully demonstrates: that he's running the risk of outsmarting himself, and that a lot of areas he saw as black-and-white really exist in different shades of gray. When the ground is pulled out from under him, Frank has to choose where to stand, and that process is the heart of "Human Resources'" powerful drama.

NEW YORK POST, 9/15/00, p. 66, Lou Lumenick

This provocative French film looks incisively at a subject that's practically unknown in American movies—labor-management relations.

Jalil Lespert, the sole professional actor in the cast, plays a young business-school graduate who accepts an internship in the human resources department at the factory where his father (Jean-Claude Vallod) has worked for 30 years.

When he proposes polling the workers as part of negotiations for a restructured work week, senior management slyly uses the naive young man—and his connection with his father's colleagues—as a way to usurp the factory union.

He eventually learns to his horror that management's goal is to replace a dozen older workers—including his own father—with machines.

He's faced with a choice of going along with the plot to secure his own future with the firm, or exposing it out of respect for his father and his co-workers.

Though it gets rather talky, "Human Resources" has very involving, well-drawn characters, including Danielle Melador as a feisty union representative and Lucien Longueville as a honey-tongued supervisor with the heart of a viper.

NEWSDAY, 9/15/00, Part II/p. B6, Jan Stuart

Movies about labor unrest tend to be written off in America as too much of a busman's holiday: Who needs to spend one's leisure hours slogging through the muck of the workaday world?

It should come as no surprise then that a piercing film that touches the nerve endings of clock punchers everywhere should come out of France, a country well versed in the science of labor strikes and the art of socially alert cinema. Eschewing that country's fastidious attention to film aesthetics in favor of a straight-gazing reality, "Human Resources" is hardly what you would call a pretty-looking film. But it doesn't let us take our eyes off of it for a moment.

"Human Resources" is the canny writing/directing debut of Laurent Cantet, who employs a largely nonprofessional cast to relate the ironic tale of a young man who so successfully educates himself beyond his father's level that he inadvertently contributes to the shattering of his family's equilibrium. A business-school graduate basking in the glory of his academic triumphs in Paris, Frank (a winking name for a French protagonist if there ever was one) takes on a trainee job in the very heartland factory where his father has been manning the same machine for 30 years.

Superbly played by Jalil Lespert (the only professional actor in the cast) with a residue of smugness that keeps foaming to the surface despite his best efforts to keep it down, Frank charges confidently into the fray of a labor dispute over a 35-hour workweek. Shrugging off the combative union leadership, he initiates a referendum over the issue that divides an already suspicious work force as it pleases the top brass. When the results are manipulated by his boss to treacherous ends, Frank is forced to reconsider the role he has chosen for himself in this prickly class warfare.

Cantet uses the schematic setup to expose some difficult truths about the dance of dominance and submission carried out between administrators and their workers, as well as the negative effects of being educated out of one's class. "Human Resources" speaks potently to anyone with a parent who has made sacrifices for their children's own betterment, anyone who has ever had their wrist slapped for pulling rank, anyone who has ever made the soul-corroding choice of going along to get along.

The ensemble of nonprofessionals is amazing, so comfortable in the skin of their characters that their lines would seem to have been written with their own blood. Especially fine are Danielle Melador as the caustic union leader and the implacably walrus-faced Jean-Claude Vallod as Frank's father. When he is berated by a supervisor in front of Frank for shuffling on the job, it is all you can do to keep from crawling under your chair from the silent shame shared between a father and son.

SIGHT AND SOUND, 12/00, p. 50, Ginette Vincendeau

Normandy, the present. Frank, a young business-school graduate, starts work experience in the office of the factory where his father has worked all his life. Befriended by management, he is shocked by his father's meek attitude and by the combative stance of the Communist-backed CGT union, led by Madame Arnoux. Frank's brief is to study the introduction of the government's 35-hour week scheme. His idea to canvass workers' opinion by questionnaire is taken up by the managing director, but angers the union. Outside the factory, Frank alienates his childhood friends.

When a confidential letter informs him that management is about to fire 12 workers, including his father, Frank tells his family, Madame Arnoux and Alain, a young worker he has befriended.

At night, he and Alain print copies of the letter which they post over the factory entrance. After he is dismissed, Frank joins workers and the union in planning a strike. His father refuses to follow the strike, prompting a major row with Frank. At a picnic outside the factory gates during the strike, Frank tells Alain he is moving back to Paris.

Marked by a concern for social issues and notable for its pared-down naturalistic *mise en scène*, *Human Resources* offers a refreshingly unusual picture of France and of French cinema. While the film is a break from narcissistic Parisian petit-bourgeois agonising and gorgeous recreations of French heritage, *Human Resources'* tale of industrial strife in a Normandy factory does relate to the socially aware agendas of Young French Cinema, as seen in the films of Bruno Dumont and Erick Zonca, similarly set among the northern unemployed. But where Dumont and Zonca harness their interest in social matters to auteurist strategies, newcomer Laurent Cantet harks back to post-May 1968 documentaries (such as Marin Karmitz's collectively conceived *Coup pour coup*, 1972) and to the films of Ken Loach, to which *Human Resources*, predictably, has been predictably compared.

Cantet's self-effacing *mise en scène* foregrounds his attention to the social realm through unglamorous real locations (local cafes, the factory) combined with unflashy camerawork and a non-professional cast (with the exception of Jalil Lespert as Frank, a graduate on work experience in the factory) relying on mainly improvised dialogue. Unlike most social-fiction films (French poetic realism in the 30s, say, or Italian neorealism in the 40s), here the characters' status as workers is less a background detail, there to enliven essentially melodramatic personal conflicts, than the very subject of the film. This does not mean that *Human Resources* is without tension or drama: Cantet's film is classically structured, bracketed between Frank's arrival in his home town and his imminent departure, and there are obvious narrative devices, such as his confrontation with old school friends, the appearance of a secret letter and his sudden change of camps from management to workforce, signalled by his pivotal phone call to union organiser Madame Arnoux. Remarkably, Cantet is also able to build suspense into such mundane events as Frank's first day at the factory.

And underlying the whole story, of course, there's the generational conflict between Frank and his father, who has worked in the factory all his life. But here again this most universal of dramas is brilliantly shaped by the social mould: Frank's father has given him the means of elevating himself socially; but having achieved a measure of success, Frank has distanced himself from his father and his family. One of the achievements of the film is that we feel emotionally Frank's agonising mixture of pain, anger and shame at seeing his father's humiliation and, more damagingly, acquiescence in his own oppression, but we also understand the situation intellectually. The irresolvable nature of this socio-Oedipal drama is illustrated by the lack of reconciliation between the two at the end of the film (if there's ever a Hollywood remake, it will no doubt include a climactic scene where father and son express their love for one another).

More obviously, *Human Resources* dramatises the larger issue of the 35-hour week which has agitated France over the last year or so. The brainchild of Socialist politician Martine Aubry, it is often seized by management as an excuse to extract more from workers in less time, rather than for the stated (and genuine) aim of job creation; hence the grassroot opposition which the naive Frank is initially unable to grasp.

Cantet has rightly attracted a lot of attention for his accomplished handling of his mostly non-professional cast, especially admirable in a first feature. It is hard to know whether to praise Lespert for appearing as genuine as the rest of the players, or whether to praise the others for seeming as professional as Lespert. Jean-Claude Vallod, as the father, is heartbreaking without being sentimental, but Danielle Mélador as Arnoux is the standout, partly because of her natural acting ability, partly because she has the best lines, notably her great put-down to the management: "Perhaps you'd like me to be a capitalist."

Human Resources is not without its unsubtle touches. The personnel manager is a little too much of a caricature, and in real life young Frank is unlikely to have chosen to work in the same factory as his father. One might also query the choice of a black character to help Frank reach his true feelings (as a North African character did in Coline Serreau's *La Crise)*. Nevertheless, *Human Resources* is generous, sensitive and innovative. it is a film in which, in the widest possible sense, the personal is political.

VILLAGE VOICE, 9/19/00, p. 120, Amy Taubin

Restrained, tough, and subtle enough to be as engrossing on the second viewing as it was on the first, Laurent Cantet's *Human Resources* is a film that both Godard and Ken Loach might envy. It combines an eternally alluring subject—the father-son relations—with one that's a more difficult sell: blue-collar work and the conflict between labor and management.

Human Resources is set in a French factory town where the changeover to the 35-hour week (the real-life current event to which the film is hitched) has the kind of life-or-death urgency that Hollywood screenwriters are paid millions to invent. Frank (Jalil Lespert), an eager-beaver business school student majoring in "human resources," returns home for a management internship at the factory where his father has worked on the assembly line all his adult life. Frank sees himself as the embodiment of enlightened capitalism. He believes that workers and bosses can cooperate toward their mutual benefit, and that, as a worker's son, he's an ideal mediator. But when his pet project—a questionnaire about the 35-hour week—is used as a justification for laying off the oldest workers, his father among them, he burns his bridges with his boss by providing the feisty, unflappable union rep (Danielle Mélador) with enough evidence of management's duplicity to fuel a strike.

Caught between his ambition and his desire to save his father, Frank discovers a working-class consciousness he didn't know he possessed. His father, however, is far from pleased at his son's transformation. Totally identified with his job (he boasts with Stakhanovist pride that he can turn out 700 parts in an hour) and with the working-man ethos, the father nevertheless wants his son to have a better life. Seeing him lunching with the managers is both revenge and a vindication for a lifetime of swallowing shit—although he'd never admit as much to himself. And his own loss of livelihood troubles him less than the possibility that Frank has thrown away his career.

The father is played with remarkable nuance and vulnerability by Jean-Claude Vallod, a bulky but worn middle-aged man with stubborn eyes and a slightly pouting lower lip just discernible beneath his bushy mustache. Like all the actors in the film, with the exception of Lespert, he's a nonprofessional. Cantet filled his cast with workers whom he found in the unemployment office. Using a method similar to Mike Leigh's, he rehearsed with them for about a year before writing a final script based on the characters they developed through improvisation. Across the board, the actors perform with an intelligence and conviction that grows out of their real-life experience. It's an adage that acting is reacting; the most difficult thing for an actor is to react with mixed emotions and contrary desires. Cantet bases his editing scheme on reaction shots, and they draw us into the film by conveying much of what is left unsaid about the power structure that defines life in the factory and in the family.

Just as compelling and tangled as the connection between father and son is the friendship Frank forms with a black worker, Alain (Didier Emile-Woldemard), who's equally alienated but has more insight into the situation. Alain's able to make the case for Frank's father and the pride he takes in his job, so we're able to see him as more than a toady. And it's through him also that Frank comes to an understanding of his own outsider position.

Human Resources was shot on location in a Renault factory, and the actors operate the heavy machinery as only those who've done it for a living can. Like the Dardenne brothers' *Rosetta* and *La Promesse* (which also couples oedipal with class struggle) and Olivier Assayas's recent Cannes entry *Les Destinées Sentimentales*, *Human Resources* is part of a growing trend in French-language films to make work and the workplace a central concern.

Also reviewed in:
CHICAGO TRIBUNE, 9/15/00, Friday/p. I, John Petrakis
NEW YORK TIMES, 9/15/00, p. E10, Stephen Holden
NEW YORKER, 9/25/00, p. 101, Anthony Lane
VARIETY, 10/4-10/99, p. 87, David Rooney
WASHINGTON POST, 9/15/00, p. C1, Stephen Hunter

HUMAN TRAFFIC

A Miramax Films release of an Irish Screen presentation of a Fruit Salad Films production. *Executive Producer:* Renata S. Aly. *Producer:* Allan Niblo and Elmer McCourt. *Director:* Justin Kerrigan. *Screenplay:* Justin Kerrigan. *Director of Photography:* David Bennett. *Editor:* Patrick Moore. *Music:* Roberto Mello and Mathew Herbert. *Music Editor:* Kenny Clark. *Sound:* Martyn Stevens. *Sound Editor:* Glenn Freemantle. *Casting:* Sue Jones and Gary Howe. *Production Designer:* Dave Buckingham. *Art Director:* Sue Ayton. *Set Dresser:* Ed Talfan and Riana Griffiths. *Costumes:* Claire Anderson. *Make-up:* Tony Lilley. *Running time:* 84 minutes. *MPAA Rating:* R.

CAST: John Simm (Jip);   Lorraine Pilkington (LuLu);   Shaun Parkes (Koop);   Nicola Reynolds (Nina); Danny Dyer (Moff); Dean Davies (Lee); Peter Albert (Lulu's Uncle Eric); Jan Anderson (Karen Benson); Terence Beesley (Moff's Father); Sarah Blackburn (Jip's Ex #2);   Anne Bowen (Moff's Grandmother); Neil Bowens (Asylum Doorman); Peter Bramhill (Matt);   Jo Brand (Reality); Stephanie Brooks (Fleur);   Richard Coyle (Andy);   Carl Cox (Pablo Hassan);   Nicola Davey (Jip's Ex #3);   Roger Evans (Inca); Bradley Freegard (Tyler); Helen Griffin (Jip's Mother); Emma Hall (Trixi);   Elizabeth Harper (Jip's Ex #1);   Carol Harrison (Moff's Mother); Jennifer Hill (Jip's Secretary); Tyrone Johnson (Hip Hop Junkie); Justin Kerrigan (Ziggy Marlon);   Nicola Heywood-Thomas (TV Interviewer);   Nick Kilroy (Herbie);   Andrew Lincoln (Felix);   Howard Marks (Himself);   Robert Marrable (Casey); Louis Marriot (Cardiff Bad Boy); Danny Midwinter (Tyrone);   Millsy in Nottingham (Millsy From Roath);   Robbie Newby (Karen Benson's Boyfriend); Ninjah (Tom Tom's MC); Cadfen Roberts (Jip's Mother's Client);   Mad Doctor X (Koop's Workmate);   Phillip Rosch (Jip's Manager);   Jason Samuels (Bad Boy);   Mark Seaman (Jeremy Faxman);   Lynne Seymour (Connie); Patrick Taggart (Luke);   Giles Thomas (Martin);   Menna Trussler (Lulu's Auntie Violet);   Larrington Walker (Koop's Father);   Anna Wilson (Boomshanka);   Eilian Wyn (Doctor).

LOS ANGELES TIMES, 5/5/00, Calendar/p. 19, Kenneth Turan

"Human Traffic" was a huge hit in Britain last year. But unless young Americans are able to make an instant and unquestioning identification with its Cardiff, Wales, youth who live for weekends of drugs, dancing, clubbing and partying they may notice how generic everyone is and how the film rarely slips below its hard, flashy surface.

This 1999 debut feature of Cardiff's 25-year-old Justin Kerrigan is nothing if not derivative: "Trainspotting," "Saturday Night Fever" and even "Thank God, It's Friday" come swiftly to mind, along with a slew of British films dealing with young people stuck in dead-end jobs.

Starting the story in motion is Jip (John Simm), a clothing store clerk who pals around with lovely, blond LuLu (Lorraine Pilkington). Jip is sexually blocked because his loving mother is a prostitute. He sees LuLu as strictly a friend, but she may be viewing him differently. Jip's best friend, Koop (Shaun Parkes), a record store clerk with terrific selling skills, dreams of DJ stardom and is quick to become jealous over his girlfriend Nina (Nicola Reynolds), an inherently touchy-feely type, a would-be college philosophy major who abruptly quits her job at McDonald's.

This is the weekend she intends to introduce her 17-year-old kid brother Lee (Dean Davies) to Ecstasy; also part of this group is Moff (Danny Dyer), a bright, volatile kid constantly at war with his conservative family, especially his policeman father.

All these young people are formidably articulate, Moff and Jip in particular, and most of them are near-incessant talkers. (It's sometimes easy to overestimate British pictures because so many people in them have such a firm command of language.) They certainly do express discontent and angst with a ferocious profanity. Kerrigan constantly punctuates their remarks with vignettes depicting their thoughts, imaginings, fears and frustrations.

He is emphatically energetic: His film is constantly on the move at a frantic pace, music blasting away and with a flourish of camera trickery. The film is nothing if not frenetic, so much so that as it unfolds you start suspecting that Kerrigan is instinctively keeping everything revved up to keep us from noticing that what's going on is pretty inconsequential. For all their fulminations and passions, which occasionally are comical, these people are difficult to become involved with because there's really nothing very distinctive about them—which, ironically, may make it easier for audiences who are their contemporaries to project themselves into their lives.

Through Moff in particular, Kerrigan does suggest, if only lightly, that there can be a comedown with drug-taking, which he views as a recreational activity, a phase you outgrow along with the whole rave scene. It's possible to disagree with his view without getting indignant about it; since the film doesn't dwell on the actual taking of drugs you find yourself oddly more concerned by the young people's virtual chain-smoking.

Ultimately, it's not the hard living these young people are doing that's disturbing per se—after all, it's hardly uncommon—but that apart from some drug-induced highs, they may not be having as much fun as the film seems to be insisting they are. There's an underlying emptiness to "Human Traffic," and it's difficult to say for sure whether Kerrigan fully acknowledges it.

NEW YORK POST, 5/5/00, p. 52, Jonathan Foreman

"Human Traffic" is an attempt to make a "Saturday Night Fever" for Britain's "chemical generation" of rave-obsessed kids by crossing "Trainspotting" with the comic oeuvre of Woody Allen.

Though it contains some very funny, cleverly written comic sketches, "Human Traffic" shares with other drug movies the problem that watching other people on drugs is not interesting.

Set in Cardiff, Wales, the film follows five young friends over a weekend of pubs, clubs, drugs and sex.

All they share is a yearning for the artificial togetherness and empathy they get from ecstasy, or "E."

Although first-time writer/director Justin Kerrigan presumably intended otherwise, "Human Traffic" paints a remarkably unflattering picture of the rave-generation as aimless hedonists.

Nevertheless, it's basically a sweet-natured exercise, the music is terrific and Kerrigan shows off a mastery of stylistic tricks.

Among the effective, real-looking cast, Lorraine Pilkington stands out as a talent to watch.

NEWSDAY, 5/5/00, Part II/p. B7, John Anderson

For all the time-lapse, stop-time, fourth-wall-breaking, "Real World"-evoking, fantasy-indulging, drug-abusing, rave-exploring energy of Justin Kerrigan's "Human Traffic," it's really a very traditional movie.

Like every other teen flick, the main male, Jip (John Simm) and his "best mate," LuLu (Lorraine Pilkington) keep circling each other with amorous intent, without ever getting down to business (well, not exactly ever). The entire cast is stuck with McJobs they hate, parents they distrust, futures they fear. They take sales jobs and then whine because people treat them like clerks. Like its characters, the movie acts like it discovered sex and treats the subject accordingly.

Character-wise, it's not exactly a freewheeling group of spirits: Koop (Shaun Parkes) can't stop conjuring up images of his girlfriend Nina (Nicola Reynolds) with other men; Moff (Danny Dyer) drowns his lack of career opportunities in Extasy and phone sex; Jip is saddled with a severe impotency problem. Who'd they make this movie for? Bob Dole?

Director Justin Kerrigan uses archival footage (of riot police, at one point), climbs around inside his characters' heads and employs narration over frozen tableaux, all of which enables him to get by with no story at all (outside of the genital collision course embarked upon by Jip and LuLu). There's an interesting analysis of a drug party with some on-target portrayals of high people and their subsequent crash. Otherwise, the movie is more or less style run amok.

That one of the characters mentions "Trainspotting," from which Kerrigan lifts a great deal of technique, is, one supposes, the postmodern method of acknowledging that you're ripping off another movie. "Human Traffic," however, is really "Trainspotting Lite": The drugs are milder, the squalor is less squalid, and the characters are striving toward a solidly middle-class stability while being thwarted by an economy that views them as fodder. The likely complaint with this film, as it was with "Trainspotting," will be that amid all of the hedonism, there's no redeeming message. Which in fact there is: You can do what Jip, LuLu, Koop, Moff and Nina do, but then you'd be boring, too.

SIGHT AND SOUND, 6/99, p. 46, Xan Brooks

One wild weekend in present day Cardiff. Jip is a shop worker in his twenties, embarrassed by his prostitute mother and insecure after failing to perform sexually during several one-night stands. LuLu is a uninhibited club minx, and Moff a laid-back dope dealer on income support who deals from his home, despite the fact that his father is a policeman. Koop works in a record shop and is obsessively jealous of his long-term girlfriend Nina.

On Friday night, the five friends, together with Nina's younger brother Lee, drop the drug ecstasy and set off for the Cardiff club scene. When Moff fails to get a ticket into top club The Asylum for LuLu, Jip gives her his and blags his way in by pretending to be a journalist from *Mixmag* magazine.

Inside, Jip confides his sexual worries to LuLu. The gang move on to a party at a country home, and become progressively more stoned on various drugs. Returning to LuLu's house, Jip and LuLu have sex. Nina and Koop make peace, while across town Moff masturbates in his bedroom and is discovered by his mum. On Sunday, Jip takes flowers to his own mother. That evening, he and LuLu wander hand in hand through Cardiff's city centre as *bona fide* boyfriend and girlfriend.

On the face of it, the cinematic appeal of clubland is easy to see. It's loud, it's visual. Its dramatic landscape is a cauldron of surface emotions. The scene serves up a ready-made menu of free-loving youngsters, and is liberally garnished with an energetic contemporary soundtrack—sex and drugs and drum 'n' bass.

But first impressions can be deceptive. Film-makers who try to fit the essence of club culture into a dramatic straitjacket are liable to find it sliding through their fingers, because club culture like art, like music, like film itself—is an autonomous and organic mode of expression. The disciplines are mutually exclusive. Bernardo Bertolucci may have described his recent film *Besieged* as "a piece of chamber music," but it remained, basically, a film about chamber pianist. Likewise, while *Human Traffic* may arrive billed as "a blinding rave movie" (by *Heat* magazine), it is, rather, a film about ravers. Its formal attempts to duplicate the rave experience are far and away the picture's weakest aspects.

Human Traffic labours hard to look like a film under the influence. Edited in an amphetamine rush, its fly-on-the-wall dramatics are interspersed with Day-Glo fantasy sequences. The dialogue apes the kind of bumper-sticker soundbites you find in the "House Nation" vox pops inside *Mixmag* magazine (a publication to which the film shrewdly cosies up). Its lead characters often deliver their lines to camera, presumably in an attempt to break the division between screen and viewer, to usher us all into the filmic party. Meanwhile, spasmodic attempts are made to hook *Human Traffic*'s microcosmic shenanigans into a wider *Raison d'être* (cue a cameo from former drug dealer-turned-cult hero Howard Marks, newsreel footage of Direct Action protesters, plus an impromptu rendition of an "alternative national anthem" that must rank as one of the most excruciating scenes I've seen all year). Stylistically, *Human Traffic* is hardly radical. For much of its run, Justin Kerrigan's debut views like a cross between *The Monkees* and those snazzy commercials that building societies use to target young investors.

Kerrigan is more effective when keeping to the subtler, more human parts of his canvas. His portraits of the interrelationships between his five principles, for instance, are often beautifully done. Kerrigan has cited Richard Linklater as a major influence and in its best moments *Human Traffic* manages to match the airy rhythms of films like *Dazed and Confused* and *Before Sunrise*. These characters are wasted but likable; the performances (from the male trio of John Simm, Shaun Parkes and Danny Dyer in particular) are consistently charming. You have a sense that beneath all the bullshit, the strutting, the jockeying for position, they all genuinely love each other. Their self-conscious back chat frames real and deep-seated emotions.

Good acting gives *Human Traffic* its soul. If Kerrigan had given his players more room to breathe, one suspects, he might have produced something truly special. As it stands, *Human Traffic* unrolls as a frustrating hodge podge: its spine of authenticity overladen with so many ham-fisted gimmicks and gestures at cool that it irritates as much as it allures. In the end its reach exceeds its grasp. As a film about clubbers, *Human Traffic* rings sweet and true. As an essay on club culture in general, it feels half-cut: pure narcotic padded out with talcum powder.

VILLAGE VOICE, 5/9/00, p. 134, Amy Taubin

Sweet, ribald, and even inspired in an off-the-cuff way, *Human Traffic* provides a bit of a contact high—the kind where you're stoned and bored at once. First-time feature director Justin Kerrigan follows five twentysomething friends on a routine weekend of drugs, clubs, and mating games. Setting the film in his hometown of Cardiff, Wales, he makes his knowledge of the local club scene evident in every frame. Kerrigan establishes an intimate tone by having his characters introduce themselves directly to the camera. Jip (John Simm) is having a little impotency problem—maybe because of his troubled relationship to his mother, who's a prostitute, and maybe because he feels as if he's being screwed by the manager of the jeans shop where he works. Kerrigan literalizes the metaphor by having the boss stick it to Jip, herky-jerky from behind. The scene establishes how reality and fantasy will morph into each other for the rest of the film.

The plot, such as it is, involves Jip and his club mates: the promiscuous LuLu (Lorraine Pilkington), with whom he discovers true love before the weekend is over; Koop (Shaun Parkes), a black DJ with more enthusiasm than talent and an irrational fear that his adoring girlfriend, Nina (Nicola Reynolds), is lusting after other men; and Moff (Danny Dyer), who deals drugs from his home even though his father is a cop. The five start dropping Ecstasy on Friday night and don't come down until Sunday. Coming down is a bummer, but not bad enough to keep them from pledging to do the same thing the next weekend. What's most refreshing about *Human Traffic* is that it's not a cautionary tale.

Kerrigan edits the film as if amphetamines were his drug of choice, and his use of extremely wide or telescopic lenses combined with Day-Glo colors is pleasantly delirious. There are some amusing set pieces—an extremely explicit conversation about sex between the two girls and three opportunities to get inside the head of Moff, including an obsessive conversation with a taxi driver about Travis Bickle. Dyer is exceptionally vivid even when catatonically stoned. Focusing on its motley crew, *Human Traffic* isn't exactly a rave movie, since the club scenes are minimal. The movie is lively enough while it's going on; afterward, it's all a blur.

Also reviewed in:
CHICAGO TRIBUNE, 5/12/00, Friday/p. A, Mark Caro
NEW YORK TIMES, 5/5/00, p. E16, Elvis Mitchell
VARIETY, 6/14-20/99, p. 34, Derek Elley
WASHINGTON POST, 5/12/00, p. C5, Alona Wartofsky

HUMANITÉ

A Winstar Cinema release of a 3B Productions/ARTE France Cinéma/PRAV co-production with participation of CNC/Canal Plus/Procirep and aid from the Nord Pas de Calais region. *Producer:* Jean Bréhat and Rachid Bouchareb. *Director:* Bruno Dumont. *Screenplay (French with English subtitles):* Bruno Dumont. *Director of Photography:* Yves Cape. *Editor:* Guy Lecorn. *Music:* Richard Cuvillier. *Sound:* Jean Pierre Laforce. *Sound Editor:* Mathilde Muyard. *Casting:* Bruno Dumont and Claude Debonnet. *Production Designer:* Muriel Merlin. *Set Decorator:* Marc Philippe Guerig. *Special Effects:* Main Street. *Costumes:* Nathalie Raoul. *Make-up:* Férouz Zaafour. *Running time:* 148 minutes. *MPAA Rating:* Not Rated.

CAST: Emmanuel Schotté (Pharaon de Winter); Séverine Caneele (Domino); Philippe Tullier (Joseph): Ghislain Ghesquière (Police Chief); Ginette Allègre (Eliane, Pharoan's Mother); Daniel Leroux (Nurse); Arnaud Brejon de la Lavergnée (Conservationist); Daniel Pétillon (Jean, the Cop); Robert Bunzi (English Cop); Dominique Pruvost (Angry Worker); Jean Luc Dumont (CRS); Diane Gray and Paul Gray (British Travelers); Jean Beulque (Guide); Bernard Catrycke (Nadège's Father); Marthe Vandenberg (Grandmother); Amanda Goemaere and

Honorine Douche (Children);   Marie Thérèse Cadet and Denis Claerebout (Parents);   Suzanne Berteloot (Nurse);   Sylvie Perel (Domino's Friend);   Malik Haquem (Dealer);   Alain Beaufromé and Pierre-Olivier Thery (Pharaon's Colleagues); Frédéric Engelaere (Young Worker); Marie Hélène Aernout (Aline);   Lucien Hallynck (Man Wearing Beret);   André Geloen (Gardener); Jean-François Carpentier (Fisherman);   Théophile Boidin,   Jérôme Pollet, and Sébastion Muselet (Bathers);   Géry Laforce (Bus Driver);   Grégory Ryckewaert and Hamid Bouderja (Museum Technicians);   Stéphanie Wyts (Barmaid);   Philippe Duriez, Ivanne Duriez, and Alexis Duriez (Customers).

CHRISTIAN SCIENCE MONITOR, 6/2/00, p. 15, David Sterritt

The French drama *L'Humanité*, by Bruno Dumont, which was roundly booed by Cannes audiences—and promptly honored by the festival jury, which gave it the second-highest prize, as well as acting awards for both of its stars, neither of whom had appeared in a movie before.

At the heart of the brouhaha was the movie's unusual content. The main character is a provincial French policeman trying to solve the horrifying murder of a young girl. His investigation is drawn out over 2½ hours of aggressively slow cinema, culminating in a deliberately ambiguous ending that suggests the stubbornness of human sin and the possibility of spiritual transcendence.

Admirers find the movie a philosophical study in the manner of Robert Bresson, a towering French filmmaker with strong religious interests.

Detractors find it a bore, and a sexually graphic one at that. While critics have been divided over it, thoughtful commentators have commended the seriousness of its concerns even when they've found its pacing problematic and its acting less compelling than its festival awards suggest. It may irritate and even infuriate the American audience that's about to discover it, but it will give them plenty to think and talk about.

LOS ANGELES TIMES, 7/7/00, Calendar/p. 4, Kevin Thomas

Bruno Dumont, who made a standout debut three years ago with "The Life of Jesus," returns with "Humanite," in which he once again selects a quiet, small French town as the setting for a savage act of violence—in this instance the brutal rape and murder of an 11-year-old girl. In outline "Humanite" sounds like a classic policier, but Dumont brings such breadth and depth to its telling that it emerges a compelling contemplation of the interplay of good and evil, and of sexuality and violence.

So broad is Dumont's perspective that you begin thinking that the grisly act will serve as a grim metaphor for life's random cruelties. News of the death hits Pharaon de Winter (Emmanuel Schotte), a police inspector in a picturesque and town in northern France. Pharaon is a 30-something man with dark eyes of haunting expressiveness. He is in a state of anguished loneliness; we later learn he lost the woman in his life and their child two years earlier, perhaps in a difficult childbirth. Yet on occasion he can rise to a wistful smile.

He lives in a brick row house with his mother Eliane (Ginette Allegre), several doors from Severine Caneele's Domino, a young factory worker exuding a ripe sensuality. She is caught up in a red-hot affair with Joseph (Philippe Tullier), a rugged school bus driver. Our first impression is that Domino includes Pharaon in her dinners and outings with Joseph as an act of kindness to a man clearly still grief-stricken.

But Eliane senses that Domino, even though in the throes of an intense romance, is nonetheless drawn to her son. In comparison to Joseph, Pharaon seems all the more physically unprepossessing: homely and out of shape with poor posture. But Pharaon, a man given to long gazes and much reflection, has a capacity for gentleness and tenderness way beyond that of Joseph. Pharaon is smitten with Domino, and she knows it, yet you don't see anything, given the circumstances, happening between them.

What you do see is a man accepting his unfulfilled desires and a woman enjoying her sexuality to the fullest. Domino is not at all shy about making it clear to a man when she is attracted to him. Dumont is quite explicit about the sexual ecstasy Domino and Joseph experience with one another, but their relationship is primarily one of raw, uncomplicated sex. You begin to sense Domino sees in Pharaon the very qualities that Joseph lacks.

Just as Dumont is beginning to explore the distinction between sex and love, he brings us back to the rape-murder as Pharaon and his, superior, the local commandant (Ghislain Ghesquiere) proceed methodically with their investigation of a crime that revolts both; interrogations for them are as painful for those they question: parents and their children, who were the last known people to see the dead girl alive. The film's contemplative first part and its police-procedural middle then fuse in a powerful, extended conclusion in which we're confronted with an evil that Dumont suggests is beyond rational explanation.

Like "Life of Jesus," "Humanite" offers vast pastoral vistas and ancient streets, and their beauty sets off a depiction of everyday life that is routine, uneventful and soul-withering, just the sort of listless atmosphere in which sex and violence can converge joltingly. Within this context Dumont confronts the mystery and power of female sexuality, and the ways in which it affects men. "Humanite" surely must have been a most demanding experience for its flawless cast.

It is, in turn, demanding itself, resulting in a film of stunning impact.

NEW YORK POST, 6/14/00, p. 56, Hannah Brown

Maddeningly pretentious and often slow to the point of tedium, "Humanite" is also hauntingly original and truly strange.

It's a movie that should be seen by all film buffs, but avoided like the plague by anyone with a short attention span.

Using a cast of non-professional actors, French writer/director Bruno Dumont has constructed a twisty detective story with the menace and atmosphere of a dream.

Emmanuel Schotte plays Pharaon De Winter, a very dim police officer investigating the murder and rape of an 11-year-old girl in a working-class, rural town in northern France.

Pharaon, the grandson of a famous local painter whose name he bears, lives with his mother, having lost his girlfriend and baby in some kind of a tragedy that is mentioned but never explained.

He is infatuated with a neighbor, Domino (Severine Caneele), a tough, big-boned factory worker who lets him hang around with her and her boyfriend, Joseph (Philippe Tullier).

The extraordinarily passive Pharaon seems to disintegrate gradually throughout the film, raising the question: Is he simply disturbed by his horrible discovery of the girl's body in the opening scene—or is he the murderer?

The tension raised by this question rescues the film from its director's pretensions, which at times threaten to overwhelm the action, and adds much-needed suspense.

The ambiguous ending of "Humanite" generated a great deal of controversy at the 1999 Cannes Film Festival, where the movie won the Grand Jury prize as well as awards for Best Actor and Best Actress (Schotte and Caneele).

It may make you want to track down the director and shake him until he reveals who the murderer is, which he has repeatedly refused to do in interviews.

Even more disturbing than the ending is the lingering shot of the dead girl's bloody corpse.

But those with the patience to sit through "Humanite" will be rewarded with a complex story that will give them something to think and argue about long after most movies have faded from memory.

NEWSDAY, 6/14/00, Part II/p. B11, John Anderson

When the non-actor Emmanuel Schotte accepted his Best Actor prize at Cannes '99 for his work in "L'Humanite, " his nearly stupefied demeanor had members of the jury looking at each other in embarrassed amazement. "It wasn't an act," they seemed to be saying, before giving the movie the Grand Prix and Best Actress award as well.

While some people were livid about all this institutional gushing over Bruno Dumont's maddeningly elusive movie, some people, as they will be from time to time, were wrong. Composed with both a precision and a poetry, possessed of a cumulative emotional and psychological effect that might be termed extravagant, "L'Humanite" is a movie that's as fascinating in its singularity of intent as it is for its numbingly pretty French countryside. Triggering a hunger for something inarguably beautiful, it elevates us through disappointment.

While Schotte's unlikely police detective Pharaon DeWinter is an anti-hero—a morose sad sack who moves almost trance-like through the film—so is the movie an anti-film, at least in the sense of what we've been trained to expect from a tale of crime and punishment.

Only on its periphery does it seem concerned with the rape-murder of an 11-year-old girl, or the search for her killer. Likewise, there are several shards of character history that aren't given enough attention to even qualify as subplots. Pharaon has a peculiar third-wheel relationship with the promiscuous Domino (Severine Caneele) and her obnoxious boyfriend (Philippe Tullier), his unrequited lust for Domino being as strange as his habit of sniffing suspects for a sense of guilt.

While plot points orbit, "L'Humanite" mostly dwells in a sea trench of loss and desire, qualities as intangible as the film itself. Despite being about a murder, its melodramatic aspects are nil—when Pharaon and his superior (Ghislain Ghesquiere) visit the home of a witness, and the witness won't talk, they leave. Then their car won't start and Pharaon has to fix it. The center of the film is in the moments when nothing but everything happens, when its characters gaze off in mortified impotence and pure longing for—what? The cessation of pain? The onset of passion? Yes. And the other way around as well.

SIGHT AND SOUND, 10/00, p. 46, Tony Rayns

Bailleul, Flanders. Police lieutenant Pharaon de Winter's car radio summons him to an emergency: local schoolgirl Nadège Smagghe has been found raped and murdered. The town police station is too small (and de Winter's superintendent too incompetent) to cope with the case; the investigation is later taken over by officers from Lille.

Left two years earlier by his partner and their child, de Winter lives with his mother Eliane and dotes on his near-neighbour Domino, a factory worker in a relationship with bus driver Joseph. Aware of de Winter's feelings, Domino frequently invites him to join her and Joseph for dinners and excursions. The jealous de Winter often finds Joseph irritating, while Joseph considers the policeman boring. Eliane asks Domino to keep more distance from her son.

De Winter's enquiries focus on the school bus which dropped off the victim shortly before she was murdered, the Eurostar train which passes close by the crime scene, and the local mental hospital. Suddenly Joseph is arrested and held as the prime suspect. De Winter embraces him in custody and tries to console Domino. Some time later, though, it is de Winter who sits handcuffed in the superintendent's interrogation chair.

Bruno Dumont's follow up to La Vie de Jésus his 1996 study of boredom in a small town in northern France, is a virtual remake with an odder protagonist: the same unreadable landscapes, the same off-kilter film grammar, the same spasms of frantic sex, similar lonely and taciturn characters and similar dramatic situations (an adult son living with his irritating mother, a woman who startles her nervous admirer by proffering her vagina). Most of all, L'Humanite reprises the earlier film's quest for humanist warmth in a cold climate, again with secular spiritual implications. This time, of course, the film takes its overall shape and structure from a police investigation into a paedophile murder, but Dumont's indifference to both genre and the nuts and bolts of police procedure erases any narrative tension. The reason Pharaon de Winter is a cop is simply that it gives him a licence to stare at people and things.

Discussion of the film's causes and effects has to start from the unemphatic revelation in the penultimate shot that Pharaon de Winter is the target of his own enquiry—less an Agatha Christie twist than a perverse (or at least idiosyncratic) grace note. The denouement retrospectively makes sense of much of de Winter's eccentric behaviour, from his slowness in responding to the emergency call to his silent cry for help in front of a canvas of a little girl by his ancestor and namesake (a real-life painter of the late 19th/early 20th century) and his reaction to the idea that his 'rival' Joseph, the lover of de Winter's neighbour Domino, could be a scapegoat for the crime. But the first time viewer, unaware of the burden of guilt on de Winter's back, is presented with one of the most bizarre protagonists in film history: a slow-witted, inarticulate sad sack whose heightened emotional responses are always printed across his face, a man who confronts the world with a wide-eyed stare but sometimes turns utterly inward, apparently overwhelmed by his own thoughts and impulses. And even when the viewer knows the truth about de Winter, his inner life—and consequently many of his actions— remains unfathomable.

Midway through the film there's a strange scene in the police station. Left alone with an Algerian who admits to dealing drugs, de Winter clasps hold of the man, rubs the back of his head and presses his own face against the man's, nosing his cheek and neck as if trying to assimilate his 'evil'. The Algerian is left near-traumatised when de Winter breaks off and leaves. The only thing clear about the scene is that some kind of moral struggle is going on; whether it's between the two men, within de Winter or out there in the objective world is moot. It's the first concrete intimation of the film's underlying moral drama, although the drama itself remains teasingly abstract.

Thankfully, Dumont seems to realise that the scene could equally be read as an absurdist take on police interrogation techniques. And it later turns out that the scene has another function: it sets up de Winter's final scene with Joseph, which replays the physical action but with some important differences. Joseph has been arrested and is sitting despairing in the superintendent's office; de Winter comes in, expressing incredulity, and gives him the same treatment he gave the Algerian—with the supplement of an extended kiss on the mouth—before dropping Joseph back in the chair. Understandably baffled, Joseph seems to take this as an unexpected homosexual overture. For de Winter, though, it seems more like a benediction cum-leave-taking, a gesture which at last frees him to approach Domino, whom he dotes on.

There are no more answers here than there were in La Vie de Jésus, it's not even sure whether non-actor Emmanuel Schotté is giving an amazing, fearless performance as de Winter or simply being himself. Dumont amplifies the moral and spiritual questions through an editing syntax which robs the strong and very physical imagery—allotment flowers, human genitals, a sweat-soaked shirt collar—of its expected certainties: fades to black at moments when de Winter's problems are closest to the surface, point-of-view shots which fail to match the perspective of the gazer, cuts which link apparently disparate things. The overall project to construct an intellectual framework around the generally squalid lives of inarticulate working-class folk brings to mind the stance that Lindsay Anderson and his Free Cinema friends adopted in the late 50s and early 60s. But despite its portentous title, L'Humanité knocks films such as This Sporting Life (1963) off the screen. Shot entirely on location with a non-professional cast, it dares to go as far beyond 'realism' as The Matrix.

VILLAGE VOICE, 6/20/00, p. 149, J. Hoberman

Where Time Regained [see Hoberman's review] feels effortless and supple, the scarcely less ambitious Humanité makes a more muscle-bound bid for greatness. Bruno Dumont's outrageously deadpan police procedural—a scandal at the 1999 Cannes Film Festival, where it won second prize to Rosetta—flirts boldly with the ridiculous in bringing a Bressonian gravitas to life on the coastal plain of northeastern France.

Site of battlefields and massacres, this is a landscape to drive the peasants mad. Set in what could be the same bland red-brick town as Dumont's 1998 Life of Jesus—a place as tense and empty as an audition stage—Humanité exudes a similar sense of belligerent time-wasting. But where Life of Jesus was strong, classical filmmaking, a subtly stylized form of low-key naturalism, Humanité is more visually grandiose. For most of its two and a half hours, the film walks the line between the abstract and the concrete, opening with the tiny figure of the protagonist—an ununiformed policeman named Pharaon—running across the wide-screen windswept ridge. The images are bracingly crisp and sometimes, as when Dumont cuts first to Pharaon slipping in the mud and then to the violated corpse of a prepubescent girl, unforgettable.

Pausing periodically so that the frustrated Pharaon can observe the long, graphic sex scenes between his young friends Domino and Joseph, Humanité is confidently absurd. Pharaon rides a bicycle into the countryside, arrives home, chomps down on an apple, and, in more or less real time, begins retching into the sink. Is he simpleminded or merely sensitive? The detective's method for interrogating a suspect is to grasp him by the shoulders and sniff like a dog—which may be the way Dumont finds the extraordinary nonactors who populate his films.

Dumont's performers seem to have crawled from the margins of a Bosch painting, and thanks largely to them, Humanité is a movie of intense physicality. (It's the meta that's the matter.) Séverine Caneele, who shared the best-actress prize last year at Cannes for her uninhibited portrayal of Domino, is a big-shouldered girl with a jaw to match and eyes set deep in a Cro-Magnon brow. No less a human potato spud, Cannes best actor Emmanuel Schotte's Pharaon looks perpetually dumbfounded—as well he might be. *Humanité* suggests that the cop is, above all, searching for himself.

The inert thereness of Schotte's being and Caneele's body holds the screen, but the illumination of inner life is a flickering candle at best. As the filmmaker told the audience at the Toronto Film Festival, "All characters partake of the allegory." His own role is something like a cosmic caption writer. Unlike Bresson, Dumont burdens his creatures with announced significance and leaves them on camera to take the rap.

Also reviewed in:
CHICAGO TRIBUNE, 6/23/00, Friday/p. J, Michael Wilmington
NATION, 7/10/00, p. 44, Stuart Klawans
NEW REPUBLIC, 7/31/00, p. 26, Stanley Kauffmann
NEW YORK TIMES, 6/14/00, p. E1, Stephen Holden
NEW YORKER, 6/12/00, p. 110, David Denby
VARIETY, 5/31-6/6/99, p. 28, Lisa Nesselson
WASHINGTON POST, 8/18/00, p. C12, Stephen Hunter

I DREAMED OF AFRICA

A Columbia Pictures release of a Jaffilms production. *Producer:* Stanley R. Jaffe and Allyn Stewart. *Director:* Hugh Hudson. *Screenplay:* Paula Milne and Susan Shilliday. *Based on the book by:* Kuki Gallmann. *Director of Photography:* Bernard Lutic. *Editor:* Scott Thomas. *Music:* Maurice Jarre. *Music Editor:* Dina Eaton and Michael Higham. *Sound:* Clive Winter and (music) Jonathan Allen. *Sound Editor:* Ian Fuller. *Casting:* Pat McCorkle and Patsy Pollock. *Production Designer:* Andrew Sanders. *Art Director:* Ben Scott. *Set Decorator:* Maggie Gray. *Set Dresser:* Mark Joubert. *Special Effects:* Dave Harris. *Costumes:* Shirley Russell. *Make-up:* Caroline Noble. *Make-up (Kim Basinger):* Ronnie Specter. *Stunt Coordinator:* Jason White. *Running time:* 120 minutes. *MPAA Rating:* PG-13.

CAST: Kim Basinger (Kuki Gallmann); Vincent Perez (Paolo Gallmann); Liam Aiken (Seven Year Old Emanuele); Garrett Strommen (Seventeen Year Old Emanuele); Eva Marie Saint (Franca); Daniel Craig (Declan Fielding); Lance Reddick (Simon); Connie Chiume (Wanjiku); James Ngcobo (Luka); Joko Scott (Mirimuk); Sabelo Ngobese (Young Mapengo); Zacharia Phali (Mapengo, Early Teens); Nick Boraine (Duncan Maitland); Susan Danford (Esther Maitland); Ian Roberts (Mike Donovan); Susan Monteregge (Karen Donovan); Jessica Perritt (Lady Diana Delemere); Steven Jennings (Vincenzo); Patrick Lyster (Sven); Winston Ntshona (Old Pokot Chief); John Carson (Pembroke Headmaster); Shannon Esrechowitz (Siri); Michael Brosnihan (14-Year Old Charlie); Theo Landey (21-Year Old Sam); Nick Lorentz (Aiden Whittaker); Valeria Cavalli (Marina); Allison Daugherty (Luciana); Paolo Lorimer (Carlo); Federico Scribani Rossi (Roberto); Sophie Hayden (Gabriella); Giselda Volodi (Rachel); Daniela Foa (Maria); Nathi Khunene, Patrick Bokaba, and Dominic Dimba (Bandits); Ernest Ndlovu (Man in Boot); Patrick Mofokeng (Young Police Officer); Kenneth Kambule and Rayburn Sengwayo (Somali Poachers); Emma Vaughan Jones (3-Year Old Sveva); Dixie Cornell (Baby Sveva); Frances Slabolepzy (Hannah Maitland); Frances Nacman (Nurse); Nadine MaharaJ (Ema's Friend).

CHRISTIAN SCIENCE MONITOR, 5/5/00, p. 15, David Sterritt

Movies as different as "Out of Africa" and countless "Tarzan" epics demonstrate the perennial appeal that Africa holds for Western filmmakers. If you're going to tell a story with an African setting, though, it's best if you have meaningful ideas that help audiences understand the continent's multifaceted nature in new and useful ways.

"I Dreamed of Africa" falls this test by using the landscapes and inhabitants of Kenya not as subjects of intrinsic interest, but merely as picturesque backdrops for the sort of photogenic white characters that Hollywood almost always turns its attention to.

Based on real events, the story centers on Kuki Gallmann, a European woman who moves from Venice to Kenya with her husband and young son, faces more harrowing challenges than she ever expected, and ultimately decides to spend the rest of her life there despite the daunting experiences it has heaped upon her.

This is promising material, but the filmmakers focus so exclusively on their attractive heroine, played by Kim Basinger with more commitment than credibility, that the story loses any real connection with Africa beyond its value as a beautiful background and a source of jolting plot twists.

Among many other questions, alert viewers may ask why so few black faces are visible in a region populated mainly by black people—and why they're shoved into the margins of the screen when they do appear, the better to enhance the picture-perfect features of Basinger and company.

Moviegoers looking for exotic scenery and a good cry may find the picture enjoyable.

Others should wait for an African excursion that lives up to its title.

LOS ANGELES TIMES, 5/5/00, Calendar/p. 1, Kenneth Turan

Hollywood movies about Africa are available in both high- and low-culture varieties, and its refined, literary title alone signals that "I Dreamed of Africa" does not want to make common cause with the likes of "Africa Screams," "Africa—Texas Style!" and "Tarzan and the Slave Girl." Perish the thought.

Rather, director Hugh Hudson has constructed a reverential, forbiddingly genteel epic that makes as high-tone a film as "Out of Africa" play like "Zulu Dawn." This is a Laura Ashley on Safari meditation on bored rich people searching for fulfillment and a new life among the photogenic wildlife of Kenya. Just wake me when it's over.

"I Dreamed of Africa" is based on the memoir of the same name by a privileged Italian woman named Kuki Gallmann (regally played by Kim Basinger), who in reality doubtless led a very fulfilling life with her young son and new husband on a 100,000-acre cattle ranch called Ol Ari Nyiro.

But director Hudson (whose last adventure in Africa was the none too thrilling "Greystoke") and screenwriters Paula Milne and Susan Shilliday have, except for its uncharacteristic closing episode, leeched all the inherent excitement out of the situation. What's been substituted is reverence and awe, making for a film whose tone is so hushed it feels like it's been shot in a church. This is not so much bad as stodgy and emotionally uninvolving.

Basinger looks majestically beautiful as Kuki, a woman who apparently ages not at all (that African climate must be great for the skin), though her son grows so much that two actors are needed to play him. It's understandable why Basinger chose "I Dreamed of Africa" as her first part since winning a well-deserved Oscar for "L.A. Confidential," but it's still kind of a shame.

After a career doing solid work in not always memorable films, Basinger may have wanted to use her Academy Award clout to at last get a Meryl Streep-type role, to do something that positively reeked of class. While this may be her dream, as Africa was Kuki Gallmann's, the reality is that, as opposed to her wonderful performance in "L.A. Confidential"—where she really was a star—here she's simply acting the way she thinks a star should act.

Kuki is introduced as an aristocratic divorced mother in her native Italy, one of a group of posh high-society types who top off a Venetian night at the opera with a nightcap at Harry's Bar. In a trice, however, tragedy strikes, and Kuki simultaneously almost loses her life and gains a handsome and devoted admirer in Paolo (French actor Vincent Perez).

Not only is Paolo great with Kuki's young son, Emanuele (Liam Aiken), he shares with her both a restlessness and a fascination with Africa, a place her father always talked about and where he himself lived when he was younger. The suddenness of the potential move worries Kuki's mother (Eva Marie Saint), but Kuki has the perfect modern rationalization for her decision. "I've stopped growing," she says in complete seriousness, and no one has a comeback to that.

Kenya, the new family's destination, looks in Bernard Lutic's cinematography as beautiful as everyone hoped it would, and soon enough they settle into the African colonial-style equivalent of a fixer-upper, complete with devoted servants who conveniently happen to live in the neighborhood.

While Kuki keeps saying things like "I've never felt so alive" as her blond hair blows in the wind, life on the ground is a bit more than she anticipated. For one thing, husband Paolo begins spending most of his time drinking Scotch and hunting with his layabout pals in an I'll-never-grow-up evasion of responsibility. "Out there, there is just the moment, I need that," he whines to Kuki, and while she accepts this as the male equivalent of "I've stopped growing," audiences may be less tolerant of these self-centered antics.

Because Paolo is always gone, Kuki is forced to become increasingly self-reliant. Soon she is chasing off elephants, dealing with marauding lions, even palavering with local dignitaries in fluent Swahili. "I am surrounded by Africa," she says, turning into a veritable Mother Courage of the Great Rift Valley. "I am surrounded by life."

While, absent an investigation by Hurricane Carter's disaffected lawyers, one can presume all of this happened, that doesn't make it especially believable. Hudson's terribly earnest style robs everything of its reality, and immediately following a scene of a house nearly toppled by fierce winds with its miraculous repair doesn't help.

With lines like "Why does love cost us so much?," what we are left with is a "woman's plight" romantic fantasy for the bored and comfortable. The very things Kuki was looking for in Africa—adventure, emotional connection, the taste of life—are missing from the film about her. While "I Dreamed of Africa" does take a more serious turn in its final section, it's too late to do anything but discombobulate whatever portion of the audience has managed to remain awake.

NEW YORK, 5/15/00, p. 69, Peter Rainer

In *I Dreamed of Africa*, Kim Basinger plays the real-life Kuki Gallmann, who, in 1972, left her life of patrician privilege in Venice to settle with her husband (Vincent Perez) and young son in rural Kenya. In the beginning, the hardships are routine, but by the time a lion mauls the family dog, we're pretty sure things will only get worse. And do they ever. "Why does love cost us so much?" Kuki asks in one of her periodic inspirational voice-overs. We're supposed to see her sacrifice as the price one pays for finding meaning in life, but it's difficult to suppress the notion that she and her family would be a lot better off far away from all the poachers and puff adders. The film, lackadaisically directed by Hugh Hudson, never really makes it humanly clear what keeps Kuki going, but the African vistas are breathtaking—you were expecting otherwise?—and so is Kim Basinger, whose lily-of-the-valley loveliness is incandescent amid all the sun-baked earth tones. She gives Kuki's indomitability a poetic force; Africa for this woman is one long ravishment.

NEW YORK POST, 5/5/00, p. 52, Lou Lumenick

The beautiful but fatally vague "I Dreamed of Africa" reminds me of the oft-repeated line in "White Mischief," another, better, movie set on that continent: Every so often, a bored white colonist remarks (and I paraphrase slightly), "Another freaking beautiful sunrise."

I was starting to feel the same way about this film after two hours of stunning sunrises, sunsets and verdant vistas, shots that surpass even those in "Out of Africa," the 1985 Oscar winner.

But "Out of Africa," which was so bland I'd almost forgotten it, packs a dramatic wallop compared with the enervated storytelling in "I Dreamed of Africa."

Ace French cinematographer Bernard Lutic also sumptuously worships star Kim Basinger, whose hair and makeup are rarely less than perfect, whether she's operating a tractor, wading through mud, wrestling a python, or delivering hokey eulogies.

She's playing Kuki Gallman, who, after surviving a ghastly automobile accident that provides the film's only drama, moves to a remote farm in Kenya with her young son (Liam Aitken) and her new husband (Vincent Perez).

I've rarely seen a movie more evasive about its characters' nationalities (possibly because Gallman is Italian, an impossible stretch for all-American Basinger) or even when the action is taking place.

Hugh Hudson, who directed another overrated 1980s Oscar winner, "Chariots of Fire," helms his first major American film since 1985's disastrous "Revolution."

But he hasn't exactly made a stunning comeback. The movie drifts along aimlessly between scenic panoramas, almost entirely lacking in dramatic momentum.

Screenwriters Paula Milne and Susan Shilliday, adapting Gallman's memoirs, half-heartedly sketch in conflict between the heroine and her husband, who leaves her for days at a time to go hunting, and between Gallman and her mother (Eva Marie Saint), who's concerned with her safety and wants her to return to Italy.

The native African characters are so underwritten they're almost condescending.

Basinger doesn't have much to work with in her first movie since her Oscar-winning role in "L.A. Confidential," and there's absolutely no chemistry between her and Perez ("The Crow: City of Angels"), whose character is even more hazily conceived than hers.

"I Dreamed of Africa" ends up a nightmare of a star vehicle.

NEWSDAY, 5/5/00, Part II/p. B3, John Anderson

Watching "I Dreamed of Africa" might best be compared to looking through a photo album. A family photo album. Of someone else's family. The pictures may be postcard-pretty, the people, too. But the emotions connecting the images—and whatever narrative lay behind them—pose the kind of mystery that cries out for no solution whatsoever.

Which is too bad, I guess, because the eponymous memoir by conservationist Kuki Gallmann apparently has inspired any number of people, including producer Stanley Jaffe. His wife, Melinda (it is suggested by the Columbia Pictures press material), lobbied him for years to turn the 1991 book into a movie. And it shows: Any objectivity among the filmmakers about whether "I Dreamed of Africa" was effective as a drama, or even as a travelogue, seems to have been trampled under the elephantine enthusiasm the filmmakers seem to have had for the, uh, project.

We're betting on less enthusiasm among audiences who, if they've read the book, can probably fill in whatever blanks keep "I Dream of Africa" from possessing any fundamental substance. Otherwise, they'll be dreaming of Meryl Streep.

Instead, of course, there's Kim Basinger as Kuki, an ivory goddess framed by a dark continent—with all that suggests. Basinger is earnest and seems to have her heart in the right place as she brings Kuki along from her suffocating existence in decadently sumptuous Italy to the verdant plains of Kenya, to which she runs off with her young son and Paolo (Vincent Perez), the love of her life.

First, however, Kuki has to get by her let's-wear-Guccis-during-rainy-season mother, played by the infrequently seen Eva Marie Saint, who is not only the worst-lit person on screen, she has the worst lines. Maybe. "You're responsible for a child now," she informs Kuki, although the washed-out-looking child in question (Liam Aiken) is about 8 years old, so one assumes Kuki has been aware of his existence for some time. For Kuki's part, when she explains their upcoming move to Africa to young Emanuele, she tells the boy, "I've stopped growing." No "I Dreamed of Africa" is heroically directed by Hugh Hudson ("Chariots of Fire," "My Life So Far"), and one says heroically because Hudson is hamstrung by a script that strives to touch on every episode in Gallmann's life (or book) without knitting them into a coherent whole—something, in other words, to suggest why we should be interested. After all the initial struggles and tragedies catalogued in "I Dreamed of Africa," Gallmann was to become a fierce advocate for the preservation of elephants and rhinos, whose poaching is one of the film's more disturbing aspects (visually as well as philosophically). This might have made for a drama with actual drama. But the mundane crises of a new family in Africa are relatively trivial, which is why Hudson seems compelled to direct our emotional response to each minor triumph by having a character assume an arms-extended "Rocky" pose, or by pumping up Maurice Jarre's score.

Although Basinger takes the standard African movie attitude to its other extreme—rather than feel superior to every black African she meets, she seems to feel ridiculous—there's no escaping the feeling that, pre-Kuki, Africa never really existed.

"Why does love cost us so much?" Kuki asks. Better question: Why do movie tickets cost us so much?

VILLAGE VOICE, 5/9/00, p. 138, Dennis Lim

Another scenic quest for self-knowledge, [the reference is to *Up at the Villa*], *I Dreamed of Africa* bloats the real-life story of conservationist Kuki Gallmann to widescreen-travelogue proportions. After an accident puts Kuki (Kim Basinger, glazed and weirdly distant) in touch with her adventurous side ("Look at me," she implores, "I've stopped growing"), our heroine flees Venice for a ranch in Kenya, accompanied by her new husband (Vincent Pérez), her son from a previous marriage, and presumably a trunkful of beauty products. (Battling wild beasts, poachers, and natural calamities, Basinger's Kuki emerges fetchingly windswept and at worst a little flushed.) Confronted with the exotic majesty of Africa, Kuki doesn't exactly grow so much as attain a narcotic giddiness, scribbling awestruck journal entries (which Basinger delivers in an absurdly listless monotone). Similarly anesthetized, director Hugh Hudson keeps the movie rambling and episodic, deferring to the imposing backdrop whenever possible. He stirs from his slumber only when unfathomable tragedy strikes and the opportunity for manipulation presents itself-true to form for the director of *Chariots of Fire*. Reaching for grief then uplift, Hudson fails to understand that his film is by nature trivializing.

Also reviewed in:
CHICAGO TRIBUNE, 5/5/0, Friday/p. E, Mark Caro
NEW YORK TIMES, 5/5/00, p. E27, Stephen Holden
VARIETY, 5/1-7/00, p. 29, Emanuel Levy
WASHINGTON POST, 5/5/00, p. C12, Stephen Hunter
WASHINGTON POST, 5/5/00, Weekend/p. 47, Michael O'Sullivan

ICE RINK, THE

An Interama release of an Anne-Dominique Toussaint and Pascal Judelewicz production in association with Les Films des Tournelles/Les Films de l'Etang/Le Studio Canal Plus/RTL/TV1 and Fandango.   *Producer:* Anne-Dominique Toussaint and Pascal Judelewicz. *Director:* Jean-Philippe Toussaint.   *Screenplay (French with English subtitles):* Jean-Philippe Toussaint. *Director of Photography:* Jean-François Robin. *Editor:* Ludo Troch. *Sound:* Philippe Baudhuin and Xavier Griette.   *Casting:* Stéphane Zito.   *Art Director:* Javier Po.   *Costumes:* Claire Gerard.   *Make-up:* Kaatje Van Damme.   *Running time:* 87 minutes.   *MPAA Rating:* Not Rated.

CAST: Tom Novembre (Director);   Mireille Perrier (Assistant);   Marie-France Pisier (Producer);   Bruce Campbell (Actor);   Dolores Chaplin (Actress);   Jean-Pierre Cassel (Ice Rink Director);   Dominique Deruddère (Cinematographer);   Gilbert Melki (Stand-in for Actress);   Aleinikovas Pierre Belot (Banker).

LOS ANGELES TIMES, 7/21/00, Calendar/p. 18, Kevin Thomas

Jean-Philippe Toussaint's "The Ice Rink" is a trifle as delicate as a soap bubble. It's kept bouncing along by the whimsical wit of Toussaint, a noted French novelist, who celebrates the timelessness of visual comedy. In this regard it could not be a more fitting debut for Dolores Chaplin, the tall and lovely granddaughter of the great Charlie. The film is also a valentine to the demanding and unpredictable craft of making movies.

It is set mainly in a French ice skating rink, where a very tall director (Tom Novembre) is attempting to make a definitive sports opus, utilizing the actual Lithuanian ice hockey team. It also works in a star-crossed romance angle involving one of the skaters, played by a good-looking, self-important Hollywood actor named Sylvester (Bruce Campbell), who becomes smitten with an ill-fated beauty in a strapless red evening gown, played by Chaplin.

Just how the movie-within-a-movie plot works is wisely and amusingly never made clear, but we're told that the ice hockey team faces a sudden-death playoff that is somehow intended to serve as a metaphor for "Europe's predicament," whatever that means. In any event, the director is to turn out his opus with the speed of lightning because his anxious producer (Marie-France Pisier) is determined that it should be ready to make the deadline for entry into the upcoming Venice Film Festival.

A great deal of the humor, not surprisingly, grows out of trying to shoot a movie on ice, with men and machinery colliding into one another, and the film's crew struggling simply to stay on its feet. There's another complication as well: The director finds himself falling for his beautiful leading lady, maintaining a wistful silence, just as she embarks on a fling with her handsome co-star, who makes his seduction of her the first order of business.

In the meantime, Toussaint hints that the director's indefatigable and dedicated assistant Veronique (Mireille Perrier) could just be in love with the director himself. Also on hand constantly is the ice rink's debonair proprietor (Jean-Pierre Cassel), who loves to go on and on about his days as a figure skating star but is not so self-absorbed as to prevent him from making a pass at Pisier.

Everything pales, however, before the collective struggle to make Venice's entry deadline, which requires a hectic flight by helicopter to Rome, which has unintended consequences for a sword-and-sandal spectacular shooting at Cinecitta. Toussaint tips his hat to the unflagging dedication of the director and his crew, and while "The Ice Rink" records one calamity after another, it never slips up.

NEW YORK POST, 2/11/00, p. 56, Hannah Brown

A slight but amusing French comedy about making a movie, "The Ice Rink" will suffer from the comparisons that will inevitably be made to another film with a similar theme, François Truffaut's "Day for Night." While Truffaut's film was a masterful look at the movie-making process and the illusions that shape people's lives, "The Ice Rink," directed by Jean-Philippe Toussaint, is far more modest.

The running joke in this sweet-natured slapstick farce is that the director, the crew and even some of the cast can barely skate, so there are pratfalls galore. These are funny at first, but the joke soon wears thin.

For reasons never made clear, the director of the film-within-a-film (Tom Novembre), a pretentious, black-clad intellectual, has decided to make a movie using the idea of "sudden-death overtime" in a hockey game as a metaphor for a unified Europe.

But the movie he's making is also a love story starring Sylvester (Bruce Campbell), an American action star.

The female lead, Sarah, is played by Dolores Chaplin, granddaughter of Charlie Chaplin and Oona O'Neill.

Obviously enjoying herself in the role of a flighty young diva, Chaplin, who has the magical bone structure that runs in her family, takes the most charming spill on the ice, dressed in a gorgeous red evening gown.

Two veterans of French cinema make appearances here, Marie-France Pisier (the star of Truffaut's "Antoine and Colette") as the film's producer, and Jean-Pierre Cassel (who starred in Bunuel's "The Discreet Charm of the Bourgeoisie") as the manager of the ice-skating rink.

For movie-goers in the mood for a silly movie with a French accent, "The Ice Rink" will do the trick.

VILLAGE VOICE, 2/15/00, p. 126, Elliott Stein

Belgian cult novelist Jean-Philippe Toussaint's *The Ice Rink*, a droll and breezy but uneven comedy about the mishaps of a Parisian director as he shoots his new flick, is marked by a wryly heartfelt affection for the process of filmmaking. Its slim plot boils down to the protag's race against the clock to get his picture in the can in time for the Venice Film Festival. Our auteur (Tom Novembre) has to contend with a Lithuanian hockey team unaccustomed to the rigors of retakes, a temperamental leading lady who holds up production while she balls her egomaniacal Hollywood costar, and a klutzy French crew who get in everyone's way as they shoot a doc about the making of the film within the film.

A number of the gags are on target—in one memorably loopy turn, clueless Novembre lectures the Lithuanian hockey bit players (who don't understand a word of French) about Bresson's theories on the cinema. *The Ice Rink* is, however, plastered with pratfalls, and the amount of fun to be had watching people land on the ice on their butts is fairly limited. The film's strong suit is to be found in the interplay of its spirited international cast, including *The Evil Dead*'s hunky Bruce Campbell, perfect as the meathead from Tinseltown, and Dolores Chaplin (granddaughter of Charlie), fresh-faced and seductive as his ditsy prima donna. Two irresistible veteran French stars in supporting roles, Jean-Pierre Cassel (the doddering rink owner) and luminous Marie-France Pisier (producer of the film within the film) are icing on the cake.

Also reviewed in:
CHICAGO TRIBUNE, 2/18/00, Friday/p. Q, John Petrakis
NEW REPUBLIC, 2/21/00, p. 28, Stanley Kauffmann
NEW YORK TIMES, 2/11/00, p. E15, Stephen Holden
VARIETY, 5/10-16/99, p. 64, Dennis Harvey

IDIOTS, THE

A USA Films release of a Zentropa Entertainments2 presentation of a Zentropa Entertainments2, ApS, and DR TV Danish Broadcasting Corporation production in co-production with Liberator Productions S.a.r.l./La Sept Cinéma/Argus Film Produktive/VPRO Television, Holland/ADF/ARTE with the support of Nordic Film and Television Fund/COBO Fund, Holland in collaboration with SVT Drama/Canal+ (France)/RAI Cinema Fiction/3 Emme Cinematografica. *Executive Producer:* Peter Aalbaek Jensen. *Producer:* Vibeke Windelov. *Director:* Lars von Tier. *Screenplay (Danish with English subtitles):* Lars von Trier. *Director of Photography:* Lars von Trier. *Editor:* Molly Malene Stensgaard. *Sound:* Kristian Eidnes Andersen and Johan Winbladh. *Casting:* Rie Hedegaard. *Production Designer:* Lene Nielsen. *Running time:* 115 minutes. *MPAA Rating:* R.

CAST: Bodil Jorgensen (Karen); Jens Albinus (Stoffer); Louise Hassing (Susanne); Troels Lyby (Henrik); Nikolaj Lie Kaas (Jeppe); Henrik Prip (Ped); Luis Mesonero (Miguel); Louise Mieritz (Josephine); Knud Romer Jorgensen (Axel); Trine Michelsen (Nana); Anne-Grethe Bjarup Riis (Katrine); Paprika Steen (High-Class Lady); Erik Wedersoe (Svend, Stoffer's Uncle); Michael Moritzen (Man from Sollerod Municipality); Anders Hove (Josephine's Father); Jan Elle (Waiter); Claus Strandberg (Guide at Factory); Jens Jorn Spottag (Boss at Advertising Agency); John Martinus (Man in Morning Jacket); Lars Bjarke, Ewald Larsen, and Christian Friis (Rockers); Louise B. Clausen (Rocker Girl); Hans Henrik Clemensen (Anders, Karen's Husband); Lone Lindorff (Karen's Mother); Erno Muller (Karen's Grandfather); Regitze Estrup (Louise, Karen's Sister); Lotte Munk (Britta, Karen's Sister); Marina Bouras (Axel's Wife); Julie Wieth (Woman with Two Kids); Kirsten Vaupel, Lillian Tillegreen, and Brigitt Conradi (Art Class Ladies); Albert Wickmann (High-Class Man); Peter Froge (Man in the Swimming Pool); Bent Sorensen (Taxi Driver); Jesper Sonderaas (Svendsen at Advertising Agency); Ditlev Weddelsborg (Severin at Advertising Agency); Iris Alboge (Qualified Carer).

LOS ANGELES TIMES, 6/23/00, Calendar/p. 6, Kevin thomas

"The Idiots" suggests that if Danish iconoclast Lars von Trier's films are getting tougher, they're also continuing to reward the patient.

It is yet another film made according to the rules of Dogma 95, the Copenhagen film collective that insists on location shooting, direct sound, hand-held cameras, no camera trickery, no superficial action sequences, no use of genre, no black-and-white film, no special lighting. The director is not supposed to be credited, but how could von Trier be considered anything but an auteur? (That's like Ingmar Bergman famously describing himself as anonymous as an artisan helping build a medieval cathedral.)

A pretty though worn-looking young woman, Karen (Bodil Jorgensen), is sitting alone at a tastefully upscale restaurant, apparently somewhere in suburban Copenhagen, when an obstreperous young man Stoffer (Jens Albinus), seemingly retarded, grasps her wrist as his companion Susanne (Louise Hassing) tries to usher him out. He won't let go, and Karen, for good reasons of her own, is not in a fighting mood.

This is how she ends up with a group of young people occupying an elegant but vacant villa with beautiful grounds not too far from the restaurant.

We're thrust in medias res into a group of 11 people that's formed a kind of makeshift commune dedicated to sending its members to public places pretending that they are retarded and sometimes also somewhat physically disabled. (They call what they do "spassing about.")

There's no getting around that many audiences will be offended by such behavior, but the group's intent is not to insult those physically or mentally challenged in any manner of degree but, rather, to disturb middle-class types as much as they possibly can.

Much of this behavior is unexplained, repetitive and seemingly pointless, but eventually where the film is going becomes clearer. There is a great deal of improvisation of the unselfconscious kind, and all 11 of the film's principals clearly must have reached deep within themselves to make so powerful an impression on the screen.

Whether this "spassing about" actually accomplishes much for those the group targets is debatable, it clearly begins to show positive effects upon members of the group. In trying to stir up others out of their complacent, conventional existences, the group finds it has lots of fun making mischief. Its people start getting in touch with themselves and each other. People begin triggering authentic emotions in each other, yielding moments of tender bonding in the face of an increasingly technological society that tends to isolate individuals from each other.

The venture, so informal, so provisional in nature, is just not designed to last—it's more in the nature of an experiment than a totally committed way of life, despite the insistence otherwise of Stoffer, its natural leader. When a man, cold and determined, arrives to take home with him the daughter who had been experiencing schizophrenic behavior but now seems calm and content, the group begins breaking up, almost inevitably.

The time in short has come for these people to test their "inner spass"—to see whether they can hold on to the changes they feel within themselves when they reenter "normal" life. Gradually, the focus returns to Karen, as Susanne accompanies her back to the life she dropped out of so abruptly and, as it turns out, so understandably.

A film that has seemed rambling to the point of numbness has, in fact, already begun unobtrusively to gather focus and build tension and suspense as Karen, more significantly than all the others, approaches her moment of truth.

Interestingly, rather than cut his film to avoid the dreaded NC-17 rating, von Trier simply blacked out genitals in the film's more frolicsome moments, which actually works as an amusing critique of censorship.

NEW YORK POST, 4/28/00, p. 53, Jonathan Foreman

The most remarkable—and shocking—thing about "The Idiots" is the disgustingly hypocritical way it was censored by the Motion Picture Association of America.

Though the film still contains plenty of full-frontal female nudity, director Lars von Trier was forced to remove all male genitalia or be penalized with an NC-17 rating, so he responded by putting black boxes over the offending parts.

Aside from the ludicrous sight of waggling black boxes, the film is a tedious, pretentious bore.

It's about a commune of loathsome young Danes who try to make some kind of Dada-ist point about bourgeois complacency and heartlessness by "spazzing"—or pretending to be retarded—in public places and in the suburban house where they live.

These "idiots" are ultimately shown to be obnoxious, but the film adores their prankishness.

It's shot according to the "Dogma vow of chastity": hand-held cameras, natural light, etc., in faux-documentary style, and much of the dialogue seems to be improvised.

If you make it through this all but unwatchable exercise, you may find it hard to believe that the same filmmaker did "Breaking the Waves."

NEWSDAY, 4/28/00, Part II/p. B7, John Anderson

Given that he'll be debuting his big-budget, Bj"rk-powered musical "Dancer in the Dark" at the Cannes Film Festival next month, auteur-provocateur Lars von Trier seems to have permanently left the church of Dogma '95, whose spartan commandments he and a handful of disciples have followed oh-so-loosely, in a fit of pique against Hollywood artifice.

Finding a parallel between Dogma and "The Idiots"—in which a group of young Danes rebel against their uptight society by acting like morons—is certainly easy enough, if not quite that simple. Purposely ephemeral, built on a foundation of crashing insignificance, the film has the rough texture of any Dogma film: handheld camerawork, natural lighting, no incidental music, a narrative devoid of melodrama. But "Idiots" also makes a pretty effective statement about societal priorities, the power of cults, the obsession of converts and the discomfiture of the comfortable.

"Searching for their inner idiot," von Trier's communal performance artists—emotionally bookended by the militant Stoffer (Jen Albinus) and the fragile Karen (Bodil Jorgensen)—practice drooling idiocy in public places. Karen is, at first, merely an innocent witness to one of their performances in a restaurant; but by exposing herself—by helping people whom she thinks are genuine mental deficients—she initiates her journey into public embarrassment.

We, of course, are meant to be made uneasy—and are—by both the reactions of the group's victims, and our own reactions. Fittingly, though, the group cannot ultimately make the crossover that Stoffer demands, that they go back to their normal lives and continue "spazzing." They can't do it, except for Karen, whose revealed history turns "The Idiots" completely around, from something extraordinarily trivial into a story of epic sadness.

What's less sad than idiotic is the awkward black-masking of the male nudity that occurs when the group dynamic shifts into group sex. (Female nudity? No problem.) But such inadvertent irony is just a bonus in "The Idiots," which in its efforts to avoid an NC-17 rating is no longer just a cry against sanctimony but an example of it.

SIGHT AND SOUND, 5/99, p. 50, Xan Brooks

Denmark, the present. A timid woman named Karen joins a band of "idiots", able-bodied students and dropouts who play-act being mentally impaired. Led by Stoffer, and based at his uncle's vacant and for-sale suburban home, the idiots (Susanne, Henrik, Jeppe, Ped, Miguel, Josephine, Axel and Nana) test the town's attitudes to the disabled. They take trips to local restaurants, factories and swimming baths. When prospective buyers visit the house, Stoffer introduces them to the idiots in order to sabotage any hope of a sale. The band functions like a religious cult and members are tested on their committment to the cause. When the local council offers to rehouse the idiots, Stoffer flies into a rage. To cheer him up, the housemates organise a "spass party" in his honour which culminates in group sex. The next morning, the frail Josephine is forcibly 'rescued' from the group by her father. Stoffer concludes that the point of his experiment lies in individuals' ability to return to their outside lives and "spass" there, so the group disperses.

Karen returns to her family's apartment with Susanne. Once there, Susanne learns that Karen ran out on her relatives and her husband Anders after the death of her infant son. Over tea and cake, Karen starts to "spass" and Anders hits her. Karen and Susanne leave the apartment together.

The second film to be released under the Dogma 95 code of conduct, The Idiots is a curious and haphazard creature, more daring thematically than Thomas Vinterberg's gripping but essentially conventional Festen yet more wild and woolly too. From its opening title (rendered as chalk marks on a parquet floor), this essay in social deviance positively wallows in semi-contrived amateurism. Writer-director Lars von Trier has stated that the principal purpose of both Dogma and The Idiots is to allow film makers to relinquish artistic control, and make a push towards an ideal dramatic state that's closer to camcorder voyeurism than to the sanitised gloss of mainstream cinema. So The Idiots breaks away from the formal precision its creator showed in his previous feature, Breaking the Waves, and adopts a guerrilla aesthetic. Von Trier's baby jives to a rhythm of jump cuts, using ill-focused camera movements (handheld, naturally) and scene changes that arrive abruptly, unheralded by audience-friendly establishing shots. At one point a boom microphone's shadow chases the characters up a sunlit gravel drive. Fluffed lines and technical gaffes are proudly flaunted. The whole thing runs on a kind of whoops!-accidentalism.

All of which would surely turn *The Idiots* into the cinematic equivalent of ready-ripped jeans were it not for the fact that the film's form fits so snugly with its content. The picture's opening half views like nothing so much as a dramatic (and X-rated) extension of such downmarket, fly-on-the-wall television shows as *Candid Camera* and *Beadle's About*. It functions like a controlled social experiment, a hard-and-fast study in behavioural science. The opening scenes find von Trier's group of middle-class youngsters running amok through straight society, "spassing" or playing the "idiot" to tease, test and bait the 'normal' people they encounter. They gorge themselves on a free meal at a chichi restaurant, disturbing their fellow diners in the process. They are ushered around an insulation plant by an accommodating factory foreman. At a busy local swimming pool, the vixenish Nana (Trine Michelsen) bares her breasts, and ringleader Stoffer (Jens Albinus) sprouts an erection in the communal showers. Unsettled by these antics, new recruit Karen (Bodil Jorgensen) initially views them as cruel student japes, a way of getting at people. "You poke fun," she comments disapprovingly.

Throughout its second half, however, *The Idiots* grows more layered and contemplative. The dubious shenanigans of its opening minutes become the raw data for a wider thesis. While the simple thrill of transgression seems to be the appeal for many of the idiots (Nana in particular), others prefer to regard themselves as a band of renegade anthropologists striving for a new Utopia. Pocket-demagogue Stoffer contends that, "idiots are the people of the future," and claims that the point of his experiment is the "search for the inner idiot". In this way, the characters' embrace of idiocy is portrayed as a blend of druggy transcendence and primal-scream therapy. The previously sceptical Karen reverts to murmuring infancy in a swimming-pool sequence that's shot to look like a new dad's video recording of a water birth. Later Josephine (Louise Mieritz) and Jeppe's (Nikolaj Lie Kaas) spass love-making shifts imperceptibly from play-acting into a fumbling real-life union. (Josephine's subsequent removal from the group—by her father who claims, "she is seriously ill"—further blurs the lines between phoney mental instability and the real McCoy.)

The trouble is that in following this dictate through to its logical conclusions, von Trier pilots his film into a tricky cul-de-sac. On its most basic level, *The Idiots* pushes a message that idiocy equals the inner-child; that real mentally handicapped people represent an unsullied human essence, people who operate at the business end of their emotions: who love, fight, fuck and eat without regard for social etiquette. Dramatically, this is fraught with problems. On the one hand, it risks sentimentalising the mentally impaired, conjuring them into generic emblems of saintliness. This, incidentally, looks to be a recurring pitfall for von Trier. *Breaking the Waves* employed Emily Watson's guileless heroine as a sacrificial lamb, while his generally masterful serial *The Kingdom* suffered from the use of a Down's syndrome couple as a visionary Greek chorus within the narrative.

More crucially, *The Idiots'* inner-child message is a banal and well-worn one. Within US cinema, in particular, it has run down the years as a more sugary variation on the *Rebel without a Cause* (1955) template. In modern times it has found its perfect expression in the oeuvres of Jim Carrey and Robin Williams, two actors who have carved a profitable niche playing wild and wacky buckers of convention. Frustratingly, *The Idiots'* final scenes reveal von Trier at his most conservative. The genuinely unstable Josephine finds spiritual balm from play-acting the idiot (before being torn away by her authority-figure dad). The broken and tragic Karen exorcises the ghosts of her past by spassing during a tense encounter with her estranged family. While never vacuous or feel-good, this closing segment annoyingly attempts to tie *The Idiots'* diffuse and colourful threads into a uniform little bow. But as a nominal embrace of chaos, this is—ironically—too neat, too secure. It undoes a lot of the raw-cored disorder which came before.

Ultimately, *The Idiots* emerges as a truly fascinating folly, an all-but-impenetrable muddle with glimmers of genius running from top to tail. Von Trier claims he wrote it at speed (four days) and shot it at a sprint in order to pin down that butterfly spirit of improvisation, of tumult, that is *Dogma 95*'s lifeblood. This undeniably results in a film of crazy-paved surfaces and deep puddles of ambiguity. But what it also does is offer an X-ray of its creator's ideals and aesthetic. Von Trier sets up his laboratory, ignites his chemicals and watches them burn. But try as he might to distance himself from his experiment, there remains a strict methodology to his madness:

man's moral code is unbreakable, it hungers for dramatic resolution, reasserting itself at the finish. The result is less a filmic revolution than an Aesop's fable for anarchists. In its dying moments, *The Idiots* cleans off the cum and transgresses to a purpose. It all ends tidily.

VILLAGE VOICE, 5/2/00, p. 125, J. Hoberman

Publicity, as all good modernists should know, is the lifeblood of any successful avant-garde. It may be a bit of a stretch to term the refurbished, mock-militant neorealism of Dogma '95 a vanguard, but the movement cofounder and best-known exponent, Danish bad boy Lars von Trier, is nothing if not an impressive self-promoter.

Dogma's restrictions—no tripods, no background music, no artificial lighting, no special effects—may be less a serious polemic than a canny branding gimmick. The so-called Dogma Brothers' "Vow of Chastity," allegedly dashed off by a giggling von Trier in half an hour, reinforces its author's position as European cinema's most relentless stunt-meister in the several decades since Werner Herzog was hypnotizing the cast of *Heart of Glass* or schlepping a steamboat through the rain forest for *Fitzcarraldo*.

The main thing that distinguishes Dogma's vaunted realism from that of cinema verité is the presence of actors. Hence von Trier's most notorious provocation to date, finally opening here nearly two years after it grossed-out half the Cannes Film Festival, is a self-reflexive jape. *The Idiots* is a movie about acting... out. Operating under some obscure philosophical imperative, the youthful members of a Copenhagen commune confound the local bourgeoisie with a form of dada guerrilla theater, engaging in wildly regressive, sometimes disgusting behavior in public places—what they call "spassing."

Von Trier pushes beyond punk paeans to pinheads and cretins to stage the comic spectacle of adult normals drooling, thrashing, disrobing, and otherwise mimicking the extreme agitation of the mentally disabled. On one hand, this politically incorrect telethon run amok is a further development of the Down's syndrome chorus that von Trier employed in *The Kingdom* or even his heroine's sexually "idiotic" behavior in *Breaking the Waves*. On the other hand, it's the essence of Dogma theatrics. The last two Dogma films to open in New York, Harmony Korine's *julien donkey-boy* —shot, like *The Idiots*, on video—and Soren Kragh-Jacobsen's *Mifune* , both trade heavily on the entertainment value of having actors play morons.

Designed to provoke laughter at the unlaughable, *The Idiots* opens with a manifestation in which some communards harass the patrons of a genteel restaurant while others pretend to be their embarrassed caretakers. The scene directly addresses the very issue of table manners, which anthropologist Claude Lévi-Strauss famously saw as the bedrock of civilization; it also provides the commune with an ongoing foil. Thanks to their performance, the idiots pick up a lonely diner named Karin—a strategy that drops this viewer-surrogate in the midst of various infantile antics as they stage a field trip to a factory or invade a public swimming pool.

For the most part, the idiots resemble a gaggle of untalented Harpo Marx imitators. Meanwhile, a dogged wet blanket, Karin keeps trying to understand the meaning of what they are doing. (Their vaguely '60s ideology is never really explained, although as semi-serious performance artists, the group holds postmortem discussions complete with psychobabble references to their "inner idiots" and earnest manifestos like "Idiots are the people of the future.") Von Trier, who is credited as director of photography, further ups the ante by shooting the movie in a documentary frenzy of smear-pans and camera-flails.

The filmmaker can occasionally be heard offscreen asking questions, and the fictional nature of his film is further complicated by several pranks that seemingly involve innocent bystanders, as when the idiots go door-to-door in a wealthy neighborhood attempting to sell their homemade, hilariously stunted Christmas ornaments. There is also a birthday gang bang, which to judge from *The Idiots'* early reviews, included actual penetration. The U.S. release print obscures this by employing floating black rectangles (often ridiculously outsize) to conceal the actors' genitalia. This outlandish discretion is but one of *The Idiots'* old-fashioned elements. Von Trier uses the orgy as a prelude to a more tender—if scarcely less regressive—one-on-one love scene. (The corniness is further compounded when one participant's father shows up to take her home, explaining that she's a real schizophrenic gone off her medication.)

Von Trier's elaborate metaphor for filmmaking was itself the subject of a feature-length documentary, Jesper Jargil's *The Humiliated*—also a Dogma project, shot like most of *The Idiots* with a digital camcorder—aptly described by its maker as "a day in von Trier's puppet theater." I caught *The Humiliated* (shown last fall in the Walter Reade's Danish series) before seeing *The Idiots*. Then it seemed an effective teaser for von Trier's film; now, it appears that, in promoting the documentary, the master may have upstaged himself.

Like *Burden of Dreams*, the Les Blank account of Werner Herzog's travails in the jungle making *Fitzcarraldo*, *The Humiliated* is more powerful than the movie it documents—as well as more successfully Dogmatic. Including most of *The Idiots'* key scenes (without added fig leaves) and more, *The Humiliated* makes clear that von Trier's film was a pretext to make something happen in life as much as on film. Jargil includes not only audio tapes of von Trier's on-set rantings but the spectacle of the artist's idiocy, directing without his trousers and convulsed with laughter at his own mischief.

Ending amid the detritus of the shoot, *The Humiliated* strongly intimates that *The Idiots* was a failed experiment. Of course, von Trier suggests as much with his own ending. Having failed to re-enter society as idiots, the commune breaks up—only to discover, in a scene of quiet horror, that, liberated by example, their little fellow traveler is the greatest idiot of all. In the fiction of the movie, life trumps art; in the reality of the film, however, it is precisely the reverse.

Also reviewed in:
CHICAGO TRIBUNE, 9/22/00, Friday/p. F, Michael Wilmington
NATION, 5/29/00, p. 35, Stuart Klawans
NEW YORK TIMES, 4/28/00, p. E14, A. O. Scott

IF YOU ONLY UNDERSTOOD

A First Run/Icarus Films release of a Luna Llena Producciones production. *Producer:* Rolando Diaz and Ileana Garcia. *Director:* Rolando Diaz. *Screenplay (Spanish with English subtitles):* Rolando Diaz. *Director of Photography:* José Manuel Riera. Editor: Jorge Abello and David Baute. Sound: Jorge Luis Chijona. *Running time:* 87 minutes. *MPAA Rating:* Not Rated.

CHRISTIAN SCIENCE MONITOR, 1/7/00, p. 17, David Sterritt

[*If You Only Understood* was reviewed jointly with *Life is to Whistle*; see Sterritt's review of that film.]

NEW YORK POST, 1/7/00, p. 44, Hannah Brown

Two recent Cuban films opening today at the Walter Reade Theater present an intriguing and at times surprising portrait of contemporary life in that country.

"If Only You Understood," the more affecting film of the two, is a documentary that tackles the controversial issue of racism in Cuba.

A kind of Cuban "A Chorus Line," the film details director Rolando Diaz's struggle to cast a black woman for the lead in a musical he plans to make.

He doesn't actually have the money to make the musical yet, he explains, but he wants to get a cast together, and so he assembles a group of 10 young women who want to he dancers and singers, each more beautiful than the next.

As they rehearse and tell their stories, compelling characters emerge, as does a sense of Havana and its decay. There's Joanni, a model with looks to rival Naomi Campbell's, who lives in a small, rundown apartment with her parents, siblings and grandmother (who disapproves of her risqué nude shots).

The unemployed Anais, abandoned by both parents as a child and raised by her grandmother, is sullen and threatens to quit the show, in spite of her talent. Ivette, an engineer trained in the former Soviet Union, nevertheless lives in grinding poverty and would like to give musical comedy a try.

All these young women complain that black actresses are rarely given a chance in the theater and hint at a more subtle but insidious form of racism that clouds their daily lives,

Interviews with passersby, who are asked to suggest a plot for the musical, give a sense of the fascinating racial diversity of Cuba, and of the disappointment and bitterness many of its citizens feel towards their government.

"Life Is to Whistle," the story of three friends from an orphanage whose lives intersect on the Day of Santa Barbara (also known as the African Saint Chango, believed to rule destinies), starts out promisingly but soon loses focus.

It's narrated by Bebe (Bebe Perez), an 18-year-old orphan who whistled before she learned to speak.

Bebe tells about Mariana (Claudia Rojas), a sensual ballerina who makes a vow of chastity when she is given the starring role in a production of "Giselle," and Elpidio (Luis Alberto Garcia), a charming con artist who contemplates leaving Havana with a German environmentalist who has fallen in love with him.

In a particularly heavy-handed bit of symbolism, the mother who abandoned Elpidio is named Cuba. Told in the magic-realist style favored by many Latin American authors, the film has a few lyrical moments but gets bogged down in fuzziness and lazy plotting.

After seeing "If Only You Understood" and learning a little about the realities of life in present-day Havana, it's hard not to become frustrated with the whimsy of "Whistle."

NEWSDAY, 1/7/00, Part II/p. B9, John Anderson

To exiled nationals and recidivist Marxists, Cuba is the home to either the Antichrist or the Last Defender of the Faith. The rest of us think of it—when we've thought of it recently—as the once-and-future homeland of 6-year-old Elian Gonzalez, the birthplace of the 80-odd-year-old Buena Vista Social Club, and the object of decades-old presumptions that should be altered by two Cuban films guaranteed to brighten the gray days of January.

"If You Only Understood" and "Life Is to Whistle" are very different from each other, but they share a surprisingly frank attitude about life in current-day Cuba. There's no articulated loathing of Fidel Castro or his woefully failed experiment—the filmmakers likely couldn't go that far even if they chose to—but neither is there any sugarcoating of the island's problems. Both films are remarkably frank about the difficulties of Cuban life, remarkably affectionate about it, too, and remarkably artful about doing what they do.

At the beginning of "If You Only Understood" (the title comes from a well-known Cuban song), director Rolando Diaz makes a confession that should rankle the ranks of nonfiction filmmakers everywhere: Although he wants to make a movie, a musical, he says, "I don't have a theme, resources, or actors...so I decided to make this documentary." His objective, however, is provocative, somewhat subversive and—almost inadvertently—totally charming. Passing on professional performers, he seeks out his actresses and dancers on the street, interviewing women who are mostly untrained—as well as unvarnished, uncensored and unafraid—drawing out their histories, hopes and resentments, and painting a sort of sidelong portrait of Cuba that looks behind the tattered-but-intact facade of the besieged, embargoed nation. Racism, for instance, is revealed to be a hugely influential factor in Cuban life (a contradiction of the popular image). So is an almost casual acceptance of poverty and its byproducts, such as prostitution.

The women, all of whom are introduced with Diaz' sobriquets—Alina the Party Girl, Joanni the Model, Anais the Unemployed, Ivette the Engineer—are the shining stars of the film, flawed but substantial women who in their conflicted lives and struggle for survival are totally real, thoroughly endearing.

"Life Is to Whistle," on the other hand, is a mischievous, allegorical fantasia that mixes magic realism, sex, Freud, Santeria and Catholicism in telling its three-sided story about self-defeat and, only indirectly, the plight of individuality under a Castro regime. The sylph-like Mariana (Claudia Rojas), a dancer in love with movement and men, makes a vow of celibacy to Jesus if she can only dance "Giselle." Elpidio (Luis Alberto Garcia) is a small-time hustler pining for the mother who demanded too much and then abandoned him (her name, symbolically enough, was Cuba). Julia (Coralla Veloz) is an aide in a senior home who has trouble staying awake and faints when she hears the word "sex." The hub of these three human spokes is an orphanage where all their stories were once joined; that they get back to that point is less interesting than the fluid and (defensively) facetious manner in which director Fernando Perez gets them there without overtly criticizing Cuba, religion or sexual conservatism.

It's a crafty dance, done with a great deal of musicality, existentiality and affection.

VILLAGE VOICE, 1/11/00, p. 112, Elliott Stein

Both the Cuban-Spanish coproductions in the Reade's "Love Letters to Cuba" program are simpatico and engaging. Fernando Perez's *Life Is to Whistle,* a striking blend of absurdist humor and mystical magic realism, is the more formally adventuresome of the two. The story of three Havana loners, it's narrated by teenager Bebe (Bebe Perez), who pops up throughout the film in a number of odd locations, often underwater. Two of these characters are Bebe's buddies from the orphanage where she was raised; the third, a frustrated nursing home employee, has a crush on her shrink and faints whenever she hears the word "sex." Her tale is entwined with that of Elpidio (Luis Alberto Garcia), a dreadlocked petty thief with an Oedipus complex, who steals money from women tourists and falls in love with one of his marks, a Greenpeace marine biologist who has dropped into town on a balloon. Nymphomaniac ballerina Mariana (Claudia Rojas), the most intriguing of the group, gets her comeuppance when, after making a vow of chastity to the Virgin in exchange for a career break, she's given the lead in a new ballet and promptly falls in love with her hunky partner. The lives of this angst-ridden trio finally intersect on the day of the African saint Chango, ruler of destinies.

Perez's film is shot through with loopy charm and handsome, often oneiric visuals, inspired by Magritte. The exhilarating musical score of Bola de Nieve and Benny Mord goes far to soothe away the heartaches.

Rolando Diaz, who lives in self-imposed exile in the Canary Islands, had plans for a musical set in Havana, but the deal fell through. Instead, he made *If You Only Understood,* a "dramatized documentary" about the casting call for a fictitious musical that requires a young black actress for its lead. Ten candidates are interviewed and they all discuss their lives at length, including racism, poor housing, and unemployment. It's a gutsy flick; these subjects are not often publicly discussed in Cuba. It's also mostly a relentless—and somewhat repetitious—talking-heads affair that would have been twice as effective at half its length.

Also reviewed in:
CHICAGO TRIBUNE, 1/28/00, Friday/p. I, John Petrakis
NEW YORK TIMES, 1/7/00, p. E26, Stephen Holden
VARIETY, 3/22-28/99, p. 38, Leonardo Garcia

I'M THE ONE THAT I WANT

A Cho Taussig Productions and Vagrant Films release of a Cho Taussig Productions production. *Executive Producer:* Margaret Cho and Karen Taussig. *Producer:* Lorene Machado. *Director:* Lionel Coleman. *Screenplay:* Margaret Cho. *Editor:* Robyn T. Migel. *Music:* Joan Jett and The Blackhearts. *Director of Photography:* Lionel Coleman. *Editor:* Robyn T. Migel. *Sound:* Michael Emery. *Sound Editor:* Glenn T. Morgan. *Production Designer:* Ron Barker   *Set Decorator:* Christian T. Andrews. *Running time:* 96 minutes. *MPAA Rating:* Not Rated.

WITH: Margaret Cho (Herself).

LOS ANGELES TIMES, 8/4/00, Calendar/p. 21, Kevin Thomas

"I'm the One That I Want," a deftly made concert film from Margaret Cho's acclaimed one-woman show, the comedian recalls the dramatic and improbable ups and downs of her life and career with scabrous humor.

She emerges as a triumphant survivor, a veritable poster girl for the painful process of self-discovery, acceptance and affirmation.

Raised in San Francisco by Korean immigrant parents who ran a bookstore on Polk Street, Cho grew up repressing her urge to perform, told by her parents that an Asian girl had no chance in show business.

Rebelling at 16, Cho began her career in stand-up. Years later, she found herself starring in TV's first Asian American sitcom, "All American Girl," only to be ordered to lose weight and listen to a consultant on how to be "more Asian."

When the short-lived series was canceled, Cho was so overcome by a sense of failure, she nearly lost her life to drink and drugs until she hit rock bottom and began the long climb back to her roots, regaining the voice—i.e., identity—her erstwhile boyfriend Quentin Tarantino told her she was losing, and emerging as the vibrant, pleasingly plump, healthy-looking woman she is today at 31.

In telling her story with a darkly hilarious, ultra-raunchy sense of humor, Cho repeatedly impersonates her mother with great affection as she looks back on family life and pays tribute to the gay community in whose midst she grew up and which has supported her steadfastly. Identifying herself with other minorities (whose members she mimics outrageously), Cho shatters racial and sexual stereotypes with merciless wit.

"I'm the One That I Want" was filmed unobtrusively and judiciously by Lionel Coleman while Cho was in performance at San Francisco's venerable Warfield Theater last November. At the end of its local premiere last week, Cho appeared in person, telling an appreciative audience that she made her film "for people who feel they don't belong."

NEWSDAY, 8/4/00, Part II/p. B6, Gene Seymour

By the time Margaret Cho's autobiographical, one-woman performance piece, "I'm the One That I Want," rolled into her home town of San Francisco for this filmed record, it had made Cho into the nationwide phenomenon that she and many others hoped she'd become when her ill-fated ABC-TV sitcom, "All-American Girl," premiered just six years ago.

Yet, as many times as Cho has done this show, which played 11 weeks Off-Broadway and toured in 40 cities, one can't help but hear the tripwire of pain that jostles Cho's voice ever so slightly as she mimics the network executive who told the Korean-American comic that her "face was too fat" for TV and that she had to lose weight if she expected her series to last.

It's a tiny tremor in a performance that makes you laugh a lot more than cry. Yet it's more than enough to show how some scars stay red and raw no matter how much time they're allowed to heal.

In a way, part of the fascination of watching "I'm the One That I Want" comes in seeing Cho running several laps ahead of the agony stalking her life after that sweet moment when she became the first Asian-American to star in her own weekly TV comedy show. That moment came, Cho tells her audience, on Mother's Day—an occasion that allows her to bring out one of her signature characters: her mom, whose depiction throughout this act is broad, outrageous and leavened with tenderness. (As is much of the show.)

Everything, Cho says, went downhill from there. She went on a crash diet to please the network and had to be hospitalized. (Her depiction of an overbearing nurse is one of the few riffs in the film that gets driven beneath the ground.) She also agreed to let the network bring in experts to help her become "more Asian"—until, predictably, someone decided she was "too Asian." The show collapsed within a year from the weight of such specious tinkering, and its failure left Cho stricken with depression and a near-suicidal addiction to drugs and alcohol.

It's 'the kind of story that would sound maudlin and narcissistic by half if it weren't for Cho's vibrant, shrewd sense of self-deprecation and—most important—her stinging digressions into the socio-cultural stereotyping of Asians and, for that matter, the "weight-challenged," that contributed to her debilitating self-doubt. Some only grasp at linking the personal with the political. Cho is one of the few who pulls it off.

Comparisons made with Richard Pryor and Lenny Bruce should be carefully withheld, however. "I'm the One That I Want" is an impressive testament to struggling with and triumphing over personal demons. But I'd like to see where Cho takes this reassembled self of hers before I'm ready to place her among legends.

VILLAGE VOICE, 8/8/00, p. 140, Dennis Lim

Purposeful with a vengeance, Margaret Cho's one-woman show belongs to the environmentally friendly branch of celebrity self-exploitation that repackages gruesome showbiz-carnage details as cathartic, inspirational, celebratory confessionals—therapeutic and rehabilitative in one fell swoop. Relying heavily on Cho's twin specialties—race and fag-haggery (she's better on the former than the latter)—and on detailed accounts of the sleazy network games that thwarted her 1995 sitcom, *All-American Girl*, the no-frills stand-up movie *I'm the One That I Want* (or *I Will Survive*, or *I Am What I Am*) has a respectable laugh-to-cringe ratio. But Cho's tendency to attenuate jokes (she repeats punch lines and derails them with bouts of face-pulling) gets in the way of some of her wittiest material, and the time-outs from wisecracking—invariably, to impart a simplistic self-esteem lesson or two—feature the most awkward silences you're likely to endure in a comedy routine.

Also reviewed in:
CHICAGO TRIBUNE, 8/11/00, Friday/p. D, Allan Johnson
NEW YORK TIMES, 8/4/00, p. E22, Stephen Holden
VARIETY, 7/10-16/00, p. 25, Dennis Harvey

IN CROWD, THE

A Warner Bros. release of a James G. Robinson presentation of a Morgan Creek production. *Executive Producer:* Jonathan A. Zimbert and Michael Rachmil.   *Producer:* James G. Robinson. *Director:* Mary Lambert.   *Screenplay:* Mark Gibson and Philip Halprin. *Director of Photography:* Tom Priestley.   *Editor:* Pasquale Buba.   *Music:* Jeff Rona.   *Music Editor:* Brian Richards.   *Sound:* Steven R. Smith and (music) Alan Meyerson.   *Sound Editor:* Michael E. Lawshe.   *Casting:* Pam Dixon Mickelson.   *Production Designer:* John Kretschmer.   *Set Designer:* Colleen Balance and Geoffrey Grimsman.   *Set Decorator:* Steve Davis.   *Costumes:* Jennifer L. Bryan.   *Make-up:* Nicki Lederman.   *Stunt Coordinator:* Cal Johnson.   *Running time:* 110 minutes. *MPAA Rating:* PG-13.

CAST: Susan Ward (Brittany Foster);   Lori Heuring (Adrien Williams);   Matthew Settle (Matt Curtis);   Nathan Bexton (Bobby);   Ethan Erickson (Tom);   Laurie Fortier (Kelly); Kim Murphy (Joanne);   Katharine Towne (Morgan);   Daniel Hugh Kelly (Dr. Henry Thompson);   Tess Harper (Dr. Amanda Giles);   Jay R. Ferguson (Andy);   A.J. Buckley (Wayne);   Charlie Finn (Gregg);   Erinn Bartlett (Sheila);   Peter MacKenzie (Bob Mead); Heather Stephens (Tayna); Joanne Pankow (Milena);   Taylor Negron (Luis); David Reinwald (Dr. Beck);   Scot M. Sanborn (Jack Simmers);   Tonya Smalls and Julia Wright (Pedicurists);   Michael J. Young (Dinner Patron);   Ron Clinton Smith (Desk Guard); Brenda Onhaizer (Nurse);   Ronald McCall (EMS Technician);   Teresa "Tree" Lynn O'Toole (Chicken Fighting Girl);   Keith Kuhl (Dancer at Club);   Leland Jones (Photographer); Mary Elias (Dr. Thompson's Date).

LOS ANGELES TIMES, 7/21/00, Calendar/p. 16, Kevin Thomas

"The In Crowd" is out of it. The earnest efforts of director Mary Lambert and her cast cannot keep this languid psychological drama, set at a posh Southern resort, from seeming trite and uninvolving.

Lori Heuring plays the lovely Adrien, whose mental institution doctor (Daniel Hugh Kelly) is confident that she is well enough to leave and take a job as a waitress at the resort, which attracts a slew of rich college kids who seem to spend their entire summer vacation there. The gist of Mark Gibson and Philip Halprin's seriously under-inspired script is that just as Adrien has arrived at the point of putting a troubled past behind her, she is confronted with a lethal psychopath in the form of a glamorous Southern belle, Brittany (Susan Ward).

Brittany has been driven crazy by her late sister, who was popular but a nasty piece of work underneath; the same could now be said of the once-overlooked Brittany, who, in effect, has taken her sister's place.

Brittany makes a huge fuss over Adrien, seemingly fearing that even though Adrien is a waitress she just might be personable and pretty enough to threaten her queen bee status. Brittany can be highly seductive with men and women alike, but you have the feeling that she really isn't interested in sex at all but rather in taking pleasure in manipulating people.

Nothing much happens the first hour, with Brittany constantly giving Adrien the rush, and Adrien in turn being warned that Brittany is trouble. At long last Brittany goes over the edge, triggering a bloody finale.

You sense that we're supposed to see Brittany's craziness as a reflection of distorted, cliquish values of the country club set, but there isn't enough characterization and observation in the script for Lambert to pull it off. Indeed, most of us would be driven crazy by the sheer boredom of these rich kids' indolent summer existence. Heuring has sufficient poise and presence, but most everyone else is merely a type rather than an individual, though Ward certainly gives the role of Brittany her best shot.

Lambert's determination to take Adrien and Brittany seriously is admirable in this era of genre spoofs, but to no real avail.

NEW YORK POST, 7/20/00, p. 42, Jonathan Foreman

A laughably bad B-thriller aimed at the teenage market, "The In Crowd" promised to be a sexed-up sleaze fest in the enjoyably shameless tradition of "Wild Things."

But that film had the advantage of star power in the form of Kevin Bacon and Matt Dillon, as well as several nastily noir-ish plot twists that weren't obvious from the start.

This movie, on the other hand, features a lot of weak unknowns, speaking increasingly ridiculous dialogue in the laborious service of a by-the-numbers plot that becomes sillier and lamer as it goes on.

It lacks even the conviction of its own sleaziness: Director Mary Lambert fails to make the most of her nubile, scantily clad cast, and the climactic cat fight is so badly shot and lit, it's actually boring.

And because the film is so poorly paced, you start noticing irritating details like continuity errors, the illogic of the ending, and the perfect hair and make-up worn by various characters even in the mental hospital.

Adrien (Lori Heuring), a nice blond girl who's just been released from the institution, gets a job (through her shrink) at an ultrafancy beach club. There she meets and has to serve a crowd of absurdly spoiled twentysomethings. The leader of this "in crowd" is the powerfully seductive Brittany (Susan Ward).

For no apparent reason, she takes Adrien under her wing, inviting her to parties, buying her dresses and lending her golf clubs. Brittany's former best friend, Kelly (Laurie Fortier), gets jealous and says catty things about partying with the help, but because Adrien is good-looking and athletic, she fits in pretty quick.

But when Matt (Matthew Settle), one of the many indistinguishably good-looking guys at the club, takes an interest in Adrien, Brittany—who has a quasi-supernatural ability to be anywhere people are talking about her—starts showing her sinister side. And it's very sinister indeed.

The most interesting thing about "The In Crowd" turns out to be the way it's cast with look-alikes: Lori Heuring looks like a seventh-generation Xerox of Sarah Jessica Parker with straight hair, and Ward is an amazing dead ringer for Denise Richards.

Unfortunately, while Ward can play sexy and devious with the same facility as Richards, Heuring is unable to make her increasingly absurd lines sound anything but unintentionally funny.

NEWSDAY, 7/21/00, Part II/p. B7, John Anderson

The tagline on the ads for "The In Crowd" is "what would you do to get in?" The better question is "What would you give to get out?" Eye teeth? Right arm? First born?"

Moving with precisely the same burning narrative urgency as a daytime soap opera and making even less dramatic sense, "The In Crowd" opens in the mental institution where diagnosed "erotomaniac" Adrien Williams (Lori Heuring) has been kept since attacking her therapist (and isn't that unfair). But with the support of the sympathetic Dr. Thompson (Daniel Hugh Kelly), she's released to work at his posh country club, where the boys wear plaid shorts and drink martinis, the girls indulge in sapphic obsessions and the worst thing that can happen is to have teen queen Brittany Foster (Susan Ward) pretend to be your friend.

Connoisseurs of "Baywatch" will appreciate the totally nuance-free rhythms and techniques employed by director Mary Lambert, who doesn't seem capable of letting a woman enter a room without the camera panning up from crotch level. It's hard to say that Lambert's lumbering, faux-gothic beach movie is advertising itself falsely—Adrien does have to suffer the snobbery of the club's spoiled regulars. But then she never seems to do any work either, so the trade-off seems reasonable.

That is, until people start dying and the movie starts turning into "Scary Movie" without the dirty jokes. There's a gaslighting-of-Brittany sequence that's just ridiculous and an ending that suggests the possibility sequel. No one involved in this thing could have taken any of it that seriously, you hope—Ward's acting, to cite just one offending party, makes "902 10" vet Tiffany Amber Thiessen look like Dame Judith Anderson playing Lady Macbeth. However, it might be worthwhile to get on the phone to your senator and see if legislation is possible to prevent such a thing from happening.

SIGHT AND SOUND, 8/01, p. 46, Edward Lawrensen

South Carolina, the present. At the instigation of her doctor, Henry Thompson, Adrien Williams is released from *St Anastasia's,* the psychiatric hospital where she has been held since assaulting her former psychiatrist. Thompson has set up a summer job for Adrien at Cliffmont, an exclusive beach-side club. There, Adrien is befriended by Britanny Foster, one of the rich students who spend their summers at Cliffmont. Adrien and Britanny grow close. Kelly, a Cliffmont regular, warns Adrien to stay away from Britanny. That night, Kelly is injured when she loses control of her moped, which has been tampered with.

Adrien chances on a photograph of Britanny and her sister Sandra, who looks very similar to Adrien. Bobby, Kelly's ex boyfriend, explains that Sandra went missing after dumping Matt, the Cliffmont tennis coach. Adrien meets Matt, to whom Britanny is attracted; they are spotted talking together by Britanny, who later accuses Adrien of betraying her. Kelly tells Adrien that Britanny and Sandra didn't get on, unaware that Britanny is eavesdropping. Adrien begins to suspect Sandra is dead, not missing, and that Britanny murdered her. Later, Britanny kills Kelly, making the murder look like a boating accident.

Having spotted Adrien searching for incriminating evidence relating to Sandra's murder, Britanny kills Dr Thompson, pinning the blame on Adrien. Confined again at *St Anastasia's,* Adrien is visited by Bobby, who tells her he thinks Britanny killed Kelly. Bobby helps Adrien escape. Confronting Adrien, Britanny admits to killing her sister because she was jealous of her popularity. The two women fight, ending up in the Cliffmont pool where they are interrupted by guests. Revealed as a multiple murderer, Britanny ends up in *St Anastasia's.*

In director Mary Lambert's *The In Crowd,* the teenage heroine Adrien Williams starts a summer job at an exclusive, super-rich country club, and gets into trouble when she begins mixing with the preppy, coldly amoral guests her own age. Before taking her on, the manager warns her about the perils of social mobility: "Know your place, and you'll do well."

The film hardly endorses the snobbish attitude underlying this opening gambit—the high-society friends Adrien makes include a multiple murderer and a date-rapist, after all. But just as Adrien is dazzled—and nearly undone—by the exalted company she keeps, notably the amorous Britanny, Lambert's film hankers after a bit of cinematic class.

Specifically, it attempts to enliven its routine plot by referring to superior psychological thrillers. The primary influence is Hitchcock: from the drugged hot drink Adrien gives her psychiatrist (shades of *Notorious),* to Britanny's attempt to dress Adrien up as her missing sister *(Vertigo),* Hitchcock's films are invoked throughout. In doing so, however, Lambert points up her film's comparative failings. For instance, the script seems to suggest that Adrien's stay in a psychiatric hospital was the result of false memory syndrome—a ploy Hitchcock would have relished. But here, the concept is swiftly ditched in the hurry to advance the (increasingly silly) plot. Likewise, the rushed editing of the scene in which Adrien blags her way into Britanny's house and creeps up the grand staircase—a very Hitchcockian architectural feature saps any potential for tension.

By the final reel, the film gives up on Hitchcockian complexity in favour of more straightforward thrills, handled efficiently enough by Lambert, whose previous work includes *Pet Sematary*. But the script isn't taut enough to generate any great suspense: the fate of Britanny's missing sister is easily guessed at, while the plot relies too heavily on coincidence as a structuring device—Britanny eavesdrops on so many crucial exchanges you begin to suspect she's omnipresent. In a few places, Lambert gets the lazy arrogance of her pampered, Gatsby-esque characters just right—Nathan Bexton's droll performance as Bobby is the standout—and there are some well-drawn scenes of the guests, picked out against the sandy beach in their impeccably white linen slacks, relaxing by the sea. This said, Lambert's camera at times seems overly fixated on the exposed flesh of her teenage cast; this can make for some immaculately framed images, but the overall impression is odd, like an episode of *Baywatch* directed by Bruce Weber. The film's most raucous scene comes at the end, when Adrien and Britanny, their expensive frocks ripped to shreds, mud-wrestle next to the open grave of Britanny's sister: it's pure trash, of course, but it also happens to be the film's single arresting image—the one scene of which Hitch, who knew a bit about morbid sensationalism, would have approved.

Also reviewed in:
NEW YORK TIMES, 7/20/00, p. E5, Elvis Mitchell
VARIETY, 7/24-30/00, p. 46, Godfrey Cheshire

INTERN

A Cowboy Booking International/Moonstone Entertainment release of a Giv'en Films/Moonstone Entertainment production. *Executive Producer:* Randy Simon. *Producer:* Galt Neiderhoffer, Etchie Stroh, and Daniela Soto-Taplin. *Director:* Michael Lange. *Screenplay:* Caroline Doyle and Jill Kopelman. *Director of Photography:* Rodney Charters. *Editor:* Anita Brandt-Burgoyne. *Music:* Jimmy Harry. *Sound:* Damian Canelos. *Sound Editor:* Shawn Ian Kerkhoff. *Casting:* Richard Hicks and Ronnie Yeskel. *Production Designer:* Jody Asnes. *Art Director:* Luna Hirai and Cherish Magennis. *Set Decorator:* Jocelyn Mason. *Running time:* 90 minutes. *MPAA Rating:* Not Rated.

CAST: Dominique Swain (Jocelyn Bennett); Ben Pullen (Paul Rochester); Peggy Lipton (Roxanne Rochet); Joan Rivers (Dolly Bellows); David Deblinger (Richard Sinn); Dwight Ewell (Gustave); Billy Porter (Sebastian Niederfarb); Leilani Bishop (Resin); Anna Thompson (Antoinette De la Paix); Paulina Porizkova (Chi Chi Chemise); Kevin Aucoin, John Bartlett; Philip Bloch; Kenneth Cole; Simon Doonan; Frédéric Fekkai; Donna Hanover; Tommy Hilfiger; Gwyneth Paltrow; Cynthia Rowley; Elizabeth Saltzman; Richard Sinnott; Andre Leon Talley; Diane von Furstenberg; Rebecca Romjin-Stamos; Narciso Rodriguez; Stella McCartney; Marc Jacobs; Neil Campbell; Amy Ashley; Gretchen Gunlocke; Marina Rust; Deda Coben; Jennifer Jackson; Susan Kittenplan; Carmen Bogonova; Cricket Burns; Pamela Fiori; Pauline Alguilera (Themselves); Victor Varnado (Messenger); Aleksia Landeau (Bianca); Mike Hawkins (Mr. Delveccio); Tristine Skyler (Debra); James Urbaniak (Olivier); Anson Scoville (Alex); Bill Raymond (Deep Throat); Rocco Sisto (Pierre).

NEW YORK POST, 8/11/00, p. 46, Jonathan Foreman

This movie, which is not about the Clinton-Lewinsky scandal, but rather a romantic comedy set in the world of women's fashion magazines, is half-baked and amateurish in almost every way.

There are some good, sharp jokes here and there amid the over-the-top performances and the lame, ultra-predictable plot, but overall it's a criminal waste of a juicy satirical target and of the many fashion-world personalities who appear in cameo.

Jocelyn (Dominique Swain) is an intern at a glossy fashion magazine called Skirt. Like all interns everywhere, she's expected to perform tedious drudgery and to kiss up to bosses.

Because it's a women's magazine, all of Jocelyn's bosses are either gay men, or women who suffer from phoniness and/or bulimia.

One of Jocelyn bosses is a spy for Skirt's chief rival, Vogue, and one of Jocelyn's assignments is to find out who the traitor is.

Director Michael Lange, in his feature debut, gets a dreadful performance out of Swain (who here bears a strange resemblance to Melissa Joan Hart of TV's "Sabrina") and almost all of his professional cast, in particular Paulina Porizkova.

But it's only fair to give some of the blame to screenwriters—and former fashionistas—Caroline Doyle and Jill Kopelman.

The only exception to the general awfulness of the acting are Kathy Griffin and Joan Rivers, who manage to be funny without overdoing it like students in a bad high school play.

VILLAGE VOICE, 8/15/00, p. 124, Michael Atkinson

Starting out as a mock doc as well, TV director Michael Lange's cheap indie *Intern* practically drops a grenade down its drawers with an early musical number, but recovers into a smartly written, unevenly executed *Network* on the fashion industry, complete with vanity immolations, inter-mag espionage, glamour accidents, Joan Rivers, Paulina Porizkova, and Peggy Lipton, as a head honcho editor with an exploded breast implant and a Deep Throat spy contact with Tourette's. Center stage is lemon-chiffon-sweet Dominique Swain as a fresh-faced, impudent intern who has romantic dilemmas that drown the movie's satire, which, as it is, targets barreled ducks the size of Cape buffalo.

Also reviewed in:
NEW YORK TIMES, 8/11/00, p. E13, Stephen Holden
VARIETY, 3/27-4/2/00, p. 28, Emanuel Levy

INTERVIEW, THE

A Cinema Guild release of a Pointblank Pictures production. *Producer:* Bill Hughes. *Director:* Craig Monahan. *Screenplay:* Craig Monahan and Gordon Davie. *Director of Photography:* Simon Duggan. *Editor:* Suresh Ayyar. *Music:* David Hirschfelder. *Sound:* John Wilkinson. *Art Director:* Richard Bell. *Costumes:* Jeanie Cameron. *Running time:* 103 minutes. *MPAA Rating:* Not Rated.

CAST: Hugo Weaving (Eddie Rodney Fleming); Tony Martin (John Steele); Aaron Jeffery (Wayne Prior); Paul Sonkkila (Jackson); Michael Caton (Barry Walls); Peter McCauley (Hudson); Glynis Angel (Robran); Leverne McDonnell (Solicitor); Libby Stone (Mrs. Beecroft); Andrew Bayly (Prowse); Doug Dew (Beecroft).

VILLAGE VOICE, 6/20/00, p. 156, Mark Holcomb

Starting off in a promisingly gloomy, Kafka-via-David Fincher mode, first-time director Craig Monahan's cop thriller, *The Interview*, ends up stumbling over its preoccupation with procedural verisimilitude and dreary departmental squabbling. Monahan sacrifices a potentially intriguing, if not stunningly original, setup (a tightly wound detective charms, seduces, and cajoles a confession from a deceptively placid suspect) in favor of a tiresome law-and-order screed.

Set almost entirely in a dingy Melbourne police station, *The Interview* works best during the cat-and-mouse exchange between its two leads. Jobless sad sack and ostensible car thief Edward Fleming (Hugo Weaving, the aggressively antiseptic Agent Smith in *The Matrix*) and outwardly calm Sergeant John Steele (Tony Martin), who has Fleming in mind for more horrific crimes, square off for a quietly riveting battle of wits. These sharply observed scenes make up for the film's static setting, until the focus inexplicably shifts to Steele's troubles with a police ethics committee over alleged goon-squad tactics. The tenuous link between his and Fleming's culpability is uninspired, and when Fleming is released on a trumped-up technicality, *The Interview* flirts dangerously with a quasi-*Death Wish* mentality.

When it works, *The Interview* is effective in the style of television's late, great *Homicide: Life on the Street*, with its tense, is-he-or-isn't-he byplay and moral fuzziness. That's hardly faint praise, but Monahan also reveals a preference for the kind of downtrodden supercop twaddle that drives the execrable *NYPD Blue*. The two extremes never quite meld.

Also reviewed in:
CHICAGO TRIBUNE, 3/17/00, Friday/p. H, John Petrakis
NEW YORK TIMES, 6/16/00, p. E25, Elvis Mitchell
VARIETY, 8/17-23/98, p. 37, David Stratton

INTO THE ARMS OF STRANGERS

A Warner Bros. Pictures release of a Sabine Films production.   *Producer:* Deborah Oppenheimer. *Director:* Mark Jonathan Harris. *Screenplay:* Mark Jonathan Harris. *Director of Photography:* Don Lenzer. *Editor:* Kate Amend. *Music:* Lee Holdridge. *Music Editor:* Stan Jones. *Sound:* Peter Miller and (music) John Richards and Gary Rydstrom. *Sound Editor:* Shannon Mills. *Production Designer:* Michael Lewis. *Running time:* 90 minutes. *MPAA Rating:* PG.

CAST: Judi Dench (Narrator); Lorraine Allard, Lory Cahn, Hedy Epstein, Kurt Fuchel, Alexander Gordon, Eva Hayman, Jack Hellman, Bertha Leverton, Ursula Rosenfeld, Inge Sadan, Lore Segal, and Robert Sugar (The Kinder). Miriam Cohen, (Foster Parent); Franzi Groszman (Lore Segal's Mother); Nicholas Winton and Norbert Wollheim (Rescuers).

LOS ANGELES TIMES, 9/15/00, Calendar/p. 4, Kenneth Turan

A child's-eye view can be lucidity itself, seeing things with a clarity and a gift for the telling detail that is powerfully instructive. Because "Into the Arms of Strangers" is as much a story about childhood as it is about the Holocaust, it's an especially moving and effective piece of work.

As its subtitle indicates, this documentary is intent on telling "Stories of the Kindertransport," a British rescue mission that, in the nine months leading up to World War II, saved 10,000 children, mostly Jewish, living in German territory.

It's an uplifting story but a wrenching one, too, when you factor in the grief of parents voluntarily relinquishing their children to save their lives and the agony of children who often discovered after the war that their parents had, in fact, died in concentration camps.

At least one other documentary, "My Knees Were Knocking," has dealt with the Kindertransport phenomenon, but this one makes more of an impact. As produced by Deborah Oppenheimer, who made the film into a kind of crusade after discovering that her late mother was one of the rescued children, and directed by Mark Jonathan Harris, who last did the Oscar-winning "The Long Way Home," this is a polished piece of work that slowly but convincingly builds its involving story.

Making the film as strong as it is are the testimonies of its witnesses, not only the former children, now old and gray, but some of the people who were adults when the story unfolded, including Franzi Grossman, the 95-year-old mother of Lore Segal, one of the children transported, who says simply but painfully of giving up her daughter: "The hurt is unbelievable. That cannot be described."

Carefully shot by cinematographer Don Lenzer, "Strangers" makes good use of a consistent visual backdrop for its interviews, enabling us to more easily focus on what its people are saying. Speaking six decades after the fact, the trauma is still alive inside these survivors, and it is gripping to experience how much they feel things, how intense the emotion remains. "I still have dreams," one woman says, "and old as I am, I wake up sobbing."

Growing up in Germany and Austria, these children freely admit to being pampered, even spoiled by indulgent parents. The gravity of their changed situation once Hitler came to power dawned on them slowly—a birthday party no one attended, a beating outside school—but after Kristallnacht, there could be no doubt that their world had been obliterated.

That night, Nov. 7, 1938, illustrated here by some rare and devastating home movie footage, saw the mass destruction of Jewish businesses and synagogues. Moved by the clear danger, the British government, in what the film calls "an act of generosity and charity almost without parallel," agreed to admit refugee children ages 17 and under. (A similar bill, it's worth noting, died in committee in the U.S. Congress. Separating children from their parents, one conservative opponent said in pre-Elian Gonzalez days, was contrary to the laws of God.)

"Strangers" is especially strong on the world-turned-upside-down chaos parents and children faced in having only a few days to prepare for a journey into the unknown that might separate them from each other forever. Things were worst of all at the train stations on the day of departure: One woman, Lory Cahn, recalls that her father was so distraught at seeing her depart that he reached through the open car window and literally pulled her off the moving train. (Cahn survived the war, though her parents did not, but at age 20 she weighed only 58 pounds after years spent in eight camps.)

The children's shock on arriving in the safe haven of Britain, not knowing the culture or the language, was quite high. "I cried for years," one woman remembers, "I never dreamed one could be so lonely and go on living." But most children made the transition, some even arranging for their parents to come after them. And Kurt Fuchel still remembers the euphoria of his first day with his new friends, coming home and proclaiming, with the exuberance only 7-year-olds have: "Somebody who's not Jewish wants to see me tomorrow." It's details like that that make "Into the Arms of Strangers" a memorable experience.

NEW YORK, 9/25/00, p. 62, Peter Rainer

The documentary *Into the Arms of Strangers: Stories of the Kindertransport*, directed by Mark Jonathan Harris, confronts a relatively unexamined aspect of the Holocaust: For nine months prior to World War II, Britain, alone among the world's nations, took advantage of the Nazis' then-policy of forced emigration and brought over some 10,000 children, mostly Jewish, from Germany, Austria, and Czechoslovakia. The children were told by their parents that they would all soon be reunited, but most of the rescued never saw their families again.

What distinguishes Harris's film, which was produced by Deborah Oppenheimer, the daughter of a rescued child, is the rarity of some of its archival footage, and its gallery of witnesses. Interviewed by the filmmakers, the grown-up *kinder* speak of the unspeakable, and as they do, their faces seem to deliquesce into those of the children they once were. Their recollections have a harrowing, kid's-eye immediacy and sense of detail. The writer Lore Segal describes how the matter-of-fact way her mother described the transport was belied by her flushed face; she remembers the panicky discomfort in seeing her neighborhood streets suddenly filled with the red flags of the Reich and soldiers in crisp new uniforms. (Segal was one of the lucky ones: As a child, she later managed to secure menial jobs for her parents in Britain and thus rescue them in return.)

Many children sent to England by their parents felt betrayed, abandoned; with just four days allowed to pack their sons and daughters off, the parents had to scrunch into that brief time together a lifetime of counsel. *Into the Arms of Strangers* is at least by Holocaust standards, a success story, but it doesn't really feel that way, nor is it intended to be. The *kinder* were forced to lose their faith in people and then regain it at a time when most of them could barely comprehend what was at stake. Many of them still stare out at us fixed in incomprehension.

NEW YORK POST, 9/15/00, p. 55, Lou Lumenick

There have been many documentaries about the Holocaust in recent years, but this one really stands out.

It's the fascinating, little known story of the Kindertransport, a remarkable 1938 rescue mission that relocated over 10,000 children—mostly Jewish—to Britain from Germany, Austria and Czechoslovakia.

Most never saw their families again. As this documentary reminds us, an additional 1.5 million children died in the Holocaust.

In a series of remarkable and deeply touching interviews, the survivors—now in their 60s and 70s and all incredibly articulate and well-chosen—tell their stories in vivid detail.

They recall the wrenching experience of being separated from their parents, their often hard lives in England (some were forced into labor as domestics, others were deported to internment camps in Australia when they came of age) and their usually heartbreaking efforts to rescue their parents from the Nazis.

We also hear from the man who organized the Kindertransport (in a segment filmed just six weeks before his death), but whose own family ended up in concentration camps; a woman who ended up in several camps after her grief-stricken father plucked her from the window of a Kindertransport train just before it parted; a British foster mother; and a woman who sent her daughter to safety in England, only to be reunited six horrifying years later.

Writer-director Mark Jonathan Harris, who won an Oscar for his previous Holocaust documentary "The Long Way Home," sketches in the historical background with some truly amazing archival footage, including color home movies and newsreels.

There are a few re-enactment scenes, gimmicks that just aren't necessary when you have material this riveting.

NEWSDAY, 9/15/00, Part II/p. B7, John Anderson

The stories of the kinderstransport, the process by which England absorbed more than 10,000 German, Austrian and Czech Jewish children beginning in 1938, have been told before, but certainly no more poignantly than in "Into the Arms of Strangers." As good as its stories are, however, and as fresh as its subjects' pain may often seem, "Into the Arms" parts company with most other Holocaust documentaries because if s not just a document, it's a cinematic triumph.

Any documentary is limited by what its director shoots; the archival documentary by what he or she finds. Harris—director of the Oscar-winning "The Long Way Home"—bases his movie on interviews with former kinder, who've been living with their experiences for more than 50 years but can still make you feel the fear or embarrassment or anger of being a Jewish child in Nazi Germany, or of being an uprooted and sometimes barely welcome "guest" of 1930s England. But it's in the period footage Harris uses that he elevates his movie beyond mere testimony and it soars into an almost ethereal realm of memory. The fragments of film we see—children skating in a Berlin park or the pedestrian swarm of a non-Nazi afternoon or, later, trains leaving for camps—have been restored to such a crispness and luster you imagine they might have been shot specifically for this project. Adding to this are the choices Harris makes, which almost never result in mere embellishment or weak stabs at authenticity. They are specific as well as beautiful, evoking the often idyllic childhood lived by the soon-to-be-shipped-off children or the smug intimidation of an SS patrol.

"Into the Arms of Strangers" is, of course, a Holocaust movie about people who didn't die—although most of their families did—and the stories told by Harris' subjects are always told with a mix of sadness, sometimes bitterness and always an element of regret at surviving. What seems peculiar is how moving the movie can be whether the incident being revisited is banal or horrific. A woman remembers how no one came to her birthday party, because the once-popular girl was now only a Jew. Another recalls her father, maddened with love, retrieving her through the window of a kinderstransport train and ensuring her later trip to Auschwitz. An English mother recollects how her little adoptee would rise to check the front-door lock every night.

One of the transport organizers remembers the last time he saw his "then wife and child." Nearly as breathtaking as "Into the Arms of Strangers" itself is the fact that Warner Bros. is distributing the film. The people who bring you Kevin Costner six or seven times a year, releasing a documentary? Unheard of, but attributable to the studio's relationship with prolific producer Deborah Oppenheimer ("The Drew Carey Show"), whose mother was aboard the kindertransport and whose grandparents died in the camps. Producers don't usually get a lot of credit in film reviews but, for Oppenheimer, this was obviously a labor of love. She should share credit not only for the quality of the movie, but the fact that a lot of people are going to be able to see it.

SIGHT AND SOUND, 12/00, p. 51, Stella Bruzzi

This film documents the events surrounding the *Kindertransport* the transportation of Jewish children out of Germany and its occupied lands to Britain immediately prior to the German invasion of Poland in 1939. Following *Kristallnacht*, the anti-Jewish riot which occurred in Berlin in November 1938, a British cabinet committee decide that Britain can take in unaccompanied Jewish refugee children under the age of 17. The first train leaves Berlin for Britain in December 1938. Soon trains are leaving from Austria and Czechoslovakia. Many of the children sought to save their parents too by trying to find them work or sponsors in Britain, but most failed to bring them over. Few children were reunited with their parents after the war. *Into the Arms of Stranger's* is a compelling, gruelling documentary about the British government's attempt to provide asylum for refugee Jewish children from Germany and its occupied lands just before World War II. Here director Mark Jonathan Harris (whose previous documentary *The Long Way Home* investigated the plight of Holocaust survivors) uses archive footage, the compassionate narration of Judi Dench and, most importantly, interviews with survivors to describe what became known as the *Kindertransport*

Despite the simplicity and familiarity of this format, *Into the Arms of Strangers,* in keeping with the tonal complexity of recent, particularly US, film treatments of the Holocaust, is a feel-good tragedy: the film satisfies our primary urge to be affected by the horror of the Nazi atrocities while sustaining the myth that, had we been there, we would have either survived or helped save those who otherwise were killed. A dualism is at work in *Into the Arms of Strangers* on the one hand, there is the sentiment expressed by Norbert Wollheim, an organiser of the *Kindertransports* in Berlin, that "survival is an accident"; on the other, the view of Alexander Gordon who, having been orphaned, sent to England and arrested, survived the torpedoing of the *HMT Dunera* and reckons he "was meant to survive".

Harris' film is imbued with Gordon's optimistic view rather than the pessimistic idea that survival is a matter of random selection. Predicated on the notion of an identification between the figures on screen and the film's spectators, the recent run of US Holocaust films configure historical realities as survival fantasies, as if giving credence to the superstitious supposition that if we dream of our own deaths we die. *Into the Arms of Strangers* isn't a fictionalisation as such but it is an idealisation into which we can insert our emotions and our experiences.

Perhaps it's no surprise then that the film is most powerful when focusing on individual testimonies rather than the big historical picture. Despite Harris' claim that he experimented with ways to defamiliarise well-known archive footage, much of the library material here has been seen elsewhere, with the exception of an image of balloons imprinted with swastikas being sold in the street and the newsreel clip showing the interviewee Lore Segal getting off her boat. The film richly evokes the child's-eye view of Nazism and of arriving for the first time in England; Harris also gives us stylised reconstructions of the events many of the children experienced: the terror of hiding from the SS, packing before leaving, receiving letters from their parents. The montage of teddies, shoes, fine clothes and mementos being lovingly pressed into leather suitcases before leaving for Britain conveys with economy and beauty the parents' pain and fear at seeing their sons and daughters go and the children's own lack of historical perspective.

The interviews at the heart of the film are all shot in intense close-up. Towards the end Lore Segal, author of *Uther People's Children* a novel recounting her experience as a refugee, comments that the events of her life have proved a writer's "gift". This may seem naive and lacking in recognition of the torment and death suffered by others, but Segal's optimistic observation encapsulates the tone of Harris' documentary. All the stories of the *Kindertransport* survivors are presented as if they are gifts, each interview a treasure to be treated with reverence. More than anything else, one comes away from *Into the Arms of Strangers* with a vivid image of these interviewees and the specific terms they use to evoke their experiences: one talks of shedding a "cloak of lead" as her train arrives in Holland, another of losing his capacity to speak German after reaching England. Put into words, such memories convey the essence of their experience as no archive footage or voiceover can.

TIME, 9/25/00, p. 102, Richard Schickel

It is one of World War II's least known stories: in late 1938 and through much of 1939, the Nazis permitted some 10,000 Jewish children and adolescents to escape to England via trains and then boats. Why the Nazis did so remains something of a mystery, though surely the world's shocked response to *Kristallnacht*, when Hitler's thugs burned hundreds of synagogues in a single night, had something to do with it. They wished briefly to place a human face on National Socialism. *Into the Arms of Strangers*, an extraordinarily fine and understated documentary, written and directed by Jonathan Mark Harris, at last gives coherent voice to those who endured this remarkable experience.

It is a voice often cracked by remembered pain. Once selected for the *Kindertransports*, these kids had just days to pack their bags and say what some of them knew was their final farewells to their parents. The latter tried desperately to cram a lifetime's moral instruction, not to mention unsunderable love, into those hasty moments. One of the film's most heartbreaking stories is of a father who, running alongside a departing train, could not bear the separation. He yanked his daughter through an open window—and ultimately into a concentration camp. She survived. He did not.

Not that life in England was easy for the *Kinder*. There were not enough foster homes for them, and many lived for months in unheated summer-vacation camps. A few were exploited; many were troubled. One could argue that these 10,000 were pathetically few compared with the 6 million lost in the Holocaust. But one of the *Kinder*, novelist Lore Segal, makes this poignant point: "None of the foster parents with whom I stayed, and there were five of them, could stand me for very long, but all of them had the grace to take in a Jewish child." That was a quality singularly lacking elsewhere (particularly in the U.S.). Still, this moving tribute to a handful of candles flickering in the darkness has the power to summon us—one prays—to our better selves.

VILLAGE VOICE, 9/19/00, p. 122, Elliott Stein

It's Beastly German week at the movies with the arrival of two feature docs: Mark Jonathan Harris's *Into the Arms of Strangers*, about the flight of Jewish children from the Third Reich, and Rob Epstein and Jeffrey Friedman's *Paragraph 175*, on the Nazi persecution of homosexuals. [see Stein's review of *Paragraph 175*.]

Harris's accomplished film is concerned with the "Kindertransport," a rescue operation that took place shortly before the outbreak of World War II. In an act of mercy unequaled elsewhere, Great Britain opened its doors to over 10,000 Jewish children from Germany, Austria, and Czechoslovakia. They left with the hope that their parents would follow; within a few years, most of the parents departed from the same railway stations on their way to the death camps. In this country, a congressional bill that would have allowed entry to the young refugees was killed in committee as Washington's powerful anti-immigration lobby opined that "accepting children without their parents is contrary to the laws of God."

Strangers is largely devoted to the moving testimony of witnesses—a dozen of the surviving "Kinder," together with a few of their rescuers—and although much of it observes the unobtrusive talking-heads format of a TV movie, it's worth shelling out to see this doc on a theater screen: The enthralling archival footage of Germany in the 1930s is rare stuff indeed, of superb photographic quality.

Also reviewed in:
CHICAGO TRIBUNE, 10/13/00, Friday/p. G, Mark Caro
NEW YORK TIMES, 9/15/00, p. E10, A. O. Scott
VARIETY, 9/11-17/00, p. 24, Emanuel Levy
WASHINGTON POST, 9/15/00, p. C8, Rita Kempley
WASHINGTON POST, 9/15/00, Weekend/p. 46, Desson Howe

INTO MY HEART

A Jean Doumanian/Mars Films release of a Jean Doumanian production in association with Mars Film and Sweetland Films. *Executive Producer:* Letty Aronson and J. E. Beaucaire. *Producer:* Jean Doumanian. *Director:* Anthony Stark and Sean Smith. *Screenplay:* Anthony Stark and Sean Smith. *Director of Photography:* Michael Barrow. *Editor:* Merril Stern and Robert Reitano. *Music:* Michael Small. *Music Editor:* David Carbonara. *Sound:* Antonio L. Arroyo and Dan Ferat. *Sound Editor:* Dan Sable. *Casting:* Sheila Jaffe and Georgianne Walken. *Production Designer:* Ford Wheeler. *Art Director:* Amy Beth Silver. *Set Decorator:* Cathy Niles, James Clauer, and David Schlesinger. *Set Dresser:* Eric Bianchini. *Costumes:* Stephanie Maslansky. *Make-up:* Joanne Ottaviano. *Stunt Coordinator:* Tony Guida. *Running time:* 93 minutes. *MPAA Rating:* Not Rated.

CAST: Claire Forlani (Nina);   Rob Morrow (Ben);   Jake Weber (Adam);   Jayne Brook (Kat); Sebastian Roché (Chris);   Nora Ariffin (Waitress);   Nelson Martinez (Doorman); John Doumanian (Chestnut Vender);   Harvey Madonick (Paramedic).

NEW YORK POST, 5/5/00, p. 53, Lou Lumenick

"Into My Heart" is yet another movie that tries to pass actors in their 30s as teenagers— and in which 15 years elapse with no change in clothing or hair styles.

That's the least of the problems with this under-produced, four-character adultery drama, which looks less like a movie than an evening of bad theater—and ominously opens with a suicide attempt.

Flashback to 1982, when we meet Ben (Rob Morrow, real age 38) and Adam (Jake Weber, who appears to be in his mid-30s) as Columbia University freshmen, on the day John Belushi's death is headlined on the front page of The Post.

The sweet-natured Adam quickly hooks up with classmate Nina (Claire Forlani, real age 28), while the charming but sleazy Ben stumbles from one romantic fiasco to another—or so at least we're told.

Ten years later, Ben, a successful lawyer, is married to Kat (Jayne Brook), a beautiful, workaholic mayoral aide.

But during a weekend in the Berkshires, he begins a flirtation with Nina—long married to Adam, a writer—that culminates with his sleeping with his best friend's wife.

(The happily married Nina's motivation for the affair isn't even hinted at.)

We know from the opening scene this will bring disaster—especially since we've been told that Adam "has never developed emotional scar tissue"—a claim that would seem to be contradicted by the eye he lost in a childhood accident.

Jointly written and directed by the team of Anthony Stark and Sean Smith, "Into My Heart" brings absolute implausibility to a story that's been told better in many previous films.

NEWSDAY, 5/5/00, Part II/p. B6, Jan Stuart

The names of John Cheever and Martha Stewart are dropped self-mockingly by the privileged young adults of "Into My Heart," and they seem to know from what they speak. Reared with a sense of entitlement from their prep school days, they studiously reproduce the colonial New England resplendence of their parents' lifestyles in their city apartments. And they wallow in the Cheever-size angst that comes along with the family legacy as well.

"Into My Heart" simmers with authenticity, and it's not just the clapboard flooring and tasteful antiques. The story of a betrayal between two guys who have been best buddies forever, it has been cooperatively written and directed by two guys who have been best buddies for almost forever. A press kit interview says there are essential parallels between teamworking auteurs Anthony Stark and Sean Smith and their two male protagonists, but they stop short of the fundamental moral transgression committed in their debut film.

Ben (Rob Morrow) and Adam (Jake Weber) are the sort of joined-at-the-hip childhood chums who follow each other dutifully to the same university and take a vested interest in each other's girlfriends. If Ben is wary of Adam's choice, a pub waitress named Nina (Claire Forlani), he rises above his initial disapproval so successfully that he engages her in an adulterous affair well after they are all happily married off.

Essentially a chamber piece for four actors (the fourth being Jayne Brook, who plays Ben's adoring wife, Kat), "Into My Heart" unfolds at a maddeningly deliberate pace, like a lab experiment arduously planned to forestall any unexpected results. It operates in an odd sort of limbo: neither clinical nor ultimately moving, transcending its stagy potential yet lacking a firm enough sense of style that would give the picture its own cinematic stamp.

There is a psychological alertness to the relationships that is reinforced by the four actors, who are all splendid. Forlani's Nina is a smart, effervescent object of desire worthy of the dueling attention she gets. Fine New York stage actor Jake Weber gives Adam a brooding, balled-up energy, while Jayne Brook effectively projects the uneasiness of an outsider. Morrow has perhaps the hardest task as the perpetrator of multiple crimes against friendship, and he makes us shudder with empathy.

VILLAGE VOICE, 5/9/00, p. 138, Jessica Winter

The anemic *Into My Heart* shares a titular coronary focus with Ms. Portman's junker as well as a fatal narrative reliance on cosmic comeuppance. [The reference is to *Where the Heart Is*; see Winter's review.] The fallout from a man's affair with his best friend's wife becomes an unwitting study in cognitive dissonance: A woman in an impossibly serene marriage commits adultery for no apparent erotic or psychological reason; a man forever marked by a horrible childhood accident is said to have "no emotional scar tissue—he's never been hurt" (subsequent events prove this conclusion correct); and a mawkish script and glacial pacing butt heads with some fine, understated performances. The droll rapport between Rob Morrow's cad and Jake Weber's cuckold feels especially live-in, recalling the effortless deadpan rhythms of *Wonder Boys* but throwing *Into My Heart*'s forced operatics into sharper relief.

Also reviewed in:
NEW YORK TIMES, 5/5/00, p. E28, Elvis Mitchell
VARIETY, 9/28-10/4/98, p. 46, Lisa Nesselson

ISN'T SHE GREAT

A Universal Pictures and Mutual Film Company release of a Lobell/Bergman production. *Executive Producer:* Ted Kurdyla, Gary Levinson, and Mark Gordon. *Producer:* Mike LoBell. *Director:* Andrew Bergman. *Screenplay:* Paul Rudnick. *Based on the article "Wasn't She Great" by:* Michael Korda. *Director of Photography:* Karl Walter Lindenlaub. *Editor:* Barry Malkin. *Music:* Burt Bacharach. *Music Editor:* Todd Kasow. *Choreographer:* Adam Shankman. *Sound:* Don Cohen and (music) Tim Boyle. *Sound Editor:* Paul P. Soucek. *Casting:* Kathleen Chopin, John Lyons, and Rosina Bucci. *Production Designer:* Stuart Wurtzel. *Art Director:* Raymond Dupuis. *Set Decorator:* Frances Calder, Susan Macquarrie, and Amy Burt. *Set Dresser:* Jean-Guy Leblanc and Jacques Pellerin. *Special Effects:* Steve Kirshoff. *Costumes:* Julie Weiss. *Make-up:* Linda Devetta. *Stunt Coordinator:* Minor Mustain and Benoit Gauthier. *Running time:* 90 minutes. *MPAA Rating:* R.

CAST: Bette Midler (Jacqueline Susann); Nathan Lane (Irving Mansfield); Stockard Channing (Florence Maybelle); David Hyde Pierce (Michael Hastings); John Cleese (Henry Marcus); John Larroquette (Maury Manning); Amanda Peet (Debbie); Terrence Ross (Radio Actor); Jeffrey Ross (Shecky); Christopher MacDonald (Brad Bradburn); Paul Benedict (Professor Brainiac); Dina Spybey (Bambi Madison); Pauline Little (Leslie Barnett); William Hill (Passerby); Mal Z. Lawrence (Mort); Adam Heller (Howie); Ellen David (Sylvia); Daniel Ziskie (Guy's Doctor); Anna Lobell (Receptionist); David Costabile (Junior Editor); Brett

Gillen (Man with Bicycle); Olga Merediz (Mrs. Ramirez); Jacklin Webb (Nurse); Clebert Ford (Claude); Dick Henley (Doorman); Sonia Benezra (Manicurist); Richard Litt (Buddy); Maurice Carlton (Orderly #1); Edward B. Goldstein (Eddie in Lindy's); Larry Block (Herbie); Jack Eagle (Waiter); Le Clanché du Rand (Lissy Hastings); Elizabeth Lawrence (Mimsy Hastings); Helen Stenborg (Aunt Abigail); John Cunningham (Nelson Hastings); Charles Doucet (Teamster); John Moore (News Anchor); Richard McConomy (Harry Gladrey); Lisa Bronwyn Moore (Irma Gladrey); Steven McCarthy (Book Nook Clerk); James Villemaire (Jim Morrison); Karyn Quackenbush (TV Cook); Sam Street (Truman Capote); Peter Blaikie (David); Sheena Larkin (Saleswoman); Frank Vincent (Aristotle Onassis); David Lawrence (Steve Lawrence); Debbie Gravitte (Eydie Gorme); Mickey Toft (Guy at 6); Ricky Mabe (Guy at 14); Robin Andrew Wilcock (Stage Murderer); Jude Beny (Skeptical Housewife); Jean-Guy Bouchard (Wolf Whistle Teamster); Carl Alacchi (Orderly #2).

LOS ANGELES TIMES, 1/28/00, Calendar/p. 4, Kevin Thomas

"Isn't She Great" is just the movie Jacqueline Susann deserves—and that is no put-down. In telling the story of the publicity-hound author of "Valley of the Dolls," director Andrew Bergman and writer Paul Rudnick give Susann's life mythical dimension in a mix of fact and fictionalized supporting characters that allows them to create a satire of popular culture and the flowering of celebrity worship from the '40s through the '70s that is as affectionate as it is hilarious.

Within their warm, amused embrace, Bette Midler as Susann and Nathan Lane as her devoted publicist-promoter-husband Irving Mansfield—ah, what glorious casting!—are able to create a couple who are outrageous, endearing and, finally, heroic. It's a tricky business to have fun with your characters yet have them taken seriously as admirable human beings, but "Isn't She Great" works faultlessly on both levels. We come away entertained by Susann's colorful saga, moved by her courage and made aware of why she was important after all.

When "Valley of the Dolls," cited by the Guinness Book of Records as the best-selling novel of all time, was published in 1966, Susann took the popular novel to new levels—or is it depths?—of lurid candor. It was the substance-abusing saga of three young women seeking love and success in New York City. One character was clearly based on Judy Garland, with a fourth character, an older woman, inspired unmistakably by Ethel Merman. Susann's prose style was wretched, but she was a helluva storyteller because she wrote about—and believed in—what she knew of show business and of human nature.

As her first publisher's assistant (Amanda Peet) remarks: "She knows what she's doing." Susann knew she was hardly a great literary talent, and extravagant praise drew from her a silent fish-eyed response that said, "You must be out of your mind." Guided by Mansfield, Susann also revolutionized the way in which books were sold. Barnstorming the country, they promoted "Valley" like the movie it inevitably became and pushed the book with the salesmanship and personal touch of Estee Lauder descending upon a department store cosmetics counter.

As Bergman and Rudnick tell it, Susann was a seriously failing actress when she met Mansfield. The two were clearly made for each other. All Susann knows is that she wants to be famous—"I need mass love!" she declares—and it takes quite a while for Mansfield—whose belief in her is as complete as his love for her—to hit upon the idea that her best shot at fame and fortune is as a writer. In fact, as early as 1946 she had published articles, and her first real success, in 1963, was "Every Night, Josephine," in which Susann's life was seen through her pet poodle.

What her public did not know until after her death at 56 in 1974 was that Susann and Mansfield were quietly and devotedly coping with a son, Guy, their only child, so severely autistic that early on he had to be institutionalized and remains so to this day. (The Mansfields' mutual devotion, drive and commitment to succeed place their marriage in vivid contrast to the decadent and destructive relationships Susann depicted in her novels.)

What her fans also did not know was that throughout her celebrity years, Susann, a heavy smoker, was living on borrowed time, having been stricken with breast cancer in 1962 that would recur and spread. Susann was given to addressing God directly and asked him to give her 10 more years to accomplish all that she wanted to—and that's exactly the length of time that was left to her. (She also wanted to ensure that her son would receive the best care possible for the rest of his life.)

If Susann's novels made a direct hit with predominantly female readers around the world, she herself became a gay icon, and there have been successful—and hilarious—stagings of the script of the "Valley of the Dolls," notably with drag performer Jackie Beat cast as the Ethel Merman character Helen Lawson, played in the movie by Susan Hayward, a last-minute replacement for Judy Garland. Susann was campy, she was kitschy, but she was also tough and silently brave in the face of tragedy. And she was honest, and at heart she and Mansfield are shown to be humble, ever-grateful for any and all good fortune that comes their way and uncomplaining when confronted with life's cruelties; clearly, it was a matter of pride and responsibility that they maintained an upbeat image to everyone.

All these are qualities that allow Midler and Lane to bring Susann and Mansfield so vibrantly and endearingly alive. Lane's Irving is unwavering in his belief in his adored wife, and her Jackie is a smart, shrewd wisecracker, strong enough to allow herself to be vulnerable and trusting with her husband and friends—in particular, a chic, earthy and loyal actress, played with delicious panache by Stockard Channing; her Florence Maybelle is a descendant of Auntie Mame's pal, Vera Charles.

Susann is also loud and gaudy, Pucci'd and Gucci'd to the max. The lesson of her life is that success makes you happy and helps you ward off life's inevitable sorrows. Susann and Mansfield are absolute believers in the power of celebrity to make you even happier, so much so that when she enters the hospital for the last time, Mansfield comforts her by telling her that she'll be in the very suite where "Elizabeth Taylor had her pneumonia"; surely, she was cheered by this. You are glad for Susann that she made it all the way to Aristotle Onassis' yacht—with that other Jackie.

"Isn't She Great" broadly and amusingly plays Susann against her first editor, Michael Hastings (David Hyde Pierce), an uptight, aristocratic WASP who is initially horrified by her manuscript, which was handed to him by her publisher (John Cleese), who would seem to have taken his flashy Nehru-jacketed style from one of those guys who wrote "Hair." But inevitably he's won over by her indomitable brashness and ability to connect with a wide range of people. (The film is based—"inspired" is more accurate—on a touching and amusing 1995 homage to Susann in the New Yorker by Michael Korda, her editor on her second novel, "The Love Machine"; some incidents concerning the fictional Hastings are drawn from Korda's own experiences with Susann.)

What the filmmakers are doing is pitting exuberant Jewish nouveau riche vulgarity with anemic traditional WASP propriety and boring good taste. It can only be regarded as healthy and refreshing that in recent years movies have felt comfortable in acknowledging that Jews can be just as vulgar as anyone else; after all, they have also long been major arbiters of lowbrow show biz as well as high culture. In any event, it's fun to hear Susann enter a Sardi's-like restaurant with Mansfield and Hastings and tell the headwaiter that their party consists of "two adults and a Gentile."

Naturally, "Valley of the Dolls" and "The Love Machine," which were followed by "Once Is Not Enough," got lots of bad reviews, and on TV we get a reprise of Truman Capote putting down Susann, adding famously that she "looks like a truck driver in drag." If there is one thing to carp about "Isn't She Great" it's that it leaves out Susann's equally famous comeback. When a talk-show host, possibly Johnny Carson, asked her what she thought about Truman, she unhesitatingly replied: "I think Truman will go down in history as one of our greatest presidents." Susann deserved to have this riposte included in her own movie.

Not surprisingly, the filmmakers don't stint on the visual aspects of their satire, with Julie Weiss' costumes and production designer Stuart Wurtzel's contributions almost as strong as those of Midler and Lane. Burt Bacharach is an inspired, period-perfect choice to compose the film's score, which deftly echoes the music, and in particular, the theme song of the "Valley of the Dolls" movie. That clothes and decor are exaggerated contributes substantially to the myth of Susann that's being projected—a myth that allows truths about her and her times to stand out in relief all the more.

When all is said and done, "Isn't She Great" leaves you suspecting that it takes a lot of taste to depict vulgarity without either condescending or succumbing to it.

NEW YORK, 2/7/00, p. 52, Peter Rainer

Isn't She Great, starring Bette Midler and Nathan Lane, is billed as a biopic about the life and hard-driving times of Jacqueline Susann, but the actual film is something else again. It's more like a camp fantasia that turns Susann into a naughty-but-nice lollipop who is royally catered to by her gummybear-ish husband—press agent Irving Mansfield. The inanity of the project is staggering. At one point, when Susann is in the throes of creation on *Valley of the Dolls*, she asks her husband if it's okay to write about orgasms. She might as well be asking him if she can write about waffles. I realize that the filmmakers—director Andrew Bergman and screenwriter Paul Rudnick—were under no obligation to give us the "real" Jacqueline Susann, but it would have helped if they had at least given us the real *somebody*.

It's kind of funny reading all the recent stories about Susann being rediscovered as a feminist icon—the high priestess of trash who brought out all the rowdy, lewd stuff—in women's lives that the big-boy pulpsters left out. She and Irving Mansfield are also being credited, if that's the right term, with starting the whole take-no-prisoners approach to book promotion. Popular culture must be pretty hard-up for heroes these days. Only in a win-win culture like ours—and, more specifically, only in Hollywood—would anyone celebrate a character who says unabashedly, "All I ever wanted was to be famous." This declaration in the movie is presented with only the lightest of ironies. Fame—any fame—is good.

The success game has never seemed so squeaky-clean. In place of the pill-popping, Pucci-appareled swaggerer who had scads of affairs and worked her personal vendettas into romans à clef, we are given an essentially kindhearted dame whose celebrity was, literally, divinely ordained. The film is punctuated by scenes in which Susann, with Mansfield dutifully in tow, looks up through the trees in her favorite spot in Central Park and talks to God. We're supposed to find these scenes adorable—God as the ultimate William Morris agent. But we're also meant to see Susann as essentially child-like—in a good way. She wishes upon a star, and the star twinkles back.

Even her heartbreak twinkles: When her baby boy turns out to be autistic, she's bummed out but pretty much snaps out of it with the help of her wisecracking actress friend Florence (Stockard Channing). When a lump in her breast is discovered, it's only a matter of time before we get the scene in which, during treatment, she pulls out a copy of *Valley of the Dolls* for her radiation technician. I suppose we should be grateful that we're not watching a big squishy sobfest, but there's something anaesthetizing about the way everything in this movie—the sorrows as well as the kicks—is made to seem silly.

The skimpiness of the conception extends to the showbiz milieu that the film is supposedly celebrating. The scenes in Lindy's, for example, might as well be taking place in cloud cuckooland. We don't get any of the hustle of the Broadway-Hollywood idiom, and the New York book scene is just so much wacky derring-do. John Cleese, whose talent, along with just about everybody else's, seems to have gone into hibernation during this film, plays the visionary publisher who recognizes the dollar signs embedded in Susann's wretched prose. Susann's editor, played by David Hyde Pierce doing his snippy Wasp thing, chafes at that prose until the numbers start racking up; he does a victory jig, which we're supposed to join in on, when Susann's sales reach the top of the best-seller list. So much for standards.

As an artist, Bette Midler began her movie career at the top, with a performance in *The Rose* in which she seemed capable of doing anything. Her raucousness and misery flowed into each other; she was like a free-form force of nature, and it remains one of the finest debut performances in movies. But then her acting career took a sharp turn into blowsy-diva comedy, and as long as she was in films like *Down and Out in Beverly Hills* or *Ruthless People*, who could complain? Like Katherine Hepburn, she was a rarity: great in tragedy and great in comedy. But as time went on, Midler's comic antics turned into shtick, and her tragic force, in movies like *Beaches* and *Stella* and *For the Boys*, dissolved into goop. Playing Jacqueline Susann should have recharged her batteries by indulging her gift for knockabout tragedy, except that the role, as written, is pure piffle. The current resurgence of interest in Susann—the magazine and newspaper articles, the reissues of her best-sellers, and all the surrounding hype—is supposed to be her last laugh on all the denigrators who said she'd be forgotten. But having the trashiness of her life turned into more trash isn't really much of way to be remembered.

NEW YORK POST, 1/28/00, p. 43, Lou Lumenick

"Isn't She Great" is the second comedy in a month about a dead, semi-forgotten show-biz figure—trashy '60s novelist Jacqueline Susann, a part that fits Bette Midler like a sequined glove.

The film takes even more liberties with the facts than the Andy Kaufman biopic "Man on the Moon," but it's amusing, light entertainment on its own terms.

Drawing as much inspiration from 1950s "women's pictures" as from a Michael Korda article in The New Yorker, "Isn't She Great" paints a glossy portrait of Susann, who died of cancer in 1974.

A minor Broadway, radio and TV actress best known for embroidery commercials in the '50s, Susann achieved her dream of international celebrity with the publication of "Valley of the Dolls" in 1966.

The movie wildly rearranges the chronology of her life and favors glamour, laughs, tears and romance, greatly downplaying the heavily autobiographical show-biz types of Susann's novels, characters who are often addicted to booze and sex.

A well-cast Nathan Lane plays Susann's husband, Irving Mansfield, a Runyonesque Broadway press agent and producer who devoted himself to promoting her into one of the top-selling authors of all time.

"I need mass love!" wails Susann, portrayed by Midler in bawdy top form. She teaches her white-shoe publishers how to hustle books—and helps usher in the era of the celebrity author.

Outfitted in an eye-popping series of outfits, Midler's Susann suffers with style. Her own only son is institutionalized with autism, and she's diagnosed with breast cancer just as she finishes her masterwork.

"Were you having a bad day?" she demands of God, from whom she demands a spot on the best-seller list from beneath a tree in Central Park. "You owe me big time!"

The movie conveniently ignores the fact that Susann had already published a best seller, "Every Night Josephine," about her pet poodles. It also leaves out her many celebrity pals and enemies—though it does recreate Truman Capote's famous description of her as resembling "a truck driver in drag."

Despite the serious aspects, director Andrew Bergman ("Honeymoon in Vegas") and screenwriter Paul Rudnick ("Addams Family Values") mostly play it for laughs.

Some of the most hilarious scenes involve Susann's interactions with an exasperated book editor (David Hyde Pierce as a character partly based on Korda), who is appalled by her near-pornographic manuscript and takes the Susann and Mansfield to Connecticut to work on the book.

Stockard Channing also scores as a tippling, man-chasing actress pal who memorably recounts her abortive stint as a guest star on "The Adventures of Ozzie and Harriet."

"Isn't She Great" isn't great, but it's an enjoyable if overly discreet and romanticized look at a long-vanished show-business world.

NEWSDAY, 1/28/00, Part II/p. B3, Jan Stuart

Late into "Isn't She Great," the broadly romanticized biography of trash novelist Jacqueline Susann and her manager-husband, Irving Mansfield, the show-biz couple attend the Hollywood premiere of "Valley of the Dolls." Bette Midler and Nathan Lane, as Susann and Mansfield, watch from the audience as Patty Duke rips Susan Hayward's wig off in one of that film's more restrained moments. A look of disgust creeps over Midler's face. She leans over to Lane and mutters, "I hate this movie!"

Had anyone connected with "Isn't She Great" been able to smell the warning smoke early enough, they would have never allowed this scene past the first draft. As it is, the spectacle of a character in one of the most dismayingly bad movies, of the past decade disdaining one of the most enjoyably bad movies of the 1960s amounts to a self-critique so naked and on-the-money as to border on the grotesque.

Based on a New Yorker profile by Susann's editor, Michael Korda, and debased by screenwriter Paul Rudnick, "Isn't She Great" is literary biography as burlesque, as shrill and stop-at-nothing as that suggests. Rudnick and director Andrew Bergman probably figured that a full-on Bette Midler comedy was the only way to honor the flamboyant author of such purple classics as "Valley of the Dolls" and "The Love Machine." What they never entirely absorbed was that there was a person beneath the blinding op-art gowns. Whatever evidence Korda offered to that effect is hyped here into kitsch histrionics Susann herself would have been hard-pressed to equal.

Fleshing out real human beings has never been a forte of Rudnick, who hit his screenwriting stride with such jokey satires as "In and Out" and "Addams Family Values." Tailoring Susann's flashy persona to the boisterous talents of Midler, Rudnick creates a Midler parody, which amounts to a caricature of a caricature. It's not The Divine Miss M he apes, however. Rather, it's Vickie Eydie, Midler's irrepressibly vulgar lounge act.

In a voice only louder than the look-at-me '60s wardrobe Julie Weiss has designed for her, Midler shrieks from a waist-deep perch in Central Park's duck pond over her failure as an actress. No sooner has Susann's lover dumped her ("He left me for his wife!" she cries, tipping us off to the film's Minsky-low wit) than she is being courted by Mansfield, who obviously sees something in her that we have to take on faith.

As the tirelessly adoring Mansfield, Lane is the only actor in the film who is not required to parody himself. Mostly, he stands sweetly in the shadows while Midler flattens everyone in her path or makes helpful remarks such as, "Hang in, the lox is coming." In one of the film's more ludicrous running conceits, he must indulge Midler while she stands in Central Park, talking to God, represented by sunlight through a tree. Periodically, the camera places the audience in God's treetop perspective, from where we are able to conclude that He is at least as mortified by what He hears as Lane.

Elsewhere, worthy actors struggle to keep a lid on their over-the-top assignments. Stockard Channing wrestles admirably with her Kay Kendall role as Susann's glamorous actress buddy, while John Cleese misfires big-time as Susann's eccentric publisher. David Hyde Pierce plagiarizes his priggish "Frasier" shtick as the Korda-inspired editor, in a lampoon of Connecticut WASP-iness that lost its freshness after "Auntie Mame." The chief point of interest in Korda's piece—the fiery editing sessions between Susann and Korda—are nowhere to be seen.

Neither Midler nor director Bergman are able to navigate the queasy shifts from camp cartoon to bathos, as Susann sputters in denial over her cancer and autistic son. When a beaming Susann upstages Steve Lawrence and Eydie Gorme (Tony Lawrence and Debbie Gravitte) at a Waldorf party in her honor, we are meant to bask in her triumph over the naysayers, but her ferocity and desperation makes us shift in our seat.

With any luck, Midler will triumph over this latest fiasco and live to see the day when a movie is made about her life. If good sense prevails, they will spare us the career-nadir moment in which Midler attends the premiere of "Isn't She Great" and looks on in horror as Midler looks on in horror at "Valley of the Dolls."

SIGHT AND SOUND, 8/00, p. 49, Charles Taylor

Manhattan, the late 50s. Jacqueline Susann is a determined but untalented actress trying to make it in New York. Irving Mansfield sees her on stage and is immediately smitten. He proposes to become her agent and her husband; Jackie accepts both offers. Despite Irving's belief in her talents, she still struggles as an actress. Deciding that his wife will have a better future as a writer, Irving persuades Jackie to write a novel based on the scandalous showbusiness stories she's heard over the years. The result, *Valley of the Dolls,* becomes a smash despite the derision of the literary world.

Meanwhile Jackie gives birth to a severely autistic son and is diagnosed with breast cancer. She prays for more time to prove that the success of *Valley* wasn't a fluke and lives just long enough to see her next two books follow it to the top of the best-seller list.

How many movies deal with *happy* marriages? Clumsy in execution but very sharp in its understanding of its subject, *Isn't She Great* uses the lifestory of trash novelist *par excellence* Jacqueline Susann as material for a comedy of happily devoted married life. The title itself was the oft-repeated phrase of Susann's adoring husband and manager Irving Mansfield. Director Andrew Bergman *(Honeymoon in Vegas)* and screenwriter Paul Rudnick rely on Bette Midler to convey the self-promoting brassiness that made Susann's persona as big a hit as her books. But the heart of their movie lies in the contented rapture that emanates from the eyes of Nathan Lane's Irving whenever he gazes at his wife.

Isn't She Great starts badly. As Jackie shuttles from commercials to game-show panels trying to make her mark, Bergman's staging is both broad and imprecise. But as soon as Jackie starts writing *Valley of the Dolls* the movie's canniness smoothes out all the unevenness.

Valley of the Dolls, Susann's novel inspired by the scandals she'd heard about true-life celebrities, was a massive hit when first published and Rudnick views the public's appetite for the book and the literati's contempt for it as a classic battle between the vulgar vitality of pop culture and the stifling propriety of approved culture. The latter is represented by David Hyde Pierce (from television's *Frasier* and one of the most gifted farceurs around) as the preppy editor Hastings assigned to whip Jackie's manuscript into shape. The winner in this rivalry is never in doubt. From the moment this Wasp finds himself lunching with these two garrulous New York Jews, he doesn't stand a chance. Rudnick and Bergman do a nifty job of foreshadowing just how strongly the public will capitulate to Susann when Hyde Pierce's character takes Jackie and Irving to his family's Connecticut house. ("Ya got slaves?" Jackie asks when she takes a gander at the sprawling country home.) In no time at all, the editor's prim Yankee grandmother and businessman father have fallen for Jackie and devoured her manuscript. The film-makers bring the friendship between the author and her editor to a satisfying close with one lovely detail: when he visits the dying Jackie, Hastings has abandoned his Brooks Brothers suits for suitably modern attire.

Roundly panned when it opened in America, *Isn't She Great* is nonetheless raucously funny and good-natured. Indeed, there's something ironic about the dismissive treatment the film received from 'serious' critics on its US release: vividly embodied by Midler, Susann epitomises the brash pop energy that attracts us to the movies in the first place. And like the lush melodramas of George Cukor and Douglas Sirk, sniffed at by critics on their first release, now given serious consideration, her novels get their emotional resonance from focusing on the disappointments in the lives of women in the pre-feminist era.

Rudnick's script avoids juicier titbits like Jackie's reputed bisexuality. He's dead on, though, about the mixture of narcissism and generosity that fuelled her self-promotion. (Her determination to hide the facts of her son's autism and her cancer are the exact opposite of the way celebrity tragedy is now used as PR capital.) Midler's performance is an astute combination of warmth and monstrousness. But it's Lane who nearly makes off with the film. From voicing the cat in *Stuart Little to* his baggy-pants brio *in Love's Labour's Lost,* Lane has one of the movies' most dependable and delightful comic presences. He's never been as touching as he is here. Even instructing a bus full of schoolchildren to ask for *Valley of the Dolls* for Christmas ("It's better than milk!") everything he does is in service of Jackie. Lane does more with his eyebrows than most actors do with their entire faces. They arch together to express sudden scepticism, or, in blissful adoration, form a steeple over his lovestruck expression. Lane's Irving is a man buoyed by love, and the actor's roly-poly frame takes on a swain's lightness. *Isn't She Great* is as much Irving's fairy tale as Jackie's. He's the putz who became a prince.

VILLAGE VOICE, 2/8/00, p. 137, J. Hoberman

More arch than satiric, *Isn't She Great* is a brazenly lightweight, genially amusing portrait of Jacqueline Susann, author of the '60s shlockbuster and quintessential dishathon *Valley of the Dolls,* and her adoring husband-cum-publicist Irving Mansfield. The movie aspires to be both stylish and coarse, camp and vulgar—which is pretty much how Bette Midler plays it.

Directed by Andrew Bergman from Paul Rudnick's screenplay, *Isn't She Great* is a slumming biopic in the *Ed Wood* mode—although the filmmakers don't have the same reverence for the super-successful Susann that Tim Burton had for his subject's transcendent failure. Basically, Bergman and Rudnick tell the same joke over and over: The author of the best-selling novel ever written was a loudmouth yenta who brilliantly parlayed her own neediness into a real-life star vehicle. Talent, schmalent. This was a woman capable of flogging her book to the nurse administering her chemotherapy.

Susann would doubtless have preferred to be impersonated by a glamorous fellow-writer like Joan Collins—indeed, as Jackie's best girlfriend, Stockard Channing is surely closer to Susann's tough-broad personality. Midler, a tiny terror of saucy oomph, clowns her way through the movie, basking in the approval of Nathan Lane's Irving ("Isn't she great!"). A matching pair of middle-aged garden gnomes planted in the *Sweet Smell of Success* universe of Broadway flacks, Jackie and Irving are caricatured caricatures. Theirs is a sensibility that exists beyond taste.

Whether announcing Jackie's pregnancy to the cheesecake-chomping multitudes at Lindy's or cackling at the plantation-style facade of an haute Connecticut mansion, the couple are foot soldiers in the immigrant Jewish assault on established American civility. Indeed, Jackie is something of a Hebrew prophetess who, no less than Martin Buber or Tevye the Dairyman, enjoys an I/Thou relationship with God. Once Irving has placed the call, so to speak, she addresses her creator from a knoll in the midst of Central Park. (Irving to a curious passerby, "Excuse us, we're in a meeting.") Showbiz rules: Even before Jackie has completed her opus, these visionaries have the whole glitzkrieg sales plan in their heads—commando book tours, surprise personal appearances ("If you love the Old Testament, you'll love *The Valley of the Dolls*"), TV tie-ins to culminate in Johnny Carson's *Tonight Show.*

Isn't She Great is based on the memoir Michael Korda published five years ago in *The New Yorker* to jump-start the current Susann revival. Korda, who edited her second novel, *The Love Machine,* isn't a character here—nor, sad to report, is Ethel Merman, with whom, so it has been reported, Jackie enjoyed a lesbian love affair. Instead, the filmmakers have recruited David Hyde Pierce, the self-important snob who serves as younger sibling foil for TV's blustering Frasier, to play visitor from the Valley of the Dull. Raising the movie's sitcom level, the Pierce character stands in for the uptight WASP literary establishment—confounded by Susann, who refuses to discuss her manuscript until he changes into Irving's eye-searing plaid sports jacket.

Back in the day, this might have been truly entertaining. The movie's leads and generic Burt Bacharach score notwithstanding, it's a musical without music. The closest thing to a production number is the lavish party that consecrates Jackie's rise to the top of the bestseller list. As the author is serenaded by Steve and Edie, her inner Midler cuts loose, singing along, swanning around with her own hand mike as poor Irving wanders off. *Isn't She Great* is not without elements of pathos—Jackie's cancer, the autistic child whose existence she and Irving conceal from the world—but it's too cool for heartbreak. Nor does it quite elevate its heroine to the full culture studies divadom she's recently obtained.

A failed actress, sometime TV pitchwoman, and occasional Broadway groupie, Susann was clever enough to grasp Cosmo's "Sex and the Single Girl" zeitgeist and dogged enough to deconstruct Harold Robbins's *The Carpetbaggers,* creating juicy romans à clef that, as Korda put it, offered "romance with tears *and* oral sex." Although some fans have compared her to bad-girl performance artists like Karen Finley, Bergman and Rudnick are disinclined to make such grandiose claims. *Isn't She Great* merely proposes Jackie Susann as the Gertrude Stein of Central Park South, the woman who invented postmodern celebrity-worship—the self-promoter who incorporated literature into showbiz rather than vice versa.

Still, the movie is not without its pungent blasphemies. Bergman and Rudnick do allow their Jackie to browbeat God as though she were Harry Cohn and he a particularly maladroit publicist. "Fuck you!" she begins, and winds up screaming: "You owe me . . . big time! Get on the phone now! Make me famous!"

Also reviewed in:
CHICAGO TRIBUNE, 1/28/00, Friday/p. A, Michael Wilmington
NATION, 2/21/00, p. 34, Stuart Klawans
NEW YORK TIMES, 1/28/00, p. E1, Elvis Mitchell
NEW YORKER, 2/7/00, p. 97, David Denby
VARIETY, 1/31-2/6/00, p. 31, Emanuel Levy
WASHINGTON POST, 1/28/00, p. C1, Rita Kempley
WASHINGTON POST, 1/28/00, Weekend/p. 38, Desson Howe

IT ALL STARTS TODAY

An Independent Artists Group release of a Le Studio Canal+/Les Films Alain Sarde/Little Bear/TF1 Films Productions production.   *Producer:* Alain Sarde and Frédéric Bourboulon.

Director: Bertrand Tavernier. *Screenplay (French with English subtitles):* Dominique Sampiero, Tiffany Tavernier, and Bertrand Tavernier. *Director of Photography:* Alain Choquart. *Editor:* Sophie Brunet and Sophie Mandonnet. *Music:* Louis Sclavis. *Sound:* Michel Desrois, Gérard Lamps, and (music) Didier Lizé. *Sound Editor:* Elisabeth Paquotte. *Art Director:* Thierry François. *Set Decorator:* José Moréno. *Costumes:* Marpessa Djian. *Make-up:* Agnès Tassel. *Running time:* 117 minutes. *MPAA Rating:* Not Rated.

CAST: Philippe Torreton (Daniel); Maria Pitarresi (Valeria); Nadia Kaci (Samia); Véronique Ataly (Mrs. Lienard); Nathalie Bécue (Cathy); Emmanuelle Bercot (Mrs. Tievaux); Françoise Bette (Mrs. Delacourt); Lambert Marchal (Rémi); Christine Citti (Mrs. Baudoin); Christina Crevillén (Sophie); Sylviane Goudal (Gloria); Didier Bezace (Inspector); Betty Teboulle (Mrs. Henry); Gérard Giroudon (Mayor); Marief Guittier (Daniel's Mother); Daniel Delabesse (Marc); Jean-Claude Frissung (Director's Colleague); Thierry Gibault (Police Inspector); Philippe Meyer (Council Member); Gerald Cesbron (Mr. Henry); Michelle Goddet (Beaten Child's Mother); Stefan Elbaum (Beaten Child's Uncle); Nathalie Desprez (Mrs. Bry); Françoise Miquelis (Mrs. Duhem); Frédéric Richard (Mr. Bacheux); Johanne Cornil-Leconte (Mrs. Bacheux); Sylvie Delbauffe (Woman with Baby); Mathieu Lenne (Jimmy); Rémi Henneuse (Kevin); Corinne Agthe (Mrs. Paquotte); Dominique Bouchard (Doctor); Benoît Constant (Daniel's Father); Patrick Courteix (Mrs. Henry's Neighbor); Véronique Dargent (Mrs. Loiseau); Valérie Dermagne (Nurse); Lilyane Discret (Young Mother); Leila Duhem (Mrs. Polliaert); Yamina Duvivier (Mrs. Chimot); Séverine Fernand (Angeline's Mother); Catherine Gorosz (Mrs. Daumise); Christophe Guichet (Daniel's Brother); Nadia Ikisse (Mrs. Mimouni); Marie-Madeleine Langlois (Neighbor's Wife); Nelly Larachiche (Mrs. Legrand); France Leroy (Cafe Owner); Claude Liénard (Mrs. Henry's Doctor); Marcelle Loutre (Guegdan's Mother); Kelly Mercier (Laetitia); Jacky Meunier (Valeria's Father); Cécile Montagnon (Mrs. Lamart); Michèle Niewrzeda (Mrs. Bornat); Vincenza Orologio (Valeria's Mother); Marie-Françoise Prette (Mrs. Marchal); Linda Prudhomme (Mrs. Dupuis); Monique Quivy (Dining Hall Lady); Claude Ronnaux (Colleague); Françoise Sage (Mrs. Mériaux); Pascale Verdière (Nanny).

CHRISTIAN SCIENCE MONITOR, 9/8/00, p. 16, David Sterritt

[*It All Starts Today* was reviewed jointly with *Pola X*; see Sterritt's review of that film.]

LOS ANGELES TIMES, 9/29/00, Calendar/p. 16, Kevin Thomas

Bertrand Tavernier's superb "It All Starts Today" is set in a small mining town in northern France, but it could just as easily be taking place in America's Rust Belt. The mines have closed, leaving much of the population unemployed, and its mayor trying to promote its slag heaps into tourist attractions.

This means that the town's kindergarten, part of France's national preschool educational system, already minimally funded, is heavily strained, with parents leaving their young children all day as they search for work. Some cannot afford even the minimal financial contribution expected; in some dire instances they are unable to send off their youngsters with lunch.

Attempting to meet the day-to-day, indeed moment-to-moment, challenge of keeping this kindergarten up and running is the dynamic and creative Daniel Lefebvre (Philippe Torreton). Supply shortages and broken-down plumbing confront Daniel regularly as he attempts to stimulate the imaginations of the very young as he teaches and serves as principal and inspiration to an admirably dedicated staff. Given the school's community, it is impossible for him and his colleagues to stick to the school room and the playground. "It All Starts Today" is inspired by the experiences of Tavernier's son-in-law Dominique Sampiero, who collaborated with his wife Tiffany and her father on the script.

The film does a terrific job of showing the toll exacted by economic hardship upon a hard-pressed town's youngest inhabitants in the form of malnutrition, abuse and myriad health, developmental and behavioral problems. For 25 years Tavernier has sustained an illustrious career as a filmmaker of passionate commitment, an artist who is never afraid to speak out but who could never be labeled a message director. His films grow out of his characters' emotions, beliefs and drives, and they tend to range wide and deep.

Thus Daniel's fervent commitment to the children drives him to step over the line continually into the province of the social worker, which brings him into fiery conflict with a frequently hidebound, entrenched and self-serving government bureaucracy. The key issue is a family that has been without heat for half a year, sending the despairing mother to drink as her truck driver/crane operator husband must constantly go abroad for whatever short-term jobs he is able to land. Daniel and his colleagues, plus a young novice social worker (Nadia Kaci), struggle mightily to prevent the family from being strangled to death in red tape.

Although there is real pain and suffering "It All Starts Today," it is too impassioned, too brisk and too embracing of life and human foibles to be depressing. It also tells another story, that of Daniel's evolving relationship with his beautiful lover (Maria Pitarresi), a sculptor who supports herself as a waitress, and with her son (Lambert Marchal), who never knew his actual father but has trouble accepting Daniel as a parent. Daniel, a native to the town, in turn is coping with his aged parents; his father, a brutal, dour man, counterpart to the often harsh environment depicted on the screen.

Daniel is a life force, and to play him Tavernier turned to the Comedie Francaise's Torreton, who also starred in the director's "L.627," "Fresh Bait" and "Captain Conan." Toffeton's Daniel has boundless enthusiasm and energy, but he is unafraid to show the man as being somewhat full of himself. Torreton clearly understands that Daniel would have to have a sizable ego to tackle a job that requires him to try to succeed against all odds.

Yet Daniel is a warm, immensely appealing man, aware that taking responsibility means risking making mistakes and owning up to them when he does. Torreton never flags and simply becomes Daniel, and Tavernier surround him with an array of formidable supporting players, typical of the director. "It All Starts Today" glows, as do all Tavernier films. It's another gem in an ever-lengthening string of accomplishments from one of the world's major filmmakers.

NEW YORK POST, 9/8/00, p. 47, Lou Lumenick

Bertrand Tavernier's new film is a damning indictment of unfeeling bureaucrats in a small town in northern France, and by extension, everywhere.

A wonderful actor named Philippe Torreton plays Daniel, the almost saintly principal of a kindergarten and pre-K school.

It's a tough environment: The local unemployment rate is 34 percent and many parents are either seething with anger or downright apathetic about the plight of their kids.

In one telling scene, the blank-eyed parents of one kindergartner explain his tardiness by saying it's tough to set an alarm clock to go off in the morning when you don't have a job to go to.

Elsewhere, a veteran teacher vents her frustration at students who barely know how to talk with adults.

Daniel stoically copes with a series of heartbreaking work crises: The school is trashed by teenage vandals, yet another child is being abused by his parents and a mother tearfully explains she can't afford $5 for an activities fee because she needs the money to feed her kids for the week.

But Daniel snaps when a desperate mother abandons her 5-year-old son and a baby at the school. Daniel takes them back home, only to discover the family lives in a hovel where the electricity for heat has been cut off in the dead of winter because of a bureaucratic snafu.

Defying his superiors and ignoring advice from other educators that only a portion of his young students can be saved, Daniel launches a crusade, with the help of his artist fiancée (Maria Pitarresi) and a sympathetic social worker (Nadia Kaci).

"It All Starts Today," which Tavernier wrote with his daughter Tiffany and her husband, Dominique Sampiero, a longtime teacher, somewhat dilutes its impact as an angry, documentary-style polemic with melodramatic subplots involving the girlfriend's son and Daniel's parents—and an ending that seems a tad too upbeat in this context.

But it's well worth seeing for the terrific performances. You'll believe Torreton, a magnetic performer, has been teaching for years, and Tavernier gets fabulous work from the nonprofessional kids, who are actually students at a school like the one depicted in the movie.

NEWSDAY, 9/8/00, Part II/p. B7, John Anderson

Here's a short list of people who probably shouldn't go to see Bertrand Tavernier's "It All Starts Today," lest they have to reassess their worldview: Members of "taxpayer groups" devoted to savaging school budgets.

Parents who neglect their children and then launch holy wars when those same children get in trouble.

Politicians who talk about "our kids" out of one side of their mouth and tax cuts out of the other.

Again, this is just the short list. It might also include those who put capital above community, or educators who evaluate their students according to mathematical formulas because, after all, they can't save them all.

But we have to leave someone off the list, so there will be someone to see this movie. Why? Because a film so passionate and passionately made reminds us, in this season of empty cinematic calories, what a stirring thing a movie can be. Directed by France's Mr. Versatile, Bertrand Tavernier ("Round Midnight" "Capitaine Conan"), "It All Starts Today" is a social indictment that plays out like epic drama.

It's decidedly French in its milieu and attitudes, but only the thickest of wits should have a problem translating it into any other language or locale.

The movie's point is that those who seek political, professional or financial gain through the underserving of children are the worst kinds of cowards. How it makes that point is the stuff of real cinema.

Based on the real-life experiences of co-writer Dominique Sampiero, "It All Starts Today" stars Tavernier's Capitaine Conan—Philippe Torreton—as Daniel, a kindergarten teacher-school director constantly thrust into the unwanted role of social worker and surrogate parent. It's a hard-luck town. Most of his students are named after soap opera characters; their mothers are sullen when chastised, shamed by their poverty, overwhelmed by their children, unsure what to do. As the veteran teacher Mrs. Delacourt (Francois Bette) observes, their leaky school's children were always poor—but at least they were on time and washed. Now, she says, "we have to teach them everything." But it's the bureaucrats, with their useless regulations and virtuoso buck-passing, who really infuriate Daniel, and Torreton brings a similar ferocity to fighting child welfare authorities that he employed cutting Balkan throats in "Capitaine Conan." Daniel is the teacher everyone's child should have—firm, affectionate and selfless. It seems a bit odd that he's virtually the only male teacher in France. But his singularity of vocation fits his singular sense of mission.

Tavernier, whose considerable documentary work has included recent films on France's incendiary immigrant issue, effortlessly balances Daniel's nonstop series of crises and at the same time monkeys with convention. That Daniel has a girlfriend, Valeria (Maria Pitarresi) is no surprise, nor is the fact that she's an artist; that her son (Lambert Marchal) resents Daniel seems positively trite. And when Samia (Nadia Kaci), a firebrand pediatric nurse, allies herself with Daniel, you can smell triangle in the wind.

But things don't quite work the way you expect. Sometimes they're better; sometimes they're tragically worse. Mostly, Tavernier suggests a situation and establishment that rigorously resist change, although his climactic embrace of pure joy makes us believe in happy endings almost as much as we believe in Daniel.

SIGHT AND SOUND, 8/99, p. 46, Kevin Jackson

Hernaing, in northern France: a former mining town with 34 per cent unemployment. Daniel Lefebvre is an idealistic principal of an infant school and a would-be writer. He struggles to do his best for his young charges but is constantly thwarted by the incompetence or indifference of the regional authorities, the hostility of his superiors and the apathy or despair of the parents themselves. Escorting five-year-old Laetitia home after her drunken mother, Mme. Henry, collapses in the schoolyard and runs off, Daniel finds their flat in a state of freezing squalor. His attempts to do something about this crisis and others have mixed results. With the help of social worker Samia, he effects some small improvements, but his tendency to rage at bureaucrats brings down on him a school inspection.

Meanwhile, his ex-miner father suffers a near-fatal stroke. The sullen son of his girlfriend Valéria helps some thugs to break into the school to vandalise it. Valéria resents his apparent unwillingness to give her another child. Beset by problems, he momentarily neglects the Henry family, who have had all their benefits cut off. Mme. Henry kills herself and her children with an overdose of Phenobarbital. The Henrys are given an elaborate funeral by the local authorities which Daniel refuses to attend. Instead, Valéria, Daniel and the schoolchildren organise a festival at the school. Daniel agrees to try for a child with Valéria. At his parents' house, his mother reads to his father from a manuscript Daniel has written, a poetic tribute to the uncrushable spirit of their region's people

According to interviews Bertrand Tavernier has given to the French press, *It All Starts Today* all began with tales told by the fireside. The director was on holiday with his daughter Tifffany Tavernier, and listened with fascinated dismay to her new boyfriend Dominique Sampiero, the headmaster of an infant school, as he described events from his working life. Sampiero told him about a mother from whom he was trying to collect a subscription of 30 francs (about £3), who couldn't pay because she had only 30 francs to last her for the rest of the month; about another young matron who turned up hours late to collect her child and then collapsed in the playground, dead drunk. It struck Tavernier, he says, that he hadn't seen too many stories of this kind in French cinema lately, and he set about helping to fill the gap himself. He wrote *It All Starts Today*'s screenplay in collaboration with Sampiero and Tiffany Tavernier (who have since married, so this film about troubled families is itself a family affair) and both those sad tales have made it into the final cut.

It's worth stressing the factual and personal origins of Tavernier's film to disarm, or at least qualify, some of the objections it will surely provoke in cynics and miserabilists on this side of the Channel. Not only is its hero a smouldering, macho-but-sensitive hunk (admirably played by Philippe Torreton, on his fourth outing with Tavernier after *L.627*, *L'Appât* and *Capitaine Conan*), but he also moonlights as a lyric poet whose macho-but-sensitive *aperçus* blossom here and there in the soundtrack. Not only is his waitress girlfriend as beautiful as a French movie actress—as Maria Pitarresi, in fact—but she spends her own leisure hours with welding goggles and blowtorch, making avant-garde metal sculptures.

In a putatively serious-minded study of social deprivation, this arty stuff looks several shades too glamorous; more unkindly, it looks silly. (I was not the only one who giggled at the first ominous sighting of sculpture.) Surely Tavernier is far too canny to believe audiences capable of responding enthusiastically to, say, Ken Loach's *Raining Stones* are still in need of such quaint narrative sweeteners? Does he think we can only sympathise with underclass characters if coaxed into the mood by a hero and heroine who are egregiously comely and artist to boot? Probably so and in Tavernier's defence, it must be stressed that life can be as contrived as art, since Daniel's original, Sampiero, is indeed a poet with a dozen slim volumes to his name who, judging by his photographs, scores fairly highly himself on the macho-but-sensitive scale.

Yet to understand all is not always to forgive all, and even after one concedes that some of the more improbable elements of this film are faithful enough to reality, it continues to seem an uneasy marriage between social realism and soap. Although Tavernier has said, no doubt, rightly, that he couldn't have made a documentary on this material because the real-life families would have refused "from timidity or pride" to take part, a lot of the most memorable and telling passages in the film are its quieter moments shot in documentary or pseudo-documentary style. In the most haunting of these, an older colleague of Daniel's talks to an unseen interlocutor in standard news-gathering interview format, jump-cuts and all, about the frightening decline she has witnessed in her pupils' most elementary skills. Nowadays, "they don't even know how to talk."

There are other sequences which have something of this quality of unforced observation as Tavernier slackens his narrative reins and allows us the chance to ponder his widescreen images; the seasonal transformation of the northern French landscape from mid-winter starkness to summer lushness (a plain but adequately tactful parallel to the emotional expansion taking place in Daniel, who seems poised to father a child after all and maybe break through as a writer); the wretched domestic interiors with the odd quasi-genteel memento of more prosperous days, such as a useless barometer; the clumsy, faltering rhythms of children at their play-work; and Daniel coaxing them along with a generosity and fairness that is more impressive, more a work of art, than his rather overwrought scribblings. Had the whole film been made in this spirit, it might have been some species of masterpiece. But for all its virtues of heart and mind, *It All Starts Today* has the whiff of unduly conscious artifice, and is mainly impressive when trying least hard to impress.

VILLAGE VOICE, 9/12/00, p. 156, Michael Atkinson

Cursed with a résumé free of sensational style and thematic homogeneity, Bertrand Tavernier may be among movie culture's consummate undersung masters—or may have recently become so, with a bruising camera eloquence and heart-throttling naturalism arrived at only in the last decade, with *L.627, L'Appât, Capitaine Conan,* and now *It All Starts Today.* Always a serious filmmaking intelligence (he is perhaps second only to Scorsese in the vastness of his inner archives), Tavernier never mistakes sentiment for character, or melodrama for reality—and his topicality never cloys.

It All Starts Today (Ça Commence Aujourd'hui) is certainly packed with explosives—it's a rambunctious, maddened portrait of a kindergarten principal (Philippe Torreton) trying to do right by his students in a small French town fraught with systemic poverty, unemployment, and abuse. But look how Tavernier shoots it: His roving camera is, terrifyingly, often a *what's-that* step away from the action, and approaches it in a panicked run (along with the principal). Just a handful of such moments gives the movie a ballistic urgency, so that every day at pickup and drop-off we expect the volcano to blow.

It blows, but without a sound. Torreton is his own kind of volcano; forever erupting in *Capitaine Conan,* here he boils, his violence successfully lidded by an impeccable professionalism. Focused on Torreton's Daniel—as at ease with the children as he is responsibly confrontational with parents and social service workers—the movie is essentially didactic, down to its repetitive episodism. (The kids, surprisingly, are given short shrift, despite the Truffaut-esque coda.) The script, cowritten with Tavernier's daughter, Tiffany, and longtime teacher Dominique Sampiero, has little momentum of its own, and its shapelessness is nearly camouflaged by the director's prowling presence. There are purposefully joyful interludes, but Tavernier supplies the sense of secret doom it's hard not to get about some children—what do you do when parents neglect their kids? Dynamic but preachy (there are plenty of free-form Loachian policy discussions, and many in the cast are actual teachers), *It All Starts Today* has no answers where there aren't any and that's the final source of its outrage.

Also reviewed in:
CHICAGO TRIBUNE, 10/6/00, Friday/p. F, Michael Wilmington
NEW REPUBLIC, 9/25/00, p. 30, Stanley Kauffmann
NEW YORK TIMES, 9/8/00, p. E14, A. O. Scott
NEW YORKER, 8/18/00, p. 155, David Denby
VARIETY, 2/22-28/99, p. 56, Derek Elley

IT'S THE RAGE

A Silver Nitrate and Scanbox Danmark release of a Scanbox Entertainment production. *Executive Producer:* Will Tyrer, Chris Ball, Mark Gordon, Gary Levinsohn, and Mark Vernieu. *Producer:* James D. Stern, Peter Gilbert, Ash R. Shah, Anne McCarthy, and Mary Vernieu. *Director:* James D. Stern. *Screenplay (Adapted from his play):* Keith Reddin. *Director of Photography:* Alex Nepomniaschy. *Editor:* Tony Lombardo. *Music:* Mark Mothersbaugh. *Sound:* Peter V. Meiselmann. *Sound Editor:* Markus Innocenti. *Casting:* Anne McCarthy and Mary Vernieu. *Production Designer:* Jerry Fleming. *Art Director:* Jim Donahue. *Set Decorator:* Rona De Angelo. *Costumes:* Edi Giguere. *Running time:* 103 minutes. *MPAA Rating:* R.

CAST: David Schwimmer (Chris); Joan Allen (Helen Harding); Jeff Daniels (Warren Harding); Robert Forster (Chris Tyler); Andre Braugher (Tim Sullivan); Bokeem Woodbine (Agee); Anna

Paquin (Annabel Lee);   Wayne Morse (Clerk);   Josh Brolin (Tennel);   Gary Sinise (Norton Morgan);   Deborah Offner (Secretary);   Barb Wallace (Diana);   Kevin Crowley (Ed);   Robert Peters (Phil);   Alex Watson (Guard);   Giovanni Ribisi (Sidney Lee);   Muse Watson (Todd);   Dan Anders (Coroner);   Dan Petterersson (Ambulance Drive);   Lynne Oropeza (Woman in the Bar).

LOS ANGELES TIMES, 7/7/00, Calendar/p. 8, Kevin Thomas

In 1974, the Emmy Award-winning writing-and-producing team of Richard Levinsohn and William Link made an unforgettable TV movie, "The Gun," in which they traced the history of a single handgun as it passed from person to person. Swift, economical and devastating under John Badham's terse direction, it was as entertaining as it was a powerful, implicit plea for gun-control legislation.

It's impossible to watch "It's the Rage" without recalling "The Gun" because the new film, which has already aired on Cinemax but opens in theaters today, is everything that the older film was not. Adapted by Keith Reddin from his play and directed by James D. Stem as if it was still a theater piece, it is implausible, contrived and tedious despite the best efforts of a prestigious ensemble cast.

The message it sends, intended or otherwise, is that guns should be kept out of the hands of the crazed and the unstable. Surely even the National Rifle Assn. would agree to that.

The story is set in motion when a jealous, nasty husband (Jeff Daniels) lies in wait to shoot to death his business partner, who is having an affair with Daniels' wife (Joan Allen). Daniels' attorney (Andre Braugher) gets him off, persuading a jury that Daniels mistook the man for an intruder, but Braugher himself makes the mistake of coming on to a clearly crazed young blond (Anna Paquin); Braugher has an unbalanced lover (David Schwimmer) who's just bought some guns; and Paquin has an even crazier, ultra-possessive brother (Giovanni Ribisi).

What's more, Allen, having left Daniels, accepts a job with an eccentric computer genius (Gary Sinise) who lives in a virtual reality universe and, suffering from information overload, has cut himself off from the world. Josh Brolin plays Allen's predecessor in Sinise's employ; he becomes a video store clerk unknowingly endangering his life when he develops a crush on Paquin. The only reasonably normal people on hand are Allen and Robert Forster as a veteran cop on the verge of retirement but certain that Daniels is a cold-blooded killer who got off scot-free.

"It's the Rage" is too wordy and uninspired, too theatrical and directed with too heavy a hand to play as a pitch-dark comedy commenting on the absurdity of the easy accessibility of guns. Only Allen is able to suggest much dimension or credibility; Sinise's bravura turn might have worked on a stage. But "It's the Rage" misfires badly as both an entertainment and a message movie.

NEW YORK POST, 7/14/00, p. 47, Lou Lumenick

Sometimes a movie is less than the sum of its parts. There is a wonderful scene in "It's the Rage," in which Gary Sinise plays Morgan, a people-phobic computer billionaire—Bill Gates crossed with Howard Hughes.

He's interviewing Helen (Joan Allen) for a job as his assistant—leaving her totally baffled as he interacts with his fantasies on room-size computer screens, avoiding any kind of eye contact.

Sinise and Allen, who co-founded Chicago's legendary Steppenwolf theater, are mesmerizing together—as are Andre Braugher and Anna Paquin as, respectively, Tim and Annabel Lee, a gay lawyer and a street urchin who have an equally confusing and hilarious encounter in a luxe hotel suite.

The problem is that the scenes seem to be taking place in separate movies with wildly divergent tones—and that neither Morgan nor Tim seem remotely like characters who would ever pick up a gun, much less point it at someone.

Yet that's precisely what they do in this curious black comedy which argues for gun control—but ends up shooting itself in the foot.

Helen links several other gun-wielding men: her estranged husband, Warren (an uncertain Jeff Daniels), who shoots an intruder who turns out to be his business partner; Tim, Warren's lawyer; Chris (David Schwimmer, who's terrible), Tim's lover; Tyler (Robert Forster), a police detective investigating Warren; and Sidney (Giovanni Ribisi), Annabel's psychopathic brother.

That virtually all of these characters are near-certifiable undercuts the arguments about limiting access to guns.

Keith Redden, adapting his play for the screen, seems to be intending it not only as "La Ronde" with guns instead of sex—but partly a spoof of "Pulp Fiction."

That being the case, he probably shouldn't have included a scene in which Warren (whose full name is Warren Harding) complains about that movie to a video store clerk (Josh Brolin) who happens to be Morgan's former assistant.

Director James D. Stern also includes clips from "Pepe Le Moko," "Twentieth Century" and "His Girl Friday" in this infuriating grab-bag of a movie.

NEWSDAY, 7/14/00, Part II/p. B7, John Anderson

Although the cast seems to be paying off a bet, "It's the Rage"' has a loosey-goosey anti-gun message that should find a hearing with everyone who doesn't consider AK-47s or Kevlar-piercing bullets to be sports equipment. Of course, unless you think of July Fourth sparklers as deadly weapons, you'll realize the whole thing is bushwah.

Too tongue-in-cheek to make any serious commentary on our, shall we say, gun problem (the phallic references in the opening montage are pointed enough), "It's the Rage" shoehorns a number of famous actors into an ersatz Altmanesque collision. The inaptly named Warren Harding (Jeff Daniels) kicks things off by killing an intruder at 5 in the morning, an intruder who just happens to be his business partner—and whom the chronically jealous Warren thinks has been sleeping with his wife, Helen (Joan Allen). When Warren walks after a self-defense plea, he prompts a couple of cops (Robert Forster and Bokeem Woodbine) to tail him around town and ticks off Helen to the point she leaves home to work for the Howard Hughes-ish software tycoon Morgan (Gary Sinise) who, coincidentally, also keeps a large calibre handgun in his desk.

Meanwhile (gasp!), Warren's lawyer Tim (Andre Braugher) is juggling relations with his unstable gay lover Chris (David Schwimmer)—who buys them matching Nancy Reagan-style pistols—and a bleached-blond street tart named Annabel (Anna Paquin), whose brother (Giovanni Ribisi) has a tendency to shoot people who come on to her.

Determined to achieve spontaneous wackiness, "It's the Rage" goes everywhere at once, to the point of making its gun arguments (which are sophomoric, didactic and obvious) subordinate to the pageant of losers who decorate the movie. James Stern, who has a wide range of credentials as a stage and screen producer, makes his directing debut here and gets a couple of good performances out of—let's face it—very reliable actors. Allen, notably, wrings genuine sympathy out of an absurdist plotline and Forster is solid. Schwimmer, on the other hand, seems to be having a lot of fun convincing us he's a straight guy acting gay. Paquin, coming off a very similar role in the film version of "Hurly-Burly," has a real future playing the lighter side of Christina Ricci. Braugher, appropriately to the story, makes us feel he'd rather be elsewhere. And so will you.

VILLAGE VOICE, 7/18/00, p. 122, Amy Taubin

It's the Rage is more commendable as social protest than as filmmaking. With a script adapted by Keith Reddin from his own play, James D. Stern's directorial debut is an impossibly stagy treatise on why it's bad for guns to be as easily available as they are in the U.S. The film weaves together several story lines, each of them involving at least one character with a low boiling point, caught in a stressful situation and in proximity to a handgun. There are a couple of cops and one or two felons, but most of the characters are seemingly solid, successful citizens. The film's point seems to be that most of us are less rational and more violent than we want to admit, so it's only good sense to limit access to lethal weapons.

Not to belabor the obvious, but the difference between a play and a film is that the former is more dialogue-driven than the latter. Stern attempts to compensate for the wall-to-wall chatter with elaborate camera moves and flashy intercutting. On the other hand, he seems to have directed the actors to speak the lines as if there were quote marks around them (the Mamet approach) and as if they needed to project their voices over great distances. Thus, even Jeff Daniels and Joan Allen look as if they've never been in front of a camera before. Playing a post-psychotic-break version of Bill Gates, Gary Sinise pops his eyes, screws up his face, and goes so bonkers that you have to be awed by his chutzpah, not to mention his immaculate comic timing. *It's the Rage* attempts to engage with its built-in hybridity, but it fails to develop into one thing or another.

Also reviewed in:
NEW YORK TIMES, 7/14/00, p. E22, A.O. Scott
CHICAGO TRIBUNE, 7/21/00, Friday/p. J, Michael Wilmington
VARIETY, 10/18-24/99, p. 42, Todd McCarthy

JAUNDICED EYE, THE

A Som-Ford Entertainment release of a Fifth Estate Productions/Pyedog Productions presentation. *Executive Producer:* Amy Sommer Gifford. *Producer:* Dan Gifford. *Director:* Nonny de la Peña. *Screenplay:* Nonny de la Peña. *Director of Photography:* Bestor Cram. *Editor:* Greg Byers. *Music:* Michael Brook. *Sound:* John Osborne. *Running time:* 90 minutes. *MPAA Rating:* Not Rated.

WITH: Stephen Matthews; Melvin Matthews.

LOS ANGELES TIMES, 9/24/99, Calendar/p. 14, Kevin Thomas

Nonny de la Peña's "The Jaundiced Eye," a documentary chronicling a terrible miscarriage of justice strung out over a decade, is a real-life family horror story. A father and son in a quaint, Norman Rockwell-like Michigan town are caught between a collision of two emotionally charged forces in American society: a lingering homophobia and a growing concern about child abuse.

In his teens, Stephen Matthews, before coming out as gay, fathered a child by his girlfriend; she raised their son, and Stephen had visitation rights. This workable relationship was shattered when the mother acquired a new boyfriend. When Stephen found his son had a black eye, he and the boy's grandfather, Melvin, who runs the family live bait shop, grew suspicious and did sufficient investigating to become convinced that the boyfriend had given the child the injury.

Stephen warned the boyfriend about ever laying a hand on his son again—and the boyfriend, not identified by name, is heard on the soundtrack admitting he came from and believes in a "disciplined family." Shortly thereafter, the boy, by then 5, accused his father and grandfather and implicated even his grandmother of repeated sexual molestation and torture. Although charges against the grandmother were dropped, Stephen and Melvin, who were inadequately defended by their attorney, were swiftly convicted primarily on the boy's testimony—and no physical evidence.

In prison, Melvin turned to bodybuilding and religion for sustenance, while Stephen became a jailhouse lawyer, discovering shocking lapses in the handling of their trial, which eventually led to their release. Nonetheless, father and son, years later, faced the prospect of a retrial.

Fueled by the ignorant but widespread belief that gays are, by their very nature, pedophiles, the plight of Stephen and his father (who is straight) reflects how the issue of child abuse has become so hot—and correctly so—that the rights of the accused have in many instances become eroded drastically. You can't see this documentary without being reminded of the McMartin case in Manhattan Beach.

Of the many child-abuse experts De la Peña has on camera, the most illuminating and crucial is Kate Hart, head of the National Child Abuse Defense Center; one of her many telling points is that once a child has become convinced that he has been molested, it's all but impossible to change his mind.

While driving home the care needed in the prosecution of child-abuse cases, "The Jaundiced Eye" also becomes a portrait of an entire family bearing up under a long and terrible ordeal, one they will never really be able to put behind them. De La Peña is resourceful in re-creating their ordeal, taking us to the courtroom, the jail, the prison and all other salient locales while we hear testimony on the soundtrack, plus interviews from those willing to speak for the record but not be filmed. Comprehensive and thoughtful, "The Jaundiced Eye" is as compelling as it is illuminating.

NEW YORK POST, 3/3/00, p. 52, Lou Lumenick

When Stephen Matthews came out as a gay man and moved from Michigan to California, it didn't sit too well with his ex-girlfriend, who was also the mother of his child.

She lodged lurid, homophobic child-abuse charges against not only Stephen, but also various members of his family, setting off a decade-long nightmare.

At its best, Nonny de la Pena's "The Jaundiced Eye" makes provocative points about how the rights of accused child abusers can be compromised by coerced testimony from victims, overly aggressive law enforcement and inept defense attorneys.

Stephen Matthews and his straight father, both interviewed extensively, spent several years in prison after being convicted largely on the basis of medical tests that were later thrown out—along with the charges—as unreliable.

VILLAGE VOICE, 3/7/00, p. 134, Dennis Lim

As suggested by its title (derived from an Alexander Pope epigram, "All is yellow to the jaundiced eye"), Nonny de la Peña's documentary concerns the perils of colored perspective—the tendency, as one talking-head psychiatrist here puts it, to see what you're looking for, not what you're looking at. The film presents itself as a made-for-*Dateline* investigation into an outlandish sexual abuse charge, which nearly a decade ago sent a Michigan family into a tailspin, but, more than a mere miscarriage-of-justice exposé, it ends up illustrating some valuable points about how a personal prejudice (in this case, homophobia) can spill over into harmful, seamlessly delusional behavior, and how the high emotions inextricably entwined with a subject like child abuse can prove ultimately self-defeating.

In 1990, Stephen Matthews, a gay man, and his father Melvin were accused by Stephen's ex-wife of molesting their five-year-old son. Despite the absence of physical evidence, and rickety testimonies from the boy comprised of leading questions and seemingly coached answers, both father and son were found guilty. After nearly four years in jail, Stephen discovered that the chlamydia test on his son was incorrectly administered; he and his father were released but found themselves facing a second trial in a matter of months. The film's main weakness is its reliance on staged inserts as punctuation (clanging cell doors, thumping gavels, and most bizarre of all, a machete ominously embedded in a tree), a suspect TV-newsmagazine technique that detracts from the cumulative force of the interviews.

Also reviewed in:
NEW YORK TIMES, 3/3/00, p. E23, A. O. Scott
VARIETY, 10/11-17/99, p, 62, Emanuel Levy

JESUS' SON

A Lions Gate Films and Alliance Atlantis relase of an Evenstar Films production. *Executive Producer:* Steven Tuttleman. *Producer:* Elizabeth Cuthrell, Lydia Dean Pilcher, and David Urrutia. *Director:* Alison Maclean. *Screenplay:* Elizabeth Cuthrell, David Urrutia, and Oren Moverman. *Based on the book by:* Denis Johnson. *Director of Photography:* Adam Kimmel. *Editor:* Geraldine Peroni and Stuart Levy. *Music:* Joe Henry. *Music Editor:* Annette Kudrak. *Sound:* John Gooch and (music) Rick Will. *Sound Editor:* Warren Shaw. *Casting:* Laura Rosenthal and Ali Farrell. *Production Designer:* David Doernberg. *Art Director:* Andrea Stanley. *Set Decorator:* Geri Radin. *Costumes:* Kasia Walicka Maimone. *Make-up:* Nicki Ledermann. *Stunt Coordinator:* Douglas Crosby. *Running time:* 105 minutes. *MPAA Rating:* Not Rated.

CAST: Billy Crudup (FH);   Samantha Morton (Michelle);   Denis Leary (Wayne);   Jack Black (Georgie);   Will Patton (John Smith); Greg Germann (Dr. Shanis);   Holly Hunter (Mira); Dennis Hopper (Bill);   Robert Michael Kelly (Salesman);   Torben Brooks (Car Crash Driver); Dierdre Lewis (Driver's Wife);   Jimmy Moffit (Car Crash Doctor); Antoinette Lavecchia (Dead Man's Wife);   Steve Buck (Richard);   Ben Shenkman (Tom); Scott Oster (Stan);   Brooke Shive (Beatle);   Mark Webber (Jack Hotel);   John Ventimiglia (McInnes);   Jess Weaver, Jr. (Carl); Mike Shannon (Dundun);   Todd Berry and Bill Thompson (College Kids);   Elizabeth Cuthrell (Diner Waitress);   Joanne Bradley (Mary); Evita Sobel (Bartender);   Ronald Croy (Big Guy in Fight);   Yvette Mercedes (E.R. Nurse); Denis Johnson (Terrance Weber);   Christine Mourad (ICU Nurse);   John Clement (Medical Assistant);   Katie Rimmer (ICU Nurse 2);   Carol Florence (Abortion Clinic Nurse);   Ron Van Lieu (Counselor);   Alan Davidson (Snakeskin); William Salera (Man in Laundromat); Miranda July (Black-Eyed Nurse);   Omar Koury (E.R. Doctor);   Lee Golden (Isaac);   Boris McGiver (Max); Susanne Case-Sulby (Beverly Home Head Nurse);   Kevin Carroll (Chris); Michael Bove (Interpreter);   Clista Townsend and David Tuttleman (AA People);   Rebecca Kimball (Mennonite Woman);   David Urrutia (Mennonite Husband);   Christine Cowin (Young Nurse).

LOS ANGELES TIMES, 6/23/00, Calendar/p. 2, Kenneth Turan

In an age of known quantities, "Jesus' Son" is almost indefinable. In a sea of one-note symphonies, this touching feature is bleak and comic, heartbreaking and affirmative, romantic and tragic, gimlet-eyed and sympathetic, all at the same time. It's the sweetest, most punishing of lowlife serenades, a crawl through the wreckage created by, protagonist FH informs, "people just like us, only unluckier. "

"Jesus' Son" is true to the off-center vision of Denis Johnson, a poet of the feckless and dispossessed whose celebrated literary collection is its source. Those linked short stories set in the '70s took their title from a line in the Velvet Underground drug anthem "Heroin," so it's not a shock that FH doesn't stand for "Fat Head." Not quite.

FH, frankly, earned his name by his penchant for screwing up. But to see him only as an addict and a sneak thief, while accurate enough, is to miss what director Alison Maclean and her trio of writers (Elizabeth Cuthrell, David Urrutia, Oren Moverman) intuitively understand. With his shambling, shuffling walk and radiant smile, FH is a kind of holy innocent who never loses his childlike thirst for life no matter how much it confuses and betrays him.

The notion of a befuddled junkie saint is not a new one, but it's almost never played with the kind of grace, humor and wistful vulnerability that Billy Crudup ("Without Limits," "Waking the Dead") manages in his best performance to date. An actor of enormous, unforced likability, Crudup carries us with him as perhaps no one else could on FH's erratic journey around America, trying to find a way out of merely staying afloat on life's roughest seas.

"Jesus' Son" is also a major success for director Mclean, who hasn't managed a feature since "Crush," her acclaimed 1992 New Zealand debut. Mclean's feel for the American heartland in the 1970s is exact down to the music on the soundtrack. She gets disciplined, on-point performances from the excellent supporting cast (Samantha Morton, Holly Hunter, Dennis Hopper, Denis Leary, Will Patton and Jack Black, among others), and, most important, she is able to cherish these people without sacrificing the ability to see them and their killing imperfections with complete clarity.

FH tells his own story, but his voice-over, like that of a man telling an elaborate tale from a bar stool, is meandering, even circular. He starts in the middle, then jumps back to the beginning before reaching the end. At the center, always, is Michelle (a compelling Morton, Oscar-nominated as Sean Penn's mute foil in "Sweet and Lowdown"), the woman of his feverish dreams.

FH meets Michelle in Iowa City in 1971, at a druggy party at an outlying farmhouse. They don't get together until a year later, and their love-among-the ruins romance, complicated by a mutual dependence on heroin, pills and whatever else is handy, is the film's core.

"There was something wrong with us," FH says distractedly at one point, "and we didn't know what to do about it."

When it's not following this relationship, "Jesus' Son" trails FH and his peculiar acquaintances on the kind of strange, almost defiantly comic escapades (like working in a hospital emergency room when someone comes in with a hunting knife sticking out of his head) that only junkies seem to have. These exploits rarely play well on the screen (or on the page, for that matter), but the combination of Mclean's direction, Johnson's original vision and the gifts of that trio of screenwriters makes a considerable difference here.

Mclean strikes the right matter-of-fact tone with the hallucinatory aspects of FH's story, like the time he saw a nude woman floating by on a parachute. More critically, the film has the feel of being told from the inside, by an articulate survivor. "There is a price to be paid for dreaming," FH says at one point, and "Jesus' Son" is always aware of what that means.

NEW YORK, 6/26/00, p. 128, Peter Rainer

Jesus' Son, based on the episodic 1992 Denis Johnson book, is set in the seventies, and it looks as if it was made in the seventies, too. It has the scruffiness and saintly hippie aura that one associates with films from that era; Jack Nicholson might once have found himself well cast in it. Billy Crudup, who has something of the young Nicholson's arrant verve and hyperbright eyes, plays a doper who goes by the nickname Fuckhead, or FH for short. Moving back and forth in time, the film follows FH from Iowa to Chicago to Phoenix, and his odyssey, from the pits of junkiedom to redemption, is, of course, intended symbolically. It's a stoner's Stations of the Cross.

FH attaches to himself a host of depraved malcontents: a man (Denis Leary) who destroys his own house in order to sell its scrap iron to pay for a few drinks; a zonked hospital orderly (Jack Black, from *High Fidelity)* who casually pulls a knife from the eye socket of a patient whose wife brutally attacked him; a sanatorium denizen (Dennis Hopper) whose mate has left tattoolike bullet-hole entry and exit marks on his face; a recovering alcoholic (Holly Hunter) whose men have all come to bizarre bad ends; a junkie waif (Samantha Morton) who shoots up in her run-down motel room while watching cartoons. FH presses on while everybody around him OD's or skids into oblivion. He seems blessed, and yet the blessing itself is a joke: Why is *this* smiley goofball spared? He's living proof of God's wit.

Alison Maclean, who directed, has a nice feeling for the poetics of disarray and a generous, intuitive way with actors. Parts of this film play like good, early Gus Van Sant, particularly *Drugstore Cowboy*, which also had a screwy blastedness. As the junkie Michelle, Samantha Morton still has the fragile intensity she demonstrated in *Sweet and Lowdown* and *Dreaming of Joseph Lees,* but added to it is an urchin's spunk and a frighteningly sensual pathos; this snaggletoothed doper always seems to be very close to us and yet far away. Billy Crudup lifts the film out of the flossy oh-wow-ness that it otherwise often sinks into. The great thing about FH is that though he's a woozy drifter, his eyes, his face are always shockingly alive. Crudup has a great physicality, and he gives FH's gangliness a loose-limbed lyricism.

Jesus' Son is pretty frazzled stuff whenever Crudup and Morton aren't around. Not all of that seventies scruffiness was such a good thing, even in the seventies; and I can't say that I'm terribly nostalgic for something I wasn't all that crazy about to begin with. What's missing from this new film is the perspective that might make it function as more than an artful memory jog. *Jesus' Son* is like something that came out of a time capsule, and it's a bit soon to be excavating, and celebrating, the artifacts of that era.

NEW YORK POST, 6/16/00, p. 52, Jonathan Foreman

When it starts with a dopey-looking Billy Crudup thumbing a lift in the rain, "Jesus' Son" seems set to be another film celebrating the cliched obsessions of indie filmmakers. Not only is it set in the '70s, in the supposed cultural and moral wasteland of Middle America, it's about those ultimate figures of hipster fascination: skanky, scabby heroin addicts. With sideburns and wide-lapel leather jackets.

But this film transcends ironic grunge-glamour and achieves a beguiling combination of dark comedy and genuine sweetness.

It does so partly thanks to vivid performances and a screenplay (co-written by Elizabeth Cuthrell, David Urrutia and Oren Moverman) that sticks closely to the book of linked short stories by Denis Johnson.

It's also directed by Alison Maclean with surprising economy for a film that inevitably contains surreal visions.

In the end, the film's flaws have much more to do with its episodic structure and the uneven heft of the underlying stories than its familiar subject matter.

The narrator and protagonist (Crudup) is called F -- - head, or FH for short. He's a passive, none-too-bright screw-up in a world of losers. But he's more observant and more gentle than most of the dope heads around him.

What you see are scenes from five years of FH's life, in the kind of mixed-up, slightly repetitive order you'd expect from a guy whose circuits have been damaged by drink and drugs.

Crudup gives a confident, rather showy performance—adopting a strange shambling, stumpy gait—as the junkie who eventually finds a kind of grace by helping other people.

But it is Samantha Morton, the English actress who was so good in "Dreaming of Joseph Lees" and Woody Allen's "Sweet and Lowdown," who steals the movie (while proving she can carry off a convincing American accent).

Denis Leary, the always enjoyable comedian turned actor, gives another confident performance. And there are amusing, effective cameos from Will Patton, Dennis Hopper, Holly Hunter and Greg Germann (of "Ally McBeal").

Jack Black, the sarcastic vinyl salesman in "High Fidelity," is perfectly cast as Georgie, a pill-popping hospital orderly, in the film's funniest sequence.

The title "Jesus' Son" comes originally from a line in the song "Heroin," by Lou Reed, but there is nothing glamorous about the junk use shown here: People are always throwing up and dying of overdoses.

NEWSDAY, 6/16/00, Part II/p. B6, John Anderson

Director Alison Maclean skips so blithely along the borderline between pathos, bathos and baggy-pants comedy you wouldn't think "Jesus' Son" would offer up a single defining moment—and it doesn't, although the one involving frosted cereal, old cartoons and heroin seems to sum things up well enough.

Based on the quasi-autobiographical book of stories by Denis Johnson, "Jesus' Son" uses Johnson's chapter headings but weaves in and out of them, flashing back and forth in a seamless Pilgrim's Progress of one F.H. (Billy Crudup)—whose unprintable nickname sums up his status as screwup, among screwups. An Iowa drifter, a guileless child-man, F.H. lacks the imagination for a life other than his drug-addled and otherwise idle state of existence. What he's not is evil, although he can't seem to get out of its way.

There's Christian imagery everywhere—at one point, filmed through a diner window, F.H. seems to be wearing a crown of thorns. But the allegorical stuff is never heavy-handed, nor should it be: F.H. is a tough sell as a savior, even if he does seem to be the repository of the abuse and bad luck of everyone around him.

Crudup, whose career seems to be taking forever to meet the media's expectations, simply gives a heartbreaking performance and, like his director (best known for 1992's "Crush"), does a balancing act that works. F.H. is self-indulgent, shiftless, virtuous and beatific. And we believe it all.

Around him circle some truly amazing characters, each of whom occupies one or more of the movie's various episodes: Georgie (Jack Black), who views his job as a hospital orderly as a free pass to the pharmaceuticals, has an interesting encounter with a patient whose wife has left a knife in his eye. Wayne (Denis Leary) hires F.H. to help him destroy the house he's lost to his ex-wife, who flies by the place topless, attached to a windsail. Mira (Holly Hunter) has lost multiple husbands and innumerable boyfriends to gruesome death and seems to have her eye on F.H. And, of course, Michelle (Samantha Morton), who's the love of his life and saves it as well.

The era is evoked through the worst music and the worst fashions—F.H.'s wardrobe seems to consist of corduroy jeans and big-collared shirts, and "Oh, Sweet Pea" is a song I could have lived happily ever after never hearing again. But "Jesus' Son" isn't supposed to be about joy. Sometimes it just feels that way.

SIGHT AND SOUND, 8/00, p. 50, Danny Leigh

Iowa City, the early 70s. Fuckhead, or FH, a drug addict in his early twenties, is involved in a car crash while hitchhiking. He returns to his apartment and is visited by his ex-girlfriend Michelle. He then reminisces about his life so far, starting with his first meeting with Michelle at a party. Ignoring the attentions of her boyfriend McInnes, Michelle seduces Fuckhead. Months after the party, the two move in together and nurture their heroin habits. McInnes is shot by one of his house mates; he's driven to hospital by Fuckhead, but dies on the way. Fuckhead and Michelle move into a cheap hotel. Fuckhead agrees to help Wayne, an alcoholic, strip a derelict house for salvage. Having made $40, the two men buy heroin. That evening, both overdose: Wayne dies, but Fuckhead is revived by Michelle. Fuckhead gets a job at a hospital, where he and his colleague Georgie steal various medication; later, Georgie saves a patient's life. Tripping, Fuckhead and Georgie drive into the country. When Fuckhead returns home, Michelle tells him she is pregnant. The baby is aborted. Michelle leaves Fuckhead for another man.

Following his car crash, Fuckhead gets back together with Michelle. After arguing with Fuckhead, Michelle dies from an overdose. Grief-stricken, Fuckhead overdoses himself, and is sent to a rehab clinic. Five months later, he is working at a hospice in Arizona; there, he finds peace among his terminally ill charges.

For a director as seemingly talented as Alison Maclean, the seven years since her last feature—the taut, unsettling *Crush* (1992)—must have been hard to endure. She spent some of the time working in US television, on such series as *Homicide Life on the Street* and *Sex and the City*. But *Jesus' Son* shows how much she relishes her return to cinema. With its exquisitely muted colours, its aura of woozy narcosis and its defiantly fractured narrative, *Jesus' Son* pointedly resembles a compendium of things you're not allowed to do on mainstream television. And if her main aim was to get as far as possible from network strictures, what better source material could she have than Denis Johnson's 1992 collection of short stories, addled, disjointed tales about a young heroin addict and his drifter friends?

Yet fitfully faithful as Maclean and screenwriters Elizabeth Cuthrell, David Urrutia and Oren Moverman are to Johnson's smacked-out lyricism, it emerges here as something of a mixed blessing. On paper Johnson's fleeting insights are immaculate, peppering a bottomless, opiate, first-person fugue. And the temptation to have Billy Crudup's drug addict Fuckhead simply recite chunks of interior monologue has not been resisted. But while Crudup's recitations *sound* great, they often leave the film looking uncomfortably like an illustrated narration. The sense of displacement is almost too palpable. Maclean can't seem to make up her mind between honouring the skewed nature of Johnson's vignettes—by punctuating each segment with title cards—and trying to mould them into a coherent, viewer friendly narrative. Take, for instance, the key character of Michelle. Despite Samantha Morton's fine, funky performance she seems an arbitrary and strangely hollow figure. It quickly becomes clear that her role is a composite of Johnson's numerous anonymous female characters, one designed to bind several threads into a conventional storyline.

Yet this hesitancy hardly negates the otherwise astute and idiosyncratic charms of *Jesus' Son*. Maclean's camera perfectly captures a mood of euphoric listlessness which is at once a homage to Johnson and a tribute to her and her teams sensitivities. If the scriptwriting mechanics of unifying Johnson's yarns prove troublesome, the potentially jarring disparities in tone are handled with greater ease. The film segues seamlessly from absurdist comedy (Crudup blankly watching a naked middle-aged woman paragliding), to documentary detail (Denis Leary's broken alcoholic Wayne mopping up a spilt scotch, then sucking on the napkin) to understated tragedy (his subsequent death from an OD). In a medium increasingly confused by the idea of pushing more than one emotional button at once, Maclean's fluency is startling, and her images achieve a cracked, off-kilter kind of beauty.

Her handling of heroin, though indulgent in terms of screen time, is otherwise strictly matter-of-fact. Rather than the ostentatious fetishism of drugs chic in, say, *Trainspotting* or *Drugstore Cowboy*, smack here is as regular and uneventful an activity as eating. People get high; sometimes they die. This uncondescending fatalism means that, when a doped-up Fuckhead wanders through a drive-in showing the 1962 horror film *Carnival of Souls* convinced he's actually in a vast, sprawling cemetery, the effect is captivating.

All of which is enhanced by the accomplishment of the performances. Billy Crudup is a dazed, ruined presence whose poise gives the project its anguished heart. The supporting turns—particularly Morton, Leary and the inspired Jack Black—are equally impressive. The sublime interplay between Black and Crudup in the darkly comic segment 'Emergency', set in a blood-soaked casualty ward ("What am I gonna do about these fucking shoes, man? Listen to how they *squish...*"), is just one memorable scene in a film of many. Moments such as these leave you hoping Maclean doesn't have to wait another seven years for her next big-screen outing.

VILLAGE VOICE, 6/20/00, p. 156, Michael Atkinson

Alison Maclean's chilly, mopey materialization of Denis Johnson's story cycle *Jesus' Son* might be the supreme screen portrait of 70s drug culture, except there's very little culture. The film's lovable dopenik, referred to only as Fuckhead and embodied in a guileless trance by Billy Crudup, spends the movie of his life between places, waiting for something, waking up in the dead center of nowhere, or wandering rain-sodden highways. Talk about unreliable narrators: FH hallucinates, jumbles his time line, chases after free-associative memories, and focuses on ephemera, and the film leaps and lollygags with him. An opening car crash doesn't get completely told until deep into the first hour; like most things about *Jesus' Son*, its narrative frazzling is ingenious and smart but self-consciously so. (Example: the split screen Maclean uses to show Fuckhead getting rescued from an OD as a buddy dies in another room.) The blowing-leaf form of *My Own Private Idaho* had an organic, risky quality that Maclean misses here, and for all of its charming messiness, Fuckhead's odyssey of cheap rooms and scag buddies leaves no pressing questions unanswered.

The vignettes have a hilarious integrity, particularly the hangout with a Stetson-sporting hot dog (Denis Leary on fire) who takes our easygoing hero to rip out an empty house's wiring and sell the copper for a fix, and the deadpan sketch-comedy of Fuckhead and a pill-scarfing buddy (Jack Black) working as very stoned hospital orderlies the night a man calmly wanders in with a hunting knife buried in his eye. (Sequences with recoverers Dennis Hopper and Holly Hunter are impeccably performed but negligible.) Much of Fuckhead's tribulations, however, focus on Michelle (Samantha Morton), an evasive junkie sprite whose romantic demands deaden the movie's nerves long before her beleaguered boyfriend goes to rehab.

Filthy with talent though he might be, Crudup seems attracted to passive characters, and here as before he's accomplished (with a sublimely retarded walk) but never dazzling. He didn't have much of a chance: Like so many novels that beckon filmmakers, Johnson's is largely attitude and rumination, and though Maclean uses every trick available to make up for the missing inner voice, we never get into Crudup's mellow loser like we should. Maclean's got an incisive eye, but it's poised on the outside of the terrarium looking in.

Also reviewed in:
CHICAGO TRIBUNE, 7/7/00, Friday/p. G, John Petrakis
NEW YORK TIMES, 6/16/00, p. E11, A. O. Scott
VARIETY, 9/20-26/99, p. 88, Todd McCarthy
WASHINGTON POST, 7/7/00, p. C5, Stephen Hunter
WASHINGTON POST, 7/7/00, Weekend/p. 34, Michael O'Sullivan

JOE GOULD'S SECRET

A USA Films release of an October Films presentation of a First Cold Press/Charles Weinstock production. *Executive Producer:* Michael Lieber and Chrisann Verges. *Producer:* Elizabeth W. Alexander, Stanley Tucci, and Charles Weinstock. *Director:* Stanley Tucci. *Screenplay:* Howard A. Rodman. *Based on "Professor Seagull" and "Joe Gould's Secret" by:* Joseph Mitchell. *Director of Photography:* Maryse Alberti. *Editor:* Suzy Elmiger. *Music:* Evan Lurie. *Music Editor:* David Carbonara. *Sound:* William Sarokin and (music) Tom Lazarus. *Sound Editor:*

Bob Hein. *Casting:* Ellen Lewis and Kathleen Chopin. *Production Designer:* Andrew Jackness. *Art Director:* David Stein. *Set Decorator:* Catherine Davis. *Set Dresser:* Anthony Baldasare, Harvey Goldberg, Doug Fecht, Joanna Hartell, and Henry Kaplan. *Costumes:* Juliet Polcsa. *Make-up:* Carla White. *Running time:* 108 minutes. *MPAA Rating:* R.

CAST: Ian Holm (Joe Gould);   Stanley Tucci (Joe Mitchell);   Hope Davis (Therese Mitchell); Sarah Hyland (Elizabeth Mitchell);   Hallee Hirsh (Nora Mitchell);   Celia Weston (Sarah); Patrick Tovatt (Harold Ross); Susan Sarandon (Alice Neel); Patricia Clarkson (Vivian Marquie); John Tormey (Harry Kolis);   Jack O'Connell (Chef);   Jerry Mayer (Minetta Bartender);   Nell Campbell (Tamar, Hostess);   Ron Ryan (Jack);   Allan Corduner (Francis McCrudden);   Merwin Goldsmith (Monsieur Gerard);   Laura Hughes (Dr. Kim Maxwell);   Steve Martin (Charlie Duell);   James Hanlon (Mike, Cop at Coffee Shop);   David Wohl (Max Gordon); Julie Halston (Sadie Gordon);   Aida Turturro (Waitress);   Alice Drummond (Helen);   Justine Johnson (Mrs. Bagly);   Gordon Joseph Weiss (Man at Flophouse);   Andrei Belgrader (Teddy);   Gabor Morea (Pawnbroker);   Ben Shenkman (David);   Katy Hansz (Margaret);   Mark Cassella (Cop at the Building Site);   Harry Bugin (Newsman);   Lauren Ward (Anne);   Jessica Walling (Betsy);   Ted Blumberg (Phil, The Writer);   Ben Jones (Southern Man at the Party);   Peter Francis James (Man at Party);   Richard Litt (Bartender);   Tom Joseph Foral (Man in Gallery);   Leigh Carlson (Janet).

LOS ANGELES TIMES, 4/7/00, Calendar/p. 2, Kenneth Turan

Exuberantly played by Ian Holm, Joe Gould is the loudest man in the quiet, carefully modulated namesake film, "Joe Gould's Secret," but he'd be loud even in a noisy one. A boisterous real-life bohemian in 1940s New York, a demanding presence always creating a ruckus, Gould was a significant bum, a street person with a pedigree, and wherever he went attention had to be paid.

It was the life's work of journalist Joseph Mitchell (played with remarkable stillness by Stanley Tucci, who also directed) to pay attention to people like Gould. A faultless writer ("Up in the Old Hotel" was his final collection) of the kind of character studies that made the New Yorker the New Yorker, Mitchell turned out a pair of profiles about Gould published 15 years apart. Those two stories and what they say about the relationship between the two men are the basis for this graceful, small-scale but insightful film.

Homeless, disheveled-looking, carrying everything that mattered to him in a large, ratty portfolio, Gould is as distinctly an urban character as Mitchell's urbane, top-coated writer, and the film's opening voice-over goes out of its way to intentionally blur the distinction between the two.

"In New York City," a soothing Southern voice begins, "in Greenwich Village, down among the cranks and the misfits and the one-lungers and the has-beens and the might've-beens and the would-be's and the never-wills and the God-knows-whats, I have always felt at home." Who's speaking about whom? The next lines tell us it's Mitchell (who turns out to be from North Carolina) we're listening to, and something more as well. "Joe Gould told me that when I was first writing about him, not knowing I felt the same. As time went on, I would learn that this was not the only thing we had in common."

"Joe Gould's Secret" has more on its mind than commenting on these unlooked for parallels. Elegantly written by Howard A. Rodman (with uncredited work by Tucci), "Secret" deals in its meticulous way with questions like the surprising, often unwieldy nature of reality as well as the always complex relationship that can develop between a writer and a subject.

Mitchell first spies Gould in a neighborhood coffee shop in the village, absolutely demanding a free bowl of soup and then pouring most of a bottle of catsup into it. Played with marvelous brio and a hint of madness about the eyes by Holm (also memorable in "Big Night," co-directed by Tucci and Campbell Scott), the tempestuous Gould has a fierce but erratic temper, an inability to accommodate to civilization and a great sense of his own importance. "Don't think me stupid," he pointedly tells Mitchell, "just because I am unclean."

The picture of conventionality in his own life as the husband of photographer Therese Mitchell (Hope Davis) and father of two young daughters, Mitchell is mesmerized by Gould's modus operandi. He's even more fascinated when he learns about the homeless man's patrician background and a life's work that has garnered support from such intellectual bellwethers as e.e. cummings, Ezra Pound and painter Alice Neel (a Susan Sarandon cameo).

For Gould has dedicated himself to what he calls "The Oral History of Our Time," preserving on paper what ordinary people were saying day in, day out for years. Gould likes to think of it as the "informal history of the shirt-sleeved multitude," the fruit of thousands of overheard conversations carefully written down in composition books stashed around town for safekeeping. Its current length, the compiler says proudly, is 1.2 million words, three times longer than the Bible.

Gould makes no bones about considering himself an artist, and thoughts about an artist's place in society are among "Secret's" most interesting passages. "Only the artist is free because he is single of purpose," the monomaniacal Gould insists. "He knows what he wants and wants only that and that frightens people."

Once the first New Yorker piece came out, Gould got some of the recognition he thrived on, but things got more complex for Mitchell, who increasingly had to deal with the way Gould's personal trajectory called forth uncomfortable echoes of his own life unrecognized dreams and adventures confronting reality. As wife Therese astutely puts it (and as every journalist eventually comes to know), "Stories don't end just because the writer is finished writing."

Tucci, working with production designer Andrew Jackness and cinematographer Maryse Alberti, has taken care to set his story in a meticulously re-created Manhattan. Though even Holm can't quite give this delicate story the oomph of "Big Night," "Joe Gould's Secret" is, like that earlier Tucci film, a series of subtly interlocking character studies. While many directors are after the big bang, Tucci is after something quieter, and ultimately more meaningful. It's the silences, the spaces between sentences when souls communicate without words being exchanged, that interest him the most.

NEW YORK, 4/17/00, p. 78, Peter Rainer

At its best, *Joe Gould's Secret*, starring Ian Holm and its director, Stanley Tucci, and based on a pair of legendary *New Yorker* profiles by Joseph Mitchell, has some of the same qualities as Mitchell's prose: plangent intelligence and an empathy that's practically a state of grace. Mitchell's profiles of Gould, the Harvard-educated Greenwich Village cadger and layabout and crackbrained philosopher, were written 22 years apart, with "Professor Seagull" appearing in 1942 and "Joe Gould's Secret" in 1964, seven years after Gould's death. Gould claimed to be compiling the longest book ever written, *An Oral History of the World,* which would give voice to everyone he encountered, especially the lowlifes and the dispossessed and the banished. He fancied himself a gutter Gibbon, and his antics, such as imitating seagulls, whose speech he believed he had deciphered, or performing a Chippewa dance in the middle of a Village soirée, were also his shtick. In the forties in New York, it was possible for someone like Gould to play the performing monkey for radical bohemia and make just enough to get by. He was even welcomed as a regular into some of the local clubs and hangouts because his "authenticity" drew in the tourists looking to do a little slumming with the art set. He got close to the likes of e. e. cummings, who wrote a poem about him, and a snatch of his musings was once published in the magazine *The Dial,* which first published *The Waste Land.*

In the movie, which was scripted by Howard A. Rodman, Ian Holm's Joe Gould isn't quite as yammery as he appeared on the page. It would have been off-putting if he were. Gould lives in Mitchell's prose as a "character"of genius—the Flying Dutchman of the Village—but on the screen his yowlings have been brought down to a manageable level. Holm's Gould is a character, all right, but he's also a believable person. The art of Holm's performance, of the entire movie, in fact, is in the way it humanizes the guy's weirdnesses and caterwaulings so we can spot the man beneath the grimy, exfoliating beard and rheumy eyes. There is no more satisfying moment in current movies than the one here where Mitchell first walks over to Gould for an interview and the old sot's face expands into delight like one of those speeded-up shots of a flower unfolding.

There is a tendency in movies of this sort to place a nimbus around such a man, and *Joe Gould's Secret* doesn't entirely escape that trap. Gould is portrayed not just as a figure of resonant derangement but also as something more: a too sensitive soul who suffers for our bourgeois sins. Gould may be a dissembler in the particulars, but mainly he is shown to be a truth-teller, which is what we, too, would be if we weren't hemmed in by fuddy-duddy convention. In fact, so goes the movie, if we look within ourselves, we may perhaps discover our own inner Joe Gould. "He's a freak," says a cop about him to the proprietor of a diner Gould frequents. "We're all freaks," comes the reply. This is a disservice to Joe Gould, who could out-freak just about anybody.

The film also sets up a simpatico relationship between Gould and Mitchell—the two Joes—that's a bit too freaky-deaky. We're supposed to see both men as loners who feel at home only among other loners. Gould is an expatriate of illustrious Massachusetts lineage; Mitchell is a refugee from the South, from North Carolina, and he retains a Southerners slow-cooked courtliness. Mitchell is shown with his wife (Hope Davis) and two daughters in scenes of snuggly harmony but, perhaps unintentionally, these moments feel weightless, as if we were observing a charade of what domestic bliss should be. Still, the hokiness of this lonely-hearts-club stuff is greatly alleviated by the extraordinary subtlety of the performers, particularly Tucci, who manages the extraordinary feat of turning a sounding board into a feeling, full-fledged character. There is a moment halfway through the film when Mitchell, weary of being hounded by Gould, hides from him in the *New Yorker* building while a receptionist lies about the writer's whereabouts, and the riven look on Tucci's face shows you how hollow Mitchell feels at that moment. Very few movies have ever dramatized as well as this one how a subject can take over a writer. Gould gets to Mitchell, not just as the subject of a profile but on a deeper, more elusive level; he's spooked by him, by the unreachableness of him. Gould is like some avenging imp who challenges Mitchell's complacencies about his profession. In approaching Gould and writing about him, Mitchell has entered into another person's life, and now, both literally and figuratively, he can't shake the guy. Noting at the end that Mitchell, who died in 1996, never published anything after his final Gould piece, the filmmakers make perhaps too large and sentimental a presumption about the men's relationship, but the presumption also has the ring of truth. If Joe Gould in this film is a bit like one of the mad, delusional barflies in *The Iceman Cometh*, then Joseph Mitchell is like that play's Larry Slade, who, alone in the end, is stripped of all illusion. He knows Joe Gould's secret, and he's stricken by it.

NEW YORK POST, 4/7/00, p. 56, Jonathan Foreman

"Joe Gould's Secret" is the ambitious, unlikely adaptation of two extraordinary essays by Joseph Mitchell, the celebrated writer for The New Yorker during the '40s, that are among the great achievements of modern American literature.

Mitchell (Stanley Tucci) doesn't know that Joe Gould (Ian Holm) is a Greenwich Village legend, when he first sees the apparent hobo pouring ketchup into his soup at a diner and haranguing the chef, who's giving him the meal for free.

Mitchell seeks out and meets Gould and in return for contributions to the "Joe Gould fund" is told about the ragged Harvard graduate's great literary project, "The Oral History of Our Time."

According to Gould, the manuscript is more than a million words long, and the composition books that contain it are either distributed with friends all over New York or buried on a farm somewhere on Long Island.

Despite being a malodorous, bad-tempered, drunken bum, Gould has impressive friends and financial supporters including Ezra Pound; e.e. cummings; artist Alice Neel (Susan Sarandon), who has painted him nude; and gallery owner Vivian Marquie (Patricia Clarkson).

Mitchell writes a profile of Gould in The New Yorker that turns the Village eccentric into a celebrity and elicits financial gifts from the readers that enable Gould to give up the homeless life.

But Gould becomes more annoying than ever and starts turning up constantly at Mitchell's New Yorker office. These visits don't just irritate the courtly scribe, and make him wonder if Gould has any intention of finishing his project, they also make him doubt his own path in life.

Tucci gives a fine measured performance as the Southern-bred Mitchell, and the oddly beautiful Hope Davis is as strong and intriguing as ever as Mitchell's photographer wife, Therese. But it's Ian Holm's movie, and the English actor is superbly convincing as the cantankerous and not very likable Gould.

Far more successful than "The Impostors," the last movie directed by Tucci, this handsomely shot period piece suffers mainly from a stately pace that drags even more once Gould achieves his celebrity.

NEWSDAY, 4/7/00, Part II/p. B3, John Anderson

Joseph Mitchell joined the New Yorker in 1938 and during the next four decades—on subjects as diverse as McSorley's alehouse, the New York shellfish business and bridge-paintingMohawks with no fear of heights—turned out what may be the best nonfiction pieces ever written. For two decades after that, Mitchell showed up at the New Yorker daily and never published another word.

Why? If you go by Renata Adler's recent book "Gone," it was due in part to the cult of longtime editor William Shawn, under which actually publishing somehow became declasse. Given that Shawn was known to withhold Adler's own pieces, though, a far more likely theory is the one proposed by Stanley Tucci, in his very thoughtful "Joe Gould's Secret"—that Mitchell was undone by his most famous subject, the wildly eccentric Joe Gould.

Based on two Mitchell stories—"Professor Seagull," published in 1942, and "Joe Gould's Secret," the followup that appeared in 1964—"Joe Gould" stars Ian Holm as the title character, a habitue of Greenwich Village saloons, streets and flophouses, and the reputed author of "The Oral History of Our Time," a millions-of-words-long revolutionary work that Gould refuses to let Mitchell see. As directed by Tucci, "Joe Gould's Secret" is clearly the work of a Mitchell devotee, although in the compression of two stories into one, there doesn't seem to be a lot of secrecy about Joe Gould's secret.

Oddly enough, the film is also, in its way, an anti-writer movie. Well, maybe not so oddly. Producer Michael Lieber—who got the film rights from Mitchell only after six years of asking (Mitchell died in 1996)—was inspired to read Mitchell through the work of Janet Malcolm, who has written extensively and angrily on the responsibility of journalists to their subject. As Mitchell, Tucci is clearly in awe of the power of the photographs taken by his Therese (the fabulous Hope Davis)—not an unlikely position for a filmmaker to take, of course. What Tucci and screenwriter Howard A. Rodman suggest in "Joe Gould's Secret"—and not so subtly—is that by bringing notoriety to Gould, by making him the minor celebrity he became, that Mitchell subsequently was saddled with a guilt he couldn't write his way out of.

True or not, Tucci makes it so with his very understated portrayal of Mitchell, which carries a convincing power even in the shadow of Holm's Joe Gould, a riotous combination of energy, egomania, alcoholism and poetry ("In winter, I'm a Buddhist/In summer, I'm a nudist..."). Only in tandem, however, do they make it all work as well as it does: "Joe Gould's Secret" being as much about Mitchell as it is about Gould.

NEWSWEEK, 4/17/00, p. 65, David Ansen

Joe Gould, a legend in Bohemian circles in New York in the early 1940s, "looked and lived like a bum," as Joseph Mitchell wrote in the second of his two New Yorker profiles on Gould. No ordinary scavenger, this Harvard grad hailed from one of the oldest families in New England. Though dirty, demanding and an exhibitionist, his flamboyant eccentricities (he often squawked like a seagull) and flashes of brilliance gave him entrée into the homes and hearts of Greenwich Village's artistic elite, who eagerly awaited the *magnum opus* Gould had been working on for decades. It was called "The Oral History of Our Time," and it was rumored to be the longest book ever written.

The role of the half-mad Gould is a gift you'd want to give only to the most worthy actor, and Ian Holm does it extravagant justice. This great English actor makes Gould hilarious, scary, tragic, pitiable and exasperating, sometimes all at once. "Joe Gould's Secret"is the story of his long relationship with Mitchell (Stanley Tucci), whom he loftily refers to as "my biographer." We react to Gould with much of the complexity Mitchell does: fondness and awe alternating with distaste.

Tucci, who directed and did a rewrite on Howard Rodman's smart screenplay, is investigating the tangled interplay between a journalist and his subject "A story doesn't end just because a writer has finished writing," cautions Mitchell's wife (Hope Davis) when her husband is fed up with Gould's invasion of his life. When Mitchell's profile of him is published, the brush with fame inflames Gould's already unruly ego. People, the reporter discovers, have the unfortunate habit of refusing to be stories. "Joe Gould's" reach sometimes exceeds its grasp. It has a stop/start rhythm. Unlike Tucci's "Big Night,"this one never rises to a full boil. Yet few films have captured the look and feel of '40s New York with such quiet assurance. This literate, nuanced miniaturist history dusts off a quirky corner of our past and brings it to life with wit and TLC.

VILLAGE VOICE, 4/10/00, p. 153, J. Hoberman

There's mass culture and then there's the authenticity mass-cult's always looking for, the stuff happening on the street. *Joe Gould's Secret* and *Black and White* are both tributes to that fascination. Different as they are, both celebrate New York as the fantasy place where—as one ancient pop song put it—the words of the prophet are written on subway walls.

Less obvious a movie subject than *Black and White*'s touristic hippity-hop, *Joe Gould's Secret* is a quietly ambitious, well-wrought, and tastefully poignant treatment of two local literary legends. The first is ace *New Yorker* reporter Joseph Mitchell, played by the film's director, Stanley Tucci; the second is the Greenwich Village eccentric Joe Gould, panhandler extraordinaire and putative author of a million-word manuscript entitled *The Oral History of Our Time*. Mitchell first profiled Gould in 1942 as Professor Sea Gull and wrote about him again, more troublingly, some years after Gould's death.

"A blithe and emaciated little man" was how Mitchell first described Gould, wearing cast-off clothes with a "forlorn, Chaplinesque rakishness." This undiscovered genius seemed to personify a kind of flophouse modernism. Back in the Freudian '40s, someone suggested to Mitchell that Gould might be the medium through which New York's unconscious was attempting to speak. In Tucci's movie, the reporter discovers his subject (Ian Holm) at a lunch counter ranting and riffing as he empties an entire bottle of ketchup into his free bowl of soup. Intrigued, Mitchell learns that Gould is a homeless Harvard graduate who's been working for 26 years on a magnum opus based on overheard conversations.

Gould shows Mitchell his clips—including endorsements from Ezra Pound, e.e. cummings, and William Saroyan—and Mitchell enters Gould's orbit, tagging along as this extravagantly voluble character crashes genteel poetry readings, cadges drinks from Village tourists, dives for cigarette butts, and otherwise makes his rounds soliciting contributions to the Joe Gould Fund. Shot mainly on location, the movie works hard for its period look and—although there's no sense of life during wartime—it's remarkably good at coaxing a lost 40s-ness out of the Manhattan streetscape, as well as providing a frame for Holm's massive performance.

As written by Howard A. Rodman, *Joe Gould's Secret* is the tale of two Joes, pitting the loud, irascible Gould (a New England Yankee) against the hesitant, self-effacing Mitchell (a courtly Southerner), played by Tucci as though suffering a case of terminal indigestion. Holm's terrible-tempered Gould is, by contrast, in perpetual high dudgeon when not translating Longfellow's "Hiawatha" into seagull caws or performing his Chippewa stomp. Gould is pleased to recite sections from the *Oral History*, but the more interest Mitchell shows in the manuscript, the cagier Joe becomes, his evasions climaxing in a classic phone-booth performance.

When the *New Yorker* profile finally appears, Gould is transported to celebrity heaven, chatting up college girls and hanging around Mitchell's office. He attracts a mystery patron and even meets a posh publisher (Steve Martin) who inadvertently puts Gould on the spot, thus alerting Mitchell to his subject's eponymous secret. Gould might be a smelly old bum and Mitchell a proper paterfamilias with two small daughters and a tart but understanding wife (Hope Davis) who is an artist in her own right, but the movie might really have been called *Joe Gould's Secret Sharer*.

As a writer, "the great artist/reporter of our century" per *Vogue*, Mitchell also has difficulty letting go—he's a perfectionist who subjects his prose to continual revisions. Tucci's most discomfiting scene places Mitchell at a cocktail party talking up his own unwritten novel, which sounds suspiciously like a version of the *Oral History*. (Ultimately, Mitchell succumbed to permanent writer's block, publishing nothing after his revisionist "Joe Gould's Secret" in the mid '60s, although he continued to come to work daily for the next 32 years.)

Tucci's film might have been less genteel. Perhaps in tribute to the old *New Yorker*, he's overly solicitous of his audience, downplaying the conditions of mental illness and softening the transference of one Joe's problem to the other. Still, from a writer's point of view, this is a true cautionary tale—the haunting story of what happens when the hunter gets captured by the game.

Also reviewed in:
CHICAGO TRIBUNE, 4/14/00, Friday/p. H, Michael Wilmington
NATION, 4/24/00, p. 42, Stuart Klawans
NEW REPUBLIC, 4/17 & 24/00, p. 62, Stanley Kauffmann
NEW YORK TIMES, 4/7/00, p. E13, Stephen Holden
NEW YORKER, 4/10/00, p. 100, David Denby
VARIETY, 1/31/-2/6/00, p. 30, Todd McCarthy
WASHINGTON POST, 4/14/00, Weekend/p. 45, Desson Howe

JUDY BERLIN

A Shooting Gallery release of a Caruso/Mendelsohn production. *Producer:* Rocco Caruso. *Director:* Eric Mendelsohn. *Screenplay:* Eric Mendelsohn. *Director of Photography:* Jeffrey Seckendorf. *Editor:* Eric Mendelsohn. *Music:* Michael Nicholas. *Sound:* Eric Susch and (music) Cynthia Daniels. *Sound Editor:* Stephen Altobello. *Casting:* Laura Rosenthal and Ali Farrel. *Production Designer:* Charlie Kulsziski. *Art Director:* Dina Varano. *Set Decorator:* Paula Davenport. *Costumes:* Sue Gandy. *Make-Up:* Kim Behrens. *Running time:* 93 minutes. *MPAA Rating:* Not Rated.

CAST: Barbara Barrie (Sue Berlin); Bob Dishy (Arthur Gold); Edie Falco (Judy Berlin); Carlin Glynn (Maddie); Aaron Harnick (David Gold); Bette Henritze (Dolores Engler); Madeline Kahn (Alice Gold); Julie Kavner (Marie); Anne Meara (Bea); Novella Nelson (Carol); Peter Appel (Mr. V); Marcia DeBonis (Lisa); Glenn Fitzgerald (Tour Guide); Marcus Giamatti (Eddie Dillon); Judy Graubart (Ceil); Arthur Anderson (Dr. Stern); Margaret Mendelson (Cathy); Keith Mulvihill and Bob DeMarco (Gast Station Attendents); Jeffrey Howard (Spirio); Sylvia Kauders (Woman on Bench); Diane Tyler (Neighbor in Window); Louise Millmann (Denise); Julie Kessler (Alice's Neighbor); Ellen Baer (Nurse); Louisa Shafia (Chatting Nurse); Dennis Roach (Gus); Renee Guest (P.A. Announcer); Vic Caroli (TV Announcer); Stephanie Goldberg (Stephanie).

CHRISTIAN SCIENCE MONITOR, 2/25/00, p. 15, David Sterritt

As usual in the midwinter season, movies from the independent and international scene are helping to fill American screens while Hollywood prepares the coming wave of spring releases. Ifs not surprising that a picture like "Judy Berlin" would arrive at this time of year, brushing off the dust it accumulated during nine months on the shelf since its première at the Cannes film festival last May.

Modest in every way, from its suburban setting to its black-and-white cinematography, *Judy Berlin* takes place in a Long Island town during what must be the longest solar eclipse in history. The main characters are a loosely connected group of ordinary people, including discontented spouses, well-meaning schoolteachers, and—central to the story—a young man who's returned home with broken dreams, and a young woman who's leaving home with great expectations. A conversation between them provides a quirky, wandering framework for the quirky wandering movie.

It's hard to say whether "Judy Berlin" is energized more by its creative acting, its unpredictable plot, or the subtly dreamlike mood that gets farther under your skin as the eclipse stretches beyond the limits of physical possibility.

Ultimately, it's the way first-time director Eric Mendelsohn combines these factors that makes the picture so engaging. "Judy Berlin" is a true original, and a welcome sign that the American independent film movement remains alive and flourishing.

Other countries also have innovators who want to shake-up the cinematic status quo, and none have gained more attention in recent years than the Dogma 95 directors in Denmark, who follow an artistic "vow of chastity" by giving up studio fakery in their films. The movement's major achievements so far have been "The Celebration" and "The Idiots," both from Denmark, and "Julien Donkey-Boy," an American offshoot.

Americans now have another chance to assess the Dogma approach in "Mifune," a Danish comedy-drama named after one of Japan's most legendary actors. The protagonist is Kresten, a Copenhagen businessman who becomes the reluctant guardian of his brother, Rud, a mentally slow fellow whose eccentricities include a huge enthusiasm for Toshiro Mifune, the Japanese movie star. Kresten leaves his brand-new wife to put Rud's life in order after the death of their father, but finds his task complicated in unexpected ways, especially when a newly hired housekeeper turns out to be a prostitute on the run.

"Mifune" benefits from the stripped-down Dogma style, which offers a refreshing change from Hollywood techniques through its emphasis on vigorous performances and streamlined filmmaking techniques. It is as solidly written and photographed as "The Celebration," the movement's most popular film. Movie fans who share Rud's affection for "Mifune" may enjoy it even more. Soren Kragh-Jacobsen directed.

"Not of This World" hails from Italy, where some moviemakers plug into Dogma-like traditions of gritty "neo-realism" while others choose more flamboyant styles. Dipping into both of these territories, director Giuseppe Piccioni tells the story of a seemingly bland dry-cleaning entrepreneur whose life changes when he meets a nun trying to find the parents of an abandoned infant.

Handling comic and dramatic scenes with equal confidence, Piccioni weaves this basic situation into a surprisingly complex tapestry involving a varied cast of secondary characters, some of whom are at least as interesting as the heroes of the tale. Already the recipient of several international prizes, "Not of This World" is a healthy reminder of Italy's still-vibrant cinematic heritage.

LOS ANGELES TIMES, 2/25/00, Calendar/p. 28, Kevin Thomas

Eric Mendelsohn's "Judy Berlin" is a comedy of the most delicately balanced perfection, rueful yet radiant, every moment calibrated with exquisite precision for just the right effect. And yet it never seems less than spontaneous.

It is a film permeated with the feeling that its maker knows exactly where he's headed, all the while overflowing with a sense of revelation. It's as if this first-time feature director confidently allowed himself to discover his film's meaning as he went along, resulting in a freshness, perceptiveness and tenderness that can only be described as extraordinary.

It's the second day of school in the pleasant town of Babylon, Long Island. Arthur Gold (Bob Dishy), principal of the local elementary school, is off to work, leaving behind his wife Alice (the late Madeline Kahn), a woman who seems to be in a constant state of apprehension in the face of a fairly empty existence, and their 30-year-old son David (Aaron Harnick), recently returned from his failure to make it as a filmmaker in Hollywood and who is overcome with a depressed indifference. As we meet one Babylon resident after another, we discover that most of them seem to be living lives of quiet desperation as an eclipse of the sun looms; it is to occur shortly before 1 p.m.

As the sky darkens, David runs into a former high school classmate, Judy Berlin ("The Sopranos'" Emmy-winning Edie Falco) and experiences his first sense of connection with another human being since he returned home. Judy is his polar opposite, a struggling actress of such boundless, bubbling optimism, despite no significant accomplishments, that later on this day she is to fly off to Hollywood. She wants to try her luck in movies and TV despite a singularly paltry resume, the high point of which may be her appearance in a commercial for a local furniture store.

David receives such a lift from their encounter that he decides to follow her to a nearby historic village, the local Williamsburg, where she's winding up her part-time job costumed as an early Colonial, depicting what women's lot was in that period. David is as beguiled by Judy's effervescence as he is ultimately alarmed by her naivete, his feeling that she's a lamb about to throw herself to the wolves, heading to a ruthless town where she has not a prayer of making it.

The great thing about "Judy Berlin" is that Mendelsohn doesn't treat the mysteriously prolonged eclipse as a time of doom or of magic—as Alice, in wandering about her neighborhood, would like it to be—but rather an interlude just enough out of the ordinary to spin the Babylonians out of their routines, to be open to new emotions and experiences. Under the spell of darkness, for example, Judy's schoolteacher mother Sue (Barbara Barrie), a brittle woman of superior intelligence but not a lot of warmth, at last dares to declare an unrequited love. Mendelsohn isn't concocting miracles that transform lives. But Mendelsohn is suggesting, modestly, how people might get a new and possibly redemptive perspective on their lives if they leave themselves open to opportunities.

Mendelsohn views his film's inhabitants with tremendous affection and respects their fears and frustrations in dealing with everyday life. He sees the humor in the absurdity of the human condition but never at the individual's expense. In celebrating a buoyant spirit in the face of despair, Mendelsohn has two key accomplices: cinematographer Jeffrey Seckendorf, who creates a poetically darkening world in black-and-white, and composer Michael Nicholas, who counters this vision with a tinkly, upbeat score.

No one actor can be singled out from this dazzling ensemble, which includes Anne Meara and Julie Kavner as a pair of gossipy workers at Arthur Gold's school and Bette Henritze as a retired teacher slipping into a senile dementia. There is so much pure joy and so much confused anguish in Henritze's Dolores Engler that she could be said to epitomize the spirit of "Judy Berlin." That is, to warmly embrace that chronic state of contradictory feelings will seem to be forever sorting out.

"Judy Berlin" marks an auspicious launch for a joint venture of the independent film company the Shooting Gallery with Loews Cineplex Entertainment, to present a 12-week series of six venturesome films in 17 markets, with the Cineplex Fairfax serving as the Los Angeles showcase.

NEW STATESMAN, 12/4/00, p. 43, Jonathan Romney

Eric Mendelsohn's *Judy Berlin*; could loosely be described as a small-town idyll—and, these days, not many reputable American films fit that description. We are so used to seeing small towns and suburbs portrayed as hotbeds of lurid dysfunction that this portrayal of a place where people sleepwalk through unexceptional, quiet, routinely troubled lives comes as a shock. The film takes place over one day when these lives come not to a cataclysmic standstill, but to a gentle, contemplative pause.

However, don't mistake this black-and-white, low-budget comedy for one of those cloyingly benevolent studies in Americana that used to sweep the board at the Sundance Film Festival (does anyone now remember *The Spitfire Grill*?). *Judy Berlin* did in fact, win Mendelsohn the director's award at Sundance in 1999, since when the film has not been much talked about. But it gets a long-overdue British release this month and, watching it again, I realise that what I had taken to be a charming anomaly is, in fact, a rich and subtle minor masterpiece. Note "minor"—these days, only a fool bandies around that other m-word, but *Judy Berlin*'s very minor-ness is what makes it exceptional.

A tolling bell accompanies a series of delicately composed shots of some genteel Nowheresville at dawn. Babylon, Long Island, seems to be no more than the sum of its gas station, telegraph poles, deserted junctions and empty schoolrooms. Then people wake to the sound of that mythical American presence—the passing train, hooting in a way that sounds deliberately archaic. It suggests the archetypal small-town movie scenario: someone is leaving, or has just arrived.

The one who has recently returned is David (Aaron Harnick), a young would-be film-maker, back living with his parents after some sort of crisis of self. About to leave is Judy (Edie Falco), dreaming of Hollywood stardom and whiling away her last day at the local history theme park, where she mimes farm work in a Puritan bonnet. This sort of image would be par for the kitsch course in most suburban-madness films, but it is about as flamboyantly eccentric as *Judy Berlin* gets; daft as it is, it is treated as nothing more than a job of work.

Meanwhile, David's parents are having their usual quietly tormented day. Alice (Madeline Kahn) is a hypersensitive belle, a skittish suburban Blanche DuBois desperate for reassurance; Art (Bob Dishy), a delicate, anguished headmaster, secretly carries a mutual longing for the brittle teacher Sue (Barbara Barrie). And Sue, Judy's disappointed mother, still nurses a wistful dream of a cultured, *New Yorker*-reading home life.

These days, a film such as *Judy Berlin* is considered commercial folly. There is very little story, most of the characters are middle-aged, weary and unglamorous, and even the younger duo are integrated into the ensemble rather than taking centre stage. Mendelsohn shoots them all as if they were phantoms, wandering around a ghost town—which Babylon effectively becomes when it is plunged into darkness by an inexplicably prolonged eclipse. These sequences of day turned night have an eerie, strangely festive mood: Alice wanders round suburban streets on a dark afternoon, whooping with childlike glee: "We're moon explorers!" The town's sudden plunge into night magically suspends events from their daily course, evoking a kind of sleepwalking state, a suburban *Midsummer Night's Dream*.

One thing that makes the film special, apart from Mendelsohn's witty script, is Jeffrey Seckendorf's soberly beautiful photography, especially the sky and landscape shots that make the everyday setting distant and extraterrestrial. The other is an extraordinary cast, who avoid all stereotypes and fill in the script's well-placed gaps with their own suggestive silences. The most exuberant is Edie Falco in the title role; getting to do rather more than in recent episodes of *The Sopranos*, she persuades us that, despite Judy's self-deception, this loud, immature wannabe could have exactly what it takes to succeed. Barbara Barrie's twitchy, punctilious Sue suggests flickers of melancholy electricity under the crisply self-deprecating shell. She has a whole subliminal telegraphy of quizzically twitching eyebrow and nostril, especially in her scenes with Bob Dishy, whose Art is a big, sad, tactful man bristling with secret delicacy.

As for the late Madeline Kahn, we know her as the flamboyant farceuse from Mel Brooks's films; but, here, she gives Alice a whole register of actressy neurosis and concealed hurt, all evoked in flighty gestures and a curious singsong diction. Some of the film's performances, especially when staged in empty rooms, come across as theatrical, but that is exactly the point. Life has turned these people's personalities into parts to be acted each day; and the stagy tone, making the film all the more hallucinatory, paradoxically makes it all the more cinematic.

So many American small-town movies seem the work of mocking urbanites, but Mendelsohn's intentions are different. At one point, David imagines making a documentary about a small town, with no plot and no sarcasm, and we can take Mendelsohn almost at his (or David's) word. *Judy Berlin* is entirely without sarcasm, but it is gently, intelligently ironic. It is an extraordinary film, daring to be so undemonstrative that it risks being overlooked altogether. Way out on its own elegant, elegiac limb, this is a study of small-town America that, for once, owes less to David Lynch than to Chekhov.

NEW YORK, 3/6/00, p. 58, Peter Rainer

Judy Berlin, the first feature from writer-director Eric Mendelsohn, arrives on a wave of goodwill from last year's Sundance festival. This modest, all-the-lonely-people comedy, set on Long Island and shot in pearly black-and-white, has its compensations: a funny-sad performance by Madeline Kahn, her last, as a spurned housewife; the warm, owlish presence of Bob Dishy, playing her husband, an elementary-school principal; and, best of all, Edie Falco's touching, deliciously nut-brain turn as Judy Berlin, an aspiring actress who works as a settler in a local historic village, milking imaginary cows and shearing imaginary sheep. (Her boredom with the job gives her a look of great gravitas.)

But the film, which takes place largely during a midday solar eclipse, often seems, perhaps intentionally, as tinny and underpopulated as a no-budget fifties sci-fi flick, and many of the little-people vignettes are trite—more cut-rate Chayefsky than Chekhov.

NEW YORK POST, 3/26/99, p. 62, Thelma Adams

There's nothing remarkable about "Judy Berlin." As played by rising star Edie Falco ("The Sopranos"), she's a Long Island fixture. She's the girl you knew in high school whom you never thought about once you got on the LIRR and left for good. While you wee off seeking the real world, whatever that was, she stayed behind, working nowhere jobs, hanging out with friends and nurturing the impossible dream of making it as an actress.

In his debut feature, a black-and-white bittersweet comedy, writer-director Eric Mendelsohn treats Berlin, and her native Babylon, with extraordinary tenderness and insight.

Judy is the center of gravity for a group of ordinary heroes—her mom (Barbara Barrie), a divorced schoolteacher who pines for the married principal (Bob Dishy), his isolated wife (the brilliant Madeline Kahn) and their son (Aaron Harnick), a filmmaker besieged by a walking nervous breakdown.

In one tightly structured day, as school reopens and Judy prepares to leave Babylon by the afternoon train for Hollywood, a solar eclipse hits. The event captures Babylon under a snow globe, revealing suburbia's hidden beauty, the wide quiet streets, the sloping lawns, the enfolding arcs of tree trunks.

Radical in its rejection of sarcasm, in its refusal to shoot suburban fish in a barrel, "Judy Berlin" poignantly points to the possibility of hope in the hinterland, to the idea that real life is where we make it, not where we take it.

NEW YORK POST, 2/25/00, p. 56, Jonathan Foreman

"Judy Berlin" boasts several fine performances and some elegant, eerie black-and-white photography.

But the most impressive thing about this gentle, slow-moving ensemble film from first-timer Eric Mendelsohn may be the relative affection it shows for suburban Long Island.

So many recent movies have aimed snide cheap shots at suburbia that merely avoiding a similar swipe requires non-conformist courage as well as honesty.

The same openness and maturity enable writer-director Mendelsohn to depict middle-aged desire with rare respect, and to explore the notion that the people who work in an elementary school are a community bound by a kind of unspoken love.

The film starts on the morning of the second day of the school year in a town called Babylon.

Arthur Gold (Bob Dishy) plays the sad, ineffectual principal of the local elementary school. It's clear that he no longer feels much for his wife, Alice (Madeline Kahn).

But Sue Berlin (Broadway actress Barbara Barrie), one of his senior staff members, is absolutely desperate for him.

Gold's sullen son David (Aaron Hamick) is a failed filmmaker who has come back home at 30 and now spends most of his time lying around the house.

Wandering around the almost-deserted town, David bumps into Sue Berlin's estranged daughter Judy (Edie Falco), who is about to leave for "the Coast," where she plans to become an actress.

Soon after they meet, all of Babylon goes dark, as a total eclipse of the sun descends on the town.

In rather "Twilight Zone"-esque fashion, the eclipse doesn't come and go but settles like a blanket, prompting the inhabitants to behave in unusually spontaneous or uncharacteristic ways that will change their lives.

The symbolism isn't subtle, and there are times when the film moves so slowly you want to scream. But the dialogue is often funny in a cerebral way, and Mendelsohn gets some wonderful performances from his cast, especially the terrific Barbara Barrie and the late Madeline Kahn.

Sadly, Falco is the film's weakest link. The actress—so wonderful on TVs "Oz" and "The Sopranos"—is hard to believe as a naive, zany 30-year-old.

NEWSDAY, 2/25/00, Part II/p. B6, John Anderson

The particular band of magic that courses along the leafy streets and strip malls of "Judy Berlin" is not the kind that defies gravity. Or logic. Or even possibility. Yes, there's a solar eclipse and a fictional place called Babylon, LI, and a score by Michael Nicholas that suggests a circus calliope playing the theme from "To Kill a Mockingbird." But that's not it.

No, the eerie enchantment of "Judy Berlin" is born of a familiarity with a place and its people so strong that it can't be overly affectionate any more than it can be baldly cruel. Director-writer Eric Mendelsohn, shooting in a purposeful pearly black and white, gives us a Babylon (actually, Farmingdale, Plainview and his old hometown of Old Bethpage) that is possessed of a child's-eye radiance for places remembered only well. On a purely textual level, Mendelsohn's is a suburbia of stunted love affairs, short-sheeted careers, unappreciated   devotion and immunity to change—the first thing he lets you hear is a Long Island Rail Road whistle. It's also, of course, a place that never stops changing. And up to here, one might well be describing a western.

But "Judy Berlin" is definitely an eastern. Go West! young men were told, to find your fortune; Go East! when you don't find it. David Gold (Aaron Harnick), a 30-ish failed filmmaker, has had to move back from Hollywood to the family's too-small Long Island house. Once there, he chafes against his school principal father, Arthur (Bob Dishy), while becoming increasingly bemused by his Blanche Dubois-ish mother, Alice (the late, great Madeline Kahn). Love-starved by Arthur, Alice has soliloquies in her bathroom mirror (David cries into his). She relates the most painfully Oedipal dreams to her son, who looks on in horror. "There's no 'sub' to it," he tells her. "You're all liminal!"

Among the old schoolmates David meets while roaming Babylon is Judy Berlin (Edie Falco, currently of "The Sopranos"). Judy, with adult braces that are as subtle as that LIRR whistle, tells David all about her plans for Hollywood. And how she had a crush on him in high school. David, for whom such a confession is rare and unsettling, manages to suppress his horror at the starry-eyed Judy's doomed plans and keeps making excuses to see her.

In one way, "Judy Berlin" is about sex that never happens, and a career that hasn't happened, and love affairs that almost don't happen—between David's dad, Arthur, and Judy's mother, Sue Berlin (a fabulous Barbara Barrie). Sue is the kind of consummate professional loathed by her fellow teachers, who says "no biggie" when she means the opposite. In another way, "Judy" is a film about parallel motions—Alice is leaving her sanity, Judy is leaving her town. Mrs. Engler (Bette Henritze), an unstable but still inspiring teacher, is looked upon by Sue as the shade of things to come. David and his father are obvious antagonists, the reasons why being deep and sad.

Why should Mendelsohn set his comedy precisely here, at the crossroads of failure, probable failure, frustrated love and illicit romance, painting suburbia as a place of intransigence and stasis? Because his heart is torn between affection and revulsion for a place that seems intended to be abandoned, a nest from which the birds refuse to be evicted. In the end, the real magic of "Judy Berlin" is that Mendelsohn made precisely the movie he wanted to make, with no compromises and no facile answers, something of a miracle in itself.

SIGHT AND SOUND, 12/00, p. 51, Philip Kemp

Babylon, Long Island, the day of a solar eclipse. Alice Gold, a housewife recovering from a drink problem, sees off her husband Arthur to the school where he's the principal. Her son David, recently returned from a failed career in Hollywood, sits at home sunk in deep depression. Sue Berlin, a teacher at Arthur's school, prepares her class to view the eclipse. She's interrupted by ex-teacher Dolores Engler, now suffering from Alzheimer's, who disrupts the class. When Sue tries to intervene, Dolores slaps her,

Wandering the streets, David meets an old classmate, Sue's daughter Judy. An aspiring actress, Judy is about to leave for Hollywood. They lunch together. The eclipse happens, and the darkness doesn't lift for hours. As Arthur comforts the distressed Sue they sense their unspoken attraction. Meanwhile, Alice and her cleaner Carol explore the dark streets.

David warns Judy she stands little chance in Hollywood. She takes offence and walks off. Arthur and Sue share a tentative kiss. David rushes to the station where Judy is catching her train to the airport and they bid each other an affectionate farewell. Sue arrives too late to see her daughter off. Meeting Dolores in the street, she speaks gently to her.

"There wouldn't be a plot," says *Judy Berlin*'s protagonist, failed film-maker David Gold, outlining his idea for a documentary about his home town. "It would just be about how it is when nobody's looking." David's project doesn't exist; it's a spur-of-the-moment excuse devised to cover his ignominious return home after failing in Hollywood. What he's describing, though, is clearly enough the film we're watching except for documentary, read feature.

Writer director Eric Mendelsohn's first full-length film, shot in the Long Island suburb of New Bethpage where he grew up, all but dispenses with plot in favour of an atmospheric study in mood and character, and like David's fictitious film, there's "nothing sarcastic" about it. Spurning cheap shots at American suburbia, Mendelsohn portrays his town's inhabitants with affection, setting out to show "the melancholy and complexity of the people who choose to live there." There's something in common herewith Steve Buscemi's 1996 directorial debut *Trees Lounge*, likewise set in the film-maker's Long Island home town. Buscemi's film, though pitched more towards comedy, shares Mendelsohn's wistful sense of dead end lives and his unpatronising generosity towards his characters.

Shot in elegant black and white, *Judy Berlin* establishes a mood of dreamlike clarity even before the onset of the prolonged eclipse. The members of this largely Jewish community (which Mendelsohn renames Babylon, city of exile) are mostly leading, in Thoreau's famous phrase, "lives of quiet desperation"; there's a sense of deferred reality about them, of holding life at one remove for fear of having to acknowledge its bitterness and disappointments. Teacher Sue Berlin and school principal Arthur Gold both display the downturned mouths and slumped shoulders of diminished expectations, and their love scene together is touching in its wary, inarticulate tenderness. His wife Alice (Madeline Kahn in her final role) meanwhile wanders the streets chanting her rubric: "I wish, I wish, I wish in vain, I wish I was 16 again." Compulsively loquacious—"There's no sub with you; it's all liminal," her son observes wearily—she's elated rather than unnerved by the prolonged darkness, finding in it a strangeness to match her own.

The motif of the eclipse risks coming across as glibly symbolic, but Mendelsohn heads this off by putting the idea into the mouth of a lunkhead ex-schoolfellow of David's who burbles that the darkness would be "like a metaphor—a comment on the suburbs". Instead, Mendelsohn and his director of photography Jeffrey Seckendorf use the night-for-day chiaroscuro to create a sense of suspended time in which the familiar swaps with the bizarre. As the camera lingers on everyday trivialities, they come to seem impossibly exotic, and David's fixation on the yellow patio chairs of his childhood ("Where does something like that go?" he laments) starts to make perfect sense.

Mendelsohn draws oblique, understated performances from his cast, letting his characters' feelings emerge in the play of emotions across their faces and the gaps between what they say. (just before Arthur kisses Sue he gently brushes a speck from her coat, a gesture far more eloquent than his fumbling words.) Amid these lives of subdued defeat, aspirant actress Judy stands out for her defiant, doomed optimism. Superbly played by Edie Falco (the disaffected Mafia wife from television's *The Sopranos),* she's always just a touch too bright, too eager, like a light bulb about to blow. As she hams her way through her role at the town's low-rent historical theme park, miming cow-milking and butter-churning, it's all too clear that David is right: she doesn't stand a chance in Hollywood and will probably, like him, end up back home with all her illusions busted. But Mendelsohn treats her vitality as admirable, however insecurely based, and hints that enough of it may have rubbed off on David to lift him out of his depression. "Make a movie!" she tells him as she boards her train, her wide-eyed grin like a benediction. And just maybe he will.

VILLAGE VOICE, 2/29/00, p. 107, J. Hoberman

One of the most-praised dramatic features of the 1999 Sundance Festival, *Judy Berlin* has intimations of soft apocalypse. Eric Mendelsohn's debut film is a carefully assembled, quasi-autobiographical mood-piece that, shot in meditative black and white, aspires to place a mid-Long Island suburb in the light of eternity. (Alas, Babylon—I knew it well.)

David Denby exhorted historically minded distributors to "seize the chance to be a part of Eric Mendelsohn's future" in his *New Yorker* Sundance report. *Judy Berlin* is, however, more a wistful look back at the artist's past. Not as caustic in his suburbanations as fellow SUNY Purchase grad Hal Hartley, Mendelsohn embodies his ambivalence in two thirtyish showbiz wannabes. The cheerfully crass aspiring actress Judy Berlin (*Sopranos* star Edie Falco) is finally leaving Long Island for L.A. even as her glum erstwhile classmate David Gold (Aaron Harnick) winds up back home, nursing some unrevealed psychic wound and dreaming of unmade movies.

Gently schematic, *Judy Berlin* unfolds on the afternoon of a total eclipse that—the cosmic clock having frozen—plunges Babylon and environs into hours of unscheduled darkness. It's a scenario for the end of the world but Mendelsohn's dramatic structure more suggests a class excursion to a petting zoo where a few harmless animals roam free. David's high-strung mother sings of being 16 again. (Making the most of her last screen role, Madeline Kahn gives her unstable character a poignant, strident edge.) Meanwhile a retired teacher in the early stages of memory loss revisits her old classroom and there causes a scene. Judy wanders around town saying her goodbyes; David merely wanders until the inevitable: "David Gold? This is so freaky!"

Mendelsohn is acute on the embarrassment of reencountering a high-school ghost some dozen years after graduation supposedly exorcised them all. He's less convincing on the chemistry that's meant to exist between these antithetical types. Judy's a gregarious extrovert, David's depressed and judgmental. The actors, perhaps encouraged to play dumb, overheat the connection until the movie blows a fuse. Harnick's morose theatricality serves to encourage Falco's wild face-pulling. She widens her eyes to accentuate her outsized features, flashing a foolish clown smile to show off her adult braces.

Drawn to Judy's vulgar energy, David visits the local History Village where she works as a colonial milkmaid, and together they experience the magical eclipse. David is still puzzled that Judy, who wears her costume throughout, was a high-school tough girl: "I mean—aren't you Jewish?" Less successful for being overly stagy, a parallel interaction involves David's father (Bob Dishy), the defensively dithering principal of the elementary school, and Judy's dourly officious mother (Barbara Barrie), who is a teacher there. Invoking a lifetime of might-have-beens, their scenes have a discordant Broadway polish. "Do you understand that I don't know what I'm doing?" he asks. Indeed, she does.

David, however, knows exactly what he's doing. His dark secret is that he has always yearned to make a documentary about daily life in an American suburb, something celebratory—"nothing sarcastic." This would-be symphony of the quotidian—the town lovingly photographed and dusted with sparkly harpsichord music—is his dream film. And, conveniently disappearing into the night, Judy is the bravely deluded muse who inspired him.

Also reviewed in:
CHICAGO TRIBUNE, 2/25/00, Friday/p. J, John Petrakis
NEW REPUBLIC, 3/13/00, p. 34, Stanley Kauffmann
NEW YORK TIMES, 2/25/00, p. E30, Stephen Holden
VARIETY, 2/1-7/99, p. 58, Dennis Harvey
WASHINGTON POST, 2/25/00, p. C1, Stephen Hunter
WASHINGTON POST, 2/25/00, Weekend/p. 47, Desson Howe

JUST LOOKING

A Sony Pictures Classics release of a Jean Doumanian production. *Producer:* Jean Doumanian. *Director:* Jason Alexander. *Screenplay:* Marshall Karp. *Director of Photography:* Fred Schuler. *Editor:* Norman Hollyn.   *Sound:* T.J. O'Mara.   *Casting:* Georgianne Walken. *Production Designer:* Michael Johnston.   *Art Director:* Mark Ricker. *Set Decorator:* Andrew Baseman. *Costumes:* Karen Perry.   *Running time:* 97 minutes.   *MPAA Rating:* R.

CAST: Ryan Merriman (Lenny);   Joseph Franquinha (John);   Peter Onorati (Phil); Gretchen Mol (Hedy);   Patti Lupone (Sylvia); Amy Braverman (Alice);   Ilana Levine (Norma);   Richard V. Licata (Polinsky);   Allie Spiro-Winn (Barbara);   John Bolger (Dr. Flynn);   Robert Weil (Guido);   Alex Sobel (Marty);   Deirdre O'Connell (Mrs. Braverman);   Colin Martin (Driver); Chevi Colton (Mrs. Crescetelli);   Marcell Rosenblatt (Mrs. Edelberg);   Shirl Bernheim (Mrs. Glantz);   Heather Hopwood (Myrna).

LOS ANGELES TIMES 10/13/00, Calendar/p. 12, Gene Seymour

[*The following review by Gene Seymour appeared in a slightly different form in* **NEWSDAY, 10/13/00, Part II/p. B12.**]

If you want to stretch as an artist, it's probably be easier if you have never achieved fame in a long-running sitcom. Jason Alexander may have been feeling this burden from the time he set out to direct "Just Looking." There have been—and doubtless will be—many moviegoers smirking at the very notion of "Seinfeld's" wormy sociopath George Costanza directing a feature film.

Matters probably won't be helped by the fact that the protagonist of "Just Looking," a 1950s coming-of-age story, is a 14-year-old Bronx klutz named Lenny (Ryan Merriman), whose idea of sating his raging hormones is to be able to watch two people in the act of copulating. As someone remarked at a preview screening, "Yes, well, that's just the kind of creepy story you'd expect from George."

Oh, dry up! In the first place, there's nothing in the Costanza genes to suggest that this—hello!—imaginary character is capable of directing a story so humane and sweet that even its flaws are ingratiating. In the second place, the script is by ex-ad man and TV sitcom writer Marshall Karp, who keeps the wisecracks jumping off the griddle—often at the expense of pace and depth.

And in the third place, Alexander displays in his second time in the director's chair (the first was the 1996 dud "For Better or Worse" which ended up on Showtime) a finely tuned approach to the movie's period setting and an ability to coax bright, sassy performances from his actors, including Patti LuPone as Lenny's mom and Peter Onorati as the uncle from Queens who takes Lenny in for the summer of 1955.

If nothing else, "Just Looking" may someday be remembered as the movie that finally brought out the juice and energy in Gretchen Mol, cast here as a nurse and former brassiere model who becomes a focal point of Lenny's inchoate desires. Mol's Hedy comes across not as a mysterious or worldly wise Older Woman so much as someone who is, in her way, every bit as awkward and vulnerable as Lenny.

It spoils little to mention that she will, unwittingly, break his heart. That's what you expect from stories like this. But there are enough grace notes and gentle surprises strewn along this well-trod path to make "Just Looking" just good enough to justify Alexander's career move.

NEW YORK POST, 10/13/00, p. 65, Jonathan Foreman

The most interesting thing about "Just Looking" is the opportunity it affords Gretchen Mol, a starlet who has not been lucky or wise in her choice of parts, to shine in a decent role.

It's really the only thing that makes it a shame that so few people are likely to see this generic memoir of lower-middle-class "white ethnic" life in the '50S.

Director Jason Alexander (George Costanza of "Seinfeld") gets decent performances from his cast—with the lethal exception of Ryan Merriman (young Jarod in TVs "The Pretender"), who plays the central character without nuance.

VILLAGE VOICE, 10/17/00, p. 140, Leslie Camhi

The Bronx in 1955 is also something of a battleground [the reference is to *Billy Elliot*; see Camhi's review] in *Just Looking*, where 14-year-old Lenny (Ryan Merriman) struggles to expand his knowledge of sexuality beyond the confines of his Jewish neighborhood. His father died a year ago; his mother (Patti LuPone) has remarried an overbearing kosher butcher. The newlyweds, needing time to adjust, pack a resentful Lenny off to the pastoral wilderness of Queens for the summer. There, his Italian Catholic uncle (Peter Onorati), some local kids who've formed a "Sex Club," and a shapely neighbor (Gretchen Mol) provide Lenny with an education he can't get in the Bronx. Marshall Karp's script is clever and funny, though studded with anachronisms. As a director, Jason Alexander (who played George on *Seinfeld*) seems to have encouraged performances that leave little to the imagination, at times overly emphatic and (in Merriman's case) marred by professional self-consciousness.

Also reviewed in:
CHICAGO TRIBUNE, 12/15/00, Friday/p. G, Loren King
NEW YORK TIMES, 10/13/00, p. E24, Stephen Holden
VARIETY, 12/6-12/99, p. 83, Oliver Jones

JUST ONE TIME

An Alliance Atlantis and Cowboy Booking International release in association with Danger Filmworks. *Executive Producer:* Marcus Hu, Charlotte Mickie, and David R. Ginsburg. *Producer:* Lane Janger, Jasmine Kosovic, and Exile Ramirez.   *Director:* Lane Janger.

Screenplay: Lane Janger and Jennifer Vandever. *Story:* Lane Janger. *Director of Photography:* Michael St. Hilaire. *Editor:* Mitch Stanley. *Music:* Edward Bilous. *Casting:* Billy Hopkins, Suzanne Smith, and Kerry Barden. *Production Designer:* Stephen J. Beatrice. *Costumes:* Melissa Bruning. *Running time:* 9 minutes. *MPAA Rating:* Not Rated.

CAST: Joelle Carter (Amy);   Guillermo Diaz (Victor);   Jennifer Esposito (Michelle);   Lane Janger (Anthony);   Vincent Laresca (Nick);   Domenick Lombardozzi (Cyrill);   David Lee Russek (Dom).

NEW YORK POST, 10/20/00, p. 50, Jonathan Foreman

"Just One Time" is a smarmy, smirky but ultimately boring film about a guy whose fiance agrees to make love to a woman in front of him—on the condition that he sleeps with another man.

You might expect that even a witless, gutless flick based on such a premise—lifted without credit from a Candace Bushnell "Sex and the City" story—would provide at the very least some cheap laughs and sex. But "Just One Time" is merely a bad '50s sitcom crudely updated to include open homosexuality.

NEWSDAY, 10/20/00, Part II/p. B6, Gene Seymour

"Just One Time" began life as a short subject, and there are times during Lane Janger's elongated version of his original film when you wish he'd kept the whole thing light, bright and tight. He's piled so many convolutions upon this exemplar of the boundary-crossing romantic comedy that you can feel its legs wobble and strain, especially toward the end.

Nevertheless, the clever conceit at the movie's core maintains its edge. What if, the movie asks, a happy heterosexual guy with naughty fantasies about three-way sex with two women decides to ask his fiance to prove her love by "doing it" with another woman?

In this case, it's a firefighter named Anthony (Janger) submitting his quirky request to his beautiful-but-uptight betrothed, a basketball-playing lawyer named Amy (Joelle Carter). She reluctantly agrees, but only if Anthony agrees to "date" their gay neighbor Victor (Guillermo Diaz), who happens to have a crush on Anthony.

Several wrenches are tossed into this premise, notably the mixed reactions of Anthony's firehouse buddies to this mondo-weird prenuptial pact and the ancillary presence of Victor's carpenter friend Michelle (Jennifer Esposito) who, wouldn't you know, is gay herself.

The actors lighten the load quite a bit, especially Diaz, who brings affecting tenderness to his comic-foil role, and Esposito, whose predatory swagger and sloe-eyed insinuation may, by themselves, arouse unhealthy fantasies in audiences, whatever their sexual preferences.

VILLAGE VOICE, 10/24/00, p. 152, Jessica Winter

Director-producer-writer-star Lane Janger exhibits a passionate faith in his own dubious studliness in the belabored sitcom *Just One Time*, an arthritic exercise in self-pleasure that finds his East Village fireman, Anthony, itching for a three-way with his fiancée and a second woman. Anthony panics, though when she turns the tables and another guy gets involved in the miserable couple's fits of passive aggression. Janger has no idea where a camera should be placed or how human beings interact (most folks wouldn't spend five seconds with the insufferable Anthony, much less a lifetime or a single sticky evening), and his reactionary ideas about sex and desire are frightfully clueless; the courage of his convictions rests upon his own stripped-down bod, showcased in shot after adoring shot—a mirror-snogging John Ritter for a new generation.

Also reviewed in:
NEW YORK TIMES, 10/20/00, p. E26, A. O. Scott
VARIETY, 11/8-14/99, p. 43, Emanuel Levy

KADOSH

A Kino International release of an Agav Hafakot/M.P. Productions/Le Studio Canal+ coproduction. *Producer:* Michel Propper and Amos Gitai. *Director:* Amos Gitai. *Screenplay (Hebrew with English subtitles):* Amos Gitai, Eliette Abecassis, and Jacky Cukier. *Director of Photography:* Renato Berta. *Editor:* Monica Coleman and Kobi Netanel. *Music:* Louis Sclavis. *Sound:* Michel Kharat and (music) Cyril Holtz. *Sound Editor:* Gil Toren, Erez Byni, Elran Dekel, and Ofer Ziv. *Casting:* Perry Cafri, Aviv Giladi, Levia Hon, and Rodika Elkalay. *Production Designer:* Miguel Markin. *Costumes:* Laura Dinulesco. *Make-up:* Ziv Katanov. *Running time:* 110 minutes. *MPAA Rating:* Not Rated.

CAST: Yal Abecassis (Rivka);   Yoram Hattab (Meir);   Meital Barda (Malka);   Uri Ran Klausner (Yossef);   Yussef Abu Warda (Rav Shimon);   Sami Hori (Yaakov);   Lea Koenig (Elisheva);   Rivka Michaeli (Gynaecologist);   Samuel Calderon (Uncle Shmouel);   David Cohen (Shlomo);   Orian Zacay (Sara);   Adi Aisenman (Sharon);   Keren Vaza (Haya);   Oren Eliyahu (Cantor);   Amos Gitai (Man in Bar).

CHRISTIAN SCIENCE MONITOR, 2/18/00, p. 15, David Sterritt

It's an excellent week for imported movies, with a trio of new releases arriving on American screens. "Kadosh," one of the rare Israeli productions to gain widespread attention beyond its native country, deals pungently and poignantly with complex intersections of religious and political thought. "Not One Less," directed by Chinese master Zhang Yimou, takes a low-key look at issues of youth and education. Last but far from least, "Kirikou and the Sorceress" tells a timeless folk tale in an atmospheric African setting.

"Kadosh"—directed by Amos Gitaï, today's best-known Israeli filmmaker—focuses on deeply rooted conflicts between personal and political concerns. Rivka is a Jewish woman whose inability to bear children threatens her marriage to an ultra-Orthodox man. Although her husband doesn't want to break up their household, his rabbi argues that childless marriages must be ended if Israel's great "enemy" is to be defeated. The enemy he has in mind is Israeli Jews who oppose ultra-Orthodox rule for their nation. These Israeli Jews will become a political minority if Orthodox families have lots of offspring as quickly as they can.

Rivka's experiences are echoed by those of her sister, Malka, who has tried to please her family by marrying a devout but unfeeling man who treats her with appalling insensitivity. Gitaï handles his potentially melodramatic material with unfailing taste and compassion, encouraging his audience to think long and hard about the moral dilemmas his film intelligently explores.

"Not One Less" begins in a rural Chinese town, where difficult living conditions bring extra challenges to everyday tasks like education. When the local teacher goes on leave, there's nobody to replace him but a 13-year-old girl. She's determined to earn the additional pay promised if none of her 28 pupils becomes a grade-school dropout. When a mischievous 10-year-old vanishes, she goes to the nearest city in search of the elusive kid.

"Not One Less" recalls one of director Zhang's greatest films, "The Story of Qiu Ju," starring Gong Li as a woman who travels from her home to seek justice in a criminal case. "Not One Less" has the same documentary-type style, and goes a step further by filling the cast with people who have never acted before. This lends authenticity to the film, which benefits greatly from the natural-born charm of its performers. The movie displays less verve and imagination than its predecessor, though.

The animated fantasy "Kirikou and the Sorceress" comes from French filmmaker Michel Ocelot, who based it on a West African story. The hero is a very small but very wise youngster who helps his village overcome a dangerous witch by ridding the woman of her own inner pain. The animation is striking, employing nudity that suits the African setting without diminishing the dignity or propriety of the characters. Many times more African than "Tarzan" and "The Lion King' combined, "Kirikou and the Sorceress" is one of the best movies so far in this very young year.

LOS ANGELES TIMES, 3/17/00, Calendar/p. 14, Kevin Thomas

Amos Gitai's somber, elegiac "Kadosh," which means "sacred" in Yiddish, takes us into the sequestered world of Mea Shearim, the Orthodox Jewish quarter of Jerusalem, where its devout citizens are committed to preserving an ancient way of life. It is a profoundly patriarchal society in which many of its men devote their lives to the study of the Talmud while the women run the households and raise the children.

Meir (Yoram Hattab) and Rivka (Yael Abecassis) are such a couple. After 10 years of marriage they share a deep and passionate love, but they have not been blessed with children. They are happy together but now Meir's father, the community's rabbi, declares that because their marriage has produced no offspring it is illegitimate. Rivka must leave and Meir must marry another woman.

Citing Abraham's fidelity to the barren Sarah and other biblical examples to his father, Meir attempts to preserve his marriage, but his father will not hear of it. Meir and Rivka are thrown into terrible conflict with their allegiance to their religion and to each other.

Although Gitai shot his interiors on sets, he filmed extensively in Mea Shearim, having gained the community's trust. That he treats the Orthodox way of life with the utmost reverence and respect actually makes his film all the more devastating. Simply by showing a couple yielding to authority the way they are supposed to becomes an implicit criticism of their plight, especially of the community's women, who may be cherished and revered by their men but who ultimately have no freedom and no defense when their spirits are being systematically crushed, as is the case with Rivka, who slides into silence in the seclusion of a rented room.

Ironically, her despair is doubtlessly made immeasurably deeper because of what would surely be construed as an act of defiance in her community: She discreetly consults a non-Orthodox female gynecologist who finds that she is in fact quite capable of bearing children. The doctor herself realizes that for Meir to submit to examination for a probable low sperm count or to consider artificial insemination or any other means of making child-bearing possible would be unthinkable. What, you have to wonder, will the rabbi say when the new wife proves to be no more capable of producing an heir than Rivka was?

Gitai has created a film that is as beautiful as it is all but unbearable to watch, for in a very real sense Rivka acquiesces, participates even, in her dire fate. Yet there is some respite in that the film is really the story of two sisters, with Rivka's devoted, caring younger sister Malka (Meital Barda) gathering the courage to resist an arranged marriage with a man she does not love and commit to the man (Sami Hori) who has left the community to pursue a career as a rock singer.

Clearly, Gitai is in awe of the Orthodox community in its stubborn survival in the face of the Holocaust and every sort of historical displacement and incursion from the modern world. Yet he leaves us feeling that the rigidity that thus far has helped the Orthodoxy to survive may ultimately prove to be its undoing.

NEW YORK POST, 2/16/00, p. 46, Hannah Brown

Unfortunately, director and co-writer Gitai, a secular Jew, focuses so intently on making his points without showing disrespect to observant Jews that the film is more praiseworthy than engrossing.

The tension between religious and secular Jews in Israel is such a divisive issue that Gitai, a well-known director of both feature films and documentaries, seems inhibited by the subject.

The main characters, while familiar, are not trivialized or clichéd, but they speak slowly, in hushed tones, like a parody of an Ingmar Bergman film.

It's as if Gitai believes that whispered, halting speech is a sure sign of true piety.

While most details of life in this community are on target, the supposedly learned discourse among yeshiva scholars is absurdly literal and superficial.

"Kadosh" (Hebrew for "holy") centers on two sisters, Rivka (Yael Abecassis) and Malka (Meital Barda), who live in Jerusalem's ultra-Orthodox enclave of Mea Shearim.

Rivka is married to Meir (Yoram Hattab), a brilliant and sensitive Talmudic scholar who loves her deeply. But the two, who have been married for over 10 years, have no children.

Rabbi Rav Shimon (Yussef Abu Warda), the spiritual leader of their community, pressures Meir to divorce Rivka and marry another woman who presumably would be able to give him children.

But Meir and Rivka want to stay together and resist the rabbi. This storyline provides a sensitive look at how childless women are marginalized in this community.

Less successful is the story of Malka, who is in love with Yaakov (Sami Hori), a man who has left the fold to serve in the army and become a musician.

She allows herself to be pressured into marrying a crude man whom she doesn't respect, Yossef (Uri Ran Klausner). Malka, who gets little support from her family, seems annoyingly passive in her decision not to marry the handsome Yaakov.

Hattab and Abecassis, the latter an actress with extraordinary beauty (she looks like a Middle Eastern Andie MacDowell), give outstanding performances.

For viewers with the patience to overlook its flaws, "Kadosh" gives a close and often accurate look at a community rarely portrayed on film.

NEWSDAY, 2/16/00, Part II/p. B9, John Anderson

Subtly storming its way across the thin ice of Israeli sectarian politics Amos Gitai's "Kadosh" ("Sacred") is a film that both grieves and seethes. Although its clinical style owes much to Gitai's earlier documentaries—work that ranged from Thai labor ("Bangkok Bahrain") to Dole pineapples ("Ananas")—make no mistake: "Kadosh" takes no pains to be objective.

It does strive for realism, however, and for a measured pace that belies its anger. In portraying the ultra-Orthodox of current-day Jerusalem, and the organized dissolution of a loving marriage, Gitai doesn't overtly ridicule the sacraments and belief of the Hasidim. He does something more damaging: fetishizes them.

Religious ritual becomes celebration of self; ego, under the guise of godliness, runs roughshod over love. Talmudic debate becomes a game; prayer, a plea for attention. The contradictions inherent in most fundamentalist belief systems—the worshipful oppression of women, most prominently—connect with Gitai's lingering-going-on-languorous observations, intended to stress the onanistic quality in much orthodox routine.

To call Gitai anti-religious might not be quite right, but he's certainly of the opinion that divorcing human concerns from godly ones is inherently wrong. In the very first scene, Meir, the disappointed scholar played by Yoram Hattab, is seen methodically, endlessly tying on the tefilin, in a room where he seems to be alone (which is the point). He's not. Rivka (Yael Abecassis), his sleepy, sensuous wife, rouses herself from slumber, talks to Meir and we learn about their marriage: childless after 10 years; a source of shame to their community and, more and more, to Meir as well; physical love without children is a sin.

Abecassis makes Rivka so abundant in love and physical appetite that the message—even before we get a medical opinion—is that she's far from sterile. "Sometimes women are barren because they have disregarded the laws of purity," Rivka is told. Yes, and sometimes they're burned as witches.

Rivka's parallel is Malka (Meital Barda), who loves Yaakov (Sami Hori), but has instead been told to marry Yossef (Uri Ran Klausner), a brutish fanatic who bellows his prayers, exhorts other Israelis on the street via his mobile PA system ("Why are you afraid? We're all Jews!") and makes not-so-veiled threats against the secular government of Israel. Yossef and Malka's wedding night is one of the saddest things you've ever seen.

Can someone die of grief? Of shame? To will one's self to die to make a loved one happy? "Kadosh" proposes one can. And that Jerusalem-captured tragically in the film's last frames—is a city not just of multiple religions, but impossible divisions.

SIGHT AND SOUND, 8/00, p. 51, Simon Louvish

Jerusalem, the present. Meir, a religious Jew, and Rivka live in an ultra-orthodox quarter of the city where the strict laws of the Torah hold sway. They have been married for 10 years and still love one another. They are also childless and Meir is under pressure from his rabbi to divorce his wife, which Jewish law permits if, after 10 years, she hasn't given birth to any children. Meanwhile Rivka's unmarried sister, Malka, is being matched with one of Meir's colleagues, Yossef, a fanatic who calls on secular Jews to "return" to religion.

Despite being in love with a young man, Yaakov, Malka accepts the arranged marriage. Meir argues with the rabbi about his edict on Rivka, but the rabbi insists, telling him that only child bearing women can help the community defeat the threat of secularism. Meir agrees to divorce Rivka and marry a new wife, Haya. Meanwhile Rivka visits a gynaecologist who tells her she is fertile and the problem must lie with her husband. Malka marries Yossef, the wedding night is a bleak and brutal encounter. Rivka moves out of Meir's house to live on her own. Meir visits her in a drunken state, but he still knows he will marry Haya. Malka has a tryst with Yaakov in a local bar. When she returns to Yossef, her husband beats her. She leaves him. Rivka visits Meir for a last night together, but when he wakes in the morning she is lifeless and he weeps over her body.

Israeli film-maker Amos Gitai has gained a reputation internationally as Israel's foremost director, not least because of the stubborn way in which he has managed to make film after film, year on year, both fiction and documentaries, where other Israeli film-makers have struggled over protracted periods to complete just one movie. Having cut his teeth on radical documentaries about the Israeli-Palestinian conflict, and other global subjects, he embarked, from a French base, on a series of fiction films, such as *Esther* and *Berlin-Jerusalem* applauded by some for their distinctive approach to narrative, criticised as overly didactic by others. Having returned to Israel in 1993, Gitai hasn't slackened his productivity, but he has adopted a more traditional, character-based style of narrative. The best of this batch so far has been his 1998 film *Yom Yom (Day after Day)* portraying his native city of Haifa through a tale of an Arab-Jewish mixed marriage. Focusing on the marriages of two ultra-orthodox couples (one loving but childless; the other miserable and occasionally violent) *Kadosh* is an attempt to portray another city, Jerusalem, as a microcosm of the Israeli secular religious divide.

The problem Gitai faces with *Kadosh* is his application of modern secular standards to a community that lives by a Biblical code last revised by Talmudic scholars almost 1000 years ago. A minority within a minority, who mostly shun the Israeli state, the ultra-zealous Jews who live in Jerusalem's Mea Shearim quarter adhere to a strict interpretation of the Torah, one that's increasingly challenged not only by the surrounding secular society but by other observant religious communities. The film, featuring some fine and poignant acting, presents a forceful argument with which few secular viewers would disagree. These men treat 'their' women abominably, maintaining their power by enforcing rules that view females as chattels, little more than baby factories. But this itself raises the question of why thousands of women would choose to remain in such communities and accept their strictures in the first place, an arguably more intriguing conundrum, but one which Gitai's film never really addresses.

The point, which comes across only partially in the film, is that to all these people, men and women, the burden of the commandments *(ol mitsvot)* is exactly that—a burden, explicable only by the layers of tradition that present the strictest adherents as the purest guardians of God's will. Everyone suffers a life of self-denial and hardship (except those who abuse their power in the community for financial gain, a vital sore completely ignored here), leavened only by the bursts of intense joy which accompany religious festivals. But even these moments are downplayed in *Kadosh*: everything is reduced to Gitai's critique of the cheerlessly repressive nature of this fanatically religious existence.

The greatest irony is that Gitai relies on a secular methodology—dramatic narrative—in his portrait of a community that recognises only one narrative, the Torah, discussed and reviewed endlessly by the film's characters. The ultra-orthodox Jews whose lives Gitai attempts to depict will never see his film, as they shun the visual culture of cinema and television. Our own disapproval of their way of life may be strengthened, but it isn't elucidated; an opportunity to see the world through their eyes has been missed.

VILLAGE VOICE, 2/22/00, p. 144, Jessica Winter

Set in the ultra-Orthodox quarter of Jerusalem called Mea Shearim, *Kadosh* (meaning "sacred") studies two sisters enduring the ironhanded restrictions of their tiny, airtight society, and marks Amos Gitaï's first effort in employing a fabricated narrative after 20 years of documentaries and semifictional film "essays." The result carries the sharp sting and the enduring chill of the hardest truth.

Gitaï bestows on his film a tenacious attention to routine, to the habits and daily tasks that provide a steadying cadence amid miscellaneous upheavals but that also, piecemeal and almost imperceptibly, add up to the story of a life: Rivka (Yaël Abecassis) wipes away tears as she chops onions for dinner; sister Malka (Meital Barda) gasps for air as the stern hand of her mother dunks her, over and over, into a ritual bath because she is unclean. Ritual amounts to an unseen but omnipotent character in *Kadosh*'s world, since rigid interpretations of Talmudic law govern everything from lovemaking to tea-taking, and formulate women as little more than childbearing bodies; after Rivka and Meir (Yoram Hattab) have been married 10 years without conceiving, they receive an anonymous letter that reads, "A woman without a child is no better than dead." Husband and wife make a loving, devoted couple, but a menacing pack of religious, societal, and familial pressures all but devour the marriage, recalling Dariush Mehrjui's equally devastating *Leila*.

Malka, more headstrong and less devout than her outwardly serene older sister, loves a Mea Shearim deserter named Yaakov (Sami Hori), but she's finally cornered into marriage to Yossef (Uri Ran Klausner), a puffing bully who tools around in a truck blaring God's teachings through a bullhorn. The Yossef character remains for the most part a monstrous abstraction, a point of entry into Malka's mounting anguish, rage, and claustrophobia. (*Kadosh* is composed mostly of close interiors; outdoor scenes, excepting a final, transcendent overview of Jerusalem, emanate a furtive, forbidden air.) Watching Malka hysterically laugh and weep at her reflection as she hacks off her beautiful long hair is almost as unbearable as the brutal ordeal of her wedding night, which Gitaï renders in one long, static, unwavering shot.

One of Gitaï's greatest assets in *Kadosh* is such stillness, which leaves facile outsiders' judgment out of the frame and thereby deepens our immersion in the narrative. He patiently contemplates his actresses: Barda's stunned, stricken look during Malka's marriage ceremony, as the female guests circle around her in a dirge-like wedding dance, lends her the breathless panic of someone being sucked into a vortex. And Abecassis's tranquil mien slowly fades as Rivka is edged out of her society—her eyes cloud over and her facial muscles slacken, like someone being strangled from the inside. Indeed, *Kadosh* makes the strong suggestion—one perhaps secular to a fault but no less compelling for it—that Rivka and Malka's crises have their origins from within as well as without, that they can choose their fates. The choice, as we see though we want to look away, requires their every reserve of strength, and might well be a matter of life or death.

Also reviewed in:
CHICAGO TRIBUNE, 5/12/00, Friday/p. H, John Petrakis
NEW REPUBLIC, 2/14/00, p. 30, Stanley Kauffmann
NEW YORK TIMES, 2/16/00, p. E1, Stephen Holden
VARIETY, 5/17-23/99, p. 53, Lisa Nesselson

KEEPING THE FAITH

A Touchstone Pictures and Spyglass Entertainment release of a Koch Co./Norton-Blumberg production. *Executive Producer:* Gary Barber, Roger Birnbaum, and Jonathan Glickman. *Producer:* Hawk Koch, Edward Norton, and Stuart Blumberg. *Director:* Edward Norton. *Screenplay:* Stuart Blumberg. *Director of Photography:* Anastas Michos. *Editor:* Malcolm Campbell. *Music:* Elmer Bernstein. *Music Editor:* Ken Karmen. *Sound:* Tom Nelson and (music) Dan Wallin. *Sound Editor:* J. Paul Huntsman and Patrick Dodd. *Casting:* Avy Kaufman. *Production Designer:* Wynn P. Thomas. *Art Director:* Chris Shriver. *Set Decorator:* Leslie E. Rollins. *Set Dresser:* Dennis Swanson, Stephen Swanson, Peter Decurtis, Denis Zack, John M. Basile, and Gary Ahroni. *Special Effects:* John Ottesen. *Costumes:* Michael Kaplan. *Make-up:* Carla White. *Make-up (Jenna Elfman):* Ann Masterson. *Stunt Coordinator:* George Aguilar. *Running time:* 129 minutes. *MPAA Rating:* PG-13.

CAST: Ben Stiller (Jake);   Edward Norton (Brian);   Jenna Elfman (Anna);   Anne Bancroft (Ruth);   Eli Wallach (Rabbi Lewis); Ron Rifkin (Larry Friedman);   Milos Forman (Father Havel);   Holland Taylor (Bonnie Rose);   Lisa Edelstein (Ali Decker);   Rena Sofer (Rachel Rose);   Ken Leung (Don);   Brian George (Indian Bartender);   Catherine Lloyd Burns (Debbie);

Susie Essman (Ellen Friedman);   Stuart Blumberg (Len);   Sam Goldberg (Jake as a Teen); Blythe Auffarth (Anna as a Teen);   Michael Roman (Brian as a Teen); Jonathan Silver (Alan Klein);   Brian Anthony Wilson (T-Bone);   Juan Piedrahita (Omar);   Kelly Deadmon (Woman in Bar);   Raphael M.A. Frieder (Cantor);   Bodhi Elfman (Casanova);   Christopher Gardner and Santi Formosa (Basketball Kids);   Francine Beers (Greta Mussbaum);   Rena Blumberg (Chaya); Ellen Hauptman (Roz Lentz);   Liz Larsen (Leslie);   Matt Winston (Matt);   Nelson Avidon (Joel); David Wain (Steve Posner);   Donna Hanover (Woman #1, Confessional);   Wai Ching Ho (Woman #2, Confessional);   Howard Greller (Doctor);   Brenda Thomas Denmark (Nurse); Marily Cooper ("Don't Walk" Lady);   Hawk Koch (Rabbinical Professor); Craig Castaldo (Radio Man);   Keith Perry (Old Man Hit with Censor);   John Arocho (Bully);   Derrick Eason (Co-Worker);   Ray Carlson (Monsignor);   Barbara Haas (Mother in Synagogue Reception Room); Sunny Keyser, Lorna Lable, and Paula Raflo (Mothers); Hillary Brook Canter, Dana Lubotsky, and Alexandra Rella (Daughters); Eugene S. Katz (Mohel);   Tony Rossi (Hot Dog Vendor);   John P. Duffell (Father Duffell);   Keith Williams (AIDS Patient).

LOS ANGELES TIMES, 4/14/00, Calendar/p. 6, Kevin Thomas

A mainstream production that's nonetheless made with considerable care and imagination, "Keeping the Faith" also offers more than a little humor and marks an astute directorial debut for actor Edward Norton.

Arriving just a week after "Return to Me," "Keeping the Faith" is another romantic comedy with a potentially smarmy premise that's all the more rewarding because of the challenge the material presented. Norton and screenwriter Stuart Blumberg introduce us to lifelong friends Jake (Ben Stiller), a rabbi, and Brian (Norton), a priest, and drop into their midst Anna, their best pal from eighth grade at Manhattan's P.S. 184. The two men haven't seen her for 16 years, when she moved to California with her family. What we end up with is an "Abie's Irish Rose" for the 21st century.

Both young men are well-established in their work. Brian is content with his life's choice, and the innovative Jake is in line to assume the post of chief rabbi at a large, upscale temple. It is true that Jake is in need of a wife to cinch the promotion, and he's constantly besieged by the eligible young women of his temple. When Anna, now a corporate executive charged with shaping up the New York office, arrives at the airport in the stunning form of Jenna Elfman, both men are transfixed.

At first it's like old times, but the three are no longer kids. A spark ignites between Jake and Anna, who tell themselves they can handle a discreet fling without falling in love. And Brian, unaware of their affair, tells himself that he's comfortable with his celibacy and is in no danger of falling in love with Anna himself.

Of course these people are kidding themselves, but Blumberg deftly works out their increasingly complicated emotional dilemmas. Anna, who's not particularly religious, is probably Catholic and certainly not Jewish. She is not exactly the ideal candidate for a rabbi's wife, and while Jake's mother, Ruth (Anne Bancroft), adores Anna, she has not spoken to Jake's older brother since he married a Gentile.

A thicket of incidents, comic and serious, most assuredly ensues, but Blumberg to his credit makes some worthwhile points: that there are times in our lives when we sell people short by not having faith in their capacity for understanding, that a religious life is a choice that must come from deep within the individual and is subject to constant reaffirmation, and finally that religion ought to unite people rather than divide them.

Significantly, Jake, Brian and Anna are all busy, committed people, but Anna is a self-acknowledged workaholic who's just beginning to wonder whether she's gotten her priorities straight. Blumberg and Norton show affection for Jews and Catholics and respect for their beliefs and customs.

"Keeping the Faith" is the kind of wishful make-believe that takes lots of star power to put over, and all three leads have charisma to bum. Anna in particular must have a blazing impact to throw two dedicated men of the cloth into a tailspin, and Elfman exudes beauty, sex appeal and self-confidence made irresistible by that sure-fire combination of wit, intellect and directness.

Meanwhile, Stiller and Norton never lose our sympathy as Jake and Brian wrestle with questions that will affect the rest of their lives, not to mention their friendship.

The stars have terrific support, most crucially from Bancroft, whose Ruth is wonderfully forthright and astringent, and from Eli Wallach and Milos Forman, wise ecclesiastical counselors to Stiller and Norton, respectively. Ron Rifkin, Holland Taylor, Rena Sofer, Brian George and Ken Leung round out the excellent key supporting players.

Cinematographer Anastas Michos and a raft of top craftspeople present a Manhattan so glowing you want to grab the next plane for New York, and Elmer Bernstein's lovely score sets the mood for sophisticated romance. "Keeping the Faith" actually does that on its own, and works out its plot with more honesty and less contrivance than you would have thought possible for an expensive entertainment conceived for wide appeal.

NEW YORK, 4/24/00, p. 132, Peter Rainer

Keeping the Faith feels like it started out in a script conference as the setup to a bad joke about a rabbi and a priest. It ends up that way, too. Edward Norton, who also directed, is the hotshot Upper West Side priest playing opposite Ben Stiller's hotshot Upper West Side rabbi. Friends since childhood, they reconnect with a heartthrob (Jenna Elfman), now a corporate honcho, they haven't seen since she moved away in eighth grade. Romantic triangulations ensue, and as much as Norton wants us to think Noël Coward, it's Aaron Spelling who comes to mind. The filmmakers seem to be aware of this, too: Spelling's name is even invoked at one point, as if that lets them off the hook. In the past, Norton has given his average-guyness an edgy allure, and his choice of acting roles has often been daring. Why he would want to kick off his directing career with this ecumenical dud, God only knows.

NEW YORK POST, 4/14/00, p. 57, Lou Lumenick

When Huey Lewis sings "It's Hip to Be Square" (currently on the soundtrack of "American Psycho"), he could be referring to Edward Norton's hugely entertaining directing debut, "Keeping the Faith."

One of our best and edgiest actors, Norton surprises us with a sweetly old-fashioned comedy that's a cross between Francois Truffaut's two-guys-and-a-gal classic "Jules and Jim" and "Abie's Irish Rose," the prototypical stage farce about interfaith romances.

The laughs are nearly nonstop in this extremely well-acted story about Upper West Side rabbi Jake Schram (Ben Stiller) and Roman Catholic priest Brian Finn (Norton), who re-encounter grown-and-gorgeous childhood pal Anna Reilly (Jenna Elfman).

Both clerics promptly get hot under their collars, causing unholy complications: Brian because he's celibate, and Jake because Anna's a *shiksa* (a non-Jew)—and every mother in his congregation is pushing her unmarried daughter at him.

Jake, seen on hilariously bad dates with a fitness freak (Lisa Edelstein) who goads him into punching her in the stomach and a gorgeous ABC anchorwoman (Rena Sofer), finally succumbs to Anna, a hard-driving corporate executive.

He's risking the wrath of his mom (Anne Bancroft) and the cranky congregation president (Ron Rifkin) who's already irked about the rabbi's use of standup comedy, group meditation and gospel choirs.

Brian, who's unaware of the budding romance, is wrestling with his own demons with the help of his superior and mentor (played by director Milos Forman). Norton's part is notably smaller than Stiller's, but he opens the film by giving himself a lengthy drunk scene that's an affectionate homage to another romantic-triangle classic, "The Philadelphia Story."

Stiller is sexy, intense and even more hilarious than he was in "There's Something About Mary," but the real surprise is Elfman, who commands the big screen in a characterization that's 180 degrees from her work on TV's "Dharma and Greg."

Screenwriter Stuart Blumberg (a buddy of Norton's from his Yale days) provides the cast with plenty of Woody Allen-style zingers that keep the laughs coming.

Norton, who acted in Allen's "Everyone Says I Love You," shows his influence with excellent use of Manhattan locations, photographed in fairy-tale style by Anastas Michos. Too bad Norton didn't learn more about editing from Allen; he needed to lose about 15 minutes.

Still, "Keeping the Faith" ain't exactly chopped liver. It's the ideal date movie for the Passover-Easter season and beyond, guaranteed to keep audiences rolling in the pews.

NEWSDAY, 4/14/00, Part II/p. B6, Gene Seymour

The premise of "Keeping the Faith" is naughty enough to tickle the nerve endings of the adventurous moviegoer. But its execution is nice enough to send your grandmother home happy.

How curious that a maiden directorial effort by Edward Norton should be so cozy and equivocal. Norton the actor is a masterly trickster-savant, using his fresh-scrubbed preppy persona to lead audiences to believe he's a passive, easygoing guy before giving their expectations a hotfoot.

There are times, both as actor and director in "Keeping the Faith," when Norton makes you believe he's going to goose the juice once again. As with the movie itself, Norton's portrayal of the Rev. Brian Finn has a few tantalizing nettles poking beneath its placid, earnest surface. When, toward the movie's midsection, his hip Catholic priest tumbles onto a shattering revelation, Norton runs through a beautifully timed sequence of slow-burning anxiety. It's a neat bit of work. But by then, you already know he's not taking things toward the edge.

And going to the edge is just about the only thing that "Keeping the Faith" isn't straining to do. It's a full-service, feel-good romantic comedy with a set-up that whispers more mischief than it delivers. See, there's this priest (Norton) and this rabbi (Ben Stiller) who grew up best friends in Manhattan and shared the same winsome blond confidante-buddy (Jenna Elfman) from childhood.

"What?," you say. "No golf course? No St. Peter waiting at the gate?" Nope. It's not that kind of priest-rabbi joke. In fact, it's no joke to Stiller's Rabbi Jake Schram, who's searching desperately for the kind of nice Jewish wife who would please both his congregants and his demanding mom (Anne Bancroft). When Elfman's Anna Reilly, who returns to New York as a buffed-up, no-nonsense corporate superstar, hooks up with her two buddies, she and Jake end up in bed. They agree to keep their affair a secret—even from Brian, who suspects nothing, even as he's working with Jake to set up an interfaith karaoke bar and subduing his own romantic feelings toward Anna.

Stuart Blumberg's script veers frenetically between lowbrow farce and middlebrow philosophizing about transacting across religious and cultural boundary lines. The film is most appealing when it shuts up about such issues and just revels in New York's myriad multicultural anomalies, embodied by such hilarious fringe characters as Brian George's Indian proprietor of an Irish bar and Ken Leung's hyperbolic karaoke salesman.

"Keeping the Faith" also appeals when its three leads kick back and feed each other straight lines to bat away like line drives. Although it's hard to imagine the intense Stiller playing anyone for whom, as Brian says of Jake, "things come easily," his dry ice spritzing is fun to watch. And it's nice to see Elfman finally getting a big-screen role that gives free rein to her wily humor and laid-back sexuality. It's just too bad that this wisenheimer trio is locked into a by-the-numbers romance that cops out on itself with a crowd-pleasing—and utterly unsurprising climax.

SIGHT AND SOUND, 10/00, p. 48, Philip Kemp

Aged 13, Jake Schram, Brian Finn and Anna Reilly were best friends at school in Manhattan until Anna moved to California. Some 15 years later, Jake is a rabbi and Brian a Catholic priest. Anna returns to New York as a high-powered corporate executive. The three renew their friendship, but Brian is constrained by his cloth while Jake, soon to succeed the aged Rabbi Lewis, is under pressure to marry a Jewish woman.

On a date with television reporter Rachel, Jake invites Brian and Anna along as a supposed couple to ease the situation. All three are confused by their feelings. Having seen Rachel home, Jake goes to Anna's apartment and they fall into bed together. They keep their affair secret from Brian and everybody else, although the pressures of Anna's work and Jake's congregation put the relationship under strain.

About to be moved to San Francisco, Anna tells Jake she loves him. He refuses to commit and they break up. Anna calls Brian; when he learns what's been happening he violently confronts Jake. The two are later reconciled, but Jake keeps away from Anna. His mother Ruth tells him he should follow his heart. Jake announces at the synagogue he's in love with a Gentile; after some debate he's approved as the new rabbi. He rushes to Anna's office. They show up together at the inauguration of Brian and Jake's ecumenical social centre. Anna reveals she's been taking instruction from Rabbi Lewis.

Religion has always enjoyed a pretty easy ride from Hollywood; even when it's taken as a subject for comedy, the jokes about priestly celibacy, rebellious nuns or even God himself have lacked any real satirical bite. For years religion in Hollywood meant the Catholic Church, since the Jewish studio heads preferred to keep all mention of Jewishness off the screen. But since Judaism became an acceptable movie topic it's been treated with much the same respectful jocularity.

Keeping the Faith Edward Norton's directorial debut, carries on this tradition, playing like a descendant of such bland comedies as *Going My Way* (1944) in which Fr Bing Crosby joshed with the Mother Superior. The wrestlings with conscience may go a little deeper, and the references to sex are a lot franker, but in the end no boats are seriously rocked. The rabbi enjoys an affair with a *shiksa* but finally that's OK because she's studying to convert. The priest suffers pangs of jealousy, but conscience prevails and he conceals his urges beneath his soutane. For a while it looks as if the girl may start bedding both rabbi and priest, which could have made for a rather more interesting film; but Stuart Blumberg's script backs off and plays it safe.

Within these cautious confines the comedy is mostly fresh and diverting, with some shrewd insights into the use of faith as a displacement strategy. "Jews want rabbis to be the kind of Jews they don't have time to be," observes Jake, the rabbi who falls in love with his childhood friend Anna. "And Catholics want priests to be what they don't have the discipline to be," responds his priest friend Brian. Norton, who also plays Brian, draws likeable, lively performances from his cast, though Jenna Elfman as Anna takes a while to ease into her role and Norton's own abrupt character shift from good listener to brash conclusion-jumper feels awkwardly plot-driven.

But though it sidesteps the key issues in favour of a cop-out ending, *Keeping the Faith* can claim one major virtue: its wholehearted embrace, and indeed celebration, of the joys of a multiracial society. In one of the film's funniest moments, Jake enlivens the singing in his synagogue by introducing a black Gospel choir to join in. Most of the action is told in flashback, with Norton's priest recounting events to the traditional sympathetic barman, except that this stock character turns out to be a half-Punjabi "Sikh Catholic Muslim with Jewish in-laws". ("'I am reading *Dianetics,*" he adds.) And in the final scene, by way of a throwaway gag, we catch a glimpse of the Jewish television reporter Jake briefly dated—now with her new Afro-American boyfriend. It's a reprise of the message Norton put across in his Oscar-nominated performance in *American History X*—but conveyed here with far more good humour.

VILLAGE VOICE, 4/18/00, p. 158, Amy Taubin

As an actor, Edward Norton is full of surprises. He has a gift for catching you off-guard, mostly because he seems so little like a performer. Who would expect this unassuming, slightly awkward guy with the stuck-in-the-throat voice to be capable of the passionate expression of deeply held beliefs (his big speech at the end of *The People vs. Larry Flynt*) or the deftly timed self-mockery of his entire split-psyche performance in *Fight Club?* Norton is a master of mind/body disjunction and other out-of-sync behaviors, the comic emblem of which is the double take.

Late in *Keeping the Faith*—basically a two-hour-long priest-and-rabbi joke with New Age flourishes, including a gospel choir rendition of the Jewish holiday standard "Ein Kelohainu"—Norton, who plays the priest, discovers something that shatters the fantasy he's finally worked up the courage to enact. He responds with a series of double takes, one of which involves dumping a pot of water over his own head. Suddenly the film, which has been mushy and predictable, becomes fun to watch. Norton, the actor, rises above his material.

But Norton, the first-time director, does not, having chosen a script so mainstream and superficial it must have gladdened the hearts of Disney execs. *Keeping the Faith* has been calculated to seem controversial but to offend no one—an ideal conversation piece for the upcoming Passover and Easter family gatherings.

Jake (Ben Stiller) and Brian (Norton) have been best friends since their school days when they were both in love with Anna, a girl with more moxie than the two of them put together. When Anna moves to California, the boys fall back on their other common interest: religion. After graduating from seminary school, they are both assigned to congregations on the Upper West Side. Soon the rabbi and the priest, who sport identical black leather jackets and who have a similar talent for stand-up comedy, are, as Brian puts it, "playing to packed houses" and trying to get their multi-faith karaoke club off the ground. Then Anna (Jenna Elfman) returns to put the monkey wrench into their friendship and their respective religious callings. Anna has metamorphosed into a corporate power broker—a chiseled, golden-skinned wonder woman with a cell phone grafted to her ear or, on festive occasions, nestled in her black lace garter.

Jake and Brian are smitten all over again, all the more so because Anna is off-limits to both of them—to Brian because of his vow of celibacy and to Jake because he believes that a rising rabbi must acquire a proper Jewish wife. Nevertheless, Jake and Anna have an affair, which they keep secret from Brian. *Keeping the Faith* uses the romantic triangle to avoid getting too embroiled in religion and vice versa. When Jake tells his congregation that, rather than weighty subjects like the future of Israel, he'll use his Yom Kippur sermon to come clean about his affair with Anna, he gives away the film's game as well as his own. The priest, the rabbi, and the shiksa who came to dinner are so enthralled with themselves that there's no room in their self-congratulatory world for such potentially divisive issues as women in the clergy, same-sex marriage, or the homeless down the block—modern religion here is a celebration of narcissism. *Keeping the Faith*'s hipness is limited to a couple of one-liners. Its exploration of faith and love is skin deep.

Also reviewed in:
CHICAGO TRIBUNE, 4/14/00, Friday/p. J, Mark Caro
NEW YORK TIMES, 4/14/00, p. E16, Elvis Mitchell
NEW YORKER, 4/24 & 5/1/00, p. 221, David Denby
VARIETY, 4/3-9/00, p. 32, Emanuel Levy
WASHINGTON POST, 4/14/00, p. C1, Stephen Hunter
WASHINGTON POST, 4/14/00, Weekend/p. 43, Desson Howe

KESTREL'S EYE

A First Run Features release.   *Producer:* Mikael Kristersson.   *Director:* Mikael Kristersson. *Screenplay:* Mikael Kristersson.   *Director of Photography:* Mikael Kristersson.   *Editor:* Mikael Kristersson.   *Sound:* Tomas Krantz and Gabor Pasztor.   *Sound Editor:* Bo Leveren and Mikael Kristersson.   *Running time:* 86 minutes.   *MPAA Rating:* Not Rated.

CAST: Caisa Persson (Cyclist).

NEW YORK POST, 1/27/00, p. 83, Hannah Brown

"Kestrel's Eye" is the perfect film for anyone who feels that the Dogma 95 directors, that group of mostly Scandinavian filmmakers who produce bleak, hard-hitting movies according to a Manifesto, have gotten too commercial.

This austere documentary follows two falcons (also called kestrels) that live on the roof of a church in rural Sweden. There is no narration or music, since presumably these would have added an artificial element.

Director Mikael Kristersson certainly achieves his goal of focusing exclusively on the birds and their world. Unfortunately, this approach doesn't make for the most diverting 86 minutes ever captured on film, though much of the photography is extraordinary.

The main problem is that these birds are not terribly expressive. Falcons, like fashion models, may look great, but they never betray the slightest emotion, whether soaring, snacking on a mouse, mating or watching a funeral procession in the churchyard below.

VILLAGE VOICE, 2/1/00, p. 122, Joe McGovern

Near as any contemporary film has come to rendering the Rorschach inkblot test, Mikael Kristersson's *Kestrel's Eye* takes an expressionless tableau and converts it into a metaphor for labor, language, and the nature of nature itself. Set principally in a church tower overlooking a mild Swedish hinterland, this patiently observed reverie portrays the seasonal conduct of two European falcons as they build shelter, lay eggs, hunt mice, and peep-peep on the preoccupied homo sapiens floundering below. A meditative piece in the lyric tradition, the 86-minute film is distinguished from a Discovery special by its uniquely fowl-minded aesthetic. Via the unaffected soundtrack (no narrator or score) and bird's-eye point of view, the audience viscerally experiences the kestrel's world: an airplane overhead, a car alarm, a scampering cat, and, most strange and unnatural, a village marching band. Courtesy of a motor-equipped hang glider, we even get a sense of the bird's flight. The film's gaze allows us to consider ourselves as well—a simultaneity made most poignant when the kestrel's freshly hatched nuclear family perch themselves to watch a human parent assembling a camping tent with his children. The scene accentuates a link between two species of nest-builders, lighting a spark in our eyes, not to mention the kestrel's.

Also reviewed in:
CHICAGO TRIBUNE, 5/19/00, Friday/p. H, John Petrakis
NEW YORK TIMES, 1/26/00, p. E5, Lawrence Van Gelder
VARIETY, 1/31-2/6/00, p. 32, Oliver Jones

KIKUJIRO

A Sony Pictures Classics release of a Bandai Visual/Tokyo FM/Nippon Herald/Office Kitano production.   *Producer:* Masayuki Mori and Takio Yoshida.   *Director:* Takeshi Kitano. *Screenplay (Japanese with English subtitles):* Takeshi Kitano. *Director of Photography:* Katsumi Yanagishima.   *Editor:* Takeshi Kitano and Yoshinori Ota.   *Music:* Joe Hisaishi.   *Sound:* Senji Horiuchi. *Casting:* Takefumi Yoshikawa. *Production Designer:* Norihiro Isoda.   *Art Director:* Norihiro Isoda and Takayuki Nitta.   *Set Decorator:* Tatsuo Ozeki.   *Costumes:* Fumio Iwasaki. *Make-up:* Mitsuyo Miyauchi.   *Running time:* 116 minutes.   *MPAA Rating:* R.

CAST: Beat Takeshi (Kikujiro);   Yusuke Sekiguchi (Masao);   Kayoko Kishimoto (Kikujiro's Wife);   Yuko Daike (Masao's Mother);   Kazuko Yoshiyuiki (Masao's Grandmother);   Beat Kiyoshi (Man at Bus Stop);   Great Gidayu (Biker/Fatso);   Rakkyo Ide (Biker/Baldy);   Nezumi Mamura (Traveling Man);   Fumle Hosokawa (Juggler Girl); Akaji Maro (Scary Man);   Daigaku Sekine (Yakuza Boss); Yoji Tanaka, Makoto Inamiya, and Hisahiko Murasawa (Yakuzas);   Taro Suwa and Hidehisa Ejiri (Hucksters);   Kenta Arai (Masao's Friend).

LOS ANGELES TIMES, 5/26/00, Calendar/p. 9, Kevin Thomas

When a Takeshi Kitano picture opens with little boys walking down a busy Tokyo street and changing their route to avoid a group of older bullies, you have every reason to anticipate that this will deliver them right smack into the hands of kidnappers. However, with "Kikujiro," Kitano, nonpareil portrayer of world-weary cops and gangsters in his stylish—and bloody—films noir, is taking us in a different direction. The result is a heart-tugger made totally irresistible because of the combination of Kitano's wry, sly sense of humor and his rigorous detachment.

The smaller of the two boys, Masao (Yusuke Sekiguchi), lives with his grandmother (Kazuko Yoshiyuiki), who works at a nearby sushi stand, but as a lonely summer descends upon him he feels a renewed longing for his mother; his grandmother has told him that his mother is working hard on his behalf at a job in a distant city and his father was apparently killed in an accident.

When he discovers a picture of the mother and her address, he prepares to run away to find her. Before he can do that, he winds up with one of his grandmother's friends, who gets her irascible, gambling husband, Kikujiro (Beat Takeshi, Kitano's performing name), to accompany him.

Feisty and combative, Kikujiro is a guy who's always working an angle that more often than not backfires on him. He's a gruff, tough guy who doesn't take anything from anybody—even if it leaves him beaten to a pulp. He's not so fearless as simply hotheaded and headstrong, a guy who often acts before he thinks. He'll get lucky gambling only to gamble away his winnings, which leaves him and Masao broke and forced to hitchhike their way to their destination, which makes for some highly comical encounters with strangers along the way.

In a deliberately roundabout way, Kitano is building to a moment of truth that is a knockout and allows Kikujiro to see himself in a completely different way in relation to Masao. Kitano's craggy, rough-hewn face, with its features perfect for playing stoics, is the ideal countenance to set off the paternal feelings Kikujiro begins to feel. As a filmmaker and as an actor, Kitano gives a unique, distinctive impact to a classic father-son type relationship.

If Kitano's vision is comical, it is also discreetly distanced in dealing with serious feelings. Kitano understands the pain of loss and longing; he respects the sacredness of the most intense emotions, the ways in which they render us vulnerable and how we crave and deserve privacy when they hit.

With its largely rural and spacious settings, "Kikujiro" is a beautiful, warm and inviting film with a distinctive structure and composition—and a totally captivating score by Joe Hisaishi. Kitano and Sekiguchi are pretty captivating too. The film runs at least 15 minutes too long but is so appealing it's easy to overlook. (This is one of those times when you feel even the most talented of auteurs might benefit from a strong producer.)

NEW YORK POST, 5/26/00, p. 50, Lou Lumenick

Looking around me during a screening of "Kikujiro," I discovered I had plenty of company—lots of people were stifling yawns and watching their wristwatches.

True, the latest effort by Japanese talk-show-host-turned-writer-director-actor Takeshi (Beat) Kitano has some beautiful imagery and some interesting situations, even a few laughs.

But the pacing of this slight and whimsical two-hour film is so painfully slow, it's like watching saki ferment.

Taking a break from the ultra-violent gangster-cop dramas that have made him an international cult figure, the expressionless Kitano plays Kikujiro, a hardened tough guy who agrees to accompany a 9-year-old, Masao (Yusuke Sekiguchi), on a journey to meet his mother for the first time.

A liar and a crook who verbally abuses everyone he meets, Kikujiro loses Masao's money on bike races, then berates the boy for not picking winning numbers.

They hitchhike across Japan at a painfully slow rate, since Kikujiro tends to demand rides and hurl rocks at the vehicles of those who don't comply with his requests. Stopping cars with nails in the road doesn't help much, either.

But Kikujiro softens after Masao's heart is broken by his estranged mother.

"Kikujiro" isn't for kids, even those with extraordinary attention spans. This R-rated comedy contains an explicit encounter between Masao and a child molester, and some male nudity that most American parents would consider inappropriate viewing for youngsters.

NEWSDAY, 5/26/00, Part II/p. B6, Gene Seymour

To devotees of Takeshi Kitano's resonant, brutal crime thrillers (the best of which, 1997's "Fireworks," may well have been his masterwork), "Kikujiro" has thus far come as a surprise in the year or so since its premiere at Cannes. And not, in many of these fans' eyes, a pleasant one, given its seeming 180-degree turnaround from a dry, merciless Kitano to a gooey, sentimental one.

But just as "Fireworks" teased the merciless conventions of cop melodrama with subtle heart-tugging, "Kikujiro," takes a formulaic plot of grizzled sourpuss shamed into helping a forlorn little boy and infuses it with unexpected quirks and offbeat tension.

Kitano, who is once again the writer-director-star, portrays the title character, a wastrel whose wife ridicules him as a cautionary example to the young neighborhood slackers. They live not far from Masao (Yusuke Sekiguchi), a 9-year-old boy living alone with his grandmother. With school over for the year, soccer practice suspended and all his friends away on vacation, an especially dismal summer break seems all but inevitable.

Then, one afternoon, Masao comes across a package that offers clues as to the whereabouts of his mother-of whom he knows little except what his grandmother tells him, that "she's working hard somewhere else for you." He sets off on his own to see for himself. But it's a long way from home, and he hasn't any money. So Kikujiro's wife gives her husband 20,000 yen and orders to take Masao where he wants to go.

The first thing Kikujiro does is lose all their travel money at the bicycle race track. So they're forced to make their way as best they can, on foot or with their thumbs. Their misadventures veer from the whimsically silly (losing battles with a hotel swimming pool) to the vaguely menacing (a brush with a pederast). As his bond with Masao warms up, Kikujiro doesn't become nicer so much as more diffident and impulsive in more creative ways.

It is a tribute to Kitano the actor that he convincingly grounds his character's evolution within the confines of his bullying, capricious personality, which you suspect will never change no matter how many nice things he does for Masao. It is a tribute to Kitano the filmmaker and showman that he is able to sustain a narrative rhythm that, as in his previous films, implies more than displays.

SIGHT AND SOUND, 7/00, p. 47, Tommy Udo

Tokyo, the present. Masao, an only child, lives with his grandmother. His only friend leaves for his summer holiday. Finding a photograph of his mother with an address, Masao sets out to find her. Miki, a friend of his grandmother's, makes her husband, yakuza Kikujiro, accompany the child on his quest. Their first stop is the bike races where Kikujiro loses all his money, but Masao picks three winners. Kikujiro blows the winnings on an absurd cycling outfit for the boy and the rest in a hostess bar. The next day Masao is unable to repeat his trick, leaving them broke. Setting out on foot, their journey is a series of mishaps involving a paedophile who tries to molest Masao, a stolen taxi and a bus stop in the middle of nowhere. They also encounter help along the way from a hotel manager, a punk couple and a wandering poet.

Arriving at his mother's home, Masao sees her with her husband and daughter. Kikujiro tries to comfort the boy, first taking him to a fun fair where the gangster gets beaten up, and then to a bizarre beach camp with the poet and two bikers whom he makes play a series of games to amuse Masao. Kikujiro goes off on a quest of his own to see his mother who is in a home nearby. They return to Tokyo and part.

Takeshi Kitano suggested in interviews that *Kikujiro* would be a break from the post-modern gangster films that established his reputation outside Japan. Though this is true in terms of action, his eighth feature does focus on yet another washed-up yakuza and reprises many favourite scenes and motifs. In fact, as the director's most autobiographical movie to date, *Kikujiro* could be seen as a key to all of his work. Kitano's own father, a largely absent drunk also named Kikujiro, was once forced to spend a summer with his son, much like the character Kikujiro with the parentless boy Masao here. However, it would be unwise to read too much autobiography into a work by such a notoriously unreliable and media-savvy narrator, especially one that feels lighter and less personal in tone than *Hana-Bi*.

Like *Sonatine* and *Hana-Bi* before it, *Kikujiro* taps into a deep-seated Japanese strain of sentimentality The two central characters maintain a respectful distance throughout their tribulations, whereas the film's Hollywood antecedents—Charles Chaplin's *The Kid* (1921), Peter Bogdanovich's *Paper Moon* (1973) and even Barry Levinson's *Rain Man*—can't resist touchy-feely cathartic hugs. It is this constant, quiet, formal respect and politeness between gangster and child that gives the final scene—a shot of the boy's angel-winged backpack as he runs over a bridge, also the first shot of the film—its emotional resonance.

Kikujiro marks Kitano's sixth collaboration with director of photography Katsumi Yanagijima, who shoots the film like a series of still images. Much of Kitano's comedy derives from this technique, explicating a scene through a series of tableaux. For instance, during Kikujiro and Masao's stay at a hotel, one shot shows Kikujiro floating face down in the water, unmoving. A cut shows Masao and the staff looking on; the next paramedics reviving Kikujiro, all producing a deadpan effect. Kitano has often used the same method to deal with violence, whether for comic or dramatic ends. Similar treatment is given here to the sequence depicting a paedophile luring Masao to a public toilet, where he persuades the boy to undress. Kikujiro arrives in time to save the kid and in a series of cutaways beats the molester up. And when Kikujiro is attacked by heavies at a fairground, we don't see the kicks and punches, only their effect on his bloodied face.

Takeshi specialises in playing stoic, often monosyllabic hard men, relying on his exquisite range of looks, head movements, nose rubbings and twitches. Nishi in *Hana-Bi* barely uttered a word in the first half of the film, allowing the other characters to drive the action. Kikujiro, by way of contrast, is a loud-mouthed thug who bullies, threatens and dominates those around him (with the exception of his wife) and swells out in the second act so as to overpower everyone else. As with *Sonatine,* in which gangsters played at sumo wrestling, *Kikujiro's* most memorable images are of games on a beach, of hard men engaged in childish play. Two bikers are made to dress up as fish or aliens for Masao's entertainment, while Kikujiro barks instructions at them, as if he or Kitano was trying to recreate some lost world of childish innocence for both of them.

It remains to be seen if Kitano's forthcoming Hollywood directorial debut *Brother* will bring him popular success on a par with the critical acclaim heaped on his two best films to date, *Sonatine* and *Hana-Bi.*   In the meantime, *Kikujiro* leaves you with the sense that he is consolidating previous work, even treading water. That said, it's a beautiful and engaging film with vivid scenes which linger in the memory long after they've faded from the screen.

VILLAGE VOICE, 5/30/00, p. 125, J. Hoberman

Anyone who knows Takeshi Kitano only from *Violent Cop, Boiling Point,* or *Sonatine* might be understandably bewildered by the sugary pink seraphim that flutter through the credits of his latest feature, *Kikujiro.* But, however deadpan, Japan's king of all media is a man with more than one face: There is Kitano the tough guy and Kitano the rank sentimentalist. *Fireworks,* which allowed him to impale an enemy's eye with a chopstick as well as nurse his wife through a terminal illness, was an attempt to synthesize the two. *Kikujiro,* which was unfairly dissed last year at Cannes, does much the same thing, albeit in a lighter mode.

Kitano has made inspirational movies about deaf-mute surfers and lonely teenagers, as well as dramas of rogue police officers and crazed yakuza. *Kikujiro* concerns a sad little nine-year-old boy (played with abysmal cuteness by TV actor Yusuke Sekiguchi) taken on a summer vacation to find his long-lost mother. His escort on this trip is the least likely of guardian angels, Kitano himself. Although the journey is carefully structured as a series of episodes, the personal connection is blithely casual. Kitano has been volunteered for the job by his acerbic wife, an acquaintance of the boy's caretaker-grandmother.

The loudmouthed, hectoring Kitano, who may be a retired yakuza, agrees only to take the boy to the beach—which actually means a day spent at the track, gambling the kid's travel money on the bicycle races. Kitano stages a 24-hour celebration when the boy, Damon Runyon-style, picks a winner. Unfortunately, his pint-sized good-luck charm fails to repeat the trick—to Kitano's mounting, voluble frustration. It's a richly comic sequence with a discomfiting denouement. The kid wanders off and "Mister," as the child respectfully calls Kitano, has to rescue his charge from a predatory pedophile.

This unpleasant bit of business is a necessary inoculation, as the boy is a largely self-contained and passive foil for Kitano's own brand of (mainly verbal) abuse. Let no one suspect Kitano's motives. *Kikujiro* is intended to be a man-boy odyssey in the tradition of Chaplin's *The Kid,* De Sica's *Bicycle Thief,* and Adam Sandler's *Big Daddy.*   What gives the movie its edge is Kitano's abrasive personality. Far from lovable, he's a relentless bully and an opportunistic sneak as well as a genuine oddball. The movie is divided into sections, one of which is simply titled "Mister Is Strange." He's also pretty funny—impulsive, scurrilous, and barely socialized.

After dissipating what's left of the winnings on a luxury hotel, Mister takes the boy hitchhiking into the countryside. This leisurely sequence affords additionally dubious antics, seemingly designed by Kitano to mock what he sees as the timid self-absorption of his Japanese audience. Kitano feigns blindness in order to get a lift; he's not only ignored but actually run down by a car, which quickly speeds away. Infuriated by the failure of this ploy, Kitano tries a more drastic way of securing a ride, inadvertently creating an accident that sends him scampering off for cover.

These gags work because Kitano has created an intrinsically funny character and because he has perfect timing and a terrific sense of construction. Not unlike Albert Brooks, Kitano is an impressively classical filmmaker who favors clean compositions, deliberate camera movements, and precise sequences. Most of the jokes are purely visual. Kitano, who edits his own films, enjoys cutting from cause to effect, leaving out the transition for comic payoff. More gratuitous, but no less elegant, is his taste for stunt camera-placement, which, in *Kikujiro,* includes the interior of a champagne flute. (Kitano also trains his camera on a spinning hubcap and throws on a lens to simulate an insect's-eye view of a scene.)

Failing to reunite the boy with his mother, Kitano creates a surrogate, all-male family composed of a wandering writer and two hapless bikers, whom he relentlessly harasses for their blue-angel charm and consequently bullies into endless games to entertain the kid. This prolonged Peter Pan setup, a good half hour of plotless pranks, recalls the extended vacation riffs in *Fireworks* and, especially, *Sonatine*—an example of what Sigmund Freud called "taking pleasure in nonsense." It's as if Kitano simply decided to switch from one TV mode to another, ending his movie with an elaborate vaudeville coda.

Kikujiro is assembled as a memory album, and even when the movie does finally turn maudlin, the formal values remain intact. Caught cheating at a rural fairground, Kitano is beaten up off-camera. With characteristic understatement, the title for this sequence is "Mister Fell Down the Stairs." The same discretion extends to the surprise visit he pays his aged mother in a rest home. For all its Hello Kitty-ism, *Kikujiro struck* me as less cloying and perhaps more audacious than *Fireworks.*

Fireworks was a violent movie that meditated on mortality and was infused with unexpected mawkishness; *Kikujiro* is an overtly saccharine fairy tale of abandonment that is subverted by its own comic brutality. It's oddly affecting—which is to say, sad in a way that its maker might not have intended.

Also reviewed in:
CHICAGO TRIBUNE, 6/30/00, Friday/p. N, Michael Wilmington
NEW YORK TIMES, 5/26/00, p. E19, A. O. Scott
VARIETY, 5/24-30/99, p. 65, David Rooney

KIPPUR

A Kino International release of an MP Productions/Agav Hafakot/Le Studio Canal+/Arte France Cinema and R & C Produzioni co-production in association with Canal+/Telad/Eldan and Tele+. *Producer:* Michel Propper, Amos Gitai, and Laurent Truchot. *Director:* Amos Gitai. *Screenplay (Hebrew with English subtitles):* Amos Gitai and Marie-José Sanselme. *Director of Photography:* Renato Berta. *Editor:* Monica Coleman and Kobi Netanel. *Music:* Jan Garbarek. *Sound:* Eli Yarkoni. *Production Designer:* Miguel Markin. *Special Effects:* Digby Milner. *Costumes:* Laura Dinulesco. *Make-up:* Moni Mansano. *Running time:* 117 minutes. *MPAA Rating:* Not Rated.

CAST: Liron Levo (Weinraub); Tomer Ruso (Ruso); Uri Ran Klauzner (Klauzner, the Doctor); Yoram Hattab (Yoram); Guy Amir (Gadassi); Juliano Merr (The Captain); Ran Kauchinsky (Shlomo; Kobi Livne (Kobi); Liat Glick Levo (Dina).

CHRISTIAN SCIENCE MONITOR, 11/3/00, p. 15, David Sterritt

As its title suggests, "Kippur" deals with the Yom Kippur War of 1973, in which Gitai himself fought while still in his early 20s. The movie focuses on a small military group formed almost by accident in the early days of the conflict. Unable to reach their proper unit because of congested roads, two soldiers join an army physician assigned to rescue wounded troops from combat areas.

Their helicopter team brings them to one Golan Heights battlefield after another, subjecting them to a dizzying variety of challenges. While this whirlwind of activity is depicted in painstaking and often frightening detail, the film's main interest lies less in the physical violence of combat than in the psychological violence inflicted on the exhausted people forced to slog through this endless series of traumas and ordeals. Rarely has a movie captured the mental costs of warfare with such keen insight and relentless energy.

"Kippur" gains much of its credibility from Gitai's first-hand experiences with combat, and also from his insistence on filming the picture in the Golan Heights, where the action takes place.

Yet this is ultimately not a war movie at all, in the traditional sense of a guts-and-glory epic highlighting the heroism of valiant fighting men. Nor is it an antiwar movie, preaching a lesson against organized bloodshed and hatred. In the end its a movie against war movies, scuffling their second-hand celebrations of battlefield bravery so as to portray combat's real nature: hard, tedious work performed by drained, tired soldiers whose overloaded minds are numbed almost to the vanishing point by trauma and fatigue.

Beneath its mercilessly realistic surface, "Kippur" has the surreal resonance of the eeriest nightmare you can imagine. It cant be real, and yet it is. And therein lies its deepest lesson.

LOS ANGELES TIMES, 12/1/00, Calendar/p. 12, Kevin Thomas

Amos Gitai's "Kippur" is a classic war film, at once elegiac and immediate, that takes you smack into the chaos of combat yet is marked by a detached perspective.

Already acclaimed at major festivals, the film is drawn from Gitai's experiences serving in the 1973 Yom Kippur War, in which Egypt and Syria launched attacks on Oct. 6, in the Sinai and the Golan Heights, respectively. Gitai, therefore, has had 27 years to stand apart from what he witnessed, and he brings it alive to us with clarity and reverence.

Gitai has no propaganda axes to grind. His mission is to convey what he experienced firsthand and let that sink in. The overwhelming sensation so eloquently evoked by Gitai and his formidable cameraman, Renato Berta, is that of sheer fatigue; indeed, Gitai has predicted that the Mideast conflict will resolve itself only when all sides are at last overcome by exhaustion.

From the first frame, Gitai establishes a sense of ease and authority. The Day of Atonement has emptied streets, and Gitai's alter ego Weinraub (Liron Levo)—Weinraub is Gitai's middle name—is in the midst of passionate lovemaking when sirens go off. Gitai creates an acute sense of how war swiftly overtakes an individual's life. Taking off in his secondhand Fiat 128, Weinraub picks up his friend Ruso (Tomer Ruso), and they head for the Golan Heights, where they are to meet with their unit. Traffic jams and detours delay them until the Syrian advance forces them to turn back.

Sleeping in the car by the side of a road, they are awakened by a doctor, Klauzner (Uri Ran Klauzner), whose own car has stalled. They take him to his destination, the air force base at Ramat David, where within the hour they've become members of a seven-man helicopter team, charged with rescuing the battlefield wounded and downed pilots.

Gitai has said that he and Berta wanted to make "Kippur" "without leaving the human face and without being carried away by the spectacular dimension of war films." And that is precisely what they've done.

Weinraub and Ruso, both vigorous young men, plunge right into the rescue operation, along with the others, focusing entirely on saving lives as rapidly as possible. They encounter many fatalities, many men hideously injured, and they just keep going until they're able to grab some rest back at the base. They are forming bonds in the face of danger that are likely to last a lifetime—however long a span that will prove to be.

There's no time for us to learn much about these men, and conventional exposition, beyond some brief self-revealing remarks by Glaumer and by Yoram Hattab, the helicopter's pilot, would destroy the film's overpowering sense of reality. (Gitai has already made a documentary, "Kippur: Memories of War," in which the real-life surviving members of his team recount their experiences.)

There are no self-conscious heroes among these men; they are all men who are doing the best they can, and that means giving one another comfort and support in overcoming fear, exhaustion and facing down the horror of all that surrounds them. Gitai and Berta take us into the eye of the storm, with many lengthy and continuous takes, following the men on the fields and back into the whirling copter that swoops them up and takes them back to the base. "Kippur" is one of those handful of films that makes you feel what war is really like, made by individuals who resist glorifying and mythologizing battle.

The war experience inspired him to abandon architecture for filmmaking—"I needed to learn a profession that would allow me to apprehend society and history around me," he has said. After 23 years of filmmaking, Gitai, now 50, achieved international renown only recently, first with "Kadosh," his stunning drama set in Jerusalem's ultra-Orthodox community, Mea Shearim. With "Kadosh" and "Kippur," Gitai became the first Israeli director to have two films selected for competition at Cannes.

NEW YORK POST, 11/3/00, p. 50, Jonathan Foreman

The Duke of Wellington said after Waterloo that the only thing more terrible than a victory is a defeat.

It's a point that Israeli filmmaker Amos Gitai makes over and over again in his autobiographical film "Kippur."

Although deeply self-indulgent and sometimes unforgivably slow, "Kippur" is an undeniably powerful, grimly fascinating movie, original both in its setting (it's the first feature made about the October 1973 war) and in the way it approaches the subject.

There's little dialogue, you never get to know much about the characters and you find out even less about what is going on.

Almost the entire "action" of the film takes place in the immediate aftermath of combat.

On the Day of Atonement, Weinraub (Liron Levo), a silent artist with Marxist inclinations, is making paint-spattered love to his girlfriend in a Tel Aviv apartment.

When war breaks out, he gets into his Fiat, picks up fellow soldier and friend Ruso (Tomer Ruso), and drives to the their base in the Golan Heights. But huge traffic jams mean that their unit has already left when they arrive at base.

After spending the night in the Fiat, the two soldiers take a hitchhiking air force doctor to a nearby air base. There they join a helicopter rescue team that makes repeated trips to the combat area to pick up the wounded.

The chaotic war that Weinraub and Ruso find is not what they expected—nor what you might expect from the reputation of the Israeli armed forces: They and the rest of their shaggy team of reservists are so undisciplined, so uncoordinated as they haul hideously burned casualties out of tanks, across muddy fields and into helicopters, you wonder how the Israelis managed to win in the end.

But certainly the scenes of battlefield triage give you a poignant sense of the price Israel paid for its survival.

Shot in the Golan Heights, the film feels strikingly authentic despite a low budget.

The lack of dialogue (presumably the men are stunned into silence) combined with the difficulty of knowing what's going on, why or when, is an effective tool of Gitai's realism.

But its harder to see why he and co-screenwriter Marie-Jose Sanselme go to such lengths to avoid placing these events in context (a news radio broadcast that might do so is not translated by the subtitles.)

You certainly don't get any sense of the desperation that accompanied the early Yom Kippur war, when a massive Syrian attack overran Israeli defenses.

But then Gitai has given interviews that suggest his decade as a much-feted exile in France has caused him to forget the terrifying Syrian invasion, with the invaders' tendency to castrate and murder their Israeli prisoners.

NEWSDAY, 11/3/00, Part II/p. B10, Gene Seymour

"Kippur's" languid opening sequence of a nude young couple with painted bodies, rolling around on a white sheet, is enough to alert you to the tendencies of director Amos Gitai toward self-indulgence and calculated obscurity. But when viewed in the full context of what turns out to be one of the more agonizing and grimly evocative war movies in recent memory, Gitai's soft-core abstraction looks almost as daring as it tries to be.

The young man in bed is Weinraub (Liron Levo), whose expectations of a lazy Yom "Kippur" holiday with his girlfriend have been thwarted by historical events. It is October, 1973, and Syria has mounted an armed offensive against Israel in the Golan Heights. Weinraub leaves for the front in his battered, hippie-ish Fiat to join his medical evacuation unit, a motley assortment of technicians, doctors and vaguely academic types who look as out of place on a movie battlefield as a maitre d' in a Burger King.

Gitai, who based his story on his real-life experiences as a paramedic in the 1973 war, shifts between mind-numbing tedium and blood-curdling terror with a seeming off-handedness that makes this war film feel more authentic than most others. It takes so long for Weinraub and his buddies to see action that one is tempted to wonder whether Gitai knows what he's doing. But when they first arrive on the scene of a just-completed firefight, surrounded by the dead and wounded, their reactions of uncertainty, dread, surprise and wariness become one's own.

This is a narrative of haunting, ruminative sequences, each flowing into the conscious mind like paint dripping on a canvas. And no, it's not at all like watching that paint dry. Only toward the end is this tense, sordid drift through blurred killing fields disrupted by a jolting mishap that will forever change the recovery team's lives.

Sometime before then, the most extraordinary and emblematic of "Kippur's" battle scenes has lodged in one's memory banks: The team is struggling, agonizing its way out of a slippery mud hole to carry the body of a wounded soldier to a helicopter. They stagger, howl, fumble and stumble their way through the slimy muck for what seems like hours and manage to get their cargo to the chopper. By which time, of course, he is dead. Silence.

Helplessness. Stupor. "Can't we take him with us anyway?" one of the team members asks plaintively. No dice.

All one needs to know about the futility of war—anywhere, anytime, for any reason—can be found in that sequence. And if the rest of "Kippur" rarely reaches such a pinnacle, the movie comes close enough, often enough to get within reach of the classic war stories.

VILLAGE VOICE, 11/7/00, p. 130, J. Hoberman

Kippur, which—with sobering timeliness—has its theatrical premiere this week, confirms Amos Gitai's earnest claim to be the most iconoclastic of Israeli directors. This first Israeli feature to depict the Yom Kippur War of October 1973 is far more daring than Gitai's previous film, the colorful if tendentious *Kadosh*. It is one thing to attack the hypocritical pieties of the ultra-Orthodox; it is another to advance so viscerally matter-of-fact and doggedly absurdist a vision of warfare in a society as militarized and defensive as Israel's.

Gitai, a filmmaker more highly regarded in the cafés of Paris than those of Dizengoff Square, is no stranger to outlandish intellectualizing. *Kippur* opens with shots of empty Tel Aviv streets and a young couple apparently celebrating the Day of Atonement by making love while finger-painting each other's bodies. The sound of a solo saxophone provides a jazzy shofar to complete the ritual flavor. A ridiculous bid to short-circuit the movie before it even starts, this sequence is clumsy but not entirely ahistorical. If nothing else, Gitai's five-minute "happening" does serve to remind that, thanks in part to the follow-up OPEC oil embargo, the Yom Kippur War marked not only the end of Israeli "invulnerability" but also the end of the '60s. War intrudes as a most unwelcome reality principle.

Gitai's alter ego, Weinraub (Liron Levo), quickly established as a reader of Herbert Marcuse as well as a practitioner of allegorical art sex, drives his battered Fiat north to join his unit at the front, along with his gung-ho buddy Ruso (Tomer Ruso; most of the actors play characters named for themselves). Given Israel's parameters, it's not a long trip, although the men do have to work their way through a snarled *Weekend*-like traffic jam to emerge into full-fledged military disorder—much aimless firing and running around amid reports of a Syrian advance. After giving a lift to the stranded medic Klauzner (Uri Ran Klauzner), Weinraub and Ruso wind up in an aerial rescue unit-flying a helicopter to the Golan Heights and behind enemy lines to gather up casualties and bring them back.

Closely based on Gitai's own combat experience during the Yom Kippur War and filmed with the utmost attention to detail, this mission is the movie—as well as the most radical narrative filmmaking of Gitai's career. Framing the action at some distance, he orchestrates lengthy shots of choppers landing at the front or the medics scrambling, under bombardment, amid the tanks.

Nothing is directly explained. The unit's activities seem at once purposeful and random—one more contribution to an unfathomable form of organized chaos.

Order and orders are barely present, although the constant shouting underscores the continuous backbeat of mortar fire. As these long choreographed takes are deliberately uninflected, Kippur, which covers a period of several days, blends horror and tedium to achieve an abstract, modernist quality. In the most blatant example of existential anxiety, the men struggle and stumble in the mud, while attempting to carry a single casualty back to their helicopter. (When they fall facedown in the muck, dropping the wounded soldier in the process, the parallel to the painting sequence is abundantly evident.) One guy cracks up. In the end, it's not even clear if the casualty is alive or dead.

Gitai's strategy encourages the viewer to ponder the logistics of war—as well as those of filming war. Are the underpopulated battlefields a function of Kippur's frugal budget (or do they reflect the overinflated budgets of more conventional combat movies)? The field hospital is even more oddly uncrowded—it's busy but not half as crazed as the precommercial rush on the average episode of E.R. Here, the traumatized wounded chat about their injuries with a single overworked doctor. Kippur is always coming up against its own limitations. The ensemble acting sometimes falters, and due to Gitai's camera placement, it can be difficult to distinguish between the various characters—although Klauzner establishes an indelible identity in a brief moment of downtime when he discusses his childhood in Europe during World War II.

As suggested by the complete absence of a visual enemy, Gitai is attempting to make a new sort of war film. In his interviews he has referred to the influence of the erstwhile World War II dogface Sam Fuller, who shot his quasi-autobiographical infantry epic, The Big Red One, in Israel in 1979. Fuller is the greatest proponent of the antiwar war film, once answering a questionnaire on the subject with the observation that "you can't show war as it really is on the screen, with all the blood and gore. Perhaps it would be better if you could fire real shots over the audience's head every night, you know, and have actual casualties in the theater."

Perhaps it would be best to have war movies made only by those who have been baptized under fire. In the Fuller spirit, Kippur is at once shockingly vivid and overwhelmingly antiheroic. Whether flying over a muddy tank-track-ridden battlefield or driving through the depopulated countryside, Gitai deploys chunks of real time—then disrupts them with some unexpected assault on human body tissue. In some respects, Kippur is a structural film. It ends as it starts—leaving the viewer to decide whether war is an aberration or all in a day's work.

Also reviewed in:
CHICAGO TRIBUNE, 1/5/01, Friday/p. E, John Petrakis
NATION, 11/20/00, p. 42, Stuart Klawans
NEW REPUBLIC, 11/27/00, p. 22, Stanley Kauffmann
NEW YORK TIMES, 10/5/00, p. E1, A. O. Scott
VARIETY, 5/22-28/00, p. 26, David Stratton

KIRIKOU AND THE SORCERESS

An ArtMattan Productions release. *Producer:* Didier Brunner, Jacques Vercruyssen, and Paul Thiltges. *Director:* Michel Ocelot. *Screenplay (French dialogue dubbed with English):* Michel Ocelot. *Director of Photography:* Daniel Borenstein. *Editor:* Dominique Lefever. *Music:* Youssou N'Dour. *Sound:* Pascal Lemaire. *Animator:* Inga Riba. *Running time:* 74 minutes. *MPAA Rating:* Not Rated.

VOICES: Theo Sobeko (Kirikou));   Antoinette Kellermann (Karaba);   Kombisile Sangweni (The Mother);   Mabuto Sithole (Old Man/Viellard);   Fezele Mpeka (Uncle).

CHRISTIAN SCIENCE MONITOR, 2/18/00, p. 15, David Sterritt

[*Kirikou and the Sorceress* was reviewed jointly with *Kadosh*; see Sterritt' review of that film.]

NEW YORK POST, 2/18/00, p. 54, Hannah Brown

Based on a West African folk tale, "Kirikou and the Sorceress" is an original and mesmerizing animated film with a dreamlike look reminiscent of traditional African art.

The movie is set in a remote village plagued by the evil sorceress Karaba (Antoinette Kellermann), who dries up the villagers' spring and kills their crops. She's also devoured all the men except one.

But a village woman gives birth to a fearless baby named Kirikou (Theo Sebeko), who sets off to help his uncle fight Karaba. Soon Kirikou fights Karaba on his own, undertaking a dangerous trip to discover the cause of Karaba's evil nature.

The film's haunting images of Kirikou fulfilling his destiny may scare or confuse young children. And director Michel Ocelot, to achieve an authentic look, has drawn the women topless and the children naked, which may disturb some parents.

Though the film's not appropriate for all kids, adult fans of animated films should definitely not miss "Kirikou."

NEWSDAY, 2/18/00, Part II/p. B6, Gene Seymour

Having made a splash at a handful of international film festivals, including last fall's African Diaspora Film Festival held throughout New York City, "Kirikou and the Sorceress" now eases its way into limited theatrical release like a stealth weapon. Its impact sneaks up on you even while you're watching it.

As with the finest live-action movies from Africa, "Kirikou" tells a deceptively simple story that takes place on a harsh landscape with elemental characters. Both spare and lush in design, "Kirikou" is a singular work of animation. Nothing like this in what's classified as "family entertainment" can be found anywhere else—which, for reasons to be enumerated later, may pose a problem for some.

In any case, the story takes place in a small West African village plagued by the vindictive magic of a beautiful and wicked sorceress named Karaba. She has reduced the water supply to a pathetic trickle and captured practically every able-bodied male. The remaining villagers, almost all women and children, are helpless to stop even worse things from happening.

Into this dreadful situation tumbles (literally) a newborn baby named Kirikou, who springs from his mother's womb able to speak in complete sentences and run faster than the Warner Bros. Road Runner. His shrewdness and courage are 10 times greater than those of the put-upon villagers, who can't quite believe their eyes when he nimbly dismantles most, if not all, of Karaba's dreadful curses.

Animator Michel Ocelot, who grew up in Guinea, uses many colorful motifs of African art to tell his engaging story. There is a warm glow within the story that challenges the conventional dualities of good and evil characterizing animated adventures of similar range and ambition.

However, none of that will placate those in the audience who may be put off by the fact that the movie's hero is naked and its women clothed only from the waist down. This was reportedly a dicey area for American distributors, concerned as to whether such depictions would cause unneeded controversy. They're right. There is no need for this controversy. It doesn't matter what the characters wear or don't wear. Every child of any age should see this movie.

Also reviewed in:
CHICAGO TRIBUNE, 3/10/00, Friday/p. C, John Petrakis
NEW YORK TIMES, 2/18/00, p. E26, Elvis Mitchell
VARIETY, 1/11-17/99, p. 115, Lisa Nesselson

KNOCKOUT

A Renegade Entertainment release of a DMG Pictures production. *Executive Producer:* Steve Stevens Sr. *Producer:* Simone Sheffield and Lorenzo Doumani. *Director:* Lorenzo Doumani. *Screenplay:* Mark Stevens and Lorenzo Doumani. *Director of Photography:* Thomas Del Ruth and Hisham Abed.. *Editor:* Dayle Mustain. *Music:* Sidney James. *Fight Choreographer:* Jimmy Gambina. *Sound:* James P. Slinghuff. *Casting:* Thom Klohn and Katy Wallin. *Production Designer:* John Hernandez and Justin Mulchy. *Art Director:* Nick George. *Set Decorator:* Nick George and Jeff Higinbotham. *Special Effects:* Albert Lenudi. *Costumes:* Sylvia Vega-Vasquez. *Make-up:* Heidi Rust and Jay Wejebe. *Stunt Coordinator:* Jimmy Gambina and Lenny Gambina. *Running time:* 100 minutes. *MPAA Rating:* PG-13.

CAST: Sophia-Adella Hernandez (Isabelle);   Eduardo Yáñez (Mario);   Fredia Gibbs (Tanya 'Terminator' Tessaro);   Gina La Plante (Sandra Lopez);   Paul Winfield (Ron Regent); Erick Vazquez (Enrique);   Maria Conchita Alonso (Carmen Alvarado);   Tony Burton (Segent Hawkins);   Ralph Cooper (Chris);   Lorenzo Doumani (Ring Announcer);   Phil Hawn (Fight Spectator);   Jim Jenkins (Sports Commentator);   Ben Lira (Referee);   William McNamara (Michael DeMarco);   Tony Plana (Chuck);   Steve Stevens, Sr. (Farmer's Corner).

LOS ANGELES TIMES, 2/4/00, Calendar/p. 6, Kevin Thomas

"Knockout" can't be said to live up to its title—it's too predictable and formulaic for that. But this story of an East L.A. Latina determined to follow in her father's footsteps to the boxing ring does pack a punch.

The point of this picture is that it's high time for more Latinas to believe that they can pursue their dreams without sacrificing the possibility of love and marriage. When Carmen Alvarado (Maria Conchita Alonso) discovers she's dying of a malignant brain tumor, she tells her young daughter Belle (Sophia-Adella Hernandez) that she shouldn't have to give up what she wants to do with her life for the one she loves—in her mother's words, "to let her light shine." Carmen had given up her dancing career to marry her husband, Chuck (Tony Plana), who had been a Golden Gloves champ when he gave up boxing for steadier work as a policeman.

Although Carmen had been horrified to learn from her husband that their daughter had shown some boxing ability at the gym, where he coaches troubled youths in the ring, she also told him to let Belle pursue her dreams. Initially, Chuck is equally horrified to learn after his wife's death that his daughter wants to take boxing seriously, but he ultimately yields to his promise to his late wife. With backing from him and shy, handsome Mario (Eduardo Yanez), himself a rising boxer, Belle gives boxing a serious shot. She will of course be thrown a jolting curve in the course of her progress, but you can't seriously imagine that anything really could stop her on her way to becoming a champ.

Mark Stevens & Lorenzo Doumani's script is on the elementary side, but their people are engaging, and Doumani draws warm, vigorous portrayals from his sterling cast, which includes William McNamara as Belle's slick young manager and Paul Winfield as a shrewd, seen-it-all boxing promoter. "Knockout" looks good and sounds good, boasting a vibrant, eclectic soundtrack.

Also reviewed in:
NEW YORK TIMES, 2/25/00, p. E20, Stephen Holden
VARIETY, 2/7-13/00, p. 50, Robert Koehler

LA BUCHE

Empire Pictures release of a Le Studio Canal +/Les Films Alain Sarde/Studio Images 6/TFI Films Productions production. *Executive Poducer:* Christine Gozlan. *Producer:* Alain Sarde. *Director:* Danièle Thompson. *Screenplay (French with English subtitles):* Danièle Thompson and Christopher Thompson. *Director of Photography:* Robert Fraisse. *Editor:* Emmanuelle Castro. *Music:* Michel Legrand. *Sound:* Jean-Pierre Duret. *Production Designer:* Michèle Abbé-Vannier. *Costumes:* Elisabeth Tavernier. *Running time:* 106 minutes. *MPAA Rating:* Not Rated.

CAST: Sabine Azéma (Louba);   Emmanuelle Béart (Sonia);   Charlotte Gainsbourg (Milla);
Françoise Fabian (Yvette);   Jean-Pierre Darroussin (Gilbert);   Christopher Thompson (Joseph);
Claude Rich (Stanislas);   Isabelle Carré (Annabelle);   Samuel Labarthe (Gilbert); François Brion
(Janine);   Hélène Fillières (Véronique);   Thierry Hancisse (Florist);   Marie De Villepin
(Marie); Didier Becchetti (Escort Boy);   Jean-Pierre Marino (Cardiologist);   Neil Ingle (Arthur);
Liliana Delahaye (Mathilde);   Matteo D'Amico (Régis);   Nicholas De Angelis (Georgie);
Bertrand Cervera (Vlado);   Pierre Chollet (Professor);   Andrea Schieffer (La femme de l'homme
d'Affaires Allemand);   Jorg Schnass (L'homme d'Affaires Allemand);   Catherine Erhardy
(Françoise);   Lola Zajdermann (Béa); Lily Galland (Angélique);   Bernard Lannes (Le Motard);
Céline Caussimon (Woman in the Square);   Valérie Labro (Nurse);   Antoine Blanquefort
(Doctor Bazin);   Julie Leibowitch (La Vendeuse Lancel).

LOS ANGELES TIMES, 12/1/00, Calendar/p. 10, Kevin Thomas

"La Buche" takes its title from a French Christmas cake, shaped like a log, heavily frosted and
decorated with sparklers. It's the piece de resistance of the Christmas meal, and this holiday treat
of a movie is hard to resist too.

It marks the directorial debut of Daniele Thompson, who as a writer has collaborated on the
scripts of some of France's most popular pictures for more than 30 years. Most recently,
Thompson, the daughter of actor-turned-director Gerard Oury, has collaborated with director
Patrice Chereau, on the ambitious historical epic "Queen Margot" and "Those Who Love Me Can
Take the Train." Now, she has collaborated on her script with her actor-son Christopher
Thompson, who appears in the film.

Those earlier films had large casts, as does "La Buche," and Thompson shows, with ease and
assurance, that she can direct actors as well as she writes for them. Marital infidelity, longtime
liaisons outside marriage, indeed every form of love in defiance of convention are staples of the
French cinema, and Thompson has wedded this topic with another, the Christmas gathering.

It arrives after considerable wry comedy and no small amount of suspense as to who will show
up and whether a family will be able to put aside differences and not spoil the grand occasion.

This is not going to be so easy for the family of Stanislas Roman (Claude Rich), a retired
violinist and Russian Jew who emigrated as a child. He has played Gypsy music in every Russian
cabaret in Paris and seemingly never missed a chance to have an affair, despite being married
once to a beautiful former movie actress, Yvette (Francoise Fabian), with whom he had three
children. (Stanislas is based on family legends about Thompson's own Russian immigrant
grandfather.)

A quarter of a century has passed, and four days before Christmas Yvette's second husband is
buried, having died suddenly. Not wanting to leave her father alone, Stanislas' eldest daughter,
Louba (Sabine Azema), invites him to Christmas dinner, to be held at the home of her sister Sonia
(Emmanuelle Beart).

Neither Stanislas nor Yvette is eager to see each other, to say the least, but this is just the
beginning of the challenges the festive occasion presents. The film's focal point is Louba and her
just-discovered dilemma. Struggling to make ends meet as a singer in a Russian restaurant and
giving Russian lessons, Louba is astonished to discover, at age 42, that she is pregnant by her
married lover of 12 years (Jean-Pierre Darroussin).

In the meantime, Sonia, who has married well, is contemplating leaving her husband (Samuel
Labarthe) after discovering his infidelity. Milla (Charlotte Gainsbourg), the youngest daughter,
a computer specialist wary of romance, finds herself drawn to the equally cautious young man
(Christopher Thompson) living in her father's old studio-workshop—and estranged from his wife.

What concerns Thompson is the price love outside marriage can cost—the strain of lying, the
pain of betrayal discovered, and the question of where allegiance ultimately lies. Thompson
neither moralizes nor judges. Rather, she reveals the pain as well the joy that following one's
heart can exact, and suggests that, sooner or later, people have to be prepared to take
responsibility for their actions.

Beyond this, Thompson wonders just how far family ties can go in sustaining people as they
thrash through emotional conflict. Thompson is serious about these issues, but that doesn't prevent
her from treating them with humor as well as a warm, mature wisdom. Thompson's long

experience in highly commercial movies and those of a more personal bent serves her well in creating holiday entertainment that possesses wide appeal and sophistication.

In a film of one intense encounter after another, there is a standout sequence in which Yvette and Stanislas, having made a dinner date, have their first actual conversation in 25 years. Yvette suggests that they might as well let down their hair, and as it turns out, while she surely has not had as much casual sex as her ex-husband, she may have had more romance. In any event, they both have had no shortage of amour in their lives, and in their mutual candor they discover they're able to retrieve some of the affection they once had for each other. Theirs is a love-hate relationship tempered now by an amused mutual acceptance of each other's failings.

With its lovely images of wintertime Paris and its lyrical Michel Legrand music, "La Buche" does take the cake.

NEWSDAY, 11/17/00, Part II/p. B6, John Anderson

Those for whom the holidays loom like six dentist appointments may find "La Buche, the perfect antidote—although certainly no anesthetic. Writer-director Daniele Thompson doesn't think the yuletide season is unimportant. Far from it. She just knows, as many suppose, that what simmers for 11 months of the year comes to a rolling boil on Christmas Eve.

Thompson, the celebrated French screenwriter ("Queen Margot," "Those Who Love Me Can Take the Train") and now first-time director, builds her film around three sisters—although any resemblance to Chekhov, Woody Allen or Nora Ephron is entirely coincidental. Neither are they anything like female Maji. Louba (Sabine Azema), teacher of Russian and faux-Gypsy performer, is pregnant by Gilbert (Jean-Pierre Darroussin), her married lover of 12 years. Sonia (Emmanuelle Beart), the designated hostess-queen of holiday overkill, is on the verge of an ugly divorce. And Milla (Charlotte Gainsburg), computer genius and malcontent, adds one plus one and gets her lonely self.

Thompson, a tart humorist as well as a keen observer of human interaction, kicks things off with a flurry of holiday "cheer"—streets filled with shoppers, mechanical window displays in full, epileptic throttle, a torrent of clicking and clacking all to cloying American carols—then segues into a funeral. If you haven't laughed yet, the upcoming cell phone joke will kill you.

But with her introductions to the family, we get a portrait of people who are joined together by accident of blood (and maybe not even ...) and whose perspectives are formed by life, not upbringing. The affection they feel and fight off may be genuine, but the clashes of temperament, or even just taste, are what family togetherness seems to be all about.

Each character, including the semi-mysterious Joseph (Christopher Thompson) and the three women's long-divorced parents—Stanislas (Claude Rich) and Yvette (Francoise Fabian)—relate their own short stories directly to the camera. This is risky—as are the various loose ends Thompson leaves dangling about—but it works. What each soliloquy reveals says much about the characters themselves, but also about what people in a family know about each other and never tell.

VILLAGE VOICE, 11/21/00, p. 140, Amy Taubin

Set in Paris during the countdown to Christmas Eve, Danièle Thompson's by turns hilarious and wounding *La Buche* disproves the cliché that adultery is what holds French marriages together. Thompson wrote Patrice Chéreau's *Those Who Love Me Can Take the Train,* and like that film, her directorial debut feature is an intricate web of secrets, lies, and revelations. Tracking who's who and what they've done to each other will keep you on your toes and even make you a bit giddy. Much of the viewer's pleasure comes from putting bits of the puzzle together before the people on the screen do. Knowledge is power; leavened with mystery, it feels like love.

The title refers to the traditional French Christmas dessert, La Buche de Noël, a buttercream-slathered cake shaped like a Yule log. Like the decorations blanketing the city's architectural beauty and the omnipresent holiday music, it awakens memories, most of them mixed. "Christmas cake makes me gag," says the youngest of the film's three sisters as she defiantly leaps into a love affair that's not as transgressive as she believes. Nostalgia nauseates because it's based in the conflicted oral impulses of childhood; the youngest sister has to choke back the memories of Christmas past, lest they plunge her into what the middle sister calls "a holiday-hostile depression." And since the sisters are members of an extended part-Jewish family living in a Catholic country, Christmas delivers a double whammy of alienation.

Children of a musician and an actress (played by Claude Rich and Françoise Fabian), the sisters have incorporated the passion and betrayal that defined their parents' bitterly failed marriage into their own love lives. The oldest sister (Sabine Azéma) works as a gypsy singer in a Russian nightclub and is pregnant by the lover who has been promising for 12 years to leave his wife when his two daughters are grown. What she doesn't know is that he and his wife now have four children with another on the way. Not that the film takes a judgmental position against him or the relationship. Rather, Thompson suggests that love is messy, torturous, and occasionally joyous, and that the joy is worth fighting for.

The middle sister (Emmanuelle Béart) gave up a promising career to marry a rich man who's about to leave her for a younger woman. Sublimating her anxiety into organizing a Christmas Eve dinner for the entire family, she shops, cooks, and decorates with an intensity that makes Martha Stewart look like a slacker. The youngest sister (Charlotte Gainsbourg), who refuses to be distracted from her career by love, can't help but be drawn to the beautiful young man (Christopher Thompson, the director's son and screen-writing partner) who rents a room from her father. Like everyone else in the film, he is in the midst of a family crisis.

Beginning with a funeral and ending with two characters poised on the brink of the kind of fairy-tale romance that life seldom delivers, *La Buche* is an emotional shape-shifter that captures the manic-depressive intensity of the holiday season. Thompson keeps her focus (and ours) on the actors, most of whom have never been as luminous as they are here. How can you resist a film that features Azéma, the habitually arch, intellectual darling of French cinema, belting out "My Yiddishe Mama"?

Also reviewed in:
CHICAGO TRIBUNE, 11/22/00, Tempo, p. 4, Michael Wilmington
NEW REPUBLIC, 12/4/00, p. 30, Stanley Kauffmann
NEW YORK TIMES, 11/17/00, p. E22, A. O. Scott
VARIETY, 1/3-9/00, p. 82, Lisa Nesselson

LADIES MAN, THE

A Paramount Pictures release in association with SNL Studios of a Lorne Michaels production. *Executive Producer:* Erin Fraser, Thomas K. Levine, and Robert K. Weiss. *Producer:* Lorne Michaels. *Director:* Reginald Hudlin. *Screenplay:* Tim Meadows, Dennis McNicholas, and Andrew Steele. *Director of Photography:* Johnny E. Jensen. *Editor:* Earl Watson. *Music:* Marcus Miller. *Music Editor:* Terry Wilson. *Sound:* Doug Johnston and (music) Thomas Vicari. *Sound Editor:* Ron Eng and Beth Sterner. *Casting:* Rick Montgomery. *Production Designer:* Franco de Cotiis. *Art Director:* Cheryl Toy. *Set Decorator:* Zeljka Alosinac. *Costumes:* Eydi Caines-Floyd. *Make-up:* Marlene Aarons. *Stunt Coordinator:* Marco Bianco and Steve Lucescu. *Running time:* 90 minutes. *MPAA Rating:* R.

CAST: Tim Meadows (Leon Phelps); Karyn Parsons (Julie Simmons); Bill Dee Williams (Lester); Tiffani Thiesen (Honey DeLune); Lee Evans (Barney); Will Ferrell (Lance deLune); Sofia Milos (Cheryl); Jill Talley (Candy); John Witherspoon (Scrap Iron); Ken Campbell (Al); Rocky Carroll (Cyrus Cunningham); Tamala Jones (Teresa); Kevin McDonald (Mail Man); Julianne Moore (Audrey); Eugene Levy (Bucky Kent); David Huband (Frank); Sean Thibodeau (Hugh Hefner); Mark McKinney (Mr. White); Chris Parnell (Phil Swanson); J'Marie Luke and J'Avie Luke (Newborn Leon); Taye Thomas and Treye Thomas (Baby Leon); Ryan Field (Leon Aged 12 years); Patrick Patterson and Diane Fabian (Older Lovers); Susan Aceron and Phil Guerrero (Young Lovers); April Mullen and Dennis McNicholas (Teen Lovers); Ardon Bess (Stage Manager); Robin Ward (Gil Stewart); Joan Massiah (Nun); Hadley Sandford (Merle); Barbara Barnes-Hopkins (Edna); John Stoneham, Jr. (VSA Driver); Boyd Banks (C & W Station Manager); Jim Codrington (Soul Station Manager); Arthur Eng

(Silver Suit Man);   Aaron Berg (Brian);   Michelle Maria Silveira (Houseboat Cutie);   Inna Korobkina (Hef's Girl);   Rebecca Weinberg (Hef's Best Girl);   Robyn Palmer (Playboy Bunny); Simone Stock (Playboy Photographer);   Reginald Hudlin (Aloysius);   Destri Yap (Leon, Jr.).

LOS ANGELES TIMES, 10/13/00, Calendar/p. 4, Gene Seymour

[The following review by Gene Seymour appeared in a slightly different form in **NEWSDAY, 10/22/00, Part II/p. B7.]**

Of the many dimwitted ego-trippers and self-deluded goofballs who pop up repeatedly on "Saturday Night Live," the one character who seemed least likely to carry a feature-length film on his own is Leon, a.k.a. "The Ladies Man." As with most sketch characters, Tim Meadows' crafty evocation of a cognac-sipping, incense-burning "lonely hearts" advisor with an overreaching libido and an obsession with black-macho cool (circa 1974) is funny in five-minute bursts. Thirty minutes or more is another matter.

So it's a pleasant surprise to find that "The Ladies Man," the movie, manages to sustain a sweet, funny groove for, say, 65 of its 85 minutes. That may sound like praise with faint damnation, but compared with such overstuffed trifles as "It's Pat," "Stuart Saves His Family" or "A Night at the Roxbury," it's almost (but not quite) a slam-dunk.

One reason for "Ladies Man's" relative success is Meadows, who also co-wrote the script. Though his tenure on "SNL" has been long and solid, he rarely gets the credit he deserves for his impeccable timing and understated wit, neither of which are qualities easily embraced within the prevailing bluster of "post-boomer" comedy. As Leon, Meadows nimbly balances faux suavity and preening cluelessness. He's good enough to make you wish he used his talents on developing a character as opposed to filling in a caricature's blank spaces.

But then, blank spaces thrive in the dubious intellect of the Ladies Man, here given a Chicago address (on a tacky lakefront houseboat) and a job as a host of an after-hours radio talk show. His faithful, plucky producer Julie (Karyn Parsons from "The Fresh Prince of Bel-Air") is apparently the only woman in the universe immune to Leon's moldy, lisping come-ons. The cuckolded husbands of Leon's conquests, led by fellow "SNL" stalwart Will Ferrell as an ambiguously gay wrestler, have banded together to chase down Leon—with show-stopping dance tunes to boot.

Reginald Hudlin directs this good-natured, frequently hilarious gag bag with a light touch and a winking appreciation for the "mack-daddy" 1970s milieu gently mocked by Meadows' creation. Having Billy Dee Williams around as a narrator-confidant-mentor-figure is an especially cozy touch. Such homespun graces aren't enough to keep "The Ladies Man" from losing what little edge it has toward the end. But it's still a reasonably pleasant ramble.

NEW YORK POST, 10/13/00 p. 52, Lou Lumenick

"The Ladies Man," an alleged comedy about a cognac-swilling 70s-style Lothario, is arguably the limpest film yet spun out from a "Saturday Night Live" sketch.

This shlocky-looking mess runs out of mojo roughly five minutes into its 85-minute running time, after a mildly amusing flashback showing how Leon Phelps (Tim Meadows) was raised as a foundling at the Playboy Mansion in Chicago—until he bedded Hugh Hefner's favorite lady and got tossed into the street.

The slight story line has the Ladies Man getting tossed from his job as a radio talk show host for his smutty comments.

His attempts to find a new gig ("I'm good at filling slots," he tells one prospective employer) include a disastrous stint at a Christian station where he interviews a nun, who makes the mistake of telling Leon she's accepted a "missionary position" in Bangkok.

Leon then abandons his job hunt to track down a rich former lover (Tiffani Amber-Thiessen). Unfortunately, she's the wife of a wrestler (Will Ferrell who heads a group of vengeance-seeking guys who have been cuckolded by the Ladies Man.

Meanwhile, Leon is too dim to realize he really loves his producer Julie (Karyn Parsons), who isn't amused by his retro antics—a sentiment likely to be shared by audiences.

This is basically a movie for people who find it hilarious that Leon lives on a houseboat named the "Skank Tuary" and that his taste in fashion and décor have barely evolved past the Austin Powers era.

It also helps to have a tolerance for a leading man who affects a heavy lisp throughout—and has so little charisma he who can barely hold his own in a scene with the movie's director, Reginald Hudlin ("Boomerang").

The latter has a cameo as Julie's ex-boyfriend, who is tricked into eating human feces—perhaps an unwitting comment on Hudlin's latest directing assignment.

Meadows is utterly upstaged by Billy Dee Williams (charming but wasted as a bartender) and Julianne Moore, who makes the year's most embarrassing appearance by an Oscar nominee (as a randy clown).

Meadows is mostly absent from the most elaborate sequence, a song-and-dance number called "Its Time to Kill The Ladies Man." Amen. Unfortunately, the time to kill this sucker was at the script stage.

SIGHT AND SOUND, 8/01, p. 49, Keith Perry

Chicago, the present. Leon Phelps is sacked as a radio host after one too many obscene remarks. His producer Julie Simmons is also fired. No other radio station will hire Leon. After receiving an unsigned letter from a past lover promising sex and money, he begins to track her down through a process of elimination. Meanwhile, a group of men cuckolded by Leon have formed a self-help group, and are intent on castrating him.

After a fruitless search, Leon confesses to Julie that he is tired of his ladies man persona. He seems on the point of settling down with her. However, he suddenly realises that the mystery woman is Honey DeLune, wife of Lance, who leads the self-help group. When Lance interrupts the pair having sex, he challenges Leon to a wrestling match. Leon defeats him. Julie arrives, and Leon leaves with her.

When it comes to cinema spin-offs, US television sketch show *Saturday Night Live* has a patchy track record, which runs from *Wayne's World* all the way down to *A Night at the Roxbury*. The latest from the *SNL* mill, *The Ladies Man*, centres on comedian Tim Meadows' creation Leon Phelps, a buffoonish lady-killer and radio sex therapist.

Meadows—affected lisp aside—has a sharp ear for the rhythms of speech, which he's honed during his two years on *SNL* Leon is a likeable, innocent braggart, his face often springing from deep thought to misplaced joy But in this feature-length vehicle Leon seems an inconsistently drawn character. He's presented as an object of ridicule for the viewer, but the film also strikes up an admiring attitude towards his sexual prowess: Leon has cuckolded so many husbands that he's responsible for a support group—the Victims of the Smiling Ass (a reference to the tattoo glimpsed on Leon's retreating backside)—whose plans to take revenge, by castration or sublimated rape (via a Greek wrestling match), form the central plot. Later on, when cornered, Leon's explanation to the VSA that he's merely listening to their wives' needs (just as they should be doing) seems like a criticism of unyielding machismo. And yet it's made clear Leon's sizeable penis is the real key to his success.

The Ladies Man runs along the same faultlines as many other films inspired by *SNL* sketches: the material originally developed for a punchier, shorter format seems stretched. The writers (Meadows, Dennis McNicholas and Andrew Steele) use all the best routines (including a nun inadvertently sending Leon into a sexual paroxysm) in the first half, then devote the rest of the film to charting the romance between Leon and his producer, Julie. The plotting doesn't deepen Leon's character; it just dilutes it.

The Ladies Man is part of a recent wave of comedies which forsake complex burnout in favour of enticing splutters of incredulity from their audience—much in evidence when Leon smoothly urges his listeners to "Do it up the butt." Director Reginald Hudlin brings the same unsubtle approach to sexual and racial politics that he demonstrated in his 1990 debut *House Party*. Here, Leon's sexism is ameliorated by the most predictable trick in the book—he is a throwback to the 70s, living in a world of waterbeds, Afros and chocolate-brown suits. A flashback might depict his boyhood as a parody of *Sweet Sweetback's Baad Asssss Song* (1971), but it's played out in a caricature of Hugh Hefner's Playboy mansion rather than the black bordello of Melvin Van

Peebles' angry blaxploitation film: on the whole Leon's act is closer to the kitschy excess of Austin Powers than, say, the cool conduct of John Shaft.

This playing down of race ironically leads to Leon, who is black, having on-screen sex with a white character, something of a coup for a mainstream movie, especially in the increasingly conservative cultural climate of George W. Bush's America. The woman chaser is an old perennial, but the note of affectionate ridicule struck here suggests a guilty yearning for the sexual politics of the 70s—a sign, perhaps, that the love affair between many male viewers and that wonderful, horrible decade looks set to continue.

Also reviewed in:
NEW YORK TIMES, 10/13/00, p. E27, A. O. Scott
WASHINGTON POST, 10/13/00, p. C2, Rita Kempley

LAST SEPTEMBER, THE

A Trimark Pictures and Scala release of a Scala Thunder production in association with Bord Scannan Na and Radio Telefis Eireann with the participation of BSKYB and British Screen/Ima Films/Canal +. *Executive Producer:* Nik Powell, Neil Jordan, Stephen Woolley, and Peter Fudakowski. *Producer:* Yvonne Thunder. *Director:* Deborah Warner. *Screenplay:* John Banville. *Based on the novel by:* Elizabeth Bowen. *Director of Photography:* Slawomir Idziak. *Editor:* Kate Evans. *Music:* Zbigniew Preisner. *Choreographer:* Cindy Cummins. *Sound:* Dan Birch. *Casting:* Leo Davis. *Production Designer:* Caroline Amies. *Art Director:* Paul Kirby. *Costumes:* John Bright. *Make-up:* Christine Beveridge. *Stunt Coordinator:* Patrick Condren. *Running time:* 104 minutes. *MPAA Rating:* R.

CAST: Michael Gambon (Sir Richard Naylor); Tom Hickey (O'Brien); Keeley Hawes (Lois Farquar); David Tennant (Gerald Colthurst); Richard Boxburgh (Daventry); Gary Lydon (Peter Connolly); Maggie Smith (Lady Myra); Maeve Kearney, Francine Mulrooney, and Christina Wilson (Maids); Lambert Wilson (Hugo Montmorency); Jane Birkin (Francie Montmorency); Jonathan Slinger (Laurence Carstairs); Fiona Shaw (Marda Norton); Emily Nagle (Livvy Connolly); Catherine Walsh (Doreen Hartigan); Bernie Downes (Nora Hartigan); Mikel Murfi (Sergeant Wilson); Arthur Riordan (Black and Tan Soldier); Kieran Ahern (Daniel Connolly); Miles Horgan (Postman); Aaron Harris (Captain Vermont); Lesley McGuire (Mrs. Vermont); Mal Whyte (Second Officer); Tamsin MacCarthy (Marci Mangan).

CHRISTIAN SCIENCE MONITOR, 4/21/00, p. 15, David Sterritt

The early chapters of Elizabeth Bowen's intelligent novel "The Last September" are preoccupied with a get-together of family and old friends. There's much description of clothes and furnishings and personalities—and tucked in around the edges, there are hints that all is not as safe and secure as the characters would wish: Is it safe to sit on the front steps after dark? Who's driving that unseen truck down the nearby road? Has someone been burying guns on the edges of the estate?

The movie adaptation of "The Last September" starts with the same unsettling touch, plunging us into the social details of a bygone period and letting us gradually discover a dark dimension that the characters themselves are tying their utmost to ignore. The impossibility of their efforts lends their story much of its poignancy.

At the same time, one cant help being impatient with a gang of privileged, prosperous people who should be more adept at facing the bluntest realities of their era.

It's 1920s Ireland, where the recent Republican uprising has caused havoc for both Irish and British interests. The main characters are Anglo-Irish aristocrats who occupy an in-between position with regard to the escalating troubles. On one hand, they're fully aware of their English ancestry. On the other, they live in Ireland and consider themselves as genuinely Irish as their neighbors. Most of them would rather overlook the political climate and get on with their comfortable lives. But violence is coming closer to their doorstep and denial is growing more difficult by the day.

As visualized by Deborah Warner, an English stage director in her filmmaking debut, "The Last September" is a deeply nostalgic story that tends to favor atmosphere over plot and character. The acting is articulate in a manner long associated with British movies—veterans Maggie Smith and Michael Gambon are ably supported by Keeley Hawes and other younger talents—and the cinematography is so picture-perfect it may distract from the film's deeper themes.

Some viewers might wish more vigor had been placed into the tale's most dramatic thread—an Anglo-Irish woman caught between a British soldier and an Irish rebel; others might wish they'd pursued the plot's historical angles more directly. But anyone seeking a low-key blend of the personal and the political need search no further than this gently photographed fable.

LOS ANGELES TIMES, 4/28/00, Calendar/p. 20, Kevin Thomas

"The Last September," a luminous, piercing film from the Elizabeth Bowen novel, richly evokes a world of privilege on the verge of disintegration.

The time is the fall of 1920 in County Cork, and the setting is a grand country estate of the Anglo-Irish aristocracy, caught between the British forces who will soon be defeated by the Irish rebels fighting for independence, bringing an end to British rule in Southern Ireland. Ironically, these wealthy descendants of English immigrants consider themselves to be Irish.

At this particular estate, Sir Richard Naylor (Michael Gambon) and his wife, Lady Myra (Maggie Smith), carry on like the aristocrats of Chekhov's "The Cherry Orchard."

Sir Richard is aware of what's going on, predicts—and hopes—the Irish will prevail but has not come to terms with what might be the fate of his exalted way of life. Lady Myra, a terrific snob, goes on about her social life as if she were deaf to the none-too-distant gunfire. A guest observes in amazement that she even stages an elaborate tennis party in the midst of war.

The Naylor estate, with its spacious and exquisitely decorated rooms, is also home to Sir Richard's 19-year-old niece Lois (Keeley Hawes) and to Lady Myra's nephew Laurence (Jonathan Singer), a foppish Oxford undergraduate.

The Naylors have just been descended upon by old family friends Hugo and Francie Montmorency (Lambert Wilson and Jane Birkin). We learn that the Montmorencys are impecunious professional house guests in their elite circle and actually have no home of their own.

The presence of the handsome Hugo, who is somewhat younger than the fragile but gallant Francie, attracts from England his elegant, sophisticated old flame Marda (Fiona Shaw), who wants to see if she has any feeling left for him before marrying her rich fiance.

Meanwhile, Lois is being pursued by Gerald (David Tennant), a deeply smitten British army captain, but as "The Troubles" escalate, Lois finds herself increasingly drawn to her childhood friend Peter (Gary Lydon), an Irish freedom fighter hiding in an old mill on her uncle's estate.

Bowen's source novel has provided director Deborah Warner and writer John Banville a considerable number of sharply drawn individuals to interact as war draws closer. The central figure is Lois, a coltish young woman who loves to dance a la Isadora Duncan—as well as the maxixe—across the estate's vast lawns. Lois is sheltered but eager to discover romance and the world beyond her uncle's exclusive realm. She is ready to lose her innocence in every sense of the word, and Marda emerges as the pivotal figure in her destiny.

Marda is further a figure of ambiguity: At the story's climactic moment she gives a reply to a question leaving us wondering if it has been made in innocence or with deliberate malice. In any event, it gives this beautifully wrought drama a resonant finish.

Performances are impeccable in their inflections and nuances. There is a cold viciousness in the Naylors' obtuse snobbery that prevents you from caring what happens to them or to their way of life, and, of course, Gambon and Smith provide the couple with bleakly amusing shadings. Hawes is deft at expressing the occasional awkwardness and gaucheness of the likably naive but imaginative Lois. Tennant, Wilson, Birkin, Lydon and others lend faultless support, but the film's dazzler is Shaw, she of the unsettlingly direct gaze, undisguised intelligence and angular beauty—her features might be those of Mary Astor stylized by Modigliani.

John Bright's period costumes are as exquisite as they are accurate, and those for Shaw's Marda rightly look toward a sleeker future. The film's sense of time and place could not seem more authentic, thanks to painstaking production designer Caroline Amies, and Slawomir Idziak's lush, dark-hued camera work, which captures the beauty of this special world.

By the time this splendid film is over, not only do you understand how these Anglo-Irish aristocrats earned the enmity of both ordinary Irish people and the British military but also come to share this view.

NEW YORK, 5/1/00, p. 57, Peter Rainer

Adapted from Elizabeth Bowen's novel and set in 1920 in County Cork, *The Last September* has a graceful, fated tone, and a real subject: the fading away of the Anglo-Irish aristocrats in the wake of the war for Ireland's independence. The best moments seem practically Chekhovian, and the cast, especially Maggie Smith, Michael Gambon, and Fiona Shaw, bring to their characters' every gesture a whole universe of feeling. Some of the other players, including Keeley Hawes as the ingenue niece, are rather blank, and director Deborah Warner's imagery, with its overuse of mirrored reflections, is perhaps too precious an approximation of Bowen's crystalline prose.

NEW YORK POST, 4/21/00, p. 49, Lou Lumenick

"I should like something to happen—something real," complains one of the characters in "The Last September," a tepid adaptation of Elizabeth Bowden's 1929 British novel.

It's a sentiment likely to be shared by audiences through much of this slow and overly genteel film, directed by British stage veteran Deborah Warner with more pregnant pauses than a season of Harold Pinter and enough raindrops on windows for a year's worth of student films.

It's 1920 in County Cork, Ireland, and the descendants of British settlers are counting the days until Irish rebels end their aristocratic reign.

But "the troubles" are pushed far into the background of John Banville's blah script, which focuses without much drama on a young English-Irish girl (the bland Keeley Hawes) torn between an English soldier (David Tennant) and an IRA terrorist (Gary Lydon).

Acting legends Maggie Smith and Michael Gambon—paired for the first time—are delightful as her snobby aunt and philosophical uncle, but they're sadly underused.

Fiona Shaw fares much better as a flirtatious middle-aged spinster who decides to renew her acquaintance with an old fiancé (Lambert Wilson), much to the consternation of his wife, a ravaged-looking Jane Birkin.

Overall, "The Last September" is a real snooze.

NEWSDAY, 4/21/00, Part II/p. B12, Jan Stuart

If you are inclined to shrink from civilized entertainments in which genteel folk hold tennis parties, clatter fine china and communicate with ironic glances, you may want to give a wide berth to "The Last September." Adapted from a novel by Elizabeth Bowen, it is the sort of Chekhovian elegy to a passing way of life that trundles along with all the vigor and velocity of a sigh.

Set in the County Cork of 1920, "The Last September" suggests the incipient submission of Anglo-Irish aristocrats to an insurgent Irish independence movement through one gentrified household. Embodying this transition is a vivacious 19-year-old named Lois Farquar (Keeley Hawes) whose affections for a British Army captain (David Tennant) are challenged by her attraction to an Irish freedom fighter (Gary Lydon).

As Lois waltzes with the Brit and makes whoopee with his enemy in the old mill, her aunt, Lady Myra (Maggie Smith), and uncle, Sir Richard Naylor (Michael Gambon), putter with their hobbies and entertain guests. Chief among them is Anglo-Irish sophisticate Marda Norton (the radiant Fiona Shaw), who fires up the embers of a past romance one last time before she gives herself over to a loveless, but secure, marriage.

"The Last September" is as much about freedom of the heart as it is a drama of cultural independence. Firebrand British stage director Deborah Warner translates the impressionistic beauty of Bowen's prose into snapshots that are as elusive as they are occasionally luminous. You may feel the need to curl up for a nap on the divan long before it's time for high tea.

SIGHT AND SOUND, 6/00, p. 46, Kevin Maher

A private estate in Cork, Ireland, 1920. Sir Richard and Lady Myra Naylor welcome their English visitors, Hugo and Francie Montmorency. Sir Richard's niece Lois is dancing flirtatiously in the garden with Captain Gerald Colthurst, an English soldier. That night Sir Richard laments the worsening Irish political situation. The next day the group welcome another visitor, Marda Norton, and organise a tennis party. Meanwhile Peter Connolly, a local Republican, kidnaps and shoots dead an English sergeant.

Hugo, Marda and Lois go for a walk to a ruined mill. Here Lois discovers Peter Connolly's hiding place. Hugo declares his affections for Marda while Lois secretly brings food to Peter. Peter attempts to rape Lois but he flees when Gerald arrives. Gerald later announces to Lady Myra his intention to marry Lois, but she protests his unsuitability. Undeterred, Lois returns to the mill to see Peter who forces himself on her but is once again disturbed by Gerald. This time he kills Gerald. Hugo and Francie leave the next morning. Marda then leaves for London, taking Lois with her.

"We're Irish!" says Marda to the clearly bemused English Captain Colthurst, "We look like you and we speak like you, but we're not like you!" It's a thematic motif (a national identity crisis among the Anglo-Irish ascendancy in the 20s) that writer John Banville crudely hammers home throughout his uneven adaptation of Elizabeth Bowen's subtle novel. Later Lois is erroneously told to go back to England, while Sir Richard explains to the still bemused Colthurst that both the IRA and the Naylors are proudly Irish. Here Banville unfortunately displays a political didacticism that's absent from Bowen's novel. What is allusive and simmering under the surface in Bowen becomes explicit in his screenplay. Hence we have the appearance of the film's Irish rebel, Peter Connolly. In the novel, Connolly's unseen presence casts a menacing shadow over the high-society dances and tennis parties Bowen's characters attend. In elevating Connolly to a major dramatic character in his own right, Banville and debut feature director Deborah Warner, an established theatre director, have unfortunately fallen back on stock IRA-movie cliches. As played by Gary Lydon, Peter can trace his lineage to earlier on-screen IRA figures portrayed by actors such as Dirk Bogarde in *The Gentle Gunman* (1952), Stephen Rea in *Angel* and even Brad Pitt in *The Devil's Own*. In other words, he is taciturn, dashingly attractive (in an animalistic way), and can display sudden flashes of psychopathic menace. His intrusion into the central romance of Lois and Gerald is not only less than convincing, but also destructive to the story's dramatic momentum—Lois goes to the mill, almost gets raped, comes back, goes to the mill again, almost gets raped again and comes back again.

Lumbered with this stilted narrative (the screenplay is long on stagy declamatory speeches, but short on action), Warner has instead concentrated on the film's visual style. With the aid of regular Krzysztof Kieślowski cinematographer Slawomir Idziak, she has created a richly detailed portrait of decay. Lugubrious autumnal yellows and browns merge with the putrid green wallpaper (often peeling away) covering the interior of the Naylors' home. Meanwhile the same lime-green light falls through half-open shades, as if to hint at an encroaching Irish nationalism. And it's with impressive visual panache that Warner reveals several key moments through the sepia-tinted iris of Lois' spyglass. Clearly bound to Lois' sexual desire, it allows her to observe Peter with impunity, then falls on her own lips and then her body during her first sexual encounter.

Lois herself is played with coquettish enthusiasm by Hawes. The rest of the cast get by with often sketchily underwritten roles (David Tennant's bemused English officer is an especially unforgiving part). Add an eerie tintinnabulating soundtrack from other Kieślowski collaborator Zbigniew Preisner and you have a well crafted but sadly stagnant period drama.

VILLAGE VOICE, 4/25/00, p. 138, Leslie Camhi

Romantic ruins, Shetland ponies, luscious lawns, and rose gardens—for the English, Ireland had everything. But by 1920, the natives were restless, and the Anglo-Irish aristocrats who ruled the land from their grand estates were beginning to sense that the end had come. *The Last September*, an adaptation of Elizabeth Bowen's novel and theater director Deborah Warner's screen debut, is set at the end of that summer on one such property, where Sir Richard (Michael Gambon) and Lady Myra (Maggie Smith) live with assorted relatives.

"How I'd like to be here when this house burns," says Myra's nephew Laurence, a disaffected Oxford intellectual. "We'll all be so careful not to notice." More obviously troubling to this clan than the growing Irish rebellion is the presence of a young British captain (David Tennant) who's forever mooning over Richard's niece Lois (Keeley Hawkes). House guests (Jane Birkin and Lambert Wilson as a pathetic married couple and Fiona Shaw as a worldly single woman) tiptoe around both subjects. Meanwhile, British soldiers are summarily executed, their naked bodies tossed from riverbanks, and Lois's childhood playmate becomes a hunted insurgent.

Warner captures Bowen's luminous prose in deft strokes of light and color. John Banville's sharp screenplay renders the divided loyalties of a people whose roots are in Ireland, though their immense privileges are owed to the crown. (He strikes a false note with the one bit of action he introduces into the novel's heady atmosphere.) Among the gifted cast, old-timers Smith and Gambon stand out, Shaw is brilliantly arch (though less effective when she tries to be moving), and Hawkes appears convincingly fresh and unformed. The film's pathos lies not with people who have justice on their side, but with those who don't know where they belong, or who find themselves pawns in a broader game of history.

Also reviewed in:
CHICAGO TRIBUNE, 4/28/00, Friday/p. P, John Petrakis
NEW REPUBLIC, 5/8/00, p. 25, Stanley Kauffmann
NEW YORK TIMES, 4/21/00, p. E18, A. O. Scott
VARIETY, 5/31-6/6/99, p. 34, Todd McCarthy
WASHINGTON POST, 4/28/00, p. C5, Rita Kempley

LEFT LUGGAGE

A Castle Hill Productions release of a Trident Releasing presentation of a Flying Dutchman Productions/Shooting Star/Favourite Films/Greystone Films co-production. *Executive Producer:* Craig Haffner and Brad Wilson. *Producer:* Ate de Jong, Hans Pos, and Dave Schram. *Director:* Jeroen Krabbé. *Screenplay:* Edwin de Vries. *Based on the novel "The Shovel and the Loom"* *by:* Carl Friedman. *Director of Photography:* Walter Vanden Ende. *Editor:* Edgar Burcksen. *Music:* Henny Vrienten. *Music Editor:* Michael Kreple. *Sound:* Leo Fransen and (music) Frans Hendrix. *Sound Effects Editor:* Glen Auchinachie. *Casting:* Susie Figgis. *Production Designer:* Peter Jan Brouwer. *Art Director:* Hemmo Sportel. *Costumes:* Yan Tax and Bernadette Corstens. *Make-up:* Winnie Gallis. *Running time:* 100 minutes. *MPAA Rating:* Not Rated.

CAST: Isabella Rossellini (Mrs. Kalman);   Maximilian Schell (Mr. Silberschmidt, Chaja's Father);   Laura Fraser (Chaja Silberschmidt);   Jeroen Krabbé (Mr. Kalman);   Marianne Sägebrecht (Mrs. Silberschmidt, Chaja's Mother);   David Bradley (Concierge);   Adam Monty (Simcha Kalman); Chaim Topol (Mr. Apfelschnitt); Heather Weeks (Sofie); Miriam Margolyes (Mrs. Goldblum); Lex Goudsmit (Mr. Goldblum);   Krijn Ter Braak (Grandfather);   Mieke Verheijden (Grandmother);   Noura van der Berg (Selma);   Lana Broekaert (Chaja, age 7);   Koen de Bouw (Father, age 20);   Edwin de Vries and Bart de Vries (Hasids);   Benjamin Broekaert (Dov); Ben Glanz (Avrom);   Jair Houteman and Jolien Claessen (Esva);   Ann Petersen (Landlady);   Luc van Mello and Gideon Rijlnders (Police Officers);   Luc d'Heu (Restaurant Owner);   Marc Lauwrys and Ben van Ostade (Cooks);   Huw Garmon (Car Driver);   Ben Rottiers (Resistance Fighter);   Alex de Jong (Cantor);   Antonie Kamerling (Peter);   Michael Pas (The Cook).

LOS ANGELES TIMES, 10/20/00, Calendar/p. 8, Kevin Thomass

"Left Luggage," after a prologue set at the outbreak of World War II, shifts to Antwerp in 1972. Chaja Silberschmidt (Laura Fraser), ostensibly a philosophy student, is a determined free spirit typical of the era. She's headstrong, independent and impetuous, and when she comes home to visit, she and her parents (Maximilian Schell, Marianne Sagebrecht), who are Holocaust survivors, sometimes clash. At just the moment Chaja is asserting herself, her father is beginning to feel the past wash over him.

Before being overtaken by the Nazis, Mr. Silberschmidt managed to bury two large suitcases with his family's treasures in the yard of a "safe house" in which he had found refuge for only one night. He previously had been so preoccupied with rebuilding his life after the war that he had no time to think of buried treasure, but now that he's slowed down he's becoming obsessed with digging up Antwerp backyards.

Meanwhile, his wife has dealt with the dark past by never mentioning it and doing her level best to stave off all painful memories. Consequently, their daughter has scant personal frame of reference for the Holocaust and has little sympathy for her father's efforts.

This is about to change, for Chaja, in need of a job, accepts the position of nanny to the five children of a Hasidic couple, the Kalmans (Isabella Rossellini and Jeroen Krabbe, the latter of whom also directed the film). Chaja's adjustment to her new job is formidable, but she persists. She and Mrs. Kalman manage to bond, despite their widely differing views.

Chaja is especially drawn to little Simcha (Adam Monty), who has normal hearing yet does not speak, almost certainly on account of his thundering, overbearing father. But in Chaja's nurturing company the 5-year-old starts to talk. Through her concern for Simcha, Chaja begins discovering her identity as a Jew, a process that will have profound impact upon her and her relationship to her parents.

With an adorable child at its center, "Left Luggage" becomes disarmingly warm and even a little folksy at times, but Edwin de Vries' script proves devastatingly deceptive. Its modest, though solid core gives way to unexpected starkness.

As you would expect from such proven veterans, Rossellini (who received, for her quietly powerful performance, one of the four prizes "Left Luggage" won at the Berlin Film Festival), Schell, Sagebrecht and Krabbe, plus Chaim Topol and Miriam Margolyes in supporting roles, are most effective.

Fraser, who resembles Julia Roberts, is a little too arch, even for the initially flouncy Chaja, but rises to the occasion as the film assumes an increasingly somber aspect. The persistent evil of anti-Semitism is embodied in David Bradley's exceptionally nasty concierge at the rundown apartment house where the Kalmans live.

NEW YORK POST, 9/22/00, p. 50, Jonathan Foreman

Good-hearted but heavy-handed, this is the story of a free-spirited teenager (Laura Fraser) who goes to work as a nanny for a Hasidic family (Isabella Rossellini and director Jeroen Krabbe) in 1970s Belgium.

The experience teaches her to understand her eccentric Holocaust survivor parents and to appreciate her own heritage. In the meantime, the nanny's modernness and openness to life inspire the Hasidic family's apparently mute 7-year-old son (Adam Monty) to speak.

After a dreadfully clunky start, "Left Luggage" picks up and becomes quite moving.

NEWSDAY, 9/22/00, Part II/p. B10, Gene Seymour

Its movie-of-the-week dimensions notwithstanding, "Left Luggage" evokes a raw authenticity about the postwar emotional fabric of Western Europe that wears down your resistance. Because it is an actor's movie (veteran heavy Jereon Krabbe directs), "Luggage" also is carried along by broad and not always subtle performances aimed for the gut. Here, too, you end up surrendering to brute force, even though you never forget that you're being worked over.

Besides, how many movies do you know are set in Antwerp, Belgium, in 1971?

It is where Chaja (Laura Fraser), a cheeky philosophy student, drops her part-time jobs as fast as she can pick them up. She could live at home with her Holocaust-survivor parents (Maximilian Schell, Marianne Sagebrecht). But she's uncomfortable with their divergent-yet-frenzied methods of dealing with the past; Dad by digging for his lost suitcases all over town, Mom by baking as fast as she can to stoke her denial.

Chaja eventually finds a job she can't walk away from. She accepts work as nanny for a Hassidic family living in a run-down apartment building. Being a "with-it" '70s girl, Chaja can't quite connect with the family's customs and has a difficult time with the parents (Krabbe, Isabella

Rossellini). What keeps her on the job is the family's terminally cute 5-year-old boy, who isn't able to say a word.

Fraser holds the center of the story with fire and sensuality, while Rossellini capably assumes a pose of melancholic stoicism. The movie also spikes the customary reflections on the Holocaust's impact with some hard-edged, yet savvy observations on the anti-Semitism that, postwar recriminations aside, lingers in the European soul like a festering boil.

SIGHT AND SOUND, 11/98, p. 55, Simon Louvish

Antwerp, Belgium, the early 70s. Chaja Silberschmidt is a philosophy student living apart from her parents, Jewish Holocaust survivors still traumatised by their experiences. Her father is still searching for two suitcases of family artefacts he buried somewhere in the city just after the war, while her mother takes refuge in small talk. Chaja takes on a job as a nanny to the Kalmans, an Orthodox-Hassidic Jewish family, tenants in a house dominated by an anti-Semitic doorman. Chaja finds the Kalmans' world alien and irrational, but adores their apparently mute four-year-old child Simcha. Mr. Kalman is hostile to Chaja's presence. The Kalmans are also perturbed at Chaja's direct challenge to the doorman's harassment.

Simcha begins to talk, and Chaja becomes more committed to the Kalman family. Chaja secretly coaches Simcha in the Passover Four Questions but, reciting them at the Passover meal, the boy trips up, and is reprimanded by his father. Chaja confronts Mr. Kalman with his apparent lack of love for his son, only to be shown a photograph of Mr. Kalman's father and brother, killed in the Holocaust, to whom Simcha bears an uncanny resemblance. Chaja stops working for the Kalmans, but is devastated when little Simcha drowns in the park pool they used to visit. Visiting the Kalmans to console them she is blamed for the tragedy by the men, but Mrs. Kalman embraces her as a "true daughter of Israel". Now more able to understand the pent-up emotions of her own parents, Chaja helps her father in his futile attempts to find his lost suitcases.

Directed by actor Jeroen Krabbé, *Left Luggage* is an attempt to depict a community (Hassidic Jews) that lives apart from the material values of our times, seen through the eyes of secular Jewish woman. Having won several awards at film festivals, it obviously has supporters who are more willing than this reviewer to accept its sentimentality and simplistic format. It doesn't help that the film is voiced in English, native neither to some of the actors nor to the film's Antwerp milieu. Everybody 'spiks like ziss', conjuring up a kind of comic-opera Judaism not helped by the script's stereotypes, such as the obsessive father or the cake-baking mother. Neither Maximilian Schell nor Marianne Saegebrecht (as the protagonist Chaja's parents) can survive their mediocre lines, to say nothing of Chaim Topol's apple-checked mentor Mr. Apfelschnitt. The anti-Semitic doorman is a one-tone oaf, and even Isabella Rossellini (as a Hassidic wife) seems to be struggling to get under the skin of her character.

At every level, the film is superficial. Whenever true drama threatens, the director opts for a thick syrup of schmaltz; at one point, a child runs into Chaja's arms in slow motion. Only Laura Fraser is able to surmount the kind of direction which requires her to look doleful, puzzled, loving, tearful, or devastated by numbers. There's an old movie adage that emotion in a film should be earned. It is not enough simply to dangle guilt-inducing elements—persecuted Jews, the Holocaust, the Yellow Star, the trauma of survivors—before an audience which feels it must respond to the underlying power of these historical horrors.

The director seeks to trump us by killing off a child, a tragic device which might be reminiscent of the sentimentalities of classic Yiddish films such as *Vu Is Mayn Kind* (1937) or *Matecika* (1939). But *Left Luggage* lacks the interlocking force of actors and crew working within a coherent cultural context in a marginalised and genuinely endangered universe, which still gives those 30s movies a special punch. At one point in the movie, Mr. and Mrs. Kalman address each other in Yiddish. The movie comes alive for an instant, but the dialogue is not translated, perhaps to match Chaja's incomprehension. The protagonists' culture is reduced back to jargon. The film's essential dishonesty lies in the fact that it is not concerned in any real sense with either religion or culture, but with ethnicity, the simple, and simple-minded bonding of Jews against the invariably anti-Semitic gentiles.

The subject matter brings to mind director Eli Cohen's neglected *tour de force, The Quarrel* (1991), in which two friends (both Holocaust survivors)—a secular writer and a Hassidic zealot—debate with searing passion the impassable personal and existential gulf that lies between them despite their shared cataclysm. In *Left Luggage,* however, neither writer nor director demonstrates the ambition or the ability to look shrewdly at the characters of their own story, to gauge the depths of their rebellion against the course of history, or to humanise them in the complexity of their own internal, seething anxieties.

VILLAGE VOICE, 9/26/00, p. 152, Leslie Camhi

Only a surrealist would cast Isabella Rossellini as an ultra-Orthodox Jewish woman. But in *Left Luggage,* Dutch actor-director Jeroen Krabbé's debut feature, the former Lancôme model turns in a credible performance as Mrs. Kalman, a Hasidic mother of five children. In Antwerp during the '70s, Chaja (Laura Fraser), a philosophy student and the daughter of Holocaust survivors, takes a job as the Kalmans' nanny. Though flummoxed by Orthodox regulations, she's drawn to four-year-old Simcha (Adam Monty), a mute cherub in a yarmulke and sidecurls.

Chaja's mother (Marianne Sagebrecht) seems drugged or possessed—spouting a steady stream of complaints and advice ("Tight jeans will give you cancer"), maniacally cutting cakes with her tattooed wrist in close-up. Chaja's father spends his days trying to locate the spot where, during the war, he buried suitcases filled with family photographs and silver; Maximilian Schell brings to the role a whiff of classic Hollywood. Locked in their memories, these two are almost as uncommunicative as Simcha, but sometimes they seem to belong to different movies.

Krabbé himself plays Mr. Kalman, who remains for the most part a wooden patriarch. As a director, Krabbé alternates exaggeration with sentiment, but the main characters are relatively complex, and its surprise ending is genuinely affecting. Most films about Hasidic life are filled with caricatures of a pitilessly hidebound people. This more nuanced view is appreciated.

Also reviewed in:
NEW YORK TIMES, 9/22/00, p. E26, Stephen Holden
VARIETY, 2/23-3/1/98, p. 80, David Stratton

LEGEND OF BAGGER VANCE, THE

A Dreamworks Pictures and Twentieth Century Fox release of a Wildwood/Allied production. *Executive Producer:* Karen Tenkhoff. *Producer:* Robert Redford, Michael Nozik, and Jake Eberts. *Director:* Robert Redford. *Screenplay:* Jeremy Leven. *Based on the novel by:* Steven Pressfield. *Director of Photography:* Michael Ballhaus. *Editor:* Hank Corwin. *Music:* Rachel Portman. *Music Editor:* Bill Abbott. *Choreographer:* Robin Stockdale and Diane Stockdale. *Sound:* Peter F. Kurland and (music) Gary Summers. *Sound Editor:* Gary Rydstrom and Richard Hymns. *Casting:* Debra Zane. *Production Designer:* Stuart Craig. *Art Director:* W. Steven Graham. *Set Designer:* Julia Starr Sandford, Thomas Minto, Adam Scher, Jack Ballance, and Geoffrey S. Grimsman. *Set Decorator:* Michael Seirton and Jim Erickson. *Set Dresser:* Eric Luling, Patrick Fuhrman, Andrea Sywanyk, Bennet Silver, Michael Shapiro, Chris Arias, John Bromell, Scott A. Lawson, Hugh W. Griffith III, Hal Gardener, Gordon McVay, and Clifton T. Cooper. *Special Effects:* Burt Dalton. *Visual Effects:* Richard Chuang. *Costumes:* Judianna Makovsky. *Make-up:* Gary Liddiard. *Make-up (Matt Damon):* Dennis Liddiard. *Make-up (Will Smith):* Judy Murdock. *Make-up (Charlize Theron):* Deborah Larsen. *Running time:* 127 minutes. *MPAA Rating:* PG-13.

CAST: Will Smith (Bagger Vance); Matt Damon (Rannulph Junuh); Charlize Theron (Adele Invergordon); Bruce McGill (Walter Hagen); Joel Gretsch (Bobby Jones); J. Michael Moncrief (Hardy Greaves); Peter Gerety (Neskaloosa); Lane Smith (Grantland Rice); Michael O'Neill (O. B. Keeler); Thomas Jay Ryan (Spec Hammond); Trip Hamilton (Frank Greaves); Dermot Crowley (Dougal McDermott); Harve Presnell (John Invergordon); Danny Nelson (McManus); Bob Penny (Laidlaw); Michael McCarty (Delahunty); Carrie Preston (Idalyn Greaves); Turner Green (Eugene James); Blake King (Wilbur Charles); Andrea Powell (Mary Jones); E. Roger Mitchell (Aaron); Charles Ward and George Green (Men); Julie

Jones (Woman);   Valanie Lang (Girl);   Bernard Hocke (News Photographer);   Dan Beene (Willy);   Elliott Street (Carter);   Wilbur T. Fitzgerald (Roy);   Sonny Seiler (Sonny the Boarder);   Joseph Reidy (Photographer);   Tannis Stoops (Anna Mae);   Dearing Paige Hockman and Erika Mounts (Hagen Girls);   Neil Gonzaga, Ronald Steppe, and Hugh Baggett (Bar Patrons);   Jabulani Brown (Jones' Caddy); Vijay Patel (Hagen's Caddy).

CHRISTIAN SCIENCE MONITOR, 11/3/00, p. 15, David Sterritt

There are lots of reasons why "The Legend of Bagger Vance" should have been a good movie. Matt Damon and Will Smith, who play the main characters. are interesting stars. Robert Redford, who directed it, is a Hollywood giant who's put much time and energy into supporting the independent film movement and its new approaches to screen entertainment. And the story has a very good heart, using low-key suspense and romance to suggest that our lives are most enriched when we put principles and generosity ahead of our own selfish interests.

Unfortunately, there are also lots of reasons why "The Legend of Bagger Vance" hasn't turned out to be a good movie. The characters are cardboard figures instead of three-dimensional personalities. The camera work is more pretty than persuasive, like a two-hour parade of picture postcards. And the dialogue is dogged by clichés, with entire scenes sounding as if they were clipped from sentimental greeting cards.

How could Redford and company have miscalculated their material so badly? The answer may be in the movie's title. "Legend" is an enticing word but a dangerous one, leading some artists to explore the realm of archetypes and ideals, but tempting others to replace the realities of human experience with generalities and platitudes. Jeremy Leven's screenplay does exactly this, turning a potentially uplifting tale into a sadly self-satisfied sermon.

Damon plays Rannulph Junuh, a young Southern golfer whose promising career is hobbled by World War I and the horrors he encounters there. Morose and cynical, he retreats into sin and self-indulgence until his former fiancée calls on him to play in a tournament she's organizing. He accepts this opportunity to renew his life, but his downward trajectory proves hard to reverse—until he meets Bagger Vance, a mysterious black caddy who cloaks wise words in a humble disposition. Little by little, Bagger's teachings reach the cynic's heart, leading him—and the movie—to a predictably happy finale.

There's nothing wrong with the basic thrust of Bagger's advice—he's like a club-carrying Yoda, doing a guardian angel's job with a court jester's flair—and few would argue with the movie's basic message about the value of honesty integrity, and being true to your own best instincts. The trouble lies in its stereotypical style, its schmaltzy emotionalism, and its romanticized view of a white man's world in which it's taken for granted that even the most enlightened African-American must be a servant as well as a sage.

None of this means the movie wont be a hit, of course. Smith has a huge following, as do Damon and costar Charlize Theron, who are acquiring true Hollywood panache after their promising starts in the indie production scene. Viewers may like the picture's leisurely pace and general avoidance of trendy vulgarities. But this said, Redford's latest represents a lost opportunity. It aims only at our heartstrings and tear ducts, when it could have touched our minds and consciences.

LOS ANGELES TIMES, 11/3/00, Calendar/p. 1, Kenneth Turan

No golf course In America is as carefully manicured as "The Legend of Bagger Vance." A highly polished genteel fantasy about the game of golf and its relation to, yes, the game of life, "Bagger Vance" is so meticulous in its craftsmanship and so earnest in its storytelling that it feels both physically and spiritually airbrushed.

Coming after "The Horse Whisperer" and "A River Runs Through It," "Bagger Vance" confirms producer-director Robert Redford as the most passionately old-fashioned of filmmakers, a determined classicist who likes his films to be so well-made even the cobwebs look buffed and polished.

This is not necessarily a bad thing, and "Bagger Vance" is not without virtues. But Redford's passion for tidiness extends to the story as well, which is such a smoothly rigged piece of business, as square and uplifting as a Sunday sermon, that there is nowhere compelling for it to go.

Fighting against this schematic quality is a mostly well-selected cast that brings a semblance of life to these self-satisfied proceedings. Matt Damon fits snugly into Rannulph Junuh, a tarnished golden boy like so many of Redford's heroes, and 12-year-old J. Michael Moncrief is winning as the child through whose eyes the tale is told. Better still is the completely charismatic Will Smith, who shows a more restrained but equally irresistible side of himself as the mysterious title character.

After a present-day framing device centering on an aging golfer (an unbilled Jack Lemmon), "Bagger Vance" recedes into the past, to a meticulously re-created Savannah, Ga., between 1916 and 1931 and a story told by boy narrator Hardy Greaves (Savannah native Moncrief, whose natural accent puts everyone else's store-bought versions to shame).

Young Hardy grows up idolizing fellow Savannian Junuh (Damon), on track to become perhaps America's greatest golfer before his shock at the carnage he witnesses during World War I turns him into his native city's most celebrated recluse, living a dissipated life in a derelict old house.

This is especially disconcerting to Adele Invergordon (Charlize Theron, trying too hard), the daughter of the wealthiest man in Savannah and Junuh's now-abandoned prewar bride. (This is a predictable change from Steven Pressfield's novel, the basis of Jeremy Leven's script, which does without romance entirely.)

But Adele has other problems besides an absent husband. She's in serious financial trouble, needing money to save the failing Krewe Island Golf Resort her late father built just before the Great Depression. Nothing if not determined, she manages to set up an exhibition match between the two greatest golfers of the day, high-minded Bobby Jones (Joel Gretsch) and the profligate Walter Hagen (Bruce McGill). When local businessmen insist a Savannah player be included, it's soon determined that Junuh, next door to a reprobate though he might be, is the man for the job.

Just about half of "Bagger Vance" follows that two-day, 72-hole contest (filmed at South Carolina's Kiawah Island, where a new 18th hole was built from scratch, the Colleton River Plantation in the same state, and Georgia's Jekyll Island Club Hotel). It's undeniably pleasant to see these re-creations of the legendary Jones and Hagen, played by golfing actors who put a lot of effort into duplicating their characters' styles. Those who believe golf deserves to be mythologized as "a game that can't be won, only played" are clearly this film's target audience.

Bagger himself may have said that, but if he didn't he certainly says a lot of other things. From the moment he materializes out of an evening's darkness and offers to caddy for a shaky Junuh for $5, win or lose, the man is never at a loss for a pithy comment.

Part Zen philosopher talking about "the place where everything that is becomes one," part golf whisperer advising "you can't make the ball go in the hole, you've got to let it," part one-man therapy group, Bagger has a knack for words that's especially noticeable in a movie where other people are reduced to saying things like "he couldn't whip a dead possum off a gunny sack" and "you've got the gumption of a corn fritter."

Master psychologist that he is, Bagger notices at once that, both physically and metaphysically, Junuh has lost his swing, a condition no doubt related to Billy Crystal losing his smile in "City Slickers." The search for it is enough to occupy the golfer, the town of Savannah and the film itself for the duration.

Just as the natural lift of Bagger's presence helps Junuh, Will Smith's moments consistently elevate the film. Though "Bagger Vance" is determined to lay on the sentiment thick as enamel paint (notice, as if you had a choice, the angelic choirs in Rachel Portman's score), Smith's easy charm has the power to dissolve a lot of it. He can't humanize the entire film, but he and the boy do their best.

NEW YORK, 11/13/00, p. 76, Peter Rainer

Among a youngish generation of film buffs, Robert Redford, the director of *The Legend of Bagger Vance*, is perhaps as renowned today for being the founder and guru of the Sundance Film Festival as he is for his Hollywood career. The odd thing about that career is that he appears in, and directs, movies that are far glossier and more traditional than anything in the American independent-film tradition. This, in itself, is not a bad thing. In his acting prime, Redford epitomized movie-star glamour tempered by sharp intelligence, and certainly no one would wish him into most of what passes for "independent" in the cinema these days: hackneyed shoestring-budget movies serving as résumés for hackneyed big-budget work. But Redford's directing career, at least in his pastoral-romantic mode, is glossy in the safest and sappiest of ways. Almost nothing in *A River Runs Through It* or *The Horse Whisperer* engages anything but the eye.

The Legend of Bagger Vance—which is already being sarcastically referred to as *A Fairway Runs Through It,* because golfing is its backdrop—is another lusciously produced, emotionally clammy Redford enterprise—forced, phony mythmaking filled with tinged sunsets and full moons. It's adapted by screenwriter Jeremy Leven from a novel by Steven Pressfield that I have not read, largely because I fear the cranium can store only so many feathers.

The mythic belief at the heart of this movie is that "inside each and every one of us is our one true, authentic swing, something that's ours and ours alone." This bit of Zen wisdom, and a dozen koans like it, are delivered by Bagger Vance (Will Smith), a scruffy caddy who appears mysteriously in the star-filled night for the purpose of aiding Savannah, Georgia's former golf whiz Rannulph Junuh (Matt Damon). Bagger seems to know exactly what Junuh needs: not just his authentic swing but his very own authentic self (in the movie's terms, they are the same thing).

Before he went off to World War I, Junuh had been paired with Adele (Charlize Theron), daughter of Savannah's wealthiest citizen; traumatized by battle, he slinks into disreputable anonymity after the war. What brings him back onto the links is the chance to redeem himself. He accepts an offer by the city's publicity-crazed civic boosters to take on golfs two greatest players, Bobby Jones (Joel Gretsch) and Walter Hagen (Bruce McGill), at Savannah's Krewe Island golf resort, which was built in prosperous times by Adele's father and, in the wake of the Great Depression, became his ruination. Adele, with her eyelash-batting wiles, pushes the deal through. Like Junuh, she is looking for redemption, too. So is the young Savannah boy Hardy (J. Michael Moncrief), who functions as a kind of Jiminy Cricket alongside Bagger's Yoda. Hardy, who as an old man (played by an uncredited Jack Lemmon) narrates the movie in flashback, is supposed to represent the wide-eyed kid in all of us: the kid we were before we bogeyed into adulthood.

Although Bagger is the film's wise one, the massa-servant overtones in his pairing with Junuh are off-putting; parts of the film play out like *Song of the South* retold by Buddha. (What helps the audience over this racial discomfort is the knowledge that Tiger Woods could kick any of these golfers' asses. Redemption indeed!) Will Smith has a trickster's gleam in his eye that downplays the docility of his role, but he still seems like someone out of one of the more oracular *Twilight Zone* episodes (like the famous one, which seems similar to this film in its sticky tonal uplift, in which a very young, Pepsodent-smiley Redford played Death). Matt Damon, searching in vain for an authentic swing in his performance, seems uncomfortable being the center of all this mythic mumbo-jumbo, while Charlize Theron carries on with a flouncy giddiness that makes the belles in *Dr. T & the Women* seem cloistered by comparison.

The Legend of Bagger Vance wants to do for golf what *Field of Dreams* did for baseball: Turn our boyish nostalgia into a creed of life. We're told that winning isn't what living is all about; life is about having the courage to play the game. But the filmmakers have it both ways; they dismiss the crassness of victory but opt just the same for a rousing finale. And this bull about finding one's perfect swing! As long as we're getting philosophical here, since when does authenticity guarantee goodness? Bagger's mantra about being true to oneself ignores the question of who that self belongs to. Surely some of the scurviest people in our midst are also entirely true to themselves. The deep-think in *The Legend of Bagger Vance* is a fancy way of saying nothing.

NEW YORK POST, 11/3/00, p. 51, Lou Lumenick

Perhaps the best way to describe Robert Redford's beautifully crafted but uninvolving new movie is to note the story is narrated by an elderly golfer (Jack Lemmon) dying of a heart attack on the fairway.

Perhaps that's why its so utterly vague and mystical—or, to be unkind about it, so slow the movie itself seems to be suffering from a hardening of the arteries.

The bulk of the action, and that may be too strong a word, takes place in 1931, when the narrator, Hardy Greaves (played as a youngster by the cloying J. Michael Moncrief) is 10 years old.

Savannah, Ga. is in the grip of the Great Depression and beautiful Adele Invergordon (Charlize Theron) is struggling to hold onto the golf resort that her late father sank all of the family's money into.

She comes up with the idea of a publicity-generating exhibition match, with a $10,000 purse, and signs up the two biggest names in the sport: Bobby Jones and Walter Hagen.

But for reasons that are not awfully clear, Savannah's city fathers take up young Hardy's suggestion that she also invite the greatest local golf legend, even though he hasn't picked up a club in 15 years.

That would be Adele's former fiancé, Rannulph Junuh (Matt Damon), an alcoholic who never returned to the game after returning from World War I a shellshocked wreck.

She tries, to seduce Rannulph into playing (the movie's best scene), but he says no. Helping him "find his swing" and the confidence to compete falls to Bagger Vance (Will Smith), a mysterious stranger who is apparently Rannulph's guardian angel.

More than 90 minutes is devoted to the match itself, and if you're a golf fan (which I definitely am not), don't miss it. Others may prefer doing their laundry.

Redford seems to be aiming for a golf version of "The Natural," which had no small amount of mystical pretensions of its own but had a lot more energy. For most of us, golf is a much less exciting sport to watch than baseball—especially, as is the case here, the outcome never seems remotely in doubt.

Damon rarely connects with Rannulph as a character, and I'm not sure it's his fault. We know hardly more about him (except a passing reference that he was the sole survivor of a wartime battle) than we know about Bagger Vance, about whom we know exactly nothing.

The best that can be said about Smith's Bagger is that he dishes out the screenplay's line of new-age hooey with a light hand. But still, the sight of one of Hollywood's biggest black stars playing a caddie—and delivering cringe-worthy lines like "sho' is some storm abrewing"—is not a little depressing.

As a director, Redford has made several films about golden boys and their struggles, though he's rarely come close to "Quiz Show," which had more sharply drawn characters, situations and performances than his more recent efforts like "The Horse Whisperer."

Aside from Theron's deeply felt Adele and Bruce McGill's entertaining turn as the flamboyant Walter Hagen, which periodically pierce the metaphysical fog, the most memorable thing about "The Legend of Bagger Vance" are Michael Ballhaus' golden-hued cinematography and the flawless period costumes.

While not as aggressively manipulative as "Pay It Forward," the pointlessness of Redford's film is sadly summed up in a single line of dialogue: "The meaning of it is that there's no meaning."

NEWSDAY, 11/3/00, Part II/p. B3, Jan Stuart

What goes on inside the head of Robert Redford? From all appearances an intelligent and thoughtful man, he seems to regard movie production as a "do as I say not as I do" proposition. As an advocate for independent filmmakers, he has invested a sizable chunk of his energies nurturing an annual festival to help reward and market innovation. Left to his devices, however, the messiah of Sundance squanders his own artistic resources on something as bland and pasteboard as "The Legend of Bagger Vance."

Adapted from a novel by Steven Pressfield, this Depression-era golf saga is one of those over-inflated progenies of "Field of Dreams" that insist upon elevating competitive sport into the realm of religious experience. In these movies, it is not enough to merely hit a home run or sink a hole in one. The ball must be powered by some mystical state of oneness between the player and the cosmos.

If this were indeed the case, one would think neophyte athletes everywhere would be foregoing sports scholarships in favor of four years in a monastic order. That is certainly what might be recommended to Matt Damon's character, Rannulph Junuh, a budding golf star from Savannah who responds to the battle traumas of World War I by retreating into seclusion of a more inebriated and self-destructive sort.

Rannulph is catapulted out of his malaise by young fan Hardy Greaves (J. Michael Moncrief) and wealthy ex-girlfriend Adele Invergordon (Charlize Theron), who initiates a championship golf match to fire publicity for her father's failing luxury hotel. Hardy suggests native son Rannulph to go up against the two reigning national pros. But does the dissolute Rannulph have the right stuff anymore?

Enter "Bagger Vance" (Will Smith), a black hobo who appears quite mysteriously out of the dark of night bearing enough penny-ante philosophy to start a New Age fortune cookie factory. While an unsteady Rannulph practices his swing, Bagger intones such inspirational mantras as "A man's grip on his club is like his grip on his world" and "The rhythm of the game is just like the rhythm of life." That, and a Tiger Woods-caliber swing, earn Bagger a job as Rannulph's caddy.

Who is he? Where is he from? What is he on? Only more irritating than Will Smith's Cheshire-cat grin and Bagger's ersatz Confucianisms is his self-serving tendency to hold back on the advice till Rannulph reaches crisis mode. This is ostensibly Redford and screenwriter Jeremy Leven's way of tiptoeing around the racial issue: An indigent black man who flaunted his prowess in 1931 Savannah society might not be looked upon kindly. But it's finally just a device to scrounge up whatever tension can be eked out of a marathon golf match whose outcome is a foregone conclusion.

Mercifully, Redford and Leven refuse to reduce Rannulph's competitors (Bruce McGill and Joel Gretsch) to figures of easy derision. That honor is reserved for the commentators, who encapsulate the dumbest tendencies of sports hyperbole with nuggets such as, "He had a way of making the difficult shots look easy, and the easy shots even easier." In between matches, voluptuous Theron alternates between two moods (hurt and kooky/vivacious) and 10 times as many outfits.

Redford piles on the expensive period costumes and the detailed decor, while the Rachel Portman music labors to tap into the script's every last feel-good impulse. But it's a feel-nothing movie, too calculated and cautious to locate anything that might resemble a genuine or spontaneous life moment. "The Legend of Bagger Vance" is not the worst movie of the year, just one of the more unnecessary.

NEWSWEEK, 11/6/00, p. 79, David Ansen

Rannulph Junuh (Matt Damon) has lost his swing. A golden boy of golf with infinite promise, he left Savannah, Ga., to enlist in World War I, and returned, years later, a broken man. Now it's 1931, in the depths of the Great Depression. Junuh's long-abandoned girlfriend, Adele (Charlize Theron), desperate to save the country club her rich, dead father has left behind, brings together the two greatest golfers in the world, Bobby Jones (Joel Gretsch) and Walter Hagen (Bruce McGill), in an exhibition match. (These were the real golf giants of the era.) But to succeed she needs the long-vanished local hero to come out of his funk and return to the green. Enter the mysterious Bagger Vance (Will Smith), part-time caddie and spiritual guru, to teach the shattered Junuh how to regain his "authentic swing."

This is the premise of Robert Redford's "The Legend of Bagger Vance," a handsome, pleasingly mushy tall tale whose outcome is never in doubt. Adapted from a Steven Pressfield novel by Jeremy Leven, it's the story of how a man rediscovers his soul and overcomes adversity, yet its brooding hero is oddly underdeveloped. We know about his crisis because the narrator (Jack Lemmon) tells us, and because, in the movie's shorthand for despair, he drinks, doesn't shave and plays cards on the wrong side of the tracks. Damon is quietly compelling in the part, but we'd like a few more details, thanks. A similar sketchiness afflicts the love story. Theron, not at her best playing a spunky Southern belle, seems to be doing just fine without her beau, and the lack of chemistry between her and Damon doesn't convince us otherwise.

The real sparks are between Damon and the mischievously enigmatic Smith, who dispenses wisdom like a cross between Krishnamurti and Uncle Remus. And also between Damon and a scene-stealing 12-year-old named J. Michael Moncrief, a Junuh worshiper who grows up to be the movie's aged narrator. Redford, no fool, knows what will put a lump in your throat. Tonally reminiscent of both "The Natural" and "Field of Dreams," lushly appointed and shot in burnished golden tones, this is the sort of movie in which a great golf shot is accompanied by the "In Paradisum" section of Fauré's "Requiem." If that sounds like your cup of spiritual tea, "Bagger Vance" serves it up with extra lumps of sugar.

SIGHT AND SOUND, 3/01, p. 53, Edward Lawrenson

Savannah, the present. Elderly golfer Hardy Greaves suffers a heart attack. Ailing fast, his mind casts back to his childhood days.

Savannah, 1928. John Invergordon and daughter Adele build a golf course, the Krewe island resort, on land by the ocean. When the depression hits, Invergordon, deep in debt, commits suicide. Refusing to sell the course to developers who want to build a paper mill, Adele pledges to stage a three-day golf tournament to raise Krewe island's profile, She secures the participation of top golfers Bobby Jones and Walter Hagen. When some eminent townsfolk demand that the event include a local player, 10-year old Hardy suggests they approach Rannulph Junuh, a golfer whose promising career ended after he returned traumatised from World War I. Adele, whose relationship with Junuh was also cut short when he returned from combat, persuades him to compete. A few days before the tournament, a mysterious man introduces himself to Junuh as Bagger Vance and offers to caddy for him. Vance later takes on Hardy as his assistant.

On the first day of the tournament Junuh plays badly. The next day, Vance encourages Junuh to play better; by the end of play, he is only one shot behind Jones and Hagen. On the last day, Junuh, whose relationship with Adele is back on track, sinks a hole in one. On the final hole the three players are even. Despite declaring a foul, which puts him one behind, Junuh holes a putt that wins him the title. As the crowd cheer Junuh's victory, Vance disappears into the night.

Of all the major sports, golf is perhaps the hardest to turn into satisfying film drama. Whereas team sports provide film makers with grounds for exploring group dynamics and one on one contact sports such as boxing allow for bold, climactic showdowns, golf is essentially a solitary pursuit, one where performance hangs exclusively on the individual efforts of each player. Inevitably the game involves a competitive element, but in the end, as Will Smith's caddie Bagger Vance makes clear here, "It's just you and the ball." This singularly intense relationship between a player and his or her game might explain the sport's popularity as a televised event, but successful film narratives tend to require a more complex set of interactions, not least between those on the fairway and those off it—a point not lost on Ron Shelton, whose fine golf movie *Tin Cup* ends with hero McAvoy blowing his lead in the final hole by firing a succession of shots into the water trap. Having spent time with McAvoy off the course, we can put his defeat in perspective, recognising that it's only a game; a televised version of the same match would permit no such moral lesson, because it rests on the conviction that the game is the *only* thing worth bothering about.

Unlike *Tin Cup, The Legend of Bagger Vance* leaves the self-involved nature of the sport unchallenged—and ends up pushing it to absurd degrees. Taking place during a three-day tournament in 20s Savannah, it's hard to tell where golf ends and therapy begins. Director Robert Redford and his editor get the pace of the game just right—they should, given that their film is over two hours long—but the film gets stuck in the rough by conflating golfer Rannulph Junuh's fluctuating fortunes during the game with his attempt to grapple with the psychological scars he sustained fighting in World war I. The conceit of pegging Junuh's psychological progress to a golf match would probably seem ludicrous in any hands. But Redford's stiff approach makes a particularly botched job of it (the best he can do to remind us of Junuh's traumatic past is to treat us to some banal flashbacks when the golfer loses a ball in the woods). And as Junuh, Matt Damon's performance is too straight edged to suggest inner turmoil.

Caddie Vance's gnomic utterances only exacerbate the film's ponderous brand of solipsism. The involvement of Smith has raised the hackles of Spike Lee, who doubted that a black caddie would have been permitted on a course in the South in the 20s. It's a fair point, but one Redford's film happily glosses over. Not only does Redford avoid touching on the racial realities of the time, but his one significant black character Vance is assigned an otherworldly, mystical aura that robs him of shading or depth—at one point, he expresses empathy with the ground beneath him, standing on a putting green in barefoot. Far from raising the spectre of segregation, Redford prefers a version of the South in which the adulation of poor, largely black folk dissuades Junuh from pulling out of the competition. The fleeting presence of Savannah's poor does at least remind us there's a depression going on. But such moments are few, and rarely allowed to get in the way of the film's central concern, the fiery, all consuming affair between a man and his golf ball.

TIME, 11/6/00, p. 113, Richard Schickel

Golf being the sort of game most of its players rather romantically seem to think it is—a lonely struggle with one's inner demons—it has inspired a good deal of quasi-mystical writing. *The Legend of Bagger Vance* is based on one of the novels—an uneasy blend of self-help and soft-core spirituality—that golfers solemnly pass from hand to hand. It is essentially the story of Rannulph Junuh (Matt Damon), a local golfing great in Savannah, Ga., whose awful experiences in World War I have caused him to "lose his swing." As a result, he spends more than a decade drunk and disorderly. Then, with the Depression on (the action is set in 1931), his erstwhile girlfriend Adele Invergordon (Charlize Theron)—improbably named characters nearly always signal an improbable narrative—decides to hold an exhibition match to publicize her moribund golf club. She lures two golfing legends, the gentlemanly Bobby Jones (Joel Gretsch) and the roughneck Walter Hagen (Bruce McGill), into playing. But Savannah insists, for reasons the movie strains to make plausible, on having its own champion to cheer in the match.

Junuh resists Adele's sexual blandishments but is putty in the hands of Will Smith's Bagger Vance. Bagger appears out of the night, looking like an itinerant caddie but rather obviously a visitor from some higher plane, spouting contradictory golfing aperçus. On one hand, he insists that you can't find a lost swing; you have to let it find you. On the other hand, he insists that we are all born with an authentic swing, which it is our business to rediscover. Of course, he warns, golf is never a game you can win. You can only play it. In that sense, it's a lot like life, don't you think?

Or maybe not. Maybe it is, metaphorically, more like celebrity life. As Junuh starts his 72-hole struggle with self, Jones and Hagen, he at first duffs unconfidently along. Then he finds his groove, and the crowd starts murmuring approval, This leads to arrogance, a downfall and then a confrontation with himself in the woods where one of his errant shots has landed. These woods are a lot like the ones in France where he was traumatized. But this time he has the magical caddie to whisper steadying words to him—*Zen and the Art of Locker Room Twaddle*—and he goes on to...

Well, let's put it this way—an ending that is not entirely unpredictable. Whether or not it is satisfying depends largely on your tolerance for extremely long golf matches. The director, Robert Redford, aiming for something a little bit unearthly, leans toward special effects, weird angles and diffusion filters to lend some visual interest—and an air of spurious spirituality—to the film. But they are often just plain annoying. And the swell of choral music under Junuh's hole in one is laughable. The actors, especially the ever appealing Smith, do what they can to ground the movie in reality, but it stubbornly remains dawdling, remote and pretentious.

VILLAGE VOICE, 11/7/00, p. 136, Amy Taubin

A lovely-looking fairy tale of a movie in which almost every scene is washed with pink-gold light, Robert Redford's *The Legend of Bagger Vance* is easy to mock. You could start with the fact that its stars—Will Smith, Matt Damon, and Charlize Theron—all have conspicuously pug noses and exceptionally large, white teeth. You might mention that it's conveniently set at the beginning of the Great Depression—before people were forced to sell off their clothes and before poverty put lines on their faces. You might also note that although the location is Savannah, a city where everyone seems to wake up humming "Dixie," the N-word never crosses a single pair of lips. And it might occur to you that World War I and the Depression are treated as natural disasters, rather than as political and social events in which human agency played a part. In other words, you would need to suspend everything except wishful thinking to fall under the spell of this movie, which uses golf as a metaphor for life and provides a basic lesson in finding your authentic swing.

Once a teenage golfer of great promise, Rannulph Junuh (Damon) returns from the war burdened with the guilt of being the only survivor in his squadron. Junuh lives like a recluse until he's pressured to represent Savannah in a tournament that his former fiancée, Adele Invergordon (Theron), has organized to save her late father's golf resort from being taken over by the bank. Junuh is about to refuse when out of the woods one moonlit night comes Bagger Vance, a black man with a small suitcase, a rakishly cocked, big-brimmed hat, and a prodigious knowledge of the game. Bagger drops some hints about how they must find the swing Junuh has lost, and, suddenly, the space before Junuh's eyes seems to shift as if it were being simultaneously stretched and squeezed and every blade of grass were illuminated from within and every cricket had its own amplifier. Junuh takes a swing, and while it's not perfect, it's so much closer to what it was in the days before he became plagued by "should'ves and would'ves" that he commits to playing in the match with Bagger as his caddie. The last 40 minutes unfold on the golf course, where Junuh conquers first his fear of failure and then his smug overconfidence to reach the place where "you can play the game that only you were born to play and that was given to you when you came into the world."

Smith delivers such inspirational nuggets with a casual grace that makes them less embarrassing than they appear on the page. Indeed, this is a film filled with graceful performances, graceful camerawork, graceful art direction, graceful sound design, and graceful everything else. It's also something of a personal film, because Damon's vocal delivery and physical mannerisms—not to mention his blue eyes and golden hair—are so reminiscent of Redford, and because it references half a dozen Redford films from *The Natural* to *The Great Gatsby* to *The Horse Whisperer*. I would be dishonest if I didn't admit to being choked up by the way the light filtered through the trees in conjunction with all that talk about the mystery of the creative process. But for the most part, *The Legend of Bagger Vance* is more mushy than mystical. Redford's authentic swing has a harder edge. It takes material like *Ordinary People* or *Quiz Show* to bring it to the fore.

Also reviewed in:
CHICAGO TRIBUNE, 11/3/00, Friday/p. A, Michael Wilmington
NEW REPUBLIC, 12/4/00, p. 30, Stanley Kauffmann
NEW YORK TIMES, 11/3/00, p. E1, A. O. Scott
NEW YORKER, 11/6/0, p. 111, David Denby
VARIETY, 11/6-12/00, p. 19, Todd McCarthy
WASHINGTON POST, 11/3/00, p. C1, Rita Kempley
WASHINGTON POST, 11/3/00, Weekend/p. 41, Desson Howe

LEGEND OF DRUNKEN MASTER, THE

A Miramax Films and Dimension Films release of a Golden Harvest Company Ltd/Hong Kong Stuntman Association/Paragon Films, Ltd. production. *Executive Producer:* Leonard Ho. *Producer:* Eric Tsang and Edward Tang. *Director:* Lau Ka-Leung and Jackie Chan. *Screenplay (Cantonese, dubbed into English):* Edward Tang, Tong Man Ming, and Yuen Chieh. *Director of Photography:* Tong-Leung Chung, Cheung Tung-leung, Wong Man-won, and Jingle Ma. *Editor:* Peter Cheung. *Music:* Michael Wandmacher and Wu Wai Lap. *Choreographer:* Lau Ker-leung and (Martial Arts) Jackie Chan. *Sound:* Val Kuklowsky. *Sound Editor:* Scott Koué. *Production Designer:* Eddie Ma and Ho Kim Sing. *Costumes:* Ching Tin Qu and Suki Yip. *Running time:* 87 minutes. *MPAA Rating:* R.

CAST: Jackie Chan (Wong Fei-hung); Ti Lung (Wong Kei-ying); Anita Mui (Madame Wong); Felix Wong (Tsang); Lau Kar-Leung (Master Fu Min-chi); Ken Lo (John); Chin Ka-lok (Fo Sang); Ho Sung-pak (Henry); Tseung Chi-kwong (Tso); Hon Yee Sang (Hing); Andy Lau (Counter Intelligence Officer); Louis Roth (Consul); Therese Renee (Terese); Vincent Tuatanne (Bruno); Mark Houghton (Smith); Ho Wing-Fong (Fun); Lau Kar-Ying (Marlon); Lau Siu-Ming (Chiu); Suki Kwan (Chiu's Wife); Evonne Yung and Chan Wai Yee (Ladies in Coffee Shop); Shing Wong (Larry); Chan Kwok Kuen (Curly); Tai Po (Moe); Chan Kui Ying (Lily); Pao Fong (Cook); Ha Chun Chau and Wah Lung Szema (Seniors in Restaurant); Pak Yan (Mrs. Chan).

LOS ANGELES TIMES, 10/20/00, Calendar/p. 18, Kenneth Turan

When "Shanghai Noon" was winning friends for Jackie Chan a few months back, one troublesome critic (no names, please) grumbled that it was bittersweet that these new fans couldn't get a chance to see the Asian action superstar in his prime. Now, with the arrival of "The Legend of Drunken Master," they can.

Originally released in 1994 as "Drunken Master 2," this is one of the films that made Jackie Chan Jackie Chan. No less an authority than Thomas Weisser, author of "Asian Trash Cinema," claims it contains "some of the most extensive, jaw-dropping stunt work and martial arts magic ever amassed together in one feature. In addition to the new title, "Drunken Master" appears with a bright new print and has been serviceably dubbed into English. Chan does his own dubbing and participates in numerous exceptional action sequences that illustrate why he really ought to be considered the hardest-working man in show business.

"Drunken Master" is set in a photogenic re-creation of early 20th century China, but its plot is not something a whole lot of attention need be paid to. It starts when Wong Fei Hung (Chan), traveling with his renounced herbalist father, decides to hide a valuable ginseng plant in someone else's luggage to avoid paying duty.

That someone else turns out to be a nefarious Western ambassador who's intent on selling carloads of China's cultural treasures to the British Museum. Not a good thing. "Today they plunder a seal," Wong is told, "the next thing you know the Great Wall will be gone."

"Drunken Master's" other plot thread concerns, not surprisingly, the drunken school of kung fu boxing, apparently a real fighting style that uses inebriation to loosen the body and increase the pain threshold. Wong's father, fearful his son will become an alcoholic, wants him to just say no to drunken boxing, but it turns out to be a hard habit to break.

"Drunken Master" nicely showcases the two aspects of Chan's persona that combine to create his wide appeal. He is first of all one of the most limber of men, a model of acrobatic athleticism. who twists, dodges and twirls his lithe body almost faster than our eyes can follow.

But while many action heroes, Asian and Western alike, come off like automatons, Chan, always ready to break into a wide grin, specializes in bright, unquenchable enthusiasm. Chan may have the sunniest disposition of any performer since Shirley Temple, more boyish in his own way than the somber (and much younger) Haley Joel Osment.

But just because he'd as soon smile as fight, that takes nothing away from the eye-widening nature of Chan's on-screen battles. "Drunken Master" features several memorable encounters, including a spear fight in a confined space and an attack by what seems like hundreds of ax-wielding hooligans. Best of all is a staggering finale in a steel mill that was filmed over four months and features a climactic struggle with the high-kicking bad guy played by Ken Lo, formerly Chan's personal bodyguard.

"Drunken Master" also has a great deal of the unapologetically broad and silly comedy that Chan greatly enjoys. There are also I Love Lucy"-type moments involving Wong's mah-jongg addict of a stepmother (Anita Mui) and an unconvincing confrontation with that disapproving father.

All of this is simply the price that must be paid to experience the kind of thrilling, non-computer-generated stunt work that is becoming increasingly rare anywhere in the world. How dangerous this stuff can be is vividly illustrated in outtakes of action moments gone wrong, which, in Chan's signature gesture, are on view at the end. You don't see stunts like this every day, not even from Jackie Chan.

NEW YORK POST, 10/20/00, p. 52, Lou Lumenick

Martial-arts aficionados know there are two, and lately three, Jackie Chans. There's the star of popular Hollywood adventures like "Shanghai Noon," and the somewhat less inhibited Jackie Chan who's starred in, and sometimes directed, a long line of comic epics made in his native Hong Kong.

"The Legend of Drunken Master" belongs to a burgeoning third category: the Hong Kong epics that have been repackaged, re-edited and dubbed into English for American audiences who wouldn't even think of going to see a subtitled movie in Mandarin, no matter how exciting.

Taken on those terms, this is quite an eyeful—Chan's most impressive achievement.

Though he was pushing 40 when "Drunken Master" was made in 1993, Chan plays Wong Fei Hung, a legendary kung fu master, as a man in his early 20s. (He's older than Anita Mui, the very skilled comic actress who plays his mother).

The silly but fun plot has him accidentally mixing up a box of his father's ginseng with an ancient Chinese artifact that a group of British aristocrats and their Chinese flunkies are planning to smuggle out of late 19th-century Hong Kong.

That kicks off a series of ever-more spectacular martial arts battles, many of which Chan performs in the "drunken" style—bleary-eyed and wildly flailing at platoons of adversaries (in one scene, 20 axe-wielding villains) while under the influence.

It's a fabulous showcase for Chan, who combines the comic timing of Buster Keaton with the athletic grace of Gene Kelly in several breathtaking sequences. The most eye-popping is the lengthy finale that reportedly took four months to shoot.

That bravura battle—which memorably pits Chan (who is dragged through live coals at one point) against lighting footed Ken Lo, Chan's real-life bodyguard—has to be seen to be believed.

Purists may want to compare this version with the subtitled, somewhat longer video version of the original movie. It's called "Drunken Master II," because Chan originally appeared in the role (played by many Hong Kong stars, including Jet Li) in his first big hit in 1978.

Direction is attributed to Lau Ka Leung, who also plays a government official who fights with Chan under a train in the opening sequence. Chan reportedly took over the helm during shooting—and whoever's responsible, it's an amazing achievement.

VILLAGE VOICE, 10/31/00, p. 178, Jessica Winter

The joys of dubbing are probably best reserved for Sunday afternoons on the couch with a kung fu triple feature, so it's a shame about the English-synching for the mass-market rerelease of Jackie Chan's 1994 fireworks show *The Legend of Drunken Master* (perhaps timed to piggyback on the advance hype for December's *Crouching Tiger, Hidden Dragon*. But the most pertinent sounds in Chan's 140-plus movies usually fall within the range of bish-thwack-ow, and this sequel to 1978's *Drunken Master* is no exception; Chan has always seemed like a silent-screen virtuoso self-catapulted into modern times. Blithely brazen as ever, he plays affable Chinese folk hero Wong Fei-Hong, who apparently hasn't aged a day since the first film—he's still failing spectacularly at avoiding fights, still drinking to win, still slacking it at home with his despotic father and roguish stepmom (Andy Lau and Heroic Trio member Anita Mui, respectively seven and nine years younger than Chan!).

The uncertain plot somehow concerns ginseng and stolen objets d'art; the main thrust is acrobatic slapstick with a decided antipatriarchal twist (theorists take note: Jackie Chan subverting the male gaze!). The star's renowned exhibitionist masochism, usually reserved for the closing blooper reel (this one sports spouting noses and singed hands), bleeds heavily into the action. Chan freaks his way through a soused pair of Incredible Hulk-style wig-outs worthy of *Bullet in the Head*; a scene in which Wong *guzzles kerosene*, blows fire, *guzzles more kerosene*, pukes, and then kicks 20 guys' asses is typical (the movie deserves its own drinking game). Game director Lau Ka Leung packs all the flying bodies he can into his teeming frame, and the climactic, heedlessly extended pas de deux between our hero and the lithe, angular, almost contortionist baddie Ken Lo seems hallucinatory in its physical pyrotechnics. Meanwhile, audience surrogate Anita "Tung, Wonder Woman" Mui takes her boy's boozing and contusing in stride; when Fei-Hong packs away a jug of rice wine in one go during a marketplace smackdown, she reassures worried onlookers, "Don't worry, it gives him power."

Also reviewed in:
CHICAGO TRIBUNE, 10/20/00, Friday/p. F, Mark Caro
NEW YORK TIMES, 10/20/00, p. E30, Elvis Mitchell
VARIETY, 10/23-29/00, p. 41, Joe Leydon
WASHINGTON POST, 10/20/00, p. C5, Stephen Hunter

LIES

An Offline Releasing Film release in association with Cowboy Booking International of a Shincine Communications production in association with Korea Films. *Executive Producer:* Keon Seop Park and Moo Ryung Kim. *Producer:* Chul Shin. *Director:* Sun Woo Jang. *Screenplay (Korean with English subtitles):* Sun Woo Jang. *Based on the novel "Tell Me a Lie" by:* Jung Jang Il. *Director of Photography:* Kim Woo Hyung. *Editor:* Go Ji Park. *Music:* Dal Palan. *Sound:* Suk Won Kim. *Art Director:* Kim Myeon-Kyeong. *Costumes:* Park Shin-Yeon. Make-up: Jin Jang and Mi Sook Song. *Running time:* 115 minutes. *MPAA Rating:* Not Rated.

CAST: Sang Hyun Lee (J); Tae Yeon Kim (Y); Jin Jeon Hye (Woori); Choi Hyun-Joo (G. J's Wife); Shin Min-Soo (Young J); Han Gwan-Taek (Y's Brother); Kwon Hyun-Poong (J's Senior); Jung Myung-Keum (Senior's Wife); Cho Young-Sun (J's Father); Ahn Mi-Kyung (Noodle Shop Owner); Yeom Kum-Ja (Short Rib Shop Owner); Choi Boo-Ho (Motel Owner); Goh Hye-Won (Motel Owner's Wife); Kwak Chul-Jin and Lee Jin-Ho (Taxi Drivers). Jun Jae-Sup and Yim Mi-Ran (Noodle Shop Customers).

LOS ANGELES TIMES, 12/8/00, Calendar/p. 21, Kevin Thomas

Jang Sun Woo's "Lies" is a no-holds-barred odyssey of sexual obsession, a work of honesty and artistic integrity that nonetheless will be difficult to watch for many viewers.

Although sexually explicit, to put it mildly, it is not pornographic in that it is not designed to arouse viewers but rather to explore sexual passion at its fullest—and darkest. Indeed, its tone is clinical rather than sensual as it traces ever-shifting power within a relationship between a man and a woman.

Adapted from a novel by Jang Jung Il, it unfolds as a recollection of the male protagonist, known only as J (Lee Sang Hyun). J is a wiry fortysomething Seoul sculptor clearly of some renown—as apparently Lee is in real life.

A pretty 18-year-old, Y (Kim Tae Yeon), whose best friend has been seeing J, is so turned on by the sound of his voice on the telephone that she decides that he's the man to relieve her of her virginity. About to enter college as a statistics major, Y wants to have sex with a man for the first time on her own terms—because both her sisters lost their virginity through rape.

The attraction between J and Y is as instantaneous as it is overpowering. J conducts Y's rite of passage confidently and so effectively that he is soon introducing flagellation as a prelude to sex. The mingling of pain and pleasure so intensifies their affair that it threatens to reel out of control, and as they trade the dominant role back and forth you begin to wonder who will finally go too far.

The filmmakers, however, ultimately are concerned with revealing that one of the partners is actually working through a liberation of self, leaving the other enslaved by an indelible love.

The hitch is that an awful lot of what J and Y are engaged in, in a seemingly endless number of hotel rooms, is not what lots of us would choose to watch, even if Jang Sun Woo's stated intentions of breaking down distinctions between good and evil, beauty and ugliness, and his overall anarchic spirit and its implications, do engage us intellectually.

The infliction of pain and the welts it raises on the bodies of J and Y might be a turn-on for them but a turnoff, to say the least, for lots of viewers—not to mention other kinky stuff they engage in. In short, you find your civil-libertarian self defending Jang Sun Woo's right to exercise his freedom of expression to make and show his movie, while your own sensibilities are declaring that you are repulsed and wearied by much of what it depicts.

NEW YORK POST, 11/17/00, p. 56, V.A. Musetto

Veteran South Korean director-screenwriter Jang Sun Woo intended "Lies" to shock and to deliberately challenge film censorship in his homeland.

After all, the novel upon which it is based, "Tell Me a Lie," was banned in South Korea a few years back, and its author was tossed into jail as a "pornographer."

"Lies" was allowed into South Korean moviehouses only after it gained international respect as part of the official competition at the high-profile Venice Film Festival.

And the version released in Korea was substantially chopped. (The edition that opens here today has not been cut.)

"Lies" is the story of the bizarre relationship between a 38-year-old married sculptor, a character identified only as J, and a teenage schoolgirl, known as Y, who is anxious to be deflowered. .

More than half of the film consists of explicit, hotel-room sex between the two, including S&M and coprophilia.

Jang gives "Lies" a semi-documentary feel, using audition tapes to introduce the characters. At one point, the camera pulls back from an out-of-control fight scene to show crew members trying to break it up.

Hand-held camera work adds to the documentary flavor.

Both lead characters are played by non-professionals—fashion model Kim Tae Yeon as the girl and Lee Sang Hyun, a real-life sculptor, as the man.

They give realistic, believable performances, and never seem embarrassed by the sexual high jinks.

In fact, both actors have said that they actually enjoyed some of the beating scenes, and Lee added that he fell in love with his leading lady while the film was being shot. (She didn't reciprocate).

It would be a disservice, however, to think of "Lies" as nothing more than a sexfest.

Jang's screenplay is playful, unpretentious and filled with subtle humor. Best is the scene in which the couple rummage through a construction site, looking for implements of torture, while oblivious workers go about their day.

Some people will condemn this film sight unseen. That's their right. But they should not be allowed to impose their views on others.

For when all is said and done, "Lies" is just good, dirty fun.

NEWSDAY, 11/17/00, Part II/p. B10, Jan Stuart

A match made in heaven, or some crazy place. He's a sculptor. She's a schoolgirl. He's married. She doesn't care. He's old enough to be her father. She wants to lose her virginity. He says "to-may-to." She says "to-may-to" He says "po-tay-to," she says "whatever."

In truth, vegetables are one of the few implements the two lovers in "Lies" don't pound each other with. Who has time to go to the grocers when you're locked up in some hotel room, reinventing the Kama Sutra by way of the Marquis de Sade?

Directed by Jang Sun Woo, the self-styled bad boy of Korean cinema, "Lies" is an appropriately obsessive movie about obsession. Two people meet, fall in lust, and the lust transforms to love through a shared fondness for sadomasochistic sex and a mutual willingness to shrug off their lives in the name of round-the-clock gratification.

A 38-year-old sculptor J (Lee Sang Hyun) meets a high schooler Y (Kim Tae Yeon) through her best friend. By the standards of Y's abuse-prone home life, J's insatiable need for S&M sex offers her the possibility of love that is tame by comparison and perversely comforting in its familiarity. Before long, J and Y are engaging in endless couplings that push the envelope of pain and leave both with welts. The further they take it, the happier they are.

Sound fascinating? It is, for about 10 minutes. Stretching on for almost two hours, "Lies" reasserts how tedious the naked actor can become without a story to play. Neither of Jang's leads had ever acted before, and the most interesting segments of the film capture them as themselves, pondering the graphic nature of their assignments.

Unsurprisingly, true intimacy eluded the two neophytes. Says the director in the press notes, "The man told me that he really did fall in love with Y during the shoot, although he wasn't sure if it was with the actress or the character. The actress, conversely, didn't warm to him during the shoot and sometimes found the whole thing very difficult. She now says that she likes him very much, but the shoot, of course, is over."

There is always the sequel.

SIGHT AND SOUND, 3/00, p. 48, Tony Rayns

When her classmate Woori starts doting on the work of the sculptor J, smalltown high-school girl Y impulsively phones the artist in Seoul and finds herself proposing a blind date. They rendezvous in Andong, and the 18-year-old willingly and voluptuously surrenders her virginity to the 38 year-old man in a 'love motel'. They begin a series of sexual assignations. On their second day Y allows J to whip her during foreplay. Soon, strenuous beatings and whippings form a large part of their love play.

J spends three months in Paris where his wife G studies art. While he is away, Y enters college to read Statistics. The liaison resumes when J returns, but when Y cries during a beating J invites her to beat him instead. This sets the pattern for their future lovemaking. Still living at home, Y grows irritated by her brother's interference in her life. J is invited back to Paris to lecture, but returns to Korea early.

Y's brother discovers the affair and sets fire to J's house. Y joins J on a cross-country odyssey, hiding in hotels and living on savings and borrowed money. One day Y carves "My love" on J's inner thigh. But when Y learns that her brother has died in a road crash (she earlier sabotaged his motorbike), she abruptly announces she will go home and resume her college courses. The abandoned J is devastated.

Some time later J is living with G in Paris when he gets a call from Y. She is in CdG airport, en route to Brazil. He drops everything to join her and finds she's travelling with nothing but her old school uniform and the pole from a garden hoe to administer a beating. Later, J reflects forlornly that he never saw Y again and recalls that when G asked about his inner-thigh 'tattoo' he began to tell her lies.

Jang Sun-Woo's deliciously witty film deals with the polarities which underlie all relationships: honesty and dishonesty, trust and distrust, bravery and cowardice. But since Jang explores these issues in the main through sex and fladge scenes, early reactions to the film have followed the pattern set when Oshima premiered *In the Realm of the Senses* 25 years ago; little discussion has risen above the level of asking whether or not it's boring to watch naked people beating each other and having sex—or asking whether or not the film is a turn-on. Some viewers may well find *Lies* erotic (after all, some viewers find Laurel and Hardy films titillating), but that really isn't the point.

Lies was intended by its producer Shin Chul as a deliberate challenge to Korean censorship; the novel (Jang Jung-Il's fourth) was banned, recalled and pulped less than a month after it was published in 1996, and the author subsequently had to serve two months in jail as a "pornographer". Jang Sun-Woo had already filmed an adaptation of Jang Jung-Il's second novel *(To You From Me/Neo-ege Narul Bonenda* 1994, an acid satire of social climbing, creativity and plagiarism in the Korean literary scene) and was initially reluctant to tackle another for fear of repeating himself. Talked into making the film, Jang approached it as a voyage of discovery. Working with two remarkably brave non-actors, both of whom volunteered for the project after reading the script, he took it as a quasi-documentary about an evolving 'outlaw' relationship which happens to involve whips, birch twigs, ropes and poles. Visibly unfaked, the fladge scenes are more a record of the actors' inventiveness and fortitude than prurient celebrations of sado masochism. Their DIY qualities couldn't be further from the sleek fetishism and scrotum-nailing of Barbet Schroeder's *Maîtresse*.

J and Y's retreat into their own sexual fantasies has a real transgressive force in a Confucian work-ethic society such as Korea, underlined by the scenes in which marginal characters (hear-no-evil taxi drivers, morally flexible motel managers, fellow passengers on trains and subways) react to the couple's frank and overt interest in sex. In one of the few loaded lines of dialogue, Y remarks that she doesn't want to sign a public petition because she doesn't want to be just one of a million: "I'd rather live in a society which respects individuality."

But the thrust of the story is more psychological than social. J (whose backstory closely resembles author Jang Jung-Il's biography) throws himself into an illicit, adulterous relationship in which he feels increasingly comfortable with the 'passive' role—but is nonetheless poleaxed by the discovery that his love object can deliver the 'sadistic' *coup de grace* by dispensing with his services. J speaks most of the film's intermittent voiceovers, oscillating between first- and third-person references to himself and once even citing the novel in which he is a character

("According to the book this happened in Taegu, but it could have been any large city..."). Insofar as this overgrown adolescent travels a trajectory, it's towards the Buñuel-like realisation that 'lies' are all but indissoluble from the lineaments of gratified desire.

For Jang Sun-Woo, though, 'lies' are also synonymous with 'fiction'. He roots the film in documentary, using clips from audition tapes to introduce the two lead actors in the opening minutes and in one early scene pulling back from the action to show the crew intervening to stop an improvised fight scene which has gone a little too far. These strategies mesh with Kim Woo-Hyung's deliberately informal, handheld cinematography to give the entire film a non-fiction undercurrent.

At the same time, he uses every playful device at hand to italicise the film's storytelling functions, from quirky voiceovers and chapter headings to slow-motion and bleached-out images. His own trajectory (already amply suggested by his earlier films, from the neorealist *Lovers of Woomuk-Baemi/Woomuk-Baemi ul Sarang*, 1989, to the Buddhist myth rethought as social critique which is *Hwa-om-kyung*, (1993) is towards lies which tell credible truths. This splendid film confirms him as one of contemporary cinema's most persuasive liars.

VILLAGE VOICE, 11/21/00, p. 135, J. Hoberman

I read someplace (it might even have been last week's *Village Voice*) that Korean food was the cuisine du jour. If so, it's appropriate that Jang Sun Woo's *Lies*—nothing less than the hottest movie in South Korean history—opened at the Screening Room, Tribeca's fashionable movie house cum restaurant.

Lay on that five-alarm kimchi: *Lies* tells the tale of the virginal schoolgirl "Y" and the 38-year-old sculptor "J," who embark on an obsessive affair that, beginning with a graphic three-orifice defloration in a cramped hotel room, escalates into full-blown amour fou, complete with consensual s&m slugfest. Some things were meant to be. By the second passionate tryst, J is asking Y if he can beat her; afterward, she happily shows her friend the welts. (Not long after, she starts setting the erotic agenda.) *Variety* estimates that 90 percent of *Lies* is devoted to sex scenes. There's an abundance of action—kinky and otherwise—which, voyeuristically shot by a roving camera and characterized by a naturalistic struggling out of clothes, doesn't entirely seem to be faked.

Does the camera not lie? Jang, who maintains that both performers confided in him that "they could enjoy the whippings and beatings" and that this "probably lent [their scenes] a certain credibility," is the arch transgressor of South Korea's increasingly daring filmmakers. (His previous feature, a quasi-documentary on Seoul street kids, had the flavorsome title *Timeless Bottomless Bad Movie*.) *Lies* was made to shock, as well as to challenge local censorship—based, as it was, on a notorious Korean novel that was published in 1996 and immediately banned and pulped as pornographic. The author Jang Jung Il (no relation to Jang Sun Woo) was sentenced to six months in prison.

Intermittently, *Lies* complicates its truth with self-reflection. J provides a voice-over, even at one point referring to the novel in which he is a character. There's a scene that's broken up by the director and an introduction in which the principals, Lee Sang Hyun (a real-life sculptor) and Kim Tae Yeon (a fashion model), neither of whom had ever acted in a movie before, are interviewed as to their feelings about appearing, mainly nude, in so explicit a drama. Y's avid, bemused personality—or is it Kim's?—complements J's dogged single-mindedness. So does the film. Jang ignores the interlude in which J leaves for three months in Paris, picking up the narrative only with the sculptor's return to Korea, where J goes straight from the airport to the college campus where Y is studying statistics.

Appropriate to its celebration of antisocial individualism, *Lies* is shot in a loose, semi-vérité style; it has a jagged construction and a fresh, jazzy look. Jang is fond of using a wide-angle lens in narrow spaces or shooting a scene from the perspective of an elevator surveillance camera. The music pulsates; the sex scenes are sometimes pixelated to enhance their mania. The movie is not without perverse humor. Nor is it entirely devoid of tenderness—even when the beatings, now administered by Y, get a bit more extreme. After Y's jealous brother burns down J's house, the couple—who often suggest a pair of sulky babies—begin a voyage from motel to motel, living on sex, fladge, and J's maxed-out credit card.

At once distanced and heedless, *Lies* manages to be lighter and less pretentious than any description suggests. The movie's playful aspect can't be denied. There's a priceless scene wherein J and Y are rummaging around a construction site, oblivious to the workaday world in their search for a suitable thwacker. Not for nothing has Jang described the couple's total self-absorption as a failed utopia, the "dream of living, eating, and fucking without having to work."

Also reviewed in:
NEW YORK TIMES, 11/17/00, E31, Elvis Mitchell
VARIETY, 9/20-26/99, p. 89, David Stratton

LIFE IS TO WHISTLE

A New Yorker Films release of an ICAIC and Wanda Distribution S.A. production. *Director:* Fernando Pérez. *Screenplay (Spanish with English subtitles):* Fernando Pérez, Humberto Jiménez, and Eduardo Del Llano. *Director of Photography:* Raúl Pérez Ureta. *Editor:* Julia Yip. *Music:* Edesio Alejandro. *Sound:* Ricardo Istuete. *Costumes:* Miriam Duenas. *Make-up:* Maria Elena Del Toro. *Running time:* 106 minutes. *MPAA Rating:* Not Rated.

CAST: Luis Alberto García (Elpidio Valdés); Coralia Veloz (Julia); Claudia Rojas (Mariana); Bebé Pérez (Bebé); Isabel Santos (Chrissy); Rolando Brito (Dr. Fernando); Joan Manuel Reyes (Ismael); Mónica Guffanti (Mme. Garces); Luis Ubaldo Benítez (Settimio); Jorge Molina (Bicitaxista); Miguel A. Daranas (Director Asilo).

CHRISTIAN SCIENCE MONITOR, 1/7/00, p. 17, David Sterritt

The political and economic barriers cutting Cuba off from the United States have not kept Cuban movies entirely away from American audiences.

Cuban films have been a rare commodity, though, despite the many viewers who might welcome them if given a chance. Recent years have seen only a few releases on US screens, and only the late Tomis Gutiérrez Alea has gained recognition as a world-class director on a par with giants of European and Asian film.

This may be changing. New York's influential Film Society of Lincoln Center has paid commendable attention to Cuban cinema during the past year, helping to raise Cuba's profile within the American film community. Now its Walter Reade Theater is continuing the trend by hosting the theatrical premières of two major productions that will soon go into national release.

While these movies differ in tone and quality, both exemplify key characteristics of Cuban films made after the Communist revolution four decades ago. One expresses fascination with ordinary people living ordinary lives. The other—also reflected by "Buena Vista Social Club," the recent Wim Wenders documentary—has a hearty appreciation of how art and culture can enrich everyday experience.

The more exciting of the new releases, "Life Is to Whistle" by Fernando Pérez, is an adventurous blend of high drama, low comedy, and experimental storytelling techniques. The narrator is a teenage girl whose hyperactive imagination churns out a string of interlocking tales. Among the characters she dreams up are a young ballerina who vows to give up men if she can dance a cherished role; a worker whose mysterious fainting fits turn out to have an amusing cause; and various others who cross one another's paths in unexpected ways.

As its title suggests, "Life is to Whistle" sees music and fun as essential parts of human fulfillment, even if these admirable activities aren't always as readily available as we'd wish.

Music is also at the heart of "If You Only Understood" by Rolando Diaz, a "musical documentary" about a Cuban filmmaker prowling Havana in search of a black woman to star in his next picture.

Painting a multifaceted portrait of contemporary Cuban life, the film doesn't hesitate to criticize the racism, sexism, and economic inequality that cause daily unhappiness for many of the women—a nurse, an engineer, a playwright, and others—who candidly discuss their lives before the camera. Although it will appeal most strongly to moviegoers with a special interest in Cuban culture, "If You only Understood" is recommended viewing for anyone seeking a deeper understanding of this rich and varied society.

NEW YORK POST, 1/7/00, p. 44, Hannah Brown

[*Life is to Whistle* was reviewed jointly with *If Only You Understood;* see Brown's review of that film.]

NEWSDAY, 1/7/00, Part II/p. B9, John Anderson

[*Life is to Whistle* was reviewed jointly with *If Only You Understood*; see Anderson's review of that film.]

VILLAGE VOICE, 1/11/00, p. 112, Elliott Stein

[*Life is to Whistle* was reviewed jointly with *If Only You Understood*; see Stein's review of that film.]

Also reviewed in:
CHICAGO TRIBUNE, 6/9/00, Friday/p. K, John Petrakis
NEW YORK TIMES, 1/7/00, p. E12, Stephen Holden
VARIETY, 7/26-8/1/99, p. 36, Jonathan Holland

LIFE AND TIMES OF HANK GREENBERG, THE

A Cowboy Booking International release of a Ciesla Foundation presentation. *Producer:* Aviva Kempner. *Director:* Aviva Kempner. *Screenplay:* Aviva Kempner. *Director of Photography:* Thomas Kaufman, Jerry Feldman, Kevin Hewitt, Tom Hurwitz, Christopher Li, and Scott Mumford. *Editor:* Marian Sears Hunter. *Music:* Henry Sapoznik. *Sound Editor:* Ira Spiegel. *Running time:* 95 minutes. *MPAA Rating:* Not Rated.

CAST: Ira Berkow, Alan M. Dershowitz, Bob Feller, Charlie Gehringer, Hank Greenberg, Kenesaw M. Landis, Carl Levin, Walter Matthau, Michael Moriarty, Hal Newhouser, Maury Povich, Shirley Povich, Dick Schaap, (themselves);   Franklin Delano Roosevelt (uncredited/archive footage).

CHRISTIAN SCIENCE MONITOR, 1/14/00, p. 15, David Sterritt

Who could resist a movie that begins with a rousing chorus of "Take Me Out to the Ball Game,"sung by actor Mandy Patinkin—in Yiddish?

Its an appropriate opening pitch for "The Life and Times of Hank Greenberg," a warmly human look at the career of major-league baseball's most famous Jewish star.

Hailed by some as a Moses of the athletic world, Greenberg was also attacked by bigots with anti-Semitic agendas inside and outside the ballpark.

He took the best and worst of it in stride, emerging as a hugely popular figure who embodied the best that sports have to offer. Aviva Kempner's movie pays exactly the sort of tribute he deserves without making exaggerated claims for him as a personal or professional icon.

Greenberg entered pro baseball in the early '30s, becoming a superstar in 1938 when he almost broke Babe Ruth's record for hitting the most home runs in a season. He left the playing field after 1947—an unwanted move from the Detroit Tigers to the Pittsburgh Pirates helped speed his retirement—and spent several years as a front-office executive.

Although his outlook on life was secular rather than religious, he recognized his status as a Jewish role model and cultivated a suitable public image. Should he play on Rosh Hashana, violating a holy day but helping his team cinch the pennant? Yes, said a rabbi who advised him, and who surely cheered when Greenberg's two homers helped win the game. Should he play on Yom Kippur, the year's holiest day? Greenberg went to his synagogue instead—earning a different kind of cheer from his admirers, even though the Tigers lost that game without him.

It took an umpire to stop members of the Chicago Cubs from hurling anti-Jewish slurs at Greenberg during a World Series game in 1935, but he seemed strengthened by such experiences. When the legendary Jackie Robinson broke the color barrier during Greenberg's last year as a player, drawing a barrage of racist hostility, the Jewish-American star knew what the African-American rookie was facing. In later years, Robinson, remembered Greenberg as the first player from an opposing team to give him moral and practical support.

Kempner captures her hero's career in its social and political context, but never loses sight of baseball's sheer fun and Greenberg's simple humanity. Additional color comes from on-screen interviews with fans as different as lawyer Alan Dershowitz, politician Carl Levin, and actor Walter Matthau, who recalls joining a country club just to hang out with his big-league acquaintance,

In short, you don't have to be a baseball fan to enjoy "The Life and Times of Hank Greenberg."

LOS ANGELES TIMES, 5/19/00, Calendar/p. 6, Kenneth Turan

Firebrand attorney Alan Dershowitz thought this man would be America!s first Jewish president. Carl Levin, senator from Michigan, said he validated the American dream. And Walter Matthau joined the Beverly Hills Tennis Club even though he didn't play in the hopes of having the occasional lunch with him. Such was the power and charisma of Henry Benjamin Greenberg, also know as Hammerin' Hank.

As revealed in "The Life and Times of Hank Greenberg," Aviva Kempner's warm and intelligent mash note to a man who clearly deserved it, Greenberg was not only the best kind of heroic personality—charming, unassuming, quietly confident—but a legend to two different groups.

To baseball fans, Greenberg had the kind of accomplishments that made his election to the Hall of Fame a formality. A lifetime .313 hitter, he had 183 RBIs in 1937, just one short of the record at that time, and the following year he hit 58 home runs, coming within two of Babe Ruth's then-record. Baseball's initial $100,000 earner, he was also the first person to be selected as a league most valuable player at two positions (first base and outfield). And, says Detroit Tiger teammate Charlie Gehringer, if he could select a single player from the sport's history to be at bat when a run was needed, he'd pick Greenberg over anyone, Joe DiMaggio and Ted Williams included.

To America's Jews, however, Greenberg was more than a great player, he was the baseball Moses. Called the first major Jewish celebrity to be famous for athletic abilities, Greenberg defied the stereotypes of what a Jew could and could not do at a time when Nazism was on the rise and domestic anti-Semitism was being fomented by Henry Ford and Father Coughlin. Not a religious man, he was nevertheless unapologetic about his Judaism, and his determination to be himself at all times and all costs made other Jews feel like giant killers by proxy.

Writer-director-producer Kempner, whose first film (as co-writer and producer) was "Partisans of Vilna" about Jewish resistance during World War II, worked 13 years on this affectionate portrait of a very different kind of hero, a 6-foot-4 slugger who swung three bats to warm up and played at a time when, one fan remembers in awe, "no one ever saw a Jew that big."

The son of immigrant parents who were not initially thrilled to have a potential ballplayer for a son, Greenberg grew up in the Bronx with a thirst for baseball in general and driving in men in scoring position in particular that never left him. "Women, food, home runs, they were fine," says someone who knew him. "But RBIs were the thing he lived for."

Signed by the Detroit Tigers, Greenberg's first year in organized ball was with Beaumont in the Texas League, where one teammate was shocked to meet a Jew who did not have horns on his head. This was the early 1930s, when a New York cop who stopped the young man for running a traffic light could insist, "Who in the hell ever heard of a Greenberg being a baseball player?"

In fact, Greenberg was not a graceful player, but he was extremely hard-working, a student of the game given to studying himself obsessively in mirrors until his swing became a potent offensive weapon. "When Hank comes up to the plate, Ball, you're going to be out late," ran one popular song about his hitting. "Goodbye, Mr. Ball, goodbye."

Greenberg was just as determined to shrug off the racial slurs that were a constant refrain while he was on the field, with some teams even bringing up especially virulent bigots from their farm teams to ride Greenberg from the bench during crucial series.

The baseball and Jewish sides of Greenberg's celebrity came together at the end of the 1934 season, when he decided to play on Rosh Hashana, the Jewish New Year, on the advice of a rabbi who is said to have consulted the Talmud before giving his OK. Greenberg hit two home runs, the Tigers won the pennant, and the Detroit Free Press printed "Happy New Year" in Hebrew as its headline. When Greenberg sat out the even holier day of Yom Kippur, his stock as a man of principle soared.

Filmmaker Kempner tells this and other tales with the help of rarely seen archival footage, a pair of on-camera conversations Greenberg did a few years before his death in 1985, and nearly 50 other interviews. Some of these, with teammates and family members (include his divorced first wife, department store heiress Caral Gimbel) are expected, while others, like talking to actor Michael Moriarty, the grandson of a man who umpired several of Greenberg's key games, are fascinatingly not.

In one of the story's most potent coincidences, Greenberg's last year in the majors, 1947, was the first for a young player named Jackie Robinson. The intense razzing Greenberg took paled before what Robinson was to experience, and when the two men literally collided on the field (Greenberg spent his final season in the National League) the older player took the time to give his younger colleague some encouragement. Robinson's comments on that moment is an eloquent coda to this involving, heartfelt film. "Mr. Greenberg," he told reporters at the time, "has class. It stands out all over him." Indeed it does.

NEW YORK POST, 1/12/00, p. 47, Lou Lumenick

More than a sports documentary, "The Life and Times of Hank Greenberg" makes a good case that the baseball Hall of Famer was "the most important American Jew of the 1930s," as Alan Dershowitz calls him.

Greenberg was not the first member of his faith to play in the major leagues, but he was the first Jewish star, and a deeply principled man who, as one elderly fan remembers in the movie, "wore his Jewishness on his sleeve."

And that was extremely important to a lot of people during his playing years, 1933 to 1947, which coincided with Hitler's rise to power and World War II. As Dershowitz puts it: "He was what they said we couldn't be."

Though in 1938, with 58 dingers, he came within a single home run of matching Babe Ruth's single-season record. Greenberg is probably equally well-remembered for sitting out a crucial pennant-race game on Yom Kippur.

Raised in The Bronx, Greenberg turned down an offer from the Yankees (his favored position, first base, was nailed down by Lou Gehrig) and spent most of his playing career in Detroit, a city rife with such notorious anti-Semites as Henry Ford and Father Coughlin.

The taunts, Greenberg recalls in an interview filmed 50 years later, were "a spur to me to do better—I could never fall asleep on the ball field."

Greenberg enlisted in 1941, and served in World War II. He returned to Detroit in 1945 for two more brilliant seasons, before he was traded to Pittsburgh.

Writer-director Aviva Kempner crafted this love letter to Greenberg by imaginatively weaving interviews with great footage from newsreels and feature films.

The main flaws? The film gives short shrift to Greenberg's post-playing life, which included front-office jobs in Cleveland and Chicago. Kempner is also vague about her subject's romantic life.

"The Life and Times of Hank Greenberg," the rare baseball film that doesn't focus on New York players, hits one out of the park.

NEWSDAY, 1/12/00, Part II/p. B9, John Anderson

When Hank Greenberg entered the minor leagues in Beaumont, Texas, he surprised at least one teammate, who thought all Jews had horns. Early in his 13-year career with the Detroit Tigers, an inquisitive traffic cop refused to believe that anybody named Greenberg could be a professional ballplayer. And during the 1935 World Series with Chicago, an umpire had to stop a game because of the volume and velocity of the anti-Semitic slurs being pitched at Greenberg by the opposing bench.

Greenberg happened to be one of the premier home run hitters in the major leagues. (He hit 58 in 138, two shy of Babe Ruth's then-record.) He was voted the American League's most valuable player in 1935 and '40, had a lifetime batting average of .313 and in 1956 became the first Jewish player in the National Baseball Hall of Fame. But the point of Aviva Kempner's "The Life and Times of Hank Greenberg" is not that Greenberg could hit fastballs. It's that he managed to survive and thrive despite the double burden of religious bigotry and unbridled adoration.

Greenberg was the "Moses" of baseball—No. 5 may mean Joe DiMaggio to much of New York, but to young Jewish fans (a number of whom grew up to testify in Kempner's film), it signified Hankus Pankus. As Kempner's celebrity talking heads (Walter Matthau, Alan Dershowitz) make clear, Greenberg defied Jewish stereotypes and in doing so became an idol of epic proportions. That he did it during Fascism's golden age is not an irony lost on anyone; that he could come back from World War II—after four years away from baseball—and hit a pennant-winning grand slam on the last day of the '45 season gives his story the heroic proportions of myth.

But "The Life and Times of Hank Greenberg" is about a seemingly very normal person, a sad-eyed, good-natured Everyman of considerable modesty—a first baseman for most of his career, he declined to join the Yankees because he couldn't imagine displacing Lou Gehrig. Greenberg also had to work harder than most for what he achieved: Former teammates recall Greenberg hiring hot-dog vendors—or anyone else who was around—to pitch to him for extra batting practice. And although not remembered as a particularly devout Jew, he took his responsibilities as a symbol seriously; During the '34 pennant race, he played on Rosh Hashanah only because of a rabbi/baseball fan's convenient interpretation of the Talmud. On Yom Kippur, when he went to services instead of the ballpark, he got a standing ovation from the congregation.

Kempner has been working on this film for years, and as a result it has a kind of time-capsule quality. Certainly, the interview footage of Greenberg himself is at least 14 years old (he died in 1986), but some of the more recent subjects have aged so since Kempner filmed them that they and Greenberg seem almost contemporary. Nevertheless, "The Life and Times..." unspools with great affection and, unlike most documentaries, a real sense of drama. Greenberg may never have let it bother him much, but social conditions made his entire career an uphill battle. That he won, and continues to win in Kempner's movie, will make you cheer.

VILLAGE VOICE, 1/18/00, p. 111, J. Hoberman

An instance of Depression-era heroism, Aviva Kempner's *The Life and Times of Hank Greenberg* sings the song of major league baseball's first Jewish superstar. Slugging firs-baseman Hank Greenberg (1911-86) was born in the Bronx but, never a Yankee, powered the Detroit Tigers past the Bombers to consecutive American League pennants in 1934 and 1935 (with one more a decade later).

Greenberg was twice the American League's most valuable player but this scarcely describes his significance for co-religionist fans. No hyperbole is too great. This six-foot-four-inch "King of the Bronx"—"My God, nobody ever saw a Jew that big!"—was a "messiah," another "Moses," hailed here by no less an authority than Alan Dershowitz as the "single most important Jew to live in the 1930s." Playing in a city that was, as Kempner points out, the base for the two most vocal anti-Semites in America, Henry Ford and Father Coughlin, Greenberg endured a fair amount of abuse. But, where other Jewish ballplayers might have changed their names to conceal their identities, Greenberg actually refused to play on Yom Kippur—during a pennant race no less!

The first ballplayer to earn $100,000, Greenberg spent the 1938 season chasing Babe Ruth's home-run record. Dershowitz expresses gratitude that Greenberg fell two short. Better he be perceived as hitting his homers against Hitler—Greenberg was the first baseball star to join the army, enlisting even before Pearl Harbor. Although scarcely observant, Greenberg was both a paradigm of Jewish pride and proof of Jewish acceptance in America. In this, his equivalent is Bess Myerson, a somewhat younger daughter of the Bronx who, declared Miss America in September 1945, symbolized the post-World War II transformation of the immigrant Jew from "oriental" Other to white American. Ignominiously traded to the Pittsburgh Pirates, Greenberg played his last season in 1947, as Jackie Robinson embarked on his first—a historical coincidence that Kempner usefully illuminates.

Treating its hero as sui generis, Kempner's film ignores the existence of the Jewish strongman Zisha Breitbart, contemporary boxers like heavyweight champ Max Baer, quarterback Sid Luckman, and even the period's other Jewish ballplayers; (Moe Berg, "Harry the Horse" Danning, Sid Gordon), let alone the longing for Jewish power expressed in the Zionist call for new *Muskeljuden*. In the absence of any greater cultural context, the ritual reiteration of Greenberg's greatness grows wearisome. Full of fans, family, and too much "Bei Mir Bist Du Schoen," *Hank Greenberg is* a cozy affair that leaves the impression of a filmmaker too close to the material.

Also reviewed in:
NEW YORK TIMES, 1/12/00, p. E5, Lawrence Van Gelder
VARIETY, 7/19-25/99, p. 29, Dennis Harvey
WASHINGTON POST, 5/26/00, p. C1, Stephen Hunter
WASHINGTON POST, 5/26/00, Weekend/p. 52, Desson Howe

LIFESTYLE, THE: GROUP SEX IN THE SUBURBS

A Seventh Art Releasing release of a Dan Cogan/Good Machine/Swinging T Productions production. *Executive Producer:* Ted Hope, James Schamus, and Mary Jane Skalski. *Producer:* Dan Cogan. *Director:* David Schisgall. *Director of Photography:* Peter Hawkins. *Editor:* Andrew Hafitz. *Music:* Byron Estep and Eddie Sperry. *Sound:* David McJunkin. *Sound Editor:* Rick Freeman. *Running time:* 78 minutes. *MPAA Rating:* Not Rated.

NEW YORK POST, 3/16/00, p. 50, Jonathan Foreman

One of most provocative documentaries to come along in years, this daringly explicit journey into the world of suburban swingers is by turns hilarious, touching and just plain weird. If only Stanley Kubrick could have seen "The Lifestyle: Group Sex in the Suburbs" before he made "Eyes Wide Shut."

At the very least, he would have learned from the middle-aged swingers interviewed—and shown in full-frontal action—that real orgies are held in suburban houses, not castles, that the participants tend to prefer karaoke to pseudo-religious rituals, and that "People always bring a potluck."

Director David Schisgall's fascinating, provocative documentary, the kind that keeps you arguing for hours afterward, makes it clearer than ever that the inhabitants of Middle America's suburbs can be kinkier and weirder than the most decadent New Yorkers.

At times hilarious, it has some sad and even grotesque moments. But in the end you're struck by the diversity and decency of these middle-aged, middle-class sexual outlaws—and impressed that so many of them have marriages that can apparently withstand the corrosive stresses of swinging.

Still, perhaps most shocking about "The Lifestyle" is the way it shatters one of the great taboos of American popular culture—the notion that only the young, beautiful and toned should engage in sexual activity—by showing older people with sagging bodies actually doing it, and doing it a lot.

"The Lifestyle" concentrates on one group of swingers in conservative Orange County, Calif., though there are swing clubs in every state of the union except North Dakota. (Who knows why?) The director also visits a "lifestyle" convention in Las Vegas.

There's no narration: Unlike so many documentarians, Schisgall resists the temptation to make it a film about himself and allows his subjects to speak for themselves.

Some of them reveal more than they intend about their marriages—especially as one spouse is invariably keener on swinging than the other.

But few of these people—all of them extraordinarily conventional in everything but their sex lives—are as debased or dishonest as the pathetic exhibitionists you see on TV talk shows like "Jerry Springer."

There are questions that "The Lifestyle" leaves unanswered—like why swinging should be an activity confined mainly to the middle-aged and older.

But even so, if s a welcome and satisfying antidote to the glossy, fake Hollywood version of sexuality: It reveals the sheer ordinariness of even extraordinary sex and contrasts it with the things that these swingers really care about: friendship, love and (naked) barbecues on the Fourth of July.

VILLAGE VOICE, 3/21/00, p. 144, Michael Atkinson

David Schisgall's *The Lifestyle*, subtitled *Group Sex in the Suburbs*, tells us more than we ever wanted to know about America's lumpy, lumpen middle class staging everythingathons and crowing proudly about it. Like an endless episode of HBO's *Real Sex*, Schisgall's movie dallies enough with loveless sport-fucking to make it depressing, particularly when you consider the padded playrooms, basement bars, and preponderance of overweight Barbara and George Bush-like couples wearing "Hi My Name Is" stickers. Monogamy never looked so good.

Also reviewed in:
NEW YORK TIMES, 3/16/00, p. E3, Stephen Holden
VARIETY, 4/26-5/2/99, p. 47, Todd McCarthy

LIGHTHOUSE

A Unapix Films release of a Tungsten Pictures/Winchester Films production.   *Executive Producer:* Chris Craib and Gary Smith. *Producer:* Mark Leake and Tim Dennison.   *Director:* Simon Hunter. *Screenplay:* Simon Hunter.   *Director of Photography:* Tony Imi.   *Music:* Paul Green and Debbie Wiseman. *Production Designer:* Simon Bowles. *Special Effects:* Paul Hyett. *Costumes:* Linda Alderson. *Running time:* 95 minutes. *MPAA Rating:* R.

CAST: James Purefoy (Prisoner Richard Spader); Rachel Shelley (Dr. Kirsty McCloud); Chris Adamson (Leo Rook); Paul Brooke (Captain Campbell); Don Warrington (Prison Officer Ian Goslet);   Chris Dunne (Chief Prison Officer O'Neil);   Bob Goody (Weevil); Pat Kelman (Spoons);   Norman Mitchell (Brownlow);   Jason Round (Spitfield);

NEW YORK POST, 2/4/00, p. 55, Lou Lumenick

"Lighthouse," a rare example of a slasher movie from Britain, is several cuts above the norm for the genre.

Debuting writer-director Simon Hunter makes clever use of his novel setting, a remote lighthouse hundreds of miles off the English coast.

When a prison boat sinks nearby, the half-dozen survivors who make their way to shore discover that a serial killer (Chris Adamson), having escaped undetected from the vessel, has already decapitated the lighthouse staff.

The killer soon turns his attentions to the group trapped in the disabled lighthouse, most prominently a plucky but troubled psychologist (Rachel Shelley) and a convicted murderer (James Purefoy of "Mansfield Park") who proclaims his innocence at regular intervals.

A scene in which a potential victim hides from the white-shoed killer in a toilet stall is as suspenseful as any in recent memory.

Hunter doesn't stint on the gore, but his artfully composed and edited images help compensate for the coincidence—heavy plot and colorless performances by a cast with thick British accents.

"Lighthouse" should delight fans of the genre—and may well land Hunter a Hollywood project.

Also reviewed in:
NEW YORK TIMES, 2/4/00, p. E12, Stephen Holden

LITTLE GIRL WHO SOLD THE SUN, THE

A California Newsreel release of a Maag Daan/Waka Films/Renardes Productions co-production. *Producer:* Djibril Diop Mambety. *Director:* Djibril Diop Mambety. *Screenplay (French and Wolof with English subtitles):* Djibril Diop Mambety. *Director of Photography:* Jacques Besse. *Editor:* Sarah Taouss Matton. *Music:* Wasis Diop. *Running time:* 45 minutes. *MPAA Rating:* Not Rated.

CAST: Lissa Baléra (Sili); Tayerou M'Baye (Babou); Oumou Samb (Crazy Woman); Moussa Bald (Boy in Wheelchair); Dieynaba Laam (Grandmother); Martin N'Gom (Gang Leader).

NEW YORK POST, 4/26/00, p. 50, Hannah Brown

[*The Little Girl Who Sold the Sun* was reviewed jointly with *Throne of Death*; see Brown's review of that film.]

VILLAGE VOICE, 5/2/00, p. 125, J. Hoberman

If *The Idiots* [see Hoberman's review] plumbs the depths of smirky neo-primitivism, the two short features paired this week are exemplary instances of the sophisticated primitivism that used to be called *Third Way* cinema. Senegalese filmmaker Djibril Diop Mambety's *The Little Girl Who Sold the Sun* and Indian director Murali Nair's *Throne of Death* are both sardonic, stylized parables of underdevelopment in which vivid nonactors perform, as though partaking in village rituals, against documentary backdrops of tropical splendor.

Throne of Death, which won the Camera d'Or for best first film last year at Cannes, is a satire of Indian politics. Caught stealing coconuts to feed his starving family, a hapless tenant farmer is jailed and falsely accused of an old, unsolved murder. Because it is an election year, his case becomes an issue. The local Communist hacks take a break from pondering the situation in Kosovo to organize a mass meeting—although once these comrades read about the new "electronic chair" imported from America (with the help of a World Bank loan), they shift from demanding the farmer's freedom to insisting on his right to enjoy a modern "blissful" death. The movie has bite, although its paradisal setting (in the southern state of Kerala) mitigates much of the pain. The village may lack electricity and running water but the palm tree beachscape exudes utter tranquility—not least in framing the farmer's grotesque apotheosis.

Considerably more affirmative, *The Little Girl Who Sold the Sun* is framed as a marketplace legend: "This story is a hymn to the courage of street children." Sili, an indomitable crippled girl, the granddaughter of a blind street singer, reinvents herself as a vendor of the local newspaper *Soleil* (hence the title). To spread the news, as it were, she must prevail over mercenary cops and the bullying of jealous rivals. A live wire bent to some new design, Sili galvanizes the neighborhood. In one scene, a group of girls dance behind her, imitating her hobbled gait in a form of celebration. (The wonderful percolating score is by the filmmaker's younger brother, the singer Wasis Diop.)

A bold, vibrant, and splashy 45 minutes, *The Little Girl Who Sold the Sun* was the last film completed by the talented Mambety before his death in Paris two summers ago. His legacy is similarly concentrated—two remarkable features, *Touki Bouki* and *Hyenas*, which will be showing as part of the Sixth African Film Festival next month.

Also reviewed in:
NEW YORK TIMES, 4/26/00, p. E5, Stephen Holden
VARIETY, 3/22-28/99, p. 42, David Stratton

LITTLE NICKY

A New Line Cinema relase of a Happy Madison production in association with the RSC media. *Executive Producer:* Robert Engelman, Adam Sandler, Michael De Luca, and Brian Witten. *Producer:* Robert Simonds and Jack Giarraputo.   *Director:* Steven Brill. *Screenplay:* Tim Herlihy, Adam Sandler, and Steven Brill.   *Director of Photography:* Theo Van De Sande. *Editor:* Jeff Gourson. *Music:* Teddy Castellucci. *Music Editor:* J.J. George and Stuart Grusin. *Sound:* James Sabat, David Kelson, and (music) Gabe Veltri.   *Casting:* Roger Mussenden. *Production Designer:* Perry Andelin Blake.   *Art Director:* Alan Au and Don Woodruff. *Set Designer:* Luis Hoyos, Greg Hooper, Gary Lee, Domenic Silvestri, Patte Strong-Lord, and Robert Woodruff.   *Set Decorator:* Rick Simpson. *Set Dresser:* William Maxwell, Gary Kudroff, Benton E. Tedlie, Joe Pfaltzgraf, and Adam Austin.   *Special Effects:* Terry Frazeee.   *Visual Effects:* Dave Moulder.   *Costumes:* Ellen Lutter.   *Make-up:* Michael Mills.   *Make-up (Patricia Arquette):* Debbie Zoller.   *Stunt Coordinator:* Jeff Imada.   *Running time:* 84 minutes.   *MPAA Rating:* PG-13.

CAST: Adam Sandler (Nicky); Patricia Arquette (Valerie); Harvey Keitel (Dad); Rhys Ifans (Adrian); Tommy "Tiny" Lister, Jr. (Cassius); Rodney Dangerfield (Lucifer); Allen Covert (Todd); Peter Dante (Peter); Jonathan Loughran (John); Robert Smigel (Beefy); Reese Witherspoon (Holly);   Dana Carvey (Referee);   Jon Lovitz (Peeper);   Kevin Nealon (Gatekeeper);   Michael McKean (Chief of Police);   Quentin Tarantino (Deacon);   Carl Weathers (Chubbs); Blake Clark (Jimmy the Demon); Rob Schneider (The Townie); John Witherspoon (Street Vendor); Clint Howard (Nipples); Leah Lail (Christa); Jackie Titone (Jenna);   Mannie Jackson (Harlem Globetrotters Coach);   Frank Sivero (Alumni Hall Announcer); Lewis Arquette (Cardinal); George Wallace (Mayor); Christopher Carroll (Hitler); Ellen Cleghorne (Mom); Reggie McFadden (Dad); Philip D. Bolden (Son); Laura Harring (Mrs. Dunleavy);   Isaiah Griffin (Scottie Dunleavy);   Brandon Rosenberg (Baby Zacariah);   Kevin Grady (Fitzie);   Jodi Outman (Roney);   Erinn Bartlett (Fenner);   Sal Cavaliere (Sal the Demon);   Henry Winkler, Ozzy Osbourne, Bill Walton, Regis Philbin, and Sylvia Lopez (Themselves);   Sid Ganis (Weatherman);   Todd Holland and Gerard "Sheck" Bugge (Reformered Demons);   Mary Brill (Church Woman);   Suzanne Frydman (Pregnant Woman); John Kirk (Young Man); Tom McNulty (Screaming Man); Michael Giarraputo (Half Court Shot Fan); Fred Wolf (Fan); David Sardi (Popeyes Cashier); Tom Winkler and John Farley (Human Dartboards);   Tim Young (Cop);   Troy Brown (Beating Cop);   Eli Wolstan (Vendor Cop); Michael Charles Roman, Peter Tambakis, and John White (Kids); Jeff Imada (Chinese Delivery Guy);   Radioman (Bum in Alley);   Mary Diveny (Lady in Park); Stuart Rudin (Bus Shelter Bum); Ng Thanh Nhan (Korean Vendor); Michael Goldfinger (Nut Vendor);   Peter Linardi (Fat Guy);   Ricco Bueno (Gardener);   Lynn Wilson (Mother with Carriage); Lillian Adams (Old Lady at Game); Andrew L. Mensch (Boy); Gwendolyn G. Yeager (Fan); Joe Griffo (Evil Little Person); Cindy Sorenson (Female Little Person); Jake McKinnon (Big Bird);   Michael Deak (Gary the Monster);   J. Graysen Stubbs (Church Kid); Ruth Annesi (Woman in Audience); Vincenetta Gunn (Angry Woman); Howard Berger, Luke Khanlian, and David Wogh (Puppeteers).

LOS ANGELES TIMES, 11/10/00, Calendar/p. 1, Kenneth Turan

What can you say about Adam Sandler that hasn't been said before? To restate the obvious:

(a) He's one of the most popular of comic actors, an entertainer whose last film, "Big Daddy," had an opening weekend gross (the word is used advisedly) of more than $40 million.

(b) As a performer, he's not without ability or appeal, but the bedrock of his success is an uncanny aptitude for pandering to the gross-out appetites of teenage boys.

(c) It's to be hoped that, as Jim Carrey did with "The Truman Show," he finds a less age-restricted vehicle that makes use of his gifts.

(d) "Little Nicky" isn't it. Not even close.

A deeply unfunny fantasy comedy about a family feud between the devil's three sons, "Little Nicky" is not a dangerous movie, just a stupid one. When one of its characters says, "You will see things more horrible than you can possibly imagine," he's being more truthful than he knows.

Basically a vanity project that not only stars the comedian but is co-executive produced and co-written (with longtime collaborator Tim Herlihy and director Steven Brill) by him as well, "Little Nicky" takes you deeper Inside Adam Sandler than you may want to go. We get to see what he finds funny, what he takes seriously, what makes him choke back a tear. A visit with the Dalai Lama it's not.

The kindest thing that can be said about Sandler's sense of humor is that it's unapologetically juvenile.

Though the actor took a stab at stretching with "The Wedding Singer," "Little Nicky" caves in completely to his adolescent fan base. Who else, after all, is going to laugh at animals having sex, at a mass accident involving people in wheelchairs, or a gag shot of the title character defecating on a Manhattan street? (Yes, this film is rated PG-13. Couldn't you tell?)

Not only is the humor unrelentingly puerile (at one screening, not so much as a chuckle came from anyone old enough to vote), but "Little Nicky" also has the unnerving ability to turn its stupidest conceits into running jokes. A ponderous riff on an encounter between a pineapple and a part of Adolph Hitler's anatomy (remember, we're talking PG-13 here) was deemed good enough to reprise, and the plight of one male character with breasts on the top of his head (don't ask) gets brought back again and again and again.

"Little Nicky's" plot, such as it is, is basically skit material and not the firmest foundation for an 89-minute movie filled with millions of dollars in special effects. After a nonsensical opening involving Jon Lovitz as a Peeping Tom, we're deposited in hell, where the devil (Harvey Keitel), having ruled the nether regions since the retirement of his father (Rodney Dangerfield), is trying to decide who will be in charge for the next 10,000 years.

Mr. Evil has three sons, bad Cassius (Tommy 'Tiny' Lister Jr.), badder Adrian (Rhys Hans) and Nicky (Sandler). Nicky is the offspring no one takes seriously, especially since his brothers hit him in the head with a shovel, leaving the kid with a partially paralyzed face, a speech impediment and the general demeanor of a hopeless dweeb.

Even in the context of the other characters Sandler has played, Nicky's maladroit sick puppy persona (Ann Pala gets a "Adam Sandler's Look Created By" credit, and she earned it) makes someone like "The Waterboy" look like John Wayne. Likely influenced by "The Hunchback of Notre Dame's" Quasimodo, Nicky is such a tedious, hopeless individual, it allows every doofus in the audience to feel superior, which is probably the idea.

Eager for a place to rule on their own, Adrian and Cassius leave Hades for New York (yes, they can tell the difference), but their departure, for reasons too contrived to go into, turns out to be a threat to the devil's very life. Hapless Nicky, who loves his dad, has to follow them to Manhattan and spirit them back to the underworld in order to prevent, well, all hell from breaking loose.

Helped by a talking bulldog named Mr. Beefy and distracted by a crush he develops on an art student named Valerie (Patricia Arquette) and the rages of a blind deacon (Quentin Tarantino), Nicky finds he has to release both his inner evil and his inner goodness to get the job done. Even from a movie this misbegotten, getting a lesson in morality from Adam Sandler is one heck of a strange experience.

NEW YORK POST, 11/10/00, p. 55, Lou Lumenick

Adam Sandler's latest makes me feel like one of those cartoon characters, with an angel and a devil perched on each shoulder, whispering in each ear.

Angel: Yuck. This is a really dumb and crude movie that speaks to the lowest common denominator.

Devil: So what? "Little Nicky" speaks to your inner 12-year-old—and it made him laugh a lot.

Angel: So you laughed at what? The devil (Harvey Keitel) doing unspeakable things to Hitler with a pineapple?

Devil: That rocked! And so did the talking dog!

Angel: You seriously want to recommend a movie with a potty-mouthed talking dog named Mr. Beefy?

Devil: Hey, he was the best thing in the movie.

Angel: Which proves what? That Adam Sandler as Nicky, the devil's nerdy, speech-impaired son—sent to earth to save his father—is less compelling than the talking dog who helps him?

Devil: Compelling? What are we talking about, "Faust" or an Adam Sandler teen comedy? It was rather generous of Adam (and his co-screenwriters) to give all the best lines to the dog—and to Rodney Dangerfield, who plays his grandfather.

Angel: He certainly didn't give any good lines to Rhys Hans or Tommy "Tiny" Lister Jr., who play his evil brothers, who conspire to take over their father's throne by taking up residence in New York City.

Devil: Who cares? There are some awesome special effects, like Adam turning into a horde of insects.

Angel: Talk about dubious technical achievements.

Devil: Between the depiction of a pre-Giuliani New York and the guest appearances by Henry Winkler, Regis Philbin and especially Ozzy Osbourne, it reminded me a lot of "Ghostbusters."

Angel: It seemed to me it was more like a reverse-rip-off of that famous Jack Benny flop, "The Horn Blows at Midnight," in which he played an angel sent to New York to destroy the world, then he meets two fallen angels.

Devil: Speaking of angels, wasn't Reese Witherspoon terrific as Nicky's mom, who meets the devil at a heaven-hell mixer?

Angel: If only. She was doing a takeoff of Alicia Silverstone in "Clueless." But she did have more of a role than Patricia Arquette, as Nicky's putative love interest.

Devil: Patricia *was* pretty lame, and what was the point of dressing a babe like her as unattractively as Adam? Jeez, Adam had more chemistry with Allen Covert, who played his Judy Garland-loving actor roommate.

Angel: The stereotypical gay character, you mean.

Devil: So he was funny, shoot me! You're so P.C.! Didn't you like anything?

Angel: I certainly didn't like the devil's aide with mammary glands on the top of his head. This is supposed to be a PG-13 movie!

Devil: Lighten up. You would have raved about it if it was in a movie directed by Robert Altman, instead of Steven Brill.

Angel: I will give you one thing. It's funnier than "Bedazzled," which isn't saying much.

Devil: I thought Liz Hurley made a much more heavenly devil than Harvey Keitel.

Angel: To hell with you.

Devil: Same to you, buddy.

NEWSDAY, 11/10/00, Part II/p. B6, Gene Seymour

To make the stygian depths of Hades into a cozy synthesis of surrealist frat house and suburban game room is exactly the kind of challenge that Adam Sandler was born to assume. Whatever Dante and Milton had in mind for decor, one feels safe in saying that it didn't include Metallica LPs or Rodney Dangerfield as Lucifer, moaning about not getting respect even Way Down Below.

Dante. Milton. Sandler. Why are you making faces like that? Who are we to say that "Little Nicky" won't someday be analyzed and exegesis-ized as much as anyone else's vision of Hell? As with just about every other component of Sandler's motley oeuvre, the future may well be the only place one can imagine this sizzling Big Mac of a movie comedy being treated as a classic. Or, anyway, as an arcane curiosity.

Sandler's standard-issue nitwit persona is squeezed into the twitchy, nervous body of "Nicky," the half-angelic youngest son of the Prince of Darkness (Harvey Keitel in an unusually avuncular mood) who, after 10,000 years of ruling the Underworld, is near retirement. Nicky's bullying big brothers Adrian (Rhys Ifans from "Notting Hill") and Cassius (Tommy (Tiny) Lister Jr. from "Friday") can't wait to get their hands on the controls. But Satan decides to keep things status quo for a while longer.

Incensed, Adrian and Cassius bolt for New York City, which seems especially ripe for their demonic mayhem. Their departure upsets the balance of Good and Evil, causing Satan to begin a slow, grisly death that can only be stopped if Nicky bottles his brothers and returns them home.

This may sound like too much backstory for the average Adam Sandler fan to take in at once. But those connoisseurs are given a lot of nasty stuff to laugh at from the very beginning. Very little of it can be safely described in a family newspaper. (Here are a few cryptic hints: Mammary glands as headwear, Hitler, a dress, a very big pineapple.) The rumor is blunt and inelegant with a vengeance. Though it's an improvement over "Big Daddy," it's still not as consistently lowbrow funny as "Happy Gilmore."

That said, there's something impressive about Sandler's clout that is large enough to top-load his movie with hip and retro-hip personalities. Not just the aforementioned Dangerfield and Keitel, but also Quentin Tarantino (is this where he's been all this time?), Carl Weathers, Patricia Arquette, Henry Winkler (smothered by bees) and Reese Witherspoon as Nicky's mom. Right. His mom. Hey, it's like a Metallica single. Don't think. Just rock with it.

SIGHT AND SOUND, 1/01, p. 52, Mark Olsen

The depths of Hell. Nicky, one of the devil's three sons, spends his days in his room listening to heavy-metal music, avoiding his two brothers, one of whom hit him in the face with a shovel, permanently disfiguring him. When the devil calls his sons to a meeting about his potential successor, he tells them he will continue to rule. His job is to maintain the balance of good and evil; Nicky, he explains, is too kind to do this, and his brothers Adrian and Cassius too evil.

Adrian and Cassius hatch a plot to make Earth the new Hell, a domain they alone will rule. In escaping they freeze the gates of Hell, so that no new souls may enter, which causes the devil's powers to weaken. Only Nicky has the power to bring them back. He must trap them within a magic flask and return them before the devil perishes. Arriving in New York, Nicky is immediately hit by a subway train, returning him to Hell. On his next trip back, he meets a talking dog, Mr. Beefy, who is a friend of his father's assigned to assist Nicky in his mission.

The brothers, posing as politicians and religious leaders, have launched a campaign to corrupt as many souls as possible. Nicky successfully captures Cassius in the flask and with the help of his new roommate, two metalheads and a female design student, Valerie, nearly captures Adrian as well. However, due to his kind heart, Nicky has landed in Heaven while Adrian returns to Hell. Nicky meets his mother, an angel, but must return to Earth for a final showdown with Adrian, who, having seized the throne of Hell, has emerged in Central Park to collect his souls. Following a final confrontation, Nicky saves his father and returns to Hell. His father sends him back to Earth to live with Valerie.

If his previous film *Big Daddy* was an attempt to move comedian Adam Sandler's persona into the more grown-up world of romantic comedy, *Little Nicky* returns him to more familiar terrain; here he plays a curious man-child, the eponymous Nicky, locked in his room, fogged by adolescent insecurities, tormented by his older brothers and in need of the affections of his dear old dad. While his dad happens to be Satan and his brothers have hatched a plan to upset the balance between the forces of good and evil on Earth, the story still follows the basic Sandler format: lovable loser solves all kinds of problems and gets the girl in the end.

Director Steven Brill (also a co-writer, along with Sandler's frequent collaborator Tim Herlihy) does best when staying out of Sandler's way. He is unable, though, to give the film much in the way of visual flair (he's at a loss when handling the extensive special effects or trying to capture the feel of production designer Perry Andelin Blake's seemingly impressive Hell sets). As in all of Sandler's films, the supporting cast provides a gallery of oddball performances that take some of the pressure off the star to deliver all the laughs, but also create the proper sense of good-time bonhomie on which the films flourish. Of particular note are Harvey Keitel and Reese Witherspoon, who seem to be enjoying themselves as Nicky's parents, and Peter Dante and Jonathan Loughran as metalheads overjoyed to meet the dark prince.

But for all its spirited performances and funny moments, *Little Nicky* still feels a little disappointing, if only because it could in fact be funnier. Sometimes it seems Sandler's bemusement at himself, the endless affection he has for scatological jokes, bad taste rock and funny voices leaves him seeming self-satisfied. (Laughing at his own act was one of the trademarks of Sandler's breakthrough performances on the US television show *Saturday Night Live*, here he has at least learned that he only needs to smirk a little to let the audience know he's in on the joke.) That Sandler has stuck to such a rigid formula—which requires him effectively to reprise the same role from film to film raises the question of whether or not he wants to stretch his acting abilities. But ultimately what's 'wrong' with Adam Sandler in this film is interwoven with everything that makes him a unique and likeable talent. Though he is purportedly being courted by indie heavyweights P. T. Anderson and Quentin Tarantino (who makes an appearance in this film) for upcoming projects, Sandler here sticks firmly to the comic schtick that has served him well in the past, laughing all the way to the bank and, like Rodney Dangerfield, who plays Nicky's Grandpa Lucifer, getting no respect.

VILLAGE VOICE, 11/21/00, p. 135, J. Hoberman

Given its Satanic premise, *Little Nicky*—the latest and most elaborate vehicle for reigning box-office monster Adam Sandler—is a relatively painless pop culture eyesore. Indeed, in some respects, this special-effects comedy (really a live-action cartoon), in which Sandler plays the spawn of the devil on the loose in contemporary Manhattan, may be the most sensible Hollywood attempt to cash in on millennial jitters. The gags are plenty vulgar but not too degrading; the requisite racial vaudeville and gay-baiting never get grossly out of hand.

Rigorous in its arrested development, Sandler's own performance is fairly self-effacing. The star has recruited a sizable *Saturday Night Live* posse plus Quentin Tarantino in various cameo roles, as well as such classy performers as Harvey Keitel and Reese Witherspoon. (I don't know how much longer she can go on playing high school seniors, but though she's no Kim Tae Yeon, she's without question the best actor in that role—not to mention the funniest in the movie.) *Little Nicky* is certainly Sandler's most ambitious work. It's not just a bid for respectability but a genuine allegory.

Also reviewed in:
CHICAGO TRIBUNE, 11/10/00, Friday/p. A, Michael Wilmington
NEW YORK TIMES, 11/10/00, p. E10, A. O. Scott
VARIETY, 11/6-12/00, p. 19, Robert Koehler
WASHINGTON POST, 11/10/00, p. C1, Rita Kempley
WASHINGTON POST, 11/10/00, Weekend/p. 45, Desson Howe

LITTLE THIEF, THE

A New Yorker Films release of an AGAT Films & Cie. production in association with La Sept-Arte. *Executive Producer:* Gilles Sandoz. *Producer:* Pierre Chevalier. *Director:* Erick Zonca. *Screenplay (French with English subtitles):* Erick Zonca and Virginie Wagon. *Director of Photography:* Pierre Milon and Catherine Pujol. *Editor:* Jean-Robert Thomann. *Sound:* Jean-Jacques Ferran. *Production Designer:* Kristina Zonca. *Costumes:* Cecile Berges. *Make-up:* Laurence Grosjean. *Running time:* 65 minutes. *MPAA Rating:* Not Rated.

CAST: Nicolas Duvauchelle ("S"); Yann Tregouet (Barruet); Jean-Jérôme Esposito (The Eye); Martial Bezot (Chacal); Jean-Armand Dalomba (Mathias); Joe Prestia (Tony); Ingrid Preynat (Leila); Véronique Balme (Tina); Olivier Gerby (Vampire); Emilie Lafarge (Sandra); Dominique Abellard (Chef Boulanger); Gilber Landreau (Employé Boulangerie).

NEW YORK POST, 3/1/00, p. 47, Lou Lumenick

"The Little Thief" is the second feature by French director Erick Zonca, who captured international attention with his debut, "The Dreamlife of Angels."

This gritty 65-minute feature is altogether a more low-key affair than "Angels."

Like that film, "The Little Thief" is about young French people scraping by, a theme virtually unknown in contemporary American movies.

Nicolas Duvauchelle plays Esse, a skinny young man barely out of his teens who's fired from his job as a baker's apprentice.

Tired of dead-end jobs, he robs his girlfriend and moves to Marseilles, where he falls in with a gang of small-time thieves.

Esse fancies himself a gangster, but he lacks the stomach for robbing villas.

His face fills with terror when he spies a sleeping woman, and he panics when he tries to rob an old lady he's been working for.

Shooting with hand-held cameras, Zonca—who directed commercials in New York before returning to his native France—doesn't glamorize the criminal life but rubs it in the audience's face.

On the same program is a more arresting short film that Zonca directed before "The Dreamlife of Angels."

The 34-minute "Alone" features a memorable Florence Loiret as a teenager who descends from being fired as a waitress to a life of criminal desperation.

VILLAGE VOICE, 3/7/00, p. 128, Amy Taubin

It's work, not love, that perplexes, frustrates, and infuriates the young women and men in Erick Zonca's films. How do you earn a living without dwindling into a wage slave? How do you make the transition from the fantasies and small freedoms of childhood to the actuality of 50 years of nine-to-five?

With their impressionist palette and vivid acting, Zonca's films have a visual beauty and emotional intimacy not usually associated with the problem of labor. But that is the subject at the core of *The Dreamlife of Angels,* Zonca's breakout 1998 feature, and his two short films, *Alone* and *The Little Thief.* Though neither of the shorts is quite as rich as *Dreamlife,* they're a provocative double bill.

Made in 1997, the 34-minute *Alone* is the sketch from which *Dreamlife* developed. In the space of an hour, a young woman (Florence Loiret) loses her waitressing job, her apartment, and all her possessions save those in her beat-up shoulder bag. When a gun literally falls at her feet during a police raid, she tries to hold up her landlord (Philippe Nahon, the brutish star of Gaspar Noé's *I Stand Alone*), who laughs at her ineptitude and slams the door in her face. During her rapid descent into homelessness and starvation, the gun presents itself (to her and to us) more as a threat than a way out. In the hands of a lesser director, it would be too crude a narrative ploy, but Zonca savors both the contingency of its appearance in the girl's life and its tactile presence—the way this hard, efficiently tooled object looks in the hands of a fragile, confused woman.

Like the eponymous heroine of the Dardenne brothers' *Rosetta,* she is willing to do a man's job, and like Rosetta, she hasn't a clue why she can't get one. She has no awareness of the number one rule of the workplace: You can't let your anger show even when the boss or the customers are abusing or rejecting you. But physically and emotionally, this girl has little in common with Rosetta. Rather, she resembles, as does Natacha Regnier's suicidal young woman in *Dreamlife,* the shame-filled, masochistic adolescents in Robert Bresson's later films.

The hour-long *Little Thief* was made immediately after *Dreamlife* and turns the tables with a male protagonist. S. (Nicolas Duvauchelle) quits his job as a baker's apprentice for a get-rich-quick life of crime. Although he seems an unlikely candidate, he's recruited by a Marseilles mob and slowly works his way up the hierarchy from being a break-and-entry lookout to taking care of the boss's aged mother to guarding prostitutes to chauffeuring the boss himself. After the boss shoves a gun down his throat and then rapes him, our hero realizes that labor relations are worse in the criminal world than in the straight world. *The Little Thief* lacks the complex characters of *Dreamlife,* but it extends the range of Zonca's filmmaking with scenes of punishing, visceral violence.

Also reviewed in:
NATION, 3/27/00, p. 34, Stuart Klawans
NEW YORK TIMES, 3/1/00, p. E5, Lawrence Van Gelder
NEW YORKER, 3/6/00, p. 99, Anthony Lane
VARIETY, 5/10-16/99, p. 63, Dennis Harvey

LITTLE VAMPIRE, THE

A New Line Cinema and Cometstone Pictures release in association with Comet Film/Avrora Media/Stonewood of a Comet Film and Stonewood Communications co-production. *Executive Producer:* Alexander Buchman, Anthony Waller, and Larry Wilson. *Producer:* Richard Claus. *Director:* Uli Edel. *Screenplay:* Karey Kirkpatrick and Larry Wilson. *Based on "The Little Vampire" novels by:* Angela Sommer-Bodenburg. *Director of Photography:* Bernd Heinl. *Editor:* Peter R. Adam. *Music:* Nigel Clarke and Michael Csányi-Wills. *Sound:* Roberto Van Eijden and (music) Gerry O'Riordan. *Sound Editor:* Andreas Musolff. *Casting:* Joyce Nettles. *Production Designer:* Joseph Nemec III. *Art Director:* Nick Palmer. *Set Decorator:* Jille Azis. *Set Dresser:* Ingrid Preisner and Charlotte Kistenmacher. *Special Effects:* Die Nefzers. *Costumes:* James Acheson. *Make-up:* Leendert Van Nimwegen and Katja Reinert-Alexis. *Stunt Coordinator:* Tom Delmar. *Running time:* 95 minutes. *MPAA Rating:* PG-13.

CAST: Richard E. Grant (Frederick); Alice Krige (Freda); Rollo Weeks (Rudolph); Anna Popplewell (Anna); Dean Cook (Gregory); Jim Carter (Rookery); Ed Stopppard (Von); Jonathan Lipnicki (Tony Thompson); Pamela Gidley (Dottie Thompson); Tommy Hinkley (Bob Thompson); John Wood (Lord McAshton); Jake D'Arcy (Farmer Mclaughlin); Iain De Caestecker (Nigel); Scott Fletcher (Flint); Johnny Meres (Teacher); Georgie Glen (Babysitter Lorna); Elizabeth Berrington (Elizabeth); Harry Jones (Caretaker).

LOS ANGELES TIMES, 10/27/00, Calendar/p. 8, Jan Stuart

[The following review by Jan Stuart appeared in a slightly different form in
NEWSDAY, 10/27/00, Part II/p. B7.]

Poor child actors. They aren't allowed the same latitude for growth as regular kids. Where we find wonder in each developmental change in our own kids, we tend to be dismayed when we see a once-adorable child star advance in years and lose that natural kid energy that made them so appealing from the start.

Such is the case with Jonathan Lipnicki, that bespectacled 5-year-old boy who softened granite hearts as Renee Zellweger's son in "Jerry Maguire." His cuddly quotient began to melt in "Stuart Little," and he's skating on very thin ice in "The Little Vampire," in which he is called upon to carry a pleasant but unremarkable bedtime story on his shoulders.

Based on characters from Angela Sommer-Bodenburg's novels and boasting a pedigree that includes screenwriters of "Chicken Run" (Karey Kirkpatrick) and "Beetlejuice" (Larry Wilson), "The Little Vampire" gives us Tony Thompson (Lipnicki), a 9-year-old San Diego boy who is transplanted to Scotland where his dad has taken a job designing a golf course. Tony is bullied and ostracized by the local kids, but wins the favor of a kid vampire named Rudolph (Rollo Weeks), who accidentally flies into his bedroom one evening.

Rudolph takes an ecstatic Tony on bat-flying adventures and Tony reciprocates by helping Rudolph and his family (Richard E. Grant, Alice Krige and Anna Popplewell) locate a missing amulet that would rescue them from the world of the undead. There are sundry complications courtesy of an inept vampire hunter named Rookery (Jim Carter) and the stuffy Lord McAshton who employs Tony's dad.

One would love to know what sparked the decision to bring in "Last Exit to Brooklyn" director Uli Edel to film such a confection, but he approaches the material with a straightforward hand that is refreshingly free of hipness or camp. The movie's assertive naivete plays to kids Tony's age or younger, who will take comfort in the benign portrayal of vampires. Older kids and grown-ups looking for more sophisticated humor will have to content themselves with a running gag about vampire cows, which could have been funnier than Edel makes it here.

As for the once-adorable Lipnicki, he is pressed into the service of mugging and shtick that would test the mettle of Roberto Benigni. As you bear witness to the disintegration of one child actor's charms, it may leave you in the sort of funk you haven't felt since Hayley Mills found herself in the family way.

NEW YORK POST, 10/27/00, p. 49, Lou Lumenick

Kids love scary stories, especially around Halloween, but there are very few fright flicks being made these days that can be recommended for them without huge reservations. This, happily, is one of them.

Based on a popular series of children's novels by Angela Sommer-Bodenburg, the beguiling "The Little Vampire" follows the adventures of Tony (Jonathan Lipnicki), a 9-year-old American living in Scotland, where his father is constructing a championship golf course.

Tony dreams about vampires, draws them and talks about them in class, much to the annoyance of his teacher and the classmates who pick on him daily.

One evening, the lonely Tony is visited by a large bat who turns into Rudolph (Rollo Weeks), a grave young vampire who takes Tony flying above the countryside and becomes his friend.

Rudolph eventually enlists the American's help in his quest. He's been 9 years old for the last 300 years, he complains. He and his family want to leave the undead and return to the world of the living, where Rudolph can grow up.

To accomplish this, the boys have to find a magic amulet before a comet passes behind the moon. They also must elude a comic vampire hunter (Jim Carter) determined to drive stakes through their hearts, not to mention their suspicious parents.

A plot that may seem complicated to the non-"Harry Potter" set (the screenplay is attributed to Karey Kirkpatrick and Larry Wilson, who between them collaborated on "Chicken Run" and "Beetlejuice") is negotiated with more than enough laughs, thrills and chills to delight pre-adolescents.

Uli Edel ("Last Exit to Brooklyn") directs with an agreeably light touch and a genuine respect for parents who don't want to take their kids to a movie that will keep them awake at night.

Though a scene where Tony is trapped in a sarcophagus might be a bit much for more sensitive pre-schoolers, there's no realistic violence or bloodshed here. These vampires, who are presented as innocent victims of human persecution, almost exclusively limit their consumption to blood from animals.

The mostly British supporting cast—including Richard E. Grant and Alice Krige as Rudolph's aristocratic parents and Anna Popplewell as his sister, who develops a crush on Tony—is excellently chosen.

The bespectacled Lipnicki, the young star of "Jerry Maguire" and "Stuart Little," again shines here, and newcomer Weeks is the perfect foil as his undead pal, who has a hard time getting used to being addressed as "dude."

With plentiful allusions to "E.T." and "Peter Pan," as well as flying cows and a prominently featured blimp, The Little Vampire" is a guaranteed crowd-pleaser for the whole family.

SIGHT AND SOUND, 11/00, p. 57, Christopher Hawkes

Tony Thompson has recently moved with his parents from America to Scotland. Friendless, bullied and troubled by strange dreams, he becomes fixated on vampires. One evening a young vampire Rudolph flies into Tony's room; after hiding him from vampire hunter Rookery, Tony befriends Rudolph.

The following night Rudolph introduces Tony to his family. Their initial suspicions dissolve when Tony shares a vision with Rudolph's father about the whereabouts of an amulet which can lift the curse of vampirism when held up to a comet due to pass Earth in the next week. After saving the family from two attacks by Rookery, Tony hides them in his cellar.

Rookery presents proof of vampirism to Lord McAshton, owner of the estate where Tony's father works, and both men visit an ancestral tomb in search of the amulet. Rookery then locks Tony, who has followed them, inside the tomb. Tony calls for Rudolph and his sister Anna with a whistle and the children search another tomb. The amulet, though, is missing. During a second vision, Tony realises the jewel is hidden in his bedroom. The two boys, and the eavesdropping Rookery, race back to the house. Tony discovers the amulet but he is captured by Rookery. Rudolph rescues Tony with the aid of a herd of vampire cows and they race to the cliff top where the vampire clans have convened for the comet's passing. After Rookery is dispatched by his parents, Tony wishes for the curse to lift and the vampires disappear. Soon after Rudolph and his family—now human—move in next door to Tony.

In adapting German novelist Angela Sommer-Bodenburg's *The Little Vampire* novels, director Uli Edel *(Christiane F)* and screenwriters Karey Kirkpatrick and Larry Wilson have created a brisk children's adventure detailing a vampire family's quest to become human. This approach forfeits one of the chief pleasures of the books in that the vampire children are no longer empowered by their condition, free from overt parental influence. In the film they're part of a closely knit family, driven underground by the prejudice of humans—only with the assistance of an innocent little boy can they lift the curse and become human themselves. As such, the film adopts a much more moral tone, promoting tolerance ("I bet they're foreigners," says Tony's father of his son's disruptive friends) and the power of imagination. These moral greens may be somewhat difficult to swallow at times (the preview audience became fidgety during the parental lectures), but for the most part *The Little Vampire* is very palatable fare, thanks to some accomplished action scenes and a likeable line in mischievous burnout.

The performances are uniformly well executed. The adult parts are pantomimed for laughs: the parents are worrisome and clueless; the fearless vampire killer gets battered and outdone; and the stuffy English aristocrat is eventually dispatched by the Scottish crematory watchman-turned-vampire. The young vampires, Rudolph and his sister Anna, are played charmingly, but most of the film rests on the performance of Jonathan Lipnicki *(Jerry Maguire)* who stumbles endearingly through his part as the vampire-fixated Tony.

Evocative of Tim Burton's work, the Scottish locations appear as a kind of ghoulish theme park full of ancient stately homes and mouldering, curse-ridden crypts. The special effects emphasise this enjoyably creaky atmosphere: the flying scenes provoke a nostalgic twinge for the pre-CGI days of blue-screen work and there's a neatly sustained visual gag in the form of a digitised herd of cows which turn into red-eyed vampires—first shuffling away from sunlight, later swinging upside down from the barn roof.

The Little Vampire is also warmly allusive. The story of a little boy who befriends and protects an alien recalls *E. T*, especially in the penultimate scene where Rudolph disappears into the ether, and the influence of *The Neverending Story* is apparent when Tony revenges himself on the school bullies with help from his supernatural friend. There are also more knowing references: Anna declares her affections to Tony by adapting Lauren Bacall's famous line in *To Have and Have Not*, 1944 ("You know how to whistle, don't you? You just put your lips together and blow"); and in those scenes where he experiences visions, Tony does a hilarious imitation of Danny Torrance's psychic seizures in *The Shining*.

Also reviewed in:
CHICAGO TRIBUNE, 10/27/00, Friday/p. A, Michael Wilmington
NEW YORK TIMES, 10/27/00, p. E28, Lawrence Van Gelder
VARIETY, 8/28-9/30/00, p. 34, Derek Elley
WASHINGTON POST, 10/27/00, p. C5, Rita Kempley
WASHINGTON POST, 10/27/00, Weekend/p. 38, Michael O'Sullivan

LIVE NUDE GIRLS UNITE!

A First Run Features release. *Executive Producer:* Gini Reticker. *Producer:* Julia Query and John Montoya. *Director:* Julia Query and Vicky Funari. *Screenplay:* Julia Query and Vicky Funari. *Editor:* Heather Weaver. *Director of Photography:* Julia Query, John Montoya, Sarah Kennedy, and Vicky Funari. *Music:* Allison Hennessy and Kali, Alex Kort, Blaise Smith, Dale Everingham, and Khayree Shaheed. *Sound:* Jennifer Ware. *Sound Editor:* Ethan Derner, Andrea Plastas, Cari Campbell, and Barbara McBane. *Running time:* 70 minutes. *MPAA Rating:* Not Rated.

NEW YORK POST, 10/20/00, p. 50, Jonathan Foreman

Julia Query's first-person documentary about the battle of a group of San Francisco strippers to organize a union and win a contract battle with their employers won't win any awards for cinematography.

But it's a funny, fascinating and at times really quite moving story, and Query and her co-director deftly weave it together with the tale of Query's dramatic coming out to her mother—not as a lesbian (mom has no problem with that) but as a stripper in a peep show club.

Query and her pals feel empowered by their work; what they hate is the poor working conditions, their lack of sick days or benefits, and their mostly female management's insistence on making scheduling decisions based on ethnicity and breast size.

VILLAGE VOICE, 10/24/00, p. 146, Amy Taubin

"Two, four, six, eight. Don't go in to masturbate," chant the strippers who are picketing the entrance to San Francisco's Lusty Lady Theater. In 1997, after a lengthy, combative labor negotiation, the Lusty Lady became the first unionized strip club; its workers were organized as the Exotic Dancers Union, a chapter of the Service Employees International 790.

Writer and stand-up comedian Julia Query worked at the Lusty Lady to pay the rent. Although she had never made a film before, she decided to document the strippers' struggle to unionize. After working on the project for about a year, she brought in experienced documentarian Vicky Funari as codirector. Their film, *Live Nude Girls Unite!*, should put to rest the canard that feminists have no sense of humor. From the opening shot of Query strolling past that legendary temple of male beatitude, the City Lights Bookstore, to the closing Emma Goldman quote, "If I can't dance, I don't want to be part of your revolution," *Live Nude Girls Unite!* is wickedly funny. Its subversive comic style is an antidote to the absence of humor in two films that must have been on Query's mind: Barbara Kopple's classic labor doc, *Harlan County, U.S.A.*, and, at the opposite end of the political spectrum, Paul Verhoeven's glossy sexploitation fiasco, *Showgirls*.

Query incorporates her stand-up routines as a way of commenting on the events at the Lusty Lady. "I never before worked with so many women with college degrees, most of them in feminist studies. They realized what to do about patriarchy: Make them pay." Nearly a decade before the Lusty Lady strippers fought to become unionized, sex workers led by Scarlett Harlot tried to get the labor relations board to recognize them as full-time, union-eligible workers rather than as independent contractors. The board ruled against them, explaining that if they had been farm laborers they might have had a case. Which isn't so different from the lawyer for the Lusty Lady's owners objecting to the use of the word "pussy" in the contract the strippers propose, claiming that "they were sexually harassing themselves."

The film zeros in on the doublethink and institutionalized misogyny behind such statements, but it's even more provocative when it goes after the divisions within feminism around the issues of sexuality, sex work, and the ways women deploy and depict their bodies. "I like dancing in a room with other women. It's like a weird pajama party," says one of the strippers, making us aware of the camaraderie, pleasure, and power the women experience as they perform, not only for the Lusty Lady's patrons but also for Query's camera.

Query's mother is Dr. Joyce Wallace, celebrated for her efforts to promote safe sex among New York prostitutes. Having learned her feminism at her mother's knee, Query didn't hesitate to come out to her as a lesbian, but she kept her sex work a secret. When she discovers that she and Wallace are both scheduled to speak at a conference on prostitution, she decides to tell all to her mom with the camera running. "I'm going to use it as a plot device," she says flippantly, but her anxiety is apparent. Dr. Wallace is horrified by the news; to her credit, she never asks that the camera be turned off. "I don't want people to know my daughter is in the smut industry," she says tearfully. For her, sex workers are victims. She can't accept that a woman with as many career options as her daughter would choose to be stripper. Query, who clearly has no taste for Oprah-like confessionals, handles the mesh of personal and political in her conflict with her mother a bit too gingerly. It's the big flaw in *Live Nude Girls Unite!*, a film that finds liberation in irony and uplift in ribald wit.

Also reviewed in:
NEW YORK TIMES, 10/20/00, p. E 17, A. O. Scott
VARIETY, 5/8/00, p. 66, Dennis Harvey

LIVE VIRGIN

A Granite Relasing release of a Vertigo Productions-MG Films co-production with the participation of TPS Cinema. *Executive Producer:* Jean-Pierre Marois. *Producer:* Aissa Djabri, Farid Lahouassa, and Manuel Munz. *Director:* Jean-Pierre Marois. *Screenplay:* Jean-Pierre Marois and Ira Israel. *Director of Photography:* Agle Egilsson. *Editor:* Georges Klotz. *Sound:* Stephan von Hase and (music) Didier Lizé. *Casting:* Owens Hill and Sharon Howard-Field. *Production Designer:* Christiaan Wagener. *Art Director:* Lisa Robyn Deutsch. *Set Decorator:* Lisa Robyn Deutsch. *Set Dresser:* Trish Sacchi, Guillaume DeLouche, and Brian A. Deitch. *Special Effects:* J. D. Streett. *Costumes:* Deborah Everton. *Make-up:* Tracy Warbin. *Stunt Coordinator:* Gary Jensen. *Running time:* 87 minutes. *MPAA Rating:* R.

CAST: Bob Hoskins (Joey Quinn); Robert Loggia (Ronny Bartoloti); Mena Suvari (Katrina Bartolotti); Gabriel Mann (Brian); Bobbie Phillips (Raquel); Sally Kellerman (Quaint McPherson); Alexandra Wentworth (Mitzi); Lamont Johnson (Nick); Vincent Schiavelli (Cab Driver); Rick Peters (Tommy); Olan Jones (Kim); Michael Milhoan (Larry); Freda Fo Shen (Marge); Michael Cudlitz (Bob); Brian Bloom (Brad); John Roarke (George Bush/Jerry Springer/Maury Povitch/Tom Snyder); Esai Morales (Jim the Director); Mark Adair-Rios (Secutiry Guard); Jason Bercy (Messenger); Jim Czarnecki (Teacher); Life Garland (Crip); Penny Griego (Anchorwoman); Elizabeth Guber (Operator); Carrie Ann Inaba (Hiromi); Ira Israel (Ira); Ron Jeremy (Desk Sergeant); Curt Kaplan (George); Cynthia Lamontagne (Gloria); Kristin Minter (Susie); Jane Morris (Buela Snarp); Lori New (Tina); Kristin Norton (Nancy); Kira Reed (Naked Actress); Jed Rhein (Paul); Kim Robillard (Jail Officer); Mary Jo Smith (Security Guard); Octavia Spencer (Agnes Large); Fernando Sulichin (Hispanic Driver); Ken Taylor (Anchorman); Ashlee Turner (Laurie); Thomas G. Waites (Grip); Billy Williams (Blood); Gina-Raye Swensson (Jury Member).

NEW YORK POST, 6/2/00, p. 46, Jonathan Foreman

"Live Virgin"—a comedy set in the wacky world of porn moviemaking—would probably seem hilarious if photographer turned director Jean-Pierre Marois had made the film in France, or at least in his native French. Its cheesy cheapness might well have seemed charming and Gallic.

Instead, it is a bad film with some oddly charming moments, and one that would almost certainly have gone straight to video—despite the presence of serious actors Robert Loggia and Bob Hoskins—had not "American Beauty" and "American Pie" turned Mena Suvari into a star.

Suvari plays Katrina Bartoloti, teenage daughter of porn director Ronny Bartoloti (Robert Loggia).

As the film opens, Katrina has plotted with her father's longtime rival, Joey Quinn (Bob Hoskins), to lose her virginity, live, on a virtual reality linkup.

Joey is particularly keen on the idea because Ronny stole his plastic-surgery-addicted ex-wife.

Ronny is the kind of dad who's uncomfortable with his daughter wearing skimpy outfits, so when he sees Katrina and Joey promoting the live defloration on a crass talk show (hosted by Sally Kellerman), he goes ballistic.

With his bodyguard/sidekick Nick (Lamont Johnson), Ronny sets out to prevent the broadcast from taking place by any means necessary.

Katrina's ex-boyfriend, Brian (Gabriel Mann), is also determined to stop her from losing her virginity in the company of millions of voyeurs. But Katrina and Joey are determined that the show will go on.

Loggia, Hoskins and Suvari are neither impressive nor awful; they're just trapped between the lines of a rather primitive script. Writer-director Marois and his co-screenwriter, Ira Israel, seem not to have the knack of writing dialogue that sounds like anything a real person would say.

But the movie is scattered with clever little jokes—some of them purely visual—that will have particular appeal for those whose familiarity with the adult film world goes beyond "Boogie Nights."

There's even a funny cameo appearance by porn legend Ron "The Hedgehog" Jeremy as a grumpy police officer.

NEWSDAY, 6/2/00, Part II/p. B9, Jan Stuart

That dubious subgenre of post-"Boogie Nights" movies that takes us inside the porno industry plumbs moronic depths with "Live Virgin." Ostensibly a satire on our shock-craving culture, it stars Bob Hoskins as a porn king who hopes to push the envelope of group thrills by staging a live sex act that observers will experience vicariously by wearing a special body suit that is wired up to the two participants.

The fair maiden Hoskins has chosen to feature in this stunt happens to be the teenage daughter (Mena Suvari of "American Beauty") of his chief competitor (Robert Loggia). This prompts an ear-splitting succession of chases, brawls, car crashes and sadistic acts in which Suvari's callow ex-boyfriend and Loggia attempt to dissuade her. As the big show approaches, Loggia screams, Hoskins gloats, Loggia shrieks, Hoskins shrugs, Loggia roars, Suvari sulks, Loggia screams some more.

For all the caterwauling, director Jean-Pierre Marois' unique sensibility is perhaps best conveyed by a moment in which the audience gazes up at Suvari from the inside of a toilet bowl as she is about to throw up. If you don't happen to own a special body suit with which to savor the je ne sais quoi of "Live Virgin," a blindfold and a set of earplugs will do in a pinch.

Also reviewed in:
NEW YORK TIMES, 6/2/00, p. E16, Stephen Holden
VARIETY, 7/31-8/6/00, p. 25, Lisa Nesselson

LONG NIGHT'S JOURNEY INTO DAY

An Iris Films/Cinemax Reel Life release of a Reid-Hoffman production. *Producer:* Frances Reid. *Director:* Frances Reid and Deborah Hoffmann. *Screenplay (English, Xhosa and Afrikaans with English subtitles):* Antijie Krog. *Director of Photography:* Frances Reid and Ezra Jwili. *Editor:* Deborah Hoffmann and Kim Roberts. *Music:* Lebo M.. *Sound:* Victor Mzwandile Njokwana. *Running time:* 94 minutes. *MPAA Rating:* Not Rated.

WITH: Peter Biehl; Linda Biehl; Mongezi Manqina; Evelyn Manqina; Easy Nofemela; Eric Taylor; Nomonde Calata; Nyameka Goniwe; George Bizos; Robert McBride; Sharon Welgemoed; Thapelo Mbelo; Jann Turner; Desmond Tutu; Pumla Gobodo-Madikizela.

VILLAGE VOICE, 4/3/00, p. 132, Dennis Lim

Nursing the raw wounds of decades of institutionalized racism, the South African government in 1994 formed the Truth and Reconciliation Commission, allowing those who committed politically motivated crimes—both to uphold and to protest the country's apartheid regime—to step forward and apply for amnesty. The TRC operates on a case-by-case basis, and the painstaking, inevitably painful process assumes the form of public hearings—not so much trials as forums that bring together victims and perpetrators, reliving trauma in an act of communal catharsis. This unique judicial procedure derives meaning not merely from uncovered facts or unexpectedly pointed apologies but from its extremely public nature. Broadcast live on radio, each session unfolds before a visibly emotional audience, often on a stage. As someone remarks in

Long Night's Journey Into Day , Frances Reid and Deborah Hoffmann's documentary on the TRC, the surreal sense is of "an ancient, tragic play."

With four case studies, this Sundance prizewinner makes amply clear the infinite complications inherent in the TRC's mission. The film opens with a hearing that involves, for many Americans, the most well-known apartheid fatality, Amy Biehl, a Fulbright scholar who was murdered in Cape Town in 1993. Four years later, Peter and Linda Biehl testify before the TRC, determined to honor their daughter's humanitarian beliefs. Not only do the Biehl's choose not to oppose the killers' amnesty applications, they request a meeting with the family of Mongezi Manqina, the young man who fatally stabbed her. Establishing a best-case scenario with this remarkable, enormously moving display of strength and compassion, the film goes on to show that absolution is, more frequently, far from forthcoming (as is genuine contrition at times) and that each conciliatory attempt rests on a singular, unpredictable foundation of remorse and resentment.

A white ex-security forces officer, Eric Taylor, says it was simply part of his job description when he assassinated Fort Calata, a rural anti-apartheid activist. Taylor expresses guilt and claims new perspective (which he attributes to Nelson Mandela's autobiography and—a detail so startling it takes a moment to fully register—the 1988 movie *Mississippi Burning*), but Calata's grieving widow, Nomonde, remains suspicious and unmoved. Robert McBride, an ANC freedom fighter who bombed a Durban bar, killing three white women, rues his naive political fervor, but Sharon Welgemoed, the sister of one of the victims, is rankled by the cockiness she perceives in McBride's TRC testimony. *Long Night's Journey* saves its most intricate case for last, the 1986 "Gugulatu 7" incident, in which seven young black men were shot dead by police in an "anti-terrorist operation." Only two of the 25 officers involved have since applied for amnesty—one a white sergeant who denies that the victims were specifically targeted, the other a black government operative, Thapelo Mbelo, who admits he was assigned to entrap the men.

Maintaining a respectful distance (in every sense), Reid and Hoffmann's elegantly constructed documentary argues that the TRC, an unwieldy experiment in "restorative justice," is not only successful on its own terms, but desperately necessary—a conclusion that may surprise, not least because this model of therapeutic confrontation as been routinely cheapened by touchy-healy American talk shows over the years. Spare, direct, and devastatingly effective, the film puts fuzzy, big-word concepts like absolution and redemption into an agonizingly vivid context. When, at the end of the film, a distraught mother spontaneously forgives her son's killer, it's a heartbreaking, heartening moment that you count yourself fortunate to have witnessed. In more ways than can be said of most films, *Long Night's Journey Into Day* is essential viewing.

Also reviewed in:
NEW YORK TIMES, 3/29/00, p. E6, Elvis Mitchell
VARIETY, 2/14-20/00, p. 44, Emanuel Levy

LOOKING FOR AN ECHO

A Regent Entertainment presentation of an Echo Productions/Steve Tisch Company. *Executive Producer:* Steve Tisch. *Producr:* Martin Davidson and Paul Kurta. *Director:* Martin Davidson. *Screenplay:* Jeffrey Goldenberg, Robert Held, and Martin Davidson. *Director of Photography:* Charles Minsky. *Editor:* Jerrold L Ludwig. *Music:* Ken Weiss. *Music Editor:* Stephen M. Galvin and Patrick M. Griffith. *Sound:* Dan Ferat. *Sound Editor:* Andrew Lackey. *Casting:* Stephanie Corsalini. *Production Designer:* Andrew Bernard. *Costumes:* Sandy Davidson. *Stunt Coordinator:* Jery Hewitt. *MPAA Rating:* R. *Running time:* 97 minutes.

CAST: Armand Assante (Vince); Diane Venora (Joanne); Joe Grifasi (Vic Spidero); Tom Mason (Augie); Anthony John Denison (Nappy); Johnny Williams (Pooch); Edoardo Ballerini (Anthony); Christy Romano (Tina); David Vadim (Tommie); Monica Trombetta (Francine); David Margulies (Dr. Ludwig); Fanni Green (Nurse Fowler); Paz de la Huerta (Nicole); Gena Scriva (Arlene); Gayle Scott (Renee); Ilana Levine (Sandi); Cleveland Still (Derelict); Peter Jacobson (Marty Pearlstein); Murray Weinstock (Orchid Blue Lead); Amanda Homi and Machan

Notarile (Orchid Blue Singers); Michael Cooke Kendrick (Jason); Kresimir Novakovic (Waiter); Mike J. Alpert (Street Vendor); Lisa France (Nurse); Rick Faugno (Young Vince); Johnny Giacalone (Young Vic); Tommy J. Michaels (Young Augie); Eric Meyersfield (Young Nappy); Danny Gerard (Young Pooch); Norbert Leo Butz (Vocals for Anthony).

LOS ANGELES TIMES, 12/8/00, Calendar/p. 12, Kevin Thomas

Martin Davidson's "Looking for an Echo" offers a warm and sensitive study of a decent man coping with midlife crisis while also paying tribute to the nostalgic pull of doo-wop music of the '50s and '60s.

A film unafraid of wearing its heart on its sleeve, "Looking for an Echo" recalls Davidson's and Stephen Verona's 1972 "Lords of Flatbush," which gave career boosts to Sylvester Stallone and Henry Winkler among others, and his two "Eddie and the Cruiser" movies, about a rock group of the '60s whose charismatic lead singer (Michael Pare) may—or may not—have died in a 1964 New Jersey car accident. All these films are permeated by the potent sound of vintage pop music.

As it happens, 1964 was also the year in which Bay Ridge's Vinnie and the Dreamers had their hit single, "This I Swear," a heartfelt love song with which 16-year-old Vinnie Pirelli made teen girls swoon. Today, Vinnie (Armand Assante, never better) is a bartender about to turn 50, with two sons, Anthony (Edoardo Ballerini), a promising singer in his own right, and Tommy (David Vadim), a married NYPD cop.

Widowed for a decade, Vinnie also has a 14-year-old daughter Tina (Christy Romano) hospitalized with leukemia. The prognosis for Tina, however, is promising, and she is to return home shortly. A deeply loving though volatile family man, Vinnie has settled into a groove, happily so, he insists to himself and others. Underneath is a man still grieving for his wife and profoundly embittered by the collapse of his singing career, which left him nearly broke, his group, like so many others of the era, cheated out of royalties.

But change and challenge, which Vinnie has scrupulously avoided, are coming upon him, whether he likes it or not. He won't admit it, of course, but he's overcome by jealousy over the encouraging progress of Anthony's career and downright upset when Anthony sings "This I Swear" with terrific impact.

When his pal since sixth grade and a fellow Dreamer, Vic Spidero (Joe Grifasi), who has a small band that plays for weddings and bar mitzvahs, organizes a Vinnie and the Dreamers reunion as part of a surprise 50th birthday party for Vinnie, Pirelli reacts with surprise and pleasure. But the gathering will bring to the surface his long-standing conflicting emotions in regard to the past and its losses personal and professional. (Vinnie and the Dreamers in song are voiced by Kenny and the Planctones.)

Luckily for Vinnie, Tina has a nurse, Joanne (Diane Venora), so lovely and vibrant—and currently single—that Vinnie cannot help but be stirred by her. They make a striking couple, for Vinnie is still in his prime, though he has been out of the dating game so long he needs Anthony to check out his appearance when he's dressing for his first date with Joanne. (He buys Joanne a white carnation corsage, as if he were taking her to the senior prom rather than out to dinner at one of Bay Ridge's more posh restaurants; Joanne's teenage daughter (Paz de la Huerta) tells him it belongs either in a vase or a time capsule.)

Assante, in a decidedly reflective role, and Venora are thoroughly engaging, with Assante gradually revealing the various facets of a man more complex, more regretful than he, his family and friends realize. The always reliable Grifasi heads the solid supporting cast, in which Ballerini emerges as a most promising young actor. The film's locales have an appealing authentic feel to them, and everything from decor to music contributes to making "Looking for an Echo" an appealing heart-tugger.

NEW YORK POST, 11/10/00, p. 58, Lou Lumenick

This well-meant but rambling little indie melodrama, set in Bay Ridge of the 1990s, revolves around Vince Pirelli (the dour Armand Assante), the lead singer for a doo-wop group that charted a No. 1 song in 1964.

Now Vinnie tends bar and plays keyboard at bar mitzvahs and weddings, never granting requests to sing with more than a few bars in his famous falsetto. His life revolves around his children—a cop (David Vadim), a 14-year-old with leukemia (Christy Romano) and his younger son (Edoardo Ballerini), an aspiring musician.

A glum widower for a decade, Vinnie reluctantly meets his daughter's tough-talking new nurse (Diane Venora, by far the best thing in the movie), who pursues him romantically.

Except for their love scenes, most everything in the script (co-written by director Martin Davidson of "Eddie and the Cruisers" fame) feels forced and contrived—especially the Miller-time reunion between Vinnie and his former bandmates.

NEWSDAY, 11/10/00, Part II/p. B6, Gene Seymour

"Loooking for an Echo" is an especially ham-handed contribution to the growing subgenre of movies about "one-hit wonders." The "wonder" in this case is a doo-wop vocal group from the early 1960s called Vinnie and the Dreamers, which, to hear the folks in the movie talk, were kinda, sorta the 'N Sync of the Kennedy era. But the ride ended as fast as it started, as it always does. The dream faded, voices change, kids grow up. Know what I mean?

Vince (Armand Assante), formerly Vinnie, the defunct group's lead singer, knows, but he doesn't want to talk about it. Now 50, Vince is a moody cuss, tending bar in his South Brooklyn neighborhood and playing keyboards in a wedding band led by another ex-Dreamer named Vic (Joe Grifasi). These gigs keep him from moping around his house, where he and his long- dead wife raised two sons—one of them a cop (David Vadim), the other a pop musician (Edoardo Ballerini) seemingly on the same career track as his dad—and a perky young daughter (Christy Romano), who's battling cancer.

Assante's Vince keeps grimacing from the strain of all this baggage. His daughter's warm-and-fuzzy nurse (Diane Venora) seems receptive enough to whatever it is that's bugging him. And whenever these two fiery actors get together on screen, "Echo" promises to become that rare commodity: a believable, middle-aged romance. Indeed, the movie so often sidesteps the contrivances expected from such "heartwarming" fare that one regrets its thick accumulations of corn and soap.

Producer-director Martin Davidson's previous foray into 1950s Brooklyn street culture, "The Lords of Flatbush" (1974) turned out to be such a small, polished gem that one even forgives that movie for boosting the public profiles of Sylvester Stallone and Henry Winkler. This one feels overinflated by contrast. But give him credit for at least including music by Jay and the Americans' co-founder Kenny Vance that sounds as if it really could have poured out of somebody's transistor radio in 1960.

VILLAGE VOICE, 11/14/009 p. 140, Alexander Clare

Vince (Armand Assante) is a widowed 50-year-old Brooklyn bartender whose life revolves around his two sons and his leukemia-stricken daughter. He is embarrassed of his youthful days as the lead singer for Vinnie and the Dreamers, a doo-wop troupe that crooned its way to the top of the charts in the mid '60s.

Thirty years later, the middle-aged ex-bandmates share forlorn recollections of their former stardom ("fucked-up memories," in Vince's case); a reunion with the group and a new love (Diane Venora) revives Vince's enthusiasm and encourages him to appreciate his past. Helped by strong supporting performances (notably by David Vadim and Christy Romano), *Echo* offers a convincing portrayal of nostalgia for lost glory days and a considered take on a father's relationship with his children. But the stream of sentimentality is endless and often sickly, and the warm afterglow is decidedly manufactured.

Also reviewed in:
NEW YORK TIMES, 11/10/00, p. E27, Stephen Holden
VARIETY, 10/25-31/99, p. 41, Dennis Harvey

LOSER

A Columbia Pictures release of a Cockamamie production. *Executive Producer:* John M. Eckert. *Producer:* Amy Heckerling and Twink Caplan. *Director:* Amy Heckerling. *Screenplay:* Amy Heckerling. *Director of Photography:* Rob Hahn. *Editor:* Debra Chiate. *Music:* David Kitay. *Music Editor:* Jeanette Surga. *Choreographer:* Mary Ann Kellogg. *Sound:* Greg Champ. *Sound Editor:* Michael O'Farrell. *Casting:* Lynn Kressel. *Production Designer:* Steven Jordan. *Art Director:* Andrew M. Stearn. *Set Designer:* Barry Isenor. *Set Decorator:* Patricia Cuccia. *Special Effects:* Martin Malivoire. *Costumes:* Mona May. *Make-up:* Patricia Green. *Stunt Coordinator:* John Stoneham, Jr. *Running time:* 93 minutes. *MPAA Rating:* PG-13.

CAST: Jason Biggs (Paul Tannek); Mena Suvari (Dora Diamond); Zak Orth (Adam); Tom Sadoski (Chris); Jimmi Simpson (Noah); Greg Kinnear (Professor Edward Alcott); Dan Aykroyd (Dad); Twink Caplan (Gena); Bobby Slayton (Sal); Robert Miano (Victor); Mollee Israel (Annie); Colleen Camp (Homeless Woman); Andy Dick (City Worker); Steven Wright (Panty Hose Customer); Brian Backer (Doctor); Meredith Scott Lynn (Dog-loving Girl); Stuart Cornfield (Foreman); Taylor Negron (Photographer); Andrea Martin (Professsor); Scott Thomson (Cell Phone Guy); Kedar Brown (Jay); Catherine Black (Military Jacket Girl); Rick Demas (Bouncer); Sanjay Talwar (Convenience Cashier); Tracy Dawson (Drug Saleswoman); Carolyn Goff (Kristen); Mike Beaver (Boy at Concert); Richard Blackburn (Security Guard); Billy Otis (Prisoner); Jenny Kim (Student Worker); Alison Sealy-Smith (University Official); Martin Roach (Veterinarian); Heidi Weeks (Saks Saleswoman); Daniela Olivieri (Store Tailor); Nicholas Michael Bacon (Beer Store Clerk); Valerie Boyle and Colleen Reynolds (Aunts); Jack Jessop (Grandfather); Mallory Margel (Paul's Sister); Patrick Mark (Bloody Nose Guy); Tanja Jacobs and Darrin Brown (Partygoers); James Barret (Guy); Robert Tinkler (Bar Patron); Geoffrey Antoine (Coffee Counter Guy).

LOS ANGELES TIMES, 7/21/00, Calendar/p. 8, Jan Stuart

[The following review by Jan Stuart appeared in a slightly different form in **NEWSDAY, 7/21/00, Part II/p. B7.]**

It takes a lot of chutzpah to recycle Simon & Garfunkel's "Scarborough Fair" for a plaintive movie interlude, almost as much as it takes to title your movie "Loser." That's about as far as nerve takes writer-director Amy Heckerling in her formulaic new teen opus, which is unique mostly for its refusal to indulge the hard-sell, gross-out desires of its intended youth market.

There are a number of losers in "Loser," most prominently the NYU freshman played with disarming affability by "American Pie" alum Jason Biggs. Sporting a forceps-style haircut (a la Shemp of the Three Stooges) that always springs back to life no matter how much he presses it down with a dorky sheepskin hat, Paul inspires derision wherever he goes. Primarily, he suffers from a surfeit of Gomer Pyle congeniality in an MYOB metropolis. But it's enough to invoke the wrath of his roommates, a trio of losers (Zak Orth, Tom Sadoski and Jimmi Simpson) in the guise of cool rich kids.

Paul's no-win campaign to gain their acceptance collides with his misguided efforts to seduce fellow student Dora Diamond (Mena Suvari). Smart and sexy in the over-cosmeticized style of Heckerling heroines in "Clueless" and "Fast Times at Ridgemont High," Dora is the It girl of Paul's dreams. But Dora's reality is something else again, as she struggles with a cheesy, sleep-depriving nightclub job and an equally degrading affair with English lit professor Edward Alcott (Greg Kinnear, laying on the smarmy older-guy butter with a trowel).

Underlying the schematic setup are some very credible truths about the conformist pressures and financial-aid issues that beset college-age kids—this is prime Heckerling territory, after all. But the pretensions of her antagonists lack the satirical snap that characterizes her best movies: Professor Alcott prefers his tea in cups, not mugs, thank you very much, while Paul's three contemptible roommates loll around in improbable beauty salons like Clare Luce's gossiping society women.

Just as unlikely are the gyrations Heckerling puts her hero through to demonstrate his purity of heart. As Biggs works admirably to underplay Paul's anti-hip energy, we are asked to believe that he would give Dora flowers and then attribute the gesture to the loutish Kinnear, all in the name of true love. Does such selflessness exist, at any age? Paul hails from some rural middle-American community, not the little town of Bethlehem.

Presumably Heckerling was suffering a bad hair day when she decided to tack on the embarrassing what-happened-to explanations of each character's fate at the end of the film. Sendups of true-story epilogues are as corny as Kansas in August, which is also when this summer fluff ball should blow away from multiplexes everywhere.

NEW YORK, 8/7/00, p. 67, Peter Rainer

Loser, writer-director Amy Heckerling's first film since *Clueless*, is about two sweet college ne'er-do-wells, played by Jason Biggs and Mena Suvari, who discover in the end that they are right for each other. It takes them much too long.

NEW YORK POST, 7/21/00, p. 51, Lou Lumenick

Just how big a loser is the aptly named "Loser"? So dumb that a college professor (Greg Kinnear) remarks, "I'm sure if she were alive, Betty Friedan would applaud your epiphany"—oblivious to the fact that Betty Friedan is still very much alive and probably consulting her lawyers right now.

So ridiculous that when penniless Paul (Jason Biggs) and Dora (Mena Suvari) sneak into the second act of "Cabaret" on Broadway, they end up seeing the show's famous opening number.

So sloppily made that, in one scene, Paul picks up a pizza while carrying a video. In the very next scene, Paul, minus the pizza, picks out the video he was previously carrying.

So mind-numbingly witless that you wish there were a Society for the Prevention of Cruelty to Actors.

Poor Suvari ("American Beauty"), who wears a look of utter misery throughout, is forced to endure a rat's-nest hairdo, nearly as much mascara as Tammy Faye Bakker and a Hollywood costumer's hideous idea of grunge wear.

Biggs ("American Pie"), who doesn't look much happier, has to wear a plaid hunter's cap and what looks like one of Burt Reynolds' old toupees.

He struggles to play a socially challenged Regents scholar (like, right) who, at one point, explains to Dora that maybe it isn't such a great idea being a human egg donor to make money—because it will increase her risk of cancer.

Paul and Dora are students at a New York City institution of lower learning that might as well be called Freddie Prinze Jr. University. Writer-director Amy Heckerling's schmaltzy dramedy bears an unfortunate resemblance to several of Prinze's lame college vehicles, most notably "Down to You."

Paul's a hick from the sticks who ends up sleeping in the campus veterinary clinic after his party-hearty dorm-mates (womanizers who inexplicably dress and behave like stereotypically flamboyant gay males) throw him out. In a confounding leap of logic, even by teen-movie standards, Paul allows them to throw a party in his new digs.

When Dora suffers an overdose at the party, she ends up moving in with Paul—though she's having a clandestine affair with an unctuous literature professor played by the wildly miscast Kinnear.

That Biggs and Suvari exhibit all the chemistry together of car-wreck survivors is almost beside the point.

They're gifted performers who should find agents who keep them out of movies packed with stale references to "Seinfeld," Axl Rose and Al Goldstein.

Heckerling was responsible for two Left Coast teen classics, "Fast Times at Ridgemont High" and "Clueless," but her depiction of New Yorkers is, well, clueless.

"Loser" is filled with continuity errors, terrible puns and nonsequiturs that remind us she also directed such laughless bombs as "Johnny Dangerously" and "National Lampoon's European Vacation."

In that notorious video-store scene, Paul rents a copy of "Simon Birch." Even that dubious choice is better than paying $9.50 to see this bomb.

SIGHT AND SOUND, 12/00, p. 52, Mark Olsen

Paul Tannek's acceptance by New York University makes him the first member of his Midwestern farming family to attend college. Once in the city he has a hard time fitting in. Even his own roommates, a group of spoiled, rich party boys, shun him. After a mishap in the classroom of Professor Alcott, Paul meets and falls for fellow student Dora Diamond. Unbeknown to him, Dora is having an affair with Alcott.

After his room-mates conspire to have him kicked out, Paul is forced to live in the animal shelter where he works. Dora tries to meet her tuition fees by working nights as a cocktail waitress in a seedy nightclub. Despite professing his love for her, Alcott is insensitive to Dora's predicament. Paul buys tickets for himself and Dora for a rock concert the same night that his former roommates plan to stage a party in his animal shelter. When Dora stops by at the party before the concert, one of the room-mates secretly slips her a pill in hopes of taking advantage of her. She misses the concert; later, a dejected Paul returns home to find Dora passed out in his shelter, which is wrecked from the party. Not wanting to upset Dora while she convalesces, Paul—who now knows about her affair with his professor—lies that Alcott is concerned about her recovery. When she learns the truth about Alcott, Dora realises her true feelings for Paul.

On paper *Loser* seems like a sure-fire winner. Some of the brightest young acting talent in contemporary Hollywood (Jason Biggs from the smartly risqué *American Pie,* Mena Suvari from the arthouse crossover *American Beauty,* Greg Kinnear from the mainstream pleaser *As Good As It Gets*) join writer-director Amy Heckerling, here making her first film since the surprise success of *Clueless.* But despite this promising lineup, *Loser* loses something along the way; what aspires to be a fresh and lively take on collegiate life and the pressures of the early adult years comes out as a tiresome mush filled with cut-outs for characters. For Heckerling, whose reputation is built largely on *Clueless* and her 1982 high school comedy *Fast Times at Ridgemont High*, it seems she has become the one thing a purveyor of youth culture can never be: out of touch.

The film's premise is promising enough, as Biggs' young Paul ventures from rural Midwest to New York City, the first member of his family to attend college. Once there, he encounters Suvari's Dora, a worldly, troubled young woman whose exotic mystique attracts the naive farm boy. Complications arise in the form of Paul's uncaring dormmates and Dora's illicit affair with one of their professors (the blatantly uninterested Kinnear).

Loser switches between outdoor scenes shot in well-known New York locations and indoor scenes filmed largely on sound stages in Toronto. The difference in look and feel between the two is palpable and a constant distraction. During a number of scenes apparently inspired by Billy Wilder's sparkling 1960 comedy *The Apartment*—where Paul and Dora sit in his shabby room and talk, straining to connect, one can see the film *Loser* wants to be be poke out from behind the glossy veneer. But for Biggs and Suvari, such genuinely lively moments are few and far between. The film's final scene, presumably the product of last-minute reshoots, finds Biggs with a different haircut and visibly many pounds lighter. Though the actors awkwardly exchange lines explaining his appearance, it's hard not to find such obvious patchwork jarring. It would probably be beyond the means of any film-maker to bring such a messy movie to a graceful conclusion, but the forced romantic coupling and outlandishly unfunny end-title cards explaining the characters' futures (a popular patch-and-fix solution) are particularly off-putting.

The numerous shortcomings of Heckerling's film are a real disappointment considering her place in the development of the teen movie. At a time when *Fast Times* and *Clueless* are considered high-water marks as honest representations of teen mores, *Loser* seems to fancy itself as an antidote to such blandly generic teen films as *Boys and Girls*. But the project repeatedly strains for laughs by pushing itself to cartoonish extremism, notably through the trite villainy of Paul's room-mates and Dora's sleazy professor, so any honestly earned sympathies are lost. Failing even to muster the faux authenticity of *American Beauty, Loser* ultimately looks down its nose at those it should be helping to lift up.

VILLAGE VOICE, 8/1/00, p. 112, Amy Taubin

A more conventional coming-of-age comedy [the reference is to *New Waterford Girl*], Amy Heckerling's *Loser* is slighter than her groundbreaking *Fast Times at Ridgemont High* or her deft Jane Austen update, *Clueless*. Still, it's the most progressive, good-hearted studio film of the summer.

The setting is an undisguised NYU, where brainy but decidedly uncool Paul Tannek (Jason Biggs) is having a hard time fitting in. Tortured by his rich, bratty roommates and terrified of falling behind in his studies and losing his scholarship, Paul takes refuge in the only off-campus housing he can afford—the back room of an East Village animal hospital. The sole bright spot in his life is Dora Diamond (Mena Suvari), who seems to like him, if only as a friend. Dora, who dresses in gothic grunge, works full-time as a waitress in a topless bar to put herself through college. Paul saves Dora when she OD's on roofies, fed to her by those same horrible roommates, who can't score unless the girl's unconscious. But Dora's having an affair with their pompous lit-crit professor (Greg Kinnear), who tells her that she's his soul mate and treats her like shit.

Heckerling is at her most subtle in showing how Dora slowly falls in love with Paul while remaining obsessed with the exploitative professor. There's a definitive moment when Dora sees Paul shirtless and is surprised and knocked out by his beautifully muscled torso. When he catches her looking at him, Paul quickly slips his Sarah McLachlan T-shirt over his head, as if to counter the impression that he's a sexy guy.

Heckerling went to NYU about 30 years ago, and throughout the film you can sense her looking askance at the current generation of students. There's a bigger gap between the good guys (Paul and Dora) and the bad guys (pretty much everyone else in the movie) than in *Fast Times at Ridgemont High*. Sean Penn's stoned surfer wasn't mean, and even the ticket scalper who betrays his best friend had a conscience. But in *Loser*, New York (which looks as clean and bright as the Beverly Center) is overrun with users and abusers, all with grandiose senses of entitlement. *Loser's* spot-on depiction of its villains would have made for a depressing movie if it weren't so funny to see them get their comeuppance.

Also reviewed in:
CHICAGO TRIBUNE, 7/21/00, Friday/p. B, Mark Caro
NEW YORK TIMES, 7/21/00, p. E8, A. O. Scott
VARIETY, 7/24-30/00, p. 46, Dennis Harvey
WASHINGTON POST, 7/21/00, p. C12, Stephen Hunter
WASHINGTON POST, 7/21/00, Weekend/p. 34, Desson Howe

LOST SOULS

A New Line Cinema release of a Prufrock Pictures production. *Executive Producer:* Betsy Stahl, Pierce Gardner, Donna Langley, and Michael De Luca. *Producer:* Nina R. Sadowsky and Meg Ryan. *Director:* Janusz Kaminski. *Screenplay:* Pierce Gardner. *Story:* Pierce Gardner and Betsy Stahl. *Director of Photography:* Mauro Fiore. *Editor:* Anne Goursaud and Andrew Mondshein. *Music:* Jan A.P. Kaczmarek. *Music Editor:* Christopher Kennedy. *Sound:* Kim II. Ornitz and (music) Rafal Paczkowski. *Sound Editor:* Paul P. Soucek and Larry Kemp. *Casting:* Mindy Marin. *Production Designer:* Garreth Stover. *Art Director:* Chris Cornwell. *Set Designer:* Jason Weil, Conny Marinos, Sloan U'ren, and Carl Stansel. *Set Decorator:* Larry Dias and Andrea Fenton. *Set Dresser:* Timothy Steinouer, William Acedo, James Hurd, Mark Boucher, and Chris Coulson. *Special Effects:* Clay Pinney. *Costumes:* Jill Ohanneson. *Make-up:* Katherine James. *Special Make-up and Animatronic Effects:* John Rosengrant. *Stunt Coordinator:* Doug Coleman. *Running time:* 102 minutes. *MPAA Rating:* R.

CAST: Winona Ryder (Maya Larkin); Ben Chaplin (Peter Kelson); Sarah Wynter (Claire Van Owen); Philp Baker Hall (Father James); John Hurt (Father Lareaux); Elias Koteas (John

Townsend);   Brian Reddy (Father Frank);   John Beasley (Mike Smythe); John Diehl (Henry Birdson);   Paul Kleiman (Paramedic);   Robert Clenendin (Mental Patient);   Oliver Clark (Mr. Silberman);   Michael Mantell (Kleiman);   Brad Greenquist (George Viznik);   Ming Lo (Michael Kim);   Anna Gunn (Sally Prescott);   W. Earl Brown (William Kelson);   Cyd Strittmatter (Susan Kelson);   James Lancaster (Father Jeremy);   Susan Mosher (Receptionist); Maureen Grady (Secretary);   Anne Betancourt (Mrs. Quintana);   Robert Castle (Josef the Doorman);   Anna Berger (Mrs. Levotsky);   Kai Ephron (Guard);   Lil Henderson (Cranky Woman);   John Prosky (Orderly);   Rob Moore (Young Man);   Ursula Brooks (Lauren);   Rainer Judd (Second Party Woman);   Uri Ryder (Second Party Man);   Ashley Edner (Gina);   Connie Ray (Mother);   Jan Triska (Melvin Szabo);   Ayo Haynes (Day Care Worker);   Joe Clark (Store Owner);   Victor Slezak (Father Thomas);   Cynthia Darlow (Directionless Woman); Joseph Lyle Taylor (Irked Motorist);   Julie Ariola (Reader); Kaity Tong (Herself);   Tom McCleister (Father Malcolm);   Dan Finnerty (Technical Director);   Xanthia Decaux (Production Assistant);   Eden Byrd (Waitress);   Charlotte L. Fleming (School Secretary);   Daniel Jones (School Kid);   Kim Harris Ornitz (Joe the Orderly);   Victor Ralys (Lithuanian Priest);   Norman Smith (Waiter); Terry Van Zandt (Mental Patient #2);   Buddy Quaid (Buddy the Waiter);   Jamie Denbo (Sharon, Leslie Grant Show);   Jodi Daley (Leslie Grant, Leslie Grant Show);   David Raymond Wagner (Joe, Leslie Grant Show);   K.K. Dodds (Deputy);   Drew Snyder (Doctor);   Kate Beahan (Flirtatious Girl);   Rebecca Hobbs (Publicist);   Jon Stahl (Voice of Psychiatrist).

LOS ANGELES TIMES, 10/13/00, Calendar/p. 4, Kevin Thomas

"Lost Souls" is lost all right, a dreary tale of supernatural horror featuring Winona Ryder doing battle with Satan. Like her most recent previous film, "Autumn in New York," an old-fashioned tear-jerker that opened sans press previews, "Lost Souls" is set in Manhattan, ravishingly photographed in virtual sepia. Maybe the talented Ryder should head back to California about now and steer clear of genre material for a while.

Ryder plays Maya, saved from demonic possession by John Hurt's Father Lareaux, whom she now assists in exorcisms. An institutionalized mass murderer (John Diehl) asserts his right to request an exorcism over the strong reservations of the facility's skeptical director (Alfre Woodard, unbilled).

This time the ceremony goes awry, the priest is left near death, and Maya decodes the mass murderer's endless rows of numbers to discover that the devil is about to possess Peter Kelson (Ben Chaplin), author of a book about mass murderers that concludes they are only extreme examples of narcissistic manipulation. Kelson holds that true evil does not exist, and Maya finds herself determined to convince him otherwise before Satan overtakes him on the moment of his swiftly approaching 33rd birthday.

The problem with the film, which marks the directorial debut of cinematographer Janusz Kaminski, who won Oscars for his superb cinematography in "Schindler's List" and "Saving Private Ryan," is not that it takes the devil seriously—remember how chillingly convincing "Rosemary's Baby" was? It's rather that its characters are so colorless and uninvolving that it's hard to take them seriously.

Pierce Gardner's woefully underdeveloped script is further undermined by stretches of unintentionally amusing dialogue. Neither scary nor even suspenseful, the picture is swiftly a turnoff, and stunning cinematography by Mauro Fiore and elaborate production design by Garreth Stover do no compensate for the many flaws. Instead, they bring them sharply into focus.

NEW YORK POST, 10/13/00, p. 53, Jonathan Foreman

There are phenomena that defy rational explanation, that tempt even the most skeptical of us to a belief in dark, supernatural forces. For instance, what else but a satanic conspiracy of agents, managers and studio executives could possibly have induced a cast including not just Winona Ryder but a team of top acting talents—John Hurt, Elias Koteas and Alfre Woodard (mysteriously uncredited)—to take part in a project like "Lost Souls." Yet another mostly unscary, occasionally comical "Exorcist" knockoff?

Ryder, looking quite beautiful and grown-up with long hair, plays Maya, a schoolteacher and daughter of murder victims who assists Father Lareaux (Hurt) and Deacon John Townsend (Koteas) in exorcisms. (As a child, she was once possessed.)

Maya, Townsend and Father Lareaux take a trip to a hospital for the criminally insane to exorcise the demon from convicted mass murderer Henry Birdson (John Diehl). The exorcism, opposed by the rationalist psychiatrist in charge (Woodard), is not only unsuccessful, it causes Father Lareaux to have an incapacitating stroke.

And even though Maya discovers that Birdson, using a numeric biblical code, has been spelling out the name of the man who will be the antichrist, the church orders all of Father Lareaux' assistants, including Maya, to drop their investigations.

The man who will be the human vessel for the antichrist turns out to be Peter Kelson (Ben Chaplin), a best-selling New York author of books about serial killers and a handsome dark-haired, dark-eyed fellow in the "Omen" tradition. Though raised as a Catholic by his uncle, Father James (Philip Baker Hall), after his parents were murdered, Kelson doesn't believe in good and evil. Maya contacts Kelson, proves to herself, and all but persuades him, that he is indeed the devil's chosen one, and then tries to prevent the transformation that will take place on his imminent 33rd birthday. To its credit, you occasionally get a sense in "Lost Souls" that the filmmakers, even if they may not be religious believers, do take their theology relatively seriously. But, as usual, the Catholic Church is wrongly depicted as not taking possession or exorcism seriously, and, as usual, there's an underground army of Satanists waiting for the apocalypse.

There are some good creepy morrients, most of them a good hour into the film. But, too often, the tension is undermined by a screenplay (credited to Pierce Gardner) that contains crude expository writing and fails to flesh out Kelson's character, and by the film's impressive but distracting visual flash (including the now-standard MTV-style bursts of slow motion).

First-time director Janusz Kaminski was Steven Spielberg's Oscar-winning cinematographer on both "Schindler's List and "Saving Private Ryan," and he shoots this film with a grainy, desaturated palette that recalls "Seven" and makes secular New York look properly defenseless against supernatural evil. But he fails to get sufficient drama from the question of whether Maya is insane or, the only person who can save the world from the devil's machinations.

NEWSDAY, 10/13/00, Part II/p. B7, John Anderson

Muttered Latin. Cryptic numbers. Stylized crucifixes shot at grotesque angles. Deuteronomy. Exorcisms. You know what this means. Hollywood's got that ol' time religion again.

The best one can say for the end-of-the-world movie "Lost Souls"—in which Winona Ryder's got the whole world in her hands—is that it doesn't begin with an archaeological dig in the Middle East, the discovery of ominous relics and a brace of Rhodesian ridgebacks howling for their daddy, Satan. No, "Lost Souls" takes place in the hell-bent limbo of New York City, a place that could use a few Ghostbusters, 'cause there's a whole lotta evil afoot. Or, perhaps, ahoof.

When an actor turns director, what happens is the actors are indulged and an otherwise flawed movie can be buoyed by the performances. When a cinematographer turns director, it's more problematic. Janusz Kaminski, the Oscar-winning shooter behind "Schindler's List" and "Saving Private Ryan," makes his directorial debut by overindulging the visuals. The look of "Lost Souls" is very high-grained, bled of much of its color, and makes the impression of being one long flashback. It's eerie, it's beautiful, but eventually the faux-Gothic texture of the image imposes an archness on the movie as a whole, because nothing else is as well-thought-out or executed.

And that's putting it mildly. Ryder, whom Kaminski repeatedly shoots from a heightened angle so her raised eyes can better imply waifish uncertainty, is Maya Larkin, a kind of consultant to the Church, whose own exorcism some time before (seen in a flashback that looks like the rest of the movie) has endowed her with a gift for sniffing out fire and brimstone. She and her allies (John Hurt, Elias Koteas) determine through the seemingly meaningless scribblings of a mass murderer/agent of the devil (John Diehl) that the Antichrist is coming, in the body of crime writer Peter Kelson. The problem is, Kelson doesn't have any idea and approaches crime as a strictly secular event. "I don't believe in evil with a capital E," he says. And you know what that means.

There are some inadvertently hilarious occurrences and some abominable acting, although the sound of the film is first-rate and delivers what chills there are. The sound hardly redeems the movie, however, which should be exorcised from your weekend schedule. Amen.

SIGHT AND SOUND, 2/01, p. 42, David Jays

New York, the present. Maya Larkin, a young woman saved from demonic possession, assists at an exorcism with her mentor Father Lareaux. They attempt to release murderer Henry Birdson from possession, but the ritual fails, leaving Lareaux incapacitated. Maya, Lareaux and deacon John Townsend believe the devil will soon attempt to become incarnate through a human body and bring evil to the world. Maya deciphers a message in Birdson's papers suggesting that Satan's intended victim is Peter Kelson, a writer whose books argue against the existence of evil.

Maya, spurred by malignant visions, attempts to warn him, but he is sceptical, especially when she suggests that he is the son of an incestuous union (one of Satan's requirements). John, impatient with delay, attempts to shoot Peter, but is himself killed. Gradually Peter's resistance softens: he discovers that his girlfriend Claire conceals a huge pentangle below his bed; that his priestly uncle Father James is actually his father and the leader of a satanic congregation. Lareaux seems to recover, but Maya realises that he is himself possessed; the subsequent exorcism kills him. Peter shoots his uncle. At the very moment of transformation, Maya shoots Peter.

In *Lost Souls* writer Peter Kelson, whose body the devil plans to possess, endeavours to "demystify" evil, but he doesn't stand a chance in this relentlessly mystifying picture. The very air is filmy with turpitude, and light sources shed diffuse, powdery beams that obscure as much as they illuminate. Maya, the young woman who tries to warn Peter that the devil has designs on his body, has occasional flashbacks to when she herself was possessed, memories bleached out by a harsh white glare. Light here frequently serves as set-dressing (the twinkle of massed church candles) or deliberately inadequate tool (etiolated torch beams creeping through a deserted house).

In this apocalyptic horror, director Janusz Kaminski sees the world through a glass, darkly. Vision is occluded, mediated by intervening surfaces—rain-spattered car windows, the mesh of a two-way mirror, frosted bathroom glass. At times, the camera is like a prowling avatar of the omni-sneaky devil. Kaminski and his director of photography Mauro Fiore continually search for unexpected angles, as if lurking in corners, ready to trap unwary souls. At one point, the lens slithers down a possessed man's hairy arm, across his porous cheek to gaze into his demon-afflicted eye.

Although making his first feature, Kaminski has frequently been Steven Spielberg's director of photography, and the experience tells not only in the virtuosic camerawork, but also in the desaturated patina of portent. The colour-bled settings of *Saving Private Ryan* are echoed in this muted palette. Soulless interiors squelch with tones of mud, mushroom and grey, pricked by accents like the rosewood gleam of Peter's desk. Grim autumn shades were also a feature of *The Exorcist* (1973), although Pierce Gardner's plot channels William Friedkin's theatrics of possession into an apocalyptic scenario closer to the millennial *Stigmata* or *End of Days*.

Dripping coffee machines provide a steady supply of the devil's brew, for Maya and Peter both run on caffeine, sucking edgily at coffee and cigarettes. Only the agents of darkness have any appetite, with Peter's sullen brother stuffing his face even after an attempted murder, and his Satan-worshipping girlfriend Claire toying with sterile tablets of sushi. The film sets up other early associations between the antagonists—Peter's courtroom note taking is echoed, for instance, by the scratch of Maya beavering at her numerical ciphers.

Although the atmospherics are fearsomely suggestive, the film lacks coherence and pace, and Kaminski's imagination falters when it comes to envisioning satanic presence. Only someone as tremulous as Winona Ryder's Maya would be spooked by such workaday hallucinations as supernatural graffiti. In a wardrobe of limp cardigans, Ryder gives another of her post-traumatic performances, doe-eyes cavernous with darkness. She and Ben Chaplin, who plays Peter, twitch, halt and stammer through Gardner's dialogue, as if trying to iron character into its flat surface. Only Philip Baker Hall, as Peter's devilish parent, gets to relish properly hammy lines such as "They've had their two thousand years now it's our turn."

VILLAGE VOICE, 10/24/00, p. 152, Jessica Winter

The Vatican's latest recruitment film, *Lost Souls*, bitch-smacks the fear of Linda Blair into hapless nonbelievers, proposing agnosticism as the real opiate of the Satan-prone masses. Catholic-school teacher Winona Ryder, lifting Angelina Jolie's hair and makeup from *Girl, Interrupted*, moonlights as a "secular adviser" to a crack team of exorcists (including a discomfitingly hammy John Hurt as a priest), who conclude that poor Ben Chaplin's faith-challenged true-crime author "has an inner emptiness that allows him to become a vessel for evil" (as the zealous, creepy press notes put it).

Longtime Spielberg cinematographer Janusz Kaminski makes his directing debut with an evocative putty-colored palette and grainy, desaturated stock, but his choppy narrative style only garbles the nakedly fundamentalist arc of the story. So does the crippling lack of spatial continuity—Ben and Winona (who sure does spend a lot of downtime with somebody who may already be walking on cloven hooves) magically appear inside rooms or stumble into secret Masses like they're navigating the endless corridors of a haunted Nintendo mansion. Stealing every trick in the *Repulsion* handbook but crash-landing in *Ghostbusters II*'s visual terrain, *Lost Souls* can be blamed foremost on its fire-and-brimstone screenwriter, Pierce Gardner. Inadvertently hilarious as the film becomes (the abrupt, oh-fuck-it ending is its own punch line), the last thing American popular culture needs right now is a dogma-grounded argument for a moral spectrum that only comes in two shades.

Also reviewed in:
NEW YORK TIMES, 10/13/00, p. E12, Elvis Mitchell
VARIETY, 10/9-16/00, p. 22, Lael Loewenstein
WASHINGTON POST, 10/13/00, p. C5, Stephen Hunter
WASHINGTON POST, 10/13/00, Weekend/p. 45, Desson Howe

LOUIS PRIMA: THE WILDEST

A Historic Films release of a Blue Sea Productions/Historic Films production. *Executive Producer:* Don McGlynn and Celia Zaentz. *Producer:* Joe Lauro. *Director:* Don McGlynn. *Director of Photography:* Steve Wacks, Randy Drummond, and Alex Vlacos. *Editor:* Christian Moltke-Leth and Don McGlynn. *Sound:* Steve Wacks. *Running time:* 82 minutes. *MPAA Rating:* Not Rated.

WITH: Keely Smith; Sam Butera; Gia Maione; Jimmy Vincent; Lou Sineaux; Bruce Raeburn; Will Friedwald; Leon Prima; Madeline Prima; Louis Prima, Jr.; Lena Prima.

NEW YORK POST, 3/3/00, p. 52, Hannah Brown

If Louis Prima were alive today, he'd be a rapper. The extraordinarily versatile musician's career spanned the jazz, swing and rock eras to become a huge presence on the cultural landscape.

His influence is still felt today, but his name has faded.

"Louis Prima: The Wildest"—a lively documentary directed by noted music documentarian Don McGlynn—tries to bring Prima back into the public eye.

As he tells Prima's story, McGlynn provides a vibrant, breezy history of popular music from the '20s through the '60s.

Prima would have been "on the Mount Rushmore of Italian-Americans," comments one of Prima's cronies and admirers.

Younger viewers may be familiar with Bill Murray's Las Vegas lounge singer parody from "Saturday Night Live," but they're probably not aware that Prima both created this persona and actually began to parody it himself.

Clips of him on stage in Vegas warbling "Just a Gigolo" with Keely Smith, his poker-faced partner and wife, illustrate just how unusual his act was.

The much-married Prima became so identified with this song that lines from it grace his tomb. Prima was born in a close-knit Italian community in New Orleans in 1911, and became a trumpet player, composer and singer.

Discovered by Guy Lombardo, Prima moved to New York, and then to Los Angeles, where he appeared in a few films and romanced movie star Jean Harlow.

In the mid-'30s, he composed the swing classic "Sing Sing Sing"—made famous in a version by the Benny Goodman Orchestra with a Gene Krupa drum solo—possibly the best-known swing tune of all time.

But Prima, who in addition to his musical gifts had a sixth sense about his commercial prospects, understood when the big-band era was coming to a close and shifted his energies to the growing Las Vegas scene.

He capped his career by moving into early rock 'n' roll, even making a Twist dance-craze movie, and he did the voice of the King Louie character in Disney's "The Jungle Book."

This documentary goes heavy on the music, but it could have done with even fewer talking heads and more songs.

One blast from Prima's trumpet is worth a thousand words from critics explaining his place in music history.

VILLAGE VOICE, 2/29/00, p. 107, J. Hoberman

Those in search of an energy fix could do worse than Don McGlynn's *Louis Prima: The Wildest*, a big smoochy valentine to one of the most resilient American entertainers of the 20th century. Born in New Orleans, the wildly energetic Prima was a trumpet-playing, hoarse-voiced scat singer—a white disciple of Louis Armstrong (whom I don't believe the movie ever mentions). Discovered by Guy Lombardo in the '30s, Prima helped establish 52nd Street as a Dixieland mecca. He wrote the swing blockbuster "Sing, Sing, Sing," relocated to Hollywood, and dated Jean Harlow. A crony recalls his response to the actress's untimely death: "I think he was sad."

The movie is similarly taciturn on other biographical subjects, but Prima's call and response clowning has near universal appeal. Always looking for an audience, he recorded in Italian, played the Apollo, and made the transition from big-band swing to proto-rock 'n' roll. Most spectacularly, Prima reinvented himself as a Las Vegas hepcat, abetted by the impassive vocalist Keely Smith and frantic saxophonist Sam Butera. He was still limber enough to jump on the Twist and even provide Walt Disney with a star vocal turn in *The Jungle Book*. Nor was that the end. McGlynn's performance-rich doc appears to have been made too soon to acknowledge Prima's posthumous assist to the most successful Gap ad in history.

Also reviewed in:
NEW YORK TIMES, 3/3/00, p. E26, Stephen Holden
VARIETY, 10/25-31/99, p. 40, Dennis Harvey

LOVE & BASKETBALL

A New Line Cinema release of a 40 Acres and a Mule Filmworks production.   *Executive Producer:* Andrew Z. Davis, Jay Stern, and Cynthia Guidry.   *Producer:* Spike Lee and Sam Kitt. *Director:* Gina Prince-Bythewood.   *Screenplay:* Gina Prince-Bythewood.   *Director of Photography:* Reynaldo Villalobos.   *Editor:* Terilyn Shropshire.   *Music:* Terence Blanchard. *Music Editor:* Lori Slomka and Michael Dittrick.   *Sound:* Willie Burton and (music) Don Murray.   *Casting:* Aisha Coley.   *Production Designer:* Jeff Howard.   *Art Director:* Susan K. Chan.   *Set Designer:* Ron Wilkinson.   *Set Decorator:* Dena Roth.   *Set Dresser:* Glenn Roberts. *Costumes:* Ruth Carter.   *Make-up:* Anita Gibson.   *Make-up (Omar Epps):* Laini Thompson. *Stunt Coordinator:* Manny Perry.   *Running time:* 118 minutes.   *MPAA Rating:* PG-13.

CAST: Sanaa Lathan (Monica Wright); Omar Epps (Quincy McCAll); Dennis Haysbert (Zeke McCall); Debbi Morgan (Nona McCall); Alfre Woodard (Camille Wright); Harry J. Lennix (Nathan Wright); Regina Hall (Lena Wright); Kyla Pratt (Young Monica); Glenndon Chatman (Young Quincy); Naykia Harris (Young Lena); Jess Willard (Jamal); Chris Warren, Jr. (Kelvin); Gabrielle Union (Shawnee); Tyra Banks (Kyra Kessler); Shar Jackson (Felicia); Charles O'Bannon (Reggie); Al Foster (Coach Hiserman); Boris Kodjoe (Jason); Christine Dunford (Coach Davis); Erika Ringor (Sidra O'Neal); April Griffin (Dorsey High School Player); Nathaniel Bellamy (High School Referee); Terry Cummings, Chick Hearn, Stu Lantz, Dick Vitale, Robin Roberts, and Trevor Wilson (Themselves); Jesse Corti (Coach Parra); Leticia Oseguera (Luisa); Kara Brock and Aichi Ali (College Girls); Dion Basco (College Student); Lisa Barkin Oxley (Bank Officer); Rebecca Patterson (Nurse); James Dumont (Reporter); Colleen Matsuhara (UCLA Coach); Andre Bellinger (College Referee); Elimu Nelson (Partygoer); Jimmy Lennon, Jr. (Sports Announcer); Monica Calhoun (Kerry); Marta Bou Morera, Marta Crespo, and Raquel Hurtado (Spanish Girls); Jordi Clemente (Security Guard); Steve Spencer (Lakers Trainer); Madison Duvernay (Lena's Baby); Sandra von Embriqs and Yolanda Higgins.

LOS ANGELES TIMES, 4/21/00, Calendar/p. 10, Eric Harrison

Choosing "Love and Basketball" as a title for a movie is a bit like slapping a "Hops and Barley" label on a can of beer. It either grabs you with its bare-bones audacity or else sits there, dumbly, while your eyes wander past.

Like its title, this charming movie skirts the line between no-brainer directness and the sort of wise restraint that suggests an active, mischievous mind at work. Impressively, it stays pretty consistently on the side of wisdom.

The movie is smarter than it has to be, but it's the sort of low-key smart that can be easily overlooked. Writer-director Gina Prince-Bythewood doesn't care if you recognize how hard it is to juggle two distinctly different types of movies (make that three, since the romance and sports elements here don't obscure the feminist fable that is the film's heart). And it's OK with her if you don't fully appreciate the difficulty of her following her lover-athletes from the age of 11 to their mid-20s or showing the way painful and complex relationships with parents can influence the trajectory of a child's life.

Accomplishing all of this in her first movie is about as challenging as making a three-point shot from center court at the buzzer with the score tied and Magic Johnson on defense. Prince-Bythewood very nearly pulls it off. She wants to be noticed—she's not above striking a fancy pose or two—but she'd be content with the audience growing and staying involved with her two likable main characters.

The title says "Love and Basketball," but for much of the movie, Quincy (Omar Epps) and Monica (Sanaa Lathan) seem to think the "and" is an "or." They are driven ballplayers, middle-class next-door neighbors who for different reasons value the game above all else. Childhood sweethearts (for about two minutes), it takes them years to realize that they really are in love. They have difficulty, though, balancing their dedication to the game and each other. Even when, during their senior year of high school, they become lovers, the bliss doesn't last. A wedge is driven between them that keeps them apart for years as they each pursue professional basketball careers.

This is an extremely well-acted movie. Lathan in particular is a marvel, guiding her character from her awkward teenage tomboy years to womanly self-possession with seamless ease. She's the movie's emotional center, and her work here should make her a star. And not only is her acting first-rate, she couldn't play basketball before getting the role yet you'd think she grew up on the court.

The acting, though, is only one of the qualities that gives this film, despite its occasional tilts toward sentimentality, an underlying sense of authenticity. Prince-Bythewood gets the details right—nuances of speech, behavior, the humor. The film is tethered too tightly to the reality of daily experience to stray too far into contrivance.

This is Prince-Bythewood's first feature film as both a writer and director, and she shows admirable command of her craft. A writer for television shows such as "A Different World," "South Central" and "Felicity," she earned an Emmy nomination for writing and directing a "CBS

Schoolbreak Special" in 1994. She drew upon her own background as a high school and UCLA athlete for this movie.

Watching "Love and Basketball," you realize how rare it is to see a high school or college dance in a movie that doesn't ring false or to see middle-class black people—in a film aimed at mass audiences—portrayed without regard to audience expectation. They're just people. Like the characters in Spike Lee's more realistic efforts (Lee is a producer of "Love and Basketball"), ethnic details are presented matter-of-factly.

An incident involving Quincy's relationship with his pro ball player father (Dennis Haysbert) provides a major plot point. Monica's difficult relationship with her mother (Alfre Woodard) is just as important to the movie on a thematic level, but it isn't as well integrated into the story and so feels tacked on. It's also hard to understand why—beyond the needs of the plot—Quincy remains so aloof from Monica long after it should be clear that they belong together. Clearly Prince-Bythewood is straining to set up a climactic basketball contest that only works if everything is riding on the outcome.

These and other quibbles aside, "Love and Basketball" is an admirable achievement. Mirroring Monica's growth, the film evolves as it goes. For most of its two-hour length, it involves us in the concerns of the very young—dating, goal-setting, athletic competition, fitting in. By the fourth quarter, though, it has blossomed into something more moving and more mature. As the clock runs out, the stakes get suddenly higher. A mark of this movie's accomplishment is how much we care about seeing the players win.

NEW YORK, 5/1/00, p. 57, Peter Rainer

[*Love & Basketball* was reviewed jointly with *The Virgin Suicides*; see Rainer's review of that film.]

NEW YORK POST, 4/21/00, p. 50, Jonathan Foreman

"Love and Basketball" is part of a welcome revolution in the way Hollywood depicts African-Americans, in that most of the film takes place in the upscale L.A. neighborhood of Baldwin Hills (known as the "black Beverly Hills").

It's also a movie that effectively conveys the excitement of basketball from a player's point of view.

So it's all the more unfortunate that it's a mawkish, predictable, mechanically written love story peppered with the kind of stale, fake-sounding dialogue you only find in the cheesiest TV movies.

It's a double shame because Sanaa Lathan is terrific in the lead role, and the cast includes major talents like Dennis Haysbert (once again playing a philandering husband) and the wonderful Alfre Woodard—here forced to play a crude feminist's cartoon of an old-fashioned, stay-at-home mom.

The story is told in four uneven quarters.

It starts in 1981, when 12-year-old Monica and her parents move in next door to young Quincy and his folks, and he discovers that a girl can play ball just as well as a boy.

The next quarter finds the neighbors as high school seniors and stars of their respective basketball teams.

For Quincy (heavy-lidded Omar Epps), now a smooth campus stud, winning a scholarship to USC is a breeze—despite his short stature. Tomboyish Monica (Lathan) is equally talented, but her hotheaded behavior on the court doesn't endear her to college recruiters.

Monica has long had a crush on Quincy, but he doesn't notice her until the senior dance, when her mother (Woodard) and sister give her a makeover and put her into a dress.

Quincy and she get it together, and by the time both get to USC for the film's third quarter, they are boyfriend and girlfriend.

At college, Monica becomes a top team-player under the tutelage of a tough coach.

But Quincy's worldview is shaken when he discovers his father has been cheating on his mother. He's explaining his crisis to Monica when she has to return to her dorm—if she violates the curfew set by her coach, she'll be thrown off the team.

Quincy feels betrayed and breaks up with her. And writer-director Gina Prince-Blythewood treats this selfish response as if it's perfectly sensible and sane.

The final quarter mainly deals with Monica's lonely post-college exile playing women's basketball in Europe, and her battle to win Quincy back upon her return to California.

For some reason, this otherwise feminist movie takes the amazingly reactionary position that it's up to the woman to make whatever sacrifices are necessary to make a relationship work.

NEWSDAY, 4/21/00, Part II/p. B2, John Anderson

When Fred and Ginger danced together, the operative metaphor was sex: furtive gestures, accelerated contact, a crescendo of synchronized slithering and a deep, collective exhale.

In "Love and Basketball," the metaphor is b-ball: In the climactic game of one-on-one between Quincy (Omar Epps) and Monica (Sanaa Lathan)—the two cagey lovers who've harbored a hostile affection since childhood—there's too much pent-up heat and anger for the game to mean much else.

Fortunately, we don't have to deal with the psycho-sexual symbolism of three-point shots or technical fouls. Unfortunately—or not—debuting director Gina Prince-Bythewood has made a movie about basketball (and love) that's best when it's sitting still. Whether lacking the financial wherewithal or the expertise (although she's apparently a gifted player herself), Prince-Bythewood doesn't offer anything like the kind of court scenes her co-producer, Spike Lee, shot for "He Got Game." Instead, she does her best work when her characters are merely interacting, and actors like Epps and the very interesting Lathan can provide the human embellishment to a story that's heading in a very obvious direction. And taking its sweet time getting there.

Monica and Quincy grow up in adjacent houses, their rooms facing each other across the yard in Los Angeles, where Quincy's father Zeke (Dennis Haysbert) plays for the Clippers and his mother Nona (Debbi Morgan) sits around at night, waiting for Zeke to come home. Quincy has dreams of playing in the NBA; so does Monica. And elusive as that dream may be, so is her dream of Quincy, who's a bit obtuse when it comes to the adoring girl next door.

"Love and Basketball" is, in part, an ugly duckling story. And therein lies the problem. The film, showcased at this year's Sundance Film Festival (and, not surprisingly, developed at its lab), showcases Prince-Bythewood's innovative, if irregularly innovative, eye; one of her best touches occurs when she shifts to Monica's POV during a crucial game, riveting us to the scene and eliminating the need for much on-court choreography. But these moments are relatively few, sublimated to the director's self-empowerment message, which seems contradicted when the movie makes the spring dance such a live-or-die event in Monica's life. How seriously can we take Monica as New Woman when she's so nervous about what to wear?

Or for that matter, when she throws herself at "Q," who's selfish, self-absorbed and ultimately self-destructive. Monica is, although inadvertently, a perfect symbol for what Prince-Bythewood wants to say about how and why and on whom women waste their time—and for the concept that, largely, men are dogs. The ending of "Love and Basketball" is supposed to be happy—everyone gets what they want, almost—but a close reading seems to indicate a director in conflict, one who couldn't quite free herself from the commercial possibilities of her movie to make the film she really wanted to make.

SIGHT AND SOUND, 8/00, p. 52, Stephanie Zachrack

Suburban southern California, 1981. Eleven-year-old Monica, a newcomer in a middle-class neighbourhood, elbows her way into a basketball game with a group of local boys. She proves she's just as good a player as they are, and young Quincy, whose father is a professional basketball player, is impressed. The two become friends, although this friendship is strained when they become teenagers. At the end of their senior year in high school, after both of them have been basketball scholarships at the University of Southern California, they start dating.

While at USC, Quincy discovers his father has been seeing other women behind his mother's back. He breaks up with Monica, feeling that she's too wrapped up in basketball to give him the attention he needs. He then decides to drop out of college to become a professional basketball player.

Later, in 1993, Monica is a star player with the International Women's Basketball Association in Barcelona. Back in the US, Quincy seriously injures himself during a game; Monica returns home and visits him in hospital where she learns that he's engaged to another woman. Having given up basketball to work in a bank, Monica musters the courage to tell Quincy that she still loves him. He realises that playing ball isn't everything, and that he wants Monica back. The two marry and Monica returns to pro basketball.

There's nothing particularly daring about the way writer director Gina Prince-Bythewood has put together her debut feature *Love & Basketball*. But it's a fine example of a conventionally made picture which follows all the rules yet still emerges as fresh and original. This may sound a little strange in the light of the film's final reel, which sees a talented and intelligent black woman get the career she's always wanted—playing professional basketball—only to discover that what she's been missing all along is a man. Sure enough, Prince-Bythewood might have finessed the last act of her film a little more gracefully—it's hard, for instance, to fathom precisely what Sanaa Lathan's Monica finds so unforgettable about Omar Epps' Quincy, a stud with a decent heart but not much depth—but *Love & Basketball* moves along smoothly and features enough careful details to keep it deeply satisfying.

The basketball sequences are beautifully shot and edited: there's a lively sense of momentum to them, but there's also a layered, thoughtful dimension to Prince-Bythewood's *mise en scène*. In one sequence she cuts between a men's game at USC and a women's, subtly underscoring the difference between the facilities (the women's gym is a bare-bones affair) and the density and energy levels of the crowds. The film features an adroit use of pop music, too; in an early scene we see the young Monica shoot hoops to the sound of New Edition's exhilarating 'Candy Girl,' a track which captures her effervescence perfectly.

Sanaa Lathan's performance as the adult Monica has a no-nonsense poise about it, both on the court and off, even Monica's moments of self-consciousness have a certain gangly beauty. In the scene where she's awkwardly dressed up for a school dance, she finds herself starting to relax—and automatically slouches forward in her chair, her elbows resting on her knees as if she were taking a break on the bench.

In its own unassuming way, Prince-Bythewood's film tackles a number of issues that other film-makers—particularly African-American ones—don't care to touch. For one thing, it's not set in the inner city but among America's black middle class, a sector with its own problems and prejudices. Perhaps most significantly, it plainly acknowledges sexism among black men without either defending or crucifying them—Quincy looks set to lead the same philandering life as his father and he refuses to acknowledge that Monica's ball-playing career is as important as his. Prince-Bythewood would seem to have no use for clichés, yet she ruefully admits that sometimes stereotypes have a grounding in certain social realities. But the film finishes with a wry acknowledgement that no one has to remain a stereotype forever. Incomprehensible as it is that Monica would rush back to the US from Barcelona to pursue a guy like Quincy. In the last shot we see of him, he's on the sidelines at one of Monica's games, holding their little girl.

VILLAGE VOICE, 4/25/00, p. 138, Amy Taubin

On a late summer afternoon in 1981, outside a sprawling modern house in the upper-middle-class, largely black Los Angeles neighborhood of Baldwin Hills, a group of 11-year-old boys is playing basketball. Another kid, new on the block, asks to join the game. The boys consent to a tryout, only to discover that the interloper is a girl. Ignoring their jeers, she grabs a pass, drives on her defender, and makes the layup. Thus begins Gina Prince-Bythewood's *Love and Basketball,* and, already, it's a turn-on and a heart-stopper, and it stays that way right to the buzzer.

And no, you don't have to be a fool for basketball, or for women's sports, to love this movie. You don't even have to be a woman, although it probably helps. *Love and Basketball* is the most passionate, clear-sighted movie ever made about women in sports (not that there's much to choose from), but, as its title proudly proclaims, it's also a film about love, specifically about romantic love between two highly competitive people playing in the same arena. And maybe you have to be a fool to believe that two such people, especially when one's a woman and the other a man, can get together in bed and stay together in marriage. Prince-Bythewood is that kind of fool, and for two hours, she convinced me that it's the best kind you can be.

Spanning 15 years, *Love and Basketball* is a girl-gets-guy, girl-loses-guy, girl-gets-guy picture that turns the formula upside down by pairing a girl who refuses to fit the mold with a guy who happily does until she teaches him to know better. Monica Wright (Sanaa Lathan) fell in love with Quincy McCall (Omar Epps) in that first moment of going eyeball-to-eyeball with him on her way to the hoop. Monica, who wears Magic's number 32 on her shoes, wants to be the first woman to play in the NBA. Quincy also has NBA point guard dreams, not in the least because his father is really a player in the league (albeit for the lowly Clippers). Quincy's imagination is captured by the tomboy next door whose passion for the game matches his own, though he doesn't see her as girlfriend material until she shows up at the high school senior prom with another guy.

For a brief moment, all is bliss. They are both recruited for basketball at USC, and they become the freshmen stars of their respective teams. But their love affair comes apart when Quincy has an emotional crisis and Monica refuses to give up a game to hold his hand.

If this sounds like you've seen it before, forget it, you haven't. Much of the thrill of *Love and Basketball* is in the details, the stuff that doesn't show up in the box score. Prince-Bythewood, a high school athlete who turned filmmaker at UCLA, understands the ambivalence with which women in sports are treated in both their professional and personal lives, and every scene is inflected with Monica's struggle not to internalize that ambivalence. But the movie also reflects the changes that have come about in the past 20 years. Monica's childhood dream becomes a reality because there finally is a WNBA.

Like its hero, *Love and Basketball* mixes punch and tenderness. Prince-Bythewood gives the film a style that's easy on the eye but also has muscle—on and off the court. And she gets terrific performances from her actors. Lathan is a remarkably convincing basketball player, but what's even more impressive is the way she switches between defense and offense in the big emotional scenes. And while less than believable as a star athlete, Epps gets extra points: for agreeing to play the boyfriend role (i.e., not the hero) and for delivering without showboating down the stretch.

Also reviewed in:
CHICAGO TRIBUNE, 4/21/00, Friday/p. A, Mark Caro
NEW YORK TIMES, 4/21/00, p. E16, Elvis Mitchell
VARIETY, 2/7-13/00, p. 54, Emanuel Levy
WASHINGTON POST, 4/21/00, p. C1, Stephen Hunter
WASHINGTON POST, 4/21/00, Weekend/p. 45, Desson Howe

LOVE & SEX

A Lions Gate Films release of a Behaviour Worldwide presentation of a Bogart/Barab/Wyman production. *Executive Producer:* Mark Damon. *Producer:* Timothy Scott Bogart, Martin J. Barab, and Brad Wyman. *Director:* Valerie Breiman. *Screenplay:* Valerie Breiman. *Director of Photography:* Adam Kane. *Editor:* Martin Apelbaum. *Music Editor:* Scott Kolden. *Sound:* Matt Nicolay and (music) Christopher J. Roberts. *Casting:* Dan Shaner and Michael Testa. *Production Designer:* Sara Sprawls. *Set Decorator:* Nancy Clements. *Costumes:* Sara Jane Slotnick. *Make-up:* Luisa Abel. *Running time:* 82 minutes. *MPAA Rating:* Not Rated.

CAST: Famke Janssen (Kate Welles); Jon Favreau (Adam Levy); Noah Emmerich (Eric); Cheri Oteri (Mary); Ann Magnuson (Ms. Steinbacher); Josh Hopkins (Joey Santino); Robert Knepper (Gerard); Vincent Ventresca (Richard); Kristen Zang (Savannah); Elimu Nelson (Jerome Davis); Yvonne Zima (9-year-old Kate); Will Rothhaar (9-year-old Bobby); David Steinberg (Tiny Man); Don Brunner (Police Officer); Melissa Fitzgerald (Melanie); Rob Swanson (Blind Date); Rance Howard (Earl); Ron Kochevar (Man); Angela Marsden (Peaches); Troy Blendell (Frank); Nicolette Little (Michelle age, 6).

LOS ANGELES TIMES, 8/25/00, Calendar/p. 8, Kevin Thomas

"Love & Sex" leaves you with the feeling that writer-director Valerie Breiman has lived through the rocky road of romance, and that Breiman is committed to her people. She hopes you care about them because they're worth caring about to her.

"Love & Sex" hasn't a strong, distinctive style, but what sets it a cut above many similar films is that for all its surface humor it has substance and emotional depth. Breiman has written roles for Famke Janssen and Jon Favreau in which they can show how relationships and the individuals within them constantly shift and change whether they realize it or not.

When we meet Janssen's Kate Welles she's single and cynical. She's submitted to her editor (Ann Magnuson) at an L.A.-based women's magazine a blunt piece implying sexual skill guarantees a woman nothing. The outraged editor, known behind her back as "the anti-Christ," gives Kate 24 hours to knock out an upbeat piece in its place about love and sex.

As Kate dictates a memo to herself her banalities fill up the soundtrack as we flash back to what her love life was really like. After a string of dead-end romances—how is it that so attractive and poised a woman as Kate can get mixed up with such jerks?—she is stopped in her tracks at an art gallery by the painter, Adam Levy (Favreau), whose work is on display. The paintings are very Francis Bacon in their tormented images, yet Adam comes across as a mensch. Kate has hit him like a ton of bricks and he pursues her with determined ardor.

Kate and Adam are swiftly caught up in a grand romance, but as they start living together and the first bloom of passion ebbs, they start getting on each other's nerves. Kate especially dreads the specter of repeating her parents' marriage, which she views as 15 years of love followed by 20 years of indifference.

Kate is not very good at grasping that relationships have to be worked at, or that a sad turn of events between her and Adam must be dealt with if their love is to endure and grow. Eventually, Adam throws in the towel, but his stance of proud indifference swiftly crumbles.

"Love & Sex" now gets underway in earnest, as both embark on inconsequential affairs that only underline how much they miss each other. They hadn't realized that along the line they had become friends as well as lovers, but can they be friends without being lovers—or vice versa?

Lots of romance movies turn upon the immaturity of men, but Breiman sees in Kate no less a need to grow up and understand the futility of expecting perfection in others—especially when there is no way she can live up to such a standard herself. Adam certainly can be overbearing and indeed downright obnoxious, but there's no questioning that his love for Kate is unshakable and inescapable. He lives in a state of torment wanting her back.

Breiman is consistently able to see the humor as well as the pain in Kate and Adam's predicament. Both Janssen, whose beauty becomes tinged with gauntness and strain, and the stocky Favreau, who has a warm teddy bear charm, have a chemistry all the more credible because initially she seems a little too glamorous, a little too striking, for him. The more we see them together, however, the more they seem right for each other.

Both Janssen and Favreau make strong impressions, showing us the many facets, moods and contradictions of Kate and Adam that draw them together as well as drive them apart. The film belongs to them, but Josh Hopkins proves a scene-stealer as a sweet-natured, hunky minor martial arts star, given to bad impressions of his hero, Robert De Niro. He's a sizzling lover for Kate but none too smart and adamantly unreflective.

"Love & Sex" is not quite original enough to make much of a dent in the marketplace, but it shows its stars to advantage and marks a solid start in features for Breiman.

NEW YORK POST, 8/25/00, p. 50, Jonathan Foreman

There are some enjoyably sharp, close-to-the-bone observations in "Love & Sex," the latest in a series of unusually sophisticated Generation-X romantic comedies ("High Fidelity," "The Tao of Steve") that put cruder big-studio romantic comedies to shame.

But while "Love & Sex" generally rises above the easy clichés you find in most such movies, it is also marred by some soppy sections, casting that undermines the story's believability and a kind of self-consciousness that makes it hard to really care about the characters.

Kate (Famke Janssen) is a beautiful magazine writer in what looks like downtown L.A.

She's in trouble with her bosses for writing a piece about oral sex that's way too explicit. To save her job, she must come up with the definitive article about thirtysomething women, love and sex.

Inevitably, she draws on her own less-than-ideal love life for inspiration, and as she dictates notes into a tape recorder, you get to see, in brief, her early relationships, and then, in more detail, the story of her romance with Adam (Jon Favreau).

Adam is a burly artist who wisecracks in the tradition of Woody Allen and Albert Brooks. He picks up Kate at one of his own gallery openings and, before long, they've moved in together.

Unlike so many men in romantic comedies, Adam has little fear of commitment. But he's insecure about Kate's having had so many sexual partners in the past, and when disaster strikes their household, the relationship falls apart.

Both of them start dating other people, but both know they're right for each other.

Janssen, a former supermodel, proved she could act in "Celebrity," "X-men," etc., and she has no problem handling a Sandra Bullock/Julia Roberts part like this one.

Bravely, she's willing to look less than perfect in the role. But she's still a little too spectacular: It makes it that much harder to suspend disbelief when you see this implausibly gorgeous yet freakishly tall and thin girl walking through offices and down streets, and no one around her does so much as a double take.

It's also hard to believe that a babe like her would be with a relative schlump like Jon Favreau's artist.

NEWSDAY, 8/25/00, Part II/p. B6, Jan Stuart

You don't call your movie "Love and Sex" unless you intend to put across some basic truths about relationships.

Here are some basic truths according to Valerie Breiman, the writer and director of this new romantic comedy: 1. Couples fight over what movie to rent at video stores; 2. The guys invariably want an action flick, while the women desire something more meaningful; 3. The fight is never really about the video.

If you're nodding your head, you needn't wait for "Love and Sex" to reach the video stores. This jovial and knowing aperitif of a movie is a charming example of what has come to be known as the date movie—i.e., a picture that enables people who are beginning to date, have been dating too long, or wish they were dating again, to gather ceremoniously and murmur an affirming "Uh-huh." And then go home and fight about it.

The film's presumed stand-in for its filmmaker is Kate Welles (Famke Janssen), a smart and svelte women's magazine writer who is busily contemplating the trajectory of her love life as she prepares a related article. Her recollections are just the sort of confidential-but-not-pornographic musings one might expect from a rag called Monique: the first childhood love, the teenage deflowering at the hands of the high school French teacher, the fling with the married man who looks suspiciously like Bill Clinton.

The guy who stands out from the muck is Adam Levy, an unremarkable-looking artist whose affability allows him to get away with the sort of blunt remarks that would seem like pie-throwing from less heartfelt sources. As played by Jon Favreau, he comes off as a next-generation Albert Brooks, without the neuroses. Adam's so grounded and funny—amiable in a Pooh-Bear sort of way—it's mildly incongruous that he churns out paintings that suggest Lucien Freud with a migraine.

Kate and Adam are so cozily right for one another that they naturally have to go around the block several times before they discover it for themselves. Their courtship is far more interesting than the romantic detours each of them takes during a breakup, in part because Breiman doesn't allow them lovers who are proper threats (Kate goes for a thick Italian-American actor who idolizes De Niro, while Adam gets a perky harp player whom Kate dismisses as a "bimbo savant").

Janssen effects just the right balance of sweet-and-sour as Kate, a self-described "relationship leper." "Love and Sex" scores enough basic truths that one can readily identify oneself as a resident of the colony.

SIGHT AND SOUND, 10/00, p. 49, Ronald McLean

In a school playground young Kate Welles experiences her first romantic tryst, and a subsequent break-up with classmate Bobby Norton. Years later, in present-day LA, Kate arrives late at the women's magazine where she works to discover she's been fired. Kate's editor says she'll be reinstated if she delivers upbeat copy by the end of that day.

Beginning work, Kate reminisces about past relationships. She recalls an exhibition where she dumped her date for artist Adam. Adam is later shocked to discover Kate has had 13 previous lovers, compared to his two. Kate remembers losing her virginity to her high-school French teacher, as well as her relationship with Eric, who turned out to have a wife and children. She moves in with Adam. On their first anniversary, Kate discovers that she is pregnant, but she later miscarries.

As their relationship loses excitement, Adam suggests they split up. Kate meets B-movie actor Joey, with whom she begins an affair. Adam is jealous and asks Kate to reconsider. She refuses, and holidays with Joey, but beyond physical attraction the two have little in common. She and Joey fall out in a cinema.

Kate decides her assignment is pointless and resigns. Preparing for a blind date, she ends up chatting up a Jehovah's witness. At his latest show, Adam rejects a fan's advances. Kate arrives, the couple reunite and end up in bed, still teasing one another.

Like Stephen Frears' recent *High Fidelity, Love & Sex* opens with a sequence depicting its lead character's first experience of love. And like *High Fidelity*, this pre-pubescent prelude is a sweetly sad episode, that primes its protagonist, in this case Famke Janssen's journalist Kate, for the more crushing disappointments of adult love. But whereas in Frears' film the mood darkens as John Cusack's Rob fumbles from one relationship to another, the mood of debut writer-director Valerie Breiman's film doesn't stray from the light, somewhat fey tone of its opening moments. All of which makes for pleasant enough viewing—Breiman's screenplay has a few genuinely sharp one-liners (Kate witheringly dismisses one of her ex-partner's girlfriends as a "bimbo savante"')—but the refusal by former actor Breiman (she had a part in John Hughes' 1988 film *She's Having a Baby)* to confront the messier adult realities of the dating game makes for a fairly banal experience.

Perhaps the film's most telling moment is an uncredited cameo by *Friends* star David Schwimmer. Diverting but lightweight, *Love & Sex* is reminiscent of a feature-length sitcom: the bulk of the humour is dialogue-driven and the characterisation broad (a basketball-playing fling of Kate's is obsessed with women's backsides; another boyfriend, actor Joey, is like his namesake in *Friends* dim but loveable). And as with television sitcoms, the film is mostly made up of interior scenes, although Breiman has some fun with the decor here: the bedroom of Kate's high-school French teacher, to whom she loses her virginity, is suitably seedy, and a poster for a low-budget action film Joey starred in carries the irresistible tag line: "It was a war no-one thought they could win In a land no-one thought they could find."

To its credit, *Love & Sex* does feature two likeable leads: Jon Favreau, who starred in *Swingers,* to which this film is being pitched as a female equivalent, veers enjoyably between confident buck and wounded boy as Kate's on-off soulmate. Despite some tentative moments where she's torn between sniping and smouldering, Janssen relaxes into the role of the pointedly far-from-perfect Kate. Reflecting on her past failed loves, she concludes "Love is ecstasy and agony," but ultimately Breiman's film is far too innocuous, longing to be adored—like the kitten which wakes Kate up one morning, interrupting her dreams of wild sex—to deliver either of these two extremes.

VILLAGE VOICE, 8/29/00, p. 140, Jessica Winter

Though it lacks any sense of place (best guess is L.A.), the nasty, lonely world of *Love & Sex* exudes as much gloom and doom as *Solomon & Gaenor*'s Wales, owing to whiny thirtysomethings who never have any friends except for their current significant others and who start a majority of sentences with "I'm a...": Famke Janssen's high-strung women's-mag writer says, "I'm a floater; I float through life," Jon Favreau's guy's-guy painter says, I'm a guy—I fuck, I don't fall in love," and so on. Built upon a shaky framing device that proves incoherent, *Love & Sex* is all solipsistic jaded-*Cosmo* patter, in which the principals—self-obsessed but not self-aware—are angry that their lives are not perfect, and said principals' anger is promptly assuaged.

Also reviewed in:
CHICAGO TRIBUNE, 9/8/00, Friday/p. B, Mark Caro
NEW YORK TIMES, 8/25/00, p. E18, Lawrence Van Gelder
VARIETY, 1/31-2/6/00, p. 37, Todd McCarthy
WASHINGTON POST, 9/8/00, p. C12, Rita Kempley

LOVE MACHINE, THE

A Crystal Pictures release of an Olympia Pictures production. *Executive Producer:* Louis Robles and Ruth Nobles. *Producer:* Steven G. Menkin. *Director:* Gordon Ericksen. *Screenplay:* Gordon Ericksen. *Director of Photography:* Hiro Wakiya. *Editor:* Michael J. Dominico. *Music:* Mike Dominico. *Sound:* Noah V. Timan and Jacques Durand. *Art Director:* Carveth Martin. *Running time:* 83 minutes. *MPAA Rating:* Not Rated.

CAST: Marlene Forte (Becca); Gary Perez (Julio); Tomo Omori (Shino); Jun Suenaga (Akira); Elizabeth Wunsch (Beverly); Chip Garner (Chip); John Chidiac (Marcus); Will Keenan (Mike); Mariana Carreno (Cecilia); Kayoko Takahashi (Kyoko); Al Rodriguez (Javier).

NEW YORK POST, 5/11/00, p. 67, Lou Lumenick

"A movie about the Internet?," asks a character in "The Love Machine," a low-budget mocumentary about online hanky-panky. "How boring."

"The Love Machine" isn't exactly boring, but it isn't a great movie either, thanks to excessive glibness and the vague motivation of its main character, who claims to be an "investigative journalist."

She's probing a Web site called "The Love Machine," which subtitles itself a "virtual community of free spirits (that is, amateur perverts)" and is being surreptitiously operated out of a computer lab at New York University.

Becca (Marlene Forte) tracks down the anonymous posters on the site and confronts them with their fantasies.

Julio, a Latin-studies prof who goes by the screen name "Macho Time," posts naked pictures of his current and former student-girlfriends, including his wife.

Others include a very closeted gay student (Jun Suenaga) who plans to return to Japan to marry his fiancée—and a middle-aged grant administrator (Elizabeth Wunsch) who details steamy sessions with a pair of teenage boys named Tom and Jerry.

Writer-director Gordon Ericksen apparently intended this as a media satire, but it's never clear who Becca works for—if anyone—or what she's after with her confrontations, and why so few of her victims are Caucasian.

"The Love Machine" has some lively scenes—including one fairly explicit sequence featuring a pair of self-styled exhibitionists—but it's too glib for its own good.

VILLAGE VOICE, 5/16/00, p. 140, Amy Taubin

A mockumentary about the Internet, made in the late '90s, during what history will regard as its primitive phase, *The Love Machine* mixes computer-wonk sophistication with old-fashioned 16mm, the medium that director Gordon Eriksen still prefers. The combination of nonglitzy filmmaking, techno-hip subject matter, humanist progressive politics, and sleazy, near-pornographic imagery is unsettling and oddly satisfying. Evading easy categories, *The Love Machine* slipped through the distribution cracks, despite winning an enthusiastic audience on the festival circuit. The new Pioneer Theater is opening it for a run, as well as showing in repertory the four features that Eriksen codirected with his partner, Heather Johnston. *Lena's Dreams* and *The Big Dis* should not be missed.

Also reviewed in:
NEW YORK TIMES, 5/11/00, p. E12, Stephen Holden
VARIETY, 5/17-23/99, p. 60, David Finnigan

LOVE'S LABOUR'S LOST

A Miramax Films release of an Intermedia Films and Pathe Pictures presentation in association with The Arts Council of England, Le Studio Canal +, and Miramax Films of a Shakespeare Film Company production. *Executive Producer:* Guy East, Nigel Sinclair, Harvey Weinstein, Bob Weinstein, and Alexis Lloyd. *Producer:* David Barron and Kenneth Branagh. *Director:* Kenneth Branagh. *Screenplay:* Kenneth Branagh. *Based on the play by:* William Shakespeare. *Director of Photography:* Alex Thomson. *Editor:* Neil Farrell and Dan Farrell. *Music:* Patrick Doyle. *Music Editor:* Gerard McCann. *Choreographer:* Stuart Hopps. *Sound:* Peter Glossop and (music) Nick Wollage. *Sound Editor:* Peter Pennell. *Casting:* Randi Hiller and Nina Gold. *Production Designer:* Tim Harvey. *Art Director:* Mark Raggett. *Set Decorator:* Celia Bobak. *Costumes:* Anna Buruma. *Make-up:* Amanda Knight. *Stunt Coordinator:* Ray De Haan *Running time:* 95 minutes. *MPAA Rating:* PG.

CAST: Kenneth Branagh (Berowne); Richard Briers (Nathaniel); Richard Clifford (Boyet); Carmen Ejogo (Maria); Daniel Hill (Mercade); Nathan Lane (Costard); Adrian Lester (Dumaine); Matthew Lillard (Longaville); Natascha McElhone (Rosaline); Geraldine McEwan (Holofernia); Emily Mortimer (Katherine); Alessandro Nivola (King); Anthony O'Donnell (Moth); Stefania Rocca (Jaquenetta); Alicia Silverstone (Princess); Timothy Spall (Don Armado); Jimmy Yuill (Dull); Alfred Bell (Gaston); Daisy Gough (Isabelle); Graham Hubbard (Eugene); Paul Moody (Jaques); Yvonne Reilly (Beatrice); Iain Stuart Robertson (Hippolyte); Emma Scott (Celimene); Amy Tez (Sophie).

CHRISTIAN SCIENCE MONITOR, 6/9/00, p. 15, David Sterritt

[*Love's Labour's Lost* was reviewed jointly with *Hamlet*; see Sterritt's review of that film.]

LOS ANGELES TIMES, 6/9/00, Calendar/p. 6, Kenneth Turan

Writing musical theater was not an option for William Shakespeare, but Kenneth Branagh hasn't let that trouble him. He's turned Shakespeare's "Love's Labour's Lost" into a 1930s-style romantic musical comedy, garnished with retro dance numbers and classic songs by Cole Porter, Irving Berlin and George and Ira Gershwin. It ought to be delightful, but it isn't.

For while the idea is a charming one, in execution "Love's Labour's Lost" feels clumsy and jerry-built. Neither Shakespeare nor a musical and nowhere near as witty or effervescent as it pretends, this fusion is too leaden to be more than sporadically alive on screen.

What could be wrong with a film in which evergreens like "The Way You Look Tonight," "Let's Face the Music and Dance," "Cheek to Cheek" and "They Can't Take That Away From Me" are featured? Start with the performers, many of whom, like co-stars Branagh and Alicia Silverstone, did not make their names as interpreters of melodies. While the vocalizing falls between the pain caused by the legendary "At Long Last Love" and the mild pleasures of Woody Allen's "Everyone Says I Love You," it's not exactly scintillating.

The same is true for the amateurish and second-hand dancing numbers (a failed Busby Berkeley extravaganza in a swimming pool is especially weak) that are unlikely to cause anyone to jettison their Fred Astaire-Ginger Rogers tapes. When one of this film's producers says, "We had no practical experience of shooting a musical number," he's not just being modest.

It doesn't help either that the starting point is not one of Shakespeare's premier comedies. Set in the kingdom of Navarre (and updated to Europe on the eve of World War II), "Lost" focuses on the principality's king (Alessandro Nivola) and his boon companions Berowne (Branagh), Longaville (Matthew Lillard) and Dumaine (Adrian Lester).

As detailed by the relentlessly upbeat faux newsreels of Navarre Cinetone News (one of the film's few amusing touches), king and company are about to embark on a monastic three years' study of metaphysics and philosophy. To prove to the world that they're serious about this endeavor, the quartet vow to ban women from their very sight.

Unfortunately for their resolve, a delegation headed by the Princess of France (Silverstone) and ladies in waiting Rosaline (Natascha McElhone), Katherine (Emily Mortimer) and Maria (Carmen Ejogo) are about to arrive and too important to ignore. The men say they will hardly notice, but in fact the king falls for the princess, his pals do likewise with her attendants, and the games of love's passions and deceptions begin.

While this isn't Shakespeare's most scintillating scenario, the screen version of "Love's Labour's Lost" does not benefit by being cut, its text consultant advises, to about 25%-30% of its original length. That kind of severe truncation makes what's left seem jagged and choppy and doesn't leave enough of the language for us to get comfortable with.

Also, a lot of what's left of the play is pitiful slapstick and failed farce, the kind of burlesque humor that helped kill burlesque. Most of this involves a barely comprehensible subplot employing a clown named Costard (Nathan Lane), chatty Spanish nobleman Don Annado (Timothy Spall) and the beautiful Jaquenetta (Stefania Rocca), all of whom have appeared to better effect elsewhere.

Worst of all perhaps is "Lost's" smug air of pleasure at how clever it thinks it's being to fit those wonderful songs into that venerable play. The cast members may want us to believe, as the newsreel puts it, "they're in the love business and there's no business like it," but the evidence on screen points the other way.

While the cast varies in its ability to handle the Shakespearean language, the person who does it best, not surprisingly, is Branagh himself. He has a true gift for making 400-year-old words seem bright and accessible, and watching him is a reminder that his direction of Shakespearean films used to exhibit the same characteristics.

In "Henry V," his 1989 debut, and 1993's "Much Ado ABout Nothing," Branagh set a modern standard for making Shakespeare approachable and comprehensible. The problem is not with that excellent intention, it's that Branagh is having more and more trouble trying to fulfill it.

NEW YORK, 6/19/00, p. 60, Peter Rainer

If ecstasy is the drug of choice in *Groove* [see Rainer's review] then Kenneth Branagh's *Love's Labour's Lost* seems to be high on Halcion. He's taken Shakespeare's peerless piece of frivolity and revamped it into a frothy thirties-Hollywood musical complete with song-and-dance numbers by Cole Porter and Gershwin. The froth quickly curdles.

NEW YORK POST, 6/9/00, p. 51, Jonathan Foreman

From Julie Taymor's brilliant "Titus" to Michael Almereyda's gimmicky but leaden "Hamlet," this has been a year of ambitious Shakespeare movie adaptations.

Kenneth Branagh's version of the early comedy "Love's Labour's Lost" may be the most ambitious of them all.

The actor/director has attempted to replace chunks of the original text with classic songs from Broadway musicals of the 1930s and '40s by Cole Porter, Irving Berlin and the Gershwins.

It must have seemed like a clever idea at the time. But the resulting hybrid is something grotesque, like some flailing, unfortunate beast created by H.G. Wells' Dr. Moreau out of a tiger and an ostrich.

While Branagh tries hard to get young Hollywood stars like Alicia Silverstone and Matthew Lillard both to speak Shakespearean verse like Olivier and to sing and dance like Rogers and Astaire, most of his cast is not up to the task. (The only one who can really dance is Adrian Lester from "Primary Colors.")

And, in any case, the juxtaposition of the two art forms could hardly be more jarring.

"Love's Labour's Lost" is an ornate, sophisticated comedy about a failed attempt to suppress sexual love in order to further the life of the mind. The language is extremely dense, though often very beautiful, as you can tell whenever Branagh himself speaks it. (He's always had an amazing ability to make Elizabethan English seem as clear and simple as our own.)

In 1939, the King of Navarre (Alessandro Nivola) and his three best pals, Longaville (Lillard), Dumaine (Lester) and Berowne (Branagh), swear an oath to give up women and other pleasures for three years so as to devote their lives to study.

The idea is that "the mind shall banquet, the body pine." Women are not even allowed in their presence.

But no sooner have the four signed their pledges when Berowne remembers that the Princess of France (Silverstone) is about to arrive on a vital diplomatic visit with three beautiful ladies in attendance: Rosaline (Natascha McElhone) Maria (Carmen Ejogo) and Katherine (Emily Mortimer).

The King agrees to meet them outside the gates of the city, and of course he and his three friends immediately fall in love. Each secretly pursues the object of his desire, despite their solemn oaths.

Silverstone is charming as always, with her trademark frown and trembling lips. But she's the weakest singer and dancer of the troupe, and her hair mysteriously turns brown during the shamefully amateurish synchronized swimming scene.

Overall, the dancing is messy with a distinctly collegiate feel. It's mostly a matter of rehearsal rather than inferior choreography. Branagh trained his actors for three weeks; the men who made the great movie musicals would train their people for months.

Besides Branagh, the star of the film is the ravishing McElhone. The actress, who has mostly played Irish terrorists, not only looks like a '40s movie star with her enormous eyes and prominent cheekbones, she can also sing and dance.

Nathan Lane, the Broadway star, shows everyone else up with a superb rendition of "There's No Business Like Show Business."

NEWSDAY, 6/9/00, Part II/p. B2, Gene Seymour

There's not a whole lot of narrative meat in Shakespeare's "Loves Labours Lost." Yet it is so heavily seasoned with the Bard's most aromatic language that it has tempted many scholars to suggest it be turned into an opera.

So imagine, then, how the synapses of Kenneth Branagh must have been charging as his quixotic endeavor to get all of Shakespeare on the big screen pulled to a stop at this festive little romp:

Well (hey, kids!), if we're making a movie of this romantic comedy, why not give it the look and feel of one of those classic romantic musical comedies from the 1930s? We'll make it all bright and shiny the way MGM used to. We'll even get Stanley Donen, the man who co-directed the greatest movie musical of all time ("Singin' in the Rain" and we'll argue about it later), listed as a presenter to give it cachet. Give it legitimacy.

Unfortunately, Donen's name alone isn't going to put wings on the feet of Branagh, Alicia Silverstone, Matthew Lillard and the other earnest plodders compelled to make their way through this noble misfire.

One very much wants to give Branagh the benefit of the doubt by assuming that the rough edges of his troupe's singing and dancing may have been as much the point here as it was in Woody Allen's comparably scattershot 1996 musical, "Everyone Says I Love You." If so, the point isn't well taken.

Nor is the somewhat ham-handed placement of the production in 1939 Europe with war clouds hovering over the mythical land of Navarre, whose king (Alessandro Nivola) decides to make a pact with his three best buds (Branagh, Lillard, Adrian Lester) to swear off women and devote themselves to hermetic philosophical study.

Their resolve is shaken by the arrival of the Princess of France (Silverstone) and her drop-dead-gorgeous court (Natasha McElhone, Emily Mortimer, Carmen Ejogo), whose diplomatic mission becomes a mating ritual of customary Elizabethan folly.

Branagh's Berowne is supposed to be the play's philosophical center and he plays it with such perfect archness that you regret it when, as frequently happens, he and/or the other boys and girls break into song in mid-dialogue.

Not that there's any complaint about the songs themselves. (Who could gripe about Porter or Gershwin?) It's just that the antic mood seems a little forced, the set pieces too awkward for comfort. Branagh's not a bad song-and-dance man. (He's a whole lot better than the embarrassing Lillard and Silverstone.) But he's not as good as Lester, McElhone, Geraldine McEwan (who's a dry-martini wonder as the tutor) or Nathan Lane, who does his best to lift the enterprise, whenever he's on screen.

SIGHT AND SOUND, 4/00, p. 54, David Jays

Britain, the 30s. The King of Navarre proposes to three companions that they join him in an oath to study rigorously for three years, during which time they will fast regularly and abjure female company. Dumaine and Longaville accept the terms readily; Berowne is reluctant, but eventually agrees. One stipulation is immediately broken when waiting women (Rosaline, Maria and Katherine) arrive for treaty negotiations with the king. Despite themselves, the men begin to fall for their visitors.

Navarre's other courtiers experience the effects of love—eccentric Spaniard Don Armado falls for Jaquenetta, and even the mature Holofernia and Nathaniel are not immune. The men confess they have contravened their oath, and seek to woo the women through a variety of entertainments which are interrupted when the princess learns of her father's death. The women leave, insisting on testing their suitors' constancy during a year's absence. War prolongs the separation but eventually the lovers are reunited.

Love's Labour's Lost is one of the few Shakespeare plays not previously adapted for cinema, although the sportive courtship rituals dappled with melancholy have inspired an opera (W. H. Auden and Chester Kallman wrote the libretto for Nicolas Nabokov's score in 1973). Here, Kenneth Branagh fashions a 30s-style musical out of the play, studding it generously with popular standards. You can see how it might have worked. The plot, tweaked by leisure and misunderstanding, is as featherlight as an Astaire Rogers movie—as in *The Gay Divorcee* (1934) or *Top Hat* (1935), guys struggle to prove they deserve the dames—and the mature camp followers surrounding the lovers would have fitted such players as Eric Blore, Edward Everett Horton or Helen Broderick perfectly. Shakespeare's relentless allusiveness also suits such blithe lyrical name-droppers as Cole Porter and George Gershwin.

Unlike his uncut version of *Hamlet* Branagh prunes away almost three-quarters of the original text. Newsreel interludes explicate the plot, with jovial Pathé-style voiceovers keeping us up to speed. Between numbers, Patrick Doyle's glutinous score cossets the lovers' barbed exchanges, robbing them of tension. When Rosaline pulls Berowne short by insisting he try his japery in a hospital "to move wild laughter in the throat of death?" he recoils—the gravity of the challenge is belied by a balm of strings. If the peppery repartee is smoothed, Branagh extols his cast for "a certain rawness in the singing and dancing" (the actors sing with their own voices, *pace* Woody Allen's *Everyone Says I Love You*). Despite Branagh's affection for stalwart amateur theatricals (evident in *Peter's Friends* and *In the Bleak Midwinter*), the numbers are tentatively performed. When Adrian Lester's Dumaine brings a velvet voice and soft shoe to 'I've Got a Crush On You', his chair-toppling ease allows a rare glimpse of emotional and physical relish. Elsewhere, there's an Esther Williams-style bathing number and an excruciating take on Gene Kelly's virile balletic interludes, all white vests, fishnets and red smoke.

The script's banter produces agitated flutters of reaction shots, and DP Alex Thomson keeps the camera circling as it did for his and Branagh's paranoid *Hamlet*. Wide, shallow shots recur: the snag with tracing four couples who negotiate identical stages of courtship is that dance numbers need to involve them all. Fine for Busby Berkeley and his beaming blonde assembly lines; here, you lose focus and the couples remain strung out over the width of the screen. It's like watching a row of bunting do the carioca. The film inhabits a lovingly artificial Oxbridge of courtyards and autumnal leaves drifting towards flagstones, into which the women introduce arresting dabs of colour, from their vermilion lips to hats like whorls of flirtation. Anna Buruma's costumes point up the pairings through colour coded ties and accessories. Colour creeps in as

Cupid advances; the circular library reveals an ultramarine trim, and when the camera swoops up for a fantasy sequence, the ceiling emerges as a vivid dome.

Shakespeare's text is suffused with the sweet smoke of rhetoric—quibbles, poems, puns that chase their own tails—but only Geraldine McEwan's tutor in sturdy brogues really frolics with the language, swooping phrases like "begot in the ventricle of memory" around her Big-Dipper vocal range. Natascha McElhone brings welcome asperity to Rosaline, but as in *Much Ado about Nothing*, comedy provokes Branagh himself into whinnies and grimaces. Alicia Silverstone, deliciously serious in *Clueless*, falls back on a coy gurgle.

The princess' bereavement, augmented by the outbreak of war in Europe, prompts the courtship's denouement, postponed for a year and a day. "That's too long for a play," comments Berowne, but the film flashes forward without difficulty, so an airstrip parting is followed by a grainy montage of wartime footage until the reunion. It's a sweet conclusion to a harmless movie. Cinematic Shakespeare has been with us since snippets of *King John* were shot in 1899, and Branagh stands in the enthusiastic Franco Zeffirelli tradition. But Baz Luhrmann's *Romeo & Juliet* surely discredited the notion that mediocre popularisation was an interesting future for the Shakespeare film.

TIME, 6/12/00, p. 82, Richard Corliss

We come to bury Branagh, not to praise him. Sorry, wrong play and all, but as Kenneth Branagh turns 40 this year—and as he presents *Love's Labour's Lost*, his fourth Shakespeare film as star and director—it's time to wonder what happened to this Great Hope of the British Theatre, this jack-of-all-arts, this next Olivier. By his mid-20s Branagh had earned raves as Henry V at the Royal Shakespeare Company, staged and fronted an acclaimed *Romeo and Juliet* and starred in the miniseries *Fortunes of War* with his future wife Emma Thompson. It all seems so very long ago when a new Branagh project was an event. Now it is a vague threat, and he is just another performer whose industry overwhelms his genius and sizzle.

After his burly film of *Henry V*, his al fresco *Much Ado About Nothing* and his all-the-words *Hamlet*, Branagh devises a high-concept *Love's Labour's Lost*. Hey, kids, let's cut most of the text, put in 10 classic show tunes and set the story in a mythical European kingdom at the start of World War II. He has cast it with young actors, many of whom have done little Shakespeare and less musical theater. So the *Clueless* Alicia Silverstone is the princess; *Scream's* Matthew Lillard and *Face Off's* Alessandro Nivola join Branagh and the gifted Adrian Lester to complete a quartet of severely dimpled swains. The assumption—here as in Woody Allen's *Everyone Says I Love You*—is that singing and dancing are not so much skills as attitudes. Anyone can do it. Just open your mouth, and pick up your feet. Well, no, it ain't so. To stumble through *Cheek to Cheek* and *Let's Face the Music and Dance* is to hobble their meaning and resonance.

Most of the people couldn't be prettier. The ladies' dresses are glamorously revealing (this is one of the most bosom-obsessed movies since Russ Meyer retired). There's a nice use of the Anglo-African actors Lester and Carmen Ejogo; Branagh pairs them off with white co-stars. And in the director's familiar long takes, some of the dance numbers do work up a pleasing tension.

But this is a sloppy job, both in little goofs (lyricist Dorothy Fields' name is misspelled in the opening credits; one character reads a letter, and the same text she is "reading" is visible on the other side) and in the cast's gung-ho amateurism. It's like Shakespeare done by the *Fame* kids. Even such old pros as Nathan Lane and Timothy Spall are made to perform their face-contorting comedy so close to the camera that mugging becomes assault.

Shakespeare will survive this distortion. So will Branagh; he is, above all, an energetic entrepreneur. But we must look elsewhere for an actor of classical grace and modern power who will be not the next Olivier but the next Ken Branagh.

VILLAGE VOICE, 6/13/00 p. 155, J. Hoberman

Having impersonated a nattering Woody Allen in the execrable *Celebrity*, Kenneth Branagh goes the master one better with a high-flown equivalent of Allen's musical wannabe, *Everyone Says I Love You*. Branagh's cloddish adaptation of *Love's Labour's Lost* recasts the play as a faux 1930s musical—albeit one that suffers mightily for the absence of a few pimps and 'hos.

Branagh is not the first to imagine a musical version of *LLL*. The composer antihero of Thomas Mann's Dr. *Faustus* contemplated the play as the basis for an anti-Wagnerian opera. Branagh's own deal with the devil dictates that he alternate Irving Berlin anthems with severely shortened Shakespearean speeches, and stage them both with fart jokes so insipid they would embarrass Benny Hill. The result is a double travesty—a triple one, actually, if you consider the quality of the singing and dancing.

Hamming shamelessly as Berowne, Branagh is overseasoned for his part; leading his colleagues in a swishy version of "I'd Rather Charleston" or declaiming "I Won't Dance" (no such luck), he's as desperate as a veteran social director at a Catskills hotel about to fold. Alicia Silverstone, concentrating to the max as the Princess of France, handles her tongue-twister dialogue better than her musical numbers. Although her valiant surplus of chin-action gives a poignantly confessional spin to the line "A heavy heart bears not a nimble tongue," she's upstaged by her lady-in-waiting Rosaline, willowy Natascha McElhone, who can actually put across a song. Branagh's conception is so gratingly jolly that even a natural cutup like Nathan Lane is rendered tiresome—required to recite the first few choruses of "There's No Business Like Show Business" as a dirge before the bewigged chorus prances on.

Triple travesty? Why not a quadruple bypass? When the long-simmering war finally breaks out, Branagh orchestrates a tap dance in combat boots and pastiches the last scene of *Casablanca*, making a segue to actual World War II footage as his cast solemnly sings "They Can't Take That Away From Me." Ah, but they can. Remarkably tolerant to this point, the largely German audience with whom I saw *LLL* at the Berlin Film Festival seemed properly perplexed to find the destruction of their city (among other wartime horrors) accompanied by Branagh's lachrymose invocation of "the way you sing off-key."

Also reviewed in:
CHICAGO TRIBUNE, 6/16/00, Friday/p. A, Mark Caro
NEW REPUBLIC, 7/10 & 17/00, p. 32, Stanley Kauffmann
NEW YORK TIMES, 6/9/00, p. E12, A. O. Scott
VARIETY, 2/21-27/00, p. 36, Derek Elley
WASHINGTON POST, 6/22/00, p. C1, Rita Kempley
WASHINGTON POST, 6/23/00, p. C12, Stephen Hunter
WASHINGTON POST, 5/23/00, Weekend/p. 39, Desson Howe

LOVING JEZEBEL

The Shooting Gallery release of an Encore Entertainment/Lancaster Productions/Starz! production. *Producer:* David Lancaster. *Director:* Kwyn Bader.   *Screenplay:* Kwyn Bader. *Director of Photography:* Horacio Marquinez.   *Editor:* Tom McArdle.   *Music:* Tony Prendatt. *Production Designer:* Franckie Diago.   *Costumes:* Arjun Bhasin.   *Make-up:* Katherine James and Joanne Ottaviano.   *Running time:* 85 minutes.   *MPAA Rating:* R.

CAST: Hill Harper (Theodorous); Laurel Holloman (Samantha); Nicole Ari Parker (Frances); Sandrine Holt (Mona), David Moscow (Gabe); Elisa Donovan (Salli); Andre Blake (Neeco); Phylicia Rashad (Alice Melville); Larry Gilliard, Jr. (Walter); John Doman (Pop Melville); Justin Pierre Edmund (Little Theodorous); Lysa Aya Trenier (June); Jean-Christophe Emo (François); Heather Gottlieb (Nina Clarise); Diandra Newlin (Nikki Noodleman); Faith Geer (Mrs. Harp); Barry Yourgrau (Mr. Leone); Eugene Ashe (Man in Car); Makeda Christodoulos and Abigail Revasch (Israeli Girls); Judah Domke and Jason Hefter (Customers); Gregory Grove (Waiter); Angel Brown (Rita); Ray Frazier (Skip); Crystal Rose (Beth); Bryant Clifford (Steve); Debra Venedam (Club Patron); Jan Triska (Melvin Szabo).

NEW YORK POST, 10/27/00, p. 46, Lou Lumenick

"Loving Jezebel," the month's second flick about a guy who covets other guys' women, isn't as relentlessly vulgar or cartoonish as "The Ladies Man"—nor is it a whole lot more realistic.

Amateurishly directed by Kwyn Bader and populated by misogynistically grotesque beauties, its sole virtue is star Hill Harper, a thirtyish actor who maintains his sense of humor, even when he's forced to play the hero as a 17-year-old with a retainer.

NEWSDAY, 10/17/00, Part II/p. B6, Gene Seymour

As with many "calling card" features by young directors, "Loving Jezebel" wears its patches and frayed edges with a callow blend of cockiness and self-consciousness. This first feature by Kwyn Bader also seems carried away with its own winsome romanticism, inspired in part by such masters of lyric, nebbish-in-love comedies as Woody Allen and Francois Truffaut.

But part of what makes "Loving Jezebel" worth seeing, if only for curiosity's sake, is that both Baker and his nerdy lover-fool of a protagonist are African-American. It's also worth noting that neither the film nor its hapless hero, Theo Melville (Hill Harper from TV's "City of Angels"), are as unparticular about the ethnic backgrounds of the women he falls for as he is about the fact that all of them are attached to other lovers. Such openness to possibility is both ingratiating and infectious, and almost (but not quite) make the movie's technical shortcomings irrelevant.

It's rare these days for any film, domestic or foreign, to wander into the once-fertile sub-genre of "young rake's progress." This is especially true if the "young rake" has Theo's many foibles, chief of which are an approach to women so goofily earnest and over-the-top that it's a wonder he scores with such enchanting beauties as Mona (Sandrine Holt), a sultry West Indian waitress who's dating his college friend, or Frances (Nicole Ari Parker), a fellow jazz lover and student whose cuckolded boyfriend is the first—and not the last—to come after Theo with a firearm.

"You want what you can't have" is the not-terribly profound diagnosis administered to Theo by his one remaining male friend. Which helps explain why the most unattainable of all Theo's romantic interests—a married poet named Samantha (Laurel Holloman)—is also the one woman who understands the roots of Theo's frenetic dating patterns.

This is a young man's movie in just about every sense of the word, including the too-typical struggle to mediate a balance between the urge to throw his glands out in public and the impulse to gloss over his less flattering aspects. But it's that very awkwardness that lends "Loving Jezebel" its fascinations and its charms. Bader is one of a handful of emerging African-American filmmakers who are taking bold, ragged dares like this. He needs encouragement. And bears watching.

VILLAGE VOICE, 10/31/00, p. 178, Jessica Winter

The simpering, sanctimonious Theodorous (Hill Harper) exerts his own mysterious powers over other men's women in Kwyn Bader's *Loving Jezebel*, an oafish wish-fulfillment wankfest. The only comeuppance provided for the exhausting, entitlement-warped protagonist is that his Don-wan magnetism attracts a racially diverse but psychologically homogenous parade of loony shrews.

Also reviewed in:
CHICAGO TRIBUNE, 10/27/00, Friday/p. Q, Loren King
NEW YORK TIMES, 10/27/00, p. E16, Elvis Mitchell
VARIETY, 11/15-21/99, p. 92, Lisa Nesselson

LUCKY NUMBERS

A Paramount Pictures release of a Dream Works SKG/Mad Chance/Paramount Pictures/Studio Canal production. *Executive Producer:* G. Mac Brown. *Producer:* Andre Lazer, Jonathan D. Krane, Sean Daniel, and Nora Ephron. *Director:* Nora Ephron. *Screenplay:* Adam Resnick.

Director of Photography: John Lindley.   *Editor:* Barry Malkin.   *Music:* George Fenton.
Choreographer: Jo Ann Fegalette.   *Sound:* Charles Wilborn.   *Sound Editor:* Ron Bochar.
Casting: Francine Maisler.   *Production Designer:* Dan Davis.   *Art Director:* James F. Truesdale
and Thomas Fichter.   *Set Designer:* Greg Berry and Gerald Sullivan.   *Set Decorator:* Tracey
A. Doyle.   *Special Effects:* Kevin Hannigan.   *Costumes:* Albert Wolsky.   *Make-up:* Michael
Eitz.   *Running time:* 100 minutes.   *MPAA Rating:* R.

CAST: John Travolta (Russ Richards);   Lisa Kudrow (Crystal);   Tim Roth (Gig);   Ed O'Neill
(Dick);   Michael Rapaport (Dale);   Daryl Mitchell (Chambers);   Bill Pullman (Lakewood);
Richard Schiff (Jerry Green);   Michael Moore (Walter);   Michael Weston (Larry);   Sam
McMurray (Chief Troutman);   Maria Bamford (Wendy);   Caroline Aaron (Nurse Sharpling);
John F. O'Donohue (Bobby);   Colin Mochrie (Jack);   Nick Loren (Father);   Jake Fritz (Sam);
Emmy Laybourne (Process Server);   Ken Jenkins (Dan Schuff);   Andrea Walters (Heidi
Zimmer);   Denalda Williams (Dottie);   Ginger Williams (Larry's Girlfriend);   Craig Lally
(Cop);   Andy Siegel (Kippy);   Frank Riccardi, Jr. (Dale's Partner);   Carole Androsky (Judy);
Pat Jordan (Larry's Mother);   Scott Mosenson (Paramedic);   Dawn McMillan (Carol);   Katrina
Law, Kim Stutzman, and Susie Ewing (Teen Girls);   Nancy Hopewell and Carmen Ashby
(Waltzing Crab Patrons);   Chris Palmer (Mitch Robertson);   Margaret Travolta and Toya A.
Brown (Nurses);   Tony Carreiro, Stephanie Erb, and Alfonso Gómez-Rejón (Reporters);   J.J.
Sacha (Game Show Announcer).

LOS ANGELES TIMES, 10/27/00, Calendar/p. 2, Kevin Thomas

In the clever and diverting dark comedy "Lucky Numbers," John Travolta's Russ Richards is
the king of all he surveys—even if it isn't much of a kingdom. He's an ebullient Harrisburg, Pa.,
TV weatherman, and his throne is his special booth at a Denny's. He's a world-class schmoozer
who plays the local celebrity bit to the hilt, but he has set his sights higher: His dream is to be
a game-show host. (Watch, out, Bob Barker.)

Meanwhile, Russ is facing a major crisis. A chronic spendthrift, he has invested in a
snowmobile dealership just when Harrisburg is facing an exceptionally mild winter. He's teetering
on the brink of financial ruin when, a couple of deft plot twists later, Russ and the station's Lotto
Girl (Lisa Kudrow) figure out a way to rig the state lottery to make them both rich. Naturally,
there's a hitch.

Taking inspiration from a 1980 rigging of the Pennsylvania state lottery's daily number drawing,
writer Adam Resnick has come up with a consistently witty and ingenious comedy of broad
appeal. Right from the start, Resnick and director Nora Ephron establish Russ as a likably brash,
reckless guy who's foolishly gotten himself in a jam so that we hope he can somehow
miraculously emerge relatively unscathed while most everyone else emerges as amusingly craven
types caught up in a comedy of avarice.

The filmmakers wisely avoid sentimentality, the better to let the greedy folk stand out all the
more sharply. Kudrow's shapely Crystal is a sexy dame conveniently devoid of a conscience
engaged in relationships with both Russ and their boss (Ed O'Neill) that are strong in lust and low
in emotion.

There are fine comic parts for some sterling supporting players: Tim Roth's Gig is a strip-joint
proprietor and shady schemer who blissfully faces every disaster with yet another dubious scheme
that will take care of everything painlessly. Michael Moore, memorable maker and star of the
documentary "Roger & Me," plays Crystal's doofus cousin Walter, who declares that, should
there actually be a pie to slice, he wants to give half of his portion to his church—and use the
other half to open an adult book store.

Michael Rapaport's Dale is one of the Keystone State's least stable robbers; Bill Pullman is
surely Harrisburg's laziest cop, about to drive his conscientious young partner (Daryl Mitchell)
crazy. Like most everyone else on hand, Russ' young snowmobile salesman Larry, amusingly
played by Michael Weston, has his eye on the main chance.

Fast-paced and unpretentious, the film effectively reteams Travolta and Ephron, who directed
him in the equally plEasing comedy "Michael," in which he played a decidedly earthy angel. While

you could wish that Resnick had been able to come up with a pow-in-the kisser finish, "Lucky Numbers" resolves itself in satisfying fashion with no small amount of ingenuity.

NEW YORK POST, 10/27/00, p. 48, Jonathan Foreman

It isn't easy to wring good comedy out of unsympathetic characters. The Coen brothers did it with "Fargo" and Gus Van Sant did it with "To Die For." On the strength of "Lucky Numbers," director Nora Ephron and screenwriter, Adam Resnick just aren't up to the task: The movie is as lifeless and unfunny as a corpse on a slab.

They also seem to be mistakenly entranced by their own metropolitan sophistication; much of this film's attempted humor is about smugly but bluntly mocking the provincials of Harrisburg, Pa.

Russ Richards (a puffy-looking John Travolta) is a big fish in a small town, with his own reserved table at the local Denny's restaurant. Not only is he a star TV weatherman, he's head of the local Rotary Club and the owner of a snowmobile dealership.

But the Christmas weather has been unseasonably warm, Russ has been spending too much money in Atlantic City and he's about to go broke. So he hatches a plan with Crystal (Lisa Kudrow), the Lotto-ball girl at the TV station—with whom he's having a casual affair— to rig the lottery and win $6.4 million.

Crystal gets her schlumpy cousin Walter (former documentarian Michael Moore) to buy the ticket before she and Russ fix the draw. But after the numbers are drawn, Walter decides he wants a bigger share of the loot, and Crystal has little choice but to draw on a surprisingly deep ruthless streak to get him out of the picture.

This first killing provokes a series of deadly crimes that involve Russ' shady strip-club-owning pal, Gig (Tim Roth); Gig's enforcer, "Dale the Thug" (Michael Rapaport); Gig's bookie, Jerry (Richard Schiff); and the manager of the TV station (Ed O'Neill), with whom Crystal is also having an affair.

A lazy, dumb cop, played without his usual conviction or wit by Bill Pullman, also comes into the plot. As the story grinds on, time seems to slow down until the second hand of your watch has all but stopped.

Travolta has often been very funny—in relatively straight roles ("Face Off," "Broken Arrow," "Pulp Fiction," etc.); here, he mugs and preens to no avail.

Of course, he's saddled with an underwritten and unbelievable character that you never care about, and he's overshadowed by Kudrow, who at times seems to be channeling Teri Garr to fine effect.

Her apparent inability to suppress entirely the tics you associate with her "Phoebe" character on TVs "Friends" (the pauses, the aborted hand gestures) serves to make the Crystal character surprisingly winning.

NEWSDAY, 10/27/00, Part II/p. B7, John Anderson

Why do so many people in the so-called hinterlands hate New York? Because of movies like "Lucky Numbers." And characters like Russ Richards.

Richards, played by John Travolta in a haircut that makes him look like a tonsured monk, is living high on the proverbial hog. He's stopped at red lights by screaming teenage girls. His special booth at the town's best boite is girdled by velvet ropes. He has the appetites and attitude of Kubla Khan. The man is a star.

And the star is a TV weatherman. The town is Harrisburg, Pa., circa 1988. His restaurant is Denny's. His house has the distinctive elegance that can only be procured through Garden State Brickface and Stucco. The guy is a schnook. And so, by implication, is everyone around him.

It's perverse, in a way, because it's likely that amid much of Middle America, Nora Ephron's brand of urban comedy ("You've Got Mail" to cite one egregious example) is the height of sophistication, accessorized by Meg Ryan's crinkling nose. "Lucky Numbers," from a script by Adam ("Cabin Boy") Resnick, is, apparently, what she thinks of Middle America. It's the easiest kind of comedy, comedy of derision. No joke about the rubes is left alone. And no obvious plot twist is, either.

So, as it would follow, the high-living Russ is in trouble. His house is in foreclosure. He's losing his Jag. And his snowmobile dealership—wouldn't you know it, it hasn't snowed in weeks. You don't need this weatherman to know which way the wind blows.

The main thrust of the film is the rigging of the state lottery by Richards and Lotto girl Crystal (Lisa Kudrow), based on a real Pennsylvania case from 1980. It takes, however, miles to go to get there, with enough detours to amuse six snowmobilers. Ephron fashions her usual stew—a glorified situation comedy/stand-up routine, in which the story is subordinate to the comedic rhythms. But "Lucky Numbers," is much darker, sometimes alarmingly violent given the context and mean-spirited to the point of distraction. She might have been thinking about Travolta in "Get Shorty," but even as he kills them off, Elmore Leonard has far more respect for his characters.

The classic big fish in the small pond, Russ knows everybody, including Gig (a good Tim Roth), the owner of a seedy local strip club who suggests Russ have his dealership robbed to collect the insurance money. Gig, of course, wants a piece of the action and, after he gets caught for the robbery, so does Dale the Thug (Michael Rapaport). Since Russ' scheme to defraud the lottery involves Crystal, and she enlists her athletic/ asthmatic cousin Walter (Michael Moore) to cash the ticket, that's two more shareholders. Russ' boss Dick (Ed O'Neill), who's annoyed that Crystal has moved from his bed to Russ', wants half the money. Only Max Bialystock could sell this many shares of a project.

The only one in Harrisburg who seems oblivious to the caper is the local cop (Bill Pullman). But it's that kind of tiresome movie.

VILLAGE VOICE, 11/7/00, p. 138, Melissa Anderson

From the auteur who assaulted us with *Sleepless in Seattle* comes a more punishing film—this time set in Harrisburg, Pennsylvania, in 1988. Unlike Nora Ephron's previous cloying paeans to cutesy coupledom, *Lucky Numbers* smugly announces itself as a dark comedy. John Travolta plays, with woeful hamminess, Russ Richards, an unctuous snowmobile dealer/television weatherman/local celebrity who needs cash fast. Russ teams up with potty-mouthed, gold-digging Lotto Lady Crystal Latroy (Lisa Kudrow, devoid of her usual pluckiness) to rig a $6.4 million lottery drawing. A crew of lumbering minor characters—including Ed O'Neill as an extorting station manager and Crystal's part-time fuck buddy, Tim Roth as a gnomic strip-joint owner, and Michael Rapaport as a commemorative-bat-wielding thug—does little more than add plot complications.

Writer Adam Resnick—a former scribe for Chris Elliott's TV show *Get a Life*—fancies his references to no-brow television a meta-narrative device, delivering the ersatz *Network* message that TV makes you stupid. (Russ dreams of being represented by the same agent as Gene Rayburn of *Match Game*.) Yet something is terribly amiss when a *Circus of the Stars* clip of Carol Channing training a monkey comes as quasi-cinematic relief from the puny big-screen performances of Vinnie Barbarino, Phoebe Buffay, and Al Bundy. By film's end, Russ flees Harrisburg for Florida, driving past the ominous cooling towers of Three Mile Island—reminding us of *Lucky Numbers'* own toxicity.

Also reviewed in:
CHICAGO TRIBUNE, 10/27/00, Friday/p. A, Michael Wilmington
NEW YORK TIMES, 10/27/00, p. E16, Elvis Mitchell
VARIETY, 10/23-29/00 p. 42, Todd McCarthy
WASHINGTON POST, 10/27/00, p. C1, Stephen Hunter
WASHINGTON POST, 10/27/00, Weekend/p. 41, Michael O'Sullivan

LUMINARIAS

A New Latin Pictures release of a Sleeping Giant production in association with July Street Entertainment. *Executive Producer:* Joel Ehrlich, Evelina Fernádez, and Jose Luis Valenzuela. *Producer:* Sal Lopez. *Director:* Jose Luis Valenzuela. *Screenplay:* Evelina Fernandez.

Director of Photography: Alex Phillips. Jr.   *Editor:* Terilyn Shropshire, Jeff Koontz, and Ivan Ladizinsky.   *Music:* Eric Allaman and John Koenig.   *Sound:* Sergio Reyes and Mike Hall.   *Production Designer:* Patsy Valdez.   *Art Director:* Christine Perez Pena.   *Costumes:* Dyana Ortelli.   *Make-up:* Ken Diaz.   *Running time:* 100 minutes.   *MPAA Rating:* R.

CAST: Evelina Fernandez (Andrea);   Scott Bakula (Joseph);   Marta DuBois (Sifua);   Angela Moya (Lilly);   Dyana Ortelli (Irene);   Seidy Lopez (Cindy);   Robert Beltran (Joe);   Sal Lopez (Pablo);   Cheech Marin (Jesus);   Fidel Gomez (Joey);   Angelina Estrada (Tia Concha);   Lupe Ontiveros (Tia Tonia);   Mike Gomez (Frank Chavez);   Liz Torres (Judge Sanchez);   Geoffrey Rivas (Carlos/Carmela);   Andre C. Kim (Lu);   Pepe Serna (Rick);   Richard Coca (Tony; Aiysha Sinclair (Laura Johnson);   Sab Shimono (Lu's Father);   June Kim (Lu's Mother); Barbara Niven (Jan);   Alma Beltran and Mary Beltran (Mary);   Elena Lopez (Sofia's Mother).

LOS ANGELES TIMES, 5/5/00, Calendar/p. 20, Kevin Thomas

"Luminarias" takes us into a world all too rarely seen on the big screen: that of upwardly mobile Los Angeles Latinas.

Instead of barrio poverty, gangs and drugs, we're introduced to four women, longtime friends, whose favorite meeting place is the Monterey Park restaurant that gives the film its name. They are Evelina Fernandez's Andrea, a successful attorney; Marta Du Bois' Sofia, a titian-haired Westside therapist; Angela Moya's Lilly, an artist; and Dyana Ortelli's Irene, a clothing designer with her own shop. The film's title clearly also applies to these vibrant women, who light up the screen.

If "Luminarias" sounds like a classic women's picture with a Spanish accent, that's about right. (It's been called a "Latina twist to 'Waiting to Exhale.'") But because these women are Latinas, it offers a fresh perspective on women's universal concerns and grapples in particular with long-festering hostility toward Anglos that persists even as society is changing and becoming more inclusive.

Adapted by Fernandez from her play and directed by her husband, Jose Luis Valenzuela, a UCLA drama professor in his feature directorial debut, "Luminarias" makes a graceful transition from stage to screen. Some moments are overly theatrical, but "Luminarias" is consistently entertaining and offers some sharp observations of the Latino experience.

Andrea and her husband, Joe (Robert Beltran), live in a mansion, where they are celebrating their wedding anniversary when the film begins. In the course of the evening, Andrea and her pals catch Joe embracing a blond (Barbara Niven). We learn that Joe is a womanizer who may see his philandering as a macho birthright. Andrea throws him out, but this time when he returns, it's not to ask for forgiveness but to tell her that he wants a divorce.

In time, Sofia sets up the stunned, depressed Andrea with a blind date, who turns out to be the attorney (Scott Bakula) representing a husband in a divorce case in which Andrea is representing the wife, her receptionist, Cindy (Seidy Lopez). Cindy is suing on grounds of spousal abuse.

That Andrea and Bakula's Joseph have begun an affair already makes things doubly complicated—doubly because Andrea has deep-seated rage toward Anglos. The film is really about a successful, intelligent woman struggling with reverse racism, and her struggle is echoed in various ways. We witness Andrea's entire Latino world maneuver the often painful, sometimes funny, process of integration and acceptance of those who happen to be different.

Lilly plunges into a romance with a handsome Korean American (Andrew C. Lim), only to find that his parents are shocked because she is a Mexican American.

Sofia has practiced assimilation diligently but has come up empty- handed in the romance department. She's beginning to respond to the ardent pursuit of a Luminarias waiter (Sal Lopez, also the film's producer), wondering if she can bridge their socioeconomic gap. Irene, who serves mainly as the film's comic relief, is struggling with having given up sex for Lent—and with accepting that her brother (Geoffrey Rivas) not only is gay but also a transvestite.

As a writer, Fernandez is on sure ground when she's confronting serious issues and strong emotions, but sometimes her comedy touches are too theatrical or sitcom for the big screen. This is especially true of Irene and her carryings-on. Much more effective is a sequence set at a backyard family barbecue, where Andrea introduces Joseph to her relatives; here Fernandez can mine the humor in the inherent self-consciousness of the occasion, especially when there are such pros as Cheech Marin, Lupe Ontiveros and Pepe Serna cast as members of Andrea's family.

Andrea and Joseph's romance reflects the complexity of their situation, socially and professionally, and in its development only once does Fernandez strike a false note, when she has Joseph, presented as a decent, sensitive man, cast a slur upon receptionist Cindy.

Valenzuela's direction has the occasional self-consciousness and unevenness of the first-timer, but on the whole, it keeps us absorbed. Performances are solid, starting with that of Fernandez herself.

The film is intriguing on yet another level: It dares to suggest romance is not over for middle-aged women. What's more, noted Mexican cinematographer Alex Phillips Jr. gives the film a rich, high- contrast look that's not always flattering to the actresses but has an honesty to it.

If "Luminarias" succeeds at the box office, it could open up the screen for more forthright depictions of contemporary Latino life.

NEW YORK POST, 10/6/00, p. 57, V.A. Musetto

Four middle-aged, successful Latina women hunt for love and sex (not necessarily in that order) in East L.A.

Director Jose Luis Valenzuela and writer Evelina Fernandez (who also appears as one of the women) have the best of intentions—to debunk the Hollywood stereotype of Latinos as either gang members or low-paid workers.

But their movie comes off as nothing more than a TV soap opera, with overwrought acting, simplistic dialogue and a generic plot.

If gags about the size of white men's endowment turn you on, you might want to take a look at "Luminarias." Otherwise, skip it.

VILLAGE VOICE, 10/10/00, p. 138, Edward Crouse

Chock-full of feisty-frank go-girl sextalk speculating on white guys' underplayable size (a myth vanquished by Scott Bakula's unsheathed—though unseen—épée), *Luminarias* can give the impression of Latino drag queens ad-libbing between lip-synch numbers. Four Latina professionals have interclass and interracial romantic skirmishes (including a Jewish lawyer and a Salvadoran waiter), eventually becoming worldly wise. It looks better than it should considering the microbudget, though the flying camera is bouncing around an L.A. checklist of clunky issues. Still, in some moments—as when Andrea (writer Evelina Fernández) and Joseph (Bakula) reprise the old "jew"/"you" pronunciation gag (also a staple of Charo's banter with Jerry Lewis on his telethon)—*Luminarias* can produce conversations somewhat more lifelike than the Lifetime channel.

Also reviewed in:
CHICAGO TRIBUNE, 8/11/00, Friday/p. M, John Petrakis
NEW YORK TIMES, 10/6/00, p. E20, Lawrence Van Gelder
VARIETY, 10/11-17/99, p. 48, David Rooney

LUMINOUS MOTION

An Artistic License Films release.   *Executive Producer:* Eric Rudin.   *Producer:* Anthony Bregman and Ted Hope.   *Director:* Bette Gordon.   *Screenplay:* Robert Roth.   *Based on his novel "The History of Luminous Motion":* Scott Bradfield.   *Director of Photography:* Teodoro Maniaci.   *Editor:* Keiko Deguchi.   *Music:* Lesley Barber.   *Sound:* Eugene Gearty.   *Casting:* Ellen Parks.   *Production Designer:* Lisa Albin.   *Art Director:* Paul Avery.   *Set Decorator:* Alisa Grifo.   *Costumes:* Melissa Toth.   *Running time:* 94 minutes.   *MPAA Rating:* Not Rated.

CAST: Eric Lloyd (Phillip);   Deborah Kara Unger (Mom);   Terry Kinney (Pedro);   Jamey Sheridan (Dad);   James Berland (Rodney);   Paz de la Huerta (Beatrice);   June Stein (Ethel); Bruce MacVitte (Norman).

LOS ANGELES TIMES, 6/23/00, Calendar/p. 8, Kevin Thomas

As Bette Gordon's seductive "Luminous Motion" commences, we hear via voice-over its young protagonist recalling a ghostly memory of childhood of "blurred images and nightmares." It's an indication that he ultimately will have difficulty distinguishing between what was real and what was not.

Gordon, best known for "Variety," maintains this tension for us in a manner that is at once engaging and provocative. "Luminous Motion" is as rigorous as it is sensual. As it is envisioned from the point of view of a 10-year-old, we cannot rely upon the accuracy of what we're seeing, which in some incidents may entirely be a figment of a boy's imagination. Stick with the film, and you'll come away with the sense of experiencing a rite of passage of both considerable intensity and darkness.

"Life was perfect," we're told by our unseen narrator as he recalls his existence on the run with his adored mother (Deborah Kara Unger). A sultry blond, Mom picks up guys, takes them to motels and leaves them robbed. Mother and son are constantly on the move, and precocious little Phillip (Eric Lloyd), who pores over biology and physics textbooks in his mother's Chevy, hopes that they will be able to continue this reckless, carefree existence forever.

He does not count on Mom developing a need to settle down and is horrified that she is about to give it all up to settle down with a kindly carpenter (Terry Kinney), who does his level best to be a loving and conscientious father to Phillip. When Philip's resistance takes a drastic turn, mother and son are on the road again, but Phillip may well have met his match when his actual father (Jamey Sheridan) turns up to reclaim his family.

You could say that Phillip is in the throes of an Oedipal complex that could have potentially dire consequences in its resolution, but the film, which Gordon based on the Scoff Bradfield novel, "The History of Luminous Motion," is too sly and jaunty—too outright kinetic—to let itself become bogged down in Freudian analyses. It's all about being open to experience, real or imaginary; you either survive it or you don't. You either accept the inevitability of change and loss as a part of growing up, or you're destroyed by them.

Gordon calls her film "the story of paradise lost, of one child's fall from heaven to earth, from Eden to banality," and that about sums up this offbeat fable, at once lyrical and brutal. Gordon directs her cast to play individuals who are nonchalant but nevertheless determined to be themselves. By the time "Luminous Motion" is over, Phillip is just beginning to see the light, beginning to grasp how being grown up is about taking responsibility for the consequences of all your actions.

That everything Gordon depicts with such clarity, ease and precision may or may not be actually happening ultimately becomes beside the point. For what counts here is the acute psychological validity with which Gordon evokes a coming of age that's seen with a darkly outrageous sense of humor—and no small amount of compassionate detachment.

NEW YORK POST, 5/19/00, p. 44, Lou Lumenick

"Mom was beyond judging," says Phillip, the 10-year-old protagonist of "Luminous Motion," an indie film that combines road movie, psychological thriller, feminism and fantasy to overall depressing effect.

Phillip (Eric Lloyd) watches happily as Mom (Deborah Kara Unger), who has fled Phillip's controlling dad, wanders the back roads of New Jersey in an old Chevy Impala in a semi-drunken stupor, supporting the two of them by selling her body in a succession of cheap motel rooms.

But his "idyllic"—and Oedipal—odyssey with Mom is threatened when she decides to settle down with Pedro (Terry Kinney), a creepy Hackensack hardware-store owner. Acting on fantasy instructions from Dad (Jamey Sheridan), Phillip slips Pedro some chili spiked with barbiturates and kills him with a power tool.

Mom whisks them away to Staten Island, where Dad turns up (apparently for real this time) and takes charge—and Pedro's ghost starts giving the increasingly addled Phillip suggestions about what to do with Dad.

"All of Mom's energy and her inner life had been sucked into this black hole called Dad," Phillip says in the self-consciously literary narration, needlessly underlining the movie's man-hating agenda.

Though the screenplay is attributed to two men (Robert Roth and Scott Bradfield) and based on an acclaimed novel by a third (Scott Bradfield's "The History of Luminous Motion," which was set in California), the overriding sensibility is that of director Bette Gordon, whose last film, "Variety" (1985), is considered in some quarters to be a feminist classic.

Gordon, a Columbia University professor, does best in the opening scenes, dreamily shot by Teodoro Maniaci, of mother and son on the road. But even stronger actors than Lloyd (the kid in "The Santa Clause") and Unger (one of Rubin Carter's Canadian saviors in "The Hurricane") would have a tough time selling her dubious political arguments.

NEWSDAY, 5/19/00, Part II/p. B7, Jan Stuart

Since "Tumbleweeds" and "Anywhere But Here," it seemed as if America's highways were teeming with renegade moms and their precocious daughters, surviving by their wits and moving wherever their wanderlust took them.

Imagine, then, a dark variation, in which the amiable, sisterly bond of mother and daughter is replaced by a homicidal, Oedipal axis of mother and son. Such is Bette Gordon's "Luminous Motion," a seductive and macabre story of family dysfunction on wheels.

Mom (Deborah Kara Unger) is footloose, resourceful and at least as sultry as Michelle Pfeiffer. Ten-year-old son Phillip (Eric Lloyd) is brainy, quick-witted and utterly enamored of his mother. Together, they tear about the country in a withering Chevy, living off the loot she bags from one-night stands and keeping two steps ahead of the law.

Larceny, promiscuity and a tendency to let her boy take the wheel as she recovers from her occasional drunks barely skirt the sins of this loving but ultimately disastrous mom. The full impact of her reckless lifestyle only begins to make itself felt, however, when they stop moving and settle in with a big-spirited white knight named Pedro (played by Terry Kinney, perfect in both angel and devil modes), who rescues them from an accident. Within days, Phillip is hatching monstrous plans to foil, and finally extinguish, the competition.

Told from Phillip's point of view, "Luminous Motion" utilizes jittery, disorienting camera effects to convey the boy's frequent disassociation from reality. The technique keeps the audience off balance as Phillip's world expands to embrace an eerily idealized Dad (Jamey Sheriden) and two trenchcoat mob-like teenagers named Rodney (James Berland) and Beatrice (Paz de la Huerta). Teodoro Maniaci's stark, nocturnal photography sets just the right illusory tone.

The odd juxtaposition of characters and unnerving pileup of events begs for a measure of irony that is missing from Robert Roth and Scott Bradfield's meticulous but sober screenplay. The actors are excellent, particularly the comely trio playing Mom, Dad and Phillip. Unger, Sheridan and Lloyd, who could easily moonlight as Abercrombie & Fitch models, elastically convey the disturbances that can lurk beneath the surface of American beauty.

VILLAGE VOICE, 5/23/00, p. 146, Amy Taubin

"My childhood seems like a ghost town... When I look back, I know my memory is hopelessly flaw, tangled with my imagination." Bette Gordon"s *Luminous Motion* opens with these words, spoken by a boy with a high, earnest voice better suited to pitching breakfast cereal than narrating a film as subtle and complicated as this one.

Adapted from Scott Bradfield's much lauded first-person novel, *The History of Luminous Motion,* Gordon's film attempts the difficult task of projecting the inner world of an emotionally disturbed child onto the screen. *Luminous Motion is* shaped entirely from the point of view of Phillip (Eric Lloyd), a 10-year-old locked in a symbiotic relationship with his boozy, beautiful, narcissistic mom (Deborah Kara Unger). The boy is a case study in arrested development, fixated at the oedipal stage. His vision of Mom is intensely eroticized; she is for him the source of all pleasure, all life. Gordon expresses this essentially preverbal experience in images that are at once lush and intangible, as in a dream. When son and Mom take to the road in a big old sedan as cluttered as the bathroom in *Eyes Wide Shut*, *Luminous Motion* fully lives up to its title.

But as the Kubrick film proved, it's difficult for contemporary audiences to accept that what they're seeing on the screen might have as tenuous a connection to so-called reality as their own fantasies. I suspect that *Luminous Motion* will meet just as much resistance as *Eyes Wide Shut;* despite differences of size and style, they inhabit a similar psychosexual landscape. Like Tom Cruise's journey into his traumatized unconscious, Phillip's attempts to keep his mother all to himself—by bumping off her boyfriend and trying to poison his own father—are a teasing mixture of memory, desire, and actuality. That said, there's nothing in Lloyd's screen presence, not to mention his dutiful, stilted performance, to suggest that this child has any imaginative life whatsoever.

If Lloyd's performance is the film's near-fatal flaw, Unger's is its saving grace. As she revealed in Cronenberg's *Crash,* Unger is most electric when she's most somnolent, most magnetic when she's most self-absorbed. Actors are, by definition, narcissistic, but Unger's self-absorption is so pure and extreme it's a revelation. We watch her suck on a pear, teeth gently piercing the skin—her blue-painted nails and blue-tinted sunglasses in perfect color-balance with the yellow-brown fruit—and we perceive why the child wants this moment to last forever and why he will look for her in all his future lovers. He can't separate from her because she can't admit the existence of anyone outside herself; he can capture her attention only by staying wrapped in her narcissistic cocoon. There's a painful psychological truth in this relationship, and the film lets us understand more about it than the boy does, even though we see it only through his eyes. *Luminous Motion* has more problems than Lloyd's performance (the narration is too literary, the ghost-effects clunky), but in its evocation of the pleasures and dangers of the maternal bond, Gordon's film is utterly fascinating and convincing.

Also reviewed in:
CHICAGO TRIBUNE, 7/21/00, Friday/p. J, John Petrakis
NEW YORK TIMES, 5/19/00, p. E14, A. O. Scott
VARIETY, 9/7-13/98, p. 76, Derek Elley

MADADAYO

A Winstar Cinema release of a Daiei Studios/Dentsu/Kurosawa production. *Producer:* Hisao Kurosawa. *Director:* Akira Kurosawa. *Screenplay (Japanese with English subtitles):* Akira Kurosawa. *Based on the book by:* Hyakken Uchida. *Director of Photography:* Takao Saito and Masaharu Ueda. *Editor:* Akira Kurosawa and Ishiro Honda. *Music:* Shin'ichiro Ikebe. *Art Director:* Yoshiro Muraki. *Running time:* 134 minutes. *MPAA Rating:* Not Rated.

CAST: Tatsuo Matsumura (Professor Uchida); Kyoko Kagawa (Professor's Wife); Hisashi Igawa (Takayama); George Tokoro (Amaki); Masayuki Yui (Kiriyama); Akira Terao (Sawamura); Asei Kobayashi (Reverend Kameyama); Takeshi Kusaka (Dr. Kobayashi).

LOS ANGELES TIMES, 9/3/99, Calendar/p. 19, Kevin Thomas

Although Akira Kurosawa did not intend "Madadayo" to be his final film, he could not have made a more fitting finale to one of the greatest careers in the history of the cinema. A gentle, humorous contemplation of the inevitability of old age and mortality, "Madadayo" celebrates the enduring joys of camaraderie and the rewards of kindness and opens a month-long Turner Classic Movies retrospective on the director ["Madadayo" has not played in a Los Angeles area theater.]

For his 30th film in a half-century of directing, Kurosawa returns to the concerns of one of his classics, the 1952 "Ikiru" (To Live). Actually, the hero of the earlier film, a government office worker who does not learn how to live until he learns that he is terminally ill, becomes the man that "Madadayo's" hero already is. The year is 1943, and Hyakken Uchida (Tatsuo Matsumura, in a masterful portrayal), a revered professor of German, announces to his all-male class that at age 60 he is retiring because he has reached the stage where he can support himself on his scholarly books. A humorist and philosopher, Uchida has won his students' hearts as their frequent drinking companion. He has given them his time and concern, and they in turn feel that they have learned from him "much more than German."

His students help him and his wife (Kyoko Kagawa) move in to a fine old, traditional-style home in a beautiful, woodsy Tokyo neighborhood that no scholar could hope to afford today. In short order, the house is bombed, and the Uchidas uncomplainingly move to a gardeners' shack on the estate of a nobleman whose mansion has also been destroyed by bombs. Never fear, a group of Uchida students are swiftly on the spot to provide their professor with whatever he needs—and they clearly will remain vigilant to the end of his life. No movie star or monarch could inspire more steadfast devotion. Kurosawa finds some humor in their fervor, yet Uchida radiates such warmth and wisdom, expressed with a jaunty light touch, that you can understand how he could be accorded such fidelity.

With each passing year, the professor, who has his own alumni association, is honored with a birthday banquet at which he invariably exclaims "Madadayo!," which translates as "not yet," meaning he's not ready to pass from this life. Uchida continues to lecture from time to time, and his life settles down into a pleasant routine. He's thrown into a crisis when a stray cat he's taken in disappears; it takes time and effort for him to come to terms with the feelings of mortality the loss of the pet unexpectedly signifies, but in working through his over-reaction he emerges tranquil and accepting of whatever the future holds for him.

"Madadayo" flows like a forest stream, and it risks seeming slow and sentimental on the surface when it is in fact leisurely in the most positive sense. So effortlessly does it unfold that you scarcely notice how evocative, even profound, is its impact by the time it is over.

NEW YORK, 9/4/00, p. 54, Peter Rainer

Akira Kurosawa's thirtieth and last film, *Madadayo*, was completed in 1992 and, criminally, is only now being shown in the U.S. (He died in 1998.) It's customary to call a master director's final film a summation, or a leave-taking, but most often this sentiment is bunk: Artists don't get to pick their moments with such precision. And yet certain lucky filmmakers do manage to pull off what amounts to an orchestrated valedictory. John Huston did it when he made *The Dead*, which is voluminously rich in its intimations of mortality. *Madadayo* is similarly concerned with the approaches of death, and of what it means to have lived a good life.

It's an extremely formalized work, a series of mostly stationary set pieces, and it will disappoint viewers who still think of Kurosawa as the thunderous, supple master of films like *Seven Samurai* and *Yojimbo*, or a later work like *Ran,* which, by a fine piece of timing, is currently in national rerelease. Kurosawa has always somewhat mistakenly been called the most Western of Japanese directors. Partly this is because a number of his movies were remade by Hollywood, or were derived from writers ranging from Shakespeare and Dostoevsky to Ed McBain, but it's also because his vigorous, multi-camera technique in his most famous movies broke with the traditional orthodoxies of masters like Yasujiro Ozu. You can go through an entire festival of Ozu films without spotting a single tracking shot; his imagery has a stilled, sacramental quality. And yet Kurosawa's imagery can have this quality, too, and no more so than in *Madadayo,* in which a lifetime of moviemaking—Kurosawa was 83 when he made it—seems to have pared down his technique to its essentials. We are looking at the work of a director who no longer needs to charge the screen with dynamism in order to achieve his effects. He's reaching for something more quietly ineffable, a rigorous splendor. He asks his audience to contemplate, in a kind of communal silence, the beauty of the imagery, and the beauty of the emotion behind the imagery.

Madadayo is a celebration of a professor beloved by his university students. It begins in 1943 as Hyakken Uchida (Tatsuo Matsumura) announces to his class his plan to retire, after 30 years of teaching, in order to write books. Professor Uchida was a real person who taught German literature and wrote novels and essays and haiku on subjects ranging from locomotives to the wartime Tokyo air raids, but Kurosawa doesn't provide us with the contours of an academic life; his professor is not so much an actual person as a vivid essence. Uchida is an idealization of grace, and Kurosawa's identification with him is total: This man, we are made to feel, is the fulfillment of the director's own best self.

The film is marked by a series of birthday tributes to Uchida put on by his students, starting with the professor's 60th and culminating in his 77th and, perhaps, last. In the years between, in a variety of mostly dry, sweetly comical situations, we see Uchida and his wife (Kyoko Kagawa) play host to the students, who at first cannot stand to see their *sensei* living in such cramped circumstances and organize to find him more spacious quarters. They are honored to watch over him. When Uchida's much-doted-upon cat is lost, sending him into a deep depression, the students form a search party. They never think to make light of his grief. He suffers because, as one of the pupils says with pride, "his sensitivity and imagination are beyond us." And yet the students also recognize what Uchida's wife realizes, too: He has never really grown up. Uchida is revered by his students both for his calm wisdom and for his childlike bemusement, which is perceived as a kind of holy innocence. Uchida makes his final birthday speech to the children and grandchildren of his students, and in this moment he seems a perfect fusion of man and cherub; his rapport with these young ones is without a trace of condescension. "Find something in life you are able to treasure," he tells them. Uchida is a man whose kindness has saved him from despair.

It is poetically perfect that Kurosawa closes the film with a dream of Uchida's in which the old man imagines himself as a boy. Kurosawa's dream sequences have always been transcendent, and this brief final scene is so quietly devastating that it summons up, in a rush, the profoundest melancholy. Throughout the film we have seen the students and Uchida play a children's game: They ask him if he is ready to pass into the afterlife and he responds heartily, "Madadayo," which means "No, not yet." In his dreams Uchida conjures this hide-and-seek game between children and that boy, and the screen at the end is filled with a lustrous wash of colors. They are the colors of a sky in which the sun could be rising—or setting.

NEW YORK POST, 9/1/00, p. 43, V. A. Musetto

Akira Kurosawa's 30th and final film, "Madadayo," made in 1993, is finally getting a release in New York. Viewers expecting one of the samurai thrillers for which the Japanese filmmaker is famous will be disappointed.

"Madadayo" is a sentimental, leisurely piece about an old man wrestling with forebodings of his own death, by a director obviously obsessed with the same thoughts.

Kurosawa died, at age 88, five years after shooting the film.

"Madadayo" covers 17 years in the life of a beloved professor of German, starting with his retirement at age 60 ("This is the day I become a genuine old man," he proclaims happily.)

It ends with a banquet for his 77th birthday, where he takes ill in front of his former students and their children and grandchildren.

The title of the film is translated as "not yet," as in, "I'm not yet ready to die." It's an expression that crops up throughout the film.

The professor, portrayed by Tatsuo Matsumura, is a stand-in for Kurosawa, just as the late Toshiro Mifune was his alter-ego in the many films they made together.

Not much happens during the course of "Madadayo." The professor and his devoted wife (who has a minor role in the film) twice move into a new house, they have numerous get-togethers with friends, and the couple's cat, Nora, disappears, an incident that brings the old man to tears.

"Madadayo" is as devoid of action as Kurosawa's samurai epics are riddled with it.

It's as if he knew this would be his screen good-bye and he was going to be as shamelessly sentimental as he wanted, whether we approve or not.

As it happens, we approve. "Madadayo" will never be confused with Kurosawa classics such as "Rashomon" and "The Seven Samurai," but in its quaint way it is a fond and fitting farewell.

NEWSDAY, 9/1/00, Part II/p. B6, John Anderson

Until his death in September, 1998, and for about 50 years previously, Akira Kurosawa was America's favorite Japanese director—which made sense, since he was the most American of Japanese directors. A virtual Japanese John Ford, his forte was the battle scene. His sense of historical time was acute. And neither quality has any place in his final film.

"Madadayo," which is basically awful and has taken about seven years to find a release here, is an homage to the real-life professor Hyakken Uchida who, as he is paid tribute over the years by his relentlessly adoring pupils, is asked "Mahda-kai? (Are you ready?)" To which he answers "Madadayo! (Not yet.)" It is, in a word, cute. Not so the movie.

Introduced in 1943, as he is about to begin his writing career after decades as a professor of German, Uchida (Tatsuo Matsumura) is held in fearful esteem by his students. We never understand why, particularly: During the unreasonably numerous tributes paid him by his former students, Uchida holds forth like the pedant he is, his limp jokes evoking uproarious laughter from his disciples but leaving the viewer with the impression of a man used to a lifetime of speaking without any interruption.

It's entirely possible that Kurosawa, having made "Madadayo" immediately after his elegiac Nagasaki film, "Rhapsody in August," was editorializing on heroes and hero-worship. Having reached a point in his career where his most minor efforts were acclaimed as masterpieces, he may have found ironic comfort in lampooning the qualified adoration paid to the Uchida he created.

On the other hand, maybe not. Although he helped enormously to advance the cause of Japanese cinema in the West, Kurosawa was dwarfed by the talents and intellect of his seniors, Kenji Mizoguchi and Yasuhiro Ozu. Neither was Kurosawa appreciated much in Japan, a country where his films were too western. Strange then that his final film should be so deliberately Japanese and not so strange that, in the wackier moments between Uchida's aging students, Akira Kurosawa's direction should recall no one so much as Preston Sturges.

VILLAGE VOICE, 9/5/00, p. 113, Amy Taubin

Madadayo, the last film of Akira Kurosawa, is unabashedly personal and uncool. I don't know if Kurosawa, who was 83 when he made the film, admitted to himself that it would be his last, but he must have known he was near the end of his life. In their late works, great artists sometimes risk breaking the rules—taboos even—that govern the making of art: Thou shalt not be sentimental; thou shalt not expose your desire to be loved; and, in the particular case of Kurosawa, thou shalt not be so un-Japanese as to express transcendence through the music of Vivaldi. *Madadayo,* which opens here seven years after its initial release, was pretty much dismissed for all these infractions by both the pro- and anti-Kurosawa critical camps, but between you and me, dear reader, I love it to death.

Gently ironic, *Madadayo* evokes baldly personal feelings and deeply held, easy-to-ridicule beliefs at one remove. The film is a meditation on the life and writings of the essayist and novelist Hyakken Uchida, who in middle age retired from teaching German literature to write full-time. Among his finest works is a collection of essays entitled *Nora, My Lost Cat.* Thus, the protagonist (Tatsuo Matsumura) of *Madadayo* (English translation: "Not Yet") is a German-lit professor who retires in 1943—smack in the middle of World War II , and the very year that Kurosawa directed his first film—and spends the rest of his life at home writing (not a very cinematic activity). His companions are his wife (Kyoko Kagawa) and two cats who enter his life consecutively, and ever in attendance are his devoted former pupils—each year, on the anniversary of his retirement, they throw a banquet in his honor.

Madadayo is basically a film structured as three set pieces with lots of picture-perfect downtime in between. The development of postwar Japan is suggested by the difference between the scruffiness of the first anniversary banquet and the respectable opulence of the 20th, both hilariously drunken affairs. The centerpiece of the film is an extended sequence in which Nora, the professor's much doted-upon cat, goes missing. The professor frantically searches for her and obsesses over her fate, long past the point of what would be considered rational. Through the images of Nora that completely occupy the professor's imagination—either she's happily leaping about the garden or miserably trapped in bombed-out rubble—we realize that the entire film is about identification and attachment, and the separation and loss inscribed within them. In other words, eros and thanatos. Or maybe it's just an unembarrassed reflection on a man and his cat.

Also reviewed in:
NEW REPUBLIC, 9/18/00, p. 28, Stanley Kauffmann

NEW YORK TIMES, 9/1/00, p. E6, A. O. Scott
VARIETY, 5/24/93, p. 47, David Stratton

MALÈNA

A Miramax Films and Medusa Film release of a Medusa Film/Miramax Films production. *Executive Producer:* Bob Weinstein, Teresa Moneo, Fabrizio Lombardo, and Mario Spedaletti. *Producer:* Harvey Weinstein and Carlo Bernasconi. *Director:* Giuseppe Tornatore. *Screenplay (Italian with English subtitles):* Giuseppe Tornatore. *Based on a story by:* Luciano Vincenzoni. *Director of Photography:* Lajos Koltai. *Editor:* Massimo Quaglia. *Music:* Ennio Morricone. *Music Editor:* Fabio Venturi. *Sound:* Getano Carito, Roberto Moroni, and (music) Fabio Venturi. *Sound Editor:* Benedetto Atria. *Casting:* Adolfo Onorati. *Art Director:* Francesco Frigeri. *Set Designer:* Bruno Cesari. *Set Decorator:* Nello Giorgetti. *Special Effects:* Antonio Corridori. *Costumes:* Maurizio Millenotti. *Make-up:* Alessandro Bertolazzi. *Running time:* 94 minutes. *MPAA Rating:* R.

CAST: Monica Bellucci (Malèna Scordìa); Giuseppe Sulfaro (Renato Amoroso); Luciano Federico (Renato's Father); Matilde Piana (Renato's Mother); Pietro Notarianni (Professor Bonsignore); Gaetano Aronica (Nino Scordìa); Gilberto Idone (Lawyer Centorbi); Angelo Pellegrino (Political Secretary); Gabriella Di Luzio (Baron's Mistress); Pippo Provvidenti (Dr. Cusimano); Maria Terranova (Dr. Cusimano's Wife); Marcello Catalono (Lieutenant Cadei); Elisa Morucci (Lupetta); Domenico Gennaro (Pharmacist); Vitalba Andrea (Pharmacist's Wife); Pippo Pattavina (Magistrate); Franco Catalano (Storekeeper); Daniele Arena (Agostino); Giovanni Litrico (Pinè); Gianluca Guarrera (Nicola); Michel Daniel Bramanti (Sasà); Giuseppe Zizzo (Tanino); Totò Borgese (Fascist Soldier); Emanuele Gullotto (Record Store Owner); Rori Quattrocchi (Brother Owner); Claudia Muzii, Ornella Giusto, and Conchita Puglisi (Prostitutes); Noemi Giarratana (Sister Renato); Paola Pace and Lucia Sardo (Lynching Women); Adelaide Alessi; Angelo Battista; Vanni Bramati; Claudio Castrogiovanni; Alessandro Cremona; Lazzaro Crocey; Francesco Drago; Patrizia De Libero; Maria Teresa Di Clemente; Giovanni Febraro; Fabrizio Ferracane; Sebastiana Fichera; Sebastiano Fisichella; Angelo Fortuna; Antonio Fulfaro; Turi Killer; Giuseppe Luciano; Chiara Marchese; Salvatore Martino; Giovanni Martorana; Antonio Pellegrino; Claudio Piano; Antonello Puglisi; Carmela Pulvirenti; Adriana Rizza; Giada Salesi; Sergio Seminara; Orio Scaduto; Agostino Scuderi; Fausto Siddi; Vincenzo Terranova; Agatino Ursino.

LOS ANGELES TIMES, 12/25/00, Calendar/p. 8, Kevin Thomas

After the bravura esoterica of such films as "A Pure Formality" and "The Legend of 1900," Giuseppe Tornatore, with "Malena," returns to the wide appeal of his classic "Cinema Paradiso."

Once again we're in an enchanting, ancient Sicilian city; once again Tornatore is dealing with a coming-of-age theme. But "Malena" is a much tougher, riskier movie than "Cinema Paradiso," yet just as successful as his 1990 Oscar winner.

Three things happened to 12½-year-old Renato Amoroso (Giuseppe Sulfaro) on July 10, 1940: He was given his first bicycle; Mussolini declared war on France and Great Britain; and he laid eyes on Malena Scordia (Monica Bellucci) for the first time. The last of these three events was by far the most important, for Renato is hit simultaneously with the full onslaught of sexual desire and grand passion. Malena is an awesomely beautiful young woman with a spectacular figure. Her husband is already off to war, leaving Malena with her aged, deaf father.

Malena needs only to stroll through town on her ankle-strap wedges to cause an uproar. Every male between adolescence and senility openly lusts after her; every woman, consumed with envy, loathes her and besmirches her reputation. Fired by the movies he loves as much as the somewhat younger hero of "Cinema Paradiso," Renato imagines he is Tarzan to her Jane, among other couples of the silver screen.

Unlike the other males of the seaside town of Castelcuto, Renato loves her even more than he lusts after her. He projects onto her a nobility of spirit, a purity of heart, that are actually qualities he possesses himself.

We have here all the makings of a classic brief encounter between the gorgeous but lonely "older"—Malena is but 27—woman who inducts a sensitive youth into manhood. But "Malena" is no "Summer of '42," and while Renato becomes swiftly obsessed with the object of his passion to the extent that he spends all his free time spying on her, she does not seem to be aware of his existence. Mussolini may be of vastly less importance to Renato than Malena, but not to Tornatore.

Drawing from a short story by veteran screenwriter Luciano Vincenzoni, the movie shows the citizens of Castelcuto to be ardent admirers of Il Duce—Renato's leftist father seems the rare exception—thrilled to hear his declaration of war.

Indeed, the film equates the subsequent fate of Malena with that of Italy in general and Sicily in particular. The townspeople are ignorant in their view of both Mussolini and Malena. As the war progresses the aloof dignity Malena rigorously maintains becomes harder and harder to sustain in the face of escalating poverty and deprivation, making her ever more vulnerable to gossip-mongers. By the time Castelcuto is bombed you can't help but feel it is just punishment for its evil treatment of her.

But Tornatore takes a much larger view, and the warm embrace of his wide scope is what makes the film such a triumph. Tornatore fills the screen with people who are small-minded and who behave horribly but whom he views with humor and loving forgiveness. If in fact he didn't love his people so passionately, you would be hard put not to hate them.

Yet this film is an expression of faith that people can undergo a change of heart, leaving us to hope that good can come from evil after all—and that surviving war may serve to dent the Sicilians' zealous puritanism.

Tornatore has at his command those grand operatic gestures that are at the heart of the classic Italian cinema; it's easy to imagine that he, like other maestros, could wring tears from a stone. But unlike the recent hit "Life Is Beautiful," "Malena" is relentlessly clear eyed instead of shamelessly manipulative, and it builds to an emotional crescendo that brings to mind the finales of the Neo-Realist classics. He would seem to have the artistry plus the depth of emotion to get by with just about anything.

"Malena" the film is as beautiful and seductive as its heroine, with its ravishing Lajos Koltai cinematography and sweepingly romantic Ennio Morricone score. Sulfaro mainly registers pain, longing and finally chagrin with his dark expressive eyes, and Bellucci has only a handful of words in the entire film. Yet so cinematic is Tornatore that they both can be said to give heroic portrayals.

There seems little doubt, too, that Bellucci will create an international sensation. She has the impact of the great Italian stars, her face recalling that of the late Silvano Mangano and her figure that of Sophia Loren.

NEW YORK POST, 12/22/00, p. 54, Jonathan Foreman

"Malena" begins like an unusually picturesque adolescent sex comedy, strongly reminiscent of "Summer of '42" (but translated from Long Island to Sicily), and then turns into something much, much darker: a portrait of small-town cruelty and hypocrisy given extra bite by its setting in a time of war and occupation.

It is 1941, and Renato Amoroso (Guiseppe Sulfaro) is 13 when Mussolini declares war on Britain and France. The declaration has little effect on his seaside village of Castelcuto—except that it takes away to Africa the soldier husband of Malena (Monica Belluci), the most gorgeous woman in town.

Renato and his friends follow the ravishing young woman as she does her errands and visits her deaf schoolteacher father. And they hear all the gossip which has this impossible beauty betraying her husband with this or that married man. Castelcuto's adults are convinced that Malena is as loose as she is stunning.

It's not true, as Renato realizes from the increasingly obsessive watch he keeps on Malena. But when her husband is reported dead, the rumors intensify, and so do the efforts of several prominent men of the town to get her into bed.

Unfortunately, poverty forces Malena to make compromises that only exacerbate her reputation and the hatred felt for her by Castelcuto's womenfolk.

Eventually, they take "revenge" on Malena in a horrifying scene that marks a jarring shift in the film's overall tone. This jagged transition tends to undermine both the comedy of the first half of the film and the drama of the second.

As a result, "Malena" too often seems like a slightly silly film about the dangers of being too beautiful, when director Giuseppe Tornatore ("Cinema Paradiso") presumably intended it more as an indictment of a people who cheerfully welcomed Fascist, German and, finally, American overlords but were only too happy to brand unpopular outsiders as "collaborators."

To the extent that "Malena" works, it's largely thanks to Monica Belluci, a star in the high-glamour tradition of Sophia Loren, who manages to convey a remarkable amount with her eyes and her gait (she has very little dialogue).

It's all prettily photographed by Lajos Koltai (there are moments when the loving shots of Malena in various states of undress approach a soft-core voyeurism). But chunks of the film, especially the sequences featuring Renato and his family, are very obviously—and irritatingly—dubbed.

NEWSDAY, 12/22/00, Part II/p. B15, Gene Seymour

"Malena" is, essentially, "Cinema Paradiso" with more dirty jokes, the same over-the-top characterizations and far less warmth or lyricism. Writer-director Giuseppe Tornatore is responsible for both of these coming-of-age stories and somewhere between 1988's "Paradiso" and now, his romantic vision of the past has become constricted and superficial.

Not that there isn't anything to hold your attention in "Malena," beginning with the title character herself. As played by Monica Bellucci, Malena is arguably the most stunning and inscrutable natural wonder living in her small Sicilian village during the 1940s.

She is first beheld by 13-year-old Renato (Giuseppe Sulfaro) on the same day that Mussolini declares war against England and France. From that day forward, Renato is at one with the village's heterosexual male population—old, young, married or single—who gape in wonder whenever Malena strolls through the town square. The women, meanwhile, speculate that no one who wears such tight dresses can be trusted to be devoted to her husband, who's off fighting for the Fascists.

Malena is depicted throughout as little more than a blank space upon which others project their fantasies and prejudices. This is especially true of the hopelessly smitten Renato, who spies on her, dreams about her, imagines having her under his lifelong protection, especially after her husband is reported missing in action and presumed dead.

Bellucci is indeed a magnetic presence, evoking memories of Ava Gardner, Jeanne Moreau and other legendary screen goddesses. But the coarseness of the movie's humor and the predictability of its situations (Of course, the kid gets to go to a brothel with his father!) overwhelm what little human dimension she's permitted to have, especially after her attempts to stave off loneliness lead to her consorting with Nazi soldiers—and her horrific postwar humiliation.

The balance between broad ribaldry and gritty tragedy is so off-kilter that you really don't care what life lessons Renato has learned in the end. If anything, you're left feeling that if you never see another awkward adolescent "coming of age" through an older woman's obscure magic, it'll be too soon.

SIGHT AND SOUND, 3/01, p. 55, Edward Lawrenson

Castelcuto, Sicily, 1940. As war gets under way, Renato, a young teenager, develops a crush on 27-year-old Malèna Scordia, whose husband Nino is fighting overseas. Renato takes to spying on Malèna at night. After Nino is reported dead, Malèna is viewed with suspicion by some of the local women, wary of the hold her beauty has over their husbands. Malèna strikes up a friendship with a soldier, Lt Cadei; leaving her place one night, Cadei runs into one of Malèna's most fervent admirers, a married dentist, who attacks the officer. Represented by lawyer Centorbi, Malèna is cleared of having an affair with the dentist. In return for his services, Centorbi starts sleeping with Malèna; following the disapproval of his mother, he ends the relationship.

Malèna's father is killed in a bombing raid by allied aircraft. Faced with destitution, Malèna dyes her hair blonde and begins to consort with the German soldiers who are garrisoned in the town. Renato, meanwhile, is taken by his father to a brothel where he loses his virginity.

When US soldiers liberate Sicily, the local women beat Malèna up in the public square for collaborating with the Germans. Malèna leaves for Messina. Nino—falsely reported dead—arrives back in town, looking for his wife. Renato slips him a note which says he was the only man Malèna loved and tells of her whereabouts. A year later, Malèna and Nino return to the town, where she is treated cordially by the locals.

The opening moments of Giuseppe Tornatore's *Malèna* toy with the director's reputation as cinema's foremost purveyor of slick but treacly nostalgia. Like his breakthrough film *Cinema Paradiso*, this one is framed by an act of remembrance: as the camera swoops down from the roof-tops of a narrow alleyway—a canyon of sandy yellows and sun-dried reds—coming to rest at its teenage protagonist Renato's eye level, an adult voice, the older Renato, sets the scene, saying of his Sicilian home town at the outbreak of World War II: "Everyone was happy we were going to war." The loving, idealised retrospective gaze here is familiar enough from *Cinema Paradiso*, but when applied to such sombre events as preparations for war—a fascist rally has the air of a summer carnival—Tornatore's trademark sentimentality is invigorated by a dose of historical irony.

But Tornatore isn't an accomplished enough film-maker to balance these two registers (unlike, say, Federico Fellini, whose 1973 film *Amarcord*—unwisely invoked throughout *Malèna*—deftly combined a portrait of his boyhood years with an account of the rise of fascism). So the political context of Tornatore's tale soon fades into the background, often serving as little more than an expedient way to mark out the good guys from the bad as in Renato's unmotivated destruction at school of a bust of Mussolini's head. Instead, Tornatore prefers to concentrate on Renato's obsession with local beauty Malèna. And it's here that the director's talent for wistful nostalgia and creamy visuals is given full rein. "Time has passed," the adult Renato tells us at the end of the film, "and I have loved many women. The only one I have remembered is Malèna."

Unfortunately, the image Tornatore serves up of Malèna is refracted entirely through his adolescent protagonist's infatuated gaze. At one point Renato, whose masturbatory fantasies involve him together with Malèna in black-and-white recreations of famous movies, is accused of being a fetishist by his father; the charge could equally apply to Tornatore, whose camera drips with hormonal longing when turned on Malèna. And admittedly Malèna, played by former model Monica Bellucci, is a startling presence, but Tornatore rarely lets his actress do anything with the character: she's all look and no depth, an inscrutable blank on to which the local men project their desires and the women a certain guarded hostility. Indeed, one of the film's most memorable sequences follows Malèna's elegant catwalk stride through the local *piazza*, as she earns admiration and spite in equal measure.

In robbing Malèna of substance, Tornatore may be commenting on the limiting effect all this retching has on her suitors, notably the lawyer Centorbi, a portly figure with frizzy tufts of hair on each side of his cue-ball head and a twitchy moustache the size of a postage stamp, are ridiculous creations. But Tornatore softens this implicit critique by being just as salivating as Malèna's many admirers, striking a particularly salacious note when Renato fantasises about giving Malèna a consoling snog as she grieves, half undressed on her bed, for her dead husband. Even the film's most poignant scene, when Malèna is violently set upon by the local women for collaborating with the Nazis, is conducted as an attack on her beauty, as if that's her sole defining feature: dragged into the *piazza*, her clothes torn, her knee gashed, her long hair cut short, Malèna, whom Tornatore gives only a few lines of dialogue in the film, is allowed only a scream to articulate her feelings at this public humiliation.

VILLAGE VOICE, 12/26/00, p. 148, Dennis Lim

Set in fascist-era Sicily, Giuseppe Tornatore's *Malèna* begins as a nostalgic coming-of-age sex comedy tastefully lecherous enough to indicate that its intended demographic is several decades past puberty. When 13-year-old Renato (Giuseppe Sulfaro) first sets eyes on delectably curvaceous Malèna (Monica Belucci), the camera zeroes in on a ceremonious erection bursting through his shorts. More cringesome than cute, the groin-driven hijinks soon yield to an ostensibly weightier concern: the venomous envy roused in the small-minded townsfolk by Maléna's transcendent va-va-va-voom-ness. Like *Chocolat* , Miramax's other Christmas feel-good (about yourself) offering, this is a double-barreled attack on piety that fights fire with a giant blowtorch.

Speaking of which, the Mafia reportedly burned down sets because of the production's unsanctioned use of extras, though they could just as well have been reacting to the uniform depiction of locals as bellowing goons. Overassisted as ever by crescendo-happy Ennio Morricone, Tornatore botches his almost mute heroine's martyrdom with a brutally protracted humiliation sequence. It's a despicably lazy signal that spectators should adjust the nature of their objectifying gaze—from lust to pity.

Also reviewed in:
NEW REPUBLIC, 1/15/01, p. 21, Stanley Kauffmann
NEW YORK TIMES, 12/25/00, Pp. E5, Stephen Holden
VARIETY, 10/30-11/5/00, p. 22, David Rooney
WASHINGTON POST, 12/22/00, Weekend/p. 42, Michael O'Sullivan
WASHINGTON POST, 12/25/00, p. C4, Stephen Hunter

ME AND ISAAC NEWTON

A First Look Pictures release of a Michael Apted film. *Producer:* Jody Patton and Eileen Gregory. *Director:* Michael Apted. *Director of Photography:* Maryse Alberti. *Editor:* Susanne Rostock. *Music:* Patrick Seymour. *Running time:* 110 minutes. *MPAA Rating:* Not Rated.

CAST: Gertrude Elion (Pharmaceutical Chemist);   Ashok Gadgil (Environmental Physicist); Michio Kaku (Theoretical Physicist);   Maja Mataric (Computer Scientist);   Steven Pinker (Cognitive Scientist);   Karol Sikora (Professor of Cancer Medicine);   Patricia Wright (Primatologist/Conservationist).

NEW YORK POST, 11/10/00, p. 58, V. A. Musetto

Director Michael Apted interviews seven key scientists about their work and their inspiration.

Michio Kiku, a theoretical physicist, credits Albert Einstein and the old "Flash Gordon" TV series for his interest in science. Nobel winner Gertrude Elion, a cancer researcher, comments, "The real reward is not the prize. The real reward is having someone come up to me and thank me for their child's life." Primatologist Patricia Wright traces her interest in saving the rain forest to a pet monkey she bought in the East Village.

The most impressive thing about the seven eggheads are their humility, dedication and passion.

The same can be said for Apted, whose work ranges from the acclaimed "7-Up" documentary series to "Coal Miner's Daughter" to James Bond. He's a filmmaker with eclectic tastes and boundless curiosity, and "Me & Isaac Newton" makes for fascinating viewing.

NEWSDAY, 11/10/00, Part II/p. B6, Jan Stuart

Perhaps only a scientist could say something as self- congratulatory as, "If scientists don't save the world, I don't know who will."

And yet, by the time one of the specialists featured in "Me and Isaac Newton" makes that claim, you are inclined to agree. The seven giants of the science world who are profiled in this inspiring documentary from Michael Apted are doing about as much to keep the world from self-destructing as humanly, if not superhumanly, possible.

You don't have to be a rocket scientist to get, or to love, "Me and Isaac Newton." A British filmmaker who invented his own cinematic niche of social science with the "7 Up" documentary series, Apted furthers a proud tradition of British directors and writers (e.g. Hugh Whitmore's "Breaking the Code" and Michael Frayn's "Copenhagen") who know that there is nothing more thrilling or elucidating than listening to a scientist rattle on passionately about what he or she knows best.

Apted's film takes its title from a scene in which theoretical physicist Michio Kaku explains how he goes ice skating whenever he hits a logjam in his research. "When I'm on the ice, it's just me and Isaac Newton, free of constraints." In a sense, Kaku and company are perpetually teetering on ice. The septet Apted follows have forged brilliant careers free of the usual constraints of what is possible or conceivable.

What separates them from the pack is the sense of civic responsibility that has propelled their passions into action. Primatologist Patricia Wright went to Madagascar to study lemurs and found herself saving an entire rain forest. Environmental physicist Ashok Gadgil implemented his purification innovations in ridding South Africa of water-borne disease. And Kaku has galvanized the nuclear disarmament movement with his informed commitment to the peaceful utilization of nuclear science.

Apted's magnificent seven talk with captivating humor and humility about the childhood roots of their careers, the practical applications of their work, the chanciness and frustrations research. "It's a lot of little eureka moments," says Nobel Prize-winning chemist Gertrude Elion. "It's never the kind of thing in movies or books where suddenly the light dawned. It's not that sudden. It's years of suddenness."

They may study robots, but there is nothing robotic about these folks: Apted taps into a common through-line of humanity. "If it doesn't work," says Gadgil of the risk-taking factor of science, "you have to pick yourself up, dust yourself off, and what?" You gotta love an environmental physicist from India who quotes Ira Gershwin, even if he can't remember the whole lyric.

VILLAGE VOICE, 11/14/00, p. 140, Michael Atkinson

As Thomas Dolby used to cry, *Science!* Books and TV shows exploring scientific issues and processes proliferate on all levels, but movies generally approach that branch of knowledge by tossing sci-fi water balloons. Michael Apted's new doc *Me & Isaac Newton* goes at the state of things with a straight face and Sagan-esque glow, profiling seven scientists about their methods, inspirations, and ambitions.

Grandmotherly Nobel laureate chemist Gertrude Elion regales us with tales of years measuring pickle acidity before beginning leukemia research; Bombay-born environmental physicist Ashok Gadgil gives us a tour of Indian poverty as he tries to cheaply disinfect their water supply; theoretical physicist Michio Kaku waxes rhapsodic about string theory; primatologist Patricia Wright chats about her impromptu career as a lemur observer; and so on.

Who wouldn't love to make this movie sound sexy—for once, high-achieving individuals who actually deserve media attention are getting some—but it's a TV show and a facile one at that. Steering clear of anything technical, Apted gluts up the movie with MTV cutaways and impressionistic doodlings, not-so-obliquely implying that scientific accomplishment isn't sufficiently interesting on its own. Apted wants to document his subjects' synapses firing rather than actually explore the work. So, the scientists are encouraged to talk more about their feelings than their findings; I would've liked to hear Karol Sikora explain how his gene therapy stunts cancer growth, or Steven Pinker focus his engaging manner on the specifics of his language cognition research. However well-articulated the philosophies, it's a long way off from Carl mooning up at the fake stars on PBS all those years ago, explaining relativity to high schoolers and making it sing.

Also reviewed in:
NEW REPUBLIC, 11/20/00, p. 24, Stanley Kauffmann
NEW YORK TIMES, 11/10/00, p. E16, Stephen Holden
VARIETY, 10/18-24/99, p. 41, Eddie Cockrell

ME MYSELF I

A Sony Pictures Classics release of a Gaumont production. *Producer:* Fabien Liron. *Director:* Pip Karmel. *Screenplay:* Pip Karmel. *Director of Photography:* Graham Lind. *Editor:* Denise Haratzis. *Music:* Charlie Chan. *Choreographer:* John O'Connell. *Sound:* Guntis Sics and Phil Judd. *Sound Editor:* Livia Ruzic. *Casting:* Shauna Wolifson. *Production Designer:* Murray Picknett. *Art Director:* Diaan Wajon. *Costumes:* Paul Warren and Ariane Wise. *Make-up/Make-up (Rachel Griffiths):* Noriko Watanabe. *Running time:* 104 minutes. *MPAA Rating:* R.

CAST: Rachel Griffiths (Pamela Drury); David Roberts (Robert Dickson); Sandy Winton (Ben); Yael Stone (Stacey); Shaun Loseby (Douglas); Trent Sullivan (Rupert); Rebecca Frith (Terri); Felix Williamson (Geoff); Ann Burbrook (Janine); Maeliosa Stafford (Max); Terence Crawford (Allen); Christine Stephen-Daly (Deirdre); Kirstie Hutton (Sally); Donal Forde (Young Christian); Frank Whitten (Charlie); Mariel McClorey (Harriet); Maurice Morgan (Stripper); Adam Ray (Restaurant Photographer); Lucinda Armour (Pregnant Woman); Lynne McGimpsy (Security Guard); Peter Brailey (Roger); Andrew Caryofyllis (Harry); Anthony Issa (Passing Student); Lenore Munro (Sophie); Phaedra Nicolaidis and Billie Prichard (Self Defence Girls).

LOS ANGELES TIMES, 4/7/00, Calendar/p. 24, Gene Seymour

[The following review by Gene Seymour appeared in a slightly different form in **NEWSDAY, 4/7/00, Part II/p. B7.**]

The moment you hear single, 30ish investigative journalist Pamela Drury (Rachel Griffiths), the doughty, disaffected heroine of "Me Myself I," complain to one of her stroller-pushing buddies about the tick-tick-tick of her biological clock, you feel this overwhelming need to reach for a remote control button. Even those who identify strongly with Pamela's anxiety will roll their eyes and wonder if there's a game on somewhere. Anything, in short, that they haven't seen many times, many ways before.

Since there's no way to change the channel on a theatrical release, you then sigh and wonder how or whether writer-director Pip Karmel can apply a different spin on this situation. It comes after a grim survey of living alone and hating it in contemporary Sydney. Put another way, it comes after Pam dates a loser on her birthday, weeps over turning down a marriage proposal from one Robert Dickson (David Roberts) some 13 years before, finds out her dream guy is already taken and attempts suicide only to be foiled by a power failure.

The next morning, a car blindsides Pam as she's crossing the street. When she wakes up, she finds that the driver is Pamela Drury. Only it's a Pamela Drury who said yes to Robert and ended up in a cozy suburban house with two small boys and a teenage girl. Soon, the Pamela who was hit by a car finds herself the only Pamela in the house. She's not dead, she's not dreaming and now she has to help the youngest child wipe his bottom.

You just know from the start that what follows is going to be one roller coaster of a learning experience for Pam and her alternate-universe household. And once again, you wonder: How is this fish-out-of-water-lifestyle-wish-fulfillment fantasy any different from what you've seen a million times before on prime-time TV?

There are a couple of answers to this question, beginning with Griffiths herself. To say that Karmel is fortunate to have her in the lead is understating matters greatly. At once supremely confident and winsomely vulnerable, Griffiths' Pam holds your attention without any gratuitous mannerisms or broad asides. It's a sleek, rangy performance that all but redeems the hackneyed familiarity of the premise.

The other thing "Me Myself I" has going for it is a beguiling attention to detail in many of the domestic sequences. There's a near-disorienting yet engaging intimacy, for instance, in the scenes between Pam and her moody 14-year-old daughter (Yael Stone) when the latter gets her first period. (Gratifyingly little is made of the fact that Pam finds herself saying the exact same thing to the daughter that her own mother said to her at the same biological moment.) The love scenes between Pam and Robert likewise conclude with a satisfying ambivalence. (She's not sure what to think of it all, except that she thinks she still loves him.)

And one supposes that there are more than a few in the audience who will be helped along by the film's message: If you want to change your life, the best thing to do is imagine yourself in somebody else's.

Perhaps a movie made less slickly than "Me Myself I" could have made this point seem fresher than it does here. But who knows whether anyone would have wanted to see it?

NEW YORK POST, 4/7/00, p. 56, Jonathan Foreman

Remarkable only in its rare insistence on dealing with the nitty-gritty of toilet training young children—and the blitheness with which it harvests old clichés about choosing between family and a career—"Me Myself I" is easily the worst of the recent crop of "what if" comedies.

Pamela (Rachel Griffiths) is a successful investigative journalist in her 30s who lives a frantic but lonely single life in a box-filled apartment in Sydney, Australia.

She not only laments her lack of a mate but also wonders if she didn't ruin her life by refusing a marriage proposal 13 years earlier.

You see her getting smashed alone after a bad blind date and then picking up a conveniently handy box containing a 13-year-old photograph of Robert Dickson (David Roberts) her "one true love."

A few days later, by an unexplained miracle, she encounters herself as she would have been in an alternative universe in which she married him.

Before Pamela One can say anything, she finds herself stranded with three badly-behaved children; a distant, overworked, unenlightened husband, a suburban house; a dog; and a part-time gig writing for women's magazines.

You don't get to see how Pamela Two is doing back in the other universe, but, of course, both Pams learn the grass is always greener on the other side, and bring equally predictable lessons back into their real lives.

Griffiths, so good in "Hillary and Jackie" has more than enough screen presence to hold your attention, but is surprisingly mannered as an Aussie Bridget Jones character.

This Australian-French co-production is the feature debut of writer-director Pip Karmel, who does a tolerable job with some Steven Soderbergh-style jump-cutting, but often seems to have forgotten what real life looks like.

SIGHT AND SOUND, 9/00, p. 44, Geoffrey Macnab

Pamela Drury, a successful journalist in her thirties, is single and regrets turning down college sweetheart Robert Dickson's marriage proposal 13 years ago. Pamela is now attracted to crisis counsellor Ben but thinks he's already married and is put off asking him out.

After almost being run over, Pamela meets a woman who looks remarkably like her. This doppelganger turns out to have married Dickson and is living a seemingly idyllic life with three kids. Startled to meet her alternative self, Pamela is even more perplexed when her double vanishes, leaving her to look after the children.

Pamela soon realises that married life has its problems. Robert, an overworked businessman, is always too tired to have sex and the kids are a handful. When Pamela discovers Robert's been unfaithful, she has a fling with Ben, the crisis counsellor she met in her 'other' life, now a journalist. In a local restaurant, Robert proposes that he and Pamela renew their marriage vows. While she's in the bathroom, her double (who has been living her old life) turns up. They both return to their old lives. Single once more, Pamela meets Ben and, learning he is divorced, arranges to see him again.

Given its identity-swapping scenario, in which Pamela, a single journalist in her thirties, encounters her double and assumes her role as a suburban wife and mum, it's not surprising that *Me Myself I* seems schizophrenic. The pitch is superficially similar to that of *Sliding Doors* or *La Double Vie de Véronique*, but writer-director Pip Karmel (who edited *Shine*) is only interested in telling one side of the story. We're never shown how Pamela's double copes with the transition from housewife to city-based hack. Nor is the switch ever properly explained. Instead, her film follows Pamela as she adapts to family life.

In the early scenes, as she swigs vodka, goes on disastrous dates and bemoans her solitary lifestyle, Pamela comes across as a comic version of the singles bar addict Diane Keaton played in *Looking for Mr Goodbar* (1977). At one point, she rails against the men who have let her down ("Bastard, coward, misogynist, commitment phobe, dental surgeon"), then later attempts suicide. But if she finds singledom miserable, she soon realises the family life she yearns for is equally oppressive.

In his documentary *A Personal Journey with Martin Scorsese through American Movies*, the director discussed how such 50s melodramas as *All That Heaven Allows* and *Bigger Than Life* showed the "psychotic undercurrents" of American family life—"the sugar and the poison," as Scorsese put it. In its most unsettling moments, *My Myself I* does something similar with the Australian suburbs. Pamela is a stranger, taken for granted by the family whose lives she has moved into. Her husband is patronising, chauvinistic and snores, one son is constantly rude to her and the teenage daughter is sarcastic and hostile. If this is what she has missed out on by pursuing her career so single-mindedly, she's had a lucky escape.

Karmel's screenplay is more tricksy than ingenious. She never explains how Pamela is able to pick up so quickly on her double's lifestyle and to strike up an instant rapport with three children she has never met before. The real 'Mr Right', crisis counsellor Ben, seems unattainable until the final-reel contrivances throw him into Pamela's lap. The plotting may be feeble, but Karmel at least has a nice line in barbed one liners and sight gags. There's an earthiness to the humour that you rarely find in Hollywood's romantic comedies. Bodily functions are always to the fore: the youngest of the children, for instance, is incapable of wiping his backside without Pamela's help.

With a less spiky star, all this might have seemed grossly self-indulgent, but Rachel Griffiths is too strong an actress to allow Pamela to turn into yet another fey Bridget Jones clone. This said, *Me Myself I*'s determination to deliver a happy ending runs against the grain of much of the film. Karmel has spent so long detailing both the horrors of suburbia and the shortcomings of the single lifestyle that the upbeat finale rings hollow. Both Pamelas, one suspects, won't be happy for long.

VILLAGE VOICE, 4/10/00, p. 162, Dennis Lim

A cozy, affirmative fantasy, *Me Myself I* relies on shopworn metaphysics to illustrate any number of cockeyed truisms about destiny and regret—or, more likely, to disguise their sheer banality. The movie collapses philosophical conundrums it barely understands into a fixed smile and a pat on the back: Whatever choice you make, it insists with the sinister, obstinate vapidity of a self-help manual, is the right one. In short, its answer to "What if?" is "Who cares?"

Pamela (Rachel Griffiths) is a driven Sydney journalist, a thirtyish single woman in the Ally/Bridget mold—angsty, mouthy, unlucky in love—and first-time writer-director Pip Karmel outlines her protagonist's initial plight in crude, smeared shorthand. A colleague plonks down an award on Pamela's desk in the first five minutes; she runs around busily investigating a story ("It's about girls today," she announces with mystifying smugness). But her personal life is a wash—she celebrates her birthday with an abortive blind date, then goes home to cry over an old boyfriend. Just in time, a freak accident sends the borderline-suicidal Pamela crashing through a sliding door on the space-time continuum; she ends up face-to-face with a different version of herself—married to the one that got away and raising three brats with him in suburbia. What follows is a grindingly obvious mix of mild fish-out-of-water comedy and grass-is-always-greener awakening.

A versatile, unshowy actor, Griffiths keeps the movie watchable, but Karmel elbows her screenplay's questionable assumptions into bold relief. *Me Myself I* positions itself as a women's film, but its attempts to explore the tensions between career and family are hamstrung by its central gimmick, which presents the two as mutually exclusive. The movie's title says plenty—supposedly evocative of Pamela's identity crisis but more suggestive of terminal self-absorption. *Me Myself I* promotes the kind of skewed introspection that has time only for uplift—it's a feel-good, fatalist placebo, and the coating of New Age goop makes it even more difficult to swallow.

Also reviewed in:
CHICAGO TRIBUNE, 4/21/00, Friday/p. F, Michael Wilmington
NATION, 5/15/00, p. 34, Stuart Klawans

NEW YORK TIMES, 4/7/00, p. E14, Stephen Holden
VARIETY, 9/13-29/99, p. 43, Todd McCarthy
WASHINGTON POST, 4/21/00, p. C12, Rita Kempley

ME, MYSELF & IRENE

A Twentieth Century Fox release of a Conundrum Entertainment production. *Executive Producer:* Charles B. Wessler and Tom Schulman. *Producer:* Bradley Thomas, Bobby Farrelly, and Peter Farrelly. *Director:* Bobby Farrelly and Peter Farrelly. *Screenplay:* Peter Farrelly, Mike Cerrone, and Bobby Farrelly. *Director of Photography:* Mark Irwin. *Editor:* Christopher Greenbury. *Music:* Peter Yorn and Lee Scott. *Music Editor:* Lee Scott. *Sound:* Jonathan Earl Stein and (music) Michael C. Ross. *Sound Editors:* John Joseph Thomas and Vanessa Ashley Lapato. *Casting:* Rick Montgomery. *Production Designer:* Sidney J. Bartholomew, Jr. *Art Director:* Arlan Jay Vetter. *Set Designer:* Richard Fojo. *Set Decorator:* Scott Jacobson. *Set Dresser:* Kenneth Weinberg, James M. Schneider, Shawn Gamache, Rafael M. Fraguada, Peter Letzelter-Smith, and William Bonn. *Special Effects:* Robert Vazquez. *Costumes:* Pamela Withers. *Make-up:* Cindy Williams. *Make-up (Jim Carrey):* Sheryl Leigh Ptak. *Make-up (Renée Zellweger):* Bernadette Mazur. *Make-up Effects:* Tony Gardner. *Stunt Coordinator:* Rick Barker. *Running time:* 100 minutes. *MPAA Rating:* R.

CAST: Jim Carrey (Charlie Baileygates/Hank); Renée Zellweger (Irene Waters); Anthon Anderson (Jamaal); Mongo Brownlee (Lee Harvey); Jerod Mixon (Shonté Jr.); Chris Cooper (Lieutenant Gerke); Michael Bowman (Whitey); Richard Jenkins (Agent Boshane); Robert Forster (Colonel Partington); Mike Cerrone (Officer Stubie); Rob Moran (Trooper Finneran); Daniel Greene (Dickie Thurman); Tony Cox (Limo Driver); Andrew Phillips (Lee Harvey, Age 9); Jeremy Maleek Leggett (Jamaal, Age 9); Justin Chandler (Shonté Jr, Age 9); Zen Gesner (Agent Peterson); Steve Sweeney (Neighbor Ed); Traylor Howard (Layla); Lenny Clarke (Barber Shop Car Owner); Herb Flynn (Herb the Barber); Heather Hodder (Jump Rope Girl); Tracey Abbott (Grocery Store Mom); Jackie Flynn (Trooper Pritchard); Steve Tyler (Maternity Doctor); Googy Gress (Guy on the Street); Joey McGilberry (Helicopter Agent); Sean P. Gildea (Kid's Father); Anna Kournikova (Motel Manager); Bob Mone (Officer Delicato); Richard Tyson (Gun Shop Owner); Dan Murphy (Agent Steve Parfitt); Cam Neely (Trooper Sea Bass); Brian Hayes Currie (Soda Machine Man); Nikki Tyler Flynn (Trooper Maryann); Mark Leahy (Vermont Police Officer); Kevin J. Flynn (Barber Shop Wiseguy); Conrad Goode (Softball Player); John Mark Andrade (Handsom Barber Shop Guy); Scott T. Neely (Trooper Neely); Shannon Whirry (Beautiful Mom); Jerry Parker (Paramedic); Heather Dyson (Reporter); Christine DiCarlo (TV Reporter); Marc R. Levine (Golfer); John-Eliot Jordan (Pizza Boy); Bob Weekes (Train Conductor); Ezra Buzzington (Disabled Guy); Will Coogan (Disable Guy's Aide); Rex Allen, Jr. (Narrator).

LOS ANGELES TIMES, 6/23/00, Calendar/p. 1, Kenneth Turan

The Farrelly brothers have been dumb and they've been dumber, and "Me, Myself & Irene" definitely falls into the second category. Even if you laughed despite yourself at the unspeakable shenanigans in "There's Something About Mary," this is one to leave for the hard-core gross-out crowd. The tasteless jokes come in as thick and fast as German ordnance in "Saving Private Ryan," and dealing with so much relentless transgression has become exhausting more than entertaining.

This despite the presence of the remarkable Jim Carrey, starring as a Rhode Island state policeman with a split personality, both of whom, the cheerful Charlie as well as the churlish Hank, are heedlessly in love with the sylph-like Irene Walters (Renee Zellweger).

As wild a comic actor as Carrey is, he's almost underutilized with but two personalities to play. The sequence when be uses little more than facial contortions to transform good guy Charlie into a Hank who acts and sounds like Clint Eastwood's Dirty Harry is a remarkable one.

But for all his gifts, noticeable warmth has never been one of Carrey's strengths, and that's the area where the shadow of "Something About Mary" falls heaviest. While the presence of Cameron Diaz in particular and Ben Stiller and Matt Dillon to a lesser extent softened the outrageous humor of co-directors Bobby and Peter Farrelly and made it surprisingly palatable, no one manages to perform that function here.

Without this leavening humanity, the Farrellys' trademark foul humor (the script is by the brothers and boyhood friend Mike Cerrone) feels haphazard and strained. Too many people are trying too darn hard to make light and frothy humor out of material (anal sex with realistic dildos, to pick a random example) that was taboo once upon a time.

Jokes also tend to repeat themselves from earlier films (the dog who won't die in "Mary" becomes a resilient cow in "Irene") and what was once a surprise is now predictable: Bring an angelic tyke into the frame and you know she's going to end up cursing like, well, a trooper.

The first part of "Irene" is an extended flashback to 18 years in the past, showing why and how Charlie Baileygates (the name has a Frank Capra echo) squandered the potential to be one of the best state troopers in Rhode Island history. It all had to do with a woman.

Charlie was in love with the attractive Layla (Traylor Howard) but a chance wedding day encounter with Tony Cox's brainy dwarf black limousine driver (this is the Farrellys, after all) ends up ruining his marriage. Ever the good sport, Charlie becomes a kind and loving stepfather to the triplets the limo driver fathered who grow up to be huge, trash-talking geniuses.

That plot strand is typical of how the Farrellys' mix-and-match taboo-breaking humor does and doesn't work. It is initially unexpected and amusing to see and hear these three guys (played by Anthony Anderson, Mongo Brownlee and Jerod Mixon), but that surprise value disappears well before they do, leaving us with repetitive and finally cliched characters whose addiction to nonstop profanity does not wear particularly well.

Given that his small Rhode Island town misses no opportunity to laugh at him behind his back, it's not a surprise when Charlie finally snaps and time-shares his body with the hostile, aggressive Hank, the man who does all the things Charlie has been repressing for years.

Irene, a winsome expert in turf management, enters the picture when the Rhode Island troopers have to escort her back to Rochester, N.Y., where, it turns out, her ex-boyfriend is involved in a criminal scheme too complex to ever be fully understood.

Charlie gets the assignment, but he forgets his schizophrenia medication and eventually both he and Hank are courting Irene in their zealous and very distinctive styles. While Zellweger's performance is pedestrian—she's more or less just along for the ride—Carrey's gift for chaotic physical humor does manage to create the occasional amusing moment.

Natives of Rhode Island, the Farrellys are enviably loyal to their home state, not only filming there but also calling their state police "the best darn law enforcement agency in the country" and using old pals in small roles. They even devote the closing credits to visually identifying bit actors who got cut out of the final film. It's a funny and amusing notion, but like a lot of "Me, Myself & Irene," it goes on for too long.

NEW YORK, 7/10/00, p. 51, Peter Rainer

After going on a walkabout into Oscarland with *The Truman Show* and *Man on the Moon*, Jim Carrey is back at his frenzied near-best in *Me, Myself & Irene*, the latest gross-me-out from the Farrelly brothers. He plays a Rhode Island trooper with a split personality: One is a Milquetoast, the other insanely bullying, his voice a Dirty Harry rasp. There's nothing here as blissfully satisfying as the best bad-taste parts in *Dumb and Dumber* or *There's Something About Mary*, but Carrey is a phenomenal whirling dervish of a performer who could probably have added another four or five personalities to the mix without breaking a sweat. If he and Eddie Murphy, another performer who likes to split himself up, ever decide to make a movie together, the blur of guises will induce mass vertigo in the audience.

NEW YORK POST, 6/23/00, p. 47, Lou Lumenick

Dwarfs, albinos, defecation, urination, vaginal preparations, dildos and Jim Carrey. Writers-directors Peter and Bobby Farrelly don't miss much in their first gross-out comedy since "There's Something About Mary."

"Me, Myself & Irene" doesn't quite reach the heights—though it does plumb the depths—of its hugely popular predecessor. But it will have an enormous, appreciative audience doubled over with belly-busting laughs.

Carrey has never been funnier than as Charlie Baileygates, a veteran Rhode Island state trooper with a dual-personality disorder.

A meek fellow, Charlie has long suppressed his rage over his wife's running off with a black dwarf chauffeur who fathered the couple's three now-grown sons.

When a colleague remarks, "Did ya notice your kids sorta have a year-round tan?" Charlie just swallows hard.

One day, Charlie, whose extreme avoidance of confrontation has turned him into the Rodney Dangerfield of law enforcement, snaps. He turns into the hyper-aggressive Hank, whose first act is to shove a little girl who refuses to stop skipping rope into the nearest outdoor fountain.

Shrinks give Charlie medication to suppress his Hank attacks, but things start to go wackily wrong when Charlie is assigned to accompany a suspect named Irene Waters (Rene Zellweger) back to her home in Massena, N.Y.

After Irene is attacked by bad guys (following a bizarre encounter with a cow), Charlie loses his medicine—and hilariously zigzags back and forth between his two personalities.

Even when the Farrellys' script starts degenerating into a generic chase movie at the midway point, Carrey, triumphantly returning to flat-out comedy after flirting with drama in "The Truman Show" and "Man on the Moon," gives an outrageous physical and verbal performance worthy of Buster Keaton—complete with a Clint Eastwoodish snarl as Hank.

Zellweger, who's Carrey's real-life squeeze, has real on-screen chemistry—attracted to Charlie, repelled by Hank—though she never quite keeps up with his frenetic comic pacing.

She fares better than Chris Cooper (the dad next door in "American Beauty"), who's criminally wasted as a rogue FBI agent trying to frame Irene in an incomprehensible plot, as is Robert Forster ("Jackie Brown") as Charlie's sympathetic superior.

In fact, the real standouts are three young black actors who play Charlie's sons—the ubiquitous Anthony Anderson ("Big Momma's House," "Romeo Must Die"), Mongo Brownlee and Jerod Mixon—massive, trash-talking geniuses who for no logical reason accompany the FBI in pursuit of Charlie and Irene.

Also guaranteed to double over audiences are Tony Cox as the dwarf who cuckolds Charlie in the prologue and Michael Bowman as an albino waiter named, well, Whitey.

Grossly insensitive to the mentally ill as well as other groups too numerous to catalog, "Me, Myself & Irene" delivers laughs by the gross for Carrey and Farrelly brothers fans, including several scenes deploying an industrial-size dildo—not to mention a novel use of a live chicken.

Though it's too long and rambling, it's hard not to love a movie that quotes Woody Allen's notorious "60 Minutes" interview, the newsreel of the Hindenberg disaster and the tarantula scene in "Dr. No.

And it's all wrapped up in folksy narration by Rex Allen Jr.—whose mellifluous western tones will instantly strike a chord with boomers who heard his sound-alike father narrate countless Disney nature films in the 1950s.

NEWSDAY, 6/23/00, Part II/p. B3, John Anderson

As Rhode Island's answer to Noel Coward, the Farrelly Brothers have been associated from the beginning of their career with the scatological, the reproductive, the flatulent, the comically handicapped, flying hair gel, bowling and all things eagerly offensive. It seems rather obvious that, were they to make a movie about a schizophrenic, said schizophrenic would be portrayed with something less than the sensitivity customarily accorded a person with a serious mental condition.

It's obvious, too, given that the price of publicity is eternal vigilance, that groups such as the National Mental Health Association and National Alliance for the Mentally Ill would want to help advertise such a movie by decrying its inaccuracy (he's not really a schizophrenic), to say nothing of its callousness and cruelty (words that should have Farrelly fans barreling out of the woodwork). The real question, however, is who. Who are these preposterous people who will take Jim Carrey's performance in "Me, Myself & Irene" seriously? Get their names. If they buy the house next door, move.

Otherwise, grab an air-sickness bag and sit back. Relax. Remember, the guy with the real gripe should be Eddie Murphy, whose "Nutty Professor II: The Klumps" isn't due till late July, but whose shtick has been co-opted already this summer by two separate movies: the tottering "Big Momma's House," with Martin Lawrence clad in Klump-ish fat, and now "Me, Myself & Irene," in which Jim Carrey's alter ego (Jim Carrey) is a badge-wearing, gun-carrying, law-enforcing Buddy Love.

Love was, of course, the other side of Seymour Klump (and Jerry Lewis), a manifestation of his host psyche's suppressed needs and repressed humiliations—quantities Charlie Baileygates (Carrey) has in abundance. Left by his wife to raise their three sons—who are, though Charlie seems not to notice, black—the dedicated state trooper is laughed at behind his back, treated by his fellow townsfolk the way a baby treats a diaper and after one slap in the face too many, releases his inner Hank—and, after several clinical diagnoses, is put on medication.

As narrated by Rex Allen Jr., the veteran voice of a million movies even if I can't seem to name one, "Me, Myself & Irene" is given the hearty tone of a nature film, maybe one about a wayward puppy struggling to find its way home. Charlie is a puppy. Hank's an oversexed greater Swiss mountain dog. Together—while at war with each other—they try to protect/seduce Irene Waters (Renee Zellweger), whose old boyfriend (Daniel Greene) is part of a corruption scandal and whose cop partner (Chris Cooper) wants Irene dead.

The story is basic, but the Farrellys adorn it with one outrageous gag after another, some of which go by so fleetingly they're hardly noticed. Is it a coincidence that Charlie and all his cop friends look like the Village People? Is it funnier that his sons—Jamaal (Anthony Anderson), Lee Harvey (Mongo Brownlee) and Shonte Jr. (Jerod Mixon)—look like Run DMC, or that they talk about atomic weights and German syntax? (Ali, there lies the real potential offense of "MM&I".) Is it funnier that Hank shoots a cow—a clearly mechanical cow—six or seven times in the head? Or that the cow is, as Robert Forster's Capt. Partington says, "lucky to be alive."

In the end, Zellweger is adorable, Carrey is unhinged but the Farrelly Brothers may still end up disappointed. They've gotten the mental health advocates aroused. But what about PETA? The PBA? The Family Research Council? Sex therapists? Manufacturers of marital aids? The Nation of Islam? The Aryan Brotherhood? Dr. Laura Schlessinger? G. Gordon Liddy? What about Eddie Murphy?

NEWSWEEK, 7/3/00, p. 60, David Ansen

There is always a "Could you believe?" moment in a Farrelly brothers movie. The shot that goes so far beyond any notion of good taste that you gasp before you laugh. Everyone knows what they were in "There's Something About Mary." The zipper. The hairgel. The dog. The most indelibly twisted sight in "Me, Myself & Irene" is not, as some would have it, the scene where an extra from "Chicken Run" is seen dangling from the nether regions of a bound and gagged cop. The concept is simply too outrageous to hit a personal nerve. No, my nominee would be the startling moment when Jim Carrey, as the long-suffering Rhode Island policeman Charlie, morphs into his raging alter ego Hank, and in his rampage goes down on his knees in the street to feast his ravenous mouth on the enormous breast of a nursing mother. When he comes up for air, his triumphantly aggressive smile is haloed with milk. Discomfort, titillation, surprise and revulsion colliding into a comic bombshell that leaves you slightly woozy with laughter. At a moment like this, Peter and Bobby Farrelly earn their stripes as the four-star generals of gross-out comedy. In an era when gross reigns supreme, this is no mean feat.

"Mary" is a tough act to follow. For "Me, Myself & Irene" they've refurbished an old screenplay co-written with Mike Cerrone and cast the great elastic man of comedy to play their split-personality hero, a sweet-tempered soul who has eaten so much crow in his life that when he finally snaps he turns into a model of machismo run amok. The father of three brilliant, trash-talking African-American sons (his wife left him for a black midget Mensa member, played by Tony Cox) Charlie/Hank is diagnosed with "advanced delusionary schizophrenia with involuntary narcissistic rage." Nonetheless, he is ordered to shepherd the lovely Irene (René Zellweger)—who is being pursued by her gangster boyfriend—to her home. During this voyage he loses his meds, resulting in a situation in which both sides of his personality are fighting over the same woman.

Even for the creators of "Dumb and Dumber" and "Kingpin" this is a farfetched premise, and the movie pays a price for it. The saving grace of "Mary" was its grounding in recognizable human yearnings. "Me, Myself" is grounded in the yearning to get a guffaw at any cost. Sure, the combination of Carrey's zealous contortionism and the Farrellys' fearlessly low humor will make you laugh (see Jim wrestle a dying cow, see him locked in mortal combat with himself, see him pee all over the wall). But you feel the effort behind the gags. There's more chemistry between Carrey and Carrey than between him and his costar, and the woman-on-the-run-from-killers plot is strictly from hunger.

There was a sweetness underlying "Mary" that put all the offending bodily fluids in a benign perspective. "Me, Myself & Irene" isn't nasty, but the aftertaste is hollow. The brothers are straining this time.

The Farrellys didn't invent gross-out humor, but such images as Jeff Daniels's diarrhetic explosion in "Dumb and Dumber" upped the ante and opened the floodgates. In teen comedies from "American Pie" to "Austin Powers: The Spy Who Shagged Me" to "Road Trip" no orifice goes uninvaded, no bodily substance goes untasted, no obscenity is left unsaid. Can we blame it on the' 60s, as right-wing ideologues love to do? Can we blame it on the infantilizing of American culture? Can we blame Canada? For the moment, let's blame Mel Brooks. Some 26 years ago, in his hilarious "Blazing Saddles," he gathered a bunch of cowpokes around a campfire, filled them up with beans and let loose a sound that changed the face of comedy. Everyone had heard it before, but not up there on screen. To this day, there is no easier way to make an American audience laugh than with a fart joke. It is, simply, the cheapest but most cost-effective weapon in the comic arsenal.

OK, maybe Jonathan Swift and Rabelais beat Mel to the punch, but neither of them had a three-picture deal at Fox. From the start, the movies were uniquely equipped to convey the shock of the gross in stomach-turning ways writers could only envy. You could describe in words a razor blade cutting an eyeball, but when Luis Buñuel and Salvador Dali showed it in their 1928 surrealist "Un Chien Andalou," they knew they had found the best medium to *épater les bourgeois*. Little did they know that by the end of the century the great middle class of moviegoers, far from being outraged, would be lined up to see a man dive into the most unsanitary toilet in all of Scotland ("Trainspotting") or convulsed with laughter at the most ferocious display of projectile vomiting ever filmed—the exploding Mr. Creosote in "Monty Python's The Meaning of Life."

The Buñuel-Dali philosophy of grossness—to use shock as a weapon against the status quo—hasn't died out, but it's always been more at home in Europe than Hollywood. Art-house directors such as Marco Ferreri (men eating themselves to death in "La Grande Bouffe"), Japan's Nagisa Oshima (the erotically explicit "In the Realm of the Senses") and Pier Paolo Pasolini (whose "Salò" features boys forced by Fascists to eat feces) still had faith in the power of shock to shake up a complacent society. American filmmakers, whether subversive or crassly commercial, were more inclined to giggle. When John Waters had his diva Divine nibble on dog poop at the climax of "Pink Flamingos," it was meant as a gesture of liberation as well as offense: a black comic announcement that the cinema and the subculture were going to let it all hang out.

But grossness isn't what it used to be; with the exception of the surprisingly political "South Park," the stinky-poo outrages of recent Hollywood fare have no higher agenda than coaxing rowdy laughter from randy teenagers. Gross equals grosses; crass is mass market. In America, bad taste is democratic: it's for everyone to share and enjoy. We're all Jim Carrey, lapping up the culture's mother's milk, an idiot's grin on our faces.

SIGHT AND SOUND, 10/00, p. 50, Leslie Felperin

Rhode Island, 1983. Good-natured teenager Charlie Baileygates marries his high-school sweetheart Layla, but her infidelity with a black dwarf produces non-identical triplets, whom Charlie accepts as his own. Layla leaves him; Charlie raises his sons—Jamaal, Lee Harvey and Shonté Jr—by himself. Seventeen years later, Charlie has become a Rhode Island state trooper, but no one respects his authority because he's too nice. Suddenly, he develops an aggressive alternative personality named Hank.

After being placed on medication, Charlie is charged with escorting attractive Irene P. Waters to upstate New York to face trumped-up charges: Irene's ex-boyfriend Dickie Thurman is in cahoots with federal agent Boshane and local policeman Gerke to stop her rumbling their illegal scheme involving the development of a golf course. Both Charlie's personalities fall in love with Irene, and when he loses his medication, Hank emerges and struggles with Charlie over her. The two/three of them go on the run, pursued by Dickie, Boshane and Gerke as well as the Rhode Island state troopers and Charlie's sons (who are able to track down their father). Along the way, Irene and Charlie hook up with an Albino named Casper who claims to have killed his parents. Hank fools Irene into thinking he's Charlie in order to have sex with her, but Irene comes to love Charlie. Charlie learns to express his anger, putting an end to Hank's influence. Boshane and Gerke are exposed and Thurman arrested, after a struggle with Charlie. Irene tries to leave Rhode Island, but is stopped from doing so by state troopers and she is happily reunited with Charlie.

Me, Myself & Irene goes out of its way to shock its audience with the bizarre and socially unacceptable antics of its protagonist, centres on a love triangle involving two halves of a man with a split personality who at one point literally beats himself up, and hinges thematically on frustrated male rage. When you get down to it, it's *Fight Club* with extra slapstick, although *Me, Myself & Irene* isn't nearly as self-important—or, admittedly, as relentlessly inventive. Having said that, both films suffer from a certain debilitating bittiness, a failure to add up to a more satisfying whole than might be expected from the brilliance of their individual parts.

This is more noticeable in *Me, Myself & Irene*, which at its worst feels like a collection of comic off-cuts from such earlier Farrelly Brothers' films as *Dumb & Dumber* and *There's Something about Mary*. As with these films, *Me, Myself & Irene*'s narrative structure is essentially picaresque—therefore bitty by nature. (The film follows lovers-on-the-run Charlie, a split personality, and Irene, escaping her gangster ex-lover whose crimes are so sketchily described it's difficult to tell how they fit into the plot.)

The virtue and vice of the Farrellys' movies are that the have so much crammed into them. The directors are capable of dazzling, audacious gags, but their habit of not knowing when to quit can be annoying (as when Charlie makes repeated attempts to kill a cow, a joke that recalls the treatment meted out to the ferocious dog in *Mary*). The minor characters have so much vitality and detail they can be distracting (Lee Evans' boffin in *Marv*, Charlie's three jive-talking genius sons here). It's the kind of comedy that plays well on video or, better yet, DVD, where you can fast forward or skip to your favourite moments (the scene in which a chicken is stuffed up a cop's rear end seems destined to become a favourite at university halls of residence).

In terms of grossness, the so-called shocking material here is hardly any more audacious than that found in recent Farrelly imitations such as *American Pie*, *Me, Myself & Irene* just has a lot more of it. The film has caused particular controversy in the US for its depiction of mental illness (which hardly seems more frivolously used here as a plot device than it is in, say, *Fight Club)*, ethnic minorities and differently-abled people. In the end, one of the film's great virtues, true of the Farrellys' work as a whole, is that it pays tribute to otherness by depicting it with humour rather than patronising solemness. Increasingly, mainstream Hollywood cinema can only present black characters as wise, noble and good. In *Me, Myself & Irene*, Charlie's three black sons are intellectually gifted but also foul-mouthed, and blithely converse in the misogynist argot of hip-hop discourse. ("No bitches after 11 o'clock," their dad admonishes them when he leaves on his trip.)

Me, Myself & Irene won't go down in history as the great screwball-slapstick comedy it could have been, a standard *There's Something about Mary* almost attains. The real weakness of the film is how little Renée Zellweger's Irene has to do, apart from hitting a guy over the head with a dildo and reacting to Jim Carrey's *tour de force* physical performance as Charlie—and strong female characters are the skeleton of good screwball. Like *Fight Club*, this is a guy film.

TIME, 6/26/00, p. 71, Richard Corliss

The National Alliance for the Mentally Ill accused the makers of *Me, Myself & Irene* of "insensitivity" to schizophrenics for its portrayal of a cop (Jim Carrey) with dueling dual personalities. But the makers are Peter and Bobby Farrelly, auteurs of *Dumb & Dumber*, *Kingpin* and *There's Something About Mary*. If they had any sensitivity, they wouldn't be at the top of Hollywood's gross-comedy heap. They'd be back in Rhode Island asking if you want fries with that. So NAMI will have to get in line behind albinos, African-American dwarfs, dead cows, live chickens and anyone possessing that vestigial appendage known as taste.

If you are none of the above, you are hereby absolved of all guilt when you laugh your ass off in the first half of the film—when the Farrelys exploit their gift for tossing sweet guys into wildly frustrating situations. Carrey plays Charlie, whose wife has left him with three fat black babies (we'll explain another time); he smiles and copes. But by repressing his rage, Charlie has let a demon grow inside him; finally it bursts out in an alter libido named Hank. That makes him bad company for Irene (Renée Zellweger), whom he must escort to upstate New York. You see, he's fallen in love. Both of him.

For his first real comedy in three years, Carrey is all manic ingenuity. His eyebrows tango; he sports dry mouth and a milk mustache; he executes a quintuple spit take. It's not that he'll do anything to get a laugh. It's that he has the timing and gall to earn it—as in his metamorphosis from Charlie to Hank in one shot and with no special effects. You don't need ILM when you have JIM.

But comedy needs a climax. Long before that *MM&I* goes slack and desperate. And a chicken in a man's butt isn't all that hilarious. Maybe filmgoers need a lobbying group too: a Society for the Propagation of Promising Comedies That Actually Deliver on Their Promises. Care to join?

VILLAGE VOICE, 6/27/00, p. 151, J. Hoberman

The uneasy reunion of two formidable comic talents, *Me, Myself & Irene* combines the Farrelly brothers' requisite jerk-off jokes with Jim Carrey's post-superstar interest in, as Jon Lovitz used to put it, "acting." *Me, Myself & Irene* is more chuckle time than laff riot but no less vulgar than one might expect. This is the first movie I've ever seen—porn included—in which a guy gets coldcocked with a dildo.

The gag might have occurred to Aristophanes—but I don't imagine him choreographing a scene around a toilet bowl and a jism-encrusted urethra. Maintaining their trademark cruddy look (the finished movie might be an untimed slop print), the Farrellys add a soupçon of slapdash violence to the mix. Meanwhile, as in *The Mask,* Carrey plays a split personality—his character, a Rhode Island motorcycle cop named Charlie, is diagnosed with "advanced delusionary schizophrenia with involuntary narcissistic rage."

Charlie, whose wife's tryst with a black dwarf genius has left him single father to a nest of outrageously oversized, trash-talking brainiac triplets, suffers from a case of advanced affability. His three humongous "whippersnappers" may love this inanely cheerful naïf, but outside the home Dad gets no respect. Indeed, Charlie is the town joke until an incident at a supermarket checkout counter triggers his long suppressed rage. This fabulously insulting and obnoxious new personality, initially signaled by the onset of Carrey's *Cable Guy* voice, shifts in moments from the hilariously snide to the wantonly destructive (and, because this is a Farrelly production, bad Charlie's decision to defecate on his neighbor's lawn invites a cut to a close-up of chocolate soft-serve ice cream).

Subdued with medication, good Charlie is charged with escorting attractive young prisoner Irene back to her home in upstate New York. Hardly a bimbo, she is played by Renée Zellweger, whose puffy-faced squint is a superb instrument for exacting spectator sympathy. Still, as Carrey is essentially a solo performer, *Me, Myself & Irene* lacks the romantic pathos that made *There's Something About Mary* the *Wuthering Heights* of gross-out comedy. What remains is pathology: Complications that include dead cows, the Environmental Protection Agency, and Irene's gangster boyfriend, as well as the loss of Charlie's prescription, conspire to turn the friendly lamebrain into his creepy alter ego, "Hank," a tough guy who hisses like Dirty Harry and is mean enough to steal candy from a baby.

Irene gamely travels with both dudes, occasionally punching one of them out to bring back the other. The Farrellys do contrive a scene in which Charlie learns to integrate his personalities (or Hank figures out how to fake being Charlie) in order to sleep with Irene, but the best material naturally involves the struggle between the two Carreys. "I'm not through with you," Hank or Charlie shouts at his mirrored reflection before breaking into a complex slug and auto-choke fandango that—more extensive, if less graceful, than the split-persona pas de deux Steve Martin performed in *All of Me*—reaches its climax when the star is compelled to throw himself out of the very car that he is driving.

Somewhat less than the sum of its parts, *Me, Myself & Irene* is overlong and choppy. The movie's surreal bits of business keep things lively, but just as Carrey's changes are inconsistent, his vehicle suffers from a related sense of multiple personality disorder. As in *There's Something About Mary*, albeit to lesser effect, the premise has an underlying therapeutic aspect—living out his yuckiest fears, the male character works through some sexual trauma. The difference is that while the Ben Stiller character in *Mary* becomes a mensch, Carrey's fulfills himself as a star.

The film's most shocking castration joke is its most violent image: Carrey's thumb is shot off in close-up, although, thanks to the Farrelly fondness for prosthetic devices, he's compensated with a Kirk Douglas cleft chin.

Also reviewed in:
CHICAGO TRIBUNE, 6/23/00, Friday/p. A, Michael Wilmington
NATION, 7/17/00, p. 35, Stuart Klawans
NEW YORK TIMES, 5/23/00, p. E12, A. O. Scott
NEW YORKER, 7/3/00, p. 89, David Denby
VARIETY, 6/19-25/00, p. 23, Todd McCarthy
WASHINGTON POST, 6/23/00, p. C12, Rita Kempley
WASHINGTON POST, 6/23/00, Weekend/p. 37, Desson Howe

MEET THE PARENTS

A Universal Pictures and DreamWorks Pictures release of a Nancy Tenenbaum Films and a Tribeca production. *Producer:* Nancy Tenenbaum, Jane Rosenthal, Robert De Niro, and Jay Roach. *Director:* Jay Roach. *Screenplay:* Jim Herzfeld and John Hamburg. *Story:* Greg Glienna and Mary Ruth Clarke. *Director of Photography:* Peter James. *Editor:* Jon Poll. *Music:* Randy Newman. *Music Editor:* Bruno Coon. *Choreographer:* Julie Arenal. *Sound:* Tod A. Maitland and (music) Frank Wolf. *Sound Editor:* George Anderson. *Casting:* Ellen Chenoweth. *Production Designer:* Rusty James. *Art Director:* John Kasarda. *Set Decorator:* Karin Wiesel. *Set Dresser:* Chris Ferraro, Jeffrey S. Rollins, Judy Gurr, Gary Levitsky, Alan Muzeni, Rick Nelson, and Raymond C. Polak. *Special Effects:* Jonathan C. Brotherhood. *Costumes:* Daniel Orlandi. *Make-up:* Michal Bigger. *Make-up (Robert De Niro):* Ilona Herman. *Make-up (Ben Stiller):* Carla White. *Stunt Coordinator:* G. A. Aguilar. *Running time:* 105 minutes. *MPAA Rating:* PG-13.

CAST: Robert De Niro (Jack Byrnes); Ben Stiller (Greg Focker); Teri Polo (Pam Byrnes); Blythe Danner (Dina Byrnes); Nicole DeHuff (Debbie Byrnes); Jon Abrahams (Denny Byrnes); Tom McCarthy (Bob Banks); Phyllis George (Linda Banks); James Rebhorn (Larry Banks); Owen Wilson (Kevin Rawley); Kali Rocha (Flight Attendant); Bernie Sheredy (Norm the Interrogator); Judah Friedlander (Pharmacy Clerk); Peter Bartlett (Animal Shelter Worker); John Elsen (Chicago Airport Security); Mark Hammer (Hospital Patient); Amy Hohn (Ticket Agent); William Severs (Father O'Boyle); John Fiore (Kinky); Marilyn Dobrin (Lost Luggage Clerk); Frank Santorelli (Courier); Russell Hornsby (Late Night Courier); Patricia Cook (Little Girl); Cody Arens, Cole Hawkins, and Spencer Breslin (Little Boys); Ina Rosenthal (Wedding Worker); Kim Rideout (Nurse); Kresimir Novakovic (Airport Policeman); John Joseph Gallagher and G.A. Aguilar (Cops); Lynn Ann Castle (Security Guard).

LOS ANGELES TIMES, 10/6/00, Calendar/p. 1, Kenneth Turan

"Hollywood Boulevard," the outlandish 1976 Joe Dante-Allan Arkush satire on the movie business, featured a studio called Miracle Pictures whose motto was, not surprisingly, "If it's a good picture, it's a miracle." In that spirit, and in the best possible sense, "Meet the Parents" is something of a miracle itself.

This buoyant, giddy comedy of catastrophe is the funniest film of the year so far, possibly the most amusing mainstream live-action comedy since "There's Something About Mary." But what's really striking about this story of a prospective son-in-law meeting the father-in-law from hell is the way it came into the world.

Most funny pictures these days, especially ones that come from studios, have the easily identifiable imprint of one key creative force, whether it be writer-director combos like the Farrelly brothers on "Mary" or an actor like Mike Myers for the two "Austin Powers" films that were previous credits for "Parents" director Jay Roach.

This film, however, apparently got developed the old-fashioned way, with individual pieces coming together as they rarely do successfully anymore. A sharp producer named Nancy Tenenbaum ("sex, lies, & videotape," "The Daytrippers") acquired the rights to a short film (story credit going to Greg Glienna & Mary Ruth Clarke) and hired comedy writer Jim Herzfeld to turn it into a feature. Director Roach liked an early draft, and once stars Robert De Niro and Ben Stiller were added on, a second writer, John Hamburg, was brought on to help fit the script to their verbal styles. It's the kind of studio-coordinated process that has ruined more films than it's helped, but here it worked, well, miraculously.

How "Meet the Parents" gets its laughs is equally traditional: an old-fashioned emphasis on shrewd casting, well-timed line readings and clever, on-target acting. Nicely complementing the light and genial but very sure touch Roach provides is an elaborate plot featuring visual and verbal gags that are worked out to a remarkable degree.

Even "Parents'" premise is time-honored and durable. Take an inevitably awkward situation—a young man eager to make a good impression on the couple he hopes will be his future in-laws—and ratchet the embarrassment factor up through the roof. The result is a series of insanely improbable but genuinely comic situations, a cacophonous 48 hours only some very devilish screenwriters could devise.

Stiller stars as Greg Focker, a deeply sincere male nurse, clean-cut but something of a worrier. Going out with schoolteacher Pam Byrnes ("Felicity's" adept Teri Polo) has made the past 10 months in Chicago the happiest of his life, and he's nervously plotting and planning for just the right way to ask her to marry him.

Literally at the last moment, however, Greg accidentally discovers that the politic thing to do would be to ask Pam's father's permission before he asks Pam. An expert in rare flowers who lives in tony Oyster Bay, N.Y., Jack Byrnes is, his daughter assures Greg, "the sweetest man in the whole world." And since Pam's sister is about to be married, a trip to meet the parents seems the natural thing to do.

As soon as Jack opens the door and Greg sees a serial killer look-alike scowling suspiciously as only De Niro can scowl, the young man knows there's been a break in communication somewhere. A prickly human minefield who's so strong-willed he took exactly one week to train his beloved Himalayan cat Jinx to use the toilet, Jack is clearly not the person Greg has been led to believe.

De Niro has ventured into comedy many times before, and not always with the happiest results. "Meet the Parents," however, is a different story. With a part that allows him to draw on and spoof his previous sinister roles, it's the dead-on funniest the actor has ever been. Who else could make the benign concept of "a circle of trust" sound as comically threatening as he does here?

As the man who feels so threatened, Stiller is little short of ideal. Always a gifted comic actor, he's the engine of earnestness that drives the film, a Jew in a nest of WASPs (something mentioned in passing and then smartly used only as subtext) who simply can't catch a break. Greg's gift for saying and doing the wrong thing rises to the level of genius, and as things go from bad to unimaginably worst he's well within his rights when he says, "I feel like this is not going well at all."

With Blythe Danner as Jack's happy-face wife and Owen Wilson formidably funny as Pam's obscenely wealthy ex-boyfriend, "Meet the Parents" is finely cast (by Ellen Chenoweth) and always outrageous in depicting Greg's misery and the unintentionally chaotic payback he delivers to his tormentors. Love never had more calamities to conquer, or got more laughs in the process.

NEW YORK, 10/16/00, p. 89, Peter Rainer

I had a good time at "Meet the Parents", even though the ratio of clinkers to yucks is disproportionately high. Ben Stiller plays a male nurse who is spending an extended weekend with his girlfriend (Teri Polo) at her Waspish parents' home, where he hopes to impress the father, played by Robert De Niro, with his qualifications as a potential son-in-law. A fair amount of the film plays out like an extended version of a similar setup in *Annie Hall*, but the filmmakers—director Jay Roach *(Austin Powers)* and screenwriters Jim Herzfeld and John Hamburg—wisely don't milk the Jewish-Gentile material. They're too busy milking everything else, including aberrant house cats, male-nursedom, caca jokes, and the last name of Stiller's character: Focker.

What keeps all of this engaging for those of us who have already been shaving for a while is the comic rapport between Stiller and De Niro. Stiller's character—an ardent patsy—is familiar by now from his many other comedies, but he's never played it better; there's a whole vortex of calculation behind that wall-eyed stare of his. De Niro, playing a martinet patriarch who once worked as a psychological profiler for the CIA—his daughter calls him "a human lie detector"—turns every one of his dialogue sequences into a nut-brain debriefing. When he hooks Stiller up to a polygraph machine, we're watching a family-initiation nightmare of the ripest sort.

NEW YORK POST, 10/6/00, p. 49, Jonathan Foreman

"Met the Parents," a very funny movie directed by Jay Roach ("Austin Powers"), is part sitcom, part comedy of manners but it lacks the courage to deal honestly with class and ethnicity.

Greg (Ben Stiller), a Chicago nurse, is preparing to ask his girlfriend, Pam (Teri Polo from TVs "Felicity"), to marry him when she happens to mention her sister's engagement—and how it became possible when their father gave his permission.

It occurs to Greg it might be a good idea for him to win Pam's father's approval, so he agrees to go back to her family's house on Long Island for the sister's wedding. To Greg's discomfort and surprise, it turns out Pam's family are old-fashioned WASPs and her father, Jack Byrnes (Robert De Niro), is a judgmental patriarch suspicious of any man who thinks he's good enough for his beloved "Pam-cakes."

Greg, who is Jewish (from Detroit) and, for some reason, completely insensitive to atmosphere, gets off to a lousy start with the Byrneses when he immediately shows himself to be a helplessly bad-mannered slob, failing to help Pam with her coat and presuming he can call her parents by their first names.

Then, as Jack's humorlessness and evident paranoia make Greg increasingly nervous, Greg puts more and more energy into saying what he supposes (in his clueless way) Jack wants to hear.

One white lie necessitates Another, and the speed and obviousness with which Greg tells untruths not only provokes Byrnes' hostility, it also upsets Pam, who apparently hasn't encountered his shifty side before.

Then Greg finds out Jack Byrne is not, in fact, a retired horticulturist, but a former CIA interrogator.

As the weekend progresses, Greg goes beyond social faux pas: His klutziness is responsible for a fantastic amount of physical destruction. And his desperate, secretive efforts to make things better only make them far worse.

Stiller is more or less reprising his "There's Something About Mary" character. But he makes a fine comic foil for De Niro, who is wonderfully relaxed and at the same time entirely persuasive.

Blythe Danner is perfect as Pam's sweetly accommodating but probably deeply neurotic mother. And Owen Wilson steals several scenes as Pam's successful, handsome, athletic ex-boyfriend. (Not that Greg has anything to worry about; Pam reassures him that their relationship was "mostly physical.")

The main thing that prevents "Meet the Parents" from approaching the sustained comic brilliance of "Mary" is that you just don't care enough about whether this couple ends up together.

It might have helped a little if Teri Polo's Pam were played by a star with the dazzle of Charlize Theron, but the part itself is so underwritten, it would be hard for anyone to make her more than pretty face under blonde hair.

Nor does it help that Stiller's Greg isn't just a socially inept klutz like his character in "Mary"; he's also a sneak, a liar and a coward. Of course—and this really tells you something about

Hollywood—you're supposed to think all his dishonest behavior is really OK because it's done in a good cause: getting what he wants.

In fact, if screenwriters Jim Herzfeld and John Hamburg wern't so blithely unaware that their hero is a slimeball by non-Hollywood standards, you might suspect the filmmakers of good, old-fashioned anti-Semitic stereotyping.

NEWSDAY, 10/6/00, Part II/p. B3, John Anderson

In and around the rickety framework of "Meet the Parents," you can still hear the echoes of the pitch meeting that birthed it. "Let's make a movie about a Ben Stiller type whose girlfriend's father is a Robert De Niro type. And we'll cast Stiller and De Niro!" Hooray. "And then," they said, "we'll get a script."

If ever there was a movie that felt like it was built backward, it's "Meet the Parents," inspired by comedian Greg Glienna's short film and subsequently stretched like meatloaf by screenwriters Jim Herzfeld and John Hamburg. Logically, perhaps, the movie gets better as it goes along—but only because of the cumulative horrors of lover boy's meet-the-parents weekend, which come to resemble a series of plagues, delivered not on the oppressors, but on the one Jew in the movie.

The screenwriters get more overt mileage out of Greg's occupation (he's a nurse) than his religion, but the ethnic conflict comes through loud and clear. The writers, ostensibly assigned to pump up Glienna's short, have also taken Woody Allen's nightmare sequence in "Annie Hall"—the one in which Alvy Singer is envisioned by Annie's grandma as a Hasid—to the scale of a bloated epic.

A disaster of biblical proportions? You start to think so. Remember back in lit class, when Oedipus was told he was going to kill his father and marry his mother? The solution always seemed simple: Oed, baby, don't get into fights and don't get married. Likewise, the thing for Stiller's unhappily named Greg Focker to do is sit on his hands for the whole weekend—not climb on the furniture, explore hidden rooms, show up at breakfast in his pajamas, have a smoke on the roof, let the toilet run so the septic tank overflows or snuggle with his girlfriend in her father's house. Because, after a while, even an idiot knows everything is going to go wrong. And you can only have so much sympathy for an idiot.

Why this particular idiot wants to marry schoolteacher Pam Byrnes (Teri Polo) in the first place is sort of a mystery—she's oblivious to Greg's plight, and an ice cube besides. But if you accept that Herzfeld-Hamburg are perpetrating an anti-assimilation theme, the Pam-as-shiksa-goddess thing makes sense. So does the idea that Greg is simply cursed: When he accompanies Pam home to Oyster Bay on the weekend of her sister's wedding, the airline (think American) loses his bag, a baby throws up on his sweater and his initial meeting with Jack and Dina Byrnes (De Niro and Blythe Danner) is marked not by the fact that he's the predatory male, but that his ironic sense of humor is so out of place in WASP-ville.

Stiller and De Niro never really inhabit their characters, but there really aren't structures to inhabit. Judging by his work on the two "Austin Powers" films, director Jay Roach's strongest instinct is to get out of the way of the script, regardless of its quality. Here, the screenplay happily sacrifices plausibility for the quick gag (few of which are genuinely funny). Jack Byrnes' personality careens from irrational hostility to blubbery sentiment in a way that suggests mental disorder. Greg, on the other hand, is mostly a cipher, a hapless dweeb to whom things happen. Both actors may be perfectly cast. But that, in and of itself, is not funny.

NEWSWEEK, 10/9/00, p. 73, David Ansen

Ben Stiller is the anti-Houdini of humiliation: he's always getting himself tied into embarrassing knots he can't get out of. Once again he endures a marathon of shame in "Meet the Parents," a comedy that sends him off, full of foolish hope, to meet his future in-laws. His name is Greg Focker: his first mistake. That name gets mispronounced by everyone just the way you think it will. A bigger problem is his girlfriend's dad, Jack Byrnes (Robert De Niro), who never met a prospective son-in-law he could abide. In "This Boy's Life," De Niro was terrifying as a sadistic father; this is the comic version—he's a CIA man (Greg's been told he's a florist) whose interrogatory social style should be banned by the Geneva Conventions.

Focker is a nurse, a job Jack considers fit only for women. Focker is a dog lover, a species the cat-loving Jack considers "emotionally shallow." Focker is a Jew, and you have only to look at Jack's face as Focker bluffs his way through saying grace to know how much *that* delights him. "Meet the Parents" is a one-joke movie—an escalating degradation derby—but the comedy never wears out its welcome. Director Jay Roach ("Austin Powers") has a keen sense of comic timing, and the script keeps finding clever new ways to mortify our poor hero. The rest of the cast is fine (Teri Polo, Blythe Danner), but it's the Stiller and De Niro show we've come to watch: as elemental a battle as Punch and Judy, and a lot funnier.

SIGHT AND SOUND, 1/01, p. 54, Danny Leigh

Chicago, the present. Eager to marry girlfriend Pam Byrnes, male nurse Greg Focker is about to propose when Pam announces her sister Debbie is to wed, after her partner asked Byrnes' father Jack's permission. Greg decides to follow suit. Two weeks later, the pair arrive in genteel Oyster Bay for Debbie's wedding. En route, Greg's bag which contains an engagement ring is lost. Greg immediately creates a terrible impression when he insults Jack's treasured cat Jinx. That evening, Greg is further humiliated when he smashes an urn holding the ashes of Jack's mother. Spending the night in Jack's study, Greg chances on a room full of intelligence paraphernalia. Discovering him, Jack admits he was once a CIA operative, before forcing Greg to sit a polygraph test.

The next morning, Greg borrows a jacket from Pam's younger brother Denny; Jack finds a marijuana pipe in its pocket, which he assumes is Greg's. The family visit the palatial home of Kevin, Pam's former fiancé, where Greg accidentally breaks Debbie's nose. On their return, he inadvertently floods the Byrnes' garden before setting fire to the house and losing Jinx. Desperate to regain Jack's favour, he secretly buys a replacement pet, only for the real Jinx to be found hours later. Greg leaves for Chicago, alone and in disgrace, but—after Pam confronts her father over his intolerance—Jack follows him to the airport, where he finally gives Greg his blessing.

Last seen mugging and grimacing through Harold Ramis' less-than-inspired mob romp *Analyze This,* Robert De Niro's periodic excursions into comic acting have, of course, been a longstanding cause for consternation among even his fiercest acolytes *(We're No Angels* was a particularly misjudged effort). But in Jay Roach's *Meet the Parents* his casting as the nightmarishly exacting Jack Byrnes, first glimpsed looming at the window of his picturesque homestead like a smirking WASP Rottweiler, provides him with an opportunity to do what he's best at: radiate a gestural sense of hugely ominous self-possession. Despite the pungent crackle of his dialogue "So, you prefer an emotionally shallow animal?" he enquires of aspirant son-in-law Greg, played by Ben Stiller, after he confesses a fondness for dogs), De Niro's performance—and the film as a whole—takes flight in the spaces between the one-liners: the pregnant pauses and subtle glowers which De Niro's previous comic outings have buried in a slew of slapstick face pulling.

Set against De Niro's unexpected accomplishment, Stiller's admirable portrayal of hapless suitor Greg Focker cannot help but fade into the background; which is unfortunate, given that he delivers a fine essay in humiliation and incipient rage. It's certainly strange witnessing what was obviously intended as the film's central turn become a sideshow, but that transformation is to De Niro's credit rather than to Stiller's detriment.

Such is the malevolent charm of De Niro's performance that you find yourself forgiving the somewhat limp trajectory the narrative pursues. The problem is fundamental: as with any great, one-joke idea, the possible extrapolations are finite. Thus while the ingenuity of the trials doled out to Stiller during the film's first hour remains impressive in its gleeful, unrelenting absurdity (rarely can the logistics of milking cats have been such a pivotal cinematic motif), Roach's momentum flags badly as the story predictably resolves itself.

That said, it would be churlish not to acknowledge the genuine streak of dark intelligence running through the material, a comic honesty which—until the sappy, hurried finale—rescues the enterprise from potential saccharine excess. In the relationship between Stiller's Greg Focker and De Niro's Jack Byrnes, the subtext is seldom far from the surface: while the overt cause of Greg's exclusion by Jack and his extended family may be his propensity for epic pratfalls, its roots lie firmly in an innate hostility to an urban Jewish American gatecrashing their riot of comfy woollens and Norman Rockwell domesticity. In Jack's transition from sardonic amusement to splenetic, accusative fury (spitting the name Focker as if it were a synonym for all that is alien and invasive), *Meet the Parents* briefly emerges not just as a well-executed mainstream comedy, but as an acute, insightful commentary on a perennially riven America.

TIME, 10/9/00, p. 110, Richard Schickel

Let's say the stern father has just read a perfectly ghastly memorial poem to his dead mother. Now let's say the young man courting his daughter has just made a little joke about the urn on the dining-room mantle. It does not take a great comic mind to imagine that it contains grandma's remains.

Now let's arm that young man with a bottle of cheap, celebratory Champagne. When he uncorks it, can you guess where the cork is going to fly? And what it must do to the precariously placed urn? If you have a taste for farce, you can.

Let us now introduce into the equation a beloved family cat, whose excretory habits have already been the subject of slightly strained discussion. Can you predict what he might do, when confronted with a nice, fresh pile of ashes in the midst of a nasty hubbub in which his needs are being ignored? If you can, then you have a taste for something in short supply lately—farce that is divinely invented and perfectly orchestrated.

And you had better skid, slide and stumble as fast as your flailing limbs can carry you to *Meet the Parents*. It is the work of director Jay Roach, whose *Austin Powers* movies were intermittently funny but not what anyone would call intricately constructed machines. What those movies needed was a couple of skilled tool-and-die makers like Jim Herzfeld and John Hamburg, who wrote this screenplay. And a bunch of actors, led by Robert De Niro and Ben Stiller, who understand that palpable reality will always trump frenzied fantasy when it comes to getting laughs.

De Niro is Jack Byrnes, formerly (or maybe not so formerly) a CIA operative, projecting an air of sweet reason from his suburban colonial home. That it contains a secret lair equipped with a lie detector is nobody's business. That the lyrics of his favorite song, *Puff the Magic Dragon*, may contain a hidden metaphor comes as an unwelcome surprise to him. That a suggestion that his affection for his daughters, especially Pam (Teri Polo), may be touched by feelings that would make Oedipus blush could earn you termination with maximum prejudice—as the beta male candidate for her affections, the unfortunately named Greg Focker (Ben Stiller), learns.

He's the kind of guy who would rather be a male nurse than a doctor. Also the kind of guy whose luggage the airline is bound to lose. And the sort you know is going to end up on Jack's roof, chasing a cat, holding a live wire in one hand, putting out a leaf fire with one foot while trying to pretend the overflow in the septic tank down below is not his fault. De Niro is getting awfully good at comic menace (see *Analyze This)*, and Stiller, a handsome guy who never alludes to his good looks, is a deliciously preoccupied innocent.

But then, preoccupation may be the key to this movie's success. All the members of the family are trying to focus on the wedding of Pam's sister, which means they would prefer Greg, the outsider, to be the fly on the wall, not the fly in the ointment. Alas, poor Focker. He can't help himself. And we can't help ourselves from falling about, equally helpless, at this superbly antic movie.

VILLAGE VOICE, 10/10/00, p. 134, Jessica Winter

Meet the Parents waters down *There's Something About Mary*'s pre-prom martyrdom sequence to feature length, capitalizing on Ben Stiller's unfailingly inventive, often quite touching abilities as an all-occasion punching bag. Here Stiller, playing a smitten nurse named Greg Focker, suffers at the hands of his girlfriend Pam's family during a visit to Oyster Bay for her sister's wedding. Shaken by the immediate and brutally pure lack of rapport that he shares with the titular parents, dotty Dina (Blythe Danner) and maniacally protective Jack (Robert De Niro), and bereft of both his luggage and his temporarily contraband cigarettes, Greg commences cramming his foot in his mouth and sputtering pointless lies. That Greg is a Jewish kid from Detroit in a decidedly unmacho profession doesn't help his standing in this condescending, old-moneyed milieu. *Meet the Parents'* potential as an altogether loopier movie is pointed up in the casting of De Niro as a sweatered WASP paterfamilias, not to mention Owen Wilson—with his magnificent busted nose and perpetual Zen-stoner squint—in the Brett Favre role as Kevin, the wealthy, church-loving golden boy whom Pam (Teri Polo) let get away. (Upon hearing that Greg is Jewish, Kevin is unfazed: "Well, so was JC!")

Greg's own stations of the cross spin out of control before the film backpedals into sentimental resolution; director Jay Roach sabotages punch lines with setups that honk and sputter like oncoming trucks, and tends to stage Farrelly-aspiring chaos only to cut away skittishly before the whole rig explodes. But watching Ben get the girl or be seriously injured trying always has its dry, keening pleasures, and Greg Focker is the richest cinematic exemplum of men in the nursing profession since Philip Seymour Hoffman's angelic guardian in *Magnolia*.

Also reviewed in:
CHICAGO TRIBUNE, 10/6/00, Friday/p. A, Michael Wilmington
NEW YORK TIMES, 10/6/00, p. E10, Elvis Mitchell
VARIETY, 9/25-10/1/00, p. 59, Todd McCarthy
WASHINGTON POST, 10/6/00, p. C1, Rita Kempley
WASHINGTON POST, 10/6/00, Weekend/p. 45, Desson Howe

MEN OF HONOR

A Fox 2000 Pictures release of a State Street Pictures Production. *Executive Producer:* Bill Cosby and Stanley Robertson. *Producer:* Robert Teitel and Bill Badalato. *Director:* George Tillman, Jr. *Screenplay (based upon the life of Carl Brashear):* Scott Marshall Smith. *Director of Photography:* Anthony B. Richmond. *Editor:* John Carter. *Music:* Mark Isham. *Sound:* David Obermeyer and (music) Stephen Krause. *Sound Editor:* Lawrence H. Mann. *Casting:* Mary Vernieu. *Production Designer:* Leslie Dilley. *Art Director:* Lawrence A. Hubbs. *Set Designer:* Erwin "Mick" Cukurs, Scott Herbertson, Daniel Maltese, and Jim Wallis. *Set Decorator:* Kate Sullivan. *Set Dresser:* Brad Turner, Marco Lopez, Douglas McKay, Drew Pinniger, and Ivo Vergara. *Special Effects:* Bruno Van Zeebroeck. *Costumes:* Salvador Perez. *Make-up:* Stacye P. Branche. *Make-up (Robert De Niro):* Ilona Herman. *Make-up (Charlize Theron):* Deborah Larson. *Stunt Coordinator:* Ernie Orsatti. *Running time:* 128 minutes. *MPAA Rating:* R.

CAST: Robert De Niro (Billy Sunday); Cuba Gooding, Jr. (Carl Brashear); Charlize Theron (Gwen); Aunjanue Ellis (Jo); Hal Holbrook (Mr. Pappy); Michael Rapaport (Snowhill); Powers Boothe (Captain Pullman); David Keith (Captain Hartigan); Holt McCallany (Rourke); Joshua Leonard (Isert); Dennis Troutman (Boots); Joshua Feinman (DuBoyce); Theo Pagones (Mellegrano); Ryan Honey (Yarmouth); David Conrad (Hanks); Chris Warren, Jr. (Young Carl); Lester B. Hanson (Admiral Yon); Jack Frazier (Read Admiral French); David Richard Heath (Medical Officer); Demene E. Hall (Mrs. Biddle); Alimi Ballard (Coke); Shawn Michael Howard (Junie); Troy Lund (Blonde Gate SP); Henry Harris (Rescued Pilot); Matt Dotson (Marine Guard); Carl Lumbly (Mac, Carl's Father); Lonette McKee (Ella, Carl's Mother); Glynn Turman (Chief Floyd); David Meyers (Dr. Cudahy); Richard Perry Turner (Dr. Dinkins); George "Chick" Rankins (Cab Driver); Richard Sanders (Bartender); Nasir Najieb (Black Inductee); Dennis Bateman (Navy Instructor); Eric Newsome (Naked Grunt); Steven Clark Pachosa (Navy Recruiter); Marilyn Faith Hickey (Pinch-faced Woman); Bruce Burkhartsmeier (Presiding Officer); Michael Tyrone Williamson (Waiter); Michelle Guthrie (Therapist); Michael Patrick Egan (Sailor); Scott Kraft (Ropeleski); Tim Monsion (News Reporter); Dulé Hill (Red Tail); Timothy McCuen Piggee (School Master); John J. Polce (Hospital Security); The Count (Band Leader); Allen Gerbino (Aerial Coordinator/Pilot #1); Art Gotisar (Pilot #2); Robert Blanche (Shore Patrolman); Ivory L. Dilley (Frantic Girl); Chad W. Smathers (Drowning Boy); Wayne Morse (Navy Orderly); Rachel Jahn (Candy Striper); Jon Du Clos (Sunday's Assistant); Leon Russom (Decker); Richard Radecki (Fan Tail Chief); Randy Flagler (Bomb Chief); Jeremy Taylor (Deckhand); Jason Bailey (Sonar Man).

CHRISTIAN SCIENCE MONITOR, 11/10/00, p. 15, David Sterritt

"Men of Honor" is an old-fashioned title for an old-fashioned movie that tells a true-blue tale—full of heroism, adversity, and human interest—through formulas Hollywood perfected decades ago. It holds few surprises, but it's just the ticket if you're in the mood for two hours of proudly traditional entertainment.

Cuba Gooding Jr. plays Navy diver Carl Brashear, whose real-life story inspired the film. He's a young African-American of the 1940s who refuses to forget the hard life led by his father—a black sharecropper in the segregated South—and decides a military career is the best route to something better. Combining his talent for swimming with his impressive store of tenacity, he sets his sights on becoming a master diver, trained to plunge into the sea on rescue and salvage missions.

This might not be an exceptional ambition today, but Brashear faces the realities of a different era. For one thing, diving is an arduous occupation in a cumbersome "hard hat" rig that bears little resemblance to lightweight scuba gear.

More important, the Navy has just been racially integrated for the first time, and plenty of Brashear's fellow sailors are infuriated at living and working with a black man. Even his superiors are against his best interests—including his training officer, a rough-hewn redneck named Billy Sunday, who'd be perfectly content to see what he perceives as an uppity Negro fail at everything he's set out to accomplish. But the young recruit soon shows that nothing will keep him down, and all but his worst enemies are eventually impressed by his unstoppable spirit.

George Tillman Jr. has directed this stirring yarn in a suitably stirring manner, alternating with clockwork regularity between scenes of adversity and unfairness (our hero gets harassed by bigots, challenged by his job, disabled by an accident) and scenes of spunky human triumph (our hero overcomes, faces down, or rises above these trials). There's not a shred of originality in sight, but what the movie lacks in novelty it makes up for in sincerity, most notably in the later scenes, involving a tragic accident and a courageous decision that proves Brashear's mettle beyond the shadow of a doubt.

Gooding brings Brashear alive with heartfelt acting, and Robert De Niro is even better as Billy Sunday, the movie's most complex character. Charlize Theron makes the most of her tiny role as Sunday's wife, and Michael Rapaport and Hal Holbrook have persuasive moments as very different Navy men. Anthony B. Richmond did the slick cinematography and Mark Isham composed the music, which underscores every emotion with the subtlety of Sunday on a particularly bull-headed rant.

LOS ANGELES TIMES, 11/10/00, Calendar/p. 2, Kevin Thomas

In 1948, Harry Truman ended segregation in the armed forces, but it did not fade away overnight any more than it did in other American institutions. What Jackie Robinson endured in breaking the color line in baseball and what a clutch of brave African American students faced in integrating Southern schools is well-known, but "Men of Honor" tells us what it was like for Carl Brashear, son of a Kentucky sharecropper, to become the first African American Navy diver in the early 1950s.

It needs to be made clear right at the top that "Men of Honor" was inspired by the life of Brashear, but that as writer Scott Marshall Smith has stated, "This is not a connect-the-dots biography." In other words, this film is part truth, part invention—don't go thinking you're seeing a biopic.

What fledgling screenwriter Smith and director George Tillman Jr. ("Soul Food") have done is give Brashear's story a heart-tugging mythological status, anchored by a rousing struggle of wills played out powerfully by a pair of Oscar-winners, Cuba Gooding Jr. as Brashear and Robert De Niro as Billy Sunday, a composite of various Brashear foes. The film is further enlivened by a series of spectacular and suspenseful undersea action sequences. Brashear's life clearly is the stuff of a big, stirring screen saga, and "Men of Honor" gives it the full-throttle Hollywood treatment.

What Brashear endures in his determination to become a Master Chief Navy Diver is at times so extreme that the effect would be comically absurd if his ordeal didn't ring so loud and so true. "Men of Honor" is relentlessly larger-than-life and unsubtle in making a superhero of Brashear and adversary of Sunday. Luckily, Gooding and De Niro have the talent and personality to pull it off, and the film emerges as a dynamic entertainment with the punch of an especially spectacular sports event—yes, a World Wrestling Federation match does come to mind.

Brashear's father (Carl Lumbly), weary with the knowledge that no matter how hard he works he will never be able to own the land he cultivates, sends his son off to the post World War II Navy with the admonition to "be your best." Automatically consigned to the galley on a ship in the South Seas, young Carl yearns for better. Whites swim in the ocean on Fridays, blacks and other minorities on Tuesday, but on one especially sweltering Friday, Carl decides what the hell and jumps into the sea along with all the whites; he most likely knew he would be able to beat out everyone else in a race to a buoy.

He ends up in the brig for violating segregation rules but only momentarily, for he has impressed a captain (Powers Boothe) sufficiently for the officer to get him transferred to the Navy diving school in Bayonne, N.J. Brashear has his work cut out for him in learning how to become a salvage expert. His presence, as the sole African American, empties the barracks, except for a stuttering kid from Wisconsin (Michael Rapaport).

The kid is promptly bounced from the diving program by De Niro's Billy Sunday, no relation to the famed 30s evangelist of the same name, but just as fiery, a tough, rebellious, hard-living redneck who automatically resents Brashear because, as he says, black sharecroppers would always work cheaper than whites. Not helping matters is that the base commander (Hal Holbrook) is a crazy, reclusive old racist who reminds Sunday that as long as he is around, no black man is to be allowed to graduate from the diving program.

The labors of Hercules—or Harry Houdini—are child's play as to the feats of strength and will that Brashear must perform at diving school and in a dramatic true-life incident later on. Gooding tempers Brashear's physical prowess and single-mindedness with an affably winning modesty and clear intelligence. De Niro's Sunday is a crusty old salt finally too smart, too untrammeled a spirit, to be able to deny any longer Brashear's soaring superiority, an acknowledgment that could transform him from the small-minded man Brashear has shown him to be. "Men of Honor" keeps chugging along, building to an all-stops-out finish, accompanied by one of those inevitable triumph-of-the-human spirit scores, this one composed by Mark Isham.

Gooding and De Niro, both blessed with innate humor, are most emphatically the film's stars, with Charlize Theron as De Niro's somewhat improbable rich, young glamour girl wife, who proves to be more staunchly devoted to him than you might have imagined, and Aunjanue Ellis as Brashear's premed student fiancee who helps him overcome his seventh-grade education. David Conrad coolly plays a man-you-love-to-hate type, a relentless Navy bureaucrat who reminds us how racism can flourish in very high places. Production designer Leslie Tilley and his staff evoke the '50s with an authenticity that, unlike other aspects of the picture, is beautifully understated.

"Men of Honor" is socially critical pop mythology at its most exuberantly potent, but it leaves you wondering what the life of the real Carl Brashear, born in 1931 and very much alive, has really been like. (Pitting him against the fictitious Sunday has the effect of making the film almost as much Sunday's story as Brashear's—and De Niro is in fact top-billed.) Brashear really deserves to become the subject of a comprehensive documentary. "Men of Honor" leaves you wanting to know more, and that's not a bad thing.

NEW YORK, 11/20/00, p. 98, Peter Rainer

The son of a Kentucky sharecropper, Carl Brashear (Cuba Gooding Jr.) becomes the first African-American to become a master diver for the Navy in *Men of Honor*, a rah-rah reality-based movie that looks like it was made by the Navy. Even though the institutional racism impeding Carl's rise is amply noted, we're never in doubt that the innate goodness of the country will prevail.

Brashear enters the Navy just as President Truman has desegregated the armed forces, but he still finds himself relegated to the kitchen. His swimming skills convince him he can make it as a diver, but the Navy Salvage School in New Jersey, under its head trainer, Master Chief Diver Billy Sunday (Robert De Niro), does everything it can to keep things lily-white: Carl's fellow trainees, with one exception, a stuttering good guy played by Michael Rapaport, refuse to bunk with him, and leave him threatening notes; he's assigned ridiculously difficult tasks, which he indomitably completes. Predictably, the crackers in his class develop a grudging respect for Carl.

So does Billy, whose hazing tactics come close to ending the young man's life a few times. The only real holdout is the school's dotty, ultraracist commander (Hal Holbrook), who, in a nice touch, is shown polishing his military medals by rubbing them with booze.

The testimonial-like tone of this movie, which was directed by George Tillman Jr. and written by Scott Marshall Smith, undercuts its supposed realism. Heroism in the movies—at least heroism based on actual events—is always at its most believable when the hero in question is something less than a saint. Because of the racism he had to counteract, Carl's single-mindedness is portrayed as the highest valor. No quitter he. When a naval accident mangles his leg, he simply orders it sawed off and becomes the first amputee to return to active duty.

If the filmmakers had bothered to delve into the monomania of such a man and dropped the inspirationalism, they might have made a truly disturbing movie instead of a glorified recruitment poster. The sort of man who, against all military advice, would voluntarily have his leg amputated in order to qualify as master diver is, I would say, a questionable role model. But because Carl's ambition is placed in a racial context, his life choices are never seriously challenged by the filmmakers. The all-white military brass who go against his decision to amputate and return to duty are portrayed for the most part as craven and corrupt, even though their concerns about his safety seem eminently reasonable. Carl's wife's concerns seem more than reasonable, too, but we know that it's only a matter of time before Carl, in a military courtroom, silences his detractors by hauling himself for twelve heavy paces inside a diving suit weighing almost 300 pounds while balancing on his one good leg as his wife and young son's eyes brim with devotional tears.

I'm not sure why movies, specifically in the racial realm, are once again proffering civics-lesson heroes in a way they haven't since the heyday of Sidney Poitier. Is it because the heroes in our political life are so unheroic? Just last month we had Denzel Washington in *Remember the Titans* playing the first black coach of a previously all-white high-school football squad replete with racists. That story was also based on real events, but like *Men of Honor,* it didn't do justice to the fanaticism of its hero, or the rage that must have burned just beneath the surface.

However uplifting these stories are designed to be, they don't draw out the artistry of the performers involved, who are required to dampen their dramatic power for a higher good. Cuba Gooding Jr., who can be rousingly freewheeling, is encased in righteous intentions in *Men of Honor,* and those intentions weigh him down more than any diving gear. Robert De Niro, in a role that reportedly is a composite of Carl's several real-life tormentors, keeps a lid on his talent, too. Despite some *Cape Fear*-style glowering, there is never any doubt that deep down, this corn-cob-pipe-smoking martinet is a decent sort. The people involved in this movie are using high principles as a bailout for low inspiration.

NEW YORK POST, 11/10/001 p. 59, Lou Lumenick

Niro and Cuba Gooding Jr. provide the oxygen for this extremely shipshape biopic of Carl Brashear, the Navy's first black diver.

The son of a poor Kentucky sharecropper, Brashear (Gooding) joins the just-integrated Navy in the late 1940s. But when he's relegated to duty as a cook because of his race, he fights for an appointment to diving school.

There Brashear encounters institutional racism in the form of Billy Sunday (De Niro), a corncob-pipe-smoking redneck instructor who employs every trick in the book to wash out his new trainee.

Though shunned by white sailors and verbally brutalized by Sunday, Brashear remains unwavering in his determination, persuading a young Harlem librarian who will become his wife (excellent newcomer Aunjanue Ellis) to help him study to pass his tests.

When the racist commanding officer (a weird turn by Hal Holbrook) orders Sunday to flunk Brashear by sabotaging his chances in a crucial underwater test, the undeterred Brashear spends hours in freezing water—and an impressed Sunday defies the brass to pass him, destroying his own career in the process.

But the highly entertaining "Men of Honor" is only half over. Now it's 1956 and Sunday is an alcoholic wreck. Brashear, meanwhile, becomes a national hero by recovering a nuclear warhead lost at sea—and saving a pair of sailors in a deckboard accident that leaves one of Brashear's legs severely mangled.

Navy bureaucrats pressure him to retire, but Brashear is determined to reach the rank of master diver. His unlikely ally is a sobered-up Sunday, who suggests Brashear could return to duty. One-legged Brashear is required to demonstrate his fitness for duty by walking 12 steps, unassisted, in a 300-pound diving suit—with Sunday bellowing encouragement—is the kind of scene that wins Oscars.

For De Niro, Sunday—an embittered, scary sociopath with a hidden noble streak—marks a return to full-throttle acting after a string of comedies. And it's his best work in years.

But the real revelation here is the deeply affecting Gooding, who was beginning to look like a one-hit wonder in a raft of poor roles and movies that followed his Oscar win for "Jerry Maguire."

It's the vibrancy of their acting that turns a somewhat obvious script (attributed to Scott Marshall Smith) from what could have been a glorified movie of the week into an inspiring, must-see movie-going experience that will have audiences cheering in their seats.

Major credit also goes to director George Tillman Jr. ("Soul Food"), who plows through the clichés and stock situations with such gusto, he makes them seem brand-new. He also helms the several exciting underwater rescue sequences with a sure hand.

Too bad he's the latest director to fall under the spell of the ubiquitous Charlize Theron, whose screen time in the role of De Niro's beautiful wife is once again out of all proportion to the character's significance.

But that's a small complaint in a movie that floats as smoothly as "'Men of Honor."

NEWSDAY, 11/10/00, Part II/p. B3, John Anderson

A sow's ear made from a silk purse, "Men of Honor" is the based-on-real-life story of Carl Brashear, the sharecropper's son who became the Navy's first black salvage diver, master diver and master chief, the branch's highest rank for enlisted men.

There's no denying that Brashear's life is worthy of the big screen treatment, or even an impersonation by Cuba Gooding Jr. at his most actorly. But it's a soggily embarrassing affair. As wave after wave of earnestness and nobility come crashing down upon you, you realize that, yes, of course, this has to be a fact-based story. No one would have the gall to jam this many heroics or high-minded orations into any simple piece of fiction.

Ostensibly, the movie is a tribute to Brashear and his spirit. A product of the landlocked South, saddled with a seventh-grade education, driven by a dream of going to sea, he fought the institutionalized racism of the '50s military elite to become the man he dreamt of being. So isn't it strange that what was formerly titled either "Navy Diver" or "The Diver" is now " Men of Honor"? Yes, except that "Men of Honor" is plural. And we wouldn't want to devote an entire title to a black man, would we? And certainly not an entire movie.

So "Men of Honor" also gives us Billy Sunday (Robert De Niro), a "composite" character created by screenwriter Scott Marshall Smith to represent all the racist nut jobs Brashear ran into on his way up the greased ladder into the ocean. Sunday is one of those raving lunatics whose motives are obscure and/or irrational, but who enables De Niro—who seems to have become as selective about his roles as John Heard—to let loose all those pent-up Max Cady-Jake LaMotta impulses stifled by moneymakers like "Meet the Parents," and then reform by the end of the film. But what "Men of Honor" is really about is a race-switched version of "An Officer and a Gentleman." Except that neither is an officer, and only one is a gentleman.

Sunday, for all De Niro's overheated shenanigans, is a cipher. He's the maverick master diver whose insubordinate, injury- sustaining heroics inspire the young Brashear to join the salvage corps in the first place. He's also the instructor who makes Brashear's life miserable while training on the banks of beautiful Bayonne, N.J. Sunday's not alone, of course: Mr. Pappy (Hal Holbrook), the training center's mad-hatter-in-chief, is obsessed about keeping Brashear out (as a metaphor, Pappy's OK, but not in this movie). No white candidate will even bunk with Brashear—except for Snowhill (Michael Rapaport), whose stutter evidently gives him an innate camaraderie with black naval outcasts.

It's clear that director George Tillman Jr. ("Soul Food") was working on the austerity plan. He creates some real tension during various under-financed underwater crises, but the '50s Harlem where Carl meets his future wife, Jo (Aunjanue Ellis), looks like a high school production of "Guys and Dolls." Similarly, other crowd scenes—the bar, for instance, where Sunday, Brashear and Sunday's wife, Gwen (Charlize Theron), have their Waterloo—are underpopulated and underfurnished.

Sometimes, Tillman is just silly: When Brashear suffers one of his various social defeats, he flips on the homemade radio his father built, only to hear "...and Jackie Robinson has just struck out..." As Oscar Wilde said of the death of Dickens' Little Nell, only a person with a heart of stone would fail to laugh at a moment like that.

Still, such intellectual sloth is symbolic of the whole. As portrayed by Gooding, Brashear is a New Millennium guy dropped into a '50s and '60s world. He acts as if he knows that Rosa Parks, the Civil Rights Act and affirmative action are just around the corner—which makes Brashear's struggle look easy. And that's certainly no tribute to either the martyrs of the civil rights movement or a courageous pioneer like Carl Brashear.

SIGHT AND SOUND, 4/01, p. 52, Philip Strick

Born in 1931 to an impoverished family in Sonora, Kentucky, Carl Brashear sets his heart on joining the US navy. Recruited in 1948, just as segregation is abolished in the armed forces, he discovers a passion for deep-sea diving. Refusing to be excluded from the navy's diver training school at Bayonne, New Jersey, because of continuing racial prejudice and his limited education, Carl is accepted there in 1952. Largely ostracised by his fellow trainees, he also encounters a bitter opponent, the school's sadistic master chief Billy Sunday, who is supervised by commanding officer 'Mr' Pappy, a vituperative racist.

Carl behaves impeccably, rescuing a colleague who gets into difficulties during a training session and studying at a Harlem library with the help of a young medical student, Jo. Gradually earning Sunday's respect, Carl passes the school's toughest challenges. Pappy furiously 'fires' Sunday, who becomes an alcoholic, constantly at odds with his superiors, while Carl marries Jo and embarks on a triumphant career. But in 1966, while aboard the *USS Hoist* in the Mediterranean, he loses part of a leg in an accident.

Carl sets out to prove he is still capable of continuing as a diver. With the support of the now-recovered Sunday, he prepares to face a special-tribunal of evaluation headed by Lieutenant Hanks, one of Sunday's more merciless enemies. Strapped in a diving rig at the hearing, Carl is goaded by Sunday into an agonised display of tenacity and determination, winning him the right to return to active duty.

Although based on the true story of Carl Brashear, whose career as a diver is one of only a handful preserved in the US navy's archives, *Men of Honor* strangely avoids any clear explanation of Brashear's obsession with underwater salvage. An early hint, nothing more, comes when, as a kid, he plunges into a river and discovers a sunken car wreck. And there is a touch of instant fetishism in his first sighting of a diving rig, with its gleaming helmet, its array of buckles and straps, and its capaciously sculpted boots. A particular attraction could be the retinue of attendants, squires in service to an armoured knight: the robing ceremony is interestingly re-enacted for Brashear's concluding duel with his navy superiors, determined to end his career. But these superficial attractions have little to do with the dark realities of diving itself, consistently shown here as a succession of near fatal emergencies. On this evidence, Brashear's only claim to fame lies in a stubborn foolhardiness.

"It's always about you," complains the hero's wife, exasperated that nothing seems to deter her husband from rushing back to sea. And this, the restrictions of respectful biography being what they are, is as accurate as the film allows itself to be in restaging the perky intransigence of Brashear, ingratiatingly played by Cuba Gooding Jr. Partly, we may gather, he is driven by a promise to his father, and partly—closer to the bone—he is pitching a battle against elitism and exclusion. "I can't fail," is his simplest explanation. "I want this because they said I couldn't have it." This actually rings truer than his near saintly disregard of racism, his astonishing nine-and-a-half-hour underwater endurance test, or his brisk recovery from the loss of a leg, items which, if presented as fiction, would invite some disbelief. Drawing our fire, *Men of Honor* gives us instead a kind of Faustian pact between the 'real' Brashear and the wholly fictitious character Billy Sunday, played by Robert De Niro.

Their two lives running in parallel, Brashear and Sunday suffer similar crises and disabilities except that Sunday gets the worst of them and, being played by De Niro, also makes the most of them. He contrives to embody all the alternatives to Brashear's successes as if this was his story, the unexpurgated version. While a trifle short on honour, Sunday is finally redeemed in true De Niro style (witness *Meet the Parents* and *Flawless*) by the concluding showdown, in this instance with a repellent officer who, from unbridled spite, would clearly like to consign both navy veterans to some distant desk job. This indecipherably malignant lieutenant echoes the film's many other eccentrics, a diverting crew headed by Hal Holbrook's deranged segregationist. Together, they comprise a demented universe in which Brashear is less of a loner than he might have imagined.

George Tillman Jr, who wrote and directed the rather undernourishing *Soul Food*, rivets this one together with an appropriately dogged air of perseverance and a sure eye for visual clichés. The scenes of Brashear's share-cropping childhood are brutally free of charm, all toiling plough and platitude, but a persistent cheerlessness also infects much of his later quest. There's not a lot to be done these days with training-camp scenes—even with De Niro doing the shouting—but when it comes to romance the only novelty Tillman can offer is a dose of slow motion as boy and girl first touch and before our astonished gaze a key changes hands. Without belittling a remarkable personal history, awash with orchestral fanfares and culminating with an inevitably triumphal salute from fact to fiction, Tillman hasn't done it many favours either.

TIME, 11/13/00, p. 112, Richard Schickel

There are times when less would not be more, when it would just be regrettably ... less. Umberto Eco has argued, for example, that *Casablanca* works because it evokes every convention of the romantic-adventure genre. If it had missed even one or two of them, he suggests, it would have been just another forgettably routine wartime movie.

That idea applies neatly to *Men of Honor*. It is one of those dramas of peace-time military service in which a determined individual attains what he wants—in this case, master-chief rank and to be a master diver in the U.S. Navy—and in the process surmounts his own shortcomings and the completely predictable prejudice and near deadly hostility of the brass.

Inspired (a word that is bound to make realists queasy) by the real-life story of a man named Carl Brashear, who is played by Cuba Gooding Jr., the film is feverish in its desire to reduce his experiences to a compendium of clichés. Carl is, to begin with, the son of a black sharecropper. He joins the Navy in 1948, when the military is officially desegregated yet still confines men of his race to the galley. But he sees Navy divers being heroic and decides to join their ranks.

Diving school is commanded by a god-like lunatic (Hal Holbrook) who never leaves his tower office but knows what he hates, which is a black man striving for élite status. All but one of Carl's barracks mates move out rather than sleep in the same room with him. Day-to-day training is under the command of Billy Sunday (Robert De Niro), a drunken, brawling redneck who, if he can't drive Carl out of school, would just as soon kill him.

But that's just the beginning. In need of help with his book learning, Carl wins the support of the dubious local librarian (an appealing Aunjanue Ellis). Can love and marriage be far behind? Not in this movie. Will Carl attain his goal and Billy's reluctant respect? Why are we bothering to ask?

A certain novelty arises when Carl's leg is shattered in an accident. The Navy wants him to retire. Instead he orders the leg amputated, thinking a prosthesis will be less of a handicap to him on duty. We may never have seen courage expressed in quite that way, but it's also an excuse to bring a sobered-up Billy back to help Carl prove to a review board that he can return to active service. This, naturally, he does, presumably with the thanks of a grateful nation.

By now, you would think that even a nation with the U.S.'s uncanny taste for inspirational improbability might be fed up with *Men of Honor*. But that may not be so. There's something refreshing about its utterly unembarrassed embrace of the familiar. The director, George Tillman Jr., either doesn't notice or doesn't give a hoot about the way Scott Marshall Smith's script piles up clichés. He just keeps driving his movie right on through them. What's true of him is true of his actors too. De Niro pitches his performance on the edge of psychopathy, where menace and comedy very effectively coexist. But it is Gooding who does the most to redeem the movie, tempering his determination with a patient sweetness and casually stated masculine conviction that's thoroughly winning. To borrow a phrase, "Here's looking at you, kid."

VILLAGE VOICE, 11/21/00, p. 144, Dennis Lim

Based on the experiences of Navy man Carl Brashear, *Men of Honor* often seems less concerned with believability than *Red Planet*. [See Lim's review of *Red Planet*.] Cuba Gooding Jr. plays Brashear, a Kentucky sharecropper's son who strives to become the first black deep-sea diver in American military history. "As a dramatist I sometimes took it up a level," screenwriter Scott Marshall Smith explains in the press notes. Meaning he tells big honking lies—none more flagrant than the "composite" character of Master Chief Billy Sunday, Brashear's racist-sadist nemesis (later repentant ally), played by an obliviously gung ho Robert De Niro. Smith and director George Tillman Jr. are less interested in credibly dramatizing a real-life story than in drawing belabored parallels and nurturing imagined bonds between Brashear and this preposterous caricature—in the process, the filmmakers at once coarsen and dilute a fascinating life into a lumpy puddle of punishing inspirational hokum.

Also reviewed in:
CHICAGO TRIBUNE, 11/10/00, Friday/p. A, Michael Wilmington
NEW YORK TIMES, 11/10/00, p. E13, A. O. Scott
NEW YORKER, 11/20/00, p. 106, David Denby
VARIETY, 9/18-24/00, p. 29, Todd McCarthy
WASHINGTON POST, 11/10/00, p. C1, Stephen Hunter

MICHAEL JORDAN TO THE MAX

A Giant Screen Sports, James D. Stern Productions, and NBA Entertainment release. *Executive Producer:* David Falk, Curtis Polk, Adam Silver, and Gregg Winik. *Producer:* Don Kempf, Steve Kempf, and James D. Stern. *Director:* James D. Stern and Don Kempf. *Screenplay (narration):* Jonathan Hock. *Director of Photography:* James Neihouse and John Bailey. *Editor:* Jonathan Hock. *Music:* John Debney. *Sound:* Greg Smith. *Sound Editor:* Arya Shirazi and Roderick Beltran. *Running time:* 45 minutes. *MPAA Rating:* Not Rated.

CAST: Laurence Fishburne (Narrator); Michael Jordan, Phil Jackson, Doug Collins, Bob Greene, Dean Smith, Deloris Jordan, Fred Lynch, Walter Iosss, Jr., Bill Murray, Bob Costas, David Falk, Ken Griffey, Jr., Johnny "Red" Kerr, Steve Kerr, Spike Lee, Willie Mays, Stan Musial, Jack Ramsay, Ahmad Rashad (Themselves).

LOS ANGELES TIMES, 5/4/00, Calendar/p. 36, Kevin Thomas

If ever there was an athlete made for the Imax screen, it is Michael Jordan. James Stern and Don Kempf's 45-minute documentary, "Michael Jordan: To the Max," opening Friday at the Universal Studios and Edwards Imax theaters, not only celebrates Jordan's incomparable skill but also suggests that his stature as a man of character more than matches his physical height. There could be no finer role model for youngsters, and the film has been made with such verve and clarity that you don't have to be a basketball fan to enjoy it.

When you think of Jordan, you think of the winner who has everything: great looks and cool charisma besides awesome athletic skills and intelligence. Yet, he says quietly to the camera, "I've failed over and over again. That's why I succeeded." The first setback, the one that galvanized him, occurred when he failed to make his high school basketball team the first time around, as incredible as that sounds today. As the filmmakers cover his final year, 1998, with the Chicago Bulls, we see not only tremendous skill and grace on the court, highlighted in slo-mo sequences, but we sense the extra willpower and push needed from him to go out a champ. In between these action sequences, especially impressive on the Imax screen, we see Jordan in many other contexts, especially in his work with children and with his teammates, inspiring and teaching them how to be the best they can be.

Jordan is too smart to permit an invasion of the privacy of his family life, but he speaks of reverence and gratitude for his father, murdered in 1993. He tells us that he cannot see a father and son together without thinking of his loss and explains that when he dropped out of basketball for a year he wanted to see if he could become the baseball player his father always thought he could be. He proved, famously, not to be as gifted on a baseball diamond as on a basketball court yet gave it his very best shot, as the film makes clear, returning to basketball more appreciative than ever of his great gifts in that sport.

NEW YORK POST, 5/5/00, p. 53, Hannah Brown

A lot has been written about Michael Jordan's phenomenal skill on the basketball court, but seeing him slam dunk the ball in slow motion, eight stories high, is worth more than a thousand words.

This dramatic image, captured in "Michael Jordan to the Max," an documentary, is just as spectacular as seeing the view from Everest or other natural wonders caught by the IMAX technology.

Using state-of-the-art techniques, including the so-called bullet-time, high-definition slow motion featured in "The Matrix," co-directors James Stern and Don Kempf have created the most exciting live-action movie ever.

Focusing on the 1998 NBA playoffs, the climax of Jordan's last season, the filmmakers manage to build tension as to whether he will finish his career on a high note.

It's actually a good enough film so that it would be watchable even if it were shown on a regular screen, a rarity for a movie produced for IMAX theaters.

The portrait of Jordan is unabashedly puffy—it's a love letter rather than an attempt at a real biography.

Information given about his life is sketchy (the fact that he's married with children is never mentioned, for example), but he does talk in detail about his playing philosophy.

While Jordan's comments are succinct and compelling, the other talking heads brought in to affirm his status as one of the 20th century's greatest athletes are less so.

Watching Jordan play is the real drama here, and "Michael Jordan" is photographed so well that it will appeal even to people who aren't particularly interested in basketball.

NEWSDAY, 5/5/00, Part II/p. B7, Gene Seymour

Given IMAX' affinity for unique spectacle and natural wonders, it was only a matter of time before Michael Jordan joined Mount Everest, dolphins and the space shuttle as a subject worthy of the biggest of big screens. And given the formidable technology at IMAX' disposal, you would expect to get a tour of Jordan's career-capping 1999 NBA title run that brings you as close to pro hoop action as you can get without being on the court.

You would, of course, be wrong.

There are close-ups, to be sure, of Jordan from just about every conceivable angle, in every possible predicament. Watching Jordan slashing and slicing his way through New Jersey, New York, Indiana and Utah toward a sixth championship reminds you of how the late sports columnist Red Smith once characterized a similarly gifted and comparably important African-American athlete, named Jack Roosevelt Robinson: "the unconquerable doing the impossible."

Yet however wide its angles, however blinding its colors, "Michael Jordan to the Max" gives off about as much penetrating insight or emotional texture as the coffee table book it was intended to resemble. I know how this sounds, but it's not necessarily a negative attribute. As the present NBA season, its second without Jordan, rumbles to its conclusion, you can be forgiven for being grateful for any sustained view of the greatest athlete of the 20th Century's... final quarter. How's that, you fans of Jim Thorpe, Babe Ruth and Muhammad Ali?

If there are any visual surprises to be found in "Jordan," they're in the offhand moments between valedictory statements. When watching a playoff crowd on an IMAX screen, you really get a strong—nay, creepy—sense that they're staring back at you. And Bill Murray once again saves the franchise by offering all of us an IMAX view of a barrel of popcorn. Which looks, you won't be surprised to learn, like a huge barrel of popcorn.

Also reviewed in:
NEW YORK TIMES, 5/5/00, p. E16, A. O. Scott
VARIETY, 5/8-14/00, p. 49, Robert Koehler
WASHINGTON POST, 5/14/00, p. C1, Kevin Merida

MIDNIGHT

A Winstar Cinema release.   *Producer:* Pierre Chevalier and Carole Scotta.   *Director:* Daniela Thomas and Walter Salles.   *Screenplay (Portuguese with English subtitles):* Daniela Thomas, Walter Salles, and João Carneiro.   *Director of Photography:* Walter Carvalho.   *Editor:* Felipe Lacerda.   *Music:* Antônio Pinto, Eduardo Bid, and Nana Vasconcelos.   *Art Director:* Carla Caffé.   *Running time:* 64 minutes.   *MPAA Rating:* Not Rated.

CAST: Fernanda Torres (Maria);   Luiz Carlos Vasconcelos (João);   Mateus Nachtergaele (Chico);   Nelson Sargento (Vovo);   Carlos Vereza (Pedro);   Tonico Pereira (Carcereiro); Aulio Ribeiro (José);   Luciana Bezerra (Rosa);   Antonio Gomes (Antonio);   Nelson Dantas (Farmaceutico).

NEW YORK POST, 3/10/100, p. 56, Jonathan Foreman

Like last year's "Central Station," "Midnight" shows how visually rich Brazilian cinema has become.

But despite being co-directed by "Central Station's" Walter Salles, "Midnight"—which depicts the fateful collision of three lives in Rio on New Year's Eve 1999—is a more predictable, less substantial film.

There's police informer Chico, who extorts money from an arms dealer, money he plans to give his estranged wife in the slums. There's Chico's imprisoned friend Joao, who is sprung from prison on condition that he murder Chico. And then there's Maria (Fernanda Torres, daughter of Fernanda Montenegro), an attractive speech therapist, abandoned by her lover. Plunged into depression she resolves to kill herself.

"Midnight" seems longer than it really is because several scenes are too drawn out, the action is slowed by some mechanical dialogue, and because in the end there is no real point to the story. It's a shame because the acting is never less than convincing, and the Brazilian backgrounds are fascinating.

VILLAGE VOICE, 3/14/00, p. 126, Michael Atkinson

Paling beside La Sept Arte's "2000 as Seen By . . . " series standouts Don McKellar's *Last Night* and Tsai Ming-liang's *The Hole,* Walter Salles and Daniela Thomas's *Midnight (O Primeiro Dia)* works its millennial angst like community chewing gum. In fact, since it shares its climactic image with McKellar's startled farce, you'd think there was some archetypal significance to the image of desperate lovers/strangers swapping death for love atop a twilit urban rooftop. But where McKellar was ruefully witty, Thomas and Salles are earnest and melodramatic; like Salles's *Central Station, Midnight* could've used a screenplay less proud of its clichés. Judiciously fragmented, the movie's too few threads eventually knot up, but not before they fray to nothingness.

I didn't think my path would cross fatefully with any suicidal gun-toters on New Year's Eve, and it didn't, but apparently everybody else was knee-deep in ironic serendipity. Although it opens with enthusiastic slimeball Chico (Mateus Nachtergaele) tossing a Liv-a-Snap to a doggish junkyard bum and extorting money from another lowlife, *Midnight* largely consists of the hardly inevitable collision between Maria (Fernanda Torres), a speech therapist whose live-in boyfriend evaporates on December 30 and leaves her life a quaking void, and Joao (Luiz Carlos Vasconcelos), a con who escapes prison during a riot with the purpose of executing the rat who put him there—Chico.

Not much more than an hour long, *Midnight* takes the calendar-roll at face value—everyone's always frantically explaining how, since "all of the nines will turn to zeros, and the one will become a two," everything will change. ("Killers will be saints!" someone questionably maintains.) Salles and Thomas don't have any idea why it might be so, or have any kind of absurdist intent. Rather, the film (like *Central Station*) has a marvelously tangible relationship with the Brazilian landscape, from anti-industrial outland to cluttered Rio casbah to the late-evening hills. Salles can shoot his country; he just can't seem to write it.

La Sept Arte's project was, at any rate, something of a conceptual nonstarter, shackling the filmmakers to an arbitrary and instantly dated calendrical apocalypse that, because it was virtually universal, carried little metaphoric charge. McKellar saw impulse romance defying The End, and Tsai occasioned an allegorical water rot, but *Midnight* never looks beyond the stroke of 12, and never seems to understand the moment's meaninglessness.

Running with and somewhat overshadowing *Midnight*, Elizabeth Schub's short, *Cuba 15* , is an impressionistic, pig-in-shit vision of Cuban adolescence. Millennial in its own buoyant, hot-blooded way, Schub's movie focuses on one Tzunami Ortega Coyra, an entrancingly confident *quinceañera* who explains right off the bat she was named for a Pacific tidal wave "that caused much destruction. In spite of that, I dislike my name." Schub's movie follows Tzunami's impish example and, after briskly sketching the girl's happy place and time, culminates in a veritable dancing tour of Cuban landscapes, with Tzunami providing the moves before a Che billboard.

Also reviewed in:
NEW YORK TIMES, 3/10/00, p. E22, A. O. Scott
VARIETY, 9/7-13/98, p. 76, Derek Elley

MIFUNE

A Sony Pictures Classics release of a Nimbus Film production in cooperation with Zentropa Entertainments, DRTV, and SVT Drama. *Producer:* Brigitte Hald and Morten Kaufmann. *Director:* Soren Kragh-Jacobsen. *Screenplay (Danish with English subtitles):* Soren Kragh-Jacobsen and Anders Thomas Jensen. *Story:* Soren Kragh-Jacobsen. *Director of Photography:* Anthony Dod Mantle. *Editor:* Valdis Oskarsdottir. *Music:* Nulle Og Verdensorkestret. *Sound:* Morten Degnbol and Hans Moller. *Casting:* Stine Brüel. *Production Designer:* Signe Jensen. *Running time:* 99 minutes. *MPAA Rating:* R.

CAST: Anders W. Berthelsen (Kresten); Iben Hjejle (Liva); Jesper Asholt (Rud, Kresten's Brother); Sofie Grabol (Claire, Kresten's Wife); Emil Tarding (Bjarke, Liva's Brother); Anders Hove (Gerner); Paprika Steen (Pernille); Mette Bratlann (Nina); Susanne Storm (Hanne); Ellen Hillingso (Lykke); Sidse Babett Knudsen (Bibbi); Soren Fauli (The Voice); Soren Malling (Palle the Pimp); Keld Norgaard (Claire's Father); Kirsten Vaupel (Claire's Mother); Torben Jensen (Greying John); Klaus Bondam (Priest); Lene Laub Oksen (Hooker #1); Line Kruse (Hooker #2); Sofie Stougaard (Woman in Bakery); Rasmus Haxen (Gerner's Friend #1); Ole Mollegaard (Gerner's Friend #2); Esben Pedersen (The Dead Father); Christian Sievert (Herning); Arthur Jensen, Albert Pedersen, and Morten Flyverbom (Rud's Friends); Christian Gronvall (Bartender); Jens Basse Dam (Fat Redneck Businessman); Peter Rygaard and Dan Paustian (Horny Business Types).

CHRISTIAN SCIENCE MONITOR, 2/25/00, p. 15, David Sterritt

[*Mifune* was reviewed jointly with *Judy Berlin*; see Sterritt's review of that film.]

LOS ANGELES TIMES, 3/3/00, Calendar/p. 8, Kevin Thomas

Talk about bad timing. The hero of Soren Kragh-Jacobsen's brutally funny "Mifune" has just married the daughter of his boss, a Copenhagen business tycoon, and given her an ecstatic bridal night when he receives a phone call that his own father, whose existence he has denied, has just died.

Anders W. Berthelsen's Kresten has blotted out his past in his determination to make it to the top in Copenhagen. His mother's life came to an inexplicably tragic end, and Kresten has been out of touch with his father for a decade. He knows he has no choice but to return to the family farm, for his father has been caring for his mentally impaired brother Rud (Jesper Asholt).

Leaving his perplexed bride (Sofie Grabol) with as brief an explanation as possible and the promise of a swift return, he takes off. Once he arrives at his birthplace you just know his life is about to unravel. The setting is idyllically beautiful, but the family's handsome old manor stands dilapidated. Kresten will soon discover that the interior is a veritable pig sty—and that his father in his decline after his wife's death simply let all his livestock die. Kresten's past has caught up with him with a vengeance.

Meanwhile, we cut to a young Copenhagen call girl, Liva (Iben Hjejle), who's reached the end of her rope. On the one hand she's tormented constantly by an obscene phone caller and on the other she's outraged at discovering that one of her clients is the same man who viciously caned her young brother Bjarke (Emil Tarding) in the private school, the school she pays for by being a prostitute. In short, she's in the perfect mood to respond to an ad seeking a housekeeper at a farm.

The moment you see Kresten, a tall, strapping fellow, and Liva, whose loveliness cannot be hidden by her current stress, together you realize they make a most attractive, well-matched couple. They are both strong, resilient individuals with a good sense of humor, and Liva is instinctively kind and patient with the childlike, easily frightened Rud, who confuses her with the heroine in a favorite comic strip. When the troubled—and troublesome—Bjarke joins the group we see the outlines of a family forming, with Kresten and Liva responding to living close to nature—and, gradually, each other as well.

The obstacles to any such love and happiness, however, are constant, calamitous and at times downright savage. Yet in his no-holds-barred manner Kragh-Jacobsen is able to see the humor—as knockabout, bleak and corrosive as it can be—in Kresten and Liva's ever-shifting predicament. A hard-edged urban ruthlessness in both of them begins to fade in the countryside, and in no time Kresten and Liva engage our sympathy and concern.

"Mifune" does in fact take its title from the late, great Toshiro Mifune, a screen hero revered by Kresten and Rud, who identifies his brother with the Japanese actor, from the time they fell under the spell of "Seven Samurai" as youngsters.

Lars von Trier and Thomas Vinterberg asked Kragh-Jacobsen to make the third Dogma 95 film, and "Mifune" is the result, which means that among other conditions it had to be shot with a hand-held camera without artificial lighting; Anthony Dod Mantle, who photographed "The Celebration" for Vinterberg, again does the honors. Kragh-Jacobsen certainly puts his actors through their paces in demanding fashion but they come through, as does the equally demanding "Mifune," a pow-in-the-kisser kind of movie.

NEW YORK POST, 2/25/00, p. 56, Jonathan Foreman

"Mifune," the dreadfully named third movie to come out of the Danish Dogma Collective, turns out to be a delightful, fresh dark comedy.

The Dogma "vow of chastity" mandates hand-held cameras and forbids artificial lighting, studio filming, props from outside locations and all "superficial action" such as gunplay and murders.

Writer-director Soren Kragh-Jacobsen shows that the Dogma strictures can co-exist with stories that aren't filled with pessimism or Scandinavian gloom.

You meet Copenhagen yuppie Kresten (Anders W. Berthelsen) just as he ties the knot with his boss' daughter Claire (Sofie Grabol).

Things go noisily well on their wedding night, but the next morning Kresten gets a phone call informing him that his father is dead. The news comes as a particular shock for Claire, because Kresten has never admitted to having any living relatives.

Kresten leaves town for his father's run-down farm, where he finds his severely retarded younger brother Rud (Jesper Asholt)—whom he has also kept secret from Claire—hiding near their father's corpse.

Rud is hysterical, but Kresten calms him down with a game that they've played since childhood: Kresten pretends to be Japanese actor Toshiro Mifune in "The Seven Samurai" (hence this film's dreadful title).

While telling various lies to prevent his wife from coming out from Copenhagen, Kresten advertises for a housekeeper to look after both Rud and the filthy homestead.

Much to his surprise, the person who answers the ad turns out to be a beautiful young woman.

What Kresten doesn't know is that Liva (Iben Hjejle) is actually a high-class hooker—she turns tricks to pay for her younger brother's school fees—who is fleeing the city to get away from both her pimp and a scary telephone stalker.

Within days, the obnoxious brother is expelled from school and joins this strange menage, and its then that things start to go wrong.

All the Dogma films feature strong acting, and "Mifune" is no exception. Iben Hjejle (who strongly resembles Robin Wright Penn) is particularly good.

"Mifune" is superior to Dogma predecessors "The Celebration" and "The Idiots" in that it doesn't make a distracting or self-conscious fetish out of its (remarkably smooth) hand-held camerawork and natural lighting.

It's this very unpretentiousness that makes "Mifune"—the Danish nominee for the Best Foreign Language Film Oscar—the best advertisement so far for Dogma's stripped-down, inexpensive brand of filmmaking.

NEWSDAY, 2/25/00, Part II/p. B7, John Anderson

Danish director Soren Kragh-Jacobsen's first film was "Do You Want to See My Beautiful Bellybutton?" and he's spent much of his subsequent career in the so-called "youth genre." I say so-called, because Kragh-Jacobsen's latest does little to establish much difference between reputed adults and ostensible children.

Take the following exchange:

"We must give Dad a fine funeral."

"Does your car have a sunroof?"

The first line is uttered by Kresten (Anders W. Berthelsen), an up-and-coming urbanite who leaves his wealthy new wife on their honeymoon to return to his family's farm and bury the father his new wife never knew he had. The second line is spoken by Rud (Jesper Asholt), the mentally impaired brother she also didn't know he had.

Kresten, it seems, was under the impression that he could abandon a family that embarrassed him, pass himself off as an orphan and marry the boss' daughter without anyone ever being the wiser. Rud, the manchild, simply wants to know if he can look out the roof of the car.

While it's often uncertain who the adult is in "Mifune," the title character is definitely Toshiro Mifune, the late Japanese actor who is not in this movie, but was in, among others, "The Seven Samurai." That movie was a favorite of the two brothers when they were little boys. Rud is essentially still a little boy. And now he's Kresten's.

Meanwhile, a lovely call girl named Liva (Iben Hjejle) is being phone-stalked by someone who manages to get her number every time she changes it. Her brother Bjarke (Emil Tarding) is being kicked out of his prep school. Liva's just had an on-the-job encounter with the schoolmaster who caned Bjarke and ended it by moistly defacing his Persian carpet. She needs to hide out. So she answers an ad for a housekeeper at—where else?—Rud and Kresten's farm.

As a family—the ad-hoc family that coalesces over the course of the movie—the central characters of "Mifune" are like some early Robert Rauschenberg collage, all found objects and fractured parts. A tire. A blanket. A coffee can. And maybe they're also a bit like Kurosawa's samurai, distinct individuals on a mission they're not quite sure about.

Kragh-Jacobsen is a signatory to the Danish film compact Dogma '95, meaning "Mifune" is Dogma 3 (Lars von Trier's unreleased "Idiots" is 1, Thomas Vinterberg's "The Celebration" was 2; Harmony Korine's "Julien, Donkey-Boy" is apparently 4). As per Dogma's 10 commandments, "Mifune" is shot without artificial light, in present time, with no imposed music or artificial action (murders, weapons, etc).

It's also shot entirely with hand-held cameras and this turns out to be "Mifune's" saving grace. The unsmooth surfaces of Kragh-Jacobsen's images and the picture's rapid, rough-hewn style are perfect means of evading the mawkishness that might have encrusted the movie had it ever stopped moving. Unlike "Rain Man," which was often played for laughs, the relationship between one troubled adult and another—presumed to be impaired but somehow savant—seldom becomes sloppy or sticky. Nor does the romance that blossoms between Kresten and Liva, who have their respective children to look after, even if it may really be the other way around.

SIGHT AND SOUND, 10/99, p. 52, Mark Sinker

Kresten has just married Claire, the daughter of his wealthy boss in Copenhagen, without telling them he has family back in rural Lolland. Their honeymoon is interrupted by news of his father's death. Kresten returns home to sort out the ruined family farm. Once there, he realises his idiot brother Rud cannot fend for himself, and advertises for a housekeeper

Liva, a prostitute, takes the job. She has been whoring to pay for the welfare of her younger brother Bjarke, but is fleeing a persistent phone pervert in Copenhagen. Claire, arriving unexpectedly, takes Liva to be Kresten's mistress and leaves outraged. Bjarke, expelled from school, also comes to the farm. After learning Claire is seeking a divorce, a drunken Kresten forces himself on Liva. Bjarke, miserable at what he sees as her return to whoring, reveals he is the phone pervert. The next day, Liva walks out and goes to turn tricks at an nearby inn. She returns still angry, intending to return to Copenhagen, but while whitewashing she and Kresten make up. Three locals seeking Liva's professional service attack Kresten. She tends Kresten's wounds and they make love. Afterwards, as she sleeps, her prostitute friends arrive from Copenhagen: believing Kresten has just raped her, they also beat him up and whisk her off. When he regains consciousness, everyone is gone. After searching for Rud, who seems to have been kidnapped by aliens, Kresten arrives back at the farm to discover Liva, Rud and Bjarke waiting for him.

Directed by Danish youth-movie veteran Soren Kragh-Jacobsen, the third Dogma release Mifune seems to consider the Dogma 95 manifesto's claims to chastity, not as a commitment to genuine aesthetic or cultural purity, as publicity-stunt come-on of minor consequence. For if the manifesto were a critique of Hollywood or of anything else, the manifesto's eighth rule ("Genre films are unacceptable") would surely disallow any story centred on a whore-with-a-heart-of-gold. A whore, moreover, whose honest love redeems a man, freeing him from false idols and fear of his past. This is whiskery stuff, and while Dogmatic dodges with camera and lighting help Mifune stay amusing (and indeed watchable and fresh-looking), it's nevertheless a surprisingly conventional film, and so perhaps a faintly deflating addition to the canon. The arrival, too soon, of Dogma Lite.

The two previous Dogma movies, Festen and The Idiots, with their underfelt of edgy improvisation, made games-playing their subject and strategy. Mifune features a few sidelined games—Liva works as a dominatrix, Kresten's old neighbour and rival acts out as a rural bachelor Lothario—but there's little here to upset viewer expectations. Rud the idiot brother is (inevitably) a kind of savant; Bjarke the brat is, once given love, sensible, sensitive and perspicacious; and Kresten and Liva are decent through and through. The flat Lolland setting potentially a very bleak region, of loneliness, ignorance and even madness proves to be an emotional haven, its down-at-heel prettiness an unspoiled bedrock, a fictional dreamspace with flyblown decor.

Despite its look, in other words, everything is true to the film's sentimental film-world cliché. As a result, the various dilemmas and dangers can sometimes seem paper-thin. Just as Rud is never going to be abandoned or put in a home, we feel we know rather too early on that everything will turn out pretty well. As for the various worst possibilities we may entertain (such as the horrible plot that suggests itself during Rud's dive into a pond) we're generally importing expectations created elsewhere, particularly from our encounters with the darker imaginations of Vinterberg or von Trier.

None of it is intrinsically bad. The performances are universally engaging and plenty of scenes—the prostitutes as a girl-gang at a funfair, Rud's wrongfooting the priest at the funeral, the yokel tea party with flamenco guitar—are in and of themselves inventive pleasures, even if they serve mostly to reduce characters that, in other settings, would seem to promise a different and perhaps revelatory species of drama. But here too, expectation is bleeding in from outside. For it's not as if we've not been warned by the film's content and style. *The Idiots* arrived with an advance guard of scandal about its orgy scene. *Mifune*'s bedroom stuff is played purely for farce, with decorous sheets draped in all the right places. *Festen* had a look, that scummy, shot on-video look that dripped the poison of postmodern confessional nightmare into television slapstick (as in those *You've Been Framed* clips where the wedding goes wonky, and it's all captured on handicam). Mifune, by contrast, is shot on film, and very quickly comes across as unthreateningly solid and emotionally superficial.

Though only original in brief lurches, *Mifune* is never tiresome. In its way it's as meaninglessly diverting as the game Kresten plays with Rud, dressing up as Toshiro Mifune in *The Seven Samurai* (1954) and roaring round the house. But if disappointment arises mainly from the hopes that its subtitle *Dogma 3* fosters, we should remember that we'd probably never have looked out for this film without it.

VILLAGE VOICE, 2/29/00, p. 118, Dennis Lim

Mifune, a/k/a Dogma 3, hews about as closely as its forerunners to the collective's tenfold Vow of Chastity (i.e., kinda), but it differs in one key respect. Dispensing with the signature anarchic posturing, not to mention any pretense of back-to-basics innovation, *Mifune* is in fact provocatively unprovocative. For all the Dogmatic emphasis on rawness and immediacy (location shooting, natural light, no post-dubbed sound, et cetera), the film, directed and cowritten by Soren Kragh-Jacobsen, feels painfully inorganic—a slapdash pastiche of tropes and tics that would be scorned arriving off a Hollywood conveyor belt but, gussied up with a bogus Euro-art-film respectability, was enough to nab a prize at Berlin a year ago and precipitate a distributors' scuffle.

Like Dogma 1, Thomas Vinterberg's melodramatic farce *The Celebration* (a masterwork by comparison), *Mifune* takes as its starting point the family as a source of shame. A Copenhagen yuppie (Anders W. Berthelsen) who keeps his humble origins a secret marries his boss's daughter; on their honeymoon, he receives word of his father's death and is called away to the family farm, where his mentally retarded brother (Jesper Asholt) awaits. (The consistently ignored 10th Dogma tenet, "The director must not be credited," might as well be replaced with "Mental illness must feature prominently"— see also #2, *The Idiots*, and #4, *julien donkey-boy*.) A search for a housekeeper results in the arrival of a beautiful, kindhearted hooker (Iben Hjejle) and her bratty adolescent brother.

The alternative-family happily-ever-after is so plainly preordained, and the script's dawdling attempts to postpone it are so disingenuous, that *Mifune* grows increasingly slack and silly. (Having your characters remark on the "triteness" of their tidy fate is a particularly worthless form of self-consciousness.) No one deviates from type. The yuppie's new bride, vigorous and loud in bed on their wedding night, is instantly established as a shrew. The idiot is a fount of comedy, pathos, and, above all, insight. (The title comes from an incidental quirk of the character's a fixation with Toshiro Mifune and samurai tales.) Resident Dogma cinematographer Anthony Dod Mantle shoots on film and makes the most of some conspicuously golden sunlight, but his digital-video work in both *The Celebration* and *julien donkey-boy* was less decorous and more inventive.

One Dogma rule stipulates that "genre movies are not acceptable"; while what exactly constitutes a genre is arguable, it's safe to presume that the basic underlying idea is to discourage the reliance on timeworn blueprints. *Mifune*, however, is beholden to the lazy character shorthand and cleanly mapped narrative trajectories of the most formulaic Hollywood fare. Maybe it's all a sick joke—there is an undeniable tragicomedy in the notion that a return to cinematic purity should produce something that suggests the union of *Rain Man* and *Pretty Woman*.

Also reviewed in:
CHICAGO TRIBUNE, 4/21/00, Friday/p. A, Mark Caro
NATION, 3/13/00, p. 36, Stuart Klawans
NEW REPUBLIC, 3/20/00, p. 25, Stanley Kauffmann

NEW YORK TIMES, 2/25/00, p. E20, A. O. Scott
VARIETY, 2/22-28/99, p. 54, David Stratton
WASHINGTON POST, 4/7/00, p. C3, Rita Kempley

MISS CONGENIALITY

A Warner Brothers and Castle Rock Entertainment release in association with Village Roadshow Pictures and NPV Entertainment of a Fortis Films production. *Executive Producer:* Marc Lawrence, Ginger Sledge, and Bruce Berman. *Producer:* Sandra Bullock. *Director:* Donald Petrie. *Screenplay:* Marc Lawrence, Katie Ford, and Caryn Lucas. *Director of Photography:* Laszlo Kovacs. *Editor:* Billy Weber. *Music:* Edward Shearmur. *Music Editor:* Lee Scott. *Choreographer:* Scott Grossman. *Sound:* John Patrick Pritchett and (music) Chris Fogel and Dan Wallin. *Sound Editor:* David Hankins. *Casting:* Denise Chamian. *Production Designer:* Peter Larkin. *Art Director:* Ray Kluga. *Set Decorator:* Leslie E. Rollins, Randy Smith Huke and Barbara Haberecht. *Set Dresser:* John Parker, Mark Hanks, Robert Tate Nichols, Christopher Stull, Karen Luzius, Terri L. Wright, Thomas Young III, Patricia Dillon, and Ken-E-Ray. *Special Effects:* Larz Anderson and Randy Moore. *Costumes:* Susie De Santo. *Make-up:* Dorothy Pearl and Carla E. Palmer. *Make-up (Sandra Bullock):* Pamela Westmore. *Stunt Coordinator:* Jack Gill. *Running time:* 105 minutes. *MPAA Rating:* PG-13.

CAST: Sandra Bullock (Gracie Hart); Michael Caine (Victor Melling); Benjamin Bratt (Eric Matthews); William Shatner (Stan Fields); Ernie Hudson (McDonald); John DiResta (Agent Clonsky); Candice Bergen (Kathy Morningside); Heather Burns (Cheryl "Rhode Island"); Melissa De Sousa (Karen "New York"); Steve Monroe (Frank Tobin); Deirdre Quinn (Mary Jo "Texas"); Wendy Raquel Robinson (Leslie "California"); Asia DeMarcos (Alana "Hawaii"); Ken Thomas (Agent Harris); Gabriel Folse (Agent Grant); Christopher Shea (Agent Jensen); Mary Ashleigh Green (Young Gracie); Cody Linley (Tough Boy); Eric Ian Goldberg (Alan); Daniel Kamin (Krashow); Konstantin Selivanov (Ivan); Mona Lee (Russian Waitress); Sergei Levtsuk, and Johnny Caan (Russian Bodyguards); Debbie Nelson (Pageant Announcer); Don Cass (Pageant Director); Laurie Guzda (Assistant Director); Jimmy Graham (Backstage Security Guard); Ruperto Reyes, Jr. (Security Guard); Bernadette Nason (Pageant Matron); Stephen Bruton (Bartender); Jessica Holcomb (Beth); Jennifer Gareis (Tina); Ellen Schwartz (Herself); Cassandra L. Small (Starbucks Cop); Marco Perella (Starbucks Guy); Cynthia Dorn (Preliminary Judge); Catenya McHenry (Newscaster); Paige Bishop (Warehouse Dentist); Lucien Douglas (Warehouse Hair Stylist); Georgia Foy (Miss United States); LeeAnne Locken (Nebraska); Pei-San Brown (Alaska); Isamari White (Florida); Kimberly Crawford (Maine); Jamie Drake Stephens (Maryland); Dyan Conner (Massachusetts); Kelly Bright (Minnesota); Dee Dee Adams (Missouri); Shana McClendon (Nevada); Janie Terrazas (New Mexico); Holly Mills (Ohio); Angela Van DeWalle (Oregon); Tarah Bartley (South Carolina); Farrah White (Tennessee); Summyr Miller (Utah); Jessica Hale (Vermont); Pam Green (Washington).

NEW YORK POST, 12/20/00, p. 52, Jonathan Foreman

Sandra Bullock's abundant talent as a comedienne has never been more apparent than in "Miss Congeniality." Which makes it more of a shame that this fish-out-of-water comedy is such a sad illustration of the decline in Hollywood screenwriting.

Part of the problem, of course, is that—either because they are too self-satirizing in themselves or too obvious a target—beauty pageants are hard to make into good comedy: Witness awful flicks like "Drop Dead Gorgeous" and "Beautiful." The last good pageant movie was 1975's "Smile."

FBI special agent and kung-fu expert Gracie Hart (Bullock) is a lifelong tomboy with a snorting laugh, appalling table manners and no clue about hair, makeup or clothes.

But she's the only person in the bureau physically suitable for an undercover role as a contestant in the Miss United States Beauty Pageant, an institution recently threatened by a criminal mastermind called "The Citizen."

The pageant organizers, led by former beauty queen Kathy Morningside (Candice Bergen), reluctantly agree to fix the pageant so that Grace—renamed Gracie Lou Freebush from New Jersey—gets into the top five.

Grace's fellow agent Eric Matthews (Benjamin Bratt), who's entrusted with leadership of the undercover op, is perfectly aware that Grace is temperamentally and sartorially unsuited to take part in a beauty pageant. So he hires retired consultant Vic Melling (Michael Caine) to perform an instant Henry Higgins-style transformation.

Despite overwhelming odds, Vic is so successful that "Gracie" fits in just fine with her fellow contestants (even though she's in her mid-30s) and actually begins to enjoy her role.

The script by Marc Lawrence cannot make up its mind whether or not beauty pageants are dumb and offensive bimbo rituals, or something sweet to be admired. And the kind of verbal sparks you expect to fly when a feisty female agent meets a fluffy "bunch of bikini stuffers who only want world peace" never materialize. The blossoming romance between agents Hart and Matthews is even more of a damp squib.

Still, "Miss Congeniality" has some entertaining moments, thanks mainly to Bullock herself, who is surprisingly glamorous as well as endearing.

In the supporting roles, Michael Caine makes the most of his role in fine, understated style, while Candice Bergen seems oddly strained and uncomfortable.

NEWSDAY, 12/22/00, Part II/p. B8, John Anderson

Maybe it's the season. Maybe our immune system is misfiring. Maybe hell is freezing over. Whatever the factors, "Miss Congeniality" is adorable.

There's no concrete reason for anyone to come to this conclusion. The direction, by Donald ("My Favorite Martian") Petrie, is all but nonexistent. (The veteran Hugh Wilson reportedly backed out of the project somewhere along the way.) The script is what you might call lumpy, with a few really smart jokes bobbing up among the mush. The story, about an ugly duckling FBI agent transformed when she infiltrates a beauty pageant-romance! self-confidence! the ability to walk in heels!—makes you wonder if chimps really are running the studios.

And costar Benjamin Bratt, as the inevitable colleague who sees our heroine's worth only when she puts on eyeliner and falsies, is irritatingly shallow—but, then, so was every other actor who's played the same, ever-recurring role.

No, "Miss Congeniality" is almost entirely about its star, Sandra Bullock, whose agent Gracie Hart attempts to redeem herself and her career by going under cover at the Miss United States beauty pageant. The pageant, which has received a threat linked to the same serial bomber who has been terrorizing the rest of the country, has plenty of other problems, including an obsessive director (Candice Bergen), a washed-up host (William Shatner, who has morphed into Merv Griffin) and a late entry (re)named Gracie Lou Freebush, Miss New Jersey and undercover agent.

Bullock, who has a producer credit on the film, is not really a physical comedienne. The scenes in which the wobbly Gracie gets tutored in the pageant arts by the very queenly Vic Melling (the always reliable Michael Caine) contain no more comic grace than the rest of the film. But when Bullock—or Caine—deliver some of the script's better lines, the result is hilarity. When Bullock goes through the waxing, plucking, tweezing and teasing of Pageantland, the good humor is contagious.

Bullock is just plain funny, but she gets a lot of help (and a run for her money) from Heather Burns, who plays the ditsy, virginal Miss Rhode Island and becomes Gracie's pal during the prelude to the pageant. Yes, it's cheap to steal good lines from movies, but here's one, from Miss Rhode Island's onstage interview:

"What's your definition of the perfect date?"

"Oh, I guess I'd have to say April 25..."

OK, maybe we're coming down with something. But charm isn't something you can really explain anyway.

SIGHT AND SOUND, 5/01, p. 54, Katy Wilkinson

New Jersey, 1982. Gracie Hart, a little girl in the school playground, punches a boy picking on another child. Years later, the adult Gracie is an FBI agent. On an assignment in a bar, she makes a wrong move which results in a colleague getting shot. Although subsequently relegated to desk duty, Gracie desperately wants to work on the case of the Citizen, an anonymous terrorist whose next target will be the imminent Miss United States pageant. Despite her reservations about dressing up, Gracie is persuaded by fellow agent Eric Matthews to go undercover as a pageant contestant.

Two of the pageant's organisers, Kathy Morningside (a former beauty queen herself and Stan Fields, who reveals he's soon to be fired, are aware Gracie is undercover. Consultant Victor Melling is hired to oversee Gracie's make-over. Pageant preparations begin but Gracie, who's having difficulty relating to her fellow contestants, tells Eric she's quitting; he manages to talk her out of giving up. Intending to gather more information about the case, she goes on a night out with the girls, bonds with them and overhears rumours that Morningside is also about to be fired. When the FBI claim to have found the Citizen (in another part of the country), the unit is disbanded. Unconvinced, Gracie carries on investigating. When Eric refuses to back her up, she resigns. In her office, Morningside discusses her plan to blow up the pageant with her assistant Frank, actually her son.

As the competition gets under way, Eric uncovers Frank's criminal past and returns to help Gracie. Realising the pageant crown contains a bomb, Gracie wrestles it off the winner. Frank and Morningside are arrested. Gracie is declared a hero and gets together with Eric.

Miss Congeniality stretches our credulity at the best of times, but the biggest demand it makes on its audience comes at the beginning when we're expected to believe in Sandra Bullock playing a plain-looking, unsophisticated FBI agent. As the dowdy Gracie Hart, Bullock strains to convince us that she's just one of the boys, eating junk food and drinking beer with her fellow agents, adopting an ungainly swagger, and so on. Bullock's seeming discomfort in the role merely reinforces our established perception of her as one of Hollywood's most stylish stars, so much so that when her transformation from tomboy to beauty-pageant contestant—staged unsubtly to the strains of 'She's a Lady'—finally comes, it seems inevitable.

Not only is it easy to see where the plot is heading (Gracie has to enter a beauty pageant undercover to find out who's behind a bomb threat), but the central and supporting characters in *Miss Congeniality* remain frustratingly undeveloped. The script, by Marc Lawrence, Katie Ford and Caryn Lucas, never explains why Gracie is so involved with her job (to the point of having no social life); nor is there any attempt to provide sufficient motivation for her sudden change in attitude towards her fellow contestants, previously the object of contempt, now accorded full respect. This shift is especially hard to take since the film seems to view the contestants as one-dimensional creatures, milking easy laughs from such stock characteristics as their desire for "world peace". In aspiring—and failing—to emulate the classic screwball comedies of the 30s, director Donald Petrie (*Grumpy Old Men*) only leaves you wondering what more accomplished hands could have made of the material: the Svengali-like relationship between beauty consultant Victor and Gracie, for instance, would have been exploited to the full had, say, Howard Hawks been directing.

The glitz of the pageant itself—as gruesomely fascinating here as they are in real life—is captured by respected cinematographer Laszlo Kovacs, but the overall look, like the plot, holds no surprises. Despite Gracie's conclusion that there's more to beauty queens than meets the eye, *Miss Congeniality* ultimately promotes a disappointingly superficial image of the beauty business. Gracie might be applauded for solving the case (the result of traditional detective work), but she receives an equal measure of credit for her physical transformation; in this day and age, when beauty is all, the fact that she's learnt to walk in high heels and use a hairbrush properly is seen as the real achievement.

Also reviewed in:
NEW YORK TIMES, 12/22/00, p. E17, A. O. Scott
VARIETY, 12/18-31/00, p. 26, Robert Koehler

WASHINGTON POST, 12/22/00, p. C5, Rita Kempley
WASHINGTON POST, 12/22/00, Weekend/p. 43, Michael O'Sullivan

MISSION: IMPOSSIBLE 2 (M: I-2)

A Paramount Pictures release of a Cruise/Wagner production. *Executive Producer:* Terence Chang and Paul Hitchcock. *Producer:* Tom Cruise and Paula Wagner. *Director:* John Woo. *Screenplay:* Robert Towne. *Story:* Ronald D. Moore and Brannon Braga. *Based on the TV series created by:* Bruce Geller. *Director of Photography:* Jeffrey L. Kimball. *Editor:* Christian Wagner and Steven Kemper. *Music:* Hans Zimmer. *Music Editor:* Marc Streitenfeld and Zigmund Gron. *Choreographer:* Antonio Vargas. *Sound:* Bob Renga, Craig "Pup" Heath and (music) Alan Meyerson. *Sound Editor:* Mark P. Stoeckinger. *Casting:* Deborah Aquila, Greg Apps, and Sarah Halley Finn. *Production Designer:* Tom Sanders. *Art Director:* Dan Dorrance. *Set Decorator:* Kerrie Brown and Lauri Gaffin. *Special Effects:* David Kelsey. *Costumes:* Lizzy Gardiner. *Make-up:* Robert McCann, Paul Pattison, and Mary Burton. *Special Make-up Effects:* Kevin Yaher. *Stunt Coordinator:* Brian Smrz, Rocky McDonald, Bob Hicks, and Bob Brown. *Running time:* 120 minutes. *MPAA Rating:* PG-13.

CAST: Tom Cruise (Ethan Hunt);   Dougray Scott (Sean Ambrose);   Thandie Newton (Nyah Nordoff-Hall);   Ving Rhames (Luther Stickell);   Richard Roxburgh (Hugh Stamp);   John Polson (Billy Baird);   Brendan Gleeson (McCloy);   Rade Sherbedgia (Doctor Nekhorvich);   William Mapother (Wallis);   Dominic Purcell (Ulrich);   Matthew Wilkinson (Michael);   Nicholas Bell (McCloy's Accountant);   Kee Chan (McCloy's Chemist);   Kim Fleming (Larrabee);   Alan Lovell, Karl McMillan, and Bret Partridge (Biocyte Security Guards);   Christian Manon (Doctor Gradsky);   Lester Morris (Bookie);   Kelly Ons, Candice Partridge, Natalie Reis, Adriana Rodriguez, Sandra Rodriquez, Cristina Brogeras, and Nada Rogic (Flamenco Dancers);   Nicholas Papademetriou (Prison Guard);   Antonio Vargas (Senor De L'Arena);   Dan Luxton (Relief Pilot); Anthony Hopkins (Swanbeck).

CHRISTIAN SCIENCE MONITOR, 5/26/00, p. 17, Stephen Humphries

Talk surrounding the release of any new Tom Cruise movie usually revolves around how much the world's most bankable actor earned for his latest role. Not so with the release of "Mission: Impossible 2" ("M:I-2"). This time tongues will be busy speculating about the actor's life-insurance premiums after watching Cruise dangling precariously from the edge of a cliff.

Cruise reprises his earlier role as Ethan Hunt, an agent of the secretive Impossible Missions Force. In keeping with the template of the original "Mission Impossible" TV series, he receives a recorded message—with the requisite self-destruct mechanism—detailing a new mission objective.

Agent Hunt's boss (Anthony Hopkins) warns that an Australian pharmaceutical company has developed the antidote to a lethal virus that they will sell to the world after releasing the bacteria. Worse, a menacing colleague of Hunt's, Sean Ambrose (Dougray Scott), has decided to blackmail the tycoon behind the scheme. Hunt must recruit Nyah Hall (a slightly out-of-her depth Thandie Newton), an old flame of Ambrose, to infiltrate Ambrose's operation.

Naturally, Agent Hunt falls for the girl. This romantic subplot is flatter than "M:I-2's" shots of the Australian outback, while a woefully underdeveloped plot implies that Hunt's conscience is troubled by recruiting Nyah.

As in the first movie, Cruise's character is a complete blank, possessing no discernible individuality other than an insouciant self-assuredness. Indeed, one weakness of the film is that despite facing all manner of spectacular obstacles, Hunt is such a superman (rock-climbing sequence aside) one never feels there are any real "kryptonite" moments from which he won't be able to extricate himself.

"M:I-2" also lacks scenes that'll put sweat on your armrest like the famous CIA heist sequence in the first movie, and little of the ingenuity of the TV series remains. "M:I-2" does boast spy gadgetry that would have James Bond raising his eyebrow.

Like the TV series, this movie borrows from the 007 formula, right down to the last exotic setting. That said, this sequel ably succeeds as a crowd-pleaser on account of the sheer creativeness of its fabulously executed stunts.

Credit must go to the patented style of director John Woo ("Face/Off"), dean of the Hong Kong school of action movies. Woo's crisp editing punctuates lovingly composed shots of doves emerging from fiery carriages and people diving in slow motion while firing two guns simultaneously.

Cruise also executes graceful "Air Jordan" leaps before he somersaults his way into karate kicks. These impressive acrobatics overly prolong the last fight sequence—a common weakness of Woo movies—but they fail to spoil a thrilling blockbuster.

LOS ANGELES TIMES, 5/24/00, Calendar/p. 1, Kenneth Turan

Except for irredeemably artistic types like Taiwan's Hou Hsaio Hsien or Iran's Abbas Kiarostami (though even they might have been tempted), star-producer Tom Cruise could have gotten any director in the world to do the sequel to his very successful "Mission: Impossible." The man asked was John Woo, and the result, now cryptically titled "M:I-2," lavishly displays the reasons for that choice all over the wide screen.

Woo, who parlayed a legendary career as a Hong Kong actionmeister into domestic extravaganzas "Broken Arrow" and "Face/Off," is a master of movement and chaos. Though they feature cascades of bullets and fists of fury, his films are more about the plasticity of the medium than pedestrian concepts like blood and violence. A director without limits who respects neither the laws of physics nor those of probability, Woo, in marvelous cult items like "The Killer," "A Better Tomorrow" and "Hard-Boiled," has made some of the most delirious films imaginable.

Once Woo unleashes his bad self and ignites the proceedings here, once the glass shatters, the flames erupt, the gunshots ricochet and the doves fly, all is well with "M:I-2." While one of the film's drawbacks is that it takes awhile until that feverish point is reached, everyone tries hard and mostly successfully to keep us occupied until the killer moments arrive.

Cruise himself, obviously, is one of "M:I-2's" strongest weapons. Looking a bit shaggier but still appropriately steely-eyed in this new incarnation of special agent Ethan Hunt, Cruise is involved in a lot of running and jumping but very little standing still, taking on stunts ranging from climbing a sheer cliff face in Utah to doing things with a motorcycle that would have intimidated Steve McQueen.

Also demanding attention is the film's Robert Towne plot, a basically simple tale told with so much artful misdirection and disinformation that it takes a bit of time to figure out. You may not understand what's happening from moment to moment, but with Woo setting the pace, you may not have the opportunity to care.

"M:I-2" opens with scientist Vladimir Nekhorvich (Rade Sherbedgia) injecting himself with a mysterious substance and sending a Delphic message to agent Hunt that ultimately proves to be the key to the plot: "The search for a hero begins with something that every hero requires, a villain."

Speaking of bad guys, "M:I-2's" is former agent Sean Ambrose, played by "Ever After's" Dougray Scott, so ruthless he is capable of using a cigar cutter to remove the fingertip of one of his own men. Though fans of "Face/Off" may feel that Nicolas Cage's style of florid criminality was better suited to Woo's operatic sensibility, Ambrose's more controlled evil proves to be a good match for Cruise's coolly heroic Hunt.

The link between these two rivals is the oh-so-beautiful and spirited Nyah Nordhoff Hall, puckishly named after the men who wrote the "Mutiny on the Bounty" trilogy and played by Thandie Newton ("Jefferson in Paris," "Beloved"). A master thief who looks good in designer clothes, Hall is recruited for the operation by Hunt at the insistence of his boss (an unbilled and not particularly energetic Anthony Hopkins), who neglects to say what her job will be.

Turns out that Hall is the ex-flame of the turncoat Ambrose, and the boss wants her to function as a seductive Trojan horse in the evil one's compound, finding out exactly what nefarious plots are being hatching behind those surveillance-proof walls. Hunt, who in the interim has fallen for

Nyah himself, says that will be difficult. "This is not Mission: Difficult, this is Mission: Impossible," the top guy dryly notes.

Helping everybody do their jobs in "M:I-2" is a whole lot of gadgetry, so much computer and electronic gear that the film plays at times like a James Bond extravaganza without the smug '60s overlay. Though agent Luther Stickell (Ving Rhames) returns from the last film, he spends so much time tediously sitting in front of the computer you start to wonder if he had a hand in the "I Love You" virus.

Even when "M:I-2" is at its exposition-heavy early stages, Woo's marvelous visual sense is always an asset. Working with cinematographer Jeffrey Kimball, Woo brings a showy flair to the most potentially pedestrian situations. Woo's films, and this one is no exception, are also characterized by an over-the-top emotionalism that amplifies all feelings to mythological status. The power of film to irrationally transform and exalt is almost a religion to Woo, and another reason why he was the natural go-to guy for this lucrative movie franchise.

NEW YORK, 6/5/00, p. 102, Peter Rainer

Mission: Impossible 2 is a fairly expert piece of star packaging, which is not necessarily the same thing as a good movie. Directed by John Woo and written by Robert Towne, it sets itself off from Brian De Palma's *Mission: Impossible* by serving up its luminary, Tom Cruise, as an adventurer with soul. His Ethan Hunt is no longer just a guy who lives by his stopwatch and swoops down from high places tethered to cable ropes; he's also a man in love. You can tell this because his gaze has a wall-eyed burn and his longish hair streams poetically, especially when he's buzzing in his motorbike around dead man's curves. This guy *cares*. The object of his caring, Nyah Hall (Thandie Newton), is a thief-turned-mission-impossiblist,and she's all dreamy, enigmatic smiles and melancholia—a swoon in motion. "I'm not going to lose you!" Ethan informs her during one particularly dicey moment in the action, but it's not clear when exactly he ever had her. For all the deep yearning on display, for all the slo-mo shampoo-commercial-style sensuality, their love match isn't really on a much higher level than what usually goes on between 007 and his Bond Girl. Ethan will surely get over her. Wanna bet Nyah's a no-show in *M:I-3?*

The Bond reference is apt because so much of this film, even more than its predecessor, is patterned on the prefab tropes of that series. I guess no mission is too impossible if you have the right template. Somehow, this sort of patterning works better when Mike Myers is running the show; Austin Powers is a much more entertaining pseudo-Bond than Ethan, and, given Ethan's boring predilection for basic black, Austin's a better dresser too. The villains aren't quite up to snuff, either. Sean Ambrose (Dougray Scott) is a standard-issue scowler whose gnarliest moment comes when he slices off the tip of his henchman's finger with a cigar cutter. Depravity, where is thy sting? Ernst Blofeld would have had this guy for lunch. Ambrose's scheme is to launch a deadly virus into the world and then market its antidote, thereby reaping billions. It's not a bad scheme, actually, but badness of this caliber needs more panache. We are told several times in the movie that a hero is only as good as his villain, but the filmmakers haven't taken their own counsel.

Which means that Tom Cruise, who also produced the movie, is pretty much the whole show. He has his usual all-business intensity (he even does most of his own stunt work), but despite Cruise's attempts here to be Byronic, there's something strenuous about his soulfulness; he turns everything, even repose, into calisthenics. It's not enough that he's a great big movie star; he has to be taken as something more, the CEO of his own destiny. But this carefully calibrated new star vehicle of his, even though it will probably be a monster hit, doesn't do him any real favors. He's loosened up a bit as an actor in recent years—I'm thinking particularly of *Jerry Maguire* and *Magnolia*—and yet for all the flowing hair, his return to Ethan Hunt marks a return to stick-figure land. It's possible to play pulp action heroes and still deliver a performance—Sean Connery, of course, did it—but that means giving yourself over to the stylishness of schlock, and Cruise is too humorless an actor for that.

John Woo indulges the humorlessness. When he made his Hong Kong pulp fantasias starring Chow Yun-Fat, the hyperviolent excessiveness was a source of wit. Woo doesn't bring that same comic delirium to his American films (the closest he came was in *Face/Off*, which his new movie borrows from), but he's retained the mythic-shmythic stuff—the slowed-down ceremoniousness of the fight scenes and the hero-villain dualisms and the doves winging into frame at crucial moments. It's all a bit much to hang on this slender thread. Brian De Palma, who, like Woo, has had some smashing successes in the realms of pulp mythos, didn't attempt to glorify *Mission: Impossible* when he took it on; although that first film was so carelessly plotted it might have been called *Mission: Incomprehensible,* it had a couple of set pieces that, taken simply as theater, were like buzz cuts to the brain. The action scenes in *M:I-2* don't have that charge; they're woozier and yet more conventional, full of skidding U-turns and fireballs and explosions of splintered glass. The climactic kung-fu clobberfest between Ethan and Sean seems surprisingly tame after everything that came before, and it also pales in comparison with similar scenes in *The Matrix,* a movie that, ironically, was heavily influenced by Woo. And yet, for all the movie-star engineering and digitizing and Dolbyized kabooms, there's something endearing about the way Woo finishes the movie with just two guys slugging it out. It's Woo's version of minimalism, and it's not a bad way to go. Future franchisers of this series, take note.

NEW YORK POST, 5/24/00, p. 47, Lou Lumenick

Mission accomplished. Director John Woo's "Mission: Impossible 2" keeps audiences on the edge of their seats for much of its two-hour running time, lavishing enough thrills and eye candy to eclipse the fact it's instantly forgettable.

The last half-hour—an extended motorcycle chase wherein Tom Cruise's Ethan Hunt barrels through a wall of fire, firing bullets while riding on one wheel, capped by a kickboxing climax—is simply incredible.

Also enormous fun to watch is Ethan's opening scene, where he's seen dangling by his fingers off a sheer rockface in Utah, jumping in midair to another peak.

Also sure to get audiences pumped is a flirtatious mountain car chase between Ethan and Nyah Hall (Thandie Newton), the beautiful thief he recruits for his latest mission—keeping her ex-boyfriend, rogue IMF agent Sean Ambrose (Dougray Scott), from unleashing a killer virus.

Ethan falls in love with the light-fingered Nyah, but is forced to send her back into the arms of the psychopathic Sean—who registers his displeasure with an associate by using a cigar cutter on one of his fingers.

The screenplay—attributed to multiple Oscar-nominee Robert Towne but apparently the work of a high-priced committee—only halfheartedly follows through on the love-and-betrayal theme after a suspenseful racetrack sequence.

There are references to "North by Northwest" throughout the film, most notably Sean's striking house in Sydney, where most of the film takes place.

"Mission: Impossible 2" also quotes liberally from Woo's last American film, the more exhilarating "Face/Off," which had much better acting and moved much more quickly throughout.

This sequel to the 1996 "Mission: Impossible" bogs down midway in lengthy exposition that doesn't do much to explain why, for instance, Sean needed to blow up an airliner in the film's opening moments.

Sean isn't anywhere near as interesting a villain (or Scott as compelling an actor) as the bad guys in the first film, played by Vanessa Redgrave and Henry Czerny.

Besides Cruise, only Ving Rhames as computer whiz Luther Stickell returns from the original cast, and he doesn't have much to do beyond lowering Ethan from a helicopter into a microbiology lab, in a scene laboriously copied from a more suspenseful sequence in the original film.

Newton pretty much disappears from the second half of the film. Not that there's much chemistry between her and Cruise, whose Ethan seems much too self-absorbed to connect with anyone else.

Cruise, who overplays the scenes in which Ethan is supposed to be concerned about Nyah's fate, looks less like a covert operative than a fashion model, with stylish long hair and designer clothes complementing his impossibly chiseled looks.

At one point a character asks, "Do you have any idea what he's talking about?" Much of the time you won't, but check your brains at the popcorn stand and hang on for a spectacular ride.

NEWSDAY, 5/24/00, Part II/p. B2, Jan Stuart

The sexual connotations of classy sports cars have never been more in-your-face than in an early scene in "M:I-2," as Tom Cruise stalks his babe of the moment on a daredevil chase up a narrow mountain strip. "If you want me, you'll have to catch me!" she shouts to him from her curvy roadster at 70 mph. And they're off, burning rubber, banging sides, their chassis hugging tight as they twirl in ecstatic slow-motion.

So much for Oscar nominations and lofty intentions. In "M:I-2," Tom Cruise reverses gears toward trivial pursuits of yore with a kind of superstar panic that makes one feel as if Stanley Kubrick and Paul Thomas Anderson were scary little detours never to be traveled again.

The million-dollar Cruise smirk and famous Cruise torso on ample display in "Eyes Wide Shut" and "Magnolia" are back, minus the irony and self-commenting that turned narcissism into acting. The star's bankable assets are almost beside the point, however, and the smugly acronymic title says it all. "M:I-2" has little to do either with Cruise, a sophisticated television series called "Mission: Impossible" or a stylish Brian DePalma film, and everything to do with the blunt, crash-and-bum movie school of director John Woo.

Between the first preposterous shot of Tom Cruise rock-climbing on a southwestern peak and the final showdown by the sea, Woo will explode at least as many vehicles as the Ford Motor Co. does in its annual safety tests, indulging us in the thrill and beauty of destruction by slowing the camera down to a voyeuristic crawl. Woo cartoons up the "Mission: Impossible" formula into a video game in which actors are a necessary evil.

Woo seems key to a master plan to simplify, simplify, simplify. Presumably hoping to avoid the script wrangling and plot convolutions that haunted the first film, co-producer Cruise has also recruited A-list screenwriter Robert Towne, whose most famous film ("Chinatown") is a lesson in maze-like clarity. The Towne solution here, however, is an Espionage for Dummies formula that revives three standard ploys: unscrupulous Russian scientists, viruses that kill within a short time and anti-virus antidotes that cure within a shorter time.

It's only too bad that Towne does not heed the oft-repeated dictum of his own script: "Every hero needs a villain." There is a bad guy, to be sure, but he lacks the oversized villainy worthy of superman-agent Ethan Hunt (Cruise) and a virus that can wipe out Sydney, Australia, before the next surf is up. Hoping to use the virus to bribe his way toward billions in stock options, the Irish-brogued Sean Ambrose (Dougray Scott, an emaciated Schwarzenegger type) is merely very unpleasant: He throws dirty punches and keeps his stooges in line with a cigar cutter.

Cruise's conduit toward his foe is Ambrose's former girlfriend, the beauteous jewelry thief Nyah Hall (Thandie Newton, an African-English siren with pyramid eyebrows and come-hither lips). The creative team would appear to have chosen Newton (so weirdly splendid as the eponymous "Beloved") for a dermatological perfection that suggests she bathes in the most expensive extra-virgin olive oil; the mere idea of her being threatened by a skin-ravaging virus is easily more horrific than Fay Wray in the clutches of King Kong.

But the director objectifies his leading lady in much the same way he does his exploding cars, capturing her in absurd slow-motion profiles that savor every silken strand of her brown hair as it flutters in the wind. The result is somewhere between a Clairol ad and soft-core pornography, effectively canceling out our pleasure at seeing an intelligent black actress go up against Tom Cruise.

Where "Mission: Impossible," director DePalma created an eerie character out of its Prague setting, Woo tosses off Sydney as another sunny place to swoop above with a helicopter. With every fiery explosion, "M:I-2" moves further from its source inspiration and closer toward a preadolescent action orgy. This so-called sequel prefers to take its cue from its chief beneficiary of product placement, Avis Rent-A- Car: When you're number two, you have to try harder.

NEWSWEEK, 6/5/00, p. 69, David Ansen

The first time Tom Cruise rips off his latex mask and turns out to be someone else, it's cool. The next time someone else rips off his face and turns out to be Tom Cruise, it's still a kick. By the third and fourth time this ploy is used, you're not only miles ahead of the trick, you are beginning to resent it. What is this, "Face/Off-2"?

If only it were. Now, that was a real John Woo movie, both exhilaratingly ridiculous and ridiculously exhilarating. "M:I-2," as the new "Mission: Impossible" is tagged, is a slick, expensive, bullet-ridden thriller that is oddly dull—the last thing you'd expect from Hong Kong action maestro Woo. It makes one nostalgic for Brian De Palma's first M:I. The plot may have been incomprehensible, but while you were lost in its seductive hall of mirrors, it didn't seem to matter.

The plot of "M:I-2" is simple enough: there's a very bad virus that could wreak worldwide havoc, and Ethan Hunt (Cruise) has to get it out of the hands of the villains. This time he needs the help of a woman he has inconveniently fallen for (Thandie Newton). She was once the girlfriend of the chief bad guy (Dougray Scott), and Ethan has to ask her to sacrifice her virtue for the good of the cause. This gives Cruise many opportunities to furrow his brow and look agonized, but for all the gnashing of shiny teeth, his concern never becomes ours. (Someone should have studied the similar dynamic between Cary Grant and Ingrid Bergman in "Notorious" for a lesson in the power of understatement.)

Woo's movie bursts out of the gate with James Bondish raffishness. But the tongue-in-cheek style suits neither Cruise's earnest, muscular emoting nor Woo's supercharged balletic carnage, and is quickly dropped. Many car and motorcycle chases ensue. Since these are rather shopworn thrills in the post-"Matrix" era, Ethan Hunt suddenly acquires an acrobatic gift for leaping into the air and thrashing his foes with his legs and feet. Strange: here is Mr. Woo imitating the two white brothers who directed "The Matrix" who were imitating the Hong Kong action style at which Woo was once peerless. But the poetic urgency behind Woo's best work is missing here. In "M:I-2" everyone seems to be going through the motions.

SIGHT AND SOUND, 7/00, p. 51, Andrew O'Hehir

The present. Dr Nekhorvich is flying from Australia to Atlanta carrying Chimera, a man-made virus, and its antidote known as Bellerophon. Sean Ambrose, a renegade agent from the Impossible Missions Force, steals Nekhorvic's briefcase, then escapes. IMF agent Ethan Hunt is instructed to recover the stolen virus. In Seville, he recruits Nyah, Ambrose's ex-lover, to help him. Ethan and Nyah fall in love.

Nyah agrees to return to Ambrose in Australia to pass on information to Ethan. Realising that all he stole from Nekhorvich was Bellerophon, Ambrose attempts to sell the antidote to McCloy, a pharmaceutical tycoon who owns the only supplies of Chimera. Ambrose becomes suspicious of Nyah. Ethan breaks into McCloy's Sydney headquarters to destroy the last of the Chimera. Ambrose anticipates this and corners Ethan, holding Nyah hostage. Nyah injects herself with the last syringe of Chimera. Ambrose must keep her alive to hold on to the virus, but she will die if not injected with Bellerophon within 20 hours. Ethan and Ambrose both escape a shootout in McCloy's building. Ambrose plans to take over McCloy's company, use Nyah to start a Chimera epidemic in Sydney and profit from selling Bellerophon to the afflicted. Ethan breaks into Ambrose's island compound and escapes with Bellerophon. Ambrose pursues him; Ethan kills him in hand-to-hand combat, finds Nyah before she kills herself and injects her with the remedy.

During one of *Mission: Impossible II*'s typically elaborate action sequences, someone at the back of the Manhattan theatre where I saw the film called out: "These guys have been watching too much Matrix." I don't know whether the heckler was ignorant of the historical relationship between John Woo and the Wachowski brothers, or was making an ironic wisecrack about the confusing state of contemporary Hollywood action cinema. It's a telling remark either way. To paraphrase what Manohla Dargis wrote about *Face/Off* (S&S September 1997), as Woo's sensibility has conquered Hollywood, so Hollywood's sensibility has seemed to conquer him.

By any reasonable measure *Mission: Impossible II* is a successful action-adventure film, and even a casual fan of Woo's work will recognise his trademark flourishes: slow-motion firearm callisthenics, overblown emotion and enough motor-vehicle eroticism to make J. G. Ballard blush. There are also a few of the surpassingly beautiful moments only he can provide, when something enormous seems to stir in the lives of apparently superficial characters. There's a meditative, almost mystical sequence as Nyah approaches Ambrose's waterfront compound outside Sydney—as ever Woo lovingly fetishises the lifestyles of the evil rich—that ranks with anything in his Hong Kong movies. Thandie Newton strides up the pier in slow motion, her olive features and raven hair framed by the preternatural blue of Sydney harbour. Dougray Scott meets her with a purposeful gleam in his eye, and as the scarf around her neck is about to slip away, he reaches out and catches it. You can argue that this is clichéd symbolism—Beauty captured by the Beast—but at least it's wonderfully executed.

But viewed in the context of Woo's other films, *Mission: Impossible II* looks like a muddy, compromised film. The director seems hemmed in by his star, by a lacklustre script and by a franchise that has abandoned its Cold War origins for generic action-adventure formula. If our waggish friend in the back row contends that this is not quite as good a Woo film as *The Matrix,* one could retort that it's no worse a Bond film than *The World Is Not Enough.* Our hero favours the casual look and motorbike leathers rather than immaculately pressed dinner jackets, but the lovely girl, the smooth-operator villain and the tangled, unconvincing doomsday plot are all in place.

Tom Cruise as agent Ethan certainly comes off as a game, athletic performer (or at least his stunt double does), but his disarmingly low-key acting style is most effective when he's given time to steep in the role. His early scenes with Newton have the appealing tenderness of two inscrutable characters who have found each other, and their giddy seduction ritual, a Porsche-vs-Audi motor race through the Spanish mountains, provides the film's sexiest thrills. But as *Mission: Impossible II* shifts its focus to Ethan's battle with Ambrose, Cruise increasingly seems like a good natured guy going through the motions. Similarly, while Woo makes good use of Dougray Scott's handsome visage as a design element, Ambrose is never more than a collection of villainous mannerisms; neither of these actors is capable of the meaty excess Nicolas Cage and John Travolta brought to *Face/Off.* Like all Woo films, *Mission: Impossible II* concludes with an extended action sequence of almost hallucinatory intensity. The finale—where Cruise and Scott face each other alone—is probably enough to ensure that mass audiences will go home sated. But Woo's fans may see the climax as an almost desperate litany of images and ideas downloaded from his earlier films. Is he trying to convince himself, or us, that he is still capable of things his imitators—almost everyone working in action cinema—are not? Or did his western admirers, snobbishly seduced by the subtitles, exotic locations and seemingly antiquated moral codes of his Hong Kong films, see something in John Woo that was never there?

VILLAGE VOICE, 6/6/00, p. 139, J. Hoberman

Unlike such philosophically grounded early-summer rivals as the Aurelian *Gladiator* and the Hubbardist *Battlefield Earth, Mission: Impossible 2* is refreshingly devoid of metaphysical ideas. John Woo's sequel to the 1996 blockbuster, designed to promote Tom Cruise as a viable action icon, is a vaguely absurd epidemiological thriller filled with elaborately superfluous setups and shamelessly stale James Bond riffs.

The Cold War is long over; Austin Powers has more than exhausted the spy genre's comic possibilities. All that remains is Woo's capacity for choreographed mayhem and king-sized clichés. Crash a plane before the credits; introduce the secret agent hero (Cruise or his stunt doubles) dangling by three fingers off a canyon wall. Cut to a back-lot Seville patched together from old issues of *National Geographic* to initiate the action courtship between Cruise and international jewel thief Thandie Newton—a meet-cute that plays somewhere between a lap dance and a demolition derby.

M:I-2 doesn't even care much for technology. Woo is content to posit a perfunctorily gadgetized world in which satellites and computers combine to create an atmosphere of Dr. Mabuse-like surveillance so total that a laptop can be used to supply a flashback when needed by the narrative. The baddies are threatening to unleash a hideous plague of gene-spliced influenza and then sell the world its antidote—in a nice instance of irrational exuberance, the villain (Dougray Scott, distinguished mainly by a thick brogue) wants stock options as well as money. Robert Towne, who diddled David Koepp's *Mission: Impossible* screenplay, supplied the script himself this time, but one doesn't attend a Woo film to hear Sir Anthony Hopkins vent his self-contempt by drawling, "This is not Mission Difficult—it's Mission Impossible."

Nor will the movie do much for the *Magnolia*-enhanced Cruise image. Bulked up but still boyish, Cruise is so theatrically hyperalert, nimble, and noble he might be starring in a grade school production of *Hiawatha.* Ultimately, Woo turns Cruise into a stalking, stomping, punch-and-pummel machine, but for most of the movie, the star-producer stands alone. (Given the director's track record, it seems likely that he would have wished to do more than employ latex face masks to facilitate the identity melding of hero and bad guy.) Ving Rhames's ace hacker is less a sidekick than a viewer surrogate. For much of the movie, he watches the action on his screen as though it were a primitive video game: "Hope he kills all the bugs before the yellow dot gets to the red one." Newton is an appropriately forlorn stray cat, never too stressed to wear a midriff-bearing T-shirt until, two-thirds of the way through, she takes a drug that turns her back into Beloved.

Woo pays homage to the midair stunt that was the centerpiece of Brian De Palma's even less interesting *Mission: Impossible,* but he doesn't pull out the stops until the bio-lab pulverization shoot-out, with Cruise skidding fearlessly across a glass-and-debris-strewn floor, both guns blazing. Never let it be said that John Woo is afraid to pour on the cheese—Cruise and Newton exchange supercharged looks across a room crowded mainly by the back-bending arabesque of the flamenco performer at center stage; Scott is used to balefully reflect a detonating grenade in his contact lens; the hero bursts through a flaming door accompanied by a swelling chorale and a crescendo of flapping pigeons.

For all this hoopla, *M:I-2* is less outrageous than *Broken Arrow* or *Face/Off* (let alone Woo's Hong Kong movies). Still, once all narrative pretense is suspended in the final 40 minutes, the director is contagiously content to riff on his own particular brand of action pyrotechnics. A somersaulting dead-shot with motorcycle getaway sets up the Evel Knievel jump across a burning bridge, allowing Woo to juxtapose a Mack truck broadside with Newton's solemn preparations for a cliff-top swan dive, then cut back for Cruise's no-hands swerve-and-skid across the path of a tumbling SUV.

The climactic seaside chopper joust has its share of explosions and near-miss eye gouges. It's a credit to Woo's relentlessly fanciful action ballet, however, that the coup de grace is a relatively low-tech (but utterly impossible) flying double kick to the head.

Also reviewed in:
CHICAGO TRIBUNE, 5/24/00, Tempo/p. 1, Michael Wilmington
NATION, 6/19/00, p. 35, Stuart Klawans
NEW YORK TIMES, 5/24/00, p. E1, A. O. Scott
NEW YORKER, 6/5/00, p. 82, Anthony Lane
VARIETY, 5/29-6/4/00, p. 19, Dennis Harvey
WASHINGTON POST, 5/24/00, p. C1, Stephen Hunter
WASHINGTON POST, 5/26/00, Weekend/p. 51, Desson Howe

MISSION TO MARS

A Touchstone Pictures release of a Jacobson Company production. *Executive Producer:* Sam Mercer. *Producer:* Tom Jacobson. *Director:* Brian De Palma. *Screenplay:* Jim Thomas, John Thomas, and Graham Yost. *Story:* Lowell Cannon, Jim Thomas, and John Thomas. *Director of Photography:* Stephen H. Burum. *Editor:* Paul Hirsch. *Music:* Ennio Morricone. *Music Editor:* Suzana Peric and Nick Meyers. *Choreographer:* Adam M. Shankman. *Sound:* Rob Young and (music) Dan Wallin. *Sound Editor:* Lon E. Bender and Maurice Schell. *Casting:* Denise Chamian. *Production Designer:* Ed Verreaux. *Art Director:* Thomas Valentine and Andrew Neskoromny. *Set Designer:* Peter Clemens, John Dexter, Kathleen Morrissey, Marco Rubeo, Carl Stensel, Janice Clements, Gary A. Lee, Richard Reynolds, Domenic Silvestri, Chris Stewart, and Suzan Wexler. *Set Decorator:* Lin MacDonald. *Set Dresser:* Cary Cooper, Jamie Westbury, Denyse Nelson, Gord Stewart, Steve Rowland, and John Werner. *Special Effects:* Hoyt Yeatman and John Knoll. *Costumes:* Sanja Milkovic Hays. *Make-up:* Charles Porlier. *Make-up (Gary Sinise):* Benjamin Robin. *Make-up (Tim Robbins):* Jeanne Van Phue. *Stunt Coordinator:* Jeff Habberstad and Melissa R. Stubbs. *Running time:* 113 minutes. *MPAA Rating:* PG.

CAST: Gary Sinise (Jim McConnell); Tim Robbins (Woody Blake); Don Cheadle (Luke Graham); Connie Nielsen (Terri Fisher); Jerry O'Connell (Phil Ohlmyer); Peter Outerbridge (Sergei Kirov); Kavan Smith (Nicholas Willis); Jill Teed (Reneé Coté); Elise Neal (Debra Graham); Kim Delaney (Maggie McConnell); Marilyn Norry, Freda Perry, Lynda Boyd, and Patricia Harras (NASA Wives); Robert Bailey, Jr. (Bobby Graham); Jody Thompson, Lucia Walters, and Pamela Diaz (Pretty Girls); Sugith Varughese (2nd Capcom); Story Musgrave (3rd Capcom); Mina E. Mina and Carlo Rota (Ambassadors); Dmitry Chepovetsky (Technician); Tracy Waterhouse (Sobbing Technician); McCanna Anthony Sinise (Young Jim McConnell); Chantal Conlin (Young Maggie); Jukka Joensuu (Priest).

CHRISTIAN SCIENCE MONITOR, 3/10/00, p. 15, David Sterritt

Despite a new millennium ahead, some normally adventurous filmmakers are turning back to time-tested formats.

"Mission to Mars" is inspirational fantasy with more than a touch of "2001: A Space Odyssey" woven into its plot. "The Ninth Gate" is an old-fashioned thriller that Boris Karloff or Bela Lugosi might have skulked through in bygone years. [See Sterritt's review of "The Ninth Gate."]

Movie fans think of many things when Brian De Palma's name is mentioned: violent thrills, over-the-top style, Hitchcockian suspense. What doesn't come to mind are streamlined science fiction and New Age clichés—yet "Mission to Mars" has plenty of both, filling the screen with equal measures of eye-dazzling grandeur and mind-numbing sentimentality.

The picture focuses on two missions to Mars. The first reaches an enigmatic end when its astronauts stumble onto a mysterious structure in the red planet's desolate landscape. Then a backup group tries to discover what happened. They encounter the same cryptic object, but their different response leads to a very different outcome.

"Mission to Mars" works best when De Palma cuts off the dialogue's oxygen supply and allows Stephen Burum's shimmering camera work to soar, transforming the clankily written screenplay into a striking visual experience. It's hardly an original movie, echoing ideas from "Forbidden Planet" and "Chariots of the Gods," to name just a couple of sources. But its cinematography is literally dizzying at times, proving that De Palma can still put on a good show even when its material isn't the freshest he might have found.

LOS ANGELES TIMES, 3/10/00, Calendar/p. 1, Kenneth Turan

"Nobody ever wanted Mars the way you two did."

"The control module doesn't have enough thrust."

"Come on, people, work the problem."

"Is that what I think it is?"

"Luke needs us now."

"He would have wanted you to have this."

"I didn't come 100 million miles to turn back in the last 10 feet."

Had enough yet? If you haven't, there's a whole lot more clunky, unconvincing and just plain bad dialogue left to sample in "Mission to Mars," a movie as cold and distant as the Red Planet itself

A notably lifeless film about the possibilities of life on Mars, "Mission" was written by Jim Thomas & John Thomas and Graham Yost from a story by Lowell Cannon and the Thomases. Between them these writers—and it's rumored that there were more—have credits on films such as "Predator," "Broken Arrow," "Hard Rain" and "Wild Wild West," so maybe the pained looks on actors Gary Sinise, Tim Robbins and Don Cheadle shouldn't come as any surprise.

Not listening very hard to these inept conversations was director Brian De Palma. Known for his virtuoso visual style, De Palma was understandably enthralled by the many technical challenges a story set almost exclusively in space vehicles and on the surface of another planet presented. As a result, "Mission to Mars" is often beautifully composed and worth looking at even when you're wishing there was some way you could turn off the sound.

Set in the near future of the year 2020, "Mission to Mars" begins, typically, with some of De Palma's trademark roving camera work servicing the dramatic dead zone, in this case a backyard barbecue and goodbye party for a team of astronauts headed for Mars.

Here's Mission Cmdr. Luke Graham (Cheadle), a caring scientist. Here's Woody Blake (Robbins), as much of a square-shooter as his "Toy Story" namesake, whose wife, Terri Fisher (Connie Nielsen), is an astronaut as well. And here's comic-relief colleague Phil Ohlmyer (Jerry O'Connell), trying without success to get unattached women to make his last night on Earth a memorable one.

The only person not here, in fact, is hotshot cover-of-Time-magazine pilot Jim McConnell (Sinise, looking, in his leather jacket and sports car, like the junior varsity version of Sam Shepard). Jim finally shows, but it's with a tear in his heart. And who could blame the guy: After training with his wife for 12 years to be the first couple on Mars, she was stricken with cancer and Jim could do no more than watch while the poor woman "wasted away in front of his eyes."

Luke goes to Mars with Jim's blessing, but then, wouldn't you know it, something sinister and inexplicable happens up there. Investigating a mysterious formation on the planet's surface, Luke and his team fall afoul of a fierce and unfriendly energy force that allows no more than a garbled message for help to reach the World Space Station.

Garbled or not, the message energizes Luke's pals Woody, Phil and Terri, who are determined to mount a rescue mission, no matter what the risk. And they insist on having grieving Jim, the space jockey's space jockey, sitting in the co-pilot's seat.

Of course, a whole variety of troublesome situations bedevil this intrepid crew once it's airborne. Even though the events surprise Woody, Phil, Terri and Jim, they will be more than familiar to anyone who's experienced even a bit of science fiction. All the film's plotting has a pro forma feeling to it and, without the kind of pizazz the "Star Trek" movie series manages to bring to similar material, the effect is deadly.

De Palma, working with his longtime cinematographer and editor (Stephen H. Burum and Paul Hirsch, respectively) and a veteran production designer (Ed Verreaux) who is new to his team, likely spent most of his energy trying to create luminous images out of "Mission to Mars'" numerous logistical challenges.

The film's press material, much more intriguing than what's on the screen, lets you know what was involved. Interior shots were done in a facility so large that parts of the Golden Gate Bridge were once constructed there, and 55 acres of the Fraser Sand Dunes outside of Vancouver were transformed into Mars with the use of thousands of square yards of "shotcrete, a sprayable form of concrete" and then spray-painted with "100 gallons of environmentally friendly Mars Red latex paint per minute. A total of 120,000 gallons of paint were used on the Martian surface."

The most striking images are those within the space vehicles themselves. One visual inside the recovery ship's living quarters used a 3½-story spinning wheel to simulate the spaceship's continual turning while the astronauts go about their daily business. It's a wonderful piece of filmmaking, but once any mouth is opened the magic is immediately tarnished. "Critical systems alert," one of the on-board computers announces at one point, and it's hard not to respond with a heartfelt "No kidding."

NEW YORK POST, 3/10/00, p. 57, Jonathan Foreman

If "Mission to Mars" weren't so boring it would have the fascination of a Dr. Moreau medical experiment gone hideously wrong.

A sickly hybrid of "2001: A Space Odyssey" (itself an overrated movie, especially when seen without the benefit of mind-altering drugs) and "The Right Stuff," it features well below par writing, acting, direction, special effects and music, while oozing a nauseating New Age sentimentality that undermines any tension in the underlying story.

The film starts with a crudely written barbecue scene introducing the main characters—all astronauts—together with their adoring spouses and cute kids. You learn that it's 2020, and host Luke Graham (Don Cheadle) is about to lead the first mission to the Red Planet.

As captain, Graham has taken the place of his pal Jim McConnell (Gary Sinise), who's still dealing with the death of his wife, a fellow astronaut (played in flashback by Kim Delaney of "NYPD Blue").

The mission is launched from an orbiting space station and lands successfully on Mars. But soon Graham's crew locates a strange geological formation; there's a gigantic wind storm (using effects left over from "The Mummy"); three of the four crew members are killed; and NASA loses contact with Graham.

The rescue mission immediately sent from Earth is led by Woody Blake (Tim Robbins), whose crew includes his wife, Terri (Connie Nielsen), a younger, wise-cracking astronaut named Phil (Jerry O'Connell) and the now rehabilitated McConnell.

All sorts of things go desperately wrong on the way to Mars, but thanks to the ingenuity and courage of the crew, they make it down to the surface. There they find Graham still alive—and discover a mountain in the shape of a giant face.

This version of the monolith in "2001 " could contain the secrets of Mars' history and of the origin of the human race.

The problem is not just the (literally) unspeakable writing, but also some atrocious acting. Robbins is particularly bad: He lacks a single believable moment on screen. But even fine actors like Cheadle and Sinise seem in a hurry to finish the job and get their paychecks.

The special effects are expensive but neither especially effective nor interesting.

Director Brian De Palma made his reputation with a series of cynical but witty homages to Hitchcock, but in this film neither he nor his trio of screenwriters seems to have a clue about science fiction.

NEWSDAY, 3/10/00, Part II/p. B6, Jan Stuart

Creationists and product placement police will be standing in line to fling mud at "Mission to Mars," a science-fiction pageant that puts forth a godless new theory for the earliest days of Earth and a shameless new strategy for goosing sales of Dr Pepper and M&M's.

Junk food flies all over this expensive Touchstone production through the combined forces of zero gravity, sublevel dialogue and weightless sentimentality. And as directed by Brian (Carrie-and-The-Untouchables-Wreak-Havoc-in-Slow-Motion) De Palma, it flies very, very languidly, simulating in its peppier moments the speed of a lava lamp bubble at the end of its tether.

The year is 2020, just far enough into the future that we can imagine NASA putting men and women on the red planet but not so far that Touchstone's wig department would have to freak out reinventing hairstyles. Three quarters of an international crew of astronauts have been wiped out by a spectacular cyclone-like eruption on Mars (in actuality sand dunes south of the Canadian planet of Vancouver, standing in with the help of red latex paint). one of them (Don Cheadle) remains alive.

As anyone who saw De Palma's "Mission: Impossible" knows, a first mission crew is entirely dispensable as long as a second, more charismatic crew remains to clean up the mess they left behind. So off goes a recovery team composed of veteran Jim McConnell (Gary Sinise), who pioneered Mars exploration with his late wife, Maggie (Kim Delaney, in gooey video flashbacks); Jim's buddy Luke Graham (Tim Robbins), Luke's beloved Terri Fisher (Connie Nielsen) and baby-faced Phil Ohlmyer (Jerry O'Connell, filling the pretty-boy slot that once gave us Fabian).

There is much mishegas impossible as the crew nears its destination. A series of awful mishaps and selfless heroics prompt such tense, Flash Gordon lines as "If we don't make it-!" "We don't have time!" "We're decompressing fast!" "It's not possible!" "It's impossible!" As rendered stoically possible by scriptwriting brothers Jim and John Thomas (those amazing "Predator" guys) and Graham Yost ("Speed"), "Mission to Mars" also promises a field day for fans of stiff-lipped techno-talk in the mode of "Seismic normal!" "Anamometer stopped!"

It's a wonder our pulses keep going. The more the crew hyperventilates, the more sluggish we become. The best visual effects happen in the film's first 20 minutes, leaving us to slog through an hour and a half before the big payoff, which turns out to be a demure Martian who resembles some cross between E.T. and Shirley Eaton in "Goldfinger" after the paint job.

One only hopes that Brian De Palma has been rewarded with cases of Dr. Pepper and M&M's to dine on while he considers his next oeuvre. Something more nutritious would be in order for his leading man, who is looking the worse for wear. Millions of dollars thrown at special effects, and they can't fix the bags under Gary Sinise's eyes.

NEWSWEEK, 3/20/00, p. 69, David Ansen

It's a shame that Brian De Palma's "Mission to Mars" is, on so many levels, a risibly bad movie. The characters are hackneyed, the dialogue is dismal and the concept takes the most overused ideas from such New Agey science-fiction fables as "Contact" and "The Abyss" and old Arthur C. Clarke novels and turns them into a mushy extraterrestrial Hallmark greeting card.

In the year 2020, a NASA mission to Mars encounters a mysterious phenomenon that wipes out the crew. A rescue mission (Gary Sinise, wearing too much eyeliner, Tim Robbins, Connie Nielsen and Jerry O'Connell) is sent to search for the one possible survivor (Don Cheadle). Once there, they encounter strange messages emanating from a giant metallic face buried in Mars's craggy soil. I won't reveal more except to say that whoever designed the spindles, cartoonish great-great-granddaughter of the "Close Encounter" aliens should be sent to bed without dinner.

Still, this is no ordinary bomb. It's a gorgeous bad movie, the folly of a great visual stylist. De Palma, relishing the optical possibilities of a weightless spacecraft and a barren Red Planet, pulls off one dizzingly elegant camera move after another. Great care has gone into the sets, the FX, the soundtrack, the lighting. At its best, this "mission" can cast a dreamy, hypnotic spell. Too bad movies have to have a story. And people talking. It would have made a swell silent.

SIGHT AND SOUND, 5/00, p. 54, Philip Strick

June 2020. Following the sudden death of his wife Maggie, astronaut Jim McConnell is replaced by Luke Graham as commander of *Mars One*, NASA's first manned flight to Mars. Landing 13 months later, Luke and his team report to Ray Beck at Mission Control that they plan to investigate a mysterious mountain in the Cydonia region. As they approach, the mountain explodes, killing Luke's colleagues. He manages one last scrambled message before being stranded on the planet with the mountains secret, a vast sculpted face.

NASA rushes the completion of *Mars Two* for a hastily assembled rescue mission, headed by Woody Blake, who insists on Jim McConnell as his co-pilot. Completing the team are Woody's wife Dr Terri Fisher and mission specialist Phil Ohlmyer. A year later, they reach Martian orbit but the ship is wrecked by meteorites. During their transfer to *Mars One*'s resupply module, Woody drifts uncontrollably away. Rather than burn up in the Martian atmosphere he removes his helmet and dies instantly.

Reaching Luke's encampment beside *Mars One*'s ERV (Earth return vehicle) the *Mars Two* survivors find Luke alive in a makeshift greenhouse. Studying the information he has assembled about the giant face, they theorise the structure has been broadcasting the equivalent of a DNA pattern. When they respond, an entrance suddenly opens. They venture inside the face, discovering a breathable atmosphere and a huge hologram of the solar system. A holographic alien 'guide' shows how, following a cataclysmic meteor impact in the distant past, most of the original Martians escaped to a remote galaxy. A few came to Earth, evolving over millions of years into the human race. Accepting the invitation to go "home", Jim is absorbed into the Martian ship stored inside the face and hurtles away into space. Terri, Luke and Phil set out on their return journey.

Originally spotted in 1976 by a Viking probe, the Face of Cydonia was identified as either an accident of lighting or a giant Martian artefact, according to preference. Especially when computer-enhanced, the Face demanded investigation no matter how many later probes recast it into the random dunes of its origin. Now that the Moon, while not exactly trodden flat, has become familiar and mundane, not a monolith in sight, it must suit NASA's ambitions and budgeting to encourage hints of fresh mysteries on the red planet where (regardless of such base parodies as Paul Verhoeven's *Total Recall* or Tim Burton's *Mars Attacks.*) signs of ancient wisdom might yet be uncovered.

While the end credits of *Mission to Mars* absolve NASA of any blame for the film's contents, there's a detectable element of self-promotion here, counterbalancing the dismal record of failures among the Mars missions so far. Although the physical NASA presence is confined to a glum, uncredited Armin Mueller-Stahl, the astronauts themselves embody all the heroism and resourcefulness of updates from *The Right Stuff*, while the grandeur of the space walks and planetary exploration sequences is like an exotic travel commercial, a refurbished *Destination Moon* to inspire a new generation of stargazers.

The irony of this vivid and highly pleasing display is that it embroiders and disguises a whole string of disasters, a process not without precedent in director Brian De Palma's work. Much of the story, in fact, happens offstage (such as the gaps between the opening Fourth of July picnic, the reunion months later and the entire flight of *Mars One)*, leaving us simply with selected highlights and cryptic references to what we haven't seen. Such abbreviations lead to an increasing puzzlement. Setting aside the delicate question as to how the presence of a married couple would affect unmarried crew members over a six-month confinement, there are symptoms of screenwriters' desperation in the business of *Mars Two's* vulnerability to a single burst of meteorites, and the seemingly effortless repair of what remains of *Mars One.*

Above all, the film's splendidly sculpted face—which, as will be expected by all post *2001: A Space Odyssey* (1968) observers, does indeed contain an alien message—remains crammed with unyielded secrets. It can't have been left by the original Martians as its educational video about evolution is too recent, although the surface was presumably carved sufficiently long ago to become deeply buried. The few Martians (who sensibly aimed for Earth instead of perversely undertaking the unimaginably arduous trip to some distant galaxy) seem in any case to have been fish-like, contriving with remarkable enterprise to evolve into dinosaurs and human beings by way of the buffalo. Now slightly resembling Disney cats and capable of shedding gentle tears, they are understandably silent amid the bedlam of Morricone's soundtrack. Their open invitation to join them among the stars, however, involves a preliminary drowning (a debt here to *The Abyss)* and is consequently rather less persuasive than the similar offer made to the pensioners of *Cocoon.*

That it is accepted nonetheless by Jim (Gary Sinise, well qualified to space out thanks to *Apollo 13)* gives the whole affair some kind of circularity, although De Palma was clearly thwarted from using some alien miracle to resurrect Jim's lost wife (too much like *Contact).* Instead, the departing spaceman is given glimpses from the film's earlier scenes, ending with a close-up of his wife giving a speech about life reaching for life. Combined with the spurious urgency of a threatened tempest, *Mission to Mars* concludes ingloriously with the catchphrase, "Have a great ride, Jim", a curious trivialisation of what could have been a memorable adventure. There's some throwaway fancy camerawork at the beginning and a repeat of his shock-shot trick from *Raising Cain,* but otherwise De Palma's own ride appears to be largely on autopilot, at its best when floating in space and when the cast is cavorting upside down to Van Halen's 'Dance the Night Away'. Whether the Face-makers have anything comparable remains to be seen.

VILLAGE VOICE, 3/21/00, p. 135, J. Hoberman

Among its many interesting factoids, *Spectres of the Spectrum* [see Hoberman's review] reveals that Nikola Tesla believed he was receiving signals from Mars. Too bad he didn't transmit them to Brian De Palma.

Mission to Mars is a movie to warm John McCain's heart—a rescue saga full of a touchy-feely esprit that's predicated on equal parts Buck Rogers bravado and backyard barbecue, the whole burnt burger drenched in Ennio Morricone's elegiac western-style score. Despite one unmistakable De Palma gag—a visual joke evoking the *Challenger* explosion—the project is scarcely more personal than *Mission: Impossible* . Who would have imagined the director would show so little interest in the Tinkertoy surveillance tractors used to explore the Martian terrain? Nor does he have much fun with sociological extrapolation. To judge from the fashions, music, and slang, the year 2020 is in the grip of a powerful '90s revival.

Suavely shot by De Palma's frequent collaborator Stephen H. Burum, *Mission to Mars* has its sensuous aspect. The weightless camera moves under, over, sideways, down. Everything is aestheticized. (Even the—here extremely—red planet might be the site of Constantin Brancusi's greatest project.) De Palma almost never cuts when he can use a slow dolly to close-up. The performances are less limber. Don Cheadle, Tim Robbins, and, most anxiously, Gary Sinise rush around pretending to be soldiers—although no one is as awful as Armin Mueller-Stahl as their blustering CO.

Despite an ending that out-Spielbergs the master, *Mission to Mars* mainly coarsens *2001* in its mix of cosmic consciousness and "naturalistic" product placement (Dr. Pepper bloblets and multicolored M&M's floating around the cockpit). As in the Kubrick trip, the middle voyage is best. Halfway through, De Palma literally explodes his narrative to orchestrate a superb deep-space float-opera replete with runaway modules, high-tech lassos, dramatic self-sacrifice, and, in the most surprising maneuver, a montage-driven modicum of actual suspense.

Also reviewed in:
CHICAGO TRIBUNE, 3/10/00, Friday/p. A, Michael Wilmington
NEW YORK TIMES, 3/10/00, p. E20, Elvis Mitchell
NEW YORKER, 3/20/00, p. 143, Anthony Lane
VARIETY, 3/13-19/00, p. 21, Todd McCarthy
WASHINGTON POST, 3/10/00, p. C1, Rita Kemply

MR. RICE'S SECRET

A Panorama Entertainment and Horizon Entertainment release of a New City Productions/Panorama Entertainment production. *Executive Producer:* David Forrest and Beau Rogers. *Producer:* Colleen Nystedt. *Director:* Nicholas Kendall. *Screenplay:* J. H. Wyman. *Director of Photography:* Gregory Middleton. *Editor:* Ron E. Yoshida. *Music:* Simon Kendall and Al Rodger. *Sound:* Ralph Parker. *Casting:* Carol Kelsay. *Production Designer:* Jillian Scott. *Art Director:* Eric Norlin. *Set Decoration:* David Birdsall. *Costumes:* Gregory Mah. *Stunt Coordinator:* Leslie Spongberg. *Running time:* 93 minutes. *MPAA Rating:* PG.

CAST: David Bowie (Mr. Rice); Bill Switzer (Owen Walters); Teryl Rothery (Marilyn Walters); Garwin Sanford (Stan Walters); Zachary Lipovsky (Funnel Head); Jason Anderson (Veg); Richard de Klerk (Simon); Tyler Thompson (Gilbert); Campbell Lane (Mr. Death); Tyler Labine (Percy); Eric Keenleyside (Ray); Colleen Rennison (Molly); Kyle Labine (Jonathan); Tim Dixon (Priest); Juno Ruddell (Cindy); Frank C. Turner (Thin Man); Shayn Solberg and Shayne Zwickel (Baseball Kids); D. Neil Mark (Coach); Peter Bryant (Umpire); P. Lynn Johnson (Doctor Vogel); Terry David Mulligan (Potential Buyer); Merrilyn Gann (Veg's Mom); Kevin Blatch (Mr. Death's Assistant).

NEW YORK POST, 12/20/00, p. 52, V.A. Musetto

This is an earnest, well-meaning film about a mysterious, centuries-old William Rice—played by none other than David Bowie—who befriends a 12-year-old boy (Bill Switzer) suffering from cancer, helping him cope with his fear of death.

Unfortunately, the narrative for this Canadian indie (originally called "Exhuming Mr. Rice") depends almost entirely on implausible plot twists and some unanswered questions, such as why Rice suddenly dies after being kept alive for 395 years by a glowing, blue elixir.

If you're in the mood for a centuries-old Bowie, check out the 1983 vampire flick "The Hunger" instead.

NEWSDAY, 12/22/00, Part II/p. B14, Jan Stuart

You have to tip your hat to any filmmaker who would hazard the thorny territory of children coping with terminal illness. But deference is about as much enthusiasm as one is able to muster for "Mr. Rice's Secret," a stilted Canadian mix of supernatural and reality in the connect-the-dots vein of after-school television specials.

Bill Switzer plays Owen, a precocious boy of 12 or so years who is losing the battle to remain upbeat as he struggles with Hodgkin's disease. He tries his best to be one of the guys, despite the fact that his energy level is unpredictable and his hair is significantly depleted from chemotherapy. And his one ray of light, a beatific neighborhood mystic named Mr. Rice (David Bowie) who tried to show Owen how to embrace life, has just passed away.

As Owen wrestles with the remainder of his own mortality triggered by his mentor's death, he embarks upon an elaborate treasure hunt of riddles and messages that Mr. Rice has left behind for him to decode. Owen's search is emotionally complicated by the specter of death that he sees everywhere, most notably in the rapidly diminishing health of Simon (Richard de Klerk) a cancer-clinic buddy with leukemia.

Owen's hostility toward Simon is the one glimmer of credibility in this hokum-drenched film, which plays off such stereotypical adolescent terrors as fat bullies and dour morticians who scowl like Jacob Marley's ghost.   J.H. Wyman's wooden script has Owen holding impassioned conversations with tombstones and his best friend saying such things as, "Owen, I hope you find whatever it is you are searching for."

Polly Draper's superb "The Tic Code," about a boy Owen's age with Tourette's syndrome, demonstrated that it was possible to make a movie about kids and disease with subtlety and sophistication. "Mr. Rice's Secret" may have a future as a staple of those dreaded assemblies one was always herded to in junior high school. Given its worthy subject matter, one wishes its creators appreciated Ms. Draper's secret, which is that kids are smarter than this.

Also reviewed in:
NEW YORK TIMES, 12/22/00, p. E28, Elvis Mitchell
VARIETY, 7/10-16/00, p. 27, Ken Eisner

MOON SHADOW

A Promofest release of a Les Films du Dauphin/Odusseia Films and Sidereal Productions presentation. *Producer:* Roberta Manfredi and Alessandro Olivieri. *Director:* Alberto Simone. *Screenplay (Italian with English subtitles):* Alberto Simone. *Director of Photography:* Roberto Benvenuti.   *Editor:* Enzo Meniconi.   *Music:* Vittorio Cosma.   *Sound:* Remo Ugolinelli. *Production Designer:* Andrea Crisanti. *Costumes:* Beatrice Bordone. *Running time:* 82 minutes. *MPAA Rating:* Not Rated.

CAST: Tcheky Karyo (Lorenzo); Nino Manfredi (Salvatore); Isabelle Pasco (Luisa); Jim van der Woude (Agostino); Johan Leyson (Titto); Mimmo Mancini (Filippo); Paolo Sassanelli (Michele).

NEW YORK POST, 12/1/00, p. 53, Lou Lumenick

The de-institutionalization of mental patients is the theme of "Moon Shadow," a very sentimental 1995 Italian film making its belated American bow at Cinema Village.

Tcheky Kayro, the Turkish-born actor who played the French officer in "The Patriot," stars as Lorenzo, an emotionally distant Milanese mathematician who inherits a crumbling villa in Sicily.

He wants to unload the property quickly as it carries unhappy childhood memories, but it isn't that simple. He hires a crew to fix up the place, led by Salvatore, a crusty old handyman played by the great Italian actor Nino Manfredi ("Bread and Chocolate").

It turns out that Salvatore's workers, including his son, are part of a community of mentally ill people led by a doctor whose unconventional therapy eschews drugs and confinement.

This first film written and directed by Alberto Simone, who has a background in advertising and psychology, contains some fine performances—particularly Isabelle Pasco as Luisa, a member of the community whose affections Lorenzo ethically can't reciprocate.

But its four-hankie climax goes way over the top.

NEWSDAY, 12/1/00, Part II/p. B6, Jan Stuart

If "Cinema Paradiso" and "Life Is Beautiful" are any evidence, few countries can make us lunge for our Kleenex at the sight of a loving father and son as quickly, or with as much abandon, as Italy.

The father-son pairing that cajoles our tears in "Moon Shadow," much like the one that drives "Cinema Paradiso," is actually a surrogate relationship. Thirty-nine-year-old mathematician Lorenzo (Tcheky Karyo) has spent the better part of his life without a father, who died when he was a child. And the elderly peasant worker Salvatore, whom he ends up befriending (Nino Manfredi), has a grown son of his own.

The conspiracy of fate and the heart that can transform strangers into family propels these two together in "Moon Shadow." When Lorenzo is pulled away from his research on black holes to repair damage at his family's abandoned country villa, he is exasperated by the laid-back work regimen of his enlisted helper Salvatore and his trio of childlike assistants. Soon, it becomes clear that the three assistants (who include Salvatore's son, Agostino) are tenants of a nearby mental clinic.

The clinic's maverick director Titto (Johan Leyson) encourages Lorenzo to volunteer his talents in the clinic's programs, which include music, art and video-making therapy. But the overly controlled Lorenzo is frightened by the anarchic impulses of the patients and resists the doctor's overtures. As the uptight mathematician becomes friendlier with the warm-spirited Salvatore and observes his selfless devotion to the unstable Agostino, Lorenzo's reserve begins to melt and he begins to uncover long-buried places in the heart.

If you aren't able to write this movie after the first 10 minutes and are not put off by movies that fawn over the innocence of the mentally challenged, then perhaps this one is right up your alley. What keeps "Moon Shadow" from being a total piece of sentimental claptrap are the integrity of performances and the direction by Alberto Simone, whose video-mediated monologues for the clinic patients lend them a much-needed dimensionality. It's a sweet-tempered little picture, hard not to like and just as hard to get excited about.

VILLAGE VOICE, 12/5/00, p. 141, Jessica Winter

Alberto Simone's *Moon Shadow* is partly inspired by the work of the late psychiatrist Franco Basaglia, who in the early '70s founded a series of neighborhood clinics for the mentally ill in northeastern Italy, in order to provide an alternative to the massive asylum where patients were previously treated. Basaglia's success is re-created in the film with a fairly tranquil community residence in Sicily, stumbled upon by "city slicker" Lorenzo (Tcheky Karyo) when he returns to his childhood house to oversee its renovation. Contrived symmetries begin accumulating upon his arrival: Though Lorenzo is a scientist who studies black-hole theory, he soon learns—with the aid of his wry handyman, Salvatore (Nino Manfredi)—that hypothetical bodies in far-off space are of small importance compared to the concrete concerns of both their troubled young neighbors and the salvaging of Lorenzo's home.

Moon Shadow offers lovely, reverent shots of the azure seaside and the verdant decrepitude of Lorenzo's estate. But the script's relativity-of-knowledge pretensions extend uncomfortably to its portrayal of the mentally ill, who are provided with rote flashes of profundity. Simone lacks the matter-of-factness that the material would seem to require: Both the very existence of the clinic and the fact that Salvatore has a son among its patients are introduced as big-secrets-revealed, but none of the faintly condescending attentions paid to the mentally ill characters can mask their narrative purpose as a simple means for Lorenzo to wake up to the world outside his study. That said, if *Moon Shadow* does sometimes overcome its sentimentalism and faulty parallels, it's because the film is altogether unburdened by cynicism.

Also reviewed in:
NEW REPUBLIC, 12/18/00, p. 22, Stanley Kauffmann
NEW YORK TIMES, 12/1/00, p. E25, A. O. Scott
VARIETY, 2/20/95, p. 83, David Rooney

MOST TERRIBLE TIME IN MY LIFE, THE

A Viz Films/Tidepoint Pictures release of a Film Detective Office/For Life Records/Shutter Pictures production. *Executive Producer:* Yutaka Goto and Yoshiharu Saga. *Producer:* Shunsuke Koga, Kaizo Hayashi, and Yu Wei Yen. *Director:* Kaizo Hayashi. *Screenplay (Japanese with English subtitles):* Kaizo Hayashi and Daisuke Tengan. *Director of Photography:*

Yuichi Nagata.   *Editor:* Nobuko Tomita.   *Production Designer:* Takeo Kimura.   *Art Director:* Takeo Kimura.   *Costumes:* Masae Miyamoto.   *Running time:* 92 minutes.   *MPAA Rating:* Not Rated.

CAST: Masatoshi Nagase (Maiku Hama); Kiyotaka Namba (Hoshino); Shiro Sano (Masaru Kanno); Yang Haitin (Yang Hai Tin); Hou De Jian (De Jian); Kaho Minami (Bai Lan); Akaji Maro (Lt. Nakayama); Shinya Tsukamoto (Yamaguchi); Jo Shishido (Joe); Haruko Wanibuchi (Lily Hama); Mika Ohmine (Akane Hama); Masako Miyachi (Masako); Kenji Anan (Kitamura); Zen Kajiwara (Iwasaki).

NEW YORK POST, 8/25/00, p. 59, Jonathan Foreman

The best thing that can be said about this kitschy, black-and-white pastiche of '50s B thrillers—that fairly brims with the Japanese equivalent of smirky film-student movie references—is that it's stunningly lit.

It also touches on a subject rarely talked of in Japan: the difficulties Asian immigrants face in a homogenous, often xenophobic, society.

But thanks to wildly variable direction, dialogue and performances, it's mostly an unfunny, rather dull affair.

VILLAGE VOICE, 8/29/00, p. 140, Dennis Lim

Drunk on B-movie love, Kaizo Hayashi's gumshoe homage *The Most Terrible Time in My Life* offers welcome evidence in the post-*Austin Powers 2* age of nth-degree reflexivity that the art of retro-kitsch plunder doesn't have to be mere necrophilia. Made in 1993, this black-and-white CinemaScope curio boasts an impeccable pedigree: It reaches back not only to classic noir but (more so) to nouvelle-vague attitude-fests and to the nuttily anarchic yakuza variants cranked out by Japanese studios throughout the '60s, most famously by polymorphous genrefucker Seijun Suzuki. Hayashi's protagonist is a Yokohama private eye and onetime juvenile delinquent called Maiku "Mike" Hama (his real name, he insists). His office doubles as the projection booth of a repertory theater (where, in a title-providing incidental, *The Best Years of Our Lives* is playing), and the clerk downstairs browbeats Maiku's clients into buying tickets, greeting their protests with harrumphing incomprehension: "If you don't see movies, you're finished."

Maiku, it's safe to say, not only sees movies but commits them to memory. As played by art-movie displacement icon Masatoshi Nagase (who drifted through Memphis in *Mystery Train,* Hong Kong in *Autumn Moon,* Iceland in *Cold Fever),* our hero—with his nifty threads, lacquered hair, perfectly angled cigarette, and sunglasses at night—is an endearingly loopy vision of monochrome cool. Driving around in a shiny vintage Metropolitan, spurred on by a bachelor-pad bongos-and-brass soundtrack, Maiku works hard at a Spillane-worthy exterior, though it crumbles with amusing ease and regularity. The poor klutz sheepishly endures all manner of physical and verbal abuse—from low-life tough guys, a growling-cop nemesis, his demented mentor (a cameo by Seijun Suzuki regular Shishido Jo), even his teenage sister. (The director studied to be a detective, and the film comes with a puzzling "recommendation" from the Japan Association of Detective Agencies.)

The violence has a prominent absurdist component—when an irascible thug lops off Maiku's finger, the severed digit has to be retrieved from a drooling mutt. But the japes eventually cede to a surprisingly sober and ruminative portrait of bloody gang warfare. Substituting male bonding for femme fatale obsession, Hayashi hinges the noirish plot on Maiku's kinship with a seemingly naive Taiwanese waiter, who hires him to find his long-lost brother. Consequent entanglements with a ring of naturalized immigrants known as the "New Japs" allow for a pointed study of xenophobia in the multiethnic port city. Playfully deploying exaggerated angles and dramatic chiaroscuro, Hayashi—as he previously proved with the vaudeville parable *Circus Boys*—delights in genre pastiche. But for all its rampant cine-snob knowingness, this is, at heart, a work of infectious, unironic affection. *Most Terrible Time,* the first of a trilogy, redresses its solemn conclusion with the most uplifting possible coda: a trailer for *The Stairway to the Distant Past,* the second Maiku Hama adventure.

Also reviewed in:
CHICAGO TRIBUNE, 6/30/00, Friday/p. G, John Petrakis
NEW YORK TIMES, 8/25/00, p. E10, Dave Kehr
VARIETY, 5/23/94, p. 59, Dennis Harvey

M. V. P: MOST VALUABLE PRIMATE

A Keystone Releasing release of a Keystone Family Pictures presentation of a Funk Monkey production. *Executive Producer:* Robert Vince, Michael Strange, and Anne Vince. *Producer:* Ian Fodie. *Director:* Robert Vince. *Screenplay:* Anne Vince and Robert Vince. *Director of Photography:* Glen Winter. *Editor:* Kelly Herron. *Music:* Brahm Wenger. *Sound:* Sebastian Salm. *Sound Editor:* Marc Chiasson. *Casting:* Ellie Kanner and Lorna Johnson. *Production Designer:* Brian Davie. *Art Director:* Liz Shelton. *Set Decorator:* James Willcock. *Special Effects:* Bill Ryan. *Costumes:* Cali Newcomen. *Make-up:* Dana Hamel. *Running time:* 93 minutes. *MPAA Rating:* PG.

CAST: Kevin Zegers (Steven Westover); Jamie Renee Smith (Tara Westover); Russell Ferrier (Darren); Rick Ducommun (Coach Marlowe); Oliver Muirhead (Dr. Peabody); Lomax Study (Dr. Kendall); Alexa Benette Fox (Jane); Jane Sowerby (Julie Beston); Ingrid Tesch (Susie Westover); Philip Granger (Mark Westover); Aaron Smolinski (Pete); Shane Vajda (Moose); Trevor Roberts (Larry); Ray Galletti (Magoo); Myles Ferguson (Waterboy); Stanley Katz (Einsteen); Dave Thomas (Willy Drucker); Patrick Cranshaw (Super Fan); David Lewis (Organist); Miles McNamara (University Dean); Nick Misura (Ticket Master); John B. Lowe (Conductor); Kirby Morrow (Tiger #1); Debra Donohue (Reporter); Dolores Drake and Christine Willes (Ladies); Jay Brazeau (Harry); Darryl David (Referee); Ralph J. Alderman (Fred); Frank C. Turner (Bart); Ann Warn Pegg (Lucy); Campbell Lane (Melvin); Lois Dellar (Teacher); John Harris (Vikings' Coach); Helen Honeywell (Secretary); Rob Lee (Ticket Agent); Jim Hughson (Don); Mark McConchie (Sam Richard/Coach of Senior League Team); Aaron Moore (Hockey Player); Ryan Northcott (Stosh).

LOS ANGELES TIMES, 10/20/00, Calendar/p. 6, Gene Seymour

[The following review by Gene Seymour appeared in a slightly different form in NEWSDAY, 10/20/00, Part II/p. B7.]

Word has leaked all over my neighborhood of what I do for a living. Even the animals at the zoo are on to me now. It's a problem.

"Do you realize," the senior baboon in the ape house chided me this past summer, "how long it's been since there's been decent roles for monkeys in movies?"

I start making a faint case for "George of the Jungle," but the baboon would have none of it. "That was some twit in a monkey suit," he snorted.

"So was King Kong," I said, but I knew that wouldn't shut him up.

"Cheetah," the baboon sighed. "Now there was a true star. Doesn't anyone in Hollywood respect tradition?"

It was a waste of time to argue. Indeed, the whole conversation was a waste of time, and the only reason I bother remembering it now is because "MVP: Most Valuable Primate" made me think that maybe—just maybe—we've all missed real apes in movies more than we'd realized.

The title character is, ostensibly, a real chimpanzee named Jack (played, according to the movie's credits, by three chimps named Bernie, Mac and Louie), who has been living the plush life as the subject of a college behavioral experiment.

When the experiment suddenly ends, the school wants to ship Jack, who is by now something of a mental marvel, to a biological testing center. Instead, a "friendly janitor" packs up Jack and sends him on a train back to his nature preserve in Northern California.

Wouldn't you know? Jack sleeps past his stop and ends up way up in snowy northern British Columbia, where the Nelson Nuggets, a minor-league hockey team, are about to begin another season of futility.

So what does one have to do with another? The movie takes a painfully long time to get to that answer, but what happens is that Tara (Jamie Renee Smith), a young deaf girl, finds Jack in the woods. Tara and her hockey-playing brother Steven (Kevin Zegers) discover Jack has a way with the skates and stick, and somehow he's allowed to play with the Nuggets, who, of course, begin beating back everyone in Jack's path.

Not even my baboon friend would agree that the world was desperate for an amalgam of "Mystery, Alaska" and "E.T. the Extra-Terrestrial." Still, pacing aside, "MVP" is a pleasant way for 5 to 11-year-olds to pass the time and relatively painless for anyone older to endure. The humor may be as low and broad as King Kong's ankles, but if it aimed any higher it would be embarrassing to anyone, regardless of their place on the evolutionary food chain.

NEW YORK POST, 10/20/00, p. 50, V.A. Musetto

Remember those "Air Bud" movies about dogs that play basketball and football? Now, from the same producers, comes this sweet little comedy about a hockey-playing chimpanzee.

His name is Jack and he's part of a college study of how primates and humans interact. Thanks to a series of improbable mishaps, he finds himself in snowy Nelson, Canada, where he joins a pathetic high school ice hockey team and brings happiness to a lonely little girl (adorable Jamie Renee Smith) with a hearing problem.

From the start, adults won't have any trouble predicting where the movie is going. Kids won't be as savvy. And they'll enjoy watching Jack (portrayed by three chimps preparing breakfast, playing checkers, getting tucked into bed, and gliding across the ice as he makes a monkey (ugh!) out of opponents.

Even parents might find themselves having fun.

Also reviewed in:
CHICAGO TRIBUNE, 10/20/00, Friday/p. G, Patrick Z. McGavin
NEW YORK POST, 10/10/00, p. E26, Lawrence Van Gelder
VARIETY, 10/23-29/00, p. 43, Robert Koehler

MY DOG SKIP

A Warner Bros. release of an Alcon presentation of a Mark Johnson/John Lee Hancock production. *Executive Producer:* Jay Russell and Marty Ewing. *Producer:* Mark Johnson, John Lee Hancock, Broderick Johnson, and Andrew A. Kosove. *Director:* Jay Russell. *Screenplay:* Gail Gilchriest. *Based on the book by:* Willie Morris. *Director of Photography:* James L. Carter. *Editor:* Harvey Rosenstock and Gary Winter. *Music:* William Ross. *Music Editor:* Jim Harrison and Sherry Whitfield. *Sound:* Steve C. Aaron and (music) Robert Fernandez. *Sound Editor:* Charles Maynes. *Casting:* Mindy Marin and Marshall Peck. *Production Designer:* David J. Bomba. *Set Decorator:* Tracy A. Doyle. *Special Effects:* Stephen Bourgeois and Matthew Zeringue. *Costumes:* Edi Giguére. *Make-up:* Pamela Roth. *Stunt Coordinator:* Jeff Habberstad. *Running time:* 95 minutes. *MPAA Rating:* PG.

CAST: Frankie Muniz (Willie Morris); Diane Lane (Ellen Morris); Luke Wilson (Dink Jenkins); Kevin Bacon (Jack Morris); Mark Beech (Army Buddy); Susan Carol Davis (Mrs. Jenkins); David Pickens (Mr. Jenkins); Bradley Coryell (Big Boy Wilkinson); Daylan Honeycutt (Henjie Henick); Cody Linley (Spit McGee); Lucile Doan Ewing (Aunt Maggie); Polly Craig (Grandmother Mamie); John Stiritz (Grandfather Percy); Caitlin Wachs (Rivers Applewhite); Elizabeth Rice (Rivers' Friend); Nate Bynum (Man on Street); Stacie Doublin (Woman on Street); Bill Butler (Barney); Winston Groom (Mr. Goodloe); Katherine Shoulders (Mrs. Applewhite); Nathaniel Lee (Sammy); Joann Blankenship (Miss Abbott);

Hunter Hays (Accordion Boy);   Cannon Smith (Bible Boy);   Courtney Brown (Snake Girl); Brian Witt (Armpit Boy);   Clint Howard (Millard);   Peter Crombie (Junior Smalls);   Jerome Jerald (Waldo Grace);   Jordan Williams (Lt. Hartman);   John Sullivan and Stuart Greenwell (Hunters);   Harry Hood (Baseball Coach); Gordon Swaim (Umpire);   Owen Boutwell and Chaon Cross (Spectators); Jim Fraiser (Veterinarian); Graham Gordy (Pump Jockey); Michael Berkshire (Older Willie);   Wayne Wimberly (Older Spit);   Josh Yates (Older Henjie);   James Thweat (Older Big Boy); Harry Connick, Jr. (Narrator).

LOS ANGELES TIMES, 1/12/00, Calendar/p. 5, Kevin Thomas

Based on Willie Morris' 1995 memoir, "My Dog Skip" is a standard-issue Hollywood family film about a boy and his dog growing up in a Southern small town during World War II. As such, it fills the bill without transcending it. It's a little too glossy, Skip a bit too much the trained performer—he's played by two perfectly matched Jack Russell terriers—and William Ross' omnipresent score far too syrupy and trite.

A big plus, however, is the naturalism of Frankie Muniz as the 8-year-old Willie, a lonely only child, the son of an overprotective yet taciturn father (Kevin Bacon), embittered by losing a leg in the Spanish Civil War and, luckily for him, an independent and imaginative mother (Diane Lane), who defies her husband's wishes in giving her son a dog for his 9th birthday.

The father believes that something is sure to happen to the animal and will only cause his son heartbreak he thinks the boy is not mature enough to handle. His wife considers this nonsense, and the dog, swiftly adored by one and all, in fact proves a vital catalyst in helping her son to relate to other children and build self-confidence. The usual adventures and life lessons ensue.

Of course, "My Dog Skip" is heavy on the nostalgia, and production designer David Bomba deserves much credit for a flawless period re-creation; the '40s are just near enough and far enough away in time to be treacherous. Bomba understands that the impact of the Depression, especially in a small Mississippi town, means that its citizens are not going to have much that is new, so he goes easy on the Streamline Modern and even Art Deco. He also realizes that even after Pearl Harbor there aren't many signs yet that we are at war, at least in rural Mississippi.

As the picture progresses, however, director Jay Russell and writer Gail Gilchriest let younger generations in on a secret: If you are about the same age as Morris, the distinguished editor and author who died of heart failure at 64 last August, you know that World War II was a wonderful time to be a child—provided its grimmer battlefront realities didn't affect your family directly. Indeed, the selfless sharing that permeated American society "for the duration," creating close-knit extended families and friendships, gave kids a false impression of a seamlessly harmonious and unified America. In that light, it's to "My Dog Skip's" credit that it deftly acknowledges—and deplores—segregation.

Bacon and Lane are fine in what are definitely supporting roles, as is Luke Wilson as a local athlete hero who discovers in battle that he is not afraid to die but has no taste for killing. "My Dog Skip" ends with a flash-forward to Morris leaving home to attend Oxford, where he was a Rhodes scholar after graduating from the University of Texas. Morris later became the youngest ever editor of Harper's, at age 32. He later returned to the South and became a prolific and prestigious writer until his death.

NEW YORK POST, 1/12/00, p. 49, Lou Lumenick

You might be tempted to walk out during the first 10 minutes of "My Dog Skip," an often lovely adaptation of late magazine editor Willie Morris' memoir of his 1940s childhood in Mississippi.

But resist the urge.

Introducing sleepy Yazoo City as "10,000 souls and nothing doing," the omniscient narrator (Harry Connick Jr.) recalls that "the cotton grew tall that summer of 1942—but I sure didn't."

And this: "My father was stern and overbearing ... it seemed like along with the leg he lost [in the Spanish Civil War], he also lost a piece of his heart."

Finally, after many more such groan-worthy observations, the narrator shuts up long enough to let the camera and actors tell the story of how shy, bookish Willie's life was transformed—by Skip, a Jack Russell terrier he received as a present on his ninth birthday.

Employing a notably lighter touch than Gail Gilchriest's screenplay, director Jay Russell (a documentary maker whose only previous feature was the underrated "End of the Line") offers finely observed anecdotes of a boyhood in a long bygone era, including a brush with moonshiners in a cemetery.

Young Frankie Muniz is very authentic and touching as Willie, who grew up to become a Rhodes scholar and the legendary editor of Harper's magazine (he died last year). With Skip's help, Willie becomes accepted by his peers and even gets to hold hands with the prettiest girl in school (Caitlin Wachs).

Kevin Bacon and Diane Lane give subtle, rounded performances as Willie's concerned parents. Luke Wilson is even better as a star-athlete neighbor who Willie idolizes—until he returns from World War II as an AWOL drunk.

The movie is on less firm footing when it comes to racial matters, alternatively condescending to blacks and attempting to explain segregation by observing that "dogs are a whole lot smarter than men."

On the whole, "My Dog Skip," splendidly photographed in glowing colors by James Carter, grows on you like kudzu.

NEWSDAY, 1/12/00, Part II/p. B9, Jan Stuart

The yearning that oozes through "My Dog Skip," the new film version of Willie Morris' childhood memoir, is dense enough to cut with a Swiss army knife. The opening credit sequence alone is a sigh-filled nostalgia crawl past every icon of lost American boyhood imaginable: a spinning top, a slingshot, a copy of "Huckleberry Finn," a leather catcher's mitt, a photo of a boy and his dog and, unless memory fails, a Swiss army knife.

It is not long before we realize that the longing expressed by this roasted marshmallow of a movie is for a time when flicks about boys and their dogs mattered. Dogs still count, for sure: the live-action "101 Dalmatians" made a splash as recently as 1996, but little boys were largely irrelevant in a scenario in which the chief lure continued to be a villainess with big hair and a baroque fashion sense. And as anyone who kissed off last year's remake of "A Dog of Flanders" will tell you, that old soft spot for boys and their dogs has given way to a hard respect for boys and their desktops.

Set in the sleepy Yazoo City, Miss., of 1942, "My Dog Skip" finds the former Harper's Magazine editor Willie Morris as a wimpy 8-year-old, slight-framed, bookish and friendless but for the big-brother camaraderie of the high school idol who lives next door (Luke Wilson). As played by Frankie Muniz, of the freckly faced Alfalfa school, Willie exudes the sort of slick orator's charisma during a show-and-tell presentation that makes you slightly sympathetic to the class bully who constantly plagues him.

Against the will of his cranky war-vet father (a prune-faced Kevin Bacon), he is given a Jack Russell terrier pup by his mother (Diane Lane) for his birthday. Presto change-o, Willie comes alive, the chubby bully cozies up and the local butcher showers the dog with slices of bologna. In real life, Skip was an English fox terrier, but producers invariably haul out the Jack Russells whenever they want an impish, non-threatening creature who can jump like a Mexican bean, imitate their owners in adorable ways and make the audience sigh "awwwww" in unison.

The now-classic 1983 "A Christmas Story," which also harked back to a writer's 1940s childhood, broke the mold on how to present a family reverie that flatters the kids in its audience as it amuses their parents. Watching "My Dog Skip" is akin to falling into a Saturday Evening Post cover of your wooziest imaginings: The banal voice-over narration by Harry Connick Jr., combined with the gooey score and feckless direction adds up to a sterilization of American life that makes Norman Rockwell look like Diane Arbus.

SIGHT AND SOUND, 9/00, p. 44, Amanda Lipman

Yazoo, Mississippi, 1940. Willie is a shy only child, who is bullied by his peers. His closest friend, local sporting hero Dink, sets off to fight in World War II. On Willie's ninth birthday, his mother gives him a puppy, which he names Skipper. With his dog at his side, Willie makes friends with a little girl, Rivers.

Forced by his former bullies, whom he has befriended, to spend a night in the cemetery, Willie chances on a couple of bootleggers who threaten to kill Skip if the boy gives them away. Dink returns home from the war, a reclusive drunk. Playing baseball, Willie is on bad form. When Skip leaps on to the field, Willie hits him. Skip runs off, Willie spends the rest of the day looking for him. Skip hides in the cemetery where he breaks all the bootleggers' bottles. One of them attacks him with a spade, just as Willie arrives with Dink who knocks the bootlegger out. Skip recovers. As an adult, Willie recalls how Skip and he remain inseparable until he left for university at Oxford. There, Willie gets a letter from his parents saying Skip has died.

Based on Willie Morris' memoir of growing up in the 40s, *My Dog Skip* is a glowing slice of nostalgia, all sleek cars, corner drugstores and crisp shirts. Here everyone, from the poor white trash to the segregated black families, gleams with an unassailable wholesomeness. If director Jay Russell raises prickly issues, he soon smooths them over to concentrate on the main action, the relationship between young Willie and his dog Skip. So while we see white folk going to the cinema through one door and black folk through another and hear Willie's white friends jeer when he becomes a keen supporter of Waldo Grace, a local black sports hero, it's all rather uncontroversial. Everything is seen through Willie's innocent eyes, without concession to the sensibilities and expectations of a critical modern, adult audience.

In this safe American idyll, Adolf Hitler is no more than a joke, a name at which Willie trains Skip to growl. Admittedly, Willie's world becomes a little more complicated when his friend Dink returns from the war an alcoholic wreck, only to be lambasted by the townspeople as a coward. There are hints of Boo Radley, the shy but kindly figure in *To Kill a Mockingbird* in this reclusive, evasive war veteran, whom nobody except a child understands, and who is forced, thanks to the determined effort of this child, to growl finally that it wasn't the dying he was afraid of during the war but the killing. But the film's focus on the relationship between the boy and his dog keeps such darker moments to the background. This central storyline has its share of strong scenes, particularly those in which Willie visibly relaxes, loses his habitual scowl and sheds his little old man cares—largely because of the cute antics of the effervescent Jack Russell playing Skip, who responds to all Willie's commands eagerly but wrongly.

Kevin Bacon—who featured in Russell's 1988 film *End of the Line*—plays Willie's sensitive, rather depressed father who lost a leg in the Spanish civil war and can't help being over-protective of his son. He and Diane Lane, as Willie's feisty but tender mother, do their be with the little they are given. But it's hard to get a sense of how they fit into Willie's world, perhaps because the boy is so focused on his dog. In one scene, as father and son walk through the countryside Willie asks his dad about his losing a leg. But the moment of intimacy is lost: instead the scene centres on Willie's first encounter with death as a deer is shot. The rite of passage is particularly poignant for showing how Willie's father can't protect him from bad things in life. But the strength of this scene also, owes a lot to the fact that in *My Dog Skip* such moments are rare.

Also reviewed in:
CHICAGO TRIBUNE, 3/3/00, Friday/p. O, Monica Eng
NEW YORK TIMES, 1/12/00, p. E1, A. O. Scott
VARIETY, 1/10-16/00, p. 109, Robert Koehler
WASHINGTON POST, 3/3/00, Weekend/p. 45, Desson Howe

NEW EVE, THE

A Sceneries Distribution release of a Centre National de la Cinématographie/Gémini Films/La Sofica Sofinergie/Le Studio Canal+/Madragoa Films/Arte France Cinéma production. *Producer:* Paulo Banco. *Director:* Catherine Corsini. *Screenplay (French with English subtitles):* Catherine Corsini and Marc Syrigas. *Director of Photography:* Agnes Godard. *Editor:* Sabine Mamou. *Sound:* Dominique Gaborieau and Laurent Poirier. *Sound Editor:* Regis Muller and Waldir Xavier. *Casting:* Brigitte Moidon and Richard Rousseau. *Production Designer:* Solange Zeltoun. *Art Director:* Solange Zeitoun. *Set Decorator:* Yves Jouen, Arnaud Puman, and

Christian Sapet. *Special Effects:* Christophe Messaoudi. *Costumes:* Anne Schotte. *Make-up:* Sylvia Carissoli. *Running time:* 94 minutes. *MPAA Rating:* Not Rated.

CAST: Karin Viard (Camille); Pierre-Loup Rajot (Alexis); Catherine Frot (Isabelle); Sergi Lopez (Ben); Mireille Roussel (Louise); Nozha Khouadra (Solveig); Laurent Lucas (Emile); Valentine Vidal (Sophie); François Caron (Le psy); Frédéric Gélard (Octave); Jean-François Gallotte (Sophie's Father); Gisèle Joly (Sophie's Mother); Alain Baudy and Emmanuel Quatra (Frisés); Philippe Lehembre (Old Man); Vincent Winterhalter (Gilles); Morgane Lombard (Fabienne); Pierre Baux (Denis); Simon Bakhouche (Doctor); François Forêt (Waiter at the Café); François Sakalauskaite (François); Christopher Loizillon (Costume Man); Hélène Alexandridis (La Femme PS); Olivier Jahan (Shy Man); Aurélia Petit (Blond Girl); Dominique Charpentier (Woman); Michel Jeanjean (Hypermarché Employee); Louise Moureau and Jeanne Moureau (Daughters of Alexis); Benoît Penven and Tibault Penven (Twins); Thibault Boitier (Child); Charly Sital (Brother); Vanessa Sital (Sister); Isabelle Hetier (Florence); René Hernandez (Lecher); David Léotard (Alexis's Twin); Olivier Bouthillier (Barrois); Emmanuel Doucet (Man in Sex Shop).

LOS ANGELES TIMES, 8/4/00, Calendar/p 18, Kevin Thomas

When the headstrong heroine of the shrewd romantic comedy "The New Eve" says she believes in always speaking the truth, she isn't kidding. Karin Viard's Camille is an attractive Parisian perhaps in her mid-20s who works as a lifeguard during the day and parties hard at night. Camille tends to go too far, drinking too much, staying out too late and getting sick as a result. Self-absorbed and reckless, she is a frequent pain in the neck to her friends, but she is also bright and vivacious.

One day in the street, a man, Alexis (Pierre-Loup Rajot), notices she is clearly unwell and asks if he can help her. This simple act of human kindness has more of an impact upon her than any of her countless casual affairs. When she meets him again at her brother's home, she knows she has fallen in love as never before.

Alexis is trim, 40-ish, bald, neither handsome nor homely but clearly sensitive and intelligent. He is a Socialist Party official, and in no time Camille is attending party meetings, where she is not shy about speaking up—even when she has no idea what she's talking about. Alexis finds her amusing and one evening invites her to his apartment for a warm beverage. Anticipating romance, Camille is shocked to discover that he is married to an elegant and attractive economics professor (Catherine Frot) and has two small daughters.

Devastated but unable to resist becoming a part of Alexis' life, Camille declares her love for him. Director Catherine Corsini and her co-writer Marc Syrigas have well spent nearly half of their film getting to this point, introducing us into Camille's world, that of the single, free-spirited modern woman—the "New Eve."

Camille can be exasperating, but she's also engaging in her determination to be her own person and to place honesty before politeness. Alexis is much lower-key but is capable of candor, pointing out to Camille that she puts people down without committing herself to anything, pushing herself too far so that she becomes ill and has to be taken care of by friends, and loves their attention.

So begins Camille's journey of self-discovery, sometimes funny, more often painful—which Corsini suggests is what all adults must be prepared to undergo if they are to be truly liberated and responsible for their lives.

Viard, who won a best actress Cesar for the not-yet-arrived "Haut Les Coeurs" ("Chin-Up"), meets the challenge of playing Camille wholeheartedly and without playing for undue sympathy. Rajot's Alexis is persuasive as a mature man surprised to discover he may not know himself as well as he thought, and Frot is spot-on as a wife who may feel a little too secure in her marriage.

Husky Sergi Lopez, so good as the traveling shoe salesman in Manuel Poirier's memorable "Western," plays Alexis' truck-driver friend, who sees himself as Camille's Mr. Right. Mireille Roussel and Nozha Khouadra play a lesbian couple, Camille's best friends, a source of stability in her life.

"The New Eve" is a beautiful film that flows with a luminous ease and assurance.

NEW YORK POST, 5/5/00, p. 52, Jonathan Foreman

"The New Eve" is a dryly funny French take on "Fatal Attraction" that comes down firmly on the side of an obsessive "other woman."

Unpretentious and often witty, it's emotional punch is weakened by spotty performances, especially from Karin Viard in the lead role.

Camille (Viard)—who looks like a cross between Diane Keaton and Barbra Streisand—is a willful, determinedly single Parisian who works at a swimming pool.

Her personal life mainly consists of getting drunk and then having sex with strangers.

Then she meets political activist Alexis (Pierre-Loup Rajot, one of those unconventionally handsome French leading men) and falls in love before learning that he's married, with children.

Alexis loves his wife, Isabelle (Catherine Frot), and has no interest in an affair. But Camille stalks him, even joining the Socialist Party just to be near him.

Eventually, the two do pair up, but Alexis breaks it off.

Camille is in despair, but because it's a French movie she doesn't try to kill anyone.

Instead she returns to her life of debauchery—at one point getting punched out in a lesbian bar—and then gets married to a former lover, a sado-masochistic truck driver named Ben (Sergi Lopez).

VILLAGE VOICE, 5/9/00, p. 134, Amy Taubin

Stubborn and demanding, impulsive and libidinous, Camille (Karin Viard), the hero of Catherine Corsini's *The New Eve*, is not an easy woman to like, let alone love. Camille is not, as such characters are often described, a force of nature or a manifestation of pure id. Rather, she is in rebellion against culturally prescribed feminine behavior. Her rebellion is conscious and willed, although not always controlled, and hardly ever strategic. At family gatherings, Camille proclaims her hatred of couples, monogamy, and the hypocrisy of a bourgeois, settled life. In sexual situations, she insists on being the aggressor. Of course, Camille is not as independent or impervious to other people's feelings as she'd like to be. She wants to be loved and cherished, but only on her own terms. Alcohol gives her false courage. At parties, she drinks herself into a stupor, relying on her best friends, a lesbian couple (Mireille Roussel and Nozha Khouadra), to put her to bed and clean up the vomit.

Coming home from a doctor's visit, muttering to herself like a bag lady, she stumbles in the street, sending bottles of antidepressants flying in all directions. A man comes to her rescue, helping her to her feet and gathering up her parcels. In gratitude, she flings herself weeping into his arms. The more he tries to disengage, the more she clings to him. For her, it's love at first sight. The man, Alexis (Pierre Loup Rajot), turns out to be a friend of her brother. That he's married and has two children does not discourage her relentless pursuit. She refuses to give up, even when Alexis tells her flat out that he's not interested in either leaving his wife or taking a mistress.

If this sounds vaguely familiar, it's because *The New Eve* is an update on Howard Hawks's sublime screwball comedy *Bringing Up Baby*, albeit more earthbound and sexually explicit. Camille is the willful, outrageous Katharine Hepburn character, but without the physical delicacy, scatterbrain act, and upper-class sense of privilege. Alexis is the repressed, professorial Cary Grant character, duty-bound to his wife just as Grant's character was to his fiancée, Miss Swallow. Corsini is interested not in the physical comedy that makes *Bringing Up Baby* such a joy but rather in the mutual attraction of a woman and a man with diametrically opposite personalities. She's a hysteric; he's an anal retentive. They irritate and infuriate each other, but they're also never so alive as when they're together. *The New Eve* is less about a woman's struggle for independence than about her fear of losing that independence by committing to a man. Since there are no easy answers to this dilemma, the film has an ending that befits a romantic comedy and yet is sufficiently ambivalent to qualify as feminist and progressive.

Slight and prematurely balding, Rajot is no Cary Grant, but he's a great foil for Viard, who won a César—the French equivalent of the Oscar—for her performance. Viard is tall, angular, and rather clumsy, with wary eyes, a hungry mouth, and more nervous tics than Parker Posey. The actress's courage—her downright recklessness—is similar to that of the character she plays. Viard never compromises Camille's abrasiveness or her scary mood swings in the interest of making herself more attractive. *The New Eve* takes its shape from her performance, which is as big as life.

Also reviewed in:
NEW YORK TIMES, 5/5/00, p. E27, Stephen Holden
VARIETY, 2/15-21/99, p. 61, Lisa Nesselson

NEW WATERFORD GIRL

An Alliance-Atlantis release of a Sienna Films/Imagex production. *Executive Producer:* Christopher Zimmer, Ted East, and Victor Loewy. *Producer:* Jennifer Kawaja and Julia Sereny. *Director:* Allan Moyle. *Screenplay:* Tricia Fish. *Director of Photography:* Derek Rogers. *Editor:* Susan Maggi. *Music:* Geoff Bennett, Longo Hai, and Ben Johannesen. *Sound:* Alastair Gray. *Sound Editor:* Paul Virostek. *Production Designer:* Emanuel Jannasch. *Set Decorator:* Norma Jean Sanders. *Costumes:* Debra Hanson. *Running time:* 97 minutes. *MPAA Rating:* Not Rated.

CAST: Liane Balaban (Agnes Marie "Mooney" Pottie); Tara Spencer-Nairn (Lou Benzoa); Andrew McCarthy (Cecil Sweeney); Mary Walsh (Cookie Pottie); Nicholas Campbell (Francis Pottie); Cathy Moriarty (Midge Benzoa); Darren Keay (Lexter Pottie); Kevin Curran (Joey); Krista MacDonald (Betty-Anne Pottie); Cassie MacDonald (Darlene Pottie); Adrian Dixon (Felix Pottie); Patrick Joyce (Darcy Benzoa); Lorne Pardy (Father Madden); Mark McKinney (Doctor Hogan); Susan Laney Dalton (Sandra); Stacy Smith (Lisa); Zach Fraser (Meeker); Jody Richardson (Mickey); Dave Frances (Pickles Kavanaugh); Sarah Whittier (Tammy); Patricia Zentilli (Patty); Mike MacPhee (Derek); Lori LeDrew (Bonnie); Ida Donovan (Mrs. Roach); Rudy Pilchie (Karl); John Dunsworth (Roddy); Gordon White (Angelo); Maynard Morrison and Bette MacDonald (Fry Cooks); Gordon Gammie (Businessman); Marguerite McNeil (Elderly Woman & Boxing Mom #1); Tricia Fish (Noreen); John Goodrich (Twitchy Guy); Stephen Gillis (Guy #1); Laurel MacDonald (Charlene); Colleen MacIsaac (Canteen Clerk); Sarah Loveridge (Red Haired Woman); Aaron Armstrong (Sandy MacPhee); Blair Boone (Referee); Ashley MacIsaac (Town Fiddler); Sam White (Announcer); Dugald McLaren (Hockey Player).

NEW YORK POST, 7/26/00, p. 57, Jonathan Foreman

"New Waterford Girl" presents yet more proof that independent cinema can be as prone to recycled cliché as Hollywood, and that Canada's industry has a particular tendency to churn out predictable, edgeless, politically correct fare, oddly reminiscent of TV's movies of the week here in the U.S.

It's a coming-of-age story about an arty, black-wearing outsider (yawn) in a tiny, gritty Irish-Catholic mining town on the attractively windswept coast of Nova Scotia.

Mooney (Liane Balaban) is a smart, cultured 15-year-old (though, of course, she looks 21), who cannot bear the rubes and morons she has grown up with.

The only person in New Waterford on her wavelength is her teacher, Mr. Sweeney (Andrew McCarthy), a refugee from the big city who lives in a trailer on a cliff. He's trying to get Mooney a scholarship to art school in New York.

Mooney's life is changed when Lou (Tara Spencer-Nairn), a spirited girl from The Bronx, turns up in town with her dance-instructor mother (Cathy Moriarty, once again looking and sounding like a drag queen).

Lou and Mooney become pals and together come up with a plan to get Mooney out of New Waterford.

The dialogue by Tricia Fish, who actually grew up in New Waterford, sounds authentic but tends toward the achingly obvious.

Under the direction of Allan Moyle ("Pump up the Volume"), Nairn, McCarthy and Balaban give confident, believable performances but overacting plagues the rest of the cast.

NEWSDAY, 7/26/00, Part II/p. B11, Jan Stuart

Ever since Duddy Kravitz took an apprenticeship at the school of hard knocks, the coming-of-age film has upstaged smoked salmon as a favored export from Canada. Lea Pool's marvelous "Set Me Free" was the happiest recent surprise in an endless wave of teen-angst pictures that seem to speak for a maturing Canadian film industry that is itself coming into its own.

Allan Moyle's lively but self-conscious "New Waterford Girl" offers evidence that all Canadian coming-of-age films are not created equal. Set in a scenic but hardscrabble Nova Scotian coal mining town in the mid-1970s, it follows the burgeoning friendship between a bookish 15-year-old misfit named Mooney Pottie (Liane Balaban) and a tough-skinned new girl in town named Lou (Tara Spencer-Nairn).

Any film that calls its characters Mooney Pottie and Cookie Pottie (Mooney's conservative-minded mother) is flirting with precious comic territory. Writer Tricia Fish presses down hard on the whimsy pedal. "New Waterford" is the sort of rough-and-tumble Irish Catholic community where nasty girls are reduced to saps at the sight of a Virgin Mary statue and folks are so poor that a woman is likely to hold her husband's wake at her daughter's wedding to cut expenses.

In this milieu, the Bronx emigre Lou becomes a surrogate Joe Palooka, punching out guys who have done their girlfriends wrong. With her aid, Mooney does her best to subvert her good-girl reputation without ruining it. Both actresses look older than their supposed mid-teen years, a fact barely camouflaged by the ruinous pigtails foisted on Balaban and the mopey internal monologue she recites. Fish-eye lens effects are also used in the hard-sell attempt to make this otherwise striking actress look gawky. There are echoes of a young Audrey Hepburn in "Sabrina" and Rita Tushingham in "Girl With the Green Eyes," but the overall impression she makes is unconvincing and irritating. Andrew McCarthy comes off best in a subtle performance as a schoolteacher whose self-repressed ardor for Mooney registers as testiness.

VILLAGE VOICE, 8/1/00, p. 112, Amy Taubin

Mooney Pottie puts sparkles on her science-class diagrams of fallopian tubes, which isn't the only reason that everyone in the small Nova Scotia town of New Waterford regards her as a bit mental. A wildly imaginative 15-year-old, Mooney lopes around town with her face in a book and her long-limbed body wrapped in thick oversized sweaters and ankle-length skirts. As played by newcomer Liane Balaban, whose dark-haired Pre-Raphaelite beauty could stop traffic in Nolita, she looks like a Brontë or Yeats heroine—those are clearly her role models despite her talent for foul-mouthed repartee. Mooney is determined to get out of New Waterford, and when her parents forbid her to accept a scholarship to an art school in New York, she comes up with a plan of escape that's "devious, sinful, and inspired."

Directed by Allan Moyle, who showed his affinity for creative, eccentric kids in the underrated *Pump Up the Volume* and *Empire Records* and for the chemistry between teenage girls in *Times Square, New Waterford Girl* is a tender and hilarious vision of female adolescence. The script by Tricia Fish, based on her memories of growing up in New Waterford during the '70s, privileges Mooney's point of view. She's alienated from her family and schoolmates, all of whom regard her as a freak, but her desire to leave is tinged with ambivalence. New Waterford may be a one-street town, but the Nova Scotia coast has a rough, romantic beauty, and the closer Mooney comes to getting out, the more she feels the pull of the place. Moyle shows us Nova Scotia through Mooney's eyes—a gray sky softly edged with pink at sunset, a brilliantly blue wooden house, a brick alley where pimply boys grope girls they've known since childhood and sometimes get them pregnant.

In too many recent movies, when girls bond, murder and mayhem soon follow. But when Lou Benzoa (Tara Spencer-Nairn) and Mooney Pottie get together, they bring out the best in each other. Lou and her mother (Cathy Moriarty) have moved from the Bronx to hide out until, as Lou puts it, "the stink wears off." The stink has something to do with Lou's boxer father, who taught her a move or two before he was sent to jail. Lou is as extroverted and impulsive as Mooney is defensive and introspective. The two of them ride around in Lou's beat-up convertible, and

Mooney starts to live in the here and now, instead of escaping into her head. If Mooney is looking for a way out, Lou is trying to learn the rules and adapt to life in a small Irish Catholic town, where just a mention of the blessed Virgin is enough to make potential sinners stop dead in their tracks. The local girls peg Lou as a "fuckin' Toronto lesbo bitch" (they can't imagine that she's come from as far away as New York), but she wins them over by using her fists to punish their two-timing boyfriends.

Balaban is a remarkably concentrated actor with a mercurial intelligence, a quick tongue, and an ability to communicate what's left unsaid. *New Waterford Girl* is her film, but in their scenes together, Spencer-Nairn is fully her match. Moyle has a gift for putting young actors at ease, and he also gets subtle comic performances from Mary Walsh and Nicolas Campbell as Mooney's parents and Andrew McCarthy as the teacher who nurtures her talent and is also madly in love with her. Just before they go their separate ways, he grabs Mooney and kisses her. By then, there's probably no one in the audience who isn't longing to do the same.

Also reviewed in:
NEW YORK TIMES, 7/26/00, p. E1, A. O. Scott
VARIETY, 9/20-26/99, p. 87, Brendan Kelly

NEXT BEST THING, THE

A Paramount Pictures and Lakeshore Entertainment release of a Lakeshore Entertainment production.   *Executive Producer:* Gary Lucchesi, Ted Tannebaum, and Lewis Manilow. *Producer:* Tom Rosenberg, Leslie Dixon, and Linne Radmin.   *Director:* John Schlesinger. *Screenplay:* Thomas Ropelewski. *Director of Photography:* Elliot Davis. *Editor:* Peter Honess. *Music:* Gabriel Yared. *Music Editor:* Andrew Dorfman. *Choreographer:* Kim Blank. *Sound:* Douglas Axtell and (music) John Richards. *Sound Editor:* Terry Rodman. *Casting:* Mali Finn. *Production Designer:* Howard Cummings. *Art Director:* David S. Lazan. *Set Designer:* Noelle King, Barbara Mesney, and Randall Wilkins. *Set Decorator:* Jan K. Bergstrom. *Costumes:* Ruth Myers. *Make-up:* Mary Burton. *Running time:* 107 minutes. *MPAA Rating:* PG-13.

CAST: Madonna (Abbie);   Rupert Everett (Robert);   Benjamin Bratt (Ben);   Michael Vartan (Kevin); Josef Sommer (Richard Whittaker);   Malcom Stumpf (Sam);   Lynn Redgrave (Helen Whittaker);   Neil Patrick Harris (David);   Mark Valley (Cardiologist); Suzanne Krull (Annabel); John Carroll Lynch (Abbie's Lawyer);   Fran Bennett (Judge);   Illeana Douglas (Elizabeth Ryder);   Stacy Edwards (Finn);   Ricki Loez (Angel);   Ramiro Fabian (Flavio);   Tiffany Paulsen (Young Mother);   Joan Axelrod (Bel Air Matron);   George Axelrod (Bel Air Man); Jack Betts (Vernon);   William Mesnik (Ashby);   Irene Roseen (Lena); Gavin Lambert (Ricky); Thomas Bankowski (Omar);   Glenn Sakazian (Glen);   Terrance Sweeney (Priest at Funeral); Anna Garduno (Coffee Shop Waitress); Frank James (Dad at Airport);   Linda Larkin (Kelly); Tom Burke (Tom, Annabel's Husband);   Benjamin Koldyke (Kelly's Boyfriend);   Marie Chambers, Lee Lucas, and Glenn Tannous (Party Guests);   Caitlin Wachs (Rachel);   Maxx Tepper (Kyle);   Jesssica Sara (Kid 3);   Katelin Petersen (Kid 4);   Holly Houston (Yoga Student);   Kimberly Davies (Hostess);   Alvin H. Einbender (Male Diner);   Laurent Schwaar (Restaurant Manager);   Patrick Price (Maitre d');   Michael Arnon (Waiter);   Jay Karnes (Kevin's Lawyer).

CHRISTIAN SCIENCE MONITOR, 3/3/00, p. 15, David Sterritt

[*The Next Best Thing* was reviewed jointly with *What Planet Are You From?*; see Sterritt's review of that film.]

LOS ANGELES TIMES, 3/3/00, Calendar/p. 6, Kenneth Turan

Trying to cheer up gay best pal Robert (Rupert Everett) after the AIDS-related death of one of his friends, Abbie (Madonna) takes a kitchen moment in "The Next Best Thing" to say she knows just what she wants in the way of funeral arrangements. "Cut me up," she says gaily, "and stuff me in this freezer next to those frozen pizzas for the next 100 years."

Any room in that freezer for this inadequate, unauthentic, indigestible film? Chopped up or whole, that's where it belongs.

A misguided romantic serio-comedy aimed at women and gay men that ends up caricaturing both, "The Next Best Thing" takes what could have been a real situation and fills it with bogus, badly written moments. And its sourness about human relationships is remarkable in a film that's nominally celebrating inclusiveness and new kinds of families.

While Everett and Madonna, good friends in real life, have been eager to work together, the pairing does credit to neither one. Playing an ordinary citizen (albeit one described as "smart, beautiful, a good cook and great in bed"), Madonna is less believable than she was as a dictator's wife ("Evita") or a wax-dripping dominatrix ("Body of Evidence").

The plain truth is that being a convincing actress is not among Madonna's considerable talents, and, in a kind of Gresham's Law of Cinema, her deficiencies are a drag on the good work of Everett, usually one of the most charming and irresistible of actors. But not here.

On the other hand, Madonna is as much a victim as her co-star is of Thomas Ropelewski's trite script and John Schlesinger's disconnected direction. How much could any actress do with lines like "I'm cowering behind a flowerpot in my courtyard"? As for Schlesinger, who's made some of the most memorable films of the past decades ("Midnight Cowboy," "Darling") and some of the least ("Honky Tonk Freeway," "Madame Sousatzka," "Pacific Heights"), his emotional tone-deafness brings to mind director Arthur Hiller's late, unlamented "Making Love."

"The Next Best Thing" opens with a standard cross-cutting introduction of Robert and Abbie at their respective occupations. He's a handsome L.A. landscape architect and she's a supple yoga instructor who's not above baby-sitting her students' children while she's teaching a class.

Herself a committed yoga student and workout fiend (the film provides some discreet glimpses of the results of her dedication), Madonna has to pretend to be a woman worried about being too old and over the hill to attract and hold a man. Typecasting this is not.

While Abbie's in the dumps about the breakup of her latest relationship with music business hotshot Kevin (Michael Vartan) and Robert's mourning the death of his friend, the two spend an inebriated Fourth of July together and end up having sex just as the fireworks go bang. (No, I am not making this up.)

Naturally, Abbie gets pregnant, and when she decides to keep the baby it's Robert who's faced with a decision. Should he commit to full-time parenthood with Abbie or should he have a V-8? His gay friends, her female friends, his barely there parents (Lynn Redgrave and Josef Sommer) all have different opinions, but Robert agrees with the person who says, "There's a certain crazy logic to this," and decides to seize the opportunity and create a new style of family unit.

Even at these preliminary stages, when everything is light and fluffy, no one seems to realize how callow and unappealingly self-absorbed these characters tend to play. Abbie gets drunk and encourages Robert to completely wreck his employers' house, but we're supposed to be charmed by their insouciance. Ditto when Robert pretends to be an effeminate queen to completely humiliate Abbie's ex, guilty only of breaking up with her. How completely amusing. It's a tendency that only gets worse.

Six years now pass so magically that, though neither Abbie nor Robert look as much as a single day older, in the blink of an eye they now have a handsome young son (Malcolm Stumpf). Robert, who has had boyfriends, tells Abbie to do the same. "You're not just a mother," he says with a straight face, "you're a woman." Later, Abbie pulls at the skin around her eyes to see if she can make her wrinkles disappear. Unfortunately for the scene's dramatic punch, the camera hasn't allowed her to have any in the first place.

Then, mistaking her mellow ashram for a power gym, handsome Ben ("Law & Order's" Benjamin Bratt) walks into Abbie's life. He's a hotshot New York investment banker out on the coast to close a big deal. Suddenly these unlikely love birds have eyes only for each other. But what about Robert? Has anyone thought about him? Has anyone thought about anything except him or herself?

"The Next Best Thing" has designs on getting serious at this point, but because it's neglected to put in any kind of foundation the story can't bear the additional weight.

With characters so reluctant to consider other points of view, it's difficult to even pretend to care as they get loud and unpleasant and cope with fake crises and even more fake resolutions.

It's like watching an "Afterschool Special" trying to transform itself into "The Sopranos." Not in this lifetime.

NEW YORK, 3/13/00, p. 87, Peter Rainer

As a pop performer and recording artist, Madonna still bestrides the world like a colossus, but she's never been a movie star. The brassy sass that makes her a pop-cult diva seems to work against her on film. She's one of the least sexy of screen presences, because there's no vulnerability to her, no softness. When she tries to play someone who's yielding and caring and hurt, as she does in John Schlesinger's *The Next Best Thing*, she turns into a mopey blank; the hard sheen of her allure doesn't lend itself to softer shades. As Abbie, an unlucky-in-love yoga instructor whose gay best friend, Robert (Rupert Everett), has presumably fathered her child, Madonna never gets a chance to show off her vaunted chemistry with her co-star; she's too busy being winsome and victimized. And victimization has never worked well for her in the movies. (It doesn't work for Sharon Stone, either, another vamp diva best observed in the predatory mode.)

As a result, Rupert Everett has to carry the movie pretty much on his own, something he seems revved up to do anyway. With *My Best Friend's Wedding* and now this, Everett has officially become Hollywood's Designated Gay Actor; he snaps out the film's sitcom-ish comedy lines as if he were still appearing in the film version of Oscar Wilde's *An Ideal Husband,* and when the film takes a weepy turn as Robert and Abbie battle for custody of the boy he has raised with her, he sparkles with a four-carat anguish. Everett is an entertaining hambone, but too much of a case should not be made for the sexually liberating effects of his screen persona. Camp is camp, whether it's aboveground or underground, and as for *The Next Best Thing*, it mostly plays like a none-too-inspired multiple-choice variation on Hollywood's standard parenthood-and-custody playbook.

NEW YORK POST, 3/3/00, p. 45, Jonathan Foreman

There hasn't been a Hollywood "message" movie as smug or cheesy as "The Next Best Thing" in quite a while. The film's main idea is to teach all the narrow-minded folk in the audience to be more tolerant of "different" families and to push for adoption laws friendlier to gay people.

Then there's the movie's apparent secondary mission: to advertise the benefits of yoga as evidenced by Madonna's impressively defined—and constantly exposed—shoulders and triceps.

If the movie were funny, the implicit sermonizing would be more tolerable, but apart from four or five good one-liners, "The Next Best Thing" is a thudding failure as a comedy.

In some sequences, the cast's timing is so bad you could be watching a high school play. Not that it's necessarily the actors' fault. After all, they and director John Schlesinger are saddled with a dreadful, cloying screenplay by Thomas Ropelewski ("Look Who's Talking Now.")

Every fag-hag cliché is here (most straight men are jerks or boors), and at the same time, the movie is even less comfortable with—or courageous about—gay sex than "Inside Out."

Straight Abbie (Madonna) and gay Robert (Rupert Everett) are best friends who've reached their late 30s without finding Mr. Right. One drunken night after a friend's funeral, they end up having sex.

Abbie later discovers she is pregnant and decides Robert would make the perfect father. He accepts the challenge, and they move in together. Before you know it, their child, Sam (Malcolm Stumpf), is 6 years old and flourishing in the middle of a happy menage.

Robert continues to date men, but they come second to the demands of fatherhood; Abbie is celibate.

But when handsome investment banker Ben (Benjamin Bratt) turns up at her yoga studio, Abbie falls for him, Robert gets jealous, and the household starts to fall apart.

Abruptly, the movie shifts its point of view from Abbie to Robert, and Abbie suddenly morphs into a spiteful, selfish witch. Robert has to sue Ben and Abbie for custody of his son, and it's only a matter of time until a climactic "Kramer vs. Kramer" courtroom confrontation.

For the first half of the movie, Madonna speaks with an unexplained English accent that draws attention to the singer's apparent inability to read a line. By comparison, Everett's performance seems pretty good, though he has the acting range of a pet rock.

The whole movie takes place in a fake Hollywood world of perfect and vast, multimillion-dollar houses, even though Madonna and Everett respectively play a yoga teacher and a landscape gardener.

NEWSDAY, 3/3/00, Part II/p. B2, Jan Stuart

Fifteen years after exhorting us to get into the groove, Madonna is still desperately seeking screen legitimacy. Perhaps desperation is too severe a term to describe the pop superstar's movie quest, which she has pursued with the same sort of try-anything brashness with which she has modeled her concert work. For all her efforts—and there have been some creditable ones—Madonna has yet to find her movie groove.

Unlike songbirds Barbra Streisand and Bette Midler, whose histrionic vocalizing translated naturally and effectively into dramatic roles, Madonna rarely acted in her recordings. Her most charismatic film appearances have been those that reflected the metallic limitations of her singing: the emotionally remote and overproduced "Evita," the strident "Dangerous Games" (a docu-style drama in which she plays an actress making a movie), and "Dick Tracy," in which she confidently embodies a cartoon chippie who tosses off such self-kidding zingers as "You don't know whether to hit me or to kiss me—I get a lot of that." Madonna could be a newfangled Carole Lombard, if only there were a writer prickly enough to feed her the ammunition.

Such a wizard is absent from "The Next Best Thing," in which she impersonates a lovelorn yoga instructor named Abbie who begets a son with her gay best pal, a gardener named Robert (Rupert Everett, exuding the ease and cockiness we have come to expect from him). Abbie and Robert are the latest step in that comic bonding dance popularized by "The Object of My Affection": the heterosexual gals and homosexual guys who dress each others' wounds suffered on the battlefield of romance. Men, these Wills and Graces sigh as they clink martini glasses: You can't live with 'em and you can't live without 'em.

In the case of Robert, one too many drinks with Abbie leads to a temporary meltdown of sexual orientation and a very permanent baby boy. Initially put off by the idea of parenthood, Robert moves in with Abbie, embracing his fatherly role to the point of abandoning a love life altogether. Everything is hunky-dory until Abble swoons for one of her students, Sam (Benjamin Bratt), a corporate go-getter with a physique that makes Madonna's arduously buffed body look like a wax figurine left out in the sun too long.

Written by Thomas Ropelewski, "The Next Best Thing" initially has the listless air of a comedy that wants to get by on the strength of its gay-positive cheer alone. Dry humor is Rupert Everett's Wheaties: When Ropelewski pitches him a couple of peppy lines, he handily bats them out of the park. But director John Schlesinger bungles the script's awkward leaps between insouciance and respectful gravity toward Robert's gay milieu. An AIDS funeral cogently points up the tensions between a gay man's family and extended family; by contrast, the freewheeling drunk that leads to Abbie's pregnancy is depressingly unfunny.

"The Next Best Thing" completely unravels when Abbie falls in love and Robert inexplicably turns into the gay brother from another planet. As he goes ballistic with insecurity, the film undermines its own assertion, which is that gay men can make great parents. Suddenly, we're in an ugly courtroom scene—ripped off lock, stock and barrel from a fine Martin Donovan vehicle called "Hollow Reed"—where we wonder: who are these people? Is it possible that these mature, renegade parents never discussed the inevitability of partners coming into their lives?

Left with scraps while her real-life chum Rupert Everett gets the choice morsels, Madonna is charmless and plastic. She has our sympathies. How is a material girl supposed to compete when all the Carole Lombard parts are now being written for guys?

NEWSWEEK, 3/13/00 p. 66, David Ansen

Rupert Everett is making a habit of playing a straight woman's friend. Playing more or less the same gay role in "The Next Best Thing" he did in "My Best Friend's Wedding", Everett once again waltzes away with the picture. But this time the perfect friendship runs into trouble. Everett is the L.A. landscape architect Robert. His best friend is single yoga teacher Abbie (Madonna). On a night of too many cocktails and '30s show tunes, Robert and Abbie become lovers for the first and last time. Lo and behold, she becomes pregnant, and the two soulmates agree to raise their child together. They will live together as mom and dad, but not as husband and wife.

It's a rich subject for a movie but the glossy, schizoid "The Next Best Thing" has little clue what to do with it. Initially, John Schlesinger's movie aims for romantic-comedy insouciance. This is a tone Everett could master in his sleep, but Madonna, for all her other talents, has never been an effortless screen presence. She acts as if she were pumping iron—with grim determination. The two stars may be great pals in life, but there's little magic in their on-screen partnership.

For the first six years, Abbie and Robert's design for living is a smashing success. (The messy early years of their son's life disappear in an abrupt cut from Sam's birth to his 5th birthday.) So where's the dramatic conflict? It arrives, with a vengeance, in the form of nice investment banker Ben (Benjamin Bratt), a very slick but none-too-interesting fellow who falls in love with Abbie and threatens to take her and the boy with him to New York. Devoted dad Robert freaks; suddenly (and implausibly) a thin but amiable comedy morphs into a courtroom custody-case tearjerker. From this point on screenwriter Thomas Ropelewski piles one silly plot contrivance upon another, and the characters start behaving like nitwits. Why don't these old and true friends work out a compromise? Silly question. If they did, the movie wouldn't have a third act.

SIGHT AND SOUND, 8/00, p. 53, Kevin Maher

Los Angeles, the early 90s. Abbie, a yoga teacher, is dumped by her boyfriend Kevin. She complains to her gay best friend Robert, a gardener, that she's getting old and wants a baby. The next day, after attending a funeral, they drunkenly have sex. Abbie soon discovers she's pregnant. She asks Robert, whom she says is the baby's father, to live with her and raise the child. He agrees; Abbie later gives birth to a son, Sam.

Six years later Abbie meets Ben, an investment banker. She brings him home to meet Robert, who is hostile. Ben and Abbie fall in love and plan to get married. Robert worries that this will weaken his relationship with Sam and protests. Ben is offered a job in New York; Abbie decides to leave with him and take Sam. Robert sues Abbie over custody of Sam. She reveals to Robert that her ex-boyfriend Kevin is actually Sam's biological father. Robert tells Kevin. In Court Kevin demands time to get to know his son. The judge adjourns the case. Robert, Abbie and Ben accidentally meet each other outside Sam's school. They reconcile their differences. Abbie allows Sam to have dinner with Robert.

Like so many movies starring Madonna, *The Next Best Thing* fetishises her wearily iconic body. When Abbie, the yoga teacher that she plays in director John Schlesinger's romantic comedy, stands semi-naked in her bedroom, her drooling boyfriend Kevin pays homage to her "fantastic body". Then, soon after, Abbie's best friend Robert (Rupert Everett) tells her, "You are the most beautiful woman I know!" During the many yoga scenes that feature throughout, the camera lingers over Madonna's contorted frame, beguiled by her entwined, self-enfolded limbs. The cumulative effect is that, as in the historical musical *Evita,* the erotic thriller *Body of Evidence* and even the baseball movie *A League of their Own* Madonna remains resolutely 'Madonna'. As a protean vessel into which the pop-cultural anxieties of the past two decades have been poured, she has an enduring symbolic appeal. But her performance here proves once more that she can't deliver in close-up. Her line readings are flat, seemingly stifled by the weight of being Madonna. Such lines as "Look at me, I'm not 24 anymore!" seem irritably inimical to her.

Admittedly, Madonna isn't helped by Thomas Ropelewski's preposterous screenplay (he directed and co-wrote *Look Who's Talking Now*). Characters inhabit *The Next Best Thing* as they would a promotional video for a new-age lifestyle product. Here the limits of being are defined by tan, muscle development and the amount of incense sticks in the bathroom. When Abbie and new boyfriend Ben have a first date, it's no surprise that they discuss "finding muscles in your body that you never knew existed." There's a childish simplicity to the dialogue that often verges on the bizarre. When Ben, the investment banker, describes his job, he proudly declares that he "takes sick companies and makes them well". Even when the script occasionally demands pathos, it is delivered via ineffably hollow lines—Robert remembers a lost love, announcing, "I miss him;

he was totally me!" Or later at the platitudinous courtroom climax, he shouts, "Being a real parent takes more than DNA!"

Dramatically, Ropelewski and Schlesinger spend the entire movie constructing a nebulous middle ground where all parties in the custody battle ultimately deserve to parent Abbie's precocious son Sam. Unfortunately this drains the court scenes of any tension. Sam himself is an empty cipher, a perky child golem who automatically adjusts to every traumatic turn in his life. (He has a similar function to the child-as-catalyst character in *Big Daddy*.)

As in many recent romantic comedies *(The Object of my Affection, Three to Tango)*, *The Next Best Thing*'s depiction of its gay characters is decidedly inane. But here the 'witty gay sidekick' (similar to Everett's role in *My Best Friend's Wedding)* has a pivotal narrative function, which makes his clichéd characterisation slightly more problematic. When a director of Schlesinger's stature, a filmmaker adept at depicting alienation and subculture *(Midnight Cowboy*, 1969; *Day of the Locust*, 1974), can produce no better, it becomes unforgivable.

VILLAGE VOICE, 3/14/00, p. 130, Dennis Lim

The newly pop-culture-friendly gay man/straight woman paradigm—rendered invariably as a wellspring of waggish repartee and mutual you-go-girl empathy—reaches a hall-of-mirrors dead end with real-life tag team Rupert Everett and Madonna. Going at least one convolution further than the likes of *Will and Grace* and *The Object of My Affection*, *The Next Best Thing* saddles its homo-hetero best friends with a baby.

Robert, a gardener, and Abbie, a yoga instructor, are what you might call soul mates—both are shrill, maudlin, narcissistic creatures who speak in wilted epigrams. Their accidental reproduction adventure begins in a haze of boozy self-pity. The script offers the drunken duo the excuse of a friend's recent death (his funeral occasions an a cappella version of Madonna's new single "American Pie"), but the real catalyst for their surprise fuck is a nobody-loves-me wallow session. In behavior that movies evidently deem typical of fag-and-hag camaraderie, they bitch toothlessly about a beauty pageant on TV ("Her national costume is too tight!") and get misty-eyed over lost loves ("I don't miss being first runner-up").

For nearly an hour, *The Next Best Thing* passes itself off as a celebration of alternative families—with Abbie and Robert raising their son together, a living arrangement whose built-in complications seem not to have crossed their minds—then takes it all back with a surge of *Kramer vs. Kramer* histrionics. When Abbie falls for a New York banker (Benjamin Bratt), the movie morphs into a custody-battle melodrama, complete with kidnap-panic scene and tearful courtroom testimonials.

An embarrassment to rival her "Ray of Light" death-yodel at the MTV awards two years back, Madonna's performance here consists of feigning an English accent, for no apparent reason and only when it occurs to her to do so. Everett, who registers more than ever as a butch Hugh Grant, deserves even greater blame, having apparently tailored the screenplay for himself and Madonna (the witless mess remains credited to Thomas Ropelewski, whose most notable previous work is *Look Who's Talking Now)*. Whether in screwball-gaysploitation or issue-of-the-week mode, the movie—directed in hands-off fashion by the increasingly doddery John Schlesinger—favors crude dramatic devices over even the most basic character psychology. This is, of course, a problem lost on Madonna and Everett, who have approached *The Next Best Thing* as a vanity project—hell-bent on playing barely human characters as themselves, they've created something quite bewilderingly ugly in the process.

Also reviewed in:
CHICAGO TRIBUNE, 3/3/00, Friday/p. A, Michael Wilmington
NEW REPUBLIC, 3/27/00, p. 26, Stanley Kauffmann
NEW YORK TIMES, 3/3/00, p. E16, Stephen Holden
VARIETY, 3/6-12/00, p. 32, Dennis Harvey
WASHINGTON POST, 3/3/00, p. C1, Stephen Hunter
WASHINGTON POST, 3/3/00, Weekend/p. 45, Michael O'Sullivan

NEXT FRIDAY

A New Line Cinema release of a Cubevision production. *Executive Producer:* Michael Gruber and Claire Rudnick Polstein. *Producer:* Ice Cube. *Director:* Steve Carr. *Screenplay (based on characters created by Ice Cube and DJ Pooh):* Ice Cube. *Director of Photography:* Christopher J. Baffa. *Editor:* Elena Maganini. *Music:* Terence Blanchard. *Music Editor:* Lori Slomka. *Sound:* Walter Anderson and (music) Jim Anderson. *Sound Editor:* Lisle Engle, Dorian Cheah, and Mark Hunshik Choi. *Casting:* Kimberly R. Hardin. *Production Designer:* Dina Lipton. *Art Director:* Keith Neely. *Set Designer:* Christopher S. Nushawg and Susan E. Lomino. *Set Decorator:* Suzette Sheets. *Set Dresser:* Peter J. Bates, James E. Hurd Sr., Quentin Schierenberg, Chris Villarreal, and Harry Frierson. *Special Effects:* Dave Kelsey. *Costumes:* Jacki Roach. *Make-up:* Debra Denson. *Stunt Coordinator:* Keith Woulard. *Running time:* 93 minutes. *MPAA Rating:* R.

CAST: Ice Cube (Craig Jones);   Mike Epps (Day-Day);   Justin Pierce (Roach);   John Witherspoon (Mr. Jones);   Don "D.C." Curry (Uncle Elroy);   Jacob Vargas (Joker); Lobo Sebastian (Lil Joker); Rolando Molina (Baby Joker);   Lisa Rodriguez (Karla);   Tommy "Tiny" Lister, Jr. (Debo); Kym E. Whitley (Suga);   Amy Hill (Miss Ho-Kym);   Tamala Jones (D'Wana);   Robin Allen (Baby D');   Carmen Serano, Maria Arce, and Vanessa White (Girls); Clifton Powell (Pinky); Michael Blackson (Customer #1);   Ronn Riser-Muhammad (Stanley); David Waterman (Sheriff #3);   Cheridah Best (Sheriff Lady);   Ronn Riser-Muhammad (Mystery Guest);   Sticky Fingaz (Tyrone);   Shane Conrad (Real Estate Man);   Keebo (Pinky Chaffeur).

LOS ANGELES TIMES, 1/12/00, Calandar/p. 4, Gene Seymour

[*The following review by Gene Seymour appeared in a slightly different form in* NEWSDAY, 1/12/00, Part II/p. B2.]

One of my chief regrets of the previous year was that I wasn't able to get to as many of last August's Urbanworld Film Festival screenings as I would have liked. Still, the few films I did see at that annual Manhattan-based showcase of African American and Latino movies were enough to convince me that there are sexy, smart and fresh movies by minority filmmakers that, with enough promotion and attention, could find an audience.

Last I checked, those films were still wandering the wilderness in search of distributors. Meanwhile, "Next Friday" gets green-lighted, packaged and shipped into the multiplexes in a relative heartbeat.

Somebody please remind me that this is supposed to be a golden age for movies.

In cold-blooded, capitalistic terms, "Next Friday's" existence makes perfect sense. It is a follow-up, after all, to the surprise hit (at least in video) "Friday" (1995), which served as a breakthrough for its director, F. Gary Gray, and its hyperbolic comic relief, Chris Tucker, neither of whom is involved in this sequel.

That movie was also something of a breakthrough in the way it used slacker slapstick to deflate "hood" movie conventions. Add some down-home, after-hours raunchiness to the dopey (in more ways than one) mix, and you have a cult. And some cults, alas, breed offspring.

So it's now five years later and Craig Jones (writer-producer Ice Cube) still lives at home with his dogcatcher dad (John Witherspoon) and still doesn't have any prospects for work. There is one prospect that could get Craig out of the house: the jailbreak of Debo (Tommy "Tiny" Lister Jr.), the gargantuan neighborhood bully Craig helped put on ice in the last movie.

Dad thinks it's a good idea to move Craig to the relative safety of a fancy suburban neighborhood where he can crash with Uncle Elroy (Don "D.C." Curry), who moved out of South-Central L.A. after winning the lottery. Elroy, putting it gently, is a self-indulgent pig. But his son Day-Day (Michael Epps) works hard to maintain his black BMW. Their neighbors include an elderly Asian woman (Amy Hill), who's fluent in new-jack jive, and a trio of Latino brothers, guarded by a fierce English bulldog.

Cube (who wanders the movie in a near-incredulous stupor) and director Steve Carr seem content to let things happen to these and other characters. What results is all setup and no follow-through. There is plenty of nasty patter and aimless jokes about hard-core sex, soft-core drugs, dog feces and flatulence to keep you occupied while you wait, in vain, for any reason to laugh out loud. If there's anything that's remarkable about "Next Friday," it's the way it manages to make Witherspoon, one of the funniest men in America, into a crashing bore.

If there were any justice, "Next Friday" would be the last "Friday." Somehow, I fear the first weekend grosses will make that unlikely.

NEW YORK POST, 1/12/00, p. 49, Jonathan Foreman

"Next Friday" is a slack sequel to 1995's "Friday," a video hit about street life in South Central L.A., that helped launch the career of Chris Tucker. Here Tucker is replaced by comic Mike Epps as Ice Cube's manic sidekick.

The jokes are remarkably crude (toilet smells are a recurring theme) even by the raunchy standards of the so-called "chitlin'" genre—a genre aimed at a young, urban, African-American audience, and which includes comic gems like "Booty Call" and even "Ride."

But the real problem with "Next Friday" is that the whole movie is so ineptly written and directed that its 90 minutes seem to take twice as long.

There are four or five good laughs, but by the time the movie crawls to its climax, you've all but forgotten them.

Craig (Ice Cube)—who's supposed to be a teenager—is sent by his father (John Witherspoon) to stay with his Uncle Elroy (Don "D.C." Curry) in the suburb of Rancho Cucamonga, when word comes down that Craig's enemy Debo (Tommy "Tiny" Lister Jr.) has busted out of jail.

Elroy himself moved out of the 'hood with his son Day-Day (Mike Epps) when he won the lottery.

Craig likes the suburbs and his panicky cousin Day-Day. But he discovers that Uncle Elroy has been too busy getting high and engaging in S&M sex with his hefty, dissatisfied girlfriend to pay his taxes, and will lose the house unless they can all come up with $3,800 by the next day.

Once again, much of the movie is about smoking dope. But Ice Cube's labored screenplay includes scenes involving vicious dogs, slutty "hoodrats," a cute Latina love interest (Lisa Rodriguez), and a pair of violent young women who are determined to wreck Day-Day's BMW.

Ice Cube, so good under David O. Russell's direction in last year's "Three Kings," is oddly bland as the straight man here. Video director Steve Carr, making his feature debut, seems unable to maintain any dramatic tension at all.

SIGHT AND SOUND, 4/00, p. 60, Keith Perry

South Central, LA, the present, Friday. Craig Jones is unemployed and living with his father. Local criminal Debo breaks out of jail, hell-bent on revenge against Craig, who beat him in a fight four years earlier. After a confrontation with Debo, Craig leaves for the suburbs to stay with his lottery-winning uncle Elroy and cousin Day-Day. Day-Day warns Craig about the brothers living next door, headed by ex-con Joker. Craig flirts with Joker's sister Karla, before being chased away by their dog. Craig discovers there is a repossession order on the house. He goes to the shop where Day-Day works to tell him, but Day-Day reveals that all the winnings have been spent. The pair get high with co-worker Roach, and lock up when Day-Day's pregnant ex-girlfriend D'Wana arrives. Following a fight between Craig and the shop's owner, Day-Day and Roach are sacked.

Craig suspects Joker is a drug dealer, and plans a cash robbery to help Elroy. Roach distracts the dog while Craig steals the money. Mr Jones, Craig's father, arrives, with Debo stowed away in his van. Joker discovers the theft, and takes Day-Day and Roach hostage; Elroy, Craig and Mr Jones rescue them. The police arrest Debo and the brothers. Elroy keeps the house. Craig says goodbye to Karla and returns to South Central.

After building a successful career as a rapper in which he maintained that South Central was a concrete jungle of police brutality, drive-by shootings and ever circling helicopters, Ice Cube went on to depict the area as a slackers' paradise in *Friday* (which he co-wrote and starred in). *Next Friday* picks up four years after the events of the previous film. Former music-video director Steve Carr has wisely debuted on a movie with minimal narrative thread, but maximum posture and sun-drenched colour. The anti-gun, pro-family messages of the first film are gone, but as before we have a sketch format, with well-timed laughs built around soft drugs and bodily functions, all edited to a continuous soundtrack from well-known rap artists. Now that Chris Tucker has gone on to bigger things, stand-up comedian Mike Epps plays Craig's sidekick Day-Day. His natural charisma goes a long way towards compensating for Day-Day's feeble characterisation, but Epps' gangly charm is no match for Tucker's controlled physical flexing or unique verbal shape throwing. All of which makes things easier for Cube, whose teddy-bear rotundity and scowl have always enabled him to flip from huggable to intimidating via a simple close-up.

Apart from the leading players, all the men and women on show are visitors from that ripple-and-jiggle world familiar from Russ Meyer's sex comedies. Cartoonishness should not, of course, be confused with harmlessness; in fact here it seems to sanction a casual violence not seen in *Friday* (where the climactic fight is provoked by Debo punching two "females"). Joker's rough treatment of the women at a party is capped off by a "Call me!", queasily attempting to disperse the moment with a laugh. What's missing throughout is sexual sassiness—a quality only brought into a film by lively female roles—and hence any real sexual sparring. The mothers and sisters of *Friday* are absent; the character of D'Wana is almost all bad, while her friend Lady of Rage is not developed beyond Carr's initial framing of her enormous, traffic-halting rear end.

Next Friday's most mendacious trick is that it is not the fish-out-of-water tale it pretends to be. Those expecting a scenario similar to the television series *The Fresh Prince of Bel Air*—in which Will Smith's character uproots from his Philadelphia inner-city home for life with his middle-class relatives in LA—will be disappointed. Craig arrives in his uncle's pastel-coloured cul-de-sac, only to discover a group of armed drug dealers next door—hardly a typical suburban storyline. What follows could easily have taken place back in South Central. There's a degree of wish-fulfilment in the film's depiction of the suburbs as a place as volatile as the projects. The device diminishes the respective guilt and envy of the residents of both and contributed, perhaps, to *Next Friday*'s massive US success. After all, if, as the film's poster tells us, "the suburbs make the 'hood look good", then we can all go home happy.

VILLAGE VOICE, 1/18/00, p. 116, Gary Dauphin

It's the rare cash-in sequel that's worth the price of full admission, so it's no surprise that *Next Friday* (part of the minifranchise that includes 1996's *Friday* and an upcoming, NYC-set version tentatively titled *Stoops)* isn't quite the picture its predecessor was. Where last *Friday* was a loopy, hard-to-categorize lark, the bigger-budget *Next Friday* is a calculated teen gross-out flick that owes more to *American Pie* than its own progenitor.

As in the first flick, *Next Friday*'s fog of riffs, gags, and barely connected events swirls around Craig (played by cowriter and producer Ice Cube), a generally put-upon, jobless South Central layabout who's tough enough to stand up to bullies but sensitive enough to woo brainy wannabe buppies like Nia Long. Craig's misadventures in the first flick had a meandering, doped-up circularity that went perfectly with the larger "getting high on Friday" theme; the antigun slogans ("Real men fight with fists") were quaint, doggedly sentimental touches that managed to come off like sincere attempts at moral instruction. This time around, such curious little moments are streamlined into formal nods—like flashbacks or Craig's voiced-over observations—that reference *Friday* without really reliving its high points. That forces this picture to rely almost entirely on the comic strengths of a cast that's been significantly weakened by the absence of the shrill but energetic Chris Tucker.

Next Friday's main action involves Craig's transfer—Fresh Prince-like—to the suburban home of his Uncle Elroy (Don "DC" Curry), a rotely freaky lottery winner who lives in gaudy nouveau riche splendor in the hills over L.A. Which just means a new set of oddballs to gawk at, including a sad-sack cousin (an able Mike Epps), an oversexed aunt, a foul-mouthed Asian grandmother, and the Joker Brothers, three Latino drug dealers who are immediately marked as last-reel villains. (No ethnic group is spared, but the Mexican stereotypes pile up pretty high.) Writers Ice Cube and DJ Pooh have broken the first movie's weed and fart set pieces into a number of gags involving dog doo-doo, comedic BDSM sexcapades, and ethnic humor directed at non-African Americans, all of that adding up to give *Next Friday* a significantly cruder vibe than the last. Curry and John Witherspoon work hard to liven things up with extended stand-up riffs, but since both men are fluent in only two basic notes (boasting and cracking), they average out after a while, becoming an ongoing BET *Comic View*-type drone—scatological, down-home, aging, and ultimately rather boring. As for Ice Cube, he has the distracted, there-not-there look of a man on a forced vacation, which might be what Craig is experiencing, but doesn't exactly make *Next Friday* anything to look forward to.

Also reviewed in:
CHICAGO TRIBUNE, 1/12/00, Tempo/p. 1, Monica Eng
NEW YORK TIMES, 1/12/00, p. E5, Lawrence Van Gelder
VARIETY, 1/17-23/00, p. 50, Joe Leydon
WASHINGTON POST, 1/14/00, Weekend/p. 35, Michael O'Sullivan

NIGHT LARRY KRAMER KISSED ME, THE

A Film Next/Montrose Pictures release.   *Producer:* Michael Caplan and Kirkland Tibbels. *Director:* Tim Kirkman.   *Screenplay (based on his play):* David Drake.   *Director of Photography:* James Carman. *Editor:* Caitlin Dixon. *Music:* Steve Sandberg. *Sound:* Michael Boyle. *Production Designer:* Anna Louizos. *Running time:* 79 minutes. *MPAA Rating:* Not Rated.

WITH: David Drake.

NEW YORK POST, 7/14/00, p. 46, Hannah Brown

There's enough wit, intelligence and theatrical intensity at work in "The Night Larry Kramer Kissed Me" to overcome an occasional tendency toward politically correct smugness.

David Drake's long-running 1992 one-man show (which both stars and was written by Drake), "Kramer," has been brought to the screen so imaginatively by director Tim Kirkman that it never becomes static.

In fact, "Kramer" invites comparisons to the best filmed monologues and concerts, such as Jonathan Demme's "Swimming to Cambodia" and "Stop Making Sense."

Buoyed by Drake's superb acting and phenomenal energy, "Kramer" is a look both at Drake's own experience as a gay man and the life of the entire gay community, starting during Drake's childhood in the late '60s through the AIDS plague.

It concludes with a hysterically funny but bittersweet epilogue set in 2018—after AIDS has been cured (and after Matt Damon and Ben Affleck have starred in a remake of "The Way We Were").

The title refers not only to a literal kiss (although playwright Larry Kramer did kiss Drake once at an Act-Up demonstration), but to the feeling of catharsis Drake got in the mid-'80s after seeing Kramer's play about AIDS, "The Normal Heart," at a time when few were discussing the devastating effect of AIDS on the gay community honestly.

Drake is at his best in the sketches about AIDS, which are the most deeply felt, original and moving. Others, especially those about trying to pick up guys at the gym and at a bar, go on much too long.

But the candlelight vigil sequence and scene where he sings "Lullaby of Broadway" as he reads the obituaries will resonate with anyone who has ever lost a friend to AIDS.

VILLAGE VOICE, 7/18/00, p. 126, Jessica Winter

The original finale for David Drake's 1992 *The Night Larry Kramer Kissed Me*, the longest-running one-man stage production in New York theater history, was set in 1999 and celebrated a cure for AIDS (the eponymous smooch refers to Kramer's 1985 watershed play *The Normal Heart)*. The film adaptation bumps it up to 2018 and adds to its prognostications a Damon-Affleck remake of *The Way We Were*. If a few pockets of Drake's seven-part, semiautobiographical narrative of growing up, coming out (with the aid of Swim Team Tim, Drake's best sketch), acting up, and sleeping around—and of constant, terrible loss—seem a bit dated, his writing is so cogently personal and his performance so versatile that *Larry Kramer* could have debuted yesterday. Director Tim Kirkman clutters up the spare production with capricious use of slo-mo, camera shakes, chop-chop editing, and an almost comical number of angles; the live audience ends up sounding like a laugh track. But the camera's pothering is only minorly distracting; once Drake reaches the candlelight vigil that acts as his penultimate set piece, he sustains an impossible balance between mordant wit and articulate bewilderment.

Also reviewed in:
NEW YORK TIMES, 7/14/00, p. E21, Lawrence Van Gelder
VARIETY, 7/17-23/00, p. 27, Robert Koehler

NINTH GATE, THE

An Artisan Entertainment release of an R. P. Productions/Orly Films/TFI Films Production/Kino Vision/Origen Producciones Cinematograficas production with participation of Bac Films/Canal Plus and Via Digital. *Executive Producer:* Wolfgang Glattes and Michel Cheyko. *Producer:* Roman Polanski. *Director:* Roman Polanski. *Screenplay:* John Brownjohn, Enrique Urbizu, and Roman Polanski. *Based on the novel "El Club Dumas" by:* Arturo Pérez-Reverte. *Director of Photography:* Darius Khondji. *Editor:* Hervé de Luze. *Music:* Wojciech Kilar. *Music Editor:* Suzana Peric. *Sound:* Jean-Marie Blondel and (music) John Timperley. *Sound Editor:* Laurent Quaglio. *Casting:* Howard Feuer. *Production Designer:* Dean Tavoularis. *Art Director:* Gérard Viard. *Set Decorator:* Philippe Turlure. *Special Effects:* Gilbert Pieri. *Costumes:* Anthony Powell. *Make-up:* Paul Le Marinel and Liliane Rametta. *Stunt Coordinator:* Dominique Fouassier and Jean-Claude Lagniez. *Running time:* 133 minutes. *MPAA Rating:* R.

CAST: Johnny Depp (Dean Corso); Lena Olin (Liana Telfer); Frank Langella (Boris Balkan); James Russo (Bernie); Jack Taylor (Victor Fargas); José López Rodero (Pablo & Pedro Ceniza); Allen Garfield (Witkin); Barbara Jefford (Baroness Frieda Kessler); Emmanuelle Seigner (The Girl); Tony Amoni (Liana's Bodyguard); Willy Holt (Andrew Telfer); Jacques Dacqmine (Old Man); Joe Sheridan (Old Man's Son); Rebecca Pauly (Daughter-in-Law); Catherine Benguigui (Concierge); Maria Ducceshi (Secretary); Jacques Collard (Gruber); Dominique Pozzetto (Desk Clerk); Emmanuel Booz (Baker); Lino Ribeiro de Sousa (Hotel Porter); José López Rodero (First and Second Workman); Asil Rais (Cabby); Bernard Richier and Marinette Richier (Café Owners).

CHRISTIAN SCIENCE MONITOR, 3/10/00, p. 15, David Sterritt

"The Ninth Gate" takes Roman Polanski back to the supernaturally tinged territory he explored so memorably in "The Tenant" and "Rosemary's Baby" years ago. The hero is an unscrupulous rare-book expert (Johnny Depp) scavenging Europe for two obscure volumes penned by the devil himself. His adventures are structured like a traditional detective tale, with the sharp-witted antihero assembling the pieces of a sinister puzzle.

Polanski spins the yarn with a generally straight face, adding an occasional self-satirizing touch to let us know he's as aware as we are that the whole shebang doesn't make a shred of sense. It goes on too long and doesn't have much of a payoff, but Polanski's directing is marvelously assured and the story has enough surprises to keep chiller fans happy.

LOS ANGELES TIMES, 3/10/00, Calendar/p. 27, Kenneth Turan

Better than Harrison Ford, John Travolta or even Leonardo DiCaprio, getting the devil involved in your picture is a sure way of getting it made. Not necessarily as a producer or financial backer (though that probably wouldn't hurt) but merely as a subject. From 1899's "Chorus Girls and the Devil" (little more than the title survives, unfortunately) to the current "The Ninth Gate," Satan has always been the movie business' go-to guy.

Adapted (quite loosely, apparently) from "El Club Dumas," a literary thriller by Spanish novelist Arturo Perez-Reverte, "The Ninth Gate" is at least the second encounter with the evil one for Roman Polanski. The director of the classic "Rosemary's Baby" still has a liking for the outre and the bizarre, but that's as far as the parallels between the two films go.

For though "The Ninth Gate" is well-crafted with a genteel and moody air, it's best understood as a kind of anti-thriller. Lacking noticeable energy or drive, its almost visceral distaste for dramatic momentum is puzzling, especially in a film about the black arts. It's got an old-fashioned European sensibility—most of it is set on that continent—all well-mannered style and very little involving passion.

It's hard to tell whether star Johnny Depp was a contributing factor to this lethargy or merely found it to his liking. Wearing glasses and a small goatee, with his hair graying at the temples, Depp quietly disappears inside the chain-smoking character of Dean Corso, a protagonist so buttoned-down he's always difficult to read.

Which is ironic in a way, because Corso plays a book detective, a specialist in finding and procuring very old and rare volumes for collectors willing to pay extravagantly for them. An elegant, soulless weasel who finds a reputation for unscrupulousness to be a professional asset, Corso is proud to say he believes only in "my percentage." That's just fine with client Boris Balkan (Frank Langella), who himself believes "no one is more reliable than a man whose loyalty can be bought for hard cash."

Balkan is a fabulously wealthy collector with a twist. "All my rare editions have the same protagonist," he tells Corso with an appropriately icy smile. "The devil." The pride of his collection, just bought from recently deceased rival Andrew Telfer, is a 17th century item called "The Nine Gates of the Kingdom of the Shadows."

Published in 1666, "The Nine Gates" is no ordinary antiquarian volume. Its author, Aristide Torchia, took the trouble to adapt it from a book supposedly written by the devil himself (who knew he had the time?) and was burned at the stake for his pains. Only three copies are known to exist, Balkan says, and he believes only one of them is genuine. Authenticity is important because the real book is said to have the power to summon the devil himself from the terrifying nether world.

Devotees of this book are understandably rabid about getting their hands on it, so when Corso accepts Balkan's commission to go to Europe and examine the other two copies, it's a given that: a) sinister forces will be unleashed in his path and b) because it's a movie after all, beautiful women will factor into the equation.

First to reveal herself is Liana Telfer (Lena Olin), the coolly seductive widow of previous owner Andrew Telfer. Then there is a character known only as the Girl, an enigmatic blond wearing a parka, jeans, running shoes and mismatched socks. Played by Emmanuelle Seigner (Polanski's wife), the Girl knows a heck of a lot about the book and appears and disappears almost at will. You figure it out, because Corso is in no hurry to.

Those similarly in the mood for something languorous and atmospheric will not be angry with "The Ninth Gate." Working with dark side cinematographer Darius Khondji ("Seven," "The City of Lost Children") and veteran composer Wojciech Kilar, Polanski has concentrated on the subdued and the spooky. And he's thrown in some bizarre acting touches, like having veteran production manager Jose Lopez Rodero play both Pablo and Pedro Ceniza, identical twin book dealers.

Because its several libraries were created by expert production designer Dean Tavoularis and his team, book collectors will be pleased by the film's visual tribute to old and beautiful volumes, its habit of bathing them in the kind of warm and flattering light usually reserved for actresses like Madonna.

Finally, however, "The Ninth Gate" is too laid-back and unconcerned about the pacing of its story to be satisfying. Polanski and his co-writers Enrique Urbizu and John Brownjohn seem supremely indifferent about bringing things to any kind of dramatic conclusion, and while a thriller that's not high-powered is an intriguing concept, in reality it can hold our attention for only so long.

NEW STATESMAN, 6/5/00, p. 48, Jonathan Romney

The Devil may have all the best tunes, but he isn't always so lucky when it comes to film scripts. Roman Polanski's *The Ninth Gate* could be fairly described as creaky, and yet, inept and archaic as the film seems, you feel that Polanski knows it perfectly well, and is simply mocking our indulgence.

Polanski's work over the past few years has generally lacked conviction, as if he were half-heartedly cooling his heels in Europe while regretting the chances missed as an exile from Hollywood. *Frantic* (1988) was by-the-book, cod Hitchcock; *Death and the Maiden* (1994) was a prosaic adaptation of Ariel Dorfman's chamber drama. In between, however, he made one remarkable film—*Bitter Moon* (1992), a moral tale of sexual obsession, the self-mocking subtleties of which were on the whole grievously misunderstood (I saw it with an audience that tittered from start to finish).

It seems futile for Polanski to engage with the Devil again, since he spun his definitive satanic tale *Rosemary's Baby* (1968), which, with its rich dream content of psychosexual and bodily anxieties, evoked the possibility of knowing the Devil from the inside. A glib, debased take on the same theme, *The Ninth Gate* is a strictly external quest, a detective story about book-learning; it might as well be about searching telephone directories for Old Nick's private number.

Based on a novel by Arturo Perez Reverte, the story has Dean Corso (Johnny Depp) tracking down variant copies of agrimoire for a powerful collector. He goes shuttling around Europe: to a leafy, antique corner of Portugal; to a semi-medieval Madrid; and to a France where the cafes have lace curtains and jaunty accordion music. Polanski's New York is no more real, its cramped brownstone apartments and basement bookshops echoing the 1940s and 1950s horror films of Jacques Tourneur—notably *Night of the Demon,* another bibliophile tale of doom and dusty shelves.

The Ninth Gate constantly signals its borrowings, with its Bondish globe-trotting, Chandleresque legwork, and Mickey Spillane sleaziness. Lena Olin is a lingerie-flashing, *femme fatale;* Emmanuelle Seigner (aka Mme Polanski) is a mystery woman, constantly flitting in and out. There are some fruity villains: Barbara Jefford has a rare old time as a posh German satanist, and Frank Langelia, in Billy Bunter specs and Tom Baker's booming voice, rounds it all off by yelling: "Yes! Yes! The enigma is solved at last!" This is by no means an atypical line in the script, yet there's something heartening about the level of cliché. Who wouldn't feel a warm glow at the line, "Coincidences, or something more?"? The film appears utterly foolish, yet Polanski is certainly no fool. The accumulation of clichés gives the film a peculiar dream quality. The story follows a false trail within a hermetic world that seems to shrink the further its hero travels; the outcome is grandiose bathos, after which Seigner smirks into the camera as if to say that she and Polanski have put one over on us again. As in *Bitter Moon,* Polanski wants to take us for a ride, but here he under estimates our intelligence. We're usually several steps ahead of Corso; we see through the wilfully thin architecture too soon.

What is most striking about *The Ninth Gate* is its curious nostalgia—this is perhaps the first film of the 2000s to hark back to the possibilities of 20th-century storytelling. For who now cares a damn about Satan, that discredited, posturing melodrama villain? And, in the internet age, who could be impressed by a story about books? Everything seems an echo of once-resonant narrative gambits. *The Ninth Gate* is a cynical, hollow film about its own cynical hollowness.

Admittedly, it has certain more straightforward qualities. If for no other reason, you might want to see it for the contribution of Darius Khondji, a French cinematographer capable of burnishing the tawdriest material *(Evita, In Dreams)* as well as the best *(Seven).* Khondji here favours mildewed greens and golds, as well as the odd strident red. He shoots a wonderfully ominous early scene in Langella's modernist mausoleum of a library overlooking Manhattan at night; there is a startling attention to sound here, too, with the rasp of hushed voices against the rustle of old paper.

This scene, rich in narrative promise, reminded me of Stanley Kubrick's *Eyes Wide Shut.* Both films are shaggy-dog stories about quests that cannot be fulfilled, including the viewer's own quest for a satisfying narrative conclusion. Yet for all its flaws and inconsistencies, Kubrick's film genuinely perplexes and fascinates: it has a real subject, as well as faith in its ramifications.

Polanski's film, however, is finally a game with no real stakes, designed purely to prove that the director is diabolically adept at spinning narrative webs with no centre and no end. It may be a gem for connoisseurs of Flawed Cinema, that damned genre, but fascinating flaws are rarely enough. *The Ninth Gate* wants to lead us a merry dance up the brimstone path, but a long, arduous crawl it proves to be.

NEW YORK, 3/20/00, p. 21, Peter Rainer

In Roman Polanski's *The Ninth Gate*, Johnny Depp plays Dean Corso, an unscrupulous New York book dealer with a reputation for tracking down the rarities and exotica his posh clients crave. As Dean says, a bad reputation is good for business, but, job description aside, he'd probably be bad anyway. He enjoys infiltrating the world of rare books with his scamp's manners; it's a form of one-upmanship.

The best thing about *The Ninth Gate* is that it locates a relatively new setting for old claptrap. Dean is a species of detective, and in the course of his quest, we're treated to a rogues' gallery of effete desiccation: Many of the book collectors on view have a sallow countenance, the look of faded parchment. The film should be much better than it is; as is often the case with Polanski's work over the past several decades, the build-up and the atmosphere are more compelling than the end result. But cold craftsmanship is better than no craftsmanship, and parts of *The Ninth Gate* have a caustic, cackling humor.

Polanski is the kind of director who keeps one eye on his audience at all times. Every camera move and every cut is conceived in cat-and-mouse terms. Like Dean Corso, Polanski enjoys one-upping those who depend on him. The undercurrent of sadism in his films comes not just from the recurring queasy subject matter but also from the ways in which we are made to feel like puppets on a string. The story goes that Polanski, against the objections of his producers, once set up a shot for *Rosemary's Baby* in which a half-opened door partially blocked our view into an adjoining room; he argued that the shot was designed so that when the film was finally projected in theaters, everybody would be craning their necks in unison to see around the door, and, of course, that's exactly what happened. Sometimes this sort of tweaking can be pleasurable. Hitchcock, for example, turned audience manipulation into sport, and we enjoyed being fooled with: it meant that Hitchcock thought enough of our smarts to try confounding them. His relationship with his audience is based on an essentially English sense of wryness. Even in the savagery of *Psycho* there is a sense in which he is toying with our frights; there is wit in the blood. The black joke in that film is how it overturns our conventional scary-movie expectations and becomes truly gruesome.

Polanski's horrors come out of a different tradition from Hftchcock's, much more Eastern European and Jacobean. His gamesmanship is closer to blood sport. Like Hitchcock's, Polanski's audience-response maneuvers have sometimes been interpreted as a sign of artistry when they're often just high-end gimmickry. But, also like Hitchcock, Polanski is a special case. His best movies have a way of blurring the line—which is mostly artificial anyway—between the manipulations of a fright-master and those of an artist. The dread that pervades, say, *Chinatown*, or even the uneven *Frantic*, which is almost intolerably anxiety-provoking for its first, seemingly uneventful half-hour or so, goes beyond pulpishness into richer realms of unease. These films are saying that while the stories we are watching are unhinged and full of fear, the real world in which they were created is even more so. (Inevitably, if unfairly, we regard Polanski's harrowing life and his movies as all of a piece.) The existential dislocation is total. Movies are not just movies; they're emissaries of a deeper disorder.

In *The Ninth Gate*, books are agents of disorder, too. Dean is hired by the publisher Boris Balkan (Frank Langella) to seek out in Spain, Portugal, and France the two surviving editions, besides his own, of a seventeenth-century tome illustrated with nine engravings that, combined with the text, are said to summon the Devil. Balkan's climate-controlled library consists entirely of books about Satan, and the man himself seems climate-controlled: Langella looks as if he were preserved in formaldehyde. His oily, orotund pronouncements—"I'm entering uncharted territory!"—are a shade too regal for camp, but his performance, like most of the movie, isn't to be taken entirely seriously. The comic effects are uneven, perhaps because Polanski is too much the martinet to achieve the florid levity he's often reaching for here. In what amounts to violent slapstick, Dean evades torchings and bashings and gougings; he steals his way into a Satanic-cult gathering at a mansion in the French countryside that recalls the scene in *Eyes Wide Shut* in which a masked Tom Cruise infiltrates a mansion of incanting orgiasts. (I do not intend this comparison as a compliment.) Polanski is torn between making a horror film and a horror spoof, in the end succeeding at neither.

And yet there are brilliant, unsettling moments throughout. As Dean tracks down the editions, he crosses paths with a magnificent array of grotesques, including a wheelchair-bound baroness (Barbara Jefford) and a French-born widow (Lena Olin) who slithers sultrily and then claws at him when she doesn't get what she wants. The women in this movie all come on like she-devils, none more so than the blonde (Emmanuelle Seigner) who mysteriously turns up as Dean's guardian angel. Seigner looks like a more brutish version of Dominique Sanda, and her eroticism is hellfire. She wears flames the way some women wear Dior.

When he was no longer able to make movies in Hollywood, Polanski lost the armature of the studio system that reined in his excesses. The commercialism of the Hollywood approach had a salutary effect on Polanski's artistry that is rare for émigré directors. Away making movies in Europe since *Chinatown,* he has become a director of bits and pieces (with the exception of *Tess*), and while the oddments are still the work of a distinctive talent, the films come across less as fully realized achievements than as squanderings. That certainly holds true for *The Ninth Gate,* a movie with some fire and lots more ash.

NEW YORK POST, 3/10/00, p. 57, Jonathan Foreman

For admirers of the work of Roman Polanski, "The Ninth Gate" is a painful experience.

Not only does it contain little or no evidence of the talent that saw such wonderful expression in movies like "Chinatown," "Repulsion" and "Rosemary's Baby," it's the worst occult film to star big-name actors in many years, and a startlingly inept and unsatisfying piece of storytelling.

Like "Eyes Wide Shut"—which it resembles in many ways (not least in its almost identical orgy scene)—"Gate" feels like a film made by somebody who has been out of touch with popular culture for decades.

Dozens of occult/devil flicks, some of them really cheap movies by second-rate hacks, have done a better and scarier job with the same basic material.

Manhattan rare-books dealer Dean Corso (Johnny Depp) is hired by a sinister, super-wealthy collector named Boris Balkan (Frank Langella)—this being the kind of film in which every character has a silly, portentous name—to find out if his is the only genuine copy of "The Nine Gates of the Kingdom of Shadows," a 17th-century satanic manual and a book said to have been co-authored by the devil himself.

Corso's mission requires him to take Balkan's book and compare it with the other two extant copies, both of which are in European collections.

But as soon as he gets hold of the volume, strange stuff starts happening around him. For a start, he is followed by a black man with scary blond hair, and he keeps bumping into an enigmatic blond girl (Emmanuelle Seigner).

Then there's the visit from Liana Telfer (Lena Olin from "The Unbearable Lightness of Being"), the sexy, witchy, garter-belt wearing widow of the book collector who sold Balkan his copy of the book.

Even more disturbing is the murder of one of Corso's pals, a slaying committed in the manner of one of the illustrations in "The Nine Gates."

As an expensively dressed, ruthless book dealer, Depp does his usual passive hero shtick—while looking slightly ridiculous in a goatee intended to make him appear more serious and less prettily boyish.

Langella seems more comfortable as he channels Christopher Lee in any number of Hammer horror films.

Seigner (Polanski's wife) plays a character who is able to fly—but all she has to do is send knowing but opaque glances in Depp's direction and look good in her one nude scene. She pulls both off with confidence.

All the action in this throwback to the religious horror flicks of the 1970s is accompanied by cheesy music, and most of the dialogue sounds like it's been translated from a foreign language (people are always saying things like, "I have solved the enigma").

The editing is in the European style—everything takes much, much longer than it should. The only original flourish is a car chase that involves a Rolls-Royce and a Range Rover.

NEWSDAY, 3/10/00, Part II/p. B3, Jan Stuart

The world of Roman Polanski's seductively entertaining thriller is an antiquarian's heaven, chockablock with oak-walled libraries, oriental carpets, potted palms and museum-caliber furniture that has probably been smudged by some pretty royal fingerprints in its day. And since this is Polanski, it is also populated with emissaries from Hell, who make no bones about burning it all to cinders if an unwitting soul dares to trespass where angels fear to tread.

Johnny Depp is quietly forging a mini-industry playing these hapless mortals who stray out of their depth, but his character Dean Corso in "The Ninth Gate" is a shnook of a very different color from his nerdy Ichabod Crane in "Sleepy Hollow." The goateed and bespectacled Corso is a trader in rare books who bilks his clients with cutthroat efficiency. As he flimflams a trusting rube out of a priceless edition of "Don Quixote," he's the sort of slippery operator who makes you think twice about all those crocodile-smiling appraisers on "Antiques Roadshow."

Corso gets in over his neck swimming with sharks after he is approached by Boris Balkan (Frank Langella), a scholar in demonology, to authenticate a volume of satanic liturgy acquired from a collector who mysteriously committed suicide. There are only three extant copies of this book, according to Balkan, and only one of them is the real McCoy.

Thus begins an old-fashioned gumshoe hunt that has Corso stalking down a droll assortment of bibliophiles, demonologists and other garden-variety strange people, many of whom meet unpleasant fates, as rendered in the book's woodcut engravings. Balkan notwithstanding, Corso's most formidable antagonists tend to be women. This is, we are quick to recall, from the same famously paranoid director who gave us Catherine Deneuve in "Repulsion" and Ruth Gordon in "Rosemary's Baby."

The most fatales of Polanski's femmes are Lena Olin, as the predatory widow of the suicidal collector (dig that viper tattoo), and Barbara Jefford, who steals the second half of the movie as a one-handed, wheelchair-bound baroness who compensates for her physical limitations with a wicked tongue and a scary-looking secretary. Far less interesting is an elusive, beautiful blonde with green eyes who perpetually rides to Corso's rescue on a motorcycle and says things like, "Someone's playing a game with you. You are part of it, and you are getting to like it." She is portrayed by French actress Emmanuelle Seigneur, whose fabulous body is no excuse for her line readings.

If Polanski and his co-screenwriters Enrique Urbizu and John Brownjohn fall down on the job whenever the girl with the green eyes rolls around, they succeed in lifting the rest of the movie's familiar conventions with a dry humor and surfeit of style that is too often absent from this brand of claptrap.

But for Seigneur, Polanski also benefits from supporting cast members who seem to know instinctively how to keep their over-the-top assignments just under the top. In addition to Jefford and Langella (who can do this sort of thing in his sleep), there is a charming cameo by longtime film production manager Jose Lopez Rodero, making his acting debut as a pair of twin bookbinders who finish each other's sentences.

As befits its musty library ambience, "The Ninth Gate" is the movie equivalent of the comfort read: the overstuffed Gothic thriller one hunkers down with by the fireplace. And true to those books, it overstays its welcome by 20 minutes or so, just long enough for us to begin to feel a little silly for having so much fun.

SIGHT AND SOUND, 9/00, p. 45, Philip Strick

Dean Corso, a rare books specialist, is hired by demonologist Boris Balkan to authenticate his copy of *The Nine Gates of the Kingdom of the Shadows,* a book which reputedly reveals a means of entry to the Underworld. Corso intends to compare the two existing copies with Balkan's volume, whose previous owner, Andrew Telfer, committed suicide. Corso discovers that Telfer's widow, Liana, is determined to recover the book. His apartment is ransacked, and a colleague temporarily looking after the book is murdered.

In Spain Corso learns from the antiquarians the Ceniza brothers that some of the book's nine engravings are signed 'LCF', perhaps meaning 'Lucifer'. Comparing the book with the copy owned by Victor Fargas, Corso notes a number of variations in the engravings. Fargas is murdered and the engravings are removed from his copy. Rescued from attack by a mysterious girl, Corso inspects the third surviving edition, held by Baroness Kessler in Paris. He notices discrepancies before the Baroness is killed. Corso realises that the secret of *The Nine Gates* is to be found in a combination of all three copies.

Liana Telfer obtains Balkan's copy. Corso follows Liana to the mansion where she is to officiate at a Satanist ceremony. Balkan bursts in, strangles Liana, seizes the engravings and the book and prepares to enter Satan's domain. But the invocation is faulty and he dies in a welter of flames. Urged on by the girl, Corso receives the final authentic engraving from the Cenizas and advances through the ninth portal in a blaze of light.

In co-adapting Spanish writer Arturo Pérez-Reverte's novel *The Dumas Club* into his latest film *The Ninth Gate,* director Roman Polanski has settled, not unreasonably, for only half the story, an ingenious 'spot the difference' murder mystery tricked out with fancy artwork and obscure Latin tags. As its title suggests, the rest of the novel concerns itself with the genesis and popularity of *The Three Musketeers*. In deleting all mention of Alexandre Dumas while filching bits from his share of the narrative, Polanski has created problems for himself. The serious-literary gathering of Dumas admirers, for example, has been translated into a curiously anaemic coven of devil worshippers, while the urbane Balkan, who employs antiquarian Corso to authenticate a book reputed to reveal an entrance to the Underworld, is an uneasy composite of two characters in the novel.

One of the novel's most teasing ambiguities is the suggestion that the mysterious girl, played by Emmanuelle Seigner, who follows Corso has a supernatural origin. Polanski cheerfully substantiates this with close-ups of her peculiar eyes and startling glimpses of the woman in flight, but then seems at a loss what to make of a demon who bleeds like everybody else and reads *How to Make Friends and Influence People*. Passionately embracing Corso outside a burning castle, presumably to seduce his recruitment to the armies of damned, Satan's envoy then has nothing more useful to offer than a note on Corso's windscreen sending him back to Toledo. The clumsy accident, again a Polanski invention, that puts the final engraving in his hands, completing the mysteries of the three books, brings Corso scurrying back to the castle, where a Satanist ceremony is taking place, on an inexplicably Faustian mission under a repellently lurid sky. Making no obvious sense—how would he gain access to the Ninth Gate if the guidebooks have all been burned?—this ugly image leaves the story in an anticlimactic limbo.

It's no worse, of course, than the dustcart ending of Polanski's 1988 Paris-set thriller *Frantic,* of which, putting aside the sorcery, *The Ninth Gate* is something of a re-run. Not only is its journey more interesting than its arrival, but also, like *Frantic, The Ninth Gate* uses Emmanuelle Seigner as an unfathomable distraction, an undeclared agent for some malevolent conspiracy. Her verbal contests with Corso even echo the abrasive exchanges of another Polanski couple, the duellists of *Chinatown* (1974), with Johnny Depp in Jack Nicholson's role—although, it's Lena Olin, as Satanist Liana, who first updates Faye Dunaway with the iconic shot of an open cigarette case.

Polanski clearly enjoys such references and diversions, and *The Ninth Gate* is generously spiced with humorous detail, from a Tex Avery call-sign to the Arab disguise assumed by the girl. The entry code to Balkan's apartment incorporates the number 666, while the picture of a mansion in flames, glimpsed inside, is—like the opening pan around the New York skyline—an image from *Rosemary's Baby* (1968). A disarmingly frivolous moment briefly gives Corso four eyes when a bottle is smashed over his head, while some effects trickery create two Ceniza brothers (both played by José López Rodero) out of one. It's a nice touch that, living up to their name (Spanish for ash), the Cenizas scatter fag-ends over the priceless pages they examine.

Sternly rejecting any link between his private predicaments and his films, Polanski remains a supreme technician and, perhaps unknowingly, a champion of the dispossessed, his stories told in transit. A Polanski scene is typically in the back of a car, in a hotel foyer, or on the uneasy threshold of someone else's territory. He loves corridors, doorways and sprawling apartments, his cast advancing to camera across the gulf from distant entry-points, and in this sense the massive doors featured on every engraving in *The Ninth Gate* would seem to offer a special fascination. Not particularly liked at first outing—partly because Johnny Depp, in fake grey temples, personifies the odious Corso of the book a little too accurately—the film is intricately well-made, deserves a second chance despite its disintegrations, and in time will undoubtedly acquire its own coven of heretical fans.

VILLAGE VOICE, 3/21/00, p. 135, J. Hoberman

Barely releasable hokum, stuffed with cheesy blah-blah, Roman Polanski's tongue-in-cheek occult thriller *The Ninth Gate* stars a solemn and dapper Johnny Depp as a rare-book hustler hired to track down a 17th-century satanic tome for billionaire collector Frank Langella.

Depp's leisurely quest leads through a posh, stodgy landscape of libraries, lecture halls, and back-alley biblio troves atingle with hissed warnings "Some books are dangerous!" The path is strewn with red herrings and dead bodies; eventually, Depp realizes that he's picked up witchy Emmanuelle Seigner as his guardian angel. Uninspired yet incongruously jaunty, *The Ninth Gate* never quite becomes unwatchable. Indeed, one could take perverse pleasure in a contemporary exercise in supernaturalism whose most impressive special effect is the satanic tattoo on Lena Olin's backside.

If *Mission to Mars* manages an astonishing 30 minutes, *The Ninth Gate* barely provides 30 seconds. For confessional pathos, it's a toss-up between the scene in which an elderly French baroness in a motorized wheelchair brandishes her stump and tells Depp that her "orgy days are over" and the desultory black mass (seemingly in Swedish) that Langella disrupts with heartfelt cries of "mumbo-jumbo."

Also reviewed in:
CHICAGO tRIBUNE, 3/10/00, Friday/p. A, Michael Wilmington
NEW REPUBLIC, 4/3/00, p. 25, Stanley Kauffmann
NEW YORK TIMES, 3/10/00, p. E22, Elvis Mitchell
NEW YORKER, 3/20/00, p. 144, Anthony Lane
VARIETY, 8/30-9/5/99, p. 50, Lisa Nesselson
WASHINGTON POST, 3/10/00, p. C1, Stephen Hunter

NON-STOP

A Shooting Gallery release. *Executive Producer:* Moto Seta. *Producer:* Masaya Nakamura. *Director:* Sabu. *Screenplay (Japanese with English subtitles):* Sabu. *Director of Photography:* Syuji Kuriyama. *Editor:* Shinji Tanaka. *Music:* Yamamoto Kato. *Fight Choreographer:* Hideo Saito. *Sound:* Daisuke Okamoto and Nobuo Komine. *Casting:* Naoto Kano. *Production Designer:* Mitsuo Endo. *Make-up:* Chieko Shimizu. *Running time:* 82 minutes. *MPAA Rating:* Not Rated.

CAST: Tomoro Taguchi (Yasuda); Diamond Yukai (Aizawa); Shinichi Tsutsumi (Takeda).

CHRISTIAN SCIENCE MONITOR, 11/10/00, p. 15, David Sterritt

"Non-Stop," directed by the Japanese filmmaker Sabu, brings to mind a hit movie more recent than Hitchcock's classic: the German picture "Run Lola Run," which explored a series of hyperactive events through an unconventional storytelling structure.

A similar sense of kinetic energy surges through this tragicomic tale of three low-life men—a gangster, a bank robber, and a drug-abusing clerk—pursuing one another down Tokyo streets until their brains are so scrambled they can hardly remember who's chasing whom and for what.

"Non-Stop" doesn't have the super-charged brilliance that made "Run Lola Run" so memorable, but it's one of the season's quickest-moving films, and action fans should enjoy it. It premiered in the Shooting Gallery Film Series, which brings offbeat fare to cities around the United States.

LOS ANGELES TIMES, 11/10/00, Calendar/p. 6, Kevin Thomas

"Non-Stop" is a dark, sly Japanese action comedy that plays like a "Run Lola Run"—times three. Cleverly structured, with a slam-bam score and style to burn, it marks the razzle-dazzle directorial debut of the actor known only as Sabu. Yes, it is violent, but the bloodshed is part of a sendup of yakuza mayhem.

Yasuda (Tomoro Taguchi) plays a boyish-looking young Tokyo restaurant kitchen helper, bullied outrageously and finally fired; he thereupon decides to rob a bank in desperation. Just as zero hour in his carefully worked out timetable approaches, he realizes he forgot to bring along a mask to hide his identity.

Luckily, there's a large convenience store near the bank, but, perhaps to save time, he foolishly tries to lift a mask, only to be spotted by the clerk, Aizawa (Diamond Yukai, who also composed the film's score), a husky, long-haired guy who is actually a flash-in-the-pan rock star who has hastened his skid with hard drugs. Forgetting all about his holdup plan, Yasuda starts running, with Aizawa in close pursuit. Alas, Aizawa collides with the handsome yakuza thug Takeda (Shinichi Tsutsumi), to whom he owes big bucks. The collision between the two has a domino effect that triggers an underworld war and sends Takeda running as well.

In short order, "Non-Stop" has three men chasing through the nighttime streets of Tokyo, so long and so hard that surely they lose sight of what they're running from—or toward. This shifts them into a state of mental limbo that leads to a payoff as clever as the way in which the plot is set up in the first place. For Yasuda the running has an exhilarating, liberating effect of freedom and confidence that he has never before experienced. Without being forced to take flight, Yasuda would most likely never been transformed—you have the feeling that the holdup almost certainly would have gone wrong one way or another had he actually gone through with it.

"Non-Stop" is slight but sure-fire fun, too brutal for kids even though the context is comical. Sabu, who appeared in the curiously titled "World Apartment Horror," a big hit in Japan, proves to be a real dynamo behind the camera with "Non-Stop."

NEW YORK POST, 11/10/00, p. 58, Lou Lumenick

This 1996 Japanese chase comedy, making its American premiere, has such an irresistible premise that you wonder why it hasn't been remade by Hollywood as a vehicle for, say, Martin Lawrence.

Baby-faced Yasuda (Tomoro Taguchi) is a hapless would-be robber who arrives at a Tokyo bank only to discover he's forgotten his mask. He tries to shoplift a kiddy mask, but he's confronted by a clerk named Aizawa (Diamond Yukai) and tries to shoot his way out.

This leads to a foot chase through the streets of Tokyo—and the two men eventually are joined by Takeda (Shinichi Tsutsumi), a drug dealer to whom Aizawa owes a substantial amount of money. Soon these three are being followed in cars by Takeda's fellow yakuzas, as well as a squad of rival gangsters.

This fresh, fast and funny movie was written and directed by Hiroyuki Tanaka, a Japanese actor who goes by the name Sabu. He's directed three more films since "Non-Stop" and I hope they make it to the United States in the near future.

NEWSDAY, 11/10/00, Part II/p. B6, Jan Stuart

If there could be said to be an international film language at the moment, it is spoken by such movies as Germany's "Run Lola Run" and the American independent "Go," breathless crime comedies in which strangers bump up against one another through some odd confluence of split-second timing, fate and bad luck. These films are a noisy, assertively visual breed that compels us to reflect upon, once the smoke clears, how whimsical our lives tend to be and how in thrall we are to events not of our making.

The latest addition to this subgenre is Sabu's "Non-Stop," a marginally clever but ultimately lamebrain crime satire from Japan. Sabu's anti-heroes are a human food chain of tiny fish chasing after even tinier fish. There are three in all: a kitchen worker-turned-bank robber who gets caught shoplifting his burglar's mask in a convenience store, the down-and-out rock singer behind the store counter who tries to foil the would-be thief and the gangster who is after the rock singer to make good on his drug debts.

The three chase each other through the streets far into the night and the next day, tailed by a sundry array of gang leaders and cops with serious Dirty Harry aspirations. Director-writer Sabu intends to satirize the macho affectations of those movies and the post-adolescent culture that venerates them. For all the crafty editing and "Go"-like repetition of scenes revealing new information about the same incident, however, "Non-Stop" winds up being just as stupid as the movies it purports to be sending up.

VILLAGE VOICE, 11/14/00, p. 131, J. Hoberman

A less distinguished example of Asian pop, [The reference is to *Suzhou River*; see Hoberman's review of that film.] *Non-Stop* is a strenuously crazy little action comedy that has been hustling around the international film festival circuit for the past few years under the title *Dangan Runner*. No less then *Suzhou River*, this first feature by the Japanese actor turned filmmaker Sabu celebrates a local neighborhood in the global village.

An inept dishwasher who keeps a gun in his refrigerator is on his way to rob a bank when he decides at the last minute to shoplift a gauze mask. This ill-advised maneuver compels him to take a wild shot at the convenience store clerk, who, after the hapless robber has dropped his gun, picks it up and begins pursuing him through the back alleys of Tokyo. These two soon collide with a cowardly yakuza to whom the clerk (a dope-addled musician) owes money, and he too joins the parade.

As this trio of losers run through the city (a sequence that must account for at least half the film), Sabu riffs on their respective subjectivity. In one quintessential urban encounter, all three successively fantasize about the same woman they dash past. Although the original reason for the pursuit is forgotten, this bongo-scored, endorphin-fueled, totally pointless chase culminates in a generic movie scenario: The trio barge into a yakuza universe, a convergence that convention dictates must litter the screen with corpses.

Japanese reviewers found Sabu's debut to be impressively Tarantino-esque. Others suspect that *Non-Stop*, which was shown to great enthusiasm at the 1997 Berlin Film Festival, may have inspired the following year's *Run Lola Run*. *Non-Stop* is some sort of high-concept contraption, but the bravado of its title is undermined by an exceedingly slow setup and the even more tediously static sequence that effectively terminates the movie well before its official running time.

Also reviewed in:
CHICAGO TRIBUNE, 11/10/00, Friday/p. P, Michael Wilmington
NEW YORK TIMES, 11/10/00, p. E24, A. O. Scott
VARIETY, 3/3-9/97, p. 70, Derek Elley
WASHINGTON POST, 11/10/00, p. C5, Stephen Hunter

NOT LOVE, JUST FRENZY

A Jour de Fête Films release of a Canal+ España/Fernando Colomo Producciones Cinematográficas S.L./Películas Frenéticas production. *Producer:* Fernando Colomo and Beatriz de la Gandara. *Director:* Alfonso Albacete, Miguel Barden, and David Menkes. *Screenplay (Spanish with English subtitles):* Alfonso Albacete, Miguel Bardem, and David Menkes. *Director of Photography:* Nestor Calvo. *Editor:* Miguel Angel Santamaria. *Music:* Juan Bardem. *Sound:* José Antonio Bermudez. *Sound Editor:* Pepín Fernández. *Casting:* Amelia Ochandiano. *Production Designer:* Alain Bainee. *Art Director:* Alain Bainee. *Special Effects:* Reyes Abades, Ana Casanova, Ricardo G. Elipe, and Ursula Garcia. *Costumes:* Paloma López and Angel Schlesser. *Make-up:* Pablo Robledo. *Running time:* 103 minutes. *MPAA Rating:* Not Rated.

CAST: Nancho Novo (Max);   Cayetana Guillen Cuervo (Monica);   Ingrid Rubio (Yeye); Gustavo Salmeron (Alberto);   Bibi Andersson (Cristina);   Javier Albala (Alex);   Beatriz Santiago (Maria);   Javier Manrique (Luis);   Liberto Rabal (David);   Juan Diego Botto (Carlos); Daniel Mirabal (Divva);   Juanfra Becerra (Dolly);   Paloma Tabasco (Jacky);   Nuria Gallardo (Clara); Carlos Bardem (Miguel);   Ernesto Alterio (Marcos);   Maite Pastor (Raquel);   César Vea (Julio);   Blanca Sanromán (Elsa);   Maria Esteve and Mónica Bardem (Chica Girls); La Calva (Ciberpunk);   Carlos Olivares (Porter);   Fernando Colomo (Fernando);   Luca Iezzi (Choreographer).

LOS ANGELES TIMES, 3/31/00, Calendar/p. 14, Kevin Thomas

"Not Love Just Frenzy" lives up to its title. This fast and funny tale of three young Madrid women and their gay pal confusing love and sex, but having plenty of adventures in the process, offers much of the uninhibited energy of early Almodovar. But unlike Almodovar even at his friskiest, this picture has nothing serious in mind beyond a good time, which is exactly what its trio of writers-directors—Alfonso Albacete, Miguel Bardem and David Menkes—deliver in smart and lively fashion.

Yeye (Ingrid Rubio), an exquisite brunet, and Maria (Beatriz Santiago), who wears a scarlet wig, are roommates of unexpected naivete and eager for experience. They are art students, as is their gay friend Alberto (Gustavo Salmeron), and they all hang out at a disco where Monica (Cayetana Guillen Cuervo), a hard-edged blond, works as a bartender while trying to launch an acting career.

Yeye pines for an absent Lothario, Max (Nancho Novo), and Maria pines for a fellow student, Carlos (Juan Diego Botto), whom she can see in his apartment from her own. Meanwhile, Alberto has a steamy encounter with Alex (Javier Albala), hoping it won't be just a one-night stand but also zeroing in on a model, David (Liberto Rabal), in his and Yeye's painting class.

On the run from a messy business in Barcelona, Max, a professional call boy working for the ruthless Cristina (Bibi Andersson, an Almodovar favorite), turns up at the bar where Monica works, seeking Yeye, but is swiftly waylaid by Monica. Despairing of Carlos seeing her as other than a friend, Maria tries the personals columns, only to confuse a Barcelona cop, Luis (Javier Manrique), posing as a journalist in his search for Max, with someone responding to her ad. Complications escalate amid a respectable amount of sex, drugs and rock'n'roll. Weaving in and out of the plot are a trio of dizzy drag queens, Divva (Daniel Mirabal), Jacky (Paloma Tabasco) and Dolly (Juanfra Becerra).

The film's cast is youthful, capable and great-looking. Its trio of writers-directors, who call their company Frenetic Films, know where they're going and how to get there with style and dispatch. They have a sure sense of how much emotion their material can sustain, and then briskly move on with the story, accompanied by a dynamite, eclectic soundtrack. Individually or together we should be hearing more from the "Frenetics," but don't hold your breath: It took this film four years to land on American screens.

VILLAGE VOICE, 2/1/00, p. 122, Dennis Lim

More sudsy nonsense. *Not Love, Just Frenzy:* The title reads like an indictment—but of what, exactly? A huge hit in Spain, this squalid trawl through Madrid clubland is less titillating than it is unpleasantly in-your-face. The setup suggests a low-rent *Friends:* When three neatly differentiated female roommates (man-eating bitch, loveless doormat, nominal heroine) look for a fourth, they end up with a possibly serial-killing gigolo who used to date one of them. The mode is loud and assaultive: rank Eurotechno soundtrack, sub-*Wong Foo* drag queens, an egregiously gory shooting, a violent black-comic finale involving corpse disposal. Absurdly, it took three men to write and direct this. You imagine it's the sort of thing the young Almodövar came up with in his sleep—and discarded without a second thought.

Also reviewed in:
NEW YORK TIMES, 1/28/00, p. E21, A. O. Scott
VARIETY, 10/14-20/96, p. 60, David Rooney

NOT ONE LESS

A Sony Pictures Classics release of a a a Columbia Pictures Film Production Asia presentation of a Guangxi Film Studios & Beijing New Picture Distribution Company production. *Executive Producer:* Zhang Weiping. *Producer:* Zhao Yu. *Director:* Zhang Yimou. *Screenplay (Mandarin with English subtitles):* Shi Xiangsheng. *Editor:* Zhai Ru. *Director of Photography:* Hou Yong. *Music:* San Bao. *Sound:* Wu Lala. *Sound Editor:* Wang Dong and Lin Qian. *Art Director:* Cao Jiuping. *Costumes:* Dong Huamiao. *Running time:* 106 minutes. *MPAA Rating:* Not Rated.

CAST: Wei Minzhi (Zhelingbao Village Middle School Student); Zhang Huike (Toubaozi Village Primary School Student); Tian Zhenda (Mayor Tian); Gao Enman (Primary School Teacher); Sun Zhimei (Longmensuo County Middle School Student); Li Fanfan (TV Host); Zhang Yichang (Instructor Yanching County Sports Bureau); Xu Zhanqing (Brick Factory Owner); Liu Hanzhi (Zhang Huike's Mother); Ma Guolin (Bus Station Man); Wu Wanlu (TV Station Manager); Liu Ru (Train Station Announcer); Wang Shulan (Statonery Store Clerk); Fu Xinmin (TV Station Director); Bai Mei (Restaurant Owner).

CHRISTIAN SCIENCE MONITOR, 2/18/00, p. 15, David Sterritt

[*Not One Less* was reviewed jointly with *Kadosh*; see Sterritt's review of that film.]

CINEASTE, Vol. XXV, no. 3, 1999, p. 46, Richard James Harris

Zhang Yimou's *Not One Less* is an elegant film which, if viewed in isolation from contemporary Chinese cinema and the social realities of today's China, makes for an enjoyable, somewhat easygoing viewing experience. It is a good story well-told, and the performances of the nonprofessional cast are exemplary. But the charm of this small-scale morality tale belies the fact that Zhang's choice of story promotes a view of a kindly and caring modern China—a view which ignores the very real social problems that underlie its subject matter. Unfortunately, this saddles an otherwise appealing film with propagandist overtones.

After the frantic urban story *Keep Cool* (1996), *Not One Less* sees Zhang return to his favorite beat, the rural drama. Zhang, who spent his formative years during the Cultural Revolution working the land in the rural province of Shanxi, has always seemed most comfortable when dealing with the inhabitants of the small towns and villages of the countryside. Even in *Shanghai Triad* (1995), with a title that suggests cosmopolitan urbanity, Zhang adopted the point of view of a country boy, swiftly relocating the action to a small island. Zhang has generally preferred a simple, storyteller-like exposition that neatly fits this chosen milieu. So the simple dynamics of *Not One Less*, adapted for the screen by Shi Xiangsheng from his own novel, fit Zhang like a glove. Shi's screenplay provides Zhang with the framework to explore some favorite themes: the resilience of the Chinese people and the continued effects of the new capitalism on Chinese society.

The story focuses on the tenacious Wei Minzhi, a thirteen-year-old who takes the job of substitute teacher at the village school when Teacher Gao is called away for a month to tend his sick mother. Children in rural schools are often needed for extra labor so that their families can make ends meet, and Gao's class has consequently shrunk from forty pupils to twenty-eight. The mayor of the village, a somewhat gruff but well-meaning official, promises Wei an extra ten *yuan*—still a substantial enough bonus in rural China—if she can keep all twenty-eight pupils in class until Gao returns.

A forty-five-minute preamble expertly establishes the predominant characters—the stern and stony-faced Wei, and her schoolboy nemesis Zhang Huike, the "king of troublemakers"—and allows space for some cute turns from the supporting cast of young schoolchildren. The rural school is nothing more than a bare room with a blackboard and desks, and is lacking, among other things, a plentiful supply of chalk. The young Huike gets his relationship with the young teacher off to a bad start by accidentally breaking the small stock of chalk the previous teacher cleverly obtained and rationed out to Wei. Incidents like these set the tone for the string of small events which make up the story.

When the eleven-year-old Zhang Huike disappears to the nearest city in search of work—as his family is poor and his mother is finding it difficult to make ends meet—the story proper gets underway. Wei decides to go off and find him. This allows Zhang to stage some appealing scenes with the children, which include Wei and her class frantically moving piles of bricks in an attempt to raise money for the bus fare to the city, and a scene in which the young teacher uses all the mathematical skills of her charges to calculate how much money she will need for the trip.

From then on, the plot evolves in a simple manner, as Wei overcomes a number of obstacles to complete her task. She finally persuades the receptionist of a TV station to allow her inside to make a televised appeal. The spanking new TV station is a fine example of today's modernized China, with its bland anchorwoman reminiscent of a CNN anchorperson. Wei gets in front of the cameras, delivers a shy, tearful appeal, and Zhang Huike is quickly found.

Not One Less sees Zhang continue to warn against allowing China to become a society in which financial gain is the sole arbiter of worth and value. As are many older Chinese, Zhang is concerned that traditional, age-old Chinese ideas of community are being obliterated by the influx of a crude capitalism (ideas which, whether real or imagined, extend back far before the Chinese Communist Party's rule). Zhang first properly addressed this theme, by reference to the 1930s, in *Shanghai Triad*. In *Not One Less*, Wei's search initially is motivated by money, having already lost one student to an athletics school and worried about her bonus if she loses yet another.

This desire for self-gain is soon replaced by a genuine concern for the missing Zhang Huike; the bonus is forgotten and humanism ultimately wins out over cash. But the director keeps the country's relatively newfound obsession with making money in the foreground throughout by continually stressing that everything, even helping another human being, has a monetary value in today's China. For instance, one of Zhang Huike's family demands payment for her time spent helping Wei search for him, while other adults—like a stationery shop owner—are sometimes helpful, but still eager to relieve Wei of her money. Our sympathy easily falls in with the tenacious Wei, whose desire to do the right thing risks being stalled by penny-pinching at every step.

Problems arise when the political undertones of the film swell up to drown out Zhang's humanism. Following in the footsteps of millions of other Chinese rural dwellers, the story sees Zhang Huike head for the city to find work. The film is, therefore, primarily concerned *not* with the problems of the education system, but with the economic gap between rural villages and cities. Villages can still be very poor, whereas the bustling, urban centers of the 'New China'—which are the legacy of Deng Xiaoping and the economic reforms he launched in 1979—are becoming increasingly affluent.

In Zhang Yimou's vision, this growing gap between town and country is something that can be bridged by the caring nature of the mass of Chinese people. All of the characters that stand in the way of Wei's attempt to find Zhang Huike—the "threshold guardians"—are grumpy and irritable, but ultimately benign. In the end, they take time out from their busy moneymaking schedules to help Wei find Zhang Huike, who has meanwhile been taken in by a feisty but kind noodle shop owner.

But in China proper, a floating population of millions of displaced rural workers, who have flooded into the cities in search of work (a situation addressed in such films as Wang Xiaoshuai's once-banned *So Close To Paradise/The Girl from Vietnam*), makes it clear that the migrant worker problem is too deeply rooted to be solved by good-natured citizens alone. In fact, it's endemic to the economic planning of the Chinese Communist Party, which has promoted the modernization of urban areas while effectively leaving rural areas to fend for themselves. Even the smaller cities, like the one in *Not One Less* (actually Jiangjiaku in Hebei Province) have seen an influx of migrant workers.

The core philosophy of *Not One Less*—hat everything is all right, really, the Chinese people just have to pull together—plays right into the hands of the Authorities. The notion is, after all, something that the party has wheeled out time and again to placate the population during numerous crises. The overriding impression is that Zhang's humanism has somehow been used to show China in a better light than it deserves.

Compromise is, of course, part and parcel of legal filmmaking in China, where scripts and negatives must be approved by the Film Bureau. It is true that part of the disappointment with the film stems from the fact that it is the great Zhang Yimou who has compromised. (A new director like Shi Runji, who brings with him no historical baggage, can make an entertaining film, *A Beautiful New World*, with a similar message and get praised for it.) But one always looks upon Zhang Yimou as a paragon of honesty and honor, a man whose integrity transcends the political machinations which surround him. Although he has never been one to actively court controversy, Zhang has never shied away from a conflict with the Chinese authorities in defense of his art. He has always told the truth as he sees it and has taken the consequences. Here, it seems that Zhang, who has been suspect in the eyes of the authorities since he made the banned *Lifetimes/To Live*, has submitted a politically acceptable script simply to get a film approved and made.

Interestingly, the way Zhang focuses on a group of schoolchildren to allude to a more general theme brings to mind the cinema of Iran, another country which is tough on its filmmakers. It comes as no surprise to learn that Zhang had been watching Iranian movies before he made *Not One Less*. Indeed, the arid courtyard of the school even recalls Ebrahim Fouruzesh's *The Jar* (1992), which details the problems a teacher suffers while trying to repair his school's leaky water jar. The neo-realist technique of *Not One Less*, first used by Zhang in *The Story Of Qiu Ju* (although there, unlike here, he used professional actors), also is a hallmark of Iranian cinema and is used well by the Chinese director. Zhang is so skillful directing the nonprofessional child actors that they barely seem to notice the camera.

Zhang could have avoided the problems of *Not One Less* by paying closer attention to his Iranian influences. He has angrily denounced politically-oriented readings of his film, claiming that Western critics harp too much on the political content of Chinese films, know too little about China, and ignore their other merits. This is, sadly, all too often the case. But the problem with *Not One Less* is that, in spite of its charm, it does have a political subtext, and, therefore, must be analyzed in a political context. By contrast, Iranian films have rarely dealt with politics but have instead zeroed in closely on individuals in order to make metaphysical, intellectual, or humanistic points. If Zhang had wanted to ensure an easy passage through China's strict censors, he might have been better advised to make a film which, like those of his Iranian counterparts, promoted humanism with no reference to the wider political arena.

LOS ANGELES TIMES, 2/18/00, Calendar/p. 2, Kenneth Turan

It's characteristic of great chefs that even the simplest dishes they create bear the mark of their gift and their skill. It's the same with film directors, which speaks to the success, and the surprise, of Zhang Yimou's "Not One Less."

An unadorned, sentimental story about schoolchildren in rural China, "Not One Less" has a warmth and sweetness that is especially hard to resist because its director is such a skillful filmmaker and because his interest in this neorealistic tale is so evident.

At the same time, it's difficult not to notice how different "Not One Less" is from the previous work of a creative force who, along with Chen Kaige ("Farewell, My Concubine," "The Emperor and the Assassin") and Tian Zhuangzhuang ("The Blue Kite"), is one of the most gifted of China's celebrated Fifth Generation group of directors.

Zhang is best-known for visually opulent, emotional melodramas like "Red Sorghum," "Raise the Red Lantern" and "Shanghai Triad," films that were also united by the presence of actress Gong Li, who was the director's real-life partner.

Now that these two are no longer an item, either personally or professionally, Zhang has changed his focus. "Sometimes you miss what you have not been eating," he pithily informed the New York Times. "I decided to make films about little people; ordinary, common people."

Certainly "Not One Less" fits that description. Set in the hardscrabble village of Shuiquan, it details the varying crises that result when the local instructor, Teacher Gao, has to leave the area for a month to care for his ailing mother.

The only substitute the town's beleaguered mayor can scrounge up is a 13-year-old girl named Wei Minzhi, not the ideal caretaker for a group of 28 rambunctious, cute-as-the-dickens students.

Though he's dubious, Teacher Gao gives newcomer Wei the benefit of his experience. Words written on the blackboard "should be as big as a donkey's turd," be advises, and chalk is at so much of a premium that no more than one piece can be used per day. And, because education is not a priority for rural students, the teacher promises Wei a bonus if all the pupils, "not one less," are in the classroom when he returns.

Wei Minzhi does not appear to be top teacher material, but she has a stubborn spunkiness that serves her well. And she's so determined to earn her bonus she even tries to sabotage the transfer of one of her athletically promising students to a prestigious sports program in the big city.

But Wei Minzhi's greatest crisis comes when the class scamp, the troublemaking Zhang Huike, is pulled out of school because of economic necessity and shipped off to the city of Jiangjiakou to help support his sick mother. Determined to get him back, Wei Minzhi has to fall back on her own resources and her class for support, a process that proves to be educational all the way around.

Director Zhang, working from a screenplay by Shi Xiangsheng, has done several things to enhance his film's connection to real life, starting with casting the project entirely with nonprofessionals. He's also used individuals, like the village mayor, who do the same thing in real life they do on screen, allowed people to keep their real names in the movie, and at times used hidden cameras to help his cast forget that they're acting.

As with the new wave of neorealistic Iranian films, "Not One Less" is slow getting started. But, helped by unexpected emotional moments like a tiny student's ode to Teacher Gao's passion for chalk, it builds to an involving, albeit earnest conclusion.

Though the film does take a few relatively mild shots at rural poverty and the shortcomings of the country's education system, "Not One Less' " modified gee-whiz nature makes you wonder if the director's past difficulties with the Chinese authorities was an unspoken factor in his making this kind of film today. For an artist with Zhang's scope, this Chinese version of the old Soviet "boy loves tractor" movies, no matter how deftly and lovingly executed, has to feel like an unnerving departure.

NEW STATESMAN, 6/12/00, p. 47, Jonathan Romney

The world over, film-makers bemoan their lot—having to suffer heavy-handed producers, being misunderstood by critics, not getting final cut. All due respect, but most of them don't know they're born: they should try working in China. There, film-makers have to worry about a government that has its own ideas about the national images that China should export. In the late Eighties and early Nineties, a group of film-makers—the so-called "Fifth Generation" directors, including Chen Kaige and his former cinematographer Zhang Yimou—put mainland Chinese cinema back on the world map, but not always with official blessing.

Zhang's lush 1920s dramas *Ju Dou* and *Raise the Red Lantern* proved eminently exportable, providing an international art-house icon in his glamorous lead actress Gong Li. But both films were initially banned in China; the government tends not to explain its reasons, but among them were certainly the films' heated, if demure, sexual content, their images of personal rebellion and what could be construed as a depiction of a former "primitive" China (the film minister at the time complained of seeing "too many bandits, eunuchs, prostitutes and spies" on screen).

Zhang subsequently made *The Story of Qiu Ju,* a more sober exercise in present-day realism, only to be accused by some critics of cynically appeasing the government. But his problems didn't stop there—he has repeatedly been prevented from attending international festivals and, last year, he pulled two films from Cannes, claiming that he was tired of the west reading his films as either political statements or apologies for the government. Whatever prompted his complaint, one can see his point: it's tough enough to cope with official pressures without worrying about approval from the Croisette crowds.

Zhang's most recent British release suggests that this is a debilitating quandary. *Not One Less* is even more back-to-basics than *Qiu Ju*—a low-key provincial tale with a non-professional cast, worlds away from the opulently staged passions of his early work. It's a benign vignette about a gauche 13-year-old girl, Wei Minzhi, who is drafted as a substitute teacher in a village school. Only two years older than her charges, she's barely up to the job: asked what she knows, she haltingly recites two lines of a song, then clams up. She's useless at discipline, preferring to hide at the back of the school shack, which doubles as accommodation for her and several pupils. Then the class rebel, a boisterously grinning lad called Zhang Huike, escapes to the city looking for work to pay his mother's debts. In a sudden fit of responsibility, Wei Minzhi decides to go to retrieve him.

However authentically Chinese it feels, *Not One Less* has the same shape as many school stories in western cinema, from *To Sir with Love* to *Dangerous Minds* the teacher and her pupils are redeemed by learning to face a common challenge. Wei Minzhi's first problem is to raise the bus fare to town, so she takes the children to earn cash at the local brickworks. Soon, they're working out how many bricks they must shift to bring the boy back. The moral: a problem shared can provide even the most inexperienced teacher with ample material for a maths class.

The film's first half has a spontaneous drive which comes largely from Zhang's casting of non-professionals in parts so close to life that they effectively play themselves. The mayor really is a village mayor; Wei Minzhi really is a gauche, blushing, grouchy-looking 13-year-old called Wei Minzhi. When her pupils crowd into the classroom for their first gawp at her, or bicker behind her back, the film has a raw, anarchic spontaneity that can't be faked.

Then things turn mawkish, to an excruciatingly soapy flute theme. Wei Minzhi's spends the night at the city bus station, eking out her precious ink to write handbills. She waits a day outside the TV centre after the concierge refuses to help her. Eventually, the station manager (a station manager in real life) ticks off the jobsworth (in reality, a ticket-office clerk), who replies: "I just follow the rules." As in *Qiu Ju,* minor officials may be pedantic or abusive, but those up top are magnanimous enough to help the people directly. In the end, a helpful Esther Rantzen-style TV host (a real-life TV presenter) not only reunites teacher and pupil, but also publicises the fate of underfunded village schools and brings the class a welcome windfall of coloured chalk.

A loose, pithy comedy carved out of the everyday becomes a crude public service announcement, critical of a pressing social problem, but expressing confidence in authority to correct matters. *Not One Less* feels all the more awkward considering a parallel that is especially visible in the first half: Zhang has claimed the influence of Iranian filmmakers, notably Abbas Kiarostami, as an object lesson in achieving wonders despite restrictive conditions. But compared to the complex and open-ended miniatures achieved by Kiarostami, Jafar Panahi *(The White Balloon)* or Makhmalbaf *père et fille (A Moment of Innocence, The Apple),* Zhang's film looks schematic and faux-naive.

Mainland Chinese cinema is moving on. The most urgent, lucid voices belong to younger, independent directors such as Wang Xiaoshuai *(The Days)* and Jia Zhangke *(Xiao Wu),* often working outside state-approved structures, even resorting to pseudonyms if necessary.

Meanwhile, Chen Kaige, abandoning his increasingly overblown historical epics, recently announced, of all things, an erotic thriller set in London. And Zhang, whatever restraints he faces, appears to have lost his way. As for his erstwhile superstar Gong Li, she has become one of the international faces of L'Oréal, and good for her—because she's worth it.

NEW YORK, 2/21/00, p.100, Peter Rainer

The Chinese director Zhang Yimou has a rare gift for dramatizing highly theatrical stories in highly naturalistic settings. His greatest film, *The Story of Qiu Ju,* was a carefully prepared fable, and yet it had the free-form look of something caught on the sly as a part of life's ongoing bustle. His new movie, *Not One Less,* has something of the same quality, but it's simpler and even more emotionally affecting. The mayor of a small village in western China replaces the local schoolteacher, away for a month, with a 13-year-old substitute barely older than her unruly students. Wei Minzhi—played by a real-life middle-school student using her own name—has a wide-open face with flushed cheeks. It takes a while to warm up to her, because she seems all too well adapted to her role as martinet. Her drive is a little frightening in someone so unformed, but she becomes a true heroine when a student, Zhang Huike (also his real name), is forced into the city to earn money for his family. Minzhi, who has been promised a bonus by the mayor if all her students remain enrolled, connives her way into the city to bring back Huike, a student with a naughty urchin's grin who has given her nothing but trouble.

The village scenes and the city scenes have a mysterious connectedness. Together they seem to take in the whole range of quotidian life. Minzhi's search for Huike, seen at various points in the story alone and scavenging for food, becomes her passion; we can see how all her pride and devotion and willfulness are wrapped up in this little boy's plight. Seemingly unlocatable in the urban sprawl, Huike has no idea he is being searched for. When Minzhi, hoping to spread the word, manages to get herself interviewed on a television news program, she clams up at first, but then her concern and sorrow break through and Huike, seeing the spectacle on TV, cries along with her. It's one of the most improbably satisfying love scenes on film, but Zhang Yimou doesn't milk the moment. He's a stringent sentimentalist, and so, when our emotions well up, we don't feel like we're being played for fools. His feeling for these children is deep, and he honors them with the full measure of his respect. They have the mettle to survive poverty, and it shows in their brazen, lyrical faces.

NEW YORK POST, 2/18/00, p. 54, Jonathan Foreman

Contemporary Chinese movies are invariably filled with gorgeous photography, and "Not One Less" —a winner of the Golden Lion at the Venice Film Festival and the first major film by the great Zhang Yimou ("Ju Dou," "Raise the Red Lantern") not to star his beautiful ex-girlfriend Gong Li—is no exception.

You can almost smell the dust on the country roads and feel the cool dawn breeze blowing through empty city streets.

And unlike some of the ponderous historical epics that have come out of that country in the last couple of years, this film uses what looks like a sentimental story about children to make telling points about the kind of country China has become since the ruling Communists unleashed the forces of free-market capitalism.

This economic revolution has been an even bigger shock for China's rural poor than for her city-dwellers. And like the director's 1992 film "Qiu Ju," "Not One Less" is about a villager who is forced to depend on the unpredictable mercies of urbanites when she leaves her poor village on a mission to the city.

In this case, the voyager is Wei Minzhi (played by an actual villager of the same name, as are all the roles). She's a 13-year-old girl who happens to be the recently appointed substitute teacher of a crumbling one-room primary school.

Wei gets the job after Teacher Gao (Gao Enman) leaves his post for a month to look after his mother.

Before leaving town, Teacher Gao tells Wei that the school has been losing pupils and that her prime responsibility is to make sure that there are still 28 students attending classes upon his return. If she succeeds, she'll get a bonus from the mayor.

Wei isn't much of a teacher, and her job is made no easier by the insolence of 10-year-old Zhang Huike (Zhang Huike), the class troublemaker. But things get much worse when Zhang doesn't turn up to school one day.

Wei discovers that his indebted mother has sent the child to the big city to find work. Panicked at the thought of losing a pupil, Wei determines to go and bring the boy back.

Some of the acting, given that it's all done by real schoolchildren, mayors, bureaucrats, etc., is very poor—Teacher Gao is especially weak— but much of it is surprisingly convincing and fresh, particularly the work of Wei Minzhi and the kids at the school.

NEWSDAY, 2/18/00, Part II/p. B13, John Anderson

At A rural schoolhouse, where Teacher Gao is taking a month off to care for his sick mother, the Mayor brings in a substitute: Wei Minzhi, 13 years old. She's agreed to take the job for 50 yuan, but the only thing anyone mentions is her caring for the children and keeping the already dwindling class together—Teacher Gao promises an extra 10 yuan if upon his return there's "not one less."

Faced with an underfinanced schoolroom, students who learn by rote—and treat the teacher like a sister—and one box of chalk that's supposed to last at least a month, Minzhi grows into her job, and into herself. When the mayor arrives one day with an Olympics trainer to appropriate one of Minzhi's students—a sprinter who trained herself to run so she wouldn't wet the bed—Minzhi sees only her small, unpaid fortune fading.

But when the troublesome Zhang Huike, her worst cutup, leaves school to go work in the city, the money is almost beside the point. She goes after him—by bus, with little money, no map and few ideas—to bring him back into the fold.

As one of China's leading filmmakers, Zhang Yimou has been condemned in the past for his deft use of historical epic to shed harsh light on current-day China. Here, he just goes for the real thing: the shameful accomplishments of China's public education system (whose number of uneducated children is no doubt deflated), and a country that's changing, not for the better. The people Minzhi encounters as she makes her way through the strange city are little help to her, although one brusquely suggests she stop drawing wanted posters for Huike and go to the local television station.

There, although Minzhi is rudely dismissed by a receptionist, she proceeds to hold a vigil at the station's gates, waiting for the station master, who understands the public relations nightmare Minzhi is about to create. The station becomes altruistic but, in Zhang's view, the catalyst of change is as much about western marketing as it is about human benevolence.

Relating the story of Minzhi and Huike, Zhang keeps a documentarian's distance, shooting crisp, flat pictures of what needs no embellishment anyway. His mood is more important: We followed Minzhi so matter-of-factly from her classroom to her travels to the near-destitution of her life on the street that the emotional catharsis becomes totally breathtaking. "Not One Less" may be a movie that demands something of the viewer, but going home unhappy isn't one of them.

NEWSWEEK, 3/6/00, p. 68, David Ansen

"Not One Less," the latest film from Zhang Yimou, China's foremost director, has an almost spartan simplicity. Following the historical epic "To Live" and the lush, gilded "Shanghai Triad," it feels like a palate cleanser. Zhang has returned to the harsh countryside of "The Story of Qiu Ju." As in that Gong Li film, his heroine is a stubborn, obsessive woman who journeys to the city on a monomaniacal mission.

Wei Minzhi is a 13-year-old schoolgirl who has to fill in as a substitute teacher in her village's one-room schoolhouse. Only a year or two older than her charges, she hasn't much knowledge to pass on, or interest in teaching. Before he leaves to tend to his sick mother, the regular teacher exhorts her to prevent any of the students from dropping out: in this impoverished area, kids are always leaving to find jobs to help their families. He promises her a bonus if she succeeds. Wei fixates on this task, so when 10-year-old Zhang Huike vanishes from her class to search for work in the city, she trains her mulish will on the job of finding him and bringing him back. Why does she care so much? That's the mystery at the heart of this touching tale.

There isn't a professional actor in the movie. In most cases, Zhang has cast people in the roles they play in life—a village mayor plays a village mayor—and the characters are given the actors' names. This gives his fable of perseverance a documentary texture. "Not One Less" is the most emotionally direct of Zhang's films. Its upbeat ending seems almost propagandistic. But its charm is deceptive. Underneath the surface, the portrait of China and its people that emerges is bleak: example after example of poverty, desperation and indifference. Wei's triumph does not come easy.

SIGHT AND SOUND, 8/00, p. 53, Philip Kemp

Provincial China, the present. Teacher Gao, who runs a primary school in the village of Shuixian, needs a month's leave to tend his dying mother. The mayor finds a substitute, 13-year-old Wei Minzhi. Gao doubts Minzhi can do the job, but no one else is available. Already children are leaving; the former class of 40 is down to 28. Gao promises Minzhi a financial bonus if numbers are no lower when he returns.

Minzhi makes her pupils copy lessons from the blackboard while she keeps guard outside. Zhang Huike, a bright but disruptive boy, causes frequent trouble. Sports officials come to take away Ming Xinhong, a promising runner. One morning Zhang Huike fails to appear, his mother has sent him to the city to work.

Determined to bring Huike back, Minzhi enlists her pupils' help in raising money for the trip to the city. There, she spends her last funds on some fruitless notices. A passer-by suggests she try the television station for help, but Minzhi is refused admittance. Determined, she haunts the gates for a day and a half until the station manager hears about her and allows her to make an appeal for Huike on a current affairs programme. The show is seen by the manageress of the café where Huike is working. Reunited, the two are taken back to Shuixian by a television crew. The school is inundated with gifts of money, and Huike writes "Teacher Wei" on the board.

Not One Less' director Zhang Yimou made his name with a run of lavish, highly coloured period melodramas starring his then partner Gong Li: *Red Sorghum, Raise the Red Lantern, Shanghai Triad* and the like. But midway through this sequence of opulent, historical films came *The Story of Qiu Ju,* a contemporary drama in realistic style, in which Gong Li drabbed herself down to play a peasant woman fighting for justice for her husband after he is assaulted by the village headman. With *Not One Less,* Zhang returns to the low-key realism of *Qiu Ju.* Once again a lone female from a peasant village travels to the city and through sheer persistence achieves her goal in the face of bureaucratic obstacles. But where the earlier film assigned the lead roles to professionals, using non-professionals in support, *Not One Less* is cast entirely from non-professionals, nearly all playing what they are in life: the village mayor is a real mayor, the stationery-store clerk works in a stationery-store and so on.

This leads to occasional awkward moments: the mayor in particular has trouble with eyelines, not always looking at the person he's talking to (but presumably at Zhang for direction). In general, though, there's an appealing freshness about the performances, especially in the classroom scenes. Altogether the first half of the film, prior to Wei Minzhi's departure for the city (where she is determined to locate her ex-pupil Huike) works well, featuring a wealth of vivid detail. Teacher Gao, worried Minzhi will waste the poverty-stricken school's supply of chalk, tells her that words on the blackboard should be only "as big as a donkey's turd". Initially sullen and indifferent, Minzhi is increasingly engaged with her pupils as they work out the practical maths involved in raising her bus fare to the city or troop off on an expedition to the local brickworks to earn the money.

But on reaching the city, the film turns steadily more schematic and predictable. Shots of Minzhi and Huike separately wandering the streets, each gazing at food stalls, or of Minzhi asleep on the pavement as pedestrians stride past, are pure Victorian cliché. It's no surprise, then, when the equivalent of the kindly old gentleman—a stock figure in sentimental Victorian literature—shows up. Trying to enter the local television station, Minzhi is blocked by a jobsworth demanding her ID. But when the station manager finds out, he rebukes his employee, sits Minzhi down in his office with a bowl of food and puts her on television to broadcast her appeal. Occasional minor officials may be callously inflexible, but rest assured, those in charge are always ready to help.

Qiu Ju, made after Zhang had run into trouble with the authorities in Beijing, also pushed a message calculated to warm the hearts of the Chinese leadership. But *Not One Less,* being partly funded by a subsidiary of US based Columbia Pictures, has two masters to please. So we not only get a clumsy scene where Minzhi and her class share Cokes at the village store ("Coke tastes good," they enthuse), but a feel-good ending that might embarrass Hollywood at its most shameless. Beaming peasants, kindly television crew, cartloads of coloured chalks with which the kids can write suitable ideograms ("Home - Happiness -Diligence") on the blackboard—and a sententious end-title telling us that, while poverty forces a million Chinese children each year to leave school, voluntary contributions have helped 15 per cent to return. All that's missing is the address we should send donations to.

VILLAGE VOICE, 2/22/00, p. 140, Leslie Camhi

The school as microcosm of society is part of a long cinematic tradition, from the little anarchists of *Zéro de Conduite* to the proto-fascists of *Mädchen in Uniform* to the '60s rebels of *If....* Well, the nation is one big classroom in Zhang Yimou's *Not One Less,* a disarming parable about who's in charge in contemporary China.

Zhang, best known for a string of lush historical melodramas starring Gong Li, employs a far dustier style for this story of a 13-year-old substitute teacher in a rural village school. Wei Minzhi (played by a schoolgirl of the same name) is recruited for this unpopular job by the local mayor when the regular teacher leaves town for a month to tend his ailing mother.

She's no matinee idol, but she has a certain sulky, recalcitrant charm, as she stands guard over her slightly younger students. She's also not much of a pedagogue. "Copy the lesson!" she barks to her 28 squirmers, then storms outside and draws with a stick in dirt. Is it any wonder that when the leader abdicates responsibility, trouble soon follows? Zhang Huike, a 10-year-old with an iron will and a winning smirk, is one of trouble's prime movers. But after he disappears to the city to earn money to pay back his family's debts, class and teacher rally, and the real learning begins.

With *Not One Less*, Zhang Yimou has fashioned what feels like an uncannily accurate portrait of a culture where Communist ideology has vanished like a brief dream, as traditional community values clash with the burgeoning cult of money. (Adding to the film's aura of transparency, almost all the actors are nonprofessionals who are mayors, teachers, students, et cetera in real life.) In the nameless city where Wei Minzhi follows Zhang Huike, and where she is nearly as lost as he is, acts of charity are rare, and most people are preoccupied with maintaining their position or making their next yuan. The bureaucrats she encounters would flourish under any system, but the new wealth is accompanied by new forms of poverty. When she stares at a television camera in a mute appeal to find her student, her despair at losing him is mixed with profound alienation in the face of technology. The film's occasional dips into sentimental cuteness and its too-pat ending can't cancel the gap that yawns ever wider between rural and urban society.

A few months ago, an upscale New York furniture emporium was selling little wooden desks from a rural school in China. Somebody had wagered that their patina of age and fragility would appeal to cash-flushed sensibilities. Perhaps our taste for the exquisite poverty revealed in national cinemas like that of Iran and China is just another symptom of our decadence. But in those places, a battle is still being waged; here it's already been won.

Also reviewed in:
CHICAGO TRIBUNE, 3/17/00, Friday/p. F, Michael Wilmington
NATION, 2/28/00, p. 32, Stuart Klawans
NEW REPUBLIC, 2/14/00, p. 30, Stanley Kauffmann
NEW YORK TIMES, 2/18/00, p. E24, A. O. Scott
VARIETY, 9/20-26/99, p. 89, Deborah Young

NOT OF THIS WORLD

An Entertech Releasing Corporation release of a Lumiere & Company production in collaboration with RAI Radiotelevisione Italiana. *Executive Producer:* Rosanna Seregni. *Producer:* Lionello Cerri. *Director:* Giuseppe Piccioni. *Screenplay (Italian with English subtitles):* Giuseppe Piccioni, Gualtiero Rosella, and Lucia Maria Zei. *Director of Photography:* Luca Bigazzi. *Editor:* Esmeralda Calabria. *Music:* Ludovico Einaudi. *Sound:* Amedeo Casati. *Sound Editor:* Filippo Bussi. *Casting:* Beatrice Kruger. *Production Designer:* Marco Belluzzi. *Costumes:* Carolina Olcese. *Running time:* 104 minutes. *MPAA Rating:* Not Rated.

CAST: Margherita Buy (Sister Caterina); Silvio Orlando (Ernesto); Carolina Freschi (Teresa); Maria Cristina Minerva (Esmeralda); Sonia Gessner (Mother Superior); Stefano Abbati (Jogger); Giuliana Lojodice (Caterina's Mother); Alessandro Di Natale (Gabriele, the Policeman); Marina Massironi (Marina); Francesco Foti (Policeman); Silvano Piccardi (Man with Wig).

CHRISTIAN SCIENCE MONITOR, 2/25/00, p. 15, David Sterritt

[*Not of this World* was reviewed jointly with *Judy Berlin*; see Sterritt's review of that film.]

NEW YORK POST, 2/25/00, p. 56, Lou Lumenick

"Not of This World," Italy's entry for the Best Foreign Language Film Oscar, didn't get nominated—though it's superior to last year's winner in the category, the maudlin "Life Is Beautiful."

The main character is a novice nun, but the depiction of her in this poignant, bittersweet comedy is light years from Hollywood stereotypes.

Caterina's life is changed when a jogger hands her an abandoned baby boy he's found in a park. She turns the baby over to the authorities, but the experience has awakened Caterina's maternal instincts.

Obsessed with finding the baby's mother, she traces a sweater that the boy was found wrapped in to a dry-cleaning establishment owned by Ernesto, a lonely middle-aged man.

Ernesto very gradually admits he may be the father of the child, who was born to one of his former employees. But he's deeply ambivalent about assuming responsibility for the boy's care. In a lesser movie, Caterina might renounce her vows and raise the child with Ernesto, but "Not of This World" isn't so predictable or sentimental.

Director Giuseppe Piccioni (who wrote the excellent script with Gualtiero Rosella) treats Caterina's crisis of faith with respect, generosity and gentle humor—and depicts the working-class milieu with great affection.

He draws a luminously layered performance from Margherita Buy as Caterina, who questions her choices in life with a subtlety practically unknown in American movies.

Silvio Orlando, who bears an uncanny resemblance to the late Peter Sellers, is very funny as Ernesto, a bundle of neuroses and phobias who struggles to connect with people.

"Not of This World," is the best foreign film released here since "All About My Mother."

NEWSDAY, 2/25/00, Part II/p. B6, Gene Seymour

The movies' recharged romance with serendipity is apparently not limited to America's shores. While neither as ambitious nor as dazzlinq as "Magnolia," "Not of This World," an award-winner in its native Italy, is nonetheless more convincing about destiny's capricious and unexpected impact on seemingly disparate lives.

Those lives in question belong to a young nun named Caterina (Margherita Buy), a dry-cleaning store owner named Ernesto (Silvio Orlando) and a baby with no name who almost literally falls into Caterina's hands, wrapped in an old blue sweater. Her only clue to the baby's origins is a laundry tag attached to the sweater, which in turn leads her to Ernesto's business.

Yes, Ernesto says, he recognizes the sweater as his. But he also remembers that it was last seen on a former employee, a teenager named Teresa (Carolina Freschi) who, because of a one-night fling, is barely more memorable to Ernesto than the other women who work for him.

Caterina and Ernesto forge an odd investigating tandem in search of Teresa, who is shown aimlessly wandering the streets in search of shelter and work. Ernesto, a dour, lonely guy with not much else besides his business occupying his life, alternates between his fears (or hopes) that he may be the baby's father and a nascent fascination with Caterina—portrayed by the luminous Buy as a lapsed sensualist with some unresolved issues of her own brought to the surface by the mystery infant.

Director Giuseppe Piccioni handles the emotional complexities of this story with a deceptively light touch. Less-assured hands would have pressed some buttons a lot harder than he does. When, for instance, Teresa flinches from the embrace of her creepy stepfather, we are left with little more than our own presumptions—valid ones—about what happened. Piccioni, who co-wrote the script with Gualtiero Rosella, trusts both his actors and the audience to fill in the blanks with their imaginative resources. By doing so, "Not of This World" proves you can probe a lot deeper into emotional terrain with simple tools and elemental strokes.

VILLAGE VOICE, 2/29/00, p. 118, Nico Baumbach

A young nun, a Laundromat owner, and a teenage girl: lonely individuals living in protective shells, drawn together by capricious circumstance. This year's Italian Oscar entry might be called *Life Is Bittersweet*. As it is, the title *Not of This World* means to convey a kind of poignant irony: We all feel that we are not of this world, which makes us so emphatically of this world. Searching for the identity of an abandoned baby, the nun, Caterina (Margherita Buy), follows her only clue—the baby's wrap—to the Laundromat of deeply repressed Ernesto (the superb Silvio Orlando). Meanwhile, it's not hard to guess that Teresa (Carolina Freschi), the frail and frumpy teenage girl wandering Milan, is the baby's mother, or that once you wash that face, she'll look like Ally Sheedy at the end of *The Breakfast Club.*

Giuseppe Piccioni's patient, affectedly unaffected style is reminiscent of recent Belgian and French naturalism. He refrains from explicit psychologizing, but drops helpful hints that flatter the viewer—Caterina uncovers a telltale photo of Ernesto with his arm around a woman; when Teresa's stepfather hugs her, she flinches, but oh so slightly—scenes unpunctuated and brief enough to give the impression of subtlety. The film is patently rigged, but particularly when Ernesto's profoundly morose features start to relax, its restrained humanism can be hard to resist.

Also reviewed in:
NEW YORK TIMES, 2/25/00, p. E33, Elvis Mitchell
CHICAGO TRIBUNE, 2/2/01, Friday/p. I, John Petrakis
VARIETY, 4/5-11/99, p. 34, David Rooney
WASHINGTON POST, 9/15/00, Weekend/p. 47, Michael O'Sullivan

NOWHERE TO HIDE

A Lions Gate Films release of a Taewon Entertainment production. *Executive Producer:* Kang Woo-Suk and Yoo Jeong-Ho. *Producer:* Chung Tae-Won. *Director:* Lee Myeong-Se. *Screenplay (Korean with English subtitles):* Lee Myeong-Se. *Director of Photography:* Jeong Kwang-Seok and Song Haeng-Ki. *Editor:* Ko Im-Pyo. *Music:* Cho Sung-Woo, Kim Dae-Hong, and Choi Young-Hoon. *Sound:* Chae In-Young, Park Young-Shin, and (music) Yoo Dae-Hyeon. *Production Designer:* Lee Myeong-Se. *Art Director:* Ooh Sang-Man. *Set Decorator:* Chung Sang-Hyeok. *Special Effects:* Kim Cheol-Seck. *Costumes:* Lee Soo-Jung and Kim Hyang-Hee. *Make-up:* Hwang Hyuang-Kyoo. *Running time:* 200 minutes. *MPAA Rating:* Not Rated.

CAST: Park Jung-Hun (Detective Woo); An Seong-Ki (Chang Sungmin); Jang Dong-Keon (Detective Kim); Choi Ji-Wu (Juyon); Do Yong-Koo (Detective Chang); Shim Cheol-Jong (Detective Chu, "Viper"); Lee Won-Jong (Detective Park "Sleepy"); Park Seung-Ho (Detective Lee); Ki Joo-Bong (Chief); Song Young-Chang (Murder Victim); Kwon Yong-Wun (Fishhead); Park Sang-Myeon (Meathead); An Jae-Mo (Yongbae); Lee Hye-Eun (Woo's Sister).

LOS ANGELES TIMES, 12/22/00, Calendar/p. 26, Kevin Thomas

"Nowhere to Hide" reveals that in Lee Myung-Se Korea has a filmmaker with enough razzle-dazzle and visceral appeal to rival Hong Kong's—and Hollywood's—John Woo. Like Woo, Lee doesn't resort to flashy technique merely to show off but instead to pull us into the heart of what his hero is feeling and experiencing. And what Inchon homicide detective Woo (Park Joong-Hoon) lives through is fast and furious, savage and dangerous.

A middle-aged drug boss emerges from an unmarked doorway in a nondescript building alongside the hilly port city's landmark 40 Steps stairs—and is immediately stabbed to death by a ruthless rival, Chang Sungmin (Ahn Sung-Ki). Woo can break into a warm smile and a hearty manner for pals, but his boyish looks mask a zealot. Woo lives only for his job, and he's a lot quicker to take the law into his own hands than even Dirty Harry.

"Detectives do whatever it takes to get the job done," he remarks unapologetically, and the film shows him interrogating suspects with such brutality that we start feeling guilty at enjoying the breathless kinetic energy of Lee's bravura style. (Lee employs two cameramen for this most visually expressive of films—his sixth.)

Fortunately, this proves to be part of Lee's strategy: As Woo begins to close in on the elusive Chang, he is brought more and more in touch with the violent side of his nature. We learn that as a youngster Woo had his own scrapes with the law and that his father managed to steer his aggressive son into police work. Lee in no way condones Woo's brutality but creates circumstances in which Woo can't escape his true self.

Consequently, "Nowhere to Hide" gains in substance as it moves through richly atmospheric settings, shot mainly at night and in the rain, with Woo encountering a clutch of film noir types, including Chang's bar hostess girlfriend (Choi Ji-Woo). Throughout, the manic Woo is counterpointed by his calm partner Kim (Jang Dong-Kun), a rational, balanced family man.

For all his mastery of his medium, Lee is no less effective in directing actors than in creating images. Ahn is Korea's most distinguished veteran star, and he conveys chang's sinister strength through sheer presence, for in this film he is seen far more than he is heard.

"Nowhere to Hide" represents a new peak for Park Joong-Hoon, who among Korean movie actors comes closest to being an internationally renowned star. American audiences have had a chance to see him in the hugely popular and appealing "Two Cops" (1993), a classic policier, and the delightful romantic comedy "My Love, My Bride" (1991).

NEW YORK POST, 12/22/00, p. 55, V. A. Musetto

The South Korean neo-noir actioner "Nowhere to Hide" opens with a tribute to Sergei Eisenstein's Odessa Steps sequence in "Potemkin": A drug lord is viciously stabbed to death on the Forty Steps, a steep, out-door staircase in the port city of Inchon.

As the Bee Gees sing "Holiday" on the soundtrack, the killer flees into the torrential rain with a briefcase full of cash.

The killing sets off a police manhunt for another drug kingpin.

Heading the search is a sadistic maverick detective named Woo (after John Woo, of course), who isn't adverse to twisting the law (and bodies) to suit his own needs.

As directed by Lee Myung-Se, a leader of the Korean New Wave of the late 1980s, "Nowhere to Hide" is light on story and dialogue but heavy on atmosphere: Lots of rain and snow, neon-lit streets, shadows on walls, bloodied bodies, and slow-motion.

The action sequences are stunning, especially a rain-drenched fistfight on railroad tracks.

Explaining his inspiration, Lee says he was intrigued by World Cup soccer,

"I thought that if I could express the furious sweating of athletes... perhaps I could depict a new type of action," he notes.

But that doesn't mean Lee (who also scripted) doesn't have a soft side. When you least expect it, he throws in moments of great tenderness.

The entire film is a feast for the eyes that brings to mind the work of Hong Kong ace Wong Kar-Wai.

Don't let the glut of high-profile movies opening this weekend keep you from seeing "Nowhere to Hide."

NEWSDAY, 12/22/00, Part II/p. B15, Gene Seymour

Ah, for the days when detectives were lean, hawk-nosed men of intellect and cultivation! Detective Woo (Park Joong-Hoon), the "hero" of "Nowhere to Hide," is squat, broken-nosed and slovenly. He's not likely to fight crime through keen observation and sharp insight. Sweaty fists and sharp sticks are more like it. You don't assign such an ornery critter to solve a case. You open a cage and get out of his way.

Hard as it may be to imagine, Woo's quarry in "Nowhere to Hide" is far more deranged than he is. Chang Sungmin (Ahn Sung-Ki) is a drug lord, elegant and lethal as a switchblade, who slaughters his main rival in rainy daylight on Inchon's Forty Steps. (The Bee Gees' soft-rock 1960s ballad, "Holiday" is juxtaposed against this bloody sequence. It's the most effective cinematic use of that pop group's music since "Saturday Night Fever.") In trying to bring Chang to whatever passes for justice in this hallucinatory South Korean landscape, Woo browbeats and bullies through so many citizens that it's hard to tell whether the policeman or the killer is the greater menace.

From what's been described, you might think that "Nowhere to Hide" is your typical bad-cop-doing-good-work-in-spite-of-himself genre piece. But writer-director Lee Myung-Se's approach to this material is anything but typical.

Vacuum-packed with flashy crosscuts, visual smears, abstract angles and abrupt tempo shifts, "Nowhere to Hide" is acid-rock moviemaking without apology. Lee's not the least bit interested in such niceties as "theme" or "issues," or even "context." As with many of Asia's most daring moviemakers, he wants to more than push the envelope of the thriller genre. He wants to blow the envelope up and reassemble the torn pieces into something that approximates, but doesn't match, its traditional prototype.

How much you enjoy the head-flipping distortions and gut-wrenching violence may be as much a matter of endurance as appreciation. Whatever your preference in such things, it's certain that your eyes won't let you turn away from "Nowhere to Hide's" hyperkinetic imagery and pile-driver pacing. Even if you aren't ready to buy Lee's approach as the wave of the future, you wonder how much an American pop counterpart such as the latest "Shaft" movie would have benefited from even a little of "Nowhere to Hide's" recklessness.

SIGHT AND SOUND, 7/01, p. 46, Andy Richards

Inchon, Korea, the present. When a gang steal a briefcase full of cash, murdering two men in the process, veteran detective Woo and his younger partner Kim are called to lead the police investigation. They chase and interrogate Fishhead, a drug runner who tips them off about Meathead, one of the participants in the murders. After further arrests and interrogations, the detectives find the phone number of the gang's leader, Chang Sungmin. A computer search of Sungmin's phone records reveals that he frequently calls a young woman, Juyon.

The detectives stake out Juyon's house. Sungmin and his men arrive, and a fight breaks out. Woo chases Sungmin through the hillside neighbourhood, but he escapes. Woo and Kim are sent to apprehend an underworld contact of Sungmin's. During the confrontation, Kim shoots the contact dead. Kim is anguished, and Woo tries to console him.

After 72 days of investigation, the detectives go undercover on a train where Sungmin, in disguise, is reckoned to be participating in a drug's deal. Woo recognises Sungmin, and a fight breaks out. Sungmin escapes, after seriously wounding Kim. The briefcase of cash is lost in the fight.

Woo finally tracks Sungmin down to a village where he is attending his mother's funeral. They fight furiously, with Sungmin repeatedly knocking Woo to the ground. The fight gives the police time to arrive in force, and Sungmin is arrested. Kim recovers in hospital.

South Korean cinema has been gathering a fair head of steam in the last couple of years. This newfound sense of confidence is evident in such domestic blockbusters as Kang Jae-Kyu's *Swiri* and Park Chan-Wook's *Joint Security Area*. Lee Myeong-Se's *Nowhere to Hide* is an accomplished action thriller that steals liberally from the canon of both western and eastern action films, while managing to bring some distinctive variations of its own.

Lee's story of a pair of cops tracking down a vicious drug lord owes a debt to the *Lethal Weapon* franchise, though its focus on the methodology of protracted stake-outs harks back to William Friedkin's *The French Connection* (1971). Park Jung-Hun's Detective Woo also bears a distinct resemblance to Clint Eastwood's Dirty Harry, not least in his maverick approach to police business. While his younger partner Kim is devoted to his wife and daughter, Woo is a loose cannon whose awkward visits to his married sister only serve to emphasise his loneliness. His obsessive dedication to his policework keeps him sane; he points out to one of the characters that his becoming a cop, as opposed to a gangster, was almost arbitrary (the thin line between the hunters and hunted is emphasised by several scenes featuring brutal police interrogations). As in Michael Mann's *Heat*, a professional respect is established between Woo and his adversary, Chang Sungmin; their final showdown is played out as a rain-drenched Leone Western, with Morricone motifs played on the soundtrack.

The film's strengths lie not so much in the broad strokes of its predictable plotting, but in the distinctive treatment of both its action set-pieces and its more reflective interludes. The violent opening murder scene is carefully choreographed in slow-motion to a cover of the Bee Gee's 'Holiday', and builds to a heightened sense of lyricism as the victims' blood mixes with the falling rainwater. Elsewhere, Lee makes some unexpected switches in tone, to refreshing effect. A fight scene among clotheslines is presented as shadow-play slapstick, the combatants silhouetted behind sheets. During a nocturnal stake-out, Woo and Kim describe to each other the food they crave, their fantasy dishes superimposed above their heads. Visual hyperbole creates the occasional moment of humour: at one point the camera focuses, in slow-motion close-up, on a bead of sweat as it drips from the end of a cop's nose and falls on to his shoe.

Lee takes particular delight in playing with filmic time. A visit to a nightclub is presented as a series of impressionistic freeze frames, while a subsequent chase scene is shown in an unconventionally long tracking shot, as Woo slowly and painfully closes the gap with his quarry. As the case drags on, bullet-ridden title cards appear to mark time. If the film's pop stylisation sometimes threatens to overwhelm proceedings, *Nowhere to Hide* remains tethered by Park's charismatic performance as Detective Woo. From behind his shabby clothes and care-worn slouch, he radiates a coiled energy born from years of tough graft and hard knocks—a performance of soulful intensity which adds a touch of class to the film's formal and technical accomplishments.

VILLAGE VOICE, 12/26/00, p. 148, Dennis Lim

Korean director Lee Myung-Se's genredespoiling policier *Nowhere to Hide* opens with a smear of boldly abstracted slapstick violence, segues into a confidently ridiculous assassination sequence scored to the Bee Gees' "Holiday," then catapults itself into a mockingly inconsequential nonnarrative in which brawls morph abruptly into shadow plays or waltzes or oil paintings. Lee's trickery is dazzling in flashes but also monotonously strenuous—the derangment factor is high but there's little evidence of authentic lunacy.

Also reviewed in:
CHICAGO TRIBUNE, 1/5/01, Friday/p. A, Michael Wilmington
NEW YORK TIMES, 3/27/00, p. E5, Elvis Mitchell
VARIETY, 11/14-21/99, p. 93, Derek Elley

NURSE BETTY

A USA Films release of a Gramercy Pictures presentation in association with Pacifica Film Distribution of a Propaganda Films/ab'-strakt pictures/IMF production. *Executive Producer:* Philip Steuer, Stephen Pevner, Moritz Borman, and Chris Sievernich. *Producer:* Gail Mutrux and Steve Golin. *Director:* Neil LaBute. *Screenplay:* John C. Richards and James Flamberg. *Based on a story by:* John C. Richards. *Director of Photography:* Jean Yves Escoffier. *Editor:* Joel Plotch and Steven Weisberg. *Music:* Rolfe Kent. *Music Editor:* Nick South. *Sound:* Felipe Borrero and (music) Tim Boyle. *Sound Editor:* Richard E. Yawn. *Casting:* Heidi Levitt and Monika Mikkelsen. *Production Designer:* Charles Breen. *Art Director:* Gary Diamond. *Set Designer:* Henry Alberti and Stan Tropp. *Set Decorator:* Jeffrey Kushon. *Set Dresser:* Rhonda Paynter, Heidi Hublou, Fred M. Paulsen, Jimmy Simeone, and Werner Hoetzinger. *Costumes:* Lynette Meyer. *Make-up:* Desne Holland. *Make-up (Morgan Freeman):* Michael A. Hancock. *Make-up (Renée Zellweger):* Sharon Ilson. *Make-up (Chris Rock):* Lisa Deveaux. *Stunt Coordinator:* Charlie Brewer. *Running time:* 112 minutes. *MPAA Rating:* R.

CAST: Morgan Freeman (Charlie); Renée Zellweger (Betty Sizemore); Chris Rock (Wesley); Greg Kinnear (Dr. David Ravell/George McCord); Aaron Eckhart (Del Sizemore); Tia Texada (Rosa); Crispin Glover (Roy); Pruitt Taylor Vince (Ballard); Allison Janney (Lyla); Kathleen Wilhoite (Sue Ann); Elizabeth Mitchell (Chloe); Susan Barnes (Darlene); Harriet Sansom Harris (Ellen); Sun Hi Lee (Jasmine); Laird Macintosh (Dr. Lonnie Walsh); Steven Gilborn (Blake); Jenny Gago (Mercedes); Sheila Kelley (Joyce); Matthew Cowles (Merle); Wayne Tippit (Doctor); George D. Wallace (Grandfather); Lesley Woods (Grandmother); Cynthia Martells (Chief Nurse); Alfonso Freeman (ER Doctor); Kevin Rahm (Friend #1); Steven Culp (Friend #2); Deborah May (Gloria Walsh); Michael Murphy (Studio Guard); Tina Smith (Waitress); Mike Kennedy (Cook); Irene Olga Lopez (Rosa's Mother); Steve Franken (Administrator); Kelwin Hagen (Deputy); Joshua Dotson (Parking Valet); Dona Hardy (Woman Patient); Paul Threlkeld (Grip).

LOS ANGELES TIMES, 9/8/00, Calendar/p. 2, Kenneth Turan

"Nurse Betty" is a masquerade that doesn't work. A noticeably sour fairy tale that mixes violence and cynicism with once-upon-a-time qualities, it was never fated to be "Snow White." But having Neil LaBute as the director has made the worst of the situation.

As demonstrated by "Your Friends & Neighbors" and "In the Company of Men," pictures LaBute has written and directed, this filmmaker has an ice-cold sensibility that divides its bemused contempt between the characters he creates and the audiences who have to spend time with them.

"Nurse Betty" marks the first time LaBute has taken on a script he didn't write himself but, in a perverse tribute to the auteur theory of directorial authorship, his frigid fingerprints can be found all over it.

Given that the film includes bloody shootouts and a graphic scalping, "Nurse Betty's" John C. Richards and James Flamberg script (which managed to win a prize at Cannes) always had designs on being as edgy as it is fantastical.

But with the addition of a director whose sensibility does not connect with all aspects of the material, who has to be dragged more or less kicking and screaming toward the film's minimal needs for warmth and humanity, "Nurse Betty" seems more like a charade than it should. Though it manages to be involving and even amusing in fits and starts, its warped, disconnected sensibility makes for an oddly distant piece of work.

Likely recognizing its potential shortcomings, "Nurse Betty" tries to compensate by casting Renee Zellweger (whose innate good-hearted decency is the very thing the film lacks) as Betty Sizemore of Fair Oaks, Kan., the title character.

The kind of perky and accommodating waitress who makes the Tip Top the place to eat in Fair Oaks, Betty wanted to take nursing classes once upon a time, but that was one of many dreams that got deferred when she married Del Sizemore of Del Sizemore Motors (LaBute veteran Aaron Eckhart), an oafish cretin, philanderer and all-around heel.

"Nurse Betty" opens not with Betty but in a hospital operating room, where world-class heart surgeon Dr. David Ravell is facing another crisis. It takes a minute or two for us to realize this isn't life, this is a "General Hospital"-type soap called "A Reason to Love," but in those few moments we get to see the daytime drama the way Betty does, as more real and involving than her everyday world.

So unsophisticated she says "the Europe?" when someone mentions having been there, Betty is such a big fan of "A Reason to Love" and George McCord, the actor who plays Ravell (a consistently amusing Greg Kinnear), that her pals at the Tip Top can think of no better birthday present for her than a life-size cardboard cutout of the handsome surgeon in his scrubs.

Naturally, Del is dubious about the value of soaps: "People with no lives watching other people's fake lives" is his verdict. It turns out to be his final verdict, because nefarious doings soon remove him from the scene, leaving Betty so disturbed she enters a post-traumatic altered state doctors call "a dissociative fugue."

What that means in terms of plot is that Betty, who can no longer distinguish television from reality ("Survivor," anyone?) not only thinks that Dr. David Ravell is a real person but also that he's her ex-fiance and just the guy she should be visiting. So she commandeers one of Del's cars and heads to California to find him, telling anyone who notices, "This is the biggest thing I've ever done and I've got to do it."

Noticing very much are a pair of philosophical hit men (more thoughtful people apparently work as killers than in university philosophy departments) who have professional reasons for wanting to catch up to Betty. Charlie (the always excellent Morgan Freeman) is the affable veteran, trying to teach the business to his snide young protege Wesley (Chris Rock). Charlie's motto: "Three in the head, you know they're dead."

All this may sound charming in a twisted kind of way, and so it might be in an ideal world. But Charlie's character goes places no one will buy, and Betty may be plucky, but demented people, no matter how chirpy, are involving for only so long.

So it falls to young gun Wesley to set "Nurse Betty's" tone. Surly, amoral, dissatisfied, he's the perfect on-screen voice for a director who is indifferent to his characters' fates, who can't even begin to squelch the mockery he feels for everyone in his frame. Maybe, if we believe as hard as Betty, we can change reality and make this distant slice of cinema go even further away.

NEW YORK, 9/11/00, p. 170, Peter Rainer

The romantic comedy *Nurse Betty* was directed by Neil LaBute but not written by him, which may explain why it lacks his distinctive note of noxious misanthropy. *In the Company of Men* and *Your Friends & Neighbors,* his two previous directorial efforts, were talked up in serioso circles as movies that dared to tell the truth about how we live. They were hailed as ritual dismemberments of bourgeois manners and male piggery, and if we recoiled from them, it's only because we could not face the Truth. But LaBute's worldview—to give it a grandiosity it doesn't deserve—is rigged. He sheds crocodile tears over the lack of value in our lives, but the lives he shows us belong to dolts and simps and psychos. It's existentialism adolescent-style, Mamet for Dummies, and probably he was right to plot a new course for his latest feature.

But LaBute's earlier, vise-like camera setups and syncopated nastiness at least had theatrical flair. Those first two movies looked like they were taking place inside a crypt, whereas *Nurse Betty* brings LaBute onto the open road, in the open air. It's all rather sweet and blobby. The flip side to LaBute's cheapjack cynicism, as it turns out, is a cheapjack romanticism. They're equally counterfeit.

Instead of raking the human race over the coals, LaBute and his screenwriters, John C. Richards and James Flamberg, are playing a fantasy-and-reality game about a wide-eyed waitress, Betty Sizemore (Renée Zellweger), from Fair Oaks, Kansas, who is entranced with a character named Dr. David Ravell (Greg Kinnear) from a *General Hospital*-style soap, *A Reason to Love.* Betty's crumbum husband, Del (Aaron Eckhart), is a car salesman who believes that people with no lives watch people with fake lives. When a drug deal goes bad, Del is executed by a pair of hit men, the sonorous Charlie (Morgan Freeman) and his loudmouth protégé, Wesley (Chris Rock). Witnessing the whole thing, Betty goes into a fugue state: Imagining Del to be alive and unharmed, she runs out on him and heads for Hollywood to connect with the soap star she believes is a real person.

Betty is less a character than a concept: She's the one person in the movie who dreams the right dreams, and her innocence is used as the standard by which all else is judged. Whomever she comes into contact with is transformed, usually for the better. The soap star, when he finally meets her, is, of course, smitten. (Implausibly, it never occurs to him that she might be some smiley species of stalker.) Charlie, who trails Betty cross-country intent on killing her, becomes stuck on her instead, and goes a bit gaga; her grace and poise melt him. Wesley, on the other hand, resents her. "Is she too poised to pee?" he inquires. (It seems like a fair question.) LaBute is promoting Betty as the patron saint of all those lost souls who pine for fantasy lovers while playing out their miserable little-people lives.

Renée Zellweger is the right actress to play Betty, because her sweetness has always had its blotto side; there's something a bit amnesiac about her screen presence. But she can't completely disguise the condescension built into *Nurse Betty,* It's doubtful that anybody who really cared about so-called common folk would depict them as commonly as LaBute does here. They're lifelessly virtuous. Even the usually magnificent Morgan Freeman seems neutered by all the goodwill. The wised-up types such as Wesley and the soap writer-producer played wickedly well by Allison Janney shine by comparison. LaBute regains his appetite whenever there's bile on the menu.

If the filmmakers really empathize with Betty, then why do they demonstrate so little pathos for her pathological condition? If one argues that this is just a dainty little fable, then why does LaBute shows us Del's murder in garish, head-scalping close-up? This Tarantino-esque paroxysm seems all wrong for the movie—unless it's there to imprint Betty's fears upon us. Which it does, but then LaBute doesn't follow through. He doesn't take Betty seriously enough to give her a plausible psychology. Instead, her willed amnesia, which suppresses the memory of her husband's murder, is presented to us as a state of grace. "I know there's something special out there for me," she says, in a line taken from her favorite soap, and it becomes her mantra. When Betty breaks out of her fugue state, it's only into a more enlightened form of niceness. She becomes more comprehensively bland.

We're supposed to think of *The Wizard of Oz* when we watch this film. Betty's odyssey has taken her from Kansas to L.A.—the Oz of illusions—where her dreamboat is revealed to be merely an actor. But instead of discovering there's no place like home, our heroine realizes she doesn't need anybody because she's got herself. Her triumph over her false pop dreams is meant as a celebration, but it looked to me like yet another pipe dream. Our relationship with pop culture, and how we perceive its reality or falseness, is far more complicated and compelling than the Goody Two-shoes wish-upon-a-star fatuity of this film. LaBute just isn't very good at selling cheer.

NEW YORK POST, 9/8/00, p. 47, Jonathan Foreman

It's a weird miracle that "Nurse Betty" is as enjoyable as it turns out to be.Here you have a stew of theoretically incompatible movie clichés: philosophical hit men out of "Pulp Fiction," a sweet none-too-bright nut job everyone thinks is fine ("Being There"), eccentric but decent small-town folk, characters whose lives start to imitate their favorite soap opera and a girl who isn't in Kansas anymore ...

And all of it is under the control of Neil LaBute, best known for writing and directing two irritatingly overpraised indies: "In the Company of Men," that smug, fraudulent film about the evil nature of yuppie males, and the equally strident wallow in misanthropic cynicism, "Your Friends and Neighbors."

Yet, this oddly cheerful, decreasingly dark comedy actually works and can boast some of the most enjoyable performances of the year. Everyone in it is on an exuberant roll.

And Renee Zellweger is not only better here than in anything she's done since "Jerry Maguire," she's so good, she could be in the running for an Oscar nomination.

She plays Betty, a coffee shop waitress in a small Kansas town, condemned to a sad, empty existence with Del (Aaron Eckhart), her abusive, unfaithful husband. Del is a car salesman with a sideline in drugs. Instead of a life, Betty has her beloved day time soap, "A Reason to Love," set in a mythical L.A. hospital, Loma Vista.

One night, while Betty's watching a tape of the show and mooning over its hero, Dr. David Ravell, Del—who has stolen drugs from the mob—gets his just deserts in the next room.

When the police arrive, Betty's already in what the production notes call a "fugue state," believing she's a nurse and the long-lost love of Dr. Ravell.

Almost immediately, she sets off for California to find Dr. Ravell, who's played by handsome but selfish actor George McCord (Greg Kinnear). Once there, crazy Betty not only lands a real job as a nurse and a new roommate/best friend (Tia Texada), she manages to meet McCord, who takes her declaration of love as a brilliant extended audition for a role on the show.

But Betty's sudden departure from Kansas has made local authorities suspicious. And because she unwittingly took the car containing Del's stolen drugs, she's also the target of two garrulous mob enforcers, Charlie (Morgan Freeman) and his protégé, Wesley (Chris Rock).

The two of them have particularly good comic chemistry. But LaBute gets strong, funny performances from everyone in his cast, including Kinnear, who gets better with every film he does; (the always excellent) Allison Janney; Crispin Glover; and Pruitt Taylor Vince.

The clever screenplay by John C. Richards and James Flamberg deservedly won a prize at this year's Cannes Film Festival.

NEWSDAY, 9/8/00, Part II/p. B3, John Anderson

Would you believe us if we told you that the entire "reality TV" phenomenon this summer had been a set-up for "Nurse Betty"? No? Well, what if we told you Renée Zellweger was Deep Throat? Well then, let's put it this way: While "Betty" serves as a kind of companion piece to "The Truman Show" and "EDtv" in the TV-reality dissection, only "Betty" wonders why we bother to tell the difference.

This makes Nell LaBute's film even darker than the others (more on that later) although it still tries to operate as straight comedy. Betty Sizemore, played with excruciating sweetness by Zellweger, is that stalwart of movie romance, good woman in bad marriage. When she witnesses the contract killing of her loutish husband, Del (Aaron Eckhart), she takes the last step in the direction she's already been heading: total psychic surrender to her favorite soap opera, "A Reason to Love" (whose "real-life" promotional Web sites and videos have made the counterfeit reality shtick even more cloying).

Betty's infatuation with its leading character, Dr. David Ravell, played by actor George McCord (played by actor Greg Kinnear) is so total it makes her reality as valid as anyone else's. And it leads the two hit men on her trail (Morgan Freeman and Chris Rock) to believe she's either the most sincere and angelic woman on the planet, or a heinous conniver who deserves what's coming to her.

Nurse Betty" has moments of low-key humor and a certain amount of charm.

More interestingly, perhaps, is the fact that Betty's path from Kansas to L.A. is about as darkly crooked as director Neil LaBute's. When he unveiled "In the Company of Men," that light romp through sadism and misogyny, at the '97 Sundance Film Festival, distributors headed for the hills; mostly male, they thought their wives would kill them. But women responded to the film, probably because they thought it was a documentary. And it became one of the more profitable films Sony Classics ever picked up in Park City.

LaBute, thinking he'd done something right, then made "Your Friends and Neighbors," an expertly made film about painfully ugly people (more reality programming, some might say). The bloom was off the rose. So along comes "Nurse Betty," the first film LaBute has directed that he didn't write; the John C. Richards-James Flamberg script won the best screenplay prize at Cannes this year.

What the results show is that you can take the boy out of the dark but you can't take the dark out of the boy. Although everyone involved is likable, especially Zellweger, the elements don't mesh: The violence, when it comes, is disconcertingly brutal. Betty's delusion is sweet, at times, but descends into uncomfortable pathos when she actually hooks up with Ravell/McCord. The ongoing subplot about Charlie and Wesley (Freeman and Rock) is underwritten and unfunny, in spite of Rock's efforts to milk laughs out of dry lines.

It can be a mystery why some movies work, but usually less of one why they don't. LaBute is a talented director, but his intention seems to have been to revamp both the road movie and the romantic comedy. With hit men. Is this reality? Wake me when they reach the island.

NEWSWEEK, 9/11/00, p. 66, David Ansen

Renee Zellweger has never been totally of this world—you can't help but suspect there's cotton in with her gray matter. That ethereal, pixilated quality makes her perfect to play the heroine of "Nurse Betty," a sweet, naive Kansas waitress who witnesses an event so gruesome and shocking (the scalping and murder of her no-good husband) that she enters a "fugue state," where reality is what she wants it to be.

What Betty wants is to be a nurse; even more, she wants to be the lover of Dr. David Ravell, who happens to be her favorite character on the TV soap opera "A Reason to Love." Director Neil LaBute ("In the Company of Men") follows his deluded heroine as she heads for Los Angeles in a borrowed Buick to fulfill her dreams. The Buick, unfortunately, contains the money her husband's assassins (hit-man team Morgan Freeman and Chris Rock) are determined to collect. The chase is on.

There are inspired moments in this edgy, unstable comedy, such as the scene when she meets her dream doctor at a Hollywood benefit, oblivious to the fact that he's soap star George McCord (a wonderfully smarmy Greg Kinnear). He assumes she's a desperate actress auditioning for a part in the show. "That is just great improv!" he says, wowed by her ability to stay in character.

Up to a point, we happily suspend our disbelief. But the script (by John C. Richards and James Flamberg) pushes its luck too far. Kinnear's blindness to Betty's madness goes on too long; Freeman's obsession with the woman he's chasing neatly parallels her romantic fantasies, but it doesn't ring true. Swerving from viciousness to whimsy to dubious feminist fable, "Nurse Betty" doesn't jell.

Still, with a cast as charmed as this, it comes oh so close.

SIGHT AND SOUND, 10/00, p. 53, Philip Kemp

Fair Oaks, Kansas. Waitress Betty Sizemore, who dreams of becoming a nurse, is a fan of the television hospital soap A *Reason to Love,* whose lead character is Dr David Ravell. Unknown to her, her car dealer husband Del is running drugs. Two hitmen, Charlie and Wesley, pay Del a visit, during which the car salesman is killed. Witnessing his murder, Betty is shocked into a fugue state; believing herself the ex-fiancée of Dr Ravell she sets out for California to find him, driving a Buick containing the drugs the hitmen are after.

While Sheriff Eldon Ballard and reporter Roy Ostrey investigate the murder, the hitmen set off after Betty, with Charlie increasingly fascinated by his quarry. In LA, Betty lucks into a hospital job by saving an accident victim, and finds lodgings with his sister Rosa. At a ball attended by the stars of *A Reason to Love,* Betty meets George McCord who plays Dr Ravell and starts treating him as her lost love. George, imagining she's improvising, gets her a part in the soap. Confronted by cameras, Betty is shocked out of her fugue.

The hitmen track Betty down to Rosa's house, ahead of Eldon and Roy. While Wesley holds the others at gun point, Charlie discovers Betty knew nothing of the drugs. A gun battle erupts: Wesley is killed and Charlie wounded. The police arrive. Betty, who has seized Charlie's gun, returns it so he can die with dignity. Betty lands a role in the soap.

Neil LaBute has been widely accused—not without reason—of revelling in misogyny, misanthropy and cruelty. Given this, *Nurse Betty* may come as a surprise. True, some fairly unpleasant things happen, but mostly to characters who deserve them: the repellent Del Sizemore gets scalped and shot dead for being not only a used-car salesman, drug dealer and abusive husband, but for sporting a hideous mullet. It's surely no coincidence that he's played by Aaron Eckhart who took the role of chief predator Chad in LaBute's first film *In the Company of Men.* LaBute has said that letting Chad get away with his loathsome behaviour in that film made it "more potent"; having Del meet his comeuppance so decisively signals that we're in a rather different kind of movie.

For although LaBute can't resist injecting the occasional acidic squirt, his latest film ends up as a fair simulacrum of a romantic comedy-thriller where the good end happily and the bad unhappily—this being, as Oscar Wilde reminded us, the definition of fiction. Which is appropriate enough, since *Nurse Betty* repeatedly zeroes in on the crossover point where fiction shades into fantasy, television-fed fantasy in particular. Knowingly scripted by ex-stand-up comedian John C. Richards and music editor James Flamberg, the film at once mocks and purloins the narrative conventions of daytime soap. When, in the final shoot-out, Charlie reveals that his fellow hitman Wesley is his son, it's precisely the sort of melodramatic bombshell soaps depend on; but it also makes sense dramatically, for why else would the professional Charlie put up with hot-headed Wesley?

Throughout, *Nurse Betty* plays this kind of juggling game. The central plot conceit of Betty's fugue—which Renée Zellweger's waitress is shocked into when she witnesses the murder of husband Del—is a latter-day take on amnesia, that reliable old standby of soap writers; and more than once, as we're about to chortle at some especially crass line of dialogue, it's revealed to be a quote from the soap within-the-movie, *A Reason to Love.* Following soapland's penchant for providing running updates for new viewers, the film's characters constantly define each other in neat encapsulations: Charlie talks of Betty as "sort of a wholesome Doris Day figure" and describes himself as "a garbage man of the human condition".

Where the film most clearly locks into LaBute's former preoccupations is that people's assumptions about each other are shown to be essentially unreliable. Betty's grasp of the supposed love of her life Dr Ravell, the character played by actor George McCord in *A Reason to Love,* has as much depth as the life-size cut-out of him she totes around, while George admiringly tells her "You're so real" just when she's most deeply mired in fantasy.

With more than one nod to *The Wizard of Oz* (Betty quits drab Kansas for West Coast Neverland, with Ravell/McCord as her phoney wizard), *Nurse Betty* seems to suggest that most of us end up creating our own delusional refuge from reality, and that finding it in a soap is no worse an option than most. Adopting a more fluid camera style than usual, courtesy of DP Jean Yves Escoffier *(Good Will Hunting),* LaBute draws nuanced performances from his cast, giving Greg Kinnear his best role yet as McCord, while Zellweger keeps a shrewd rein on the ditziness. But while *Nurse Betty* proves that LaBute has more than one string to his bow, you can't help thinking that he makes more memorable cinema when revelling in misanthropy.

TIME, 9/11/00, p. 114, Richard Schickel

It isn't every day that you see your husband bloodily scalped (and then shot to death) in the living room. Maybe feckless Del Sizemore, sleazy used-car salesman and inept drug dealer, had it coming, but still—it's bound to have an effect on a girl.

In the case of Betty Sizemore (a divinely innocent Renée Zellweger), the effect is a spectacular one. A hash-house waitress in Fair Oaks, Kans., she has always been a fan of *A Reason to Love,* a television soap opera of the *General Hospital* type. Traumatized, in what the shrinks call a fugue state, she completely enters the soap's slightly tacky alternative reality. Convinced that its leading hunk, Dr. David Ravell (the amusingly actorish Greg Kinnear), is her long-lost fiancé, she sets off for Los Angeles, intent on rekindling this imaginary old flame.

Unfortunately her vehicle of choice, a 1997 Buick LeSabre, is the very one in which Del stashed his stolen drugs. Equally unfortunately, the guys who offed him (Morgan Freeman's pensive Charlie and his kick-ass protégé, Chris Rock's Wesley) are in hot pursuit, intent on recovering the goods and silencing the only witness to their crime.

You could say that *Nurse Betty* is a road picture. You could also call it a meditation on how the media scramble easily impressionable brains. Or a study in obsession, since Charlie, working his last job before retirement, conceives a passion for Betty that fully matches hers for David—and is another product of a simmering imagination.

But none of those descriptions quite covers the case. To begin with, John C. Richards and James Flamberg have actually written a screenplay instead of merely structuring one, which is what most American screenwriters do these days. It is full of quirky yet weirdly believable turns—and wacky, revealing dialogue. "I'm glad they got those casinos," says the parodistically psycho Rock as he reflects on the injustices endured by Native Americans. "I haven't felt like this since I was with Stella Adler in New York," says Kinnear—all actor, all self-absorption—when he finally acknowledges his attraction to Betty. Their feelings may be stunted, but in their way they are pure, even heartfelt.

And the director, Neil LaBute, is attentive to them, in a way that he was not when he was directing his own screenplays—*In the Company of Men, Your Friends and Neighbors*—which were so claustrophobic, so tense with the desire to hurt and shock. Here he makes time for minor characters—barkeeps, small-town newsmen, cops—whose dreamy oddness he catches in a few sly, nonjudgmental glances.

Put that another way: his work is relaxed without being slack, affectionate without going sentimental. Above all, he leaves his actors room to breathe, to live, as it were, between the script's lines. Zellweger blooms in this context. Her naiveté is radical, of course, but that imparts a fierce serenity to her quest. Mostly, the people she encounters on the road and in Los Angeles quickly come to understand that she is off her rocker—except the soap-opera folk, who think she's an actress going to any lengths for a job—but there is such sweetness in her determination, such an endearing faith in the destiny she alone perceives, that they help her along. Zellweger is lovely in the role.

Freeman's Charlie is a more complicated figure. The Polaroid pictures of Betty he carries take on talismanic power for him, and he keeps referring to her as a Doris Day type, which somewhat oversimplifies her—and also, perhaps, betrays his age and his longing for the more coherent times in which he was raised. He may be a hit man, but he's a cultivated one. He claims to read books and listen to symphonies; he manifestly loathes yet loves the volatile Wesley. This is a great, understated performance, wistful and funny, by a superb actor, and maybe one that will win him the Oscar he has so long deserved.

All in all, *Nurse Betty* is a wonderful movie, unpredictably alive to the fact that the American citizenry is a lot stranger than we like to admit—tossing restlessly in dreams that are at once brutal and sad, yet, like Zellweger's heroine, full of an eagerly chirping life. What's best about this movie is that it plays our abnormalcy as normalcy. It lets its people live (and occasionally die) with their lunacies gloriously intact uninstructed by superior attitudes or indulgent patronization.

VILLAGE VOICE, 9/12/00, p. 147, J. Hoberman

Something like *The Truman Show* in reverse, Neil LaBute's *Nurse Betty* has the most provocative high-concept premise since *Being John Malkovich.* The movie—in which a Kansas naïf wills herself into the Emerald City of network tele-reality—was written by John C. Richards, a onetime stand-up comedian, and his partner, James Flamberg; would-be wacky and amiably twisted, it's temperamentally antithetical to the nastiness of LaBute's own scripts.

Betty (the infinitely sympathetic Renée Zellweger) is a friendly small-town waitress with big, messy hair, nursing-school dreams, and a monstrous soap-opera jones. Specifically, she's obsessed by the handsome Dr. Ravell (Greg Kinnear) in *A Reason to Love.* Her husband (Aaron Eckhart), a swinish car dealer with a haircut to match, has projected himself into a less wholesome scenario. Having run afoul of some big-city dope dealers, he's confronted by a pair of enforcers: conscientious Morgan Freeman and volatile Chris Rock. The scene turns ugly, although, hidden in the den watching *A Reason to Love* on tape, Betty escapes the carnage in the next room, and does not seem at all put out. Enacting the American, she takes off for the coast in her husband's LeSabre with the hit team in pursuit—her state helpfully diagnosed in the press notes as a dissociative fugue, "a combination of amnesia and physical fright" in which "the individual flees from his customary surroundings toward the assumption of a new identity."

In this case, that new identity is a role in *A Reason to Love*—literally. Once in L.A., Betty dons her nurse's uniform and goes looking for a job in the soap's imaginary hospital; after she's set up to see the actor who plays Dr. Ravell, she begins improvising with his character, much to his fascination. For a time, Betty suggests a contemporary Maria Montez—effectively deforming reality to the dimensions of her own imagination. She even casts a spell on one of her pursuers, who, much to his colleague's disgust, is mesmerized by their quarry's presumed Doris Day wholesomeness. Like *Being John Malkovich, Nurse Betty* is a movie about image and acting. LaBute successfully constructs a world that can encompass the Martian histrionics of Crispin Glover and the bland snarkiness of Greg Kinnear.

After spending three hours with Betty, Kinnear's character exclaims that he hasn't felt so real since he was "with Stella Adler in New York." But, whether or not Betty sustains her character, the movie fails to maintain its own. The scenario falls apart. *Nurse Betty* initially suggests that anything is possible; the final burst of bloody confusion and conventional wish-fulfillment makes it clear that nothing is.

Also reviewed in:
CHICAGO TRIBUNE, 9/8/00, Friday/p. A, Michael Wilmington
NATION, 10/2/00, p. 42, Stuart Klawans
NEW REPUBLIC, 9/18/00, p. 28, Stanley Kauffmann
NEW YORK TIMES, 9/8/00, p. E1, Stephen Holden
NEW YORKER, 9/11/00, p. 104, Anthony Lane
VARIETY, 5/15-21/00, p. 28, Emanuel Levy
WASHINGTON POST, 9/8/00, p. C1, Rita Kempley
WASHINGTON POST, 9/8/00, Weekend/p. 41, Michal O'Sullivan

NUTTY PROFESSOR II: THE KLUMPS

A Universal Pictures and Imagine Entertainment release of a Brian Grazer production. *Executive Producer:* Jerry Lewis, Eddie Murphy, Tom Shadyac, Karen Kehela, and James D. Brubaker. *Producer:* Brian Grazer. *Director:* Peter Segal. *Screenplay:* Barry W. Blaustein, David Sheffield, Paul Weitz, and Chris Weitz. *Story:* Steve Oedekerk, Barry W. Blaustein, and David Sheffield. *Director of Photography:* Dean Semler. *Editor:* William Kerr. *Music:* David Newman. *Music Editor:* Tom Villano and Jim Harrison. *Sound:* Jose Antonio Garcia and (music) John Kurlander. *Sound Editor:* Michael Hilkene. *Casting:* Pamela Basker and Joanne Koehler. *Production Designer:* William Elliott. *Art Director:* Greg Papalia. *Set Designer:* John Berger, Patricia Klawonn, Kristen Pratt, Masako Masuda, and John Warnke. *Set*

Decorator: John Anderson. *Set Dresser:* Dale E. Anderson, Frank Anderson, Sam Anderson, Mark Boucher, Larry Haney, J.D. Smith, James Malley, C.J. Maguire, Desmond J. O'Regan, Phil Calhoun, John Rankin, Tony Piller, Jerry Tirado, and John Horning. *Special Effects:* Dan Sudick. *Visual Effects:* Jon Farhat. *Costumes:* Sharen Davis. *Make-up:* Nena Smarz. *Make-up (Janet Jackson):* Shutchai Buacharern. *Special Make-up Effects:* Rick Baker. *Stunt Coordinator:* Mickey Gilbert and Alan Oliney. *Running time:* 105 minutes. *MPAA Rating:* PG-13.

CAST: Eddie Murphy (Sherman Klump, Buddy Love, Granny Klump, Mama Klump, Papa Klump, Young Papa Klump, Ernie Klump and Lance Perkins); Janet Jackson (Denise Gaines); Larry Miller (Dean Richmond); John Ales (Jason); Richard Gant (Denise's Father); Anna Maria Horsford (Denise's Mother); Melinda McGraw (Leanne Guilford); Jamal Mixon (Ernie Klump, Jr.); Gabriel Williams (Isaac); Chris Elliott (Restaurant Manager); Duffy Taylor (Restaurant Trainee); Earl Boen (Dr. Knoll); Nikki Cox (Ms. Stamos); Freda Payne (Claudine); Sylvester Jenkins (Old Willie); Wanda Sykes (Chantal); George King (Stripper); Charles Walker (Preacher); Enya Flack (Bridesmaid); Andrea C. Robinson (Party Guest/Bridesmaid); Kym E. Whitley (Party Guest); Selma Stern (Mrs. Dudikoff); Julia Schultz (Receptionist); Barry W. Blaustein and David Sheffield (Men in Bathroom); Ralph Drischell (Zeke); Myles Mason, Jeffrey Michael Freeman, and Maurice Colquitt (Baby Buddies); Bill Applebaum and Harry S. Murphy (Boardroom Members); Tom Jourden (Guy in Elevator); Kevin Michael Mondane (Buddy at 15); Viola Kates Stimpson (Sweet Old Lady); Naomi Kale (Buxom Student); Kente Scott (Fraternity Student); Justin Urich (Lecture Student); Sonya Eddy (Heavyset Woman); James D. Brubaker (Krusty Reporter); Richie Palmer (Cab Driver); Charles Napier (Four Star General); Steve Kehela and Miguel A. Nunez, Jr. (Scientists); Renee Tenison (Dog Owner); Richard Saxton (American Newscaster); Peter Segal and William Kerr (Scared Popcorn Men); Michael Ewing (Hot Dog Vendor); Nicole Segal (Scared Little Girl).

CHRISTIAN SCIENCE MONITOR, 7/28/00, p. 15, David Sterritt

Eddie Murphy's remake of "The Nutty Professor" struck gold four years ago, and "Nutty Professor II: The Klumps" is poised to do the same. It might even outgross its predecessor, since it serves up Murphy in no fewer than eight roles—enough to delight his fans, although it may drive his detractors as nutty as the title character himself

Murphy's first "Nutty Professor" centered on a bashful scientist named Sherman Klump, whose newly discovered elixir turned him into a foul-mouthed womanizer. The most talked-about scene matured Murphy as Sherman's entire family, comporting themselves around the dinner table with the kind of unrestrained vulgarity that summertime audiences adore. The sequel stretches this sequence into a whole movie, drowning the earlier picture's most interesting angle—the complex relationship between the best and worst aspects of Murphy's own persona—in a swamp of sex jokes and bathroom humor.

It's ironic that Jerry Lewis is one of the film's five executive producers. Lewis originated "The Nutty Professor" in a 1963 comedy that generates Jekyll-and-Hyde laughs with far more intelligence and a notable absence of the elaborate prostheses, special effects, and other gimmicks that Murphy and company rely on from start to finish. These cosmetic devices contrast with Jim Carrey in his recent movies, which return to Lewis's great tradition of body-based acting skills.

What interested Lewis in the '60s was the tension between our private selves and the public roles we play for the people in our lives. What interests Murphy today is how far rudeness and crudeness can be pushed without cracking the profitable PG-13 rating barrier. There's nothing nutty about his financial ambitions, but his over-the-top energy isn't enough to make this numbingly repetitious farce worth watching.

LOS ANGELES TIMES, 7/28/00, Calendar/p. 1, Kenneth Turan

"Nutty Professor II: The Klumps" is all Eddie, all the time. When the cast list appears at the end of this benighted sequel, the active Mr. Murphy is credited with eight roles. While this surely has its advantages (fewer star trailers to park, no arguments about billing, fewer salaries to negotiate—and to pay), being funny is no longer among them.

This is a waste of talent and a surprise, because Murphy's ability to simultaneously portray all five members of the hefty and contentious Klump family in two brief but hilarious dinner scenes was the highlight of his first "Nutty" venture and even won him the best actor award from the snooty National Society of Film Critics.

"The Klumps" does show flashes of that original bravura, but the thrill is definitely gone, leaving a disappointing and unpleasant mess in its place. All the Klumps are back, as is Professor Sherman Klump's ostentatiously nasty alter ego Buddy Love, but several factors combine to make meeting up with them again more of a chore than a pleasure.

On the simplest level, seeing Murphy, helped by three to five hours per day in makeup plus impressive special-effects technology, play elaborate scenes with himself loses the element of surprise the second time around. If familiarity hardly breeds contempt—this kind of wizardry is too much of an accomplishment for that—it does make the proceedings seem more like a stunt than a pleasure.

Also, while no one was exactly clamoring to "Break up the Klumps," that was the result of the film's decision to give family members their own subplots. As those original dinner scenes proved, in unity there is strength for the Klumps, and seeing them a few at a time in their own little dramas instead of en masse is less amusing almost by definition. Five Klumps are definitely better than one or two.

Both of these problems might have been overcome if it wasn't for the film's decision to compete fiercely in Hollywood's trendiest contest, the Gross-Out Derby. Putting aside the question of how a film whose repertoire includes erection, flatulence and anal rape jokes qualifies for a PG-13 rating (the MPAA is truly the most mysterious organization since the Rosicrucians), the crude and juvenile sense of humor displayed by veteran Murphy writers Barry W. Blaustein & David Sheffield and "American Pie's" Paul Weitz & Chris Weitz corrupts everything it touches.

This is a shame, because Murphy brings a surprising amount of empathy to his portrayal of the brilliant but poundage-challenged Sherman Klump, scientist and shining light of Wellman College's biological research center. And Peter Segal, whose direction is indifferent at best, does seem to want to include some gentler moments. The film's die-hard tastelessness, however, ruthlessly trumps all its better intentions.

"Nutty II" begins where the first film left off, albeit substituting Janet Jackson for Jada Pinkett in the role of a fellow Wellman professor who is also the sweet-natured woman of Sherman's dreams. Then, as now, Sherman is on the verge of another staggering discovery, and, then as now, he is locked in mortal combat with his thin evil twin, Buddy Love.

It's a fountain-of-youth drug Sherman has come up with this time, an elixir so potentially potent that Wellman's scheming dean (a returning Larry Miller) sells it sight unseen to a grasping pharmaceutical company for $150 million. All Sherman has to do is prove it works at an upcoming public demonstration.

The scientist himself, however, is grappling with a much more personal problem. He may have vanquished the physical Buddy, but the man lives inside him like a monster from the id, causing Sherman to say the most embarrassing things at the most inopportune moments.

Though Sherman clearly needs an exorcism, the professor, either because he's a man of science or because Max von Sydow was unavailable, chooses another route. He uses an untested method to extract the gene to which Buddy is attached, a procedure that leads to all manner of strange complications, including Buddy's reappearance as a man with marked canine characteristics. Don't ask.

Meanwhile, Sherman's relatives have relationship problems of their own. Papa and Mama are not connecting in the bedroom, while sexually active Granny (Murphy's most out-there creation) tries her darndest to seduce, of all people, Buddy Love. There is something surreal about seeing Murphy in effect flirting with himself, but, like everything else about "Nutty II," it's not as funny as it sounds.

NEW YORK, 8/14/00, p. 65, Peter Rainer

Eddie Murphy once again divides himself into an entire family in *Nutty Professor II: The Klumps,* and the result is an amazingly virtuosic, lived-in piece of acting that deserves to be more than the centerpiece in what is essentially a racially oriented gross-out teen pic. Murphy's characters here seem to personify both his best and worst images of himself, as well as the ways in which blacks traditionally have been caricatured in Hollywood. He needs a movie to match the artist he has become.

NEW YORK POST, 7/28/00, p. 45, Jonathan Foreman

There are long gaps between the halfway decent jokes in this surprisingly poor sequel to Eddie Murphy's 1996 comeback triumph, "The Nutty Professor" (a remake of the 1963 Jerry Lewis flick). "Nutty Professor II: The Klumps" lacks both the comic exuberance and the underlying sweetness of the first film.

To be sure, Murphy once again displays his extraordinary talent for multiple impersonation, but what stays with you is the script's repetitive reliance on jokes about sagging breasts, horny elderly women and middle-age impotence.

In fact, it's extraordinary that a movie so dependent on explicitly sexual humor should have been rated PG-13.

Given the ratings board's strictness when it comes to nudity, this shameful, irresponsible lenience to a movie guaranteed to embarrass parents who bring their children, is so hypocritical it makes you wonder if the ratings process is as incorruptible as the Motion Picture Association of America claims.

Murphy once again is the lovable but massively overweight scientist Sherman Klump. The professor is about to get married to his lovely colleague, Denise Gaines (Janet Jackson).

Denise not only loves the brilliant professor, she actually likes his grotesque family, all of whom—Mama, Papa, brother Ernie and Granny—are played by Murphy in a series of amazingly seamless ensemble scenes.

But Sherman's obnoxious alter ego, Buddy Love (Murphy without prosthesis) keeps popping into Sherman's head, prompting him to say embarrassing and inappropriate things.

Worried that his Buddy persona might wreck his marriage plans, Sherman uses Denise's experimental genetic technology to remove the Buddy Love genetic material from his DNA.

But the experiment goes wrong. Buddy is not just removed from Sherman's system, he comes to life as a separate person. And he immediately plots to steal the professor's amazing youth serum.

Meanwhile, the operation has the side effect of eroding Sherman's intelligence. Unless the rapidly declining Sherman can pull something off, he could lose not just his bride, but his job.

For a big-studio movie, "The Klumps" contains some appalling continuity errors, especially in the all-you-can-eat restaurant scene. And chunks of dialogue are so mumbled by the Klump family that you cannot hear what the characters are saying.

Pop star Jackson ("Poetic Justice"), sporting some serious cleavage, plays a professor of genetics with about the same verve that Denise Richards and Nicole Kidman brought to their on-screen impersonations of nuclear physicists. She looks fine, but lacks the fire and range of expression that Jada Pinkett brought to the love interest role in the first "Nutty Professor" film.

This is another movie that illustrates how even a comic talent as powerful as Eddie Murphy, under the capable direction of Peter Segal ("Tommy Boy," "Naked Gun 33⅓"), can be sunk by a ragged, inadequate script (by Barry W. Blaustein & David Sheffield and Paul & Chris Weitz).

NEWSDAY, 7/28/00, Part II/p. B3, John Anderson

It's entirely possible that Sherman Klump, the big fat teddy bear of "The Nutty Professor," is the most accomplished character Eddie Murphy has ever created. Warm, wise, guileless and affectionate, Sherman is not only completely believable, he's completely alien to anything else Murphy's ever done.

So you kind of wish there was a little more Sherman and maybe a little less of those other Buick-sized Klumps—Mama, Papa, Ernie and Granny—who share the billing in "Nutty Professor II." Sure, playing a cast of six characters that includes Buddy Love—Sherman's chemically released and lustful alter ego—is a great showcase for Murphy's talents. But the result is a movie that's not as funny as the first (excuse us, second) and has too many subplots to be anything besides a vehicle for gags—which, in turn, are all too often about body parts/fluids/functions/malfunctions and various graphic manifestations of gastro-intestinal distress.

Last time around, Sherman's Jekyll-and-Hydish experiments brought out of hiding the libidinous Buddy, the dark, id-ish side of the repressed and romantically challenged Sherman. This time, Sherman's research has him close to discovering a virtual Fountain of Youth—a potion that can reverse the aging process, if only momentarily.

As his college's Dean Richmond (Larry Miller) gets ready to go public with the news, Sherman starts to exhibit signs of Tourette's—except that it's really Buddy doing the talking.

The Sherman story is fine. You kind of wish the lumbering love story would simply go away, the one between him and Denise Gaines (Janet Jackson, who has two expressions). You wish that when she takes Sherman home to meet her parents, he didn't have to zip the tablecloth into his pants and drag dinner onto the floor, which feels like a joke older than Granny herself.

But in this Peter ("Tommy Boy") Segal sequel to the 1996 Tom Shadyac film—which was, of course, a remake of the classic Jerry Lewis-directed original of 1963—there are simply too many storylines to contend with. As well as various and dubious objects of ridicule: the oversexed (Granny); the undersexed (Papa); the overfed (Ernie and Ernie Jr., played by Jamal Mixon); the elderly and therefore disgusting (Granny again), and the stupid, which is what Sherman becomes once Buddy is freed from his genetic material and attempts to steal the youth potion so he can sell it on his own.

Some of Murphy's most creatively manic moments are as Buddy, whose abnormal genetic material has managed to metamorphose into Buddy himself only by coming in contact with DNA—in this case, a dog's. So Buddy is part dog. And when he's sniffing around a room, chasing a cat or playing fetch with sherman, Murphy is a howl. When he puts newspaper on the floor it's not so funny.

The movie has four writers, which is never a good sign. It also has no sense of momentum, or rhythm, or, very often, taste (two of the authors are "American Pie's" Chris and Paul Weitz, so there are obvious suspects). Dean Richmond's rape by a giant hamster, for instance, certainly seems like fine family fare—it must be, since the movie's rated PG-13. One of the more thrilling experiences of youth is getting the opportunity to watch your parents gag.

There are funny moments; of course, there are. In fact, aided by multiple-Oscar winner Rick Baker and his astonishing makeup, Murphy's performance is a tour-de-force of impersonation and comic timing. It's just too bad he had to carry so much of the water in this soggy vehicle himself.

NEWSWEEK, 8/7/00, p. 72, David Ansen

Playing the sweet, massive science professor Sherman Klump and his sleek, demonic doppelgänger. Buddy Love in 1996's "The Nutty Professor,"Eddie Murphy took comic chameleonism to some rare, wiggy heights. The frosting on the cake was his all-in-one appearance as the entire Klump clan—lascivious Granny, ebullient Mama, grumpy Pop and grousing Ernie. The Klumps almost stole the picture, so it seemed a great idea to give the whole brood costarring status in the sequel alongside Sherman and Buddy, who are now battling over the profits on Sherman's fountain-of-youth formula.

Well, this time it isn't just Sherman who has swallowed the wrong formula—it's the filmmakers. What was a ragged but often hilarious charmer has been genetically altered into a deafening and desperate mutant. Everything has been ratcheted up six notches. You liked the flatulence in the first movie? When someone passes wind in director Peter Segals's sequel, an entire restaurant catches on fire. A dream sequence that parodies "Armageddon" and "2001" seems to have been included just so "The Blue Danube" waltz can be punctuated with farts. But the result is at least six times *less* funny than the first.

Murphy is still undeniably amazing. The bizarre thing about "The Klumps" is how little it seems to matter: you can rise only so far over material this base. And the technical difficulties of having to play out scenes entirely with other versions of himself throws the comic timing off. Nothing is allowed to build—every joke, every line, is shot out of a cannon. Add David Newman's arm-twisting score *(Laugh, dammit!)* and you get a comedy with all the nuance of a jackhammer.

Janet Jackson, smiling prettily, is on hand as Sherman's unlikely girlfriend—but who's paying attention in a movie that throws in a giant mutant hamster to rape the dean of the college? Of course no movie with this much Murphy can be entirely devoid of laughs. His horny grandma—who puts the moves on Buddy—is pretty irresistible. When a dog's DNA gets mixed in with Buddy's (don't ask), I laughed out loud at a couple of Murphy's sudden transformations into compulsive canine behavior. More often, sad to say, it's the movie that's the dog.

SIGHT AND SOUND, 11/00, p. 59, Charles Taylor

US, the present day. Science professor Sherman Klump is working on an anti-ageing serum. Later, at a family dinner, he insults his father; tests show that Sherman has an abnormal gene which he believes is a trace of Buddy Love, the obnoxious alter ego he thought he was rid of. When Sherman tries to propose marriage to genetics professor Denise Gaines, he suffers another outburst. He extracts the Buddy Love gene, and the following evening successfully proposes to Denise.

Buddy, however, is recreated as a separate entity after an accident at the lab and asks for his share of the youth serum. Sherman is later offered $150 million from Phleer Pharmaceuticals for the serum. Finding his apartment ransacked by Buddy, Sherman hides the serum at his parents' house. Papa Klump drinks the anti-ageing agent and is rejuvenated; when Buddy sees him, he guesses the whereabouts of the serum, which he steals.

Buddy later sets up a meeting with Phleer which has called off the deal with Sherman. After tests show that his brain is deteriorating since his separation from Buddy, Sherman tells Denise they can't marry. Determined to rejoin with Buddy, Sherman interrupts his meeting with Phleer and gives him the youth serum. Buddy turns into genomic fluid. Sherman gives chase but the Buddy fluid evaporates next to a fountain. Denise finds Sherman. A tear drops from her eye on to Buddy's DNA and into the fountain. He drinks from the fountain and regains his old intelligence levels. Sherman and Denise marry.

Eddie Murphy's performance in the 1996 remake of *The Nutty Professor* was perhaps the sweetest example of self-loathing ever seen in the movies. In the original 1963 film, Jerry Lewis reputedly turned his character's alter ego Buddy Love into a parody of Dean Martin. But Murphy's Buddy Love was his worst nightmare of himself: a loud-mouthed narcissist, Love was almost an exaggerated version of the persona that made Murphy a star. When, as the movie's hero Sherman Klump, Murphy suffered the taunts of a television comedian, he seemed to be blaming himself for spawning a crass strain of black stand-up comedy. In the film, audiences learned to hate the very qualities they once loved in Murphy, while falling for his endearing, tubby character, Sherman Klump. The actor may have been hiding inside Sherman's latex bulk but he was as emotionally open as he'd ever been; and, as critic Elvis Mitchell recently noted, Murphy knew how to act through the prosthetics. It's one of the great comic performances in recent American movies.

This sequel manages to be just as funny though much cruder and not as sweet. Sherman's relation to Buddy has become even more complex: here, Buddy is literally a parasite whom Sherman expunges from his genetic makeup. It's hard not to feel that Murphy is addressing his own ambivalence about the new, friendlier persona which brought him his greatest success. By banishing Buddy, Sherman risks becoming permanently enfeebled, and that seems to suggest that Murphy is afraid to—or can't—let go of his old ways. And yet Buddy is made even more hateful here; each of his appearances makes us feel ever more protective of Sherman.

Nutty Professor II: The Klumps capitalises on the first movie's most virtuosic turn, Murphy's impersonation of Sherman's entire family—a turn that's heir to a tradition in African-American comedy of loving, observant humour about family life that never turns homiletic. Each Klump, particularly Sherman's adoring, big-hearted mother, is a distinct creation. And if some are played just for laughs—such as Sherman's horny grandmother, the source of the movie's most outrageous and funniest jokes—others are so real they take on a life of their own. For a director who doesn't hesitate to push the scatological humour (the best bit being a fleeting parody of Kubrick's overrated *2001: A Space Odyssey*), Peter Segal *(Naked Gun 33 1/3* is surprisingly capable of some graceful moments, such as the scene where Sherman uses fireflies to spell out his marriage proposal to Denise and the touching climax where he is saved by his beloved shedding a tear—a moment that genuinely deserves the overworked appellation 'Chaplinesque'.

VILLAGE VOICE, 8/8/00, p. 144, Brian Parks

Eddie Murphy is back in college, but his *Nutty Professor II: The Klumps* suffers from a serious case of sophomore slump. The last time we saw Professor Sherman Klump, in 1996's *The Nutty Professor*, he'd invented a formula that jiggered fat people's DNA to make them thin. Despairing at how his girth kept him from romance, Sherman downed a vial of the brew—which made him skinny indeed, but also transformed the sweet-souled researcher into his obnoxious, testosterone-fueled alter ego, Buddy Love. The movie's big conceit, though, was Murphy—in elaborate fat prosthetics—playing five members of the garrulous, overweight Klump family. Their profane dinner repartee was often hilarious.

This time around, Sherman has invented a fountain-of-youth potion, which the college dean wants to sell to raise cash. After a lab accident, Buddy Love springs free of Sherman's body and plots his own scheme to peddle the concoction—causing mayhem for the school and derailing Sherman's relationship with new girlfriend Denise (a dewy Janet Jackson). Meanwhile, Sherman's family carries on its ribald ways, complicated by Papa Klump's ingestion of some of Sherman's secret sauce (which looks suspiciously like the cough syrup I've been swilling all week).

Murphy's first *Nutty Professor* was a funny, even charming effort. Sherman was a surprisingly sympathetic creature, his family an entertaining dystopia. Murphy's new chronicle of higher education is pitched louder and cruder, but to much less effect. The Klumps are still an amusing crew, but the gag gets tired despite Murphy's wonderful multiple-personality theatrics. Swamped by tit jokes and a numbingly busy plot, Sherman's romantic woes only seem saccharine here, not endearing.

Please note that *The Klumps* depicts a staple of faculty life rarely written up in *Lingua Franca:* anal rape by giant hamster. Department chairs may wince, but the eight-year-old sitting next to me found it especially droll.

Also reviewed in:
CHICAGO TRIBUNE, 7/28/00, Friday/p. A, Michael Wilmington
NEW YORK TIMES, 7/28/00, p. E14, Elvis Mitchell
NEW YORKER, 8/7/00, p. 76, Anthony Lane
VARIETY, 7/31-8/8/00, p. 23, Joe Leydon
WASHINGTON POST, 7/28/00, p. C1, Rita Kempley
WASHINGTON POST, 7/28/00, Weekend/p. 37, Desson Howe

O BROTHER, WHERE ART THOU?

A Touchstone Pictures and Universal Pictures release in association with Studio Canal of a Working Title production. *Executive Producer:* Tim Bevan and Eric Fellner. *Producer:* Ethan Coen. *Director:* Joel Coen. *Screenplay by:* Ethan Coen and Joel Coen. *Based upon "The Odyssey" by:* Homer. *Director of Photography:* Roger Deakins. *Editor:* Roderick Jaynes and Tricia Cooke. *Music:* T-Bone Burnett. *Music Editor:* Sean Garnhart. *Choreographer:* Jacqui Landrum and Bill Landrum. *Sound:* Peter Kurland and (music) Mike Piersante. *Sound Editor:* Skip Lievsay. *Casting:* Ellen Chenoweth. *Production Designer:* Dennis Gassner. *Art Director:* Richard Johnson. *Set Designer:* Thomas Minton. *Set Decorator:* Nancy Haigh. *Set Dresser:* Jimmy Meehan. *Special Effects:* Peter Chesney. *Costumes:* Mary Zophres. *Make-up:* Jean Black. *Stunt Coordinator:* Jery Hewitt. *Running time:* 143 minutes. *MPAA Rating:* PG-13.

CAST: George Clooney (Ulysses Everett McGill); John Turturro (Pete); Tim Blake Nelson (Delmar); John Goodman (Big Dan Teague); Holly Hunter (Penny); Chris Thomas King (Tommy Johnson); Charles Durning (Pappy O'Daniel); Del Pentecost (Junior O'Daniel); Michael Badalucco (George Nelson); J.R. Horne and Brian Reddy (Pappy's Staff); Wayne Duvall (Homer Stokes); Ed Gale (The Little Man); Ray McKinnon (Vernon T. Waldrip); Daniel Von Bargen (Sheriff Cooley); Royce D. Applegate (Man with Bullhorn); Frank Collison (Wash Hogwallop); Quinn Gasaway (Boy Hogwallop); Lee Weaver (Blind Seer); Milford Fortenberry

(Pomade Vendor); Stephen Root (Radio Station Man); John Locke (Mr. French); Gillian Welch (Soggy Bottom Customer); A. Ray Ratliff (Record Store Clerk); Mia Tate, Musetta Vander, and Christy Taylor (Sirens); April Hardcastle (Waitress); Michael W. Finnell (Interrogator); Georgia Rae Rainer, Marianna Breland, Lindsey Miller, and Natalie Shedd (Wharvey Gals); John McConnell (Woolworths Manager); Isaac Freeman, Wilson Waters, Jr., and Robert Hamlett (Gravediggers); Willard Cox, Evelyn Cox, Suzanne Cox, Sidney Cox, Buck White, Sharon White, and Sheryl White (Themselves); Ed Snodderly and David Holt (Village Idiots).

LOS ANGELES TIMES, 12/22/00, Calendar/p. 12, Kenneth Turan

The Coen brothers did not make their reputation by taking things too seriously, and in that sense "O Brother, Where Art Thou?" is of a piece with what's come before. An eccentric, picaresque Southern period comedy, "Bonnie & Clyde" as told by Monty Python, "O Brother" is rife with the kinds of genial madness only writer-director Joel and writer-producer Ethan can come up with.

The Coens, however, have treated one element with respect this time around, and that's made quite a difference. Fans of traditional American music, country, blues and bluegrass, they've worked with composer T Bone Burnett to select nearly 20 prime examples and seen them superbly recorded by top-of-the-line contemporary musicians such as Emmylou Harris, Alison Krauss, Gillian Welch (who has a cameo as a record buyer) and Ralph Stanley.

As a result "O Brother's" music is more than pleasant background; it is a living presence, and with apologies to an excellent cast, just about the star of the picture. By enlivening things to an unprecedented extent, the songs turn "O Brother' into perhaps the warmest production in the Coens' repertoire.

"O Brother's" inspiration and story line are a typically eclectic Coen brothers mix. The film's title and its opening 1930s chain-gang setting are a tip of the hat to Preston Sturges' classic Hollywood comedy "Sullivan's Travels," but what "O Brother' is really riffing off is something different. With whimsical glee, it cross-pollinates two vivid and distinct mythologies, contrasting the ancient Greeks with the cliched movie South.

"Based Upon 'The Odyssey' by Homer" reads an opening title card, and, like another deadpan card the Coens considered but rejected ("Portions Also Based on 'Moby-Dick'), it is as true as it is amusing.

Here's a hero named Ulysses Everett McGill (George Clooney) who sets out on a long and difficult journey, encountering along the way a bad-tempered Cyclops named Big Dan Teague (John Goodman), a trio of honey-tongued sirens (sung but not acted by Harris, Krauss and Welch), even a wife named Penny. It's enough to make you want to rent the old Kirk Douglas-starring "Ulysses" to compare and contrast plot points and adaptation styles.

Just as much fun to notice are the endless chestnuts about the Old South that dot the landscape, mocking our thirst for standard plot elements. Ignorant farmers, mass riverside baptisms, burning crosses, crooked politicians and more, they've all made it into the Coens' rambling plot.

"O Brother' also delights in working up connections between the music and the mythology. So, spoofing the legends surrounding blues giant Robert Johnson, there's a singer named Tommy Johnson (Chris Thomas King) who talks of meeting the devil by a crossroads. And Charles Durning's irascible singing governor Pappy O'Daniel, host of the "Pass the Biscuits Pappy O'Daniel Flour Hour," brings to mind Jimmy Davis, the real-life singing governor of Louisiana and the author of the "You Are My Sunshine" song that is Durning's theme.

The story all these references get worked around begins with a trio of manacled convicts fleeing a Mississippi chain gang. With a fondness for Dapper Dan hair pomade and a misguided belief in his own powers of persuasion, Clooney's McGill may be dumb, but his fellow escapees Pete (John Turturro) and Delmar (Tim Blake Nelson) are dumber and dumbest, respectively.

All three have departed the chain gang in search of a $1.2- million stolen treasure McGill has secreted in a cabin that is in imminent danger of being flooded by a dam. Trying to get the money and avoid the law, our boys take time out to cut a record as Jordan Rivers and the Soggy Bottom Boys and cross paths with everyone from manic-depressive bank robber George "Don't Call Me Baby Face" Nelson (Michael Badalucco) to Homer Stokes, the Reform candidate for governor (Wayne Duvall), an enemy of O'Daniel who is such a friend of the little man he his own little man accompany him on campaign swings.

Helped by computers able to desaturate color, cinematographer Roger Deakins has given "O Brother" an old-fashioned patina that matches its music. "It's a fool who looks for logic in the chambers of the human heart," one character says, and while it may be equally foolhardy to look for logic in a Coen brothers film, this one makes it most pleasant to try.

NEW YORK, 12/18-25/00, p. 170, Peter Rainer

O Brother, Where Art Thou? is set in Depression-era Mississippi, but its real locale is that rarefied and icy-hot postmodern nowheresville peculiar to the Coen brothers. This time around, though, the Coens' usual arch deliberateness isn't quite as deliberate, and there's an appealing shagginess to some of the episodes and performances. The plot is a variation on *The Odyssey*, with three escaped convicts from a chain gang, played by George Clooney, John Turturro, and Tim Blake Nelson, encountering sirens, a blind prophet, and a cyclops (John Goodman as a jolly, homicidal Bible salesman wearing an eye patch).

In most of the Coens' movies, it seems as if the brothers are up in the clouds taking potshots at their people, but here they seem more indulgent and affectionate. The paradox of *O Brother, Where Art Thou?* is that it's a facetious tall tale that still manages to mix in the most unreasonably beautiful country-folk music, including a rendition, by Ralph Stanley, of "O Death" that is doubly shattering because the character doing the singing is a Klansman. This is the Coen brothers' most emotionally felt movie, and that's not meant as faint praise.

NEW YORK POST, 12/22/00, p. 53, Jonathan Foreman

If you liked "Fargo" and "Blood Simple" and the hilarious, grievously underrated "The Big Lebowski," then you're likely to get a big comic kick out of the Coen brothers' latest and perhaps lightest film, "O Brother, Where Art Then?" a picaresque, loose update of Homer's "Odyssey" (set in Depression-era Mississippi) that clatters along amiably like a Model T on a bumpy country road.

Equally, if you are not a fan of the Coen brothers' movies with their quirkiness and playful allusions to film classics, then it's a sure bet that you won't like "O Brother." The title is a reference to the proposed movie-within-a-movie in Preston Sturges' "Sullivan's Travels," even though much of "O Brother" seems like a cunning satirical attack on all those '70s films that looked with affection on life in Depression-era South.

But "O Brother" is too jokey to be thematically consistent or even to be quite as clever as it thinks it is. Fortunately, if you're in the right mood it doesn't much matter: The performances by George Clooney and Coen regulars like John Goodman and John Turturro are simply a delight, the music is strange and the Coen brothers' amazing control of tone has never been so pitch perfect.

Ulysses McGill (Clooney) is serving hard time on a Mississippi chain gang when he escapes while shackled to moody Pete (Turturro) and doltish Delmar (Tim Blake Nelson).

A con man obsessed with his fine head of hair and with his talent for high-falutin' talk, Ulysses has promised Pete and Delmar that he knows where a fortune in treasure is buried. But it's going to take a long journey on the backroads of Mississippi before the three of them get anywhere near this burial spot, and Ulysses is able to reunite with his wife (Holly Hunter) and family.

Along the way they meet fabled bank robber Babyface Nelson (played as a manic-depressive by Michael Badalucco) and Tommy Johnson (Chris Thomas King) a black blues musician who has sold his soul to the devil (and who looks a lot like fabled bluesman Robert Johnson).

All the while Ulysses and his friends are pursued by the sinister Sheriff Cooley (Daniel von Bargen). But they also encounter danger in strangers loosely inspired by Homeric characters like Circe the sorceress, the Sirens who lure sailors to their death, and Polyphemus the Cyclops. For instance, there's Dan McTeague (John Goodman, in another terrific Coen brothers turn), the brutal one-eyed Bible salesman...

Their odyssey also takes in an amazing Busby Berkely-style KKK meeting, (that flirts with bad taste and evokes memories of both "Blazing Saddles" and "The Wizard of Oz") and an election campaign that contrasts Southern populism at its darkest with a merely venal political regime headed by one Pappy O'Daniel (brilliantly played by Charles Durning).

Shot beautifully by Roger Deakin, the film is worth seeing for George Clooney's performance. More than ever he seems like a Clark Gable for our time.

NEWSDAY, 12/22/00, Part II/p. B9, John Anderson

A Coen Brothers movie based on Homer? The obvious question is, "Simpson?" Director Joel and producer Ethan can be the smuggest of smart alecks, as apt to turn out a "Big Lebowski" as a "Fargo," or claiming their new movie is based on "The Odyssey," while also boasting they never even read it.

But "O Brother" is an epic of a kind, an attempt to amalgamate a trove of southern myths and movie tropes into a comedy that doesn't feel like an overly ambitious undergraduate thesis. Which doesn't always work. But it doesn't really matter. Depending on your tolerance for Coen-style smarminess, and whatever day of the week it is, "O Brother, Where Art Thou?" is hilarious, homely, infuriating, ingenious, literary and looney. There's also too much alliteration. But the music's fabulous.

For the most part, so is the cast. As Ulysses Everett McGill, a hybrid of Clark Gable and Cliff Klaven, George Clooney reasserts his star quality and willingness to do the unexpected. The Moe to John Turturro's Larry and Tim Blake Nelson's Curly, the always dapper Ulysses leads his fellow escaped convicts across the Depression-era South as they impersonate not just the Stooges, but the Tin Man, Scarecrow and Cowardly Lion, and three Ishmaels afloat on a coffin.

When "O Brother" premiered at Cannes, neither Coen wanted to discuss the title (the name of the "serious film" Joel McCrea wants to make in Preston Sturges' 1941 "Sullivan's Travels"). Their refusal seemed ill-considered, implying an all-too-frivolous attitude toward their own work. But it may have been self-defense: The movie is so overstuffed with references and allusions that to open the analytic can of worms would have distracted from the overall movie. And it is, in its way, a serious movie.

Scored by T-Bone Burnett and featuring a first-rate, high-lonesome soundtrack of blues, bluegrass and Appalachian folk songs, "O Brother" really rides on its rootsy music. The rendition of "Man of Constant Sorrow" by the so-called Soggy Bottom Boys—Ulysses, Peter (Turturro), Delmar (Nelson) and Tommy Johnson (Chris Thomas King), the soul-selling bluesman they pick up at a crossroads—could be a hit today, just as it is in "O Brother's" South. As the boys travel to Ulysses' Penelope-Penny Wharvey (Holly Hunter), who's about to be remarried—the movie is grounded by its score, while kept off-kilter by southern caricature.

There's also something up with the number three. Three heroes instead of Homer's one. Three episodes that can really be linked to "The Odyssey"—the Sirens, Cyclops (John Goodman's one-eyed Big Dan Teague) and return to Ithaca—plus a tendency for the tamest lines to be repeated three times. The rest of "O Brother's" apparatus, such as Charles Durning's Wizard of Oz-like Gov. Pappy O'Daniel (singing "You Are My Sunshine," a la its composer, Louisiana governor Jimmie Davis), is a collection of free-floating political-cultural myths that the Coens have harvested and wed to literature. The result, as they probably intended, is an American "Golden Bough" as written by Groucho Marx.

SIGHT AND SOUND, 10/00, p. 54, Kevin Jackson

Mississippi, the 30s. Three convicts—Everett, Delmar and Pete—escape and head off across country in search of a hoard of $1.2 million. En route, they encounter a bluesman, Tommy Johnson, the local governor and a record producer, for whom they record a song that becomes a hit across the South. The convicts are seduced by three women they encounter; waking up, Everett and Delmar mistakenly believe Pete has been turned into a frog. After being robbed by salesman Dan Teague, Everett and Delmar discover Pete was handed back to the authorities by the women; later, they help him escape. Everett admits there isn't any buried treasure; his motive for breaking out was to get back to his former wife, Penny, who is about to marry her suitor, the campaign manager for the governor's rival, Homer Stokes.

The trio discover Homer is involved with the Ku Klux Klan and rescue Penny from a lynching. Later, they expose Homer and secure pardons from the governor. Penny insists she won't marry Everett until he recovers her wedding ring from their shack. When the four friends go there, they are caught by the cops. As they are about to be hanged, the area is flooded by the TVA. The four survive; Everett rejoins his wife.

One of the earliest gags thrown out (and apparently away) by the Brothers Coen is their po-faced title-credit claim that *O Brother, Where Art Thou?* is based on the *Odyssey*. Aha, you think, typical smart-alecky college-boy spoofery... and then darn it if the Homeric parallels don't start coming thick and fast. A hero called Ulysses heading back home to see off the suitors for his wife Penny/Penelope; a one-eyed and hence suitably Cyclopean bad guy in the corpulent form of John Goodman, crooked Bible salesman and KKK goon Big Dan Teague; a trio of exquisitely sexy sirens, who coax our crew, three escapees from a chain gang on the trail of a cache of buried money, to the river and oblivion with sweet song and spiked hooch, and even manage to turn one of them—or so his superstitious pals believe—into a frog; blind men prophesying signs and wonders and a guy called Homer.

None of which would appear to have very much point, other than in adding a certain quality of bookish gamesomeness to the proceedings for those in the know, just as a movie buff's knowledge of the film's undeclared source, Preston Sturges' 1941 comedy *Sullivan's Travels* (in which the idealistic director played by Joel McCrea yearns to make a socially conscious epic entitled *O Brother, Where Art Thou?*), will give a little extra relish to the scene in which a chain gang is marched into the local cinema for their weekly dose of motion entertainment. Disparate as they otherwise are, though, the two classic sources of Sturges' *Travels* and Homer's *Odyssey* do have at least one thing in common: they share the basic structure of the episodic adventure journey—a form which can have the virtue of mating a reasonably strong narrative drive with a pleasingly wide and promiscuous range of subject matter.

The better part of a century ago, both James Joyce and Ezra Pound twigged to the usefulness of the *Odyssey* as a clothes line for hanging your obsessions on, and though the Coens are neither as universally compendious as Joyce nor as nastily deranged as Pound, their film is also a bit of an encyclopaedic rag-bag or cabinet of curiosities, stuffed to bursting point with the minutiae of American popular culture and folk memory. At one point or another, their film invokes more or less directly all of the following and more: the satanic legend of blues guitarist Robert Johnson, the career of Louisiana governor Huey Long, *The Wizard of Oz*, the modernising and devastating activities of the Tennessee Valley Authority, bank robbers Bonnie and Clyde, *The Grapes of Wrath*, Southern novelist Flannery O'Connor's religious zealots and hucksters, writer James Agee and photographer Walker Evans' account of the Depression years *Let Us Now Praise Famous Men* and the Lord alone knows what else.

Above all, it's a compendium of American musical styles of the period, from blues and gospel to bluegrass and back again, comparable in spirit and sheer enjoyment value to Harry Smith's celebrated anthology of American folk music of the 20s and 30s, re-issued on CDs a couple of years ago to ecstatic reviews and brisk sales. (Did the Coens join the rest of us in snapping it up?) Simply, *O Brother, Where Art Thou?* has one of the richest and most satisfying soundtracks I've heard in years: hats off to T-Bone Burnett, who arranged and produced it, as well as recruiting a lot of the performers.

So much for the encyclopaedic rag-bag. As for the narrative clothes line: well *O Brother...* certainly isn't as funny as one of the top-flight Preston Sturges movies—no shame there, since almost nothing is—but it's more than funny enough sometimes unexpectedly charming into the bargain. George Clooney, who's been made into a strikingly good ringer for Clark Gable, is agreeably relaxed and understated in the slightly image-tarnishing role of Everett Ulysses McGill, a bit of a blue-collar fop who is almost pathologically concerned with the state of his hair (there is much play with nocturnal hairnets and cans of a gentleman's pomade by the name of "Dapper Dan"), a bit of a pompous and sesquipedalian word-spinner, a bit of a coward and a bit of a cad. Clooney also does a terrific job of lip-synching to 'I Am a Man of Constant Sorrow', the song that unknowingly catapults him and his fellow escapees, in the guise of a hillbilly outfit called the Soggy Bottom Boys, to the top of the redneck hit parade.

Clooney's character holds the film together as much as such a digressive narrative can be held together, and few viewers are going to be much bothered by the implausibilities and grandstanding vignettes which threaten to pull it apart from time to time. As you'd expect from the Coens, *O Brother...* is rich in visual jokes, from very simple slapstick stunts (chained together, the convicts try to jump on to a train one after another; Everett goes first, only to be yanked back into the dust by his less athletic peers) to less readily encapsulated effects, such as the neatly shot moment in which the siren-drugged cons wake up and see that nothing is left of their friend Pete (John Turturro) but a carefully laid-out set of clothes. The torch-lit Klan rally, which the gang eavesdrop, is a particularly strange piece of virtuoso staging, which manages to be at once camp and authentically sinister.

Time to raise and, if possible, lance the old objection levelled against the Coens by unbelievers: yes, they are clever, very clever, too clever by half, but where is the substance, the warmth, the passion? One answer, this time around, is that it is obviously possible to love some of the things you mock (to mock them partly because you love them), and that the treatment of American music in *O Brother*... even silly yodelling American music, is in the end far more loving than mocking, just as it was in Robert Altman's *Nashville* (1975).

And what is true of the music is true of the culture which produced that music: it would be hard for film-makers with no real attachment to Americana to produce a movie so besotted with the bric-a-brac of their nation's half-forgotten folk ways. It was always clear that the Coens were film-fed boys, but less clear how reverent they felt to their pop-cultural roots. Maybe, like Ulysses or Odysseus, they've finally come home to Ithaca. In any event, *O Brother, Where Art Thou?* is a finely wrought entertainment film, one which any con might be pleased to see on his afternoon away from the chain gang.

TIME, 12/25/00-1/1/01, p. 148, Richard Corliss

Three cons (Clooney, Turturro and Nelson) are on the lam in '30S Mississippi. A blind prophet intones, "You shall see a cow on top of a cotton bale, and many other startlements." Startlements are indeed in store: a one-eyed, toad-squishing salesman (Goodman); three maidens washing their laundry in a stream. These, and the name of the bombastic schemer Clooney plays—Everett Ulysses McGill—should be sufficient clues to identify the film's source: "Based on *The Odyssey* by Homer."

While *tout* Hollywood purloins comic books for its scenarios, Joel and Ethan Coen raid noble antiquity: not just Homer's fabulous travelogue in verse but Preston Sturges' *Sullivan's Travels* (for the movie's title) and MGM's *The Wizard of Oz* (for a delirious production number starring the Ku Klux Klan). Toss in enough gorgeous blue-grass music to make the movie's CD a must-have, and you get prime, picaresque entertainment. It celebrates the chicanery of the human spirit, the love of raillery and rodomontade. But don't ask us for reasons; we just liked it. As Clooney, who never radiated more star quality, opines, "It's a fool that looks for logic in the chambers of the human heart."

VILLAGE VOICE, 12/26/00, p. 137, J. Hoberman

For the unadulterated Olympian perspective, look to the Coen brothers. In *Fargo* and *The Big Lebowski*, these ferociously clever siblings took the risk of investing in a character to whom they did not feel absolutely superior. That strategy is abandoned in *O Brother, Where Art Thou?*, a protracted Little Moron joke in which three white idiots (George Clooney, John Turturro, and Tim Blake Nelson) escape from a chain gang into the wilds of late-'30s Mississippi. As the filmmakers take pains to point out, their plot occasionally intersects with *The Odyssey*—Clooney plays one of the few Southerners since the Civil War to be named Ulysses. The unwieldy title, however, alludes to the "serious" movie within the movie in *Sullivan's Travels*. It's a jab at anyone who expects the Coens to ever be less than facetious.

Basically, *O Brother* warms up a tepid gumbo of Deep South clichés: brainless Gomers, zombie Baptists, the colored boy who sells his soul to the devil to play the blues, the loudmouthed bank robber who turns out to be Baby Face Nelson. The art direction is impeccable, but this is a pop-up book that I was impatient to slam. Scampering through an ensemble whose acting is confined largely to pulling funny faces, Clooney has the oily charm of middle-period Burt Reynolds. An excellent, mainly traditional bluegrass score is placed at the service of the three stooges, who turn out to be great natural entertainers. (They sold their soul to the Coens.) Replete with Homer and Jethro two-stepping and *Hee Haw* high-kicks, music triumphs over racism—if not rampant rube-baiting.

The epitome of the Coens' po'mo' puppet show is placing the high mournful sound of Ralph Stanley's "Oh Death" in the mouth of a murderous KKK kleagle. In terms of nihilistic mix-and-match, I'd love to see Spike Lee make a mess of this fastidiously smug scenario even more than I'd enjoy watching the Coens impose their cruel order on the chaos of *Bamboozled*.

Also reviewed in:
CHICAGO TRIBUNE, 12/29/00, Friday/p. A, Michael Wilmington
NEW YORK TIMES, 12/22/00, p. E1, A. O. Scott
VARIETY, 5/22-28/00, p. 19, Todd McCarthy
WASHINGTON POST, 12/29/00, p. C1, Stephen Hunter
WASHINGTON POST, 12/29/00, Weekend/p. 41, Desson Howe

ON THE RUN

A Phaedra Cinema release of an Arco Films/CLT-UFA International/Le Studio Canal +/MGN Filmes/Sunday Films production. *Producer:* Tino Navarro and Bruno de Almeida. *Director:* Bruno de Almeida. *Screenplay:* Joseph Minion. *Story:* Bruno de Almeida and Jonathan Berman. *Director of Photography:* Igor Sunara. *Editor:* Beatrice Sisul. *Music:* Frank London. *Sound:* David Pastecchi. *Sound Editor:* Coll Anderson. *Casting:* Sheila Jaffe and Georgianne Walken. *Production Designer:* Andrew Bernard. *Art Director:* Jordan Jacobs. *Set Decorator:* Sara Baldocchi. *Special Effects:* Alex Weil. *Costumes:* Catherine Marie Thomas. *Make-up:* Nuria Sitja. *Running time:* 94 minutes. *MPAA Rating:* Not Rated.

CAST: John Ventimiglia (Louie); Michael Imperioli (Albert); Drena De Niro (Rita); Agnès Jaoui (Kirstin); Joaquim de Almeida (Ignácio); Nick Sandow (Jack); Victor Argo (Man Shaving); Tom Gilroy (Tom); Joseph R. Gassascoli (Burly Guy); Suzanne Shepherd (Lady in Travel Agency); Sara Graça (Vicky); Jason Pabon (Young Albert); Saul Negron (Young Louis); Arthur J. Nascarella (Irwin); Sharon Angela (Tina); Paul Lazar (Cabbie); Anthony Zaccaro (Cop in Apartment); Tino Navarro (Homeless); Kate Lunsford (Waitress); L. B. Williams (Cop in Coffee Shop); Joel Rooks (Bartender); Luís Fontes and Miguel Ferreira (Bodyguards); Gary Perez (Cop in Havana Club); Dwight Ewell (Rasta); John Frey (George); Bronson Dudley (Dr. Shapiro); Paolina Weber (Nurse); Eddie Branquinho and David Callegati (Cops in Hospital); Lou Tiano (Man in Bathroom).

NEW YORK POST, 9/15/00, p. 54, Lou Lumenick

This rambling, Portuguese-financed, New York-filmed indie has (understandably) been on the shelf so long that a character goes looking for Frank Sinatra (who died in 1998) and the millennium is being anticipated as an upcoming event.

The movie starts promisingly with witty, sharply designed animated opening credits. Then things rapidly go downhill in this pinch-penny production, which has an exceedingly amateurish supporting cast.

It's about a shy travel agent (Michael Imperioli) whose life is turned inside out by the appearance of a wildly extroverted childhood pal (John Ventimiglia) who's just escaped from prison.

The travel agent could easily dispose of his unwanted pal at several points, but he doesn't. This leads to a series of increasingly contrived comic mishaps in bars and a Times Square porno shop that seem a fairly desperate attempt by screenwriter Joseph Minon to recapture the glory of "After Hours," which he wrote 15 years ago.

But director Bruno de Almeida is no Martin Scorsese (the earlier film's director), to put it mildly. Almeida has little idea of when to end a scene or when an actor is going too far over the top.

VILLAGE VOICE, 9/19/00, p. 126, Jessica Winter

[*On the Run* was reviewed jointly with *Turn It Up;* see Winter's review of that film.]

Also reviewed in:
NEW YORK TIMES, 9/15/00, p. E24, Lawrence Van Gelder
VARIETY, 5/3-9/99, p. 84, Lisa Nesselson

ONCE IN THE LIFE

A Lions Gate Films release of a Cinema Gypsy Productions and The Shooting Gallery production. *Executive Producer:* Larry Meistrich, Stephen Carlis, and Donald C. Carter. *Producer:* David Bushell, Helen Sugland, and Laurence Fishburne. *Director:* Laurence Fishburne. *Screenplay (based on his play "Riff Raff"):* Laurence Fishburne. *Director of Photography:* Richard Turner. *Editor:* Bill Pankow. *Music:* Branford Marsalis. *Music Editor:* James Flatto. *Sound:* Tom Brandau. *Sound Editor:* Ahmad Shirazi and Stuart Stanley. *Casting:* Bonnie Tmmermann. *Production Designer:* Charley Beal. *Art Director:* Diann Duthie. *Set Decorator:* Paul Cheponis and Jordan West. *Costumes:* Darryle Johnson. *Stunt Coordinator:* Jalil Jay Lynch. *Running time:* 93 minutes. *MPAA Rating:* R.

CAST: Laurence Fishburne (20/20 Mike); Titus Welliver (Torch); Eamonn Walker (Tony); Dominic Chianese, Jr. (Freddie Nine Lives); Paul Calderon (Mann Rivera); Gregory Hines (Ruffhouse); Annabella Sciorra (Maxine); Michael Paul Chan (Buddha); Andres "Dres" Titus (Hector); Tiger Chen (Chino); Harsh Nayyar (Cab Driver); Sue Costello (Sergeant Kneeley); Nick Chinlund (Mike Murphy); Tim White (Little Billy); Wanda De Jesus (Jackie); Justin Pierre Edmund (Little Mikey); Jim Breuer (Pizzaman); Huey Morgan (Carlos); Madison Riley (Precious); Allan Francis (Strip Club Patron).

LOS ANGELES TIMES, 10/27/00, Calendar/p. 16, Kevin Thomas

Laurence Fishburne wastes no time plunging us into the precarious world of his absorbing and edgy "Once in the Life." In his deft and imaginative adaptation of his 1994 play "Riff Raff," Fishburne also plays Mike, a slick New York dude who crosses paths with his half-brother Torch (Titus Welliver), whom he barely knows, in a police station, where both have been held briefly.

Mike invites Torch to join him in a drug deal. Mike, who thinks he's way smarter than he is, prides himself on the acute powers of observation that have earned him the nickname "20/20" because it seems he has eyes in the back of his head. Yet he assumes the clearly high-strung and seedy-looking Torch has a bad cold when, of course, he's a junkie in dire need of a fix.

And sure enough, Mike foolishly lets himself be drawn into a scam with a flunky (Dominic Chianese Jr.) of a drug kingpin, Manny (Paul Calderon). The scam goes awry when the jittery Torch guns down a couple of the young hotshots the flunky has set up for robbery.

Wounded in his hand, Torch is taken to a hide-out in an abandoned building by Mike, who now waits for his ex-con pal Tony (Eamonn Walker) to arrive to help out the brothers, who managed to escape with the drug haul. What Mike doesn't know is that Tony, who he believes has gone straight, not only works for Manny but also that the heroin was earmarked for Tony to distribute.

In short order Fishburne has set up a predicament riddled with conflicting emotions. Tony, whose jailhouse poetry and friendship had sustained Mike when they were prison cellmates, is the most intelligent of the three, a man who loathes the life of crime but is resigned to his fateful place in it, supporting his staunch wife (Annabella Sciorra) and their young daughter (Madison Riley).

Mike says he would like to get out, too, but is no thinker, as his strung-out but much brighter brother observes. As Tony ponders how he's going to spare his friend's life and yet not cross his boss, Mike and the increasingly sick Torch start forming the fraternal bond they never had.

Themes of friendship, family and loyalty interplay as the situation grows tenser, yet the time these men spend in their secret oasis presents a human face to individuals who might be dismissed as dangerous scum. Not unlike the saloon in "The Iceman Cometh," the abandoned apartment is an oasis in which these losers can for a moment indulge themselves in the illusion that a better life is possible.

All the while, waiting on the street below are two of Manny's ruthless enforcers (Gregory Hines and Michael Paul Chan) who are there to ensure Tony satisfies Manny's demand. The two consider themselves very funny guys—and in a way they are, even though their thuggish skills are no laughing matter.

Fishburne excels in his triple-threat roles as actor, director and adapter of his own play, and his cast glows under his direction. In this handsome, graceful film, Fishburne has found the stuff of tragedy in an urban, streetwise melodrama.

NEW YORK POST, 10/27/00, p. 48, Lou Lumenick

Laurence Fishburne's debut as a writer-director doesn't do much to disguise its origins as his grim, three-character off-Broadway play from 1994, "Riff Raff." Sure, there are brief appearances by characters only referred to by dialogue in the play, such as a sadistic henchman (a most unlikely Gregory Hines) and a kidnapped wife (Annabella Scicorra).

But basically it's an acting exercise—a one-set rendition of that-old stage and movie standby, the ex-convict struggling to go straight who's tempted to attempt one last score.

For "20/20" (played by Fishburne), whose nickname reflects his supposed street instincts, temptation arrives in the form of his long-estranged half brother, a junkie nicknamed "The Torch" (Titus Welliver).

Things go horribly wrong when they intercept a drug shipment. "The Torch" is seriously injured, and it turns out the stolen heroin belongs to a very vengeful crime boss (Paul Calderon), who leans on "Tony the Tiger" (Eamonn Walker), an ex-cellmate of "20/20's" to get it back.

Fishburne is solid as usual as an actor, but as a director his notable achievement is capturing a searing, affecting performance by Welliver as a pathetic, drug-addled character that at its best recalls Dustin Hoffman's Ratso Rizzo in "Midnight Cowboy."

It would easily qualify for an Oscar nomination if it were in a movie that was a bit less like canned theater and more cinematic, like the even more harrowing "Requiem for a Dream."

NEWSDAY, 10/27/00, Part II/p. B8, Gene Seymour

Actor Laurence Fishburne's conviction to shine a warm light to those trapped on society's seamier margins managed to burn through many reviewers' qualms over his 1994 Off-Broadway play, "Riff Raff." And though his three-character drama about a jittery, improbably clueless ex-con, his heroin-addicted half brother and his former cell mate who may or may not be out to kill them both over stolen drugs was awash in in-your-face speeches, jailhouse rhymes and overdone motifs, there was enough energy in Fishburne's writing to make one think this formidable actor could pass on his day job for a while if he wanted to.

But in opening up his play for a filmed version, "Once in the Life," Fishburne may have only succeeded in magnifying the flaws of his original. He has saddled—or, more accurately, sandbagged—his tale with back-story material about brothers "20/20" Mike (Fishburne) and Torch (Titus Welliver, from the original play) and how they happened to hook up for the truly inspired notion of ripping off neighborhood drug kingpin Manny Rivera (a scary Paul Calderon).

Having stolen a shipment of dope in a bloody transaction, the pair hole up in an abandoned Brooklyn building to await the arrival of Mike's old cellmate, Tony the Tiger (Eamonn Walker from "Oz"). What Mike doesn't know—and Torch rightly suspects—is that Tony's been dispatched by Manny to retrieve his merchandise and slaughter the pests.

Walker's magnetic presence makes Fishburne's decision to magnify Tony's role in the film a sound one. But what's the point of adding the comparably magnetic Annabella Sciorra as Tony's beleaguered wife or Gregory Hines as an even-quirkier-than-usual leg breaker if you're going to make them peripheral decorations for the three-character story? Which, by the way, seems lumpier and more leaden here than one recalled from the stage.

VILLAGE VOICE, 10/31/00, p. 174, Michael Atkinson

Director Laurence Fishburne could hardly control his hammier instincts with his filmization of his play *Riff Raff*, and *Once in the Life* is hot-tempered theatrical combat, punctuated by supposedly cool jailhouse doggerel that scans like "Casey at the Bat," and blanketed with a Branford Marsalis score that plugs, wails, and finger-snaps along regardless of what's happening. Always commanding, Fishburne miscasts himself as 20/20 Mike, a jabbering, somewhat spineless hood with a slight case of self-declared precognition; after he meets his long-lost (and white) half-brother Billy (Titus Welliver) in the overnight tank, they decide to rip off a local drug lord, leaving them terrified and oozing blood in an abandoned hideout. Once Mike's joint buddy Tony (Eamonn Walker) shows up to help and/or cap them, the stage is set for teary speeches and gun-to-the-temple face-offs. While the line-readings are often dead-on, Fishburne's movie suffers from the usual one-room claustrophobia and Mametian repetitions (you hear "Don't call me that!" 50 times), and cutting to cameo roles by Gregory Hines, Annabella Sciorra, and Paul Calderon doesn't help much.

Also reviewed in:
CHICAGO TRIBUNE, 10/27/00, Friday/p. F, Michael Wilmington
NEW YORK TIMES, 10/27/00, p. E24, A. O. Scott
VARIETY, 10/30-11/5/00, p. 22, Robert Koehler

ONE

A Shooting Gallery release of a Two Nine Productions presentation in association with 3 Ring Circus. *Producer:* Wendy Cary. *Director:* Tony Barbieri. *Screenplay:* Tony Barbieri and Jason Cairns. *Director of Photography:* Matthew Irving. *Editor:* Jeffery Stephens. *Sound:* Alan B. Samuels. *Sound Editor:* Malcolm Fife and Kim B. Christensen. *Casting:* Malia Levine. *Production Designer:* Wendy Cary. *Art Director:* David Bjorngard. *Costumes:* Wendy Cary. *Make-up:* Ginger Damon. *Running time:* 88 minutes. *MPAA Rating:* Not Rated.

CAST: Kane Picoy (Nick Razca); Jason Cairns (Charlie O'Connell); Autumn Macintosh (Sarah Jenkins); Ed Lynch (Johnny the Bartender); Gabriell Ruvolo (Iris Razca); Paul Herman (Ted Razca); Muhammed Hasan (Dan the Parole Officer); Willie La Nere (Coach Gus); Cassandra Braden (Helen); Kara Michaels (Joan); Rainy Jo Stout (Nancy); Heather Gomoll (Girl with Balloon); Robbie Lanzone (Small Boy on Couch); Kathryn Matthews (Small Girl in Wheelchair); Colette Ibanez (Stripper); Tito Barbieri (Scout 1); Rick Bruno (Scout 2); Mike Gilliam (Scout 3); Jonsen Vitug (Faceless); Tom Williamson and Socrates Delianides (Dice Players).

LOS ANGELES TIMES, 10/13/00, Calendar/p. 12, Kenneth Turan

American independent films don't qualify as rare, but ones like "One" definitely are. Subtle yet stylish, carefully and rigorously made, it assumes intelligence and sophistication on the part of the audience. A haunting character study of two longtime friends who reach a point where the bonds between them are as senseless as they are unbreakable, this is serious and uncompromising filmmaking in the best sense of the words.

More impressive still, "One" is the debut film for director Tony Barbieri (who co-wrote with co-star Jason Cairns). A filmmaker who understands the drama inherent in deliberateness and repose, Barbieri uses the rarest of qualities, nuance and restraint, to get under our skin with a simple yet complex human drama. And, rarer still, he makes the film's visual style a key component in his storytelling arsenal.

Admittedly influenced by European films as diverse as "The Conformist" and the classics of neo-realism, Barbieri and cinematographer Matthew Irving use spare, telling imagery combined with delicate music to draw us in. There is a confident, hypnotic classicism about the film's compositions and slow pans, about the way, for instance, the camera slowly changes focus in a key scene from two actors talking to a burning cigarette in the ashtray beside them.

Convincingly set in blue-collar San Francisco, "One" starts with its two mid-20s protagonists being alone. Nick Razca (Kane Picoy), hanging in his neighborhood bar, is a gifted ex-minor-league baseball player who washed out for mysterious reasons and still has the disaffected air of a prince in exile.

Nick is next seen picking up his oldest, closest friend Charlie O'Connell (Cairns) on his release from prison for an unstated crime. Without a family, without a place, Charlie will be staying at Nick's parents' house, where his friend still lives, and working with Nick as a sanitation man.

As a community service condition of his parole, Charlie goes to work for attractive Sarah Jenkins (Autumn Macintosh), whose company brings medical supplies to disabled children. Something in Charlie is touched by this work, but Nick, typically, speaks contemptuously of "deliveries to the retards and the cripples."

That gap in perception indicates a larger problem. Though neither one wants to acknowledge it, their time apart has done something to both men and their relationship to each other. While Charlie, who never cared about school, enrolls in junior college and seems intent on making something of himself, Nick becomes even more embittered and dismissive, aggrieved that the world has not given him what he feels entitled to. When Charlie's determination finally forces Nick into a kind of action, the results are complex and unforeseen.

There's a quiet desperation about these unfulfilled lives, a sense of sadness and melancholy that makes "One" distinctive. Both men find themselves haunted, even imprisoned, by their pasts; Charlie by what happened during his time in prison, and Nick by his minor league experience. Their frustrations with each other play at times like a disguised lover's quarrel, as both men find how impossible it is to live either with or without the other.

Perhaps what's most impressive about how "One" deals with this material is its sureness, its belief in itself. Finely acted across the board, largely by unknowns, this is a film that never pushes, that takes its time revealing its secrets, confident that its exactly calibrated effects will be worth the wait.

Speaking of waiting, though "One" greatly impressed critics at Sundance in 1998, it's taken 2½ years to reach theatrical screens (as part of the excellent Shooting Gallery series that previously brought us "Croupier" and "Human Resources") because of doubts about its ability to attract an audience. If you care about the best kind of independent filmmaking, if you want the option of experiencing artistic films when you go to the movies, missing out on "One" is not an option. When a film like this appears, attention should be paid.

NEW YORK POST, 10/13/00, p. 65, Lou Lumenick

A rare dud in the Shooting Gallery series, this is another painfully earnest little indie about a just-released jailbird, Charlie (Jason Cairns), who's been doing time for euthanizing his grandfather.

Charlie moves in with his best friend, Nick (Kane Picoy), and Nick's parents in San Francisco, where they consume endless plates of spaghetti. Nick is a talented but sullen ballplayer who gets sacked by a Triple A team for slugging a coach and works as a garbage collector.

Will Charlie make a new life for himself or get sucked into Nick's downward spiral?

There's one particularly frustrating sequence that points up the missed opportunities in this film: an eager Charlie takes his pretty boss (Autumn Macintosh, a notably better actor than the guys) out on a date—which ends abruptly because she's forced to fire him for not following the rules.

But instead of lingering on the characters' pain, writer-director Tony Barbieri cuts away and continues on a predictable, well-worn path.

NEWSDAY, 10/13/00, Part II/p. B6, John Anderson

The penultimate scene in Tony Barbieri's "One"—murder under a streetlight, outside the Lucky Cafeteria—appears like some unknown Edward Hopper painting, sick in its soul, produced out of inescapable loneliness. What has happened during our journey through the film isn't surprising. Far from it. But the echoing sense of inevitability is far more unsettling than any tortuous plot twist could possibly be.

On one hand, "One" is the story of childhood friends with nothing else in common. Nick (Kane Picoy) is an embittered ex-baseball player who self-destructed on his way to a big-league contract. Charlie (Jason Cairns) has just finished serving time for the euthanasia killing of his grandfather, a victim of Lou Gehrig's disease, and Charlie's only family. Nick's father (Paul Herman) takes Charlie in and treats him like family, while treating Nick with contempt. And you feel for him: Nick had it all, took everyone down with him and is looking for someone else to blame. Charlie did what he had to do. And at his center, he's almost serene.

The two leads give first-rate performances; the story is almost archetypal in its rustic profundity. But Barbieri's cinematic instincts kick the film up a few notches. Maybe it's the proximity of the two films' openings, but "One" suggests Edward Yang's "Yi Yi" (or the work of Yang's Taiwanese compatriot, Hou Hsiao-hsien)In the way Barbieri addresses his characters so indirectly, creating distance and isolation through deep focus and obscured perspective. Characters are barely glimpsed (but always heard) through doorways, from outer rooms, via skewed points of view. The sense we get is of a universal insulation, not hostility, but resignation to the idea that we're born alone and are certainly going to die alone.

No, it's not a popcorn movie, but "One" has its rewards—in the acting, the way the story unfolds with such effortless ease and, not so incidentally, the introduction it proffers to that rarity of rarities, a born director.

VILLAGE VOICE, 10/17/00, p. 136, Amy Taubin

If *Ratcatcher* [see Taubin's review of that film], is unmistakably an art film (it even has subtitles that translate the Glasgow dialect for American audiences), Tony Barbieri's first film, *One*, is the kind of hybrid that too often falls between the cracks. This twisted buddy movie has a hint of Antonioni in its wide-screen compositions, but its blue-collar milieu strips the glamour from alienation.

Once a promising player for a Yankee farm team, Nick (Kane Picoy) destroyed his career by slugging the manager. Now he lives with his parents and works as a garbage collector. When his childhood friend Charlie (cowriter Jason Cairns) is released from jail (he served hard time for assisting the suicide of his terminally ill grandfather), Nick offers him a place to stay. Nick desperately needs to connect emotionally, but Charlie is wary of his friend's dependence. Feeling abandoned and betrayed when Charlie moves out and gets involved with a woman, Nick turns his anger on himself. Their relationship careers downhill until it's blown apart by an event no one could have predicted.

Nick and Charlie look enough alike to be brothers, but psychologically they're the opposites who attract. Charlie seems to have absorbed The *Little Engine That Could* as a child, but since the film offers almost no information about his upbringing, his optimism and balanced sense of self seem almost as miraculous to us as they do to Nick. In contrast, Nick's problems have almost everything to do with his father and mother, and they have ample screen time to exhibit their bad-parenting maneuvers. Nick's delusions of grandeur and fear of failure are the result of his father's demands and the contempt he shows his son for not measuring up.

Unlike the vast majority of Amerindies, in which waving the camera around is the correlative of desire, inner conflict, and just about everything else associated with drama, *One* uses strategically composed fixed-camera images to express Nick and Charlie's loneliness and their frustrated desire for something or someone that will make them feel complete. Barbieri favors compositions in which either Nick or Charlie is placed near the side of an otherwise empty frame. The image is conspicuously unbalanced. It needs another person to fill the space on the other side. Even more than the subtlety of the writing and acting, it's this sophisticated and emotionally potent visual strategy that suggests Barbieri's promise as a filmmaker and lifts *One* above the low-budget indie heap.

Also reviewed in:
NEW YORK TIMES, 10/13/00, p. E24, Stephen Holden
VARIETY, 2/16-22/98, p. 58, Emanuel Levy

100% ARABICA

An ArtMattan Productions release of a Fennec Productions, Les Films de la Toison d'Or, and Incoprom co-production. *Producer:* Mahmoud Zemmouri. *Director:* Mahmoud Zemmouri. *Screenplay (French with English subtitles):* Mahmoud Zemmouri, and Marie-Laurence Attias. *Director of Photography:* Noel Very. *Editor:* Youcef Tobni. *Music:* Khaled, Cheb Mami, Tak Farinas, Sage, Mohammed Hamhni, Cheb Tahar, Cheb Fethi, Cheb Tarik, and Nrodine Marsaoui. *Costumes:* Mahadevi Apavou. *Running time:* 86 minutes. *MPAA Rating:* Not Rated.

CAST: Khaled (Rachid); Cheb Mami (Krimo); Mouss (Slimane); Majim Laouriga (Madjid); Farid Fedjer (Kamel); Youssef Diawara (Sylla); Patrice Thibaud (Bernard Lemercier); Mohamed Camara (Salem); Nedjma (Zoubida).

NEW YORK POST, 6/23/00, p. 50, Jonathan Foreman

"100% Arabica" is the nickname of a friendly Parisian ghetto peopled by Algerian and other African immigrants who don't pay rent and who are rarely visited by the frightened local cops.

Some of the local kids led by Rachid (played by Khaled) and Krimo (Cheb Mami) have turned from petty crime and founded Rap Oriental, a band that combines traditional Algerian rai music with rap.

They are loved by everyone in their community, except for the comically hypocritical and corrupt local imam, Slimane (Mouss).

Slimane preaches that music is forbidden by Islam, partly because the rap 'n' rai concerts draw his congregants away from evening prayers, and partly because he's subsidized by the local French mayor and he thinks the mayor won't approve of concerts in the ghetto.

There's not much plot, the pacing is slow and both the dialogue and the acting are fairly crude.

The fundamentalist-vs.-musicians conflict is so one-sided and over-the-top you would almost feel sorry for the "fundies," if the music wasn't so enjoyable—and if you didn't know that many rai musicians have been persecuted or driven out of their native land by fundamentalist critics. (The "Prince of Rai," Cheb Hasni, was murdered in Algiers in 1997).

VILLAGE VOICE, 6/27/00, p. 154, Edward Crouse

A North African rent-controlled *banlieu* outside Paris is a not-quite-slapstick battleground for cops, immigrants, a fundamentalist Muslim little Caesar, and a cuddly rap group in *100% Arabica*. The film works as a B musical consecrated to Rai (a polyglot North African music smelted with Western rap) and not much else. Rachid and Krimo (real-life singers Khaled and Cheb Mami) lead Rap Oriental, a local group that soothes, amps, and grooves said hood, while a prickly, waddling Holy Roller named Slimane greases up the mayor with guarantees of community submission and shakes down local merchants for tithes. Above all, the ban on music and dancing, defied by seemingly 99 percent of the town, must be maintained, in order to assure both the bureaucratic French mayorship and the Muslim that crime is down.

The slight story, broadly and declaratively played, consists of various joyful takes on petty ghetto delinquency (stripping cars for spare parts and bootlegging music seem to be the dominant modes). The whizzy opening shots of three roller-blading punks—slashing their way through Parisian boulevardiers and eventually ditching a police blockade with a searing jump—are about as adventurous, visually and otherwise, as the film gets.

Curiously, most of the Rai/rap tunes in *100% Arabica* are not subtitled, leaving the viewer to register the music's antiauthoritarian stance purely on the basis of its community populism (i.e., that it empties out Slimane's uptight and evil mosque). Rachid's swaying, raspy warbling agreeably contrasts with Krimo's sweeter, near-crooning balladeer style; their songs, the movie's strength, are barely enough to subsume the mostly glazed, one-note acting. A kindlier *La Haine* crossed with a world-music retread of Vanilla Ice's film debut, *Cool as Ice, 100% Arabica* is best taken lightly, according to its own advice: "This a neighborhood party, not a circumcision."

Also reviewed in:
NEW YORK TIMES, 6/23/00, p. E12, Stephen Holden
VARIETY, 10/6-12/97, p. 59, Deborah Young

102 DALMATIANS

A Buena Vista Productions release of a Walt Disney Pictures production. *Producer:* Edward S. Feldman. *Director:* Kevin Lima. *Screenplay:* Kristen Buckley, Brian Regan, Bob Tzudiker, and Noni White. *Story:* Kristen Buckley and Brian Regan. *Based on the novel "The One Hundred and One Dalmatians" by:* Dodie Smith. *Director of Photography:* Adrian Biddle. *Editor:* Gregory Perler. *Music:* David Newman. *Music Editor:* Jim Harrison. *Sound:* Chris Munro and (music) John Kurlander. *Sound Editor:* Michael Silvers. *Casting:* Priscilla John. *Production Designer:* Assheton Gorton. *Art Director:* John Ralph. *Set Decorator:* Joanne Woollard. *Special Effects:* Chris Corbould. *Visual Effects:* Jim Rygiel. *Costumes:* Anthony Powell. *Make-up:* Patricia A. Cameron. *Stunt Coordinator:* Steve Dent. *Running time:* 101 minutes. *MPAA Rating:* G.

CAST: Glenn Close (Cruella De Vil); Gerard Depardieu (Le Pelt); Ioan Gruffudd (Kevin); Alice Evans (Chloe); Tim McInnerny (Alonso); Ben Crompton (Ewan); Carol MaCready (Agnes); Ian Richardson (Mr. Torte); Jim Carter (Detective Armstrong); Ron Cook (Mr. Button); Timothy West (Judge); David Horovitch (Doctor Pavlov); Dick Brannick (Pavlov's Assistant); Mike Hayley (Constable); Nicholas Hutchison (Reporter); Tim Willcox (ITN Reporter); June Watson (Prison Warden); Tony Bluto (Photocopier Repairman); Tessa Vale (Ticket Seller); John Styles (Punch & Judy Man); Kerry Shale and Thierry Lawson (Le Pelt's Assistants); Hugh Futcher (Brakeman); Charles Simon (Lord Carnivore); Dorothea Phillips (Mrs. Mirthless); Delphine Annaiis (Paris Poodle Lady); Eric Idle (Voice of Waddlesworth).

LOS ANGELES TIMES, 11/22/00, Calendar/p. 1, Kevin Thomas

"102 Dalmatians" is 101 too many, but that's not likely to deter anyone who enjoyed the 1996 "101 Dalmatians," which in turn was a lavish live-action remake of Disney's much-loved 1961 animated classic. Still, you can't help but feel that Disney has delivered a turkey for Thanksgiving.

If sets and costumes were everything, this even more lavish sequel and the 1996 film would have it made. But Kevin Lima directs with as heavy a hand as Stephen Herek did the last time around—and with a script even more contrived. Alice Evans and Ioan Gruffudd, who supply the love interest this time, are less pallid than 1996's Joely Richardson and Jeff Daniels, but the main attractions are of course a screen full of adorable dogs—and Glenn Close as Cruella De Vil, the only real excuse for going live-action with the familiar story.

When you watch Close in Cruella's bizarre wardrobe and her half-black, half-white wig and her crazed hauteur, you cannot help but think that Close's justly acclaimed Norma Desmond, in the "Sunset Boulevard" stage musical, beat the rap for shooting Joe Gillis, pleading temporary insanity, and has made her silver-screen comeback as Cruella. In short, Close is high camp, and you can be thankful for that in a family movie that lays everything on thick.

You have to wonder how Cruella, as an awesomely successful London fashion designer, designs for other women. Anthony Powell's delirious costumes—he also did Close's gowns as Norma—black-and-white ensembles with the occasional red outfit, seem like dominatrix street-wear crossed with the post-World War II New Look carried to an eye-boggling extreme—wasp-waisted, long skirts, spike heels.

The only other woman you can imagine wearing Cruella's clothes is the late Gladys Towles Root, a colorful longtime local criminal attorney who wowed juries with gets-ups not that different from Cruella's.

Production designer Assheton Gorton and his crew have come up with an estate for Cruella with interiors as grandiose as those in Miss Desmond's mansion, and they've created numerous other settings of much charm and imagination. If not much else, "102 Dalmatians" certainly looks great—how it sounds is another matter, thanks to David Newman's bombastic score.

As is so often the case, "102 Dalmatians" seems more a reworking than a sequel. Having served three years for dognapping, not to mention converting a stolen Siberian tiger into a coat, Cruella leaves prison a changed person, thanks to aversion therapy.

However, the gongs of Big Ben and the sight of the Dalmatians belonging to her parole officer (Evans) unhinges her; by golly, she's going to have that cloak made of Dalmatian puppy skins that so far has eluded her—only this time she wants 102 instead of 101 because she now wants it to have a hood.

Because she's not supposed to have anything to do with any kind of fur or animal skins as a condition of her parole, she turns to her former design rival, another fur lover, Paris' Jean-Pierre Le Pelt (Gerard Depardieu), to help her execute the design as well as the 102 dogs. (Depardieu, heavier than ever and utterly unintelligible in English, in leopard-skin hot pants and a punk haircut, is not a pretty sight.)

In line with her supposedly reformed image, super-rich Cruella comes to the rescue of Gruffudd's Kevin, hard-put to keep running his London animal shelter-cum-children's puppet theater. Since Evans' Chloe and Kevin both love Dalmatians, romance blossoms as adventure beckons, with Cruella up to her old tricks.

They're aided by Kevin's clever, opinionated green winged macaw—voiced by Monty Python's Eric Idle—who thinks he's a dog. That Le Pelt maintains a sweatshop in an ancient building next to an equally ancient bakery in the Paris suburbs makes for a quaint though elaborate finale.

What goes on there, however, and all the physical abuse Cruella's long-suffering valet (Tim McInnerny) endures in the course of the film really does strain the film's G rating. In a sense it's cartoon violence, but this is a live-action film with its inescapably stronger aura of realism. You can only hope the awesome ingenuity of the animals, in overcoming human evil, will register more strongly with the youngsters for whom " 102 Dalmatians" is intended.

NEW YORK POST, 11/22/00, p. 43, Lou Lumenick

Can Cruella De Vil change her spots? That's the amusing question at the heart of "102 Dalmatians," which opens with the prison release of a timeless two-toned villainess, played again with great malicious gusto by Glenn Close.

She's freed on the testimony of a psychiatrist named Pavlov, who swears Cruella has been cured of her obsession with Dalmatian puppies, and their use in coats.

But Chloe (Alice Evans), her sweet, Dalmatian-owning probation officer, is skeptical—particularly after Cruella decides to sponsor a down-at-the-mouth dog shelter run by the naive Kevin (Ioan Gruffudd).

When Dalmatian puppies start disappearing all over London, Cruella frames Kevin—and once again, it's the pups to the rescue.

It turns out Cruella is conspiring to make the ultimate Dalmatian coat with Jean Pierre Le Pelt, a fur designer played in goofy, high-slapstick style by the French screen legend Gerard Depardieu.

"102 Dalmatians" is the rare family movie that works on two levels.

Kids will get a kick out of the simple story, basically a variation on "101 Dalmatians" (which stuck pretty close to the original animated version) and be delighted by the dogs, some of them representing descendants of the original's Pongo and Perdy.

Dozens of them—real and digitally animated—as well as a talking parrot who *thinks* he's a dog, appear in stunt sequences that have been expertly staged by director Kevin Lima, who co-helmed the animated "Tarzan." "102 Dalmatians" plays much like an animated movie (and would be better in cartoon-like length rather than a somewhat protracted 101 minutes). It certainly has cartoonish performances by Close, Depardieu and Tim McInnerny (the only other returning cast member from "101" as Cruella's long-suffering manservant who suffers more physical abuse than Wile E. Coyote.

The romantic leads (especially Gruffudd, last seen in the Jewish-Welsh soap opera, "Solomon and Gaenor") are even blander than in "101," but it hardly matters when Close's Cruella is plotting behind every corner.

Close gets to wear a vast array of outlandish outfits that are even more over the top than her Cruella. She also delivers a few nifty lines, as when she consoles the fur-shorts-wearing Le Pelt after he's splashed with red paint during a PETA-style protest.

"Demonstrators?" she cackles. "I thought they were critics."

"102 Dalmatians" is the kind of movie that is beyond criticism.

NEWSDAY, 11/22/00, Part II/p. B3, Gene Seymour

Cruella De Vil (Glenn Close) is out of jail! That's the good news. The bad news is that some behavioral quack named Dr. Pavlov (Dogs. Get it? Laugh, like, whenever you feel the need.) has managed to bleach all the fur-loving, dog-hating pathology out of her. In short, all the stuff that made Cruella so much gee-golly fun has been replaced by an overbearing earnestness. Not only does she no longer want to turn Dalmatian puppies into cold-weather wardrobe, but she even gives most of her fortune to a shelter for ne'er-do-well doggies.

Even the new, improved Cruella is frightening enough to make her parole officer, Chloe (Alice Evans), suspicious. And more than a little nervous, since she happens to own a small family of Dalmatians whose patriarch, Dipstick, is the son of Pongo and Perdy and thus a veteran of Cruella's 101-member hit list. Chloe isn't at all convinced that Cruella has changed her-um-spots.

And through circumstances far too silly to mention here, Cruella does indeed revert back to her wicked ways. With the reluctant help of her incredulously faithful servant Alonso (Tim McInnerny returns to take more punishment), and the far more enthusiastic assistance of hotshot furrier Jean Pierre Le Pelt (Gerard Depardieu, looking like a lumpy cross of Liberace, Billy Idol and Otto the Circus Strongman), she begins a scorched-earth campaign to make her long-awaited Dalmatian coat.

All of which is about as inevitable as the existence of "102 Dalmatians" itself. The unlikely, yet indelible success of its 1996 predecessor, "101 Dalmatians," ensured yet another puppy party. Here as before, Close, all lips, incisors, two-toned hair and blue eyes, is the best reason to attend—though she's not nearly as outrageous as her wardrobe. Indeed, even after she switches her dials back to evil, Close's Cruella retains a candy sweetness that almost, but not quite, keeps her predatory claws reined in.

This version also adds a wiseacre parrot (voice by Eric Idle), who thinks he's a rottweiller. He's funny enough to make you wish that he and the unctuous "reformed" Cruella had teamed for a different movie than this, since the puppies, while cuter than anything and impressively trained, seem almost like background decor. Personally I would have liked to have seen far more of the incomparably smarmy Ian Richardson as Cruella's attorney, Mister Tort. (No, really, go ahead and laugh! No charge.)

Director Kevin Lima, whose previous work is limited to such full-length animated features as last year's "Tarzan," tries admirably to limit the "Home Alone"-like sight gags that overly cluttered the climax of "101." But the visual pacing in "102" errs in the opposite direction, with a chase sequence as airy and goopy as the substance that brings about Cruella's downfall. No fair asking what it is, but don't get any nasty ideas. This is—so to speak—Disney's world, after all.

SIGHT AND SOUND, 1/01, p. 56, Amanda Lipman

London, the present. After a time in prison, former dog snatcher Cruella De Vil is set free a reformed woman thanks to therapy. Her probation officer, Chloe, owns Dipstick, one of the puppies Cruella originally stole; the dog has now sired four puppies of his own. Chloe is mistrustful of Cruella, who takes over an ailing dog shelter run by Kevin. When the chimes of Big Ben reverse the effect of Cruella's therapy, she revives her plot to make a fur coat from Dalmatian pelts, and enlists the help of fellow designer Le Pelt and her manservant Alonso.

When puppies are stolen Cruella pins the blame on Kevin, who is put in prison. She invites Chloe to dinner and throws her into her dungeon, while Le Pelt steals three of Dipstick's puppies. With animal help, Chloe and Kevin escape from their jails and, aided by the dogs' night-time barking, track the puppies down to Le Pelt's parisian workshop. Set free, the puppies escape into a bakery, where Cruella pursues them. But the dogs start up the machinery and Cruella is turned into a huge cake before being arrested.

What can a sequel to *101 Dalmatians*, the 1996 live-action adaptation of Dodie Smith's children's book, offer that we haven't seen already? Not much, since director Kevin Lima (who co-directed Disney's 1999 cartoon *Tarzan*) makes sure that *102 Dalmatians* sticks to the best bits from the first film. Glenn Close is still in fantastically nasty form as Cruella De Vil, the villain of the piece who kidnaps Dalmatian puppies in order to make a fur coat from their pelts. Never fully convincing as a gentle animal lover—thanks to a spell of therapy in prison—she bounces back to life, hair fizzing, talons popping out of her gloves, in a hallucinatory sequence where the world goes Dalmatian spotted as she turns evil again. At one point she laughs like some mad horror queen as she feeds dog-shaped feasts to her startled guests' pets at a banquet that turns into a bizarre orgy of eating. Then there are the many dogs, trotting dutifully through another adventure in front of picture-postcard scenery of London and, this time, Paris. The 102 of the title refers not just to the fact that this is a sequel but to Cruella's overarching greed: here she requires not just 99 puppies for a coat but three more for a hood. As in any tragedy, it's this hubristic desire that triggers her downfall.

Picking up on Cruella's horrified reaction in the first film to the fact that new-born Dalmatian pups have no spots, the sequel turns her disgust into an ongoing nightmare as she encounters Oddball, one of her probation officer Chloe's Dalmatian puppies whose spots do not develop. Oddball, too, is sensitive about her coat, but against the grain of any affirmative message about diversity, the mutt is finally rewarded with spots.

As fashion designer Le Pelt, who helps in the dognapping, a monstrous leopardskin-clad Gérard Depardieu tries to relish his role but never hits the mark, ending up like an inflated Jean-Paul Gaultier without the spry camp. The obsequious Alonso, Cruella's servant, undergoes a transformation, finally tiring of his mistress' evil ways. Fighting the massive bulk of Le Pelt, he asserts his desire to be a good man; there seems to be a subtext here in which Cruella's desexed male cohorts only escape her influence when they establish their masculinity through wrestling one another. Cruella, meanwhile, despite her tailored outfits and trappings of femaleness, is not unlike the masculinised *Spitting Image* Margaret Thatcher puppet, ending up a terrifying zombie-like creature when she is fed through cake-making equipment in a Parisian bakery. Just as in *101 Dalmatians*, where she is drenched in farm muck, we have to see her suffer, and, because she is inhuman, feel no pain. Only here, the emphasis has switched to sexuality: once she has been rendered powerless, she emerges as a grotesque parody of femininity, an enormous iced cake.

VILLAGE VOICE, 11/28/00, p. 138, Richard Gehr

Quelle surprise to discover that Disney's own seasonal product might have been titled *102 Dalmatians in Paris*. Coco LaBouche is mirrored by Glenn Close's scenery-chewing, fashion-flaunting Cruella De Vil, while LaBouche's beleaguered assistant, Jean-Claude (John Lithgow), has his own counterpart in ferocious French furrier Jean Pierre Le Pelt (Gerard Depardieu). Cruella is once again bent on collecting enough puppy skins to fashion the frock of her dreams. And once again, yawn—this time in a strangely industrial patisserie—she is foiled by those cute li'l canines themselves. Guess which filmmakers didn't have the smarts to license "Who Let the Dogs Out"?

Also reviewed in:
CHICAGO TRIBUNE, 11/2/00, Tempo, p. 1, Michael Wilmington
NEW YORK TIMES, 11/22/00, p. E15, A. O. Scott
VARIETY, 11/27-12/3/00, p. 17, Todd McCarthy
WASHINGTON POST, 11/22/00, p. C1, Stephen Hunter

OPPORTUNISTS, THE

A First Look Pictures and Flashpoint release in association with Prosperity Pictures of a Eureka Pictures/Clinica Estetico/Kalkaska production.   *Executive Producer:* Jonathan Demme, Peter Saraf, Edward Saxon, David Forrest, and Beau Rogers.   *Producer:* John Lyons and Tim Perell.

Director: Myles Connell.   *Screenplay:* Myles Connell.   *Director of Photography:* Teo Maniaci. *Editor:* Andy Kier.   *Music:* Kurt Hoffman.   *Sound:* Thomas Varga.   *Casting:* Kathleen Chopin. *Production Designer:* Debbie De Villa.   *Art Director:* Nicolas Berry.   *Set Decorator:* Stobain Flaherty.   *Set Dresser:* Laura Ballinger and Daniel Maldonado.   *Special Effects:* Drew Jiritano. *Costumes:* Kasia Walicka Maimone.   *Make-up:* Mia Thoen.   *Running time:* 89 minutes.   *MPAA Rating:* R.

CAST: Christopher Walken (Victor Kelly);   Peter McDonald (Michael Lawler);   Cyndi Lauper (Sally Mahon);   Vera Farmiga (Miriam Kelly);   Donal Logue (Pat Duffy);   Jose Zuniga (Jesus Del Toro);   Tom Noonan (Mort Stein);   Anne Pitoniak (Aunt Diedre);   Olek Krupa (Ted Walikaki);   Paul D'Amato (Dylan);   Wally Dunn (Harry);   Patrick Fitzgerald (Kevin);   Chuck Cooper (Arnon Morris);   Claudia Shear (Gladys);   Kate Burton (Rest Home Sistr);   Jim Mayzie (Rest Home Priest);   Jerry Grayson (Tom Hansome);   John Ortiz (Ismail Espinoza);   Rosalyn Coleman (Kevin's Partner).

LOS ANGELES TIMES, 8/18/00, Calendar/p. 16, Kenneth Turan

Given the number of indifferent films that leave the Sundance Film Festival loaded with honors, it's something of a shock to come across a small gem that played the event but somehow slipped in under everyone's radar. That's the case with "The Opportunists."

A character-driven, neo-noir crime drama, "The Opportunists" is a spare and classical piece of work, made with deliberation and pared down to essentials. For first-time filmmaker Myles Connell, who wrote as well as directed, it's an extremely promising debut; for veteran star Christopher Walken, it's one of the best, most compelling performances in a long and active career.

Working in the Sunnyside, Queens, neighborhood where he grew up, Walken gives a beautiful display of nuanced, minimalist acting as Vic Kelly, owner/proprietor/sole employee of Vic's Garage, a decent guy with a shady past trying to straighten out his life.

Over the course of 40 films during a 20-year-plus career, Walken has learned to make his ghostly face into a subtle, expressive instrument. An ex-con who doesn't smile much and says less, someone almost submerged in worry and concern, Walken's Vic still makes a powerful emotional connection. His somber affect seems to attract catastrophe; you know things will inevitably go wrong for him, it's just a question of how wrong.

Vic definitely has things to be worried about. Though he's clearly a good mechanic—the film's opening sequence showing him working on a vintage Buick Riviera leaves no doubt of that—Vic can't seem to catch a break financially. Always strapped for cash, his habit of bouncing checks has made "wait a day and it'll be good" into a much-repeated mantra, exasperating both his daughter, Miriam (an excellent Vera Farmiga), and his tavern-owner girlfriend, Sally Mahon (an unexpected Cyndi Lauper).

Then, out of nowhere, Michael Lawler (Peter McDonald) shows up and things get worse. (Not out of nowhere exactly but direct from Dublin, director Connell's birthplace as well.) Michael says he's a distant cousin, but it's not family that's attracted him, it's Vic's reputation as a major professional thief.

The truth is more mundane. Vic was recently released from prison after serving 8½ years for burglary and is not eager to go back. But, like a baby-faced tempter, the aggrieved and irritating Michael not only keeps egging Vic toward crime but also makes common cause with a neighborhood lout named Pat Duffy ("The Tao of Steve's" Donal Logue), who says he knows about a sweet job that can't miss.

Not unexpectedly, circumstances force Vic to take the plunge; "the regular citizen thing," he memorably admits, "is not going too well." With the help of been-around former associate Mort Stein (a wonderful cameo from Tom Noonan), he starts to practice his safecracking skills.

"The Opportunists" is not shy about spending time on the mechanics of crime, and those sequences, tense and compelling, are among its best. But robbery is only the turning point, not the climax of this carefully made film, which is always more concerned about the people behind the action.

If anything characterizes filmmaker Connell's style, it's the care with which he's done everything. No word of dialogue is excessive or out of place, no character is anything less than convincingly cast. While some of the plotting is without a doubt familiar, Connell has treated everything he touches with so much old-fashioned care and concern that the results click together as smoothly as the tumblers of an old-fashioned safe. The kind that's built to last.

NEW YORK POST, 8/11/00, p. 47, Lou Lumenick

It isn't often you see a movie these days where (a) Christopher Walken plays a normal human being; (b) the main character is a master safecracker and (c) where a Queens resident is played by a real-life Queens native.

But writer-director Myles Connell's debut film has more going for it than novelty value.

Walken gives a beautifully understated performance as a financially hard-pressed ex-con who is coaxed back into the criminal life by a shady young Irish immigrant (Peter McDonald) who claims to be his cousin.

The movie's high point is their heist—cracking the safe at a security company where they know the owner is skimming the take from his customers.

But "The Opportunists" is no hair-trigger thriller like "Rififi" or "The Asphalt Jungle," though Connell pays homage particularly to the latter movie.

It's a more layered seriocomic character study of quiet desperation—colorfully depicted in the Irish enclave of Sunnyside, Queens.

Cyndi Lauper, a bona-fide Queens native like Walken, gives her best screen performance to date as his no-nonsense girlfriend, from whom he refuses to accept a loan—with dire consequences.

The fine ensemble also includes Vera Farmiga and Anne Pitoniak as Walken's concerned daughter and elderly aunt, respectively. Tom Noonan has a showy cameo as his criminal mentor, who can see disaster looming.

The only discordant note is struck by a pre-"Tao of Steve" Donal Logue, whose accent as a crooked security guard is a few hundred miles off.

NEWSDAY, 8/11/00, Part II/p. B10, Jan Stuart

Myles Connell makes an impressive directing debut with "The Opportunists," one of those contemporary noir dramas in which we are compelled to care about a character whose main talent seems to be for wearing out the welcome mat wherever he goes.

The anti-hero of the moment is Victor Kelly (Christopher Walken), a hapless car mechanic who has done his best to submerge his jailbird history (which entailed a botched robbery) and be an attentive family man. When a young cousin arrives out of the blue from Ireland (Peter McDonald), debts are closing in on Victor that may force his mother out of a nursing home, as well as lead to the eviction of him and his grown daughter, Miriam, from their modest home in Sunnyside, Queens. Suddenly, a heist that friends have been contemplating seems like the only way out, and the Irish cousin seems oddly eager to nudge Victor back into crime.

It's a hoary noir formula, but it feels fresh here, thanks to an uncommonly potent ensemble of actors who lend deeper resonance to sketchily observed characters. Pop singer Cyndi Lauper, simmering with yearning and frustration as Victor's barmaid girlfriend Sally, has heart and charisma to spare. She's got a great movie face and a tender-tough Gloria Grahame thing going that is perfect for both the milieu and the genre. Vera Farmiga makes us sit up as the protective Miriam, as does Donal Logue ("The Tao of Steve") as the genial shnook who masterminds the theft, and Tom Noonan as the no-nonsense locksmith who schools Victor in the art of cracking safes.

The actors are so engaging and the photography (by Debbie DeVilla) so rich that the robbery, when it happens, almost seems secondary. That it matters as much as it ultimately does owes to Walken, giving his most sympathetic performance to date as a decent, old-school kind of guy whose inability to lean on the women in his life threatens his survival. Walken brings gravity and weight to Victor with a minimum of actorly effects: He takes as much care in camouflaging his craft as his character takes in concealing his woes. He's a pleasure to watch.

VILLAGE VOICE, 8/15/00, p. 120, Amy Taubin

Another darkly brilliant song-and-dance man, Christopher Walken, gets a chance to show the regular-guy side of himself in Myles Connell's nifty little heist movie, *The Opportunists*. Walken stars as Vic Kelly, a reformed safecracker who's having a hard time making ends meet. Vic's car repair shop doesn't generate enough income to pay the rent on the shabby Queens house where he lives with his grown-up daughter (Vera Farmiga) and also cover the fee for keeping his elderly aunt (Anne Pitoniak) in a nearby private nursing home. Vic takes his responsibilities seriously enough to risk going to prison again and losing the love of his long-term girlfriend (Cyndi Lauper), who owns the neighborhood bar. When a couple of old acquaintances (Donal Logue and Jose Zuniga) and another young man (Peter McDonald)—recently arrived from Ireland and claiming to be Vic's cousin—invite him to join them in a robbery that requires his special safecracking skill, he agrees.

A highly promising first-time director, Connell has a fine-tuned sense of the film's working-class, Irish American, outer-borough milieu and of the people who've lived there all their lives. (The film's only false note is the overly chic cinematography by the usually dependable Teodoro Maniaci.) Although Vic is the focal character, *The Opportunists* is largely an ensemble piece, and Connell, blatantly appreciative of his terrific cast, allows them to riff off one another in every scene. Both Walken and McDonald seem like men who keep their own counsel, but Walken's gravity and tenderness is amusingly matched to McDonald's boyish impulsivity. And as usual, Logue impresses by seeming more like a real person who wandered onto the screen than like an actor.

More crucial to the success of a heist movie than the timing, logic, and mechanics of the robbery is that the audience be on the side of the robbers, that something of ourselves is at stake in whether or not they pull off the job. *The Opportunists* delivers an anxious five minutes when we worry that the Robin Hood-like Vic might not get away with what is essentially a victimless crime. Filled with vivid and likable characters, *The Opportunists* could be the basis for a TV series as captivating as *The Sopranos*.

Also reviewed in:
CHICAGO TRIBUNE, 8/11/00, Friday/p. K, Mark Caro
NEW YORK TIMES, 8/11/00, p. E13, Elvis Mitchell
VARIETY, 3/27-4/2/00, p. 28, Joe Leydon

ORFEU

A New Yorker Films release of a Rio Vermelho Films production. *Producer:* Renata Almeida Magalhaes and Paula Lavigne. *Director:* Carlos Diegues. *Screenplay (Portuguese with English subtitles):* Carlos Diegues. *Screenplay Collaborator:* Hermano Vianna, Hamilton Vaz Pereira, Paulo Lins, and Joao Emanuel Carneiro. *Based on the play by:* Vinicius de Moraes. *Director of Photography:* Affonso Beato. *Editor:* Sergio Melker. *Music:* Caetano Veloso. *Sound:* Mark Van Der Willigen. *Production Designer:* Clovis Bueno. *Carnival Art Director:* Joaozinho Trinta. *Costumes:* Emilia Duncan. *Running time:* 110 minutes. *MPAA Rating:* Not Rated.

CAST: Tony Garrido (Orfeu); Patricia França (Euridice); Murilo Benício (Lucinho); Zezé Motta (Conceição); Milton Gonçalves (Nacío); Isabel Fillardis (Mira); Maria Ceiça (Carmen); Stepan Nercessian (Pacheco).

LOS ANGELES TIMES, 9/8/00, Calendar/p. 15, Kevin Thomas

Carlos Diegues' "Orfeu" is such an original and intoxicating creation in its ownright that it should not be considered a remake of "Black Orpheus."

That 1959 French classic also loosely transposed the Greek myth of Orpheus to Rio de Janeiro's enduring shantytown, Carioca Hill, as the five days of Carnaval unfold. Whereas the '50s film was drenchingly romantic in the tradition of fatalistic French cinema, "Orfeu" is a veritable folk opera of such intense, stylized theatricality and dynamic cultural fusions that only a filmmaker of Diegues' stature and experience could still come through with a film that would be no less vivid.

World-renowned composer Caetano Veloso produced the film's seductive, insistent and haunting music, and cinematographer Affonso Beato captured sequences of the actual Carnaval in the richest of colors. "Orfeu" is totally captivating, as seductive as a samba.

Orfeu (Toni Garrido) is the King of Carioca Hill, a young singer-composer whose songs have mesmerized audiences far beyond his neighborhood. He could afford to leave but prefers to stay, true to his roots. He is good-looking, kind but, not surprisingly, also a devastating ladies' man. He's involved with a gorgeous, ambitious model, Mira (Isabel Fillardis) but is instantly swept off his feet by Euridice (Patricia Franca).

Euridice has just arrived from the Amazon in the wake of her gold miner father's death. She's staying temporarily with her glamorous but embittered aunt, Carmen (Maria Ceica), who was Orfeu's very first love—and who has never gotten over it. The arrival of the beautiful Euridice, alas, does not go unnoticed by Lucinho (Murilo Benicio), the handsome but morose leader of the worst gang of drug traffickers that have made life in Carioca Hill dangerous, constantly triggering brutal raids by corrupt police.

"Orfeu" seethes with dark portents while throwing itself into the spirit of Carnaval, with Orfeu leading the local Carioca samba school's elaborate entry into the parade, which passes through Rio's vast open-air Sambadrome in a blinding array of glitteringly costumed samba dancers and equally bespangled floats. Orfeu's vibrant mother, Conceicao, is played by Zeze Motta, a longtime Diegues regular.

"Orfeu" is heady and exaggerated, so rigorously stylized with star-crossed lovers so appealing and music so irresistible that its fairy-tale world—charged with all-too-real contemporary social ills—comes vividly alive. Drawing from—and updating, in the process—the play by Vinicius de Moraes, the great Brazilian poet, Diegues (best known for "Xica" and "Bye Bye Brazil") reaffirms his dominant position in Latin American cinema.

NEW YORK POST, 8/25/00, p. 59, V.A. Musetto

File veteran Brazilian director Carlos ("Bye Bye Brazil") Diegues' film under U—for Unnecessary Remakes.

Actually, his reworking of French helmer Marcel Camus' 1959 Oscar winner, "Black Orpheus"—which was based on a play that transposed the Greek myth of Orpheus and Eurydice to contemporary Rio de Janiero—has its pluses.

The lead actors—pop star Toni Garrido as Orfeu and Patricia Franca as Euridice—are personable, Grammy winner Caetano Veloso's sound track is listenable and the scenes of Carnaval in Rio are colorful.

But eye and ear candy alone can't carry a movie. When all is said and sung, Diegues' film falls to deliver the dramatic punch that has made Camus' version a favorite.

NEWSDAY, 8/25/00, Part II/p. B13, Jan Stuart

If you harbor fond memories of "Black Orpheus," Marcel Camus' samba-happy retelling of the Orpheus legend that won an Oscar in 1959, get rid of them. This minute. Or at least before you see Carlos Diegues' sobering new update, "Orfeu."

Expectations can get in the way of appreciating Diegues' vision, which is not a remake so much as a reconsideration. As Diegues points up, the vivacious Rio of the earlier film is even more of a chimera now than it was then. The stratification of Brazilian society allows for staggering poverty that defies romanticizing. Shantytowns are riddled with orphans, disease and lean-to shacks held together with chewing gum and a prayer. Crime reigns, artillery rules.

Diegues clues us into these changes from the opening shot, in which a jet plane cuts across a gleaming full moon. The technologically informed world of "Orfeu" is one in which lilting bossa novas are composed on computers and drug operations are conducted over cell phones. Orpheus ("Orfeu" here) can still make the sun rise with his dreamy guitar playing, but he and the other characters have taken on noticeably darker shadings.

No longer the happy-go-lucky trolley conductor of Camus' film, Orfeu (Toni Garrido) is a womanizing songwriter whose stylish gear and flowing, corn-rowed hair make him stand out like a pop god in his hillside ghetto. His jealous girlfriend Mira (Isabel Fillardis) is now a hooker and Playboy model. Instead of a Carnival-costumed specter of Death, we have Orfeu's former childhood friend, Lucinho (Murilo Benìcio) terrorizing the neighborhood with his drug operation while playing judge, jury and executioner in the local lynch-mob justice. Only Orfeu's beloved Euridce (Patricia Franca), arriving on that jet plane from a remote country village, maintains a modicum of the old innocence.

Diegues' assertive reality check can be psychologically tantalizing (Orfeu's possessive mother encourages his promiscuity so that he will never get married), but is a little too heavy-handed to be entirely convincing. Criminals and cops alike snarl with a kind of movieland hyperbole. Teasing glimpses of the Carnival beauty queens as they booze it up backstage are a cliched form of anti-cliche.

"Orfeu" builds to a potent climax that leaves us to ponder an operatic tableau of despair. "Black Orpheus" fans may miss the throbbing rhythmic pulse of that film, replicated only in a beautifully edited Carnival parade sequence. Caetano Veloso's purring melodies, when they come, are a respectable replacement for the now-classic tunes of Antonio Carlos Jobim (one of which is paid homage here). But this is a distinctly straight-up Orpheus, for better and for worse.

VILLAGE VOICE, 8/29/00, p. 140, Dennis Lim

With *Orfeu*, cinema novo pioneer Carlos Diegues takes another stab at the Orpheus myth, adapting the play by poet Vinicius de Moraes that inspired the 1959 Rio-in-Carnaval extravaganza *Black Orpheus*. Diegues's admirable intent is to reclaim one of Brazil's most enduring cultural exports and replace its touristy exoticism with a harsh, contemporary social context (the earlier film was directed by Frenchman Marcel Camus). Orfeu (played here by pop star Toni Garrido) is once again a samba composer and lady-killer whose gentle guitar strums make the sun rise, and his love for new-in-town country girl Euridice still arouses the ire of jealous women throughout the favela. But Death, some guy wearing a black leotard in *Black Orpheus,* is here embodied by a quietly ominous drug lord. On the soundtrack, the soothing bossa nova of the original finds a complement in a few mellifluous Caetano Veloso ballads, supplemented by an energizing blast of local hip-hop. Seemingly overawed both by the operatic pitch of the central love story and the kaleidoscopic enormity of Carnaval, Diegues's update hovers between mythic poetry and earthbound grit; the result is an inert, drably florid spectacle.

Also reviewed in:
CHICAGO TRIBUNE, 9/22/00, Friday/p. B, Michael Wilmington
NEW YORK TIMES, 8/25/00, p. E10, A. O. Scott
VARIETY, 10/11-17/99, p. 56, Todd McCarthy

ORIGINAL KINGS OF COMEDY, THE

A Paramount Pictures release of an MTV Films and Latham Entertainment presentation of a 40 Acres and a Mule Filmworks production. *Executive Producer:* Van Toffler. *Producer:* Walter Latham, David Gale, and Spike Lee. *Director:* Spike Lee. *Director of Photography:* Malik Sayeed. *Editor:* Barry Alexander Brown. *Music:* Linda Cohen. *Music Editor:* Maisie Weissman. *Sound:* Rolf Pardula. *Sound Editor:* Jeffrey Stern. *Production Designer:* Wynn P. Thomas. *Art Director:* Tom Warren. *Special Effects:* Abby Okin. *Costumes:* Janet Melody. *Make-up:* Herita Jones. *Running time:* 117 minutes. *MPAA Rating:* R.

WITH: Steve Harvey; D. L. Hughley; Cedric the Entertainer; Bernie Mac.

LOS ANGELES TIMES, 8/18/00, Calendar/p. 8, Kevin Thomas

No wonder "The Kings of Comedy" tour, organized in 1997 by producer Walter Latham, has become the highest-grossing comedy tour in history, with ticket sales exceeding $37 million. Any of its four Kings—Steve Harvey, D.L. Hughley, Cedric the Entertainer and Bernie Mac—in a solo performance would be hilarious, so you can well imagine that the laughter just keeps building as one comedian follows another to create an unforgettable evening.

Spike Lee, no less, has created a dynamite concert film, called "The Original Kings of Comedy," shot in February during a pair of performances in Charlotte, N.C. The convergence of these sensational comedians is reason enough to film them in performance on the same bill. But this concert film par excellence hopefully will serve another purpose: to allow these Kings of Comedy, all familiar presences on the tube, to reach beyond black audiences and let others know what they've been missing by not seeing these guys perform live.

Their humor is of course based on the African American experience, and these men tell it like it is—and how! Their audiences not only deserve honesty, but surely wouldn't sit still for anything less. (Audiences at Harlem's landmark Apollo Theater are famous for being as tough as they are enthusiastic.) The Kings use language that TV would never allow but is common in everyday life. Addressing hard-pressed, hard-working black people, they touch upon universal truths about joy and sorrow. Their audiences are not shy about expressing their exhilaration at their sense of recognition in everything these men comment upon in such inspired comic fashion. You recognize too the towering presence of such fearless predecessors as Richard Pryor, Redd Foxx and the one and only Jackie "Moms" Mabley.

The comics share bluntness and a capacity for finding humor in a wide range of circumstances, but their personalities are distinct. Harvey has the smoothness and the maturity—early middle age—to summon memories of popular music of his high school days 25 years ago for an inspired skewering of rap music. Hughley displays an awesome command of comic ammunition, fired in a dizzyingly rapid delivery. His speed also allows him to get away with just about anything, but his colleagues, in their own styles, are no less bold. Cedric the Entertainer offers a fluid drollness, and Bernie Mac has a strong masculine presence but can be as wide-eyed as Mantan Moreland of an earlier era, as he comments on the realities of 25 years of married life.

Not surprisingly, all four comedians find a rich source of humor in comparing the black man or woman with the white man or woman. (It is striking how often these men refer to their mothers and grandmothers—those matriarchal Big Mamas—but scarcely if ever to fathers and grandfathers.) We get a picture of ourselves as making too much of a fuss over trivial matters and of being slow to respond to danger. In short, we see how insulated most white people are to life's harsher realities and injustices. Hughley tellingly comments on white people's need to seek out sports for excitement. Black people, he explains, don't need to go looking for excitement; just driving past a police station and hoping not to get stopped does the trick. Yet the show is distinguished by its lack of anger and bitterness. It's not that these men don't harbor such feelings, but rather it's their particular genius to transform their life experiences into fodder for laughter. "The Original Kings of Comedy" ranks right up there with Pryor's "Live on Sunset Strip," Eddie Murphy's "Raw" and Martin Lawrence's "You So Crazy."

NEW YORK POST, 8/18/00, p. 53, Jonathan Foreman

The four African-American stand-up stars of this concert film are unashamedly vulgar and exuberantly politically incorrect.

And while that vulgarity eventually gets wearing, parts of their acts are so funny your cheeks hurt. But "The Original Kings of Comedy" also reminds white folks just how culturally different black America can be.

Not that black America is homogenous. In fact, it very quickly becomes clear that "The Original Kings of Comedy" is aimed at a relatively conservative, relatively middle-aged, middle-class crowd that prefers "old school" '70s music to hip-hop.

The concert was filmed with unobtrusive skill by Spike Lee (with deft editing by Barry Alexander Brown and photography by Malik Sayeed) at two nights of the hugely successful "Kings of Comedy" tour. Performers Steve Harvey, D.L. Hughley, Cedric the Entertainer and

Bernie Mac have distinct styles, but share a taste for shiny suits, a pre-rap sensibility and a fondness for the word "motherf---er."

The all-purpose adjective/noun/adverb gets such a workout here that when the film's 117 minutes are over, you too may find yourself using it every other word.

You may also find yourself thinking all kinds of politically incorrect thoughts, because, like all good stand-up, "Kings of Comedy" offers the liberating pleasure of hearing things said (about blacks as well as whites) that people think but never say.

Steve Harvey of the "WB's "Steve Harvey Show"—who bears a striking resemblance, vocally as well as physically, to Richard Pryor—is the emcee and gets the most time on screen. In his best riff, he imagines what would have happened if the Titanic had been full of black folk.

Then there's D.L. Hughley, of TV's "The Hughleys." He engages in some rapid-fire improv with the audience and takes aim at black people with a less than ideal work ethic, as well as the usual white targets.

Cedric the Entertainer (a regular on the Harvey show) is particularly good when riffing on music. Like Harvey, he feels a pronounced nostalgia for youth pop culture of the '70s, but it's when he imitates a friend of his, "Big Mama," singing a gospel song with lyrics from old TV shows, that he raises the roof

Bernie Mac—the only one of the four who hasn't had major TV success—turns out to be the funniest. But his is also the material most likely to offend, with his outrageous views on child rearing (if you're old enough to talk back, he claims, you're old enough for a beating) and his unapologetic use of terms like "faggot."

NEWSDAY, 8/18/00, Part II/p. B3, Gene Seymour

It never fails to amuse your correspondent to watch politicians and pundits of many colors pretending to know what African-Americans really talk about when they talk among themselves. Of course, such presumptions only become important when something big and/or bad happens to People of Color. But that's a whole other story.

The point to be made here is that you don't need a cardiologist to take black people's collective pulse. All you have to do is listen to what the hard-core African-American comedians have to say about manners and morals. By hard-core, I'm talking about the men and women skilled in piercing an after-hours din of whiskey and cigarette smoke with lightning streaks of sky-blue raunch and drive-by insight. Redd Foxx is their patron saint. Robin Harris is their martyred prince. Richard Pryor is their god of gods. And so on, so forth.

Whether you see these folks in cable television's headlights or punching the sitcom time clock, there's usually something formulaic about the context. People expect to see them being dumb or dirty. No surprises allowed.

And what makes "The Original Kings of Comedy" such a joy to behold is watching hard-core pros Steve Harvey, Cedric the Entertainer, D.L. Hughley and Bernie Mac unleashed from shackles of family-hour network conventions or gratuitous late-night toilet jokes.

Well, actually, there's quite a bit of the latter to be found in Spike Lee's filmed record of a "Kings of Comedy" tour stop at the Charlotte Coliseum in North Carolina. But there are just as many jokes aimed well above the groin.

The head, for sure, is a major target. Hughley's rueful observations about the economic squeeze on working-class folks in these so-called prosperous times connect like a major league batter on a hitting streak. Harvey, whose performance here will be quite a revelation to those who know him only from his eponymous WB-network sitcom, also grabs the collective heart of his predominantly black audience with a trenchant and passionate screed for "old-school" '70s soul ballads over the present-day dominion of rap. It's backyard-barbecue rifting transfigured to elemental performance art. Harvey's friend Cedric doesn't quite reach such heights, but he's still fun to watch. His recital about the perils of public smoking will click with those who smoke and those who don't.

The climax, fittingly, belongs to the relatively unheralded Bernie Mac, who proves himself to be the most hard-core member of this Fab Four with a staggering display of after-hours pyrotechnics. Lee's cameras seem so transfixed by Mac's physical presence that they're afraid to stray from his laser-beam, bulging-eyed gaze.

Mac fires his comic salvos with the authoritative ease of a champion boxer, By the time he reaches the end of a hilarious shaggy-dog tale of a stammering boy who's always left behind by the school bus, you feel drained, but deliriously happy. It's the best massage your nerves will ever get.

SIGHT AND SOUND, 1/01, p. 57, Danny Leigh

A documentary record of a comedy gig held in Charlotte, 1999: compere Steve Harvey introduces D.L. Hughley, Cedric The Entertainer and Bernie Mac who perform in front of a packed auditorium.

For anyone familiar with Spike Lee's brassy, innovative movies, *The Original Kings of Comedy*—with its pointedly A-to-B DV camerawork—may come as a shock. His account of one evening in the life of America's most popular black comedy troupe was envisaged for cable television—and it shows, with its bloodless colour scheme and woozy focus. Neither does the movie deliver any insight into its stars' off-stage existences, its few behind-the-scenes vignettes offering little beyond textural punctuation.

None of which is meant as criticism, as the film's stripped-down sensibility lends a raw immediacy to the business at hand, namely four hugely talented stand-ups in full, frequently inspired flow. What the anonymity of Lee's direction says most clearly about his subjects is that they are best observed in their element, before an audience—just as the film's unexpected US box-office success says more about the commercial legitimacy of black comedy than any earnest, straight-to-camera soliloquy on the subject.

The film plays like a masterclass in the art of slick, arena-scale stand-up. When Lee sporadically pans around the Kings' North Carolina venue, what strikes you is the sheer size of the place and, by implication, the skill of all four comics in creating an almost casual intimacy. The result is as impressive a display of comic technique as one could expect from, say, Jerry Seinfeld, which, given the accessibility of the respective *shticks,* is not such an inapposite comparison. While each routine touches on the highs and, more pertinently, lows of the African-American experience (Hughley, for example, boggles at the notion of extreme sports: "You know what I do for extreme sports? Drive past the police and try not to get my ass whipped"), the collective source material is often that of plain-and-simple observational comedy: childhood memories, the absurdities of sex, and nostalgia. Indeed, it's this preoccupation with what compere Harvey refers to as the "old school" (essentially, a time before hip-hop) that provides perhaps the most emblematic scene of the entire film: Harvey taking a break from baiting audience members to lead a mass, wryly affectionate sway to the strains of Kool and The Gang.

And while show-closer Bernie Mac breaks with the mood of his predecessors to essay a line in scabrous nihilism (on his plans to open a childcare centre: "I will fuck your kids up"), there's an air of traditionalism running through his act too: in essence, the wild-eyed profanity of the 'blue' club comic. Laden with dark autobiographical hints, his performance brings to mind Richard Pryor at his most audacious; bizarrely, it also recalls the foul-mouthed iconoclasm of Bernard Manning.

All of which means, irrespective of race, that a UK audience should be as comfortable with the project as a US one. Certainly, those crazy white folks come in for any amount of ridicule; yet the movie's most delicious confrontation is when Harvey singles out a young black spectator in the front row. Told that his victim earns his living at "computer school", there's an expert snort of derision as the comedian gazes at his prey and muses, "Now, nothing about you says computer. Or school. C'mon, what d'you *really* do?" Perhaps, with its equal opportunity acerbity (a feature of the director's canon since *Do the Right Thing), The Original Kings* is more of a Spike Lee joint than it might at first appear.

VILLAGE VOICE, 8/22/00, p. 138, Gary Dauphin

There is a particular cut of suit favored by black men of a certain age, girth, and means—a long, three-quarter-ish jacket paired with loose-fitting slacks that provide extra room for big asses. As young, small-framed, or unemployed African American men tend not to wear the Suit, it not only conveys a certain sartorial sensibility but confers a kind of survivor gravitas that middle age and prosperity bring to folks who are commonly expected to achieve neither. Everything a man wearing the Suit says is important, even when it isn't. Don't tell him he's an aging overweight clown, though, because if *The Original Kings of Comedy* is any indication, he'll threaten to get "ghetto-ish on your ass."

In *Kings,* a concert film featuring the stand-up talents of Steve Harvey and Cedric the Entertainer (both of the WB's *The Steve Harvey Show*), D.L. Hughley (UPN's *The Hughleys),* and Bernie Mac (of countless bug-eyed supporting roles), the Suit is definitely in the house, prowling the stage while the men inside serve the standard Def Jam Comedy Hour riffs to the audience. The material hews to a familiar range of topics—"Whatever Happened to Big Mama?" "Why Kids Today So Crazy?" "My Mama Wore a Housecoat All Day," "Funny Shit White Folks Do," and of course, that great universal, "How I Ain't Got No Pussy Since I Got Married." Although this is ostensibly a Spike Lee Joint, the direction is unobtrusive and sparely functional, very unlike the Suits.

But the actual performances do feature small amounts of individuation, variations on the theme of being a pissed-off aging black man with money. Harvey wears his suit extra long and shiny, and has an older man's penchant for complex tall tales involving church and a dislike of that hip-hop foolishness. Youngblood Hughley, clad in an agitated canary yellow, delivers similarly high-energy, staccato outbursts that suggest a man with too many jokes but too little time. Cedric the Entertainer takes the greatest risk with his suit—no arms!—and has the most technically proficient onstage persona (he's the most accomplished physical comic of the bunch). As there can only be one king, the crown goes to Bernie Mac, a goggle-eyed marvel of old-school Chicago weirdness whose basic gimmick is drumming the audience into a frenzy about how it's time to bring back "beatin' our chillrun." Just about every word out of his mouth is simultaneously hilarious and reprehensible, a situation Mac understands given his admissions that he's only saying what "you think but are afraid to say." Not really, but you (don't tell him that to his face unless you're wearing a bigger and shinier suit.

Also reviewed in:
CHICAGO TRIBUNE, 8/18/00, Friday/p. A, Michael Wilmington
NEW YORK TIMES, 8/18/00, p. E12, Elvis Mitchell
NEW YORKER, 9/4/00, p. 88, David Denby
VARIETY, 8/14-20/00, p. 17, Scott Foundas
WASHINGTON POST, 8/18/00, Weekend/p. 36, Michael O'Sullivan

ORPHANS

A Shooting Gallery release of an Antonine Green Bridge production for Channel Four Films, The Glasgow Film Fund and The Scottish Arts Council. *Executive Producer:* Paddy Higson. *Producer:* Frances Higson. *Director:* Peter Mullan. *Screenplay:* Peter Mullan. *Director of Photography:* Grant Scott Cameron. *Editor:* Colin Monie. *Music:* Craig Armstrong. *Sound:* Peter Brill and (music) Paul Hulme. *Sound Editor:* Hilary Wyatt. *Casting:* Doreen Jones. *Production Designer:* Campbell Gordon. *Art Director:* Frances Connell. *Special Effects:* Stuart Brisdon. *Costumes:* Lynn Aitken. *Make-up:* Anastasia Shirley. *Stunt Coordinator:* Nick Powell. *Running time:* 95 minutes. *MPAA Rating:* Not Rated.

CAST: Gary Lewis (Thomas); Douglas Henshall (Michael); Rosemarie Stevenson (Sheila); Stephen McCole (John); Frank Gallagher (Tanga); Alex Norton (Hanson); Dave Anderson (Uncle Iam); Deirdre Davis (Alison, Carole's Mom); Maureen Carr (Minnie, in Basement); Laurie Ventry (Henry, in Basement); Malcolm Shields (DD Duncan); Eric Barlow (Mr. Bell); Jan Wilson (Sandra, Woman in Bar); Sheila Donald (Mrs. Finch); Ann Swan (Rose Flynn, Mother of Family); Gilbert Martin (Frank); Lenny Mullan (Julian, Bar Manager); June Brogan (Mona); Paul Doonan (Lenny, Duncan's Brother); Linda Cuthbert (Evelyn, Waitress in Bar); Lex Keith and Hugh Ferris (Themselves); Joel Strachan (Neil, Lad in Toilet); Tom White (Alistair, Taxi Driver); Vanya Eadie (Maria, Receptionist at Evettes); Dorothy Jane Stewart (Margaret); Michael Mallon (Rab, Cheeky Boy in Street); James Casey (Peachy, Cheeky Boy in Street); Alan Gracie (James, Cheeky Boy in Street); Jim Twaddale (Liam, Bus Driver); Frances Carrigan (Mrs. Bell); Judith A. Williams (Amanda, Baby Sitter); Michael Sharpe (David Flynn, Michael's Son); Laura O'Donnell (Carole); Lee-Ann McCran (Anne Marie, Paper Girl); Debbie Welsh (Melissa, Paper Girl); Donna Chalmer (Bernadette, Paper Girl); Sarah Hepburn (Louise, Carole's Sister); Martha Leishman (Alice); Catherine Connell (Angela Flynn, Michael's Daughter); Joan Commeford (Ed, Carole's Dad); Stephen Docherty (Alastair, Barman in Pub); Steven Singleton (Seamus, in Basement); Kate Brallsford (Deaf Boy's Mum); Luka Kennedy (Fraser, Deaf Boy); Helen Devon (Jessica, Woman in Tube); Josie Aitken Sheridan (Duncan's Baby); Seamus Ball (Father Fitzgerald); Robert Carr (Mr. Litch, Undertaker); Jenny Swan (Aunt Geraldine).

CHRISTIAN SCIENCE MONITOR, 3/10/00, p. 15, David Sterritt

Hollywood's penchant for glittering stars and extraordinary events has a tendency to limit the screen exposure of ordinary people. Independent and international movies help balance the equation. A vivid example is the British drama "Orphans," directed by Peter Mullan, the fine actor who recently impressed American audiences In "My Name is Joe."

In his first movie as a director, Mullan deals not with orphaned children—this is no "Cider House Rules" clone—but with grown-ups discovering how ill-equipped they are to handle the emotional fallout from their mother's death. Before the funeral, her three Glasgow sons allow grief and anger to run away with them. Meanwhile their disabled sister faces challenges of her own.

"Orphans" is not a happy tale. It's not very original, either, with its string of banal events that bring the clan closer together. The acting is consistently strong, though.

Mullan has a sharp eye for compelling images, often putting his camera to a discreet distance that modifies the movie's potentially melodramatic excesses. He's a promising addition to the growing list of talented actors—Tim Roth, Gary Oldman, Sean Penn—who launched their directorial careers with stories of family strife.

LOS ANGELES TIMES, 3/10/00, Calendar/p. 4, Kevin Thomas

"Orphans" begins with a ritual, as three adult brothers and their sister bid formal farewell to their dead mother in her Glasgow, Scotland, row house bedroom as they prepare her for her funeral the next day. But what comes next swiftly careens into chaos.

By the time we learn that Rose Flynn had died suddenly, at 61 of a heart attack the day before, we have already experienced the full and devastating impact her death has had upon her children. We are also left wondering if she didn't love them a little too well, a little too possessively. Yet in its dark and calamitous way, "Orphans"—which marks the feature writing and directing debut for actor Peter Mullan—is a comedy.

Once Mum has been properly laid out, the four Flynns head for the neighborhood pub. Thomas (Gary Lewis), the eldest brother, a pious mama's boy, feels compelled to sing a song in his mother's memory, breaking down in tears. But not before a guy in the pub has jeered poor Thomas' maudlin dirge. Michael (Douglas Henshall), a shipyard welder estranged from his wife, does a slow burn at the man's disrespect for his eldest brother and finally explodes. Immediately realizing he has been stupid to lose his self-control, he winds up knifed in the abdomen in the ensuing fracas. Michael's injury, in turn, enrages his younger brother John (Stephen McCole), a college student, who swears he will kill the man (Malcolm Shields) who laughed at Thomas and then stabbed Michael.

Recently seen as the recovering alcoholic in Ken Loach's "My Name Is Joe," Mullan depicts a domino effect as the Flynn siblings' lives spin out of control in the course of the 24 hours leading up to their mother's funeral, accompanied appropriately by a violent storm. Mullan has thus set in motion what would seem to be an intensely theatrical film, even to observing Aristotle's dictum in regard to the span of time a drama should cover. Mullan plays against this premise with much psychological insight and an impressive capacity for drawing from his cast full-throttle portrayals that could go sailing way over the top had he not held firm control of them.

"Orphans" is a rowdy, raucous, risk-taking business with much figurative tearing of hair, gnashing of teeth and beating of chest as the four confront their grief, yet Mullan makes high dudgeon pay off, for he is able to see in such excess humor as well as pain.

All four take off on separate adventures. Michael decides that if he can staunch the bleeding he can pass off his wound the next morning as an industrial injury that just might yield as much as 10,000 pounds in compensation—if he doesn't bleed to death first. John seeks out his cousin Tanga (Frank Gallagher), who at 35 is stuck delivering Chinese food, not realizing his relative has reserves of anger just ripe to be tapped in service of a lethal act of revenge. Thomas has vowed to his priest that he will spend the night in the chapel, maintaining vigil over his mother's coffin until the funeral takes place.

Since Sheila (Rosemarie Stevenson) is in a wheelchair because of cerebral palsy, Thomas expects her to stay with him throughout the night. But she becomes bored and restless and sets out for home in her power-driven wheelchair alone—but not before ramming Thomas in anger, which causes him to topple a larger-than-life plaster statue of the Virgin Mary. It's at this moment we start realizing that it's OK to laugh at "Orphans."

"Orphans" deliberately keeps you in a state of uncertainty as to whether or not to laugh, and our hesitance echoes that of Mullan's people, who need to learn how to pause to think before yielding to an all-consuming anger. Clearly, it is Mullan's hope that if people can see how laughable they can be when consumed with wrath, then perhaps they wouldn't follow through in drastic acts that in an instant will ruin their lives and those of others. (Think of the perils of giving in to road rage.)

For the record, "Orphans" comes equipped with subtitles to help us cut through thick Glaswegian accents—but not so thick as to hide four-letter words.

NEW YORK POST, 3/10/00, p. 56, Jonathan Foreman

For its first 45 minutes, "Orphans" looks like yet more evidence that severe restrictions should be placed on British actors who want to write and direct films.

Unlike American actors turned auteurs, serious Brit actors who go behind the camera—such as Tim Roth and Gary Oldman with "The War Zone" and "Nil By Mouth"—are invariably convinced that audiences need a brutal and unsentimental reminder that all life is pain and ugliness, occasionally mixed with tedium.

Then "Orphans" turns into a story of family love and grief that deftly and disturbingly mixes humor and horror, social realism and surreal whimsy.

Director Peter Mullan, who gave a magnificent performance as the title character in Ken Loach's "My Name Is Joe" sets this story in a hellish working-class Glasgow, filled with characters so violent and degraded—drunk, stupid and endlessly foul-mouthed—that if Mullan weren't a Scot, you might see this film as one long ethnic slur.

It begins with an agonizingly long scene in a chapel as four orphans in their 20s and 30s attend their dead mother's funeral, then finally repair to the local pub.

There the oldest brother, Thomas (Gary Lewis), a none-too-bright religious fanatic, sings a lugubrious song in memory of their mother.

While he's singing, some youths make fun of him, so the next brother, Michael (the excellent Douglas Henshall), starts a fight. He is stabbed in the chest before being ejected from the pub by the bouncers. Thomas just keeps on singing.

After a taxi driver, worried about blood on the seats, refuses to take him to the hospital, Michael decides to use the wound to fake a workplace accident the next day (for the compensation money).

But his younger brother, John (Stephen McCole), a hitherto respectable college boy, resolves to avenge the stabbing. He hooks up with his cousin Tanga (Frank Gallagher), and the two of them plan to get a gun.

Meanwhile, Thomas goes to the church with their sister Sheila (Rosemary Stevenson), who is wheelchair-bound from cerebral palsy. For some reason, Thomas has promised the priest to stay awake by the body all night.

Sheila, bored, wants to go home. He won't take her so she hums off in her motorized wheelchair, which then breaks down in an alley. Then some children in fancy dress come along and take her with them to a party.

The rest of the film follows the four siblings through the night as a huge storm hits the city. There are moments when the grotesquerie goes too far and seems just plain self-indulgent.

But Mullan evokes such superb performances from his cast that you can forgive many of the weaknesses in his writing, and in the end, "Orphans" manages to be a moving and original experience.

NEWSDAY, 3/10/00, Part II/p. B7, Gene Seymour

The Shooting Gallery's admirable effort to throw some light upon offbeat, under-recognized independent and foreign films follows up "Judy Berlin" with another dark, funny and melancholy tour through several hours of painfully human confusion.

And, as with "Judy," the darkness in "Orphans" is literal as well as stylistic, because most of writer-director Peter Mullan's gritty, harrowing comedy takes place through a long black night in Glasgow.

It is, to be specific, the long dark night before a woman's funeral. Her four grown children—Thomas (Gary Lewis), Michael (Douglas Henshall), John (Stephen McCole) and Sheila (Rosemarie Stevenson)—are each driven by grief to emotional extremes so volatile that it severs their bonds with each other hours before the service. A barroom brawl after the wake leaves Michael with a stab wound in his side, making youngest son John angry enough to seek out and kill his brother's antagonist.

Even Thomas, the relatively laid-back eldest son, is compelled by an overzealous sense of duty to his mother's bier to shove his wheelchair-bound sister Sheila from the chapel and into the streets to make her own long way home beneath threatening skies.

Somehow she ends up as a guest at a surprise birthday party given by people she doesn't know, while not far away, John has hooked up with his delivery-boy cousin Tanga (Frank Gallagher)—who's got serious stress-management issues of his own—to find the proper sidearm with which to carry out his vendetta. Michael, meanwhile, is wandering the streets, drinking, getting into more trouble at pubs and bleeding profusely from his side as he waits for the morning to arrive so he can go to work at the docks and claim his injury was work-related.

The Glasgow locale, Scottish accents and semisurreal incidents might lead one to assume "Orphans" to be "Trainspotting" without the heroin. But Mullan's night's-journey-into-day structure gives his film a tightness and shape more conducive to well-rounded characterization and humane viewpoint. He's helped considerably in this effort by an outstanding cast, including Henshall, whose admixture of drollness, defeat and barely contained rage both anchors and informs the movie's psychic turbulence.

There are subtitles provided in case you can't quite cut through the thick accents. But whether the story takes place in Scotland, Sierra Leone or Colombia (where it could have easily been imagined by Gabriel Garcia Marquez in a down-and-dirty mode), anyone can connect with this movie's touching, seriocomic view of a family in crisis.

SIGHT AND SOUND, 5/99, p. 54, Edward Lawrenson

Glasgow, the present. On the eve of his mother's funeral, Thomas Flynn sings a tribute to her at a local pub, attended by his siblings Michael, John and Sheila. Duncan, a local youth, laughs and is attacked by Michael for his disrespect. In the ensuing fight, Michael is stabbed. John vows to kill Duncan. He tracks down his cousin Tanga and asks him to find him a gun. Thomas spends the night with his mother's coffin in the church. When he refuses to take his wheelchair-bound sister Sheila home, she leaves alone, but her wheelchair becomes stuck. Passer-by Carole comes to her aid and takes her to meet her family. Tanga procures a gun without bullets for John. They make a return visit to Mr Bell, one of the regular customers Tanga delivers carry-out meals to. Tanga forces himself into the house and threatens to rape Bell's wife, but John makes him leave.

After dressing his wounds, Michael goes to a pub. When he mildly protests at the landlord Hanson's rudeness, Hanson locks him in the beer cellar with three other unruly customers. They break the door down, tie up Hanson and help themselves to drink. A storm rips off the church roof. The next morning Michael turns up at work and tries to pass off his stab wound as an industrial accident. Weakened by blood loss he falls in the River Clyde. Having acquired some bullets, John fires on Duncan but misses when he notices the baby he's carrying. They fight; John flees. Turning up at the makeshift funeral, John encounters an ailing Michael who collapses and is taken to hospital. Later, the family are reunited by their mother's grave.

Early on in *Orphans*, Thomas, the eldest of the four Flynn siblings, mounts the stage of his local pub to croon a mawkish love song in honour of his deceased mother. His drunken audience are torn between two responses: do they sit in silence out of respect for his grief or, like the grinning Duncan, openly deride Thomas' off-key and laughably bad performance? Watching Peter Mullan's debut film you recognise their dilemma. Mixing harrowing scenes of a family at grief with high comedy (the film contains moments of sustained knockabout which play like *Rab C. Nesbit* out-takes) *Orphans* doesn't so much tread a delicate line between these two modes as career wildly back and forth between them like a drunken mourner. Given this, *Orphans* makes for difficult viewing.

The bleak austerity of the opening scene, in which we're introduced through long takes to the Flynns ranged around their mother's open coffin, recalls the determinedly dour sensibility of Scottish director Bill Douglas. But Mullan audaciously follows this up with a Farrelly Brothers-type ejaculation gag and pokes fun at Thomas' piety. Such humour could so easily have trivialised his attempts to depict the painful business of grieving. Thomas, comment on deciding to carry his mother's coffin to her grave singlehandedly—"She ain't heavy, she's my mother"— is a clanger which perhaps betrays Mullan's experience as a sitcom writer. But then the easy laughs and flat irony offered here are trumped by the following image of Thomas, grimacing with pain, emotionally and physically crushed under the weight of the coffin. it's a fine balancing act that Mullan and his acrobatic actor Gary Lewis pull off, giving us a deft piece of physical comedy, but, like the bulk of *Orphans,* one that is underpinned by a palpable and very raw sense of loss.

An acclaimed short-film director accustomed to the form's visual economy, Mullan has an eye for quietly affecting, connotatively rich visuals. A wheelchair-bound Sheila stuck down an alley as threatening noises-off fill the soundtrack; a drunk, clad only in jeans and a T-shirt, blithely strolling down a storm-lashed street as braver souls take shelter: Mullan's image of Glasgow is built out of these bizarre nocturnal encounters and strangely resonant narrative and visual fragments. It's a little reminiscent of (but not quite as full blown as) the alternate reality painted by Alasdair Gray's landmark novel *Lanark*. However, when Mullan does veer into Gray's baroque territory, ripping the roof from the church where Thomas is spending the night, it feels like a hand-of God intervention from a director out to grab attention.

Orphans quietly assured surrealist slant places it in a Scottish tradition diametrically opposed to the hard-boiled realism of such writers as William McIlvanney and Peter McDougall. Indeed, that traditions insistently masculine bias—and the lasting stereotype of the Glasgow hardman it has perpetuated—is slyly subverted throughout *Orphans*. Just as the film's tone feels fractured, so the surface sheen of quiet sufferance, of manly endurance which the three brothers set great store by also cracks spectacularly. Most obviously, John's attempt to play the tough guy comes to nothing when his obdurate vow to shoot Duncan is let down, first by inadequate equipment (he has a gun, but no bullets), second by compassion. But the traditional and rigidly male roles his two other brothers have set themselves also prove elusive: elder brother Thomas' attempt to play the patriarch ends up alienating everyone; and Michael's plan to be a breadwinner for his estranged family consists of a botched attempt to win compensation for a faked industrial accident.

Mullan is best known for his lead role in Ken Loach's *My Name Is Joe*. Unsurprisingly, the powerful and sensitive performance he gave there finds echoes in the work of his cast, particularly Douglas Henshall as Michael and a quietly touching turn from first-time actor Rosemarie Stevenson as Sheila. But Mullan is more than an actors' director. When, wearing workers' overalls soaked in his own blood, Michael falls into the river where he works, the camera follows him as he floats serenely past a deindustrialised Clyde. It's an image of male vulnerability, but it also plays like an oblique elegy to the shipyards that once stood there. In an instant, the film reverberates with the passion and anger of Loach's far more politicised movie. It's a measure of Mullan's success (and confidence) that even by the end of his rough and ambitious film, he's still not ready to give up on surprising us.

VILLAGE VOICE, 3/14/00, p. 122, Amy Taubin

Peter Mullan's volatile, ultimately cathartic debut feature suggests a combo of Scorsese's *After Hours* and Cassavetes's *Husbands* transposed to Scotland. On the night before their mother's funeral, four siblings wander through the dark, crumbling streets and buildings of Glasgow as if they were passages into the depths of their psyches. Mourning makes them crazy; their emotions blast through behavioral restraints and catapult them in unpredictable directions. What makes the movie funny and scary at once is that, given their loss, their extreme reactions have a logic beyond reproach—for them and for us.

Having completed the funeral arrangements for their mother (custom dictates that they each cut a lock of hair and place it in the coffin), the brothers Thomas (Gary Lewis), Michael (Douglas Henshall), and John (Stephen McCole) and their wheelchair-bound sister, Sheila (Rosemarie Stevenson), repair to their local pub. Things quickly get out of hand when Thomas, the eldest, gets up to sing a mournful love ballad in his mother's honor and is heckled by a bunch of drunks. A fight breaks out and Michael is stabbed in the gut. Instead of going immediately to the hospital, he decides to try to stay alive until morning so he can say he was injured on the job and claim workmen's comp. John rushes off to find a gun, vowing to kill his brother's assailant. Thomas retreats with Sheila to the church to keep watch over their mother's body. As the night deepens, the four become enmeshed in increasingly violent and baroque adventures; when the roof flies off the church during the course of a fierce rainstorm, *Orphans* turns a corner into a Buñuel-like surrealism.

Mullan handles this treacherous shift in tone and the even more difficult crosscutting among the four story lines as if it were the most natural way to put a film together. *Orphans* pulls you in as if you were dreaming it yourself, and yet you can sense its allegorical underpinnings. The siblings act out their grief through anger, but that anger seems to have afflicted most of the population of Glasgow as well. It's the expression of a larger sense of abandonment—the loss of what Mullan has referred to as "Mother socialism," the welfare state, the economic safety net. The picture Mullan paints of Glasgow is ugly and violent, but the violence is not gratuitous or sexy. It's the expression of need and pain. And it can be resolved at least in part through the expression of that need. "I want my mummy," cries the thirtysomething Michael as he faints from blood loss.

An actor himself, Mullan keeps his focus on his marvelous ensemble of actors, all of whom seem as egoless as the film itself. Shot largely at night and on a bare-bones budget, *Orphans* has a murky beauty that puts to shame the flash of *Trainspotting* and *Shallow Grave*, regarded as the cornerstones of the New Scottish Cinema. (Mullan appeared in both.) The film's finest achievement is its combination of cultural specificity and universal humanism. Everyone knows that it's hard to lose a mother (even a mother from whom you're estranged), but few non-Glaswegians will be able to fully understand the dialect. Hence *Orphans* is being released as an English-language film with subtitles. Be warned, however: The "translation" is not nearly as obscene or hilarious as what comes out of the characters' mouths.

Also reviewed in:
CHICAGO TRIBUNE, 3/10/00, Friday/p. C, John Petrakis
NEW YORK TIMES, 3/10/00, p. E24, Stephen Holden
NEW YORKER, 3/20/00, p. 145, Anthony Lane
VARIETY, 7/27-8/2/98, p. 57, David Rooney

OUTLAW!

An Adriana Chiesa Enterprises release of a Hera International Film production. *Executive Producer:* Mino Barbera. *Producer:* Gianfranco Piccioli. *Director:* Enzo Monteleone. *Screenplay (Italian with English subtitles):* Enzo Monteleone. *Based on the autobiography by:* Horst Fantazzini. *Director of Photography:* Arnaldo Catinari. *Editor:* Cecilia Zanuso. *Music:* Aldo de Scalzi. *Sound:* Gaetano Carito and Antonio Barba. *Casting:* Fabiola Banzi and Lorella

Chiapatti. *Production Designer:* Simona Garotta. *Costumes:* Andrea Viotti. *Running time:* 95 minutes. *MPAA Rating:* Not Rated.

CAST: Stefano Accorsi (Horst Fantazzini);   Giovanni Esposito (Lance Corporal Di Gennaro); Emilio Solfrizzi (Brigadiere Lo Iacono);   Fabrizia Sacchi (Teresa Fantazzini);   Antonio Petrocelli (Ridolfi, Prison Manager); Antonio Catania (Assistant Public Prosecutor); Alessandro Haber (Horst's Lawyer);   Francesco Guccini (Libero Fantazzini).

NEW YORK POST, 2/2/00, p. 47, Hannah Brown

Based on the true story of Italy's "gentleman bandit" of the 1970s, "Outlaw!" is a low-key reworking of "Dog Day Afternoon" that isn't as compelling as it should be.

It tells the story of Horst Fantazzini (Stefano Accorsi), a polite but nervous young man who has trouble supporting his young wife and children.

So Fantazzini goes on a bank-robbery spree—always using toy guns—and is caught and jailed. In a montage of '70s newsreel footage and newspaper headlines, we learn how he breaks out of prison yet is recaptured over and over again.

Finally sent to a maximum security prison, he spends five years behind bars, living as a model prisoner before he gets someone to smuggle him a real pistol in a pound of hard cheese (this is an Italian prison movie, remember).

Pulling the gun on some guards, he panics, shooting three and taking two others hostage. The rest of the film is the story of the standoff that ensues.

The film is at its best when it's less predictable, particularly when focusing on a subplot involving Fantazzini's father (Francesco Guccini), a former partisan and anarchist, who is terribly disappointed with his son.

But the film—with an unimaginative screenplay by writer and director Enzo Monteleone—doesn't do much with this original storyline and the pacing drags as we wait for the inevitably tragic final confrontation.

In the end, hostage taking Italian-style turns out much the same as the American variety.

NEWSDAY, 2/2/00, Part II/p. B9, Jan Stuart

The spin doctors called him "the gentleman robber." He held up banks with a toy pistol, treated his victims with the utmost deference, and even handed back money to the teller if the amount was so paltry that the institution appeared to be strapped for cash.

As it happens, the courtly crime spree of Italian bandit Horst Fantazzini makes up only the pretitle sequence of "Outlaw!," the engaging and oddly touching film that has been adapted from his memoirs. Instead, it zeroes in on a fateful day in 1973 when Fantazzini attempted to cut short his 22-year prison sentence by busting out. Before the ineptly executed escape attempt was over, three guards with whom he enjoyed respectful relations would be left seriously wounded, two more would be taken hostage and Fantazzini would effectively paint himself into a life-or-death-sentence corner.

written and directed by Enzo Monteleone (whose "Mediterraneo" won the Oscar for Best Foreign Language Film in 1991), "Outlaw" amasses a surprising collection of nuanced characters given the story's concentration of time and place. Not the least of these is Fantazzini himself, played by goateed charmer Stefano Accorsi with a skin-deep stealth that puts across a sense that he's making up his moves as he goes along.

The son of a former anarchist, Fantazzini suffers under the misperception that he's carrying on his father's traditions. In the film's single most moving moment, he receives an unexpected call from his father, who cures the 30-year-old thief of his illusions in one shattering stroke.

The larger share of "Outlaw!" operates on a frothier plane, alternating scenes of Fantazzini's evolving sympathies with his two captors (who argue mindlessly over the radio's hit parade) with his fruitless phone negotiations with a hierarchy of officials (including a prison director who natters at him like a flustered parent). The human foibles of all of Monteleone's characters are gently kidded without reducing anyone to cartoons.

For all its alternations in tone, "Outlaw!" generates a considerable amount of genre-type suspense in the final clinch. Where it succeeds as a seriocomic prison-break drama, it sidesteps any deeper explanations of Fantazzini's eccentric pathology beyond a misguided paternal attachment and an understandable yearning to get back to his beautiful wife. If every prisoner were motivated to extremes by a conjugal itch, correctional officers would be working overtime subduing all the inmates scratching at the gates.

VILLAGE VOICE, 2/8/00, p. 137, J. Hoberman

Horst Fantazzini established an image as Italy's "gentleman bank robber," a self-identified anarchist pulling his jobs with a toy gun, taking only as much money as he needed, and sending flowers to a teller who fainted mid-heist. *Outlaw!*, directed by Enzo Monteleone from Fantazzini's memoirs, is set on a single day during the summer of 1973 when the bandit ineptly attempted to escape the prison where he had been incarcerated for five years.

Because Fantazzini took two guards hostage *Outlaw!* has been compared to *Dog Day Afternoon*. But unlike Sidney Lumet's docudrama, *Outlaw!* is less a celebration of social banditry than a good-natured bureaucratic comedy. It's well-made but slight, precisely staged and populated by gregarious stock characters—the self-absorbed warden (brought back from a beachside vacation), the officious police commander, the taciturn sniper, the lovable sad-sack hostages, and the befuddled Fantazzini himself.

Fantazzini quote Brecht when he tells his hostage that it's "more of a crime to found a bank than rob one," but cries when his father berates him on the phone, calling him an idiot and not an anarchist. That's as emotional as the movie gets, although, goosed by a manic Balkan brass score, it's still sufficiently taut to work as a hostage procedural.

Also reviewed in:
NEW YORK TIMES, 2/2/00, p. E5, A. O. Scott
VARIETY, 5/17-23/99, p. 57, David Rooney

PAN TADEUSZ: THE LAST FORAY IN LITHUANIA

A FilmArt Hanka Hartowicz Productions release of a Heritage Films and Les Films du Losange production in association with Canal and Polska and Le Studio Canal +.   *Executive Producer:* Michael Szczerbic and Amira Chemakhi.   *Producer:* Lew Rywin and Margaret Menegoz.   *Director:* Andrzej Wajda.   *Screenplay (Polish with English subtitles):* Andrzej Wajda, Jan Nowina Zarzycki, and Piotr Weresniak.   *Based on the poem by:* Adam Mickiewicz.   *Director of Photography:* Pawel Edelman.   *Editor:* Wanda Zeman.   *Music:* Wojciech Kilar.   *Sound:* Philippe Senechal, Thierry Lebon, Jean-Pierre Halbwachs, and Nikodem Wolk-Laniewski.   *Production Designer:* Allan Starski.   *Art Director:* Wieslawa Chojkowska.   *Set Decorator:* Wieslawa Chojkowska.   *Costumes:* Magdalena Teslawska-Biernawska and Malgorzata Stefaniak.   *Make-up:* Maria Dziewulska.   *Running time:* 120 minutes. *MPAA Rating:* Not Rated.

CAST: Boguslaw Linda (Bernardin Robak);   Daniel Olbrychski (Gervais);   Andrzej Seweryn (Judge Soplica);   Grazyna Szapolowska (Telimene);   Marek Kondrat (Count Horeszko); Michal Zebrowski (Tadeusz);   Alicja Bachleda-Curus (Sophie);   Krzysztof Kolberger (Adam Mickiewicz);   Sergei Chacourov (Rykow);   Jerzy Binezyeki (Mathias de Dobrzyn);   Jerzy Gralek (Wojski);   Marian Kocıniak (Protais);   Krzysztof Globisz (Major Plut);   Henryk Baranowski (Napoleon Bonaparte);   Piotr Cyrwus (Maciej Konewka); Lech Dyblik (Szlachcic); Jozef Fryzlewicz (Kniaziewicz Karol Otto);   Piotr Gasowski (Rejent);   Wladyslaw Kowalski (Jankiel); Dorota Naruszewicz (Ewa Horeszkowna);   Marek Perepeczko (Maciej Chrzciciel); Krystyna Zachwatowicz (Kawiarka).

VILLAGE VOICE, 1/25/00, p. 132, Elliott Stein

Andrzej Wajda's career has been inseparable from themes of Polish history. His new film, *Pan Tadeusz*, the *Last Foray in Lithuania* (did Mel Brooks supply the title?), is based on an epic poem by Adam Mickiewicz, set in Lithuania on the eve of Napoleon's expedition into Russia in 1812. It concerns a family feud among the Polish country nobility. Tadeusz (Michal Zebrowski), an orphan of 20 with pure soul and virile charm, comes to stay with his uncle, Judge Soplica. He's not really an orphan. Daddy has become a monk to expiate his sins. There's a lot of expiating to be done, for the Soplicas, and their neighbors, the Horeszkos, are the Hatfields and McCoys of Polonized Lithuania and have been at each other's throats for generations. After tons of byzantine plot, not often easy to follow, and a good many scenes of cruelty to man and beast Tadeusz woos and weds Sophie (Alicja Bachleda-Curus), who is a Horeszko on her mother's side, putting paid to the bitter feud.

Bachleda-Curus is a tad too modern as the Romantic heroine, Zebrowski is a winning hero, but the film is stolen by Daniel Olbrychski as the monstrous Gervais, a rabble-rousing fanatic who urges Count Horeszko to acts of vengeance. Olbrychski was chosen by Wajda to play the lead in *Ashes* (1965) when the actor was 20. His angelic good looks have been put to good use in a number of Wajda's films since then. It's a shock to see him here as a spooky, decrepit old man who speaks with an otherworldly voice and seems a character out of the Middle Ages, and whose scalp bears scars from a dozen saber wounds.

This is a talky film, but if you lift your eyes up from the subtitles from time to time, you'll note that it's also quite handsomely turned out. There are echoes of *Smiles of a Summer Night* and *Rules of the Game*, but they're faint echoes—it's not in their league. Wajda has made some great movies, but he's an erratic talent and this is one of his lesser works. It becomes a lumpy melange of revenge melodrama, low comedy, and pale romance; far too much time is taken up by the dull humor of village dolts. Wajda completists will not want to miss it, but *Tadeusz* is unlikely to make any converts.

Also reviewed in:
NEW YORK TIMES, 1/22/00, p. B16, Lawrence Van Gelder
VARIETY, 2/28-3/5/00, p. 44, David Stratton

PAPA'S SONG

An ArtMattan Productions release of a Luna Blou/St. Aves production. *Producer:* Norman de Palm and Mark Stekelenburg. *Director:* Sander Francken. *Screenplay (Dutch and Papiamento with English subtitles)* Norman de Palm and Sander Francken. *Director of Photography:* Rogier Stoffers. *Editor:* Herman P. Koerts. *Music:* Rob Hauser (score), Roy Louis (songs), and Bibi Provence (theme song). *Sound:* Wim Vonk. *Running time:* 95 minutes. *MPAA Rating:* Not Rated.

CAST: René Van Asten (Nico); Romana Vrede (Shirley); Lisette Merenciana (Magda); Victor Bottenbley (Hugo); Tyronne Meerzorg (Juan); Vergill Ford (Roy).

NEW YORK POST, 3/30/00, p. 83, Hannah Brown

"Papa's Song" squanders an intriguing premise—tensions among black immigrants from the Antilles living in Holland—and ends up as little more than a movie-of-the-week soap opera.

Director Sander Francken aspired to make a psychological thriller and came up with a plot that at least sounds interesting.

"Papa's Song" is the story of Shirley (Romana Vrede), a black hairdresser married to a white Dutch judge, Nico (Rene Van Asten).

Shirley, who can't have children, has been taking care of her sister Magda's young sons while her sister tries to repair her failing marriage back in their native Antilles.

When Magda (Lisette Merenciana) shows up in Holland to stay with them, she's a threat to the Europeanized Shirley's complacency. Magda is a flamboyant singer who dresses in Afro-Caribbean clothes that are at odds with Shirley's understated chic style.

Shirley is also upset that Magda plans on taking her boys back home with her to her abusive husband, Hugo, with whom she has reconciled.

As if this weren't enough plot for one movie, Francken throws in several portentous subplots that overheat and overload the movie.

There's a whole incest storyline. Was Shirley involved in an incestuous relationship with her father? And did she kill him to protect her younger sister, or out of jealousy?

By this point, the film has gotten so talky, so trite and so predictable that the supposedly tumultuous flashbacks are more tedious than either titillating or shocking.

There are hints of mystery and tension throughout "Papa's Song," but they're buried by the unconvincing psychodrama.

VILLAGE VOICE, 4/3/00, p. 126, Michael Atkinson

Sander Francken's *Papa's Song* is a culture-dash stealth bomb that, in the end, shoves culture aside in favor of the psychological war game born of warped siblinghood. We haven't seen many movies about the head-butt between the Dutch bourgeois and Netherlands Antilles immigrants, but Francken wastes little time on socioeconomics and dives into the snake pit of barely repressed menace and bitterness between two Curaçao sisters, one married childlessly to an honest, white Dutch judge, the other a pop-diva mother of two running from an abusive husband. The mysteries of their manic-depressive relationship are riveting as long as they're mysteries; by now, explaining away "family secrets" is subject to diminishing returns, and the final toe-to-toe is outlandishly savage. But like its judge-hero, *Papa's Song* spends so much time caught in these vivid women's crossfire that the postcolonialist exoticism lurking under the surface ends up signifying everything married couples don't know about each other.

Also reviewed in:
NEW YORK TIMES, 3/30/00, p. E5, A. O. Scott

PARAGRAPH 175

A New Yorker Films release of a Telling Pictures production. *Producer:* Michael Ehrenzweig, Janet Cole, Rob Epstein, and Jeffrey Friedman. *Director:* Rob Epstein and Jeffrey Friedman. *Screenplay:* Sharon Wood. *Director of Photography:* Bernd Meiners. *Editor:* Dawn Logsdon. *Music:* Tibo Szemzo. *Sound:* Al Nelson. *Running time:* 81 minutes. *MPAA Rating:* Not Rated.

CAST: Rupert Everett (Narrator).

LOS ANGELES TIMES, 2/23/01, Calendar/p. 14, Kevin Thomas

When filmmakers Rob Epstein and Jeffrey Friedman went to the 1997 Amsterdam premiere of their documentary "The Celluloid Closet," based on Vito Russo's landmark survey of how gays and lesbians have been depicted in the movies, they met Dr. Klaus Muller, a German historian and European project director for the U.S. Holocaust Museum. They then embarked upon a collaboration with Muller, who had been researching gay survivors of the Nazis since the early '90s.

The result is their prize-winning new documentary, "Paragraph 175," which takes its title from the German anti-gay law passed in 1871 and enforced in East Germany until 1968 and West Germany until 1969.

At once illuminating, poignant and heartening, "Paragraph 175," eloquently narrated by Rupert Everett, calls attention to the fact that the Third Reich systematically targeted gay men as well as Jews, Gypsies, Communists and anyone else it deemed undesirable.

That gays were rounded up and sent to concentration camps, required to wear pink triangles, just as Jews had to wear yellow Star of David patches, is not all that well-known. A 1993 survey commissioned by the American Jewish Committee revealed that only half of the adults in Britain and only one-fourth of American adults knew that gays were victims of the Nazis.

What's more, the 20th century ended without any effort on the part of the German government to offer reparations to gay survivors, whose fate went unnoticed at the Nuremberg trials. Muller, who looks to be thirtysomething, tells us he grew up in Germany unaware of the Nazi treatment of gays.

In the course of the 12 years of the Third Reich, about 100,000 men were arrested for homosexuality. Roughly half were sent to prisons and 10,000 to 15,000 were sent to concentration camps. Since most gay men were Gentiles, they were not slated for execution but were made slave laborers or subjected to medical experimentation; their death rate, however, is estimated to be as high as 60%—the highest percentage for non-Jewish victims of the Nazis.

By 1945, only 4,000 had survived. By the time "Paragraph 175" was shot, only 10 were known to be still alive, with two declining to participate. We meet six of them, with one man appearing only long enough to protest, "Oh, I've talked about this so much," and then refusing to say more.

While the Nazis regarded male homosexuality as contagious and therefore a threat to the Third Reich, they curiously viewed lesbianism as a "temporary, curable" condition. Only five lesbians are on record as having been sent to concentration camps, although the Nazis closed down lesbian bars as swiftly as gay bars and gathering places. Also participating in the film is Annette Eick, a lesbian and a Jew, who speaks of her miraculous escape to England while losing her entire family to Auschwitz. The Nazis were soon not only enforcing Paragraph 175, but also extending it. Gossip and innuendo were enough to have a man arrested and imprisoned without trial.

Through a treasure trove of vintage stills and archival footage the filmmakers evoke the glittering high life of Weimar Republic Berlin, a center of avant-garde art and literature and a mecca for gays and lesbians, who could live openly at a time when pioneer gay activist Dr. Magnus Hirshfeld, founder of the prestigious Institute of Sexual Science, was leading a campaign to repeal Paragraph 175. Even with the rise of Hitler, gays, like many Jews, considered themselves Germans first, which in many instances slowed their response to danger. Many gays were also given a false sense of security when Hitler, shortly after coming to power, stood by Ernst Roehm, his burly chief organizer of the fearsome storm troopers, when Roehm came under fire for his well-known homosexuality. However, in the following year, 1934, during the notorious Night of the Long Knives, Roehm was murdered after he refused to commit suicide.

Gad Beck, Heinz Dormer, Pierre Seel, Heinz F. and Albrecht Becker, ranging in age from late 70s to mid-90s, recall with pleasure and amusement sexual adventures of long ago, many of them carried out in a spirit of defiance and at high risk. These men come across as sturdy survivors, which provides uplifting and crucial contrast to the terrible stories they have to tell. Alsatian Seel recounts, among other atrocities, witnessing a concentration camp friend being eaten alive by German shepherd dogs.

Especially moving is the dignified Heinz F., who beginning in 1935 spent nearly nine years in concentration camps, returning home to help his brother run the family store without ever speaking of his ordeal until, at age 93, he recounts for this documentary his experiences for the first time. There are tears shed for the dozen friends he witnessed being summarily shot to death, but at the end of his account, he says with a smile, "I've got a thick skin, no?" As for Heinz Donner, not only did he spend nearly a decade behind bars for Paragraph 175 violations, being released only with the war's end in 1945, he spent another eight years in prison for post-World War II arrests.

Reparations, should they ever be made, seem unlikely to arrive in time for these men. Muller, however, has seen to it that the experiences of gays during the Third Reich have been acknowledged and preserved at the U.S. Holocaust Museum.

NEW YORK POST, 9/13/00, p. 48, Lou Lumenick

The title of the movie "Paragraph 175" refers to Germany's anti-sodomy law of 1871, which was expanded by the Nazis to justify the arrest of as many as 100,000 men they suspected to be homosexuals, only eight of whom are still known to be alive.

Six of them—ranging in age from 78 to 94—tell their stories in this absorbing documentary by Rob Epstein and Jeffrey Friedman ("The Celluloid Closet"), which begins with a vivid portrait of what one survivor calls the "homosexual Eden" of the Weimar Republic, where gays openly proclaimed their preferences.

But things turned horrific with the rise of Hitler, whose response to accusations that some of his top lieutenants were closeted gays was to add male homosexuals to the list of those being shipped off to concentration camps—along with Jews, Gypsies and political dissidents.

Partly because most of them were gentiles, few gays ended up in the gas chambers. But as many as 15,000 died while being used as forced labor or for hideous medical experiments. (Lesbians were spared arrest because their sexual preference was considered a temporary, reversible condition—but they were forced underground or left the country altogether).

One of the men, a resistance fighter, recalls posing as a Hitler Youth to rescue his Jewish boyfriend (both were 18)—who perished when he refused to leave his family, who were sent to a death camp.

Another bitterly recalls his unsuccessful, decade-long struggle to receive compensation for the unspeakable torture he suffered from the German government, which has never acknowledged the persecution of gays. (Paragraph 175 remained on the books until 1969).

Narrated by Rupert Everett with well-chosen archival footage, "Paragraph 175" is a worthy addition to the growing canon of Holocaust documentaries.

NEWSDAY, 9/13/00, Part II/p. B9, Jan Stuart

In the perverse hierarchy of victimization that governed the Nazi concentration camps, homosexuals fell in line at the very bottom. Even the pink color of their identifying triangle badges (political prisoners wore red, gypsies brown, Jehovah's Witnesses purple, criminals green, and Jews yellow Stars of David), was intended to connote weakness and frailty.

Before the patches came into effect, the 10,000 to 15,000 homosexual men who were incarcerated at the camps by the Nazis were identified either by the word "homo" on the back of their jacket or "Paragraph 175." The latter referred to the German penal code passed in 1871 that dictated, "An unnatural sex act committed between persons of male sex or by humans with animals is punishable by imprisonment..." Largely ignored in the swinging Berlin of the post-World War I era, the code was enforced by Hitler with a terrible vengeance.

"Paragraph 175," the new documentary that reveals the depth of Hitler's animus toward homosexuals, is a stirring reminder that just when you think you've borne witness to the Holocaust from every conceivable angle, there is something essential that has been left out.

The stories related by a half-dozen homosexual camp survivors to filmmakers Rob Epstein and Jeffrey Friedman went untold for decades, in part due to a sense of shame they assimilated from the culture at large and in part because no one wanted to listen. Unlike other camp survivors who eventually received reparations and were accorded a measure of dignity and sympathy, the gay campmates who did make it out alive were reclassified as criminals and thrown back into prison after the war.

Friedman and Epstein (his stunning documentary "The Times of Harvey Milk" was re-released at the Film Forum in a digitally restored print), are led to these five aged men and one woman by Holocaust researcher Klaus Muller.

As they open up-some with sputtering rage, others with tearful reserve—it is interesting to note the elements of their experience that echo that of the Jews. Like many Jewish-German prisoners, gay inmates had thought themselves immune from persecution because they identified themselves as Germans first. Unlike Jews, they were not subject to the gas chambers, because most of them were Christians. Instead, they were tortured and castrated in human experiments, many of which were carried out at Dachau. Only 40 percent of homosexual prisoners survived.

The memories of the film's survivors are heart-stopping and occasionally squirm-inducing, imbued with a humanity and an unexpected humor that should give pause, if not shame, to the factions that have attempted to deny homosexuals their day in Holocaust commemorations. Given the extent of psychic and physical scars (one survivor was left disabled after being raped with a block of wood), the humor they are able to summon is an important reminder of what is required, at the end of the day, to survive a waking nightmare.

VILLAGE VOICE, 9/19/00, p. 122, Elliott Stein

Paragraph 175 was launched after a meeting of Rob Epstein and Jeffrey Friedman *(Common Threads, The Celluloid Closet)* with historian Klaus Muller, a project director for the U.S. Holocaust Memorial Museum; Muller had been researching the persecution of homosexuals under the Third Reich. He serves as interviewer in their film, which is built around the striking, often devastating accounts of a half-dozen elderly survivors.

The doc opens with carefree scenes of Berlin nightlife during the Weimar Republic, when gay men and women lived openly. Everything changed with the Nazis' assumption of power and the enforcement of paragraph 175, an anti-sodomy provision of the penal code that dated from 1871. Between 1933 and 1945, 100,000 men were arrested for homosexuality; some were imprisoned, others sent to the camps. Far from being Manichaean, the directors' expert multilevel narrative reflects their attraction to the gray areas of the story. They touch on gay resistance fighters and victims, but also gay Nazis and sympathizers. The tales told are bitter, horrific in detail—yet often leavened with irony and humor (Rupert Everett's low-key narration serves the film well). An indelible high point is the salty recollection by irrepressible octogenarian Jewish resistance fighter Gad Beck of his first visit to a gay bar.

Also reviewed in:
NATION, 10/2/00, p. 42, Stuart Klawans
NEW YORK TIMES, 9/13/00, p. E5, Lawrence Van Gelder
VARIETY, 2/7-13/00, p. 53, Dennis Harvey

PARIAH

An Indican Pictures release of a Poor Boy Productions production. *Producer:* Shaun Hill and Vince Rotonda.   *Director:* Randolph Kret.   *Screenplay:* Randolph Kret.   *Director of Photography:* Nils Erickson.   *Editor:* Bill Deronde.   *Music:* Scott Grusin.   *Music Editor:* Tom Brennan.   *Sound:* Darryl Patterson.   *Sound Editor:* Scott Grusin.   *Art Director:* Shaun Hill and Jordan Steinberg. *Special Effects:* Patrick Sullivan.   *Costumes:* Julie Colella and Carrie Niccol.   *Running time:* 105 minutes.   *MPAA Rating:* Not Rated.

CAST: Damon Jones (Steve);   David Oren Ward (Crew);   David Lee Wilson (David Lee); Elexa Williams (Sam);   Aimee Chaffin (Sissy);   Angela Jones (Angela);   Anna Padgett (Lex); Brandon Slater (Doughboy);   Dan Weene (Joey);   Ann Zupa (Babe);   Jason Posey (Kevin); Joe Virzi (Man in Car); Candy Ass (Drag Queen);   Clint Curtis (Preacher);   Teresa Durant (Party Goer);   Nils Erickson (Red Car Seller);   Orlando Estrada (Aaron);   Jay Giankabutuka (Hey); Scott Grusin (Joe's Buddy);   Crew Hamilton (New Skinhead Recruit); Robert Hargett (Rob); Tracy House (Tracy); Chris Jarecki (Tall Guy);   Tom Kaminski (Kegmaster);   Lisa Keller (Girl Assaulted);   Raymond Kuhar (Ray);   Kevin Mangold and John Sunseri (Whin);   Kelly McCrary (Steve's Sister);   Lynn Odell (David Lee's Mother);   Jan Reese (Sam's Mother);   Jean Rose (Grandma);   Vince Rotonda (Vinny);   Jaime Schene (Tattoo Artist);   J.J. Snyder (Prostitute); Josef Snyder (Jewish Beating Victim);   Dan Stanley (Clerk);   Bill Stevens (Bill);   Cat Tabor (Friend);   Ray Wadsworth (Bobby);   Terence Washington (Mario);   Dylan Wood (Dylan); Tyrone Young (Ty).

NEW YORK POST, 2/18/00, p. 55, Hannah Brown

Anyone who already has a negative opinion of racist thugs will want to skip "Pariah," which features many scenes of graphic violence in portraying life among American neo-Nazis.

It will turn off most viewers without offering insights into the thugs' behavior.

"Pariah" is about a young white man, Steve (Damon Jones), and his black girlfriend, Sam (Elexa Williams), who are viciously beaten by skinheads, who also rape her. She then commits suicide and he becomes obsessed with getting revenge.

So he poses as a skinhead by shaving his head and tattooing swastikas on himself. He joins a gang, but then doesn't strike back, for reasons that are never explained.

This shallow, repetitive film is notable only for the scary performance of David Lee Wilson as the sickest of the psychos.

VILLAGE VOICE, 2/22/00, p. 135, Michael Atkinson

"Look who it is—Mr. Jigaboo!" is one of the first spittings from the mouth of David Lee (David Lee Wilson), an L.A. skinhead hitting the ceiling over his mother's black boyfriend, and in no time flat you get a clear idea of how broadly painted and platitudinous Randolph Kret's *Pariah* is. Kret opens the riot hose of neo-Nazi clichés; five minutes don't go by without a beating, perpetrated either by the chrome-domes or upon them by the movie's four black characters or a retaliatory posse of bat-wielding queers. The story is unoriginal and static—an interracial couple gets assaulted, and after the girl's suicide, her boyfriend shaves his head and infiltrates the group with mayhem on his mind, flipping his Iron Cross-emblazoned lighter like an extra in *Grease*. The actors labor, but the dialogue sits like wads of old gum in their mouths. "I hate fags," says one of the girlfriends casually. "They gave my brother AIDS." During a rape, the punks even get to hum "The Ride of the Valkyries." And the inclusion of a retarded skinhead is as inappropriate as the lifts from *A Clockwork Orange*. Kret clearly has his heart in the right place: Hate Is Bad. If only being right were all you needed.

Also reviewed in:
NEW YORK TIMES, 2/18/00, p. E18, A. O. Scott
VARIETY, 1/26-2/1/98, p. 72, Leonard Klady

PASSION OF MIND

A Paramount Classics and Lakeshore Entertainment release of a Lakeshore Entertainment production in association with Ron Bass Productions. *Executive Producer:* Gary Lucchesi, William Kepper, Ted Tannenbaum, and Sigurjon Sighvatsson. *Producer:* Carole Soctta, Tom Rosenberg, and Ron Bass. *Director:* Alain Berliner. *Screenplay:* Ron Bass and David Field. *Director of Photography:* Eduardo Serra. *Editor:* Anne V. Coates. *Music:* Randy Edelman. *Music Editor:* Jay Richardson and David J. Bondelevitch. *Sound:* Ludovic Henault and (music) Elton Ahi. *Sound Editor:* David Giammarco. *Casting:* Deborah Aquila and Sarah Halley Finn. *Production Designer:* Pierre-Francois Limbosch. *Art Director:* Daniel Ouellette. *Set Decorator:* Philippe Léveque and Anne-Charlotte Vimont. *Set Dresser:* Todd Cole, Matt Duncan, George Krivobok, and Alan Mamet. *Costumes:* Valerie Pozzo Di Borgo. *Make-up:* Judith Gayo. *Stunt Coordinator:* Philippe Guégan. *Running time:* 112 minutes. *MPAA Rating:* PG-13.

CAST: Demi Moore (Marie/Martha Marie "Marty" Talmadge); Stellan Skarsgard (William Granther); William Fichtner (Aaron Reilly); Sinead Cusack (Jessie); Peter Riegert (Dr. Peters); Joss Ackland (Dr. Langer); Eloise Eonnet (Jennifer); Chaya Cuenot (Sarah); Gerry Bamman (Edward Youngerman); Julianne Nicholson (Kim); Hadrian Dagannaud-Brouard (Jean-Pierre); Hélène Cardona (Newscaster).

LOS ANGELES TIMES, 5/16/00, Calendar/p. 10, Eric Harrison

In "Passion of Mind," Demi Moore plays an emotionally detached career woman who believes that, when she falls asleep each night in Manhattan, she wakes to a completely different life as a widow and loving mother in France. Or is it the other way around?

She might be dreaming, as acquaintances on both continents keep telling her, but if she is, which life is real?

Such a quandary could keep a platoon of psychiatrists busy for years. But if Moore's twin characters are disoriented, think about the audience. Watching "Passion," our own sense of reality buckles and warps. Are we dreaming, or have we already seen this film two or three times before? How did Gwyneth Paltrow, who starred as two same-but-different characters in the lighter-hearted "Sliding Doors," manage to morph into Moore? And what was Paltrow's movie, anyway, but a dim (and diminished) reflection of "The Double Life of Veronique"?

"Passion" is like a hall of mirrors, casting back at us distorted images from other movies. It even calls to mind "The Sixth Sense" in the way that the ending is meant to spin us around, make us replay the film in our minds to find the clues we overlooked the first time. The difference is that we cared about the characters in "The Sixth Sense," but until "Passion" wades into the ontological murk of its "surprise ending," it isn't engaging in the least.

Switching back and forth between New York and France, we're fed slivers of two essentially static stories. Marty and Marie, Moore's twin selves, meet and fall in love with two men so sensitive and lovably eccentric that they seem the stuff of dreams. But mostly she sits around with anyone who will listen, muttering variations of lines like "I have a whole other life in France" and "That's the problem with all you guys—you all think you're real."

In this, Belgium-born director Alain Berliner's ("Ma Vie en Rose") first English-language film, nobody behaves the way a real person would. Long after anyone else would've concluded she was mad, Marty/Marie's suitors (Stellan Skarsgard and William Fichtner) continue their pursuit. And when Marty wakes up one morning in her sterile Manhattan apartment, still panting and writhing from Marie's passionate encounter in Provence, convinced that the lover and the sex were as real as the sheets that entwine her, does she check herself into Bellevue? Nope. She just continues her moping and fretting.

For reasons I can't explain without giving too much away, "Passion" plays like a distaff version of "Frequency," the current Dennis Quaid film in which a man and his long-dead father communicate with each other through time. This is emotionally rich material, which "Frequency" takes full advantage of for a time, but both movies seem afraid of challenging audiences. Apparently to avoid confusing anyone, "Passion" has its characters reiterate Marty/Marie's dilemma over and over until there's hardly time left for a real story—she lives two lives, but she does very little actual living.

NEW YORK, 6/5/00, p. 103, Peter Rainer

Passion of Mind, which was completed almost a year ago, has one of those dreary reality/fantasy plots that tour-de-force-starved movie stars are partial to. Demi Moore, looking for a comeback role, plays a woman with alternate identities. Which one is real? She might be a New York literary agent, childless, tense, or she might really be an earth-mother émigré living in Provence and reviewing books for the *Times*. One's a dream of hers, one isn't, and at least I can reveal to you that the film finally coughs up an answer. But not before we've been served a full casserole of women's-movie clichés courtesy of Hollywood's reigning women's-movie scribe, Ron Bass *(How Stella Got Her Groove Back, What Dreams May Come, Waiting to Exhale, When a Man Loves a Woman).* Ibsen must be spinning in his grave over this guy. The film might at least be fun if we were given some clues about which woman was the real McCoy, but the two halves of her life are equally dull, in different styles of dullness, with matching dull performances. Considering how much trouble Hollywood has differentiating the real world from the dream world, it probably should not come as a surprise that this film is such a muddle. Though not so much of a muddle that you fail to notice the fact that the career woman isn't fulfilled in the way that the earth mother is. And the men in her lives are the ones who force her to make a choice—pretty backward notions for such a supposedly liberated scenario. One of those men, incidentally, played by Stellan Skarsgard, is a novelist who falls in love with Demi notwithstanding her pan of his book in the *Times*. To my mind, this is hands-down the most fantastical element in the movie.

NEW YORK POST, 5/26/00, p. 50, Lou Lumenick

Demi Moore plays two roles in the stilted romantic thriller "Passion of Mind"—and it's definitely a case of Moore is less.

Her first release since 1997's "G.I. Jane" is an altogether more low-key and artsier affair, shot largely in Europe, with a Belgian director. For once, she keeps her clothes on.

But her latest exploration of post-post-feminist empowerment, Hollywood style, is in its own way as loopily misguided as its predecessors "G.I. Jane," "Striptease" and "The Scarlet Letter."

With the same level of authenticity she brought to the military, exotic dancing and early America, Moore plays Marty, a hard-driving Manhattan book agent.

Marty keeps falling asleep and waking up as a woman named Marie—a widow with two young daughters living in a chateau in the Provence region of France who dashes off book reviews for the New York Times between trips to the *boulangerie.*

Who's real? Marty or Marie? Marie and Marty both have psychiatrists who assure them the other woman is a manifestation of her unfulfilled desires, though Marty's shrink (Peter Riegert) helpfully adds that she's "as mad as a hatter."

Marty falls in love with a shy, disheveled accountant (William Fichtner), while Marie gets involved with William (Stellan Skarsgard), an older writer whose novel she once panned.

"He's a chance to love again," Marie's friend Jessie tells her in one of innumerable clunky lines devised by screenwriters Ron Bass ("Rain Man") and David Field ("Amazing Grace and Chuck").

Astonishingly, neither man flees when they learn of Marty/Marie's dual existence, which plays more like a shallow metaphor for women's choices than as a dramatically satisfying situation.

Moore sleepwalks through both parts, sometimes making it possible to tell the two women apart only by their hairstyles and wardrobes. Both have lavishly overdecorated homes straight out of Martha Stewart Living, and Marie's children are pretty much treated like part of the furniture.

It's difficult to believe this dull and humorless exercise was directed by Alain Berliner, who helmed "Ma Vie en Rose," a delightful film about a little boy who's convinced he's a little girl.

"Passion of Mind" is marginally better than the last women's picture to explore a dual existence, the dreadful "Me Myself I," but worse than the one before that, Gwyneth Paltrow's "Sliding Doors." Call this one "Sliding Bores."

NEWSDAY, 5/26/00, Part II/p. B3, Jan Stuart

Imagine, then, that you are carrying on simultaneous relationships with two different people on two different continents without so much as boarding a plane in either direction. One of them is your real lover, the other is a dream. But each of them seems so immediate and palpable that you don't know which is which. Both lovers bear equally upon your heart, both elicit a comparable degree of attention. Just how many hours of therapy are we talking about here?

For the dual characters played by Demi Moore, plenty, and then some. In fact, she has two therapists, one for each of her double lives. As Marie, she is a widowed writer nestled with her children amid the agrarian splendor of the south of France, where she is pursued by a dashing novelist (Stellan Skarsgard) whose book she has recently reviewed. As Marty, she is a high-powered literary agent in New York City, where she has an appropriately edgier romance with one of her clients (William Fichtner). Each identity comes and goes with vexing predictability: She goes to sleep in France, wakes up in New York, and vice versa.

And Marie/Marty really makes these boys work for her love. A psychoanalyst could have a field day with her conundrum, which anyone who has been fixated on more than one person at once (as opposed to being borderline crackers, like Marie/Marty) can relate to. Each of Moore's personas enjoys a lifestyle that would be a fantasy trip for the other; each of them exerts control over her man both professionally and romantically.

The set-up is steeped in an air of Freudian mystery alternately operatic and mundane, leading us to expect a kind of hybrid "The Three Faces of Eve" and Hitchcock's "Spellbound." Moore throws herself into her dual assignments with energy and conviction, but the screenplay concocted by Ron Bass and David Field is much like Moore's character(s): too uptight for its own good—and dismayingly absent of tension. The movie tick-tocks woozily back and forth between pastoral France, where Skarsgard sweeps Moore off her feet Clark Gable-style, and the waterways of Manhattan, where Fichtner takes her on boat rides and makes her wear outlandish Brooklyn Bridge earrings that are probably the source of all her problems.

Perhaps the greater mystery is how did such an earthbound movie come out of Alain Berliner, the gifted Belgian director whose debut film ("Ma Vie En Rose") splendidly juggled the effervescent fantasy world of an unusual boy and his duller domestic reality? "Passion of Mind" may not be devoid of passion—Moore and Skarsgard work up a genuine romantic heat that makes you want to hop the next flight to Provence—but the mind is left oddly unpleasured.

VILLAGE VOICE, 5/30/00, p. 130, Dennis Lim

The psychopathology of choice at the movies—the split-personality syndrome that helped Gwyneth Paltrow find true love in *Sliding Doors,* transformed Edward Norton into Brad Pitt in *Fight Club,* resolved Rachel Griffiths's career/family conflict in *Me Myself I,* and facilitates Jim Carrey's precipitous mood swings in next month's *Me, Myself & Irene*—has an especially discombobulating effect on poor Demi Moore. "I don't know who I am anymore," the distraught diva mumbles in the opening voice-over to her cred-seeking vehicle, *Passion of Mind.* Half the time, she's Marie, a widowed mother of two living in the south of France; but Marie falls asleep every night to awake as Marty, a single New York literary agent. And so on. The delusion is seamless: Marty/Marie is fully cognizant of her two lives (she sometimes refers to herself in the third person) but unable to accept that one of them is imagined. A reality check takes the form of competing lovers: suave novelist Stellan Skarsgard and diffident accountant William Fichtner.

Oddly distracted and enervated, *Passion of Mind* is an out-of-body experience for its viewers as well as its heroine. Belgian director Alain Berliner reprises the vivid color scheme, if not the light, emphatic touch, of *Ma Vie en Rose,* flip-flopping between warm, saturated tones for Provence and chilly gray-blues for the big city. If there's a chief culprit here, it's Ron Bass, who wrote *Passion of Mind* years ago before becoming the Hollywood automaton responsible for *My Best Friend's Wedding* and *Dangerous Minds.* Too spacey for psychodrama, too sludgy for magic realism, Bass's script (he reportedly disallowed changes) is encrusted in so many layers of cryptic cornball it seems to have forced Berliner into a defensive torpor. (Fighting the two-pronged assault of daftness and languor, the mind wanders.... What happens if Demi takes a nap? Is she instantly plopped down into her other existence? If she stays up all night in one life, does she fall behind a day in the other? If she oversleeps, does she miss a day? Does she really sleep at all? If not, why are there no bags under her eyes? If *I* go to sleep now, what are my chances of waking up at a different movie?)

Most of the actors, taking Berliner's cue, exhibit a laid-back resignation. Supremely at ease, Skarsgard proves immune to the encroaching idiocy (this must have been good practice for *Time Code*); Fichtner affects an endearingly helpless deadpan as a morose, weaselly suit. But the star herself reverts to type, making up for her lack of instincts with steely focus and dogged exertion—the very reasons she was effective in *G.I. Jane.* The most galling aspect of the movie isn't its harebrained premise (a short story by Ken Kalfus turns an identical scenario into a gem of existential-metaphysical comedy) but its decision to free Demi from her plight with a flood of psychobabble. Intentionally or not, *Passion of Mind* at least parlays this climactic epiphany into its version of a money shot—a gloriously bonkers sequence in which Demi and her estranged demi-psyches finally kiss and make up.

Also reviewed in:
CHICAGO TRIBUNE, 5/26/00, Friday/p. A, Mark Caro
NEW REPUBLIC, 5/29/00, p. 29, Stanley Kauffmann
NEW YORK TIMES, 5/26/00, p. E12, Elvis Mitchell
VARIETY, 5/22-28/00, p. 21, Emanuel Levy

PATRIOT, THE

A Columbia Pictures release of a Mutual Film Company production and a Centropolis Entertainment production.   *Executive Producer:* William Fay, Ute Emmerich, and Roland Emmerich.   *Producer:* Dean Devlin, Mark Gordon, and Gary Levinsohn.   *Director:* Roland Emmerich.   *Screenplay:* Robert Rodat.   *Director of Photography:* Caleb Deschanel.   *Editor:* David Brenner.   *Music:* John Williams.   *Music Editor:* Ken Wannberg.   *Sound:* Lee Orloff and (music) Shawn Murphy.   *Sound Editor:* Per Hallberg.   *Casting:* April Webster and David Bloch.   *Production Designer:* Kirk M. Petruccelli.   *Art Director:* Barry Chusid.   *Set Designer:* Randy Wilkins, Chad S. Frey, Greg Papalia, Noelle King, Sloane U'Ren, and Clare Scarpulla.   *Set Decorator:* Victor J. Zolfo.   *Set Dresser:* John D. Maskovich, Michael Hansen, and Richard

Brunton. *Special Visual Effects:* Stuart Robinson. *Costumes:* Deborah L. Scott. *Make-up:* Thomas Nellen. *Make-up (Mel Gibson):* Patty York. *Make-up Effects:* Bill Johnson. *Stunt Coordinator:* R. A. Rondell. *Running time:* 158 minutes. *MPAA Rating:* R.

CAST: Mel Gibson (Benjamin Martin); Heath Ledger (Gabriel Martin); Joely Richardson (Charlotte Selton); Jason Isaacs (Colonel William Tavington); Chris Cooper (Colonel Harry Burwell); Tcheky Karyo (Jean Villeneuve); Rene Auberjonois (Reverend Oliver); Lisa Brenner (Anne Howard); Tom Wilkinson (General Cornwallis); Donal Logue (Dan Scott); Leon Rippy (John Billings); Adam Baldwin (Loyalist/Captain Wilkins); Jay Arlen Jones (Occam); Joey D. Vieira (Peter Howard); Gregory Smith (Thomas Martin); Mika Boorem (Margaret Martin); Skye McCole Bartusiak (Susan Martin); Trevor Morgan (Nathan Martin); Bryan Chafin (Samuel Martin); Logan Lerman (William Martin); Mary Jo Deschanel (Mrs. Howard); Jamieson K. Price (Captain Bordon); Peter Woodward (Brigadier General O'Hara); Grahame Wood (Redcoate Lieutenant); Beatrice Bush (Abigale); Shan Omar Huey (Joshua); Hank Stone (Rollins); Kirk Fox (Skunk); Jack Moore (Curly); Mark Twogood (Danvers); Colt Romberger (Colt); Terry Layman (General George Washington); Shannon Eubanks (Mrs. Simms); Bill Roberson (Loyalist Simms); Charles Black (Matthew); Andy Stahl (General Greene); Kristian Truelsen (Hardwick); Kanin Howell (Postrider); Mark Jeffrey Miller (Wounded Continental); Zach Hanner (British Field Officer); Dara Coleman (Redcoat Sergeant #2); Randell Haynes (Patriot Middleton); John Storey and Greg Good (Cowpens Militiamen); John F. Dzencelowcz II (Continental Soldier); John Curran (Redcoat Sergeant #1); Kyle Richard Engels (Billings' Son); John Bennes (Speaker); Roy McCrerey and P. Dion Moore (Redcoats); Tyler Long (Page Boy); John H. Bush (Abner); Gil Johnson (Militiaman); Scott Miles (Patriot Private); Derrick B. Young (Slave Boy); Samuel Brown, Jr., Samuel Brown Sr., Lillie L. Harris, and Braima Moiwai (Gullah Musicians); Le Roy Seabrook (Gullah Minister); Patrick Tatopoulos (French Naval Officer).

CHRISTIAN SCIENCE MONITOR, 6/30/00, p. 15, David Sterritt

The hero of "The Patriot" is a South Carolina farmer, a devoted family man, a veteran of the French and Indian War, and a believer in liberty for all.

But first and foremost, he's a Mel Gibson character, and the movie swirling around him—all $80 million worth—is dedicated to the proposition that watching Gibson shoot guns is one of the great American pastimes. Judged as an action-movie spectacle, it's passable fare. Judged as a lesson in American history, it's as deep as you'd expect from the director of "Godzilla" and "Independence Day."

Not that Roland Emmerich doesn't know his craft. He moves the adventure at a reasonably swift pace, and his carefully aimed cameras keep Gibson squarely in view for most of the picture. This makes good economic sense, since a quarter of the movie's budget reportedly entered the star's pocket. It also ensures that we'll see plenty of what we came to see: Gibson shooting guns.

Or muskets, to be precise. They're the firearm of choice for well-regulated militias in 1776, when our story begins on Benjamin Martin's plantation. He sympathizes with members of the Charleston Assembly who want to drive away the British and organize a new nation, but he's a widower with seven kids to feed. He'd rather stay home—until Redcoats barge onto his land and slay one of his youngsters. Cue the film's first round of crackling musketshots, adroit guerrilla manouvers, and bloody demises of every Englishman in sight. Benjamin is a warrior again, so deft and deadly that his enemies think he's literally a ghost.

"The Patriot" pays lip service to the idea that war breeds violence and excess on all sides, even allowing that Benjamin himself participated in an atrocity during his previous combat tour. But the movie works differently on an emotional level, suggesting that the Colonial lads are basically decent sorts while the Redcoats harbor more than their share of monsters.

What might have been a treat for history buffs and a refresher course for the rest of us turns into just another occasion for watching a gun-toting Gibson—who also throws knives, and swings tomahawks, and wreaks other kinds of havoc on adversaries we've been primed to hate.

Some may call it patriotism, but a more accurate label is Hollywood flimflam with a vengeance.

LOS ANGELES TIMES, 6/28/00, Calendar/p. 1, Kenneth Turan

"How could it come to this, an army of peasants, rabble?" commander Lord Gen. Cornwallis wonders from the losing side of the Revolutionary War. The British, as it turns out, committed the one mistake no armed force, no matter how powerful, can afford to make: They stepped on Mel Gibson's last nerve.

At least this is the case made by "The Patriot," an epic look at America's war for independence that has designs on being a better film than it finally is. Not completely successful in its attempt to blend a broad canvas with an intimate family story, "The Patriot" does benefit from Gibson's charisma and is more serious and skillful than might be expected from the team responsible for "Independence Day" and "Godzilla." Whether it is quite good enough is another question.

One reason "The Patriot" is a noticeable improvement over those predecessors is that the otherwise capable team of director Roland Emmerich and producer Dean Devlin has stopped (God willing, forever) penning its own scripts. Robert Rodat, who soldiered on through a reported 38 drafts, is the writer here, and, for both better and worse, his script echoes the Oscar-nominated work he did on "Saving Private Ryan."

As with "Ryan," "The Patriot" is strong on depicting the dark side of combat and the hellishness of the wartime experience for soldiers and civilians. You can tell how serious this film wants to be by its nearly two-hour-and-40-minute length and the number of key characters it allows to die. "Why," Gibson's Benjamin Martin asks pointedly when the talk turns to glory, "do men feel they can justify death?"

With expert cinematographer Caleb Deschanel ("The Black Stallion," "The Right Stuff") handling the visuals, "The Patriot" has a good sense of spectacle and is quite successful at re-creating a period that has not been brought to the screen with much success recently.

The film is especially strong at re-creating the look of combat in the 18th century, not a surprise given Rodat's predilections. Making use of computer wizardry and reenactors (hobbyists who take part in re-created battles), "The Patriot" shows us the bloody, chaotic, hand-to-hand denouement of clashes that begin with armies stiffly approaching each other across open fields in carefully arranged ranks.

"The Patriot" also deals with philosophical conflicts about a war that inevitably pitted neighbor against neighbor and was not as obvious a situation as hindsight would make us believe. It's Gibson's Martin, in fact, who strongly comes out against a confrontation with Britain, saying, with enviable foresight (he's the hero, after all), "Mark my words, this war will be fought among our homes, the innocent will die with the rest of us."

But if "Private Ryan's" weakness was a willingness to sentimentalize, that is true here as well. Included are an awkward romance for Martin, a gushy young love subplot, some pious stuff about racial brotherhood, and more along the same lines. In fact, "Patriot's" main difficulty is reconciling its extremes of maudlin emotion and graphic violence: It's hard to know what to make of a film that wants to feature winsome grins from gaptoothed kids as well as a graphic shot of a cannonball taking a man's head off. It's an ungainly mixture, to say the least.

Doing his best to meld these conflicting tendencies is Gibson as South Carolina plantation owner Martin. It's his hands we see first, placing a sinister-looking tomahawk in a chest as his voice-over talks mysteriously of sins returning to visit him. Clearly, if this guy ever takes the tomahawk out again, everybody within throwing distance better watch out.

A widower with seven children, Martin is living an unimaginably bucolic life in 1776. Yes, like Clint Eastwood's character in "Unforgiven," some dark secret from his past hangs over him, something to do with the bloody Ft. Wilderness campaign in the French and Indian War, but otherwise he's such a paragon that the film arranges for his entire plantation to be worked not by slaves but what must be the most contented group of freed black men in the entire South.

Having experienced war, Martin speaks out against it when the Carolina Assembly meets. His idealistic eldest son, 18-year-old Gabriel (Heath Ledger) sees things differently and promptly joins the Continental Army.

Two years pass, the colonials are losing, and Martin is still determined to stay out of the war. Then, after a battle practically in his frontyard, a bearskin-hat-wearing dragoon colonel named William Tavington (Jason Isaacs), the vilest, most reprehensible man in the British army, rides into view. A smirking sadist and a wonderfully convincing villain, perhaps the year's best, Col. Tavington does things that Martin finds unforgivable. That's right, it's tomahawk time.

Though it comes relatively early in the film, the scene of Martin's terrible act of vengeance is Gibson's strongest, the lodestone of a performance that ranks among the actor's most convincing. We see a restrained man turn into a complete berserker, a killing machine covered in blood and gore. His own children look at him with genuine fear when it's over, and no wonder.

Leaving those children in the care of a sister-in-law (Joely Richardson) who is always making cow eyes at him, Martin picks up the nickname of "The Ghost" and becomes the leader of a band of guerrilla militia whose assignment is to bottle up the snobbish Cornwallis (Tom Wilkinson) and his army in the South until enough promised French military aid comes to turn the tide of the war. With independence hanging in the balance, they sure asked the right guy.

Besides those mentioned, Gibson is supported by a number of strong actors, including Chris Cooper as an American officer, Tcheky Karyo as a French liaison and Rene Auberjonois as a fighting padre. Yet for its real virtues, "The Patriot" is never completely satisfying. Having aims that exceed its reach makes this a better film than it would otherwise have been, but they also inevitably point out where things fall short of expectations.

NEW YORK, 7/10/00, p. 50, Peter Rainer

The ad for *The Patriot*, set in 1776, features an immense, close-cropped portrait of Mel Gibson's famous head, and his longish sideburns are the only real clue that the man might not be up-to-date. Accepting Gibson in a period setting has never been difficult, but the period here is a movie no-no: the Revolutionary War era. Maybe it's all those powdered wigs, or maybe the genre is too close to a high-school history class; in any event, the few movies that have taken the period on, such as *Revolution* and *Jefferson in Paris*, had most of the audience pining to be saved by the bell. *The Patriot* gets around the historical mustiness by turning itself into a high-minded revenge thriller that consciously echoes *Braveheart* when it isn't invoking the *Mad Max* series. It's a Mel Gibson action anthology in Colonial drag.

The period decor and costuming and production design may be in the overhoned Hollywood classic style, but the plotting is pure melodrama: Someone *important* is killed, revenge is taken, another biggie is offed, prompting further revenge, and so on—a daisy chain of vengeance. Gibson's Benjamin Martin is a widowed father of seven who, word has it, committed unspeakably bloody deeds during the French and Indian War and now, repentant, lives only to peaceably preserve his brood and his South Carolina plantation. (The blacks who work the plantation are not slaves, conveniently eliminating a rather nettlesome issue.) Benjamin is introduced to us not as a patriot but as a father, and the movie initially makes the large and unconvincing point that the two are mutually exclusive. Refusing to join the Continental army to fight the British, Benjamin ends up watching one son murdered by the redcoats under the command of Colonel Tavington (Jason Isaacs), who makes Vlad the Impaler look like a charm-school graduate. His eldest boy, Gabriel (Heath Ledger, who has a teen-heartthrob stalwartness), is then carted off for hanging, whereupon Mel goes into Thunderdome mode for the rescue operation. It's as if *Little House on the Prairie* suddenly went ninja; with two preteen musket-toting sons spotting him, Benjamin slaughters an entire squadron with wraithlike finesse.

When he finally joins the militia and the revenges pile up, he seems to be engaged in a battle against the British that is more about class than about Colonial independence. Benjamin's ragtag warriors show off their earthiness and love of liberty by baring their bad teeth and their bad grammar while the British, led by General Cornwallis (Tom Wilkinson), are sleek snoots who can't wait to get back to their gold chandeliers and Chippendale. (After routing the Colonials, Cornwallis laments that fighting these rustics takes the honor out of victory.) I hope it won't be misinterpreted as unpatriotic if I point out that the British come across about as bad in this movie as I've ever seen—even worse than in *The Messenger*, where a British soldier is shown raping a French girl after killing her. The atrocities perpetrated here by Tavington, especially one involving a churchful of townspeople, don't appear to bear much resemblance to recorded history; but even if they do, it seems remiss to turn the Revolutionary War into the kind of hero-villain confrontation that might be better suited to a Sega video game. The director Roland Emmerich made *Godzilla* and *Independence Day*, so perhaps this approach should come as no surprise, but the screenwriter Robert Rodat wrote *Saving Private Ryan*. What's his excuse?

The French, on the other hand, who have generally been viewed in American movies as a race of Pepe Le Pews, get what amounts to a free pass in *The Patriot*. A Lafayette-ish character played by Tchéky Karyo is made fun of—he insists on looking good even in battle—but it's the kind of affectionate needling that lets you know we're all brothers under the skin (or at least under the epaulets). The sympathy quotient in this movie is so skewed in favor of the French over the British that one suspects it's the result of a studio demographic survey: Did Sony Pictures determine the English market to be a write-off for this material and therefore decide to fall in with the French?

As in *Braveheart*, Mel Gibson turns himself into a great big sufferer, and boy, does he get a lot to suffer about. The scenario is ruthlessly punitive; as his friends and family are systematically eliminated, Benjamin seems to bloat with pain. There's an uncomfortable element of masochism in the way Gibson serves up these recent heroes of his; the camera lingers a bit too lovingly on the racked ruination of his stellar visage. He can be powerful, but his fondness for grandiose displays of martyrdom has its unseemly side. Gibson is better when he's not so balled up in anguish; when, as in *Conspiracy Theory*, he lets some screwiness and wit and ardor come through.

Humorlessness, however, is a trademark of historical epics, and *The Patriot* is full of speeches where Colonials talk about building a new world where all men are created equal (although, presumably, only white land-owning men need apply). Meanwhile, the audience hangs in for the wide-screen battles and the inevitable close-ups of heads being sheared off. The filmmakers want to make an anthem about the founding of this country, but they also want to rack up the gross-outs. How very American of them.

NEW YORK POST, 6/28/00, p. 45, Jonathan Foreman

"The Patriot" was directed by Roland Emmerich, the German director of "Independence Day" and "Godzilla."

While the film contains some terrific, realistically bloody battle scenes, it has a distinctly Germanic feel, both in its epic heaviness and in the peculiar way it revises the history of the American Revolution.

The fact that the Revolution was fought for a political ideal rather than blood and soil seems to have passed by both Emmerich and screenwriter Robert Rodat.

The "patriot" of the title goes to war because insanely malevolent and brutal bad guys in red coats have attacked his family and his farm.

A widower with seven children, South Carolina plantation owner Benjamin Martin (a stolid Mel Gibson) is a veteran of the vicious French and Indian War.

He doesn't want to get involved in the impending Revolutionary War, but his oldest son, Gabriel (Heath Ledger), joins the Continental Army against his father's wishes.

After Charlestown falls to the British, a wounded Gabriel takes refuge on the family farm. But psychopathic British cavalry officer Col. Tavington (Jason Isaacs) turns up and takes him away to be hanged.

When one of Martin's younger sons tries to stop Gabriel's arrest, Tavington guns him down on the spot.

Now motivated to join the war, Martin takes his two preteen boys into the woods, and in an implausible but thrilling scene, takes on a 20-man British detail and rescues Gabriel.

He then hides his kids with his dead wife's sexy sister (Joely Richardson), joins the rebel militia and becomes "The Ghost," leading a platoon of mountain-men irregulars against British supply lines.

Martin is based on several real-life rebels, in particular Francis Marion, "The Swamp Fox," an effective guerrilla leader (and notorious slaughterer of Indians) against loyalist forces in the Carolinas.

Martin's archenemy, Col. Tavington, leader of the Green Dragoons, is a version of Banastre Tarleton, a British cavalry officer who led a partly American (loyalist) force, also called the Green Dragoons.

Even if you allow for some poetic license (while exploding cannonballs look good on film, they sure didn't exist in the 18th century), there are problems with the film's picture of the American Revolution.

"The Patriot" turns the war into a kind of Vietnam, with Americans as the Viet Cong and the British committing one atrocity after another.

One scene features redcoats rounding up American rebel civilians, locking them in a church and roasting them alive. Nothing like it took place during the Revolution—although it's the exact atrocity committed by the SS Death's Head division in France in 1944.

Making the redcoats into cartoon SS men misses the whole point of the Revolution: It was truly about political ideals.

But instead, the movie delivers a lot of New Age, baby-boomer sentimental guff about family—combined with a pretend horror at the nastiness war brings out even in good guys.

The film plays down the Southerness of South Carolina, scrupulously eschewing Southern accents and turning Southern gentlemen into guys who could be Northern college profs.

And there's a problem with the way the film portrays race and slavery.

Not since "Gone with the Wind" has there been such a ludicrous, dishonest depiction of happy, loyal black folk down on the plantation. (Many slaves were quick to join the British.)

On the other hand, the film delivers a wonderfully real sense of the terrors of 18th-century battle, when highly drilled armies formed lines and the side that could absorb the most musket volleys without breaking ranks was the winner.

NEWSDAY, 6/28/00, Part II/p. B2, John Anderson

While it may not seem so by the time the end credits roll, "The Patriot" is not, in fact, longer than the Revolutionary War. On the other hand, every significant moment of the Revolutionary War wasn't played out in slow motion. Or directed by Roland Emmerich. If it were, we would still be paying a stamp tax.

For the benefit of those who've been on Mars, this lumbering wooden vehicle stars Mel Gibson, father of many children, as Benjamin Martin, father of many children and a variation on real-life Revolutionary hero Francis (the Swamp Fox) Marion. Opposed to war with England on the basis of paternal instinct and the atrocities he committed during the French and Indian War, Martin is driven to join the Colonials only after the callous murder of his second son by a dragoon commander of the British army (Jason Isaacs).

In terms of giving away too much, please be reassured that telling you all this is like divulging that "Aida" is set in Egypt. The opera is yet to come.

Muscular, obvious and leaving no sentiment unturned, "The Patriot" is one of those movies that seems to be opposed to violence, but whose only memorable moments are those in which life and, especially, limb are being lost. Those sequences are electrifying, particularly Martin's virtually single-handed attack on a British patrol that's escorting his eldest, Gabriel (Heath Ledger), to his execution. Martin's ferocity does more than hint at his own war experiences. It actually suggests something about the sating of bloodlust and the soul of war.

The thoughtfulness is short-lived and the way "The Patriot" deals with slavery is just insulting, but the fighting resembles nothing if not the innovative butchery of "Braveheart." Surely that's no coincidence. Emmerich ("Godzilla") may be the director of record, but Emmerich has never won an Oscar and Emmerich is not the poster boy for "The Patriot." We love Mel, but the conclusion one draws after seeing the film is that a showdown between Shaquille O'Neal and Phil Jackson would be settled by the Lakers firing Jackson.

"The Patriot" makes ample use of computerized backgrounds and imposed scenery, most of which is thoroughly suspect. Cannonballs seem to be flying in from the last "Star Wars" movie; the ships in the harbor and other deep-set backdrops look like they were done on a paint by numbers set. Overall, "The Patriot" is the computer-era equal of those very early talkies in which actors lean over a table to deliver their dialogue because the microphone was hidden in the flower bowl.

People fight, people die. People love: Gabriel and young Anne Howard (Lisa Brenner) manage to court and spark amid ongoing catastrophe; Benjamin Martin warms up to his dead wife's sister (Joely Richardson), whose bodice is ripe for ripping. Unfortunately, Ben's too busy turning the strategic tables on Lord Cornwallis (Tom Wilkinson), recruiting guerrillas or cultivating his beef against Colonel Tavington (Isaacs), who himself is busy slaughtering the citizenry wholesale.

Each death, each scream, each act of indiscriminate cruelty is not only processed through the filmmakers' slo-mo sensibility, it's accompanied by the strain(s) of composer John Williams, who has never thought that a point wasn't so obvious it couldn't be made twice. The script by Robert ("Saving Private Ryan") Rodat is just ponderous.

A 40-minute segment of "The Patriot" was shown to selected press about six weeks ago, which seemed to mean that the studio (Sony) was so eager to let the world in on the movie it would expose an unfinished version to critical scrutiny. What it means now is that, at 40 minutes, "The Patriot" worked. At two hours and 40 minutes, you feel a little like the guy who gets his head shot off with the cannonball.

NEWSWEEK, 6/26/00, p. 58, David Ansen

Benjamin Martin (Mel Gibson), the hero of Roland Emmerich's two-hour-and-40-minute American Revolution epic "The Patriot," was once a hero of the French and Indian Wars, but he's seen enough of fighting not to want to bloody his hands again. A widower with seven children, he refuses to join with his fellow South Carolinians in the battle for independence. We know, of course, that it won't be long before he changes his mind. All it takes is a sadistic British colonel (the wonderfully malevolent Jason Isaacs), who, without batting an evil eye, kills not only the wounded soldiers Benjamin is sheltering on his farm, but Benjamin's 15-year-old son. Our hero arms himself with muskets and hatchet, hands firearms to his preadolescent sons and heads for the woods in search of revenge. *This time it's personal...*

"The Patriot" comes to brutal life in the ensuing slaughter—savage, bloody, shocking. Benjamin's rage turns him into a beast, hacking way at already dead bodies, and for a moment it seems as if this epic may take us into unchartered waters, presenting us with an unhinged hero whose barbarism is indistinguishable from his heroism. The moment passes quickly, however. Just hours after arming his children and undergoing a psychotic episode, a quickly recovered Benjamin is trying to stop his 18-year-old son Gabriel (Heath Ledger) from riding off to war, and acting as if nothing has occurred. Except now Benjamin has joined the cause and will become a legend leading his brave band of militiamen against the Redcoats.

Gibson gives the part his all, but he can't create a coherent character: the movie won't let him. This handsome, impressively mounted, sometimes gripping studio production has a split personality. It has so many agendas to fill and so many demographics to please that it often feels as if it were written by a committee of studio executives and not by the credited screenwriter, Robert ("Saving Private Ryan") Rodat. A harrowing battle scene (for the boys) will be followed by a tepid romantic interlude (teen idol Ledger's dull courtship of Lisa Brenner, for the girls). Shameless sentimentality is presented back to back with unblinking scenes of the mass extermination of women and children. Comic relief is sprinkled in small, regular doses (collapsing rocking chairs, foppish Brits). Demonstrations of the nightmare of war go hand in hand with flag-waving paeans to patriotism, stirred up by a John Williams score working overtime for uplift.

Great attention may have been paid to the accuracy of the uniforms, but "The Patriot" is stamped from beginning to end with a 21st-century sensibility. A subtheme dealing with the freed slaves who served in the Revolutionary Army is presented with civics-lesson condescension (the reformed racist soldier telling his black comrade in arms it's an honor to serve beside him). If the South Carolina of 1778 looked like this House and Garden version—gentrified, spick and span, wealthy—you'd wonder why anyone would feel the need to fight a revolution. If you didn't know any better, you'd come away thinking the War for Independence was caused by a couple of rotten-apple British officers whose nastiness pushed the Colonies over the edge.

Yet there's no denying that Emmerich's film, though a good halfhour too long, keeps us watching. For all the expensive window dressing, it's a Mel Gibson revenge melodrama at heart, and its drawing card is violence. The single most memorable shot is of a cannonball tearing the head off an unknown soldier. Emmerich ("Independence Day") and editor David Brenner give us massive battle scenes that demonstrate the suicidal folly of 18th-century warfare—those formalized engagements where rows of tightly bunched soldiers offered themselves up for certain oblivion. Benjamin knows better: his militia is successful because it has mastered the guerrilla-style art of ambush. The writer of "Private Ryan" may want to sound a cautionary note about the horror of war, but it's these visions of carnage that get our blood racing. Up until now, movies about the American Revolution have been regarded in Hollywood as a box-office kiss of death. If "The Patriot" breaks the curse, it's because its really "Lethal Hatchet, Part One."

SIGHT AND SOUND, 9/00, p. 46, Philip Strick

South Carolina, 1776. As the 13 colonies of North America prepare to fight for independence from the British, plantation-owner Benjamin Martin refuses to become involved. His eldest boy Gabriel, however, joins the Continental Army; Benjamin's friend, Colonel Harry Burwell, promises to keep Gabriel out of harm's way. But when the war reaches Charleston, Gabriel comes home wounded. His brother Thomas tries to protect him and is shot dead by Colonel Tavington, commander of the Green Dragoons.

Helped by his two youngest boys, Benjamin slaughters the British soldiers holding Gabriel prisoner, and releases his son. Leaving his children with his sister-in-law Charlotte, he joins Gabriel and witnesses the disastrous Battle of Camden before being appointed by Burwell to head a regiment of militia. Tavington captures a number of Benjamin's men; Benjamin tricks General Cornwallis, head of the British forces, into releasing them. Furious, Cornwallis authorises Tavington to use any means to crush the colonials. Tavington herds the villagers of Pembroke into their church and burns it down. Among the victims is Gabriel's young bride, Anne.

Gabriel pursues Tavington, who kills him. Benjamin considers abandoning the struggle but returns to the militia and leads them into battle at Cowpens where the British forces fall into his trap. In the thick of the fighting Benjamin and Tavington confront each other: Benjamin is narrowly the survivor. Cornwallis orders retreat and surrenders to the French at Yorktown in 1781, while Benjamin and the children plan a new life with Charlotte.

With his goofy charm and collapsing home-made rocking-chairs, the hero of *The Patriot* is of much the same calibre as director Roland Emmerich's previous reluctant adventurers—the travel-sick computer virologist of *Independence Day,* say, or the worm specialist of *Godzilla.* Launched against a sea of troubles, these forlorn lateral thinkers, astonishingly resourceful in an emergency, suffer romantic deficiencies that can only be resolved after extreme crisis. The crisis itself, seldom involving anything less than planetary destruction, can be occasioned by swarms of dinosaurs or flying saucers. In the case of *The Patriot* it's an infestation of British soldiers.

There has been much indignation over the way these invaders behave, but in fact their Britishness is largely irrelevant. A near-faceless mass, they do and die as instructed while their leaders conform to other Emmerich scapegoats—such as the Mayor of New York in *Godzilla* or the President's bureaucrats in *Independence Day*—driven by good old-fashioned causes like career-advancement, discipline and survival. In *The Patriot* General Cornwallis, who heads the British forces, is inclined towards leniency and is more concerned about protecting his memoirs than about the rustics who oppose him. The true villain of the piece, cavalry commander Tavington, reliably child-killing, church-burning, and repeatedly returning from the dead, is in reality Emmerich's latest Universal Soldier, a stateless militarist, unchangingly evil throughout. He is too ludicrous an opponent to personify anything but warfare in general, a global insanity.

His antecedents, as it happens, have helped to define almost the entire career of Mel Gibson, who has been taking arms against sneering wrongdoers since the days of *Mad Max,* a crusade incorporating the paranoia of *Hamlet, Ransom, Conspiracy Theory,* and particularly closely his own *Braveheart.* Cutting through the enemy ranks at full slow-motion stride, Gibson's colonialist has a familiar wildness bordering on parody, his dementia little different from that of the beyond-control cop of the *Lethal Weapon* series. And since Emmerich as far back as his 1989 science-fiction film *Moon 44* has been a blatant plagiarist, *The Patriot* not only exploits the Gibson image but also packs itself with the habitual predicaments of Western classics, a good chunk of *Shenandoah* (1965) intermingled with Clint Eastwood's 1976 *The Outlaw Josey Wales* (both set during the Civil War), a headlong rush through the woods courtesy of *The Last of the Mohicans,* and a sunset graveyard and battling preacher courtesy of John Ford.

This said, Emmerich also makes a virtue of the unexpected, his films setting frequent ambush for his audience. Here, his virile hero turns anti-hero by refusing to fight, only to become in turn a killer so terrible that members of his own family are dumbfounded. There is the business of the bullet, specially prepared as if to destroy a vampire, that simply misses its mark, and of the tomahawk that vanishes ineffectually into the serum of battle. And reversal plays a crucial role in the final conflict, both for the two duellists at its heart and for the armies that surround them, struggling to contend with a retreat that isn't, then is, then isn't...

The main irony, of course, lies in the film's title, which suggests that the absurdly flag-waving activist should be taken at face value despite the ample evidence that defending his country is the last thing on his mind. Robert Rodat's script, echoing his argument in *Saving Private Ryan*, proposes that patriotism entails a lethal interruption to more important matters. His script, appealingly written despite a glib approach to the slavery issue, also finds room for Emmerich's trademark Frenchman—Tchéky Karyo's militia member Villeneuve is both an action man and a figure of fun (see Jean Réno's Roaché in *Godzilla*)—and remind us that the War of Independence was actually won by the French fleet, for whom patriotism would have had a rather different significance. The film's main attraction, the spectacular battle scenes, finds Emmerich at both his best and his worst (the cannonball fired straight at the audience is a cheap trick), but the appallingly detailed carnage exhaustively follows the unwritten rule of epics that they should appear to last twice as long as the original events.

TIME, 6/26/00, p. 69, Richard Schickel

It has everything you want in an epic: sweep, scope, wild reversals of fortune and plenty of bold, basic emotions. It offers a stalwart hero and a sneering villain, bloody battles and daring rescues, tender love, heedless cruelty and, above all, scores of attractive human beings who have pledged their lives, fortunes and sacred honor to a desperate but noble cause.

What's not to like about *The Patriot?* Well it certainly suffers from irony deficiency. It is four-square for democracy and decency, and this, of course, will cause a certain amount of superciliousness among the postmodernist swells. Since it is a story about the American Revolution, it will suffer from the age-old suspicion of movies in which guys wear knee britches and write with quill pens. But if the mass audience can get behind *Gladiator*, why shouldn't it take a flier on more recent history? You telling us Russell Crowe is cuter than Mel Gibson? Or in his picture suffers more than Gibson does? Get outta here.

Gibson is cast as a grieving widower named Benjamin Martin. In the French and Indian War he was a gallant, not to say legendary, commander, but something bad happened in its course—a preventable atrocity, we eventually learn—and he is determined to raise his numerous progeny in peace and prosperity on his South Carolina plantation. In the state assembly he votes against raising troops and money for a war of independence. This alienates his son (charmingly played by Heath Ledger), who joins the Continental Army. And it reckons without the relentless cruelty of Colonel William Tavington (whom Jason Isaacs plays with ferocious candor, offering neither excuses nor a single redeeming grace).

One day, in hot pursuit of retreating rebel soldiers, Tavington comes riding up to Martin's plantation at the head of a cavalry troop. Insouciantly, even rather jauntily, he orders all the Americans—most of them wounded—to be shot, the plantation fired, and for good measure, he marches Gabriel (by this time a dispatch rider for the valiant Colonel Harry Burwell, played by Chris Cooper) off to be hanged. When one of Martin's other sons tries to rescue his brother, he is coldly murdered.

It is this psychopathy that begets Martin's patriotism. With two of his other boys, he rescues Gabriel from the hanging party in what is surely director Roland Emmerich's most dashing set piece. This action establishes Martin, whose character is surely based in part on Francis Marion, the not-as-nice "swamp fox" of the Revolution, as a great, almost ghostly guerrilla leader. Also, it personalizes the war for him. At some point, we know, he must confront the hateful Tavington *mano a mano*.

Before that can happen, a lot of war will have to be fought. Fought seriously. Fought painfully. And it is here that *The Patriot* often transcends the clichés of the epic form, not to mention director Emmerich's previous work (the mysteriously successful *Independence Day* and the seriously miscalculated *Godzilla*). This is possibly because the script is by Robert Rodat, who wrote the unblinking *Saving Private Ryan*. He and Emmerich stress two things. The first is the brutal reprisals the British take against the families of the men fighting with Martin. You cannot help comparing what happens in this movie with what we have been horrified to see, the day before yesterday, in the Balkans. Civil wars—which our Revolution was—are even more relentless and unforgiving than other kinds of war, Rodat and Emmerich insist.

They are, however, also aware of the formal conventions of 18th century warfare, which were peculiarly sanguinary: two armies lined up neatly, marched toward one another until they were at virtually point-blank range, then fired. It is the sort of battle in which war's deadly essence is thrown into the highest possible relief.

One has to wonder if today's audience, out for summer fun, will appreciate all this. The movie, though it is never less than surprising in its willingness to confront human ugliness and sometimes more than inspiring in its embrace of our better natures, is long-almost three hours. And some people won't be able to dig out the poignant reality beneath what looks superficially like rather old-fashioned spectacle.

But that, perhaps, is why Mel Gibson was placed on earth. He is hard pressed here—by family losses, by the unrelieved harshness of this nasty, backwoods war, by the demons that haunt his character. Yet we are never unaware of the actor's fundamental good nature, reflected in Martin's fierce, sweet love of family, the casual ease of his action passages. He is unquestionably a star who can open a picture. Now we will see if he can, as he did in the even more unlikely *Braveheart*, narrow the distance between the modern audience and far-off history. It is by no means a sure shot. On the other hand, it would be almost unpatriotic to bet against him.

VILLAGE VOICE, 7/4/00, p. 121, J. Hoberman

Will Roland Emmerich's evocation of the American Revolution supplant Roland Emmerich's *Independence Day* as the greatest July 4th attraction in the history of civilization? Don't bet on it.

The Patriot is an earnest, inanely robust, and reasonably gory Mel Gibson vehicle, but try as it might to Nazify the British army, it never establishes the sense of panicky territorial imperative that underscored the gooey intraspecies armageddon (and interethnic solidarity) of *ID4*. Still, even if *The Patriot* fails to unite the nation before the spectacle of American cultural hegemony, it is likely to be Hollywood's first Revolutionary War hit in the six decades since John Ford directed *Drums Along the Mohawk*.

What does it take to sell the American Revolution? *The Patriot* is a movie of cornball sentiment, humorously anachronistic dialogue, and expensive Colonial Williamsburg sets. With a house full of cute kids (the fruit of a deceased, saintly wife), Gibson's South Carolina planter would seem a prime candidate for the father of his country. (The apparent slaves working in his fields turn out to be freedmen.) Still, despite the outrage of British tyranny, he doesn't want to fight—he's too worried about his motherless children (and too haunted by his own savagery in the French and Indian War). Engaging his fellow South Carolinians in what amounts to a one-man debate on the necessity for revolution, he explains his logic: "I'm a parent—I haven't the luxury of principle."

The boys, however, do want to kick some royal butt, and, as Gibson predicts, the war comes home—right into his front yard and up on the porch. Gibson's veranda serves first as an American field hospital and then as a stage on which the British enact their storm-trooper atrocities. Led by Jason Isaac's pale-eyed, lank-haired, sneering psycho, these Brits are a plummy lot—torching plantations, deporting slaves, murdering civilians, slaughtering prisoners, targeting children, and riding their horses right into the center of a colonial church.

The home attack does the trick, and, aided only by a pair of tots, Gibson ambushes and decimates an entire British platoon. The terrified redcoats call this mysterious superhero "The Ghost," although Bloody Hatchet would be a more accurate description. Gibson's character seems modeled on the Swamp Fox, a/k/a Francis Marion, a South Carolina planter and Indian-fighter turned revolutionary guerrilla. But screenwriter Robert Rodat, who scripted *Saving Private Ryan*, has performed a similar feat in stripping the Revolutionary War of its historical basis and making it a matter of emotional bonding. Even while organizing a militia to terrorize the Brits, Gibson is still trying to enforce his will over his son (Heath Ledger). "I'm losing my family," he complains.

Less plodding than Emmerich's *Godzilla*, *The Patriot* features some effective battle scenes. There's ample evidence of post-*Private Ryan* naturalism, as American regulars march in formation across an open field to get their heads blown off by the more disciplined British troops. "These rustics are so inept—it really takes the honor out of victory," Lord Cornwallis (Tom Wilkinson) whines. These effete Brits pretend to believe in honor. *The Patriot* has no such illusions, ransacking the screen-epic playbook to lift scenes from *The Birth of a Nation* and *Barry Lyndon*, as well as Gibson's Oscar-winning *Braveheart*. (Indeed, as the story of an unwilling dad who reconnects with his inner savage, *The Patriot* seemingly mimics Clint Eastwood's *Unforgiven* without addressing any of the issues raised by that vastly more troubling meditation on American history and the Hollywood-mediated American character.)

Gibson (who, always best when playing the spry lunatic, is somewhat less convincing here than as the voice of a claymation rooster in *Chicken Run)* fights tears, as well as the British, throughout. He's burdened with the success of the American Revolution—not to mention Columbia's summer schedule—but family always comes first. The most shamelessly heartwarming episode has the Gibson clan seeking refuge—and discovering their own most tender feelings—among the dumbstruck Gullah people of some nearby Club Med. Of course, Ledger has already promised to fight to end slavery. ("Equal... sounds good," the movie's token black volunteer muses.)

Opening July 4th on the last election year, *Independence Day* had no competition and was even endorsed by both candidates for president. But this time, we have the makings of an E! channel plebiscite: Emmerich's war movie versus Wolfgang Petersen's *Perfect Storm*. Will the revolution run aground in digitally enhanced big weather? Should you batten down the hatches or perform your patriotic chore? Vote for an Act of God pseudo-event or the virtual Rights of Man? The choice is yours. As nominal love interest Joely Richardson coyly tells Gibson, "It's a free country—or, at least, it will be."

Also reviewed in:
CHICAGO TRIBUNE, 6/28/00, Tempo/p. 1, Michael Wilmington
NEW YORK TIMES, 6/28/00, p. E1, Elvis Mitchell
NEW YORKER, 7/3/00, p. 87, David Denby
VARIETY, 6/19-25/00, p. 23, Todd McCarthy
WASHINGTON POST, 6/28/00, p. C1, Stephen Hunter
WASHINGTON POST, 6/30/00, Weekend/p. 43, Desson Howe

PAY IT FORWARD

A Warner Bros. Pictures release in association with Bel-Air Entertainment of a Tapestry Films production. *Executive Producer:* Mary McLaglen and Jonathan Treisman. *Producer:* Steven Reuther, Peter Abrams, and Robert L. Levy. *Director:* Mimi Leder. *Screenplay:* Leslie Dixon. *Based on the novel by:* Catherine Ryan Hyde. *Director of Photography:* Oliver Stapleton. *Editor:* David Rosenbloom. *Music:* Thomas Newman. *Music Editor:* Bill Bernstein. *Sound:* Mark Hopkins McNabb and (music) Joel Iwataki. *Sound Editor:* J. Paul Huntsman and Christopher Aud. *Casting:* Geraldine Leder. *Production Designer:* Leslie Dilley. *Art Director:* Larry Hubbs. *Set Designer:* Mick Cukurs, Gary Speckman, and Marcos Alvarez. *Set Decorator:* Peg Cummings. *Special Effects:* Burt Dalton. *Costumes:* Renée Ehrlich Kalfus. *Make-up:* Tania McComas. *Stunt Coordinator:* Jeff Dashnaw, Buddy Joe Hooker, and Johnny Martin. *Running time:* 155 minutes. *MPAA Rating:* PG13.

CAST: Kevin Spacey (Eugene Simonet); Helen Hunt (Arlene McKinney); Haley Joel Osment (Trevor McKinney); Jay Mohr (Chris Chandler); James Caviezel (Jerry); Jon Bon Jovi (Ricky); Angie Dickinson (Grace); David Ramsey (Sidney); Gary Werntz (Thorsen); Colleen Flynn (Woman on Bridge); Marc Donato (Adam); Kathleen Wilhoite (Bonnie); Liza Snyder (Michelle); Jeannetta Arnette (Nurse); Hannah Werntz (Thorsen's Daughter); Tina Lifford (Principal); Loren D. Baum, Nico Matinata, and Zack Duhame (Rough Kids); Shawn Pyfrom (Shawn); Alexandra Kotcheff (Alexandra); Bradley White (Jordan); Christi Colombo (Christi); Phillip Stewart (Phillip); Justin Parsons (Justin); Myeshia Dejore Walker (Myeshia); Brenae Suzanne Davey (Brenae); Molly Kate Bernard (Molly); Andrew Patrick Flood (Andy); Tameila N. Turner (Tameila); Julian Correa (Julian); Carrie Ann Sullivan

(School Girl);   Patricia Deanda (Change Girl);   Ryan Berti and Gabriela Rivas (Hallway Kids); Carric O'Quinn (Man in Window);   Stephanie Feury (Woman in Window);   Bernard White (Cop);   Tom Bailey, Tim Dezarn, and Jonathan Nichols (Liquid Men);   Ron Keck and John Powers (Lowlifes); Bob McCracken (Creepy Middle-aged Man);   Frank Whiteman (Doctor); Eugene Osment (Cop Who Gives Directions);   Kendall Tenney (Male Newscaster);   Sue Tripathy (Female Newscaster); Rusty Meyers (News Stand Guy);   Leslie Dilley (Governor).

LOS ANGELES TIMES, 10/20/00, Calendar/p. 1, Kenneth Turan

Is it live or is it Memorex? Is it a diamond or is it authentic cubic zirconium? Is the feeling in "Pay It Forward" genuine or is it a carefully created emotional forgery, the kind of fake tinsel that's been a Hollywood specialty forever? In each case, it's awfully hard to tell the difference.

For it's the not inconsiderable accomplishment of "Pay It Forward" to win us over, much against our better judgment, to its sentimental, inspirational brand of fantasy. Difficult as it is for a multimillion-dollar Hollywood movie that bangs the drum for selflessness and idealism to be taken at all seriously, the combination of restrained writing and direction and top-of-the-line acting is enough to make even confirmed agnostics want to believe in this unashamed fairy tale.

Starring Kevin Spacey and Helen Hunt as damaged people in need of connections and the remarkable Haley Joel Osment as the small child who leads them, "Pay It Forward" is adapted from a novel by Catherine Ryan Hyde that is so brazenly sentimental it has real glitter on its cover and actually boasts of being "in the tradition of the successful and inspirational television show 'Touched by an Angel.' "

It was the task of screenwriter Leslie Dixon, as it was with Richard LaGravenese on "The Bridges of Madison County," to put a leash on the novel's extremes of sentimentality, and she's done an excellent job. Typically adept is the change of the book's setting from a generic California town to the intriguing locale of working-class Las Vegas.

Mimi Leder builds on what Dixon has done and takes it further. A director who adds human texture to generic blockbusters "Deep Impact" and "The Peacemaker," she works especially hard and with surprising success using tact and restraint to overcome the story's patness and sentimentality. "Pay It Forward" is notable for where it doesn't go as where it does, for avoiding the missteps of bathos and piling on that almost invariably mar these kinds of three-hankie studio productions.

Without the quality of acting "Pay It Forward" attracted, this would not have been possible. Cast by Geraldine Leder, the film is strong through its main supporting roles, which include Jay Mohr as a curio journalists James Caviezel as a homeless man with a drug problem, Jon Bon Jovi as an absent husband and Angie Dickinson as a decidedly unglamorous street person. But the film gets the most out of its three stars who bring more carefully calibrated emotion to their parts than could rightfully be expected.

Spacey, always especially good at characters who are half-hidden inside themselves, is Eugene Simonet, middle school social studies teacher (the character was African American in the novel) whose terrible burns disfigure his body and motivate his guarded outlook on the world. The sight of Eugene painstaking ironing his own shirts is the film's opening shot, and it encapsulates the controlled, repetitive way he has chosen to live his life.

Arlene McKinney, naturally, has exactly the opposite temperament. A harried, disorganized single mother who works two jobs to earn a living, she is also an alcoholic troubled by self-doubt who needs more than the stars on her fingernail polish to brighten her life. Hunt, one of the most empathetic of actresses, smoothly draws us into the life of this convincingly haggard and uncertain woman.

Eleven-year-old Trevor McKinney, Arlene's son and Mr. Simonet's student, is the link between these two people. The de facto adult in his family, Trevor has a steeliness and a fierce determination that Osment is completely comfortable with. The substance and strength he brings to the part, his ability to match intensity with both Spacey and Hunt, show, in case anyone had any doubts, that Osment's performance in "The Sixth Sense" was hardly a fluke. Young as he is, this is quite an actor.

Responding to Mr. Simonet's assignment to think of a way to change the world and put it into action, intrigued Trevor comes up with the "pay it forward" notion, the idea that you do really big favors for people, and instead of paying it back, the recipients pay it forward to others similarly in need of help.

(Classic movie buffs will recognize that idea as a variant of a concept that was old when Douglas Sirk utilized it in his 1954 remake of the 1935 "Magnificent Obsession," which in turn came from a 1933 Lloyd C. Douglas novel. The idea there, put into practice by a character whose death gets the plot into gear, is that the correct response to someone doing good for you is to "pass it along" to someone else.)

While we watch the ways Trevor tries to put his idea into practice—guess what, it's harder than he thinks—we also follow a reporter tracing how the notion the young boy has started has made its way into the world.

The point about "Pay It Forward" is not that the film isn't as contrived as it sounds—it is—but that the way it's been made enables us to forget that if we're so inclined. The ultimate recycler, Hollywood doesn't have much success inventing new kinds of stories; its strength is coming up with ways to reuse the old ones.

NEW YORK, 10/30/00, p. 92, Peter Rainer

Pay It Forward is a heavy heaping of inspirationalism that manages to work in child abuse, single-motherhood, violence in the schools, homelessness, wife battering, the effects of divorce on children, alcoholism—and that's just for starters. It has the ungainly heft of a political-party platform. You can tell from this fable's drawn-out deliberateness that something momentous is being imparted to us, but what? A fable should be lucid in its meanings. With its smorgasbord of moralizings, *Pay It Forward* is a confusing welter of sentiment. Our compassion becomes gridlocked.

Back for another tour of duty as a precocious junior sufferer who sees into the hearts of suffering adults is Haley Joel Osment as Trevor McKinney, a seventh-grade latchkey child whose single mother, Arlene (Helen Hunt), a Vegas barmaid and casino change girl, is not very effectively fighting off her drinking problem. Trevor's new social-studies teacher, Eugene Simonet (Kevin Spacey), whose face bears burn scars, is hypercontrolled and reclusive and prone to uttering words in class requiring the use of a dictionary for his students to grasp. (Ever helpful, he hands out pocket dictionaries for this purpose.) He offers up to his class his traditional beginning-of-the-school-year extra-credit assignment—*Think of an idea to change our world and put it into action*—and darned if Trevor doesn't come up with a doozy: If a favor is done to you, don't pay it back to the donor; pay it forward to three people in need, who in turn help three others in need, and so on until the world is linked by a chain of do-goodness.

The film's idea of doing good is solidly Hollywood: Our first example which the story, confusedly, flashes back from comes when a newspaper reporter (Jay Mohr), whose Mustang has been totalled, finds himself the instant recipient of a flashy new Jaguar from a well-to-do passerby. It's unclear to me how bestowing a Jaguar on somebody results in a better world, except perhaps for Jaguar dealers, but one accepts this gesture as the purest case of showbiz altruism. Trevor's first act of generosity is to bring home a derelict (James Caviezel) and feed him, and no doubt if this film is a hit, its producers will want to follow suit and pay forward some of its gross points to the homeless.

It's not enough that Trevor is a sad, spunky kid with an ache for a happy family life; he must also be turned into an angelic martyr whose fate seems rather farfetchedly aligned with Christian theology (as if this film needed any more bloat). Director Mimi Leder and screenwriter Leslie Dixon, adapting a novel by Catherine Ryan Hyde, play into the fashionable movie trend of portraying children as adults-in-miniature, and vice versa. Trevor isn't just precocious; despite his tantrums and action toys, he's practically a spirit guide, while his mother and Eugene are blighted by the badness of the big bad world and their own childlike fears. Arlene can't cope without Trevor's interventions, while Eugene, whom the boy tries to set up with his mother, is so creepily recessive that he seems one degree away from pod-personhood. Eugene's scars are, of course, both literal and symbolic, and it's nice to see Kevin Spacey playing someone with a quiet vulnerability for a change; but we are asked to mourn this character's benighted life without ever getting much of a life to mourn.

The sympathy between Eugene and Trevor might have had some resonance if the film had pared down the metaphors and mythology and instead shown us how a gifted teacher can inspire a student and make a difference in his life no matter how dismal the circumstances.

But why settle for *The Corn Is Green* or *Dead Poets Society* when you can create your very own New Testament? *Pay It Forward* offers itself up as a religious experience couched in the vernacular of self-help psychobabble: These people suffer because they won't allow themselves to be loved, they can't always see what they need, and so on. The failures that result from Trevor's pay-it-forward campaign occur because we don't have enough faith in each other. We're not *ready* for such goodness. Or are we? By film's end, the movement seems to be catching on, especially, natch, in L.A. Is it too late for the presidential candidates to appropriate this movie? A chicken in every pot and a Jag in every garage. Pass it on.

NEW YORK POST, 10/20/00, p. 47, Jonathan Foreman

For self-consciously inspirational Oscar-bait, "Pay It Forward" works unexpectedly well for its first three quarters. Director Mimi Leder ("Deep Impact," "The Peacemaker") works her sentimental material with surprising, effective restraint.

The main problem—until the last act twist in the tale and mawkish climax—is the romance at the heart of the story, a romance rendered unbelievable by the lack of physical chemistry between Kevin Spacey and Helen Hunt, and by Leslie Dixon's script's failure to show what might bring these two unlikely people together.

Spacey plays Eugene Simonet, a schoolteacher with a badly scarred face (in corny movie fashion, the scars aren't too disfiguring—they trace the areas where a beard would be). Hunt is Arlene a single mom who works as a waitress in a stripper bar. Her son Trevor (Haley Joel Osment) is in Simonet's class.

Simonet gives his class a year long assignment, to do something that will make the world a better place. Trevor, one of those movie kids repellently wise and serious beyond his years, comes up with "Pay it Forward" a kind of chain letter of goodness. The idea is that you do a good deed and the recipient must pay it forward to three other people.

Naturally the idea takes off and does begin to change the world. But Trevor's own good deeds are rather less successful. Jerry (James Cavaziel from "Frequency") a junkie homeless whom Trevor adopts, feeds and cleans up, falls back into his own ways. And his efforts to help his alcoholic mother fix up her life by fixing her up with his Mr. Simonet don't quite come off either. At least at first.

Meanwhile, in a parallel story, Los Angeles reporter Jay Mohr is trying to find out who inspired the Pay it Forward movement. His efforts bring him to Las Vegas where he meets Arlene's street person Mom (Angie Dickinson).

Hunt, wearing deliberately bad eye make-up, a push up bra and short skirts (revealing terrific legs) is just about believable as Arlene. Spacey makes a fine damaged teacher.

Like those bumper stickers that urge you to practice random acts of kindness and beauty, the tale of the Pay It Forward movement harks back to the 80's when boomers like Steven Spielberg made movies about the power of childish innocence to save a corrupt world. Yet the parts of the film that deal with exploding altruism are actually the most enjoyable—even if you're tempted to see it all as a guilty rich person's fantasy about the effects of charity and the gratitude felt by its recipients.

It makes it a shame that it's so hard to care about whether or not Simonet and Arlene will make it as a couple. In this movie both Spacey and Hunt have the sex appeal of a fish on a slab, and you don't buy their attraction for a second.

A musical theme semi-cribbed from "American Beauty" does "Pay it Forward" no favors.

NEWSDAY, 10/20/00, Part II/p. B3, John Anderson

As John Lennon once said, instant karma's gonna get you, although it's unlikely he was thinking of the kind of Kwik-Grits version you get in "Pay It Forward." Or that anyone based on the feel-good ad campaign surrounding the film, will be expecting its peculiar brand of unrelenting darkness. Think Frank Capra, but from the point of view of Mr. Potter.

Much, much-much-acting goes on here, by Kevin Spacey as the burn-scarred teacher Eugene Simonet, by Helen Hunt, as single-mom-waitress-drunk Arlene McKinney and, as her son, Trevor, by young Haley Joel Osment, who still seems to be seeing dead people. These characters carry so much emotional luggage and dramatic apparatus—the scars, the bottle, the hunched, fearful look of the small kid in middle-school hell—that it's tough to get handle on the point of the story: the idea of "paying it forward," aka rewarding acts of gratuitous kindness by doing so unto others.

Trevor seems to be the one who comes up with the idea, after the supercilious Eugene assigns his social studies class to find some way to "change the world." I say "seems," because early in the film there's a flashback to "four months earlier" and unless I just blanked on something, it totally confused the plotline. In any event, what Trevor practices down in his junkie-fied neighborhood of Las Vegas is the Golden Rule, in one form or another a tenet of every major religion on Earth. "Pay It Forward" would like us to think it's something new. In Hollywood, it probably is.

The sluggish pace and unwieldy structure of the film are the real problems, as is the fact that director Mimi Leder has no sense of proportion. In "Deep Impact," she made TV broadcaster Tea Leoni's career arc as important as the killer asteroid screaming toward Earth. "The Peacemaker" was a light romantic comedy built around Balkan terrorism. "Pay It Forward" keeps zigging and zagging between plots and subplots that don't really matter: the obnoxious reporter Chris Chandler (Jay Mohr) sniffing out this mysterious "pay-it-forward" movement" (a guaranteed laugh line), or Jerry (James Caviezel), the homeless addict redeemed by young Trevor, who, at one point, tries to talk a potential female suicide down off a bridge railing. Since she's still up there when the film pulls away, she may in fact have jumped.

Meanwhile—there are many meanwhiles—Trevor is trying to fix up Mom with Eugene, both of whom he sees as ripe candidates for his largesse. It isn't easy. Eugene's reticence, due partly to his scars and partly to what his scars have made of him, won't let him take the step toward Arlene that Arlene desperately wants—even though you know they're going to hook up eventually, and that Trevor's delinquent father (Jon Bon Jovi) is going to complicate things once they do. And that all this persistent resistance is just a way of killing time. In fact, there's so much romantic bobbing and weaving you almost expect a bell to ring.

Warner Bros. has made its biweekly request that the press not reveal the ending of the film that (with the exception of "The Perfect Storm") we never do anyway. Suffice to say that the climax is characteristic of a film that, on one hand, wants to make everything kind of nice—Angie Dickinson, for instance, is the best-kempt homeless alcoholic you've ever seen—and, on the other, tries to surprise us with brutality. What's really worrisome about "Pay It Forward" is that it comes at the time of year when studios start to release their "better" movies. If this is any indication, New Year's can't come fast enough.

NEWSWEEK, 10/30/00, p. 84, David Ansen

Hectoring Hollywood to straighten up and fly right is the popular political sport of the season. As if on cue, the life-affirming "Pay It Forward" arrives on the scene, swelled up with good intentions and garlanded with three recent Oscar-contending actors. Its hero is an 11-year-old boy, Trevor (Haley Joel Osment), who is inspired by his seventh-grade teacher to practice random acts of kindness. The teacher, Mr. Simonet (Kevin Spacey), a man whose face is disfigured with burn scars, exhorts his class to "think of an idea to change the world, and put it into action." Trevor, a solemn, sensitive lad whose mother is an alcoholic Las Vegas cocktail waitress (Helen Hunt), devises a plan to do three good deeds. Each of the three recipients of his selfless acts must "pay it forward," performing three good deeds in turn. Thus begins a movement with the potential to change the world.

There are many different ways a premise like this could play out (imagine what the sardonic Spaniard Luis Buñuel, for whom no good deed went unpunished, could have done with this). However, we are stuck with the movie that director Mimi Leder and screenwriter Leslie Dixon have concocted from the novel by Catherine Ryan Hyde. If this is what Hollywood considers serious, important filmmaking, maybe the movie industry should stick to the low road. Directed with the in-your-face subtlety of a sitcom, the tone of the movie is weirdly miscalculated from the get-go. When Leder isn't milking the material for inappropriate laughs, she's desperately tugging at the heartstrings.

Neither ploy works. It's bad enough when a shameless tear-jerker like "Remember the Titans" puts a lump in your throat; even worse is the tear-jerker that can't raise a sniffle.

The first of Trevor's good deeds is to take in a homeless heroin addict (a badly used Jim Caviezel, all of whose scenes ring false). His second is to hook up his backsliding mom (who has a weakness for abusive men) with Mr. Simonet. The unlikely romance begins to bloom, in spite of the self-protective, emotionally and physically scarred teacher's fear of relationships, and Mom's bad habits. While Hunt has been encouraged to stridently over-act (especially in her bad-girl phase, before she gets a cosmetic and moral makeover), Osment and Spacey manage to achieve some moments of honesty amid the melodramatic hokum. But it's an uphill battle: Spacey is saddled with a tragic family backstory (his abusive father was even worse than Trevor's) that echoes the boy's all too neatly. Osment demonstrates again that he's uncannily gifted, but it would be nice if someone gave him a part where he could lighten up and act his age. His do-gooder's role seems designed not just to win him a nomination, but canonization. (To keep Oscars in the viewer's mind, Thomas Newman has been asked to produce a faded carbon copy of his haunting "American Beauty" score.)

"Pay It Forward" piles on enough domestic horrors to fill a month's worth of Jerry Springer shows. This is the sort of movie where as soon as Trevor, running away from home, enters a bus station, he's approached by a child molester. Adding to the clutter is the parallel tale of a reporter (Jay Mohr) who is trying to track down the "pay it forward" phenomenon. These scenes take place at a later date than the running story, making a bumpy ride even bumpier. For the sake of those who might enjoy this high-minded sermon (and from the scattered applause, some will), I won't give away the ending: but for truly egregious sappiness, it's hard to beat.

SIGHT AND SOUND, 3/01, p. 56, Philip Kemp

Eleven-year-old Trevor McKinney lives with his mother Arlene in Las Vegas. Arlene works as a waitress in a strip club and change-girl in a casino, and drinks. On the first day of term, civics teacher Eugene Simonet gives Trevor's class an assignment to come up with an idea to change the world. (Four months later in LA, a reporter, Chris, has his car totalled at a crime scene. He's amazed to be given a new Jaguar by a stranger.)

Trevor comes up with the concept of Pay It Forward—to do gratuitous favours to three people, each of whom must do something for three more. He invites a down-and-out, Jerry, home for food. Jerry fixes Arlene's truck, but later reverts to his drug habit. Trevor tries to get his mother together with Eugene, who's lonely and sensitive about the burn scars on his face, but their mutual mistrust gets in the way. Trevor's third plan is to help his classmate Adam, who is picked on by school thugs, but he chickens out. (Chris locates the man who gave him the car, hears about Pay It Forward and starts working his way back up the chain.)

The budding affair between Eugene and Arlene is interrupted by the return of Ricky, Trevor's feckless dad; but when Ricky threatens Trevor with violence, Arlene kicks him out. She also makes peace with her estranged mother Grace, a bag lady. Grace and Eugene attend Trevor's twelfth birthday party. Chris arrives, having pinpointed Trevor as the source of Pay It Forward, and interviews him for television. Seeing Adam getting beaten up, Trevor goes to help and is stabbed to death. As Eugene comforts Arlene, a crowd gathers with flowers and candles outside the McKinney house.

Pay It Forward might seem something of a departure for Mimi Leder, who with her two previous features, action spectaculars The Peacemaker and Deep Impact, looked to be carving out a niche as a female director capable of handling the big-bucks slam bang stuff. But both films, for all their apocalyptic imagery and CGI explosions carried an oddly reassuring subtext about the innate goodness of most people, and in the present movie that message gets to take centre stage—so much so that the characters are subordinated to it.Much of the time Pay It Forward feels like a story created to illustrate a thesis in this case, the Readers Digest-like truism that the world would be a better place if we tried being nice to each other.

The actors fight back valiantly against being sidelined. Helen Hunt as struggling mother Arlene, her sharp features subtly shifting from shrewish to tender, builds on the streetsmart/vulnerable persona she established in As Good As It Gets, while Haley Joel Osment's watchful gaze, with its hint of suppressed tears, carries conviction to the role of her son, the psychologically abused Trevor. As Trevor's teacher Eugene, Kevin Spacey is landed with the task of animating two Hollywood clichés: the brilliant, bookish but socially inept teacher, and the use of disfiguring facial scars as an index of emotional withdrawal. Negotiating all the pitfalls with delicacy, Spacey unleashes a sense of long-buried fury in his key speech to Arlene, when he reveals how he got the burns.

This and other isolated moments are moving, despite the contrivances surrounding them, and occasional touches of the unexpected—especially a scene in a hospital waiting-room—go some way to lightening the load. In the end, though, Spacey and the rest of the cast are defeated by a concept-driven story that rarely allows them room to breathe. Angie Dickinson, in particular, never gets enough screen time to flesh out her crusty-but-good-hearted bag lady, and the episode when her relationship to Arlene is revealed is almost drowned out by the sound of prefabricated plot points clicking neatly into place.

Any residual tolerance that *Pay It Forward* might have earned is dissipated by the triple whammy of its final reel. Trevor's appearance on television, in which everything the film has been saying is spelled out in large letters, is followed by a 'shock' plot twist, delivered by three young thugs whose sole aim in life seems to be bullying Trevor's friend. After which, we're slugged with an ending whose glutinous excess—enhanced by Jane Siberry crooning 'Calling All Angels' on the soundtrack—makes the Princess Di sobfest look like an exercise in stiff-upper-lip restraint.

TIME, 10/23/00, p. 82, Richard Schickel

Something's wrong with Kevin Spacey's face. At first you think it's just a case of bad lighting. But soon you realize this is scar tissue—not enough to turn him into a grotesque, but plenty to explain why his Eugene Simonet, a junior high social-science teacher, is prissy, overintellectual and socially withdrawn.

He is, of course, a victim of the Joan Crawford syndrome: messed up, but as curable, psychologically speaking, as the scarred stars of ancient weepies always were. Like them, he just needs to be loved. And Arlene McKinney (Helen Hunt) is the girl to do it. She, naturally, has her own problems. She's a single mom, a waitress working extra shifts at a topless bar while she struggles with alcoholism; she hides her bottle in a chandelier, just as Ray Milland did in *The Lost Weekend*. But there's good stuff in her too.

Better still, she has a saintly son, Trevor (Haley Joel Osment), who is eager to bring these two damaged creatures together for purposes of mutual redemption. He also has bigger plans. Responding to an assignment from Mr. Simonet, who asks his students to come up with a plan to improve the world, he invents the Pay It Forward plan. His idea is to do good deeds for three people, each of whom does the same for three more individuals and so on—until, presumably, peace is established in the Middle East. This is not dissimilar to Frank Capra's John Doe movement and, indeed, the movie ends on a populist-sentimental note that's in Capra's vein, but shamelessly so. It's Capracorn without the Capra craft.

These antique movie references are not coincidental. Surely Mimi Leder, the director, and screenwriter Leslie Dixon had them in mind. They are, however, of interest largely to students of clichés and their maddening persistence in popular culture. Leder and Dixon are more up to date. Theirs is an epic of au courant abuse and unlikely but inspirational redemption.

How did Eugene come by his scars? Why, long ago, his evil father dumped a can of gasoline on him and lit a match. Why is Arlene a drunk? Well, you see, her mother was a bag lady and her former husband a wife beater. Why is Trevor such a shy and skittish little do-gooder?

Because he's afraid his nasty dad will return—can you guess whether he does or not?—and start hitting him too.

The makers of *Pay it Forward* know misery must be occasionally relieved. They give Spacey some funny curmudgeonly lines to snap in his *American Beauty* way. They let him hide his worst scars under his shirt, so they are revealed only when Hunt finally, gently touches them in the half-light of her bedroom. And Osment gets a couple of moments to reveal his inner Beaver.

We're supposed to feel sorry for these people, and be inspired by their brave struggles to recover from all those wounds. But some of us are bound to take umbrage at the film's vulgar manipulations. Set in terminally tacky Las Vegas, *Pay It Forward* is as rigged as a casino slot machine, preying on people's hopes but paying off only for the house.

VILLAGE VOICE, 10/31/00, p. 174, Dennis Lim

Just in time to placate the quadrennial Beltway snipers, Warner Bros. prostrates itself before John McCain with the inbred Gump relation *Pay It Forward,* an overflowing septic tank of chicken-soupy sanctimony that proceeds from casually offensive hypocrisy to wretchedly inapt religiosity. The studio has requested that reviewers collude in its brain-dissolving assault on the moviegoing public and not disclose the end of the film, and a critic would, under normal circumstances, be professionally honor-bound to comply. But Hollywood manipulations as virulent, cynical, and phonily wholesome as this (the filmmakers have gone so far as to position this godsploitation atrocity as an object lesson) require drastic responses, and it would be equally irresponsible for a critic not to discuss the egregious twist with which *Pay It Forward* concludes (turn away now if you care): The kid from *The Sixth Sense*—he dies, croaks, buys the farm, ceases to exist, meets Joe Black. *They knife him. To death.* Because Haley Joel Osment, in the dangerous, harebrained scheme of this grievously misguided passion play, is Jesus. After two hours of mawkish do-gooding, the precocious tyke is stabbed in the ribs by a playground bully. He falls to his knees, arms flailing, in slow motion. Director Mimi Leder, a Spielberg protégé, dutifully provides an aerial shot.

The title refers to the chain-reaction exponential-goodwill scheme devised by HJO in response to a tauntingly ambiguous assignment by his burn-scarred social studies teacher Kevin Spacey ("change the world"). The little scamp fixes up his alcoholic, Vegas-topless-bar-waitress single mother (Helen Hunt) with Spacey, and helps out a startled junkie (James Caviezel); before long, the charity outbreak has reached L.A., where a journalist (Jay Mohr) decides to sniff out the origins of the "pay it forward" movement. Compassion is confused throughout with pity and condescension, even when it comes to the central romance (Hunt, throwing herself at Spacey: "Something is being offered to you here"), and the movie's class and racial politics are indefensible. The Spacey character in the original novel was black and a Vietnam vet; here the source of his tasteful scars is ostentatiously skirted around and guarded like a state secret for so long that when he finally projectile-vomits his miserable backstory into your lap, it lands with extra force. While I'm at it, I might as well tell you: His dad did it.

Also reviewed in:
CHICAGO TRIBUNE, 10/20/00, Friday/p. A, Mark Caro
NEW YORK TIMES, 10/20/00, p. E12, A. O. Scott
NEW YORKER, 11/6/00, p. 110, David Denby
VARIETY, 10/9-15/00, p. 21, Todd McCarthy
WASHINGTON POST, 10/20/00, p. C1, Rita Kempley
WASHINGTON POST, 10/20/00, Weekend/p. 41, Desson Howe

PERFECT STORM, THE

A Warner Bros. release of a Baltimore Spring Creek Pictures production in association with Radiant Productions. *Executive Producer:* Barry Levinson and Duncan Henderson. *Producer:* Paula Weinstein, Wolfgang Petersen, and Gail Katz. *Director:* Wolfgang Petersen. *Screenplay:* Bill Wittliff. *Based on the book by:* Sebastian Junger. *Director of Photography:* John Seale. *Editor:* Richard Francis-Bruce. *Music:* James Horner. *Music Editor:* Jim Henrikson. *Sound:* Keith A. Wester and (music) Simon Rhodes. *Sound Editor:* Wylie Stateman. *Casting:* Janet Hirshenson and Jane Jenkins. *Production Designer:* William Sandell. *Art Director:* Chas Butcher. *Set Designer:* John Leimanis, Doug Meerdink, Bill Taliaferro, and Bruce West. *Set Decorator:* Ernie Bishop. *Special Effects:* John Frazier. *Costumes:* Erica Edell Phillips. *Make-up:* Susan Cabral-Ebert. *Special Effects Make-up:* Matthew Mungle. *Visual Effects:*

Stefen Fangmeier. *Stunt Coordinator:* Doug Coleman and Daniel W. Barringer. *Running time:* 129 minutes. *MPAA Rating:* PG-13.

CAST: George Clooney (Billy "Skip" Tyne);   Mark Wahlberg (Bobby Shatford);   John C. Reilly (Dale "Murph" Murphy);   Diane Lane (Christina Cotter);   William Fichtner (David "Sully" Sullivan);   John Hawkes (Michael "Bugsy" Moran);   Allen Payne (Alfred Pierre); Karen Allen (Melissa Brown);   Bob Gunton (Alexander McAnally III);   Christopher McDonald (Todd Gross);   Dash Mihok (Sgt. Jeremy Mitchell);   Josh Hopkins (Captain Darryl Ennis); Michael Ironside (Bob Brown);   Cherry Jones (Edie Bailey);   Rusty Schwimmer (Irene "Big Red" Johnson);   Janet Wright (Ether Shatford, "Ma");   Mary Elizabeth Mastrantonio (Captain Linda Greenlaw);   Todd Kimsey (Lt. Rob Pettit);   Chris Palermo (Flight Engineer Borgers); Wiley Pickett (Sgt. Millard Jones);   Hayden Tank (Dale Murphy, Jr.);   Merley Kennedy (Debra Murphy, Murph's Ex-Wife);   Jennifer Sommerfield (Alfred Pierre's Girlfriend); Joseph D. Reitman (Douglas Kosco);   Sandy Ward (Quentin, the Old Timer);   Melissa Samuels (Pam, Todd Gross' Assistant); Steve Barr (Commander Brudnicki);   J. Scott Shonka (Communications Officer);   Patrick Foley (Falcon Jet Pilot);   Lloyd Malone (Falcon Jet Co-Pilot);   Billy Mayo and Mark Adams (C-130 Co-Pilots);   Tim Trotman (C-130 Navigator);   Barry Turstein (C-130 Engineer); Patrick Stinson and Terry Anzur (TV Newscasters);   Katelyn C. Brown and Miles Schneider (Carrot Top Kids);   James Lee (Helmsman);   Jim Argenbright (Quartermaster); Michael Spaseff (Look-out).

CHRISTIAN SCIENCE MONITOR, 6/30/00, p. 15, David Sterritt

"The Perfect Storm" is a perfect formula movie. Looking for originality, creativity, and real surprises rather than superficial shocks? Then fish somewhere else.

But if you're in the mood for a tried-and-true entertainment that delivers all the obligatory goods—turbulent action, corny romance, and enough wave-churning seascapes to make "Titanic" seem landlocked—then this is the place to sink your anchor for 127 minutes of fact-based adventure.

Well, not quite 127 minutes. The movie begins with a great deal of slow-moving drama intended to make us care about the seafaring heroes as human beings. Or at least as stereotypes—the Aging Skipper who's losing his touch, the Eager Rookie determined to prove his worth, the Feuding Fishermen itching for a fight. And so on, not forgetting the Loyal Womenfolk who wait faithfully on shore and the Crusty Oldtimer who comments on events behind a grizzled beard.

My favorite is the Amazed Meteorologist who ponders a pile of charts, realizes that three devastating weather systems are converging off the coast, and utters the line we're hungering to hear: "This doesn't look good!"

The movie picks up when the heroes head to sea. It picks up more when the ice machine breaks down on the fishing boat, forcing the skipper to make an Awesome Decision many miles from land: Should he let his cargo rot, or should he steer into the Biggest Storm Ever and race for home? It's an easy call—perishing in the waves is clearly better than living with stinky swordfish—and from this point the picture bobbles from one water-drenched crisis to another.

"The Perfect Storm" packs a cinematic wallop during its best sequences, full of towering surf and improbable derring-do made vivid by split-second editing. The acting is adequate to the occasion, with George Clooney's skipper nicely balanced by Mark Wahlberg as the rookie and by John C. Reilly and William Fichtner as seamen with chips on their shoulders.

You may get tired of watching them flounder around, but for variety there's a Coast Guard rescue team that also flounders around. Wolfgang Petersen became a star director with "Das Boot" in 1981, and apparently the briny deep still lures him. "The Perfect Storm" will hardly enhance his reputation, but it stays afloat as well as anything Hollywood has launched so far in this rather soggy season.

LOS ANGELES TIMES, 6/30/00, Calendar/p. 1, Kenneth Turan

"The Perfect Storm" didn't get its name by being nice. Rather, as Sebastian Junger's book explained, this was "a storm that could not possibly have been worse," a marine event with 120-

mph winds, rain so intense it drowned birds in mid-flight and waves of a size "few people on Earth have ever seen." When meteorologists began calling this the storm of the century, no one thought to argue.

Taken from Junger's enormously popular book (3.5 million copies in print) about the October 1991 Atlantic juggernaut and the people with the dreadful luck to be at sea when it struck, "The Perfect Storm," like its namesake, overwhelms the obstacles in its path.

Directed by Wolfgang Petersen and starring George Clooney as the captain of the swordfish boat Andrea Gail out of Gloucester, Mass., "The Perfect Storm" has noticeable problems with characterization and dialogue. But once that awesome storm, one of the most terrifying ever put on film, gets cranked up, it's hard to remember what those difficulties were, let alone care too much about them.

Elaborate watery disasters have been shot as far back as 1929's "Noah's Ark," which created a flood so realistic it reportedly cost the lives of several extras. But the ferocious storm sequences here are even more unnerving thanks to modern movie technology and a director who knows how to use it.

Even if you didn't know weather this threatening was on its way, the pre-maelstrom segments of "The Perfect Storm" would play like marking time, which is what they are. Written by Bill Wittliff ("Legends of the Fall," the "Lonesome Dove" miniseries), "Storm" has no choice but to depart in places from Junger's gripping book, not always with the best results.

Great chunks of the printed work, for instance, are filled with fascinating but unfilmable scientific information and storm lore. Junger also only lightly characterizes the six-man crew of the Andrea Gail, and he doesn't speculate overly much on what happens to them aboard ship.

But since the film is increasingly concerned with these men's fates, screen time is spent on an understandable but largely inept attempt to create back stories that will provide them with reasons to go out to sea and us with reasons to care if they come back or not.

For the Andrea Gail's Capt. Billy Tyne (Clooney), who apparently went out to fish on that trip because fishing is what he did, the film clumsily concocts an added incentive in the form of a challenge to his manhood by the ship's owner, who needles Billy for his lack of productivity until the captain snaps, "I'm gonna bring you more fish than you ever dreamed of."

As for the Andrea Gail's crew, all of whom need the money an extra trip to the Grand Banks fishing grounds would provide, they are given the equivalent of cuddly stuffed animals back home. New guy Bobby Shatford (a convincing Mark Wahlberg, who grew up scant miles from Gloucester) has an intense relationship with Christina Cotter (Diane Lane, effective as always). The divorced Murph (John C. Reilly) has a small son he's devoted to. Alfred Pierre (Allen Payne) has an inexhaustible string of girlfriends. Even the loveless Bugsy (John Hawkes) contrives to meet a woman just before the ship departs.

"The Perfect Storm" also provides numerous "is this trip necessary?" premonitions from everyone from Linda Greenlaw (Mary Elizabeth Mastrantonio), a friendly rival captain, to Bobby's mother, who says, "The Grand Banks are no joke in October" with a straight face. And as rushed as the men are to get out to sea, there's still time for a completely silly "You're a god --- sword-boat captain, is there anything better in the world?" elegy to his profession by Capt. Billy. Aye, aye to that, sir.

These flimsy constructs turn out to be more irritating than necessary. We'd care about Saddam Hussein in the grip of this storm of storms, a meeting of three independent weather systems that causes an amazed TV meteorologist to say, in tones usually reserved for horror and science-fiction films, "Oh my God, it's happening."

Once the maelstrom hits, "The Perfect Storm" smartly goes back and forth between the Andrea Gail and Capt. Billy, acting more and more like a defiant Ahab the stronger the storm gets, and the smaller Satori, a sloop embarked on what it innocently thought would be a pleasure cruise to Bermuda.

The Satori's story is especially potent because it involves a Coast Guard rescue ship and the awesome Air National Guard rescue junipers, remarkable individuals who voluntarily leap out of cozy helicopters into rolling pitch-black seas to save lives. Their exploits are the most nerve-racking "The Perfect Storm" provides and probably deserve a film of their own.

The storm of the title is as awesome as it is, with destructive torrents of water and waves that look as big as the Chrysler Building, because of director Petersen's great gift (remember "Das Boot") for physical verisimilitude, not to mention the interaction of men in confined spaces.

Also, the film benefits from the way it combines traditional and modern special effects. Most of the filming was done on the largest sound-stage tank in the world, 100 feet by 95 feet and 22 feet deep, with a full-sized ship attached to motion-inducing gimbals. Then the genies at ILM, led by visual effects supervisor Stefen Fangmeier, added whatever computer-generated imagery was necessary to make things seem super-real. So real, in fact, that survivors of the film may conclude that leaving the house in a heavy drizzle is way too much of a risk.

NEW YORK, 7/10/00, p. 51, Peter Rainer

The Perfect Storm, directed by Wolfgang Petersen and written by William Wittliff (based on the Sebastian Junger nonfiction best-seller), has an impressive assortment of computer-generated monstro-waves and lots of hollering between shipmates trying to be heard above the crash of those waves. The film is about what happened, or may have happened, when a swordfishing boat departing in the fall of 1991 from Gloucester, Massachusetts, ran into perhaps the biggest storm in modern marine history. George Clooney is the skipper whose crew includes Mark Wahlberg and John C. Reilly, and you can literally see his thin dark beard go grayish as the waves start to hit. He's the kind of hard-bitten guy who feels the need to explain that he's "never good at doing things the way they were meant to be done." Of course. If he were, there wouldn't be a movie.

There's practically no way to respond to *The Perfect Storm* except as spectacle. The filmmakers are so intent on setting up the fishing trip as a heroic-mythic quest that they shortchange the more obvious question of why these men would risk so much for thrills and pride and a paycheck when, with far less difficulty, they could have made their way to safety. The audience, with good reason, is much more conflicted in the end about this voyage than the crew, and so we are put in the unfortunate position of feeling superior to these men. Heroism without much of an undercurrent—that's what this movie is selling. Pyrrhic gestures work best when the gestures don't appear to be so dunderheaded.

NEW YORK POST, 6/30/00, p. 43, Lou Lumenick

This is one perfectly terrifying movie, an instant classic. Based on Sebastian Junger's best seller about the October 1991 "Storm of the Century," it brilliantly captures the fearsome majesty of a sea with 100-foot waves.

Computer-generated effects, location shooting and studio tank shots are blended so seamlessly—and to such utterly visceral effect—that this adaptation of Junger's best seller will have you on the edge of your seat for nearly two hours.

Buoying this white-knuckle ride are beautifully understated, Oscar-caliber performances by George Clooney and Mark Wahlberg as fishermen waging the fight of their lives.

Clooney is Billy Tyne, the down-on-his-luck captain of the Andrea Gail, a swordfishing boat out of Gloucester, Mass. Billy needs to make a big score to hold onto his boat—and he pushes the envelope by heading into a very remote area of open sea called the Flemish Cap in search of fish.

He finds swordfish aplenty, but then the ship's ice machine breaks down. The only way to bring the fish to market—and make a killing—is to gamble by running the boat straight through a "perfect" storm formed by the rare confluence of a hurricane and two other weather systems.

Meanwhile, a Coast Guard helicopter is attempting an extremely risky rescue from a sailboat caught in the storm—a heart-stopping sequence that more than justifies the price of admission on its own—even as its pilots risk having to ditch their craft because of its the near-impossibility of mid-air refueling during 120-mph winds.

But "The Perfect Storm" is much more than a $120 million special-effects machine.

Fleshing out Junger's often highly speculative narrative, screenwriter William Wittliff (TV's "Lonesome Dove") etches such memorable portraits of the Andrea Gail's crew and their women before they set out that we care deeply about their fates.

Besides Clooney's gruff captain (the best role he's ever played) and Mary Elizabeth Mastrantonio as a friendly rival captain, the huge, extremely well-chosen cast includes a terrific

Wahlberg as Bobby, a younger man looking for one last score before settling down with the love of his life Christina (Diane Lane).

There's also the incomparable John C. Reilly ("Magnolia") as the bearish Murph, who yearns for reconciliation with his estranged wife and son; William Fichtner as a last-minute replacement who Murph despises; Allen Payne as Alfred Pierre, the crew's sole black member; and John Hawkes as Bugsy, a lovable loser who finally finds a woman (Rusty Schwimmer) to wait for him.

What could have seemed soap opera-ish in less capable hands proves to be tremendously moving under the helm of director Wolfgang Petersen, who returns to the ocean for the first time since his submarine classic "Das Boot."

There are long stretches with little or no dialogue—stage star Cherry Jones, in a relatively small part as one of the sailboat crew (Karen Allen and Bob Gunton are the others) says more with one terrified glance out a porthole than many actors could accomplish in a two-minute scene.

The movie brilliantly conveys why swordfishing is one of the most dangerous occupations in the world: before the storm even hits, we see a shark attack, a crew member snagged by a hook and dragged underwater and the boat nearly swamped by a rogue wave.

"The Perfect Storm" is a see-worthy epic in the same league as "Jaws" and "Titanic."

NEWSDAY, 6/30/00, Part II/p. B3, John Anderson

They die.

Die die die die die.

Of course they die. The focus of Sebastian Junger's 1997 book, a gripping, enormously popular piece of pure reportage, is the Gloucester swordfisher Andrea Gail, which disappeared with barely a trace around Halloween, 1991, amid one of the most ferocious storms on record. It takes a certain gall to make a movie out of a blockbuster like Junger's and then ask people to keep the ending a secret. From whom? The one potential ticket-buyer who lives in a terrarium? Junger's already told the story on every talk show in existence; a night hasn't gone by recently that some synergistic TV report hasn't barnacled itself to the "Perfect Storm" hype machine. All the wishful thinking in the world isn't going to make it otherwise.

But wishful thinking is at the heart of "The Perfect Storm"—a special-effects tour de force, if a rather shallow study of character. Sure, we want Captain Billy Tyne (George Clooney) to somehow snatch victory from the watery jaws of death. We want ardent lovers Bobby Shatford (Mark Wahlberg) and Chris Cotter (Diane Lane) reunited back in Gloucester ("Glawstuh"). And we want Dale Murphy (John C. Reilly) to get home to his son and ex-wife, maybe even make a family again.

But far stronger than our yearning is the burning desire on the part of the filmmakers to have changed the story. So we get about eight endings, each one a progressively cruel false victory, each one accompanied by James Horner's strident score (which swells more than any sea), each one corroding the nobility Junger bestowed on his lost souls, by never supposing anything.

Tragedy has never been subordinate to comedy in the history of theater—tragedy is ennobling, poignant and essential. And within the conflict of "The Perfect Storm" is the germ of classic tragedy—man defeated by his own hubris, defying nature and perishing. But Hollywood has such an allergy to unhappy endings, you're surprised they didn't bring Junger's real-life victims back from the dead—and the fact they want the ending a secret implies they thought about it.

It was clear in Junger's book that Tyne and his crew were typical of thousands who have fished and died out of Gloucester, an active port since 1623 and the oldest in the country. And Junger manufactured nothing: no "recreated" dialogue aboard the Andrea Gail, no action contrived to make a better read. Everything was fashioned out of interviews with friends, family, survivors of the 1991 storm, survivors of lesser storms. It all might have happened—but didn't necessarily.

Of course, you can't make a movie with Clooney (who should make everyone forget the Mel Gibson version that was originally planned) or Wahlberg (bad rapper, good actor) without giving them something to do. So we get screenwriter Bill Wittliff's on-board melodramatics, which included a near-lethal feud between Murphy and shipmate Sully (William Fichtner), which is resolved in the most cliched fashion, as well as a shark attack, for which Horner lifts a few notes from "Jaws." There's an implied romantic buzz between Billy Tyne and his fellow swordfisher Linda Greenlaw (Mary Elizabeth Mastrantonio) that Mother Nature nips in the bud. And there's a legacy of blame around the Andrea Gail that certainly was missing from the book, but which the producers obviously felt was necessary for dramatic effect.

There are other questionable digressions from Junger's work, none of which would have meant very much if "The Perfect Storm" wasn't caught in its own conflict, between the story that was and the happy ending that might have been. What occurs in the confusion is that the real people of the Andrea Gail become typical movie characters, which is hardly a tribute.

NEWSWEEK, 7/10/00, p 64, David Ansen

Wolfgang Petersen's movie of Sebastian Junger's non-fiction best seller "The Perfect Storm" promises excitement on the high seas, and you can't say it doesn't deliver. Once the sword-fishing boat Andrea Gail runs into heavy weather (about an hour into the story), and the special-effects waves begin to roil, there's little danger you'll be bored. Petersen ("Das Boot," "Air Force One") is an action pro, and he's been given control over all the computer-generated tricks that money can buy. As Hurricane Grace and two other weather fronts collide to generate this legendary 1991 storm, the movie tracks not just the crew of Billy Tyne's (George Clooney) fishing boat but a yacht caught in the treacherous drink, and the astonishing efforts of Air Force and Coast Guard rescue teams to pluck the small crafts three endangered sailors from the jaws of catastrophe.

Oddly, this helicopter rescue turns out to be the most thrilling episode in the film. What's strange is that we have no idea who these three minor characters—or their rescuers—are. It's an indication of what has gone wrong with Petersen's movie, which is at once spectacular and anemic. The discrepancy between the sophistication of the special effects and the rudimentary dramaturgy results in a $140 million film that may raise your blood pressure, but leaves the rest of you distinctly unengaged.

Something feels off from the get-go. The first half hour introduces us to the Andrea Gail's crew, their wives and girlfriends at the Crow's Nest, a Gloucester, Mass., bar, where they work off their tension with booze and sex. Petersen's doom-laden, portentous direction does not allow any of his fine actors (Mark Wahlberg, Diane Lane, John C. Reilly, William Fichtner) any naturalistic wriggle-room. Yes, they have a dangerous job, but the elegiac tone suggests they are going off to war rather than a fishing trip. The only way to explain how peculiarly everyone is acting is that they've all read Junger's book.

The script, credited to Bill Wittliff, is a blunt instrument. "This doesn't look good!" announces the alarmed TV weatherman: a fair indication of the screenplay's finesse. The human element is completely overwhelmed by the movie's need to cattle-prod the audience with regular doses of (often fictionalized) peril—sharks, fishing accidents, titanic waves. "The Perfect Storm" is impersonal Hollywood filmmaking at its most paradoxical. It keeps you glued to your seat, and leaves no aftertaste whatsoever.

SIGHT AND SOUND, 9/00, p. 47, Andrew O'Hehir

Gloucester, Massachusetts, October 1991.   Billy Tyne, captain of the *Andrea Gail, a* swordfishing boat, returns to port with another disappointing catch. Although his crew want to stay home for a while, Billy decides to return to sea to fish the Grand Banks of the north Atlantic. One crewman quits and Billy recruits Sully, an old friend, to join Bobby, Murph, bachelor Bugsy and West Indian ladies' man Alfred Pierre. Fishing is poor on the Grand Banks and Billy heads east to the waters of the Flemish Cap. Murph and Sully fight. Murph is swept overboard in an accident and Sully saves him.

A massive storm brews; a hurricane and two hostile weather fronts collide along the Atlantic seaboard. A Coast Guard helicopter unit saves the crew of a foundering sailboat. When the helicopter crew tries to find the *Andrea Gail,* they run out of fuel and must ditch at sea. Its crew are rescued but one man is lost. Hoping to save the catch after the ice machine fails, Billy decides to drive through the storm back to Gloucester. Realising he can't make it, he attempts to return east. But a huge wave capsizes the *Andrea Gail* and all hands are lost.

A harrowing nautical adventure driven by dazzling special effects and fuelled by equal measures of human folly and heroism, *The Perfect Storm* seems made to order for some old-fashioned Hollywood yarn spinning. It has the peculiar grandeur of a story whose ending we know before it starts; we watch fisherman Billy Tyne's fatal mistakes as if through the eyes of God, or perhaps as Athenian audiences watched *Oedipus Rex*. Early box-office returns suggest that audiences have responded, silencing industry sceptics who doubted the public would flock to such a downbeat story. (Presumably, they forgot about the box-office splash made by *Titanic* and its similarly doomed passengers.)

But for all the commendable work of its cast and crew, *The Secret Storm* is a great tragedy suffocated by tyrannical sentimentality. Sebastian Junger's non-fiction best-seller, on which the film is based, relies principally on ascertainable facts about the North Atlantic storm of 1991 and the fate of the *Andrea Gail;* it doesn't presume to speak for the dead. In contrast, Bill Wittliff's portentously awful screenplay flogs us, from its first lines, with a sense of maudlin predestination (underscored by the weeping and shuddering of James Horner's music).

Never a subtle film-maker, even at his best, director Wolfgang Petersen goes along with Wittliff's programme, from the early shot of the City Hall plaque memorialising Gloucester's lost seamen onwards. Gloucester is evidently the most doleful town on Earth, all foreboding dreams, divorced dads' wrenching goodbyes and worried women gazing at their doomed mariners and murmuring, "The Grand Banks are no joke in October,' or, more directly, "Don't go, Bobby. I got a bad feeling." Then there's Billy's long, lyrical monologue about the route from Gloucester harbour out to sea, delivered to a rival captain and potential love interest: "You know what?" he concludes, "You're a goddamn swordboat captain. Is there anything better in the world?"

Seemingly continuing their on-screen relationship from *Three Kings,* George Clooney, as Tyne, and Mark Wahlberg, as crewman Bobby, are once again exemplars of decent American guyness. Both are appealing and talented actors, and, along with the smashing storm cooked up by Petersen and his technical team, they very nearly make *The Perfect Storm* worthwhile. Clooney is, of course, the restless, twinkling rogue, while Wahlberg, like Russell Crowe in *Gladiator,* thinks only of the woman he left behind. This pattern suggests that Hollywood has rediscovered one of its grossest but most effective axioms: appeal to male audiences with heroes who love the woman they just met, and to female audiences with heroes who love the woman they already know.

There's a squishy, uncomfortable dishonesty to *The Perfect Storm*'s discourse about class and money, and portraying Billy and Bobby as happy-go-lucky salts in worn flannels, grubby anoraks and three-day stubble does nothing to redeem it. Maybe the real Billy Tyne loved his job, but there are surely better things in the world than the choice he apparently faced: becoming either a broke swordboat captain or a dead one. In deciding to sail to the Flemish Cap and then to head directly into the storm, the Billy given us by Wittliff and Petersen briefly seems like an obsessive sea captain in the Ahab and Queeg tradition. But he is played by Clooney, Hollywood's reigning purveyor of sensitive masculinity, after all, and not even his disastrous greed and arrogance can shake the love of his men. In their last moments together on screen, Bobby tells Billy he has made the right decisions; the film-makers apparently do not intend this to be ludicrous. One almost hopes the real Bobby had time for something more along the lines of "Nice work, asshole."

VILLAGE VOICE, 7/11/00, p. 119, J. Hoberman

If *Blood Simple* is forever young, *The Perfect Storm* is instantly old. Wolfgang Petersen's $140 million adaptation of Sebastian Junger's best-selling account of a Gloucester fishing boat lost in the great nor'easter of '91 opens with a squall of anticipatory clichés, busily stowing away human interest to be used once the shit hits the fan—or, rather, the big blue screen.

Captain Billy Tyne (George Clooney) is in a slump. His last catch was a record low, and so, although it's dangerously late in the season, he ships back out for one last job, browbeaten crew in tow. The money is as lousy as the risks are great, and as a long scene in a rowdy fishermen's bar makes clear, the romance of the sea is a less potent hook than working-class heroism and everyday aspiration. The filmmakers are particularly anxious to make sure we understand that Bobby Shatford (Mark Wahlberg) and Christina Cotter (Diane Lane) are more than the town's hottest couple. These are lovers whose transcendent passion would make that of Leo and Kate seem a fickle flirtation.

The barroom scene is full of portents, and the omens continue once Captain Billy takes the *Andrea Gail* back out. A stray shark grabs Bobby's leg; another member of the crew gets yanked overboard with a hook through his hand; a "rogue wave" knocks the old tub on its keister. Meanwhile, even as the *Andrea Gail* heads east of the Grand Banks toward what's colorfully known as the Flemish Cap (a place where, as one old salt informs the bar, there's "lots of fish and lots of weather"), an inexplicable sailboat, *Mistral,* is turning somersaults in a hurricane off Bermuda and the TV weatherman tracking events in the North Atlantic is gleefully predicting "a disaster of epic proportions."

Given that *The Perfect Storm* is a relatively concise 129 minutes, we don't have to wait too long for the action-which, for my money, is marginally more fun than the lugubrious slaughter offered by its July 4th rival, *The Patriot.* The *Andrea Gail* heads right into the mad vortex of the colliding storm systems and then has to execute the "turnaround of all time." Still, *The Perfect Storm* rains on its own parade. Clooney has less authority than attitude as the foolhardy captain, while the largely convincing effects are somewhat weakened by a puzzling slackness in the crosscutting between the two boats, various rescue vehicles, and their respective maelstroms.

Although *The Perfect Storm* is based on one of the most widely read nonfiction books of the past few years, Warners has requested that the press not reveal the film's ending. Suffice to say that the big "You'll Never Walk Alone" conclusion of *Carousel,* to cite an earlier exercise in the New England mawkish, is dry-eyed by comparison.

Also reviewed in:
CHICAGO TRIBUNE, 6/30/00, Friday/p. A, Michael Wilmington
NATION, 7/24/00, p. 43, Stuart Klawans
NEW YORK TIMES, 6/30/00, p. E1, Stephen Holden
NEW YORKER, 7/10/00, p. 77, Anthony Lane
VARIETY, 6/26-7/9/00, p. 21, Todd McCarthy
WASHINGTON POST, 6/30/00, p. C1, Rita Kempley
WASHINGTON POST, 6/30/00, Weekend/p. 43, Desson Howe

PIECE OF EDEN, A

A Film Acres/GS Entertainment/RGH/Lions Share Pictures release of a Film Acres production. *Executive Producer:* Robert J. Hiler.   *Producer:* John Hancock.   *Director:* John Hancock. *Screenwriter:* Dorothy Tristan.   *Director of Photography:* Misha Suslov.   *Editor:* Christopher S. Baird, Michael Benson, and Dennis M. O'Connor.   *Music:* Angelo Badalamenti. *Sound:* James Thornton.   *Sound Editor:* Mark Choi, Perry Robertson, and Frederick H. Stahly. *Casting:* Susan Willett.   *Art Director:* Wendy Jo Martin.   *Set Decorator:* Kathy Glesser, Vi Krentz, and Jeannette Washluske.   *Special Effects:* Mike Menzel.   *Costumes:* Rochelle Zaltzman.   *Make-up:* Jeni Zaharian.   *Stunt Coordinator:* Gary Jensen.   *Running time:* 106 minutes.   *MPAA Rating:* Not Rated.

CAST: Marc Grapey (Bob Tredici);   Robert Breuler (Franco Tredici);   Jeff Puckett (Greg Tredici);   Rebecca Harrell (Happy Buchanan);   Tyne Daly (Aunt Aurelia);   Frederic Forrest (Paulo Tredici); Tristan Rogers (Victor Hardwick); Andrea Katsulas (Giuseppi Tredici); Irma St. Paule (Maria at 90); Marshall Efron (Andres);   Julia Swart (Claire Tredici);   Regnin Altay (Maria at 30);   Lara Phillips (TV Reporter);   Jeannette Washluske (Nurse);   James Ferguson (Teenage Franco); Tracy Lopresto (Bob's Mother);   Jesse Giuliani (Young Franco);   Kevin Hundt (Young Paulo); Aknnastecia Spano (Young Aurelia);   Matthew T. Mender (Bob at 9); Kiva Wenig (Bob at 4); Brittany Miser (Nikki);   Christian Porod (Anthony);   Beth Behler (Mr. Hardwick's Assistant); Mary Wagner (Mrs. Hofmeister);   Claudette Harrison (Hofmeister's Daughter);   Glenn Hutchinson (Farm Salesman);   Don Varda (Computer Delivery Man);   Jim Quartuccio (Chauffeur);   Brooks B. Barnes (Fish Truck Driver);   Diana Glasgow (Shirley); Theresa Bowen (Female Fan);   Colleen Davenport (Female Customer);   Ted Grice (Male Customer); James R. Lewis (Big Jack Hurley);   Jake Christner (Teenage Paulo);   Brandi Keehn (Teenage Aurelia).

NEW YORK POST, 9/15/00, p. 54, V. A. Musetto

John Hancock, best known for the 1973 hit "Bang the Drum Slowly," directs this sentimental comedy about a New York yuppie (Marc Grapey) who returns to Indiana to take over the family farm after his dad is injured in an accident.

He brings along his daffy secretary, Happy, to pretend she's his pregnant wife. Seems Dad wants a "family man" to inherit the business.

There's more sap here than in anything since Frank Capra called it quits. There's even a steal from his classic "It Happened One Night."

Still, it is hard to dislike such a wholesome, well-meaning movie, which has some very funny moments and a lovable cast.

Our fave is pixieish Rebecca Harrell as Happy. She's a star waiting to be discovered.

VILLAGE VOICE, 9/19/00, p. 120, Edward Crouse

Mushy and musty itself, *A Piece of Eden* takes an eternity—this time to cheat and shortcut its way to lesser Frank Capra moments without the gritty touch of, say, a Garry Marshall. It starts with a schlubby New York publicist watching a clock in his office, an act that a viewer is likely to take up. Very soon, with his secretary, Happy, in questionable, sleazy tow, he's gone to find himself by making up with an ailing dad during apple blossom time. *A Piece of Eden* unfolds in an alternate universe where glazed Hallmark nuggets—magical-realist Corsican grandfather revisitations, Happy smeared in homey honey, a folksy cherry-spitting contest that seems to take an hour—are served ad nauseam and eventually sew themselves into a suffocating quilt.

Also reviewed in:
CHICAGO TRIBUNE, 4/21/00, Friday/p. H, John Petrakis
NEW YORK TIMES, 9/15/00, p. E24, Dave Kehr
VARIETY, 10/9-15/00, p. 24, Robert Koehler

PITCH BLACK

A USA Films release of a Gramercy Pictures presentation of an Interscope Communications production. *Executive Producer:* Ted Field, Scott Kroopf, and Anthony Winley. *Producer:* Tom Engelman. *Director:* David Twohy. *Screenplay:* Jim Wheat, Ken Wheat, and David Twohy. *Story:* Ken Wheat and Jim Wheat. *Director of Photography:* David Eggby. *Editor:* Rick Shaine. *Music:* Graeme Revell. *Music Editor:* Josh Winget. *Sound:* Paul "Salty" Brincat and (music) Mitch Zelenzy. *Sound Editor:* Robert Shoup. *Casting:* Ann Robinson. *Production Designer:* Graham "Grace" Walker. *Art Director:* Ian Gracie. *Set Designer:* Jacinta Leong and Martin Ash. *Set Decorator:* Michael Rumpf. *Set Dresser:* Scott McMaster. *Special Effects:* Brian Cox. *Visual Effects:* Peter Chang. *Creatures Designer:* Patrick Tatopoulos. *Costumes:* Anna Borghesi. *Make-up:* Margaret Stevenson. *Stunt Coordinator:* Chris Anderson. *Running time:* 107 minutes. *MPAA Rating:* R.

CAST: Vin Diesel (Riddick); Radha Mitchell (Fry); Cole Hauser (Johns); Keith David (Imam); Lewis Fitz Gerald (Paris); Claudia Black (Shazza), Rhiana Griffith (Jack/Jackie); John Moore (Zeke); Simon Burke (Owens); Les Chantery (Suleiman); Sam Sari (Hassan); Firass Dirani (Ali); Ric Anderson (Total Stranger); Vic Wilson (Captain); Angela Makin (Dead Crew Member).

LOS ANGELES TIMES, 2/18/00, Calendar/p. 18, Kevin Thomas

"Pitch Black," a routine sci-fi/horror action-adventure, takes us where we've been countless times before—a forbidding distant planet—and offers nothing new along the way. Director David Twohy, who co-wrote the script with Jim and Ken Wheat, seems to understand this because he brings maximum razzle-dazzle and energy to the film, which is certainly the way to go with such trite material, even if ultimately a flashy technique is not enough.

Twohy does have an ace in the hole in his star, Vin Diesel, a tall, New York-based actor who has an intelligence and authority to match his imposing physical presence. Without Diesel, "Pitch Black" wouldn't be worth watching.

Diesel's Riddick is a smart, cynical and decidedly dangerous prisoner who's had a "surgical shine on my eyeballs" that makes them glow in the dark—don't ask why. He's in the custody of Johns (Cole Hauser), a self-proclaimed lawman with a macho swagger and drawl. They are among the passengers aboard a spacecraft that pilot Fry (Radha Mitchell) is forced to crash-land on a desert-like planet with three suns to keep the temperature scorching.

The small group come upon an abandoned laboratory complex, where Fry discovers one of those models of the cosmos suggesting that as blindingly bright as the sunlight is now, a total eclipse is in the offing—precisely the most dangerous circumstances for Riddick. Meanwhile, the whole party comes to the realization that, predictably enough, They Are Not Alone!

Shot in the Queensland, Australia, outback, "Pitch Black" is as relentlessly efficient as it is mechanical, and its steadfast craftsmanship may make it acceptable to die-hard sci-fi fans. Its appeal, however, is limited because of its blah characters—with the exception of Riddick—and almost total absence of humor. As a result, "Pitch Black's" biggest plus is to serve as a calling card for Diesel, who made a strong impression in "Saving Private Ryan" and as the voice of "The Iron Giant," and who's clearly ready to carry bigger and better projects.

NEW YORK POST, 2/18/00, p. 55, Jonathan Foreman

"Pitch Black" is essentially a mediocre but nonetheless entertaining copy of the "Alien" films, with the action transferred from a leaky and rusty spaceship to a spectacular desert planet that becomes a killing ground when night falls.

With their shark's-fin heads, the nasty creatures that prey on the human heroes in "Pitch Black" even look like the ones from the "Alien" franchise—crossed with raptors from "Jurassic Park." The main difference is that these monsters can fly, and they don't like the light.

A space freighter crash-lands on the planet, killing the captain. Among the survivors, who must form a team despite their differences, are the pilot Fry (Radha Mitchell), lawman Johns (Cole Hauser) and Riddick (Vin Diesel), the convicted murderer in his charge.

Once it becomes clear that only Riddick's lethal, prison-honed talents can protect the castaways from the aliens, these three vie for leadership of a rapidly diminishing group that includes a couple of Australian geologists and a Muslim priest (Keith David).

There are also some young acolytes and a persnickety, effeminate antique dealer (Lewis Fitz-Gerald) who seems to be channeling Dr. Smith from "Lost in Space."

By far the best thing about "Pitch Black" is the cool-looking lighting and photography.

Director David Twohy plays lots of inventive and effective "Three Kings"-style tricks with filters and different kinds of film stock to make the burning planet with its three suns look properly strange and otherworldly.

Diesel is compelling in a one-note role as a deep-voiced psychopath with a good heart buried beneath his huge muscles, and it's always a pleasure to watch talented Aussie actors like Mitchell (so good in "Love and Other Catastrophes" and "High Art") and Claudia Black (from TV's "Farscape"), who plays a tough miner.

On the other hand, with the exception of Mitchell, those members of the Australian cast who are supposed to be doing American accents don't always pull it off.

Unfortunately, the shaky accents are a minor fault compared with the clunky lines everyone has to deliver.

NEWSDAY, 2/19/00, Part II/p. B7, Jan Stuart

Keep your eye on the skinhead. He's a killer. He sports black goggles over mercury-glazed eyes. His tank-top shirt flatters a chest that has been bench-pressed to within an inch of its life. He speaks with a gravel-throated insolence that seems to have been cultivated in the bad-boy neighborhood of Eric Bogosian. He's out for blood, and you gotta love him.

In timeless Hollywood tradition, the bad guy steals the show in "Pitch Black," a sci-fi action thing that delivers the goods with breakneck velocity and road-warrior force. The thief of the hour is the aptly named bruiser Vin Diesel, starring as Riddick, an escaped convict who menaces the passengers and crew of a spaceship that has crash-landed on an arid, nightless planet.

Chief among the survivors in this land with three suns and one water fountain are Australian actress Radha Mitchell, doing the Sigourney Weaver bit as the tough-as-nails crew leader; pretty-boy Cole Hauser as a truculent mercenary; Keith David as an imam with a retinue of Muslim followers: Lewis Fitz-Gerald as an effete antiquarian and Rhiana Griffith as a runaway punk teenager.

We never entirely understand why this motley crew is gathered on this aircraft, but we don't have much time to think about it as they defend themselves against the slithery Riddick and a battery of creatures that thrive on darkness. An eclipse offers all the encouragement these creepy-crawlies need. Once the lights go out, "Pitch Black" becomes a field day for fans of things that go chomp in the night.

Director David Twohy ("The Arrival") seems to appreciate that if there is anything scarier than squiggly monsters, it is squiggly monsters you can barely glimpse. Twohy and editor Rick Shaine floor the goosebump pedal with fleet cutting, combined with some crafty nocturnal lighting. If the landscape gives you that old deja vu feeling, it's because you're seeing the same Australian desert used in "Mad Max." Cameraman David Eggby lends the terrain an extraterrestrial spin with excellent overexposed photography.

Where "Pitch Black" falls off is in the predictable arc of its body count and a twist on the sexual identity of one of its characters that was so thuddingly obvious from the outset as to elicit hoots of laughter from the audience. But there are dandy visual effects galore and that prowling murderer with the East Village sex appeal. Vin Diesel, indeed.

SIGHT AND SOUND, 8/00, p. 54, Daniel Etherington

Space, the future. A spaceship is hit by fragments of cosmic debris and crashes on a desert planet. Pilot Fry, bounty hunter Johns, and his captive, Riddick, are among the survivors. When a survivor is found dead, Riddick is blamed. Fry stumbles across a cave where she escapes being killed by alien creatures.

In a deserted camp, Riddick concludes that the planet's last human inhabitants were all killed when an eclipse occurred. The resourceful Shazza repairs a solar-powered vehicle which allows the group to transfer fuel cells from their ship to a craft at the camp. As they head off, an eclipse begins. A swarm of flying creatures kills Shazza. Riddick, whose eyes are altered for night vision, sees larger creatures fill the sky before the group retreat to the crashed ship.

With the vehicle useless, the group carry the fuel cells, using lights to keep the creatures—which can only survive in darkness—at bay. Antiquarian Paris accidentally destroys the main light source. Johns proposes to use Jack, a female passenger, as a decoy. Riddick and Johns fight; the bounty hunter loses and is killed by a creature. Fry, Muslim holy man Iman and Jack take shelter, Riddick presses on without them. Fry follows using phosphorescent bugs for light and convinces Riddick to help the others. Fry is killed but the rest escape.

From its shipwreck-in-space scenario, which recalls *Robinson Crusoe on Mars* (1964), to its throngs of vicious cave-dwelling aliens, which bring to mind the deadly insect-like creatures in *Starship Troopers*, *Pitch Black* plays like an amalgamation of some of the most familiar tropes in science-fiction film. The film's clearest stylistic debt, though, is to the *Alien* series, and its hybrid of horror and sci-fi. Not only do Patrick Tatopoulos' creatures, which pick off the survivors of the crashed spacecraft, resemble H. R. Giger's razor-toothed predators, but pilot Fry's reluctant, ultimately fearless brand of heroism follows the template set by Ripley in *Alien* and its three sequels.

David Twohy (who made good use of a low budget on his debut, the sci-fi film *The Arrival* directs with a vigour that compensates for *Pitch Black*'s more derivative elements. just as *Alien*'s shadowy *mise en scène* tantalised us with glimpses of its monster, *Pitch Black* initially holds back from showing us its predatory creatures (the first victim is killed off screen). Indeed, this stock horror device, which plays on our desire to see all against our wish to be spared the gore, is given a twist by the nocturnal nature of the attacking aliens. (In the best horror traditions, the characters are at their most vulnerable when the lights fail.) When not shrouded in darkness, the Australian locations are given a subtle sense of otherworldliness by production designer Graham Walker (who gave the cutback a futuristic makeover in *Mad Max Beyond Thunderdome*).

Pitch Black features some lovingly crafted effects—notably director of photography David Eggby's bleached colour palette—and some vivid characterisation. There's an intriguing moral ambiguity, for instance, which surrounds convicted murderer Riddick. With his opaque, inscrutable eyes (Riddick has enhanced night vision), gravelly intonation and reluctance to look after anyone but himself, Vin Diesel's Riddick puts you in mind of the lone, ungiving figures of films by Sam Peckinpah and Sergio Leone. Though some sexual frisson between this consummate outsider and Fry is introduced, Twohy refuses to soften Riddick's hardened exterior, thereby imbuing this predictable plot turn with an uneasy charm of its own.

VILLAGE VOICE, 2/22/00, p. 144, Justine Elias

A spaceship crash-lands on a harsh desert planet. Who among the survivors will emerge as the natural leader? The obnoxious, brutal cop (Cole Hauser), the brawny imam (Keith David), or the ruthless criminal (Vin Diesel)? In the future posited by *Pitch Black,* things really have progressed, because everybody falls into line behind the copilot, Fry (Rad Mitchell), who wears the de rigueur action heroine costume (tank top) but looks about as fierce as the toughest seventh grader on a suburban school bus. Resourceful as Fry is, though, she's uncomfortable in her new role—particularly when the planet's *Mad Max*-like landscape, thought to be uninhabited, suddenly turns treacherous. The hapless humans have aroused the wrath of something weird and hungry.

Director David Twohy, who made the aliens-among-us thriller *The Arrival* keeps things moving, even if the screenplay (by Twohy and Jim and Ken Wheat) doesn't contain many surprises about who among the Red Shirt victim-class will get chomped. Just as *Pitch Black* begins to seem tiresome familiar, things change: The lights go out, thanks to a welcome lift from Isaac Asimov's *Nightfall,* and the balance of power among the survivors begins to shift. Mitchell, who was so effective in *High Art,* seems to be struggling with her character's contradictions, while her more charismatic costar Claudia Black (of the Sci-Fi Channel's *Farscape*) doesn't get to do much. The real marvel of *Pitch Black*—aside from the eerie, burnt-orange light shining from the planet's trio of suns—is Diesel, whose voice seems to be emanating from some scary sci-fi sub-basement. (Voicing the title character in *The Iron Giant* can't have been much of a stretch.) His Riddick, a silver-eyed, musclebound escape killer, is the most sequel-worthy sci-fi creation since the Terminator.

Also reviewed in:
CHICAGO TRIBUNE, 2/18/00, Friday/p. H, Barbara Shulgasser
NEW YORK TIMES, 2/18/00, p. E12, Stephen Holden
VARIETY, 2/14-20/00, p. 40, Emanuel Levy
WASHINGTON POST, 2/18/00, Weekend/p. 47, Desson Howe

PLACE VENDÔME

An Empire Pictures release of an Alhenia/Studio Canal Plus/Les Films Alain Sarde/Studio Images 3/TF1 Films co-production. *Executive Producer:* Christine Gozlan and Alain Sarde. *Director:* Nicole Garcia. *Screenplay (French with English subtitles):* Nicole Garcia and Jacques Fieschi. *Director of Photography:* Laurent Dailland. *Editor:* Luc Bannier and Françoise Bonnot. *Music:* Richard Robbins. *Choreographer:* Chris Gandois. *Sound:* Jean-Pierre Duret, Dominique Hennequin, and (music) Didier Lizé. *Sound Editor:* Marie-Christine Ratel, Cécile Ranc, and Emmanuele Lalande. *Production Designer:* François Menny. *Set Designer:* Thierry Flamand. *Costumes:* Nathalie du Roscoat and Elisabeth Tavernier. *Make-up:* Cédric Gérard and Sylvie Duval. *Running time:* 105 minutes. *MPAA Rating:* Not Rated.

CAST: Catherine Deneuve (Marianne Malivert); Emmanuelle Seigner (Nathalie); Jean-Pierre Bacri (Jean-Pierre);   Jacqués Dutronc (Battistelli);   Bernard Fresson (Vincent Malivert); François Berléand (Eric Malivert); Dragan Nikolic (Janos); Otto Tausig (Samy Balin); Laszlo Szabo (Charlie Rosen); Elisabeth Commelin (Pierson); Philippe Clévenot (Kleiser); Eric Ruf (Philippe Terence); Nidal Al-Ashkar (Saliha); Larry Lamb (Christopher Makos); Julian Fellowes (Wajman); Michael Culkin, Nick Ellworth, and Antoine Blanqueforth (De Beers Men); Coralie Seyrig and Carmen Roman (Malivert Shop Assistants); Martine Erhel (Louise); Arnaud Xainte, Aristide Demonico, and Paolo Capisano (Malivert Employees); Germaine Labarthe (Shop Customer); Eric Landau (Diamond Expert); James Oliver (Advocate); Sylvie Flepp, Hélène Otternaud, and Saliha Fellahi (Clinic Nurses); Pierre Mottet (Doctor); Michel Huby, Paul Chevillard, and Catherine Cretin (Dinner Guests); Delphine Blamont (Chambermaid at the Ritz); Pierre-Jean Le Gregan (Bellhop); Pascal Renault (Hunter); Myikhaël Georges-Schar (Hilton Concierge); Phillippe Giblin (Jean-Pierre's Assistant); Arno Feffer (Musician Behind with the Rent); Cécile Camp (Musician's Wife); Rahal Jawahir (Mini-Market Manager); Mehdi Mengal (Manager's Son); Jean-Claude Perrin (Priest); Albert Goldberg (Poker Player); Georges David and Henri Leon Bakon (Samy's Friends); Beatrice Demachy (Rosen's Secretary); Jacques Michel (Kleiser's Associate); Patrick Colucci (Café Manager); Paul Kawan (Broker at Antwerp Exchange).

LOS ANGELES TIMES, 9/8/00, Calendar/p. 8, Kevin Thomas

"Place Vendome" takes its title from one of the most elegant public squares in the world. In the heart of Paris, it is framed by superb 18th century buildings, many of them housing ultra-luxe jewelry stores. One of the most prestigious is Malivert et Cie., but it's quietly crumbling behind its ornate facade. Vincent Malivert (Bernard Fresson), its stocky, 60ish proprietor facing bankruptcy, has been humiliated by De Beers for having allowed a huge uncut diamond stolen from them to pass through his hands.

Actually it has stayed with him, secretly cut into several spectacular gems and secreted in his home. He shows the jewels to his alcoholic wife Marianne (Catherine Deneuve), just back from being dried out for the umpteenth time at an exclusive clinic. Already Marianne is slipping back to the bottle, but he sees no way out but to end his life.

This complex, sophisticated and increasingly suspenseful tale of love and betrayal, intrigue and redemption, is as elegant as its star and its settings. It is the third film as director (and in this instance, co-writer, with the veteran Jacques Fieschi) for the exquisite actress Nicole Garcia, and it's tailor-made for Deneuve, who has yet another demanding role as a woman convincingly emerging from an alcoholic haze to regain control of her life and destiny.

The fire and glow of those magnificent diamonds rekindle Marianne's spirit. No, she is not going to try to save the family firm, although she's not about to rubber-stamp its sale to a Bombay-based conglomerate, a deal engineered by her brother-in-law (Francois Berleand), who does not bother to hide his contempt for her drinking. But in going forward with her life Marianne finds herself confronting her past and her drinking, which had so impaired her from seeing her husband's desperate state.

As part of her plan of action she reaches out to Nathalie (Emmanuelle Seigner), one of Vincent's most ambitious staffers. Marianne sees herself in Nathalie and would like to save her from the mistakes she herself made. Indeed, the crucial man in Marianne's past, the shadowy and unscrupulous Battistelli (Jacques Dutronc), has taken the same role in Nathalie's life. The man Nathalie has just left, the dark, intense Jean-Pierre (Jean-Pierre Bacri), a disbarred lawyer turned repo man, has just started pursuing Marianne professionally—and, inevitably, romantically. Meanwhile, Russian Mafiosi want to get their hands on those diamonds in Marianne's possession.

Garcia manages to get all this plot to emerge from her well-drawn characters, to create a fatalistic atmosphere of romance and danger and to offer an adult reflection on the interplay of character and emotion in the conduct of relationships. "Place Vendome" is also an implicit comment on the need of women, in youth and maturity, to break free from men who would control and exploit them; but Garcia plays fair: A man may be as capable of self-sacrifice as a woman.

This is a rich, dense film, its bits and pieces gradually coming together with clarity and allowing the timelessly beautiful Deneuve the range and depth, subtleties and nuances, she demands of her roles and fulfills so glowingly; she won the best actress prize at the Venice Film Festival for her performance. Catherine Deneuve, quite simply, is an enduring glory of world cinema, never resting on her laurels or her looks, seeking always fresh challenges.

NEW YORK, 8/28/00, p. 133, Peter Rainer

Catherine Deneuve plays the alcoholic widow of a debt-ridden diamond merchant in the moody, well-paced *Place Vendôme*, directed by Nicole Garcia, and she's captivatingly seedy. Deneuve has acquired a world-weariness in her recent movies that seems more lived-in than her usual decorous rue. Watching her fill up her glass with the half-filled drinks of others at a party is a sight to behold: She's a radiant slattern slumming in her own sadness. Later, when she becomes involved in a scheme to sell her husband's stolen stash of diamonds, the film turns into a thriller of redemption. Crime, it appears, is good for the soul, and also not a bad way to kick the sauce.

NEW YORK POST, 8/18/00, p. 52, Jonathan Foreman

"Place Vendome" is a labored, remarkably crude attempt to make one of those grown-up, noirish psychological thrillers the French were so good at back in the 1970s and early '80s.

But where those films (like Claude Miller's "Garde a Vue") were smart and subtle, this one is mostly heavy-handed, predictable and almost completely unbelievable.

Its lugubrious tone is supposed to evoke a tragic coolness, like a Joan Didion novel; instead you get something that feels both dreary and utterly phony.

To be fair, there are some good scenes, especially in the second half, and it's hard to get less than interesting performances from a cast this good (with the exception, of course, of the beautiful but robotic Emmanuelle Seigner, Roman Polanski's current paramour).

"Place Vendome" centers on the secretive and supposedly glamorous gem business.

Marianne (Catherine Deneuve) is the wrecked, alchoholic wife of top jeweler Malivert (Bernard Fresson). Foolishly, he's been dealing stolen diamonds, and when the folks at the DeBeers cartel (depicted as a shadowy, multilingual London-based cabal) find out, he commits suicide.

After his death, Marianne finds his stash of amazing rocks and, all of a sudden, starts to get herself together. Despite having spent years in a drunken haze, she is able to outwit not just her brother-in-law, who's taken over her husband's firm, but also DeBeers and the Russian mafia.

It's always hard to know who is who and what's going on (bad lighting doesn't help), but Marianne breaks out of her haute-bourgoise world by hooking up with a repo-man (Jean-Pierre Bacri), who happens to be the ex-boyfriend of her husband's mistress, Nathalie (Seigner).

Nathalie is now living with Marianne's own former love, the renegade jewel dealer Battistelli (Jacques Dutronc), who years ago tricked her into taking the rap for an illegal transaction.

There's almost nothing in the film that isn't a cliché: There's corruption and greed behind the elegant facades of fashionable Paris; there's the neurotic upper-middle-class lady who finds herself when confronted by widowhood and adversity; there's the strange bond between wife and mistress.

Worse still, if you think American films have problems depicting the world of work, writer-director Nicole Garcia is so clueless about it—and about the social world of wealthy people—that it's almost laughable.

There's even one of those ludicrous scenes where people drop names of cities—"blah blah New York, blah blah Munich, blah blah Rio"—and you're supposed to think "Ah, the glamorous world of international business."

NEWSDAY, 8/18/00, Part II/p. B10, Jan Stuart

You know the world is taking a turn for the worse when Catherine Deneuve stops wearing diamonds and starts selling them. But here is the embodiment of 14-carat screen elegance, consorting with a host of slippery men as she traipses around kingdom come with a lode of rocks to flog.

In "Place Vendome," Catherine Deneuve gets to be everything filmmakers rarely allow her to be: declass, noisy, vulgar and drunk. She's played psychopathic killers and prostitutes with the best of them, but always with such cool and tasteful reserve one can only imagine she encouraged a better class of people to take up those professions.

You couldn't convince a double-A battery peddler on the subways to go into the diamond trade after Nicole Garcia's "Place Vendome," a dreary tale of intrigue and betrayal among very well-dressed people. Deneuve plays Marianne, a former jewel-trade maven and the dissolute, alcoholic wife of one of the most respected diamond merchants in the business.

Why is she so unhappy? We don't really know at first, but when her husband kills himself amid despair over debts and dirty dealings, she perks up pretty quickly. The drinking stops, and her dormant skills rise to the fore as she tries to unload a small trove of huge (and probably hot) diamonds.

Marianne's efforts bring her into contact with a number of folk who have the word "shady" all but plastered on their kissers, including a repo man named Jean-Pierre (Jean-Pierre Bacri), his ex-girlfriend Nathalie (Emmanuelle Seigner), who is also the top saleswoman in Marianne's husband's business, and a diamond broker named Battistelli (Jacques Dutronc), who is profoundly implicated in Marianne's past.

These are the recurring faces in an overpopulated film that is so convoluted and humorless in the telling, it is all you can do to figure out who is doing what to whom—and if you should care. Deneuve gets down and messy with a self-conscious lack of self-consciousness that alerts us that glamorous actors are Acting. She's always very watchable, but the film around her makes us work much too hard for the privilege.

SIGHT AND SOUND, 8/99, p. 51, Keith Reader

Vincent Malivert directs a jewellery business in Paris' Place Vendôme. His wife Marianne was once an ambitious dealer, but she slid into alcoholism. Vincent's business is riddled with debts and his creditors are closing in. Realising his position is hopeless, he shows the now sober Marianne seven magnificent diamonds he is proposing to hide from his creditors. Vincent's assistant Nathalie is in the process of leaving her lover Jean-Pierre for jewel-dealer Battistelli. Vincent commits suicide, leaving Marianne at the helm of the business but she refuses to surrender the stones to her husband's creditors.

In Antwerp, she discovers Battistelli is also trying to get his hands on them. She and Jean-Pierre become lovers. A flashback reveals that many years ago Marianne had been in love with Battistelli. He used her to pass on some stolen gems and abandoned her, thus precipitating her alcoholism. Marianne makes an appointment to meet Battistelli, ostensibly to sell him the diamonds which the creditors will then discover about his person. She tells Battistelli the creditors are lying in wait for him, and the two flee to Ostend, where they spend a night in separate beds in a hotel room, admitting they were not made for each other. The creditors turn up, tipped off by Battistelli who believes he can negotiate his way out of trouble with them. Later, Marianne is pursued by Jean-Pierre on the beach; she asks if he always runs after women who run from him.

Although she's best known as an actress, Nicole Garcia has directed four feature films including *Place Vendôme*. In *Un week-end sur deux* she drew a superb turn from Nathalie Baye, playing a fraught but powerful woman similar to Garcia's own best-known role in Resnais' *Mon oncle d'Amérique*. Catherine Deneuve here belongs to the same family, giving a performance that ranks as one of the finest of her middle age.

As in André Téchiné's *Ma saison préférée,* the bodily filling-out characteristic of that time of life serves to give her character more gravitas than in many previous incarnations. Eyes and gesture do most of the work—hers is not a verbose role—in her evocation of the iconically named Marianne, whose initial near-catatonia gives way to assertiveness. By the end she is multiply in charge: restored to solvency; capable of dealing with former lovers, whether defaulters from the past (Battistelli) or pursuers in the present (Jean-Pierre); and even (supposedly impossible for a recovering alcoholic) capable of social drinking in moderation. The other performances inevitably tend to look like mere foils to Deneuve's. Emmanuelle Seigner's mannered flouncings irritated this reviewer, but Jacques Dutronc exudes a convincingly disreputable air as Battistelli. Jean-Pierre Bacri deserves credit for his masochistic cragginess, confirming after *Un air de famille* that he has what it takes as actor as well as screenwriter.

But *Place Vendôme* is more than a jewelcase for performers. It is subtly scripted, making discreetly resonant use of doublings: Nathalie with Marianne in her youth; Marianne and the disbarred lawyer Jean-Pierre brought together through a shared professional disgrace; Battistelli and Vincent as respectively treacherous and supportive father figures to their trophy lover/wife. The film also puts on screen a world scarcely seen other than as the backdrop to Jules Dassin's *Du rififi chez les hommes* (1955)—one whose elegance is matched by its menace, rendered all the more sinister by the fact that no gun is drawn and no violence apart from Vincent's suicide takes place on screen. If the complexity of the intrigue and the genre stereotypes evoke the world of *noir*, the decor is at its antipodes—thick carpets, luxuriously panelled rooms, expensive cars. Nor could we be further from the gritty *banlieue* film or the all-gloss *cinéma du look*.

In a curious way *Place Vendôme* has affinities with the heritage movie, reassuring us that the uppermost echelons of Parisian chic—the eponymous square and Catherine Deneuve—are still as potent as before. Garcia deploys her silky men in designer suits sparingly, making the frisson they generate all the more palpable (though the references to the Russian mafia, a seemingly inescapable component of end of-the millennium *noir*, appear clichéd). We see surprisingly little of the city for a largely Paris-set film, reinforcing the sense that the real action is elsewhere in the echoing corridors and suave international train and car journeys of a ruthlessly stylish world.

The colonnaded elegance of the Place Vendôme is a spatial counterpart of Deneuve the ice maiden, but not until the very end do we find an equivalent for her character's fragility issuing in wonderfully understated strength. That is emphasised by the scrubby Ostend dunes of the final sequence, deserted save for Marianne and the limpet-like Jean-Pierre, whose desperate loyalty has provided an ironic counterpart to her development throughout. Altogether, *Place Vendôme* is a film whose performances and settings yield immense pleasure.

VILLAGE VOICE, 8/22/00, p. 134, Amy Taubin

There's a libidinal undertow in *Place Vendôme* that would be Hitchcockian if it weren't so unmistakably female. Director Nicole Garcia and star Catherine Deneuve have created a character unique enough to compensate for the film's narrative deficiencies. Deneuve plays Marianne, an alcoholic middle-aged woman married to the director of a Paris jewelry firm located in an elegant 18th-century building on the Place Vendôme. Behind the facades of houses erected during the Age of Reason, corruption and greed is rampant. When her husband, Vincent (Bernard Fresson), commits suicide, Marianne puts away the bottle and takes control of her life and his company. Once a gem trader herself, Marianne was left by her lover (Jacques Dutronc) to take the rap for a deal involving stolen diamonds. Vincent saved her from jail and later married her, but their relationship infantilized her. Now, with no one to rely on but herself, she rediscovers long-buried resources and desires.

Like the Place Vendôme, the smooth-surfaced, well-appointed Marianne is prey to dangerous impulses within herself. And unlike Hitchcock's heroines, she has a palpable awareness of her lived-in body. Deneuve's performance is remarkably physical—from the angry little shake she gives her head to clear away an alcoholic haze to the way she positions a bare arm so you notice the slight sag in the fullness. As she's aged, Deneuve has lost some of her emotional inhibitions as an actress, but she's never before spilled so much of herself on screen.

What makes Marianne so fascinating is the internal conflict between her self-destructive and her survival impulses. But the film's thriller-styled narrative isn't expansive enough to contain her. Given Marianne's reckless behavior—she walks around Paris openly carrying a fortune in stolen diamonds—you'd think she would be murdered before the film is half over. Hitchcock knew how to camouflage flaws in logic, but Garcia isn't as skillful. Inept as a thriller, *Place Vendôme* nevertheless intrigues.

Also reviewed in:
CHICAGO TRIBUNE, 10/13/00, Friday/p. F, Michael Wilmington and John Petrakis
NEW YORK TIMES, 8/18/00, p. E12, Dave Kehr
VARIETY, 9/14-20/98, p. 36, Lisa Nesselson
WASHINGTON POST, 2/2/01, p. C1, Stephen Hunter
WASHINGTON POST, 2/2/01, Weekend/p. 43, Desson Howe

PLAY IT TO THE BONE

A Touchstone Pictures/Shanghai'd Films release. *Executive Producer:* David Lester. *Producer:* Stephen Chin. *Director:* Ron Shelton. *Screenplay:* Ron Shelton. *Director of Photography:* Mark Vargo. *Editor:* Paul Seydor. *Music:* Alex Wurman. *Music Editor:* Jim Harrison. *Boxing Choreographer:* Darrell Foster. *Sound:* Art Rochester and (music) Michael Verdick. *Sound Editor:* William Jacobs. *Casting:* Kim Coleman and Victoria Thomas. *Production Designer:* Claire Jenora Bowin. *Art Director:* Mary Finn. *Set Designer:* Theodore Sharps. *Set Decorator:* Danielle Berman. *Special Effects:* Gary D'Amico. *Costumes:* Kathryn Morrison. *Make-up:* Steve LaPorte. *Make-up (Woody Harrelson):* Fred C. Blau. *Running time:* 124 minutes. *MPAA Rating:* R.

CAST: Antonio Banderas (Cesar Dominguez); Woody Harrelson (Vince Boudreau); Lolita Davidovich (Grace Pasic); Tom Sizemore (Joe Domino); Lucy Liu (Lia); Robert Wagner (Hank Goody); Richard Masur (Artie); Willie Garson (Cappie Caplan); Cylk Cozart (Rudy); Jack Carter (Dante Solomon); Aida Turturro (Mad Greek Waitress); Louie Leonardo (Freddy Green); Slade Barnett (Vegas Cop); Cameron Milzer (Vegas Paramedic); Julio Garcia (Chiquito Rosario); Johnny Ortiz (Gym Owner); Jordy Oakland (Julie); Will Utay (Sal); Joseph Arsenault (Bobby); Fred Lewis and Maurice Singer (Vegas Lawyers); Robert Sale (Robert Velario); Joe Cortez (Garden Referee); Bruce Buffer (Garden Ring Announcer); Teddy Atlas (Cesar's Garden Trainer); Dana Lee (Man with Ferrai); Rob Ingersoll (Jesus); Robby Robinson (Skeeter Lewis); Mitch Halpern (Vince's Big Fight Referee); Chuck Hull (Vince's Big Fight Ring Announcer); Al Bernstein and Reynaldo Rey (Sportswriters); Eloy Casados (Vince's Trainer); Henry G. Sanders (Cesar's Trainer); Vasil Chuck Bodak (Cesar's Cutman); Jacob "Stitch" Duran (Vince's Cutman); Al Benner (Cesar's Cornerman); Pat Barry (Vince's Cornerman); Steve Lawrence (Himself); George Foreman, Jim Lampley, nd Larry Merchant (HBO Commentators); Mike Tyson (Himself); Darrell Foster (Referee); Michael Buffer (Ring Announcer); Rod Stewart (Himself); Bill Caplan (Dr. Velvil Ginsberg); Marc Ratner (Boxing Commissioner); Jane Broadfoot and Carlos Padilla (Timekeepers); Debbie Caplan and Elizabeth Caplan (Press Assistants); Denise Pernula and Veronica Becerra (Ring Card Girls); Tamara Gibler, Fulvia Sanchez, and Faye Mangabang (Fantasy Girls); Alison Walsh (Bartender); Ana Divac (Grace's Party Friend); Tom Todoroff (Croupier).

LOS ANGELES TIMES, 12/24/99, Calendar/p. 16, Kevin Thomas

Ever since he made his directorial debut with "Bull Durham," Ron Shelton has displayed a winning way of taking us into the contemporary world of sports—even for those whose interest in them is minimal at best. In athletes' lives Shelton finds humor, lust, courage and no small degree of poignancy, and this is especially true of his latest, "Play It to the Bone," a wonderfully entertaining, raunchy, hilarious and savage foray into the lives of a couple of beat-up middleweight boxers who get a second chance.

Woody Harrelson, who got his breakthrough movie role in Shelton's "White Men Can't Jump," and Lolita Davidovich, who played stripper Blaze Starr in Shelton's "Blaze," are joined by Antonio Banderas, in what is arguably his most challenging role ever and perhaps the richest since his collaborations with Pedro Almodovar. They may be cast as a trio of losers, but their performances are certainly winning

Banderas' Cesar is a Madrid-born boxer now out of Philadelphia, living in L.A., where he has become best pals with Harrelson's Vince, a Texas-born fighter and a born-again Christian constantly upbraiding himself for taking the Lord's name in vain. Both guys had a shot at the big time that backfired, and now well into their 30s they're hanging in as sparring partners, but just barely.

When hours before yet another Las Vegas "Fight of the Century" Mike Tyson bout, both fighters on the undercard—the semi-main event—become unavailable, fight promoter Joe Domino (Tom Sizemore) turns to Cesar and Vince as replacements. They're astonished at this quirk of fate but know enough to hold out for title shots for both of them. When the shock wears off—and after Vince bungles negotiations for their price—the friends suddenly realize they will be fighting each other.

The first half of the film is a road movie, with Vince's former girlfriend—and Cesar's current lady—Grace (Davidovich) driving them to Vegas in her spiffy lime-green 1972 Olds convertible. Grace is sharper than the guys, a tireless promoter of self and of an array of "product ideas" for which she is constantly seeking backing. She tells the highly emotional Cesar that their romance is over, but shrewdly sets up both men to do their best when she tells each of them privately that he is the better lover—but lesser fighter.

There's lots of sexy bantering between Grace and both men that intensifies greatly when freewheeling 20-year-old Lia (Lucy Liu) hitches a ride. Lia is an up-front party girl eager to get down night now with Vince, swiftly confronting him with the old bedeviling question of whether or not an athlete should have sex before the big competition.

Awaiting their arrival with tough-guy Domino is a colorful array of henchmen. Suave casino owner Hank Goody (Robert Wagner in another amusing comic role) is a steely operator in a Brioni wardrobe and a well-practiced surface charm. Domino and Goody's key aides are the shrewd, unflappable Rudy (Cylk Cozart) and canny ex-fighter Artie (Richard Masur); their attorney (Jack Carter, in a nifty turn) is not the kind to inspire trust.

Cesar and Vince are in the thrall of a pack of sharks and know it, but we're in good hands, thanks to spot-on performances across the board—and that includes Aida Turturro's warm but take-no-nonsense waitress at a road-side cafe. We're in Damon Runyon land, brought up to speed for a sleeker, utterly ruthless present.

When Cesar and Vince step into the ring "Play It to the Bone" starts living up to its title. This second chance, dubious as it is at best, fires up Cesar and Vince to go all-out. Shelton evokes not the mythical fantasy of "Rocky" but the gritty spirit of George Bellows' classic 1909 painting "Stag at Sharkey's" in capturing the enduring visceral appeal of boxing, exciting in its suspense, deplorable in its brutality. Vince and Cesar go for a lengthy, bloody, old-fashioned slugfest, complete with colorful ring attendants and a celebrity-studded audience who are unexpectedly getting their money's worth.

This match is absolutely convincing, with Banderas and Harrelson and their fight doubles undetectably blended. The entire free-for-all is sustained unflaggingly by Shelton, who uproariously and daringly intermingles Cesar's and Vince's sex fantasies, which wash over them between rounds. Vince starts envisioning as topless the voluptuous, scantily clad women who hold up cards announcing the rounds, while Cesar has flashes of the match's trim referee (Darrell Foster) in the nude.

Yes, you read right. On the ride to Vegas Cesar has casually admitted to a homosexual phase in the wake of his big setback of years before. So maybe the phase isn't entirely over, which allows Shelton to create the sense that anything is possible between Cesar, Vince and Grace by the time he reaches his ending.

"Play It to the Bone" is surely going to be too raw for some audiences, but it does pack a punch, and no small degree of its pleasure is in its assured craftsmanship. Alex Wurman's outstanding score has an elegance that works well for the film, even if elegance may be an unexpected quality for a fight picture. Its songs are uncommonly apt, with "Here's to Life" sounding just the right note under the end titles. By the time the lights go up "Play It to the Bone" has become a love story.

NEW YORK POST, 1/21/00, p. 51, Lou Lumenick

What can you say about a boxing movie in which the most convincing blows are landed by Lolita Davidovich and Robert Wagner—instead of leads Woody Harrelson and Antonio Banderas?

"Play It to the Bone" doesn't have a bad premise. It was inspired by a true story of two best friends, washed-up fighters who get enlisted as last-minute replacements on the undercard for a championship bout.

In writer-director Ron Shelton's enervated, drawn-out version, long-forgotten middleweights Vince Boudreau (Harrelson) and Cesar Dominguez (Banderas) get the frantic call when one fighter dies in a car crash and the other overdoses on drugs—the very day they were scheduled to be the top undercard match on a Mike Tyson fight in Las Vegas.

They agree to fight each other—but only after extracting a promise from sleazy promoter Joe Domino (Tom Sizemore) that the winner will get a title bout with the middleweight champ.

For no logical reason, the duo spend the day driving from Los Angeles to Las Vegas with Grace Pasic (Davidovich)—Vince's ex-girlfriend, who chooses the occasion to inform her current paramour, Cesar, that she's dumping him, too,

This prompts a full 90 minutes of tedious bickering, tiresome reminiscences and lackluster performances as they cross the desert. The sequence includes Cesar's admission that he experimented with homosexuality after a gay fighter ended his career.

The confession prompts a homophobic tirade from Vince, who suffers from religious visions that Shelton thoughtfully shares with the audience.

Things aren't helped much by the arrival of Lia (Lucy Lau of "Ally McBeal"), a sexy young hitchhiker who takes a fancy to Vince—at least until Davidovich demonstrates a better hook than we'll see when Vince and Cesar finally get around to fighting.

This decking prompts one of the film's many groan-worthy observations from the wildly misogynistic Vince: "Any guy with any gal is a mismatch—we're just not equipped to go the distance."

Neither is this movie. The fight scenes are flat and poorly staged, no matter how much the sound of punches is goosed on the soundtrack and how much fake blood is applied to the combatants. The bout—the last round of which is played out in slow-motion—is a bloody bore.

Not even a slew of cameos (an over-the-hill gang that runs the gamut from Steve Lawrence to Rod Stewart) helps much. The brief participation of Kevin Costner is a sad reminder that Shelton once directed the great "Bull Durham" and Wesley Snipes turns up momentarily to represent another far livelier Shelton sports movie, "White Men Can't Jump."

And then there is the venerable Robert Wagner, who has a larger role as the owner of the hotel where the match is being held. He sets out to seduce Grace, an inventor who's trying to sell him a periscope for watching TV in bed.

"I knew Brigitte Bardot" Wagner boasts, trying to impress the younger woman.

"I bet you did," she replies, with timing sadly lacking in most of the movie. He makes a pass, she slaps his face—and he decks her.

That's about as entertaining as "Play It to the Bone" ever gets. Otherwise, it's bone tired.

NEWSDAY, 1/21/00, Part II/p. B2, John Anderson

Director-writer Ron Shelton is obsessed with sports, more precisely its snake-bit losers ("Bull Durham"), fringe dwellers ("White Men Can't Jump") and lunatics ("Cobb"). Like Kevin Costner's golf pro in "Tin Cup," however, Shelton has no idea when to walk a batter, call a timeout or punt. If movies were a chess game, he'd be Jake LaMotta.

Aptly enough, "Play It to the Bone" is about the sensitivity and camaraderie of two guys whose only hope for success is beating each other's brains out. Journeyman Cesar Dominguez (Antonio Banderas) lost his one title bout by being completely, utterly and unquestionably knocked out—an outcome that came as a total surprise to boxing kingpin Joe Domino (Tom Sizemore), resulting in Cesar and his career languishing somewhere on the outskirts of Palookaville.

Cesar's buddy, sparring partner and fellow dreamer, Vince Boudreau (Woody Harrelson), also lost his one big fight, but by a decision so criminal that Vince can't quite get over it. Neither can his career. Both men harbor the wish inevitable to both boxing and boxing movies—one more chance at the title. So when Domino asks if they'll take $50,000 each to fill the undercard on that night's Mike Tyson fight in Las Vegas—one scheduled boxer OD'd; the other was permanently KO'd by a light pole—the guys make a few pathetic attempts to negotiate a better deal, beg Cesar's girlfriend Grace (Lolita Davidovich) to drive them to Vegas and hit the highway.

Shelton has a solid grip on the endemic corruption of the boxing game, knows how fighters are exploited and seems to know who's to blame. Some of the suspects even get cameos in the film. The rest are lampooned; Robert Wagner's leering casino owner Hank Goody, for example, is such an obvious parody of a certain egomaniacal presidential candidate it's a wonder Shelton bothered with a pseudonym.

Despite Shelton's savvy, there's this weird convergence in "Play It to the Bone" of the amorality of big-time sports and its counterpart in Hollywood. You have to wonder whether any of those friends and acquaintances Shelton sprinkles throughout the movie—from boxing despot

Bob Arum to George Foreman to HBO announcers Larry Merchant and Jim Lampley—realize they're being tarred by the same big brush with which Shelton paints boxing. Or care. I think they're just so thrilled to be in a movie, they don't have a clue. Either way, the idea of Hollywood wagging its finger at boxing for being stupid and corrupt is more than preposterous, and "Play It to the Bone" is a good example of how and why.

En route to the film's climactic matchup, which feels longer than the 75-round Sullivan-Kilrain bare-knuckle bout of 1889, we get the real film. Showing an almost Hawksian instinct for exploiting the space between men and woman—and men and men, for that matter—Shelton provides the trio's life stories and mutual lusting during that day-long desert drive to Nevada. It's amazing, in fact, how long we can watch three people talking in a car without realizing what we're doing. But between Harrelson's likable brutishness, Banderas' charm and Davidovich's tough-cookie-with-the-heart-of-mush, the trip isn't nearly as arduous as it might have been.

Getting there, however, turns out to be more than half the fun. In addition to a gay subtext that's played for crude laughs, the gratuitous addition of Lucy Liu as a Japanese nymphomaniac/ethnic joke and the overall coarseness of Shelton's script, the three main contenders wind up cast as losers—disposable humans in a story that tries way too hard to make you think it's being honest. "Play It to the Bone,, is like a fighter with a good right, no left and maybe a little too much roadwork: You're not sure when, or why, but eventually he's going to apply a face-block to the floor mats.

SIGHT AND SOUND, 10/00, p. 54, Geoffrey McNab

Las Vegas, the present. The promoters behind a Mike Tyson match learn that two of the boxers on the undercard are indisposed. In need of replacements, they call the gym in Los Angeles where Cesar and Vince work out. Both are fighters who have never fulfilled their potential. They accept the terms offered. $50,000 each and a shot at the title.

Cesar's girlfriend Grace (who used to go out with Vince) agrees to drive them to Vegas. En route, they joke, argue and fret about the fight. A hitchhiker whom they pick up has sex with Vince behind a gas station.

Once in Vegas, Cesar and Vince sign their contracts and square up against one another in the ring. Their riveting 10-round bout is judged a draw, which means neither gets a shot at the title, although the promoters, who short-change the boxers, hint at a possible rematch. Vince and Cesar blow a large part of their winnings in the casino. Grace, who has been trying to whip up interest in various business schemes, meets a businessman who tries to seduce her, then hits her. The trio leave Vegas together and drive back to Los Angeles.

Writer-director Ron Shelton's sports movies rarely celebrate winners. A former minor-league baseball player, he is preoccupied with the sporting world's more marginal figures, old-timers who have squandered or been denied their shot at glory. In *Tin Cup,* for instance, an over-the-hill golfer blows his chance of becoming US Open champion by blasting ball after ball into the water, while in *Cobb* legendary baseball star Ty Cobb is exposed as a racist misanthrope. But while Shelton seems to understand the tawdry politics and dirty business of sport, his films still stubbornly preserve a sense of child-like idealism.

Play It to the Bone is typical Shelton in this regard. He spends much of the film revealing just how corrupt the professional boxing world really is. The promoters and Vegas bigwigs treat their fighters with contempt—if a boxer inconveniently dies, they simply send for another. And the fighters—in need of money, or desperate for a stab at the title—allow themselves to be abused. Vince and Cesar, both coming to the end of their careers, jump at the chance to fight each other at a few hours' notice on Mike Tyson's undercard. They're best friends and past their prime—one has a detached retina—but nothing can stop them from beating each other up.

Play It to the Bone is as much a road movie as a fight film. As Shelton follows the fighters and Grace, the woman they both love, driving from LA to Vegas—they're too poor to fly—his dialogue captures the bravado, childishness and nostalgia of the two men. Both have their foibles: Vince is a born-again Christian who keeps thinking he has sighted Jesus on the sidewalk; Cesar is naive and diffident. When Vince announces that "all the great ones get laid before a fight" and disappears behind a garage with a female hitchhiker, Cesar, who is copying everything he does, tries forlornly to talk Grace into having sex with him. As with so many buddy movies, there is an erotic undertow to the two men's friendship, one which Vince's homophobic rants only bring closer into focus.

Once the fighters reach Vegas, the film begins to rehash old sports-movie clichés. The boxing commissioners, bent lawyers and stony-faced corner men, are familiar types, whose equivalents can be found in Ring Lardner stories and countless other boxing movies. Tom Sizemore gives an outrageously hammy performance as the cigar-chomping, Don King-like promoter who's putting the bill together. The fight itself is brutal, bloody and expertly choreographed. It lasts for a small eternity and teeters on the verge of absurdity throughout, but the outcome—which sees the judges declare a draw between Cesar and Vince—is a missed opportunity. It would surely have made for a more interesting, ambiguous movie had Shelton singled out one of his two heroes as the winner.

Whereas John Huston's *Fat City* (1971)—arguably the most honest boxing movie ever made—feels like a film directed by an insider, somebody who understands at first hand the squalor, pathos and macabre comedy of the sport, *Play It to the Bone* ends up as an old-fashioned wish-fulfilment fantasy. Here the fighters' innate decency transcends the corruption of the professional boxing world they inhabit. It's an amiable, low-key yarn which suggests that Shelton, like the athletes whose exploits he celebrates, is a perennial underachiever.

VILLAGE VOICE, 1/18/00, p. 116, Dennis Lim

Ron Shelton's new sports comedy, *Play It to the Bone,* suggests that the director's most successful blueprint—over-the-hill jock inspired by sexy oddball muse and screwed over by corporate evil—may have finally calcified into crass formula. The movie takes the form of an interminable road trip (from L.A. to Vegas) and, presumably as compensation, climaxes with a 10-round boxing match bloodier and more punishing than anything in *Fight Club* (though less likely to inspire pious fulminations). Washed-up pugilists Vince (Woody Harrelson) and Cesar (Antonio Banderas) get one last shot at glory when the sleazoid promoters of a Mike Tyson pay-per-view event call them in as last-minute undercard (i.e., opening-act) replacements. For unexplained reasons, Vince and Cesar, who happen to be best friends, decide to drive to Vegas. And they get Grace (Lolita Davidovich), whom they both happen to be in love with (she used to date Vince and is currently seeing Cesar), to drive them.

Shelton's road-movie antics are designed to provide the emotional context for the culminating fight, but the journey is a yawn—an outpouring of backstory, punctuated by cute episodic diversions and ill-advised running gags. Grace dumps Cesar, leaving the boys on seemingly equal footing. Vince and Cesar take turns revealing fall-from-grace sob stories. They pick up a hitchhiker—Lucy Liu (vixenish, naturally)—who fucks Vince and gets into a crowd-pleasing catfight with Grace (Shelton might want to try women's tennis next). None of this feels like it matters, so, with increasing desperation, Shelton leans hard on the quirks: Vince is a newly born-again Jesus freak; Grace invents things and hopes to sell patents in Vegas. Most intriguing of all is Cesar's confession (to Vince's utmost horror) that he "became a fag for a while" after he was beaten by one. Shelton makes a show of toying with the homophobia and homoeroticism of male sporting worlds, but there's no follow-through: Cesar's disclosure serves mainly as an excuse for Vince's potty-mouthed blue streaks, which Harrelson, best in the business at rednecks, handles with his usual panache.

Shelton's most satisfying films—*Bull Durham, Tin Cup, White Men Can't Jump*—are not only snappily written but oddly enhanced by a kind of baggy shapelessness. The dull-witted *Play It to the Bone* might as well have been constructed with a geometrical kit. Grace is less a character than a fulcrum in a lazily symmetrical setup; the cop-out ending stops short of proposing a *Design for Living* threesome. The most troubling aspect of the movie is the bone-crunching slugfest. Shelton indulges boxing-movie clichés (slo-mo punches, reaction-shot celeb cameos, lavish sprays of sweat, blood, and spit) and even attempts comic relief by visualizing the concussed boxers' increasingly dopey hallucinations. But the sheer viciousness of the bout is baffling—both men leave the ring with blood streaming down their faces. Shelton reserves his scorn for the corrupt, cartoonish Vegas honchos (Tom Sizemore, Robert Wagner, and Richard Masur—maniacal, oily, and hoarse, respectively), but the match is shot, cut, and scored with an unmistakable bloodlust: *Play It to the Bone* ends up less an indictment of sporting exploitation than of the sport itself.

Also reviewed in:
CHICAGO TRIBUNE, 1/21/00, Friday/p. A, Michael Wilmington
NEW YORK TIMES, 1/21/00, p. E24, Stephen Holden
VARIETY, 1/3-9/00, p. 80, Robert Koehler
WASHINGTON POST, 1/21/00, p. C5, Rita Kempley
WASHINGTON POST, 1/21/00, Weekend/p. 44, Michael O'Sullivan

POKEMON THE MOVIE 2000

A Warner Bros. release of a Warner Bros., Kids presentation of a 4Kids Entertainment production. *Producer:* Norman J. Grossfeld. *Director:* Kunihiko Yuyama (Japanese Production) and Michael Haigney (American Production). *Project Supervisor:* Gail Tilden. *Screenplay:* Takeshi Shudo. *Adapted by:* Norman J. Grossfeld and Michael Haigney. *Production Designer:* Gail Tilden. *Music:* Ralph Schuckett and John Loeffler. *Running time:* 85 minutes. *MPAA Rating:* G.

VOICES: Ikue Otani (Pikachu); Veronica Taylor, Rachael Lillis, Eric Stuart, and Addie Blaustein (various roles).

LOS ANGELES TIMES, 7/21/00, Calendar/p. 12, Gene Seymour

[*The following review by Gene Seymour appeared in a slightly different form in*
NEWSDAY, 7/21/00, Part II/p. B6.]

I got the early word from the grade-school pundits who talk about semiotics, chaos theory and Quidditch strategy between kickball games. Within months, these guys told me with customary assurance, Pokemon will be, like, so over, that you'll barely notice it existed at all.

Does this mean, I asked, that all those candy-colored critters with the bubble-headed names will be consigned to a corner with the Mighty Morphin Power Rangers and other discarded playthings of the postmillennial generation, left for the postmillennial tykes to bop around and break at will?

Uh, yeah, we guess, they said, before heading off to the mall to see if they could scrounge up any canceled tickets for the 'N Sync tour.

Really, though, it didn't take a grand intuitive leap to sense that last November's jackpot take for "Pokemon the Movie" signaled both an apotheosis of the craze that sold millions of trading cards, plush toys and key rings, and the beginning of its long, slow trip down the pop-phenomenon water slide.

Not even a whole "universe" such as the one regularly depicted on the "Pokemon" Saturday morning TV series can withstand the effect of being chewed and swallowed by a far more omnipresent universe of media saturation and fly-speck attention spans.

After seeing "Pokemon the Movie 2000," the inevitable sequel, one is surprised to say that, if the whole thing is as, like, over, as smarty pants of all ages say it is... well, it's kind of sad.

Yes, sad. Because this freshly baked and frosted big-screen "Pokemon" goes down with a sweetness that charms without talking down to its audience.

Moreover, unlike its predecessor ("Pokemon: The First Movie"), "Pokemon 2000" doesn't assume that everyone who sees it will know how to tell Togepy from Balbasaur or Squirtle from Pikachu. Sure, I know now, but I'm not telling because I don't have to.

All you have to know is that there's this avaricious Pokemon collector named Lawrence III who travels the globe in a Jules Verne-like aerial contraption, grabbing and caging whatever Pokemon he can. His latest conquests are three giant, powerful birds, each of which holds dominion over an island named for fire, ice and lightning.

This piracy pitches Earth into meteorological chaos and—wouldn't you know?—the only one who can set things right is that plucky kid Pokemon trainer, Ash Ketchum.

Leaving aside its cheesier jokes (even those made at the expense of its real-life avaricious collectors), "Pokemon the Movie 2000" is better looking and better wrought than its full-length predecessor. OK, so that's not saying much.

But one shouldn't be too hard on a kid franchise that, foaming hype and all, at least tried to persuade its younger audience to be careful with living things that are their responsibility—even if those things are turquoise, orange and purple and shoot fire though their noses.

NEW YORK POST, 7/21/00, p. 50, Hannah Brown

They're back! Just when you thought it was safe to go to the movies, the new 84-minute commercial for Pokemon merchandise, "Pokemon the Movie 2000" opens today at a theater near you.

It features several new monsters to add to the 150-plus Pokemon (pocket monster) roster and cards that thousands of children have slavishly collected, and these also are now available at a toy store near you.

Anyone who's read this far into the review is most likely the parent of a child who hasn't yet heard that the Pokemon phenomenon is dead.

Well, the news isn't good. A couple of wisecracks, even a reference to Weight-Watchers, have been added to appeal to adults and older Pokemaniacs, but none of it is worth staying awake for.

The filmmakers have tried hard to come up with an original plot, but somehow this film is actually duller than the first Pokemon movie, which played exactly like an extended episode of the TV series.

The story concerns the sinister Pokemon trainer Jiraldin, who wants to control Lukia, the beast of the sea. In order to capture Lukia, he has to first capture three rare Pokemon birds that live on remote islands. In order to achieve his goals, he unleashes terrible storms on Earth (shades of "The Perfect Storm").

Ash, a young Pokemon trainer, has to save the world and prove himself by finding and taming the rare Pokemon birds and Lukia.

The great innovation here is that Ash actually does something, instead of standing around the way the human characters in the Pokemon world usually do, while their monsters explode like angry little bowling balls and do all the fighting and all the work.

There are a few knowing references to the whole Pokemon craze. At one point, Jiraldin says, in his James Bond movie villain voice, "I am a collector. I started with one Mew card and now I have all this." However, no one will confuse this movie with "South Park."

"Pokemon the Movie 2000" lacks even the hip-hop soundtrack that was one of the few tolerable features of the original film. A cloying song that plays often features the refrain, "We all live in a Pokemon world." If this film is a hit, that will certainly be proven true.

It opens with a short starring Pikachu, the cutest Pokemon, which will appeal most to the youngest Pokemon fans.

Also reviewed in:
CHICAGO TRIBUNE, 7/21/00, Friday/p. A, Michael Wilmington
NEW YORK TIMES, 7/21/00, p. E10, Elvis Mitchell
VARIETY, 7/24-30/00, p. 45, Robert Koehler
WASHINGTON POST, 7/21/00, p. C1, Rita Kempley
WASHINGTON POST, 7/21/00, Weekend/p. 35, Desson Howe

POLA X

A WinStar Cinema release of an Arena Films/Pola Production/Théo Films/France 2 Cinéma/Pandora Filmproduktion/Euro Space/Vega Film co-production. *Executive Producer:* Albert Prévost and Raimond Goebel. *Producer:* Bruno Pesery. *Director:* Léos Carax. *Screenplay (French with English subtitles):* Léos Carax, Lauren Sedofsky, and Jean-Pol Fargeau. *Based on the novel "Pierre; or the Ambiguities") by:* Herman Melville. *Director of Photography:* Éric Gautier. *Editor:* Nelly Quettier. *Music:* Scott Walker. *Sound:* Jean-Louis Ughetto, Béatrice Wick, Jean-Pierre Laforce and (music) Geoff Foster. *Casting:* Antoinette

Boulat. *Production Designer:* Sylvie Barthet and Dschingis Bowakow. *Art Director:* Laurent Allaire. *Set Decorator:* Régine Constant. *Costumes:* Esther Walz. *Make-up:* Bernard Floch. *Running time:* 134 minutes. *MPAA Rating:* Not Rated.

CAST: Guillaume Depardieu (Pierre Valombreuse); Katerina Golubeva (Isabelle); Catherine Deneuve (Marie); Delphine Chuillot (Lucie de Boisieux); Laurent Lucas (Thibault); Patachou (Marguerite); Petruta Catana (Razerka); Mihaela Silaghi (The Little Girl); Sharunas Bartas (The Boss); Samuel Dupuy (Fred, Houseboy); Mathias Miekuz (TV Presenter); Dine Souli (Taxi Driver); Miguel Yeco (Augusto); Khireddine Medjoubi (Café Owner's Son); Mark Zak (Romanian Friend); Anne Richter (Chef's Wife).

CHRISTIAN SCIENCE MONITOR, 9/8/00, p. 16, David Sterritt

Movies from France have been flourishing on American screens, with more French productions and coproductions playing between January and June than in all of 1999, according to Unifrance, which promotes French films around the world.

Two more arrive today, representing opposite poles of the cinema spectrum.

"Pola X," directed by Leos Carax, is so aggressively offbeat that even art-film audiences may find it daunting. "It All Starts Today," directed by Bertrand Tavernier, tells a story of children and grown-ups that should have near-universal appeal.

Carax's film is based on Herman Melville's novel "Pierre, or, the Ambiguities," published in 1852. This explains the movie's name: "Pola" is an acronym for the book's French title (*"Pierre, ou, les ambiguités"*) and the "X" tells us that Carax wrote 10 drafts of the screenplay before rolling his cameras.

Like the novel, "Pola X" tells the dark-toned tale of a young man (Guillaume Depardieu, son of Gérard Depardieu) whose comfortable life is jolted when he meets a half-sister he never knew about. Leaving his devoted mother (Catherine Deneuve) and attractive fiancée, he takes his sibling to the big city and begins writing a book meant to uncover the secrets of his increasingly confused soul.

Carax updates the story in spirit as well as time—where the novel gives us an eccentric theologian, for instance, the movie gives us a bizarre cult—and adds a sexual explicitness that would have been unthinkable in Melville's day.

Melville is currently in style with French filmmakers. Claire Denis's drama "Beau Travail," based on the classic "Billy Budd: Foretopman," is one of the best recent movies from France or anywhere else. But the delirious "Pierre" was a disaster for Melville, whose desire to translate the heart's deepest ambiguities into a series of gothic, psychological adventures struck readers as a misguided effort that the writer of "Moby Dick" should never have attempted.

"Pola X" has received a similarly skeptical response. Carax is used to controversy—his greatest film, "The Lovers on the Bridge," earned both applause and catcalls at its Cannes premiere nine years ago—but even sympathetic critics (like me) have acknowledged that the new picture takes on far more than it's prepared to handle. Its hyperactive visual style is a strained equivalent for Melville's explosively romantic prose, and while Depardieu certainly looks right as Pierre, his acting seems derivative and uninspired.

This said, it must be added that "Pola X" makes up in courage what it lacks in common sense. Moviegoers with a sense of adventure (plus a tolerance for graphic sex) will find much to ponder. Those who want to explore Carax's work further will be pleased to learn that his first two features are also coming to the United States: the 1984 drama "Boy Meets Girl," about the ill-starred relationship of a young couple, and the 1986 fantasy "Bad Blood (*Mauvais Sang*)," about crooks, lovers, and a medical potion. Both are inventive excursions recalling the New Wave movement that revolutionized French film in the '60s.

Tavernier is a different kind of director, taking a more humanistic approach during his quarter-century of filmmaking. "It All Starts Today" continues this tradition with its hard-hitting story of a provincial kindergarten teacher who risks his career by defying a failing education system. The acting is intense, the story is vivid, and the theme is urgent: Even societies that pride themselves on compassionate policies have underprivileged children in their midsts, and nobody should rest easily when their welfare is in jeopardy.

LOS ANGELES TIMES, 10/13/00, Calendar/p. 8, Kevin Thomas

The Europeans, especially the French, can still carry off the big, serious romantic movie, and no one is doing it better, or with such bravura, as Leos Carax.

The cost of replicating Paris' Pont Neuf for his "Lovers on the Bridge," which drove its budget upward of $25 million, and its initially cool reception sidelined Carax for seven years. But that has not stopped him from pulling out all the stops—at least in regard to complexity of style and theme—in the clearly less costly "Pola X." It works on several levels of meaning and panache, yet it undoubtedly will leave behind those unable to go along with its unabashed heartiness.

Guillaume Depardieu, Gerard's tall, handsome son, stars as a privileged young man living an idyllic existence in a grand Normandy chateau on the banks of the Seine with his beautiful mother Marie (Catherine Deneuve), with whom he has so warm a relationship as to border on incest. He also has a devoted, beautiful and aristocratic fiancee, Lucie (Delphine Chuillot), of whom his mother clearly approves. To top it off, he has written a bestseller hailed as the cult novel of his generation. Then he starts having disturbing dreams of a furtive dark-haired young woman (Katerina Golubeva) who materializes in his waking hours, her appearance truly cataclysmic in impact.

When Depardieu's Pierre finally catches up with her, she tells him in her broken, strongly accented English that she is Isabelle, his older half-sister who was actually in residence at the chateau when he was born but was banished soon afterward. It would seem that Isabelle is the result of a romance of Pierre's late father, a once-eminent French diplomat stationed in the Balkans. Or is Isabelle an impostor like Anna Andersen, the German woman who, not long after the Russian Revolution, falsely proclaimed that she was the Romanov princess Anastasia and had somehow survived the firing squad?

In any event, Pierre loses his heart to Isabelle in an instant. He feels so repulsed by his parents' rejection of Isabelle that he runs off with her to Paris, where his next book will "reveal the great lie hidden behind everything." The couple takes shelter in a vast abandoned complex outside Paris, either a former power station or factory, that has become the refuge of a group of rock musicians/terrorists. (Scott Walker's industrial-strength rock score is just right for the movie, as is cinematographer Eric Gautier's grand, sweeping camera movement).

"Pola X" plays out the notion of the forces of light being inexorably drawn to those of darkness, of the older generation betraying the younger and maybe even an indictment of European indifference to the Balkans' agony. The film is also a notably dizzying romance, its key love scene shadowy but discernibly graphic.

Above all, it's a portrait of the artist determined to express himself truthfully at all costs. Surely, Carax must identify with Pierre, especially in the wake of his "Lovers on the Bridge" debacle. Carax need not worry: In going for broke with "Pola X," he pulled off a personal triumph.

Depardieu bears no physical resemblance to his crooked-nosed, beefy father, yet he reveals a similar stamina and passion in playing a challenging role. Golubeva's Isabelle is as loving as she is enigmatic, and Deneuve lends dignity and ballast, along with beauty and presence. "Pola X" takes its title from "Pierre, or the Ambiguities," the 1852 Herman Melville novel that inspired it. "Pola" is an acronym for the French title ("Pierre ou les Ambiguites"); the "X" refers to the fact that its shooting script represents Carax's 10th draft. Ambiguity suffuses the film, eluding and menacing Pierre, who can't accept it as inevitably part of life.

NEW YORK, 9/11/00, p. 171, Peter Rainer

Pola X, Leos Carax's free-form imagining of Herman Melville's *Pierre; or the Ambiguities*, accomplishes what all successful literary adaptations must: It conveys the emotions we felt when we read the novel. (*Pola* is an acronym for the book's title in French; the X stands for the tenth and final draft of the script.) Too simply stated, Pierre is about a young writer who is fated to destruction with his half-sister. Begun by Melville just after he completed *Moby-Dick*, it's a dense and despairing dungeon of a book, blooming with the most beautiful night flowers. You read it with a heightened consciousness, because Melville gets at things no one ever attempted before in American literature, about the sorrows and aberrations of the artist's life.

Carax sexualizes Melville's meanings, bringing out the incest latent in the novel. Updated from New York to modern-day Paris and Normandy, the narrative seems right at home both in the chateaux on the Seine and in the city warehouses where radical sects split the air with heavy-metal sounds. (I could have done with a little less ear-splitting.) Carax chooses his actors—Guillaume Depardieu (Pierre), Delphine Chuillot, Catherine Deneuve, Katerina Golubeva—as much for the deep resonance of their faces as for their acting. They appear before us as illustrious masks. As he amply demonstrated in his last film, the mesmerizing, interminable *Les Amants du Pont-Neuf,* Carax can be madly self-indulgent; but I never get the feeling he's showing off just to preen or to get written about in *Cahiers du Cinema*. He's an outlaw filmmaker who is interested in making outlaws of us, too.

NEW YORK POST, 9/8/00, p. 46. V. A. Musetto

Asked once why his movies never received commercial runs here, French renegade director Leos Carax blamed "an old man at the New York Times."

The gentleman in question long ago stopped reviewing movies, and today Carax's latest, "Pola X," opens in New York.

As with most of Carax's films ("Lovers on the Bridge," for instance), "Pola X" is frantic and out of control—and great fun to watch.

Blond Guillaume Depardieu (son of you know who) is Pierre, a writer who lives in a manor with his mother (Catherine Deneuve) and is engaged to the proper Lucie (Delphine Chuillot).

Along comes a raggedy young Eastern European woman (Katerina Golubeva) who claims to be Pierre's long-lost cousin Isabelle. It doesn't take much to convince Pierre to abandon his plush life and run off with Isabelle.

They find a home with a band of terrorists living in a vast, rundown warehouse, where Pierre wildly sets to work on a new book.

Depardieu gives a crazed performance, becoming grungier with each scene. Wearing a tattered overcoat, he's a sight to see as he staggers along the street.

Deneuve is as classy as ever, even though she doesn't have much to do. The remainder of the cast is fine.

Carax ignores just about every narrative rule—but, as someone once said, rules are made to be broken.

The visuals are superb, as with "Lovers on the Bridge." And there's a daring scene with Pierre and Isabelle *really* having sex (using body-doubles).

Some will dismiss "Pola X," which is based on a little-known book by Herman Melville, as pretentious. It is. But that doesn't mean that it can't be savored for just that very reason.

NEWSDAY, 9/8/00, Part II/p. B10, Gene Seymour

Like its vainglorious hero-savant, "Pola X" dares you to hate its guts as it staggers around, lost in its beauty and stewing in its romanticism. The guess here is that the movie, unlike that aforementioned protagonist, knows how self-indulgent it is and, ultimately, doesn't care whether you back off from or dive into its outrageous excesses.

Which makes sense when you consider who made it. Leos Carax fashioned this contemporary adaptation of Herman Melville's 1852 novel, "Pierre, or the Ambiguities," after years of wandering the wilderness trying to sell his impassioned 1991 dare, "The Lovers on the Bridge," to bewildered distributors and reluctant audiences.

Those who know both that movie and its backstory can't help but connect Carax' over-the-top willfulness with that of Pierre (Guillaume Depardieu), a glamorous novelist living the good life in Normandy with his widowed mother (Catherine Deneuve). His engagement to a woman (Delphine Chuillot) with both hair and body similar to mom is the first not-so-subtle sign of Pierre's subconscious wish to blow apart the fragile veneer of gilded ease cloaking his life.

He gets his chance when he encounters a vagrant named Isabelle (Katerina Golubeva), an Eastern European refugee who claims to be a half-sister abandoned by Pierre's mother. The revelation shakes Pierre, who renounces his pampered existence and takes Isabelle and some of her fellow transients to the lower depths of Paris where be intends to write Truth-with-a-capital-T to a shallow world.

It seems clear to even the most callow observer that Pierre's own self-absorption makes his rebellion as shallow as whatever it is he thinks he's fighting. Yet, it's hard to tell from the moping and whining of Depardieu (yes, that's Gerard's son) whether he or his director are in on the joke. The intensity of vision and the audacious, often-poetic sense of visual composition make you want to give Carax the benefit of the doubt. He does know how to hypnotize, especially in scenes that are both implicitly and explicitly erotic.

Even the movie's caresses are powerfully seductive.

In the end, Carax' lunge for significance, even with his ironies showing, causes his movie to trip over itself into maudlin contrivances and overcooked red herrings. Still, if you dug the go-for-broke recklessness of "Lovers on the Bridge" for its own sake, then it's as hard to reject this inchoate, lumbering mess as it is to spurn a lost, pregnant mongrel on a winter's night.

SIGHT AND SOUND, 6/00, p. 51, Gavin Smith

France, the present. Wealthy young Pierre Valombreuse lives in Normandy with his mother Marie on the family's estate. He is the author of the best-selling novel *In the Light*. Pierre divides his time between visiting his fiancée Lucie and writing his second novel. When Lucie's brother Thibault returns after a long absence, he and Pierre have an uneasy encounter. Pierre becomes aware of a mysterious homeless woman who seems to be following him.

One night, he comes across the woman, Isabelle, wandering down a country road. Isabelle describes the atrocities she has witnessed in an unspecified Eastern European country and explains she is the illegitimate daughter of his late father, a celebrated diplomat, long kept a secret by Marie. Stunned, Pierre renounces his former life and leaves for Paris with Isabelle and her companions, refugee Razerka and her young daughter. But after the death of Razerka's daughter, he and Isabelle move in with a commune in a warehouse where he is left alone to concentrate on his writing. Marie dies in a motorcycle accident. Lucie finds Pierre, but gradually realises he and Isabelle are now lovers. Pierre finishes his manuscript but it is rejected by his publisher. At wit's end, Pierre steals a gun from the commune's leader, tracks down Thibault and kills him. As he is being led away by the police, Isabelle throws herself in front of an emergency vehicle and is killed.

Whether one regards *Pola X* as a preposterous self-indulgent fiasco or as an improbable triumph of romantic audacity—in fact it's a bit of both—there's no denying Léos Carax's intense visual imagination and commitment. His act of hubris and commercial perversity in updating and transposing to contemporary France Herman Melville's critically savaged 1852 novel *Pierre, or the Ambiguities* may be freighted in more ways than one. As a not-so-distant scion of the Dupont dynasty, Carax himself hails from a background similar to Pierre's. Carax has indicated that the book has been an important one to him for many years and it's not such a great leap to discern some degree of over-identification with Melville's critical and commercial misfortunes. The film's very title, an acronym of the book's French title *(Pierre, où les Ambiguitiés)*, foregrounds the act of adaptation, bringing us back to authorial will. On one level the film is an unmistakable if masochistic act of self-parody comparable to Melville's. Even without the comedy of Pierre's metamorphosis from graceful novelist of leisure into caricatured starving artist, there's little doubt the publisher's evaluation of his manuscript ("A raving morass that reeks of plagiarism,") is a just one. On another level, the film, in all its deranged grandeur, represents a defiant refusal to capitulate to the dictates of commerce after the failure of *Les Amants du Pont-Neuf* and nearly ten years in the wilderness.

At the same time, more than in any of his previous films, Carax invests the narrative with highly charged subtext. Pierre's relationships with his mother and Thibault are visibly fraught with intimations of prior or latent sexual interest. Pierre and Marie address one another as "brother" and "sister" and enjoy an unusual level of intimacy. Pierre's blonde cipher-fiancée Lucie and the dark waif Isabelle seem equally passive manifestations of Pierre's implicit psychosexual crisis. Lucie is little more than a projection of Pierre's own narcissistic aristocratic entitlement, but as his cousin and a mirror image of his mother, she represents the next best thing to Marie herself.

Isabelle by contrast is a projection of Pierre's guilt and self-loathing, a return of the repressed in both personal and historical terms. As his half-sister, she represents an opportunity to succumb to his desire for an "unnatural" (incestuous) relationship. At the same time she is a reproachful spectre, an incarnation of the unspeakable suffering that has underwritten a century of European genocide in which his father and his class are implicated. This is made manifest in the film's stunning prologue montage: an image of the earth from space accompanied by a voiceover quotation from *Hamlet* ("The time is out of joint..."), smash-cuts to dropping bombs. From this Carax cuts to the paradise of the Valombreuse estate, making an explicit connection between Pierre's privilege and the horrors of 20th-century war.

Carax doesn't idealise Pierre or the world he falls from any more than the cold industrial urban hell he descends into. In fact, the film's most remarkable formal aspect is its bold use of visuals to balance the two realms. In one of the film's pivotal scenes, Isabelle's audaciously over-extended monologue explains her backstory as she and Pierre make their way through the woods at twilight. Carax tests legibility and exposition to breaking point in this scene, and its visual liminality becomes a metaphor for the contradictions in the director's uniquely self-defeating talent. His narrative and formal risk-taking are indistinguishable from failure.

VILLAGE VOICE, 9/12/00, p. 147, J. Hoberman

Neither genius nor poseur, the aging enfant terrible who calls himself Leos Carax can be seen to best advantage in *Pola X* . This moody, rapturous adaptation of *Pierre*, Herman Melville's gothic follow-up to *Moby-Dick,* is never less than seriously romantic.

Melville supposedly wrote *Pierre* in a few weeks and a state of "morbid excitement." *Pola X* encourages you to believe it. Events unfold in a headlong rush even when nothing much happens. The movie begins by quoting Shakespeare ("time is out of joint") and reveling in newsreel footage of World War II aerial bombing—most spectacularly, an exploding graveyard. After this violent Caraxysm signifying the resurrection of the dead, the camera gently descends upon an idyllic Normandy chateau where the promising young writer Pierre (Guillaume Depardieu, Gerard's son) lives in innocent bliss with his incestuously doting mother (Catherine Deneuve), next door to his adoring fiancée, Lucie (Delphine Chuillot).

Were it not for Pierre's motorbike, the summery landscape would be perfectly 1800. Indeed, Carax hews closely to Melville's tale, in which Pierre's discovery of a dark and mysterious half-sister named Isabelle, the embodiment of his late father's secret sin, leads him to renounce pretend incest for the real thing. Carax, however, eschews the sarcasm with which Melville skewered his principled, if confused, protagonist. ("The book is full of irony but I'm not gifted for that," the filmmaker told interviewer Dave Kehr on the occasion of *Pola X*'s premiere at the 1999 Cannes Film Festival.)

Conventionally regarded as a heroic literary failure about heroic literary failure, *Pierre* is a subject close to Carax's heart. ("Pola" is the acronym of the novel's French title; the "X" signifies Carax's 10th draft.) The film reiterates the same outlaw love story that has characterized Carax's three previous features—and, as the novel followed the commercial disaster of *Moby-Dick*, so *Pola X* is the follow-up to Carax's would-be blockbuster *The Lovers on the Bridge*. Perhaps his time has come, if it has not been usurped by the calculated whimsy of Patrice Leconte's locally successful faux Carax *Girl on the Bridge*.

Carax has more grit in his *amour fou.* Depardieu's Pierre has a slightly brutish quality; his hulking near-constant motion contrasts with Isabelle's succubus passivity. As played by Katya Golubeva (the Russian actress who appeared in Claire Denis's *I Can't Sleep),* Isabelle is a sepulchral presence—mournful and hollow-eyed with a high toneless voice that shades into a piercing cry. Carax suggests that she's a reproachful Balkan ghost. (In Melville, Isabelle is a daughter of the French Revolution.) The movie is too anachronistic to make any but the most sweeping social statements, but once Pierre relocates to Paris with Isabelle and her familiars—a mother and daughter, perhaps Gypsies—Carax adds a critique of French xenophobia to the general hysteria.

Pola X may be pretentious and self-indulgent, but it's not the least bit literary. As Jean-Luc Godard once said of Brian De Palma, Carax "works from the image." Pierre pursues Isabelle's lurking specter through the woods in a sequence so harshly lit it seems to have been printed on negative stock. Elsewhere a motorcycle crack-up is shot from a foot off the pavement with the bike spinning down the road—Carax cuts just before it hits the camera. The movie is as visually convulsive as the long, graphic sex scene played out between Pierre and Isabelle in the cold shadows of their clammy Paris hovel.

As Carax approaches this material in total identification with Pierre's noble ambition, so *Pola X* has been released by WinStar, the nervy distributor of Hou Hsiao-hsien and *Humanité*. WinStar has also boldly acquired the two movies that made Carax's precocious reputation as a cinematic Rimbaud. Scarcely seen here since their New York Film Festival showings, *Boy Meets Girl* (1984) and *Mauvais Sang* (1986) was screened at the Walter Reade.

Also reviewed in:
CHICAGO TRIBUNE, 10/6/00 Friday/p. K, Michael Wilmington
NEW YORK TIMES, 9/8/00, p. E14, Stephen Holden
VARIETY, 5/17-23/99, p. 55, Derek Elley

POLLOCK

A Sony Pictures Classics release of a Brant-Allen Films production. *Executive Producer:* Peter M. Brant and Joseph Allen. *Producer:* Fred Berner, Ed Harris, Jon Kilik, and James Francis Trezza. *Director:* Ed Harris. *Screenplay:* Barbara Turner and Susan J. Emshwiller. *Based on the book* "Jackson Pollock: An American Saga" by: Steven Naifeh and Gregory White Smith. *Director of Photography:* Lisa Rinzler. *Editor:* Kathryn Himoff. *Music:* Jeff Beal. *Music Editor:* Sharon Smith. *Sound:* Scott Breindel. *Sound Editor:* Richard King and Peter Drake Austin. *Casting:* Todd Thaler. *Production Designer:* Mark Friedberg. *Art Director:* Peter Rogness. *Set Decorator:* Carolyn Cartwright. *Special Effects:* Steve Kirshoff and Mark Bero. *Costumes:* David C. Robinson. *Make-up:* Marilyn Carbone. *Stunt Coordinator:* George Aguilar. *Running time:* 117 minutes. *MPAA Rating:* Not Rated.

CAST: Ed Harris (Jackson Pollock); Marca Gay Harden (Lee Krasner); Any Madigan (Peggy Guggenheim); Jennifer Connelly (Ruth Kligman); Jeffrey Tambor (Clement Greenberg); Bud Cort (Howard Putzel); John Heard (Tony Smith); Val Kilmer (Willem DeKooning); Stephanie Seymour (Helen Frankenthaler); Tom Bower (Dan Miller); Robert Knott (Sande Pollock); Matthew Sussman (Reuben Kadish); Sada Thompson (Stella Pollock); Norbert Weisser (Hans Namuth); Sally Murphy (Edith Metzger); Molly Regan (Arloie Pollock); Moss Roberts (Ted Dragon); Eduardo Machado (Alfonso Ossorio); Katherine Wallach (Barbara Kadish); Annabelle Gurwitch (May Rosenberg); Isabelle Townsend (Mercedes Matter); Claire Beckman (Vita Peterson); Kenny Scharf (William Baziotes); Barbara Garrick (Betty Parsons); Everett Quinton (James Johnson Sweeney); Stephen Beach (Jay Pollock); Jill Jackson (Alma Pollock); David Leary (Charles Pollock); Donna Mitchell (Elizabeth Pollock); Sondra Jablonski (11-Year-Old Jeremy Pollock); Frank Wood (Frank Pollock); Julia Anna Rose (Marie Pollock); Kyle Smith (8-Year-Old Jonathan Pollock); Eulala Grace Harden (Arloie's Baby); John Rothman (Harold Rosenberg); Tom McGuinness (Franz Kline); Cassandra Klewicki (Kadish Child); Sloane Shelton (Dot Miller); Robert O'Neill (Herbert Matter); Jennifer Piech (Young Redhead); Rebecca Wisocky (Dorothy Seiberling); Linda Emond (Martha Holmes); Tony Palazzolo (Delivery Man); David Cale (William Wright); April Petroski (Karen Pollack); Nicholas Petroski and Noah Petroski (Jason Pollack); Bob Harris (Veterinarian); John Madigan (Voice of News Broadcaster).

CHRISTIAN SCIENCE MONITOR, 12/15/00, p. 15, David Sterritt

Sometimes an actor gets a part he was born to play, and sometimes he goes out of his way to make this happen. The latest example is Ed Harris as Jackson Pollock, who revolutionized modern painting in the 1940s. "Pollock" has been a labor of love for Harris over the past 10 years, during which he prepared the picture with thought, research, and yes, painting lessons.

Not that Harris does the only bravura acting. He dominates the movie with his sensitive portrayal of an artist who dared to cultivate an unprecedented style based on a love of abstraction with a skill for dripping and pouring paint with finely tuned control. But others expertly support him, including Jeffrey Tambor as critic Clement Greenberg and Marcia Gay Harden as Pollock's gifted wife, painter Lee Krasner.

Harris's directing sinks into clichés at times, as when Pollock's breakthrough into "drip painting" is announced through trite images of the artist's piercing eyes and the huge, blank canvas he's about to fill. But the movie is enriched by its respect for an innovator whose influence still permeates contemporary art.

CINEASTE, Vol. XXVI, no. 2, 2001, p. 46, Leonard Quart

A biopic about a celebrity painter like Pollock—the first avant-garde artist to break through to the larger public—could easily have made all the wrong esthetic and intellectual choices. It could have turned into a bloated, romanticized portrait of a demonic artist whose destructive, pathological conduct is absolved or seen as attractive because it's the behavior of a genius. The film could also have made the creation of art into an almost divine act, not a result of concentrated, disciplined daily work, but a set of inspired epiphanies that come almost magically to the artist. It would then have been the kind of kitschy Hollywood film that gives us a tormented, brooding painter, who after being blocked for weeks cries, "I've got it," and in two days or so knocks out a number of masterpieces.

Luckily, the director/producer and star of *Pollock,* the fine underrated actor Ed Harris, understands what the artistic process and Pollock's painting are all about. For over a decade Harris has been working the ideas for this film over in his mind. And though he provides at least one of those eureka moments that Hollywood loves—and Pollock is an alcoholic, tortured figure like most of the painters portrayed in films—Harris generally avoids melodrama, realistically observing the painter taking his time, quietly contemplating an empty canvas and then purposively setting to work. Harris has written: "One thing I learned about Mr. Pollock's art ... is that Jackson fully believed and lived by 'I don't use the accident, because I deny the accident.' One cannot even approximate Pollock's work unless every stroke, every pour, every slap, every fling, every shake, every splash, every flick has a special intention."

In *Pollock,* Harris, who is making his directorial debut, chooses to leave out the artist's formative years—no scenes of an alienated, angst-ridden young Pollock finding his way in California to his calling as a painter, or of the family turmoil and dysfunction he grew up with. Instead, Harris opens the film with a flashback to Pollock's first meeting with his wife-to-be—the painter Lee Krasner (Marcia Gay Harden). Harden may overdo the Brooklyn accent, but she gives an extremely strong, shaded performance as a painter who puts her own career on hold, and gives herself up to supporting Pollock's genius—Krasner acting as his agent, mother, manicurist, therapist, and intellectual adviser. It's a volatile relationship, with a tough, direct, more intellectually sophisticated Krasner able to hold her own emotionally with a sometimes violent, out-of-control Pollock who is utterly dependent on her. Krasner is no passive doormat; she exudes intellectual and emotional authority. It's the postwar era, however, and even a woman like Krasner—a painter and bohemian, who lived a very different life from more conventional women of the time—submerged her needs and career to the man she was committed to.

The relationship between Krasner and Pollock is one of the film's prime motifs, but what is most striking is the portrait of Pollock as painter. Harris successfully captures Pollock's need to create an art that derives from his inner self, not from the mastery and synthesis of art/historical influences. Pollock wanted, in his own words, "to literally be in the painting." In one overhead shot, the film observes Pollock moving gracefully like a dancer around an immense blank canvas on his studio floor. In other scenes, the camera follows Pollock in medium close-up around his studio, as he skillfully drops swirls of paint and then consciously shapes it, in all its labyrinthian complexity, into a unity based on the flow of energy. (Harris practiced painting like Pollock, and mimicked Pollock's physical movements and gestures—the ones he used in the Hans Namuth documentary that helped create the Pollock myth.) The only time in the film that the inarticulate, anguished Pollock is at ease is when he is painting—making order on canvas of the raw feeling and fury that he often couldn't control in his daily life. Pollock's most emotionally stable periods seem to have occurred when he was most creative: he produced a number of his great "drip" paintings from 1948-50 when he had stopped drinking and was relatively happy living with Krasner in East Hampton.

Without offering any psychological explanations, Harris gets to the heart of Pollock's personality. Harris's Pollock is taciturn, depressive, socially awkward, profoundly insecure, and filled with coiled rage. As a result, he goes on drunken jags, sleeping in the street or emotionally exploding by screaming and throwing over tables filled with food. Pollock is also filled with self-doubt and has a desperate need for approval, craving praise, overreacting to criticism, seeking fame, and needing to see himself as a great genius—a painter better than Picasso. He's even wary of his celebrity, not sure that he isn't just a phony. Towards the end of the film, a tight close-up of Pollock, at the height of his celebrity, captures his utter desolation.

Still, despite his deep-set neuroses, Pollock was a risk-taking artist, who had sufficient self-confidence to pursue his own vision of art. And Harris has always been an actor who conveys unself-conscious manliness, self-assuredness, and physicality without turning it into posturing machismo. Wearing paint-splattered jeans, a worn black jacket, and work shoes, he feels utterly right as Pollock. He embodies the taut, monosyllabic painter who doesn't speak the language of art crit and who vigorously struggles to move from paintings built on mythic, biomorphic forms and idiographic signs to a gestural and 'drip' painting that was stylistically revolutionary.

Where the film is problematic is in its too elliptic depiction of Pollock's large family and mother. The film clearly suggests that something has gone wrong in his relationship with them—a family visit elicits anger from his relatives at Pollock's self-absorption. His mother (Sada Thompson), whom he seems to love and wishes to please, feels utterly remote from him, and he is self-conscious and uncomfortable around her. It's all dramatically opaque, however, with family members appearing and disappearing and almost all of the psychic undercurrents left undefined.

The film also fails in its evocation of the social and intellectual worlds of the abstract expressionists. A brief, stagy scene set in a smoky Cedar Tavern of Pollock sitting and drinking with his fellow artists, De Kooning, Tony Smith, and William Baziotes reveals nothing either about who they were as people, or about the nature of their artistic vision. We do get some smart art talk from Krasner and Clement Greenberg, but even they provide no real sense of the artistic breakthrough made by the abstract expressionists. (A fictional film cannot provide us with a long disquisition about the esthetic significance of the New York school, but a touch more of the historical context wouldn't have hurt.) In addition, besides the perfunctory depiction of a couple of art openings, the film captures little of the Forties Village scene.

Still, Amy Madigan makes an animated, idiosyncratic appearance as imperious art patronness Peggy Guggenheim, who was the main financial support of Pollock's painting in the mid-Forties. Unfortunately, Jeffrey Tambor as Clement Greenberg, the art critic for *The Nation*, and Pollock's friend and critical champion (he sententiously declared that Pollock was "great"), gives a much too mannered performance. Greenberg tended to be oracular and prescriptive, and Tambor partially succeeds in providing us with an intelligent, dogmatic, somewhat comic figure who sees himself as both pulling the strings and being the ultimate judge of the artists' careers. Watching Tambor, however, one is too conscious of him playing a part, working too hard at conveying the mixture of perceptiveness and arrogance that gave Greenberg his critical cachet.

Pollock's strength as a film lies in its depiction of Pollock as painter, man, and husband to Lee Krasner. There are emotionally riveting and painful scenes where Krasner and Pollock erupt in volcanic arguments. One of them involves Pollock's desire to have children, which elicits from Krasner a furious tirade, asserting that taking care of one disruptive child is enough.

Pollock's last years were ones of decline. He becomes involved with a woman the film portrays as a banal art groupie, who offers him youth, beauty, and uncritical admiration. He drinks heavily, grows fat, and his painting loses its edge. By 1953, he had abandoned his 'drip' technique and moved to anatomical abstractions whose origins were in his early mythic pictures. The arguments between him and Krasner grow more painful and frequent: Pollock, red-faced, breaking chairs, and cursing her out as a "bitch," vents all his frustrations about his waning talent on her; she—the woman who probably kept him alive—ultimately responding by taking off to Europe, leaving Pollock without his main emotional and artistic support. The film's final scene trenchantly captures an emotionally depleted Pollock on his suicidal last car ride, heedlessly killing another young woman who was riding in the car with him.

Harris has made a modest, intelligent film that avoids most of the pitfalls into which artist biopics fall. Yes, *Pollock* is about a suffering artist, but the film unfolds in an understated, unsensational, and utterly real manner. Predictably, Harris's strength as a director is in eliciting impressive, nuanced performances, especially from himself and Marcia Gay Harden, that never reduce Pollock and Krasner to one or two notes. Otherwise, his direction eschews the virtuosic for the solidly functional, though there is one silent, strikingly composed scene of a more sexually active Krasner undressing a passive, lost-looking Pollock when they go to bed together for the first time (both of them framed and silhouetted by a doorway in a full shot).

Pollock may lack the exhilarating camera movements and expressionist camera angles of *New Life Lessons* (one of three sections of *New York Stories),* Martin Scorsese's comic/tragic film about an abstract painter who needs to churn himself into an emotional frenzy to paint. But Harris has created an indelible portrait of a painfully uneasy and self-destructive painter, depicted here without a touch of sentimentality or self-aggrandizement. Pollock was an original, a great improvisatory painter who painstakingly gave America a new way of seeing, and Harris has made him come alive without a false move.

LOS ANGELES TIMES, 12/15/00, Calendar/p. 6, Kenneth Turan

Jackson Pollock, one of the key figures in Abstract Expressionism and America's first postwar art star, was a man destined to be consumed by his own internal fires. As insecure as he was gifted, a full-blown alcoholic prone to frightening rages, he was often on the edge of agony, a prisoner of demons he could no more identify than control.

Putting a figure like this on film, someone so close to the stereotypical Hollywood view of the artist as tormented and self-destructive, is a chancy enterprise. Though it's taken him nearly a decade of involvement to make it happen, Ed Harris, working as star and producer as well as first-time director, has managed to bring it off successfully.

It's not that "Pollock" doesn't have its share of standard, conventional elements—it does. But the intensity of Harris' performance—the best of his career, and that's saying a lot—and his gift for guiding co-star Marcia Gay Harden and cameo performers like Amy Madigan to an equally high level make everything else less important.

More than that, "Pollock" stands out among creative bio-pics for an ability to show art being made in a way that's as realistic and exciting as it's ever been on screen. To watch Lisa Rinzler's expressive shots of Harris as Pollock create his paintings, especially the famously acrobatic drip canvases, to Jeff Beal's Aaron Copland-influenced music is little short of thrilling.

Harris was first attracted to Pollock when his father pointed out how much he looked like the artist, but the actor hasn't stopped with a physical resemblance that is in truth uncanny. Harris has invested himself completely in the part, even changing his cigarette brand and building a studio behind his house so he could throw himself into practicing action painting, finally inhabiting Pollock with an intensity and force of life that is almost frightening.

Going along with this integrity, the film's solidly built albeit old-fashioned Barbara Turner and Susan J. Emshwiller script doesn't try to explain how Pollock got the way he was. Aside from a brief reference to the artist being classified 4F for being "too neurotic," it takes an ecce homo (here is the man) approach to his torments, refreshingly avoiding the kind of psychological theorizing that tends to be facile and simplistic.

Harris' Pollock is a complicated man, wary, restless and almost bursting with so much physicality and controlled energy he's as happy breaking a door down as unlocking it. Pollock also radiates the kind of fragility that can be terrifying, displaying enough congenital desperation to cause one character to say, "You remind me of a trapped animal." And he has a way of looking out at the world that is haunted more often than not.

That look confronts us in the film's opening sequence, set in 1950 at a packed Manhattan gallery opening at the height of Pollock's fame, after Life magazine had anointed him America's premier artist and every canvas sold as soon as he touched it. Yet the artist has the face of a man who's seen a ghost, and, we soon learn, the ghost was quite likely himself.

"Pollock" then flashes back nine years, to the artist as a mentally unstable alcoholic living in Greenwich Village with his brother and his brother's disapproving wife. Everything changes for him when a knock on his door reveals fellow painter Lee Krasner (Harden in easily the strongest performance of her career), cheekily introducing herself, as she puts it, to the only Abstract Expressionist in New York she hasn't met.

Raised in Brooklyn, from a Russian Jewish background, Krasner is in many ways Pollock's opposite: She's verbal and self-assured and faces the world with confidence. Both parties immediately sense the possibility of a relationship, but there is a tension as well as a complicity between them, the intuitive knowledge that whatever transpires will be as dangerous as it will be life-changing.

Once they are together, Krasner becomes Pollock's tireless advocate and propagandist. She encourages him in his work, does the best she can with his alcoholic binges, even masterminds his introduction to the eccentric but influential collector Peggy Guggenheim (a dark-haired Madigan in a superb cameo). And she is the driving force in the couple's move to Long Island, where Pollock does his best and most influential work.

Though the film has no shortage of dramatic confrontations or cameos of celebrated people (Val Kilmer, the man of a thousand accents, plays Willem De Kooning; Jeffrey Tambor is influential critic Clement Greenberg; Jennifer Connelly is the beautiful and willing Ruth Kligman), it is to the painting that it always in and most successfully returns. Even occasional on-the-nose lines like "You've done it, Jackson, you've cracked it wide open" can't hurt that focus.

Whether it's Harris warily sizing up an enormous blank canvas, looking at it for weeks before picking up a brush, or the eureka moment when he discovers drip painting and then uses it in a way that the film emphasizes is anything but casual and accidental, "Pollock" has an innate feeling for the process of painting that its subject would appreciate. Even in his darkest moments, when success would mock him as even failure never had, Pollock always respected the work, and Ed Harris' film is as successful as it is because it passionately follows the artist's lead.

NEW YORK, 12/18-25/00, p. 169, Peter Rainer

Ed Harris has wanted to make a film about Jackson Pollock for more than a decade, and now that he's finally made it, you can see why. Harris has always been an intensely kinesthetic performer as well as the rough-hewn inheritor of the Brando-Dean tradition of action acting. Pollock, flexing his Ab Ex muscles, was the archetypal action painter, and his doomy, boozy persona, as much as his art, was an icon of postwar bohemianism. He would sometimes paint straight from the tube, and his life seemed to come straight from the tube, too, he poured everything out and yet could also seem furiously inhibited and forbidding. He was an inchoate orgiast, and Harris, who both directed and stars in *Pollock*, captures the artist's divided soul. Harris doesn't go in for a lot of great-man posturing, and there aren't many of the *Aha*! moments one might expect from a Hollywood film about a famous painter. (Pollock's discovery of his "drip technique" is admirably underplayed.)

Instead we get an almost punishingly exact portrait of a pathologically thin-skinned genius who reacted to the slights and upheavals of life with an almost feral intuitiveness. The real Jackson Pollock was cannier about the way he played into the American public's perception of the artist-as-outlaw than the Pollock of this picture. Harris's Pollock is all instinct, and you can see in his raging, self-dramatizing physicality what fascinated and repelled his coterie of lovers and admirers and hangers-on. He's an immensely, insufferably liberating force, and one of the film's great achievements is its depiction of the ardent purgatory of Pollock's marriage to Lee Krasner (Marcia Gay Harden, who is very fine in a difficult role).

As a first-time director, Harris isn't as powerfully expressive as he is as an actor; the script, by Barbara Turner and Susan J. Emshwiller, is rather conventional, and Harris doesn't attempt to come up with a visual or emotional equivalent to his subject's art (which is what Robert Altman achieved in his Van Gogh movie, *Vincent & Theo*). The result is somewhat confounding: a methodical, straightforward movie about a hair-trigger iconoclast. But Harris as an actor does justice to his long-term passion to play Pollock. When you think of his performance and then think back to the famous Hans Namuth movies of Pollock at work, they merge together in the mind. They share the same swagger and creepy, closed-off intensity.

NEW YORK POST, 12/15/00, p. 59, Lou Lumenick

There are few more thrilling sights around than watching the great Ed Harris furiously hovering over a canvas in "Pollock," his flawed but fascinating portrait of abstract art legend Jackson Pollock.

Giving the performance of his career in this labor of love (he also directed and produced the film, which took a decade to bring to the screen), Harris is frighteningly convincing as Pollock, whose ground-breaking "drip" technique made him America's first star artist, though he struggled for two decades with self-doubt and the bottle.

Pollock is a hugely challenging subject for a first-time director, much less an actor, and Harris is most triumphant when it comes to the performances, starting with his own jeans-and-T-shirted Pollock, who exudes the raw sensuality and pain of the contemporaries the painter was sometimes compared with in the '50s, Marlon Brando and James Dean.

Marcia Gay Harden, too, gives an Oscar-caliber performance as Lee Krasner, a painter Pollock met in Greenwich Village, in the early '40s and eventually married. She gives a very moving portrait of a woman who appreciates Pollock's potential so deeply that she puts her own promising career on the back burner, and endures his drunken rages and infidelities to be his muse.

Harris' crowded canvas includes exquisite cameos by Amy Madigan (the real-life Mrs. Harris) as Pollock's sponsor, the heiress Peggy Guggenheim; Bud Cort as her art scout, Howard Putzel; Jeffrey Tambor as Clement Greenberg, an influential critic who helped put Pollock on the map, then turned against him; and Val Kilmer, as rival artist Willem De Kooning.

The film also boasts gorgeous camerawork totally appropriate to the subject, by Liza Rinzler, and one of the best evocations I've ever seen of '50s settings, by production designer Mark Friedberg and costume designer David Robinson.

The big drawback to "Pollock" is the screenplay by Barbara Turner and Susan Emshwiller, which shies away from probing Pollock's psychological problems (alternatively boastful and tremendously insecure, he probably suffered from bipolar disorder).

Perhaps because the movie was made with the cooperation of Krasner and Pollock's latter companion, Ruth Kligman (who's sued the filmmakers, despite a very careful portrayal by Jennifer Connelly, the film too often falls back on the tortured-artist clichés so familiar to connoisseurs of biopics from the '40s and '50s.

There is also too much tin-eared dialogue and way too much exposition explaining why Pollock was a great artist. We don't need someone roughly every 10 minutes telling Pollock, "What you re doing is the most original and vigorous art in this country."

Pollock's bold canvases, which are displayed at length, speak far more eloquently. So do the masterful acting and production values that make "Pollock" a tantalizing near-miss.

NEWSDAY, 12/15/00, Part II/p. B6, Gene Seymour

Rarely has a raucous force of nature like Jackson Pollock been as tightly contained as in "Pollock," Ed Harris' biopic of abstract expressionism's whirlwind fatalist. Those who come to this movie expecting to see the rampaging grizzly of mid-20th-Century legend acting out his volcanic mood swings and sating his bottomless appetites will not be disappointed. They may wonder, however, why the movie isn't as wild and daring as his paintings were.

But then, the tension between Pollock's mercurial, volcanic personality and "Pollock's" cool, even-tempered tone may well be what makes Harris' film so daring. The movie forces you, as few of its kind ever do, to see the fruits and spoils of genius framed against the gritty, banal canvas of normal life.

Capturing a sense of whatever "normal life" was in the 1940s and early '50s—the era of Pollock's meteoric rise, decline and untimely death at 44 in a 1956 car crash—is one of the things the movie does exceptionally well. Harris the director shows a realist's conscientiousness in making sure that even the crates of beer are given labels in sync with the specific time period. It's possible to wish for an overall vision of the era as less selective and evocative and more cacophonous and Dickensian. But the balance between subject and background is so neatly established that you almost worry what would happen if things got noisier.

Harris' artistry is even more conspicuous in the title role. He plays Pollock as if he were an untamed animal wandering the forest of his life by raw instinct, gazing cockeyed at every if he or she posed a threat.

When Pollock's mood swings enter the red zone, Harris makes his personality disorders seem tangibly, ominously dangerous to every living thing in their vicinity. But when he paints, the scattered energies are focused; what is irrational makes sense. Watching Harris-as-Pollock move his brushes toward harmonic convergence is not only inspiring, even to nonartists, it also helps explain what his art was all about.

As Lee Krasner, Pollock's wife, enabler and agent-promoter, Marcia Gay Harden complements Harris' volatility with a steely force that brings her performance to his high level. She provides such gravitational magnetism that when, after one tantrum too many, Jackson runs Lee out of their Hamptons home, you feel the ground beneath his feet—and the movie's—getting soft and moist.

It's their story as much as—if not more than—his alone.

Which doesn't take anything away from Jennifer Connolly's shrewdly observed turn as Ruth Klingman, the young woman who was with Pollock, literally and figuratively, at the end of his life. There are vivid portrayals throughout "Pollock," notably Amy Madigan's hilariously high-strung collector-patron Peggy Guggenheim and Jeffrey Tambor's bullish and vaguely bullying art critic Clement Greenberg.

SIGHT AND SOUND, 6/02, p. 47, Michael Bracewell

Greenwich Village, 1941. Jackson Pollock is a struggling painter sharing an apartment with his brother and wife. Fellow artist Lee Krasner introduces herself to Pollock. The two start dating.

When Pollock's brother gets a job in Connecticut (to avoid the draft), Pollock and Lee move in together. Reuben Kadish, a drinking friend of Pollock's introduces him to art dealer Howard Putzel. Putzel shows Pollock's paintings to wealthy art patron Peggy Guggenheim. In 1943 Pollock gets a show at Peggy's Art of the Century Gallery, where he meets influential art critic Clement Greenberg. He is also commissioned to paint a mural for Guggenheim's New York home. At a party at Peggy's, Pollock's drinking gets out of hand and he urinates into the fireplace (later that night, he has fumbled sex with Peggy). Soon after, Pollock goes missing on a drinking binge, at the end of which he returns to Lee.

Now married, Pollock and Lee move to a small town in Long Island in 1945. Lee puts her artistic ambitions on hold to concentrate on looking after Pollock, who spends most of his time painting. She firmly turns down Pollock's suggestion they try for a child. In 1947 Pollock works on a new technique (so-called action painting) on a series of large-scale canvases. The paintings are a success: Greenberg champions the work and *Life* magazine do a feature on the artist, turning him into a media star. He also gives up drinking. Deflated by having to recreate his spontaneous methods for a documentary in 1950, Pollock starts drinking again.

Five years later. Pollock's relationship with Lee is strained because of his drinking. Having found out he has a mistress, Ruth, Lee goes to Venice for a break. Ruth arrives to stay with Pollock, bringing her friend Edith. Driving home from a party, a drunken Pollock crashes his car, killing himself and Edith. Ruth survives.

Writing in *Art News* in 1964, the critic Thomas Hess described Jackson Pollock as "Rodeo Rimbaud". The tag was a good one, like critic Clement Greenberg's ambiguous description of Pollock's early abstraction as "apocalyptic wallpaper". The accent was on rugged masculinity and elemental forces, and in his own time Jackson Pollock was more enshrined in myth than almost any other artist—with the possible, and in Pollock's opinion debatable, exception of Picasso. Pollock, it would seem, was a walking minefield of brilliance and neuroses, and these are the qualities which Ed Harris' visceral and perceptive life of the artist sets out to examine.

The lives of great artists, in fact, tend to make irresistible cinema because of their very affinities with melodrama and myth—most of them possessing "the whole kit", as Tom Wolfe might say, of a classical five-act tragedy. When the form goes wrong—Julian Schnabel's *Basquiat* for instance, seemed like one long advert for an isotonic cola—it goes horribly wrong, but in recent years both Derek Jarman's sumptuous *Caravaggio* and John Maybury's Francis Bacon portrait *Love Is the Devil* have been involving and to some extent informative. Ultimately, they maintain our fascination with genius.

A defining moment in the genre, and one which would not seem out of place in *Pollock,* could perhaps be found in Kirk Douglas' portrayal of Van Gogh in Vincente Minnelli's somewhat overheated 1956 biopic *Lust for Life:* as the tortured artist struggles to paint in a scorching cornfield, demonic crows sweep down on him, driving him to literally rage against his own abilities to capture nature on canvas. The image is both moving and slightly comic; but it also seems to summarise, like some kind of allegorical *mise en scène*, that all-too human awkwardness—physical and spiritual clumsiness, even—which so often attends the near-cosmic struggle between a great artist, their vision and their work.

Such bruising physicality, set against an almost unbearably acute refinement of sensibility—the Rodeo Rimbaud, in fact—is one of the principal tensions that make Harris' film so compelling and eerily real. There are times within the film—Pollock's drunken attempt to cycle carrying a crate of beer on the handlebars, for instance—which have all the disturbing intimacy of a documentary. As a consequence of this acuity, *Pollock* raises some enduring questions about the mythologies, often male in origin, of creativity or genius.

For many critics, it was as much the mythology which grew up around Pollock in his own lifetime—the pioneer woodsman of modern art, all furrowed brow and cigarette smoke—as his actual painting which was credited with displacing the progress of modernism from Europe to America. In Harris' film, therefore, as Pollock discovers his signature style of 'dripping' paint (the myth's dynamo, so to speak), there is a satisfying sense of epiphany which just manages to skirt the safe side of cheesy by remaining relatively understated. As the art historian Brian O'Doherty has written of that moment, in relation to the mythology of Pollock: "The drip, of course, in the canon of Pollock's myth, represents cutting the Gordian knot of his difficulties." In *Pollock* the movie, the drip can also be seen as the beginnings of a whole new set of problems for Pollock as a person riddled with self-doubt.

As Harris both stars and directs, playing Pollock as a man wide open to all the human frailties of mood and temper, part shaman, part ego-maniacal monster, one is struck by his uncanny physical resemblance to his subject. The athletic low brow, broad mouth and square jaw, which made the younger Harris so persuasive as astronaut John Glenn in Philip Kaufman's *The Right Stuff* (1983), have now become more weathered in their intimation of muscular heroism. The eyes seem darker too, as we first encounter Harris as Pollock in a remarkable flash-forward—a scene which seems slowed down and submarine, as though destiny itself were stilling the moment—to a private view of his paintings at the zenith of his fashionability in the early 1950s. All that was honourable and upright in Harris' portrayal of Glenn as a great American hero can be seen as a troubled, skewed version of itself in his acting of Pollock as a great American anti-hero. The champion is seen as weighed down by his very strength—simian, clumsy, disturbed.

Pollock's compensatory drunkenness for the condition in which his abilities as an artist leave him as a human being is both joyless and boorish—alcohol is almost a character in the film, the fuel and poison of the myth. The Cedar Tavern machismo (of which Andy Warhol would write: "I mean, how corny") leads only to a kind of emotional castration and sexual misery. The latter point is well made in a scene where Pollock, riding high and roaring drunk, attempts a clumsy fuck with his patron Peggy Guggenheim. Bent double with premature ejaculation and self-loathing, Pollock stumbles from the room as Guggenheim, who has predicted disaster from his first drunken lunge, looks on with a mixture of pity, embarrassment and exasperation. Guggenheim herself is a towering inferno of studied hauteur, as though Ethel Scull had tutored with Edith Sitwell.

Alcohol and women become the factors in Pollock's life—his milk and his mother—the need for which entwines to coil a mainspring of domestic tension. Marcia Gay Harden's portrayal of his wife, the artist Lee Krasner, is nothing less than an essay in sexual politics as they are lived within the twin arenas of art and marriage. And if Krasner is seen at times to be little more than the handmaiden to Pollock's genius, then that role is more than questioned by the film's sympathy to both partners. As Anne Wagner has written in *Krasner's Presence, Pollock's Absence:* "The point is not to dispute the relevance of particular biographical circumstances, but rather how to recognize how and when any one account hardens those circumstances into stereotype."

In *Pollock* the account is primarily one of addiction: how do Lee and Jackson survive within their addictions, to substances, to other people, and most of all to each other. Krasner, for example, is crystal clear that she wants to marry Pollock in belief of his genius, but equally clear that she does not consider either of them capable of being parents. And as Pollock lashes out against the nearest breakable object when she tells him this, so she stops him dead in his tracks with a burst of chilling conviction: "I refuse to bring another human life into—this." Withering her husband's violence with a look, she forces him to realise that his own actions—his infantilist mess—prove her point.

As Pollock once said of himself, "I am Nature", so Harris' film describes a confrontation between genius and human frailty, acting out the stations of art's particular cross in a plain cold world of booze and envy. As such it tracks a mythology of creativity which runs from Caravaggio to Patti Smith, and is running still, unended.

TIME, 12/25/00-1/1/01, p. 150, Richard Schickel

There are two things you have to say about Jackson Pollock: he figured out a way to paint as no one before him ever had, and he was, as a human being, a shambles—drunken, depressed, disloyal and near to moronically inarticulate. The only way to approach his short and miserable life (he died in a possibly suicidal car crash at age 44) is as an insoluble mystery, and that's precisely what Harris, the star, director and co-producer of *Pollock,* does.

The script by Barbara Turner and Susan J. Emshwiller offers no explanation of the painter's dysfunction or his genius. We meet him pretty much when his wife Lee Krasner (the excellent Harden) does: hanging around Greenwich Village in the 1940s, struggling to break away from his imitative work. Then we see him achieve his breakthrough and watch his burgeoning celebrity do him in. There has never been a more antiheroic biopic than this one. Or a better portrait of the artist as a hopeless mess.

Harris' great performance has a kind of blank grimness; it contains not a single moment of charm or self-awareness. Harris never allows his exhibitions of Pollock's inexplicable gift to soften or redeem the man's monstrousness. The result is a harrowing film, impossible to "like" in any conventional way, hypnotically impossible to turn away from.

VILLAGE VOICE, 2/20/01, p. 131, J Hoberman

Genius or con? That was the question implied by the three-page color spread *Life* published in August 1949 under the title "Jackson Pollock: Is he the greatest living painter in the United States?"

The market has long since rendered such speculation irrelevant. Now it's Jackson Pollock hot, Jackson Pollock cool, or Jackson Pollock: the Movie? Reopening after its one-week Oscar-qualifying run last December, Ed Harris's self-directed vehicle has as its very first image a copy of *Life* thrust forward for an autograph as subliminal flashbulbs illuminate the artist's haunted visage. It is a gallery opening—or, rather, a "premiere." The art star has been born.

Pollock follows the Van Gogh paradigm, up until a point. The artist is misunderstood and tormented; he has sexual problems and is haplessly self-medicated. But unlike Van Gogh, Pollock achieved celebrity in his lifetime—and then died. He's an American who, as with the subject of Julian Schnabel's underrated *Basquiat,* could handle neither failure nor success.

More than any previous American painter, Pollock *was* his personality. (Even better, he was a personality with a trademark: "Jack the Dripper," *Time* dubbed him.) But he also auditioned for a role on the stage of history. Pollock's dreams of art-world domination were focused on a struggle with a powerful adversary. After the opening scene, *Pollock* immediately flashes back eight years to show the hammered painter collapsing in a tenement stairwell, shouting, "Fuck Picasso!" at his sleeping neighbors. No one tells him to pipe down.

As Pollock was himself a sort of method actor playing a genius, Harris's emphatically *pas mal* movie is itself a multiple performance. Star and director in this hall of mirrors, Harris is working every moment. (The most complex example comes with his re-creation of the Hans Namuth movie of Pollock painting and the artist's subsequent explosion—thus we have the actual filmmaker harassing the actor playing the filmmaker with the mantra "I'm not the phony, you're the phony!") Alternately swaggering and staggering, Harris's Pollock is a selfish lout, obnoxious and sullen between manic outbursts as well as one of the least charming drunks ever put center screen in an American movie. In one unforgettable scene, the artist employs a knife and fork to beat time along with a radiocast of Gene Krupa—prelude to a bender after which he wakes up screaming in a Bowery flophouse.

The brutish Marlon Brando who galvanized Broadway in the 1947 production of *A Streetcar Named Desire* reminded more than one member of the New York art world of Pollock; two years later, *Life* introduced Pollock to America as something like the Brando of abstract art. Harris, of course, is a product of the same Actors Studio epitomized by Brando; there are multiple Marlons in his inarticulate, tormented, highly physical, man's-man performance.

The uncanny resemblance between the actor and the acted in *Pollock* suggests that anatomy is destiny. So too, the screenplay, written by Barbara Turner and Susan J. Emshwiller, albeit in a different way. Brand-name title and star turn notwithstanding, *Pollock* is what *Variety* calls a two-hander. The movie is a portrait of a marriage. Pollock the painter is introduced when fellow artist Lee Krasner (Marcia Gay Harden), a humorless noodge with a Bettie Page hairdo, drops by his East Village apartment studio uninvited. "I thought I knew all the abstract painters in New York," she muses in rich Brooklynese, having discovered that this lout of mystery is exhibiting alongside her in a group show. Some weeks later, Pollock reciprocates her visit and thereafter, until the movie's coda, they are unhappily inseparable. When he slowly runs his hand a half-inch over the surface of her canvas, she's receiving his most sensitive caress. When he tells her that she's "pretty damn good for a woman painter," the overdramatized reaction shot given to Harden's wince is only the first of many indignities that her Krasner will suffer.

Carter Ratcliff described Pollock and Krasner as "an intense and dreary couple." Harden more than matches Harris with her wide-eyed determination. Krasner takes charge of Pollock's career—introducing him to the man who introduces him to patron Peggy Guggenheim (wittily played by Amy Madigan). Squeezing paint directly from the tube to the canvas, Pollock is totally intuitive; Krasner's free association is largely verbal. She's the earnest, somewhat badgering intellectual who provides Pollock's theory and plays culture to his nature. She explains his work when even critic Clement Greenberg deems it pretentious "mud."

Scarcely the "allover" blitz of a Pollock canvas, Harris's movie is carefully schematic. The first act—four years of the barely mentioned World War II in claustrophobic New York City—is followed by six years by the beach on outermost Long Island (among other things, Pollock and Krasner invent "East Hampton"). During the good times, nature takes root in nature. Pollock communes with animals, plants a garden, listens to Billie Holiday. It all comes crashing down when he suggests to Krasner that they "make a baby." As she makes clear, in Harden's show-stopping scene, he is her baby.

The brief final act is suffused with pain. Pollock, fat and bearded living in a house full of Pollocks, is a raging bull ready for crack-up. He argues with Greenberg and curses Krasner, taking with a gorgeous groupie (Jennifer Connelly) who, as part of the spooky prelude, is first seen handing him *Life*, which is to say death. The film overwhelmingly suggests that, as much as he may have resented her, Pollock literally could not live without Krasner.

"Yes—I don't think it's so *hot,*" Jeffrey Tambor's Clement Greenberg opines in a superb line-reading of '40s slang. To a degree, *Pollock* thrives on amusing impersonation (Val Kilmer's button-bursting Willem de Kooning) and entertaining anecdote. Avant-garde grand dame Guggenheim has to twice climb the five flights to the Pollock-Krasner tub-in-kit; the painter then enlivens her New Year's Eve soiree by pissing in the fireplace. Full of arty shop talk and dated critical jargon, the movie is high middlebrow fun. "You're retreating into imagery again, Jackson," Greenberg warns. "Paint is paint."

Be that as it may, in Pollock's attempt to embody the modern, he transformed painting into psychodrama. Although Harold Rosenberg was more inclined to bury Pollock than praise him when he wrote his 1952 essay on action painting, Pollock was inevitably cast as the existential hero who understood painting as "an arena in which to act—rather than a space in which to reproduce." Thus, Harris contemplates the empty canvas as though it were a dressing-room mirror. There's an obligatory flurry of Coplandesque fanfares when, cigarette dangling, his Pollock "creates" action painting by knocking off a mural for Peggy Guggenheim in a single night. The riff is repeated later when, working in his Long Island shack, he accidentally discovers the drip. These epiphany scenes notwithstanding, Harris's painting is surprisingly graceful.

Even more unexpected, his spare direction intermittently projects the crazy excitement of people on the edge. ("We're *painters,* Jackson," Harden pleads proudly in her big scene.) The movie's best moments evoke the thrill of doing something new. Even if it fails to make clear how an artist like Pollock might truly have believed himself a world-historical force, *Pollock* convincingly retails the beauty and originality of the painter's best work—it may not be an intellectual adventure, but it does represent one.

Also reviewed by:
CHICAGO TRIBUNE, 2/16/01, Friday/p. A, Michael Wilmington
NEW YORK TIMES, 12/15/00, p. E15, Stephen Holden
NEW YORKER, 3/5/01, p. 104, Anthony Lane
VARIETY, 9/11-17/00, p. 27, David Rooney
WASHINGTON POST, 2/23/01, p. C1, Stephen Hunter
WASHINGTON POST, 2/23/01, Weekend/p. 34, Michael O'Sullivan

POP & ME

A Seventh Art Releasing release of a Fish Eggs production.   *Producer:* Richard Roe and Chris Roe.   *Director:* Chris Roe.   *Director of Photography:* Erik Arnesen and Chris Roe.   *Editor:* Jesse Negron and Chris Roe.   *Music:* Steve Edwards and Mazatl Galindo.   *Sound:* Jesse Negron.   *Running time:* 90 minutes.   *MPAA Rating:* Not Rated.

WITH: Chris Roe; Richard Roe.

LOS ANGELES TIMES, 6/9/00, Calendar/p. 4, Kevin Thomass

"Pop & Me," an edgy probing of the father-and-son relationship, won the audience award at the recent Los Angeles International Film Festival for good reason: It's a documentary made with rigor, humor and no small amount of honest emotion.

A bearded, good-looking man of 55 and the father of three handsome sons, Richard Roe found himself in a triple-threat mid-life crisis: His longtime marriage broke up and both his parents died just as his successful career (as a bond trader) began to falter. He wound up coming to stay in Santa Monica with his middle son Chris, a graphic designer.

A gregarious man with a forceful personality, Richard discovered that what he wanted to do most was to take another trip around the world, for his previous 1979 trip, with his wife and three boys, represented the happiest time of his life. He would dip into his savings not only to make this six-month journey but also offer to take along Chris (plus cameraman Erik Arnesen) and underwrite a film of their travels.

The result is no mere travelogue, for the film is first of all a collection of interviews with fathers and sons around the world about their relationships with each other. Beyond that it delves into Richard and Chris' own relationship, which proves to be problematic and is put to the test time again during their long and at times grueling odyssey.

That Chris intends to delve beneath the superficial becomes clear right away. Following a brief visit to the pleasant suburban Philadelphia home where the Roe family once was happy, Chris and Richard proceed to a Bronx tenement where Richard lived in poverty with his mother. Richard's father was an alcoholic who would be institutionalized with dementia for decades. Richard speaks movingly of seeing his father for the first time in 33 years and giving him his forgiveness for so many years of neglect.

The vast majority of the fathers and sons the Roes interview speak with teary-eyed mutual devotion, but there are several standout variations on the theme. A recovering alcoholic in South Africa tells of the hell he put his family through before he sobered up; the love between an Egyptian general and his policeman son is palpable, but their relationship is based on the father's absolute dominance and the son's total obedience.

But the Roes' real coup was in coming upon Julian Lennon on a beach in Monte Carlo and having Lennon speak forthrightly of his feeling of abandonment once his parents divorced (in his infancy) and his father, John Lennon, had married Yoko Ono. "As a father, I don't have much respect for him at all. He gave the world more love than he did to me," Lennon says.

As the film progresses, relations between the extroverted Richard, not shy about telling his son how to make his movie, and Chris become strained. A brief visit with his oldest son reveals in a flash that Richard shows him more respect than he does Chris and an equally short encounter with his youngest son shows a closeness to him that he and Chris do not share.

"Pop & Me" leaves you feeling that Richard and Chris' relationship is a work in progress, but one that seems heading in the right direction. It would be harder to imagine a film that audiences could identify with more readily.

NEW YORK POST, 6/9/00, p. 50, Hannah Brown

If you've ever taken a road trip with a parent or child and got on each other's nerves, you'll identify with the journey in the documentary "Pop & Me."
Whether you'll want to go along for the ride is another question.
Chris Roe, an aspiring filmmaker, decided to make a movie about the 'round-the-world trip he took with his father, Richard, and a cameraman.
The gimmick is that the Roes attempt to straighten out their relationship by interviewing fathers and sons all over the globe.
They did manage to snag an interview with Julian Lennon. But other than this gem, and one or two other touching interviews, the film is a self-indulgent chronicle of Chris Roe's whiny power struggle with his father over where to eat dinner in various exotic locales.

VILLAGE VOICE, 6/13/00, p. 158, Amy Taubin

Americans are notoriously more oriented toward geography than history. Unlike *Sunshine* [see Taubin's review], which examines a lineage of fathers and sons over a period of 125 years while seldom moving outside of Budapest, *Pop & Me*, like a pint-size *M:I-2*, jets around the world in six months on the impossible mission of restoring the tattered relationship between Chris Roe, an aspiring filmmaker, and his father, Richard Roe, a self-made millionaire. The elder Roe is in the throes of a midlife crisis, exacerbated by having just lost most of his money and having been divorced by his wife. The father wants to revisit the happiest time of his life—a 1979 trip around the world taken in the company of his wife and three young sons. Chris seizes on his father's invitation to accompany him as an opportunity to break through the anger that separates them. It's also a way of making a documentary about fathers and sons on his fathers dime. The last of Dad's fortune is spent on plane tickets and food and travel expenses, not just for two, but also for the cameraman whose constant presence is a guarantee against the intimacy that the son and father both claim to desire. For the purpose of this indie documentary, the Roes visit families in about 20 countries, but they are so blinded by their own neurotic power struggle that they are only capable of viewing other relationships in terms of their own. Tears flow, but the most revelatory moment is provided not by the spectacle of the Roes clinging to each other on a bungee cord, but by Julian Lennon, who pops up on the beach in Monaco to give a terse evaluation of his father: "He loved the world more than he loved me."

Also reviewed in:
CHICAGO TRIBUNE, 6/16/00, Friday/p. K, no reviewer given.
NEW YORK TIMES, 6/9/00, p. E21, Stephen Holden
VARIETY, 4/26-5/2/99, p. 46, David Finnigan

PRAISE

A Strand Releasing release of an Emcee production. *Producer:* Martha Coleman. *Director:* John Curran. *Screenplay (based on his novel):* Andrew McGahan. *Director of Photography:* Dion Beebe. *Editor:* Alexandre de Franceschi. *Music:* Anthony Partos. *Sound:* Phil Tipene. *Casting:* Nikki Barrett. *Production Designer:* Michael Philips. *Art Director:* Anne Beauchamp. *Costumes:* Emily Seresin. *Make-up:* Paul Pattison. *Running time:* 98 minutes. *MPAA Rating:* Not Rated.

CAST: Peter Fenton (Gordon); Sacha Horler (Cynthia); Marta Dusseldorp (Rachel); Joel Edgerton (Leo); Yvette Duncan (Molly); Ray Bull (Vass); Gregory Perkins (Raymond);

Loene Carmen (Cathy);   Skye Wansey (Helen);   Richard Green (Dave);   Lynette Curran (Sexual Health Worker);   Susan Prior (Sophie);   Paul Lum (Darren);   Fiona Mahl (Darren's Girlfriend);   Damon Herriman (Skinhead);   Mick Innes (Taxi Driver);   Jamie Jackson (James); Stephen Shanahan (Steve);   Karen Colston (Mary);   Jason Clarke (Frank);   Basil Clarke (Footless Old Man);   Ken Shorter (Male Nurse);   Joy Hruby (Old Woman).

LOS ANGELES TIMES, 7/14/00, Calendar/p. 10, David Chute

The impressive Australian import "Praise" isn't a "sex movie" in the conventional sense. It certainly isn't puerile or exploitative. But it is largely a movie about sex—about the role of sexual chemistry in relationships, and about the toll that a clash of erotic temperaments can exact, even when (or perhaps especially when) the partners are helplessly addicted to each other.

The film's central characters, Gordon and Cynthia, could easily have been stereotyped as rootless young urban slackers. Instead they are irreducibly specific personalities who can't be explained away as instances of an alarming social trend.

Hard-drinking Cynthia (Sacha Horler) is always heedlessly in motion, usually pursuing raw pleasure. Glum Gordon (Peter Fenton), a chain smoker who seems to be playing chicken with his chronic asthma as if daring the disease to flatten him, is almost catatonically inert.

In dreary Brisbane, Cynthia stalks hungrily from thrill to thrill, while Gordon slouches through life in a dingy flophouse full of bickering old men. Gordon barely has enough drive to hoist himself out of bed in the morning, so he's no match for Cynthia's gale-force appetites.

What's most startling about "Praise" isn't the graphic visual content but the almost claustrophobic emotional intimacy. We are drawn so close to these characters so quickly that we never feel like mere onlookers. Because the lovers don't seem to be performing for our benefit, the director, John Curran, can get at the things that people really say and do to each other in the clinches, in their most unguarded moments, without provoking either grimaces or giggles. There's no hidden voyeuristic agenda.

The performers, like the characters they play, are egregiously mismatched, but in a way that works for the movie. Cynthia pursues sensation with the shameless desperation of a junkie, as a form of anesthesia, and she's literally thin-skinned, with a case of eczema that leaves her cracked and bleeding. A character this extreme should be almost impossible to watch, but Horler is the real thing, the kind of actor who can go all out emotionally without losing control even for a second. We never lose sight of Cynthia's bruised humanity.

Fenton, on the other hand, isn't an actor at all. He's the lead singer of the Australian rock band Crow and had no prior film experience. Fenton seems to slip in and out of focus as we're staring at him. He has a formless, fuzzy screen presence, but it's the point of the movie, in a way, that Gordon is just about impossible to pin down. He is presumably a stand-in for the author of the movie's autobiographical-source novel, Andrew McGahan, who also wrote the screenplay.

But when McGahan, like Gordon, took a pass on the upper-middle-class life that had been mapped out for him, he did it for a reason: He had bigger fish to fry. We never get a clue what Gordon might have cooking, if anything. When Cynthia explodes at him in impotent frustration, we know exactly how she feels.

"Praise" is a lovely piece of movie making: precisely controlled but with a lived-in scruffiness. Curran has a remarkable sensitivity for the textures and rhythms of ordinary life. But there are also some nagging limitations. Gordon and Cynthia may look like hyper-realistic characters, but they are also much more limited than any of the real people we know. They seem to be completely defined by their "personalities," without any higher interests or aspirations. They have been boiled down to their basic instincts.

NEW YORK POST, 6/30/00, p. 47, Jonathan Foreman

Like most of the recent crop of Australian films, "Praise" depicts life in Oz as bleak and depressing.

But this story of a doomed twentysomething relationship, much of it taking place in a grungy boarding house, has going for it a bracingly raw and honest approach to sex that marks it out from similar films on either side of the Pacific. (Unusually, the female characters in the movie are all hornier than the male ones.)

"Praise" follows the intense sexual affair between a short, over-weight sex-crazed young woman with a bad skin condition, and an unemployed asthmatic but hard-smoking 25-year-old boy.

Gordon (Peter Fenton) lives in the sweaty, run-down boarding house. He's bored with his existence until he meets Cynthia (Sacha Horler), who pulls him into her life of sex, heroin and Scrabble.

Despite the frustrations caused by Gordon's premature ejaculation problem, things basically go OK until Rachel, his high school love, turns up in town and Cynthia starts becoming increasingly possessive and demanding.

Both the central performances are as strong as the relatively thin script (adapted by Andrew McGahan from his prize-winning novel of the same name) will allow.

The film's earthy frankness is refreshing, but there's something merciless about its relentless portrayal of human weakness.

NEWSDAY, 6/30/00, Part II/p. B6, John Anderson

In this world there are only two tragedies, said Oscar Wilde. One is not getting what one wants, and the other is getting it. In "Praise"—which is a bit like Oscar Wilde meets "Sid and Nancy"—our hero manages to do both.

Gordon (Peter Fenton, frontman for the Australian band Crows) is adrift in unemployment and the lonely community of his squalid boarding house. Gordon is the anti-stud, sexually unsure of himself and self-deprecating to the point of disappearance. Cynthia (Sacha Horler) has a raft of her own problems—including a checkered sexual history, a rampaging skin problem and an affinity for everything that makes it worse ("oil, dust, soap, beer..."). A most unlikely matchup, but Cynthia sees in Gordon malleable potential. In Cynthia, a flummoxed Gordon has stumbled onto a sexual Club Med.

Director John Curran's debut feature—marked by terrific, naked performances by Fenton and Horler—is a rollicking, darkly funny and in-your-face movie that mixes its hot and cool impulses with a great deal of grace. It's also a remarkably honest film about sexual obsession—remarkable because the obsession so frankly masks everything else that's wrong with its characters, and honest because, in their ultra-grungy fashion, even the characters know the truth.

The way the world works is perverse, "Praise" says. Cynthia, in her tortured bluntness, may represent some people's idea of liberation; for others, she's pathetic. Gordon may find himself in one man's version of the ultimate male fantasy, but the fact remains that too much cake can make you sick. The sad truth within "Praise" is that, for many people, contentment can be found only in disorder and uproar—or in the mad search for love, rather than its discovery. It's a pretty oily subject, but one that "Praise" makes more than palatable.

VILLAGE VOICE, 7/4/00, p. 121, J. Hoberman

A far superior character-driven romance [the reference is to *Trixie*], the Australian film *Praise* chronicles the love affair between a pair of dissolute slackers living day-to-day in a state of dazed, drug-enhanced marginality.

Gordon (Australian rock star Peter Fenton), an unemployed convenience-store clerk, is a good-looking paradigm of passivity who chain-smokes to treat his asthma. His erstwhile coworker Cynthia (Sacha Horler) is a loud-mouthed potato-sack of need with a case of eczema so severe that, when it's inflamed, her skin bleeds to the touch. He's diffident and a bit repressed, she's furiously forward and sexually voracious. Initiating the relationship, Cynthia moves into Gordon's room in a too-tidy flophouse, where they play Scrabble and (mainly) make love. Gordon is so laid-back that heroin improves his sexual performance.

Praise—which Andrew McGahan (the dean of Australian "grunge literature") adapted from his prizewinning novel—has no narrative beyond the trajectory of their relationship. First-time, American-born director John Curran presents his suffering principals with good humor and heartfelt tenderness, framing Cynthia and Gordon's self-consciously dysfunctional codependence in somewhat antiseptic squalor. (The movie's commercial lighting is more suggestive of romantic comedy than a kitchen-sink melodrama.) The acting, however, is refreshingly bold. The lovers' Jack Sprat coupling, which usually features avid Cynthia riding Gordon roughshod, is as wryly explicit as their general disaffection with life's other aspects.

Memorably embodied by Fenton and (especially) Horler, Gordon and Cynthia go deeper into their respective pathologies—the movie only improves as their affair founders on the reef of unintended pregnancy (and genital warts). *Praise* flirts with cute irreverence and the overwrought, overbright look of certain Australian comedies released here by Miramax. Still, neither as uplifting nor as downbeat as it might have been, the movie projects a confessional frankness about human relationships that has the messy feel of truth.

Also reviewed in:
CHICAGO TRIBUNE, 11/17/00, Friday/p. P., Michael Wilmington
NEW YORK TIMES, 6/30/00, p. E13, Elvis Mitchell
VARIETY, 9/28-10/4/98, p. 42, Leonard Klady

PRICE OF AIR, THE

An Artistic License Films release.   *Executive Producer:* Lauren Wild and Lisa Larrivee. *Producer:* Zachary Matz, Thomas Garvin, and Michael Madsen.   *Director:* Josh Evans. *Screenplay:* Josh Evans. *Director of Photography:* Rufus Standefer. *Editor:* Sabine El Chamaa and Fritz Feick. *Music:* Goldie. *Sound:* Garrard Whatley. *Running time:* 85 minutes. *MPAA Rating:* Not Rated.

CAST: Josh Evans (Paul); Charis Michelsen (Anne); Michael Madsen (Mr. Ball); Dick Van Patten (Mr. Rye); Michelle Phillips (Mrs. Rye); Sticky Fingaz (D); Goldie (Greaser); Allison Lange (Amy Rye); Alexis Arquette (Willy); Jenna Hoffman (Thumpy); Badja Djola (Sugar); Gary Chazen (Sr. Dontra); George Randall (Zuma).

LOS ANGELES TIMES, 11/3/00, Calendar/p. 6, Kevin Thomas

For his third independent feature, "The Price of Air," writer-director Josh Evans expands his vision but at a loss of impact. Whereas his first two films, "Inside the Goldmine" (1994) and "Glam" (1997), were harrowingly personal, this film ventures from a strong core relationship to a conventional crime plot that does not play out as effectively as it might.

Evans goes for a finish that demands a tone of dark irony or absurdist humor to keep it from seeming either too easy or merely preposterous; instead, he plays it too dead-on. Evans is no less promising a talent for the drawbacks of this film, but simply has yet to learn how to incorporate the generic within the personal imaginatively.

Evans begins with a fusillade of fragmented moments that more or less connect eventually. Evans also stars, giving a persuasive portrayal as the naive but likable slacker, Paul, whose streetwise best pal D (Sticky Fingaz) is wary of him agreeing to serve as a courier for the crooked Mr. Ball (Michael Madsen). D is to deliver Mr. Ball a new drug, sniffed like cocaine but said to be "more addictive than air."

Not surprisingly, things go disastrously wrong, with Paul ending up on the lam with a young woman (Charis Michelsen) with whom he has a romantic idyll in the desert and in Las Vegas, where they feel they must return to face the music.   They are ill-equipped for any sort of confrontation, despite being strengthened by their evident love for each other, but fate plays into their hands with extraordinary, indeed, awesome generosity.

Evans' plotting is virtually free of exposition, he's fearless in his use of coincidence, and remains a wry commentator on L.A. angst and excesses. He gets high-energy performances from his cast, but Madsen's bad guy and Michelle Phillips and Dick Van Patten as a couple as rich as they are corrupt need to come across as more distinctive individuals in order to engage our interest.

The score by Goldie, with additional music from Sticky Fingaz, Seal, Eve and the Butterfly Species is rich and atmospheric—as stylish as Evans' direction. "The Price of Air," smartly shot in digital and transferred to 35 mm, suggests that Evans needs more seasoning to make genre conventions and characters work for him rather than against him.

NEW YORK POST, 9/29/00, p. 54, Lou Lumenick

The latest vanity production to take up residence at the Empire (as well as the Village East), this is apparently the first film by Hollywood brat Josh Evans to darken a theater outside his native Los Angeles.

"Inside the Goldmine" (1994) and "Glam" (1997) may have gotten decent notices from the company-town press, but on the evidence of the numbingly self-indulgent "The Price of Air," nobody in New York is going to be clamoring to see his earlier work anytime soon.

Evans, the son of Ali McGraw and producer Robert Evans, gives new meaning to the phrase triple-threat as the star, as well as the writer-director of this sorry drug melodrama.

He delivers a singularly monotonous performance as Paul, a small-time dealer who double-crosses his boss (Michael Madsen of "Reservoir Dogs") in Orange County, Calif.

That triggers Paul's flight to Las Vegas and Zion National Park with porno star Anne (Charlis Michelsen), and a mounting body count. Besides the hip-hoppers Sticky Fingaz and Goldie (whom Evans worked with in his day job as a music-video director), the victims include Paul's girlfriend Amy (Allison Lange), who succumbs to an overdose.

Amy's parents are played by Dick Van Patten and Michelle Phillips, who hit new career lows here. There's certain perverse entertainment value in watching the erstwhile star of "Eight Is Enough" trash his image by cavorting in sadomasochistic gear and the former Mamas and the Papas member jeeringly try to seduce Paul at gunpoint—not to mention Jenna Hoffman's frightening cameo as Anne's lesbian lover.

But it's not worth suffering through 85 excruciatingly slow minutes of exceedingly ugly digital-video images.

NEWSDAY, 9/29/00, Part II/p. B6, Jan Stuart

What wouldn't we have given to be able to have sat in on a meeting where someone said, "What the world needs now is another ultraviolent underbelly-of-L.A. picture in which two alienated young adults fall in love and get mixed up with evil drug dealers and sadistic hit men and smarmy porno producers and everyone ends up blowing each other away by the final reel except the two romantic leads."

Perhaps it would have not been too late to put a stop to "The Price of Air," an 85-minute exercise in shopworn amorality that looks like a ludicrous "Saturday Night Live" parody of Quentin Tarantino and Oliver Stone shoot-'em-ups called "Natural Born Losers." But then again, there might have been no getting through to Josh Evans, the film's star, writer and director, who seems hell-bent on squandering the talent and influence gleaned from being the son of producer Robert Evans and actress Ali MacGraw.

At the very least, we would have had the opportunity to ask Evans why we are supposed to give a fig for his character Paul, a punky creep who mistakenly agrees to act as courier for a new, rarefied high called "blue," or for his bisexual porno-actress girlfriend Anne (Charis Michelsen). Or why we are supposed to think they are any worthier of our sympathies than the vulgar exemplars of L.A.'s corrupt power brokers (Michael Madsen, Dick Van Patten and Michelle Phillips, snarling and foaming at the mouth like rabid dogs) that they are rebelling against.

It is doubtful that even Evans could explain why his distaste for humanity is so all-encompassing-to accuse him of misogyny and homophobia would be an oversimplification. He is not untalented, and perhaps someday when he gets over himself he will make a movie that someone else besides his therapist would like to see. As it is, "The Price of Air" is worth only the price of the soundtrack, which features intriguing primal-sounding music by some guy named Goldie.

VILLAGE VOICE, 10/3/00, p. 238, Michael Atkinson

Josh Evans's *The Price of Air* starts out temptingly: Shot on digital video, the movie doesn't tell its story so much as toss it in the air like loose cash. Evans (son of Ali McGraw and Robert Evans) plays scofflaw with rudimentary syntax like establishing shots and matching eye lines, and initially his movie has a rowdy, fractured, shake-'n'-bake looseness that meets the needs of his characters: drug dealers. But it doesn't take long before the fog evaporates and Hollywood-brat self-indulgence becomes the film's primary lingo. What seems to thrum with naturalism quickly becomes arch and posturing, hardly helped by the macguffin: a new drug called "blue" that is reportedly "more addictive than air."

Or so says Michael Madsen as the resident bloated drug honcho, cronying around with the Porky-ish likes of Dick Van Patten as an L.A. magnate married to Michelle Phillips (rest assured, Evans dresses her up in a bustier and garters before we're through) and prone to hanging out in a local s/m club sporting a spiked collar. *(Eight Is Enough* fans, we never knew ye.) Evans himself plays, rather adroitly, a young layabout who moves some of the dope for quick cash, and when Madsen's men decide to off him, he sees his best buddy (Sticky Fingaz) take a bullet, and consequently hits the bricks.

But being on the run from the mob here means wandering around, sightseeing Vegas, and eventually retiring to a hotel room with a bewitching young thing (Charis Michelsen) to do some of the shit until a hit man (Goldie) shows up, inexplicably, to remove one of Evans's kidneys. ("Promise me you'll take him to the hospital right away," he tells the girl.) Meandering, listless, and more than a little condescending (wealthy Beverly Hills movie kids making yet another movie about down-and-out losers with idyllic dreams), *The Price of Air* culminates in a second bing-bang-boom triple shoot-out that effectively cancels out the shreds of remaining plot but is shot and cut like a sixth grader's Super-8 struggle for Woo-ness. If digital video's acceptance as a public medium means that celebrious incontinence will become a rank wave of its own, let's start holding out for the true emulsion.

Also reviewed in:
NEW YORK TIMES, 9/29/00, p. E16, Dave Kehr
VARIETY, 10/2-8/00, p. 21, Scott Foundas

PRICE OF GLORY

A New Line Cinema release of an Esparza-Katz production in association with Arthur E. Friedman productions. *Executive Producer:* Carolyn Manetti, Stephanie Striegel, and Loretha Jones. *Producer:* Moctesuma Esparza, Robert Katz, and Arthur E. Friedman. *Director:* Carlos Avila. *Screenplay:* Phil Berger. *Director of Photography:* Affonso Beato. *Editor:* Gary Karr. *Music:* Joseph Julian Gonzalez. *Music Editor:* Lisé Richardson. *Sound:* Stephen Halbert and (music) John Whynot. *Sound Editor:* Benjamin Cook. *Casting:* Rick Pagano. *Production Designer:* Robb Wilson King. *Art Director:* Amy Martin. *Set Designer:* Pamela Klamer. *Set Decorator:* Lance Lombardo. *Set Dresser:* Otniel Gonzalez, Marc Martin Del Campo, Vartan Tashjian, George C. Atamian, and Tim Savatgy. *Visual Effects:* Richard Malzahn. *Costumes:* Ruth Carter. *Make-up:* Mark Sanchez. *Stunt Coordinator:* Benny "The Jet" Urquidez. *Running time:* 100 minutes. *MPAA Rating:* PG-13.

CAST: Jimmy Smits (Arturo Ortega); Maria Del Mar (Rita Ortega); Jon Seda (Sonny Ortega); Clifton Collins, Jr. (Jimmy Ortega); Ernesto Hernandez (Johnny Ortega); Ron Perlman (Nick Everson); Louis Mandylor (Davey Lane); Sal Lopez (Hector Salmon); Danielle Camastra (Mariella Cruz); Paul Rodriguez (Pepe); Ulysses Cuadra (Young Sonny Ortega); Marlo Esquivel (Young Jimmy Ortega), Gilbert Leal (Young Johnny Ortega); Muni Zano (Chivo); Jack Rader (Marata); Carlos Palomino (Oscar); Matt Cedeno (Young Arturo Ortega); Irene De Bari (Mrs. Cruz); Paco Farias (Luis Cruz); Joshua Ponce de Leon (Little Oscar); Jeff Langton (Referee); William Marquez (Machado); Jose Yenque (The Hood); Tony Genaro (Malave); Harley Rodriguez (Young Hector Salmon); John Verea (Azamar); Patrick Outlaw (Dupree); Matthew Kimbrough (TV Announcer); Michelle Bonilla (Grace Chavez); John La Fayette (Dr. Bill Ward); Katrina Gibson (Young Rita Ortega); Jimmy Lennon, Jr. (Ring Announcer); Tom Simmons (Salesman); Craig Love (Rex Macon); Leyna Nguyen (TV Newscaster); John Capodice (Priest); Bill Ryusaki (Silver Gloves Official); Noel Gugliemi (Angel); Clayton Landey (Boxing Official); Ernesto Macias (Saraceno); Zitto Kazann (Dr. Cardinal); Larry Strauss (Ringside Doctor).

LOS ANGELES TIMES, 3/31/00, Calendar/p. 6, Eric Harrison

Just as the endings of the big, climactic fight scenes in boxing movies all are preordained, so, too, are the plot mechanisms that get us there. A degree of predictability is built into the genre. How well these movies work for us, then, depends in large part on how much life filmmakers can breathe into ossified conventions.

On that score, "Price of Glory" wins points simply by virtue of its premise—the movie is set in a modest Chicano community in Arizona. For almost as long as Hollywood has existed it's spun out stories about urban Irish, Italian and, more recently, African American pugilists fighting their way out of their respective ghettos. You don't see many fight movies about Chicanos in tiny border towns.

That alone isn't reason enough to recommend it, but, luckily, "Glory" has more going for it than that, not least of which is a powerful and nuanced performance by Jimmy Smits as Arturo Ortega, the overbearing patriarch of a family that lives and breathes boxing.

Ortega's own promising career was cut short when a greedy manager put him in the ring with a raging dynamo before he was ready. Beaten badly—he's initially shown many years after that bout with a twitch that miraculously vanishes—Arturo has placed all of his ambitions and dreams in his three sons.

That disappearing twitch is indicative of the kind of clumsiness that mars this movie, which sometimes looks and sounds like a less-than-distinguished television production. But the material is elevated by the acting (former Golden Globes boxer Jon Seda and Clifton Collins Jr. are also quite good as two of the sons) and by its visceral power, of the fight scenes especially. "Glory" also packs an emotional wallop that sneaks up on you like an uppercut.

The movie's central focus is the way Arturo's single-minded pursuit of glory via the vehicle of his sons comes close to tearing the family apart. Its central weakness is a script (by former New York Times sportswriter Phil Berger) that goes badly off track midway.

First-time director Carlos Avila moves "Glory" swiftly in the early going through the boys' youth, showing how Arturo drove them mercilessly, often expressing his love in a way that looks more like cruelty. Then the boys grow up. Arturo still tries to dominate and mold their lives, but they have developed wills of their own.

One son has gotten married and pulled away somewhat from his dad; another rebels and goes into a tailspin; and the third, the youngest (played by newcomer Ernesto Hernandez), becomes the superlative fighter Arturo wants him to be. An unscrupulous boxing promoter (Ron Perlman) and his henchmen add a sinister and deadly twist.

Like Arturo, the movie doesn't allow any of the sons enough room to develop. It tries to juggle too many story lines while also keeping Smits front and center. The narrative thread frays and very nearly breaks.

Whether it regains its footing for you will depend on how powerfully the concluding fight scene and the emotional buildup to it connects. That will vary with the individual, but it tore me up.

It's common to talk of the "crossover potential" of movies like this. "Glory" sprouts so clearly out of the bedrock of American myth and culture that to speak of it as somehow marginal or specialized offends common sense. The film deals with notions—fathers and sons, the resilience of family, a child's longing to break free—to which anyone can relate.

To watch the way Arturo's excessive pride and need for control edge close to destroying his family is to witness nothing less than a contemporary American spin on Shakespearean themes. The specificty of "Glory's" setting and ethnicitiy of its characters enrich the story without moving it one iota away from a mainstream frame of reference.

NEW YORK POST, 3/31/00, p. 55, Lou Lumenick

Clichés fly faster than fists in "Price of Glory," an old-fashioned boxing movie that can't really go the distance.

Jimmy Smits tries hard—and often connects—as a stubborn Mexican immigrant in Arizona, a failed middleweight contender who trains his three sons for the ring with results ranging from tragedy to triumph.

"You think I want them to end up like me?" he asks, over and over as the film drones on for nearly two hours.

"Everything I've ever done is for you boys!" he exclaims all too often.

Screenwriter Phil Berger covered boxing for the New York Times and collaborated on biographies of Joe Frazier and Larry Holmes, but what he's done here is to basically take a Warner Bros. boxing film of the 1930s and change the ethnicity from Irish to Latino. Its as if "Rocky" and "Raging Bull" never happened.

This sometimes painfully sincere movie is clearly a labor of love for all involved, including director Carlos Avila, whose extensive TV experience is apparent in his flat handling of scenes: many fights, many arguments, a wedding and a funeral.

Jon Seda, Clifton Collins Jr. and Ernesto Hernandez are fine as Smits' sometimes restless sons, but some of the supporting performances—especially Ron Perlman as a ruthless boxing promoter—are less than convincing.

"Price of Glory" isn't an embarrassment on the order of the last major boxing movie, "Play It to the Bone," but its not especially worth intercepting on its way to the video racks.

NEWSDAY, 3/31/00, Part II/p. B7, John Anderson

Having amassed a total of 10 Emmy nominations for his work on "L.A. Law" and "NYPD Blue," Jimmy Smits should feel right at home in "Price of Glory," which is essentially a better-than-average TV movie with a strong streak of Hispanic pride. As a boxing movie, of course, the film carries the paradoxical burden of most of its ilk: glorifying the ring while at the same telling us what a filthy business it is.

But as written by ex-New York Times fight writer Phil Berger, "Price of Glory" comes equipped with a better-than-average take on the mechanics of the game and maybe even what makes its practitioners tick—guys like Arturo Ortega (Smits), who had his own fight career cut short by crooked management and is determined to raise his sons to be champs. If this seems paradoxical, it is: The scenes of Arturo's sons in their peewee boxing garb suggests a troupe of JonBenet Ramseys in protective headgear.

But if Arturo is an obsessive, and his thirst for vicarious glory rooted in his own frustrated career, he's also a crafty trainer and an honest judge of talent: He knows that his son Johnny (Ernesto Hernandez), with whom he shares the strongest bond, is the real thing; that Sonny (Jon Seda) is also a contender, but that Jimmy (Clifton Collins Jr.) will never be a champ (if this were "The Godfather"—which in many ways it is—Jimmy would be Fredo).

With Arturo trying to maneuver his sons' careers, the family is rent by internal conflicts that are as easy to see coming as the weekend and that make "Price of Glory" feel more than recycled.

That it was developed with the help of the Sundance Institute is interesting—Sundance must have been much more interested in the Hispanic aspects of the film than its structure, story or message, all of which are fairly routine.

The triumphant ending, which is close to hysterical, should have embarrassed someone, but apparently not.

And where's Mom in all this? Played by Maria Del Mar, Arturo's wife, Rita Ortega, is a pretty passive sports madre, rarely showing concern about the damage her sons incur in the ring; that seems more than a little strange, although in the overwhelmingly patriarchal scheme of "Price of Glory," it probably makes perfect sense.

SIGHT AND SOUND, 6/01, p. 51, Edward Lawrenson

Mariposa, Arizona, 1990. Thirteen years after the end of his professional boxing career, Arturo Ortega spends his spare time coaching his two elder sons Sonny and Jimmy for the Silver Gloves trials. Jimmy wins the state wide competition while Arturo's youngest son Johnny, who hasn't fought before, takes the place of a competitor who had to pull out from his match.

Ten years later, Arturo still coaches his sons. Johnny attracts the attention of boxing promoter Nick Everson. Wary of outside interference, partly because his own manager exploited him during his boxing career, Arturo refuses Everson's offer to sign up his sons. In the lead-up to his first televised bout, Sonny announces he is to marry his girlfriend Mariella. Arturo agrees to a match between Jimmy and one of Everson's fighters Davey Lane, the champion of his weight league, and hints that he's prepared to have Sonny and Johnny fight for the promoter at a later date. Jimmy, the least talented of the Ortega brothers, is beaten by Lane; after the fight, Arturo turns down Everson's suggestion that Sonny fight Lane. Angered that Arturo has gone back on his word, the promoter then signs up Jimmy, who has ignored Arturo's advice to give up boxing, and puts him up against another of his fighters, Junior Dupree.

Former boxer Pepe attempts to persuade Johnny of the benefits of being under contract to his boss Everson. Loyal to his father, Johnny beats Pepe up. Later, in a scuffle with a tough guy whom Pepe has hired, Johnny is shot dead. Resentful towards Arturo, Sonny signs with Everson, who plans to pit him against Lane. Having given up boxing, Jimmy persuades Arturo to train Sonny for his fight with Lane. Reconciled with his father, Sonny wins his bout with Lane, and is declared champion.

Price of Glory is a stolid and earnest family drama revolving around the world of professional boxing and marked by a dutifully understated central performance from Jimmy Smits. The results are efficient, but woefully underwhelming. Curiously for one of the most machismo-driven sports, boxing has provided the subject matter for a good few emotive tearjerkers, and there's certainly potential in *Price of Glory*'s premise for some ripe melodrama along the lines of *The Champ* or *Rocky*: with a botched career as a professional boxer behind him, Smits' middle-aged family man Arturo makes up for his sense of failure by trying to turn his three teenage sons into prize fighters, causing varying degrees of triumph and tragedy along the way. But debut director Carlos Avila's workmanlike approach, entirely untouched by the brash showmanship that characterises the best boxing movies as well as the sport itself flattens his material into bland, unengaging fare. Even the clichés of the genre, such as when Arturo tells his son Jimmy, "You are this close to being a contender", seem strangely unfamiliar thanks to their deadeningly dull delivery.

Part of the problem is the uneven casting. Chosen from open casting sessions, Ernesto Hernández looks the part as Johnny, Arturo's youngest: in the ring, his punches seem quick and powerful, and he's fast on his feet; even on the other side of the ropes, he looks like he's gearing up for a fight, his heavy-set features arranged into a goading scowl. But he falters when required to do the dramatic stuff; his line delivery is particularly clumsy, which makes his scenes with the other actors seem stilted. Jon Seda, meanwhile, a former New Jersey boxer who reportedly switched to acting because it was less dangerous, is less convincing in the ring, and the staging of his climactic showdown with title holder Davey Lane, a nicely arrogant cameo from Louis Mandylor, is choppy and awkward. Smits' performance as Arturo is an admirable effort. But given that the script is replete with such trite dialogue as "I need to talk to you different, not like your fighter, like your son", it's hardly surprising he's not given the chance to build on those few occasions (the fine scene, for instance, when Arturo manages to alienate nearly everyone at a family Thanksgiving dinner) which explore the darker side to his drive to see his kids succeed as fighters.

VILLAGE VOICE, 4/10/00, p. 162, Michael Atkinson

But what price glory? Whatever the cost, it's a debt unpaid by the platoon of guileless hacks who assembled *Price of Glory* —not that the title or ads are fooling anyone. ("For every dream there is a sacrifice"—guess whose?) An exasperating ordeal by cliché and schmaltz, Carlos Avila's Chicano Rocky saga begins in a punch-drunk stumble: Failed boxer Arturo (Jimmy Smits) bullies his three prepubescent sons into the ring, and we're subjected to a symphonically hallowed montage of their training that would shame John Avildsen. The three sons grow up (to be stoic Jon Seda, testy Clifton Collins Jr., and oaken Ernesto Hernandez) and get caught in a variety of mild conflicts with their glowering papa (so ill-conceived as a character he launches into hot-headed tirades for no apparent reason) on their way to tragedy or title fights or both.

Phil Berger, a former *New York Times* sportswriter, wrote the script, but the boxing in the movie is vintage-'80s crap—the winners hit, the unguarded losers get hit, and all of the boys' nasty opponents are balding—and the rise and fall of attempted dramatic action suggests tectonic-plate movement. Contrived and contrived sloppily, this self-adoring soap even manages to make its all-Hispanic cast seem unconvincing—except for Seda, everyone sounds as if they learned their accents from watching *The Perez Family*.

Also reviewed in:
CHICAGO TRIBUNE, 3/31/00, Friday/p. J, Michael Wilmington

NEW YORK TIMES, 3/31/00, p. E15, Lawrence Van Gelder
WASHINGTON POST, 3/31/00, p. C5, Rita Kempley
WASHINGTON POST, 3/31/00, Weekend/p. 45, Desson Howe

PRINCE OF CENTRAL PARK

An Avalanche Home Entertainment and Keystone release of an Abe Hirschfeld presentation of a Seagal/Julius R. Nasso production. *Executive Producer:* Abe Hirschfeld, Karen Poindexter, and Phillip B. Goldfine.   *Producer:* Steven Seagal, Julius R. Nasso, and John Gulino.   *Director:* John Leekley.   *Screenplay:* John Leekley.   *Based on a novel by:* Evan K. Rhodes;   *Director of Photography:* Jonathan Herron.   *Editor:* Philip Steinman.   *Music:* Ted Shapiro.   *Music Editor:* Jay B. Richardson and Lisa Jaime.   *Sound:* Jeff Pullman.   *Sound Editor:* Jay Nierenberg.   *Casting:* Ellen Parks.   *Production Designer:* Deana Sidney.   *Art Director:* Betsy McDonald.   *Costumes:* Laura Jean Shannon.   *Stunt Coordinator:* Kristopher Medina.   *Running time:* 111 minutes.   *MPAA Rating:* PG-13.

CAST: Kathleen Turner (Rebecca Cairn); Danny Aiello (Noah Cairn); Cathy Moriarty (Mrs. Ardis); Frankie Nasso (J. J. Somerled); Harvey Keitel (Guardian); Lauren Velez (Rosa Sanchez); Jerry Orbach (Businessman); Mtume Gant (Easy); Tina Holmes (Annalisse Somerled); Carmen Moreno (Sophia); Svetlana Efremova (Sophia's Mom); Francesco Vittorio (Young JJ); Michael P. Moran (Security Guard); Stephanie Berry (School Principal); Frank Anthony (Carousel Operator); Larry Clarke and Vincent Rocco (Cops); Dan Ziskie (City Planner); John P. Gulino (Deputy Mayor); Ted Arcidi (Construction Worker); Philippe Mao (Maitre D'); Martha Ryan (Nurse Yeager); Pamela Stewart (Nurse Kohanek); Jaliyl Lynn (Dominique); Frank Bongiorno (Judge); Lexie Sperduto (Little Girl); Todd Wall (Joe).

NEW YORK POST, 9/22/00, p. 50, Lou Lumenick

This elaborate vanity production boasts no fewer than four Oscar nominees and high production values—all in support of a minimally expressive youngster named Frankie Nasso, the son of producer Julius R. Nasso. Young Frankie runs away from his abusive foster mother (Cathy Moriarity) to live in Central Park, where a troll (Harvey Keitel) protects him until he's adopted by a wacko rich lady (Kathleen Turner) and her estranged husband (Danny Aiello).

Directed by John Leekley at a funereal pace, this bomb is based on a 1974 novel by Evan Rhodes that was previously turned into a 1977 TV movie and a flop Broadway musical. Eccentric mayoral candidate Abe Hirschfeld gets an associate producer credit here.

NEWSDAY, 9/22/00, Part II/p. B6, Gene Seymour

The only enchantment to be found in "Prince of Central Park" is in the quaint coarseness of its visuals. Not since the 1960s has New York City looked as garish and gritty in Technicolor as it does here. Those of us old enough to remember dreaming of Manhattan in that long-ago decade, whether inspired by "The World of Henry Orient" or "Coogan's Bluff," may feel a warm whisper of nostalgia from this self-styled urban fairy tale.

Otherwise, it's a hackneyed dirge about a sensitive, musically gifted 14 year-old boy named J.J. (Frankie Nasso), who has been abandoned by his ailing mom and living in malign neglect with a Staten Island slattern (Cathy Moriarty), who's into the foster-care thing purely for the money. After taking one body blow too many, J.J. crosses the river to the magic island of Manhattan and to the forest primeval of Central Park.

There, he meets a "troll" living under a footbridge. Actually, it's a noisy, oracular bum (Harvey Keitel), who agrees to protect J.J. from muggers and other predators if the kid will scrounge for their supper. Of course, there's also a dog. There always is.

If this makes the grown-up in you wince, you should see some of the overcooked hamming served up by Keitel, Moriarty and Kathleen Turner, who plays an uptown matron whose sugar-rush dottiness has driven her husband (Danny Aiello) from their posh digs. Nasso, a relative newcomer, outshines them all with an unaffected confidence and beguiling honesty that almost saves the movie from its suffocating coyness.

VILLAGE VOICE, 9/26/00, p. 152, Michael Atkinson

Remaking *Prince of Central Park* hasn't helped anybody. A stinky dumpster for sentimental dung about homelessness and the magical mecca that isn't Manhattan, John Leekley's boogie thru the old Evan Rhodes chestnut can make your corneas ache. Frankie Nasso is the orphan who escapes his venomous foster mother (Cathy Moriarty) to live in Central Park under the tutelage of a pointy-bearded troll who lives in a secret cave (Harvey Keitel, I swear to God), and eventually warms to an emotionally fractured mom (Kathleen Turner). If you're not seduced with the prospect of Moriarty and Turner whiskey-growling at each other in court over the boy, you're somewhere else.

Also reviewed in:
NEW YORK TIMES, 9/22/00, p. E16, Dave Kehr
VARIETY, 5/17-23/99, p. 58, Brendan Kelly

PROOF OF LIFE

A Warner Brother release of a Castle Rock Entertainment presentation in association with Bel-Air Entertainment of an Anvil Films production. *Executive Producer:* Steven Reuther and Tony Gilroy. *Producer:* Taylor Hackford and Charles Mulvehill. *Director:* Taylor Hackford. *Screenplay:* Tony Gilroy. *Inspired by the Vanity Fair article "Adventures in the Ransom Trade"* by William Prochnau *and by the book "Long March to Freedom" by:* Thomas Hargrove. *Director of Photography:* Slawomir Idziak. *Editor:* John Smith and Sheldon Kahn. *Music:* Danny Elfman. *Music Editor:* Ellen Segal. *Sound:* Ivan Sharrock and (music) Dennis Sands. *Sound Editor:* Per Hallberg. *Casting:* Nancy Klopper. *Production Designer:* Bruno Rubeo. *Art Director:* Steve Carter. *Set Decorator:* Steve Shewchuk. *Set Dresser:* Miriam Bell-Irving. *Special Effects:* Yves DeBono. *Costumes:* Ruth Myers. *Make-up:* Luigi Rocchetti. *Make-up (Meg Ryan):* Karen Kawahara. *Stunt Coordinator:* Gary Davis. *Running time:* 135 minutes. *MPAA Rating:* R.

CAST: Meg Ryan (Alice Bowman); Russell Crowe (Terry Thorne); David Morse (Peter Bowman); Pamela Reed (Janis Goodman); David Caruso (Dino); Anthony Heald (Ted Fellner); Stanley Anderson (Jerry); Gottfried John (Eric Kessler); Alun Armstrong (Wyatt); Michael Kitchen (Ian Havery); Margo Martindale (Ivy); Mario Ernesto Sanchez (Fernandez); Pietro Sibille (Juaco); Vicky Hernandez (Maria); Norma Martinez (Norma); Diego Trujillo (Eliodoro); Aristóteles Picho (Sandro); Sarahi Echeverria (Cinta); Carlos Blanchard (Carlos); Raul Rodriguez (Tomas); Mauro Cueva (Rico); Alejandro Cordova (Rambo); Sandro Bellido (Mono); Miguel Iza (ELT officer); Roberto Frisone (Calitri); Tony Vazquez (Fred/Marco); Claudia Dammert (Ginger); Rowena King (Pamela); Michael Byrne (Luthan); Jaime Zevallos (Nino); Gilberto Torres (Raymo); Flora Martinez (Linda); Laura Escobar (Cara); Marcos Bustos (Alex); Jorge Medina (Berto); Gerard Naprous (Pierre Lenoir); Alexander Balueyev (Russian Colonel); Dimitri Shevchenko (Russian Sergeant); Zbigniew Zamachowski (Terry's Driver); Said K. Saralijen (Chechen Leader); Oscar Carrillo, Pedro Martinez Laya, and Wolframio Benavides (Trial Honchos); Alonso Alegria (Master of Ceremonies); Merlin Hanbury-Tenison (Terry's Son); Stefan Gryff (Bank Official); Yolanda Vazquez (Notary).

LOS ANGELES TIMES, 12/8/00, Calendar/p. 2, Kenneth Turan

It may be unfair, but it's inevitable that "Proof of Life" is going to be seen, at least in the short run, through the lens of the off-screen romance that developed on location between co-stars Meg

Ryan and Russell Crowe. The affair that unleashed a flood of tabloid headlines is simply too fitting a viewpoint to resist in our scandal-and celebrity-crazed age.

Partly that's because the film's story line, which to some extent involves a forbidden love that develops between a crack "K&R" operative (that's kidnapping and ransom to you civilians) and someone else's wife (in this case the wife of the man he's trying to extract) has some parallels to what happened in life.

But it's also partly because this Taylor Hackford-directed, Tony Gilroy-written film, solidly and professionally made though it is, is nowhere near as engrossing as looking for signs of life between the two lead performers, trying to see if we can spy a genuine relationship developing in front of us. The movies may be fantasy, but a touch of the authentic never hurt anything.

Which is why, even though the film's climactic action sequences are briskly done, the biggest gasp one preview audience gave was when Ryan and Crowe finally join for a brief but noticeably passionate kiss. Everyone felt, or imagined they did, that it was for real.

Based initially on a Vanity Fair article about men who specialize in getting back kidnapped business executives, "Proof of Life" is an ambitious film that aims to examine the human equations behind the abductions. But for all its good intentions, it's not as subtle as it might be, and it's finally pitched too broadly to achieve the level of emotional truth it aims for.

To familiarize us with the world K&R men consider home, "Proof of Life" uses its opening credits sequences to eavesdrop on the exploits of Terry Thorne (Crowe), one of Luthan Risk International's best operatives, as he negotiates for and then rescues a man abducted by the Chechen rebels. A proactive, essentially nerveless individual who if need be could probably use his teeth to latch onto a departing helicopter, Thorne is not a person to be trifled with.

Another of the world's trouble zones turns out to be the mythical South American country of Tecala, where the usual corrupt oligarchy runs things and fights for power with a rebel movement called the ELT. This used to be an idealistic Marxist organization but devolved into a thuggish group more devoted to drug trafficking and kidnapping for profit than ideology.

Though they live in Tecala, neither American engineer Peter Bowman (David Morse) nor his spunky wife Alice (Ryan) know much about this. He's a naive humanitarian, trying to build a dam for an oil company that regards his project as do-gooder window-dressing, while she is too involved in a recent personal loss to have even learned to speak Spanish.

Then, more by happenstance than careful planning, Peter gets kidnapped by the ELT. Once they find out that he works for a multinational corporation, the rebels insist on a $3-million ransom, a figure that flabbergasts both Alice and Peter's overbearing sister Janis (Pamela Reed), who flies down to be of assistance.

It takes no great stretch of imagination to figure out that Terry is going to get involved in the attempt to pry Peter loose from his captors, but, movies being movies, all kinds of obstacles to his taking the job arise and almost half of the film's running time elapses before, with the help of fellow negotiator Dino (David Caruso) he's firmly in charge.

Once that happens, "Proof of Life" cuts back and forth between Terry saying calming things to Alice like, "This is a game you play whether you like it or not" and Peter being carted around the countryside by a not-very-together ELT. Unfortunately, a lot of what Peter attempts in the name of heroic resistance seems irritatingly childish, and though he is supposed to be more of an audience surrogate than Terry, his churlishness, albeit understandable, makes that an awkward fit.

Instead, audiences may prefer to identify with and/or fantasize about Crowe. Well-matched by Ryan's feistiness and in a role halfway between "The Insider" and "Gladiator," Crowe uses his top-of-the-line masculine presence and the ability to pour considerable emotion into the simplest looks to create interest in his character and his situation. Terry doesn't have to say, "I'm for real," but when he does, no one will be asking for a second opinion.

NEW YORK, 12/18-25/00, p. 168, Peter Rainer

A good subject is thoroughly and methodically wasted in Taylor Hackford's *Proof of Life*, starring Meg Ryan and Russell Crowe, which is about the kidnapping of an American engineer in a South American country and the attempt by a professional ransom consultant to negotiate his release. Apparently it is now big business for terrorists—mostly mercenaries and drug lords with dubious revolutionary political ties—to abduct high-level American executives from their foreign-based posts. (The film takes off from a *Vanity Fair* article, "Adventures in the Ransom Trade," by Bill Prochnau, and Thomas Hargrove's autobiography.) American corporations doing business overseas routinely factor into their insurance policies the costs of abduction, spawning in the process a new industry of kidnap negotiators consisting mainly of ex-CIA, SAS, KGB, and FBI agents.

In *Proof of Life,* the abducted engineer (David Morse) is left stranded when the corporation he works for goes belly-up, and so it falls to Russell Crowe's Terry Thorne, a tight-lipped former SAS commando turned hostage negotiator, to bring him out of the jungles alive. Meg Ryan's Alice is the engineer's wife, and the pre-kidnap scenes with her husband convey the all-too-convenient revelation that her marriage is wobbly. Being in a bad marriage allows Alice to shoot smoldering glances at Terry and still retain audience sympathy, even as her spouse, growing progressively hairier as the film lugs along until he resembles a woolly mammoth, is repeatedly battered and tortured for our delectation.

Ryan and Crowe, despite all the real-life publicity surrounding their pairing, never get to indulge in anything more than a chaste kiss, and so all the strong-silent simmering between them seems kind of a cheat; after all the teeth-gritting and hacked limbs, we have a right to expect from this romance more than a wimpy Casablanca-style fade-out. But the political-thriller genre has been in the doldrums since the end of the Cold War. *Proof of Life* tries to resuscitate the Cold War mentality by portraying former communist rebels as hepped-up, doped-up curs; they make the banditos who converged upon Humphrey Bogart in *The Treasure of the Sierra Madre* seem statesmanlike by comparison. The only proof of life in this moribund movie comes from Pamela Reed's brief turn as Alice's sister. She packs so much intensity into every line and gesture that she gives her cameo the fullness of a starring role.

NEW YORK POST, 12/8/00, p. 55, Lou Lumenick

Let's get the important, tabloid stuff out of the way first.

No matter what hanky-panky is alleged to have been going on off the set, the characters played by Meg Ryan and Russell Crowe aren't seen doing the nasty in the final cut of "Proof of Life."

Months following their alleged real-life affair, the protagonists are glimpsed exchanging just one, relatively innocent, kiss. The film's adultery angle has apparently been played way down, and a steamy Ryan-Crowe bedroom scene reportedly ended up on the cutting room floor.

What's left is a disappointingly routine kidnapping thriller with soap-opera trimmings and some very strong acting—though nothing in the way of on-screen chemistry between Crowe and Ryan. Ryan plays Alice, an unhappily married American in a Latin American country. Her husband, Peter (David Morse), an engineer, is abducted by guerrillas who are asking a $3 million ransom.

After her husband's bankrupt employers leave her to her own devices, Alice hires Terry (Russell Crowe), a crack kidnapping and rescue negotiator out of London.

Terry's approach is methodical—it's all about the money, he assures Alice, as he slowly negotiates the ransom sum downward—but the process takes months, as her husband suffers imprisonment in a remote mountain camp peopled by offensively stereotyped South Americans.

There's ultimately a commando-style raid to free David—lots of gunfire and explosions, but pretty much by-the-numbers stuff.

Director Taylor Hackford ("An Officer and a Gentleman") has generally been more interested in romance than action, but real-life events and nervous studio executives may have tied his hands here.

The on-screen relationship between Alice and Terry in the finished film is so circumspect that the "Casablanca"-style ending doesn't make a whole lot of sense.

Working hard to flesh out an underwritten role, Crowe once again demonstrates he's one of the best actors working today. Ryan, saddled with a soggy subplot about her thwarted maternal ambitions, hardly seems to be in the same movie as Crowe. She struggles, with mixed results, to tone down her dithery mannerisms enough to be entirely credible as a woman in crisis.

David Morse ("The Green Mile") is once again impressive as the workaholic husband and the tortures he endures in his lengthy, prison-camp scenes are remarkably convincing.

But the most vivid presence is David Caruso, as a hot-dog hostage negotiator who masterminds the prison-camp raid. It's the first time his movie work has come close to matching the reputation he's built as a TV actor.

The title "Proof of Life" refers to a negotiator's demand for proof a hostage is still alive. As it lumbers past the 120-minute mark, you may start wondering the same thing about the movie.

NEWSDAY, 12/8/00, Part II/p. B3, John Anderson

Letting a scowl be his umbrella, Russell Crowe has segued from neo-Nazi lunatic ("Romper Stomper") to suspect-thumping obsessive ("L.A. Confidential") to limb-lopping Roman ("Gladiator") and it's probably a sign of his burgeoning success that as rescuer-for-hire in "Proof of Life" he gets to crack a smile.

Now he wants to be nice?

It's OK. We understand. As one of Hollywood's hottest properties, Crowe has to prove he can be sensitive, so he can play the kinds of roles upon which he hasn't based his career. He's got to be nice, more or less, and make the transition smoothly. So in "Proof of Life" his character is a loving father, good-hearted soul and corporate mercenary whose usual playmates are Chechnyan rebels, drug lords and professional kidnapers.

The problem is that "Proof of Life"—in which director Taylor Hackford more or less plays advance man for U.S. drug czar Barry McCaffrey and the upcoming, $7.5 billion mud-wrestling match called Plan Colombia—is far better as a pure action picture than the star-crossed romance it wants to be.

It does, however, provide a solid hard-case-with-heart-of-gold part for Crowe: Terry Thorne, a gentleman soldier who can brief corporate boards or play bag man for the Chechnyans. His son by an ex-marriage attends an Eton-like school near London; he's a world traveler with an obvious taste for the finer things—which don't include "Tecala, South America," where Peter Bowman (David Morse), an engineer for a mega-U.S. oil company, has been abducted by guerrillas and taken into the Andean hills.

Terry, it turns out, is in Tecala by accident. The well-intentioned Peter, who was there to design a dam (which was fronting for an oil pipeline), was not covered by kidnap insurance. So Terry tells Peter's wife, Alice (Meg Ryan), sorry, but there's nothing he can do. And catches the next plane home.

...And shows up at her door a few hours later. We have no idea about the status of Terry's 401 (k), but he's apparently quit the firm and taken on the nonprofit cause of Peter Bowman—and this is even before he falls for Alice.

Hackford bookends his movie with some terrific action sequences, but the center is a void. The on-screen chemistry between Terry and Alice (played by real-life lovers Crowe and Ryan) is all but nonexistent. Having seen Peter and Alice play out their marital woes, a la Edward Albee in a screamfest replete with thwarted dreams and dead children, the fact that Alice's memory keeps Peter going through his months-long ordeal with his for-profit, ex-Marxist captors is a little hard to stomach. Nobody suffers quite like Morse, but Ryan and her character's sister-in-law, played by the usually reliable Pamela Reed, are literally unbelievable. Did they lose a loved one? Or a parking space?

Crowe gives a solid performance and has some good scenes with David Caruso, who plays rival "K&R" specialist Dino, who teams up with Terry on the Bowman case and has all the markings of the best friend who gets killed at the last possible moment. We won't say what happens, but losing Caruso would be losing the one piece of "Proof of Life" that has much life at all—except for those shoot-'em-ups, in which a lot of brown people get slaughtered wholesale, mostly for the crime of being poor and exploited.

NEWSWEEK, 12/11/00, p. 75, David Ansen

Taylor Hackford's thriller "Proof of Life" leaves a lot to be desired, but it's got its hands on a fascinating subject. Inspired by a Vanity Fair article by William Prochnau and a book by former hostage victim Thomas R. Hargrove, it gives us a peek into the world of K&R (kidnap and ransom). As organized kidnapping has become a big business, it has given rise to K&R insurance policies, routinely taken out by multinational corporations on behalf of their endangered employees. The insurance companies in turn employ professional negotiators—many of whom are former CIA, FBI or Interpol agents—to bargain for the lives of the hostages spirited off by mercenary rebel forces.

That's the job of London-based Aussie Terry Thorne (Russell Crowe), a former soldier with a calm, cool bedside manner. In "Proof of Life" Thorne finds himself holding the hand of Alice Bowman (Meg Ryan), whose engineer husband, Peter (David Morse), has been abducted by drug-running guerrillas in the fictitious South American country of Tecala. Making matters worse for Peter, his failing company has canceled its insurance policy. Thorne, who prides himself on his strictly-business professionalism, at first turns his back on the job, but we know better. We also know, this being a Hollywood movie, that his emotional detachment will be compromised by his growing attachment to his attractive client.

To be fair, Tony Gilroy's screenplay keeps the romance on the back burner. The focus alternates between the captive's ordeal in the mountains (the gorgeous locations are actually Ecuador), where he is at the mercy of young, trigger-happy rebels, and Thorne's attempts to bring the $3 million demand down to a manageable 600 grand.

Thorne is the most compelling aspect of "Proof of Life," thanks to Crowe's quiet, hard-bitten charisma. It's a part Bogart once would have played—the amoral tough guy who rises to the moral occasion—and Crowe gives it just the right note of gravel-voiced masculinity.

But neither Crowe, Ryan nor the topical subject keeps "Proof of Life" from feeling recycled. For all the up-to-the minute research, the movie still gives off the musty scent of Hollywood contrivance. Haven't we seen these stereotypical wild-eyed guerrillas and shifty-eyed corporate types a hundred times before?   Instead of maximizing the tale's urgency, the melodramatic flourishes just make it seem more generic. The wonderful Pamela Reed injects a splash of spiky, unexpected feeling as Peter's busybody sister; you wish there were more moments when somebody made a move you couldn't second-guess. This slick, handsomely produced thriller only gets the pulse half racing.

SIGHT AND SOUND, 3/01, p. 57, Geoffrey Macnab

American engineer Peter Bowman is kidnapped by guerrillas in Tecala, a volatile Latin American country. Terry Thorne, a kidnap and ransom expert, flies out from Britain to conduct negotiations and ensure Peter's safe return. When he learns that Peter's company is not properly insured, he has to quit the job.

Back in Britain, Thorne, an Australian-born ex-SAS officer, is stricken with remorse. If only for the sake of Peter's wife Alice, to whom he is attracted, he returns to Tecala and offers her his services. Alice dismisses the local security expert she had hired, then Thorne attempts to barter down the hostages to a price Alice and her relatives can afford. Unknown to Thorne, Peter has made an escape attempt. He is recaptured, but a fellow hostage, German missionary Eric Kessler, escapes. He has a hand-drawn map with details of where Peter is held. Negotiations for Peter's release stall. Thorne and his fellow kidnap-and-ransom expert Dino (who knows an Italian businessman is being held in the same place) decide to mount a rescue expedition. Just before setting off, Thorne and Alice kiss. Thanks to an elaborate decoy, most of the terrorists have been lured out of their camp. After a gun battle which leaves several of the remaining captors dead, Peter and the Italian are freed. Thorne and the team return to base. Peter is re-united with Alice. Thorne instructs them to leave the country. As they depart, Thorne and Dino talk about going into business together.

Inspired by a *Vanity Fair* article about "the ransom trade" and by *Long March to Freedom*, Tom Hargrove's book about his kidnapping by FARC guerrillas in Colombia, *Proof of Life* suffers from a severe identity crisis. Director Taylor Hackford seems uncertain whether he is making an action adventure about mercenaries, a romantic melodrama, or a Costa-Gravas-style docudrama about a westerner missing in Central America. The film begins spectacularly enough, with "kidnap and ransom" expert Terry Thorne, played by Russell Crowe, defying Chechen militia and Russian soldiers to rescue a kidnapped businessman. Shot in he same grey, desaturated fashion as the opening battle in *Gladiator,* the sequence suggests that Crowe is once again playing an action hero, having swapped swords and breast-plates for guns and grenades.

This overture belies what follows. As the scene shifts to Central America, where US engineer Peter Bowman has just been taken hostage, the film assumes an unlikely solemnity. The kidnap comes just as Bowman's marriage, to Meg Ryan's Alice, is under severe strain, and the boy's own heroics of the opening scene are briefly forgotten as Hackford attempts to explore the cracks in the relationship. His treatment of the guerrillas who kidnap Bowman is relatively even-handed,

But ultimately he is beholden to his two stars. What really matters here is not the missing American or the drug trade, but the dynamics between Ryan and Crowe. Both play characters who sublimate their feelings for one another: Ryan curbs her instinct for comedy, while Crowe, sent to Latin America to get Alice's husband back, not to replace him, displays a stiff-upper lipped selflessness rarely seen since *Brief Encounter* (1945).

The most dispiriting aspect of *Proof of Life* is its creeping jingoism. The film might be set in a fictional country, but that hardly excuses its stereotypical portrait of South America. Most of the locals are depicted in a resolutely negative light: there is the corrupt security expert, the oleaginous politician, the sadistic peasant who hates his hostage. Hackford throws in a few corrupt Texan businessmen to counter balance the slimy locals, but this seems like tokenism. The engineer's life may be sacred; those of his captors are clearly not. As if tiring of the negotiation process, Hackford throws in a wham-bang finale in which Thorne, an ex SAS man, and his old buddy fly into the jungle, guns blazing, and kill countless guerrillas. You half suspect that the escapade is Thorne's way of venting his frustration at not getting any further with Alice.

As the final credits begin to roll, to one of Van Morrison's more maudlin ballads, Alice and Peter are hot footing their way out of Tecala, while Thorne is planning his future as a mercenary for hire. It's a glib ending to a film which falls down as a love story (the affair between Thorne and Alice is arrested before it begins), as a *Wild Geese*-style boy's own adventure (the action sequences are fleeting) and most of all as a piece of reportage.

TIME, 12/11/00, p. 103, Richard Corliss

This one came in with a funny smell: the perfume of illicit passion, domestic upheaval and smoldering guilt. (O.K., forget that last bit; we're in the post-guilt age, at least in Hollywood and Washington.) *Proof of Life*, a romantic thriller with Meg Ryan and Russell Crowe, is coming out in the wake of the two stars' affair and the fracturing of Ryan's marriage to Dennis Quaid. The all-American blond is now a Jezebel, her cuddlings with Crowe sprayed across gossip-mag covers and on tabloid-tale TV shows. The eventual film looked destined to be remembered as Exhibit A in the trial of adulterous love.

So the first thing to say about *Proof of Life* is that it makes the problems of three show people seem less important than the drama of three compelling characters on a big movie screen. Inspired by a *Vanity Fair* article about a U.S. businessman kidnapped in Colombia, Tony Gilroy's script imagines that engineer Peter Bowman (the excellent David Morse) is seized by terrorist rebels, taken to an Andean prison aerie and held for a $3 million ransom. His wife Alice (Ryan) finds that Peter's company will not pay for the services of Terry Thorne (Crowe), an expert negotiator; she must hope Terry takes the job pro bono. Even if he does, he'll have to juggle the demands of Alice, the guerrillas and his own bruised but open heart.

Under the commando-efficient direction of Taylor Hackford (*The Devil's Advocate*), the film intelligently deploys familiar thriller elements: chases; shoot-outs; high-level duplicity; terse, sassy dialogue; and a cast having a high time playing preening villains and wily good guys. Even Ryan, with too much attitude and nonstop nutating, finally gets into the film's burly spirit. All this is enough to stoke the action engine, but the movie has a fuller agenda—to give its characters flesh and a meaningful melancholy.

The film's first big set piece is, surprise, all talk. Peter and Alice have one of those marital arguments—a wrangle about career frustration, principles and office politics, money and kids—found all too often in life and almost never in movies. He's had a bad day, she's not sufficiently sympathetic, and the tension escalates like *Bolero*, stopping just short of a declaration of war. Soon after, Peter is abducted. In most movies, someone who is to be killed or imperiled gets a soppy farewell scene. This jarring confrontation gives *Proof of Life* another reason to bring Peter back alive—so he and Alice can forgive each other.

Terry is a more standard-issue hero-strong, smart and caring—but Crowe gives him the burden of a wise realist. His hard-earned awareness of the world's wicked ways presses down on his sturdy shoulders and at the corners of his sensitive lips. Crowe displayed this moral weight in *The Insider* and *Gladiator*, it makes him the thinking man's grunt, and it grounds his can-this-be-love scene with Ryan. "Just tell me you know how much you mean to me," she says dewily. His reply shows a tough man's brusque vulnerability: "Then we're even."

Insider and *Gladiator,* it makes him the thinking man's grunt, and it grounds his can-this-be-love scene with Ryan. "Just tell me you know how much you mean to me," she says dewily. His reply shows a tough man's brusque vulnerability: "Then we're even."

Yes, it's the old *Casablanca* triangle: an idealist, his conflicted wife and the adventurer who can save a life by breaking a heart. *Proof of Life* isn't quite at that level of romantic melodrama, but its wit, vigor and rue make it a superior entertainment—and a lot more illuminating than the real-life romance it sparked.

VILLAGE VOICE, 12/19/00, p. 141, J. Hoberman

Dubya may appear hopelessly inadequate, but the cool JFK exhibited on Day Nine of the missile crisis [The reference is to *13 Days*; see Hoberman's review of that film.] is nothing compared to the presence of mind which Russell Crowe   simultaneously bamboozles Russian tanks and Chechen insurgents to liberate a hostage and pull himself into an airborne chopper under rocket fire in the precredit sequence of *Proof of Life.*

Crowe's next assignment is to free David Morse, playing an idealistic American engineer abducted by the ski-masked narco-guerrillas of a pseudo Colombia code-named "Tecala." That the kidnapping occurs one scene after Morse's big quarrel with wife Meg Ryan adds a bit of psychological piquance to the otherwise mechanical proceedings. Crowe's character is a man of absolute faith and unblinking realism who explains to naive Ryan and her obnoxious, hysterical sister-in-law (Pamela Reed) that the issue is not revolution but money. Taking hostages is a third-world business. As in American electoral politics, "the end of the Cold War changed everything."

Its nonsensical narrative complications fleshed out with lazy stereotypes (the locals are mainly nightclub fascists or crazed Communists; the scariest moment has Crowe replaced by some Tecalano jerk), *Proof of Life* derives its emotional coherence from generic models. It's *Rambo* with a split hero—Morse absorbing punishment and Crowe wreaking vengeance—as well as a *Casablanca* triangle with Crowe as Bogie. There's a key moment when the star kisses his pretty client and she swoons. To judge from the heat, their much publicized on-set romance could have been a desperate PR stunt to promote an otherwise undistinguished movie.

Also reviewed in:
NEW YORK TIMES, 12/8/00, p. E8, Stephen Holden
VARIETY, 12/4-10/00, p. 26, Todd McCarthy
WASHINGTON POST, 12/8/00, p. C1, Stephen Hunter
WASHINGTON POST, 12/8/00, Weekend/p. 45, Desson Howe

PSYCHO BEACH PARTY

A Strand Releasing release of a Strand/New Oz and Red Horse Films production.   *Executive Producer:* John Hall.   *Producer:* Ginny Biddle, Jon Gerrans, Marcus Hu, and Victor Smyris. *Director:* Robert Lee King.   *Screenplay (based on his play):* Charles Busch.   *Director of Photography:* Arturo Smith.   *Editor:* Suzanne Hines.   *Music:* Ben Vaughn.   *Sound:* Tim Walston, Pat Toma and (music) David Tobocman.   *Sound Editor:* Jay Nierenberg.   *Casting:* Laura Schiff.   *Production Designer:* Franco-Giacomo Carbone.   *Art Director:* Alberto Gonzalez-Reyna.   *Set Decorator:* Ann Shea.   *Special Effects:* Dan Walker.   *Costumes:* Camille Jumelle.   *Make-up:* Wendy Lynn Allison.   *Running time:* 95 minutes.   *MPAA Rating:* Not Rated.

CAST: Lauren Ambrose ("Chicklet"/Florence Forest);   Thomas Gibson (Kanaka); Nicholas Brendon (Starcat);   Kimberly Davies (Bettina/Diane);   Matt Keeslar (Lars); Charles Busch (Capt. Monica Stark/Writer);   Beth Broderick (Mrs. Forest/Mom);   Danni Wheeler (Berdine); Nick Cornish (Yo Yo);   Andrew Levitas (Provoloney);   Amy Adams (Marvel Ann); Kathleen Robertson (Rhonda);   Nathan Bexton (T.J.);   Buddy Quaid (Junior);   Jenica Bergere (Cookie); Channon Roe (Wedge Riley);   Stephen Wozniak (Johnny);   Ruth Williamson (Pat); David

Chokachi (Eddie);   John Cirigliano (Vince);   Jolie Jenkins (Angel);   Mike Malin (Bobby); Charlie Finn (Ped Brolin);   Nick D'Agosto (Drive-In Counterman);   Richard Fancy (Dr. Westworth/Dr. Edwards);   Michael Manasseri (Boy);   Rona Benson (Girl);   Tera Bonilla (Go-Go Girl);   Madison Eginton (Young Florence).

LOS ANGELES TIMES, 8/25/00, Calendar/p. 10, Kevin Thomas

"Psycho Beach Party" has to be twice as funny a play as it is as a movie.It's too much filmed theater to come alive fully on the screen, and it doesn't help that spoofing schlocky movies of the '50s, '60s and even '70s is not exactly virgin territory. What's more, deliberate camp like this film presents a special challenge: It must generate and sustain a high level of energy or it will swiftly fall flat. The latter is too often the case here.

Charles Busch displays a wild imagination in conflating motifs from various film genres of the eras in dizzying fashion and can certainly write amusingly absurd dialogue, but he didn't turn out to be the best person to adapt his own play for the screen. What was needed is someone who could substitute chunks of dialogue with action and then a director who could jump-start the convoluted plot and keep it racing along.

Robert Lee King's workmanlike direction is not what unabashed silliness needs to keep it bubbling. "Psycho Beach Party," set in an affectionately evoked 1962, could sure use a jolt of John Waters' "Cecil B. Demented."

Perky, redheaded Lauren Ambrose plays Florence, nicknamed Chicklet, a teen with multiple personalities a la "Three Faces of Eve," but that doesn't stop her from trying to get the boys at Malibu to teach her how to surf. She eventually wins over the king of the beach, Kanaka (Thomas Gibson). Amid all the shenanigans, a serial killer also is simultaneously stalking the teens, and all the key figures are so eccentric that any of them may be the culprit. (In the midst of riding a big wave, Kanaka breaks into a danse du ventre, a wacky throwaway visual touch that the movie could use lots more of.

Among the kooks are Berdine (Danni Wheeler), Lauren's brilliant, nerdy best pal, a seemingly latent lesbian who becomes a girl friday to a horror picture starlet, Bettina (Kimberley Davies), who's living in a supposedly haunted beach house—the scene of a mass murder—and who is herself apparently a dominatrix in her private life.

Then there's Lauren's man-hating but sex-starved widowed mother (Beth Broderick) and Lars (Matt Keeslar), a dim Swedish exchange student, and even the nice guy (Nicholas Brendon) Chicklet should end up with if she ever gets a grip on all those personalities. About the only people formidable police captain Monica Stark (Busch in drag) can pretty much rule out as suspects are ultra-buff surfer dudes Provoloney (Andrew Levitas) and Yo Yo (Nick Cornish), who have only eyes for each other but in keeping with the times try to play straight.

NEW YORK POST, 8/4/00, p. 52, Lou Lumenick

Charles Busch's spoof of beach-party movies and psychological thrillers, an off-Broadway hit 13 years ago, stubbornly refuses to entertain in this unrelentingly dull film version.

Drag legend Busch originally wrote the lead role for himself—Chicklet, a 16-year-old misfit with multiple personalities who becomes the main suspect when someone begins killing off members of her surfer crowd.

In the screen version, written by Busch and directed with minimal flair by Robert Lee King, Chicklet is played by a bona-fide female—the hapless, pouting Lauren Ambrose—and Busch instead shaves his legs to portray Capt. Monica of the LAPD, who is investigating the murders.

Neither of them is more than passable, but Thomas Gibson ("Dharma and Greg") and other members of the supporting cast playing sexually confused characters—none of whom seems sure whether to camp it up or play it straight—are even bigger drags.

VILLAGE VOICE, 8/8/00, p. 140, Dennis Lim

Psycho Beach Party, based on Charles Busch's 1987 play, conflates the cheapo surf movie with the cheapo slasher movie, and simply leaves the two '60s exploitation high-water marks to duke it out—they win, you lose. If nothing else, Busch (who wrote the screenplay) prefigured the current cinematic plot device of choice—the multiple personality—with his Gidgety confection about Chicklet, a troubled tomboy who, when she sets eyes on any circular object, slips into one of her two alternate personas: a finger-snapping homegirl or a dominatrix who may be responsible for a series of gory slayings.

In the stage production, Busch played Chicklet; Robert Lee King's film loses one of the original jokes by casting biological female Lauren Ambrose in the lead (Busch plays a policewoman who resembles David Duchovny in *Twin Peaks)*. Confronted with this awkward combination of garish set decoration and muffled humor, the viewer is left to ponder the number of levels on which this counts as a pointless exercise—a parody of parodic movies, a deconstruction of transparent genres, a self-negatingly knowing example of camp ...

Also reveiwed in:
NEW YORK TIMES, 8/4/00, p. E16, Stephen Holden
VARIETY, 3/13-29/00, p. 27, Dennis Harvey

PUPS

An Allied Entertainment Group release of a Fire Heart Films Inc./Team Okuyama/Allied Entertainment Group production. *Executive Producer:* Kazuyoshi Okuyama, Sachie Oyama, and Boro Vokodinovic. *Producer:* Ash and Daniel Berger. *Director:* Ash. *Screenplay:* Ash. *Director of Photography:* Carlos Arguello. *Editor:* Michael D. Schultz. *Music:* Spring Aspers. *Sound:* Bill Foster.   *Casting:* Stephanie Chao.   *Production Designer:* Daniel M. Berger. *Costumes:* Merrie Lawson. *Make-up:* Brian McManus. *Running time:* 100 minutes. *MPAA Rating:* Not Rated.

CAST: Cameron Van Hoy (Stevie); Mischa Barton (Rocky); Burt Reynolds (Daniel Bender); Adam Farrar (Wheelchair Man); David Alan Graf (Bank Manager);   Kurt Loder (Himself); James Gordon (J.P.); Darling Narita (Joy); Ed Metzger (Mr. Edwards); Suzie Gordon (Rio); Jonathan Coogan (Security Guard);   Uri Ryder (Pizza Man);   Matthew Fairchild (Rocky's Father);   Hsa Mann and Johnny Hawaiian (Puppy Sellers);   Kevin Kennedy (Field Reporter); David N. Preston, Bea Pompa, and Stanley Herman (Studio Reporters);   Hardia Madden (Agent Hardy);   C.C. Bechloff (Agent C.C.);   Alex Lui (Officer);   Matt Roth (Bank Worker); Natascha Cobar (Bank Customer); Dara Tomanovich (Bender's Wife/Stevie's Mom); Matthew Cory Dunn (MTV Camera);   Ashley Darrow (Phoebe); Julieanne Young (Field Reporter).

LOS ANGELES TIMES, 3/31/00, Calendar/p. 14, Kevin Thomas

Two days before the Columbine, Colo., massacre last year, "Pups" screened at the Los Angeles Independent Film Festival to wide acclaim, but the high school shooting spree derailed the film's distribution a full year. The irony is that "Pups" is a serious film that confronts some of the issues raised by the shootings: the lethal combination of guns and youthful rage in a media-manipulative world. As in his first film, "Bang," the British-born filmmaker known simply as Ash, taps the paranoia and danger that lurk just beneath the surface in everyday life.

Not only is he an acute, wide-ranging observer but he also inspires his actors to attempt the most demanding portrayals yet and make them seem as wholly spontaneous as his edgy, restless films appear. Shot by the resourceful Carlos Arguello with a Steadicam, "Pups" feels as if it's been shot on the run yet is a most graceful, adroitly paced work. What's more, Ash plays off youthful newcomer Cameron Van Hoy and old pro Burt Reynolds to the advantage of both, who are surrounded by a strong supporting cast.

The film takes place in the perfectly ordinary suburban Chatsworth. Van Hoy's 13-year-old Stevie is bright, dreamy and TV-and-games saturated, like most youngsters. But as we meet him, he's toying with hanging himself when he's interrupted by an asthma attack. In an instant he's off on another tack, playing detective it would seem, and in rooting around his mother's bedroom—she is apparently a single parent—he comes across a handgun.

By the time his girlfriend, Rocky (Mischa Barton), arrives to go off with him to school, Stevie has had a call from his mother saying she won't be home for dinner, which triggers—or revives—an anger within him. You feel he's a latch-key kid, that his mother is often absent from his life. While Rocky is far from thrilled with the idea, Stevie is determined to take the gun with them as they leave for school. As they approach a bank, Stevie—armed and angry, well-primed for the obvious inspiration derived from a zillion movies, TV shows and newscasts—holds the place up.

All of this is staged with a disarming casualness that gives the film a terrifying aura of authenticity that Ash sustains throughout. Rocky as well as Stevie has a momentary "Bonnie and Clyde" sense of exhilaration with this sudden and dramatic rush of empowerment. But Stevie is also plenty scared over what he's gotten into, and the thrill wears off swiftly for Rocky. Steeped in conflicting emotions, Stevie grows increasingly hysterical as he waves his gun at the handful of people he has taken hostage.

They are the varied group you would expect to find there, but none really communicates with Stevie except an embittered young man (Adam Farrar), a Gulf War vet left paraplegic, who asserts that he wouldn't mind Stevie putting him out of his misery.

Consequently, it's really left to Rocky, so engagingly played by Barton, and Reynolds' FBI agent Daniel Bender, whose men have surrounded the bank along with a thicket of onlookers, to try to calm Stevie down. Stevie repeatedly baits Bender, who's too disciplined to let Stevie know how angry and frustrated he is over the standoff.

Ash, who illuminates rather than preaches, carries off "Pups" with aplomb. It's not that Ash raises brand-new issues but that he brings to them a freshness and an emotional impact. We'll be hearing more from him, for sure.

NEW YORK POST, 2/11/00. p. 56, Lou Lumenick

"Pups" effectively considers the awful consequences of a 13-year-old finding what Clint Eastwood's Dirty Harry once called "the most effective handgun in the world."

Stevie, played with astonishing intensity by newcomer Cameron Van Hoy, is a skinny, asthma-stricken Southern California teen who makes videos about mock suicide attempts.

When he and his girlfriend, Rocky (Mischa Barton), find a .44-caliber Magnum in his divorced mom's closet and accidentally fire a shot into the wall, the effect is exhilarating and scary.

Rocky reluctantly goes along when Stevie decides, as a lark, to rob a bank on the way to school. Stevie copies all the moves from movies and TV shows, but things don't go according to script.

A guard ends up wounded and hostages taken. Squads of police sharpshooters take up position outside the bank, along with hordes of media.

It's "Dog Day Afternoon" with a pair of 13-year-olds—complete with takeout pizza, to which Stevie adds orders for beer and condoms.

Working in extended sequences, Van Hoy and the more experienced Barton (she had small parts in "The Sixth Sense" and "Notting Hill") give high-energy performances of rare authenticity as Stevie and Rocky, who are alternately scared and petulant as circumstances spiral out of their control.

Except for an impressive film debut by Adam Farrar (Leonardo DiCaprio's step-brother) as a bitter, wheelchair-bound Gulf War vet who sides with the teens, the adult characters—bank employees and customers taken hostage—tend toward the stereotypical.

Burt Reynolds is barely OK as a sympathetic FBI negotiator who keeps breaking into obscenities, but MTV's Kurt Loder has a droll, self-deprecating cameo as himself. Crude but memorable, "Pups" was inspired by the Jonesboro, Ark., school shootings. Offered for sale right after the Columbine High School massacre, it frightened away major distributors and is now opening at a single theater in Manhattan. Which is a shame; this movie deserves a wider audience.

Ashley Baron Cohen, the 36-year-old British writer-director who goes by the name Ash, and who directed the well-received "Bang" for only $20,000, offers deft social commentary about kids, guns and the media without ever preaching.

"Pups" isn't perfect, but it makes a similar, much more elaborately produced studio project—last year's "Light It Up"—look phony and pathetic by comparison.

VILLAGE VOICE, 2/15/00, p. 130, Jessica Winter

Going to extremities is the 13-year-old aspiring outlaw Stevie in *Pups,* the second feature from British-born director Ash, whose $20,000 debut, *Bang* (not starring Annabel Chong), also pivoted on the discovery of a gun and the resulting domino string of consequences over the course of a sweltering Los Angeles day. Thug-posturing, asthma-plagued Stevie (Cameron Van Hoy) finds his mother's pistol and, with girlfriend Rocky (Mischa Barton) in tow, impulsively decides to hold up a bank because, as he later explains to MTV's Kurt Loder (in a startlingly self-flagellating cameo), "It was on the way to school." Ash trips up with Burt Reynolds's blustering FBI negotiator, but the hyperreal performances he elicits from his two young leads, the complex dependencies that develop between the hostages and their captors, and his deft, unshowy doc-style camerawork all cohere and combust, borrowing from *Dog Day Afternoon* to debate the effects of media violence on youth. Didactic but not pedantic, Pups had both the prescience and the bad luck to premiere at the Los Angeles Film Festival 48 hours before Columbine, and was then shelved; no pundit since has come close to answering the questions it raises.

Also reviewed in:
NEW YORK TIMES, 2/14/00, p. E5, Lawrence Van Gelder
VARIETY, 4/26-5/2/99, p. 47, Robert Koehler

QUARRY, THE

A First Run Features release of a Man's Film/Tchin Tchin/Studio Nieuwe Gronden/Wanda Films production. *Producer:* Marion Hansel. *Director:* Marion Hansel. *Screenplay (English and Afrikaans with English subtitles):* Marion Hansel. *Based on a novel by:* Damon Galgut. *Director of Photography:* Bernard Lutic. *Editor:* Michele Hubinon. *Music:* Takashi Kako. *Sound:* Dominique Hennequin. *Sound Editor:* Henri Morelle. *Costumes:* Yan Tax. *Make-up:* Dick Naastepad. *Running time:* 112 minutes. *MPAA Rating:* Not Rated.

CAST: John Lynch (The Man); Jonny Phillips (Captain Mong); Serge-Henri Valcke (The Reverend); Oscar Petersen (Valentine); Jody Abrahams (Small); Sylvia Esau (The Woman).

CHRISTIAN SCIENCE MONITOR, 1/14/00, p. 15, David Sterritt

[*The Quarry* was reviewed jointly with *The Terrorist*; see Sterritt's review of that film.]

NEW YORK POST, 1/21/00, p. 49, Lou Lumenick

Good moviemaking is often about editing: Knowing which of your favorite scenes to leave out is frequently as important as knowing what to put in.

This is illustrated by "The Quarry," a decent drama by Belgian director Marion Hansel that's plagued by narrative overkill.

This 112-minute multinational production, filmed mostly in English, begins with an endless tracking shot of an escaped prisoner (John Lynch) walking down the road, and ends with a series of climaxes, each less credible than the one before.

In the middle, there's the well-acted, intriguing story of the unnamed prisoner, who kills a minister who gives him a lift, buries the minister in the quarry of the title, and impersonates him at the minister's new church in a remote South African town.

Like the hero of "Les Miserables," the prisoner takes enthusiastically to his new role, but then the body is discovered—and police Capt. Mong (Jonny Phillips) won't rest until he's nailed the culprit.

The movie contains fine performances, particularly by Lynch, an Irish actor seen in "Sliding Doors," and Sylvia Esau as the racist Mong's black mistress. But "The Quarry" is in need of cutting.

NEWSDAY, 1/21/00, Part II/p. B10, Jan Stuart

Talk about your rotten luck. It's bad enough to get a flat tire in the middle of nowhere. But to break down within inches of a runaway criminal who happens to be the only other person around for God-knows-how-many-miles is the height of born-loserdom.

We don't know who this vagrant is, where he has come from or what crime he had committed when he accosts a traveling minister near the opening of Marion Hansel's "The Quarry." But it is only a matter of hours before he has stolen the unfortunate clergyman's identity and assumed his role in a remote South African parish.

Unlike that other identity thief of the moment, Matt Damon's Mr. Ripley, this fellow is not very talented at concealing his own culpability. Invested with feverish intensity by Irish actor John Lynch, Hansel's con man is a living mask of guilt and remorse. In keeping with the archetypal nature of the tale, he has no name other than that of the minister he is impersonating.

For all of her South African location trappings, Belgian filmmaker Hansel is working in a time-honored tradition familiar to readers of Dostoevsky's "Crime and Punishment." In the scheme of morality yarns like "The Quarry," it is not a question of if this con man will give himself away, but how and when.

Paced so deliberately that it pauses to give metaphoric weight to a fly on a cafe table, "The Quarry" thickens with ironic complications: A pair of footloose brothers, both black (Oscar Petersen and Jody Abrahams), accidentally implicate themselves in the pseudo-minister's crimes. Hansel scores some pungent racial points as the local Afrikaaner police captain (Jonny Phillips) trusts the white film-flammer implicitly, at the expense of the hapless brothers.

Evocatively photographed with an austere, CinemaScope lens by Damon Galgut, "The Quarry" is an absorbing tale of fate that begs our indulgence for coincidence one too many times and belabors the foregone conclusion by tying up every loose end in sight. Even so, this honorable film is well worth retrieving from the mire of overhyped holiday releases.

VILLAGE VOICE, 1/18/00, p. 120, Jessica Winter

Notable if only for a lead performance delivered by John Lynch with agonized focus and intensity, Marion Hansel's *The Quarry* bears a striking resemblance to the recent, scarcely released *The Broken Giant*, which likewise encompassed fallen clergymen, fleeing Job figures, and purgatorial fire scorching dusty ground. Hansel's terrain is a rural South African township, where an Irish drifter known only as the Man (Lynch)—who seems to be fleeing from the police—gets a ride from a minister en route to his new church. The preacher isn't as reverend as he first appears, and a gratuitous if basically innocent act of self-defense by the Man leaves him with another?) body on his hands. When two young black locals rob the deceased's van, they realize the Man has assumed the minister's identity just as they implicate themselves in his crime—an arrangement that suits the bigoted white police captain just fine. Meanwhile, churchgoers seem puzzled but endeared by their autistic-savant newcomer, who's nearly speechless when he's not at the pulpit and given to quoting Lamentations when he is.

Hansel's overlong film is hobbled by distracting technical gaffes and a sometimes cringingly earnest script; troubling too is why Hansel has left the time period uncertain—the ambiguity undermines any sense of social context. Emotional context, however, is provided by Lynch. With his perpetually startled eyes, hoarsely confessional voice, and cowed, scarecrow limbs, he embodies a soul in limbo, choked and bewildered by his own grief and guilt.

Also reviewed in:
CHICAGO TRIBUNE, 4/21/00, Friday/p. H, John Petrakis
NEW YORK TIMES, 1/21/00, p. E27, Lawrence Van Gelder
VARIETY, 9/14-20/98, p. 90, Leonard Klady

QUILLS

A Fox Searchlight Pictures release of an Industry Entertainment/a Walrus & Associates Ltd. production in association with Hollywood Partners. *Executive Producer:* Des McAnuff, Sandra Schulberg, and Rudulf Wiesmeier. *Producer:* Julia Chasman, Nick Wechsler, and Peter Kaufman. *Director:* Philip Kaufman. *Screenplay:* Doug Wright. *Based on the play by:* Doug Wright. *Director of Photography:* Rogier Stoffers. *Editor:* Peter Boyle. *Music:* Stephen Warbeck. *Music Editor:* Robin Lee, Andy Glen, Tony Lewis, and Matt Barr. *Sound:* John Midgley and (music) Chris Dibble. *Sound Editor:* Frank Eulner. *Casting:* Donna Isaacson and Priscilla John. *Production Designer:* Martin Childs. *Art Director:* Mark Raggett and Steven Lawrence. *Set Decorator:* Jill Quertier. *Special Effects:* Stuart Brisdon. *Costumes:* Jacqueline West. *Make-up:* Nuala Conway. *Stunt Coordinator:* Jim Dowdall, Andy Bradford, Nrinder Dhudwar, and Richard Hammatt. *Running time:* 120 minutes. *MPAA Rating:* R.

CAST: Geoffrey Rush (Marquis de Sade); Kate Winslet (Madeleine); Joaquin Phoenix (Coulmier); Michael Caine (Dr. Royer-Collard); Billie Whitelaw (Madame LeClerc); Patrick Malahide (Delbené); Amelia Warner (Simone); Jane Menelaus (Renee Pelagie); Stephen Moyer (Prouix); Tony Pritchard (Valcour); Michael Jenn (Cleante); Danny Babington (Pitou); George Yiasoumi (Dauphin); Stephen Marcus (Bouchon); Elizabeth Berrington (Charlotte); Edward Tudor-Pole (Franval); Harry Jones (Orvolle); Bridget McConnel (Madame Bougival); Pauline McLynn (Mademoiselle Clairwil); Rebecca Palmer (Michette); Toby Sawyer (Louison); Daniel Ainsleigh (Guerin); Terry O'Neill (Gaillon); Diana Morrison (Mademoiselle Renard); Carol Macready (Sister Noirceuil); Tom Ward (The Horseman); Richard Mulholland (Fop); Ron Cook (Napoleon); Julian Tait (Pawnbroker); Tessa Vale (Sister Flavie); Howard Lew Lewis (First Vendor); Andrew Dunford (Second Vendor); Lisa Hammond (Prostitute); Matthew Fraser (Lunatic Band Member); Jamie Beddard (Lunatic at Play).

CHRISTIAN SCIENCE MONITOR, 11/24/00, p. 15, David Sterritt

Call it a sign of the new millennium, but 2000 has given us no fewer than two new movies about the Marquis de Sade, one of the most notorious miscreants of the past few centuries.

"Sade," a French production, is a rather tame affair that hasn't yet found American distribution. But the more abrasive "Quills" is opening with a Hollywood-style flourish, evidently meant to offset the picture's unsavory content by calling attention to its respected stars. They are eccentricity specialist Geoffrey Rush as the aging anti-hero, "Titanic" veteran Kate Winslet as the laundress he loves, Joaquin Phoenix as the priest who runs the asylum where he's incarcerated, and Michael Caine as the doctor who aims to cure him but may secretly be as sadistic as the Marquis himself.

Directed by Philip Kaufman from Doug Wright's screenplay, "Quills" is designed to strike different moviegoers in different ways. In many respects it's an exercise in Grand Guignol grotesquerie that presents the Marquis and company in the sort of self-consciously lurid manner associated with horror pictures. It's also a deliberately toned-down account of the Marquis's true artistic and intellectual ideas, abridging them so much that they're hard to recognize at times.

This double-faced approach is a clever compromise, allowing some spectators to praise the picture's blunt naturalism while others defend it as "only a movie" and find solace in its fundamentally conservative view of art's ability to stir up a society's most evil impulses.

Still, you can't help wondering why the Marquis's story is worth telling at all if it isn't worth telling accurately. If the actual transgressions of his life and work were laid bare on the screen, the result would hardly be a studio moneymaker. But it might be a useful lesson in the raging horrors that swept through European culture during an 18th-century epoch so momentous that its influence is still felt on both sides of the Atlantic.

Like most dramas centering on Sade's career, "Quills" takes place at the Charenton asylum where the Marquis was imprisoned in the later part of his life.

The plot depicts his complex relationship with the servant Madeleine, and his conflicts with the increasingly exasperated clergyman and physician who have authority over him within the institution.

The movie's basic message seems to be that the power of these professionals—and of the less imposing individuals who are promoting the terrors of the French Revolution outside Charenton's walls—has corrupted them so much that Sade has little edge over them when it comes to cruelty, malice, and perversion.

This is hardly an original idea, and its impact is further reduced by the anemic account of Sade's writing, which is quoted at enough length to seem awfully naughty but not enough to appear genuinely subversive. Ditto for the picture's depiction of sadistic violence, which may shock the unwary but is little more gruesome than a '50s monster yarn from Hammer Films.

If there's any real value in "Quills, it's the story's emphasis on the potency attributed to written words before the media-drenched excesses of our own postverbal time. When the Marquis risks safety, sanity, and life itself in order to scrawl a few outlandish sentences that may someday reach a reader, it's a salutary reminder that language once mattered a lot more than it appears to in the age of "Quills."

LOS ANGELES TIMES, 11/22/00, Calendar/p. 4, Kenneth Turan

Not content to simply explore the life and philosophy of the celebrated Marquis de Sade, "Quills" soon becomes a sadistic experience in its own right. Experiencing this pretentious wallow—overwritten, under-thought and overdone—is a very sophisticated form of torture.

For if the marquis, his scabrous thoughts on pleasure and pain notwithstanding, was nothing if not genuine, "Quills" is a smug fraud that indulges in the worst kind of pretense. It would like you to believe it's about such high-minded notions as the power of words, the risks of free expression and the price of censorship, but in fact what director Philip Kaufman has come up with is a crude and shameless melodrama weighted down with sham pieties. This film isn't challenging, it's self-congratulatory in the most meretricious way, over-ripe contrivance masquerading as high art.

"Quills" certainly has the right ingredients for this charade. Stars Geoffrey Rush, Kate Winslet, Joaquin Phoenix and Michael Caine are all respected; Kaufman himself remains a critical favorite, though his last unalloyed success ("The Unbearable Lightness of Being") is deep in the past; and screenwriter Doug Wright based the script on his Obie-winning play. But credits don't make films, people do, and everyone on the "Quills" team has betrayed their talent by participating in this fiasco.

Wright's script is a good place to start the search for unindicted co-conspirators. It's annoyingly and artificially theatrical, rife with bogus philosophizing and wink-wink lines like "the price is every bit as firm as I am," and, worst of all, it's got a sense of character about as subtle as "Sgt. Preston of the Yukon."

In his zeal to make his right-thinking points about the horrors of stifling creativity, Wright hasn't known or cared how much his characters pander to our preconceptions, how much they are obvious, over-familiar heroes and villains whose heroism and venality (and this is where Kaufman comes in) couldn't be written more clearly on their faces if they had capital Hs and Vs stamped on their foreheads.

After a brief prologue illustrating the French Revolution at the height of the Paris Terror, "Quills" shifts to the Charenton Asylum and its most infamous inmate, the marquis. (Filmgoers with good memories will remember this same institution as the site of "Marat/Sade," the 1966 Peter Brook-directed version of the Peter Weiss play.)

A tireless scribbler who considers himself "a writer, not a madman," the marquis (Australian actor Rush, "Shine's" Oscar winner) wears out quill after quill in a cell liberally decorated with what is probably the greatest collection of Oriental sex toys in all France.

Madeleine (Winslet), charmingly described in the press notes as "a ravishing young laundress," gets a kick out of flirting with the nasty old marquis. She also helps him out by smuggling his manuscripts to Paris, that hotbed of perfidy, where back-street publishers can't print them fast enough for a public that doesn't have the Spice Channel to distract it.

Unfortunately, a copy of the marquis' latest, "Justine," reaches the hands of Napoleon (played, with characteristic heavy-handedness, as someone whose short, childish legs don't reach the floor when he sits on the throne). The emperor, no surprise here, is not amused, and decides to put a tough-love advocate in charge of the marquis' asylum.

That would be Dr. Royer-Collard (an unsmiling Michael Caine), a "man of iron resolve" who considers idealism "youth's final luxury." Sternness itself, Royer-Collard is the kind of guy who takes it as a deserved compliment when people call him old-fashioned and barbaric.

Currently in charge of Charenton is the doctor's opposite number, the idealistic young Abbe Coulmier (Joaquin Phoenix), a godly man who believes in reason, compassion and therapy. He lets the inmates put on plays, paint, even, in the marquis' case, put his thoughts on paper as "a purgative for the toxins of his mind" (though becoming the Jackie Collins of Paris was not part of the bargain). He also has his eye on young Madeleine, but what with his being a priest and her being a ravishing laundress, it's a complicated relationship.

Royer-Collard, for his part, considers inmate theater "playing dress-up with cretins," so a battle with the saintly abbe is in the cards. If you're naive enough to expect a fair fight, you'll be disappointed. The doctor it turns out, has taken a child bride of just 16 (Amelia Warner) literally straight from a nunnery, and the way he treats her on their wedding night would not make fellow physician Dr. Ruth Westheimer happy. My God, the man is a hypocrite. What a revelation.

The celebrated marquis, the center of all this attention, turns out to be a terrible showoff as well as a spoiled brat. Rush's portrayal of him is occasionally amusing, but though its excessiveness is what the director wanted, it's much too gaudy a performance to be meaningful and the great man's endless smugness does not wear at all well.

The closer "Quills" gets to its ponderous ending, the more impossibly heavy-handed it becomes, throwing in dark and stormy nights, a panting would-be rapist, even an aren't-we-sophisticated scene of sex with a corpse in a church that is pitiful in its childish determination to stick its tongue out at convention. "A malcontent who knows how to spell," is what the abbe calls the marquis in the film's one and only good line. It's a judgment that fits the filmmakers just as well.

NEW YORK, 11/27/00, p. 130, Peter Rainer

Quills, about the Marquis de Sade, is a voluptuous impasto. Everything in it—the colors, the locations, the people—seems swirled with a mixture of decadence and grace. American movies don't often delineate with such rich ambiguity the demarcation between angels and demons, and the lack of clear-cut borders here can seem heady yet profoundly unsettling. Philip Kaufman, directing from a script by Doug Wright expanded from his Obie-winning play, makes a vivid, if finally somewhat compromised, show out of these ambiguities; he revels in them because he understands that his film is ultimately an attempt to describe what it means to be human.

Humanity's depraved, annihilating force is represented by the Marquis (Geoffrey Rush), the aristocratic libertine who barely survived the terrors of the French Revolution only to find himself incarcerated in its aftermath at the Charenton asylum for the insane, where he lives in a book-lined, velvet-draped bedchamber. A bewigged fop whose finery becomes ever more ragged, he uses Madeleine (Kate Winslet), a young laundress, to smuggle his scurrilous writings to a waiting public—much to the embarrassment of Napoleon. The emperor dispatches to Charenton Dr. Royer-Collard (Michael Caine), whose "treatments" for the insane are widely viewed as barbaric. Royer-Collard and Sade are linked by a deep, almost incestuous understanding of each other. Sade intuitively grasps the depravities strengthening Royer-Collard's iron will. The doctor, in turn, recognizes the subversion that Sade represents; he recognizes his Antichrist posturings, his masochistic obsession to draw out the torturer in his enemies. The black comedy of *Quills* is that the more Sade is crushed and humiliated, the more thrillingly righteous he gets; his abasement is a horror that doubles as erotic pleasure.

The intermediary in this face-off is Charenton's overseer, the abbé Coulmier (Joaquin Phoenix in yet another first-rate performance this year), whose benevolence toward his inmates has allowed Sade to stage theatricals in which they lewdly prance and chortle. In a series of quick philosophical exchanges with Sade, Coulmier tries to coax his illustrious tenant into exhibiting in his writing the good parts of life; he considers the Marquis his friend, incorrigible but not abhorrent. Sade, of course, interprets Coulmier's kindness as a veiled request to be brought into the illicit, and Coulmier's unadmitted love for Madeleine, which racks him, gives credence to Sade's suspicions.

Kaufman, who also directed *The Unbearable Lightness of Being* and *Henry & June* (the first studio film to receive an NC-17 rating), knows how to bring together intellectualism and carnality without losing the carnal bite. Sade is, for him, perhaps the archetypal protagonist, since the Marquis, despite all his ravenous carryings on, is a species of philosopher Sade needs to play to an audience, which is why, when the doctor's intercessions deprive him of his writing implements, he can justifiably howl, "I've been raped!" Sade, even in rags, expects aristocratic privilege, and without a readership for his works, he sees himself brought down to commonness—a mere diddler. This is why he rages for his right to continue spewing his salacious screeds and why he ultimately obliterates himself rather than relent. In Kaufman and Wright's scheme, it doesn't really matter if Sade is a great artist or just a depraved scribbler; the point is that he has within himself the inextinguishable impulse to create, which summons all of the filmmakers' anguish and awe. (Wright, drawing an implicit parallel between then and now, wrote his play in 1996 in response to attacks on the NEA. Marquis de Sade, meet Andres Serrano.)

Quills isn't very seductive; nor does it try to be. Seductiveness implies a level of human interplay that is far more shared and intimate than anything on view here. Sade may be a libertine, but he is sealed off from everybody else by his own voraciousness. He has the spirited dullness of a pornographer in the grips of compulsion. For him, every interaction contains a sexual secret, and where none exists, he creates one. Geoffrey Rush brings an extraordinary density to Sade; between his tantrums and harangues one can glimpse a man crazed by self-deceit and the wastefulness of his life (and perhaps, although it's not discussed, venereal disease). When Sade's wife, Renée (Jane Menelaus, Rush's real-life wife), is brought into his cell, we are at first startled at her poise and concern; this is not the kind of woman we would have expected him to marry. Renée mourns the wastefulness, too, and her reasoned sorrow gives us a new window on her husband. It exposes him—humanizes him.

Michael Caine so often plays characters who are sympathetic and good-natured that it's easy to forget how truly terrifying he can also be (as in *Mona Lisa*). What's horrifying about Royer-Collard is the placidity of his belief in his own barbarism—which, of course, he sees as benevolence. Caine understands the self-justifying nature of villainy. The doctor fears and loathes Sade because the Marquis is the one man who sees through that self-justification. Chaos for Royer-Collard, as for Coulmier, is an abyss to be avoided at all cost; but, unlike the abbé, he isn't tempted by degradation. Or by beauty either. His pretty, virginal young bride (Amelia Warner) is for him a "rare bird" he intends to keep caged in his clutches. Royer-Collard's understanding of baseness is perhaps as profound as Sade's. The difference between them is that Sade aches for liberation while Royer-Collard is all about repression. He suspects everyone of degeneracy, and those suspicions keep him in command. When his bride makes a fool of him, we get a momentary flash of the beast within; it's as if a statesman had suddenly gnarled himself into a gargoyle.

Kaufman goes deep in *Quills,* but in the end he may stand back from the abyss, too. He's a bit too much of the civil libertarian to do full justice to Sade, who, for all his preening decadence here, is never depicted in the full measure of his atrociousness. Sade catalogued and exulted in practically every perversion imaginable, but the words we hear spoken from his works are for the most part weak derivatives of the real thing; likewise Sade's monstrous crimes, while alluded to, are not emphasized. These crimes, which included the torture and mutilation of young women, with possible intent to murder, were at least as responsible for getting Sade repeatedly locked up as anything he wrote.

Quills is one of the few really good American movies of the year, and it's bursting with intellectual energy and standout performances and good old-fashioned Grand Guignol theatrics. But for all its attention to ambiguity, it's also pushing a rather neat formulation: In order to know virtue, we must know vice. The film is offered up to us as a kind of curative. But since Sade's vice has been adulterated by the filmmakers, our ensuing knowledge of virtue is a bit too easily won.

Kaufman doesn't completely avoid the deranging implications of Sade's words on others; in a riotous scene near the end, his words help bring about the death of someone close to him. Neither does Kaufman avoid those implications for the Marquis himself. The film practically says that Sade died for our sins. But his writing also occasions a lot of bawdy guffawing and groping among the groundlings and the hired help, and there's something a bit self-congratulatory about such scenes: They seem to be saying, "Look at how unshocked we are," when in fact there's nothing much that's spoken here to be shocked about. Madeleine, representing, it would appear, all free spirits, calls Sade's works her salvation. They allow her to fantasize: If she wasn't such a bad woman on the page, she says, she couldn't be such a good woman in real life. This is a dear conceit, and Kate Winslet's radiance as Madeleine—she has the soft glow of idealized youth—saves it from ickiness. But still. Kaufman may believe no man is beyond redemption; he may believe it necessary, as a formidable artist in his own right, to promote art as salvation, much as Coulmier did to salve his mad inmates. But in doing so he links art to the bromides of therapy and denies blackness its truest sheen.

NEW YORK POST, 11/22/00, p. 47, Jonathan Foreman

Monster and rotten writer though he was, even the Marquis de Sade doesn't deserve to be memorialized by a costume drama as ludicrously crude as "Quills."

The author of "Justine," that classic of rape and torture, was a cultivated man who would have despised this film's smugness and vulgarity—and the way it shamelessly, confusedly rips off several genuinely brilliant works of art, including the classic 1964 play "Marat/Sade" and 75's "One Flew Over the Cuckoo's Nest."

Marat/Sade," also inspired by Sade's incarceration at the Charenton insane asylum, was a '60s masterpiece about repression, revolutionary violence and art.

This, on the other hand, is an exercise in self-congratulation pretending to be brave statement for art, free expression and sexual liberation.

The result resembles a period version of "The Rocky Horror Picture Show"—played dead straight.

It's all there: a dark and stormy night, scenery-chewing performances and Geoffrey Rush as Sade channeling Tim Curry's Dr. Frank N. Furter, bringing polymorphous sexual liberation to the uptight folk of Napoleonic France.

The asylum where Sade is luxuriously imprisoned is under the control of the idealistic Abbe Coulmier (Joaquin Phoenix).

Coulmier lets the Marquis put on plays starring asylum inmates, and allows him to write sadistic pornography as part of his therapy. He doesn't know that Madeleine (Kate Winslet), his favorite busty laundry-woman, is smuggling Sade's writings out to a mysterious horseman who arranges their publication in Paris.

There, they are such a success that Napoleon himself wants Sade silenced, and sends Dr. Royer-Collard (Michael Caine) to take over the asylum. Royer-Collard is an authoritarian sadist who immediately seeks to stifle Sade's creative output.

As if this weren't bad enough, Royer-Collard is also a sexually inadequate hypocrite who has just bought a teenage virgin wife (Amelia Warner) from a nunnery. It's only a matter of time before she's corrupted by the Marquis' works, and the battles between the doctor, priest and prisoner end in a bloody climax.

Rush hams it up as Sade, and Caine is little better as the Ken Starr-like Royer-Collard. Winslet, who's incapable of a bad performance but lately only appears in pretentious stinkers, is hamstrung by Doug Wright's over-wrought but underwritten script.

Blame for the way "Quills" feels like a Masterpiece Theater spoof must go also to director Philip Kaufman, who once made films like"The Wanderers" but has been on a downward slide since "Henry & June."

NEWSDAY, 11/22/00, Part II/p. B7, John Anderson

If insanity is defined as an inability to tell right from wrong, Philip Kaufman's "Quills" is certifiable. Based on the Marquis de Sade's post-revolution sabbatical at the Charenton Asylum (1803 till his death in 1814), it's an ostensible plea for freedom of expression and a critique of censorship—but it also advances the theory that mere prose actually can incite sex crimes, promiscuity and arson.

The print ads could include quotes from Larry Flynt and Jerry Falwell.

A personification of pure mischief is how screenwriter-playwright Doug Wright paints de Sade (played by Geoffrey Rush), who flirts outrageously with his laundress-ally Madeleine (Kate

Winslet), has a Buddy Sorel-Mel Cooley relationship with the beleagured Abbe (Joaquin Phoenix) and directs the lunatic imates in "therapeutic" productions of plays. He's also smuggling out, with Madeleine's assistance, pages of manuscript, which are assembled elsewhere into such notorious novels as "Justine" and sold on Parisian streets like heroin.

The old Marquis, for those of you not wearing leather corsets or carrying riding crops, is the namesake of sadism, a writer whose prose includes vigorous portrayals of coprophilia, necrophilia, pedophilia and recreational disembowelments, hallmarks of de Sade's oeuvre that, for purposes of propaganda, are not-so-strangely missing from Kaufrnan's movie.

The beatification of de Sade seems to be in vogue; besides several recent sympathetic books, there is French director Benoit Jacquot's "Sade," as yet unreleased in the United States, which paints the Marquis as the avuncular Dolly Levy of the French Revolution, bringing unhappy young kids together for a pre-guillotine roll in the hay. Like Kaufman, Jacquot doesn't quote too liberally from de Sade's books, lest the intended image of martyrdom be diluted by the work itself.

But using de Sade strictly as a metaphor, disregarding historical accuracy, is OK. It's just eminently unclear what Kaufman and Wright intend his symbolism to mean. Certainly he's a martyr, although his persecution doesn't really begin until the Abbe calls in Dr. Royer-Collard (Michael Caine), a proto-psychologist who begins his own little reign of terror by depriving de Sade of his tools (the quills of the title) and thus sets up the movie's central motif: de Sade, no matter what they do, will find a way to write—be it with wine, blood or excrement. He's a crazy Christ figure, whose mission is a world free for licentiousness.

De Sade's improvisations on pen and paper—and the decor of Charenton itself—provide Kaufman ample opportunity to create his own mischief and Rush a character with which to run dramatically amok. The doctor, predictably enough, is set up as hypocritical counterweight to the marquis. His new wife, Simone (Amelia Warner), is taken fresh out of the convent, sexually brutalized by Royer-Collard and set up as a trophy through which de Sade gets his revenge—Simone is eroticized to the point of nymphomania by a smuggled copy of "Justine," which is funny enough, but helps demolish the politics of the film.

Winslet, the most consistently intelligent and believable actress on the screen today, is terrific, but has a much easier time of it than Rush, whose de Sade is jerked back and forth so many times between agent-provocateur and crucified artist it's a wonder he gets as firm a grip on the role as he does. If Caine had a mustache, he'd twirl it; Amelia Warner is a sumptuous tart, and Phoenix, as usual, is expert and precise. Also watchable. So is "Quills," if you've got the stomach. It's just a little bit mad.

SIGHT AND SOUND, 2/01, p. 45, Philip Kemp

1804. The Marquis de Sade is held in the Charenton asylum near Paris, under the care of the Abbé Coulmier. With the help of Madeleine, a young laundress, he smuggles out his latest novel *Justine*. Its explicit passages anger Napoleon, who orders that Dr Royer-Collard, an alienist known for his draconian methods, be installed at Charenton as overseer.

At first Coulmier manages to protect de Sade, having made him promise no further publication. But de Sade stages a play in the asylum theatre, poking bawdy fun at Royer-Collard and his teenage bride Simone. The theatre is closed down, and Coulmier confiscates de Sade's writing materials. But the Marquis writes a story on his bedsheets, which is published. Royer-Collard orders de Sade's cell stripped bare; de Sade writes on his clothes in his own blood.

Madeleine comes to Coulmier at night, desperately tempted, he rejects her. Simone, who has been reading *Justine*, runs off with a young architect. Royer-Collard tortures de Sade with his medical machines. Madeleine is to be sent away; de Sade tells her one last story, relayed verbally via other inmates. Excited by the story, an inmate murders Madeleine. De Sade's tongue is cut out; naked in a dungeon, he writes on the walls with shit. When Coulmier offers spiritual comfort, de Sade swallows the crucifix and chokes to death. A year later, Royer-Collard is in sole charge at Charenton. The subdued inmates are printing the works of de Sade on the asylum press. Coulmier, a hopeless case, remains locked in his cell.

In the pre-credit sequence of *Quills*, a hulking executioner prepares a young female aristocrat for the guillotine, and the Marquis de Sade gazes down from the window of his asylum cell, half titillated and half appalled, as the blade severs her delicate neck. "How easily, dear reader," he muses in urbane, teasing voiceover, "one changes from predator to prey." This sequence (after which the action jumps forward some 10 years) prefigures the whole film in miniature: the disquieting mix of erotically tinged comedy and blood-thirsty horror and the underlying political subtext.

The risky interface between romanticism and dissidence has always intrigued Philip Kaufman, himself something of a maverick among US filmmakers; for him, as for Arthur Penn, "the measure of a society is how it treats its outsiders." This is the second time that Kaufman has taken the creation of hardcore erotica as his test-case, but *Henry & June* was weighed down by the solemn self-importance of Henry Miller and Anaïs Nin, the film's subjects. *Quills*, as befits its subject, is a far more full-throated and subversive affair, and incidentally shows up Milos Forman's *The People vs. Larry Flynt* for the fudged exercise that it was.

Doug Wright's screenplay, adapted from his own stage hit, plays fast and loose with historical fact (de Sade was never tortured or mutilated in the Charenton asylum; his wife was supportive of him), but then *Quills* makes no pretence at being a straight biopic. De Sade stands for the creative instinct at its most extreme, both in terms of what he writes and of his uncrushable compulsion to express himself. "My writing is involuntary," he proclaims, "like the beating of my heart."

Steadily the tone of the film darkens, its visual texture thickens and coarsens. Plush draperies are stripped down to bare wood and stone as de Sade is reduced from using the eponymous quills to chicken bones, glass shards dipped in blood and finally his own fingers scrawling in his own shit scatology in the most literal sense. His opponents, notably his strict overseer Royer-Collard, are likewise pushed to extremes by the logic of their stance, visiting on him tortures as cruel as those he created in his imagination. But unlike Forman, Kaufman and Wright don't take the easy liberal option of declaring freedom of expression an unmixed good. It's one of de Sade's stories that directly causes the death of Madeleine, the asylum's laundress and one of de Sade's most avid readers, by arousing an inmate to murderous frenzy. To give the irony a further twist, the killer is Bouchon, the former executioner from the opening scene, society's licensed murderer.

As played by Geoffrey Rush, de Sade is a man driven by his own contradictions, at once caustic and tender, engaging and repellent, triumphing in his final anguish as he sees his tormentors dragged down to his own level. It's an audacious performance, verging on high camp and always pushing to the edge of excess, and it says a lot for his fellow players that they hold their own so effectively—especially Kate Winslet's warm, sensuous Madeleine, Joaquin Phoenix's tormented Coulmier, the devout asylum head, and Michael Caine, giving a superbly controlled display of cold clinical venom as Royer-Collard. The sets by Martin Childs *(Mrs. Brown, Shakespeare in Love)* feel lavish but sleazy, like a fine satin gown drabbled in dirt, and along with the livid greenish tones of the lighting by Rogier Stoffers (who shot the Dutch film *Character)* create a disquieting sense of encroaching decay.

TIME, 11/27/00, p. 93, Richard Schickel

At the Charenton Insane Asylum, the Marquis de Sade (Geoffrey Rush) has a nice life—good food, good wine, the ability to smuggle his dirty books out to his publisher via a sympathetic chambermaid (Kate Winslet). But he offends Napoleon, who orders an alienist (Michael Caine) to cure him or kill him.

First he's robbed of his writing instruments (the quills that give this movie its title). Undaunted, he uses his blood for ink, his clothing as paper. Stripped, he manages to write a story in his excrement on his cell walls. Finally, his tormentors rip out his tongue. *Quills* is not, obviously, your standard biopic.

It is actually a fantasy only vaguely based on the facts of the case—a distinctly postmodern fantasy insistently exploiting the paradox that De Sade is a victim of sadism as wretched as any he might have imagined. Other matters are also ironically explored: What is freedom; What is power—that sort of thing. The film's creators—director Phil Kaufman, writer Doug Wright (adapting his own play)—seem to think they have made a black comedy. But Kaufman, who displayed a gift for sexy literacy in *The Unbearable Lightness of Being,* here succumbs to an unbearable heaviness of spirit. His approach to this material is brutally horrific, vulgarly unamusing. And Rush wears the desire for another Oscar nomination on his sleeve in a puffed up, unfelt performance.

The film poses a smug challenge: If you don't like our merry little prank, that makes you square and unhip. O.K., we'll bite. This is soft-gore porn, obvious in its strategies, witless in the play of its ideas, absurdist only in its pretense to seriousness.

VILLAGE VOICE, 11/28/00, p. 133, J. Hoberman

"Dear reader, I have a naughty little tale to tell ..." So begins *Quills*, Philip Kaufman's earnestly overblown celebration of the Marquis de Sade, adapted for the movies by Doug Wright from his Obie-winning exercise in intellectual Grand Guignol.

Assuming a fun, rowdy tone from the get-go, *Quills* opens in 1794 Paris with a brief pastiche of Sade's catalog of atrocity *Juliette* and a blade's-eye view of a liberated young woman being whacked by the guillotine. Sade, at this point our narrator, gazes down from his prison window on the bloody terror—as though he were at once product and prophet of the French Revolution. Having paid homage to Madame Tussaud, the film leaps a decade or more into the future and the marquis's internment at the Charenton insane asylum.

It is here that Sade (Geoffrey Rush) is freest to be himself—confined with his monstrous ego and the means to indulge it. Coulmier (Joaquin Phoenix), the young abbé who administers the hospital, is a man of the Enlightenment; he believes in art therapy, explaining to one pyromaniac how much better it is to paint fires than set them. Hence Sade, comfortably ensconced in a cell stocked with moldy sex toys, is encouraged to stage theatricals and write stories—which, unbeknownst to Coulmier, the institution's comely laundress, Madeleine (Kate Winslet with a mild Cockney accent), has been smuggling out to Sade's avid publishers.

Reading the marquis's outrageous manuscripts aloud to her friends (who are inspired by what they hear to spontaneously form a threesome), virtuous Madeleine is the sweetheart of the loony bin—she's variously pursued by a feebleminded 300-pound wanker, yearned for by Coulmier, and continually propositioned by Sade, all the while maintaining her virginity. (Although Madeleine's chastity is considered admirable and even necessary to the movie's argument, the filmmakers assume a modern, anticlerical tone toward Coulmier, who is shown as worse than a fool for not following through on his sexual feelings for the girl who so admires him.)

Wright's script takes more liberties with history than Sade does with Madeleine. Still, it's essential to the premise that Sade's anonymous books attract a popular audience and even make money. When a few humorous passages from *Justine* are read aloud to Napoleon, France's newly crowned emperor demands that the book be burned and its author shot. Cooler heads prevail, and instead, the stern Dr. Royer-Collard (Michael Caine) is dispatched like an 18th-century Lynne Cheney to oversee overly permissive Charenton. Greeted by a gaggle of singing inmates, the doctor tartly remarks that "playing dress-up with cretins sounds like a symptom of madness, not a cure"—the best one-liner given to anyone in the movie other than Geoffrey Rush.

A ridiculously incorrigible roué crowned with a long, ratty gray wig, Rush's strutting, winking, leering Sade sends each delicious bon mot out into the world with lip-smacking glee. This Sade is far less philosophical than the more urbane Divine Marquis played by Daniel Auteuil in Benoit Jacquot's rival production *Sade* (not yet acquired for U.S. release), and also a tad less blasphemous-although he does at one point spit on the Bible. Indeed, the biggest sadist in *Quills* is, of course, Dr. Royer-Collard.

Living out his own tawdry gothic novel while Sade's "crimes" are limited to his imagination, Royer-Collard claims his orphan child-bride from a compliant convent and installs her in the barred-window boudoir of a renovated castle as his prisoner of love. This juicy information soon spreads through Charenton and Sade takes it as the subject for a farce, which is performed for Dr. and Madame Royer-Collard by a troupe that proves to be remarkably accomplished, given that they haven't had the benefit of any rehearsal or even a read-through prior to the play's world premiere.

Rising to Sade's bait, the irate Royer-Collard shuts down the theater and commands the hapless Coulmier to prohibit the miscreant Sade from any further writing. Deprived of his quills, the diabolical author forges on using wine and a chicken bone to inscribe a tale of necrophilia on his bedsheets—and that's just for starters.

It's striking that both *Sade* and *Quills* humanize the marquis by having him cast his spell on innocent young girls. *Quills,* however, goes further in conceptualizing Sade's audience as essentially female. Madame Royer-Collard is one such fan, who, in effect, seals Sade's fate when she slips her well-thumbed copy of *Justine* to the handsome young architect who is redecorating the castle—then leaves the book behind as evidence for her cuckolded hubby to find. For her part, Madeleine is proud to play Jeanne d'Arc to Sade's dauphin. She is publicly flogged for aiding and abetting his writings, but her devotion to the cause leads her to ask the marquis for one last tale of baroque debauchery—relayed from Sade's cell to hers telephone-style by a helpful network of inmates.

The effect is grossly overstimulating. Even the weather turns stormy and the entire asylum runs amok in a full Shock Corridor of rape, mutilation, self-flagellation, necrophilia, and coprography (if that's the scientific term for writing with human feces). All this is quite risible until it turns actively unpleasant. I'm inclined to agree with my colleague Michael Musto, who suggested that the reason various characters have their tongues ripped out is to prevent the actors from chewing away the scenery.

Ultimately, Kaufman's Sade is less the "freest man who ever lived" (as the Surrealists thought him) than an artist deprived of his art—a First Amendment martyr. Less ambiguous on-screen than onstage, *Quills* is an anticensorship manifesto—even a defense of Hollywood. (Kaufman's far sexier *Henry and June* was the movie that first compelled the industry to invent the scarlet NC-17 and then unfairly suffered the consequences for it.) *Quills* argues that, when it comes to culture, downtrodden workers like Madeleine need the rough stuff to hold their interest. Moreover, for healthy people—although not necessarily the unstable inmates of Charenton—Sade's hyperbolic, even pornographic, tales of rape and torture provide a useful form of sublimation.

As Madeleine explains to the abbé when he questions her taste in literature, "If I wasn't such a bad woman on the page, I couldn't be such a good woman in my life." I look forward to hearing some young movie fan paraphrase that line during the next round of congressional hearings.

Also reviewed in:
CHICAGO TRIBUNE, 12/15/00, Friday/p. A, Michael Wilmington
NEW REPUBLIC, 12/18/00, p. 22, Stanley Kauffmann
NEW YORK TIMES, 11/22/00, p. E1, Elvis Mitchell
NEW YORKER, 11/27/00, p. 181, Anthony Lane
VARIETY, 9/11-17/00, p. 26, Todd McCarthy
WASHINGTON POST, 12/15/00, p. C1, Stephen Hunter

RATCATCHER

A First Look Pictures release of a Merchant Ivory Productions presentation of a Pathe Pictures/BBC Films in association with the Arts Council of England/Lazennec and Le Studio Canal+ of a Holy Cow Films production. *Executive Producer:* Andrea Calderwood, Barbara McKissack, and Sarah Radclyffe. *Producer:* Gavin Emerson. *Director:* Lynne Ramsay. *Screenplay:* Lynne Ramsay. *Director of Photography:* Alwin Küchler. *Editor:* Lucia Zucchetti. *Music:* Rachel Portman. *Sound:* Richard Flynn and (music) Chris Dibble. *Casting:* Gillian Berrie. *Production Designer:* Jane Morton. *Art Director:* Robina Nicholson. *Costumes:* Gill Horn. *Stunt Coordinator:* Paul Heasman. *Running time:* 94 minutes. *MPAA Rating:* Not Rated.

CAST: William Eadie (James Gillespie); Tommy Flanagan (Da); Mandy Matthews (Ma); Michelle Stewart (Ellen Gillespie); Lynne Ramsay, Jr. (Anne Marie Gillespie); Leanne Mullen (Margaret Anne); John Miller (Kenny); Jackie Quinn (Mrs. Quinn); James Ramsay (Mr. Quinn); Anne McLean (Mrs. Fowler); Craig Bonar (Matt Monroe); Andrew McKenna (Billy); Mick Maharg (Stef); James Montgomery (Hammy); Thomas McTaggart (Ryan Quinn);

Stuart Gordon (Tommy);   Stephen Sloan (Mackie);   Molly Innes (Miss McDonald);   Stephen King (Mr. Mohan);   John Comerford (Insurance Man);   Jimmy Grimes (Mr. Mullen);   Anne Marie Lafferty (Rita);   Bess McDonald (Elderly Lady);   Leanne Jenkins (Kitten Girl);   Ian Cameron and Brian Steel (Soldiers);   Dougie Jones and Joe McCrone (Scavengers);   James Watson (Bus Driver);   Stephen Purdon (Boy on Bike);   Marion Connel (Jessse);   Robert Farrell (Boy);   Donnie McMillan (Artie);   Lisa Taylor (Anne Marie's Friend).

LOS ANGELES TIMES, 11/1/00, Calendar/p. 3, Kenneth Turan

Bleak childhoods make for the best cinema, and "Ratcatcher" stands at the head of the class.

From acknowledged favorites like Francois Truffaut's "The 400 Blows" to underappreciated works like the Robert De Niro-Leonardo DiCaprio "This Boy's Life" and Jean-Claude Lauzon's French-Canadian "Leolo," films that let us into the push and pull of difficult young lives have a power to create emotion like almost nothing else. Even in that company, Scottish writer-director Lynne Ramsay's exquisite feature debut is something special.

A knockout in its premiere at Cannes (where Ramsay had previously won two Prix du Jury for her short films), "Ratcatcher" is not only made with unhurried artistry and unblinking assurance, it also combines two very different and usually mutually exclusive kinds of filmmaking.

Hearing that "Ratcatcher" is set in one of Glasgow's poorest neighborhoods during a 1973 sanitation strike that led to massive garbage pileups and a major rodent explosion, it would be simple to assume that it's wholly in the tradition of socially conscious directors like Ken Loach, that it can be summed up simply as, in Ramsay's words, "another grim film from up north." Nothing could be less true.

It's not that the writer-director, herself a Glasgow native, doesn't tear at your sympathies with her depiction of this pitiless environment, where tragedies strike quickly and uncaringly, where chances for tenderness are rare and elusive. With her ability to give every moment its correct emotional weight and an unwillingness to trespass on the realities of lower-class life, Ramsay shows the kind of empathy and concern that is heir to Loach's.

But, and this is especially rare for socially conscious directors, Ramsay also has a remarkable visual imagination, a gift for putting vivid, poetic images on the screen. Working with the same creative team (cinematographer Alwin Kuchler, editor Lucia Zucchetti, production designer Jane Morton) she's used since film school, Ramsay creates unexpected, even daring shots of lyrical beauty that go right to the heart.

Typical is "Ratcatcher's" striking opening sequence. It's unsettling and hard to read at first, and then we realize we're watching the slowed-down sight of a boy completely enveloped by and twirling around in his mother's curtains. The background sound is muted, as it would be for a boy in what has to be a sort of dream state, one of the few escapes from a troubling reality open to someone like him.

Out of the curtains comes 12-year-old James Gillespie (William Eadie, like many of the film's child actors, a nonprofessional). His incongruously large ears bookend what has to be called a tragic face, one that seems to know instinctively the kind of unhappy life fate is planning for him.

It's typical of "Ratcatcher's" nerve that James' first post-curtains scene not only locates him unmistakably in his environment but also sets a powerfully disconcerting tone. No matter what happens to James during the troubling summer vacation that lies before him, what we've seen at the start never leaves our minds, or his. Living with his parents, his older sister Ellen (Michelle Stewart) and his younger sister Anne Marie (Lynne Ramsay Jr., the filmmaker's niece), James feels trapped by his surroundings, his actions, his very life. He's the kid nobody wants around, not his siblings, not the neighborhood gang, not even his hard-pressed parents.

It's indicative of "Ratcatcher's" sensibility that its character judgments are not schematic. His mother (Mandy Matthews) is overworked, his father (Tommy Flanagan) a problem drinker and a philanderer, but the love that once animated their relationship is quite visible when it's not overmatched and exhausted by the extent of their problems. The only hope the family has of escaping suffocation is a potential move to new community-sponsored housing out in the suburbs.

As for James, the only friends he manages to connect with are misfits and outcasts like himself. There's Kenny (John Miller), a mentally slow animal lover, and 14-year-old Margaret Anne (Leanne Mullen), the neighborhood's abused and victimized sexual mark. The unlikely bond she forms with James answers the need they both have for simple childhood innocence that is available to them nowhere else.

Ramsay's imaginative shot-making gifts make for a sublime result, creating a different sort of magical realism than we're used to seeing. "Ratcatcher" is clearly the work of a natural film artist, and experiencing her debut (helped by subtitles that the thick Glasgow accents mandate) is as much a privilege as it is a pleasure.

NEW YORK POST, 10/13/00, p. 65, Lou Lumenick

This is your typical, wildly over-praised festival-circuit film, which one British critic actually gushed "oozes with raw realism." Don't say you weren't warned.

There are some good things in Lynne Ramsay's debut feature, which follows the adventures of James (William Eadie, who isn't bad), a 12-year-old urchin in a garbage-strewn Glasgow slum in the early '70s.

Already guilt stricken over the accidental death of a pal in a scummy canal, James copes manfully with his drunken dad (scar-faced Tommy Flanagan, who played Russell Crowe's servant in "Gladiator") and loses his virginity to the local slut (Leanne Mullen), all the while dreaming of life in a new housing project.

"Ratcatcher" has its moments, but overall the effect is uneven, second-rate Ken Loach, with lots of rats and Scottish accents so impenetrable that subtitles have been added for U.S. audiences.

NEWSDAY, 10/13/00, Part II/p. B6, John Anderson

We're on pretty familiar, working-class British ground with "Ratcatcher," director Lynne Ramsay's debut and a harrowing/ whimsical coming-of-age film set in '70s Glasgow. Look closely: You might spot the ghost of Lindsay Anderson having a pint with Ken Loach at the local pub. Or the cast of "Secrets and Lies" just ambling about the council flats.

But Ramsay adds more than a touch of poetry to her portrait of the city and of James (William Eadie), a 12-year-old who watches a friend drown, keeps it secret and then spends the rest of the movie trying to reconcile his life and his guilt. It's grim—the festering refuse of a garbage strike is piling up around them all, just in case you missed the point of waste and claustrophobia. And James' family isn't exactly the Bloomsbury Group. His father (Tommy Flanagan) possesses the distinct air of brutality. Ma (Mandy Matthews) is kind, but ineffectual. James finds consolation with Margaret Anne (Leanne Mullen), an unpopular local girl whose gawkiness is leading her to promiscuity. They take a bath together. It's the least erotic thing you've ever seen.

But none of this is easily tossed off by Ramsay. Her characters are rich, her atmosphere is genuine, her problems are mundane, perhaps, but not to the people who have them—James' family, for instance, is wracked by apprehension over whether the local council will give them a bigger apartment, one with indoor plumbing.

There's a real sense of life being lived; humor, awkwardly but persistently, shoots up between the cracks in the concrete. And the occasional pastoral image suggests hope for James, even if the unavoidable implication of "Ratcatcher" (with a bounty on rats, catch, the garbage strike creates a windfall) is about what James will become. Not the sensitive man his boyhood seems to suggest. More like another extra in a Ken Loach movie.

SIGHT AND SOUND, 11/99, p. 50, Charlotte O'Sullivan

Glasgow, the 70s. A dustmen's strike is on. Two boys, Ryan Quinn and James Gillespie, fight in a canal. Ryan drowns, James survives. James notices an older girl, Margaret Anne, being picked on by Matt Monroe's gang and the pair become friends. One day James decides to follow his sister Ellen when she takes a bus ride. Instead of finding out what she's up to, he discovers a new housing estate being built in the countryside. James' friend Kenny falls into the canal and is rescued by James' dad. Plans are afoot to relocate some of the families on James' estate to the new houses, but when the inspectors visit his house is in chaos. James' dad receives a bravery award for rescuing Kenny. Going home, he's beaten up by a gang of boys and at home hits James' mother.

The army arrive to clear up the refuse. James returns to the estate in the country, but the houses are no longer accessible. Back home he discovers Margaret Anne having sex with the older boys and begins rowing with Kenny, who blurts out that he saw James "kill" Ryan. Later James jumps into the canal, but images also show the family arriving at the new house with their possessions.

You can't help liking *Ratcatcher*. Like the canal that dominates so much of the film, Lynne Ramsay's painterly portrait of childhood drags you in. You believe in 12-year-old James, all Prince Charles ears and snappable wrists. You adore his mousy mother. You're glued to his sister Anne Marie (her bouts of giggles erupt like the foam around a shaken bottle of pop). But does it work? Ultimately *Ratcatcher* is most successful when scribbling in its own margins. The beginning, for instance, is a triumph, precisely because it isn't a beginning but an end. We follow the progress of Ryan, an intense little boy who all of a sudden dies. James' mother hugs him, saying, "I thought it was you," her skin shining with relief. The audience might say the same thing. We are temporarily dumbfounded, assuming our hero, our narrative centre, is dead. Ramsay has shown us a horrible possibility right from the start. We obey the Darwinian principle: we want to back a winner.

It's when the film tries to be linear that problems arise. James' father's rescue of Kenny leaves him in a stupor. As a result, when the council inspectors pop by, he and the flat are a sorry sight. And for some reason this jeopardises the family's chances of relocation. Why this should be so is never quite made clear, but Ramsay seems desperate to push home a grim message: good deeds are rewarded only by punishment. In the same way, Mrs Quinn's sweet request for James to have Ryan's shoes results in destruction (a box of possessions is smashed). Still more importantly, when James' dad helps a little girl by holding her kitten, he attracts the jeers of some macho lads and is beaten up.

Another message seems to be that good people are masochists. When James saves his friend Kenny's mouse Snowball from Matt Monroe's gang, Kenny himself then tries to impress the boys by attaching the mouse to a balloon and letting Snowball drift into the sky. Unprotected, doomed Margaret Anne also chooses to go with the older, abusive boys rather than stay loyal to James. Most crucially, James' mother takes back his dad after she's battered. Not only is the world a predictably bad place, but everyone in it seems wilfully self-destructive. In justifying the grim ending, the plot feels contrived. As central narratives go, it's just too neat.

Even more disappointing is James' relationship with Margaret Anne. In a scene in which they share a bath the pathos feels strained and she fails to become distinctive—she could be any giggling, uneasy-bodied girl. So when we see her betray James with Monroe's gang she really does seem a faceless victim, the "poor cow" that Kenny dubs her. (The reference to Loach's 1967 film seems particularly inappropriate. In *Poor Cow,* Joy's need for leery male attention is allowed to exist as a banal, pleasurable kink in her character, not a pathetic flaw.)

This is a shame, since James and Margaret Anne's relationship begins so well. There's one gorgeous scene, for instance, where Margaret Anne, having been poked by all the other boys, receives young James. In one of the film's many powerful silences we see him lying on top of her, as if he'd been there for ever, his brain as well as his body at peace. And yet the real tension in his character remains intact. As usual, his small-adult desire to protect—he's covering up Margaret Anne's body from the other boys' lecherous gaze, keeping her warm, like a rug or an extra layer of clothing.

This brings us back to what Ramsay's feature debut does best. *Ratcatcher* makes you see the world with bigger eyes, revealing the layers beneath every surface. We're frequently asked to notice materials in conjunction with each other: flesh beneath curtain fabric, a bathtub beneath plastic, a toe beneath nylon, spectacles beneath water. These don't cancel each other out, the mystery, blurring our perceptions. The pugnacious Ryan, who begins the film twisted in a net curtain, is visible but we don't know whether he's in pleasure or pain—from the twists and turns of his dancing mouth, his mood seems enigmatically extreme.

The film works in the same way, providing an impression of intensity without judgement. Thus what appear to be an easy distinction—contaminated rubbish versus pure countryside—is made complex. The rubbish is dangerous, but it's not aberrant. It's merely another layer, partially but never entirely obscuring the view. The council workers make us realise this when they judge the Gillespies' flat negatively. They assume the family are also rubbish and can't see the mess as simply the surface of the Gillespies' existence. And it's the council people therefore, who are exposed as superficial.

In the radiant scene when the mother cleans the flat we fall into the same trap, assuming this is the start of good, wholesome things, but the family is as fractured as before. Similarly, and most importantly, the dream that closes the film—a dream of life, wealth and nature—is as real (or unreal) as James' possible death. *Ratcatcher* has two beginnings; it also has two ends. The dream is a layer of James' consciousness that neither covers up nor is covered by the matter of his drowning. A layer of material can read as a shroud: a preparation for, and protection from, the ultimate nakedness of death. William Faulkner would have loved the slow burn of *Ratcatcher*, a film that won't choose life or death, but makes perfect sense of the phrase *As I Lay Dying*.

VILLAGE VOICE, 10/17/00, p. 136, Amy Taubin

The first image in *Ratcatcher*, Lynne Ramsay's haunting evocation of a horrific Glasgow childhood, is of a preadolescent boy wrapping himself in a window curtain as if it could protect him from the toxic world outside. Five minutes later, Ryan is dead—drowned in the brackish canal that's as close as this poverty-stricken neighborhood comes to a playground. The curtain, in retrospect, seems like his shroud.

Ryan drowns while horsing around in the canal with his friend James (William Eadie). His death is accidental, but James blames himself for pushing Ryan in the water and then running away in a panic; his guilty secret makes an already bleak life more terrible to bear. James is a thin-faced, frail-shouldered boy with clownishly large ears that do nothing to offset the gravity of his demeanor. *Ratcatcher*, which has the feel of a film made from the inside out, burrows under his skin to the place where perception and imagination meet. If James lives in a world of abjection, he is not an abject character like Bresson's Mouchette. James's anger, his emerging sexual desire, his nurturing impulses, and, most of all, his hope of escaping from the darkness to the light keep him from falling victim to his circumstances. But only for so long.

James lives with his parents and two sisters in a dank council flat where the vermin have gotten the upper hand. *(Ratcatcher* is set during the national garbage strike of the mid '70s, which made a large number of neighborhoods hazardous for humans but heaven for rodents.) Da (Tommy Flanagan), a bad drunk who, on at least one occasion, hits his wife, is more interested in soccer than his kids, but we've seen fathers far worse. Worried and worn though she is, Ma (Mandy Matthews) is still capable of affection. There's a lovely scene in which she jitterbugs with James, but she lavishes even more attention on him when she combs the lice out of his hair. James, in turn, performs the same service for Margaret Anne (Leanne Mullen), the slightly older girl he tries to save from the teenage toughs who've issued themselves a free pass to her vagina.

Sitting next to Margaret Anne on a stone wall above the canal, James is mesmerized by the angry red scrape on her knee. "Do you want to touch it?" she asks, and James places a tentative hand over the wound. The image is both visceral and suggestive. The bloody skin is a metaphor for the girl's masochistic sexuality and also for James's sense of being rubbed raw by life.

Ratcatcher is full of images that are similarly immediate and allusive, their poetry heightened by Ramsay's elliptical editing style. Ramsay's short film *Gasman* (1997) turned on a young girl's realization that she was not the only object of her father's affection; it was reminiscent of Jane Campion's early short films in its combination of anthropological detail with extremely subjective camera angles and editing so fragmented it gave the film the feeling of a dream. In *Ratcatcher*, Ramsay uses the same film vocabulary in shaping a full-length narrative to a child's subjective vision. As spare and unflinching as Alan Clarke's *Christine*, and as poetic as Jean Vigo's *Zero de Conduit, Ratcatcher* is a film in which viewers still close to the experience of childhood will be able to recognize themselves. It's also the most audacious debut feature of the year.

Also reviewed in:
NATION, 11/13/00, p. 34, Stuart Klawans
NEW YORK TIMES, 10/13/00, p. E27, Elvis Mitchell
VARIETY, 5/17-23/99, p. 61, David Rooney

READY TO RUMBLE

A Warner Bros. release in association with Bel-Air Entertainment of an Outlaw production in association with Tollin/Robbins Productions.   *Executive Producer:* Steven Reuther and Mike Tollin.   *Producer:* Bobby Newmyer and Jeffrey Silver.   *Director:* Brian Robbins.   *Screenplay (based on World Champion Wrestling characters):* Steven Brill.   *Director of Photography:* Clark Mathis.   *Editor:* Ned Bastille and Cindy Mollo.   *Music:* George S. Clinton.   *Music Editor:* Mike Flicker and Helena Lea.   *Sound:* Ed Novick and (music) John Whynot.   *Sound Editor:* George Simpson.   *Casting:* Marci Liroff.   *Production Designer:* Jaymes Hinkle.   *Art Director:* Alan Muraoka.   *Set Designer:* Mark Poll.   *Set Decorator:* Carla Curry.   *Special Effects:* Joe DiGaetano.   *Costumes:* Carol Ramsey.   *Make-up:* Mindy Hall.   *Stunt Coordinator:* Joel J. Kramer.   *Running time:* 107 minutes.   *MPAA Rating:* PG-13.

CAST: David Arquette (Gordie Boggs);   Oliver Platt (Jimmy King);   Scott Caan (Sean Dawkins); Bill Goldberg, Diamond Dallas Page, and Steven "Sting" Borden (Themselves); Rose McGowan (Sasha);   Joe Pantoliano (Titus Sinclair);   Martin Landau (Sal Bandini); Richard Lineback (Mr. Boggs);   Chris Owen (Isaac);   Carolina Rhea (Eugenia King);   Tait Smith (Buddy King); Ellen Albertini Dow (Mrs. MacKenzie); Kathleen Freeman (Jane King); Lewis Arquette (Fred King);   Ahmet Zappa (Cashier);   Chad Carr, Darby Wilson, and Joey Deters (8-Year-Old Kids);   Max Daniels (Stu);   John Ennis (Stan);   Jill Ritchie (Brittany); Melanie Deanne Moore (Wendy);   Catherine Paolone (Mrs. Boggs);   Wendy Jean Wilkins (Gabby Boggs);   Ric Mancini and Bruce-Robert Serafin (Front Row Fans);   Greg Collins (Crusty Veteran Cop);   David Ursin (Fire Chief);   Earl H. Bullock (Cop 1);   Floyd Levine (Floor Manager);   Pete Blincoe (Video Cameraman);   Richard Karron (Sanitation Guy);   Alex Skuby (Young Doctor);   Tim Sitarz (Fireman Fred);   Tony Penello (Gus);   Jeff Podgurski (The Chewer);   Adam Tomei and Jason Kassin (Siamese Twins);   Philip Pavel (Happy Young Man); Julia Schultz (Kitty);   William E. Daley (Bill Silverman).

LOS ANGELES TIMES, 4/7/00, Calendar/p. 10, John Anderson

[The following review by John Anderson appeared in a slightly different form in NEWSDAY, 4/7/00, Part II/p. B7.]

"Loser! "
"Would a loser have two tickets to Monday Night Nitro, live from Cheyenne?"
"Yes."
There you have it, folks. I wanted to like "Ready to Rumble." Really. I think David Arquette is the thinking man's Adam Sandler. Professional wrestling isn't on TV enough. Stars like Gorilla Monsoon, Haystacks Calhoun and Gorgeous George never got the recognition they deserved. The current craze will ensure immortality for serious wrestling artists of the future.

But a movie made for wrestling fans that makes fun of wrestling fans? That cuts a little too close to the vicarious masochism at the heart of pro wrestling's core constituency. Also, it's not funny.

It is disgusting though, which may be enough. The best scene was when our dimly lit heroes, Gordie (Arquette) and Sean (Scott Caan)—whose movie-long mission is to bring the defeated Jimmy King (doughboy Oliver Platt, of all people) out of forced retirement—take a break from emptying portable toilets in Wyoming and eat lunch behind their leaking truck. Well, it's the best scene we can actually describe. A number of real-life wrestling stars (Diamond Dallas Page, Bill Goldberg, Sid Vicious, Bam Bam Bigelow) as well as the Oscar-winning Martin Landau are in the picture. They should all be very proud.

NEW YORK POST, 4/7/00, p. 57, Lou Lumenick

We've seen lots of toilet humor in recent movies, but the wrestling farce "Ready to Rumble" plumbs new depths: its two heroes empty portable johns for a living.

"You guys are as dumb as paint," someone tells Gordie (David Arquette) and Sean (Scott Caan), who spend their days fantasizing about World Championship Wrestling.

Gordie's dad, a state trooper, doesn't encourage his son's aspirations.

"You got trouble wrestling your -- out of your trousers to take a leak," he says in one of endless scatological quips that pepper the script by Steven Brill (the "Mighty Ducks" author, not the Court TV founder).

Gordie and Sean leave tiny Lusk, Wyo., to devote themselves to resurrecting the career of Jimmy "The King" King (Oliver Platt), a washed-up WCW star who gets banned after a run-in with WCW head Titus Sinclair (Joe Pantoliano in a takeoff on WWF head Vince McMahon).

"You mean the King is a Queen?" Sean asks Gordie after they discover their hero hiding out from bill collectors while disguised in drag in a trailer home he's "borrowed" from his disgruntled parents.

Despite their disillusionment—the King's estranged wife tells them "all I got to remember him by is an itchy crotch"—the boys press on and manipulate him into a rematch with another WCW star, Diamond Dallas Page.

Page, Goldberg and other WCW stalwarts play themselves. Rose McGowan appears as the league's head dancing girl, who relieves Gordie of his virginity, and Martin Landau is funny as a coach the boys hire to whip the King into shape.

Directed with an emphasis on vulgarity and head-banging action by Brian Robbins ("Variety Blues"), this infomercial for the WCW (a corporate cousin to Warner Bros., which is releasing the movie) defies criticism.

"Ready to Rumble" has its moments of interest, including two excruciating vocals by Arquette and Caan—and a George Clinton score that contains a theme eerily similar to that of "American Beauty."

SIGHT AND SOUND, 1/01, p. 57, Andy Richards

Wyoming, the present. World Championship Wrestling fans Gordie and Sean attend a title defence match by their hero, Jimmy 'the King' King. Behind the scenes, fight promoter Titus Sinclair has decreed that the King will lose to Diamond Dallas Page. When the King is knocked senseless by Diamond Dallas and his crew Gordie and Sean are devastated. Having resolved to track their hero down and mastermind his comeback, they find him washed up in a trailer park and take him to retired wrestling great Sal Bandini for coaching. Gordie meets WCW dancer Sasha, and they become lovers until Gordie discovers that she has been sent by Sinclair to sabotage the King's recovery. Under pressure from his family to take his police exams, Gordie feels unable to help the King any more.

In Las Vegas, the King and his team take on Diamond Dallas and his crew in a three-cage fight. Gordie reappears and joins the King's team. The King reclaims his championship belt, and Sinclair is beaten up by members of the crowd. The King invites Gordie to be his tag-team partner, and Sean to be their manager.

World Championship Wrestling, the backdrop to *Ready to Rumble*, was created by media mogul Ted Turner as a rival to Vince McMahon's World Wrestling Federation. Given Turner's subsequent strategic alliance with media conglomerate Time-Warner, that Warners has made a film promoting the joys of WCW should come as no surprise. Considering the brazen cartoonish hyperbole that is a feature of televised wrestling matches, the filmmakers have a relatively easy time poking affectionate fun at the sport, while simultaneously making sure that the movie plays as an unabashed endorsement of wrestling as an exciting, empowering pursuit for a certain type of American male.

The film's two resplendent representatives of this male mindset are David Arquette's Gordie and Scott Caan's Sean, two slackers in the mould of Beavis and Butt-Head, but with considerably less appeal, as their hectoring banter is crude, charmless and—worst of all—unfunny. Heading straight for the jugular of its built-in demographic, the film wastes no time at all in cranking out a succession of throwaway scatological gags, before settling into its main plot: their quest to regain their favourite wrestler the King his throne. Oliver Platt, though, is woefully miscast in this role; his physique just doesn't match that of the *bona fide* pro wrestlers he faces in the ring (his arch-rival, for instance, is played by the real Diamond Dallas Page). At least the supporting cast enjoy the pantomime spirit: Martin Landau as the King's coach gets to sneer "Who's your daddy, bitch?" at his opponents, while Joe Pantoliano's performance as the Machiavellian promoter masterminding the WCW's soap operatics feels like a caricature of WWF's Vince McMahon.

Unlike Barry Blaustein's 1999 documentary *Beyond the Mat,* in which McMahon appeared, *Ready to Rumble* is so determined to demonstrate what fun it's having that it seems wholly unwilling to probe its subject more deeply. Where the female characters could have critiqued the men's obsessive fandom (as they did in *High Fidelity),* the only women here are the King's abandoned wife (who complains of the crabs he's bequeathed her) and duplicitous sex-bomb Sasha (a wasted Rose McGowan). Neither is there any scrutiny of the cult of violence. Indeed, it's hard not to feel that the film's bloody violence is excessive, in particular in the climactic three-cage deathmatch which after all isn't 'scripted' in the way the fight which robbed the King of his title was, and this ruptures the cartoonish tone of the other set-piece fights.

Yet if wrestling fans will be gratified by the way director Brian Robbins (*Varsity Blues)* stages some of the fight scenes, non-believers will doubtless be left just as nonplussed by the sport and its constituent appeal. It seems ironic that the film's deathmatch is grounded in the kind of unrehearsed, unfaked contest that is seldom to be found in the real game. Meanwhile, the line between appreciating wrestling as a balletic pantomime and relishing it as a sadistic blood sport seems as blurred as ever.

VILLAGE VOICE, 4/18/00, p. 162, Emily Bobrow

If you have a weakness for butt jokes, flatulent nuns, or old ladies saying, "Bitch-slap him like the two-bit crack whore that he is," *Ready to Rumble* will split your sides. Sean (Scott Caan) and Gordie (David Arquette in a familiar turn as a bug-eyed charismatic idiot) are a couple of small-town ne'er-do-wells and wrestling fanatics. After a hard day cleaning out portable toilets and driving a septic truck, a typical night for these two involves poring over some glossy wrestling magazines, slurping slushies, and regaling youngsters with stories of their hero: World Championship Wrestling titleholder Jimmy King (Oliver Platt). When King, a deadbeat turned mythical icon, is dethroned in an ambush orchestrated by the federation's mastermind (there are no oppressive corporate conglomerates here, just a nasty man with a ponytail), Sean and Gordie take it upon themselves to nurse their beer-guzzling idol back to power. Employing a sense of humor that pubescent boys keep locked away in their ids, *Rumble*'s aim is low and dirty. Not even the reliable Martin Landau, as a sadistic wrestling coach, can save this film from itself.

Also reviewed by:
CHICAGO TRIBUNE, 4/7/00, Friday/p. A, Allan Johnson
NEW YORK TIMES, 4/7/00, p. E31, A. O. Scott
VARIETY, 4/10-16/00, p. 43, Dennis Harvey

REAR WINDOW

A USA Films release of a Universal Studios presentation.   *Producer:* Alfred Hitchcock. *Director:* Alfred Hitchcock. *Screenplay:* John Michael Hayes. *Based on the short story "It Had To Be Murder" by;* Cornell Woolrich. *Director of Photography:* Robert Burks. *Editor:* George Tomasini. *Music:* Franz Waxman. *Sound:* Loren L. Ryder, Harry Lindgren, and John Cope. *Art Director:* Hal Pereira and Joseph MacMillan Johnson. *Set Decorator:* Sam Comer and Ray Moyer. *Special Effects:* John P. Fulton. *Costumes:* Edith Head. *Make-up:* Wally Westmore. *Running time:* 114 minutes. *MPAA Rating:* PG.

CAST: James Stewart (L. B. "Jeff" Jeffries); Grace Kelly (Lisa Fremont); Wendell Corey (Tom Doyle); Thelma Ritter (Stella); Raymond Burr (Lars Thorwald); Judith Evelyn (Miss Lonely Hearts); Ross Bagdasarian (The Composer); Georgine Darcy (Miss Torso, the Dancer); Jesslyn Fax (Miss Hearing Aids, the Lady Sculptore); Rand Harper (Honeymooner); Irene Winston (Mrs. Thorwald); Havis Davenport (Newlywed); Sara Berner (Woman on Fire

Escape);   Frank Cady (Fire Escape Man);   Marla English and Kathryn Grandstaff (Party Girls); Alan Lee (Landlord);   Anthony Warde (Detective);   Benny Bartlett (Miss Torso's Friend);   Fred Graham and Edwin Parker (Stunt Detectives);   Harry Landers (Young Man);   Dick Simmons (Man);   Iphigenie Castiglioni (Bird Woman);   Ralph Smiley (Waiter);   Len Hendry and Mike Mahoney (Policemen).

CHRISTIAN SCIENCE MONITOR, 1/21/00, p. 15, David Sterritt

Movie buffs can disagree about almost anything, and even the great Alfred Hitchcock has critics who consider his style too precise, his characters too passive, his images too artificial.

Hitchcockians far outnumber Hitchknockians, though, and his reputation seems to grow more lofty with every passing year. This trend isn't likely to change as we head into 2000, especially since the new century is beginning with a burst of renewed interest in one of the director's greatest works: "Rear Window," first released in 1954 and now returning to theaters in a freshly restored edition so resplendent that you'd think the movie rolled out of the studio just yesterday.

If anyone's memory needs jogging, "Rear Window" stars James Stewart as an injured photographer who spends his days dozing in his wheelchair, fending off a gorgeous girlfriend (Grace Kelly) whose refined habits don't suit his adventurous tastes, and snooping on neighbors across the courtyard from his Greenwich Village apartment. When a salesman's nagging wife disappears from her customary place, our hero decides foul play must be afoot—but he has trouble convincing a skeptical detective, who thinks the trouble is all in the overstimulated imagination of his voyeuristic friend.

This is an ingenious plot, adapted by John Michael Hayes from a Cornell Woolrich story. But what makes "Rear Window" a masterful movie is the way Hitchcock uses its suspenseful narrative to examine areas of human experience that preoccupied him throughout his life. Chief among these is the power of vision—it provides us with our most vivid knowledge of the world, yet is capable of leading us astray by throwing illusion, confusion, and misperception into our paths.

"Rear Window" also played to Hitchcock's fondness for exploring bold stylistic and technical ideas. He realized the challenge of turning traditional cinema on its head—limiting an entire movie to a single room and the view from its window, and filming nearly all the suspense scenes in long-distance shots with a minimum of comprehensible sound.

In the hands of a lesser talent, this might have become a self-conscious stunt, but in Hitchcock's it has the tightly wound perfection of a flawless sonnet or sonata.

"Rear Window" is one of several movies—the outrageous "Rope" and the profound "Vertigo" are also among them—that Hitchcock eventually withdrew from theaters in the hope that rarity would increase their market value. They were reissued in the middle 1980s to great acclaim, but the copies had lost some of their nuances due to careless storage.

Since then, Universal Studios has commissioned the team of Robert A. Harris and James C. Katz to restore a number of classic films, including Orson Welles's brilliant "Touch of Evil," that have suffered the ravages of time. The refurbished "Rear Window" is their latest project. Some of their decisions have been controversial in the past; there has been criticism of the restored sound in "Vertigo," for instance, which some experts find too aggressive for the dreamlike atmosphere Hitchcock had in mind. But their overall contribution has been extremely valuable.

"Rear Window" benefits enormously from their skilled work, filling the screen with rich (colors and unimpeded rhythms that lend a whole new life to one of Hitchcock's supreme achievements.

NEW YORK, 1/24/00, p. 63, Peter Rainer

Alfred Hitchcock's *Rear Window*, which was re-released at the Film Forum in a marvelously restored print supervised by Robert Harris and James Katz, features James Stewart as the cinema's most famous Peeping Tom and is often described as the ultimate movie about voyeurism. Since watching a movie is, in itself, a form of voyeurism, Hitchcock's film has also been called the ultimate movie about moviegoing. There may be some truth to this, but, like so much academic Hitchcock criticism, it doesn't really describe our feelings when we watch the movie; it doesn't convey our sheer enjoyment.

For much of his career, Hitchcock was categorized as a "mere" entertainer—the master of suspense. Then along came the *Cahiers du Cinema* crowd and the Brits to tell us that Hitchcock was the supreme Catholic artist for our age of anxiety and a rival to Poe and Baudelaire. This revisionism was, I think, overscaled, but I remain sympathetic to its intent; more riches, after all, are camouflaged by popular entertainment than by most of what passes for high art. With Hitchcock there was always, even in his most minor entertainments, a residue of fear, of dread, that was more expressive and unsettling than, strictly speaking, it needed to be. Perhaps more than any other director, Hitchcock controlled down to the minutest detail the environment of his moviescape; and yet the great theme of his best movies is the horror visited upon us by a loss of control. The extreme manipulation in Hitchcock's films, the sense we have that he has already anticipated our every response, can seem coldly calculating, but it probably helps to recognize that, deep down, he was just as frightened as we were.

Rear Window, which was released by Paramount Pictures in 1954, is perhaps the clearest example of a Hitchcock movie that functions on dual levels. It's both mousetrap and abyss. Contrast this with *Vertigo* (1958), also restored a number of years back by Harris and Katz, in which the mousetrap, for perhaps the only time in Hitchcock's career, is entirely gone, and what we get instead is pure, obsessive trance. *Vertigo* is a great walkabout of a movie, with delirium at its core. What disturbs viewers about it is that Hitchcock is supposed to be the director who makes us all, at least for the time that we are in the theater, a little crazy, and yet in this film the moviemaker himself seems unmoored. In *Rear Window,* Hitchcock never lets himself go like that, but the movie has a morbid, spectral atmosphere that links it with that later work, and Stewart's performance is almost a warm-up for what he would accomplish in *Vertigo.* In both films, his characters dally with a suspicion that ultimately engulfs.

Stewart's Jefferies in *Rear Window* is a news photographer laid up in his Greenwich Village apartment with his leg in a cast, the result of an on-the-job mishap. Peering into the windows of his neighbors across the courtyard, he begins to imagine—first as diversion, then as obsession—that a white-haired, barrel-chested salesman, Lars Thorwald (Raymond Burr), has murdered his ailing wife and disposed of her body in pieces. Jefferies's amateur sleuthing impresses no one at first, not his smart-aleck nurse, Stella (Thelma Ritter), or his police-detective friend, Tom (Wendell Corey), or his marriage-minded high-society girlfriend, Lisa (Grace Kelly), who makes her first real appearance in the movie as a luminous profile sliding with sensuous slowness into a kiss with the dozing invalid. Jefferies, who can't get himself to commit to her, complains that Lisa is "too perfect," and, actually, she is. (That was always the problem with Grace Kelly.) But Hitchcock understood that dry ice can sting, too. The blonde ice queens who often were his heroines embodied his aesthetic: tight control on the surface and smolderings underneath.

Rear Window has a ghastly, comic subtext: Jefferies's obsession with the supposed murder is also a projection of his own desire to be rid of Lisa and her gold-plated ministrations. (She does things like ordering up to his apartment dinner and champagne from "21.") Virtually the entire movie is shot from Jefferies's vantage point inside his cramped apartment, and the people who pass through it often register as intrusions. They distract Jefferies from the real show going on across the courtyard—the summertime mini-dramas glimpsed through unshaded windows involving not only Thorwald but a childless couple doting on a pet dog, a flirtatious dancer, newlyweds, a sculptor, a composer, and a sad spinster who sets the dinner table for two and eats alone. These window-framed vignettes are trite, perhaps deliberately so, but they offer up a quintessentially urban phenomenon. In the city, every window is a portal into an incompletely understood story. (Psycho, remember, opens with the camera's entry into a randomly chosen window) Hitchcock captures our compulsion to transform our surroundings into a narrative, a cyclorama, not only for our amusement but for our sanity.

He also recognizes how much we want the worst to happen: Like Jefferies, we want the murder to be real. If it isn't, then we are merely voyeurs, and that's too sordid to contemplate. Even if it *is* real, even if we turn out to be saviors instead of peepers, there's still a sordidness about the enterprise. If you break into people's carefully constructed worlds, you can expect to come undone, too. Jefferies puts Lisa and, ultimately, himself in mortal danger, and yet the most plaintive and powerful moment in the movie comes when Thorwald confronts Jefferies in his apartment and cries out, "What do you want from me?" In the world of *Rear Window,* even murderers are entitled to a little privacy.

NEWSDAY, 1/21/00, Part II/p. B13, Jan Stuart

When Alfred Hitchcock's delicious Gotham masterpiece "Rear Window" was released in 1954, New York City phone numbers began with letters, artists could still afford to live in Greenwich Village and a landlord could bounce you out on your nose if he caught you shacking up without a marriage license. And, if one is to believe the urban sociology as captured by screenwriter John Michael Hayes, folks slept out on the fire escape when the nights really baked.

We could be just imagining things, but the summer evenings feel hotter than ever before in the print of "Rear Window" that has been lovingly restored by Robert A. Harris and James C. Katz. Maybe it's the sunsets that have been freshened up to a blazing Sunkist orange or the shmuts that has been removed from a window thermometer, revealing a band of mercury that hovers at 94 degrees Fahrenheit.

But it's the heat of primal lust that really makes itself felt in this, the most deliriously sexed-up of Hitchcock's thrillers. James Stewart, as an action photographer homebound by a broken leg, looks out his living room window over a courtyard named Desire. Every window he peers into with his brazenly phallic telephoto lens frames a scenario of passion bottled up or uncorked: a tireless newlywed couple, an old maid pantomiming a fantasy date, a curvaceous dancer who entertains multiple suitors at a time like some metropolitan Penelope.

As the invalid hero sublimates vicariously through his neighbors, is it any wonder that he can't work up any romantic interest in his society girlfriend? Well, given the fact that the girlfriend is played by Grace Kelly at the apex of her porcelain-skin radiance (Hitchcock poses her in every scene like a high-priced call-girl-turned-Vogue model), Stewart's indifference is arguably more incredible than the murder case that begins to unravel across the courtyard.

Inspired by an elegant Cornell Woolrich short story and two lurid real-life murders, the consummately voyeuristic "Rear Window" swings pendulum-style between the repressed Stewart-Kelly mating dance and the dirty doings in neighbor Raymond Burr's apartment. As Stewart zooms in on Burr's comings and goings, Hitchcock sets up a tantalizing conundrum: How and when do we cross the line that separates being one's brother's keeper from being one's neighbor's intruder?

"Rear Window" is daringly low-burning suspense, almost an art-house movie by today's high-decibel, pulverize-the-audience standards. The restoration also clarifies the complex layering of chat and music emanating from each apartment.

Hayes' script sings with the sort of vervy wit one associates with the '50s New York City it portrays. It's a play, really: Even the window blinds ascend, theater-curtain style, over the opening credits, as if we were about to see a performance.

The film's unsung hero is the redoubtable Thelma Ritter, of the scouring-pad lungs and the Rolex precision timing. As Stewart's morally circumspect nurse, she is a hilarious reflection of our own tendency to take the lower ground when a good, nasty crime story falls in our lap.

VILLAGE VOICE, 1/25/00, p. 123, J. Hoberman

Immobilized in his Greenwich Village apartment with a broken leg, photojournalist L.B. "Jeff" Jeffries (James Stewart) amuses himself by spying on his neighbors. Inevitably, observation becomes obsession. Jeff imagines that he has uncovered a murder in an apartment across the courtyard.

Alfred Hitchcock's *Rear Window* which opened in a print newly restored to its original Technicolor grandeur, was one of the master's greatest stunts. Not only is this a thriller without on-screen violence or a visible (human) corpse, but virtually the entire movie unfolds in a single room, albeit facing out on one of the largest, most elaborate sets ever built on Paramount's back lot.

Steeped in fetishism, concerned with l'amour fou, and structured by dream logic, *Vertigo* is Hollywood's surrealist masterpiece; *Rear Window* showcases another side of Hitchcock's vulgar modernism. It's a blatantly conceptual movie, self-reflexively concerned with voyeurism and movie history, the bridge from Soviet montage to Andy Warhol's vacant stare, as well as a construction founded on the 20th-century idea of the metropolis as spectacle—or, more specifically, on the peculiar mixture of isolation and overstimulation the big city affords. Reveling in the simultaneity of the 8 million stories in the Naked City, *Rear Window* is the slyly alienated precursor of multiple narratives like *Short Cuts or Magnolia.*

As Jeff's wisecracking nurse (Thelma Ritter) tells him, "We [have] become a race of Peeping Toms," and like Buster Keaton's Sherlock Jr. or, in another sense, Dziga Vertov's *The Man With a Movie Camera, Rear Window* is one of the great allegories of cinephilia. No less than any viewer of the movie, Jeff is immobile and transfixed. Observing without being observed, at once godlike and impotent, he treats other people's daily lives as though they were his show.

The photographer not only spies on his neighbors, treating himself to close-ups by using the telephoto camera lens his nurse calls a "portable keyhole," but gives them names and invents little backstories. These dramas are, necessarily, staged in highly emphatic pantomime style, and, as in silent movies, music—almost always supplied by the handy composer who lives across the courtyard—substitutes for dialogue. (The movie's complex sound mix has been considerably brightened in the restoration.) A pair of newlyweds keep vanishing "off-screen." The statuesque blonde Jeff calls Miss Torso affords a primitive peep show in contrast to the pathetic fantasies enacted by the character he's named Miss Lonelyhearts. And then there is the unhappy domesticity unfolding in the Thorwald apartment ....

Contemplating the courtyard, Jeff is the warden of his own panopticon, and yet it is he who is in a state of heightened anxiety. Does the hypervigilant photographer suspect that, just as he spies on his neighbors, they might be observing him? "I wonder if it's ethical to watch a man with binoculars," he muses. "Course, they can do the same thing, watch me like a bug under a glass." *Rear Window* has a definite paranoid edge. Placing his neighbors under surveillance, Jeff is a freelance agent for the national security state who seems taken aback when a cop explains the need for a search warrant. But mainly, *Rear Window* is a demonstration (two decades before cine-theorist Christian Metz) that the spectator identifies with the camera, and that the entire cinema machine is predicated on what psychologists call the scopic drive.

Absorbed in his neighbors' lives, the world of images and vicarious experience echoed by the photos on his walls, Jeff has a marked aversion to intimacy—most obviously in his ambiguous relationship with his "too perfect" lady friend Lisa (Grace Kelly, who, as befits a movie about voyeurism, may be the most gorgeous creature to appear in any Hitchcock film). Only slightly less neurotic here than he would appear in *Vertigo,* Stewart projects a mixture of defensive normality and sexual ambivalence. If he is obviously discomfited to hear his nurse wonder if Lisa's father is "loading up the shotgun" to insure their wedding, his anxiety reaches comic proportions once Lisa proposes to spend the night. "I just have one bed," he protests.

When Lisa closes Jeffs window shades ("the show's over for tonight") and changes into a filmy nightgown (delightfully announced as a "preview of coming attractions"), she draws attention to the movie's two narratives, the murder mystery playing across the courtyard and the love story acted out in the apartment, as fictional constructions. It remains for the viewer to make the connection.

Hitchcock considered *Rear Window* his "most cinematic" movie and, by way of explanation, paraphrased the famous Soviet montage experiment known as the Kuleshov effect: "Mr. Stewart is looking out into the courtyard and—let's say—he sees a woman with a child in her arms. Well, the first cut is Mr. Stewart, then what he sees, and then his reaction. We'll see him smile. Now if you took away the center piece of film and substituted—we'll say—a shot of the girl Miss Torso in a bikini, instead of being a benevolent gentleman he's now a dirty old man. And you've only changed one piece of film, you haven't changed his look or his reaction."

Like the Soviets, Hitchcock understood movies as a machine to evoke a series of conditioned responses, and *Rear Window,* one of his most commercially successful movies, was almost universally hailed when it opened during the summer of 1954. Despite the blatant metaphoric content, no contemporary reviewer seems to have seen it as anything more than a superior entertainment—although *The New York Times's* Bosley Crowther surely did protest too much in declaring that "Mr. Hitchcock's film is not significant. What it has to say about people and human nature is superficial and glib."

The only critics to take *Rear Window* seriously were the movie-mad writers of *Cahiers du Cinema.* "One can see *Rear Window* again and again, even when one knows the denouement," André Bazin observed, while Claude Chabrol plumbed the dark side of Jeff's "amorous fixation," noting that "in the end one no longer knows whether the crime may not have been made a reality simply by Stewart's willing it." From here it is a small step to proposing that what happens in the Thorwald apartment is but the most extreme fulfillment of Jeff's desire to be rid of Lisa. ("For all you know, there's something a lot more sinister going on beyond that window," she had kidded about the Newlywed Show.)

Rear Window has enjoyed a long classroom run as Exhibit A in Laura Mulvey's canonical "Film and Visual Pleasure," an essay suggesting that cinema is founded on the pleasure derived from looking, unseen, at another person as an erotic object. Movies, Mulvey argued, allow men to gaze upon women within the context of illusionist narrative—and this sense of control compensates for the very castration anxiety exemplified by Jeff's helpless state. Lisa does perform for Jeff throughout *Rear Window* (and just as his voyeurism is rationalized by his profession as a photojournalist, so her exhibitionism is underscored by her career in fashion), but for most of the movie, he has more fun watching his imaginary movies than relating to his girlfriend.

Jeffs aesthetic distance is shattered, however, when intrepid Lisa materializes in the theater of the Thorwald apartment. Suddenly, the voyeur is reacting like the most naive spectator, shouting a warning to a figure who cannot possibly hear him: "Lisa, what are you doing? Get out of there!" Lisa's appearance on the screen is paralleled by Thorwald's evolution from a distant silent actor to the all-too-real creature who, as in some Pirandellian nightmare, enters Jeff's space hissing, "What do you want of me?" In a denouement Time correctly identified with Mack Sennett slapstick, the movie turns interactive—although, by this time, the joke is on the audience.

Thorwald's question is really addressed to the spectator. (Lisa speaks for all when she tells Jeff they are "ghouls" for being "plunged into despair [to] find a man didn't kill his wife.") Jeff's pad is just one more window. As always in Hitchcock, there is no pleasure without guilt.

Also reviewed in:
CHICAGO TRIBUNE, 2/25/00, Friday/p. A, Michael Wilmington
NEW YORK TIMES, 8/5/54, p. 18, Bosley Crowther
VARIETY, 1/17-23/00, p. 48, Todd McCarthy
WASHINGTON POST, 2/18/00, p. C5, Stephen Hunter

REBELS WITH A CAUSE

A Zeitgeist Films release of a Shire Films production. *Producer:* Helen Garvy. *Director:* Helen Garvy. *Screenplay:* Helen Garvy. *Editor:* Helen Garvy. *Director of Photography:* Emiko Omori. *Sound:* Witt Monts. *Running time:* 110 minutes. *MPAA Rating:* Not Rated.

WITH: Jane Adams; Bill Ayers; Carolyn Craven; Carl Davidson; Benardine Dohrn; Alice Embree; Dick Flacks; Todd Gitlin; Carol Glassman; Juan Gonzalez; Alan Haber; Casey Hayden; Tom Hayden; Sharon Jeffrey; Mark Kleiman; Sue Eanet Klonsky; Steve Max; Carl Oglesby; Robert Pardun; Bob Ross; Vivian Leburgh Rothstein; Judy Schiffer Perez.

CINEASTE, Vol. XXV, no. 4, 2000, p. 35, Paul Arthur

"We were *very serious* organizers; we intended to change the world, and our business and our life was about changing the world." So declares Sharon Jeffrey, a prime mover in the fledgling Students for a Democratic Society, near the start of Helen Garvy's engaging documentary history, *Rebels with a Cause*. Just as you don't need a weatherman to gauge the windiness of our current political season, you needn't be a veteran of the Sixties to know the sensational story of how SDS, at its peak a youth organization of unprecedented influence, disintegrated amid factionalism, outrageous government harassment, and a propensity for counterproductive violence. It is to Garvy's credit that, without glossing over the tumultuous final days, *Rebels* offers a remarkably clear-eyed account of the group's gradual, emblematic—historically inevitable?—march from grass-roots multi-issue organizing to a mass movement galvanized around antiwar protest. The tone throughout this briskly edited collage of interviews, still photos, and archival material maintains a delicate balance between wistful self-valorization and shrewd self-critique. But aside from hard-won lessons in organization building and its discontents, what makes the film required viewing, especially for a younger generation of activists, is the aura of passionate, ongoing commitment to social justice exuded by its graying cadre. These are people you want to break bread with, if you haven't done so already.

Lacking conventional trappings of 'disinterested' narration or academic commentary, the perspective in *Rebels* is unabashedly partisan: Garvy and executive producer Robert Pardun were in the first wave of membership; with notable absences, the twenty-eight interviewees represent a substantial segment of SDS national leadership, both less-known figures and familiar faces such as Tom Hayden, Todd Gitlin, and Jane Alpert; end credits list an even wider circle of New Left contributors. As a result, despite a carefully stitched chronology of events and issues, the overall narrative is presented as if it were a first, and unimpeachable, telling. There is surprisingly little interest in rebutting dominant media myths about who or what SDS was in its heyday, nor is there much acknowledgment of the wider combustion of political and cultural forces that helped propel—were in turn propelled by—the SDS dynamo. Proper credit is given, however, to black Civil Rights struggles which served as a training ground for key honchos and from which they derived moral urgency plus an initial repertoire of organizing tactics.

As prelude to rehashing the 1962 conference that ratified the Port Huron Statement, the organization's formidable founding document, speakers offer telling anecdotes about Cold War defense drills, sexism in Little League baseball, routine segregation in Southern department stores, and so on. The impression is that original members were 'innocent of ideology,' that they translated youthful experiences of oppression and alienation into direct action without the mediation of intellectual influences, political theories, or models of praxis (save for the Civil Rights movement). This is an appealing and not entirely disingenuous canard—a sort of left equivalent of the hippie injunction 'Do it because it feels good.' Although hoisted as an egalitarian, anti-Old Left banner at the time, the notion of an autochthonous program for change has since been questioned in writings and interviews with the Port Huron crowd, as well as by historians of the movement such as James Miller in his excellent *"Democracy Is in the Streets"* (1987). To be sure, the sixty page Statement is nearly devoid of Marxist rhetoric—albeit bristling with analyses of "capitalism," "militarism," and "unreasoning anticommunism"—yet bears the distinct imprint of a tradition of American social thought from Emerson to Dewey to C. Wright Mills.

Weak on intellectual origins, somewhat evasive about the core group's racial composition and class background (an intertitle citing the Statement's opening sentence, "We are people of this generation ... looking uncomfortably at the world we inherit," manages to leave out the phrase "bred in at least modest comfort"), *Rebels* soars during reminiscences of the formative period of urban interracial projects to combat poverty and racism. Returning home from voter registration drives in 1963, stalwarts targeted nine Northern cities, with Newark as a test case, for actions ranging from rent strikes to demonstrations around bank redlining and apartheid. For college-age political mavericks, the euphoric edge of face-to-face encounters, of acting on rather than merely studying our society's rife inequalities of class and race, created individual transformations so powerful they echo through testimony given thirty-five years later. From a certain angle, SDS's version of participatory democracy was never more cohesive, politically innovative or, perhaps, effective than when it was focused on a localized multi-issue campaign.

As one organizer asserts, "For us, all the issues were connected." At first, the accelerating incursion into Southeast Asia was regarded as part of a larger nexus of government-corporate malfeasance. Yet the rapid growth of campus SDS chapters was spurred less by concern with poverty than by increased military involvement and the threat of the draft. Within months of mobilizing a 1965 march on Washington, SDS had ceased to be a cozy 'neighborly community,' its agenda now bent toward a single cause. The strategic shift from antiwar protest to resistance, from applying symbolic pressure to end the war to selectively stalling the draft process—summarized in the exchange of slogans "Hell no, we won't go!" to "Hell no, nobody goes!"—reached its well-publicized climax with a brief shutdown of the Oakland Induction Center in 1967. As recounted by several speakers, this is a stirring episode though it was soon eclipsed in the national imagination by the march on the Pentagon, the Columbia 'revolt,' and police riots at the 1968 Democratic Convention.

Because SDS dwarfed adjacent student organizations in size and influence, because its leadership was so vocal and articulate, it became a highly visible target for FBI interference via the infamous

COINTELPRO. As several key figures admit, not only did they underestimate the government's use of illegal tactics, they began to recognize that "There were no non-violent options." Not unexpectedly, leaders of the Weatherpeople now deplore their rhetoric and tactics as "self-righteous, judgmental, arrogant, elitist," but *Rebels* also provides a glimpse into their understandable desperation: as Elizabeth Stanley recalls, "Peaceful protest wasn't getting us anywhere ... I felt that my life was worth risking in order to make this stop." By mid-1969, the organization had split into several militant factions, not counting vestiges of an "Old Guard," vowing in slightly different terms to "Bring the War home!" By the following year, the national office in Chicago had shut down and an explosion of bomb-making materials in a New York City townhouse had killed three radicals, forever linking the image of SDS with self-annihilating adventurist violence.

Like other films about misunderstood and underdocumented movements of American insurgents, *Rebels* places too much emphasis on developments for which SDS was at best a peripheral player while undervaluing other facets of its influence. For instance, a 1965 paper written by Casey Hayden and Mary King, "Sex and Caste, " is implicitly credited as a crucial instigation in the rise of the women's movement, even though Bernardine Dohrn voices a more familiar, and credible, complaint: "Being a woman in the middle of these social movements was thoroughly contradictory." For many, militant feminism evolved despite or in reaction to the gendered division of power within the New Left rather than as an adjunct to it. Similarly, there is no room in the *Rebels* account of the Sixties for acknowledging the work of parallel, at times antagonistic but also mutually inflecting, groups such as the Free Speech Movement, Liberation News Service, Newsreel, Trotskyite spinoffs like the Worker-Student Alliance, Yippies, and the Black Panther Party. Anyone familiar with the period's protean energies will remember numerous instances of productive, if agonized, alliance.

On the other hand, there is practically no discussion of SDS's social or cultural impact. As Jeff Shero, a founding editor of the underground newspaper *Rat*, confides: "We knew at a grass roots level that SDS was growing because it was connected to the culture"-i.e., to rock music, drugs, movies. Yet aside from a smattering of musical clips by Phil Ochs, Country Joe, and CCR, and despite an explicit mandate to heal the rifts between politics and personal life, the idea of 'participatory democracy' as a model for liberatory social relations or collective cultural activity is roundly ignored. (On a personal note, a leader in my campus SDS chapter, and one-time editor of *New Left Notes,* was also a prominent avant-garde filmmaker.) Thus, there is considerable irony in the film's constant display of eye-popping buttons and poster art.

As a cinematic construction, *Rebels* adheres closely to the conventions of interview/archival footage documentaries. A series of discrete interviews, employing the same studio backdrop, are merged to form a continuous narrative with contrapuntal voices addressing a given event or issue. Dissolves shuttle the viewer back and forth from talking heads to vintage photos from the Sixties of the same speaker. With a few minor exceptions, like contrasting statements by Casey Hayden and Dohrn on the position of women in the movement, the verbal thrust of reminiscence is nearly univocal. What is gained in pacing and historical clarity by this format, however, eventually emerges as a weakness. Put simply, *Rebels* is a bit too seamless, too uncontentious to honor the spontaneity and heady dissonance of its subject. Perhaps it would have been unwieldy to have had six former comrades present at the same interview, and there might have been problems in situating, say, Dohrn and Gitlin—who refers to her in a 1987 book as "chorus-line figured" and "the object of many an SDS male's erotic fantasy"—on the same couch. Nonetheless, it seems a shame, especially for viewers already familiar with the basic historical trajectory, to have skipped the potential for spirited debate or even contradictory reflection.

That said, *Rebels with a Cause* is a more than adequate primer. As in Connie Field and Marilyn Mulford's similarly structured but more fulfilling *Freedom on My Mind* (1993), there is rousing coda in which participants offer summary affirmations of their involvement. While some take the opportunity to wax grandiose—"We were the conscience of America. We saved the soul of America by protesting against Vietnam" (Shero)—others are content with assertions of obdurate defiance—"I'm still here" (Junius Willliams). Under the final words of each speaker a subtitle indicates their current vocation; it is moving testament to the collective aspirations and struggles of Sixties' radicals that in nearly every case a continuing commitment to the process of social change remains undimmed.

NEW YORK POST, 11/10/00, p. 58, Jonathan Foreman

This nostalgic but compelling oral history of the SDS—Students for a Democratic Society, one of the most important New Left/antiwar groups of the 1960s—makes no attempt to appear objective or to put the organization's activities in context.

None of the activists interviewed by director and former member Helen Garvy (including Tom Hayden, Bernadine Dohrn, Todd Gitlin and several bearded fiftysomethings) have had any interesting second thoughts on SDS. And Garvy rather obviously chooses to highlight the heroic early years of movement rather than the entropy of the late '60s or the extremist violence of the Weather Underground.

Nor do you get enough about the social and sexual aspects of the movement—it's clear from the photographs that the female SDS leaders were disproportionately attractive young women.

But even if this film may irritate some people who remember "the movement" differently, it's nevertheless a fascinating and often moving document of recent history.

VILLAGE VOICE, 11/14/00, p. 136, Amy Taubin

Helen Garvy's *Rebels With a Cause* is a history of Students for a Democratic Society (SDS), the vanguard organization of the New Left formed in 1960 by a few dozen college students who believed in the Bill of Rights and were horrified by TV news footage of police mauling civil rights demonstrators in the South. In the early '60s, SDS focused on community activism, but as American involvement in Vietnam grew, it was drawn into the antiwar struggle. In 1970, SDS membership had grown to 100,000, but the leaders—deeply divided over tactics and burnt out on a decade of activism—disbanded the organization. "We were caught up inside our own psychodrama," says Bernardine Dohrn, one of the most articulate SDS leaders interviewed in the film. Dohrn was also a leader of Weatherman (or the Weather Underground), the militant breakaway group that decided to oppose the war "by any means necessary." Weatherman was decimated when three of its members blew themselves up building a bomb in a Greenwich Village townhouse.

Besides offering a comprehensive picture of the development of SDS, *Rebels With a Cause* corrects the popular misperception that SDS and Weatherman were one and the same. Through interviews with more than 20 former members, most still involved in political activism and education, the film testifies to the legacy of SDS. Notable in its absence is any discussion of how these veterans, some of the most vibrant and intelligent fiftysomethings to grace a movie screen, view the left today, particularly the demonstration in Seattle last fall. Garvy has worked hard to weave the interviews into an exciting narrative, but the focus is perhaps too narrow for the film to be as politically effective as it could have been.

Also reviewed in:
NEW YORK TIMES, 11/10/00, p E16, A. O. Scott
VARIETY, 7/31-8/6/00, p. 28, Ken Eisner

RED PLANET

A Warner Brothers release in association with Village Roadshow Pictures and NPV Entertainment of a Mark Canton production. *Executive Producer:* Charles J.D. Schlissel and Andrew Mason. *Producer:* Mark Canton, Bruce Berman, and Jorge Saralegui. *Director:* Antony Hoffman. *Screenplay:* Chuck Pfarrer and Jonathan Lemkin. *Story:* Chuck Pfarrer. *Director of Photography:* Peter Suschitzky. *Editor:* Robert K Lambert and Dallas S. Puett. *Music:* Graeme Revell. *Music Editor:* Ashley Revell. *Sound:* Paul "Salty" Brincat and (music) Mark Curry and Wolfgang Amadeus Mozart. *Sound Editor:* Dane A. Davis. *Casting:* Lora Kennedy. *Production Designer:* Owen Paterson. *Art Director:* Hugh Bateup. *Set Designer:* Judith Harvey. *Set Decorator:* Brian Dusting. *Special Effects:* Tad Pride. *Visual Effects:* Jeffrey A. Okun. *Costumes:* Kym Barrett. *Make-up:* Deborah Lanser. *Stunt Coordinator:* Guy Norris. *Running time:* 110 minutes. *MPAA Rating:* PG-13.

CAST: Val Kilmer (Gallagher);   Tom Sizemore (Burchenal);   Carrie-Anne Moss (Kate Bowman);   Benjamin Bratt (Santen);   Simon Baker (Pettengil);   Terence Stamp (Chantilas); Jessica Morton and Caroline Bossi (Website Fans);   Bob Neill (Voice of Houston).

CHRISTIAN SCIENCE MONITOR, 11/10/00, p. 15, David Sterritt

Movie distributors give critics propaganda packets—whoops, I mean production information—to accompany their new releases, but these materials aren't always as effective as the studios hope.

Take the information for "Red Planet" given out by Warner Bros. at preview screenings. "Though loaded with more than 900 visual effects," it read, "it was the film's human element that most intrigued [director Antony] Hoffman."

Yeah, right. Here's a science-fiction epic with a walloping budget, a gigantic special-effects crew, and a list of producers who include pictures like "The Matrix" and the "Lethal Weapon" series among their credits. And we're supposed to believe it's all about the "human element" rather than action, adventure, runaway robots, and creepy-crawly aliens?

The heroes are an astronaut crew sent to Mars in 2050 to find out why Earth's preparations for colonizing the planet have mysteriously failed. An emergency landing wrecks their well-laid plans, deluging them with deadly threats including a dwindling oxygen supply, an escape vehicle too small for them all to fit in, and a robot assistant that looks like a mechanical dog but acts like a ninja warrior when its circuits get scrambled. Who will live and who will die? Look for the guy and gal aiming love-struck gazes at each other, and rest assured they'll be around when the final credits roll.

The screenplay by Chuck Pfarrer and Jonathan Lemkin spices its science-fiction clichés with occasional pop-theology clichés giving the tale a nebulous New Age touch; but the movie has as much genuine concern for spirituality as for the "human element" touted by the press kit. Look for "Red Planet" to crash as resoundingly at the box office as its heroes do on Mars.

LOS ANGELES TIMES, 11/10/00, Calendar/p. 10, Kevin Thomas

If looks were everything, "Red Planet" would have it made. On the visual level, this space epic is completely convincing in its depiction of the barren landscape of Mars, the mission there to save mankind from an over-polluted Earth, and all the elaborate equipment and technology involved in the undertaking.

When it comes to special effects, the filmmakers have spared no expense. But when it comes to the story, audiences have been shortchanged. "Red Planet" plays flat: There's precious little sense of adventure, suspense or excitement and no sense of fun. Chuck Pfarrer and Jonathan Lemkin's script and Antony Hoffman's direction is as mechanical as all the machinery involved.

In voice-over, mission commander Kate Bowman (Carrie-Anne Moss) tells us that by 2025 Earth has become so polluted that a project has been launched to harvest algae on Mars to generate enough oxygen to make it habitable. By 2056, as Earth continues to die, oxygen readings suddenly cease transmitting. Hence Bowman and her fellow astronauts—mechanical systems engineer Gallagher (Val Kilmer), scientific analysis team leader Burchenal (Tom Sizemore), Air Force captain Santen (Benjamin Bratt), youthful scientist Pettengil (Simon Baker) and chief science officer Chantilas (Terence Stamp) take off for Mars, along with AMEE, a robot that looks like a giant metallic spider.

A solar flare cripples the ship, which leads to a crash-landing of its shuttle containing the crew, leaving Bowman alone in the space ship. One catastrophe leads to another and on to the eerie truth of what happened on Mars with Kilmer emerging as the superhero who must solve the crisis on Mars and try to get back to the ship alive.

There's no denying that as space exploration has become a reality, it gets tougher to make space adventure movies because filmmakers feel pressured to be as authentic as possible—something that George Melies didn't have to contend with nearly a century ago when he made his timelessly delightful "A Trip to the Moon." The scarcely unique problem with "Red Planet" is that the technology, much of it incomprehensible to the layman, overwhelms plot and characterization. Moss, fresh off "The Matrix," and the seasoned Kilmer manage a strong, credible presence, even overcoming a first encounter that has Kilmer inadvertently happening upon her in the nude as she steps out of a shower. (She orders him to think of her as he would a sister!)

Sizemore, playing a crude but decent guy, is solid, but Bratt has little chance to register anything except machismo, and Baker, a lack of confidence and cowardice. This crew is on the whole so lacking in personality that it seems conceivable that "Red Planet" might just play better with the dialogue track turned off.

NEW YORK POST, 11/10/00, p. 59, Jonathan Foreman

"Red Planet" isn't as bad as the year's first abysmal Martian movie, "Mission to Mars," but it's pretty close.

Slackly directed by first-timer Antony Hoffman, it has only the sketchiest characterization, some of the worst writing of any recent big-budget release (the screenplay is credited to Chuck Pfarrer and Jonathan Lemkin but could have been assembled by robots), and some poor acting—including an atrocious performance by Terence Stamp.

"Red Planet" seems to be set in a time when humanity has abandoned common sense. It does things like send astronauts to Mars without back-up radios, weapons, a buggy like the Apollo heroes had on the moon, or a back-up plan.

The year is 2050. Earth is so polluted it will have to colonize Mars for the human race to survive. Though we don't have the technology to clean up our own planet, we do have the means to "terraform" another one with a carbon dioxide atmosphere.

When the project hits a snag, five dim but good-looking astronauts led by Bowman, (Carrie-Anne Moss) are sent to fix it.

Bowman's team includes a bio-engineer (Tom Sizemore), a handsome handyman (Val Kilmer), an older guy keen on philosophy (Terence Stamp), an arrogant Air Force captain (Benjamin Bratt), and a last-minute replacement (Simon Baker).

One of the odd pleasures of good science-fiction movies can be the way they depict the energies and tensions of people working in jobs that require team-work. But there's nothing here to convince you the crew in "Red Planet" has spent months together in space.

Instead, the filmmakers come up with some hopelessly dumb debates about whether science or religion holds all the answers, and a scene in which Kilmer's Gallagher walks in on Bowman in the shower, thereby establishing sexual tension.

When she's not naked, Bowman is to be found wearing tank tops—now de rigueur in the movies for female members of spaceship crews—or a fetching slip.

When the ship is crippled by solar flares as it approaches Mars orbit, Bowman orders the four men down to the planet's surface while she stays on board to make repairs. They crash-land, breaking most of their equipment, with the exception—of course—of their military robot dog.

Everything that happens next is turgidly predictable and straight from the Joseph Campbell box of ready-made themes.

The best things about "Red Planet" are the landscapes—the film was shot in Jordan and Australia—and Carrie-Anne Moss, who makes the best of a bad job.

NEWSDAY, 11/10/00, Part II/p. B7, John Anderson

At one point "Red Planet" was vying with "Mission to Mars" to be the first post-Voyager Mars movie to hit the big screen. Turns out it was a contest as critical to contemporary culture as the Bud-vs.-Bud Lite playoff of 1994.

What's the problem? Sci-fi is always a delicate balance of fantasy and fact, and "Red Planet" has based most of its "fact" on other sci-fi movies. The hardware is all pretty familiar. The heroic music gives it all a Kubrickian echo. And the spaceship is dimly lit—much like the script.

Earthlings have poisoned their planet—again—and rather than find a way to muzzle the lobbyists for either Detroit or Monsanto, humans of the year 2050 have opted for an algae-based overhaul of the Martian atmosphere and mass relocation. Uh huh. And the advance team will accomplish its mission of prepping the planet, our narrator tells us, because of the unconquerable human spirit and because "I'm leading the mission."

That the voice belongs to mission commander Kate Bowman (Carrie-Anne Moss of "The Matrix") is meant to make you say, "Wow, a female in space." Somebody call Sigourney Weaver. The thought that actually crosses your mind is that you're in serious narrative trouble.

Any movie that requires this much narration—background, plot line and introductions to each and every character—is as deprived of oxygen as outer space.

Kate has a motley collection of geniuses behind her: Burchenal (Tom Sizemore), a biologist with a Biosphere-sized ego; Capt. Ted Santen (Benjamin Bratt), the kind of guy who snapped wet towels at you in gym class; the nervous Dr. Chip Pettengill (Simon Baker), and chief science officer Chantilas (Terence Stamp), who long ago stopped looking to science for answers to "the really serious questions." He's the resident spiritualist, though the philosophical discourse in "Red Planet" sounds like it was written by people who rob gas stations.

There's also Gallagher (Val Kilmer), who supplies technical support, sex appeal and a love interest for Kate, who spends much of the movie in regulation-uniform cotton tank top. The gist of "Red Planet" (which has no connection with either "Red Planet Mars" of 1952 or "Angry Red Planet" of 1959) is the great sci-fi paradox: People as a group are stupid enough to trash an entire world, but as individuals can manage to return from other planets via a box of baking soda and a Zippo lighter.

Kate and Co. get separated en route to the planet's surface: She stays aboard while the rest try to find the "Hab" that's been sent there ahead of them, while being pursued by a robot that's gone native. The robot, Amee, is the best invention in the movie, a slinking, feline piece of machinery that's genuinely scary. But why is it female?

Likewise, what's up with that bit of business at the end of the movie? Kate, connected to her ship by a lifeline, and the egglike space module carrying Gallagher perform a docking maneuver that seems straight out of sex ed. "Red Planet" may not offer much, but its sexual point of view is priceless.

SIGHT AND SOUND, 2/01, p. 46, Philip Strick

In 2050, as overpopulation on Earth reaches critical levels, the first manned spaceship to Mars investigates the failure of the Terraforming Project intended to render the planet habitable. After a six month journey under the command of Kate Bowman, the only woman aboard, *Mars-I* reaches orbit but sustains severe damage from a solar flare. The ship's five-man crew crash land on the planet's surface, leaving Bowman in orbit to attempt repairs. One of the crewmen, Chantilas, is fatally wounded; the others search for supplies but find only wreckage from previous missions.

As their oxygen runs out, their co-pilot Santen is killed, but the remaining trio discover the Martian air is breathable. They are being hunted, however, by the expeditions robot AMEE, its controls locked into killing mode. Having restored *Mars-I*, Bowman reports that two of the men might be able to lift off in a Russian probe grounded nearby. One of them, Pettengil, convinced he'll be left behind, sneaks ahead under cover of a storm. AMEE cuts him down.

His body becomes infested with roach-like insects; the bioengineer Burchenal realises they are oxygen producers and potential saviours of humankind before he too is consumed. The remaining astronaut, Gallagher, manages under Bowman's guidance to reactivate the Russian probe, using a battery snatched from AMEE's circuits. Soaring back into orbit, he is rescued by Bowman.

Doubtless in deference to the bewildered explorer of *2001: A Space Odyssey* (1968), the central character of *Red Planet* is called Bowman, a cheerful acknowledgement that the film, which charts a disaster-ridden expedition to Mars, is hardly exploring territory where nobody has gone before. Directed by newcomer Antony Hoffman after more than a decade of prize-winning commercials, with effects supervised by Jeffrey A. Okun *(Sphere, Stargate)*, the production also employs a number of the talents responsible for *The Matrix*, granting it an unarguable state-of-the-art calibre. Despite this, *Red Planet*, while satisfyingly spectacular, is not out to dazzle with *Matrix*-style acrobatics; apart from a few enjoyable if unnecessary moments inside a robot's head, the film has a persuasive realism in keeping with Hoffman's original training in documentaries. Thanks to the striking choice of desert locations (in Jordan and Australia), Mars itself could hardly look more authentic.

The most prominent recruit from *The Matrix*, in fact, is Carrie-Anne Moss, playing the aforementioned Bowman, the expedition's commander and a recognisable successor to the indestructible Ripley of the *Alien* series. In something of a feminist triumph, it is Bowman's commentary that introduces us to the crew and provides a final summary that leaves no doubt about her plans for the one she has reeled in like a fish on a line. Over-ruling the ship's pleasingly defeatist computer (the evocatively named Lucille), Bowman dodges fireballs and other hazards single-handedly to convert the lifeless mothership into usable transportation, to restore contact with Mission Control, and to guide and encourage the stranded crew on the planet below. That she manages it all in a state of gasping panic renders her the more appealing, by contrast with her clumsy male subordinates who focus on a predictable mixture of alcohol, petty feuding and innuendo.

Their leader apart, these wisecracking specialists are a throwback not only to the motley crew of *Alien* but further, to George Pal's chauvinistic space movies of the 50s. That was a decade which, in the wake of the Pal-produced *Destination Moon,* theorised that astronaut teams would inevitably include one rough-diamond comic one slightly crazed visionary, one scholarly 'expert', and one or two salt-of-the-Earth expendables. Its personnel lightly reshuffled for *Red Planet*, the purpose of the mission another Pal-produce science-fiction film *Conquest of Space* (1954) is resurrected here in two fundamental respects, apparently unchanged in half a century: to solve Earth's overpopulation problem and to find evidence of divine existence. Aboard ship, both topics are aired ("Science," they conclude, "can't answer any of the really interesting questions"), but after the disastrous landing on Mars there is no time for theology. "What are we going to do?" asks one agnostic astronaut. "Look out for rocks marked 'Made by God'?"

Constructed rather too schematically as a succession of last-minute rescues, *Red Planet* strains plausibility to such an extent that a benevolent intervention from above—at least by the scriptwriter—actually seems the only explanation. It appears unlikely, for instance, that without considerable effort from *a deus ex machina* the plight of an overflowing Earth, at six months' distance away from these astronauts, could be resolved by simple pest-control. Why, in any case, has the creation of a breathable Martian atmosphere by homicidal roaches (whose origin, of course, is a mystery) gone unnoticed by monitors of the Terraforming Project?   More immediately, we might be sceptical that the elegantly designed spacesuits of the castaways have no provision for testing the oxygen content of their environment or that the superb sound quality of inter-suit communications appears to cut out immediately when two astronauts get into an argument. There is also a miraculous coincidence when the power-battery of an ultra-modern mechanoid proves to be compatible with the circuitry of a derelict Russian probe.

Its thunder somewhat stolen by *Pitch Black*—which similarly uses a catastrophe in space, livid colours under an alien sky and swarms of lethal wildlife—*Red Planet* is a respectable if simplistic venture, nicely played, and with the extra attraction of the sinuous robot AMEE. An enviable piece of unreliable hardware, cunningly animated, this wanton device is dedicated to cutting men down to size. Naturally referred to as female, she deserves to be long remembered.

VILLAGE VOICE, 11/21/00, p. 144, Dennis Lim

A pale, patchy amalgam of the year's two unfairly reviled interplanetary adventures, *Supernova* and *Mission to Mars*, the lunkheaded *Red Planet* distinguishes itself with a touching pretense of scientific veracity. New Age mysticism is kept to a minimum, and the life-on-Mars discovery is as absurdly mundane as De Palma's was histrionically Spielbergian. Such committed understatement can only be counterproductive in the sci-fi realm (star Val Kilmer, for the record, proudly classifies *Red Planet* as "science fact").

An ungainly voice-over spells out the boilerplate premise: Earthly eco-disaster prompts deep-space colonization, and scientists dispatch clumps of algae to oxygenate the Martian atmosphere. When the green stuff mysteriously vanishes in 2050, NASA sends a manned expedition: tank-top clad commander Carrie-Anne Moss, smirky engineer Kilmer, chiseled blowhard Benjamin Bratt, wisecracking geneticist, um, Tom Sizemore, and chin-strokingly spiritual elder Terence Stamp (who delivers the token what-if-God-was-a-spaceman rumination).

Cinematographer Peter Suschitzky, a longtime Cronenberg collaborator, capably renders the mythologized dread of the pockmarked Martian surface—the Australian outback and Jordanian desert shot through blazing vermilion filters. But nothing here comes close to the Kubrick homages De Palma uncorked midway through *Mission,* and excepting a clamorous crash landing in which the male crew members are catapulted onto the planet in a giant pod, first-timer Antony Hoffman directs with a studious lack of imagination. The movie complies slavishly with the space-thriller model of cast attrition—the demises are, in predictable succession, quietly noble, accidental, karmic, and heroically gruesome. Kilmer complicates his line readings with a weirdly contemptuous Malkovich-affect; Moss remains in orbit for the duration, issuing panicky instructions to her shipwrecked crew ("Avoid pressing anything that says 'Ignition'!"). As in *The Matrix*, her contained beatitude acquires a sudden auroral luminosity in the dying moments, crystallizing her role into a single, transcendent feat of hero resuscitation.

Also reviewed in:
CHICAGO TRIBUNE, 11/10/00, Friday/p. A, Mark Caro
NEW YORK TIMES, 11/10/00, p. E13, Stephen Holden
VARIETY, 11/13-19/00, p. 24, Todd McCarthy
WASHINGTON POST, 11/10/00, p. C5, Rita Kempley
WASHINGTON POST, 11/10/00, Weekend/p. 45, Desson Howe

RED STUFF, THE

An Intercinema-Art Agency presentation of a Novoe Kino production.. *Producer:* Pieter van Huystee. *Director:* Leo de Boer. *Screenplay (Russian with English subtitles):* Leo de Boer. *Director of Photography:* Peter Brugman. *Editor:* Berenike Rozgonyi. *Music:* Micha Molthoff. *Running time:* 78 minutes. *MPAA Rating:* Not Rated.

VILLAGE VOICE, 10/17/00, p. 131, J. Hoberman

It's a show-business truism that the gravitas of the American presidency has been sadly diminished by the fall of the Evil Empire. *The Red Stuff,* harks back to that lost era-from the other side of the looking glass.

Made for Dutch television, this jovial documentary on the Soviet space program begins by conjuring phantoms of parades gone by in an otherwise empty Red Square. Interviews with a number of the now elderly surviving cosmonauts are juxtaposed with their official socialist realist portraits. Gazing toward the radiant future, the men seem invulnerable—if only because their chests are ridiculously bedecked with layers of medals.

Coinciding more or less with the reign of Nikita Khrushchev, the glory days of the Soviet space program lasted from the October 1957 Sputnik launch through the March 1965 first-ever space walk. (Thereafter, the U.S. took the lead and held it.) *The Red Stuff* may have its greatest appeal for those who lived through these events and can be stirred by their evanescence. The movie is basically a nostalgic assemblage of Jetsonesque monuments to interplanetary travel, triumphalist newsreels, commemorative china plates, and pop anthems proclaiming "The Eaglets Learn to Fly!"

Although filmmaker Leo de Boer has exhumed some remarkable footage of the three cosmonauts who died in a 1971 accident, the far more devastating (and perhaps still classified) launchpad explosion of October 1960 is never cited. The movie is evocative but ahistorical. There's no mention made of the proto-cosmonaut propaganda generated around the Soviet aviators of the 1930s. (These were "Stalin's falcons" rather than Nikita's eagles.) Nor is much attention paid to the political implications of the space race. Two days after Yuri Gagarin became the first man to orbit the earth, a wavering JFK decided to sign off on the CIA-organized invasion of Cuba; a few months later, Gherman Titov's follow-up 17-orbit trip contributed nearly as much to the war hysteria of August 1961 as did the following week's erection of the Berlin Wall.

In the Museum of Cold War Culture, *The Red Stuff* would make a resonant double bill with *Space Cowboys*. Rounding out the Film Forum program, however, is Aki Kaurismäki's more sardonic *Total Balalaika Show,* which, shot in 1993, documents the "outrageous spectacle" of the once mighty Red Army Chorus appearing in concert with those outlandish Finnish "tundra rockers," the Leningrad Cowboys, before 70,000 flag-waving fans in Helsinki's Senate Square. Both groups are in uniform, which in the case of the Cowboys means gargantuan pointy pompadours and mile-long shoes.

Basically an exercise in post-imperial humiliation, *Total Balalaika Show* begins with the hapless Russians signing a contract for all 160 of their singers, musicians, and dancers to perform as the Cowboys' backup. In a gesture of friendship, they open the concert with the Sibelius ode "Finlandia"; the Cowboys then join them to sing "Happy Together" (in English, as are all their songs). Thereafter it's schlock around the clock-"Volga Boatmen" gives way to the no less bombastic Tom Jones hit "Delilah"; a ripe "Orchi Chornye" is trumped by "Sweet Home Alabama."

Playing cardboard tractor-shaped guitars or doing a kozotski across the stage during "Kalinka," the Cowboys play the Chorus for a colossal stooge. This cathartic commercialization of the Red Army is a minor exercise in Sots Art—the equivalent of using Lenin to endorse Coca-Cola. The joke is funny but it wears thin even before the ensembles combine to cover the English-language version of the old Russian vodka-swiller "Those Were the Days."

Also reviewed in:
NEW YORK TIMES, 10/11/00, p. E3, Lawrence Van Gelder

REINDEER GAMES

A Dimension Films release of a Marty Katz production. *Executive Producer:* Harvey Weinstein, Cary Granat, and Andrew Rona. *Producer:* Marty Katz, Bob Weinstein, and Chris Moore. *Director:* John Frankenheimer. *Screenplay:* Ehren Kruger. *Director of Photography:* Alan Caso. *Editor:* Tony Gibbs and Michael Kahn. *Music:* Alan Silvestri. *Music Editor:* Dan DiPrima and Kenneth Karman. *Sound:* Larry Sutton and (music) Dennis Sands. *Sound Editor:* Mike Le-Mare. *Casting:* Mali Finn. *Production Designer:* Barbara Dunphy. *Art Director:* Helen Jarvis and Eric Fraser. *Set Decorator:* Elizabeth Wilcox. *Set Dresser:* Matt Reddy, Gordi Brunner, and Patrick Kearns. *Special Effects:* Bill Orr. *Visual Effects:* Crystal Dowd. *Costumes:* May Routh. *Make-up:* Victoria Down. *Make-up (Ben Affleck):* Charles Porlier. *Make-up (Gary Sinise):* Benjamin Robin. *Make-up (Charlize Theron):* Deborah Larsen. *Stunt Coordinator:* Joe Dunne and Jacob Rupp. *Running time:* 99 minutes. *MPAA Rating:* R.

CAST: Ben Affleck (Rudy); James Frain (Nick); Dana Stubblefield (The Alamo); Mark Acheson (Mean Guard); Tom Heaton (Ugly Staffer); Isaac Hayes (Zook); Michael Sunczyk and Douglas H. Arthurs (Distant Inmates); Dean Wray and Ron Sauve (Guards); Ron Hyatt (Prisoner); Hrothgar Mathews (Exit Guard); Charlize Theron (Ashley); Clarence Williams III (Merlin); Donal Logue (Pug); Danny Trejo (Jumpy); Gary Sinise (Gabriel); Dennis Farina (Jack Bangs); Gordon Tootoosis (Old Governor); Lee Jay Bamberry (Young Governor); Frank Jones (Security Boss); Jimmy Herman (Bartender); John Destry (Fat Guy); Ashton Kutcher (College Kid); Ana Paul Piedade (Portuguese Woman); Enuka Okuma and Eva De Viveiros (Cocktail Waitresses); Joanna Piros (TV Newscaster); Robyn Driscoll (Desk Clerk); Lonny Chapman (Old Timer); Alonso Oyarzun (Casino Dealer); Rod Wolfe and Marcus Hondro (Cashiers); Sam Bob (Video Guard); Jacop Rupp and David Jacox (Park Rangers); Anna Hagan (Mother); Ken Camroux (Father); Terry O'Sullivan (Aunt Mary); Michael Puttonen (Bill); Paula Shaw (Aunt Lisbeth); Don S. Williams (Uncle Ray); Jenafor Ryane (Jill); James Hutson (Mike); Wendy Noel (Stacey); Blair Slater (Sam)

CHRISTIAN SCIENCE MONITOR, 2/25/00, p. 15, David Sterritt

[*Reindeer Games* was reviewed jointly with *Wonder Boys*; see Sterritt's review of that film.]

LOS ANGELES TIMES, 2/25/00, Calendar/p. 1, Kenneth Turan

"Reindeer Games" is genre all the way, a standard brand updated with the requisite modern touches. Its twisty film noir world of down-on-their-luck men and unfathomable women is vintage B-picture material, but, in the grand B tradition, the games it plays are more ambitious than successful.

For though dazzling B's like 1945's "Detour" are justly idolized, it's often forgotten that many of those low-budget second-rung films featured a capable director trying to make the best of miscast stars and not the most plausible of scripts. Which, decades later, is still more or less the case.

"To tell you the truth, I've never been much for the holidays," Rudy Duncan (Ben Affleck) says in classic wised-up voice-over to begin things as director John Frankenheimer has his camera linger over shots of dead men in Santa suits. Immediately we flash back six days to upper Michigan's bleak Iron Mountain prison, the kind of unfriendly place that specializes in cafeteria riots, sadistic guards and psychos unwisely let loose from solitary confinement.

Rudy, in for grand theft auto, and his best prison pal and cellmate Nick (British actor James Frain) are Just three days shy of a Christmastime release and talking over what they'll do with their first taste of freedom. Rudy says a mug of hot chocolate is all he's after, but Nick has something more romantic in mind.

For Nick has been corresponding with Ashley (Charlize Theron), an attractive pen pal he met while behind bars. Her pictures fill the space above his bed and thoughts of her dance like sugarplums in his head. "I'm going to walk right into a relationship," he says, content.

But movies being movies, events conspire in such a way that Rudy walks out of the joint alone. He sees Ashley, and she's such a hot ticket that he does what men always do: He lies and tells her that he in fact is the Nick she's been waiting for.

After engaging in one of those frenzied, acrobatic sexual bouts that have become standard big-screen fare, Rudy's guilt about the deception pretty much disappears. But then he meets Gabriel (Gary Sinise), Ashley's long-haired sadistic lunkhead of a brother who is called, not without reason, Monster.

Gabriel and his equally thuggish crew have their own reasons for being happy to see the man they think is Nick. For the real Nick, gleefully addressed as "Convict," once worked security on a Native American-owned gambling establishment called the Tomahawk Casino. Gabriel and friends are counting on Nick's expertise to get them inside the vault, and they don't particularly care how they access it.

If this sounds complicated, it is the merest beginning to a baroque plot devised by Ehren Kruger, whose debut film was the similarly convoluted "Arlington Road." Kruger has a gift for this kind of thing, but also a tendency to so pile surprise on surprise that succeeding revelations run the risk of deadening audiences as much as exciting them.

Also problematical is the film's star casting, starting with Affleck as the tough, resourceful ex-con Rudy. Though the actor is excellent as a suit-wearing shady character in the current "Boiler Room," it's difficult to buy him as the kind of hard-boiled amoral type he's supposed to be here. No amount of wicked tattoos or prison-built muscles can make Affleck look like anything but the prep school version of Robert De Niro's Max Cady in Martin Scorsese's "Cape Fear."

Similarly out of place is Theron as the woman in Rudy's life. Though her performance in "The Cider House Rules" was lovely, the actress seems to have been placed in a role she isn't suited for simply because, like Affleck, she's a current hot commodity that moviegoers are presumably interested in seeing.

Though "Reindeer Games" is not as compelling as "Ronin," the veteran Frankenheimer's last outing, the director does a brisk, no-nonsense job here, bringing his usual visual energy and professionalism to the table. He knows the difference between the things he can control and those he can't, like the way the film's wealth of Christmas music ("Games" was originally scheduled for December) feels out of place in a February release. Here's hoping the former outweighs the latter next time around.

NEW YORK POST, 2/25/00, p. 49, Lou Lumenick

"Reindeer Games" opens with an image of a dead Santa Claus lying on the hood of a car. How apt: This Christmas-themed thriller is brain dead on arrival, a full two months after the holiday. Bah, humbug, indeed.

There's nothing quite as dispiriting as listening to Ben Affleck's a capella rendition of "The Little Drummer Boy" in late February—unless it's a script that piles on ridiculous plot twists like so many discarded Christmas trees.

More naughty than nice is the severe miscasting of the boyish, clean-cut Affleck as Rudy, a tough ex-con who's released from Michigan prison after a stretch for auto theft.

Rudy impulsively decides to pass himself as his cellmate, Nick—a murderer who had been corresponding for months with a beautiful young stranger named Ashley (Charlize Theron) before his demise in a prison riot just before his impending release.

Rudy and Ashley (who demonstrate less sexual chemistry than Mr. and Mrs. Claus) no sooner finish making love to the accompaniment of Dean Martin's "Let It Snow" in a motel room, when in bursts her psychotic truck-driver brother Gabriel (Gary Sinise).

Gabriel intends to force Rudy, who he thinks is Nick, to help him use his supposed inside knowledge to plot a heist at a casino on an Indian reservation where Nick used to work as a security guard.

Scriptwriter Ehren Kruger ("Arlington Road, "Scream 3") comes up with ever-more desperate contrivances to explain why (1) Rudy can't prove his real identity, (2) Rudy can't get away from Gabriel and his gang and (3) Gabriel doesn't kill Rudy as soon as he gets the information he's seeking.

Affleck, so impressive in "Boiler Room," flounders badly between wisecracks ("I had better sex in prison," he complains at one point to Theron) and masochism as Rudy, who endures a dip in a freezing lake and serves as a human dart-board for Gabriel.

The beautiful but bland Theron ("The Cider House Rules") isn't remotely convincing as the kind of woman who would send love letters to a murderer in prison, much less one with the absurd secrets revealed in the movie's home stretch.

Sinise, sporting a Charles Manson hairstyle, is way overqualified to play Gabriel, a barely one-dimensional character. The only performance of note is the underrated Dennis Farina, who generates most of the movie's intentional laughs as a casino manager.

The legendary John Frankenheimer ("The Manchurian Candidate" and, more recently, "Ronin") directs at a furious pace, staging vigorous action sequences and deploying his wintry Canadian locations with great expertise.

But in the end, it's a waste of effort.

Without any believable characters or situations, "Reindeer Games" is about as appealing as leftover Christmas fruitcake.

NEWSDAY, 2/25/00, Part II/p. B3, Jan Stuart

No one does mean and thuggish quite like Gary Sinise. To judge from the mounting evidence presented by "Ransom," "Snake Eyes" and, now, "Reindeer Games," Sinise must spend hours upon hours in front of a gym mirror, bench-pressing his trigger finger and flexing his snarl.

The Gary Sinise snarl goes up against the Ben Affleck smirk in John Frankenheimer's "Reindeer Games," a brutal action thriller that ladles on twists and reversals in the seeming hope that you won't notice how preposterous it all is. It also piles on the acts of sadistic violence. While Affleck's smart-alecky charms continue to elude many of us, his detractors would never go so far as to throw darts at his belly. Sinise, who does the tossing, has obviously been training at the dartboard as well.

Overwritten by Ehren Kruger, "Reindeer Games" is a quintessential mistaken-identity tale of a not-so-innocent innocent schnook who is taken for a bad ride by a band of nasty gangsters. Affleck plays Rudy (as in the red-nosed creature of song), a quick-witted car thief who is sprung from the clink just two days after his best cell buddy, Nick (James Frain), is murdered in a prison riot.

In one of the many wrong calls that Rudy will make over the next hour and a half, he passes himself off as Nick to the gal whom his dead friend courted by mail from behind bars. As embodied by Charlize Theron (in a redheaded makeover from "The Cider House Rules"), Ashley would appear to be the pen pal of a jailbird's wildest fantasies: gorgeous and accessible, needy but gainfully employed, vulnerable yet sexually aggressive.

She is also a good listener who doesn't know when to shut up. Once Ashley has confided in her vicious gunrunner brother Gabriel (Sinise) about Nick's former employment at a gambling joint, Rudy finds himself shanghaied by Gabriel and his gang, who strongarm the reluctant ex-con into abetting them in a casino heist.

As the Midwestern Christmas snow pummels the landscape, "Reindeer Games" muscles the audience into rooting for Rudy, not because we care for the one-note Affleck, but because Gabriel and his three stooges (Clarence Williams III, Donal Logue and Danny Trejo) are so insufferably over the top in their malevolence they would have been hooted off even the campy "Batman" TV series back in the '60s.

Gabriel, who talks a pretty florid talk for an ex-trucker, turns out to be too stupid an adversary to make these "Reindeer Games" competitive. He shares with most B-movie flunkies a fatal tendency to ramble so long while holding a gun on someone that the intended victim can easily wriggle himself out of the jam. If Rudy had a dollar for every snowdrop that falls, every bullet he dodges and every sucker punch he throws Gabriel, he could have bought the casino.

Veteran director Frankenheimer keeps the reins taut up to a harrowing chase on the ice midway, then lets the action dissolve into an assembly-line bloodbath. In a half-hearted attempt at aping the great screen adaptations of James Cain novels, the screenwriter endows Rudy with a citrusy narrator's voice, then promptly forgets about it. Just when the audience is wondering why in God's name Rudy doesn't seek help from the police, Affleck chimes in grimly over the soundtrack, "Being on parole, going to the police wasn't an option." Apparently, armed robbery was.

The one solid film-noir touch is Theron, who cagily morphs into the sort of crafty femme fatale who would do Lana Turner and Barbara Stanwyck proud. It's a tricky, if not impossible, assignment, but Theron's eyes convey a stunning ambiguity of intent that keeps us off-kilter throughout. "Reindeer Games" offers the discomfortingly mixed pleasure of watching a rising star's talents come together, while the career of Sinise, spilling into self-caricature, threatens to self-destruct.

SIGHT AND SOUND, 8/00, p. 43, Geoffrey McNab

US, the present. Rudy, a convicted car thief, and Nick are cell mates. Nick is pen pals with Ashley, a beautiful young woman he has never met. During a riot in the dining hall, a prisoner with a grudge attacks Rudy. Nick is stabbed trying to defend Rudy and appears to die.

Rudy is released. He sees Ashley waiting outside the prison. He pretends to be Nick, for whom she is waiting. They become lovers. Ashley's psychopathic truck-driver brother Gabriel knows that Nick used to work in a Michigan casino. Using Nick's inside information, Gabriel and his gang plan to rob the casino. They refuse to believe Rudy when he tells them he is only impersonating Nick. Realising that they'll kill him otherwise, he carries on the deception. He learns that Ashley is actually Gabriel's lover and co-conspirator.

The thieves, each dressed as Santa Claus, turn up at the casino. They find the money, but the heist goes wrong. In the ensuing shoot-out, only Gabriel and Ashley escape, with Rudy as their prisoner. They are about to kill him when the real Nick appears. He reveals that he staged his own death and, together with Ashley, plotted the robbery. Nick and Ashley now kill Gabriel. Rudy foils Nick and Ashley's attempt on his life and kills them both. Left with all the money and still dressed as Santa Claus, he makes his way home.

Lightness of touch is not exactly director John Frankenheimer's trademark. Whether dealing with global terrorism *(Black Sunday,* 1976) or international car racing *(Grand Prix,* 1966), his films tend to take themselves very seriously. Even his two classic Cold War dramas, *The Manchurian Candidate* (1962) and *Seven Days in May* (1963), were portentous affairs. Perhaps inevitably, then, his directorial touch has a deadening effect on *Deception.* With more plot twists and narrative sleights-of-hand than David Mamet's playfully convoluted thriller *The Spanish Prisoner,* Ehren Kruger's script is—you can't help thinking—partly tongue-in-cheek; but if this is the case, the jokes and attempts at self-parody have gone unnoticed by Frankenheimer.

Deception begins promisingly enough, with young thief Rudy behind bars. "That's me... menace to society," he tells us in a self-deprecating voiceover. Thanks to the austere lighting and martial music, the prison scenes have an intensity which the rest of the film lacks. The dining-hall fight scene, in particular, is staged with real flair. (After *Birdman of Alcatraz,* 1962), one guesses prison riots are second nature to Frankenheimer.) Unfortunately, once Rudy is released, matters begin rapidly to unravel. It doesn't help that none of the main protagonists is plausible and their behaviour often seems irrational. Genial, clean-cut Ben Affleck, who plays Rudy, is more like a preppy college student than a hardened con. He gets the best one liners ("I had better sex in prison" he taunts the movie's femme fatale Ashley when she betrays him), but seems uncertain whether he is playing a light romantic lead or an all-out action hero.

The characters aren't developed in any depth, either. All we know about Rudy is that he used to steal cars, his greatest craving on being released from jail is hot chocolate and he wants to be home for Christmas. The apparent brains behind the casino heist Gabriel has a self-pitying monologue in which he bemoans the plight of the overworked American truck driver, but we learn little about him. As the double-crosses come thick and fast, it's hard to retain much curiosity about or sympathy for any of the film's duplicitous protagonists.

"When writing and talking about the film," producers Miramax/Dimension enjoin journalists in the press kit, "we would appreciate that you protect its unexpected plot developments so that the audience can enjoy them for the first time." But these "unexpected plot developments" are, perversely, what make the film so predictable. Once the ground rules are established—namely that everyone is cheating everyone else and that Frankenheimer will pull the carpet from beneath the audience's feet as often as he can—the tension drains out of the storytelling. The result is that the (final) surprise ending isn't so much ingenious as hugely contrived—yet one more cheap trick in a film that abounds in them.

VILLAGE VOICE, 3/7/00, p. 128, Amy Taubin

Punishing, visceral violence is the key element of *Reindeer Games,* in which Ben Affleck suffers more grievous bodily harm than the protagonists of any Scorsese film, De Niro in *Raging Bull* and Dafoe in *Last Temptation of Christ* included. Affleck is bound and beaten to a bloody pulp so often that even viewers heavily invested in the s/m aspect of action flicks will be bored silly. (The scene in which his body is used as a dartboard does little to break the monotony.)

Directed with throwaway skill by veteran John Frankenheimer but hampered by a clichéd script that becomes more illogical with every twist, the picture teeters between parody and pretentiousness. Dimension Films, the producer and distributor of *Reindeer Games,* has urged critics to "protect its unexpected plot developments so audiences can enjoy them for the first time." It might have escaped your notice that Bruce Willis was dead in *The Sixth Sense,* but you'll know where *Reindeer Games* is headed long before the end credits roll.

Rudy (Affleck), a naive auto thief newly released from prison, is kidnapped by a gang of gunrunners who plan a Christmas Eve robbery of a gambling casino located on an Indian reservation in the frozen wilds of northern Michigan. It's Rudy's forbidden lust for Ashley (Charlize Theron, looking remarkably like Ashley Judd), his former cell mate's pen pal, that's gotten him into this fix. Gabriel (Gary Sinise), the head gunrunner, has some relationship to Ashley that would be too complicated to get into here, even if Dimension Films hadn't cautioned me against letting even the smallest cat out of the bag. Dimension is a division of Miramax, and if this film is evidence of how they treat Affleck, one of their most valued stars, then who am I to risk their displeasure? On the other hand, I doubt that Harvey Weinstein is going to be working the phones trying to plug up leaks the way he did years ago for *The Crying Game.*

Affleck has learned a bit of action-film technique since his embarrassing turn in *Armageddon.* His best performance is still as the jock with artistic leanings in Mark Pellington's *Going All the Way.* Here, he seems less like an actor than the host of a bad party who suffers his ill-tempered guests with a certain grace. Sinise, however, engages in much teeth gnashing before he gets down to chewing the scenery. I admit a weakness for Frankenheimer's huge low-angled close-ups and the way he can send a body or two hurtling down a snowy mountain. Still, that's precious little on which to pin a movie.

Also reviewed in:
CHICAGO TRIBUNE, 2/25/00, Friday/p. A, Michael Wilmington
NEW YORK TIMES, 2/25/00, p. E20, Elvis Mitchell
VARIETY, 2/28-3/5/00, p. 40, Todd McCarthy
WASHINGTON POST, 2/25/00, p. C1, Stephen Hunter
WASHINGTON POST, 2/25/00, Weekend/p. 48, Desson Howe

REMEMBER THE TITANS

A Walt Disney Pictures/Jerry Bruckheimer Films release of a Technical Black production. *Executive Producer:* Mike Stenson and Michael Flynn. *Producer:* Jerry Bruckheimer and Chad Oman. *Director:* Boaz Yakin. *Screenplay:* Gregory Allen Howard. *Director of Photography:* Philippe Rousselot. *Editor:* Michael Tronick. *Music:* Trevor Rabin. *Music Editor:* Will Kaplan. *Choreographer:* Joann F. Jansen. *Sound:* Mary H. Ellis and (music) Steve Kempster and Dennis Sands. *Sound Editor:* Robert L. Sephton. *Casting:* Ronna Kress. *Production Designer:* Deborah Evans. *Art Director:* Jonathan Short. *Set Decorator:* Anne Kuljian. *Set Dresser:* William Butler. *Special Effects:* Robert M. Shelley Sr. *Costumes:* Judy Ruskin Howell. *Make-up:* Lynne Eagan. *Make-up (Denzel Washington):* Carl Fullerton. *Running time:* 113 minutes. *MPAA Rating:* PG.

CAST: Denzel Washington (Coach Herman Boone);   Will Patton (Coach Bill Yoast);   Wood Harris (Julius "Big Ju" Campbell);   Ryan Hurst (Gerry Bertier);   Donald Faison (Petey);   Craig Kirkwood (Rev);   Ethan Suplee (Lewis Lastik);   Kip Pardue (Sunshine);   Hayden Panettiere (Sheryl Yoast); Nicole Ari Parker (Carol Boone);   Kate Bosworth (Emma);   Earl C. Poitier (Blue Stanton);   Ryan Gosling (Alan Bosley);   Burgess Jenkins (Ray Budds);   Neal Ghant (Glascoe);   David Jefferson, Jr. (Cook); Preston Brant (Jerry Buck);   Michael Weatherly (Kirk Barker);   Gregalan Williams (Coach "Doc" Hinds);   Brett Rice (Coach Tyrell);   Richard Fullerton (A. D. Watson);   J. Don Ferguson (Tor);   Krysten Leigh Jones (Nicky Boone); Afemo Omilami (Mr. Campbell);   Andrew Masset (Col. Bass);   Tim Ware (Mr. Bosley);   Tom Turbiville (Captain Hal);   Tom Nowicki (Coach Ed Henry);   Jim Grimshaw (Coach Taber); David Dwyer (Coach Tolbert, Groveton);   Walter Benjamin Keister (Kip Tyler, Groveton;   Lou Walker (Ferdinand Day);   Marion Guyot (Mrs. Bertier);   Rhubarb Jones (Radio Announcer); Bob Neal (Colorman);   Dan Albright (Doctor);   Mike Pniewski (Cop);   Sharon Blackwood (Nurse);   Paula Claire Jones and Kelly C. Cheston (White Girls); Walker Jones (White Kid); Ronald L. Connor and Courtney James Stewart (Black Kids);   E Y Coley and John Wesley Register (Officials);   B. Keith Harmon (Crooked Official);   Andy Francis (Quarterback); Stuart Greer (Marshal Assistant Coach);   Derick Marshall (Davis); Scott Miles (Fred Alderson);   Steve Barnes (Titan Supporter);   Shanda Besler (Emma's Friend); David Devries (Parent);   Andrew Collins (Black Newspaper Man);   Steve Martin and Matt Adams (Hecklers); Marcus M. Moore (Special Teams Coach);   Ryan Duncan (Opposition Quarterback).

LOS ANGELES TIMES, 9/29/00, Calendar/p. 1, Kenneth Turan

You can tell by its mock-epic title, one that hints at heart-stirring endeavors. You can tell by the advertising material, with its soft-focus image of star Denzel Washington looking heroically off into the distance. You can tell by the fact that Denzel Washington is in this in the first place. Yes, it's true, "Remember the Titans" finds producer Jerry Bruckheimer in an inescapably serious mood.

Apparently not happy at being typecast as, in the words of his official bio, "one of the most successful producers of all time... with worldwide revenues of over $11 billion in box office, video and recording receipts, more than any other producer in history," Bruckheimer is determined, he says, to develop "smaller films, cutting-edge stories that explore issues not generally seen in mainstream filmmaking."

So "Remember the Titans" does without car chases, explosions and the other crowd-pleasing staples that characterize Bruckheimiana. It's not about the end of the world but about how two high school football coaches, one black, one white, brought racial harmony to a divided community. It's even based on a true story, but to little avail: The result remains transparently a Jerry Bruckheimer film from beginning to end. Which means that anyone expecting anything cutting-edge will have to settle for "Guess Who's Coming to Dinner" in cleats.

Though critics are not usually his biggest fans (a situation the producer seems to relish), being a Bruckheimer film is not all a bad thing. Like the best of the rest of his output, "Remember the Titans" (directed by indie veteran Boaz Yakin in classic Bruckheimer style) is a shrewd, pulpy crowd-pleaser. Engagingly cast, with a lively soundtrack and glossy cinematography (by Oscar winner Philippe Rousselot), it also features Washington, as big a plus as a film can have.

Someone who never sets a foot wrong, Washington is an actor it's impossible to remain unmoved by. Even in a conventional role as one tough hombre of a football coach, a straight-talking, square-shooting 1970s family man who says things like "you're overcooking my grits" when he's irked, Washington makes us believe no matter how cornball the situations become.

Of course, the shameless moments in "Titans" do come in thicker and faster than footballs from a shotgun offense. With signpost dialogue (Gregory Allen Howard has the writing credit), characters of a single dimension and more male bonding than a Super Bowl's worth of beer commercials, this story is no less predictably cliched for being unconcerned and easygoing about it. It's almost as if the more honest "Titans" tries to be, the sillier it gets.

Though most of the film takes place on a football field, "Titans" opens at a cemetery in 1981, and then, with the help of a voice-over by the adult version of one of the characters, flashes back to Alexandria, Va., in 1971, a time when "high school football was a way of life, bigger than Christmas."

That was also the year when, by court order, T.C. Williams High School became integrated. This news was taken especially hard by the all-white football team, whose players made free with sentiments like "I don't want to play with any black animals."

Worse, however, was yet to come for these good old boys. The team's beloved white coach Bill Yoast (Will Patton) was going to be replaced by Hennan Boone (Washington), a black coach who had come up from South Carolina expecting to be an assistant. Yoast's 8-year-old wiseacre tomboy daughter Sheryl (Hayden Panettiere) is especially peeved at this turn of events, but in truth both Yoast and Boone are as equally unhappy at the arbitrariness of the school board-mandated decision as she is.

But when those hostile white players threaten to sit out a year and thus harm their chances for college scholarships, Yoast swallows his pride and accepts Boone's offer to coach the team's defense. This is the first hint of one of "Titans" themes: These guys, despite differing skin color, have an awful lot in common. Imagine that.

Not that they don't have their differences. For one thing, Boone is so much of a strict disciplinarian that the more kindly Yoast is moved to say, "There's a fine line between tough and crazy and you're flirting with it." But when Boone marches his exhausted charges to the Gettysburg battlefield (yes, that Gettysburg) during summer football camp and makes a stirring peroration about the necessity of coming together to avoid destruction, Yoast knows he's working for the right man.

Though that camp forges the beginnings of unity on the team, the small-minded, kissing-cousin-to-the-Klan nature of Alexandria society (at least as it's portrayed here) threatens to tear things apart when the boys come back home. Can the team stay together despite the hatred and turmoil swirling around them, can they fight racism by their good example, can they learn that there is no I in team? No, those are not trick questions.

As "Remember the Titans" goes along on its predetermined way, crowded with familiar types like overweight white lineman Lewis Lastik (Ethan Suplee), no racist because he was raised in New Jersey, and can't-keep-from-singing Blue (Earl C. Poitier), it's hard not to wish that life was as, shall we say, black and white as it is portrayed here. It's not that these problems don't occur in real life, it's that things always seem so wonderfully, naively simple in Bruckheimer movies. And that, as likely as not is where that $11 billion in receipts really comes from.

NEW YORK, 10/9/00, p. 90, Peter Rainer

The syrupy, inspirational *Remember the Titans*, set in 1971, is a race-relations drama that's about as far removed in tone from *Bamboozled* as you can get. Denzel Washington's Herman Boone becomes head coach of the T.C. Williams High Titans in Virginia, the school board having passed over the expected choice, Bill Yoast (Will Patton), after being forced to integrate an all-black school with an all-white school. Whites and blacks, initially at odds, learn to respect one another, and at each sign of respect the music swells. The story is based on real incidents, but the uplifting tone is laid on so thick that it's difficult to believe a minute of it. Because this is a Disney movie, the N-word is never used, although its substitutes here, *monkey* and *coon*, sound even worse in context. It's time for Denzel Washington to stop essaying role models for a while.

He's beginning to confuse playing an admirable human being with giving an admirable performance.

NEW YORK POST, 9/29/00, p. 51, Lou Lumenick

This is a civics lesson about integration very artfully—and entertainingly—disguised as an upbeat family sports movie. Once again, Denzel Washington is starring in a movie about race relations in America—but this time, it's not filled with breast-beating speeches, as were "Malcolm X" and "The Hurricane."

And though it depicts racial hatred, this PG-rated Disney production doesn't get any more violent than a rock thrown through a window.

But, in its way, "Remember the Titans" is no less effective for communicating its characters' feelings (noble and not so noble), largely through telling glances and gestures.

That's especially true of Washington, who gives another wonderfully nuanced, Oscar-worthy performance as the first black high school football coach in Alexandria, Va.

It's 1971 and the city, still a bastion of institutional racism, has been ordered to finally integrate its schools. That process includes installing Herman Boone (Washington), a new hire from South Carolina, as coach, in place of Bill Yoast (Will Patton), the hugely popular incumbent.

The courtly Yoast swallows his pride and accepts a position as assistant to Boone, whose much more aggressive tactics—and tough-love approach to the players—he has misgivings about. But Yoast's reservations are minor compared to those of his white players, who initially balk at even playing on the same team as blacks.

The black team members are equally leery, and it's Boone's task to bring them together at a no-holds-barred boot camp, where they're forced to bunk together and where he delivers the movie's only major inspirational speech, during a 3 a.m. forced march through the battlefield at Gettysburg.

Even when the players do begin to bond, the white players have to face hostility from family and friends who see cooperation as a threat to their way of life—something Gregory Allen Howard's screenplay manages to depict without turning them into racist caricatures.

In his first big-studio film, director Boaz Yakin ("Fresh," "A Price Above Rubies"), gets uniformly winning performances from the little-known actors cast as the players.

Among them are Wood Harris as a black quarterback who views the whites with suspicion, Ryan Hurst as the white team captain with increasingly divided loyalties, Donald Faison as the upbeat wide receiver, and the massive Ethan Suplee and hunky Kip Pardue as the team's utterly different non-Southern whites (from New Jersey and California, respectively), who can't understand what all the fuss is about.

Patton, who's wonderfully understated as his character faces a crisis of principle, beautifully complements Washington. And young Hayden Panettiere is delightful as Yoast's football-crazy daughter.

It's fashionable for movie critics to sneer at "family" entertainment and at movies that rework real-life events (the Titans' drive to the state championship, and how they served as an example to the sports-mad population of Alexandria) to make them dramatically satisfying.

And I'll bet some of my colleagues will dismiss this just because of its producer, Hollywood hit-meister Jerry Bruckheimer, none of whose previous films were remotely this subtle—though, to be sure, it has its share of manipulative moments.

Ignore them, please, and take your kids to see "Remember the Titans," so they can see that as recently as 30 years ago, blacks were being refused service in restaurants in an American city, and how that changed. It's certainly a lesson I want to share with my daughter.

NEWSDAY, 9/29/00, Part II/p. B2, Gene Seymour

"Remember the Titans" gets in your face from start to finish like the loudest gym teacher you ever had in life. There's no room, mister, for subtlety or delicacy in this movie! You will learn how to love your neighbor as yourself. You will learn to recognize and hate racism in all its pernicious forms! You will believe that three-a-days can make a difference! You say you won't leave your doubts at the door? Drop and give us fifty!

Well, what do you expect? Any Jerry Bruckheimer production is an aerobic workout for the senses, and football, even high school football with a social conscience, is tailor-made for his blunt, bring-the-noise aesthetic.

That said, "Remember the Titans," as Bruckheimer productions go, can surprise you at times with its sensitivity toward the era it chronicles. Which is, essentially, the later civil-rights era, when the residue of southern institutional segregation was being scraped away.

Specifically, it's 1971 and Alexandria, Va., has been ordered to integrate its public schools. What that means, in particular, for all-white T.C. Williams High School is that its beloved Titans football team will have to assume a surplus of African-American players. Worse still, the school's popular coach, Bill Yoast (Will Patton) has been ordered to step aside and make room for Herman Boone (Denzel Washington), a black Lombardi-esque dynamo from South Carolina.

Even if you don't know the true story behind this film, its outcome is never in doubt from the title sequence. Yet you will still have to endure the pain of watching petty cruelties and nasty manners inflicted upon and exchanged between the races, even from Yoast's young daughter (Hayden Panettiere), who, like the white players, bitterly resents her daddy's demotion.

Still, as good football teams must, the players, led on the black side by Julius Campbell (Wood Harris) and on the white side by Gerry Bertier (Ryan Hurst), band together as a unit.

And, by the way, they become unbeatable on the field, knocking down like bowling pins every team it meets. Maybe, the town starts thinking, this integration stuff isn't so bad ...

Such rapprochement can't possibly be as quick and easy as the movie makes it sound. But even with the heavy-handed plot dynamics, the movie still manages to inject some pointed observations about lingering sensitivities among the black players and the still- festering resentment among the white grownups. Such moments may be attributed to director Boaz Yakin, best known for films such as "Fresh" (1994) and "A Price Among Rubies" (1998) that addressed racial and ethnic subcultures with style and cunning.

The role of Herman Boone requires Washington to be little more than a snarling ramrod. The actor's core sweetness almost, but not quite, prevents you from believing he could be a martinet. But his confidence on camera pulls off the star turn that's required of him. Patton, given the high-profile role that his talent has long deserved, is the movie's pulsing core. As a man torn between his personal dreams and history's demands, Patton lets you see not only Yoast battling his conscience, but a whole culture coming to grips with change.

In the end, "Titans" resembles nothing so much as a rookie defensive lineman: All heart, big muscles and not a whole lot of gray matter upstairs. Still, once in a while, it shows itself to be just smart enough to make a key play.

SIGHT AND SOUND, 4/01, p. 55, Matthew Leyland

Alexandria, Virginia, 1971. Herman Boone, a black football coach from South Carolina, takes up his appointment as head coach of the Titans at the newly integrated TC Williams High School. Boone replaces the popular white coach Bill Yoast, who is offered and accepts the position of his assistant.

The Titans depart for training camp, where the imperious Boone strives to mould them into a highly disciplined, and mutually tolerant, winning team. Initially hostile, the black and white team members grow to respect and like one other; white captain Gerry Bertier and black quarterback Julius Campbell form a particularly strong bond.

Returning to school, the unified team is disheartened to find that racial prejudice is still rife in the community. Despite his team's run of victories in the Virginia schools tournament, Yoast's nomination for the state Hall of Fame is thrown out when he defies a group of officials conspiring to get rid of Boone. Bolstered by their sense of unity, the Titans continue to win games and are embraced by the community. A road accident leaves Gerry paralysed from the waist down. Ending the season undefeated, the Titans become state champions. In 1981, the players and coaches assemble for the funeral of Gerry, who was killed in a drunk driving incident.

The sports drama *Remember the Titans* announces itself from the off as an atypically earnest, message-centred drama from action-movie *über*-producer Jerry Bruckheimer. Based on the true story of an integrated high-school football team whose success reportedly eased racial tensions in Alexandria in the early 70s, it begins with crisply photographed close-ups of autumn leaves. These opening moments suggest a reflective, thoughtful tone—and the notion, perhaps, that on offer here is something more grown-up than the wilful superficiality of such summer action pantomimes as *Con Air, Armageddon* and *Gone in Sixty Seconds* that Bruckheimer tends to churn out.

But though *Remember the Titans* may mark the producer's most prominent attempt at high-minded earnestness (at least since 1995's *Dangerous Minds)*, its ambitions to be a serious, thought-provoking social-conscience film are fatally undermined by the incessantly feel-good aspirations of its script (credited to Gregory Allen Howard). The film's final act, which sees team captain Gerry paralysed in an accident on the eve of a big match, segues into melodrama and features an interminable succession of crowd-stirring moments including the tearful consolidation of the friendship between bed-ridden Gerry, who's white, and his star quarterback Julius, who's black, a handshake between Julius and Gerry's formerly racist girlfriend, and the Titans' victory in the state final, which, in time-honoured football movie fashion, is decided by a touchdown in the last play Such moments are so nakedly calculated to be moving that they're virtually affectless; the cloying sentimentality on display does serve to remind us, though, that *Remember the Titans* is a Disney film as well as a Bruckheimer one.

More effective are some of the smaller, less conspicuous narrative asides: when the black coach Boone, played by Denzel Washington, hands a banana to a bigoted rival coach, who's white; when a cop stops Julius in a white neighbourhood—in order to congratulate him. It's here, perhaps, that the influence of director Boaz Yakin (whose last film A *Price above Rubies* was a restrained drama set among Brooklyn's Hasidic Jews) on proceedings is most apparent. Any directorial subtlety, however, is undercut by Howard's sententious dialogue, which trots out such platitudes as "Trust the soul of a man, not the look of him" with wearisome regularity.

With the Titans' on-pitch action disappointingly routine, the film's most rewarding aspect emerges in Denzel Washington's performance. Following on from *The Hurricane,* another liberal sports drama, Washington resists the temptation to sleepwalk the role and laudably offsets some of the picture's preachy worthiness by accentuating Boone's authoritarianism. Both he and Bruckheimer regular Will Patton lend delicacy to the difficult relationship between Boone and assistant coach Yoast—although their climactic moment of post-victory conciliation is marred by an exchange ("You were the right man for the job!"; "You're Hall of Fame in my book!") that summons up the gung-ho spirit of Bruckheimer's 1986 *Top Gun.*

TIME, 10/9/00, p. 111, Richard Schickel

In 1971, T.C. Williams High School in Alexandria, Va., was integrated, and the usual ugly protests ensued. Perhaps the bitterest blow to the school's racist spirit was that its popular football coach, Bill Yoast (Will Patton), was demoted to defensive coordinator and replaced by a black man, Herman Boone (Denzel Washington). How Boone, a tough-love sort of guy, got his racially mixed team playing so well that it went on to an undefeated season and the state championship is the substance of *Remember the Titans.*

Producer Jerry Bruckheimer says the screenwriter, Gregory Allen Howard, first heard this story in a Virginia barbershop many years after the Titans' famous victories and instantly decided that latter-day America needed to contemplate it. The producer, who is normally associated with high-tech action movies, is inordinately proud of the result, despite the bruising direction of Boaz Yakin. Bruckheimer seems to think they've made an art film.

The film's heart is surely in the right place, though it's hard to think how you could misplace its ticker and still have a releasable movie. In its way, it beats solidly too, following the rhythms of well-established clichés. First the team is ridden with mutual prejudice; then it starts to pull together. The two coaches' relationship is first gnarly, then affectionate. There's a goofy kid who learns to play, a star who is grievously yet inspirationally hurt in an accident and, of course, a kid who comes off the bench to help win the big game. Maybe it's all true. But one is always a little discomfited when life, or a movie, imitates weary melodramatic patterns this slavishly.

VILLAGE VOICE, 10/3/00, p. 232, Dennis Lim

"I'm not a savior," Denzel Washington cautions early on in *Remember the Titans.* Don't worry, he's lying. Dragging his team out of bed for a 3 a.m. run, Washington's Herman Boone, the new football coach at a recently integrated high school in 1971 West Virginia, leads them to

Gettysburg and, as a momentous early-morning fog conveniently rolls in, messianically urges them to "come together on this hallowed ground." And so, the T.C. Williams High Titans settle in for a crash course in race relations—black and white teammates begin to regard each other not with fear and suspicion but as, well, charmingly different (the black kids' habit of launching into spontaneous, soulful song and their off-color jokes about each other's mothers are a source of particular bemusement). Based on (or rather, inflated from) a true story, *Remember the Titans* is apparently producer Jerry Bruckheimer's idea of a serious, small-scale movie, but by any reasonable standard, it's still boorish and flatulent. There's plenty of downtime before the come-from-behind victory, so director-for-hire Boaz Yakin cranks up Trevor Rabin's randomly rousing earache of a score and engineers a shameless moment of courageous-athlete poignancy that wouldn't be out of place on NBC's doggedly lachrymose Olympics coverage.

Also reviewed in:
CHICAGO TRIBUNE, 9/29/00, Friday/p. A, Michael Wilmington
NEW YORK TIMES, 9/29/00, p. E10, A. O. Scott
VARIETY, 10/2-8/00, p. 20, Todd McCarthy
WASHINGTON POST, 9/29/00, p. C1, Stephen Hunter
WASHINGTON POST, 9/29/00, Weekend/p. 43, Michael O'Sullivan

REPLACEMENTS, THE

A Warner Bros. Pictures release in association with Bel-Air Entertainment of a Dylan Sellers production. *Executive Producer:* Steven Reuther, Jeffrey Chernov, and Erwin Stoff. *Producer:* Dylan Sellers. *Director:* Howard Deutch. *Screenplay:* Vince McKewin. *Director of Photography:* Tak Fujimoto. *Editor:* Bud Smith and Seth Flaum. *Music:* John Debney. *Sound:* Edward Tise. *Casting:* Mary Gail Artz and Barbara Cohen. *Production Designer:* Dan Bishop. *Art Director:* Gary Kosko. *Set Decorator:* Maria Nay. *Costumes:* Jill Ohanneson. *Stunt Coordinator:* Allan Graf. *Running time:* 105 minutes. *MPAA Rating:* PG-13.

CAST: Keanu Reeves (Shane Falco); Gene Hackman (Jimmy McGinty); Brooke Langton (Annabelle Farrell); Orlando Jones (Clifford Franklin); Jon Favreau (Daniel Bateman); Rhys Ifans (Nigel Gruff); Faizon Love (Jamal Jackson); Michael "Bear" Taliferro (Andre Jackson); Ace Yonamine (Jumbo Fumiko); Troy Winbush (Walter Cochran); David Denman (Brian Murphy); Michael Jace (Earl Wilkinson); Jack Warden (Edward O'Neil); Gailard Sartain (Leo Pilachowski); Art LaFleur (Christopher Banes); Brett Cullen (Eddie Martel); John Madden (Himself); Pat Summerall (Himself).

LOS ANGELES TIMES, 8/11/00, Calendar/p. 1, Kenneth Turan

The British can relax. Collectively distraught at being depicted as the bad guys in a spate of recent pictures, they've been supplanted by Hollywood's latest candidate for villain du jour: unionized workers.

Not content with being a cliche-ridden, stereotype-driven comedy about average guys following their dream of football glory, "The Replacements" (inspired, if that is the right word, by the 1987 NFL strike) can't resist making sour jokes about how whiny athletes are for even thinking about walking off the job.

Even if it's acceptable to have that as a starting point, the film can't get enough of portraying striking players as the kind of bullying thugs who make cruel fun of a deaf athlete and say things like "I know $5 million sounds like a lot of money, but do you have any idea what insurance on a Ferrari costs?" This from well-paid writers and actors who are thinking of going on strike themselves and would be shocked if anyone told them they should shut up and be grateful for what they have.

It would be conveniently glib to say that "The Replacements" shows what happens when replacement writers and directors get to make films, but the harsh truth is that the reverse is true.

Both director Howard Deutch ("Grumpier Old Men") and writer Vince McKewin (everything from "Rush Hour" to "Operation Dumbo Drop") are veteran Hollywood players, and the result is a haphazard film about half as sophisticated as the average beer commercial.

As for the actors, every single one of them, even star Keanu Reeves, has been noticeably better in previous work. Jon Favreau and Brooke Langton were better in "Swingers," Orlando Jones was better in "Liberty Heights," Rhys Ifans was better in "Notting Hill" (as Hugh Grant's dotty roommate). As for Gene Hackman, it's not so much that he's been better elsewhere (that's a given) as that his performance as Washington Sentinels Coach Jimmy McGinty is such a pale copy of the memorable work he did as Robert Redford's coach in "Downhill Racer."

When McGinty gets hired by owner Edward O'Neil (the venerable Jack Warden) to assemble and coach the replacement Sentinels for the final four games of the season, he is not without ideas of his own about player selection. "We're gonna go a different way," he tells his boss, by which he means hire a bunch of misfits and weirdos, each of whom has one particular talent. For instance: Clifford Franklin (Jones), a super speed demon who can't hold onto the ball; Nigel "The Leg" Gruff (Ifans), a Welsh place-kicker who drinks, smokes and gambles to excess; Daniel Bateman (Favreau), an L.A. cop prone to excessive violence; Jumbo Fumiko (Ace Yonamine), a bulky Japanese sumo wrestler.

When you add in a nasty African American felon as well as a painfully macho attitude toward women epitomized by the often-repeated mantra "that's why girls don't play the game," you get a film that wouldn't know where to begin without stereotypes of all kinds to lean on.

Speaking of women, one of the oddities of "The Replacements" plot is that the team's cheerleaders seem to have walked off along with the players, leaving head cheerer Annabelle Farrell (Langton) to recruit replacements from local lap dancers and exotic performers. From then on, the film's philosophy becomes, when in doubt—which is often—cut to shots of the gyrating cheerleaders.

Though she doesn't date football players, Annabelle can't keep her eyes off the team's new quarterback, Shane Falco (Reeves), nicknamed "Footsteps" because his confidence was destroyed by a bad performance in the Sugar Bowl. Vow or no vow, Annabelle is soon rubbing yam extract onto Shane's bruises, and their romantic arc is as predictable as the homilies of TV commentators John Madden and Pat Summerall (who may yet regret agreeing to play themselves).

Since McGinty's idea of coaching is throwing platitudes like "winners always want the ball when the game is on the line" at Falco, you know the quarterback has gotten the hang of things when he tells his guys, "Pain heals, chicks dig scars, glory lives forever." Any replacements for that line will be gratefully accepted.

NEW YORK, 8/28/00, p. 133, Peter Rainer

The Replacements deserves a historical footnote for being the most blatantly anti-union movie in memory. A pro-football strike necessitates the hiring of a bunch of lovably goony, ragtag players, headed by quarterback Keanu Reeves, to replace the spoiled-rotten zillionaire professionals looking for another notch in their bank account. The substitute coach for the Washington Sentinels, played by Gene Hackman in a performance that can most charitably be termed minimalist, sides with the scabs because they, unlike their overpaid counterparts, still have a hunger for the sport. Since Hollywood is riven with current and impending labor strikes these days, you have to wonder how this sort of thing will play in Burbank, not to mention Peoria. Obviously somebody decided the time was ripe to cash in on fan resentment of star salaries and star egos, but there's still something a bit bloodcurdling about this nudnick celebration of strike-breaking in which not a single pro player is portrayed as anything more than pond scum. If *The Replacements* turns out to be a commercial success, can we next expect a Reagan-righteous movie about the glory days of the air controllers' strike?

NEW YORK POST, 8/11/00, p. 43, Jonathan Foreman

For all its pleasures, "The Replacements" won't replace "North Dallas Forty" "Semi-Tough" or even "The Longest Yard" in the canon of classic football movies. But despite a slow start, a shamelessly formulaic plot and what looks like some heavy-handed last-minute editing (here and there, you see the beginnings and endings of vanished subplots), it manages to be great fun—indeed, one of the most enjoyable entertainments of the summer.

It achieves this by recycling and binding into a genial and effective whole tried and true elements from "Slap Shot," "The Bad News Bears," "Longest Yard" and various other successful sports films and inserting them into a story line inspired by the 1987 NFL strike.

Even the pounding sound track is such a compilation of popular "jock jams" that there are times when the movie feels like a long music video. Still, although every sports cliché you've ever seen is here (especially "heart" triumphing over talent), it somehow doesn't matter: You end up cheering for Keanu Reeves and his motley crew of scab players.

With the playoffs approaching, the Washington Sentinels have just gone on strike. So owner Ed O'Neil calls in Jimmy McGinty (Gene Hackman), a coach he once fired, to recruit a team of amateurs, has-beens and coulda-beens happy to cross a picket line.

McGinty has an amazing memory for once-promising high school and college players, and quickly assembles a wacky, multicultural group, including Bateman (Jon Favreau), a dumb super-aggressive cop, and Wilkinson (Michael Jace), a hardened criminal allowed out of the penitentiary just to play football.

There's also a sumo wrestler (Ace Yonamine), a lightning-fast but cowardly and butterfingered ghetto thief (Orlando Jones), a talented but stone-deaf wide receiver (David Denman) and gun-toting twins who work as music industry bodyguards (Michael Taliferro and Faizon Love).

But the team's stars are Reeve's quarterback, Shane Falco (where do moviemakers get these names?) and chain-smoking soccer player turned kicker Nigel "The Leg" Gruff, ("Notting Hill's" Rhys Ifans).

There seems to be a cheerleaders' strike, too, because Annabelle, the head of the squad (Brooke Langton), is forced to recruit a bunch of sexy stripper/hookers to do the job.

Can Reeves unite the team and control his own tendency to choke at key moments? Will he persuade the lovely Annabelle to break a self-imposed ban on dating players? Will the replacement Sentinels be able to withstand the harassment of the horrible, arrogant regular players? (Of course, unlike those greedy millionaire players, the billionaire owners are just in it for the game ...

Reeves is as stolid and likable as ever. Hackman, as always, brings an amazing amount of class and conviction to a skimpily written role. And Langton (TV's "Melrose Place" and "The Net") is so natural and appealing as Annabelle that she's a sure bet for future female leads on the big screen.

The football scenes are choreographed and directed by Allan Graf, the master who made the game look so exciting in "Any Given Sunday" and "Jerry Maguire."

The only thing in the film that leaves a slightly sour taste in your mouth—especially with Hollywood unions considering a strike next summer—is the way it glorifies scabs and unabashedly takes the side of management, painting pro-football players as overpaid and spoiled brats who during the strike "return to their castles and private jets."

It conveniently ignores the fact that most players aren't millionaire superstars, and are finished and semi-crippled by 40.

NEWSDAY, 8/11/00, Part II/p. B3, Jan Stuart

Write you own review—A dozen dirty questions:

1. In "The Replacements," Keanu Reeves plays a washed-up football player who has retired after disgracing himself at a Sugar Bowl game. During his retirement, Reeves (A) takes beginner's acting lessons (B) takes advanced grunting lessons (C) has an excellent adventure (D) scrapes barnacles off the bottom of a boat.

2. Deja vu moment #341: When hired to coach a replacement team for the striking players of the Washington Sentinels football team, Gene Hackman hires a motley crew of street criminals and flunkies. Motley crews who go on to triumph also can be found in (A) "The Dirty Dozen" (B) "The Bad News Bears" (C) "The Full Monty" (D) all of the above, and then some.

3. Among the motley crew hired for Hackman's team is (A) a member of Les Ballets Trockadero de Monte Carlo (B) a toll booth clerk at the Triborough Bridge (C) Tatum O'Neal (D) none of the above.

4. When the replacements are thrown in jail for brawling in a bar, they (A) plan a breakout (B) are given a welcome-home party by the guards (C) trade recipes (D) line dance to Gloria Gaynor's disco hit "I Will Survive."

5. Reeves has a generic romance with a generic perky head cheerleader played by a generic babe. The babe's name is (A) Brittany Murphy (B) Britney Spears (C) Brittany B. Brittany (D) I can't remember.

6. Miss Perky Head Cheerleader hires a replacement team of cheerleaders from among (A) the surviving cast members of "Debbie Does Dallas" (B) the Daughters of the American Revolution (C) the sons of Flubber (D) a local lap-dancing club.

7. Fill in the cliche. Hackman to Reeves, "I look at you and see two men: the man you are and the man "(A) that got away (B) who fell to Earth (C) who fell over his lines (D) you ought to be.

8. When the Sentinels' teamwork begins to slide after Reeves is laid off, Hackman tells a reporter, "You gotta have heart." Recruiting Keanu Reeves when you need heart is like getting (A) Sandra Bernhard to do "The Sound of Music" (B) Bart Simpson to play "Pinocchio" (C) taken (D) all of the above.

9. Pop songs are inserted repeatedly into the movie in very literal ways so the slow learners in the audience will know (A) when the characters are sad (B) when the characters are falling in love (C) to buy the collected-hits soundtrack (D) all of the above.

10. Howard Deutch is credited with the direction, but "The Replacements" has the distracted, listless air of a movie put together by (A) a beached tuna (B) an electric can opener (C) Strom Thurmond (D) a beached South Carolina senator opening a can of tuna fish.

11. Hackman presumably agreed to do this movie because he needed (A) a new house (B) a new swimming pool (C) a new agent (D) to be humbled after a long, distinguished career.

12. (D) is the correct answer to all of the above questions. D is for (A) dumb (B) dumber (C) dese, dem and dose (D) don't, as in "What part of 'don't bother' don't you understand?"

VILLAGE VOICE, 8/22/00, p. 138, Jessica Winter

Tossed on the August dog-days movie heap like last season's frayed uniform, *The Replacements* is an amiable, lackadaisical mouth-breather, lame even by triumph-of-the-underdog sports-comedy standards. Close cousins include the greed-and-gridiron half-satire *North Dallas Forty,* not to mention the Scott Bakula paragon *Necessary Roughness* (though another ancestral line might be the David-and-Goliath stick-action giggler: *Slap Shot; The Mighty Ducks; Mystery, Alaska;* the 1980 Olympic ice-hockey finals; etc.).

After the Washington Sentinels go out on strike, aging coach Gene Hackman comes on board to assemble a multiculti patchwork quilt of ne'er-do-well shadow talents: a lightning-fast convenience-store employee who can't catch (Orlando Jones); a sumo wrestler (Ace Yonamine, shot frequently from low angles, much like Richard on *Survivor);*a drunk Welsh soccer player (Rhys Ifans) who can kick the length of a field; a borderline-psychotic cop (Jon Favreau, doing his best Vin Diesel impression). Hackman's most coveted recruit, a former college football star named Shane Falco, harbors the most ambivalence about returning to the game, but this only adds to his noble luster. The second former Ohio State quarterback in Keanu Reeves's oeuvre, Falco is somewhat of an inversion of *Point Break*'s Johnny Utah, whose career-ending busted shoulder only led him to the illustrious path of law enforcement and transcendentalist surfing, while Falco's humiliating 45-point loss in the Sugar Bowl dumped him in a marina where he scrapes the gunk off yuppie boats and sleeps alone. But Falco may set off typecasting alarms: His principled reluctance, his (career) resurrection, his selfless leadership on and off the field (a Shane-induced pub fight finally brings the bickering ragtags together), his martyrdoms in the line of duty (more sacks in one game, it would seem, than Archie Manning incurred in his whole career)—it all recalls Reeves's Jesus figure in *The Matrix.* Falco's Costas-like grace in spinning a sports aphorism ("That's some deep shit Shane," a teammate testifies) only enhances his aura as the Chosen One.

Our Keanu ambles through Howard Deutch's slow-paced, thick-tongued production with his usual dazed beatific grace, and both he and Hackman seem embarrassed, which gives their scenes together a special poignancy. Eventually, girls are gotten and face is saved, but *The Replacements* offers only two new wrinkles in the annals of sports culture. One is a flat rejection of cheerleaders as mere superfluous eye candy; these tongue-lolling pom-pom ladies, who dress like the former Ginger Spice, prove a valuable source of distraction to the Sentinels' opponents. The other concerns the ongoing relationship between players, spectators, and affirmational gay disco anthems. Much as Yankees fans bump and grind each home game to "Y.M.C.A.," these Replacements, during a long night in prison after the aforementioned bar scrape, do a choreographed ass-shaking to "I Will Survive." Which is terrific, but aren't these the guys who did "Bastards of Young"?

Also reviewed in:
CHICAGO TRIBUNE, 8/11/00, Friday/p. A, Mark Caro
NEW YORK TIMES, 8/11/00, p. E13, Elvis Mitchell
VARIETY, 8/7-13/00, p. 16, Joe Leydon
WASHINGTON POST, 8/11/00, p. C1, Stephen Hunter
WASHINGTON POST, 8/11/00, Weekend/p. 33, Michael O'Sullivan

REQUIEM FOR A DREAM

An Artisan Entertainment and Thousand Words release of a Sibling/Protozoa production in association with Industry and Bandeira Entertainment. *Executive Producer:* Nick Wechsler, Beau Flynn, and Stefan Simchowitz. *Producer:* Eric Watson and Palmer West. *Director:* Darren Aronofsky. *Screenplay:* Hubert Selby, Jr. and Darren Aronofsky. *Based on the novel by:* Hubert Selby, Jr. *Director of Photography:* Matthew Libatique. *Editor:* Jay Rabinowitz. *Music:* Clint Mansell. *Music Editor:* Stephen Barden, Jay Rabinowitz, and Matt Mayer. *Sound:* Ken Ishi and (music) Dann Michael Thompson. *Sound Editor:* Nelson Ferreira. *Casting:* Freddy Luis and Jennifer Lindesmith. *Production Designer:* James Chinlund. *Art Director:* Judy Rhee. *Set Decorator:* Ondine Karady. *Special Effects:* Drew Jiritano. *Costumes:* Laura Jean Shannon. *Make-up:* Judy Chin. *Make-up (Special Effects):* Louie Zakarian. *Make-up (Prosthetic Effects):* Vincent J. Guastini. *Stunt Coordinator:* Pete Bucossi. *Running time:* 102 minutes. *MPAA Rating:* Not Rated.

CAST: Ellen Burstyn (Sara Goldfarb); Jared Leto (Harry Goldfarb); Jennifer Connelly (Marion Silver); Marlon Wayans (Tyrone C. Love); Christopher McDonald (Tappy Tibbons); Louise Lasser (Ada); Marcia Jean Kurtz (Rae); Janet Sarno (Mrs. Pearlman); Suzanne Shepherd (Mrs. Scarlini); Joanne Gordon (Mrs. Ovadia); Charlotte Aronofsky (Mrs. Miles); Mark Margolis (Mr. Rabinowitz); Mike Kaycheck (Donut Cop); Jack O'Connell (Corn Dog Stand Boss); Chas Mastin (Lyle Russel); Ajay Naidu (Mailman); Sean Gullette (Arnold the Shrink); Samia Shoalb (Nurse Mall); Peter Maloney (Dr. Pill); Abraham Abraham (King Neptune); Aliya Campbell (Alice); Te'ron A. O'Neal (Young Tyrone); Denise Dowse (Tyrone's Mother); Bryan Chattoo (Brody); Eddie De Harp (Brody's Henchman Victor); Scott Franklin (Voice of Jailer); Peter Howard (Sal the Geep); Brian Costello (First AD); Abraham Aronofsky (Newspaper Man on Train); James Chinlund (Space Oddity); Olga Merediz (Malin Block Secretary); Allison Furman (Malin Block Office Woman); Robert Dylan Cohen (Paramedic Greenhill); Ben Shenkman (Dr. Spencer); Keith David (Big Tim); Dylan Baker (Southern Doctor); Shaun O'Hagen (Ward Attendant Seto); Leland Gantt (Ward Attendant Penn); Bill Buell (Court Doctor); Jimmie Ray Weeks (Prison Guard); Greg Bello (ER Doctor); Henry Stram (ECT Technician); Stanley B. Herman (Uncle Hank); Hubert Selby, Jr. (Laughing Guard); Liana Pai (Angelic Nurse).

CHRISTIAN SCIENCE MONITOR, 10/6/00, p. 15, David Sterritt

"Requiem for a Dream" takes its cue from Hubert Selby Jr.'s fierce novel "Last Exit to Brooklyn," which etches a hard-edged picture of the wages of sin. The movie's main characters are New Yorkers with different kinds of addictions: an aging woman hooked on fantasies of fame, and two young men hooked on drug dealing as a route to easy cash.

This is the American dream at its darkest, and director Darren Aronofsky probes it with relentless energy. Solid acting helps it stay earthbound when the filmmaking gets addicted to its own flashy cynicism, but the picture sometimes seems as dazed and confused as the situations it wants to criticize.

Aronofsky made an impressive showing in his 1998 fantasy "Pi," a blend of scientific and religious ideas. That brand of human-scaled cinema suits his talents better than the hyperactive gyrations of this grim "Requiem."

LOS ANGELES TIMES, 10/20/00, Calendar/p. 12, Kevin Thomas

Hubert Selby Jr. has said of Darren Aronofsky's startling film of Selby's 1978 novel "Requiem for a Dream" that it brought him to tears, adding that he believed that "anybody who has lived on this planet will recognize something about themselves in this story."

Even if you agree wholeheartedly with Selby, who first found recognition with his unforgettable—and unrelenting—"Last Exit to Brooklyn," you have to add an important qualification: provided you're willing to submit to a film that is as unremittingly bleak as it is brilliant. You really have to be up for—and open to—this most harrowing of films that dazzles with Aronofsky's acute command of his medium and of his actors, from whom he demands the utmost and then some.

The great theme here is how the American capacity for a naive self-deception can pack the destructive force of a tornado. In her comfortable if faded Brighton Beach apartment, near that rotting fantasy land, Coney Island, Sara Goldfarb (Ellen Burstyn), a lonely widow, glues herself to her TV—when she's not having to buy it back from a junk dealer to whom her son Harry (Jared Leto) sells it regularly. Sara constantly watches Tappy Tibbons (Christopher McDonald), an unctuous TV weight-loss guru, whose twin mantras are "No red meat! No refined sugar!"

One day Sara's mail brings her the news that she's among a group of people who have been selected to appear on a game show, assuring her that "You're already a winner!" The letter doesn't say when she may be summoned to appear, but it never occurs to Sara that she may well never hear from the show again. In an instant Sara is lifted from her despair and becomes a heroine to her neighbors.

Casting back to her happiest memory, she takes out of the closet the bright red dress she wore to her son's high school graduation. As she can no longer get into it, she goes to a neighborhood weight-loss doctor. Sure enough, she starts losing the pounds swiftly from taking all those little pills, but she also starts losing her mind as well, from the dangerous drugs, most likely amphetamines, that she has been prescribed.

Mother and son, it seems, have started down similar paths. Harry is a good-looking but aimless young man who thinks he's going to hit it big peddling drugs with his pal Tyrone (Marlon Wayans) and his new girlfriend Marion (Jennifer Connelly). But they're also users, which enhances Harry and Marion's rush as they fall in love. When Tyrone and Harry score some high-grade stuff, Tyrone persuades a dubious Harry—they're already getting high a lot—that they should have "just a little taste, to know how well it's cut. It's business."

Aronofsky, who made a knockout debut with the virtuoso "Pi," draws upon grammar of the experimental film—extreme close-ups, strobe cuts, split screen, rapid crosscutting, fast-forwards—to link the remorseless parallel downward spirals of mother and son, and the son's lover and friend. For them, euphoria has been the cruelest, most destructive of illusions, prompted by that aching longing to get back to that moment of joy that we have lost—or to get hold of a happiness we never had.

Sara's dream is so humble—to be able to wear that red dress again for her eagerly anticipated appearance on "national television." And here's Harry the drifter, experiencing an overwhelming first love with a young woman who's been discarded by her wealthy family, left just enough money to allow Harry and Tyrone to have initial success in dealing drugs.

At this late date, it's not easy to work up sympathy for drug addicts, but Aronofsky, in drawing from a writer as pure, raw and steadfast as Selby, thrusts us right into the psyches of these people. They have been brought to vivid, aching life by his cast, especially Burstyn, whose transformation from pleasant-looking matron to crazed, terrified wraith comes from deep within herself, way beneath all the surface tricks of makeup and movie wizardry that Aronofsky has at his disposal.

Indeed, "Requiem for a Dream" does get harder and harder to take as these four continue their downward paths with escalating swiftness. But Aronofsky is so compelling, so visionary a filmmaker, he keeps us riveted to his film as tightly as Sara is to her TV set.

There's no easy way out for these sad cases, so betrayed by their most human longings. But "Requiem for a Dream," superbly designed and photographed, by James Chinlund and Matthew Libatique, respectively, is a work of art whose beauty has the eternal power of redemption.

NEW YORK POST, 10/6/00, p. 48, Jonathan Foreman

"Requiem for a Dream," the second film (after "Pi") by highly praised indie director Darren Aronofsky turns out to be a powerful fable about love and addiction that manages to be darkly humorous when it isn't graphic or harrowing in the extreme.

Among other qualities, "Requiem" boasts a courageous performance by Ellen Burstyn that could well win her an Oscar nomination if enough Academy members see the movie.

It's also a visual tour de force. In an era when flashy, empty, MTV-style gimmickry is all too common in independent film, Aronofsky makes wonderfully effective and intelligent use of a variety of visual devices— split screens, speeded up film, fish-eye lenses, digital effects, even special riggings attaching cameras to the actors bodies.

The film begins on a sunny Coney Island morning with Harry (Jared Leto) taking his mother's TV to pawn it for the drugs he craves along with his best friend, Tyrone (Marlon Wayans, who shows he's the real actor in the Wayans clan), and his girlfriend, Marion (Jennifer Connelly).

Harry's mother, Sara (Burstyn), patiently buys it back from the pawnbroker.

She herself is obsessed with a TV program that combines a game show with Anthony Robbins-style personal motivation.

When she gets a call from the show, saying she might be invited on as a guest, she embarks on a quest to lose weight, eventually getting a prescription for diet drugs that do strange things to her mind.

When Harry and Tyrone lose their drug supplier in a gang war, it becomes almost impossible for them to feed their habits.

Soon their desperation for drugs sends Marion and Harry on separate but equally destructive spirals, mirrored by the devastating effects of Sara's diet pills. Mostly, the dark humor of the piece keeps it on the good side of melodrama. But there are times when "Requiem" does feel a little like a feature-length, unusually hard-hitting public service announcement.

And the parallel between illegal drug abuse and the use of dangerous prescription drugs can seem both a little forced and a little anachronistic.

But Aronofsky gets strong performances from everyone, including Connelly, who shows once again that she's much more than the mere beauty she seemed to be in early films like "The Hot Spot."

NEWSDAY, 10/6/00, Part II/p. B7, John Anderson

Being released unrated, rather than with the dreaded NC-1 7, "Requiem for a Dream" proves a number of things: the audacity of director Darren Aronofsky's eye, the brilliance of Ellen Burstyn's acting and an apparent poverty of discernment or intelligence on the MPAA ratings board.

Either that, or the Motion Picture Association of America's ratings have to change again, because the stigma of X—and the prohibitions on advertising and screens across what chief censor Jack Valenti once called "this free and loving land"—is now attached to NC- 17. And that seems to mean that a movie as gloriously adult as "Requiem for a Dream" will inevitably be ghettoized by the system.

The irony is that Aronofsky's first feature since his award-winning "Pi" is first a cautionary tale about addiction, as personified by its four leading characters: Sara Goldfarb (Burstyn), widow, TV-junkie, devourer of candy and would-be game-show contestant; Harry (Jared Leto), Sara's junkie son, who periodically pawns her TV; Harry's girlfriend, Marion Silver (Jennifer Connelly), with whom Harry develops a sub-addiction of love; and Tyrone C. Love (Marlon Wayans), Harry's partner in crime and dreamer of large dreams.

Having found a correlation between heroin and television—via Hubert ("Last Exit to Brooklyn") Selby Jr.'s novel—probably makes Aronofsky into Entertainment Industry Enemy No. 1. Still, "Requiem," is as visceral and uncompromised a movie about the seduction-cum-terrors of substance and brain abuse as has ever been filmed.

And filmed it is: Aronofsky's devices—his hallucinogenic machine-gun rifts on shooting up, the multiple split-screened images, the rattling of FrankenFridge after Sara's diet-pill addiction runs amok—combine to create a mood of genuine horror, as well as a story that's thoroughly involving, thanks in part to the splendid acting of its cast. It's particularly unfortunate that Burstyn's performance might not get the exposure it deserves because it's truly of Oscar caliber (whatever that means). Her costars, too, are first-rate. Leto embodies doomed junkie-hood. (The scene in which he fires a dose into his abscessed arm may never leave my mind.) Connelly is better than she's ever been and Wayans, although his role is a bit underwritten, makes the most of it.

"Requiem" is a director's film, of course—Aronofsky fires both barrels to create a movie that haunts and disturbs. Apparently, he disturbed the MPAA to the point of panic.

SIGHT AND SOUND, 2/01, p. 48, Xan Brooks

Brighton Beach, New York, the present. Widowed Sara Goldfarb leads a lonely life eating chocolates in front of her favourite television game shows, while her junkie son Harry wanders the neighbourhood hunting highs alongside his girlfriend Marion and partner-in-crime Tyrone. After Sara receives a telephone call informing her that she may be selected to appear on a television game show her social status among her neighbours rockets. In her efforts to lose weight, Sara becomes addicted to dieting pills and is plagued by hallucinations.

Meanwhile, Harry and Tyrone set themselves up as drug dealers, but are using more than they sell. When their supply dries up, tensions break out within the gang. Marion is persuaded into sleeping with her former shrink Arnold to obtain money for drugs while Harry and Tyrone plan a trip to Florida to take possession of a major shipment. Tired of waiting to appear on television, Sara storms the network studio and is carted off to a psychiatric hospital where she receives electro-convulsive therapy. Abandoned by Harry, Marion turns for help to a dope dealer who forces her to take part in a sex party. On the road to Florida, Harry is troubled by an infected track mark on his arm and is admitted to hospital where the arm is amputated. Tyrone is arrested and forced into a chain gang. Lying in her hospital bed, Sara fantasises about an idyllic appearance on a television game show.

Requiem for a Dream begins in Brooklyn and ends in hell; or rather, it ends in four distinct circles of hell occupied respectively by its quartet of lead characters. In this, Darren Aronofsky's film differs from other recent junkie fables which, like some playful God, dipped their protagonists into the abyss only to pluck them back out again (think Renton's assurance that he's going to be "just like you" at the close of *Trainspotting,* or Matt Dillon's reformed junkie's ambulance trip in *Drugstore Cowboy).* By dumping the traditional last-minute upswing, *Requiem* bows out with an extended, accelerated plunge into the inferno. Despite the voguish trappings, its final tone is thunderously Old Testament.

At least Aronofsky is staying true to his source material. His adaptation of Hubert Selby Jr's 1978 novel takes few liberties with the text, while simultaneously hot-wiring it with his own array of directorial flourishes. If anything, Aronofsky's second film is even more visually jazzy than his first, the monochrome puzzle picture *Pi.* It runs on a flurry of split-screens, extreme close-ups and rapid edits (the average feature boasts between 600 and 700 cuts; this one has 2000). The result is highly impressive: a swooping, gut-churning assault on the senses, all underpinned by Clint Mansell's mesmerising string score. But behind the fireworks you wonder if the picture is quite as radical as it paints itself.

For a start, its governing thesis—that junk culture, in particular television, is as dangerous a drug as class-A narcotics—is a claim that feels worn from overuse; insufficient (at least in such a parroting, unquestioning form) to support the weight of an entire movie. Second, Aronofsky's dazzling way with an edit and a camera move often threatens to obscure his actors. Jared Leto proves faintly colourless as Harry, the tale's nominal hero, while Jennifer Connelly as his junkie girlfriend Marion is reduced to decoratively wasted eye-candy (although her crooked, cynical urchin grin still whips up some voltage). Only Ellen Burstyn appears able to function unimpeded as the doomed Sara Goldfarb, Harry's lonely television-obsessed mother. Harassed, timid, flashing a scared smile at the world at large, her performance hits home with a humanity that the rest of the film can only dream of. It's a role that reminds the viewer just how Hollywood has squandered her in the years since her 70s heyday.

The real problem with *Requiem for a Dream* is that it treats its characters with a queasy blend of sentiment and cruelty. Aronofsky invites us to weep for Sara, Harry and Marion's thwarted little lives in a harsh world and then proceeds gleefully to send them to the slaughter. The film's final montage is harrowing, but not for all the right reasons. In it, the director cross-cuts the amputation of Harry's infected arm with scenes of Sara undergoing ECT. He throws his beautiful white princess Marion under the wing of a wicked black pimp-cum-pusherman and then counters any taint of racism by having the film's sympathetic black man, played by Marlon Wayans, brutalised by a gang of redneck cops. Technically brilliant, the finale still reeks of cynicism. One is left with the impression that the preceding 90-odd minutes was just the loving arrangement of dolls in preparation for a mammoth toy smashing session. In setting the torch to his play things, Aronofsky turns drunk on his own rush for destruction.

VILLAGE VOICE , 10/10/00, p. 138, Michael Atkinson

Out of breath, dizzy with migraine frustration, and shuddering with an undeniable energy, Darren Aronofsky's torpedo-shot through Hubert Selby Jr.'s fourth novel may be the definitive scag movie, in part because there's no kicking the habit for Selby's lost ones—just descent. Aronofsky shows no signs of giving up the visual spasms he exploited in *pi;* if anything, *Requiem for a Dream* ups the dosage. More expressionistically funkadelic than *Trainspotting* (if not as witty), *Requiem* comes packing something the Danny Boyle team didn't have: a point, and one that reverbs. For Selby, dope and television are two heads of the same American-escapist ogre, and so the (by now) familiar agony of stringing out and hunting for a fix is conjoined with the plummet of the hero's blowsy Brooklyn mom (Ellen Burstyn) into a diet-pill inferno fueled by the promise of game-show contestantship and scored by a maniacal infomercial in which the studio crowd keeps bellowing, "Be! Excited! B! E! Excited!"

Aronofsky doesn't get by without misfires—the risk of literalizing pharmaceutically warped inner states is large, and flourishes like a perambulating refrigerator and a recurring seaside hallucination never pay off. You may not see a more self-conscious movie this decade, down to the split screens and chest-strapped cameras. Instead of heaping in Selby's prose as narration, Aronofsky shapes the movie as one long, carefully constructed seizure—shoot-ups are fast, explosive wham-bam montages of needles, bloodstreams, and eyeballs, and the soundtrack is a percussive fury of thing-noises, like the opening of Pink Floyd's "Money" times 20. (It's ironic how movies about heroin tend toward hyperventilation.) Just when you think it's going to settle into sobriety, the film jumps off another cliff.

As a trio of Brighton Beach dopeniks, Jared Leto, Jennifer Connelly, and Marion Wayans are all subsumed by the formal hootenanny; they're figures in a storm, scheming to buy, cut, and sell dope in order to "be on Easy Street" but quickly devolving from the handsomest junkies you ever saw to hollow-eyed wastrels. But the star of the show has to be Burstyn, if only for her perhaps naive trust in Aronofsky's fish-eye lens and makeup team. Starting out at a mannered maternal pitch suitable for *Playhouse 90,* Burstyn ends up a jabbering banshee left over from *Marat/Sade;* though she's never quite convincing, her ordeal is. Of course, the entire movie is contents under pressure, tear-assing toward a climactic Götterdämmerung montage split four ways, punching in between shock treatment, prison farm withdrawal, the most heinous systemic infection in movie history, and a public dance with a KY-slathered Louisville Slugger of a dildo that, though it may be a fun Saturday night for some people, is shot like it has its own circle in hell.

Iced with a genuinely felt, Springsteenian-loser-teen heartbreak, *Requiem for a Dream* may be an elaborate stunt, a bungee jump, but even so, it's forceful enough to leave a rare palpitating residue. How many movies can Aronofsky make this way? Critical mass will be easy to reach, but the better question is: How many other recent American movies demand to be seen?

Also reviewed in:
CHICAGO TRIBUNE, 11/3/00, Friday/p. A, Michael Wilmington

NEW YORK TIMES, 10/6/00, p. E27, Elvis Mitchell
NEW YORKER, 10/9/00, p. 101, Anthony Lane
VARIETY, 5/22-28/00, p. 24, Todd McCarthy
WASHINGTON POST, 11/3/00, p. C5, Stephen Hunter
WASHINGTON POST, 11/3/00, Weekend/p. 43, Desson Howe

RESTAURANT

A Palisades Pictures release or a Chaiken Films/Giv'en Films/Palisades Pictures production. *Executive Producer:* Michael Brysch, Galt Niederhoffer, Gary J. Palermo, and Mark D. Severini. *Producer:* H.M. Coakley, Shana Stein, and Eric Bross   *Director:* Eric Bross. *Screenplay:* Tom Cudworth. *Director of Photography:* Horacio Marquinez.   *Editor:* Keith Reamer.   *Music:* Theodore Shapiro.   *Sound:* Robert Ghiraldini.   *Sound Editor:* Kevin Lee. *Casting:* Joseph Middleton.   *Production Designer:* Steven McCabe.   *Art Director:* Shawn Carroll.   *Set Decorator:* Nick Evans.   *Costumes:* Elizabeth Shelton.   *Make-up:* Sandy Molina.   *Stunt Coordinator:* Arthur M. Jolly.   *Running time:* 108 minutes.   *MPAA Rating:* R.

CAST: Adrien Brody (Chris Calloway); Elise Neal (Jeanine); David Moscow (Reggae); Simon Baker-Denny (Kenny); Catherine Kellner (Nancy); Malcolm-Jamal Warner (Steven); Jesse L. Martin (Quincy); Vonte Sweet (Marcus); John Carroll Lynch (John English); Sybil Temchen (Lenore); Lauryn Hill (Leslie); Michael Stoyanov (Ethan); Elon Gold (Kurt); Lori Heuring (Donna); Avery Waddell (Al-Tarique); Tai Bennett and Matthew Black (Waiters); Jeff Bond (Drunken Frat Boy); Karey Butterworth (Girl at Bar); Robert Capelli, Jr. (Mike D'Amato); Bill Golodner (Party Goer); Lauren Nadler (Casting Director).

LOS ANGELES TIMES, 1/28/00, Calendar/p. 20, Kevin Thomas

"Restaurant" does something special and does it beautifully: It charts the course of a contemporary interracial romance within the larger context of an integrated social situation. It takes place in an upscale Hoboken eatery with a youthful staff for whom the Manhattan skyline seems so near yet so far—the perfect symbol of their dreams.

Director Eric Bross and writer Tom Cudworth drew from their own experiences in the making of this film, and it shows in its incisive, highly personal quality. Edgy, funny and emotionally wrenching, "Restaurant" glows with vital writing, acting and direction.

Adrien Brody, tall and thin with remarkably expressive eyes, has in rapid succession gone from one notable film to the next, most recently "Liberty Heights" (which ironically also featured a blossoming interracial relationship). In "Restaurant" he arguably has his most challenging and substantial role to date as Chris, the head bartender. Chris is also a playwright, one who can take scarce pleasure in the production of his highly autobiographical play, for his stage alter ego is played by a glib, handsome co-worker, Kenny (Simon Baker-Denny).

Kenny has had a fling with Chris' now ex-lover Leslie (Grammy Award-winning singer Lauryn Hill) that has left Chris in a state of emotional anguish. Yet along comes a new waitress—and talented aspiring singer—Jeanine (Elise Neal), who is swiftly drawn to Chris. Too swiftly—for Jeanine finds herself falling in love with Chris, even though he has not freed himself from his feelings for Leslie. As it happens, both Jeanine and Leslie are beautiful, charismatic African American women.

By and large the restaurant staffers are as close as they are diverse, but tensions emerge beneath surface harmony. Chris doesn't hesitate to put his job on the line to insist that the hard-working Steven (Malcolm-Jamal Warner), an African American, get a shot at bartending when the restaurant's proprietor (John Carroll Lynch) threatens to pass him over in favor of a less dedicated, young white guy. A tragic incident triggers a latent racism within Chris, who is the child of a blatantly racist father.

Brody takes us through all of Chris' painful self-discovery in an illuminating manner, and Neal is easily his equal as Jeanine, who is as vulnerable as she is lovely. Also key in a splendid cast is David Moscow as Brody's reckless pal Reggae, Catherine Kellner as a waitress who drinks too much and, unlike most of the others, has no drive. And, in a comparatively small yet pivotal role, hip-hop superstar Hill makes Leslie an unexpectedly sympathetic character.

"Restaurant" surely can't have cost much—in film relative terms—but it looks great and flows well. "Restaurant" marks the second collaboration for Bross and Cudworth, who made their feature debut with "Ten Benny" in 1998. It augurs well for them, their cast and their crew.

NEW YORK POST, 1/28/00, p. 50, Lou Lumenick

"Restaurant" is the year's first low-budget sleeper, a wonderfully acted ensemble piece set in a busy Hoboken eatery.

Adrien Brody, who's establishing himself as the most interesting young actor around (starring in both high-profile films like "Summer of Sam" and "Liberty Heights" as well as indie projects like "Oxygen") gives another affecting, layered performance as Chris, a troubled bartender.

Chris has just finished writing a play that's being produced by a local theater, but he sleeps through auditions because of a drinking problem. Much to his chagrin, the autobiographical lead part goes to Kenny (Simon Baker-Denny), an insufferable waiter-cum-actor at the restaurant.

Meanwhile, Chris, who's white and hasn't gotten over his black ex-girlfriend, drifts into a relationship with another black woman, Jeanine (Elise Neal), a beautiful young co-worker.

Tom Cudworth's slightly melodramatic screenplay contains several subplots, the most interesting of which incisively explores the racial politics of the restaurant, where black staff members tend to be relegated to behind-the-scenes, lower-paying jobs.

Director Eric Bross, who collaborated with Cudworth (they were waiters together in New Jersey) on the little-seen indie mob comedy "Ten Benny," stages even stock dramatic situations with an assurance that makes them seem fresh.

Bross draws consistently fine performances from his fresh young cast, which includes Malcolm-Jamal Warner (of "Cosby" fame) as a busboy who aspires to a bartending job and David Moscow as a wisecracking line cook.

Hip-hop diva Lauryn Hill appears briefly but effectively as Chris' ex-girlfriend. Perhaps because of her presence, "Restaurant," which was shot several years ago, is playing at uptown action-movie houses.

A tasty treat, "Restaurant" is better than 95 percent of the indie product being shown downtown these days.

VILLAGE VOICE, 2/1/00, p. 118, Amy Taubin

Restaurant has been sitting on the shelf for a few years. It was shot before Lauryn Hill, who plays a small but pivotal role, became Lauryn Hill. You'd think that Hill's name in the credits of an indie film that's a bit more serious than most of the stuff out there would have hooked at least some small distributor, but nothing doing. Not to mention that the film stars Adrien Brody as the anguished, alcoholic bartender of a Hoboken hot spot.

Set in a familiar world of actors, singers, and writers temping in restaurants until they get their big break, *Restaurant* takes on the difficult subject of race as it plays out in the daily life of twentysomethings. Chris (Brody), an aspiring playwright, is pining over Leslie (Hill), his gorgeous ex-girlfriend, while putting moves on a new waitress (Elise Neal). Chris's obsession with black women adds a sexual charge to a workplace where African Americans have been limited to the low-paying jobs. During the course of the film, the restaurant hires its first African American bartender.

Chris, who grew up in a racially mixed, low-income Newark neighborhood (this is an insider's New Jersey film), knows that his guilt over his father's bigotry has something to do with his choice of girlfriends, but he's too angry and neurotic to understand what's going on inside him. The film tries to explore the complexity of white racism, but it falls into a whites über alles trap when Chris's ex returns to tell him that she'll never love her black fiancé as much as she loves him. Why not one but two stunning black women should fall for this angry young white man is a mystery that the film fails to engage. Despite this contradiction, *Restaurant* raises provocative issues, particularly for white audiences, and it's sad that it has the gatekeepers for that audience—festival programmers and indie distributors—running scared.

Director Eric Bross has a smooth nonstyle that serves him well until the screenplay turns melodramatic at the end. Attempting to ratchet up tension, Bross relies on forced crosscutting and stagey clichés. The ensemble cast is pleasant enough, and Brody performs with his usual intensity, even when Bross and screenwriter Tom Cudworth lose track of the fact that this is a film about relationships, and not one white boy's show.

Also reviewed in:
CHICAGO TRIBUNE, 3/31/00, Friday/p. K, John Petrakis
NEW YORK TIMES, 1/28/00, p. E27, A. O. Scott
VARIETY, 4/27-5/3/98, p. 60, Todd McCarthy

RETURN TO ME

A Metro-Goldwyn-Mayer Pictures release of a JLT production. *Executive Producer:* C. O. Erickson and Melanie Greene. *Producer:* Jennie Lew Tugend. *Director:* Bonnie Hunt. *Screenplay:* Bonnie Hunt and Don Lake. *Story:* Bonnie Hunt, Don Lake, Andrew Stern, and Samantha Goodman. *Director of Photography:* Laszlo Kovacs. *Editor:* Garth Craven. *Music:* Nicholas Pike. *Music Editor:* Michael Jay. *Sound:* Scott D. Smith and (music) Dan Wallin. *Sound Editor:* Robert Grieve. *Casting:* Mali Finn. *Production Designer:* Brent Thomas. *Art Director:* Dave Krummel. *Set Designer:* Craig Jackson. *Set Decorator:* Daniel Clancy. *Special Effects:* Rodman Kiser. *Costumes:* Lis Bothwell. *Make-up:* Ron Berkeley. *Stunt Coordinator:* Rick LeFevour. *Running time:* 116 minutes. *MPAA Rating:* PG.

CAST: David Duchovny (Bob Rueland);   Minnie Driver (Grace Briggs);   Carroll O'Connor (Marty O'Reilly);   Robert Loggia (Angelo Pardipillo);   Bonnie Hunt (Megan Dayton);   David Alan Grier (Charlie Johnson);   Joely Richardson (Elizabeth Rueland);   Eddie Jones (Emmett McFadden);   James Belushi (Joe Dayton);   Marianne Muellerleile (Sophie);   William Bronder (Wally Jatczak);   Brian Howe (Mike);   Chris Barnes (Jeff);   Adam Tanguay (Adam Dayton);   Karson Pound (Karson Dayton);   Tyler Spitzer (Tyler Dayton);   Laura Larsen (Laura Dayton);   Austin Samuel Hibbs (Austin Dayton);   Dick Cusack (Mr. Bennington);   Joey Gian (Singer);   Tom Virtue (Doctor Senderak);   Holly Biniak (Big Hair);   Tamara Tungate (Celia);   Kevin Hunt (ER Doctor);   Tom Senderak and Jennie Lew Tugend (Paramedics);   David Pasquesi (Tony);   Claire Lake (ER Nurse);   Carol Hunt (Nurse Alice);   Patrick Hunt (Danny);   Lindsay Allen (Delivery Girl);   Don Lake (Transplant Man);   Holly Wortell (Marsha);   Becky Veduccio (Shari);   Peter B. Spector (Valet Guy);   Darryl Warren (Father Rudy);   Alice Hunt (Nancy);   Franklin E. Jones (Chester);   Tom Hunt (Tom);   Jack Cooper (Ballroom Bartender);   Tim O'Malley (Patrick);   LaTaunya Bounds (Zebra Girl);   Harry Teinowitz (Ice Cream Clerk);   Walt Jacobs (MC);   Romano Ghini (Cappuccino Man);   Gabriella Arena, Paola Sebastiani, and Lilliana Vitale (Nuns).

LOS ANGELES TIMES, 4/7/00, Calendar/p. 6, Kevin Thomas

"Return to Me" is the kind of big romantic movie Hollywood used to make with such seeming ease. This means you actually can care about the lovers, there's a fine sense of balance between humor and pathos in their story, and far from existing in a vacuum, they are surrounded by a substantial number of endearing types who recall the beloved character actors of the studio era.

This very contemporary charmer should further consolidate stardom for David Duchovny ("The X-Files") and Minnie Driver ("Good Will Hunting"). It also provides Carroll O'Connor with a worthy return to the big screen after a nearly 25-year absence, and marks a triple triumph for Bonnie Hunt, who not only plays Driver's sister but also directed the film, her first, and co-wrote it (with Don Lake).

Hunt, a versatile veteran of stage and TV as well as screen, grasps well two fundamentals that are essential to all else that she and her colleagues achieve: Luminous Hollywood escapist fare requires a seamless mix of fantasy and reality, and you've got to have a clever plot twist upon which your love story is to turn.

Actually, the gimmick is out-and-out shameless, but Hunt follows the Hitchcock dictum of letting the audience know what it is upfront, letting suspense build as to how her key people will be inevitably dealing with it. "Return to Me" goes to show that the most outrageous of coincidences can be milked for all they're worth if you know—and believe in—what you're doing and where you're going.

Duchovny's Bob Rueland is a highly successful young Chicago builder, a designer-contractor whose happiness is shattered when his beloved wife, the radiant Elizabeth (Joely Richardson), is killed in a car crash. A year after her death, Bob meets Driver's Grace Briggs, when she waits on him, while on a disastrous blind date.

An aspiring painter, Grace works at her grandfather's cheery neighborhood cafe, O'Reilly's Italian Restaurant, as its name implies, an Irish Italian eatery owned by her grandfather Marty (O'Connor) and his partner (and chef) Angelo, (Robert Loggia), his late wife's brother. Grace is beautiful, but her poise as a waitress belies a shyness and inexperience. She's only recently had a heart transplant; her life had been restricted by heart disease since the age of 14. A deeply religious widower, Marty tends to be overly protective of the granddaughter he nearly lost at an early age, as he had her mother.

Bob and Grace click swiftly and deeply, but they proceed with understandable caution, for grief is just beginning to lift for Bob while the possibility of love and romance are clearly new for Grace. In so many modern screen romances the lovers seem not only to live in a world of their own but also are concerned exclusively with their emotions. Bob and Grace, in refreshing contrast, get to know each other in a much larger, well-populated context.

Hunt gets lots of warmth and humor from O'Connor (who's very Pat O'Brien in the best sense) and Loggia and their cronies, played deliciously by Eddie Jones and William Bronder, and from Marianne Muellerleile as the restaurant's good sport longtime waitress, the kind you always wish were waiting on you.

Grace in turn has a good idea of what wedded bliss can be like, as her sister Megan (Hunt) and brother-in-law Joe (James Belushi, never better), a local cop, deal with a brood of lively kids with affectionate good humor, not letting them get too much in the way of their abiding love for each other. After a solitary year of bereavement that his pal Charlie (David Alan Grier) tries hard to free him from, Bob finds himself responding to the kind embrace of Grace's extended family and friends.

Hunt and her sterling cast get us so wrapped up in these lovely, loving people that she's well-prepared for the moment of truth that we know is coming. When it occurs she directs it with credibility, sensitivity and an impeccable sense of timing and structure so that she can send us home not merely happy but with a sense of happiness earned.

"Return to Me" has an appropriately burnished glow, thanks to cinematographer Laszlo Kovacs. Its production design is elegant without being overdone and its score is rightly romantic without being treacly. Duchovny and Driver have distinctive good looks and they both combine attractiveness with talent and intelligence. Best of all, they possess that essential quality all screen lovers must have: terrific chemistry.

NEW YORK POST, 4/7/00, p. 49, Lou Lumenick

"Return to Me" is the cinematic equivalent of meat loaf—comfort food that's reassuring in its utter lack of sophistication and surprises.

Well, it does have one surprise—the novelty of David Duchovny as a romantic lead, apparently trying for a part as far as he could find from his FBI agent on "The X-Files."

Though he's not bad, in a sub-Richard Gere sort of way, he shouldn't give up his day job just yet.

Minnie Driver is much more appealing as the object of his desire, a reclusive young waitress who's just received a heart transplant—from Duchovny's wife (Joely Richardson), who died in an off-screen automobile accident.

Talk about meeting cute—though it will be more than an hour before Driver and architect Duchovny discover their shared cardiovascular secret, much less their feelings for each other.

This is the sort of movie where you know what's going to happen well before it does—and believe me, debuting director Bonnie Hunt (who also collaborated on the corny screenplay and plays Driver's sister) takes her sweet time getting there.

On the other hand, Hunt has a genuine affection for the movie's Chicago locations, its working-class milieu and the walking clichés who populate it—including such expert crowd-pleasers as Carroll O'Connor (in his first movie since the Archie Bunker days), and Robert Loggia as Driver's grandpa and uncle, respectively, who run a too-cute-for-words Italian-Irish tavern.

With nothing stronger than one use of the "s" word and a discreet kiss, this PG-rated trifle is the perfect movie to take your parents to see without fear of embarrassment.

In fact, I took my 83-year-old mom and her older sister and brother-in-law to a paid sneak preview of "Return to Me" to celebrate his 88th birthday.

The eightysomethings agreed it was a three-star movie—good, but no "Moonstruck," which the new picture vaguely tries to emulate with its Dean Martin-heavy soundtrack.

NEWSDAY, 4/7/00, Part II/p. B2, John Anderson

Making her directing debut with the romantic comedy "Return to Me" is Bonnie Hunt, she of the gin-dry delivery and wry intelligence, one of the funniest actresses in movies, the best female second banana since Joan Blondell. So you wish that amid all its old-fashioned goodness and bare-knuckle fantasy, her movie contained a little more Hunt and a little less formula.

But what's really missing are three little words.

In Chicago, Bob and Elizabeth Rueland (David Duchovny and Joely Richardson) are living a rather idyllic urban existence. Nice house, nice dog (great dog), solid romance, solid jobs: He's the designer of big-shouldered buildings, she's a primatologist raising money for an expansion of the zoo's gorilla facility. Grace Briggs? Played by Minnie Driver, she's a transplant candidate waiting for a heart, which is supplied when a car crash kills Elizabeth on the very night of her major fund raiser.

You see where this is going, I trust (although you'd never get an inkling of the plot from the TV ads, which suggests some coronary trepidation on the part of MGM). Boy meets girl, boy likes girl, boy and girl have crisis, boy and girl go to Italy. And yet, through the process of getting Bob introduced to Grace—and their falling in love, and their coming to grips with the transplant issue—Hunt makes a movie that's as simultaneously frank and sentimental as Dean Martin (the main attraction on a soundtrack that includes Frank Sinatra and the Jackie Gleason orchestra).

On one hand, Carroll O'Connor plays Grace's grandfather and is the Irish-est Irishman since Barry Fitzgerald. Robert Loggia is her barely less stereotypical uncle—together, they run O'Reilly's Italian restaurant, which is the kind of low-flying joke that infiltrates the movie.

On the other hand, Bob and Grace make their way through the formalities of budding romance without the usual gymnastics—"Would you go out with me?" "Yes. "Can I hold your hand?" "Yes." It's very refreshing. While the comic efforts Grace makes to hide her surgery scar seem to go on ad infinitum, in a way she's a concession to modern times—only a life-threatening heart condition contracted at the age of 14 could account for a virgin her age.

Hunt appears, as Grace's best friend, Megan, and she and Jim Belushi, as Megan's husband, have some really funny bits as the parents of what seems like 25 kids. And those three little words? Well, considering that Bob and Grace meet completely by accident, fall in love and she turns out to have his wife's heart, you'd think someone would have said, "What a coincidence!" But no. Amid the often pleasant dreamworld of "Return to Me," these kinds of things apparently happen all the time.

SIGHT AND SOUND, 7/00, p. 52, Kay Dickinson

Chicago, two years ago. Driving home from a charity dinner with husband Bob, Elizabeth Rueland is killed in a car crash. Her heart is transplanted into a woman called Grace. A year later, Bob is reluctantly persuaded by his friend Charlie to go on a double date. They dine at O'Reilly's, an Irish-Italian restaurant co-owned by Grace's grandfather. Bob quickly realises that he dislikes his date Marsha and has more rapport with their waitress, Grace. He leaves early, forgetting to take his mobile phone. When he returns to pick it up, he asks Grace on a date.

The romance blossoms. Grace is nervous about consummating their relationship because she is ashamed of her surgical scars. On the night she has chosen to explain her medical history to Bob, she stumbles across a letter she anonymously sent him via an agency to thank him for his wife's organ donation. She leaves without explanation. The following day, Grace tells him she has Elizabeth's heart. He leaves her and she flies to Italy for a painting holiday. Before long, he makes the journey to Europe and sucessfully wins her back.

With its big-band theme song (the same as the film's title), the sudden death of Bob's beloved wife, an operation in which her heart is transplanted into the sickly Grace, and its grief-stricken leading man, you don't need to be an aficionado of romantic comedies to recognise the generic world to which *Return to Me* belongs. Having established her debt to such films as *Sleepless in Seattle* and *Moonstruck* in the first 15 minutes, debut director Bonnie Hunt doesn't offer any great surprises—the film builds to a happy-ever-after finale which inevitably requires Grace's newly acquired palpitating muscle to do a whole lot more than pump blood from A to B. But it does offer a share of incidental pleasures along the way.

As with so many romantic comedies, it's the script (co-written by Hunt and Don Lake) which really carries the film, dexterously balanced between the cloying sentiment of, say, *Stepmom* —which similarly dealt with grief and romance in US suburbia—and the all-too-easy cynicism of such recent films as *Happiness* and *Your Friends & Neighbors*. That said, there are some rather syrupy slow-motion flashbacks to Elizabeth, whose death prompts the family dog to pine for her by the door in the hope that she'll return. The film's central hangout, the Irish-Italian restaurant O'Reilly's, also houses a cringe-worthy roster of characters from both *The Quiet Man* school of Irishness and television pizza commercials. Thankfully Grace (played by Minnie Driver) is on hand to sprinkle a fair few spicy wisecracks around this otherwise characterless milieu. But the film's liveliest moments are more reliably provided by Grace's tender-yet-cynical friends Joe (Chicago personified, Jim Belushi), Megan (Grace's confidante, played by Hunt herself) and their Catholic families whom they both vainly try to protect from their cursing and canoodling.

Even the undercharged charisma of David Duchovny as Bob is well cushioned by the film's refreshingly zesty script. "It's like a garden!" he gasps with impressive observational skill as he takes stock of Grace's garden, before collapsing into everyone's worst nightmare of flirting ineptitude. He similarly bolts the door on any pity we might feel for him when Grace confronts him with the truth about her surgery: "Phew, I thought you were going to tell me you used to be a man!" he exclaims with relief. Duchovny doesn't quite get away with more demanding emotions such as grief or frustrated wrath, but thanks to the kindly script and some deft, sensitive direction these shortcomings manage to pass themselves off as assets. As Richard Gere admirably demonstrated in *Pretty Woman,* a clever romantic comedy can turn stiffness (and a pair of endearingly squinty eyes) to its advantage. In *Return to Me,* Duchovny's actorly range—a weakness in most other films—exudes coy slightness rather than limitation. Whether he's playing awkward or is simply being awkward hardly matters here.

VILLAGE VOICE, 4/10/00, p. 158, Jessica Winter

First-time director Bonnie Hunt pays slavish adherence to the Nora Ephron rules of assembly for the prefab rom-com: emotion-cueing whitebread soundtrack, ostentatious attention to given urban landscape—here it's Chicago—that renders a bland, mall-bought local flavor, and sentimental longing for the "chaste" relationship comedies of the '30s and '40s, necessitating some prudish gimmick designed to leave our predestined lovers laissez-faire. In *Return to Me,* it's Minnie Driver's self-consciousness about her heart-transplant scar that keeps widower architect David Duchovny out of her blouse. He stays out long enough, in fact, to discover that Minnie received his dead wife's heart (the creepiest high-concept date-movie twist since, um, *Kissed*). Missing from the Ephron stew, however, is the usual smarmy bourg air of entitlement, since Hunt makes gimpy efforts at some working-class heroism (Driver works with her extended brood at a restaurant dive; Duchovny might carry a cell phone, but he drives a truck and wears a hard hat to work), leaving us with less to hate but not more to like.

Also reviewed in:
CHICAGO TRIBUNE, 4/7/00, Friday/p. A, Mark Caro

NEW YORK TIMES, 4/7/00, p. E14, Elvis Mitchell
VARIETY, 3/27-4/2/00, p. 19, Emanuel Levy
WASHINGTON POST, 4/7/00, p. C5, Stephen Hunter

ROAD TO EL DORADO, THE

A DreamWorks Pictures release. *Executive Producer:* Jeffrey Katzenberg. *Producer:* Bonne Radford and Brooke Breton. *Director:* Eric Bergeron and Don Paul. *Screenplay:* Terry Rossio and Ted Elliott. *Editor:* John Carnochan and Dan Molina. *Music:* Elton John, (lyrics) Tim Rice, (score) Hans Zimmer and John Powell. *Music Editor:* Adam Smalley. *Sound:* Greg King and (music) Alan Meyerson. *Sound Editor:* Yann Delpuech. *Animators:* William Salazar (Tulio); Serguei Kouchnerov and Bob Scott (Miguel); Rodolphe Guenoden (Chel); Kathy Zielinski (Tzekel-Kan); Frans Vischer (Chief Tannabok); Kristof Serrand (Altivo/Cortes); Sylvain Deboissy (Jaguar); Nicholas Marlet (Armadillo); Patrick Mate (Sailors/Ballplayers); Erik Schmidt (Miscellaneous Characters). *Running time:* 89 minutes. *MPAA Rating:* PG.

VOICES: Kevin Kline (Tulio)); Kenneth Branagh (Miguel); Rosie Perez (Chel); Armand Assante (Tzekel-Kan); Edward James Olmos (Chief Tannabok); Jim Cummings (Cortes); Frank Welker (Altivo); Tobin Bell (Zaragoza); Duncan Marjoribanks (Acolyte); Elijah Chiang and Cyrus Shaki-Khan (Kids); Elton John (Narrator).

LOS ANGELES TIMES, 3/31/00, Calendar/p. 1, Kevin Thomas

"The Road to El Dorado" not only sounds like an old Bob Hope-Bing Crosby "Road" movie, it plays like one—never mind that it is a splashy work of up-to-the-minute animation. It's fitted out with Elton John-Tim Rice songs that are entirely pleasant and appropriate to the story without being particularly memorable—which pretty much sums up this lavish DreamWorks presentation. It's reasonably diverting, but don't count on it lingering in your memory.

When we first meet blond Miguel (Kenneth Branagh) and black-haired Tulio (Kevin Kline), you think Siegfried and Roy, and in the way they've been drawn they even somewhat resemble the Vegas magicians. But we quickly discover they're a pair of klutzes looking to get rich quick who stow away on Cortes' ship bound for the New World. Many mishaps later they, in fact, do stumble onto the legendary El Dorado, fabled for its vast treasure in gold.

Tulio and Miguel may not be the swiftest guys on the block, but they're smart enough to try to pass themselves off as gods to the natives with the help of a sexy local, Chel (Rosie Perez)—the Dorothy Lamour role—who has an eye on the main chance and agrees to help the guys grab the loot, provided they provide her safe passage to the outside world she craves to see—and a substantial portion of the gold.

Much of the film's shenanigans have to do with Tulio and Miguel passing muster with El Dorado's high priest Tzekel-Kan (Armand Assante, the film's richest "voice"), a great believer in ruling by fear instilled by human sacrifice rituals. In these politically correct, ethnically sensitive times, writers Ted Elliott and Terry Rossio present El Dorado's citizens, including their benevolent chief (Edward James Olmos) as kindly, highly civilized types in the thrall of the evil Tzekel-Kan, who possesses terrifying supernatural powers. To be sure, by the film's end the guys have acquired less materialistic values, and they've saved El Dorado from Cortes, who in an earlier era would have been treated on the screen as a conquering hero rather than a genocidal villain.

The look of the film, which was directed by Eric "Bibo" Bergeron and Don Paul in lively fashion, is lush and amusing. When it comes to evoking a pyramid-dominated city-state, the film summons images from those Mexican calendars featuring lurid depictions of the ancient gods and monuments. El Dorado recalls the Mayan Theatre more swiftly than Chichen Itza, for example, and that's fun. Indeed, in its colorful jungle atmosphere and pagan ritual stuff, "The Road to El Dorado" resembles nothing so much as a Maria Montez Technicolor epic like "White Savage."

You have to wonder, though, whether the filmmakers intended this outing to be as campy as it is.

In any event, youngsters should find plenty to divert them—one of the liveliest sequences involves a sport that seems a cross between soccer and basketball in which it's absolutely essential for some reason that Tulio and Miguel demonstrate their prowess to Tzekel-Kan. The film's use of bold colors is frequently stunning and, as amusing as the production design deliberately is, the imagery has considerable beauty and grace. If you decide to take a chance on "The Road to El Dorado," just don't go expecting to experience the impact of an animation classic. Yes, it has Elton John and Tim Rice songs, but "The Lion King" this ain't.

NEW YORK, 4/10/00, p. 88 Peter Rainer

DreamWorks' latest animated feature, *The Road to El Dorado*, has a few sequences with real swoop and glide; a few semi-forgettable Elton John-Tim Rice ditties; some unmistakably Rosie Perez-ish line readings by Rosie Perez, playing a native and enough shimmering gold surface make you believe the Yucatan is an adjunct of Trump Tower.

NEW YORK POST, 3/31/00, p. 55, Lou Lumenick

"The Road to El Dorado" is lined with visual and vocal treats—but ends up taking enough detours to keep DreamWorks' latest animated epic from striking cinematic gold.

A knowingly hip update of the old Bob Hope-Bing Crosby "road" movies of the 1940s, it scores with the positively inspired teaming of Kevin Kline and Kenneth Branagh as the voice talents behind a pair of none-too-bright con men in 17th-century Spain.

When they win a map to the legendary city of El Dorado in a crooked dice game, ifs off to old Mexico, where the natives mistake them for gods—and start showering them with gold.

To help with the swindle, the duo enlists the help of the sexy and much smarter Chel (think Dorothy Lamour with Jennifer Lopez's hips and Rosie Perez's voice), who ingeniously rescues them from scrapes with the high priest (Armand Assante), his rival the native chief (Edward James Olmos) and Cortez the conquistador (Jim Cummings).

The initially witty script (credited to Ted Elliott and Terry Rossio of "Aladdin") flattens out disappointingly into what seems largely an excuse for admittedly spectacular special effects, including a Godzilla-like monster whose rampage may prove frightening for very young viewers.

Kids will be oblivious to the movie's rather extensive gay subtext, which begins with a brief and tasteful skinny-dipping scene with the self-described "partners"—and culminates in a decidedly ambiguous snit on the part of Branagh's somewhat swishy Miguel when Kline's Tulio decides to forsake El Dorado to return to Spain with Chel.

The Elton John-Tim Rice ballad about their "friendship" can also be read more than one way, though it's as elevator-ready a knockoff of their "Lion King" tunes as most of the other numbers warbled by John.

The movie's musical high point is easily the show-stopper by Kline and Branagh ("Who am I to bridle/If I'm forced to be an idol?"), who really should have been given more numbers together.

The animation itself (Eric Bergeron and Don Paul co-directed) is eye-popping and very richly detailed, with especially amazing water sequences.

"The Road to El Dorado" is well worth traveling with the kids, though most adults will find it a somewhat less rewarding trip than DreamWorks' last, the "The Prince of Egypt."

NEWSDAY, 3/31/00, Part II/p. B3, John Anderson

A Hope-Crosby road movie with better-looking actors, "The Road to El Dorado" is another no-holds-barred bid by DreamWorks to be the animation studio. With songs by the multimillion-dollar men—Tim Rice and Elton John, of "The Lion King" and "Aida"—and an all-star lineup of vocal talent topped by Kevin Kline and Kenneth Branagh, "El Dorado" could easily have been subtitled "The Continuing Revenge of Katzenberg."

That would be Jeffrey Katzenberg, who with Steven Spielberg and David Geffen owns DreamWorks SKG and was the executive producer of the studio's previous blockbuster, "The Prince of Egypt." If anyone's looking for gold in "El Dorado," I think they're going to find it.

The film, about two con men named Tulio (Kline) and Miguel (Branagh) who escape the explorer Cortes and stumble into the lost city and its indigenous people, "El Dorado" owes more to Disney—especially latter-day Disney—than just its songwriters and former honcho Katzenberg. The sense of humor, the landscapes, the pratfalls, all are redolent of "Tarzan," and even in a way, the "Toy Story" films. It's also indebted to every buddy movie ever made, to say nothing of Kipling's "The Man Who Would Be King"—Tulio and Miguel are passed off as gods by the High Priest Tzekel-Kan (Armand Assante) in a bid to seize power from the Chief (Edward James Olmos). How they maintain the ruse provides the tension and most of the laughs.

Starring in the Dorothy Lamour role, if not the sarong, is Rosie Perez as Chel, an oversexed-looking little animatrix who matches Tulio and Miguel scam for scam as the clock winds down on their elaborate deceit. Chel may be why the movie is rated PG instead of G.

Despite all the appropriations, "El Dorado" is a cut above most action-adventure animated movies because of the integration of Kline and Branagh's comedic talents with their cartoon selves. Neither Tulio nor Miguel look that much like the real actors, but their personalities are infused with them, Kline-ized and Branagh-fied. If, like this reviewer, you wish both men (particularly Kline) would make more movies, this is the next best thing. And if, like this reviewer, the charm of Rice and John's music thoroughly eludes you, the best that can be said is that the songs don't impose themselves too rigorously.

SIGHT AND SOUND, 9/00, p. 50, Leslie Felperin

1519, Spain. Petty criminals Tulio and Miguel obtain a map leading to El Dorado, the fabled city of gold in the Americas. They accidentally stow away on a ship bound for Mexico, commanded by the conquistador Cortes. Through a series of misadventures they end up washing ashore on a boat with a horse named Altivo. Encountering some Native Americans from El Dorado who mistake them for gods, Tulio and Miguel are taken to the city and worshipped. They dissuade their hosts, led by Chief Tannabok, from offering a human sacrifice in their honour, angering high priest Tzekel-Kan. Tulio and Miguel demand gold instead, and plan to leave. Native girl Chel rumbles their deceit and insists on going with them.

Tulio falls in love with Chel, breaking an agreement he made with Miguel not to get romantically involved with any of the natives. Miguel is enraptured by the city's friendly occupants. Having deduced the Spanish opportunists are mortal when he sees Miguel bleeding from a cut, Tzekel-Kan summons a monster from the spirit world to attack Chel and Miguel. The Spaniards defeat this creature; banished from the city, Tzekel-Kan chances on Cortes and his men, and agrees to guide them to El Dorado. As Tulio and Chel leave the city on a ship filled with gold, the citizens attempt to seal up the access route to the outside world, thereby protecting their city from Cortes. Miguel—who planned on staying in El Dorado—joins Tulio and Chel on board and helps block the entrance to the city. They escape unharmed.

While all movies are engaged, consciously or not, in a dialogue with films from the past, some are more talkative than others. The latest animated feature from DreamWorks SKG, *The Road to El Dorado,* is positively garrulous, invoking the spirits of its ancestors with near superstitious fervour. For starters, the business of having the invaders mistaken for gods, then seduced by the land they came to exploit is a nod to *The Man Who Would Be King,* John Huston's 1975 adaptation of Rudyard Kipling's story, featuring Sean Connery and Michael Caine. *El Dorado* even steals the plot point of a bleeding forehead betraying the gods' mortality and a jump from a bridge which echoes Connery's swan dive in Huston's film.

More significantly, its title is a self-conscious wink in the direction of the Bob Hope-Bing Crosby *Road to...* franchise in which the bantering duo found themselves in antic scrapes with quaint cultural stereotypes from central casting. Thus, *The Road to El Dorado* features two amiable rogues, Tulio and Miguel (voiced by Kevin Kline and Kenneth Branagh respectively), whose picaresque pursuit of riches takes them to exotic Latin America, a familiar Hope-Crosby haunt, especially during World War II when Hollywood was encouraged by the US government to forge stronger cultural links with the neighbouring continent. The film industry needs no such encouragement today when there's a vast international market to be tapped.

But the most important template for this movie is the monstrously successful films *El Dorado*'s executive producer Jeffrey Katzenberg used to make at Disney such as *The Lion King*. Having performed flatly at the box office with their two earlier cartoon efforts, *Antz* and *The Prince of Egypt*, each of which deviated slightly from the Disney formula, DreamWorks played it by the rules this time: from the swooping ballads, penned by Tim Rice and Elton John (who collaborated on *The Lion King*), to the trippy montage sequence showing the leads' infatuation with their new-found kingdom. As with the films Katzenberg oversaw at Disney, *The Road to El Dorado* even features its share of cute animals, including a friendly horse and helpful armadillo. In truth, *El Dorado* is as good as most recent post-Katzenberg Disney films, and certainly with its stylised characterisation and bursts of witty dialogue—a great deal better than the Mouse's turgid mega-budget epic *Dinosaur*. Unfortunately for DreamWorks, *El Dorado* flopped in the US. One can't help seeing a certain similarity between Katzenberg and the scheming high priest at the end of the film: frustrated in his efforts to wrest back the kingdom, he gnashes his teeth for losing paradise.

Also reviewed in:
CHICAGO TRIBUNE, 3/31/00, Friday/p. A, Michael Wilmington
NATION, 4/24/00, p. 42, Stuart Klawans
NEW YORK TIMES, 3/31/00, p. E10, Stephen Holden
VARIETY, 4/3-9/00, p. 35, Todd McCarthy
WASHINGTON POST, 3/31/00, p. C1, Stephen Hunter
WASHINGTON POST, 3/31/00, Weekend/p. 43, Desson Howe

ROAD TRIP

A DreamWorks Pictures and The Montecito Picture Company release of an Ivan Reitman production. *Executive Producer:* Ivan Reitman and Tom Pollock. *Producer:* Daniel Goldberg and Joe Medjuck. *Director:* Todd Phillips. *Screenplay:* Todd Phillips and Scot Armstrong. *Director of Photography:* Mark Irwin. *Editor:* Peter Teschner and Sheldon Kahn. *Music:* Mike Simpson. *Music Editor:* Roy Prendergast. *Sound:* Jonathan "Earl" Stein. *Sound Editor:* Cameron Frankley. *Casting:* Nancy Nayor and Ann Goulder. *Production Designer:* Clark Hunter. *Art Director:* Max Biscoe. *Set Decorator:* Traci Kirshbaum. *Set Dresser:* Alice Nisbet. *Special Effects:* Burt Dalton. *Costumes:* Peggy Stamper. *Make-up:* Donna Premick. *Stunt Coordinator:* Gregg Brazzel. *Running time:* 91 minutes. *MPAA Rating:* R.

CAST: Breckin Meyer (Josh); Seann William Scott (E.L.); Amy Smart (Beth); Paulo Costanzo (Rubin); D J Qualls (Kyle); Rachel Blanchard (Tiffany); Anthony Rapp (Jacob); Fred Ward (Earl Edwards); Tom Green (Barry); Andy Dick (Motel Clerk); Ethan Suplee (Ed); Horatio Sanz (French Toast Guy); Rhoda Griffis (Tour Group Mom); Marla Sucharetza (Sperm Bank Nurse); Ellen Albertini Dow (Barry's Grandma); Edmund Lyndeck (Barry's Grandpa); Jessica Cauffiel (The Wrong Tiffany); Kohl Sudduth (Mark); Wendell B. Harris, Jr. (Professor Anderson); Rini Bell (Carla); Jaclyn DeSantis (Heather); Aliya Campbell (Wendy); Kim Fox (Target Clerk); Patricia Gaul (Cookie Edwards); Richie Dye (Dutty); Mary Lynn Rajskub (Blind Brenda); Tim Ware (Officer Bortz); Julia Wright (Joyce); Paula Claire Jones (Stephanie); Richard Peterson (Michael); Phe Caplan (Boston Coed); Avery Kidd Waddell (Jeff); Omar J. Dorsey (Lawrence); Preston Brant (Chris); Mia Amber Davis (Rhonda); Jimmy Kimmel (Corky the Dog); Bethany Sacks (Lisa); Charlie McWade (Brian); Todd Barry and Bill Rowell (Campus Security); Bill Gribble (Bomb Squad Detective); Matthew Paul Walsh (Crime Scene Photographer); John Ross Bowie (Waiter); Cristen Coppen (Kim); Cleo King (Woman on Bus); Bridgett Wise and Aerica D'Amaro (Barry's Girls); Todd Phillips (Foot Lover); Deborah Zoe (E. L.'s Girlfriend).

LOS ANGELES TIMES, 5/19/00, Calendar/p. 2, Kevin Thomas

[The following review by Kevin Thomas appeared in a slightly different form in **NEWSDAY, 5/19/00, Part II/p. B6.]**

"Road Trip" marks the major studio debut for director Todd Phillipps and his co-writer Scot Armstrong, and it's an auspicious, sometimes outrageous way to start. They've come up with an uproarious college comedy for DreamWorks, which is releasing it at the perfect moment, just as summer is nearing but before moviegoers are inundated with seasonal blockbusters.

Ivan Reitman produced "National Lampoon's Animal House" 20 years ago, and "Road Trip"—which Reitman co-executive produced with Tom Pollock—continues that rowdy tradition.

During a tour of Ithaca College in upstate New York, someone complains to the guide, Barry (Tom Green), that the school seems a dull place; Barry replies by telling the amazing adventure that becomes the story line of "Road Trip."

Barry, a sly cynic himself, has a pal Josh (Breckin Meyer) who has sworn to stay faithful to his girlfriend Tiffany (Rachel Blanchard). He's known her since they were kids, but she's gone off to college in faraway Austin, Texas.

The likable Josh is low-key in contrast to his aggressive friends and perhaps that's why he attracts Beth (Amy Smart), a blond beauty who's all but stalked by a nerdy, nasty philosophy department teaching assistant, Jacob (Anthony Rapp).

Josh succumbs to Beth's charms but only after he hasn't been able to get Tiffany to return his calls for several days; her evil roommate, instead of explaining that Beth's unexpectedly away for her grandfather's funeral, implies she's dumped him. Josh also consents to Beth's desire to videotape their encounter. One of Josh's well-meaning pals mails the tape to Tiffany, mistaking it for another, gushy romantic tape Josh intended to send to her. So naturally with the weekend coming up, Josh and his buddies head out on a "road trip" to intercept the tape at Tiffany's dorm before she can get her hands on it.

Phillips and Armstrong have thus cleverly set up a sturdy premise for all the shenanigans Josh and pals will encounter in their journey—an adventure that for all its hi-jinks is not without a maturing effect on everyone concerned. Along for the ride is E.L. ("American Pie's" Seann William Scott), a fearless and unabashed hedonist; Rubin (Paulo Costanzo), more brainy than zany; and Kyle (DJ Qualls), a skinny, unprepossessing outcast cajoled into joining in because he has a car (it works out nicely for him; he's exuberantly liberated along the way).

Meanwhile, Barry, who stays behind, has been charged with feeding white mice to Josh's pet python. This duty sets up an elaborate and ultimately gratifying gag, but the filmmakers dwell too long on Barry enjoying holding up a little mouse by its tail, squirming to get free; one relatively quick dangle of the mouse should be enough before Barry gets his comeuppance as a tormentor. It suffices to say that just about everything you might imagine happening to the travelers on the road does happen—and then some, much of it raunchy and inspired by films such as "American Pie," "There's Something About Mary" and even "Porky's."

"Road Trip" is consistently funny, but, to be sure, it's undergraduate-guy humor, hilariously gross and sometimes unfeeling. Yet on the whole it works because its over-the-top humor is supported by the filmmakers' ability to view life with a clear-eyed lack of sentimentality. They recognize that life is full of treacherous villains and poke tart fun while cheering on those daring to overcome every obstacle in pursuit of their goals.

Even so, some women will not see "Road Trip" as the thigh-slapper most men of all ages will. Smartly produced and consistently lively, the film shows its young actors to terrific advantage, and there is every reason to expect that "Road Trip" will jump-start their screen careers.

NEW YORK POST, 5/19/00, p. 45, Lou Lumenick

"Road Trip" is this season's slice of "American Pie"—a cheerfully crude, well-cast (and frequently uproarious) campus comedy in the tradition of "There's Something About Mary."

How crude? The movie's most memorable scene involves a sperm bank nurse (Marla Sucharetza) who deploys a gloved finger so expertly that a grateful male character remarks, "That was... awesome."

As anyone who's seen the coming attractions knows, there is also a classic gross-out gag that should send French toast sales plummeting—and a mouse-eating scene.

Not to mention the white protagonists' memorable visit to a black fraternity house—a neat twist on "Animal House," another very major source of inspiration for first-time feature film director Todd Phillips, who helmed the award-winning documentary "Frat House."

The action starts at Ithaca College, where Josh (Breckin Meyer of "54") assumes his longtime, long-distance girlfriend, Tiffany (Rachel Blanchard), is cheating on him. Josh allows himself to be seduced by Beth (Amy Smart), who records their lovemaking on video.

Josh learns he was very mistaken about Tiffany's fidelity—but not before his stoner roommate Rubin (Paulo Costanzo) has accidentally mailed the incriminating videotape to her at her college in Austin, Texas.

So Josh sets out for Austin to retrieve the tape, accompanied by Rubin, party-hearty E.L. (Seann William Scott of "American Pie") and the nerdy Kyle (big-eared D J Qualls, who's virtually a walking sight gag), who's along for the ride only because they've commandeered his car.

Along the way, the guys trash the car, steal a bus from a school for the blind, encounter a Viagra-crazed senior and Kyle's angry dad (Fred Ward)—and, oh, Kyle is relieved of his virginity by a large coed.

Back in Ithaca, the boys' buddy Barry (MTV's Tom Green) is so obsessed with feeding a live mouse to Josh's pet python that he sends poor Beth on a mistaken odyssey to Boston (instead of Austin), where she wreaks havoc on another Tiffany.

The borderline-obnoxious Green has a smaller role than the ads imply, and the movie is better for it.

Mostly he's deployed as the demented on-screen narrator—who at one point defends the frequent toplessness of the female cast members.

"Road Trip" takes a well-traveled highway, but the drivers know exactly what they're doing.

SIGHT AND SOUND, 11/00, p. 61, Keith Perry

New York State, the present. On a tour of Ithaca University, visitors are intrigued by a story mature student Barry recounts about a long-time couple Josh and Tiffany: Josh, studying at Ithaca, begins to doubt the fidelity of Tiffany, who studied at Austin; he has sex with classmate Beth and videotapes the event. The next day, it emerges the tape has been mistakenly mailed to Tiffany. With friends E. L. and Rubin, Josh heads for Austin in the car of acquaintance Kyle to intercept the package. The car is soon destroyed, but E.L. steals a school bus and the four continue their journey. Fearing a kidnap, Kyle's violent father, Earl, begins a search for his son.

Barry reveals to Beth that Josh has a girlfriend but then inadvertently directs her to Boston University. Josh retrieves the package in time, but Earl arrives soon after, and there is a ruckus. Tiffany later suggests to Josh that they should see other people. Beth calls for Josh, and while the two are talking, Tiffany views the tape, but Barry has recorded over the sex scene.

Back in the present, Barry reveals to the visitors that Beth and Josh are now together.

In *Road Trip*, a foursome of male students drive from upstate New York to Texas in order to retrieve a videotape revealing the infidelity of one of their number before it reaches his unsuspecting girlfriend. But it would be wrong to think that the film is a melding of road movie and fraternity comedy. This is merely a youth comedy on wheels; a series of set pieces in the tradition of *Animal House* (1978), intercut with a car or bus speeding up the freeway. It even ends right back where it started. Curiously, when applied to the current run of scatological comedies, the law of diminishing returns does not seem to be operating. Debut feature director Todd Phillips has a CV that includes *Hated*, a documentary about the late excrement-eating punk G. G. Allin, while the film's narrator, Barry, is played by Tom Green—a Canadian comedian known for publicising his testicular cancer on MTV. The presence of either should have pushed the envelope, but nothing here is as outrageous as *American Pie*, which in turn was less daring than *There's Something about Mary*. The only boundary all three of these ruinously moral films break is the delicate one of taste. Highlights here include Barry's grandfather complaining about the effects of Viagra after knocking over ornaments with his pajama-stretching erection, Green letting a real mouse crawl around inside his mouth and the smarmy E. L. chatting up a nurse at a sperm bank, who responds by milking his prostate. Much of this visual comedy is amusing, but the script (by Phillips and Scot Armstrong) should have been whipped into sharper peaks; too many scenes are capped with a bathetic "cool" or "awesome" instead of a punchline. Barry, meanwhile, emerges as someone ruled by heart not head—obsessed both with the true love between guilty fornicator Josh and girlfriend Tiffany, and the mortality of the mice he must feed to a friend's python. Green's delivery is flat, but his comedic tone tends towards wall-eyed surrealism, which douses some of the saturnalian mugging around him.

Of course, the teen comedy genre has its obligations, like any other. In *Road Trip,* the frat-house party, girls' shower scene, car trashing and soft-drug banter are all present and correct, as are the personality types: the fascistic dad, the jock, and the pasty masturbator. As is now standard, the central female characters are all sexually responsible and pro-active; depicting them as being driven by their hormones—like the boys—would be a genuine transgression. All of which reinforces the familiarity of the genre's elements and will no doubt contribute to the end of this current cycle.

VILLAGE VOICE, 5/30/00, p. 130, Jessica Winter

Unclean! Unclean! The existence of *Road Trip*—which belches up Grampa's-boner gags, wayward-prostate jokes, a hot-chick auction, unclothed nymphets straddling fully clad boys, and other college-trash staples with an alacrity that Adam Sandler would cherish—proves that Porky yet goes unrevenged. The titular death march across the U.S.A., commencing after Breckin Meyer accidentally mails his girlfriend a tape of himself humping Amy Smart, gets a lurching spring in its step whenever Tom Green shows up to, say, cram a live mouse in his mouth, or when DJ Qualls, making his movie debut, gets any decent screen time. Inhabiting a naive, dorky tagalong with uncommon gangly grace, Qualls—with his scarecrow frame, mud-flap ears, and goofy crooked smile—shouldn't miss Harmony Korine's next casting call.

Also reviewed in:
CHICAGO TRIBUNE, 5/19/00, Friday/p. C, Mark Caro
NEW YORK TIMES, 5/19/00, p. E23, Stephen Holden
VARIETY, 5/15-21/00, p. 26, Joe Leydon
WASHINGTON POST, 5/19/00, p. C1, Rita Kempley
WASHINGTON POST, 5/19/00, Weekend/p. 45, Desson Howe

ROMEO MUST DIE

A Warner Bros. release of a Silver Pictures production. *Executive Producer:* Dan Cracchiolo. *Producer:* Joel Silver and Jim Van Wyck. *Director:* Andrzej Bartkowiak. *Screenplay:* Eric Bernt and John Jarrell. *Story:* Mitchell Kapner. *Director of Photography:* Glen MacPherson. *Editor:* Derek G. Brechin. *Music:* Stanley Clarke. *Music Editor:* Jennifer Nash and Bradley A. Segal. *Sound:* Rob Young and (music) Dan Humann and Frank Wolfe. *Sound Editor:* Dane A. Davis. *Casting:* Lora Kennedy. *Production Designer:* Michael Bolton. *Art Director:* Jim Steuart. *Set Designer:* Jay Mitchell. *Set Decorator:* Rose Marie McSherry. *Special Effects:* Tony Lazarowich. *Costumes:* Sandra J. Blackie. *Make-up:* Taylor Roberts. *Stunt Coordinator:* Conrad E. Palmisano. *Running time:* 110 minutes. *MPAA Rating:* R.

CAST: Jet Li (Han Sing);   Aaliyah (Trish O'Day);   Isaiah Washington (Mac);   Russell Wong (Kai);   Henry O (Ch'u Sing);   D. B. Woodside (Colin O'Day);   Edoardo Ballerini (Vincent Roth);   Jon Kit Lee (Po Sing);   Anthony Anderson (Maurice);   DMX (Silk);   Delroy Lindo (Isaak O'Day);   Matthew Harrison (Dave);   Terry Chen (Kung);   Derek Lowe (Chinese Messenger);   Ronin Wong (New Prisoner);   Byron Lawson (Head Guard);   Kendall Saunders (Colin's Girlfriend);   Benz Antoine (Crabman);   Keith Dallas (Bouncer);   Taayla Markell (Po's Girlfriend);   Chang Tseng (Victor Ho);   Tong Lung, Richard Yee, and Colin Foo (Overlords); Lance Gibson (Doorman);   Grace Park and Jennifer Wong (Asian Dancers);   Manoj Sood (Cab Driver);   Fatima Robinson (Lori);   Gaston Howard and Clay Donahue Fontenot (Maurice's

Crew);   Ryan Jefferson Lowe (Young Po);   Jonross Fong (Young Han);   Alonso Oyarzun (Alonso);   Samuel Scantlebury (Paperboy);   François Yip (Motorcycle Fighter);   Alvin Sanders (Calvin);   William S. Taylor (Harold);   Morgan Reynolds (Morgan);   David Kopp (Delivery Man);   Aaron Joseph (Kid in Boutique);   William MacDonald (Officer);   Oliver Svensson-Tan (Gate Guard);   Candice McClure (Store Clerk);   W.J. Waters (Hardware Store Clerk);   Cesar Abraham (Park Bench Kid);   Jerry Grant (Bartender);   Tonjha Richardson (Store Clerk);   Chic Gibson (Taxi Driver);   Jody Vance (Sportscaster);   Perry Solkowski (Anchor);   Ann Gwathmey (Shopper).

LOS ANGELES TIMES, 3/22/00, Calendar/p. 5, Kevin Thomas

"Romeo Must Die" may take its inspiration from Shakespeare, but in a Jet Li martial-arts action thriller it's more likely that Li, as the hero, will be the last man standing. So don't take that title too seriously, though certainly there are plenty of characters who are most eager to see Li removed from the scene, permanently.

The scene happens to be the Oakland waterfront, four choice acres controlled by Delroy Lindo's Isaak O'Day and Henry O's Ch'u Sing. The African American and the Hong Kong emigre are intense rivals but have much in common, as both are rich businessmen whose fortunes have been built ruthlessly on criminal activities.

O'Day, hungering to go legit, wants to grab all that land, a site for a proposed stadium demanded by an NFL team, but needs Ch'u to help him deliver it. The truce between the underworld titans, both living in elegant suburban mansions, is so tense that when Ch'u's younger, spoiled-playboy son defies orders to leave a black club, it sets off a chain reaction that threatens to bring down Ch'u's dynasty as well as O'Day's.

When Ch'u's older son Han (Li), in a Hong Kong prison, hears his brother has been killed, he goes berserk and breaks out of maximum security in a flurry of martial artistry. It seems that he is actually a cop who had promised his late mother he would always look after his brother and has taken a fall for his gangster father, who had fled the former British crown colony.

Landing in the Bay Area to avenge his brother's death, he swiftly—and amusingly—crosses paths with Trish (Aaliyah), Isaak's lovely young daughter who has turned her back on her father and lives on her own in a modest apartment while running a gift shop. The attraction between Han and Trish is instant and develops into a relationship their respective fathers are less than thrilled about.

Body counts run high in this genre, but "Romeo Must Die," which marks Li's first English-language starring role, tries for some depth and sophistication. The fathers, especially Lindo's Isaak, possess intelligence and dimension, and O and Lindo both capably evoke pathos. The film is a new step for both Li, who hopes to break out with it, and for recording star Aaliyah, in an accomplished film debut. Han and Trish are appealing and attractive.

However, the couple's fathers are both lamentably unperceptive about their second-in-commands. From the get-go it's obvious that Kai (Russell Wong), Ch'u's handsome, cocky enforcer, and Mac (Isaiah Washington), Isaak's nakedly ambitious protege, are not guys long on loyalty and are swift to resort to violence to get their way.

Although you can almost immediately tell that the film was shot in Vancouver rather than Oakland, "Romeo Must Die" has a great look and an edgy feel, along with some broad swaths of humor, most of it supplied by Isaak's thickheaded strong-arm, Maurice (Anthony Anderson), who is on hand purely for comic relief.

This Warners release marks a confident directorial debut for noted cinematographer Andrzej Bartkowiak, working from a shrewd Eric Bernt-John Jarrell script, adapted from a Mitchell Kapner story. Glen MacPherson's cinematography is sleek and jazzy, and J. Michael Riva, no less, has served as visual consultant. The film's kinetic energy is well-matched by Stanley Clarke and Timbaland's terrific score, which incorporates lots of hip-hop numbers.

NEW YORK POST, 3/22/00, p. 53, Jonathan Foreman

Almost as cool as you'd hope from its trailer, "Romeo Must Die" is a hip, slick fusion of Asian and Hollywood action genres. It boasts spectacular acrobatic fight scenes equaling the best combat sequences in "The Matrix"—a film that, not coincidentally, was also produced by Joel Silver.

As you would expect from what is essentially a martial-arts movie crossed with a gangsta flick (both genres themselves are heavily influenced by westerns and Japanese samurai films) "Romeo" won't win any prizes for dialogue or plot originality.

Nor does it make much of the Romeo and Juliet theme, except to borrow the basic plot structure. It also moves along at a surprisingly leisurely pace between the action sequences.

Control of the Oakland waterfront is divided between African-American and Chinese crime families. They are constantly at war, although their respective bosses, Isaak O'Day (Delroy Lindo) and Ch'u Sing (Henry O), are collaborating on a plan to bring a football franchise to the area.

Sing's rude, arrogant son causes a fracas in a local black-owned nightclub and is discovered dead the next morning. The Chinese suspect O'Day's lieutenant, Mac (Isaiah Washington). but O'Day, desperate to keep the football venture alive and move into the straight business world, swears to Sing that his men had nothing to do with it.

Sing's other son Han (Jet Li, the villain from "Lethal Weapon IV:) a former cop who went to jail in Hong Kong to save his brother and father, hears about the killing and, in an amazing sequence, breaks out of a "beating room" and then his prison.

He turns up in San Francisco the same day that O'Day's only son, Colin (D. B. Woodside), is thrown out of window.

By pure chance, Han meets O'Day's daughter Trisha (Aaliyah), who owns a clothing store and has just had a vulgar and annoying bodyguard forced upon her by her father. She and Han hit it off.

Together they try to solve the mystery of who killed their respective brothers. But once they join forces, the each become the target of killers sent by someone from their own crime family.

Li is no Chow Yun-Fat in the looks department, but he's an amazingly graceful and athletic martial artist. His co-star, the singer Aaliyah, is a revelation, easily holding her own in her acting debut.

It's a shame that the movie lacks the courage to be explicit about their interracial romance, settling instead for a flirtation and affection.

Lindo, unjustly overlooked for his role in "The Cider House Rules" in this year's Oscar nominations, is effective as ever, if a little too cuddly to believe, as Oakland's black Godfather.

And Anthony Anderson from the sitcom "Hang Time" makes the most of his role as an unusually verbal and witty Mafia soldier. But it's Russell Wong, playing Ch'u's handsome, ruthless lieutenant, Kai, who steals every scene he's in.

The martial-arts action is breathtaking but heavily reliant on wire work and unlikely to please aficionados who prefer their kung fu battles to be remotely plausible.

NEWSDAY, 3/22/00, Part II/p. B9, Gene Seymour

Surprise. There's nobody named Romeo in all of "Romeo Must Die." You're allowed to recover from your astonishment while we tell you that the title—coolness quotient notwithstanding—refers to the vague connections shared by the plot of this hip-hopping, Kung Fu-fighting gangster melodrama with Shakespeare's "Romeo and Juliet."

On one side of Oakland's multicultural divide is the O'Day clan, whose patriarch, Isaak (Delroy Lindo), wants to buy up all the businesses on the city's waterfront in order to build a pro football stadium. On the other side is the Sing clan, whose warlord, Ch'u (Henry O), has similar designs on the same stretch of real estate. Neither family has much in common besides appalling ruthlessness in their business dealings and superb taste in threads.

As in Shakespeare's version, there are two attractive star-crossed kids from both families caught in the crossfire. Isaak's "little girl" Trish (Aaliyah) is a tough, smart businesswoman who wants no part of daddy's dirty dealings, while Ch'u's son Han (Jet Li) is an ex-cop taking the fall in a Hong Kong jail for a crime someone else in the family committed. Both join forces to stop the madness. And no, they don't exactly fall in love, unless you consider fluttering eyelashes at each other and sharing ice cream constitutes romantic commitment.

But forget what the "Romeo" stuff means, OK? Just the mention of Jet Li's name is enough to make clear that this so-called plot is merely an excuse for some serious martial arts.

And at the beginning, anyway, the movie delivers on its promise with a sensational fight sequence in the basement of the Hong Kong jail in which Li's Han is hoisted to the ceiling on one chained leg. The elaborate, startlingly ingenious manner in which he breaks out of this predicament is the movie's high point. Too bad there's still about an hour and 45 minutes left to go.

With the exception of a couple of other eye-popping set pieces (love those quick X-ray cuts of bone breaking), the rest of "Romeo Must Die" is a fairly tepid exemplar of street-hoods-in-suits melodrama. The serpentine menace conveyed with chilling perfection by henchmen Russell Wong and Isaiah Washington is offset by some comic relief by Anthony Anderson as a klutzy O'Day retainer.

It's surprising that this feature debut by cinematographer-turned-director Andrzej Bartokowiak has so many out-of-focus, out-of-rhythm shots. Still, he knows what he's doing when he focuses on Aaliyah. The camera eats her up like a rich dessert. And Li brings electricity and grace to the job of action hero. There's no question he's got the goods to become as big a star on this continent as Jackie Chan, Chow Yun-Fat and other Asian movie icons. All he needs, like them, are surroundings that are at once more commodious and more contained.

NEWSWEEK, 3/27/00, p. 74, N'Gai Croal & Ana Figueroa

If Chow Yun-Fat is the Cary Grant of Hong Kong action movies and Jackie Chan their Buster Keaton, Jet Li is their Fred Astaire. But we're pretty sure that Astaire never used Ginger Rogers as a lethal weapon. In just one of the incredible action sequences in "Romeo Must Die," Li takes R&B songbird turned actress Aaliyah and whirls her around so that her fist and feet slam repeatedly into their female opponent for a stylish pas de death. "[My] character wouldn't hit a girl" he explains. "So I thought, Why not use the girlfriend?'" At a time, when special effects are so commonplace that they're no longer special, Jet Li is a one-man "Matrix." The 36-year-old Li is downright modest about the buzz surrounding "Romeo Must Die," as if he were afraid to jinx this latest stage of his up-and-down-career. His first high kick came at the age of 7, when he began studying the martial art of *wu shu*, eventually becoming a five-time all-China champion. In 1988, with several movies under his belt, he made his first attempt to scale the Hollywood gates, but failed due to bad scripts and his broken English. Fortunately, director Tsui Hark selected him to play a Cantonese folk hero with blink-and-you'll-miss-'em moves in the 1991 Hong Kong epic "Once Upon a Time in China," a role that propelled him to regional super-stardom. After three sequels, Li's triumphant return to Hollywood as the villain in the 1998 hit "Lethal Weapon 4" won him the lead role in "Romeo Must Die."

Even though the entertaining "Romeo" pinches its plot outline from the Bard—Li and Aaliyah meet cute as their crime families go Uzi to Uzi—it doesn't have the poperatic brilliance of Li's best Hong Kong films. Even Li acknowledges that if there's any art here, it's decidedly corporate. "Joel Silver said, 'We've done the research,' after 'Lethal Weapon 4.' They discovered that an urban audience like my movies. This is why we decided to put martial arts and hip-hop music together." But even if it's more "Titus Destructus" than "Shakespeare in Love," at the movie's giddy center is Li, who balances his outrageously inventive fight scenes with a gift for comic timing that more than compensates for his wobbly English. When asked if he plans to branch out into romantic comedy, he flashes a mischievous smile. "What would make someone want to pay $7 to see Jet Li; It's not because he is so handsome, or so high [tall]," he says with a laugh, gesturing above his head. "They want to see Jet Li in martial-arts films, so I'll stay with that. We think he's selling himself, well, short, but no matter. With that many moves in his repertoire, Li's certain to come out on top.

SIGHT AND SOUND, 11/00, p. 62, Dave Haslam

US, the present. Escaping from a Hong Kong jail, ex-cop Han Sing arrives in Oakland to avenge the death of his younger brother Po, killed in the battle between Chinese and African-American gangs over the ownership of several waterfront properties. In conflict with his father Ch'u, who heads a coalition of Asian gangs, Han is thrown together with Trish O'Day, daughter of rival gang-leader Isaak, who dreams of going into legitimate business.

When Trish's brother Colin is murdered amid attacks on local business premises, Han suspects that insiders are involved. It transpires that a shady development consortium is intent on obtaining the land for a football stadium. Before the deeds can be signed, Trish informs her father that

Mac, his right-hand man, has gunned down a local club owner whose property was the last to be acquired. Admitting his desire to replace him as crime boss, Mac shoots Isaak while boasting of how he murdered Colin. Mac also reveals Han's brother was assassinated by someone in his own gang. Han hunts down Po's bodyguard Kai, who confesses to the murder. After killing Kai, Han confronts Ch'u with ordering his son's death, obliging the old man to commit suicide.

In an age of aggressively coordinated media campaigns, high-speed digital editing and bludgeoning urban beats, the commercial potential of the martial-arts movie would appear to be limitless. Fast, tough and stylish, with a generous side order of street credibility thanks to the success of top rap acts such as the Wu-Tang Clan, the genre appeals as both an object of pop-cult veneration and as arthouse entertainment. Adapting its conventions to mainstream western audiences is another matter entirely. Before successfully casting Jet Li (or Jet Lee as he then chose to spell his name) as Wong Fei-Hung, a legendary Cantonese folk hero who is the subject of a string of Hong Kong movies from the 40s onwards, in *Once upon a Time in China* (1991), Tsui Hark directed him in a radical update of the role, relocated to the west coast of America. Originally released in 1989, *The Master* may have been filmed entirely in Los Angeles, but it still took place on Li's own turf. A five-times world wushu champion, Li had always displayed greater skill as an athlete than as an actor, but the African-American street kids who followed his character about here respected his spiritual self-discipline and fighting technique. Nearly ten years on, and the predominantly young cast of *Romeo Must Die* seem too preoccupied with grid-iron football, real estate and flashing around their status symbols to pay Li's latest hero Han much mind.

At times playing like a feature-length promotional video for its own soundtrack album, the film looks as if Andrzej Bartkowiak, making his directorial debut after photographing Li in *Lethal Weapon 4*, had decided to assemble the whole piece around the star without actually telling him what was going on. This might have explained the total lack of romantic chemistry between Li and singer Aaliyah. Our star-crossed lovers are so emotionally off-channel, it's easy to forget the origin of the film's title; together they make Tom Cruise and Nicole Kidman in *Eyes Wide Shut* look like Rhett Butler and Scarlett O'Hara.

With such a gaping chasm at its heart, *Romeo Must Die* relies on a strong supporting cast to get by. Russell Wong brings a malevolent energetic charm to gang member Kai, while Isaiah Washington exudes taut fury as the villain Mac. Playing Han's father, Henry conducts his scenes opposite Li, presented in subtitled Chinese, with a fluid intensity. Unfortunately, the same can't be said of the fight sequences. Devised and choreographed by Li and Corey Yuen, they suffer from fussy editing and unimaginative camerawork. The insertion of animated X-ray images, showing bones being broken, and a spine shattering, offers some moments of flair, but there should be more going on beneath the skin than this.

VILLAGE VOICE, 3/28/00, p. 126, Dennis Lim

Romeo Must Die opens with a late-night drive across the Golden Gate Bridge, into deepest Oakland, the music turned way up, the gleaming, gliding, saturated-blue images cut and spliced to mirror the signature syncopation of the accompanying Timbaland-produced number. For a few brief moments, the movie is thrilling, in the way Timbaland beats are thrilling—skittish yet propulsive, weirdly unstable and fearless about it. The sensory high evaporates soon enough (in the next scene, to be precise, which cuts to a dance floor and a teasing glimpse of Asian Lesbian Action with gratuitous tit shot). *Romeo Must Die* delivers routine kicks without living up to its iconic casting: Hong Kong martial-arts superstar Jet Li paired with hip-hop princess Aaliyah. The movie makes a show of crossing racial lines, but it's hardly political (or even enamored with culture clash, à la Jarmusch or Wu-Tang), just demographically astute. The wall-to-wall rap score is as kinetic as the acrobatic fight choreography, and nothing else matters.

When an Asian mob boss's son is found hanging from a tree, his brother Han (Li) breaks out of a Hong Kong jail and travels to SF to avenge his death-blamed on a black gang led by Isaak O'Day (Delroy Lindo). The whole sorry mess has something to do with coveted waterfront property and the NFL. Against the backdrop of an escalating gang war, Han strikes up a friendship with O'Day's daughter Trish (Aaliyah). The directorial debut of Andrzej Bartkowiak, a cinematographer whose credits include *Speed*, *Romeo Must Die* keeps the fight scenes—most of which involve an airborne Jet Li and some queasily convincing sound effects—frequent and fairly elaborate. Still, the movie fills too much of its downtime with silly mawkishness. One unbelievable flashback has Han remembering a childhood trauma shared with his brother: The two boys, adrift at sea, hold on for dear life to a basketball (the artifact that triggers the memory) and float "toward the lights of Hong Kong."

Romeo Must Die tries to have it both ways: Race is the movie's gimmick and its willful blind spot. Conspicuously cautious in its delineation of a racial gang war, the script ensures that the distribution of villainy is evenhanded. Meanwhile, the romantic angle promised by the title is barely acknowledged. Some Romeo—by the final scene, Han and Trish have barely worked their way up to holding hands. As modern star-crossed lovers, Jet Li and Aaliyah would have been hard to beat; it's a shame the Hollywood powers who brought them together didn't have the nerve to one-up Leo and Claire.

Also reviewed in:
CHICAGO TRIBUNE, 3/23/00, Tempo/p. 6, Rene Rodriguez
NEW YORK TIMES, 3/23/00, p. E3, Elvis Mitchell
VARIETY, 3/20-26/00, p. 25, Todd McCarthy
WASHINGTON POST, 3/22/00, p. C11, Stephen Hunter
WASHINGTON POST, 3/24/00, Weekend/p. 41, Michael O'Sullivan

ROOM FOR ROMEO BRASS, A

A USA Films release of an Alliance Atlantis and BBC Films presentation in association with the Arts Council of England of a Company Pictures/Big Arty production supported by the National Lottery through the Arts Council of England. *Executive Producer:* András Hámori and David M. Thompson. *Producer:* George Faber and Charles Pattinson. *Director:* Shane Meadows. *Screenplay:* Paul Fraser and Shane Meadows. *Director of Photography:* Ashley Rowe. *Editor:* Paul Tothill. *Music:* Nick Hemming. *Choreographer:* Paul Fraser. *Sound:* Colin Nicolson and (music) Paul Hamblin. *Sound Editor:* Catherine Hodgson. *Casting:* Abi Cohen. *Production Designer:* Crispian Sallis. *Costumes:* Robin Fraser Paye. *Make-up:* Pebbles. *Stunt Coordinator:* Glenn Marks. *Running time:* 90 minutes. MPAA Rating: R.

CAST: Andrew Shim (Romeo Brass); Ben Marshall (Gavin "Knock Knock" Woolley); Paddy Considine (Morell); Frank Harper (Joseph Brass); Julia Ward (Sandra Woolley); James Higgins (Bill Woolley); Vicky McClure (Ladine Brass); Ladene Hall (Carol Brass); Bob Hoskins (Steven Laws); Martin Arrowsmith (Dennis Wardrobe); Dave Blant (School Pianist); Darren Campbell (Darren); Shaun Fields (Male Nurse); Nicholas Harvey (Neighbor Lad 2); Shane Meadows (Fish and Ship Shop Man); Joel Morris (Park Lad 1); Johann Myers (Clifford); Tanya Myers (Headmistress); Sammy Pasha (Ambulance Man); Jamahl Peterkin (Neighbor Lad 1); James Tomlinson (Park Lad 2); Paul Fraser (Psysiotherapist).

LOS ANGELES TIMES, 10/27/00, Calendar/p. 17, Kevin Thomas

"A Room for Romeo Brass" is a classic coming-of-age story that swiftly and compellingly assumes the form of a parable of innocence and evil.

This engaging English film, set in a suburban Nottingham blue-collar tract, focuses on two 12-year-olds, Romeo (Andrew Shim) and Gavin (Ben Marshall), next-door neighbors and lifelong friends. They complement each other well: Romeo is a strong, solid boy while the spindly Gavin is about to undergo back surgery that causes him to limp slightly. Both are bright, especially Gavin, and they share a well-developed sense of humor, an effective armor in coping with oncoming adolescence.

The boys look to be friends for life, yet they become estranged with shocking abruptness. Some older boys start picking on them when a stranger, Morell (Paddy Considine), comes to their rescue. Morell is a wiry, ungainly, shabby man of about 25, a bit eccentric in a comical way, and he and the boys take to each other instantly. Morell, in turn, is quite taken by Romeo's older sister, the lovely Ladine (Vicky McClure), who works in a trendy clothing store.

Gavin prankishly maneuvers Morell into purchasing an outlandish sports outfit intended to impress her. When it predictably has the opposite effect, Morell flies into a rage at Gavin, venting dire threats while Romeo is out of earshot. Thoroughly terrified, Gavin retreats, keeping to himself as he awaits surgery.

As fate would have it, Romeo's errant father Joe (Frank Harper), a big, burly guy eager to be welcomed back into his family after a fling with another woman has ended, turns up at this particular moment. Clearly, there is bad blood between father and son, which Morell exploits, making Romeo feel protected and cared about. The irony is that Joe is the one adult who has had the opportunity to see Morell as dangerously deranged, not merely a harmless, comical weirdo who feels more comfortable around kids than adults. In the meantime Morell, fixated totally on Ladine, intends to use Romeo to further his desperate pursuit of his sister while trying to instill in him his profoundly sociopathic views.

In telling this story director Shane Meadows and his co-writer Paul Fraser draw upon their own lifelong friendship. They deftly depict the chilling vulnerability of the normal to the crazy; of the difficulty children have in communicating their fears to their parents when they don't believe they will be taken seriously or are simply too terrified to do so; and of the way even conscientious parents, saddled with multiple responsibilities and distractions, may be maddeningly slow to pick up the sinister aspects of those who associate with their children.

"A Room for Romeo Brass" is an assured, graceful instance of effective screen storytelling, and Meadows draws splendid performances from his cast, especially from the young Shim and Marshall, and from Considine, alternately scary and pathetic. What Meadows and Fraser are celebrating is family solidarity—and the dangers that lurk when those bonds are frayed.

NEW YORK POST, 10/27/00, p. 46, Lou Lumenick

Is there a law in Great Britain requiring that 50 percent of their movies have to be coming-of-age stories? For every "Billy Elliot," there are 50 dreary kitchen-sink-realism exercises like this made-for-TV movie that's inexplicably getting a theatrical release.

Writer-director Shane Meadows' fairly shapeless story is about a black youth with an abusive dad, and his white buddy with a bad back. You can guess the rest. A promising newcomer named Paddy Considine provides brief distraction as a creepy neighbor.

SIGHT AND SOUND, 2/00, p. 52, Mark Kermode

Nottingham schoolchildren Romeo Brass and Gavin "Knocks" Woolley are neighbours and best friends, helping each other through the trials of an absentee father and damaged spine respectively. When a limping Knocks is bullied by local thugs, Romeo intervenes but is himself saved from a beating by twentysomething misfit Morrell.

Morrell drives Romeo home and meets his mother and sister Ladine. He becomes infatuated with Ladine. Morrell befriends Romeo and Knocks, who gives him jokingly misleading advice on how to dress to impress Ladine, resulting in humiliation for Morrell. Romeo's father Joe returns home, unwelcomed by his son and former partner, and confronts Morrell who continues to pursue Ladine. On a day trip to the beach, Morrell threatens Knocks, who subsequently withdraws from Romeo. As Knocks is admitted to hospital for back treatment, Romeo moves in with Morrell, whose attempted seduction of Ladine ends in angry confrontation. Rejected, Morrell throws Romeo out of his house, and attacks one of Ladine's suitors. When Morrell attacks Knocks' father, Joe intervenes, beats him and sees him off, thereby precipitating a family bonding. Romeo and Knocks are reunited, and perform a magic show together.

If there is indeed such a thing as a British film tradition it probably owes less to the Laura Ashley loveliness of the Merchant Ivory period romps which sell so well abroad than to the lower-budget work of film-makers like Shane Meadows, who is fast becoming to cinema what Morrissey once was to pop. Refining the blend of realism and romance which characterised *24 7*, Meadows again proves himself one of our most intriguing visual poets with this engaging picture of English mores. At once insightful and inspirational, it reminds us that it's possible to make extraordinary movies about apparently ordinary people.

Whatever else it may seem to be, *A Room for Romeo Brass* is first and foremost a love story, played out between a succession of odd couples: two young boys, an estranged husband and wife, a misfit and his unattainable siren. Indeed, during one musical interlude, Meadows even plays Sunhouse's "If This Is Love" against a montage of the lost souls, at odds with their partners, to drive the point home. In other hands it could be monstrously corny, but somehow the earthiness of the characters, the believable quirkiness of their relationships and the unsentimental eye through which Meadows spies them all (accompanied by an edgily endearing soundtrack of Beck, Ian Brown, Billy Bragg and others) prevent the project from sliding into mere pop video clichés.

Instead, what we have here is a cinematic slice of life filtered through 30 years of British popular culture. From its *Kes*-style opening, to its classic television sitcom closing credits, *Romeo Brass* hits the nostalgic home-grown touchstones with ease, but crucially avoids cosiness at every turn. Like Ken Loach and Les Blair before him, Meadows possesses an unflinching eye which does not need rose-tinted spectacles to find delightful sights. What marks Meadows' work apart from that of many of his contemporaries is his ability to negotiate the change from significance to insignificance, drama to comedy, and humour to horror with ease, allowing each element to flow into the next as if each were an individually observed moment. On at least two occasions (most notably, Morrell's attempted seduction-cum-rape of Ladine) the juncture between laughter and violence is crossed so subtly that the audience is left genuinely shocked.

As before, Meadows is aided and abetted by a handsomely accomplished cast, with newcomers Andrew Shim and Ben Marshall delivering the sort of confidently accomplished youthful performances that only come from actors who have been genuinely put at their ease by their director. The parents also hit the right note throughout, thanks (apparently) to some on-camera improvisation, jokey outtakes of which are tacked on at the end presumably to leave the audience feeling good about these people, which we do. Special mention is due to Paddy Considine whose repressed nasal Morrell lurches from sad misfit, to jestery goon, to hateful bully with consistent conviction, encapsulating the wide emotional range of the entire eccentric movie.

VILLAGE VOICE, 10/31/00, p. 170, Amy Taubin

Shane Meadows's *A Room for Romeo Brass,* a slight, semiautobiographical saga of adolescent boy friendship, is enhanced by a fabulous soundtrack that runs the gamut from the Specials to J.J. Cale, with Hank Williams, Beck, Belle and Sebastian, and lots of others in between. Like Meadows's *Small Time* and *TwentyFourSeven*, the film draws on Meadows and screenwriter Paul Fraser's memories of growing up poor in the English Midlands.

Romeo Brass (Andrew Shim) and Gavin "Knocks" Woolley (Ben Marshall) are inseparable until Romeo falls under the influence of the much older Morell (Paddy Considine), a serious sicko who's using Romeo to get into his sister's pants. A chubby black 12-year-old with an enormous appetite for junk food, Romeo is flattered by Morell's attention. Knocks, a fragile white boy with a lively intellect and a damaged spine, is terrified by Morell's violence and angry with Romeo for abandoning him when he needs him most. After Knocks has back surgery, Romeo doesn't even come to visit. *A Room for Romeo Brass* is so low-key it could be mistaken for a throwaway. But Meadows's understanding of childhood fears and fantasies and the yearning, heartfelt performances he draws from his two young actors should not be underestimated.

Also reviewed in:
CHICAGO TRIBUNE, 11/3/00, Friday/p. D, Loren King
NEW YORK TIMES, 10/27/00, E28, Stephen Holden
VARIETY, 8/30-9/5/99, p. 55, Derek Elley
WASHINGTON POST, 11/3/00, p. C5, Stephen Hunter
WASHINGTON POST, 11/3/00, Weekend/p. 43, Desson Howe

RUGRATS IN PARIS: THE MOVIE

A Paramount Pictures release and Nickelodeon Movies release of a Klasky-Csupo/Nickelodeon Movies Rugrat production. *Executive Producer:* Albie Hecht, Julia Pistor, Eryk Casemiro, and Hal Waite. *Producer:* Arlene Klasky and Gabor Csupo. *Director:* Paul Demeyer and Stig Bergqvist. *Screenplay:* David N. Weiss, J. David Stem, Jill Gorey, Barbara Herndon, and Kate Boutilier. *Editor:* John Bryant. *Music:* Mark Mothersbaugh. *Music Editor:* Michael Baber, Jennifer "Jiffy" Blank, and Kim Naves. *Sound:* James Bolt and (music) Jonathan Allen. *Sound Editor:* Cameron Frankley and Beth Sterner. *Casting:* Stephán A. McKenzie and Barbara Wright. *Production Designer:* Dima Malanitchev. *Art Director:* Gena Kornyshev. *Animation Supervisor:* Brice Mallier. *Running time:* 78 minutes. *MPAA Rating:* PG-13.

VOICES: E. G. Daily (Tommy Pickles); Tara Charendoff (Dil Pickles); Cheryl Chase (Angelica Pickles); Christine Cavanaugh (Chuckie Finster); Cree Summer Franck (Susie Carmichael); Kath Soucie (Betty DeVille/Lil DeVille/Phil DeVille); Michael Bell (Drew Pickles); Tress MacNeile (Charlotte Pickles); Casey Kasem (Wedding DJ); Joe Alasky (Grandpa Lou Pickles); Debbie Reynolds (Lulu Pickles); Michael Bell (Chas Finster); Jack Riley (Stu Pickles); Susan Sarandon (Coco La Bouche); John Lithgow (Jean-Claude); Marlene Mitsuko Wamene, Darrell Kunitomi, and Goh Misawa (Villagers "Princess Spectacular"); Julia Kato (Kira Watanabe); Melanie Chartoff (Didi Pickles); Margaret Smith (Stewardess); Philip Simon (Animatronic Bus Driver); Phil Proctor (Howard Deville); Paul Demeyer (Dog Catcher); Mako (Mr. Yamaguchi); Tim Curry, Kevin Richardson, and Billy West (Sumo Singers); Dionne Quan (Kimi Watanabe); Richard Michel (French Worker); Paul Demeyer (Street Cleaner); Phillippe Benichou (Ninja); Darryl Wright (Cafe Owner); Lisa McClowry (Princess); Charles Fathy (Photographer); Dan Castellaneta (Priest).

LOS ANGELES TIMES, 11/17/00, Calendar/p. 12, Robin Rauzi

In the history of American cinema, sequels that match or surpass the quality of their predecessors are not unheard of. Many critics preferred "The Empire Strikes Back" to "Star Wars." "The Godfather, Part II" is always ranked right alongside the first installment. And despite a seven-year gap between them, "Aliens" showed no stylistic drop-off from "Alien."

Alas, "Rugrats in Paris: The Movie" does not fall into this category.

This will matter not one lick to 6-year-olds. Plots just don't seem obvious to first-graders. They generally don't complain, later, over a grande apple juice, "You know, I didn't think Coco LaBouche was a fully developed character." They will be mostly entertained for most of the movie's 80 minutes and leave the theater shouting, "Who let the dogs out? Woof Woof-woof" Woof-woof-! "—the song used in the movie (and just about everywhere else in the world).

So the rest of this is not for our first-grade readers, but for their guardians who are wrestling with options: Take the kids myself, pawn them off on some friend's parent, or hold out for the video.

"The Rugrats: The Movie"—a $ 100-million hit in 1998—had a certain charm. Much like a newspaper comic strip, it viewed everyday life through the eyes of babies. Tommy Pickles (voiced by E.G. Daily), age 1, and his diaper-donning crew tried to rustle him up a baby sister. He wound up with a bawling baby brother instead, who was such a pain that the Rugrats tried to take him back. It was tightly plotted with a lot of action and a nice message about the responsibility of being a big brother. The TV show had been on Nickelodeon since 1991, yet the movie worked so well that one would believe the series was spun off the film.

"Rugrats in Paris: The Movie," on the other hand, feels like a half-hour TV show inflated into a feature film. The prominent placement of the Baha Men's song "Who Let the Dogs Out," is a completely tangential sequence. About half the running time is spent setting up why the Rugrats and their families are in Paris, how they got there, and who the new characters are.

The emotional thread is 2-year-old Chuckie (Christine Cavanaugh, who was also the voice of "Babe") and his quest to find a new mommy to marry his widowed father. For some reason this takes place in a Japanese-style theme park—Reptarland, based on a toy by Tommy's dad—in Paris.

Cold, calculating Coco LaBouche (voiced by Susan Sarandon) runs the park with assistance from the unscrupulous Jean-Claude (John Lithgow) and the kind Kira (Julia Kato). To get a promotion in her kid-oriented business, Coco plots to acquire an instant family: Chuckie and his dad, Chas (Michael Bell).

Yet for all the machinations and theme-park attractions, the plot doesn't cover much ground. The babies still speak in amusing malapropisms—"over my dad's potty" for "over my dead body"—but this Parisian edition offers few observations that will be clever to parents. The animation itself is unremarkable; the hand-painted and the computer-generated parts sometimes don't blend well.

But the appeal of "Rugrats" was never based on the quality of its animation, and all of this film's faults are nearly forgiven for the short but memorable scene of sumo wrestlers singing a karaoke version of "Bad Girls." Fortunately, the lyrics for that Donna Summer song will probably go over 6-year-old heads.

NEW YORK POST, 11/17/00, p. 56, Lou Lumenick

Hey call it "Rugrats in Paris: the Movie," but really, what exactly is the point of setting a movie in the City of Light if almost all the action takes place in a Japanese theme park?

Maybe I'm being a bit of a grinch and yes, it is only an animated cartoon, but is it really asking too much for children's film to show enough imagination to keep adults from squirming in their seats?

Sure, this second feature based on the popular Nickelodeon series has some bright ideas, like casting one of my all-time favorites, Susan Sarandon, as the voice of the villain, and even giving a number to her "Rocky Horror Picture Show" co-star Tim Curry, as a singing Sumo wrestler waiter at the theme park. (But they're not in a scene together, I'm sorry to report).

The opening parody of "The Godfather" is fun, too—but too much of what follows is by-the-numbers cartoon plotting and video-game-like action unlikely to engage anyone over the age of say, 7.

When a mechanical reptile malfunctions at EuroReptarland, the selfish, mean-spirited manager, Coco La Bouche (Sarandon as a sort of road-company Cruella de Ville) summons its inventor Stu Pickles to Paris, along with his family and friends.

Coco needs a husband and child, quick, to secure a promotion from her Japanese boss—and Stu's mischievous daughter Angelica gives her the idea of pursuing the father of her 2-year-old friend Chuckie, whose mother is in heaven."

The toddler Rugrats (who mostly take a backstage to Angelica and Chuckie) get wind of the situation and race to rescue the father from a planned wedding at Notre Dame—pursued all the while by Coco's devious personal assistant Jean-Claude (voice of John Lithgow).

While "Rugrats in Paris" has its moments (like their first encounter with a bidet—"wow, a potty that squirts you back!"), it doesn't have enough of them, even if the voice work and animation is much better than the first "Rugrats" movie, which made more than $100 million.

With so few films aimed at this segment of the audience, it's a shame that "Rugrats in Paris" (like "Dr. Seuss,' the Grinch that Stole Christmas") seems more like a merchandising ploy than a successful attempt to entertain kids and their parents.

NEWSDAY, 11/17/00, Part II/p. B6, Gene Seymour

At what point is one "too grown-up" for "Rugrats"? I'm only asking because I figured that, by now, I'd be sick of green goo, jokes about smelly diapers and fantasies about climbing out of playpens into scary alternate universes. I also was sure that I'd have had more than enough of goody-goody Tommy, snooty-greedy Angelica and sniffly sniveling Chucky to make the prospect of their second feature-length movie, "Rugrats in Paris," a dreary prospect.

Maybe it's not time to let go of these guys just yet. Despite its occasional indulgence in brassy noise and crass sentiment, "Rugrats in Paris" turns out to be just as charming as—and more impressively animated than—its predecessor. The inner 8-year-old in all of us will cruise with the digitally enhanced giant toys and nonabrasive, gross-out humor. Meanwhile, the budding sophisticate in each child may be intrigued by parents' chuckles over the movie's well-conceived parody of the wedding scene from "The Godfather."

And it's pretty darned hard to dismiss a movie in which French-speaking sumo wrestlers perform "Bad Girls" behind Angelica's lead vocals at a sushi restaurant.

With that to pique your interest, why should you care that the whole reason those toddlers are in Paris is that Tommy's dad, Stu, has to fix a malfunctioning giant robot lizard at EuroReptarland, a theme park managed by the evil Coco LaBouche (voice by Susan Sarandon)? Told by her Japanese bosses that she has to prove her kid-friendliness to keep her job, Coco schemes to convince Chuckie's widowed dad, Chas, to marry her immediately. Chuckie, desperate for a new mom, nonetheless thinks (rightly) that Coco is just another thing to be scared of.

Sarandon seems to be having a good time with her gig, and while John Lithgow's work as Coco's henchman, Jean Claude, isn't as noticeable, it's good to have him among the show's regulars, including E.G. Daily (Tommy), Cheryl Chase (Angelica), Christine Cavanaugh (Chuckie) and Kath Soucie (Phil and Lil, whose customary unflapability is even more pronounced here).

If there's a real star here, it's the music. Not only does composer Mark Mothersbaugh provide his customary mix of tin-toy whimsy and coy melodramatics to the show, but there's a motley assortment of songs by the likes of Sinead O'Connor ("When You Love"), T-Boz Watkins ("My Getaway"), Gerri Halliwell ("These Boots Are Made for Walking") and Isaac Hayes ("Chuckie Chan") that will help ensure another big payday for producers of the soundtrack album.

SIGHT AND SOUND, 4/01, p. 56, Matthew Leyland

US, the present. Two-year old Chuckie Finster misses his dead mother and wishes he had a new one. Stu Pickles, the father of Chuckie's best friend Tommy, is summoned to EuroReptarland, a Japanese theme park in Paris, to repair Reptar, his robot dinosaur invention. Stu's family, accompanied by Chuckie and his dad Chas, plus the families of twins Phil and Lil and Tommy's cousin Angelica, travel to Paris and meet Coco La Bouche, the careerist manager of EuroReptarland. Coco's boss, Mr Yamaguchi, informs her that he is looking for a family-oriented person to replace him when he steps down. Angelica offers to set Coco up with Chas in return for a few favours.

Pretending to be child-friendly, Coco manages to dupe Chas into marrying her. On the day of the wedding, Chuckie and his friends are held captive in EuroReptarland by Coco's right hand man Jean Claude. Angelica confesses her deal with Coco and the children escape in the now repaired Reptar. After defeating a giant robot snail controlled by Jean Claude, the children arrive at Notre Dame cathedral, where Coco's deception is exposed and she is fired from her job. Later, back in the US, Chas marries Coco's assistant Kira.

Crammed to the hilt with bodily-function jokes and displays of infant anarchy designed to sate its target audience of two- to-11-year olds, *Rugrats in Paris* the second film spin-off from the Nickelodeon cartoon series about a group of unruly toddlers, is nonetheless as smartly allusive, satirical and adult friendly as its 1998 predecessor *The Rugrats Movie*. Its first gag is aimed squarely at cine-literate grown-ups: a pin-sharp parody of *The Godfather* (1972), featuring the line "I believe in the playground..." and the discovery by one of the toddlers of a hobby-horse head in his crib. And throughout, there are similarly canny references to the likes of *King Kong* (1933), *Enter the Dragon* (1973) and *A Few Good Men* (1992).

Most of the action is confined to EuroReptarland—a Paris-based Japanese theme park—but when the film does roam beyond its gates, it typically takes the opportunity, physically or verbally, to defame such Parisian landmarks as the Eiffel Tower or Notre Dame cathedral ("Wake me if you spot a hunchback," says one unimpressed adult visitor to the latter). The park itself, based around the robot monster invented by Tommy's dad, is an obvious dig at Disney, with its Small World send-up, Ooey Gooey World (an amusingly surreal boat-ride celebration of viscosity), and stage-show power ballad pastiche 'Reptar, I Love You'. The incongruity of a Japanese theme park bang in the middle of the French capital is explained by the script as a nod to globalisation ("It's the 21st century!"), but it seems equally likely that the filmmakers are acknowledging the influence such fads as Pokémon, which originated from Japan, have lately exerted on western kids' imaginations.

EuroReptarland is dominated by a giant representation of Katsushika Hokusai's famous drawing *The Great Wave* (one of debut feature director Paul Demeyer's neatest graphical touches), but thankfully the movie is largely untouched by the tsunamis of glutinous sentiment that usually overwhelm children's movies. Toddler Chuckie's quest to find a new mother is handled with judicious sensitivity, while the story's wedding coda eschews homiletic schmaltz in favour of a reprise of the earlier *Godfather* gag and a raucous cake fight.

On the downside, it's a pity given the considered characterisations of the television show that the scriptwriters have opted lazily for a Cruella De Vil clone as their villain (albeit one voiced enthusiastically by Susan Sarandon). Also, young *Rugrats* fans may be disappointed by how the show's ostensible front-baby Tommy is given little to do here, aside from dispensing nuggets of pre-school wisdom to Chuckie on the topic of bravery. There's small doubt, though, that children will be consistently engaged by this hurtling, vibrant adventure. The animation is a riot of rich colours and employs computer technology to produce beguiling effects such as the faces Chuckie sees—of himself and his late mother—in the clouds above. And the toilet humour is occasionally as instructional as it is crude: "Wow," gasps an awed tot on his first encounter with a bidet, "a potty that squirts you back!"

VILLAGE VOICE, 11/28/00, p. 138, Richard Gehr

Nine years old and still growing strong, Arlene Klasky and Gabor Csupo's animated *Rugrats* remains a merchandise machine with heart, maintaining its freshness with the gradual addition of new characters to its core group of "dumb babies" lorded over by three-year-old Angelica. So where 1998's *Rugrats: The Movie* introduced Tommy Pickles's baby brother, Dill, this sequel navigates a potentially dicier psychological minefield as the 'rats assist timid, motherless Chuckie Finster in his quest to bond with the animatronic "princess mommy" he spies on a Matterhorn-like edifice in EuroReptarland, a Japanese theme park in Paris. Chuckie does acquire a new mommy and stepsister, but only after destroying most of the city.

Rugrats has always spoofed the merchandising hand that feeds it. In *Rugrats in Paris,* though, Nickelodeon launches a comedic assault on the Disney empire's tired formulas. Susan Sarandon voices Coco LaBouche, a pointy, sinister corporate climber, dressed in hilariously parodied Japanese high fashion, who drags Chuckie's father down the aisle (of Notre Dame, no less) to prove to the park's owners that she's kid-friendly enough to run EuroReptarland. Former Devo leader Mark Mothersbaugh detonates the Disney tear-jerking ballad with "Reptar I Love You," while Disneyland's small-world banality is slimed in Reptarland's Ooey Gooey World ride.

A colorful theme park of a film, *Rugrats in Paris* nicely conveys a family trip abroad as seen from both the exhausted-parent and bewildered-infant points of view. And it pushes the viscosity button hard for extra verisimilitude, with countless pee, poop, vomit, and drool jokes that add a documentary aspect to the frantic family fare.

Also reviewed in:
CHICAGO TRIBUNE, 11/17/00, Friday/p. I, Loren King
NEW YORK TIMES, 11/17/00, p. E31, Elvis Mitchell
VARIETY, 11/13-19/00, p. 23, Robert Koehler
WASHINGTON POST, 11/17/00, Weekend/p. 49, Desson Howe
WASHINGTON POST, 11/18/00, p. C10, Rita Kempley

RULES OF ENGAGEMENT

A Paramount Pictures release in association with Seven Arts Pictures of a Richard D. Zanuck/Scott Rudin production. *Executive Producer:* Adam Schroeder and James Webb. *Producer:* Richard D. Zanuck and Scott Rudin. *Director:* William Friedkin. *Screenplay:* Stephen Gaghan. *Story:* James Webb. *Director of Photography:* Nicola Pecorini and William A. Fraker. *Editor:* Augie Hess. *Music:* Mark Isham. *Music Editor:* Tom Carlson. *Sound:* Russel Williams II and (music) Stephen Krause. *Sound Editor:* Steve Boeddeker and Mike

Szakmeister.   *Casting:* Denise Chamian.   *Production Designer:* Robert Laing.   *Art Director:* William Cruse.   *Set Decorator:* Rick Simpson.   *Special Effects:* Paul Lombardi.   *Costumes:* Gloria Gresham.   *Make-up:* Robert Ryan.   *Stunt Coordinator:* Buddy Joe Hooker.   *Running time:* 123 minutes.   *MPAA Rating:* R.

CAST: Tommy Lee Jones (Colonel Hays Hodges);   Samuel L. Jackson (Colonel Terry Childers);   Guy Pearce (Major Mark Biggs); Bruce Greenwood (National Security Adviser William Sokal);   Blair Underwood (Captain Lee);   Philip Baker Hall (General H. Lawrence Hodges);   Anne Archer (Mrs. Mourain);   Mark Feuerstein (Captain Tom Chandler);   Ben Kingsley (Ambassador Mourain);   Dale Dye (Major General Perry);   Amidou (Doctor Ahmar); Richard McGonagle (Judge);   Baoan Coleman (Colonel Cao);   Nicky Katt (Hays III);   Ryan Hurst (Corporal Hustings);   Gordon Clapp (Harris);   Hayden Tank (Justin);   Ahmed Abounouom (Jimi);   William Gibson (Hodges' Radio Man);   Tuan Tran (Translator);   John Speredakos (Lawyer); Scott Alan Smith (Another Lawyer); Jilhane Kortobi (Little Girl); David Lewis Hays (Bailiff, NCO);   Peter Tran (Cao's Radio Man);   Bonnie Johnson (Mary Hodges); Jason C. West (Childers' Radio Man);   Attifi Mohamed (Tariq);   Zouheir Mohamed (Aziz); Chris Ufland (Ambassador Aide);   Thom Barry (Chairman Joint Chiefs of Staff);   Kevin Cooney (4 Star General);   Helen Manning (Sarah Hodges);   David Graf (ARG Commander);   Conrad Bachmann (Secretary of Defense);   Aziz Assimi (Little Boy);   Robert Pentz, Jr. (Courtroom Spectator);   Laird MacIntosh (Radio Op);   Baouyen C. Bruyere (Colonel Cao's Grandaughter); Todd Kimsey, Lawrence Noel Larsen, and Stephen Ramsey (Officers);   G. Gordon Liddy (Talk Show Host).

LOS ANGELES TIMES, 4/7/00, Calendar/p. 1, Kenneth Turan

"Rules of Engagement," as this courtroom-combat drama takes pains to explain, are a set of regulations that let soldiers know what the military can and cannot do when it comes to using deadly force. Wouldn't it be nice if there were similar rules governing what Hollywood can and cannot do when confronted with what's potentially an involving, invigorating subject?

Directed by the veteran William Friedkin and starring Tommy Lee Jones, Samuel L. Jackson and an impressive Guy Pearce, "Rules" is a passable, moderately diverting dramatic entertainment that raises all kinds of thought-provoking questions it's not really interested in answering. Though we all know that situations in the real world are complex while those in the movies are simple, it's always frustrating when a film hints at the former before ending up with the latter.

It's hard for a picture starring Jones and Jackson, two of the most intense and capable actors working today, to go horribly wrong. Few performers look as natural as Marine officers, and seeing them both in the jungle in Vietnam in the film's 1968 prologue makes us wonder how the hell we ever lost the war.

Close combat buddies, Hays Hodges (Jones) and Terry Childers (Jackson) get separated before a blistering fire fight and Childers has to make a fateful decision about some Viet Cong captives that may mean life or death for his pal. Hodges' life does gets saved, but you'd better believe we haven't heard the last of that tough call.

Cut to 28 years later, in Camp Lejeune, N.C., where the two men are reunited at Hodges' retirement celebration. Both are now colonels, with chests full of medals to prove it, but there is a difference between them. Since being wounded in combat, Hodges has been a desk-bound Marine attorney while Childers, known to intimates as "the warrior's warrior," is about to get an important field command.

That command turns out to involve leading a squadron of helicopter-borne Marines from an aircraft carrier to the U.S. Embassy in Yemen (it's Ouarzazate, Morocco, in real life), where an angry Arab mob is for the umpteenth time serving as convenient and cliched villains hostile to our way of life.

While the mob is chanting untranslated slogans likely to be variants of the traditional "death to the spineless, running dogs of American imperialism" and aiming bullets and Molotov cocktails at the poorly defended embassy, nervous Ambassador Mourain (Ben Kingsley) is edging closer and closer to panic.

Not so the cool Col. Childers. Does he take a moment to calm down the ambassador's understandably terrified small son? You betcha. Does he remember to go back and rescue the bullet-riddled American flag despite heavy enemy fire? Roger that. Does the seriously rattled ambassador mean it when he vows eternal gratitude before he flies away? Don't hold your breath.

Only one thing gets Col. Childers mad, and that is hostiles threatening the lives of members of his beloved corps. It's a complicated crowd he's left to deal with in front of the embassy, some taking pot shots at the building, others content to merely chant those snappy slogans. Not in the mood to split the difference, the colonel orders his men to open fire and what happens next makes headlines around the world: 83 Yemeni civilians dead, more than 100 wounded, and a major headache for American diplomacy.

Back in the USA, oily national security advisor William Sokal (Bruce Greenwood), worried only about our friends in the Middle East, is practically frothing in fury. He insists that Col. Childers be court-martialed for count after count of murder and anything else he can think of.

Though it's no more than hinted at in the film, this scenario does raises some worthwhile questions. Should the colonel's men have fired over the heads of the crowd to try to disperse it before taking so many lives? What exactly is necessary force? Does Childers represent all that is wrong or all that is right about the military? Is it true, as someone says, that the difference between a hero and a murderer is a very fine line?

Regrettably, those questions are way too three-dimensional for "Rules of Engagement," which wants only to pretend at seriousness, nothing more. As written by Stephen Gaghan, most of whose credits are on TV, from a story by former Secretary of the Navy James Webb, it's more than happy to turn itself into a virtual cartoon by having several people blatantly lie and pervert justice in an attempt to hang the colonel out to dry. Childers, however, has a secret weapon on his side. It's old pal Hays Hodges, whom he picks for his attorney because he doesn't want "a Starbuck's drinker who's never seen combat" to defend him.

Of course, this being a movie, no one knows Hodges is a secret weapon. To the world and even to himself and members of his immediate family he appears to be a mess, a weak attorney on the way to retirement who barely survived a drinking problem and a messy divorce. But, hey, this is Tommy Lee Jones we're talking about, and anyone wanting to bet against him making a rousing summation to the jury would probably have picked "Wild Wild West" to win an Oscar.

Unfortunately neither Jones nor Jackson is really used to his fullest capacity here. Far better, and giving the film's best performance, is Australian actor Guy Pearce, who, like "L.A. Confidential" co-star Russell Crowe, is proving a master at reinventing himself for each new role.

Pearce's Maj. Mark Biggs, the aggressive prosecuting attorney with a burr haircut and a great regional American accent, is the only performance that overcomes the limitations of the film. While the rest of "Rules of Engagement" is acceptable, it doesn't have the chops or the ambition to wrestle with the questions it raises.

NEW YORK POST, 4/7/00, p. 57, Jonathan Foreman

Proof that star power really can work magic, "Rules of Engagement" is a cut-and-paste combination of "A Few Good Men" with "Courage Under Fire."

As mechanical and predictable as a cuckoo clock, it shouldn't work half as well as it does.

But thanks to the always terrific Tommy Lee Jones and Samuel L. Jackson, and some powerful (if bloody) combat scenes, it ends up being as entertaining as anything released this season.

The underlying story by "Fields of Fire" novelist (and former Navy Secretary) James Webb is certainly promising: A Marine combat hero is court-martialed after foreign civilians are killed in an incident with overtones of the street battles in Mogadishu, "Bloody Sunday" in Northern Ireland and America's hostage humiliation in Tehran in 1979.

So it's unfortunate that the movie is burdened by a screenplay (by Stephen Gaghan) so hackneyed you have literally heard every line before and seen almost identical situations in other movies.

The film opens in Vietnam in 1968, with the squad of Lt. Hodges (Jones) pinned down in a swamp, and that of Lt. Childers (Jackson) capturing an enemy command post on a nearby hill. By shooting one prisoner in cold blood and threatening to kill another, Childers forces the captive CO to order his troops away from the swamp—and saves the life of his friend.

Cut to 28 years later: Both men are now colonels, but Hodges (who was wounded in the firefight) is a Marine lawyer on the brink of retirement, while the much-decorated Childers commands a Middle East expeditionary force.

Childers is sent on a helicopter mission to evacuate the U.S. Embassy in Yemen, which is being attacked by violent demonstrators and rooftop snipers.

He rescues the cowering ambassador (Ben Kingsley) and his wife (Anne Archer). Then, as his Marines come under heavy fire, he orders them to open fire on the crowd, killing 80 men, women and children.

Childers is charged with murder on his return to the United States, and turns to Hodges to lead his defense in the court-martial.

The courtroom scenes—with the wrinkly, rumpled lawyer going up against a crisp young whippersnapper—could come straight out of an episode of "Matlock."

(Except that the film-makers seem unaware that both sides in a trial get to see all evidence before proceedings start.)

Logical problems abound, and even though everything the characters feel is made explicit (buttoned-up Marine officers say things like "I goddamn hate myself'), lots of things make no sense.

Director William Friedkin ("The Exorcist") elicits some terrible line readings from his cast, but does a good gory job with the combat scenes.

And to his credit, he has made a contemporary war movie that is neither hostile to nor obviously ignorant of military culture: People who have served in the armed forces should be able to watch it without choking.

NEWSDAY, 4/7/00, Part II/p. B3, John Anderson

Like the words "Miranda decision" as muttered by Dirty Harry Callahan, the title "Rules of Engagement" is meant to inspire a smirk. How can a code devised by pencil-necked bureaucrats justly govern the behavior of the military in combat situations? How can people who've never seen warfare pass judgment on those who have? In fact, while we're at it, why should the military answer to civilian rule at all?

William ("The Exorcist") Friedkin doesn't go quite that far. His latest very high-toned, high-gloss and not particularly highbrow movie—which is blessed by the performances of both Tommy Lee Jones and Samuel L. Jackson—contains enough righteous indignation for a talk radio station and, as a battlefield-courtroom-buddy movie, doesn't leave an emotional stone unturned. But it's clear at this point that Friedkin has a decided taste for order over law—his 1971 "The French Connection" was an early good indication of that; "Rampage," his bloody 1992 screed about the insanity defense and capital punishment, was pure hand-wringing hysteria.

So it's no surprise that "Rules of Engagement," like most of its ilk, assumes that all government officials are evil dweebs, that the less educated are morally superior to people from Ivy League schools, that only those who've been in combat can judge war crimes and that good will triumph over evil if given enough screen time. In "Rules of Engagement," the good is Col. Terry Childers (Jackson), who orders his men to open fire on a crowd containing women and children during an attack on the U.S. Embassy in Yemen. Since there are no witnesses except Childers who saw guns in the crowd, the national security adviser (Bruce Greenwood) decides that Childers—who has been in every U.S. combat situation since the Vietnam War, if you can believe that—will take the rap for what becomes an international outrage.

Showing a lack of judgment so profound he should be discharged from the service immediately, Childers goes for help to old buddy Col. Hays Hodges (Jones), who is about to retire after the uninspired legal career he took up after his maiming in Vietnam (Friedkin's attempt to open his film "Private Ryan"-style makes one appreciate Steven Spielberg). Ex-drinker, ex-husband, bad lawyer. You have to ask yourself: If Childers' case is so essential to U.S. standing in the Middle East—and all about public relations anyway—why would a guy like Hodges be allowed to handle the case? I mean, if everything is a conspiracy anyway.

You also want to know why Guy Pearce, who plays the Marine prosecutor, sounds like Stanley Kowalski Esq., and whether they really serve beer and whiskey on Yemenite airplanes full of fundamentalist Muslims (providing Hodges the fuel for falling off the wagon). Or whether Friedkin really needed to put guns in the hands of Yemenite children (in scenes actually filmed in Morocco). Does he really believe his audience believes the innocent don't get killed in war? Maybe. What he never answers is why he apparently thinks individual glory should be accorded battle heroes, but not individual responsibility. Oh well: Tommy Lee Jones gives a great courtroom summation. And when Childers gets indicted, the look of pain on Jackson's face might make you forget that what you're watching is a really stupid movie.

SIGHT AND SOUND, 9/00, p. 50, Mark Kermode

Vietnam 1968. Approaching Ca Lu, US Marine Terry Childers executes a Vietcong soldier, terrifying the Vietnamese Colonel Cao into calling off an ongoing attack on his platoon, thus saving the life of wounded comrade-in arms Hays Hodges.

Present day. Colonel Childers leads an airborne mission to the besieged US Embassy in Yemen. Having evacuated Ambassador Mourain and his family, Childers orders his men to open fire on a crowd of demonstrators, killing 63 Of them. Back in the US, Childers is charged with murder and asks Hodges to be his defence council. National Security Adviser William Sokal destroys a tape from Yemen Embassy security cameras showing the crowd firing weapons and insists Childers was under fire only from rooftop snipers. Hodges travels to Yemen, where he meets children crippled by gunfire and observes the undamaged security camera from which the tape is now missing.

In court, prosecutor Mark Biggs paints a damning picture of Childers, calling Cao to testify as to his illegal warfare tactics. Hodges argues that Childers was protecting US territory, and that the disappearance of the surveillance tape points towards a cover up. He gets Cao to agree that he would have done the same as Childers in Ca Lu were circumstances reversed. The jury finds Childers guilty of breach of the peace but not guilty of murder. Outside the courtroom, Childers and Cao salute one another.

After some years in the Hollywood wilderness, director William Friedkin returns to big box-office form with this unevenly edgy and exciting film. Pitched somewhere between thoughtful courtroom drama and gung-ho actioner, *Rules of Engagement* fires off in numerous directions simultaneously, hitting only some of its intended targets, but spraying enough explosively scattershot cinematic shells to draw flak away from the cracks in the design. Most of these cracks are the result of flaws in the screenplay which lacks a degree of cohesive credibility despite—or perhaps because of—several rewrites. But reliably rugged performances from Samuel L. Jackson as Childers, the US colonel accused of firing on innocent Yemeni demonstrators, and Tommy Lee Jones as Hodges, the officer charged with defending him, provide a solid foundation for the drama. Guy Pearce, whose cadaverous features are used to show-stealing effect, contributes a mincingly menacing turn as the prosecutor Biggs and a brace of well chosen cameos add international spice, most notably Amidou (seen previously in Friedkin's underrated *Sorcerer,* 1977), whose melancholy gravitas lends a powerful emotional pull to his few fleeting scenes.

As is usual with a Friedkin film, *Rules of Engagement* attracted a fair deal of controversy when it was released in the US. Public battles between James Webb (who served in Vietnam and receives a story credit on Stephen Gaghan's final screenplay) and military technical advisor Dale Dye were reportedly patched up during production, thus side-stepping potentially damaging claims of inauthenticity. Later, skirmishes flared between the film-makers and Yemeni officials who condemned an allegedly racist bias, provoked doubtless by the use of such provocative sights as a little Arab girl brandishing a machine gun or a Vietcong colonel saluting an American officer.

It is ironic, then, that a film which has been labelled racist should be distinguished by a cinematic gaze which lavishes so much love on its non US locations, far more, indeed, than on its American ones. Nicola Pecorini's haunting views of Morocco (doubling for Yemen) provide the visual core of the film, showcasing Friedkin's flair for the exotic. Like the lyrical Iraqi opening sequence in Friedkin's *The Exorcist,* (1973) the long-lensed images of Arabic faces and facades in *Rules* give the impression of observation without intrusion. Even during the action-packed siege sequence, Friedkin seems more interested in shooting the big picture than nailing the specifics of the crossfire, unlike the Vietnam sequence (shot with aplomb entirely in North Carolina), in which the location is little more than a bland canvas on which to paint the bloody violence of warfare.

For the courtroom sequences, William Fraker displaces Pecorini (who himself replaced an uncredited Dariusz Wolski), lending a more polished sheen to the close up showdowns. Ironically this underlines the protagonists' claim that clean-cut legal niceties have little to do with the nuts-and-bolts nastiness of the battlefield. Although this change to his crew was unplanned, Friedkin seems to thrive on the tensions it produced, conjuring a crackling sense of conflict between the rules and realities of engagement. It is on this level that *Rules* works best, reminding us what an exceptional eye the director possesses, and how much his film-making has depended on gut reaction rather than calculatedly clinical cutting.

It is a shame, therefore, that for all his visual brilliance, Friedkin rarely finds scripts worthy of his attention. Although Webb and Gaghan's work is an improvement on the drooling drivel of Joe Eszterhas' *Jade* (1994), it is a far cry from the rigorous writing of William Peter Blatty's *The Exorcist*, the free-form improvisation of *The French Connection* (1971) or even the incohesive rambling of Friedkin's own script for *Cruising* (1980). Perhaps it's a mark of changing audience expectations that a film which would doubtless have ended in despair and disarray in the 70s (witness the detective Doyle's conclusively hopeless off-screen gunshot in Friedkin's police thriller *The French Connection)* must now win viewer approval by neatly tying up all its loose ends. Still, although the arrival may be ultimately unsatisfying for die-hard cynics, there is enough about this journey that is unsettling and eye-opening to make it worth the fare.

VILLAGE VOICE, 4/18/00, p. 162, Michael Atkinson

Duck and cover: Finally for big-budget Hollywood, it's Giuliani time. William Friedkin's bathetic flag-fucker *Rules of Engagement* is as dogged and concise an apologia for using militarist might to control civilians as any City Hall publicists could ever concoct. Here, the Diallos in question are 83 Yemeni civilians, mowed down from a rooftop by marine honcho Samuel L. Jackson during an embassy evacuation. Lip service is paid to the pile of corpses, or at least to the one or two presumably innocent Arabs among them (the rest are merely yowling wogs), but the movie concentrates on the poor schlubs with the ordnance, and the holy obligation to use it. Friedkin and writers Stephen Gaghan and James Webb train in on the old-'Nam-buddy bond between Jackson and Tommy Lee Jones's laconic lawyer (looking a few Rhesus years older than his movie mom Bonnie Johnson), and the clichés lap like bay waves, from the salutes to the brotherly brawl to the olive-oil tear streaks semipermanently painted down Jackson's cheeks.

Like an evil lawyer, the movie withholds the scenario's crucial information, just as the evil U.S. federal bureaucrat (Bruce Greenwood) does so that Jackson's seasoned hothead will take the fall. But the buried evidence is logistically and morally meaningless, making the hell-bent prosecutor (Guy Pearce, doing an impression of someone doing an impression of Christopher Walken) sound like the voice of reason even though he's intended to be the punkass pencil pusher. While studio films usually strive to slouch left, occasionally we're witness to reactionary bunco like this, rallying round the flag as it marks its own cards—we're even treated to a close-up of an evil five-year-old Yemeni girl shooting an automatic pistol. Even the chickenshit needs of government are secondary to the noblesse oblige of firefight-scarred marines. (G. Gordon Liddy even makes a cameo as a talk-show host.) "Innocent people always die!" Jackson hollers in court—for all he cares. War is, of course, hell, but for Friedkin and troops, it's not because the innocent die (as it is in all war = hell movies from *Arsenal* to *Attack!* to *The Thin Red Line*) but because we have to kill them. Poor us. Who's talking this neo-con psycho-talk, exactly—Friedkin, producers Scott Rudin and Richard Zanuck? Probably no one—there's no limit to how cynical you should be about Hollywood.

Also reviewed in:
CHICAGO TRIBUNE, 4/7/00, Friday/p. A, Michael Wilmington
NEW YORK TIMES, 4/7/00, p. E14, Elvis Mitchell
VARIETY, 4/3-9/00, p. 32, Todd McCarthy
WASHINGTON POST, 4/7/00, p. C1, Stephen Hunter

RUNNING FREE

A Columbia Pictures release of a Reperage production. *Executive Producer:* Alisa Tager and Lloyd Phillips. *Producer:* Jean-Jacques Annaud. *Director:* Sergei Bodrov. *Screenplay:* Jeanne Rosenberg. *Story:* Jean-Jacques Annaud and Jeanne Rosenberg.. *Director of Photography:* Dan

Laustsen. *Editor:* Ray Lovejoy. *Music:* Nicola Piovani. *Sound:* Conrad Kuhne. *Sound Editor:* Rodney Glenn. *Casting:* Janet Meintjies. *Production Designer:* Wolf Kroeger. *Art Director:* Jonathan Hely-Hutchinson and Zak Grobler. *Set Decorator:* Emelia Roux Weavind. *Special Effects:* David J. Brown. *Costumes:* Jo Katsaras-Barklam. *Make-up:* Pia Cornelius. *Running time:* 82 minutes. *MPAA Rating:* G.

CAST: Chase Moore (Young Richard);   Jan Decleir (Boss Man);   Maria Geelbooi (Nyka); Lukas Haas (Narrator);   Arie Verveen (Adult Richard);   Graham Clarke (Mine Supervisor); Patrick Lyster (Officer);   Morne Visser (Groom);   Dan Robbertse (Colonel); Nicholas Trueb (Hans, Boss' Son);   Robin Smith (Blacksmith);   Iluce Kgao (Nyka's Friend).

LOS ANGELES TIMES, 6/2/00, Calendar/p. 14, Kevin Thomas

Sergei Bodrov's sweeping family adventure "Running Free," as beautiful as it is harsh, tells the story of how herds of wild horses came to roam the red sand dunes of Namibia's vast desert—and what it reveals about humans in their treatment of animals. Written by "The Black Stallion's" Jeanne Rosenberg (from a story she wrote with the film's producer, "Quest for Fire's" Jean-Jacques Annaud), "Running Free" is a stunner marred by its central figure, a colt named Lucky, having been voiced (by Lukas Haas).

The animal's observations not only are trite but also redundant, for Bodrov, director of the superb Oscar-nominated "Prisoner of the Mountain," and his cinematographer Dan Laustsen know how to tell the story visually. The anthropomorphization of Lucky, furthermore, blurs the important distinction between human and animal behavior.

Though it's true that the narration provided by Haas will certainly be helpful to children in keeping track of what's going on, youngsters really ought to be accompanied by adults in the first place, despite the film's G rating. That's because "Running Free" is unflinching in its depiction of the brutality with which humans treat each other as well as animals.

This handsome, period-perfect Columbia release opens dramatically in 1914 with an overhead shot of a large number of horses clattering over a cobblestone street in a German port city, where the animals are to be shipped off to Namibia to work in a copper mine, a large, grueling operation overseen by a stern boss (Jan Decleir). Lucky is born mid-passage to a gray mare aboard a German supply ship, but mother and child become separated, with the foal ultimately rescued by Richard (Chase Moore), an orphan stableboy at the mining camp.

The tie between boy and the colt grows strong, but their situation, always dicey due to human indifference and cruelty, abruptly turns critical when this German outpost is bombed with the spread of World War I to Africa. At this point Richard must do everything in his power to ensure that Lucky will survive on his own with the imminent abandonment of the community by the survivors of the bombing.

Bodrov and trainer Sled Reynolds' 10-man team have done a totally persuasive job of making the horses behave as naturally as the film's cast of humans, which includes Maria Geelbooi as Nyka, a pretty and resourceful girl from a bushmen tribe, and Arie Verveen as the adult Richard. "Life Is Beautiful" composer Nicola Piovani's score is lyrical and emotionally charged, and it goes a long way toward negating the effects of the voice-over narration we're asked to accept.

NEW YORK POST, 6/2/00, p. 46, Lou Lumenick

Imagine "The Black Stallion" if it were narrated by Mr. Ed, and you get a rough idea of this lame children's movie, which suffers from terminal hoof-in-mouth disease.

Sappy wall-to-wall narration destroys the potentially interesting story of Lucky, a horse born aboard a ship carrying workhorses from Europe to an African mining town.

Separated from his mother—"Why didn't anyone understand that I needed to be with my mother?" needlessly whines Lucky, impersonated on the soundtrack by Lukas Haas—he's befriended by a stableboy named Richard (the charmless Chase Moore).

But mom dies and World War I separates Richard and Lucky ("I suddenly realized they were taking my boy away from me"). The colt flees into desert, proclaiming: "It was time for me to set out into an unknown world, where I would be as wild and free as in my dreams."

Lucky returns to lead abandoned horses into the wild after a contrived showdown with a thoroughbred stallion ("I didn't know if I was strong enough to win, but I was strong enough to try")—and eventually has a ridiculous reunion with the grown-up Richard.

Endless cloying new-agey talk—not to mention a mushy musical score—wastes some gorgeous location footage that outdoes last month's dud, "I Dreamed of Africa."

"Running Free" is directed by Sergei Bodrov (Russia's "Prisoner of the Mountain") with a visual grace totally at conflict with the hokey narrative concocted by producer Jean-Jacques Annaud ("The Bear") and screenwriter Jeanne Rosenberg ("The Black Stallion").

NEWSDAY, 6/2/00, Part II/p. B9, John Anderson

A class fable set among the horsey set—literally—"Running Free" is produced by Jean-Jacques Annaud (director of "The Bear") and based on a story he wrote with screenwriter Jeanne Rosenberg. So it shouldn't be much of a surprise that the film achieves such convincing characterizations of its animal cast, or the boy's-book heroics of Walter Farley ("The Black Stallion") or, occasionally, the poignancy of "Dumbo."

Unfortunately, "Running Free" is also saddled with actor Lukas Haas, who delivers a lifeless first-person-or first-horse-narration, the very existence of which will have some audiences thinking "Mr. Ed."

"I was born at a time when many horses were being sent to Africa to work in the copper mines," recalls our hero, Lucky (Nisha), who as a fuzzy red colt is shipped off with his old gray mother to the near-desert of South Africa's outback. Once there, the two will be separated and "Running Free," will follow the classic narrative tradition of not just "Dumbo" but "Babe," "Bambi" and "David Copperfield."

It's truly a Dickensian horse story. Like Oliver Twist, Lucky is the son of an unwed mom, loses her and is hobbled by his uncertain social status: Caesar (Fat Albert), the villainous and pampered top horse at the copper mine, tolerates no strangers in his paddock nor near his daughter, Beauty (Noodle). "I was only the stable boy's horse," Lucky laments. "I wasn't good enough to play with his daughter." Lucky is befriended by that stable boy (Chase Moore) and a young girl from a local tribe (Maria Geelbooi), but it's mostly a one- horse show, with Lucky growing into the kind of red stallion (Aladdin) worthy of his own film.

"Running Free" equates species-ism with racism and racism with fascism; the mine boss (Jan Decleir) is a Boer, but might as well be a Nazi; his young son (Nicholas Trueb), a white-blond Pugsley, seems ready to sing "Tomorrow Belongs to Me." The unfortunate thing about "Running Free," which seems a good bet for young and especially horse- crazed kids, is that it didn't need Haas. The visual storytelling is so strong it would have told the tale quite adequately, without resorting to the horse's mouth.

Also reviewed in:
CHICAGO TRIBUNE, 6/2/00, Friday/p. A, Monica Eng
NEW YORK TIMES, 6/2/00, p. E18, A. O. Scott
VARIETY, 5/29-6/4/00, p. 19, Robert Koehler

SANTITOS

A Latin Universe release of a Spingall Pictures production. *Executive Producer:* John Sayles. *Producer:* Alejandro Springall and Claudia Florescano. *Director:* Alejandro Springall. *Screenplay (Spanish with English subtitles):* Maria Amparo Escandón. *Director of Photography:* Xavier Pérez Grobet. *Editor:* Carol Dysinger. *Music:* Carlo Nicolau and Rosino Serrano. *Sound:* David Baksht. *Casting:* Claudia Becker. *Production Designer:* Eugenio Caballero and Salvador Parra. *Special Effects:* Alex Vázquez. *Costumes:* Mónica Neumaier. *Make-up:* Carlos Sánchez. *Stunt Coordinator:* Gerardo Moreno. *Running time:* 90 minutes. *MPAA Rating:* R.

CAST: Dolores Heredia (Esperanza); Fernando Torre Lapham (Padre Salvador); Juan Duarte (Fidencio); Ana Bertha Espin (Soledad); Maya Zapata (Blanca); Roberto Cobo (Doña Trini); Georgina Tabora (Hospital Receptionist); Demián Bichir (Cacomixtle); Alberto Estrella (Angel); Pedro Altamirano (Public Minster); Mónica Dionne (La Morena); Josefina Echánove (Professor); Felipe Ehrenberg (Alto); Maria Amparo Escandón (La Adicional); Flor Eduarda Gurrola (Paloma); Pilar Ixquic Mata (La Flaca, the Skinny One); Paco Morayta Olímpico (Don Arlindo, Manager of the Angel); Regina Orozco (Vicenta Cortés); Darío T. Pie (César); José Sefami (Dr. Ortiz); Luis Felipe Tovar (Doroteo); Claudio Valdés (San Judas Tadeo).

LOS ANGELES TIMES, 1/31/00, Calendar/p. 5, Kevin Thomas

"Santitos" is pure enchantment, a beguiling tale of love, faith and self-discovery told in a colorful, effortless folkloric style by Alejandro Springall. It's from a script by Maria Amparo Escandon that she developed from her novel at the Sundance Screenwriters' Lab, where she met Springall.

"Santitos" is the first film to be distributed by Latin Universe, which claims that it is "the nation's first Spanish-language film distribution company catering exclusively to the Latino entertainment marketplace."

"Santitos," which lists John Sayles as its executive producer and boasts excellent English subtitles, has the same kind of humor, charm and sensuality that made "Like Water for Chocolate" the most popular foreign-language film until "Life Is Beautiful" came along.

Dolores Heredia stars as Esperanza, a beautiful and devoutly religious young widow who lives in the quaint Veracruz town of Tlacotalpan with her beloved teenage daughter, Blanca. One day Blanca undergoes a tonsillectomy, and the next thing Esperanza knows, her daughter has died, the victim of an unknown virus. The distraught mother is not allowed to see her daughter's body.

On the glass window of her kitchen oven, Esperanza experiences a vision of a plaster statue of St. Jude, who suddenly speaks, telling her not to believe those who would tell her that her daughter is dead. That her daughter's doctor leaves the hospital the day after Blanca's reported death understandably heightens Esperanza's anxiety. With the support of the kindly, understanding local priest (Fernando Torre Lapham), Esperanza commences a long odyssey, convinced that Blanca has been sold into slavery.

Esperanza takes a job as a maid at a local brothel as a starting point for gathering clues about Blanca's fate. The most slender of tips sends her off to Tijuana, where there is supposed to be a highly secret bordello called the Pink House.

Esperanza reluctantly but bravely becomes one of the stable, only to end up the exclusive, well-paid lover of a kindly, good-looking, middle-aged San Diego judge (Rudger Cudney), who smuggles her into Los Angeles when she receives another tip about Blanca's possible whereabouts. In L.A., she is swept up into a romance with a tall, handsome wrestler (Angel Galvan) who bills himself as the "Angel of Justice."

What Esperanza is unexpectedly experiencing is her reawakening as a woman while searching for her daughter, a quest that she will not relinquish until she either finds Blanca or receives a sign that she is in fact dead, presumably safely ensconced in heaven.

Tone is everything in such a film, and cast and crew alike clearly understand that they are engaged in depicting a woman unwittingly caught up in the process of balancing the spiritual with the physical in her life. Never does the film mock Esperanza's faith—or religion itself, for that matter—and it embraces her quest with affection and respect. Ultimately, "Santitos" celebrates the unity of the flesh and the spirit in a thoroughly refreshing manner.

NEW YORK POST, 1/28/00, p. 51, Hannah Brown

"Santitos" aims to be a magic-realist comedy, but the premise is so sad it's impossible to chuckle at the often heavy-handed humor.

A "saint" appears in the oven grime to tell young Mexican widow Esperanza (Dolores Heredia) that her 13-year-old daughter—who died during routine surgery—is still alive.

Esperanza embarks on a quest to find her daughter, who she believes is a prostitute in Tijuana. Mom journeys from Tijuana to L.A. and—for reasons never clear—becomes a whore along the way.

"Santitos" is often entertaining, but it's hard to laugh. The beautiful Heredia and the supporting cast perform admirably. Too bad its creators didn't think through the premise a little better.

VILLAGE VOICE, 2/9/00, p. 146, Dennis Lim

Bestowed the widest Spanish-language opening since *Like Water for Chocolate, Santitos* concerns a grieving young Mexican woman who embarks on a bittersweet, therapeutic dream-voyage after Saint Jude appears to her in her grimy oven. Aspiring toward magic realism, Alejandro Springall's first feature is in essence a formulaic heal-thyself inspirational, a feel-better fantasy that, for all its gaudy Catholic flourishes, seems touched mainly by the hand of Oprah. The screenplay was incubated at the Sundance writers' lab—a not entirely dissimilar institution, one might argue—and writer Maria Amparo Escandón has already converted her script into a novel, *Esperanza's Box of Saints,* in both English and Spanish.

Shortly after Esperanza's daughter dies, supposedly from a mystery virus contracted during a routine tonsillectomy, the saintly apparition tells her that the girl is in fact still alive. Confiding in a half-exasperated, half-fascinated comic-relief priest (much of the movie takes the form of flashback confessions), the devout, headstrong heroine, charmingly played by Dolores Heredia, leaves her village, first for Tijuana, then Los Angeles, convinced that her child has been sold into prostitution. She soon falls into a spiral of dubious, God-motivated whorishness (à la *Breaking the Waves),* and—her path strewn with unidimensional, moderately malevolent kooks—suffers a crisis of faith, which is assuaged by the timely intervention of an angel. To be exact, by a masked wrestler who calls himself the Angel of Justice.

Lavishly mounted but directed with no particular flair (a fetish for mirror images notwithstanding; there's even a kaleidoscopic peephole), *Santitos* has trouble getting past its pat ideas about grief and healing. The filmmakers' solution is to crank up the whimsy, but the harder they try, the more obvious it is that there's no gold dust to be found here, just an awful lot of stick-on glitter.

Also reviewed in:
NEW REPUBLIC, 2/28/00, p. 26, Stanley Kauffmann
NEW YORK TIMES, 1/28/00, p. E18, Anita Gates
VARIETY, 2/8-14/99, p. 82, Leonardo Garcia Tsao

SASAYAKI: MOONLIGHT WHISPERS

A Viz Films/Tidepoint Pictures release of a Nikkatsu Corporation production. *Producer:* Masaya Nakamura. *Director:* Akhiko Shiota and Hiroyuki Negishi. *Screenplay (Japanese with English subtitles):* Akihiko Shiota and Yoichi Nishiyama. *Based on the comic strip "Gekko no Sasayaki" by:* Masahiko Kikuni. *Director of Photography:* Shigeru Komatsubara. *Editor:* Yoshio Sugano. *Music:* Shinsuke Honda. *Sound:* Kenji Sakagami. *Production Designer:* Norifumi Ataka. *Running time:* 100 minutes. *MPAA Rating:* Not Rated.

CAST: Kenji Mizuhasi (Takuya Hidaka); Tsugumi (Satsuki Kitahara); Kota Kusano (Tadashi Uematsu); Harumi Inoue (Shizuka Kitahara); Chika Fujimura (Satsuki's Friend); Yoshiki Sekino (Maruken).

NEW YORK POST, 11/22/00, p. 46, V.A. Musetto

Less than a week after the opening here of "Lies," the controversial South Korean film about the bizarre S&M relationship between a schoolgirl and an older man, comes yet another kinky Asian film.

This time the subjects are a seemingly average boy and girl in Japan—Takuya and Satsuki, respectively—whose high school romance drifts into sadomasochism.

The on-screen sex, however, is much less explicit than in "Lies," and the S&M consists more of mind games (such as Satsuki forcing Takuya to listen as she makes love to another man) than physical abuse.

Newcomer Akihiko Shiota shows talent as a director, but he allows "Sasayaki" to go on too long. The final few scenes could have been dropped without taking away from the film's erotic charm.

Now if someone will program "Lies" and "Sasayaki" as a double-feature . . .

VILLAGE VOICE, 11/28/00, p. 138, Dennis Lim

Like Unbreakable Bruce, teenage Hidaka (Kenji Mizuhashi) has a high threshold for pain. Kendo practice is an excuse for much pleasurable bruising at the hands of playmate Kitahara (Tsugumi). "I like it when you strike me on the head," he informs her. Later he breaks into her locker, discovers a pair of shorts, and greedily inhales. Akihiko Shiota's first feature, *Sasayaki,* dryly and quietly notes the improbable progression of a coquettish courtship into s&m mindfuck. Kitahara first suspects a lurking fetish when her new beau expresses profound envy for her dog (a blast of the Stooges would at this point have been preferable to the cutely tinkling soundtrack). When he takes to tape-recording her in the bathroom, she freaks and dumps him. But Hidaka's tenacious passivity continues to anger, excite, and scare her; she responds by humiliating him, which only turns her on more. The movie stagnates midway, and the second half plays out with rote variations, predictably accelerated. Still, up against the screechy, sexless theatrics of *Quills* and the hardcore purity of the bravura Korean fuckfest *Lies,* this dreamy, languorous farce offers a manageable strawberry-flavored alternative, a mildly kinky Hello Kitty sadomasochism.

Also reviewed in:
NEW YORK TIMES, 11/22/00, p. E8, A. O. Scott

SAVING GRACE

A Fine Line Features release of a Portman Entertainment presentation in association with Sky Pictures and Wave Pictures of a Homerun production. *Executive Producer:* Cat Villiers and Xavier Marchand. *Producer:* Mark Crowdy. *Director:* Nigel Cole. *Screenplay:* Craig Ferguson and Mark Crowdy. *Story:* Mark Crowdy. *Director of Photography:* John de Borman. *Editor:* Alan Strachan. *Music:* Mark Russell. *Sound:* John Midgley and (music) Gerry O'Riordan. *Sound Editor:* Alan Paley. *Casting:* Gail Stevens. *Production Designer:* Eve Stewart. *Art Director:* Tom Read. *Costumes:* Annie Symons. *Make-up:* Rose Ann Samuel. *Running time:* 93 minutes. *MPAA Rating:* R.

CAST: Brenda Blethyn (Grace Trevethan); Craig Ferguson (Matthew); Martin Clunes (Doctor Bamford); Tchéky Karyo (Jacques); Jamie Foreman (China McFarlane); Bill Bailey (Vince); Valerie Edmond (Nicky); Tristan Sturrock (Harvey Sloggit); Clive Merrison (Quentin); Leslie Phillips (Vicar); Diana Quick (Honey); Phyllida Law (Margaret); Linda Kerr Scott (Diana); Denise Coffey (Mrs. Hopkins); Paul Brooke (Charlie); Ken Campbell (Sergeant Alfred); John Fortune (Melvyn); Philip Wright (Nigel); Darren Southworth (Terry); Magnus Lindgren (Tony); Dean Lennox Kelly (Bob); Johnny Bamford (Removal Boss); Bill Hallet (Postman); Alison Dillon (Secretary); Bill Weston (John Trevethan); Jonathan Kydd and Mark Crowdy (Presenters); Jay Benedict (Master of Ceremonies); Ben Cole (Man at Checkout).

CHRISTIAN SCIENCE MONITOR, 8/4/00, p. 15, David Sterritt

The punningly titled "Saving Grace" takes us to the Cornish coast of England, where middle-aged Grace is facing more than her share of hardships: Her husband has died, her debts are enormous, and if her financial picture doesn't improve she'll lose her beloved home. Putting together two of her remaining assets—a talent for gardening and a few shady acquaintances—she sets up a marijuana farm in her greenhouse, hoping for a quick profit to end her woes. The enterprise veers in unexpected directions before the happy ending, which restores Grace's basic decency and provides endorsement of traditional values.

"Saving Grace" gets much of its charm from the first-rate acting of Brenda Blethyn, already known for "Little Voice" and "Secrets & Lies," among other British pictures. She brings her character alive with a canny blend of subtlety and gusto, keeping the movie bright even when the plot occasionally sags. Add a sturdy supporting cast and some very funny visual moments, and you have a minor but engaging entertainment.

LOS ANGELES TIMES, 8/4/00, Calendar/p. 19, Jan Stuart

[The following review by Jan Stuart appeared in a slightly different form in **NEWSDAY, 8/4/00, Part II/p. B10.]**

For those who have not partaken of marijuana and would never consider it, the makers of "Saving Grace" are here to tell you what it's all about.

It makes you giggle.

That's the dark, dirty secret. You giggle. You giggle again. You put on novelty store spectacles with big eyeballs that pop out on springs and you giggle some more. And then you eat a case of cornflakes.

"Saving Grace," otherwise known as "Brenda Blethyn Gets the Munchies," is about as benign a marijuana comedy as one could imagine. Set in the sort of pristine Cornish village where one might expect to find Miss Marple poking the hedges for clues, it features the twice-Oscar-nominated Blethyn ("Secrets & Lies" and "Little Voice") as a middle-class widow who turns to growing marijuana crops in her greenhouse to pay off the staggering debts left by her husband.

That's the tall and the short of it. What lends this one-joke comedy a measure of interest are the ways in which writers Craig Ferguson (who co-stars as Blethyn's faithful gardener) and Mark Crowdy avoid the adorable-stoned-Mrs.-Minivertrap for Blethyn (although there are a couple of those dithering about on the sidelines). Instead of the blowzy or weepy gals who have made her famous, Blethyn gives us here a woman of dignity and comeliness who is compelled by necessity toward nefarious means.

Sporting the sort of pragmatic but fashionable ensemble of plaid blouse and leather vest one would expect to find in a Marks and Spencer catalog, her Grace Trevethan accords her illegal green crops the same loving attention as her orchids. The locals set up lawn chairs to watch the light show emanating from her greenhouse each night, and everyone keeps mum about her activities. This is a village where folks look out for their own, and the upstanding town doctor (Martin Clunes) is the biggest stoner for miles around.

The complications don't amount to a hill of buds. What saves "Saving Grace" from its ineffectual tendencies is Blethyn, dressing up as a big white day lily to peddle her crops on the streets of London or facing down a dangerous French dealer (Tcheky Karyo) in an absurd subterranean den (the interiors are great throughout). Blethyn is the model of a middle-aged movie star: relaxed, intelligent, quietly handsome, full of grace.

NEW YORK POST, 8/4/00, p. 62, Lou Lumenick

It isn't easy to make a comedy that has audiences rooting for a supplier of illicit drugs, but this uproarious British farce manages, with laughs to spare.

Basically a "Full Monty" for the cannabis crowd, it features a thoroughly winning performance by the great Brenda Blethyn ("Secrets & Lies") as Grace Trevethan, a sheltered middle-aged widow driven into the pot trade by financial circumstances.

Heavily in debt after her husband's death in a sky-diving accident, she has only one marketable skill: She's the most gifted gardener in a tiny, remote (and very scenic) town in Cornwall.

Grace's Scottish pot-smoking handyman, Matthew (Craig Ferguson), suggests she apply her talents to growing industrial quantities of hemp, which she does with spectacular—and consistently hilarious—results.

Sympathy for Grace's plight is such that everyone from the vicar (Leslie Phillips) to the constable (Ken Campbell) turns a blind eye to Grace's increasingly conspicuous activities—and a greenhouse that spectacularly lights up the night sky.

Blethyn's tour-de-force performance puts over the wilder twists in Ferguson's script, which has Grace trolling London's tony Notting Hill district looking for a buyer—which she finds in a suave drug dealer (Tcheky Karyo, the Frenchman in "The Patriot").

In the movie's funniest scene, Grace discovers the joys of pot smoking, and soon much of the village—including the old biddies in the garden—are joining in the fun.

There is excellent supporting work by Martin Clunes as the toking village doctor and Bill Bailey as a hippie dope dealer.

Beautifully shot on location with sure comic timing by director Nigel Coles, "Saving Grace" is a real high in a season filled with unfunny comedies.

SIGHT AND SOUND, 6/00, p. 53, Edward Lawrenson

Port Liac, Cornwall, the present. Amateur gardener Grace Trevethan discovers her deceased husband John ran up debts without her knowledge and had a mistress, China. She makes her gardener Matthew redundant, but this isn't enough to stop Quentin, a London-based businessman, from threatening to repossess her cottage. Grace suggests a business proposition to Matthew, a casual pot smoker: they will grow marijuana in her greenhouse and sell the harvest to drug dealers. Matthew agrees. Promising Matthew's pregnant partner Nicky she will keep Matthew out of trouble, Grace goes to London to sell the drugs. Her attempts to sell a sample on the street land her in jail. China bails her out and introduces Grace to drug dealer Vince, who reluctantly takes her to French crime boss Jacques, a potential buyer. Aware of a mutual attraction, Grace strikes a bargain with Jacques.

Jacques' thuggish associate follows Grace to Port Liac. As Grace harvests the marijuana, Quentin arrives to stake his claim on the house. Mistaking Jacques' henchman for a poacher, local policeman Alfred follows him to Grace's house and discovers her stockpile of weed. He advises her to destroy it before more police arrive. Grace burns the weed. Some time later, Grace is a successful novelist, married to Jacques.

The best thing about *Saving Grace* is the trouble the film-makers went to in order to ensure the authenticity of Grace's marijuana plants. The producers actually secured permission to get hold of all this gear from the Ministry of Agriculture. While a film as casually pro-soft drugs as this isn't likely to earn a commendation from Home Secretary Jack Straw, it says something for *Saving Grace*'s innocuous charm that the producers gained Crown dispensation in the first place. It's hard, for instance, to imagine Donald Cammell making a similar approach when he shot *Performance* (1970).

In fact, the comparison with *Performance* isn't too ludicrous. *Saving Grace*'s final sequence—where the police, Jacques' henchmen and a couple of old dears from the Womens' Institute fall under the influence of Grace's dope, disrobe and run naked through her garden—does suggest a suburban spin on *Performance*'s assault on established conventions. Except, like everything else in this film, this rather strained scene is less a moment of pure carnival, deliriously upturning codes of normality, than an innocent bit of fun. It's certainly no more shocking than when real-life WI members went nude and were photographed last year to shake up their organisation's rather stuffy reputation. This benignly tolerant attitude envelops all of *Saving Grace*. not only does her local community accept Grace's career in drugs, she ultimately escapes any charges, gets to keep her house and marries Jacques—a rosy outcome which would be next to heresy in the morally upright Ealingesque world director Nigel Cole consciously evokes. Even a brush with the criminal underworld has its endearingly ordinary, if not solidly respectable side. "Can I go now," small-time drugs dealer Vince says, trying to wheedle his way out of a potentially dangerous situation, "I've got to pick my daughter up from flute practice."

All of which makes for a film with a certain unfocused amiability. But in trying too hard to convince us what good eggs his characters are, Cole creates a shapeless, dramatically unengaging movie. Grace and China's descent into the criminal underworld, for instance, is about as tense as a stroll through Harvey Nichols, and the prolonged mistaken-identity finale is like a Ray

Cooney farce with the timing out of whack. Cole would have done well to remember the best Ealing films were never this nice: think of the caustic bite of *Whisky Galore!* or the black humour of Charles Crichton's crime capers.

This said, Brenda Blethyn's performance as Grace who blossoms into the Delia Smith of hemp cultivation stands comparison with a line of such indomitable Ealing women as Googie Withers and Katie Johnson. Dressed in Ascot attire circa 1977, her attempts to sell a sample of dope to the bewildered residents of London's Notting Hill *(Performance*'s stomping ground) almost make up for the film's flabbier moments.

VILLAGE VOICE, 8/8/00, p. 140, Dennis Lim

Constipated English whimsy for the easily tickled, *Saving Grace* treats its thin, smugly eccentric premise—upstanding small-town widow turns marijuana farmer—as a comic gold mine, when its attempts at humor can be boiled down to three basic concepts:

1. Smoking pot is naughty.
2. Growing pot is naughtier.
3. Smoking pot causes one to regress to a state of preverbal buffoonery.

Inanely upbeat and grindingly obvious, the movie amounts to a checklist of inevitable tee-heeing scenarios that surface on cue, only to wilt instantly before your eyes: the transportive first inhalation, the choked-back mouthful of smoke in the presence of authority figure (here a vicar), the accidental ingestion (daft biddies brew some "tea"), the resultant hunger pangs (stoned daft biddies pig out).

All too game (though mercifully not as game as in *Little Voice),* Brenda Blethyn plays the titular heroine, whose husband's death leaves her in debt and in danger of eviction. Egged on by her handyman (Craig Ferguson, the film's cowriter, already accountable this year for the hairdressers-in-kilts fiasco *The Big Tease),* Grace turns her attention from orchids to a more profitable crop, converting her greenhouse into a hemp plantation, outfitted with blinding high-intensity lamps that, to the bewilderment of the local yokels, illuminate the night sky like aurora borealis.

Old-school parochial quaintness with a self-congratulatory hint of subversion (though it owes plenty to the original Ealing contraband farce, Alexander MacKendrick's far superior *Whisky Galore!), Saving Grace* in the end keeps up appearances, copping out as decisively as you'd expect. It's clear that under no circumstances will Grace be allowed to cash in her bumper harvest (her financial troubles are instead resolved in a tossed-off fairy-tale epilogue). Directed by Nigel Cole, who deflates his gags even as he's setting them up, *Saving Grace* was wildly acclaimed at Sundance this year, where it won the audience award for best *foreign* film and, in the festival's costliest transaction, was picked up by Fine Line for $4 million—a chain of events that lends a new dimension to the notion of reefer madness.

Also reviewed in:
CHICAGO TRIBUNE, 8/4/00, Friday/p. A, Michael Wilmington
NEW YORK TIMES, 8/4/00, p. E25, A. O. Scott
VARIETY, 1/31-2/6/00, p. 33, Joe Leydon

SCARY MOVIE

A Dimension Films release of a Wayans Bros. Entertainment, Gold-Miller, Brad Grey Pictures production. *Executive Producer:* Bob Weinstein, Harvey Weinstein, Cary Granat, Peter Schwerin, Brad Grey, Peter Safran and Bo Zenga. *Producer:* Eric L Gold and Lee R. Mayes. *Director:* Keenen Ivory Wayans. *Screenplay:* Shawn Wayans, Marlon Wayans, Buddy Johnson, Phil Beauman, Jason Friedberg, and Aaron Seltzer. *Director of Photography:* Francis Kenny. *Editor:* Mark Helfrich. *Music:* David Kitay. *Music Editor:* Charles Martin Inouye. *Sound:*

Richard D. Lightstone and (music) Danny Wallin. *Sound Editor:* John Leveque. *Casting:* Mary Vernieu, Anne McCarthy, and Christine Sheaks. *Production Designer:* Robb Wilson King. *Art Director:* Lawrence F. Pevec. *Set Decorator:* Louise Roper. *Set Dresser:* Jim McGill, Steve Lamare, Cornel Maris, J.P. Bagshaw, and Richard Beech. *Special Effects:* Gary Paller. *Visual Effects:* Brian Jennings. *Costumes:* Darryle Johnson. *Make-up:* Stan Edmonds. *Stunt Coordinator:* J.J. Makaro. *Running time:* 88 minutes. *MPAA Rating:* R.

CAST: Carmen Electra (Drew); Dave Sheridan (Doofy); Frank B. Moore (Not Drew's Boyfriend); Giacomo Baessato, Kyle Graham, and Leanne Santos (Trick or Treaters); Mark McConchie (Drew's Dad); Karen Kruper (Drew's Mom); Anna Faris (Cindy); Jon Abrahams (Bobby); Rick Ducommun (Cindy's Dad); Regina Hall (Brenda); Marlon Wayans (Shorty); Shannon Elizabeth (Buffy); Lloyd Berry (Homeless Man); Cheri Oteri (Gail Hailstrom); Matthew Paxman (Annoying Guy); Chris Robson (KOMQ Reporter); Susan Shears (Female Reporter); Peter Bryant (Black TV Reporter); Lochlyn Munro (Greg); Shawn Wayans (Ray); Andrea Nemeth (Heather); Craig Brunanski (Road Victim); Dan Joffre (Cameraman Kenny); Kelly Coffield (Teacher); Kurt Fuller (Sheriff); David L. Lander (Principal Squiggy); Reg Tupper (Beauty Pageant MC); Tanja Reichert (Miss Congeniality); Kendall Saunders (Miss Thing); D.M. Babe Dolan (Grandma); David Neale and Nels Lennarson (Policemen); Nicola Crosbie and Ian Bliss (Reporters); Chris Wilding (Shorty's Roomate); Trevor Roberts (Dookie); Glynis Davies (Buffy's Mom); Jayne Trcka (Miss Mann); Peter Hanlon (Suicdal Teacher); Ted Cole (Older Man in Theater); Doreen Ramus (Old Lady in Theater); Lee R. Mayes (Amistad II Captain); Keenen Ivory Wayans (Slave); Mark Hoeppner (Whipmaster/Slavemaster); Jessica Van Der Veen (Woman in Theater); Jim Shepard (Young Man in Theater); Marissa Jaret Winokur (Garage Victim); Dexter Bell (Shorty's Friend); Ted Gill (Store Clerk).

LOS ANGELES TIMES, 7/7/00, Calendar/p. 1, Kevin Thomas

When Dimension Films stated firmly that "Scream 3" would be the last in the series, that didn't mean it couldn't be spoofed. "Scary Movie" not only sends up the "Scream" franchise but also the whole Dimension horror catalog and beyond—including even "The Blair Witch Project." There's not a real fright in sight in "Scary Movie," but no problem: Its blatantly clear intent is to stir up as much raunchy, gross-out humor as an R rating can withstand.

The result, while undeniably silly and violent in a cartoon-like manner, is by and large a hilarious skewering of the cliches of teen pix.

Director Keenen Ivory Wayans has kept everything fast and light; even a momentary slackening of pace or heaviness of touch could have proved disastrous in handling all the outrageous shenanigans dreamed up by a raft of writers headed by Wayans' brothers Shawn and Marlon. In any event, a lively, lowdown laff riot is always welcome amid a plethora of summer blockbusters.

Basically, the plot pretty much crosses the original "Scream" with "I Know what You Did Last Summer." A small-town high school is terrorized by a hooded killer with a mask inspired by the tormented visage of Edvard Munch's famous "Scream" painting. The film focuses on three couples, principally Cindy (Anna Faris), whose comfortable suburban home is supported by her dad's drug dealing, and Bobby (Jon Abrahams), intent on persuading her to go all the way.

Cindy and Bobby are archetypal teens, whereas Shannon Elizabeth's beautiful Buffy and Lochlyn Monroe's hunky Greg supply the glamour. Much of the humor comes from Shawn Wayans' Ray, a handsome football star of amusingly ambiguous sexual orientation, and from his girlfriend Brenda (Regina Hall), who has an unfortunate tendency to talk out loud at the movies.

Brenda's brother Shorty (Marlon Wayans) is the film's chronic stoner; Dave Sheridan's Doofy, a seriously slow-witted cop (who is also Buffy's brother) and Cheri Oteri's Gail Hailstorm, a ruthless TV reporter, are sendups of David Arquette and Courteney Cox Arquette's characters in the "Scream" series. Kurt Fuller is the local sheriff, more preoccupied with scoring than with crime-solving. Carmen Electra, gorgeous and a world-class good sport, appears in the opening sequence as the unknown killer's first victim.

The story gets underway when the three couples start getting notes reminding them that someone knows what they did last summer, keying a flashback of inspired knockabout comedy.

"Scary Movie's" R is a real envelope-pusher, and much of what happens to accomplish this, while very funny, defies description in a family newspaper. The film is not afraid to be politically incorrect yet remains essentially good-natured in spirit.

As with other Dimension movies, "Scary Movie" is a good showcase for a talented, youthful cast, and the film is carried with aplomb by newcomer Faris, a fearless comedian and an appealing ingenue.

NEW YORK POST, 7/7/00, p. 53, Jonathan Foreman

You don't have to have seen any of the "Scream" movies or the "I know What You Did Last Summer" series to enjoy "Scary Movie"—the gleeful teen-horror spoof that proves that the Farrelly brothers have no monopoly on outrageous, politically incorrect comedy.

In fact, the movie's best jokes tend to be incidental to the scene-for-scene parody: Instead, they deal with race and sex in ways that are bracingly politically incorrect.

Directed by Keenan Ivory Wayans ("I'm Gonna Git You Sucka"), "Scary Movie" is a feast of laughs that are juvenile, cheap, silly, aimed below the belt or all four—but effective.

It's only in the last 20 minutes or so that you begin to think the material could easily have been condensed into a one-hour cable special.

More daring and definitely more memorable—if generally dumber and less coherent—than "Me, Myself & Irene," it's a movie that all sorts of people could find deeply offensive, especially those who found the Wayans brothers' TV series, "In Living Color," too much to take.

Amusing jabs at recent movies, including "The Sixth Sense," "The Blair Witch Project," "The Matrix" and the whole self-conscious oeuvre of Kevin Williamson (not to mention references to "American Pie" and "Riverdance"), are combined with low-brow verbal and visual jokes about pot, flatulence, breast implants, snot, semen and penises.

Indeed, the director and six-man screenwriting team use the latter in ways (once as a weapon) that would have been guaranteed to earn an NC-1 7 before "There's Something About Mary."

The plot follows that of "Scream" almost exactly (with a few nods to "I Know What You Did..."). Carmen Electra plays Drew, the Drew Barrymore character who gets attacked after a creepy phone call in the first scene.

Anna Farris is the Neve Campbell virgin type. Cheri Oteri is the reporter who will do anything to get a story and Dave Sheridan plays Doofy (the David Arquette role), the cop she manipulates for inside information—except here, that character's moronism is taken to gross extremes.

Shawn Wayans and Lochlyn Munro play football stars burdened with personal secrets that would be unmentionable in the "Scream" flicks.

It's a well-chosen, well-directed cast: Everyone plays his or her part with just enough unself-conscious seriousness for the jokes to work.

NEWSDAY, 7/7/00, Part II/p. B3, Jan Stuart

Caution. You are entering a brain-free zone. Anything resembling taste, wit or political correctness is strictly prohibited. This area is rated R for raunch, which means adults should be accompanied by someone 17 or pubescent at heart.

You don't have to be a high school flunkie to revel in the carnival of bodily function and sex jokes that is the Wayans Brothers' rambunctiously rude "Scary Movie." It speaks to the out-to-lunch in all of us. Like a class clown trying to get a rise out of an uptight teacher, it ambushes the fuddy-duddy in our souls, stopping at nothing to render us defenseless.

Directed with devilish irreverence by Keenen Ivory Wayans from a script by brothers Shawn and Marlon and a small army of the shameless, "Scary Movie" sends up slasher movies ("Scream,") anti-slasher movies ("The Blair Witch Project"), gross-out movies ("There's Something About Mary") and any other pop culture phenomenon it can get its slippery little hands on.

"Scary Movie," launches in with a funny takeoff on the pre-credit Drew Barrymore murder in "Scream," aping the get-the-bimbo ambience of Wes Craven's blockbuster down to the starkly lit suburban kitchen. But as the famously black-cowled serial killer trail a gang of teenagers who share a dark secret, parodic accuracy takes a back seat to prurient gags.

As impresarios of pushing the envelope, the Brothers Wayans make the Brothers Farrelly look like the Brothers Osmond. Their teenage heroes are hormonally active to an orgiastic fare-thee-well, and trash begets trash. Flatulence and amorality rule in their all-American burg, a place where the locals are so busy mowing each other down on the streets and in the movie theaters that the masked killer's work is all but done for him.

Outrageousness is an end unto itself in "Scary Movie," in which sexual anatomy has a way of popping out in untoward ways and the recent teen-pic craze for semen humor is inflated to apocalyptic proportions. The youthful cast, which includes Marlon and Shawn Wayans, displays rubber-faced comic instincts that belie their generic "Baywatch" beauty. Everyone looks like somebody more famous; in the instance of Dave Sheridan, who plays a Jim Carrey-like doofus, the resemblance seems intentional.

The only thing scary about "Scary Movie" is the extent to which it underscores the depth of American neuroses regarding relations sexual and racial. Its tongue-'n-cheek pileup of cavalierly violent acts against women and obsessive jokes about homosexuals quickly becomes its own cliche. In the name of honesty, they should have called it "Summer Movie."

SIGHT AND SOUND, 10/00, p. 55, Kim Newman

US, the present. Drew Decker, a senior at B.A. Corpse High School, is pestered by a masked phone prankster who then kills her. The killer's next target is teenager Cindy Campbell, already traumatised because she and her friends—boyfriend Bobby, couple Ray and Brenda, Greg and Buffy—caused the death of a stranger last Halloween. Television reporter Gail Hailstorm arrives and flirts with Officer Doofy to get the inside scoop on the case.

When Cindy survives an encounter with the stalker, Bobby is arrested but released once the killer is seen elsewhere. The killer murders Greg, Buffy, Brenda, Gail and Ray. Cindy surrenders her virginity to Bobby. Bobby, apparently attacked by the slasher, is revealed to be a killer himself, with his secret lover Ray, who turns out to be alive and is embittered because of the cancellation of the Wayans Brothers' television show. The killers have also abducted Mr. Campbell, Cindy's drug-dealing father, whom they plan to murder. However, the masked murderer shows up and kills Bobby and Ray before engaging in a martial-arts fight with Cindy. As the police interrogate Cindy, she realises that the clues point to Officer Doofy, who walks away, shedding his disguise. As Cindy rants at the unfairness of it all, she is run over by a car.

And so cycles turn inevitably to spoof. In the late 40s, a decade and a half after Universal made a name for itself with a string of horror movies, Abbott and Costello met the studio's pantheon of movie monsters. Then, in the early 80s, only a few years after the teen slasher genre exploded with *Halloween* (1978) and *Friday the 13th* (1980), a clutch of *Airplane!*-style skits came along: from *Student Bodies* to *Saturday the 14h*. Arriving barely months after the alleged conclusion of the *Scream* series, which it parodies, and far out-grossing its inspiration, *Scary Movie* may well be the most commercially successful spoof yet, as well as the quickest off the mark. Indeed, *Scary Movie* has been such an immediate hit that it must have clicked more with mainstream audiences who appreciate the Farrelly Brothers—whose style of gross-out humour is in evidence throughout—than with the sizeable but cult crowd who saw *Scream*.

A major problem with *Scary Movie* is that it seems to have been made by people who didn't especially care for *Scream* which was humorously intended in the first place. Director Keenen Ivory Wayans—assisted here by his brothers Shawn and Marlon as co-writers and performers—has previously ventured into parody with the blaxploitation spoof *I'm Gonna Git You Sucka!*. The Wayans' half of the script was developed in two versions, one hewing close to the whitebread conventions of the slasher movie and the other with mostly black characters. In the event, you're left feeling that they would have been happier filming the second script—there are a couple of wry race jokes, notably the cut from the announcement "white woman in trouble" to the arrival of hordes of police cars—but have been forced to stick with the first.

After the opening riff on the Drew Barrymore killing from *Scream*, *Scary Movie*'s model provides rather thin material for skitting. Some of the parody is so abstruse as to be subliminal: echoing *Scream*'s casting of Henry Winkler, who starred in *Happy Days*, as the school principal, this casts David L. Lander from the *Happy Days* spin-off *Laverne and Shirley* in a similar role.

Scenes taken from *Scream*—Buffy's sarcastic confrontation with the killer, for instance—are played more broadly than in the original, but actually aren't as funny.

Wayans is on safer ground lampooning *I Know What You Did Last Summer,* a more po-faced slasher than *Scream,* and screws a few laughs out of the hit-and-run victim who keeps insisting he's all right as the teens argue about disposing of his corpse. Otherwise, *Scary Movie* has to yank in bits from other films not so much for parodic effect as for the shock of recognition, cueing limp variations on sequences from *The Blair Witch Project* and *The Matrix* (Cindy riverdancing in mid-air).

The air of desperation is emphasised by the insistence on padding out horror-movie gags with crude Farrelly-style humour a hairy-chinned gym mistress with dangling testicles, a penis-through-the-brain murder that mimics a moment in *Scream 2* and an ejaculation that splatters Cindy against the ceiling in a rare nod to pre-*Scream* horror (*A Nightmare on Elm Street*). This sort of material initially gets big, shocked laughs but soon wears thin, especially without the Farrellys' streak of sentiment. Indeed, it hardly seems all that daring in a summer that finds a college dean being sodomised by a giant hamster in a PG-12 movie (*The Nutty Professor.* A rare instance of real humour is the murder of Brenda at the hands of an audience for whom she has ruined *Shakespeare in Love* by talking loudly—and even that's similar to a gag in *Silent Night Deadly Night Part 2.*

VILLAGE VOICE, 7/18/00, p. 130, Michael Atkinson

As the introductory, Drew Barrymore-ish victim of the Wayans brothers' *Scary Movie,* Carmen Electra qualifies her idea of horror films to the gravelly voiced mystery caller with an incredulous "Ever seen Shaq act?" By the time the berobed psycho stabs her in the breast, extracting a fat silicone implant bag, I'm thinking Dennis Rodman is destined to show up under the *Scream* mask. Parodying self-parody has become something of a bottom-shelf cultural staple for American entertainment media; if you accept that many original slasher movies already began with a clear idea of how absurd they were, then the Wayans boys (stars and coscripters Marlon and Shawn, director Keenan Ivory) are working at several removes from their proposed ground zero. Indeed, the redundant *Scary Movie* (Kevin Williamson's original *Scream* script title) is a big, stupid bull with bodacious tits, but that's not to say it doesn't dish out some lite hardy-hars, particularly when Shannon Elizabeth (as the school ditz) sasses the killer even as her head comes off and self-denying football queer Shawn dresses his girlfriend up in helmet and gear and calls her "Brendan" in mid hump.

But labored, *Naked Gun*-ish quotes from *The Matrix, The Blair Witch Project,* and *The Usual Suspects* merely congratulate us for recognizing them, and the only thing the Wayans have to spike is the new teen films' tendency toward sexless, dopeless whitewash. Crazy with penises and spliffs, *Scary Movie* is actually closer to American teendom, though hardly close enough to dissuade some future numbskull from continuing the circle jerk and parodying genre parodies, and so on.

Also reviewed in:
CHICAGO TRIBUNE, 7/7/00, Friday/p. A, Mark Caro
NEW YORK TIMES, 7/7/00, p. E8, A. O. Scott
VARIETY, 7/10-16/00, p. 19, Joe Leydon
WASHINGTON POST, 7/7/00, p. C5, Rita Kempley

SCREAM 3

A Dimension Films release of a Konrad Pictures production in association with Craven/Maddalena Films. *Executive Producer:* Bob Weinstein, Harvey Weinstein, Cary Granat, and Andrew Rona. *Producer:* Cathy Konrad, Kevin Williamson, and Marianne Maddalena. *Director:* Wes Craven. *Screenplay:* Ehren Kruger. *Based on characters created by:* Kevin Williamson. *Director of Photography:* Peter Deming. *Editor:* Patrick Lussier. *Music:* Marco Beltrami. *Music Editor:*

Bill Abbott and Adam Kay. *Sound:* Jim Stuebe and (music) John Kurlander. *Sound Editor:* Todd Toon. *Casting:* Lisa Beach. *Production Designer:* Bruce Alan Miller. *Art Director:* Tom Fichter. *Set Designer:* Nancy Deren, Anthony D. Parrillo, Barbara Ann Spencer, and Sloane U'Ren. *Set Decorator:* Gene Serdena. *Set Dresser:* Josh Elliott, J. Michael Glynn, Peter Angles II, Brian Derfer, Edward Tamayo, and Robert W. Anderson. *Special Effects:* Ron Bolanowski. *Costumes:* Abigail Murray. *Make-up:* Lesa Nielson. *Make-up (Neve Campbell):* Angela Levin. *Make-up (Richmond Arquette and Courteney Cox Arquette):* Beth Katz. *Stunt Coordinator:* Rick Avery. *Running time:* 116 minutes. *MPAA Rating:* R.

CAST: Liev Schreiber (Cotton Weary); Beth Toussaint (Female Caller); Roger L. Jackson ("The Voice"); Kelly Rutherford (Christine); Neve Campbell (Sidney Prescott); Courteney Cox Arquette (Gale Weathers); Julie Janney (Moderator); Richmond Arquette (Student); Patrick Dempsey (Mark Kincaid); Lynn McRee (Maureen Prescott); Nancy O'Dell (Female Reporter); Ken Taylor (Male Reporter); Scott Foley (Roman Bridger); Roger Corman (Studio Executive); Lance Henriksen (John Milton); Josh Pais (Wallace); Deon Richmond (Tyson Fox); Matt Keeslar (Tom Prinze); Jenny McCarthy (Sarah Darling); Emily Mortimer (Angelina Tyler); Parker Posey (Jennifer Jolie); Patrick Warburton (Steven Stone); David Arquette (Dewey Riley); John Embry (Stage Security Guard); Lawrence Hecht (Neil Prescott); Lisa Beach (Studio Tour Guide); Kevin Smith (Silent Bob); Jason Mewes (Jay); Erik Erath (Stan); D. K. Arredondo (Office Security Guard); Lisa Gordon (Waitress); Heather Matarazzo (Martha Meeks); Jamie Kennedy (Randy Meeks); Carrie Fisher (Bianca); C. W. Morgan (Hank Loomis).

LOS ANGELES TIMES, 2/4/00, Calendar/p. 1, Kevin Thomas

"Scream 3" brings to a blood-drenched, bravura conclusion (hopefully) the hugely successful horror trilogy about a serial killer decimating a small town. From the outset, director Wes Craven and writer Kevin Williamson established that the "Scream" movies would also be a running commentary on themselves and the horror genre in general. This has given them a smart, sharp edge and set off reverberations, especially in this complex movie-within-a-movie finale, in which the film being shot—"Stab 3: The Return to Woodsboro"—and the film we're watching play off and deeply affect each other.

The body count is horrendously high and there's much that's grisly, but "Scream 3" is also genuinely scary and also highly amusing. Craven, horror veteran supreme, and writer Ehren Kruger have come up with a razzle-dazzler that delivers the goods for horror fans. Be warned—and not just on account of the violence—that if you've not seen the first two films you will likely be confused, and even if you have seen them, be prepared to stay on your toes to keep track of a heavily populated, highly convoluted plot.

The prologue is a jolter, a cinematic tour de force that sets the tone—and the standard—for all that is to come. The camera picks up Liev Schreiber's Cotton Weary, once wrongly sent to prison as the elusive killer, ever-hidden by a black shroud and a mask emulating Edvard Munch's famous painting "The Scream." Now the host of a nationally syndicated TV talk show who's set to do a cameo in "Stab 3," Cotton is stuck in traffic near the Hollywood Bowl when, via his cell phone, he learns his girlfriend (Kelly Rutherford) is in acute danger in her elegant, vintage apartment not so far away.

Cotton jumps the curb for a hair-raising rush to rescue her, only to wind up in an elaborate trap; the whole point is that he refuses to disclose to a menacing caller the whereabouts of Sidney Prescott (Neve Campbell), whose mother's murder 3½ years earlier set a murderous rampage in motion. Sidney, we learn soon enough, has been living in seclusion in a Northern California wilderness, where, under an alias, she's a phone-in counselor for a hotline for women in crisis.

Sidney, however, will soon be heading for Hollywood to help the Los Angeles Police Department's Det. Kincaide (Patrick Dempsey), assigned to catch the unknown killer. With the aid of advanced electronic technology, the murderer mimics voices throwing the cast and crew of "Stab 3," currently shooting, into a state of total terror and confusion. This is all you need to know of the plot.

As before, Campbell's Sidney, a lovely, intelligent young woman, must confront evil yet another time—just like Sigourney Weaver and those aliens. Also back are David Arquette as Dewey Riley, hapless Woodsboro cop, and Courteney Cox Arquette as Gale Weathers, the most ruthless TV newscaster of all. Dewey and Gale experienced a bit of opposites attracting each other in the past, and the sparks are likely to fly all over again. Arquette and Cox Arquette met and married during the "Scream" series, and the way in which they play off each other gives the film a much-welcome warm and good-humored resonance.

Dewey has signed on "Stab 3" as a technical advisor, and Gale smells a story in the making. Dewey's "Stab 3" counterpart is played by the more glamorous Matt Keeslar while Gale is played by Parker Posey as the gauche Jennifer Jolie, determined to be more aggressive than Gale already is (though Jennifer is not nearly as smart as Gale).

Lance Henriksen is cast as "Stab 3" producer John Milton (!), whose lavish 1920s Hollywood Hills estate brings to mind Norma Desmond's all but identical mansion in "Sunset Blvd." and serves perfectly as the complicated baroque setting of the film's climactic sequences. Jenny McCarthy is amusing as a 35-year-old actress still stuck in starletdom, playing 21-year-olds, and rounding out a substantial and effective cast are Tyson Fox, Angelina Tyler and Patrick Warburton (as the Steven Seagal of celebrity security guards).

Ehren Kruger has come with a persuasive back story to explain away what triggered the carnage of all three movies. Marco Beltrami's high-energy score and Peter Deming's superior camera work add to "Scream 3's" vitality and punch. Be on the lookout for cameos by producer Roger Corman and Carrie Fisher.

NEW YORK POST, 2/4/00, p. 47, Lou Lumenick

He's b-a-a-a-a-c-k! The ghost-masked killer of the first two "Scream" movies has turned up in Hollywood and started skewering people again.

"I'm starting to see why Tori Spelling and David Schwimmer didn't want to come back," complains one of the cast members of the film-within-the-film at the center of "Scream 3," referring to her predecessors.

Production has been shut down on "Stab 3" as the real-life survivors of the Woodsboro massacre arrive on the set—Sidney Prescott (Neve Campbell), who's been in hiding as a telephone crisis counselor, and hard-boiled newswoman Gail Weathers (Courteney Cox Arquette).

Dewey Riley, the dorky ex-deputy sheriff, is also at the studio. He's a technical adviser for the movie and is dating Jennifer Jolie (the delicious Parker Posey), the actress who plays Gail, whom he still loves.

The most entertaining parts of "Scream 3"—an unnecessary but quite tolerable attempt to wrap up loose threads and maybe make another $100 million or so—are the constant bickering between Gail and Jennifer.

Gail doesn't like Jennifer's strident (but accurate) interpretation of her—and Jennifer is no less sarcastic about Gall's work as a reporter.

David Arquette is endearing as the very earnest Dewey, who rhapsodizes about Gail's "lost and lonely little girl inside" while protecting her and the very jealous Jennifer.

It's the chemistry between the Arquettes (they met on the first film and married after the second) and their rapport with Campbell that sustains "Scream 3" through its overly convoluted plot, which involves the dark past of Sidney's mother.

The solid cast also includes Liev Schreiber, briefly and hilariously reprising his role as the wrongly accused Cotton Weary from the earlier films; Jenny McCarthy as an aging Hollywood bimbo; Patrick Dempsey as a detective whose interest in the case may border on the obsessive; and Scott Foley and Lance Hendrikson as the director and producer of "Stab 3 " and possible suspects in the killings.

Kevin Williamson, who wrote the inescapably fresher first two installments, has been succeeded by screenwriter Ehren Kruger ("Arlington Road"). Kruger manages some good jibes ("Hollywood is full of criminals with flourishing careers," one character observes), but the climax is silly—even by standards of the genre.

Director Wes Craven is adept at providing shocks as ever, though he should have borrowed the killer's knife and hacked away at the movie's excessive 116-minute running time.

It won't matter much to appreciative fans that he did the movie-within-a-movie thing much more effectively in "Wes Craven's New Nightmare."

Truth be told, anyone who claims they're going to see this very violent and gory "Scream 3" for its hip irony should be viewed as skeptically as those people who claim they read Playboy for the articles.

NEWSDAY, 2/4/00, Part II/p. B2, Gene Seymour

When does a parody of a formula become as formulaic as what it's parodying? Apparently, director Wes Craven and others responsible for the "Scream" series of slasher-movie send-ups have answered that question by declaring in advance that "Scream 3" will be the last installment.

Right. And I'm Freddy Krueger and you look like you could use a nap.

In a spirit of hope and trust, however, let's take Craven and company at their word and say that "Scream 3" feels very much like the stretch run toward a finish line.

And not a moment too soon, because, by now, the series' smirking inquiry into its genre's dumb conventions seems very much beside the point. The teen horror boom that came in the wake of the stunning success of "Scream" four years ago has all but bottomed out. Both that film and "Scream 2," released a year later, have shrewdly-and successfully-neutered the impact of cheesy splatter fests. But they've also neutralized their own capacity to surprise, even with their own self-referential jokes.

Hence the deja-vu-all-over-again feel of this installment, which finds three of the series' mainstays pretty much the same as they ever were, only in different places.

Stoic, sad Sidney Prescott (Neve Campbell), haunted by the bloodshed of her lost teen years, is hiding out in a remote, heavily secured northern California compound. Ace TV reporter Gale Weathers (Courteney Cox Arquette), still a rhymes-with-witch on wheels now plies her mean and merciless trade on an entertainment-news show. (The "60 Minutes II", thing fell through. Poor baby!)

And former deputy Dewey Riley (David Arquette), as sweet- natured and clue-challenged as ever, has a new Hollywood gig as technical adviser on "Stab 3: Return to Woodsboro," the latest effort by horror mogul John Milton (Lance Henriksen) to exploit the bad stuff that happened to Sidney in what passes for "real life" in this universe.

Oh, almost forgot about Cotton Weary (Liev Schreiber), wrongfully accused of murder in "Scream 2," who has parlayed his exonerated status into his own syndicated talk show, 100% Cotton."

There isn't a heckuva lot more to say at this point without spoiling things for you and for Dimension Films, whose request for minimum disclosure of plot developments will be honored here.

What can be said is that screenwriter Ehren Kruger ("Arlington Road") picks up on "Scream" creator Kevin Williamson's laid-back, genre-subverting style without any real lapses. And that once more, the game of what-happens-next is leavened with red herrings, false turns and over-the-top show-biz satire.

Indeed, the cast members for this "Stab 3" movie make up an inventory of E! magazine case studies, including Tyson Fox (Deon Richmond), who struggles to bring "dignity" to his role as a black video-store geek; Sarah Darling, (a prim, barely recognizable Jenny McCarthy), a bimbo weary of being consigned to bimbo roles, and Jennifer Jolie (Parker Posey), an ambitious actress taking a break from "must see TV" to play Gale. (Nudge-nudge, wink-wink, say no more!)

Even such Pirandello-esque touches seem so familiar that you can see the languor beginning to creep over the actors, faces like smog. No mas, they seem to be saying beneath the din of slashing and yowling. And, while the whole ride's been fun, you can't help but agree.

SIGHT AND SOUND, 5/00, p. 59, Kim Newman

Hollywood. Cotton Weary, a talk show host once unjustly convicted of the murder of Maureen Prescott, is killed by someone masked like the murderers who have terrorised Maureen's daughter Sidney. Producer John Milton is working on *Stab 3: Return to Woodsboro* (the latest film in a series based on the murders that have revolved around Sidney), with music video director Roman Bridger making his first feature, Dewey Riley working as a technical advisor and actresses

Jennifer Jolie and Angelina Tyler cast as real life figures Gale Weathers, a news reporter, and Sidney.

When actors Sarah Darling and Tom Prinze and a security expert are killed, *Stab 3* is shut down. Gale digs further into the story and Sidney comes to help. It turns out that Maureen was once a starlet at the studio, leaving Hollywood after an orgy at one of Milton's parties. At Roman's birthday party, the killer strikes again, murdering Roman, supporting actor Tyson Fox, and Jennifer and Angelina. Sidney confronts the masked maniac, who turns out to be Roman (who faked his own death), her long-lost half brother. Having prompted the original Woodsboro killings, he has been taking his rage out on the family he feels cheated out of. Sidney kills Roman.

In one of the wittiest moments in *Scream 2* (film nerd Randy, explaining the rules of sequels, wound up his argument with "and if you want your sequel to turn into a franchise, never ever..." only to have his thought cut off before his wisdom could be delivered. Randy pops up again here via a video-diary entry. Explaining what happens when your sequel turns into a trilogy, Randy tells us to expect any character could be the killer and survivors from the earlier instalments will end up dead. Sadly, *Scream 3* is not nearly ruthless enough to go through with this delicious warning/promise.

With original screenwriter Kevin Williamson now pursuing a directorial career, series director Wes Craven is here partnered by screenwriter Ehren Kruger *(Arlington Road)*. There's a sense that Craven's emotional investment was in his significantly named 'personal' project *Music of the Heart,* completed last year, leaving this to come together by itself. Has Sidney Prescott been so abused in two *Scream* movies that she has herself become the new killer? Is her dead mother, whose murder kicked the whole thing off, coming back as a ghost to add a supernatural twist? Will Riley and Gale, fake-killed several times in the earlier entries, finally die for real, or get to be unmasked as the secret fiends behind it all? The disappointing revelation here is that a new character with far less dramatic weight than the killers in the first two films is guilty, and Sidney gets to gun him down for a pat wrap-up.

The Hollywood setting allows for a pleasant succession of in-references and gags. Jenny McCarthy has a great set-up-for death speech as she complains about being a 35-year-old playing a 21-year-old who takes a shower before getting killed, and there's a neat cameo from Carrie Fisher as a studio functionary who claims not to have won the part of Princess Leia because she didn't sleep with George Lucas. The best thing in the film is the bickering between Cox Arquette's Gale and Parker Posey as the Method actress who thinks she's better at being Gale than Gale herself. With the exception of a chase through a soundstage, Craven rarely exploits the potential for suspense of his Hollywood setting. Mostly, his visual imagination seems stretched thin; the stalk-and-slash scenes are directed merely with anonymous competence. A warning to the avaricious: if Randy the movie geek has left another video testament, it might well cite *Omen IV* and *Halloween IV* Through *H20* as dire examples of what happens when your trilogy is complete but the producers go back to the well. If you want your trilogy to become a franchise, make something grander than *Scream 3*.

TIME, 2/14/00, p. 78, Richard Schickel

Scream 3 is no mere sequel, it's makers want us to understand. It is, they insist, something more self-consciously thought out—the grand, concluding chapter of a "trilogy." This means, they tell us, both from the screen and in the publicity, that it is not ruled by the horror film's generic conventions, that anything can happen.

Well, yes, it can, but will it? The survivors of the first two episodes in the series—they are not many—are now in Hollywood, where a movie version is being made of the unfortunate occurrences in Woodboro a few years back. David Arquette's deputy Dewey Riley is marginally less dorky than he was, and Courteney Cox Arquette is marginally less bitchy as hard-charging TV newshen Gale Weathers. On the other hand, Neve Campbell's overbite remains as fetching as ever, and she and the other victims, real and potential, of the slasher in the ironic mask—they are many—continue to put up game, liberated fights for their lives.

This is good. And so are director Wes Craven's inventive stagings of these set-tos. Not so good is the absence of hip cross-references to the classic horror tropes. Instead there are edgy exchanges, which are not very funny, between the "real" *Scream* characters and the actors playing them in the movie. This perhaps indicates the figure that really should have survived all three iterations is screenwriter Kevin Williamson. He has been replaced by Ehren Kruger, whose work is more competent than inspired—not that one imagines that afflicting the grosses.

VILLAGE VOICE, 2/15/00, p. 126, Michael Atkinson

Deliver us from midwinter.

Distributor shelves are cleared, projectors choke on misassembled junk, tumbleweeds haunt the empty theater corridors. Among this cruelest-season's gifts is *Scream 3,* the latest fulfillment of Wes Craven's efforts at living up to his own name. The *Scream* series is that rare horror-genre text that cannot for the life of it muster even a ghost of a subtext; it's as barren as the moon. Indeed, the laborious button-pushing and pandering make you understand all too well the fried/bored brain-states of electrode-wired lab rats. Of course, the series' main flourish is its "self-reflexivity," which at least in this case translates to being so self-involved the movie seems to be looking up its own ass. (Compare it to the infernal dreaminess of Craven's *New Nightmare.)* Giving Roger Corman one line, and having the killer follow a film script, is as cerebral as it gets.

Plot?! If we know anything about the travails of Sidney Prescott (Neve Campbell), Gale Weathers (the consumptive-looking Courteney Cox), the interchangeable cast of bodies, and the voice-mimicking knife-wielder in the robe and rubber mask, it's that what happens doesn't matter. Whatever happens, "a preponderance of exposition" (as a guest-appearing Jamie Kennedy intones on video when describing the trilogy effect) will arrive to arbitrarily rewrite it all. Logic, motivation, suspense-anything that might make the film frightening or resonant-is buried under Dolby blams, medulla-shaming dialogue, and a rain of overdubbed hunting-knife schwings that grate like a 3 a.m. car alarm. The setting has moved to L.A., where the latest *Stab* movie is shut down after a few corpses (Jenny McCarthy's, for one) show up, etc. But it's basically the old chase-&-stab. One might suggest that Craven go watch and absorb Michael Powell's *Peeping Tom,* but why would a hit-making millionaire want to do something crazy like that?

Also reviewed in:
CHICAGO TRIBUNE, 2/4/00, Tempo/p. 1, Mark Caro
NATION, 3/6/00, p. 34, Stuart Klawans
NEW YORK TIMES, 2/4/00, p. E14, Elvis Mitchell
VARIETY, 2/7-13/00, p. 48, Joe Leydon
WASHINGTON POST, 2/4/00, p. C1, Rita Kempley
WASHINGTON POST, 2/4/00, Weekend/p. 41, Desson Howe

SCREWED

A Universal Pictures release of a Robert Simonds/Brad Grey production. *Executive Producer:* Brad Grey and Ray Reo. *Producer:* Robert Simonds. *Director:* Scott Alexander and Larry Karaszewski. *Screenplay:* Scott Alexander and Larry Karaszewski. *Director of Photography:* Robert Brinkmann. *Editor:* Michael Jablow. *Music:* Michel Colombier. *Music Editor:* Richard Ford. *Sound:* David Husby and (music) Steve Durkee. *Sound Editor:* Richard Legrand, Jr. and Gary Gerlich. *Casting:* Stuart Aikins *Production Designer:* Mark Freeborn. *Art Director:* Sandi Tanaka. *Set Decorator:* Rose Marie McSherry. *Set Dresser:* Keith Burk and Rich Hachey. *Special Effects:* Reg Milne. *Make-up:* Lisa Love. *Stunt Coordinator:* Charles Andre. *Running time:* 90 minutes. *MPAA Rating:* PG-13.

CAST: Norm Macdonald (Willard Fillmore); Dave Chappelle (Rusty P. Hayes); Elaine Stritch (Miss Crock); Danny DeVito (Grover Cleaver); Daniel Benzali (Detective Tom Dewey); Sherman Hemsley (Chip Oswald); Sarah Silverman (Hillary); Malcolm Stewart (Roger); Lochlyn, Munro (Officer Richardsen); Helena Yea ("Aunt Mabel"); Lorenzo Campbell (Tito); Damon Thornton (Tito's Henchman); Lorena Gale (Angry Momma); Sue

Astley (Morgue Operator);   Mark Acheson (Mr. Kettle);   Joanna Piros (National Anchor Woman); Samantha Ferris (Local Anchorwoman);   Brian Arnold (News Anchorman);   Ted Friend, Claire Riley, and April Telek (News Reporters);   Lois Dellar (Policewoman);   Ken Kirzinger and Charles André (Cops);   Camille Sullivan (Flower Shop Clerk);   D. Harlan Cutshall (Sharp Shooter); Ben Derrick (Cop at Pile Up);   Ann Warn Pegg (Meter Miad);   Brent Butt and Anthony Harrison (Buddies);   Robert Moloney (Vice President);   Lloyd Berry (Willard's Uncle);   Dee Jay Jackson (Garbage Man); Tygh Runyan (Cussing Guy);   Georgina Hegedos (Russian Lady);   Khaira Le (Ticket Agent);   Laurie Bekker (Chicken Girl);   Martin Amado (Chicken Shack Worker);   Irene Miscisco (Lady in Beauty Shop);   Tom Heaton (Morgue Janitor); Tony Morelli and Jim R. Dunn (ND Cops).

LOS ANGELES TIMES, 5/15/00, Calendar/p. 8, Kevin Thomas

"Screwed": That's exactly what you're likely to feel if you try to watch this relentlessly unfunny loser, a candidate for the short list of the year's worst major studio release.

Pros like Elaine Stritch and Danny DeVito are always fun, but even their presence can't make a dent in this disaster.

Amazingly enough, it was written by Scott Alexander and Larry Karaszewski, who have "The People vs. Larry Flynt" and "Man on the Moon" to their credit—and, alas, chose to make their directorial debut with this picture.

Their premise is that in these prosperous times a chauffeur-houseman (Norm Macdonald) would stick it out 15 years working for an imperious, cranky Pittsburgh cookie tycoon, Miss Crock (Stritch), who's such a skinflint that Macdonald's Willard is still wearing the same uniform he inherited from his late father along with the job. At last reaching the end of his tether, Willard decides to snatch his employer's cherished little dog and hold it for a huge ransom.

Naturally, the scheme misfires big time, with Willard and his pal Rusty (Dave Chappelle) getting into increasingly bigger trouble.

Now Willard and Rusty are none too bright, to put it kindly, and while many a comedy has turned upon the antics of numskulls, these two are colorless and charmless and simply too stupid and dull to care about. Dummies have to seem somehow endearing if we're to be concerned with what happens to them, but this pair is hopeless.

Sherman Hemsley is Miss Crock's top aide and DeVito is a weirdo morgue worker who also happens to be an officer of the Jack Lord Fan Club. Daniel Benzali is the police detective trying to sort everything out.

Alexander and Karaszewski bring a sledgehammer touch to their script, which does it no favors. The only smart thing about "Screwed" was Universal's decision not to screen the picture in advance for the news media so as to avoid scalding opening-day reviews.

NEW YORK POST, 5/13/00, p. 19, Hannah Brown

"Screwed" is the title of a new comedy that sneaked into theaters yesterday without advance screenings for critics, and screwed is how you'll feel if you pay good money to see this unfunny flick.

It stars Norm Macdonald as Willard, a chauffeur so mild-mannered he doesn't protest when his super-bitch boss Miss Crock (Elaine Stritch) forces him to scrub her dentures—and her toilets.

Miss Crock, who owns a huge baked-goods factory and is known in public as a sweet old lady, dotes on her mean-tempered lapdog and her boyfriend Chip (Sherman Hemsley).

She's the kind of battle-ax who parades around in front of Willard in her girdle and laughs at him when he asks for a new uniform for Christmas.

Fed up with years of mistreatment, Willard and his pal Rusty (Dave Chappelle) come up with a scheme to kidnap her dog and ransom him for $1 million.

In a slapstick scene that borrows heavily from "There's Something About Mary," but lacks any real laughs, they manage to botch the kidnapping, but leave the house in such chaos that Miss Crock thinks Willard has been abducted.

While this might not be a terrible premise for a comedy, the actors go through their paces as if they're sleepwalking. Daniel Benzall barely registers as a bumbling detective.

But the real disappointment is Danny DeVito as a creepy coroner.

His scenes in the morgue, which involve licking items removed from corpses' colons, are so inept and witless it's hard not to spend the rest of the movie wondering why he agreed to participate in this mess.

If you want to see a truly funny movie about a botched kidnapping, go rent the Coen brothers' "The Big Lebowskl," but skip "Screwed," which will be coming soon to a video store near you.

Also reviewed in:
CHICAGO TRIBUNE, 5/15/00, Tempo/p. 2, John Petrakis
NEW YORK TIMES, 5/13/00, p. B15, Stephen Holden
VARIETY, 5/22-28/00, p. 31, Joe Leydon

SCULPTRESS, THE

A Plus Entertainment and Phaedra Cinema release of a Plus Entertainment/D & S production. *Executive Producer:* Denis Shusterman. *Producer:* Tony DiDio. *Director:* Ian Merrick. *Screenplay:* Ian Merrick. *Director of Photography:* David Scardina. *Editor:* Jeffrey Stephens. *Music:* Tim Jones. *Sound:* David Silberman. *Sound Editor:* Roy Braverman and Timothy J. Borquez. *Casting:* Erica Arnold and Mia Levinson. *Production Designer:* Don Day. *Art Director:* Doug Freeman. *Set Decorator:* Dee Jour. *Costumes:* Marian Astrom de Fina. *Special Effects Make-up:* Jeff Farley. *Running time:* 96 minutes. *MPAA Rating:* R.

CAST: Jeff Fahey (Matthew Dobie); Patrick Bauchau (Professor Giraud); Katie Wright (Sarah); Emmanuelle Vaugier (Sylvie); Allen Cutler (Chris); Vivis Colombetti (Madame Cleo); Miriam Babin (Mrs. Broelli); Katriona Browne (Isabelle); Johanna Falls (Marie); Bridget Nelson (Celeste); Stone Man (Bill).

VILLAGE VOICE, 10/31/00, p. 170, Nick Rutigliano

A line of inquiry into the appearance of *The Sculptress* anywhere but on Cinemax might be raised, but why bother? "Dark Man [psycho neighbor] + Dreams + Gargoyles + Evil Spirits = Incubus!" is how one character sums up the troubles of clay-scrunching naïf Katie Wright, and it's as clear a description as any. Sadly, most of the endless blather's way less loopy, and Wright's "British" accent elicits the only shudders.

Also reviewed in:
NEW YORK TIMES, 10/27/00, p. E28, A. O. Scott
VARIETY, 10/30-11/5/00, p. 22, Sheri Linden

SET ME FREE

A Merchant Ivory Films and France Film release in assocation with Artistic License Films of a Cité-Amérique/Catpics/Haut et Court production with the participation of Sodec/Canada Television Fund/Telefilm Canada/Harold Greenberg Fund/Quebec Government/Canadian Government and Super Ecran. *Executive Producer:* Louis Lavardière. *Producer:* Alfi Sinniger, Lorraine Richard, and Carole Scotta. *Director:* Léa Pool. *Screenplay (French with English subtitles):* Léa Pool, Monique H. Messier, Nancy Huston and Isabelle Raynault. *Based on an original idea by:* Léa Pool *Director of Photography:* Jeanne Lapoirie. *Editor:* Michel Arcand. *Music:* Jan Garbarek, Ketil Bjornstad, David Darling, Michel Legrand, and Ben E. King. *Music Editor:* Gabriel Hafner. *Sound:* Christian Monheim and (music) François Musy. *Casting:* Lucie Robitaille. *Production Designer:* Lucie Bouliane. *Set Designer:* Catherine Labrecque. *Set Decorator:* Serge Bureau. *Set Dresser:* Stéphane Brunelle, Pierre Bédard, Bruno Charlebois,

Nichola Corbo and Roger Pilon. *Costumes:* Michèle Hamel. *Running time:* 94 minutes. *MPAA Rating:* Not Rated.

CAST: Karine Vanasse (Hanna);   Pascale Bussières (Hanna's Mother);   Charlotte Christeler (Laura);   Nancy Huston (Teacher);   Miki Manojlovic (Hanna's Father);   Monique Mercure (Hanna's Grandmother);   Alexandre Mérineau (Paul, Hanna's Brother);   Anne-Marie Cadieux (Prostitute);   Marie-Helene Gagnon (Landlady);   Jacques Galipeau (Hanna's Grandfather);   Carl Hennebert-Faulkner (Martin);   Neil Kroetsch (Preteur);   Michel Albert (Security Guard);   Gary Boudreault (Boulanger);   Suzanne Garceau (Nurse);   Normand Canac-Marquis (Hanna's Client); Jerome Leclerc-Couture (Claudio);   Sébastien Burns (Sébastien);   Serge Dionne (Motard);   Claude Desparois (Grocer); Michel Antonelli (Barber);   Sylvain Rocheleau (Patron de l'usine);   Paul Kunigis (Joueur d'échec);   Daniel Monastess (Pimp);   Michel Rochon (Client Refusé);   Sacha Bourque (Waiter at the Party);   Marco Ledézma (Man on a Bicycle);   Jacques Brouillet (Curé); Sandrin Michon (Sandra);   Marie-José Tremblay (Elyse, student);   Frédéric Zacharek (Employee of the Grocery).

CHRISTIAN SCIENCE MONITOR, 3/10/00, p. 15, David Sterritt

There's more subtlety in "Set Me Free," [The reference is to "Orphans;" see Sterritt's review.] directed by Léa Pool, a French-Canadian filmmaker with a rising reputation. Hanna is a 13-year-old girl with very different parents—her father is an inward-looking Jew, her mother a Roman Catholic with a delicate disposition. There's also a schoolteacher who strikes Hanna as a role model who could change her life.

"Set Me Free," originally called "Emporte-moi," tells Hanna's coming-of-age story with imagination and restraint. The most exquisite scene occurs when she goes to the movies and sees Jean-Luc Godard's masterly "My Life to Live," a 1963 drama that touches her to the depths of her being with its sad revelation of life's bitter complexities. It's as fine a moment as any recent film has given us.

NEW YORK POST, 4/14/00, p. 57, Lou Lumenick

Blame Canada?

Not if you've seen "Set Me Free" ("Emporte-moi"), a lyrical and beautifully acted export from our neighbors to the north.

Young Karine Vanasse is extraordinary as 13-year-old Hanna, whose onset of puberty only adds to her confusion about her identity in 1963 Quebec.

Asked to give her religion at school, she offers an embarrassed explanation that her father is a Polish Jew and her mom, to whom he's not married, is a Catholic of French descent.

Things are not happy at home. Dad (Miki Manojlovic), an embittered, abusive leftist and Holocaust survivor, can't keep a job and spends his days playing chess. Mom (Pascale Bussieres), an overworked seamstress, is on the verge of a nervous breakdown.

The film is a triumph for writer-director Lea Pool, who handles Hanna's crises with rare sensitivity and restraint. This is nowhere more obvious than in a sequence where Hanna gives into advances by a flirtatious female classmate (Charlotte Christeler) she meets at a dance.

Pool also offers a very effective homage to Jean-Luc Godard's 1962 film "My Life to Live" ("Vivre Sa Vie"). Hanna is seen several times watching the film's flickering black-and-white images in a darkened theater and identifying with its heroine, a doomed prostitute played by the beautiful Anna Karina, who resembles Hanna's teacher (Nancy Huston).

"Set Me Free," which was featured at last year's New York Film Festival, tells its story so effectively through pictures it's barely necessary to read the subtitles.

NEWSDAY, 4/14/00, Part II/p. B7, Jan Stuart

There are as many memory films about dysfunctional upbringings as there are filmmakers in therapy, but the genre is always worth returning to when a film is as freshly minted and vividly detailed as "Set Me Free." Opening the same day the Film Society of Lincoln Center launches a three-week tribute to Canadian movie-makers, this abundantly felt drama from Montreal director-writer Lea Pool provides further evidence that Canadian cinema is a force worthy of its own niche on the international film circuit.

The heroine and presumed director's surrogate of this 1963-set tale is Hanna (the disarming Karine Vanasse), a 13-year-old who gets caught up in the mercurial passions that govern her parents' relationship. Her father (Miki Manojlovich) is a Polish-Jewish poet and Holocaust escapee. Perpetually unemployed, he takes his discontents out on his Catholic wife (Pascale Bussieres), an overworked seamstress.

Hanna finds solace in the almost-incestuous attentions of her brother Paul (Alexandre Merineau) and the movies, where she is mesmerized by the prostitute character played by Anna Karina in Godard's classic new wave film "Vivre Sa Vie" (My Life to Live). She develops youthful crushes on women who project the Karina je ne sais quoi: a supportive schoolteacher (Nancy Huston) and a hormonally precocious schoolmate, Laura (Charlotte Christeler).

Given the extent of unhappiness and adolescent angst engulfing Hanna, the film that Pool has fashioned around her floats with a buoyancy and an abiding faith in the basic goodness of humanity that carries us over the bumpy spots along with its heroine. Characteristically, Pool has Hanna's volatile father present her with a copy of "The Diary of Anne Frank," whose optimism provides a life-affirming alternative to the fatalistic existentialism offered her by the Godard film.

Pool is aptly named: She reveals a deep wellspring of patience for all of her characters (with the possible exception of a Jew-baiting schoolgirl) and a feel for the sorrowful push-and-pull of adult relations redolent of Diane Kurys' "Entre Nous." And she has a compelling star performer in Vanasse, a fresh-faced young actress with an inner radiance that grows on you. Stick around for the closing titles while Vanasse serenades us with "Sidonnie" on the acoustic guitar. It's a lovely coda to a lovely film.

VILLAGE VOICE, 4/18/00, p. 164, Jessica Winter

The most exuberant set piece in the acutely sensitive *Set Me Free* finds two girls blithely spurning the puppy-dog attentions of the boys at a dance party to hold hands and exchange gazes. As in much of her autobiographical coming-of-age tale, director Léa Pool uses long, steady close-ups to limn the girls' discovery of each other, coaxing tender, unaffected performances from her two young actresses. They stand on the precarious threshold of adolescence, when physical love has not yet divided into erotic and platonic categories.

Set Me Free ponders how a young person can make a livable home out of this liminal space yet flee its restrictions as quickly as possible. Karine Vanasse, as the protagonist Hanna, is perfectly cast because she has the body of a woman and the sweet, sexless face of a child. Her character, growing up in Montreal during the early '60s, craves embrace, and she seeks it out from her parents, teacher, brother, and best friend Laura—these last two and Hanna even form a spin-the-bottle love triangle. Not yet 14, Hanna is already searching for an escape hatch from her loving but claustrophobic and emotionally volatile household, where her delicate mother (Pascale Bussières), a Catholic with something of a martyr complex, works long hours as a seamstress to support her children and husband (Miki Manojlovic), a Polish Jew and combative aspiring poet who all but refuses to work a paying job. Seeking refuge in the cinema, Hanna becomes obsessed with the existential Parisian prostitute Nana in Godard's *Vivre Sa Vie,* memorizing lines, mimicking her carriage, even finding Anna Karina's doppelgänger in her sympathetic teacher (Nancy Huston). With generous excerpts from *Vivre Sa Vie* woven throughout, *Set Me* Free becomes a movie within a movie, but Pool's meta-narrative leanings always serve empathic character study. Her film is a tribute to cinema love and all of its engendering possibilities. The movies made Hanna, for better and worse, and by the end of *Set Me Free,* Hanna is making movies.

Also reviewed in:
CHICAGO TRIBUNE, 5/12/00, Friday/p. I, Michael Wilmington
NEW YORK TIMES, 4/14/00, p. E16, Lawrence Van Gelder
VARIETY, 2/22-28/99, p. 62, Brendan Kelly

SEX: THE ANNABEL CHONG STORY

A Strand Releasing and Greycat Films release of a Coffee House Films production. *Executive Producer:* Kathleen Curry and Suzanne Bowers Whitten. *Producer:* Hugh F. Curry, David Whitten, and Gough Lewis. *Director:* Gough Lewis. *Story Consultant:* Greg West. *Director of Photography:* Jim Michaels, Kelly Morris, Gough Lewis, and Tony Morone. *Editor:* Kelly Morris. *Music:* Peter Mundinger. *Sound:* Konrad Skreta. *Running time:* 86 minutes. *MPAA Rating:* Not Rated.

CAST: Grace Quek (Student);   Annabel Chong (Porn Star);   John Bowen (Director, World's Biggest Gang Bang 1 & 2);   Ed Powers (Director/Performer "Dirty Debutante" Series);   Walter Williams (Professor of Anthropology, U. of Southern California);   Charles Conn and Monica Moran (Friends/Classmates);   Dick James (President, Annabel Chong Fan Club);   Steve Austin (Talent Agent, World Modeling);   Jim South (Talent Agent/Porn Director);   Al Goldstein (Publisher, "Screw" Magazine/Host, "The Midnight Blue Show");   Ron Jeremy (Porn Star);   Lanisha Shanthi Easter (Friend and Former Lover);   Mr. Quek and Mrs. Quek (Parents);   Allen Wong (Best Friend);   Frank Sanford (Publicist, Scoop Snydication);   Seymore Butts (Porn Director/Performer);   Ona Zee (Porn Performer/Director);   Chi Chi LaRue (Porn Director);   Michael J. Coxx, Donna Warner, Jack Hammer, and Dick Nasty (Porn Performers);   Calvin Teo (High School Friend);   Robert Black (Porn Producer/Director);   Israel Gonzales (Porn Designer/Production Assistant);   David Carr (Art Instructor/Author);   Chuck Zane (Porn Producer);   Jasmin St. Claire (Porn Performer/Exotic Dancer);   Elana Craig (The HIV Clinic);   Raynard Tan (Cousin);   Susan James (Student Affairs Counselor).

NEW YORK POST, 2/11/00, p. 56, Hannah Brown

Watching "Sex: The Annabel Chong Story," a documentary about a porn star who had sex with 251 men in 10 hours, is like staring at an animal that has just been run over by a truck.

You know you should look away, but there's something undeniably fascinating about the blood and guts and mess.

Chong (whose real name is Grace Quek) has made a career out of playing with this obsession people have with the more extreme and grotesque aspects of human sexuality.

The film starts out promisingly, with a clip of a dolled-up Chong being interviewed on the "The Jerry Springer Show" to discuss her 251-men feat (which was filmed and made into a best-selling porn flick). Never at any moment in the course of "Sex" (including during brief clips from her sex marathon) does she project as much sensual enjoyment as she does when she's appearing before a TV audience of millions.

But instead of exploring Chong's need for attention, director Gough Lewis simply accepts her explanation of her actions at face value, and "Sex," while never boring, is superficial. He is similarly shy when she describes, and then shows, how she cuts her arms repeatedly with a razor blade.

"There's so much pain inside, but you can't let it out because you're so numb," is all she has to say about it.

Unfortunately, the director of "Sex" let himself become almost as numb as shis subject, and what could have been an intriguing look at a bizarre and complex woman plays like just another cog in the Annabel Chong publicity machine.

NEWSDAY, 2/11/00, Part II/p. B7, Jan Stuart

The place where Grace Quek is observed going to work at the end of "Sex: The Annabel Chong Story" is a red-brick fortress: stark, air-tight, its front door windows shrouded in brown packaging paper. It's the factory that dare not speak its name, a pornographic-movie mill, where Quek is returning to ply the only assembly-line skills she knows.

In 1995, Quek (aka porn star Annabel Chong) performed the ultimate assembly-line stunt for a woman in her trade: She performed 251 sexual acts with 70 men in 10 hours. She would have done 49 more to make it an even 300 but had to call it quits after an overly enthusiastic partner jabbed her with a fingernail.

Anyone hoping to get his jollies from Gough Lewis, head-spinning documentary would do better to rent a Chong video such as "More Dirty Debutantes #37" or "I Can't Believe I Did the Whole Team!" There is far less prurient content than one would expect from a movie called "Sex: The Annabel Chong Story," and what remains is so clouded in the self-delusions of its protagonist as to become altogether alienating.

Lewis and his camera crew trailed Quek for two years, following her from the classrooms of Southern Cal (where she attended the School of Fine Arts) to the debating halls of Cambridge to her parents home in Singapore. There is even a visit inside a porn-movie studio, where a buxom rival is attempting to trounce Annabel Chong's record for number of onscreen partners.

What emerges is a riveting and ultimately very saddening portrait of a young woman who claims to be turning stereotypes of female passivity and victimization on their head, but who gradually reveals herself to be the quintessential victim.

The only child of middle-class parents, Quek boasts of her sexual feats with desperate glee on "The Jerry Springer Show" but conceals her livelihood from her parents back in Singapore in fear of hurting her mother. Cheated by a producer of the $10,000 she is owed, she lives out of a cramped Los Angeles apartment, where she plays dress-up with her drag-queen best buddy. Interestingly, the only person with whom Quek appears to have had a deep relationship is another woman, who testifies as a "former lover." Before the final fade, Chong has become so desensitized by her multi-partner occupation that she commits self-mutilation to see if she can feel any pain.

Quek took her stage surname from an ill-fated Edgar Allen Poe heroine, and she owns a sense of doom with pride. Even after coming clean in an HIV test and vowing to her mother in a tearful confession that she will reform, Grace Quek goes back to her red-brick sex factory. When the director plays "Amazing Grace" over the end credits, the refrain crashes with irony. Once she was "blind," saw for a moment, and appears to be blind once more.

SIGHT AND SOUND, 5/00, p. 60, Linda Ruth Williams

Grace Quek (aka Annabel Chong), a student at the University of Southern California, engages in the record-breaking feat of having sex with 251 men in 10 hours. The experience is filmed by John Bowen as the hardcore video *The World's Biggest Gang Bang*.

Quek's life is discussed by her family, her friends and her colleagues in the porn industry. She attends a porn convention in Las Vegas, and speaks at the Cambridge University Debating Society. Jasmin St. Claire, another porn performer, has sex with 300 men, breaking Quek's record. Quek is still owed $10,000 for *The World's Biggest Gang Bang*. She is tested negative for HIV. Quek decides to leave the porn industry and returns to London, where she was once gang raped. During a visit to her family in Singapore her mother discovers what Grace does in the US. One year later, back in Los Angeles, Quek returns to the porn industry.

Some of the many contradictions which riddle *Sex The Annabel Chong Story* are present in its title. Gough Lewis' documentary claims to be the story of Annabel Chong but it is also the story of Grace Quek, or rather the story of a multiple entity who is both Quek and Chong, student and sex worker, daughter and classmate, Asian and American. This is no single-subject biopic. It also becomes clear that at the film's centre is not sex, but rather a struggle for identity in which pornography is used as a canvas.

If the project of the porn industry was to turn Chong into a purely sexual object, then the project of Gough Lewis' film is to take an already divided identity and prise open its fissures to see what emerges. Lewis' fragmented directorial technique presents an astute diagnosis of its contrary hybrid subject. Formally, the film is part cut-up novelisation, part postmodern docu-drama, chopping backwards and forwards in time and across a variety of media: Quek/Chong's media appearances, porn performances, interviews with friends and family, and the developing narrative of the day she did 251 men, itself documented in the film within-the-film *The World's Biggest Gang Bang* (directed by John Bowen).

The result is both difficult to watch and utterly compelling, having all the forbidden fascination of a freak show. Appropriate as this multi-strand approach is to *Sex*'s star, Quek/Chong does not emerge as the postmortem schizo-heroine she clearly would like to be. Rather, as the film progresses she seems to slide from one popular cultural identity (star of hardcore) to another (crumbling psyche of the talk show), which gives this film the narrative trajectory of a car crash. Beginning with Quek's appearance on *The Jerry Springer Show, Sex* then clicks into *Jerry Springer*-like confessional mode when it eavesdrops on moments such as Grace's mother finally finding out what her daughter does in the US.

At the heart of the film is the issue of how we read Chong's record-breaking feat of fucking 251 men in 10 hours. Chong explains that she did it to shake up stereotypes about women being passive sex objects. This fantasy of female appetite is reinforced by the film's publicist at the event, who says she just wants to fuck and go (but then he would, wouldn't he?). Yet the record Chong breaks isn't that of how many orgasms a woman can have in 10 hours but how many men can penetrate her. Just whose fantasy this really is isn't hard to guess, especially when the sordid details of the shoot emerge. Once the idea, inspired by Quek's anger at a feminist theory class (wouldn't you just love to know what they teach them at USC?), is picked up by the porn industry it becomes anything but a girl-power statement. The pathetic narrative which emerges from the cracks between Quek's straight to-camera justification, the *Gang Bang* shoot and the explanatory subtitles suggests she is just as much of a victim of male appetite (this time for the profits of Bowen's film) as any other girl in the history of patriarchy. Not only was she under the false impression that the men she partnered had all been Aids tested, she is also still owed $10,000 for her participation in the film.

So why watch this film? And who is its audience? *Sex* is as slippery about its viewers as it is about its star. Even if you wouldn't actually watch *The World's Biggest Gang Bang,* there is still something salaciously compelling about the way Lewis' film charts the progress of Bowen's filming. This art documentary shadows hardcore porn so doggedly that it makes you wonder about the difference. *Sex* shows us the action, as it were, only from the waist up, so that the real focus of Bowen's spectacle (cum and penetration shots) is tantalisingly denied in Lewis'. But perhaps because we don't get the money shots, we feel even more acutely the desire to see beyond the margins, such is the magnetic pull of off-screen space. This is art cinema which gets into bed with porn but keeps one foot on the floor. As documentary viewers plunged into the heart of a hardcore spectacle yet denied the most revealing shots, we are peculiarly visually disenfranchised. *Sex* seems to offer the arthouse viewer free entry into the porn cinema, but then leaves her standing at the door.

Yet do we really believe any of this? Perhaps the final question this film raises is that of its own credibility as fact or fiction. I was reminded of the sentiment at the heart of the documentary on Madonna *Truth or Dare* (aka *In Bed with Madonna*) that there would be no point in its star doing anything off camera since she only exists on it. Here, both sides of the Chong/Quek persona perform with equal unbelievability for the camera, yet neither seems to be able to exist without it. Whether there is a real truth at stake here is uncertain: feminism's heroine or patriarchy's victim, Grace Quek or Annabel Chong, Sex cannot decide whose story it's telling. Whether Grace chose truth or dare when she agreed to make this film, we'll never know.

VILLAGE VOICE, 2/15/00, p. 130, Jessica Winter

At first, Gough Lewis's *Sex: The Annabel Chong Story* affects heavy-lidded ironic bemusement as Chong, queen of the World's Biggest Gangbang, visits with her beer-bellied fan club president; as *Oral Majority* star Michael J. Coxx complains that Chong's record-breaking feat "gives porn a bad name"; as her mum back in Singapore speaks proudly of her daughter, having no idea that the biggest-selling porn video of all time features Annabel having sex with 251 men in 10 hours. But the film's smug smirk fades as another personality comes into focus: that of Grace Quek, earnest, tomboyish gender-studies student and creator/performer of the Annabel Chong character. Quek improbably envisions her Caligulicious stunt and her other porn work (selected filmography: *All I Want for Christmas Is a Gangbang, I Can't Believe I Did the Whole Team!, Sgt Pecker's Lonely Hearts Club Gangbang*) as what she calls "a piss take on masculinity"—she wants to reposition, as it were, the promiscuous female, recasting "slut" as "stud."

Her proporn postfeminism challenges a truism that's already weathered and hobbled, but Quek is compelling not for her ideas but the tangled path by which she came to them. Lewis sketches adolescent chafing against her conservative Singapore milieu, guilt-edged devotion to her unwitting family, and a gang rape at 19, the obvious parallels of which Quek declines to draw. Sex's initial facile smarm begins to appear as a strategy by which the audience will draw easy, soon-dispelled conclusions about Quek/Chong—we'll see the same lip-smacking dragon lady ("I'm Annabel Chong, porn's newest fortune cookie") as do Lewis's long, hairy parade of adult-movie producers, one of whom calls her "a babbling idiot." The movie is still a cheat, cutting ethical corners, seeking cheap laughs and cheaper sentiment. Quek herself, however, is fascinating in all her contradictions, in her extreme-sports quest to chase down and obliterate an outmoded ideal.

Also reviewed in:
CHICAGO TRIBUNE, 8/4/00, Friday/p. I, Michael Wilmington
NEW REPUBLIC, 3/6/00, p. 26, Stanley Kauffmann
NEW YORK TIMES, 2/11/00, p. E27, Lawrence Van Gelder
VARIETY , 3/8-14/99, p. 64, Todd McCarthy

SHADOW BOXERS

A Katya Bankowsky release of a Swerve Films production. *Producer:* Katya Bankowsky. *Director:* Katya Bankowsky. *Screenplay:* Katya Bankowsky. *Director of Photography:* Tony Wolberg and Anthony Hardwick. *Editor:* Katya Bankowsky. *Music:* Zoel. *Sound:* John Bucher. *Running time:* 72 minutes. *MPAA Rating:* Not Rated.

WITH: Lucia Rijker; Michael Bentt; Jill Matthews; Freddie Roach.

NEW YORK POST, 5/12/00, p. 50, Hannah Brown

The idea of women boxers strikes people as either distasteful, laughable or liberating.

"Shadow Boxers," a compelling and beautifully photographed documentary, makes a strong case for women's participation in this sport, though director Katya Bankowsky does not shy away from the grittier side of the game.

Bankowsky opens the film by showing inexperienced amateurs being beaten silly at the 1995 Golden Gloves tournament in New York, the first major competition open to women.

It's disconcerting, to say the least, to see some of these small-boned women being pounded against the ropes.

Even as spunky Jill Matthews, winner of the Golden Gloves in her weight division, basks in her glory, she has to face a question from a reporter no male athlete is ever asked: "Why?" as in, "Why bother to compete?"

"Why do you want to be part of making history?
Figure it out!" she snaps back.

The film then shifts to Lucia Rijker, a charismatic figure who's held the Women's World Champion title in the lightweight class since 1997.

Born in Holland, Rijker has exotic looks, a soft, smoky voice and obvious intelligence.

A kick-boxing champ for over 10 years, she has risen quickly to dominate women's pro boxing since moving to Los Angeles in the mid-'90s.

As she spouts the inspirational psychobabble that's inevitable in sports documentaries, it becomes clear she faces her bouts with special feminine insight: "In every fight I learn something about myself, and that wisdom I can pass on to a new generation."

Her Zen-influenced philosophy is a far cry from the conventional "win-at-all-costs" sports mentality.

Rijker's dignity, athleticism and charm gradually erase the memory of the battered Golden Gloves amateurs, and the film begins to seem more like a valentine to Rijker than a serious look at the sport as a whole.

By focusing on Rijker and avoiding issues such as steroid use—hinted at but never explored—Bankowsky glamorizes the sport more than necessary.

The most outstanding aspect of the film is the striking cinematography. Boxing hasn't been shown this creatively on screen since "Raging Bull."

VILLAGE VOICE, 5/16/00, p. 140, Amy Taubin

As smooth and powerfully packed as its protagonist, Katya Bankowsky's documentary *Shadow Boxers* focuses on Lucia Rijker, widely considered the greatest female fighter in the world. Bankowsky met Rijker in 1995 when she fought in the Golden Gloves, which had only recently been opened to women. The filmmaker, briefly an amateur fighter herself, followed Rijker as she turned pro and won the Women's International Boxing Federation World Title in 1997. Rijker is not only a boxing champion—she holds the screen like a star, and she's even thinking about a career in movies when she retires from the ring.

Shadow Boxers opens with vignettes about half a dozen women boxers as they experience the adrenaline rush of their first matches. Winners or losers, they are almost all hooked on the experience. "Why wouldn't I want to make history?" a clownish former gymnast says to an interviewer who wonders what attracts her to boxing. Bankowsky undercuts the romance with a glimpse of an older male fighter commenting that he wouldn't let his daughter or son box.

This prologue sets us up to see Rijker in a class apart from these other women boxers. Not that the adrenaline rush is absent, but her immersion, dedication, and dazzling skill is the equivalent of a great ballerina who lives to dance or a great musician who lives to play. Rijker is also particularly attuned to the existential confrontation that occurs in the ring—one with the self rather than the opponent. "Because you can get hit, because you can get hurt, because you can get knocked down, it's like real life. In every fight, I learn something new about myself." The woman who admits that her ferocious anger could have made her a danger to others outside the ring centers herself for a fight by chanting the Lotus Sutra.

Rijker was born in Amsterdam to a white mother and a black father. An athlete from childhood, she became the European women's kick-boxing champ in her teens and defended her title for 10 years. In 1994, she moved to Los Angeles and began boxing. Her potential was obvious, and she was quickly signed by powerful promoter Bob Arum (who says he has no interest in women fighters except for Rijker) and trainer Freddie Roach, who rates her as one of the greatest fighters—male or female—that he's ever known. Roach wants Rijker to fight for a couple of years, make some money, and retire while she's still on top. Rijker keeps two pictures on her wall—one of herself as a child and one of a boxer who died in the ring. She says she doesn't want to turn into one of those boxers who are so addicted to fighting that they keep trying to make comebacks. A brilliant career can end tragically in a blood sport—that awareness is what gives the film poignancy and dramatic tension.

Bankowsky's boxing experience serves her well. The matches are filmed with exceptional insight into the ritual preparations, the entrance into the ring, the sizing up of the opponent, the fight itself, and the moment of triumph. Rijker narrates the fight sequences in voice-over, and her precise memory of what she was doing and feeling adds immeasurably to our understanding of the person and the sport. The film, which was shot over a period of three years—focusing on the six fights that led to the championship—switches fluidly between color and black-and-white, and the handheld camerawork is all the more impressive for being so invisible. The emergence of women in boxing has inspired several documentary and fiction films; *Girlfight*, the Sundance winner opening this fall, showcases a stunning young actress, but Rijker is more fabulous than any fiction.

Also reviewed in:
NEW YORK TIMES, 5/12/00, p. E22, Stephen Holden
VARIETY, 6/21-27/99, p. 78, Ken Eisner

SHADOW HOURS

A CanWest Entertainment release of a Newmark Films prentation in association with 5150 Productions, Inc. *Executive Producer:* Andrea Mia and Michael Thomas Shannon. *Producer:* Peter McAlevey and Isaac H. Eaton. *Director:* Isaac H. Eaton. *Screenplay:* Isaac H. Eaton. *Director of Photography:* Frank Byers. *Editor:* Annamaria Szanto, Clayton Halsey, and Bill Yarhaus. *Music:* Brian Tyler. *Sound:* Giovanni Di Simone. *Sound Editor:* Dean Hovey. *Casting:* Cathy Henderson and Dori Zuckerman. *Production Designer:* Francis J. Pezza. *Set Decorator:* Laura Roberts. *Costumes:* Luke Reichle. *Running time:* 93 minutes. *MPAA Rating:* R.

CAST: Balthazar Getty (Michael Holloway); Peter Weller (Stuart Chappell); Rebecca Gayheart (Chloe Holloway); Peter Greene (Detective Steve Adrianson); Michael Dorn (Detective Thomas Greenwood); Richard Moll (Homeless Man); Frederic Forrest (Sean); Brad Dourif (Roland Montague); Corin Nemec (Vincent); Johnny Whitworth (Tron); Arroyn Lloyd (Mickey); Clayton Landey (Announcer); Julie Brown (Speaker); Christopher Doyle (Sweeny); Tan McClure (Keesha); Cheryl Dent (Serena); Sonny King (Manager, Nude Bar); Steve Hulin (Willie Wilson); Mark Ginther (Eli Houston); Monty Freeman, De'voreaux White, and Joseph Reilich (Transvestites); Aloma Wright (Nurse Johnson); Yareli Arizmendi (Dr. Marshall); Josephine Bailey (Desk Clerk); Philippe Bergeron (Antoine); Daniel Faraldo (Santos Armando); Gregory Scott Cummins (Johnny); Daniel Alexander (Pete); Beau Starr (Jeremiah Walker); Leroy Thompson (Dealer); Byron Chief-Moon (Chatuga); Ilia Volokh (Russian); E.J. Callahan (Man with Handicap Sign); Maral Nigolian (Neighbor); Hans Howe (Bum); Frank Novak (Husband); Diane Robin (Wife); Chris Weber (Hitchhiker); Charles Sergis (Newscaster); Eric Strausz (Cop with Bulletproof Vest); Ron Athey (Man with Hooks in Face); Crystal Cross and Stosh J. Fila (Women in Suspension Room); Bernard Elsmere (Man in Suspension Room); Cyril Kuhn and Tom Bliss (Male Huffers); Darryl Carlton (Male Guard); Kari French (Female Tripper); Jake Miller (Fingered Man); Mistress Ilsa (Elegant Woman); Pleasant Gehman (Lingerie Woman); Marcy Johnson (Nazi Mistress); Joey Jaramillo (Bavarian Puppet Boy); Luke Reichle (Butler); Selene Moreno (Small Woman); Amber Cannon (Pale Woman); Jade Semiprecious (Chopsticks Woman); Russ Glazer (Man Sucking Toes); Michelle Muloney (Seductress, Wicked Chamber Club); Chris Colvin and Alex Livingston (Boys, Wicked Chamber Club); Abby Travis (Member of Punk Rock Band); Ginger Moon and Austin St. Croix (Exotic Dancers).

NEW YORK POST, 7/14/00, p. 46, Jonathan Foreman

Despite any number of speeded-up shots of nighttime traffic on the L.A. freeways, "Shadow Hours" is one of the most boring films of the year.

A movie that purports to the show the underside of nightlife L.A., it comes alive only when the characters deliver lines of dialogue that are so comically bad, you begin to wonder if it isn't meant to be a spoof.

Michael Holloway (Balthazar Getty) is a recovering addict who works nights as a gas station attendant. His gorgeous wife, Chloe (Rebecca Gayheart) is expecting their baby.

One day Holloway is befriended by Stuart Chapell (Peter Weller) a mysterious, elegant man driving a Porsche. Stuart says he's a writer and wants someone to accompany him on a tour of L.A.'s underside.

You can tell he's evil, because he's wearing a suit and seems to know something about expensive wine.

Michael allows Stuart to buy him some sharp threads and off they drive, very fast, with techno music in the background, to all sorts of supposedly shocking secret places like strip clubs, leather bars, gambling dens and—gasp!—even clubs where people get themselves pierced.

As Stuart says, "I've seen things in this city that make Dante's 'Inferno' look like Winnie the Pooh."

At the same time you hear that a serial killer is on the loose. But the main question is, will Michael be seduced back into a life of drugs and decadence?

Writer-director Isaac Eaton introduces you to the seedy side of L.A., with the slack-jawed gawp of someone who has spent his whole life in an Amish village. The only shocking thing about "Shadow Hours" is that a script this lame actually made it to the screen.

NEWSDAY, 7/14/00, Part II/p. B6, Jan Stuart

Like that vigilante mob of Canada-hating matriarchs in the "South Park" movie, there must be a group of Mothers Against Los Angeles behind "Shadow Hours." Set in a nocturnal L.A. in a lamented near- past when a gallon of unleaded cost a mere $1.23, this juicy little thriller depicts the City of Angels as a devil's paradise that lures young dreamers with wicked temptations and spits them out without so much as a talent agent to show for themselves.

It would be harder to find more innocent-looking prey than Balthazar Getty, a moon-faced young actor who resembles a year-old baby with a month-old goatee. He gives a fine, knotted-up performance as Michael Holloway, a recently reformed substance abuser who is trying to stay straight with the help of an adoring wife (Rebecca Gayheart) and a graveyard shift at an all-night filling station.

The gas station offers a recovering addict more than his share of challenges, attracting as it does the creme de la down-and-out of L.A.'s losers. With all the addicts and derelicts who conspire to make Michael's work routine miserable, he is susceptible to the bait of a well-heeled customer who offers the promise of an easier lifestyle.

Identifying himself as a writer in search of material, Stuart Chappell (Peter Weller, doing a terrific creepster turn) smooth-talks the wary gas attendant into his graces. Chappell proves to be the ultimate hedonist and the ultimate cynic, the kind who savors a bottle of '68 wine by commenting, "That was the year they shot Martin." Chappell spirits him off on a Dante-esque odyssey through L.A.'s lower depths: fight clubs, opium dens, S&M joints and piercing parlors.

The allegory-minded writer-director Isaac H. Eaton offers us two sides of the same coin in explaining the mysterious Chappell: He is either a Mephistopheles, luring the weak into hell toward their ruin, or a benevolent Virgil guiding them through hell toward their redemption. "Shadow Hours" is a noir thriller for 12-steppers, a finger-wagging warning against the dangers of recidivism.

Eaton keeps the moralizing at bay and lays on the B-movie atmosphere, giving "Shadow Hours" the lurid kick of a virtual reality ride through L.A.'s twilight zone. There is plenty of the overbaked dialogue one expects from the genre, much of it coming from Holloway's prosaic boss Roland (Brad Dourif, prince of eccentric cameos), who says things like, "This town is full of lost souls running on empty who, for whatever reason, end up here in search of transmission fluid."

The film could use a couple of more hothouse flowers like Roland to realize its full noir-ish potential. On its own terms, "Shadow Hours" is a solid voyeur's night out.

VILLAGE VOICE, 7/18/00, p. 122, Amy Taubin

If nothing else, *Two Women* and *It's the Rage* are admirable for their social conscience, [See Taubin's reviews of these films.] *Shadow Hours*, however, is too enthralled with its own hipness to have anything else on its mind. Balthazar Getty (looking like a more catatonic Charlie Sheen) stars as a recovering coke addict who's tempted from the straight life by Peter Weller, playing—well, there's no getting around it—the devil. Since being clean and sober involves a job pumping gas and a whining, pregnant fiancée (Rebecca Gayheart), you can't fault the guy for slipping.

The devil drives a fast car, is probably a serial killer of women, and has a free pass to most of the after-hours hot spots in L.A., including a gambling den where Russian roulette is the game of choice and an s/m parlor where you may spot performance artist Ron Athey hanging from the hardware piercing his eyebrows. Given the film's faux naïveté, even Athey's transgressive art seems reduced to mere exploitation (his own and the viewers').

Fashionably photographed by Frank Byers in the manner of too many low-budget independent films, *Shadow Hours* would be at least nice to look at if its near-phosphorescent greens, reds, and flesh tones weren't so blatantly ripped off from Nan Goldin. Isaac Eaton wrote and directed; he evidences little talent in either department.

Also reviewed in:
CHICAGO TRIBUNE, 7/14/00, Friday/p. G, Achy Obejas
NEW YORK TIMES, 7/14/00, p. E12, Lawrence Van Gelder
VARIETY, 2/7-13/00, p. 57, Todd McCarthy

SHADOW OF THE VAMPIRE

A Lions Gate Films release of a Saturn Films presentation of a Long Shot Films production in asociation with BBC Films and DeLux Productions. *Executive Producer:* Paul Brooks and Alan Howden. *Producer:* Nicolas Cage and Jeff Levine. *Director:* E. Elias Merhige. *Screenplay:* Steven Katz. *Director of Photography:* Lou Bogue. *Editor:* Chris Wyatt. *Music:* Dan Jones. *Choreographer:* Françoise van den Bruck. *Sound:* Carlo Thoss and (music) Martin Astle and Dan Jones. *Sound Editor:* Nigel Heath. *Casting:* Carl Proctor. *Production Designer:* Assheton Gorton. *Art Director:* Christopher Bradley. *Special Effects:* Ricky Wiessenhaan. *Costumes:* Caroline de Vivaise. *Make-up:* Ann Buchanan. *Stunt Coordinator:* Ricky Wiessenhaan. *Running time:* 94 minutes. *MPAA Rating:* R.

CAST: John Malkovich (Frederick Wilhelm Murnau); Willem Dafoe (Max Schreck, "Count Orlok"); Cary Elwes (Fritz Arno Wagner, Cameraman); John Aden Gillet (Henrick Galeen, the Writer); Eddie Izzard (Gustav von Wangerheim, "Hutter"); Udo Kier (Albin Grau, Producer/Art director); Catherine McCormack (Greta Schröder, "Ellen"); Ronan Vibert (Wolfgang Müller, Cameraman); Marja-Leena Junker (Innkeeper's Wife); Sacha Ley (Drunken Woman); Nicholas Elliott (Paul); Milos Hlavak (Innkeeper); Derek Kueter, Norman Golightly, and Patrick Hastert (Reporters); Marie Paule von Roesgen (Old Woman).

CHRISTIAN SCIENCE MONITOR, 12/29/00, p. 15, David Sterritt

Silent-movie buffs, rejoice! No, your old favorites aren't on their way to the local multiplex. But the next best thing has arrived: "Shadow of the Vampire," a new picture that spins a comic nightmare around the making of "Nosferatu." the 1921 classic that introduced Count Dracula to the silver screen.

"Nosferatu" was directed by German genius F.W. Murnau in the "expressionist" style, using weird and wild images to convey a weird and wild story about a vampire who brings death and destruction to a peace-loving little town. It starred German actor Max Schreck as the monster, whose name was changed to Orlock so the producers wouldn't have to pay copyright fees for Bram Stoker's great "Dracula" novel.

The premise of "Shadow of the Vampire" is that Schreck was an actual vampire, whose price for starring in the movie was a bite of the leading lady's neck after her scenes were filmed. His acting gives Murnau all the authenticity a director could want, but his evil ways cause havoc on the set when he decides to vampirize a few other personnel during the shoot. This is pure fantasy, of course—the real Schreck was a real actor who followed "Nosferatu" with many other films—but it gives a mischievous new twist to the current craze for pictures like "Scream" that spin horror-movie ideas around and around horror movies themselves.

"Shadow of the Vampire" was directed by E. Elias Merhige, a gifted filmmaker whose 1991 feature "Begotten" was a memorable avant-garde journey into uncharted realms of fear and desire. He stays within the bounds of Hollywood storytelling this time, but scene after scene gains freshness and originality from the imaginative qualities of Steven Katz's screenplay and a host of inventive performances. The best of these come from John Malkovich as Murnau and especially Willem Dafoe as his spooky star, who succeeds brilliantly at the tricky task he takes on here—being an actor playing a vampire playing an actor playing a vampire! Oscar, are you watching?

CINEASTE, Vol. XXV, No. 4, 2000, p. 34, David Sterritt

In his influential book *From Caligari to Hitler: A Psychological History of the German Film*, critic Siegfried Kracauer credits director F.W. Murnau with a "unique faculty of obliterating the boundaries between the real and the unreal." That certainly applies to Murnau's most widely seen movie, *Nosferatu—A Symphony of Horrors*, based on Bram Stoker's novel *Dracula*, with the title changed to protect the unauthorized adapters from a copyright suit. In some ways, *Nosferatu* is as dreamlike and deranged as *The Cabinet of Dr. Caligari*, its spookiest predecessor in the German Expressionist sweepstakes of the silent-film era—replete with supernatural overtones, aggressively grotesque images, and a protagonist only a horror fan could love. But unlike the stagebound *Caligari*, which draws much of its power from patently theatrical scenery and lighting, *Nosferatu* pays homage to the actual world, using real locations and deriving some of its imagery from traditions of landscape painting that infuse the ultra-creepy plot with pictorial elements that would have been comfortably recognizable to contemporary viewers. Even the specifically cinematic effects that separate *Nosferatu* most definitively from *Caligari*, including stop-motion photography and use of negative footage, must have seemed fascinatingly physical as well as eerily supernatural to early-Twenties spectators still enchanted by cinema as a material process.

In sum, Kracauer is right to note Murnau's penchant for blending everyday reality with "a halo of dreams and presentiments." Murnau faces stiff competition in this area, though, from some of his present-day admirers. One is German filmmaker Werner Herzog, who directed Klaus Kinski in a *Nosferatu* remake in 1979. And now there's American director E. Elias Merhige, who uses Murnau's classic as the starting point for a different sort of yarn. Packed with cinematic in-jokes and postmodern paradoxes—a symphony of ironies, you might call it—his entertaining *Shadow of the Vampire* blends film-historical pastiche with an inventive visual style and crafty performances by John Malkovich as Murnau and Willem Dafoe as his mysterious leading man. It deserved its slot in the Director's Fortnight program at last spring's Cannes International Film Festival, where it had its world premiere, and should become a perennial favorite among movie buffs who don't mind sacrificing a large amount of historical accuracy in order to have a larger amount of amusing situations and sardonic laughs.

The story begins in 1921 in Berlin, where Murnau is shooting studio scenes of *Nosferatu* and looking forward to going on location, where he will further discombobulate the distinction between naturalism and supernaturalism. To play the undead Orlock he has engaged Max Schreck, an actor so deeply in tune with his role that he remains 'in character' at all times. The others wonder who this weirdo is, unsatisfied with vague reports that he's a Stanislavsky man from Max Reinhardt's famous troupe. The truth turns out to be more exotic: He's a full-fledged vampire, discovered in an abandoned monastery Murnau stumbled on during a location hunt. Schreck has agreed to subsist on bottled blood and an occasional animal until shooting is complete, whereupon the photogenic neck of costar Greta Schroeder, will be discreetly placed at his disposal. You can't keep a good vampire down, though, and Schreck's bad habits get the better of him long before the final scenes are in the can.

Isolated on the remote island where Murnau plans to wrap the picture, an increasingly scared Greta prepares for the climactic scene, when her character tempts Count Orlock into staying up past dawn so the sun will turn him to dust. With her are macho cinematographer Fritz Arno Wagner and their increasingly obsessed director, who complicates matters by drugging his leading lady so her gyrations won't mess up his compositions. This leads to a wry twist on the notion of the satiated vampire, since the morphine in Greta's bloodstream sends Schreck into a trancelike stupor of his own. In the end Murnau gets his shot, Weimar cinema gets a completed masterpiece, and we get the most imaginative cinematic spoof in recent memory.

Shadow of the Vampire was written by newcomer Steven Katz, who got some of his inspiration from a photo of Murnau and his real-life crew shooting a scene in lab coats and goggles, as if filming were an exercise in scientific documentation (or perhaps alchemical transformation) by its very nature. Merhige follows up on this idea nicely, creating a neat visual counterpoint between the eye of the camera and the eyes of Murnau lurking behind flat, opaque lenses as his performers go through their paces. Malkovich gives a subtly emotional performance while making the most of Katz's amusing dialog, putting impressive zest into everything from Murnau's glee at getting out of the studio—"Thank God, an end to this artifice!"—to his exasperated quarrels with collaborators who find Schreck much too creepy for comfort.

Shadow of the Vampire ultimately belongs to Dafoe, however, and it's hard to imagine a better casting choice, the late Kinski aside. While his face is a little too full to evoke the "walking phallus" that Schreck's iconic Orlock has been likened to, he has every other aspect of the role brilliantly nailed down—no mean achievement when you consider the complexities of being an actor playing a vampire playing an actor playing a vampire. There's ample opportunity for pitch-dark humor, of course, as when Dafoe gives a sinister lilt to Schreck's announcement that he wants to vampirize another crew member ("I don't think we need the writer any longer") or improvises an inappropriate line during a scene. ("We'll give the lip-readers a thrill," quips Murnau, deciding to print the take.)

But what's most unexpected about his acting, and about Katz's screenplay, is the way real emotion finds its way into the picture. Dafoe is positively chilling when Schreck responds to a physical threat from Murnau by growling with grim conviction, "Tell me how you would harm me, when even I don't know how I could harm myself." And he's genuinely touching when two members of the production team archly ask his opinion of Stoker's novel. "It made me sad," Schreck mournfully murmurs, telling how disheartened he was by the loneliness and forgetfulness that beset Dracula in his centuries of solitude. Dafoe's physical acting is equally impressive, drawing on the bodily agility he's cultivated in his stage work with the Wooster Group, whose unflinching experimentation has been good preparation for the challenges of Schreck.

The richest humor in *Shadow of the Vampire* comes from its look at the perplexities of Method acting—Schreck is the ultimate Stanislavsky man, inhabiting his role all too thoroughly—and at the relationship between creative performers and the camera that mechanically records their work. We discover that Murnau enticed Schreck into their bargain by promising not only Greta's neck but also the prospect of "everlasting life" through cinema—a prospect that André Bazin might applaud, but must surely be superfluous to a vampire! This implicates the camera as a vampire in its own right, as Greta hints in her remark that "a theatrical audience gives me life, while this *thing* merely takes it from me." Schreck certainly finds the camera a companionable toy, and the projector, too, which he uses at one point to cast a flickering image directly into his invulnerable eye. On some levels the entire movie can be read as a bemused reflection on cinema's dual existence as "material ghost," in critic Gilberto Perez's phrase. The tension between physicality and ephemerality is amusingly summed up when two of Murnau's partners sit over a bottle of schnapps and try to recall the most memorable thing they've ever seen. One describes a spiritualist who pulled ghostly ectoplasm out of his mouth, and the other says he saw the luscious Greta naked. "That beats ectoplasm, " admits the first.

As a satire, *Shadow of the Vampire* has license to bend the film-historical facts, and it does so with abandon. Scholars will find many a flaw, from details of dialog (Eisenstein is mentioned as a master director, although in 1921 he hadn't yet made a film) to the movie's blithe disavowal of the actual Schreck's life—including the inconvenient fact that he appeared in well over a dozen movies after *Nosferatu,* hardly possible if he disintegrated in the daylight while Murnau's camera rolled! Other small blemishes also mar the picture, such as a trite montage of Weimar decadence that Merhige perfunctorily inserts near the beginning, as if no visit to Berlin in the Twenties could be complete without one.

But these are cavils. In most respects *Shadow of the Vampire* is sharp and savvy, and although far less avant-garde than Merhige's amazing 1991 debut film—the unique *Begotten,* which spins a Beckett-like tale of desolation and delirium through images literally scraped and scratched into submission—it is still a notably inventive and at times wildly original comic nightmare.

LOS ANGELES TIMES, 12/29/00, Calendar/p. 1, Kenneth Turan

Rare as a crucifixion in Dracula's lair is a film opening for Oscar consideration in the last days of the year that actually has something in it worth considering. Willem Dafoe's performance in "Shadow of the Vampire" is so irresistible it not only breaks that cycle but turns an otherwise just adequate film into something everyone will want to take a look at.

Though it was ineligible for a prize, Dafoe's work was generally considered the best male performance at Cannes earlier this year and has already won the Los Angeles Film Critics' best supporting actor award. His role may sound like a stunt, but Dafoe imbues it with enough of a variety of emotional colors to make it poignant as well as mesmerizing.

The idea behind "Shadow" is an intriguing one. Imagine that the 1922 silent classic "Nosferatu," the cinema's first great vampire film, was more of a documentary than anyone knew. Imagine that without alerting the rest of his east F.W. Murnau, the film's obsessive director, found an actual vampire to take on the name of actor Max Schreck and play the king of the undead.

Directed by E. Elias Merhige and written by Steven Katz (who came up with the idea), "Shadow" has difficulty living up to its potential. The film has a mannered, pretentious air about it, a self-consciousness that's only encouraged by having a super-aware actor like John Malkovich playing Murnau and saying things like "our battle, our struggle is to create art, our weapon is the motion picture."

Even though we initially don't know what we're waiting for, "Shadow" marks time during its opening Berlin sequences. There we see Murnau shooting some of the early scenes of "Nosferatu" (a familiarity with the original adds amusement but isn't necessary) and doing his particular version of getting star Greta Schroeder ("Braveheart's" Catherine McCormack) into the mood for what's to come. "The ultimate expression of love," he tells her, "is the most exquisite pain."

Producer Albin Grau (veteran Udo Kier) has other things on his mind. "We have to talk about the vampire," he tells his director as they prepare for their location shoot in Eastern Europe. Who will play him, what clothes will he need, what makeup? Not to worry, Murnau says. The actor Max Schreck will appear in full makeup and costume, and, sounding like an early Stanislavski adept, will agree to be filmed only at night.

Once Dafoe's vampire, complete with the elongated fingernails he habitually clicks together, makes his appearance, it's impossible to do anything but watch him. Simultaneously silly and sinister, pleased with himself yet nervous about this unaccustomed movie work, Dafoe's Schreck combines crazy dignity, towering presence and an unstoppable blood lust to create the kind of presence you just don't see every day.

All talk of being deeply into character notwithstanding, Schreck's otherworldly aura unsettles the rest of the cast. Though the vampire makes no secret of viewing the beautiful Greta as more than just a feast for the eyes, he has no intention of being a fussy eater in the interim. "I don't think we need the writer anymore, he says at one point, literally licking his chops in a way even the most cutthroat producers can't match.

All this drives Murnau the director into a grumpy rage, and a series of uninspired plot devices follows, none of which would be worth experiencing if they didn't allow us to see more of Dafoe's completely realized performance as this petulant, thousand-year-old Peck's Bad Boy.

"Even in the most naturalistic parts, I'm always searching for a mask, because a mask is liberating," Dafoe, who required a minimum of three hours daily to have his makeup applied, said in Cannes of his performance. "For an actor, giving over to something that feels outside of yourself is the purest kind of performing." And for an audience, the purest kind of pleasure.

NEW STATESMAN, 2/12/01, p. 45, Jonathan Romney

Shadow of the Vampire is what you might call a biopic of a film. It is a fictionalised "making of", a fanciful account of how the great German silent film director F W Murnau shot his 1922 vampire movie, *Nosferatu*. But who, apart from historians and the more fetishistic of cinema buffs, cares how a film was made? Some films, however, are extraordinary, such miraculous freaks of culture, that you just cannot help wondering about the background history.

Nosferatu is a perfect case for study: horror is the genre in which there is the greatest discrepancy between the mystique of the image and the mundane graft of getting the image on screen in the first place. Think of the vampire casting his long-fingered shadow on a wall, then imagine the dreary industrial process of lighting and framing a posturing actor. This is the divide explored in *Shadow of the Vampire*.

Murnau's star was Max Schreck, to this day one of the most talented German film actors of Weimar cinema which was a direct precursor to Nazi ideology. Here is the auteur as autocrat, deigning to explain himself to no one and muttering instructions to his actors during takes, like a hypnotist/puppet master, a cinematic Caligari.

Shadow of the Vampire is a preposterous conceit that never quite hits its full potential for comic fruitiness. Often, it is pure farce, one step away from Mel Brooks, with the cast exploring a range of hammy German accents (bizarrely, even Udo Kier, who really is German, seems to be trying it on). At the centre is the fevered play-off between Murnau and Schreck, and although Malkovich gives it his florid all—vaulting from effete whispers to petulant barks, always with his gimlet stare—he is out acted for once. Willem Dafoe at least has a good excuse. The make-up artist, Katja Reinert, sticking close to Schreck's original, has fabricated a truly repellent wraith, with nasty tufts of white hair on an elongated, egg-like skull. Dafoe breathes fetid life into the role, grunting, sniffing and wielding long, grubby nails that variously resemble tendrils, lobster claws and castanets. He is as funny as he is gruesome.

But Merhige and the screenwriter, Steven Katz, seem uncertain whether to play for laughs or for poetic unease. For all his pastiche expressionist effects, Merhige never overcomes the cut-price look sufficiently to create the other-worldly, silent-screen mood at which he gestures. Katz at times indulges in lushly purple philosophising about the moving image, and at others seems anxious to produce witty bites of dialogue: "In my old age," says the vampire, "I feed the way old men pee—sometimes all at once, sometimes drop by drop." There is, however, an inspired and rather moving moment when Schreck explains why he found *Dracula* such a poignant novel. Stoker's solitary vampire, he explains, has no servants to aid him: can he remember how to select cheese?

Ultimately, the whole curious exercise is made somewhat redundant by Werner Herzog's underrated 1979 remake of *Nosferatu*, which starred an actor quite as bizarre in his own right as either Murnau's or Merhige's Schreck. Behind all his eye-rolling and verminous whimpering, there was little doubt that Herzog's nemesis, Klaus Kinski, was indeed essentially being himself—a mad, feral monster that no amount of effects or make-up could ever equal.

NEW YORK, 1/8/01, p. 48, Peter Rainer

W. Murnau's 1922 Dracula movie, *Nosferatu,* is one of the most unsettling movies ever made—maybe the most. The actor who plays its vampire, Max Schreck, was given a look—bat-shape ears, tapered fangs, and spidery fingers—that has served as something of a template for all who have followed in his hurried, silent footsteps. (The ghastliest homage was Klaus Kinski's in Werner Herzog's 1979 *Nosferatu.)* Not much is known about Schreck; his surname, which means "terror' in German, was apparently made up. The conceit of *Shadow of the Vampire*, which stars John Malkovich as Murnau and Willem Dafoe as Schreck, is that Schreck, as is known only to Murnau, is a real vampire, enlisted by his director to provide maximum frights. The actor's payoff: the blood of his co-star (Catherine McCormack, whose alabaster neck beckons throughout the movie). It's a marvelous, resonant joke that never quite succeeds: Stretches of the film resemble a Dario Argento horrorfest crossed with a Mel Brooks spoof. But the director, E. Elias Merhige, and his screenwriter, Steven Katz, occasionally bring some rapture to the creepiness, and Dafoe's vampire, with his graceful, ritualistic death lunges, is a sinewy, skull-and-crossbones horror who seems to come less out of the German Expressionist tradition than from Kabuki. He's also—sickest joke of all—the ultimate Method actor.

NEW YORK POST, 12/29/00, p. 43, Jonathan Foreman

Elias Merhige's "Shadow of the Vampire"' is a clever, funny, extended joke about ruthless directors, method actors and the power of the cinema, based on the making of the first vampire movie: F.W. Murnau's silent 1922 masterpiece, "Nosferatu: A Symphony of Horrors."

The inspired conceit of screenwriter Steven Katz is that Murnau's sinister-looking star, Max Schreck—who came from nowhere to play the vampire, Count Orlock—was a real vampire.

The obsessive perfectionist Murnau found him and persuaded him to play an actor playing a vampire in exchange for the neck of his lovely leading lady, the cabaret diva Greta (Catherine McCormick), once shooting was done.

Murnau (a relatively understated John Malkovich, using a convincing German accent) explains the strangeness of Schreck (Willem Dafoe) to his producer (Udo Kier) and crew by announcing that Schreck is a follower of Stanislavsky, and that his method requires that he stay in character until the film is complete.

The problem is that Schreck is unable to contain his urges, and his nightly predation at the movie's remote Slovakian location begins to threaten the production.

The photographer Wolfgang (Ronan Vibirt) collapses and has to be replaced by the dashing but deeply decadent Fritz Wagner (Cary Elwes).

And when filming moves from the ruined Slovakian monastery where Murnau found Schreck to a small Baltic island, Murnau finally realizes he cannot control Schreck. The question remains, though, whether Murnau is so dedicated to making this film that he's willing to risk everyone's lives, especially Greta's.

Dafoe is simply superb as the rat-faced, pointy-eared, long-fingernailed and occasionally child-like Schreck. English comedian Eddie Izzard does a very funny impersonation of big, bad silent-movie acting as Schreck's co-star, Gustav von Wangerheim.

Despite a small budget, director Merhige is remarkably successful at conveying both the heady atmosphere of the German expressionist filmmaking in its heyday and a sense of how wonderful those films actually look, even today.

NEWSDAY, 12/29/00, Part II/p. B2, Gene Seymour

"Nosferatu," that horrific fever dream of movie masterpieces, has haunted the imaginations of all those who have seen it. F.W. Murnau's seminal 1922 epic was, for all intents and purposes, the first vampire movie ever made. And, in the opinion of many, it is still unsurpassed after dozens and dozens of Dracula movies.

The making of Murnau's film is, in some ways, as shrouded in legend and shadow as vampire folklore itself, tempting the imagination to fill in some of the blanks. The biggest of these blanks is the personality of Max Schreck, who played the movie's wild-eyed, pointy-eared vampire, Count Orlock. This German actor was unknown when he got the role—and relatively little was heard from him afterward. Yet, his big, bald bloodsucker with the long fingernails and maniacal expression remains the most frightening—and hence, believable—nightmare ever given cinematic form.

So here's "Shadow of the Vampire" bearing a "what if?" premise so obvious that it's amazing it's taken this long to draw a coherent story out of it. Maybe Schreck (Willem Dafoe) wasn't just "acting" a part. Maybe he was the Real Deal.

In this spin on film history, Murnau (John Malkovich) is the only one who's in on the secret. Being as much a wild-eyed, mercurial monster as his movie's villain, Murnau is so obsessed with making Art that he's oblivious to the risks of having an honest-to-goodness vampire in the cast.

How to justify or explain Schreck's sudden, bloody attacks on cast and crew members? Murnau says it's just a heightened form of naturalistic acting. Everyone associated with the project pretty much buys this explanation, from airhead leading man Gustav Von Wangerheim (Eddie Izzard) to urbane producer Albin Grau (Udo Kier), all of whom are in awe of what they perceive as Schreck's impassioned "dedication" to his role.

Schreck doesn't need their praise. He wants to eat. And he's expecting Murnau to follow through on his part of the bargain: delivering leading lady Greta Schroeder (Catherine McCormack) to him for a climactic blood feast.

The cleverness of the conceit in Steven Katz' script barely holds up for an hour and a half, and E. Elias Merhige's direction keeps even the most gripping moments contained within frames too tightly compacted. But with a project such as this, it's the two central performers who should run with the ball, and they both come through like champs.

Murnau's intense, freaked-out obsession is a perfect fit for Malkovich's twitchy, off-center persona, and his scenes with Dafoe's Schreck are irradiated with nervy energy. But Dafoe's performance is the movie's whirling dynamo, making you flinch and giggle in the same way that Marlon Brando did in the early 1950s. This is a movie that's less about movies than it is about acting, and Dafoe's outrageous demonstration of the craft's divine mysteries is an aromatic, nutritious gift to audiences as hungry for artistic daring as "Shadow's" vampire, is for blood.

SIGHT AND SOUND, 2/01, p. 50, Philip Kemp

Berlin, 1921. Film director F. W Murnau is shooting the initial scenes of his vampire film *Nosferatu* at the Jofa Studios. Albin Grau, his producer and art director, badgers him for details of the actor cast as the vampire Count Orlok, but Murnau isn't telling. Together with scriptwriter Henrik Galeen, cameraman Wolfgang Müller and leading man Gustav von Wangerheim, the unit travels to the location in Slovakia.

There Murnau introduces his Orlok, Max Schreck, explaining that the actor, who trained with the Russian theatre director Stanislavsky, will remain in character throughout the shoot and act only at night. In fact Schreck is a real vampire; Murnau has induced him to appear with the promise that at the end of shooting he can sink his fangs into Greta Schröder, the film's leading lady. Giving vent to his impulses, Schreck preys on Müller, who falls ill. Murnau flies him back to Berlin and hires a replacement, Fritz Arno Wagner.

The unit flies to Heligoland for the final scenes. Greta, terrified by Schreck, refuses to act with him; Murnau has her pumped full of morphine to play the scene. Eagerly biting her neck, Schreck falls into a drugged stupor. When he wakes dawn is breaking. Realising he has been tricked, he kills Grau and Wagner and advances on Murnau, who calmly keeps filming. Daylight floods in and the vampire disintegrates. Murnau has captured the scene; his film is complete.

F.W. Murnau's classic silent vampire movie *Nosferatu* (1922) isn't just the first, but by common consent still the scariest Dracula movie yet made. (Murnau changed the title when he failed to gain the rights to Bram Stoker's novel.) Its power derives largely from the chilling presence of the actor Max Schreck, who plays Murnau's vampire. Bald, cadaverous, bat-eared and rabbit-toothed, moving stiffly upright as though still cramped by the coffin he sleeps in, Schreck seems at once terrifying and pitiable in the urgency of his need for blood. Beside him all other screen Draculas, even Christopher Lee, feel crudely overstated.

Given so compelling a performance, it's not too difficult to suspend disbelief in the central conceit of Elias Merhige's film: that Schreck really was a vampire, cast by the megalomaniac Murnau in the cause of artistic verisimilitude and bribed with the promise of his leading lady Greta Schröder's blood. The film blithely disregards historical fact: far from dying during the shoot of *Nosferatu,* producer Grau and cameraman Wagner went on to make more films, as indeed did Schreck. Nor does the loving recreation of early movie-making technique aim at total accuracy: the slow filmstock of the period would certainly have needed far stronger lighting than we see being used, and the 'night' scenes in *Nosferatu* were in any case shot day-for-night.

But accuracy is beside the point. Music-video director Merhige's second feature (his first, the 1991 experimental film *Begotten,* has an impressive cult reputation) is at once an affectionate homage to the silent era and an ironic metaphor: cinema is the vampire, sucking the blood of those who serve it. "A theatrical audience gives me life," says Schröder, gesturing with distaste towards the camera. "This thing merely takes it from me." Murnau, making what might qualify as the first snuff movie, is far more of a monster here than Schreck; the vampire acts from compulsion, the film director from artistic hubris. Addressed by his colleagues as "Herr Doktor" and attired in a long white coat and goggles, Murnau often seems to be playing the archetypal mad scientist. Indeed, he even refers to himself and his crew as "scientists engaged in the creation of memory," and at the film's climax, set on the North Sea islet of Heligoland, we've clearly reached the Island of Dr Murnau.

Willem Dafoe, though a touch too broad in the face, makes an eerily convincing Schreck, and much of the film's humour derives from the mutual upstaging between him and John Malkovich's Murnau. "I don't think we need the writer any longer," insinuates Schreck, visibly salivating, to which the director responds, "I am loath to admit it, but the writer is important." Dafoe also catches much of Schreck's pathos, mournfully quoting Tennyson ("Left me maimed/To dwell in presence of immortal youth") or voicing his sympathy with Stoker's Dracula. In one of the film's best gags, he breaks off from this heartfelt speech to snatch a live bat out of the air and snack on it like a chocolate bar.

Merhige is at pains to recreate Murnau's atmosphere. Each time Murnau starts filming, colour drains (or should that be bleeds?) from the frame, and it's sometimes hard to tell whether we're watching a facsimile or a clip from the original. What the film misses, perhaps not surprisingly, is the poetry and the compassion that Murnau brought to his material. To some extent Merhige's film is undermined by its own unevenness of tone, so that the ending, with the destruction of the vampire, can't hope to equal the emotional impact of its source. Still, like Bill Condon's rather more accomplished *Gods and Monsters, Shadow of the Vampire* stands witness to the enduring iconic potency of the great classics of the horror genre.

VILLAGE VOICE, 1/2/01, p. 101, J. Hoberman

Premised on the notion that F. W. Murnau's silent horror classic *Nosferatu* was actually a documentary, *Shadow of the Vampire* manages to turn a highly dubious concept into a subtle and deliciously mordant comedy.

The movie, directed by E. Elias Merhige from Steven Katz's script, joins Jim Shepard's 1998 novel, *Nosferatu,* as the second recent fiction to feature the German filmmaker as a tormented protagonist. But, unlike Shepard, Katz has only a casual interest in the historical Murnau. His protagonist has been reinvented for the movie as an overbearing Herr Doktor and heterosexual of the s persuasion. Of course, this, as well as numerous other liberties, anachronisms, and historical inaccuracies (Sergei Eisenstein invoked as a "master" of the medium three years before he made his first film), is minor compared to the movie's insistence that Max Schreck, the Reinhardt actor who played the indelibly feral Count Orlock, was actually a centuries-old Carpathian vampire typecast by a filmmaker driven to go beyond "artifice."

Shot largely on location, Murnau's *Nosferatu* was an experiment in open-air" expressionism. That *Shadow of the Vampire* is itself so predicated on artifice is part of the joke; that the 1922 *Nosferatu was* an authorized adaptation of Bram Stoker's *Dracula* is only the movie's first instance of blood-sucking. Murnau's leading lady, Greta Schroeder (played by Catherine McCormack as a far greater vamp than the potato dumpling who appears in Murnau's film), complains to Herr Doctor that she prefers the theater: the audience gives her life while the camera takes it from her. The creepy suggestion, eventually to be literalized, that the cinema is an inherently vampiric medium is hilariously self-serving in a movie as parasitic as this one.

As played by John Malkovich, Murnau is most impassioned as an apostle of the moving picture: "We are scientists engaged in the creation of memory that will neither blur nor fade." Perhaps taking this to heart, Merhige (directing his first feature since his own poetic horror film, 1989's remarkable *Begotten*) has created a near perfect replica of Murnau's original footage. This facsimile is even more fastidious than Tim Burton's (in *Ed Wood)* it's suggestive that Merhige, like the actual Murnau, came to this project as a hired gun. (The driving force behind *Nosferatu* seems to have been the art director Albin Grau, played in the movie by an uncharacteristically restrained Udo Kier.)

Merhige's simulacrum is all the more amazing in the scenes of the filmmaker at work. He revels in the crazy logistics of nighttime shoots, which are necessary for the mysterious Max (Willem Dafoe), Murnau's latest discovery, who, so the cast is informed, will remain in character throughout the production. Dafoe is the most uncanny aspect of Merhige's pastiche. On one hand, the filmmaker goes in and out of *Nosferatu* re-creating Murnau's original sequence to introduce Max or showing Murnau cleverly setting up the scene in which the Count's spooked visitor inadvertently cuts his hand with a bread knife. On the other, he plays with the backstage notion of the vampire's secret vanity and on-screen "innocence."

During a break in the production, the hissing star holds forth on Bram Stoker's *Dracula,* offering poignant insight into the feelings of a lonely vampire compelled to plan and prepare dinner for a human guest when he himself hasn't eaten food in centuries. Grau and screenwriter Henrick Galeen (Aden Gillet) are astonished by the dedication the actor brings to his role, particularly after he snatches a bat out of the air and devours it. "Max, the German theater needs you," the writer exclaims in admiration. (Murnau has explained that his vampire is a disciple of Konstantin Stanislavsky (a joke comparable to the Coneheads' claim that they have pointy craniums because they come from France.)

Ultimately, the movie becomes the battle of the vampires. "You and I are not too different," Max tells Murnau, as they struggle for possession of the project. In fact, *Shadow of the Vampire* belongs to Dafoe. Where the real Max Schreck gave a remarkably focused expressionist performance, Dafoe's is pure Wooster Group (its rigorous precision is part of its underlying humor.) Sniffing and snorting, sucking on his fangs and nervously clicking his claws, Dafoe treats Malkovich as his straight man. There's a wonderful buildup for the last scene. Annoyed Greta can't quite take her slavering costar seriously. Is he a crazed fan or what?

The original Schreck gave one of the most iconic performances in silent cinema. Dafoe not only invokes but enriches and, paradoxically, humanizes it. In a lovely bit of business, the vampire is left alone with the cinematic apparatus and, cranking the projector by hand, makes his own shadow play. It's particularly apt that this evocation of eternity and fake paean to the veracity of camera-based art would materialize at the dawn of the digital animation that will reduce the camera to mere graphic tool. More than a footnote scrawled in the margins of film history, *Shadow of the Vampire* is a footnote whose philosophical weight allows it to make light of that history.

Also reviewed in:
CHICAGO TRIBUNE, 1/26/01, Friday/p. A, Michael Wilmington
NEW YORK TIMES, 12/29/00, p. E1, A. O. Scott
NEW YORKER, 1/15/01, p. 99, Anthony Lane
VARIETY, 5/22-28/00, p. 25, Todd McCarthy
WASHINGTON POST, 1/26/01, p. C1, Rita Kempley
WASHINGTON POST, 1/26/01, Weekend/p. 38, Desson Howe

SHAFT

A Paramount Pictures release of a Scott Rudin/New Deal production. *Executive Producer:* Adam Schroeder, Paul Hall, and Steve Nicolaides.   *Producer:* Scott Rudin and John Singleton. *Director:* John Singleton. *Screenplay:* Richard Price, John Singleton, and Shane Salerno. *Story:* John Singleton and Shane Salerno. *Based on the movie "Shaft" (1971 and the novel by:* Ernest Tidyman. *Director of Photography:* Donald E. Thorin. *Editor:* John Bloom and Antonia Van Drimmelen. *Music:* David Arnold and Isaac Hayes. *Music Editor:* Nic Ratner, Dina Eaton, and Joseph Lisanti. *Sound:* Danny Michael and (music) Robert Fernandez. *Sound Editor:* Skip Lievsay and Paul Urmson.   *Casting:* Ilene Starger.   *Production Designer:* Patrizia von Brandenstein.   *Art Director:* Dennis Bradford.   *Set Decorator:* George De Titta, Jr. *Special Effects:* Steve Kirshoff.   *Costumes:* Ruth Carter.   *Make-up:* Bernadette Mazur.   *Stunt Coordinator:* Nick Gillard. *Running time:* 110 minutes. *MPAA Rating:* R.

CAST: Samuel L. Jackson (John Shaft); Vanessa Williams (Carmen Vasquez); Jeffrey Wright (Peoples Hernandez);   Christian Bale (Walter Wade, Jr.);   Busta Rhymes (Rasaan);   Dan Hedaya (Jack Roselli); Toni Collette (Diane Palmieri); Richard Roundtree (Uncle John Shaft); Ruben Santiago-Hudson (Jimmy Groves);   Josef Sommer (Curt Fleming);   Lynne Thigpen (Carla Howard); Philip Bosco (Walter Wade, Sr.); Pat Hingle (Hon. Dennis Bradford);   Lee Tergesen (Luger);   Daniel Von Bargen (Lieutenant Kearney);   Franciso "Cogui" Taveras (Lucifer);   Sonja Sohn (Alice);   Peter McRobbie (Lieutenant Cromartie);   Zach Grenier (Harrison Loeb);   Richard Cocchiaro (Frank Palmieri);   Ron Castellano (Mike Palmieri); Freddie Ricks (Big Raymond); Sixto Ramos (Bonehead); Andre Royd (Tattoo); Richard Barboza (Dominican);   Mekhi Phifer (Trey Howard);   Gano Grills (Cornbread); Catherine Kellner (Ivy);   Philip Rudolph (Uniform Sergeant);   Angela Pietropinto (Mrs. Anna Palmieri); Joe Quintero (Assistant D.A. Hector Torres);   Lanette Ware (Terry);   Stu "Large" Riley (Leon); Mark Zeisler (D.A. Andrew Nicoli); Capital Jay (Golem); Bonz Malone (Malik); Ann Ducati (Aunt Toni DeCarlo); Lisa Cooley (News Anchor);   Elizabeth Maresal Mitchell and Scott Lucy (Troy's Friends);   Chris Orr, Evan Farmer, Will Chase, and Jeff Branson (Walter's Friends);   Jerome Preston Bates (Desk Sergeant); John Elsen (Uniform Cop in Metronome); Nadine Mozon (Abused Woman); Lawrence Taylor (Lamont); Caprice Benedetti (Karen); John Cunningham (Judge);   Louie Leonard, Tony Rhune, and Fidel Vicioso (Pistoleros);   F. Valentino Morales (Enforcer); Myron Primes and Unioversal (Young Bloods); Travis Brandon Rosa and Matthew Wallace (Fighting Boys); Luis Torres (Fat Man); John Wojda (Construction Worker).

LOS ANGELES TIMES, 6/16/00, Calendar/p. 1, Kenneth Turan

"Do you know my name?" Samuel L. Jackson's detective John Shaft asks people every chance he gets. "What's my name?" he insists, or "Remember me?" As if anyone could forget.

Though it came out nearly 30 years ago, the original "Shaft"—directed by Gordon Parks, with Richard Roundtree as the New York private eye who was "Hotter Than Bond, Cooler Than Bullitt"—has never slipped from memory. Streetwise and sexually active, Shaft had an easy and confident manner that helped make him a success at the box office (there were even a pair of sequels and a TV series) as well as a new kind of African American hero.

Things have changed in Manhattan since 1971, however, and even Times Square, where the old Shaft hung out, is much too gentrified for a detective's office. The current version, directed by John Singleton and written by Richard Price, Shane Salerno and Singleton, tries awfully hard but with little success to create a "Shaft" for this day and age. The classic Isaac Hayes theme music has been kept (how could it not be?), but much else has changed, including a seriously diminished sex life for our hero.

The main thing the new "Shaft" gets right is casting for the title role. The always excellent Jackson has the presence of a force of nature, and his John Shaft, tough, to quote Raymond Chandler, the way other people think they're tough, is a galvanic presence. It's too bad the rest of the film doesn't hold your attention the way he does.

A detective on the NYPD when the film opens and described as the nephew of the original (Roundtree has a substantial cameo, and even Parks makes an appearance), the new-model Shaft—slick, powerful, angry—comes off more like RoboCop in a black leather Armani coat than his predecessor did.

While the first Shaft was a person before he became an icon, Jackson has upped the voltage and taken the role way past mythic. An avenging angel who makes his own law on and off the force, this Shaft is so indestructible you half-expect to encounter laser beams instead of eyes when he discards his sunglasses. When he resigns from the force, he hurls his badge across a courtroom like a stiletto; when he says, "Don't move," you better listen; when he fires a bullet, a man dies. That's right, Shaft never misses.

A plot to challenge a hero like this is hard to imagine, but "Shaft" doesn't even break a sweat in that direction. With few exceptions, the characters the detective encounters, whether good or evil, are standard-issue, neither interesting nor involving, and the same is true for the story line and the direction.

Filmmaker Singleton has had an erratic career since his "Boyz N the Hood" debut ("Poetic Justice," "Higher Learning" "Rosewood"), and the jumbled work on view here is not going to help his reputation.

The problem is not that Singleton has chosen to do genre material, it's that he's done it (compared, for instance, to what Steven Soderbergh did with "Out of Sight") with so little inspiration.

The film begins with the murder of a young black man, beaten to death by a racist swine named Walter Wade Jr. who seems to think he can get away with it because his father, Big Walter Wade, is a major real estate developer. As played by Christian Bale, in a role that could be called "American Psycho, too," Walter is a wall-to-wall smirk, a rotten rich kid who thinks he can beat the system. You can imagine how that irritates Shaft.

The only witness to the crime, a pasty-faced waitress named Diane Palmieri (Toni Collette) who looks like she's survived a 24-hour "Battlefield Earth" marathon, promptly disappears. And, aided by typical rich white guy machinations, Walter evades the law for a time as well.

While waiting for that case to jell, Shaft teams up with fellow officer Carmen Vasquez (Vanessa Williams) and ends up tangling with Peoples Hernandez, a Dominican drug lord so named, no kidding, because he always takes care of his peoples. As played with eccentric brio by Jeffrey Wright, unrecognizable to those who remember him as the artist of the title in "Basquiat," Peoples goes over the top at times, but he's still the only character aside from Shaft that is any fun to watch.

Eventually, rich punk Walter resurfaces and, unlikely as it sounds, hooks up with the unorthodox Peoples in a kind of anti-Shaft jihad. Having two villains instead of one makes things more confusing and less focused without managing to give Shaft a worthy rival.

With its hero pingponging on and off the police force (and being more effectively violent in the off position), "Shaft" ends up with a strong and unsavory streak of vigilantism. Fed up with the system, Shaft and company reason that if you know who the bad guys are, it's more reliable to take care of them yourself. It's "Death Wish" all over again, and not any more fun the second time around.

NEW YORK, 6/26/00, p. 128, Peter Rainer

Samuel L. Jackson walks manfully through much of the new *Shaft* in the latest NYPD-issue Armani. He's a clotheshorse cop who appreciates a sense of style in the criminals he collars, but who could possibly match up to him? You get the distinct feeling that John Shaft is outraged more by the dress-down couture of his crooks than by their crimes. The first *Shaft*, starring Richard Roundtree and directed by Gordon Parks, was slapdash except for the sleekness Roundtree brought to it; the film was set up as a black private-eye thriller, but its real subject was stylishness as a form of militancy, and that was a pretty good and sustaining racial joke at the time. It still is. The so-called blaxploitation-movie cycle of the seventies turned the race-baiting tactics of white Hollywood inside out. Whites were demonized and marginalized in ways that blacks so often had been in the movies, but in the end the new approach wasn't any more appetizing than the old approach, except perhaps as payback experienced by black and bleeding-heart white audiences.

The current *Shaft*, directed by John Singleton and co-written by Singleton, Richard Price, and Shane Salerno, preserves the race-baiting essence of the genre, but it's cannier about it; the film's chief villain, played by *American Psycho*'s Christian Bale in what amounts to an encore performance, is a spoiled rich scion who might look best modeling an Armani Klan hood. Shaft's righteous fury in nabbing this guy is given *Dirty Harry* overtones: The corrupt justice system protects these moneyed scorpions, so Shaft's only recourse is to toss his badge and go vigilante. At one point he says he's "too black for the uniform and too blue for the brothers," and it's a good line except that it remains just a line—the dilemma is never dramatized in the movie. Despite a tossed-off comment about Mayor Giuliani, there's no real reference to New York's racial police politics either. In other words, the new *Shaft* is just as much a fantasyland as the old *Shaft*. The big difference is that now Shaft is so burned-up about everything, he doesn't have time to be a sex machine. Under the circumstances, the revived Isaac Hayes theme song seems more like a taunt than a tribute.

NEW YORK POST, 6/16/00, p. 47, Jonathan Foreman

"Shaft" is what summer action flicks should be. It is every bit as slick and exciting as "M:1-2" and "Gone in 60 Seconds," but more satisfying than either, thanks to superior writing, acting and direction.

The perfect casting of Samuel L. Jackson, and the kind of authentic, intelligent writing about urban crime and punishment that you would expect from a script co-written by the Oscar-nominated novelist/screenwriter Richard Price, ensure that this part remake/part sequel to the 1971 blaxploitation classic simply exudes coolness.

The James Bond-style opening credits proclaim the filmmakers' intention to initiate an action franchise.

And the film works so well that if Samuel L. Jackson is willing, this could be the first of a whole new series of "Shaft" movies.

Leather-coat-wearing Detective John Shaft is the most expensively dressed cop in the NYPD, if not the world, and a man who projects a tremendous, dangerous presence.

He is also the nephew and protégé of John Shaft, private eye (Richard Roundtree)—who keeps urging him to leave the force and join the PI business.

When a young black student is killed by racist WASP rich kid Walter Wade (Christian Bale), it's Shaft who makes the arrest—and who socks the perpetrator in public. Partly because of the beating, Wade is given bail and promptly flees the country.

Despite the frustrations of dealing with bigoted superiors and a corrupt justice system, Shaft continues keeping the streets clean. This brings him into particular conflict with a Bronx-based Dominican drug lord, Peoples Hernandez (the excellent Jeffrey Wright, sporting an over-the-top accent).

When Wade comes back to the United States, Shaft rearrests him. But, being one of those untouchable rich white guys, Wade makes it out on bail *again*—after having made contact with Peoples in the Tombs.

The two baddies from opposite sides of the tracks then hatch a plan to kill Shaft and to silence the only witness to Wade's original crime, a waitress named Diane Palmieri (Toni Collette), who has dropped out of sight.

Infuriated by Wade's bail, Shaft quits the police force and becomes a cunning, ruthlessly brutal vigilante, resolving to find Diane and put Wade away.

He's aided in an unofficial capacity by Detective Carmine Vasquez (Vanessa Williams—the movie's main Latino characters are all played by non-Latino African-Americans) and by an informer and small-time crook, Rasaan (Busta Rhymes).

The Black Power politics and rampant sexism of the original film have been dropped in favor of a more nuanced—if all too predictable—concern with white racism and corruption in the NYPD.

Unlike Roundtree's original Shaft, who was always being badly beaten, Jackson's a superhero who never gets scratched, even when the car he's driving flips over. Every bullet he fires finds its target.

For an accomplished movie actor like Jackson, playing an action hero like this is a walk in the park. But it's clearly a role he enjoyed: You can almost see him relishing the character's combination of humor and physical threat.

Bale is essentially playing a tougher version of his yuppie character in "American Psycho." Once again, his accent is flawless and his good looks make him an effective villain. But he pales as a miscreant next to Wright's funny, vivid—if slightly stereotypical—Dominican gangster.

NEWSDAY, 6/16/00, Part II/p. B3, John Anderson

No one can resist "Shaft"—the theme song, that is. "Badabump. Badabump. Badabump. Bahhhhhhh..." During the opening credits, at least, the groove is on.

Likewise, it's hard not to like Samuel L. Jackson as rogue police detective John Shaft (or Nephew of Shaft), since the original, Richard Roundtree, shows up to play his old self). What other current candidate could play "the private dick who's a sex machine to all the chicks," as Isaac Hayes has been groaning since '71? Well, Don Cheadle would have been interesting. Taye Diggs? Denzel? No, Jackson is fine, especially when exercising his specialty brand of dangerous cool.

But while this "Shaft," directed by John Singleton ("Boyz N the Hood," "Rosewood"), doesn't pretend to be any other "Shaft," the situation begs comparison, if only for what it says about politics, race and the politics of race. What it says is, the new "Shaft" loses on all counts. More racially polarized than the first, even less nuanced than the first and far less intelligent than the first, it's not even as well-shot as the first—a renowned photographer, Gordon Parks had never directed a film before, but at least he knew something about composing a picture. Singleton's movie wears its punk attitude like a badge of honor—in a cheap ploy for cheers, Shaft punches out the movie's handcuffed villain not once but twice, 10 minutes into the movie. But it basically punks out when it comes to saying something strong.

The producers and writers and director of "Shaft" have no particular obligation to have a social conscience or to promote a message any wider than the one they wave around, which is a very valiant resistance to a very street-level kind of racism. But the movie nimbly avoids saying anything about systemic bigotry or the alleged downside of "Giuliani time" (a slogan, when uttered by Shaft, the cop, that provides one of the screenplay's more surreal moments).

Its story line is, in short, inconsequential. The suspect who gets Shaft's blood boiling is Walter Wade (Christian Bale), a rich white boy (their term, not mine) and a lone attacker, who lethally assaults a lone black male outside a nightclub. There are no witnesses save one (Toni Collette). And since she's disappeared and Wade's father (Philip Bosco) is a big-time developer (see: Trump), Walter gets off on bail. The filmmakers are shocked—shocked!—to find that money talks in court. They need to read more newspapers.

Certainly, the attack is a vicious crime. A catastrophe for the victim's mother (Lynne Thigpen). And a blight on New York City. But when Wade is released on bail, and Singleton constructs a courthouse scene and a public outrage that resembles the outcry over Amadou Diallo, he's trivializing actual tragedy. Also, it's a little hard to buy.

So is the film's portrayal of virtually all white people as racists, cowards and/or morons, and virtually all the Hispanics as both stupid and criminal. Most spectacularly cartoonish is Peoples Hernandez (Jeffrey Wright), a machismo-mad, chew-looking-at-me- style Latino mobster, who wants Shaft's blood after a public dissing and allies himself with Wade—partly because Wade is paying Peoples to kill the witness, partly because Wade can provide entree to the downtown enclaves where Peoples craves acceptance. He's suffering a bad case of class envy—possibly, ethnic self-loathing. It's a nasty little portrayal. But it plays into Singleton's agenda nicely.

Excitement? Thrills? Action? Yeah, even if the director choreographs every shootout the same, like ducks in a carnival. They line themselves up, and Shaft mows' em down. Much as Singleton does with good taste, character development, racial understanding and the idea of bringing any grace or style to a cultural icon who deserved both.

SIGHT AND SOUND, 10/00, p. 57, Andrew O'Hehir

New York, the present. John Shaft, a police detective, investigates the murder of a young black man outside a nightclub. The obvious suspect is Walter Wade Jr, son of a white billionaire. Shaft arrests Wade, who skips bail and flees to Europe. Diane, a waitress at the club who witnessed the killing, also disappears.

Two years pass. Wade returns from Europe to face the murder charge. While in jail, he meets Peoples Hernandez, a drug lord arrested by Shaft and his partner Carmen. When Wade is granted bail, Shaft quits the police force in anger. Worried that Shaft will find Diane, Wade approaches Hernandez and asks him to kill her. But when Wade comes to Harlem with $40,000 for Hernandez, Shaft and an accomplice steal the money and plant it on two corrupt cops who work for Hernandez, making it appear they stole it. Shaft finds Diane, but so does Hernandez. In the ensuing shoot-out, most of Hernandez's crew are killed, but he, Shaft and Diane escape alive. Shaft hides Diane in the apartment of Rasaan, his sidekick and driver. Another shoot-out and car chase end with Shaft killing Hernandez. Diane is injured but survives to testify against Wade. But the murder victim's mother kills Wade outside the courthouse.

What sense would one make of John Singleton's erratic *Shaft* remake if gossip magazines had not helpfully explained that the production was plagued by infighting between the director, co-writer Richard Price and star Samuel L. Jackson? My own theory is that Singleton *(Boyz N the Hood)* has carried his loyalty to the blaxploitation genre of the 70s to an illogical extreme, emulating the nonsensical plotting and incomprehensible scenes of violence of many films of that era. The (barely) updated musical theme by Isaac Hayes remains enjoyable, and Jackson, as the new Shaft, cuts a dashing figure in his shades and black Armani leathers. But Gordon Parks' 1971 film, however awkward it may appear in hindsight, struck audiences at the time as both daring and angry, a standard this *Shaft*—episodic, fatally confused, only intermittently entertaining—fails to live up to.

Given the atmosphere of growing concern over police abuse of minority citizens in US cities, especially New York, there were bound to be some uneasy moments in this story about a cop, the original Shaft's nephew, who feels "too black for the uniform, too blue for the brothers." Singleton and company never address this issue directly; instead, they work in a cryptic reference to the real-world case of Abner Louima, a Haitian immigrant who was brutalised in a New York station house, and generally depict their policeman hero and his colleagues as reckless and incompetent thugs. After arresting drug lord Hernandez, Shaft warns him to expect an "ass-whipping" on the way to the station. Later he viciously beats a teenage drug-dealer merely to ingratiate himself with a potential informant. As Shaft is pistol whipping this youth, a white patrolman drives by. He doesn't intervene in the assault; a long look passes between him and Shaft before the cop nods and departs. Ironically, while it is true that undercover police use codes to identify themselves on the streets, this episode echoes one that ended quite differently a few years ago in New York when a black undercover cop pursuing a suspect was shot by a white officer who took him for an armed felon.

Shaft's angry resignation from the police after racist killer Wade's second bail hearing is undoubtedly meant to show that he's had enough of the legal system, but it makes little sense in context. Wade has voluntarily returned from overseas to stand trial; that he is released on bail should surprise no one. Similarly, the final plot twist, in which the victim's saintly, grey-haired mother avenges herself on Wade, can be read as symbolising African-Americans' legitimate mistrust of the US judicial system. But it also renders Shaft's labours meaningless: he has pursued, cajoled and protected witness Diane, and killed Hernandez and virtually his entire family—all, it seems, for nothing.

Just as the movie itself feels jittery and unfocused, Jackson himself never settles into the role, for all his feline grace and easygoing charm. The screenplay (credited to Singleton, Price and Shane Salerno) gives him little time to relax between action scenes, but one utterly irrelevant mood piece set in Harlem's historic Lenox Lounge gives us just a taste of how much fun *Shaft* could have been. Parks and Richard Roundtree (here, reprising the title role of the original film) put in appearances, and Jackson seems suddenly in his element, half-ironically purring at a comely waitress: "It's my duty to please the booty." (Trust me, British readers, it rhymes.)

Throughout, Singleton never seems sure whether he wants a high-style spectacle or down-at-heels realism in the 70s tradition, so the film lacks not only a consistent visual tone but a well-defined sense of time and place. Instead, *Shaft* simply ends up looking cheaper than any big-budget Hollywood entertainment should. It will draw audiences based on the irreducible charisma of its star, but it does no favours to him, to its one-time-wunderkind director, or to the legacy of Parks' film, for all its flaws a true landmark in American popular cinema.

TIME, 6/26/00, p. 70, Richard Schickel

The new Shaft, played by Samuel L. Jackson, is different from the old one, portrayed in the '70s by Richard Roundtree, in two significant ways. He is no longer a private eye—if you can believe it, he's now a New York City cop—and though plenty of foxy chicks sashay across his eyeline, his interest is mainly in chatting them up, not in bedding them down.

This is not necessarily an improvement, but it's not a total disaster either. Jackson is as fast with a contemptuous quip as he is with his fists; and if he is not quite the cool sexual outlaw that his predecessor was, that's all right too, since "blaxploitation" was never more than a passing fad—a more or less genial way of asserting black studdishness while giving white liberals the jimjams.

But it at least had an attitude, and that's what director John Singleton's *Shaft* lacks. It begins by focusing on an upper-class racist murderer (Christian Bale) whose motives we don't quite believe. So the movie quickly shifts its attention to a sly, brutal, self-regarding Latino drug dealer (Jeffrey Wright). You can understand only about one in three words he speaks, but you catch his very scary drift.

Wright's a wonder, playing a role that was—deservedly—built up during production. But that leaves a lot of other actors among them Vanessa Williams, Toni Collette and Roundtree himself (as Shaft's beamish uncle)—shortchanged. It also leaves Jackson to play yet another cop rebelliously disgusted with the system and Singleton with yet another urban action piece, well enough made but not essentially different from a hundred other movies just like it.

VILLAGE VOICE, 6/27/00, p. 151, J. Hoberman

Made on the cheap by MGM to capitalize on the market revealed, during the spring and summer of 1971, by Melvin Van Peeble's infinitely more incendiary *Sweet Sweetback's Baadasssss Song*, the original *Shaft* generated two quick sequels, a short-lived TV show, a series of paperback novels, and a long-running Burger King commercial. This black private eye had all the James Bond franchise essentials—guns and pulchritude, a one-syllable brand name with trademark attitude, and a theme that's been inscribed on the world's DNA. You tell me why it's taken 27 years for Hollywood to follow up on *Shaft in Africa*.

That said, John Singleton's *Shaft* update—with Samuel L. Jackson taking over the family business from his Uncle John (the original "bad mutha," Richard Roundtree)—is no less mediocre than the original, which, even in its day, was outclassed by *Superfly* and *Across 110th Street*. Still, the icon remains: Resplendent in his leather duster, Jackson (who has long since established himself as Hollywood's Mr. Volatility) stalks through the movie with a hard stare and a major chip on his shoulder—at one point marching off down a midtown Manhattan avenue in the fire lane, against traffic.

An NYPD detective rather than a private dick, the new Shaft resigns from the force to become a righteous trickster vigilante dude. That his real home is showbiz is made clear with a scene at an all-star Harlem bar whose resident bon vivant is Uncle John and whose other patrons include Gordon Parks (director of the first two *Shaft* movies), a former Giants football star, and one of the second-string doctors from *ER*. The bartender is poet Sonja Sohn, apparently rendered speechless when the script dictates that Jackson lean over and leer, "It's my duty to please that booty."

Shaft is basically a posture-fest fueled by ethnic jive and racist invective—Christian Bale's American Psycho has been transposed to this world as a ready-made villain. Jackson's credibility is not enhanced by the Fu Manchu beard that appears to have been painted on his face like military camouflage—it's even upstaged by the elaborate wig-sideburns-tattoo ensemble sported by Jeffrey Wright's Washington Heights coke lord. Indeed, as a Spanglish-hissing bantam with social aspirations, Wright steals the movie in the most hilarious bit of method acting since Lincoln Center honored Al Pacino. (On the other hand, the white extra required to exclaim, "This is wack!" has nothing on Jim Carrey's reading of the same line in *Me, Myself & Irene.*)

As an action flick, *Shaft* is clumsy out of the gate and overfond of hurtling stuntmen through windows. As judicious editing prevails over the pointless camera moves (if not over the stiletto wipes), the various narco-bust and bumper-car segments are respectable; when all else fails, the filmmakers manage to get a rise out of the crowd by cranking up Isaac Hayes's newly gussied theme.

Also reviewed in:
CHICAGO TRIBUNE, 6/16/00, Friday/p. A, Michael Wilmington
NEW YORK TIMES, 6/16/00, p. E12, Elvis Mitchel
NEW YORKER, 7/3/00, p. 88, David Denby
VARIETY, 6/12-18/00, p. 13, Robert Koehler
WASHINGTON POST, 6/16/00, p. C1, Rita Kempley
WASHINGTON POST, 6/16/00, Weekend/p. 45, Desson Howe

SHANGHAI NOON

A Touchstone Pictures and Spyglass Entertainment release of a Birnbaum/Barber production in association with a Jackie Chan Films Limited production. *Executive Producer:* Jackie Chan, Willie Chan, and Solon So. *Producer:* Roger Birnbaum, Gary Barber, and Jonathan Glickman. *Director:* Tom Dey. *Screenplay:* Alfred Gough and Miles Millar. *Director of Photography:* Dan Mindel. *Editor:* Richard Chew. *Music:* Randy Edelman. *Music Editor:* John LaSalandra. *Sound:* David Lee and (music) Elton Ahi. *Sound Editor:* Tim Chau. *Casting:* Matthew Barry and Nancy Green-Keyes. *Production Designer:* Peter J. Hampton. *Art Director:* Jeff Ginn. *Set Decorator:* Bryony Foster. *Special Effects:* Neil N. Trifunovich. *Costumes:* Joseph Porro. *Make-up:* Rosalina Dasilva. *Make-up (Owen Wilson):* Ann Pala. *Stunt Coordinator:* Brent Woolsey. *Running time:* 110 minutes. *MPAA Rating:* PG-13.

CAST: Jackie Chan (Chon Wang); Owen Wilson (Roy O'Bannon); Lucy Liu (Princess Pei Pei); Brandon Merrill (Indian Wife); Roger Yuan (Lo Fong); Xander Berkeley (Van Cleef), Rong Guang Yu, Cui Ya Hi, and Eric Chi Cheng Chen (Imperial Guards); Walton Goggins (Wallace); P. Adrien Dorval (Blue); Rafael Baez (Vasquez); Stacy Grant (Hooker in Distress); Kate Luyben (Fifi); Jason Connery (Andrews); Henry O (Royal Interpreter); Russel Badger (Sioux Chief); Simon Baker (Little Feather); Cliff Solomon (Medicine Man); Alan C. Peterson (Saddle Rock Sheriff); Rad Daly (Saddle Rock Deputy); Lee Jay Bamberry, Stephen Strachan, and Tim Koetting (Van Cleef Deputies); Rick Ash (Jedadiah); Valerie Planche (Jedadiah's Wife); Tom Heaton (Saloon Bartender); Ben Salter, Terry King, and Michele Fansett (Saddle Rock Townsfolk); Joyce Doolittle, Randy Birch, and Andrew Krivanek (Carson City Townsfolk); Christopher Hunt (Apothecary Shopkeeper); Jody Thompson (Margie); Eliza Murbach, Kendall Saunders, and Jenafor Ryane (Dream Sequence Hookers); Chang Tseng (Pei Pei's Father);

Sherman Chao (Emperor's Cousin);   Regent Or (Emperor); Howard Rothschild (Drunken Doctor); Tong Lung, Grace Lu, and Elise Lew (Chinese Workers); Melvin Skales (Hangman); Jimmy Carver (Bordello Doorman); Dallas Dorchester and Jason Glass (Blind Drivers); Lisa Stafford (Blonde on Train).

LOS ANGELES TIMES, 5/26/00, Calendar/p. 1, Kevin Thomas

The hilarious, knockabout "Shanghai Noon," Jackie Chan's best American picture to date, breathes fresh life into the virtually dormant comedy-western. It also marks the relaxed and confident directorial debut of Tom Dey, working from a consistently funny, inventive and perceptive script by Alfred Gough and Miles Millar, whose previous major screen credit was "Lethal Weapon 4."

To top off all these pluses, Chan has a sensational sidekick in Owen Wilson and a beautiful and intrepid leading lady in Lucy Liu. All in all, it's a kick in more ways than one.

The film opens like "The Last Emperor," in Beijing's Forbidden City in all its vast grandeur, pomp and ceremony. It's 1881, and the exquisite Princess Pei Pei (Liu), who's been reading "The Sleeping Beauty" in English and longing to live happily ever after, resists being married off to the emperor, a goofy 12-year-old.

She naively allows herself to be spirited away by a young Briton (Jason Connery) who delivers her to an evil ex-Imperial Guard, Lo Fong (Roger Yuan), who runs a Nevada mine with Chinese forced labor. He sends word that the princess' safe return depends upon receiving a treasure in gold. Imperial Guardsman Chon Wang (Chan) winds up in a party dispatched to Carson City to ransom the princess.

Mayhem comes fast and furious when the train carrying the Imperial party, dressed in their elaborately embroidered silk robes, is held up by rowdy bandit Roy O'Bannon (Wilson) and his really nasty henchmen (headed by Walter Goggins). O'Bannon, a tall, rangy blond guy and a classic western good-bad man, and the rugged Chon strike up a wildly seesawing relationship, squaring off repeatedly but with O'Bannon gradually ending up Chon's sidekick.

Roy is much amused when he finally learns Chon's name, which comes out of his mouth sounding like "John Wayne," a name O'Bannon finds comically inappropriate for a frontiersman. (Never mind Roy's real name.)

When Chon, in one of his literally countless grand flourishes of martial arts, rescues a small Sioux boy from some Crow warriors, the Sioux chief (Russell Badger) treats Chon to a peace pipe so powerful that he finds himself waking up the next morning betrothed to the chief's gorgeous daughter (Brandon Merrill).

"At least he's not a white man," shrugs the chief philosophically, in one of the film's amusing multicultural asides.

Chan and his colleagues must have decided at the outset to have some fun while engaging in the hard work an action-filled western demands. (It's an attitude that has always permeated Chan's films.)

Gough and Millar have created a sterling script that allows Dey, a seasoned commercials director, to keep things moving along with a spaciousness that inspired zaniness demands. The script is good-natured yet sharp, filled with deft characterizations like Wilson's Roy, who comes across like a laid-back California surfer dude who's both reckless and canny.

In its own lighthearted way, the film is quite candid about racism on the frontier, which older Hollywood westerns rarely, if ever, were. There's an essential dignity, too, in the depiction of the Chinese and a respect for their ancient traditions, even if the regal but independent-spirited Princess has no intention of returning to her cloistered existence.

One dazzling feat of derring-do follows another, defying descriptions in the speed and bravura of Chan's martial artistry, in particular, and in all the action sequences in general. Yet the moment that just could become a classic finds Roy and Chon getting drunk while soaking in adjacent tubs in a fancy brothel and singing the craziest songs you'll ever hear.

No action picture is complete without just the right setting for the big showdown—in this instance, the dashing and virile villains Lo Fong and crooked sheriff (Xander Berkeley), whose name is Van Cleef, surely an homage to the great heavy Lee Van Cleef. It happens to be a fine old Spanish Mission-era church, with a belfry put to the best use since Hitchcock shot "Vertigo" in a similar tower structure.

For all the easy-going quality of "Shanghai Noon," it is a work of impeccable craftsmanship, with splendid cinematography by Dan Mindel (with Alberta, Canada, standing in for Nevada) and impeccable costumes by Joseph Porro and faultless production design by Peter J. Hampton; period authenticity often goes out the window in comedy-westerns but not here. Randy Edelman's score rounds out the buoyant, effervescent delight that is "Shanghai Noon."

NEW YORK POST, 5/26/00, p. 51, Jonathan Foreman

A sure-fire summer crowd-pleaser, and the most enjoyable western comedy since "Blazing Saddles," "Shanghai Noon" is a cheerful, good-hearted delight.

First-time director Tom Dey deftly mixes Jackie Chan's Buster Keaton-inspired genius for physical comedy with Owen Wilson's talent for the deadpan one-liner, to fashion a fast, smart, very funny buddy flick.

It obviously helps that the two stars have such sparkling chemistry, but they are also working from an uncommonly smart, dryly irreverent script by Alfred Gough and Miles Millar.

The movie starts in Peking's Forbidden City in 1881. The beautiful Princess Pei Pei (Lucy Liu of "Ally McBeal") is about to be married off to the fat, toadlike, 12-year-old emperor.

With the help of her English tutor (Jason Connery) she runs off to America, only to be delivered to an evil Chinese traitor (Roger Yuan) who has become a mining magnate using Chinese labor, and who threatens to kill her unless the imperial court pays a massive ransom.

A crack team of imperial guards is dispatched to Carson City, Nev., with a chest full of gold to ransom the princess. Accompanying them only because his uncle is the official interpreter is Chan, as the bumbling imperial guard Chon Wang pronounced "John Wayne."

The train on which they're traveling to Carson City is robbed by an outlaw gang led by the ultra-laid-back gangster Roy O'Bannon (Owen Wilson), who's really only in the crime game to impress the girls. Because one of his new gang-members is a psychopath who doesn't get O'Bannon's rules of nonviolent train robbery, the heist goes badly wrong.

Chon's uncle is killed, and Chon and O'Bannon find themselves alone and at each other's throats in the desert.

Of course, after various misadventures and brawls, and an episode in which Chon is adopted by a party of Sioux warriors, he and the feckless O'Bannon end up working together to rescue the princess.

Jackie Chan's English is now good enough to showcase the charm and charisma the star has to spare. One of his funniest moments—a drinking scene with Wilson in a bordello bathroom—doesn't even involve any stunts.

There are times, in fact, when you almost wish that the movie took more time to show off his amazing acrobatic abilities (Chan choreographs and performs his own stunts).

Despite all the hilariously anachronistic dialogue, the filmmakers take care to respect the plot and visual conventions of the western.

They deal lightly with issues of race and culture without any of the politically correct point-scoring so common in revisionist westerns. It's also a very well-photographed film that makes the most of some stunning Alberta, Canada, locations.

The lovely Native American model Brandon Merrill plays Falling Leaves, Chon Wang's Sioux wife.

NEWSDAY, 5/26/00, Part II/p. B2, Gene Seymour

If summer movie season is the postmortem equivalent of the traveling circus, then Jackie Chan is a one-man big top, his own ringmaster, acrobat troupe and clown act. He may give tent shows compared with the arena-rock phantasmagoria routinely delivered by James Cameron or Jerry Bruckheimer. But within his self-defined limits, Chan works with both dogged conviction and an unapologetic, ingratiating affection for elaborate silliness.

So what, then, if Chan's latest, "Shanghai Noon," isn't as good a western as "Rio Bravo" or as laugh-out-loud funny a western spoof as "Blazing Saddles"? As filmed circus acts go, it's a lot more fun than the "Cirque du Soleil" show now oozing its way through the IMAX circuit. The jokes are broad and dumb, just as they're supposed to be in a sideshow. Its settings, both in imperial China and the Wild West of the 19th Century, are the exotic stuff of old-fashioned carnival romance. Who needs a plot to connect it all?

Nevertheless, there is one. It is 1881 and Princess Pei Pei (Lucy Liu) decides to bolt China's Forbidden City for the United States, rather than marry a royal-blooded dolt as pre-arranged by her family. It turns out that she's been set up for a kidnaping by a renegade imperial guard (Roger Yuan) now exploiting Chinese immigrants' labor on the American railroads.

Back in China, a far less terrifying palace guard named Chon Wang (Chan) begs to accompany three of his comrades to Carson City, Nev., with the ransom. The train they're riding is attacked by a gang of outlaws led by genial Roy O'Bannon (Owen Wilson), whose sole reason for becoming a desperado is roughly equivalent to those held by more than a few aspiring rock stars: It impresses the heck out of the womenfolk.

In the ensuing chaos, Chon Wang is separated from his party, battles one tribe of Indians while being embraced by another and ends up in a like-hate alliance with Roy, who's about as adept in the frontier as this greenhorn from the Far East.

This fish-out-of-water scenario served Chan well in 1998's "Rush Hour" and once again, his wide-eyed charm and befuddled stoicism are given plenty of space to operate. The movie also has plenty of space to display the patented Chan panache with inanimate objects in the midst of rapid-fire martial arts sequences. On the shady side of 40, Chan is still in fighting, twirling trim. These days, the real surprises are found in Chan's non-combative moments, such as the well- timed Keatonesque way he deals with a horse that insists on following him into a saloon.

Wilson may provide a less drastic comic foil for Chan than "Rush Hour's" Chris Tucker. But his off-kilter hayseed persona is given what may be its most attractive setting to date and he makes the most of it with an inspired exhibition of goofball cool.

"Shanghai Noon's" title is only the first of its many gratuitous nods to Hollywood's western heyday. Say "Chon Wang's" name out loud and you'll know why you're supposed to laugh. Wilson's O'Bannon is moved to say, "What kind of name is that for a cowboy?" It's funnier the first time than it is the second. Which proves that western spoof is now as stodgily ritualized as what it used to mock. Still, you have to admire the cheek of any western, funny or otherwise, where Indians are placed in the role of the calvary, that is, "saving the day."

SIGHT AND SOUND, 10/00, p. 58, Andy Richards

1881, China's Forbidden City. Attempting to escape an arranged marriage, Princess Pei Pei is unwittingly sold by her unscrupulous English tutor to Lo Fong, a renegade ex-Imperial guard running a mining operation outside Carson City, Nevada. The Emperor dispatches his three best guards to deliver her ransom of 100,000 gold pieces, accompanied by an interpreter and his nephew, guard Chon Wang.

Crossing the Nevada desert by train, the Imperial entourage is hijacked by robbers led by Roy O'Bannon. Chon's uncle is killed by one of the robbers. Chon sabotages the robbery. Separated from the other guards, Chon finds Roy, abandoned by his gang and buried up to his neck in sand. Chon leaves him some chopsticks to dig himself out.

Continuing his quest to find the princess, Chon rescues a young Sioux boy from a party of Crow warriors. He is treated as a hero, and given the Sioux chief's daughter, Falling Leaves, as a wife. Chon chances on Roy in a saloon and a brawl develops. They are both thrown in jail, where Chon tells Roy about the kidnapped princess. They escape with the help of Falling Leaves and head to Carson City, where posters reveal that they are now both wanted men. They have a run-in with Van Cleef, the town's corrupt sheriff, and narrowly escape his posse. Chon and Roy bond in a bath house. They rescue the princess and defeat Lo Fong and Van Cleef. The princess falls in love with Chon, while Roy and Falling Leaves become a couple.

Shanghai Noon is an accomplished follow-up to Jackie Chan's first big-budget US film *Rush Hour*. Admittedly, the film (directed by Tom Dey whose past credits include episodes of the television horror series *The Hunger*) plays it safe by transplanting the fish-out-of-water scenario of *Rush Hour* to the Old West—here, Chan takes the role of a Chinese Imperial guard sent to Nevada to rescue a young princess. But this time the gags are sharper, the stunts slicker and, crucially, the dynamic between Chan and his co-star is much more effectively developed. While in *Rush Hour* Chan played straight man to Chris Tucker's motor-mouth LA cop (occasionally creating the impression that they were acting in different films), in *Shanghai Noon* he is given strong comic moments (his introduction to the narcotic joys of the peace-pipe, for instance) and some fine duets with Owen Wilson, who plays cowboy Roy. Their infectiously amusing drunken scene in a bordello bath house, where they thrash out a Chinese drinking song in between bouts of melancholic ponderings and bubble-blowing, is a particular stand out. Perhaps best known for co-writing the excellent *Rushmore*, Wilson's partly improvised contribution is *Shanghai Noon*'s real trump card: cowardly and laconic, he's more laid-back Californian surfer than weather-beaten cowpoke.

As in the majority of Chan's films, the plotting here is somewhat slapdash: it's less a coherent narrative than a series of well-staged but loosely connected set pieces, including Roy's showdown with sheriff Van Cleef and a bar-room brawl between Roy and Chon. The lack of narrative polish can be frustrating—Chon's bride Falling Leaves disappears for great tracts of the film, appearing only to rescue the heroes from jail. Lucy Liu, whose comic talents are on show in television's *Ally McBeal* is also underused as a conventional embattled damsel, while the film's ending, in which Chon abruptly partners up with Liu's character while Roy is palmed off with Chon's Sioux' "wife" Falling Leaves, is bafflingly throwaway and curiously distasteful. The dialogue, though, is consistently witty, not only having fun with genre conventions (Chon Wang is a phonetic muddling of John Wayne), but also demonstrating a wry awareness of the racial issues thrown up by the film's scenario (unlike Barry Sonnenfeld's *Wild Wild West* in which Will Smith's racial identity went largely unexamined). In one scene, a homesteader reassures his wife that the trio of Imperial guards are not Indians but Jews, and bids them shalom. Mystified, they shalom back.

TIME, 6/5/00, p. 82, Richard Schickel

They probably sold the idea with the pitch meeting's first phrase: "Jackie Chan in the Old West." Surely the deal was sealed when they mentioned his characters name: Chon Wang. It may be, as someone in the film says, a terrible name for a cowboy, but soften that g, and it sounds a lot like that of a certain massive movie star who won immortality playing Western heroes.

Chan, of course, is a smallish, sweet-smiling man whose sense of humor irresistibly enlightens his martial artistry. In *Shanghai Noon* he's a guard in China's Forbidden City who intrudes himself on a mission to rescue Princess Pei-Pei (Lucy Liu), who, avoiding an arranged marriage, has run far, far away to Carson City, Nev. There she is enslaved by Lo Fong (Roger Yuan), an unredeemable bad guy who is exploiting Chinese railroad workers, smuggling dope and demanding a ransom for her.

Eyeing his traditional Chinese garb, pioneers wonder why Chon is dressed like a girl. Others think he's Jewish. The slightly spaced-out Indian tribe that adopts him is just happy that he is visibly not another rapacious white guy. We can be happy that he links up with Roy O'Bannon (Owen Wilson), a train robber with the anachronistic manners of a surfer dude—a little too politely countercultural for his line of work and not half as clever as he thinks he is. He looks like a young Robert Redford (the movie makes a nice satirical reference to Butch Cassidy and the Sundance Kid), but his genial self-regard--assailed by amusing self-doubt when he actually gets into a classic gunfight--is all his own. He's a terrific sidekick to Chan's funny, earnest, often victimized righteousness. This kid could be a star.

The West that he and Chan inhabit is more generic than authentic—come to think of it, a lot like the B-picture West in which the real John Wayne toiled through his early years. It's the kind of place where the subsidiary gunmen have no real motives—other than bad breeding-for their depredations, where barroom brawls blow up for no good reason and where plains, mountains and deserts are mixed without any particular geo-logic. This, of course, frees the director, Tom Dey, to play fast and loose with other kinds of logic. In his West, horses sit down when you need them to be up and doing, Indian princesses are as sportively knowing as any of the gals in *Sex and the City*, and a guy buried up to his neck in sand manages to dig himself out with a pair of chopsticks.

Structurally, *Shanghai Noon* is not exactly a tribute to narrative coherence. But that's all right. It's meant to be a fantastic stage for Chan's quick hands and fast feet. The man is a human special effect. And as always, he gives a full measure of devotion to his blindingly choreographed action sequences.

Increasingly, though, we go to Jackie Chan movies not for the stars good moves but for his good nature. He's the kind of guy you could ruin with slickness and overmounting, the sort of performer who flourishes in the hip-casual context that screenwriters Alfred Gough and Miles Millar have provided him here.

Everyone's having a good time, but they're not winking at us either—making us parties to their in-jokes. As a result, we have a swell time too.

VILLAGE VOICE, 5/30/00, p. 130, Jessica Winter

Jackie Chan's latest shotgun marriage of martial-arts action and buddy-pic slapstick suffers from a script less written than treated, scenes less directed than strong-armed into semicoherence, and a scarifying premise: a Chinese imperial guard and a ne'er-do-well American petty criminal team up in Nevada to rescue a kidnapped princess (Lucy Liu). *Shanghai Noon* is also unstintingly funny—far more so than the wince-worthy trailer—owing to Chan's pairing with droll indie eccentric Owen Wilson, as his would-be gunslinger sidekick.

Wilson could have walked straight off the set of *Bottle Rocket* —the sweet, cockeyed, rigorously understated heist comedy he starred in and cowrote with Wes Anderson before they penned *Rushmore*—and into *Shanghai Noon*, where his gentle, faintly delirious, wholly idiosyncratic presence provides winning absurdist counterpoint to his frenetic surroundings and to the self-effacing whirling dervish Chan. The pair's affectionate, rat-tat-tat chemistry seems to spring from mutual fascination and, no doubt, from the fact that Wilson was allowed to improvise. Chan, now into his late forties, is bearing up astonishingly well, but his twilight years of defying gravity and good common sense have so far gone ill-recorded. As in *Rush Hour,* the action sequences are so tightly framed and haphazardly edited that your eye can't follow his breathtaking balletic bang-pow.

That Chan and Wilson deserve better seems beside the point. A solid spit-your-popcorn lowbrow comedy comes along only so often, so don't think it's damnation by faint praise to say that the best scene in *Shanghai Noon* involves two grown men screaming their way through an apparently untranslatable Chinese drinking game while enjoying a bubble bath together.

Also reviewed in:
CHICAGO TRIBUNE, 5/26/00, Friday/p. A, Michael Wilmington
NEW YORK TIMES, 5/26/00, p. E12, A. O. Scott
VARIETY, 5/22-28/00, p. 21, Joe Leydon
WASHINGTON POST, 5/26/00, p. C5, Stephen Hunter
WASHINGTON POST, 5/26/00, Weekend/p. 51, Desson Howe

SHOWER

A Sony Pictures Classics release of an Imar Film production. *Executive Producer:* Sam Duann. *Producer:* Peter Loehr. *Director:* Zhang Yang. *Screenplay (Mandarin with English subtitles):* Zhang Yang, Liu Fen Dou, Huo Xin, Diao Yi Nan, and Cai Xiang Jun. *Director of Photography:* Zhang Jian. *Editor:* Zhang Yang and Yang Hong Yu. *Music:* Ye Xiao Gang. *Sound:* Lai Qi Zhen. *Art Director:* Tian Meng. *Costumes:* Hao Ge. *Running time:* 92 minutes. *MPAA Rating:* Not Rated.

CAST: Zhu Xu (Master Liu); Pu Cun Xin (Da Ming); Jiang Wu (Er Ming); He Zheng (He Bing); Zhang Jin Hao (Hu Bei Bei); Lao Lin (Li Ding); Lao Wu (Feng Shun).

LOS ANGELES TIMES, 7/7/00, Calendar/p. 10, Kevin Thomas

Zhang Yang's beguiling and poignant "Shower" opens with a shot of a young man placing himself in a sleek high-tech device that functions like a carwash for humans. The next shot finds him in an old-fashioned Beijing bathhouse, whose proprietor, Master Liu (Zhu Xu), is surprised to find that this busy young man has for once found time to partake of its more leisurely comforts.

Most of Master Liu's customers are elderly men like himself, and the bath, located in an old, run-down yet charming section of the city, functions as a community center. The warm camaraderie it offers is clearly its most precious commodity. A quick collage of shots shows us just what you can get there: a massage, a back scrub, a pedicure, a shave and a cup of tea. Master Liu can even snap a dislocated shoulder back in place.

Master Liu one day receives an unexpected visit from his older son Da Ming (Pu Cun Xin), an upwardly mobile businessman in distant Shenzhen. Da Ming has received a postcard from his mentally disabled younger brother Er Ming (Jiang Wu) with a drawing that suggests their father is laid out for a funeral rather than upon a massage table. While relieved to discover his father is still alive, Da Ming, a low-key type, has clearly grown distant from his parent. Da Ming plans to return home the next day, but as you might well suspect, his stay will prove to be considerably longer.

"Shower's" sentimental veneer, with its folksy comic touches and flashbacks to Master Liu's childhood, proves deceptive. As the film unfolds, we discover that this veneer throws into relief Zhang's clear-eyed view of universal themes and issues.

The gradual reconciliation of son and father, and of the older son coming to understand the importance of taking responsibility for his childlike younger brother, provides plenty of sure-fire heart-tugging. But Zhang s also concerned with the inevitably of change, and most specifically, the relentless erosion of a sense of community in modern urban life everywhere.

Even Master Liu, hale and hard-working, cannot live forever, and his neighborhood is the kind that eventually becomes targeted for urban renewal. No longer will the neighborhood's elderly men have a place to gather, no longer will the community have the use of Master Liu's array of services dedicated to the well-being of the spirit as well as the body.

In short, "Shower" is easy to identify within the personal and social issues it raises.

"Shower" gains immeasurably from its authentic key setting, a no-frills yet inviting bathhouse, which looks to date back to the' '30s or '20s, just as it benefits strong from its distinguished stars. Zhu Xu, last seen in Wu Tianming's "The King of Masks," is a veteran master of his craft.

Like Zhu, Pu Cun Xin is a major star on stage as well as screen, best know for "The Blue Kite." Jiang Wu, a young actor on the rise, has already starred in Zhang Yimou's epic "To Live" opposite Gong Li. In only has second feature, Zhang Yang shows that he knows how to move an audience.

NEW YORK POST, 7/7/00, p. 53, Lou Lumenick

This stunning comedy-drama from China comes as close to perfect as any movie I've seen lately.

Acted, written, directed and photographed with extraordinary skill, the touching "Shower" grabs your attention with a stunning opening sequence and doesn't stop until a climax that will wring tears from the most jaded moviegoers.

Director Zhang Yang, who wrote the script with Liu Fen Doug, Huo Xin and Diao Yi Nan, offers an engrossing portrait of a China in transition, as personified by a Beijing businessman, Da Ming (Pu Cun Xin).

Da Ming is first seen using a high-tech, coin-operated public shower that resembles nothing so much as a car wash for humans.

It's an incredible contrast to the life of his elderly father, Master Liu (Zhu Xu), who runs an old-fashioned bathhouse in distant Szechuan with Da Ming's retarded younger brother, Er Ming (Jiang Wu).

Da Ming, who's deeply embarrassed by his family, comes to visit because of his father's declining health and gradually comes to appreciate the traditions embodied by the run-down bathhouse, which caters to a mostly elderly clientele given to beetle racing.

Master Liu dispenses towels and marital advice while providing Er Ming with fatherly love that can only make his older brother jealous.

But the old man is sick, and the bathhouse is scheduled to be torn down as part of a renewal project.

And Da Ming must come to terms with his younger sibling, in a situation more glibly portrayed in the American film "Rain Man."

The acting is superlative—especially Jiang Wu as the cheerfully simple-minded brother.

"Shower" is full of memorable scenes, including one where Er Ming comes up with an ingenious way to help a patron who has trouble singing outside the shower.

NEWSDAY, 7/7/00, Part II/p. B6, Jan Stuart

At the decaying men's bathhouse of Master Liu, getting clean is almost beside the point. It is one of those outposts of fading civility where clients come to have their souls massaged along with their shoulders. There, you can play chess, gossip, fritter away an afternoon over cricket fights, repair an ego bruised from a troubled marriage. Master Liu opens your pores, and the ills accrued from an uncaring world come rushing out.

As the regulars unwind in the corroding oasis at the center of Zhang Yang's "Shower," you know it is only a matter of time before the shopping-mall developers knock on the door and blow it all away. But not before the kindly Master Liu (a deeply affecting Zhu Xu) attends to his customers' emotional aches and puts his own house in order for one last time.

In this new film from China that is as gentle and spirit- cleansing as its wrinkled protagonist, the usurping of the old ways by a fast-paced modern world becomes personalized through generational family tensions. When Master Liu's hotshot son, Da Ming (Pu Cun Xin), returns from the big city for a brief visit, you can read the disdain in his eyes for his father's occupation and the provincial life he left behind. But the son hangs in a while, drawn in part by the weight of familial responsibility imposed by his retarded brother, Er Ming (Jiang Wu).

Over the ensuing days, Da Ming will get a crash course in humanitarian values, as his father and simpleton brother solve the problems of a variety of customers. They include a self-styled Enrico Caruso who only has the nerve to sing in the shower and a get-rich-quick schemer whose creditors threaten the tranquility of Master Liu's bathhouse.

Corny? Yes. Sentimental? You betcha. Predictable? Down to the final fadeout. We also get a little nervous about the way in which it rides a recent trend in movies to glorify the innocence of the mentally challenged.

But just as Master Liu instills in his city son a regard for the old ways, "Shower" reminds us of the pleasure of time-tested scenarios played out with almost archetypal simplicity (but for clumsily inserted flashback sequences). So much of what makes "Shower" interesting comes from its almost self-conscious universality. Anyone who has seen August Wilson's wonderful play "Jitney" in recent months should appreciate that there is nothing so divergent between Chinese and American lives that couldn't be bridged by an afternoon whiled away at Master Liu's.

SIGHT AND SOUND, 4/01, p. 58, Tony Rayns

Disturbed by an ambiguous postcard from his retarded brother Erming, Shenzhen businessman Liu Darning hurries to Beijing, where their elderly father runs the Qingshui public bathhouse. He finds his father well but less than delighted to see the son who turned his back on the family business. Darning feels the need to improve his relationship with his father, so he delays his return and starts pulling his weight in the running of the bathhouse.

Regular customers include electrician and would-be entrepreneur Hezheng, the irascible Zhang who is constantly arguing with his wife Old Wu, the owner of champion fighting crickets, and Miao Zhuang, an amateur tenor who practises 'O sole mio' in the showers. All of them solve their problems with Mr Liu's help.

Soon after learning that the neighbourhood will be demolished in a redevelopment scheme, Mr Liu dies peacefully in the bath. After the funeral, as neighbours and regulars begin to move away, Darning worries about looking after Erming. An attempt to place him in a nursing home is disastrous, and it proves hard to convince him that the Qingshui has actually closed down. When workmen arrive to remove the fittings, Erming scares them away with a water hose. Moving away, Miao Zhuang gives Erming a tape of 'O sole mio' as a goodbye present. Erming sings along with the aria in the now empty Qingshui.

It may seem ironic that it has taken an émigré American to reinvigorate China's moribund film industry, but it's a fact that Peter Loehr's Imar Film Co has very quickly established itself as a key force for change in methods of production, distribution, exhibition and promotion. Independent producers are still obliged to work in partnerships with the country's remaining film studios (which generally contribute nothing but their trademarks—and expect to be paid for doing so) and Film Bureau censorship remains an intractable obstacle, but Imar has already managed to notch up four lively and in some ways innovative entertainments which have drawn audiences and turned profits. Loehr develops projects designed to appeal to the young urban audience and works with youngish directors from the music-video and advertising industries. Neither the company nor its output ventures far beyond the mainstream, but it has no rival in sight for the current middle ground of the market.

Shower, Imar's third production but the first to be released in Britain, is actually the company's least youth-oriented film so far: a melancholy comedy about vanishing traditions, the price of economic development and getting back in touch with one's roots and core values. Its central premise is topical and correctly observed. Large parts of 'old' Beijing have been and are being torn down in the name of urban renewal and community institutions such as public bathhouses are either disappearing or turning into up-market saunas and 'health centres'. The mix of men shown congregating in the fictional Qingshui bathhouse—pensioners, local tradespeople, underachievers, gangsters and loansharks—seems about right sociologically and the details of bathhouse management and services (from body-scrubs to moxibustion) are accurate and well captured. As a muted protest against the loss of such institutions and the dispersal of the communities they served, the film can stand justifiably proud.

Curiously, though, director Zhang Yang and his four co-writers have grafted various other agendas on to this essentially simple stem. First, they venture in the general direction of mysticism by suggesting that the bathhouse and its presiding spirits (the saintly Mr Liu and his retarded son Erming, a 'holy fool') can cure all ills the flesh is heir to. When regular patron Mr Zhang confides that his marriage is on the rocks and implies that his anger towards his wife has left him impotent; the bath becomes the arena for their reconciliation and the healing of their problems. Similarly, Mr Liu saves Hezheng, another of his customers, from vengeful heavies by bringing out their latent politesse and Erming saves Miao Zhuang, who also uses the bathhouse, from public humiliation by improvising the shower jets which give him the (confidence he needs to sing. It must be said that this torrent of wish-fulfilment is less convincing than the film's sociological bent.

Second, the writers forge a bizarre connection with the 'Fifth Generation' cinema of the 80s by giving Mr Liu flashbacks to a bathless childhood in the arid north-east of China. He recalls going for weeks without bathing, and then later describes a great journey across epically inhospitable landscapes in search of a distant pool. It's hard to see why Zhang felt his film needed this element running through it, but it's even harder to see why he shot the flashbacks as if they were outtakes from Chen Kaige's *Yellow Earth* and Tian Zhuangzhuang's *Horse Thief*. Most Chinese directors of Zhang's thirtysomething generation disavow any interest in or enthusiasm for such films, seeing them as overly poetic and portentously allegorical.

And third, the writers insist that the film's Betjeman-like nostalgia for vanishing Beijing be linked with businessman Daming's moral regeneration as a son and as a materialist go-getter. Insofar as the film has an overarching theme, it's precisely Daming's progress from denizen of the free-market fleshpots of the south to Good Samaritan and paragon of filial virtue. The open ending leaves him poised to return to his unseen girlfriend in Shenzhen, probably with his brother Erming in tow, and makes it clear that he will go back a changed man.

If any or all of these alien agendas is a misjudgement, then all three can be forgiven and forgotten in the light of the wonderful opening sequence, worth the price of admission on its own. In what turns out to be Hezheng's daydream as he lazes on the massage table, we see a vision of the bathhouse of the future: the human equivalent of a car-wash. It's hilarious, and it gets the less pretentious side of the film off on just the right foot.

VILLAGE VOICE, 7/11/00, p. 119, J. Hoberman

Winner of audience awards at festivals from Rotterdam to Thessaloniki, the hit of this year's "New Directors/New Films" series, Zhang Yang's *Shower* has proven to be a dependable crowd pleaser. The second feature by the onetime music-video director uses an old-fashioned Beijing bathhouse as the site for a family reconciliation between the old China and the new. Will a modern son abandon his lucrative business in the boom-boom south to take his traditional dad's place alongside a mentally retarded brother in operating what amounts to an irreplaceable neighborhood mental health clinic?

Even if you can't guess the answer (or anticipate the film's moral), you may not be surprised to learn that this sentimental tribute to humble pleasures and the healing power of aqua therapy is amply stocked with lovable oddballs. (Perhaps that's why the script required five writers.) Predictable as it is, *Shower* has a few quirks—as well as a flinty performance by veteran actor Zhu Xu as the old bathhouse proprietor—but it's far too soggy a confection for my taste. Someone is surely considering a Hollywood remake that would allow Tom Hanks to play either (or both) of the brothers.

Also reviewed in:
CHICAGO TRIBUNE, 7/28/00, Friday/p. A, Michael Wilmington
NEW YORK TIMES, 7/7/00, p. E16, Stephen Holden
NEW YORKER, 7/17/00, p. 89, David Denby
VARIETY, 9/13-19/99, p. 52, Derek Elley
WASHINGTON POST, 8/4/00, Weekend/p. 38, Desson Howe

SIMPATICO

A Fine Line Features release in association with Emotion Pictures and Le Studio Canal+ of a Jean-François Fonlupt/Dan Lupovitz/Zeal Pictures production in association with Kingsgate. *Executive Producer:* Joel Lubin, Greg Shapiro, and Sue Baden-Powell. *Producer:* Dan Lupovitz, Timm Oberwelland, and Jean-François Fonlupt. *Director:* Matthew Warchus. Screenplay: Matthew Warchus and David Nicholls. *Based on the play by:* Sam Shepard. *Director of Photography:* John Toll. *Editor:* Pasquale Buba. *Music:* Steward Copeland. *Music Editor:* Sharyn Tylk. *Sound:* Pawel Wdowczak and (music) Jeff Seitz. *Sound Editor:* Lance Brown. *Casting:* Daniel Swee. *Production Designer:* Amy B. Ancona. *Art Director:* Andrew Laws. *Set Decorator:* Ellen Brill. *Special Effects:* Burt Dalton. *Costumes:* Karen Patch. *Make-up:* Edouard F. Henriques III. *Stunt Coordinator:* Ernie Orsatti. *Running time:* 106 minutes. *MPAA Rating:* R.

CAST: Nick Nolte (Vincent "Vinnie" T. Webb); Jeff Bridges (Lyle Carter); Sharon Stone (Rosie Carter); Catherine Keener (Cecilia Ponz); Albert Finney (Darryl P. Simms, "Ryan Ames"); Shawn Hatosy (Young Vinnie); Kimberly Williams (Young Rosie); Liam Waite (Young Carter); Whit Crawford (Jean); Bob Harter (Louis); Angus T. Jones (5-year-old Kid); Ken Strunk (Charlie); Ashley Gutherie (Kelly); Maria Carretero (Airport Attendant); Nicole Forester (Female Flight Attendant); Joseph Hindy (Dan, the Bartender); Lloyd Catlett (Pete, the Male Passenger); Brigitta Simone (First Class Flight Attendant); Christina Cabot (Waitress); Mack Dryden (Rosie's Father); Kristen Knickerbocker (Beck, Lyle's Secretary); Barb Rossmeisl (Woman 1); Roxana Brusso (Checkout Girl); Jeannine Corbo (Ostario Attendant); Malina Moye (Receptionist); Dan Willoughby (Official); Trevor Denman and Allan Bochdahl (Race Callers).

CHRISTIAN SCIENCE MONITOR, 2/4/00, p. 15, David Sterritt

It takes more than a great cast to make a great picture.

"Simpatico" features a whole stable of stars, from Nick Nolte and Jeff Bridges to Sharon Stone and Catherine Keener, with the great Albert Finney thrown in for good measure. All do respectable work, and Keener does better than that—her award-winning performance in "Being John Malkovich" is no fluke—but in the end they're no more memorable than the movie around them.

Named after a race horse, "Simpatico" centers on a criminal escapade planned by three young friends who stop being so friendly after their caper falls apart. The movie shuttles between the bygone scheme and a period much later, when the reunited trio must come to terms with events of the past.

This isn't a bad story idea, and if the movie doesn't have as much impact as its credentials lead you to expect, it's less because of specific shortcomings than a general failure to make the most of promising material.

Matthew Warchus directed it from a screenplay he wrote with David Nicholls. It is based on a play by Sam Shepard, whose own career has become progressively less interesting—see his unimaginative acting in "Snow Falling on Cedars" for an example—since his early years as a feisty artistic rebel.

"Simpatico" is worth seeing to keep up with Keener's evolving excellence and Stone's continuing effort to stretch her range. But the picture isn't likely to linger in your mind once the closing credits have rolled.

LOS ANGELES TIMES, 12/15/99, Calendar/p. 3, Kevin Thomas

"Simpatico," a neo-noirish tale of deception and redemption, finds a sleek, rich Kentucky racehorse breeder (Jeff Bridges) in negotiations to sell a Triple Crown winner (which gives the film its title) when he's interrupted by an urgent call from an unkempt man (Nick Nolte) at a pay phone not far from Cucamonga. Reluctantly, Bridges' Carter departs the meeting for what is supposed to be a quick emergency trip to California. But it becomes a devastating journey into the past.

Nolte's Vinnie has a hold on Carter and insists that he personally persuade a young supermarket cashier (Catherine Keener) not to press charges of sexual harassment against him. When Carter has a meeting with Keener's perplexed Cecilia he quickly learns that although she's been seeing Vinnie for a while, he's no more than kissed her—and that just once. The next thing Carter knows, Vinnie, who has been parked across the street from Cecilia's apartment, drives off in Carter's rented car. A role reversal has just commenced.

The flashbacks begin, introducing us to the Vinnie (Shawn Hatosy) and Carter (Liam Waite) and their pal Rosie (Kimberly Williams) of 20 years before. They are a trio of young sharpies with a get-rich-quick horse-racing scam that involves substituting a slow horse for a fast one and cashing in by betting high odds.

It also involves buying a horse-racing commissioner's silence by setting him up with Rosie for some rough sex and then blackmailing him. (So traumatized is Rosie by the encounter that, for good measure, she makes a couple of phone calls that destroy the commissioner's career and marriage.)

Carter has become the success he intended, but at a price. Over the years he's forked over several hundred thousand dollars to Vinnie, with a clutch of incriminating evidence, to keep him silent. Rosie (Sharon Stone) has ended up Carter's hard-drinking, chain-smoking wife, with whom he shares a vast faux chateau, the acme of nouveau-riche vulgarity, in Lexington.

After all these years, Vinnie has become a virtual derelict, posing as a private eye and living in a messy cottage—entirely at Carter's expense. But at long last Vinnie has had it and tells himself he can reclaim the past. He's discovered that the racing commissioner (Albert Finney) has changed his name and become a bloodline agent, tracing racehorses' genealogy for a fee and living not far from Carter. Vinnie assumes Finney's Simms will be only too happy to buy a box of incriminating photos; in the meantime, Carter has persuaded Cecilia to go to Simms in his behalf and ask him to name his price, for they have the potential for destroying the lives of both Carter and Rosie.

The cast of "Simpatico" is so good that you wish debuting director Matthew Warchus, who with co-writer David Nicholls adapted Sam Shepard's play of the same name, could have pulled off the with less strain and more clarity. Although it's true that you would never guess that the film had begun as a play, it's also true that Warchus can't quite meet the challenge of involving us with three people whose innocence was lost well before we meet them. They may have been naive in their youth about the long-term consequences of their actions, but they are completely aware of their own criminality.

Nolte, Bridges and Stone (who doesn't appear until one hour into the film but, once there, gets to tear into some all-stops-out Barbara Stanwyck histrionics) are adept at conveying the toll exacted from living lives built on lies and destruction. But for their—and Finney's—solid contributions to pay off, the film needs to seem more anchored in real life and less derived from other movies. Keener has considerable charm as the plucky but unsophisticated Cecilia, who hasn't a clue as to what she's getting into.

Much effort and expertise have gone into the making of "Simpatico," but, while it's entertaining, it's not as persuasive as it needs to be to succeed fully.

NEW YORK POST, 2/4/00, p. 55, Lou Lumenick

"Simpatico" is, in racetrack terminology, a non-starter. A barely adapted version of Sam Shepard's 1994 play about three people haunted by a long-ago racing scam, it's a textbook example of what happens when movie stars try to deliver stage-style dialogue.

The results aren't pretty.

Nick Nolte is beating a dead horse as Vinnie, a middle-aged California barfly who's long been supported by his childhood pal Lyle (Jeff Bridges), a wealthy Kentucky horse owner.

Lyle's efforts to pull off another swindle—selling his prized Triple Crown-winner Simpatico, a sterile horse he knows will be useless for breeding— are interrupted by an urgent phone call from Vinnie.

In an attempt to clear his guilty conscience, Vinnie is threatening to spill the beans on the original scam in 1970—they switched horses in several races and blackmailed a racing commissioner to cover it up. A panicky Lyle flies to L.A., where Vinnie steals his plane ticket and flies to Kentucky with a shoe box full of incriminating photos under his arm to track down the commissioner, who's working as a breeding expert under an assumed name, and offers to clear his name.

For reasons that are totally unclear and unconvincing, Lyle elects to remain in Vinnie's ramshackle trailer and assume his disheveled lifestyle. He talks a friend of Vinnie's, a supermarket checkout clerk named Cecilia (Catherine Keener) into flying to Lexington and making the commissioner a large cash counteroffer.

The venerable Albert Finney, who plays the commissioner, is the only cast member who's remotely comfortable with Shepard's dialogue and he alone finds the humor in his character. It's a rounded, lively performance.

The same can't be said for a tentative Keener—so good in "Being John Malkovich"—or Sharon Stone. The latter appears an hour into the movie as Rosie, Lyle's wife and Vinnie's ex-girlfriend, the brains behind the original scheme.

At best, Stone's over-the-top performance suggests a bad imitation of Shepard's companion Jessica Lange, who at least would have made a decent stab at the material.

British stage director Matthew Warchus ("Art"), who makes his shaky movie debut here, also collaborated on the screenplay with David Nicholls—and it's way too talky and ill-suited to the stars.

The major change, flashbacks to 1970, with younger actors playing Vinnie, Lyle and Rosie, only serves to elongate an already draggy picture.

"Simpatico," which could badly use some racing sequences to punch up its flabby narrative, pulls up lame way before the stretch.

NEWSDAY, 2/4/00, Part II/p. B7, John Anderson

The play's the thing, as Laurence Olivier once said, but it's also the thing that drives film directors cuckoo. Exhibit A? "Simpatico," in which Nick Nolte and Jeff Bridges look for adulthood, Sharon Stone looks for her lost innocence and Matthew Warchus doesn't seem to have looked at the play he's directing.

In the metamorphosis from play to movie, the level of desperation a director displays in trying to distance himself from the stage is a diagnosis—sometimes of the director, sometimes of what he/she has to work with. Olivier and Orson Welles didn't seem to have any concerns about the stage-rootedness of "Hamlet" or "Macbeth," but the past few years have seen some real head-on collisions of material and ego: Julie Taymor ("Titus"), laying the set design on so thick that Shakespeare got lost; Anthony Drazan, translating "Hurlyburly" into one long close-up; Andy Tennant, throwing piles of money at "Anna and the King."

More successfully, Oliver Parker played Oscar Wilde's "Ideal Husband" safe and smart, and Mike Figgis managed to exploit all the space to be found within the one-room confines of Strindberg's "Miss Julie." But the matchup of director and play is a question of temperament and intelligence. In making his directorial film debut, Britain's Warchus has simply chosen the wrong play.

Sam Shepard's "Simpatico," which opened at the Public Theater in November, 1994, is essentially about the suppressed guilt and rage of three people who betrayed each other while fixing a horse race 20 years earlier: Carter (Bridges), who's become a millionaire and is about to sell his Triple Crown winner, Simpatico; his wife, Rosie (Stone), who was once used as bed-bait to compromise the racing commissioner, Simms (Albert Finney); and Vinnie (Nick Nolte), who was once in love with young Rosie (Kimberly Williams) but has since become a broke-down drunk.

Warchus' most energetic moments, logically enough, come at the beginning, as he races around furiously, trying to convince us we're not watching a play. The film only starts to make sense, however, when he settles down to Shepard's story, a tale full of contrivances that might work (it's not his best play) only when seen and heard within the artificial confines of a black stage set. There, reality has already been suspended and the characters can be seen—if one chooses—as allegorical, if not idealized, imprints of fractured souls.

The realism warchus imposes makes Shepard's lines ludicrous, and there's no plot turn that doesn't seem forced. Finney is fine and has a better sense of the play than Warchus; Catherine Keener, playing dumb for once, has some good moments as the vacuous Cecilia.

Still, it's little wonder "Simpatico" was released in the dead of winter, although putting the play on film does have its payoffs, of sorts. There are those repetitious and meaningless flashbacks to the young trio of race-fixers.

(Shawn Hatosy does a sly, if brief, Nolte impersonation.) Stone gets to throw some incriminating pictures across her bedroom in slo-mo outrage. (It's hilarious.) And, of course there are those incriminating pictures, which seemed far more ominous when you never got to see them.

And when you do? Oh, good Lord, Rosie and Simms had sex. Just like on TV. What will the movies think of next?

SIGHT AND SOUND, 2/00, p. 53, Geoffrey Macnab

Lyle Carter is a millionaire businessman who breeds and trains thoroughbreds on his estate in Lexington, Kentucky. He is about to sell Simpatico, a highly valued stallion, when he receives a call from his old friend Vinnie who claims he has been arrested. Years before, Vinnie and Carter collaborated on a horse-racing scam. Their plan was rumbled by racing commissioner Simms, but they blackmailed him by photographing him having sex with Rosie, Vinnie's girlfriend at the time. Rosie informed the racing authorities Simms was crooked and his career was ruined.

Vinnie, now living in squalor in Cucamonga, Ca., wants to make up with Simms. Worried this might jeopardise his business empire, Carter flies out to California to stop him. Vinnie steals Carter's plane ticket and flies back to Kentucky where he tracks down Simms who is annoyed and wants nothing to do with him. When Carter realises what Vinnie is up to, he persuades Vinnie's friend Cecilia to meet Simms with a suitcase full of money to keep Simms quiet. Simms is charmed by Cecilia. Carter, meanwhile, stays at Vinnie's place, gradually turning into a bum himself. Vinnie confronts Rosie, now Carter's wife. Carter had been planning to sell Simpatico to stud for a fortune, despite knowing he's incapable of siring any foals. Rather than let this happen, Rosie rides off on the horse and shoots him. Months later, Cecilia turns up to meet Simms at the Kentucky Derby.

Unlike other films about horse-racing, which tend either to strike a light Damon Runyonesque comic tone California Split, 1974 for example) or to play out along the lines of a Dick Francis thriller, Simpatico unfolds with all the solemnity of a Greek tragedy. Adapted from a Sam Shepard play, the film features three protagonists who have unleashed the furies on themselves through their own misdeeds. "There's no running away any more," Rosie snarls at one co-conspirator. "You're in your hell and I'm in mine."

The film starts out reminiscent of Wim Wenders' *Paris, Texas* (scripted by Shepard). This time, instead of Harry Dean Stanton's Travis wandering through the desert, the dishevelled loner Vinnie is a bum living in a rundown LA bungalow beside the freeway. Just as Travis was eventually reunited with his ex-wife, Vinnie has a painful, final-reel reunion with his former girlfriend Rosie, now married to Carter. In *Paris, Texas* Wenders used home-movie footage to evoke happier times between Travis and his wife. Here, director Matthew Warchus (best known for his work on the London stage) and his co-writer David Nicholls resort to flashbacks in which we see younger versions of the three leads.

What might have been a fast moving *noir* thriller, touching on blackmail and race fixing, is weighed down by its own gravitas. Vinnie, Carter and Rosie are so consumed with guilt they cast a pall of gloom over the film. Jeff Bridges' resilient yuppie Carter may seem the model of the successful businessman, but from the first time we see him with Vinnie (Nick Nolte, in a performance which rekindles memories of the tramp he played in *Down and Out in Beverly Hills*), it is obvious both men are damned, and that each offers a distorted reflection of the other. It is no surprise how easily they switch identities.

In a drama like this, where almost everybody is tainted, there is invariably one holy innocent. Here, Catherine Keener takes on the thankless role as the Pollyanna like check-out girl Cecilia. Her scenes with Simms, the disgraced racing commissioner, sum up just why the film finally seems so inconsequential. His response to her bribe is an offer of a day at the races. While Vinnie, Carter and Rosie tear themselves up with Euripidean angst, Simms simply isn't bothered. His indifference makes their antics seem absurd; if he doesn't care that they ruined him, why should they?

Like fellow British theatre director Sam Mendes with *American Beauty*, Warchus allows his actors plenty of space to develop their characters. Jeff Bridges, Nick Nolte and Albert Finney, all in typically belligerent form, have their share of close-ups and monologues. There's a striking cameo, too, from Sharon Stone as the blowzy, hard-drinking Rosie, spitting out sarcastic one-liners. Warchus succeeds in opening out Shepard's play for the screen, but ultimately the problem is that the material just doesn't have the emotional resonance of Sam Shepard's very best work.

VILLAGE VOICE, 2/8/00, p. 144, Michael Atkinson

At this late date, Sam Shepard's brand of symbol-strewn American Dreamism seems to require a little electroshock, and that could be said twice over for the narrative pulsation of plays-on-film. Matthew Warchus's *Simpatico* suffers obliviously beneath both burdens. A decked-out mediocrity with a high-octane cast and enough respect for Shepard's lightly stylized dialogue to treat it realistically, Warchus's movie cannot quite overcome its theatrical sclerosis. We have two old friends, Vinnie the textbook whiskey-guzzling, unwashed waste case (Nick Nolte) and Carter the uptight billionaire entrepreneur (Jeff Bridges), both of whom we immediately learn have a common closet skeleton that Carter, with so much more to lose, is in constant dread of Vinnie revealing. Nervously summoned to California from his Kentucky estate by a lying Vinnie, Carter is soon left holding little more than his sports jacket as a semi-deranged Vinnie steals his rental car and flies back to Kentucky with a proverbial black (shoe) box of dark secrets. Enter both Cecilia (Catherine Keener), a sweetly naive supermarket clerk who serves as a go-to girl, and Simms (Albert Finney), a crotchety old bloodstock agent (the macguffin is horse racing, and a particular horse-racing scam). Of course, somewhere amid this country-mouse/city-mouse routine, the protagonists begin to switch identities, and Carter begins to swill whiskey and sleep on Vinnie's loamy sofa.

It's a shame Nolte and Bridges weren't cast as brothers, because the two have similar rumpled-suede faces and irritated-bark delivery. They're dynamite together, but too much time is spent on their separate trajectories into symbolhood. Sharon Stone, as the requisite rich Southern souse-wife, doesn't show up until more than an hour in, and then chews her lines like they were martini olives. Predictably, she gets to deliver the play's Big Secret, but in a moment of horrifying melodramatic slo-mo. (Warchus can rarely resist a moment of hysteria, or a chance to cut to a rosy-cheeked flashback of the characters as young buckaroos.) *Simpatico* takes on the free-floating guilt of the American enterprise, but the movie's squinting cynicism is facile. In fact, it's preachy as hell; only Keener's bubblehead is untortured by shame. In a climactic howler, maddened couch potato Bridges pitches his nagging cell phone into the void, not because it doesn't work but because it works all too well. Apparently it would've said less about Our Soullessness if he'd just turned the thing off.

Also reviewed in:
CHICAGO TRIBUNE, 2/4/00, Friday/p. A, Michael Wilmington
NEW REPUBLIC, 2/28/00, p. 26, Stanley Kauffmann
NEW YORK TIMES, 2/4/00, p. E17, Stephen Holden
NEW YORKER, 2/14/00, p. 85, Anthony Lane
VARIETY, 9/20-26/99, p. 85, Dennis Harvey

6TH DAY, THE

A Columbia Pictures and Phoenix Pictures release of a Phoenix Pictures presentation of a Jon Davison production. *Executive Producer:* Daniel Petrie, Jr. and David Coatsworth. *Producer:* Mike Medavoy, Arnold Schwarzenegger and Jon Davison. *Director:* Roger Spottiswoode. *Screenplay:* Cormac Wibberley and Marianne Wibberley. *Director of Photography:* Pierre Mignot. *Editor:* Mark Conte, Dominique Fortin, and Michel Arcand. *Music:* Trevor Rabin. *Music Editor:* Jeanette Surga and Richard Harrison. *Sound:* David Husby and (music) Steve Kempster. *Sound Editor:* Tony Lamberti and Lon E. Bender. *Casting:* Judith Holstra. *Production Designer:* James Bissell and John Willett. *Art Director:* Patrick Banister, Chris Burian-Mohr, and Doug Hardwick. *Set Designer:* Andrea Dopaso, William Hawkins, Martha Johnston, James Philpott, Jim Ramsay, Steve Schwartz, and Easton Smith. *Set Decorator:* Peter Lando. *Special Effects:* Michael Lantieri. *Visual Effects:* Tom Leeser. *Costumes:* Trish Keating. *Make-up:* Jeff Dawn. *Make-up Effects:* Alec Gillis and Tom Woodruff, Jr. *Stunt Coordinator:* Steve Davison and Jacon Rupp. *Running time:* 124 minutes. *MPAA Rating:* PG-13.

CAST: Arnold Schwarzenegger (Adam Gibson); Michael Rapaport (Hank Morgan); Tony Goldwyn (Michael Drucker); Michael Rooker (Robert Marshall); Sarah Wynter (Talia Elsworth); Wendy Crewson (Natalie Gibson); Rod Rowland (Wiley); Terry Crews (Vincent); Ken Pogue (Speaker Day); Colin Cunningham (Tripp); Robert Duvall (Dr. Griffin Weir); Wanda Cannon (Katherine Weir); Taylor Anne Reid (Clara Gibson); Jennifer Gareis (Virtual Girlfriend); Don McManus (RePet Salesman); Ellie Harvie (Rosie); Don S. Davis (Cardinal de la Jolla); Jennifer Sterling (Virtual Attorney);   Steve Bacic (Johnny Phoenix); Christopher Lawford (Police Lieutenant); Mark Brandon (RePet Spokesman); Walter Von Huene (Virtual Psychiatrist); Chris Cound (Snowboarder); Ben Bass (Bodyguard); Robert Clarke and Michael Budman (Zealots); Warren T. Takeuchi, Claudine Grant, and Alex Castillo (Reporters); Peter Kent (Duty Officer); Hiro Kanagawa (Team Doctor);   Mi-Jung Lee (Newscaster); Gillian Barber (Doctor); Gerard Plunkett (Technician); Claire Rile (Webcaster); Andrew McIlroy (Scott Moore); Norma Jean Wick and Paul Carson (Announcers); Graham Andrews (Cab Driver); Benita Ha (Teacher); Andrea Libman (Voice of SimPal Cindy).

LOS ANGELES TIMES, 11/17/00, Calendar/p. 2, Kenneth Turan

Hollywood, which has been cloning action-adventure movies for years, has gotten around to making an action-adventure movie about cloning. It's called "The 6th Day," and whom does it star? Arnold Schwarzenegger. Twice.

Even before computers improved the process in films like the Michael Keaton-starring "Multiplicity," actors sharing the screen with themselves was not a new phenomenon. Still, it's an arresting sensation, something that seems almost contrary to nature, to see Schwarzenegger playing against Schwarzenegger.

For the man is so sui generis, so preeminently himself, that seeing him twice is like going to Yellowstone National Park and finding a pair of Old Faithfuls sharing the same plot of land. Even the idea of Schwarzenegger playing Danny De Vito's identical twin in "Twins" was not half so strange.

Aesthetic considerations aside, of all the guys to clone without his knowledge, don't the villains know better than to pick on Our Arnold? Aren't they familiar with the track record, couldn't they predict that the closest he's going to get to a serious wound is a nick while shaving? And once you've gotten the big guy riled, you might as well have challenged John Wayne to a barroom brawl. Or Shane to a gunfight.

In all fairness to the villains, Schwarzenegger's Adam Gibson does seem like quite the family man, down to his loving wife (Wendy Crewson) and adoring daughter. And though "The 6th Day's" press notes describe Adam as a "decorated fighter pilot in what was known as the Rainforest War," none of that has made it into the film, so how were the bad guys to know how potentially lethal a character he was?

In a further attempt to distance Adam's character from Arnold's Terminator image, "The 6th Day" (written by first-timers Cormac Wibberley & Marianne Wibberley and directed by the veteran Roger Spottiswoode) opens with our hero celebrating a birthday and worriedly scanning his face for wrinkles. Not to worry, even a year older he's still capable of making a muscle that could incapacitate a horse.

Since "The 6th Day" is eager to have a "ripped from today's headlines" feeling, it puts headlines about the cloning of Dolly the sheep and the mapping of human DNA right up on the screen. The film is set in the near future, where things look pretty much, but not totally, the same.

It's a world where your refrigerator automatically keeps track of your family's milk needs, and where Adam's pal Hank (Michael Rapaport) enjoys the favors of a virtual girlfriend. And it's a world where a company called RePet is taking animal cloning to new levels.

With advertising slogans like "cloning is love" and "where love means no surprises," RePet will duplicate your recently deceased companion and do such a good job of it that even the replacement animals have no idea they are not the real thing.

An old-fashioned kind of guy, Adam Gibson wants nothing to do with any of this. He doesn't even want to give his daughter a super-realistic doll called the Sim-Pal Cindy that never shuts up (an idea that came from writer John Sayles). Death, he says, is part of the natural process of life, and it ought to stay that way.

Michael Drucker of Replacement Technologies (an effective Tony Goldwyn), the world's most powerful human, sees things differently. Though human cloning is illegal, he's been collaborating with scientist Griffin Weir (an underused Robert Duvall) to make it happen, and let's just say they've made a lot of progress. Just how much progress becomes clear to Adam when he comes home one night and finds what looks suspiciously like a clone version of himself getting all the presents at what had been billed as his own birthday party.

Adam is, not surprisingly, perplexed by this turn of events. "I know it sounds crazy," he tells a disbelieving police officer. "I can't hardly believe it myself." Once the villains realize that Adam knows what they've been up to, they think it'll be easy to eliminate him. Obviously, these guys have not been to the movies much the past 20 years.

One of "The 6th Day's" devices is the notion that its awfully hard to tell a clone from the original person, and though this leads to some wry humor ("Doesn't anyone stay dead anymore," Adam asks plaintively at one point), it's also confusing and saps our interest. Given how generic everything else about "The 6th Day" is, from its standard-issue action to its halfhearted dialogue and acting, that's one situation even two Schwarzeneggers aren't enough to solve.

NEW YORK POST, 11/17/00, p. 57, Jonathan Foreman

Despite a large budget and jazzy special effects, "The 6th Day" harkens back to Arnold Schwarzenegger's trashy but enjoyable "B" pictures like "Running Man" and "Commando"—except the violence has been toned down for a PG-13 rating and the straight dialogue increased.

This otherwise undistinguished thriller about cloning is the most entertaining movie from the aging action star for some time (remember "End of Days," "Batman and Robin" and "Jingle All the Way"?).

The story takes place in a near future where people still drive pick-up trucks that look like 2000 models, but refrigerators tell you when to buy more orange juice, cigars are an illegal drug, guns shoot fiery "Star Wars"-style bolts, cars drive themselves and you can clone your dead pet.

Cloning humans, however, is forbidden by the "6th Day" law.

But a sinister biotech company run by Michael Drucker (Tony Goldwyn) has developed the technology to do so with ease.

Thanks to scientist Dr. Graham Weir (Robert Duvall), you can not only clone a living or recently deceased human, in a few minutes you can grow them in tanks to the exact age and appearance of the original model.

Another amazing technology developed by Weir can somehow read the entire contents of your brain through your eyes and record them on a computer disc, to be downloaded into your clone.

Adam Gibson (Schwarzenegger), a veteran of the "rainforest war," is a pilot for a helicopter-jet charter company. One day the company gets the commission to take Drucker on a fateful heliboarding trip.

At the list minute, Gibson hands the job over to his partner and best friend Hank (Michael Rapaport).

When Gibson arrives home that night, a little late for the surprise birthday party he knows his wife has planned, through a window he sees a duplicate of himself cutting a cake.

Seconds later, in the first of many fights and chases, Adam is fleeing black-clad assassins from Drucker's company (the always reliable Michael Rooker and Australian looker Sarah Wynter).

Director Roger Spottiswoode responsible for "Tomorrow Never Dies" and "Stop or My Mom Will Shoot") keeps the pace taut, but annoying computer graphics divide one scene from another.

It's a shame old Arnold hits so many philosophical lines about cloning because his leaden, heavily accented delivery too often jerks you out of the film.

Fans of early Schwarzenegger should know Arnold keeps his shirt on and—unlike Jean-Claude Van Damme or Jackie Chan in movies where they play identical twins—never gets to fight himself.

But Tony Goldwyn, who also has a part in this week's "Bounce" and directed last year's "A Walk on the Moon," makes a convincingly intelligent and cold-blooded villain.

NEWSDAY, 11/17/00, p. B6, John Anderson

The argument against human cloning—theoretically, since it's never actually articulated in "The 6th Day,"—is that such blasphemous science would make human life cheap. Which makes sense. Life has always been cheap in Arnold Schwarzenegger movies.

Schwarzenegger is back (he said he'd be) as Adam Gibson, a helicopter pilot sometime "in the near future" who finds himself cloned and his life, wife (Wendy Crewson) and daughter (Taylor Anne Reid) stolen away, all by a malodorous corporate entity engaged in the reproduction of human beings. It's a practice banned by law in this technologically advanced society, but that doesn't stop Replacement Technologies, its CEO Michael Drucker (Tony Goldwyn) or its chief scientist Griffin Weir (Robert Duvall) from creating humans with impunity. Adam becomes a victim of corporate security, but obviously they do not know who they are dealing with.

Taking anything too seriously in a movie as cretinous as "The 6th Day" ("On the sixth day God created man..." etc.) is a big mistake: Each time you think someone's actually done some thinking, they'll prove you wrong. Still, the concepts are provocative enough: If a human is replicated as exactly as its done here—to the point where memories of one's own death could be genome ically programmed into one's clone—what are the moral implications? The movie makes it simple: Shoot 'em down like dogs.

"The 6th Day" isn't the most violent movie Schwarzenegger has ever made. (What would be? "Conan the Barbarian"?) Much of it consists of image-manipulated, computer-game-inspired nonsense; the slo-mo shots probably add 15 minutes to the picture. But the fact that this is a PG-13 movie is more proof that the tectonic plates of the Motion Picture Association of America have shifted and that Jack Valenti may in fact be a clone of King Ludwig of Bavaria.

Enforcement of the R rating has been toughened, so subsequently we're getting more PG-13 movies that skirt the line of propriety—for instance, "The 6th Day" has only one F word, since two gets you a mandatory R. Isn't it interesting that in a film with so many Schwarzenegger trademarks—the cigars, the Humvee, the atrocious puns—fundamentalists would be the heroes, fighting on biblical grounds against cloning of any kind? Meanwhile, the prominently conservative Republican star helps produce a movie that violates the spirit of Hollywood's own law.

SIGHT AND SOUND, 2/01, p. 51, Andrew O'Hehir

North America, the future. Animal cloning has become routine, and new techniques permit a cloned pet to share the memories and characteristics of its predecessor. Human cloning is illegal, but Michael Drucker, a tycoon, is secretly cloning famous athletes and politicians. Adam, a charter pilot, has been assigned to take Drucker on a snowboarding trip, but switches identities with his friend Hank so Adam can spend the day with his family. Drucker and Hank are assassinated by an anti-cloning fundamentalist, and Dr Weir, Drucker's chief scientist, creates clones of Drucker and Adam, believing Adam to be the dead pilot.

After Adam returns home to discover another version of himself with his family, he is hunted by a squad of Drucker's henchmen who seek to eliminate evidence of the illegal cloning operation. Hank is also cloned, but the fundamentalist kills him. Dr Weir turns against Drucker after his wife's clone dies and he learns that Drucker has implanted genetic defects in the clones to control them. Adam confronts his clone only to learn that he himself is the clone and the other Adam is the original. The two Adams join forces to destroy Drucker and his cloning lab. The original Adam returns home to his family while the clone goes off to sea.

Employing Arnold Schwarzenegger's unlikely physique as a vehicle for exploring what it means to be human no longer carries the resonance it used to. Where Schwarzenegger once struck commentators as the semi-official deity of postmodern Hollywood, he now seems unmistakably mortal, not least because the world of spectacle cinema has drifted away from him. *The 6th Day,* a crisp and agreeable futuristic adventure that references many of his earlier films, therefore seems faintly, even sweetly imbued with nostalgia. Roger Spottiswoode, who breathed new life into the James Bond franchise with *Tomorrow Never Dies,* tries to do the same here for Schwarzenegger's career. It's certainly the star's most effective action film since James Cameron's *True Lies,* but the film's dismal US box office results suggest that the decline in Schwarzenegger's commercial fortunes may be irreversible.

If you're willing to accept the claptrap about clones inheriting the memories and personalities of their genetic predecessors, the screenplay by Cormac and Marianne Wibberley is, by genre standards, witty and sophisticated. Its elements of social satire and its central plot device—a man isn't who he thinks he is and cannot rely on his own memories—will remind viewers of the 1990 Schwarzenegger vehicle *Total Recall,* directed by Paul Verhoeven; in fact, Spottiswoode has made a more convincing job of fusing futuristic science with action aesthetics here than Verhoeven himself did with his recent film *Hollow Man.* In *The 6th Day* cloning, it seems, has been insidiously integrated into everyday life. Schwarzenegger's character Adam is offered a choice of nacho-flavoured or "regular" bananas by his daughter, who then insists that he take their dead dog to RePet ("Where love means no surprises"), a company that will imprint a defunct pet on to a genetic blank and return it to you, full-grown, in a few hours. Tobacco has become illegal and is considered a powerful aphrodisiac; as tycoon Drucker's agents pursue Adam and his family, his wife worries, "It's not because of the cigars, is it?"

Schwarzenegger's acting has not improved with age, and the scenes where Adam and his identical clone are together on screen are especially leaden. (His daughter's ominous android doll SimPal Cindy seems more lifelike.) But Spottiswoode has packed the picture with enjoyable character actors who play things for laughs: perhaps the best of these is lantern-jawed Michael Rooker as Marshall, Drucker's principal thug, who growls at his oft-cloned minions after one fight scene, "All right, knock it off. We've all been killed before." Tony Goldwyn plays Drucker as a smug baby boomer with a distinct resemblance to a certain Seattle computer billionaire, and Robert Duvall brings his customary grace to the formulaic role of Dr Weir, the misguided man of science.

There's nothing original about *The 6th Day*'s litany of chase and action sequences—one goes through a suburban house and out the other side, while another features not one but two Schwarzeneggers dangling from a helicopter—but Spottiswoode and cinematographer Pierre Mignot *(Pret-a-Porter)* manage them with considerable success. The film is never dull, although its ending seems confused and its ultimate view of the cloning issue is murky. Unlike John

Woo's *Mission: Impossible II*, the film doesn't descend into an incomprehensible onslaught of sound and vision either.

Still, the impression it leaves behind is nearly pathetic, that of an ageing action star trying to assert his continued virility and relevance in the face of time's relentless march. Unlike Mel Gibson and Bruce Willis, Schwarzenegger was never a romantic leading man and cannot easily reconfigure his action-man persona to suit middle age. One of the jokes in *The 6th Day* has Adam telling the RePet salesman, "Maybe I'll be back." Maybe he will (in John McTierman's planned *Terminator 3*, for instance). But time is not on his side.

VILLAGE VOICE, 11/28/00, p. 140, Michael Atkinson

No less a residue of World War culture than Boyd, [The reference is to *The Trench*; see Atkinson's review.] Arnold Schwarzenegger couldn't be mistaken for an icon anymore, much less an organic reality. But in the endtimes of Jackie Chan's Americanization and Cameron Diaz's butt-shaking the mega-budgeted action rerun into a Pixy Stix sugar high, what's an aging, tongue-twisted Austrian cyborg to do? Stretch Armstrong, that's what, and *The 6th Day*—a genetic-engineering thriller in which Arnold gets to utter the timeless chestnut "I will not clone my dog!"—is everyone's favorite semihuman's latest effort at seeming a little less James Cameron and a little more Philip K. Dick. But instead, cloning simply offers director Roger Spottiswoode a chance to have the worst actor in Beverly Hills play scenes with himself, scenes that come off like a pair of Rock 'Em Sock 'Em Robots guest-starring on *MacGyver*. As with *End of Days*, the context seems flexible, but Arnold himself is a chrome-plated trailer hitch aspiring to be the galaxy's goddamnedest family man.

In the "sooner-than-you-think" near future, human cloning is illegal, but replication of organs and animals is big business—the script's few witticisms involve the mail store RePet, and the frequency with which evil mogul Tony Goldwyn's henchmen get killed and cloned anew, complaining about their death traumas and retrieving jewelry from their old corpses. There's even a mall-sold synthetic child someone has to behead to shut up. Mostly, though, it's a standardized quip-shoot-and-run, assembled by Spottiswoode with the requisite proficient inefficiency, with moments of bio-dread showing through the cracks: cloning expert Robert Duvall watching his cloned wife die a second time, a wounded Goldwyn's last-minute, half-baked clone (looking like Ross Perot covered with Vaseline) getting off the table and roughly undressing the bleeding original. "We've all been killed before," bad guy Michael Rooker grunts once; in an Arnold movie, supporting players have few other options. The star has fewer himself as the years press on; I prescribe a sitcom, or a talk show.

Also reviewed in:
CHICAGO TRIBUNE, 11/17/00, Friday/p. N, Mark Caro
NEW REPUBLIC, 12/4/00, p. 30, Stanley Kauffmann
NEW YORK TIMES, 11/17/00, p. E20, Elvis Mitchell
NEW YORKER, 11/20/00, p. 107, David Denby
VARIETY, 11/13-19/00, p. 23, Todd McCarthy

SKULLS, THE

A Universal Pictures and Original Film/Newmarket Capital Group release of a Neal H. Moritz production. *Executive Producer:* William Tyrer, Chris J. Ball, and Bruce Mellon. *Producer:* Neal H. Moritz and John Pogue. *Director:* Rob Cohen. *Screenplay:* John Pogue. *Director of Photography:* Shane Hurlbut. *Editor:* Peter Amundson. *Music:* Randy Edelman. *Music Editor:* Joanie Diener. *Sound:* John Nutt, Glen Emile Gauthier and (music) Elton Ahi. *Sound Editor:* Christopher Emerson. *Casting:* Mary Vernieu and Anne McCarthy. *Production Designer:* Bob Ziembicki. *Art Director:* Peter Grundy. *Set Designer:* Neil Morfitt. *Set Decorator:* Steven Shewchuk and Clive Thomasson. *Special Effects:* Ted Ross. *Costumes:*

Marie-Suylvie Deveau. *Make-up:* Leslie Sebert. *Stunt Coordinator:* Branko Racki. *Running time:* 100 minutes. *MPAA Rating:* PG-13.

CAST: Joshua Jackson (Luke McNamara); Paul Walker (Caleb Mandrake); Hill Harper (Will Beckford); Leslie Bibb (Chloe); Christopher McDonald (Martin Lombard); Steve Harris (Detective Sparrow); William Petersen (Ames Levritt); Craig T. Nelson (Litten Mandrake); David Asman (Jason Pitcairn); Scott Gibson (Travis Wheeler); Nigel Bennett (Doctor Whitney); Andrew Kraulis (McBride); Derek Aasland (Sullivan); Jennifer Melino (J.J.); Noah Danby (Hugh Mauberson); Mak Fyfe (Laurence Thorne); David Christo (Shawn Packford); Shaw Madson (Chad MacIntosh); Jesse Nilsson (Kent Hodgins); Shawn Mathieson (Jonathan Payne); Steven McCarthy (Sweeney); Matt Taylor (Medoc); Henry Alessandroni (Strain); James Finnerty (Preppy Freshman); Cyprian Lerch (Student in Lunch Line); Dominic Kahn (Regatta Judge); Ken Campbell (Starting Judge); Pedro Salvin (Lodge Butler); Derek Boyes (Assistant District Attorney); Katherine Trowell (Sanctuary Administrator); Connie Buell (Waitress); Steve Richard (Furniture Mover); Kevin Allen (Sturtevant Security Guard); Paul Walker, III (Boxing Coach); Jason Knight (Police Techie); Amanda Goundry (Coo-ed in Caleb's Car); Malin Akerman (Co-ed in Caleb's Apartment).

LOS ANGELES TIMES, 3/31/00, Calendar/p. 9, Robin Rauzi

"If it's secret and elite, it can't be good."

Those words of warning come about 30 minutes into "The Skulls," but any moviegoer with a pulse will have suspected as much from the first frames.

This junior thriller from director Rob Cohen comes across as "The Firm" turned into a very special episode of "Dawson's Creek." Its underlying theme of the perils of elitism is never really dealt with and it contains, perhaps, one pinkie-toe bone of surprise in its skeleton of cliche.

New Haven townie Luke McNamara (Joshua Jackson), a senior and captain of the rowing team, is tapped for membership in the most selective of the secret societies at Yale. Membership looks like the key to success—they'll pay for law school, give him connections among the East Coast power brokers.

All that changes after the mysterious suicide of Luke's roommate and best friend, Will (Hill Harper), the same person who issued the warning about the secret and elite.

As created by screenwriter John Pogue, the characters are each of a type. Luke, the climber who has neglected his friends on the wrong side of the tracks. Will, the nosy student journalist. Chloe (Leslie Bibb), the wealthy socialite non-character. Caleb (Paul Walker), the second-generation Skull who can't live up to his father. They also all live in "dorm rooms" that would be suitable for ballroom dancing.

The Skulls are loosely based on Skull and Bones—one of five well-known secret societies at Yale. It counts among its inductees former President George Bush and aspiring president Texas Gov. George W. Bush.

Truth is indeed stranger than fiction. Or at least in this case, more interesting. The real group dates back hundreds of years and has been suspected by the conspiracy-minded of trying to impose a New World Order.

"The Skulls" has pretensions of seriousness. One professor asks if America is a meritocracy or ruled by the wealthy elite. Such questions drop from scrutiny in favor of a campus cover-up. But then, who would expect a serious critique of elitism from filmmakers who—their biographies point out—went to Harvard and Yale?

"The Skulls" instead is simply more fuel for the hot-burning teen market bonfire, and it'll likely serve that purpose for Universal Studios. As a breakout role for W. B. star Jackson, "The Skulls" doesn't fare as well. Not that he's untalented; the material just doesn't take him far enough from the shores of TV's "Dawson's Creek. "

Director Cohen, who also made "Daylight" and "Dragon: The Bruce Lee Story," seems to think subtext would be lost on his under-22 audience—and that hurts his actors as well. In the more adult roles, Craig T. Nelson as the head Skull and William Petersen as a senator come off as more marionettes than flesh-and-bone humans. Cohen keeps the plot, as predictable as it may be, moving right along, but veers away from what could have been a truly dark ending.

Director of photography Shane Hurlbut gives the whole film a hazy, golden glow. That may be fitting for the ideal-Ivy-League-college opening, but it grows increasingly at odds with the dark plot. But give credit to him, Cohen and editor Peter Amundson for cutting together what may be the only exciting crew race in a movie this year.

NEW YORK POST, 3/31/00, p. 54, Jonathan Foreman

Shot from one of the worst scripts to make it to the big screen in recent memory, it represents the sludge at the bottom of the Hollywood barrel.

Everything about "The Skulls" looks and feels fake, especially the action sequences. The story is so preposterous—yet unimaginative—there are times when you wonder if it isn't turning into a spoof.

Luke McNamara (Joshua Jackson) is a former townie in his senior year at an Ivy that's clearly supposed to be Yale (the name is never actually mentioned, presumably for legal reasons, but the school's teams, like Yale's, are called the Bulldogs)

Oddly, in the moviemakers' version of New Haven, Conn., the city is a hangout for senators, judges and other government bigwigs.

Luke is a candidate for membership in an ancient secret society called the Skulls by virtue of his success as an oarsman. His best pal, Will (Hill Harper), and his lissome love interest, Chloe (Leslie Bibb from TVs "Popular"), are against the idea.

But once you're in, the Skulls give you a flashy car, cash and a letter guaranteeing you a place at any law school of your choice. Its 300-odd alumni run the country, if not the world.

Luke is "tapped" and happily inducted in an unintentionally campy, Monty Python-esque ceremony at the society's gothic/high-tech headquarters.

The head of the society—which gives oddly unsecret white-tie parties on its private island, with sleek (secret?) babes shipped in for the pleasure of the boys—turns out to be Judge Mandrake (Craig T. Nelson).

You know that when student journo Will breaks into the Skulls' HQ to take photographs, and is promptly killed, Judge Mandrake will oversee the coverup. You also know that Luke will do whatever it takes to expose or take vengeance on the killers.

NEWSDAY, 3/31/00, Part II/p. B7, Jan Stuart

You will be surrounded by wealth and privilege. Accorded inside favors. Showered with sporty cars, natty clothes and wristwatches classy enough for an oil tycoon. All this will be yours, when you are elected to an Ivy League secret society.

But first, you have to answer a ringing pay phone. If you buy into a piece of hyped-up malarkey called "The Skulls," then no review is going to weaken your resolve. You may perhaps be one of those ruthless SUV drivers who likes to terrorize smaller cars, as happens in a climactic chase scene. You may be a fan of Joshua Jackson, a doughy-faced actor from "Dawson's Creek." You may be the mother of Joshua Jackson.

Jackson plays Luke McNamara, a working-class townie who has obviously made it into a cushy college by dint of hard work, brains and athletic prowess. Despite his wiser instincts, he allows himself to be drawn into the school's ancient secret society, The Skulls. It seems to be the only way to win the favor of gorgeous rich girls such as Chloe (Leslie Bibb) and the company of dashing classmates like Caleb Mandrake (Paul Walker) or the blueblood scion of powerful judge and Skull alumnus Litten Mandrake (Craig T. Nelson)

All might be well, until Luke's best buddy, Will (Hill Harper), goes sticking his cub-journalist's nose into The Skulls' unsavory business. Things get messy. Murder and blackmail happen; that SUV goes on a rampage. As the dust clears, one is left wondering how it is that such an ineptly run operation as The Skulls lasted the length of the movie, let alone 200 years.

"The Skulls" was written by John Pogue, a Yale graduate and former secret society member who knows his way around this world. He could have written something trenchant about the corruptive potential of class, but he has obviously been around Hollywood long enough to also have learned that when it comes to box office, the ruling elite is not the old-boy network but the teenage-boy network. He garnishes his story with action, opulence, pretty girls and specious sentiments on the order of "when it comes to friendship, there is no middle ground."

Undemanding teen audiences may well eat this stuff up. It may be worth the inflated cost of a date to learn what many of us have learned the hard way: Anyone who picks up a ringing pay phone gets what he deserves.

SIGHT AND SOUND, 12/00, p. 55, Xan Brooks

Luke McNamara is a student from an impoverished background attending an Ivy League college. An athletics ace and top flight law student, he is inducted into the elitist, top-secret society the Skulls, much to the disgust of his roommate, journalism student Will and his friend Chloe. As a Skull, Luke is given money and a sports car. He befriends Senator Levritt, a senior Skull, and fellow member Caleb Mandrake, whose father, Litten, is chairman of the society. Will, who is researching an exposé of the Skulls, is found dead in his room, apparently having committed suicide.

Caleb admits that he inadvertently killed Will in a struggle at the Skulls headquarters, where he caught him researching his story. With the help of Chloe and his friends from the days before he went to university, Luke obtains a surveillance tape which reveals that Litten ordered his henchmen to murder the injured Will after Caleb had left the building. Luke hands the tape to the police inspector investigating Will's death, only to realise that he is in cahoots with the Skulls. Luke is shipped off to a mental institution. Chloe informs Caleb that his father was responsible for Will's death, and later rescues Luke with the aid of Senator Levritt. Luke challenges Caleb to a duel, during which the enraged Caleb shoots his father. Luke realises that he has been used as a pawn in a plan by Levritt to seize control of the Skulls. He declines Levritt's offer to rejoin the society and sets off to begin a new life with Chloe.

There's a glorious moment near the start of The Skulls in which Leslie Bibb's WASP love interest unveils a machine programmed to squirt paint randomly at a canvas a la Jackson Pollock. "Am I the artist or is the machine?" she wonders.

"Maybe it's just chaos in its purest form." Tweak this question a little and it could apply to the film as a whole. Who's the artist here: director Rob Cohen (making his first feature since Daylight, 1996) or the Hollywood machine? Either way, the end result is chaotic. Clankingly schematic in its first half, The Skulls proceeds to suffer a protracted nervous breakdown about midway through.

A college-set conspiracy thriller (think Enemy of the State by way of Varsity Blues), The Skulls affects to lift the lid on American elitism with a tale of a secret society obviously based on Yale's clandestine Skull and Bones (which counts both Bush senior and junior among its members). Its opening scenes set up a ready-made class tension. Luke (Joshua Jackson, graduate of televisions Dawson's Creek) is a "townie" kid from the wrong side of the tracks who attracts the notice of the club's posh-boy fraternity by dint of sheer ability (he wins a boat race from a seemingly hopeless position). But while Luke is intrigued by the wealth and power of the Skulls, his best friend Will (a journalism student played by Hill Harper) is more sceptical: "If it's secret and elite it can't be good."

This, in essence, is The Skulls' moral. The trouble is that the film is fatally compromised, at least half way in love with the culture it purports to criticise. Throughout the film, Cohen adopts a trusty tabloid tack: shout it loud and then condemn it. He rubs the viewers' nose so lavishly in the cash and cars and career opportunities that follow Luke's entrée into the Skulls that the resulting fall-out (Will's murder) comes across as a minor price to pay More significantly, it is this turn of fortunes that heralds the film's sudden plunge towards oblivion. Until then The Skulls is merely risible (arcane ceremonies and jocks wearing cowls). After Will's death it becomes positively barmy; afflicted by a fit of plot twists that culminate in the sight of Luke drooling in an institution like some extra from One Flew Over the Cuckoo's Nest

Through pure mismanagement, The Skulls bungles a rich seam of material. There is a potentially fine drama to be made about secret societies like Skull and Bones—those breeding grounds of the American class system, with their ersatz model of age old rituals thrown down on a new, supposedly libertarian landscape. The Skulls —at once airbrushed and untidy, contrived and confused—is emphatically not that movie.

VILLAGE VOICE, 4/10/00, p. 158, Jessica Winter

Centuries of Ivy League entitlement get an energetic and thoroughly brainless dressing-down from *The Skulls*, in which Joshua Jackson plays an ambitious Yale student with little money or family support who's invited to join a powerful secret society festering with murder and intrigue. The movie (filmed in Toronto) nails New Haven's Disney-Gothic architecture, our Pacey flings himself agreeably into the proceedings, and plenty of compelling motifs help pass the time. Top Gun-style shirtless bonding between the recruits (all male, all WASP, all the time); celebrations of Mr. Jackson's superhuman strength (he outruns a speeding Jeep—at length); and one Skulls alum—a corrupt-but-lovable, teen-girl-chasing, honey-throated Southern senator—who bears enough resemblance to our commander in chief that *The Skulls* begins to resemble a roman à clef (to get you started, Craig T. Nelson plays Kenneth Starr). The preview audience chatted happily all the way through the movie, indicating its destiny as a perennial rental favorite for frat-house living rooms across the U.S.A.

Also reviewed in:
CHICAGO TRIBUNE, 3/31/00, Friday/p. A, Michael Wilmington
NEW YORK TIMES, 3/31/00, p. E22, Dave Kehr
VARIETY, 4/3-9/00, p. 35, Godfrey Cheshire
WASHINGTON POST, 3/31/00, p. C5, Stephen Hunter

SMALL TIME CROOKS

A DreamWorks release of a Sweetland Films presentation of a Jean Doumanian production. *Executive Producer:* J. E. Beaucaire. *Producer:* Jean Doumanian. *Director:* Woody Allen. *Screenplay:* Woody Allen. *Director of Photography:* Zhao Fei. *Editor:* Alisa Lepselter. *Sound:* Gary Alper. *Sound Editor:* Robert Hein. *Casting:* Juliet Taylor and Laura Rosenthal. *Production Designer:* Santo Loquasto. *Art Director:* Tom Warren. *Set Decorator:* Jessica Lanier. *Special Effects:* John Ottesen and Ron Ottesen. *Costumes:* Suzanne McCabe. *Make-up:* Rosemarie Zurlo. *Running time:* 95 minutes. *MPAA Rating:* PG.

CAST: Woody Allen (Ray Winkler); Carolyn Saxon (Candy Salesperson); Tracey Ullman (Frenchy Winkler); Michael Rapaport (Denny); Tony Darrow (Tommy); Sam Josepher (Real Estate Agent); Jon Lovitz (Benny); Lawrence Levy (Dynamite Dealer); Brian Markinson (Cop); Elaine May (May); Dana Tyler (TV News Reporter); Steve Kroft (Himself); Brian McConnachie (Paul Milton); Riccardo Bertoni (Winklers' Butler); Isaac Mizrahi (Winklers' Chef); Kristine Nielsen (Emily Bailey); Larry Pine (Charles Bailey); Hugh Grant (David); Julie Lund (Linda Rhinelander);   Teri Black, John Doumanian, and Phyllis Burdoe (Winkler Party Guests); Maurice Sonnenberg (Garth Steinway);   Richard Mawe (Anthony Gwynne); Karla Wolfangle and Rob Besserer (Modern Dance Performers); Frank Wood (Oliver);   Ruth Laredo (Concert Pianist); Julie Halston (Concert Party Guest); Anthony Sinopoli (Frenchy's Chauffeur);   Jesse Levy (Church Cellist);   Josephine Calabrese, Cindy Wilks, and Trevor Moran (Churchgoers); Peter McRobbie and Douglas McGrath (Frenchy's Lawyers);   Elaine Stritch (Chi Chi Potter); Howard Erskine (Langston Potter);   Ramsey Faragallah (Potters' Walter); Scotty Bloch (Edgar's Wife); George Grizzard (George Blint); Marvin Chatinover (Dr. Henske).

LOS ANGELES TIMES, 5/19/00, Calendar/p. 4, Kevin Thomas

Woody Allen's "Small Time Crooks" is such delicious, giddy fun that it matters little that in its final moments it goes flat. Somehow in the staging, timing and perhaps the writing of the ending Allen has allowed the film's energy to slip through his fingers. It's no big deal in relation to the film as a whole, and if anything, it suggests how like quicksilver Allen's art is and what a tricky business it is to sustain all that lovely fizz.

Allen casts himself as Ray, an ex-con dishwasher married to Frenchy (Tracey Ullman), a former topless dancer he met when he was a minor player in the numbers racket. A botched attempt to hold up a bank landed him a two-year stretch in prison. However, his desire to whisk off the souring Frenchy to a life of Miami luxury and his delusions of criminal genius convince him that he and his pals can get it right this time. All they have to do is rent an empty store near a bank and start tunneling their way into it.

While Ray and his cohorts (Michael Rapaport, Tony Darrow and Jon Lovitz) dig away in the basement, Frenchy will serve as a front, baking and selling cookies in the store. As the guys dig away—in the wrong direction yet—Frenchy's cookies start bringing home the bacon. Soon she has to hire her cousin May (Elaine May) to help out.

In short order Frenchy's cookies lead to an immense factory, a gaudy Park Avenue penthouse—and Frenchy's ambitious social aspirations. Since she knows little about being classy, she turns to Hugh Grant's suave but impecunious art dealer for guidance. More "Born Yesterday's" Billie Dawn than "Pygmalion's" Eliza Doolittle, Frenchy has natural intelligence and craves an education and sophistication. She and Ray are at heart innocents, and as they start drifting apart, they leave themselves open for big trouble.

The protean Ullman makes Frenchy tremendously endearing, a tough talker with a loving heart and a forthright capacity for taking responsibility for her actions. Ray, a beer-and-TV guy, is similarly able at last to admit that he's not remotely as smart as he thinks he is; if he and Frenchy can get back together they could survive just about anything. Allen and Ullman have teamed twice previously, and they play off each other as easily as a George Burns and that other Allen, Gracie. Amazingly, Elaine May has never worked with Allen before, and she is ever the delight: You can never predict whether her May is going to be spacey or shrewd—or both.

Grant, the master at polished self-deprecation, is the perfect guide to acclimate Frenchy to high society and high culture. Frenchy is certainly smitten with Grant's charming David, but he's too wise to undercut his status as an arbiter of taste by playing the gigolo as well. Allen as usual fills the screen with wonderful people, among them Elaine Stritch as an elegant Manhattan grande dame. (Just imagine, Allen, May and Stritch on the screen at the same time.)

"Small Time Crooks" is handsome as all Allen films are, and it proceeds with the brisk, sophisticated air of throwaway confidence and lack of pretense that we expect from the contemporary master of grown-up comedy. That minor glitch at the picture's end can serve as a reminder: The quality of effortlessness that makes Allen movies so tonic most surely must be the result of much hard work.

NEW YORK, 5/29/00, p. 102, Peter Rainer

Small Time Crooks isn't just minor Woody Allen. It's minuscule Woody Allen. It harks back not to the great, anarchic "early funny" movies like *Bananas* and *Sleeper* but even farther back, into the Milquetoast recesses of *Take the Money and Run.* Allen began his moviemaking career taking very small baby steps, and now, perhaps to draw a wider audience, or maybe just to blow a few bubbles in between his usual deep-breathing exercises, he's gone back to pure piffledom. Which would be fine if at least the piffles had some bounce. *Small Time Crooks* is mildly enjoyable and has its scattered, hilariously aberrant moments, but mostly it's cranked up and overextended, a one-joke movie predicated on a not particularly fragrant joke.

Woody Allen is playing Ray Winkler, a whiny two-bit swindler who recently spent some time in jail and now works as a dishwasher. His brassy wife, Frenchy, played by Tracey Ullman, used to be an exotic dancer known as the Topless Wonder. She indulges—just barely—his harebrained get-rich-quick schemes while churning out his favorite meal, spaghetti and turkey meatballs. Allen presents these two as a screw-loose variant on the Kramdens from The *Honeymooners;* she rolls her eyes at him, and he threatens to clonk her. When Jackie Gleason did this sort of thing with Audrey Meadows, the hostilities at least had some flint. The Kramdens were playing out a marital comedy of prole dissatisfaction, and the contrast between Ralph's raucous grandiosity and Alice's stern, level gaze was essential to the joke. We were never put in the position of feeling superior to their working-class gripes or their itch for upward mobility; we weren't congratulated for having better taste than the Kramdens. The show was too juicy and knockabout to be playing those high-low games. *Small Time Crooks* makes it a point to play up Ray and Frenchy's proletarian bad taste, and when they strike it rich, their taste, especially hers, goes from bad to worse while we are encouraged to snicker.

In order to make this tired gag work, you need a filmmaker with a deep affinity, even affection, for both schlockiness and the fineries of the upper crust (a filmmaker like, say, Preston Sturges). But Woody Allen's comic affinities are somewhere in between, which is perhaps why the working-class humor in this film seems so labored and the hoity-toity comedy so routine. His way of ribbing the Winklers and their crook cronies, played by Jon Lovitz, Michael Rapaport, and Tony Darrow, is to have everybody speak with a Noo Yawk accent a mile wide. At the opposite extreme, he can't fully satirize the Winklers' nouveau-richness because he doesn't care enough to be drawn in by it. He doesn't want to be tainted by it. And so what we get are excruciating close-ups of the couple's Park Avenue penthouse with its bronze lilies on the winding staircase; we get jokes involving truffles and fey chefs and tony cocktail parties. All of this succeeds, on a fairly low level, but Allen doesn't give nouveau-richness its comic due; he doesn't show us how even a grouch like Ray might succumb to gaudiness. Hugh Grant plays a swank operator who is supposed to tutor the Winklers in the finer things, and you look forward to some classic scenes on the order of the sequence in *Silver Streak* where Richard Pryor taught Gene Wilder how to be "black." But Allen won't entertain the notion that Ray might have anything to learn from this snoot. Money doesn't change Ray. Nothing does. This may be an admirable characteristic in a man, but it doesn't do much for a comic hero.

The best reason to catch *Small Time Crooks* is for the occasional actors' grace notes, most of them supplied by Elaine May, as Frenchy's addled cousin May. Despite Allen's vaunted reputation for casting the best actors, he has an annoying habit of employing them as glorified bit players; it's like sitting down to a full-course meal and getting fobbed off with hors d'oeuvre. (I'm still recovering from the now-you-see-her-now-you-don't cameo by Blythe Danner in *Husbands and Wives*.) I was afraid this sort of thing was going to happen with Elaine May in *Small Time Crooks,* because she appears early only to disappear for a long stretch. Fortunately, she comes back into the picture and gives it an addled warmth. Her May is a blotto kook with a sweet-tempered genius for doing the wrong thing, and yet she sees more clearly into the ongoing inanities than anybody else. She's a holy fool as a supremely gifted revue-sketch artist might imagine her.

Elaine May even brings out some fellow feeling from Woody Allen, who tones down Ray's whininess whenever she's around. He's truly responsive in his scenes with her, and suddenly, the movie doesn't seem so minuscule anymore. I recently wrote in these pages that Mike Nichols's absence from the screen since his stunning performance in the 1997 film version of *The Designated Mourner* has deprived us of a great actor. The same sentiment applies to Elaine May, who hardly ever performs in films. Maybe it's time for the two of them to work together as actors again, in the movies.

NEW YORK POST, 5/19/00, p. 44, Lou Lumenick

"Small Time Crooks" is Woody Allen's very self-conscious attempt to return to what he once referred to as his "earlier, funnier" comedies.

After decades of typecasting himself as a neurotic intellectual to ever-decreasing box-office returns, Allen retreats to his (more commercial) past, playing a clueless bank robber—essentially a geriatric version of his character from "Take the Money and Run," the Woodman's 1969 debut as a director-star.

Ray Winkler is an ex-con who doesn't get any respect—especially not from his wife, Frenchy (Tracey Ullman), a sarcastic exotic-dancer-turned-manicurist with whom he trades insults straight out of "The Honeymooners."

She's even more skeptical than usual when Ray announces he has come up with a scheme to make enough money so they can retire to Florida: Open a cookie store next to a bank, tunnel into the vault and help themselves to the loot.

Things go awry when Frenchy's cookie-making talents turn her into another Mrs. Fields, spawn a vast franchising empire, and make them and their partners in crime (including Jon Lovitz and Michael Rapaport) millionaires.

Ray is happy watching TV and playing poker with his cronies, but the newfound wealth awakens Frenchy's social aspirations, which she tries to further by enlisting the help of a socially connected (if sleazy) art dealer, David (Hugh Grant, who horribly overplays).

Smitten with David, Frenchy dumps Ray, who finds solace in the company of her famously dim cousin (Elaine May), with whom he can share Chinese food and old movies—yes, a woman Allen's own age.

The good news here is that Allen, for the first time in a while, isn't doing an *hommage* to Fellini or Bergman. His sources here are no loftier than Garson Kanin, who wrote "Born Yesterday," and S.J. Perelman—the bank-tunnel plot is straight from one of his plays that was turned into a minor Edward G. Robinson vehicle, "Larceny Inc."

The bad news is that "Small Time Crooks," isn't anywhere near as hilarious as I hoped it would be. Allen's one-liners provoke fewer chuckles than the garish outfits worn by Allen and Ullman, who tries hard (maybe too hard) to flesh out a one-dimensional character.

Through no fault of his own, Allen is showing every one of his 64 years—so it's as creepy as it is amusing when we glimpse bits and pieces of the young Woody mugging, as when Ray repeatedly tries to sneak upstairs at a society party to pull off a scam with May (whose attempt to play a nitwit at times is even more labored than Allen's is.)

"Small Time Crooks" is petty larceny—but Allen's fans won't want to miss this lowbrow caper.

NEWSDAY, 5/19/00, Part II/p. B7, Jan Stuart

Elaine May commits an act of screwball larceny in "Small Time Crooks," smoothly wresting every scene she is in from such comic titans as Woody Allen, Tracey Ullman and Elaine Stritch.

In Allen's raffishly funny new prank May plays May, a blunt-spoken gal whose slushy delivery and wanton lack of tact gives the impression that there is little activity going on between the ears. The joke, of course, is that she is more alert than anyone around her; she has a talent for landing on both feet when everyone else is tripping over himself. May brings to the role a calculated spaciness that is all her own, recalling her inspired improv creations with ex-partner Mike Nichols.

As Elaine May returns triumphant to her performing roots, her writer-director would appear to be coming full circle as well. "Small Time Crooks" is a blithe cartoon immorality tale of the kind that Allen fans have pined for since "Take the Money and Run" (1969). Indeed, Allen once more plays a wrong-way Corrigan of the petty criminal world with a weakness, if not a genius, for knocking off banks.

As Ray Winkler, a former racketeer and professional loser, Allen takes all the nagging and linguine and meatballs his manicurist wife Frenchy (Ullman) can dish out. Enlisting her aid along with three bozo buddies (Jon Lovitz, Tony Darrow, Michael Rapaport), he purchases a pizza joint a few feet down from a bank. As the boys burrow their way toward everything but the vault, Frenchy fronts upstairs, reinventing the pizza place as a cookie shop.

The heist is a botch, but the cookie business is a hit, so much so that Frenchy has to bring her cousin May to handle the rush. Before you can say Famous Amos, the whole gang is franchising to the tune of millions. Ray and Frenchy are living in gaudy Park Avenue splendor, requiring a seemingly well-bred art dealer (Hugh Grant) to school her and Ray in the finer things in life.

Despite the superficial link to "Take the Money and Run," Allen's latest owes more to the spirit of "The Lavender Hill Mob" and the Ealing Brothers comedies of Britain's yesteryear: affable, ironic confections in which best-laid plans invariably go astray or average Joes react clumsily in the face of a sudden financial windfall. But Allen saves his twists for the beginning and the end, leaving longueurs in the middle of the film. At such times, Ray and Frenchy strike us as tired conceits, over-the-top incarnations of the vulgarians Allen himself ostensibly left behind when he hit pay dirt and moved uptown.

If "Small Time Crooks" is a trifle, taking a place between such on-again-off-again larks as "Bullets Over Broadway" and "Manhattan Murder Mystery," there is no one around who gives and takes such pleasure in being silly as Allen. When things slow down, he sprinkles in another vintage one-liner, the best of which he saves for his classy third banana, Elaine May. "I think this whole evening was apocalyptic," she says, groping for the wrong word after a good date. "Small Time Crooks" is precisely that: The big bang that follows whenever people apply a stick of dynamite to bust through the inertia of their lives rather than the low flame of honest grunt work.

NEWSWEEK, 5/22/00, p. 73, David Ansen

Woody Allen is confused with the characters he plays more than any other performer, but "Small Time Crooks" should give that game a rest. No one is likely to mistake him for the hapless con man Ray Winkler, a bank robber so inept he and his gang of equally dimwitted thieves (Jon Levitz, Mark Rapaport, Tony Darrow) dig a tunnel into a clothing store, missing the bank altogether. But if Ray is a loser, he's lucky in his choice of a wife. Frenchy (Tracey Ullman), an ex-stripper, has a gift for baking. She's fronting the cookie store where the gang is doing its tunnel work, and her sweet confections turn out to be an unexpected gold mine. Instead of jail, Ray, his wife and the gang that couldn't dig straight find themselves rolling in dough. Their sham store turns into a national franchise that Krispy Kreme might envy, and soon the nouveau riche Winklers are confronting the horror of getting everything they ever dreamed of. The incurably vulgar Frenchy suddenly fancies herself a socialite and patron of the arts and starts dragging her husband—who just wants to sit in front of a VCR and eat burgers—on a forced march from museum to ballet to opera. Can their marriage survive?

This is an amiable and quite conventional comedy. The biggest problem is that it's not all that funny. The whole movie, with its rather antiquated notions of the lower classes, feels as if it were inspired by another era. This may be Allen's attempt to pay homage to his idol Bob Hope. You can feel Hope's influence in Woody's unusually physical performance. "Small Time Crooks," his first movie for DreamWorks, gives off a slight scent of mothballs.

Still, considering that the basic joke is how dumb and uncultured its characters are, the comedy is surprisingly benign. It could have reeked of condescension (as "Mighty Aphrodite" often did). Ullman, who can underplay even the most broadly written part, magically invests this paragon of bad taste with a no-nonsense humanity that rescues her from stereotype. And as the dumbest character of them all, Frenchy's cousin May, Elaine May makes total stupidity totally irresistible. When she's around, this tepid jest is laugh-out-loud funny.

SIGHT AND SOUND, 1/01, p. 59, Leslie Felperin

New Jersey, the present. Ex-con Ray Winkler plans to rob a bank by leasing nearby shop premises from where he will tunnel into the vault. He enlists the help of fellow criminals Denny, Tommy and Benny in digging up the basement while his wife Frenchy opens a cookie store upstairs as a front. Frenchy's cookies prove popular and she hires her cousin May to help serve. After the tunnel takes a wrong turn, Ray and Frenchy concentrate on the cookie business.

A year later, Ray, Frenchy and their criminal cronies have become rich through the cookie business. Frenchy decides she wants to become a "patron of the arts" and throws a dinner party for her wealthy upper-class acquaintances. Overhearing some guests' disparaging comments about her apartment, she enlists the help of David, an art dealer, to teach her and Ray about culture. As Frenchy becomes more upwardly mobile, she drifts away from Ray who seeks solace in the company of May. David plots to marry Frenchy for her money, but he dumps her when he discovers Frenchy's accountants have embezzled company funds, leaving her penniless. Ray tries and fails to steal a necklace from a rich heiress. Frenchy and Ray reconcile; Frenchy then reveals that she has stolen an expensive cigarette case from David, which she originally bought him as a gift.

Sour, broadly comic, and yet the most financially successful film he's made for years, Woody Allen's *Small Time Crooks* has been hailed by some as a resurgence of the comic form of his early films, such as *Take the Money and Run* (1969) and *Sleeper* (1973). Judging from its reception, it's as if Allen is courting those fans whom he disparaged in *Stardust Memories* (1980). There, the director plays an auteur who, much like Allen, shunned the buoyancy of his "earlier, funnier movies" in favour of darker themes and arthouse aesthetics.

In fact, although it has few witty one-liners, *Small Time Crooks* is less a return to form than a mean-spirited combination of early-Allen comic schematics and late-Allen misanthropic snobbery. Allen and Tracey Ullman's New Jersey couple Ray and Frenchy Winkler—the eponymous small-time crooks who set out to rob a bank and end up striking rich in the cookie business only to come undone at the end—are little more than piñatas of vulgarity, sneered at for their attempts to ingest abstract art and fancy *hors d'oeuvres*. Fate and the director bash them with a contempt second only to that reserved for the stereotyped Manhattan elitists they meet (particularly Hugh Grant's foppish slimeball David). What spills out of their eye-searing Versace duds is pure straw, not the sweet candy of likeability some of the earlier Allen protagonists are made of. Allen himself has described *Small Time Crooks* as a parable about the perils of getting what you wish for, but it comes off as a cautionary tale against self-improvement, a breeding-will-out allegory seemingly written by a sarcastic eugenicist. Only Elaine May as the sweetly gormless cousin May manages to hew two dimensions from her character. The rare chance to see this gifted comedian on screen is one of the few compelling reasons to see the film.

Made after his marriage to his former stepdaughter Soon-Yi Previn, Allen's recent films *Deconstructing Harry, Celebrity* and *Sweet and Lowdown* have been apologies for genius, arguing that talented people have monstrous morals which, implicitly, we have to forgive for the sake of their art. *Small Time Crooks* plays like the flipside of this argument; here people of only plebeian skill (Frenchy is a baker) are unjustly elevated to fame and then supposedly justly brought low. But *Small Time Crooks* hasn't the structural ingenuity of *Deconstructing Harry* or the nuanced performances that elevated *Sweet and Lowdown*. Unlike Frenchy's cookies, the film leaves a bad taste in the mouth.

VILLAGE VOICE, 5/23/00, p. 141, J. Hoberman

It's my pleasure to report that Woody Allen's *Small Time Crooks* doesn't pretend to be anything more than a well-executed caper. Eschewing payback, Allen's funniest, least sour outing in nearly a decade is a small movie with a tidy payoff.

Unlike last year's *Sweet and Lowdown*, *Small Time Crooks* isn't a period piece, but given its old-fashioned virtues, it could be. The movie, which opens with a burst of Chick Webb's "Stomping at the Savoy" and a proletarian Woody peering over his *Daily News,* maintains a distinct, if imaginary, '30s flavor throughout. This is one Woody Allen comedy that does not cozy down in the lap of bourgeois comfort. The premise is irredeemably lowbrow: Ex-con dishwasher Ray Winkler (Allen) and his dull-witted partners (Michael Rapaport, Jon Lovitz, Tony Darrow) conceive a scheme to rob a bank, using a cookie store operated by Ray's wife, Frenchy (Tracey Ullman), as their cover.

Ray prides himself on having been dubbed "the Brain" in stir, although as a colleague argues, this may have been an instance of cell-block sarcasm. His plan naturally goes awry, not least because Frenchy's cookies begin to sell like crazy. As in some fairy-tale enchantment, the dough really turns out to be dough; the crooks prosper even after Frenchy's gloriously dim-bulb cousin May (Elaine May) blurts out the truth to a cop. A year and many franchises later, the gang is being profiled on TV as a "corporate culture that has business readers scratching their heads."

Small Time Crooks strikes a balance between situation and character. The filmmaker himself plays a skinny, querulous old man; as an actor, he has better rapport trading one-liners with the nasal, rubber-faced Ullman's quick-witted harridan than with any costar since he went one-on-one with the similarly voluble Bette Midler in Paul Mazursky's *Scenes From a Mall.* Newly resplendent in blue jacket and yellow pants, Ray begins modeling clothes so loud they nearly drown out Frenchy's parvenue hysterics. The jaw-dropping decor of the couple's Park Avenue penthouse seems beyond the nouveau imagination of the Jacqueline Susann character in *Isn't She Great*—it even trumps the crystal-palace fantasia of Tavern on the Green.

The movie's garish set piece is the party, catered by Isaac Mizrahi, that Frenchy throws to launch herself in New York society. Wearing a creation that might have been ripped from the wall of the current Whitney Biennial, she overhears her guests dishing her vulgarity and, soon after, hires an upper-class hustler (Hugh Grant) as a tutor in taste. Thus, *Small Time Crooks* makes an artful segue from the precincts of *Big Deal on Madonna Street* to those of *Born Yesterday*. Throughout, however, the movie's colorful cast, class-based satire, and controlled slapstick suggest the secondario-crammed comedies of Preston Sturges. Elaine May, who gets her own party scene to preside over, all but steals the show as a single-minded fount of empty-headed yammer. (May also demonstrates impressive chemistry with the Woodman, particularly in the art of conversational shouting.)

As if to acknowledge that May plays a better Gracie Allen than Gracie herself, Allen's script tips its hat to the sitcoms of the '50s: Ray greets his wife in the manner of Desi Arnaz; his last line is a variant on Jackie Gleason's "Baby, you're the greatest." Greatest or not, at least Frenchy manages to upgrade her wig by film's end. Hilariously designed, vibrantly shot, and deftly paced, *Small Time Crooks* is a conventional fable but a generous screwball comedy. The movie gives vulgarity a good name.

Also reviewed in:
CHICAGO TRIBUNE, 5/19/00, Friday/p. A, Mark Caro
NATION, 6/19/00, p. 35, Stuart Klawans
NEW YORK TIMES, 5/19/00, p. E14, Stephen Holden
NEW YORKER, 5/22/00, p. 99, Anthony Lane
VARIETY, 5/15/-21/00, p. 25, Todd McCarthy
WASHINGTON POST, 5/19/00, p. C5, Rita Kempley
WASHINGTON POST, 5/19/00, Weekend/p. 47, Desson Howe

SMILING FISH AND GOAT ON FIRE

A Stratosphere Entertainment release. *Executive Producer:* Sheilah Goldman and Thomas W. Lynch. *Producer:* Derick Martini, Kevin Jordan, and Steven Martini. *Director:* Kevin Jordan. *Screenplay:* Kevin Jordan, Derick Martini, and Steven Martini. *Director of Photography:* Fred Iannone. *Editor:* Kevin Anderson and Ryan Rothmaier. *Music:* Chris Horvath, Steven Martini, and Bill Henderson. *Set Designer:* Karyn Burgner and Deana Aho. *Running time:* 90 minutes. *MPAA Rating:* R.

CAST: Derick Martini (Chris Remi); Steven Martini (Tony Remi); Christa Miller (Kathy); Amy Hathaway (Alison); Bill Henderson (Clive Winter); Rosemarie Addeo (Anna); Heather Jae Marie (Nicole); Nicole Rae (Natalie); Wesley Thompson (Burt Winter).

CHRISTIAN SCIENCE MONITOR, 8/25/00, p. 15, David Sterritt

From its title, you'd think "Smiling Fish and Goat on Fire" is a fairy tale, or maybe a native-American legend. In fact, it's a contemporary story about two ordinary men coping with everyday situations. It's not particularly memorable, but it provides fresh evidence that independent filmmaking remains alive and well.

The main characters are Chris and Tony, brothers who share a Los Angeles house. They get along, but there's an undercurrent of mild tension arising from deep-down differences in their personalities. This is reflected in the movie's title, taken from nicknames their grandmother gave them as children. Chris does well at work (he's an accountant), but has a rocky relationship with his girlfriend. Tony likes his girlfriend, but hasn't yet turned his career (he's an actor) into something to boast about.

The plot thickens when each brother falls for a new woman, and it thickens more when Chris strikes up a friendship with an elderly African-American man whose soulful ideas and colorful memories give Chris a new perspective on life.

The film derives its energy from the day-to-day interactions of these crisply etched characters. It also benefits from the liveliness of its screenplay, written by director Kevin Jordan with the real-life brothers Derick and Steven Martini, who play the title roles.

LOS ANGELES TIMES, 9/1/00, Calendar/p. 2, Kevin Thomas

If you can get past the stay-away title of the year, "Smiling Fish and Goat on Fire," you'll find an endearing little picture hiding behind it.

Chris (Derick Martini) and Tony (Steve Martini) are mid-to-late-twentysomething brothers, who have recently lost their parents in a freeway crash, and for now are living in the old L.A. Craftsman cottage in which they grew up. One of their grandmothers was half-Italian and half-Native American, and she bestowed the nicknames Smiling Fish and Goat on Fire on the sunny-natured Chris and the sober Tony, respectively.

Still, you could wish the brothers Martini—who wrote the script with their director, Kevin Jordan—had simply called their movie "Chris and Tony" for want of a more inspired title. At any rate, as adults they've stayed true to their natures. Easy-going Chris is an aspiring actor, losing no sleep over not setting the world on fire while Tony sticks to his dull office job and an even duller relationship with his high school girlfriend (Amy Hathaway) who reacts to his dogged devotion with undisguised indifference and even contempt.

Both brothers are about to meet women who could change their lives—provided they are up to the challenge. Tony meets the gorgeous Anna (Rosemarie Addeo), an Italian-born animal wrangler for movies and TV shows, and Chris finds himself taken with his lovely postal carrier, Kathy (Christa Miller), whom he runs into at an audition for her young daughter Natalie (Nicole Rae). Natalie has enjoyed some success back in Wyoming in TV commercials and stage productions, and Kathy, a single mother, is letting her daughter give Hollywood a shot.

The brightest spot in Tony's everyday life is Clive, who is amusingly played by Bill Henderson, the veteran actor and jazz vocalist, who also contributed to the film's score. Clive, the uncle of his ultra-uptight boss (Wesley Thompson), is an elderly pioneer motion picture sound engineer, mourning the death of his beloved wife and nudging Tony to loosen up and live a little.

Chris and Tony, while different in temperaments, are sweet-natured, thoughtful guys, and the film is really a portrait of them in transition in the wake of their shared loss—of how they discover within themselves how much potential they have for change and growth.

This is a deliberately modest movie of modest goals, but having said that, Jordan, the Martini brothers and their colleagues are committed to realizing the potential for humor, emotion and enlightenment in its every moment. This is a film of much gentleness, tenderness and keen observation into the way laughter and pain have a way of colliding into each other. It takes a while for it to find its own rhythm, but by the time it does, you're hooked. Now if they could just change that title ....

NEW YORK POST, 8/25/00, p. 59, Lou Lumenick

This inexplicably overpraised flick is much less a satisfying movie than an intermittently funny 90-minute acting audition, with a title referring to nicknames bestowed on the two main characters by their Italian-Native American grandmother.

The fish is Chris (Derick Martini), an irresponsible actor who's a poster child for arrested development.

The goat is his brother Tony (played by Derick's real-life brother, Steven Martini), a much put-upon accountant whose unvarying routine is symbolized by repeated orders of corned-beef sandwiches. Neither is very interesting.

The very slight story (by the Martinis) follows the brothers, who share a house in Los Angeles, as they depart dead-end relationships for new ones during the Christmas season.

Kevin Jordan, a pal of the Martinis making his feature directing debut on a shoestring budget, tends to let his camera wander and his actors flounder.

NEWSDAY, 9/1/00, Part II/p. B6, John Anderson

Before we proceed, the title of "Smiling Fish and Goat on Fire" seems to demand some kind of explanation. So:

As nicknamed by their Native American grandmother, brothers Tony and Chris Remi (brothers Derick and Steven Martini) are, respectively, Smiling Fish and Goat on Fire—the former fair and sunny, the latter darker and serious. Chris is an accountant, Tony an actor. Chris has romance trouble because he tries too hard; Tony because he doesn't try at all. Otherwise, you'd think they were related.

Actually, they're more alike than not and the real-life fraternity that the Martini brothers bring to their roles makes the film—hereafter referred to as "Fish/Goat"—a naturally loose, friendly, goofball romantic comedy that may even restore your faith, had you spy to begin with, in the low-budget, low-concept, highly personable indie film.

Personality, ultimately, is what "Fish/Goat" is all about. Alongside the buoyant Martinis is a supporting cast of charmers: Christa Miller of "The Drew Carey Show" is devastatingly unglamorous as Kathy, the mail lady who becomes Tony's special delivery. As Anna, the imported Italian animal wrangler—this does take place in Hollywood, after all—Rosemarie Addeo provides an alluring antidote to Chris' breakup from his long-suffering, longtime girlfriend. And little Nicole Ray, as Kathy's daughter Natalie, is extremely fresh and extremely likable.

But it's the veteran actor Bill Henderson as the salty Clive who balances the recipe. As the 80-year-old uncle of Chris' boss, Henderson delivers vulgarity with an aplomb rarely heard and gives the movie the gravitas it needs: As he tells Chris in a series of reminiscences, he met the great love of his life while working as a sound man in the black film industry. And when he mixes his tales of love with anecdotes about Paul Robeson, there's a substance created that elevates the entire film.

Director Kevin Jordan makes a fairly auspicious debut, although there are some fatuous antics that cry out for cutting. And while "Fish/Goat" is described as "a film by Kevin Jordan"—in accord with irritating recent custom—it seems to be far more a collaboration than an auteurist effort. And if they all got together again, it wouldn't be the worst thing in the world.

VILLAGE VOICE, 8/29/00, p. 140, Edward Crouse

Smiling Fish and Goat on Fire is named for the supposedly polar personalities of two brothers, as christened by their half-Native American grandmother. This conceit, like many things in the movie, is dropped and never pursued. The movie's slacker tempo is set by the Christmas season, which, in this blandly accurate L.A., reads as bleachy and lonely. Life has fallen into routine for Chris and Tony (real-life siblings Derick and Steven Martini), as the opening coital crosscutting reveals. The elder Chris (the goat) lies benumbed atop his longtime girlfriend; in the next room, Tony (the fish) boisterously knocks boots with Nicole, whose discovery of an alien condom wrapper fragment highlights the former's philandering. Chris, the accountant and breadwinner (Tony's an actor), is then called on to chauffeur his boss's Uncle Clive around, and—poof—this wizened black guru has the answers to his romantic impasse: something called "magnetic perfection," which he claims can be heard on the soundtrack of a Paul Robeson movie on which he was the boom man.

The rest of the movie plays ping-pong with these regular dudes as they recalibrate their lives around new women. In this visually malnourished film, quirks substitute for character. Roast beef dribbles out of a meat-slicer while Chris stares blankly, thinking of his girlfriend's pregnancy and his future. This wince-worthy emasculating suggestion is but one of several animal-sexual-gastronomic bits—the better ones involve Clive (great character actor Bill Henderson, playing with laid-back, lumpy verve), whose donut diet will form a cholesterol bridge to the afterlife and back to his true love. Less tolerable are the jazz Muzak score and the intermittently deployed accents. Are the characters or the actors New York transplants? Why does the Italian's dialect suggest Roseanne Roseannadanna?

Also reviewed in:
CHICAGO TRIBUNE, 10/6/00, Friday/p. I, Mark Caro
NEW YORK TIMES, 8/25/00, p. E18, Dave Kehr
VARIETY, 9/27-10/3/99, p. 40, Eddie Cockrell

SNOW DAY

A Paramount Pictures and Nickelodeon Movies release. *Executive Producer:* Raymond Wagner. *Producer:* Albie Hecht and Julia Pistor. *Director:* Chris Koch. *Screenplay:* Will McRobb and Chris Viscardi. *Director of Photography:* Robbie Greenberg. *Editor:* David Finfer. *Music:* Steve Bartek. *Music Editor:* Will Kaplan. *Sound:* Garrell Clark and (music) Robert Fernandez. *Sound Editor:* Cameron Frankley and Beth Sterner. *Casting:* Mary Gail Artz and Barbara Cohen. *Production Designer:* Leslie McDonald. *Art Director:* Ken Rempel. *Set Decorator:* Carol Lavoie. *Special Effects:* Mike Vezina and Gordon Davis. *Costumes:* Wendy Partridge. *Make-up:* Gail Kennedy. *Stunt Coordinator:* Tom Glass. *Running time:* 89 minutes. *MPAA Rating:* PG.

CAST: Chris Elliott (Snowplowman);   Mark Webber (Hal Brandston);   Jean Smart (Laura Brandston);   Schuyler Fisk (Lane Leonard);   Iggy Pop (Mr. Zellweger);   Pam Grier (Tina); Chevy Chase (Tom Brandston);   John Schneider (Chad Symmonz);   Zena Grey (Natalie Brandston);   Emmanuelle Chriqui (Claire Bonner);   David Paetkau (Chuck Wheeler);   Jade Yorker (Chet Felker); Connor Matheus (Randy Brandston);   Damian Young (Principal Weaver); Josh Peck (Wayne Alworth);   J. Adam Brown (Bill Korn); Chilli (Nana);   Tim Paleniuk (Mailman);   Josh Sealy (Ben's Son);   Orest Kinasewich (Ben);   Andrea Engel (Phillis, TV Newscaster); Katharine Isabelle (Marla);   Carly Pope (Fawn);   Kea Wong (Paula);   Desiree Lindsay (Patty);   Lorena Gale (Radio Mother);   Jeff Watson (Kid);   Daniel Cuthbertson (Snowployboy);   Alex Hudson (Braces Kid);   Renee Christianson (Make-up Person);   Frank Takacs (Technician);   Dan Wilmott (Crossing Guard);   Shaye Ganam (Sportscaster);   Gepert Myers (Dad);   Bob Chomyn (Editor); Rick Ash (Producer);   Terry King (Diner Dan);   Stevie Mitchell (Scout 1);   Leon Frierson (Odd Ball Kid);   Chad Gosgrave (Steve); Colt Cosgrave (Greg).

LOS ANGELES TIMES, 2/11/00, Calendar/p. 4, Robin Rauzi

Southern California exports filmed images of sunshine to the eyeballs of kids around the nation, so it's only fair that snowy upstate New York gets its chance at being the locale of childhood fantasies.

However, "Snow Day," a harmless co-production of Nickelodeon Movies and Paramount Pictures, may be a hard sell in places where kids have never experienced the joy of a surprise day off school—or at least one that wasn't caused by the violent shaking of the earth. But it is not completely without charms, most notably that rare thing, a girl protagonist.

The presence of Chevy Chase, Pam Grier, Chris Elliott and Jean Smart might suggest that there is more in "Snow Day" for adults than there really is. Chase is preoccupied with a slight subplot that pits his meteorologist Tom Brandston against a rival weatherman played by John Schneider (hardly recognizable from his "Dukes of Hazzard" days), which doesn't allow for much goofing off. If Grier, who plays his boss, didn't complete filming on all her scenes in one day, her time was wasted.

The plot instead focuses on two of the Brandston children. High schooler Hal (Mark Webber) is trying to make inroads with immensely popular Claire Bonner (Emmanuelle Chriqui) despite threats from Chuck Wheeler (David Paetkau), her ex-boyfriend who refuses to allow a breakup. Meanwhile, Natalie Brandston (Zena Grey) and her posse of fellow 10-year-olds are trying to secure a second snow day by stopping the dreaded Snowplowman (Chris Elliott) from clearing the streets.

In the production notes, Elliott, like most of the adult cast, expressed some pleasure at making a film he could watch with his children. But neither Elliott nor Chase seemed excited enough to do anything interesting with their short parts. Elliott's role in particular could've been played by any scruffy yellow-toothed grunting actor.

"Snow Day" isn't for teens, it's for the kids who aspire to be teens. Nonetheless, Webber and Schuyler Fisk, who plays his best friend, are a welcome relief from the teenager-cum-fashion models who populate so much of entertainment. That's not to say they're unattractive, but they have a naturalness that, even in a film as contrived as "Snow Day," suggests a career beyond such material.

The writers and director are feature-film rookies out of Nickelodeon's farm team—which makes sense. The cable network is already the most consistent provider of children's broadcast entertainment. Director Chris Koch and writers Will McRobb and Chris Viscardi worked on the network's shows "The Adventures of Pete & Pete" and "KABLAM!" Not surprisingly, "Snow Day" has the took and feel of a slick network production—and the Nickelodeon seal of approval.

The film could—and probably will—run on Nickelodeon as-is. There's nary a swear word heard nor an inappropriate patch of skin revealed. The 15-year-olds here seem only distantly related to the PG-13 high schoolers of "10 Things I Hate About You," let alone their R-rated brethren in "American Pie." It's all good, clean—if slightly dull—fun.

NEW YORK POST, 2/11/00, p. 57, Lou Lumenick

"Snow Day" is sort of a "Groundhog Day" for the Nickelodeon set—a gentle but funny family comedy that will tickle kids and bring smiles to their parents' faces.

Like "Groundhog Day," it has a goofy weatherman—this time played not by Bill Murray but by another "Saturday Night Live" veteran, Chevy Chase.

And Chris Elliott, who co-starred in "Groundhog Day," is on hand again—except this time, he has the best role, and top billing for the first time since "Cabin Boy."

He's hilarious as an evil snowplow operator determined to keep a blizzard that's socked in Syracuse from turning into an extended school holiday.

As this movie is basically aimed at kids, the adult stars are subsidiary to the engaging young performers who play Chase's children.

Hal (Mark Webber), the oldest, is a 10th-grader who uses the snow day to moonily pursue the girl of his dreams (gorgeous Emmanuelle Chriqui)—all the while ignoring the female friend (Schuyler Fisk, Sissy Spacek's real-life daughter) who quietly pines for him.

His younger sister, Natalie, played by the spirited Zena Grey, is busy rallying the neighborhood kids to stop Elliott's Snowplow Man, who carries a crow in his 10-ton rig and whose teeth are badly in need of a flossing.

The film doesn't neglect their toddler brother (Connor Matheus), whose desire to play in the snow is frustrated by their mom's determination to close a business deal.

In his most understated performance in years, Chase does slow burns as his boss (Pam Grier, a long way from "Foxy Brown") forces him to don outlandish costumes—including a Jack Frost outfit—to pump up his anemic ratings. When he finally confronts and exposes his know-nothing-but-highly-rated TV rival (the toothy John "Dukes of Hazzard" Schneider), it's delightful.

Other incidental pleasures include recurring snowball attacks on the high school principal (Damian Young) and an ice-rink deejay (Iggy Pop) whose playlist is limited to the collected works of Al Martino.

Chris Koch, a veteran TV director for Nickelodeon (which produced this movie), directs with a pleasingly light touch and brisk pacing: The movie clocks in a painless 88 minutes.

Filmed in Canada, "Snow Day" makes the most of its wintry settings and never insults the audience's intelligence—no mean feat for a family film. It's a real crowd-pleaser.

NEWSDAY, 2/11/00, Part II/p. B7, John Anderson

Given that "Snow Day" is a Nickelodeon-Paramount co-production and the mean age of its target audience is 6, it would be unseemly to harp on the predictability of its story line and plot devices. After all, when you're 6, you really haven't seen this stuff a hundred million trillion times.

However: During the sequence when the fat kid (there's always a fat kid) has ketchup poured on his coat in order to simulate blood so he can stop Snowplowman (Chris Elliott) from clearing the roads and preventing a second snow day, a kid behind me, circa 6 years old, said, "He's gonna dip his fries in the ketchup." Sure enough, Snowplowman took one look at the kid and dipped his fries in the ketchup. When 6-year-olds can forecast plot points, you've got trouble.

But "Snow Day," directed by the debuting Chris Koch, certainly is a family-friendly film, with an attractive cast that includes: Mark Webber as Hal Brandston; Emmanuelle Chriqui as Hal's dream girl Claire; Schuyler Fisk as his best girl-pal Lane (you know immediately where this is going) and Jean Smart as Hal's mom, a more benign version of Annette Bening in "American Beauty."

And although casting any movie for kids with both Elliott and Chevy Chase is the cinematic equivalent of child abuse, Chase plays the fool once again as Hal's dad, a weatherman forced to wear hula skirts and snowman suits in order to wage a ratings war with his more attractive and successful rival (John Schneider).

The two-pronged story line involves the longed-for Snow Day and the longed-for Claire: while Hal chases the latter—and incurs the wrath of Claire's loutish boyfriend Chuck (David Paetkau)—his sister Natalie (Zena Grey) and her pals try to keep Snowplowman from opening the roads. It's inane, of course, but goofy enough to keep kids occupied, even if they can guess what happens next.

SIGHT AND SOUND, 7/00, p. 55, Edward Lawrenson

US, the present. Fifteen-year-old Hal Brandston has a crush on his classmate Claire Bonner. His 10-year-old sister Natalie wishes for snow the next day in the hope that her school will have to close. That night, her father Tom, a television weatherman, forecasts snow.

The next day the town is covered in a blanket of snow. Hal and Natalie get a day off school. Natalie conspires with her friends to scupper the attempts of the resident snow-plough operator—known as Snowplowman—to clear the snow from the streets in the hope of securing another day off; Hal resolves to ask Claire out; Tom broadcasts weather reports dressed in ludicrous outfits (much to his shame); and Tom's wife Laura takes a day off work, where she had an important meeting, and looks after her youngest child Randy.

Snowplowman takes one of the children hostage; Natalie negotiates his release. Making use of an interruption during one of Tom's live weather reports, Hal woos Claire on-air; later, having been pursued by her boyfriend Chuck, he kisses her, but then realises he's actually attracted to his friend Lane. Hal tracks down Lane to ask her out. Laura loses a big contract but realises she should spend more time with her family; Natalie and her friends prevent Snowplowman from clearing all the streets free of snow. Having exposed a rival weatherman—who claimed he forecast the freak snow storm—Tom earns respect in his job.

Towards the end of its short-lived existence, the UK film magazine *Neon* ran a regular item which asked celebrities to name their favourite Chevy Chase film (the majority went for *Caddyshack)*. Chase might seem an unlikely hero, especially considering the straight-to-video freefall his career recently experienced, thanks largely to a string of sloppy and forgettable efforts. But *Snow Day,* a hit in the US, reminds us that *Neon*'s tribute wasn't so misplaced after all. A natural physical comedian, Chase brings a nicely unruffled elegance to the various pratfalls and acrobatic shtick the script requires of him. The gags might be as unsubtle as those in the innumerable kids' cartoons the television channel Nickelodeon—one of *Snow Day*'s backers—broadcasts, but they're at least given a lift by Chase's reliably deadpan performance.

As the deceptively stoic weatherman Tom Brandston, Chase recalls the father he played in *National Lampoon's Vacation* But whereas the *National Lampoon* movies from the early 80s revelled in frat-house humour and casual sexism, *Snow Day* is geared towards the family audience. To this end, the film has its fair share of wholesomely anodyne moments (notably, Tom's son Hal's teen romance with Lane). But appropriately enough in a film that celebrates children at play, debut director Chris Koch introduces an endearing unruly streak into the mix (Tom's daughter Natalie's rotund friend can't help breaking wind when faced with even the slightest of dangers; Natalie has, in her armoury of snowballs, one that's coloured urine-yellow). While the pre-teen crowd is likely to appreciate these irreverent moments (at times, the film plays like watered-down Farrelly brothers), there are enough incidental pleasures to keep adults amused: notably Iggy Pop as an Al Martino-obsessed DJ and a deliciously tacky sequence where Hal fetishises his would-be girlfriend's bracelet in his bedroom to the soft-rock chords of Foreigner's "Waiting for a Girl Like You".

Breezy and good-natured throughout, *Snow Day*'s one sour note is its portrayal of Tom's career wife Laura. Rushing off to yet another meeting, she happily admits to her family, "OK I'm a terrible mother." Whereas the rest of the Brandstons end the film having achieved their stated goals (Tom gets respect in his job; Hal a girlfriend; Natalie another day off school), it's Laura who has to make a sacrifice—she loses a big contract at work—in order to prove her worth in the family.

Also reviewed in:
CHICAGO TRIBUNE, 2/11/00, Friday/p. F, Lou Carlozo
NEW YORK TIMES, 2/11/00, p. E16, A. O. Scott
VARIETY, 2/7-13/00, p. 50, Lael Loewenstein

SOFT FRUIT

A Fox Searchlight Pictures and The Australian Film Finance Corporation release in association with The New South Wales Film and Television Office of a Helen Bowden Production. *Executive Producer:* Jane Campion. *Producer:* Helen Bowden. *Director:* Christina Andreef. *Screenplay:* Christina Andreef. *Director of Photography:* Laszlo Baranyai. *Editor:* Jane Moran. *Music:* Antony Partos. *Sound:* Sam Petty. *Casting:* Alison Barrett and Nikki Barrett. *Production Designer:* Sarah Stollman. *Costumes:* Jane Holland. *Running time:* 101 minutes. *MPAA Rating:* R.

CAST: Jeanie Drynan (Patsy); Linal Haft (Vic); Russell Dykstra (Bo); Genevieve Lemon (Josie); Sacha Horler (Nadia); Alicia Talbot (Vera).

LOS ANGELES TIMES, 4/7/00, Calendar/p. 25, Kevin Thomas

"Soft Fruit" asks us to spend 101 minutes with people most of us would take pains to avoid in real life.

The difference between this film, a first feature for writer-director Christina Andreef, and works by her executive producer, Jane Campion, is that Campion can take blue-collar Australians and New Zealanders at their crassest levels and involve us in their fates. Andreef's people are, by and large, as off-putting at the end as they are at the beginning, and they stubbornly remain types rather than emerging as individuals.

Andreef tries for laughter amid tears as a rowdy clan in a small town gathers to be with hearty matriarch Patsy (Jeanie Dryden). At the outset Patsy seems perfectly fine, but she is facing a swift decline and death from some unspecified form of abdominal cancer.

Patsy has been married a long time to Vic (Linal Haft), an irascible and violent Russian immigrant. Her eldest daughter, Josie (Genevieve Lemon), arrives from the United States with her small children, promising herself she won't squabble with her sisters, Nadia (Sacha Horler) and Vera (Alice Talbot). Patsy's son Bo (Russell Dykstra), a drug-abusing biker, has won early parole from prison—we don't know precisely what put him there, but he's clearly the reckless type—but his father has sworn not to let him in the house.

Patsy seems a pleasant-enough woman with a passion for Jacqueline Kennedy that she defends as a harmless flight of fancy, and who would argue with that? Her daughters are all pretty women who are also overweight, so there's much concern among them about what the bathroom scales will reveal. They spar a bit, carry on a lot, but it's crystal-clear they're basically nice women who will pull together to care tenderly for their mother. The clash between Vic (who's not above giving a grown daughter a hard smack if she says something that displeases him) and Bo is predictably violent, but we never do get a clue as to why Vic is such a relentless, thick-headed brute.

The ability to play boisterous comedy against impending tragedy effectively is beyond Andreef's reach, and the entire family comes across as loud and tiresome. None of its behavior is convincing because none of these people seems completely real in the first place. A poor man's "Sweetie"—alas, Andreef was that film's assistant director—"Soft Fruit" is soft-headed.

NEW YORK POST, 3/17/00, p. 49, Jonathan Foreman

"Soft Fruit" is yet another Australian film about the vulgar ghastliness of middle-class Australian families. Writer/director Christina Andreef is a protégé of Jane Campion (who executive produced), so it's has a fine feeling for place—and a particular loathing for Aussie men.

A swiftly moving story about four adult siblings—three squabbling, overweight daughters and a druggy-but-decent jailbird brother—who come home to be with their dying Jackie Kennedy-obsessed mother, Patsy (Jeanie Drynan), it's not especially well-written: It shifts uneasily between grotesque humor and pathos.

It's also compromised by weak performances from Genevieve Lemon as Josie, the Americanized daughter who lives in San Diego, and Linal Haft as a stereotypically uptight and brutal East European father.

NEWSDAY, 3/17/00, Part II/p. B7, Gene Seymour

As with any long-term stay at another family's house, how much you're able to enjoy or endure "Soft Fruit" depends on how long—or whether—you can stand being around the people you're visiting.

Writer-director Christina Andreef, who apprenticed under fellow Australian filmmaker Jane Campion, doesn't make things easy for herself or her audience. She brings us into a suburban household whose seemingly normal state of tumult and tension is being pushed into the red zone by the fall of Patsy (Jeanie Drynan), long-suffering wife to Vic (Linal Haft) and a devoted mum to a burly, surly brood of case studies.

Elder daughter Josie (Genevieve Lemon from Campion's "Sweetie") has been transformed by marriage and motherhood in the United States into the essence of all-American status buffoonery. She is most at odds with her sassy sister Nadia (Sacha Horler), who doesn't let single motherhood slow down her active libido. By contrast, shy Vera (Alicia Talbot) casts about for a way to get pregnant while bypassing sex altogether. Then there's big bad Bo (Russell Dykstra), fresh out of the slammer and leaking trouble whenever he's too far away from his sweet mum's vicinity.

Pa and the kids struggle to subdue their vices—food, drugs, sex and fights—for Patsy's sake. But her own appetite for life is mildly aroused to the point where she and Bo go off for a day at the beach and get high on fresh air and morphine. It's for moments like these that you endure the rest of the movie's frequent indulgences in sentiment and caricature. The latter extreme is especially apparent with Lemon's Josie and even with Patsy, whom Drynan invests with a hint of slyness lacking in her otherwise beatific conception.

Of the rest of the family, Horler's Nadia is given the most dimension and subtlety, while Dykstra's Bo, like the movie itself, veers too sharply between rowdy exuberance and sullen torpor. Still, it's hard to fault Andreef for daring to show a family with all its sags, bags and blotches on display. There's also something to be said for cinematographer Laszlo Baranyai's lushly textured view of Australian suburbia.

VILLAGE VOICE, 3/21/00, p. 144, Jessica Winter

Christina Andreef worked as assistant director on Jane Campion's first three films, and *Soft Fruit*, Andreef's feature-length debut, is a mutant strain of her mentor's domestic horror-comedies (such are the perils of inbreeding, since Campion also executive-produced). Bursting with grotesque burlesques of household relations that make Kate Winslet's clan in *Holy Smoke* look like the Dashwoods and attempting a Campionesque dialectic between bodily functions and family dysfunction, it hurls its humanity at you like rotten tomatoes. To nurse their saintly, dying mother through her last days, four grown siblings descend on their parents' home: Vera, a shy, bovine nurse (Alicia Talbot); Bo, a boorish ex-con (Russell Dykstra); Nadia, a wry, horny young mother (Sacha Horler, thankfully playing in three dimensions); and Josie, an ostentatious, aggressively stupid American transplant. This last coxcomb is provided by Genevieve Lemon, whose overacting makes this simple suburban caricature into more of a monster than the title role she played in Campion's *Sweetie*.

Andreef (aided by DP Laszlo Baranyai) shows more aplomb with place than with people. The family's house is surrounded by lush greenery—Australia has rarely looked so verdant on film—that provides perhaps too sharp a counterpoint to the claustrophobic melodrama within; when Mum is in the yard in her hammock, you can feel the light and the breeze on your face. And when Vera and Bo sneak their mother out of their cramped abode (made the more insufferable by their abusive father) for a restorative, morphine-aided road trip, the fresh air does the film good too. Then it returns inside for a concluding three-ring carnival of grief, the operatics of which are meant as harsh, shit-happens honesty. Andreef, at the least, is never mean, an accusation that can sometimes be leveled at Campion; however, bathos is its own kind of contempt.

Also reviewed in:
NEW REPUBLIC, 4/10/00, p. 29, Stanley Kauffmann
NEW YORK TIMES, 3/17/00, p. E12, A. O. Scott
VARIETY, 6/28-7/11/99, p. 72, David Stratton

SOLAS

A Samuel Goldwyn Films-Fireworks Pictures release in association with Canwest Entertainment of a Maestranza Films production. *Producer:* Antonio P. Pérez.   *Director:* Benito Zambrano. *Screenplay (Spanish with English subtitles):* Benito Zambrano.   *Director of Photography:* Tote Trenas.   *Editor:* Fernando Pardo.   *Music:* Antonio Meliveo.   *Sound:* Jorge Marín and Carlos Faroulo. *Production Designer:* Lala Obrero.   *Running time:* 98 minutes.   *MPAA Rating:* Not Rated.

CAST: Ana Fernández (Maria);   María Galiana (Mother);   Paco De Osca (Father);   Carlos Alvarez-Novoa (Neighbor);   Juan Fernández (Juan);   Antonio Dechent (Doctor).

LOS ANGELES TIMES, 9/29/00, Calendar/p. 4, Kevin Thomas

"Solas," a film that attests to the timeless power of simplicity, marks the feature debut of writer-director Benito Zambrano, destined to take his place in the front ranks of Spanish filmmakers. "Solas," whose title refers to two women, a mother and daughter, both alone in their own way, is one of those quiet, unassuming little movies that sneaks up on you and knocks you for a loop.

Ana Fernandez is the daughter, Maria, 35 and single. She's just moved into a once-elegant but now-faded apartment house in the dangerous, run-down neighborhood of San Bernardo in Seville. The hard-drinking Maria might be beautiful were she not so gaunt-looking and embittered. She lands a job as a cleaning woman working the night shift in a luxe office building—clearly the best work she can hope for.

She is one of four children of a brutal, drunken peasant (Paco De Osca), who is in a nearby hospital recovering from surgery. Her siblings have all moved to northern Spain, leaving her to cope with a father she justifiably hates and with a mother, Rosa (Maria Galiana), she cannot respect for having put up with him.

Maria has seriously underestimated her mother, who has accompanied her husband from their village and who has been welcomed by her daughter with an undisguised lack of enthusiasm. Rosa is a plump, plainly dressed woman who looks to be in her late 60s. She may well have been a beauty in her youth and continues to radiate an inner glow—should you take the trouble to notice.

She is a traditional-minded woman who long ago has learned to accept her lot in life, to look inside herself for the strength to endure and to tap into her moral imagination for sustenance. We are never told whether she is devoutly religious or not, but Rosa is a woman of towering spiritual strength, refusing to slide into the bitterness and cynicism consuming her daughter, accepting people and situations as she finds them.

One of the key recipients of Rosa's attentiveness is her daughter's neighbor, a handsome, dignified older man (Carlos Alvarez-Novoa), a lonely widower who has only his dog for a companion. As Maria copes with the consequences of having becoming involved with a virile but cruelly cold truck driver, a man surely not unlike her father, Rosa awaits the recovery of her husband, who berates her as a stupid old woman but cannot escape intimations of his own mortality.

Rosa is drawn into a friendship with her daughter's courtly neighbor, who treats her with kindness and respect from a man for the first time in her life. In the most overpowering of several extraordinary sequences, Rosa calmly copes with the neighbor's diarrhea, good-humoredly preserving his dignity, getting him into his shower and making his bed. So serenely in command of her every gesture is Galiana that her Rosa becomes for a moment the eternal nurturing wife and mother figure. The neighbor and Rosa exchange a glance that tells us in an instant the depth of their mutual feelings.

The sheer implacability of Rosa's glowing serenity cannot help but ultimately impact upon her daughter, and the way in which Zambrano resolves "Solas" reveals his mastery of his medium and his grasp of human nature. Alternately heart-wrenching, dismaying, raw and even funny, "Solas" is ultimately a wonderfully warm and embracing experience.

NEW YORK POST, 9/8/00, p. 46, Jonathan Foreman

"Solas" (it means "alone" in Spanish) is a lovely, intelligent film from Spain about recognizable human beings with real-life problems.

Mother (Maria Galiana), an elderly woman from a country village, has come to the city where her nasty jealous, abusive husband (Paco De Osca) is having an operation. During his convalescence in the hospital she stays with their angry, alienated 35-year-old daughter Maria (Ana Fernandez).

Somehow Maria's mother has remained a decent, kind person and she is recognized as such by Maria's courtly septuagenarian neighbor downstairs (Carlos Alvarez-Novoa) who lives alone, but not unhappily, with his dog Achilles.

While Maria struggles with the knowledge that she's pregnant, her mother and the neighbor form a restrained, polite but romantic bond.

In a subtle layered way, and without inspiring depression, first-time writer/director Zambrano contrasts two kinds of loneliness: that of an abused wife in a rural community and that of her single friendless daughter in a big anonymous city.

It's a shame that the ending feels so rushed and that Fernandez' emotional range seems limited to rage and sullen silence, because Galiana gives an absolutely superb and moving performance in the film's central role.

NEWSDAY, 9/8/00, Part II/p. B10, Gene Seymour

The temptation, when encountering such a movie as "Solas," is to grab your head and bury it in your lap in order to keep your senses from absorbing yet another grimly realistic family drama with subtitles. Yet there is much about writer-director Benito Zambrano's film that makes it stand out from other efforts, with or without subtitles, to depict simple people with complicated problems.

Yes, the set-up is familiar, often painfully so: Maria (Ana Fernandez) is in her mid-30s and living alone in a squalid neighborhood in a dismal Spanish city. She is mad at the world in general and at her parents in particular, whom she blames for having little to took forward to except jobs cleaning houses for rich people and doomed relationships with men she regards as losers at first sight.

It's Maria's miserable luck that her father (Paco De Osca), who's as much a wretch as she is, needs surgery in a nearby hospital. Having nowhere to go while her husband recovers, Maria's mother (Maria Galiana) stays with her daughter, who has just discovered that, on top of everything else, she's pregnant.

Back in 1950s England, this type of story would be called "kitchen sink melodrama" with the emphasis on "kitsch." But Zambrano, who studied at Gabriel Garcia Marquez's Havana-based Cinema School of San Antonio de Banos, displays both keen observation and a soft touch that keep his story grounded in reality without swerving into soapy bathos. "Solas," which is Spanish for "alone," uses the dynamics of this normally claustrophobic genre to inquire about the subtle but important distinctions between loneliness and being alone. And it does so without turning its characters into attitudes-with-clothes.

His actors greatly help this process along. As the dotty elderly widower who lives next door with a smarter-than-average dog, Carlos Alvarez-Novoa carries himself with the kind of graceful aplomb you tend to expect from a professional dancer. Fernandez has spiky energy to burn as Maria. All are upstaged by the seemingly unassuming conviction of Galiana's performance as the mother. The strength that builds from her character's passive surface illuminates all of "Solas" by the time it ends.

Also reviewed in:
CHICAGO TRIBUNE, 9/22/00, Friday/p. B, Michael Wilmington
NEW REPUBLIC, 10/2/00, p. 30, Stanley Kauffmann
NEW YORK TIMES, 9/8/00, p. E10, Stephen Holden
VARIETY, 3/29-4/4/99, p. 74, David Stratton
WASHINGTON POST, 10/20/00, Weekend/p. 42, Desson Howe

SOLOMON & GAENOR

A Sony Pictures Classics release of an S4C/Film Four presentation with the Arts Councils of England and Wales of an APT Film & Television production. *Executive Producer:* Andy Porter and David Green. *Producer:* Sheryl Crown. *Director:* Paul Morrison. *Screenplay (English, Welsh and Yiddish with English subtitles):* Paul Morrison. *Director of Photography:* Nina Kellgren. *Editor:* Kant Pan. *Music:* Ilona Sekacz. *Sound:* Richard Dyer and (music) Gerry O'Riordan. *Sound Editor:* Danny Longhurst. *Casting:* Joan McCann. *Production Designer:* Hayden Pearce. *Art Director:* Frazer Pearce. *Special Effects:* Richard Reeve. *Costumes:* Maxine Brown. *Make-up:* Gill Rees. *Running time:* 110 minutes. *MPAA Rating:* R.

CAST: Ioan Gruffudd (Solomon); Nia Roberts (Gaenor); Sue Jones Davies (Gwen); William Thomas (Idris); Mark Lewis Jones (Crad); Maureen Lipman (Rezl); David Horovitch (Isaac); Bethan Ellis Owen (Bronwen); Adam Jenkins (Thomas); Cyril Shaps (Ephraim); Daniel Kaye (Philip);   Elliot Cantor (Benjamin);   Steffan Rhodri (Noah Jones);   Emyr Wyn (Reverend Roberts); Julian Lewis Jones (Wyn); Arwyn Davies (Huw); Dai Morgan (Geraint); Rhys Evans (Rhys); Helen Griffin (Aunt Myfanwy); Gwyn Vaughan Jones (Trefor Lloyd); Alan Schwartz (Uncle Mennasseh); Anne Sessions (Aunt Sadie); Olivia Simova (Naomi); Barry Davies (Mannie Silvergilt); Daniel Levy (Rabbi Wolfe); Derek Smith (Jewish Man); Jane Manuel (Jewish Woman); Daniel Pruchnie (Jewish Child); Ri Richards (Glass Woman); Gill Griffiths (First Woman); Manon Eames (Welsh Woman at Door); Dafydd Wyn Roberts (Old Tramp); Ceri Evans (Ceridwen); Huw Emlyn (Barman Alun); Winston Evans (Postman); Siôn Hopkins (Sleepy John).

LOS ANGELES TIMES, 8/25/00, Calendar/p. 8, Kevin Thomas

By the time the heavy-handed "Solomon & Gaenor" is over, it has become such a punishing exercise in the self-evident that one is left numb and eager for escape.

The precious few Welsh pictures that surface in the U.S. show a country gorgeous and populated by people of nobility and good humor. This is not one of those pictures. Although the countryside is as beautiful as ever, it is populated by people puritanical and narrow-minded in the extreme.

The setting for this 1999 Oscar nominee for best foreign-language film is a 1911 coal-mining town, the kind familiar from "The Corn Is Green" and "How Green Was My Valley." On the other side of a mountain is another community, in which an ever-increasing number of Jews from Eastern Europe has settled.

Among them is a family from Lithuania that runs a pawnshop, where it also sells fabric. One day the store's regular outside salesman, who crosses over the mountain to the coal town to sell cotton fabric door-to-door, is unavailable, and the family's studious eldest son, Solomon (Ioan Gruffudd), is sent in his place.

In the course of his rounds, he knocks on the door of a row house, the home of a miner's family, and its eldest daughter, Gaenor (Nia Roberts), answers. She is lovely and demure; he is handsome, shy, romantic. It is completely natural that the attraction between them should be mutual and nearly instantaneous.

Both come from oppressively strict religious families, and Solomon's parents would no more accept Gaenor than hers would accept Solomon, who reflexively passes himself off as a Gentile, calling himself Sam Livingstone.

You understand Solomon's urge to rebel and Gaenor's equally strong urge to respond to him. You comprehend how a romance could develop so swiftly between the two of them that Solomon could lose his bearings.

Even so, what's hard to understand is that Solomon risks getting Gaenor pregnant without telling her that he is a Jew. Honesty on his part would have given them the chance to weigh carefully the depth of their love for each other and deal with the reality that commitment to each other would result in both being cast out by their families and necessitate a workable plan of escape and survival.

But, sad to say, Solomon proves to be a coward and a fool, and his silence sets in motion near-inevitable tragedy that writer-director Paul Morrison stretches out for another increasingly depressing and ponderous hour.

This is lamentable, for Morrison has actually painstakingly laid the foundation for a much stronger and more original film. He sets his story in motion with economy and style, and he adroitly makes implicit the point that people for whom life is hard and uncertain cling all the more tightly to their religion for sustenance, becoming increasingly intolerant of all other beliefs.

"Solomon & Gaenor" recalls Bo Widerberg's 1967 art-house hit "Elvira Madigan," in which a married army officer runs off with a tightrope walker in 19th century Sweden. They were as much outcasts as Solomon and Gaenor in early 20th century Wales.

But Widerberg, a socially conscious filmmaker if ever there was one, knew how to play up a doomed romantic idyll and avoid weighing it down with more commentary than it could bear. Besides, he had the wisdom to have the whole ill-starred romance play out to the strains of Mozart's Piano Concerto No. 21 (Second Movement).

NEW YORK POST, 8/25/00, p. 59, Lou Lumenick

"Romeo and Juliet" live again in this tepid tale of star-crossed lovers in 1910 Wales.

Welsh heartthrob Ioan Gruffudd plays Solomon, who meets the beautiful Gaenor (Nia Roberts), a coal miner's daughter, while selling cotton goods door to door.

Solomon decides to hide his Jewishness from Gaenor because his parents, who are Orthodox, wouldn't approve of his relationship with a gentile girl.

Neither would Gaenor's family, Protestants who view Solomon, who calls himself Sam, with deep suspicion anyway.

Things go from terrible to tragic when Gaenor becomes pregnant with Solomon's child.

Even with a mini-pogrom and a strike, director Paul Morrison's film—curiously Oscar-nominated for Best Foreign-Language film this year (about half the dialogue is in Yiddish and Welsh)—is more interesting than compelling, thanks to performances that are way too restrained for the semi-melodramatic material and pacing that's positively funereal.

NEWSDAY, 8/25/00, Part II/p. B/13, Jan Stuart

Cinema's crowded population of star-crossed lovers makes room for an arresting pair of newcomers in "Solomon and Gaenor," a tearjerker that provides a heady ethnic wrinkle on the Romeo and Juliet formula.

Poverty and anti-Semitism are the gulfs that separate the two families at the center of this period love story set in Wales around 1911. Solomon (Ioan Gruffudd) hails from a devout Orthodox Jewish family that cobbles together a living running a pawnshop and drapery business. Gaenor (Nia Roberts) is one of four children in a churchgoing Welsh mining family. The two meet when Solomon makes his door-to-door rounds peddling cotton samples in Gaenor's neighborhood.

The romance that quickly evolves is steeped in deception. The aggressively inhospitable climate for Jews compels Solomon to conceal his real identity from Gaenor. Using a pseudonym, he stashes his ritual undergarments behind a rock before their rendezvous and fabricates stories about his family when meeting Gaenor's family.

The familiarity of their archetypal romance is offset to a certain degree by the sheer novelty of the cultural clash that portends its doom. Writer-director Paul Morrison lends a convincing measure of authenticity to his depiction of a Jewish family fleeing from Russian pogroms, only to find the same-old-same-old in their country of refuge. Surely you would have to wait a long time before you would again hear Yiddish and Welsh and English spoken in the same movie; for this achievement alone, "Solomon and Gaenor" might have earned its Oscar nomination for Best Foreign Film.

"Solomon and Gaenor" may well find its strongest supporters among audiences gratified to see a validation of Jewish emigre life that reaches beyond the usual borders. For others, the predictable vein of prejudice and melancholy running through the film may seem like old news. It's the sort of well-crafted and sincerely performed downer that defies criticism. As with an arduous round of exercise, you know it's good for you, even as you wish there was a bitter pill you could swallow to get the job done quicker.

SIGHT AND SOUND, 5/99, p. 56, Simon Louvish

In a small village in the Welsh valleys, around 1911, a young Jewish peddler (or 'pacman') named Solomon meets Gaenor, the eldest daughter of a local family of mineworkers. There is an instant attraction between them. Gaenor doesn't realise Solomon is Jewish and calling himself Sam he pretends to be a Christian from across the valley. Solomon's parents Isaac and Rezl run a pawnshop-drapery. Smitten by Gaenor, Solomon makes her a dress, and soon they become lovers.

Gaenor asks to meet Solomon's parents, but he cannot now reveal his Jewish faith. The village is embroiled in an industrial dispute with the mine's owners, and both Gaenor's father and her brother Crad are involved in the miners' response. Gaenor's world is shattered when her new fiancé Noah denounces her in the chapel as a fornicator, pregnant by a stranger. She is put under the care of her family, and will be taken to her distant aunt to give birth after which she'll be forced to give up her baby. Gaenor tracks down her lover's home and, discovering his Jewishness, tries to speak to his parents, but they cannot accept that the child she is carrying is their grandchild.

As industrial unrest and poverty increase in the valley the hotheads march on Jewish shops, accusing the Jews of enriching themselves at their expense. Isaac and Rezl's shop is razed, and they have to seek shelter elsewhere. Isaac warns Solomon, in the midst of the unrest, that if he persists in seeing the gentile girl he will be disowned. Solomon nevertheless tries to see Gaenor, and is beaten severely by Crad. Refusing to give up on Gaenor, Solomon finds out her whereabouts and treks, bleeding, through snow and storm, across the valley, to the remote farmhouse where she is confined. Reunited, they perform their own Jewish wedding together but he dies in her arms. That same night Gaenor gives birth to her child. Gaenor is taken to a chapel where she has to give up her baby. Idris and Crad transport Solomon's coffin back to the valleys.

Set before World War I, in a period of raw industrial conflict, Paul Morrison's film focuses on two communities at the bottom of Britain's class hierarchies, whose proximity in harsh economic circumstances drives them to hostility. The Jewish migrants who came to England, Scotland and Wales at the turn of the twentieth century were fleeing hardship and persecution in Europe, much as today's developing-world migrants seek asylum in what they hope will be a tolerant place. But for a younger generation, represented here by Solomon and Gaenor, the rigid faiths of both communities make building an individual bridge all but impossible.

Solomon and Gaenor is impeccable in its liberal intentions—respectably produced, nicely photographed, reasonably well acted in most cases—and appeared to induce a proper modicum of cathartic tears at the screening I attended. It is courageous in taking on a less than entertaining prospect: the self-destructive dourness both of the chapel-ridden Welsh and the law-ridden Orthodox Jewish families whose very identity is formed by their respective separation from the wider world. In one poignant scene Solomon and Gaenor's Welsh family exchange well-memorised Biblical quotations. Both communities derive their faith from the same source, but this is not enough to bring them together.

However, the movie is unable to escape from the conventions of its own filmic heritage. Despite the protestations of the director and producers that they didn't wish to make a typical BBC type period piece, this is exactly what the film most resembles. Like many of the current crop of Lottery-funded and television-backed movies, *Solomon and Gaenor* appears (by choice or necessity) to have followed the prevailing formulas beloved of media commissioners, with predictably bland results. There is little evidence of directorial flair which would bring the plodding script to life. What the film lacks most is a darker subtext below the surface of the conventional craft

Ioan Gruffudd makes an attractive lead, but neither script nor direction appears to have considered a different slant on his doomed amour. In the context of the period, as a Jew who seduces a gentile girl without revealing his true identity, he has in fact set her up for ruination in her own prejudiced society. But the film only sees his tragic destiny, not his internal flaws. (Or does he die for his sins? Perhaps there is more of the Orthodox spirit here after all.)

Much better and more ambivalent is Mark Lewis Jones as Gaenor's brother Crad, a brooding hulk of a man visibly torn up by his repressed rage as a worker subject to the whims of distant bosses, searching for scapegoats among the closest strangers. Nia Roberts as Gaenor gives a moving performance within the limits of the stereotyped victim supplied to her by the script, and

David Horovitch as Solomon's father achieves a melancholy dignity. But Maureen Lipman should be banned from playing Jewish mothers until at least 2010.

VILLAGE VOICE, 8/29/00, p. 140, Jessica Winter

The majority of U.K. releases that enjoy art-house runs on these shores fall into one of two categories: the heartburning comedy hawking daft Britquirks or the stiff-limbed costume downer plowing cursed love and bleakly gorgeous soggy vistas. *Solomon & Gaenor* falls into the latter column; despite an acute eye for detail in rendering a coal-mining Welsh town in 1911, Paul Morrison's relentlessly unsurprising staging of a Romeo-and-Juliet story fetishizes its accelerating tragedies with morbid solemnity.

Solomon (Ioan Gruffudd) is a thoughtful, kindhearted packman out of the early chapters of a Thomas Hardy novel (Morrison's plottings and deployment of landscape nod to *The Return of the Native* and *Jude the Obscure*). The boy is also an Orthodox Jew, which he conceals from chapel-going Gaenor (Nia Roberts) when he comes to her door selling his wares. He woos the bashful, fidgety girl by making a dress for her; this endearing bit of courtship strategy is sweet and unforced, but only impels candlelit pans of forbidden hayloft missionary-position sex. Disastrous disclosures and betrayals begin accumulating long before Solomon's real identity comes to light, but the multiple conflicts of class and culture (the miners are on strike, and economic strain only worsens already existing religious tensions) are hastily sketched and the dialogue drags with awkward exposition. Solomon & Gaenor does work up a lather during its deliriously pitched last reel: a bloody interlude worthy of *Fight Club*, a body-horrific sex/birth/death smashup aching for a Bruno Dumont remake, and a coda purloined from *Au Hasard Balthazar*. Indeed, the only dramatic suspense of *Solomon & Gaenor* lies in wondering which of the pair will end up as the sacrificial donkey on love's stone-cold altar.

Also reviewed in:
CHICAGO TRIBUNE, 10/27/00, Friday/p. E, John Petrakis
NEW YORK TIMES, 8/25/00, p. E10, Stephen Holden
VARIETY, 3/15-21/99, p. 43, Derek Elley
WASHINGTON POST, 9/15/00, p. C5, Stephen Hunter
WASHINGTON POST, 9/15/00, Weekend/p. 47, Desson Howe

SOUND AND FURY

An Artistic License and Unapix Entertainment Inc. release of an Aronson Fil Associates/FilmFour/Public Policy Productions production in association with Thirteen/WNET and Channel 4. *Producer:* Roger Weisberg. *Director:* Josh Aronson. *Director of Photography:* Brian Danitz, Kenny Gronningsater, Mead Hunt, Gordy Waterman, and Brett Wiley. *Editor:* Ann Collins. *Music:* Mark Suozzo. *Sound:* Jose Aviles, Daniel Brooks, Brian Buckley, Francisco Latorre, John Murphy, Robert Reed, Juan Rodriguez, and Dean Sarjeant. *Sound Editor:* Dow McKeever and Marsha Moore. *Casting:* Liz Lewis. *Running time:* 80 minutes. *MPAA Rating:* Not Rated.

CAST: Scott Davidson (Voice of Peter Artinian).

CHRISTIAN SCIENCE MONITOR, 10/27/00, p. 15, David Sterritt

When is a disability not a disability? This paradoxical question is explored by filmmaker Josh Aronson in "Sound and Fury," the most riveting documentary to arrive in theaters this year.

The film centers on two branches of a Long Island, N.Y, family. One of the fathers is deaf, the other can hear, and both have young children diagnosed with hearing disorders. Searching their consciences and discussing the issue with their wives and others, they wrestle with the question of whether to accept a surgical procedure that may allow their youngsters to hear. Two of the parents lean toward giving their offspring greater chances of a normal life. But the others feel differently, arguing that deafness is not a handicap or limitation at all, and that choosing to hear betrays the "deaf culture" they and their friends have learned to cherish.

Aronson's straightforward filmmaking conveys the complexity of the social, political, and medical issues connected with these matters; and just as important, it etches a vivid portrait of the bedrock human emotions aroused by endless debates involving a wide range of family members and outside experts. The result is gripping, touching, and enlightening.

LOS ANGELES TIMES, 11/17/00, Calendar/p. 22, Kevin Thomas

Josh Aronson's "Sound and Fury," as illuminating and comprehensive as it is heart-wrenching, is an example of what the documentary can accomplish at its most vital and engaging. There is such a sense of immediacy to the film that it is as if we are watching life unfolding before our very eyes. In a way we are, for Aronson and his associates spent a year and a half recording the lives of the extended Artinian family as it undergoes a crisis that will tear it apart.

Peter and Chris Artinian are brothers, family men in their 30s who live near each other and their parents on Long Island. Peter; his wife, Nita; their bright 6-year-old daughter, Heather; and their two infant sons are all deaf. Chris, like his parents, has normal hearing, as do his wife, Mari, and their eldest child. But one of their twin baby sons, Peter III, is deaf, as are Mari's parents.

Chris and Mari are eager to have little Peter undergo a cochlear implant as soon as possible, because this relatively new device is more effective the earlier the child receives it. Meanwhile, Heather—who signs, as do all the Artinians, deaf or not—says that she would like to have a cochlear implant so she can communicate better with her playmates who have normal hearing. Her parents, while wary, initially are open-minded about the procedure, with Nita going so far as to investigate undergoing the procedure herself, until she learns that her age works against her.

The more Nita and Peter investigate a cochlear implant for Heather, the more defensive they become. They fear losing her to the world of normal hearing; they feel that those with normal hearing fail to respect deaf culture and consider the deaf and especially their education to be inferior and their opportunities limited.

The flash point occurs when they learn from a mother with normal hearing whose daughter has adjusted well to a cochlear implant, that Heather will be encouraged not to use sign language for fear that it will become too much of a crutch for her. The woman speaks in a respectful manner but without realizing how devastating her words will be to Peter and Nita.

Their fears escalate to the extent that they end up moving to Frederick, Md., site of a 130-year-old school for the deaf and center of a large, closely knit deaf community. It doesn't look like Heather will be getting a cochlear implant any time in the near future. Peter's parents, his mother especially, and sister-in-law Mari try mightily to get through to him and Nita in arguing that Heather, with her exceptional intelligence, will have a richer life with greater options with an implant—if it is done soon. They say early on they want Heather to move easily between the world of hearing and that of deafness, but are so soon in retreat that they fail to see Mari as a fine example of this, a woman with normal hearing who since infancy has communicated with her parents in sign language.

"Sound and Fury" has got to be a consciousness-raiser for one and all, but it has special meaning and impact for those of us who have firsthand experience with deafness in the family. The challenge "Sound and Fury" illuminates so thoroughly is for all the institutions and professionals involved in dealing with the hearing-impaired to join in creating a climate in which deaf parents can feel secure that permitting cochlear implants for their children does not mean that they will lose them.

"Sound and Fury" ends on an encouraging note: The National Assn. of the Deaf is reconsidering its negative stand on the implants.

NEW YORK, 11/6/00, p. 85, Peter Rainer

Josh Aronson's *Sound and Fury*, a documentary about two families contemplating the controversial use of cochlear implants to boost their deaf children's auditory capabilities, gets at the intense divisions within the deaf community over the ways in which their handicap is to be perceived by both the hearing and non-hearing worlds. These divisions, which run as deep as any long-standing rift between countries and can be just as hurtful, are given a fair airing.

NEWSDAY, 10/25/00, Part II/p. B11, John Anderson

The question seems simple enough: Say your child were deaf and there was a way to allow that child to hear. Would you do it?

The question sounds foolishly simple. So let's complicate it: Say you were deaf yourself, your entire identity, culture and world view inalterably tied to the silent, signing world of the deaf Would your child's removal from that world be tantamount to abandonment and betrayal?

Such are the contrapuntal aspects of "Sound and Fury," Josh Aronson's intimate, wrenching documentary centered on the Artinian family of Glen Cove and their coming to terms—or not—with the controversial cochlear implant. Before addressing the convoluted arguments over implants, however, one needs to address the convoluted structure of the Artinians themselves.

At the center of the story is 5-year-old Heather, an intelligent, precociously self-possessed little girl who announces to her parents, Peter and Nita, both deaf, that she wants to hear. Meanwhile, Peter's hearing brother, Chris, and his hearing wife, Mari (whose parents are both deaf), have twin boys, one of whom, also named Peter, is also born deaf

Director Aronson doesn't venture into the genetic, generation-hopping deafness among the various Artinians, but he's right in the thick of their philosophical wrangling. While Chris and Mari are unflinching in their support of an implant for their son—despite Mari's mother's hysterical accusation that the implant is commensurate with maternal rejection—the elder Peter balks at one for Heather. She'll never have a deaf culture, he says, and at the same time never really be part of the hearing world.

You can't say he doesn't have a point. Or a passion that's irresistible. But it seems clear enough that his anguish is rooted in a fear that his child will no longer be his own.

Aronson seems to be everywhere. A verbal Waterloo waged at a family barbecue by Peter and his mother, Marianne—the ultimate voice of reason in this movie—is too close for comfort. That Marianne, and Chris, tearfully accuse Peter of child abuse shows the level of heat at which the arguments rage.

Perhaps the most revealing of episodes Aronson captures is Nita's own consultation on the cochlear implant—for herself. Once told how much lower the success rate is for adults, however, her attitude changes—and so, not mysteriously, does Heather's.

There are no unsympathetic characters in "Sound and Fury," just ideas that both inform and inflame. Ambiguity is a co-star of the movie, although it's hard to imagine that one scene—the testing of baby Peter's implant a few weeks after surgery—will do anything but bring tears to your eyes.

VILLAGE VOICE, 10/31/00, p. 170, Amy Taubin

Josh Aronson's thoroughly engrossing documentary *Sound and Fury* is as much about children's rights as it is about the impact of cochlear-implant technology on a family in which deafness runs through three generations. Peter Artinian, his wife, Nita, and their three children are all deaf. When their five-year-old, Heather, asks to have a cochlear implant, they feel betrayed by her desire to become part of the hearing world. But they try to keep an open mind while investigating this new technology, which uses tiny computers to enhance hearing. The earlier the procedure is performed, the more effective it is in enabling speech acquisition. The conflict between Heather's parents and the hearing members of the Artinian family becomes more heated when Peter's hearing brother and sister-in-law, Chris and Mari, decide to give their 18-month-old deaf son the implant despite the protests of Mari's deaf parents.

Peter and Nita believe that cochlear implants are a threat to the survival of the culture in which their identity is based. Many of the deaf people in the film share their views. "I was happy when my children were born deaf," says Peter. "Silence is peaceful. Signing is more expressive than speech." To their hearing relatives, however, it seems as if Peter and Nita are acting against their daughter's best interests, not to mention her desires, to affirm their own identity. And *Sound and Fury,* which gives both sides of the Artinian family a forum to debate their views, seems weighted in favor of the implants. Aronson translates sign language into voice-over that interprets not only what deaf people say but the emotional charge behind their words—which, paradoxically, reinforces the barrier between the hearing members of the audience and the deaf people in the film. (The version showing at Film Forum also has subtitles.) Heather, who never seems totally convinced by her parents' arguments and warnings against "the cochlear," emerges as a tragic figure whose desire to hear, and thus to move between the worlds of the hearing and the deaf, is suppressed by her parents' need to mold her in their own image.

Also reviewed in:
CHICAGO TRIBUNE, 1/12/01, Friday/p. L, John Petrakis
NEW YORK TIMES, 4/8/00, p. B16, Anita Gates
VARIETY, 4/3-9/00, p. 60, Joe Leydon

SOUTHPAW

A Shooting Gallery release of a Bord Scannan na Eireann/The Irish Film Board/Radio Telefis Eireann/Channel 4 presentation of a Treasure Films production. *Executive Producer:* Clare Duignan and Rod Stoneman. *Producer:* Robert Walpole and Paddy Breathnach. *Director:* Liam McGrath. *Director of Photography:* Cían De Buitléar. *Editor:* James E. Dalton. *Music:* Dario Marianelli. *Sound:* Simon J. Willis. *Sound Editor:* Annette Stone, Anthony Litton, and Gráinne D'Alton. *Running time:* 77 minutes. *MPAA Rating:* Not Rated.

CAST: Francis Barrett (Himself);   Chick Gillen (Coach);   Tom Humphries (Sports Writer); Colum Flynn (Ennis Boxing Club); Nicolas Cruz Hernandez (Irish Boxing Coach, Barcelona Olympics);   Gerry Callan (Sports Writer);   Jim McGee (Sports Commentator); Eamonn Hunt (Narrator).

LOS ANGELES TIMES, 4/7/00, Calendar/p. 16, Kevin Thomas

Francis Barrett of Galway would seem to be a young man with everything going for him. At 19 he's handsome, well-spoken, has a radiant smile and winning personality and is a boxer of great promise. Yet he grew up a social pariah in his native Ireland, for he is a Traveller.

"Southpaw," Liam McGrath's engaging documentary on Barrett, obviously was not made for the international audience, for it assumes we know all about the Travellers. They are an ancient group of itinerant people whose history is lost in time and who today live in trailer communities on open land which they do not own and from which they are periodically expelled. They apparently subsist on odd jobs and once were tinkers, repairing pots and pans. It would seem that their American equivalents on the social ladder would be so-called "trailer trash" or squatters. We are repeatedly told how the Travellers are spat upon in the streets of Ireland and are subject to other forms of blatant discrimination.

It's impossible to understand how the Irish are able to identify Travellers outside their trailer communities, for they look just like them. Travellers seem not to have any traces of continental Gypsy ancestry, and in fact it is said that Travellers consider being called a Gypsy a slur.

In short, for an American audience, it's a shame McGrath spent no time at all in exploring this unique, marginalized culture that shaped Barrett, a modest, neatly dressed young man of such likability and civility that he could easily dine with the queen.

This documentary concentrates principally on Barrett's relationship with Chick Gillen, a Galway barber and former fighter (it's never made clear whether he's a Traveller). He is Barrett's mentor, a sturdy and loving father figure who coaches him so effectively that Francis becomes the first Traveller ever to represent Ireland at the Olympics. He boxes in Atlanta in 1996, where he wins his first match and loses the second but returns home a champ and local hero. (That did not prevent the Galway City Council from ordering the eviction of Francis' 17-trailer community from the Hillside section of town.)

Upon his return we follow Francis' amateur career as he goes after Irish and English titles. He's encouraged by his pretty bride, Kathleen, with whom he moves to a London Traveller encampment. A sophisticated, champion Afro-Cuban boxer (we'd love to know more about him too) pops up from time to time to lend Francis crucial advice; he opines that Francis has outgrown Chick and must seek a more experienced coach if he is to gain success this summer at the Sydney Olympic Games. "SouthPaw" is warm and appealing, but there clearly was a far more informative and comprehensive film to be made of the life and world of Francis Barrett.

NEW YORK POST, 4/7/00, p. 55, Lou Lumenick

"Southpaw" is a minor addition to the recent plethora of fiction and non-fiction films about boxing.

There may well be a good feature lurking in the story of Francis Barrett, an Irish gypsy fighter who, at the 1996 Atlanta Olympics, became the first of his people to compete internationally.

Those possibilities are barely hinted at in Liam McGrath's earnest and pedestrian little documentary, which is interesting but not particularly involving.

McGrath extensively employs unfocused interviews with journalists and news footage, which does little to explain the background of Ireland's gypsies, the Traveling Community.

Barrett's achievement was especially notable because he constantly faced eviction from the trailer camp where he was living without heat or hot water.

"Southpaw" does not offer much in the way of exciting boxing footage.

Its greatest selling point is the 19-year-old Barrett, who is charming and articulate, but whose thick accent may be somewhat challenging for American ears.

NEWSDAY, 4/7/00, Part II/p. B7, Gene Seymour

"Southpaw" is as mild-mannered and as good-natured as its subject: Irish light-welterweight boxer Francis Barrett, whose failure to win gold at the 1996 Olympics made him no less of a hero to the "Traveller" community from which he came. Those with intimate knowledge about contemporary Ireland understand that to be a Traveller—a group of gypsies who camp out in trailer parks on the outskirts of Galway—is to be consigned to the lowest, most despised tier on the social strata.

So the fact that Barrett competed at all in Atlanta was considered something of a sociocultural breakthrough. And the fact that Barrett thrashed one of his international opponents (a victory watched by the folks back home with near-startling reserve) elevated the 19-year-old to a higher competitive plateau.

But as Liam McGrath's documentary demonstrates in gentle but firmly directed strokes, the odds that Barrett faces in his advancement are tall, wide and stiff. As his post-Olympic bouts frequently demonstrate, Barrett's reach is as short as he is (though his left, when it connects, is a mini-bazooka). Moreover, he lives in a community that lacks running water or electricity. So, as you can imagine, his home training facilities are less than ideal.

He does have, in his corner, a full-time barber and part-time coach named Chick Gillen, whose paternal solicitousness and Buddha toughness are reminiscent of the late, legendary American trainer Cus D'Amato. Gillen brought "Frankie" in from the trailers to his Olympic Boxing Club, whose grand name belies its scruffy, low-rent surroundings. He exhorts Barrett to take no prisoners in the ring with the tenderness of a veteran hit man. Yet by film's end, it's clear that Barrett's scrappy courage isn't enough to take him to the next level. Journalists and boxing touts in London and Galway hint that Barrett may have to leave Chick's nest altogether if he wants to reach the top.

Exactly how Barrett himself feels about all this remains curiously out of reach. Apparently, it isn't in the kid's nature to reflect or react too demonstrably about either the social or athletic forces affecting his life. And while you're curious about the coiled-steel will that props up Barrett's ingratiating personality, the film leaves you grasping at phantoms where revelation should be. Still, it's a graceful effort, spiced with subtle humor and vivid photography, especially—and oddly—away from the ring.

SIGHT AND SOUND, 3/99, p. 53, Geoffrey Macnab

This documentary depicts two years in the life of Francis Barrett, a young traveller from Galway. Coached from an early age by Chick Gillen, a local barber, Francis shows a rare talent for boxing. Despite training in a rickety gym outside the caravans where his family live, he qualifies for the Irish Olympic team for Atlanta in 1996 and gets to carry the Irish flag during the opening ceremony. He wins his first bout easily. Although beaten in his second, he is already a national hero and relishes the chance to represent the travelling people in the media glare.

After the Olympics, Francis marries and moves to London. He works in a variety of casual jobs and starts training at a new gym with a London coach. He competes in both English and Irish ABAS. Barrett wins the English title but is defeated in the Irish final. Although tempted to turn professional, his mind is set on the Sydney Olympics. As the film ends, he still has to qualify for the Games. Advisors and journalists believe that he has come as far as he can with Chick and that he'll have to train with a new coach in order to fulfil his potential.

When Frank Launder and Sidney Gilliat made *Geordie* (1955), a film about a little lad from the Highlands who grows up to be an Olympic hammer thrower, it seemed as if they were indulging in preposterous wish-fulfilment fantasy. Liam McGrath's *Southpaw* offers a story every bit as improbable, but one that happens to be true. Francis Barrett, a young boxer, rises up the amateur ranks in an astonishingly short time to represent Ireland at the Atlanta Olympics. He carries the flag for his country at the opening ceremony, a singular achievement for somebody who grew up an itinerant traveller.

A southpaw, Barrett explains at the start of the film, is a boxer who leads with the right hand and punches with the left, who gets in under an opponent's guard and makes matters awkward. On a metaphorical level, the travellers do something similar. Local councillors regard them as an irritant, a drain on taxpayers' money. Rarely allowed to settle in one place for more than a few months, they are treated as malingerers and underachievers, and encounter discrimination on a day-to-day basis. This is what makes Barrett's success all the more unlikely. He trained in a rickety old homemade gym and sparred with his brothers in the yard. Whereas Sylvester Stallone's Rocky had the wizened old Burgess Meredith as mentor, Francis is guided by Chick, a kindly boxing-loving barber.

On one level, *Southpaw* is a sporting fairytale. Barrett, clean-cut and enthusiastic, is immediately likable. Just by being in the public eye, he counters long-held prejudices about the travellers. However, his story is not quite as gilt-edged as it may at first seem. Relatively early in the film Barrett wins his first fight at the Atlanta Olympics, but is comprehensively beaten in his second. Back in Galway, a huge crowd of his friends and relatives look on in dismay.

The real strength of the documentary lies in its account of what happens to the returning hero. He marries, moves to London and becomes a father. After his meteoric rise, he is forced into the daily grind like any other aspiring boxer. *Southpaw* offers an insider's view of the boxing world. Barrett takes on fight after fight in his bid to win both the English and Irish ABA titles. The documentary makers are given access to the gym, to Barrett's changing room, and are even able to film Barrett's corner during bouts. We see his colourful English trainer swearing away at the referee and whispering encouragement to Barrett between rounds. Like Ron Peck's *Fighters,* the film captures the monotony of training, the tension before big fights and the camaraderie that the sport inspires.

There is nothing especially cinematic about *Southpaw,* nor does it offer a comprehensive account of Barrett's life (we barely see the other members of his family). At the end, it's not clear whether he will ever qualify for the Sydney Olympics or turn professional. His story has not grown any less interesting since *Southpaw* was completed: it was reported in the *Irish Times* in August 1998 that he was stabbed in Galway because he refused to take part in bare-knuckle street fighting. Perhaps McGrath intends *Southpaw* as the first in a series of films—a sort of boxing equivalent to Michael Apted's *Seven Up* documentaries. In the meantime, we are left with a portrait of a courageous and articulate fighter who has already changed people's attitudes towards his community. Barrett, the commentators enthuse, is an all-action boxer who never stops coming forward. That same irrepressible enthusiasm he shows in the ring is what makes him such an engaging subject, and *Southpaw* such an easy film to warm to.

VILLAGE VOICE, 4/10/00, p. 162, Michael Atkinson

Liam McGrath's doc *Southpaw* focuses on light-welter Irish boxer Francis Barrett, the piercingly modest and Wahlberg-mugged Galway teen who at 19 qualified for the Olympics and fought in Atlanta in '96. Francis's handicaps are formidable: Not only is he diminutive and short-armed (his same-weight-class opponents often loom over him), but he's a Traveller, having grown up in a trailer park with no electricity or plumbing, and with the stigma of belonging to what is apparently the most loathed minority in Ireland. Whether Barrett's Traveller clan is of actual Rom descent or tied to the "lifestyle" (as it's called) is not clear, but for Barrett there was some ambivalence in carrying the flag at the Atlanta ceremonies for, as an Irish journalist puts it, "the only country in the world that would discriminate against him."

McGrath's movie is simple and kind (and, thankfully, not shot on video but on lovely Super 16), gracefully providing us with the reality of up-and-coming boxing-five-round fights, all-important scores, no knockouts. (Someone attached subtitles as well, and they're totally extraneous.) Barrett's trajectory is exciting, but his tribe is hilariously, dryly Irish about the experience—when Francie trounces his first Brazilian opponent in Atlanta, the crowds back home barely manage to crack a smile. (McGrath's camera obviously stiffened everyone up, but there are scores of powerful goodbyes and thank-yous in which the Barrett's and Francie's coach Chick Gillen cannot bring themselves to show emotion at all.) When Francie finally loses in Atlanta, it's as if the home front knew not to get too excited, and were privately thankful that further demonstrations would not be necessary.

Also reviewed in:
CHICAGO TRIBUNE, 4/7/00, Friday/p. K, John Petrakis
NEW YORK TIMES, 4/7/00, p. E27, Dave Kehr
VARIETY, 7/19-25/00, p. 30, Joe Leydon

SPACE COWBOYS

A Warner Bros. Pictures release in association with Village Roadshow Pictures/Clipsal Films of a Malpaso and Mad Chance production. *Executive Producer:* Tom Rooker. *Producer:* Clint Eastwood and Andrew Lazar. *Director:* Clint Eastwood. *Screenplay:* Ken Kaufman and Howard Klausner. *Director of Photography:* Jack N. Green. *Editor:* Joel Cox. *Music:* Lennie Niehaus. *Music Editor:* Donald Harris. *Sound:* Walt Martin and (music) Bobby Fernandez. *Sound Editor:* Alan Robert Murray. *Casting:* Phyllis Huffman. *Production Designer:* Henry Bumstead. *Art Director:* Jack G. Taylor, Jr. *Set Designer:* Joseph G. Pacelli, Jr. *Set Decorator:* Richard Goddard. *Special Effects:* John Frazier. *Costumes:* Deborah Hopper. *Make-up:* Tania McComas and Francisco X. Perez. *Stunt Coordinator:* Buddy Van Horn. *Running time:* 105 minutes. *MPAA Rating:* PG-13.

CAST: Clint Eastwood (Frank D. Corvin); Tommy Lee Jones (Hawk Hawkins); Donald Sutherland (Jerry O'Neill); James Garner (Tank Sullivan); James Cromwell (Bob Gerson); Marcia Gay Harden (Sara Holland); William Devane (Eugene Davis); Loren Dean (Ethan Grace); Courtney B. Vance (Roger Hines); Rade Sherbedgia (General Vostov); Barbara Babcock (Barbara Corvin); Blair Brown (Doctor Anne Caruthers); Jay Leno (Himself); Nils Allen Stewart (Tiny); Deborah Jolly (Cocktail Waitress); Toby Stephens (Young Frank D. Corvin); Eli Craig (Young Hawk Hawkins); John Asher (Young Jerry O'Neill); Matt McColm (Young Tank Sullivan); Billie Worley (Young Bob Gerson); Chris Wylde (Jason); Anne Stedman (Jason's Girlfriend); James MacDonald (Capcom); Kate Mcneil and Karen Mistal (Female Astronauts); John K. Linto (Male Astronaut 1); Mark Thomason (Mission Control Tech); Georgia Emelin (Jerry's Girlfriend); Rick Scarry (State Departmen Official); Paul Pender (JBC Security Guard); Tim Halligan (Qualls); Manning Mpinduzi-Mott (1958 Press Reporter); Steve Monroe (Waiter); J.M. Henry (Centrifuge Tech); Steven West (Construction Tech); Cooper Huckabee (Trajectory Engineer); Hayden Tank (Andrew); Jock MacDonald and Artur Cybulski (Press Reporters);   Gerald Emerick (T-38 Pilot);   Reneé Olstead (Little Girl);   Don Michaelson (NASA Doctor);   Gordon Owens (Simsupe);   Steve Stapenhorst (Vice President);   Lauren Cohn (Teacher);   Michael Louden and Jon Hamm (Young Pilots); Deborah Hope (Female Engineer);   Lamont Lofton (KSC Guard);   Alexander Kuznetsov (Russian Engineer);   Erica Grant (Female Engineer).

CHRISTIAN SCIENCE MONITOR, 8/4/00, p. 15, David Sterritt

Astronauts stand high among our real-life superheroes, and movies like "The Right Stuff" and "Apollo 13" have done accordingly well at the box office.

But those pictures seem a bit dated, and we haven't exactly been flooded with more contemporary treatments of the subject. A reason is that the golden age of astronautics—the first orbital flights, the historic moon landings—lies largely in the past, replaced by the more routine missions of today's shuttle crews.

Who in Hollywood could make a story about NASA seem topical and original?

Clint Eastwood, that's who.

And he proves it in "Space Cowboys," the new comedy-drama-adventure-romance-buddy picture blasting off today.

It's an entertaining movie with intriguing twists. But successful as it is, the film bears out the difficulty of making the US space program seem exciting enough for Hollywood to take notice.

To give his astronauts a charge of freshness and novelty, Eastwood makes them as old and, persnickety as the movie stars who play them—and resurrects, the cold war for good measure, complete with a shifty Russian general and a high-flying nuclear secret.

The story centers on Team Daedalus, a quartet of hotshot test pilots who reached their peak in the 1950's, then went their separate ways. Cut to the present day, when this groups is just a hazy memory—until a vintage Russian satellite shows signs of losing its orbit, and a NASA administrator decides the best repairman would be the Daedalus veteran who designed its guidance system.

This turns out to be Eastwood's character, of course, and he agrees to leave retirement if his old teammates (Donald Sutherland, James Garner, and Tommy Lee Jones) can join in the adventure. This touches off some mildly suspenseful questions: Do these likable geezers still have the right stuff? And what's really wrong with that satellite, anyway? How did it acquire an American guidance system when the Soviets launched it during the cold war? Why don't the authorities just let it crash into the ocean, or send an ordinary crew to haul it back, or let the Russian military clean up its own mechanical mess?

The answers to these conundrums are as predictable as you might expect, but "Space Cowboys" is fun to watch anyway.

At a time when most Hollywood productions pander to the youth market, Eastwood and company have made a whole movie about old things: aging guys, outdated politics, and outmoded equipment, not to mention a string of old-fashioned clichés sprinkled throughout.

What keeps it enjoyable is amiable acting and Eastwood's peppery directing style, never showy but always smooth and lively, and mostly free of the age-based condescension that sours many movies about the elderly.

It's not "Grumpy Old Astronauts," and that alone is cause for gratitude.

Will young moviegoers flock to a movie about adventurers old enough to be their grandfathers? Watch the box office. But grandfathers will have a ball, as will Eastwood admirers of every age.

LOS ANGELES TIMES, 8/4/00, Calendar/p. 1, Kenneth Turan

It's called "Space Cowboys," but it ought to be "Space Codgers." The story of a quartet of "Leisure World aviators" who want to prove they won't be old and in the way in outer space, this is a mostly genial film that gets as much mileage as it can out of the undeniable charisma of its stars. Like many charmers, it involves us against our better judgment, but only for a while.

That "Space Cowboys'" shenanigans engage us as much as they do is a credit to the skill and good-old-boy camaraderie of Clint Eastwood (who also directed), Tommy Lee Jones, Donald Sutherland and James Garner. Between them, they have more than 150 years of screen experience, and the creation of a lightly likable guy movie ambience is comfortably within their range.

It's also pleasant to see a movie where—shall we say—mature stars work with, instead of trying to hide, their age. The Ken Kaufman & Howard Klausner script includes numerous "The Ripe Stuff" references to bad eyes, false teeth and friends who have died. Where Eastwood's characters once said things like "Go ahead, make my day," he now mutters, "I've got Medicaid, take your best shot" when ruffians cross his path.

"Space Cowboys," however, squanders its assets. Though its basic ancients-in-orbit premise is sound enough (John Glenn was older than anyone on screen when he last went into space), the Kaufman-Klausner script (the first screen credit for both) fritters away the goodwill its actors accumulate on a meandering, contrived, haphazard scenario. Even Eastwood's classicist directing style can't do much with that.

The film opens with an extended black-and-white flashback to 1958, with younger versions of the leads playing the hottest Air Force test pilots of their day, breaking records, looking longingly at the distant moon and vowing, "That's where we're going."

But fate was not kind to this Team Daedalus crew. Partly due to the antics of Hawk Hawkins (Jones), the designated "crazy son of a bitch" with a proclivity for crashing planes and pushing situations to the limit, when NASA took over the space program from the Air Force, the Daedalus bunch found itself out in the cold as regards travel into the great beyond—as did real-life prototype Chuck Yeager.

Cut to a crisis in the present day. Ikon, a venerable Russian communications satellite, is showing signs of faltering, and because of warnings that its loss could plunge that country into civil war, the U.S., in the form of arrogant NASA Administrator Bob Gerson (James Cromwell), says it will do all it can to repair the ship's ailing guidance system.

What NASA mission director Sara Holland (Marcia Gay Harden) discovers, however, upsets Gerson's equilibrium. The Russian satellite has the same internal structure as America's 1969 Skylab, a system designed by Gerson's sworn nemesis and former Team Daedalus pilot Frank Corvin, played by Eastwood.

No actor, with the possible exception of Paul Newman, has aged better on film than Eastwood, who turned 70 in May and whose lined and weathered face makes Mt. Rushmore look like the Pillsbury Doughboy. When his disgruntled Corvin snaps, "What the hell is my guidance system doing on a Russian satellite?" even Vladimir Putin would be disconcerted.

It's also passably amusing to follow Corvin as he rounds up his old team: Tank Sullivan (Garner) is now a Baptist minister, Jerry O'Neill (Sutherland) designs roller coasters and chases younger women, while Hawkins, whom Corvin hasn't spoken to in 12 years, seems to make a living just by being irascible.

Still eager for that ultimate flight and still behaving, if the truth be told, like kids who couldn't or wouldn't grow up, the Daedalus crew all appreciate Corvin's plan, which is to force old enemy Gerson to send them into space as the only team that knows enough about the outmoded system to fix it in the short time available.

That plot strand is fine as far as it goes, but it soon gets overwhelmed by more conventional and badly handled considerations.

Deciding it needs a little romance, "Space Cowboys" concocts love scenes between Jones and Harden that are painfully awkward.

Things get even worse on the mission, when the whole tone of the film changes and confusing and unconvincing jeopardy situations hijack the proceedings. Even star power can get lost in space.

NEW STATESMAN, 9/11/00, p. 42, Jonathan Romney

Let's start with a roll-call of some of Hollywood's current box-office deities: Neve Campbell, Giovanni Ribisi, Freddie Prinze Jr, Devon Sawa, Melissa Joan Hart. This is a random selection of fresh young things who have staffed in some of Hollywood's biggest recent successes. For viewers over a certain age, these names may not resound with Tin-seltown glamour. Imagine, then, how it must feel for a veteran such as Clint Eastwood, who must experience the new reign of shiny, super-callow youth as a sort of un-barbarian invasion—akin to the arrival of Bobby Vee and Sandra Dee after the golden age of gnarled, redneck rock'n'roll.

For an audience d'un certain age, as the French euphemistically say, Eastwood has returned with a film "of a certain age"—that is, of a tried-and-tested sci-fi vintage. The script of *Space Cowboys* is full of references to obsolescent machinery that only old-timers could know how to operate; similarly, the director Eastwood and his writers have cobbled together a rickety space vehicle, patching it up with goodwill and one-liners, and have somehow got it aloft in the stratosphere of mega-budget action movies. As an Old Boys' Own adventure, it passes muster, with plenty of crunching steel at the close, but at heart it's really a Neil Simon-style Third Age comedy, a Sunshine Boys in space.

In an implausible plot, four astronauts from the dawn of space exploration are brought out of retirement and sent on the journey that they were cheated out of in the Fifties. (Their politics are defrosted, too: here's a film in which a spaceship labelled "CCCP" still invokes dread and the KGB can still be accused of skulduggery.) But the stars—Eastwood, Tommy Lee Jones, Donald Sutherland and James Garner—are relatively trim and youthful; and besides, in Hollywood, old age has been replaced by extended marinaded youth. These are hardly the creakiest geezers imaginable—not like, say, Walter Matthau, George Burns, John Houseman and Wilfrid Brambell in their codgerly heyday.

With birth dates ranging from 1928 (Garner) to 1946 (Jones, Eastwood's quartet do not strike us as old, more as young men who are less young than they were, although they carry traces of that youth like shadows around their slackening jowls. In a sense, the effect is all the more shocking. No one is ever struck by Gene Hackman's age because, even in his early roles, he never seemed exactly young. But these four, in their leather jackets and hip shades, look as unsettling as those "then and now" photos of old rock bands in Q magazine—swaggering mod blades in the Sixties, today amiably sweatered greengrocers or participants in a Fairport Convention reunion.

Only Garner looks as we expect old Americans to look: gummy and jovial, ripe for golf slacks. Jones hasn't so much aged as gathered yet more malevolent pitholes, like a beaten Texas oilfield. Sutherland may look baggy-faced and ancient but, every time he opens his mouth, the stoned grin of the Sixties oddball still gleams. As for Eastwood, it's reassuring to see him still using his one defining expression—face scrunched up in a half-amazed, half-displeased scowl, like a redwood tree that has received an unwelcome telegram from the Forestry Commission.

The best sequences are the most self-mocking: the medical tests, where the men line up naked, buttock to flabby buttock. They narrowly pass sight tests, show evidence of deafness, flop from jogging; Sutherland even produces a set of false teeth. But the film is not without vanity. Its central trick is to suggest that the men's younger personae are only premonitions of their later seasoned selves. The 1958 mission, shot in black and white, has four unknown actors playing the young heroes—but dubbed with the voices of Eastwood and co today, as if the older men were already guiding spirits within the younger bodies. Later, when the team goes into space, Eastwood has younger astronauts (Loren Dean, Courtney B. Vance) along for the ride, clearly for the pleasure of reducing fresher, prettier faces to set-dressing.

The old guys still have the heyday in their blood, although Eastwood bucks the trend among vain male leads of his generation by giving his character a wife roughly his own age, still up for a tumble in the garage. More in keeping with convention, Jones enjoys a romance with a younger scientist (Marcia Gay Harden—sensible casting, in that she is no-nonsense and rather more matronly than, say, Calista Flockhart). Swings and roundabouts, however: for balance, or perhaps just narrative manipulation, one of the four turns out to have cancer, and is therefore called on to make a noble sacrifice in the final reel. This is where fantasy takes over—the spectre of mortality reassuringly exercised in generic heroism.

As a retaliation against the diaper-dominated state of Hollywood, *Space Cowboys* is an entertaining and ever-so-faintly radical gesture. But it isn't as serious, as tender or remotely as intelligent as the late Burt Lancaster vehicles, the final John Wayne essays on decline, or the best recent film to star older actors and use them creatively—Robert Benton's 1998 thriller, *Twilight*, about an ageing detective (Paul Newman), an ageing client (Hackman) and an ageing Los Angeles. Ultimately, *Space Cowboys* is a jocular pipe-and-slippers job—but then, let's see whether Freddie Prinze Jr. and Devon Sawa do any better when their time comes.

NEW YORK, 8/14/00, p. 65, Peter Rainer

Space Cowboys, directed by and starring Clint Eastwood, has so predictable a premise that there's really no reason to actually see the movie. You can sit back and imagine what it would be like and probably get just about the same results—maybe, one hopes, better. The premise, made joshingly explicit in the movie, is *The Right Stuff* meets *The Ripe Stuff*. Eastwood, Tommy Lee Jones, Donald Sutherland, and James Garner play ex-Air Force test pilots from the glory days of the fifties who finally get their chance to go into space on a mission. A chimp edged them out for outer-atmospheric-testing honors back in 1958, when NASA took over the space program, and now it's payback time. The NASA bureaucrat (James Cromwell) who once screwed them is urgently implored by the Russians to repair one of their broken orbiting satellites which otherwise will cause a total communications blackout in their country. Since the satellite has the same guidance system as the American satellite Skylab, Eastwood's Frank Corvin, who designed Skylab and is apparently the one person in the universe qualified to do the job, blackmails his old NASA nemesis into also bringing along his flight buddies for the repairs. Who would have thought we would be seeing a movie in which Clint Eastwood risked his neck rescuing the Russkies? Ah, but even that plot point has its predictable twist.

The film is one of those over-the-hill-gang buddyfests that pretend to be about teamwork and valor but are really about movie-star cronyism. Watching these actors appear together in the film as astronauts with Jay Leno isn't all that different from watching many of the same actors appear as themselves *promoting* the movie with Jay Leno. The charitable way to look at all this is that Eastwood and Co. are winking at us; we are nudged to believe that they are playing themselves. The film comes across like an action fantasy for old coots; when these actors groan and squint during their NASA physicals, we're supposed to laugh, sympathetically, at the famous men doing the groaning and squinting. (Some are longer in the tooth than others.) Eastwood, in his recent movies, has been pushing this AARP worldview, and I suppose it's a more genial solution to the problem of being an aging action-movie star than having Arnold Schwarzenegger obliviously muscle his way through yet another splatter epic, or having Sylvester Stallone, in *Cop Land,* go all pot-bellied and Methody. But Eastwood buys off too much for too little. Shouldn't the moment when the guys finally get their up-close glimpse of the universe be a transcendent one? In *Space Cowboys,* they might as well be ushers in a planetarium.

NEW YORK POST, 8/4/00, p. 49, Lou Lumenick

Clint Eastwood makes our day with the summer's most delightful surprise. Though I'm an Eastwood fan from way back, I was skeptical about what sounds suspiciously like a cross between "Armageddon" and "Grumpy Old Men"—fueled by a payload of John Glenn wish fulfillment.

It turns out to be an expertly directed, acted and written crowd-pleaser about a group of geriatric pilots who get a chance to show they have, as the movie slyly put it, "the ripe stuff."

Eastwood, Tommy Lee Jones, Donald Sutherland and James Garner play former Air Force flyers who were cheated out of their spots in the space program way back in 1958.

Forty years later, the double-dealing NASA official (James Cromwell) who passed them over—and sent up a monkey instead—is forced to come begging to Eastwood.

Clint's the only guy on Earth with the "obsolescent" skills to fix an ancient Soviet "communications" satellite whose fall to Earth will have very dire consequences.

He'll do it—but only if he gets to right the old wrong by going into space with his original, albeit wrinkled, team of fly guys.

The old pilots gamely make it through rigorous training (and some very funny sequences), an attempted double-cross and even the cancer diagnosis of one crew member.

Their characters are so well drawn—Eastwood, the steely leader; Jones, his hot-headed rival; Sutherland, the womanizing genius; Garner, the Baptist minister and quiet tower of strength—that you really care about their adventures in space and suspend disbelief to an astonishing degree.

Those space adventures are indeed spectacular, abetted by terrific special effects work that really moves the story along to a beautiful and elegiac climax that will take your breath away.

What could have been a collection of old-age clichés (Sutherland's character wears dentures and Coke-bottle glasses, and there are jokes about Ensure and adult diapers) is handled with self-deprecating wit by Eastwood, who gives his veteran cast the opportunity to shine in a film that's almost defiantly leisurely paced by current Hollywood standards.

Sutherland (Eastwood's co-star in "Kelly's Heroes" 30 years ago) hasn't been this funny since "M*A*S*H," and Garner's underplaying once again shows why he's one of the most durable of stars.

Eastwood hands the showiest role to Jones. He's notably younger than his co-stars, but pulls off a cranky geezer with aplomb, engaging in a barroom brawl with Eastwood and a romance with a NASA scientist very well played by Marcia Gay Harden.

William Devane is outstanding as the skeptical flight commander who forces Eastwood to take along younger astronauts, played by Loren Dean and Courtney Vance.

But in the end, it's 70-year-old Eastwood who puts "Space Cowboys" into orbit, with everything from a snappy black-and-white prologue (an apparent homage to "The Right Stuff") to a scene where he trades squinty-eyed quips with Jay Leno on "The Tonight Show."

It's his best directing stint since his Oscar-winning "Unforgiven"—and as an actor, Clint's comic timing is far sharper than 64-year-old Woody Allen's in "Small Time Crooks."

NEWSDAY, 8/4/00, Part II/p. B3, John Anderson

How do four Eisenhower-era astronauts cope with a trip into Clinton-era space? Depends.

Sorry, bad joke. But not entirely inappropriate when you consider how the four stars of Clint Eastwood's "Space Cowboys"—Eastwood, Donald Sutherland, James Garner and Tommy Lee Jones—seem to treat aging itself as a bad joke. As each has gotten older, his screen persona has adopted the message that getting creaky is something to be ignored, if not somehow avoided altogether. Still, here they are, old and creaky and what the hell.

And while "Space Cowboys" is something of a one-joke movie, its stars' attitude toward the inevitable makes Eastwood's occasionally draggy movie fundamentally charming.

The four members of the movie's long-retired Daedalus Team—all seem to be modeled after Air Force pilot Chuck Yeager, the flying ace cheated of his chance at outer space in "The Right Stuff"—have spent the post-'58 years in various earthbound pursuits. Frank Corvin (Eastwood) tinkers around the house; Tank Sullivan (Garner) has become a less-than-stirring Baptist preacher, ex-engineer Jerry O'Neill (Sutherland) constructs roller coasters and Hawk Hawkins (Jones), the most unreconstituted of the group, is a charter stunt pilot, willing to take birthday boys on lunch-lurching tailspins. None seems particularly satisfied. None has ever forgotten the chances he missed.

The imminent crash of a Cold War-era Russian satellite—which somehow, and very suspiciously, became equipped with a Corvin- designed guidance system—brings the boys out of retirement, to the disgruntlement of NASA bureaucrat Bob Gerson (James Cromwell), the suit who grounded them to begin with. Since the engineering is as vintage as our heroes, there's not a lot Gerson can do to stop them. Not that he won't try.

"Space Cowboys" is a confection that's a lot more appetizing while it stays grounded; once Team Daedalus is on its mission, the movie becomes a replay of every space adventure from "Red Planet Mars" through "Apollo 13." Despite some impressive special effects, it isn't top-shelf Eastwood, but it has his touch. It's fun watching Eastwood and Jones (who is at least a decade younger than his costars) lock horns, however fragile those horns may be, or to watch the way Eastwood can use effortless little gestures to flesh out his characters—such as Frank giving the most subtle of second looks at Jerry's attractive young assistant, as if it's simply the reflex action of a veteran male. Which it is.

The politics of the movie are certainly nothing new. Eastwood's movies have consistently questioned authority, sometimes to the point of paranoia, and always assumed the worst about government and its functionaries. He's never too sure about youth, either—there's certainly no reason to trust the two hotshot astronauts ("Mumford's" Loren Dean and the always wonderful Courtney B. Vance) forced on Team Daedalus by Gerson. Eastwood likes to keep his friends close and his enemies at arm's length.

Women are another story. All four fliers have their romantic interests, most poignantly Hawk and the NASA scientist played by Marcia Gay Harden, another cast member who seems a little young for AARP status. Still, as comedy, adventure or a celebration of rueful maturity, "Space Cowboys" is one of the more gracefully satisfying features of the summer. Our boys may be less Buck Rogers than Buck Codgers, but as Eastwood obviously sees it, you're as young as you act.

NEWSWEEK, 8/14/00, p. 63, David Ansen

Clint Eastwood's "Space Cowboys" is at least three different movies—high-tech thriller, low-key comedy, rumination on aging—jammed together into an implausible but very likable entertainment. The idea of Eastwood, James Garner, Donald Sutherland and Tommy Lee Jones (the first two in their 70s, one in his mid-60s and 53-year-old Jones) donning their astronaut helmets after three decades of inactivity to go on a high-risk NASA expedition into space may be farfetched, but with actors as sly and seasoned as these, who'll complain? Clint reassembles the members of Team Daedalus—whose dreams of making it to space were dashed back in the late '50s—for a mission to repair an obsolete Russian communications satellite. The old satellite has the same guidance system as one Eastwood designed: no one else, it seems, is capable of fixing it.

Eastwood's movie, written by Ken Kaufman and Howard Klausner, throws in an old bureaucratic nemesis (James Cromwell) to oversee our heroes; cranks up the pathos by giving Jones both a love interest (Marcia Gay Harden) *and* inoperable cancer, and waits until our boys are in deep space to spring some dubious last-minute surprises. These strained plot contortions aren't really necessary: the funny, amiable heart of the movie is in the scenes of these tough old duffers scamming their way through the training program. The movie itself, like these guys, is defiantly old school—confident, relaxed, professional. These four stars, with more than 260 years of experience among them, know how to get the job done.

SIGHT AND SOUND, 10/00, p. 60, Edward Buscombe

1958, some where over a desert in the American West. Two US airforce pilots, Frank Corvin and Hawk Hawkins, eject when their experimental plane begins to break up. Both are members of an elite team of flyers named Daedalus. Later, in front of assembled press, the team are humiliated by being told they will no longer be part of the space programme.

Cut to the present. A Russian communications satellite is falling out of orbit. Its guidance system is based on a design by Corvin. NASA asks him to help fix it. Despite the opposition of General Gerson, a long-time enemy, Corvin persuades NASA to allow Team Daedalus to carry out the repairs in space. Corvin and his reunited team, comprising Hawkins, Jerry O'Neill and Tank Sullivan, embark on a programme of physical and technical training. Following a medical exam, Hawkins learns he has terminal cancer, but NASA allows him to carry on with the mission.

Once in space, the team rendezvous with the satellite, only to find the Russians have secreted six nuclear missiles inside it. Acting against Corvin's orders, Ethan Grace, a young astronaut accompanying Daedalus, unwittingly activates the missiles on the satellite, which damage Corvin's shuttle. Corvin manages to fix the satellite's guidance system and arrest its descent. He then decides to propel the missiles towards the moon, although there isn't enough fuel in the guidance rocket to do this. Hawkins volunteers to stay with the missiles and fire them so they will crash harmlessly on the moon. Corvin lands the disabled shuttle back on earth.

"I don't know how to break this to you, Frank, but you're an old man." This harsh truth delivered to Frank Corvin, a retired airforce pilot, by his former commander Gerson is intended to deflate his ambition to get into space. Instead it only increases his determination. One can imagine Clint Eastwood, who plays Corvin, faced with the evidence of his own ageing, being similarly provoked. The star is, after all, 70 years old, and sometimes he looks it, the lean features now a little scrawny, the hair wispier. There's courage in facing facts, making a virtue out of necessity.

Eastwood has always liked to poke fun at himself In *The Gauntlet* (1977) Sondra Locke's character has a high old time deflating the macho ego of Eastwood's tough-guy cop, while his 1992 Western *Unforgiven* in which his character, the elderly William Munn struggles to mount his horse, anticipates much of the comedy of *Space Cowboys*. But in mocking his screen persona, Eastwood—who also directs *Space Cowboys*—avoids undermining its potency. In *The Gauntlet* he's man enough to get the job done; in *Unforgiven* he proves more than a match for the brutal Little Bill Daggett. So it is in *Space Cowboys*. The two earnest young things sent from NASA to persuade Corvin back to the fold (he knows how to fix the guidance system of a broken-down Russian satellite) discover him in *flagrante* with his wife. There's life in the old dog yet.

And in the other members of Team Daedalus, the crack flying squad which Corvin reunites. Donald Sutherland's O'Neill is still an incorrigible flirt, while Tommy Lee Jones' Hawk flies like a dream *and* romances a pretty young NASA engineer. Only Sullivan, played by James Garner, seems limited by his failing physique, huffing and puffing round the training track (although he's still a crack robotics expert). Like Eastwood's own production team, here assembled for the umpteenth time, Team Daedalus shows there's no substitute for experience.

Of course, if you've got the 'Right Stuff'—the title of Tom Wolfe's influential book about the early years of the US space programme—age would seem to be no impediment. Indeed, *Space Cowboys* ploughs much the same furrow as Wolfe's work (itself turned into a movie by Philip Kaufman in 1983). As the military-industrial complex grows ever more powerful, so there is a more urgent need to believe it is still dependent on human qualities such as courage and resourcefulness: in other words, cowboy values. Several times Frank is accused of not being a team player, but it's his individualism that sees the mission through. By contrast, the two by-the-book young astronauts accompanying the old-timers are nothing but a liability.

Only one of the quartet, Hawk Hawkins, is overtly identified as a cowboy, introduced by a shot of his fancy boots. But the dividing line between the free spirits and the suits is absolute. It's rather over-egging the pudding that Gerson, up to his neck in the murky world of internal NASA politics, turns out to be covering up for his negligence—Frank's designs were stolen by the KGB while in Gerson's care, and subsequently used in a Soviet satellite—throughout the whole operation. Not that the old guys resist the new; far from it. In an oddly moving moment Hawkins, to whom we are introduced flying a vintage biplane, lovingly strokes the fuselage of a Stealth bomber. And when Frank finally gets to look down on Earth from space, a beatific smile spreads over his face.

Despite the poignancy of old age, the mood of the film is cheerful, sustained by the high spirits of the four veterans. Even Hawkins' terminal illness is played for comedy; in the final sequence Frank and his wife look up at the night sky wondering if Hawk reached his goal; we then cut to a shot of his body lying serenely on the lunar surface as on the soundtrack Frank Sinatra croons "Fly Me to the Moon".

TIME, 8/14/00, p. 70, Richard Corliss

When F. Scott fitzgerald wrote, "There are no second acts in American lives," he was ruefully noting the early rise and fall of celebrated people. In this young country, success was a young man's game, and so was failure. But today's Americans might take Fitzgerald's jeremiad as a compliment: there are no second acts because we prolong the first act forever; we work and play hard to extend adolescence for another 40, 50 years. It's hard work, consuming all that wheat germ and Viagra, but it's worth it to stay tan, teen and terrific. Besides, the alterative is so nonattractive. To be old in America is almost as uncool as being poor.

That makes the recent films of Clint Eastwood a bracing, useful social corrective. "I don't know how to break this to you, Frank," a long-time adversary tells Eastwood in *Space Cowboys*, "but you're an old man." No need to tell Eastwood; he knows. As a sleuth in *True Crime* and *In the Line of Fire*, and as a career criminal in *Unforgiven* and *Absolute Power,* the actor-director has dramatized the perils and grace of something we all do (if we're lucky): age. His breath is short, his trigger finger is arthritic, and the young women in his life are more likely to be his daughters or his bosses than a hot amour. Yet even at 70, he's still Clint, which means he's about the best any of us can hope to be in our reclining years.

Once upon a time (in the West), Eastwood was the grizzled loner, using the Old Testament playbook to clean up Tombstone or San Francisco. Here he's surrounded by other gents of a certain age: hotdogging fly-boys of the '50s named Hawk (Tommy Lee Jones), Jerry (Donald Sutherland) and Tank (James Garner) who were pioneers in Air Force research but got passed over for the first U.S. astronaut program. An old Soviet satellite is about to crash to earth, threatening humanity; since Frank built the technology the Russkies swiped, his expertise is needed. He insists on going up to fix the damn thing and taking his pals along for a senior-citizen road trip to outer space. The Over the Moon Gang rides again, in an alter-kocker *Armageddon*.

Four guys doing something kooky—that sounds like a teen-hormone romp. But the *Space Cowboys* quartet has been alive for a cumulative 261 years, and in films for 156. They're too mature to fiddle with bra straps or play with pastry. Besides, Eastwood is a gentleman of sorts, so—except for displaying the four men's naked butts, which is quite an archaeological sight—he will embarrass neither them nor us. Directing from a script by Ken Kaufman and Howard Klausner, he finds fresh breezes in familiar vectors: the residual rivalry of Frank and Hawk, the tensions between the ancient astronauts and the modern ones, the impact of decay and disease on minds that are still bright, wills that are still strong.

For its first hour, this is an engaging rite-of-passage comedy for the *Modern Maturity* set. When the men go into orbit, so does the film. It blends tension and emotion, computer wizardry and dramatic skill in a vigorous climax—and the most impressive, haunting final shot of the movie year.

Eastwood's message is clear: he wants Hollywood to see how an old man can play a young man's game. Find a story that allows elbow room for star quality; hand the old boys some new toys; don't try to be a kid. Deep into Act 3 of his career, Eastwood still has the goods.

VILLAGE VOICE, 8/15/00, p. 115, J. Hoberman

There's no Hollywood icon—not even John Wayne—who has ever had more fun with the specter of encroaching decrepitude than that still lean and spry septuagenarian, Clint Eastwood. In *Space Cowboys,* which Eastwood both produced and directed, the veteran star plays long-retired test pilot Frank Corvin, who contrives to blast himself into space-along with his former team, Tank (James Garner, 72), Jerry (Donald Sutherland, 66), and Hawk (Tommy Lee Jones, a mere child of 54). The movie may not pack anything near the emotional punch of *Unforgiven,* but it's an entertainingly raffish action-comedy nonetheless.

A cockpit-shaking, wing-shearing, black-and-white prologue, set in 1958, establishes the team's cowboy derring-do as well as the ongoing rivalry between feisty Frank and hellcat Hawk. Indeed, Frank was supposed to be the first American in space until, he thinks, he was sandbagged by the, irresponsible Hawk and replaced by a monkey. Dissolve to present-day America, where a crisis has arisen in NASAland because no one any longer understands the obsolete technology Frank used to power an old satellite that, for reasons not yet disclosed, requires urgent attention. Called upon to do his patriotic chore, Frank declines to teach the whippersnappers how to fix the thing, exploiting the situation to reunite his old buddies. Or, as one NASA flack puts it, "We've got three weeks to put four old farts in space."

Something like *Grumpy Old Men Go to the Moon,* the scenario is amusing in a crusty sort of way. The movie has no shortage of recurring gags—including one in which the teammates regularly discover that old pals have passed away. The mode is relaxed and folksy, with occasional heartwarming bits of business—although the grinning Marcia Gay Harden, who plays a NASA mission director, seems a bit too thrilled (or is it pained?) with her part in the project. Each actor gets more than ample time to rehearse his identifying quirk and the leisurely regimen includes trading riffs with Jay Leno on TV. Eastwood is in no particular hurry. It's nearly 90 minutes before the guys board the Metamucil Express and blast out into the cosmos to lasso the malevolent fossil of Cold War hardware that's been left floating in space like a Russki time bomb.

The obvious subtext here is that Clint knows not only how to fix an obsolete satellite but how to make an old-fashioned movie. I was particularly impressed by the effectively frugal use of Industrial Light & Magic effects-despite the somewhat abrupt (and anticlimactic) landing. Eastwood signs off with a blast of generational insouciance, but if he had held off on the Sinatra until the end credits, the final shot would have had a bit more poetic pow.

Also reviewed in:
CHICAGO TRIBUNE, 8/4/00, Friday/p. A, Michael Wilmington
NEW REPUBLIC, 8/28 & 9/4/00, p. 28, Stanley Kauffmann
NEW YORK TIMES, 8/4/00, p. E16, A. O. Scott
VARIETY, 7/31-8/6/00, p. 23, Todd McCarthy
WASHINGTON POST, 8/4/00, p. C1, Rita Kempley
WASHINGTON POST, 8/4/00, Weekend/p. 34 , Michael O'Sullivan

SPECIALIST, THE

A Kino International release of a Momento! and France 2 Cinéma/Bremer Institut Film and WDR/Image Création and RTBF/Lotus Film/Amythos and Noga Communication-Channel 8 co-production with the support of Canal+, Arcapix, Editions Montparnasse, Institut National de l'Audiovisuel, Ikon TV and Humanistische, Omroep, Studio l'Equipe, ORF, Centre National de la Cinématographie, Filmsiftung Nord Rhein-Westfalia, Wiener Filmfinanzierungfonds, Israeli Film Center, MAP TV and Documentary, and Eurimages. *Executive Producer:* Armelle Laborie. *Producer:* Eyal Sivan. *Director:* Eyal Sivan. *Screenplay (Hebrew, German, and French with English subtitles):* Eyal Sivan and Rony Brauman. *Archival Footage:* Leo T. Hurwitz. *Editor:* Audrey Maurion. *Music:* Yves Robert, Krishna Levy, Béatrice Thiriet, Jean-Michel Levy, and Tom Waits "Russian Dance". *Running time:* 128 minutes. *MPAA Rating:* Not Rated.

WITH: Adolf Eichmann; Moshé Landau; Benjamin Halévy; Yitzhak Raveh; Gideon Hausner; Robert Servatius.

NEWSDAY, 4/12/00, Part II/p. B9, John Anderson

The idea that Adolf Eichmann, stationmaster of the Final Solution, was hanged in 1962 seems like a rather pathetic footnote to the Holocaust, in light of Eyal Sivan's "The Specialist". One starts to wish that Eichmann had been kept in his bulletproof terrarium—built for his own protection, ironically, when he went on trial in Jerusalem in 1961—and put on display. Scrutinized. Poked at. Preserved like a lemon. Not, at any rate, given the dignity of an execution.

But Sivan's movie is the next best thing, a deceptively simple adaptation of footage that American documentarian Leo T. Huwitz shot at Israelis behest over the course of Eichmann's eight-month trial. Although writer Hannah Arendt immortalized Eichmann and what she called his "banality of evil" (in her "Eichmann in Jerusalem"), seeing the thing up close is to immerse oneself in a fetid bath of morbid fascination. Here he is, the twitchy, bespectacled, purse-lipped bureaucrat referring to the uprooting and massacre of millions as an "unpleasantness" caused by "inadequacies" at the "local level." That 1,000 Jews were jammed onto train cars meant for 700 is easily explained: The 700 number is assumed to include soldiers with their baggage. As the Jews' belongings were stowed elsewhere, of course, more bodies could be accommodated, at which point I think someone in court screams, "Butcher!!!"

Sival has taken Hurwitz, 500 hours of footage and pared it to essentials that are frank and eloquent. He establishes the courtroom as a stage—Eichmann is giving a performance, after all. Sivan closes in on his subject during testimony, cuts to his reactions, cuts to his hands—or, in shocking aside, cuts to a faceless soundman's hands as he adjusts a playback for the court, the tattooed camp number clear on his wrist.

The film, which opens with a mute shot of the courtroom's empty seats, is interrupted frequently by shouts and disturbances from the audience, in reaction to some appalling thing Eichmann has said, which is just: Sival puts us in the gallery, but lets the Israelis of '61 be the voice of posterity.

VILLAGE VOICE, 4/18/00, p. 153, J. Hoberman

The real Adolf Eichmann—or at least his televisual form—is currently on view in *The Specialist,* an austere and fascinating documentary fashioned by Israeli director Eyal Sivan from the 500 hours of video footage shot by Leo Hurwitz during the trial.

More than the miniseries *Holocaust* or the Oscar-winning *Schindler's List* , the spectacle of Eichmann in Jerusalem introduced America—and the world—to the facts of what was, for the first time, referred to as the Holocaust. Even then, many intellectuals understood the trial's fundamental purposes to be the legitimization of Israeli authority and the creation of a Holocaust narrative. Harold Rosenberg ascribed to it "the function of tragic poetry, that of making the pathetic and terrifying past live again in the mind."

Here, the Eichmann trial itself is that pathetic and terrifying past. A performance-documentary set in a hall of mirrors, *The Specialist*—like the movie fashioned from the Army-McCarthy hearings, *Point of Order*—is about history as it is structured in court and mediated by the camera. The credits suggest a cast of actors—the first few shots are of the empty seats and stage. Excavating the event as theater, Sivan is less interested in giving voice to the many witnesses against Eichmann or showing the atrocity footage entered as evidence than in demonstrating how this evidence functioned in the trial. The material has been digitally enhanced so that the image of the audience is reflected an Eichmann's protective glass booth, and the frequent, sometimes violent, crowd reactions are now audible.

The greatest emphasis is on Eichmann's performance. His peculiar half-smile as he listens through a headset to the testimony against him is unnerving and disarming. (You should have seen the balding, bespectacled clerk—a self-identified "specialist" in forced emigration—when he was costumed in his SS uniform of absolute power.) Eichmann is clever enough to suggest that he is really a Zionist and stupid enough to insist that he improved conditions on the transports to Treblinka. He is fastidious in his language, precise in his evasions, anxious to seem reasonable, deferential to authority. This born flunky always stands to speak—one assumes he also clicks his heels—an appropriate tactic for a man who, arguing for his life, claims only to have followed his superiors' orders.

Sivan further accentuates the differing agendas of the judges, some interrogating Eichmann directly, and the show's real director, prosecutor Gideon Hausner. Aggressively trying to break down a criminal bureaucrat who had no official function apart from his mandated task of facilitating the extermination of Jews, Hausner grows increasingly sarcastic. When cornered, however, Eichmann holds his ground: "I refuse to reveal my inner feelings," he sulks, taking refuge in his own enigma as the empty suit of institutionalized evil.

Also reviewed in:
CHICAGO TRIBUNE, 8/18/00, Friday/p. F, John Petrakis
NATION, 5/8/00, p. 50, Stuart Klawans
NEW YORK TIMES, 4/12/00, p. E14, Elvis Mitchell
VARIETY, 3/1-7/99, p. 81, Eddie Cockrell

SPECIALS, THE

A Regent Entertainment release of a Brillstein-Grey Entertainment/Mindfire Entertainment production. *Executive Producer:* Mark Gottwald and Ellie Gottwald. *Producer:* Dan Bates, Mark A. Altman, and Rick Mischel. *Director:* Craig Mazin. *Screenplay:* James Gunn. *Director of Photography:* Eliot Rockett. *Editor:* Stephen Garrett and Jeremy Kasten. *Music:* Brian Langsbard. *Sound:* James H. Coburn. *Casting:* Christine Sheaks. *Production Designer:* Dorian Vernacchio. *Special Effects:* Sherry Hitch. *Costumes:* Nickolaus Brown. *Make-up:* Akiko Matsumoto. *Running time:* 140 minutes. *MPAA Rating:* R.

CAST: Rob Lowe (The Weevil); Jamie Kennedy (Amok); Thomas Haden Church (The Strobe); Paget Brewster (Ms. Indestructible); Kelly Coffield (Power Chick); Judy Greer (Deadly Girl); James Gunn (Minute Man); Sean Gunn (Alien Orphan); Jordan Ladd (Nightbird); Barry Del Sherman (Zip Boy); Mike Schwartz (U.S. Bill); Jim Zulevic (Mr. Smart); John Doe (Eight #1); Abdul Salaam El Razzac (Eight #3); Lauren Cohn (Eight #4); Tom Dorfmeister (Eight #5); Greg Erb (Eight #6); Brian Gunn (Eight #7); Chuti Tiu (Eight #2); Michael Weatherly (Verdict); Melissa Joan Hard (Sunglight Girl); Matt Champagne (Tippin); Chase Masterson (Moira Murphy); Christopher Shea (Reporter); Jenna Fischer (College Girl); Eme Gollward (Linda); Frank Medrano (Orestes); Lee Kirk (Reporter).

LOS ANGELES TIMES, 9/22/00, Calendar/p. 8, Kevin Thomas

"The Specials" is an unfortunate name for a film that's anything but. It's all talk and no action in the most literal sense, yet its title refers to a team of superhumans dedicated to putting their unusual powers the service of doing good deeds in the tradition of Superman. Alas, they are always coming in second in comparison to other such teams. When a toy conglomerate selects them for a line of action figures in the images, the Specials start feeling special again, but to be sure, there's a hitch.

Debuting director Craig Mazin, who scripted "Rocket Man" and "Senseless," and his writer James Gunn (who also plays one of the Specials) seem to be in an anti-special effects mode—or maybe they were simply constrained by their obviously low budget. In any case, it would really have helped to see the Specials in action—to see their leader, Ted the Strobe (Thomas Haden Church), shoot laser beams out of his arm—and show how his counterpart on another team does it better, for humorous effect.

Instead, the Specials sit around talking, talking, talking until a crisis erupts that will either serve to demoralize them further or to reunite them. In short, the Specials seem increasingly like mere mortals having to cope with everyday problems of marital fidelity, self-interest, etc.; the problem is that the filmmakers fail to show them as superhuman at the start, so they simply seem throughout as being inundated with standard yuppie angst over personal and professional crises.

"The Specials'" team star is the Weevil, described vaguely as a pest dispenser, and while he is as well-played as humanly possible under the circumstances by Rob Lowe, you have to feel that it's unfortunate that this hopeless little picture is surfacing just as Lowe is riding the crest of a hard-won comeback with TV's "The West Wing." "The Specials" is being promoted as "Spinal Tap" meets "Scream." Whatever that means, it certainly doesn't describe this limp loser.

NEW YORK POST, 9/22/00, p. 50, Lou Lumenick

His lame spoof is about a group of fifth-rate super-heroes who bicker about toy licensing, extramarital affairs and whether they should join rival groups. The moronic, obscenity-ridden script is by James Gunn, who plays a size-reducing character named Minute (mi-NUTE) Man.

NEWSDAY, 9/22/00, Part II/p. B6, John Anderson

The more perverse among us will be running out as fast as we can to see "The Specials," because in the grand tradition of "Beavis & Butt-head" and Pauly Shore, it's so unfunny it's funny. In a gruesome sort of way. Actually, it's precisely the kind of thing that's driving a dull knife into the tender heart of movie comedy. But what good will whining do us?

Besides, there's enough whining in "The Specials" for 18 Woody Allen movies. Remember "Mystery Men"? Ben Stiller, Janeane Garofalo, Pee-wee Herman? It was a second-rate comedy about second-rate superheroes. "The Specials" is about "the sixth or seventh greatest superhero team in the world." Speaking comparatively, you can't accuse it of dishonest advertising.

"The Specials" opens on the day the group—which includes the Great Strobe (Thomas Haden Church), Amok (Jamie Kennedy), Ms. Indestructible (Paget Brewster) and Power Chick (Kelly Coffield)—is getting its own line of action figures, all of which turn out to look nothing like them, because who, after all, would want a "Specials" action figure?

This ignites all the pent-up jealousies, hostilities and neuroses of the dysfunctional "Specials" prompts Strobe to dissolve the group and accuse the Weevil (Rob Lowe) of sleeping with Strobe's wife, Ms. I (which he is). It also leaves poor Nightbird (Jordan Ladd) wondering if she was nuts to join this outfit in the first place (which she was).

Both Coffield, a gifted comedian, and Ladd, an ingenue with real screen appeal, are oases of talent in "The Specials," which in virtually every other way is (to quote Alice Kramden) like Yucca Flats after the blast—a dry, desiccated, lifeless terrain upon which little can grow but warts.

Ironically, a movie so poverty-stricken for laughs or, quite frankly, a reason to exist, tends to make you ask questions. How did it get made? Is there a God? Only the hopelessly cynical would imagine there'd be an audience for "The Specials." It'll probably make billions.

VILLAGE VOICE, 9/26/00, p. 152, Michael Atkinson

Something like the soapbox derby car of superhero comedies, Craig Mazin's *The Specials* skirts the edge of professionalism, one-upping *Mystery Men*'s yuk factor even as it shoots for being the most crudely made indie of the year. Mazin, whose fratboy scripts were turned into the not-unamusing *Rocket Man* and *Senseless*, barely manages a charcoal-sketch fluency. But James Gunn's script must come off like a pack of firecrackers on the page, where the jokes aren't starved for oxygen. Here, the titular third-rate superhero team hang out in their scrubby suburban office, bickering and lamenting their superpowers, which they never get an opportunity to display. The only gift that The Weevil (Rob Lowe) seems to have is to attract fans and women, while stuffy team leader/electromagnetizer Strobe (Thomas Haden Church) struggles to maintain a sense of moral decorum. Amok (Jamie Kennedy) is a punky antimatter source, Deadly Girl (Judy Greer) a Goth brooder soured by her ability to summon the dead, Minute—that's mine-*oot*-Man (Gunn) a bashful self-shrinker whose name needs revamping, and so on. The movie is in clover with one-liners, delivered like one-liners: Mr. Smart (Jim Zulevic) howling behind his olfactory gadgetry ("I smell everything!"); Strobe's businessman brother (Barry Del Sherman) stumping for a normal life and still utilizing his powers ("Hey, I ran here from Yemen this morning"); the ruefully noted incidence of cancer among crusaders with stretching talents. Wittily conceived but clumsy as a newborn calf, *The Specials* has a box of ideas it never uses—here's hoping for a Gilliam remake.

Also reviewed in:
NEW YORK TIMES, 9/22/00, p. E22, Stephen Holden
VARIETY, 9/25-10/1/00, p. 62, Scott Foundas

SPECTRES OF THE SPECTRUM

An Other City Production release.   *Producer:* Craig Baldwin.   *Director:* Craig Baldwin. *Screenplay:* Craig Baldwin.   *Director of Photography:* Bill Daniel.   *Editor:* Bill Daniel.   *Music:* John Watermann.   *Sound:* Gibbs Chapman.   *Production Designer:* Matt Day and Thad Povey. *Art Director:* Matt Day, Thad Povey, Chris Santeramo, and Molli Simon.   *Running time:* 84 minutes.   *MPAA Rating:* Not Rated.

WITH: Sean Kilcoyne (Yogi);   Caroline Koebel (Boo Boo);   Beth Liseck.

NEW YORK POST, 3/17/00, p. 48, Lou Lumenick

Frank Sinatra, Chuck Yaeger, Admiral Chester Nimitz, Edward Teller, Dave Garroway, Orson Welles and Dean Martin are among the more recognizable faces that pop up in a most entertaining collection of clips—some amazingly obscure—from old TV shows, horror movies, educational films and cartoons.

Writer-director Craig Baldwin cleverly works them into this 2007-set collage of paranoid fantasies about corporate domination of electronic media.

Sean Kilcoyne and Caroline Koebel give rudimentary performances as a father and daughter named Yogi and Boo Boo who argue Baldwin's point.

VILLAGE VOICE, 3/21/00, p. 135, J. Hoberman

Made for the coffee budget of behemoths like *Mission to Mars* or *The Ninth Gate*, Craig Baldwin's conspiratorial harangue *Spectres of the Spectrum* turns their showbiz concepts upside down. Baldwin's alien world is really earth; his black magic is what we call science.

This guerrilla media-assault on the so-called national entertainment state opens Friday for a limited run at Cinema Village. (Having already played the New York Film Festival and the New York Underground Film Festival as well as being chosen for the forthcoming Whitney Biennial, R's something of a mutant blockbuster.) Baldwin, a San Francisco-based provocateur who's made some of the funniest, most political found-footage collage films of the past decade, believes that sensory overload can only be fought by more of the same. *Spectres of the Spectrum is* a rapid-fire montage with a constant barrage of information. The movie takes no prisoners and it hits the ground ranting: "Fellow earthlings, there is a spectre haunting the planet."

An appropriately crude transmission announces the paranoid scenario. By 2007, all media have come under the corporate control of the New Electromagnetic Order—a mysterious entity that plans to bulk-erase the brains of all sentent beings. "This is a real story although some of it hasn't happened yet," Baldwin's protagonist, Boo Boo, declares. The narrative, such as it is, consists of crosscutting between the desert-dwelling Boo Boo and her father, Yogi, hunkered down in his bunker. These two rebellious telepaths are not only named for TV cartoon characters but exist as symbolic constructs. Yogi was born the day *Sputnik* was launched (and Wilhelm Reich died), Boo Boo in 1984, during the Super Bowl that introduced the Macintosh computer.

After two uneven features, the historical comedy *O No Coronado!* and the documentary *Sonic Outlaws,* Baldwin has returned to the mode he invented with his 1991 masterpiece, *Tribulations 99.* *Spectres*'s narrative is less important than its bargain-basement blitz of TV kinescopes, old classroom films, and ancient Hollywood biopics. Reveling in tacky models and primitive diagrams, Baldwin transforms everything into sub-Ed Wood schlock sci-fi even while concocting an outrageously complicated backstory connecting everyone from Benjamin Franklin to Scientology founder L. Ron Hubbard.

Satirizing the didactic TV of Baldwin's childhood, *Spectres of the Spectrum* is something of an educational movie itself—an eccentric history of modern media. "The telegraph annihilates the social imaginary," an anonymous narrator declares, crediting Samuel Morse's invention with inspiring an upsurge of both utopian fantasizing and spiritualist table-rapping. Repeatedly, Baldwin links new communication technology to occult concerns while grouping their inventors with contemporary "geek hackers." A grand war pits the forces of electromagnetic control against those of electromagnetic liberation. Baldwin champions eccentric individualists Nikola Tesla and Philo T. Farnsworth over corporate moguls Thomas Edison and David Sarnoff. In one of his more provocative asides, he describes Bill Gates as Sarnoff's second coming, a businessman who transformed the Internet into a marketing tool as Sarnoff did with broadcasting.

I suspect Baldwin views himself as battling Gates for control of the image archive. In any case, Boo Boo is compelled to travel back to 1957 to retrieve a secret message her grandmother encoded in a telecast of *Science in Action.* Time is reversible mainly through the miracle of found footage. Although she blasts her trailer back 50 years, the trip is mediated by television. Her return triggers the solar power surge that is, in some respects, a metaphor for Baldwin's movie. "It has never been my intention to kiss the ass of the audience," he told *Release Print* , setting himself in opposition "to the commercial technique, where you test-market a film and conform [it] to the expectations of the audience. It seems backward to me."

Well before it ends, *Spectres of the Spectrum* has overloaded its own circuits. But this ultimately numbing demonstration of information psychosis is humanized by the filmmaker's own obsessions. (To name one, he keeps bringing on Korla Pandit—the turbaned master of the Hammond organ, at once sinister hypnotist and benign spirit of the cathode-ray tube.) Caveat emptor: *Spectres of the Spectrum* is a crank call that borders on genius.

Also reviewed in:
NEW YORK TIMES, 10/9/99, p. B19, Stephen Holden
VARIETY, 11/29-12/5/99, p. 58, Ken Eisner

SPENT

A Regent Entertainment/Dreamfactory release of a Trademark Entertainment presentation of a THF Pictures production. *Executive Producer:* Joseph Cates and Jordan Zevon. *Producer:* Rena Joy Glickman, Jordan Summers, and Gil Cates, Jr. *Director:* Gil Cates, Jr. *Screenplay:* Gil Cates, Jr. *Director of Photography:* Robert D. Tome. *Editor:* Jonathan Cates. *Music:* Stan Ridgway. *Music Editor:* Pietra Wexstun. *Sound:* Jason Maltz. *Production Designer:*

Aaron Osborne.   *Art Director:* Kristen Gilmartin.   *Costumes:* Mimi Maxmen.   *Make-up:* Francie Paull.   *Running time:* 91 minutes.   *MPAA Rating:* Not Rated.

CAST: Jason London (Max); Charlie Spradling (Brigette); Phill Lewis (Doug); Erin Beaux (Nathan); James Parks (Grant); Barbara Barrie (Mrs. Walsh); Richmond Arquette (Jay); Gilbert Cates (Mr. Walsh); Rain Phoenix (Kimberly); Margaret Cho (Shirley); Jonah Blechman (Scott); Yale Summers (Max's Father); Kim Winter (Forum Waitress).

NEW YORK POST, 8/25/00, p. 59, Jonathan Foreman

This is one of those very Hollywoodish indie movies (it's written and directed by Gil Cates Jr., son of Gilbert Cates, the director and producer of Oscar ceremonies) about young L.A. types grappling with the problems that afflict so many wealthy young Hollywoodites: addiction (in this case, to gambling and alcohol), sexual confusion and denial of same.

There's a good sex scene and the standard of acting is generally strong, but Cates' pacing is slack, and the characters are either too thinly drawn or too bereft of redeeming qualities to be sympathetic.

The film is only 91 minutes long, but it seemed to stretch out for days.

NEWSDAY, 8/25/00, Part II/p. B13, Jan Stuart

Jason London shines in "Spent" as an unemployed young L.A. actor with a serious gambling problem. His character, Max, is a consummate con artist who has learned how to finesse shell games with other people's money in order to pay off whopping debts incurred from impulse sports bets. What becomes clear to us very quickly is that Max' most masterful con is the one he plays on himself.

Written and directed by Gil Cates Jr., "Spent" is a modest but diverting film about young people in denial. Max's girlfriend Brigette (Charlie Spradling) is a daytime alcoholic who sips wine for breakfast, scotch for afternoon snacks and refuses to concede she's got a problem. His roommate, Grant (James Parks), is a deeply closeted gay man who fixes on Max' issues rather than own up to a significant part of himself that he is repressing. None of them— surprise—is particularly happy.

Funny, then, that the movie around them should work so hard to be happy. In the manner of its characters, "Spent," is an earnest message picture (honesty is the best policy) that won't admit to its own latent sitcom tendencies. Cates surrounds his protagonist with a pair of tennis buddies (Phill Lewis and Erin Beaux) who spike home the comic relief whenever matters threaten to become too heavy. In a ploy that was amusing when Lucy and Ricky tried it more than 40 years ago, Max and Brigette dare one another to live without their bad habits for a month.

The uneasy balance of clowning and gravity lend "Spent" the air of an instructional film designed to reach high school seniors before they go out into the world and mess up their lives. Given the disturbing signals sent out by its denouement, it might be a more useful tool for the show business community of Los Angeles, where it is apparently more socially acceptable to be an addict than it is to be gay.

VILLAGE VOICE, 8/22/00, p. 138, Mark Holcomb

Part broad sitcom, part strained soap opera, Gil Cates Jr.'s *Spent* is so committed to its by-the-numbers banality you wonder why it isn't part of the fall TV lineup. Hip, handsome man-boy Max (Jason London), a fledgling screenwriter and chronic gambler, clashes with his girlfriend (Charlie Spradling) over her burgeoning alcoholism. In no time, they cop to their addictions and walk hand-in-hand into rehab. In an unrelated subplot, Max's writing partner and Kramer-esque friend conspire to slip their screenplay to Jack Nicholson at a Lakers game. Cates nudges his movie toward its tidy conclusion with the agility of a seasoned network hack.

Shot in warm, bland tones in pristine L.A. neighborhoods, *Spent* could pass as a commercial for the Santa Monica tourist board: impeccably fit characters share spacious homes, drive expensive cars, and yet have no visible means of support (gambling notwithstanding). Its characterizations are just as unlikely: Brigette drinks like a fish and remains model-thin, while

Max's bookie turns up to dispense fatherly advice on how to stay out of debt. All this would amount to innocuous fluff, but in need of some galvanizing event, the film offers up Max's closeted gay roommate as a sacrifice. Suffice to say it's a nasty bit of business that makes an otherwise forgettable film hard to shake.

Also reviewed in:
NEW YORK TIMES, 8/25/00, p. E20, Elvis Mitchell
VARIETY, 7/24-30/00, p. 46, Lael Loewenstein

SPIN THE BOTTLE

A CinéBlast! Productions release. *Executive Producer:* Gill Holland. *Producer:* Jamie Yerkes, Kevin Chinoy, and Kris Hornsher. *Director:* Jamie Yerkes. *Screenplay:* Amy Sohn. *Story:* Jamie Yerkes. *Director of Photography:* Harlan Bosmajian. *Editor:* Josh Apter and Jamie Yerkes. *Music:* Ded Tomney. *Sound:* Elaine Porcher. *Sound Editor:* Matthew Fleece. *Casting:* Mary Clay Boland and Catherine Zambri. *Production Designer:* Johanna Belson. *Art Director:* Liz Carney. *Running time:* 86 minutes. *MPAA Rating:* Not Rated.

CAST: Mitchell Riggs (Ted); Kim Winter (Bev); Jessica Faller (Alex); Heather Goldenhersh (Rachel); Holter Graham (Jonah); Michael Conn (Young Jonah); Allison Gervais (Young Bev); April Harvey (Young Alex); Zachery Newland (Young Ted); Kristen Way (Young Rachel); Todd Wheel (Sledge).

VILLAGE VOICE, 5/9/00, p. 138, Jessica Winter

Making a go at the tragedy tryouts, *Spin the Bottle* sends five childhood friends—now in their late twenties—back to the summer cottage of their youth where a game of that junior high basement-party standby dredges up latent insecurities, grudges held over from eighth grade, and forbidden homoerotic longings, scattering all lives concerned into disarray. Former *New York Press* sex columnist Amy Sohn wrote the script, in which characters quip and navel-gaze as lonely yuppie singles are apparently wont to do, while the plot pirouettes on tidy gotcha reversals: The uptight lawyer turns out to be closeted, the dumbshit stud harbors a Machiavellian streak, and the sex-obsessed commitment-averse, frank-talkin' seductress bitch turns out to be the wryest, wisest, most self-aware aching soul of the bunch.

Also reviewed in:
NEW YORK TIMES, 5/4/00, p. E5, A. O. Scott
VARIETY, 4/5-11/99, p. 40, Lael Loewenstein

SPRING FORWARD

IFC Films release of a C-Hundred Film/Cineblast Productions Inc. production. *Executive Producer:* Jonathan Sehring, Caroline Kaplan, William Gilroy, and Michael Stipe. *Producer:* Jim McKay, Gill Holland, Paul S. Mezey, and Tom Gilroy. *Director:* Tom Gilroy. *Screenplay:* Tom Gilroy. *Director of Photography:* Terry Stacey. *Editor:* James Lyons. *Music:* Hahn Rowe. *Sound Editor:* Damian Volpe. *Production Designer:* Susan Block. *Make-up:* Joanne Ottaviano. *Running time:* 110 minutes. *MPAA Rating:* R.

CAST: Ned Beatty (Murph); Liev Schreiber (Paul); Campbell Scott (Fredrickson); Ian Hart (Fran); Peri Gilpin (Georgia); Bill Raymond (Don Reagan); Catherine Kellner (Dawn); Hallee Hirsh (Hope); Justin Laboy (Bobby); Kristin Laboy (Kristin); David Roland Frank (Boy with Snowblower).

LOS ANGELES TIMES, 12/29/00, Calendar/p. 2, Kevin Thomas

Tom Gilroy's debut feature, "Spring Forward," is so fully realized and so moving that you wish you could get away with merely saying: "Go see it for yourself."

Every frame attests to the power of simplicity. It affords Ned Beatty the role of a lifetime and an equally fine part for Liev Schreiber, who is swiftly emerging as one of the most accomplished actors of his generation. This modest, intimate film may be one of the last pictures to open in 2000, but it ranks among the year's best, as do Beatty and Schreiber's performances.

It begins deceptively, without any fanfare, as the camera picks up two men in work clothes riding in a pickup truck to a woodsy area. In time we learn that they are park and recreation department employees in an unnamed, enchantingly beautiful rural community—in reality, it is principally Ridgefield, Conn.

They pull up to a sizable house in the woods, where they are greeted by a preppy-looking young man of obvious influence: Fredrickson (Campbell Scott). There's a suggestion that his family is in the nursery business; in any event, the young man has a substantial load of fertilizer to donate to the city and needs it moved immediately. But the two workmen he promised would be on hand to help Beatty's Murph and Schreiber's Paul have not shown up.

Fredrickson presumes that Murph and Paul will proceed with the unappealing task anyway, not even bothering to ask them whether or not they would mind doing so unassisted. Fredrickson's casually condescending tone has ignited a slow burn in Paul from the get-go, and now he explodes at Fredrickson's presumption.

From here, the movie could go lots of ways. Paul could turn violent, with Murph inadvertently winding up on the run with him—that would be the most predictable. But the steady, even-tempered Murph succeeds in calming Paul down. The younger man, suddenly ashamed of himself, runs off and gives way to sobbing, saying he's got to quit on what is actually his first day on the job.

Paul is an ex-con, fresh out of prison, where he was sent for robbing a Dunkin' Donuts to get funds he desperately needed to buy a car so he could hold down a job. He is filled with rage over the hard luck that has dogged him all his life but even more is dismayed at himself for failing to manage his anger, as he was taught in prison. Admitting he didn't actually get the help he needed there, he has learned just enough to believe he should feel forever apologetic and impose upon himself rigid rules of behavior.

Murph has a better idea: that Paul ought to relax a little and try some self-acceptance. It is the birth of a friendship that makes this movie glow. In his 60s, Murph is old enough to have grown up in an era—the years following the Depression and World War II—when the old American tradition of lending a helping hand was intensified in one last gasp before receding in the wake of the postwar boom and all the wrenching socioeconomic changes since. Truly, Paul could have easily taken a hopelessly self-destructive course in his life, had Murph not happened to be there and actually cared what happened to him.

Murph and Paul learn about each other as they go about their jobs. Both had hard-drinking fathers, but Paul grew up in a poverty-stricken, broken home. Although a high school dropout, Paul is bright, curious and an autodidact with a susceptibility to New Age ideas that he at times carries to amusing lengths. Murph has learned to meet life philosophically, yet both admit to spiritual yearnings.

On one level, a father-son relationship develops between the men, but it is also a true friendship of equals in which innermost fears and joys are shared in an atmosphere of mutual trust. And as in all good friendships, theirs is not one-sided; indeed, Murph is as surprised as he is grateful for all that he learns from Paul.

Most significantly, "Spring Forward" is in no way the two-character play it could have been in lesser hands. Gilroy's perspective runs wider and deeper than required just to depict the development of a bond between the two men, as affecting as it is.

At all times, Gilroy, a seasoned actor, stage director and playwright, exhibits a keen awareness of nature. The film's settings and the outdoor work the characters do lend themselves to this concern, enabling Gilroy and his splendid cinematographer, Terry Stacey, to capture with subtlety the change of the seasons to evoke both the passing of time and the eternal cycle of life. This rich context lifts "Spring Forward" securely above the merely sentimental, delivering the fullest possible emotional impact.

Beatty and Schreiber become Murph and Paul to the extent that you forget they are actors giving performances. No moves, gestures, nuances or intonations suggest calculation, but rather complete naturalness, and this goes for the other actors in the cast: most important, Peri Gilpin as a likable young woman who gives Paul reason to hope he might not be so lonely in the future, and Catherine Kellner as a profoundly troubled young woman who evokes in Paul a response that reveals how thoroughly he has absorbed Murph's exemplary kindness and concern for others.

"Spring Forward" leaves one with that rarest of feelings: a heightened awareness of the human capacity for good.

NEW YORK POST, 12/8/00, p. 54, Jonathan Foreman

Most of this well-written but stagy film by New York playwright Tom Gilroy is taken up with scenes of two Connecticut parks employees shooting the breeze and getting to know each other over a year.

They're played by those excellent actors Ned Beatty (who gives the kind of superbly nuanced performance all too rare in films today) and Liev Screiber.

Beatty's character is on the verge of retirement and has a son (whom you never meet) who is dying of AIDS. Schreiber's is a neurotic but decent young man just out of prison.

But despite the high quality of the acting, "Spring Forward" is for the most part sleepy, long-winded stuff, that becomes increasingly predictable along the way, and which tends to come alive only in the moments when the two guys encounter other people, like Campbell Scott's odious rich kid, Ian Hart's drunken homeless guy, and Peri Gilpin's sexy older woman.

There's also a faintly patronizing air hanging over the whole proceedings, as if some upper middle-class filmmakers were a little bit too proud of themselves for making a film set in a working-class milieu.

NEWSDAY, 12/8/00, Part II/p. B8, Gene Seymour

Any two-character play, on stage or on film, is pushing its luck if it lasts longer than, say, an hour. And despite the occasional outsider who strays into view, "Spring Forward" is essentially a chamber piece performed by a pair of character actors working at the top of their game. Indeed, Ned Beatty and Liev Schreiber are so terrific together that they almost shut down one's qualms about writer-director Tom Gilroy's indulgence in theatrically long pauses and meandering verbal rifts.

One could also argue that such paint-drying pacing may well be what makes Gilroy's movie daring. The argument would be more persuasive if even a few of the 110 minutes were shaved away. Still, when thinking back on some of the things Beatty and Schreiber do with this material, you're hard pressed to think of what you'd take away that wouldn't disrupt the actors' finely calibrated interaction.

The movie chronicles a year in the life of two parks department field workers in a small Connecticut town. Murph (Beatty) is a world- weary veteran who's months away from retirement. Paul (Schreiber) has just been released from prison, where he did time for a half-baked armed robbery attempt.

The younger man is all too anxious to blab about both the desperation compelling him to crime and the cool spiritual stuff he's been picking up from books since his release. The older man doesn't want to hear any of it. Yet, Murph, from his relatively reserved corner of the world, has collected enough pain and rough wisdom in his own life to become a kind of Zen referee for Paul's stumbling pursuit of the straight and narrow.

After Paul's first day on the job, when he almost gets into a dustup with a snarky offspring (Campbell Scott) of the local elite, he and Murph eventually settle into a comfortable routine. Whether picking up trash, painting a fence or policing the schoolyards, Murph becomes a reluctantly attentive sounding board for Paul's inchoate yearnings. In return, Paul allows Murph to quietly blow off some steam about barely concealed troubles, one of which is his dying homosexual son.

So much of "Spring Forward's" raw material could be overplayed and cheapened for mass consumption. Yet, the tender solicitude Gilroy and his actors show for these decent blue-collar guys and what they say to each other validates even the stickier sequences. The cameos by Scott,

Ian Hart (stunning, as always, as a park vagrant) and Peri Gilpin (who makes neediness sexy as a dog-loving single gal) are all striking. But if the movie belongs to anyone, it is Beatty, who manages to display the fruits of a life's work just in the way his character slouches in front of a funeral home and gropes for words about his dead son.

VILLAGE VOICE, 12/12/00, p. 178, Michael Atkinson

Spring Forward exemplifies what American indies—so often pie-eyed with genre hypercoolness, egomania, and fatuous ambition—should be best at: modesty, attentive realism, conceptual rigor, believable performances, and a healthy, uncommercial respect for real people, real talk, and real life. An indie actor and theater hound, director Tom Gilroy has even constructed his microbudgeted movie organically: a dual-character study of two New England Parks Department workers—one aging, one young and thrumming with problems—shot in sequence over the course of a year. The easy slide into stilted speechifying and "character arc" is an ever present risk, but Gilroy keeps the reins taut—the conversational setups and delivered exposition are as sly and natural as American movies seem to be capable of. Paul (Liev Schreiber) is an uneducated ex-con who, when we meet him his first day on the job, has to gab about his crime and time; Murph (Ned Beatty), a weary, practical retiree-to-be, doesn't want to hear it. The movie simply leaps along from there, from spring to midwinter, punctuated by lovely visual haiku of quotidian routine (opening a pool, burning leaves, playing street hockey) that slow the movie down to a contemplative stroll.

The sense of continuing life is quietly remarkable. The two men are never at odds in a formulaic way, so their accumulating rapport and mutual fondness don't seem fake, even when Murph enjoys his first spliff and Paul attempts to communicate his study of Buddhism. Reuniting every few months to pick up where they left off, the actors don't struggle—time does a lot of the work, just as some plot elements (like Peri Gilpin's sexy appearance as a puppy-swamped love interest for Paul) vanish with the passing seasons. Gilroy's script isn't brilliant: Clichés have free run of the joint ("What goes around comes around"; "Haste makes waste!"), and some of the over-philosophical dialogue rings Hollywood fake. But so much of what's there sounds right; by the climactic mini-melodrama involving a battered wife standing on a frozen lake, you've gotten to know these men as men. Beatty is the movie's glue, but all he does is remind us that he might be the best natural actor in the country. Watching him listen and react (even to Campbell Scott's officious blue blood), you cannot help but become aware of how most movie acting is posturing goatcrap. With one great scene—a regretful moment of remembrance on the back porch of the funeral parlor where his gay son is being waked—Beatty steals the year's meager thunder.

Alsor reviewed in:
NEW YORK TIMES, 12/8/00, p. E16, A. O. Scott
VARIETY, 4/3-9/00, p. 43, Joe Leydon

STARDOM

A Lions Gate Films release of an Alliance Atlantis and Serendipity Point Film presentation in association with Cinémaginaire and Ciné B.   *Producer:* Denise Robert and Robert Lantos. *Director:* Denys Arcand. *Screenplay:* Denys Arcand and Jacob Potashnik.   *Director of Photography:* Guy Dufaux. *Editor:* Isabelle Dedieu.   *Music:* François Dompierre.   *Sound:* Claude La Haye. *Casting:* Deirdre Bowen and Lucie Robitaille.   *Production Designer:* Zoë Sakellaropoulo.   *Art Director:* Jean Morin.   *Set Decorator:* Louise Pilon.   *Set Dresser:* Charles-André Bertrand.   *Special Effects:* Ann Smeltzer.   *Costumes:* Michel Robidas. *Make-up:* Micheline Trpanier.   *Running time:* 102 minutes.   *MPAA Rating:* R.

CAST: Dan Aykroyd (Barry Levine);   Jessica Paré (Tina Menzhal);   Robert Lepage (Bruce Taylor);   Thomas Gibson (Renny Ohayon);   Frank Langella (Blaine de Castillon);   Charles Berling (Philippe Gascon);   Camilla Rutherford (Toni);   Patrick Huard (Talkshow Host);   Tony

Calabretta (Bernie Placek);   Alain Goulem (Bobby Veau);   Larry Day (Brian O'Connell); Danielle Desormeaux (Sheila Rinaldy);   Domenic Di Rosa (Principal);   Claudia Ferri (Ruth Levine);   Susan Glover (Claire Crosby);   Jayne Heitmeyer (Penelope Vargas);   Lisa Bronwyn Moore (Susie Tucker);   Charles Powell (Terry Pfizer);   Norm Rebadow (Detective Sam Donahue);   Janine Theriault (Irina);   François Berléand (French Accountant);   Philippe Caroit (French TV Journalist);   Rachelle Lefevre (Leslie Bloor);   Joel McNichol (Gaby Stern); Patrick Poivre d'Arvor (French TV Presenter);   Jonathan Robert Rondeau (Justin);   Joanne Vannicola; Victoria Show;   Benoît Brire;   Richard Greenblatt;   Sophie Lorain;   Macha Grenon;   Chantal Baril;   Jamie Elman.

LOS ANGELES TIMES, 10/27/00, Calendar/p. 14, Kevin Thomas

Denys Arcand's "Stardom" traces the arc of a beautiful small-town Canadian woman from hockey player to world-famous fashion model and beyond. The trouble is that French Canadian Arcand, whose memorable "The Decline of the American Empire" and "Jesus of Montreal" were both foreign-language Oscar nominees, takes us down a familiar path without discovering anything new along the way.

Arcand realizes he needs a fresh twist, but the best he can come up with is to present Jessica Pare's Tina Menzhal entirely through the lens of a film or video or TV camera. When she's not being seen in newscasts or on TV shows, she's conveniently being taped by a sympathetic fashion photographer-cum-documentarian (Robert Lepage), to whom she looks as a confidant. His constantly running camera seems for her a kind of therapy and validation of her existence, possibly even an addiction, but at times becomes, understandably, annoying.

It might have proved more profitable for Arcand to explore this ambivalence in Tina further than to devote so much time to a clutch of TV news commentators and talk-show personalities, who are consistently obnoxious and dense stereotypes. So much time is spent on them, the film's minuses outweigh its pluses.

Ironically, Pare's Tina is as beguiling as she is beautiful, an uncomplicated but resilient young woman whose fate might hold our attention without the tricky media layering.

Beauties like her seem always to become involved with thuddingly unsuitable older men. She first has an affair with the slimy French fashion photographer (Charles Berling) who propels her to professional heights; then with a trendy Montreal restaurateur (Dan Aykroyd), so besotted with her that he self-destructs—making Aykroyd look foolish in the process; and finally with a snooty, sophisticated U.N. ambassador (Frank Langella), a patent mismatch.

That Arcand regards Tina's story above all a media commentary makes it difficult for the film to come alive and become involving, and it says something Pare's poise and presence that we come to care about Tina, though not about "Stardom."

NEW YORK POST, 10/27/00, p. 46, Lou Lumenick

This is a glitzy and shallow satire about shallow people.

The stunningly beautiful Jessica Pare plays Tina, a back woods Canadian hockey player who takes the modeling world by storm. Along the way, she destroys three helplessly smitten middle-aged men.

Director Denys Arcand's level of wit is indicated by Tina's last name: Menzhal (i.e., men's hell). Laced with faux video clips, it's like an episode of "GE Theater" crossed with MTV's "House of Style."

NEWSDAY, 10/27/00, Part II/p. B6, Gene Seymour

After a while, one gets tired of writing reviews of movie satires arguing that such movies end up, intentionally or not, flattering, even glorifying, the thing they're supposed to be satirizing.

So let's just get it over with. Start talking about "Stardom" by saying that French-Canadian director Denys Arcand ("Jesus of Montreal," "The Decline of the American Empire") seems to be as caught up by the fluffy meringue of media voguing as the many glamour-obsessed men and women caught in the gravitational pull of supermodel Tina Menzahl's (Jessica Pare) meteoric trajectory through the Global Village.

And for anyone who has compulsively channel-surfed to crash-and-burn bios on VHl or the E! Network, there are plenty of salty guilty pleasures to nosh on in "Stardom's" video-scrapbook chronicle of Tina's rise from a gangly high-school hockey player from a small Canadian town to the Face of Her Time.

All the usual stops on such odysseys flash before our eyes: There's Tina, squirming during ambush interviews on daytime talk shows, and perpetually caught in the camera's clutches, like the proverbial deer in headlights. All of which only magnifies her stature, for want of a better word, in this Warholian land of fashion designers and media hucksters such as her super-cool agent Renny Ohayon (Thomas Gibson from "Dharma and Greg" in impeccably snarky form).

Ohayon's just about the only man in Tina's life who isn't reduced to violent, blathering helplessness by her pouty mouth, ice-blue eyes and sleek physique. Restaurateur Barry Levine (Dan Aykroyd) leaves his wife to follow her to New York where he spectacularly self-destructs. Later on, Blaine de Castillon (Frank Langella), Canada's seemingly unflappable ambassador to the UN, makes her a trophy wife only to find scandal and disgrace lurking just past the altar.

Arcand makes all this stuff so entertaining to watch that both you and he seem to forget that he's supposed to be making an inquiry into the ways beauty is crassly transformed by corporate-ized pop culture into commodity. When he brings up a scene or statement to dramatize that point, it comes across as far more shallow than he intends. You just can't win.

VILLAGE VOICE, 10/31/00, p. 174, Dennis Lim

If not much else, *Stardom* has a formal conceit—and clings to it for dear life. Denys Arcand's sub-Brechtian, pseudo-McLuhanesque, anti-Warholian satire charts a Canadian high schooler's fairy-tale ascent to supermodel celebrity (and her *True Hollywood Story* slide into obscurity) through a series of uniformly brainless mass-mediated images: news reports, talk shows, commercials, interviews, telethons, puff pieces. To a degree, Arcand approximates the evanescent, analgesic quality of a long, dumb channel surf—an activity that's never much fun when someone else is hogging the remote.

Stardom's purposefully blank heroine, Tina Menzhal (Jessica Pare), is discovered in a backwater ice-hockey rink; a sports photographer catches her mid-pout, and before long she's pacing the Montreal catwalks and shacked up with an unctuous French photographer (Charles Berling). Tina then goes from homewrecker (moving to New York with married restaurateur Dan Aykroyd) to trophy wife, perched uncomfortably on the arm of Canadian UN ambassador Frank Langella. As she hops from New York to Paris to London, from ski resort to Caribbean island, Arcand tracks the meaninglessness of her fame by stressing the vacuity of televisual codes and clichés. Tina's caught in numerous Springerish ambushes (an Oprah clone stages a cruel reunion with her estranged father) and interviewed or stalked by infotainment correspondents, fashion-maven creatures, breathlessly belligerent VJs. But the director also compromises his high concept with a disingenuous device: A flamboyant fashion photographer (Robert Lepage) shadows Tina for a *Truth or Dare*-style documentary, and Arcand, too timid to fully simulate the disjointedness inherent in his premise, uses the canned black-and-white mock-vérité like putty.

With a few exceptions (none more memorable than a discombobulated Langella's riotous outburst before the United Nations), most of the laughs in *Stardom* are cheap—and worse, the ideas beyond platitudinous. A newsreader interrupts a report on a cult suicide in Algeria to carry live a breaking story about Tina's hospitalization for cuts and bruises, and we're supposed to tsk in horror. The fickleness of fame, the distortions of mass media, the skewed priorities of celebrity culture—Arcand treats each truism like a hard-won insight.

Also reviewed in:
CHICAGO TRIBUNE, 10/27/00, Friday/p. Q, Michael Wilmington
NEW YORK TIMES, 10/27/00, p. E 16, Elvis Mitchell
VARIETY, 5/22-28/00, p. 30, Brendan Kelly
WASHINGTON POST, 10/27/00, p. C5, Stephen Hunter

STATE AND MAIN

A Fine Line Features release in association with Hilltop Entertainment and FilmTown Entertainment of a Green/Renzi production in association with El Dorado Pictures. *Executive Producer:* Jon Cornick and Alec Baldwin. *Producer:* Sarah Green. *Director:* David Mamet. *Screenplay:* David Mamet. *Director of Photography:* Oliver Stapleton. *Editor:* Barbara Tulliver. *Music:* Theodore Shapiro. *Music Editor:* John Carbonara. *Sound:* John Pritchett and (music) Michael Farrow. *Sound Editor:* Maurice Schell and Richard P. Cirincione. *Casting:* Avy Kaufman. *Production Designer:* Gemma Jackson. *Art Director:* Carl Sprague. *Set Decorator:* Kyra Friedman. *Special Effects:* Peter Kunz. *Costumes:* Susan Lyall. *Make-up:* Peter Robb-King. *Stunt Coordinator:* Manny Siverio. *Running time:* 102 minutes. *MPAA Rating:* R.

CAST: Alec Baldwin (Bob Barrenger, Actor); Charles Durning (Mayor George Bailey); Clark Gregg (Doug Mackenzie); Philip Seymour Hoffman (Joseph Turner White, the Writer); Patti LuPone (Sherry Bailey, the Mayor's Wife); William H. Macy (Walt Price); Sarah Jessica Parker (Claire Wellesley, Actress); David Paymer (Marty Rossen); Rebecca Pidgeon (Ann Black); Julia Stiles (Carla Taylor); Michael Higgins (Doc Wilson); Michael Bradshaw (Priest); Morris Lamore (Bunky); Allen Soule (Spud); Ricky Jay (Jack); Matt Malloy (Hotel Clerk); Tony V (Water Delivery Man); Tony Mamet (Electrician); Jack Wallace (Bellhop); Michael James O'Boyle (Chuckie); Charlotte Potok (Maude); Christopher Kaldor (Officer Cal Thompkin); Rick Levy (Gun Store Owner); J J Johnston (Stationmaster); Richard L. Friedman (Postman); Kolbie McCabe (Girl on Scooter); Emma Norman (Fisherwoman); Dee Nelson (Decorator); Brian Howe (Bartender); Robert Walsh (Trooper 1); G. Roy Levin (Salesman with Rubber Duck); Matthew Pidgeon (BBC TV Reporter); Daniel B. Hovanesian (Bailiff); Jerry Graff (Fake Judge); Timothy Jernigan-Smith (Billy on Bike); Paul Butler (Real Judge); Alexandra Kerry (Television Director); Ken Cheeseman (Trooper 2); Jordan Lage (Doc Morton); Lionel Mark Smith (Bill Smith); Vincent Gustaferro (Uberto Pazzi-Sforzo); Linda Kimbrough (Courteney); Jim Frangione (Tommy Max); Lana Bilzerian (Girl Production Assistant); Laura Silverman (Secretary); Josh Marchette (Production Assistant); Jonathan Katz (Howie Gold).

LOS ANGELES TIMES, 12/22/00, Calendar/p. 2, Kenneth Turan

Contradictory as it sounds, Hollywood is the kind of place you have to despair of to truly love. Where else can a director caught in an untruth say, "It's not a lie, it's a gift for fiction," or a producer insist, "I made $11 million last year and I don't like to be trifled with"? And where else, for that matter, can a horse be a legitimate candidate for an associate producer credit?

True, these are not real people, or a real horse, but as pungent characters in writer-director David Mamet's completely delicious show-biz satire "State and Main," they might as well be. An occasional worker in Hollywood for nearly 20 years, Mamet knows where bodies are buried and how to use the corpses to bring a smile to your face. "State and Main" is a quintessentially wised-up insider comedy, ideally cast and filled with sharp writing from start to finish (a line about associate producers at the end of the credits is especially worth waiting for).

It may be cynical, but, in another paradox, "State and Main's" story of what transpires when a major studio movie comes to a small New England town may be the warmest film Mamet has yet made. Someone once said that complaining about Hollywood is like a boxer coming out of the ring and saying, "That guy hit me." Mamet doesn't moralize, he just records it all with a can-you-believe-this kind of bemused glee.

Like the real estate office setting of his Pulitzer Prize-winning "Glengarry Glen Ross," Hollywood is ideal Mamet territory. Both worlds are filled with people who bend words to their particular uses just as they bend the rules of morality in an attempt to cope with increasingly desperate situations.

In fact, "State and Main" has a lot of Mamet's trademark characteristics, including numerous plot twists, all presented in a looser, more relaxed form than we're used to. Even his clipped, pungent dialogue isn't delivered in quite as rigid a cadence as the director usually insists on. And maybe because the movie business brings its own particular darkness and devilry with it, Mamet has felt freer to make his vision more amiable than it's ever been.

Accentuating the comedic aspects is the terrific farce situation Mamet the screenwriter has come up with. Fast pacing and intricate plotting, with endless complications bringing on recriminations, vendettas and worst-case scenarios mean that the invention and the energy never flag.

This kind of manic, antic storytelling brings to mind the classic 1940s comedies of Preston Sturges, a writer-director whose influence here Mamet acknowledges. Like Sturges, Mamet has increased the laughter by his adroit casting of a large and expert ensemble. Alec Baldwin, Charles Durning, Clark Gregg, Philip Seymour Hoffman, Patti LuPone, William H. Macy, Sarah Jessica Parker, David Paymer, Rebecca Pidgeon and Julia Stiles, take a bow. You've earned it.

Until the bucolic fictional hamlet of Waterford, Vt. had the movie business come to town, the only thing the town and its most ambitious politician Doug MacKenzie (Gregg) ever got worked up over was the new traffic light at that State and Main intersection.

Then the cast and crew of "The Old Mill," if mysteriously ejected from neighboring New Hampshire, enter the picture. First to arrive is director Walt Price, who likes what he sees. Beautifully played by Macy, Price is the pragmatic facilitator with a solution for everything. He's the good cop who could placate an aroused polar bear, who knows what to say to everyone, even sending a few words of atrociously pronounced Yiddish to his killer producer Marty Rossen (Paymer).

An attorney who just happens to travel with the statutes on statutory rape, Rossen is the bad cop, the kind of guy who says, "Don't flinch when I'm talking to you." His mandate is dealing with big problems, like placating the town's mayor (Durning) and his social-climbing wife (LuPone). And coping with whatever crises his stars will inevitably precipitate.

With female lead Claire Wellesley (Parker), it's a reluctance to take off her shirt. Yes, she signed a contract agreeing to do just that, but without an added $800,000 she's threatening to walk.

Her co-star Bob Barrenger (Baldwin), who shows up with the "I'm just here to do a job" swagger of the world's top box-office attraction, turns out to have a weakness for underage girls. "Everyone," he says by way of shameless explanation, "needs a hobby." Naturally, the presence in town of a fetching and sharp-eyed teenage waitress (Stiles) doesn't escape his notice.

Expected to be creative in the midst of this chaos is the awkward, woebegone writer Joseph Turner White (Hoffman), who starts off on the wrong foot by (a) being the writer and (b) immediately losing his typewriter.

Fortunately for him and the film, White gets a big break when he makes a connection with local bookstore owner Ann Black (Pidgeon), who's sane, sensible and smart with a pithy sense of humor thrown into the mix. Ann is the emotional center of the film, someone who makes the fictional world of Waterford not only a great place to visit, but also someplace we actually might want to live. And that, for a David Mamet setting, is saying a lot.

NEW YORK, 1/1/01, p. 81, Peter Rainer

Given how acidic David Mamet can be toward Hollywood (as in his play *Speed-the-Plow*), his new film, *State and Main*, which is about the shenanigans of a movie crew on location in a New England town, is surprisingly mild. Actually, Mamet's approach is not so much mild as it is indifferent: He doesn't lavish his customary full attention on these characters because he doesn't care enough about them or what they do (maybe indifference represents his ultimate revenge on Hollywood). Even at half-speed, Mamet still manages to pull off some marvelous, if familiar, satire of movie-business egomania, and the tip-top cast includes David Paymer as a viperish producer; William H. Macy as the glib, harried director; Alec Baldwin as a star with a fetish for underage chicks; Sarah Jessica Parker as his insecure co-star; and, in a role that indicates Mamet's worst-case image of himself, Philip Seymour Hoffman as the serious playwright turned hack screenwriter. In speaking Mamet's best lines, these performers bring out the grain in his syncopated nastiness.

NEW YORK POST, 12/22/00, p. 55, Lou Lumenick

"It's about the quest for purity," explains the screenwriter of the film whose crew has wreaked havoc in a small Vermont town in "State and Main," David Mamet's hilarious and surprisingly sweet new comedy.

The central joke—a good one with lots of resonance—is that except for the hopelessly idealistic and naive Joe White (Philip Seymour Hoffman), the filmmakers trying to realize his vision are about as pure as Manhattan slush.

Bob Barringer (Alec Baldwin), the star of this historical romance, has a well-reported yen for under-aged females ("It's my hobby," he explains) that's already gotten the company thrown out of another town in New Hampshire.

Walt Price (William H. Macy), the inventive director, is so behind schedule and over budget that he orders Joe to write an old mill out of the script to save money—even though the movie is titled "The Old Mill."

Meanwhile Marty Rossen (David Paymer), the schmoozing, take-no-prisoners producer, is threatening to blackball the female lead Claire (Sarah Jessica Parker) from the industry.

She's threatening to walk off the film unless she's paid an additional $800,000 for the embarrassment of showing her breasts—even though, as one character remarks, audiences can draw them from memory.

At the same time, a politically ambitious councilman (Clark Gregg) is scheming to hold up filming permits unless town merchants get a "three percent of the first-dollar gross."

Temporarily fired by Walt, a dazed Joe finds a soulmate in the down-to-earth Ann Black (Rebecca Pidgeon), who runs the local bookstore and helps him with broken glasses and emergency rewrites on the script.

She also comes to provide a moral compass for the clueless Joe, whose willingness to compromise in pursuit of a three-picture deal is sorely tested when he witnesses an unfortunate encounter between Bob and a smitten local teenager (Julia Stiles).

As anyone who's seen "Almost Famous" can attest, Hoffman is one of the best character actors working today, and "State and Main" shows this wonderful performer makes a quite credible romantic leading man. There is a wonderful understated chemistry between Hoffman and Pidgeon (in real life Mrs. Mamet), who is quite irresistible as Ann.

"That's absurd," says a flabbergasted Joe of the ever-crazier events at one point.

"So is our electoral process," replies the level-headed Ann in a line that's become much funnier since "State and Main" was filmed last year. "But I still believe in it."

NEWSDAY, 12/22/00, Part II/p. B8, Gene Seymour

David Mamet's spare-riffing dramaturgical style would seem an imperfect fit for the snappy rhythms and hard-charging momentum of classic Hollywood comedy. Yet maybe it takes a playwright with Mamet's spiky sense of craftsmanship to reach all the way back to the halcyon days of Preston Sturges, Leo McCarey, Howard Hawks and other masters of the wisecracking screwball farces that flourished throughout FDR's administration.

"State and Main," doesn't quite reach those exalted heights. In fact, Mamet imposes his allusive mechanics and surreptitious characterization on this culture-clash farce to the point where the film sags where it should bend (or curve) toward its next plot development. Yet, pound for pound, there are fresher wisecracks packed in "State and Main" than in just about any high-concept Hollywood comedy of recent vintage.

The concept here—movie sharpies descending upon a bucolic New England hamlet—isn't exactly bakery-fresh. But Mamet, though not as elegant in his directorial touch as Ernst Lubitsch or McCarey, nonetheless brings enough verbal ingenuity to the package to make you wonder why it isn't done more often.

The town in question is mythical Waterford, Vt., whose citizenry isn't quite sure how to feel when a troubled historical epic, forced to move its cast and crew from New Hampshire, lands in their community. Director Walt Price (William H. Macy), under the gun and frantic, makes nice with the town mayor (Charles Durning) and a skeptical, politically ambitious attorney (Clark Gregg) as he goads his screenwriter, Joe White (Philip Seymour Hoffman), to make needed changes. And fast.

Joe, diffident and shy, doesn't know quite what to do without his missing manual typewriter. But he finds both a new machine and unexpected inspiration from Ann Black (Rebecca Pidgeon), the head of the local theater group who's one of his biggest fans—and engaged to the aforementioned pol.

Meanwhile, the movie's leading man, Bob Barrenger (Alec Baldwin) arrives, carrying baggage—and not just the literal suitcases. He's known for his fatal attraction to underage girls—a reputation not lost on Carla (Julia Stiles) a teenage coffee-shop waitress willing to do anything to help the visitors.

You don't have to be Billy Wilder or Moliere to imagine the subsequent potential complications, which do manage to rapidly accumulate on Waterford's tree-lined streets and motel corridors. Mamet's script maintains tight traffic control over the colliding mishaps while managing to keep everyone in the movie from slipping into TV-cartoon flatness.

The impressive cast, of course, has as much to do with sustaining the movie's humanity. They're all good, especially Hoffman, Macy and Pidgeon, whose easygoing sensuality almost allows her to walk away with the whole enterprise.

SIGHT AND SOUND, 2/01, p. 52, Geoffrey Macnab

A movie crew arrives in Waterford, Vermont to shoot a feature. Director Walt Price needs an old mill for the film, which is set in the 19th century, but the town doesn't have one—although its tourist brochure claims otherwise. Writer Joe White is assigned to revise his screenplay to make the most of Waterford as it stands. When his manual typewriter goes missing, owner Ann Black provides him a replacement. Ann becomes friends with Joe and breaks off her engagement to Doug Mackenzie, an ambitious local politician.

Meanwhile, lead actress Claire objects to scenes requiring nudity When Joe stands up for her, she is so grateful she comes to his room and tries to seduce him. Ann sees her there, but accepts Joe's explanation for her presence. Lead actor Bob Barrenger, who has a weakness for seducing underage girls, crashes a car while out with local teenager Carla Taylor. Joe witnesses the accident.

Walt and his producer Marty Rossen offend the town mayor by failing to attend a dinner party in their honour. When he learns that Carla was involved in the car crash with Barrenger, Doug threatens to close the production down. Its future hinges on Joe's testimony. Joe initially lies about what happened, then tells the truth. With Joe's testimony, Doug could ruin the film-makers and disgrace Barrenger; but instead he accepts a massive bribe from Marty. The movie is allowed to go ahead as planned.

It's hard to work out exactly what David Mamet feels about the film industry. In his 1988 play *Speed-The-Plow* he viciously satirised Hollywood's obsession with money, sex and status, but that hasn't stopped him from working there, both as a writer-for-hire and on projects he originated himself. In his essay "A Playwright in Hollywood" (collected in his 1994 book *A Whore's Profession*), he claims that "writing for the movies taught me to stick to the plot and not to cheat." It also helped him rediscover "an abiding concern for the audience".

A wry yarn about what happens when a big film crew pitches up in a small town, *State and Main* suggests Mamet is fast becoming part of the industry mainstream. Admittedly, the film-makers here are as venal as their counterparts in *Speed-The-Plow*—the director and his terrier-like producer bully, browbeat and bribe anyone who gets in the way of the picture. Nor do they have exalted ideas about their own artistic integrity—when they are offered money to advertise an IT company in their movie, which is set in the 19th century, they immediately find a way of getting around the anachronism. But Mamet is very gentle on them: if anything, he seems to admire their resourcefulness and opportunism. His refusal to strike a censorious note even extends to the characterisation of the libido-driven star, played by Alec Baldwin (an astute piece of casting), who has sex with a minor. Mamet refuses to moralise at his expense, and the possibility that his behaviour might prompt a scandal is presented as just another problem with which the film-makers must deal.

The comedy is more whimsical than barbed, with Mamet taking soft pot shots at easy targets—the nymphomaniac actress who refuses to take her clothes off for the camera, the perfectionist cinematographer and the long-suffering assistant director are straight from stock.

Likewise, there are shades of the title character from the Coen brothers' *Barton Fink* in the nervous, solemn playwright who takes his work very seriously and is not yet accustomed to the compromises of big-budget film making. Mamet claims to have drawn on his "own adventures in Hollywood" (his first script, for Bob Rafelson's *The Postman Always Rings Twice,* had to be rewritten several times) but many of the characters and situations here echo those found in other films about film-making such as Alan Alda's *Sweet Liberty* (1985) and Tom DiCillo's *Living in Oblivion* (1995).

If the film-crew types are overly familiar, so are the eccentric townsfolk. Mamet provides us with a blustering mayor (who shares the same name, George Bailey, as James Stewart's character in Frank Capra's 1947 paean to small-town life *It's a Wonderful Life),* various old-timers making small talk in the coffee shop and a bookshop owner who seems infinitely more talented than any of the Hollywood big shots. Mamet goes to such lengths to portray the inhabitants of this sleepy pocket of Americana as folksy, neighbourly types that it's inevitable we will see a darker side. But the revelation when it comes—that the townsfolk are just as capable of subterfuge as the film crew in their midst—hardly matches the subversive punch of, say, David Lynch's portraits of seemingly idyllic small town existence.

Generally, Mamet's plots are tightly coiled affairs, but here there are some loose ends. In one scene the cinematographer destroys a plate-glass window above the fire station, a supposedly cherished historical monument—and yet nobody mentions his act of vandalism. The visual gags—the smudging of the white board, for instance, on which the film crew's invitation to dinner with the mayor is written—are likewise laboriously handled. There's none of the deftness of touch displayed by a director like Preston Sturges, whose ensemble comedies Mamet has cited as an inspiration for *State and Main.* Perhaps screwball comedy just isn't his genre: amiable in its own way, but toothless by comparison with his best work, *State and Main* ends up seeming like Mamet at half throttle.

VILLAGE VOICE, 12/26/00, p. 148, Jessica Winter

With *State and Main,* David Mamet has, against all odds, made a movie about moviemaking that bears not a trace of either cinephilia or intentional self-reflexivity. That is, unless the central dichotomy of a manic, jaded director and a depressive, idealistic screenwriter indicates that Mamet's mirror has two faces. Callous auteur Walt Price (a Spacey-esque William H. Macy) and put-upon scribe Joe White (Philip Seymour Hoffman) descend upon sleepy Waterford, Vermont, to film a period drama called *The Old Mill* , not least because the town supposedly boasts an old mill. But the brochure they're reading is decades out of date, and so seem the natives—pliant, impassive yokels all, who speak in aphorisms whittled down to Mametian abstraction (Codger #1: "It takes all kinds." Codger #2: "That's what it takes? I always wondered what it took"). A few get smothered by the smallpox blanket of Hollywood corruption: A teen (Julia Stiles) initiates an affair with the leading man (Alec Baldwin), while a politico (Clark Gregg) exploits the scandal for career gain, especially since he's lost his girlfriend (Rebecca Pidgeon) to unlikely homewrecker Joe.

Indeed, many of *State and Main*'s machinations hinge on sexual vengeance, but only Baldwin gets regular play (he thoughtfully conducts all incriminating conversations in his hotel hallway). Joe's the real prince, though, defending an infantile actress (Sarah Jessica Parker) when a reptilian producer (David Paymer; the year's most noxious anti-Semitic stereotype comes courtesy a Jewish writer-director) tries to bully her into onscreen nudity. Revealing an improbable taste for irony, the grateful starlet promptly strips for befuddled Joe, in a sequence so disjointedly assembled that you know even Mamet isn't buying it.

Much of the smugly reactionary *State and Main* strikes a similar balance between the adolescent and the puritanical. Mamet's ideal moral universe is predicated on nostalgia, so when the electricity goes out and Pidgeon lights a kerosene lamp, she's made to say, "The past comes to our rescue once again." The interlocking hijinks and homespun non sequiturs attempt homage to Sturges, but surely Preston would have inverted Mamet's scenario, in which our hero doesn't have to confess an inconvenient truth but gets brownie points for wanting to. The narrative ends up a fatuous triumph of Machiavellian thought and action; *State and Main* is a Hollywood satire as cynical and thickheaded as its supposed targets.

Also reviewed in:
NEW REPUBLIC, 1/29/01, p. 28, Stanley Kauffmann
NEW YORK TIMES, 12/22/00, p. E17, Stephen Holden
VARIETY, 9/4-10/00, p. 19, Eddie Cockrell
WASHINGTON POST, 12/22/00, p. C5, Stephen Hunter
WASHINGTON POST, 12/22/00, Weekend/p. 41, Desson Howe

STEAL THIS MOVIE!

A Lions Gate Films release. *Executive Producer:* Jon Avnet, Vincent D'Onofrio, and Ken Christmas. *Producer:* Robert Greenwald and Jacobus Rose. *Director:* Robert Greenwald. *Screenplay:* Bruce Graham. *Based on "To America with Love: Letters from the Underground"* by Abbie Hoffman and Anita Hoffman *and on "Abbie Hoffman: American Rebel"* by Marty Jezer. *Director of Photography:* Denis Lenoir. *Editor:* Kimberly Ray. *Music:* Mader. *Sound:* Douglas Ganton. *Sound Editor:* Bruce Fortune. *Casting:* Jeanne McCarthy. *Production Designer:* Richard Paris and Linda Del Rosario. *Art Director:* Phillip Tellez. *Set Decorator:* Renee Davenport. *Special Effects:* Martin Malivoire. *Costumes:* Sherry McMorran. *Make-up:* Marilyn Terry, and Edelgard Pfluegel. *Make-up (Vincent D'Onofrio):* James Ryder. Stunt Coordinator: David Stevenson. *Running time:* 108 minutes. *MPAA Rating:* R.

CAST: Vincent D'Onofrio (Abbie Hoffman); Jeaneane Garofalo (Anita Hoffman); Jeanne Tripplehorn (Johanna Lawrenson); Kevin Pollak (Gerry Lefcourt); Donal Logue (Stew Albert); Kevin Corrigan (Jerry Rubin); Alan Van Sprang (David Glenn); Troy Garity (Tom Hayden); Ingrid Veninger (Judy Albert); Stephen Marshall (Louis Wertzel); Joyce Gordon (Florence Hoffman); Bernard Kay (John Hoffman); Jean Daigle (Sheriff); Johnie Chase (Josh); Joshua Dov (Hippie Kid); Michael Cera (America Hoffman, age 7-8); Craig Ryan (America Hoffman, age 16); James Binkley, Walter Masko, and Brian King (Crew Cuts); Jim Codrington (Soldier); Merwin Mondesir (Private Kendall); Derek Murchie (Undercover Cop); Joey Pomanti (Juror); Shawn Lawrence (Stahl); Tony Meyler and Nicholas Michael Bacon (Cops); Trevor Bain (Medic); Shane Daly (Chicago Cop); Kent Staines (Richard Schultz); Ken Kramer (Judge Julius Hoffman); David Eisner (William Kunstler); Todd Kozan (Rennie Davis); Panou (Bobbie Seale); Timm Zemanek (Dave Dellinger); Keith Jones (John Frolnes); Marc Aubin (Lee Weiner); Domenico Fiore (Jury Foreman); Chad Willett (Sky); Tyagi Schwartz (Wannabe Hippie); Demore Barnes (Student Leader); Robert N. Smith (Ad Exec); Jeana MacIsaac (Unknown Woman); Scott Wickware (FBI Agent Kells); Kevin Hare (FBI Agent); Shaun Smyth (Paul Held); Jody Racicot (Cardozo); Aaron Steele (Sambini); Stuart Clow (FBI Agent in Filing Room); Rhona Shekter and Kim Roberts (Auditors); Beatriz Pizano (Mrs. Ramos); Michael Capellupo (Studio Executive); Andy Marshall (Security Guard); Jeff Pustil (Dr. Oscar Janigar); June Whiteman (Mayor at Yacht Club); Carolyn Goff (Hippie Girl); Donald Tripe and Christine Donatelli (Newscasters); Philip Craig (Police Chief); Toni Ellwand (Mother); Robert Ward (FBI Agent in Boiler Room); Michael Segovia (America Hoffman, age 4).

CHRISTIAN SCIENCE MONITOR, 8/18/00, p. 15, David Sterritt

Abbie Hoffman was such a colorful hero of the 1960s counterculture that it's surprising Hollywood hasn't capitalized on his story until now. It's also just as well, given the disappointing quality of "Steal This Movie," directed by Robert Greenwald from Bruce Graham's screenplay.

Youth-centered social protest is back in style, as events at this summer's political conventions have underscored. But neither its friends nor its foes will find much enlightenment in this uneven bio-pic.

If the '60s were a time when you couldn't trust anyone over 30, then Hoffman was over the age limit before many of his exploits took place. Born in 1936, he moved from Massachusetts to California—without shaking one of the world's thickest New England accents, judging from

Vincent D'Onofrio's portrayal—and started his activist career in the Berkeley campus protests of 1960. Equally interested in political ideas and guerrilla theater, Hoffman put his revolution-touting talents at the service of many left-leaning causes, from the free-speech and civil-rights crusades to the steadily growing effort to end the Vietnam War.

His fame peaked in 1968, when he helped establish the Yippie movement—or Youth International Party, to be a tad more formal—and used it to shake up the Democratic National Convention, already split by dissension over Vietnam and other issues. His trial with the so-called "Chicago 7" earned headlines everywhere, but his life afterward was more troubled and ambivalent, partly because of ongoing psychological problems.

Police surveillance, concern for his physical safety, and a narcotics charge led him to go underground in the mid-'70s. After several years of hiding he resurfaced in rural New York State, helping environmentalist causes under a false identity. He finally surrendered to the authorities in 1980 and went to jail for a year. He died in 1989.

Hoffman had a private life and a political calling, and "Steal This Movie" throws a frequent spotlight on the people closest to him—his second wife, his little boy, the woman he lived with in the underground years. That's a reasonable approach for the filmmakers to take, but there are problems with the way they've handled this aspect of their story.

The movie steers toward emotional cliches, oversimplifying Hoffman's public exploits so we'll have more time to gawk at his personal peccadilloes. This trivializes both his strong political convictions and the entrenched attitudes of the powers that be he tried to overthrow.

All of which raises a perennial question about movies dealing with controversial subjects. Is it permissible to streamline their events and simplify their ideas so they'll reach a wider audience? Or must one treat such material as thoroughly as possible, since a half-baked account may leave false impressions?

There's no one-size-fits-all answer to these questions, but "Steal This Movie" supports the latter position. It might be better to leave Hoffman a half-forgotten legend than to revive his fame on such superficial terms.

LOS ANGELES TIMES, 8/18/00, Calendar/p. 6, Kevin Thomas

"Steal This Movie!" is a vital and conscientious rendering of the life and times of Abbie Hoffman, one of the most charismatic figures of the '60s antiwar movement. He emerged as a countercultural hero as one of the so-called Chicago 7, placed on trial for inciting a riot at the 1968 Democratic convention, where the police launched a brutal attack on demonstrators.

Hounded mercilessly by the FBI, and arrested for selling cocaine in 1973, Hoffman would eventually be driven underground for seven years, emerge to see his name cleared and a government conspiracy revealed and denounced. Years of harassment and flight would exact their toll, however, in paranoia and manic depression that would drive Hoffman to suicide in 1989 at the age of 52.

Society needs fearless gadflies like Hoffman, who fought tirelessly for freedom of expression and social justice with inspired showmanship and a genius for making politics personal. He has been brought to life vividly, to say the least, by the protean Vincent D'Onofrio, whose Hoffman is a brilliant, larger-than-life dynamo. Hoffman met his equal in his wife, Anita, played by Janeane Garofalo as a woman as passionate, intelligent and courageous as her husband.

"If I were a woman I would be Anita," Abbie once remarked of their similar temperaments and common beliefs. They are an admirable couple, deeply in love and committed to ending the war and transforming American society. They are people of wit, style and imagination, who realize the effectiveness of presenting protest as a form of outrageous theater. They and their followers bring a lot of highly potent prankishness to the antiwar movement but in bringing down the wrath of the establishment they would pay an immense personal price.

A substantial portion of the film unfolds as flashbacks triggered by Anita at last telling her husband's story to a trusted reporter some five years into his underground period. Screenwriter Bruce Graham uses the reporter's interviews with Anita to put over a ton of expository material, which has the effect of making the film's action seem more reported upon than actually happening.

But Abbie's activities and the responses they provoked were wide-ranging and complex and their implications timeless. A whole generation has come along with little or no knowledge of

Hoffman's activities and his lasting importance, so it is understandable that producer-director Robert Greenwald, who knew Hoffman, and Graham wanted to provide plenty of context—even if it meant preventing their film from coming fully alive until it is safely past the publication of the reporter's piece.

It would have been more satisfying if the filmmakers had come up with a less heavy-handed approach, allowing us to experience more fully Anita and Abbie's story from the inside and as they are living it night from the start, but "Steal This Movie!" nevertheless generates much impact by the time it is over.

Greenwald draws from considerable archival footage that is integrated into the film's narrative, though again rather artlessly. The period is evoked well and good use is made of the popular music of the era. D'Onofrio and Garofalo are impressive in their demanding roles—D'Onofrio's part is especially taxing. His Abbie emerges as a bravura but clear-thinking rebel who raised the consciousness of countless Americans, students in particular.

Kevin Pollak as Gerry Lefcourt, Hoffman's shrewd and determined attorney, and Jeanne Tripplehorn as Hoffman's steadfast underground companion also make strong, persuasive impressions. There might have been a better, more involving method of telling Hoffman's story, but it is expressed with a firm sense of commitment to accuracy and authenticity.

NEW YORK, 8/28/00, p. 132, Peter Rainer

Steal This Movie, about Abbie Hoffman (Vincent D'Onofrio), is so hyped up that the filmmakers seem to be competing with their subject.

Robert Greenwald, who directed from a screenplay by Bruce Graham, offers a rat-a-tat scattering of Greatest Hits from Hoffman's career as political activist and court jester, and for a long time the film never settles down. The cascade of events has a rough, tawdry gangster-movie quality: the Rise and Fall of Abbie Hoffman. There's a dash of wit in this approach. Hoffman the clown prince who whammied the Pentagon and Yippied the prevailing political orthodoxies and then, pursued by the FBI, went underground is a species of gangster, all right. He's also one of the few authentic folk heroes from the sixties, perhaps because, unlike some of his cohorts at the time, he didn't become a gentleman farmer or a corporate shill or find God or turn neocon. In *Steal This Movie*, Hoffman is portrayed as a sacrificial lamb in a police state, and for those who feel compelled to see him in this light, the film will have the force of tragedy. But Hoffman's life contained more disturbing psychological crosscurrents than the filmmakers' skittering, agitprop style can account for. His life, his demons, were too custom-made for the generalized hero-worshipfuless of this movie.

Abbie's wife, Anita (Janeane Garofalo), says about Abbie at one point, "Too much is never enough with him," and that seems to be the taking-off point for D'Onofrio's gusher of a performance. D'Onofrio, a marvelous, vastly under-acclaimed actor, resembles Burt Lancaster in the way he uses his sheer physicality to heighten the emotions of his characters. In *The Whole Wide World*, he played Robert E. Howard, the Texas pulp writer who created *Conan the Barbarian*, and the young man's inchoate passions seemed to muscle out of him until he himself took on the dimensions of a raging hulkster. D'Onofrio understands how the ruinous loneliness of his larger-than-life characters causes them to boil up and become even larger. The people he creates are both more grotesque and more beautiful than anybody, including the characters themselves, might ever have imagined. In a classic horror movie, the monster is always the most awful and the most transcendent image on the screen, and this is the realm in which D'Onofrio excels: He creates sacred monsters.

Unfortunately, the power of his performance as Abbie Hoffman is repeatedly fractured by the filmmakers. Too much is also never enough for D'Onofrio, but Greenwald keeps pulling him back into careful, prearranged patterns: the life-of-the-party prankster and husband, the almost Disneyishly sweet, caring, but absent father. Beneath the scat-style narrative is a standard paean to revolutionary hippiedom and the anti-Establishment mind-set. Satisfying as this anthem may be for those primed for a sentimental journey, it doesn't really take us beyond the shibboleths of those years, and so the film often seems painfully out-of-step and flimsy. What is the point of making a movie about that era that looks like it was made *in* that era, complete with cookie-cutter reactionaries arrayed against Abbie and his sexed-up, life-affirming co-conspirators? Were the filmmakers afraid of being labeled disloyal to the cause? Hoffman is celebrated as a counterculture avatar, which he certainly was, but we don't see enough of the real man in all this hoopla. His story is both weirder and more mundane than the one we're shown here. Abbie Hoffman, the good Jewish boy who begins his activism looking so straitlaced that people mistake him for a narc, ends up hiding out from the Feds in an alternate life where he poses as "Barry Freed" and wins an award for environmental activism from Daniel Patrick Moynihan. The staged freak-outs of his Yippie prime give way to the more horrific mood swings of bipolar disorder; recreational drugs are replaced by lithium; political paranoia becomes personal paranoia and then back again. Such a black-comic jumble of a life, with ironies flashing in all directions, demands a chronicler with less stardust in his eyes. When Abbie declares that he's an outlaw in his own country, we should not be, as we are here, pressed to accept him at his word. He was an outlaw in his own mind. Probably even Abbie Hoffman, with his rampaging, carnal sense of theater, would have balked at such weak-willed hagiography. Stealing for him was a political act, a lark, and a sign of respect for what is being stolen. I doubt he would have wanted anyone to steal this movie.

NEW YORK POST, 8/18/00, p. 52, Lou Lumenick

"If you don't like his mood, wait a minute," the wife of '60s radical Abbie Hoffman advises his lover—and that sentiment applies in spades to this wildly uneven biopic.

Though he looks and sounds nothing like the Hoffman I personally encountered several times during the Age of Aquarius, Vincent D'Onofrio does capture Hoffman's charisma and nuttiness—and he's the only reason to resist the temptation to skip this exasperating movie.

The director, Robert Greenwald, has a long history in television and the final product plays very much like a movie of the week: It keeps telling you things in lines of dialogue ("Abbie was very influenced by Allen Ginsberg") that a theatrical movie would show you.

It even employs the creaky framing device of a reporter researching Hoffman's life—as interviewees recall his progression from a Mississippi Freedom Rider in 1963 to an anti-Vietnam political provocateur in 1968 to fugitive from a federal drug rap in 1972.

Hoffman, a manic depressive, committed suicide in 1989.

Among the witnesses are Anita Hoffman, the activist's wife. She's gamely played by Janeane Garofalo, who's saddled with such incredibly hokey narration as "everything about him threw my uptight middle-class a - - for a loop."

The script by Bruce Graham ("Dunston Checks In") is remarkably reticent about the Hoffmans' relationship, including Anita's tolerance for his numerous affairs, notably with activist Johanna Lawrenson (Jeanne Tripplehorn).

In its effort to cram in as many incidents as possible, it ends up treating the Chicago 7 trial (Hoffman was one of the defendants convicted of conspiring to disrupt the 1968 Democratic Convention) almost as cartoonishly as Abbie and Anita's be-in wedding in Central Park.

More seriously, it takes the paranoid Hoffman's allegations of government harassment (some of which were later backed up by declassified FBI files) totally at face value, as well as accepting Hoffman's dubious claim he acquired the cocaine that led to his arrest as research for a book he was writing.

Hoffman's attorney, Gerald Lefcourt (here played by a subdued Kevin Pollak), was one of the producers, and the whole thing has the feel of an authorized biography.

Fellow radical leader Stew Alpert (the ubiquitous Donal Logue of "The Tao of Steve") has been mysteriously renamed Stew Albert here, and the film plays down Hoffman's conflicts with Jerry Rubin (Kevin Corrigan) and Tom Hayden (played by his real-life son, Troy Garrity).

But despite considerable odds, D'Onofrio makes it matter—the most interesting parts of the movie are in the second half, when Hoffman goes underground for five years after his coke bust.

A scene where Abbie confesses his identity to his young son is so heart-rending, you truly wish it were in a better movie.

NEWSDAY, 8/18/00, Part II/p. B2, Jan Stuart

The producers of the new Abbie Hoffman screen bio couldn't ask for better guerrilla-theater advertising than the clamorous protests that have greeted the Democratic Convention in Los

Angeles this past week. The news shots of armed guards vs. unruly activists could have been lifted right out of the 1968 Chicago convention scenes in "Steal This Movie."

The pivotal Chicago clashes and the memorable Chicago Seven trial that followed are among the many greatest hits of yippie culture that are packed into "Steal This Movie," one of those entertaining but pedantic social histories that lead one to anticipate a written exam before the closing credits. Grab a Blue Book and a ragged pair of Birkenstocks on the way out the door.

"Steal This Movie" is as busy as its star, Vincent D'Onofrio, whose film "The Cell" also opens today. Sporting an Afro-like shock of curly brown hair and a jaunty New England accent, D'Onofrio gives a kinetic, three-ring circus of a performance as the self-described "long-haired revolutionary freak" who turned social unrest into a brash and occasionally bloody political carnival.

Screenwriter Bruce Graham frames Hoffman's story as a chronology of flashbacks prompted by an investigative reporter's piece in 1977, when Hoffman had been living underground for five years, in flight from a drug rap. It's an alarmingly conventional narrative ploy, given the subject matter, made even creakier by the ways in which it boldfaces its hero's achievements in the opening minutes.

"I have a long history of rubbing the authorities the wrong way," a paranoid Hoffman tells the reporter, as if he needed reminding. And we get that history, from his early anti-Vietnam War organizing to his civil rights work in Mississippi, all the way to his late-career environmental activism living under an alias.

After the clunky opening, the film slides into a reasonably compelling, "And Then I Protested..." rhythm propelled by the testimony of his adoring wife, Anita (Janeane Garofolo). Director Robert Greenwald makes some attempt at imbuing his film with the freewheeling impulses of its protagonist and his mellow-yellow era: There is a mud-sliding moment redolent of "Woodstock" and a fast-cutting Chicago trial that echoes the '60s style of "A Hard Day's Night" director Richard Lester.

But he's covering too much ground for Hoffman's alliances with his circle, which included Jerry Rubin, Tom Hayden and Bobby Seale, to resonate. For example, when Hoffman confesses to feeling betrayed by a fellow yippie who turns out to be an FBI agent in disguise, we haven't really seen that friendship evolve in a way that would make that hurt felt.

"Steal This Movie" is actually most interesting as it settles into its loping final section, when Hoffman flees the feds and takes up a benign domestic life with lover Johanna Lawrenson (Jeanne Tripplehorn) under the alias Barry Freed. It was an ironic pseudonym, given how stifled and manic-depressive the activist became in his underground years. The emotional imprisonment of a man who lived to foment change suggests a deeper psychological portrait that this particular movie is too restless to sit still for.

VILLAGE VOICE, 8/22/00, p. 129, J. Hoberman

The much maligned "Sixties" refer less to a precise decade than to a chunk of time lasting a dozen years or so when, for a host of reasons ranging from the threat of World War III to the saturation of TV to the proliferation of LSD, it seemed as though America's social and psychic reality was up for grabs.

At least, that was the fantasy. The hapless Abbie Hoffman biopic *Steal This Movie* attempts to depict this heady moment, just as John Waters's infinitely cannier, if only marginally more successful, *Cecil B. DeMented* allegorizes it. Waters grasps the essential dilemma. The '60s resist filmic representation in part because of the era's delusional quality—more than a few who lived through it imagined themselves the protagonists, or the directors, of an ongoing movie. [See Hoberman's review of *Cecil B. DeMented*.]

It's this impulse that Waters celebrates in *Cecil B. DeMented* —a satire of his own early movies like *Multiple Maniacs*, wherein dedicated bands of social-outcast "life-actors" launched outrageous guerrilla attacks on bourgeois reality. The media-savvy, hippie rabble-rouser Hoffman was himself one such life-actor-showering the New York Stock Exchange with dollar bills, nominating a pig outside the 1968 Democratic Convention, blatantly theatricalizing the Chicago Seven trial—and it's sobering to think that, if the veils of illusion were parted in the cosmic scheme of things, he might actually have been the star of something as badly directed, shot, and acted as *Steal This Movie!*

Seen without sentimentality, Hoffman was an unstable, self-promoting, highly perceptive, and genuinely funny individual whose manic temperament was magically in accord with the national mood from 1967 through 1970.Producer-director Robert Greenwald, best known for the camp debacle *Xanadu,* presents him in a historical vacuum, using the perspective of 1977 as a vantage point, with then fugitive Abbie telling his story to a lunkhead alternative press reporter he's designated for the task. The flashbacks and interviews with, among others, Hoffman's wife, Anita (Janeane Garofalo, given a real role for a change, albeit in a fake movie), are at once inflated and pitiful. Everything is a sort of spontaneous efflorescence—Abbie brawling with undercover cops at the Free Store, staging grotesque hippie soirees in the East Village, sliding around in the mud with Anita as preparation for the Yippie demonstrations in Chicago.

Crude and physically overbearing where the actual Hoffman was puckish and slight, Vincent D'Onofrio appears to take the film's title literally—although he doesn't steal the movie so much as squelch it. The actor guards each scene like a junkyard dog, obnoxiously smirking and swaggering through a world of cutouts.

Meanwhile, the filmmakers emphasize his character's hysterical paranoia. D'Onofrio's blunderbuss performance obliterates whatever wit and charm Hoffman had. To her credit, Garofalo seems embarrassed.

At once simple-mindedly didactic and utterly chaotic, *Steal This Movie!* is interspersed with fake headlines and botched history ("Nixon elected in landslide," one newspaper reports on the extremely close 1968 election), and thanks to the primitive Gumpery of the montage, even the newsreel footage looks like a cruddy restaging. The most authentic aspect is the cluttered mise-en-scène of the Hoffman loft, with its Salvation Army sofas and Indian fabrics. Confusingly, the screenplay suggests that Hoffman was the main target of the illegal FBI and CIA domestic intelligence operations that were widely written about during the early and mid '70s and even the subject of Senate hearings.

There are facts here—the infiltration of the antiwar movement by police provocateurs, the gagging of Bobby Seale at the Chicago Seven trial—that deserve reiteration. But the film's educational impulse would have been far more effectively served by a documentary. As it stands, Greenwald's barely coherent mishmash discredits itself. When it comes to misinterpreting the '60s, Ronald Reagan couldn't have done a better job. The final scene even offers its own redemptive "Morning in America" aspects.

Thanks to the successful lithium program promoted by Anita and Hoffman's underground consort (Jeanne Tripplehorn), a scrubbed and glowing Abbie makes a final Capraesque courtroom speech—complete with twanging folk guitar—to a new generation of activists. For a moment, I imagined I was watching the socialist realist hagiography that might have been made by the least talented member of the Hollywood Ten had Abbie been martyred and George McGovern elected president.

Also reviewed in:
CHICAGO TRIBUNE, 8/25/00, Friday/p. B, John Petrakis
NEW REPUBLIC, 9/11/00, p. 28, Stanley Kauffmann
NEW YORK TIMES, 8/18/00, p. E1, Stephen Holden
NEW YORKER, 8/21 & 28/00, p. 171, Anthony Lane
VARIETY, 3/13-19/00, p. 23, Robert Koehler
WASHINGTON POST, 8/25/00, p. C12, Rita Kempley
WASHINGTON POST, 8/25/00, Weekend/p. 37, Michael O'Sullivan

STELLA DOES TRICKS

A Strand Releasing release of a British Film Institute and Channel Four presentation of a Compulsive Films/Sidewalk production. *Executive Producer:* Ben Gibson. *Producer:* Adam Barker. *Director:* Coky Giedroyc. *Screenplay:* Alison Kennedy. *Director of Photography:*

Barry Ackroyd. *Editor:* Budge Tremlett. *Music:* Nick Bicat. *Sound:* Stuart Bruce. *Casting:* Simone Ireland and Vanessa Pereira. *Production Designer:* Lynne Whiteread. *Art Director:* Tim Ellis. *Set Decorator:* Joanna Tague. *Costumes:* Annie Symons. *Make-up:* Fiona Clegg. *Running time:* 97 minutes. *MPAA Rating:* Not Rated.

CAST: Kelly Macdonald (Stella McGuire);   James Bolam (Mr. Peters);   Hans Matheson (Eddie);   Ewan Stewart (Francis McGuire, Stella's Father);   Andy Serkis (Fitz);   Joyce Henderson (Auntie Aileen);   Suzanne Maddock (Carol);   Richard Syms (Donald);   Lindsay Henderson (Young Stella);   Jennifer Todd and Lisa Adam (Young Stella's Friends);   Dimitri Andreas (Greek Hotelier);   Leona Walker (Young Girl);   Andrej Borkowski (Polish Cafe Owner);   Emma Faulkner (Belle);   Shaun Williamson (Mr. Peter's Driver);   Molly Innes (Cake Shop Owner); Paul Chahidi (Chris);   Nick Stringer (Edward).

NEW YORK POST, 1/28/00, p. 51, Jonathan Foreman

"Stella Does Tricks" is worth watching mainly for its terrific central performance by Kelly Macdonald (from "Trainspotting" and "Elizabeth"). She plays a tough but essentially decent teen prostitute in a film that's brisk, sordid and effective until its strangely vague ending.

Stella (Macdonald) works the London streets with her underaged colleagues for a pimp called Mr. Peters (James Bolam).

When Stella decides to leave the business, Mr. Peters has her gang raped as an example to the rest of his stable. She eventually starts afresh, though shedding her past proves more difficult than she had imagined.

Aided by a commendable cast, "Stella Does Tricks" presents an unusually realistic picture of hustling, but the film's structure is uneven, and you never really find out how a girl as smart and self-sufficient as Stella found herself turning tricks.

NEWSDAY, 1/28/00, Part II/p. B10, Jan Stuart

There is no magic in "Stella Does Tricks," neither the rabbit-in-hat kind, the special-effects kind nor the transcendent, triumph-of-human-spirit kind. The only tricks that its wayward young protagonist knows are doughy, middle-aged men who pay her to perform the most intimate acts.

If there is any hocus-pocus to be gleaned from this tough-minded and expertly made drama from England, it is in the unexpected, occasionally brutal strategies its beleaguered heroine devises to fend off the predators who conspire to keep her down.

Stella is a Scottish girl of indeterminate teen years who has left behind a troubled upbringing in Glasgow to live the hooker's life in London. Imbued with both insolent humor and muted heart by Kelly MacDonald, she finds refuge from her ever-stalking pimp (James Bolam, oozing with paternalistic malevolence) in a chummy sorority of prostitutes and a dependent, smack-addicted boyfriend (Hans Matheson).

The script by Scottish novelist Alison Kennedy deftly blends glimpses of Stella's seat-of-pants London existence into fantasy encounters with dark influences from the past: her morally imperious Auntie Aileen (Joyce Henderson) and her sexually abusive nightclub comic father (Ewan Stewart). It's not a happy film, by any means, but director Coky Giedroyc and cinematographer Barry Ackroyd give it a constant visual dynamism that keeps its melodramatic inclinations on the run.

The lower-depths milieu, combined with high-velocity filmmaking, lend "Stella Does Tricks" more than its share of "Trainspotting" echoes. Like that film (in which MacDonald also appeared), this one is thick with often-incomprehensible Scottish accents, along with a renegade sensibility that seems determined to prove that young women can hold their own when it comes to bucking the system and vandalizing private property. Given the stark realities of Stella's life, director Giedroyc's ability to minimize the exploitative potential of the film's sex and violence borders on the heroic.

SIGHT AND SOUND, 2/98, p. 50, Melanie McGrath

Stella is a teenage prostitute. On the run from her Glaswegian childhood, she works London's streets under the aegis of her pimp, the creepy Mr Peters. Stella is haunted by memories of austere Auntie Aileen and her father, McGuire, a low-rent stand-up comedian. While turning tricks, Stella inserts a fiery Fisherman's Friend into the anus of a john, assuring him it's cannabis. She is punished by Peters, who forces her to strip and give him oral sex. A gang of youths pick up one of Stella's hooker friends, rape and then dump her. Stella meets one of the gang's hangers-on, a junkie named Eddie, who helps her set alight the gang leader's car. Breaking free of Peters, Stella is evicted from her bed and breakfast. Peters has his gang of henchmen rape Stella as he looks on.

Stella moves in with Eddie. On a trip to Glasgow, Eddie and Stella fill Auntie Aileen's garden full of condoms. Stella recalls the sexual advances made by McGuire when she was a little girl. She surprises him backstage and sets light to his penis. Back in London, Stella starts selling flowers. She shops Peters to the police. Life is semi-sweet until Eddie, who can't kick his smack habit, sells Stella's sexual services to his housemate Chris in return for drugs. Finally, Stella takes some booze and pills and dreams of herself as a little girl, wearing butterfly wings and setting fire to the pigeon coop.

Stella Does Tricks was inspired by a documentary series on homelessness, but where such inspirations are often excuses for the lazy fictive plundering we see every day in issue-led television docudramas, Stella is very much its own film. Screenwriter AL Kennedy, well regarded for her droll short stories, has created in her heroine something more than a mere cipher for an issue. This isn't a film about Stella's loss of innocence, but one about how far her innocence persists. In spite of the sexual manipulations of first her father, then her pimp, Stella still moves to her own, fundamentally decent, impulses. She decorates Eddie's room, rescues her friend and tips the local cafe owner. Stella's vulnerability lies not in her victimhood, which would have been easy, but rather in her humanity. In one illuminating scene, she clumps along in her six-inch platforms, a shot which says all that needs to be said about her vulnerability and grit.

The script is by no means faultless, though. A few rather overworked scenes follow prepared sequences rather than flowing naturally from the narrative. The odd literary turns strikes a false note and there are moments bordering on heavy-handedness. Stella's incitement to a group of street kids to have fun rather sinks under its own weight.

However, the film is saved from morbidity by its frequent (rather whimsical) flashbacks to Stella's childhood and by the sheer winning exuberance of its heroine's personality. Fragmented close-ups and handheld camera wobbles emphasise her subjectivity and the writing lives right inside Stella's mind. But what makes her truly compelling is Kelly Macdonald's gifted performance, bringing to the role a kind of tenderness not allowed to her in the cartoonishly nihilistic *Trainspotting*. Though let down by costume design (is Stella's teddy-bear knapsack truly necessary?) and by occasionally portentous dialogue ("Picture this scene," says Stella, telling one of her stories), Macdonald's portrayal of the feisty, broken teenager is so naturally numinous, it makes James Bolam's cloying, paternalistic pimp appear stolid and unconvincing. Ewan Stewart as Stella's father McGuire, on the other hand, turns in an amiably sinister performance and Hans Matheson suits the damply inarticulate Eddie, though he could do with shedding some of his self-consciousness.

Director Coky Giedroyc has remarked that she was anxious "not to stand in moral judgement" of Stella, but by doing so, she creates a film that inevitably stands in moral judgement of others. This is not a heartening film for men, who are portrayed as weak at best and perverse at worst. None of the male characters manages to embody a single unencumbered virtue. Accepting that though, if you can, *Stella* is still a potent portrait of male manipulation, making the point that sexual violence happens in the head as well as the bed. And where many lesser films would have resorted to prurient sexual displays, *Stella* says as much by what it leaves out as by what it shows. The most telling detail of Stella's rape is that in the midst of it all, she reaches out for her pimp Peters' hand.

With P. J. Harvey and C15 (a mutation of KLF) supplementing Nick Bicât's otherwise spartan score, *Stella* could have so easily been yet another pop promo masquerading as a movie. But the clean, assertive direction, the confident pacing, the subtlety of image, script and editing mark

Stella out as a mature work, bold enough to resist both unnecessary irony and resolution and wise enough to be honest without being earnest. *Stella Does Tricks* but it doesn't fall for any.

VILLAGE VOICE, 2/1/00, p. 118, Amy Taubin

Pretty Woman it's not. *Stella Does Tricks* turns an unsparing eye on the seamy, dangerous world of a teenage prostitute. Stella (Kelly Macdonald) escapes a dead-end Glasgow life and the sexual abuse of the father she once adored; but instead of the freedom she imagined she'd find on the streets of London, she winds up under the thumb of an even more vicious substitute father—a middle-aged pimp named Mr. Peters (James Bolam). Mr. Peters likes Stella to dress up like a 10-year-old (teddy-bear book bag, thigh-length plaid skirt) and jerk him off, ever so discreetly, in public places. "Now lick your hand clean and you can have your ice cream," he instructs her. It's one of many stomach-turning moments. Mr. Peters looks like a fat, white slug, as do Stella's stand-up comedian dad and most of her johns. Eventually, Stella finds a cute, skinny, young boyfriend (Hans Matheson), but he's a junkie and treats her as badly as all the others do. There are no good men in this movie—only a variety of corrupt bullies who take out their rage on women. They believe it's their privilege to do so, and their sadism is boundless.

Stella's only refuge is her imagination. At her worst moments, she escapes in her head to a place that's not necessarily happier, but where she controls the images. The film shifts abruptly between the real world and Stella's interior world of memories and fantasies. Her most pleasurable fantasies are of revenge, and what makes the film bearable is that she acts on them. She blows up cars, she throws lighter fluid on a significant part of her father's body and sets it ablaze, she tips the cops off to Mr. Peters's pedophilia and watches while they take him away. Revenge makes her jump and shout, but it doesn't set her free. The film has an ambiguous double ending, and the meaning of the last shot is unclear. Is it a final wish-fulfillment dream for Stella and for us, or is it really happening? Either way, *Stella Does Tricks* is extremely disturbing and difficult to resolve—on the screen and in the mind.

The film grew out of a documentary series on homelessness that director Coky Giedroyc made for British television in the mid '90s. Giedroyc has a documentarian's eye for detail and will to probe for the truth. She's also immensely skillful at placing the camera so that we feel the full horror of what's happening without it being shoved in our face. For all the nasty sex, the film is never sensationalistic.

The actors seem to have checked their egos off-camera. Most of them are playing loathsome characters, and they neither sentimentalize them nor make their villainy attractive. But it's Macdonald, with her strongly boned face, her quick-witted eyes that can turn from hopeful to wary and hard to dreamy in an instant, and her buoyant, purposeful way of moving, who carries the film. She makes Stella a mesmerizing bundle of contradictions. *Stella Does Tricks* would be inconceivable without her.

Also Reviewed in:
NEW YORK TIMES, 1/18/00, p. E20, Lawrence Van Gelder
VARIETY, 11/18-24/96, p. 61, Derek Elley

STRIPPERS

A Hollywood Independants release of an A.J. Productions film. *Executive Producer:* Jorge Ameer and John Greenlaw. *Producer:* Janine Gosselin, Rochelle Jefferson, and Marianne Marx. *Director:* Jorge Ameer. *Screenplay:* Jorge Ameer. *Director of Photography:* Aaron Kirsch and Gary Tachell. *Editor:* Rollin Olson. *Music:* Paul McCarty. *Sound:* John Lusitana and Lawrence Missonge. *Casting:* Antonio Saviour. *Production Designer:* Jorge Ameer. *Costumes:* Elizabeth Devue. *Running time:* 75 minutes. *MPAA Rating:* Not Rated.

CAST: Tony Tucci (Alan Gardner); John Greenlaw (Alan Gardner Credit Counselor); Jorge Ameer (Kevin); Kerrie Clark (Susan); Jeff Seal (Harry Bellman); JD Roberto (David); Linda

Graybel (Violet);   Kirsten Holly Smith (Bank Rep);   Jane Grogan (Betty); Sybile Kohn (Lesbiana);   Bob Nellis (Tadpole);   Elena Zaretsky (Nurse);   Danny Fehsenfeld (Mark); Danny Rohsenfeld (Mark); Linda Nile (Psychic);   Michael Swiney (Repo Man);   Lisa Marx (Credit Rep);   Bill Bourier (Model);   Shaun McDowell (Security); Wesley Paris (Parking Attendant);   Smitty Smith (Bar Owner);   Chika Marx (Bar Maid);   Scott Kaufman (Bar Security);   Maribel Simkin (Desk Nurse);   Chris Kase (Todd);   Torie Tyson (Nan);   Shelly Price (Reporter);   Rollin Olson (Employer).

NEW YORK POST, 12/8/00, p. 54, V.A. Musetto

No, this inept movie isn't about the men and women who take it off in public. Instead, it concerns people who, the press notes tell us, "strip others of financial belongings and emotional stability."

Although the notes don't say so, one of these strippers is Jorge Ameer, the producer-director-writer of this unbelievably awful celluloid-waster about a yuppie who loses his job, car, apartment, girlfriend and just about everything else he possesses.

Ameer, it seems, is trying to strip viewers of their hard-earned dollars at the box office. You've warned. Avoid this movie like the plague.

VILLAGE VOICE, 12/12/00, p. 178, Michael Atkinson

Jorge Ameer's *Strippers* is one of a barely acknowledged sub-breed of indie: howling-vanity amateur-work that finds its way into a theater only because the producers buy the room out for a week.

Exotic-dancer-free, Ameer's sludgy ordeal entails the Job-like wreckage of an L.A. suit's life and finances; Kafkaesque chuckles might have been the goal, but it's impossible to tell. Rave about it to someone you loathe.

Also reviewed in:
NEW YORK TIMES, 12/8/00, p. E20, Stephen Holden
VARIETY, 9/18-24/00, p. 30, Robert Koehler

SUCH A LONG JOURNEY

A Shooting Gallery release of a Film Works and Amy International Artists presentation with the participation of Telefilm Canada, British Screen, and the Harold Greenberg Fund.   *Executive Producer:* Victor Solnicki.   *Producer:* Paul Stephens and Simon MacCorkindale.   *Director:* Sturla Gunnarsson.   *Screenplay:* Sooni Taraporevala.   *Based on the novel by:* Rohinton Mistry. *Director of Photography:* Jan Kiesser.   *Editor:* Jeff Warren.   *Music:* Jonathan Goldsmith. *Sound:* Henry Embry and (music) Michael Banton Jones.   *Sound Editor:* David Evans.   *Casting:* Dolly Thakore, Tigmanshu Dhulia, and Jennifer Jaffrey.   *Production Designer:* Nitin Desai.   *Set Decorator:* Suzanne Caplan Merwanji.   *Costumes:* Lovleen Bains.   *Make-up:* Hajera Coovadia. *Stunt Coordinator:* Alan Amin.   *Running time:* 110 minutes.   *MPAA Rating:* Not Rated.

CAST: Roshan Seth (Gustad Noble);   Soni Razdan (Dilnavaz Noble);   Om Puri (Ghulam); Naseeruddin Shah (Jimmy Bilimoria); Ranjit Chowdhry (Pavement Artist);   Sam Dastor (Dinshawji);   Kurush Deboo (Tehmul);   Pearl Padamsee (Mrs. Kutpitia);   Vrajesh Hirjee (Sohrab Noble);   Shazneen Damania (Roshan Noble);   Kurush Dastur (Darius Noble); Noshirwan Jehangir (Inspector Bamji); Dinyar Contractor (Mr. Rabadi); Souad Faress (Mrs. Rabadi);   Shivani Jha (Jasmine Rabadi);   Meher Jehangir (Freny Pastikia); Aileen Gonsalves (Laurie Coutinho);   Sohrab Ardeshir (Mr. Madon);   Rashid Karapiet (Joshi);   Chatru L. Gurnani (Bhimsen);   Madhav Sharma (Peerbhoy);   Pratima Kazmi (Hydraulic Hema);   Sunny Bharti (Prostitute);   Antony Zaki (Morcha Director);   Irfan Khan (Gustad's Father);   Anahita Oberoi (Gustad's Mother); Rajesh Tendon (Gustad, 20 Yrs. Old); Meral Durlabji (Gustad, 10 Yrs. Old);   Meet Nandu (Sohrab (8 Yrs. Old));   Aloo Heerjibehedin (Gustad's Grandmother);

Anupam Shyam (Milkman); Anirudh Agarwal (Street Butcher); Nina Wadia (Sister Constance); Shauket Baig (Waiter); Viji Khote (Taxi Driver); Lovleen Bains (Worshippper); Nizwar Karanj (Nusli); Zul Valani (Kavasji); Mahabanoo Mody-Kotwal (Alamai); Rakesh Shrivastav and Arun Kanan (Municipal Workers); Noshir B. Andhyarujina (Dasturji Priest); Renur Setna (Dr. Paymaster).

LOS ANGELES TIMES, 3/24/00, Calendar/p. 6, Kevin Thomas

Roshan Seth is one of India's most internationally renowned actors, best known as the prosperous uncle in "My Beautiful Laundrette" and for appearances in such films as "Mississippi Masala" and "London Kills Me." Never in the West, however, has he had such a formidable role as in "Such a Long Journey," playing a Bombay bank clerk, a classic Everyman, who is severely tested on the eve of India's 1971 war with Pakistan.

Seth, a handsome, middle-aged man with an aura of civility, reveals the strength and wisdom within a seemingly ordinary man. In doing so, he brings a presence and authority much needed in holding together a thoughtful but uneven film, making it a rewarding experience.

Seth's Gustad Noble is a Parsi, a descendant of Zoroastrians who fled from Persia to India more than 1,000 years before to escape Muslim persecution. He sometimes daydreams about his family's lost wealth but never complains. He is content, complacent even, about his life in a dingy, crowded apartment he shares with his wife, Dilnavaz (Soni Razdan), and children. Gustad has taught himself to make the best of things and to embrace bustling Bombay street life. But all of this is about to change.

His eldest son, Sohrab (Vrajesh Hirjee), is accepted by an institute of technology but wants to stay in his current college and pursue the arts, incurring the wrath of his father, who wants his son to have a more prosperous life than he has had. Then his little daughter Roshan (Shazneen Damania) is struck with malaria, and Dilnavaz, in her concern for both Sohrab and Roshan, falls under the sway of a neighbor (Pearl Padamsee), a veritable voodoo woman.

These developments, however, pale before the danger that envelops Gustad when he receives word from a friend from the old days who wants him to agree to receive a package on his behalf. Is the friend a sincere leader in the Bengali resistance in Pakistan? Or simply a con man? In any event, Gustad reflexively agrees, bringing him into contact with a formidable mystery man (Om Puri) who, by coincidence, once saved Gustad's life in the aftermath of a traffic accident.

Canadian director Sturla Gunnarsson, in bringing to the screen Sooni Taraporevala's English-language script from Rohinton Mistry's 1991 novel, has much to keep track of—the complications outlined are only part of the story. "Such a Long Journey" lacks coherence, with too many questions raised only to be dropped for several reels; even the suspense evoked in Gustad's compliance with his old friend's request is allowed to dissipate. Furthermore, there is considerable cornball humor that strikes an artificial note, and the film, which means to be a comedy, is consistently more effective and credible in its serious moments. There's a lack of clarity in the use of flashbacks, and most everyone, with the exception of Seth, is at one time or another hard to understand through thick Indian accents.

In short, "Such a Long Journey," which has strong political overtones, is not very well-made. But Gustad is so exceptionally well-drawn, his simple humanity so staunch, and Seth's portrayal of a good man whose capacity for courage and understanding grows under duress so transcendent that the film is ultimately quite moving.

NEW YORK POST, 3/24/00, p. 50, Jonathan Foreman

Exotic in the best sense of the word, "Such a Long Journey" is an unusually well-written and satisfying multilayered drama that conveys the feel of urban India with more vivid accuracy than anything made in the subcontinent in recent years.

Moving and funny, it stars two wonderful Indian actors who have already made an international impact: Rohsan Seth ("My Beautiful Laundrette," "Indiana Jones and the Temple of Doom" and Om Puri ("City of Joy," "The Ghost and the Darkness"), and showcases a number of fine actors who deserve to be better known.

Set in Bombay in 1971, on the eve of India's third war with Pakistan, it tells the story of the practical and spiritual crises that threaten the life of struggling gentility led by Gustad Noble

(Seth), a bank clerk from a once elegant Parsee family. (The Parsees are descendants of Zoroastrians who fled Persia for India when their homeland was conquered by Muslim Arabs in 800 AD.)

Gustad is contacted by his long-lost best friend, Maj. Jimmy Billimoria (Naseeruddin Shah). Jimmy claims to be a member of RAW, the Indian secret service, and through a gangsterish go-between (Om Puri) he asks Gustad to deposit illegally a large sum of money.

At the same time Gustad's son (Vrajesh Hirjee) suddenly refuses to go to an elite college to study science, his little daughter is taken seriously ill, and his wife (the terrific Soni Razdan) becomes consumed by superstition.

Sooni Taraporevala ("Salaam Bombay," "Mississippi Masala") adapted Rohinton Mistry's prizewinning novel, and this screenplay is of considerably greater subtlety and sophistication than her previous work.

The film is deftly directed, with remarkable feeling for place, by Sturla Gunnarsson, an Icelandic-born Canadian.

It is also the first film to depict Parsee religious rituals long kept secret from outsiders.

SIGHT AND SOUND, 11/99, p. 57, Nina Caplan

Bombay, India. Gustad Noble is a Parsi bank clerk living in Bombay in 1971. His son Sohrab refuses to attend college; his friend Jimmy Bilimoria has disappeared; his wife Dilnavaz is increasingly influenced by a neighbour who practises the black arts; and the wall of their building is used as a latrine by passing drunks. Gustad is also haunted by the memory of an uncle's betrayal which bankrupted his father and hardened the young Gustad. Jimmy writes asking Gustad to collect money from the sinister Ghulam; Gustad complies, but balks at illegally transferring it to a bank account. Meanwhile, Sohrab has left home and Gustad's young daughter has caught malaria. Dilnavaz tries with increasing desperation to cure her daughter's illness and her son's rebellion by diverting the poison, via black magic, to the local madman Tehmul.

Threatened by Ghulam, Gustad enlists his colleague Dinshawji to help transfer the money. Dinshawji tells a secretary what he's done. Gustad persuades a pavement artist to paint the wall of his building; the urinating stops and a community grows up around the religious images depicted. Jimmy is arrested for fraud; Ghulam demands that the money he handled for him be returned. Dinshawji helps recover it, then dies. Gustad is reconciled with Jimmy, who is dying. Sohrab is also reconciled with Gustad. Jimmy dies. During a demonstration against the demolition of the wall Tehmul is killed. During the vigil for him, Gustad is at last able to cry.

Such a Long Tourney is like a work of art that has been painted over: you can just see the outlines underneath of Rohinton Mistry's beautiful novel. Director Sturla Gunnarsson's film charts bank clerk Gustad's journey from emotional detachment to greater tolerance as he copes with a slew of familial and historical problems. He softens and matures as his wife grows estranged from him, his son leaves home and his daughter catches malaria, but it is difficult to follow the progress Gustad makes: his journey is long in the watching, certainly, but as with many literary adaptations it's largely an internal one. Besides, his problems all have fairly straightforward solutions, and the way they're all neatly tied up by the end sits ill with the film's wry, realist tenor: as a Parsi, Gustad is a member of a minority religion in a country so uncomfortable with its multi-ethnic make-up that religious divides have brought it to the brink of war.

It is in the details rather than in the more melodramatic events that this film excels. Gunnarsson makes the dirt, smells and bureaucracy all appear equally and instantly present—an immediacy which is unnecessarily sharpened by a series of yellow-tinted, irrelevant flashbacks to Gustad's childhood. The community of Gustad's apartment block—from the old witch to the mad child-man Tehmul—is subtly rendered, as are the devotees who appear around the apartment block wall after Gustad persuades a pavement artist to draw his religious pictures there. Remarking on the faith Gustad's wife has invested in the black magic practised by her neighbour, the street artist provides the film with its most telling comment: that all life's problems begin when we look for permanence.

Such a Long Journey's problems begin when it rejects the permanent in favour of the temporarily exciting. So Gunnarsson's humorous portrait of 70s Bombay and study of a family coping with personal and political difficulties gives way to the trite thrills of a conventional crime story in Jimmy's attempts to demand illegal favours from Gustad. The final orgy of reconciliation and the predictable tears don't help.

VILLAGE VOICE, 3/28/00, p. 120, Michael Atkinson

Long absent as a source of outrage from the movies we see, the Pakistani-Indian war as it's been fought on and off since 1947 is suddenly hot, at least for Americanized Indian films like Deepa Mehta's languidly shot sermons and Sturla Gunnarsson's new *Such a Long Journey*. Acted by Indians in English, produced with British and Canadian money, and directed by an Icelander with American TV to his credit, *Journey* has an acultural lostness about it, meant for all races but expressive of none. It's a sensation bound to grow more common as globalism trods on, but Gunnarsson's movie rises above this vague dispossession, particularly in its respect for the textures of Bombay and for the Ben Kingsley-esque gravity of its star, Roshan Seth. Set on the eve of the dustup over Bangladesh in 1971, *Journey* tracks Gustad, Seth's decent-hearted banker, as he negotiates the usual changing-cultural traumas (willful teenage son, exhausted wife seduced by superstition, etc.) and tries to do a long-lost friend the favor of accepting a package that turns out to be secret-service-absconded cash.

Mistaken for a covert operation to aid the Bangladeshis (turns out the lost cash is what actually got Prime Minister Indira Gandhi in hot water in '71), Gustad's noirish plight is soon superseded by larger catastrophes. Gunnarsson's movie often feels like a mere succession of deaths and tragedies, but the filmmaking is fresh and unemphatic, and the acting is generally gripping. Om Puri (as a mysterious go-between) and Vrajesh Hirjee (as Gustad's amused but rebellious son) are excellent, but Seth is the movie; even when it's not clear what the action has to do with the war for Bangladesh, Seth makes it all one genuine, tired man's woeful business. Still, too bad no one dared shoot the movie in Gujarati, with actors we don't know from TV (faces from *NYPD Blue, Cosby,* and *Space: 1999* crop up)—it might seem less of an entertainment and more of an encounter with history.

Also reviewed in:
CHICAGO TRIBUNE, 3/24/00, Friday/p. C, John Petrakis
NEW YORK TIMES, 3/24/00, p. E25, A. O. Scott
VARIETY, 12/7-13/98, p. 57, Leonard Klady
WASHINGTON POST, 3/24/00, p. C5, Stephen Hunter
WASHINGTON POST, 3/24/00, Weekend/p. 41, Desson Howe

SUNSET STRIP

A Fox 2000 Pictures release of a Linson Films production. *Executive Producer:* James Dodson. *Producer:* Art Linson and John Linson. *Director:* Adam Collis. *Screenplay:* Randall Jahnson and Russell DeGrazier. *Based on a story by:* Randall Jahnson. *Director of Photography:* Ron Fortunato. *Editor:* Bruce Cannon. *Music:* Steward Copeland. *Music Editor:* Brent Brooks and Michael Dittrick. *Choreograper:* Toni Basil. *Sound:* Benjamin Patrick. *Sound Editor:* Ted Caplan. *Casting:* Don Phillips. *Production Designer:* Cynthia Charette. *Art Director:* Jay Pelissier. *Set Designer:* Faneé Aaron and Stephanie J. Gordon. *Set Decorator:* Robert Kensinger. *Set Dresser:* David Ladish. *Costumes:* Ha Nguyen. *Make-up:* Mindy Hall. *Stunt Coordinator:* Manny Perry. *Running time:* 105 minutes. *MPAA Rating:* R.

CAST: Simon Baker (Michael); Anna Friel (Tammy); Nick Stahl (Zach); Rory Cochrane (Felix); Adam Goldberg (Shapiro); Tommy J. Flanagan (Duncan); Jared Leto (Glen); Stephanie Romanov (Christine); John Randolph (Mr. Niederhaus); Sebastian Robertson (Busboy); Darren Burrows (Bobby); Mary Lynn Rajskub (Eileen); Maurice Chasse (Nigel); Mike Rad (Badger); Josh Richman (Barry Bernstein); Sebastian Robertson (Busboy); Dori Brenner (Doctor); Krista Allen (Jennifer); Matthew Frauman (Hobbit); Justin Ashforth (Joel); Robin Moxey (Ronny); Rainbow Borden (Butch); Marques Johnson (Toussaint); Andre

Roberson (Leroy);   Dave Lafa (Malcolm);   Garland R. Spencer (Darryl);   Ron De Roxtra (Vito);   Turtle (Turner's Counter Clerk); Kellie Waymire (Mary);   Brian Gattas (Production Assistant);   Michelle Beaudoin (Girl with Frizzy Red Hair);   Anna Berger (Older Waitress); Judy Greer (Younger Waitress);   Paul Weiss (Guitar Counter Clerk);   Ryan "Rhino" Michael (Doorman at Duncan's); Jimmie F. Skaggs (Guitar Center Owner);   Ralph P. Martin (Motel Pool Man);   Linda Lawson (Mrs. Canter);   Nowldar Alexander Winterhawk (Guitar Store Clerk #2).

LOS ANGELES TIMES, 8/11/00, Calendar/p. 16, Kevin Thomas

Since the very title "Sunset Strip" suggests sex, drugs and rock'n'roll, this intimate, reflective, even wistful little film comes as a surprise. To be sure, the above-listed elements are in evidence, but the emphasis is on the character of six individuals whose lives we follow over the course of 24 hours sometime in 1972. It's a look back at an exciting era from a mature perspective, suffused with an inevitable nostalgia but even more a compassionate wisdom.

While not stunningly original, "Sunset Strip" is nonetheless affecting and persuasive, for clearly its makers care about their people. It would have had at least a fighting chance of finding an appreciative audience as a specialized release rather than as a mainstream Fox 2000 Pictures presentation; in any event, it opened with little fanfare at the AMC Century 14.

Simon Baker's handsome, blond Michael is a 30ish professional photographer who tells us that "L.A. is a gold mine. Your life could change in 24 hours."

That's been true in many contexts throughout the city's history, but whereas Michael has responded to its eternal promise of fame and fortune, he is a mature man who takes his work as a celebrity photographer seriously. He shares an apartment near the Strip with Rory Cochrane's neurotic but brilliant Felix, the Oscar Levant of rock composers, who's had a hit in the past but is now hitting the skids while struggling to come up with another winner.

Michael works frequently with Anna Friel's Tammy, a fashion designer with a trendy shop on the Strip catering to rock musicians. Anna is attractive, vivacious and ambitious—and finds her customers often hard to resist.

Her current No. 1 customer is Tommy J. Flanagan's Duncan, a tall, sexy Scottish rock star with a wicked scar setting off his striking features. Michael has fallen hard for Tammy but is finding it hard to declare his feelings, realizing how easily she is swept off her feet by her glamorous clients. Indeed, Duncan is soon urging her to rush off with him to London "for a while."

Tammy is just beginning to realize she may have to decide soon between her career and an endless round of casual sex. In the meantime, a very young rock guitarist and singer-composer, Zach (Nick Stahl), is hoping that opening for Duncan will be his big break. Weaving in and out of the multi-strand plot is Adam Goldberg's amusingly obnoxious talent manager and Jared Leto as a currently hot and none-too-sharp rock star.

Director Adam Collis and writers Randall Jahnson and Russell DeGrazier tell the stories of all these people with wit and affection, and "Sunset Strip" moves smoothly amid a near-perfect period evocation, captured in an array of shifting moods by cinematographer Ron Fortunato. (Even the Whisky is seen again painted in its alternating squares of yellow gold and lavender, checkerboard style.)

Of course, there are a slew of vintage songs, with a complementary score by Stewart Copeland. The contributions of costume designer Ha Nguyen and production designer Cynthia Charette and her associates are outstanding, amusingly retro and all but flawlessly accurate—and absolutely crucial to making "Sunset Strip" come alive.

NEW YORK POST, 8/11/00, p. 46, Lou Lumenick

There are some decent actors and great costumes in this overly solemn compendium of rock clichés, which is receiving a token theatrical run en route to home video.

Under first-time director Adam Collis, the action in and around the legendary Whisky A Go-Go club in Los Angeles covers a 24-hour period in August 1972—and seems to go on almost that long.

Will a flirtatious costume designer (Anna Friel) choose between a rock star (Tommy J. Flanagan), a country-music singer (Jared Leto), or a colorblind photographer (Simon Baker)? Will an obsessive guitarist (Nick Stahl) and troubled songwriter (Rory Cochrane) find fame and fortune?

Also reviewed in:
NEW YORK TIMES, 8/11/00, p. E13, Dave Kehr
VARIETY, 8/14-20/00, p. 18, Robert Koehler

SUNSHINE

A Paramount Classics release of an Alliance Atlantis and Serendipity Point Films presentation in association with Kinowelt of a Robert Lantos production. *Executive Producer:* Rainer Kolmel and Jonathan Debin. *Producer:* Robert Lantos and Andras Hamori. *Director:* István Szabó. *Screenplay:* István Szabó and Israel Horovitz. *Story:* István Szabó *Director of Photography:* Lajos Koltai. *Editor:* Dominique Fortin and Michel Arcand. *Music:* Maurice Jarre. *Music Editor:* Dina Eaton. *Sound:* Glen Gauthier and (music) Shawn Murphy. *Sound Editor:* Fred Brennan. *Casting:* Leo Davis. *Production Designer:* Attila Kovács. *Art Director:* Zsuzsanna Borvendég. *Set Decorator:* Tommy Vögel. *Special Effects:* Ferenc Ormos. *Costumes:* Györgyi Szakács. *Make-up:* Erzsébet Forgács. *Make-up (Ralph Fiennes):* Jeremy Woodhead. *Stunt Coordinator:* Gyorgy Kives. *Running time:* 180 minutes. *MPAA Rating:* R.

CAST: Ralph Fiennes (Ignatz Sonnenschein/Adam Sors/Ivan Sors); Rosemary Harris (Older Valerie Sors); Rachel Weisz (Greta Sors); Jennifer Ehle (Young Valerie Sonnenschein/Sors); Molly Parker (Hannah Wippler Sors); Deborah Kara Unger (Carola); James Frain (Young Gustave Sonnenschein/Sors); John Neville (Older Gustave Sors); Miriam Margolyes (Rose Sonnenschein); David de Keyser (Emmanuel Sonnenschein); Mark Strong (Istvan Sors); William Hurt (Andor Knorr); Bill Paterson (Minister of Justice); Rudiger Vogler (General Jakofalvy); Hanns Zischler (Baron Margittay); Balazs Hantos (Aaron Sonnenschein); Adam László (Emmanuel at 12); Kathleen Gati (Josefa Sonnenschein); Vilmos Kun (Rabbi Bettelheim); Jácint Juhász (Mr. Hackl); Katja Studt (Kató); Mari Töröcsik (Kató); Kati Sólyom (Landlady in Vienna); Joachim Bissmeier (Dr. Emil Vitak); Tamás Fodor (Notary); Tamás Raj (Rabbi at Wedding); Zoltán Bognár, Sándor Simó, and János Vészi (Doctors); Attila Lóte (Count Forgach); Frederick Treves (Emperor); István Hirtling (Dr. Lanyi); Zoltán Gera (Man at Synagogue); András Fekete (Footman); Bálint Trunko (Istvan at 18); János Némes (Adam at 17/Ivan at 16); Tamás Juranics (Commander of Lenin Boys); András Stohl (Red Guard); Tamás Keresztes (1st Boy); Bence Kotany (2nd Boy); Péter Andorai (Anselmi); Zsolt László (Lugosy); Gábor Mádi (Priest at Conversion); István Szilágyi (Hungler); László Gálffi (Rossa); Zoltán Seress (Tersikovsky); István Bubik (Saray); Eszter Onodi (Secretary at Officer's Club); Sándor Dánffy (Policeman); Buddy Elias (Mr. Brenner); Károly Mécs (Defense Secretary); Adám Rajhona (Caretaker); Péter Takács (Stefano Sarto); Laszlo Szepesi (Olympic Judge); János Kulka (Molnar); Lajos Kovács (Military Police in Camp); Gábor Máté (Rosner); Israel Horovitz (Poet); Andrea Fullajtár (Agota Hofer); György Kézdi (Outraged Man); Trevor Peacock (Comrade General Kope); Péter Halász (Wild Duck); Tamás Jordan (Sommer); József Fonyo (Prison Sergeant); Frigyes Hollósi (Mr. Ledniczky); Ila Schltz (Mrs. Ledniczky); Ica Gurnik (Woman in Hospital); Eva Igó (Policewoman).

CINEASTE, Vol. XXVI, No. 1, 2000, p. 56, 2000, Catherine Portuges

Sunshine is an undeniably Central European film in focus yet decidedly global in production, with a multinational cast and crew, Canadian producers (Robert Lantos and András Hamori), a screenplay cowritten by its distinguished Hungarian director (István Szabó) and an American playwright (Israel Horovitz), shot on location in Hungary. A sweepingly ambitious epic spanning four generations of the Jewish-Hungarian Sonnenschein family, the film is at times schematic and forced to condense certain historical periods. Nonetheless, it has given rise to passionate, ongoing debate on the Internet and in the popular and academic press with regard to questions it raises about the ambiguities of Jewish assimilation, and has resonated widely with audiences, judging from the film's remarkable success in the U.S.

One of the most influential European filmmakers of the postwar period, Szabó directed *The Age of Daydreaming* (1964); *Father* (1966), a crucible for themes explored in *Sunshine; Love Film* (1970); *25 Firemen's Street* (1973); *Budapest Tales* (1976); *Confidence* (1979); and his German trilogy—*Mephisto* (Academy Award for Best Foreign Film, 1981), *Colonel Redl* (1985), and *Hanussen* (1988), which explores the period of the 1890s to the end of the 1930s in Central Europe. Like *Sunshine*, these films investigate the complex internal processes of those considered to be social outsiders and who appear to overcome that stigma by becoming blindly loyal to—and ultimately destroyed by—those very institutions and individuals from whom they so ardently desire acceptance. In 1990, Szabó directed his first English-language film, *Meeting Venus*, and, in 1991, *Sweet Emma, Dear Böbe*, a powerful narrative of two young women struggling to survive in post-Communist Budapest.

Against the unfolding backdrop of Central European history, from the twilight of the Habsburg Empire in prosperous Budapest to the fall of communism, *Sunshine*'s legendary cinematographer, Lajos Koltai, Szabó's longtime collaborator, uses luminous color to highlight sumptuous decors and magnificent costumes (by Györgyi Szakács, who designed Szabó's opera productions over the past six years) in scenes that traverse the whole of the twentieth century—through Miklós Horthy's counterrevolution of the 1920s and '30s, to the Holocaust, the Stalinist era, the anti-Soviet Hungarian uprising of 1956, and, ultimately, from post-Stalinist Hungary to the post-communist transition period of the 1990s.

Iván Sonnenschein (Ralph Fiennes), the family's last descendant, frames this family saga in voice-over, inflecting the story with his own individual perspective without disrupting its historical flow. The first section of the triptych begins in the mid-nineteenth century when, as a young boy, Iván's great-grandfather, Emmanuel (David de Keyser), leaves home for the capital when his father, the local village tavern keeper, dies in an explosion in his own distillery. Emmanuel (1828-1897) manages to take with him a black notebook containing his father's secret recipe for the herbal tonic, "Taste of Sunshine" (source of the film's Hungarian title, and a reference to the assimilated Zwack family, makers of the digestive tonic called Unicum), that eventually assures the Sonnenschein family's substantial wealth.

Most of the dialog in this segment takes place in tumultuous—sometimes melo-dramatic—discussions around the dining-room table in the family's grand-bourgeois apartment, modeled after Szabó's memories of his childhood home (where his great-grandparents also manufactured an herbal liqueur), with some sequences set in the very courtyard where he grew up. We see its opulent, well-furnished interior—textured walls, deep hues, and gold-framed paintings—gradually evolve into starkly-lit *mise-en-scène*, mirroring the decline of the family and the nation from aristocratic honor and bourgeois propriety to the sordid violence, harsh manners and language, and sexual vulgarity of the postwar years. The film's multiple, somewhat over-wrought erotic encounters reflect these shifts, from the lavishly portrayed romantic trysts between Emmanuel's son, Ignátz (Ralph Fiennes), and Ignátz's cousin, Valerie (Jennifer Ehle), in the Franz Joseph era (shot in dreamy soft-focus, with moments of stagy, overheated pillow talk) to the hurried coupling in the woods between Iván and his Gentile communist mistress during the Stalin years. With the exception of Valerie, the female characters are alternately depicted as adulterous creatures, acting out of 'natural' impulse; matriarchs, deeply attached to the family and nature; or sources of esthetic beauty, who do not participate in making history or ideology.

Ignátz (1872-1952) comes of age during the Austro-Hungarian Dual Monarchy (1867-1918), enjoying a brilliant career as a high-court judge under Emperor Franz Joseph, when Jews were well-represented in positions formerly reserved for the Christian nobility. A nation of multiple ethnic, linguistic, and religious identities—speaking a language of Finno-Ugric origin with elements from Turkish, Slavic, Latin, French, Italian, and German—Hungary has, throughout its thousand-year history, been the site of a mosaic of migrations including Serbs, Czechs, Romanians, Slovenes, Germans, Croats, Bosnians, Gypsies (Roma) and others. Conversion was often considered a plausible pragmatic strategy for Jews desiring social and professional acceptance in the milieu depicted here, often having little to do with religious persuasion. At the suggestion of his Christian patron, Ignátz changes the family name to the more Hungarian-sounding "Sors" ('fate'), when doing so was not yet fraught with the fear of persecution that would later accompany the 'magyarizing' of one's name; in fact, such a move was considered part of the 'assimilationist contract' that accorded Jews full participation in modernizing a country then considered backward. Ignátz's brother Gustave (James Frain), a doctor, and his cousin Valerie—raised as his adopted sister—join him in 'magyarizing' the family name.

One of the film's powerful narrative strategies is its depiction of erosion of the false sense of security typical of Hungarian Jews who, often ardent Hungarian patriots, were nonetheless ultimately forced to comply with the instigation of the Jewish Laws of 1938-39, which effectively excluded them from professional and cultural life. As the historian István Deák observes in *The New York Review of Books*, "Szabó's is an invented story, yet it is based on true incidents... the particular interest of the film ties in what it tells us, and fails to tell us, about Central European and Jewish life." Szabó himself explains: "Even though a lot of things in my films come from my own life, I see them more as 'biographies of a generation'...*Sunshine* is a case history of what one family went through, but many real human beings experienced the same thing in the 20th century."

Although Ignátz eventually marries Valerie (such quasi-incestuous marriages between cousins apparently not having been contravened by Jewish law), an emotional, if not sexual, love triangle among Valerie, Ignátz, and his younger brother Gustave is increasingly infused and disrupted by politics: whereas Ignátz remains loyal to Emperor Franz Joseph and the empire's 'liberal' multiculturalism, and their cousin/sister reveals Hungarian nationalist tendencies, Gustave becomes a socialist and, in 1919, joins the revolutionary government of Béla Kun.

In the second triptych, Ignátz and Valerie have two sons, one of whom, Adám (Ralph Fiennes) (1902-1944), converts to Catholicism as an adult in order to join the officer's fencing club, representing his country during the 1936 Berlin Olympics. Adám's compromises are sharply observed, suggesting that conversion was hardly a sufficient strategy for escaping the Holocaust: following the German invasion of Hungary in March 1944, nearly half a million Hungarian Jews (some two-thirds of its Jewish population) were deported and exterminated, with the cooperation of the Hungarian Arrow Cross militia.

Adám's character is, according to Deák, based on the experience of Attila Petschauer, an upper-class Jewish-Hungarian fencing champion (though not at the Berlin Olympics) who was himself a convert. The contrast between Adám's glorious Olympic victory and the atrocity of his subsequent torture and murder by Hungarian militia in a Hungarian forced-labor camp is striking: in full view of his adolescent son, Iván (1927-present), Adam is stripped and beaten, sprayed with water, and transformed into an ice sculpture, all the while insisting that he is an "officer in the Hungarian army and an Olympic medalist." As an Olympian, he would have been technically exempt from the discriminatory laws imposed upon Jews; as a member of the elite, his fate in the labor camp is far worse than that of many other members of his class. Some Hungarian viewers found the estheticized martyrdom of the Jewish figure portrayed in this scene to be unwarranted, even offensive.

Adám Sors's family are murdered by the Arrow Cross in Budapest, leaving only Iván and his grandmother Valerie (in her elder years, beautifully portrayed by Rosemary Harris) as survivors of the Holocaust by the end of the war in 1945. Out of revenge against the fascists who destroyed his family, Iván becomes a communist, a member of AVO, the dreaded secret police, resigning only in 1952, when his boss and friend, Jewish Auschwitz survivor Col. Andor Knorr (a character based on the experience of Col. Ernö Szücs, and brilliantly performed by William Hurt), is tortured and beaten to death by the communist régime of Mátyás Rákosi. Iván becomes a leader of the incipient 1956 uprising and is imprisoned for his activities.

After his grandmother's death in the 1960s, Iván discovers a letter addressed to Ignátz from the family patriarch, Emmanuel Sonnenschein, urging him to remain faithful to his family's origins and traditions; these words prompt him to take back the Sonnenschein family name, a gesture, the director suggests, in honor of Valerie, "the only one of us," as her grandson remarks, "who had the gift of breathing freely." In the film's final sequence, as the camera lingers on overhead shots of Budapest divided by the Danube, Iván's voice-over confesses that, for the first time in his life, he can breathe freely. Szabó elucidates: "Each generation loses itself in the larger fight for comfort, acceptance, conformity ... Ultimately it is Iván Sonnenschein who rediscovers the spiritual power that first led his great-grandfather to leave his village 150 years earlier ... I think this story shows how three supposedly different régimes—Imperial, Nazi, and Communist—each promise happiness but carry out dreadful acts in the name of society's betterment ... Sometimes a generation comes along that will not continue the cycle."

The conclusion—Iván's decision to take back the Jewish name, disposing of the relics of the past—is a major object of the controversy surrounding the film: if indeed one is to "remain true to family origins and traditions," we might well ask how identity is constructed when one is seen as both 'insider' and 'outsider.' Is it a constant, unchanging entity, a part of human character (Szabó's view, as expressed in a ninety-minute interview broadcast on Hungarian television)? Or rather, is identity a developmental, postmodern process, in view of the eventual end of Communism in 1989 (a historic moment unfortunately not covered by the film), that was led by the dissident descendants of Iván Sors's generation? That *Sunshine* was made in the late 1990s, when Hungarian Jewish life enjoyed a period of renewal, is significant and raises further historical questions that remain to be addressed by other European filmmakers.

Ralph Fiennes gives a virtuoso performance in the role of all three primary male protagonists, linking family history through his interpretation of grandfather Ignátz, father Adám, and son Iván, each of whom must confront the consequences of his own generation's crisis of assimilation. According to Szabó, speaking at a Columbia University symposium, "I wanted to make a film of this story because I realized how many people suffer from an identity crisis. This is not simply a question of ethnicity or race. From mobility among the various strata of society in recent Hungarian life to the waves of economic and political emigration in Europe today, people must face the challenge of surrendering the self or deliberately demonstrating their identity ... I wanted to give an example of what happens to someone who renounces his true self in order to be accepted, which can happen to anyone, anywhere, not only those who belong to a minority group."

Richly interwoven with art nouveau, secessionist-period architectural details (by Attila Kovács, who designed the sets for Szabó's previous three films), and intercut with archival footage, the film's historic Budapest locations appear throughout sequences set in the visual grandeur of the Opera House, the Museum of Applied Arts, and the Parliament Building, and such familiar settings as the Muzeum Kávéház, the Dohány Street Synagogue, and the Western Railway Station. Maurice Jarre's musical score comments hauntingly on the family's fate with variations on a melody from Schubert's "Fantasia in F Minor" and motifs from the Hungarian folk song, "Spring Wind," ("Tavászi szél") used to emphasize the family's feeling of "Hungarianness," as Szabó has indicated. Despite occasional flaws in pacing and continuity—excessive length, moments of oversimplification, and a tendency toward moralizing—*Sunshine* never loses sight of the personal, intimate details of generational identity, sexuality, and the cinematic representation of personal and national memory, transforming the tragedy of twentieth-century Jewry into a work of redemptive power.

CHRISTIAN SCIENCE MONITOR, 6/2/00, p. 15, David Sterritt

Look at the coming attractions for "Sunshine" and you'll think William Hurt is the movie's shining star. He actually has a small role, though, taking second place to Ralph Fiennes, who plays three characters in this epic tale of a Hungarian Jewish family coping with the convulsions of 20th-century history.

It was directed by Hungarian filmmaker Istvan Szabo, who won an Oscar for the more interesting "Mephisto" years ago. He gives the new movie a lot of passion but little originality or imagination. Regrettably, each of its three hours seems longer than the last.

LOS ANGELES TIMES, 6/9/00, Calendar/p. 12, Kevin Thomas

With the monumental three-hour "Sunshine," master director Istvan Szabo relates the tragic and turbulent history of Hungary in the 20th century. The story is told through the Sonnenscheins, an assimilated Jewish family whose last survivor finally accepts the futility of trying to deny one's roots—especially when he realizes that that is all he has left.

It is a superb period re-creation and boasts a formidable international cast acting in English but does not attain the high artistic level of Szabo's great trilogy exploring the theme of self-deception, "Mephisto, "Colonel Redl" and "Hanussen."

Szabo and his co-writer, playwright Israel Horovitz, tend to match every upheaval in Hungarian life with tempestuous behavior on the part of the Sonnenscheins, particularly the three generations of scions played by Ralph Fiennes. The constant compounding of personal and political turmoil is soap operatic in effect, which makes you feel that "Sunshine" would play best as a TV miniseries. It is nevertheless absorbing and illuminating in regard to the eras its spans but is also pretty wearying by the time it starts winding down. However, those of us who are steadfast admirers of Szabo—and also suckers for traditional-style period epics—wouldn't want to miss it.

"Sunshine," which is English for Sonnenschein, prophetically opens (in 1840) with an explosion in the herbal distillery of a rural tavern-keeper, killing him and his entire family except for his 12-year-old son, Emmanuel. The boy heads for Budapest with his father's secret recipe for his "Sunshine" herbal tonic, which will become the basis for the family fortune that affords the Sonnenscheins a palatial mansion. Their story begins in earnest with the dawn of the 20th century, at which time the sons of Emmanuel (David de Keyser) and Rosa (Miriam Margolyes), Ignatz (Ralph Fiennes) and Gustave (James Frain), have settled on careers in law and medicine, respectively. They have been raised with their orphaned cousin, Valerie (Jennifer Ehle), an aspiring photographer and free spirit who defiantly and successfully seduces Ignatz, whom she marries.

Under the rule of Emperor Franz Joseph, Hungarian Jews were granted unprecedented opportunities and civil rights, and the dashing Ignatz rises fast through the ranks of jurisprudence but must change the family name (to Sors, pronounced Sorsh) if he is to go all the way to the top. He's so grateful to the emperor that he refuses to notice that the government is growing ever weaker and more corrupt, with the lower classes left in such dire straits that Gustave becomes a Communist in protest.

The outbreak of World War I, the deaths of the emperor and his father on the very same day, and Valerie's disillusionment with him ensure an early grave for Ignatz. Hungary goes briefly Communist until taken over by Admiral Horthy's military regime, which ultimately collaborated with the Nazis. With the end of World War II, Hungary would endure Communist rule until 1989.

It is unclear whether in the wake of World War I the Sunshine Tonic is still being manufactured, but in any event the Sonnenscheins continue living in style in the family mansion. Ignatz's son Adam, a dedicated assimilationist and superb fencer, leads Hungary to triumph at the 1936 Olympics in Berlin, returning home a national hero and no more willing to see where the country is heading than his late father, Ignatz, was in his time.

Only Adam's sister-in-law Greta (Rachel Weisz) sees that the family needs to emigrate before it's too late. Needless to say, Adam's heroic status will mean nothing once the deportations of Hungarian Jews commence. Valerie (Rosemary Harris, having taken over for Ehle, her real-life daughter) and Adam's son Ivan survive the Holocaust, with Ivan turning Stalinist inquisitor in his mood for vengeance but emerging a hero of the futile 1956 Hungarian uprising. Ivan, too, is seduced—by an aggressive apparatchik (Deborah Kara Unger).

With his clenched intensity, Fiennes is well-cast as a series of single-minded, self-absorbed innocents who are pursued by women rather than pursuing them. The film is anchored by Ehle and Harris, equally luminous as Valerie, who possesses the strength and wisdom of a woman who always dared to be true to herself. Margolyes makes a put-upon, tradition-minded matriarch sympathetic because she can be amusing and common-sensical in her candor.

William Hurt is commanding as a man who survives Auschwitz only to meet a worse fate at the hands of rabid Stalinists, and Rudiger Vogler is an elegant and subtle Hungarian general. (Vogler in middle age recalls Melvyn Douglas at his most urbane, which is a long way from the hippie drifters Vogler played in Wim Wenders' early films.) Lajos Koltai's cinematography is glorious, as usual, and Maurice Jarre is the ideal composer for a stirring epic. Although the lives of the three generations of Sonnenscheins come across as melodramatic rather than tragic, "Sunshine" is a film of many redeeming virtues.

NEW YORK, 6/19/00, p. 59, Peter Rainer

István Szabó's highly uneven *Sunshine*, starring Ralph Fiennes in three separate roles, is an epic romance encompassing several generations of a Hungarian Jewish family as well as most of the twentieth century and its attendant political horrors. Szabó's script originally ran some 600 pages; the version that's on the screen, written in collaboration with the American playwright Israel Horovitz, lasts three hours. The results are schematic yet sprawling. We're watching the playing-out of a thesis, which could be summarized as *You can never escape your roots,* but along the way Szabó demonstrates the kind of grand-scale ambition one still sees in novels but rarely sees anymore in the movies. What I am speaking of here is *conceptual* ambition, not the bigger-is-better pomp and pageantry that most filmmakers mistake for breadth.

You certainly feel like you've been through something when *Sunshine* ends. But what, exactly? Szabó's specialty, notably in films like *Mephisto* and *Colonel Redl,* both starring Klaus Maria Brandauer, is dramatizing the bloody confluence of politics and matters of the heart. He is a fatalist who believes that history plays out our destinies. And yet he is drawn to the ways in which people fight the inevitability of their fates. He's drawn to decadence too; the most memorable moments in his movies are not the humanist ones but, instead, those passages in which the screen is wormy with terror and corruption.

The Sonnenscheins (the name means *sunshine* in German) are the family whose destiny is being played out. Emmanuel (David de Keyser), the patriarch, created the family fortune with the marketing of an herbal health tonic; his advice to his two sons, Ignatz (Fiennes) and Gustave (James Frain), is to "take nothing on trust, see everything for yourself." Gustave, in love with Ignatz's wife, Valerie (Jennifer Ehle), a first cousin raised within the family, becomes a firebrand physician who rails against the reigning Austro-Hungarian monarchy; Ignatz becomes a judge and staunch defender of the empire. With his father's blessing, he changes his surname from the Jewish-sounding Sonnenschein to Sors, an acceptably Hungarian appellation. Neglecting his wife, who despises his accommodationist cravings, Ignatz is a caricature of middle-class respectability, a poseur whose pose has become the man.

His son Adam (Fiennes), an even fiercer assimilator, grows up into a lawyer and champion fencer who converts to Catholicism in order to compete at the highest levels. A gold-medalist at the 1936 Olympics in Berlin, he ultimately is done in by the Fascist forces he refused to foresee. Adam's young son, Ivan (later played by Fiennes), who narrates the film, watches as his father is tortured and murdered before his eyes in a concentration camp, and survives to revenge himself as a Communist—before falling victim to yet another strain of totalitarianism.

Szabó carefully sets up the three characters played by Fiennes to represent the phases of a man's life: Ignatz wants power, Adam glory, Ivan redemption. He gives each of them a distinct look, too, as a beard gives way to a mustache and ultimately to a more sunken, sallow countenance. Casting Fiennes in all these roles is something of a stunt, but at the most basic level of our not confusing one man with the other, he brings it off. Missing, however, is the spellbinding performance that would unify this behemoth of a movie. Szabó's films require not only heroic protagonists but heroic actors to play them, someone like Klaus Maria Brandauer. (What has happened to him?) Fiennes's soulfulness can be wearying. He's too elegantly refined, too effete, too Dirk Bogarde-ish to carry the day. His resonant blankness doesn't allow us to see behind the mask, and in roles like these, that's a near-fatal flaw.

The meanings of this movie seemed coerced rather than arrived at. If we are meant to interpret *Sunshine* as a cautionary tale about the dangers of denying one's roots, we come face-to-face with the realization that for the Sonnenscheins, it ultimately mattered little to their survival whether they declared themselves Jews. Would a scenario in which Ignatz and Adam embraced their Jewishness have resulted in a far different fate? Name change or no, Hitler and Stalin were still waiting in the wings. In one unsubtle scene, Ivan is asked why no one among the thousands of prisoners was moved to save his father when there were only three officers in command. At times, Szabó seems to be implying that his characters' accommodations brought on the dictators. The family, starting with Emmanuel, is never shown to be terribly rooted in Jewish tradition anyway. That may be part of the point, but we are being asked to mourn a lost cultural bond that has never been fully established for us.

There's something uncomfortably punitive about the way Szabó frames this story. Ignatz's wife, now a wise old matriarch (played radiantly by Rosemary Harris, Jennifer Ehle's mother), speaks of the family's fate as a Jewish fate. Is the assimilationist dream of wanting to belong such a grievous malady? And if one takes the larger view that many of these people have indelibly compromised their individuality, then why do they yet seem so individual?

For all its scope and intermittent power, *Sunshine* ultimately seems like a family squabble that Szabó has politicized into epic proportions. The brother-vs.-brother infighting, the messing-around with each other's wives, the affairs and recriminations and capitulations would be just as likely to occur in Boise as in Budapest. Inflating their importance by presenting them against the backdrop of the Holocaust and the Gulag in the end deflates them. Whenever Szabó inserts documentary clips of the Jewish ghetto, or the Hungarian uprising of 1956, the acted-out drama is vastly diminished by comparison. Conceptual epics are wonderful things, but the concept here is as deficient as the curative powers of the Sonnenschein-family tonic.

NEWSDAY, 6/9/00, Part II/p. B6, John Anderson

Among the crimes of Adolf Hitler—a minor crime, certainly, but a crime—is the fact that any story involving 20th Century Eastern European Jewry has forever been sublimated to the Holocaust. That such a culture should be viewed merely as a prelude to tragedy, its every aspect overweighted with foreshadowing, is a cultural offense that cannot be wiped away.

You can't, however, accuse Istvan Szabo of not trying. "Sunshine," the Oscar-winning Szabo's ironically titled history of one Hungarian family, chronicles the Sonnenscheins (see title) from the late Austro-Hungarian Empire through the fall of communism, from its initial success as the producers of a popular elixir through the ravaged family's last male heir, a Holocaust survivor-turned-Party-apparatchik-turned-street-revolutionary in '56 Budapest.

Ralph Fiennes is that lonely Sonnenschein, Ivan. And he's Ivan's grandfather, Ignatz, the system-climbing judge who changes the family name to Sors, and Ignatz' son, Adam, the world-class fencer who changes the family religion to win Olympic gold. That's a lot of Fiennes, who eventually seems like a particularly dour Zelig, having been present at every significant instance of the Hungarian century.

But despite his tendency to be a bit "actorly" as well as irritatingly serious, Fiennes proves himself a splendid physical actor. You see it in the subservient hunch he assumes when Ignatz visits his superiors, and in Ignatz' studied martial strut and in Adam's not-quite-flinching regard of his anti-Semitic fellow swordsman and in the mantle of heroism, so unfamiliar, that's assumed by a late-blooming Ivan.

"Sunshine" is not the story of saints—Ignatz, for instance, will bed and wed his cousin Valerie, who's been reared as his sister (the young Valerie is played by Tony winner Jennifer Ehle, the older Valerie by Ehle's mother, the acting genius Rosemary Harris). Neither is Fiennes' performance, on the surface, the stuff of nobility. He's just very human.

Szabo reportedly started with enough script for a 10-hour film and, unfortunately, it shows. The narrative hops about from one unresolved crisis to unresolved crisis as if skipping chapters in a novel. What's here, however, despite the occasional stiffness of posture and Szabo's fondness for the unnecessary visual echo, is an epic in small scale, a movie that makes us love its characters because, not in spite, of their flawed humanity.

SIGHT AND SOUND, 5/00, p. 62, Julian Graffy

In the mid 19th century, on the death of his father, the Hungarian Jew Emmanuel Sonnenschein leaves his village and moves to Budapest, where he builds up a business selling his family's "Sunshine Tonic", marries and has two sons, Ignatz and Gustave, and also brings up his brother's daughter, Valerie. All three children change their name to the Hungarian name Sors to assist assimilation. Ignatz studies law and marries Valerie despite parental opposition. They have two sons, Istvan and Adam. Gustave, a doctor, gets involved in the socialist opposition, while Ignatz becomes a judge.

The family's life is thrown into turmoil by World War I, the collapse of the monarchy and the short-lived Communist republic, under which Gustave becomes a high-ranking official and Ignatz is arrested. With the coming of the right-wing Horthy regime Gustave flees to France. In 1930, Ignatz dies, leaving Valerie head of the family. Their son Adam, a brilliant fencer, converts to Catholicism to join the elite army fencing team and wins the gold medal at the 1936 Berlin Olympics. Both Adam and Istvan marry and have sons. But their assimilation into Hungarian society cannot save them from the ghetto and the Nazi death camps. Istvan and his family are shot in Budapest. Adam and his son Ivan are taken to a camp where Adam is tortured to death.

After World War II, Ivan returns to the Budapest house where his grandmother has survived and where his great-uncle Gustave has returned to enter politics. Ivan becomes a Communist Party official, but begins to doubt the regime when he is forced to interrogate his Jewish boss Knorr.

After Stalin's death he makes an impassioned speech at the funeral of the rehabilitated Knorr, and leads the rebels in the 1956 revolution. The re-imposition of Soviet power brings his imprisonment. After his release, Valerie dies. Ivan changes his name back to Sonnenschein. In a brief contemporary coda Ivan walks through free Budapest.

Sunshine records the trajectory of a Hungarian-Jewish family over four generations as they move from their village to Budapest, into commerce and government service of various kinds and finally into dissidence and a rediscovered sense of personal identity. Each generation, in its different historical circumstances, copes with a recurrent series of moral dilemmas. The unease of the outsider leads to an excessive desire for acceptance, but acceptance entails compromise, and for these Jews a readiness to renounce both their name and their religion. Compromise brings a seductive closeness to power and heady worldly success, but also involves hypocrisy, shame and self-delusion, laced with a constant fear of the loss of what is gained at such cost.

That the road of these lives is always the same is effectively suggested by having Ralph Fiennes play three generations: the son, Ignatz; the grandson, Adam; and the great-grandson, Ivan. It is the life of the second generation in monarchist Budapest that the film examines most amply, and where the connections between family, society and nation are most carefully delineated. With the story of the dull Adam its grasp becomes much less certain, partly because of a decision to cover the inter-war years chiefly through his passion for fencing (alas, one fencing bout is very like another), but also because director István Szabó's illustrative strategies are already becoming apparent. The final part, the post-war study of Ivan, is more securely rooted in politics and history, but by this point the film, like the viewer, is flagging and the post-1956 period is extremely skimped.

Sunshine is a film of epic scope, and it makes its material manageable by finding patterns in history. There are patterns in the life of the country, in its successive thraldom to three powerful neighbours, Austria, Germany and Russia. In each period power corrupts and leads to vengeful violence, and state anti-Semitism is ever present. There are patterns in the lives of men. Each generation of Sonnenscheins has two sons, and in each generation the central character played by Fiennes is drawn out of weakness to 'forbidden' women.

There are also patterns between the lives of individuals and the nation, for both men and country are sucked into a maelstrom of compromise and self-delusion, a connection underlined by the coincidence of key family events with those of history. But history brings change as well as repetition, and a reading of it through such rigorously applied templates is ultimately unsatisfying. The oversimplifications are accentuated by an over-insistent use of symbolic objects. The recipe for the family's Sunshine tonic, the great grandfather's watch, broken crockery, a photograph of the young Valerie recur with an eventually dismaying regularity. This excessive desire to guide the viewer is also reflected in the film's dialogue, which is strewn with sententious abstractions, and in the interpretive voiceover provided by Ivan.

Szabó has visited these historical sites before: the decline of the Empire in *Colonel Redl*, World War I in *Hanussen*, the Nazi period in *Mephisto*, World War II in *Confidence* and so on. In this sense, and also in its examination of individual fates in societies in crisis, *Sunshine* is a summation of the concerns of a long and brilliant career. And yet each of the earlier films, with its narrower focus, could inevitably achieve greater density and persuasiveness, greater urgency. All the key ingredients of the 20th-century Central European recipe—the two world wars, the Berlin Olympics, the concentration camps, the Stalin cult and the purges, the rise and fall of communism—are assembled here. But the resulting dish is slightly stolid. Near the end of our epic journey we learn, "the purpose of life is... life itself", and the sense of anticlimax is palpable.

TIME, 6/12/00, p. 82, Richard Schickel

The family name, Sonnenschein translates as Sunshine, and its bearers at first prosper in turn-of-the-20th-century Budapest, selling an herbal tonic with that cheerful word emblazoned on the bottles. But they are Jews in an endemically anti-Semitic society. By the end of Istvan Szabo's three-hour epic, which traces the family's decline through three historical epochs—the Austro-Hungarian Empire, Nazism and communism—the irony of his title is almost unbearable. There is little sunshine in *Sunshine*, only degradation.

The three principal Sonnenschein heirs are all played by Ralph Fiennes. The first of them, Ignatz, changes his name to Sors, in order to advance his career as a judge faithfully serving the empire. He ends up bitter and betrayed. His son Adam abandons his religion in order to join the right fencing club. He becomes an Olympic gold medalist, but—in the film's most haunting sequence—dies in a concentration camp denying his lost Judaism. His son Ivan becomes a communist bureaucrat, then revolts against that totalitarianism. The picture ends virtually as the century does, with Ivan melting into a crowd, all ambitions, all faiths abandoned.

Including the romantic one. None of Fiennes' characters are lucky in love either. Perhaps that's because he's always a man who cannot yield his sense of self to bruising, confident ideology. Ignatz's wife (played first by Jennifer Ehle, then by her mother Rosemary Harris) is his opposite—serene, patient an exemplary survivor. Written by Szabo and playwright Israel Horovitz, *Sunshine* is a trifle schematic. But it also makes you feel, quite poignantly, the crushing tides of history: heedless, inhuman—and tragic.

VILLAGE VOICE, 6/13/00, p. 158, Amy Taubin

On New Year's Eve, 1899, the Sonnenschein family of Budapest toasts the future. Ignatz (Ralph Fiennes), the elder son and a successful judge, predicts that the 20th century will be a time of justice, love, and peace. This is the first, and, perhaps, only dramatic irony in István Szabó's *Sunshine,* save for the title itself. *Sunshine* is a chronicle of four generations of a Hungarian Jewish family, narrated by its last surviving member, Ivan Sonnenschein. Ivan is also played by Fiennes, as is Ivan's father, Adam, son of Ignatz. If this seems confusing, it's not so on-screen, since the film plods, with devout linearity, from one generation to the next and one political regime to another. That said, Fiennes himself may well have been confused, not only in playing three characters but also in having to keep track of the four actresses who at various times play his mother, as well as four others who play his wives and lovers and with whom he engages in one urgent sex act after another, as historic catastrophes crash about them: the assassination at Sarajevo, World War I, the destruction of the Austro-Hungarian Empire, the rise of Nazism, World War II and the Holocaust, the Communist takeover of Hungary, the 10-day revolution of 1956, the Soviet invasion, and in a hasty epilogue, the fall of the Iron Curtain.

An English-language film that employs British and North American actors in the leading roles and Hungarians to play everyone else, *Sunshine* is, for its first 30 minutes, a heavy Euro-pudding, overwhelmed by generic TV lighting and theme park costumes. But it slowly gathers force as the succeeding generations of Sonnenscheins attempt to assimilate into Hungarian society by denying their Jewish identity. Advised by his mentor that no one named Sonnenschein could be appointed to the high court, Ignatz, his brother, and his cousin change their name to Sors. Ignatz's son Adam, who aspires to be on the Olympic fencing team, takes the next step and converts to Catholicism. He wins the gold medal in the infamous Berlin Olympics of 1936, but it doesn't save him from being sent to a concentration camp, where he's tortured and killed. To avenge him, Adam's son Ivan joins the Communist secret police. Ivan thrives on ferreting out Nazi collaborators, but he's forced to reconsider his options when he's asked to investigate his boss as a suspected Zionist conspirator.

Szabó is an intelligent and capable filmmaker, but despite *Sunshine*'s historical scope and multiplicity of characters, it doesn't shed half as much light on its subject—identity and anti-Semitism—as does, for example, Agnieszka Holland's claustrophobic chamber piece *Angry Harvest.* As the three Sonnenscheins, Ralph Fiennes is most alive when he's angry, which isn't often enough.

The women in the cast fare better than the men, in particular Deborah Kara Unger and Rosemary Harris. Unger, almost unrecognizable coiffed in a late-'40s blond pageboy, plays the wife of a Communist Party thug who has an affair with Ivan but refuses to give up the security of her marriage for a loose cannon. Unger's trademark narcissistic sexuality is mixed here with a powerful paranoia. Szabó uses the character to show the paralytic effect of living in a police state, and Unger's panicky sideways glances and evasive body language make the point more indelibly than any of the film's big speeches. Harris has the far more crucial role as Valerie, Adam's mother and Ivan's grandmother, who's an accomplished photographer. Valerie survives into old age with grace and equanimity because, as she explains, she hasn't much use for politics or religion and always looks for the beauty in life. Szabó puts Valerie on a pedestal, and he's lucky to have Harris to bring her down to earth.

Also reviewed in:
CHICAGO TRIBUNE, 6/23/00, Friday/p. B, Michael Wilmington
NEW REPUBLIC, 6/12/00, p. 32, Stanley Kauffmann
NEW YORK TIMES, 6/9/00, p. E12, A. O. Scott
NEW YORKER, 7/17/00, p. 89, David Denby
VARIETY, 9/20-26/99, p. 83, Eddie Cockrell
WASHINGTON POST, 6/23/00, p. C1, Stephen Hunter

SUPERNOVA

A Metro-Goldwyn-Mayer Pictures release of a Screenland Pictures/Hammerhead production. *Executive Producer:* Ralph S. Singleton. *Producer:* Ash R. Shah, Daniel Chuba, and Jamie Dixon. *Director:* Thomas Lee. *Screenplay:* David Campbell Wilson. *Story:* William Malone and Daniel Chuba. *Director of Photography:* Lloyd Ahern II. *Editor:* Michael Schweitzer and Melissa Kent. *Music:* David Williams. *Music Editor:* Terry Delsing and Bunny Andrews. *Sound:* Jim Webb and (music) John Richards. *Sound Editor:* Michael Kirchberger, Mark Stoeckinger, and Jay Wilkinson. *Casting:* Mary Jo Slater. *Production Designer:* Marek Dobrowolski. *Art Director:* Bruce Robert Hill. *Set Designer:* Luis Hoyos, Kristen Pratt, Lauren Cory, and Domenic Silvestri. *Set Decorator:* Nancy Nye. *Set Dresser:* Mara Massey, Tom Callinicos, Michael Triant, and John H. Maxwell. *Special Effects:* Thomas L. Fisher and Scott R. Fisher. *Costumes:* Bob Ringwood. *Make-up:* Gary Liddiard. *Make-up Effects:* Patrick Tatopoulos. *Stunt Coordinator:* Allan Graf. *Running time:* 91 minutes. *MPAA Rating:* PG-13.

CAST: James Spader (Nick Vanzant); Angela Bassett (Kaela Evers); Robert Forster (A.J. Marley); Lou Diamond Phillips (Yerzy Penalosa); Peter Facinelli (Karl Larson); Robin Tunney (Danika Lund); Wilson Cruz (Benj Sotomejor); Eddy Rice, Jr. (Flyboy); Knox Grantham White (Troy Larson); Kerrigan Mahan (Voice of Troy Larson); Vanessa Marshall (Sweetie).

LOS ANGELES TIMES, 1/17/00, Calendar/p. 4, Kevin Thomas

"Supernova" isn't so super, which is no doubt why MGM opened it Friday without early press previews. Despite the distinctive presences of James Spader, Angela Bassett, Robert Forster and Lou Diamond Phillips and a great high-tech look, the film is a relentlessly routine outer-space adventure further hampered by a load of technical jargon. The direction (credited to the pseudonymous Thomas Lee after Walter Hill requested that his name be taken off it) is brisk and firm, however, and the film may play OK with undemanding fans of the genre.

We're 200 years into the future, and Forster's A.J. Marley is the captain of the emergency medical rescue vessel Nightingale. Bassett's Kaela Evers is the Nightingale's no-nonsense—but very aloof and sexy—medical officer, and she's wary of Marley's new co-pilot, Nick Vanzant (Spader), who has just kicked a drug habit, having been addicted to the same future superdrug to which her ex-lover (Peter Facinelli) fell victim. Phillips, Robin Tunney and Wilson Cruz capably round out the Nightingale's crew.

No sooner has this tension between Evers and Vanzant been established than the Nightingale receives an emergency distress signal from a rogue moon, site of a mining operation where some sort of disaster has struck. After some special effect razzle-dazzle involving "dimension jumping," a celestial storm and gravitational pull from a star about to implode, the Nightingale winds up short on fuel and with a new passenger, a smirky, edgy young man, Troy (Knox Grantham White), who's the son of Bassett's former lover and clearly the harbinger of big-time trouble ahead.

Unfortunately, all of what ensues is pretty murky and dull. Writer David Campbell Wilson further hampers a hazy narrative line with minimal characterization. Even so, Spader and Bassett, equally assured and sharp, strike sparks and it would be fun to see them reteamed in more elevated circumstances.

NEW YORK POST, 1/15/00, p. 21, Jonathan Foreman

Despite reports of a troubled production and the departure of two directors, "Supernova" turns out to be a perfectly enjoyable sci-fi thriller.

Sure, its story is recycled from a number of sources—from "The Treasure of the Sierra Madre" to "Event Horizon"—but it's a combination that works in a satisfying if predictable B-movie-ish way.

Partly it's because, like a lot of post-"Alien" sci-fi pictures, "Supernova" is as much about the tensions of the workplace as it is about the dangers of galactic travel. Put some ordinary Joes and Jill—all of whom have irritating as well as attractive qualities—on a space ship for months on end and you're going to get some interesting friction.

Here, on the medical rescue vessel Nightingale 229, is a mix of intertwining stories: Capt. A.J. Marley (Robert Forster) spends his spare time working on a dissertation on 20th-century cartoons; engineer Benj Sotomejor (Wilson Cruz) has become too intimate with "Sweetie," the computer system; and Kaela Evers (Angela Bassett) serves as the ship's lonely, difficult doctor.

You also have two medical techs (Lou Diamond Phillips and the lovely Robin Tunney) who spend most of their time engaged in zero-gravity sex, and a co-pilot (James Spader) who was thrown out of the military and jailed for his drug addiction.

The Nightingale receives a distress call from an abandoned mining colony on a distant moon. After "dimension jumping hundreds of light years to the site of the call, the ship finds itself damaged and in the gravitational path of an imploding star.

The crew also rescues a strange, charismatic young man (Peter Facinelli), who turns out to have something in his luggage that threatens the whole human race.

The always enjoyable Spader (who clearly buffed up for the role) is believably tough for the first time in his career. Bassett is always a pleasure to watch—even when delivering the kind of uninspired lines that characterize much of the film's script.

And Facinelli, with his Tom Cruise-like smile (until he starts to look like one of the vampires in "Buffy"), makes a fine, seductive villain.

"Supernova" also deserves credit for its relative courage in calmly featuring an interracial relationship—something that is still all too rare in Hollywood movies, especially when the coupling involves a black woman and a white man.

NEWSDAY, 1/17/00, Part II/p. B2, John Anderson

Rising as it does out of the often blackish hole of the sci-fi genre, "Supernova" concerns an emergency medical team that takes intergalactic 911 calls. What it diagnoses is the flexibility and atrophy of the form.

Exhibit A: James Spader, perpetual ingenue and an actor who's always seemed somehow wrong for his times. In the critically under-appreciated "Stargate" (1994), he played the insouciant wiseacre to Kurt Russell's rock-jawed Buzz Lightyear clone. Here, Spader has made a somewhat uneasy transition to Clint Eastwood impersonator as Nick Vanzant, ex-pilot and recovering drug addict, who is signed on to the medical team for the "quiet" of deep space. The production of "Supernova," which wasn't screened for critics, has been what they call troubled. The director of credit, Thomas Lee, is described by MGM as "a name mutually agreed upon by Walter Hill and MGM," so one can draw one's own conclusions. "Supernova" does come equipped with a lot of recycled equipment: The eclectic crew, with its shared history/relationships. The endearing robot and/or omnipotent computer voice (no HALs here). The uneasy voyage into uncharted territory. And the seemingly unbeatable foe who defies every law of God and man and then gets what's coming to him. But at the same time "Supernova" is a decent enough thriller. The effects, designed by Digital Domain, may be all over the place, but the cast is impressive and that's the film's strength. Besides Spader, Angela Bassett offers her usual winning mix of intimidation and sexuality as Dr. Kaela Evers; relative newcomer Wilson Cruz ("Party of Five") is quite persuasive as the EMS Nightingale's computer wonk; and the all-too- rarely seen Robert Forster is Capt. Marley, whose molecules don't catch up with each other when the crew responds to a deep-space distress call.

What they find is Troy (Peter Facinelli), who claims to be the son of Karl Larson—a man Kaela describes as "the worst nightmare I ever met." What Troy has found on this derelict planet looks like a high-tech lava lamp.

"Supernova" is adequate space hoopla. The characters are compelling and that's what makes the difference between good space fare and unadulterated jetsam. That, and checking out how the space ship looks like a health club full of Stairmasters. And giggling at the makeup piled on to simulate Troy's increasing muscle mass. And an ending that suggests both a race-less fate for humankind and a genesis for Kubrick's star child in "2001."

Who says you can't have everything?

SIGHT AND SOUND, 8/00, p. 56, John Wrathall

The 22nd century. Joining the crew of deep-space medical-rescue vessel *Nightingale 299*, co-pilot Nick Vanzant gets a frosty welcome from chief medical officer Kaela Evers. The *Nightingale* picks up a distress call from a mine on an abandoned rogue moon apparently from Karl Larson, an abusive former lover of Kaela's whom she believed to be dead.

To reach the moon, the *Nightingale* has to perform a "dimension jump", during which the captain is killed. Nick takes command. The ship loses most of its fuel supply in an asteroid attack. A patrol vehicle docks carrying the sole survivor of a mining expedition, who claims to be Larson's son Troy. His vehicle is carrying an alien object which Troy dug out of the abandoned mine. Led to believe that there is fuel on the abandoned moon, Nick goes to investigate, but is left stranded there by Troy. Kaela realises that the alien object on board her ship is "ninth dimensional" and will destroy the Earth if it is taken back there. But Troy, whose body and mind have been infiltrated by an alien force, is determined to do exactly that. After killing the rest of the crew, Troy reveals to Kaela that he is in fact Karl, rejuvenated by his contact with the ninth dimension. Now he wants her back.

Kaela is rescued by Nick, who manages to return from the moon in time to blow up Karl and the ninth-dimensional object. Forced to share the only undamaged "dimensional stabilisation chamber" on the journey back to Earth, Nick and Kaela undergo a transfer of a small amount of genetic material which leaves Kaela pregnant.

The slow decline of Walter Hill as a director over the past 20 years, from *The Driver* (1978) and *The Long Riders* (1980) to his more recent *Trespass* and *Last Man Standing,* has been offset by a parallel career as producer and sometimes co-writer of one of the most successful film franchises of the era, the *Alien* quartet. That Hill chose to entrust the direction of *Alien* to the then relatively untried Ridley Scott, and its sequels to comparative newcomers James Cameron, David Fincher and Jean-Pierre Jeunet, suggested an acknowledgement on his part that science fiction wasn't his forte. So it's a mystery why Hill, some way from the height of his powers, should have chosen to direct this substandard *Alien* imitation which he apparently had no hand in writing. *Supernova* proved a disastrous experience—not just for the viewer but for Hill himself, who removed his name from the credits, replacing it with Thomas Lee. (Alan Smithee is presumably too well-known for his own good.) Extensively recut and reshot (by an uncredited Francis Ford Coppola, among others), *Supernova* bombed at the US box office earlier this year.

Like *Alien Supernova* relies on the basic set-up of alien, or in this case alien-infected human, picking off the crew of a spaceship one by one. And as with *Alien*, in which the spaceship was named after Joseph Conrad's novel *Nostromo, Supernova* toys with references to classic nautical literature, specifically Jack London's *The Sea Wolf.* In *The Sea Wolf* Larsen is the ship's captain who terrorises the castaways he rescues; here Larson is the castaway who terrorises the crew who rescue him. Alongside such literary references, there are a few interesting ideas buried in *Supernova,* notably the decision by an advanced alien race to plant a lethal "ninth-dimensional object" in a far corner of the universe as a booby trap for any species evolved enough for deep-space exploration—and thus posing a threat to their supremacy.

But like so much else in the film, this intriguing premise remains undeveloped. Whether it's the fault of the script or the re-editing, *Supernova* feels woefully rushed and bursts with loose ends and unfulfilled set-ups. In the film's incoherent first act, for instance, the spaceship's speaking computer Sweetie has to keep up a running commentary in order to give us any idea what's going on.

As for Hill, the only sign of his involvement as director is the strange, seasick camera style, forever tilting from side to side, which marred his 1995 Western *Wild Bill*. More seriously, he seems to have broken the cardinal rule that gave such early films as *The Driver* their existential charge: his avowed refusal, against received Hollywood wisdom, to give his characters backstory. Here, fatally, the whole plot depends on backstory, in particular Karl Larson's past relationship with medical officer Kaela Evers, which is what motivates him to send out his distress call to her ship. But since we're never told the terrible things Karl did to Kaela during their time together (presumably the scene where this happened ended on the cutting-room floor with so much else), the climactic revelation that Larson's son Troy is in fact the rejuvenated Karl falls hopelessly flat.

VILLAGE VOICE, 2/1/00, p. 122, Dennis Lim

The most charming thing about *Supernova*—a frivolous sci-fi adventure set in the 22nd century aboard a medical emergency spacecraft—is its giggly preoccupation with Kinky Space Sex. Couples retire to the ship's zero-gravity chamber for free-floating coitus. The medics travel from one distress call to another by "dimension-jumping," a high-risk process that requires the jumpers to cocoon themselves in a polyglass pod without any clothes on. (This occasions much frantic disrobing and the odd lingering glance.) And the romance between the ex-junkie copilot (a newly beefy, endearingly glum James Spader) and the testy doctor (a death-glare-hurling Angela Bassett) is quite a treat, with a seduction-scene discussion of how pears get into pear-brandy bottles.

Supernova has apparently fallen victim to the transparent damage-control tactics of studios in possession of perceived stinkers: a January release with no advance screenings. (Given that many reviewers are only too happy to oblige when told what to think, it's no wonder these fears are self-fulfilling.) Original director Walter Hill has removed his name—the blame now falls on the nonexistent "Thomas Lee," a bland, new variation on Alan Smithee. And yet, *Supernova* is no real cause for shame—by no means a good movie but silly and strange enough to recommend. On the one hand, it plumbs the standard deep-space-panic scenarios pioneered by *Alien* (on which Hill served as cowriter and coproducer); on the other, it shamelessly aspires to the cheap-thrill tawdriness of daytime soap—the plot loosely concerns the reemergence of a villainous type, rendered unrecognizable here thanks not to plastic surgery but to the rejuvenating powers of a glowing pink ovoid. The "alien artifact," as everyone nervously calls it, inspires much hyperventilating about ninth-dimensional matter and natural selection. Don't bother paying attention—the script's one-track mind reduces it all to a parting joke about an intergalactic impregnation.

Also reviewed in:
CHICAGO TRIBUNE, 1/17/00, Tempo/p. 2, John Petrakis
NEW YORK TIMES, 1/15/00, p. B20, Lawrence Van Gelder
VARIETY, 1/17-23/00, p. 48, Godfrey Cheshire
WASHINGTON POST, 1/15/00, p. C3, Stphen Hunter

SUZHOU RIVER

A Strand Releasing release of a Dream Factory and Essential Films presenation of a Nai An and Phillippe Bober production. *Producer:* Nai An and Philippe Bober. *Director:* Lou Ye. *Screenplay (Mandarin with English subtitles):* Lou Ye. *Editor:* Karl Riedl. *Music:* Jörg Lemberg. *Sound:* Xu Peijun and (music) Zhai Lixin. *Production Designer:* Li Zhuoyi. *Costumes:* Zhang Li Fang and Li Wei. *Make-up:* Wang Xuemin. *Running time:* 83 minutes. *MPAA Rating:* Not Rated.

CAST: Zhou Xun (Moudan/Meimei);   Jia Hongsheng (Mardar);   Hua Zhongkai (Lao B.);   Yao Anlian (Boss);   Nai An (Mada).

CHRISTIAN SCIENCE MONITOR, 11/10/00, p. 15, David Sterritt

"Suzhou River", has already acquired an impressive list of honors on the film-festival circuit, including a slot tn New York's prestigious New Directors/New Films series at the Museum of Modern Art and the prize of the Film Critics International Federation (FIPRESCI) jury at Vienna's recent Viennale festival, on which I served.

For those who think Chinese movies diverge from Western fare by their very nature, "Suzhou River" may come as a surprise. The strongest influence on it is not traditional Chinese culture but the spirit of Alfred Hitchcock, whose 1958 masterpiece "Vertigo" appears to have inspired filmmaker Lou Ye's tale of a young man who finds himself in mysterious waters when he enters a kidnapping scheme, falls in love with the victim, loses her in a moment of violence, and becomes fixated on a young woman who may or may not be his vanished lover.

Adding more layers to the story is the fact that it's narrated by a video-maker who may have lived these events, or may be spinning them from his imagination even as we watch them. "Suzhou River" is concerned as much with moods and mentalities as with actions and occurrences.

At once a poetic art film, a traditional suspense yarn, and a moody voyage through Shanghai's gritty back roads, it's a rich experience from any perspective.

LOS ANGELES TIMES, 11/10/00, Calendar/p. 14, Kenneth Turan

Whatever you think when you think about films from China (if you think anything at all), "Suzhou River" will come as a bracing surprise. An assured exercise in high cinematic style, it references a variety of film and filmmakers—Alfred Hitchcock not the least of them—but what it is preeminently is alive and dynamic. "Suzhou River" is written and directed by Lou Ye, a key figure in the young Sixth Generation of mainland filmmakers who are doing things differently than Fifth Generation giants like Zhang Yimou and Chen Kiage. Daring and edgy, it's a German co-production (critical for avoiding censorship) that's filled with intoxicating excitement of creating images for the screen.

What this love of movie-making is most reminiscent of is the bravura quality of the French New Wave. With its jump cuts, jazzy camera work and an intricate storytelling style that never stops to catch its breath "Suzhou River" exults in visual razzle-dazzle.

All this is visible in a remarkable opening sequence that would be ordinary in less deft hands. The film's nameless narrator-director (safely hidden by the camera's first person point of view, a vantage point that echoes Robert Montgomery's "Lady in the Lake") takes us on a tour of the Suzhou, a river that runs through Shanghai.

"It's the filthiest river, with an eternity's worth of stories and rubbish," the narrator says with typically neo-noir world-weariness that compliments the brooding images that flash by. "If you watch it long enough, the river will show you everything."

But "Suzhou River" is more than a jittery travelogue; it has a tricky story that convincingly rifts on Hitchcock's "Vertigo," a tale of love, voyeurism and obsession that casually plays with dramatic conventions without any sacrifice of narrative drive.

The faceless storyteller is a freelance videographer. "Pay me," he says as he paints his pager number on vacant walls, "and I'll shoot anything. But don't complain if you don't like what you see."

The owner of a divey bar—incongruously called the Happy Tavern—signs on as a client, asking for a video of the place's mermaid act, which features a girl in a blond wig swimming in a big tank. Her name is Meimei (Zhou Xun), and the videographer immediately falls for her, hard. "When she closes the door," he says, "I feel life stopping."

It's through Meimei that the videographer hears the story of Marder (Jia Hongsheng), a stoic former street tough who works as a courier and lives only for his motorbike. Partly through what he's heard, partly through his imagination, the videographer starts inventing and then refining the story of Marder and the love of his life Moudan.

A teenage girl with twin ponytails and a pixie smile, Moudan (also played by Zhou Xun) starts as a kind of delivery job for Marder. The daughter of a Shanghai smuggler, she has to be ferried to an aunt's apartment when her father entertains women, which is often. Marder does the transporting, and though he is impassive at first, Moudan's teasing—she demands he drive his bike like Arnold Schwarzenegger—finally gets him emotionally involved.

If this story sounds too pat, the videographer agrees with you. Soon, like Scheherezade, he is embroidering it yet again, adding complications to these characters' lives. Adding even more layers, Marder takes over his own story and even materializes in the flesh, creating new problems in the videographer's life that have everything to do with the fact that Moudan and Meimei look exactly alike.

Though these narrative devices are cumbersome to describe, they work with such ease on film you hardly even notice them as you're pulled along deeper into the story.

As much about style as about love, "Suzhou River" echoes a lot of films, from the Hong Kong style of Wong Kar Wei to Kieslowski's "The Double Life of Veronique," but the sum total is something with a freshness of its own.

NEW YORK POST, 11/8/00, p. 59, Lou Lumenick

"Suzhou River" is a rare Chinese movie (it was co-produced with German money) that isn't about Chinese culture or history—in fact, it's a contemporary homage to Alfred Hitchcock's "Vertigo."

The setting is a seedy, crime-infested section of Shanghai alongside the polluted Suzhou River.

The unnamed narrator (played by writer-director Lou Ye) is a videographer who meets a motorcycle courier named Mardar (Jia Hongsheng) who tells him an incredible story.

Several years earlier, Mardar was hired to look after a smuggler's daughter named Moudan (Zhou Xun). They fell in love, but then she found out he was conspiring with a couple of his criminal pals to kidnap her for money.

Heartbroken, Moudan hurled herself into the Suzhou River—and Mardar was thrown into jail for her murder.

After his release, Mardar encounters Meimei (also played by Zhou Xun), a dancer who performs in a fish tank in a nightclub wearing a mermaid costume and blonde wig (as snippets of Bernard Herrmann's "Vertigo" score play on the soundtrack).

The smitten Mardar is convinced Meimei is the supposedly dead Moudan, though Meimei insists otherwise.

So does the narrator, who says Meimei is *his* ex-girlfriend.

It would be unfair to give away much more of the plot, which has some pretty neat twists.

"Suzhou River" has a terrific lead performance by Zhou Xun as the childish Moudin and the much more sophisticated Meimei, who lives on a houseboat and finds herself ardently wooed by Mardar.

Excessive hand-held camerawork may induce, well, vertigo in some audience members. But overall, this intriguing film is the best variation on "Vertigo" since Brian DePalma's far more polished "Obsession" (1976), which ranks with the best Hitchcock knockoffs of all time.

SIGHT AND SOUND, 12/00, p. 38, Lizzie Francke

Shanghai, the present. A videographer is in love with Meimei, a performer at the Happy Tavern nightclub. He becomes intrigued by the story of Mardar, a motorcycle courier who works for a businesswoman involved in various criminal activities. One of Mardar's tasks is to ferry around Moudan, the teenage daughter of an associate of Mardar's boss. Mardar and Moudan fall in love. Mardar, though, is pressurised into kidnapping Moudan; devastated by Mardar's betrayal, Moudan escapes and jumps from one of the bridges crossing the river Suzhou. Mardar is arrested and sent to prison.

On release, he hangs out in the Happy Tavern. Glimpsing Meimei he is convinced that she is his lost love Moudan and begins to court her. After the jealous videographer arranges for Mardar to be beaten up, Mardar decides to leave town. Later the videographer receives a note from Mardar, stating that he has found the real Moudan working in a shop in the suburbs. Later still, the videographer is summoned to identify Mardar and Moudan's bodies, dragged from the river.

The videographer informs Meimei who rushes to the scene. After asking the videographer whether he loves her in the same way that Mardar loved Moudan, Meimei disappears.

Writer-director Lou Ye's second film, a tale of *amour fou* set in modern-day Shanghai, opens with shots of the swirling Suzhou river from which it takes its name. As we float past the cluttered banks of the city, the unnamed—and unseen—videographer who narrates the film ponders the many secrets the river holds. As with the muddied waterways of Taipei in Tsai Ming-Liang's *The River/Heliu*, the polluted estuary here is the powerful symbol at the film's core. A site of flux, it suggests the transient nature of the lives in the story that unfolds: the anonymous videographer, through whose lens we see much of the story; his elusive girlfriend Meimei (Zhou Xun), a nightclub performer who dresses up as a mermaid as part of her act; Mardar (Jia Hongsheng), a small-time crook and motorcycle courier; and finally Moudan (also played by Zhou Xun), the daughter of a rich businessman, whom Mardar is hired to ferry around town. The videographer tells of how Mardar and Moudan fall in love but when Mardar gets involved in a botched attempt to kidnap her, Moudan disappears. Bereft, Mardar catches sight of Meimei's act, becomes convinced she's his lost love and attempts to seduce her.

Despite the gritty, almost documentary feel Lou Ye gives these opening moments, his film steers a different course from the downbeat realism that characterises the work of his Beijing Film Academy contemporaries Zhang Yuan *(Beijing Bastards/Beijing Zazhong,*1993) and Wang Xiaoshuai *(The Days/Dong-Chun De Rizi,* 1993). Building the narrative from chance encounters and interconnected lives, Lou makes obvious nods to Wong Kai-Wai's *Chungking Express/Chongqing Senlin*. Stylistically the film also owes something to Wong's restless visual sensibility; jump cuts abound and director of photography Wang Yu's dextrous hand-held camerawork snakes like the river itself. One of the most memorable images adroitly captures the mix of observational realism and lush romanticism; as the videographer tells of how the locals explain the disappearance of Moudan, we catch a glimpse of her, dressed as mermaid—the persona she adopts for her nightclub act, complete with a long blonde wig and emerald-scaled tail—exists in an equally incongruous environment, the dingy, drinking dive the Happy Tavern. At the beginning the videographer catches only a glimpse of the coquettish Meimei as she prepares for her act, but it's clear she has beguiled him, much as her mythical counterparts were said to drive men to distraction—and to their doom.

Lou's decision to use the figure of the mermaid—which isn't part of Chinese folklore—is characteristic of the global outlook of his sixth-generation film-making contemporaries. Similarly he markedly embraces what was presumably illicit cinema history by paying a clear stylistic debt to Alfred Hitchcock's *Vertigo,* the perennial favourite of cinéphile directors worldwide. The river, the bridge, the obsessive, haunted protagonist and the girl who might not be quite who she seems; this drifting reverie of a film shares elements that have figured in countless movies inspired by Hitchcock's 1958 masterpiece from Chris Marker's arthouse sci fi *La Jetée* (1962) to Paul Verhoeven's glossy thriller *Basic Instinct* (1992). But *Suzhou River* is less a radically new spin on Hitchcock's film than a free-fall replay that revels in its lachrymose love story, as Mardar, like *Vertigo*'s hero Scottie, falls for a woman who's seemingly the double of his lost love.

Much of the film is seen through the lens of the videographer who admits to spending more time "observing" than working —and is accompanied by his pensive musings. The device brings to mind the first-person camerawork of Robert Montgomery's 1946 thriller *Lady in the Lake,* but whereas the subjective visual strategy in that movie was really only a *noir* novelty, here it deepens the dreamlike intensity and haunting, slippery sense of unreality. Narrating Mardar and Moudan's story, the videographer's voiceover often assumes a tentative, improvisory quality: against a reflection of Mardar lit by a flickering bulb, he hesitates before letting us into his backstory as if he's making it up; later, as Mardar and Moudan get to know one another, the narrative seems to stall, and the videographer asks: "What happens next?" ("Love, of course," is his answer, but he could just as honestly have added betrayal and death.)

So much of what we see is filtered through the videographer's lens that it's difficult to take things at face value. Mardar and Moudan's love story isn't exactly idealised he betrays and kidnaps her but it's more deeply felt and richly realised than the videographer's obsessive crush on Meimei. The videographer's relationship with Meimei might be effervescent, but the message underlying the narrative drift that carries Mardar and Moudan to their watery ends is hardly comforting: that true love is ever allusive and can at any point disappear into the darkness.

Ironically, given the hold they have over the videographer and Mardar, Meimei and Moudan are the least alluring aspects of *Suzhou River*. Neither is a true-blooded femme fatale in the *noir* tradition the film evokes; they're both a little too ditzy and prone to flighty behaviour, if not childlike. At various moments Moudan is seen toying with a mermaid doll as if to emphasise her girlish qualities. (At least *Vertigo*'s Scottie fell for a grown-up woman.) But while the film is at its most irritating when we follow the lovelorn videographer's record of the pouting Meimei, the unsteady first-person point of view at least foregrounds the inherent voyeurism at play. In the end, it's hard not to be swept up by the strong current of *Suzhou River*, a seductive and atmospheric conundrum that works pleasingly as an exercise in storytelling. The Chinese-box structure allows for multiple parallels, most obviously with the doubling of Meimei and Moudan, as the videographer latches on to—or for that matter invents—Mardar's tale. Meanwhile these loved ones may be only echoes of another unseen desire: with this fresh piece of film making from mainland China, Lou Ye swoons to the memory of Hitchcock.

VILLAGE VOICE, 11/14/00, p. 131, J. Hoberman

Home to the last great popular cinema of the 20th century, Hong Kong has proved a great source of inspiration. Syncretic by nature, Hong Kong movies expanded the imagination of Asian filmmakers, no less than that of the American audiences for whom the East Asian metropolis (from Seoul to Singapore) has come to be the image of globalization, if not the economic frontier of the future.

The latest in East-West fusion, Lou Ye's wildly atmospheric, cleverly low-budget *Suzhou River* is no *Blade Runner* or *Crouching Tiger, Hidden Dragon*—but this adroit, concise, and poetic city-symphony is almost too fashionable for its own good. Awash with new-wave flotsam and jetsam, *Suzhou River* (which had its premiere in last spring's "New Directors/New Films") is a movie of seductive surfaces—mainly as reflected in the queasy glamour of the polluted canal that winds through the heart of Shanghai.

In the absence of anything by Wong Kar-wai, this may be the most stylish movie currently playing lower Manhattan. Lou, a 35-year-old Shanghai native who has worked mainly in Chinese TV (and made his share of music videos), locates a plot lifted largely from *Vertigo* and a noirish first-person narration supplied by an unseen, itinerant videographer in a moody urban landscape whose sumptuous industrial dereliction would be the envy of film aesthetes from Williamsburg to Edinburgh or even Azerbaijan.

Less intractable than the season's other first-rate Chinese movie, Jia Zhangke's cool and detached *Platform, Suzhou River* revels in déjà vu. Voyeur that he is, the movie's nameless camera-I naturally falls in love with the exhibitionist Meimei (Zhou Xun), a young woman who performs in a long blond wig and a floodlit tank, impersonating a mermaid in the dank recesses of the Happy Tavern. Tapes documenting Meimei, already a vanished object, at work and play segue into the legend of Mardar—the handsome motorcycle messenger who has experienced a far more dramatic tale of love and loss.

Charged with the care of the schoolgirl Moudan, daughter of a wealthy lowlife, Mardar made the mistake of becoming emotionally involved with her. The alert viewer will quickly note that Moudan is also played by Zhou Xun, albeit as an annoyingly pert gamine. Mardar, who is not particularly bright, allows himself to be recruited by some underworld pals in a plot to kidnap Moudan and hold her for ransom. Shocked by his betrayal (as well as the apparently paltry sum that her captors are demanding), the girl seizes an opportunity to run away and hurl herself into the Suzhou, clutching—yes—a blond mermaid doll. Mardar is sent to jail and, on his return to Shanghai some years later, begins searching the urban maze for Moudan—inevitably, as well as literally, bumping into her grown-up doppelgänger at the bar of the Happy Tavern.

Suzhou River's narrative is more than a bit cornball and not overly convincing—which is to say the movie's conviction is to be found in its formal values. (The plot doesn't really kick in until quite late, once Mardar—even more obsessive than the narrator—meets the enigmatic Meimei and begins haunting her dressing room: "Am I the girl you are looking for?" she asks in a question rich with multiple meanings.) Shot with a jostling, nervous camera, *Suzhou River* looks great—the showy jump cuts and off-kilter close-ups belie an extremely well edited, even supple, piece of work.

Lou is confident even in his influences: The movie's aggressive style, its tawdry neon pink-and-green cocktail-lounge color schemes and heavy rain, are all suggestive of Wong Kar-wai. The score, by German composer Jorg Lemberg, deliberately echoes the Wagnerian rhapsody Bernard Herrmann wrote for *Vertigo*. But the lessons Lou learned from Wong and his allusions to Hitchcock are far less important than his vision of cavernous dives illuminated by naked lightbulbs or the flux of the industrial smokestacks and derelict buildings that line the canal's rubbish-strewn embankments.

This is not a film that plumbs the depths, unless it is to dredge those of the filmmaker's own melancholy. After Meimei breaks up with the camera, the Happy Tavern (that neighborhood house of fiction) shuts down. "Suddenly it was as if none of this had happened," the narrator muses. Further complications—restless spirits, additional doubles, sudden disappearances—send him drifting downstream with his camcorder, following the grimy garbage scows in search of another story.

Lou has transformed Shanghai into a personal phantom zone. Named for an urban stream of consciousness, *Suzhou River* is a ghost story that's shot as though it were a documentary—and a documentary that feels like a dream.

Also reviewed in:
NEW YORK TIMES, 3/25/00, p. B16, A. O. Scott
VARIETY, 2/14-20/00, p. 42, David Rooney

TABOO

A New Yorker Films release of a Shochiku Co./BAC Films/Le Studio Canal Plus/Recorded Picture Co. presentation in association with Kadokawa Shoten Publishing Co./Imagica/BS Asahi/Eisei Gekijo Co. *Executive Producer:* Nobuyoshi Otani. *Producer:* Shigehiro Nakagawa, Eiko Oshima, and Kazuo Shimizu. *Director:* Nagisa Oshima. *Screenplay (Japanese with English subtitles):* Nagisa Oshima. *Based on the novel "Shinsengumi Keppuroku" by:* Ryotaro Shiba. *Director of Photography:* Toyomichi Kurita. *Editor:* Tomoyo Oshima. *Music:* Ryuichi Sakamoto. *Choreographer (swordplay):* Hirofumi Nakase and Kazuhiro Hashimoto. *Sound:* Kunio Ando and (music) Fernando Aponte. *Production Designer:* Yoshinobu Nishioka. *Art Director:* Shoichi Yasuda. *Set Decorator:* Yosakichi Shimizu, Atsushi Shimamura, Keita Gohara, Nami Hoshizaki, and Toshio Fukuda. *Costumes:* Emi Wada. *Make-up:* Kunio Yamazaki, Mitsuyo Takasaki, and Ihoko Uchiyama. *Narrator:* Kei Sato. *Running time:* 100 minutes. *MPAA Rating:* Not Rated.

CAST: Takeshi "Beat" Kitano (Captain Toshizo Hijikata); Ryuhei Matsuda (Samurai Sozaburo Kano); Shinji Takeda (Lieutenant Soji Okita); Tadanobu Asano (Samurai Hyozo Tashiro); Koji Matoba (Samurai Heibei Sugano); Tommys' Masa (Inspector Jo Yamazaki); Masato Ibu (Officer Koshitaro Ito); Uno Kanda (Geisha Nishikigi-Dayu); Kazuko Yoshiyuki (The Servant Omatsu); Tomoro Taguchi (Samurai Tourjiro Yuzawa); Yoichi Sai (Commander Isami Kondo); Jiro Sakagami (Lieutenant Genzaburo Inoue); Zakoba Katsura (Wachigaiya).

CHRISTIAN SCIENCE MONITOR, 9/29/00, p. 15, David Sterritt

[*Gohatto (Taboo)* was reviewed jointly with *Yi Yi;* see Sterrit's review of that film.]

LOS ANGELES TIMES, 11/17/00, Calendar/p. 18, Kevin Thomas

When you think of samurai movies, you think of Toshiro Mifune and other epitomes of masculine heroism. When you recall director Nagisa Oshima, you're reminded of his notorious—and overrated—sex-equals-death fable "In the Realm of the Senses" (1976) and his iconoclastic, socially critic masterpieces of the '60s such as "Boy" and "Death by Hanging." So you can be sure that an Oshima samurai movie will be like no other: His first theatrical film in 14 years—he's been working in TV—is not titled "Taboo" for nothing.

Infinitely more complex than "Realm," "Taboo" is one of Oshima's finest films, recalling his prodigious early efforts but marked by a contemplative detachment. A classic Japanese period picture at its most evocative and rigorous, "Taboo" is a major work of subtle suggestiveness that lets the audience connect the dots. It is set in 1865 in an ancient Kyoto temple, headquarters of the Shinsengumi militia.

Commodore Matthew Perry's dropping anchor in the Bay of Edo in 1853 would open up isolationist Japan to trade—and thereby erode the power of the shogunate, the military dictatorship that had ruled the country for 700 years. By 1863 the shogun would need a personal militia—the Shinsengumi—to protect him.

Composed mainly of young men from peasant or poor trading families, the militia, which increased rapidly from two dozen to around 200 men, had triumphed at the Battle of Ikedaya in 1864 over the rebellious Chosu and Higo clans. But uprisings by clans, outraged by the shogun's treaty with "barbarians"—and most likely also feeling left out of the deal—continued, and by the spring of 1865 the Shinsengumi was hard-put to attract qualified recruits. (By the end of 1867 the great-grandfather of the present emperor would at last succeed in overthrowing the shogunate and restoring power to the throne.)

Had recruits been plentiful there's just no way that Sozaburo Kano (Ryuhei Matsuda) would have been accepted. From a samurai-turned-wealthy-merchant family, Kano is a skilled and confident swordsman but is so pretty that a maiko—apprentice geisha—would envy his rosebud lips. While his gestures and movements are not effeminate he continues to wear, at age 18, his hair long and in a ponytail rather than in a samurai's topknot.

The impact of Kano's mere presence, of which he is well aware, in a macho all-male environment is seismic, especially upon the confounded Shinsengumi leadership: Beat Takeshi's alert, concerned captain and Yoichi Sai's aggressive commander.

Some of the men are repelled by Kano, while others, no matter to what degree they are in denial, are stirred by his beauty. Kano is admitted to the militia along with another youth, Hyozo Tashiro (Tadanobu Asano), a free-thinking type who is instantly attracted to Kano and is quick to make a pass, only to be swiftly rejected.

It would seem that Kano is not so much in denial over his sexual orientation, which remains ambiguous, but has largely channeled his desires into the pleasure he takes in slaughter and in exerting power over others as a shameless and sometimes daring tease.

So here you have an utterly fearless samurai of stunning ability and courage—i.e, the perfect warrior—but whose appearance and selectively seductive manner not only keep the militia in a constantly unsettled state but also, inevitably, invites the slurs of enemies, which means the Shinsengumi has itself been slurred.

In short, Kano wreaks havoc in the lives of men dedicated to living up to the rigid samurai code of honor; Ryuichi Sakamoto's lush, captivating score expresses perfectly Kano's personality and its effect, sometimes darkly amusing in its consequences, other times tragic.

It takes a director with exceptional talent, skill and experience to explore ambiguity in all aspects of human nature and behavior, and Oshima has created a film of resilient, downright tensile strength that ends on a satisfyingly ironic note.

Backed by a sterling cast and the understated cinematography of Toyomichi Kurita, Oshima brings a contemporary perspective to a complex situation during an equally complex and crucial era in Japanese history.

NEW YORK POST, 10/6/00, p. 57, Jonathan Foreman

It's actually the surprisingly compelling plot and the often hilarious dialogue that keep you watching this tale of passion and murder in a Samurai militia unit—not the beautiful scenery or the elegant color palette.

The first film in more than a decade from Nagisa Oshima, the Japanese director best known abroad for the explicit scenes of sex and death in "In the Realm of the Senses," is set, in 1865, as feudal order was crumbling.

It deals with the havoc caused when Kano (Ryuhei Matsuda), a young recruit of striking, feminine beauty, is awarded a place in the Kyoto militia's rigid, ultra-traditional all-male hierarchy.

Although Kano himself seems much more interested in killing than in love or sex, just about everyone in his unit falls in love with him.

Because this is late 19th-century Japan, nobody is particularly horrified by homo-sexual desire.

But Kano and his looks do become a problem for the unit's ostensibly heterosexual leaders, especially Capt. Hijikata (Beat Takeshi), when one of Kano's lovers is found stabbed to death in the street, and an eyewitness says the killer wore the uniform of the militia.

As Hijikata investigates the crime—the first of several killings—he has to look into who has "leanings that way," and even into his own feelings for the boy.

NEWSDAY, 10/6/00, Part II/p. B11, Gene Seymour

There's nothing like the arrival of a beautiful girl alone among a pack of hyper-aggressive alpha males to create old-fashioned, hair-trigger movie tension. Leave it to Nagisa Oshima, Japan's master of gaudy insinuation (1971's "The Ceremony") and subversive passion (1976's "In the Realm of the Senses") to raise the stakes on this time-honored formula by changing the gender of this rogue element to that of a beautiful boy.

In the case of "Taboo" ("Gohatto"), adapted by Oshima from two historical novellas by Ryotaro Shiba, such tension is aroused in members of a samurai militia in 1860s Kyoto by the presence of Sozaburo (Ryuhei Matsuda), a murderously gifted enlistee possessed of an ethereal, equally lethal beauty. There isn't a man in the unit who isn't somehow affected by Sozaburo's looks, whether it's his love-struck fellow recruit Tashiro (Tadanobu Asano) or a handful of officers who become enraptured, unnerved or just plain goofy over this pretty cipher.

The tempest of jealousy and innuendo surrounding Sozaburo's magnetism soon builds to bloodshed, prompting the group's dour, relatively levelheaded captain (Takeshi Kitano) to grasp for some solution, including the hoary one of taking the kid to a nice brothel and introducing him to women. Which never works—especially in a movie such as this.

To this rough amalgam of Melville's "Billy Budd" and Oshima's own "Merry Christmas, Mr. Lawrence" (1982), the director liberally applies a gilded coating of B-movie gloss and scattered complexity, especially in the motives of its characters. The diffuse plot dynamics are apparently meant to leave certain psychological issues open-ended enough for the audience to fill in. This is especially true of Sozaburo's furtive sense of his own strength as well as the company commanders' unspoken desires. Unfortunately, such open-endedness dilutes, more than intensifies, the movie's provocative elements.

Still, the fact that "Taboo" is not quite as daring as it tries to be only enhances its cozier, old-fashioned charms. When it behaves like a straight-forward historical epic, "Taboo" be fun to watch, especially the fight sequences. Unlike other aging rebels, Oshima often demonstrates that he can pass up gratuitous shocks for no-sweat showmanship.

SIGHT AND SOUND, 8/01, p. 44, Philip Strick

Kyoto, Japan, 1865, The Shinsen-gumi militia, a samurai troop fiercely dedicate to tradition, tests potential new recruits by pitting them against crack duellist Okita. Observed by Shinsen-gumi leader Kondo and his lieutenant Hijikata, two young applicants are considered acceptable: Tashiro and Kano. A handsome 18-year old, Kano excites much admiration, particularly for his efficiency on a first assignment, the beheading of a man who has broken militia rules. Infatuated, Tashiro makes advances but is repelled at knifepoint; nevertheless, Hijikata becomes convinced some weeks later that Tashiro and Kano are now lovers.

Kondo departs on a diplomatic mission, leaving Hijikata in charge. Kano discovers that Inoue, whom he mistook for an ageing monk, is a veteran Shinsen-gumi leader, although a poor swordsman. He tries to make amends by going easy on Inoue during fight practice but their inhibited swordplay is scorned by two passing samurai, who then run off. Hijikata assigns Inoue and Kano to track down these intruders; confronting them, Kano is wounded. Tashiro is frantic with concern, as is Yuzawa, a fellow samurai who has been forcing his passion on Kano. Weeks later, Yuzawa is found murdered.

Returning, Kondo notes the tensions surrounding Kano and instructs Hijikata to restore order. Hijikata assigns his henchman Yamazaki to escort Kano to the local brothel, but Yamazaki's best efforts serve only to attract Kano's amorous devotion. Yamazaki even has to fight off an unknown 'rival', who drops a dagger; when this is identified as Tashiro's, Kondo decides that Tashiro must die. Kano is instructed to execute him; Hijikata and Okita wait nearby to assist if needed. Fighting for his life, Tashiro accuses Kano of murdering Yuzawa and attacking Yamazaki; Kano kills him and runs away. Okita sets out in possible pursuit while Hijikata, concluding that beauty is not to be trusted, fells a cherry sapling in full blossom.

With a shower of white cherry blossom, director Nagisa Oshima ends *Gohatto*—much as, 10 years ago, he framed his autobiographical documentary *Kyoto, My Mother's Place*. There, in typically ambivalent symbolism, the cascading petals were shown to prompt picnics and dancing among the citizens, a response scorned, Oshima reported, by his strong-willed and independent widowed mother, who had no time for such frivolity. Undecided as he wandered the decorated landscape whether to cherish Kyoto's temporary beauty or to burn the place down, Oshima finally admitted to defiance of maternal abstinence and proposed to get drunk. But the tension between respect for the past and concern for the future is an Oshima theme, and the emblematic cherry sapling in *Gohatto* finds him once again irresolute.

Gohatto is set in 1860s Kyoto, among the elite samurai Shinsen-gumi militia. At the simple story level, the 'death' of the sapling—felled with a single sword-swipe by second-in-command Hijikata ('Beat' Takeshi)—appears to signal that the newly recruited samurai Kano (Ryuhei Matsuda), a troublemaker too beautiful for anybody's good, has been despatched. But the fallen blossoms, a lone blaze of purity on the drizzled heathland, suggest much else, from the arguable innocence of Kano (he's accused of murdering a fellow samurai, but his on-screen admission of guilt and execution are denied us) to the chopping short of all future prospects for the military tradition the Shinsen-gumi stands for.

Underlying the story of Kano is a period of historical catharsis: 1865 was the year when western warships anchored off Kyoto to enforce a treaty that would destroy the centuries-old Shogunate system and transfer the newly empowered emperor from Kyoto to Edo (renamed Tokyo). A postscript considered for *Gohatto* pointed out that within two years of the Kano incident the samurai age was at an end, and the Shinsen-gumi militia (including Hijikata, Okita, Kondo and Inoue, four of its founders) were dead. Significantly, this perspective is omitted. As a result, Hijikata and his tree assume the stateless status of previous Oshima protagonists, with implications outside any specific time and place.

The film's final scenes, staged in studio-bound disregard for authenticity, are a jumble of imagined and 'real' encounters as Hijikata tries to work out the truth about Kano's admirers. Supposedly in hiding in order to witness Kano's attack on his lover Tashiro, Hijikata and his long-term colleague Okita stand openly nearby, surely in plain sight. The effect is both to suggest the inevitability of legend and to make us consider alternatives. The most striking of these would be that in felling the sapling Hijikata has severed himself from his own inadmissible interest in the taboo of Kano.

The wake-up call that sounds with the arrival of Kano at the Shinsen-gumi headquarters—a microcosm of the inflexibly feudal condition of Kyoto—is a familiar fanfare in Oshima's work. His earliest films, which placed him in the 1960s at the forefront of an acclaimed Japanese new wave, were replete with Godardian outsiders, among them the US fighter pilot captured by villagers in the 1961 *The Catch/Shiiku* and the amorphous Korean outcasts in the astonishingly surrealistic *Three Resurrected Drunkards/Kaette Kita Yopparai* (1968). And with increasing vehemence the primary challenge offered by Oshima's disruptive invaders was sexual, though always with political reference, culminating in the starkly confrontational *Empire of the Senses/Ai No Corrida* (1976), which left little scope for further manoeuvre. Like addenda to a complete text, *Merry Christmas Mr. Lawrence* (1982) and *Max Mon Amour* (1986) offer variations on the same theme of sexual obsession, in which the consequences of erotic rule-breaking are considered with humour and despair.

Unlike, however, the martyred Major Celliers in *Merry Christmas Mr. Lawrence,* Kano brings no apparent guilt or inhibition to his sudden absorption by a sealed community (in which sense, perhaps, he is more like Max the innocent chimpanzee). "He has something other than courage," comments Hijikata when Kano performs a relatively neat beheading, but the nature of this hidden quality is never entirely clear: Kano remains an enigma. Masked by flawlessly ambiguous features (even a slash across the brow is briskly healed) and flowing hair which he refuses to trim, he is unresponsive to the advances of fellow recruit Tashiro; the only embrace to which he is seen to submit is that of the older samurai Yuzawa, whose wild rumblings appear to evoke little more than boredom, except, perhaps, when they approach strangulation.

As if a kind of plague-carrier, himself uninfected, Kano might even be interpreted as being inspired only by violence. ("I joined the militia," he says, "in order to have the right to kill.") Properly respecting his elders—as illustrated when he makes his own swordsmanship look bad when pitted against former leader Inoue—he calmly attends to the duties assigned him. It's the rest of the Shinsen-gumi troop who are in disarray, all motives and decrees open to suspicion, all actions questioned for possible bias. Oshima makes light of most of this, even resorting to interpolated titles that read like newspaper headlines ("Rumor! Sozaburo [Kano] is still a virgin!") to update us on militia speculation. There's considerable amused chatter about people who "have the look of leaning that way", and much is made of the clownishly stolid Yamazaki, the only person for whom Kano admits affection.

Not too seriously, perhaps, the film gradually turns itself into a whodunit, only tentatively resolved by Kano's final scuttle into obscurity. That Okita goes after him (we have to assume this, as Okita doesn't admit to anything) offers a further solution, uncomfortable to Hijikata, in which Okita has observed that the presence of Kano has caused an as-yet unrecognised rift in the relationship between Kondo, the troop's present leader, and Hijikata, his lieutenant. If they have begun to compete for 'ownership' of the youth, the unity of the Shinsen- gumi organisation is in jeopardy, along with the entire Shogunate. Probably to alert Hijikata to the risks, Okita tells him the celebrated story *(Pledge of the Chrysanthemum)* of a pact between a scholar and a samurai which results in an act of ultimate loyalty when the samurai, although dead, turns up for a promised dinner party. Hijikata rather obtusely wonders if reading such stuff might signify that Okita is of dubious persuasion, but Okita quickly puts him straight: "I hate this kind of people—but I love beautiful stories. " The clear hint is that Okita, a champion of loyalty, has at the very least been both an observer and a manipulator behind the Kano affair. We might also note that Oshima, on the other hand, hates nobody and, wonderfully served by cast and camera, loves the reticence of a story immaculately told.

VILLAGE VOICE, 10/3/00, p. 227, J. Hoberman

Taboo, which has its premiere at the New York Film Festival, could be considered an event within the event. Nagisa Oshima is Japan's greatest living filmmaker, and his first theatrical feature in 14 years is an action film at once baroque and austere, hypnotic and opaque—a samurai drama punctuated by thwacking kendo matches in which the romantic swordsman keep falling in love . . . with each other.

Radically reconfiguring two novellas by Ryotaro Shiba, Japan's best-selling author of historical fiction, *Taboo* (previously billed as *Gohatto)* is an appropriately fatalistic, drolly deadpan, and elegantly precise restatement of the 68-year-old filmmaker's career-long concerns. From his aptly named *Cruel Story of Youth* (1960), through his New Left critique *Diary of a Shinjuku Thief* (1969) and his hardcore masterpiece *In the Realm of the Senses* (1976), to the unreleased *Max, Mon Amour* (1986), in which Charlotte Rampling falls in love and carries on an affair with a chimpanzee, Oshima has reveled in the spectacle of unleashed sexual frustration disintegrating the dam of a repressive social order.

One of Oshima's few period films—his last samurai film, the blatantly subversive *Shiro Amakusa, the Christian Rebel,* was made in 1962—*Taboo* is set in 1865, just before the dawn of Japanese modernization, during the final two years of the Tokugawa shogunate and its samurai supporters. The movie opens with the commander of the Shinsengumi militia and his captain (Takeshi Kitano) selecting new recruits—possibly for their looks as much as their swordsmanship. The new men include the teenage cutie Kano (Ryuhei Matsuda) and the somewhat older, confidently strutting Tashiro (Tadanobu Asano). Scarcely have they been inducted than Tashiro begins hitting on Kano: "Have you ever killed a man? Have you ever made love?"

Like *Beau Travail,* to which it has a family resemblance, *Taboo* is set in an all-male military universe. But where the Claire Denis film is a rapt meditation on the erotic obsession that one officer develops for an individual soldier, *Taboo* is more detached and analytical in its concern with love's flowering within a highly restrictive system. The soon-to-be-obsolete samurai are governed by a strict code of conduct, serving a spy state populated by informants and characterized by the regulation of dress and decor.   Under the regime of the samurai, homosexuality (repressed or otherwise) isn't the love that dare not speak its name but, as in Oshima's last military drama—and *Taboo's* main precursor—*Merry Christmas, Mr. Lawrence,* the only form of sexual passion that exists. In the end, all the principals seem to "have that leaning," as the captain is wont to say.

With his provocative bangs and rosebud lips, the enigmatic Kano is the universal object of desire—a pale, impassive vixen turning heads as he prances through the ranks. The coy lad is not only courted by Tashiro and several other samurais but obsessively observed by the captain, who, after he fights with both Kano and Tashiro, decides that they are lovers. Kano's other-worldly presence and Kitano's wryly contemporary performance, full of wheezy chuckles and bemused twitches, are but two of the subtly discordant elements Oshima throws into the mix. The film's narrative is annotated by both voiceover and intertitles; the action is set to Ryuichi Sakamoto's moody piano loop; the samurais are so fashionably attired they might have been outfitted by Commes des Garçons. (Indeed, their dojo's decor anticipates that ostentatiously underfilled Chelsea emporium.)

Oshima began his career by rebelling against the classicism of Yasujiro Ozu: "I tried to eliminate completely all scenes with characters sitting on tatami while talking." Breaking the filmmaker's own taboo, *Taboo* favors a discreetly classical mise-en-scène-balanced geometric forms, slightly off-center compositions, a lacquered look, a burnished but muted gray-brown-black-white palette. (The production design is by the venerable Yoshinobu Nishioka, responsible for such period classics as *Gate of Hell.*) There are numerous ghostly moonlit scenes but, as befits a filmmaker who programmatically banned "green" from his first color film, only a single daytime exterior.

Oshima is a visual thinker, and his studio world of painted sunsets is humanized as a thicket of rumor, innuendo, and jealousy.   Someone starts attacking Kano's real and imagined lovers—including the sergeant who has been ordered to set Kano straight and take him out whoring. (The expedition to nighttown is the movie's comic set piece.) In the end, the leadership decides to resolve the Kano question by having him fight Tashiro to the death—a clash by night in a suitably mist-shrouded kabuki-land.

Oshima's films are typically predicated on a mixture of violence and restraint. (This is most apparent in his ambivalent attitude toward militarism.) If, as is sometimes said, he is a Marxist, it is of the Reichian persuasion—the economy that fascinates him is libidinal. Thus, the seductive Kano may be "evil," but not for the reasons that the smitten captain imagines. In an offhand and uncommented-upon aside near the end of the film, the boy admits that he became a samurai so that he would be free to kill.

Also reviewed in:
CHICAGO TRIBUNE, 1/19/01, Friday/p. K, Michael Wilmington
NEW YORK TIMES, 9/30/00, p. B16, Stephen Holden
VARIETY, 5/22-28/00, p. 28, Todd McCarthy

TAO OF STEVE, THE

A Sony Pictures Classics release of a Good Machine production in association with Thunderhead Productions. *Executive Producer:* Ted Hope. *Producer:* Anthony Bregman. *Director:* Jenniphr Goodman. *Screenplay:* Duncan North, Greer Goodman, and Jenniphr Goodman. *Based on a story by:* Duncan North. *Director of Photography:* Teodoro Maniaci. *Editor:* Sarah Gartner. *Music:* Joe Delia. *Music Editor:* Brian Bulman. *Sound:* Brian Dixon and (music) Gary Solomon and Greg Curry. *Sound Editor:* Kelly L. Oxford. *Casting:* Nicole Arbusto, Joy Dickson, and Teresa Neptune. *Production Designer:* Rosario Provenza. *Art Director:* Mark

Alan Duran.   *Special Effects:* Keith McGee.   *Costumes:* Brigitta Bjerke.   *Make-up:* Charise Rives.   *Running time:* 87 minutes. *MPAA Rating:* R.

CAST: Donal Logue (Dex); Greer Goodman (Syd); Kimo Wills (Dave); Ayelet Kaznelson (Beth); David Aaron Baker (Rick); Nina Jaroslaw (Maggie); John Hines (Ed); John Harrington Bland (Priest); Jessica Gormley, Mercedes Herrrero, and Cheryl Anne Jaroslaw (Gossipy Women); Dana Goodman (Julie); Matt Hotsinpiller (Jeremy); Sue Cremin (Jill); Roxanne De Mien (Sarah); Jessica Bohan (Diane); Selby Craig (Chris); Craig D. Lafayette (Matt); Tristan Bennett (Tris); Duncan North (Duncan); Zak Garcia (Zak); Jacob Sanchez (Blond Card Shark); Cira Sandoval (Vanessa); Shane Hamashige (Corey); Jeannie Bauder (Secretary); Nicholas Ballas (Doctor); Malaika Amon (Kinko's Chick); Garland Hunter (Kelly).

CHRISTIAN SCIENCE MONITOR, 8/4/00, p. 15, David Sterritt

"The Tao of Steve" signals its thoughtful undercurrents right from the title, which is slightly misleading, since there's not much Taoism in the picture, and there's no Steve at all.

The main character is Dex, a roly-poly kindergarten teacher whose philosophy of life is a celebration of the lax, the lazy, and the lascivious. He spends his time chasing women, getting high with his buddies, and preaching the virtues of irresponsibility. He calls his ideas the Tao of Steve, referring to a pair of his favorite inspirations: the Eastern concept of harmony with the world, and the Western worship of ultracool celebrities like Steve McQueen.

Dex isn't much of a role model, but the movie about his adventures has three things to recommend it: One is the story, which introduces Dex to a relatively mature girlfriend who gets under his skin and encourages him to change his ways.

Another is Donal Logue's magnetic performance which makes Dex lovable at his best and hard to dislike even at his rascally worst. Logue is strikingly versatile, as he's shown with his chameleon-like work in such movies as "The Patriot," where he plays a soldier gradually overcoming bigotry, and the coming "Steal This Movie!", in which he plays a close friend of Abbie Hoffman, the '60s radical. He's a standout talent with a promising future.

The third redeeming element of "The Tao of Steve" is Greer Goodman's refreshingly lifelike portrayal of Dex's new love interest, which avoids the glamour-girl clichés that even non-Hollywood productions often fall into. Ms. Goodman also helped write the picture, with Duncan North and director Jenniphr Goodman, all of whom deserve applause for the originality of their comic vision.

LOS ANGELES TIMES, 8/4/00, Calendar/p. 12, Kevin Thomas

When did you last see a romantic comedy in which the man and the woman discussed Kierkegaard—and knew what they were talking about? Better yet, when did you see a leading man who's about 100 pounds overweight and is nevertheless a lady-killer?

Such a film is the sparkling and irresistible "The Tao of Steve," a movie that's as unafraid of proclaiming its smarts as it is of wearing its heart on its sleeve. It's a terrific debut for director Jenniphr Goodman, who wrote the script with Duncan North—the true-life inspiration for the film's hero—and Greer Goodman, the director's sister and the film's leading lady.

Donal Logue's Dex is a handsome, redheaded but exceedingly rotund guy in his early 30s who attends his 10-year college reunion only to be reminded of how far he has let himself go since he was the golden boy of his class.

He's about to cut out of this humiliating gathering when he crosses paths with the stunning Syd (Greer Goodman), a classmate with whom he had once been involved but does not even remember.

Syd has returned home, to Santa Fe, N.M., to design the sets for the city's famed opera company and is staying with old friends. Because her motorcycle goes on the blink she winds up sharing a truck with Dex, a part-time kindergarten teacher who passes himself off as a "forensic anthropologist" and lives in a house on the outskirts of town with a bunch of buddies.

Dex is a brilliant, self-indulgent layabout who easily rationalizes his lack of ambition. Drawing from Lao-tzu, Heidegger and Groucho Marx, he has developed a sure-fire theory of dating, which he dubs "The Tao of Steve" in honor of Steve McQueen, who never had to chase after women but always wound up with the girl. An indefatigable womanizer currently having an affair with a married woman (Ayelet Kaznelson), Dex is forever reminding his pals that "We pursue that which retreats from us."

Used to playing hard-to-get, he's now faced with Syd playing hard-to-get with him. When she points out that Don Giovanni seduced legions of women in fear of being rejected by the one he truly wanted, her words hit home with Dex perhaps more strongly than she intended.

For Syd, the problem with Dex is not that he is overweight, but that she's wary of a man so into scoring with women. How is she to know if such a man is capable of sincerely falling in love?

The filmmakers make getting to the answers to these questions much fun, for "The Tao of Steve" bristles with sophisticated wit and humor.

Logue's Dex lights up the screen as a free-spirited rogue of infinite charm—and cunning—who unexpectedly discovers how vulnerable he really is. Goodman is also a natural in front of a camera, and her Syd is a self-possessed young woman completely capable of parrying with Dex.

"The Tao of Steve" proceeds as a series of skirmishes between the two, delighting us with the artfulness and wisdom with which the filmmakers play out this duel. Inevitably, the film has to do with Dex's need to grow up if he is ever going to experience true love, but the filmmakers wisely leave this familiar concern strictly implicit.

"The Tao of Steve" is a constant, idiosyncratic pleasure that leaves us eager to see what the Goodmans and Logue will do next.

As for North, he has said making the film "was like $2 million dollars' worth of therapy."

NEW YORK POST, 8/4/00, p. 52, Jonathan Foreman

An ideal antidote to the big-budget bores that studios put out in late summer, "The Tao of Steve" is a charming, funny and refreshingly smart Gen-X romantic comedy in the tradition of "When Harry Met Sally"—with the bonus of an engagingly laid-back Southwestern flavor.

It's about an overweight underachiever in his early 30's who has an amazing talent for getting attractive women into bed. Not only is Dex (the terrific Donal Logue) no Adonis, he isn't rich or successful either. (He'd say he doesn't need to be; he scores anyway.)

Dex leads a slackerish existence in a house on the edge of Sante Fe, New Mexico, with a bunch of other bachelors. When not sleeping with waitresses or his friends' wives, he teaches kindergarten part-time, smokes pot for breakfast and spends his ample spare time playing cards or Frisbee golf.

Dex can pull this off because he is also clever, witty and charming and he runs his personal life according to a set of time-tested rules he calls "The Tao [or Way] of Steve." This approach combines the imitation of Steve McQueen (and other male pop-culture icons named Steve, such as Steve McGarrett of "Hawaii Five-O" and Steve Austin of "The Six Million Dollar Man") with Chinese philosophy.

As one of Dex's Frisbee-golf-playing friends explains, "A Steve doesn't try to impress the women but he always gets the girl... James Bond is a Steve." The trick, according to Dex, is to eliminate your own desire, to display excellence in the woman's presence and to retreat just when she's getting interested.

But at Dex's 10-year college reunion, he meets—he thinks for the first time—the beautiful Syd (Greer Goodman), a woman smart enough to be impervious to his charm. Like him she rides a motorbike, and like him she can talk about religion and philosophy.

But she's not looking to be one of Dex's conquests. For one thing, she has a handsome, slim boyfriend. She's also suspicious of Dex. Unfortunately for him, the Tao of Steve—with its "Rules"-like emphasis on manipulation—doesn't work as well with love as it does with scoring.

Director (and co-writer) Jenniphr Goodman moves the story along swiftly, with a sure hand, avoiding the predictable until the very end.

Greer Goodman (who co-wrote the sparkling screenplay with sister, Jenniphr, and Duncan North) makes a promising debut as the self-possessed Syd.

Logue ("Reindeer Games," "The Patriot") deservedly won a special jury award at Sundance for his performance as Dex.

Only the infinitely mysterious ways of the MPAA can explain why this film—which contains neither nudity nor violence—received an R rating rather than a PG-13.

NEWSDAY, 8/4/00, Part II/p. B11, Jan Stuart

For those who may have been avoiding Santa Fe because they thought It was nothing but fabulous art, innovative opera and transcendental scenery, there is reason to rejoice. "The Tao of Steve" is here to tell you that the place is littered with genial young men who do little with their lives but play Frisbee, smoke dope and trade notes about how to get to first base with women.

So, have you phoned Southwest Airlines yet?

"The Tao of Steve" (say "dow" for "tao,") is sort of the thinking fat man's version of "Women Are From Venus, Men Are From Mars." Which merely means its protagonist can talk a mean streak about Kierkegaard while advising his amigos about the female psyche, in between chomps of peanut butter sandwiches.

At 31, Dex (Donal Logue) is still the same womanizing jerk he was back in college, with the addition of perhaps 50 or so more pounds of jerk-iosity around his waistline. Despite his girth, Dex has a talent for smooth talking his way into bed with any number of women, particularly the married kind, with whom he doesn't have to get serious.

True to his own rulebook of dating do's and don'ts (named for cool-dude Steve McQueen), Dex is most attracted to the gal who offers up the most resistance. A former college fling named Syd finds Dex oddly compelling, but can't recover from the fact that Dex can't remember a tryst the two shared 10 years back. So, Dex will spend the better part of the film's 90 minutes learning how to be real, not an easy task for a self-styled Don Giovanni who has been making all the wrong moves for too long.

"The Tao of Steve" was inspired by the experiences of one Duncan North, who has roped in two women to help him on the screenplay (Greer Goodman, the film's Syd, and her sister Jenniphr Goodman, the film's director), presumably so he won't get himself into deeper mud than he already is. Because its creators have obviously studied the liberal arts and are up on Elaine Pagels, it is a hipper version of all those smarmy farces about the mating game that used to star Tony Curtis or Walter Matthau. If it plays by all the old rules of the Tao of '60s romantic comedy, it does so with some knowing, citrusy dialogue and a slyly charming performance from big bear Logue. Aging slackers who use the word "solipsistic" in a sentence will be in heaven.

SIGHT AND SOUND, 3/01, p. 59, Mark Olsen

New Mexico, the present. After having sex with Beth, his married lover, in the college library, Dex works the crowd at his 10-year student reunion. Known as a ladies' man in his day, he has since put on weight, but his charms generally still do the trick. When he is introduced to former classmate Syd he doesn't remember her.

Driving home from his part time job as a day-care worker, Dex's motorcycle breaks down. Because it will take a few weeks for a new part to arrive, he arranges to borrow a truck from a friend, with whom Syd happens to be staying. Dex and Syd work out a schedule so they can both use the truck. Though he continues his affair with Beth, he falls for Syd. When the required part arrives, he hides it to continue spending time with Syd, who seems disinterested.

Dex explains to his room-mates the essentials of being "Steve" his philosophy of cool. At a pool party he breaks his own rules and admits to Syd his feelings for her. She reveals that they slept together in college, though he doesn't remember it. By way of apologising, he fixes up a motorcycle for Syd and breaks off with Beth. Syd and Dex finally get together, but she is due to leave for New York in a few days. Later, Dex arrives in New York to see her.

The debut of director Jenniphr Goodman, and one of the nominal breakouts from the 2000 Sundance Film Festival, *The Tao of Steve* is a character piece whose belaboured quirkiness is typical of so much contemporary US independent cinema. Over-educated and under-motivated, Dex, the film's puckish, pudgy lead character, is someone who can't shake off his student lifestyle despite having left college some 10 years ago. The plot—which tells of his budding relationship with ex-classmate Syd—isn't really Goodman's central concern; what the success of her film hinges on is the viewers' willingness to be charmed by her winsome and wacky cast.

In fact, *The Tao of Steve* can be whittled down almost entirely to the showpiece lead performance of Donal Logue as Dex. His transformation from puffy slacker pleasure-seeker to responsible romantic adult is the crux of the entire film, and while Logue does a fine job of making Dex likeable, he misses a certain insecure cruelty that seems to be at the centre of the character. Dex sets his life by the effortless cool and easy going macho charm of the mythical "Steve" a conflation of Steve McQueen, *Hawaii Five-O*'s Steve McGarrett and the *Six Million Dollar Man* Steve Austin—and while this method works on hapless undergraduates, the film's main point seems to be that it doesn't help Dex in extricating himself from the go-nowhere affair he's conducting with a married woman, nor does it score him any points with Syd.

It is perhaps the film's finest, if not entirely unexpected, irony that the way of life Dex spends so much time discussing—a strange brew of religious studies, pop-cultural ephemera and various classical thinkers—is the very thing he must move beyond in order to engage in a properly adult relationship (with the more mature Syd). This final transformation, though inevitable, is a little too abrupt in story terms; in particular the romantic kismet of the film's finale leaves one with the feeling of exit-stage-left necessity rather than pleasing resolution.

One of the film's smartest jokes is the throwaway credit "Based on a story by Duncan North, based on Duncan North". While it is nice to think of the film as a homage to a lovable friend, *The Tao of Steve* ultimately comes off as blandly distant, like a story about people you don't know. Overall it's pleasant enough, but there's nothing distinctive about it, either: nice to look at, but not especially striking, amusing without being outright funny, romantic without ever being truly engaging, it never springs completely to life. To use the parlance of its lead character, there is quite simply not enough "Steve" in *The Tao of Steve*.

VILLAGE VOICE, 8/8/00, p. 144, Jessica Winter

Having garnered good word of mouth by default in the midst of an undernourished Sundance lineup, *The Tao of Steve* arrives just a few months after the festival but long past its expiration date. The movie belongs to a certain mushroom cluster of Amerindies from the mid '90s, when Park City started welcoming any young white guy with a visually anemic, obstinately single-minded relationship comedy wherein true love enables the hero to make a sentimental fetish out of toppling his cynicism and confirming his morbid sense of entitlement, while not disrupting his ability to fire off endless pop-culture-laden riffs on romance and, you know, chicks.

As it turns out, *The Tao of Steve* is directed by a chick (first-timer Jenniphr Goodman), but the alpha personality here is clearly the main screenwriter, young white guy Duncan North, who—true to his school—started with the man in the mirror to come up with his protagonist and alter ego, portly boyslut Dex. (The film's epigraph reads: "Based on a story by Duncan North/Based on an idea by Duncan North/Based on Duncan North.") A preschool teacher in Santa Fe, Dex is a proudly undermotivated sort but a freak with the ladies, no remarkable feat in itself except that, as played with flaccid nonchalance by Donal Logue, he seems less magnetic voluptuary than self-consciously loutish lech, who overcompensates for his perceived shortcomings through stultifying epigramming ("Doing stuff is overrated") and lengthy, Will Hunting-esque discourses on the intersections of dating strategy with Buddhism, Heidegger, and Steve McQueen (his effortless biker cool provides a title for Dex's courtship philosophy, and for the movie). Aggressively slacker, physically a cross between Philip Seymour Hoffman's phone stalker in *Happiness* and George from *Big Brother* but boasting a Beatty-worthy catalog of conquests, the Zen-tropic Dex is intended as a living koan, though his exploits read better as studies in cognitive dissonance.

The film finds its raison d'être in Dex's need to confront his fears of monogamy via his former college classmate and possible true love Syd (coscreenwriter Greer Goodman, Jenniphr's sister), a brittle, maddeningly fickle set designer still nursing a grudge about their long-ago one-night stand. A cloud of dreary inevitability hovers over the pair as they pretend not to flirt for *The Tao of Steve*'s 90-minute duration, and the Goodman behind the camera does little to brighten the weather: Santa Fe might as well be Jersey, and the glaring absence of a directorial schema is broken only by her proclivity for random circular pans. The threesome's script toys for a moment here and there with poor-man's *Notorious* notions about the performance of self, but *The Tao of Steve* poses only one pertinent question: Can any American filmmaker other than the Farrellys make a rom-com in which the principals engage in activities apart from the tiresomely tireless dissection of rom?

Also reviewed in:
CHICAGO TRIBUNE, 8/18/00, Friday/p. E, John Petrakis
NEW YORK TIMES, 8/4/00, p. E16, Elvis Mitchell
NEW YORKER, 8/7/00, p. 78, Anthony Lane
VARIETY, 1/31-2/6/00, p. 36, Todd McCarthy
WASHINGTON POST, 8/18/00, p. C12, Rita Kempley
WASHINGTON POST, 8/18/00, Weekend/p. 37, Michael O'Sullivan

TAVERN, THE

A Castle Hill release of a Foote Speed Productions film in association with Redeemable Features. *Executive Producer:* James Cooper and Lin Chen Tien.   *Producer:* Walter Foote. *Director:* Walter Foote. *Screenplay:* Walter Foote. *Director of Photography:* Kurt Lennig. *Editor:* Josh Apter. *Music:* Bill Lacey and Loren Toolajian. *Sound:* Ralph Kelsey and M. De Chiara. *Casting:* Jerry Beaver.   *Production Designer:* Gonzalo Cordoba.   *Art Director:* Lisanne McTernan. *Set Decorator:* Daniel Goldman. *Costumes:* Lisa Padovani. *Make-up:* Gloria Cruz. *Stunt Coordinator:* Douglas Crosby. *Running time:* 88 minutes. *MPAA Rating:* Not Rated.

CAST: Cameron Dye (Ronnie);   Kevin Geer (Dave);   Greg Zittel (Kevin);   Margaret Cho (Carol);   Tyler Foote and Lillian Foote (Dave's Children);   Jennifer Harmon (Ronnie's Mother); Frank Girardeau (Ronnie's Father);   Phyllis Esposito (Angela);   Nancy Ticotin (Gina);   Carlo Alban (Tommy);   Steven Marcus (Jerry);   Tom Ryan (Jimmy);   Michael Baker (Freddie);   Kym Austin (Sharon);   Henry Strozier, Eric Kornfeld, and John Pero (Customers);   Pete Zias (Boy); Edward K. Thomas (Cliff);   Don Creech (Shank);   Gary Perez (Miguel);   Donald Roman Lopez (Waiter);   Al Espinosa (Busboy);   Jesse Doran (Marino);   LaDonna Mabry (INS Clerk); Bruce Katzman (George);   Richard Mover (Killer);   David Runco (Jackie's Fiancée);   Simon Jutras (Frenchman);   Heather King (Jeannette);   Susan Cella (Irate Woman);   Carol Goodheart (Real Estate Agent);   Richard Petrocelli (Sal);   Robert Turano (Nick);   Sharon Mayberry (Interviewer);   Harold Alvarez (Tavern Busboy);   Bernie McInerney (John Mahoney).

LOS ANGELES TIMES, 11/10/00, Calendar/p. 4, Kevin Thomas

Walter Foote's "The Tavern" is in the finest tradition of the small, independent movie that endeavors to illuminate the struggles and dreams of ordinary people. With tenderness, insight and humor but also with a clear-eyed sense of reality and an absence of sentimentality, Foote acquaints us with two lifelong friends, Ronnie (Cameron Dye) and Dave (Kevin Geer).

A trim, nice-looking man on the cusp of middle age but with nothing to show for it, Ronnie sees his big chance in buying a popular Manhattan neighborhood tavern. It will be tough to finance the purchase, but as a start he enlists Dave as his partner. As a husband and father of two, Dave is understandably hesitant but cannot resist the opportunity to escape a soul-withering job in a Price Club mega-store. Ronnie and Dave then set about raising the cash necessary to make the deposit.

Among others he turns to his sister-in-law, Gina (Nancy Ticotin), whose police officer husband was slain in the line of duty a year earlier. Gina agrees but insists that Ronnie find some kind of after-school job for her 14-year-old son, Tommy (Carlo Alban), sullen and withdrawn since his father's death.

Glitches accrue, but Ronnie and Dave do manage to take over the tavern and start running it. At this point we get to the heart of the matter, which is how very tough it can be for decent working-class folks to be their own bosses—indeed, to have any real control over their destinies in corporate, increasingly technological America.

On the other hand, the men are also at the mercy of an older evil: the kind of people you find yourself financially entangled with when you're desperate. Dave and Ronnie would seem to be exactly the kind of men that the just-concluded presidential race seemed to target—individuals with a precarious foothold in the middle class and who become exceedingly vulnerable when they set their sights a bit higher.

These are the kinds of guys, however, whose destinies don't seem to be affected too much by campaign promises—in part because they fall between the ever-widening chasm between rich and poor, and in part because for them taking a gamble also means, perhaps inescapably, that they're getting in over their heads.

In the past, hard work, and hopefully a little luck as well, would carry the day for Ronnie and Dave, but that time seems to have passed.

In any event, Dye and Geer make Ronnie and Dave tremendously likable guys whose lack of status undermines their self-confidence at every turn but who gamely put on the best face they can in the grinding struggle simply to survive. Margaret Cho, playing absolutely straight, is Dave's wife who has her heart set on a house in the suburbs at precisely the worst time.

If "The Tavern" rings particularly true, it's surely because Foote, son of playwright Horton Foote, has had firsthand experience in taking a flier on a restaurant; significantly, his brother Horton Jr. and Horton's best friend, Michael Stewart, operate Greenwich Village's Tavern on Jane. Foote is actually a corporate attorney as well as a screenwriter and producer who is making his film debut with this picture. Foote pulls off a daring and unexpected finish for "The Tavern" that takes it to a rigorous, uncompromising level.

"The Tavern" ends up considerably more than the warm little movie it appears to be.

NEW YORK POST, 10/20/00, p. 52, Lou Lumenick

Yet *another* indie movie about lifelong buddies?

After 10 minutes of resistance, I found myself being drawn into this well-told, bitter-sweet story about two middle-aged guys who decide to defy the odds and open a tavern in Greenwich Village.

Ronnie (Cameron Dye) is the more outgoing of the partners, a bartender whose avoidance of responsibility extends to his half-hearted pursuit of Sharon (Kim Austin), an attractive salesgirl at an upscale boutique.

Dave (Kevin Geer) is the other half of this odd couple. He's sick of his job as an assistant manager at a Costco warehouse and seems weighed down by his wife (Margaret Cho) and two children, as much as he loves them.

Part of what makes "The Tavern" so engaging is that debuting writer-director Walter Foote clearly knows the territory: He and his wife ran an unsuccessful Mongolian barbecue restaurant, and his brother, Horton Jr., still operates a successful Greenwich Village establishment called Tavern on Jane.

The struggles of Tavern on Main, as the bar in the movie is called, feel like observed life. No sooner have Ronnie and Dave opened than the previous owner (Greg Zittel), who assured them he was retiring to Florida, opens a more successful, competing establishment.

The partners lure away his star chef, only to touch off an escalating war.

Foote has obviously also learned about creating characters from his father, the noted playwright Horton Foote.

Among the more interesting here is Ronnie's 14-year-old nephew (Carlo Alban) whose father has died and who becomes Ronnie's surrogate son when he takes a job at the tavern.

"The Tavern" isn't a perfect movie. There are too many subplots, Cho is under-used and it doesn't have as satisfying an emotional payoff as "Two Family House," this month's other opening-a-tavern movie.

But it's still a worthwhile choice in a crowded marketplace.

VILLAGE VOICE, 10/24/00, p. 150, Michael Atkinson

Being damned by faint praise is the lot of most releasable ultra-indies, and Walter Foote's *The Tavern* is particularly damnable—deliberately slight and modest, the movie often achieves a temperate naturalism that doesn't quite make up for the lack of ambition, depth, or originality. But naturalism is no mean feat, at least not in America. The filmmaker, a not-so-young scion of the Horton Foote dynasty, honed his narrative down to the naked basics: Two working-class buddies (Cameron Dye and Kevin Geer) decide to buy a restaurant-bar somewhere in Manhattan (though the exterior looks like a nice corner of Queens). That's it. Of course, the nine-out-of-10 failed-food-biz stat looms, and the tiny joint is beset by a series of small, believable dilemmas (loans, rival restaurateurs, errant cooks, etc.) until low volume does them in. The two heroes are affable schmucks with no secrets; Dye's gabby barkeep tries to maintain a romance with a zaftig store clerk (Kym Austin), while Geer's bald, placid family man barely tolerates his grouchy wife (Margaret Cho). Though rife with incidental plot holes, Foote's movie feels right even when nothing important is happening—which is much of the time. But it amounts to a dozy, unmemorable daydream.

Also reviewed in:
NEW YORK TIMES, 10/20/00, p. E26, Lawrence Van Gelder
VARIETY, 9/6-12/99, p. 68, Paul Power

TERROR FIRMER

A Troma Entertainment release. *Producer:* Michael Herz, Lloyd Kaufman, and Elizabeth van Merkensteijn. *Director:* Lloyd Kaufman. *Screenplay:* Douglas Buck, Patrick Cassidy, and Lloyd Kaufman. Based on the book *"All I Need to Know About Filmmaking I Learned from the Toxic Avenger"* by: Lloyd Kaufman. *Director of Photography:* Brendan Flynt. *Editor:* Gabriel Friedman. *Music:* Sean McGrath. *Sound:* Sean McGrath. *Casting:* Will Keenan. *Production Designer:* Jean Loscalzo. *Art Director:* Jim Donahue. *Set Decorator:* Rona De Angelo. *Creature Effects:* Tim Considine. *Costumes:* Stephanie Imhoff. *Special Effects:* David Bracci and Ruth Pongstaphone-Safer. *Running time:* 114 minutes. *MPAA Rating:* Not Rated.

CAST: Will Keenan (Casey); Sean McGrath (12 Year Old Retarded Boy); Alyce LaTourelle (Jennifer); Lloyd Kaufman (Larry Benjamin); Trent Haaga (Jerry); Sheri Wenden (Mysterious Woman); Yaniv Sharon (Naked P.A.); Charlotte Kaufman (Audrey Benjamin); Gary Hrbek (Toddster); Joe Fleishaker (Jacob Gelman); Ron Jeremy (Casey's Dad); Greg "G-Spot" Siebel (Ward); Mario Diaz (DJ); Mo Fischer (Andy); Lyle Derek (Asshole P.A.); Tracey Burroughs (Edgar Allan); Edouard Baer and Joseph Malerba (French Cool Cats); Roy David (Jeff/Toxie); Sean Pierce (Moose); Barry Brisco (Stephen); Darko Malesh (Nikolai); Carla Burden (Sarah, Toxie's Girl); Anthony Haden-Guest (Toxie's Father); Jen Miller (Script Girl); Eve Crosby (Jennifer's Mom); Don McGregor and Jim Salicrup (Video Company Executives); Stefanie Imhoff (Assia); Theo Kogan (Theodora); Michael Levine (Guy Beaten by Leg); Wendy Adams (Police Officer Woman); Lisa Gaye (Casey's Mom); Jonny Spanish (Mad Cowboy); Dan Truman (Nerd P.A.); Ariel Wizman (Nikolai); Becque Olson (Butcher's Wife); Trey Parker and Matt Stone (Hermaphrodites); Christopher Pierce, Douglas Weiss, and Ez Davidson (Stockbrokers in Front of Library); Lemmy (Himself).

LOS ANGELES TIMES, 10/29/99, Calendar/p. 12, Kevin Thomas

"Terror Firmer" marks the 25th anniversary of New York-based Troma Films, famed for its amusing and gory low-budget schlock. For the occasion, Troma has pulled out all the stops, which means there's more entrails, more bare bosoms, more R-rated sex, more flatulence, more mayhem, more brutality and more violence. But it adds up to less and less After a quarter of a century, the tried and true Troma formula is beginning to wear thin.

Of course all this action is patently fake, but the gross and the savage and the imbecilic aren't as funny as they used to be in Troma productions. The premise of "Terror Firmer," loaded with insider references and self-congratulatory in tone, is so slight that the constant recourse to the above-listed ingredients reveals the film's underlying severe lack of imagination. Troma partner (with Michael Herz) Lloyd Kaufman casts himself as the blind director of a typical Troma outing, featuring a crazed glamour-girl psychiatrist (Debbie Rochon) who wants to slay perennial Troma hero, the Toxic Avenger. But there's a serial killer at loose on the set, which Kaufman's Larry Benjamin won't shut down because he doesn't have a completion bond. The show must go on no matter how high the corpses pile up.

Meanwhile, production assistant Jennifer (Alyce LaTourelle) is drawn to sexy sound man Casey (Will Keenan), and special effects/makeup guy Jerry (Trent Haaga) is attracted to her. Roy David plays Jeff, the actor playing Toxie, and porn veteran Ron Jeremy turns up late in the action. As the director on both sides of the camera, Kaufman does keep "Terror Firmer's" pace up to the fast and furious Troma standard.

NEW YORK POST, 12/1/00, p. 52, Jonathan Foreman

Troma is a New York-based indie company that specializes in ultra-low-budget, heavily tongue-in-cheek shlock-horror films with a high gross-out factor.

Some of them, like "The Toxic Avenger" and "Class of Nuke 'Em High" are very funny indeed, and have clearly influenced raunchy Hollywood fare like "American Pie" and "Scary Movie."

Unfortunately, "Terror Firmer," the latest by Troma's chief auteur, Lloyd Kaufman, is a self-indulgent bore, so lacking in wit and so gross as to be almost unwatchable.

It's one of those movies about moviemaking—although the plot is really just an excuse for one over-the-top-gag after another.

Blind indie director Larry Benjamin (Lloyd Kaufman) is trying to make a Troma movie filled with blood and gratuitous T&A, but his cast and crew are being killed off by a serial killer who vaguely resembles Pam Grier's murderous hooker in "Fort Apache, The Bronx."

At the same time, a love triangle develops between Spielberg-loving soundman Casey (Will Keenan), production assistant turned actress Jennifer (Alyce LaTourelle) and special effects guy Jerry (Trent Haaga).

There are a couple of noisy sex scenes involving the use of pickles as sex toys, and if that's not wild enough, cameos from plump porn star Ron "Hedgehog" Jeremy, notorious Manhattan party animal/journalist Anthony Haden-Guest, and Motorhead frontman Lemmy.

Also reviewed in:
NEW YORK TIMES, 12/1/00, p. E16, Elvis Mitchell
VARIETY, 6/7-13/99, p. 48, Lisa Nesselson

TERRORIST, THE

A Phaedra Films release of an Indian Image Productions film. *Executive Producer:* Ravi Deshpande, Sunil Doshi, Vikram Singh, and Mark Burton. *Producer:* A. Sriram, Abhjit Joshi, and Shree Prasad. *Director:* Santosh Sivan. *Screenplay (Tamil with English subtitles):* Santosh Sivan, Ravi Deshpande, and Vijay Deveshwar. *Story:* Santosh Sivan. *Director of Photography:* Santosh Sivan. *Editor:* Sreekar Prasad. *Music:* Sonu Sisupal Rajamani. *Sound:* Suhas Gujarathi and (music) G. Shiva Kumar. *Production Designer:* Shyam Sunder. *Art Director:* Sriram. S. *Costumes:* Anu Radha. *Running time:* 95 minutes. *MPAA Rating:* Not Rated.

CAST: Ayesha Dharkar (Malli); Vishnu Vardhan (Thyagu); Bhanu Prakash (Perumal); K. Krishna (Lover); Sonu Sisupal (Leader); Vishwas (Lotus); Anuradha (Sumitra); Bhavani (Old Lady); Parmeshwaran (Vasu); Gopal (Gopal); Bala (Commando); Saravana (Traitor); Anna Durai (Photographer).

CHRISTIAN SCIENCE MONITOR, 1/14/00, p. 15, David Sterritt

Critics often chide Hollywood for its fascination with violent action, but filmmakers in other lands have also been drawn to subjects linked with violence and its challenges. When such directors take a constructive approach, the results can shed light on social and cultural issues.

"The Terrorist," an Indian production, is coming to American theaters after having its US première in the Human Rights Watch Film Festival last summer.

Although its title would fit a run-of-the-mill thriller, it's a serious and morally complex drama that raises provocative questions about how difficult it can be to sustain a sense of personal responsibility in a society destabilized by political upheaval.

The plot centers on a teenage girl whose brother has been killed in a revolutionary uprising. Playing on her tumultuous emotions, the insurgents call on her to follow in his footsteps by carrying out an assassination that will almost certainly result in her death. She agrees to this mission, but then discovers that she is pregnant and will be sacrificing the life of her unborn child along with her own.

On one level, "The Terrorist" is a psychological drama examining an agonized choice between personal and political obligations.

On another, it's a parable about the dark power of violence itself, always destructive yet forever claiming to be justified for the sake of some larger cause.

The movie emphasizes its tuneless philosophical concerns by painting its characters as generic revolutionaries rather than members of any particular movement. Capably directed by Indian filmmaker Santosh Sivan, ifs a troubling but worthwhile picture.

"The Quarry" is an international movie if ever there were one, directed in South Africa by Belgian director Marion Hansel and starring John Lynch, a talented Irish actor. He plays a drifter who meets a clergyman on a little-traveled highway, kills the minister for no reason, then assumes his identity and takes over his new job as pastor in a rural community.

A flawed movie that doesn't always make narrative sense, "The Quarry" raises questions about the nature of identity and the temptations of violence without saying anything substantial. Its willingness to grapple with ethical issues is impressive, though, and Hansel is good at building ominous moods that may linger in the mind long after the characters have faded from the screen.

LOS ANGELES TIMES, 2/25/00, Calendar/p. 27, Kenneth Turan

"The Terrorist" is a wonder several times over. Joining a compelling tale with exquisite photography and involving acting, it's a remarkable film by any standard but especially given the circumstances of its creation.

The story of a crisis of conscience in the young life of a committed revolutionary suicide bomber, "The Terrorist" is an Indian independent film, almost a contradiction in terms for a country whose passionate moviegoers are if anything more addicted to their "Bollywood" commercial cinema than Americans are to studio output.

Directed, co-written and photographed by the gifted Santosh Sivan, "The Terrorist" (though shot for $50,000 in 16 days) has a delicacy and artistry that is rare at any cost and any budget.

This is Sivan's first feature as a director, but he's not a film neophyte. He's worked as director of photography on some 20 features and twice that many documentaries and won India's National Film Award for cinematography nine times. The exhilarating visual sensibility he's brought to "The Terrorist" is the first thing you notice about it.

Exclusively using natural light in largely jungle situations, Sivan gives his settings a brighter than bright radiance. Colors are luminous (the greens especially pop out at you) and there's a crispness to his look that gives running water an extra sparkle. While images like a leaf in a stream, a glass of iced tea or a faded red guerrilla mask being river-washed may sound familiar, "The Terrorist" makes them indelible.

Though set in Sri Lanka, where the government has been contending with Tamil separatists for years, "The Terrorist" was more directly inspired by the assassination of Indian Prime Minister Rajiv Ghandi. One of its intentions is to provide insight into the mind-set of people willing and even happy to die as martyrs as well as to examine what happens when the human cost of terrorism takes on a personal dimension.

The terrorist of the title is 19-year-old Malli (Ayesha Dharkar), the veteran of 30 successful operations who opens the film by coldly executing a traitor within her guerrilla group. A woman who kills without mercy or compunction, Malli will take human life several more times and never look back.

This ability to be "a thinking bomb" is why the leader of Malli's revolutionary group chooses her from a group of equally young, equally eager volunteers, to carry out a suicide mission: Get close to an important government official and set off a quantity of explosives strapped to your waist.

"The Terrorist" is deliberately shadowy about the makeup of this group and the legitimacy of their drive for independence. The barely glimpsed leader insists that "our struggle has a purpose, justice is on our side, we will shed our blood but not our tears," and pains have been taken to make he and his cohorts sound rational and sane. No judgment is offered about the rightness or wrongness of Malli's clandestine movement, nor is providing her—and us—the easy way out by presenting her group as obviously deluded.

The leader's words make a particular kind of sense to Malli, given her background. Her father was a nationalist poet; her brother, a famous martyr, was killed when she was small. Throughout her life she has known almost nothing but the Struggle and its world of guns, violence and betrayal. "If you were a man," a besotted female comrade-in-arms says, "I'd marry you."

But as Malli makes the physical journey from the jungle to the city where her suicide bombing is to take place, she takes an interior journey as well. She meets a traumatized young boy named Lotus (Vishwas), who serves as a guide, and also has memories of an unexpected assignation with a wounded fellow fighter (K. Krishna) who touchingly tells of having buried his beloved school books with the vow to dig them up again only after freedom is won.

Though most viewers will inevitably want Malli to have second thoughts about her mission, because the film is so delicately balanced and so fair to all sides, it's perfectly plausible for the opposite to take place.

Dharkar, the Indian actress who plays Malli, is in almost every shot of the film and "The Terrorist's" success would be less without her expressive performance. With her dark and deeply penetrating eyes, she looks out at us in a way that is familiar, terribly touching and, as it should be in the final analysis, all but unknowable.

NEW YORK POST, 1/14/00, p. 49, Jonathan Foreman

Visually gorgeous despite its low budget, "The Terrorist" is a haunting film about a lovely teen girl turned into a "thinking bomb" by the guerrillas who raised her in the jungle.

It's one of a number of recent serious movies ("Earth, ""Bandit Queen") from India that breaks away from the sexist, super-patriotic conventions of Bombay "masala" musicals.

It's also sufficiently compelling to appeal to a mainstream audience.

Although the conflict the film depicts could be any of India's brutal colonial-style wars against ethnic uprisings, Santosh Sivan's tale of a girl who starts opening up to life while on a suicide mission is clearly inspired by the assassination of Indian Prime Minister Rajiv Gandhi by a Tamil suicide bomber.

And the more you know of that horrific incident—the bomber was a young girl wearing plastic explosive around her waist—the more powerful the film is.

Malli (Ayesha Dharkar) is the daughter of a slain nationalist poet and has been living in the jungle with the guerrillas since the age of 4. The film opens with her executing a "traitor," and shows her taking part in combat against uniformed troops and killing one soldier in cold blood.

Along with several other girls she is then offered a chance at martyrdoms The organization wants a suicide bomber to assassinate a VIP.

With the help of a small boy she goes downriver, avoiding army patrols before crossing what look like the straits between Sri Lanka and India. She stays with an elderly but talkative farmer and his comatose wife while preparing for her murder/suicide mission.

All during her journey and her stay with the farmer, she has flashbacks to a night she spent with a wounded guerrilla she fished out of a river and who was later kicked to death by soldiers. Those memories, combined with exposure to older and younger generations living a normal life, begin to undermine her revolutionary morale as the morning of her attack draws nearer.

The film makes no attempt—nor is one necessary—to explore the rights and wrongs of the underlying political situation.

There isn't much dialogue, but unfortunately some of it is absurdly crude ("this VIP is blocking our movement," Malli is told by her commander) and the mostly nonprofessional cast is unable to make it sound any more believable.

It's the first movie directed by cinematographer Santosh Sivan and there are too many shots of the star washing her hair, too many unnecessary close-ups and some dubbed-in heavy breathing at tense moments that becomes annoying.

Still, Sivan does a fine job of conveying the sheer monstrousness of child soldiering in the Third World, while keeping you guessing as to whether Malli will actually carry out her terrible mission.

NEWSDAY, 1/14/00, Part II/p. B7, John Anderson

"The Terrorist" is a painfully beautiful film about painfully horrible subjects: fanaticism, terrorism and the brand of slaughter meant to make the world a better place to live. Although it's clear by the end that cinematographer-cum-director Santosh Sivan's eye and conscience are a bit more developed than his sense of restraint, "The Terrorist" is a potent mix of intoxicating visuals and scourging politicals.

Think "La Femme Nikita" meets Satyajit Ray. Malli (Ayesha Dharkar) is a committed member of an Indian political splinter group (director Sivan reportedly was inspired by the 1991 assassination of India's former prime minister Rajiv Gandhi) who coolly executes a suspected traitor and as a result is given the group's highest honor: She will become its "thinking bomb," taking out a high-ranking government official during a public ceremony, killing herself in the process.

Sivan, like Terrence Malick in "The Thin Red Line," places his characters in a world so lush and ripe that the carnage they commit is nothing short of obscene. Sivan never shows the bloodletting, however (violence almost always happens off camera, but is no less potent for not being visible). Neither does he have anyone articulate a political philosophy: The professions of patriotic faith made by the various very young guns in Malli's unnamed terrorist cabal are all about the group (alias family, alias blood) and very little else.

When Malli discovers she's having a child—the father is a compatriot who died in her arms—the terrorist's poverty of selflessness couldn't be more bluntly illustrated: what's the worth of an unborn child to someone whose line of work is wholesale slaughter? Everything, it seems.

Sivan injects humor into his movie in the nick of time, via an old man named Vasu (Parmeshwaran), with whom Malli rooms and whose basic views on the sanctity of life defy every precept on which Ms. Malli has been indoctrinated. Sivan loads the second half of his film with enough life-affirming symbols to sink a ship—a fallen bird's nest, kids en route to school, Vasu's comatose wife, whom he has been nursing for years. And in the end, Sivan pulls back from the kind of ending that might have made the entire film as startling as it is provocative. Instead of just the well-meaning and perversely gorgeous thing it is.

SIGHT AND SOUND, 5/01, p. 58, Paramjit Rai

In an unnamed country, possibly Sri Lanka, Malli, a 19-year-old terrorist, shoots an informant who is responsible for her lover's death. Selected then to carry out the suicide bombing of a visiting senior politician, Malli rejoices, believing her death will make her the equal of her martyred elder brother. Travelling to the small town where the assassination is to take place, Malli is led through thick jungle by a young Brahmin boy Lotus whose family were burned alive by the army. Lotus watches in horror as Malli kills a soldier who tries to catch them unawares. Reaching the boat that will take her to the town, Malli is equally horrified as Lotus is shot dead by another soldier.

Posing as a college student, Malli takes a room in the home of Vasu. As she prepares for the assassination, she is careful to avoid revealing her mission to her landlord and his servant Gopal. Vasu realises before Malli that she is pregnant. As the day of the assassination approaches, Malli's confidence wavers. Vasu's affections for her prove to be genuine; Malli begins to see value in his simple but compassionate belief system. On the morning of the attack, rather than the bomb going off, petals fall from a garland that Malli had been carrying.

Santosh Sivan, here making his directorial debut, worked as a cinematographer on Mani Ratnam's controversial 1992-98 trilogy on terrorism and violence: *Roja, Bombay* and *Dil Se*. (the last of which featured a female suicide bomber). Picking up on some of the themes running through these three films, and reportedly inspired by the killing of Indian prime minister Rajiv Gandhi by a female suicide bomber, *The Terrorist* attempts to explore the mindset of a female terrorist, 19-year-old Malli, who willingly accepts an assignment to assassinate a visiting politician with a suicide bomb.

Ayesha Dharkar as Malli is a captivating presence. As she accepts her fatal duty, her face switches instantaneously from innocence to cold rage. Dharkar's body language is crucial throughout—at one moment she takes long, purposeful strides down a corridor to meet the shadowy leader who briefs her on her mission; at another she has the hesitant, slightly seductive gait of a peasant girl calmly walking past a row of enemy soldiers. But such scenes unfortunately give us little insight into what motivates Malli.

Malli remains inscrutably accepting of her orders. The flashbacks to her time with her lover, who was killed by their political opponents, suggest one reason behind her involvement in terrorism, but these painterly sequences have a stilted, archetypal quality that evokes the doomed love affair between Sohni and Mahival, well-known figures from Indian folk culture.

Sivan's failure to get beneath Malli's surface is most evident when she begins to question her belief in her mission. Her dilemma—whether to kill the politician or save herself and her unborn child—ought to be deeply felt and dramatically urgent. But as Malli begins to unpick her convictions, the film flags badly. You're left wondering not whether she'll kill the politician but what form Sivan's recurring water motif will take next.

Water is omnipresent in this visually arresting film—images of rain, waterfalls, even a drop of water, suspended from Malli's eyelash are all lovingly crafted. The film is humanistic and sensitive for the most part, but its visuals also feel empty at times. Sivan might be highlighting the incongruity of fighting a war (the exact cause of which is left ambiguous) in these beautiful surroundings, but the striking visuals overwhelm all other concerns, including, fatally, narrative and characterisation.

VILLAGE VOICE, 1/18/00, p. 111, J. Hoberman

Somewhere in the forests of southern India, a prisoner is being tortured by the revolutionary cell he betrayed. Tied to a tree in the pouring rain, his head is forced back into the camera; it's a disconcertingly fabulous arabesque. Finally, one of the masked figures shoots him point-blank. The mask is removed to introduce the fresh-faced 19-year-old Malli, daughter of a nationalist poet and the group's soon-to-be-anointed suicide-assassin.

The Terrorist, was inspired by the assassination of Rajiv Gandhi—although its chilling political scenario is as universal as it is specific. Directed by cinematographer Santosh Sivan, this heavily aestheticized Tamil-language movie has intimations of Carl Theodor Dreyer's *Passion of Joan of Arc,* both for its sense of spiritual anguish and the vast number of close-ups lavished on the visage of its tormented heroine (played by Ayesha Dharkar, one of the film's few professional actors).

Malli—approvingly referred to by her group's leader as "a thinking bomb"—is somber and fleshy, beautiful mainly for her tragic eyes and incongruous youth. Guided through the jungle and into the city where she is to gird herself with explosives and self-detonate in range of a targeted Indian politician, she's haunted by memories of battle and a brief interlude with a wounded male comrade. We see her kill twice more after the opening scene—and watch her watch as a child is killed in her stead.

Waiting to fulfill her mission, Malli is installed with a garrulous farmer who, naive as he may be, figures out something about her condition that even she didn't know. Although restrained in its violence, *The Terrorist* is scarcely subtle in its symbolism. Still, the movie's bold visual and psychological patterns, as well as its heavy immersion in the natural world, imbue Malli's journey with a folktale quality.

Moist and a bit melodramatic, *The Terrorist* is nevertheless taut enough to work as a thriller. (It's also sufficiently pop to engage a wide audience.) The cinematography is almost too gorgeous. Given to tilts and rack focus shots of one character or another charging away from the camera into some myopic mist, Sivan's framing hovers on the mannered. The director plants his camera in the foliage and regularly drenches his principals with water. The music can be overemphatic.

The grim subject matter is purposefully at odds with this dewy pantheism. (The strategy is not unlike Terrence Malick's in *The Thin Red Line.)* A suspense film with a transcendentalist backbeat, *The Terrorist* ultimately takes on a religious—or, at least, a metaphysical—aspect. Open-ended though it may be, Malli's journey toward death has been one long awakening.

Also reviewed in:
CHICAGO TRIBUNE, 3/31/00, Friday/p. F, Michael Wilmington
NEW YORK TIMES, 1/14/00, p. E16, A. O. Scott
VARIETY, 10/5-11/98, p. 71, Eddie Cockrell
WASHINGTON POST, 4/21/00, Weekend/p. 46, Desson Howe

THIRD WORLD COP

A Palm Pictures release of a Palm Pictures production in association with Hawk's Nest Productions. *Executive Producer:* Chris Blackwell and Dan Genetti. *Producer:* Carolyn Pfeiffer Bradshaw. *Director:* Chris Browne. *Screenplay:* Chris Browne, Suzanne Fenn, and Chris Salewicz. *Director of Photography:* Richard Lannaman. *Editor:* Suzanne Fenn. *Music:* Wally Badarou and Sly & Robbie. *Sound:* Don McGregor. *Sound Editor:* John Davies and Debby Van Poucke. *Casting:* Sharon Burke, Suzanne Fenn, and Sheila Lowe Graham. *Production Designer:* Richard Lannaman. *Art Director:* David Borely. *Set Decorator:* Raquel Anita Parke. *Special Effects:* Dwight Ramsay. *Costumes:* Michelle Haynes. *Make-up:* Carol Reid. *Special Effects Make-up:* Cecile Burrows. *Running time:* 98 minutes. *MPAA Rating:* R.

CAST: Paul Campbell (Capone); Mark Danvers (Ratty); Carl Bradshaw (Wonie); Audrey Reid (Rita); Winston Bell (Floyd); Lenford Salmon (Not Nice); Desmond Ballentine "Ninja Man" (Deportee); O'Neil "Elephant Man" Bryan (Tek-9); Andrew "Nittie Kutchie" Reid (Crime); Devon "Angel Doolas" Douglas (Razor); Winsome Wilson (Carla); Ronald "Too Small" Small (Bodyguard); John Jones (Superintendent Lewis); Kathy Owen (TV Announcer); Natalie Thompson (Port Antonio Superintendent); Lillian Foster (Mama); Clive Anderson (Jacko); Lloyd Reckord (Reverend); Robbie Shakespeare (Don Next Door); Onanadi Lowe (Pool Player); Buccaneer (MC); Donavan "Boom Dandymite" Stewart, Patrick "Harry Toddler" Jackson, and Christopher "Hawkeye" Smith (Crew in Car); Junior Frazer and Owen Williams (Detectives); Glen Campbell (Security Guard); Joslyn "Captain Barkey" Hamilton and Phillip "Cutty Ranks" Thomas (Police); Amelia Sewell (Woman); André Thompson (Red Stripe Vendor); Daniel Ellis (Marble Kid); Winston Rowe (Spoonhead); Dean Khouri (Stall Vendor); Desmond Castello (Skinny); Ricardo Barrett (Teen with Finger); Omarr Fogo (Youth on TV); Janice "Lady G" Fyffe (Entertainer); Alton "Fancy Cat" Hardware (Annoying Man); Simon Hemmings (Man on TV); Natasha Budhi, Angela Hunigan and Tesah Linton (Go-Go Dancers); Calvin Mitchell (Accused); Glenville Murphy (Drunk Man); Howard "Muggy" Williams (Crying Convict).

LOS ANGELES TIMES, 4/28/00, Calendar/p. 22, Kenneth Turan

With a crime story so old-fashioned it would have pleased Jimmy Cagney and George Raft joined to an up-to-date reggae and dance-hall soundtrack produced by Sly & Robbie, "Third World Cop" is a genial case of gangster meets gangsta on the streets of Jamaica.

Directed by Chris Browne and using many of the same people who made the earlier Jamaican hit "Dancehall Queen," "Third World Cop" has become that country's highest-grossing film ever.

While the plotting could have come out of a Dick Tracy comic strip, "Third World Cop" does offer some diverting moments plus an absorbing glimpse into the poorest, most dangerous parts of Kingston, where the film was originally shot on digital video for a bargain price of half a million dollars.

"Third World Cop" also offers a charismatic lead performance by Paul Campbell, one of Jamaica's most popular stars, as Capone, a guns-blazing, ask-questions-never kind of policeman. When he peers at you from under his ever-present black beret and over the top of his impassive sunglasses, you know you've been peered at. "Your talents are wasted here," his small-town superior archly remarks before transferring him back to Kingston, the city of his birth.

Capone is partnered with the nervous Floyd (Winston Bell), who is forever wanting to call for backup when things get hot, a scenario that fills Capone with contempt. "What do you want, an air strike?" he cracks with the acid sense of humor that allows him to snarl "Read the manual, idiot," at the corpse of a fumbling-with-his-weapon bad guy he's just eliminated.

But just because his motto is "We run things, things don't run we?" (turned into the soundtrack's most effective cut by Red Dragon), don't think Capone doesn't have a soft side. He's got a heck of a smile and a great affection for his old neighborhood, a place so tough that the local bar is called Saddam's and people prefer to be known by nicknames like Dummy, Skinny, Spoonhead, Dainty Crime and Deportee (the latter played by reggae star Ninjaman).

The two people Capone is most eager to be reunited with are his old flame Rita (Audrey Reid) and his boyhood pal Ratty. Played by the almost equally charismatic Mark Danvers, Ratty likes to promote concerts and is fond of first quoting a passage from the Bible and then tearing out the page it's printed on to smoke some serious ganja.

But though Capone doesn't know it at first, Ratty is now the right hand (no, make that the left hand) man of the one-armed local crime boss logically nicknamed Wonie. Played by Carl Bradshaw, a "The Harder They Come" veteran, Wonie takes time out from auditioning go-go dancers to smuggle arms into the neighborhood in preparation for even more criminal activity, plans that will put a heck of a strain on the Capone-Ratty relationship.

Aside from the uncomplicated pleasures of very traditional police story material (the film's script is by Suzanne Fenn, Chris Browne and Chris Salewicz), "Third World Cop's" main lure is what feels like a very authentic visual sense of the nontourist side of Kingston, where the ambience of zinc-walled shacks wallpapered with old newspapers is captured by cinematographer Richard Lannaman.

"Third World Cop" is so authentic, in fact, that the English-language film has to supply subtitles to make its dialogue (laced with frequent use of profane local expressions) understandable to non-island audiences.

Though the film lacks the elan of 1971's groundbreaking "The Harder They Come," it's good to see what another Jamaican generation is up to.

NEW YORK POST, 4/14/00, p. 55, Jonathan Foreman

This gunplay-filled Jamaican movie was a monster hit on the Caribbean isle, but the acting, camera work and writing are all crude and amateurish, even by the standards of student films.

The fact that it's shot on garish video, like a porn movie, only makes it harder to watch.

The predictable story follows a quick-firing cop named Capone (Paul Campbell) from Port Antonio to an assignment in Jamaica's notoriously violent capital of Kingston, where he has to confront former pals from his shantytown youth who have now become gun-running criminals.

The best thing about the movie is the music: a mixture of dance hall, reggae and rap.

NEWSDAY, 4/14/00, Part II/p. B6, Gene Seymour

Times have changed just a little bit since Perry Henzell's "The Harder They Come" came into being way back in 1972. The central figure of that legendary Jamaican movie with the killer soundtrack was a poor kid from the country seeking his fortune as a pop star and ends up as an outlaw in a valiant, doomed struggle against violent, corrupt cops.

It's 28 years later, and here comes "Third World Cop," boasting a killer soundtrack and directed by Henzell's nephew, Chris Browne. Guns are still fired two at a time and cops are still on the take. The difference is that the hero is not an outlaw but a hard-boiled Port Antonio police detective named Capone (Paul Campbell), who is both ruthless and scrupulous in the extreme.

After dispensing of three criminal intruders with bloody dispatch, Capone is ordered by his superiors to take his Lee Marvin scowl to a Kingston shantytown where he'd grown up with his best friends Ratty (Mark Danvers) and Rita (Audrey Reid). The old neighborhood is now rife with guns, spread surreptitiously throughout by a gang led by a sharp-dressed, one-armed viper named Wonie (Carl Bradshaw). Capone quickly, if reluctantly, figures out that Ratty is one of Wonie's lieutenants and tries to get him to go straight without getting each other killed.

Sounds like every other cop movie made since Technicolor was invented, right? Well, sure, except that every once in a while you don't mind seeing a movie that carries out a formula as tautly and efficiently as this one does, even with its glossy, shot-on-video sheen and especially with that aforementioned soundtrack, courtesy of the reggae band Sly and Robbie, throbbing in the background.

SIGHT AND SOUND, 4/00, p. 62, Peter Curran

Kingston, Jamaica, the present. Two childhood friends are reunited: Capone has become a successful police officer while Ratty is the right-hand man of a local gangster engaged in gun running. As the police attempt to capture the criminals, the two former friends agonise over their personal loyalty to each other.

Capone fails to persuade his friend to disengage from crime; Ratty's friendship with a cop makes him, in the gang's view, a police informant. After going on the run, he agrees to give evidence against his boss One Hand. Having secured immunity from prosecution and a new identity, he and Capone set out for the trial. Capone's corrupt rival in the police force sets up an ambush on behalf of One Hand, and in the confusion Ratty attempts to escape with the trial evidence, only to be shot dead by Capone.

The childhood friends/adult adversaries scenario might seem laughably clichéd in any other setting, but in the townships of Jamaica it has the same timeless ring as those biblical declamations that featured heavily on early reggae records, where good and evil were distinct and unsubtle enemies. Like the seminal Caribbean bad boy tale *The Harder They Come* (1972), *Third World Cop* is resolutely local in language and setting so you can tune into to its idiosyncratic pleasures even though you've seen virtually the same stock characters in crime movies since the 40s.

Successful detective Capone is transferred back to his old Kingston neighbourhood and enjoys moving through familiar hang-outs all the more because he got out of them. He can wear a spotless white t-shirt, while his poor lawless contemporaries are layered in designer-label sportswear. The initial encounter between cop and oldest friend Ratty is a Leone-style stand-off on a dusty football pitch. They speak with the guarded sarcasm of police and villain—the words of a mock antagonism that suddenly becomes real at the close of the movie—but then they drop the act, dissolving into laughter and easy banter.

This work comes from the same production team that made *Dancehall Queen* and shares that earlier film's easygoing immediacy. Naturalistic settings—bars, street corners, alleyways—are just a backcloth to the full-frame faces of the characters as they declare their intentions, a departure from the kind of films usually shot in Jamaica which rely so heavily on tourist-attracting countryside shots. Cinematographer Richard Lannaman comes from an advertising background and his luminously lit shots make the most of the great looking cast.

Even the rheumy-eyed gangster One Hand, toting around a vast stock of jewellery on his body, affects an air of sophistication and menace as he plays Ratty off against his other aspirant crime deputies. At the same time, debut director Chris Browne lingers on the attractive features of his hero Capone, scrambling to uncover the gun runner's plans. One senses Browne was reluctant to depend on a creaking old thriller plot to keep the audience interested and opted instead to make the film a showcase for his easy-on-the-eye leading man,

The inevitability of the plot—the double-cross, ambush and final betrayal all announce themselves noisily before entering—seems quaint rather than exasperating. The execution of these set-piece moments and the editor's fast cutting tighten the sense of excitement, particularly when the gang set out to kill Ratty as a suspected police informer. The pace is coaxed along by a rolling percussive score produced by reggae veterans Sly Dunbar and Robbie Shakespeare. As an exploration of how friendship is ultimately sacrificed for selfish ends, the film only partially succeeds, but it does deliver a handsome, atmospheric portrait of life behind the dancehall.

VILLAGE VOICE, 4/18/00, p. 158, Tina Benitez

Suggesting that punishment fits the crime, *Third World Cop* exposes the clash between gun traffickers and the police in Kingston, Jamaica. Capone (Paul Campbell), a badass celebrity cop, is transferred to his island hometown, where he discovers that his childhood friend Ratty (Mark Danvers) is the right-hand man of a ganja-loving, gun-running ganglord (Carl Bradshaw). Reciting a passage from Ezekiel to a fellow gang member about to meet an ill fate, Ratty is a philosophizing Jules from *Pulp Fiction*. As arrogant Capone attempts to cut a deal with Ratty, their icy confrontation thaws to reveal a wiser elder looking after a younger brother. The highest-grossing Jamaican film of all time (one of only 19 films made by Jamaican directors since 1951's *Father Brown Learns Good Diary*), *Cop* is an energetic portrayal of mean-street ghetto life.

Also reviewed in:
NEW YORK TIMES, 4/14/00, p. E27, A. O. Scott
VARIETY, 1/10-16/00, p. 113, Joe Leydon

THIRTEEN

A Film Society of Lincoln Center & The Independent Feature Project release of an American Independent Visions presentation of a Bellevue Films production. *Producer:* David Williams. *Director:* David Williams. *Screenplay:* David Williams. *Director of Photography:* David Williams. *Editor:* David Williams. *Music:* Cecil Hooker, Shep Williams, and Carlos Garza. *Sound:* Bernice Baker. *Running time:* 87 minutes. *MPAA Rating:* Not Rated.

CAST: Wilhamenia Dickens (Nina); Lillian Folley (Lillian); Don Semmens (Artist); Michael Aytes (Michael); Michael Jeffrey and Dawn Tinsley (Social Workers); David Scales (Lillian's Male Friend); Doug Washington (Nina's Uncle); Anisa Dickens (Kiki); Thomas Shelton (Man Working in Lillian's Yard); Mary Aytes (Babysis); Marguerita Austin (Woman Married a Long Time); Shelby Ware (Woman Worried About Boyfriend); Chichie Tascoe (Canine Designer); Nathalie Le Floch (Dog Owner); Brenda Parker (Teacher); Samuel Flynn (Insurance Salesman); Wanda Dickens (Wanda).

NEW YORK POST, 6/2/00, p. 47, Hannah Brown

Unsettling and original, "Thirteen" is a quasi-documentary that follows a painfully inarticulate African-American girl through her troubled 13th year.

Quiet and gawky Nina (Wilhamenia Dickens) doesn't have the usual stormy problems that plague teens in most movies.

Although her father is nowhere in the picture and her mother (Lillian Folley, Dickens' real-life foster mom) is a bit overbearing, she is surrounded by a large, loving extended family and lives in a pleasant house in Richmond, Va.

But she is troubled about something she can't confide to anyone, and one day, with no explanation, wanders off.

The first half of "Thirteen" shifts back and forth between Nina on the road and her anguished mother, as she answers questions posed by detectives trying to put together a profile of Nina.

As Nina tramps through the woods, accepting food from strangers but speaking to no one, "Thirteen" is reminiscent of Agnes Varda's haunting "Vagabond."

Then, as mysteriously as she left, Nina returns home. Her listlessness is replaced by a new obsession: buying a car.

She begins to come out of herself as she works at odd jobs to earn enough money to achieve her dream.

The cast of non-professionals, most of whom appear under their real names, reportedly improvised much of the dialogue.

The film alternates between scenes that feel remarkably fresh and other moments that are jarringly stilted.

Dickens' startlingly natural performance in the lead is downright disconcerting.

Watching "Thirteen" is like spending an hour and a half with a poker-faced teen who's obviously unhappy but refuses to talk about what's wrong.

The most frustrating aspect of the film is that director/writer David Williams never chooses to reveal what's really the matter with Nina. Is she just going through a typical teenage funk, or is something more serious the problem?

At times, her depression seems so deep that she seems to be suffering from an actual mental illness.

In the end, the triumph of "Thirteen" is that you begin to worry about Nina and keep thinking about her long after most teen movie prom queens have faded from memory.

VILLAGE VOICE, 6/6/00, p. 139, J. Hoberman

Opening some years after a distinguished film-festival career (which includes the 1998 "New Directors/New Films"), David Williams's *Thirteen* is a triumph of understatement. Williams's first feature is modest and thoughtful, homespun and humanist and regionally based-a sort of old-school Sundance production.

The title refers not to public television but to the heroine's age. Sometime after her 13th-birthday party, Nina (Wilhamenia Dickens) runs away from home, hitchhiking into the autumn countryside outside Richmond, Virginia. As her motivations are largely a mystery, much of *Thirteen* suggests a teenage *Citizen Kane*, with various explanatory flashbacks arising out of the interview two social workers conduct with Nina's mother Lillian (Lillian Foley). The inquiry is interrupted by Nina's casual return. Having experienced some sort of epiphany, the girl decides to earn money to buy a car-baby-sitting, pet-watching, attempting to become a real estate agent.

Wilhamenia Dickens's Nina is tall and skinny, with sad eyes and a sullen overbite. Blunt yet withholding, she's an authentic adolescent presence who makes no attempt to charm the audience. Nina is shown through her mother's eyes. Her activities are annotated, if not entirely explained, by Lillian's low-key voice-over, and her enigmas are filtered through the prism of Lillian's idiosyncratic religious faith. The two principals seem to be less acting than playing themselves, which, in a sense, they are—albeit in a fictionalized framework. (Dickens is a foster child whom Foley adopted; the filmmaker is their neighbor.)

Ending with Nina's 14th-birthday party, *Thirteen* is a youth movie without a single youth movie cliché. Highly composed and sometimes stilted, it nevertheless manages a documentary freshness. In this quietly affecting mother-daughter story, Williams has created a true imitation of life. The movie is as eloquently uninflected and filled with quirks as its star.

Also reviewed in:
CHICAGO TRIBUNE, 8/4/00, Friday/p. I, John Petrakis
NEW YORK TIMES, 6/2/00, p. E21, Stephen Holden
VARIETY, 3/9-15/98, p. 43, David Stratton

THIRTEEN DAYS

A New Line Cinema release in association with Beacon Pictures. *Executive Producer:* Thomas A. Bliss, Michael De Luca, Ilona Herzberg, and Marc Abraham. *Producer:* Armyan Bernstein, Peter O. Almond, and Kevin Costner. *Director:* Roger Donaldson. *Screenplay:* David Self. *Director of Photography:* Andrzej Bartkowiak. *Editor:* Conrad Buff. *Music:* Trevor Jones. *Music Editor:* Alex Gibson. *Sound:* Richard Bryce Goodman and (music) Simon Rhodes. *Sound Editor:* Steven D. Williams. *Casting:* Dianne Crittenden. *Production Designer:* Dennis Washington. *Art Director:* Thomas T. Taylor and Ann Harris. *Set Designer:* Julie Ray, Donald B. Woodruff, and Nancy Mickelberry. *Set Decorator:* Denise Pizzini. *Set Dresser:* John H. Maxwell, Alan Baptiste, and Michael G. Miller. *Special Effects:* Louis Lantieri. *Visual Effects:* Allen Maris. *Costumes:* Isis Mussenden. *Make-up:* Rick Sharp, Kimberly Felix-Burke, and Brad Wilder. *Special Effects Make-up:* Mathew W. Mungle. *Running time:* 140 minutes. *MPAA Rating:* PG-13.

CAST: Shawn Driscoll (U-2 Pilot);   Kevin Costner (Kenny O'Donnell);   Drake Cook (Mark O'Donnell);   Lucinda Jenney (Helen O'Donnell);   Caitlin Wachs (Kathy O'Donnell);   Jon Foster (Kenny O'Donnell, Jr.);   Matthew Dunn (Kevin O'Donnell);   Kevin O'Donnell (NPIC Photo Interpreter);   Janet Coleman (Evelyn Lincoln);   Bruce Thomas (Floyd);   Stephanie

Romanov (Jacqueline Kennedy);   Bruce Greenwood (John F. Kennedy);   Frank Wood (McGeorge Bundy);   Dakin Matthews (Arthur Lundahl);   Liz Sinclair and Colette O'Connell (Kenny's Assistants);   Karen Ludwig (Operator Margaret);   Audrey Rapoport and Marliese K. Schneider (White House Operators);   Steven Culp (Robert F. Kennedy);   Dylan Baker (Robert McNamara);   Bill Smitrovich (Gen. Maxwell Taylor); Henry Strozier (Dean Rusk);   Ed Lauter (General Marshall Carter);   Michael Fairman (Adlai Stevenson);   Walter Adrian (Lyndon Johnson);   Tim Kelleher (Ted Sorensen);   James Karen (George Ball);   Daniel Ziskie (General Walter "Cam" Sweeney);   Len Cariou (Dean Acheson);   Peter White (John McCone);   Kevin Conway (General Curtis LeMay);   Kelly Connell (Pierre Salinger);   Olek Krupa (Andrei Gromyko);   Elya Baskin (Anatoly Dobrinyn);   Timothy Jerome (Journalist);   Jack McGee (Mayor Daly);   Lamar Smith (Aide);   John Aylward (Orville Dryfoos);   Madison Mason (Admiral George Anderson);   Vivien Straus (White House Aide); Christopher Lawford (Commander William B. Ecker);   David O'Donnell (Lieutenant Bruce Wilhemy);   Gene Del Bianco (Petty Officer);   Ben Koldyke (RF-8 Pilot);   Daniel Vergara (OAS President);   Reuben Moreno (Argentine Diplomat);   Thomas Roberts (Sonar Operator);   Sean Bergin (Chief Sonarman);   Robert Munstis, Joseph Repoff, and Alex Veadov (Radio Room Operators); Michael Gaston (Captain of USS Pierce);   J. Tucker Smith (Captain of USS Kennedy);   Alan Francis (Executive Officer of USS Kennedy); Chris Henry Coffey (Officer of Destroyer);   Oleg Vidov (Valerian Zorin);   Radu Gavor (Romanian Delegate);   Zitto Kazann (Chilean Delegate); Jack Blessing (John Scali);   Tom Everett (Walter Sheridan);   Karl Makinen (Young FBI Agent); Boris Lee Krutonog (Alexander Fomin);   Charles Esten (Major Rudolph Anderson);   Charles Barrett (Air Force NCO);   Darryl Smith (Football Coach);   Alan Graf (Football Referee); Robert Miranda (RFK's Driver);   Todd Sible (RFK's Staffer);   Marya Kazakova (Soviet Woman);   Cliff Fleming (Aerial Coordinator); Craig Hosking (Pilot).

CINEASTE, Vol. XXVI, No. 2, 2001, p. 43, Art Simon

Midway through *Thirteen Days,* Roger Donaldson's love letter to the Kennedy brothers and their handling of the Cuban missile crisis, General Curtis LeMay reminds the president of a new slogan for the U.S. Strategic Air Command: "Peace Is Our Profession." However ironic that slogan is supposed to sound coming from the most hawkish of Pentagon hawks, I could not help but think of *Dr. Strangelove,* the cinema's greatest meditation on the threat of nuclear destruction. Recall that when army ground troops try to break through the defense of Burpelson Air Force Base in order to make contact with General Jack D. Ripper, Kubrick's battle sequence takes place in front of a large billboard declaring the same SAC slogan.

To even mention *Strangelove* in the course of discussing *Thirteen Days* borders on serious insult to the deceased auteur. For no two films, despite their similarity of content—a U.S.-Soviet showdown, the infighting at the highest echelon of national defense, the threat of nuclear Armageddon—could be less alike in purpose, tone, or artistry. Indeed, their Doomsday montages of mushroom cloud imagery come at exactly opposite points. *Strangelove,* of course, ends with the end of the world, the logical outcome of a failed atomic policy dependent on a warmongering military leadership. *Thirteen Days* begins with a vision of conflagration, shots of atomic explosions that have no clear link to the rest of the film. Are these images from a nightmare dreamt by Presidential aide Kenneth O'Donnell? After all, the first shot of O'Donnell, played by Kevin Costner, through whom most of the story is focused, shows him waking up in the morning. Perhaps he was dreaming about the end of the world. Indeed, for a script in which subtlety is a stranger, 'seeing the morning' is only one of several overheated narrative motifs. On the other hand, perhaps these mushroom shots simply serve as historical markers, returning us to a time when the atomic threat figured as a persistent cloud over the postwar world.

I sense these opening shots are there to alert the audience to the gravity of the story about to unfold and, as such, they are wholly consistent with a movie obsessed with its own seriousness. *Thirteen Days* may center on some fascinating history, but it is wretched filmmaking precisely because it employs every cinematic device, again and again, to declare its own significance. As if worried that a post-Cold War audience just would not understand what a suspenseful situation this is, screenwriter David Self and director Donaldson have built a film around ponderous reaction shots, trite references to the family, mostly O'Donnell's, and a clichéd musical score that is merciless in its reliance on drum rolls. So bankrupt is their imagination that the filmmakers even borrow, for no apparent reason, Oliver Stone's technique of cutting brief sequences of black-and-white footage into their color photography. Hell, it worked for one film about JFK, maybe it will work for another.

Floating amidst this oppressive style is a rather straightforward political thesis: namely, that the Kennedy brothers (Jack, played by Bruce Greenwood, and Bobby, played by Steven Culp) were able to bring about a peaceful solution to the Cuban missile crisis despite being baited at every turn by a Pentagon brass determined to use its arsenal against the Soviet Union. The Kennedy triumph here is one of balance. The brothers are men enough to stand up to the trigger-happy Joint Chiefs but wise enough to make a diplomatic solution their top priority. They are neither hawks nor doves. Their machismo enables them to stare down the Russians; their resolve ensures the national defense, but their wisdom brings them to understand the consequences of military escalation.

What distinguishes the Ivy League trio (Jack, Bobby, and Ken) from their uniformed advisors, in addition to their civilian sensibilities, amounts to good looks and family ties. The film begins and ends at the O'Donnell breakfast table, underscoring that while the Generals have their battle plans, the Kennedys and O'Donnell have their children to worry about. Family as a source for their humanity is underscored when JFK takes a fleeting glimpse outside the Oval Office window and sees his wife and kids playing out on the lawn. Duty to country takes O'Donnell away from his family (to be with his surrogate White House family), and we are left with the cliché of the lonely, resentful yet frightened wife who asks her in-the-know husband "what's going to happen?" O'Donnell's sacrifice is emphasized by the painfully obligatory scene in which he finds a spare moment to attend his son's football game. And if there were any doubt that averting atomic warfare meant saving the nuclear family, it gets put to bed quite literally toward the end of the film when news that the Russians have backed down is accompanied by a shot of O'Donnell and his wife waking up together. Their union, and that of the nation, have made it through to another morning.

Thirteen Days is less historical inquiry than a profile in courage. When Andrei Gromyko tells JFK that Soviet aid to Cuba is of a defensive nature, the President rejects this claim immediately. The film's authors do so as well. Accepting the premise that these were offensive missiles prevents *Thirteen Days* from exploring, let alone questioning, American policy toward Fidel Castro. The Bay of Pigs invasion represents a blunder to overcome rather than a possible explanation for Cuban actions. Likewise, the depth of RFK's efforts to remove Castro, while referred to briefly during an antagonistic exchange between one of the joint Chiefs and Bobby, gets elided, further eclipsing the context in which the missile crisis took place. As Gary Wills has pointed out, to an American public uninformed about their government's secret war on Castro, the location of Russian missiles on Cuban soil appeared sudden and unprovoked. For the contemporary filmgoer, the same will probably hold true.

With six hundred pages of transcripts drawn from tape-recorded discussions held by the Executive Committee of the National Security Council, the filmmakers certainly had no shortage of material. But such sources are only history in a limited sense. No matter how faithful the script may be to the high-level deliberations that took place in the White House, wedding the archive to Hollywood convention inclines toward an interpretation that always favors drama. A fuller context for the missile crisis is just not available to the chosen form of *Thirteen Days*. Thus, the background on U.S. missiles in Turkey, the implications of resumption, in 1962, of nuclear testing, the meaning of Cuba for Soviet global self image, and, of course, the history of U.S. involvement in pre- and post-revolution Cuba, are all missing. Missing, too, is any attempt at provocation. For a film that, at times, gestures incoherently toward *JFK, Thirteen Days* exhibits none of the incendiary stylistic traits that worried critics of Stone's film but that also motivated wider debate and inquiry into the events it recounts.

This is not to indict the film for what it is not, but to underscore how its focus curtails the possibility of a wider context, one that would undermine its ultimate mission to celebrate the moral toughness and political wisdom of the Kennedy brothers. Never mind that the bargain ultimately struck with Khrushchev, dismantling obsolete missiles in Turkey, resembles that suggested by Adlai Stevenson at the beginning of the crisis. Stevenson has first to be condemned as a dove, then recuperated by his tough questioning of the Soviet ambassador at the United

Nations. In fact, for all the advice they solicit, the Kennedys' triumph is presented in terms of an independence of thought. "There is something immoral," JFK tells Bobby and O'Donnell, "about abandoning your own judgment." Meanwhile, O'Donnell comes off as the brother who is not one, a trusted ally whose devotion is offered as testimony to the brothers' greatness. In one of the more annoying exchanges of dialogue, O'Donnell reassures his wife by saying, "Jack and Bobby ... they're smart guys." "You're smart too," she replies. "Not like them," he solemnly intones. The point is driven home again when Soviet Ambassador Anatoly Dobrynin tells Bobby that he and his brother are "good men."

There are points at which *Thirteen Days* almost achieves an attractive claustrophobia as O'Donnell, the Kennedys and their military advisors wrestle in close quarters over strategy. These sequences aptly suggest the invisibility of the people on whose behalf policy is supposedly being enacted. They also suggest the guessing game at the heart of decision making, since the president and his advisors are involved in constant speculation over Khrushchev's motives and methods. In fact, given how closely the narrative action is tied to the White House, it remains unable to explore the role played by the Soviet Premier in resolving the crisis. Unfortunately, the filmmakers just can't resist interrupting the deliberations with action scenes of reconnaissance jets in flight. Heaven forbid two-and-a-half hours should go by without some video-game imagery. These aerial distractions are also occasions for more irritating drum rolls and overwrought orchestration.

Two of the sequences that take us into the field, however, function strategically to assert that the Commander-in-Chief works out of the White House not the Pentagon. The first is when O'Donnell makes a direct call to one of the reconnaissance pilots. Under no circumstances, O'Donnell tells him, should he report being fired upon to his superiors. News of any firing by the Cubans, even in defense, will only set off the hawks, already anxious to invade the island. The second scene involves JFK speaking directly to a ship commander administering the blockade against Soviet vessels bound for Cuba. In both scenes, the White House succeeds at circumventing the military chain of command and, in both cases, Kennedy authority gets bolstered through the loyalty of boys at the front.

With *Thirteen Days* and *JFK*, Kevin Costner has certainly redefined the term best supporting actor—that is, performances in support of the Kennedy legend. As O'Donnell, Costner assumes a New England accent that toward the beginning brings a touch of Vaughn Meader to a role that otherwise demands little beyond a variety of stern looks. So fixed in popular memory, through archival film or still photography, are the rhythms of the Kennedy voice and the expressions of either brother's face, that playing John or Robert Kennedy is pretty much a no-win situation for any actor. To his credit, Bruce Greenwood acts rather than impersonates JFK and whatever credible drama emerges throughout the film is, in large measure, due to his performance.

Despite the film's focusing events, albeit loosely, through the eyes of the President's confidant, it is JFK who gets the final word. With the final credits, the real world replaces the reenactment as the soundtrack is given over to a recording of Kennedy delivering a speech at the American University in Washington. (It is the same speech excerpted by Stone for the opening montage of *JFK.*) Its purpose is twofold. First, the archive serves to authenticate the docudrama. Second, this speech—"Our most basic common link is that we all inhabit this small planet, we all breathe the same air, we all cherish our children's future, and we are all mortal"—presents the philosophical president, not the political one.

Meanwhile, the end of the crisis returns O'Donnell to the family breakfast table to engage in some torturous dialogue that aspires to poetry. Knowing what we now know about JFK's affection for extramarital pleasures, O'Donnell's family is a necessary substitute for a film that wants desperately to restore calm by restoring the protecting father amidst his innocent children and grateful wife. Still, I would have preferred knowing how JFK had celebrated that victorious night. But, by this point, the film's 150 minutes had indeed felt like thirteen days, and the end of the world seemed a small price to pay for its finally drawing to a close.

LOS ANGELES TIMES, 12/25/00, Calendar/p. 1, Kenneth Turan

"Thirteen Days," the crisp and involving dramatization of 1962's Cuban missile crisis, starts with shots of what might have been—rockets being fired and exploding on target, the awful mushroom clouds of nuclear holocaust. Pay attention is the message, don't forget that this is what was at risk.

If high stakes make for high drama, that near-fortnight of tension and peril--arguably the closest the world has come to being annihilated—is as dramatic a subject as anyone could want. And director Roger Donaldson and a fine ensemble topped by Kevin Costner (not your usual ensemble player) have handled it adroitly.

Someone who has talked about his vivid memories of living through those 13 days in his native Australia, Donaldson ("No Way Out," "Dante's Peak") used that personal involvement to turn out a confident, professional film that, a few problematical areas notwithstanding, is likely his best work as a director.

With a tone that sporadically ventures into the gee-whiz, "Thirteen Days" is not a film for inveterate haters of the brothers John F. and Robert Kennedy, though it should be said that its heroic point of view is something of a relief after the avalanche of partisanship the last election triggered.

Also, those who are bears for historical accuracy will be surprised at the preeminent position inevitably given to the man Costner plays, Kenneth P. O'Donnell. O'Donnell was one of JFK's closest aides but, as more of a fall-on-the-sword kind of guy than moral philosopher, probably didn't have nearly the role in the Cuban missile crisis the film gives him.

Still, David Self's careful, measured script (it's hard to believe his last credit was "The Haunting") earns our respect and our attention. For one, it's based on extensive research, including the Kennedy White House tapes and interviews O'Donnell (whose son, Kevin, is an investor in Beacon Pictures, which made the film) did with journalist Sander Vanocur. Just as important, Self and Donaldson have understood that when you're dealing with inherently dramatic material, nothing works so well as restraint.

Efficient and low-key, "Thirteen Days" takes itself just seriously enough while maintaining a powerful dramatic momentum. Its cast, including Bruce Greenwood as the president and Steven Culp as his attorney general, not only look remarkably like the people they're playing, but they've all been made to understand that individual performances have to be subservient to the good of the whole.

This even applies to Costner, whose name will sell the picture but who is smart enough to be content with his role as the window into the story. The main difficulty the actor has is with his no doubt based-on-fact but still god-awful Boston accent, a painful reminder that certain kinds of stars should avoid accents at all costs.

"Thirteen Days" starts with the U2 surveillance flight that discovered medium-range Soviet ballistic missiles in Cuba, missiles that could potentially reach as far as Washington, D.C., and kill millions of Americans. The experts' best guess is that they'll be operational in 10 to 14 days, so it's essential that a way be found to deal with them as soon as possible.

The first questions, obviously, are about the Russians. What are their intentions? What's the best way to deal with them so as not to precipitate a deeper crisis or a world war? Kennedy and company were handicapped during their deliberations by not knowing what the Russians knew, and the film smartly adds to the tension by keeping us similarly in the dark, never shifting focus to Moscow and refusing to clue us in on what the Soviets and their leader, Nikita Krushchev, were thinking.

Difficult as the Russians are, the president soon comes to feel that his nominal friends and allies in the military are giving him more trouble than his avowed enemies. While other options like blockades are suggested, one of the themes of the film, backed up by history, is how fiercely the military establishment pushed for an all-out attack on Cuba even though it would probably have led to nuclear war.

The Russian incursion, Gen. Maxwell Taylor announces, is "a massively destabilizing move" that must be countered. And Gen. Curtis LeMay (Kevin Conway) goes further. "The big red dog is digging in our backyard," he barks, "and we're justified in shooting him."

Trying to resist this stampede, the president, his brother and their supporters try hard to keep a sense of historical perspective. "We have to make things come out right," Kennedy says, always keeping in front of him the example of the start of World War I as related in Barbara Tuchman's "The Guns of August," which detailed how the momentum for military action got so strong that the war began even though none of the leaders involved really wanted it.

Kenny O'Donnell's job in all of this, if "Thirteen Days" is to be believed, was to function as a combination sage and secret agent, to be the pragmatic voice of reason ready to do what needed to be done while serving up nuggets of wisdom and kernels of plain truth. Even if not historically accurate, it's an acceptable construct the film uses as a way to increase dramatic effectiveness.

Dealing with all these crises and decisions gives "Thirteen Days" a surprising amount of tension and watchability for a story whose outcome we already know. Adding to the film's compelling nature is the unfortunate fact that the broader issues it deals with have hardly gone away. The shapes and forms may change, but as long as nuclear arsenals are a fact of life, the concerns Kennedy and his advisors had to cope with will keep reappearing time and time again.

NEW YORK, 1/1/00, p. 81, Peter Rainer

Thirteen Days recounts the moment-to-moment brinkmanship in the White House during the Cuban Missile Crisis. This sweat-it-out saga has been filmed before, notably in 1974, with ABC's *Missiles of October*, which gave us not only William Devane and Martin Sheen as Jack and Bobby Kennedy but also Howard Da Silva (!) as Khrushchev. I would wager that more potentially deployable nuclear missiles are in the world now than in 1974 or 1962, but the effect of watching *Thirteen Days* is unavoidably nostalgic anyway. Roger Donaldson, directing from a script by David Self based on the book The *Kennedy Tapes—Inside the White House During the Cuban Missile Crisis,* isn't trying for a cautionary tale here. The movie is more like a deconstruction of a bygone near-annihilation. Finally, the graying members of the boomer generation can see precisely how it came to pass that they were sent scurrying beneath their grade-school desks.

Although most of the film plays out like a docudrama, there's a fair amount of high-pressure hokum to take the starch out of the history lesson, particularly when hawks like General Curtis LeMay (Kevin Conway) are fulminating. Much of the action involves Kenny O'Donnell, a close "Irish Mafia" cohort of the Kennedys and a White House adviser to the president. He's played by Kevin Costner in a Boston accent that leaves more than a bit to be desired—even Jackie Mason's Ted Kennedy impression is closer to the real thing. But otherwise Costner doesn't stand out unduly, and his staunch reticence is admirable. He doesn't try to turn himself into the whole show, and yet it is O'Donnell's sidelong perspective that gives the film its skewed fascination. As Robert and Jack Kennedy, Steven Culp and Bruce Greenwood are better at the accent thing and creditably lifelike; each seems to be giving a performance rather than an impersonation. I much prefer the whacked-out, Dr. *Strangelove*-ish brand of political-apocalypse film to all this straitlaced you-are-there dramaturgy, which seems a throwback to the early sixties not only in time but in spirit. But what *Thirteen Days* sets out to do it does admirably.

NEW YORK POST, 12/22/00, p. 52, Lou Lumenick

Our national crisis over this year's election was small chads indeed compared to a heart-stopping two-week period in 1962, when we teetered on the brink of a nuclear showdown with Russia.

"Thirteen Days" is a highly competent docudrama portraying the Cuban Missile Crisis, precipitated when American surveillance planes discovered that Russian nuclear missiles capable of reaching 80 percent of the United States were being installed in Cuba.

Most advisers to President John F. Kennedy (well-played by Bruce Greenwood)—especially military brass still licking their wounds from the abortive Bay of Pigs invasion—urged immediate air strikes to take out the missile sites, followed by wide-spread attacks and an invasion.

But JFK's brother Robert (an uncanny impersonation by Steven Culp), the attorney general, and his top aide Kenneth O'Donnell Kevin Costner) wondered if a sneak attack wouldn't be seen in the court of world opinion as the equivalent of Japan's strike on Pearl Harbor.

As tensions steadily mounted, the Kennedys instead employed a risky naval embargo (the movie's best sequence) and desperate back-door negotiations with Soviet Premier Nikita Krushchev.

It's still as gripping a story as it was in 1973, when this real-life "Armageddon" inspired an acclaimed TV-movie,called,"The Missiles of October."

"Thirteen Days," which plays like a very good TV movie (it's quite talky and there's not much action), bends the facts by building up the role of O'Donnell, played by Costner with an annoying Boston accent in what's nonetheless one of his most effective performances in recent years.

When O'Donnell pressures a reconnaissance pilot (played by JFK's real-life nephew, Christopher Lawford) to lie to his Pentagon bosses and hide the fact he was shot at during a run over Cuba, credited screenwriter David Self pushes credulity to the limit.

The scene where O'Donnell gives dovish U.N. Ambassador Adlai Stevenson (the superb Michael Fairman) a locker-room talk before confronting Russia with his famous "Hell Freezes Over" speech is also fairly risible, if undeniably entertaining.

Short on visual flair and starpower, "Thirteen Days" is not the definitive story of the Cuban Missile Crisis, but it's an engrossing historical lesson nonetheless.

NEWSDAY, 12/22/00, Part II/p. B2, John Anderson

It's a risk attributing too much influence to the movies, but isn't it fun to think of how "Thirteen Days" might have influenced this year's presidential election? With George W. Bush repopulating Washington with old Cold Warriors, and director Roger Donaldson showing us just how blithely their ilk might have blown up the world, you simply have to wonder.

And you wonder a lot during "Thirteen Days," easily the best film Donaldson has ever made—and that includes "No Way Out," the movie that more or less unleashed Kevin Costner on the world. Reuniting the director and the star in a retelling of the Cuban Crisis, "Thirteen Days" stars Costner as Kenny O'Donnell, Kennedy administration special assistant, family friend and, later, memoirist ("Johnny, We Hardly Knew Ye").

O'Donnell, who died in 1977, was in the eye of the storm that blew around the USSR's installation of nuclear missiles in Cuba and John F. Kennedy's steel-nerved showdown with Soviet Premier Nikita Khruschev. Costner, the actor, finds himself in another kind of showdown. O'Donnell may be a real-life character, but he still feels imposed upon the story, a combination Kennedy cheerleader and fellow Irish Mafioso (and, more importantly, a character who seems to possess 20-20 foresight about the mere 27-year gap between near-annihilation in '62 and the fall of Communism in '89).

Bruce Greenwood's John Kennedy, on the other hand, is as close to perfect as any such portrayal might be. Costner is a character; Greenwood is the late president. Greenwood, who's best known for his work with director Atom Egoyan and for (yikes) "Double Jeopardy," doesn't look that much like JFK; he doesn't even sound that much like JFK. Yet, working with Kennedy's measured cadences, closeted emotions and cunning, he's more than convincing. Whatever he presents as Kennedy, we're willing to accept.

Likewise Steven Culp: He plays Bobby Kennedy as ruthless, but also as a natural tactician who doesn't even realize he's ruthless. He also portrays RFK as the eternal little brother, which adds a mournful grandeur to the proceedings whenever the president and his attorney general are left alone.

That isn't often, but that's OK. Despite his ebbing and flowing Boston accent, Costner is solid, certainly the conscience of the film and its one source of occasional mirth. At home with his wife (Lucinda Jenney) and requisite swarm of children, Kenny is asked to sign something by one of his sons. "This isn't a permission slip," he says. "This is yaw repaught cod..." It's hilarious. And certainly the last time you laugh at the movie.

On paper, it's Costner's film, because of his star power and the fact he's executive producer; in actuality, it's Greenwood's. But the balance is probably for the best, because the JFK of "Thirteen Days" becomes an even more remotely Olympian figure, tragic in retrospect, but thoroughly self-possessed in the maelstrom of '62. Donaldson has surrounded him with a first-rate cast—Dylan Baker as Robert McNamara, Frank Wood as McGeorge Bundy, Kevin Conway as a foaming-at-the-mouth Gen. Curtis LeMay and a terrific Len Cariou as ber-hawk Dean Acheson. ("Remember, the Kennedys' father was one of the architects of Munich. Let's hope appeasement doesn't run in families.")

The most ironic bit of casting has to be Chris Lawford, an actual Kennedy, as the Air Force commander who takes the photographs of Cuba's missile installation. But of course, when all is said and done, we hardly need any more irony than "Thirteen Days" already offers.

NEWSWEEK, 12/25/00-1/1/01, p. 76, David Ansen

My first reaction when I heard a movie was being made about the 1962 Cuban missile crisis was: why? Everyone knows the calamity was averted. Where's the suspense? I'm happy to say I was wrong. "Thirteen Days," a behind-closed-doors account of the nail-biting deliberations that went on inside the JFK White House, keeps you hanging on every twist and turn of its wilder-than-fiction plot.

It's an extraordinary tale of political brinkmanship played for the highest of stakes, as much about the infighting John Kennedy and his brother Bobby waged with the hawks in the military as it is about the game of dare and double dare being played with the Russians, who had planted nuclear missiles on Cuba that could have turned most of the country to dust.

Screenwriter David Self (who had access to White House tapes) does an admirable job of condensing these byzantine machinations into a charged two-and-a-half-hour film. His point of entry is presidential confidant Kenneth O'Donnell, played by Kevin Costner. Whether O'Donnell was as pivotal a figure as the movie suggests is open to historical debate. But it's not his story (and certainly not the unnecessary scenes with his wife and kids) that we come away remembering. It's the Kennedys, as usual, who steal the show—a brooding, cautious, canny JFK (Bruce Greenwood, a tad too stolid) and his brilliant, aggressive younger brother (Steven Culp), who must fend off the likes of trigger-happy Gen. Curtis LeMay (Kevin Conway) while trying to second-guess the cryptic messages coming from the Kremlin.

Director Roger Donaldson's film won't win any prizes for stylishness. It has a bland, textureless TV-movie look. But you will probably be too caught up in the drama to care. Ifs terrifying to realize how close we came in those 13 days to the nuclear edge, and sobering to contemplate how our newly elected president might navigate a crisis this dire.

SIGHT AND SOUND, 3/01, p. 60, Xan Brooks

October 1962. An American U-2 Spy plane over Cuba provides photographic evidence that the Soviet Union is planning long range nuclear-missile bases in Castro's Cuba. In Washington DC, President John F. Kennedy, attorney general Robert Kennedy and defence secretary Robert McNamara hunt a solution to the crisis. Aided by special assistant Kenny O'Donnell, the president seeks advice from those around him. On the one hand, he is urged towards air strikes by the militaristic officials from the Pentagon; on the other, towards a peaceful UN brokered solution by the liberal Adlai Stevenson.

Resisting pressure to launch air strikes, JFK decides to blockade Soviet supply ships currently heading towards Cuba. The ships turn back, but the Soviets still refuse to remove their missiles, which are now nearly operational. With the world on the brink of war, the Kennedy administration is approached in secret—through an intermediary—by Alexander Fomin, an old friend of Soviet leader Khrushchev, who is keen to broker a deal. Robert Kennedy meets with the Soviet ambassador. He privately promises that if the Soviets remove their missiles, the US will in turn dismantle its war-heads in Turkey within a six-month period. The crisis averted, Kennedy heads towards the mid-term elections.

The persistence of the Kennedy myth hinges on two key events: the 1962 Cuban missile crisis which earned the young president his spurs, and the 1963 assassination that made him a martyr. Having tackled the latter event in Oliver Stone's turbulent, paranoiac JFK (1991), Kevin Costner turns his attention to the, former in the rather more stolid Thirteen Days. This workmanlike political drama re-unites the actor with Roger Donaldson (his director on No Way Out, 1986) and casts him in the role of special assistant Kenny O'Donnell, a behind-the-scenes player prestigious enough to bully Jack and flirt with Jackie. While Donaldson's film is largely based on the book The Kennedy Tapes (edited by Ernest May and Philip Zelikow), David Self's script has inserted a human focal point. By and large, it is through O'Donnell's eyes that we view the crisis.

Costner's character may be something of a cipher (dry professional at work, loving dad at home), but his presence anchors the narrative and balances the political with the personal. Certainly Self deserves credit for the way he's ordered his brief. Thirteen Days is at once a historical re-enactment (true life figures introduced via on-screen captions), a backstage thriller (scurrying officials in smoke-filled rooms) and a portrait of a man (and, by definition, an administration) in crisis. Indeed, the film is at its most successful when mapping out the tensions between the moneyed, liberal intelligentsia encamped at Kennedy's White House and the gung-ho commie bashers over at the Pentagon.

Inevitably, though, *Thirteen Days* strays towards the airless, Madame-Tussaud's school of film making—and some of its waxworks are less convincing than others. The problem is simply that the Kennedy era has become so iconic, so endlessly documented as to remain to the fore of the public consciousness. Here, the viewer is forced towards a major imaginative leap in order to accept the physically dissimilar Bruce Greenwood's otherwise adequate impersonation of JFK. Ditto Michael Fairman as Democrat whipping-boy Adlai Stevenson. At the other end of the scale, Steven Culp proves an eerie deadringer as the bumptious Robert Kennedy, while Dylan Baker follows up his high-risk performance in Todd Solondz's *Happiness* with a pitch-perfect rendition of defence secretary Robert McNamara.

Of course, in focusing so intently on the White House, the film shelves a mass of other relevant material. *Thirteen Days* offers but fleeting glimpses of the outside world and little sense of the primary Soviet players (the Pentagon, it is suggested, is a bigger threat to world peace than Khrushchev). Yet while sceptics may scoff at *Thirteen Days'* depiction of a basically honourable JFK (no hookers or Mafiosi here), Self and Donaldson have coped well in hewing a manageable drama out of a historical monolith. For all its weighty resonance, this is essentially the tale of a cocky but inexperienced administration that suddenly found itself in hot water. Kennedy's White House, implies *Thirteen Days,* made the correct decisions during the Cuban missile crisis. By and large, the film's makers have too.

TIME, 12/25/00-1/1/00, p. 147, Richard Schickel

The interesting thing about life is that it does not come prepackaged in a three-act structure the way most movies do. It tends to lurch along like—oh, say, a disputed election in Florida. Take the Cuban missile crisis of 1962. Since we are all still here to savor this accurate reconstruction of those anguished days, we know everything came out all right in the end. But seen through the eyes of presidential aide Kenny O'Donnell (Costner), it is still a suspenseful tale. Well acted too, especially by Costner, and Greenwood as John F. Kennedy. The players don't particularly look like their historical models, but they make us feel their life-threatening pain and puzzlement.

VILLAGE VOICE, 12/19/00, p. 141, J. Hoberman

Galloping into the holiday season with a cloud of dust and a hearty "Hi-yo, Silver," *Thirteen Days* evokes a thrilling yesteryear of beehive hairdos, afternoon editions, and open-top limousines—when being president of the United States actually meant something. The veteran director Roger Donaldson and young screenwriter David Self have risen above their previous work to fashion a tense and engrossing political thriller from the transcripts of tapes made in the secretly bugged White House offices where John F. Kennedy and associates managed the potential Armageddon known as the Cuban missile crisis.

Although *Thirteen Days* runs nearly two and a half hours, it cuts immediately to the chase—October 16, 1962—with reconnaissance photographs of Soviet offensive weapons in Cuba hand-delivered to the president (Bruce Greenwood). Trusty aide Kenny O'Donnell (Kevin Costner) rushes from the warmth of his big Boston Irish family to the icy ramparts of the New Frontier: "I feel like we caught the Jap carrier steaming for Pearl Harbor" is his pithy summation. The Joint Chiefs argue for an immediate air strike to be followed by an invasion. Dredged up for advice, old Cold Warrior Dean Acheson (Len Cariou) agrees.

Thus, while figuring out how to confront the duplicitous Russians, JFK must simultaneously restrain his own military commanders. It's the suits against the brass as well as America versus the Communists. To avoid complicating this neat moral equation, *Thirteen Days* selectively obfuscates some extenuating facts. One is Kennedy's concern that Operation Mongoose, the administration's ongoing plot to terminate Fidel Castro in time for the midterm elections, remain secret; another is that CIA director John McCone had actually reported the presence of Soviet missiles in Cuba some two months before.

The Chiefs, on the other hand, exceeded Kennedy's orders to ratchet up American forces to DefCon Two, or a single step below nuclear war—a posture that the enraged JFK worries will "look like an attempted coup." With macho pilots flying low over Cuba and their commanders ranting about the rules of engagement, the situation could have easily gone out of control. Indeed, it is difficult to watch *Thirteen Days* without superimposing the *Dr. Strangelove* scenario. McNamara facing off against some crazed admiral in the war room gives a second meaning to the crisis's most celebrated sound bite, "We were eyeball to eyeball, and the other fellow just blinked."

Thirteen Days, which takes its title from Robert Kennedy's posthumously published account of the crisis, is pure existential drama. Played out largely around burnished wooden tables, the movie has aspects of high-level boardroom chicanery—but what corporate takeover can compare to this? (The week that JFK blockaded Cuba was a week, Norman Mailer later wrote, "when the world stood like a playing card on edge ...One looked at the buildings one passed and wondered if one was to see them again.") Going on television to invoke World War II to prepare the nation for World War III, Kennedy is shown as heroically cool and totally hands-on—the movie should only boost the polls that declare him the most popular of American presidents, surpassing even Ronald Reagan.

Greenwood's JFK and Steven Culp's Robert Kennedy have the appropriate body language, vocal inflections, and coiffures—as does Dylan Baker's secretary of defense, Robert McNamara. Villainy is provided by Olek Kupra's Lugosi-like Soviet envoy Andrei Gromyko and Kevin Conway's air force general Curtis LeMay, who openly taunts the president in his itchy eagerness to get "those red bastards." Heart, of course, is supplied by Costner. *Thirteen Days* puts the actor in brisk *Bodyguard* mode, but with the helpful dramatic crutch of an exotic accent. His hard-nosed op is nothing less than JFK's brain, stomach, and conscience—serving the quarterback in chief as a combination defensive lineman and cheerleader.

Costner's presence reinforces *Thirteen Days* as a sort of *JFK* prequel, while as the only real star in the wax museum, he provides a sort of friendly *Forrest Gump* effect. His Kenny is the fly on the wall who always sees what's really happening. He's the first to recognize that the Chiefs want war, the person the president dispatches to check on a potential back-channel overture, the only one who believes that Adlai Stevenson has the balls to stand up to the Russians at the UN. Vital to JFK's triangulation between hawks and doves, Stevenson (Michael Fairman) wryly calls himself a "coward" and reasonably proposes swapping the new Soviet missiles for obsolete U.S. rockets stationed in Turkey.

Although the Stevenson plan was ultimately employed, Camelot spinmeisters, including the president himself, wasted little time in casting him as an appeaser—one of the most horrific aspects of the missile crisis was that appearance was all. Given the nuclear-armed Soviet submarine fleet, missiles in Cuba did not appreciably change the balance of power—the Russians already had the capacity to reduce Washington to radioactive rubble. Moreover, despite the bogus "missile gap" that had propelled Kennedy to the presidency, America's nuclear capacity exceeded by tenfold that of the Soviets—perhaps the reason why the Russians never put their forces on military alert. (The movie downplays this for understandable dramatic reasons.)

Thirteen Days adds little to what is known about the missile crisis but subtracts quite a bit. The Cubans are barely a factor—although, according to Russian archival material published in 1997, Castro panicked and began agitating for a nuclear first strike. Soviet premier Nikita Khrushchev, the man who blundered into the crisis and who, more than anyone else, found a way to blunder out, is totally invisible. I also regret the omission of the final LeMay outburst: When the Chiefs were informed Khrushchev had agreed to remove the missiles, the general pounded the table and bellowed, "It's the greatest defeat in our history!..... We should invade today!" (McNamara remembered looking at JFK and noting that the shocked president was "stuttering in reply.")

Less comic than cautionary, *Thirteen Days* ends with the euphoric McNamara and McCone thinking about seizing the opportunity to "run the table" on Khrushchev in Vietnam. Did the successful resolution of the missile crisis pump up America for the disaster to come? The movie excludes Kennedy from this overconfidence. It was the actual O'Donnell, after all, who was most responsible for the unverifiable story—popularized by Oliver Stone, among others—that, once he was safely reelected in 1964, JFK planned to withdraw America totally from Vietnam.

Thirteen Days doesn't explain how the world came to the brink of nuclear war, only that it did... and that catastrophe was averted. But it is also a movie of its own moment. The TV docudrama *Missiles of October* was broadcast only four months after Richard Nixon's resignation and served a useful social purpose in rehabilitating the prestige of the American presidency. The timing of *Thirteen Days* is scarcely less uncanny, although the effect may not be so comforting—the film encourages the audience to ponder, if they dare, the spectacle of George W. Bush under pressure.

Also reviewed in:
CHICAGO TRIBUNE, 1/12/01, Friday/p. A, Michael Wilmington
NEW REPUBLIC, 1/29/01, p. 28, Stanley Kauffmann
NEW YORK TIMES, 12/25/00, p. E1, Elvis Mitchell
VARIETY, 12/4-10/00, p. 21, Todd McCarthy
WASHINGTON POST, 1/12/01, p. C1, Stephen Hunter
WASHINGTON POST, 1/12/01, Weekend/p. 57, Desson Howe

30 DAYS

An Arrow release of an Arielle Tepper/Araca Group production. *Producer:* Matthew Rego, Michael Rego, Arielle Tepper, and Hank Unger. *Director:* Aaron Harnick. *Screenplay:* Aaron Harnick. *Director of Photography:* David Tumblety. *Editor:* Sean Campbell. *Music:* Andrew Sherman and Stephen J. Walsh. *Sound:* Mike Woroniuk. *Casting:* Andra Reeve. *Production Designer:* Michael Fagin. *Costumes:* Juliet Polcsa. *Running time:* 87 minutes. *MPAA Rating:* Not Rated.

CAST: Ben Shenkman (Jordan Trainer); Arija Bareikis (Sarah Meyers); Alexander Chaplin (Mike Charles); Bradley White (Tad Star); Thomas McCarthy (Brad Drazin); Catherine Kellner (Lauren); Jerry Adler (Rick Trainer); Barbara Barrie (Barbara Trainer); Arden Myrin (Stacey); Mark Feuerstein (Actor); Lisa Edelstein (Danielle); Tina Holmes (Jenny); Matt W. Brooks (Party Guest); Meghan Strange (Maria).

NEW YORK POST, 9/15/00, p. 54, V. A. Musetto

Aaron Harnick suffers from a disease found much too often in starry-eyed young filmmakers: Woody envy—or the uncontrollable urge to make a Woody Allen movie.

This dumb flick opens with music and credits right out of something Allen might have done. There follows a plot that Allen has used countless times—the love troubles of a neurotic New York Jew.

The lead actor, a most annoying Ben Shenkman, is taller than Allen, but he employs (very badly) the same body language as Woody. For good measure, the cast includes Jerry Adler, who played the killer in Allen's "Manhattan Murder Mystery."

About the only thing not stolen from Woody are the shots of people sitting on the toilet. For those we have only Harnick to blame.

NEWSDAY, 9/15/00, Part II/p. B7, Jan Stuart

The New York City liquor shop the young protagonist of "30 Days" takes over from his parents boasts a nice old neon sign that is partially obscured by scaffolding. It's less than perfect, but it's what he knows. Like his trio of hangout buddies, it offers both the consolations and the antagonisms of the all-too-familiar.

Therein lies the urban reality of "30 Days," a perceptive but unmemorable comedy that follows the attempts of this befuddled and not terribly ambitious shopkeeper to romance a beautiful TV casting agent. Written and directed by Aaron Harnick (who played David Gold in "Judy Berlin"), the film seems to emulate this fits-and-starts romance in the on-again-off-again manner in which it engages our attentions.

As played by Ben Shenkman, Jordan Trainer is a well-meaning shnook who experiences the usual amount of commitment anxiety before zeroing in on Sarah Meyers (a Gwyneth Paltrow-redolent Arija Bareikis), the WASP blonde of his dreams. In between dates, he commiserates with his three buddies (Alexander Chaplin, Bradley White and Thomas McCarthy), all of whom are struggling through various stages of relationships.

As they trade barbs and insights, "30 Days" recalls the camaraderie of Barry Levinson's "Diner," minus that film's defining sense of style. There is a satirically broad ethnic bite to the film's at-home moments, suggesting that the filmmaker has also wallowed heavily in the Brooklyn-set oeuvre of Woody Allen.

Harnick elicits most of his laughs from bald one-liners and most of his emotion from musical interludes in which we are meant to feel sad for the hero as he shaves for no one in particular and chops ice from a freezer in sore need of defrosting. Jordan's pals are irritating in varying degrees, and their girlfriends are generally nondescript. The sharpest turn is delivered by the redoubtable Barbara Barrie (also of "Judy Berlin"), who deserves some sort of special award for her unswerving loyalty to neophyte film directors in need of surrogate screen mothers.

VILLAGE VOICE, 9/19/00, p. 120, Edward Crouse

After nibbling on Woody Allen zwieback in its opening credits (trad jazz, alphabetized cast list, white-on-black titles), 30 Days thuds away at the now familiar New York turf of Jews and their mating habits, throwing in a little early Fellini mama's-boyishness to complete the derivation. Struck in an anti-*Friends* mold, the film's damp yuppies (two sample names are Tad and Brad) become galvanized by the impending marriage of the most well-off couple among them. The chief nebbish, Jordan (Ben Shenkman), who still works in his parents' wine store, rubs his aching soul sore, feeling out his callow romantic condition through witless lines like "My idea of accomplishment is getting through *The New Yorker* in a month. 30 Days feels an awful lot like that month.

Also reviewed in:
NEW YORK TIMES, 9/15/00, p. E24, A. O. Scott
VARIETY, 11/8-14/99, p. 43, Eddie Cockrell

THIS IS NOT AN EXIT:THE FICTIONAL WORLD OF BRET EASTON ELLIS

A First Run Features release of a Marquee Film and Television production. *Producer:* Julian Ozanne. *Director:* Gerald Fox. *Director of Photography:* Richard Numeroff, Simon Fanthorpe, and Les Young. *Editor:* Tony Webb. *Music:* Stefan Girardet. *Sound:* Robert Briscoe, Greg Molesworth, Caleb Mose, Mario Mooney, and Tim Barker. Sound Editor: Julian MacDonald. *Running time:* 80 minutes. *MPAA Rating:* Not Rated.

CAST: Dechen Thurman (Patrick Bateman); Rachel Weisz (Lauren Hynde); Jason Bushman (Clay); Paul Blackthorne (Victor Ward); Marieclaire (Hollywood Housewife); Kelly Rogers (Evelyn); Noelle McCutchen (Blair); Natalie Avital (Anne); David Monahan (Hamlin); Michael Cavalier (Reeves); Huger Foote (MTV VJ); John Bryan (Clay's Father); Justine Melman (Junkie); Cory Travalena (Poolboy); Tamsin Pike and Vered Halkin (Girls); Casey Schacter (Muriel).

NEW YORK POST, 4/7/00, p. 56, Hannah Brown

"We're a celebrity-obsessed people," observes novelist Bret Easton Ellis, and nothing could prove his point better than the fact that he is the subject of a documentary, "This Is Not an Exit: The Fictional World of Bret Easton Ellis."

There isn't a single memorable thought or word uttered by Ellis or his admiring contemporaries in this film, which plays like an infomercial for reissue of the author's works.

Ellis, who burst onto the literary scene in 1985 with "Less Than Zero" and later gained notoriety with "American Psycho" is, at age 34, an unlikely subject for a film, because his life is already so exposed to press scrutiny, as well as being generally uneventful.

Praised by critics for his distinctive voice and success in capturing the alienation of drug-addled L.A. rich kids in "Less Than Zero," he was still an undergrad when that book came out and hit the bestseller list. But his career has been downhill from there.

In a series of interviews, Ellis displays a grating solipsism as he laments his bad reviews and other perceived mistreatment. He was, he says, "vilified" when his nightclub antics became gossip-column fodder.

The film also features what the press kit describes as "rare" interviews with his mother, high school teachers and friends, as well as a series of talking heads from the literary world who, annoyingly, are not identified.

The film ends with Ellis and two friends squealing in the back of a limousine on their way to a club—apparently, he's out to gather more material for a new, even more critical novel about his own life.

VILLAGE VOICE, 4/11/00, p. 162, Dennis Lim

A quickie release timed to coincide with the film version of *American Psycho*, *This Is Not an Exit*—subtitled *The Fictional World of Bret Easton Ellis* (why not *Me Myself I?*) and produced for British TV in 1998—is in fact the worst imaginable form of publicity for Mary Harron's already much beleaguered movie. Bret reads from his books—poolside, as if for the first time—while the camera zooms in for a close-up of his mouth; Bret discusses his formative years (words like *alienation* and *aloneness* feature prominently)—Bret runs the gamut of pretentious-celebrity-brat doublespeak, from false modesty to righteous victimhood. The dramatizations of passages from Ellis's novels—with a "cast" that includes Rachel Weisz, Dechen Thurman as Patrick Bateman, and for no reason at all, John Bryan, the man known exclusively for sucking Fergie's toes—have an airless, tone-deaf, brain-dead quality that may or may not be intentional.

Also reviewed in:
NEW YORK TIMES, 4/7/00, p. E 32, Lawrence Van Gelder

THOMAS AND THE MAGIC RAILROAD

A Destination Films and Gullane Pictures, Barry London/Brent Baum release of a Britt Allcroft film in association with The Isle of Man Film Commission. *Executive Producer:* Steve Stabler, Charles Falzon, Nancy Chapelle, Barry London, Brent Baum, and John Bertoli. *Producer:* Britt Allcroft and Phil Fehrle. *Director:* Britt Allcroft. *Screenplay:* Britt Allcroft. *Story:* Britt Allcroft. *Based on the "Railway Series" by:* W. Awdry. *Director of Photography:* Paul Ryan. *Editor:* Ron Wisman. *Music:* Hummie Mann. *Music Editor:* Yuri Gorbachow. *Choreographer:* Christine Wild. *Sound:* Nelson Ferreira and (music) David Greene. *Casting:* Karen Margiotta and Mary Margiotta. *Production Designer:* Oleg M. Savytski. *Set Designer:* Gordon White. *Set Decorator:* Cheryl Dorsey and Caroline Gee. *Special Effects:* Peter Hutchinson and David Eves. *Costumes:* Luis M. Sequeira *Make-up:* Kathleen Graham. *Stunt Coordinator:* Dave van Zeyl and Chris Lamon. *Running time:* 89 minutes. *MPAA Rating:* G.

CAST: Peter Fonda (Grandpa Burnett Stone); Mara Wilson (Lily); Alec Baldwin (Mr. Conductor); Didi Conn (Stacy); Michael E. Rodgers (Mr. C. Junior); Cody McMains (Patch); Russell Means (Billy Twofeathers); Jared Wall (Young Burnett Stone); Laura Bower (Young Tasha); Eddie Glen (Voice of Thomas); Neil Crone (Voice of Diesel 10); Colm Feore (Voice of Toby); Linda Ballantyne (Voice of Percy); Neil Crone (Voice of Splatter and Gordon); Kevin Frank (Voice of Dodge); Susan Roman (Voice of James); Kevin Frank (Voice of Henry/Bertie/Harold); Shelley Elizabeth Skinner (Annie/Clarabels); Britt Allcroft (Lady).

LOS ANGELES TIMES, 7/26/00, Calendar/p. 5, Gene Seymour

[The following review by Gene Seymour appeared in a slightly different form in
NEWSDAY, 11/22/97, Part II/p. B19.]

To those age 5 and under for whom "Thomas and the Magic Railroad" will be the first theatrical movie, the following words of encouragement are offered: It gets better. Bigger anyway, for sure. The stories will make more sense. The acting will improve. And no one will try to put anything over on you on the big screen.

All right, that last sentence is a lie. But it's as harmless as "Thomas and the Magic Railroad."

Admittedly, one begrudges the sweet wholesomeness of the whole Thomas the Tank Engine universe at one's peril, especially given the emphasis it places on the values of cooperation, imagination and—how do the steam engines of Sodor put it?—usefulness. Is that really a word? Better you should ask whether Sodor is a real place. Or, for those with no wee ones at home, what Sodor is.

As millions of PBS viewers can tell you, Sodor is a magical island mostly inhabited by means of transportation that talk without moving their lips. Prominent among the many steam engines hauling freight along Sodor's tracks is Thomas, a sweet-natured little blue engine that could—and often does.

Other engines on the island—gruff Gordon, persnickety Percy and jittery James—aren't as nice as Thomas. But none is as mean as Diesel, who wants to chomp all the steam engines into scrap metal so he can rule the rails unencumbered by the slower steamers.

Only Mr. Conductor (Alec Baldwin) can keep Diesel in line, so to speak. But the jaunty, whistle-blowing master of the mystic arts finds his gold-dust mojo on the blink and can't even make the normally easy transit from Sodor to the relative reality of Shining Time Station.

What's wrong? Apparently, it has something to do with the deep, dark funk of Burnett Stone (Peter Fonda), a hermit hiding out in a mountain with a no-longer-enchanted engine called Lady. His granddaughter Lily (Mara Wilson) tries, sort of, to get him out of his melancholy stupor and save Sodor from Diesel.

Baldwin looks like he's having a lot of fun, while Fonda looks like he's having a slow-motion stroke. It's good to see, however briefly, Didi Conn, reprising her TV role as Shining Time stationmaster Stacy Jones. (But where's Schemer?)

Britt Allcroft deserves all the honors she's received over the years for cultivating Thomas' archives. But as the writer-director of "Magic Railroad"—which blends live action, digital effects and animation—she lays thick, goopy layers of uplift on what should (one would think) be lighter on the heart and stomach.

NEW YORK POST, 7/26/00, p. 57, Lou Lumenick

Usually, it's possible to pinpoint when a movie starts going off the track, but this train-wreck of a "family" movie is skin-crawlingly awful as soon as it leaves the station.

Even very young children at the screening I attended were squirming in their seats at this pathetic attempt at dragging out the popular half-hour kiddie TV show "Shining Time Station" to feature length.

The adults looked like they'd rather be having their teeth drilled.

This is such a cheap-looking affair that Thomas the Tank Engine and the other locomotives who talk with British accents still don't move their lips—and the out-of-focus backgrounds the model trains are photographed on are downright annoying on a big screen.

Even more depressing is the spectacle of one-time Hollywood A-lister Alec Baldwin, reduced to playing the 18-inch Mr. Conductor, who uses gold dust to travel between Shining Time Station and Sodor, the land of talking trains.

Mr. C. exhausts his supply of gold dust just as Evil Diesel and his sidekicks Splatter and Dodge are planning to scrap the steam engines.

It's Thomas to the rescue—with help from Lily (Mara Wilson of "Miracle on 34th Street") and her grandpa Burnett (Peter Fonda), who get a long-lost engine going with some magic coal and enough aphorisms to propel a season of "Shining Time Station."

Baldwin, in a role that the far more suitable Ringo Starr and George Carlin played on TV, takes it way too seriously—the acting-family scion doesn't even break even a tiny smile when he reads the movie's funniest (unintentionally) line, "My family is pretty good at getting themselves out of trouble."

Fonda, whose choice of this film is equally inexplicable (he was Oscar nominated for "Ulee's Gold" just last year), doesn't take it seriously enough—in some scenes, he doesn't even deign to look at the actors he's allegedly addressing.

Writer-director Britt Allcroft, who has turned an obscure 1940s children's story into a cottage industry, has turned this quintessential British bit of whimsy into an Anglo-American mishmash, complete with some of the ghastliest children's songs since the Smurfs took early retirement.

The makers of the upcoming Harry Potter movie should be forced to watch "Thomas and the Magic Railroad" as an object lesson in what to avoid.

SIGHT AND SOUND, 9/00, p. 54, Edward Lawrenson

Thomas and his fellow steam engines live in Sodor, a magical place where locomotives speak to one another. Mr Conductor, whose supply of gold dust allows him to visit the village of Shining Town in the real world, is keeping his eye on Diesel, an evil train who has vowed to destroy a locomotive which went missing some time ago and is said to provide a link between Sodor and Shining Time. Realising his supply of gold dust is running out—and the magic of Sodor fading—Mr Conductor calls on his cousin, Junior, for help.

Lily, a young girl, goes to Muffle Mountain to visit her grandfather Burnett, a morose widower who spends his time trying to repair a locomotive called Lady. Lily befriends Patch, a local boy, who takes her to Shining Time.

Thomas discovers the entrance to a magic railroad which runs from Sodor to Shining Time. Lily encounters Junior, who uses his gold dust to take her to Sodor. Diesel kidnaps Junior; Mr Conductor, meanwhile, realises that Lady is the train which can link Sodor with Shining Time. Carrying Lily, Thomas rides to Shining Time via the newly discovered magic railroad. With the coal Thomas was carrying, Burnett stokes Lady up and rides to Sodor with Lily and Patch. Junior uses the last of his gold dust to escape from Diesel, who subsequently falls down a ravine and is carried away by a passing barge. Mr Conductor makes some gold dust from the embers of Lady's fire. The magic of Sodor is restored.

Originally written for his son Christopher, Rev. W. Awdry's Sodor railway books were disarming tales about talking steam engines. Published just as the age of steam travel was coming to an end, Awdry's stories were imbued with a certain nostalgia: his locomotives had happy, soot-free faces and childlike personalities and were run by kindly railway bosses. Writer director Britt Allcroft maintains much of this affection for steam trains in her debut film *Thomas and the Magic Railroad*. The live-action sequences—set in the rural idyll of Shining Time—contain some pretty shots of a restored locomotive, polished, fired up and charging along a stretch of railway as if on its maiden journey. And like the television series *Thomas the Tank Engine and Friends,* which Allcroft produced, the scenes depicting Thomas and his fellow locomotives are staged with models on what seems to be a vast toy train set. While there's a beguiling naivety to the model trains and surrounding landscape—the engines discharge ice-cream-white wisps of smoke; delicate bonsai-like trees line the diminutive railway—there's crudeness here, too. Given the level of CGI-fuelled sophistication at play in such films as *Stuart Little,* young audiences might be disappointed: the expressions on the faces of the trains, for instance, change only between cuts and their lips remain closed while delivering their lines. Gone too are the wonderfully onomatopoeic rhythms of Awdry's dialogue ("Pull harder, pull harder," the catty engine Gordon exhorts Thomas in one of Awdry's tales).

But Allcroft's biggest mistake is to portray Sodor as magical and distinct from a world that is recognisably real. In Awdry's stories, the idea the trains talked went unremarked by the passengers who travelled on them (in *Thomas's Train* for instance, they even forgive Thomas for being late because he's upset). Here, the steam engines seem to exist in a parallel world. Not only are the connections between Sodor and Shining Time half-hatched—a horribly tortuous plot is a massive flaw in any film intended for easily distracted kids—Allcroft's script is drenched in saccharine sentiment. Hailing from this charmed, unreal place, Thomas is able to bring grieving grandfather Burnett out of his shell and teach everyone that "helping each other brings alive the magic in all of us." Allcroft also relies heavily on other-worldly occurrences to advance her story—a rabbit, for instance, leaves clues for Alec Baldwin's conductor on where to find more gold dust—but these soon feel less like flights of fancy than expedient plot devices. At one point, after being thrown high into the air and landing on conveniently placed bags of flour, Baldwin winks at the audience. "What a perfect landing," he says. This might be a game attempt to acknowledge the inherent nonsense on screen, but if so, it comes too late. *Thomas and the Magic Railroad* derails soon after the opening credits; the rest is an inglorious wreck of a movie.

Also reviewed in:
CHICAGO TRIBUNE, 7/26/00, Tempo/p. 2, Monica Eng
NEW YORK TIMES, 7/26/00, p. E3, Elvis Mitchell
VARIETY, 7/24-30/00, p. 47, Derek Elley
WASHINGTON POST, 7/26/00, p. C5, Rita Kempley
WASHINGTON POST, 7/28/00, Weekend/p. 37, Desson Howe

3 STRIKES

A Metro Goldwyn Mayer release of an Absolute Entertainment/Motion Picture Corporation of America production in association with Lithium Entertainment Group. *Executive Producer:* Julio Caro, Benny Medina, and Brad Krevoy. *Producer:* Marcus Morton. *Director:* D. J. Pooh. *Screenplay:* D. J. Pooh. *Director of Photography:* John W. Simmons. *Editor:* John Carter. *Music:* Aaron Anderson and Andrew Shack. *Music Editor:* Jay Bolton. *Sound:* David M. Kelson. *Sound Editor:* Rod O'Brien. *Casting:* Kim Williams. *Production Designer:* Thomas Fichter. *Art Director:* Amina Allean Dieye. *Set Designer:* Charlotte Beck Taylor. *Set Decorator:* Natali Pope. *Set Dresser:* Meredith McCarthy, Yukion Frierson, Richard Ponder, and Brandon James. *Special Effects:* Dennis Petersen. *Costumes:* Tracey White. *Make-up:* Merc Arceneaux. *Stunt Coordinator:* William Washington. *Running time:* 83 minutes. *MPAA Rating:* R.

CAST: Brian Hooks (Rob); N'Bushe Wright (Juanita); Faizon Love (Tone); E40 (Mike); Starletta DuPois (Moms); George Wallace (Pops); David Alan Grier (Jenkins); Dean Norris (Officer Roberts); Barima McKnight (Blue); Meagan Good (Buela); Mo'nique (Dahlia); De'Aundre Bonds (J. J.); Antonio Fargas (Uncle Jim); Harmonica Fats (Grandpa); Mike Epps (Dee); Kurt "Big Boy" Alexander (Dre); Angela Wright (Joaney); Vincent Schiavelli (Cortino); Phil Morris (Mr. Libowitz); Jerry Dunphy (Himself); D. J. Pooh (Trick Turner); John Verea (Saldamo); Richard Fancy (Captain); David Leisure (District Attorney); Gerald O'Loughlin (Judge); Dennis Howard (Governor); Shawn Fonteno (Big Mo); Rashaan Nall (T-Bird); Yolanda Whitaker (Charita); Melanie Comarcho (Woman in Police Station); Angela Tracy (Fly Female); Bennet Guillory (Stan Wilson); D. J. Pooh and Marcus Morton (Taxi Drivers) Michele Maika (Hotel Concierge); Rod Garr (Hospital Guard); Lydell Cheshier (Orderly); Regino Montes (Old Man); Jeffrey Garcia (Valet); Bruce Fairburn, Kevin Finn, and Terence Winter (Patrol Officers); Christel Cottrell (Receptionist); Jascha Washington (Little Boy); Darreck D. Burns (Barber); King T (Liquor Store Thug).

LOS ANGELES TIMES, 3/3/00, Calendar/p. 10, Eric Harrison

[The following review by Eric Harrison appeared in a slightly different form in **NEWSDAY, 3/4/00, Part II/p. B8.]**

Yo, word up, dog. Disjoint whacked, ni...oops. Sorry. But I just saw the new rap-flavored comedy, "3 Strikes," and it takes a while for the experience to wear off. Until it does, I won't be fit for company.

This is the latest attempt by the bad boyz of hip-hop to transfer the gangsta-rap sensibility to celluloid. On that count, this movie would have to be considered a success. It's all here—gangsta rap's lewdness, the loudness, the violence, the oafish displays of self-loathing masquerading as cultural celebration. It's perfect.

The bad news is that it's also vile, not to mention sophomoric and unfunny.

Rob Douglas (Brian Hooks) is a dim but good-natured young thug imprisoned for an unspecified crime who finds himself immediately in trouble upon his release. A friend driving a stolen car picks him up from prison, then gets into a gunfight with the police.

Doug must avoid capture at all costs because he's already been convicted of two felonies. Under California's three-strikes law, he could be sentenced to life in prison if he's convicted again. Gang members also are out to get him for running away instead of staying to shoot it out with the cops.

It isn't a problem that the movie—which opened but wasn't screened for the press—depicts a casually amoral universe in which pathology is the norm and decency is unknown. That sounds like half the movies coming out of Hollywood.

But the uniformly lazy, shuffling, bellowing, brawling, stealing, oversexed, pot-smoking or alcoholic black characters who populate this movie's universe are easily as offensive as the movie stereotypes that proliferated in the pre-Civil Rights era. "3 Strikes" even has Amos 'n' Andy-style eyeball popping and double takes.

And the soundtrack song titles sound like something the Ku Klux Klan dreamed up to insult black people. "Where Dey At" is one song. "Where Da Paper At" is another.

Rappers like to say that their work merely describes life as they know it—they're chronicling the thug life, not glorifying it. And writer-director D.J. Pooh, an ex-rapper-music producer who co-wrote Ice Cube's "Friday" movie, describes "3 Strikes" in interviews as a comic critique of the judicial system.

But in movies like this, and Cube's "Player's Club" and "Friday" comedies as well as hard-core films such as "Belly" (1998), what they're really doing is draining their black characters of their humanity (turning them into monsters or buffoons) and then presenting them to audiences as representations of authentic black experience.

What's troubling is that the target audiences tend to be young people who either 1) see just enough of their own lives reflected in these movies to think the characters are fit for emulation or 2) know nothing about the lives of black folk and so walk away thinking they've been educated.

In the midst of the uproar over the paucity of nonwhite characters on television, the movies have been experiencing a mini-boom of low-budget, black-themed movies, many of them directed by, produced by or starring rappers. But I'd take invisibility over the demeaning portrayals in these movies any day.

NEW YORK POST, 3/2/00, p. 46, Jonathan Foreman

As contemporary blaxploitation comedies go, "3 Strikes" is relatively inoffensive—apart from its use of the word "nigger" in almost every line of dialogue.

The movie's crime is that it's butt-numbingly dull and almost entirely laugh-free—despite the usual complement of fart jokes, horny fat-girl jokes, etc.—thanks to a combination of bad writing, slack direction and a colorless lead performance by star Brian Hooks.

"3 Strikes" is written and directed by rap impresario D.J. Pooh—who co-wrote the hit "Friday." It tells the predictable tale of Robert Douglas (Hooks), a decent-enough fellow who has just finished serving a sentence in L.A. County jail on his second felony conviction. In the knowledge that a third strike will carry an automatic 25-year sentence, Robert has resolved to go straight.

However, when JJ (De'Aundre Bonds), a friend of a friend, picks him up from jail, it's in a stolen car. And when the highway patrol pulls them over, JJ opens fire on the cops. JJ is wounded in the buttocks and captured in the ensuing shootout; Robert escapes and gets home on foot.

Robert tries to keep the incident a secret from his family and his girlfriend, Juanita (N'Bushe Wright), but thanks to JJ's treachery, Robert's face is soon all over the TV and the cops are looking for him, led by Lt. Jenkins (David Alan Grier, whose lively competence shows up the rest of the cast).

Instead of running away, Robert takes Juanita to a fancy hotel for the night. The move keeps him out of the cops' hands just long enough for a means of clearing himself to fall into his lap.

But Robert will first have to make it to the sanctuary of the AME Church without getting shot by the police.

Antonio Fargas, who played "Huggy Bear" in the '70s TV series "Starsky and Hutch" plays Robert's flatulent Uncle Jim.

Also reviewed in:
CHICAGO TRIBUNE, 3/7/00, Tempo/p. 3, John Petrakis
NEW YORK TIMES, 3/2/00, p. E5, A. O. Scott
VARIETY, 3/6-12/00, p. 34, Joe Leydon

THRONE OF DEATH

A Flying Elephant Films release. *Producer:* Murali Nair. *Director:* Murali Nair. *Screenplay (Malayam with English subtitles):* Murali Nair and Bharathan Njarakkal. *Based on a story by:* Murali Nair. *Director of Photography:* M.J. Radhakrishnan. *Editor:* Lalitha Krishna. *Music:* Madhu Apsara. *Production Designer:* Preeya Nair. *Art Director:* Saji Varkala. *Running time:* 57 minutes. *MPAA Rating:* Not Rated.

WITH: Vishwas Njarakkal (Krishnan); Lakshmi Raman (Krishnan's Wife); Suhas Thayat (Politician); Jeevan Mitva (Krishnan's Son).

NEW YORK POST, 4/26/00, p. 50, Hannah Brown

"Throne of Death," one of two films from the Third World is an example of the kind of heavy-handed, sledge-hammer irony that somehow passes for sophisticated satire when it treats politically correct themes.

A father, Krishnan (Vishwas Njarakkal) is caught stealing coconuts from the trees of the rich landowner on whose estate he and his family live, and he is arrested.

The corrupt legal system accuses and convicts him (though there is no evidence against him) of every unsolved crime in the district, including a murder, and sentences him to death.

His wife appeals to local Communist politicians for help—and the pols turn Krishnan into a cause celebre.

But when they fail to win his freedom, they demand that he be the first prisoner in India put to death in the "electronic chair," an electric chair modeled on those used in America.

The chair is brought to the remote village with great fanfare, accompanied by a government minister. Everyone, including Krishnan and his family, is ecstatic.

The characters are utterly lacking in individuality, and it's impossible to be moved by this Mad-magazine-style critique of corruption and cultural imperialism.

Far more affecting is the companion film on the double bill, "The Little Girl Who Sold the Sun," a joyous modern fable from Senegal.

Dedicated to "the courage of the street children," it's the story of a young girl on crutches who ekes out a living begging on the streets of Dakar.

Lissa Balera gives an outstanding performance as the girl, so full of strength and genuine charisma that she is a joy to watch. This triumphant effort was the last film by acclaimed Senegalese director Djibril Diop Mambety, who died in 1998, just after completing it.

With its light-hearted tone, exuberant score by Wasis Diop and stunning lead performance, "The Little Girl Who Sold the Sun" gives an inspiring, even poetic, glimpse at the children at the bottom of the heap in a Third World city.

VILLAGE VOICE, 5/2/00, p. 125, J. Hoberman

[*Throne of Death* was reviewed jointly with *The Little Girl Who Sold the Sun*; see Hoberman's review of that film.]

Also reviewed in:
NEW YORK TIMES, 4/26/00, p. E5, Stephen Holden
VARIETY, 6/7-13/99, p. 31, David Stratton

TIC CODE, THE

An Avalanche Releasing release of a Gun For Hire Films production in association with Jazz Films, Inc. *Executive Producer:* Steven Sherman. *Producer:* Polly Draper and Sarah Pillsbury. *Director:* Gary Winick. *Screenplay:* Polly Draper. *Director of Photography:* Wolfgang Held. *Editor:* Bill Pankow, Kate Sanford, and Henk Van Eeghen. *Music:* David R. Barkley and Michael Wolff. *Music Editor:* Carl Zittrer. *Sound:* Brian Miksis and (music) Dan Wallin. *Sound Editor:* Peter Austin. *Casting:* Sheila Jaffe and Georgianne Walken. *Production Designer:* Rick Butler. *Art Director:* Darryl Glanious. *Set Decorator:* Catherine Pierson. *Special Effects:* Wilfred Caban. *Costumes:* Karen Perry. *Make-up:* Jennifer Aspinall. *Stunt Coordinator:* Douglas Crosby. *Running time:* 90 minutes. *MPAA Rating:* R.

CAST: Gregory Hines (Tyrone); Polly Draper (Laura); Christopher George Marquette (Miles); Desmond Robertson (Todd); Carlos McKinney (Chester); Richard A. Berk (Dick); John B. Williams (Spanky); Tony Shalhoub (Phil); Robert Iler (Denny); Bill Nunn (Kingston); Fisher Stevens (Morris); James McCaffery (Michael); Allison Nurse (Leilani); Peter Appel (Engineer); Carol Kane (Miss Gimpole); Pat Moya (Belinda); Ismail Bashey (Indian Man); David Johansen (Marvin); Camryn Manheim (Mrs. Swensrut); Blair Ashlee Swanson (Confident Girl); Michael Wolff (Engineer 2).

LOS ANGELES TIMES, 9/4/00, Calendar/p. 10, Kevin Thomas

"The Tic Code" is one of the toughest kinds of movies to make—those intended to enlighten the public about an often misunderstood physical affliction.

The trick, of course, is to get the message across through an involving drama. This film, which deals with the neurological disorder Tourette's syndrome, starts out self-consciously but gets better as it goes along, winding up as affecting as it is illuminating.

Christopher George Marquette's Miles is an adolescent jazz piano prodigy, a personable boy living with his divorced mother Laura (Polly Draper) in a modest Greenwich Village apartment. She supports them working as a seamstress—a profession that's a tad too heart-tugging, summoning images of early silent melodrama.

They live near the Village Vanguard, where Miles hangs out much of the time and where he meets Tyrone (Gregory Hines), a saxophonist with whom he bonds, through their passion for jazz and their disorder. Tyrone has a milder form of Tourette's than does Miles, who is given to irregular and involuntary eye blinks, shakes, twists and sometimes sounds. Even so, his is not an extreme case, and for both Miles and Tyrone their syndrome retreats when they are performing.

Miles has a staunch, protective friend in a neighbor boy and classmate, Todd (Desmond Robertson), but is nevertheless targeted by a bully, who is amusingly defused by Tyrone in a sequence that gives the film its name. (Miles must also cope with his well-meaning but rigid music teacher, played in uptight fashion by Carol Kane.)

Laura is a conscientious mother, loving but not smotheringly protective. Her biggest challenge is in trying to convince Miles that her ex-husband, a hugely successful movie composer (James McCaffery), has not left them because of his son's Tourette's.

There may be other factors in the couple's breakup, but clearly the father neglects the son, sees him rarely and acts like a complete jerk when he does show up.

The film begins to kick in when an understandable attraction develops between Tyrone and Laura, but complications swiftly arise. Laura rightly believes that talking freely about Tourette's and the challenges it presents is the best way for Miles to keep it in proportion; Miles certainly has lots going for him in regard to his personality, intellect and talent.

The trouble is that Tyrone deals with his Tourette's by refusing to talk about it. He sees himself as a weirdo and believes that the sooner Miles accepts that he is one, too, the better off he will be. This outrages Laura, which does no good for her and Tyrone's burgeoning romance.

"The Tic Code" swiftly becomes complex and emotion-charged, increasing its credibility and involvement and revealing that Laura is after all only human and can give way to the strain of raising a Tourette's child.

There are some stabs at humor that seem all too obviously contrived to offset the film's seriousness—the moments that are genuinely funny grow out of everyday life—but by and large "The Tic Code," well directed by Gary Winick, rings true.

This is not surprising, for Draper, who also wrote the script, is married to jazz recording artist Michael Wolff—it is his music, played by Alex Foster, you are hearing when Tyrone plays his sax—and Wolff suffers from a mild form of Tourette's. Tyrone and Miles' relationship is based on that of Wolff and his young cousin, an instance of an older person learning to cope with a condition from a younger person.

Draper and young Marquette are persuasive, but it is Hines' star charisma and his sensitively nuanced portrayal that makes the film come alive and glow.

It took Draper five years to get her handsomely produced film made, and for her husband, best known for his stint as bandleader on "The Arsenio Hall Show," it marked the first time he ever talked about Tourette's with another person with the syndrome. "The Tic Code" is a worthy reward for her efforts.

NEW YORK POST, 8/4/00, p. 52, Hannah Brown

The story of an 11-year-old jazz prodigy with Tourette's Syndrome, "The Tic Code" sounds bleak, but turns out to be an absorbing and lively film.

Raising it above the usual clichés are the superb jazz music and a sparkling script by lead actress Polly Draper, a regular on the erstwhile TV series "thirtysomething. "

Draper understands how kids and parents really sound and has firsthand knowledge of the jazz scene—since she's married to co-producer Michael Wolff, a jazz musician who suffers from Tourette's Syndrome. He also wrote the score.

Despite stereotypes, most Tourette's sufferers do not curse uncontrollably, but like "Tic Code" hero Miles (Christopher George Marquette), they make involuntary facial and hand movements.

Miles, a gifted jazz pianist, lives with his mother, Laura (Draper), a tailor, in Greenwich Village. His musician father, has left, partly ashamed of Miles' disorder.

Because they're too poor for a piano, Miles hangs out at the Village Vanguard, where he meets one of his idols, saxophonist Tyrone Pike (Gregory Hines), who also happens to have Tourette's. He befriends Miles and starts a romance with shy Laura.

Things come to a crisis point when Miles' father makes a brief visit to New York.

The extraordinary Marquette makes Miles' shame and anger at his uncontrollable grimaces so real and intense that "The Tic Code" is painful at times.

Hines has never been more relaxed, likable or sexy.

Draper's triumph as screenwriter is that so much of "Tic Code" is funny. Particularly witty is the title scene, where Hines tells a teasing kid that the tics are all part of a top-secret CIA code.

NEWSDAY, 8/4/00, Part II/p. B11, Jan Stuart

Rare is the drama that credibly depicts New York's jazz world; rarer still is the film that attempts to put a human face on the misunderstood neurological disorder known as Tourette Syndrome. Director Gary Winick and actress/writer Polly Draper have not only succeeded in blending the two with authority and nuance, they have risked upping the ante with interracial romance and adolescent angst.

The risk pays off. "The Tic Code" is the summer's surprise gift, a loving and humane film that rises above the season's over-hyped blockbusters like a flower poking up through the concrete.

"The Tic Code" is dominated by Christopher George Marquette, a remarkable young actor who is able to play precocious without slipping into obnoxious. Marquette is a wonder as Miles, a 12-year- old jazz-piano prodigy whose Tourette symptoms (uncontrollable jerks of the head) are a perpetual source of misery. Rejected by his estranged father and bullied at school, Miles finds solace hanging out with the jocular denizens of the Village Vanguard jazz club during the day.

His mother Laura's (Draper) attempts to lift the boy's self- image include hooking him up with a renowned sax player, Tyrone Pike (Gregory Hines), who also has Tourette Syndrome. As a relationship unexpectedly heats up between Laura and Tyrone, it becomes clear that the musician's shame over his condition makes him a turbulent]over and a less than ideal role model for Miles.

If the arc of Laura and Tyrone's romance is fairly predictable, it is made fresh by the rich infusion of jazz-world detail: the coffee-shop camaraderie of the musicians; the sardine-tight, smoke-filled sets at the Vanguard; the contentious recording sessions. Draper and Hines get as naked as we've seen them: Their need is so transparent—and the film's empathy so all-embracing-you don't know who to ache for first.

Draper would appear to have learned some lessons about crafting cogent dialogue from her days tooling scripts for TV's "thirtysomething." A subtle interchange in which Miles catches his mother out in a moment of double-standard racism exemplifies the sort of knowing edge that lifts her screenplay several notches above your average disease-of-the-week flick. The only cliche she succumbs to is the belabored notion that school bullies are fat. That "The Tic Code" has enough heart for even the fat bullies of the world reveals a generosity of spirit potent enough to transcend its own formulaic impulses.

The film's R rating is an affront. Alienated adolescents of all stripes should be able to glean its lessons in compassion and self-worth without having their hands held by an adult.

VILLAGE VOICE, 8/8/00, p. 125, Amy Taubin

Gary Winick's *The Tic Code* is a sympathetic but conventional disease-of-the-week movie about a 12-year-old jazz piano prodigy who suffers from Tourette's syndrome, an incurable neurological disorder that manifests itself in facial and body tics, loud hiccup-like sounds, and sometimes, in its advanced stages, uncontrollable, unmotivated outbursts of obscenities.

Deserted by his jazz musician father, who regards him as a freak, Miles (Christopher George Marquette) lives alone with his mother, Laura (Polly Draper, who also wrote the screenplay). In the afternoons Miles practices on the piano at the Village Vanguard, which is where he meets one of his idols, trumpet player Tyrone Pike (Gregory Hines), who's also afflicted with Tourette's. Tyrone and Laura get romantically involved, but his long-standing strategy of denying his Tourette's becomes a problem in their relationship.

Marquette handles the technical difficulties of his role with aplomb if not with absolute consistency (it's hard enough to act like a musical prodigy, let alone one with Tourette's), Draper is quite moving as a protective single mother who's insecure about her sexual allure, and Hines, despite his tendency to play to the balcony (he doesn't just walk out of a room, he makes an exit), convinces us that he's the right man for this family. The music by Michael Wolff, who is married to Draper and has a mild case of Tourette's, is not sufficiently distinguished to make us believe that either Tyrone or Miles is the jazz great he's supposed to be.

Also reviewed in:
CHICAGO TRIBUNE, 9/1/00, Friday/p. N, John Petrakis
NEW YORK TIMES, 8/4/00, p. E28, Stephen Holden
VARIETY, 3/22-28/99, p. 41, Ken Eisnor

TIGERLAND

A 20th Century Fox release of a Regency Enterprises presentation of a Haft Entertainment/New Regency production. *Executive Producer:* Ted Kurdyla. *Producer:* Arnon Milchan, Steven Haft, and Beau Flynn. *Director:* Joel Schumacher. *Screenplay:* Ross Klavan and Michael McGruther. *Director of Photography:* Matthew Libatique. *Editor:* Mark Stevens. *Music:* Nathan Larson. *Music Editor:* Denis Okimoto. *Sound:* Jay Meagher and (music) Carl Glanville.

Sound Editor: Paul Curtis.   *Casting:* Mali Finn and Emily Schweber.   *Production Designer:* Andrew Laws.   *Set Decorator:* Shawn R. McFall.   *Set Dresser:* Michael E. Hendrick, Dan Wilkerson, and Michael Fitzgerald.   *Special Effects:* Kevin Harris.   *Costumes:* Linda Gennerich.   *Make-up:* Rodger Jacobs.   *Stunt Coordinator:* Phil Neilson.   *Running time:* 110 minutes.   *MPAA Rating:* R.

CAST: Arian Ash (Sheri);   Haven Gaston (Claudia);   Nick Searcy (Captain Saunders);   Michael Shannon (Training Sergeant Gilmore);   Afemo Omilami (Sergeant Landers);   James McDonald (Sergeant Thomas);   Carl Hauser (Sergeant Cota, NCO);   Neil Brown (Keams);   Tory Kittles (Ryan);   Rhynell Brumfield (Dickson);   Chris Huvane (Barnes);   Shamari Lewis (Lukins);   Dane Northcutt (Hicks);   Thomas Guiry (Cantwell);   Russell Richardson (Johnson);   Clifton Collins, Jr. (Miter);   Shea Whigham (Wilson); Matthew Davis (Jim Paxton);   Colin Farrell (Roland Bozz);   Keith Ewell (Sergeant Oakes);   Matt Gerald (Sergeant Eveland); Stephen Fulton (Sergeant Drake);   Tyler Cravens (Sergeant MP);   Michael Edmiston (Hit the Break Driver);   Roger Floyd (Killed Truck Driver);   Ronnie Schafer (Bartender);   Frances Taylor (Bargirl);   Matt White (Sniffling Soldier);   Christy McKee and Karolyn Arnold (Hookers); James Lessick, Jr. (Hobo Vet);   Daniel Martin (Range Officer);   Marc MacCaulay (Tigerland CO);   Nubia (Girl with Bandana);   Jack Newman (Sergeant Gordon);   Gerald Jackson, Jr. (New Orleans Drag Queen);   Jonathan Hill (Drew);   Jeff Hephner (McManus);   Drew Gardner (Drunk Nixon);   Dennis Benatar (Gate to Tigerland Sergeant).

LOS ANGELES TIMES, 10/6/00, Calendar/p. 16, Kevin Thomas

"Tigerland" is a Vietnam War movie that takes place not in Southeast Asia but in a Louisiana Army boot camp in 1971, and it's a film with more psychological suspense than action. In short, it is atypical, especially for its director, Joel Schumacher, whose name is synonymous with summer blockbusters and boffo John Grisham adaptations. (He moved in a new direction with his last picture, "Flawless," which was in essence a two-character drama featuring Robert De Niro's macho ex-security guard and Philip Seymour Hoffman's drag queen.)

With this taut, spare drama, which is consistently fresh, engrossing and unpredictable, Schumacher has traveled all the way from "Batman" movies to a picture consciously made in the rigorous spirit and style of Lars von Trier's anti-glitz Dogma credo—it has that kind of grit and spontaneity. Few big-time Hollywood directors have attempted such a major shifting of gears and done it so successfully.

Armed with a top-notch script by Ross Klavan—who drew upon personal experiences—and Michael McGruther, Schumacher has turned out a film that has an exceptionally strong personal feel to it.

"Tigerland" launches a screenful of young and talented actors and wins over even those of us who frankly would rather never have to deal with the Vietnam War on the screen ever again.

We've met Colin Farrell's Bozz before, the cocky private who's smart and caring but has a real problem with respecting authority. In the conventional war picture he'd shape up by the last reel and emerge a hero. His rite of passage here is not going to be conventional, because Vietnam was not a conventional war; by 1971 it was widely felt to be a losing proposition, even if not everyone admitted it.

"Tigerland" offers a stinging picture of the Army chain of command going through the motions of barking out commands and toughening up new infantrymen in eight weeks of basic training followed by a final week in Tigerland, as close a simulation to Vietnamese jungles as possible. The difference here, and it is profound, is that these young men are being ordered to risk their lives to fight a losing war. So thick you can all but taste it, this feeling seriously erodes the up-and-down-the-line respect that any fighting unit needs.

Most of the young men, however, pretty much keep their feelings to themselves, but Bozz cannot or will not hide his sense of the absurdity and futility of the dehumanizing process he and the others are undergoing. It's not that Bozz runs off at the mouth all the time; he knows that a glance here and a couple of remarks there are all it takes in these rigid conditions to express an attitude of defiance at the risk of severe consequences.

Not surprisingly, Bozz enrages all of those in positions of command, and while becoming a hero to others, especially when he helps two hapless misfits, Miter and Cantwell (achingly well-played by Clifton Collins Jr. and Thomas Guiry). The brutally realistic and shrewd Capt. Saunders (Nick Searcy) loathes Bozz because he recognizes that he is a born leader who refuses to take responsibility or accept authority.

Bozz becomes the inevitable target of the psychopathic Wilson (Shea Whigham, whom you love to hate), yet this clash doesn't play out quite the way you predict it will any more than any other aspect of the film; Schumacher creates a lethal atmosphere in which just about anything can happen.

The film's other key character is Matthew Davis' Paxton, a college student who becomes friends with Bozz. They are poised young men, more intelligent, articulate and reflective than the others in their platoon. In comparison to Bozz, the knocked-around realist, disillusioned rather than easily cynical, Paxton is naive, not a supporter of the war effort yet willing to serve his country. He keeps a diary in the hopes of becoming another Ernest Hemingway or James Jones. All the tensions, conflicts and contradictions that have been building look to be coming to a boil under the extreme duress of Tigerland.

Farrell and Davis, with only a few screen credits under their belts, are potent discoveries who should receive key career boosts with their performances; indeed, everyone involved in the making of "Tigerland" on both sides of the camera comes out looking good. The film itself, photographed (in 16 millimeter) with stunning immediacy by Matthew Libatique, looks great, its impact punctuated by a consistently apt score composed by Nathan Larson, fresh off "Boys Don't Cry." "Tigerland" is tightly constructed and culminates with a stunningly appropriate charge of ambiguity.

NEW YORK POST, 10/6/00, p. 48, Lou Lumenick

Veteran Hollywood director Joel Schumacher's third attempt to put the big-budget glossiness of "Batman & Robin" behind him is by far the most successful.

"Tigerland," a gritty Vietnam War drama with a star-making central performance by a previously obscure Irish actor named Colin Farrell, is not only a far more coherent movie than its predecessors ("Flawless" and "8mm"), but it's Schumacher's most dramatically satisfying work since "Falling Down."

Some of the credit must go to credited screenwriters Ross Klavan and Michael McGruther, who came up with a tightly written yarn with well-defined characters, even if it covers much the same ground as such 1980s efforts as Robert Altman's "Streamers" and the excellent, little-seen "84 Charlie MoPic."

"Tigerland" is also boosted by its grainy, hand-held 16-mm camerawork by Matthew Libatique ("Pi"), shot largely with natural light. It gives the movie a documentary-like urgency (underlined by the very sparse use of music) that's really striking for studio-backed project.

But Schumacher deserves the lion's share of the praise for the extraordinary performances, particularly that of Farrell, whose Oscar-caliber work here has been accurately compared to James Dean, Montgomery Clift and the young Marlon Brando.

Farrell burns up the screen as Bozz, a rebellious draftee who stirs up trouble in his platoon during their basic training at Fort Polk, La. It's 1971, and they're about to be sent to Tigerland, a nearby jungle-like combat simulation area that will prepare them for Vietnam.

Bozz wants out of the service, and he figures his best route is to make himself a pain in the neck to his superiors. A rule-book expert, he heroically obtains discharges for a couple of his compatriots.

But the brass, stung by domestic opposition to the unpopular war, decide Bozz' scheming shows he has a leadership potential. This exacerbates the tensions between Bozz and the platoon's seriously disturbed leader Wilson (Shea Whigham) to the breaking point, in a scene that will chill your blood.

The film is narrated by Paxton (Matthew Davis), an enlistee from New York who naively hopes to become the James Jones of Vietnam—but who's saved from his writerly fantasies by Bozz is an act of self-sacrifice that strains credulity.

But even with its contrivances (and gratuitous male beefcake shots) "Tigerland" is rarely less than compelling, must-see entertainment, thanks to Farrell, Schumacher and company.

NEWSDAY, 10/6/00, Part II/p. B6, Gene Seymour

Very little in Joel Schumacher's resume, choked as it is with high-octane schlock, such as "St. Elmo's Fire" (1985) and the last two Batman movies, prepares you for the grainy texture and bleached visuals of "Tigerland." When this Vietnam-era military drama premiered at the Toronto International Film Festival, its stripped-to-the-bone pseudo-documentary style seemed such a radical departure from Schumacher's glossier efforts that many critics wondered if a mistake had been made somewhere, somehow about this director's capabilities.

But you don't really have to dig very far beneath "Tigerland's" 16-millimeter grit to find a familiar story of young men in uniform, under stress, trying to get along by getting along. Set in 1971 when that "light at the end of the tunnel" was acknowledged even by the military to be next to unreachable, the movie follows a fresh shipment of cannon fodder through an especially brutal round of basic training.

Calling this battalion a motley crew would be barely less cliched than its members. The narrator, Paxton (Matthew Davis), is a stand-up guy who scribbles down his experiences in hopes of being to Fort Polk, La., what James Jones was to Pearl Harbor, Hawaii. He's surrounded by a heavy contingent of emotionally challenged Southerners: an obligatory wild-eyed racist named Wilson (Shea Whigham); a pliable Gomer Pyle type named Cantwell (Thomas Guiry), who all but howls at the moon, and a faux macho guy from N'awlins named Miter (Clifton Collins Jr.), who joined up to "prove" something.

You've seen platoons like this many times in many wars. Yet "Tigerland's" tightly wound psyches help make one of the movie's cogent points: That, at the last gasp of a lost cause, this was just about the best they could get. Pickings are so slim that the cynical brass can't even bring itself to discharge Bozz (Colin Farrell), a hip malcontent, free spirit and "barracks lawyer" loathed by his superiors yet graced with the kind of magnetism and bravado that, in other wars, would have helped him accumulate dozens of decorations.

For all his innovative technique, Schumacher can't help submitting to formula by waylaying his narrative momentum with big speeches and long stares. Indeed, the by-the-numbers conventions of military melodrama threaten to put "Tigerland" in "St. Elmo's" queasy company were it not for its bruising, riveting power and the crackling energy of its young, mostly unknown cast.

Farrell's brooding, crookedly grinning Bozz may at times seem like an archetype from its era, a Randle Patrick McMurphy in khaki fatigues. But it's a type so rare in contemporary movies that its presence alone makes "Tigerland" a worthy addition to the Hollywood war-movie archives.

SIGHT AND SOUND, 5/01, p. 59, John Wrathall

1971. A platoon or recruits en route to Vietnam are sent for infantry training at Fort Polk, Louisiana. The idealistic Paxton, who enlisted by choice, makes friends with the cynical Bozz, who is trying to get thrown out by breaking army regulations. At the firing range, Bozz gets another recruit, Wilson, into trouble by stealing his target. Convinced that Bozz has the makings of a soldier, Sergeant Landers makes him acting sergeant in charge of the other recruits. This improves platoon morale, because everyone, except for Wilson, respects him.

On weekend leave, Bozz hints to Paxton that he knows of an escape route to Mexico. Paxton says he wouldn't escape, because that would mean someone else would have to take his place in Vietnam. Returning to barracks, Bozz is attacked by Wilson. Bozz fights back and is only prevented from killing him by Paxton. On the firing range, Wilson tries to shoot Bozz, but the gun jams. Wilson is transferred. The platoon arrives for the final week of training at Tigerland, where jungle warfare is simulated. On an exercise, they encounter Wilson, who beats up Paxton.

That night Bozz has arranged his escape to Mexico. Worried about leaving Paxton in the jungle with Wilson at large, he decides to stay. The next day Wilson fires at Bozz with live ammunition, but misses and is court-martialled. In the confusion, Bozz deliberately fires a blank in Paxton's face, injuring him just enough to get him out of the war. Bozz leaves for Vietnam. In voiceover, Paxton tells us that Bozz went missing in Vietnam, but was never reported dead. He may be in Mexico.

Like the great journeyman directors of the studio era, Joel Schumacher worked his way up through the industry, from costume designer to writer (of Motown spin-offs such as The Wiz, 1978) to director. In this last capacity he has proved bewilderingly versatile—and no less bewilderingly successful—moving from comedy *(The Incredible Shrinking Woman)* to horror *(The Lost Boys)* to John Grisham adaptations *(The Client)* to the last two Batman movies. Recently, however, the twin disappointments (creative and box-office) of *Batman & Robin* and *8mm* appear to have been something of a road to Damascus for Schumacher, pushing him away from big-budget spectaculars towards smaller, more indie fare.

As on his last film *Flawless,* the most immediate sign of this change of heart is his choice of cinematographer. Flawless was adventurously shot by Declan Quinn *(Leaving Las Vegas)*. On *Tigerland,* Matthew Libatique *(Pi,Requiem for a Dream)* provides a handheld, grainy, reversal stock look, at once modern and immediate and apt for the 1971 setting (the film takes place at a US training camp preparing soldiers for Vietnam). In the press notes, Schumacher rather improbably namechecks *Dogme* and documentarist Fred Wiseman as inspiration; more calculatingly, perhaps, the rough-and-ready style is a crucial way of distinguishing *Tigerland* from its obvious forerunner as a Vietnam training movie, the clinically composed *Full Metal Jacket*.

Either way, Schumacher seems to have embarked on his own version of basic training, purging himself of the high camp which constitutes the only consistent characteristic of his previous oeuvre. Of course, there are plenty of successful directors in Hollywood who have no distinctive style or particular thematic interests (Mike Newell, say). What distinguishes Schumacher—and is laid bare by *Tigerland*—is that he isn't a very fluent storyteller either. Based on the actual army experiences of co-screenwriter Ross Klavan, *Tigerland*—like so much semi-autobiographical material—is episodic and jerky in rhythm, alternating between choppy montage scenes of training exercises and long conversations late at night in the kitchen or the latrine. But the structural problems run deeper. At the start of the film, it's the shaven-headed training sergeant Thomas who is set up as the nemesis of our hero, the Texan free spirit Private Bozz. But as the film progresses, Thomas recedes, to be replaced by Private Wilson, who develops a homicidal grudge against Bozz for no clear reason other than to allow a retread of the good soldier/bad soldier conflict staged by Willem Dafoe and Tom Berenger in *Platoon,* complete with attempted murder in the jungle.

For all the indie trappings, unknown cast and autobiographical detail, *Tigerland* falls back on some of the hoariest clichés of the war movie: the unruly maverick who ends up making a good soldier (Bozz); the ball-breaking but deep-down humane drill sergeant (Landers); the observant college boy (Paxton) who writes it all down in his notebook in preparation for his great American novel—and, of course, delivers the voiceover. The difference is, the soldiers in *Tigerland* never see any action—which is normally what makes the clichés worth sitting through. One can't help feeling that the only audience for this unlikely project will be casting agents—at the very least, it's a fine showcase for spirited performances from a dozen up-and-coming actors, notably *Ballykissangel* refugee Colin Farrell, who makes a charismatic and convincingly Texan Bozz.

VILLAGE VOICE, 10/10/00, p. 134, Dennis Lim

A lot of time, money, and pain have gone into establishing Joel Schumacher's reputation as a well-oiled toxic-waste machine (deathless Batman and Grisham franchises, vigilante apologies, *St. Elmo's Fire)*—and all for what? Schumacher would now like you to believe that he is sorry, though not sorry enough to desist. This contrite phase apparently began with last year's low-key but clueless drag-queen/homophobe buddy movie, *Flawless,* and continues with the ostentatiously scruffy *Tigerland,* a contrived (if surprisingly well acted) martyr story set in a pre-Nam Louisiana boot camp. The modest budget and unknown cast are supposed to signal integrity, though glossy production values and name actors are not traditionally the problem with Joel Schumacher movies.

The director, who's presumably realized that small films are less easy to hate, keeps it real Dogme style, shooting in murky 16mm, with mostly natural light and a good deal of hand-held tumult. (The cinematographer is Matthew Libatique, best known for his flashy work with Darren Aronofsky.) But while *Tigerland* is the least egregious of Schumacher's recent films, it's also fatally convinced that grime equals authenticity. The movie monitors the implosion of a Vietnam-bound platoon as its members progress from brutal drills to the merciless tropical-swamp simulation known as Tigerland, "the second worst place on earth."

With its numerous instances of institutionalized sadism (some lingered on a little too fetishistically for comfort), *Tigerland* unavoidably evokes the first hour of *Full Metal*

Jacket—and, of course, its verité precursor, Frederick Wiseman's *Basic Training*—but the screenwriters are ultimately more indebted to the *Biloxi Blues* model of bonding and lesson-learning under pressure. Cocky, charismatic troublemaker Bozz (Colin Farrell) and idealistic aspiring writer Paxton (Matt Davis) form the core of the group, almost all of whom eventually benefit from Bozz's anarchic leadership; there's a sociopathic hair-trigger thrown in to liven things up. In his first major role, the Irish actor Farrell deflects the script's more dubious aspects through sheer magnetic presence. *Tigerland* is, if not much else, a casting director's triumph—a point reinforced in the current *Interview*, where the film is successfully reimagined as a homoerotic fashion spread.

Also reviewed in:
NEW REPUBLIC, 10/16/00, p. 40, Stanley Kauffmann
NEW YORK TIMES, 10/6/00, p. E14, A. O. Scott
VARIETY, 9/18-24/00, p. 29, Emanuel Levy

TIGGER MOVIE, THE

A Walt Disney Pictures release of a Walt Disney Television Animation production. *Producer:* Cheryl Abood. *Director:* Jun Falkenstein. *Screenplay:* Jun Falkenstein. *Story:* Eddie Guzelian. *Based on Characters by:* A.A. Milne. *Editor:* Robert Fisher, Jr. *Music:* Harry Gregson-Williams. *Music Editor:* Richard Whitfield, Sherry Whitfield, and Dominick Certo. *Songs:* Richard M. Sherman and Robert B. Sherman. *Sound:* Steve Kohler and (music) Michael Farrow, Frank Wolf, Cary Butler, Bill Jackson, and Ross Pallone. *Sound Editor:* Louis L. Edemann. *Animation Director:* Kenichi Tsuchiya. *Casting:* Jamie Thomason. *Production Designer:* Sharon Morrill Robinov. *Art Director:* Toby Bluth. *Running time:* 76 minutes. *MPAA Rating:* G.

VOICES: Jim Cummings (Tigger/Winnie the Pooh); Nikita Hopkins (Roo); Ken Sansom (Rabbit); John Fiedler (Piglet); Peter Cullen (Eeyore); Andre Stojka (Owl); Kath Soucie (Kanga); Tom Attenborough (Christopher Robin); John Hurt (The Narrator).

LOS ANGELES TIMES, 2/11/00, Calendar/p. 24, Charles Solomon

Disney's new animated feature "The Tigger Movie" is a brightly colored, upbeat entertainment that will please small children, its obvious target audience. Parents and older siblings, however, may grow impatient with the uneven execution that weakens the genuine charm the film sporadically exhibits.

Tigger, the energetic tiger from the Winnie the Pooh series who's spent decades proclaiming "the most wonderful thing about tiggers is I'm the only one," suddenly feels lonely. No one wants to go bouncing with him, except Roo; the other animals are tired of him breaking everything he touches.

Wishing he had a family who shared his tastes quickly turns into believing he has one, and his search for them leads to predictable disappointments and mishaps. Tigger learns the very contemporary lesson that a family is something you assemble from the people who love you, rather than a group you happen to be born into.

Director-screenwriter Jun Falkenstein and story author Eddie Guzelian make the mistake of pitting mild, familiar characters against a danger that is both inappropriate and too big for them—a fault that also weakened the recent "Pokemon" movie. For example, Tigger's yelling triggers an avalanche that threatens to sweep the entire cast over a precipice. Tigger may break furniture and annoy his friends with his rambunctious antics, but he doesn't put their lives at risk. And what's a precipice doing in the gentle English countryside of the Hundred Acre Wood?

The animation was done in Japan by the studio that produces many Disney TV shows. Pooh, Eeyore, Tigger and Roo generally look and act as they should, but Owl, Rabbit and Kanga look misproportioned and move stiffly. Animation this limited needs strong poses and careful staging to make the characters' thoughts and actions read clearly, and the artists don't always find them. Falkenstein relies too heavily on close-ups, which becomes a problem when Roo cries: The animators simply can't draw the expressions convincingly.

As Pooh, voice actor Jim Cummings comes close to re-creating Sterling Holloway's beloved interpretation from the '60s animated shorts, but he fails to capture the affectionate little growls Paul Winchell gave Tigger. In his zanier moments, Tigger sounds like Buddy Hackett with a lisp. Peter Cullen is properly dour as Eeyore; the rest of the cast is adequate, if unremarkable.

Art director Toby Bluth does an exceptional job of capturing the distinctive ink lines and watercolor washes of E.H. Shepard's illustrations for the A.A. Milne books. Richard M. and Robert B. Sherman, who crafted the songs for "The Jungle Book" and "Mary Poppins," have written six new tunes—their first for Disney in nearly 30 years. "Round My Family Tree," the inevitable upbeat production number, overflows with bright graphics and references to old films and television programs that will probably go over kids' heads. How many 6-year-olds remember Marilyn Monroe in "The Seven Year Itch"? The most effective number in the score is "Pooh's Lullabee," the charming song the Silly Old Bear uses to soothe a hive of bees who've caught him stealing honey.

"The Tigger Movie" looks and sounds better than the pedestrian "Winnie the Pooh and a Day for Eeyore" (1983), but no one would mistake it for one of the Oscar-winning featurettes made by Disney's star animators during the '60s. Its shortcomings are unlikely to bother young children, who only know the characters from the limited animation of the popular TV series, specials and last year's direct-to-video feature "Winnie the Pooh: The Seasons of Giving."

NEW YORK POST, 2/11/00, p. 57, Hannah Brown

There's nothing especially wrong with this animated musical, but it moves along slowly and the songs, while pleasant, are nothing special.

The lackluster songs are particularly disappointing, because they were written by Academy Award-winning composers Richard and Robert Sherman, brothers who wrote the music for "Mary Poppins."

But Winnie the Pooh and his cronies have amassed nearly 80 years' worth of goodwill, and audiences will arrive at theaters filled with warm feelings. There will probably be enough to carry them through "Tigger" with only a mild feeling of letdown.

The film opens promisingly with some live action shots of Christopher Robin's room, then shifts to animation.

The energetic Tigger wants to find someone to bounce with him, but no one can keep up with him. Only Roo, the young kangaroo, tries, but he's too small.

So Tigger embarks on a search for his family and sings a song, "Someone Like Me."

It's obviously intended to teach children to be thankful they have families, rather than grousing about how they can't stand their siblings.

Realizing that Tigger has no family and that he is searching in vain, Pooh and the other inhabitants of the Hundred Acre Wood write him a letter, pretending to be relatives wishing him well.

But their scheme backfires when he decides that this means they are on their way to visit him. To avoid disappointing him, they dress up in tiger costumes and pretend to be relatives.

When this scheme backfires as well, Tigger heads out into a snowstorm, determined to find his family. Don't worry, though.

It all ends at a nice party, and Tigger learns the comforting message that, as Kanga puts it, "Tigger is one of our family and as long as we care for him, he always will be."

The one imaginative Disney-style number is "Round My Family Tree," where Tigger imagines famous relatives throughout history.

In spite of its shortcomings, children love these characters and will enjoy "Tigger."

SIGHT AND SOUND, 6/00, p. 56, Kim Newman

The Hundred-Acre Wood. Although his friends are devoted to him, Tigger misses the family he has never known. Tigger approaches Owl for advice about locating his family; Owl tells him to look up his family tree. Tigger takes him literally and searches for this tree in the Wood.

Realising Tigger's predicament, Roo and his other friends—Winnie the Pooh, Piglet, Eeyore, Kanga and Owl—write him a letter purporting to be from his family to cheer him up. Tigger misconstrues this as a promise that they will come to visit.

As winter encroaches, Pooh and comrades dress up as tiggers and visit Tigger. Tigger sees through the imposture and sets out to find his real family. Rabbit leads Tigger's friends in search of Tigger; they find him by a large tree which he believes to be his family tree. Tigger's shouting causes an avalanche, but he saves all his friends by bouncing them into the tree. He is swept away and only the encouragement of Roo prompts him to save himself. Christopher Robin turns up and tells Tigger that he already has a family, his devoted friends.

The greatest moment of Tigger's screen career is in T. Graham's presumably illegal short *Apocalypse Pooh* (1987): soundtrack excerpts from *Apocalypse Now* are laid over brilliantly edited excerpts from Disney's Pooh films, and Tigger's bouncing first entrance is cut to the dialogue from the "it's a fuckin tiger" scene from Francis Ford Coppola's 1979 Vietnam epic. Sadly, nothing in this belated series entry—the first feature in a run of Disney shorts which began in 1966 with *Winnie the Pooh and the Honey Tree*—comes up to that mark. Though one dreads the addition of any further elements that would distance the characters from the Hundred-Acre Wood which writer A.A. Milne and illustrator E.H. Shepard created in the original books—an excursion into the world beyond this leafy idyll comes only in a fantasy song sequence ('Round My Family Tree') which manages to evoke divers contemporary figures such as Jerry Springer and Andy Warhol—this 75-minute crawl is such thin stuff that even a burst of rap (Tiggaz with Attitude?) would be a relief.

There is something badly wrong with the film's premise, which contradicts Milne's lessons that Tigger can't climb trees (here, he lives in one and searches for another) and that, crucially, Tigger can't be unbounced. The great appeal of the character is his emotional invincibility, yet in *The Tigger Movie* he turns all sappy and is often seen with animated tears brimming in his eyes. When Tigger stops blithely flattening things and starts yearning for a family, a great many children in the preview audience began to fidget (overheard on the way out: "He sat still all the way through *Toy Story 2"*), sensing that the toothless tiger on screen had ceased to be the Tigger they liked.

The rest of the characters are reduced to stooges, with the shrill Roo given the largest role, and, as ever, the only real laughs come from Eeyore's tonic gloom (his advice to Tigger, "Keep smiling"). A lick of contemporary satire comes with the casting of Rabbit as a survivalist whose warren is stocked for the winter like a Y2K-fearing militia man, but the character, like everything else, has been softened to the point of blandness. Richard and Robert Sherman contribute unmemorable new songs ('Pooh's Lullabee','The Whoop-de-Dooper Bounce'), and their classic 'The Wonderful Thing about Tiggers' is revived in a decidedly unbouncy new arrangement. The owners of the franchise should perhaps reread the last chapter of *The House at Pooh Corner,* which predates *Toy Story 2* in its understanding of the brief life a child's plaything can have and establishes the wisdom of knowing when to stop before something unique becomes something tiresome.

Also reviewed in:
CHICAGO TRIBUNE, 2/11/00, Friday/p. E, Monica Eng
NEW YORK TIMES, 2/11/00, p. E15, A. O. Scott
VARIETY, 2/14-20/00, p. 40, Todd McCarthy
WASHINGTON POST, 2/11/00, p. C1, Rita Kempley
WASHINGTON POST, 2/11/00, Weekend/p. 41, Desson Howe

TIME CODE

A Screen Gems release of a Red Mullet production. *Producer:* Mike Figgis and Annie Stewart. *Director:* Mike Figgis. *Screenplay:* Mike Figgis. *Director of Photography:* Patrick Alexander Stewart. *Music:* Mike Figgis and Anthony Marinelli. *Music Editor:* Richard Whitfield. *Sound:* Robert Janiger and (music) Mark Curry. *Sound Editor:* Patrick Dodd. *Casting:* Amanda

Mackey Johnson and Cathy Sandrich. *Production Designer:* Charlotte Malmlöf. *Set Decorator:* Jennifer Gentile. *Special Effects:* Ron Bolanowski. *Costumes:* Donna Casey. *Running time:* 93 minutes. *MPAA Rating:* R.

CAST: Xander Berkeley (Evan Watz); Golden Brooks (Onyx Richardson); Saffron Burrows (Emma); Viveka Davis (Victoria Cohen); Richard Edson (Lester Moore); Aimee Graham (Sikh Nurse); Salma Hayek (Rose); Glenne Headly (Therapist); Andrew Heckler (Auditioning Actor); Holly Hunter (Executive); Danny Huston (Randy); Daphna Kastner (Auditioning Actor); Patrick Kearney (Drug House Owner); Elizabeth Low (Penny, Evan's Assistant); Kyle MacLachlan (Bunny Drysdale); Mia Maestro (Ana Pauls); Leslie Mann (Cherine); Suzy Nakamura (Connie Ling); Alessandro Nivola (Joey Z); Zuleikha Robinson (Lester Moore's Assistant); Julian Sands (Quentin); Stellan Skarsgard (Alex Green); Jeanne Tripplehorn (Lauren Hathaway); Steven Weber (Darren Fetzer).

CHRISTIAN SCIENCE MONITOR, 4/28/00, p. 11, David Sterritt

The big news about Mike Figgis's new picture, "Time Code," is that it was shot entirely with digital video equipment instead of regular movie cameras and film.

The bigger news is that it was photographed in "real time," telling its story without the shot-to-shot editing that's found in almost every other movie ever made.

The biggest news is that "Time Code" isn't one movie but four movies, unfolding at the same time in four adjacent portions of the screen. Sometimes the different images complement one another showing the same action from varying perspectives, for instance—and sometimes they diverge in unpredictable ways, requiring us to figure out how they relate to one another.

Some are hailing "Time Code" as a bold experiment, a radical new vision, even a glimpse of cinema's future. Others are more skeptical, pointing out that avant-garde innovations have sprung up for decades without seducing Hollywood away from well-worn formulas and time-tested formats. Doubters also wonder if the picture's story, characters, and ideas live up to their inventive setting.

Wherever you stand on the merits of "Time Code" as a Saturday-night movie, though, you have to admit it's different from anything else around. That goes for the production process as well as the on-screen results.

Figgis has always been an adventurous director, making off-beat pictures like "Leaving Las Vegas," which earned popular acclaim despite its uncompromisingly downbeat plot, and "The Loss of Sexual Innocence," which is more a thematic exploration than a linear story. While assembling a split-screen scene for "Miss Julie," his recent adaptation of August Strindberg's classic play, he started thinking about the expressive possibilities of lengthy shots assembled side-by-side instead of one after the other. He also thought about music—he's a trained composer who often scores his own films—and his interest in improvisation by performers of all kinds.

All of which led to the unorthodox methods that brought "Time Code" into being. Figgis wrote a bare-bones story about an aspiring actress, a drug-dealing cop, various film-industry figures, and many other characters. He gave this outline to the cast, but left every detail of their performances—words, movements, costumes—up to their individual choices. Every day they improvised the entire film, photographed without interruption by four digital video cameras.

In the end, Figgis had about 60 complete versions, from which he selected the four that pleased him most. These are what "Time Code" audiences see, mounted alongside one another on a single screen, with sound coming from whichever picture most deserves our attention at the moment.

On some levels, "Time Code" builds on a string of multiple-image experiments dating back to Abel Gance's silent epic "Napoleon" and continuing through Andy Warhol's amazing "Chelsea Girls" and some of Brian De Palma's pictures, to name just a few examples. Such movies make the viewer into a central part of the creative process, since you can't sit back and passively absorb the story.

On the contrary, you have to assess differing bits of information and piece them together on a moment-by-moment basis. Since no two spectators will do this precisely the same way, "Time Code" will be a somewhat different movie for everyone who sees it—and perhaps for the same person on two different viewings.

The film's most disappointing aspect is its story, which makes little effort to get beyond standard melodramatic fare. More impressive is the cast that brings it to spontaneous life, including Salma Hayek as the actress, Jeanne Tripplehorn as her suspicious lover, Stellan Skarsgard as a sleazy executive, and Richard Edson as an anxiety-ridden director. Also on hand are Holly Hunter, Kyle MacLachlan, Julian Sands, Saffron Burrows, Laurie Metcalf, Viveka Davis, Danny Huston, and plenty of others.

Time will tell whether "'Time Code" marks a major shift in film history or a momentary blip on the cinematic radar screen. The latter prospect is more likely, and it won't be surprising if the picture prompts more term papers than ticket sales.

What's incontestable is that director Figgis and his collaborators have been brave enough to push the envelope of commercial filmmaking more vigorously than anyone else in recent memory. This deserves a rousing cheer, even if the movie's story doesn't.

LOS ANGELES TIMES, 4/28/00, Calendar/p. 10, Kevin Thomas

Mike Figgis' "Time Code" is a notably funny and inspired execution of divide and conquer. Figgis takes four intersecting stories and splits his screen into four sections, enabling the narratives to unfold simultaneously in real time for 93 minutes.

It's all in the name of the digital video revolution, but at the same time it's a clever way of providing crucial layering and heightening a hip, satirical take on bad old Hollywood ways in which beauty, talent and ambition collide with sex, power and drugs with the usual consequences. "Time Code" wouldn't pack nearly as much punch if it were told in traditional narrative style involving much cross-cutting nor seem nearly as provocative and illuminating.

It takes awhile to get used to keeping track of the four separate images, but Figgis assists by pumping up the sound in whichever segment at the moment is most important. The screen is filled by 28 actors, some familiar and some not, but all of them effective.

There are four key figures: Alex Green (Stellan Skarsgard), a film executive who's beginning to unravel when his beautiful wife, Emma (Saffron Burrows), drops by his Sunset Strip office to tell him she's leaving him despite his promise to whisk her off to a Florence or Venice without scripts, cell phones or books that can be made into movies. Despite an impending staff meeting he's almost immediately buoyed by the arrival of Rose (Salma Hayek), an actress swift to demonstrate that she will do anything to get an audition. (But no, she won't go off to Italy with him either.)

In the meantime, Rose's rich, jealous lover, Lauren (Jeanne Tripplehorn), is sitting out Rose's visit in her limo, where she's involved in some electronic eavesdropping on the actress. As if Lauren's mounting rage weren't portentous enough, Figgis throws in a series of pretty sharp earthquakes.

These four, all played with aplomb, interact with a raft of others, in and around Green's headquarters. The meetings are frequently uproarious, especially one in which a director (Richard Edson), mustached and wearing a cap, pitches an idea for a time-travel comedy to be called "Time Toilet," in which, for openers, human waste will splat John Wilkes Booth, thus deflecting that fatal shot at President Lincoln.

Then there's the executive producer (Golden Brooks) pitching an idea for a serious movie on the frustrations of a group of African American actors trying to make it in Hollywood, but when pressed for her job description at Red Mullet (the actual name of Figgis' own company) she says euphemistically that she's in charge of "urban noir."

The segmented image becomes a deft metaphor for these peoples' fragmented lives. This large cast, which includes Holly Hunter as Green's concerned business partner, working from a basic premise, improvises without a trace of self-consciousness. (Especially sly: Julian Sands as a masseur who's of course also an aspiring actor.) The multiple perspectives add dimensions to the characters, all the better to sustain the film's dark satirical tone.

The film has a style that is at once terrifically sophisticated and carefree, and if it seems all of a piece that is because it basically is. Patrick Alexander Stewart is Figgis' wizardly cinematographer, yet Figgis operated one of the four cameras himself and composed his own score—in this instance, one that's as sleek and seductive in its shifting moods as the film is itself.

In the film's set piece a fledgling digital video director, Ana (Mia Maestro), recently returned from Russia, where her rap musician boyfriend, Joey Z (Alessandro Nivola), was on his Walk

Don't Run tour (!), makes an elaborate pitch involving Joey's latest rap, to which she hums like a human Theremin. Ana then launches into a hilariously academic lecture on among other things, Sergei Eisenstein's theory of montage, the importance of going beyond "the paradigm of collage" with digital—and yes, "the need to get back to Leibniz" while we're at it.

The way this sequence plays out we can see that Ana is at once pretentious, sincere and just possibly talented. It's nifty and compassionate observation, and what's more, allows Figgis to send up all the technical hullabaloo surrounding his own quite satisfying experiment.

NEW YORK, 5/8/00, p. 70, Peter Rainer

Time Code is a novelty act posing as an aesthetic breakthrough. Director Mike Figgis shot four separate, thematically related movies, each in a single take, utilizing specially designed high-definition hand-held digital video cameras. The screen is split in four, and the correspondence between the simultaneous stories is sometimes nil and sometimes one-to-one. Actually, Figgis and his crew shot many more than four continuous movies, fifteen in all, with no two takes the same; the quartet we behold bug-eyed is presumably the one with the greatest synergy.

By themselves, none of these movies would be very exciting. Four at once isn't very exciting, either: More in this case is definitely not better. Set in an L.A. that is periodically registering earth tremors, the film has something to do with a philandering, low-rent movie executive (Stellan Skarsgard); his neurasthenic wife (Saffron Burrows); a two-timing actress (Salma Hayek) whose lover (Jeanne Tripplehorn) has secretly miked her to get the skinny; and a host of additional intersecting plot lines culminating in murder and involving the likes of Julian Sands, Holly Hunter, Laurie Metcalf, and Kyle MacLachlan.

Time Code is worth mentioning only because of the outsize claims being made for it both by the filmmakers and the press. Now that high-definition digital video equipment and desktop filmmaking and the Internet and God knows what else are making it possible for anyone to turn out feature films for zilch, we are being asked to believe that all this freedom represents some kind of *artistic* revolution. But does it? You don't have to be a Luddite to realize that technology isn't the savior of the creative spirit. At best, it's a rich relation. Did the creation of the word processor result in a higher proportion of good writers? The facility with which one makes a movie may or may not have anything to do with its value. It all depends on who is making the movie. An unfettered no-talent is still a no-talent. I don't relish the prospect of everybody with a laptop and a digital videocam converting themselves into instant auteurs; nor am I particularly interested in watching movies break through to some supposedly advanced realm of gizmology. I just wish the kind of movie we have now—the kind that plays on one screen and not four, thank you very much—was *better*.

Mike Figgis is not wrong to explore new methodologies for working cheaply and unbridled by the studio system, especially considering how corrupting that system has become for film artists. It's just that *Time Code* isn't much of a calling card. In the past, directors like Robert Altman have indeed used technological innovations, especially with sound, to bring us into a denser, closer connection with life. Others, like Francis Ford Coppola in his *One From the Heart* phase, made movies in which the technology, reaching for a greater intimacy, trumped all human feeling. It remains a time-honored belief that art and science working together will somehow forge a new unity, a new way of seeing. But the great works that have been created in the movies, as in all the other arts, are expressions of that most hallowed and mysterious and unquantifiable of conundrums: the creative impulse. And no amount of digitzing and quadrupleizing will mask its absence.

NEW YORK POST, 4/28/00, p. 54, Jonathan Foreman

Mike Figgis' "Time Code" tells four interlinked stories that take place at the same time.

It was shot using four synchronized, hand-held digital cameras, each of which ran for a single, 93-minute take (impossible with a conventional 35mm camera).

The stories run simultaneously on a screen split into four. Director Figgis ("Leaving Las Vegas") nudges you into looking at one picture over the others by playing with the sound (though the story on the top right, featuring Saffron Burrows, is so dull you almost forget it's there).

The fact that "Time Code" is shot in real time, like live TV, makes for a cute gimmick, but little more. It's Figgis' clever use of four simultaneous images that hints at the amazing possibilities of multi-channel storytelling.

But apart from its technological originality, "Time Code" is almost completely uninteresting.

In fact, for long stretches, especially during the first hour, it's as soporific as watching a bank of security cameras.

Still, "Time Code" is an important, pioneering film that should inspire less pretentious filmmakers to combine Figgis' daring techniques with good writing, acting and editing.

NEWSDAY, 4/28/00, Part II/p. B10, Gene Seymour

Since his triumphant "Leaving Las Vegas" in 1995, Mike Figgis has been an itchy, restless wanderer along the outer limits of conventional storytelling. From 1997's "One Night Stand" to last year's "The Loss of Sexual Innocence" and "Miss Julie," Figgis has taken technical and stylistic liberties with both time and space. In each case, you marvel at his nerve, even if you're at best bewildered and at worst irritated by the results.

The latest stop on Figgis' quixotic quest is "Time Code," which borrows the split-screen device he used in adapting August Strindberg's "Miss Julie" and subdivides the screen into four sections. In each screen, a story unfolds one continuous 93-minute take during which the connections each story has to the other are attached, detached and put back together again using digital video cameras. Once again, the admiration you feel for Figgis' daring is overpowered by your disappointment over how far his effort falls short of his aspiration.

Figgis, who's also an accomplished jazz musician and composer, wanted "Time Code" to come across as the cinematic equivalent of a composed musical piece, within which each of his 28 actors would improvise their performances under tight time guidelines.

The story takes place on Los Angeles' Sunset Boulevard within and outside the offices of a low-budget movie company frantically casting a slasher movie. The production chief (Stellan Skarsgard) is a lumbering grizzly, addled by booze and drugs, whose wife (Saffron Burrows) has decided to leave him.

He's makes a call to his lover, a starlet (Salma Hayek), who's trying to conceal her affair from her other lover (Jeanne Tripplehorn), who in turn is suspicious enough to plant a listening device in the girlfriend's purse. In another screen, several high-strung production execs (played by Holly Hunter and Steven Weber, among others) scatter and jabber when they're not getting rubdowns from a freelance masseur (Julian Sands in a quietly hilarious turn).

Meanwhile, another camera follows Burrows around through several aimless encounters, which like the movie, promise more than they deliver. More to the point, synchronicity is promised by "Time Code," but dissonance is what's delivered. Someday, someone, maybe even Figgis, will make it work.

SIGHT AND SOUND, 9/00, p. 56, Xan Brooks

Hollywood, the present. A screen segmented into four frames chart the overlapping experiences of a group of movie business players. The action plays out in real time and pivots around the production offices of Red Mullet films.

Emma leaves her therapy session and travels to the office to tell her partner—philandering executive Alex—that she is leaving him. Meanwhile aspiring actress Rose is being chauffered to the office alongside her wealthy lover Lauren. Convinced that Rose is having an affair, Lauren plants a surveillance device on her and listens in as Rose meets with Alex and has sex in a darkened preview theatre. Struggling cult director Lester is desperately hunting a female lead for his new production. Having unsuccessfully auditioned for the role, actress Cherine leaves the office and meets the distressed Emma.

Returning to Cherine's apartment, the two women share a kiss before Emma is disturbed by the arrival of Cherine's boyfriend and leaves hurriedly. At Red Mullet, Alex brushes off Rose's plea for an audition and is dragged into a meeting with enfant terrible director Ana. Rose prepares to leave the building but is introduced to Lester, who decides that she is perfect for the lead in his movie.

In a rage, Lauren storms into the building and shoots Alex. Lying wounded on the floor, he is filmed on Ana's digital camera and receives a phone call from Emma who admits she loves him.

Like a series of lights coming on in an uncurtained building, Mike Figgis' *Timecode* opens at quarter-strength and then builds to full illumination. With the bulk of the screen's physical space still black (though abstracted light sources occasionally streak through or flicker), a window pops up filling the upper right-hand corner. Inside, a young woman (Saffron Burrows) is recounting a dream to her therapist. Midway through their exchange, an adjacent window at the top left-hand comes alive and the viewer sees a power-dressed vixen (Jeanne Tripplehorn) storm down the steps of a Beverly Hills residence and hurriedly let down the tyre of a nearby car. And we're torn. Do we continue to eavesdrop on the low, murmurous confessional in the shrink's sanctum or switch our attention to the more nakedly subversive actions next door? Or do we attempt to keep tabs on both: snooping on the top-right square while playing peeping Tom on top-left. A moment later, two more windows of opportunity have opened up on the picture's bottom storey and we're torn again. Four frames, four narratives. A quartet of options for the discerning voyeur to choose between.

Played out on a quartered screen, in real time, with no edits, *Timecode* is an ongoing fascination. As an exercise in parallel plotting, it's endlessly inventive. As a filmic experiment, it's gloriously audacious. If the closing credits neglect to acknowledge an editor, that's in part because the viewer is implicitly encouraged to fill that role for him or herself: concentrating on the dramas and characters that grab his or her attention and tuning out the others. Admittedly *Timecode* falls some way short of attaining the Holy Grail that is the first truly interactive feature film, but it at least has its nose pointed in the right direction.

It also hits something of a high-water mark in Figgis' push towards a more formally ambitious mode of movie-making; a push that began with 1995's award-winning, low-budget *Leaving Las Vegas* and continued through last year's floridly experimental *The Loss of Sexual Innocence*. In preparing *Timecode,* Figgis (a keen musician) composed his film on music sheets, as though scoring a string quartet. He then proceeded to shoot the picture in one continuous 93-minute take. The film's four digital video cameras (operated by Figgis, James O'Keeffe, Tony Cucchiari and director of photography Patrick Alexander Stewart) were all turned on simultaneously and run on a common timecode, the electronic counter encoded on the tapes.

There was no formal script and the blocking was largely improvised. The dangers, of course, in such a no-nets mode of working are manifest. At one stage a tell-tale hand can be glimpsed holding open the door as we trail Salma Hayek's starlet into the washroom, while on several occasions where the narratives overlap two frames move into such close proximity that the cameras must be mere inches away from clashing. But on the whole *Timecode* synchronises its high-wire act with aplomb: technically, this is a virtuoso piece of work.

More crucially, the film succeeds on a dramatic level. Figgis has admitted suffering initial qualms over the viability of his split-screen, parallel-plotting device, fretting that *Timecode's* constant four-way dialogue of sound and visual information would swamp the viewer. He concluded, however, that a diet of channel-surfing and multi-media has made sophisticates of modern-day filmgoers, equipping them to process a bombardment of information thrown at them on various frequencies. Where MTV would sate its audience through frenzied editing, Figgis reasoned, *Timecode* would do so through simultaneous, real-time narratives. Formally separate, these two modes of communication are spiritual cousins. The difference is that while the dominant MTV style is traditionally accused of spoon-feeding its public, *Timecode* empowers them. It serves up four dishes and invites us to sample instances drama from each one.

Undeniably this makes for a tart and appealing diet. *Timecode* revolves around the Hollywood offices of Red Mullet films (the name of Figgis' own production company) and juggles a roster of semi-crazed *Day of the Locust* types with lots of satirical potshots at the movie industry. So we get comedic script pitches ("It's like *Shine* except the guy has a lot more problems"), forlorn mantras ("I am always in the right place at the right time") and duff green-lit projects (a director is auditioning actresses for the star role of a girl "who's sleeping her way to the top of a public-relations firm in Missouri"). The largely improvised acting is sharp and convincing (particularly from Stellan Skarsgard and Salma Hayek) and the quartet of stories feed smartly into one another.

But while *Timecode* provides some measure of viewer freedom, this is finally a freedom within limits. Throughout it all, one can never quite escape the godlike hand of Figgis (credited as writer, director, producer and composer) at work behind the scenes. In structuring the film as a piece of music, its creator shrewdly allows some frames to idle while the others combust. In overseeing the sound edit (with no room for a boom, a plethora of hidden microphones were used, following techniques pioneered by Robert Altman on *California Split*, 1974, and *Nashville*, 1975), Figgis elects to keep certain tracks low down in the mix and emphasise the dialogue elsewhere.

He even throws in a mission statement. Near the end of the film, Mia Maestro pops up as Ana, a glacial teenage prodigy who wants to throw out the trusty Eisensteinian montage in favour of a new form of cinematic language. "Montage has created a false reality," she proclaims. "Digital is demanding new expressions." Her proposed film will be played out in real time, on four cameras, in one continuous take. To Ana, the proposal is revolutionary. To Skarsgard's anguished executive it sounds like "the most pretentious crap I've ever heard".

In the end *Timecode* is never pretentious—it's too witty, too sure-footed, too infectiously exuberant for that. But it's not quite revolutionary either. In dispensing with montage, *Timecode* liberates the medium up to a point, but is still constrained by the simple need (perhaps inherent in all drama) to order its material and tell a story. Ergo, *Timecode*'s structure nudges the viewer subtly towards what Figgis regards as the important frames.

Timecode unfolds like a fantastically textured stretch of contemporary jazz. Its segmented interior is maddening, involving, often exhilarating. But there is a strict methodology behind its madness, and what sounds like free-form chaos in the opening bars soon swings into orbit around a central, unifying structure. In attempting to reconfigure the language of film, *Timecode* bends the rules beautifully yet it never quite breaks them.

VILLAGE VOICE, 5/2/00, p. 130, Amy Taub

More fashionable than innovative, Mike Figgis's *Time Code* brings the hot new technology of digital video to bear on the hippest trend in Hollywood narratives—multiple intersecting story lines à la Robert Altman (who's been doing it intermittently for 30 years, but never more purposefully or economically than in *Nashville*). Figgis's contribution to this narrative genre is to put four unedited real-time stories on screen simultaneously. The image is divided into quadrants, thus allowing viewers to switch their attention at will. Each viewer becomes an editor, charged with the task of intercutting four takes into one 93-minute cinematic experience.

Figgis used the Sony DSR-1 camera, which holds 93-minute loads, is light enough to carry for that length of time, and can be synced to other camera guaranteeing the simultaneity of all four takes. The film was mapped rather than scripted. The actors were given outlines for their characters a situations (their jobs, their ambitions, who they're fucking, who they want to fuck). The map also indicated where they had to be at crucial moments, and the performers improvised accordingly. A camera person was assigned to each of the four story lines, and the four synchronous films were shot in their entirety many times over. With no mixing and matching allowed, the only editing Figgis did was to choose one take.

A thriller-parody about the biz, *Time Code* is in every sense a process movie. Its central location is a Sunset Boulevard building in which a ragtag production company is casting a straight-to-video slasher flick. The producer (Stellan Skarsgard) is estranged from his wife (Saffron Burrows) and involved with several other women, one of whom is an ambitious actress (Salma Hayek) with a jealous lesbian lover (Jeanne Tripplehorn). Guess who the villain turns out to be.

I suspect that *Time Code* was a lot more fun to make than it is to watch. Figgis's working method is closer to theater or live television than to film. But while it may have produced an adrenaline rush in cast and crew, it also caused the actors to jabber away and ham it up incessantly. No one wants to be the person who drops the ball when it means that four 93-minute takes go into the trash. With too much responsibility and too little structure, the actors turn into boors.

Warhol, who made many definitive real-time, split-screen movies (the most famous being *Chelsea Girls*), had, among his many filmmaking talents, an eye for performers. His superstars—from the nearly silent Nico to the witty Edie Sedgwick to the motor-mouthed Viva—were riveting. When the camera rolled, they rose to the occasion, shaping our perception of time with their desires and fantasies. Everything Figgis tries to do in *Time Code* , Warhol did three decades ago, including the Hollywood parody. True, Warhol's Auricon camera could only record 33 minutes at a time and it was too heavy to carry. *Chelsea Girls,* which is composed of 12 33-minute takes, may not be as structurally pure as *Time Code,* but the purity of real time is wasted when nothing's happening in it.

Also reviewed in:
CHICAGO TRIBUNE, 4/28/00, Friday/p. A, Mark Caro
NEW YORK TIMES, 4/ 28/00, p. E1, A. O. Scott
VARIETY, 5/1-7/00, p. 29, Dennis Harvey
WASHINGTON POST, 5/12/00, p. C5, Rita Kempley
WASHINGTON POST, 5/12/00, Weekend/p. 53, Desson Howe

TIME FOR DRUNKEN HORSES, A

A Shooting Gallery release of a Bahman Ghobadi Films production with the cooperation of the Farabi Cinema Foundation. *Producer:* Bahman Ghobadi. *Director:* Bahman Ghobadi. *Screenplay (Kurdish and Farsi with English subtitles):* Bahman Ghobadi. *Director of Photography:* Saed Nikzat. *Editor:* Samad Tavazoui. *Music:* Hussein Alizadeh. *Sound:* Morteza Dehnavi, Mehdi Darabi, and (music) Nasser Farhodi. *Art Director:* Bahman Ghobadi. *Running time:* 77 minutes. *MPAA Rating:* Not Rated.

CAST: Ayoub Ahmadi (Ayoub);   Roujin Younesi (Roujin);   Ameneh Ekhtiar-Dini (Ameneh); Mehdi Ekhtiar-Dini (Madi).

LOS ANGELES TIMES, 10/27/00, Calendar/p. 12, Kevin Thomas

The intriguing title of Kurdish Iranian filmmaker Bahman Ghobadi's "A Time for Drunken Horses" comes from a practice of Kurds along the rugged Iran-Iraq border. They get their dray animals, mainly mules, inebriated in order to be able to drive them back and forth across the border in severe winter weather as they transport smuggled goods into Iraq.

Ghobadi describes his beautiful, heart-rending film, a co-winner of the Camera d'Or at Cannes 2000, as "a humble tribute to my cultural heritage."

Life is hard for these poverty-stricken Kurds, among the 20 million who live as an ethnic minority in portions of Turkey and Syria as well as Iran and Iraq. It is especially true for an adolescent brother and sister, Ameneh (Ameneh Ekhtiar-Dini) and her older brother Ayoub (Ayoub Ahmadi). Like everyone else in their village, they are engaged in smuggling to survive.

Their mother is dead, their father is often absent, and they are the linchpins for their other siblings, in particular their brother Madi (Mehdi Ekhtiar-Dini), diminutive, disabled and sickly. Madi can barely walk and is carried most everywhere by either Ayoub or Ameneh.

Worse yet, the smuggling, an operation vulnerable to ambushes, is made horrifically dangerous by myriad land mines. Some villagers cannot even farm their land because it is riddled with mines.

This is a story of tender, loving family ties with the strength of iron; Ayoub and Ameneh are prepared to make any sacrifice to pay for the operation that Madi must have within the month if he is to survive—an operation that will buy him only an additional seven or eight months of life at best.

"A Time for Drunken Horses" is a film of simplicity and power, beautifully shot and effortlessly acted by nonprofessionals. One of the few Iranian films made largely in Kurdish, it is like many other Iranian films in that it reveals and implicitly comments upon hardship, injustice and inequity through the experiences of children.

Shrewdly, Ghobadi ends his film abruptly; what he is celebrating is neither triumph nor defeat but the dogged determination of a people to survive unselfishly despite terrible circumstances not of their own making.

NEW YORK, 11/6/00, p. 84, Peter Rainer

Bahman Ghobadi, the young Iranian whose first feature is *A Time for Drunken Horses*, has a marvelous eye for children's faces. He brings out not only their innocence but also their preternatural gravity. At times, you feel as if you could look into one of these faces and see the whole life that will be imprinted upon it.

Ghobadi's film takes place near the Iraq border in the remote and mountainous Kurdish region of Iran, and the harshness of existence there strips away the artifice from people's lives. Ayoub, who struggles to survive with his three sisters and two brothers, is a fiercely resilient young adolescent portrayed without sentimentality; when his ailing, dwarf-like brother Madi requires an operation to survive, if only briefly, Ayoub places himself in great danger to raise the money for the surgery. He accepts the danger and its consequences matter-of-factly. His persistence in saving his siblings makes him a hero, though he would never think of himself in that way. We've become so accustomed to Hollywood portrayals of childhood, sappy with uplift and cant, that Ghobadi's view has a cauterizing effect. The heroism in this movie is fully earned.

NEW YORK POST, 10/27/00, p. 46, Jonathan Foreman

Like so many of the wonderful films that have come out of Iran in recent years, Bahman Ghobadi's moving "A Time for Drunken Horses" avoids government censorship by telling a story through the eyes of children, and achieves a neo-realist authenticity by using non-professional actors.

In this case, the children are Kurdish orphans who live in an impoverished village near the Iran-Iraq border where the people subsist on money made in the risky business of smuggling.

When a land-mine explosion kills their father, the oldest little boy, Ayoub, gets a job carrying heavy loads through the snow to support the family.

But Ayoub's disabled brother Madi needs an operation, and the children try to figure out another way of raising funds.

Ghobadi (himself an Iranian Kurd) takes some gorgeous shots against the snow, but his storytelling is uneven and often slow. Inadequate subtitles don't help.

But watching these kids burdened by crushing adult responsibilities is heartrending stuff, and the documentary-style picture it paints of a people and a place is fascinating.

NEWSDAY, 10/27/00, Part II/p. B8, John Anderson

The embargoes against Iraq and the countless landmines in Iran have proved mutually beneficial: The Iranians can't farm, so they smuggle truck tires into Iraq. It's like synergy.

That children should be the focus of "A Time for Drunken Horses"—whose title comes from the fact that the snow-covered border terrain is so treacherous the mules are given vodka to make them cross the mountains—is hardly unusual for Iranian cinema. Or, since writer-director Bahman Ghobadi seems to be the only working Kurdish director, it's not unusual for Kurdish cinema, either.

But as the Iranian cineaste Jamsheed Akrami has written, "Iranian children's films are so heavily imbued with melancholy and anguish that they are virtually inappropriate, if not outright inaccessible, for children." So it is with "A Time for Drunken Horses," a movie of splendid craft, about disarming poverty.

While containing imagery and photography vivid enough to set it apart from most of its compatriot cinema, the story line of "Horses" has the typically archetypal feel of many Iranian films. Ayoub (Ayoub Ahmadi), whose father is a smuggler missing along the Iraq-Iran border, has been handed responsibility for his siblings, who include young Ameneh (Ameneh Ekhtiardini), our occasional narrator, and Madi (Medhi Ekhtiar-dini), their dwarf, crippled brother. At 15 and looking 5, Madi serves as a potent metaphor for the misshapen future of his family, but for Ayoub he is very real: Surviving on pain injections and the affection of his family, Madi is mortally in need of an operation. The lengths taken to secure its price include Ayoub's own attempts at smuggling, an older sister sold into marriage, deals gone sour and a desperate flight into Iraq.

The faces of Ghobadi's characters are often beautiful, and usually eloquent: No one has to speak for the sentiments to be as plain as billboards. But there's poetry here, too, and a certain crabbed humor: Madi sitting before his gift from Ayoub, an old muscle poster of Arnold Schwarzenegger, is a caustic cultural barb, if less convincing as pathos. But where Ghobadi really stuns us is in his pictures of his country and the shadows cast by its bedraggled people.

SIGHT AND SOUND, 9/01, p. 55, Geoffrey Macnab

A rugged mountain village in Iran, close to the Iraqi border, the present. With both parents dead, Ayoub, a young Iranian Kurd, assumes responsibility for his family. Ayoub's teenage brother Madi is suffering from a crippling disease and needs constant injections and a supply of pills to stay alive. Ayoub is told by the doctor that Madi will die unless he has an operation (which Ayoub can't afford). Ayoub takes the only job available—helping smuggle goods over the mountains. Not having his own mule, he is in a poor bargaining position with his bosses. The money he makes is spent on keeping his family alive and providing his youngest sister with exercise books for school. In a pact brokered by their uncle, Ayoub's eldest sister agrees to marry an Iraqi Kurd; she has been told his family will pay for Madi's operation. When she meets her husband, her new family rejects Madi. Ayoub is given a mule as her dowry.

Ayoub resolves to cross the border (with Madi in tow) and sell the mule to pay for the operation. He and his fellow travellers are ambushed. Their mules, which are fed alcohol to help them cope with the duress of their work, are too drunk to flee. Everybody except Ayoub runs down the mountain in panic. Ayoub removes the mule's load, helps it to its feet, and carries on up the mountain, past the border.

Iranian films adopting a child's-eye view of the world are sometimes accused of sidestepping political controversy, or of trying too hard to keep the censors happy. Epic yarns about a kid trying to buy a goldfish (Jafar Panahi's *The White Balloon*) or a brother and sister sharing a pair of shoes (Majid Majidi's *The Children of Heaven*) may be affecting and beautifully observed, but they touch only obliquely on (what certain western critics perceive to be) the harshness of daily life in Iran. This is not a charge that can be levelled at Bahman Ghobadi's debut feature. Once again, we're seeing events from a youngster's perspective—here, that of the recently orphaned Ayoub, who's barely into his teens. There are numerous low-angle shots, but in the world that Ghobadi portrays—that of a small village high in the mountains of Iranian Kurdistan—the lines between childhood and adulthood are blurred. Following the death of his parents, Ayoub has had to take on responsibility for his entire family, including a handicapped younger brother racked with illness.

Ghobadi apparently knows his subject matter at first hand. The young writer-director (who also plays a leading role in Samira Makhmalbaf's *Blackboards* and was an assistant-director on Abbas Kiarostami's *The Wind Will Carry Us)* grew up in Iranian Kurdistan and was himself sent out to work from an early age; the plight of his actors (mostly young unknowns drawn from the region) matches that of the characters they play: the handicapped boy who plays Ayoub's ailing brother Madi—Ghobadi revealed in an interview—really does need an operation if he is not to die.

Ghobadi doesn't sentimentalise or provide a glibly happy ending: the young orphans here live in desperate poverty; their village has few modern amenities; the only way to make money is to embark on perilous smuggling journeys across the Iraqi border. Even the animals suffer—the climate is so harsh, the loads so heavy that the mules are given alcohol to help them do their work. Just as audiences in the early 1930s were taken aback by Buñuel's documentary *Las hurdes/Land Without Bread*, (1933) which portrayed a remote region of northern Spain that appeared stuck in medieval times, viewers today may be shocked by the austerity of the Kurds' lives.

A Time For Drunken Horses is occasionally a little clumsy in its exposition. Once the characters have been established and we've learned their problems, the narrative risks stalling. Caught in a netherworld between fiction and documentary, the film carries a searing emotional charge. The sense of helplessness that afflicts Ayoub and his family as they attempt to save Madi is particularly well conveyed. The handicapped boy is a teenager, but one with the physique of a baby; and in the course of the film, this intelligent, sweet-natured kid with huge mournful eyes becomes a symbol of the Kurds' humanity and selflessness. He is utterly dependent on others, but whatever their own problems, they refuse to abandon him. One sister is even prepared to marry in the hope that her bridegroom's family will pay for Madi's operation.

Despite the subject matter, there are moments of lyricism and quiet humour. At one stage, Ayoub buys Madi an incongruous present—a picture of a pumped-up bodybuilder flexing his pecs (it's about the only reference to western consumer culture). Even the most catastrophic scene, when the smugglers are ambushed high up near the border, with the mules too drunk to turn tail, has a perverse beauty about it. The huge rubber tyres loaded on the mules' backs are cut free; the mules stagger to their feet, but nobody can stop the tyres from careening back down the icy slopes.

Strikingly shot by Saed Nikzat on location in the mountains, excellently acted by its young cast, *A Time For Drunken Horses* has an extremely grim undertow. For all Ayoub's courage and his family members' loyalty to one another, there's no obvious solution to their problems. Throughout, the characters refuse to despair; audiences, however, are likely to prove less resilient in the face of so bleak a story.

VILLAGE VOICE, 10/31/00, p. 164, J. Hoberman

A Time for Drunken Horses, one of the two Iranian first features that shared this year's Camera d'Or at Cannes, begins with the sound of an adult interviewing a child but, compared to *George Washington,* this movie—set mainly in the Kurdish village where filmmaker Bahman Ghobadi was born—is straightforward observation.

A band of stoical children, saddled with adult responsibilities, compete for menial jobs in the village marketplace or, more arduously, serve as smugglers transporting contraband goods across the Iran-Iraq border. Gradually, it emerges that the protagonists are four or five orphaned siblings—one of whom, 15-year-old Madi, has failed to grow beyond the size of a small toddler and cries like a baby when the doctor gives him a shot. Cared for by his younger brother and sister (the performers are apparently dramatizing actual relationships), Madi is doomed to die in 10 days unless money can be raised for an operation to keep him alive for another six months.

Underdog tenacity in the face of hopeless odds is the indie credo. The 30-year-old Ghobadi, who was Abbas Kiarostami's assistant on *The Wind Will Carry Us,* also set in Kurdistan, is Iran's first Kurdish director. Perhaps the implications of this will be explained by the critic for a distinguished local weekly who, in the year's most smugly brainless review, made the "sociological" observation that Kiarostami was like a third-world pest with a useless knowledge of English. For his part, Ghobadi labors under no compulsion to explain exactly what is going on. Most scenes plunge the viewer into the middle of a situation. The smuggling is blatant and messy—when Iraqi border guards routinely impound a truck full of contraband texts, the kids scramble home in the snow, perhaps for miles. (The title for this single-minded, sometimes harrowing movie comes from the smugglers' practice of dosing their horses with vodka to keep them working in the cold.)

At one point, Madi's eldest sister betroths herself to an Iraqi Kurd, imagining that this will help arrange for the operation. Madi is literally bundled up as part of the bridal procession, but the groom's family reneges on the deal and refuses to take him. Ultimately, they buy off the bride's siblings with a mule that the youngest boy will use to smuggle Madi into Iraq. It's a bit startling to see the movie put forth the idea that Iraq is a more technologically advanced (and even safer) country than Iran. As the children brave the minefields to cross the border, the movie does as well.

Also reviewed in:
CHICAGO TRIBUNE, 10/27/00, Friday/p. I, Michael Wilmington
NEW YORK TIMES, 10/27/00, E. 16, A. O. Scott
VARIETY, 5/22-28/00, p. 26, Deborah Young

TIME REGAINED

A Kino International release of a Gemini Films/France 2 Cinema/Les Films du Lendemain/Blu Cinematografica production. *Producer:* Paulo Branco. *Director:* Raoul Ruiz. *Screenplay (French with English subtitles):* Gilles Taurand and Raoul Ruiz. *Based on the book "Time Regained" by:* Marcel Proust. *Director of Photography:* Ricardo Aronovich. *Editor:* Denise de Casabianca. *Music:* Jorge Arriagada. *Sound:* Philippe Morel and (music) Gérard Rousseau. *Sound Editor:* Vincent Guillon. *Casting:* Richard Rousseau and Adriana Sabbatini. *Art Director:* Bruno Beaugé. *Sound Effects:* Pascal Mazière. *Costumes:* Gabriella Pescucci and Caroline de Vivaise. *Make-up:* Cédric Gérard. *Running time:* 158 minutes. *MPAA Rating:* Not Rated.

CAST: Catherine Deneuve (Odette de Forcheville); Emmanuelle Béart (Gilberte); Vincent Perez (Charlie Morel); Pascal Greggory (Robert de Saint-Loup); Marie-France Pisier (Madame Simone Verdurin); Chiara Mastroianni (Albertine); Arielle Dombasle (Madame de Farcy); Edith Scob (Oriane de Guermantes); Elsa Zylberstein (Rachel); Christian Vadim (Albert Bloch); Dominique Labourier (Madame Cottard); Philippe Morier-Genoud (Monsieur Cottard); Melvil Poupaud (Prince de Foix); Mathilde Seigner (Céleste); Jacques Pieiller (Jupien); Hélène Surgère (Françoise); André Engel (Marcel as an Old Man); Georges Du Fresne (Marcel as a Child); Monique Mélinand (Marcel's Grandmother); Laurence Février (Marcel's Mother); Jean-François Balmer (Uncle Adolphe); Marcello Mazzarella (Marcel Proust); John Malkovich (Baron de Charlus); Patrice Chéreau (Voice of Marcel Proust); Pierre Mignard (Marcel as an Adolescent); Lucien Pascal (Prince de Guermantes); Jérôme Prieur (Monsieur Verdurin); Bernard Pautrat (Charles Swann); Alain Robbe-Grillet (Goncourt); Ingrid Caven (Russian Princess); Jean-Claude Jay (Duc de Guermantes); Camille Du Fresna (Gilberte as a Child); Alain Guillo (The Great Designer); Xavier Brière (Marcel's Butler); Bernard Garnier (Cambremer); Monique Couturier (Marquise de Villeparisis); Alain Rimoux (Monsieur Bontemps); Isa Mercure (Madame Bontemps); Pierre Alain Chapuis (Guermantes Butler); Jean-François Lapalus (Head Waiter, Café de la Paix); Damien O'Doul (Gaspard, Cook in Café de la Paix); Daniel Isoppo (Hotel Manager, Balbec); Patrice Juiff (Young Waiter, Balbec); Pascal Tokatlian (Hotel Bellhop, Balbec); Marine Delterme (Morel's Friend); Jean Badin (Rachel's Husband); Laurent Schwarr (Maurice); Hattou Mess (Monsieur Léon); Alexandre Soulie (Louis, Military Man); Sébastien Libessart (2nd Military Man); Fabrice Cals and Jean-Pierre Allain (Workmen at Jupien); Carl de Miranda (Sailor at Jupien); Hervé Falloux (Monsieur Redingote); Lou (Speaker); Philippe Lehembre (General); Vanzetta (Officer); Rosita Mital (Old Maid); Tatie Vauville (Old Maid's Mother); Michel Armin (Distinguished Client at Jupien); Pierre Villanova (Monsieur René); André Delmas (Priest at Jupien); Philippe Gauguet (Jupien's Chauffeur); Serge Brincat (Waiter, Café de la Paix); Yann Claasen, Bruno Guillot, and Emmanuel Crepin (Military Men, Café de la Paix); Francis Leplay (Jupien's Employee); Isabelle Auroy (Madame de Sainte Euverte); Jacques-François Zeller (Marcel's Grandfather); Serge Dekramer (Marcel's Father); Suzy Marquis (Old Woman at Gilberte); Laure De Clermont-Tonnerre (Gilberte's Daughter); Georgette Bastien-Vona (Madame de Marsantes); René Marquant (Monsieur d'Argencourt); Laetitia Colin-Vialaneix (Léa); Maxime Nourissat (Léo); Romain Sellier (Charle's Friend, Café de la Paix); Pierre Pitrou (Photographer); Alexandre Boussat (René, Morel's Friend); Sheila Irubacek (Vicomtesse de Saint-Fiacre); Bernard Barberet (One-Legged Man); Diane Dassigny (Pianist, Bal de Tête); Guillaume Choquet (Violinist, Bal de Tête); Alain Duclos (Uncle Adolphe's Valet); Raymonde Bronstein (Double, aged Gilberte); Madeleine Lechoux (Double, aged Madame Vendurin); Alberte Barbou (Double, aged Rachel); Jean Léger (Double, André Engel); Manuela Morgaine (Reader); Christian Magis (Blind Man); Daniel Beretta (Additional voice of Baron de Charlus).

CHRISTIAN SCIENCE MONITOR, 6/2/00, p. 15, David Sterritt

"Time Regained" borrows its story and themes from "Remembrance of Things Past," one of this century's greatest novels—and one of the most unfilmable, if only because its introspective tale takes thousands of pages for author Marcel Proust to tell. Some hardy cinéastes have taken a crack at it, though, including Harold Pinter, who wrote a 3½-hour screenplay that has never gone into production.

Not long ago, director Raoul Ruiz would have seemed an unlikely candidate for this enterprise, since he used to specialize in quick, inexpensive pictures. He has turned to more elaborate projects, though, and "Time Regained" is the most lavishly produced yet. Its cast is expertly chosen, and its images are splendidly photographed.

What's missing is a sense of Proust's profound human understanding and Ruiz's free-wheeling cinematic energy. In short, each artist seems held back by the other. One wishes Pinter's version, which is more intuitive and impressionistic, would somehow reach the screen.

CINEASTE, Vol. XXV, No 1, 1999, p. 43, Melissa Anderson

With its labyrinthine prose, plethora of characters, and multiple shifts in time, Marcel Proust's magnum opus *A la Recherche du Temps Perdu (In Search of Lost Time)* does not lend itself easily to film adaptation. Earlier screen adaptations of Proust's novel, one of the greatest modernist masterpieces, include Volker Schlöndorff's woefully affected *Un Amour de Swann* (1983). Yet Raúl Ruiz's skillful rendering (cowritten with Gilles Taurand) and direction of *Le Temps Retrouvé (Time Regained)*, the last book of Proust's epic, is laudable primarily for not making Proust's work *recherché*. Rather than emphasizing the preciosity of this grand novel, Ruiz—whose own films are marked by an elliptical sense of time—smartly utilizes cinematic tricks to evoke the multiple layers of memory in Proust's writing—writing which in itself anticipates a cinematographic sensibility. For those who are not familiar with Proust's sprawling novel, Ruiz's film may seem somewhat impenetrable since he wastes no time on exposition. True to Proust's esthetic, Ruiz's film plunges immediately into a series of oneiric, time-bending episodes linked by the vagaries of memory.

Although not necessarily a summation of the previous volumes of *A la Recherche* (Proust's writing remains to the very end adamantly antithetical to a conventional narrative arc), *Le Temps Retrouvé* is nonetheless concerned with the irrevocable changes wrought by World War I, death, loss, reconciliation, and, above all, the ravaging effects of aging—themes which Ruiz, by occasionally borrowing incidents from the preceding volumes of the novel, handles quite adeptly. The film begins with an ailing Marcel Proust himself (Marcello Mazzarella), haggard and gaunt, painfully dictating from his bed the sentences that will become *Le Temps Retrouvé* (which was published in 1927, five years after its author's death). After this arduous exercise, Proust examines, with the aid of a magnifying glass, a series of sepia-toned photographs of the main characters in his novel.

Here the leitmotif of Proust's scrutinizing gaze is introduced—a meticulous, often ruthlessly vicious gift of observation bestowed upon the Narrator (also played by Mazzarella), who is sometimes referred to as Marcel, Proust's literary alter-ego. As a chronicler of Paris's moribund aristocratic society, the Narrator notes later in the film, "I was X-raying them," suggesting a voyeuristic gaze as penetrating as that afforded by a camera's tight close-up. Ruiz skillfully frames this insatiable voyeurism as a peep show when the Narrator, peering through a porthole-sized window, spies on the sinisterly fey Baron de Charlus (John Malkovich) in the throes of passion when being whipped by a male prostitute.

Ruiz not only makes the connection between the Narrator's voyeurism with that of a film spectator's but also suggests that the Narrator is also a cinematographer, one whose *mise-en-scène* is composed of memory, dreams, and childhood fantasies. In one scene the young Marcel (played by Georges du Fresne, the star of 1996's *Ma Vie en Rose)* maneuvers a magic lantern, creating a gorgeous spectacle of light and color. As young Marcel says of this precinematic invention in *A la Recherche du Temps Perdu,* "[I]t substituted for the opaqueness of my walls an impalpable iridescence, supernatural phenomena of many colors, in which legends were depicted as on a shifting and transitory window." Similarly, Marcel's memories of the "legends" of Parisian society are also shifting and transitory. During the party scene hosted by the Princesse de Guermantes, Marcel mistakes Gilberte (Emmanuelle Béart) for her mother Odette (Catherine Deneuve), a mishap which suggests the conflation of characters and past and present within his memory.

In one of Ruiz's more adroit liberties with the text, the young Marcel is depicted as a film projectionist sitting high above the oblivious members of the aristocracy. His delicate face is alternately obscured and illuminated by the flickering of the images—which, appropriately enough, are early films by Georges Méliès, who was as innovative in film language as Proust was in written language. Ruiz's own cinematic innovations are glorious tribute to the moments in Proust's novel in which the laws of gravity and motion are obliterated by the more powerful laws of memory. During a recital at the Guermantes's party, entire rows of seated guests tilt left then right; trees mysteriously change position; and the Narrator himself remains stationary in front of the animated shifts from the past to the present.

Making the themes of time and memory even more poignant is the casting in the film which is as varied as the constellation of players in Proust's Parisian high society. It was particularly brilliant of Ruiz to cast Catherine Deneuve—who better represents the aristocracy of French actors?—and Marie-France Pisier—who appeared in three of the five films in François Truffaut's Proustian Antoine Doinel series—as Mme. Verdurin. "The true paradises are the ones that we have lost," muses the Narrator (in a voice-over provided by Patrice Chereau) towards the end of *Le Temps Retrouvé*. Upon first seeing the older Deneuve and Pisier, one cannot help but reflect back on their youthful incarnations during the halcyon, lionized years of French film in the 1960s—a period that is not necessarily a paradise "lost" but one that is worshipped as an era of youthful exuberance, vitality, and possibility. The faces of Deneuve and Pisier, then, become the icons—much like Proust's infamous madeleine—which evoke our own cinematic memories. This very iconicity of Deneuve and Pisier is accentuated by the lusciously surreal recurrence—spaced about an hour apart in the film—of Odette's entrance into Mme. Verdurin's salon after several years of absence from Mme. Verdurin's "little clan." This brief reunion acts as a mnemonic device on two different levels, reminding the viewer both of the significance of the two formidable characters throughout Proust's epic *and* the regal status of the two actresses in the history of French cinema.

Additionally, the presence in the film of Deneuve's own children, daughter Chiara Mastroianni as Albertine and son Christian Vadim as Albert Bloch, although certainly firmly rooting us in French cinema's present (if not its future), nevertheless also suggests the lineage of acting aristocracy. The casting of Emmanuelle Béart as Gilberte is also particularly savvy, for Béart is the 'successor' to Deneuve's reign as *grande dame* of French cinema in much the same way that Gilberte is positioned to supplant Odette.

Rather than making a tedious, costume-driven, narrative film of a text that poses many challenges to cinematic adaptation, Ruiz wisely chooses to explore the rich metaphorical connections between the reveries and memories evoked by film—the most time-bound of all arts—with those recalled by Proust in *A la Recherche du Temps Perdu*. In *Le Temps Retrouvé*, Proust writes: "So often, in the course of my life, reality had disappointed me because at the instant when my senses perceived it in my imagination, which was the only organ that I possessed for the enjoyment of beauty, could not apply itself to it, in virtue of that ineluctable law which ordains that we can only imagine what is absent." Ruiz pays the ultimate tribute to Proust by not only honoring the author's imagination but also by enriching the film with his own creative directorial flourishes.

LOS ANGELES TIMES, 7/14/00, Calendar/p. 4, Kevin Thomas

Raul Ruiz, the audacious Chilean director who has long lived in France, has pulled off his most ambitious coup yet: a mesmerizing, shimmering and amazingly successful adaptation of "Time Regained," the final two volumes in Marcel Proust's monumental "Remembrance of Things Past."

An exquisitely wrought period piece of remarkable timelessness, it is a multilayered accomplishment that does not require viewers to have read Proust, though surely it is more accessible to those who have.

The best way to approach the film is simply to allow it to wash over you; key relationships within Proust's substantial dramatis personae gradually become clear. It's not necessary to sort out the connections between everyone because Proust's implicit point is that, in the rarefied high society that was his universe, everyone was connected to everyone else one way or another.

Ruiz's "Time Regained" manages to be a lot of things all at once. It is a depiction of an old world giving way to the new as France is ravaged by World War I, and by extension a depiction of 19th century literature yielding to the introspective modern novel. It is a portrait of an artist in the process of discovering that he can transform the life of his imagination into a work of art.

Proust's subject was the eternal human comedy, and Ruiz and his co-adapter view it through the memories of the asthmatic Proust (Marcello Mazzarella) as he lies dying, nearing the completion of "Time Regained," his recollections triggered by a collection of old photographs. True paradises, Proust concludes, are those that have been lost, to be recalled only in memory.

What is crucial and inspired here is that what Proust is shown to be remembering, apart from interspersed intervals in his childhood and on his deathbed, are not the real-life events and individuals that formed the bases of his writings but the characters and incidents they inspired. In short, Proust is comforted, touched, amused and moved by what his imagination has wrought, just as we are.

This glittering world in which Proust moved so easily, as above all an observer but also a trusted confidant and advisor, has been brought to dazzling life by Ruiz in all its elegance and luxury.

It is the world of privilege and status, of gala parties and concerts and dinners and seaside vacations—a world preserved in part by the late prodigious photographer Jacques Lartigue. It is a world of sexual intrigue and social ambition and, beneath a veneer of wit and manners, it possesses a great deal more mobility than you might imagine, for all its ancient titles and formality. Beautiful women and handsome men make breathtaking progress on their looks and sexual availability.

Indeed, it was the enchanting mistress of his own uncle who captivated him and helped spark his interest in the workings of high society. She would become in "Time Regained," book and film, the agelessly ravishing Odette (Catherine Deneuve).

Her daughter Gilberte (Emmanuelle Beart) marries fashionably but unhappily to the handsome Marquis Robert de Saint-Loup (Pascal Greggory). He takes lush actress-demimondaine Rachel (Elsa Zylberstein) as a mistress and, as another lover, Morel (Vincent Perez), an aspiring concert pianist who had first been the protege of Saint-Loup's kinky uncle, Baron de Charlus (John Malkovich, with hair and a fine command of French).

One of the important achievements of Ruiz, who moves effortlessly between past and present, memory and imagination, is to depict subtly the ever so gradual intrusion of war on the privileged. The initial responses are flip and shallow, but Saint-Loup proves a noble hero in battle, as does Morel, who redeems himself after a period of scandalous desertion.

Cinematographer Ricardo Aronovich brings to glowing life a past flawlessly and richly re-created by production designer Bruno Beauge and by costume designers Gabriella Pescucci and Caroline de Vivaise, whose clothes are often the key indicators of the time in which a sequence is set.

Jorge Arriagada's score is as evocative as it is elegant.

As Proust's health fails, someone, partially overhearing gossip, asks for clarification: Is it Proust's life or novel that is over? Informed that he has completed "Remembrance of Things Past" at last but lives still, the inquirer remarks, "What then does he have to live for?"

What indeed: The man for whom his life became his work died seven months later at 51 on Nov. 18, 1922.

NEWSDAY, 6/16/00, Part II/p. B6, John Anderson

It's highly unlikely that French novelist Marcel Proust ever went to the movies, though he might have seen Chaplin, Griffith and at least one woman he'd have appreciated, Theda Bara. His epoch and the cinema's overlapped and, in a Proustian way, almost complement each other: the author was always looking back, and in his obsession modernized the novel; cinema was a step toward the future, but has always been about looking back.

In "Time Regained" (the last installment of Proust's mammoth "In Search of Lost Time"), director Raul Ruiz joins the equations, accomplishing at least one Proustian achievement: awing us with the complexity and ambition of his task. Proust's work reinvents time and place, melding memory and character in a stream of impressions and judgments, constructions and reconstructions in a seemingly endless striving toward the perfect dream and a perfect timelessness. Likewise Ruiz.

The film, even at almost three hours, is an impression of an impression, a kind of printmaking process in which something is always lost. But something is gained here as well: an artist's interpretation of a dissimilar artist's work, the dissimilarity being an edge Ruiz exploits to gorgeous advantage.

The characters parade out of Proust's novel in all their intrigues, romantic entanglements, embodied by some of France's more spectacular vessels: Catherine Deneuve, Emmanuelle Beart, Vincent Perez, Chiara Mastroianni. Also, John Malkovich as the "ladylike" Baron de Charlus, and a Narrator named Marcel (Marcello Mazzarella), who might as well be named Raul.

SIGHT AND SOUND, 1/00, p. 61, Keith Reader

Paris, after World War I. The reclusive and asthmatic Marcel Proust, all but bedridden, is finishing his opus *A la recherche du temps perdu*. He scrutinises photographs of the major figures in his life and the fictional text. The rest of the narrative oscillates between the Verdurin and Guermantes salons in Paris, Marcel's childhood in the village of Cormbray, his youthful summer vacations at the Norman resort of Balbec, later stays in Venice and the war years in Paris. From childhood to maturity, Marcel moves through an at once real and imagined world whose denizens include: the camp Baron de Charlus, Charlus' one-time lover the violinist Charlie Morel, the war-hero Saint-Loup and his wife Gilberte, the Prince de Guermantes and his wife Oriane, the brassy socialite Madame Verdurin, Charles Swann and his coquettish wife Odette (Gilberte's mother), and the actress and singer Rachel. Past and present, the experienced, the remembered and the partly forgotten overlap and flow into one another like the stream with which the film begins. At the end, the older Marcel watches as his boyhood self runs along the beach at Balbec, time at last regained through art.

The less-than-linear form of the synopsis above illustrates one of the major difficulties in filming or writing about Proust's towering classic of modernity. The story of an invalid writer facing premature death who retrieves through art his childhood anxieties and adult frivolities, the gap between the overarching narrative and the myriad smaller narratives which comprise *A la recherche* is too vast to be bridged even in a film as long as this. Earlier Proust-based films have dealt with this problem by narrowing their focus to the microcosm that is *Un Amour de Swann* (Volker Schlöndorff's film of that title), or to the final days of the historical Proust's life as he wrote against the clock of death (Percy Adlon's superb *Céleste*). For *Time Regained* Raoul Ruiz adapts a similar strategy, but goes for broke by concentrating on the work's final volume, in which its multifarious narrative strands converge and it becomes clear that its end is in its beginning. The result is richer and more inclusive in its sweep than previous adaptations and more visually spectacular. The colours—notably the gold of many of the salon scenes echoing the sands of Balbec or the architecture of Venice—are ravishing, and the movements of the camera, at once caressing and sweeping, impart a thrill rarely encountered in the cinema.

Nonetheless, *Time Regained* is anything but a heritage movie, as you would expect for a film made by a Chilean expatriate with a background in leftist politics and experimental film-making. Ruiz rewrites Proust in cinematic terms. The camera movements—particularly at the end where we move from the Guermantes salon through a 'room of memory' dotted with top hats to a terrace and the beach at Balbec—correspond to the oscillations of the written narration between the recollected and the imagined, the past and the present. In this respect the film evokes Resnais' *Last Year at Marienbad*, notably in the salon scenes (Madame Verdurin's high-pitched laugh, as if poised on the brink of hysteria, echoes Delphine Seyrig's in *Marienbad*).

Time Regained is a *tour deforce*, gorgeous yet stark. That starkness is achieved partly through the constant threat or actual presence of war which gives an edge to the scenes of brittle social comedy, partly through the unflinching way the film treats such scenes as Charlus' flagellation in Jupien's gay bordello, which offsets potential charges of voyeurism by the exquisitely simple device of framing the narrating Marcel in a window as the blows descend. The cast are on the whole splendid. Catherine Deneuve is at once queenly and raffish as Odette, Emmanuelle Béart gives the most mature performance of her career as Gilberte and Marie-France Pisier is magnificently high-camp as Madame Verdurin. If there is a false note it's struck by John Malkovich's Charlus competing, alas, with Alain Delon's magnificent performance in the

Schlöndorff film, and far too reedy voiced and mincing to carry the same weight as Proust's grotesque, but ultimately loving and loveable character.

My one anxiety concerns how accessible Ruiz's film will be to an audience with little or no knowledge of the source novel. Its extraordinary textual sweep is likely to bewilder such viewers. The brief allusions to the force of involuntary memory, notably in the 'madeleine scene', could well pass them by altogether. However, Ruiz has come closer than either of his predecessors to the superhuman task of filming Proust in his entirety, for which it would be churlish to criticise him. The audacious transposition of the finale, from an epiphany in the Gutermantes salon to one on a Norman beach, works because the waves of the sea echo time flowing stream of the beginning, in a triumphant cinematic correlative of what a leading Proust scholar once described to me as an extraordinarily happy ending. The happiest ending, for viewers unfamiliar with the original, would be for them to be drawn to it by Ruiz's masterly film.

TIME, 7/17/00, p. 72, Richard Corliss

Marcel Proust wrote great gossip. His epic novel, *A la recherche du temps perdu (In Search of Lost Time)*, is artful celebrity journalism about the beautiful people of Paris in the early 20th century. This was also when movies came of age; and the novel's shuffling of tenses, from present to past to conditional, has its film equivalent in the flashback—the lightning stroke of emotional teleportation that brings a memory instantly, poignantly, to the mind's eye.

The chic, assured film that Raúl Ruiz has made of the novel's final volume, *Le temps retrouvé (Time Regained)*, is an ideal Proust in pictures. It roams through prewar drawing rooms, attending to whispers of malice and amour. A brilliant man (Marcello Mazzarella, as Marcel) talks to a ravishing woman (Emmanuelle Béart as Gilberte) of an old wound. "Heartbreak can kill," he says, "but leaves no trace." The roué Charlus (John Malkovich) takes his sexual pleasures at the business end of a whip. These characters are often crushed by the burden of glamour, but the film isn't. It wears its gravity with a buoyant ease, seeing through walls, magically turning statues into people. It shows Marcel, as a child, watching himself as a young man—just as we all hit the replay button on our lives.

Like the turn-of-the-20th-century fantasy films of Georges Méliès, *Time Regained* reminds you that all cinema is a clever trick of the light.

At 2 hr. 42 min., *Time Regained* has its slow spots, especially during the war years, when the prime social occasions are the funerals of those lost in either war or melancholy. Even then, there are beguilements aplenty in the work of some of France's ageless actress-beauties: Béart, Catherine Deneuve, Arielle Dombasle, Edith Scob, Marie-France Pisier. In their smart frocks and pretty predicaments, they make Proust seem a fashion that could never go out of style. This is a serious filmgoer's treat: intelligence cloaked in elegance.

VILLAGE VOICE, 6/20/00, p. 149, J. Hoberman

Time Regained, the tastefully brash, subtly eccentric, and altogether triumphant Raúl Ruiz adaptation of the labyrinthian volume that brings Marcel Proust's *Remembrance of Things Past* to its magnificent conclusion, is a golden reverie on a passing age—namely ours.

Writing in the light of the Lumière brothers' cinematographer Proust sought to have his readers visualize temporality; filming at the dawn of the digital era, Ruiz allows the flow of static images through the movie projector to merge with the stream of time, while pondering the paradox of memories fixed in emulsion. *Time Regained*'s characters are introduced as the dying Proust shuffles through his collection of photos. "Then one day," he muses, "everything changes."

The movie searches for that day. A humorously shocking scene in a male bordello notwithstanding, *Time Regained*—which had its local premiere at the last New York Film Festival—is primarily a series of spectacular social gatherings through which men stroll beneath outsize hats and women glide in feathered finery. The action is set mainly during the always off-camera First World War, and everyone is living *le mode rétro*. The funerals are oddly festive; the other receptions have a comic haunted-house feel. At one, the guests obligingly turn to stone to serve as screens for the shadow play of the child Marcel's magic lantern. Elsewhere, figures are frozen and illuminated by the camera while Ruiz integrates vintage films throughout—reveling in the presence of this new entertainment machine.

Proust is a writer whose work defeated such would-be adapters as Joseph Losey, Bernardo Bertolucci, and Luchino Visconti. Volker Schlöndorff eliminated Marcel's subjective consciousness in his tepid adaptation of *Swann's Way;* Ruiz makes this observer his central character. The bedridden writer is visited by ghosts in his dreams and watched by his childhood self in his memories. A pursed and pomaded near-double for Proust, Italian actor Marcello Mazzarella makes a dapper little outsider in an ostentatiously glittering ensemble. Even the star turns—which include such once and future divas as Catherine Deneuve, Emmanuelle Béart, Marie-France Pisier, and Edith Scob—are fully inhabited performances. As the perverse Baron Charlus, John Malkovich is the personification of wit, and particularly after his character suffers a stroke, the actor's French only improves his mannerist delivery.

Given the audacity of adapting the last novel in a multi-volume series, *Time Regained* presents a few difficulties for those unfamiliar with Proust's novel—although it also serves as a superb trailer. (When the movie opened in the U.K. early this year, it elevated Proust to best-sellerdom.) As David Cronenberg did with *Naked Lunch,* Ruiz has made a film about the novel—it is a meditation on, rather than a copy of, the original. Ruiz imagines Proust as though Proust were imagining a movie. (Thanks to the model Ruiz provides, Hou Hsiao-hsien's time-twisting masterpiece, *The Puppetmaster,* becomes retrospectively "Proustian.")

Although *Time Regained* is not as aggressively cheap or provocatively lurid as standard Ruiz, the Chilean-born filmmaker has not abandoned his "underdeveloped" disrespect for European culture. At times, *Time Regained* suggests an irreverently lively, historical, and colorized version of *Last Year at Marienbad.* Playfully jumbling time and space, freezing the moment and choreographing long, fluid takes, doubling back to jump ahead, it's full of surprises. The most amazing thing is that this may be the most relaxed movie Ruiz has ever made. Would that it were the most commercially successful. The daring of the conception is matched only by the brilliance of the execution. (All hail Kino in releasing what is so far the most exhilarating movie—movie of the year.)

With misplaced nostalgia, contemporary filmmakers continue to revisit those literary classics written before there were movies. Ruiz is more creatively anachronistic. This is a 20th-century movie about a 20th-century novel. The filmmaker attempts to approximate not Proust's prose but rather the writer's modernist, multiple-perspective simultaneity. People are simultaneously old and young. Marcel wanders through the crypt after his child self. As the camera moves, statues parade through a shifting foreground. *Time Regained* is a testament to Marcel's understanding that "the true paradises are those we lost"—which is to say that the pleasure it provides is the involuntary memory of cinema itself.

Also reviewed in:
CHICAGO TRIBUNE, 7/21/00, Friday/p. F, Michael Wilmington
NATION, 7/3/00, p. 34, Stuart Klawans
NEW YORK TIMES, 6/16/00, p. E23, Janet Maslin
NEW YORKER, 6/19 & 26/00, p. 187, Anthony Lane
VARIETY, 5/24-30/99, p. 68, David Rooney

TITAN A.E.

A Twentieth Century Fox Animation release of a Gary Goldman production in association with David Kirschner Productions. *Executive Producer:* Paul Gertz. *Producer:* David Kirschner, Gary Goldman, and Don Bluth. *Director:* Don Bluth and Gary Goldman. *Screenplay:* Ben Edlund, John August, and Joss Whedon. *Story:* Hans Bauer and Randall McCormick. *Director of Animation:* Len Simon. *Editor:* Fiona Trayler and Bob Bender. *Music:* Graeme Revell. *Music Editor:* Joshua Winget. *Sound:* Marc Server and (music) John Kurlander. *Sound Editor:* Matthew Wood. *Casting:* Marion Levine. *Production Designer:* Philip A. Cruden. *Art Director:* Kenneth Valentine Slevin. *Special Effects Animation:* Peter Matheson. *Costumes:* Kym Barrett. *Running time:* 90 minutes. *MPAA Rating:* PG.

VOICES: Matt Damon (Cale);   Bill Pullman (Korso);   John Leguizamo (Gune);   Nathan Lane (Preed);   Janeane Garofalo (Stith); Drew Barrymore (Akima);   Ron Perlman (Professor Sam Tucker);   Alex D. Linz (Young Cale);   Tone-Loc (Tek);   Jim Breuer (Cook);   Chris Scarabosio (Queen Drej);   Jim Cummings (Chowquin);   Charles Rocket (Firrikash/Slave Trader Guard);   Ken Campbell (Po);   Tsai Chin (Old Woman);   Crystal Scales (Drifter Girl);   David L. Lander (Mayor);   Thomas A. Chantier (Male Announcer); Elaine A. Clark (Citizen);   Roy Conrad (Second Human);   Leslie Hedger (First Human);   Roger L. Jackson (First Alien); Shanón Orrock (Female Announcer);   Alex Pels (Soldier);   Eric Schniewind (Alien);   Stephen W. Stanton (Colonist).

CHRISTIAN SCIENCE MONITOR, 6/16/00, p. 15, David Sterritt

"Star Wars: Episode I—The Phantom Menace" didn't turn out to be much of a supérnova. As a market event it was the big bang all over again, but as an actual movie it plummeted through its own black hole with surprising speed—making hardly a ripple in the Oscar race, and vanishing from everyday conversations a nanosecond after it vanished from multiplex screens.

This doesn't diminish the walloping effect the "Star Wars" series as a whole has had on our mythologies. George Lucas's approach to science fiction—high-speed storytelling, video-game special effects, and characters based on old Hollywood formulas—has defined the rules for a generation of fantasy-film producers. The end is no more in sight than the final installment of Lucas's saga.

The latest "Star Wars" clone is "Titan A.E.," billed as "the first animated science-fiction film ... produced in the US in decades." (It seems "The Iron Giant,' one of last year's best pictures, doesn't fit this description.) As a feature-length cartoon, it obviously has differences from the live-action pictures that inspired it. But this won't matter much to the teenage boys at whom the new movie is squarely aimed. This is a "Star Wars" wannabe in everything but name—so close to the Lucas originals that if it didn't bear the imprint of 20th Century Fox, the studio that owns the franchise, the movie's sound effects would be drowned out by the din of lawyers sharpening their pencils for a cosmic copyright battle.

Set in the 31st century, "Titan A.E." blasts off when Earth is wiped out by evil aliens, leaving a handful of survivors to battle their enemies from the Titan, an elaborate spacecraft that embodies the human race's best accomplishments. (It's not clear why the title abbreviates "After Earth," but that's what the initials mean.) The protagonist is Cale, a young man who wants to be left alone but joins the struggle because, well, sometimes a guy's just gotta take a stand. (Does the name Han Solo ring a bell?) Others on board include the ship's crusty commander, an oddball navigator and first mate, and yes, the luscious Akima, a female pilot whom neither Cale nor we can stop watching, cartoon character or not.

Lucas's influence shows up in conspicuous ways—it was the first "Star Wars" movie, for instance, that upped the science-fiction body count by massacring an entire planet—and also in a zillion small details, from voice tones of characters to snazzy high-tech effects.

Young viewers will have fun identifying the famous folks (Matt Damon, Drew Barrymore) who speak the dialogue. But horizons will hardly be broadened by a movie that borrows its gimmicks from a bag of tricks we've been all too familiar with for the past 25 years.

LOS ANGELES TIMES, 6/16/00, Calendar/p. 1, Kenneth Turan

If you think homelessness is a problem today, look closely at the initials at the end of "Titan A.E." They stand for After Earth, the time in the 31st century after our planet has been incinerated. That's right, humanity has been turned into the homeless people of the universe, forced to live on drifter colonies, junk heaps cobbled together from random pieces of intergalactic trash. It's not good not to have a home.

It was the Drej, a terrifying race of stainless-steel insects, who did this to us. The nastiest master race since the Borg started picking on "Star Trek" crews, the Drej may be pure energy, but they have no gift for small talk. "Destroy the humans, destroy them all" is their most common remark, followed closely by "Eliminate the human race" and "The human threat ends now." Not anyone you want to be seated next to at a dinner party.

Though American feature-length animated science-fiction films are rare, "Titan A.E." does not lack for standard elements. Its characters are, well, cartoonish; their dialogue is of the "Hang on kid, I'm coming/Are you sure this will work?" variety; and the whole project, from the pulse of its soundtrack to the tattoo on its hero to the slinky look of it heroine, has been ruthlessly calibrated to the likes and dislikes of teenage boys.

Still, as concocted by five credited writers (story by Hans Bauer and Randall McCormick, screenplay by Ben Edlund and John August and Joss Whedon), "Titan A.E.'s" rudimentary narration does work up a certain amount of propulsion. But it's not the story that's the story here, it's the film's bravura visual look.

Under the joint direction of animation veterans Don Bluth and Gary Goldman ("The Secret of NIMH," "An American Tale," "Anastasia") and influenced, connoisseurs say, by the style of Japanese anime, "Titan A.E." does an excellent job of using computer-generated effects to create a vast and wondrous outer-space world.

Whether it's the luminous, highly explosive hydrogen trees of Sesharrim, the terrifying Ice Rings of Tegrin, or even the blast that turned the Earth into toast, "Titan A.E." is always up to generating distinctive and involving visions. And being able to put its characters through sci-fi-type action no human stunt person could match is also a plus.

Though the backdrops are 3-D, the film's characters are drawn in old-fashioned two dimensions. We first meet the gang in the year 3028, just after Earth's scientists have completed the Titan Project, mastering a universal secret so profound it has attracted the attention of the Drej—jealous in addition to their other virtues—who attack and destroy because they fear our potential.

Sam Tucker, the top Titan scientist, just has time to get his young son Cale on an escape ship before attempting to save the Titan Project. He gives the boy a ring, telling him, prophetically as it turns out, "as long as you wear it, there's hope."

The next time we see Cale (voiced by Matt Damon) it's 15 years later, and he's a muscular hunk working as a space junkman on salvage station Tau-14. A cynical, cocky, what's-in-it-for-me kind of guy, Cale has a spaceship-sized chip on his shoulder because his dad never made it back into his life.

Docking at the station at that moment, however, is his dad's old comrade-in-arms Korso (Bill Pullman), who tells Cale that the ring he is wearing is in fact genetically encoded to reveal the location of the Titan, which if found has the power to give Earth's stragglers a home.

"The human race needs you," Korso says with a straight face, but Cale is more interested in Korso's pilot, a hot number with fuchsia highlights in her hair named Akima (Drew Barrymore). A no-nonsense "in your dreams" type of woman, Akima is a product of those drifter colonies and has the kind of warm feelings for Planet Earth that gradually win Cale over.

While these characters are solid, if expected, the alien members of Korso's crew are more problematical. Intended as comic relief, Gune (John Leguizamo), Preed (Nathan Lane) and Stith (Janeane Garofalo) are way too cutesy and easily the weakest and most off-putting element in this cosmic concoction.

With Cale and Akima making eyes at each other and nothing less than the fate of the universe at stake, "Titan A.E." goes its preordained way through a very trippy version of outer space. It's the kind of film you'd like to share with a teenage boy; if one isn't available, Cheech and Chong will do.

NEW YORK, 6/26/00, p. 130, Peter Rainer

Currently in the world of animation there is a great war going on for the hearts and minds of young-adult audiences. Disney's domination was always kid-centric. Once the kids move into teenhood, the rules change, and animation, for them, is no longer considered cool. *Titan A.E.* (*Titan* is a spaceship; *A.E.* stands for "After Earth") is the latest attempt by non-Disney, or former Disney, upstarts to go toe-to-toe with the Mouse and market their own cheese. Animators Don Bluth and Gary Goldman, whose biggest previous success was *The Secret of NIMH*, are among the most adept of the anti-Disneyites, and *Titan A.E.* has a couple of sequences of surpassing beauty that rival the best work of Japanese *anime*. The storyline is a *Star Wars* mélange, and the 2-D human characters seem stick-figure-ish next to the expressive 3-D backgrounds. But the sci-fi elements, complete with the young hero Cale (voiced by Matt Damon) leading the charge of dispossessed Earthlings against the dreaded Drej monsters who destroyed their planet, are at least an attempt to bring teens into the fold. Once there, they may get their eyes widened by such scenes as the ones in which Cale and his cronies are whooshed through a forest of explosive hydrogen trees (they look like membranous cups of crimson) or locked inside a nebula of ice rings. The film's industrial-design décor and lighting, along with the heavy-metal soundtrack, are a jarring, and welcome, change from the soupiness of most American animated features, Disney or otherwise.

NEW YORK POST, 6/16/00, p. 52, Jonathan Foreman

There is no excuse for the badness of "Titan A.E."—the "Mission to Mars" of animated sci-fi—not when you have a script co-written by Joss Wheedon of TV's "Buffy the Vampire Slayer," voice performances by big-name stars like Matt Damon and all the amazing creative possibilities offered by the combination of the cartoonist's art and computer-generated imagery.

But this cliché-ridden, crudely drawn, thoroughly undramatic sci-fi epic is inferior to your average Saturday morning cartoon, and proves that Disney still knows best when it comes to animated features.

The story is set in the 31st century. Earth has been destroyed by a spindly, blue-tinged alien race called the Drej. Human beings are dispersed around the galaxy. Their one hope of being reunited, and avoiding extermination by the Drej, is a lost spaceship called the Titan, constructed just before Earth's destruction.

A young, obnoxious blond youth named Cale (Matt Damon) whose father built the ship 15 years before, has inherited—without knowing it—the key to the Titan's whereabouts.

One day, Cale gets a visit from spaceship captain Korso (Bill Pullman), who wants him to join an expedition to find the Titan. Cale refuses, but when the Drej turn up at the space station and try to kill him, he realizes he doesn't have much choice.

On board Korso's ship, Cale meets Akima, an Asian-babe pilot (Drew Barrymore), and a trio of aliens copied from "Star Wars" and "ET." The nasty, effeminate one is given voice by Nathan Lane; the tough female, by Janeane Garofalo; and the ET-type, with a funny accent, by John Leguizamo.

As they seek the hidden ship, there are some visually impressive scenes as they are pursued by the relentless Drej. But most of the hand-drawn scenes—in particular, the faces of the main characters—are remarkably crude.

Worse still, and it's odd to say this of a cartoon, the acting is mediocre to awful, the notable exception being Nathan Lane. (For really, really good voicing in an animated feature, wait for the forthcoming "Chicken Run.")

But in the end, it is inadequate, juiceless storytelling that deprives "Titan A.E." of any dramatic force: There are no surprises anywhere along the way, and, in any case, you couldn't care less what happens to any of the film's colorless, charmless characters.

NEWSDAY, 6/16/00, Part II/p. B3, John Anderson

Plenty of people would say we're doing just fine destroying the planet all on our own, but in "Titan A.E." we have help: blue meanies from space, who find human hubris a bit threatening and turn—the whole planet into what looks like a bursting sea anemone.

"Titan" is strong on imbuing disaster with beauty. Hydrogen trees, cleft moons, a post-evolutionary soup of red space and viscous skies—veteran animator Don Bluth and his onetime Disney colleague Gary Goldman have made their latest cartoon a pageant of colliding styles and ominous shape-shifting. And all of it works, more often than not, despite an inherent disharmony between the traditionally drawn human characters and the wide, wide wiggy world (or lack thereof) that Bluth-Goldman create around them.

The story, less ingeniously, is a creation myth—correction, a re-creation myth—about a new human planet and character lineup that owes more than a bit to the 'Star Wars' model..The callow Skywalker-style youth who looks like he was modeled after James Van Der Beek—is Cale (voice of Matt Damon), a disillusioned former earthling who works a salvage ship. Fifteen years earlier, he was left behind by his scientist father when the Earth went kablooie, and the experience has made him a slacker. But then he finds that Dad has left him a map to the Titan—the great spaceship that will take Earth's survivors to their new home.

So he decides to save the race with some other space vagrants: the space-war vet Capt. Korso (Bill Pullman), the princess-like wonder woman Akima (Drew Barrymore) and their eccentric sidekicks, Stith (Janeane Garofalo) and Gune (John Leguizamo). You get the picture.

Owing more than a little to the old animation classic "Heavy Metal," "Titan A.E." is loaded with action and would be fine stuff for children as long as the children are old enough not to flip out at the idea of their world's being extinct.. Personally, it was unsettling but exciting for me, so maybe it's OK for quasi-grown-ups, too.

SIGHT AND SOUND, 8/00, p. 57, Andrew O'Hehir

The 31st century. Earth is destroyed by the Drej, an alien race consisting of pure energy. The scientist in charge of the secret Titan spaceship project escapes with his ship, entrusting his young son Cale with a powerful ring and sending him into exile on a different vessel. Fifteen years later, human survivors are adrift in the universe. Cale works at a remote salvage station. Korso, a visiting trader, convinces him that his ring holds a map to the abandoned Titan, which can reunite humanity. But the Drej also know of the ring and pursue Cale, who barely escapes with Korso, a girl named Akima and their alien shipmates.

Aided by the bird-like race of Planet Sesharrim and the mysterious map on Cale's palm, the group survives many close calls. Having been betrayed to the Drej by Korso and his sidekick Preed, Cale and Akima escape to the human colony of New Bangkok, rebuild a ship and reach the Titan before Korso and the Drej do. In the final battle, Korso dies helping Cale defeat the Drej. Titan creates a new planet and populates it with all of Earth's life-forms.

Children of the 8 to 11 years old age group should find the odyssean quest of the animated science-fiction film *Titan A.E.* enthralling, especially if they have seen the original *Star Wars* fewer than a dozen times. But for many adults, the experience of watching *Titan A.E.* will be a matter of trying to ignore the simple and exaggerated style of directors Don Bluth and Gary Goldman's character animation and the inane dialogue provided by five credited writers, while focusing on the richly coloured backgrounds and lush, painterly outerspace vistas.

Bluth has of course been making animated features since the days when they were called cartoons, and the approach here is not much different from that of his earlier efforts *The Secret of NIMH* or *An American Tail*: cuddly creatures occupy the foreground, facing a big and often frightening world. Here, the bland and muscular Cale (with a voice to match by Matt Damon), whose haircut makes him look a boy band member, never really seems to belong. He's less compelling than the saucy Akima (voiced by Drew Barrymore) and less memorable, if also less irritating, than the cantankerous kangaroo-like Stith (Janeane Garofalo) or the wise tortoise Gune (John Leguizamo).

Some of Bluth and Goldman's depictions of outer space are undoubtedly delightful: the glowing hydrogen trees of Planet Sesharrim, the enormous ice crystals in which the Titan is hidden, the cloudy nebula through which Cale leads the mysterious deep-space creatures called "wake angels". But the directors also seem to distrust their audience's attention span; such scenes are undermined by an atrocious musical score that veers from faux 80s heavy metal to faux 90s trip-hop. Then there's the nonsensical plot (Korso kills an awful lot of Drej for someone in league with them) and the achingly weak dialogue with its leaden efforts to acquire a degree of street credibility. (Consecutive lines from a battle sequence run: "I'm out!"; "Let's do this!"; "It's been fun!"; "Who's your daddy?") At times, it seems that two completely different films have been superimposed on each other—against those glorious hydrogen trees, Bluth and Goldman have placed ludicrous bird-like creatures that resemble the Thanksgiving turkeys from television's *South Park*.

While the influence of the often adult-oriented Japanese anime and of its master, Hayao Miyazaki, is now widespread in animation, Bluth and Goldman's film—like almost all Hollywood cartoons—is still aimed at a pre-adolescent common denominator. Given their evident talent and flashes of visionary sensibility, this seems regrettable. But their films have consistently drawn large audiences, while the Hollywood-dubbed version of Miyazaki's *Princess Mononoke,* whose Tolkienesque fantasy was perhaps too sophisticated and dark for very young children, bombed in the US. To anyone who takes animated film seriously, *Titan A.E.*, for all its striking imagery, will seem tepid and outdated. But its core demographic should go home happily stuffed with sweets.

TIME, 6/19/00, p. 130, Richard Corliss

Well, why shouldn't Hollywood make a science-fiction adventure using animation instead of live action? The Japanese have been doing it for decades (they call it anime). Besides, in *Star Wars* and its myriad clones the characters, the acting and the plots are already on the cartoony side. So give half a chance to *Titan A.E.*, which has the retro-pioneering spirit of recent sci-fi movies.

In A.D. 3034, the universe is ruled by Drej, translucent, electric-blue beings of pure energy and malefic power. The lowest form of life is the human, including our hero Cale (voiced by Matt Damon), who has a lousy job sawing the edges off bulky space trawlers. Guess what? Cale has a great destiny in store once he hooks up with his dead dad's pal—tough, hard-to-read Korso (Bill Pullman)—and an intergalactic crew of comic villains, saintly mutants and the requisite feisty babe (Drew Barrymore).

Don Bluth has been making just-O.K. animated features for two decades; typically, he dabbles in tantalizing subjects (the immigrant experience in *An American Tail*, the historical romance in *Anastasia)* without freshening them. But Bluth's best film, *The Land Before Time*, was set in the distant past, where he was freed from his tendency for painterly realism. Here he and co-director Gary Goldman use 3-D computer technology, and some very talented designers, to dream up a world—a galaxy of marvelous sights, spaceships, planets, vistas and critters. And when it shifts into action mode, the movie can be a spectacular rush. It's the video game that plays you.

The good news: what *Star Wars* was to live action—the reimagining of an old genre with new tools—*Titan A.E.* is to animation. The bad news: dramatically, it's also the *Phantom Menace* of animation.

VILLAGE VOICE, 6/20/00, p. 156, Dennis Lim

The initials in *Titan A.E.*—about a boy and his Jesus complex—stand for After Earth. The planet is blown up sometime in the 31st century, and it turns out that Matt Damon is, not unlike Keanu Reeves in *The Matrix* or even Damon's own Godlike creation Will Hunting, the Chosen One, who will save the human race from extinction. This feature-length sci-fi cartoon by veteran animators Don Bluth and Gary Goldman is suggestive of nothing so much as Saturday-morning TV: 2-D characters frolic in 3-D CGI spacescapes, but the handiwork is uninspired, the digichicanery obviously expensive but bland, the New Age odor off-putting, and the reliance on inspirational Glen Ballard power ballads fatal.

Also reviewed in:
CHICAGO TRIBUNE, 6/16/00, Friday/p. A, Michael Wilmington
NEW YORK TIMES, 6/16/00, p. E12, Stephen Holden
VARIETY, 6/12-18/00, p. 13, Robert Koehler
WASHINGTON POST, 6/16/00, p. C1, Stephen Hunter
WASHINGTON POST, 6/16/00, Weekend/p. 47, Desson Howe

TITANIC TOWN

A Shooting Gallery release of a Company Pictures production for Pandora Cinema, BBC Films, British Screen, and the Arts Council of Northern Ireland through its National Lottery Fund. *Executive Producer:* David Thompson, Robert Cooper, and Rainer Mockert. *Producer:* George Faber and Charles Pattinson. *Director:* Roger Michell. *Screenplay:* Anne Devlin. *Based on the novel by:* Mary Costello. *Director of Photography:* John Daly. *Editor:* Kate Evans. *Music:* Trevor Jones. *Sound:* Rosie Straker and (music) Gareth Cousins. *Casting:* Sarah Trevis. *Production Designer:* Pat Campbell. *Art Director:* Dave Arrowsmith. *Special Effects:* John

Markwell. *Costumes:* Hazel Pethig. *Make-up:* Jean Speak. *Stunt Coordinator:* Andy Bradford. *Running time:* 96 minutes. *MPAA Rating:* Not Rated.

CAST: Julie Walters (Bernie McPhelimy);   Ciaran Hinds (Aidan McPhelimy);   Ciaran McMenamin (Dino/Owen); Nuala O'Neill (Annie McPhelimy); Lorcan Cranitch (Tony); Oliver Ford Davies (George Whittington);   Des McAleer (Finbar);   James Loughran (Thomas McPhelimy);   Barry Loughran (Brendan McPhelimy);   Elizabeth Donaghy (Sinead McPhelimy); Aingeal Grehan (Deirdre);   Jaz Pollock (Patsy French);   Kelly Flynn (Bridget);   Nicholas Woodeson (Immonger); Doreen Hepburn (Nora); Veronica Duffy (Mary McCoy); Cathy White (Rosaleen);   Ruth McCabe (Kathleen);   Caolan Byrne (Niall French);   Cheryl O'Dwyer (Maureen);   Maggie Shevlin (Mrs. Morris);   Timmy McCoy (Colm);   Malcolm Rogers (Uncle James);   Tracey Wilkinson (Lucy);   Billy Clarke (Gunman);   Fo Cullen (Miss Savage);   Simon Fullerton (Jimmy Cane); Duncan Marwick (Lionel Thirston); John Drummond (Sergeant); Paul Trussell (Lanky Para);   Darren Bancroft (Corporal);   Claire Murphy (Nuala Curran);   Julia Dearden (Mrs. Gilroy); Mairead Redmond (Mairead Curran); Andrew Havill (Officer); Paula Hamilton (Mrs. Brennan);   Mike Dowling (Butcher);   Robert Calvert (Bus Driver);   Jeananne Crowley (Mrs. Lockhart); Peter Ballance (Fergus); Richard Clements (Brian); Colum Convey (Interviewer);   Amanda Hurwitz (Night Nurse);   Tony Rohr (Cork Driver);   B. J. Hogg (Chair); Richard Smedley (Patrol Leader);   Alan McKee (Reporter);   Tony Devlin (Republican Youth); Andrew Downs (Ambulance Driver);   Breffini McKenna (Paramedic);   John Quinn (Publican); Packy Lee (Hijack Youth);   Catriona Hinds (TV Journalist);   Christina Nelson and Gerard Mccartney (Journalists); Karen Staples (Nurse); Kieran Ahern (Father Clancy); Brenda Winter (Mrs. Duffy);   Richard Orr (Man in Black Jacket);   Chris Parr (1st Radio Interviewee).

CHRISTIAN SCIENCE MONITOR, 9/1/00, p. 15, David Sterritt

Everyone talks about the disappointing state of Hollywood filmmaking, but nobody does anything about it—except a small number of mavericks producing and releasing independent fare.

One such group is the Shooting Gallery, a New York-based company that not only distributes non-Hollywood productions but launches them with a touch of extra fanfare.

If you live in one of the 16 cities where the Shooting Gallery Film Series is starting its second year (see www.sgfilmseries.com), you have the opportunity to see six promising new pictures between now and November, each with a discussion session on opening night. Those movies greeted with applause will go on to open-ended engagements in communities everywhere, as the well-crafted drama "Croupier" has done.

This year's first Shooting Gallery attraction is "Titanic Town," and no, it's not the sequel to a certain high-grossing Hollywood hit. Quite the opposite, it's a human-scaled look at problems in the recent past, based on the true story of a middle-aged Irishwoman who became so outraged by sectarian violence in her neighborhood that she decided to wage a war for peace, with or without the help of friends and family.

"Titanic Town" is more a personal comedy-drama than a political study or a polemical tract. It's fueled by Julie Walters's feisty performance—perhaps her best since "Educating Rita," which brought her an Oscar nomination—and an easygoing subplot about a teenager's first love affair. It's not great cinema, but it's a far cry from over-budgeted Hollywood heroics, and that's a recommendation in itself.

LOS ANGELES TIME, 9/1/00, Calendar/p. 6, Kevin Thomas

The Shooting Gallery launches its second series of worthy but neglected films with "Titanic Town," and it's likely to be a tough sell. It's well-made but conventional, and it deals with strife in Northern Ireland—which at this point may be a tough combination for anyone feeling saturated by films on the subject. What's more, Julie Walters plays its doughty, middle-aged, working-class heroine with virtually no variation on numerous similar portrayals.

Walters' Bernie McPhelimy, her husband Aidan (Ciaran Hinds) and their four children believe they're leaving their troubles behind when they move up to the pleasant tract of Andersontown in West Belfast. The community's housing consists of simple red-brick row houses placed on spacious lots with trees, unlike urban row houses built directly along the sidewalk. But the

McPhelimys have moved straight into a war zone, with constant skirmishes between the IRA and British soldiers, for the year is 1972.

When a friend looking after Bernie's young son is killed in the gunfire, Bernie is galvanized into action. Like many crusaders, her initial goal is modest: to get both sides to stop shooting at each other during the day when children are out and about.

Bernie is a strong, forthright woman with native intelligence to balance her innocence. She and her loyal friend Deirdre (Aingeal Grehan) refuse to be daunted when they attend a meeting of peace-minded local women only to discover that they are from Protestant South Belfast.

Bernie not only has placed herself in a situation that causes her neighbors to think of her as a traitor merely for attending the meeting but also takes the opportunity to state what everybody knows: that her friend was killed by a stray IRA bullet.

Uproar ensues, which makes Bernie only more determined. In short order she's meeting with IRA leaders—with the proviso that she personally present their demands to the secretary of state for Northern Ireland. In her new role as a peace broker, she hits upon the idea of suggesting to the secretary that she lead a petition drive for peace.

Bernie emerges as an instant and controversial celebrity whose fame predictably takes its toll on her family. The impetus for her becoming politically involved was to secure the safety of her loved ones, now endangered by her widely misunderstood activism.

Director Roger Michell and writer Anne Devlin, in adapting to the screen Mary Costello's autobiographical novel, strongly make the specific point that Irish Catholics and the IRA are not synonymous and the universal point that in the face of chronic conflict, somebody, sometime, somewhere is going to have to get people on both sides to start sitting down and talking to each other if the strife is ever to end.

"Titanic Town" is an admirable, thoughtful venture, but it may leave you with the feeling that you've seen it all before.

NEW YORK POST, 9/1/00, p. 42, Lou Lumenick

Making one of this season's most welcome comebacks is the delightful British actress Julie Walters, a British TV fixture who hasn't made much of an impression on American moviegoers since she was Oscar-nominated for "Educating Rita" 17 years ago.

Next month, we'll get to see Walters in the crowd-pleasing "Billy Elliott," but her galvanic presence also firmly anchors "Titanic Town," a more modest effort that opens the second season of the highly worthwhile Shooting Gallery series of premieres at Loews State.

The title ironically refers to Belfast, the city where the big liner was built and a locale that's been almost as ill-fated, seemingly forever, as Catholics and Protestants waged a bloody battle for supremacy.

Based on an autobiographical novel by Mary Costello, screenwriter Anne Devlin's story takes place in 1972 in the heavily Catholic Andersontown section of West Belfast, which has turned into a killing field roamed day and night by British soldiers and IRA snipers.

When a friend is killed by a stray bullet, working-class mother of four Bernadette McPhelimy (Walters) decides to take action.

She marches into a peace meeting organized by middle-class Protestant women, commandeers the proceedings—and infuriates many of her neighbors by admitting, on TV, that a stray bullet fired by the IRA, not British soldiers, was responsible for her friend's death.

Though she and her family are repeatedly threatened and her ulcer-stricken husband (Ciara Hinds) urges her to keep quiet for their safety, Bernie can't hold her tongue.

She agrees to a clandestine meeting with the IRA and presents their demands to the Secretary of State for Northern Ireland, who encourages her to circulate a peace petition.

As Bernie is branded a traitor by IRA loyalists, her oldest daughter Annie (Nuala O'Neill) is falling in love with a young medical student (Ciaran McMenamin) she meets when the bus they are riding on is attacked by an angry mob and set afire.

Roger Michell, who directed "Notting Hill" (a far different look at the effects of fame) after "Titanic Town" was shot in 1997, does an effective job of the capturing people living in a perpetual state of war, even if this British production has a decided anti-IRA slant some Americans will take issue with.

The supporting performances are somewhat uneven, but "Titanic Town" is well worth seeing for Walters, whose comic and dramatic gifts are showcased to very entertaining effect.

NEWSDAY, 9/1/00, Part II/p. B6, John Anderson

What the Irish quaintly refer to as "the troubles" have not been the subject of a great many motion pictures, despite their obvious dramatic potential. But fashioning fiction out of tragedy requires some distance. And there's never been much distance from the troubles.

The films that have been made include some classics—notably, John Ford's "The Informer," Carol Reed's "Odd Man Out," and "Shake Hands With the Devil," starring Jimmy Cagney—but they've generally been dramatically solid and romantically delinquent. Didn't Hollywood ever read Sean O'Casey? The slouch-hatted, revolver-wielding IRA portrayal was never much good to anyone—something both Jim Sheridan and Terry George knew, and remedied, with "In the Name of the Father" and "Some Mother's Son," movies that took some account of the cost of venerating violence.

Taking such a tack even further is Roger Michell's "Titanic Town," from the autobiographical novel by Mary Costello, the story of Bernie McPhelimy (Julie Walters) and her crusade to do something about the theater of violence in which she's trying to raise a family. She doesn't want a miracle. She doesn't even, initially at least, expect the war between Republicans and the Brits to stop. All she wants is for the shooting to be done at a decent hour—in the evening, so kids can go to school and women can look out their window without taking a rubber bullet in the face.

This is funny in a bleak, black way, but Michell ("Persuasion") is masterful in the way he so casually, naturally, exposes the way his people in '72 Belfast have learned to live their lives in and around the paths of gunfire. Sometimes, the effect is purely comic: Bernie, for instance, complaining to her daughter Anne (Nuala O'Neill) about the dust under her bed, which is exposed as British soldiers ransack their house. At other times, it's purely pathetic: While babysitting for Bernie's young son, a friend is stopped dead by a stray bullet while shopping in the middle of the afternoon—sitting down first in a way that says she can't believe what's happened.

It's this intrusion into the reality Bernie's fabricated that begins her crusade into the drawing room of the occupying British authorities and the not-so-well secured hideaways of the IRA; and along the way, she incurs the wrath of her more belligerent neighbors (no one looks particularly good in "Titanic Town"). As her husband with the ulcer, Ciaran Hinds ("Persuasion") plays Chicken Little to Bernie's often reckless stampede into the middle of a centuries-old conflict, and he does it well.

Newcomer O'Neill is convincingly petulant/sensitive as Anne, whose first love has the bad timing to come along just as her mother is making headlines; if her silent soliloquies had been scored with less emotionally obvious alt-rock, the movie would have benefitted immensely.

But it's Walters' movie, essentially, and while the actress is still probably best known here for "Educating Rita," she's become a beloved star in Britain through her seemingly relentless work for the BBC, as well as the intelligence of her acting. She doesn't really have an American counterpart as such—but then, we don't really have much work for middle-aged actresses, do we? If we're lucky, we'll get the occasional Walters appearance. And if we're really lucky, they'll all be as solid as "Titanic Town."

SIGHT AND SOUND, 1/99, p. 58, Geoffrey Macnab

Northern Ireland, 1972. Bernie McPhelimy and her family move to Anderstown, in Catholic West Belfast. Soon after they've arrived they see a running battle between an IRA gunman and the British army outside their house. Bernie's anger at the violence spilling into her backyard is exacerbated when a neighbour is dragged away by the soldiers and an acquaintance is killed by a stray bullet. After attending a meeting of local women to stop the violence, Bernie and her friend Deirdre decide to spearhead a new peace movement. Bernie provokes the wrath of the IRA with some ill chosen words to the media. A brick is thrown through her window and her children suffer at school. Bernie and Deirdre meet both the IRA leadership and the Secretary of State for Northern Ireland. They propose a peace petition. At first, no one wants to sign. Bernie's actions drive a wedge between her and her family. Her husband falls ill, while her teenage daughter Annie starts a romance with a student who—she discovers much later—is an IRA volunteer. A mob led by Bernie's bigoted neighbour Patsy gathers outside the McPhelimys' house. In the clamour, Bernie's son receives a near-fatal head wound. Bernie and Deirdre's peace petition suddenly takes off and they gather 5,000 signatures, yet Bernie begins to fear the petition will make no difference. She and her family decide to leave Anderstown.

Early on in *Titanic Town* we see a British soldier lying on his stomach in the flowerbed outside the McPhelimys' new house in Anderstown, West Belfast. It's an incongruous but telling image. He looks almost like a garden ornament, but his presence, like that of the IRA gunman a few minutes earlier, is taken as a personal affront by Bernie McPhelimy who refuses to accept the Troubles spilling into her own backyard. Repeatedly, quiet domesticity and political violence are juxtaposed: a dinner is interrupted by an explosion or a siren, a simple shopping trip or a visit to the hairdresser is blighted by a stray bullet.

All Bernie wants is peace for her family. Julie Walters plays her as the archetypal housewife. Curlers in her hair, she is intent on keeping up appearances, always bustling and fussing. Confronted with slippery British politicians and plain-speaking IRA leaders, she reacts like an angry mother discussing a child's future with dim-witted and patronising teachers. It's an engaging but mannered performance, a little like *Mother Courage* done sitcom-style. Unlike Helen Mirren's character, who became politicised when she saw how the Long Kesh prisoners were treated in Terry George's *Some Mother's Son,* Bernie won't take sides. She scolds soldiers and terrorists alike.

Anne Devlin's screenplay doesn't hide the fact that many consider Bernie a naive and meddlesome busybody. Even her husband is sceptical about her peace campaign. There is never any suggestion that Bernie's intervention is somehow going to sort out the Troubles once and for all, nor do the film makers impose a pat, happy ending. The story, after all, is set in 1972. There are running gun battles when the McPhelimy family arrive in Anderstown and the tanks are rumbling along the streets when they leave.

Titanic Town is loosely based on an autobiographical novel by Mary Costello, whose mother was involved in the Peace Campaign of the early 70S. (The area is so named because of the Harland and Wolff shipyard which built the *Titanic.)* The film, however, is not simply about Bernie's fight against sectarianism. It also doubles up as a rites-of-passage yarn about her daughter Annie. Director Roger Michell (whose next film is the *Four Weddings* follow-up, *Notting Hill)* handles the scenes between Annie and her schoolfriends and her burgeoning love affair with a medical student delicately enough. The problem is bringing the competing strands of the narrative together. At times it's as if there are two different films running side by side—one from the perspective of the mother and one from that of the daughter.

The mood oscillates wildly. When Bernie is holding forth to an interviewer on BBC Radio 4's *Women's Hour* or dropping clangers in television debates, the emphasis is on comedy. Then, an instant later, matters darken as somebody is killed or wounded. The film-makers can't resist caricature. The bigoted, loud-mouthed next-door neighbour Patsy and her malingering, thieving son are presented in an entirely negative light. Why they behave as they do is never addressed. The patronising, middle-class Protestant women are likewise used as comic targets. They're pelted with eggs, but such knockabout slapstick can't help but seem strained when, a few scenes later, Bernie's son is almost lynched by an angry mob. Unlike many films about the Troubles, *Titanic Town* isn't blighted by machismo and doesn't preach. It shifts the focus away from the politicians to the families whose lives are affected on a day-to-day level by the violence. Michell seems caught, though, in a no-man's land between gritty realism and upbeat, stylised comedy. For all its strengths, the film comes no closer to marrying its competing storytelling styles than Bernie herself does to bringing about peace.

VILLAGE VOICE, 9/5/00, p. 113, Amy Taubin

How a nightmare existence can come to seem almost normal is the most disturbing aspect of Roger Michell's *Titanic Town.* Adapted from Mary Costello's fictionalized memoir of the Troubles, it's one of the rare movies about war that focuses on the relatively nonpartisan civilians whose front yards are turned into battlegrounds.

It's 1972, and Bernie McPhelimy (Julie Walters), her sickly husband, Aidan (Ciaran Hinds), their teenage daughter, Annie (Nuala O'Neill), and their two young sons have no sooner moved to a supposedly peaceful neighborhood in West Belfast than the IRA and the British go into all-out combat mode. Bullets fly and bombs explode at all hours with no consideration, by either side, of the innocent people caught in the crossfire. When one of her friends is shot dead coming back from the butcher shop, Bernie becomes a peace advocate. All she wants, she explains to the IRA and the British, is for them to refrain from fighting during the daytime so that kids can go to school and men and women can get their work done. Bernie becomes a kind of folk hero, but she also incurs the wrath of brick-hurling neighbors who view her peacenik efforts as a betrayal of the IRA.

Titanic Town plunges us into the surreal conditions of civil war, where people pursue their needs and desires regardless of the risk involved. The fact that a kid might catch a bullet on his way to pick up a date doesn't stop girls and boys from their romantic pursuits. Annie's teenage angst has less to do with the danger she's in every day than the fact that classmates ostracize her because of her mother's supposed British sympathies. Walters and O'Neill insightfully flesh out the mother-daughter conflict, even though the longer Bernie persists in her naïveté (she'd have to be an idiot not to know she was being co-opted by the British), the less believable she is as a character. *Titanic Town* isn't convincing on every front, but as a political conversation piece, it's potentially effective.

Also reviewed in:
CHICAGO TRIBUNE, 9/1/00, Friday/p. A, Michael Wilmington
NEW YORK TIMES, 9/1/00, p. E14, Stephen Holden
VARIETY, 6/8-14/98, p. 70, David Rooney
WASHINGTON POST, 9/1/00, p. C12, Rita Kempley
WASHINGTON POST, 9/1/00, Weekend/p. 37, Michael O'Sullivan

TOO MUCH SLEEP

An Anthology Film Archives and The Shooting Gallery release of an Angelika Entertainment Corporation/Arrowhead Productions/Open City Films production. *Producer:* Jason Kliot and Joana Vicente. *Director:* David Maquiling. *Screenplay:* David Maquiling. *Director of Photography:* Robert Mowen. *Editor:* Jim Villone. *Music:* Mitchell Toomey. *Sound Editor:* David Ellinwood. *Running time:* 86 minutes. *MPAA Rating:* Not Rated.

CAST: Marc Palmieri (Jack Crawford); Pasquale Gaeta (Eddie De Luca); Nicol Zanzarella (Kate); Philip Galinsky (Andrew); Judy Sabo Podinker (Judy); Mary Ann Riel (Sandy); John Stonehill (Frankie); R. G. Rader (Jonathan); Ruth Kaye (Gert); Jon Langione (Tom Coffee); Joan Maquiling (Jack's Mother); Jack Mertz (Judy's Father); Glenn Zarr (Mel); Raj Kanithi (Mr. Raj); Peggy Lord Chilton (Mrs. Bruner); Temme Davis (Lucy); Stan Carp (Male Nurse); Sally Stat (Agnes Janarone); Anthony Trentacost (Chris Bruner); Michael Hernando and Alan Podinker (Male Dancers); Jeff Morris (Bartender); John Medina and Rocco Paolo (Bouncers); Brett Podinker (Waiter); Laurie Eng (Restaurant Hostess); Gage Dehesa (Boy); Katie Rossie (Girl); Martin Pfeffercorn (Man on Street); Anita Orlacchio (Woman at Car Wash); Nicole Orlacchio and Alexis Orlacchio (Children); Paul Sean , George Masters, Ted Boehler, and Vic Hyder (Men at Deli).

LOS ANGELES TIMES, 3/23/01, Calendar/p. 4, Kevin Thomas

David Maquiling's "Too Much Sleep" is a droll slacker comedy about a small-town New Jersey security guard whose search for his stolen pistol proves to be a depth charge: Marc Palmieri's 24-year-old Jack doesn't realize when he starts out that he's actually embarking on a maturing journey of self-discovery.

The film, part of the wonderful Shooting Gallery series, unfolds as a shaggy-dog story, full of hilarious and outrageous twists that suggest that weirdness lies just below the surface of daily life seemingly at its most ordinary.

"Too Much Sleep" is essentially slight, and Maquiling, in his feature debut, shrewdly avoids laying on too much significance, content to let us discover for ourselves just what, if any, larger meanings Jack's adventure contains. It's a modest, non-pushy little movie, one that resists hitting you over the head to get laughs. However, if you just sit back and relax you may be surprised at how frequently you find yourself laughing out loud.

Jack gets too much sleep because he's bored and his life is aimless. From the way he thinks and speaks, you sense he's been exposed to college, but somehow he's ended up back home, living with his widowed mother, never seen but heard; she's clearly a nurturer but also rightly afraid he might lose his job if he doesn't take it more seriously. In any event, Jack is riding a bus when a pretty young woman, Kate (Nicol Zanzarella) asks him if he might give up his seat to an older woman, Judy (Judy Sabo Podinker), who's not feeling well. Jack unhesitatingly complies, only to wind up losing his prized gun.

Because Jack had inherited the pistol from his father and he probably would be hard-put financially to replace it easily, he's suddenly shaken out of his aimlessness. His best friend Andrew (Philip Galinsky) advises him to have a talk with his Uncle Eddie (Pasqualte Gaeta), a retired county employee who brags of his "connections," leaving you to wonder whether he means with the law enforcement community or the underworld or both.

Eddie is a voluble guy with dyed black hair who sounds like Lou Costello. Eddie declares confidently that Jack's been the victim of a con, and he sends Jack off in search of the two women. Along the way, Eddie has one encounter after another, each individual possessed of more bizarre revelations than the last. Each has a story to tell, often revealing a philosophical take on life's craziness.

As time passes, you have the sense that it matters much more that Jack find himself than the gun. You sense that Jack has a growing realization of this as his string of encounters forces him to think about what's important to him and what his values are.

If Maquiling has a keen ear for the way people talk, he has no less a facility in inspiring his actors to go with the material, keeping a straight face no matter how absurd the circumstances. Maquiling has an admirable ease in his storytelling; he strings you along with confidence. More than anything else, he invites us to see the consequential in the seemingly inconsequential.

If "Too Much Sleep" seems unusually observant and effectively oblique in its humor and insights, it might stem from the fact that Maquiling was born in New Jersey to a Filipino emigre father and an American mother. In discovering Asian cinema, Maquiling discovered his calling and how central folk tales and legends are to culture. Consequently, Maquiling suggests in his film that it doesn't matter so much whether his people's assertions are true or not but that they believe them and act upon them accordingly.

Every moment in "Too Much Sleep" is therefore charged with ambiguity and uncertainty despite its casual air. All that really matters, the film is suggesting, is that Jack learn to believe in himself.

NEW YORK POST, 10/6/00, p. 57, V. A. Musetto

Just when I was dreading seeing another indie movie, along comes this delightful, low-budget comedy from writer-director David Maquiling.

Jack Crawford (Marc Palmieri) is a 24-year-old security guard who still lives with Mommy. While taking a bus to work one day, Jack loses his gun—which was in a paper bag—to a thief.

He never registered the weapon, which he inherited from his father, so he can't go to the cops. Instead, he turns to Eddie (a wonderful Pasqquale Gaeta), who talks like a wiseguy and is alleged to have connections in the small New Jersey town where he and Jack live.

In the resulting hunt, Jack encounters a variety of suburban oddballs, is beaten up, and lands in bed with Kate, played by the fetching Nicol Zanzarella.

Maquiling, in his feature-film debut, lets the story unfold leisurely, with each character given enough time to spill his or her guts while Jack listens patiently. It brings to mind Richard Linklater's "Slacker," except that Maguiling's slackers are middle-aged.

Maguiling, a product of Holmdel, N.J. perfectly captures the cultural and emotional wasteland that is suburban Jersey. "Too Much Sleep" reminds me why, many years ago, I fled that state for Manhattan.

VILLAGE VOICE, 10/10/00, p. 130, Amy Taubin

A wry, nearly deadpan suburban comedy, David Maquiling's *Too Much Sleep* is so good it made me wish I had kept that workhorse phrase "remarkably assured debut feature" just for it. Maquiling comes at his slacker-coming-of-age story from fresh angles in every scene.

At 24, Jack Crawford (Marc Palmieri) still lives at home with his mother in a small working-class town somewhere in New Jersey. On his way to his security guard job, his gun is stolen. Since Jack inherited the gun from his father and never bothered to register it, he can't go to the police. Instead he enlists Eddie (Pasquale Gaeta), a retired local official who still has connections. Once a minor mobster (maybe only in his imagination), Eddie likes to feel important and has nothing but time on his hands, so he agrees to help Jack. Following a roundabout trail, Jack discovers a curiosity and an initiative he didn't know he possessed.

If this narrative setup seems familiar, Maquiling's way of developing it is anything but. *Too Much Sleep* reaches its ostensible goal (the gun) through a series of digressions. Jack finds himself in unfamiliar living rooms, backyards, restaurants and parking lots, making small talk with strangers who pour out their stories to him because he seems so interested. What emerges is a cumulative picture of working-class suburbia that recalls what Richard Linklater did with the college town in *Slacker*. Maquiling has an ear for the language of this milieu, and he almost never goes for a cheap laugh. Raw-boned and apple-cheeked, Palmieri is a near double for Thurston Moore; his diffident delivery is perfectly balanced with Gaeta's staccato wiseguy patter. Maquiling has a fabulous sense of film rhythm (the way sound, music, dialogue, and actors' movements play off one another and together determine the length of shot). *Too Much Sleep* is an understated gem.

Also reviewed in:
NEW YORK TIMES, 10/6/00, p. E20, Dave Kehr
VARIETY, 3/17/97, p. 53, Emanuel Levy

TRAFFIC

A USA Films release in association with Initial Entertainment Group of a Bedford Falls/Laura Bickford production. *Executive Producer:* Richard Solomon, Mike Newell, Cameron Jones, Graham King, and Andreas Klein. *Producer:* Edward Zwick, Marshall Herskovitz, and Laura Bickford. *Director:* Steven Soderbergh. *Screenplay:* Stephan Gaghan. *Based on "Traffik" created by (originally produced by Carnival Films for Channel 4 Television):* Simon Moore. *Director of Photography:* Peter Andrews. [uncredited Steven Soderbergh]. *Editor:* Stephen Mirrione. *Music:* Cliff Martinez. *Sound:* Paul Ledford and (music) Alan Meyerson. *Sound Editor:* Larry Blake. *Casting:* Debra Zane. *Production Designer:* Philip Messina. *Art Director:* Keith P. Cunningham. *Set Designer:* Greg Berry, Maya Shimoguchi, and Barbara Ann Spencer. *Set Decorator:* Kristen Toscano Messina. *Set Dresser:* Dale E. Anderson, Brent Blom, Gary Brewer, Alan Easley, Brooke Sartorius, and Mike Malone. *Special Effects:* Kevin Hannigan. *Costumes:* Louise Frogley. *Make-up:* Kathrine James. *Stunt Coordinator:* John Robotham. *Running time:* 147 minutes. *MPAA Rating:* R.

CAST: Benico Del Toro (Javier Rodriguez); Jacob Vargas (Manolo Sanchez); Andrew Chavez and Michael Saucedo (Desert Truck Drivers); Tomas Milian (General Arturo Salazar); Jose Yenque (Salazar Soldier/The Torturer); Emilio Rivera (Salazar Soldier #2); Michael O'Neill (Lawyer Rodman); Michael Douglas (Robert Wakefield); Russell G. Jones (Clerk); Lorene Hetherington and Eric Collins (State Capitol Reporters); Luis Guzman (Ray Castro); Don Cheadle (Montel Gordon); Don Snell, Enrique Muricano, and Gary Carlos Cervantes (DEA Agents, Trailer); Leticia Bombardier (Ruiz's Secretary); Miguel Ferrer (Eduardo Ruiz); Carl Ciarfalio (Ruiz's Assistnat); Steve Lambert (Van Driver); Gilbert Rosales (Van Passenger); Corey Spears (F*****-up Bowman); Majandra Delfino (Vanessa); Topher Grace (Seth Abrahms); Erika Christensen (Caroline Wakefield); Alec Roberts (David Ayala); Catherine

Zeta-Jones (Helena Ayala); Rena Sofer, Stacey Travis, and Jennifer Barker (Helena's Friends); Dean Faulkner (Parking Valet); Albert Finney (Chief of Staff); D.W. Moffett (Jeff Sheridan); James Brolin (General Ralph Landry); Daniella Kuhn (Tourist Woman); Brandon Keener (Tourist Man); Bill Weld, Don Nickles, Harry Reed, Jeff Podolsky, Barbara Boxer, Orrin Hatch, and Charles Grassley (Themselves); Stephen Dunham (Lobbyist); George Blumenthal, Jewelle Bickford, Dave Hager, and Tucker Smallwood (Partygoers); Steven Bauer (Carlos Ayala); Marisol Padilla Sanchez (Ana Sanchez); Amy Irving (Barbara Wakefield); Dennis Quaid (Arnie Metzger); Clifton Collins, Jr. (Francisco Flores); Victor Quintero, Toby Holguin, and Ramiro Gonzalez (Salazar Soldiers); Viola Davis (Social Worker); James Pickens, Jr. (Prosecutor Ben Williams); Peter Riegert (Attorney Michael Adler); Elaine Kagan (Judge Reed); John Slattery (ADA Dan Collier); Jim Ortega (Arrested Man in Apartment); Greg Boniface and Tom Rosales (Tackled Men); Rudy M. Camacho (Customs Official); Yul Vazquez (Tigrillo/Obregon Assassin); Jack Conley (Agent Hughes); Eddie Velez (Agent Johnson); Craig N. Chretien (Director of EPIC); John Brown (Assistant Director of EPIC); Mike Siegel (DEA Representative); Joel Torres (Porfilio Madrigal); Steve Rose (Marty); Kimber Fritz (Rehab Counselor); Harsh Nayyar and Mary Pat Gleason (Witnesses); Vincent Ward (Man on Street); Benjamin Bratt (Juan Obregon); Jesu Garcia (Pablo Obregon); Gregory Estevane (Polygraph Administrator); Alex Procopio (Polygraph Assistant); Rita Gomez (Mrs. Castro); Kaizaad Navroze Kotwal (Teacher); David Jensen ("John"); Jay Fernando Krymis and Mike Malone (Waiters); Rene Pereyra (Doctor); Kymberly S. Newberry (Press Secretary); Carroll Schumacher (Ayala Security); Michael Showers (Meeting Leader).

CHRISTIAN SCIENCE MONITOR, 12/29/00, p. 15, David Sterritt

Some of today's most interesting directors are making their mark on 2000 just before the calendar runs out.

Steven Soderbergh has already graced the year with "Erin Brockovich," the most politically alert crowd-pleaser in recent memory. Now he's back with "Traffic," a more abrasive commentary on ills of contemporary life.

The new picture will probably draw smaller audiences, but may figure even more prominently in the upcoming Academy Awards race, given its impressive ensemble cast and the imaginative visual style it uses to explore its complex subject from a variety of perspectives.

That subject is drugs—or more precisely, the so-called war on drugs that the United States government has been waging for many a long and controversial year. Although its highly dramatic screenplay is based on a British television series, "Traffic" amounts to a 140-minute commentary on American efforts to stem the tide of illicit drugs through a wide assortment of varyingly effective means, from infiltration of the narcotics underworld to treatment of drug-dependent individuals.

This doesn't mean "Traffic" is an exercise in punditry. Quite the opposite, ifs one of the year's most suspenseful, gripping, and sometimes disturbing films. It begins near the Mexican border, where a Mexican cop (Benicio Del Toro) and his close partner (Jacob Vargas) are working under a military commander (Tomas Milian) whose methods are as ruthless as the enemy he wants to conquer.

The action soon switches to the United States, where a Midwestern judge (Michael Douglas) has been chosen as federal drug czar—a job he's proud to take, even though it consumes so much time that it hampers his ability to stay close with family members, one of whom (Erika Christensen) is a teenager with a hankering for narcotics.

On the West Coast, meanwhile, two officers on the drug beat (Luis Guzman, Don Cheadle) monitor the life of a wealthy woman (Catherine Zeta-Jones) whose incarcerated husband (Steven Bauer) has become a pawn in a set of dangerous intrigues.

These are only some of the characters in Soderbergh's web of plots and subplots, which run on parallel but interrelated tracks throughout the movie.

Some are more compelling than others, and portions of the action seem a bit confused, as if a too-long running time had caused necessary story material to remain on the cutting-room floor. Sentimentality creeps in a little, as well. But the tension rarely lets up, and the film's thoughtfulness is a welcome relief from the season's general run of fluff and fantasy.

And then there's the acting, much of which ranks with the best we've seen all year. Soderbergh has a gift for eliciting strong performances—he launched his career with "Sex, Lies & Videotape," a star-making vehicle if ever there was one—and he hasn't lost his touch. Douglas gives one of his most crisply etched portrayals, Miguel Ferrer and Amy Irving do first-rate work, and Del Toro reconfirms his growing reputation as one of today's most talented actors.

CINEASTE, Vol. XXVI, No. 3, 2001, p. 41, Richard Porton

Since its release last fall, Steven Soderbergh's *Traffic* has achieved the status of a fullfledged media event, a film that is as likely to be discussed on the op-ed pages of newspapers as in the entertainment section. At a time when most dispassionate observers agree that the United States' much-ballyhooed, but interminable, War on Drugs has failed miserably, Soderbergh's thriller with epic pretensions is a sexy departure point for the often dry-as-dust discussions of drug interdiction and funding for rehabilitation programs that flourish in the mainstream press and on Sunday political-chat shows. The critic for the online magazine *Feed* lauded *Traffic* as a brilliant film that is also an effective "public service announcement." Even the well-regarded Mexican daily, *La Jornada,* chimed in, claiming that *Traffic* is inspiring usually complacent American politicians to reconsider their outmoded antidrug bromides. On the other hand, disgruntled conservatives such as *Commentary's* Gary Rosen and the *Daily News's* A. M. Rosenthal denounced the film as insidious propaganda for drug legalization.

While right-wing denunciations of *Traffic* end up making it seem like a radical, or at least a liberal, manifesto, a closer look at the film reveals a more conventional form of cinematic rhetoric bogged down by generic formulas and anemic political assumptions. Many of the tonier critics, who were much fonder of *Traffic* than its schlockier Oscar rival, *Gladiator,* praised Soderbergh for achieving an Altmanesque fresco that provided a multifaceted view of the front lines of the drug war. Yet the supposed sophistication of screenwriter Stephen Gaghan's screenplay quickly evaporates if any of the narrative's three intersecting strands is held up to more intense scrutiny. In fact, *Traffic's* cannier esthetic strategies managed to camouflage its overweening flaws for the majority of viewers and critics, many of whom were all too eager to praise a flawed enterprise for ostensibly good intentions. The film ingeniously cuts from one plot line to another before viewers with short attention spans can recognize the ludicrousness of any one of its constituent parts.

In the final analysis, Gaghan's plot twists are not even completely his own, since his screenplay—and the idea of intertwined narratives—is closely patterned after the British miniseries, *Traffik,* broadcast on Channel 4 in 1990 to great acclaim. Not without its own longueurs, *Traffik* traced the movement of heroin from its point of production in Pakistan to eventual consumption in Britain with much more flair and coherence than *Traffic's* analogous examination of the trajectory of cocaine from Mexican cartels to Suburban Midwestern living rooms. Perhaps most poignantly, *Traffik* demonstrated how poor Pakistani farmers were virtually forced, given their limited economic options, to grow heroin as a cash crop. Instead of focusing on similarly inescapable economic realities in Central and South America, Soderbergh and Gaghan depict their Mexican villains (Benicio Del Toro's heroic, honest cop is the only exception) as moral lepers who lack the refinement possessed by their betters north of the border.

Traffic's revulsion towards Mexican amorality notwithstanding, the film is primarily obsessed with how drugs have befouled the American family nest. Popular culture has always treated the drug culture as a threat to the solidarity of the nuclear family, and this film's revamped liberalism is only a more baroque variation on films and television programs from the Sixties and Seventies (J.P. Miller's CBS teleplay *The People Next Door* is a seminal example) in which parents are startled to find that their children have been transformed into drug-addled aliens. For this reason, the sequences detailing drug czar Robert Wakefield's (Michael Douglas) discovery of his daughter Caroline's (Erika Christensen) drug addiction provide much of the movie's ideological ballast.

Unlike previous cautionary tales such as *The People Next Door,* however, *Traffic* shares the superficially hip propensities of other recent drug sagas like *Requiem for a Dream* and *Blow.* The filmnmakers grudgingly admit that getting high is not without its pleasurable moments. (Indeed, the film has gotten considerable mileage out of the fact that Gaghan's previous experience with addiction lends it an aura of authenticity.) In addition, politicians who pontificate about substance abuse while savoring cocktails are gently skewered. Facile ironies aside, and without minimizing the genuine devastation wrought by drug abuse, it is all too predictable that *Traffic* depicts its adolescent drug users as nihilistic empty shells and celebrates Caroline's redemption from coke-snorting and free-basing as a victory for family values. Soderbergh and Gaghan do not object to the drug war because of its devastating effect upon poor African Americans and Latinos or because inmates are languishing in jail as the result of draconian laws. Their credo, appropriately vague as well as vacuous, is summed up by Wakefield's speech resigning his position: "The War on Drugs is a war on our nation's most precious resource—our children."

The assault on childhood innocence takes some melodramatic turns during its teenage protagonists' descent into hell, but few of them are likely to be praised by academics known for their devotion to the 'melodramatic imagination.' As a case in point, honor student Caroline's fall from grace takes on the flavor of a sub-Griffith potboiler, vaguely reminiscent of silent-era movies that depicted damsels sold into the white slave trade with a combination of moralism and prurience. After this wealthy young woman escapes from the pastoral environs of a drug rehabilitation camp, she scores drugs in a seedy neighborhood and promptly becomes a street hooker to support her habit. (One wonders, however mischievously, why such a pampered young woman didn't at least become a call girl.) Falling under the influence of a black pusher cum pimp, she is punctually saved from his clutches by her father; Michael Douglas appears to be fashioning his vigilantism, as well as his persona, after several of his previous, more flamboyant roles. Being the very model of a postmodern drug movie that wants to curb its own excesses, Caroline's friend, Seth, chides Douglas for resorting to vigilantism.

The casual racism of these scenes seems almost tame when contrasted with the most wrongheaded of *Traffic*'s overlapping narratives—the saga of Javier Rodriguez, the aforementioned 'honest cop,' whose earnest spade work in the trenches of the drug war is eventually undone by his corrupt superiors. In an interview with *American Cinematographer*, Soderbergh (who served as the film's lighting cameraman, although a pseudonymous cinematographer is listed in the credits) explains that he shot the Mexican sections "through a tobacco filter" and then overexposed the film to imbue these vignettes with an oversaturated look. Mexico, therefore, becomes a miragelike, evanescent realm where life is cheap and morality is infinitely expendable. As film scholar and Latin American specialist Catherine Benamou observes, the movie "posits an historical and moral hierarchy between the postmodern United States—which has to retrieve its moral foundations and family values—and premodern Mexico, which has presumably never been able to draw the line between the law and lawlessness."

Traffic's demonization of a Mexican netherworld, moreover, is most misleading in purveying the assumption that the American bureaucratic infrastructure, particularly the DEA, is merely inept. Salazar, for example, the Mexican counterpart to Wakefield, combats the Tijuana Cartel only because he is being paid off by its rival. To be fair, the oily Salazar is based on an actual despicable Mexican bureaucrat, General Jesús Gutierrez Rebollo, whose escapades eventually landed him in jail. Unfortunately, Soderbergh and Gaghan's use of the historical record is extremely selective. While it would be silly to deny that Mexico is rife with corruption, the film, either willfully or naively, sidesteps the long history of collusion between the American CIA and members of the Elite in Central America whose best interests are served by the efficient proliferation of drugs. To cite only one example, in their invaluable exposé, *Cocaine Politics*, Peter Dale Scott and Jonathan Marshall detail how Miguel Nazar Haro, head of the DFS (Dirección Federal de Seguridad, a Mexican agency that synthesizes the functions of both the FBI and CIA) during the 1970s and a man who protected right-wing Cuban nationalists involved in the cocaine trade, maintained close ties to the DEA. Scott and Marshall also provide evidence that the CIA lent support to a drug mogul, a Cuban exile in Mexico named Alberto Sicilia Falcón, who plotted to overthrow the Portuguese government in 1974. More recently, Stefan Wray has produced evidence that American military equipment, supposedly designed to fight drug trafficking in Mexico, has actually been employed in campaigns against the Zapatista movement: the War on Drugs has become inextricable from a War on Subversion. One of Gaghan's more articulate mouthpieces insists that "in Mexico law enforcement is an entrepreneurial activity, this is not so true for the U.S.A." This kind of offhand remark is Hollywood's version of disinformation.

Given *Traffic*'s one-dimensional analysis of the drug cartels' machinations, it is almost a relief to turn to its third narrative link—the riches-to-rags and back-to-riches-again tale of Helena Ayala (Catherine Zeta-Jones). For a few brief sequences, she is shocked and devastated by the revelation that her husband, Carlos (Steven Bauer), is a slimy drug kingpin, not a respectable businessman. Emboldened in the fashion endemic to characters in mediocre films, she quickly becomes a steely matron who makes brazen demands of members of the Tijuana Cartel and gleefully orders the murder of the government informer scheduled to be the chief witness against Carlos. There are, admittedly, moments of campy bliss in these sequences (on occasion, Zeta-Jones appears to be paying homage to Ava Gardner, and a scene in which she proudly displays a doll constructed of cocaine to some drug lords might even be intentionally humorous), but they certainly seem out of place in a serious 'social-conscience' film. An analogous character played by Lindsay Duncan in the original Channel 4 series underwent a more subtle transformation and, for this reason, the melodramatic payoff was well earned and more credible.

Finally, the banter provided by a pair of wisecracking DEA agents assigned to trail Helena—African-American Montel Gordon (Don Cheadle) and Puerto Rican Ray Castro (Luis Guzman)—frequently comes off as Gaghan and Soderbergh's attempt to frame the debate surrounding the drug war within the framework of race and class. Although the partners are more like reconstituted versions of cops in movies such as *48 Hours* or the *Lethal Weapon* series than real people, they clearly relish the job of ensnaring wealthy, primarily white, criminals. Montel and Ray could be viewed as *Traffic*'s unconscious penance for its more reactionary moments. Ultimately, however, their occasionally witty jibes arc eclipsed by gunfire and a few obligatory scenes of cars exploding.

Overhyped and frequently boring, *Traffic* might well have been even worse; an article in *Brill's Content* reports that Soderbergh and Gaghan initially conceived of the Benicio Del Toro character as a corrupt cop who rises to the top of the heap as a drug king and that they discarded a scene in which Michael Douglas, out of his empathy with his daughter, lights up a crack pipe. Nevertheless, it is difficult not to view the film as a missed opportunity, a project that might have honestly explored the ravages of American drug policy without resorting to creaky generic contrivances or political obfuscation.

LOS ANGELES TIMES, 12/27,00, Calendar/p. 1, Kenneth Turan

Maybe because the opponent is so terrifying and insidious ("an allergy of the body, an obsession of the mind," someone calls it here), our desperation to win the war against drugs detailed in "Traffic" has made it the most unexamined conflict of our time, something we are more than willing to throw dollars at but not so eager to actually analyze and reconsider.

Given that, it took a certain amount of nerve to tackle the chaotic, unfocused, largely unsuccessful waste of lives and money that is the drug war today in a major motion picture with an ensemble cast including Michael Douglas and Catherine Zeta-Jones. Complex and ambitious, "Traffic" is that film, and its examination of how pervasive drugs are, how wide a swath they cut in our society, though not always completely successful, is yet another indication of how accomplished a filmmaker Steven Soderbergh has become.

Soderbergh, whose equally sure-handed but very different "Erin Brockovich" came out earlier this year, has once again opted for a change of pace. For one thing, as written by Stephen Gaghan (based on a British TV miniseries), "Traffic" effortlessly intertwines several complex stories across two countries and several cities without ever dropping a stitch.

At the same time, using the pseudonym Peter Andrews, Soderbergh has expertly shot the film himself in a neo-documentary, run-and-gun style whose emphasis on held-held camera work adds to its immediacy (Soderbergh has mentioned Costa-Gavras' "Z" as his model here).

Gaghan ("Rules of Engagement") has clearly done considerable research into the film's theme, and his script is strongest in its broad outlines, its ability to convey lots of information about the drug trade and show it to be a kind of pernicious octopus, with tentacles powerful enough to make almost everyone it touches corrupt, complicit or potentially so.

Unfortunately, "Traffic" is much less secure when it comes to dialogue and the creation of individualized characters. Some of its narrative threads are noticeably less compelling than others, and its people, no matter what social strata they occupy, have a tendency to sound a lot like standard brands.

While keeping the notion of intertwined stories from the British original, "Traffic" has sensibly changed the geographic focus from the Turkey-Britain drug trade to the more near-at-hand Mexico-U.S. situation. And by adroit use of filters and other techniques, Soderbergh has given each segment distinctive visual markings: a brown cast for Mexico, blue for Cincinnati and environs, a bright look for San Diego.

The Mexican section (in Spanish with subtitles) is by far the most effective, partially because it's got the film's best performance. That's by Benicio Del Toro, an actor ("The Usual Suspects," "Snatch") who's always been much admired for his subtle power but whose nuanced authority has never been more on view than as a state policeman who goes to work for Gen. Salazar (an effective Tomas Milian), the army's designated illicit drug fighter.

The film's biggest star is Douglas, a solid choice for Robert Wakefield, an Ohio Supreme Court judge who's just been selected as head of the Office of National Drug Control Policy. A square shooter who believes in his mission, Wakefield just happens to have a 16-year-old daughter (Erika Christensen) who, unknown to him, is a major narcotics abuser. When the judge says, "It's time to see the front lines," he doesn't realize the battlefield is his own bathroom.

Weakest of all in terms of plausibility is the section involving Zeta-Jones as Helena Ayala, a pampered wife who suddenly discovers that her husband (Steven Bauer) and his oily attorney (Dennis Quaid) are major drug players. Even with the expert assistance of Don Cheadle and Luis Guzman playing DEA agents, this plot strand takes turns that are way too questionable for its own good.

No matter what straits these people find themselves in at the film's opening, "Traffic" inexorably tightens the noose around them. If the film's plotting has a flaw, it's that, in its eagerness to make its points in an emotional way, it falls back too readily on the excesses of melodrama. Sometimes we feel we're watching an updated version of "Marijuana: The Weed With Roots in Hell," or, to go back even further, a dramatization of the titillating horrors faced by young women in the dread clutches of the white slave trade.

Finally, and perhaps inevitably, one of the difficulties with "Traffic" is that it feels like the filmmakers are tiptoeing around the implications of their good work. As a big-budget film in a controversial area, "Traffic" seems especially eager to be seen balanced, to be fair—for instance, to the hard-working and sincere anti-drug agents putting their lives at risk. So though it takes important steps in that direction, the film pulls back from what seems to be its own logical conclusion: No matter how much money we throw at the drug problem ($45 billion per annum at last count) and how heroically they're implemented by those at the front lines, current policies simply do not work.

No one expects a Michael Douglas-starring film, and one that has Sens. Orrin Hatch, Barbara Boxer and Charles Grassley playing themselves, to take the kind of strong stance for drug decriminalization that, for instance, New Mexico's Republican Gov. Gary Johnson has. Still, many of the film's stronger moments, like Douglas' character getting absolutely no response when he asks for aides to think out of the box about the problem, point in that direction.

Given what this film shows, a clearer stand on decriminalization or even treatment in place of prison seems in order. Without one, watching "Traffic," artfully made though it is, feels a little like seeing a version of "The Insider" that thought it politic to waffle on whether cigarettes were a danger to your health.

NEW STATESMAN, 1/29/01, p. 46, Jonathan Romney

In the course of his career, Steven Soderbergh has gone from being a well-meaning, low-budget tyro (*Sex, Lies, and Videotape*) to a mainstream pro-for-hire (*Out of Sight, Erin Brockovich*), with the occasional blip of personal eccentricity along the way (*Kafka*, his little-seen absurdist farce *Schizopolis*, the sublime fish-out-of-water thriller *The Limey*). *Traffic* is his most confident film to date, and the sort of grand, serious statement by which a journeyman signals to the world that he would rather be seen as an auteur—a stylist and a pensive commentator on the state of things. And maybe the odd Oscar or Golden Globe wouldn't go amiss.

Well, good for Soderbergh that his boat has come in. He is intelligent; he takes risks; he's interested in exploring structures and visual techniques—he even photographed *Traffic* himself, giving it a wide range of visual textures, from sheened Californian pastel to harsh, urgent deep blue and parchmenty yellow-brown. It's an impressive exercise; I only wish it seemed to be more heart, more urgency, or that it aspired to reimagine the world, rather than attempted such a detached, quasi-documentary view of it. It is a film with a thesis, in a peculiar sense, for it proposes that, when approaching the issue of drug use and trading in the United States, hard-and-fast theses are neither tenable nor useful.

Written by Stephen Gaghan, the film was inspired by *Traffik*, the mid-1990s Channel 4 series about the drug trade. It is structured as a panorama of the drug trade in America, suggesting that it infiltrates every corner of life. Soderbergh and Gaghan propose a collection of jigsaw fragments that gradually fit together, almost too conveniently at moments. The characters include a Mexican cop (Benicio Del Toro), his task-force boss (Tomas Milian) and, in the US, the worthy, patrician politico Robert Wakefield (Michael Douglas, whose screen gravitas is just about perfect these days). Wakefield is soon to take on the post of national drug tsar. In Cincinnati, a gang of well-heeled high-school kids sit around sampling coke and smack. In San Diego, a group of ladies who lunch chat about the dangers of cholesterol.

Little by little, the picture builds up. The fresh-faced schoolgirl (Erika Christensen) taking her first steps towards being a junkie is none other than the daughter of the drug tsar. One of the rich women (Catherine Zeta-Jones) discovers her wealthy businessman husband has just been arrested for drug dealing, with connections leading straight back to Mexico. Everyone and everything will tie up one way or another; and while this sort of self-enclosure can be gratifying in more fanciful fictions (in something as playful as *Magnolia*, say), it is uncomfortable in a film that claims to comment on the real world. It is too crushing an irony that Wakefield's daughter should become a junkie just as he is stepping up to the podium to announce his commitment to the "war on drugs". That leads to a pointed scene in which he denounces the uselessness of the military metaphor—what can it mean when you end up waging war on your own family members? Too often, the narrative seems engineered specifically so that characters can make points about moral contradictions.

The film is at its best when it dares to be fragmentary and cut corners. At one point, Del Toro's detective is despatched to the US to intercept a dangerous hood. He finds himself getting chummy with his target in a gay bar, but, just as we wonder what will come next, the miscreant is already back in Mexico, under arrest. The secret to these sprawling, thousand-and-one-story structures is that some stories should simply go untold, or merely be hinted at.

That is why the film starts to freeze when we get into the story of Wakefield and his daughter. Suddenly, it's in danger of becoming a problem-of-the-week TV movie, as Wakefield trawls through seedy hotels looking for her. The most awkward moment comes when we are simply read a lesson by an unconvincing embodiment of absolute corruption, a cynical posh boy out of Bret Easton Ellis, who reads Wakefield a street-smart lesson on inner-city economics. Much the same happens when the drug dealer Ruiz (Miguel Ferrer) lectures his captors on the futility of their attempt to control border traffic. "We on Larry King, man?" quips a cop, mercifully puncturing the didactic mood.

Overall, *Traffic* is rarely that preachy, but has many sensible, liberal points to make. It points out that corruption and compromise are so rooted in the economic system that attempts to target an easily identified and demonised enemy are meaningless and hypocritical. It takes special issue with the warfare metaphor, particularly through the too obviously sinister figure of Milian's General Salazar, who is there to show that military ideology inevitably goes hand in hand with betrayal and senseless attrition.

Nor is this a moralising film, although the moral nature of some characters is too clear-cut for it to be truly analytical. *Traffic* is gripping because it is, in effect, a melodrama, and a very well-directed and well-acted one. It pretty much avoids the hysteria that usually comes with the subject, but it doesn't quite live up to its intent to be a dispassionate, "state of things" film. But it will give pundits on Larry King and other current affairs shows plenty to chew over—and that, you suspect, was what was intended all along.

NEW STATESMAN, 2/5/01, p. 45, Keith Hellawell

Films that depict the work of individuals or organisations may well entertain, but they rarely do justice to reality. *Traffic* is no exception. It sets out to convince us that the American war on drugs is unwinnable, without actually identifying what that war is.

Traffic shows the problems created within a family by a young daughter who, influenced by her friends, becomes a drug addict. Well, that part certainly rings true, since it is often peer pressure that sets someone on the path to taking drugs, and the drugs supplier is often an acquaintance or friend.

The family in question is that of the newly appointed American drug tsar and hero of the film, played by Michael Douglas. Catherine Zeta-Jones plays the wife of one of the film's many villains, a respectable middle-class husband and father who is a secret drug-trafficker and whose family life is torn apart when he is exposed. Zeta-Jones, a token wife, all mum and apple pie, implausibly dons his criminal mantle when he is in custody and the family bank accounts are frozen. I somehow couldn't see her as the mother-turned-Messalina. The film better displays the violence and corruption within the law-enforcement agencies of Mexico and the United States, and shows how this corruption on both sides of the border contributes to the flow of drugs into the States.

The US's anti-drugs activities in other parts of South America are touched upon, but with the film's crude action approach, viewers will form little concept of the reality of US efforts to tackle drugs.

Action, I'm afraid, seems more attractive to the film's money men than real life, although they do have a stab at realism. Again, this is most notable when the daughter (played by Enka Christensen) starts to recognise her problem, having been forced into prostitution to feed her habit, and goes into treatment and rehabilitation.

There is an important message in the roles of the parents. On the verge of splitting up, they rally to support their daughter. Young people need that stability, and persuading parents and friends to provide this is a crucial part of Britain's own anti-drugs strategy.

Nevertheless, in America and the UK, there appear to have been no accurate films or documentaries on a role such as mine, or on the government's anti-drugs activities. In terms of what is happening to combat drugs, the media portrayal of anti-drugs actions is shallow and misleading.

There is a distinctive difference between my role and that of the American drug tsar, both in reality and as depicted in *Traffic*. He is largely concerned with federal powers and organisations. As these are largely law-enforcement or quasi-enforcement agencies, the emphasis—and the hype—is essentially combative. This panders to politicians, who welcome any battle cry, and comforts Middle America.

I do spend time with law-enforcement and intelligence agencies here and abroad. I have flown in and out of "war zones" under heavy guard, but such activities offer little more than endorsement for the troops on the ground and good photo opportunities. The real challenge is to change people's attitudes and behaviour, whether in our schools, our communities, or among those who govern us. Little of this is exposed in the film.

What *Traffic* does is show that the drugs tsar is human. I can closely associate with the problems caused by long absences from home, and have always been lucky to have the support of my wife and family.

The film may, however, alert people to the uncomfortable truth that their own children might be involved. It will expose that they are in danger from drugs and may be becoming addicts right under the noses of their parents. Addicts can be clever in hiding their habits, as Erika Christensen's character shows.

Traffic reveals that there is so much corruption and reward from the drugs trade that even the might of the United States cannot stop it by force of arms, but it is barren on what needs to be done. Americans at all levels of society now recognise that "the war" is unsustainable. Much is being done, and Barry McCaffrey (the real-life US drugs tsar) and I share thoughts and prospects. We share successes and failures. We share the same philosophy.

The trick will be to convince those politicians who seek simple solutions and harsh words that this is not enough. The implausibility of parts of this film, particularly when Douglas and his off-screen partner go into dangerous drugs ghettos where all others have feared to tread (they return unscathed), will only relegate the message to the realm of pop art.

Other victims of reality in *Traffic* include the key witness, a drug trafficker-turned-informant, who enters the witness protection programme but falls victim to a car bomb. Speaking as a former chief constable, if any one of my men had been involved in such slack and inefficient policing, he would have been looking for a job as an ice-cream salesman.

What I did like was the final scene, in which Douglas, due to accept the presidential nomination as drugs tsar at a press conference, walks away from the job. The administration wants him to concentrate on the "law and order" side of anti-drugs measures, to the apparent neglect of treatment and rehabilitation. They want him to "make war" on drugs, but Douglas says he cannot wage war on those unfortunates caught up in addiction; he cannot wage war on his own family, his own daughter. I said that 15 years ago. I wish I'd copyrighted it; I might be getting a percentage from the film!

Luckily, the real world, certainly as far as the UK's ten-year anti-drugs strategy is concerned, is much different. We hit the villains, we rehabilitate the addicts, we help communities get free of drugs.

So I have no intention of resigning...and I won't be calling on Michael Douglas to portray me in a British version of *Traffic*. However, if Martin Shaw were free...?

NEW YORK, 1/1/01, p. 80, Peter Rainer

Traffic is a helter-skelter mosaic about drug use in locales as disparate as Tijuana and Cincinnati's affluent Hyde Park. The various discrete stories coalesce in a single panorama; the corruption is total and cuts across all boundaries. Steven Soderbergh, who directed from a script by Stephen Gaghan loosely derived from a British TV mini-series, shot most of the movie himself with hand-held cameras, and the jittery, present-tense approach unifies the action even when the visual schemes—cool-blue hues for the upper-crust sequences, tobacco-brown tones for the Mexican scenes—clash. The fracturedness of the story lines matches Soderbergh's scattershot technique; at times we appear to be watching a new-style *policier* crossed with a documentary about dope-dealing mixed in with a TV cop show added to an inspirational anti-drug sermonette about the need for parents to listen to their troubled children.

Each separate story line is compelling if too familiar, and together they accumulate into a larger vision. Perhaps unavoidably, there's also an ungainliness to the enterprise. We keep getting yanked in and out of high-anxiety situations; it's like a serial bad trip. As with much of Soderbergh's avant-garde work, his garde isn't quite as avant as he would have us believe it is. In movies such as *The Limey* and *Out of Sight*, for example, he buffed the noir to a fine finish but the appeal remained essentially pulpy and old-fashioned. Still, Soderbergh's jazzed stylistics can be smartly entertaining. Without them, an uneven movie like *Traffic* might seem more of a mélange than it already is.

An overwrought Michael Douglas plays an Ohio Supreme Court justice and the president's new drug czar, whose daughter (Erika Christensen), as he is slow to realize, is a junkie. In another story line, Don Cheadle and Luis Guzman are San Diego DEA agents whose undercover work brings them into the world of a La Jolla drug kingpin (Steven Bauer) and his pregnant, socialite wife (an underwrought Catherine Zeta-Jones). Benicio Del Toro and Jacob Vargas are Mexican cops who, in the course of busting up one of the major drug cartels, find their scruples seriously tested by the entrepreneurial lure of Mexican law enforcement. Soderbergh is very canny about the ways in which information is imparted to us. When, for example, we see Douglas, on a fact-finding expedition, checking out the U.S.-Mexican border in San Diego, we don't need to be told how overwhelming his challenge is—it's right there for us to see, in the bunched-up rows of cars that look as if they were melting in waves of heat. Any of these vehicles could be a carrier of contraband.

Soderbergh's hit-and-run technique allows him to make his points quickly and move on. He slows down when he wants to highlight a gesture, a glance, and this is particularly helpful for an actor like Del Toro, whose performing style is like an extended slow burn. The film's most resonant and emotionally powerful moment comes when his character's modest but unmovable ambition is realized and he takes on the heavy-lidded look of someone transported into a bittersweet bliss beyond the reach of corruption. It's the only natural high in the movie.

NEW YORK POST, 12/27/00, p. 43, Jonathan Foreman

"Traffic" is a triumph on almost every level. It is breathtakingly stylish, wonderfully acted and its three interrelated tales of the "war" on drugs are brilliantly structured to form a cohesive, powerful whole.

Perhaps most impressive of all is the bracingly honest way director Steven Soderbergh presents the drug war in all its vastness (the corruption of whole governments) and at its most intimate (the destruction of an individual family), and depicts the struggle as depressingly futile, but at the same time desperately necessary.

"Traffic" is based on a successful British miniseries of the 1980s, but Soderbergh and screenwriter Steven Gaghan have shifted the action from the Pakistan-to-England heroin route to the Mexico-U.S.A. cocaine trade via California.

First you meet two Mexican cops in Tijuana, Javier (Benicio del Toro) and Manolo (Jacob Vargas), as they intercept a coke delivery, then are themselves intercepted by a Mexican army unit led by the sinister General Salazar (Tomas Milan). Soon Javier and Manolo are caught up in a terrifying web of temptation, corruption and cruelty.

Then you're introduced to Ohio Judge Robert Wakefield (Michael Douglas), the conservative about to be appointed the nation's drug czar, who doesn't yet know his clever, pretty teenage daughter (excellent Erika Christensen) is running with a druggy, preppy crowd.

You also meet two determined San Diego DEA agents, Montel (Don Cheadle) and Ray Castro (Luis Guzman) who are working on a sting operation designed to bring down local drug baron Carlos Ayala (Steven Bauer).

The sting results in the arrests of San Diego dealer Eduardo Ruiz (Miguel Ferrer) and Ayala, much to the shock of his pregnant European wife, Helena (Catherine Zeta-Jones), who always assumed her husband was a legitimate businessman.

All the story lines converge as Helena, upon the advice of her husband's sleazy attorney (Dennis Quaid), acts quickly and ruthlessly to save her husband from conviction.

Del Toro steals the film as Javier, conveying a world of frustration and fear with his eyes alone. And the great Cheadle, whose movie career took off with "Boogie Nights," shows once again why he is one of our finest younger actors.

One of the many extraordinary things about "Traffic" is the cast: The movie is reminiscent of those giant war movies "A Bridge Too Far" and "The Longest Day," in which one famous actor after another pops up in small roles.

Soderbergh has clearly become one of those filmmakers everyone wants to work with, like Woody Allen and Robert Altman.

James Brolin is the U.S. general who is Wakefield's cynical, frustrated predecessor, and Albert Finney is the president's chief of staff.

That sharp mob lawyer is Peter Riegert, the gangster's moll in Mexico City is Salma Hayek and an almost unrecognizable (and unprecedentedly good) Benjamin Bratt is the shadowy Tijuana cartel boss.

In the Washington scenes, there are cameos by Senators Orrin Hatch and Barbara Boxer, playing themselves.

In a visual flourish reminiscent of David O. Russell's "Three Kings," the Mexican scenes are all shot in bleached-out yellow tones; the Washington ones, in cold, blue ones; and the sequences involving the DEA agents, in bright colors. Soderbergh was his own director of photography on the picture.

In a daring gambit that adds to "Traffic's" authentic feel, all the Mexican scenes are played in Spanish with English subtitles.

The cleverly structured screenplay is by Stephen Gaghan, previously responsible for the unimpressive script of "Rules of Engagement."

But several scenes have that sharp, witty, unmistakably Soderberghian touch, especially those that deal with dysfunctional relationships like the one between the Douglas character and his lawyer wife (Amy Irving).

The film's two weaknesses are its excessive length and its artificially sentimental conclusion, a jarring surprise after so much uncompromising truth-telling.

Nevertheless, "Traffic" is never less than entertaining, and clearly ranks among the year's most accomplished movies.

NEWSDAY, 12/27/00, Part II/p. B2, John Anderson

Twenty miles south of Tijuana, in a desert rendered gothic byhand-held, high-grained camerawork, a couple of undercover cops (Benicio Del Toro and Jacob Vargas) bust a couple of low-level couriers in a van full of drugs. As they escort their prisoners and coke back toward civilization, "civilization" meets them halfway: Gen. Arturo Salazar (Tomas Milian) and a company of Mexican soldiers roar out of the dust in a swarm of black SUVs, relieve the pair of their cargo, compliment their work and leave them musing in the sun.

So begin our introductions—to "Traffic," Steven Soderbergh's structurally stunning dissection of the drug trade; to Javier Rodriguez (Del Toro), who'll be the real conscience of the movie, and to its director's M.O. regarding all the intersecting and not- intersecting plotlines and characters with which he composes his film's breathtaking choreography: an initial sense of unease, a rising sense of apprehension, a crisis and a sense of total disorientation. Is Javier the bad guy? Is Salazar? Is anyone? Soderbergh keeps us constantly off guard, but the ultimate effect of "Traffic" is our amazement at our personal/national naivete.

Naivete is what "Traffic" is all about. It affects Robert Wakefield (Michael Douglas), the soon-to-be-installed U.S. drug czar. (That his predecessor, played by James Brolin, looks just like Ollie North is a pretty good joke). It affects his wife, Barbara (Amy Irving), willfully blind about their own daughter's drug use. It affects Ray and Montel (Luis Guzmn and Don Cheadle), the two DEA agents who keep busting people despite the Sisyphean nature of their job. It affects Helena Ayala (Catherine Zeta-Jones), a wealthy, pregnant San Diego socialite who's oblivious to her husband's business, up until the moment he's busted.

It's curious that "Traffic" (like the drug-themed "Proof of Life") should be timed so closely to Plan Colombia, the $7.5-billion interdiction project the United States seems intent on launching against South American cocaine. But you can't really say Soderbergh is for or against it. Dramatically, the film is an almost total success; the acting is excellent, almost all the characters arc convincingly human and the meshing of episodes flawless. But like the drug issue itself, the film's message is no answer at all. Which may be all the message you need.

Can impoverished people be blamed for selling drugs, when the profit margin is so huge? Can any supply be eliminated when a demand is so great? There are few heroes in "Traffic," and few villains—the closest, really, are Caroline Wakefield (the amazing Erika Christensen), the girl with everything who nearly vanishes in a crack cloud; and Seth (Topher Grace), the obnoxious preppy boyfriend who turns her on to freebasing (and in whose mouth, perversely, screenwriter Stephen Gaghan puts some of the wisest lines). Without people like them, there'd be no drug trade.

Which is not, of course, the greatest revelation since the Dead Sea Scrolls. "Traffic" is a far more entertaining and virtuosic than it is instructional. Several of the characters, in fact, are a bit short of plausible: Wakefield, who sees the drug czar job as a stepping-stone until his daughter's crisis, knows less about the drug trade than someone who watches the evening news. (Worse: He knows less about drugs than people who produce the evening news.) Ayala is apparently too vacant to know her husband's a drug smuggler, but ends up playing patty-cake with Mexican drug lords and hiring hit men to rescue her husband.

This is, perhaps, Gaghan exposing his TV roots. (He also wrote the movie "Rules of Engagement," which is no credential.) Overall, "Traffic" is first-rate, shot by Soderbergh himself and proving that the director works with crime the way Bergman worked with shadows.

NEWSWEEK, 1/8/01, p. 62, David Ansen

In Hollywood, 2000 may be remembered as the year of Steven Soderbergh. There's a real chance he may become the first director since Francis Coppola in 1974 to have two films nominated for a best-picture Oscar, "Erin Brockovich" and his panoramic new thriller "Traffic," which takes a scorching look at the way drugs have stained every stratum of society.

Three groups have already named Soderbergh the year's best director for both films (the New York and Los Angeles critics, and the National Board of Review), and "Traffic" was crowned best picture by the New York Film Critics Circle. For the man proclaimed the great white hope of independent cinema back in 1989 for "sex, lies, and videotape," it's like a prophecy fulfilled.

Sitting in his offices in Burbank in late October, Soderbergh had no idea all these laurels awaited him. Dressed in black jeans, black T shirt and black geek-chic glasses, posters of Godard films overhead, the straight-talking, unpretentious director didn't seem a likely candidate to be the toast of Hollywood. Indeed, he was remembering that only a few years ago—after the failures of "Kafka," the underrated "King of the Hill" and "The Underneath"—he was a director at the end of his tether. "I'd lost the enthusiasm of the amateur, and that's a dangerous thing. I was heading down this path toward becoming a formalist, and it reached its nadir with "The Underneath," which is far and away the worst thing I've done. I just had to start over again."

The first step in his rejuvenation was "Schizopolis," a low-budget comic experiment that few people got to see. "That sort of unlocked me," he explains. "And then 'Out of Sight' [his sexy, funny Elmore Leonard adaptation] was the opportunity to show this new version of myself, which was much looser, much freer, much more playful. I think the movies I've made since 'Schizopolis' are just more fun to sit through."

"Traffic's" engines are already revved when it starts, with a drug bust in the Mexican desert, and it careers through its multiple stories with a documentary-style urgency that never lets up. In Mexico we follow the fraught, ambiguous journey of a Tijuana cop (Benicio Del Toro) caught between the ruthless, corrupt general (Tomas Milian) he works for and the DEA, which wants him to inform on his countrymen. The mesmerizing Del Toro, as alert and poised as a cat, keeps us wondering which side he's on. In La Jolla, a California society matron (Catherine Zeta-Jones) discovers, when her husband is carted off in handcuffs, that her fortune has been built on drug money. Determined to hold on to her lifestyle, she promptly takes over where her husband left off. The case against him rests on the testimony of a busted drug dealer (Miguel Ferrer) under the close watch of two cops (Don Cheadle and Luis Guzman). Their task is to keep him alive for his trial appearance. Meanwhile, in Washington, an Ohio judge (Michael Douglas) is about to be named the new drug czar by the president. His preconceptions, however, are tested when he discovers that his bright, privileged daughter (Erika Christensen) is strung out on crack.

Screenwriter Stephen Gaghan, using the skeleton of the British TV series "Traffik" as his guide, artfully interweaves these tales, composing a fresco of greed, courage, addiction and betrayal that underscores the futility of our government's costly War on Drugs. Soderbergh is a peerless director of actors: no one in his huge cast hits a false note. But not everything in the movie works equally well. The drug-czar/junkie-daughter skein is powerfully drawn, but it's the most form-ulaic and predictable. The most stunning sequences (which don't come from the TV series) are those in Tijuana, shot by Soderbergh in a harsh, over-exposed yellow tint. "Traffic" doesn't quite come to a full emotional boil at the end. Soderbergh is too knowing to offer easy solutions. But what a journey it takes us on: disturbing, exciting, completely absorbing.

"Traffic" is nothing if not timely. Witness the passage of Proposition 36 in California, requiring treatment, not incarceration, for drug possession. But Soderbergh isn't holding his breath that changes are imminent on a federal level. "Any politician trying to present a progressive idea about this issue is attacked for being soft on drugs, and they're screwed," he says. "There's a funny sort of disconnect about this issue. When it happens to someone in your family, it's a health-care problem. When it happens to somebody in somebody else's family, it's a criminal issue."

After two social-problem movies, Soderbergh wanted an "antidote." He's working on a star-studded remake of the heist movie "Ocean's 11" (of the Rat Pack original he quips: "It's a movie that's fondly remembered by all who haven't seen it"). No less than Brad Pitt, George Clooney, Julia Roberts and Matt Damon star. He knows that some who want him to remain the maverick who made "sex, lies" will question his choice. "The irony is that 'Ocean's' may well be, as a filmmaker, one of the more difficult things that I've attempted. I'm a run-and-gun guy, and this has to be so carefully machined." Soderbergh no longer has to prove anything to anyone. He's a born-again filmmaker, at ease, as all the classic Hollywood directors were, with the notion that art and entertainment don't have to be mutually exclusive terms. As he's proven—twice in one year.

SIGHT AND SOUND, 2/01, p. 53, Andrew O'Hehir

While arresting drug runners near the US Mexican border, Tijuana policemen Javier Rodriguez and Manolo Sanchez become involved with the National Drug Force, a unit commanded by General Salazar. Salazar instructs them to locate Francisco Flores, a hit man who works for a local drugs cartel which the general is determined to smash. In San Diego, Gordon and Castro, members of the US Drug Enforcement Agency, arrest Ruiz, a mid-ranking member of the same

Tijuana cartel, which is run by the Obregon brothers. Ruiz agrees to give evidence against Carlos Ayala, a major Obregon trafficker in San Diego. Rodriguez and Sanchez find Flores in San Diego and drive him to Salazar's base where he discloses the addresses of key members of the Obregon cartel.

With her husband in custody, Helena Ayala is shadowed by the DEA and the Obregons, who demand money that Carlos owes them. Meanwhile, newly appointed US drug czar Robert Wakefield finds out about his daughter Caroline's drug problem. In Tijuana, Helena strikes a deal with the Obregon cartel to have Ruiz killed and Carlos' debt wiped out. Flores botches the hit on Ruiz, inadvertently killing Castro before being shot dead by a hit man. Rodriguez and Sanchez discover that Madrigal, a member of the Juarez cartel, chief rival to the Obregons, who was believed dead, is alive in Mexico City and that Salazar works for the Juarez cartel. While Wakefield establishes cross-border links with Salazar, Caroline's drug problems worsen and she runs away from home. Salazar finds out that Sanchez is selling information to the DEA and has him executed. Rodriguez then passes on his knowledge about Salazar and the Obregon cartel to the Americans. With Salazar's criminal links exposed, he is murdered. Wakefield tracks Caroline down and brings her home. Ruiz is poisoned before he can testify; Carlos goes free. Wakefield resigns his post. At a party celebrating Carlos' release, Gordon forces his way into the Ayala household where he plants a surveillance device.

Although its vigorous, unaided rush of imagery and story makes for an exciting visual experience, Steven Soderbergh's *Traffic* is in the end a fatally sober film about drugs. For all the washed-out yellows of the film's Mexican desert and the midnight blues of its American Midwest, *Traffic* is a conventional cops-and-robbers melodrama, uniform in narrative texture, moralistic in tone and only intermittently in contact with the pleasure principle. None of this needs interfere with most viewers' enjoyment, and this adaptation (by Stephen Gaghan) of the Channel 4 series *Traffik* may be the most rousing Hollywood film about the drug trade since *The French Connection*.

Given the extravagant claims made for Soderbergh by many American critics, the comparison between *Traffic* and William Friedkin's genre-defining 1971 classic is instructive. Both films are innovative, at least in a limited, stylistic sense; *The French Connection* most notably for its extended car-chase scene and *Traffic* for its dizzying hopscotch from one plotline to another and its urgent seeming, quasi-documentary handheld camerawork. But *Traffic* is, if anything, less cynical or amoral in its vision than Friedkin's film. Its fictional universe seems to be one in which virtue is rewarded (or at least nobly sacrificed) and wickedness is punished. One gets the sense that Soderbergh and Gaghan want to see a tragic ambiguity in all their characters. But only the sad and soulful Benicio Del Toro as Rodriguez, the Tijuana cop forced to negotiate a series of unacceptable bargains, ever fully escapes the pasteboard action-film motivations supplied by the script.

The ironies and contradictions of *Traffic* are driven home with deadly earnest hammer blows. When Michael Douglas, as drug czar Bob Wakefield, bellies up to the bar amid a discussion with several (actual) US senators about the progress of the drug war, he asks loudly for a Scotch and soda. We can read Wakefield the moment we meet him; he is well meaning but compromised, an inattentive, borderline-alcoholic dad who must venture into terrifying neighbourhoods full of dark-skinned people to retrieve his daughter, like the father George C. Scott played in Paul Schrader's *Hardcore* (1978). Still, he's a more convincing character than his Mexican counterpart Salazar, a comically nefarious Third World caricature who all but twirls his moustache gleefully while pronouncing that addicts provide their own "treatment" by overdosing.

As Wakefield's dopehead daughter, Erika Christensen is a junior Botticelli angel who weeps for joy the first time she smokes freebase cocaine. Like the semi-tropical vegetation found throughout this film—in Southern California, Mexico City, Ohio in midsummer—she seems a symbol of lush and uncontrollable decadence, eager to escape from the restrictions of her story. But her abrupt descent into naked depravity (as represented by sex with black men), like the depiction of her high-school drug pals as dank-skinned, repellent characters, is tinged with the persistent odour of didacticism. Not for the first or last time in *Traffic,* one feels the presence of a finger-wagging adult, assuring us that just because the drug war is a failure doesn't mean we should rush out and do whatever crazy thing we want.

In the 90s, the drug trade and the drug experience played prominent roles in films by the likes of Quentin Tarantino, Darren Aronofsky and P. T. Anderson. Here, Soderbergh demonstrates that he's closer to the Dickensian moralising of mid-80s Oliver Stone than to any of them. Whatever their various flaws, those directors have sought to appreciate drug-altered consciousness as a libidinal field in which id and ego, Eros and Thanatos, come to grips with one another. Acting as his own cinematographer, Soderbergh resists any such attempt to capture subjective experience, sticking to 'naturalistic' point-of-view shots. This is a legitimate aesthetic choice and creates some striking moments, but considering the subject matter of *Traffic* it ultimately seems limited. Except for Javier, Soderbergh's characters are insufficient to lend the film human depth, and the result is a flashy entertainment that can only offer frustrating glimpses of the currents of psychology and desire far below its surface.

TIME, 1/8/01, p. 64, Richard Schickel

All Americans seem to be addicted to something that is bad for them—booze, cigarettes, excessive getting and spending. Drugs, naturally, are at the top of the hell list—they kill, they addle, they lie at the heart of a vast criminal enterprise, and the feckless "war" against them mostly wastes billions of public dollars every year. *Traffic* is the epic of our despair on this topic, an attempt to gather all the strands of the issue in one place and implicitly show how they entangle people at every level of society.

The film is well made by Steven Soderbergh, who handheld his own camera and often edits in an artless, documentary style. The picture is full of strong, soberly realistic performances; its melodramatic beats are not too many and, in context, not particularly overstated. Finally, though, *Traffic,* for all its earnestness, does not work. It leaves one feeling restless and dissatisfied.

Partly it's a structural problem. The film is telling three distinct stories. One is about a judge from Cincinnati, Ohio, Robert Wakefield (Michael Douglas), who is appointed by the President to be the new national drug czar only to discover that his own daughter (well played by Erika Christensen) is an addict, headed toward the lowest levels of degradation. Another is about an honest Mexican drug-enforcement officer (a marvelously watchful Benicio Del Toro) mystified by the cruel omnipotence of Tomas Milian, who is more or less Wakefield's Hispanic counterpart. The final story is of a San Diego material girl (Catherine Zeta-Jones) whose lifestyle is threatened when her husband is arrested for high-level trafficking. She proves to be a very tough nut when she takes over the family business.

We have left out a lot of details in this rough account of a very long and complicated narrative—for instance, Don Cheadle's smart, funny cop on perpetual stakeout, Miguel Ferrer's cynically truthful mid-level dealer—but there is a possibly predictable downside to this multiplicity of story lines: they keep interrupting one another. Just as you get interested in one, Stephen Gaghan's script, inspired by a British mini-series, jerks you away to another.

But that's not the biggest problem with *Traffic*. At one point Douglas' character convenes his staff and asks them to "think outside the box" about solutions to the drug problem. They don't come up with much, and neither do these filmmakers. "Oh, please," we murmur, seeing that Wakefield's daughter is hooked. "Oh, sure," we say when we learn that Milian's cruelty is corruption's mask. "What else?" we ask when a character is assassinated before he can testify against the higher-ups in his operation.

These are the clichés of a hundred crime movies, and bringing them all together in one place does not, finally, constitute an act of originality, no matter how interesting the details sometimes are, no matter how expertly they are presented. It may be that the magnitude of the problem is bound to strike dumb anyone who addresses it. It may also be that a mainstream movie doesn't dare consider more than offhandedly the radical alternatives to an official policy. We win tactical victories of the kind this film chronicles. But we are losing the "war" because its strategies are undiscussible.

VILLAGE VOICE, 1/2/01, p. 101, J. Hoberman

Traffic, the Steven Soderbergh dope opera that outflanked *Crouching Tiger, Hidden Dragon* and pushed past *The House of Mirth* to win the New York Film Critics Circle best picture award, is a most ambitious pop epic. Inspired by the 1989 British television miniseries *Traffik,* it brings the story closer to home, opening just south of the border with two Tijuana cops (Benicio Del Toro and Jacob Vargas) capturing a planeload of cocaine. In the first of many reversals, another agency unexpectedly takes over.

Cutting north, Soderbergh introduces a parallel pair of DEA agents (Don Cheadle and Luis Guzman) making a messy undercover bust in San Diego; a quartet of upper-class teens freebasing in Ohio; and Michael Douglas flying into Washington, D.C., to take over as the nation's latest drug czar. *Traffic* is not just an ultra-procedural—it's the Big Picture, the Whole Enchilada, complete with a complicated war between two Mexican drug cartels. The movie, which Soderbergh shot as well as directed, can be a bit exhausting in its color-coordinated parallel action, but it replenishes itself once the various melodramas begin to entwine.

Traffic puts a heavy arm on the audience to demonstrate that drugs touch us all. The effect is never more Griffithian than when the czar's golden daughter (Erika Christensen) becomes a crack 'ho. There are more than a few plodding clichés mustered among the movie's large ensemble cast, but TV writer Stephen Gaghan has scripted some excellent scenes—teenage kids trying to think and then think again when one of them goes into convulsions, Douglas's harried wife (Amy Irving) demanding that he stop babbling about his access to the president and devote some "face time" to their daughter. (This terse domestic squabble has a bitterness far beyond the smarmy histrionics in *American Beauty*.)

As it turns out, Douglas's comprehension of the Mexican situation matches his understanding of his daughter. Nothing else in his performance equals the tight fist he makes of his face when a 16-year-old preppie (Topher Grace) informs him that, down in the ghetto, crack is "an unbeatable market force." Everyone has a piece of the puzzle: A posh La Jolla matron (Catherine Zeta-]ones) comes to terms with her husband's real business; a middle-level drug dealer (Miguel Ferrer) lectures his DEA captors on how NAFTA makes their job harder. ("Are we on *Larry King* or something?" the bored cops ask.) *Traffic* may be didactic, but it's not unduly moralizing or simplistic even when Douglas tosses away the text of his big speech and tells the nation, "I don't know how you wage war on your own family."

Performing public service here for the feckless (if unconvincing) pothead he played in *Wonder Boys*, Douglas is the film's nominal star. It's Del Toro, however, who has been racking up the raves he should have received for enlivening *Basquiat* and *Fear and Loathing in Las Vegas*. Unafraid to posture (his Paul Muni parody in *The Funeral* was exceeded only by his Brando turn in *Way of the Gun*), Del Toro plays his enigmatic Mexican everyman as cocky yet thoughtful, an infinitely delicate brute. (The scene wherein he cruises a psycho hit man in a Tijuana bar is a standout non sequitur.) Fascinatingly mannered, Del Toro is not exactly giving a coherent performance, although his stunts seem to have driven Tomas Milian to his own heights of weirdness as a Mexican general.

Surely less lugubrious than if it were directed by Michael Mann, *Traffic* is exemplary Hollywood social realism. Skeptical about the War Against Drugs, it's cannily designed to make the movie industry look good—and not just because the film is serious, responsible, and half in Spanish. Watch for that D.C. party where happily co-opted Hollywood basher Senator Orrin Hatch simpers with pleasure at the prospect of hobnobbing with the likes of Michael Douglas. There's more than a shadow of Willem Dafoe's Nosferatu in the old tart's hunger to share the spotlight and more than a bit of Malkovich's Murnau in Soderbergh's willingness to oblige.

Also reviewed in:
CHICAGO TRIBUNE, 1/5/01, Friday/p. A, Michael Wilmington
NATION, 2/5/01, p. 5, Michael Massing
NEW REPUBLIC, 1/22/01, p. 22, Stanley Kauffmann
NEW YORK TIMES, 12/27/00, p. E1, Stephen Holden
NEW YORKER, 12/25 & 1/1/01, p. 154, David Denby
VARIETY, 12/18-31/00, p. 21, Todd McCarthy
WASHINGTON POST, 1/5/01, p. C1, Stephen Hunter
WASHINGTON POST, 1/5/01, Weekend/p. 36, Desson Howe

TRANS

A Screening Room release of a Yid Panther and Down Home Pictures production in association with Fig Leaf Productions. *Producer:* Martin Garner and Michael A. Robinson. *Director:* Julian Goldberger. *Story:* Julian Goldberger, Michael A. Robinson, and Martin Garner. *Director of photography:* Jesse Rosen. *Editor:* Affonso Gonçalves. *Sound:* Tom Efinger. *Sound Editor:* Damian Volpe. *Production Designer:* Sarah Wagoner. *Running time:* 83 minutes. MPAA Rating: Not Rated.

CAST: Ryan Daugherty (Ryan Kazinski); Michael Gulnac (Mike Gonzales); Justin Lakes (Justin Mallenkoff); Charles Walker and Jeremiah Robinson (Inmates/Party Rappers); Elijah Smith Trevor Thomas. Stephanie Davis (Boston Cream Girl); Daughert Edge (Bus Station Manager); Vince Kelly (Warden).

NEW YORK POST, 1/7/00, p. 44, Hannah Brown

There have been countless films about troubled teens on the run, but "Trans," a disturbing story of a boy who escapes from a detention center stands out because it gets inside his head in a way movies rarely manage to do.

Ryan Kazinski (Ryan Daugherty) has only one month left to serve of his sentence in a bleak juvenile prison in rural Florida. He spends most of his time there either locked in solitary or cleaning the highway as part a chain gang.

Ryan's thoughts, as he works or thrashes about his cell, are confused and confusing. He cares about his brother, whom Ryan injured in a pool accident when they were children. Their mother now lives in Colorado and Ryan hasn't seen her in long time; he doesn't mention their father.

While Ryan's face often has the cold, blank stare of a psycho—he admits that he feels like an alien sent to earth who doesn't understand his mission—it's hard to ignore his sadness.

"I believe that I have something to do that is very important," he says. "But you just can't get a grip on what it is."

When a fight breaks out on his work detail, he runs, although he has no idea where to go or what to do. For Ryan, acting on impulse is the only logic.

Two other boys run away with him, and for a few minutes, as they flee through the swamps, laughing and joking about alligators, the movie is like a junior version of Jim Jarmusch's "Down by Law."

But his friends ditch him, and Ryan is left on the porch of a convenience store with a bunch of locals who soon realize his predicament. Eventually, Ryan achieves a brief moment of real freedom, but his fall will be hard when it comes.

First-time director Julian Goldberger makes the audience feel what it's like to be this scared and lost.

The dreamlike visual style beautifully reflects Ryan's shifting moods. The obvious inspiration for "Trans" is Francois Truffaut's classic "The 400 Blows."

As this intense, haunting film ends, it's hard not to dread that moment of impact, and even harder to forget Ryan once it's over.

NEWSDAY, 1/7/00, Part II/p. B9, John Anderson

Early on in "Trans," Julian Goldberger's dreamlike state of a movie, there's a shot of an alligator cruising through a Florida swamp, stealth and silence only partly submerged. As fleeting as a sneeze, the scene—even calling it one is a stretch—is set against a monochromatic field that mutates from blue to fuchsia to green to sallow yellow, the black blotches shifting like a Rorschach test in motion. Death-dealing jaws become toothless against the mutating color scheme, because what's different has disarmed what's dangerous.

Goldberger's first film, which received considerable attention at the Sundance and Berlin festivals last year (including a prize at Berlin) is one of those movies—and there aren't many—that are transfixing because of what they don't do, don't say and because of what they pretend to be and aren't. Yes, there's a plot—this kid has run off from a youth offender work camp with a couple of other inmates, steals clothes, makes friends, gets hungry, gets beat up, goes home, is rejected and suffers for his freedom. Although he has a destination (a mother who has left him) this kid—named Ryan Kazinski (Ryan Daugherty)—isn't traveling through a world he knows or a world he's missed. He's made an interplanetary landing, crossed dimensions, trespassed on very foreign soil.

Time becomes indefinite; objects become art. Like post-structuralist concepts, the components are part of a conspiracy of irony.

The sense of dissociation Goldberger achieves, like some illicit pharmaceutical or Ryan's hunger, makes you lighthearted, elated, maybe morose, but also blessed by a certain clear-eyed concentration. Daugherty, who makes Ryan unlike any similar hero in any similar movie (meaning: virtually any movie in which a troubled youth makes a pilgrimage toward enlightenment) is genuinely appealing, maybe because he's antithetical to what the youth hero is "supposed" to be.

And Goldberger is a talent. The fugitive edginess that Ryan exhibits is palpable; the visual compositions the director achieves with such seeming ease are nothing short of noble. And his use of sound—from the creak of a rotating surveillance camera to the songs of Fat Mama or Lonnie Liston Smith—create an almost constant reorientation of perceptions and impressions, like that alligator in motion or all those shifting shades of meaning.

VILLAGE VOICE, 1/11/00, p. 108, Amy Taubin

Julian L. Goldberger's debut feature is a haunting portrait of a teenage boy busted out of reform school with nowhere to run. Buried in the experimental "Frontier" section at last year's Sundance, it elevated the festival for the handful of viewers that ventured away from the buzz. I caught up with it only because Richard Linklater tipped me off to how special a film it is.

Special, but no more experimental than Linklater's own debut film, *Slacker*, which also shaped film language, ever so gently, to the sensibility of a '90s generation and to the rhythms of a place that's neither a glittering urban hell nor the sanctified heartland mythologized by Hollywood. *Trans* is set in southwest Florida, where the Everglades are bounded by small towns that are merely a gas station, a laundromat, a supermarket, and a bus depot set along a highway with a few rundown houses behind them. This is the place that's home to Ryan Kazinski (Ryan Daugherty), who in his fantasy life is a space alien inhabiting a human body until he figures out what he was sent here to do.

What's most remarkable about *Trans* is how faithful it is to Ryan's consciousness and to the way it shifts between fantasy and a mesmerized response to details of the outside world: sunlight glinting on an open field, the beat-up silk on an ear of corn, the word "violation" displayed inside a parking meter. We don't know what landed Ryan in reform school—probably nothing more than petty theft or sniffing freon. A gentle, guileless kid, he acts on impulse, his attention span too fragmented to calculate consequences. With only a month left on his sentence, he goes on the lam; instead of heading out of state, he hangs around to see his kid brother and then to rescue a dog from the pound. It's not that he's totally unaware of the law closing in; he just can't stay focused on self-protection. We understand, better than he, how dire his situation is, which is why the film is so painful, particularly in its second half.

Over the subterranean narrative of the chase, Goldberger scatters a series of fragmentary scenes that map Ryan's 48 hours of freedom. Shot with a hand-held camera and occasionally rendered more dreamlike with slow or high-speed motion, the scenes are less dramatic interactions than windows onto the boy's psyche. Daugherty, who had never acted before, has a broad, snub-nosed all-American face that's in no way remarkable except when his eyes become rapt or when they seem to turn totally inward. His presence gives the film much of its immediacy and authenticity, and the large cast of nonprofessional local talent add immeasurably to the specific sense of place. It would be a slighting of *Trans*'s specifically American 1990s beauty to compare it to *The 400 Blows*, although the comparison is deserved. Better to place it among such Florida films as Victor Nunez's *Ulee's Gold* and Kelly Reichardt's *River of Grass*, which mix fragility and toughness and prove that the aspiration toward regional filmmaking that inspired American indies back in the '70s has not completely faded away.

Also reviewed in:
CHICAGO TRIBUNE, 5/5/00, Friday/p. H, John Petrakis
NEW YORK TIMES, 1/7/00, p. E24, Lawrence Van Gelder
VARIETY, 3/15-21/99, p. 43, Joe Leydon

TREASURE ISLAND

A King Pictures release of a King Pictures production. *Producer:* Adrienne Gruben. *Director:* Scott King. *Screenplay:* Scott King. *Director of Photography:* Phillip Glau and Scott King. *Editor:* Dody Dorn. *Music:* Chris Anderson. *Sound:* D.W. Harper. *Casting:* Nicole Arbusto. *Production Designer:* Nathan Marsak. *Art Director:* David Huffman. *Running time:* 86 minutes. *MPAA Rating:* Not Rated.

CAST: Lance Baker (Frank);   Nick Offerman (Samuel);   Jonah Blechman (The Body);   Pat Healy (Clark);   Suzy Nakamura (Yo-Ji); Rachel Singer (Annna);   Stephanie Ittelson (Stella); Daisy Hall (Penny);   Caveh Zahedi (Harold);   Becket Cook (The Gent);   Scot Thomas Robinson (Jimmy);   Bob Byington (Thomas);   Guinevere Turner (Evelyn).

NEW YORK POST, 3/17/00, p. 48, Lou Lumenick

"You've never seen *anything* like 'Treasure Island'" proclaim the ads. True enough, but that's hardly reason to endure this excruciating gay take on a grade-C 1940s melodrama.

This Treasure Island isn't R.L. Stevenson's but the military base in San Francisco Bay, where two World War II counterintelligence officers are assigned to write letters to accompany a body that'll be used to fool the Japanese about Allied invasion plans.

Shot in gleaming black-and-white, "Treasure Island" begins with beautiful '40s-style opening credits but quickly descends into poorly-acted, soft-core incoherence.

No director is credited, but writer-cinematographer-producerScott King probably deserves much of the blame.

VILLAGE VOICE, 3/21/00, p.144, Michael Atkinson

A beguiling, navel-focused freakazoid as original and mysterious as Sundance award winners are ever likely to get, Scott King's *Treasure Island* pretends to WW II-era hypernostalgia, but it's actually a vision of all-American movie culture as alternative psychohistory. Though it apes the noir visual palette hilariously, it's also eccentric, sexually anxious, and happy to be picking from the fields Guy Maddin and David Lynch have sowed. Far from merely doing an Ulmer or Ted Tetzlaff cover, King has created his own little cosmos, going so far as to preface his mock-feature with "King Movietone" newsreels and a fragmented episode of *John Q. Nazi,* a faux spy serial that reveals an understanding of the form George Lucas never had. Still, climaxing with images shanghaied from *Ugetsu* and *Dr. Strangelove, Treasure Island* can be thin and underrealized—Maddin's balmy conceptual assaults dwarf it.

The titular locale is actually a Frisco naval base used during wartime as a mail filter and code-breaking think tank; *Treasure Island* is thus a litter ground of secrets and unreadable messages. Depicted mostly as a single institutional room covered with scraps of paper, the central office houses Frank (Lance Baker), a reedy, Buster Keaton-eyed agent who has two problematic wives and one fiancée he cannot bring himself to fuck, and Samuel (Nick Offerman), a Borginnian man's man who spackles in his dead marital sex life by recruiting men for lifeless, tense threesomes with his wife. The two of them hatch a plan (lifted by King from an old pulp novel) to dump a John Doe corpse full of misleading tactical information in the Pacific, steering the Japanese wrong in the war's final months. They keep the freshly dead body right in the office—in a metal casket, abstrusely hooked up to a generator.

As the two men fabricate The Body's ultra-straight identity with stories that mirror their own lives, the stiff (a fey Jonah Blechman) manifests himself as a kind of gay phantom that begins to invade their dreams and then their reality. A haunted absurdity, *Treasure Island* reaches its most hypnotically harebrained when The Body shows up to double-team Samuel's wife, or takes the witness stand—in blackface—during a military hearing. Park City hoopla or no, King still had to self-release this changeling—such is the cachet of even the nerviest Sundance laurel.

Also reviewed in:
CHICAGO TRIBUNE, 10/6/00, Friday/p. F, John Petrakis
NEW YORK TIMES, 3/17/00, p. E18, Stephen Holden
VARIETY, 2/15-21/99, p. 63, Todd McCarthy

TRENCH, THE

A Film Forum release of a Blue PM/SkylineFilms/GalatéeFilms production. *Executive Producer:* Xavier Marchand. *Producer:* Steve Clark-Hall. *Director:* William Boyd. *Screenplay:* William Boyd. *Director of Photography:* Tony Pierce-Roberts. *Editor:* Jim Clark and Laurence Méry-Clark. *Music:* Evelyn Glennie and Greg Malcangi. *Sound:* Chris Munro. *Sound Editor:* Jonathan Bates. *Casting:* Jennifer Duffy and Mary Selway. *Production Designer:* Jim Clay. *Art Director:* Phil Harvey. *Set Decorator:* Val Wolstenholme. *Special Effects:* Graham Longhurst. *Costumes:* David Crossman and Lindy Hemming. *Make-up:* Ann Buchanan and Susan Howard. *Stunt Coordinator:* Tom Delmar. *Running time:* 98 minutes. *MPAA Rating:* Not Rated.

CAST: Paul Nicholls (Billy Macfarlane); Daniel Craig (Sergeant Telford Winter); Julian Rhind-Tutt (Lieutenant Ellis Harte); Danny Dyer (Victor Dell); James D'Arcy (Colin Daventry); Tam Williams (Eddie Macfarlane); Anthony Strachan (Horace Beckwith); Michael Moreland (George Hogg); Adrian Lukis (Colonel Villiers); Ciarán McMenamin (Charlie Ambrose); Cillian Murphy (Rag Rockwood); John Higgins (Cornwallis); Ben Whishaw (James Deamis); Tim Murphy (Bone); Danny Nutt (Dieter); Charles Cartmell (Harold Faithfull); Tom Mullion (Nelson); Jenny Pickering (Maria Corrigan).

NEW YORK POST, 11/22/00, p. 46, Jonathan Foreman

In film, it's not the thought that counts. And all "The Trench" has going for it is the worthy thought of commemorating the men and boys slaughtered at the Battle of the Somme in July 1916.

The British took 60,000 casualties on the first day of battle (half of them in the first hour) as they went "over the top" into a curtain of machine-gun fire from German trenches that were supposed to have been destroyed in a massive artillery bombardment.

This static, play-like movie, with its painfully doomy music and low-budget TV-style cinematography, is set on the eve of that hideous massacre.

Just as the vastly superior "Kippur" tells terrible truths about combat while showing only its aftermath, "The Trench" tries to do so by painting a picture of an inexperienced young squad enduring the 48 hours of tension before the big push.

Unfortunately, it says nothing about the horrors of World War I trench warfare that hasn't been better put in other films and in the vast literature of that conflict (the first international war to be experienced by mass-literate armies).

In fact, if you know anything about the Somme, or if you have seen any of films like "All Quiet on the Western Front" or "Paths of Glory," then"The Trench" is almost unbearably hackneyed.

There isn't a line you haven't heard or a stock character you haven't encountered before.

With grinding predictability, the young soldier who disobeys the tough sergeant and peeps at the enemy gets shot by a sniper, and the squad captures a trembling German soldier who reminds them uncannily of themselves.

But if you don't know anything about the Somme (especially the salient fact—revealed at an end title—that most of those in the first wave were wiped out) then all the film's intended ironies simply collapse.

Worse still, the kids in the squad, played by relative unknowns, feel like a writer's devices in authentic period uniforms rather than real people.

It doesn't help that they look like well-fed young actors with fashionable '90s haircuts rather than the pinched youths familiar from contemporary photographs, or that most of them have not been told how to hold a rifle like a soldier.

There are a couple of moving scenes toward the end, but nothing with the pathos of the devastating final episode of the "Blackadder" TV series.

It's hard to believe that writer-director William Boyd is the same person who authored fine novels like "A Good Man in Africa" and "The New Confessions."

NEWSDAY, 11/22/00, Part II/p. B7, John Anderson

There has been a lot written lately about golf being the perfect metaphor for life. William Boyd's got a better idea.

In a muddy trench in northern France, late June of 1916, a company of British soldiers awaits the onset of the Battle of the Somme. What you know as you watch, of course, will calibrate your sense of apprehension: The biggest offensive of the war, the Somme will result in 60,000 casualties on the first day, becoming—and remaining—the biggest military defeat in British history.

What we're looking at are dead men. They just don't know it.

They have their suspicions, though. And Boyd, the celebrated English novelist ("A Good Man in Africa") and scriptwriter ("Chaplin") makes the most of a situation guaranteed to bring out the best and worst in each of his characters—all of whom, as if to deflect comparisons with other war films, seem familiar, but aren't.

There's the Billy Buddish, underage foot soldier Billy Macfarlane (Paul Nicholls), who's in love with a prostitute's picture—a postcard he's stolen from the blowhard corporal (Danny Dyer) and whittled down to a sentimentalized cameo. His hard-bitten sergeant (Daniel Craig) is no Claggart, but rather a teetotaling professional. The too-introspective commanding officer (Julian Rhind-Tutt) is weak-willed and drinks but exhibits nobility under pressure rather than the panic you might expect.

The rest are cowards, heroes and Wellington's inevitable scum of the earth, in a war whose causes—a rat's nest of political allegiances, alliances and incompetence—you still need charts and graphs to figure out.

The First World War has always held a more prominent place in the public imagination of Britain than the United States, which entered late and never suffered what its ally did, the loss of virtually an entire generation of men. Boyd's grandfather and great-uncle both fought in the war, but don't expect solemnity—at least, not always: Told that the remains of one slain Brit could have fit in a sock, a naive soldier asks, "Did they bury the sock? In a full-size grave?"

We've seen some of the themes of "The Trench" explored before—in "All Quiet on the Western Front," and certainly "Paths of Glory." And though Boyd's film has an intensity that may not always be successful, it is certainly unique. The claustrophobic rabbit warren of the trench itself, the unseen enemy above, the long-range military blundering of the British officer corps, the mounting terror—each of Boyd's devices are distilling agents, symbols as well, but essentially the means by which each man meets himself. To march off to death is bad enough. Having one's own revealed face as a final memory gives the idea of dying in battle an added sense of horror, a horror exploited here to withering effect.

SIGHT AND SOUND, 10/99, p. 57, Tom Tunney

On the Western Front, just before the build-up to the Somme offensive of 1 July 1916, a platoon of British troops hold a section of the front line. As the deadline for the dawn attack approaches, one man, Macfarlane, is wounded by an enemy sniper and evacuated. The troops' banter turns unpleasant when Dell accuses the others of stealing one of his pornographic postcards. A senior officer arrives and tells the troops the advance will be easy because the artillery will destroy the enemy's defences. The men cheer, but Daventry dissents and is later reprimanded by Sergeant Winter.

Several of the group are killed in an adjacent trench while carrying rations. Winter and Beckwith undertake a night patrol and bring back a German prisoner whom Dell insults and attacks. The German is sent back to the rear and safety. Dell is ordered to fetch the rum ration for the men, drinks much of it himself and is caught in an explosion. He comes back drunk without the rum. Winter persuades the platoon officer Harte to share his whisky with the men. As they prepare to go over the top at dawn, one man shoots himself in the leg. Macfarlane looks at the photograph in his locket: it's a face cut from Dell's missing postcard. Winter forces the drunken Dell into the attack. Winter is hit just after leaving the trench. The others advance and are cut down by enemy fire within yards of their own front line.

Author and screenwriter William Boyd's directing debut plays more like a schools-education programme than a theatrical film. The movie's low budget is particularly glaring in the final sequence where a mere handful of men (representing an army of tens of thousands) step out into an unspoilt meadow and are cut down in slow motion one by one. Compared to the manic, visceral horrors of *Saving Private Ryan* or the sweeping battlefield tracking shots of *Paths of Glory* (1957), this austere stylisation seems both clichéd and absurdly inadequate. The studio mock-up of the British trench system fails to deliver the oppressive dirt and squalor of the genuine article and the actors—despite some impressive performances, particularly from Daniel Craig as the care-worn Sergeant Winter—always look like actors dressed up as soldiers rather than men who are actively subsisting in their long hole in the ground. Other low-budget war films, such as Joseph Losey's *King & Country* (1964), have managed to evoke the merciless, class-ridden, rituals of the British Army in World War I, but Losey felt no need to cap his film with a major battle he couldn't afford to stage.

Despite its Great War setting, Boyd's screenplay is structurally reminiscent of two British war films set in World War II: Carol Reed's *The Way Ahead* (1944) and Leslie Norman's *The Long and the Short and the Tall* (1960). The first is an optimistic platoon-focused film in which the men learn to work with each other before going into action. The second is a kind of Angry Young Man-era cynical riposte to *The Way Ahead* a pessimistic platoon film in which men constantly argue and are unprepared for the Japanese ambush which overtakes them. Boyd's film wavers indecisively between the bonding rituals of the first and the sarcasm of the second. The character of Victor Dell and his abusive treatment of the German prisoner are reminiscent of a similar scene in *The Long,* in which a Japanese prisoner is captured. But *The Trench* also emphasises the group's camaraderie, with its geographical cross-section of troops drawn from all over the British Isles. However, Boyd's script is unduly schematic. With the exception of Winter, the characters come across as writer's devices rather than real people and the funereal tones of the music score has the effect of embalming them from the start in tragic hindsight.

At least Boyd's film conveys the central failure of the generals' tactics in this war. It didn't matter whether the attacking troops were well trained or not: many would be killed before they had even fired a shot. The long dawn wait before the men finally go over the top generates a palpable tension and it is here that his direction and his cast's committed performances come into their own. That highly evocative sequence apart, the main problem with film is that it says nothing that hasn't been said more powerfully and more persuasively by other films. Although it's a useful beginner's guide to the war movie and to World War I, for real trench-level tension and terror look elsewhere.

VILLAGE VOICE, 11/28/00, p. 140, Michael Atkinson

Refreshingly, novelist William Boyd's *The Trench* doesn't gang-press WW I, virtually forgotten apocalypse that it was, into genre service or a Spielbergian redemptive strike. Rather, it's *All Quiet* all over again, taking us to the western front to simply watch the carrion accumulate. Moviewise, the Great War has few other functions. Hardly known to us by way of news footage (Boyd does include an at-the-front shooting of what could've been the world's first propaganda film), the war is by now a docket of muddy glyphs: the hallway-in-hell trench life, the helmets and sandbags, the compulsory rush toward slaughter, the fresh-faced teenagers narratively earmarked for a pointless martyrdom. Falling unceremoniously into line behind Lewis Milestone's awesome 1930 version of Remarque, Kubrick's *Paths of Glory,* and Peter Weir's *Gallipoli,* Boyd's movie thieves knowingly from all three, all the while reclaiming a few even grimmer realities, like picking tooth shrapnel out of your head and the de rigueur distribution of pre-attack whiskey to infantrymen. "They won't go five yards," the bellicose sergeant (Daniel Craig) growls, begging one of the movie's several pasty/plummy officers to contribute his own scotch.

The Trench focuses nominally on Billy (Paul Nicholls), a sensible, doe-eyed everybloke who talks too much about the romantic epiphany he never actually had with a woman. But there are over a dozen characters in the trench, stuck holding down the field in a skeleton force only days before the Battle of the Somme—which, we're reminded, was the bloodiest single day the British Army ever faced. (That is not to say the bloodiest faced by any opposition.) Gritty revisionism or not, Boyd (whose self-described "family lore" involves grandparents wounded in the green fields of France) can't help but be nostalgic—his is a safe antiwar film, executed at an entertaining remove. The stereotypes—hotheads, fat boys, cynics, brownnosers, etc.—squabble and wax working-class lyrical along the hand-dug corridor's lower depths, and Boyd shoots them almost entirely on an obvious set, with BBC miniseries lighting. The acting, by a large cast of little-known young Brits chewing on South London accents like dog bones, is uniformly splendiferous, but you can't mistake them for doughboys.

Also reviewed in:
NEW YORK TIMES, 11/22/00, p. E3, Stephen Holden
VARIETY, 6/7-13/99, p. 31, David Rooney

TRIXIE

A Sony Pictures Classics release. *Executive Producer:* James McLindon. *Producer:* Robert Altman. *Director:* Alan Rudolph. *Screenplay:* Alan Rudolph. *Story:* Alan Rudolph and John Binder. *Director of Photography:* Jan Kiesser. *Editor:* Michael Ruscio. *Music:* Mark Isham and Roger Neill. *Sound:* Rick Patton. *Casting:* Pam Dixon Mickelson. *Production Designer:* Richard Paris and Linda Del Rosario. *Set Decorator:* Brian Kane. *Special Effects:* Jak Osmond. *Costumes:* Monique Prudhomme. *Make-up:* Jayne Dancose. *Running time:* 117 minutes. *MPAA Rating:* R.

CAST: Emily Watson (Trixie Zurbo);   Dermot Mulroney (Dex Lang);   Nick Nolte (Sen. Drummond Avery);   Nathan Lane (Kirk Stans);   Brittany Murphy (Ruby Pearli);   Lesley Ann Warren (Dawn Sloane);   Will Patton (Red Rafferty);   Stephen Lang (Jacob Slotnick);   Mark Acheson (Vince Deflore);   Vincent Gale (Sid Deflore);   Jason Schombing (Ramon);   Robert Moloney (Alvin);   Troy Yorke (Cleavon Arris);   Wendy Noel (Coffee Shop Waitress);   David Kopp (Bell Boy);   Ken Kirzinger (Avery's Bodyguard);   Jonathon Young (Gas Attendant);   Terence Kelly (Mr. Lang);   Karen Elizabeth Austin (Mrs. Lang);   Andrew McIlroy (Maitre d');   Dalias Blake and Maria Herrera (Store Guards);   Brendan Fletcher (CD Thief);   Gina Chiarelli and Stephen E. Miller (Casino Security);   Robin Mossley (Casino Pickpocket);   Taayla Markell (Casino Call Girl);   Michael Puttonen (Tourist);   Kate Robbins (Tourist Wife);   Lesley Ewen (Casino Bartender);   Darrell Izeard (Casino Guard);   Alvin Sanders (Capital Building Custodian);   Peter Bryant (Cop);   Violetta Dobrijevich (Grandma);   Rondel Reynoldson (Nurse);   Norman Armour (Dr. Gold);   Blake Stovin (Valet);   Michael Cromien (Legislator on Street);   Francisco Trujillo (Forum Bartender);   Alonso Oyarzun, Tyler Labine, and Zak Santiago Alam (Gang Members).

CHRISTIAN SCIENCE MONITOR, 6/30/00, p. 15, David Sterritt

"You've got to grab the bull by the tail and look it in the eye!"

That wisdom is spoken by the eccentric heroine of "Trixie," and it applies to movie reviews as well as life in general. So let's do it.

Looking the new Alan Rudolph comedy in the eye, you see an amusing premise and a talented cast, but also a weakly constructed story and repetitious jokes.

Should audiences give the picture a chance to do its tricks? It isn't without merit, but the safest choice is to ignore it and hope it'll wander quietly away.

The story centers on Trixie, a gambling casino security guard. She meets a klutzy womanizer who tempts her into a date on a crooked businessman's boat. His friends include a state senator and a washed-up nightclub singer who lead our heroine into crime, politics, and show business.

"Trixie" will have extra interest for moviegoers who've followed the ups and downs of Rudolph's erratic filmography, from the promising "Welcome to L.A." and "Remember My Name" to the awful "Endangered Species" and "Equinox."

The new picture ranks with his middling efforts, lifted by the magnetism of Emily Watson and Nick Nolte but weighed down by a "screwball noir" story that allows humor and pathos to cancel each other out.

Rudolph has called "Trixie" his "autobiography," explaining that it's about "someone who doesn't connect with the society around them and who has a different language and different ideas and thoughts." That's an odd way for a commercial filmmaker to describe himself—how can you sell tickets if you don't connect with your society?—but it indicates a laudable ambition to work outside the familiar gaggle of Hollywood conventions.

Similar goals have long motivated Robert Altman, who produced "Trixie" and once served as Rudolph's mentor. While both filmmakers have had their share of flops, Altman has reached greater heights because he's willing to pursue his "difference" to extremes.

"Trixie" relies too much on the cliches it wants to deconstruct, suggesting that Rudolph needs to take more risks if he's going to sustain a truly distinctive career.

LOS ANGELES TIMES, 6/28/00, Calendar/p. 4, Kevin Thomas

Alan Rudolph aptly describes "Trixie," his latest ensemble piece, as "screwball noir." In the title role, Emily Watson plays a drugstore security guard who dreams of becoming a private detective and who never met a metaphor she couldn't mix. Quick thinking on the job lands her a chance to take a more promising assignment working undercover at a mountain resort casino in an unnamed state, and in an instant, she's caught up in romance and danger.

Clocking in at just six minutes short of two hours, "Trixie" is too much of a good thing. Trixie's malapropisms are laid on so thick you begin wondering if she is suffering from some disorder. Still, so much of the film is so funny, inspired and sophisticated, the performances so richly nuanced, that many viewers, Rudolph admirers in particular, will be inclined to forgive a little self-indulgence on the part of this authentic auteur.

Working the 9 p.m.-5 a.m. shift, Trixie is quickly befriended by boozy lounge entertainer Kirk (Nathan Lane), a world-weary celebrity impressionist-singer, and by Ruby Pearli (Brittany Murphy), a young glamour girl who hangs out at the bar on the lookout for a main squeeze. Trixie, in turn, is zeroed in on by a certified lounge lizard, Dex (Dermot Mulroney), a sexy dude with Valentino sideburns and abundant confidence with women.

Trixie flatly rejects his advances, only to end up agreeing to come visit him at a yacht he tends for a brash developer, Red Rafferty (Will Patton). She winds up, unexpectedly, on a boat ride with Red; Sen. Drummond Avery (Nick Nolte), a silver-haired, silver-tongued orator type; Dawn Sloane (Lesley Ann Warren), a nightclub singer of uncertain age; and a pair of Rafferty's goons, the Deflore brothers (Mark Acheson, Vincent Gale).

Rudolph understands that you can smell corruption in this group without having to spell out just how Rafferty and the senator will be slicing the pie. Not long after Trixie is back on terra firma, she's investigating blackmail and murder.

If Rudolph goes on a bit, he nonetheless is using his screen time to probe character and not just pile up plot complications for their own sake; if anything, he is so incisive that you're in danger of taking this comedy too seriously. As a director, Rudolph is most empathetic with actors; and as a writer, he has—in this instance as in many others—come up with material rich in humor and complexity.

Nolte keeps showing us more and more facets of the senator, who gleams like a highly polished, but deeply flawed diamond, a man still in his tanned and rugged prime but so rotten to the core, he's ready to implode whether he realizes it or not. What the senator has to say about Nixon and Eisenhower—and much else—to the increasingly baffled Trixie is hilarious.

Warren's Dawn is a lovely woman too mature for the flirtatious sexpot routine—and she knows it. However, she persists in doing it but is increasingly desperate to escape to a different life with a measure of security.

With Dex, Trixie brings out a basic decency that's inconvenient for him, but which he will not betray. Mulroney continues to build his reputation as a first-rate leading man with a flair for comedy, and "Trixie" offers the protean Watson a refreshing change of pace from such grim fare as "Breaking the Waves," "Hilary and Jackie" and "Angela's Ashes."

Filmed in Vancouver (as so many movies are these days), "Trixie" is a handsome, well-designed film typical of Rudolph, and it has a wonderful score by Mark Isham and Roger Neill that reflects the film's ever-changing moods.

NEWSDAY, 6/28/00, Part II/p. B13, Gene Seymour

The essence of "Trixie"—indeed, of most of Alan Rudolph's movies—can be distilled in one line of dialogue: "Do you hear yourself talking when you speak?"

The question is both asked by and posed to the movie's eponymous heroine, Trixie Zurbo (Emily Watson), a gum-snapping rent-a-cop from Chicago who wants to be a full-fledged private detective. Her yearning to break free from patrolling department store corridors is gratified when she takes a gig working plainclothes security duty for a backwoods casino.

Trixie takes no guff and is just observant enough to be effective at her job. But—let's see, how to put this?—her brain doesn't transmit words to her mouth in a logical manner. Or, as she herself would describe the malady, her cliches have their pants on upside down.

Of one suspicious character, for instance, Trixie is moved to say, "He smokes like a fish." This same character, one Dexter Lang (Dermot Mulroney), is the kind of self-deluded stud so often found in the cloud-cuckoo-land of an Alan Rudolph movie. (Think of the klutzy Lotharios played by Keith Carradine in 1984's "Choose Me" and 1985's "Trouble in Mind" and you know where Dex is coming from. And heading for.)

Kirk Stans (Nathan Lane), the casino's world-weary one-man lounge act, gives suspicious Trixie the skinny on Lang: He's an errand boy for a snarky land developer named Red Rafferty (Will Patton) who's in bed, politically speaking, with an oily state senator (Nick Nolte in what Trixie would call "high dungeon"). Dex is in bed, non-politically speaking, with singer Dawn Sloane (Lesley Ann Warren), who's apparently on the run from blackmailers in Red's employ.

Rudolph's story makes about as much sense as Trixie's thought process. Which may well be the point of this exercise in what the writer-director himself calls "screwball noir": That, as goofy as she talks, Trixie ends up making more sense, verbally and otherwise, than the cracked pots surrounding her.

How much you buy into this movie depends on how much you enjoy being tossed down one of Rudolph's rabbit holes. Usually, I can handle the fall. But while there are virtuoso set pieces galore and an enrapturing moodiness that typifies Rudolph's style, the offhandedness of the storytelling throws the movie's rhythm off-key. (As Lane's nightclub comic observes, Trixie's talk is contagious.) And though I love Emily Latella as much as the next guy, those malapropisms do get on one's nerves by the movie's end.

Yet Watson, finally granted the comic star turn her immense talent deserves, makes the whole gauzy mess worth watching. She can't help bringing along her intensity to the party. but you love watching her big blue eyes strain to get this gooey stuff in focus.

VILLAGE VOICE, 7/4/00, p. 121, J. Hoberman

Another proud symbol of America, the eponymous heroine of Alan Rudolph's Trixie is a wide-eyed working-class wacko who chews gum, toils as a casino security guard, and spouts outlandish malapropisms, roughly in that order. The big surprise is that, as courageously played by Emily Watson, this self-described "private detective" turns out to be the smartest, bravest, most sexually well-adjusted character in the movie.

Trixie's competition includes Nathan Lane's broken-down lounge comic, Dermot Mulroney's romantic klutz, Lesley Anne Warren's addled sexpot, Will Patton's ineffectual gangster, and Brittany Murphy's precocious femme fatale. Embodiment of corruption, Nick Nolte's white-maned state senator swans through the movie as though he were the John Huston character in

Chinatown—although the evil that he does consists mainly of ranting about presidential sex scandals and mouthing the blind Newt Gingrich quotes that Rudolph has worked into the dialogue. Trixie has little difficulty baffling him with bullshit. "Do I have an ace up my hole?" she wonders. Not this time. Rudolph has called his movie a "screwball noir"—elevating *The Big Lebowski* to the level of the Sistine Chapel by comparison. (Try to imagine *The Big Lebowski* directed by the Dude from a script by his bowling partners.)

Trixie is eager to please, but even mildly amusing routines are relentlessly run into the ground. The bribery-blackmail-murder mystery comes unraveled long before Rudolph can knit a narrative skein. The movie is as overlong and undermotivated as it is absentmindedly incoherent. At one point, Trixie advises someone to "fish or get off the pot." Perhaps the filmmaker should take her advice.

Also reviewed in:
CHICAGO TRIBUNE, 7/14/00, Friday/p. E, Michael Wilmington
NEW YORK TIMES, 6/28/00, p. E8, Stephen Holden
VARIETY, 3/6-12/00, p. 41, Emanuel Levy

TURN IT UP

A New Line Cinema release. *Executive Producer:* Gary Ventimiglia, Lennox Parris, and Lester Parris. *Producer:* Guy Oseary and Happy Walters. *Director:* Robert Adetuyi. *Screenplay:* Robert Adetuyi. *Based on a story by:* Ray "Cory" Daniels, Chris Hudson, and Kelly Hilaire. *Director of Photography:* Hubert Taczanowski. *Editor:* Jeff Freeman. *Music:* Frank Fitzpatrick. *Music Editor:* Richard Harrison. *Sound:* Greg Chapman and (music) Tim Boyle and David Tobocman. *Sound Editor:* Frank Gaeta. *Casting:* Robi Reed-Humes. *Production Designer:* Ina Mayhew. *Art Director:* Kei. *Set Decorator:* Jaro Dick. *Set Dresser:* Jacques Alexander Veilleux and David Orin Charles. *Special Effects:* Michael Kavanaugh. *Costumes:* Mimi Melgaard. *Make-up:* Mario G. Cacioppo and Nicki Lederman. *Stunt Coordinator:* John Stoneham, Jr. and Michael Russo. *Running time:* 100 minutes. *MPAA Rating:* R.

CAST: Pras (Diamond); Elain Graham (Rose); Chris Messina (Baz); Eugene Clark (Marshall); Harry-O (Master Mix); Ja Rule (Gage); Patrice Goodman (Jane); John Ralston (Mr. White); Jason Statham (Mr. B.); Chang Tseng (Mr. Chang); Tamala Jones (Kia); Jeff Jones (Minister); Vondie Curtis-Hall (Cliff); Melyssa Ford (Deborah); Derwin Jordan (Seamus); Leroy Allen (Security Guard); Faith Evans (Natalie); DJ Skribble (DJ); Shinehead (Smiley); Conrad Dunn (Urie); Juliana Stojkic (Pregnant Slavic Woman); Ted Clark (Crusher); Errol Gee (Tyrone); Cam Natale (Slick); Robert Dodds (JT).

LOS ANGELES TIMES, 9/6/00, Calendar/p. 6, Kevin Thomas

Debuting writer-director Robert Adetuyi's "Turn It Up" casts a harsh light on the dark side of the hip-hop scene.

In this somber but vital drama, Pras (Prakazrel Michel, a founding member of the Fugees) plays Diamond, a Brooklynite with a craving for rap stardom so strong that he and his lifelong pal Gage (Ja Rule) have for some time been working as couriers for a Manhattan drug lord, Mr. B (Jason Statham), who also operates a luxe and trendy nightclub.

Diamond and Gage see this as the only way to make the demo that will skyrocket them out of the ghetto and Diamond to the top of the charts.

As Diamond becomes increasingly wary of being involved in drug trafficking, Gage becomes more and more convinced that they have no choice.

Diamond's girlfriend Kia (Tamala Jones) not only is none too happy with her lover's being involved in shady business but also has become unexpectedly pregnant and demands to know whether Diamond is prepared to accept the responsibilities of marriage and parenthood. When Diamond's ailing mother dies, his father (Vondie Curtis-Hall), a gifted musician who tried drowning his professional disappointments in drink, unexpectedly turns up at his wife's funeral, 12 years after deserting her and his son. He strongly advises Diamond not to repeat his mistakes.

There are moments when "Turn It Up" could be more specific: Has Diamond any viable way of supporting himself, let alone a wife and child, outside crime? Is there in fact no way for him to launch a recording career without resorting to crime? And when all is said and done, we're left wondering just how successful that first recording is, considering the high toll in human lives exacted to get it made.

Even so, "Turn It Up," which benefits strongly from Hubert Taczanowksi's masterly, mood-setting cinematography, hits hard and pulls no punches in telling its brutal story.

Pras is poised and persuasive, but it is rapper Ja Rule, in his acting debut, who energizes the entire film as the doggedly loyal Gage, more realistic than Diamond yet in way over his head as well. Jones is properly feisty as the worried, plain-spoken Kia, and Hall is solid, as always.

"Turn It Up" boasts strong musical selections and an effective score by Frank Fitzpatrick. It has action and violence, to be sure, but it may prove considerably more serious and uncompromising than its audience expected.

NEW YORK POST, 9/6/00, p. 52, Lou Lumenick

"It's got no bite. It's too processed," a would-be rap star's father responds when asked his opinion of his son's music.

Which perfectly describes this highly derivative little gangsta melodrama set on the mean streets of Toronto—er, Brooklyn.

Pras Michel, a real-life rap star who founded the Fugees with Lauryn Hill and Wyclef Jean, plays Diamond, a small-time drug runner who aspires to hip-hop stardom.

Diamond is cutting his first album with help from his buddy Gage (hip-hopper Ja Rule), who raises $100,000 by stealing it from a thug who has underworld connections that cause major problems for both of them.

"When Jesus helped the blind man, did he ask how he did it?" Gage asks Diamond, who yearns to go legitimate.

Between shootouts, there are halfhearted subplots involving Diamond's estranged father (Vondie Curtis-Hall) and his pregnant girlfriend (Tamala Jones). Under Canadian writer-director Robert Adetuyi, the acting is adequate, at best.

Oddly, "Turn It Up" features less than 10 minutes of music in its mercifully brief 83-minute running time.

NEWSDAY, 9/6/00, Part II/p. B2, Gene Seymour

[*Turn it Up* was reviewed jointly with *Backstage*: see Seymour's review of that film.]

VILLAGE VOICE, 9/19/00, p. 126, Jessica Winter

Some form of distancing device would come in handy for the protagonists of *Turn It Up* and *On the Run*, both of whom suffer by the *Mean Streets-Rounders* model of guilty duty to a parasitic no-goodnik best buddy from childhood. *On the Run* is a bad one-night stand endured with a jailbroke cad and his put-upon travel-agent pal that hinges somewhat on the characters' impression that Frank Sinatra is still among us—this may or may not be a screen-writing oversight, but if it's a joke, it has no punch line. The marginally more watchable *Turn It Up* features two live pop stars: Ja Rule in the worm role and the Fugees' Pras as a silken-voiced, somewhat passive aspiring hip-hop star juggling pregnant girlfriend, prodigal dad, and nefarious business associates. The staging and performances are awkward, the frequent shoot-outs a snore, and there's no reprise of "Ghetto Supastar."

Also reviewed in:
CHICAGO TRIBUNE, 9/6/00, Tempo/p. 2, Vicky Edwards
NEW YORK TIMES, 9/6/00, p. E5, Stephen Holden
VARIETY, 9/11-17/00, p. 22, Robert Koehler

28 DAYS

A Columbia Pictures release of a Tall Trees production. *Producer:* Jenno Topping. *Director:* Betty Thomas. *Screenplay:* Susannah Grant. *Director of Photography:* Declan Quinn. *Editor:* Peter Teschner. *Music:* Richard Biggs. *Music Editor:* Nick Sound. *Sound:* Tod A. Maitland and (music) Jeff Vaughn. *Sound Editor:* Michael J. Benavente. *Casting:* Francine Maisler. *Production Designer:* Marcia Hinds-Johnson. *Art Director:* Bo Johnson. *Set Designer:* Geoffrey S. Grimsman, C. Scott Baker, and Bill King. *Set Decorator:* Debra Schutt. *Set Dresser:* Paul Cheponis and Marthe Pineau. *Special Effects:* Connie Brink. *Costumes:* Ellen Lutter. *Make-up:* Sharon Ilson and Pamela Westmore. *Stunt Coordinator:* Daniel W. Barringer. *Running time:* 110 minutes. *MPAA Rating:* PG-13.

CAST: Sandra Bullock (Gwen Cummings); Viggo Mortensen (Eddie Boone); Dominic West (Jasper); Elizabeth Perkins (Lily); Azura Skye (Andrea); Steve Buscemi (Cornell); Alan Tudyk (Gerhardt); Michael O'Malley (Oliver); Marianne Jean-Baptiste (Roshanda); Reni Santoni (Daniel); Diane Ladd (Bobbie Jean); Margo Martindale (Betty); Susan Krebs (Evelyn); Loudon Wainwright, III (Guitar Guy); Katie Scharf (Young Gwen); Meredith Deane (Young Lily); Elizabeth Ruscio (Mom); Kathy Payne (Aunt Helen); Lisa Sutton (Dr. Stavros); Joanne Pankow (Saleslady/Night Tech); Corinne Reilly (Vanessa); Andrew Dolan (Groom); Maeve McGuire (Groom's Mother); Jim Moody (Chauffeur); Christina Chang (Bridesmaid); Adam Pervis (Younger Boy at Gas Station); Dan Byrd (Older Boy at Gas Station); Ric Reitz (Father at Gas Station); Suellen Yates (Andrea's Mother); Frank Hoyt Taylor (Equine Therapist); Brittani Warrick (Traci); Elijah Kelley (Darnell); Mike Dooly (Marty); Wendee Pratt (Elaine); Bill Anagnos (NY Cabdriver).

LOS ANGELES TIMES, 4/14/00, Calendar/p. 2, Kenneth Turan

Gwen Cummings thinks being in rehab is one big joke. And no wonder. She's in a movie that believes exactly the same thing.

"28 Days," otherwise known as " 'Happy Days' Checks Into 'Wonderland,' " is a film with a jones for the obvious and an uncertainty about how seriously to take itself. Directed in breezy sitcom fashion by Betty Thomas, it wants to be real enough to get your attention but not too real to get in the way of the incessant wisecracks of Susannah Grant's script. Eager to have it both ways, "28 Days" is too glib too often to make much of an impression any way you look at it.

That is in one sense a shame, because the film squanders an empathetic, watchable star turn by Sandra Bullock as grumpy Gwen. In theory, this could have been the kind of rewarding vehicle "Erin Brockovich" (also written by Grant) was for Julia Roberts, but where that film added texture to standard material, "28 Days" falls all over itself to make everything as simplistic as possible.

If anyone has any doubts as to how much of a party animal Gwen, allegedly a successful New York writer, really is, those are soon dispelled. With the Clash's "Should I Stay or Should I Go" pounding on the soundtrack, Gwen and her British boyfriend Jasper (Dominic West) get so wasted they nearly burn their apartment down before the opening credits are over. Now that's some serious fun.

But wait, things will get even funner. Horribly hung over, Gwen and Jasper force themselves out to the wedding of her older sister Lily (Elizabeth Perkins), a stuffy type who just isn't in on the joke and keeps muttering downer things like "You make it impossible to love you."

Suffice it to say that Gwen commits such a wide and inclusive variety of atrocities at the reception and after (it's not this film's style to do anything by half measures) that a less than amused court orders her to spend 28 days in a rehabilitation facility.

That would be peaceful Serenity Glen, motto "Mind, Body, Spirit," a cheery place that believes in chanting as much as any Hare Krishna, with people getting pumped up over slogans like "Hey, hey, what do we know, pills and booze have got to go" or the equally popular "Hey, hey, what do you say, being sober is the only way."

Gwen doesn't enjoy what she calls the place's "Romper Room" tone, and she doesn't care for her counselor Cornell (a wasted, so to speak, Steve Buscemi), whom she lambastes as "a 12-stepping geek." There's nothing wrong with her, she insists, she doesn't belong in rehab, she can control herself any time she wants to.

Gwen has even less regard for her buddies in group therapy, who as a general rule are not allowed to wander too far from the nearest wisecrack. There's Andrea (Azura Skye), the teenage addict; Oliver (Michael O'Malley), who keeps ineptly trying to pick Gwen up; Gerhardt (Alan Tudyk), the painfully cliched gay man; and so on.

The only person not laughing at all these jokes is Gwen, and, for once, she's right. For one of the problems with "28 Days" is not so much that it has the temerity to attempt the mixture of comedy and serious material, but that the comedy is so lame and the nominally weighty material is too obviously a setup.

More than that, if the therapeutic methods used by Serenity Glen are such a joke, how are we supposed to account for Gwen's inevitable improvement? And why are we supposed to care when bad things happen to characters who have been presented as little more than cartoons?

Aside from Bullock, who is difficult to resist despite the mess surrounding her, "28 Days" has a few other interesting performances. British actor West works hard and successfully to turn boyfriend Jasper into a genuine person, and Viggo Mortensen is interesting as Eddie Boone, a womanizing star pitcher who watches a soap opera when he should be thinking about baseball.

That would be the mythical "Santa Cruz," an intentionally silly bit of business about characters named Falcon, Deirdre and Darian. If the choice were offered, however, most "28 Days" viewers would as soon stick with "Santa Cruz." At least it makes no bones about being a soap.

NEW YORK POST, 4/14/00, p. 56, Jonathan Foreman

For a Hollywood comedy about alcohol rehab starring Sandra Bullock, "28 Days" is much less mawkish and predictable than you might expect.

Director Betty Thomas (a former "Hill Street Blues" star), working from a screenplay by Susannah Grant, deftly avoids one corny pitfall after another and ends up with a movie that is both exuberantly funny and surprisingly dry.

Thomas directed "Dr. Dolittle," "Howard Stern's Private Parts" and "The Brady Brunch," and whenever she must choose between a scene of Robin Williams-esque sentimentality and a good joke, she goes straight for the joke.

It's also Sandra Bullock's best film in years—perhaps even the best work she has ever done.

Given her past proclivity for starring in mediocre thrillers and schlockfests, this might not sound like high praise, but the movie shows that, given the right material, Bullock has the acting chops to carry a movie in which she isn't playing the sweet girl next door.

Gwen (Bullock) is a hard-partying, wise-cracking New Yorker whose drinking has gotten so out of hand that she ruins the wedding of her square sister Lily (Elizabeth Perkins) before crashing a limo into a suburban house.

Sentenced to a month of rehab in lieu of prison, she is horrified by the chanting, singing and confessional psychobabble that greet her at Serenity Glen, not to mention the rules that forbid cell phones and coffee.

Gwen has no intention of obeying the rules. And when her charming, dissolute boyfriend (Dominic West in a dead-on performance that's already making him a new Hollywood name) comes down to visit, they steal away from the institute and get wasted.

Of course, you know that Gwen will have to lose some of her self-conscious cynicism before she can start getting better. But though the rehabilitation process involves inherent melodrama (especially during "family week") and weepy public confessions, the film never forces you to believe that a cynical, sophisticated New Yorker like Gwen would ever sing "Lean on Me" without embarrassment.

Nor do any miracles occur among her fellow inmates. The disgraced former doctor played by Reni Santoni is just as obnoxious after a month of treatment as he was before.

Bullock is surrounded by a strong supporting cast, particularly Steve Buscemi as an addiction counselor. And Gwen's therapy group includes characters played by the wonderful Marianne Jean-Baptiste ("Secrets and Lies"), Alan Tudyk ("Patch Adams") and Diane Ladd.

"A Walk on the Moon" heartthrob Viggo Mortensen is convincing as a Southern baseball star and alternative love interest, and Azura Skye plays a teenager addicted to both soap operas and heroin.

So many Hollywood movies that deal with emotionally charged subjects feel fake. This one doesn't, perhaps because addiction and rehab are the kind of phenomena that many people who work on movies like this are familiar with.

NEWSDAY, 4/14/00, Part II/p. B3, Jan Stuart

For the millions of Americans who regularly attend 12-step programs, the past year has offered a certain amount of validation at the movies but little in the way of affirmation. In "Fight Club," the most pathetic addicts were those terminally hooked on support groups. And now we have "28 Days", a new Sandra Bullock vehicle in which detox clinics are places where you go to feed a habit for dumb daytime soaps and corny pop songs from the '70s.

The best way to take "28 Days" is one minute at a time. Otherwise, expectations may do strange things to your head. You may laugh when you're not supposed to, get very solemn when you're intended to lighten up, or have other inappropriate reactions that bug the people around you.

From the moment a clinic official snaps at Bullock, "We carry our own bags here; this is not the Sheraton," you may be thinking you are in for "Private Benjamin Goes to Rehab." And certainly the first half hour of this tonally uncertain picture gives you some of those jollies. Here is Sandra Bullock, the reckless girl's Julia Roberts, in full-blast, Bullock-in-a-china-shop mode. Her character, Gwen Cummings a self-absorbed writer whose alcoholism spoils her sister's wedding, where she destroys the cake and then zips up the neighborhood with the newlyweds' limo in an attempt to replace it.

Presto, Gwen is dumped at the door of the Serenity Glen clinic, a Betty Ford-style retreat where residents croon "Lean on Me" in dead earnestness, an odd-duck patient makes silly Jerry Lewis faces at an encounter group, and folks sit around playing guess-the-addiction with every newcomer who walks through the door.

If "28 Days" wants us to sympathize with the denial and disorientation of a first-timer in rehab, it has a ham-fisted way of doing it. We're never entirely sure at first whether it is sending up the rituals of such places, sympathizing with them or both at once. What we do know for sure is that Little Miss Arrogant from New York City is going to have to hit rock bottom before she comes around to acknowledging her addiction, warming up to her fellow patients and embracing the program as laid down by the clinic honcho, played by Steve Buscemi.

As scripted by Susannah Grant ("Erin Brockovich"), Gwen's fellow patients are etched with primary-colored strokes to maximize their minimum screen time. They're like some Mad magazine Greek chorus, filtered through the American melting pot: There's a hostile Jewish tracheotomy survivor, a dorky German gay guy in horn-rimmed glasses, a petulant African-American woman, a waifish teenage heroin addict, an aging southern belle, et al. The film has a researched air about it, and yet it feels tinny and artificial at the same time.

If the grim journey of Michael Keaton in "Clean and Sober" begged for some leavening, "28 Days" shows you can't have it both ways. Director Betty Thomas ("The Nutty Professor") is a slick shtick-meister who also wants to be taken seriously. She works up a credibly boozy energy with flashback scenes of Gwen's childhood that show how she and her sister survived an alcoholic mother. But the shifts between these moments and the farcical acting out of the Serenity Glen peanut gallery come off with all the smoothness of a parachute halting a free-fall.

Screenwriter Grant, who knows how to put a high gloss on formula, gives Gwen a healthy clinic romance (Viggo Mortensen) that predictably kisses off the jerk she left behind (Dominic West). Bullock plows through it all with her usual verve, but there is something self-consciously *worthy* about her work here. You kind of wish she'd get herself out of rehab and go back to "Speed."

NEWSWEEK, 4/17/00, p. 65, David Ansen

If you thought Sandra Bullock was a wild thing in "Forces of Nature," check her out as the disheveled, alcoholic party girl Gwen in "28 Days." At her sister Lily's wedding she licks the hors doeuvres right off the tray, tumbles into the wedding cake, insults the bride and groom, hijacks their limo and crashes it into a house. Would you say this girl has a problem?

This is the movie's overstated opening, and its uncertain tone—pitched sloppily between farce and nightmare—doesn't bode well for what is to come. Director Betty Thomas and writer Susannah Grant ("Erin Brockovich") want to rehabilitate the overly familiar rehab drama ("Clean and Sober," "When a Man Loves a Woman") by injecting it with a streak of gallows humor. It's a good idea in theory, but it requires more than synthetic sitcom humor. The laughs in "28 Days" are designed to distract us from the subject, not illuminate it. This is a movie afraid of its own shadows.

SIGHT AND SOUND, 6/00, p. 57, Stephanie Zacharek

New York, the present. Gwen is good-time gal who traipses around the city with her equally lackadaisical boyfriend Jasper, getting very drunk and very loud. She sets the bedclothes on fire through carelessness, among other things. When Gwen ruins her sister Lily's wedding (while drunk she hijacks and crashes the bridal limo), she's packed off to a rehab centre where chanting and venting one's feelings are the order of the day.

Gwen rails at the centre's discipline (she's not even allowed to have painkillers), not to mention its' 'touchy-feely' atmosphere. Before long Cornell, a no-nonsense counsellor, touches a nerve and Gwen is finally able to see her life needs to change. She begins opening up to her rehab mates and engages in a mild flirtation with one of them, a sexy professional ball player named Eddie. Gwen endures a measure of heartache when her roommate Andrea commits suicide. When her term is up, she returns home and faces the changes she needs to make (including splitting up with Jasper) in order to embark on her new drug and alcohol-free life.

28 Days might very well be viewed as one of those movies that take an honest snapshot of what it's like to go through substance-abuse rehab—but that doesn't make it any good. Director Betty Thomas and screenwriter Susannah Grant (who's capable of sharp writing, if the recent Erin Brockovich is any indication) try hard to show us the transformation Gwen must undergo in order to change her life, but none of it clicks. Sandra Bullock injects the early part of the movie with a minor jolt of energy. She's most interesting when she's playing out the blithe selfishness people with substance-abuse problems inflict on others. It's funny when she shows up at her sister's wedding, dishevelled and with black bra straps showing beneath her pastel bridesmaid's dress. But it's just the tip of the iceberg in terms of her utter carelessness.

Once Bullock enters rehab, though, there's nothing to do but brace yourself for her initial resistance to it, which is of course soon to be followed by her total embrace of its philosophy. Along the way she is reconciled with her sister (the sadly underused Elizabeth Perkins) and recognises her addictions most likely stem from their mother's own substance-abuse problems. It's a wonderful, healing shock of recognition for her—bravo! But we saw it coming a mile away, and what do we get for our trouble?

Almost all of Gwen's revelations are like giant signposts rather than insights into some very deep-rooted problems. Anyone who's been through rehab in real life would be the first to tell you that there are no easy answers. But in 28 Days the most blatant realisations are treated as grand solutions. When Gwen screws up her leg and is forced to hobble around in a walking cast, her anger and frustration mount. Wise old counsellor Cornell knows just what to do: he hangs a signboard around her neck that says, "Ask me if I need help, and if I say no, give it to me anyway."

If pretty much all a movie character needs is a signboard to get to the root of what are, in real life, very subtle and difficult problems, it's safe to assume that character isn't getting much more than a good slathering of Hollywood gloss. When Gwen hangs a different signboard around the neck of her sensitive and ill-fated roommate (Drew Barrymore lookalike Azura Skye), it reads like nothing so much as a hamfisted Author's Message: "Don't ever be a slogan, because you are poetry."

That may very well be true: the poor girl is simply stuck in a movie that's a giant slogan—no poetry allowed here, because that would just be too messy and people might be likely to miss the point, which is "Substance-abuse recovery is very very hard." 28 Days is not bad enough to ruin your life, nor is it good enough to change it even remotely. In any event, you won't need more than an hour to recover from it.

VILLAGE VOICE, 4/18/00, p. 158, Dennis Lim

Irrepressible alcoholic Sandra Bullock shows up plastered at her sister's wedding, prompting the bride, Lilly (Elizabeth Perkins), to explode: "Gwen, you make it impossible to love you!" On the contrary, actually. Bullock, whose career is founded on a vaguely agreeable screen nonpresence, would never allow Gwen, even at her most pickled and loudmouthed, to be unsympathetic, let alone a truly ugly drunk. Playing it safe, *28 Days* slaps her with a DUI charge 10 minutes in, and shuttles her off for a month-long stint in rehab, where the testy, cynical Manhattanite has her cell phone and Vicodin supply confiscated, meets her match in tough-love counselor Steve Buscemi, engages in mass bonding with a Cuckoo's Nest coterie, accepts that she has a substance-abuse problem, and-crucially-realizes it can be blamed on other people. Flashbacks reveal a wrecked, party-monster mother looming over her two apprehensive daughters ("If you're not having fun, peanuts, what's the friggin' point?!"). Lilly comes around, too. "I should have helped you with your homework," sobs the equally troubled elder sister, before issuing the inevitable recantation. "Gwen, you make it impossible not to love you."

Writer Susannah Grant—doing a brisk trade in interchangeable, outsize female star vehicles, having also scripted *Erin Brockovich* keeps the tone improbably sunny. In this case, humor isn't a point of entry to a thorny subject but an escape hatch. *28 Days* is a rehab comedy insofar as it has a reflexively wisecracking heroine and a supporting gallery of eccentrics (most peculiar of all, an Andy Dick-ish German homosexual played by Alan Tudyk). Director Betty Thomas, who reportedly reworked Grant's script, moves the film along, conjuring momentum out of nothing, even indulging in distracting bits of random weirdness (Loudon Wainwright III, playing Jonathan Richman in *There's Something About Mary*). But whenever the movie takes itself seriously (and it's all downhill from the moment a crudely telegraphed tragedy is enlisted to expedite Gwen's rehabilitation), Thomas's fleet-footed approach suggests the anxious embarrassment of a director in an awful hurry to get it over with.

Also reviewed in:
CHICAGO TRIBUNE, 4/14/00, Friday/p. A, Mark Caro
NEW YORK TIMES, 4/14/00, p. E14, Stephen Holden
VARIETY, 4/10-16/00, p. 43, Todd McCarthy
WASHINGTON POST, 4/14/00, p. C5, Rita Kempley
WASHINGTON POST, 4/14/00, Weekend/p. 43, Desson Howe

TWO FAMILY HOUSE

A Lions Gate presentation of a Filbert Steps production. *Executive Producer:* Jim Kohlberg and Adam Brightman. *Producer:* Anne Harrison and Alan Klingenstein. *Director:* Raymond De Felitta. *Screenplay:* Raymond De Felitta. *Director of Photography:* Michael Mayers. *Editor:* David Leonard. *Music:* Stephen Endelman. *Casting:* Sheila Jaffe, Georgianne Walken, and Julia Kim. *Production Designer:* Teresa Mastropierro. *Costumes:* Liz McGarrity. *Running time:* 104 minutes. *MPAA Rating:* R.

CAST: Michael Rispoli (Buddy Visalo); Kelly Macdonald (Mary O'Neary); Katherine Narducci (Estelle Visalo); Kevin Conway (Jim O'Neary); Matt Servitto (Chipmunk); Michele Santopietro (Laura); Louis Guss (Donato); Rosemary DeAngelis (Marie); Anthony Arkin (Danny); Saul Stein (Anthony); Vincent Pastore (Angelo); Sharon Angela (Gloria); Ivy Jones (Tina); Victor Arnold (Mr. Cicco); Richard B. Shull (Mr. Brancaccio); Nick Tosches (Hotel Clerk); Jack O'Connell (Mr. Mahoney); Gerry Bamman (Mr. Pine); Barbara Haas (Mrs. Genova); Marshall Efron (Tiny); Joseph R. Gannascoli (Counter Guy); Robert Fitch

(Drunken Guy);   Peggy Gormley (Miss Dimunjik);   Richard Licata (Mr. Asippi);   John McLaughlin (Arthur Godfrey);   John Pizzarelli (Julius LaRosa).

CHRISTIAN SCIENCE MONITOR, 10/6/00, p. 15, David Sterritt

The biggest selling point for "Two Family House" is probably its cast, headed by Michael Rispoli and Katherine Narducci, mainstays of "The Sopranos," the popular TV series on HBO. Here they play Buddy and Estelle, a couple with a mildly troubled past.

Buddy once had a chance to become a TV crooner, but let it pass to marry Estelle and settle into a solid working-class routine—a decision he's regretted ever since. He still hopes for a more exciting life, and eventually his dream takes a new form.

He buys a run-down house big enough to set up his own neighborhood saloon—a place where its friends can congregate, his income can swell, and he can provide the entertainment with his vocal stylngs.

The only obstacle is the couple who lives there, one of whom is a pregnant, abused young woman. Buddy tries to help her, but runs into complications when this new (white) friend gives birth to an adorable (black) baby, sparking bigoted eruptions in almost everyone they know.

This plot might easily have turned melodramatic or preachy, but writer-director Raymond De Felitta dodges such dangers with his open-hearted attitude toward his characters and their flawed, but basically decent, temperaments.

LOS ANGELES TIMES, 10/6/00, Calendar/p. 20, Kevin Thomas

Raymond De Felitta's "Two Family House" is as fragile as a soap bubble—one false move and it bursts. That it never does only adds to its abundant pleasures, its rich, rueful humor, poignancy and tenderness.

Sharp judgments are demanded of De Felitta, acclaimed for his "Bronx Cheers" and "Cafe Society," every step of the way. He avoids the crippling effect of self-consciousness through the sheer dint of his love for an enclave of Italian Americans living on Staten Island in 1956. Yet De Felitta's love is never blind: People may be funny, but there's nothing amusing to him or to us, only pain and regret, when they cannot or will not transcend their narrowest views.

Michael Rispoli's Buddy Visalo, a warm teddy bear of a man, has more intelligence and imagination than his pals at Angie's neighborhood bar. He realizes this truth about himself only partially, and his wife Estelle (Katherine Narducci) and his pals, far from seeing him as their superior, regard him, with affection, as a loser.

Buddy loves to sing and when no less than Arthur Godfrey hears him perform near the end of World War II, he tells Buddy to look him up after he gets out of the Army. Estelle, his bride, convinces him he's aiming too high and talks him out of it.

Estelle, unimaginative and conservative, is so convinced of his ordinariness—indeed, she is so afraid of anything that's not in keeping with her tight ethnic community that she cannot possibly see any potential in her husband. Buddy's a machinist whose repeated failed attempts to go into business for himself constitute a perfect example of self-fulfilling prophecy.

Estelle finally allows Buddy to buy a run-down house in an Irish neighborhood, divided long ago into an upstairs and a downstairs apartment. He'll turn the ground floor into a bar, and he and Estelle will at last be able to escape her parents' home and live upstairs. The hitch is that it proves difficult for him to evict the Irish immigrant couple living upstairs (the downstairs apartment being derelict and abandoned).

Jim O'Neary (Kevin Conway) is a stubborn, raucous drunkard whose lovely wife Mary (Kelly Macdonald), young enough to be his daughter, is about to give birth Proud and defiant, Mary nevertheless touches Buddy's heart; he is not about to throw her into the street, and when she gives birth to a baby boy, this will unexpectedly and profoundly alter the course of Buddy's life, not to mention that of Mary and her baby.

Buddy starts to think for himself, and we hope that he proves to be as courageous as he is big-hearted and open-minded; he will need to be, as he gradually comes into conflict with the entrenched, collective views of family and community. In Rispoli's consummate playing, Buddy grows before our eyes; so does Mary, in the beguiling Macdonald's equally persuasive portrayal.

As splendid as they are, Narducci has the toughest role, for she must show us that Estelle is basically a good woman, deserving of sympathy in many instances. Yet she must ultimately reveal Estelle's best instincts being strangled by ignorance and prejudice in its crudest form. We feel pity rather than contempt for Estelle, no small feat and crucial to the film's aiming toward illuminating rather than merely condemning.

De Felitta manages the film's constant shifting between joy and sorrow, humor and anguish, and exudes such a sense of discovery in the alternating possibilities and limitations of human nature that his film avoids any sense of manipulation or contrivance, qualities certain to have emerged in lesser hands. "Two Family House," winner of the audience award at Sundance, is a film of rare, delicate sensibility.

NEW YORK POST, 10/6/00, p. 48, Jonathan Foreman

Raymond De Felitta's delightful "Two Family House" was one of the genuine pleasures of this year's Sundance Film Festival, where it deservedly won the Audience Award.

A charming, (mostly) briskly unsentimental love story, written, directed and acted with remarkable assurance, it's one of those small films that deserves a wider audience than a small advertising budget is likely to get it.

The story is set on 1950s Staten Island and centers on Buddy Visalo ("The Soprano's" Michael Rispoli) a young factory worker who always wanted to be a singer.

He was once offered an audition spot that might have led to greatness, but was persuaded by his pessimistic wife, Estelle (Katherine Narducci, also from "The Sopranos"), and her family not to take it.

Detesting his machine-shop job and living in his wife's parents' apartment, Buddy comes up with a variety of money-making schemes, all of which fail, confirming Estelle's belief that he's a loser, "pregnant with failure."

Finally, Buddy hits on the idea of buying a two-family house in a run-down Irish neighborhood and converting the downstairs apartment into a bar—a bar in which he'll get the chance to sing and entertain his customers. Estelle hates the idea, but goes along with it.

But when they move into the ramshackle house, they discover the upstairs apartment contains a pair of tenants who show no inclination to leave: a brutal, drunken Irishman (Kevin Conway) and his much younger, heavily pregnant wife, Mary (Kelly Macdonald, the fine Scottish actress from "Trainspotting" and "Stella Does Tricks").

When Buddy recruits a gang of his fellow Italian-Americans to evict the couple, the young Irishwoman suddenly goes into labor.

The birth is successful, but the baby looks surprisingly dark-skinned and its putative father immediately abandons mother and newborn, who turns out to be the narrator of the film.

Buddy may be no genius, but he's a generous and courageous guy. Egged on by Estelle, he proceeds with Mary's eviction. But even though Mary seems like a difficult, shrill young woman, the thought of her living in a sleazy hot-sheets hotel with her tiny baby bothers Buddy's conscience and he secretly sets her up in a little apartment he can ill afford.

Mary relaxes and visibly blossoms (Macdonald has a stunningly beautiful complexion) in her new situation, but the bond that grows between her and Buddy surprises them both.

NEWSDAY, 10/6/00, Part II/p. B6, John Anderson

Buddy Visalo, the sweetly failed dreamer/knucklehead played by Michael Rispoli in "Two-Family House," moves with the defiant strut of a guy who wants you to think he thinks he runs his life. He gives himself away, though, via the softness of his eyes: Buddy doesn't quite believe in Buddy, either. But being Catholic and Italian, he does believe in miracles.

That the miracle arrives via an indigent woman named Mary O'Neary (Kelly Macdonald) and her illegitimate child, is a little bit of Christmas. But then, Raymond De Felitta's movie is a gift. Part ethnic comedy, part domestic drama, set in an Italian-American enclave in '50s Staten Island—all of this sounds like an invitation to stay home and scrape your own teeth. Do not be misled. Confident, compassionate and wonderfully acted, it's easily one of the best movies of the year.

The film is built around Buddy; the neighborhood's Italian flavor is meant to carry with it the pungent aroma of vine-ripened machismo. "Two-Family House" is also, on the surface, about luck: how it breaks or doesn't, how we seemingly live according to a butterfly effect of fortune. In actuality, De Felitta says, there is no chance, there is no luck. It's all about love and the power of women.

After giving us an aerial assessment of Staten Island, De Felitta circles in on a dirt-brown, ramshackle house, the kind of eyesore that would elicit from the neighbors an escalating campaign of obscure comments, polite suggestions, veiled threats and an eventual act of pyromania. This is the place Buddy wants to buy so he can get out of his in-laws' house after 10 years, open a bar and live with his wife upstairs.

That the wife in question (Estelle, played by a delightfully poisonous Katherine Narducci) wants nothing to do with this place is understandable. But Estelle would have said no to Windsor Castle. Ever since she vetoed Buddy's audition with Arthur Godfrey—and his career as a singer—she's had to let him follow his dreams while reminding him of every failure.

"Two-Family House" is a cautionary tale about a mode of life that keeps people like Buddy and Estelle together. Unless something happens. What happens is the pregnant Mary, who with her belligerent, drunken husband (Kevin Conway), occupies the upstairs apartment, gives birth on her kitchen floor—to a black baby, who grows up to narrate the film. The kid is the biggest thing that's ever happened to Staten Island. Mary is the biggest thing that's ever happened to Buddy. And while the world De Felitta creates in "Two-Family House" isn't big, it's a marvel nonetheless. Because it all feels true.

VILLAGE VOICE, 10/10/00, p. 125, J. Hoberman

Two Family House is a vaudeville turn that comes off as fine and mellow (and warm) as the John Pizzarelli ballad used by writer-director Raymond De Felitta to ease his camera's descent from the heavens down to Staten Island.

Set in the year of Our Elvis, 1956, this well-wrought indie (De Felitta's second feature, after the 1995 *Café Society*) concerns a frustrated crooner. Having been scouted by broadcast personality Arthur Godfrey while he was in the army, Buddy Visalo believes that, had he followed his star, he could have been Julius La Rosa. Instead, he works in a machine shop, lives with his in-laws in the shadow of the Bayonne Bridge, and times his lovemaking to *The Perry Como Show*. As played by Michael Rispoli, Buddy has a quizzical baby face and a head full of dreams. He's not especially bright, but he's generous and, as it turns out, gutsy. Over the voluble objections of wife Estelle (Katherine Narducci, who, like Rispoli, has played a recurring character on *The Sopranos*), Buddy buys a derelict frame house on the outskirts of his Italian neighborhood, planning to live upstairs and transform the ground floor into his own personal nightclub, Buddy's Tavern.

Populated by acerbic women in cardigan sweaters and posturing men in porkpie hats, *Two Family House* conjures up an affectionately cartooned vision of Eisenhower-era white-ethnic working-class New York. The colors are slightly overbright, the squabbling elaborately volatile, and the stereotypes affectionately broad. Rheingolds are ubiquitous (although the requisite horde of cap-gun-toting kids is conspicuously absent). There's a hyperreal home-movie quality that De Felitta, who based his script on a family story, accentuates in having the film's narrator, like Tristram Shandy, begin by describing the events leading to his birth.

Having become an unwilling landlord, Buddy is compelled to evict an extravagantly deadbeat tenant (Kevin Conway) complete with pregnant missus (Kelly Macdonald, a veteran of *Trainspotting*). The process proves problematic, but the feckless O'Neary vanishes of his own accord when his Mary gives birth to an unmistakably mocha-colored baby. *Variety*, which reviewed *Two Family House* when it was shown last January at Sundance, expressed some concern for the ongoing Irish-Italian insult-fest—never more comic than in O'Neary's intentional mangling of Buddy's name—and the racial banter that Mary's baby precipitates. But these attitudes, which will scarcely shock anyone familiar with the films of Martin Scorsese or Spike Lee, are explicitly presented as expressions of insularity and fear. Buddy courts excommunication when he retrieves the splendidly querulous Mary from a flophouse and secretly rents her a room above a neighborhood *salumeria*. "You're all a race of pimps!?" she incredulously explodes, unaware that her baffled benefactor in particular has no idea of his intentions.

A fairy tale that presents love as a case of mutual enchantment, *Two Family House* is not only uniformly well acted, superbly designed, lovingly lit, and sensitively scored, it's as romantic as it is funny. This deft and touching urban fable about the neighborhood legend who "threw his whole life away" is like discovering a long-lost episode of *The Honeymooners*—the best New York movie Woody Allen never made.

Also reviewed in:
CHICAGO TRIBUNE, 10/20/00, Friday/p. F, Michael Wilmington
NEW YORK TIMES, 10/6/00, p. E20, Lawrence Van Gelder
VARIETY, 1/31-2/6/00, p. 35, Joe Leydon
WASHINGTON POST, 10/27/00, p. C8, Rita Kempley
WASHINGTON POST, 10/27/00, Weekend/p. 43, Desson Howe

TWO WOMEN

An Arta Film production in association with Arman Film.   *Director:* Tahmineh Milani. *Screenplay (Farsi with English subtitles):* Tahmineh Milani. *Director of Photography:* Hossein Jafarian. *Editor:* Mustafa Kherqepush. *Music:* Babak Bayat. *Sound:* Parviz Abnar. *Art Director:* Malek Jahan Khazai. *Running time:* 96 minutes. *MPAA Rating:* Not Rated.

CAST: Mohammad Reza Forutan (Hasan "Maniac"); Niki Karimi (Fereshteh); Atila Pesiani (Ahmad); Marila Zare'i (Roya); Reza Khandan (Fereshteh's Father).

CHRISTIAN SCIENCE MONITOR, 7/14/00, p. 15, David Sterritt

"Two Women" tells a story so powerful it might be block-buster material itself if it had a star-studded cast and a glitzy Hollywood look. This is unexpected since it hails from Iran, where a censorship-shy film industry steers away from controversial subjects. It's hard to generalize about contemporary Iranian culture, though. Anyone who perceives it in simplistic ways can get a lesson from this forceful story of a woman's struggle against oppression, told by a female filmmaker who pulls no social or political punches.

The main characters are two young women studying architecture in a Tehran university. One is especially gifted, but her progress is interrupted when a mentally disturbed man stalks her. This would be a difficult situation in any culture, but here it's intensified by prejudices against women who go into the world instead of remaining at home. The paths of the two heroines branch when one continues her studies while the other submits to an arranged marriage that protects her from physical harm but ends her career.

"Two Women" is unlike most Iranian exports in two respects. One is its unflinching concern for the plight of talented women in a male-dominated society. The other is its ability to make sociological points through heart-pounding melodrama. For expertly crafted suspense, Tahmineh Milani's "Two Women" rivals any American production of the season.

NEW YORK POST, 7/21/00, p. 50, Jonathan Foreman

Tahmineh Milani's astonishingly daring "Two Women" isn't nearly as sophisticated or technically accomplished as many of the Iranian films that have made it to these shores.

But it's fascinating and moving all the same, both in its depiction of Iranian daily life and in its powerful portrait of female oppression.

It begins in the present day with architect Roya (Marila Zare'i) directing the action on a construction site, a hard hat over her hejab (Head-scarf). She gets a call for the first time in many years from Fereshteh (Niki Karimi), her college friend.

In the first of several flashbacks, you see the two young women at school together in the early '80s. Fereshteh had been the superior student and seemed to have a brilliant career ahead of her.

But Fereshteh has a scary stalker who at one point throws acid on her cousin, mistaking him for a boyfriend.

Because it's Iran, she's blamed for the incident by her insanely unreasonable father. Her only way out of trouble is a loveless arranged marriage to a pathologically jealous man (Atila Pesiani) who resents her education and won't let her use the phone or speak to her old friends.

It's only after years of imprisonment in this marriage that destiny intervenes to bring Fereshteh into contact with her old friend Roya, who has gone on to lead the life that should have been hers.

You can understand why "Two Women" created such a sensation in Iran: It presents an angry, undeniable argument for the kind of freedoms that women in the West take for granted.

VILLAGE VOICE, 7/18/00, p. 122, Amy Taubin

Tahmineh Milani's *Two Women* places the feminist desire for equality in the center of the conflict between conservative and progressive elements in Iranian society. The film provoked controversy in Iran, but its awkward mix of polemic and melodramatics probably won't travel very well.

Fereshteh (Niki Karimi) and Roya (Marila Zare'i) meet in architectural college. Brilliant and driven, Fereshteh supports herself by tutoring her less accomplished classmates, Roya among them. The two become fast friends, but Roya's privileged, liberal background prevents her from fully comprehending how precarious her friend's independence is. Fereshteh is being stalked by an insane thug on a motorbike who threatens to carve up her face unless she marries him. When the stalker mutilates her cousin with acid, Fereshteh's father blames her for bringing disgrace on the family and drags her home. The stalker follows her there, and in trying to escape him, she's involved in a car accident that kills a child. The stalker is sentenced to 13 years in prison, and although Fereshteh is guiltless, she's given a heavy fine. Ahmad, one of her many rejected suitors, offers to pay it, but only if she'll marry him. Her father forces her to agree. This intricate setup establishes a blame-the-victim mentality in which the stalker, the father, and the suitor are all complicit.

The marriage turns out to be no better than jail. Ahmad (Atila Pesiani) is as pathological as the stalker. Like him, he's enraged by Fereshteh's independent mind and spirit, and he's determined to break her will. Both men view women as objects to be controlled and marriage as the institution that legalizes their need to dominate and oppress. Eventually, even Fereshteh's father admits that he's sold his daughter into the equivalent of slavery, but he's too weak and ashamed to stand up to her husband. Although he appears in only half a dozen scenes, the father is by far the most complex of the male characters—the only one who displays any ambivalence or mixed motives. Ahmad is potentially interesting, but Pesiani's performance verges on the ludicrous: He contorts his eyebrows the way silent-film villains twirled their mustaches.

Still, the success of *Two Women* is dependent on its female characters, and here too there's a problem. Roya is less a character in her own right than a foil for Fereshteh. Roya has a perfect marriage—she and her husband are partners in life and in their architectural firm. The first time we see her, she's on a construction site wearing a hard hat over her head scarf. "Your husband-and-wife team is the greatest," says a satisfied client. It's all too good to be true.

A more accurate title would have been *My Friend Fereshteh* , since it's Fereshteh on whom the narrative is almost entirely focused. Milani's thesis seems to be that Iran, despite certain liberal inroads, remains a conservative, misogynist society and that its wrath falls most heavily on its most brilliant and ambitious women. Played with conviction and intelligence by Karimi, Fereshteh is a compelling hero. But our belief in her plight is undermined by the film's reliance on the old-fashioned tropes of melodrama-surging music, over-the-top performances, a schematic narrative filled with forced coincidences, and a descent into madness that's right out of 19th-century opera. Unlike Moufida Tlatli, who in her great *The Silences of the Palace* turns a critical eye on the intersection of female subjectivity with Middle Eastern film melodrama, Milani embraces stylistic clichés whole-hog as a way of popularizing tough content. Or maybe her ideas just outstrip her directing ability.

Also reviewed in:
CHICAGO TRIBUNE, 3/3/00, Friday/p. O.
NEW YORK TIMES, 7/21/00, p. E10, Lawrence Van Gelder
VARIETY, 3/8-14/99, p. 67, Deborah Young

U-571

A Universal Pictures and Studio Canal release in association with Dino De Laurentiis. *Executive Producer:* Hal Lieberman. *Producer:* Dino De Laurentiis and Martha De Laurentiis. *Director:* Jonathan Mostow. *Screenplay:* Jonathan Mostow, Sam Montgomery, and David Ayer. *Story:* Jonathan Mostow. *Director of Photography:* Oliver Wood. *Editor:* Wayne Wahrman. *Music:* Richard Marvin. *Music Editor:* Daryl K. Kell. *Choreographer:* Leontine Snell. *Sound:* Ivan Sharrock and (music) Dennis Sands. *Sound Editor:* Jon Johnson. *Casting:* Carol Lewis. *Production Designer:* Wm Ladd Skinner and Götz Weidner. *Art Director:* Robert Woodruff. *Set Designer:* Gina B. Cranham, Eric Sundhal, Gregory Scott Hooper, Joseph G. Pacelli, Jr., Alessandro Santucci, Giulia Chiara Crugnola, Daniela Giovannoni, and Richard Skinner. *Set Decorator:* Bob Gould and Cinzia Sleiter. *Set Dresser:* Roberto Magagnini. *Special Effects:* Allen Hall. *Costumes:* April Ferry. *Make-up:* Luigi Rocchetti. *Stunt Coordinator:* Pat Romano. *Running time:* 120 minutes. *MPAA Rating:* PG-13.

CAST: Matthew McConaughey (Tyler); Bill Paxton (Dahlgren); Harvey Keitel (Chief); Jon Bon Jovi (Emmett); David Keith (Coonan); Thomas Kretschmann (Wassner); Jake Weber (Hirsch); Jack Noseworthy (Wentz); Thomas Guiry (Trigger); Will Estes (Rabbit); T.C. Carson (Eddie); Erik Palladino (Mazzola); Dave Power (Tank); Derk Cheetwood (Griggs); Matthew Settle (Larson); Rebecca Tilney (Mrs. Dahlgren); Carolyna De Laurentiis (Prudence Dahlgren); Dina De Laurentiis (Louise Dahlgren); Burnell Tucker (Admiral Duke); Rob Allyn (Ensign); Carsten Voigt (German Chief); Gunther Wuerger (Kohl); Oliver Stokowski (German E-Chief); Arnd Klawitter (German Hydrophone Operator); Kai Maurer (German Planesman); Robert Lahoda (German Engineer); Peter Stark (German Lookout); Erich Redman (German Bosun); William John Evans (Marine Sergeant); Robin Askwith (British Seaman); Jasper Wood (Pettty Officer); Martin Glade (Gunner Officer); Oliver Osthus (Depth Charge Officer); John William Falconer and Cory Glen Mathews (Other Sergeants); Valentina Adreatini (Mrs. Larson).

CHRISTIAN SCIENCE MONITOR, 4/21/00, p. 15, David Sterritt

You can't keep a good submarine story down. That's a message Hollywood rediscovers from time to time, and if s not surprising that the idea is surfacing again, since stories about World War II recaptured the public imagination when "Saving Private Ryan" and "The Thin Red Line" invaded the wide screen last year.

"U-571" is less ambitious. It concentrates on claustrophobic thrills found in an underwater vessel crammed with quarrelsome seamen, under fire from an enemy destroyer, headed for depths way beyond its limit, and spurting water from every rivet-lined seam. Much of the action strains credibility, but there's no denying the excitement the best scenes provide.

The story takes its cue from real-life Allied missions designed to capture German encryption secrets. The movie's own credits acknowledge that most of these were carried out by British forces, but Hollywood loves its own, so the heroes of "U-571" are Americans all the way. They've been ordered to disguise their submarine as a Nazi vessel, seize a top-secret encoding device from an actual U-boat, and make sure no Germans escape to tell the tale. Things go well up to a point, but then the Yanks find themselves inhabiting a German sub and unsure how it works.

"U-571" was directed by action specialist Jonathan Mostow, whose 1997 thriller "Breakdown" was one of the most exciting directorial debuts in recent memory. He resorts to a lot of old tricks—cut like crazy between worried faces and overheated gauges inching into the red zone—but he uses them with conviction and pizazz, helped by virile cinematography and snappy editing.

Matthew McConaughey as a skipper out of his depth and Harvey Keitel as a combat-savvy officer make strong impressions in the crash-and-bang adventure. "U-571" is a sturdy specimen of its waterlogged breed. But when is Mostow going to take on a cinematic mission that can match his talent?

LOS ANGELES TIMES, 4/21/00, Calendar/p. 1, Kenneth Turan

There's something inherently dramatic about submarines, there just is. What could be more stirring than heroic (not to mention handsome) young men under intense mental and physical stresses trapped in dangerous, claustrophobic surroundings? When you throw in those unnerving Klaxons sounding without warning and the captain screaming, "Dive! Dive! Dive!" it's hard to go too far wrong.

Though it's undernourished in terms of dialogue and character development (especially compared to the brilliant 1981 German "Das Boot"), "U-571," the first World War II sub movie from Hollywood in quite a while, gets high marks for tension and excitement. The action sequences are bracing and involving and the standard plagues of submarine life (water and fire, men cracking under pressure, the fierce impact of depth charges) are played for maximum effect.

Credit that to the brisk, professional way with traditional genre material of director and co-writer Jonathan Mostow, who showed the same traits in his little-seen 1997 debut, "Breakdown." An assured physical director, Mostow (working with "Face/Off" cinematographer Oliver Wood and a "Last of the Mohicans" editor, Wayne Wahrman) handles both the pure chaos of men firing at one another in confined spaces and the anxiety of a ship going down, down, down with welcome aplomb.

"U-5 71" is so old-fashioned it begins with a narrative crawl that could have come from decades-old submarine classics like "We Dive at Dawn," "The Enemy Below" and "Run Silent, Run Deep." It's the spring of 1942, and Hitler's U-boats are "wreaking havoc in the North Atlantic," sinking ship after ship and seriously disrupting the war effort.

The film (written by Mostow, his "Breakdown" co-writer Sam Montgomery and former submarine crewman David Ayer) opens inside just such a German killing machine, the U-571 of the title. After smartly dispatching a victim, the U-boat finds itself the target of an advancing destroyer intent on revenge.

As fans of the 1950s TV series "The Silent Service" can testify, it's those lumbering depth charges that do the most harm to a sub, and "U-571" is most in its element handling that kind of damage. An apparatus called a gimbal is used to simulate the shaking of a sub under attack, and special effects supervisor Allen Hall designed what producer Dino De Laurentiis legitimately calls "the Ferrari of gimbals," so effective in simulating both the early attack and later ones that when someone talks about depth charges capable of knocking the fillings out of your teeth, you believe it.

Afloat but disabled, the U-571 is unknown to the men of the American sub S-33, gathered to celebrate the marriage of one of their number. The only person in a less than festive mood is Lt. Andrew Tyler (Matthew McConaughey), the ship's executive officer, or "x.o.," who has just been turned down in his request to be (what else but) the captain of his own ship.

Tyler is much liked by his crew and that, the S-33's Lt. Cmdr. Mike Dahlgren (Bill Paxton) soon tells his x.o., is part of the problem. Tyler, it turns out, may be too much of a nice guy for the rigors of combat, and his commander worries that he won't be able to make the tough decisions that could cost his men their lives, perhaps unnecessarily.

Before too much wedding celebrating can take place, the S-33's shore leave is canceled and they are off on a "special op." Aided by the German-speaking Lt. Hirsch (Jake Weber) and Marine Maj. Coonan (David Keith), the S-33 is going to pretend to be a German rescue ship going to the aid of U-571. Their real mission is to capture the boat's Enigma machine, part of a German secret coding system that the Allies must decipher to have a shot at winning the war.

This is a great premise (inspired by real events, although in truth mostly accomplished by Britain's Royal Navy), and it doesn't take a genius at code to figure out that some seriously unforeseen things are going to happen along the way. It's no surprise either that Tyler ends up in command situations and gets to appreciate how difficult it is to be the man in charge.

The "U-571" script is strong on structure, alternating an endless variety of crises to keep audiences off balance. The genius of "Das Boot" was clearly on everyone's mind—a few scenes feel like quotes and that picture's production designer, Gotz Weidner, did the honors here along with William Ladd Skinner—so it's too bad that the filmmakers couldn't also duplicate that picture's sense of dramatic reality.

The physical verisimilitude that "U-571" managed with full-size replicas of World War II submarines deserts it when it comes to character and dialogue. Harvey Keitel as a veteran chief petty officer looks pained to have to say things like "I'm a sea dog, sir, I need some salt" and none of his shipmates are giants of credibility, either.

It's McConaughey, awfully handsome in his dress whites and appropriately sweaty under the strain of combat, who comes off best. He's a decent actor, now that he can be seen clearly after the fuss of his "A Time to Kill" performance has faded, and his heroic presence is exactly what this stalwart film is happiest falling back on.

NEW YORK, 5/1/00, p. 56, Peter Rainer

The World War II submarine thriller *U-571* is engagingly old-fashioned. It doesn't try to palm itself off as revisionist or indulge in the kind of jitterbug techno-moviemaking designed to rope in the short-attention-span audience. The only concession to modernity is in the eardrum-vibrating soundtrack, which converts every sonar blip and torpedo whoosh into a Wagnerian cataclysm. Watching this movie makes you feel pressurized, which is as it should be.

Director Jonathan Mostow, who co-wrote the screenplay with Sam Montgomery and David Ayer, is probably gambling that most of his viewers are either unfamiliar with the standard-issue tropes of World War II movies or else harbor an abiding affection for them. Lieutenant Commander Mike Dahlgren (Bill Paxton) is the skipper of the S-33, a World War I-vintage sub older than most of its crew; Matthew McConaughey is Lieutenant Andrew Tyler, who chafes at Dahlgren's decision not to assign him his own boat, and who, when peril strikes, rises to the occasion. The Trojan Horse mission Tyler ends up commanding involves the takeover of a battered U-boat by American sailors impersonating a German rescue party in order to seize a top-secret Nazi device for encrypting the Enigma code. As the sub wobbles through hostile waters, rattling and leaking as it dips ever downward to avoid the enemy, its hastily assembled American crew appears to be simultaneously pulling together and coming apart.

Fortunately, Mostow doesn't play up the hokiness of the assemblage in quite the way that actual WWII-era movies did; we don't feel as if we're watching a cross-section of America, or at least of white America, with its Italian, its Jew, its hayseed farm boy and its city tough, and so on. This sort of speciousness still partially survives in some of the recent war movies having to do with that era, including *Saving Private Ryan*. In *U-571* (an unfortunate title that sounds like a hemorrhoid ointment), the crew's diversity comes not from any multi-cult political correctness but from the sailors' varying responses to terror. Many of the actors playing the young crew, including Jack Noseworthy, Derk Cheetwood, Dave Power, and Thomas Guiry, are fairly new to movies, and so, thankfully, unlike with many Hollywood-action ensembles, we don't have to pick our way through a crush of famous faces who are pretending not to be famous. When some of the more recognizable actors turn up—including David Keith as a Marines munitions expert and the omnipresent Harvey Keitel as Tyler's seasoned second-in-command—their onscreen familiarity confers its own status on their roles.

One of the welcome differences between WWII-era movies then and now lies in their depiction of the adversary. Gone from many of the recent movies is the rampant stereotyping that we saw in the old films, but the enemy is still the enemy. The trick is how to convey that fact without indulging in demonization. *U-571* is unevenly successful at this. On the one hand, we have the usual scene in which a German naval officer orders the shooting of a boatload of helpless Allies. But later, when the crew led by Tyler invades the U-boat, the caught-in-the-headlights look on the faces of the German sailors matches the look of their attackers. Most of the combatants on both sides appear to be barely out of high school, and they're massed, cowering, inside the belly of this beast.

U-571 is no *Das Boot*, which told *its* sub story from the German side, but it has its share of depth-charged theatrics. (One of its production designers was art director on the German film.) Mostow made his name with the creepy road-revenge movie *Breakdown*, which also was a kind of genre throwback. He works in a somewhat sleeker style than the old-time Hollywood hands but still incorporates many of the old-time attitudes. The ad line for his new movie—"Heroes are ordinary men who do extraordinary things in extraordinary times"—pretty much sums up its spirit, which is not jingoistic, exactly, but triumphal. Still, unlike most Hollywood war movies, this one doesn't look like it was directed by the Joint Chiefs of Staff. Mostow never forgets he's spinning a yarn. *U-571* doesn't skimp on our pleasure in hearing once again lines like "Fix torpedo!" or "Take me to 200 meters!"

NEW YORK POST, 4/21/00, p. 51, Jonathan Foreman

After the disappointment of "Mission to Mars," it's a pleasure to see an old-fashioned blockbuster that can sustain some real excitement.

In "U-571," - the action never lets up.

Unfortunately, it's also a formulaic and predictable movie that combines minimal characterization with some irritating implausibility.

The story draws on real-life events in World War II—mostly involving the British Royal Navy—concerning the capture of the Enigma machine that encoded German communications.

The film opens in 1942 with a long but taut undersea combat scene strongly reminiscent of the submarine classic "Das Boot." The German submarine U-571 sinks Allied supply ships, is crippled by enemy destroyers and forced to surface.

The U.S. Navy somehow discovers that the U-571 is damaged and heading toward a rendezvous with a re-supply sub.

So an ambitious plan is developed to find it, board it, take its Enigma machine and then sink it without the German high command ever finding out.

The Navy refits one of its old submarines, the S-33, to make it look like a U-boat, and sends it out to meet the U-571. A boarding party led by Lt. Tyler (Matthew McConaughey) and marine Maj. Coonan (David Keith) is outfitted in Nazi uniforms and includes a German-speaking naval intelligence officer.

Tyler, we learn, is bitter because his skipper, Capt. Dahlgren (Bill Paxton), declined to recommend him for his own command.

The assault goes fine. But just as the sailors are rowing back to the S-33 with the captured code machine, the American sub is sunk by a German torpedo. Tyler suddenly finds himself in command of the survivors—but now he's forced back into the damaged German sub. Somehow he must get his men and the Enigma machine to an Allied base before the Germans catch on.

Fortunately, he can draw on the experience of his senior NCO, chief Klough (Harvey Keitel, fully clothed throughout) and a crewman who can read the German instructions on the sub's equipment.

Though you get a good sense of the damp claustrophobia and fragility of life on board a diesel submarine, the movie bristles with careless errors and logical holes.

You can forgive some of the technological exaggerations. But there are too many details, both big and small, that defy common sense.

None of this would matter so much if the movie made it clearer why the sub can't radio for help, why it isn't in danger from Allied ships patrolling the Atlantic or how far it is from land.

The performances are uniformly adequate, with McConaughey resembling the young Paul Newman more closely than ever.

NEWSDAY, 4/21/00, Part II/p. B3, John Anderson

It's complete hokum, and annoying hokum at that—"a memorial to all who served"? Right. Still, the submarine adventure "U-571 " does offer an interesting twist on basic math. Add together three one- dimensional actors—let's say, Matthew McConaughey, Harvey Keitel and Bill Paxton—and what do you get? One-dimensional acting. Whoever said the sum had to equal the parts?

Whoever did probably also thought that ripping off a foreign masterpiece—"Das Boot," Wolfgang Petersen's great 1981 German sub movie—was enough to rescue a stillborn project like "U-571" from the watery depths of the cheesy action thriller. There are, indeed, a couple of white-knuckle moments, each of which is inspired by an identical scene in "Das Boot," as are the grizzled Germans battling McConaughey's dress-white sailors. But the film is so smugly sure of itself, and so smugly sure of the Tom Brokaw—"Private Ryan"—induced "don't you wish we could have another World War II" nostalgia movement, that you're not quite sure which side you're on.

Director Jonathan Mostow seems to sense that, so just to make sure we know the Germans were the bad guys, he has his U-boat commander (Thomas Kretschmann) machine-gun a raft full of castaways. "Fuhrer's orders," the Kapitan sneers, although without twirling the ends of his moustache. You know, of course, that McConaughey, as Lt. Cdr. Andrew Tyler—passed over for promotion, but destined to prove himself under fire—will fish all the living bodies he can out of the roiling sea. And that the Americans will, through their innate trust and guilelessness (and petty jealousies and self-indulgent passions) almost blow the whole thing. Almost.

I'm not sure which is the funniest line in "U-571," but there are a couple of obvious candidates. When a wedding is broken up early in the movie because the sailors suddenly need to mobilize, the groom utters a plaint destined for immortality (maybe via "The Man Show"): "They couldn't give me five minutes to consummate my marriage!" The other is perpetrated by Keitel as the salty Chief, who tries to read the controls of his men's captured Nazi sub and exclaims in despair, "Everything's in German!"

Not everything. "Das Boot for Dummies" has at its center the search for the fabled Enigma machine—the real-life Nazi encoding device that would enable the Allies to crack German messages and thus halt the "wolf-pack" attacks on shipping along the U.S. East Coast.

Which means, as we're told by the meant-to-be-unlikable Lt. Hirsch (Jake Weber), who's been slipped into the chain of command between Tyler and his soon-to-be-submerged skipper (Paxton), that the men must succeed in sinking a Nazi destroyer or die trying: Capture would mean torture; torture would mean the divulgence of secret information.

So Tyler has to do everything he can to elude the German subs and warships, creeping undersea (again, a la "Das Boot") and leaping at the chance to put his men at risk. "Take her to 160 meters," he tells Chief. "That's more than 500 feet! " says Chief, recalling the scene just moments before when Mazzola (Erik Palladino)—assuming the token Italian role assumed in WWII movies by everyone from Richard Conte to John Cassavetes—showed what happens to a sub at 400 feet by cracking an egg in his bunk.

What was he doing with an egg in his bunk? Hey, get with the spirit of the thing. It is, after all, "a memorial to all who served" and if you don't like it, you probably burn American flags at Christmas and want little Elian sent home to Cuba. You commie.

SIGHT AND SOUND, 7/00, p. 57, Tom Tunney

1942, the Atlantic ocean. The German submarine U-571 is disabled by a British warship. The U-boat's radio request for assistance is intercepted by the US Navy. Impersonating a German rescue sub, an American submarine draws alongside U-571 and a heavily armed boarding party led by Lt Tyler and Major Coonan secure the enemy vessel and its top-secret Enigma coding machine. While they are on board, a German rescue submarine torpedoes the US vessel. Ship's steward Eddie and one German prisoner survive and are dragged aboard U-571.

Tyler and his skeleton crew hastily prepare U-571 for action and destroy the enemy sub. Heading for England, the submarine encounters a German warship and dives. While the submarine is being depth charged, the German captive breaks free and attempts to wreck the engine room. Recaptured, he is executed when the crew realise he has been banging Morse code messages to the warship on the side of the hull.

U-571 has only one chance to destroy the enemy vessel. Crewman Trigger swims outside the hull and successfully makes vital repairs before drowning. Tyler fires his last torpedo and destroys the warship. The Americans abandon the sinking U-571 and, with the Enigma machine, take to a raft.

U-571 is loosely inspired by a fascinating incident in May 1941 in which a German U-boat was forced to the surface in the waters of the mid-Atlantic by a Royal Navy warship. Boarding the U-boat, a British naval team secured a major coup for the Allies by chancing upon an Enigma coding machine, the top-secret device used by the German military to send encoded messages.

For U-571's director Jonathan Mostow (Breakdown) the fact that the Enigma machine was secured more through luck than any planned operation poses certain dramatic problems. The real-life event lacks narrative drive and a consistent, controlling hero. More importantly for his film's US box-office prospects, there weren't any Americans involved in the action. His unambitious screenplay thus seeks to reshape the incident along the lines of such formulaic submarine adventure movies as *Crimson Tide* and *The Hunt for Red October.*

On these terms, *U-571* is an efficient enough exercise. Sharply edited and vigorously directed and performed, the claustrophobic action scenes have a manic momentum to them—the sequence in which the Americans row slowly across to the enemy vessel is especially suspenseful. The underwater special effects are generally excellent; booming sound effects milk the dramatic power of the sundry exploding depth charges for all their worth and, as with *Saving Private Ryan,* the colour photography (by Oliver Wood) convincingly emulates the rich lustre of genuine World War II footage. The film also recalls Ryan in an extended close-quarter struggle between the US sailors and the Nazi U-boat captive, proving once again that it's always a bad idea in Hollywood war films to let the prisoner live.

But in playing out Hollywood's favourite war-movie scenario by presenting a few individuals operating against the odds, *U-571* blithely ignores historical fact. The waters of the Atlantic are erroneously depicted as wholly dominated by the German military—German aircraft and surface warships roam at will, while Allied back up units are notable only by their absence (for a corrective view see *The Cruel Sea,* 1952, and *Sink the Bismarck!,* (1960). Isolated and continually under threat, the U-boat's stoic, inclusive and self-reliant US crew—including Harvey Keitel's Chief Klough (a role that brings to mind *Star Trek's* resourceful Scottie) and Eddie, the token black crewman (the US Navy was rigidly segregated and racism was endemic at the time)—is a comic book embodiment of American heroic ideals. The film focuses on a group of exclusively American heroes, operating in a historical and military vacuum; and the German captive a villainous, unscrupulous murderer—seems to function solely as a justification for the US sailors' acts of brutality. By contrast, the surviving Nazi U-boat captain in Alfred Hitchcock's *Lifeboat* (1944) is by far the strongest character in the film; the Allies have to learn to be ruthless to dispose of him.

Keeping their crew cut off from help and in perpetual danger—*U-571* is, at times, like an underwater version of *The Alamo* (1960)—screenwriters Mostow, Sam Montgomery and David Ayer run into dramatic problems, too. Little more than a succession of discrete action sequences, their script depends on plot devices that grow increasingly implausible as the film progresses (the idea that such a skeleton crew could man a vessel they've never sailed before; repairs being made to the outside of the submarine while it's still underwater, and so on). Even U-571's opening premise raises questions: if the US Navy can locate a German submarine so easily, why does it need the Enigma machine to break the U-boat code in the first place?

VILLAGE VOICE, 4/25/00, p. 142, Michael Atkinson

Hardly a spasm of nostalgia but so old-fashioned it smells like your grandfather's socks, Jonathan Mostow's *U-571* is not the WWII submarine movie, but—endearingly—a WW II submarine movie, a patient, tight genre number that acts as if *Das Boot* never happened. It's difficult to resist Hollywood's recent anti-'80s tendency to shy away from cosmic blockbusting in favor of midcentury matinee obsessions like submarines, Vikings, giant animals, haunted houses, etc.; the modesty is ingratiating. (The Greek-myth fantasies are left, sadly, to TV.) Who said every movie has to wipe you out? Mostow's smoothly efficient white-knuckler (he applied a similarly lean-mean approach to *Breakdown)* does its work as unceremoniously as its characters do theirs, and though there are occasional bombastic timpani seizures, the propaganda is kept to a minimum.

We open with a German U-boat, equipped with an Allies-maddening coding machine, stranded in the eastern Atlantic. Quickly, an American crew is pulled off liberty to intercept it masquerading as a German rescue sub, capture the exhausted crew, and steal the coder. But the seas are littered with German boats, and when a torpedo takes out the American sub, the handful of surviving Americans still on the near-dead German ship must try to clear the waters and get out alive. The characters are familiar—hot young fearless leader Matthew McConaughey, second banana Jon Bon Jovi, seasoned sarge Harvey Keitel, Noo Yawk greaseball Erik Palladino, black cook T.C. Carson, green-horned spy Jake Weber—but the work is the story, blessed with only a single sacrificial death (offscreen, even) and no speeches. The fact that nearly everything about *U-571* has been done better elsewhere doesn't sour the fact that it's a simple pleasure watching an American movie that respects genre, knows its limitations, and genuflects at the memory of Don Siegel in the age of Spielberg.

Also reviewed in:
CHICAGO TRIBUNE, 4/21/00, Friday/p. A, Michael Wilmington
NEW YORK TIMES, 4/21/00, p. E16, Elvis Mitchell
NEW YORKER, 5/15/00, p. 107, David Denby
VARIETY, 4/17-23/00, p. 25, Todd McCarthy
WASHINGTON POST, 4/21/00, p. C1, Stephen Hunter
WASHINGTON POST, 4/21/00, Weekend/p. 47, Desson Howe

UNBREAKABLE

A Touchstone Pictures release of a Blinding Edge Pictures production. *Executive Producer:* Gary Barber and Roger Birnbaum. *Producer:* M. Night Shyamalan, Barry Mendel, and Sam Mercer. *Director:* M. Night Shyamalan. *Screenplay:* M. Night Shyamalan. *Director of Photography:* Eduardo Serra. *Editor:* Dylan Tichenor. *Music:* James Newton Howard. *Music Editor:* Thomas S. Drescher. *Sound:* Allan Byer and (music) Shawn Murphy. *Sound Editor:* Richard King. *Casting:* Douglas Aibel. *Production Designer:* Larry Fulton. *Art Director:* Steve Arnold. *Set Decorator:* Gretchen Rau. *Special Effects:* Steve Cremin. *Costumes:* Joanna Johnston. *Make-up:* Bernadette Mazur. *Stunt Coordinator:* Jeff Habberstad. *Running time:* 107 minutes. *MPAA Rating:* PG-13.

CAST: Bruce Willis (David Dunn); Samuel L. Jackson (Elijah Price); Robin Wright Penn (Audrey Dunn); Spencer Treat Clark (Joseph Dunn); Charlayne Woodard (Elijah's Mother); Eamonn Walker (Doctor Mathison); Leslie Stefanson (Kelly); William Turner (Elijah, aged 8); Johnny Hiram Jamison (Elijah, aged 13); Michaelia Carroll (Babysitter); Elizabeth Lawrence (School Nurse); Bostin Christopher (Comic Book Clerk); David Duffield (David Dunn, aged 20); Laura Regan (Audrey Inverso, aged 20); Chance Kelly (Orange Suit Man); Michael Kelly (ER Doctor); Firdous Bamji (Businessman); Johanna Day (Saleswoman); James Handy (Priest); Sally Parrish (Ancient Personnel Secretary); Richard E. Council (Noel); Damian Young (Green Army-Jacketed Man); Sherman Roberts (Physician); Whitney Sugarman (Physical Therapist); Dianne Cotten Murphy (Mother Walking Boy); M. Night Shyamalan (Stadium Drug Dealer); Sasha Neulinger (Thermometer Boy); José L. Rodriguez (Truck Driver); Samantha Savino (Peering Girl on Train); Ukee Washington (Radio Announcer); Susan Wilder (Shoplifter); Greg Horos (Slicked-Hair Man); Todd Berry (Frat Party Boy); Angela Eckert (Frat Party Girl); Anthony Lawton (Hostage Father); Julia Yorks (Hostage Girl); John Patrick Amedori (Hostage Boy); John Morley Rusk (Security Dispatcher); Joey Hazinsky (Five-Year-Old-Boy); Bill Rowe (Bar Patron); Marc H. Glick (EastRail Engineer); Kim Thomas (Hostage Woman).

CHRISTIAN SCIENCE MONITOR, 11/24/00, p. 15, David Sterritt

When a movie becomes a megahit, Hollywood is often ready to pounce with a sequel. The next best thing is a follow-up film made by members of the same creative team—which brings us to "Unbreakable," the new supernatural thriller from star Bruce Willis and writer-director M. Night Shyamalan, who gave us "The Sixth Sense," one of last year's big successes.

Pundits never quite figured out what propelled "The Sixth Sense" to such stellar box-office heights. Some said it was the Oscar-nominated performance of Haley Joel Osment as the young boy who "sees dead people." Others said it was Shyamalan's spooky cinematic style. Still others pointed to Willis's understated acting.

These are good guesses, but apparently all wrong. Osment's charm has done little for his subsequent movie, "Pay It Forward," currently floundering in theaters everywhere. Clunkers like "Breakfast of Champions" and "The Story of Us" have confirmed Willis's fallibility. And now "Unbreakable" shows Shyamalan doesn't have a magic touch either. Whatever made "The Sixth Sense" such a smash remains in the category of unsolved movie mysteries.

Adding to the puzzle is the fact that the wobbly "Unbreakable" does everything this side of outright self-plagiarism to reproduce the earlier picture's moody seductiveness. This strategy begins with the story, which focuses again on eerie events linking a thoughtful boy and a vaguely troubled man. The boy (Spencer Treat Clark) is an ordinary kid this time, but his dad (Willis) is facing a paradox: How did he get through a catastrophic train wreck without sustaining a single scratch when everyone near him was killed?

Also on hand is a third major character who diverges from the "Sixth Sense" formula: a melancholy African-American man (Samuel L. Jackson) who's been diagnosed with an illness that makes his bones so breakable he has to be careful with every step. He's convinced that he and the train-wreck survivor represent opposite ends of the same physiological spectrum. Is he onto something here? Are there supernatural reasons for the phenomenon? And do answers to these conundrums lie in the comic books he's been studying since childhood?

The most impressive aspect is Shyamalan's poetic style, unfolding the story through expressive camera movements and an evocative soundtrack that rarely shouts when a murmur or whisper will do.

The trouble with the movie is its plot, which begins with a richly enigmatic aura, then becomes more silly and superficial with every new twist. It climaxes with a surprise that's becoming Shyamalan's trademark, and while audiences may get a kick out of it—listen for millions to mutter "I should have known" and clap their foreheads—it's far more contrived than the similar "Sixth Sense" switcheroo.

The sad thing about "Unbreakable" is that Shyamalan has an interesting approach to screen storytelling, and could become a significant artist if he had material worthy of his cinematic talent. Perhaps he should direct screenplays by more penetrating writers instead of his own tales. Or maybe he should take a vacation from the Hollywood financial pressures inseparable from the Bruce Willis scene, and follow his own poetic instincts.

LOS ANGELES TIMES, 11/22/00, Calendar/p. 1, Kenneth Turan

Copycat films are a fact of life in Hollywood, and once writer-director M. Night Shyamalan's "The Sixth Sense" grossed more than $600 million worldwide and earned six Oscar nominations, it was inevitable that someone would use all the same elements to produce an inferior version. "Unbreakable" is the knockoff we've been expecting, but what's surprising is that it's Shyamalan himself who's at the helm.

It's of course unreasonable and unfair to expect any film to have the special impact "The Sixth Sense" had on audiences, but Shyamalan (who wrote, directed, produced and still found time for a cameo as a drug dealer this time around) has recycled so many of the same elements that he seems to be inviting comparisons.

Back for an encore are Bruce Willis as the star and the city of Philadelphia as the setting. Returning as well are a small boy with three names in a key co-starring role (Spencer Treat Clark in for Haley Joel Osment), a theme dealing with the supernatural and an unexpected twist at the close.

Also the same—and it's a reason why this odd, creepy movie is a special source of frustration—is Shyamalan's gift for creating tension, uneasiness and a spooky atmosphere. It would be foolish to deny that "Unbreakable" has scenes that make you jump, but without anything resonant to apply that skill to, the film has no option except squandering its technique.

The real problem here is the story line, which starts out implausible and gets increasingly more difficult to take seriously as it unfolds. It's a comic-book idea in the worst sense, and Shyamalan's decision to start the film with on-screen statistics about the popularity of comics probably stems as much from a need to justify his preposterous plot as from the prominent place comics have in it.

"Unbreakable" begins with Willis in full "I Walked With a Zombie" mode as David Dunn, a phlegmatic security guard returning by train to his home in Philadelphia. As his inept attempts to chat up his attractive seatmate demonstrate, Dunn is a listless sad sack who hasn't felt good about himself in years. He loves his son, Joseph (Clark), but his relationship with his equally depressed wife, Audrey (Robin Wright Penn), is just about over.

Into this uneventful life comes a terrible train wreck. More than 100 people die—everyone on that Philadelphia-bound train, in fact, with a single exception. David Dunn not only comes out alive, he emerges without so much as a scratch on him.

The notoriety of his survival leads directly to something left on his car windshield, an unsigned note asking if he's ever been sick. Intrigued, Dunn not only investigates the history of his own health but also tracks down the man who left the message, comic-art dealer Elijah Price (Samuel L. Jackson).

Price, as we see in flashbacks that alternate with Dunn's story, has been afflicted since birth with osteogensis imperfecta, a disease that makes his bones ridiculously easy to break. They've been shattered 54 times, leading to a hated childhood nickname of Mr. Glass. His mother (Charlayne Woodard) fosters an interest in comic books that turns into the obsession of Price's life and leads to a theory he has about why Dunn survived the wreck, a theory Dunn is not at all eager to embrace.

In addition to its plot problems, "Unbreakable" seems to have encouraged all its actors to emulate Willis' lugubrious pacing, meaning that usually vibrant actors such as Wright Penn and Jackson are not shown to their best advantage. As for young Clark, it takes nothing away from his performance to say that Osment is a tough act to follow.

Whether it means to or not, the shadow of "The Sixth Sense" hangs over "Unbreakable." If the former hadn't been as big a success as it was, this story might have been assigned to oblivion, or at least to rewrite. Although it's true that the earlier film had its share of gimmicks, it was able to use them in a surprisingly heartening, almost inspirational way, and that made all the difference.

NEW YORK, 11/27/00, p. 134, Peter Rainer

Unbreakable is the fine new film from writer-director M. Night Shyamalan of *The Sixth Sense,* and it has the same nocturnal sense of dread and largo pacing. It also has a wrap-up that is just about as satisfyingly surprising. Bruce Willis plays, with great feeling, a security guard who survived a train wreck killing 131 people. Why did he alone survive? Samuel L. Jackson plays a comic-book-art collector named Elijah, as in the prophet, and his stare could probably burn a hole through Superman's Fortress of Solitude.

NEW YORK POST, 11/22/00, p. 47, Lou Lumenick

"The Sixth Sense" was no fluke. "Unbreakable," writer-director M. Night Shyamalan's dazzling reunion with Bruce Willis confirms he's one of the most brilliant filmmakers working today.

I should stress at this point that like its predecessor, this remarkable supernatural thriller is the kind of film that will yield maximum enjoyment with as little advance knowledge as possible.

If you're willing to take it on faith (which happens to be a major theme of this film), head right for the nearest multiplex—and read the rest of this review later.

You'll know you're in the hands of a latter-day Hitchcock with the mesmerizing opening sequences.

The film opens with a prologue set in 1962 in Philadelphia, where a woman has given birth in a department store to a boy named Elijah, whose arms and legs are mysteriously broken.

We then cut to the present day and an almost equally unsettling scene on a commuter train where a married man, played by Bruce Willis, casually slips off his wedding ring and flirts with an attractive woman.

The scene, which also involves a little girl and ominous sound effects, is shot by a hand-held camera peeking through the cracks in the seats in front of them—and you just *know* something awful is going to happen any minute.

Shyamalan wisely doesn't show us. David, the man played by Willis, is the sole survivor of a crash that kills 131 people. And he hasn't got a scratch on him.

Soon David, a stadium security guard, hears from a mysterious stranger who has him trying desperately to remember if he's *ever* been injured or even sick. The stranger is the grown-up Elijah (Samuel L. Jackson), who runs a comic-book art gallery and suffers from a brittle-bone disease that keeps him confined to a wheelchair for most of the movie.

Suffice it to say that Elijah raises profound questions about David's history, his special abilities and his destiny—and that the slowly unfolding answers will keep you on the edge of your seat.

There are many terrific scenes—the sequence where David conspiratorially slides a newspaper in front of his son at breakfast is worth the price of admission alone.

The boy here is played by Spencer Treat Clark of "Gladiator," and his quietly devastating performance as the child of estranged parents (Robin Wright Penn is excellent as the wife) confirms Shyamalan's gift for directing children, even if Clark's role is not as central as Haley Joel Osment's in "The Sixth Sense."

The deliberately paced "Unbreakable," make no mistake about it, is a vehicle form-fitted to Bruce Willis' burgeoning gifts as an uncommonly subtle and affecting actor.

Willis should get the Oscar nomination he deserved for "The Sixth Sense," and Jackson's enigmatic Elijah—who has devoted his life to searching for the sole survivor of a disaster, for reasons that won't be explained here—is equally commanding in a difficult if somewhat underwritten role.

I've stopped short of giving "Unbreakable" four stars because I felt somewhat let down by the closing scene, which I suspect may be more fiercely debated than the mother of all surprise endings in "The Sixth Sense."

Does it come out of left field? Were there clues in earlier scenes? Is Shyamalan setting up a sequel? See for yourself.

NEWSDAY, 11/22/00, Part II/p. B3, John Anderson

It hardly qualifies as a plot twist that M. Night Shyamalan, whose "Sixth Sense" established him as the combination O. Henry-Rod Serling of Hollywood, would try to get lightning to strike twice. You can't blame him. Not, at least, for standing out in the rain.

But someone has to take the rap for "Unbreakable" and it might as well be him, the writer, producer and director of this inscrutable and unbearably contrived movie. Like "The Sixth Sense," it does have Bruce Willis, a kid with three names (Spencer Treat Clark) and a surprise ending—of sorts. (Some people were probably surprised that the ship sank in "Titanic.") But "Unbreakable" is far more startling for its poverty of ideas and for the degree to which Shyamalan has become a victim of his own success.

When what you expect to happen happens—in a movie whose director is presumed to be setting you up—does that qualify as astonishing? If so, "Unbreakable" is a coup. Otherwise, it's mind-bogglingly sophomoric, the product of what seems to be an infantilized artistic sensibility.

You don't want to say too much about any film's plotline, much less one that relies, even this wobbly, on the element of surprise. But you also have to get from point A to point B: Willis is woebegone security guard David Dunn, who upon returning to Philadelphia from a job interview in New York becomes the only survivor of a horrific train wreck. In fact, he doesn't have a scratch on him. This helps to salvage his all-but-ruined marriage to Audrey (Robin Wright Penn), but also attracts the attentions of Elijah Price (Samuel L. Jackson), a collector-dealer of comic-book art.

Elijah, by all indications a crackpot, was born with a brittle-bone condition called osteogensis imperfecta and subsequently has led a life of unremitting pain—and a life philosophically fashioned by the comic books he obsessed over as a kid. Elijah's oratorical explanation of why comics are history—Jackson does what he can—is just one of the more squirm-inducing elements in "Unbreakable."

Ironically, though, the film works to the degree it does precisely because Shyamalan knows how to create mood and moodiness—he did it in the faux-gothic scenes in "The Sixth Sense," and he does it with Willis in "Unbreakable," as David goes through the various tortured examinations of his life and soul and tries to figure out who he is.

But the director is also erratic and, frankly, a bit immature: A scene in which David's adoring son, Joseph (Clark), keeps piling weights on his dad's bench-press bar is genuinely funny. A scene in which an upset Joseph finds David's revolver and waves it around their kitchen is played for a degree of laughs—and to that degree is both ludicrous and offensive.

To say "Unbreakable" is symptomatic of our cinematic times may be overstating the case. Still, "The Sixth Sense" was a literally indescribable movie (and thus, apparently, unmarketable), and was virtually dumped onto the marketplace in summer '99—proceeding to embarrass its studio with success. Conversely, "Unbreakable" makes sense on paper—Willis, Jackson, a wildly successful director—except for the paper the script was printed on.

Shyamalan's film isn't unwatchable, or even unforgivable. But it does make you wonder about the workings of Hollywood, whether there's an intelligence at work in an industry that could make a movie like "Unbreakable" and not expect audiences to be shocked and disturbed, if only by its lack of substance.

NEWSWEEK, 11/27/00, p. 80, David Ansen

Even if there were no credits at the start of "Unbreakable," it wouldn't be hard to guess that it was made by the writer-director of "The Sixth Sense." There's the same tone of hushed gravity; the same gray skies and dark Philadelphia interiors; the same measured pace, the camera sitting still and staring while an atmosphere of dread settles upon the audience like a damp fog.

And here again is Bruce Willis whispering his lines with fierce concentration. Willis is not dead this time—though he ought to be. Miraculously, his character, a security guard named David Dunn, has survived a train wreck that has killed every other passenger. There's not a scratch on him. This being a thriller by M. Night Shyamalan, we know there must be more than dumb luck involved. But what?

Enter Elijah Price. Elijah (Samuel L. Jackson) is David's physical opposite. Born with a condition rendering his bones vulnerable to the least impact, he's as breakable as David seems immune to physical harm. The owner of an art gallery specializing in comic-book art, he has some weird notion that David, like the comic-book heroes who fascinate him, has been put on earth for a special reason.

"Unbreakable" is structured as a riddle that David, along with the audience, must gradually come to solve. As a director, Shyamalan unfolds his story with stately assurance, slowly upping the ante of creepiness like an anesthesiologist toying with his patient. It's the story itself that proves to be a problem. This time out, Shyamalan the writer lets Shyamalan the director down badly. Once again he's got a surprise waiting for us at the end (don't worry: I won't give anything away), but when the cat is let out of the bag, its a pretty scrawny specimen. Instead of making us look back over the tale with new illumination, it only confirms the growing suspicion that "Unbreakable" is much less than the sum of its parts.

The whole middle section of the movie is basically a stalling tactic. David, who has a Haley Joel Osment-aged son (Spencer Treat Clark) and a physical-therapist wife (Robin Wright Penn) who is about to leave him, gradually comes to believe—prodded on by Elijah—that he is no ordinary mortal. The comic-book connoisseur asks him if he's ever been ill. David has to think about it, looking up his work records to see if he's taken any sickdays. Now, don't you think if you'd never had a sick day in your life, you'd have *noticed?* And if you were gifted with psychic powers, would you be oblivious to them until someone else pointed it out? If you had emerged unscathed from a previous accident, are you likely to have forgotten this detail, as David has? Why is our hero so dense? Because if he weren't, Shyamalan couldn't stretch "Unbreakable" to feature length.

What lifted "The Sixth Sense" out of the realm of ordinary horror films was its emotional veracity. We became deeply invested in the characters. Even without the twist ending, it worked—a unique synthesis of thriller and tearjerker. "Unbreakable" has stunning sequences, but there's nothing real holding the pieces together. Who are these people? Willis and Penn don't look or act like any working-class Philadelphia couple you're ever likely to meet. Time after time, Shyamalan sacrifices sense for sensation: there's a highly dramatic scene in which someone points a loaded gun at David, but there's no reason to believe that character would hold that gun at that moment. It's just there for effect. The most exciting section in the film—a bravura action sequence, late in the movie, in which David goes after a killer—is almost totally extraneous to the plot. Dramatically, Shyamalan can't find the forest for the trees.

"Unbreakable" looks impressive, and if you're willing to be seduced by its moody surface, you might be satisfied. But it doesn't bear up under the least bit of scrutiny: it's much ado about nothing, and the abrupt final revelation only makes matters worse. Someone actually thought this screenplay was worth a record $5 million? To the Hollywood moneymen, anyone whose last movie made more than $200 million is a genius. Still, "Unbreakable" is clearly the work of a gifted filmmaker. But Shyamalan badly needs to explore new territory. He's done himself no favor making a genre movie everyone will compare with "The Sixth Sense." It falls, way short—and feels way long.

SIGHT AND SOUND, 2/01, p. 54, Kim Newman

Philadelphia, 1961. New-born Elijah Price is diagnosed with a condition that renders him susceptible to bone fractures. As a teenager, Price grows obsessed with superhero comics.

The present. David Dunn, a former football player working as a security guard in the local stadium, returns from a job interview in New York, considering a move away from his wife Audrey and young son Joseph, When David's train is derailed, he walks away, the sole survivor, free of injuries. Price approaches David with a theory—that David is endowed with an ability to withstand injuries and illness. David insists that he suffered an injury in a car crash as a youth which forced him to retire from football, but Joseph, impressed by Price's theory, encourages his father to test his strengths. Price comes to believe that the insights David has into the dangers posed by some strangers at the stadium are proof of his psychic ability. David later admits that he wasn't hurt in the car crash but used it as an excuse to quit playing because Audrey, whom he was dating at the time, was against violent sports. He does admit to almost drowning in a swimming pool when he was a kid, which, Price suggests, indicates that exposure to water is David's one weakness. Accepting his powers, David allows passersby to brush against him at the train station, intuiting their recent crimes. He follows a janitor to a home where he has murdered a father and is terrorising the wife and children. There, he defeats the killer. Thanking Price, he shakes the man's hand and realises that Price caused the train to crash.

Unbreakable opens with statistics about the popularity of comic books in America and the devotion of comic book collectors. A tale of an ordinary man who unknowingly possesses superhuman powers, the film then proceeds to alternate a very sophisticated understanding of its subject matter (the early roots of graphic narrative are signalled by a glimpse of Egyptian hieroglyphs) with strange naivety (the misconception that comics are exclusively concerned with superheroes). Perhaps hampered by Buena Vista/Touchstone's parentage, which might have given director M. Night Shyamalan access to Disney's 'funny animal' books but precious little superhero material, the film is forced to dance around its centre, steering clear of much needed discussion of actual superhero archetypes Superman and Batman, both owned by the corporate masters of DC Comics, Disney's rival Time-Warner.

Which is not to say that the film doesn't work, most of the time. Taking a premise that is at bottom little more than the original Stan Lee-Steve Ditko vision of Spider-Man (what if a real person had superpowers?), *Unbreakable* plays it out with utmost seriousness as the buttoned-down, troubled David Dunn, played by Bruce Willis, is prompted by a flamboyant comic-book expert Elijah Price to investigate his paranormal abilities. The trouble is, the film conducts itself as if no one had ever taken this approach to superheroics before, though it has actually been almost mandatory in comics since the early 80s. The location of the superhuman in a modern miserabilist environment is the cornerstone style of DC's Vertigo line of books, which tend to the rainy, near-monochrome *noir* look and introspective feel characteristic not only of *Unbreakable* but of Shyamalan's last film *The Sixth Sense*.

Though he wears his hooded slicker on his one hero mission, it is not until a newspaper runs an artist's impression that we see how like Batman David Dunn looks in his crime-fighting gear. Price, meanwhile, after an appalling tumble down the steps of a subway station retreats from traumatised eccentricity into human caricature—he styles himself "Mr Glass"—and crippled solitude, although Samuel L. Jackson's performance hints at last-minute revelation well before the (slightly rushed) *Sixth Sense*-style climactic twist. Following up this hit film with a similar-looking picture and casting the same star was a risk, and Shyamalan pulls it off by playing deliberate variations on themes. His art-film roots show in the perfectly judged domestic scenes, uncomfortable and convincing as David's family sits around a kitchen trying not to crack up, but he can also pull off unforgettable suspense such as the moment when David has to talk to his son Joseph, determined to prove his dad's invincibility, out of shooting him.

As in *The Sixth Sense*, the hero can intuit other people's stories and provide resolution for them. And where *The Sixth Sense* climaxed in a murder mystery, here David tracks down an anonymous serial killer and rescues his victims—an impressive scene staged in a threatening downpour with a memorable moment of peril as David falls on to the cover of a swimming pool which shrouds him as he sinks. David's ability to glimpse people's troubled past also leads to a powerful scene earlier: standing amid a crowd, he senses the crimes of all those who brush past him, and though he is unwilling to stir himself until he finds a suitably villainous adversary, he is still agonised by the pain and corruption revealed in the flashy little vignettes of cruelty and larceny.

With captions that wrap the film up a little too swiftly, *Unbreakable* closes on a feeling that there should be more to the story. Though David has entered into a complicit understanding with Joseph about the hero business, his wife Audrey is shut out, which suggests that while David might have found a vocation (that is, if he can get over Price's final-reel revelation) he must pursue it by continuing to be dishonest with his wife. In most superhero comics, the real meat of the story comes in issue two, with the first instalment simply devoted to explaining the origins of the hero. With *Unbreakable*, however, you get the impression that Shyamalan is laying down character material and setting up storylines, which, you suspect, he'll have a hard time paying off.

VILLAGE VOICE, 11/28/00, p. 138, Dennis Lim

Variously characterized as ingenious, cheap, or (by those familiar with '60s cult favorite *Carnival of Souls)* secondhand, the suckerpunch finale of *The Sixth Sense* served at least to divert attention from the film's soggy mysticism, nagging inconsistencies, and coarse horror-playbook jolts. But the real surprise, if you could get past the closure-seeking ghosts and therapeutic approach to exorcism, was writer-director M. Night Shyamalan's curious tendency to alternate melodramatic surge with solemn understatement, faceless blockbuster vernacular with (in the movie's more corporeal moments) a credible shorthand of fraught gestures and atmospheric pauses.

Shyamalan has spoken of his monster commercial breakthrough in terms of cracking a Spielbergian code ("All I did was become aware of the rules that no one else is aware of," he told the *London Daily Telegraph* in a canny bit of self-promotion). Essentially a backfired encore stunt, *Unbreakable* cleaves to a formula that was far from airtight to begin with: eerie metaphysical puzzle, New Age inflections, misplaced emphasis on blind-siding parting shot, atypically detailed scrutiny of agonized family relationships, and at the morose, benumbed center, a reluctant superhero who learns to post-traumatically apply himself, bursting forth from his twilight-zone cocoon with a salvo of cathartic do-gooding.

As David Dunn, a Philly security guard who, alone among 132 passengers, escapes a horrific train wreck unscathed, Bruce Willis hones the existential panic he mustered for *12 Monkeys* and the final scene of *The Sixth Sense* into a sustained hum of spooked despair. Survivor's guilt is supernaturally complicated by accruing evidence of beyond-brute strength and an indomitable immune system (traits that have generally gone unquestioned in the Willis oeuvre to date). Hints of Shyamalan's thuddingly banal intentions seep into the frame with the emergence of David's eminently breakable opposite number, Elijah Price (Samuel L. Jackson), an ominously gloved comic-book fanatic with brittle-bone syndrome. Elijah badgers David into acknowledging his superhuman prowess and attendant obligations; suffice to say, the result involves crime-fighting in an improvised cape.

Unbreakable is presumably meant to unfold at a hallucinatory remove, but it doesn't encourage credulity, let alone eventually reward it. That said, eye candy keeps it painless: This might be the handsomest Hollywood production of the year, thanks largely to a crack team that includes cinematographer Eduardo Serra *(The Wings of the Dove)* and editor Dylan Tichenor *(Magnolia).* There's a showy precision to the visual style, all story-boarded symmetries and deft, fluid stealth. (As in *The Sixth Sense*, however, James Newton Howard's rudely over-cued score is a ubiquitous irritant.) Shyamalan gravitates once again to the unruly tangle of family dynamics: David's uncomfortably starched relationship with his preadolescent son (though the scene in which the kid abruptly decides to test his dad's invincibility is inexplicable, even as comedy) and his miserable, hollowed-out marriage. The most affecting scene has the alienated couple out on a tentative, reconciliatory date, exchanging vital stats (his wife, played by Robin Wright Penn, reveals her favorite song: "Soft and Wet" by the Artist Formerly Known as Prince). But mostly, what passed for melancholic austerity in *The Sixth Sense* registers here as fetishistic, perversely shrill sobriety: *Unbreakable* is at once flagrantly absurd and stubbornly mournful. To his credit, Shyamalan sticks to his guns; the grating incongruity persists at a deafening pitch until it finally splits the film wide open. \

Also reviewed in:
CHICAGO TRIBUNE, 11/22/00, Tempo/p. 1, Mark Caro
NEW YORK TIMES, 11/22/00, p. E1, Elvis Mitchell
NEW YORKER, 12/4/00, p. 113, David Denby
VARIETY, 11/20-26/00, p. 13, Todd McCarthy
WASHINGTON POST, 11/22/00, p. C1, Rita Kempley

UNDER SUSPICION

A Lions Gate Films release of a Revelations Entertainment and TFI International production. *Executive Producer:* Gene Hackman, Morgan Freeman, Maurice Leblond, and Ross Grayson Bell. *Producer:* Lori McCreary, Anne Marie Gillen, and Stephen Hopkins.   *Director:* Stephen Hopkins.   *Screenplay:* W. Peter Iliff and Tom Provost.   *Based on "Garde à'Vue" by:* Claude Miller, Jean Herman, and Michel Audiard.   *Based on the book "Brainwash" by:* John Wainwright.   *Director of Photograpyhy:* Peter Levy.   *Editor:* John Smith.   *Music:* BT.   *Music Editor:* Roy Prendergast.   *Sound:* Simon Kaye.   *Sound Editor:* Peter Drake Austin.   *Casting:* Reuben Cannon.   *Production Designer:* Ceclilia Montiel.   *Art Director:* Michael Atwell.   *Set Decorator:* Brian Kasch and Bonita Huffman.   *Costumes:* Francine Jamison-Tanchuck.   *Make-up:* Mike Hancock.   *Stunt Coordinator:* Manny Sivero.   *Running time:* 110 minutes.   *MPAA Rating:* R.

CAST: Gene Hackman (Henry Hearst);   Morgan Freeman (Captain Victor Benezet);   Thomas Jane (Detective Felix Owens);   Monica Bellucci (Chantal Hearst);   Nydia Caro (Isabella);   Miguel A. Suarez (Superintendent);   Pablo Cunqueiro (Detective Castillo);   Isabel Algaze (Camille Rodriguez);   Jackeline Duprey (Maria Rodriguez);   Luis Caballero (Paco Rodriguez); Patricia Beato (Darlita); Sahyly Yamile (Reina); Hector Travieso (Peter);   Marisol Calero (Sergeant Arias);   Vanessa Shenk (Sue Ellen Huddy);   Gelian Cotto (Paulina Valera);   Myron Herrick (Mr. Ricardi);   Vanesa Millán and Zina Ponder Pistor (Wives);   Willie Denton (Ben); Ramón Saldaña (Raymond);   Conchita Vicéns (Ruthanne);   René Cervoni (Thomas);   Frank Rose (Drunken Acquaintance).

LOS ANGELES TIMES, 9/22/00, Calendar/p. 4, Kevin Thomas

"Under Suspicion," the latest in a long line of cat-and-mouse police interrogation movies, pits Morgan Freeman's veteran cop against Gene Hackman's rich tax attorney and affords its stars terrific roles. It's no wonder they were so eager to remake Claude Miller's superb 1981 "Garde a Vue" that they signed on as executive producers.

While you could wish W. Peter's Iliff and Tom Provost's adaptation and Stephen Hopkins' direction were as tight and dynamic as Miller's, "Under Suspicion" is absorbing, keeps you guessing right up to a wallop of a finish and offers the pleasures of a chamber drama's bravura performances from a pair of supremely accomplished pros. What's more, with admirable rigor it makes the important distinction between experiencing desire and acting upon it.

The story has been transplanted from a small seaside French town to Puerto Rico. San Juan is in the throes of a carnival, and Henry Hearst (Hackman) and his gorgeous, much-younger wife, Chantal (Monica Bellucci), are arriving at a black-tie affair at a posh hotel where Hearst is to deliver a speech to help raise funds to cope with the ravages of a recent hurricane.   He's immediately asked by Capt. Victor Benezet (Freeman) to come across the street to police headquarters to answer a few questions. Hearst has reported the discovery of the corpse of a 13-year-old girl who had been raped and murdered and left in a thicket he passed by while on a hike. He's not at all happy but is urged rather forcefully to comply.

We quickly discover that the two men know each other well, which is perhaps why Hearst doesn't swiftly ask to contact his lawyer. As it turns out, the disarming Benezet and his thoroughly nasty detective (Thomas Jane) are amassing considerable circumstantial evidence that convinces them that Hearst not only killed this girl but another of about the same age in a slum district where he freely admits he had gone to seek out a prostitute. Hearst is a well-connected public figure, tough-minded, capable of arrogance but also honesty. He admits he's attracted to girls in their early teens—and believes many men are—but that doesn't mean he or most other men actually act upon such feelings.

Yet we learn that Hearst's marriage has become a sham and that he is concerned enough about aging to wear a too-obvious toupee. For his part, Benezet has two failed marriages behind him; these two men are strong, shrewd personalities who are nonetheless not without vulnerabilities.

In the escalating psychological tug of war you start considering who will prove to be the stronger of the two as you keep wondering if Hearst, as embodied by so forceful and direct a presence as Hackman, could really be guilty of such deplorable killings.

The filmmakers take advantage of vivid Puerto Rico settings whenever the script moves outside Benezet's spacious office. Jane is convincingly hateful and ominous, and Bellucci gets more chances than you might expect to demonstrate that she is not just another pretty face. Made with more solidity than inspiration, "Under Suspicion" is nevertheless worthwhile and thought-provoking.

NEW YORK POST, 9/22/00, p. 51, Jonathan Foreman

"Under Suspicion" is a profound disappointment, given its cast and source material.

A stilted, tensionless update of Claude Miller's fine if stagy French thriller, "Garde a Vue"—for some reason, reset in Puerto Rico—"Under Suspicion" contains what may be the only bad Gene Hackman performance on film.

On the eve of a carnival in Puerto Rico (the press notes explain that it's "a small Caribbean island"), successful tax attorney Henry Hearst (Hackman) is brought into a police station for questioning.

Apparently, Hearst found the corpse of a young girl on his morning run, the second victim of two recent rape-murders on the island. But police captain Victor Benezet (Morgan Freeman), an old friend of Hearst's, is convinced Hearst is the perpetrator.

Every time Hearst tells the story of his discovery of the body, it changes slightly but significantly. The interrogation begins in friendly enough fashion, but becomes increasingly nasty and intense, and both the suspect and the detective reveal more and more about their personal lives.

Eventually the cops bring in Hearst's much younger European wife, Chantal (Monica Belluci, an oval-face, Adjani-esque beauty), who, it seems, has long suspected her husband of tendencies to pedophilia.

Director Stephen Hopkins ("Lost in Space") illustrates Hearst's recollections in a series of arty flashbacks with lots of needlessly speeded-up or slowed-down shots. But thanks to his lack of subtlety and a rickety screenplay by W. Peter Iliff ("Varsity Blues") and Tom Provost, the tension never builds the way it should.

Freeman is as good as ever and Thomas Jane ("Deep Blue Sea") holds his own as an aggressive, slightly dumb young officer. But Hackman is strangely mannered: For once, you can actually see him acting away.

The Puerto Rican setting allows some pretty views and attractive sets (Freeman's police captain has a great-looking office) but also creates a series of false notes—including a strangely Anglicized police department.

NEWSDAY, 9/22/00, Part II/p. B3, Jan Stuart

Sometimes, star power does matter.

It is hard to imagine appreciating "Under Suspicion" without actors of the clout and weight of Gene Hackman and Morgan Freeman. Much of the supreme pleasure in seeing them go at each other in this enjoyable if tricked-up investigation thriller is the way in which they reassert and expand upon their already formidable screen mystiques.

"Under Suspicion" is the assembly-line title for an artfully directed remake of the 1981 French film "Garde à Vue," in which a pillar of the community gets caught with his pants down. Hackman is the pillar, Henry Hearst, a wealthy American tax attorney dwelling in Puerto Rico who is celebrated for his charity work and his impossibly beautiful young wife Chantal (Monica Belucci in the Romy Schneider role).

Henry's idyllic island lifestyle begins to crumble when his police captain friend Victor Benezet (Freeman) calls him in on a raucous carnival evening for questioning in the rape and murder cases of two 12-year-old girls. Benezet couldn't have picked a worse time, as Henry is about to make a charity appeal at a black-tie dinner.

Abetted by a bottle of uppers and a hotheaded detective (Thomas Jane) whose attack-dog methods only succeed in pushing Henry further into himself, Benezet chips away slowly at Henry's cock-of-the-walk facade. As Benezet catches Henry in one lie after another, the taint of guilt that fills the room is so thick it all but spills off the screen with the cigarette smoke and perspiration. The audience shares in Benezet's certainty as well as his frustration: The question is never "Did he?" but rather "Why did he?" and "How did he?" and "What is going to make him crack?" Except for the occasional clunker, "Under Suspicion" has been pungently written by W. Peter Iliff and Tom Provost. Director Stephen Hopkins tries too hard to pump up what is essentially a one-set play, using zoom-and-stop videogame photography and jazzing up Hackman's monologues by inserting his interrogators into flashback testimonials. Further inflating his canvas with pulsating carnival sequences that give the film the hyperbolic feeling of a two-hour Hitchcock climax, Hopkins communicates a distrust of the audience, who ostensibly don't want a big-star movie to sit still for more than a minute at a time.

Fortunately, his stars are titans of subtlety. Hackman is a master at embodying existential isolation, be it in the guise of an implacable wiretapper ("The Conversation") or a low-lurking detective ("The French Connection"). He's sensational here, navigating a shaky tightrope between righteous indignation and shame. Freeman has honed the simmering, all-knowing observer to a fare-thee-well, and he is able to convey deeper levels of personal anguish that are only hinted at in the script.

For all the unnecessary flash, "Under Suspicion" manages to be a seductive entertainment, providing a pleasurable reminder of why its two stars are among a handful of the classiest acts Hollywood has to offer.

SIGHT AND SOUND, 2/01, p. 55, John Wrathall

Puerto Rico, the present. Wealthy lawyer Henry Hearst is preparing his speech for a charity dinner when he is summoned to the police station by Captain Victor Benezet, who has uncovered inconsistencies in the statement Hearst gave about finding the body of a murdered girl. Hearst says Benezet and his subordinate Detective Owens are questioning him because they're jealous of his wealth and his young wife Chantal. Benezet reveals that Hearst was in La Perla, an impoverished district, the night another girl was murdered there. Hearst insists he was there to deliver presents to his wife's niece Camille and her family. But he can't account for his whereabouts later that night.

Arrested, Hearst is escorted to the dinner to give his speech. He returns to the station to find Chantal being interviewed by Owens. Her testimony reveals further holes in his story. Under pressure from Benezet, Hearst confesses that he was with a prostitute the night of the first murder. His wife has refused to sleep with him since suspecting him of fondling Camille during a Christmas visit they made to her house two years ago. Believing Hearst to be guilty, Chantal allows their house to be searched. Owens finds photographs which prove that Hearst knew the two girls before they were killed. Hearst confesses—at which point a policewoman informs

Benezet that the real murderer has been caught in the act of killing a third girl, with Polaroids of the first two corpses in his car. Hearst walks free.

The prospect of those two titans of American screen acting, Gene Hackman and Morgan Freeman, locking horns for two hours in an interrogation room is an enticing one, not just for audiences but also presumably for the stars themselves, both credited here as executive producers. The actors' previous memorable confrontation was in *Unforgiven* but then they were both playing second fiddle to Clint Eastwood. This time round, there's no one else to get in their way except, alas, the director. A competent enough action director, Stephen Hopkins has worked his way up from sequels *(Nightmare on Elm Street 5, Predator 2)* to blockbusters with 1998's *Lost in Space*. But he's clearly striving for something more. Last year, rather improbably, he directed one of the nine stories comprising the British portmanteau movie *Tube Tales*. Now, with *Under Suspicion* he's staking his claim as a serious film-maker.

On this evidence, though, he remains a frustrated action director at heart. With much of the film confined to two rooms in the police station where Freeman's weary police captain Benezet gradually breaks down the defences of a suspected child murderer Hearst, played by Hackman, Hopkins seems terrified of making a slow movie. In the opening credits, with the camera swooping over Puerto Rico, he literally speeds up the footage, a trick he uses later in the film too. The rest of the movie is edited at the same furious pace, with cuts every couple of seconds to anything that may be going on in the vicinity (Hopkins is especially keen on the carnival taking place in the streets outside). The immediate problem with this approach is that a film that starts in fifth gear can only slow down. But for a project that depends for its effect on the gradual build-up of atmosphere and psychological nuance, it seems particularly wrong-headed.

This is a terrible shame, because on paper *Under Suspicion,* with its probing insight into the crumbling psyches of two outwardly forceful sixtysomethings, has the makings of an excellent film. In fact, it has already made one: Hopkins' movie is a remake of Claude Miller's 1981 *Garde à vue*, a battle of wits for two corresponding elder statesmen of French cinema, Lino Ventura (in Freeman's role) and Michel Serrault. Hollywood has a venerable tradition of inferior remakes of French originals (another Miller/Serrault *policier*, 1982's *Mortelle Randonnée*, for instance, was turned into *Eye of the Beholder* only last year). The irony is that Hopkins' obsession with speed has resulted in a movie 23 minutes longer than the original—that's an awful lot of cutaways to revellers in the street, helicopter shots and close-ups of Bacardi bottles. When, in the final lap, Benezet produces a video camera to record Hearst's statement, it provides yet another image to cut away to. But it also makes you wonder how much more compelling this might have been if Hopkins had simply set up a video camera in the corner of the room and let the actors get on with it.

VILLAGE VOICE, 9/26/00, p. 147, Dennis Lim

A no less familiar pas de deux [The reference is to *Duets*; see Lim's review of that film.] transpires during a protracted overnight interrogation in *Under Suspicion,* a sleazy police procedural with wobbly philosophical pretensions. The setting is San Juan, Puerto Rico ("a small Caribbean island," the press notes helpfully inform us). Questionably motivated detective Morgan Freeman summons bigshot attorney Gene Hackman away from a fundraiser to cross-examine him about the rape and murder of two adolescent girls. Directed with assaultive showiness by Stephen Hopkins, the film remakes Claude Miller's stagy 1980 chamber piece, *Garde à Vue* , minus clammy claustrophobia. Instead Hopkins (*Lost in Space*) substitutes a disreputable made-for-cable poshness and grotesque stylizations: Hackman's testimony is visualized in arty flashbacks, which feature a disbelieving Freeman in the role of Hackman's conscience, and appear to have been shot by a lush and edited with a shredder. Strangely, there's no thrust and parry to this potentially heavyweight mind game. The effect is more like a tennis match in which every feebly contested point ends with an unforced error.

Also reviewed in:
NEW YORK TIMES, 9/22/00, p. E14, Elvis Mitchell
VARIETY, 5/22-28/00, p. 23, Derek Elley

UP AT THE VILLA

A USA Films release of an October Films and Intermedia Films presentation of a Mirage/Stanley Buchthal production.   *Executive Producer:* Sydney Pollack, Arnon Milchan, and Stanley Buchthal.   *Producer:* Geoff Stier.   *Director:* Philip Haas.   *Screenplay:* Belinda Haas.   *Based on the novella by:* W. Somerset Maugham.   *Director of Photography:* Maurizio Calvesi.   *Editor:* Belinda Haas.   *Music:* Pino Donaggio.   *Music Editor:* Annette Kudrak.   *Choreographer:* Karole Armitage.   *Sound:* Ken Weston.   *Sound Editor:* Richard King.   *Casting:* Celestia Fox.   *Production Designer:* Paul Brown.   *Art Director:* Anna Deamer and Livia Borgognoni.   *Set Decorator:* Gianfranco Fumagalli.   *Special Effects:* Roberto Ricci, Riccardo Ricci, Claudio Quaglietti, and Silvano Scasseddu.   *Costumes:* Paul Brown.   *Make-up:* Maurizio Silvi.   *Make-up (Kristin Scott Thomas):* Nuala Conway.   *Running time:* 115 minutes.   *MPAA Rating:* PG-13.

CAST: Kristin Scott Thomas (Mary Panton);   Sean Penn (Rowley Flint);   Anne Bancroft (Princess San Ferdinando); James Fox (Sir Edgar Swift); Jeremy Davies (Karl Richter); Derek Jacobi (Lucky Leadbetter);   Massimo Ghini (Beppino Leopardi);   Dudley Sutton (Harold Atkinson);   Lorenza Indovina (Nina);   Roger Hammond (Colin Mackenzie);   Clive Merrison (Archibald Grey);   Linda Spurrier (Hilda Grey);   Ben Aris (Colonel Trail);   Anne Ridler (Lady Trail);   Anne Bell (Beryl Bryson);   Barbara Hicks (Lulu Good);   Gianfranco Barra (Peppino); Gretchen Given (Isa MacKenzie);   Mary Shipton (Dowager);   Pierantonio "Noki" Novara (Guard).

CHRISTIAN SCIENCE MONITOR, 5/5/00, p. 15, David Sterritt

More than one current movie explores the interesting plot faced by privileged people living in a time and place when their privileges are no longer in fashion.

"The Last September," portrays Anglo-Irish aristocrats failing to recognize the harsh realities of Ireland in the turbulent 1920s. And now "Up at the Villa" visits a group of Anglo-American expatriates trying to sustain romantic Italian lifestyles even as Mussolini's fascists rise in power and World War II looms on the horizon.

Coming to theaters from the San Francisco International Film Festival, where it screened as a special gala presentation, "Up at the Villa" centers on a young Englishwoman named Mary whose life has been emotionally and financially difficult since her husband's death. Her challenges will be met if she accepts the marriage proposal of an aging friend whose employment prospects—he's bound for India to be a governor—are offset by his incredibly boring personality.

Seeking one last adventure before heading off to Bengal with him, Mary spends a night with an impoverished Austrian refugee, under the misguided impression that a few hours of her charms will take the sting out of his unpleasant life. She's amazed when he shows up again the next evening, proclaiming his newfound love for her, and she's astonished when her hesitation leads him to threaten a desperate, perhaps violent, retaliation.

Things go from bad to worse, and within hours she's faced with enormous guilt and—even worse in her eyes—the possibility of a public scandal. There are only two people who might be able to help her: a fascist officer she despises and a dashing American whose assistance might actually add to her burdens.

Based on a novella by W Somerset Maugham, this tale of competing loves and thwarted passions has many old-fashioned elements, from understated British dialogue to familiar contrasts between sophisticated Europeans and jaunty American sensibilities. In a sensible decision, director Philip Haas has filmed it in a pleasantly old-fashioned way, concentrating more on visual beauty— vivid colors, attractive settings, graceful camera movements—than on the story's sordid undertones. Sex and violence are integral parts of the plot, but it's been a long while since a movie has evoked them with more eloquent restraint.

The cast is excellent, headed by Kristin Scott Thomas as Mary and Sean Penn as her American friend. James Fox is perfect as the old-line British fiancé, and as a jaded princess, Anne Bancroft gives an impeccably tuned performance that makes Maggie Smith's in "The Last September" seem flimsy by comparison.

In all, "Up at the Villa" is a splendid place to spend an evening.

LOS ANGELES TIMES, 5/5/00, Calendar/p. 16, Kenneth Turan

"Up at the Villa" is the knockoff version of a quality film. With a beautiful period look and the presence of gifted actors Sean Penn and Kristin Scott Thomas, it resembles the real thing, but a closer examination reveals that the construction is suspect and the seams won't hold.

The filmmaking team of director Philip Haas and writer-editor Belinda Haas has at least a visual gift for the past. Their earlier "Angels and Insects," taken from a work by Angela Byatt, created a striking Victorian ambience. "Villa," adapted from a Somerset Maugham novella, uses production and costume designer Paul Brown and cinematographer Maurizio Calvesi to decoratively re-create the environs of 1938 Florence, a "second-rate provincial town" struggling to maintain its equilibrium as Mussolini's Fascists are consolidating their power.

But, even more than that earlier film, "Villa" is not dramatically convincing. The melodrama of the Maugham original is too simplistic to involve, and the places the film's plot goes are so obvious that even the presence of quality actors can't create sufficient interest.

Scott Thomas, who also starred in "Angels and Insects," brings her usual beauty and intelligence to the part of Mary Panton, an impoverished young widow bone weary of being dependent on the kindness of strangers even if their generosity includes the loan of the Florentine villa she is staying in.

Her days of being as poor as a church mouse, however, may soon be over. An old friend, Sir Edgar Swift (James Fox), the stiffest upper lip in war-torn Europe, cares about her enough to think about proposing marriage. And Sir Edgar's new job as governor of Bengal in British India, is posh enough to keep Mary up to her elegant cheekbones in servants.

Taking a nosy interest in Mary's future is the Princess San Ferdinando (Anne Bancroft), an aging American fortune hunter who married shrewdly and well and who is anxious that the young woman do the same. "I hope you're not one of those who has to be in love to marry," the princess huffs, telling Mary about her many lovers, including an impoverished man she took on because she wanted to bring something beautiful into his humdrum life.

It's the princess who introduces Mary to American Rowley Flint (Penn), the smooth, cocky and, you guessed it, married playboy of the Tuscan world. They flirt beautifully, but because Mary's past has led her to look on love as a source of humiliation while Rowley lives only to "find someone who makes every nerve in your body snap," their relationship does not seem to have much of a future.

But wait. Mary gets distracted by a penniless young refugee named Karl (Jeremy Davies) while all non-Italians come under the scrutiny of local Fascist leader Beppino Leopardi (Massimo Ghini), shiny boots and all, and the film's already contrived doings take a more sinister but even less creditable turn.

Penn is an exceptional actor whose choices, though invariably interesting and unexpected, are not always successful. Here he seems to have modeled himself after Robert Mitchum, turning Rowley Flint into a monument to suavity who raises his eyebrows like a man of the world and insists, "I don't make set plans."

It's a polished but disconnected performance, with the feeling of a stunt about it, and it adds to an air of unreality in a movie where people are forever exclaiming "I say" and "by Jove." Penn and Scott Thomas do have a certain physical chemistry, but it's not enough to cancel out plot dynamics so old they creak. Beauty and bloodlessness battle it out in every frame of "Villa," and no one comes out a winner.

NEW YORK, 5/15/00, p. 59, Peter Rainer

Adapted from a Somerset Maugham novella of romance and murder set in 1938 Tuscany and directed by Philip *(Angels & Insects)* Haas, the lackluster *Up at the Villa* features actors who appear to be either exactly right for their roles—like James Fox, as the soon-to-be-appointed governor of Bengal—or exactly wrong, like Sean Penn, as an American playboy-dandy, and Jeremy Davies, as an Austrian refugee. Kristin Scott Thomas, who might seem well cast as an

English beauty in murderous straits, turns out to be all wrong, too: Her poise, which once seemed so sensual, has now reached the freezing point.

NEW YORK POST, 5/5/00, p. 53, Lou Lumenick

If Keenan ("Merchant") Ivory Wayans had directed this movie, it would have probably been called "Up at the Villa, the English Patient on the Razor's Edge wrote The Letter."

It also would have probably been a lot more entertaining than this wan adaptation of a 1940 novella—from director Philip Haas and his screenwriter wife, Belinda Haas—which serves mostly as a vague reminder of superior films derived from W. Somerset Maugham's better-known works.

The film also (weakly) evokes the Maugham-ish "The English Patient" through the mannered presence of Kristin Scott Thomas—who also starred in Haas' more assured "Angels and Insects"—as a penniless widow in fascist Italy.

Adultery has rarely seemed less fun than in the hands of Thomas' Mary Panton, who strays when her wealthy-but-older fiancé (James Fox in a virtual self-parody that wouldn't have been out of place in the costume spoof "Stiff Upper Lips") leaves the country for a few days after popping the question.

Mary rebuffs the advances of married roué Rowley Flint (Sean Penn, interestingly cast against type in a too-small role), who argues against her entering into a loveless marriage.

But she succumbs to the charms of an Austrian refugee (Jeremy Davies)—with a cutaway so discreet you almost expect one of those "Comes the Dawn" title cards used in old movies to signify a night of romantic passion had occurred.

Mary thinks it was a one-night stand, but the Austrian has other ideas—and their clumsy (and dramatically unconvincing) gunpoint confrontation makes you wish Thomas had been forced to watch Bette Davis' version of "The Letter" for some tips on how to handle a pistol.

Rowley is called in by Mary to help cover up the ensuing scandal—worrying all the while whether it will wreck her engagement to her fiancé, who's being named to a high post in Colonial India.

There are a few interesting moments, but basically "Up at the Villa" is dangerously short of sympathetic characters, except an aging, social-climbing gay expatriate (a lift from "The Razor's Edge") played by Derek Jacobi, and Anne Bancroft's entertainingly hammy old princess, who gives Mary some disastrous romantic advice.

The Haases barely hint at the dangers of El Duce's regime, weakly represented here by a corrupt fascist officer (Massimo Ghini) who also flirts with Mary.

Along with the other male characters, he keeps praising her beauty. But like Penn's ex-wife Madonna in "The Next Best Thing" (whom Thomas frighteningly resembles in some shots), the compliments don't seem based on any kind of reality.

Nor, for the most part is "Up at the Villa."

NEWSDAY, 5/5/00, Part II/p. B6, John Anderson

In anticipation of "Up at the Villa," Philip Haas' version of the Somerset Maugham story, I asked someone whether she could think of a more unlikely romantic duo than Kristin Scott Thomas and Sean Penn. "Kristin Scott Thomas and Mickey Rourke?" she asked. Exactly.

Not only did the two seem temperamentally ill-suited, there's a physical incomparability hinted at here: Scott Thomas is of a willowy insouciance; of Penn, a Maileresque pugnacity. Either way, they seemed the oddest of couples.

But the film itself proves these reservations, if not others, to be unfounded. Like many of the stories of Maugham, "Up at the Villa" is situated on the edge of decadence. Like many of the films of Philip Haas—his various art docs as well as the under-appreciated "Music of Chance"—"Villa" toys with our expectations about morality, opportunity and, in this case, romantic chemistry. Discovery—by us, by the characters—is the operating ethic.

In '30s Florence, after the black shirts have taken over, young widow Mary Panton (Scott Thomas) is being wooed by the stuffy if decent Sir Edgar Swift (James Fox), who is soon to be named a governor of the Raj. It's a future Mary views as a comfortable death sentence, but she's inclined to accept, until a dinner party changes her life.

Hosted by Princess San Ferdinando (Anne Bancroft), the party guests include rakish Rowley Flint (Penn), who immediately cocks his eye in Mary's direction. She is more sympathetic toward the restaurant's violinist (Jeremy Davies), who is so mediocre he's cut off mid-song. Inspired by a story the princess has told her earlier, Mary winds up sleeping with the boy, a destitute Austrian refugee who has the bad taste to think he's in love. When Mary tells him he's not, he kills himself in her room.

The story line, full of malevolent fascists and romantic entanglements, isn't particularly invigorating. But the fascinations engendered by "Up at the Villa" aren't about the intrigues involved when Rowley rids Mary's villa of its unfortunate dead body or when Mary returns the favor by getting Rowley sprung from jail. It's the Maughamian mischief that occurs when people break out of the atrophied shells and find people inside them they never knew existed. And in actors defying our expectations.

SIGHT AND SOUND, 6/00, p. 58, John Mount

Florence, 1936. Penniless widow Mary Panton lives in a borrowed villa and socialises with the expatriate Anglo-American community. Sir Edgar Swift, 25 years her senior, proposes marriage. Mary asks for time to decide. Sir Edgar leaves Mary his revolver for her protection. Princess San Ferdinando urges Mary to marry Sir Edgar, soon to be Governor of Bengal, and suggests she take a lover if she grows bored. At the Princess' dinner party Mary receives the unwelcome attentions of Fascist officer Beppino Leopardi and meets charming American playboy Rowley Flint. She is attracted to Rowley but rejects his advances when he escorts her home. Impulsively, she has sex with Karl Richter, an Austrian refugee. Mary rebuffs Karl when he returns the next night. Richter shoots himself with Sir Edgar's gun.

Rowley helps Mary dump Karl's body; he is arrested by Leopardi. Mary steals incriminating files on Leopardi from the Princess; in exchange for the files, Leopardi releases Rowley. Mary parts from Rowley. On being told what has happened, Sir Edgar sticks to his proposal of marriage but explains that he will have to resign. Mary rejects him. Later, she runs into Rowley.

Director Philip Haas and his co-writer/editor and wife Belinda Haas produced some interesting literary adaptations during the 90s, notably *The Music of Chance* and *Angels and Insects*. Coolly intelligent and distinguished by understated observation, both films were effective in teasing out the more unsettling aspects of their original source material. But for all the directorial polish on show, the Haases' films have tended to start promisingly but fall frustratingly short of expectations. The same is true of their latest film, based on a W. Somerset Maugham novel: *Up at the Villa* is perfectly enjoyable fare but not the stunning period drama one feels the Haases are capable of.

In late-40s Hollywood Christopher Isherwood failed to write a screen adaptation of Maugham's novel because its tale of a young widow caught between financial obligation and romantic desire was considered too sexually explicit. Having finally reached the screen, the film ironically seems too restrained, its handling of the novel too discreet to make much impact on a contemporary audience. This said, Haas shows a great deal of delicacy in his dissection of the emotional turmoil Mary suffers after her impetuous one-night stand leads her to the brink of ruin. Kristin Scott Thomas gives a customarily convincing portrayal of a romantic Englishwoman chafing against the double standards of upper-class society. And what threatens to be a clichéd romance with Sean Penn actually sputters into life, in large part thanks to Penn's performance.

Up at the Villa is less effective when augmenting the scant political background of the novel with a more explicit historical context—the film's depiction of Italian fascism, for instance, is obvious and lacks insight. Similarly some of the minor characters are portrayed a little too broadly (although Derek Jacobi's cameo as a Quentin Crisp-like Lucky Leadbetter is strangely engaging and Anne Bancroft gives a commanding queen bee performance as the Princess). Unsurprisingly, given the consummate visual style of Haas' earlier films, the lush Tuscan settings are expertly photographed, framing perfectly the sybaritic lifestyle of the expat community. Haas imbues this idyllic setting with a slow-burning sense of foreboding and occasionally hints at a more lurid, pliable morality under the genteel surface. But, like Neil Jordan's marginally more successful *The End of the Affair*, he fails to pull off the trick of depicting the period without lapsing into stiff lipped, straight-backed mannerisms and creaky lines of dialogue.

VILLAGE VOICE, 5/9/00, p. 138, Dennis Lim

Fondly memorialized by bourgie nostalgists as a panoramic playground for twittering, uptight, romance-starved expats, pre-war Italy receives one of its most waxen eulogies to date in Philip Haas's *Up at the Villa* (not to be confused with *A Month by the Lake,* which it now supplants as Most Evocatively Titled Idle-Privilege Movie). The freakishly inspired pairing of Franco Zeffirelli and Cher in last year's crack-brained *Tea With Mussolini* was enough to kill the subgenre and, in the process, unwittingly reinvent it as parody. Haas's earnest resuscitative effort suffers by comparison. Adapting a heavy-breathing Somerset Maugham novella, the director and his wife, Belinda Haas (the film's writer and editor), have fashioned a stiff self-discovery fable both decorous and ludicrous.

Mary Panton (Kristin Scott Thomas) is a proper English widow living off rich friends in 1938 Florence. A crusty colonialist bigwig and longtime acquaintance (James Fox) pops the question, and in the few days she takes to mull over his proposal, Mary (comfortably installed at the lavish titular estate) finds herself reevaluating her romantic priorities—or, more to the point, her taste in men. Natty, unflappable American Rowley Flint (Sean Penn) figures in this dilemma. So does a scruffy Austrian refugee (Jeremy Davies, fidgety as ever), with whom Mary, in but one instance of her much noted generosity, shares a night of passion. "My heart was full of tenderness and pity," the slumming patrician later explains, lip aquiver. This rationale causes the poor boy, now hopelessly enamored, to shoot himself, leaving Mary and Rowley to bond in a clumsy act of body disposal and a clumsier blackmail scheme against the local fascists.

The Haases, whose previous films *(Angels and Insects, The Music of Chance)* evinced a remote, unfussy sensibility, are a poor fit for the melodramatic contortions that the story demands. The actors appear not to have been directed: Scott Thomas shifts robotically from downcast introspection to weak smiles to glassy-eyed surprise, and there's no erotic tension to speak of, not least because Penn's performance consists of trying hard not to be noticed (and generally succeeding). By way of comic sideshow, *Up at the Villa* features two parts that might have been written with drag queens in mind: gossipy socialite Anne Bancroft and mascaraed "sodomite" Derek Jacobi. Both mug and preen with a touching lack of vanity, sadly unaware that, in the period-pudding camp-spectacle stakes, Cher has raised the bar beyond human means.

Also reviewed in:
CHICAGO TRIBUNE, 5/5/00, Friday/p. B, ???
NEW REPUBLIC, 5/15/00, p. 32, Stanley Kauffmann
NEW YORK TIMES, 5/5/00, p. E16, A. O. Scott
NEW YORKER, 5/15/00, p. 106, David Denby
VARIETY, 5/1-7/00, p. 35, Derek Elley
WASHINGTON POST, 5/5/00, p. C12, Rita Kempley

URBAN LEGENDS: FINAL CUT

A Columbia Pictures release of a Phoenix Pictures presentation of a Neal H. Moritz/Gina Matthews production. *Executive Producer:* Nicholas Osborne and Brad Luff. *Producer:* Neal H. Moritz, Gina Matthews, and Richard Luke Rothschild. *Director:* John Ottman. *Screenplay:* Paul Harris Boardman and Scott Derrickson. *Based on characters created by:* Silvio Horta. *Director of Photography:* Brian Pearson. *Editor:* John Otttman and Rob Kobrin. *Music:* John Ottman. *Music Editor:* Amanda Goodpaster. *Sound:* Richard Waddell and (music) Peter Fuchs. *Sound Editor:* Richard L. Anderson. *Casting:* Randi Hiller. *Production Designer:* Mark Zuelzke. *Art Director:* Nancy Pankiw. *Set Designer:* Pat Flood and Charles Dunlop. *Set Decorator:* Carol Lavoie. *Special Effects:* Martin Malivoire, Daniel Gibson, and Larz Anderson. *Costumes:* Marie-Sylvie Deveau and Trysha Bakker. *Make-up:* Irene Kent. *Prosthetic Make-up:* François Dagenais and Matthew W. Mungle. *Stunt Coordinator:* Shane Cardwell and Pat Banta. *Running time:* 94 minutes. *MPAA Rating:* R.

CAST: Jennifer Morrison (Amy Mayfield);   Matthew Davis (Travis/Trevor);   Hart Bochner (Professor Solomon);   Joseph Lawrence (Graham Manning);   Anson Mount (Toby);   Anthony Anderson (Stan);   Eva Mendes (Vanessa);   Michael Bacall (Dirk);   Jessica Cauffiel (Sandra); Marco Hofschneider (Simon);   Loretta Devine (Reese);   Derek Aasland (P. A. Kevin);   Jacinda Barrett (Lisa); Peter Millard (Doctor Fain);   Chas Lawther (Dean Patterson);   Chuck Campbell (Geek in Plane);   Yani Gellman (Rob);   Jeannette Sousa (Libby);   Rory Feore (Killer Flight Attendant);   Shauna Black (Blonde Girlfriend);   Leland Tilden and Joel Gorson (Jocks on Plane);   Pat Kelly (Crony in Screening Room);   Stephanie Moore (Girl in 16mm Film);   Kevin Hare and David Sparrow (Police Officers);   Clare Martina Preuss (Clapper Girl).

LOS ANGELES TIMES, 9/22/00, Calendar/p. 12, David Chute

The coolest single element in the walk-don't-run horror sequel "Urban Legends: Final Cut" may be its atmospheric setting, the actual rural campus of Trent University, in Peterborough, Ontario. With blocky poured-concrete buildings and a river-spanning bridge plopped down among wooded hills, the place is a bizarre stylistic mix of faux Frank Lloyd Wright and grim Stalinist modern; call it institutional gothic.

Trent U. must be a pretty oppressive place to spend one's college years. At the same time it should be a perfect setting for a horror film, especially one whose ostensible subjects are the anachronistic intimations of the uncanny that can still occasionally bubble up from the depths of the human brain, even in hard-edged modern environments. At the movies, of course, there's many a slip between "should be" and "is."

"Urban Legends" is the kind of franchise that producers love because the films don't have to be good to be popular—not with a premise like this, the endlessly mutating modern folk tales that even sophisticated city dwellers find irresistible. Factor in the sequel's ingenious setting, a film school packed with ambitious wannabe auteurs, and "Final Cut" has promising raw material to burn—and that's pretty much what's been done.

This killer-stalks-the-campus retread, directed by John Ottman from a script by Paul Harris Boardman and Scott Derrickson, is exactly the kind of flat-footed stalker film that the recent trend-setting hits in the genre have been making fun of. It delivers bald-faced variations on devices that were originally deployed, albeit with a redeeming glint of irony, in the "Scream" films and in "Scary Movie."

An established editor ("The Usual Suspects") and film music composer ("The Cable Guy") making his debut as a director, Ottman, at least, has a couple of career alternatives to fall back on. The hard-working young actors in the large ensemble cast may not be so lucky. Even when the performers are well-cast, like TV veteran Joseph (formerly "Joey") Lawrence, who clearly relishes his smarmy turn as a smug rich kid with family connections in the film business, the movie often leaves them stranded, floundering helplessly in unplayable situations. The lucky ones get killed off early.

Jennifer Morrison (the ghost in "Stir of Echoes") staunchly fills the inquisitive coed role occupied by Alicia Witt in the 1998 original. As a hot undergraduate directing prospect, hard at work on an urban legend-related thesis film, Morrison's smart and sensible Amy Mayfield begins to suspect that her classmates are being eliminated, permanently, from the competition for a prestigious annual award.

Amy teams up with the hunky twin brother of one of the murder victims (both siblings are played by Matthew Davis) and a two-fisted security guard (Loretta Devine, the only holdover in the cast) for some late-night sessions of perfunctory detective work.

. After sitting through a tired and tiring film like this, we're naturally tempted to write off the entire genre, to dismiss it as hackneyed or played out. But in the right hands the teen scare picture still has some life in it. Just this year, for instance, there was Glen Morgan and James Wong's "Final Destination," a smartly crafted entry with a playful, surreal atmosphere.

The "Urban Legends" concept seems tailor-made for that kind of ingenuity, for a little bit of sly wit and playfulness. Movies like "Final Cut" are bunker-mentality productions, safe, square and purely functional, like buildings made from poured concrete.

NEW YORK POST, 9/22/00, p. 50, Lou Lumenick

Did you hear the one about the masked killer stalking the cast and crew of a slasher movie? Sure you have—in "Freddie's New Nightmare," "Scream 3" and now, the proudly derivative "Urban Legends: Final Cut."

It's several, uh, cuts below its predecessors, as well as the modest hit from 1998 it purports to be a sequel to. The cast is much weaker than "Urban Legends," which featured such up-and-comers as Jared Leto, Alicia Witt and Rebecca Gayheart, as well as Robert Englund, the erstwhile Freddy Kreuger.

This time out, they've been replaced by the likes of Joey Lawrence and Hart Bochner. The only character who returns from the original is the sassy campus guard, played again by Loretta Devine—and the new movie's biggest laugh is her watching "Foxy Brown" on a bank of security cameras.

This one is set at a film school, where there's a cutthroat competition for the Hitchcock award, a stepping-stone to Hollywood success. A mysterious figure in a parka and fencing mask is killing off everyone associated with the serial-killings-inspired-by-urban-myths movie being made by Amy (the merely adequate Jennifer Morrison), the daughter of an Oscar-winning documentary maker.

Besides film brat Lawrence and professor Bochner, the suspects include the twin brother (Matthew Davis) of a student who committed suicide, a neurotic rival filmmaker (Anson Mount), Amy's chain-smoking cinematographer (Marco Hofschneider), her lesbian boom operator (Eva Mendes) and just about everyone else in the cast, including a pair of scene-stealing special effects geeks (Michael Bacall and the ubiquitous Anthony Anderson).

Even as the body count mounts, of course, Amy can be counted upon to roam deserted corridors alone in the middle of the night. The running joke for the audience (not a new one) is that we're never sure at the outset of each scene whether we're seeing "reality," a scene from one of the student films or one of Amy's nightmares.

Debuting director John Ottman (who edited "The Usual Suspects") and screenwriters Paul Harris Boardman and Scott Derickson manage a couple of modestly clever sequences, most notably an homage to Michael Powell's pioneering 1959 slasher movie, "Peeping Tom."

But you cease to care as they fall back on a catalogue of clichéd shocks, tired camera angles and an ever-mounting gore quotient, including decapitation by falling window sash and rats nibbling at a victim's corpse.

Of course, in the post-modern style of the "Scream" movies, "Urban Legends: Final Cut" contains dialogue commenting on everything from its bad acting (an actress is criticized for her performance in an airplane-restroom sex scene) to its very unoriginality. It may be the first movie where someone complains, "You stole my f---ing genre."

NEWSDAY, 9/22/00, Part II/p. B6, John Anderson

Directors of teen-horror-genre movies aren't expected to do much, but they should really be able to execute the basics. The face suddenly looming in the window/doorway/rearview mirror. The body abruptly falling out of a closet.

The virginal (or near-virginal) blonde running, running, running away from the serial killer without getting anywhere. And a simple story sold simply, but with generous amounts of precious bodily fluids.

Compared with "Urban Legends 2: Final Cut," "The Blair Witch Project" was a model of clarity, "Scary Movie" was Merchant Ivory and the original "Urban Legend" in 1998 was the lost collaboration of Alfred Hitchcock and Wes Craven.

But what's objectionable about "UL2:FC" is not so much that the movie's plot line is impenetrable, or that the very idea of urban legends is all but absent.

It's that even the easy stuff is beyond its reach.

There are more red herrings, dream sequences and false leads in "Urban Legends 2" than in a season of "Dallas" and "The Sixth Sense" combined, so giving away too much will ruin it for those who still plan to go (which, we assume, are those who simply can't read). Suffice to say, it's a dark and stormy night through most of the film, which takes place at the Orson Welles Film Center of Alpine University, where competition for the Hitchcock Award is fierce, the professors are washed-up hacks and the students all look like actors—but not the actors who are playing them.

Jennifer Morrison, who portrays our imperiled heroine, is sort of standard issue Kirsten Dunst-Michelle Williams blonde; Matthew Davis, who is both the "gifted" Travis and his twin brother, Trevor (be afraid of movies with twin brothers), looks like he just left "Dawson's Creek," and I thought I saw Anson Mount (the obnoxious Toby) in "Clueless," but apparently not. Marco Hofschneider, as the Dieteresque cameraman Simon, has some funny, German-inflected lines ("I must smoke"). And Loretta Devine, reprising her role from the original, has the genre's seemingly obligatory role of black security guard and voice of reason, in a movie where the white people can't get out of their own way, much less the killer's.

SIGHT AND SOUND, 1/01, p. 60, Matthew Leyland

Alpine University, New England, the present. In their final semester at film school, students compete to win the Hitchcock, an award given for best film that effectively guarantees its winner a Hollywood career. Amy, the daughter of a dead documentary film-maker, is inspired by a conversation with security guard Reese to make a thriller about urban legends.

Amy has her script approved by Professor Solomon. Her cinematographer, Toby, quits, and is replaced by Simon. Filming starts. Actress Sandra is killed by a masked assailant. Her death is captured on film which the crew dismiss as fake. After receiving a poor grade for his film, gifted film-maker Travis apparently commits suicide. His twin brother, Trevor, turns up. Filming continues. Simon is murdered; his death is caught on a security tape which Amy watches but then loses when the killer attacks her. Trevor, the only person who shares Amy's belief that a murderer is at large, suggests she continue filming to draw the killer out into the open. More crew members are executed.

Trevor realises that all the victims worked on Travis' film. He and Amy confront Toby. After summoning Professor Solomon, they accuse Toby of stealing Travis' film and submitting it to the Hitchcock competition under his own name. However, Professor Solomon, who blames Amy's father for his failure at film school, reveals that it was he who planned to pass off Travis' film as his own and admits to the killings. A fracas ensues in which Amy shoots Solomon. Later, Amy makes her first Hollywood movie, entitled *Urban Legends,* while Solomon ends up institutionalised.

Based on the making of a movie (a premise which is similar to that of *Scream 3),* Urban Legends Final Cut toys endlessly with the boundary between fiction and reality. It begins and ends with that time-honoured device, a sequence depicting a film-within-a-film, and includes numerous moments designed to fool the audience such as the on-set accident that turns out to be a prank and the sex-cum-stabbing scene that's just a dream. This knowing, ironic attitude, which sets the movie apart from the first *Urban Legend* film—a relatively straightforward slasher movie—may well be an attempt to teach the audience, as befits a movie set in a film school, rudimentary lessons about the illusory nature of cinema. But like so many post-*Scream* horrors, the film comes across as an exercise in empty, larkish reflexivity for reflexivity's sake.

There's one scene, though, in which the tension between fiction and reality is explored with some insight: as they watch footage of lead actress Sandra's *Peeping Tom*-style execution, unaware that what they are seeing is genuine, the crew of student director Amy's film laughingly dismiss the relatively goreless murder as phoney ("OJ left more blood than that on the Bronco!"). The scene hints at the inuring, perception-skewing effect horror movies have on their audience, but debut director John Ottman doesn't develop the idea. Instead, he focuses on cramming as many gratuitous movie references (and there's an admittedly eclectic range, from *La Nuit américaine,* 1973, to *Basic Instinct,* 1992) and noisy student slashings into the frame as possible.

Despite the prodigious tally of on-screen killings, there's just one slaying that's memorable, partly because it's the only one based on a recognisable urban legend (unlike, for instance, the cinematographer who is bludgeoned by his camera lens). A drugged female student awakens in an ice-filled bath to find her kidney missing; the killer decapitates her and feeds her removed organ to a dog. Graphic and gruesome, it highlights the ability of Ottman (who edited *The Usual Suspects)* to seize the audience's attention with gore rather than with well executed scares or suspense.

With its risible denouement, which evokes the cartoon excesses of television's *Scooby Doo*, and bland young cast, *Urban Legends Final Cut* is an intermittently entertaining but disposable slasher. One of the more intriguing aspects of its script, penned by two USC film-school graduates, is the portrayal of film-makers as, at various stages, suicidal, homicidal, embittered and obsessive-paranoid. Or, in the case of Amy: bright and promising but destined to end up churning out Hollywood schlock—a state of affairs that's easier to believe than any urban legend.

VILLAGE VOICE, 10/3/00, p. 232, Nick Rutigliano

Whatever else can be said of *Urban Legends: Final Cut*, you can't whine that they skimped on the cast: Not only is Rebecca Gayheart (you *know*, from *Urban Legend!*) back in a FULL CAMEO, but—brace yourselves kids—the chance to see JOEY LAWRENCE on the big screen has finally arrived! His humor value rests squarely on his past persona, a poignant reminder of when crap had the nerve to really be *crap*. Which, in turn, is not to say that *Final Cut* isn't shitty; it's simply less campily moronic than its predecessor, a tired kill-by-numbers. Hell, even the series' premise is barely kept afloat, low-tech kidney theft being the only UL on display that seems to have made the rounds off set (y'ever hear the one about the *real bodies* in the funhouse? Didn't think so.), though its gloomily streamlined vision of college remains intact. Thus, where earnest Ivy Leaguers once battled the evil dean, limply satirized film students now muss about top-notch sound stages, paving the way for lame nods to *Peeping Tom* and *Blair Witch*. *UL*'s security guard/Pam Grier disciple (Loretta Devine) adds a mote of continuity and awkward racial tension as she again saves various dumb white collegiate asses, and before long we're treated to no less than a triple cop-out wrap.

Also reviewed in:
CHICAGO TRIBUNE, 9/22/00, Friday/p. H, John Petrakis
NEW YORK TIMES, 9/22/00, p. E16, Dave Kehr
VARIETY, 9/25-10/1/00, p. 60, Robert Koehler
WASHINGTON POST, 9/22/00, Weekend/p. 47, Desson Howe

URBANIA

A Lions Gate Films presentation of a Commotion Pictures and Daly/Harris production. *Producer:* Stephanie Golden, J. Todd Harris, and Jon Shear. *Director:* Jon Shear. *Screenplay:* Jon Shear and Daniel Reitz. *Adapted from the play "Urban Folk Tales":* by: Daniel Reitz. *Director of Photography:* Shane Kelly. *Editor:* Randolph K. Bricker and Ed Marx. *Music:* Mark Anthony Thompson. *Casting:* Jordan Beswick. *Production Designer:* Karyl Newman. *Costumes:* David Matwijkow. *Running time:* 103 minutes. *MPAA Rating:* R.

CAST: Dan Futterman (Charlie); Alan Cumming (Brett); Matt Keeslar (Chris); Josh Hamilton (Matt); Lothaire Bluteau (Bill); Bill Sage (Chuck); Barbara Sukowa (Clara); Paige Turco (Cassandra); Megan Dodds (Deedee); Gabriel Olds (Ron); Samuel Ball (Dean).

LOS ANGELES TIMES, 9/15/00, Calendar/p. 6, Kevin Thomas

Jon Shear's "Urbania" is such a powerful experience that it is equally effective whether you have figured out from the start where it is headed or whether its denouement comes as a complete surprise.

Actor-turned-director Shear has reworked Daniel Reitz's play "Urban Folk Tales" into a daring and unnerving evocation of contemporary big-city life where sex and violence seem so frequently interlinked. It's a reminder of how illusory self-control over our destinies can be and also how transitory and fragile happiness and life itself are. These are of course timeless truisms, but Shear expresses them with such jolting freshness we find ourselves rediscovering them all over again.

"Urbania" represents a formidable directorial debut for Shear, who starred in the original stage production of "Angels in America" and appeared on Broadway in "Six Degrees of Separation."

Shear chose Dan Futterman, who replaced him in "Angels," to star as Charlie, a clearly successful young New Yorker. When we meet him he has undergone some kind of experience that has left him seriously traumatized yet determined to regain control of his life. His dislocated state of mind has left him with a heightened awareness of people absorbed in slaking desires for sex and romance but also existing in a constant state of danger in pursuit of them.

Shear plunges us into Charlie's fragmented and often terrified imagination. We soon sense that for whatever reason, someone Charlie cares for deeply is no longer in his life as he proceeds on a series of experiences over a short period of time that quickly take on the shape of a quest. Some 15 minutes into the film we discover that Charlie is gay, but by then we realize that his ordeal, in another context, could happen to anyone.

Suddenly, Charlie's eye is caught by a leather-jacketed type, the kind of guy who struts about, often accompanied by pals. He could be rough trade or just a sexy macho guy who knows his impact and flaunts it. One way or another, however, Dean (Samuel Ball) would seem to spell trouble for Charlie, determined as he is to chase him.

As Charlie's pursuit of Dean gets underway, "Urbania" draws from Reitz's other urban tales to round out Charlie's dicey sense of the universe. A kindly bartender (Josh Hamilton) relates to Charlie his story of his encounter with a formidable older woman (a sultry Barbara Sukowa), which leads to astonishing good fortune; a visit to a friend, Brett (Alan Cummings), afflicted with AIDS and whose friendship with Charlie seems as edgy as it affectionate; a showdown with his upstairs neighbor (Bill Stage) and his dimwit girlfriend (Megan Dodds) to whom it never occurred that flaunted heterosexuality could ever be carried to an offensive degree; and a less-than-thrilling tryst with a soap opera star (Gabriel Olds) with a lot of attitude and rules for Charlie to demolish.

There are glimpses of the man (Matt Keeslar) Charlie has loved and other asides: a homeless man (Lothaire Bluteau), who has a story about how he came to be mentally handicapped and a glimpse of a woman who decides to stick her beloved little dog, damp from rain, into a microwave to dry him. All these developments add to Charlie's heightened perception of the darkly bizarre.

In his own mind Charlie is turning himself into a Rambo until he arrives at a moment of truth that is boldly staged by Shear to incorporate a touching, redemptive sequence. Shear and cinematographer Shane Kelly have done a superlative job of discovering myriad ways of expressing visually all that Charlie is going through in his struggle to regain his equanimity.

Futterman, who has a starring role in the TV series "Judging Amy," in turn, registers all the changes and emotions Charlie is experiencing with conviction and empathy. Cummings lives up to the stir he first created as the emcee in the recent revival of "Cabaret." They make strong impressions as does Keeslar and, for that matter, everyone else in the film. "Urbania" manages to be quite candid—even blunt—about sex and desire and violence in the modern world, without being exploitative. Be warned, however, "Urbania" is strong stuff.

NEW YORK POST, 9/15/00, p. 54, Lou Lumenick

One rough way I use to gauge a movie is how many times I look at my wristwatch. This is one of those pictures where you can't take your eyes off the screen for even a second, as much as you might want to at times.

Actor John Shear's auspicious directing debut isn't for all tastes, to put it mildly, but those willing to take a harrowing walk in the netherworld of gay Greenwich Village will be rewarded by one of the year's best performances—by Dan Futterman.

Futterman, best known for the TV series "Judging Amy" and for playing Robin Williams' son in "The Birdcage," is in every scene of this dark, morbidly funny and quite violent movie, which plays with audience members' heads in ways many people will find quite disturbing.

He gives a tour de force as Charlie, a charming young gay man who's been traumatized by the death of his longtime partner (Matt Kesslar), the exact details of which are slowly revealed in a series of tantalizing flashbacks—until a "Sixth Sense"-style twist that dazzlingly challenges your understanding of much that came before.

During one long evening in Manhattan, Charlie pursues the elusive Dean (Samuel Ball), a menacing hunk who doesn't at all seem to share our hero's sexual predilections.

He also has telling encounters with a friendly bartender (Josh Hamilton); a soap opera actor (Randy Olds) who vehemently proclaims himself bisexual, despite considerable evidence to the contrary; a dying friend devoted to Glenda Jackson movies (Alan Cumming); a strange homeless man (Lothaire Bluteau); and Charlie's upstairs neighbors (Megan Dodds and Bill Sage), whose sexual exhibitionism he neatly puts down.

The acting is uniformly superb and often quite moving.

VILLAGE VOICE, 9/19/00, p. 120, Amy Taubin

Jon Shear's *Urbania,* adapted from Daniel Reitz's play, traffics almost exclusively in a single psychological state: anxiety. Shear wants to evoke that dreadful moment when, struggling to awake from a bad dream, you remember that your real life is more of a nightmare.

On another level, it's a film about storytelling, about the stories you tell yourself and everyone else to avoid dealing with what's really eating you up inside. The stories that preoccupy Charlie (Dan Futterman), the film's protagonist, are all urban legends: the dog exploding in the microwave; the prostitute who slips you a mickey in order to steal your kidney. Relayed through fantasy, dream, and flashback sequences, the stories camouflage the terrible event that has irrevocably changed Charlie's life, until, at a point that will differ for each viewer, it becomes clear that Charlie is gay and that he's lost his lover and that somehow violence is part of the picture.

Ambitious, if overly theatrical in its structure, the film puts a twist in noir by excavating the castration anxiety and homoeroticism that usually remain buried in the subtext. Shear suggests the hallucinatory quality of Charlie's experience by combining film and video in a way that heightens color contrast and destabilizes space. Striking cameos by Alan Cumming, Barbara Sukowa, and half a dozen others lift the burden of carrying the film from Futterman, whose lack of affect is not, I suspect, entirely attributable to playing a character suffering from post-traumatic stress. *Urbania* derails toward the end, becoming platitudinous, not to mention kitschy, but, given the Cheerios wholesomeness of most gay indies, its grief-stricken delirium is a welcome relief.

Also reviewed in:
CHICAGO TRIBUNE, 9/22/00, Friday/p. F, John Petrakis
NEW YORK TIMES, 9/15/00, p. E23, Stephen Holden
VARIETY, 2/14-20/00, p. 43, Emanuel Levy
WASHINGTON POST, 10/27/00, Weekend/p. 42, Desson Howe

VATEL

A Miramax Films release of a Legende Entreprises-Gaumont in association with Nomad/Timothy Burrill Productions Ltd./T.F.I. Films/Franco British co-production with the participation of Canal +. *Producer:* Alain Goldman and Roland Joffe. *Director:* Roland Joffe. *Screenplay:* Jeanne Labrune. *Screenplay (English Adaptation):* Tom Stoppard. *Director of Photography:* Robert Fraisse. *Editor:* Noelle Boisson. *Music:* Ennio Morricone. *Choreographer:* Corinne Devaux. *Sound:* Pawel Wdowczak, François Groult, Laurent Quaglio, and (music) Fabio Venturi. *Casting:* Gerard Moulevrier and Karen Lindsay-Stewart. *Production Designer:* Jean Rabasse. *Art Director:* Beatrice Chauvin. *Set Dresser:* Françoise Benoit-Fresco, Sabine Delouvrier, Eric Viellerobe, Julian Grisot, and Dominique Beaucamps. *Special Visual Effects:* Annie Dautane. *Costumes:* Yvonne Lassinot de Nesle. *Make-up:* Giannetto De Rossi and Mirella Sforza. *Stunt Coordinator:* Michel Carliez. *Running time:* 102 minutes. *MPAA Rating:* PG-13.

CAST: Gérard Depardieu (François Vatel); Uma Thurman (Anne de Montausier); Tim Roth (Marquis de Lauzun); Timothy Spall (Gourville); Julian Glover (Prince de Conde); Julian Sands (Louis XIV); Murray Lachlan Young (Philippe d'Orleans "Monsieur"); Hywel Bennett (Colbert); Richard Griffiths (Docter Bourdelot); Arielle Dombasle (Princess de Conde); Marine Delterme (Athenais de Montespan); Philiippine Leroy-Bealieu (Duchesse de

Longueville); Jerome Pradon (Marquis d'Effiat); Feodor Atkine (Alcalet); Nathalie Cerda (The Queen Marie Therese); Emilie Ohana (Louise de la Valliere); Sebastien Davis (Demaury); Natacha Koutchoumov (Louis de la Valliere's Maid); Nick Robinson (Colin); Patrick Saverioni (Rochefort); Julie-Anne Roth (Maidservant); Alain Stern (Sharp Equerry); James Thierree (Duc de Longueville); Geoffrey Bateman (Balmour); Nicholas Hawtrey (Lauzun's Secretary); Paul Brandey (Comte de Mirail); David Gablson (Creditor Guillaume); Louise Vincent (Woman Creditor); Andre Chaumeau (Monkey Handler); Jay Benedict (King's Commode Valet); Dominique Frot (Hysterical Woman); Leslie Clack (Whipping Courtier); David Houri (Vicomte d'Amboise); Christophe Prevost (Lantern Deliveryman); Ron Forfar (Melon Deliveryman); Albert Goldberg (Leviathan Worker); Vincent Grass (Martin's Father); Patty Hannock (Duchesse at the Banquet); Fiona Curzon (Woman at the Banquet); Adrian Pochna (Foot Servant); Jerome Duranteau (Cavalry Officer); Patrick Albenque (Soldier at Chateau Gate); Vincent Nemeth (Emissary); Edwin Apps (Fish Deliveryman); Helen Later (Servant with Flowers); Remi Roubakha (Cook); Kevin Greenlaw (Baritone); Joachim Serreau (Young Servant); Pia Lagrange (Duc d'Ambroise's Sister); Lionel Vitrant (Large Cook); Alexandre Chaussat (Cook's Apprentice); Louis Bustin (Martin); James Ney, William Hough, and Jess Gage (Colin's Friends).

LOS ANGELES TIMES, 12/25/00, Calendar/p. 6, Kevin Thomas

On April 10, 1671, according to the beginning of Roland Joffe's sumptuous yet scathing "Vatel," the Prince de Conde received a letter from a key aide to Louis XIV stating that the Sun King would accept an invitation for a visit to his estate, Chantilly—that "he wants no fuss, merely the simple pleasures of life in the country. In other words, if you value His Majesty's favor you will set no limit to the extravagance and ingenuity of the festivities."

As it happens, Conde (Julian Glover) is in dire need of Louis' favor, for his province in the west of France is on the verge of financial ruin. While he would have to go far deeper into debt to entertain Louis and his court in suitably grand fashion, he has in his master steward Francois Vatel (Gerard Depardieu) a man with the genius to pull it off.

A perfectionist, Vatel is not only a great chef with the ability to direct an enormous kitchen staff. He also is a superb designer of baroque spectacles replete with fireworks, mimes, dancers and special effects all the more awesome because they were staged two centuries before electric power and lights came into use. A nascent republican at heart, Vatel loathes the monarchy but worships Conde as a nobleman, an acclaimed general whose restoration to favor will be good for France.

Louis (Julian Sands), in turn, will need the leadership of Conde if he is to go through with his plan to invade Holland on the premise that "No King is safe from free thinkers." Conde is prepared to serve his country in battle, even though he is suffering severely from gout. Besides, he feels that fighting a war will be a piece of cake in comparison to entertaining the monarch for three days.

"Vatel" makes Conde emphatically believable. Vatel himself is like a general, marshaling an entire regiment of workers, peasants who slave away out of sight preparing and staging the exquisite meals and entertainments for Louis and his vast retinue.

Vatel is a juggler of infinite skill, resourcefully solving each and every crisis, but as his work proceeds and Louis et al arrive, "Vatel" moves from the virtual documentary to high drama.

In the royal party there is a ravishing newcomer, the regal Anne de Montausier (Uma Thurman). Not only has she caught the king's eye but also those of Vatel and the king's nasty aide the Marquis de Lauzon (Tim Roth). To the monarch and the marquis she is but a sexual conquest, but Vatel and Anne recognize the decency and honesty in each other, qualities in short supply in the rarefied world in which they move but in which they have no real status.

Vatel is middle-aged and stout, but it is wholly understandable that Anne would be attracted to him as a man of strength and character. As staunch as the relationship between Conde and Vatel is, both nobleman and his steward live in a world as precarious as that of Anne, who realistically remarks that she has no way of knowing whether she is merely a momentary diversion from the king's renowned favorite Athenais de Montespan (Marine Delterme) or whether she'll end up a duchess.

Everyone is subject to the whims of Louis, the most absolute of absolute rulers. From start to finish in "Vatel," beneath its veneer of utmost extravagance and elegance, seethes a bitter discontent that would erupt savagely into revolution some 120 years later.

In production design (by Jean Rabasse) and costume design (by Yvonne Lassinot de Nesle) "Vatel" is a landmark in world cinema not merely for sheer grandeur but also attention to dense authenticity. As superb as the settings are, Joffe and Tom Stoppard, in adapting Jeanne Labrune's original screenplay, do not let them overwhelm their people—although the scenery may crush them literally as well as symbolically.

Depardieu is perfectly cast as Vatel, an actual historic figure, at once a man of the people, a patriot and a true artist as well as an artisan of varied and highly developed skill. Thurman is equally fine as the gallant Anne, with Roth suitably nasty, Glover appropriately noble as Conde and Sands a delight as Louis, whom he plays as the shrewdest of fops. (On his best day Louis was never as handsome as Sands, but the actor hits just the right note of witty hauteur.) Arielle Dombasle is the lovely, fearless Princess de Conde. The evocative score is by none other than Ennio Morricone.

"Vatel" is arguably Joffe's strongest film since his 1984 debut feature "The Killing Fields," and significantly both deal with the terrible oppression of people living under despots.

Boldly distinctive in its depiction of individuals caught up in a veritable internal machine designed solely to give pleasure to a monarch, "Vatel" is a timeless tale of love and sacrifice in a world as opulent as it is cruel.

NEW YORK, 1/8/01, p. 49, Peter Rainer

Vatel, set in 1671 during a visit of King Louis XIV to a prince's country estate, looks as if it was made to win Oscars, though doubtless it won't cop many; it's too turgid with its own upholstered pomp. But Gérard Depardieu, as the prince's steward Vatel, is better than I've ever seen him in an English-language film: Readying the endless procession of royal ceremonies, dipping his worrying fingers into sauces, he is most convincingly a man for whom the spoils of life were created.

NEW YORK POST, 12/22/00, p. 53, Jonathan Foreman

"Vatel" is one of the most expensive French (but English-language) movies ever made and it certainly boasts handsome settings and authentic-looking 17th-century costumes.

Unfortunately, they aren't sufficient to keep your interest once you've given up caring about the skimpily sketched characters and their perfunctory relationships.

Worse, "Vatel' is even unsatisfying on a visual level: it's many sumptuous food shots look like they are photographed through filters coated in blue mold. And the music by Ennio Morricone relies heavily on the "Frere Jacques" theme.

In 1671, Louis XIV of France invites himself to stay for three days of elaborate partying at the estate of the bankrupt Prince de Conde (Julian Glover). If the visit is a success, the royal coffers will open and both Conde and his province will be saved from penury.

It all depends on Vatel (Gerard Depardieu), Conde's steward, whose task it is to design the various entertainment and to supervise the banquets for the royal entourage.

The King (Julian Sands) is bringing with him his wife, his latest mistress and several candidates for that position, including Anne de Montausier (Uma Thurman), a new lady-in-waiting.

Vatel is not just a genius with food and tableau vivants, he's also a saintly fellow who cares deeply for the plain folk who work for him. He's even willing to defy the King's gay brother, who wants one of Vatel's teenage kitchen boys for his bed.

Presumably, it's Vatel's combination of artistic talent and niceness that wins him the affection of Anne, in the face of competition from both the King and his smarmy lieutenant, Lauzon (Tim Roth, in his first wig-role since the much superior "Rob Roy").

Unfortunately, you don't believe in or care about Thurman' relationship with Vatel. She looks exotically good enough for the entire court to want to "take chocolate" with her at midnight, but she's given so little dialogue that when she starts emoting it comes out of left field.

Alone among the leads, Depardieu manages to give his character dignity and depth despite the shallowness of the screenplay (written by Jeanne Lebrune and adapted by Tom Stoppard).

Although "Vatel" is trying to say something about freedom and gilded cages, it feels more like a behind-the-scenes look at the high-end catering business.

NEWSDAY, 12/22/00, Part II/p. B14, Jan Stuart

Rural period epics have become almost an annual rite for Gerard Depardieu, whose bulbous face and porcine frame have generally seemed more sympathetic to a boar farm than a sleek tower office. As the eponymous "Vatel" in Roland Joffe's new film, he is the apotheosis of the Depardieu peasant, the uber-rustic whose native brilliance, charisma and resourcefulness make life a bowl of cherries for the royal court.

And you can be sure Vatel knows just where to get the best cherries. As the steward of the Prince de Conde (Julian Glover), Vatel runs the kitchen like the greatest chefs of Europe rolled into one, stages theatrical spectacles that would overwhelm Radio City Music Hall and makes a wax fruit centerpiece that Harry and David would swear is the real thing. If there is not enough meat for the stew or fireworks for Louis XIV's pleasure, get Vatel!

Which is precisely what the prince does when he needs to squeeze some serious francs out of King Louis (Julian Sands). Pushing Vatel's talents to the max, Conde hosts the king for a bacchanalia at his country estate. The weekend invitation brings out an entourage of hangers-on that includes a fair lady-in-waiting (Uma Thurman, doing her eye-batting Uma Thurman thing), an evil Marquis (Tim Roth, doing his snarling Tim Roth thing) and the king's predatory, homosexual brother (Murray Lachlan Young, doing a mincing homosexual thing that confirms all of "Dr." Laura's worst fears).

Vatel is the ultimate supernumerary, the unsung drudge who gets the job done. We all know such people, but Tom Stoppard's ponderous screenplay never makes it clear why we should care about Vatel until that old bugaboo—personal honor—creeps in at the 11th hour. Instead of drama, we get fabulously imagined theatrical orgies: pyrotechnics and trick sets and a deus ex machina flying overhead.

The film's greatest spectacle, however, is the vanity of the star. As he beds Thurman, Depardieu projects all the sex appeal of W.C. Fields playing Jean Valjean opposite Mae West in "Les Misrables," and yet we are to believe he has young men and women falling at his feet. "Vatel" is an improbable, if sumptuous, bore.

VILLAGE VOICE, 1/2/01, p. 101, Jessica Winter

Vatel's dudes, if nothing else, provide better sartorial eye candy. [The reference is to *Dude, Where's My Car*?]—Roland Joffés pithy Louis XIV chapter is crawling with tittering bewigged dandies draped in upholstery, not to mention Sun King Julian Sands (!) in a terrible wax-on Dali mustache. (Inveterate squeezer of nobles, Louis is introduced constipated on the pot.) As the titular master *cuisinier,* charged with preparing a massive three-day feast for the king, Gérard Depardieu manages an affecting performance against the likes of ambivalent lady-in-waiting Uma Thurman (striking High Baroque poses) and eye-rolling, tongue-lolling snake Tim Roth (in his outfit from *Rob Roy).* Vatel is drawn as an interloper across France's class chasm (the film switches nimbly between sickly greens for the bowels of Vatel's kitchen and nosebleed reds for high society), and Joffé intermittently shows an eye for grotesquely gorgeous spectacle. But he flits skittishly back and forth between blunt overkill (random magic-realist touches, lots of Uma-associated caged birds) and blandly tasteful restraint (a pivotal death barely registers) *Vatel* is dull and silly, but the holiday season doesn't offer a better sets-and-costumes workshop.

Also reviewed in:
NEW YORK TIMES, 12/25/00, p. E5, Elvis Mitchell
VARIETY, 5/15-21/00, p. 29, David Stratton

VENUS BEAUTY INSTITUTE

A Lot 47 Films release of an Agat Films & Cie/Gilles Sandoz presentation in co-production with Arte France Cinéma/Tabo Tabo Films.   Producer: Gilles Sandoz.   Director: Tonie Marshall. *Screenplay (French with English subtitles):* Tonie Marshall.   *Screenplay Collaborators:* Mario Vernoux and Jacques Audiard.   *Director of Photography:* Gérard de Battista.   *Editor:* Jacques Comets.   *Music:* Khalil Chahine.   *Sound:* Jean-Jacques Ferran and (music) Didier Lozahic and Philippe Laffont.   *Sound Editor:* Mathilde Muyard.   *Casting:* Bruno Levy.   *Art Director:* Michel Vandestien.   *Special Effects:* James Unger.   *Costumes:* Nathalie Duroscoat and Claire Gérard-Hirne.   *Make-up:* Françoise Andrejka Anastassios.   *Running time:* 105 minutes.   *MPAA Rating:* Not Rated.

CAST: Nathalie Baye (Angèle Piana);   Bulle Ogier (Nadine);   Samuel Le Bihan (Antoine Dumont);   Jacques Bonnaffé (Jacques); Mathilde Seigner (Samantha);   Audrey Tautou (Marie); Robert Hossein (M. Lachenay, the Pilot);   Edith Scob (Client with Spots on Her Hands);   Marie Rivère (Client in Fur Boots);   Hélène Fillières (Antoine's Fiancée);   Brigitte Roüan (Marianne); Lillian Rovère (Hair-Removal Client);   Claire Denis (Asthmatic Client);   Claire Nebout (Madame Buisse);   Elli Medeiros (Evelyne);   Gilbert Melki (Lover at Station);   Phillippe Harel and Patrick Pineau (Men at Self-Service Café);   Chantal Bronner (Elaine);   Sophie Grimaldi (Madame); Frédéric Andrëi (Last-Minute Client);   Micheline Presle (Aunt Maryse);   Emmanuele Riva (Aunt Lyda);   Catherine Hosmalin (Client with Sun Tan);   Florence Derive (Zizou);   Eric Petitjean and Rinaldo Rocco (Removal Men);   Martine Audrain (Angèle's Neighbor); Laurence Mercier (Madame Schmidt);   Michel Gauthier and Medhi de Lu (Waiters);   Joël Brisse (Joël, Friend from Poitiers);   Romain Goupil (Doctor Fremond);   Carole Deroo (Madame Pommerand);   Charles-Roger Bour (Pierre);   Nicholas Bomsel (Passer-by Asking for the Time); Michel Vandestien (Warehouse Owner);   Olivier Pace (Warehouse Worker);   Arnaud Dautzenberg (Cabinetmaker);   Vanda Benes (Waitress);   Alain Peyrollaz (Man on Platform); Cyril Arvenzag and Cedric Bruzac (Nadine's Sons).

CINEASTE, Vol. XXVI, No. 2, 2001, p. 44, Joan M. West

Puzzlement, impatience, and a certain unease may greet *Venus Beauty Institute* in its U.S. run, where audiences tend to prefer a 'point A to point B' kind of storytelling, with all the plot strings explained. This French film tends more towards a collage of individual moments. Furthermore, the heroine at first glance is anything but politically correct, and her erstwhile Prince Charming seems to have materialized from some lovelorn woman's dream rather than any identifiable reality. We must not forget, however, that this story takes place in Paris, city of light and magic, and that there is a woman writer-director at the helm. Viewers willing to suspend some of their preconceived notions of genre and character long enough to enter into this distinctive and largely feminine universe will discover why this refreshing little film blew away such competition as Luc Besson, Patrice Leconte, and Régis Wargnier, winning four Césars (Best Director, Best French Film, Best Screenplay, and Best Young Actress) last year from the French Film Academy.

Glowing pink and blue through the gloom of Parisian winter evenings just before Christmas, the Venus Beauty Institute and its quartet of beauticians attract an intriguing selection of clients, who are by turns realistic and fantastic, humorous and sad. The comings and goings of all these characters—signaled by a Tinkerbellesque little door chime—trace the boundaries and quality of Angèle Piana's existence.

Nathalie Baye's finely-nuanced performance as Angèle could not be more convincing. She is a 'woman of a certain age,' as the French so diplomatically phrase it, who wears the distress of love lived and lost on her sleeve. Inside the beauty institute of the film's title, she is a skilled and often-requested beautician who possesses a particular talent for listening sympathetically to her clients' stories, soothing away their tensions, and sending them back into the outside world, beautiful and refreshed once again. But after hours another personality emerges, messy and self-destructive. She appears incapable of helping herself in the way she helps others, and so lives an ugly double life, picking up men in cafeterias for one-night stands, because, as she tells a friend, she never again wishes to experience the frustration, jealousy, and pain of so-called mutual love. "Love is only another form of slavery; and in the end we all screw up and no one is happy." Such caustic observations are meant to mask Angèle's hurt; but, in fact, they do quite the opposite, and even hint where the source of her great sadness lies.

Had *Venus Beauty Institute* been construed within an entirely realist vein, we might have ended up in the same grim territory as, for example, *Looking for Mr. Goodbar*. Fortunately, director-screenwriter Tonie Marshall has a lighter touch and other ideas. One afternoon, during a coffee break at the cafe across the street and thus outside the protective cocoon of the salon, Antoine (portrayed intensely and earnestly by Samuel Le Bihan) appears. Younger by quite a bit than Angèle and a complete stranger to her, he announces, totally inexplicably, that he has fallen deeply in love with her to the point that he is abandoning his fiancée, even though he regrets the hurt this will cause. Disbelief and a touch of panic set in: she has become the pursued. This man is incredible, seemingly too good to be true, but also too sexy to be ignored. Besides, he persists in coming back, no matter what Angèle does to brush him off or disillusion him. Is this really Mr. Right? Can Angèle—like many of her compatriots and the film's director—come to believe that true love can strike like a lightning bolt from the blue? Is this emotionally wounded woman salvageable and curable? The film proceeds to straddle a delicate line between reality and fantasy without ever rigidly dividing the two.

Angèle's colleagues, variations on the film's central theme, embody various problematic relationships with men, emphasizing the loneliness one suffers when love is absent. Nadine (the incomparably perky Bulle Ogier) may be the successful owner of the salon, but she is still haunted by the problem of how to keep a man interested in her as age advances. Samantha (rising star Mathilde Seigner) is constantly changing boyfriends as soon as a more interesting prospect comes along; contrary to her tough-cookie exterior, she remains terribly alone and depressed. Marie (newcomer Audrey Tautou), gentle and sincere in her naivete, seems to be the only one to find a genuine, loving relationship with a much older man, much to the surprised disbelief of her colleagues.

The stream of clients who pass through the Venus Beauty Institute offer an extraordinary set of vignettes that range from realistic (a woman trying to choose a foundation color) to outrageous (Mme Buisse parading through the salon to the tanning booth naked and in full view of passersby in the street), from sad (the woman who would prefer her lover buy her warm boots and a winter coat rather than an expensive, weekly make-up job) to incredible (a man wanting a massage that includes the "finishing details"). For the viewer, these characters' visits (many of them bright little cameo appearances by recognizable actresses and a couple of well-known female directors) lend vitality, veracity, and occasional humor to life as portrayed within the rarefied space of the institute. For Angèle, however, these incidents with clients and the conversations she hears through the walls are only inconclusive, isolated bits of life, fleeting incidents without past or future. They add little more meaning to the quality of her pained existence than do the strings of Christmas lights, bright against the gray street outside her apartment window.

Marshall effectively utilizes the film's episodic structure to suggest her protagonist's disconnectedness from society; she is a woman so hurt in a past relationship that she has never found the courage to recommit, to 'grow up,' to accept life and its responsibilities. Indeed, Angèle constantly demurs: she ran away to Paris from a former life in the provinces; she refuses to advance in her profession, preferring to remain one of the 'girls'; she avoids emotional attachment to men; and she rebuffs Antoine, her golden chance of redemption. But this is a fable; and so, when we begin to see traces of the salon's warm peachy pinks and cool relaxing blues following Angèle home through the nighttime darkness, we begin to think that not all is lost.

The cast of this film is remarkable for the diversity of talents assembled. While the younger generation shines, it is the 'veterans' whose performances are most pleasurable to watch, in part because of the cinematic nostalgia they bring with them. Marshall was born into the cinema world, and by her own admission saw many movies when she was growing up. It is not too far-fetched, then, to believe that she was actually playing with some of her memories as she wrote her script. For example, Micheline Presle (the director's mother) and Emmanuele Riva create a delightful portrait of Angèle's sprightly spinster aunts, tucked away in the provinces, dreaming of imagined amorous conquests. How not to remember the one as a beautiful, romantic leading lady (who even worked in Hollywood), and the other as the distraught lover of Alain Resnais's

Hiroshima mon amour (1959)? And, in an evident homage to a character he played in the popular Angélique films of the 1960s, Marshall has Robert Hossein reprise the essence of that role from forty years ago in his portrayal now of the older gentleman who wins the heart of the youngest beautician. Such references to French cinematic memory add a note of elegy to *Venus Beauty Institute* that lightly underlines the theme of time passing.

Human beings' search for beauty and their efforts to arrest the effects of time can tend themselves all too easily to a satiric treatment. This is not the case in Marshall's film. Her approach to even the most potentially outlandish of the salon's clients—the woman dressed in a space suit, for instance—remains observant and nonjudgmental. This is especially true in regards to Angèle. The director refrains from criticizing her protagonist's behavior and instead makes it possible for us to observe and, especially, feel what her life is like. Marshall's essentially generous approach is particularly evident in the discretion with which she portrays Angèle's sexual encounters and the film's last sequence. She does not follow Angèle to the hotel with the man she's just picked up; nor does her camera allow us any close-up details when Angèle finally accepts Antoine as a lover. The couple is just two silhouettes filmed in chiaroscuro; and, exercising further discretion, the camera not only keeps its distance, it also does not stay with them very long. The point is not to illustrate Angèle's sex life, but rather to suggest the state of her psyche. At the end of the film, Marshall's camera moves us even further away—we watch the denouement from outside the salon, across the street, where only muffled voices can be distinguished. Seeing is enough. Words would only create an opportunity to criticize what these people are doing, and the moral this tale offers is a corrective lotion, not an indictment.

In the end, viewing *Venus Beauty Institute* may be rather like actually visiting a French beauty institute, where clients can receive both instruction in caring for beauty needs as well as actual beauty treatments: Marshall's cinematic fable acts as a restorative toner to our jaded, harried existence by inviting us into a special space outside our usual spheres. In this milieu we have the opportunity to observe the small bits of truth tucked away in the strange details of people's lives. And her fantasy-tinged view of reality offers assurance that, even though all things must pass—beauty and love in particular—and even if we've screwed up, we would be wrong to lose faith in the most powerful salve of all—love. A simple and beautiful reminder to women and men alike.

LOS ANGELES TIMES, 10/27/00, Calendar/p. 18, Kenneth Turan

While American filmmakers tend to fall back on violence and special effects if all else fails, French directors know that love is all there is. They understand that the dance of human attraction is a theme with infinite variations, that each time two people dive into those treacherous currents their story can be as new to us as it feels to them.

The enchanting "Venus Beauty Institute" tells just such a tale. The toast of last year's Cesars, the French Oscars, it took home awards for best picture, best director, best young actress and best screenplay and was a best actress contender as well for its star, the marvelous Nathalie Baye. A rueful examination of the comedy, the pain, the unexpectedness of love, this adult fairy tale may sound familiar, but the way it plays is not like that at all.

That's due to the deft and delicate touch of writer-director Tonie Marshall, the daughter of American actor-director William Marshall and French actress Micheline Presle (seen in a cameo as one of a pair of aunts.) With additional work from writers Mario Vernoux and Jacques Audiard, "Venus Beauty Institute" has more than an unexpectedly playful and pointed sense of humor, it has the gift of joining threads of sensuality, longing and anger to its comedy, tones not usually found sharing the same film.

Marshall wrote "Venus'" lead specifically for Baye, one of the great stars of modern French film, perhaps best known in this country for her role in "The Return of Martin Guerre." An alive and expressive actress, Baye uses the craft accumulated in a 50-plus feature career to turn Angele the beautician into one of her strongest performances. Sadness, anticipation, pity, fury, frankness, humor and love, all these emotions and more play across her face as Angele tries to cope with the choices life has given her.

With its hypnotic pink and blue pastel lights, harp-noted door chimes and piles of products like Serenity No-Blot and Aquaenzyme Facial, the Venus Beauty Institute, the Parisian salon where

Angele works, is almost as much of a character as the staff and the pampered, demanding clientele.

Owned by the regal Madame Nadine (an excellent Bulle Ogier, pretty much defining what's meant by a woman of a certain age), the institute is staffed by a trio of pink-smocked beauticians, as different as their uniforms are identical.

Samantha (Mathilde Seigner, Emmanuelle Seigner's sister) is a major coquette who likes to boast of having "sex ray vision." Marie (Cesar winner Audrey Tautou) is as young and naive as her braids indicate, but with a quality that attracts the attention of a widowed pilot (the veteran Robert Hossein). And then there is Angele, the oldest, the wisest and in some ways the saddest.

The institute's clients are also a various lot, and filmmaker Marshall has a graceful ability to amusingly characterize them without turning them into caricatures. We hear everyone's secrets, but it's the love lives of the beauticians we follow, and Angele's most of all.

She's 40, we hear Angele confessing to a lover at a train station just before we see what had been the briefest of relationships collapse in a welter of recriminations. Angry and tough though she can seem, there is a kind of aching desperation about Angele she won't acknowledge, a vulnerability she tries to pretend she doesn't have.

As "Venus" progresses, we learn more about this woman, about her reasons for preferring brief affairs and one-night stands (she calls them "flirts") to relationships, about what has led her to dismiss the possibility of lasting beauty in her own life. And so it might have remained, except for another man at the same train station cafe.

Seated at the table next to her, young and handsome Antoine (Samuel Le Bihan) is struck by a classic coup de foudre, failing instantly and savagely in love with Angele. He tracks her down to the salon, tells her of his passion, and then finds he has to deal with this woman's absolute contempt for love, her vehemently expressed feeling that it's simply "another form of slavery." Let the contest begin.

Though "Venus Beauty Institute" can sound schematic in outline, the combination of Baye's tour de force performance and Marshall's ability to convince us that this story has never been told quite this way before are a powerful combination. There is a sophistication about affairs of the heart, about the wisdom and the risks of romantic involvement that is more than quintessentially French. It's irresistible as well.

NEW YORK POST, 10/27/00, p. 47, Jonathan, Foreman

This slight but entertaining and occasionally touching film, mostly set at a Paris beauty salon, boasts some fine performances, in particular one by Nathalie Baye.

She plays the capable rock of the salon, whose personal life is a mess: she's a fortysomething single woman who talks too much and sleeps with lots of guys who then don't call her back.

Often funny about the absurd pseudo-medical world of skin care products, the film exudes that bracingly matter-of-fact French attitude to sex—especially between people of different generations.

SIGHT AND SOUND, 7/99, p. 56, Ginette Vincendeau

Angèle works in the Venus beauty salon run by Nadine, with two younger colleagues, naive Marie and cynical Samantha. Angèle is cool and professional during the day, but at night she picks up men in cafés and railway stations. Traumatised by the failure of her marriage, which ended by her shooting her husband Jacques, she believes love is an illusion and seeks only sex. But she is moved and disturbed by the unexpected relationship which unfolds between Marie and a much older customer, M. Lachenay, a pilot. Also, a young man named Antoine insistently pursues her, claiming he has fallen in love with her at first sight. Antoine's jealous girlfriend tries to shoot him and Angèle, but he deflects the shot and the film ends with Angèle and Antoine dancing in the salon.

With its salon's pastel blue and pink colour scheme, separated from the dreary real world by a music jingle that plays each time the door opens, *Venus Beauty* takes us into a feminine universe of massage, gossip and cosmetics. We are, however, far from the girlie fun of Susan Seidelman's *Desperately Seeking Susan* or Chantal Akerman's musical *Golden Eighties,* also set in a hairdressing salon. *Venus'* world of pampering is designed to highlight the characters' acute loneliness, melancholy and stress. A gallery of anxious female customers goes by, some funny, some tragic: a UV-tan freak, a narcissistic woman trying to erase the liver stains on her hands, a woman in increasingly outlandish costumes, another with disastrous make-up. The male characters hardly fare better: both protagonist Angèle's ex-husband and Marie's suitor Lachenay are disfigured, literalising the film's metaphor that everyone here is somehow scarred.

"Here, we only sell appearances," says Angèle. Yet *Venus Beauty* shows the recourse to cosmetics as neither demeaning as a first-wave feminist analysis would have had it, nor empowering as post-feminists would argue. As the boss Nadine, Bulle Ogier gives a superbly funny performance that captures the ambivalent tone of the film, her po-faced recitation of the virtues of this or that moisturising cream a masquerade. But when Samantha verbally attacks her, Nadine is not ridiculed—both women are given equal weight. Like many French women directors, Tonie Marshall makes films with clear lines of feminine interest, but without an obvious feminist angle—Angèle is certainly no positive role model. Humorous like Marshall's earlier (and funnier) *Pas très catholique*, *Venus Beauty* sharply observes how women are constantly subjected to the male gaze. Angèle's looks are repeatedly commented upon by men ("too thin," "lanky hair"). Her friend Marianne is devastated to find a book in which her partner has graded (out of 20) every woman he has had sex with. Marie Rivière's poor customer complains her rich lover buys her beauty treatments instead of shoes.

Upending the usual gender stereotypes, Angèle is cool and professional while Antoine cannot control himself either emotionally or physically when Angèle gives him a massage. Sexually active Angèle isn't seeking romantic attachment, but the film constantly undermines her. The first scene shows her humiliation by a two-bit macho type she's picked up, and it is precisely her vulnerability which attracts Antoine. So *Venus Beauty* constructs the unusual figure of a female sexual predator, only to characterise her as terminally melancholy. No joyful Parisian encounters around a *café-crème* here. As Marianne says, "You're the saddest girl I've ever met." Angèle talks to herself aloud on gloomy streets in a permanent winter. She has no ambition, isn't interested in politics or other people, and unrealistically tries to hang on to her youth by bizarrely washing her face in cold water on the landing. She ignores the advice of the more pragmatic Nadine, who tells her, "When you're not a girl any more, you'd better decide not to be a girl any more." A frustratingly short moment of warmth is provided by Angèle's visit to her aged aunts, played with great gusto and humour by former stars Emmanuele Riva and Micheline Presle (Marshall's mother), but the scene also pinpoints the difference between their fantasy of single life and Angèle's reality.

Throughout the 70s and 80s Nathalie Baye, with her graceful gestures and shy smile, developed the persona of the vulnerable yet determined woman, epitomised by her part in Bertrand Tavernier's *Une semaine de vacances*. In the 90s, her independent yet vulnerable image was used to great effect by such women directors as Diane Kurys in *La Baule-les Pins* and Nicole Garcia in *Un week-end sur deux*. *Venus Beauty*, like the Jeanne Labrune film *Si je t'aime, prends garde à toi* which also casts Baye as a sad sexual predator, seems to fix her further in a morose, masochistic mode.

Angèle's independence is made hollow since she gives in to Antoine at the end of his seduction campaign which many would regard as sexual harassment. Similarly, the scene in the pilot's house where he and Marie engage in an awkward erotic ritual is the only thing which turns Angèle on sexually. She may claim "reciprocated love does not exist" but contradictorily wishes for it. Personally I had hopes for the more robust Samantha until her promiscuity led her to a suicide attempt. *Venus Beauty* offers women phoney comfort (Nadine), fetishistic eroticism (Marie) and unfulfilling promiscuity (Angèle and Samantha). In this light, the provincial comfort of the aunts is positively attractive. As her direction of Ogier and Seigner shows, Marshall has a real talent for comedy. Let us hope she can leave the gloom of *Venus Beauty* and return to the zestful form evinced in *Pas très catholique*.

VILLAGE VOICE, 10/31/00, p. 170, Amy Taubin

Tonie Marshall's *Venus Beauty Institute* is a showcase for Nathalie Baye, who rode to stardom on a bicycle in Godard's 1979 *Every Man for Himself.*. Since then she has appeared in some 35 films, few worthy of her talent. Earlier this year, the deadly dull *An Affair of Love* blatantly exploited the desire of her audience to see how, at age 52, she was holding up as French cinema's most unselfconscious sex symbol.

The winner of four César awards, *Venus Beauty Institute* has a wittier, more finely tuned appreciation of Baye's appeal. First seen behind the plate glass windows of Venus Beauté, a small Paris day spa, she looks somewhat sad and wan, her hair hanging limply about the collar of her peach uniform. Baye plays Angèle, a beautician who's at least 20 years older than her coworkers. Her employer, Madame Nadine (Bulle Ogier), makes a comfortable living by convincing women that facials and dye jobs are a duty rather than an indulgence. She's perplexed that Angèle doesn't want to follow in her footsteps by opening a salon of her own. But Angèle is leery of growing up and settling down in both her professional and private life.

Once wounded in a love affair—the extravagant details of which are kept secret for most of the film—Angèle now limits herself to sexual flings that give her a sense of control, but almost inevitably result in humiliation. *Venus Beauty Institute* opens with a deftly written scene: Angèle and the pudgy suburbanite with whom she's spent the weekend are in a railroad station café. She puts herself in a vulnerable position by asking to see him again; he uses the opening to brush her off with utmost cruelty. As he piles on the insults about her "flat ass" and her "vulgar aggression," her hurt turns to anger. "This is a democracy, I have equal rights!" she yells as she follows him to his train. "You dump me, I stalk you."

This encounter has been observed by Antoine (Samuel Le Bihan), an attractive, bearish-looking man who's instantly smitten with Angèle—and wants to rescue her from this bully. (Marshall frames the scene as a triangle with Antoine watching Angèle over the other man's shoulder, to emphasize the oedipal underpinnings of his feelings.) Antoine fixates on Angèle as the love of his life and breaks up with his gorgeous 20-year-old fiancée. His protective impulse mirrors what the audience feels for Angèle and for Baye. Decorated in sherbet colors that change from pink to blue with the flick of a light switch, the salon is like a miniature movie set. We want our heroine to escape its confines even though we have no idea where she can go next.

Thanks to some brilliant casting, *Venus Beauty Institute* provokes ideas about women, movies, sexuality, and age that extend beyond its frothy fiction. At least during the first hour, the film thrives on the hilarious girl talk and cameo appearances by such luminaries as Claire Denis, Edith Scob, and especially Robert Hossein as a scarred pilot, who comes to Venus Beauté to preserve the skin that was grafted from his wife's thighs onto his face. Much to Angèle's dismay, the pilot, now widowed, becomes enamored of Marie, the youngest beautician (Audrey Tautou). Angèle enlists Antoine's help in rescuing Marie from the clutches of this much older man. Spying on the lovers, who despite their age difference are well matched, Angèle is sufficiently turned on to forget, for a brief moment, her misgivings about Antoine. Once they begin groping each other, the movie loses both subtlety and momentum, and its bittersweet tone quickly shades into melodrama. Despite the pressure of the box office, movie sex is often better kept in the head.

Also reviewed in:
CHICAGO TRIBUNE, 11/17/00, Friday/p. P, Michael Wilmington
NEW YORK TIMES, 10/27/00, p. E22, A. O. Scott
VARIETY, 2/8-14/99, p. 76, Lisa Nesselson
WASHINGTON POST, 11/22/00, p. C9, Stephen Hunter

VERTICAL LIMIT

A Columbia Pictures release. *Executive Producer:* Marcia Nasatir. *Producer:* Lloyd Phillips, Robert King, and Martin Campbell. *Director:* Martin Campbell. *Screenplay:* Robert King, and Terry Hayes. *Story:* Robert King. *Director of Photography:* David Tattersall. *Editor:* Thom Noble. *Music:* James Newton Howard. *Music Editor:* Jim Weidman, David Olson, and Richard Bernstein. *Sound:* Kathleen "Pud" Cusack and (music) Shawn Murphy. *Sound Editor:* Dave McMoyler. *Casting:* Pam Dixon Mickelson. *Production Designer:* Jon Bunker. *Art Director:* Kim Sinclair, Jill Cormack, and Nick Bassett. *Set Decorator:* Bernhard Henrich. *Set Dresser:* Brad Mill. *Special Effects:* Neil Corbould. *Costumes:* Graciela Mazon. *Make-up:* Nikki

Gooley. *Prosthetics Make-up:* Bob McCarron.   *Stunt Coordinator:* Simon Crane.   *Running time:* 110 minutes.   *MPAA Rating:* PG-13.

CAST: Chris O'Donnell (Peter Garrett); Robin Tunney (Annie Garrett); Stuart Wilson (Royce Garrett); Tom Struthers and Leos Stransky (Grunge Climbers); Augie Davis (Aziz); Temuera Morrison (Major Rasul); Bruce Kingan (Rasul Flying Double); Roshan Seth (Colonel Amir Salim); Alejandro Valdes-Rochin (Sergeant Asim); Nicholas Lea (Tom McLaren); Rod Brown (Ali Hasan); Scott Glenn (Montgomery Wick); Steve Le Marquand (Cyril Bench); Ben Mendelsohn (Malcolm Bench): Izabella Scorupco (Monique Aubertina); Bill Paxton (Elliot Vaughn); Ed Viesturs (Himself); Robert Taylor (Skip Taylor); Alexander Siddig (Kareem Nazir) Clinton Beavan (WNN Camerman); David Hayman (Frank "Chainsaw" Williams); Robert Mammone (Brian Maki); Nicole Whippy (Spanish Climber); Tiffany De Castro (Crying Woman); Campbell Cooley ("Campbell"); Alistair Browning ("Ali"); Jo Davidson (Italian Team Member); Tamati Rice, Sally Spencer Harris, and Craig Walsh Wrightson (Party Goers); Leela Patel (Mayama Wick): Gavin Craig (Summit Air Pilot); Shahid Zafar (Prayer Leader).

CHRISTIAN SCIENCE MONITOR, 12/15/00, p. 15, David Sterritt

Action and adventure are staples of movie entertainment, but they take dtfferent forms in different parts of the world. Two of this season's most eagerly anticipated films—"Vertical Limit" and "Crouching Tiger, Hidden Dragon"—illustrate some of the contrasts between action-movie styles in the East and West.

A look at their approaches to wide-screen spectacle says much about current interests in everything from media violence to the role of women in traditionally male genres. A look at their box-office performance—which should become clear in the next week—will say even more about what American moviegoers are expecting for the price of a ticket.

"Vertical Limit," directed by Martin Campbell, is a textbook example of the traditional Hollywood epic—big, boisterous, full of heroic sentiments, and populated with cardboard-thin characters. The most interesting character isn't a person at all, but a mountain: the famous K2, second to Everest in height and to no place for daunting danger.

After an opening scene of high-intensity suspense—a routine climb turns disastrous, forcing members of a loving family to make life-or-death decisions in an instant—the movie clambers into its main story, about a K2 expedition by a mix of mountaineering professionals and less-experienced adventurers.

Their trek goes sour when an overambitious climber tries for the summit as a storm approaches. This leads to a worse-case scenario that only Hollywood could dream up. Three climbers are trapped in a snow-bound cave. One is seriously ill, another is gravely injured, and the third is a creep who can't be trusted. The only person who can rescue them is the ill woman's brother, who swore off mountaineering after the calamity we saw in the opening scene.

The key to enjoying "Vertical Limit" is to understand that it's only pretending to tell a coherent story. Its real agenda is to jolt us with thrills and spills as frequently as possible, escalating its shock value without worrying whether the shocks make sense. Great care is taken with the visual effects, lending postcard-clear realism to the icy environment. But what happens there becomes more unbelievable, as characters scurry along treacherous trails and leap from peak to crag with the weightless dexterity of characters in a Disney cartoon.

See it if two hours of cinematic surprises are all you're looking for. Skip it if your recipe, for a meaningful movie includes token attention to psychology, credibility, and common sense.

"Crouching Tiger, Hidden Dragon," directed by Taiwanese-American filmmaker Ang Lee, also takes great liberties with traditional realism, but it has a good reason. As the title hints, it's less a naturalistic drama than an extravagant fable that uses action and violence to explore themes of bravery, honesty, loyalty, and the tensions between romance and reality in human affairs. While it has just as much action as "Vertical Limit," it doesn't try to fool us with claims of resemblance to the world we actually live in.

The plot centers on a martial-arts warrior who's tired of fighting; an old friend who agrees to help him retire by delivering his sword to a revered master; a young woman who's itching to enter their world of exotic adventure; and a rascally bandit who becomes her unlikely lover.

Early on, the story focuses on unhurried dialogue and character development. When action takes over, it's as stylized and choreographed as a ballet. People leap over walls, fly through the air, and trade sword-blows while perched in the branches of leafy trees. It's as realistic as a dream more mainstream projects like "Sense and Sensibility" and "The Ice Storm." which gathered large audiences even if they didn't carry the same emotional charge.

His temperament has seemed so literary that many observers thought he was joking about his longtime interest in the martial-arts genre. But he wasn't, and while "Crouching Tiger, Hidden Dragon" (in Mandarin with English subtitles) isn't as engrossing as his very best films, it combines his innate thoughtfulness with the long-standing conventions of this hyperactive movie tradition.

This blend of intelligence and action may be the film's most impressive trait, but it could also cause problems at the ticket window. The film is being marketed as a breakthrough picture with solid appeal to audiences of every kind: youngsters looking for action, adult men interested in absorbing dialogue, and women who'll appreciate Lee's liking for strong female characters.

This strategy may work—but if it fails, the film's own sophistication may be to blame. Will action-hungry youngsters put up with all that on-screen conversation? Will women sit through long martial-arts scenes just because female characters swing some of the swords? Will older folks embrace Lee's brand of mythic fantasy as readily as the cartoonish craziness of "Vertical Limit"?

"Vertical Limit" has premiered with a much larger bang, thanks to the ability of Columbia Pictures to open it in a huge number of malls and multiplexes.

"Crouching Tiger, Hidden Dragon" started to build momentum on the film-festival circuit, but even optimists expect it to acquire a mass audience at a somewhat slower pace. While the comparative success of these contrasting films won't give definitive answers as to the state of today's culture, their popularity—or lack of it—will be a revealing sign of what American audiences are looking for at the movies.

LOS ANGELES TIMES, 12/8/00, Calendar/p. 1, Kenneth Turan

A man's face fills the screen. His eyes expand in terror, his mouth opens double-wide, he screams "AVALANCHE" as if the fate of nations hung on the word. You can run, you can hide, but ready or not, "Vertical Limit" is that kind of a movie.

In theory, these high-octane extravaganzas, old-fashioned in form but bristling with up-to-the-minute special-effects technology, should be business as usual for Hollywood. In reality, making a success of high-altitude heroics is something of a lost art. Which is why getting Martin Campbell to do the directing was the right idea.

After a career largely spent doing TV miniseries in Britain, with the occasional feature thrown in, Campbell revealed an unusual gift for revitalizing traditional genre material, making films like the James Bond "GoldenEye" and "The Mask of Zorro" more crisp and exciting than anyone else could manage.

Yet Campbell's strengths are almost offset by flaws that would have hamstrung a less confident and exciting film than "Vertical Limit." The Robert King and Terry Hayes screenplay (inspired in part by the same Mt. Everest tragedy Jon Krakauer detailed in "Into Thin Air") is weighted down with fly-weight dialogue and weak characterization, dilemmas that are not helped by problematic casting and lack of a true star performance. Still, for a film with action sequences that can wind us up the way "Vertical Limit" does when the moment is right, an awful lot of trespasses can be forgiven.

Though he's personally afraid of heights, Campbell has turned out nail-biting moments of mountaintop peril, crackle and pop. While a good deal of "Vertical Limit" is undeniably by the numbers, it has become increasingly rare to see those digits whipped into this kind of shape.

The film's thrills start with its prologue introducing the brother-and-sister climbing team of Peter and Annie Garrett (Chris O'Donnell and Robin Tunney) taking their ease on a sheer rock face high above the Utah desert. That sense of calm is illusory, however, for something happens on that Godforsaken cliff that makes the next Peter and Annie meeting awkward and strained.

That would be three years later in Pakistan, at the foot of the Himalayas. Peter is now a National Geographic photographer (an excuse for some nice scenes of snow leopards at play) while sister Annie has progressed into a purposeful climber who's just completed a speedy ascent of the Eiger.

Peter finds himself sharing base camp space with a massive expedition put together by Elliot Vaughn (an effective Bill Paxton), a wealthy Texas entrepreneur with more money than sense who wants to tempt fate by climbing the notoriously temperamental K2 on a deadline as part of a publicity stunt for a new airline he's starting. Sister Annie turns out to be one of the climbers on Elliot's crack team.

It will surprise no one to learn that Elliot and friends get into trouble on the climb, big trouble. It's madness to even think of rescuing them, let alone actually try, but brother Peter, one of several people with unfinished business to settle on the mountain (not the best place for it), can't be dissuaded. Off he goes with a motley crew, including a gorgeous French Canadian medic (Izabella Scorupco) whose makeup stays fresh in gale-force conditions. And Montgomery Wick.

Just as there would be no hope for a rescue attempt without the legendary Wick, the climber's climber, so there would be much less of a film without Scott Glenn's perfectly pitched performance as the mysterious loner who knows more about K2 than any man living or dead.

Glenn not only has the ideal face for the part, as rugged and lined as a contour map of the Texas hill country, but he also completely understands the demands of playing a ghost-like Rip Van Winkle who's part force of nature, part mystical seer. And his sense of the let-'er-rip spirit of the proceedings is impeccable.

Other characters are less successfully handled. The comic-relief characters of a pair of Australian stoner brothers turn out to be neither comic nor a relief. And star O'Donnell, though a capable enough actor, feels miscast. He's too puppyish and lacks the weight of personality to be as forceful as the script demands or to add the charisma that Catherine Zeta-Jones and Pierce Brosnan provided in Campbell's last two films.

Not that "Vertical Limit" lacks the resources to mount a counterattack. These include a pounding score by James Newton Howard, relentless editing by Oscar winner Thom Noble and photography by David Tattersall that makes the film's combination of effects shots and location photography (New Zealand's Mt. Cook sits in for K2) look completely real.

As crisis follows crisis on the mountain, with people falling into crevices and dangling off cliffs left and right, this is one locale whose thrills turn out to be as merciless as its weather.

NEW YORK POST, 12/8/00, p. 55, Jonathan Foreman

One of the most thrilling—and authentic—mountain-climbing films in recent memory, "Vertical Limit" boasts a fine series of gut-wrenching, high-altitude thrills.

Unfortunately, it's also burdened by one of those every-line-a-wretched-cliché Hollywood screenplays (credited to Robert King and Terry Hayes).

The movie begins with a terrifying, fatal accident as siblings Peter (Chris O'Donnell, disappointingly bland here) and Annie Garrett (Robin Tunney from "End of Days") are climbing a sandstone tower with their father.

Four years later, we find that Peter has given up climbing to become a nature photographer in the high Himalayas, while Annie has become one of the world's top female mountaineers. Brother and sister are estranged, but they meet again when Peter comes back from a photo expedition and visits the base camp of K2, the world's second-highest—and most dangerous— mountain.

Annie is there to take part in a summit attempt by billionaire airline owner Elliot Vaughn (Bill Paxton), who plans to arrive at the top just as one of his planes flies by.

In theory, the expedition is led by top climber Tom McLaren (Nicholas Lea), but when bad weather is sighted, Vaughn overrules McLaren and insists the team continue the climb into the "death zone" above 26,000 feet, where a human being can survive for 36 hours at most. When the storm hits, Vaughn, Annie and Tom crash down into a crevasse that is soon sealed by an avalanche. Down at K2 base camp, Peter immediately starts to organize a rescue mission, recruiting a motley band of adventurers, including Monique (Swedish actress Izabella Scorupco), a gorgeous mountain nurse; Kareem (Alexander Siddig from "Star Trek—Deep Space Nine"), a Pakistani guide; and Montgomery Wick (Scott Glenn), a grizzled, stringy-haired Buddhist recluse who was once a friend of Peter's father.

The rescue mission is a race against time as well as the elements, although the writers laid on an extra obstacle in the utterly absurd form of a super-unstable high explosive: Peter has the team carry up canisters of nitroglycerin to blast out the trapped climbers.

Unlike Stallone in "Cliffhanger," the actors here all look like climbers, especially Tunney and Glenn. You can see that it really is Tunney hanging over a deep chasm and Glenn hacking his way up an ice cliff. And they struggle gamely against the script's atrocious dialogue in an attempt to bring their one-note characters to life. Glenn, unsurprisingly, enjoys the most success.

Director Martin Campbell does a perfunctory job with what are supposed to be the film's "emotional" moments (the over-the-top score by James Newton Howard only makes them feel emptier), but shows an even better and more inventive command of action here than he did in "Goldeneye" and "The Mask of Zorro." Taut editing helps.

There are cameos by famed climber Ed Viesturs and the fine Indian actor Roshan Seth, who plays a Pakistani colonel. Significantly, this is the first Western movie to depict, even as backdrop, the simmering war between India and Pakistan over Kashmir.

NEWSDAY, 12/8/00, Part II/p. B9, Gene Seymour

The Marquis De Sade can be found in another movie, "Quills," that's part of a whole different neighborhood, figuratively speaking, from "Vertical Limit." But if you have an appetite for the kind of sadomasochism of which only Hollywood at its most crass is capable, this extravagantly staged popcorn thriller will give you everything you can handle.

It isn't enough, after all, that "Vertical Limit's" relentless shots of frightened people hanging from high places (and, more often than not, falling off) are enough to make you leery of stepping off a curb for weeks. Nor is it enough that its extensive sequences of frigid people straining and wheezing their way through icy winds can make your lungs feel as if they're being stir-fried.

No, it's the insistence of director Martin Campbell and others to pile on calamities like used towels in a football game. How many times, to take one example, can a helicopter almost crash because of high winds and klutzy mountaineers? Another example: One avalanche eating human beings alive is impressive, even entertaining; two is cheesy.

And speaking of the plot: It involves a lantern-jawed climbing ace (Chris O'Donnell) who's been spooked away from the game after an accident kills his father—an accident for which he, of course, Feels Responsible. His kid sister (Robin Tunney) presses on, agreeing to help a smarmy Texas billionaire (Bill Paxton) lead a team up K2 to publicize his new airline. Needless to say, this Richard Branson wannabe is responsible for getting himself, the sister and another mountaineer trapped in a cavern at 26,000 feet with—aw, you guessed!—limited supplies and more bad weather on the way.

Not wanting another dead relative on his conscience, O'Donnell's hero organizes a— what else?—motley rescue team led by a once-prominent climber (Scott Glenn) who's now a long-haired hermit, embittered by the death of his wife and others during a previous K2 assault led by Mister Moneybags. Uh-oh! Doodly-doodly-doo-doo-doooooo.

Maybe it's asking too much of a thrill machine like "Vertical Limit" to lay off the cardboard characterizations and overripe cliches. But Campbell all but forgets to add the ingratiating good spirits and sly sense of fun that were evident in "The Mask of Zorro"—his earlier film that was also steeped in grand stunts and old-fashioned melodrama. The only traces of whimsy come from a couple of Australian retro-hippies assisting the rescue; some sardonic Pakistani soldiers who shake their heads at the silly, reckless western infidels, and Glenn himself, getting the best showcase he's had in years for his edgy, cool persona.

NEWSWEEK, 12/11/00, p. 74, David Ansen

There is one reason, and only one, for anyone to check out "Vertical Limit." The hanging-by-a-fingernail mountain-climbing sequences are spectacular. The cliffhanger is such a primal movie experience that it can turn the most sophisticated moviegoer into a writhing 12-year-old, and director Martin Campbell, stunt coordinator Simon Crane and the special-effects crew serve up several lulus. Perhaps the best comes first: a stunning prologue on the sheer-face of a Utah mountain, where brother and sister Peter and Annie Garrett (Chris O'Donnell and Robin Tunney) and their father (Stuart Wilson) find themselves dangling over the void suspended by a single fraying rope, facing a sacrificial Sophie's-like choice that, of course, will haunt the survivors for the rest of the movie. Bye, Dad.

You could leave after this opening sequence and almost feel you'd gotten your money's worth. That way you'd be spared the many risible moments that occur, with dismaying regularity, whenever there isn't an avalanche, nitroglycerin explosion, terrifying fall or other climbing catastrophe to interrupt the otherwise ludicrous story and the crummy dialogue.

Knee deep in clichés, writers Robert King and Terry Hayes send Annie up K2, the world's second highest mountain, with an arrogant billionaire (Bill Paxton) and a reluctant guide (Nicholas Lea). Of course they are trapped by an avalanche in a cavern, and given only 36 hours to live unless brother Peter and his motley team of rescuers can reach them in time. This unlikely crew includes Scott Glenn as a wizened loner with a dark agenda, a woman who would appear more at home on a fashion runway (Izabella Scorupco) and two Aussie stoners (Ben Mendelsohn and Steve Le Marquand), who look as if they could barely ascend a stairway.

"Vertical Limit" produces a decidedly split reaction in an audience. You gasp at the action sequences, then giggle at the drama, then gasp, then giggle until finally the filmmakers pile on one cliffhanger too many. By that point, the gasps have become muted by sheer disbelief.

Early on, at the base camp in Pakistan, where the international climbing crowd assembles and the air is filled with pot, hormones, beer and bravado, you get a brief taste of the movie that might have been. This is a scene we'd like to see the filmmakers explore, but any connection to the real world is quickly jettisoned for the hoariest tropes in the action-movie lexicon. Alternately generating adrenaline and ennui, "Vertical Limit" battles itself to a hard-earned draw.

SIGHT AND SOUND, 2/01, p. 56, Mark Sinker

Monument Valley, four years ago. Climbing with his children Peter and Annie, Royce Garrett is knocked from the face. At Royce's behest, Peter cuts the rope, Royce falls to his death.

Pakistan, the present. Annie is to climb K2 with millionaire Elliot Vaughn's expedition, intended to publicise his new airline. Peter, now a photographer, discovers that Vaughn's back-up team are suppressing storm warnings. He tells climb leader Tom McLaren, but Vaughn bullies McLaren into continuing. An avalanche hits: Vaughn, Annie and the injured McLaren are trapped in a crevasse. Carrying nitro-glycerine, Peter sets out to rescue them. In the crevasse, Vaughn insists they ration medication. Montgomery Wick, a maverick climber looking for the body of his wife lost during Vaughn's previous K2 attempt, splits the rescue team into three pairs. Two pairs are caught in successive nitro-glycerine blasts; nurse Monique survives, rejoining Peter and Wick. Annie finds extra medication in a half-buried backpack. Vaughn murders McLaren. Monique discovers Wick's wife's body. Wick reveals that he knows Vaughn murdered his wife. Annie calls Peter on the walkie-talkie, forgives him for Royce's death, and asks him to turn back and save himself. He presses on with Monique. The nitro works, but they can't haul Annie to safety. Wick arrives and helps. Wicks cuts the rope he and Vaughn dangle on. Only Peter, Monique and Annie get off the mountain.

In 1996 Ed Viesturs rescued wealthy Texan amateur mountaineer Beck Weathers from a storm on Everest. Rob Hall, trapped higher on the killing slopes with another paying tyro, died. A hopelessly bogus mountain movie action thriller, *Vertical Limit* boasts a laconic Viesturs cameo. It also evokes his fellow climber Hall's death when one of its fictional characters—in an act of courageous selflessness—proposes precisely that reckless, unfeasible peaks rescue that Viesturs appropriately rejected when faced with news that Hall was stranded further up on Everest.

A big-budget film that cannibalises real-life tragedy is hardly in the position to preach about how money can distort values. How will those acquainted with the events on Everest in 1996 react to *Vertical Limit?* More astounding even than the backdrops are the gusts of clumsy exposition, the blizzards of product placement, the ice storms of hypocritical yet pinheaded moralising about behaviour above the clouds— none of which makes it likely Martin Campbell's film will be praised for its sensitive reworking of its true life material.

The mountain movie reached its zenith in 1932, with director-star Leni Riefenstahl's breathtakingly goofy *Blue Light*. Since then, the genre has remained seriously under-populated. They may strive for the sublime—the heights, the perils, the sheer unbiddability of the rock, ice and tempest that define the elemental thrill of the climb—but most mountain movies tend to collapse towards implausible, fatuous drama. *Vertical Limits* visual thrills are OK by action-movie standards: five explosions, two avalanches, one (poorly staged) helicopter rotor-blade flesh-rip threat and so on. But narrative tension—which is where the action movie can best subvert its clichés—is clumsily borrowed at best. Screenwriters Robert King and Terry Hayes attempt to fuse the guessing-game format of *Ten Little Indians* with the sweaty tension of *The Wages of Fear*. as the rescue team carries nitro up hazardous cliffs, the main source of amusement is taking bets on who will die first—will it be the angelic native porter, the loutish Australians, the sullen French-Canadian blonde or the Grizzled Old Man of the Mountain?

King and Hayes have even less fun with the plot mechanics which put these stock figures in the way of such loud comedy danger. They've frantically avoided giving a sexual dimension to the motives behind the rescue attempt: here, lead character Peter risks his life to save Annie, his sister rather than a love interest. In Riefenstahl's heyday, the tack was of course extreme sublimation, with homoerotic subcurrents which probably somewhat mirrored the unexamined motivations of the climbers themselves, for whom extreme exploration was always a form of self-imposed celibacy. Try being this unexamined in the 21st century, as wised-up to the sexual unconscious as it is to genre conventions, and you'll find the audience hooting with laughter or snoring.

Where sexual tension drives so many Hollywood action movies, here the characters have to make do with mumbled pieties for motivation: Peter and Annie lay claim to a mutual sense of loyalty and anger that stems from their failure to save their father Royce's life during a climbing accident some years ago. The premise prompts some intriguing questions—why do climbers risk their lives, and how is this meant to be read by their loved ones back home? But the device just doesn't work: brother and sister might care about each other via their shared love for their dad, but we sure don't. Royce's pre-credit death is one of a dozen; he is only slightly more developed than the five unnamed bodies slung about for texture—and he's less developed than those whose deaths are staged as pure slapstick. Of course, when the McGuffins swarm, the grown-up response is to suck back every ignorant pleasure, imagine all the brilliant gags the film-makers forgot to include, and enjoy resenting the money they were paid to forget them. But sometimes maturity is the hardest climb of all.

TIME, 12/11/00, p. 103, Richard Schickel

It starts out great: a Father and his two grown children, Peter (Chris O'Donnell) and Annie (Robin Tunney), are on a practice climb in what appears to be Monument Valley. An accident occurs, and the three of them are dangling from a rope that can only hold two. Someone has to be cut loose. This turns out to be the father, and it is his son who wields the knife that sends him into deadly free fall.

All right, the sequence is a cliché. But it is well executed by director Martin Campbell *(The Mask of Zorro)*. Thereafter, though, *Vertical Limit* consists mainly of variations on a theme. If your tolerance for seeing lots of people hanging by their fingertips from icy cliffs is high, you may enjoy the film. On the other hand, when its principals are not so engaged, they are talking through painfully obvious moral dilemmas stated with laughable earnestness in the overwrought script by Robert King and Terry Hayes.

Peter, rather sensibly, quits climbing and takes up nature photography. Annie, however, joins forces with an egomaniacal mogul (Bill Paxton) for an assault on K2, said to be the world's toughest mountain to master. His inner skankiness comes out when they fall into a snow cave and have to be rescued before succumbing to altitude sickness.

Guess whose brother just happens to be in the Himalayan neighborhood, eager to save the sister who has not forgiven him for Dad's death? Now try to guess why Scott Glenn signed on to play the shaggy, half-mad old man of the mountains honchoing the rescue. It is the year's most ludicrous character part in what is likely the year's most ludicrous action movie.

VILLAGE VOICE, 12/19/00, p. 150, Michael Atkinson

However seductive the pulp-cinematic mechanics of mountain-climbing misadventures might be, it's a genre that really has only one destination (down) and one pace (glacial). Revisiting Davey-fell-in-the-well territory, Martin Campbell's movie focuses on Bill Paxton and Robin Tunney—as a smug billionaire and a climbing expert, respectively—trapped in an ice cavern (though their breath is never visible) on K2 as Tunney's bro Chris O'Donnell and renegade climbing savage Scott Glenn struggle to reach them before pulmonary edema kicks in. (The words "pulmonary edema" are repeated as many times as "pipe dreams" in *The Iceman Cometh.)* Since the trip up is littered with idylls and chitchat, there's no sense of urgency, and the script is Barney-simple (someone explains Morse code to other climbers), but *Vertical Limit*'s real problem is its digitized sheen. Every shot seems to have been CGI-enhanced, so the movie has an over-pasteurized, Velveeta-like glow-processed movie food. The stunts have all the tension of bungee-tied rock climbing in Times Square.

Also reviewed in:
CHICAGO TRIBUNE, 4/14/00, Friday/p. I, John Petrakis
NEW YORK TIMES, 12/8/00, p. E16, Elvis Mitchell
VARIETY, 12/4-10/00, p. 21, Todd McCarthy
WASHINGTON POST, 12/8/00, p. C2, Rita Kempley
WASHINGTON POST, 12/8/00, Weekend/p. 45, Desson HOwe

VIRGIN SUICIDES, THE

A Paramount Classics release of an American Zoetrope production in association with Muse Productions and Eternity Pictures. *Executive Producer:* Fred Fuchs and Willi Baer. *Producer:* Francis Ford Coppola, Julie Costanzo, Chris Hanley, and Dan Halsted. *Director:* Sofia Coppola. *Screenplay:* Sofia Coppola. *Based on the novel by:* Jeffrey Eugenides. *Director of Photography:* Edward Lachman. *Music:* Air. *Music Editor:* Richard Beggs. *Sound:* Henry Embry. *Sound Editor:* Galen Walker. *Casting:* John Buchan, Linda Phillips-Palo, and Robert McGee. *Production Designer:* Jasna Stefanovic. *Art Director:* Jon Goulding. *Set Decorator:* Megan Less. *Special Effects:* Jordan Craig and John Laforet. *Costumes:* Nancy Steiner. *Make-up:* Kathleen Graham. *Running time:* 97 minutes. *MPAA Rating:* R.

CAST: James Woods (Ronald A. Lisbon); Kathleen Turner (Mrs. Lisbon); Kirsten Dunst (Lux Lisbon); Josh Hartnett (Trip Fontaine); A. J. Cook (Mary Lisbon); Hanna Hall (Cecilia Lisbon); Leslie Hayman (Therese Lisbon); Chelse Swain (Bonnie Lisbon); Anthony DeSimone (Chase Buell); Lee Kagan (David Barker); Robert Schwartzman (Paul Baldino); Noah Shebib (Parkie Denton); Jonathan Tucker (Tim Weiner); Michael Paré (Adult Trip Fontaine); Scott Glenn (Father Moody); Danny DeVito (Doctor E.M. Horniker); Joe Roncetti (Kevin Head); Hayden Christensen (Jake Hill Conley); Chris Hale (Peter Sisten); Joe Dinicol (Dominic Palazzolo); Dan Belley (Dominic's Stunt Double); Suki Kaiser (Lydia Perl, TV reporter); Dawn Greenhalgh (Mrs. Scheer); Allen Stewart-Coates (Mr. Scheer); Sherry Miller (Mrs. Buell); Jonathan Whittaker (Mr. Buell); Michèle Duquet (Mrs. Denton); Murray McRae (Mr. Denton); Roberta Hanley (Mrs. Weiner); Paul Sybersma (Joe Larson); Susan Sybersma (Mrs. Larson); Peter Snider (Trip's Dad); Gary Brennan (Donald); Charles Boyland (Curt Van Osdol); Dustin Ladd (Chip Willard); Kirsten Fairlie (Amy Schraff); Melody Johnson (Julie); Sheyla Molho (Danielle); Ashley Ainsworth (Sheila Davis); Courtney Hawkrigg (Grace); François Klanfer (Doctor); MacKenzie Lawrenz (Jim Czeslawski); Tim Hall (Kurt Siles); Amos Crawley (John); Andrew Gilles (Principal Woodhouse); Marilyn Smith (Mrs. Woodhouse); Sally Cahill (Mrs. Hedlie); Tracey Ferencz (Nurse); Scott Denton (Mr. O'Connor); Catherine Swing (Mrs. O'Conner); Tim Adams (Buzz Romano); Michael Miglessi (Parks Department Foreman); Sarah Minhas (Wanda Brown); Megan Kennedy (Cheerleader); Sandi Stahlbrand (Meredith Thompson, TV Reporter); Neil Girvan (Drunk Man in Pool); Jaya Karsemeyer (Gloria); Leah Straatsma (Rannie); Mark Polley and Kirk Gonnsen (Cemetery Workers); Marianne Maroney (Teacher); Ann Wessels (Woman in Chiffon).

LOS ANGELES TIMES, 4/21/00, Calendar/p. 6, Kevin Thomas

Sofia Coppola shows an impressive maturity and an assured skill in adapting Jeffrey Eugenides' novel "The Virgin Suicides" to the screen for her directorial debut. As the title suggests, it's a challenging undertaking that requires a smooth passage from pitch-dark humor to a stark finish. The result is a highly affecting film unafraid to exact an emotional toll.

A never-seen Giovanni Ribisi lends his voice as the film's narrator, Tim Weiner, a man looking back to his high school days 25 years ago in leafy, upscale Grosse Pointe, Mich., a community favored by auto industry executives for generations. Tim (Jonathan Tucker) and his pals became tantalized and then obsessed with the five beautiful Lisbon sisters, ranging in age from 13 to 17. Their father (James Woods) is a math teacher at their high school, and the sisters live with their parents in one of their neighborhood's more nondescript yet spacious homes. The girls' parents, especially their mother (Kathleen Turner), are fervently religious and extremely strict with their daughters, who face the world with enigmatic smiles.

The neighborhood has long come to accept the Lisbons as distant when it is jolted by the news that the youngest Lisbon, Cecilia (Hanna Hall), has attempted suicide by slashing her wrists. Her parents are sufficiently shaken to listen to a psychiatrist (Danny DeVito) when he says Cecilia would benefit from more contact with boys, which leads to them throwing the only party they've ever given. This means the neighborhood boys will have a chance to come in closer contact with all the Lisbon sisters than has previously been possible. Soon the campus hunk, Trip Fontaine (Josh Hartnett) zeros in on Kirsten Dunst's Lux, the most gorgeous and forward of the sisters.

Trip is smart enough to ask Mr. Lisbon's permission to ask Lux to the homecoming prom, and when her mother says no, he's fast enough on his feet to suggest that he line up dates for all the sisters, thereby successfully offering the pretense of safety-in-numbers. But this night of freedom for the girls will have dire consequences. At the film's end Tim tells us that a quarter-century later he and his pals are still wondering why.

While subtle in the utmost, Coppola leaves us with an understanding of how things could turn out as they did. Most of us will conclude that the Lisbon sisters' course of action is consistent with that of young people intent upon punishing their parents regardless of the consequences to themselves.

When Cecilia slashes her wrists, a neighbor woman, secure in her well-appointed living room (heavy on the chintz, natch), suggests facetiously that it was her mother's hideous decor that drove her to it. The Lisbon home is in fact oppressively awful with dull furnishings in drab colors, its walls cluttered with tacky pictures awkwardly hung. There's none of the exuberance of the garish or the vulgar to amuse or lift the spirits but rather the clamminess of a total absence of taste and imagination.

Turner provides Mrs. Lisbon with her sultry voice and full figure; the woman's dowdiness suggests that she's so terrified of her innate sensuality that she feels compelled to repress it zealously in her daughters. There's a craziness in this woman's fervor that makes her akin to Turner's "Serial Mom" for John Waters. Woods' far from unsympathetic Mr. Lisbon is not such a bad guy, but he lets himself be dominated by his strong, shrill wife.

There are no fewer than 64 cast members in "The Virgin Suicides," and turning up in sharp cameos are Scott Glenn as the Lisbons' well-meaning priest and Michael Pare as the present-day Trip Fontaine. Dunst and Hartnett are as effective as Turner and Woods, and right down a very long line Coppola, daughter of that other Coppola, reveals a sure touch with actors. Hartnett makes witty use of his height and thinness; his Trip has a mastery of body language that is not lost on the opposite sex.

In a film in which so much is implicit rather than explicit a revealing atmosphere is crucial, and production designer Jasna Stefanovic and her team have done a masterful job of making the Lisbon home quietly dreadful; Nancy Steiner's conservative clothes for the Lisbon girls and their mother also contribute to the film's aura of repressiveness. "The Virgin Suicides" is successfully venturesome, but you need to know that it's also a real downer.

NEW YORK, 5/1/00, p. 57, Peter Rainer

Two directorial debuts have their moments: Sofia Coppola's "The Virgin Suicides," about five suburban daughters who inexplicably, poetically, kill themselves, puts a dreamy, Salingeresque spin on material not always up to such rueful mythologizing, but Coppola has a fresh, fervid eye and a way with actors, among them Josh Hartnett, Kirsten Dunst, and Kathleen Turner. Gina Prince-Bythewood's "Love & Basketball," about a female ballplayer, is mawkishly heartfelt, but actress Sanaa Lathan performs as if she were lit from within.

NEW YORK POST, 4/21/00, p. 43, Jonathan Foreman

It's hard to remember a film that mixes disparate, delicate ingredients with the subtlety and virtuosity of Sofia Coppola's brilliant "The Virgin Suicides."

Her adaptation of Jeffrey Eugenides' highly praised novel somehow combines hilarity with heartbreak, nostalgia with satire, realism with magic, and a gauzy, hazy atmosphere with sharp performances—without any of them losing their distinct flavor.

The result is a hauntingly beautiful film that makes you laugh with recognition while leaving a lump in your throat, and which captures with pinpoint accuracy both an era (the mid-'70s) and an age (adolescence.)

Indeed, no film in recent memory has caught so deftly the emotional world of teenage boys. And while we've had no shortage of movies about high school, suburban anomie, the '70s and suicide, this one manages to deal with all of these subjects without ever being obvious, crude or predictable.

The "virgins" of the title are the teenage Lisbon sisters, five dreamy golden beauties who fascinate all the males in the upscale Michigan suburb of Grosse Pointe. Their fate over a year and a half will have a powerful, permanent effect on one particular group of men, a group represented by the nameless adult narrator (Giovanni Ribisi).

The girls have strict parents. Their father (James Woods) is a math teacher at the local high school, and their mother (Kathleen Turner) is an overprotective religious fanatic. But that is the extent of the family's apparent abnormality until the youngest girl, Cecilia (Hanna Hall), attempts suicide by slashing her wrists.

A psychiatrist (Danny DeVito) suggests to the stunned Lisbon parents that their daughter might benefit from a more active social life, and in particular from the company of boys.

So they throw the sisters their first and only party, and give the transfixed neighborhood boys a chance to see the enigmatic, oddly mature girls up close. The evening ends in a way that makes the Lisbons more of a haunting mystery than ever.

When the school year begins again, the narrator focuses on the pursuit of the oldest and most nubile Lisbon sister, Lux (Kirsten Dunst, perfectly cast) by Trip Fontaine (Josh Hartnett), the snake-hipped campus stud.

Trip manages to persuade the Lisbon parents to let their daughters go out en masse to the homecoming dance. But then something happens that drives Mrs. Lisbon berserk, prompting her to take her children out of school and imprison them in the house.

The boys watch the girls through binoculars, try to make contact with them and dream of liberating them. And they become witnesses to something terrible and beyond understanding.

Coppola gets excellent performances from her cast, including an unusually restrained (and funny) turn by James Woods and strong cameos by Scott Glenn and Michael Pare (as the grownup Trip).

Her inspired use of music—a combination of well-chosen '70s pop and ethereal songs by the French group Air— fits perfectly with the wonderful photography by Edward Lachman.

NEWSDAY, 4/21/00, Part II/p. B7, John Anderson

That Sofia Coppola's Mary Corleone in "Godfather III" remains the standard by which all bad film acting is measured hasn't just been a boon to guys like Kevin Costner and Matthew McConaughey, it testifies to how cruel a move it was to put her in the movie at all. While you wouldn't want to call "The Virgin Suicides" her revenge, it's certainly a vindication of her filmmaking instincts—and nourished to its roots on the bittersweet milk of remembered innocence.

A mystery, a romance and medieval allegory in platform shoes, "The Virgin Suicides" is dreamy, rhythmically flirtatious, fatally romantic and set on the cusp of the modem feminist movement. The time frame is no accident. While the Jeffrey Eugenides novel won fans for its treatment of adolescent longing and memory, debuting director Coppola adds to this—no, distills from this—a parable of sexual power and disequilibrium.

The Lisbon sisters are five bonded blondes, '70s teenagers who dwell in a suburban split-level as well as some lofty region inaccessible to the infatuated boys who love them. When they kill themselves, it's for no apparent reason—no reason apparent, that is, to those infatuated boys, who remember them years later and confer upon the Lisbons the status of myth.

What drives Coppola's film, giving it a sad, funny magic and an absurdist sense of fun, is a sense of what the girls possessed and lost, a kind of blessed immunity from the rigors of equality. This may sound like reactionary feminist backlash, but it's far more delicate than that. The putative villain may be Mom (Kathleen Turner), who runs her house like a convent; Dad the math teacher (a brilliantly bemused James Woods) runs only modest interference. But the household in fact provides an empowering atmosphere: Unaffected by mutating mores and popular pressure to sink to the level of boys, the girls can be comfortable in their sexuality—or flaunt it, in the case of Lux (Kirsten Dunst)—without intimidation. Untouched and untouchable, the girls are cocooned in their sisterhood, which becomes a sort of fortress besieged.

Displaying a great deal of humor, more than a dash of Truffaut and a willingness to allow her metaphorical storyline to go unfettered by questions (to say nothing of answers) Coppola makes the Lisbon sisters, and her movie, ethereal. It may strain a bit at the end, but "Virgin Suicides" is an impressively confident as well as visionary debut.

SIGHT AND SOUND, 6/00, p. 59, Mark Olsen

A male narrator recounts how a group of five teenage sisters, the Lisbons, all committed suicide during his youth in a Michigan suburb 25 years ago.

After the youngest Lisbon, Cecilia, tries to slash her wrists, a psychiatrist recommends the sisters be allowed more interaction with boys. The Lisbons host a party during which Cecilia throws herself from a window, killing herself. The shock of her death causes the family to close in on itself, and the girls become a source of obsessive fascination for the boys. When the athletic Trip Fontaine courts Lux Lisbon, the girls seem within their grasp. Mr and Mrs Lisbon only allow Trip to take Lux to a dance if the girls all go. At the party, Trip and Lux are crowned homecoming king and queen. When Lux stays out all night, she brings on a parental crackdown.

The girls are taken out of school and kept at home. The boys attempt to communicate with them, and soon the girls secretly begin sending notes. Lured late one night to the Lisbon house, the boys believe it is to aid an escape. They discover the four sisters have all taken their own lives. The mysterious motivations of the Lisbon sisters haunt them into their adult years.

Making her feature-film debut directing her own adaptation of Jeffrey Eugenides' novel *The Virgin Suicides,* Sofia Coppola has essentially given herself two main goals: to portray adolescence's delicate blend of whimsy and melancholy, while recreating the soft-rock and wood-panelled-basement side of American life in the 70s. Her take is probably more in line with the actual recollections of people who came of age in that era, when suburban living had reached its decadent peak, more so than the coked-up disco-pants and haircuts imagery so commonly used to establish the period.

Moreover, that era has long been the main cultural touchstone for the casually wealthy, ultra-hip media-darling demimonde of which Coppola is very much a part. Before now she has dipped a toe into numerous endeavours, including photographer, actress and boutique owner. This diverse background makes her perfectly suited for the role of film director and perhaps the most impressive thing about her film is the way it's very much a total package. All of its elements—performance, cinematography, sound, art design—combine to illuminate not just a theme or singular idea, but to create a unified feeling and mood.

An oblong detective story of sorts, the film's unseen narrator recounts, 25 years on, one odd year in a suburb just outside Detroit. A group of five teenage sisters all kill themselves, leaving behind a group of boys whose odd fascination with the girls lingers into adulthood. Eugenides' novel and Coppola's film in turn are not concerned with explaining the exact details and motivations of the event. Tinged with a stately death-march pace that stems from the divulged outcome from the start, both film and novel are touched by a sad sympathy for the boys' obsession, while allowing the girls to remain inscrutably unknowable, inhabiting a world of rainbows and tampons where reality and fantasy intermingle. As Lux, the only sister allowed a singular personality, Kirsten Dunst brings a remarkably knowing air to her character, suggesting that oddly feline quality of young women. James Woods and Kathleen Turner as the girls' stilted and repressed parents both turn in remarkably restrained performances, cast against type. Woods in particular gives what may be the most sensitively nuanced performance of his career.

The film moves confidently through its opening sequences, establishing its characters and locale with energy and zest. Coppola frequently frames moments as if taking a still photograph, aiding the film's air of suffocating memory: a mother washing dishes, the assorted clutter of a young girl's bedroom, or a boy locked in the lonely late-night world inside his headphones. Explosions of energy—the dance, Trip's stoner-elegant swagger to the spacy wail of 'Magic Man'—and a sly, off-balance sense of humour keep the film feeling brisk even as it delves deeper into a world of silent hysteria.

Having so deftly created this overall milieu and tone, it's disappointing when the film splutters towards its finale. Following the homecoming, as the boys watch dumbfounded while the girls begin the grim slide towards their demise, Coppola doesn't quite seem to know where to go and begins to rely on trickery—time-lapse photography or split-screen effects—that feels more like straw-grasping than skilful control. The central enigma regarding the girls' inexplicable motives becomes central too late. Similarly, the ludicrously unnecessary sequence near the end in which a fashionable debutante party is celebrated with an asphyxiation theme falls too far into grotesquerie. Altogether a mixed bag, *The Virgin Suicides* is nevertheless a noteworthy debut. Coppola proves herself a director of burgeoning talent, as well as a sensitive screenwriter. If her missteps hold the film back from achieving the full grandeur it aims for, there is no denying the way it conjures a magic-realist American suburbia, rarely before brought so convincingly to life.

VILLAGE VOICE, 4/25/00, p. 142, Dennis Lim

As purposefully ambiguous as its source novel, *The Virgin* Suicides doesn't so much unfold as waft off the screen, leaving behind a vapor trail of swoony, mysterious sadness. Sofia Coppola's thoughtfully crafted portrait of lost (or embalmed) adolescence is suffused with a wistfulness so consuming it transcends nostalgia—even before the first of the five doomed teenage Lisbon sisters has offed herself, the movie already feels ghostly and strangely bereft.

Jeffrey Eugenides's novel, set in a Michigan suburb in the early '70s, casts the suicides as the defining cataclysm in the lives of the smitten neighborhood boys (the book's omniscient collective narrator), who—having spent more than two decades cataloging the physical evidence and reconstructing the circumstances surrounding the girls' baffling demise—are now grown men who find themselves more haunted than ever. Eugenides's shapely, sinuous prose seems at once generously cinematic (well stocked with eloquent, prismatic imagery) and resistant to adaptations feat of precarious composure not built to withstand even the slightest manhandling. But Coppola's transposition is canny, faithful, observant—a disarming daydream of a movie, enhanced by Ed Lachman's lovely, gauzy cinematography and the voluptuous melancholy of French lounge hipsters Air ("Playground Love," the film's recurring theme, might be as close to a piece of music has ever come to approximating a sigh).

The impression of ethereal drift is deceptive; the film slices through its dizzying succession of events with clean, swift efficiency. First, the youngest sister—Cecilia (Hanna Hall), a glum, world-weary 13-year-old-hurls herself from her bedroom window onto a spiked iron fence. The other four are dead within a year, and the traumatic intervening period centers on a fleeting romance between the most flirtatious Lisbon, Kirsten Dunst's radiant Lux (eternally illuminated by soft, celestial sunlight), and heartthrob Trip Fontaine (Josh Hartnett), introduced swaggering down a hallway to Heart's "Magic Man." When Lux breaks curfew, the girls are indefinitely grounded by their bedraggled, blankly stern mother (Kathleen Turner, suggesting *Serial Mom* after a born-again conversion and a regimen of sedatives). Dad, a wimpy math teacher, is played by James Woods, cast ingeniously against type as a downtrodden little man whose immersion in an estrogen-soaked household has left him in a diffident, emasculated daze.

In the context of contemporary American film, *The Virgin Suicides* sets off all manner of red flags—suburbia, the '70s, teens. But the movie (thanks to its writer-director's empathic, intelligent reading of the novel) approaches its themes obliquely, averting kitsch and cheap irony. Coppola looks beyond the seductive metaphysical puzzle and locates the core of Eugenides's allegory in an obsessive, almost forensic act of remembering, both futile and inexplicably essential.

Also reviewed in:
CHICAGO TRIBUNE, 5/5/00, Friday/p. A, Mark Caro
NEW REPUBLIC, 5/15/00, p. 30, Stanley Kauffmann
NEW YORK TIMES, 4/21/00, p. E16, A. O. Scott

VARIETY, 5/24-30/99, p. 67, Emanuel Levy
WASHINGTON POST, 5/5/00, p. C1, Rita Kempley
WASHINGTON POST, 5/5/00, Weekend/p. 47, Michael O'Sullivan

VISIT, THE

An Urbanworld Films and Shoreline Entertainment release of a Dawa Movies production. *Executive Producer:* Vicky Pike, Morris Ruskin, and Stacy Spikes. *Producer:* Jordan Walker-Pearlman. *Director:* Jordan Walker-Pearlman. *Screenplay:* Jordan Walker-Pearlman. *Based on a play by:* Kosmond Russell. *Director of Photography:* John Ndiaga Demps. *Editor:* Alison Learned and Jordan Walker-Pearlman. *Music:* Michael Bearden, Stefan Dickerson, Ramsey Lewis, Wallace Roney, and Stanley A. Smith. *Sound:* Mike Hall and James P. Slingluff. *Production Designer:* John Larena. *Art Director:* Andy Brittan. *Set Decorator:* Jennifer Knepschield. *Visual Effects:* Jerry Pooler. *Costumes:* Carlos Rosario. *Make-up:* Steve Ratliff. *Running time:* 107 minutes. *MPAA Rating:* Not Rated.

CAST: Obba Babatundé (Tony Waters); Rae Dawn Chong (Felicia McDonald); Marla Gibbs (Lois Waters); Hill Harper (Alex Waters); Phylicia Rashad (Dr. Coles); Billy Dee Williams (Henry Waters); Talia Shire (Marilyn Coffey); David Clennon (Bill Brenner); Glynn Turman (Al Rheingold); Efrain Figueroa (Max Cruz); Amy Stilller (Julie Bronsky); Jascha Washington (Young Alex); Christopher Babers (Young Tony); Jennifer Nicole Freeman (Young Felicia); Tim De Zarn (Guard Enheim); Charmin Lee White (Mrs. Tony Waters); Terrell Mitchell (Tony's Son); Enoh Essien (Tony's Daughter); Hugh Dane (Mr. McDonald); Jordan Lund (Photographer); Drew Renkewitz (Prison Guard); Kirk Acevedo (Parolee); Lyne Odums (Crackhouse Woman); Jaime Perry (Drug Dealer); David Roberson (Corrections Officer); Javier Silcock (Lamar); Garey McGhie (Prison Guard).

LOS ANGELES TIMES, 4/20/01, Calendar/p. 10, Kevin Thomas

"The Visit" powerfully depicts the flowering of spiritual redemption within a young man who has every reason to give in to despair. It marks the directorial debut of Jordan Walker-Pearlman, who in his adaptation of the Kosmond Russell play displays an acute sense of how to realize visually a work intended for the stage while respecting its text. In accomplishing this always challenging task he has had strong assistance from the fluid and expressive camera work of John Ndiaga Demps.

Walker-Pearlman has also been fortunate to attract a formidable cast, with Hill Harper, Billy Dee Williams, Rae Dawn Chong, Marla Gibbs, Phylicia Rashad and Obba Babatunde in the leading roles.

We first meet Babatunde's Tony Waters as he and his wife are entertaining a large number of friends in their upscale home. We then discover that this scene, a moment of high spirits in a setting that spells out considerable personal success, is occurring in Tony's memory while on a long drive that'll end at the gates of a state prison, where his younger brother Alex (Harper) is serving 25 years in prison for a rape he swears he did not commit. Before the story is underway, Walker-Pearlman has already established through the camera rather than dialogue the stark contrast between the worlds of the brothers.

Tony hasn't visited his brother in 10 months, blaming the demands of two infant children on top of his Job, but Alex, in a hostile mood because he feels so neglected, forces his brother to admit the real reason: shame. It's a shame that penetrates far deeper into their father, Henry (Williams), a stern, self-made man.

Tony had been a loving father figure to his younger brother, and when he left for college, Alex felt abandoned and then overwhelmed by Henry's expectations. Alex fell into a gang, then into drugs, and now that he's dying of AIDS he wants to make peace with his family, whom, with the exception of Tony, he has not seen since his imprisonment five years earlier.

What Alex learns, first through his prison psychiatrist (Rashad), a direct woman, and then through a childhood friend (Chong), is that this peace has to start from within and involve forgiveness. Alex doesn't realize it initially, but in reaching out to his family he has embarked on a course that will challenge him to the utmost.

Alex's loving mother, Lois (Gibbs), never believed that her son was guilty of rape. And Alex was too proud to seek his father's financial help in securing strong legal defense, and his father was too proud—and too angry over his son's lifestyle—to extend help without being asked. Consequently, when Alex was convicted, Henry, in his hurt, shame and unacknowledged guilt over his possible failures as a father, took the view that his son was guilty and deserving of being in effect disowned. Lois dared not cross her old-fashioned patriarch of a husband to try to visit her son.

The changes that begin to take place within Alex and then his family credibly come with much anguish and difficulty. "The Visit" demands and receives much from its cast, especially from Harper and Williams. Playwright Russell, drawing upon the story of his own brother, has made his drama all the stronger for having been fair to Henry. Williams reaches a career high in expressing the crushing disappointment and enraged pain of a man who strived his entire life to provide a solid middle-class upbringing for his sons, only to see his younger son throw it away.

"The Visit's" splendid ensemble cast is further enhanced by the fine actors—Talia Shire, David Clennon, Glynn Turman, Efrain Figueroa and Amy Stiller—who play the members of the parole board. This is a film that stays with you long after the lights have gone up.

NEW YORK POST, 12/15/00, p. 58. V.A. Musetto

Jailhouse dramas have come a long way since Jimmy Cagney went bonkers in the prison mess hall in White Heat" back in 1949.

The latest entry in that time-honored genre, "The Visit," is free of rioting cons, sadistic guards and other cliches.

Instead, we get the touching story of Alex Waters (Hill Harper), a 32-year-old black man dying of AIDS as he serves a 25-year sentence for a rape he strongly denies committing.

The film focuses on jailhouse visits by Alex's older, middle-class brother (Obba Babatunde), his parents (Billy Dee Williams and Marla Gibbs) and, finally, the woman (Rae Dawn Chong) who was Alex's boyhood sweetheart before she killed her abusive dad and ended up a drug addict. (She has since kicked the habit.)

Thrown into the mix are Alex's sessions with the sympathetic prison shrink (Phylicia Rashad).

"The Visit" is based on a play with the same name by Kosmond Russell, but the film's director-screenwriter, Jordan Walker-Pearlman, opens up the action just enough to keep things moving along.

Strong acting, especially by Williams and Harper, and a nice jazz score, are bonuses.

Alex's appearance before the parole board serves as an indictment of a bureaucracy more interested in following rigid guidelines than in compassion for a dying, harmless man who may very well be innocent.

He's told that the way to impress the board is to show remorse. But how can he show remorse for something he insists he didn't do?

You can't help but root for him in his Kafkaesque quest to spend his little remaining time a free man.

"The Visit" is marred, however, by sappy fantasy sequences (Alex imagines his family visiting him in his cell) and a sentimental finale that's out of step with most of the rest of the movie.

VILLAGE VOICE, 12/19/00, p. 146, Mark Holcomb

Prison dramas, as any *Oz* fan can tell you, are typically more concerned with the physics of bloodspray than with the inner lives of their characters. *The Visit*, then, comes as something of a surprise: An earnest character study that's neither sordid nor exploitative, it portrays the brutality of life behind bars without resorting to a single slit throat. Too bad it's swamped by good intentions. Structured as a series of jailhouse-visit vignettes, the film tracks the slow, knotty transformation of convicted rapist Alex Waters (Hill Harper) from intractable thug to family man. With the help of his older brother (Obba Babatundé) and a prison psychologist (Phylicia Rashad),

Alex—who's dying of AIDS—confronts his parents (Billy Dee Williams and Marla Gibbs) and childhood sweetheart (Rae Dawn Chong) in an often desperate attempt to ease the loneliness of his final days.

To director Jordan Walker-Pearlman's credit, Alex's new-found peace doesn't spring from some improbable epiphany any more than his guilt or innocence is conclusively established; until *The Visit*'s final passage, the change comes via a slow, incomplete melting away of the attitudes that have kept him frozen in resentful indifference for much of his life. Those last scenes, however, contain so many moral and spiritual turnarounds that Alex—and the film—are all but buried in the uplift. Harper, in a fierce, nuanced performance, deserves better. The other actors are generally as good, even if Rashad plays Dr. Coles more as mesmerist than shrink and a parole board sequence helmed by Talia Shire (Talia Shire!) brims with improvisational slop. The real surprise is Williams. His loveless, bullying patriarch is a heartbreakingly repellent man, and, with the exception of an unconvincing graveside coda, Billy Dee pulls no punches. Who knew?

Also reviewed in:
NEW YORK TIMES, 12/15/00, p. E26, A. O. Scott
VARIETY, 6/26-7/9/00, p. 24, Sheri Linden

WAITING GAME, THE

A Seventh Arts Releasing and Amsell Entertainment release of an Absolute Films, Inc. production. *Producer:* Mirjam Goldberg, Ken Liotti, and Jason Lust. *Director:* Ken Liotti. *Screenplay and Story:* Ken Liotti. *Director of Photography:* Richard Eliano. *Music:* Jim Farmer. *Sound:* Tammy Douglas. *Casting:* Susan Shopmaker. *Production Designer:* Sonya Gropman. *Art Director:* David Incorvala. *Costumes:* Claudia Hill. *Running time:* 81 minutes. *MPAA Rating:* Not Rated.

CAST: Will Arnett (Lenny); Debbon Ayer (Merris); Dwight Ewell (Joe); Eddie Malavarca (Derek); Terumi Matthews (Andi); Michael Raynor (Franco); Daniel Riordan (Dan); Taylor Stanley (Shannon); Donald Williams (Nick the Cook); Alice Spivak (Customer from Hell); Christopher Lawford (Barfly); Howard Spiegel (L.A. Director); Amy Marcs (Casting Director); Leslie Lyles (Therapist); Scott Wojcik (Cliff); Pam Wilterdink (Cynthia); Harvey Waldman (Ralph); John McKay (Bathroom Customer).

LOS ANGELES TIMES, 7/28/00, Calendar/p. 18, Kevin Thomas

Ken Liotti's "The Waiting Game" offers a wry take on a group of aspiring actors working in a New York restaurant while waiting for that big break.

Ultimately, Liotti focuses more on the vicissitudes of romance than show biz, as a bartender, Lenny (Will Arnett), and a waitress, Andi (Terumi Matthews), as long-time friends, find themselves in denial over their mutual attraction.

The more forthright of the two, Andi tells Lenny she wouldn't want to become involved with him because he's the only man she half-way trusts.

As emotion clashes with reason between Lenny and Andi, Lenny breaks up with his live-in girlfriend (Debbon Ayer) and Andi has a fling with a rugged construction worker (Michael Raynor). In the meantime, their co-worker Dan (Dan Riordan) puts his pals through the agony of his pretentious one-man show and he faces the humiliation of an audition that crashes when he's told that his 14½ shoe size indicates that he's automatically wrong for the role.

Liotti manages to bring a freshness and humor to an oft-told tale. "The Waiting Game" serves as a good calling card for cast and crew, especially Raynor, Arnett, Mathews and Riordan and cinematographer Rich Eliano, whose use of the film's Manhattan backdrop is graceful and unobtrusive.

NEW YORK POST, 2/24/00, p. 51, Lou Lumenick

Here's a tip: Beware any movie in which one of the characters' work is described by a critic in the film as a "masturbatory snooze fest."

In "The Waiting Game," this review is aimed at a 1-hour-and-40-minute one-man off-Broadway show, in which a waiter named Daniel delivers a pompous rant and bakes a loaf of bread onstage.

But it could equally refer to writer Ken Liotti's debut feature, an annoying romantic comedy about Daniel (Dan Riordan) and his equally self-absorbed co-workers at a Manhattan restaurant that seems far longer than its 80-minute running time.

Spouting the kind of cliches you'd expect from a third-rate sitcom, a cast of virtual unknowns serve up Liotti's boring menu of Love, Manhattan style.

They include a waitress (Terumi Matthews) who falls in love with a hunky construction worker (Michael Raynor) she's been hired to "fidelity test" by his fiancée, the busboy (Eddie Malavarca) who wonders if he might be gay—and the married waiter (Will Arnett) who steps out with a fetching colleague (Taylor Stanley).

The most decent performance—a gay waiter with a crush on the busboy—is given by the most seasoned performer in the cast, Dwight Ewell ("Chasing Amy").

Ewell plays a similar role in "Restaurant," another low-budget movie about aspiring actors that's vastly superior to the "The Waiting Game."

Also reviewed in:
NEW YORK TIMES, 3/2/00, p. E6, Lawrence Van Gelder

WAKING THE DEAD

A USA Films release of a Gramercy Pictures presentation of an Egg Pictures production. *Executive Producer:* Jodie Foster.   *Producer:* Keith Gordon, Stuart Kleinman, and Linda Reisman. *Director:* Keith Gordon. *Screenplay:* Robert Dillon. *Based upon the novel by:* Scott Spencer. *Director of Photography:* Tom Richmond.   *Editor:* Jeff Wishengrad. *Music:* tomandandy. *Music Editor:* Chris McGeary. *Sound:* Patrick Rousseau and (music) Steve Mac. *Sound Editor:* John Nutt.   *Casting:* Ronnie Yeskel and Richard Hicks.   *Production Designer:* Zoe Sakellaropoulo.   *Art Director:* Marie-Claude L'Heureux.   *Set Decorator:* Anne Galea, Simon Lahaye, and Joelle Turenne.   *Special Effects:* Bill Rivard.   *Costumes:* Renee April. *Make-up:* Diane Simard.   *Stunt Coordinator:* Dave McKeown.   *Running time:* 106 minutes. *MPAA Rating:* R.

CAST: Billy Crudup (Fielding Pierce); Bill Haugland (TV Newsman at Bombing); Nelson Landrieu (Francisco Higgens); Jennifer Connelly (Sarah Williams); Maxine Guess (Danny's Receptionist);   Paul Hipp (Danny Pierce);   Hal Holbrook (Isaac Green); Lawrence Dane (Governor Kinosis); Ed Harris (Jerry Carmichael); Robert Harding (TV Newsman #2); Janet McTeer (Caroline Pierce); Molly Parker (Juliet Beck); Larry Marshall (Angelo Bertelli); Don Jordan (Minister with Bertelli on TV); Caroline Sabourin (Little Sarah Look-Alike); Stanley Anderson (Fielding's Father); Patrica Gage (Fielding's Mother); John Carroll Lynch (Father Mileski); Bruce Dinsmore (Tony Dayton); Mimi Kuzyk (Adele Green); Tony Calabretta (Sonny Marchi);   Walter Massey (Otto Ellis);   Norris Domingue (Congressman at Isaac's Party); Dean Hagopian (Politician at Isaac's Party); Bernard Behrens (Father Stanton); Philip Williams (Al); Sharon Washington (Kelly); Ranee Lee (Woman from Fielding's Campaign); Zoe Sakellaropoulo ("Sarah" in Caroline's Flashback);   Scott Spencer (Man with Sarah in Flashback); Alan Fawcett (Reporter at Restaurant); Leah Pinsent (Reporter from Fielding's Past); Karina Iraola (Seny); Marco Ledezma (Gustavo); Walt MacPherson (Sarah's Father); John Walsh (Protest Leader Outside Sarah's Funeral); Vlasta Vrana (Priest at Sarah's Funeral); Sandra Oh (Kim);   Pasca Petardi, Leonardo Fuica, and Qariy Hendrickson, (Kids who Mug Fielding); Sandra Caldwell (Concerned Mom from Letter); Justin Bradley (Adopted Kid from Letter); Richard Hicks (Young Man from Letter); Ed Cambridge (Old Man from Letter).

LOS ANGELES TIMES, 3/24/00, Calendar/p. 2, Kevin Thomas

"Waking the Dead" is a powerful story of love and politics in the '70s and '80s and their bittersweet aftermath. It is a film of uncommon intelligence and rigor that illuminates a complex era, and the romance at its center is also one of exceptional passion and honesty. Beyond this, it establishes Billy Crudup as an authentic star who can carry a challenging film, and it offers further proof that Jennifer Connelly is a fresh, vibrant presence on the screen.

It has been adapted from Scott Spencer's novel by Robert Dillon with a consummate skill matched by Keith Gordon's direction, which mixes much care with considerable riskiness. "Waking the Dead" shifts smoothly between 1972-74 and 1982, with stopovers in between and beyond, allowing sufficient time in each period for us to become involved with what's happening at that moment.

Young Coast Guard officer Fielding Pierce (Crudup) meets Connelly's Sarah Williams in the office of Fielding's counterculture publisher-brother (Paul Hipp) in Chicago in 1972. The attraction between them is far more than sexual, strong as it is. They are idealists who deplore the Vietnam War with equal fervor, yet from Day 1 their approaches to activism differ and clash.

Fielding is the son of a union leader and he already has the U.S. Congress as his goal whereas Sarah is a fiery radical. Fielding wants to effect change within the system whereas Sarah would tear it down if it would end the war in Southeast Asia—or resolve any other military or political crises.

By 1974 their love is severely tested when Sarah participates in a dangerous mission to rescue a couple from Pinochet's Chile. While Sarah is chauffeuring the couple back in Chicago, a fire bomb kills all of them.

As devastated as Fielding is, he deals with tragedy the way most people do, by getting on with his life. Now it's 1982, and at 32 Fielding is in fact running for Congress. (Paving the way is a senator, played by Ed Harris, who resigned when caught up in a sex scandal.) Fielding is involved with the eminently suitable niece (Molly Parker) of his political mentor (Hal Holbrook). On the eve of his campaign, while on a solitary stroll, Fielding thinks he hears Sarah's voice, and as the campaign progresses he hears her more and more, and even thinks he spots her on the street. He is flooded with emotion and longing, and this haunting sense of Sarah's presence also makes him question what he thinks he can accomplish in public office.

Whether Sarah is a figment of his imagination, manifesting itself under the stress of campaigning, or a supernatural phenomenon, is unclear; either way Fielding is truly put to the test. Not only is Fielding's ordeal potentially jeopardizing his campaign by distracting him increasingly but also calls into question his very sanity. The only person Fielding feels comfortable confiding in is his sister (Janet McTeer), an artist who comforts him but urges him to concentrate on the campaign and deal with the specter—if that is what it is—of Sarah afterward.

The way in which Fielding's predicament plays out is the reason this film is so impressive and satisfying. It evokes the eras it spans and raises timeless questions of values, priorities and of the roles ideals and emotions play in the lives of those committed to making a difference, one way or another. The seeming presence of Sarah creates a special challenge for Gordon and his stars, and that "Waking the Dead" deals with it so imaginatively, makes the film all the richer and provocative an experience.

NEW YORK POST, 3/24/00, p. 51, Jonathan Foreman

"Waking the Dead" is an ambitious film that doesn't quite work. At times it descends into shameless (but effective) shlockiness. And it too often loses its momentum in overabundant flashback scenes.

But it also has two remarkable qualities that make it one of the more interesting and enjoyable movies of the season.

One is the hypnotic screen presence of Jennifer Connelly, who once again proves to have plenty of erotic chemistry with co-star Billy Crudup.

The other is its ability to sustain ambiguity both in its plot (is Connelly's character alive or is she a ghost?) and its political morality (is the electoral system so corrupt that taking part in it means selling out, or is it a valid alternative to empty, self-righteous leftist posturing?). It takes subtle, articulate writing of a kind that is all too rare in movies today to pull off such ambiguity.

An adaptation of Scott Spencer's 1986 novel, this apparently supernatural love story begins in 1972. Fielding Pierce (Crudup) is a kind of working-class, pretty-boy Al Gore: he opposes the Vietnam war, but because he wants to be president one day and must maintain his political viability, he has joined the Coast Guard.

Stationed in New York Harbor, he visits the publishing house run by his hippie brother (Paul Hipp), and there meets lovely young activist Sarah (Connelly).

Despite her radical ideals, she's willing to deal with the consequences of dating a man in a uniform, and the two of them fall in love. He goes to law school; she works for a left-wing Catholic organization that helps victims of the new Chilean dictatorship find sanctuary.

But just as Fielding gets a foothold in Chicago's political machine—thanks to cynical mentor Isaac Green (Hal Holbrook), Sarah intensifies her involvement in the sanctuary movement, and dies in a car bombing attributed to Chilean secret agents.

Cut to the early '80s and Assistant District Attorney Fielding is embarking on an election contest for a seat in the House of Representatives. Walking along the street he thinks he hears Sarah's voice. Then he seems to see her at an airport, looking through the windows of a restaurant.

Fielding thinks he must be losing his mind, perhaps out of guilt at having become part of the system Sarah always despised. His supportive sister Caroline (Janet McTeer) tells him to ignore the flashbacks and visions until after the election is over. Then it occurs to him that Sarah might really be alive—that the whole assassination may have been faked in order to further The Cause.

Writer/director Keith Gordon, whose previous efforts include "A Midnight Clear" and the less successful "Mother Night," is guilty of a number of flourishes that actually sap the strength of the narrative, including an unnecessary voice-over epilogue.

But he's good with his cast and gets a particularly strong performance out of Crudup—who does a lot of convincing weeping and is terrific in a powerful, believable breakdown scene set in a crowded restaurant.

NEWSDAY, 3/24/00, Part II/p. B3, John Anderson

What can you say about a 25-year-old woman who died? Well, it was too much in "Love Story," and in "Waking the Dead" it's still too much, even if the woman in question is a lot more interesting, probably not quite 25 and possibly not even dead.

The only thing we're sure about Sarah Williams (Jennifer Connelly) is that she's the Dorothy Day of the '70s. (We'd know it was the '70s, even if they didn't tell us, because Joni Mitchell and "Maggie May" are on the soundtrack.) She's devoted to Catholic causes and liberation theology, works tirelessly on behalf of oppressed peoples and has the best line in the movie: "I want a life of unbelievable adventure and profligacy and at the last possible moment ... sainthood. You might call her a pragmatist, if the competition didn't include Fielding Pierce (Billy Crudup).

Despite the name, Fielding is a blue-collar kid with fierce political aspirations (think Bill Clinton) whom we first see crying his eyes out as he watches the newscast of a 1974 terrorist car bombing, which reportedly killed girlfriend Sarah. Flash back to '72 and the Vietnam War years—don't worry, the movie helps you—which Fielding is spending in the Coast Guard (think the Republican leadership of the '90s). "Name one political leader who hasn't served his time," Fielding answers his skeptical and much more hippie-fied brother Danny (Paul Hipp). Fielding is a born politician, a nice cutthroat, and that he has a crisis of conscience should put "Waking the Dead" on the sci-fi rack in Blockbuster—by next week.

That's what they want us to believe, though, and it's a tough sell. But in this feature by Keith Gordon ("Midnight Clear," "Mother Night") based on the novel by the apparently hard-luck Scott Spencer ("Endless Love") they have a much bigger problem to surmount.

As his dreams of a congressional seat become more and more probable, and his indebtedness to slimy politicians such as Isaac Green (Hal Holbrook) becomes more and more permanent, Fielding starts to hear voices. "Sarah?" he asks. Well, it seems like a good guess. And then Sarah starts showing up. And Fielding starts to lose his marbles.

The problem is, Sarah really is showing up—not just to Fielding, but to others, such as his sister Caroline (Janet McTeer). The movie in other words, wants to have things both ways:

Psychological mystery, and mystery. And each cancels the other out, because you can't very well ascribe Fielding's hallucinations to his moral crisis when what he's seeing aren't hallucinations.

Ah, well. Jennifer Connelly and Billy Crudup are both very attractive performers of whom greater things have long been expected who once again find themselves in a movie without a brain. Not that we don't like brainless movies. We just don't like ones that are so insufferably prolonged and self-indulgent that you'd rather be at a wake.

VILLAGE VOICE, 3/28/00, p. 120, Jessica Winter

Waking the Dead twists time, but trips up in its herky-jerky, flashback-strewn trek across the psyche of a callow congressional hopeful haunted by the accusatory ghost of his dead lover. A strident righteous hippie who doth protest too much, Sarah (Jennifer Connelly) rattles her chains often enough to convince working-class, to-the-manor-named Fielding Pierce (Billy Crudup) that he's both sold out and gone around the bend. As shrill as its heroine, *Waking the Dead* (executive-produced by Jodie Foster) does offer one weirdly moving scene for Crudup late in the film, when he finally breaks down at what is supposed to be a celebratory family dinner. Billy gives crying in public a good name.

Also reviewed in:
CHICAGO TRIBUNE, 3/23/00, Friday/p. A, Mark Caro
NEW REPUBLIC, 4/10/00, p. 28, Stanley Kauffmann
NEW YORK TIMES, 3/24/00, p. E14, Stephen Holden
NEW YORKER, 3/27/00, p. 136, David Denby
VARIETY, 2/7-13/00, p. 55, Dennis Harvey
WASHINGTON POST, 3/24/00, p. C5, Rita Kempley
WASHINGTON POST, 3/24/00, Weekend/p. 43, Desson Howe

WATCHER, THE

A Universal Pictures release in association with Interlight of a Lewitt/Eberts-Choi/Niami production. *Executive Producer:* Patrick Choi and Paul Pompian. *Producer:* Christopher Eberts, Elliot Lewitt, Jeff Rice and Nile Niami. *Director:* Joe Charbanic. *Screenplay:* David Elliot and Clay Ayers. *Story:* Darcy Meyers and David Elliot. *Director of Photography:* Michael Chapman. *Editor:* Richard Nord. *Music:* Marco Beltrami. *Music Editor:* Chris McGeary. *Sound:* Jacob D. Collins and (music) John Kurlander. *Sound Editor:* Barney Cabral. *Casting:* Jane Alderman. *Production Designer:* Brian Eatwell and Maria Caso. *Art Director:* Jeff Wallace. *Set Designer:* Pat Raney. *Set Decorator:* Caroline Perzan. *Set Dresser:* Bruce "BJ" Johnson. *Special Effects:* Sam "Mo-Mo" Barkan. *Costumes:* Jay Hurley. *Make-up:* Suzi Ostos. *Stunt Coordinator:* Cort Hessler III. *Running time:* 93 minutes. *MPAA Rating:* R.

CAST: James Spader (Campbell); Marisa Tomei (Polly); Keanu Reeves (Griffin); Ernie Hudson (Ibby); Chris Ellis (Hollis); Robert Cicchini (Mitch); Yvonne Niami (Lisa); Jennifer McShane (Diana); Gina Alexander (Sharon); Rebakah Louise Smith (Ellie); Joe Sikora (Skater); Jillian Peterson (Jessica); Michelle Dimaso (Rachel); Andrew Rothenberg (Jack Fray); David Pasquesi (Norton); Dana Kozlov (Anchorwoman); Butch Jerinic (Flower Girl); Marily Dodds Frank (Wanda); Rebekah Arthur (Business Woman); Sheila Lahey (Wanda's Sister); Jason Wells (Computer Tech); Lisa Velten (Photo Store Employee); Frederick Garcia (Coffee Store Clerk); Mindy Bell (Supervising Agent); Ryan Oliver (Waiter); Varen Black (Female Reporter); Tamara Tungate (Young Woman); Quinn Yancy (Campbell's Secretary); Jennifer Anglin (Television Reporter); Peter Reinemann (Motel Clerk); Michael Nicolosi (Passerby); Rich Komenich (Bloody Guy); Michael Guido (Mendel); Janelle Snow (Waitress); Joe Forbrich (Bennigan's Manager); Scott Benjaminson (Guest).

LOS ANGELES TIMES, 9/8/00, Calendar/p. 12, Kevin Thomas

[The following review by Kevin Thomas appeared in a slightly different form in
NEWSDAY, 9/9/00, Part II/p. B9.]

"The Watcher" is a meticulously crafted but resolutely routine serial killer suspense thriller. While intelligently plotted and well-acted by James Spader, Keanu Reeves and Marisa Tomei, it is neither acutely suspenseful nor particularly thrilling but instead mainly numbing. You're left wishing that Oscar-winning cinematographer Michael Chapman's glorious lensing of Chicago was in the service of a far more engaging and original movie.

Spader plays Campbell, an FBI specialist in serial killers who has failed to nail the killer of 11 women in Los Angeles. He's gone into hiding in Chicago, where he's under heavy medication and regular therapy from a psychologist (Tomei). Naturally, the killer (Reeves) soon pops up in the Windy City to continue singling out largely solitary young women for strangling with piano wire. Tomei's Polly assures Campbell that, as burned-out as he is, he's still the guy best qualified to continue trying to nab Reeves' Griffin, who always dresses in black.

As time passes and Griffin still eludes Campbell, writers David Elliot and Clay Ayers begin offering a few observations, primarily that Griffin needs to feel that Campbell specifically is pursuing him. It gives him an added kick, and it would seem that he has, in a sense, fallen in love with the FBI agent—though that would scarcely stop him from killing him if he could.

The film, which has been directed with energy and dispatch by Joe Charbanic, takes its title from Griffin's careful observation of the daily routines of the women he chooses as his victims; it also allows the serial killer to make the point that "We don't notice each other anymore," thus enabling him to get away with killing largely anonymous young women, such as a clerk in a shopping mall photo developing store and a homeless young runaway, panhandling in the streets.

But that's about it for content. It's good to see an actor who radiates as much intelligence as Spader capably hold down a major role in a big action movie, but Reeves is asked no more than to be insinuatingly evil and clearly crazed, and Tomei is required little more than to register lots of empathy for Spader's Campbell. Among the supporting players, Chris Ellis is a standout as the kind of dedicated, confident cop that we wish all police officers could be.

NEW YORK POST, 9/8/00, p. 47, Jonathan Foreman

"The Watcher"—a crass, mechanical attempt at a thriller that should have gone straight to video—provides another reminder of how arty (or, at least, visually self-conscious in the MTV style) even the trashiest mainstream Hollywood thrillers have become.

It also shows how too many filmmakers seem to believe a few flashy tricks with the camera will distract audiences from a rotten screenplay.

Is it contempt for the audience, sheer bad taste or plain stupidity that allows folks like producers Christopher Eberts, Elliot Lewitt, Jeff Rice and Nile Niami to think that the lousy dialogue, the incompetently derivative plot and the lifeless characters provided by their screenwriters (David Elliot and Clay Ayers) could be the basis for an entertaining movie?

Joel Campbell (James Spader) is an FBI profiler of serial killers who has suffered a breakdown after a particularly disastrous case and moved to Chicago, where now he lives on disability payments and takes a lot of pills.

But David Allan Griffin (Keanu Reeves), the serial killer who was his nemesis back in L.A., has missed playing the cat-and-mouse game with him and relocates to Chicago just to start it again.

Once in the city, Griffin starts murdering lonely young women in their apartments, first sending Campbell photographs of his intended victims and challenging him and the Chicago PD to find them within 24 hours.

Naturally, the challenge pulls Campbell out of his stupor more effectively than his sessions with his psychologist (Marisa Tomei, almost as unconvincing a shrink as Lorraine Bracco in "The Sopranos"), but puts him—and her—in deadly danger.

Like too many serial-killer films, "The Watcher" takes a creepy, pornographic pleasure in the infliction of terror on women.

It also includes one of those now-compulsory vomit scenes and a sequence in which a helmeted SWAT team goes down a dark staircase, flashlight beams and laser sights cutting through the gloom.

Once you've stopped caring about the story, you start noticing how bad the direction is, from the lame grainy photography (plus heavy breathing on the sound track) whenever you're looking through the eyes of the killer to the pointless wannabe-cool slow-motion sequences.

There's also a rooftop chase scene that's so badly shot—you have no sense of distances or heights—that it's quite remarkable.

One hopes Mr. Reeves (at his most wooden here) and the talented Mr. Spader (who has lost his nose for good or challenging roles since 1996's "Two Days in the Valley") were paid well for slumming in "The Watcher."

SIGHT AND SOUND, 1/01, p. 61, Ken Hollings

US, the present. Suffering from acute stress brought on by hunting down serial killers, FBI agent Joel Campbell has relocated to Chicago from California following his failure to capture David Allen Griffin, psychotic murderer, who stalks and photographs his victims before strangling them. Under medication and seeing psychiatrist Polly, Campbell avoids contact with the outside world.

He discovers that Griffin has tracked him down and is now murdering women in Chicago. Sending him snapshots of his next intended victims with the time at which he will kill them, Griffin goads Campbell into trying to find him. When Campbell becomes hospitalised due to his failed attempts to prevent two further murders, Griffin kidnaps Polly. Holding her hostage on the booby-trapped top floor of a warehouse, Griffin forces Campbell to admit their mutual dependence. A police rescue attempt triggers a massive explosion that claims Griffin, while Campbell and Polly escape.

Ever since a giggling Richard Widmark garrotted a helpless old woman with a length of electrical cord taken from her own home in the 1947 *noir Kiss of Death* filmed in recognisable New York locations, the psycho-killer has represented the ultimate urban nightmare. But in debut director Joe Charbanic's remarkable feature *The Watcher*, it's alienated FBI man Campbell who stands for city living at its darkest and most deranged: dosed on heavy medication, holed up like a junkie in his dingy apartment, unable to remember names or where he's going, Campbell is the solid professional whose life has gone to hell. "If his pupils don't dilate," an FBI colleague mutters behind his back, "then we don't need him." James Spader brings a bruised humanity to his sympathetic portrayal of Campbell's drug-fuddled mental condition; when Campbell forces himself to concentrate on the photographic evidence of serial killer Griffin's next intended victim, you get a, vivid sense of the conflict between the lawman's willpower and his dissipated mental functions. By contrast, Keanu Reeves displays an easy, unreadable charm as Griffin, moving through the crowds of Chicago with assurance, as if its malls, sidewalks and payphones were created exclusively for him. In a grim social irony, faces and locations seen from Griffin's point of view are scanned and smeared to resemble images captured by a CCTV camera, now present on just about every city block in the west.

Director of photography Michael Chapman, whose past credits include *Taxi Driver* (1976) and *Hardcore* 1978), endows Chicago's shops, cafés, corridors and offices with a chilling sense of anonymity, while Richard Nord's nervy editing conveys the pervasive mood of claustrophobia. Charbanic's previous experience as a music-video director is evident in the way he gives a heady spin to the chase scenes by using excerpts of pop music, from the likes of Portishead, Sneaker Pimps and Rob Zombie. A thoughtful screenplay by David Elliot and Clay Ayers gives a strong supporting cast plenty to chew on, notably Chris Ellis as the brusque Lieutenant Hollis, a cop who can maintain a telephone conversation while putting a chokehold on a car thief. "They're going to like him," Campbell deadpans when suggesting that Hollis front a news conference.

However, it's the details of each victim's life, stark, vulnerable and unsettlingly familiar, that come through most strongly in *The Watcher*. To secure Campbell's numbed attention, Griffin abandons his strategy of targeting women without close social attachments, going instead for random faces in the crowd. One works in a mall, another panhandles on the street, and neither attracts more than a passing glance from the people surrounding her. "We're all stacked up on top of each other," Griffin comments, "but we don't really notice each other, do we?" The bodies of his victims have a hyperreal clarity to them in death. Starkly lit and carefully delineated by Chapman's camerawork, they appear to have absorbed the crazed intensity of Campbell's helpless, searching gaze.

Also reviewed in:
CHICAGO TRIBUNE, 9/8/00, Friday/p. A, Michael Wilmington
NEW YORK TIMES, 9/8/00, p. E10, A. O. Scott
VARIETY, 9/11-17/00, p. 22, Joe Leydon
WASHINGTON POST, 9/8/00, p. C12, Rita Kempley
WASHINGTON POST, 9/8/00, Weekend/p. 43, Desson Howe

WATER DROPS ON BURNING ROCKS

A Zeitgeist Films release of a Fidélité Productions/Les Films Alain Sarde production in association with Euro Sage. *Producer:* Olivier Delbosc and Marc Missonnier. *Director:* François Ozon. *Screenplay (French with English subtitles):* François Ozon. *Based on the play "Tropfen auf heisse Steine" by:* Rainer Werner Fassbinder. *Director of Photography:* Jeanne Lapoirie. *Editor:* Laurence Bawedin and Claudine Bouché. *Choreographer:* Sébastien Charles. *Sound:* Eric Devulder and Jean-Pierre Laforce. *Sound Editor:* Benoît Hillebrant. *Casting:* Antoinette Boulat. *Production Designer:* Arnaud de Moléron. *Set Decorator:* Valérie Chemain. *Costumes:* Pascaline Chavanne. *Make-up:* Gill Robillard. *Running time:* 90 minutes. *MPAA Rating:* Not Rated.

CAST: Bernard Giraudeau (Léopold Blum); Malik Zidi (Franz Meister); Ludivine Sagnier (Anna); Anna Thomson (Véra).

CHRISTIAN SCIENCE MONITOR, 7/14/00, p. 15, David Sterritt

"Water Drops on Burning Rocks" is a keenly sardonic tale adapted by French director François Ozon from a play by the late German filmmaker Rainer Werner Fassbinder. It explores the self-destructive nature of sexual gamesmanship through the story of a heedless young man caught between his beautiful fiancée and a self-absorbed male lover.

NEW STATESMAN, 10/9/00, p. 44, Jonathan Romney

Cinema's great overachiever, Rainer Werner Fassbinder had made more than 30 films by the time he died in his mid-thirties. The young French director Francois Ozon, conversely, has acquired something of a reputation as an underachiever, only because his first two features fell so far below the promise of his early shorts. One of the few French film-makers to have worked convincingly with gay themes, Ozon made a series of provocative, poly-sexual vignettes, which he then capped with *Regarde la mer*, a medium-length psychological thriller of fastidious nastiness that matched vintage Roman Polanski. Then came Ozon's first two features and, as they say in France with a perplexed shrug, "Bof!"

Sitcom was a black comedy about a bourgeois family whose buttoned-up life turns orgiastic, as if John Waters had turned his hand to the world of Claude Chabrol, but the taboos were busted with a mechanical joylessness. Then came *Criminal Lovers*, a directionless fairy tale about two homicidal teenagers lost in the dark woods: *Natural Born Killers* meets the *Erl-King*.

Fortunately, with his third film, Ozon has put on an impressive burst of confidence. Oddly enough, the story concerns a youth who comes under the spell of a charismatic older man—more or less what has happened to Ozon himself with *Water Drops on Burning Rocks*. The film is an adaptation of a stage play that Fassbinder wrote at the age of 19, and it makes fascinating viewing if you subscribe to the theory of "anxiety of influence". Young Franz (Malik Zidi) is seduced by the middle-aged businessman Leopold (Bernard Giraudeau), and becomes both his flatmate and his emotional prisoner. Franz is inevitably crushed by his mentor-oppressor, but Ozon—although apparently submitting to Fassbinder's textual and stylistic yoke—emerges replenished from the experience.

Water Drops is remarkable less for the drama itself than for what Ozon manages to do with the play's restraints. The drama, divided into acts, takes place wholly in Franz's apartment, and Ozon consistently frames his characters to remind us that the apartment is itself a stage. This is a device often decried as uncinematic, yet it can be the boldest film gambit of all: the challenge is to come right up against film's borderline with theatre, yet still make cinema. The set, by Arnaud de Moleron, seems infinitely adaptable and extendable, a suite of spaces hemmed in by heavy, dark surfaces, but always providing new corners for the action. The look could almost be a pastiche anthology of Fassbinder's sets: the bedroom an up-market love nest from *Fox and His Friends*, the austerely cosy kitchen niche right out of *Fear Eats the Soul*.

Language itself becomes part of a masquerade that is, above all, sexual. Franz starts off as the image of an idealistic student of the era, leather-jacketed and believing that what counts in life is "books, theatre, art" (trendy students into theatre—now that's retro). By Act 2, we are seeing a full-blown parody of marital domesticity, with Franz now a servile haus-pet in lederhosen, and Leopold sourly ordering him around.

We may have seen these places before, and recoiled at the high-collared tweed overcoats, but this is not a standard exercise in Seventies retro. Every visual and cultural reference is quintessentially German—more precisely, Bavarian—and Ozon stresses Germanness both in order to indulge his passion for pastiche and to distance his French audience. He doesn't Gallicise the play at all: we hear a Heinrich Heine poem in the original, and even a Francoise Hardy song has German lyrics.

The next twist comes when the women arrive: Franz's girlfriend, Anna (Ludivine Sagnier, as friskily wide-eyed as a screen ingenue has ever been), and Leopold's ex, Vera, whom Ozon has made transsexual in a nod to another Fassbinder film. Vera is an unsettling casting choice—the American actress Anna Thomson who, here, strangely resembles a haggard drag act trying to pass as Pamela Anderson.

This is, at moments, an exuberantly sexy film, and Ozon does rather more with his cast's bodies and body language than he does with the text, which seems, for the most part, to reiterate the message that (as Fassbinder called his first feature) "love is colder than death". But Ozon is most intrigued by the intricate complications of lust and style: and this is where the casting of Giraudeau is so astute. A hard-boiled matinee idol in the Eighties, Giraudeau now comes across as a faintly unsavoury roue, mixing suavity and bluff cheapness—here, polo-necked and predatory, he is like a spoiled libertine Roger Moore. Ozon presents Fassbinder's play as a dance of sex and death, and the most winning moment is when the four actors execute an incongruously nifty disco dance—a ludicrous bit of showoffery, and perhaps an over-literal metaphor, but a dizzy marvel to behold and a welcome suspension of the overall dark mood.

The end result may not be that substantial. Ozon's attention to Fassbinder's themes seems to yield less than his stylistic invention. And British viewers may, after a while, find themselves on more familiar ground than expected: by Act 3, we come remarkably close to Joe Orton territory. The tart frivolity, in the end, makes the film a touch hollow, and it still feels like something of an intermediate venture for Ozon. But he is moving on—he has already followed it with another feature, his fourth in two years. He could be a Fassbinderian overachiever yet.

NEW YORK POST, 7/12/00, p. 48, Hannah Brown

Imagine a Pedro Almodovar movie without the pizazz and you have a good idea of what it's like to sit through "Water Drops on Burning Rocks."

Based on an unproduced play by the late German movie director Rainer Werner Fassbinder, this glib and heavy-handed French film tells the story of the relationship between 20-year-old Franz (Malik Zidi) and 50-year-old Leopold (Bernard Giraudeau).

It opens at Leopold's apartment, just after he and Franz have met.

In the film's heartfelt opening sequence, the naive Franz babbles about his relationship with his fiancée and plays board games with Leopold, who eventually gets the boy to open up and discuss his homosexual fantasies.

The static, claustrophobic movie is very much a filmed play. The camera never leaves the apartment, and titles introduce each act.

In the final frame of the first act, Franz succumbs to Leopold's advances.

In the second act, they're bickering lovers, living together. Then, Anna (Ludivine Sagnier), Franz's jilted fiancée, shows up to seduce him away from Leopold.

To complicate matters, Vera (Anna Thomson), Leopold's ex-girlfriend, who happens to be a transsexual, also drops by.

The action becomes more comic as the characters play musical beds and break into a dance number, then turns unexpectedly and pointlessly tragic.

Franz and Leopold are stereotypes of the callow, effeminate young gay man and the predatory rich effeminate young gay man and the predatory rich older homosexual. Neither is especially interesting or sympathetic.

The two women simply want desperately to hold onto their men, although Sagnier shows comic flair in her thankless role as the laughably voluptuous, ultra-feminine bimbo. Her breasts steal every scene they're in.

Director François Ozon, best known for his bizarre "Sitcom" and "See the Sea," has a hard time with the flat, cynical tone of the Fassbinder play.

Although there are moments of wit here, they don't sustain interest in or affection for the characters.

NEWSDAY, 7/12/00, Part II/p. B9, Jan Stuart

Oh, that Rainer Werner Fassbinder! Eighteen years after his death from a drug overdose at 36, he's still finding novel ways to get under our skin.

In "Water Drops on Burning Rocks," the prickly Bavarian auteur receives an unexpectedly winsome treatment from French director Francois Ozon. Adapted by Ozon from a play Fassbinder wrote at the beginning of his career, this chamber piece for four players takes an oddball pleasure in the heartless games that people in love often play with one another.

A 50-year-old businessman named Leopold (Bernard Giraudeau) admittedly finds little pleasure in anything. When he brings home a 19-year-old named Franz (Malik Zidi) for an evening that has all the makings of a one-night-stand, he is momentarily charmed by the young man's inexperience and elfin beauty. But when the date improbably evolves into a long-term relationship, Leopold's irritable and latently cruel nature is unleashed on the callow Franz, who seems willing to take a lot of punishment to preserve a potent sex life.

The sado-masochistic nature of their relationship is thrown into relief when women from each of their pasts invade their squalling love nest. Leopold's wife of seven years, Vera (Anna Thomson), begins to show up at their door, running off in tears almost as soon as she arrives. She is followed soon thereafter by Anna (Ludivine Sagnier), the young fiancee whom Franz threw over to be with Leopold. Franz responds with a steeliness he could only have learned from his older lover. Leopold, in turn, plays his old seduction card on the women, demonstrating the full measure of his selfishness and narcissism.

Fassbinder ratchets up the ambiguities of dominance, control and sexual role playing by making Vera a transsexual who was a former male buddy of Leopold's before they were married. One can't help but be impressed at both the prescience and casualness with which Fassbinder was confounding notions of sexuality decades before the word "transgender" entered the vernacular.

Ozon transmits all this with a visual formality that echoes the austerity and geometric nature of Fassbinder's blueprint. Abetted by the brittle performances of Giraudeau and Zidi, the handsomely minimalist, one-set film will speak primarily to Fassbinder fans and cineasts, who will, no doubt, be fascinated by the ways in which Leopold and Franz provide contrasting surrogates for the artist in his zealous youth and in a middle age he never lived to see.

SIGHT AND SOUND, 11/00, p. 64, Richard Falcon

The Federal Republic of Germany, the 70s. Fifty-year-old insurance salesman Léopold Blum invites 19-year-old student Franz Meister to his apartment and learns of his unsatisfactory sexual relationship with his girlfriend Anna. Franz agrees to sleep with Léopold, who enacts an erotic dream of the student's by appearing in the bedroom doorway wearing a raincoat.

Six months later. Franz is now living with Léopold as his chattel. The lovers row about domestic details, but the sex keeps them together. During one of Léopold's business trips, Anna arrives and finds Franz depressed. She has had an offer of marriage but still loves Franz and is determined to win him back. They sleep together. Anna is enthused by Franz's new-found sexual confidence; Franz, though, is reluctant to leave. Léopold arrives and shows a sexual interest in Anna. Léopold's ex-lover Véra, who visited while he was away, then turns up. Léopold, Anna and Véra have sex; sidelined by Léopold and Anna, Véra joins Franz in the living room where she tells him she had a sex change to maintain Léopold's interest. Franz swallows poison and phones his mother. When Léopold and Anna discover his body, Léopold takes control. Leaving Franz's corpse in the living room, he continues having sex with Véra and Anna.

François Ozon's third feature is a treat for devotees of European film culture. In adapting for the cinema a play written in the mid 60s (but never staged) by Rainer Werner Fassbinder, Ozon conjures a complex film experience out of what would have been relatively thin—if typically provocative—theatrical material. The reasons why Fassbinder never directed the play are a matter of speculation; perhaps he considered this first work an apprentice exercise—the claustrophobically perverse sexual power dynamic between young student Franz and older sophisticate Léopold finds echoes in the relationship between the two gay protagonists of *Fox and his Friends* (1975) and the lesbian couple in *The Bitter Tears of Petra von Kant* (1972).

Having already established his credentials as a pasticheur in *Sitcom* (1998), Ozon here adopts some of the most obvious stylistic traits of mid-period Fassbinder. There is the claustrophobic single interior location (Léopold's flat) and the use of overt theatricality for specifically cinematic aims (Ozon even employs captions to introduce each act). The one exterior shot, repeated throughout the movie, isolates the characters—first Franz and Léopold, then Franz and his girlfriend Anna, then Franz and Léopold's ex-lover Véra—from each other within the apartment's window frames; and when the prowling camera rests, it entraps the characters within a constricting *mise en scène* similar to that in Fassbinder's Douglas Sirk-inspired melodramas. The result is quite an achievement, a startling homage that reflects Ozon's preoccupation with the black humour of potentially menacing power games, visible in his chilling 1997 film *Regarde la mer*, as it does Fassbinder's conviction that, in the words of one of his film's titles, love is colder than death.

The play, whose first three acts Ozon is remarkably faithful to, turns on a series of reversals. The unhappy Franz—subtly and confidently played by Malik Zidi—is first seduced by the charming Léopold (the older man even takes time to wash the drinks glasses before taking Franz to bed). By the end of the second act, it is Franz who is cleaning the glasses, looking after the flat as Léopold's live-in lover. A recurring Fassbinder pattern, in which a passive victim internalises his oppression and in turn oppresses others, looks set to establish itself when Anna arrives, wanting to rescue Franz. By the third act, though, Franz is still the victim; as Anna reciprocates the sexual interest Léopold takes in her, Franz's meagre *raison d'être* is the domestic tasks he performs for Léopold. Unlike Franz Biberkopf, the hero of *Fox*, this Franz isn't a working-class rent boy used by a middle-class gay sophisticate, but a student, while Léopold is an insurance salesman, driven by the need to earn a living. The power relations between them are initially ambiguous—Franz, for instance, chooses to succumb to Léopold in the first act. But by the end, in the land of blind desire, Léopold is king and Franz as doomed as Gregor Samsa in Kafka's *Metamorphosis*.

But Franz is not the only victim: Véra, who appears, like Marlene in *Petra von Kant*, in Fassbinder's original as a wholly subjugated and thinly sketched character, is here given a tragic backstory, taken by Ozon from Fassbinder's *In a Year with 13 Moons* (1978) she underwent a sex change, Véra tells Franz, to maintain the fickle Léopold's interest. As Véra moves into focus in the final act, so too does the difference between Ozon and Fassbinder. In performance terms, Ozon's film is polished, where Fassbinder's would have been rawer, reflecting perhaps the borderline sado masochistic relationship between the director and his cast. Here Ozon's close-ups allow us to enjoy the subtleties of Bernard Giraudeau's performance as Léopold, in some senses an embodiment of the archetypal old French roué (the character in the play is 35, not 50). Ozon uses popular music, not to illustrate bathetically the longings of the characters as Fassbinder might have, but to manipulate audience mood—there is a sudden joyous outburst as the characters start boogying to 70s Euro pop song 'Tanze Samba mit mir' by Tony Holiday before, in a moment of pure farce, Léopold claps his hands and ushers Anna and Véra into the bedroom for sex. If Ozon is necessarily self-conscious in his cross-cultural foray—ending the film with the title track

'Traüme' from Françoise Hardy's only German-language album, having Franz quote a Heine poem in German, and starting the film with a series of retro postcards of Germany—he at least proves he is far more than a tourist in Fassbinder's peculiar, and fast receding, 70s Federal Republic.

VILLAGE VOICE, 7/18/00, p. 117, J. Hoberman

It will soon be 20 years since the untimely death of R.W. Fassbinder dealt populist art cinema a stunning blow. Moving throughout the '70s from political noir and stylized melodrama to mordant studies in psychosexual sociology, Fassbinder anticipated the entire trajectory of American independent film. The loss is not just the films he might have made but the persistent erasure of those 40-plus features he did complete.

This week, however, Fassbinder rises from the dead—at least after a fashion. In *Water Drops on Burning Rocks,* a hit at the last Berlin Film Festival, French enfant terrible François Ozon (in high school when Fassbinder died) attempts a risky stunt in dusting off and filming a play that Fassbinder wrote at 19 and that was never produced in his lifetime. Like much Fassbinder, *Water Drops on Burning Rocks* is tragic farce. It's a love story that's not only unhappy but unblinking in its lack of sentimentality.

The confidently domineering Leopold (Bernard Giraudeau) has picked up and brought home a guy less than half his age. When Franz (Malik Zidi) estimates that fastidious Leo is 50, the older man is hilariously taken aback: "No one's ever said that before." The two chat briefly about the women in their lives and even more briefly play a board game before Leo cuts to the chase: "Have you ever slept with a man?" Now it is Franz's turn to act surprised. What prompted this question? He's never even thought about the possibility, although he has had this recurring dream.... Thus begins the relationship on which the movie spins.

Water Drops on Burning Rocks is at once a tribute and an appropriation. The French dialogue serves to put Fassbinder in quotation marks even as the action recalls the real thing, and Ozon has further Fassbinderized the original by adding a plot twist from *In a Year of 13 Moons. Water Drops* not only traffics in Fassbinder's themes but uses the mise-en-scène of early middle-period Fassbinder films like *The Bitter Tears of Petra von Kant* and *The Merchant of Four Seasons.* The lighting is flat, the perspective is head-on. There's a fondness for posing actors and organizing mirror shots; a tinkling music-box refrain is used for punctuation, and to add to the theatricality, the movie does not include a single exterior shot.

Indeed, *Water Drops* never leaves Leopold's apartment—it jumps ahead six months from the first scene to the spectacle of Leopold and Franz's domestic life. Franz grooms himself in preparation for Leopold's return from the business world, scurrying to greet him in cutely suspendered short-shorts. But Leopold, an insurance salesman, is an insufferable grouch and petty tyrant. He browbeats the seemingly compliant Franz (who then exacts revenge by blasting the stereo). This crabby non-idyll is further complicated when their respective former girlfriends arrive. Taking a leaf from Leopold, who's away on business, Franz orders around his lovelorn Anna (Ludivine Sagnier) while posing questions like "What is happiness?"

If Franz (whose name is a favorite Fassbinder alter ego) has certain aspects of the artist as a young man (the teenage Fassbinder was a sometime prostitute), Leopold's character looks forward to the seductive scene-maker and master manipulator that was the mature Fassbinder. The insurance man (embodied by Giraudeau in the film's most authoritative performance) returns to take charge—Anna never manages to get back into her clothes—and orchestrate the antics, which, with the arrival of his own ex-"wife," Vera (Anna Thomson), grow increasingly convoluted and ultimately fatal.

A movie of cutting humor, near-constant talk, and one show-stopping dance routine, *Water Drops* is more a diagram of human relations than a portrait of human beings, a movie fascinated less by sex than the power with which sex is invested. If the Coens can rerelease *Blood Simple,* perhaps Fassbinder's distributors will reissue *Ali: Fear Eats the Soul* or *Fox and His Friends* or *Lola.* These movies have scarcely dated. To judge from the response to *Water Drops,* the audience is more than ready.

Also reviewed in:
CHICAGO TRIBUNE, 8/18/00, Friday/p. G, John Petrakis
NEW YORK TIMES, 7/12/00, p. E1, A. O. Scott
VARIETY, 2/21-27/00, p. 39, David Stratton

WAY OF THE GUN, THE

An Artisan Entertainment release of an Aqaba production. *Executive Producer:* Russ Markowitz. *Producer:* Kenneth Kokin. *Director:* Christopher McQuarrie. *Screenplay:* Christopher McQuarrie. *Director of Photography:* Dick Pope. *Editor:* Stephen Semel. *Music:* Joe Kraemer. *Music Editor:* Lisé Richardson. *Sound:* Earl Stein, Roger Davis and (music) Armin Steiner. *Sound Editor:* Chuck Michael. *Casting:* Lynn Kressel. *Production Designer:* Maia Javan. *Art Director:* Thomas Meyer. *Set Designer:* Linden Snyder. *Set Decorator:* Les Boothe. *Costumes:* Genevieve Tyrrell and Heather Neely McQuarrie. *Make-up:* Gina Homan. *Stunt Coordinator:* Gary Paul. *Running time:* 120 minutes. *MPAA Rating:* R.

CAST: Ryan Phillippe (Parker); Benicio Del Toro (Longbaugh); Juliette Lewis (Robin); Taye Diggs (Jeffers); Nicky Katt (Obecks); Geoffrey Lewis (Abner); Dylan Kussman (Dr. Allen Painter); Scott Wilson (Hale Chidduck); Kristin Lehman (Francesca Chidduck); James Caan (Joe Sarno); Henry Griffin (P. Whipped); Mando Guerrero (Federale 1); Jan Jensen (Receptionist); Andres Orozco (Federale 2); José Perez (Federale 3); Neil Pollock (Interviewer); Irene Santiago (Sloppy Prostitute); Sarah Silverman (Raving Bitch).

LOS ANGELES TIMES, 9/8/00, Calendar/p. 6, John Anderson

[The following review by John Anderson appeared in a slightly different form in NEWSDAY, 9/8/00 Part II/p. B7.]

Since Quentin Tarantino has been making himself scarce—and Sergio Leone is dead, Howard Hawks is dead and John Woo is on Cruise control—Christopher McQuarrie has decided to fill the enormous void with "The Way of the Gun," an implement of destruction loaded with more borrowed film riffs than could be compiled by 47 clones of Robert Rodriguez.

Like a director who's budgeted a helicopter and can't bear not to use it, McQuarrie—the Oscar-winning screenwriter of "The Usual Suspects"—can't help larding his directorial debut with trimmings from far superior crime dramas, old and new ("Heat," "Hard-Boiled" and "The Big Sleep," to name a few). He may harbor an affection for the genre, but McQuarrie keeps tripping over the cluttered video library of his mind.

Either that, or he can't tell the difference between prime cut and baloney. It's possible. There's a scene at the beginning of this eventually tiresome salute to mayhem in which Mr. Parker (Ryan Phillippe) and Mr. Longbaugh (Benicio Del Toro), down-on-their-luck gunmen, have just finished semantically torturing the clerk at a sperm bank and are about to make their deposit. Then they overhear a conversation about a fabulously wealthy Southwestern couple and the surrogate mother of their child-to-be. They don't say a word, but their silent, mutual, instinctual plotting is a far more eloquent illustration of their nefarious personalities than all of Parker's windy philosophy of crime (delivered in a voice borrowed from Dan Hedaya), to which we've already been subjected quite enough, thanks so much. It's better than the shootouts too.

What Parker and Longbaugh don't know is that Ms. Surrogate, Robin (Juliette Lewis), is carrying the baby for Hale Chidduck (Scott Wilson), a leg-breaking, money-laundering "bagman" of the old school who can't produce big-time ransom money without raising a lot of federal suspicions. So Chidduck calls in his longtime associate and hired gun Sarno (James Caan) to get him out of the mess that his regular security men, Jeffers and Obecks (Taye Diggs and Nicky Katt), have managed not to avoid. Bad blood is running everywhere.

So is regular blood. And McQuarrie's violence, despite its occasionally errant choreography, provides a relief from the faux-Faulknerian dialogue and the convoluted plot, both of which are more than inspired by the byzantine "Big Sleep." Keeping track of who is connected to whom becomes as exasperating as the deliberately oblique bits of dialogue that are intended to tantalize but, ultimately, merely irritate.

By the way, "bagman," a word the movie throws around promiscuously, is supposed to denote a thug who collects money (hence the bag), not just a wise guy with a gun. You'd think McQuarrie, with all his encyclopedic knowledge of crime and drama, would have known that. But then, he subjects us not once but three times to the impaired vision of Lewis stumbling bowlegged around the movie with her prosthetic womb halfway to the floor. Anyone who'd do that doesn't have much sense. Or any mercy at all.

NEW STATESMAN, 11/20/00, p. 46, Jonathan Romney

Christopher McQuarrie's *The Way of the Gun* is a mean, nasty, brutal film, but it is in no way a dumb one. It has the skewed critical intelligence that you would expect from the writer of that quintessentially clever-dick piece of neo-*noir The Usual Suspects*. Like that film, *The Way of the Gun* is a tale of skulduggery among men, but this time the misogyny is foregrounded to become a theme in its own right. In *The Usual Suspects*, the single female character was first sidelined, then given a nasty send-off. *The Way of the Gun* begins with one of its anti-heroes casually punching a woman in the face, and it ends with a shoot-out in a Mexican brothel—while a gory caesarian delivery is being performed.

On paper, this might seem about as unpleasant as American gangster cinema can get—and that's pretty much how it comes across on screen, too. But McQuarrie should not be written off too quickly as a callous opportunist riding the tail-end of the post-Tarantino sick-kicks wave. He has more serious intentions than just to amuse us, and the real comparisons here are with the Seventies American directors of westerns and thrillers—Sam Peckinpah, Don Siegel, Walter Hill—who gave full moral weight to the power of a firearm and what it means to shoot one.

We can gather that McQuarrie is questioning the men-with-guns myth right at the start, when his two hoodlums (played by the weird, hoarse Benicio Del Toro and the tarnished pretty-face Ryan Pbillippe) introduce themselves as "Parker" and "Longbaugh"—the real names of Butch Cassidy and the Sundance Kid. Like them, they will go down outnumbered under the Mexican sun, but will have been stripped of any vestige of heroism.

Parker and Longbaugh are losers who fancy themselves as existential heroes facing their fate: choosing between "petty crime or a minimum wage". They believe in "the way things are meant to be", but it is clear from the start that the world is a chaos in which people can only pretend to be in control. They hear of a young woman, Robin (Juliette Lewis), who has been impregnated as a surrogate mother for a wealthy client, and decide to kidnap her for the ransom. But the client is a powerful mob figure, Chidduck (Scott Wilson). Once Robin is in their hands, Chidduck won't pay up, but unleashes a merciless veteran, played by James Caan, to track them down. The duo's plan comes undone in a labyrinthine imbroglio of double-dealing, in which everyone—including Robin's doctor—has their own agenda.

This is a classic example of a film in which no character is straightforwardly sympathetic. We may root for Robin but, as the film goes on, it is less as the young mother in peril, more as a tough operator who proves as remorseless and feral as her captors. By conventional standards, the idea of having a pregnant woman as the stakes in men's murderous games is simply tasteless, and McQuarrie knows it. He wants us to be shocked that real blood gets spilled, not just Tarantino's ketchup. The film's climax is at moments barely watchable, largely because of the discrepancy between the abstract action of the gunplay and the intensity of Robin's screams in labour: what is shocking is the discordant element of birth, normally an absolute taboo in this genre. Rather than letting us relish the action, the film detaches us from it and questions why we expected to enjoy it.

That may seem an oversophisticated, perhaps even overfamiliar, excuse for what is surely just a tough, brutal little crime movie. *The Way of the Gun* is just that—but as such films go, it is a pretty distinctive example. Its genre attractions are several: McQuarrie has devised some action sequences that are as effective as anything in Michael Mann's *Heat*—in particular, a slow game of tag between cars. But it also has a moral weight, a sense of the immediacy of death (its oldest gangster, played by Geoffrey Lewis, is a suicidal depressive) and a quite unique mood of careworn remorse. Its moral centre is Sarno, an old-guard foot-soldier who bears his battle scars on his neck—a wonderfully stiff turn in barrel-chested menace from Caan, who makes the film's most dangerous character also the most sympathetic. It's not just that he gets McQuarrie's most baroquely resonant dialogue ("I can promise you a day of reckoning that you will not remember long enough to never forget"). Nor is it sentimental, Kray-style nostalgia that makes us respect a hard man simply because he is older. It is more that Sarno is the professional who knows how things should work, and sees, with a pained wince, how they are going wrong.

Del Toro's Longbaugh remarks that villains aren't what they were: "These days, they want to be criminal more than they want to commit crime." Caan replies: "That's not just crime, that's the way of the world." But it is also, McQuarrie argues, the way of cinema: too many movies about guys dressed for the part, too much bonhomie and circus-style gunplay. In contrast, McQuarrie gives us birth, death, blood and maximum-impact retribution. *The Way of the Gun* is a thriller that horrifies as much as it thrills—and that, McQuarrie seems to be saying, should be the way of the world.

NEW YORK POST, 9/8/00, p. 46, Lou Lumenick

Here's a belated addition to the long list of ultra-violent, jokey and generally mediocre thrillers inspired by "Reservoir Dogs," "Pulp Fiction" and "The Usual Suspects." The Academy Award-winning writer of the latter, Christopher Quarrie, is making his debut as a writer-director with this one, so at least it's got some promising plot twists and quotable dialogue.

At one point, one tough guy asks another tough guy, "Are you the brains of this outfit?   Or is he?"

The reply: "I don't think this is a brains kind of operation."

Our heroes in what amounts to a contemporary western—specifically, a sort of twisted variation on the John Wayne-John Ford "Three Godfathers"—are a pair of hardened gunmen who call themselves Parker (pretty boy Ryan Phillippe, cast wildly against type) and Longbaugh (Benicio Del Toro of "Usual Suspects"), after the real names of Butch Cassidy and the Sundance Kid.

They are raising a little capital by selling their sperm when they overhear a conversation about Robin (Juliette Lewis), a young woman who's been hired as a surrogate mother by a very wealthy couple.

In the first of many shootouts, they abduct the very pregnant Robin from her hotshot bodyguards (Taye Diggs and Nicky Katt) and whisk her to a motel in Mexico.   When her obstetrician (Dylan Kussman, who must've entered medical school when he was 12) arrives to tend to complications, they learn Robin's employer is Chidduck (Scott Wilson), a money-laundering, union-busting bagman.

The kidnappers demand $15 million for Robin's return—not realizing that because of the nature of his business, the last thing Chidduck (who won't call the cops) can do is pay them off.

Instead, he sends his cool-headed top fixer, Sarno (James Caan), and a lieutenant (Geoffrey Lewis, Juliette Lewis' real-life dad), along with the two bodyguards, to bring back the about-to-be-born baby from south of the border.

What follows is a series of double- and triple-crosses, revealed secrets and rapidly escalating body counts. There are also more plugs for Coca-Cola than we've seen in a movie since that soft-drink company sold Columbia Pictures to Sony in the early 1990s.

The laughably miscast Phillippe aside, the performances are more than decent. Caan seems to be particularly enjoying delivering threats such as: "I can promise you a day of reckoning that you won't live long enough to never forget."

Where "The Way of the Gun" falters seriously is its too-leisurely pacing. If you're going to make a gun-heavy movie without a single sympathetic character (even the pregnant Robin is pretty sleazy), you had better make it move quickly enough that the audience doesn't have time to dwell on that fact at length.

Especially in the post-Columbine era.

SIGHT AND SOUND, 12/00, p. 56, Geoffrey Macnab

US, the present At a fertility clinic where they intend to sell sperm samples, Parker and Longbaugh, two career criminals, overhear the whereabouts of surrogate mother Robin, who is carrying the child of a wealthy couple, Hale and Francesca Chidduck. Outwitting Robin's bodyguards Jeffers and Obecks, they kidnap Robin and head for Mexico. When Parker and Longbaugh learn from Robin's doctor Allen Painter that Chidduck is a crook who will do anything to get the baby (if not the mother) back, they demand a $15 million ransom.

Jeffers, who is having an affair with Francesca, and Obecks come after them; so does old-timer Joe Sarno, Chidduck's "adjudicator". After a shoot-out in a motel, during which Obecks is shot, Jeffers takes Robin to a remote Mexican hotel; there, he plans to wait for her to give birth, kill her and take the baby. Painter is on hand to deliver the baby. Before going into labour, Robin admits that the child is hers, and that Painter is the father. Parker and Longbaugh are wounded in another shoot-out. While performing a Caesarian operation on Robin, Painter shoots Jeffers dead.

Sarno arrives with the ransom money and a small army of henchmen, with whom Parker and Longbaugh have a pitched battle. Painter delivers Robin's baby. As they lie gravely wounded, Parker and Longbaugh realise that Sarno is Robin's father.

Francesca Chidduck informs her husband that she is pregnant.

In *The Way of the Gun* the line between hero and villain is infinitesimally drawn. Parker and Longbaugh, as close as the film comes to good guys, are trigger-happy, cheerfully amoral petty hoodlums with a penchant for torture, robbery and blackmail. In the first sequence they needlessly pick a fight with a couple which ends with Parker punching out a woman. Later, they think nothing of kidnapping a heavily pregnant woman, an act for which they feel no remorse ("We didn't come for absolution. We didn't ask to be redeemed.") If they are morally ambiguous figures, the bad guys are even more unscrupulous: every character, from the criminal boss Chidduck to his sharp-suited goons, from the boss' wife to the surrogate mother who is carrying Chidduck's baby, has a hidden agenda. As in *The Usual Suspects* (scripted by *The Way of the Guns* debut director Christopher McQuarrie) we're never quite sure who is deceiving whom; and just as *The Usual Suspects* had an anonymous, all-powerful *deus ex machina* in Keyser Soze, *The Way of the Gun* boasts one character, Sarno, who is several steps ahead of everybody else. Played by James Caan, Sarno is nicknamed "the adjudicator", Chidduck's Mr Fixit whose function isn't just to bring back the baby but to tie the disparate strands of the story together. He is also, almost by default, the moral centre of the film, the one character whose motives aren't primarily selfish.

The infuriatingly complex plotting of McQuarrie's script muddies what would otherwise seem like a straightforward latter-day Western. As in late Howard Hawks, here the gunplay is interspersed with long passages in which characters sit around talking. Caan is the paternal old timer, giving advice to the two hot-headed hoodlums (a reversal from his role as a young gambler in Hawks' 1966 *El Dorado*). To emphasise the generational divide, McQuarrie casts several veteran actors opposite the young guns: the corrupt businessman Chidduck is played by Scott Wilson (one of the killers from Richard Brooks' 1967 film *In Cold Blood*) and Sarno's old partner by Geoffrey Lewis (a craggy veteran of many Clint Eastwood Westerns and the father of Juliette Lewis, who plays surrogate mother Robin).

Once Parker and Longbaugh cross the Mexican border, the film-making becomes more ritualistic and melodramatic, and McQuarrie loses his obsession with contriving elaborate plot twists. His main inspiration in these final stretches seems to be Sam Peckinpah's *Bring Me the Head of Alfredo Garcia* (1974). Just as the old patriarch in that movie puts a grisly $1 million price tag on Alfredo Garcia's head, here Chidduck promises his hoodlums untold riches if they deliver him the baby he craves. There's an extraordinary birth scene in which Robin goes into labour in a dusty hotel room with mobsters for midwives and a doctor who doesn't know what he's doing. McQuarrie avoids the temptation to have Robin's new born babe bring harmony to the proceedings, and the final shoot-out is as stylised and as far-fetched as any Spaghetti Western showdown. Not that McQuarrie downplays the effect of the violence (in one particularly gruesome scene, Parker has to pull shards of broken glass from his arm). But such brutal scenes are undercut with lyricism and deadpan wit, and make for a flamboyant, richly satisfying denouement to a film which that initially seems hobbled by its own self-consciously clever screenplay.

VILLAGE VOICE, 9/12/00, p. 147, J. Hoberman

Where *Nurse Betty* [see Hoberman's review] lifts its garrulous hitmen from *Pulp Fiction, The Way of the Gun* is an attitude noir that takes a good deal more. Written and directed by Christopher McQuarrie, who won an Oscar for scripting *The Usual Suspects*, this buzzword mantra is stocked with showy, pointless bits of business—beginning with the opening attention-grabber in which a posturing pair of philosophical petty criminals, Ryan Phillippe and Benicio Del Toro, precipitate a brawl in a suburban parking lot.

Like *Nurse Betty*, with which it shares Monument Valley as a backdrop, *Way of the Gun* is a self-consciously American odyssey. But, as befits a movie that wants to go *mano a mano* with Tarantino, Peckinpah, and the Coens, it's obsessed with genealogy. After a ludicrous attempt to become sperm donors, Phillippe and Del Toro conceive the notion of kidnapping the pregnant young woman serving as a criminal multimillionaire's hired womb. The idea of Juliette Lewis—Ms. Bad Karma—as a surrogate mother is the least of the movie's abstractions. The initial abduction stops the stillborn show with its gratuitous brutality, absurdly slow getaway, and increasingly desperate Method actors. While the coolly frantic Del Toro gives a performance in search of a character, Phillippe is implacably inert throughout. Phillippe talks like Brando; Del Toro apes the body language. Nevertheless, James Caan steals the movie as a veteran tough guy, rotating his torso around some unseen truss.

Unexpectedly, the initially clumsy exposition improves once the desperadoes head south of the border—the movie accelerating into a plot-driven rondo of convoluted relationships and hairpin power shifts. But *Way of the Gun*'s middle act, which includes the best of the film's three extravagantly choreographed shoot-outs, is dissipated by McQuarrie's big closer, a cosmic denouement in a Mexican whorehouse. It's possible that *Way of the Gun* will garner some wild kudos, but the chief villain's best line suggests that at least the film is onto itself: "It's a simple fact of life that anyone who does business with me can't be trusted."

Also reviewed in:
CHICAGO TRIBUNE, 9/8/00, Friday/p. A, Michael Wilmington
NEW YORK TIMES, 9/8/00, p. E10, Elvis Mitchell
NEW YORKER, 10/2/00, p. 148, David Denby
VARIETY, 9/11-17/00, p. 22, Emanuel Levy
WASHINGTON POST, 9/8/00, p. C1, Stephen Hunter
WASHINGTON POST, 9/8/00, Weekend/p. 41, Desson Howe

WEEKEND, THE

A Strand Releasing and Granada Films release of a Granada Film/Lunatics & Lovers production. *Executive Producer:* Pippa Cross and Janette Day. *Producer:* Ian Benson. *Director:* Brian Skeet. *Screenplay:* Brian Skeet. *Based on the novel by:* Peter Cameron. *Director of Photography:* Ron Fortunato. *Editor:* Chris Wyatt. *Music:* Sarah Class and Dan Jones. *Sound:* Thomas Varga. *Production Designer:* Bob Shaw. *Art Director:* Will Carlough. *Set Decorator:* Jacqueline Jacobson. *Special Effects:* Alan Church. *Costumes:* Edi Giguere. *Running time:* 97 minutes. *MPAA Rating:* Not Rated.

CAST: Gena Rowlands (Laura Ponti); Deborah Kara Unger (Marian Kerr); Brooke Shields (Nina); Jared Harris (John Kerr); David Conrad (Lyle); James Duval (Robert); D.B. Sweeney (Tony); Gary Dourdan (Thierry).

LOS ANGELES TIMES, 11/24/00, Calendar/p. 18, Kevin Thomas

The strongest presence at a gathering at an upstate New York country estate in "The Weekend," a film as subtle and incisive as a New Yorker short story, is that of a dead man. Exactly a year has passed since the charismatic Tony (D.B. Sweeney) has died of AIDS. Handsome and charming, Tony was gay but was equally attractive to both sexes and didn't hesitate to string women along. They never got anywhere with him sexually, but that didn't stop them from falling in love with him.

This is especially true of the reserved yet sultry Marian (Deborah Kara Unger), the wife of Tony's half-brother John (Jared Harris), to whom the estate—a large and splendid Colonial-style home alongside a river—belongs. John has always been overshadowed by the glamorous Tony, but the half-brothers, raised separately, had formed a close bond before Tony died.

Marian, formerly an art restorer at the Met, considers Tony's lover Lyle (David Conrad), an art critic and historian, her best friend. The mother of a baby son, Marian has never really acknowledged to herself, let alone her husband, a quiet man of much perception and understanding, the depth of her unrequited, passionate love for Tony.

When Lyle arrives at the estate unexpectedly accompanied by a young painter Robert (James Duval) he met only three weeks before, Marian is thoroughly disconcerted. Clearly, she had looked forward to having Lyle's company all to herself on his first visit since Tony's death to commiserate with him on their mutual loss. For Lyle, Robert represents his first involvement after a long and painful ordeal.

Meanwhile, Marian and John's friend and neighbor Laura (Gena Rowlands), a worldly and formidable widow of a celebrated Italian architect, has been invited to the Kerrs for dinner. Out of the blue her daughter Nina (Brooke Shields) a B-movie actress, has arrived with her latest boyfriend, Thierry (Gary Dourdan), an animal wrangler on her current picture.

To be sure, Marian's carefully planned Saturday night dinner will bring various subterranean tensions to a simmer—but not a melodramatic boiling over. In the privileged, sophisticated world of Peter Cameron's novel, adapted for the screen with consummate skill by director Brian Skeet, people are fundamentally decent, highly articulate and capable of being honest with themselves upon reflection, prepared to face up to thoughtless cruelty, its source and its consequences. These people are able to look at situations and themselves in a fresh way from even a slight change in perspective; it doesn't take disaster on an epic scale to do it.

"The Weekend" has been bathed in a warm glow by cinematographer Ron Fortunato, keyed to the hues of the Fairfield Porter watercolors that are part of the opening credits. "The Weekend" is saved from seeming too neatly tied up by how well-drawn its people are and how equally well-played they are by a carefully chosen ensemble cast.

Rowlands takes over most every scene she is in, and not simply because she's a highly experienced actress; Laura is at once needy of attention and infinitely skilled in commanding it.

What's surprising is how well Shields holds her own with Rowlands, which gives their scenes together punch and conviction. By effective contrast, Harris, Unger and Conrad underplay while Duval is most persuasive. Seen only in flashback, Sweeney makes it crystal-clear why the shameless Tony was such an overwhelming presence. "The Weekend" is a small film of understated impact.

NEW YORK POST, 11/22/00, p. 46, Lou Lumenick

You rarely see movies as dramatically uneven as "The Weekend," which has a dreadful, one-star first half—followed by an interesting, three-star conclusion.

The characters as initially presented are self-centered, pretentious artistic types, gathered at a weekend house in upstate New York on the anniversary of a young man's death from AIDS.

Among them are the dead man's brother (Jared Harris) and his wife (Deborah Kara Unger), new parents whose marriage is foundering; the dead man's lover (David Conrad) and his new squeeze (James Duval).

Joining them halfway through the movie are a wealthy widow (Gena Rowlands) who battles constantly with her daughter (Brooke Shields), a horror-movie actress who utters perhaps the worst line in a movie this year: "He broke my heart, not my hymen."

When writer-director Brian Skeet finally maneuvers all the principals into the same house midway through, you start to get caught up as they unburden themselves of secrets—even if they never shut up about art restoration, Italian villas, writing best-selling books, and, so help me, grape scissors.

VILLAGE VOICE, 11/28/00, p. 140, Michael Atkinson

Things descend even further [The reference is to *The Trench* and *The 6th Day*; see Atkinson's review of these films.] with the bloodless, lip-biting psycho-carnage that's supposed to be Brian Skeet's *The Weekend,* in which the entire cast inexplicably mourns the passing of D.B. Sweeney. Deborah Kara Unger was his sister-in-law/lover, Jared Harris his brother, David Conrad his lover (who we first meet reading *Art and Anarchy,* reclining on a lake-shore dock), Gena Rowlands a blowsy neighbor, Brooke Shields her slut-actress daughter, etc. Every shot of the film features someone holding a wineglass halfway to their mouth. Hudson Valley real estate porn, treacly piano music, fade-to-blue flashbacks—it's almost the awful movie Kevin Bacon wanted to make in *The Big Picture.* Here we need Arnold, and a gun.

Also reviewed in:
NEW YORK TIMES, 11/22/00, p. E3, Stephen Holden
VARIETY, 6/19-25/00, p. 32, Ken Eisner

WELL, THE

A Cowboy Booking International release of a Southern Star/Xanadu production.   *Executive Producer:* Maureen Barron, Noel Ferrier, and Errol Sullivan.   *Producer:* Sandra Levy. *Director:* Samantha Lang.   *Screenplay:* Laura Jones.   *Based on the novel by:* Elizabeth Jolley. *Director of Photography:* Mandy Walker.   *Editor:* Dany Cooper.   *Music:* Stephane Rae. *Casting:* Ann Robinson.   *Production Designer:* Michael Philips.   *Costumes:* Anna Borghesi. *Running time:* 105 minutes.   *MPAA Rating:* Not Rated.

CAST: Pamela Rabe (Hester); Miranda Otto (Katherine); Paul Chubb (Harry Bird); Frank Wilson (Francis Harper); Steve Jacobs (Rod Borden); Genevieve Lemon (Jen Borden).

NEW YORK POST, 5/19/00, p. 45, Hannah Brown

"The Well" is a heartfelt, beautifully acted film that suffers from its similarity to countless other movies. Its plot is achingly familiar: A repressed loner takes in a wild, sexy drifter. The drifter craves the security the loner can provide; the loner is infatuated with the drifter's freedom and sexuality, and for a while, they share a mutually satisfying idyll.

But it all ends badly, usually with violence and desertion, when the drifter gets restless.

The novelty in this film is its setting, a remote Australian farm.

The loner is Hester Harper (Pamela Rabe), who is what used to be known as a spinster. She walks with a limp, wears long skirts to cover her malformed legs, oversees her family's farm and cares for her senile father (Frank Wilson).

The drifter is Katherine (Miranda Otto, best known for her performance in "Love Serenade"), who is hired to keep house.

But the childish, pouty Katherine spends most of her time daydreaming and dancing when she should be cleaning.

Hester finds herself drawn to this younger woman. When her father dies, Hester gives up all pretense of running the farm and begins devoting herself full time to making Katherine happy.

She buys Katherine a TV, and some of their happiest moments are spent watching "Bonnie and Clyde" together and acting out the movie afterwards. They even begin planning a trip to Europe and America.

But there's not enough money and so, in order to keep Katherine happy, Hester sells the farm, and the two women move into a cottage on what used to be Hester's property. They keep the money from the sale hidden in a suitcase and plan their trip.

But Katherine hates hanging around the house with Hester, so they head to a local dance. Hester, of course, is a wallflower, while Katherine dances up a storm and gets drunk.

Katherine insists on driving home, and something terrible happens. How each reacts to the tragedy drives the drama for the rest of the film.

For a while, supernatural elements threaten to overwhelm the action, as if "The Well" were about to turn into an Australian "Carrie."

But director Samantha Lang and writer Laura Jones wisely realize that the real horror comes from what people do to each other in the name of love, and pull back from the cheap scare tactics just in time.

In the end, "The Well" holds few surprises, but has magnificent performances by Rabe and Otto.

VILLAGE VOICE, 5/23/00, p. 146, Dennis Lim

Knee-deep in dread, fueled by sexual repression, *The Well* is an outback gothic that resists Grand Guignol in favor of psychological suggestion and fussy symbolism. First-time Australian director Samantha Lang keeps backstory to a parenthetical minimum in this stark two-hander, a double-edged strategy that heightens the mystery and coarsens the archetypes. A lonely spinster hires a vivacious, wayward waif as her maid, and the first half of *The Well* maps the psychic terrain of their relationship, detailing its implicit agreements and calculated ambiguities; the second enlists this precarious, coded dynamic in the service of sequestered-housemate mind games.

Hester (Pamela Rabe), a dowdy schoolmarmish type who walks with a limp and wears her graying hair in a forbidding, noose-like braid, lives on a farm with her senile, cranky father. Her impulsive new employee, Katherine (Miranda Otto), is like a life force blowing through the musty household. Before long, she's assumed control of their recreational time, supplanting somber requiem singing with hard-rock wigouts and (after an evening glued to the TV set) persuading Hester to playact Clyde to her Bonnie. When Hester's father dies suddenly and the homestead is traded in for a smaller house with a portentous well on the property, their camaraderie takes on an uncomfortable element of neediness—the older woman plainly in thrall to the younger, who seems to be either losing her grasp on reality or awakening to the opportunity for manipulation.

As rendered by Mandy Walker's evocative cinematography, the craggy, desolate landscapes stand in for Hester's state of mind—the severely bleached images are a fatigued shade of cobalt, while bright primary-color objects, usually associated with Katherine, are vividly isolated in the near-monochromatic palette. Working from a script by Laura Jones (who adapted *An Angel at My Table* and *The Portrait of a Lady* for Jane Campion), Lang engineers the suspenseful interludes with complete assurance and some flair, and Rabe's performance is admirably complex; but *The Well* is still most easily defined by its unavoidable parallels to any number of lesbian-overtone psychodramas (from *Rebecca* to *The Fox*). Throughout, the familiarity of the scenario undermines the confidence of the filmmaking.

Also reviewed in:
NEW YORK TIMES, 5/19/00, p. E10, A. O. Scott
VARIETY, 5/19/97, p. 55, David Stratton

WENT TO CONEY ISLAND ON A MISSION FROM GOD...(BE BACK BY 5)

A Phaedra Cinema release of an Evenmore Entertainment production. *Producer:* Jon Cryer and Richard Schenkman. *Director:* Richard Schenkman. *Screenplay:* Jon Cryer and Richard Schenkman. *Director of Photography:* Adam Beckman. *Editor:* Richard LaBrie. *Music:* Midge Ure. *Casting:* Mark Saks. *Production Designer:* Bill Stabile. *Art Director:* Philomena Marano. *Costumes:* Deirdra Elizabeth Govan. *Running time:* 94 minutes. *MPAA Rating:* R.

CAST: Jon Cryer (Daniel); Rick Stear (Stan); Rafael Baez (Richie); Ione Skye (Gabby); Frank Whaley (Skee-ball Weasel); Peter Gerety (Maurice); Akili Prince (Julie); Aesha Waks (Cindy Goldclang); Susan Foster (Jennifer); Dominic Chianese (Mickey, the Photographer); William Wise (Sexy Larry, the Store Owner); Patricia Mauceri (Mrs. Munoz); Leslie Hendrix

(Bearded Lady); Jesse Lenat (Jojo); Brandon Espinoza (12-Year-Old Stan); Timmy Reifsnyder (12-Year-Old Daniel); Richard Acosta (12-Year-Old Richie); Laura Breckenridge (12-Year-Old Gabby); Judy Reyes (Waitress); Robert Levine (Sol); Helma Augustus Cooper (Bumper Car Operator); Justin Pierre Edmund (Kid); Fernando Lopez (Richie's Brother); Richard Schenkman (Freak Show Guy); Norbert Butz (Pawnbroker); Merceline Hugot (Homeless Woman); Roz Ryan (Nurse); Petty Pope (Mrs. Bernstein, Teacher); May Lin Pultar (Consuela); Wilson Jermaine Heredia (Darcy); Diane Cheng (Mrs. Liu); Eugene Byrd (Teenage Friend).

LOS ANGELES TIMES, 9/15/00, Calendar/p. 12, Kevin Thomas

"Went to Coney Island on a Mission From God... Be Back by Five" re-teams director/co-writer Richard Schenkman and actor/co-writer Jon Cryer, who first joined forces on the romantic comedy "The Pompatus of Love." This time they're in a more serious mood, which is not to say this deeply felt, engaging little film is without humor, although it confronts a great deal of pain and loss.

Cryer's Daniel and Rick Stear's Stan are lifelong friends in a working-class New York neighborhood. Steadfast Daniel has a modest job as a jeweler, whereas Stan is experiencing the unraveling of his life from gambling and drink. Yet they remain friends, although Dan is not yet aware of how dire Stan's predicament has become.

They take off to explore Coney Island in search of their long-missing childhood friend Richie, who is rumored to have been spotted at the once-venerable, now increasingly derelict, seaside amusement area.

Stan and Dan locate Richie (Rafael Baez) living under the boardwalk. But the story is really just beginning, and as the film moves back and forth between past and present, Schenkman and Cryer show how the high spirits of childhood, so seemingly full of promise, can so swiftly give way to mediocre adult lives.

The film has a strong, limiting sentimental streak and some loose ends, but clearly Schenkman and Cryer have come up with a film that is finally quite affecting and glows with the performances of Stear and Baez as well as Cryer. (Ione Skye is seen all too briefly as Stan's longtime girlfriend.)

Evocative and poignant, Coney Island is a powerful key setting, and the filmmakers make the most of it without letting it overwhelm the story—Adam Beckman is the film's skilled cinematographer. You find "Went to Coney Island" sticking with you long after it's over.

Also reviewed in:
NEW YORK TIMES, 9/8/00, p. E20, A. O. Scott
VARIETY, 4/27-5/3/98, p. 62, Emanuel Levy

WES CRAVEN PRESENTS DRACULA 2000

A Dimension Films release in association with Neo Art & Logic. *Executive Producer:* Wes Craven, Marianne Maddalena, Bob Weinstein, Harvey Weinstein, and Andrew Rona. *Producer:* W. K. Border and Joel Soisson. *Director:* Patrick Lussier. *Screenplay:* Joel Soisson. *Story:* Joel Soisson and Patrick Lussier. *Director of Photography:* Peter Pay. *Editor:* Patrick Lussier. *Music:* Marco Beltrami. *Music Editor:* Bill Abbott. *Sound:* Douglas Ganton and (music) John Kurlander. *Sound Editor:* Frank Eulner. *Casting:* Randi Hiller and Sarah Halley Finn. *Production Designer:* Carol Spier and Peter Devaney Flanagan. *Art Director:* Elinor Rose Galbraith. *Set Designer:* Michael Madden and Gordon White. *Set Decorator:* Peter P. Nicolakakos. *Set Dresser:* John Morrison, Joe Libanio, John Rankin, and Michael Stockton. *Special Effects:* Ted Ross. *Visual Effects:* Erik Henry. *Costumes:* Denise Cronenberg. *Make-up:* Marese Langan. *Make-up Effects:* Gary J. Tynnicliffe. *Running time:* 99 minutes. *MPAA Rating:* R.

CAST: Gerard Butler (Dracula);   Christopher Plummer (Abraham Van Helsing);   Jonny Lee Miller (Simon Sheppard);   Justine Waddell (Mary Heller);   Colleen Ann Fitzpatrick (Lucy); Jennifer Esposito (Solina);   Omar Epps (Marcus);   Sean Patrick Thomas (Trick);   Danny Masterson (Nightshade);   Lochlyn Munro (Eddie);   Tig Fong (Dax);   Tony Munch (Charlie); Jeri Ryan (Valerie Sharpe);   Shane West (JT);   Nathan Fillion (Father David);   Tom Kane (Anchor Man);   Jonathan Whittaker (Gautreaux);   Robert Verlaque (Dr. Seward);   Randy Butcher, Bill Davidson, Peter Cox, Chris Lamon, Herb Reischl, and Duncan McLeod (Stakemen); Wayne Downer (Desk Guard);   Robert Racki (Door Guard);   William Prael (Parade Cop);   Karon Briscoe (Teen Co-Worker); Scarlett Huntley (Blood Doll);   Harold Short (Black Angel of Death);   David J. Francis (Jesus);   Shimmy Silverman (Barker).

LOS ANGELES TIMES, 12/25/00, Calendar/p. 4, David Chute

"Wes Craven Presents Dracula 2000" is this film's official title, and it has a nice ring to it, seeming to promise a sly and subversive updating of one of the horror genre's pivotal myths. This is not exactly a minty fresh idea; bolder movies than this one, from David Cronenberg's "Rabid" (1977) to Abel Ferrera's "The Addiction" (1995), have deployed vampirism as a metaphor for, respectively, venereal disease and drug dependency. And on prime-time TV now the reformed Nosferatu Angel is a good guy, a brooding Byronic dreamboat. But you never know: In the age of Goth cults and promiscuous body piercing, there might be a little bright red juice left in the old boy yet, especially for a genre-twister as crafty as Craven.

A couple of sharp satiric sequences offer fleeting glimpses of the true millennial vampire movie that got away. In one of them, the film's smugly seductive Euro-trash Dracula (Gerard Butler) savors a Goth rock music video and pronounces it "brilliant." In another, he passes unnoticed through the extravagantly draped and punctured throng celebrating Mardi Gras in New Orleans—the city that has replaced London as Vampire Central in the popular imagination, thanks to the Lestat novels of Anne Rice. A revivified Dracula could indeed move like a born-again homeboy through the most ravenous parasitic subcultures of the modern world: Wall Street. A corporate law firm. Hollywood!

The big surprise, however, is that "Dracula 2000" is at heart a solidly old-fashioned cloak-and-fangs vampire flick. It honors the central traditions of the form a lot more often than it skewers them. Christopher Plummer plays Dr. Van Helsing, Vampire Hunter No. 1, in the oracular grand manner of Peter Cushing, embellishing the role with an untraceable Middle European accent. A secret panel in Van Helsing's wainscoted London office glides open to reveal an arsenal of bulky silver-spewing weaponry, which manages to look both antique and futuristic, like the side arms of a 19th century Terminator.

On the purely visceral/visual level, this is a surprisingly impressive piece of work, especially for a Dimension genre item that was dumped into theaters without press screenings. The movie certainly doesn't look as if it was cranked out on a pinch-penny budget. First-time director Patrick Lussier has worked with Craven as the editor of all the "Scream" pictures, and the man behind the camera is Hong Kong action veteran Peter Pay ("Crouching Tiger, Hidden Dragon"), a past master of the fine art of throwing things (often human bodies) right into the viewer's lap.

Lussier tries out some daringly fast, almost subliminal shock cuts in the action scenes, and he seems to know exactly how far to push this effect. Even when the pummeling vampire battles rush past in a blur of movement, they're never muddled or confusing. "Dracula 2000" has some of the best "boo" effects in the recent horror canon, and a couple of memorably icky gross-out moments involving leeches and deliquescent human tissue.

But the movie also hits some tin-eared wrong notes. Screenwriter-producer Joel Soisson squeezes together the tried and true formulas of old-school horror and the new postmortem formulas of the teen horror subgenre that Dimension has been strip-mining for years. The two styles clash repeatedly.

Jeri Ryan, who was the Borg bombshell Seven of Nine on "Star Trek: Voyager," takes a Courteney Cox Arquette retread role as a meddling journalist. Most of the heavy lifting in the anti-vampire camp is undertaken by Jonny Lee Miller, from "Hackers" and "Trainspotting," who accompanies every thrust of the stake with a would-be smart remark.

Dracula is liberated from his mossy vault by a band of bickering high-tech safecrackers, led by Omar Epps. Once bitten, these smooth dudes become wisecracking street-smart blood-suckers who instantly dissipate the ominous foggy mood whenever they appear.

The movie's central weakness, though, is the great big empty space at the heart of the story. There's a guy in the picture who calls himself Dracula, and he's well-played by Butler as a sort of lounge-lizard psycho-killer. But he's never a force of evil of mythic proportions: he seems small-minded and even whiny. The new "secret origin" story that's been cooked up for him doesn't add any depth to his legend; it's just a narrative stunt, a far-fetched twist ending that seems to explain less and less the more we think about it.

SIGHT AND SOUND, 6/01, p. 43, Kim Newman

London, 2001. Abraham Van Heising, arch-enemy of Dracula, has been keeping himself alive for a century with infusions of the vampire's blood in order to guard the coffined corpse of the apparently indestructible creature. Solina, one of Van Helsing's assistants, assumes that his highly-secure vault contains something valuable and helps a team of thieves to steal the coffin. On board a plane en route to the US, the coffin is opened and Dracula emerges, killing the thieves and transforming them into vampires. Van Helsing leaves his more trustworthy assistant Simon Sheppard to run his antiques business and follows Dracula to New Orleans, where the vampire is appearing in the dreams of Van Helsing' estranged daughter Mary, who has inherited the taint of his blood and has the potential to become his mate.

Simon turns up to help Van Helsing and tangles with the undead Solina and her comrades, learning how to kill regular vampires with silver bullets and wooden stakes. Dracula vampirises television newscaster Valerie Sharpe and Mary's best friend Lucy and pursues Mary through the Mardi Gras carnival, tempting her. When Mary finds her father drained dead by Dracula's three vampire concubines, she flees with Simon. Through her mental link with Dracula, Mary learns that the first vampire in the world is Judas Iscariot, cursed after his betrayal of Christ—hence the vampire aversion to crosses, wood and silver. Mary seems to acquiesce to Dracula, but resists, helping Simon destroy the vampire harem. Dracula is thrown off a building and hanged, the original method of Judas' suicide attempt, then burned by the rising sun. Mary becomes the guardian of the vampire's coffin in case he isn't completely destroyed.

Prefaced by the same meaningless "Wes Craven Presents" title card that introduced *Mind Ripper*, which went straight to video, and *Wishmaster*, which enjoyed only a brief theatrical showing, *Dracula 2001* (retitled for international consumption after a US release late last December as *Dracula 2000*) gets round to a quite ambitious rethink of the origins of the *King of the Vampires*. Director Patrick Lussier and screenwriter Joel Soisson (who have worked together on the similarly biblical *Prophecy III. The Ascent*) abandon the lately overworked identification of Bram Stoker's character with the historical Vlad the Impaler (as in *Bram Stoker's Dracula* and the television movie *Dark Prince. the True Story of Dracula*) to envision the first vampire in the world not only as Judas Iscariot but also as the Wandering Jew. There is a neat bit of horror-movie logic in ascribing the vampire's aversion to crosses, wood, holy water and silver (as in "thirty pieces of") to guilt over Judas' betrayal, but sunlight (which does harm these vampires) and garlic (which isn't mentioned) can't be rounded up into the theory. Given the shadow-puppet silliness of the film's depiction of the crucifixion and Judas' suicide, the ambitious stroke doesn't play well, climaxing in the bathos of Dracula arguing with a neon Jesus crucifix on the roof of a New Orleans building and finally exiting the world throttled by electrical cord. It's probably beside the point to complain that the Wandering Jew was cursed in order that he learn a lesson by eternally witnessing the sufferings of the world, whereas this Judas/Dracula has spent 2000 years *causing* the sufferings of the world; after all, this isn't Christian Fringe Mythology 101, it's a turn-of-the-century remix of Hammer Films's endearingly daffy *Dracula AD 1972* (1972).

As in that film, a group of trendy cutting-edge types, who are bound to make *Dracula 2001* look as dated in 2025 as *Dracula AD 1972* appears now, semi-accidentally resurrect the vampire (there the majestic Christopher Lee; here the bland Gerard Butler), who resumes his battle with old enemy Van Helsing (this time, the original not a descendant) by chasing after his handiest female relative (a daughter, as opposed to a grand-daughter as in *Dracula AD 1972*). As Van Helsing, Christopher Plummer is an acceptable substitute for Peter Cushing (who regularly played the role for Hammer), although he's wastefully killed off half-way through to make room for the energetic but superfluous Jenny Lee Miller. It's also a shame that the producers didn't think to cast Plummer's real-life daughter Amanda Plummer, who might have made something of Mary, the vampire hunter's estranged offspring who is torn between two blood fathers and who finally accepts the legacy of Van Helsing rather than the curse of Dracula.

A problem with the film is that all the best stuff comes before Dracula is back, with the high-tech thieves breaking into the booby-trapped Van Helsing vault on the assumption that it contains something valuable and an impressive mid-air uncoffining (slightly derivative of *The Monster Squad*, 1987) that winds up with an off-screen plane crash and a selection of young guest stars—Jennifer Esposito, Omar Epps, Colleen Ann Fitzpatrick, Jeri Ryan, Sean Patrick Thomas—transformed briefly into vampires, presumably so they can indulge their fangs and kung fu fantasies.

Once the plot gets to New Orleans, where the film manages an amazing number of product placements for Virgin Megastore, the weakness of Butler's performance undercuts the fun elements—though he is hardly helped by daft notions like Dracula being impressed by a heavy-metal video ("Brilliant!"). In the wake of television's *Buffy the Vampire Slayer* and *Angel*, it's become a convention that all vampires know Hong Kong cinema style wire-assisted martial arts and that both creatures of the night and vampire-slayers should pepper their violent confrontations with wisecracks. All this is fair enough, but it sits ill with attempts at atmosphere: New Orleans came off better in the dire *Candyman Farewell to the Flesh* than it does here, despite the regulation graveyard and Mardi Gras scenes. Like most recent vampire movies, *Dracula 2001* bounces around a lot and writhes sexually but never manages to make its vampires especially scary or seductive.

Also reviewed in:
CHICAGO TRIBUNE, 12/25/00, Tempo/p. 2, Robert K. Elder
NEW YORK TIMES, 12/23/00, p. B18, Stephen Holden
VARIETY, 1/1-7/01, p. 35, Joe Leydon

WHAT'S COOKING?

A Trimark Pictures release of a Flashpoint Films presentation with Jeffrey Taylor of a Stagescreen production developed with the assistance of the Sundance Institute. *Executive Producer:* Abe Glazer, David Forrest, and Beau Rogers. *Producer:* Jeffrey Taylor. *Director:* Gurinder Chadha. *Screenplay:* Gurinder Chadha and Paul Mayeda Berges. *Director of Photography:* Jong Lin. *Editor:* Janice Hampton. *Music:* Craig Pruess. *Music Editor:* Gregory Hobson and Jerry Gilbert. *Sound:* William M. Fiege. *Sound Editor:* Chris Welch, Doug Jackson, Chuck Neely, and Howard Neiman. *Casting:* Cathy Henderson-Martin and Dori Zuckerman. *Production Designer:* Stuart Blatt. *Art Director:* Melissa Hibbard. *Set Designer:* Steve Mitchell. *Set Decorator:* Melissa Levander. *Set Dresser:* Holly Brand. *Special Effects:* Andre Ellingson. *Costumes:* Eduardo Castro. *Make-up:* Angela Johnson. *Make-up (Alfre Woodard):* Carrie Angland. *Stunt Coordinator:* Julius LeFlore. *Running time:* 106 minutes. *MPAA Rating:* PG-13.

CAST: the avila's: Mercedes Ruehl (Elizabeth Avila);   Victor Rivers (Javier Avila);   Douglas Spain (Anthony Avila);   Maria Carmen (Sofia Avila);   Isidra Vega (Gina Avila);   Elena Lopez (Grandma Avila);   A Martinez (Daniel);   Richard Yniguez (Robert Avila);   Eva Rodriguez (Auntie Eva);   Adrian Armas (Avila Cousin);
the nguyens: Joan Chen (Trinh Nguyen);   Francois Chau (Duc Nguyen);   Will Yun Lee (Jimmy Nguyen);   Kristy Wu (Jenny Nguyen);   Brennan Louie (Joey Nguyen);   Jimmy Pham (Gary Nguyen);   Kieu Chinh (Grandma Nguyen);   Chao-Li Chi (Grandpa Nguyen);   Chad Todhunter (Luke);   Scotty Nguyen (Don);

the seeligs: Lainie Kazan (Ruth Seelig); Maury Chaykin (Herb Seelig); Kyra Sedgwick (Rachel Seelig); Julianna Margulies (Carla); Albie Selznick (Art Seelig); Suzanne Carney (Sarah Seelig); Estelle Harris (Aunt Bea); Ralph Manza (Uncle David); Andrew Heckler (Jerry);
the williams: Alfre Woodard (Audrey Williams); Dennis Haysbert (Ronald Williams); Eric K. George (Michael Williams); Brittany Jean Henry (Kristen Williams); Ann Weldon (Grace Williams); Shareen Mitchell (Paula Moore); Gregory Itzin (James Moore); Mariam Paris (Monica Moore);
Frank Novak (Governor Rhodes); Margie Loomis (Woman in Airport); Gwendolyn Oliver (TV Reporter); Charles Constant (TV Announcer); Bruce Dobos (Turkey Man); Darren O'Bannon, Jeremy Berger, and Alexandra Castro (Students).

LOS ANGELES TIMES, 11/17/00, Calendar/p. 20, Kevin Thomas

"What's Cooking?" is a sure-fire winner, an endlessly inventive serious comedy that zeros in on four Los Angeles families—the Avilas, the Nguyens, the Seeligs and the Williamses—as they prepare to celebrate Thanksgiving.

Co-writer and director Gurinder Chadha, a Kenya-born Englishwoman of Indian descent, whose first film was the delightful "Bhaji on the Beach," about a bus load of Indian women on an outing to Blackpool, has precisely the right perspective and bemused sensibility to capture our city's famous multicultural diversity. The result is a Thanksgiving treat for all seasons that you may find yourself going back to for seconds.

For so brisk and entertaining a film, sharp in its observations but light in its touch, "Cooking" has unexpected substance and is a formidable accomplishment in that it brings dimension to its nearly 40 principal characters. Chadha and co-writer Paul Mayeda Berges accomplish this by an inspired structure coupled with some of the smartest dialogue heard in an American film this year.

By cutting back and forth between the four families Chadha establishes a buoyant, lively rhythmic pacing while constantly furthering the plot. With the preparation of the Thanksgiving meal given four distinct and clearly delicious approaches, "What's Cooking?" has got to be the most savory movie since not only "Like Water for Chocolate" (1992) but also 1987's "Babette's Feast."

Each time Chadha returns to a family, she and Berges have in motion a developing situation, each loaded with unpredictable elements, that provoke responses from their characters that enable us to see them in an evolving light. The film seesaws between tradition and change with its people learning as they go what's important to hold onto and let go of. As a result, "What's Cooking?" captures the spirit of family life in contemporary Los Angeles to a degree unexpected in a mainstream movie.

Every element of the film gleams, but its script is exceptional, its wit bubbling with seeming spontaneity from what is actually a rock-solid foundation. In the finest Hollywood tradition, it touches upon serious issues and genuine emotion with an unfailing, infectious sense of humor.

All four families live in the central city along a pleasant, leafy stretch of Genesee Avenue, most likely not far from Olympic Boulevard. All live in well-maintained older homes, some more elaborate and sophisticated in decor than others, but all warm and inviting. The Williamses, who are African American, live in a large, old Spanish-style house with a sleek contemporary interior. Alfre Woodard's Audrey, a divorce lawyer, prepares her nouvelle cuisine turkey amid mounting tension. Her husband Ronald (Dennis Haysbert) has an all-consuming job as a top aide to a controversial conservative governor.

That leaves her to cope with her visiting mother-in-law Grace (Ann Weldon), an unthinking and critical traditional matriarch who worships her son but, with comical obtuseness, finds fault with the way Audrey does everything. Both Audrey and Ronald are on edge over their son Michael (Eric K. George) for an undisclosed reason and make excuses to Grace for his assumed absence from the table. The Williamses' gathering will pack plenty of surprises, some of them hilarious, others stinging.

There's also tension at the Nguyens, new to the neighborhood. Joan Chen's Trinh and her husband Duc (Francois Chau), proprietor of a video rental store, are aghast at discovering an unopened condom in a coat belonging to their unhappy daughter (Kristy Wu), refusing to buy her explanation that they're handed out at school. They should be more concerned with their headed-for-trouble son (Jimmy Pham), whom their daughter is trying to protect. The Nguyens are clinging to their Vietnamese traditions so tightly they haven't a clue how to listen to their children.

Meanwhile, at the Avilas, Mercedes Ruehl's attractive Elizabeth, whose dashing macho husband (Victor Rivers) has left her for her cousin, has found consolation with a handsome colleague (A Martinez) at work and has invited him to her family dinner. Elizabeth's son Anthony (Douglas Spain) runs into his father at a supermarket, and since poor old dad is alone now that his fling is over, invites him to Thanksgiving.

Explaining that he can't be himself at home, the eldest Nguyen son Jimmy (Will Yun Lee), a college student, has opted to spend the holiday with his new girlfriend, Elizabeth's daughter Gina (Isidra Vega), telling his parents he's busy studying.

Lainie Kazan's Ruth Seelig and her husband, Herb (Maury Chaykin), accept uneasily though lovingly the lesbian relationship their daughter (Kyra Sedgwick) has with another woman (Julianna Margulies), yet Ruth is eager to conceal it from her husband's tiresome elderly relatives (Estelle Harris and Ralph Manza, both very funny).

"What's Cooking?" affords many actors the opportunity to shine. Ann Weldon sparkles and glows, her matriarch as exasperating as she is amusing. Woodard typically dives in deeply to show us a smart, accomplished woman trying to hold herself together in the face of more strain than we had ever imagined.

Kazan's Ruth, like Woodard's Audrey, is striving unobtrusively to be the best cook and hostess possible while trying to ensure that her Thanksgiving meal goes smoothly, knowing she is faced with a potentially volatile situation. Even the smallest roles are clearly defined: Mariam Parris is a hoot as one of Audrey's guests, the outspoken counterculture daughter of one of her husband's colleagues.

In covering so much territory with such unexpected depth, "What's Cooking?" benefits crucially from Stuart Blatt's on-the-money production design with its revealing details. The Seeligs almost certainly have lived in the once lily-white neighborhood the longest, and it tells in their formal, slightly passe decor; leave it to Ruth Seelig to cover her dining room table with an old-fashioned lace cloth.

Cinematographer Jong Lin brings a lovely glow to all four households, and Craig Pruess' score enhances the film's shifting moods. Of all the films made about life in contemporary Los Angeles, "What's Cooking?" could well be the one in which the greatest number of Angelenos recognize themselves.

NEW YORK POST, 11/17/00, p. 56, Jonathan Foreman

For all its humor, and despite the occasional lapse into (mostly benign) stereotype, "What's Cooking?" is a daring and refreshing film.

It uses four Thanksgiving dinners in today's astonishingly diverse Los Angeles to celebrate in a profoundly moving way the things we have in common, as families and as Americans, in a constantly evolving culture.

Perhaps only a foreigner like British director Gurinder Chadha—born in Kenya of Punjabi extraction—who co-wrote the film with Paul Mayeda Berges, could have made a comedy so optimistic and yet so clearsighted about an America strong and flexible enough to give succor to people as superficially different as the Vietnamese Nguyens, the African-American Williamses, the Chicano Avilas and the Jewish Seeligs.

The four interlinked families are played by a terrific ensemble cast, including Joan Chen, Mercedes Ruehl, Kyra Sedgwick and Julianna Margulies (as a gay couple), Kristy Wu, Isidra Vega, Dennis Haysbert and the always superb Alfre Woodard.

What's important about these characters is not so much the way they dress their turkey to suit the old-country tastes of their grandparents, but the way they have to deal with the problems that emerge whenever families come together, whether it's a mother-in-law who tries to take over, or the arrival of a divorced mom's new love interest.

Sometimes conflict is provoked by a child's assimilation into the main-stream culture—like one of the Vietnamese kids' membership in a gang. Other times, it's just the usual tension between protective parents and rebellious teens, and in the case of the Seeligs, it's older people coming to terms with their daughter's lesbianism.

If all this sounds a bit piously multicultural, rest assured that, aside from a couple of PC moments, this film is lighthearted and smart enough to be one of the best Altmanesque ensemble comedies of the last couple of years.

And the food looks absolutely mouthwatering.

NEWSDAY, 11/17/00, Part II/p. B6, Jan Stuart

The press release for "What's Cooking?" contains recipes for Mrs. Williams' Oyster and Shiitake Mushroom Stuffing, Mrs. Avila's Tamales, Mrs. Seelig's noodle kugel and Mrs. Nguyen's Vietnamese spring rolls. It merits a place of honor on the shelf above the fridge, right next to "Joy of Cooking."

The joys of "What's Cooking?" are as bountiful and inviting as a Thanksgiving spread with all the trimmings. There are no less than four very different takes on that traditional holiday dinner in this generous-spirited family comedy from Gurinder Chadha, the director of "Bhaji on the Beach." And until the Kentucky Fried Chicken hits one of the tables, you may be tempted to pull up a chair at each one.

A Kenyan-born Englishwoman of Indian descent living in Los Angeles with an American husband of Japanese and Basque descent (Paul Mayeda Berges), Chadha is a one-woman United Nations of goodwill. The screenplay she and Berges have crafted follows the preparations and subsequent travails of four ethnically diverse families in L.A. as they celebrate Thanksgiving under their respective roofs.

In contrast with those consummate food movies "Babette's Feast" and "Eat Drink Man Woman," the menus take a backseat to the familial tensions simmering in each house. African-American matriarch Audrey Williams (Alfre Woodard) must diplomatically fend off an interfering mother-in-law (Ann Weldon) while refereeing between a rabble-rousing son (Eric K. George) and a status quo politico husband (Dennis Haysbert). Over at the Nguyens', a recently emigrated Vietnamese family, mother Trinh (Joan Chen) scapegoats her sullen teenage daughter (Kristy Wu) while her middle son (Jimmy Phan) is covertly stirring up trouble.

The Seeligs (Lainie Kazan and Maury Chaykin), a relatively open- minded Jewish couple, are biting their tongues over the homecoming of their lesbian daughter (Kyra Sedgwick) and her lover (Julianna Margulies). And a showdown is brewing for Latina mom Elizabeth Avila (Mercedes Ruehl) when her son Anthony (Douglas Spain) invites his adulterous father (Victor Rivers) to the holiday table in a misplaced attempt to get his parents back together.

The four scenarios are set up and set loose with a schematic division of attention that threatens at first to become an over-whipped sitcom. But "What's Cooking?" takes on weight and gravitas as each of the families nears its much-anticipated meal and the four carefully delineated narratives begin to overlap.

The film's inevitable detractors may accuse "What's Cooking?" of being a shopping list of gourmet ethnic jokes. But the writers observe each family with a knowing eye and a miraculously even hand that lends the jokes the ring of truth, as when a Vietnamese teenager is repeatedly met with well-intentioned compliments about martial arts master Bruce Lee, or Mr. Seelig goes on about the Jewish cast of "Bonanza" in a fumbling effort to make conversation with his daughter's lover.

Chada is abetted by what is arguably the most felicitous ensemble work of this or any season, with particularly memorable moments from Lee, Chen, Ruehl, Sedgwick, a hilariously befuddled Chaykin and the ever-wondrous Woodard. "What's Cooking?" has all the earmarks of a holiday perennial.

SIGHT AND SOUND, 9/01, p. 57, Bonnie Grier

Los Angeles, the present. Four families living on the same street prepare to host their separate Thanksgiving celebrations. Trinh and Duc Ngyuen, a Vietnamese immigrant couple who run a video store, are disappointed that their eldest son Jimmy, a student at a university in another city, can't make it. Their neighbour Elizabeth Avila is angry that her son Anthony has invited her estranged husband Javier to her Thanksgiving celebrations, and has him withdraw the offer. Elderly Jewish couple Herb and Ruth Seelig welcome their daughter Rachel, who is visiting with her partner Carla. Audrey Williams, whose husband Ronnie is kept busy working for a conservative governor, picks up her mother-in-law Grace from the airport and returns home. At the Ngyuen household, Trinh and Duc confront their daughter Jenny about a condom discovered in her coat; unbeknown to them, Jenny is dating a white youth.

Elizabeth's daughter's Gina arrives with her boyfriend—Jimmy Ngyuen. Worried that his parents wouldn't approve of Gina, Jimmy has told his family he has to stay at college over Thanksgiving. Audrey Williams' son Michael unexpectedly turns up. Ronnie receives him coldly, and tells his guests that Michael earlier threw paint over the governor to protest against his anti-affirmative-action policies. Michael in turn reveals that Ronnie recently had an affair. Javier, meanwhile, has turned up at Elizabeth's house; when Daniel, a colleague whom Elizabeth is dating, appears, Javier storms out. Over dinner, Rachel announces she is pregnant by her sister-in-law's gay brother; she and Carla are to bring up the child. Jenny discovers a gun that her brother Joey is hiding for friends. Confronted with this, the Ngyuens accuse Joey of being in a gang; as they argue with him, his youngest brother Gary accidentally fires the gun.

The shot alerts the Seeligs, the Avilas and the Williams who arrive at the Ngyuens to discover Gary unhurt. As night falls, the tensions among the various parties recede.

At the beginning of *What's Cooking?*, a tale of Thanksgiving with a twist, we see an all-American family about to celebrate the ritual annual carving of the sacred turkey However, this blond, blue-eyed 1950s vision turns out to be an advertisement on the side of a Los Angeles bus, which is full to bursting with the real, multi-ethnic representatives of the 21st-century city.

In director Gurinder Chadha's first feature, *Bhaji on the Beach,* a bus was the means of escape for the female Asian protagonists; by taking them to Blackpool, it offered an escape not only from the oppression of society at large, but also from the oppression of their own culture. The bus in *What's Cooking?* is more: a missile aimed at the heart of the Land of the Free and the Home of the Brave as portrayed by Norman Rockwell. The America depicted here is a rainbow nation, a polyglot, multi-ethnic mix of people whose lives are shaped not only by racial identity but also by excursions outside the comfort of their own ancestry and custom.

In *What's Cooking?* four families—the African-American Williams, the Latino Avilas, the Jewish Seeligs and the Vietnamese-American Nguyens—separately prepare for their Thanksgiving meal. Alfre Woodard's Audrey Williams, an elegant urban type from *Waiting to Exhale* country, is married to a spin doctor for the conservative white governor of California; her mother-in-law Grace, who believes that no woman is good enough for her son, bustles about tasting the food and commenting on Audrey's housekeeping. Mercedes Ruehl's Elizabeth Avila, a cool, self-contained teacher newly separated from her philandering husband, presides over the cooking of Thanksgiving tamales. Lainie Kazan's Ruth Seelig tries to make her noodle kugel take the place of her daughter Rachel's lover Carla, while Joan Chen's Trinh Nguyen handles the ultimate Thanksgiving Day disaster—burning the turkey—by ordering buckets of Kentucky Fried Chicken.

These kitchen sequences are lovingly done. Chadha and her cinematographer Lin Jong, who worked on *Eat Drink Man Woman*, have created the best foodie film since *Babette's Feast*. Each morsel of food, from preparation to consumption, casts California as the land of plenty, but the film suggests that the material things of this world cannot buy happiness or peace of mind. The direction is as sensual as the camerawork. Chadha's style is big and generous, displaying the wide-eyed awe of the immigrant. She peeps into every corner, lifts every lid, eavesdrops on every conversation. Hers is a full-frontal approach; there are no shadows here. She waits until the very end before pulling back, when we see that these characters who have flowed in and out of one another's lives actually live on the same street.

It is this very exuberance that unfortunately leaves Chadha's screenplay, co-written with Paul Mayeda Berges, panting behind, trying to keep up. One example: the son of Audrey and her spin-doctor husband Ronald turns out to be the young black man who splashed paint on the governor at the beginning of the film. His name, "Michael", is whispered throughout, so that we come to expect him to be the perpetrator of some dastardly deed. The revelation that he's merely committed an act of youthful protest feels like a weak pay-off.

Chadha and Berges' attention to telling details that circumvent racial cliché outweigh the film's structural problems. The African-American family, for instance, struggle not over racism, but rather over the father's belief in integration and his son's belief in black cohesion. Their contest is played out against a background not of poverty, but affluence. The Vietnamese-American daughter is a mini-skirted Valley Girl with a white boyfriend and condoms in her pocket, while her brother hides a pistol under his bed for his mates in a Vietnamese-American gang. Back at the home of the Avilas, the strong, sexy, independent Elizabeth still has to do the cooking while the men watch television, Ruth Seelig discusses important issues with her daughter while they prepare an intricate dessert, their entire relationship expressed through the way they handle the icing.

Chadha seems at home with mainstream tastes and sentiments, but is able to help her audience see themselves in a new light—a winning mode of address that, at times, almost puts one in mind of Frank Capra's populist, socially aware movies from the 30s. By bringing a British-Asian eye to that most American of festivities, she depicts a nation bursting with colour, high drama, and too much of everything for its own good.

VILLAGE VOICE, 11/21/00, p. 140, Amy Taubin

A much less successful holiday panorama, Gurinder Chadha's *What's Cooking?* [The reference is to *La Bûche*; see Taubin's review of that film.] interweaves Thanksgiving dinner celebrations at the homes of four Los Angeles families: one Latino, one Vietnamese, one African American, and one Jewish. Chadha's first feature was the ebullient *Bhaji on the Beach,* a feminist comedy set in an Indian community in the north of England—a community that Chadha knows very well and depicted with specificity and verve. But her new film trades in sitcom stereotypes and crosscuts predictably from family to family as if under the misapprehension that equal time is a dramatic principle. Among the huge cast, Mercedes Ruehl, Dennis Haysbert, Kyra Sedgwick, Julianna Margulies, and Joan Chen make the strongest impressions, but they've all been seen to better advantage elsewhere.

Also reviewed in:
CHICAGO TRIBUNE, 11/17/00, Friday/p. Q, Mark Caro
NEW YORK TIMES, 11/17/00, p. E14, A. O. Scott
VARIETY, 1/24-30/00, p. 58, Emanuel Levy

WHAT LIES BENEATH

A DreamWorks Pictures and Twentieth Century Fox release of an Imagemovers production. *Executive Producer:* Joan Bradshaw and Mark Johnson.   *Producer:* Steve Starkey, Robert Zemeckis, and Jack Rapke.   *Director:* Robert Zemeckis.   *Screenplay:* Clark Gregg. *Based on a story by:* Sarah Kernochan and Clark Gregg.   *Director of Photography:* Don Burgess.   *Editor:* Arthur Schmidt.   *Music:* Alan Silvestri.   *Music Editor:* Ken Karman.   *Sound:* William B. Kaplan and (music) Dennis Sands.   *Sound Editor:* Dennis Leonard.   *Casting:* Ellen Lewis and Marcia DeBonis.   *Production Designer:* Rick Carter and Jim Teegarden.   *Art Director:* Tony Fanning, Stefan Dechant, and Elizabeth Lapp.   *Set Designer:* Patte Strong-Lord, Pam Klamer, Alicia Maccarone, Beverli Eagan, Masako Masuda, and Beck Taylor.   *Set Decorator:* Karen O'Hara.   *Set Dresser:* James Marchwick.   *Special Effects:* T. Brooklyn Bellissimo.   *Visual Effects:* Robert Legato.   *Costumes:* Susie DeSanto.   *Make-up:* Deborah La Mia Denaver. *Make-up (Michelle Pfeiffer):* Ronnie Specter.   *Make-up (Harrison Ford):* Michael Laudati. *Stunt Coordinator:* Tim A. Davison.   *Running time:* 130 minutes.   *MPAA Rating:* PG-13

CAST: Michelle Pfeiffer (Claire Spencer);   Katharine Towne (Caitlin Spencer);   Miranda Otto (Mary Feur);   James Remar (Warren Feur);   Harrison Ford (Norman Spencer);   Victoria Bidewell (Beatrice);   Diana Scarwid (Jody);   Dennison Samaroo, Jennifer Tung, Rachel Singer, and Daniel Zelman (PhD Students);   Eliott Goretsky (Teddy);   Ray Baker (Dr. Stan Powell);   Wendy Crewson (Elena);   Amber Valletta (Madison Elizabeth Frank);   Joe Morton (Dr. Drayton);   Sloane Shelton (Mrs. Templeton);   Tom Dahlgren (Dean Templeton);   Micole Mercurio (Mrs. Frank);   Donald Taylor (EMT Worker).

LOS ANGELES TIMES, 7/21/00, Calendar/p. 1, Kenneth Turan

Claire Spencer (Michelle Pfeiffer) looks to have an enviable life. Consider the stunning Vermont lakeside house, the sympathetic friend, the spacious SUV, the swell daughter who's just off to college. And the husband, don't forget about the husband.

Norman Spencer (Harrison Ford), a brainy geneticist who heads his own university research lab, is also a ruggedly handsome type who still looks like he belongs in his Rolling Stones T-shirt. Norman and Claire make each other laugh, not to mention sharing an active romantic life. Think it's just a little too good to be true? You must have peeked at the title.

For this new film by director Robert Zemeckis is not called "On the Surface" or "Appearance Is Reality" or even "What You See Is What You Get." No, this is "What Lies Beneath," and once its more-twists-than-a-Philadelphia-pretzel plot and "Scream"-for-adults scare moments finish unfolding, an awful lot will be called into question.

In general outline, the film's Clark Gregg script (based on a story by Sarah Kernochan and Gregg) follows the classic Hollywood dynamic of presenting characters who seem better off than the audience but turn out to be in considerably more dire straits. Under the surface a lot more is going on—maybe even too much.

For "What Lies Beneath" is several different films, some even contradictory, all trying to coexist, like the Israelis and the Palestinians—or "Scream" and "Poltergeist"—in the same physical space. It's not easy.

On one hand, "Beneath" is a neo-Hitchcock suspense thriller with a Bernard Hermann-esque score by Alan Silvestri accentuating a brisk succession of bump-in-the-dark moments. But while Hitchcock in general scorned the supernatural, this film shoehorns the ingredients of an old-fashioned dark-and-stormy-night ghost story into its plot dynamic.

"Beneath's" cultural politics are equally divided. On one side you have the traditional movie exploitation of a defenseless-looking woman (well-played, as per usual, by Pfeiffer), pale and fragile in her nightgown or in a bathtub, very much in peril. But the film simultaneously takes a proto-feminist stance, implying that no horror is greater than what men do to women and mocking those who underestimate a woman's strength or try to dismiss genuine concerns as a warped bid for attention or a product of the empty-nest syndrome.

The only thing holding all this together, and it is no small task, is Zemeckis' directing skills. An Oscar winner for "Forrest Gump," Zemeckis has apparently long had a yen to do a tale of suspense, and his impressive filmmaking and storytelling gifts make this one efficient, at least from moment to moment. Working with his regular team, including cinematographer Don Burgess and editor Arthur Schmidt, Zemeckis has gotten the placement of those squeal-inducing surprises (the Audrey Hepburn-starring "Wait Until Dark" is more of a model than Hitchcock) down to such a precise science that the film feels genetically engineered. But though Zemeckis gets a lot out of this scenario, "What Lies Beneath" is not completely persuasive.

Initially, the only blemish on Claire's life, aside from the departure of daughter Caitlin (Katharine Towne), are Mary and Warren Feur (Miranda Otto and James Remar), new neighbors who have a weakness for abusive arguments in the driveway. One day, having a little cry on her own, Claire hears a sobbing Mary and has a brief conversation with what is from all appearances a quite terrified woman. Who promptly disappears.

Though the evidence seems flimsy to Norman, way preoccupied with putting the final touches on a genetic breakthrough that will put humanity deeply in his debt, Claire is soon convinced that Mary is the victim of foul play and that husband Warren is the foul player. She enlists Jody (Diana Scarwid), the flaky pal every movie heroine needs, to help her, even buying a Ouija board at the local Wal-Mart to assist with her investigations.

If nothing else, the state of things in Claire's own house would make a person suspicious. There are radios that turn themselves on, doors that won't stay closed, pictures that fall again and again, places a suspicious dog simply won't go and a bathroom that gets as foggy as 221B Baker St. With neither Sherlock Holmes nor Bill Murray's Ghostbusters available to investigate, Claire must get to the bottom of this on her own.

Spooky with a polished kind of creepiness added in, "What Lies Beneath" nevertheless feels more planned than passionate, scary at points but unconvincing overall. With questionable character motivations and a heavy dependence on happenstance and coincidence, "What Lies Beneath" pushes the envelope of plausibility too much, until we are second-guessing the film even while we're watching it. The best scary movies, like roller coasters, exhilarate as well as terrify; this one, its evident skill notwithstanding, tends more toward exhaustion.

NEW YORK, 7/31/00, p. 51, Peter Rainer

What Lies Beneath is a great big *boo*! movie involving two great big stars, Harrison Ford and Michelle Pfeiffer, and an Oscar-winning director, Robert Zemeckis, and doubtless there will be those who see this lineup as some sort of advance in the current screen-horror derby, with its *Scream* and *I Know What You Did Last Summer* entries and spoofs like *Scary Movie*. Shock pictures now are almost exclusively low-budget and schlocky, with teens their target audience. By comparison, *What Lies Beneath* comes on like a class act, even though its sex-and-terror ingredients are not that far removed from the cheapies.

I'm not convinced that a glossier version of the same old entrails is all that classy. There's something to be said for the low-grade approach to horror; at least it makes no bones about what's going on. Whenever a heavyweight director deigns to make a scare movie, we inevitably hear about how the filmmaker intends to anticipate the audience's preconceptions and "reinvent" the genre. This was the mantra when Stanley Kubrick made *The Shining*. He let it be known that we weren't going to be getting just any old pulp; we would be getting *oracular* pulp. Kubrick approached the Stephen King material as if he were a pathologist painstakingly dissecting the cadaver of an expired genre, holding each organ up to the light for inspection. Despite all this posturing, parts of *The Shining* did indeed have oracular power, but Kubrick's lugubriousness killed most of our pleasure in the essential pulpiness of it all.

There was something punishing in Kubrick's attempted makeover of the genre; he was telling audiences that the low-down frights they have come to expect from these films were beneath them—or, more to the point, beneath *him*. What he failed to grasp was that if you wish to be a master, you cannot approach the horror genre with such cold calculation, it's far too sensual an animal for that. A great scare movie is a species of ravishment in which you give yourself up to the forbidden. The terror lies not just in the knowing but in the not knowing too—in the thrill of being unmoored. Hitchcock, for all of his fanatic preplanning and tricks of the trade, always made sure the deadbolts of his narratives were fondled open by the pleasures of the illicit. His best films brought out the erotics of danger.

In *What Lies Beneath*, Robert Zemeckis appears to have adopted the same *I'll show 'em* attitude as Kubrick. He wants his new film to be not just a star-studded thrill ride but also the playbook that future scare-movie directors will be drawing on for years to come. But he hasn't rewritten the playbook, just rejiggered it. As you watch *What Lies Beneath,* you can practically see the frame-by-frame storyboards and digital stopwatches that went into its making; the film is a feat of horror engineering. And on that level, at least, it mostly delivers. The audience, adding its own Sensurround, shrieks in all the intended places, then giggles afterward. Zemeckis includes the standard paraphernalia of the genre: the hand reaching abruptly into frame, the shadows under the door, the family pet that senses something is horribly wrong, the car that won't start, the corpse that bursts alive. But in the end, it's not really such a great achievement to make an audience jump on cue. The horror cheapies are pretty adept at it, if nothing else. What's disappointing about *What Lies Beneath is* that nothing lies beneath.

Nothing, that is, except Michelle Pfeiffer's performance, which has more depth than this film deserves. Her Claire, the wife of a prominent research scientist, Dr. Norman Spencer (Ford), believes the Vermont home they inherited may be spook-infested, and she has a fragility that makes you afraid for her. Pfeiffer takes you through the paces of her character's mounting terrors and denials, and you feel that, yes, this is how a real human being would react in this situation. Pfeiffer's special gift is that she is both ethereal and supremely down-to-earth. It's the perfect combination for the role. When Claire goes to a psychiatrist (Joe Morton) for help, she tries to frame her anxiety in realistic terms, but you can see that she's enticed by her fearfulness. A former cellist, she is presented as the free-spirited contrast to her cerebral scientist husband, played by Harrison Ford with his usual solid-oak somnolence. Claire is the one who is truly in tune with the cosmos. This classic, corny art-science dichotomy is common to schlock occultism. Pfeiffer gives it a poignancy. Terror turns Claire wraith-like. As the frights heighten, her hair seems to grow munificently scraggly; at times, she resembles a Pre-Raphaelite Ophelia. In the film's most clutch-the-arm-of-your-date scene, she sits mute and immobilized in a bathtub as it fills to the drowning point, and her cat's-eyes seem to give off a lasered glow. You can believe this woman might be possessed because, after all, who *wouldn't* want to possess her?

I've been deliberately discursive in discussing this film because I don't want to give the show away (unlike the film's trailer, or even the print ads). But audiences won't be without a road map. Zemeckis and his screenwriter, Clark Gregg, draw on a whole stable of imperiled-woman warhorses, including *Wait Until Dark* and *Gaslight*; they summon up *Fatal Attraction* and *Rear Window* and *Psycho* and *The Haunting*. So much for reinventing the genre. You won't need to be that smart to figure out what lies beneath. You just need a bit of film history.

NEW YORK POST, 7/21/00, p. 47, Lou Lumenick

"What Lies Beneath" does for bathtubs what "Psycho" did for showers. My wife was clutching at my arm so insistently during Michelle Pfeiffer's climactic bathtub scenes—there are several—that I can barely read my notes.

The preview audience was shrieking, as they did through much of this season's first real scary movie.

Which is not to say that this "Fatal Attraction"-with-a-ghost thriller is a terrific movie, just one that expertly manipulates viewers with just about every scare technique in Alfred Hitchcock's—and Hollywood's—playbook.

Perhaps the biggest surprise is that "What Lies Beneath" revolves around Pfeiffer and not top-billed Harrison Ford, who has relatively little to do. He plays her husband, Norman, a grumpy genetics researcher whose name is a pretty good indicator of how far the filmmaker's tongues are in their cheeks.

Pfeiffer gives her best performance in years as Claire Spencer, who starts going to pieces after their daughter leaves for college.

Strange things start happening around their obscenely elegant waterfront home in Vermont: slamming doors, falling glass, frosty mists and teasing glimpses of a beautiful ghost (model Amber Valletta).

Claire at first suspects the apparition is mysteriously vanished wife of a neighbor, which throws her into an investigation straight out of "Rear Window." (Anyone who hasn't seen the spoiler-filled ads for the movie and wants to be surprised should probably stop reading now.)

Everyone else (thanks a lot, DreamWorks) knows that much of the movie's first hour is a red herring—the ghost is actually a graduate student Norman had an affair with.

This is the sort of movie you can easily spend an hour picking apart afterward.

Without giving anything away, let's just say that many of the twists in first-timer Clark Gregg's script don't really hold water in retrospect—they're just plot gimmicks.

The fact that you can largely suspend disbelief while actually watching the movie is a tribute to skill of director Robert Zemeckis ("Contact") who pulls out all the stops and manages to maintain an extremely tense mood, even when things get extremely hokey (when was the last time you saw a Ouij a board in a movie?) or downright ridiculous (the clichéd lady-in-peril ending).

Ford is cast effectively against type as the philandering and increasingly manipulative spouse, and his and Pfeiffer's relative stiffness together—they're two of the most humorless performers in Hollywood—actually works well for this story. Diana Scarwid provides much-needed comic relief as Claire's best friend.

Also helping greatly is Alan Silvestri's score, which closely echoes Bernard Herrmann's work for Hitchcock, and the elegant photography by Don Burgess (who shot Zemeckis' "Forrest Gump").

This is probably not a movie for people who wonder why a terrified woman would walk backward down a staircase when she knows a killer lurks at the bottom.

If you're able to check your brain at the popcorn stand, you'll stand a much better chance of enjoying this crowd pleaser.

NEWSDAY, 7/21/00, p. B3, John Anderson

What "Jaws" did for the beach and "Psycho" did for the shower, "What Lies Beneath" wants to do for your bathroom mirror. There comes a stage in Robert Zemeckis' half-anemic ghost story when you see one and you start to twitch. In fact, there are enough jolting camera movements, falling picture frames and faces looming out of the dark to make you feel like a frog clipped to a jumper cable.

Is the frog happy? Depends on the frog.

Personally, being manipulated by a supernatural thriller—even to the point of having your spine adjusted—is fun. The graveside scene at the end of "Carrie"? Deliciously scary, nightmare stuff. But do you want to sit, however tentatively, through 120-plus minutes of graveside scenes? Maybe. For others, however, a thriller's more fun if there's something at stake, less fun when you're yanking the armrests off the seat against your will.

"What Lies Beneath," which boasts the first on-screen pairing of bona fide sex symbols Michelle Pfeiffer and Harrison Ford, has a gloss befitting its stars. Pfeiffer remains one of the screen's most beautiful women as well as a first-rate actress, when she's got something to do. Under director Robert ("Forrest Gump") Zemeckis, even Ford manages to stretch, however uncomfortably, beyond the dramatic confines of his usual graying Boy Scout. But there's very little going on between the movie's moments of visceral hysteria, other than a story that might have surfaced out of some producer's bottom drawer.

Is there something off about a movie that suggests divine retribution for the wayward and wicked, and then employs ghosts and goblins to make its point? Maybe, but the movie has bigger problems than that. Claire Spencer (Pfeiffer), a year after surviving a rather serious auto crash, tearfully sees her only daughter off to college and begins suffering empty-nest syndrome of a most painful variety. When she subsequently starts seeing a wraith-like young woman in the reflection of her bathtub, and hearing voices and watching her front door open on its own—well, there's reason to think it might be in her head.

Problem is, the movie never bothers to raise any doubts about either Claire's sanity or the fact that there's going to be some connection between the haunting and Claire's husband, Nobel-level math professor Norman Spencer (Ford). He's the one with the complex about his more famous father and his unsatisfactory professional standing; she's the one who does a "Rear Window" on their bickering neighbors and then accuses the husband (James Remar)—during a college function—of murdering his wife. Oops. No wonder Norman's unsure of his status.

The Hitchcock references come fast and furious—Alan Silvestri's climactic music is a wholesale ripoff of Bernard Hermann's "Psycho" score—and Zemeckis does manage to imbue the film with a certain ongoing dread. The story, however, can't maintain the tension on its own and Zemeckis has to shore it up with the tumbling furniture and the floating faces and the villains you think are dead but who are contractually obligated to survive through the last possible contrivance.

If there's a bright spot in all this, it's Diana Scarwid, still best known as the adult daughter in "Mommie Dearest" and who brings to the best friend role in "What Lies Beneath" a snappiness and delivery that's all but missing from the rest of the film. More Scarwid! Unfortunately, what her presence points up is how helplessly adrift such stars as Pfeiffer and Ford are when they have only each other for chemical reaction. In Pfeiffer's case, "What Lies Beneath" could have used Jeff Bridges and a piano. In Ford's, a fedora, a whip and some faces from the crypt. Oops again: Make that a fedora and a whip.

NEWSWEEK, 7/24/00, p. 58, Jeff Giles

This first paragraph is specifically addressed to the most pragmatic moviegoers: people who want to see *something* on Saturday night, and just need to know if "What Lies Beneath" is worth $8.50. Given what else is out there, sure. Robert Zemeckis's Hitchcockian ghost story has a couple of movie stars, a couple of jokes and a couple of jolts. If that's all you need to know, stop reading here because what lies beneath this paragraph may spoil a few plot points.

OK, now that *they're* gone, let's really talk. "What Lies Beneath" is a slick but surprisingly empty genre movie that builds to a not particularly shocking shock. As the movie opens, Claire Spencer (Michelle Pfeiffer) packs her daughter off for college and prepares to deal with empty-nest syndrome. Only her nest isn't empty. Her second husband, a workaholic scientist named Norman (Harrison Ford), may be in the lab night and day, trying to work his way out of his famous father's shadow. But a pretty young ghost (model Amber Valletta, who has about eight seconds of screen time) keeps dropping by to knock pictures off desks, fill the tub with water and play the stereo really loud. Claire is convinced that her next-door neighbor has murdered his wife, and does some pro forma "Rear Window" snooping. Is she on the right trail? What do you think? Even the movie's marketing campaign makes it plain that the dead woman is actually someone Ford's character had an affair with—"He was the perfect husband until his one mistake followed them home"—which renders the first hour of the movie pointless.

Not that it wasn't close to pointless already. Ford and Pfeiffer are two of our chillier movie stars. Early in the movie, as they run through "cute" marital dialogue, they're so stiff and unchemical it's almost like watching a rehearsal. (He: "Wanna *fool around*?" She: "Yep!") The scares, too, are shamelessly ordinary at first—an endless series of red-herring slams and bangs that are frightening only because the music is suddenly blaring. *Boo! Nope, it's only her husband.* That kind of thing.

It goes without saying that Zemeckis ("Forrest Gump") is far from a hack. "What Lies Beneath" is full of gorgeously pale and eerie images and, while the screenplay tends toward the obvious, the characters eventually get interesting. Still, it's all in the service of banal moralizing about the misleading placidity of "happy" people's lives. (What lies are beneath! Get it?) Zemeckis's movie may well be a hit because it entertains in a way we are used to being entertained. It is worth $8.50. It is not worth remembering.

SIGHT AND SOUND, 11/00, p. 65, Philip Strick

Her nerves on edge after a car crash a year ago, Claire Spencer finds herself idle when her daughter, Caitlin, goes off to college. Claire's husband, Dr Norman Spencer, a geneticist, is loving but overworked, determined to better the achievements of his late father. Alone in her lakeside house in Vermont, Claire becomes certain that their neighbour, Warren Feur, has murdered his wife, Mary. She is also uneasy about strange happenings in the house and imagines glimpses of a phantom woman.

At the suggestion of her psychiatrist and with the help of her friend Jody, Claire attempts a seance. Shaken by its apparent result, she rushes to Norman's campus laboratory where Warren, one of the faculty tutors, is accompanied by Mary, alive and well. At home, a press cutting hidden behind a picture frame refers to a missing girl, Madison Elizabeth Frank. Tracing Madison's mother, Claire visits the girl's room and removes a memento, a braid of Madison's hair. With this and a book on witchcraft for guidance she tries to contact the dead, a process which 'transforms' her into Madison for long enough to realise that Norman had an affair with her.

Norman admits his lapse and begs forgiveness. Claire later finds a jewel-box in the lake containing Madison's pendant, and under questioning Norman admits to hiding the girl's body after her suicide. Claire insists he calls the police but he drugs her into immobility and confesses he killed Madison to prevent her ruining his life's work, as he must now kill Claire. Avoiding being drowned in the bath, Claire crashes their car into the lake, where Madison's enfolding corpse prevents Norman resurfacing.

Given that the making of *What Lies Beneath* was reportedly sandwiched between production schedules of another new Robert Zemeckis project (*Cast Away*), the extent to which the two completed films will be seen to complement each other must await future measurement. In its own right, however, there is no denying that *What Lies Beneath* is something of a disappointment after the grander designs of *Contact*. Despite the high-gloss players and lavishly tailored settings, the film contrives to be both overdressed and undernourished, a twilight-zone anecdote attenuated beyond its reasonable span. Intended as a Hitchcockian suspense thriller (one of the few genres not previously tackled by Zemeckis), it has blatant and joltingly effective allegiances but remains ultimately unconvincing.

Hitchcock's plots, while not averse to some divine intervention, scorned the supernatural as a driving force. Zemeckis, director of *Death Becomes Her* and episodes of the television series *Tales from the Crypt*, has no such qualms. His audience—primed, in fact, as much by Henri-Georges Clouzot as by Hitchcock, thanks to the copious bathroom scenes—may insist on working out a rational explanation for the film's spectral assaults, but Zemeckis gleefully complie with the current craze for being spooked by disguising his heroine's intuitive imaginings (Claire is haunted by visions of her husband Norman's dead mistress) as a story of revenge from beyond the grave. Depending on our preference, the film just about holds together as a case history of shared delusion, the ghosts only in the minds of the neurotic wife and fickle husband. And our scepticism is usefully prompted by the reminders of *Rear Window* (1954) and *Psycho* (1960), although the tearing of the shower curtain and Alan Silvestri's Hermannesque soundtrack are a bit much. It will not escape notice that the duplicitous spouse is called Norman.

Written by Clark Gregg, better known for his acting (*The Usual Suspects*), *What Lies Beneath* craftily employs two habitual Hitchcockian devices, the plot detour and the peculiar bystander. Much of the film's first half is time-wasted by the mystery of the neighbours whose violent dispute leads to the removal of a corpse-sized parcel. This lively melodrama has no bearing on the 'real' story except that, like the several predicaments unfolding in the apartments of *Rear Window,* it provides an uncanny parallel to the central relationship. Up to the point at which the villain turns indestructible and we are stuck with a gory collection of horror-film clichés, *What Lies Beneath* is a gallery of eccentrics echoing the innumerable rehearsals for marriage in Hitchcock's work. Oddly adrift, like Claire's best friend Jody or Mrs Frank and her cat, these troubled souls seem even to extend to Claire's enigmatic psychiatrist and to her daughter's withdrawn roommate. Inadvertent spirits, there but not there, they embody the sorry relics of countless lost partnerships.

Such losses are a constant in Zemecki films: what really lies beneath his flashy and ingenious surfaces has been a tide of dysfunctional families, missing parents and deprived offspring. Norman's problem, as it was for the hero of *Back to the Future* and the heroine of *Contact,* is his departed father whose house he now occupies and whose achievements he struggles to transcend. The theme of mislaid and displaced children, central to *Forrest Gump* and *Back to the Future II,* continues here in the form of the wraith herself, an unnerving substitute for the daughter who has assumed the independence of college life. At the same time, the ghostly obsessive and her anguished observer are the latest recruit to the Zemeckis army of 'driven women' pathetic in *Forrest Gump*, comical in *Death Becomes Her*, deadly serious in *Contact*. Frequently linking his characters' awakenings with a magical casket (the 'Flux Capacitor' of *Back to the Future* now becomes a revelatory jewel-box), much given to rolling his cast down flights of stairs, and showing a Tarkovskian relish for soaking them amid bursts of lightning, Zemeckis is having a grand time making his audiences jump but seems intriguingly hell-bent for matters of deeper concern.

TIME, 7/24/00, p. 65, Richard Schickel

Is the wind playing tricks? Or does the front door need a locksmith's attention? Surely the supernatural wouldn't waste its forces making a door swing open whenever the lady of the house (Michelle Pfeiffer as Claire Spencer) walks by.

For an hour or so, *What Lies Beneath* dwells in this sort of quotidian creepiness. And as long as it does, director Robert Zemeckis' movie goes like a (haunted) house afire—mysterious moans from the heating system, the hint of a stalking presence, even some strange initials on Claire's computer screen. Everyone—especially her gruffly good-natured husband Norman (Harrison Ford)—says Claire is overwrought.

With good reason. The Spencers' expensively renovated nest is empty; their only child has just left for college. Norman is temporarily neglectful; he's on deadline with an important research paper down at the college. And lonely Claire begins—nosily, obsessively—to focus on the mysterious, conceivably murderous doings of the young couple who have moved in next door.

They're red herrings, naturally. The Spencer house really is ghost-ridden. But once that fact is established, *What Lies Beneath* begins to succumb to a common genre problem. When the haunt ceases to be a set of eerie manifestations and begins to take on shape and form, all the spooky fun tends to drain out of these pictures. This one becomes a variation on the *Fatal Attraction* theme, but with more muscular action and, finally, a lot less plausibility. That's too bad, because the early wit of Clark Gregg's writing and some persuasive direction and playing are drowned out by the doomed, desperate search for a persuasive ending.

VILLAGE VOICE, 7/25/00, p. 128, Michael Atkinson

There may not be a more soulless director in Hollywood than Robert Zemeckis—his entire purpose is the manufacture of empty distractions, and his mechanical authority is precisely why his movies date more wretchedly than any other high-flyin' '80s-'90s auteur. His new non-blockbuster *What Lies Beneath* dates in the pot, as he blanches the *Sixth Sense*-style character-driven horror movie until there's nothing coming at you except cues and exposition. Before long, the movie begins to feel like a sleep deprivation trial: Obvious scenes are drawn out into perpetuity (you could sprout your first liver spot waiting for Zemeckis's camera to get to its point), and then unfailingly climax with an irrelevant, slamming soundtrack gotcha. You begin to sympathize with the rats in brilliant scientist Harrison Ford's genetics lab.

Ford's workaholic Norman is married to high-strung Claire (Michelle Pfeiffer), who begins to experience the usual movie-ghost oddness in her wealth-porn seaside manse: doors opening, radios turning on, bathtubs that fill up by themselves (not so usual, I guess), and visions of a dead girl Norman shtupped, and for whom, of course, there is hell to pay. Hardly a frame goes by without Pfeiffer, who looks day-old-dead already, and who accentuates the effect of being semi-possessed by another vapid, lynx-eyed blond with line readings worthy of a stroke victim. As it turns out, the ghost is a macguffin of sorts, and the wholly unaffecting rigmarole carries the burden of belated Hitchcockianism. (The major suspense piece involves being drug-paralyzed in a slowly filling tub antique-shopped right out of Bates Motel cabin #1.) Ostensibly a scarifying parable about wives left alone in piggish homes (the credits include a "bonsai team lead") after the kids go off to college, *What Lies Beneath* does, with Ford's presidentiality and Pfeiffer's testy relationship with middle age, suggest a Clintons-at-home scenario for 2001—haunted by the ghosts of dalliances past.

Also reviewed in:
CHICAGO TRIBUNE, 7/21/00, Friday/p. A, Michael Wilmington
NEW YORK TIMES, 8/21/00, p. E10, Elvis Mitchell
VARIETY, 7/17-23/00, p. 25, Emanuel Levy
WASHINGTON POST, 7/21/00, p. C1, Rita Kempley
WASHINGTON POST, 7/21/00, Weekend/p. 34, Desson Howe

WHAT PLANET ARE YOU FROM?

A Columbia Pictures release of a Brad Grey/Bernie Brillstein production. *Executive Producer:* Brad Grey and Bernie Brillstein. *Producer:* Mike Nichols, Garry Shandling, and Neil Machlis. *Director:* Mike Nichols. *Screenplay:* Garry Shandling, Michael Leeson, Ed Solomon, and Peter Tolan. *Story:* Garry Shandling and Michael Leeson. *Director of Photography:* Michael Ballhaus. *Editor:* Richard Marks. *Music:* Carter Burwell. *Music Editor:* Todd Kasow. *Sound:* David MacMillan and (music) Michael Farrow. *Sound Editor:* Ron Bochar. *Casting:* Ellen Lewis. *Production Designer:* Bo Welch. *Art Director:* Tom Duffield. *Set Designer:* John Dexter. *Set Decorator:* Cheryl Carasik. *Set Dresser:* Val Harris. *Special Effects:* Al Lorimer. *Costumes:* Ann Roth. *Make-up:* J. Roy Helland. *Stunt Coordinator:* John Moio. *Running time:* 115 minutes. *MPAA Rating:* R.

CAST: Gary Shandling (Harold Anderson); Annette Bening (Susan); John Goodman (Roland Jones); Greg Kinnear (Perry Gordon); Ben Kingsley (Graydon); Judy Greer (Rebecca); Danny Zorn (Randy); Harmony Smith (Rita); Richard Jenkins (Don Fisk); Linda Fiorentino (Helen Gordon); Caroline Aaron (Nadine); Nora Dunn (Madeline); Cricky Long (Janice); Camryn Manheim (Alison); Ann Cusack (Liz); Jane Lynch (Doreen); Richard Minchenberg (Dr. Weitzman); Drinda La Lumia (Drunken Lady); J. C. MacKenzie (John); Willie Garson (Brett); Marjorie Lovett (Neighbor Woman); Bil Dwyer (Husband); Cathy Ladman (Wife); Alexander Lyras (Male AA); Anastasia Sakelaris (Cheryl); Jane Morris (Charity Woman); Michael Dempsey (Baggage Handler); Stacey Travis (Woman); Walter Addison (Pilot); Brian Markinson (Co-Pilot); Octavia L. Spencer (Baby Nurse); Ana Mercedes (Older Nurse); Samantha Smith (Flight Attendant); Tom Dahlgren (Minister); Tammy Tavares (Hologram Woman); Wade Andrew Williams (Planet Man); Phill Lewis (Other MD); Minerva Garcia (Nurse); Jack Sydow (Minister); Rick Hoffman (Doctor); Tom Dorfmeister (Heavy Man);

Neil Machlis (Dr. Tom);   Mitchell Greenberg (Robotic Voice);   Jerry Punch and Mike Gottfried (Football Announcers).

CHRISTIAN SCIENCE MONITOR, 3/3/00, p. 15, David Sterritt

Parenthood is at the heart of two new Hollywood comedies. "What Planet Are You From?" and "The Next Best Thing," but viewers interested in old-fashioned family values will have to wade through a lot of irreverent humor before they'll find a hint of what they're seeking.

"What Planet Are You From?" stars Garry Shandling as a denizen of a distant planet who's sent to Earth with orders to impregnate a woman so that his all-male race can spread to our corner of the galaxy.

Disguised as a mild-mannered banker, he sets about his task with grim determination, making a pass at every woman he sees. Most of them brush him right off, but then he meets an attractive real-estate broker who wants a child as much as he does. She marries him without guessing his secret mission, and eventually her honest feelings make him realize it's more fun to be an emotion-filled Earthling than an alien with more intellect than he knows what to do with.

Although it offers a few good laughs, the movie often seems like a second-rate parody of more original pictures—starting like a sexed-up "Star Trek" episode, then traveling through "Men in Black" territory, and detouring into "Rosemary's Baby" near the end.

Its best asset is its cast, including Annette Bening as the alien's wife, Ben Kingsley as the leader of his planet, and John Goodman as an investigator on his trail. Goodman gets most of the best lines, and his brilliant comic delivery helps the movie survive its overdoses of silliness and vulgarity.

Let's hope Mike Nichols agreed to direct this throwaway farce as a temporary break from the more meaningful fare ("The Graduate," "Primary Colors") that his admirers hope for when they see his name in the credits.

"The Next Best Thing" would have been a better thing if director John Schlesinger and writer Thomas Ropelewski had decided what kind of movie they wanted to make. It's a well-meaning picture, but its uneven story and scrambled emotions ultimately doom its good intentions.

Madonna plays Abbie, a not-quite-young woman who's afraid family life will pass her by if she doesn't have a child soon, but can't find the right man to settle down with. This concern becomes moot when she discovers she's pregnant after a one-night fling with her close friend Robert, a gay man, who finds fatherhood quite agreeable once the little boy is born.

Their household is unconventional but contented until Abbie meets exactly the kind of man—handsome, successful, heterosexual—she'd longed for at the beginning of the story. She falls for him, and this is when the movie falls apart, trading its air of mischievous humor for trite sentimentality, arbitrary plot twists, and enough maudlin melodramatics to sustain a tabloid TV series.

It's starting to seem unlikely that Madonna will ever have a real movie career—even a rock 'n' roll superstar can have just so many false starts before the public gets suspicious—and after this crash-and-burn disaster she'd be well advised to stop trying, at least until a halfway decent script comes her way.

Rupert Everett fares even worse with the collection of clichés called Robert. Add a syrupy music score by Gabriel Yared and you have one of the most disappointing movies of this disappointing season.

How regrettable to find Schlesinger, of "Billy Liar" and "Midnight Cowboy" fame, at the helm of a sinking ship like this.

LOS ANGELES TIMES, 3/3/00, Calendar/p. 2, Kenneth Turan

"What Planet Are You From?" is a question this Mike Nichols-directed hybrid ought to be asking itself. Part alien sex comedy, part fake sensitive look at human relationships, its diverse parts come at you out of everywhere all at once. Imagine "Mork and Mindy" meets "The Love Boat" with a bit of "The Omen" and a lot of the randyness of burlesque humor thrown in. A disconcerting combination, to say the least.

"Planet's" idea came from star Garry Shandling, who also co-wrote the script and served as one of the film's producers. The force behind HBO's "The Larry Sanders Show," Shandling presumably wanted this to be funny but also confesses to having had "personal issues" he was eager to explore. But neither Shandling nor the trio of credited writers (Michael Leeson, Ed Solomon, Peter Tolan) who worked with him were able to consistently bring both sides of that equation to life. The result is a film that is sporadically funny, often strange and almost never poignant.

The film begins "at the far reaches of the universe," on a nameless planet four solar systems away in distance and a thousand years more advanced than Earth in technology. It's a planet inhabited only by men who've (no surprise) eliminated emotions and reproduce themselves by cloning. In the process their sexual organs, not to put too fine a point on it, first shrunk and then completely disappeared.

Now, however, Graydon (Ben Kingsley), the planet's leader, has a plan to rule the universe that makes those lost organs necessary. One of his subjects will be selected to go to Earth and father a child with one of the planet's women, facilitating an eventual "Body Snatchers"-type insider's takeover.

Before a volunteer is chosen, training has to take place, and legions of identically dressed men somberly learn puzzling techniques ("She will enjoy being told her footwear is stylish") for putting women into "receptive moods." The lucky candidate is H1449-6 (Shandling), hereafter known as Harold Anderson, outfitted with a new sexual organ and selected for his adaptability to "unpredictable" Earth women.

Once Anderson's in country as a Phoenix bank loan officer, however, it turns out that all that training has turned him into a smug and obnoxious lounge lizard, a "humongous sleazebag" whose one-track mind irritates and flummoxes more women than it attracts.

Also getting in Anderson's way is his new mechanical penis, which makes a loud humming noise at the least opportune moments. FAA investigator Roland Jones, played by John Goodman, tells his disbelieving wife that it sounds "like the refrigerator-freezer we had in that time-share up in Deer Valley."

Goodman, very much in his element as the dogged federal agent—and the only person who suspects Anderson's alien status—is funny, but little else is, even at these early stages. Shandling's bogus sincerity can be amusing, but his distant performance doesn't wear well and neither does the film's overreliance on stale sex jokes. It's an open question whether Nichols' smart but cool direction adds to the problem or simply doesn't do enough to overcome it.

As fake alien Harold Anderson, he wastes no time telling morally suspect co-worker Perry Gordon (Greg Kinnear), "I've just got to have sex, I've got to have it right away." Gordon then engineers a visit to a local AA meeting, which he views solely as "a good place to meet vulnerable women."

In fact, Anderson does meet Susan Hart (Annette Bening), sober just a couple of months. A former party animal, she bought herself a new car to celebrate her change of life, and shares the feeling that "it's going to be great to get up and remember where I parked it."

Naturally, Hart, with a history of picking the wrong men, is attracted to Anderson, for whom no one of childbearing age is the wrong woman. Bening does the best she can with this part—her peppy, pajama-clad singing of "High Hopes" is a treat—but she naturally projects more intelligence and focus than the film knows what to do with.

Except for the appearance of Linda Fiorentino, dryly humorous as Perry's libidinous wife, Helen, too much of the rest of "Planet" bogs down in weak dramaturgy about love and commitment. Truly, these are not the likeliest people for us to get all warm and cuddly about. To borrow a title from an earlier film with a similar subject, Earth women may be easy, but making movies about them is not.

NEW YORK, 3/13/00, p. 86, Peter Rainer

What Planet Are You From? is a bit like a middling *Saturday Night Live* sketch stretched to feature length. It has a fluky, mild affability and some fine performances, but it wafts into the ozone while you're watching it. Expectations for this piffle might not be so high if it were the work of a new, young filmmaker with a couple of sitcom episodes to his credit. But because Mike Nichols directed, one expects a bit more *something*. And since Garry Shandling, who also stars, is a co-screenwriter and producer, the letdown is doubled: Any old segment of *The Larry Sanders Show* had more invention and larcenous wit.

Shandling plays Harold, an alien from a planet four solar systems away populated entirely by cloned robotic males. His mission is to arrive on Earth and impregnate a woman, played here by Annette Bening, in order to carry out his planet's ambitions to colonize us from within. The jokiness works at a fairly crude level, and the sentiment, when it begins to seep in, is fairly crude, too. Along with Elaine May, Nichols brought a new, super-smart causticity to revue-sketch comedy. The comedy in *What Planet Are You From?* doesn't draw on the tradition he helped create, and it also doesn't draw on the more surefire commercialism (dolled up as social satire) of *The Graduate* or *The Birdcage*, or his Neil Simon stage and screen stewardships. Nichols's movies are often meticulously crafted to the point of parchedness, and he may have taken a swing at this Wiffle Ball as a way to limber up. I'm not complaining entirely; I'll take a Wiffle Ball over a medicine ball any day, and, after some of Nichols's more serioso entries, like *Regarding Henry* and *Wolf* who would wish for more of the same? The problem with *What Planet Are You From?* isn't so much that it's minor but that it's so cut-rate. Its cheapjack, knocked-off quality is almost a form of effrontery.

The film's pifflishness wouldn't be so bad if you didn't also get the hearts-and-flowers treatment alongside it. Nichols and Shandling are trying to set up Harold, with his emotionless demeanor and lewd, pro-grammatic pickup lines, as an intergalactic example of the way all men behave. It's a ticklish notion: Males across the cosmos are more in tune with each other than they are with any woman. But then the filmmakers turn Harold's story into a cosmic immigrant's quest for humanness, for family feeling, and it gets awfully touchy-feely. *Coneheads* covered a lot of this same territory. And it was funnier.

It doesn't help that Garry Shandling seems permanently zonked in the role. What's funny about Shandling normally is how his zonkiness camouflages the squiggles of hate and cunning that keep breaking through his big-haired Howdy Doody visage. When, as Harold, he goes on about how he doesn't know what love means and all that jazz, you keep expecting him to snap out of it—for the movie's sake, if not his own. Playing opposite Shandling, Greg Kinnear, as a lecherous co-worker in a Phoenix bank, steals most of their scenes simply because this crumbum Lothario with an intimate knowledge of the local titty bars is so unregenerately piggy. As intergalactic male exemplars go, Kinnear's character at least has a pulse, which puts him a beat ahead of Harold.

Annette Bening's performance is far and away the best thing about *What Planet Are You From?* It's so good that you wish it were in another movie. (I like her better here than in *American Beauty*, where her shrillness kept hitting you over the head.) As an AA graduate with a string of bad love affairs, Bening's Susan is a fidgety mess in search of redemption. Her early scenes with Harold reveal such a longing for a life change that you actually *want* her to hook up with the big zero. She has an ineffably charming moment when Harold comes home and she surprises him by singing "High Hopes" while performing a girlish little shimmy. Bening's full-fledged tenderness in this movie deserves a better foil. If she were playing opposite, say, Steve Martin, an actor who really knows how to communicate the ardency behind the frozen mask, the film might have been out-of-this-world in more ways than one.

A final thought: Why isn't Mike Nichols acting in the movies? His performance a few years back in *The Designated Mourner* was one of the most extraordinary extended monologues I've ever seen anywhere. His character had a voracious, sorrowful creepiness that seemed to issue entirely unimpeded from the actor's soul. On the basis of that performance alone, Nichols stands as one of our finest actors. Why deprive us of more of the same? What planet is *he* from, anyway?

NEW YORK POST, 3/3/00, p. 53, Lou Lumenick

Men are from Mars and women are from Venus, the saying goes. But the hero of "What Planet Are You From?" isn't from either planet—nor from Earth, for that matter.

Garry Shandling is hilarious H1449-6, late of "Planet 10," who's assigned to impregnate an Earth woman while posing as banker Harold Anderson of Phoenix, Ariz.

The big joke is that horny Harold is as clueless about the opposite sex as the average Earth man in this odd mixture of social satire, penis jokes and sci-fi directed by, of all people, Mike Nichols.

The leader of the all-male, all-cloned Planet 10 (Ben Kingsley) is bent on taking over Earth from the inside.

After extensive sessions in which trainees are taught to respond "uh-huh" to any remark by Earth women, Harold is equipped with a high-tech penis (which emits a high-pitched hum, the movie's best running gag) and sent to Earth.

After many failures with his crude pick-up lines, Harold hits pay dirt with the insecure, mood-swinging Susan Hart (Annette Bening), who he meets at an Alcoholics Anonymous meeting.

Harold closes the deal by agreeing to wed Susan after their first date. But the honeymoon—21 orgasms, depicted in the fountains of a Las Vegas hotel—is quickly over and she's complaining about his inattentiveness and his lack of interest in her friends.

Bening—again playing a real-estate agent, though her performance couldn't be more different than in "American Beauty"—is terrific, even when Shandling (who co-wrote the script) veers off into "There's Something About Mary" territory, tossing off one-liners with impeccable timing in his starring debut.

Greg Kinnear is effectively smarmy as Harold's co-worker, while Linda Fiorentino is wasted as his wife. John Goodman gets a few laughs in a stock role as an FAA investigator obsessed with tracking down Harold.

"What Planet Are You From?," which careens from sentimentality to an outer-space slapstick finale straight out of "Sleeper," is wildly uneven. But it's still easily the funniest movie of the year.

NEWSDAY, 3/3/00, Part II/p. B6, Gene Seymour

Garry Shandling stumbles a lot in "What Planet Are You From?" almost as if he's not quite sure of the floor plan of a movie he helped conceive. Conception being, literally, the operative word here, since Shandling plays a visitor from another planet sent by his leader (Ben Kingsley) to impregnate Earth's women as means of conquering "from within."

At one point during a painful talk with the mother of his child, played by Annette Bening, Shandling's alien stumbles into a corner, bewildered by fluid coming out of his face. "I'm bleeding," he mutters.

"No, you're not," she replies tenderly. "You're crying."

It's an awkward moment in a movie cluttered with them. But here, at least, the effect is touching because it's one of the few times when "What Planet Are You From?" stops coasting fitfully between broad comedy and pop psychology, and summons genuine emotion.

Still, even with the most refined mushiness available, you'd want a movie with a plot like this to be mostly funny. And the most disappointing thing about "What Planet Are You From?" is that, by the time it's over, you're still waiting for the potential of its high-powered cast and clever premise to be fulfilled. You're also waiting, most of the time, for something to make you laugh.

Which is the one thing that you'd think wouldn't be a problem in a comedy directed by Mike Nichols and co-written and co-produced by Shandling, whose "The Larry Sanders Show" is a landmark in television comedy. Still, there are three other guys (Michael Leeson, Ed Solomon and Peter Tolan) sharing screen-writing credit with the star and, in at least nine out of 10 cases, multiple writing credits can only mean a static, unfocused story line.

The story begins on a distant planet whose advanced technology has displaced emotion—and sexual intercourse. To ensure its exponential growth and power in the universe, the planet selects one member of its bland, utilitarian population to mate and procreate.

Shandling's alien comes to Phoenix, bearing the name Harold Anderson and a sheaf of recommendations that secure him a fast-track job with a local bank.

While there, he hooks up with a slimy co-worker, Perry (Greg Kinnear), who takes Harold on a tour of the city's best strip clubs and Alcoholics Anonymous meetings—a great place, says Perry, to pick up women.

And sure enough, it's at such a meeting that Harold meets his bride-to-be: a 40-something recovering alcoholic named Susan (Bening), who's trying to piece her scattered life back together.

As with every other woman Harold meets, Susan's a little puzzled by the mechanical humming sound he makes every time she so much as smiles at him. He can't tell her that it's his automated reproductive organs attached to his alien form. The hum, by the way, does make you laugh for the first or second time—and maybe once near the end. Mostly, it's a running gag that you wish would run offscreen for a breather.

Shandling and company probably believed, with some justification, that this sci-fi premise provided a means to show ways in which guys on this planet Just Don't Get It when it comes to connecting with women. Harold's "progress," from bluntly telling women he wants to have sex to tripping upon the complexities of his involvement with Susan, is set up as a metaphor for the primitive, non-evolved male coming to terms with his own humanity and that of the opposite sex.

The problem is that just about all the characters in "What Planet Are You From?" seem to come from other planets and none of them speak the same language. Bening once again is forced to play a tightly wound real estate agent, reminiscent of her "American Beauty" role. ("Don't laugh," she says to Harold when told of her profession. He doesn't but we do.) Kinnear's malevolence as Perry functions in a vacuum, as does the sultry lasciviousness of Linda Fiorentino as Perry's equally adulterous wife. John Goodman, as a federal agent who's figured out Harold's mission, tries gallantly to bring some focused energy to the show. But even he seems lost in another zone.

NEWSWEEK, 3/6/00, p. 68, David Ansen

Garry Shandling is an alien from outer space. On his advanced planet, which seems to be entirely populated by men, the ambitious citizens have no emotions and no sexual organs. Shandling is chosen to propagate the future of their species. Outfitted with a penis, he is sent to Earth on a mission to impregnate a woman and thus begin his planet's ultimate takeover of Earth. His destination: Phoenix. His alias: bank officer Harold Anderson from Seattle. His weapons: an arsenal of stale come-ons ("I like your shoes," "You smell good") that will only confirm a woman's suspicions that men are indeed from Mars.

The premise of "What Planet Are You From?'—dreamed up by Shandling and Michael Leeson—sounds like the basis for a raunchy farce. The comedy that Mike Nichols has directed has its fair share of phallic jokes (the best is just a sound: the whirring noise that begins every time our randy alien is aroused), but the movie wants its satire to be taken seriously. Nichols and Shandling think they've stumbled on a resonant metaphor to describe the intractable differences between men and women. Man is a heat-seeking missile only interested in sex, while woman, of course, is the relationship-seeking, nest-building species.

This is not what anybody would call a novel perception, which wouldn't matter if the movie were riotously funny. Mildly amusing at best, "What Planet Are You From?" follows a predictable trajectory as our alien moves in with a recovering-alcoholic real estate broker (Annette Bening), fathers a son and begins to suspect that human emotions may not he such a bad thing after all. Nichols always works with topflight talent (Greg Kinnear, John Goodman and Ben Kingsley play supporting roles; Janeane Garofalo pops up for a cameo; the estimable Bo Welch is the production designer), but a skit idea is a skit idea. There are funny lines scattered here and there—especially at the end—but the combination of Shandling's button-down TV sensibility and Nichols's good taste produces a film whose tone is out of sync with the simple, ribald conceit. A little more vulgarity might have helped. "Planet" seems a misuse of talent, like employing Vladimir Horowitz to play "Chopsticks."

TIME, 3/6/00, p. 72, Richard Schickel

Harold Anderson (Garry Shandling) is a visitor from a faraway, all-male, procreatively challenged planet. His mission on earth is to impregnate a woman and bring their offspring home for breeding purposes. To accomplish the task, he has been equipped with an artificial metal penis, which hums audibly when its interest is, shall we say, aroused. Why does it do that? Because "it doesn't know the words," snaps Linda Fiorentino, playing a woman immune to Harold's charms.

That's the best joke in *What Planet Are You From?* Considering the number of variations played on it, you might argue that it's the only one. Mostly, Shandling plays an over-grown adolescent of a familiar, earth-bound sort. He's befuddled and inept as he attempts to comprehend the rules of the mating game.

In other words, he's the nerd from outer space. But Shandling—also one of the film's several writers—is not enough of an actor to make him a sympathetic one. Harold does not live life; he comments on it. And that plays into director Mike Nichols' supercilious side. The producers have employed good comic actors, among them Annette Bening, John Goodman and Greg Kinnear, in an effort to take the chill off. But most of the women Harold encounters are unfunnily damaged—timorous or frigid, frenzied or alcoholic—while the men are sexist, henpecked or just clueless.

The result is a movie that is at once smug and lazy, qualities fatal to comedy. And qualities increasingly prevalent in an era enervated by the ironic ideal. (Wouldn't it be ironic if irony destroyed our ability to make one another laugh?) At some point in *What Planet Are You From?* you start to wonder how these people acquired the air of unearned superiority that makes the movie seem so old and tired.

VILLAGE VOICE, 3/14/00, p. 130, Dennis Lim

A more coherent but no more sophisticated view of the perilous modern mating game, [The reference is to *The Next Best Thing*; see Lim's review.] Mike Nichols's *What Planet Are You From?* stars Shandling as an alien sent to impregnate an earthling—the first step in an imminent takeover by his all-male planet, whose highly evolved natives possess neither emotions nor genitalia. For his mission, our dickless hero—assuming the guise of Harold Anderson, Phoenix banker—has been fitted with a mechanical penis that, when aroused, makes an alarming whirring noise (somewhere between vibrator and Cuisinart). Cruising AA meetings with sleazy coworker Greg Kinnear, Harold zeroes in on his target: mildly neurotic, sweetly patient 12-stepper Susan (Annette Bening).

Literalizing the Men Are From Mars conundrum, the movie essentially writes itself, but the performances save it from *Earth Girls Are Easy* opprobrium. An actor who never trades in half-measures, Bening actually works hard at making Susan a flesh-and-blood person; the supporting cast includes the great John Goodman, as a suspicious aviation investigator, and Linda Fiorentino, back to vamping after her mysteriously anemic turn in *Dogma*. Shandling, who also cowrote the screenplay, has no range to speak of (his fixed expression is one of severe consternation), but his knowingly piggish self-absorption prevents the movie from thickening into treacle. There's a certain satisfaction in recognizing that Harold—even when he inevitably starts to feel, just like a human—remains something of an asshole.

Also reviewed in:
CHICAGO TRIBUNE, 3/3/00, Friday/p. A, Mark Caro
NATION, 3/27/00, p. 35, Stuart Klawans
NEW REPUBLIC, 3/27/00, p. 26, Stanley Kauffmann
NEW YORK TIMES, 3/3/00, p. E23, Elvis Mitchell
NEW YORKER, 3/13/00, p. 101, David Denby
VARIETY, 2/28-3/5/00, p. 39, Todd McCarthy
WASHINGTON POST, 3/3/00, p. C1, Stephen Hunter
WASHINGTON POST, 3/3/00, Weekend/p. 46, Desson Howe

WHAT WOMEN WANT

A Paramount Pictures release of an Icon/Wind Dancer production. *Executive Producer:* Stephen McEveety, David McFadzean, and Carmen Finestra. *Producer:* Matt Williams, Susan Cartsonis, Gina Matthews, Bruce Davey, and Nancy Meyers. *Director:* Nancy Meyers. *Screenplay:* Josh Goldsmith and Cathy Yuspa. *Story:* Josh Goldsmith, Cathy Yuspa, and Diane Drake. *Director of Photography:* Dean Cundey. *Editor:* Stephen A. Rotter and Thomas J. Nordberg. *Music:* Alan Silvestri. *Music Editor:* Andrew Silver. *Choreographer:* Keith Young. *Sound:* David MacMillan and (music) Robert Fernandez. *Sound Editor:* Dennis Drummond. *Casting:* Howard Feuer and Deborah Aquila. *Production Designer:* Jon Hutman. *Art Director:* Gae Buckle and Tony Fanning. *Set Designer:* John Goldsmith, Andrew Menzies, Easton Smith, Patrick Sullivan, Beck Taylor, and John Warnke. *Set Decorator:* Rosemary Brandenburg. *Costumes:* Ellen

Mirojnick.   *Make-up:* Brad Wilder.   *Stunt Coordinator:* Lance Gilbert.   *Running time:* 123 inutes.   *MPAA Rating:* PG-13.

CAST: Mel Gibson (Nick Marshall);   Helen Hunt (Darcy Maguire);   Marisa Tomei (Lola); Mark Feuerstein (Morgan Farwell);   Lauren Holly (Gigi);   Ashley Johnson (Alex Marshall); Judy Greer (Erin);   Alan Alda (Dan Wanamaker);   Delta Burke (Eve); Valerie Perrine (Margo); Lisa Edelstein (Dina);   Sarah Paulson (Annie);   Ana Gasteyer (Sue Cranston);   Loretta Devine (Flo);   Diana-Maria Riva (Stella);   Eric Balfour (Cameron);   Andrea Taylor (Inner Voice Actress);   John Frazier (Truck Driver);   Perry Cavitt (Ogling Man);   Crystal McKinney and Jeannie Renick (Unimpressed Women);   Andrea Taylor (Office Intern);   Kathrin Lautner (Gigi's Friend);   Logan Lerman (Little Nick);   Kelly Cooper, Palmer Davis, and Katie Miller (Showgirls);   Dana Waters (Nick's Mom);   Gregory Cupoli (Male Role Model);   Alexondra Lee (Woman in Sweater);   Aviva Gale (Counter Girl);   Shirley Prestia and T. J. Thyne (Coffee Shop Customers);   Norman H. Smith (Norm);   Audrey Wasilewski (Secretary with Danish); Angela Oh (Dan's Secretary);   Robert Briscoe Evans (Ted);   Harmony Rousseau (Sloane/Curtis Receptionist);   Lisa Long (Sloane/Curtis Executive);   Cristine Rose (Sloane/Curtis Attorney); Arden Myrin (Darcy's Assistant); Rachel Duncan and Alex McKenna (Alex's Friends);   Regiane Gorski (Yoga Instructor);   Jamie Gutterman (Jogger by Lake);   Maggie Egan, Juanita Jennings, and Robin Pearson Rose (Kitchen Secretaries);   Hallie Meyers Shyer and Laura Quicksilver (Girls at Lunch Counter);   Nnenna Freelon (Nightclub Singer); Gil Hacohen (Haim);   Nancy Monsarat, Jacqueline Thomas, and Rory Rubin (Nike Executives);   Chris Emerson (Mail Room Kid); Victoria Kelleher (Secretary);   Gertrude Wong (Woman in Chinatown);   Andi Eystad (Girl at Prom);   Bette Midler (Therapist).

LOS ANGELES TIMES, 12/15/00, Calendar/p. 1, Kenneth Turan

Because his character does nothing but wrong, it's necessary to believe that actor Mel Gibson does everything right to fully enjoy his new starring vehicle, "What Women Want."

A picture constructed with Mel-aholics in mind, "What Women Want" is a vaguely amusing formulaic comedy with a premise that turns out to be more discomforting than endearing: that chauvinistic Chicago advertising executive Nick Marshall (Gibson) suddenly finds himself with the ability to literally hear what women think.

"What Women Want" is written by "The King of Queens" supervising producers Josh Goldsmith & Cathy Yuspa and directed by Nancy Meyers, who co-wrote and directed the enjoyable "Parent Trap" remake of a few years back. But despite its contemporary "women rule" window dressing, its foundations are a lot more ancient.

For one thing, the film's underlying plot of a rivalry between two advertising executives, one a hard-working woman, the other a womanizing man who takes unfair advantage of her, is rather close to the outline of that archaic 1961 Doris Day-Rock Hudson vehicle "Lover Come Back."

For another, Nick Marshall's character is such an anachronistic Rat Pack knockoff, down to the lipstick kiss on his face, his love of Frank Sinatra and his willingness to break into a Gene Kelly-influenced soft shoe at the slightest provocation, that you'll think at times you've wandered into the long-delayed remake of "Ocean's 11."

Marshall, all the women in his life (and there are many) will tell you, is a man's man who, despite his remarkable success as a seducer, doesn't get what women are about. "He's the total bachelor and the least politically correct man in the company" is the word on him at the Sloane/Curtis Agency, where Marshall's angling to be named creative director.

The good thing about having the handsome and charming Gibson in a role like this is that it's not hard to see why he might be catnip to so many. But that doesn't mean that shots of Marshall trying on panty hose or briefly pretending to be gay are automatically funny (they're not), or that we're willing to suffer through his character being several different kinds of jerk for almost the entire film so we can experience the uncertain pleasure of having the big lug finally see the light (praise be!) just before the credits roll.

Marshall's professional troubles begin when his boss, Dan Wanamaker (Alan Alda), tells him he's being passed over for that promotion he wanted. The ad game is changing, Wanamaker says; females 16 to 24 are the fastest-growing consumer group in the country, spending $40 billion per year, and Marshall's Swedish Bikini Team approach to advertising doesn't cut it with them.

Which is why the job of creative director is going to the person Marshall fears the most, Darcy Maguire (Helen Hunt), a top executive with the reputation of being "a real man-eater" (as opposed to the fake kind). Marshall takes an instant dislike to Maguire, as well as to her insistence that everyone in the agency take home a box of products for women and try to figure out new ways to sell them.

It's in the midst of getting drunk, painting his toenails, trying on panty hose, etc., that Marshall has an electrical accident and wakes up with this uncanny ability to hear what is on women's minds. At first this gift terrifies him ("It's personal, private stuff, things no one on earth is supposed to hear"), but soon a therapist (an unbilled Bette Midler cameo) inadvertently sets him straight. "If you know what women want," she tells him, "you can rule."

What this means in practice is that Marshall goes from being a chauvinist jerk to being a devious jerk, literally reading rival Maguire's mind and more or less stealing her ideas to undercut her at the office and make himself, if possible, more smug and self-satisfied than ever. Yes, there are some laughs here, but not enough to make up for the disagreeableness involved.

While working out new ways to be conniving, Marshall has to deal with the thoughts of several other women, including his estranged teenage daughter (Ashley Johnson) from a failed marriage and a desperate coffee-shop counter girl (Marisa Tomei). These other women have a less consistently Olympian view of Marshall, an attempt at giving the film the kind of comic balance it never really achieves.

"What Women Want" also takes a few shots at being poignant, but they play more like afterthoughts. In fact, it says a lot about this film that the most moving moment it provides is a Nike commercial for female runners created by the real-life Weiden-Kennedy Agency. When that's your emotional high spot, you know you're in trouble.

NEW YORK POST, 12/15/00, p. 53, Jonathan Foreman

After a slow start, "What Women Want "picks up and becomes an adequately funny but predictable sitcom, with an enjoyably sentimental third act.

But it never does anything surprising or interesting with its clever "Twilight Zone" premise: how a man might behave if he could hear women's thoughts.

Apparently women—at least the confident, super successful but lonely kind represented here by Helen Hunt—just want guys who are sensitive and humble and who can read their minds at certain key moments. As for men, well, the filmmakers seem to be completely clueless about the male sex.

Mel Gibson, in a role originally conceived with Tim Allen in mind, plays Nick Marshall, a divorced ratpack-esque Chicago ad executive who still calls women "girls' or "broads" and is supposed to be a famously successful womanizer despite his manifest insensitivity, boorishness, arrogance, etc.

Nick, who lives in a suspiciously fabulous apartment, expects to be promoted to creative director at his agency when his boss, Wanamaker (Alan Alda), tells him that the agency needs to tap the women's market and has therefore hired Darcy Maguire (Helen Hunt) instead.

Men, you see, can't sell products to women, at least in this movie world, one in which the guys at Revlon and the sons of Estee Lauder presumably never got it together.

Terrified that his career is over after all, Darcy is clearly smart and able while he has no discernible talent—Nick goes home and tries out a bunch of beauty products, and is of course caught by his teenage daughter and her boyfriend while wearing pantyhose and nail polish. He also has an accident with a hairdryer and the electric shock gives him the ability to hear women's thoughts.

At first, he's horrified. Then he realizes that the power will be extremely useful for getting women into bed and for getting rid of Darcy, his new boss, by stealing her ideas.

It's not clear, but either the power works only intermittently, or the filmmakers believe that women alternate between thinking nothing at all and coming up with unspoken comic zingers, especially in business meetings.

Of course the experience of hearing women's secret thoughts makes Nick like them more ... and he quickly becomes a more sensitive lover, father and boss (he even tries to help the suicidal office-mouse). He falls for Darcy, who begins to fall for him despite his reputation as a chauvinist.

The script is credited to the team of Josh Goldsmith and Cathy Yuspa, but director Nancy Meyers ("The Parent Trap") has claimed in interviews that much of the writing is in fact hers, in particular the yuppie—superwoman/feminist—role model character played by Hunt.

Darcy's s split from a man who couldn't handle her success, Meyers has also said, is inspired by her own from the director Charles ("Father of the Bride") Shyer.

The ubiquitous Ms. Hunt is more feminine and attractive than she has been for some time. Mel Gibson looks a little old for this character (so similar to Ben Affleck's in "Bounce") and his comic timing is rather clunky, but he does have charm and good looks to spare. And what's more, he can dance.

Marisa Tomei is on screen for too little time as a neurotic actress/coffee-shop waitress with whom Nick has an educational sexual experience.

In place of genuine wit and sophistication, Meyers swamps the movie with music that has both: Sinatra performing "Mack the Knife" and "I've Got You Under My Skin."

NEWSDAY, 12/15/00, Part II/p. B2, John Anderson

What do women want? Apparently, Helen Hunt. Radiating far more intelligence than sex appeal, Hunt is about the most nonthreatening presence currently making movies—and lots of them, including four of the biggest, if not best, of the year in pictures: "Dr. T and the Women," "Pay It Forward," the upcoming "Cast Away" and, today, "What Women Want." Just guessing, we'd say the actress has been the beneficiary of serious female-market research. Why? Because, given the same choice, most men would be voting for Carmen Electra.

And therein lies la difference, the heart and soul of Nancy Meyers' "What Women Want," in which Mel Gibson proves himself edgy, funny and willing to do just about anything for a laugh. As Nick Marshall, so-called "man's man" and advertising dinosaur, he falls into the bathtub with his hair dryer, while wearing pantyhose and too much mascara, and comes up hearing what women think.

He's not gay—although when Gibson prances around his spectacular Chicago living room to Meredith Brooks' "Bitch," the words "closet case" aren't the furthest things from your mind. Nick is, however, under pressure: His ex-wife (Lauren Holly) is getting married, his hormone-tormented daughter (Ashley Johnson) is coming for an extended stay and he's seen the writing on the wall—written there by his new boss, Darcy Maguire (who comes up with these names?), who's laid down the corporate law: It's a woman's world. And if the firm is going to survive, they've got to think pink.

Nick is a retro, Rat Pack kind of guy, which may be why Meyers—who's perpetrated such crimes against nature as "The Parent Trap" and "Father of the Bride II"—directs "What Women Want" as if it were a '60s bedroom farce. The jokes are as broad as barn doors; the attempt at screwball rhythms falls flat.

She calms down after a while, letting the movie ease into the most conventional of comedic formats, but during the time Nick is being his original self, you half expect him to run into Doris Day.

Instead—like most leading men this season—he runs into Helen Hunt, who, as Darcy, unknowingly provides Nick with the creative ideas that save his bacon and the insight into the female mind that turn him into the most sensitive of guys—albeit, a guy who's only being sensitive because he can hear the reactions of women to everything he says.

The lesson—there had to be a lesson—is that men can only "get it" in the Anita Hill sense of things by trading on insider information. But it's a wonderful concept. When he first gets his gift, Nick can hear women's flattering mental comments as he passes them by. But these are women he doesn't know. The ones that actually know him think he's a jerk. He gets better, though. And one of the more pungent and adult sequences in the movie is when Nick goes to bed with the coffee shop waitress he's been flirting with for years (Marisa Tomei) and follows her unspoken commentary like an instruction manual. That "What Women Want" is PG-13 is more proof that the ratings system is corrupt and ludicrous. But then, no one gets blown up.

It's more than disappointing that "What Women Want" doesn't sing a little more. The whole point of the movie is that men should better understand women, because women are in many ways superior, more sensitive, gentler, more intuitive. That the movie is made by a woman who can challenge any male filmmaker on Earth for ham-handed direction connotes some kind of sexual equality. But not one we should be striving for.

NEWSWEEK, 12/25/00, p. 74, David Ansen

Mel Gibson is guy's guy Nick Marshall, Chicago advertising executive and unreconstructed male chauvinist pig. One fateful night in his bachelor pad, Nick slips in the bath and gets a jolt from a hair dryer.

When he comes to, he has magically acquired the power to hear what women are thinking. At first this drives him nuts (he's astonished at how many women think he's a total jerk). But then he realizes the usefulness of his gift. Not only will he be able to steal his new female boss's (Helen Hunt) ideas and sabotage her job, it will make him an even more ruthlessly efficient lothario.

It's a farfetched but promising premise for a romantic comedy. But "What Women Want" is about half as funny as it ought to be. Once they've milked the gag for some broad laughs, director Nancy Meyers and screenwriters Josh Goldsmith and Cathy Yuspa are more interested in providing us with moral lessons than in giving us a good time. The result of Nick's journey into the hearts and minds of the opposite sex is—surprise!—to turn him into a model lover, dad and professional.

Gibson, in his first romantic-comedy role, is nothing if not game. He dances, he connives, he mugs, he sends himself up. He makes a likable heel, but you feel the effort in everything Gibson does. The ubiquitous Hunt is appealing as the woman Nick simultaneously betrays and falls for. Trouble is, the better a human being Nick becomes, the duller the movie gets.

SIGHT AND SOUND, 3/01, p. 61, Charlotte O'Sullivan

Advertising executive Nick Marshall is a chauvinist with a long list of women, including his ex-wife, daughter and maid, whom he has mistreated. Called in to see his boss Dan Wanamaker, he assumes that he is about to be made creative director at his firm; in fact, the job goes to a woman, Darcy Maguire. Nick's bosses believe she will appeal to America's growing number of female consumers. Nick's misery increases when he remembers his daughter is about to spend two weeks with him.

That night he has a freak accident. The next morning, he discovers he can hear what women are thinking. At first he's horrified, but after a visit to a shrink he realises he can use this "gift" to his advantage. Working closely with Darcy, he uses her ideas to come up with a brilliant, woman-friendly campaign for Nike. As a result, the bosses decide they don't need Darcy and give her job to Nick. By this time, he realises he's fallen in love with her. Determined to do the right thing, Nick arranges for Darcy to get her job back. Next, he goes to the home of a miserable office worker whom he's overheard planning suicide and he offers her a job. There, after being struck by lightning, he realises his gift has vanished. Undaunted, he rescues his daughter from a prom-night humiliation, then rushes to Darcy's flat and confesses all. Darcy fires him, then declares her love for him.

For reasons best known to its accountants, what this film wants is to be mistaken for a Nora Ephron-style heart warmer, as opposed to a bizarre treatise on the horrors of work, sex and identity à la Being John Malkovich. It almost succeeds: as in such hits as Sleepless in Seattle and You've Got Mail, the New York imagined here by director Nancy Meyers (who helmed the 1998 remake of The Parent Trap) harks back to a supposedly gentler time—a hymn to clean skyscraper lines and pat-a-cake croons. We must also endure precocious kids (namely, hero Nick's 15-year old daughter), and, more insidiously, a philosophy that speaks first and foremost to the privileged.

The titular reference to Freud's famous inquiry is no slip of the pen. Faced with Nick's "gift" he can hear what women are thinking—Bette Midler's therapist realises its potential: like an analyst, Nick has access to women's private monologues, but, interestingly, the talking cure doesn't work for everybody. Nick draws a blank when attempting to eavesdrop on the thoughts of his two middle-aged bimbo secretaries, women who stick out like sore (if manicured) thumbs in an office swarming with angsty Harvard graduates. The film, it seems, would have us believe that have-nots want-not.

For all that, it would be a mistake to dismiss *WWW*, because what it has to say about men in relation to middle-class women is far from conventional. The plot's trajectory may suggest that Nick is the one in control, but that's not how it's played out. Nick's gift is stronger than Nick himself and, even more than for John Cusack's character in *Being John Malkovich,* the special access our hero gains to a 'superior' being's brain leaves him intensely dissatisfied with his own self. It's a demoralisation that the film implicitly condones. Nick is literally not himself when he's in bed with Marisa Tomei's ditzy waitress—responding to her inner desires, it's as if he's a woman in a man's body. And, as in *Being,* that turns out to be a recipe for great sex. Liberation is in the detail: it's not lesbianism we're being asked to see in a new light, but masturbation.

Similar shocks are in store at the workplace. As a result of his gift, Nick stops thinking for himself, instinctively (and correctly) assuming that all of new girl Darcy's ideas are better than his own. Wanting what he hasn't got (Darcy's brain and soon Darcy herself, he copies everything she does from then on. That this works to his advantage appears almost accidental—it's Darcy's generosity that allows him to win the coveted account with Nike and the bosses' latent sexism that makes them so willing to take Nick back. More to the point, as ploys go it couldn't be more short term—without Darcy, how could he hope to hold on to his job?

In its last reel, *WWW* grows even more juicily strange. In a scene that comes right out of the blue, Nick tracks down a suicidal office worker and offers her a creative, fulfilling job. He's playing the ultimate white knight, but as the film soon makes clear, Darcy is the one with the sword. Having heard Nick's confession, plus the news that she's got her job back, she narrows her eyes and says: "If I have my job back, I think you're fired." So where does that leave the suicidal office worker? We're pretty sure Darcy will see the girl right, but it's not a given and that her goodness can't be relied upon is refreshing. So is Nick's confusion. Before rushing off to find the office worker, Nick tells his boss he wants "time out". Darcy's edict is thus both a shock (he looks stricken) and a dream come true Darcy gives him what he couldn't choose for himself.

What do men want? Just like women, they're in two minds. And can't change overnight.

TIME, 12/25/00-1/1/01, p. 150, Richard Schickel

The accident is plausible: It involves a hair dryer, a bathtub and an electric shock. The results are improbable: the victim, Gibson's Nick Marshall, an adman confronting a career crisis, is given a magical ability to listen in on womens' thoughts. As comic premises go these days, it is acceptable. One settles back to enjoy the advantages, personal and professional, that accrue to Nick as a result of his unexpected gift.

There's some good humor in the truths that he overhears, maybe even some sympathetic insights into the inner life of a sex he has exploited as God's hunky gift to womankind. Certainly it helps him ingratiate himself with Darcy Maguire (Hunt), the new creative director at his ad agency.

But something goes wrong at about the moment they start getting romantically involved. Maybe it's a failure of chemistry between Gibson and Hunt. More likely it's a failure in the script, attributed to Josh Goldsmith and Cathy Yuspa. They just can't seem to establish a consistently bantering tone between the stars. They might also want to re-examine their boring subplots involving Nick and his conventionally rebellious teenage daughter, a romance with a waitress that goes nowhere, and a relationship with a suicidal woman at the office. Meyers gets lost in these meanderings. The movie has none of the giddy wit we associate with classic romantic comedy. It just runs on and on—like a slightly stupid story you wish you hadn't overheard in a singles bar.

VILLAGE VOICE, 12/26/00, p. 142, Amy Taubin

Contrary to the title, the subject of *What Women Want* is not women's desires. Rather, this hardworking but ineffective Mel Gibson vehicle is part of a comedy genre based on the premise that men don't know exactly—to paraphrase Miss Swallow, Cary Grant's bossy fiancée in *Bringing Up Baby*—who and what they are. Failing to heed Miss Swallow's warnings, Grant's stuffy paleontologist finds himself garbed in a marabou-trimmed negligee, mockingly proclaiming, "I've just gone gay."

While *What Women Want* clearly owes something to *Bringing Up Baby*, a more direct model is Billy Wilder's transcendent gender-fuck *Some Like It Hot*. You might think that the sight of a bare-chested Gibson painting his nails flaming red and waxing his legs would trump Lemmon and Curtis fooling with their faisies and girdles. But director Nancy Meyers and writers Josh Goldsmith and Cathy Yuspa have put their star at a disadvantage. Lemmon and Curtis could use each other, not to mention Marilyn Monroe, as foils; Gibson must play his big scene with only his mirror for company.

Hollywood trendspotters could make something of the fact that in two of Christmas 2000's big studio releases, *What Women Want* and *Cast Away* [see Hoberman's review] the male star spends long stretches alone, talking to himself, while his love interest, played in both films by Helen Hunt, languishes off-screen. And though it pains me to say it, Tom Hanks, as a contemporary Robinson Crusoe, wins the soliloquy competition hands down.

Gibson's plight in *What Women Want* is less dire than being stranded for four years on a desert island. His Nick Marshall is a dedicated womanizer and the star of a Chicago advertising agency specializing in beer and car commercials. In an effort to boost an eroding bottom line Nick's boss (the avuncular Alan Alda, the only actor in the movie not to overplay his hand) decides to pursue the burgeoning female market for beauty products and hires Darcy Maguire (Hunt) as creative director. Not content to take a backseat, the competitive Nick is determined to beat Darcy at her own game. Whence comes his lengthy, lonely investigation of nail polish, leg wax, Wonderbras, and panty hose. Preceded for no discernible reason by another solo sequence in which Nick does a soft-shoe routine to a Sinatra record (a game dancer, Gibson is hardly in a league with Grant, let alone Astaire), the foray into cross-dressing climaxes with him accidentally electrocuting himself with a hair drier. Narrowly escaping death, Nick wakes to discover that the current has altered his brainwaves, so that he can hear women's thoughts as if they were spoken aloud. Once he gets over his astonishment that many women do not perceive him in a flattering light, he uses his newfound powers to secretly pick Darcy's brain and steal her job.

Like Mick Jagger, Gibson is the kind of performer who needs to go into overdrive to find a groove. As age renders him less supple, it becomes harder for him to separate energy from tension. Gibson's facial muscles are so tight that they seem to have driven his eyes into the back of his skull. This is the kind of acting problem that a perceptive director can spot and solve, but the heavy-handed Meyers is hardly the person to do it. *What Women Want* is so busy and noisy that Gibson has to work even harder than usual to make himself noticed above the din.

Gibson has never lacked chemistry with his leading ladies, from Sigourney Weaver in *The Year of Living Dangerously* to Julia Roberts in *Conspiracy Theory*, but faced with the awkward Hunt—Hollywood's bland antidote to the Lolita syndrome—he doesn't even try. What women do not want is to see Mel Gibson embarrassed and at a loss. I wish I could be sure it won't happen again.

Also reviewed in:

CHICAGO TRIBUNE, 12/15/00, Friday/p. A, Mark Caro
NEW YORK TIMES, 12/15/00, p. E15, Elvis Mitchell
NEW YORKER, 12/25/00 & 1/1/01, p. 156, David Denby
VARIETY, 12/11-17/00, p. 21, Todd McCarthy
WASHINGTON POST, 12/15/00, p. C12, Rita Kempley

WHATEVER IT TAKES

A Columbia Pictures release of a Phoenix Pictures presentation of a Paul Schiff production. *Executive Producer:* Bill Brown and Vicki Dee Rock. *Producer:* Paul Schiff. *Director:* David Raynr. *Screenplay:* Mark Schwahn. *Director of Photography:* Tim Suhrstedt. *Editor:* Ronald Roose. *Music:* Edward Shearmur. *Music Editor:* Daryl Kell and Jonathan Karp. *Choreographer:* Neisha Folkes. *Sound:* Steve Cantamessa and (music) Bobby Owzinski. *Sound Editor:* Greg Hedgepath. *Casting:* Randi Hiller. *Production Designer:* Edward T. McAvoy.

Art Director: Alan E. Muraoka. *Set Designer:* Mark Poll. *Set Decorator:* Debra Echard. *Set Dresser:* Martin Mulligan. *Special Effects:* David M. Blitstein, Mark Lilienthal, and Gary Schaedler. *Costumes:* Leesa Evans. *Make-up:* Robin La Vigne and Tracey Levy. *Stunt Coordinator:* John Robotham. *Running time:* 92 minutes. *MPAA Rating:* PG-13.

CAST: Jodi Lyn O'Keefe (Ashley); Shane West (Ryan); Marla Sokoloff (Maggie); Manu Intiraymi (Dunleavy); Aaron Paul (Floyd); Julia Sweeney (Kate Woodman); James Franco (Chris); Kip Pardue (Harris); Scott Vickaryous (Stu); Colin Hanks (Cosmo); Richard Schiff (P. E. Teacher); Kevin Ruf (Security Guard); Erin Champaign and Rachel Zerko (Shower Girls); Eric Kushnick (Stoner); Christine Lakin (Sloane); Nicole Tarantini (Marnie); Shyla Marlin (Shyla); Vanessa Evigan (Vanessa); Julie Garibaldi (Stuck Up Girl); Chantal Abbey (Swim Coach); Joe Gieb (Octopus Ride Operator); Tyrone Granderson Jones (Toothless Carnie); Mason Lucero (Sweet Kid); Stan Sellars (Teacher); Jeff Sanders (Large Football Player); Marge Anderson (Old Woman); Sam Menning (Old Man); Nick Cannon (Chess Club Kid); Hubert Hodgin (Waiter); Rachel Kaber (Miranda); Caroline Kindred (Little Girl); Romy Rosemont (Cosmo's Date); Mami Nakamura (Noriko); Jay Harrington (Cop); David Koechner (Virgil Doolittle).

LOS ANGELES TIMES, 3/24/00, Calendar/p. 12, John Anderson

[The following review by John Anderson appeared in a slightly different form in **NEWSDAY, 3/24/00, Part II/p. B7.]**

Stop me if you've heard this one: High school everyman who's a cross between David Schwimmer and Doogie Howser has a crush on the high school bombshell. She, in turn, has no reason to think twice about him. He, meanwhile, has a perfectly beautiful gal pal who's coveted by the school Lothario/lowlife and whom Mr. Howser is willing to sell out at a heartbeat for the chance to get to the aforementioned Miss Gorgeous Drawers. Everyone knows our hero and his girl-next-door will get together eventually, if only after the requisite series of degradations and humiliations.

We got it down, pretty much? Pick the movie. OK, how about this one? The aptly titled "Whatever It Takes" carries the ad line "How far will they go"—a sentiment you may feel free to apply both to the high school sex-a-thon of recent cinema as well as the race for Hollywood dollars. In "Whatever" we get a seemingly decent kid like Ryan (Shane West), who, on the chance of getting close to the overripe and all-too-obvious Ashley (Jodi Lyn O'Keefe, who played exactly the same role in "She's All That"), will sell out his best pal Maggie (Marla Sokoloff).

Teen movies are about sex—sex that never actually happens, but that informs everything that otherwise occurs in the film. To this end, the genre is unique because it can't help but render the main characters thoroughly uninteresting while giving all the comic thrust to the incidental idiots—Richard Schiff s gym coach, for instance, who seems incapable of not throwing beanballs at his baseball players. Or Floyd (Aaron Paul), the geekiest of Ryan's geek friends, who has fixated himself on the long-ago vandal who cut the neck off the school statue. It's guys like Floyd who make a movie like "Whatever It Takes" feel like high school. And the rest of the losers make it feel like a movie.

NEW YORK POST, 3/24/00, p. 50, Lou Lumenick

"Does he say anything clever or funny or even sincere?," asks a character in "Whatever It Takes," an assembly-line high-school comedy that flunks miserably in all three subjects.

The plot bears slight resemblance to "Cyrano," but seems heavily influenced by "Some Kind of Wonderful" and other works by John Hughes, the Martin Scorsese of 1980's teen flicks.

Geeky Ryan (Shane West) fantasizes about Ashley (Jodi Lyn O'Keefe), a midriff-baring mantrap at their Southern California high school.

The resident lothario Chris (James Franco), her cousin, offers Ryan pointers on landing her—in exchange for Ryan's help wooing Maggie (Marla Sokoloff), Ryan's beautiful buddy since childhood.

Screenwriter Mark Schwahn goes for cheap laughs off groin injuries, hookers, oral sex and bedpans.

Only Sokoloff ("The Practice") of the four TV-vet leads comes close to delivering a thoughtful performance. West ("Once and Again") tries too hard in a part requiring two accordion solos. O'Keefe ("Nash Bridges") and Franco ("Freaks and Geeks") are grotesquely obnoxious.

Julia Sweeney briefly represents the older generation as Ryan's school-nurse mom, delivering a safe-sex lecture with a 5-foot plastic model of a penis.

"Whatever It Takes" scores one coup—commandeering the famous retractable dance-floor over the swimming pool at Beverly Hills High School, used in "It's a Wonderful Life."

Too bad director David Raynr ("Trippin") is clueless about wringing laughs from the sight of prom-goers falling into the pool. The prom's theme, "Titanic Dreams," proves perversely appropriate for this shipwreck of a movie.

Also reviewed in:
CHICAGO TRIBUNE, 3/24/00, Friday/p. A, Mark Caro
NEW YORK TIMES, 3/24/00, p. E16, A. O. Scott
VARIETY, 3/27-4/2/00, p. 20, Robert Koehler
WASHINGTON POST, 3/24/00, p. C1, Stephen Hunter

WHERE THE HEART IS

A Twentieth Century Fox presentation of a Wind Dancer production. *Executive Producer:* Carmen Finestra and Rick Leed.   *Producer:* Susan Cartsonis, David McFadzean, Patricia Whitcher, and Matt Williams.   *Director:* Matt Williams.   *Screenplay:* Lowell Ganz and Babaloo Mandel.   *Based on the novel by:* Billie Letts.   *Director of Photography:* Richard Greatrex.   *Editor:* Ian Crafford.   *Music:* Mason Daring.   *Music Editor:* Brent Brooks.   *Sound:* Hank Garfield and (music) Michael Golub and John Richards.   *Sound Editor:* Doug Parker and Chris Winter.   *Casting:* Mali Finn.   *Production Designer:* Paul Peters.   *Art Director:* John Frick. *Set Designer:* Janet Stokes.   *Set Decorator:* Amy Wells.   *Set Dresser:* Darren Patnode, Shane Patrick, Bart Brown, Christopher Stull, and Patricia Dillon.   *Special Effects:* Margaret Johnson.   *Costumes:* Melinda Eshelman.   *Make-up:* Felicity Bowring.   *Stunt Coordinator:* Randy Fife.   *Running time:* 115 minutes.   *MPAA Rating:* PG-13.

CAST: Dylan Bruno (Willy Jack Pickens);   Ray Prewitt (Tim);   Laura House (Nicki);   Karey Green (Rhonda);   Natalie Portman (Novalee Nation);   Keith David (Moses Whitecotten);   Mary Ashleigh Green (Girl in Bathroom);   Kinna McInroe (Wal-Mart Clerk);   Laura Auldridge (Wal-Mart Assistant Manager);   Stockard Channing (Sister Husband);   Alicia Godwin (Jolene);   Dennis Letts (Sheriff);   James Frain (Forney Hull);   Richard Jones (Mr. Sprock);   Kathryn Esquivel (Mrs. Ortiz);   Ashley Judd (Lexie Coop); Mark Mathis (Reporter);   John Daniel Evermore (Orderly);   Sally Field (Mama Lil);   Linda Wakeman (Hospital Receptionist);   David Alvarado (Cellmate);   Mark Voges (Religious Man);   Angee Hughes (Religious Woman);   Todd Lowe (Troy);   Margaret Ann Hoard (Mary Elizabeth Hull);   Rodger Boyce (Officer Harry);   Gabriel Folse (Polieman #2);   Joan Cusack (Ruth Meyers);   Mackenzie Fitzgerald (Americus);   Natalie Pena (Angela Ortiz);   Yvette Diaz (Rosanna Ortiz);   T.J. McFarland (Ray);   Richard Nance (Johnny Desoto);   Tony Mann (M.C. of Banquet);   John Swasey (Jerry);   Scarlett McAlister (Kitty);   Kylie Harmon (Praline);   Cody Linley (Brownie);   Bob Coonrod (Ernie);   Heather Kafka (Delphia);   Angelina Fiordellisi (Nurse);   Cheyenne Rushing (Co-Ed).

LOS ANGELES TIMES, 4/28/00, Calendar/p. 18, Kevin Thomas

"Where the Heart Is" plays like a feature-length version of one of those folksy commercials for Wal-Mart, where customers are greeted with big smiles and warm hugs. According to this shamelessly synthetic film, a Wal-Mart is not such a bad place in which to have your baby. And, if you do, you get a shot at celebrity and the offer of a job at the Wal-Mart of your choice.

Derived from the Billie Letts novel, Lowell Ganz and Babaloo Mandel's slick, stereotypical screenplay finds Natalie Portman's 17-year-old and very pregnant Novalee Nation and her no-good boyfriend, Willy Jack Pickens (Dylan Bruno), stopping off at a Wal-Mart in a small Oklahoma town. They're driving from Tennessee to California in a ramshackle Plymouth. You guessed it: Novalee returns to the parking lot only to find that Willy Jack has ditched her, leaving behind just her Polaroid camera (which probably fell through the same hole in the car's floor her shoes did).

The upshot is that once Novalee has her baby girl, whom she names Americus, she finds shelter with the kindly recovering alcoholic Sister Husband (Stockard Channing), who shares her trailer with a fellow AA traveler she calls Mr. Sprock (Richard Jones). (Asking the blessing at supper, Sister invariably asks God to forgive her and Mr. Sprock their daily fornication.)

At the Wal-Mart, where Novalee now works, she gets encouragement in her love of taking pictures from the store's avuncular portrait photographer, Moses Whitecotten (Keith David). She strikes up a friendship with Ashley Judd's Lexie Coop, a man-chasing single mother of five—she names them after snack foods, hence Brownie and Praline—who clearly is not too interested in avoiding pregnancy. Novalee is also befriended by Forney Hull (David Frain), the shy, gentle young man who has dropped out of college to take over the job of local librarian for his alcoholic sister.

Beneath a schmaltzy, cutesy-precious, nakedly heart-tugging surface lurks what could have been an affecting portrait of a nearly illiterate but bright teenager with no family or material resources who discovers how to make something of her life. For all her hard-earned accomplishments, however, Novalee feels she's not good enough for the saintly Forney, who turns out to be the grandson of a New England governor. Portman is a lovely and gifted actress, and Frain is talented and personable too. We root for both of them.

It's too bad their contributions, and those of many others, drown in a big glop of treacle. Throughout the film, we catch up needlessly with Willy Jack, who manages to latch on to Joan Cusack's tough talent agent in his pursuit of stardom as a country singer. Naturally, he turns up in Novalee's life at the climactic moment, but the picture, like Novalee, would have been better off losing him permanently. But, to his credit, Bruno's portrayal of this dumb jerk is amusing and witty.

The film's most honest note, however, is struck by Sally Field as Novalee's shiftless mother, who ditched her years ago but turns up just long enough to cash in on the fleeting celebrity surrounding her granddaughter's birth.

Pedro Almodovar would know how to have deft, affectionate fun with the soap operatics of this film's coincidence-heavy plotting, and still make it come out as a salute to the strength and solidarity of women—that's precisely what he did in his Oscar-winning "All About My Mother."

But director Matt Williams—a veteran TV producer—takes a weighty, head-on approach filled with caricature, with its negative elements of condescension and artificiality. In comparison to "Where the Heart Is," the Wal-Mart commercials seem like cinema verite.

NEW YORK, 5/8/00, p. 70, Peter Rainer

Natalie Portman, who stars in the new comedy weepie *Where the Heart Is*, has what the young Elizabeth Taylor also had—a serenely pretty equipoise—and she adds to it a steady gleam of fierce intelligence. This is not to say that her work in the movies thus far has always been equal to her radiance. What I'm describing about her is less a function of talent than of some innate, camera-ready state of being—a state which, in the end, may be rarer than talent. As the unhappy daughter in *Anywhere But Here*, I thought Portman condescended to her character's waywardness; she wore her poise too lightly. In *Where the Heart Is*, adapted by Lowell Ganz and Babaloo Mandel from the 1995 novel by Billie Lefts and directed by Matt Williams, Portman is more free-spirited. She plays 17-year-old Novalee Nation, who starts out barefoot and pregnant and ends up in small-town Oklahoma as a species of angel. The goodness that pours out of Novalee is so generous and naively felt that it's almost comic. She doesn't seem to have worked herself up to a state of grace; it's just the way she is.

Novalee emerges almost unscathed from a string of little tragedies: Her mother (Sally Field) ditches her twice; her boyfriend (Dylan Bruno), the father of her child, ditches her early on, too; her good friend Sister Husband (Stockard Channing) gets whirled away in a tornado, and another soulmate (Ashley Judd) meets up with the wrong guy and is bloodied. Through it all, Novalee has a seraphic glow. Portman seems more unearthly here than she ever did playing Queen Amidala in *The Phantom Menace,* and she's a lot funnier. The movie isn't all that much—it's too cloyingly ramshackle—but Portman isn't playing down to her character this time around. Novalee isn't simply the kind of shopper who might camp out at Wal-Mart; she's practically its patron saint.

NEW YORK POST, 4/28/00, p. 54, Jonathan Foreman

"Where the Heart Is" is a lesson in star power. It's a generic, below-par chick flick—slow, and filled with movie-land clichés about strong, eccentric women in small Southern towns—that is raised above its material by the powerful presence of Natalie Portman (and, to a smaller but significant extent, Ashley Judd).

The exquisitely beautiful Portman plays Novalee Nation (it's one of those Southern-set movies in which everyone has a ridiculous name), a pregnant, white-trash teen who is abandoned by her boyfriend, Willie Jack (Dylan Bruno), at a Wal-Mart.

Broke and alone, she ends up living secretly in the vast department store and eventually gives birth there one night with the help of a rescuer who hears her screams and crashes through the store window.

Nation and her baby, a girl she names Americus, become instant celebrities, and they move into an unconventional household headed by the eccentric, outspoken Sister Husband (Stockard Channing).

Nation also becomes best friends with Lexie (Ashley Judd) a happy-go-lucky maternity nurse from the local hospital who names her many kids from different liaisons after snack foods.

The always winsome Judd and Portman have excellent chemistry, and you wish that Judd had more time on screen.

Bad things continue to happen to Nation, but she triumphs over these disasters and becomes a stronger person. Still, the question remains whether she's strong enough to admit her love for eccentric librarian Forney Hull (James Frain), who is devoted to her.

The film shifts uneasily from a broad to a more subtle comic tone, but a faint whiff of cynicism hovers over the whole movie. And the only decent men are the shy, freakish ones and the wise, older black guy (here incarnated by Keith David).

A side plot involving Willie Jack's rise, fall and redemption never gets off the ground, and cameos from Sally Field and Joan Cusack seem to have been cut and pasted from another movie.

NEWSDAY, 4/28/00, Part II/p. B3, Jan Stuart

There ought to be a museum commemorating some of Hollywood's more lunatic pairings of artists and material. John Huston directing "Annie." William Faulkner scripting "Land of the Pharaohs." Ava Gardner passing herself off as an octoroon nightclub entertainer in "Show Boat." Rudolph Giuliani playing a New York City mayor in "The Out of Towners."

An entire wing would have to be reserved for screenwriters Lowell Ganz and Babaloo Mandel's man-handling of Billie Letts' plain-folks weeper "Where the Heart Is." New Yorkers at heart, Ganz and Mandel specialize in the smart-talking but sensitive, guys-will-be-guys comedies that launched Tom Hanks and Billy Crystal: "Splash," "City Slickers" "Mr. Saturday Night." Even "A League of Their Own," about an all-gal baseball team, had the collegial edge of fellas gently snapping towels in a locker room.

"Where the Heart Is," the book, is earnest, rural and forthrightly feminine in its appeal. Have either Ganz or Mandel done much time at an Oklahoma Wal-Mart? That's where a pregnant 17-year-old Novalee Nation (Natalie Portman) ends up living for six weeks after she is dumped at a shopping mall by her boyfriend, Willy Jack (Dylan Bruno). But don't you fret for long. Once this dense maid from Tennessee gives birth on the floor of Aisle 6 with the help of a nervous librarian who comes crashing into the store through a plate of glass (don't ask), she has friends aplenty.

They are called things like Sister Husband (Stockard Channing) and Moses Whitecotten (Keith David) and Lexie (Ashley Judd) and Forney (James Frain). And let's not forget little miss

Americus Nation, the famous "Wal-Mart Baby" who gives Novalee her 15 minutes of fame. Together, they could write a book, "When Bad Things Happen to People with Precious Names."

One is kidnaped.

One dies in a tornado.

One has the daylights beaten out of her by her boyfriend, after he rapes her children.

One has his legs mashed by a train. One drops dead suddenly, presumably from dialogue deprivation.

The calamity overload could have a kind of camp giddiness, but first-time director Matt Williams has such a leaden feel for narrative, it's merely ponderous. Only Joan Cusack, as a Nashville agent, and Sally Field, munching scenery in a cameo as Novalee's mother, keep the egg off their faces. It's hard to know whether to blame Oprah Winfrey, who anointed Billie Letts' novel to her book club, or Ganz and Mandel, who have transformed it into a white-trash epic of sublime awfulness. Where is William Faulkner when we really need him?

SIGHT AND SOUND, 12/00, p. 57, Kay Dickinson

Six years ago, south-western America. Willy Jack and his pregnant girlfriend Novalee move out of their trailer to find a new home. They stop at a Wal-Mart general store so that Novalee can go to the toilet; she returns to discover that Willy Jack has driven off. With no money, Novalee surreptitiously moves into the Wal-Mart. One night she goes into labour and is taken to hospital by Forney, the town's librarian. She becomes a minor celebrity and her daughter Americus is dubbed the "Wal-Mart baby". When her previously absent mother visits her and steals the money she's received in gifts from the public, she moves in with Sister Husband, a woman she met in the shop. As the years go by, she builds up a photographic business living happily with Sister Husband who later dies in a tornado. She develops a close friendship with Forney and gradually realises he's in love with her. On the day of his alcoholic sister's funeral, they have sex, but after Novalee tells him she doesn't love him, Forney leaves town for university.

Meanwhile, Willy Jack has served time in prison and had a career as a country singer. Having turned to drugs and alcohol, he stumbles into the path of a train and loses his legs. Novalee reads a newspaper report about his wheelchair being stolen and visits him in hospital. He inspires her to visit Forney at college, where she tells him she loves him. They are married in the Wal-Mart.

On paper *Where the Heart Is* looks like a jaunt through melodrama's most tawdry and tragic themes: its homeless heroine Novalee gives birth in a general store, her daughter is kidnapped by militant Christians, her surrogate mother is sucked up by a passing tornado, her best friend's children are sexually abused and her ex-partner's legs are run over by a train. It's startling, then, when a movie thronging with this much spectacular bad luck turns out to be so leaden. Whether consciously dismissive or simply clueless about the ironic treats it could have offered, the film promotes teenage single parenthood and small-town warmth with the straightest of faces.

Herbert Ross' 1989 melodrama *Steel Magnolias* may have been set a little further east than this film, but otherwise there's not much to separate these two wishful mirages of neighbourhood wholesomeness. Admittedly, *Where the Heart Is'* portrait of the apple-pie idyll in which it's set does have the odd dark touch: the film, for instance, doesn't hide away its alcoholics, of which there are four, and generously welcomes them into the bosom of the community, no questions asked. But here you're left wondering why in such a supportive place, they took to the bottle in the first place. Unfortunately the crammed plot has far too much else going on to offer any such insight.

The contradiction of plugging small-town tranquillity within such a hurtling storyline is exacerbated by the appearance of a cyclone. The images of Novalee clinging on to a storm-shelter door amid the ungainly special effects that created the pewter-hued maelstrom bring to mind Douglas Sirk's melodramas, as do the characters' unnervingly speedy return to everyday life. But the sequence seems less an exercise in deliberate distanciation than a directorial misfire on the part of first-timer Matt Williams—an ill-advised attempt at a bit of CGI spectacle on a modest budget.

The movie's distinguished cast do their best; Natalie Portman even manages to coo "How can you love someone so much who you've just met?" at her character's new born without making the moment seem too risible. Unfortunately, the spirited performances (notably Stockard Channing as the benevolent Sister Husband) buckle under the weight of the implausibly overloaded script.

Knowingly playful hyperbole sneaks in courtesy of Joan Cusack's seen-it-all-before music manager and Sally Field's trampy bottle-blonde mother, a performance fuelled by an evident fervour for playing against type.

VILLAGE VOICE, 5/9/00, p. 138, Jessica Winter

Hard-luck Novalee Nation (Natalie Portman) puts a great deal of terrified faith in numerology: She was five when her momma left her, got 55 stitches in her arm the time a barfly slashed her, and receives $5.55 in change just before her scumbag boyfriend strands her—barefoot, pregnant, and 17—in an Oklahoma Wal-Mart, where she later gives birth. Likewise, the Grand Guignol-on-trailer-wheels horror show *Where the Heart Is* indulges something of a number obsession, amounting not exactly to a movie but rather a tallying of atrocities (which add up, inexorably, to Novalee triumphing over all assembled odds).

A handy index:

• *Total number of children born to Novalee and her harder-luck friend Lexie (Ashley Judd) who are abandoned by their fathers: 6*

• *Total number of fathers: 5*

• *Number of said children named either for dessert snacks or Latinizations of Italian explorers (e.g., Brownie, Praline, Americus): 6*

• *Number of cameos by Sally Field. 1*

• *Number of scenes in which Novalee sits on a bench looking forlorn until someone happens by to rescue her. 3*

• *Number of scenes in which said rescuer is played by Stockard Channing: 2*

• *Number of filmmakers liable for this bloody mess who also cocreated* Home Improvement: 2

• *Grand total of tornado deaths, alcohol deaths, instances of domestic abuse, instances of child sexual abuse, kidnappings, and legs severed by trains: 9*

• *Number of fine actresses who should know better. 3*

Also reviewed in:
CHICAGO TRIBUNE, 4/28/00, Friday/p. A, Michael Wilmington
NEW YORK TIMES, 4/28/00, p. E14, Elvis Mitchell
VARIETY, 4/24-30/00, p. 30, Todd McCarthy
WASHINGTON POST, 4/28/00, p. C1, Stephen Hunter
WASHINGTON POST, 4/28/00, Weekend/p. 51, Michael O'Sullivan

WHERE THE MONEY IS

A USA Films release of a Gramercy Pictures presentation in association with Intermedia Films and Pacifica Film Distribution of a Scott Free/IMF production. *Executive Producer:* Tony Scott, Guy East, Nigel Sinclair, Chris Sievernich, and Moritz Borman. *Producer:* Ridley Scott, Charles Weinstock, Chris Zarpas, and Christopher Dorr. *Director:* Marek Kanievska. *Screenplay:* E. Max Frye, Topper Lilien, and Carroll Cartwright. *Story:* E. Max Frye. *Director of Photography:* Thomas Burstyn. *Editor:* Sam Craven, Garth Craven, and Dan Lebental. *Music:* Mark Isham. *Music Editor:* Tom Carlson. *Sound:* Michel Charron and (music) Stephen

Krause. *Sound Editor:* Patrick Dodd. *Casting:* Randi Hiller. *Production Designer:* Andre Chamberland. *Art Director:* Martin Gendron. *Set Designer:* Jean-Pierre Paquet. *Set Dresser:* Mary Lynn Deachman, Anne Grenier, and Francis Tremblay.   *Costumes:* Francesca Chamberland. *Make-up:* Gillian Chandler. *Make-up (Paul Newman):* Monty Westmore. *Make-up (Linda Fiorentino):* Tricia Heine. *Stunt Coordinator:* Stan Barrett. *Running time:* 89 minutes. *MPAA Rating:* PG-13.

CAST: Paul Newman (Henry); Linda Fiorentino (Carol); Dermot Mulroney (Wayne); Susan Barnes (Mrs. Foster); Anne Piotoniak (Mrs. Tetlow); Bruce MacVittie (Karl); Irma St. Paul (Mrs. Galer); Michel Perron (Guard); Dorothy Gordon (Mrs. Norton); Rita Tucket (Mrs. Weiler); Diane Amos (Kitty); Dawn Ford (Cheryl, Wife #2); T. J. Kenneally (Farwell Welk); Roderick McLachlan (Lloyd the Cop); Bill Corday (Grounds Worker); Gordon McCall (Handyman); Robert Brewster and Eric Hoziel (Guys); Charles Doucet (Tom); Arthur Holden (Bob); Richard Jutras (Manager); Frank Fontaine (Cop); Janine Thériault (Girl); Frankie Faison (Security Guard); Philip Preten (Cop #2); Vlasta Vrana (Jewelry Store Employee); Heather Hiscox (TV Announcer); Michael Brockman (FBI Agent); Emily Wachtel (Waitress); Jayne Eastwood (Connie).

CHRISTIAN SCIENCE MONITOR, 4/14/00, p. 15, David Sterritt

What happens when a good movie star shows up in a bad movie?

It's a perennial question, and it's raised this time by "Where the Money Is," a lackluster comedy featuring a typically solid performance by Paul Newman, one of the few American superstars who really knows what he's doing in the acting department. He plays an aging crook who's been faking a severe illness to pave the way for a prison break. Once out of the slammer, he befriends a nurse (Linda Florentino) who saw through his ruse all along, and together with her suspicious husband (Dermot Mulroney) they plan a new caper meant to finance fresh starts for all of them.

Once you get past its slightly unusual premise, this is a painfully ordinary picture, with enough twists to stave off complete boredom but not enough to make it a strong vehicle for an actor of Newman's abilities.

In years long past, star names made the box office busy all by themselves, and news of a "Jimmy Stewart picture" or "a Bette Davis picture" was all many moviegoers needed to head for their local theaters. Today, not even the most famous Hollywood faces can write their own ticket to success. The current Exhibit A is Bruce Willis, who bombed with "Breakfast of Champions" and then failed to get an Oscar nomination for "The Sixth Sense" even when it did become a hit. If he isn't a star to conjure with, nobody is.

That includes Newman, whose magnetic face and riveting voice can't overcome the fundamental fact that "'Where the Money Is" has little going for it. Since few ears will perk up at the announcement of "a Linda Florentino picture," and since director Marek Kanievska is hardly a well-known auteur, you can expect this movie to disappear with dazzling speed. Newman deserves more auspicious surroundings, and so do as admirers.

LOS ANGELES TIMES, 4/14/00, Calendar/p. 21, Kevin Thomas

"Where the Money Is" takes its title from a famous reply legendary thief Willie Sutton gave when he was asked why he robbed banks. However, crooks would be ill-advised to stick up the box offices at theaters where this tepid caper comedy is playing, for the take is not likely to be worth the risk. Not all the star power of Paul Newman, backed strongly by Linda Fiorentino and Dermot Mulroney, can pull off this job.

Caper comedies—films that take a humorous approach to the old heist plot—are not exactly the rage, but director Marek Kanievska and his writers don't take into account that we're not still in the '60s. The only way the film could have had a prayer of working—and thereby tapping its stars' considerable strengths—is by taking a much harder edge and going for dark, even bleak humor. Instead, they turn the picture into a kind of good-natured romp.

The possibilities for a much tougher, better picture are there. Our first glimpse of Newman as Henry is of a paralyzed, mute and virtually comatose old convict in a wheelchair arriving from prison for treatment at a nursing home. When Fiorentino's Carol, his nurse, discovers that Henry is a legendary thief, she starts dreaming of ill-gotten gains—if only she can get Henry to snap out of it.

Carol is a dutiful, kindly but bored professional who was queen of her high school prom. She married its king, Mulroney's Wayne, but life has been downhill ever since when it comes to glamour and excitement. Wayne, in contrast, is settled and content in his quiet small-town existence. Wayne may be a sensible yet sexy guy devoted to his wife, but that's not enough for Carol, who fears that she may end up in a nursing home herself without ever having "lived."

Newman is so skilled an actor that it comes as a genuine surprise that Henry is faking a stroke as a way of escaping prison. By the time Henry emerges in Newman's usual fit and vigorous form, Carol is determined to become his partner in whatever criminal activity he may have in mind. Newman, Fiorentino and Mulroney are all consistently sharp, but their material becomes progressively thin and contrived.

If only Fiorentino had a chance to bring more of that lethal quality she brought so memorably to "The Last Seduction's" villainess, "Where the Money Is" might have been a different story and a much more enjoyable film.

NEW YORK, 4/24/00, p. 132, Peter Rainer

Far be it from me to give Paul Newman career advice, but here goes anyway: Don't be autumnal. In *Where the Money Is*, he plays a jailed bank robber who cons his way into a nursing home and, aided by an attendant (Linda Fiorentino) and her husband (Dermot Mulroney), pulls off a fresh scam. The film, to its detriment, draws wistfully on our memories of *The Hustler* and *The Sting*. Graceful retirement in an actor can be ennobling; so can a rage against the dying of the light. It's this wan, winsome middle ground that doesn't cut it.

NEW YORK POST, 4/14/00, p. 49, Lou Lumenick

The premise of "Where the Money Is" is enough to make you groan—Paul Newman plays a veteran bank robber who feigns a stroke to get out of jail and into a nursing home.

But though it bears some alarming similarities to the last senior-citizen caper movie—"Diamonds," which treaded water on the strength of on real-life stroke victim Kirk Douglas' star power—this delightfully low-key comedy is a whole lot more fun.

That's thanks to Paul Newman's delightfully wry, self-effacing performance as robber Henry Manning. Newman, who at 75 is threatening to retire after making one more film with his wife, Joanne Woodward, is at the top of his game here.

Few stars half his age can command the screen with such little visible effort—you can't take your eyes off his handsome, weathered face, even when he's lying motionless in a wheelchair, his eyelids drooping.

And when Henry drops the act and starts scheming, his still-boyish vigor recalls an entire catalogue of great Newman performances, from "Hud" to "The Color of Money."

"Where the Money Is" is too slight a vehicle to stand comparison with his classics—yet Newman has one of his best partners in Linda Fiorentino, who more than holds her own as Carol, a sexy nurse who sees through his scam and tries to smoke him out.

Her frantic efforts, which include a hilarious wheelchair lap dance that sounds a lot more tasteless than it actually is, finally bear fruit—and she blackmails the very reluctant Henry into helping her with a heist.

There's a third, even more hesitant participant—Carol's husband, Wayne (Dermot Mulroney), one-time prom king to her prom queen who's stuck in a dead-end job.

The Coen brothers might have done something inspired with this, but director Marek Kanievska, making his first film since "Less Than Zero," turns out a more modestly entertaining little low-budget movie (Canada stands in for Oregon) with car chases that are almost quaint by contemporary filmmaking standards.

Newman has rarely been as relaxed and assured as his is as Henry, who hijacks an armored car and impersonates a mustachioed guard on the verge of retirement. His banter as he scoops up takings from the car's route are among the movie's most delightful.

Also adding to the enjoyment is the easy chemistry between Newman and Fiorentino, the latter wasted in such recent movies as "What Planet Are You From?" It's her liveliest performance since "The Last Seduction."

"Where the Money Is," which takes its title from the famous quote by bank robber Willie Sutton (he was asked why he robbed banks) is not remotely in the same league with Newman's last caper film, "The Sting." But then, it doesn't need to be.

NEWSDAY, 4/14/00, Part II/p. B7, John Anderson

Asked why he robbed banks, legend of larceny Willie Sutton reputedly answered, "That's where the money is." Asked why he keeps making movies, the now 75-year-old Paul Newman—a kind of legend himself—might answer the same.

Not that "Where the Money Is" isn't a tight, funny, fast-moving little caper film with a Newman who looks almost as spry as he did in "Nobody's Fool" (1994). Nor has the actor, philanthropist and salsa-maker lost the roguish gleam in his eyes, or the smile that makes every glance a conspiracy. But it's a slight movie, capably—and a bit noirishly—directed by Marek Kanievska. And Mr. Newman's appearance is hard to explain, lest one refer back to the late Mr. Sutton.

But it's fun. When Newman's Henry Manning, serving a long term for armed robbery, is deposited by prison guards at a local nursing home, he bears all the physical indications of having suffered a massive stroke. But Nurse Carol Ann McKay (Linda Fiorentino) is suspicious. She knows Henry's history—that in addition to big-time theft, he once sold security systems and then robbed his customers. After she has spontaneous sex on an infirmary gurney with her husband, Wayne, the downwardly mobile security guard (Dermot Mulroney), she finds the mirrored door ajar—and positioned just so Henry could have watched. She sets her cap to blowing his cover, but Henry is good: Even a lap dance by Carol Ann doesn't bring him around.

When she finally gets him—having dumped him and his wheelchair in a river—he tells his tale of having studied tantric yoga and mind control, and gotten himself to the point where he could almost fake death, in order to get himself out of prison. Carol Ann is fascinated, but basically she's bored—with her job, her town and, particularly, her husband. And what she'd really like to do is rob a bank.

A little bit "Treasure of Sierra Madre" and a whole lotta "Atlantic City," "Where the Money Is" moves effortlessly through the planning, execution and aftermath of the crime, a $2-million armored car scam that goes off with barely a hitch. Dramatically, this is well-traveled territory. Culturally significant, though, is the sexual chemistry between Fiorentino and Newman, which could very well do a lot more for Viagra sales than Bob Dole ever did. But then, Newman is Newman, and for mere mortals to try and match his Olympian standing in the wide, wide world of sex appeal is to risk a terrible, terrible fall.

SIGHT AND SOUND, 11/00, p. 66, Kim Newman

Oregon, the present. Carol, a nurse in a home for senior citizens, cares for Henry Manning, a former bank robber who has been transferred from prison after suffering a stroke. Carol suspects Henry is faking his condition; when taking Henry out on a picnic with her husband Wayne, Carol pushes Henry's wheelchair into the river, forcing him to admit he has been shamming and plans an escape.

When the son of Henry's former criminal partner refuses to hand over his share of the proceeds of former robberies, Carol suggests the three of them team up to rob a bank depository in the area. Henry responds that they should hijack the armoured car which makes cash deliveries to the depository. The three pull off the plan, though Wayne makes a mistake and broods about it, sensing Carol has transferred her allegiance to Henry. When Henry is picked up for transfer to a prison hospital, Carol rescues him. Wayne tries to cut a deal selling Henry out to the police; Carol sides with Henry. Henry and Carol escape the police by driving a car into the river and emerge elsewhere to continue their criminal careers.

This addition to the slim Marek Kanievska filmography comes 13 years after his second directorial credit, the ill-received film of Bret Easton Ellis' *Less Than Zero,* and 16 years after his acclaimed debut *Another Country.* Whether he has been toiling all this time on fruitless projects or living out in the woods in Terrence Malick-like seclusion until the memory of *Less Than Zero* faded is hard to gauge from this entirely acceptable if fairly straight job of work. The sort of modest little film that was a Hollywood staple until the blockbuster era, *Where the Money Is* still somehow required the services of nine producers and executive producers (including Ridley and Tony Scott) to get made.

Practically a three-hander, the film affords a fine late opportunity for Paul Newman to exert blue-eyed charisma and gravelly charm as the spry senior citizen Henry who fakes drooling insensibility but is secretly scheming all the while, as revealed by a few sharp looks from those extraordinary orbs even as the mouth maintains the proper degree of slackness and the hands shake with directed palsy. Recent Newman vehicles *(Nobody's Fool, Twilight)* have played with his image, ruefully suggesting that while he may not be the man he was he's still more of a man than most. This amiable caper movie naturally harks back to the days of *Butch Cassidy and the Sundance Kid* (1969) and *The Sting* (1973) yet again, the star is the calm-headed heist man who would rather talk his way out of a situation—shaking off a couple of cops by pretending to be a born-again Christian—than use more brutal methods. When accomplice Wayne reaches for the shotgun as a guard is about to stumble on to the robbery scheme, Henry keeps talking and trusts Wayne's wife Carol to get bloodlessly past this obstacle, a neat little suspense scene that also shows how the relationships are changing.

The film also picks up from *The Last Seduction* by making good use of the too often squandered talents of Linda Fiorentino. Fiorentino's turn isn't a re-run of the criminal mastermind she played in John Dahl's acclaimed neo-*noir*, but it does call on some of the grit and cool of that role to suggest the inner growth of the kindly but discontented Carol. She also pulls off admirably a growing semi-romantic, semi-daughter-like fixation on Henry, in an amusing but tasteful lap dance and a clever coda which finds her in a jeweller's store, coaxing a clerk into helping her remove her wedding band in celebration of a divorce and also distracting the man while Henry (now posing as her father) can case the merchandise. Dermot Mulroney, stuck with the third-wheel role as Wayne, continues to do the same as he did in *Copycat* and *My Best Friend's Wedding*: avoid upstaging the leading lady while making room for character turns that rob him of any pretence at being the leading man.

Where the Money Is remains resolutely a small film, focused on its central trio and their one night of crime to the exclusion of all else. There are nice little cameos from the residents of the old folks' home, but no one really intrudes into the world of Henry, Carol and Wayne. Carol is allowed unbelievable latitude in repeatedly taking a convict out of the home, and a potential major plot thread is left unexplored as the son of Henry's old partner is allowed to get away with stealing the crook's ill-gotten gains. Anonymously set in Oregon so inexpensive Canadian locations can be used, and directed with tact rather than flair, this is a welcome entertainment, effortlessly the best thing its director has done. But Kanievska will have to pick up the pace if he's to establish anything like a career or, better yet, a personality.

VILLAGE VOICE, 4/18/00, p. 158, Amy Taubin

Paul Newman idles gracefully through *Where the Money Is,* a caper film hardly worthy of his presence. Newman plays a gentleman bank robber who fakes a stroke to escape from jail. Linda Fiorentino is the nurse who sees through his con and latches onto him as a way of escaping her dead-end life. Although Fiorentino throws sparks at Newman, he's too wary of falling into the dirty-old-man trap to reciprocate with more than a knowing glance. Only when he gets behind the wheel of a getaway car does he merge the older Paul Newman with the Paul Newman of old.

Also reviewed in:
CHICAGO TRIBUNE, 4/14/00, Friday/p. A, Michael Wilmington
NEW YORK TIMES, 4/14/00, p. E22, Elvis Mitchell
VARIETY, 4/17-23/00, p. 25, Emanuel Levy
WASHINGTON POST, 4/14/00, p. C1, Stephen Hunter
WASHINGTON POST, 4/14/00, Weekend/p. 46, Michael O'Sullivan

WHIPPED

A Destination Films release in association with Hi-Rez Films of a Peter M. Cohen production. *Executive Producer:* Anthony Armetta and Taylor MacCrae.   *Producer:* Peter M. Cohen. *Director:* Peter M. Cohen.   *Screenplay:* Peter M. Cohen.   *Director of Photography:* Peter B. Kowalski. *Editor:* Tom McArdle. *Music:* Michael Montes. *Music Editor:* Jay Bolton. *Sound:* Antonio Arroyo and (music) Kevin Halpin.   *Sound Editor:* David Alvarez.   *Casting:* Jodi Collins.   *Production Designer:* Katherine M. Szilagyi.   *Art Director:* Svetlana Rabey.   *Set Decorator:* Colette Miller.   *Costumes:* Karen Kozlowski.   *Make-up:* Claus Lulla.   *Stunt Coordinator:* Eddie Braun.   *Running time:* 82 minutes.   *MPAA Rating:* R.

CAST: Amanda Peet (Mia);   Brian Van Holt (Brad);   Jonathan Abrahams (Jonathan);   Zorie Barber (Zeke);   Judah Domke (Eric);   Callie Thorne (Liz);   Linda Udd and Beth Ostrosky (Chicks);   Kurt Williams (Cab Driver);   Bridget Moynahan (Marie);   Aviva Gale (Stacey); Taryn Reif (Bristol);   Monte Viader (Hot Girl in Park);   Peter M. Cohen (Pizza Delivery Man); Sarah Isenberg and Tanya Brown (Lesbian Dancers);   Karen Kozlowsky (Hoover Hana); Natalie Jovan and Jen (Two Hot Freaks); Tony Javed (Italian Cyclist); Lyle Kanouse (Plumber); Neriah Davis (Dreamgirl);   Billy Cordon (Geeky Boy).

LOS ANGELES TIMES, 9/1/00, Calendar, p. 4, Kevin Thomas

Peter M. Cohen's "Whipped" is way too bleak to be funny, even as a contemporary satire of the battle of the sexes. Though it's been made and promoted as a mainstream comedy, it comes off more stark than an arty independent production shot with a hand-held camera. It's hard to tell whether Cohen, in his feature debut, meant to be quite so nihilistic.

Cohen gathers three guys, friends from college and living in Manhattan, who meet every Sunday for brunch at a diner to go over the week's sexual triumphs. Brad (Brian Van Holt) is a handsome, cocky stockbroker; Zeke (Zorie Barber) is a nerdy fellow with glasses who thinks he's every bit as much God's gift to women as Brad; and Jonathan (Jonathan Abrahams) is a self-proclaimed sensitive type who's a little insecure in his sexuality.

Apparently Jonathan hangs with Brad and Zeke to shore up his sense of masculinity and pretty much goes along with his pals, who view women entirely in terms of sexual conquest.

Their talk could scarcely be more crass, reveling in the grosser aspects of sex and bodily functions. They are often joined by their friend Eric (Judah Domke), married for two years and miserable about it. These guys are full of themselves, and the way they hit on women is repellent yet, alarmingly enough, apparently often effective.

All of a sudden things start changing. In one week Brad, Zeke and Jonathan all meet a woman who sweeps them off their feet, who listens to them and makes them feel they're the greatest, in or out of the sack. Alas, they've all met the same woman, Mia (Amanda Peet). It's pretty clear early on that she's setting them up, getting them to fall for her hard in order to teach them a lesson—that perhaps through the pain of love lost they'll get wise to themselves and start growing up.

Cohen, however, goes on to make the point that when it comes to sex, women are just as coarse as men in their vulgarity, cruelty and shallowness. We learn that Mia gets pleasure from deflating a bunch of jerks who should be beneath her attention.

What does this leave us with? A screenful of thoroughly obnoxious individuals—played quite persuasively, at that—who are preoccupied with sexual gratification on its most selfish level or as a satisfying form of revenge.

Of course, the world is full of people who seem to have no more to them than Mia or her dupes. While most movies, even quite serious ones, traditionally act as a form of escape from everyday life, "Whipped" leaves you with the feeling of having at last escaped a numbing experience, trapped in the company of people too pathetic to be amusing.

It also leaves you with the feeling that human boorishness is so abundantly self-evident you scarcely need to spend 83 minutes watching it on the screen.

NEW YORK POST, 9/1/00, p. 42, Jonathan Foreman

"Whipped" is a fast-moving satirical sex comedy with some genuinely funny jokes, a couple of strong performances and some amusing insight into the dating ways of twentysomething guys. For a low-budget film, it's also remarkably good-looking.

These qualities make it all the more of a shame that the movie shifts so quickly into cliché, and then morphs into a poorly conceived and bleakly misanthropic morality tale.

Potential viewers should also be aware that Amanda Peet, though given star billing, has much less time on screen than the three guys who are the movie's real subject.

They play college pals—all three of them "types" apparently selected by the movie's costume department. There's Brad (Brian Van Holt) a smooth Wall Streeter, who, in the way of movie bankers, makes more money than God.

There's Zeke (Zorie Barber) an East Village screenwriter who hangs around in cafes all day. And there's Jonathan (Jonathan Abrahams) an arty, shy goateed fellow who wears black.

They have a pathetic married friend, Eric, who's overweight and blinks a lot and dreams of the time when they were a foursome.

The idea is that all three single guys are coarse, cheerfully conscienceless "scammers" obsessed with bedding girls—although Jonathan is generally too shy to close the deal. At brunch on Sundays, they discuss various amusing theories on picking up women—with an emphasis on how to make potential hookups feel "safe" enough to give in to desire.

Then, apparently by chance, all three men bump into Mia (Peet), date her and suspect that they have finally found a woman they can care about. She's actually interested in them and what they do.

An awkward plot device ensures they all realize at the same time that Mia is dating the others. But rather than give her up, all three risk their buddyhood and continue seeing her, each assuming that eventually she'll choose him over his two friends. All of them begin to fall in love. But what never occurs to these "players" is that they could be ones being played.

The problem with "Whipped" is its failure to establish believable motivation for the Machiavellian Mia. It would be understandable if she were using the boys for sex or money or companionship. But in a sudden pseudo-feminist turn, the script condemns the male behavior it has affectionately portrayed and would have you believe Mia is actually an agent of some kind of poetic justice.

Because the boys haven't displayed any malice or even real dishonesty, the punishment they receive feels disproportionate to the crime. And while the logic of the story would suggest they get their comeuppance via their faults—vanity, greed, etc.—Mia exploits what's decent in them: their capacity for love. It all leaves an oddly sour taste.

And in the era of "Sex and the City," the movie's presentation of female locker-room talk (here conceived as an overriding preoccupation with penis size) as something oh-so-shocking and revelatory is embarrassingly old hat.

Abrahams and Barber, both in their first feature, make impressive debuts. Peet, who seems to have gone on the Flockhart diet, cannot do much with an underwritten role.

NEWSDAY, 9/1/00, Part II/p. B3, Gene Seymour

Along with her obvious, camera-friendly attributes (a plush, sultry mouth, glow-in-the-dark grin and laser-like blue eyes), Amanda Peet also packs concealed weaponry (stiletto wit, gleaming self-possession) that, sooner or later, will conquer the world.

On big or small screens, Peet has always come across as the bratty kid sister you wish Julia Roberts would take along on all her movies. But when she almost single-handedly snatched "The Whole Nine Yards" away from the likes of Bruce Willis and Matthew Perry, Peet served notice that she was ready to carry a movie by herself. You'd never know this from watching "Whipped," except in the last eight minutes. By which time you may have decided to head for the exits. The movie may look as good as Peet does—for which writer-director Peter M. Cohen should genuflect before his cinematographer Peter B. Kowalski. But its soul is ugly and what little brains it has are shrink-wrapped in bile.

It starts out as nothing more than a bunch of Manhattan guys sitting around and talking—actually, bragging—about their sexual conquests, real and imagined. Brad (Brian Van

Holt) is a Wall Street shark whose lame pick-up routine works every time. Zeke (Zorie Barber), a screenwriter, makes his conquests in downtown coffeehouses, while the only weekend dates for sensitive guy Jonathan (Jonathan Abrahams) are in his mind. Eric (Judah Domke), the married friend, gets off on their conversations.

The entrance of Peet's enigmatic Mia into each of their lives tosses their tiny tribe into predictable chaos. Since neither Brad, Zeke nor Jonathan wishes to yield to the other, she agrees to go out with all of them at different times. For the most part, Mia is little more than an obscure object of desire and it speaks well of Peet's abilities that she gives just enough of a glint in her eye to let us know that she's not all she appears.

The crude, graphic level of conversation among her bozo suitors is meant to be somehow revelatory of the urban male psyche. But all Cohen has done is collect these attitudes and toss them on the screen like dirty pillowcases. And does he really think he's delivering us a special bulletin in showing that guys, at their basest level, travel in packs and treat women as little more than an extension of their egos? Hold page one, get me rewrite!

In terms of Peet's career, "Whipped" will serve as little more than a speed bump on her ascent to stardom. As for the rest of the world, it exists only as a misshapen signpost in the ongoing decline of love and grace.

SIGHT AND SOUND, 7/01, p. 61, Keith Perry

New York, the present. Zeke, Brad and Jonathan are three men in their late twenties who meet each Sunday to boast about the previous week's sexual encounters. Another friend, Eric, offers advice, despite being unhappily married. One Sunday all three report meeting the perfect woman. After a week of dating, however, they discover they have been going out with the same person—Mia. Initially shocked, the trio begin sharing time with Mia, although this soon destroys their friendship. Eric confronts Mia over his lost companions, and she promises to choose one of them, but a fight between the three suitors leaves the matter unresolved.

The following Sunday, all four meet up, only to see Mia flirting with a group of other men. She tells Zeke, Brad and Jonathan that her relationships with them is over. The four men go back to their old ways, and their Sunday meetings gradually end. Mia discusses with her girlfriends how she manipulated Brad, Zeke and Jonathan from the beginning, having seen their dishonest methods of seduction. She displays some regret over finishing with Jonathan, but her friends warn her off pursuing him.

Peter M. Cohen's debut feature is truly independent (financed by friends on Wall Street), very slight, and very stretched. *Whipped* comprises an anecdote that the superficially similar television series *Sex and the City* could have dispensed with in half the time: three womanisers in their twenties fall in love with the same woman, Mia, only to discover that she has used them all. Although its focus is on the heterosexual dating game as it's played out in contemporary New York, *Whipped* aspires to be universal through its archetypal characters (bearded Jonathan is driven by emotions, bespectacled Greenwich Village resident Zeke is the intellectual, while Brad is pure Wall Street id) and through Mia's final pronouncement to the audience: "Everybody fucks everybody; it's the nature of the beast."

The largely inexperienced cast acquit themselves well enough (especially Judah Domke as the neurotically blinking Eric), and there's a convincing sense of New York interiors. However, the title—with its "pussy" prefix glaringly absent—is a fair indication of the self-censoring nature of the script. Drawn directly from the experiences of Cohen's friends, the film is foul-mouthed but toothless. With *Chasing Amy* (which is cited in the production notes as a Cohen favourite), Kevin Smith proved it is possible to make a sex comedy which is explicit without being puerile. But here, there are just too many easy laughs, such as Jonathan losing Mia's vibrator down the U-bend of her unflushed toilet. (At least the Farrelly brothers would have fully explored the comic repercussions; Cohen just makes our noses wrinkle and cuts to the next scene.)

Although it sometimes feels as if Cohen is merely compiling a glossary of sex slang (the term "throwing your web" paints a lovely picture), he is wise to the motives behind male banter. These beer-lite Lotharios are not just stroking their egos; they're also comparing notes, judging each other, determining their own values and standards (threesomes: yes; rimming and wife stories: no). He also makes clear that if all this denigrating talk is adolescent, so is their idea of finding the "perfect woman".

The moral to Cohen's story (bafflingly put forward as a revelation) is that women can be as sexually devious as men. Thus *Whipped* becomes exhibit A for womanisers everywhere, and unwittingly weighs in as defence witness for Aaron Eckhart's loathsome misogynist Chad in Neil LaBute's *In the Company of Men*. But if the men do the right thing for the wrong reason, Mia does the wrong thing for the right reason. This would-be ball breaker silently endures bad sex and nerdish behaviour from the three men in order to prove a point to herself, and her arch girlfriends, about female superiority. More fool her.

This is neither sophisticated nor enlightening viewing; but did audiences ever go to sex comedies to learn something profound? Cohen knows his paying public as well as he knows his protagonists, and *Whipped* will no doubt be of comfort to this small pocket of men.

VILLAGE VOICE, 9/12/00, p. 156, Nick Rutigliano

If all-out headache-nausea-braindeath is what you crave, *Whipped*'s available. Charming as a seven-year-old who drops out at recess to show off his doodle, the main attraction (er, whatever) of Peter Cohen's take on "the New York dating scene" is its pathetic dedication to, tee-hee, DIRTY WORDS, though most of 'em are yesterday's toss-offs. Bachelor-pad euphemism "stabbin' cabin" is one exception, a tidy summary of the film's vile attitude toward women (not to mention H*O*M*O*S). Meant to skewer would-be playas, *Whipped* never bothers to explain why one liberated chick (Amanda Peet) might teach three such dipshits a lesson by following them around Manhattan and fucking them all senseless. 'Course, maybe I'm just bein' a fag—cause everybody knows girls suck even more than guys do. Huh huh, "suck"—get it?

Also reviewed in:
NEW YORK TIMES, 9/1/00, p. E14, Stephen Holden
NEW YORKER, 9/11/00, p. 105, Anthony Lane
VARIETY, 9/4-10/00, p. 20, Joe Leydon
WASHINGTON POST, 9/1/00, p. C12, Rita Kempley

WHISPERS: AN ELEPHANT'S TALE

A Walt Disney Pictures release of a Dereck and Beverly Joubert production. *Producer:* Beverly Joubert and Dereck Joubert. *Director:* Dereck Joubert. *Screenplay:* Dereck Joubert, Jordan Moffet, and Holly Goldberg Sloan. *Story:* Dereck Joubert and Beverly Joubert. *Director of Photography:* Dereck Joubert. *Editor:* Nena Olwage. *Music:* Trevor Rabin. *Music Editor:* Will Kaplan. *Sound:* Beverly Joubert. *Sound Editor:* Odin Benitez. *Casting:* Marion Levine. *Production Designer:* Heather Carr-Hartley and Kimberly Rimer. *Running time:* 72 minutes. *MPAA Rating:* G.

CAST: Angela Bassett (Voice of Groove); Joanna Lumley (Voice of Half Tusk); Anne Archer (Voice of Gentle Heart); Debi Derryberry (Voice of Whispers); Kevin Michael Richardson (Voice of Adult Whispers); Alice Ghostley (Voice of Tuskless); Betty White (Voice of Round); Kat Cressida (Princess); Joan Rivers (Spike); John DiMaggio (Tough-Tusk/Fulla Bull); Tone Loc (Macho Bull); Jeannie Elias (Stranger/Herd Elephant); L.A. Mad Dogs (Loop Group Voices); Jim Black, Joseph Molekoa, David Mabukane, and Sandor Carter (Poachers).

NEW YORK POST, 10/13/00, p. 65, Lou Lumenick

Disney has certainly wrung a lot of box-office bucks out of the young-male-animal-cruelly-separated-from-his-mother story line, from "Bambi" through "The Lion King" to this spring's "Dinosaur."

Doubtlessly counting on audiences not to have memories like a you-know-what, Disney has trotted out this yarn again (scarcely five months after "Dinosaur's" release) this time as a live-action adventure with a young elephant undertaking the quest to prove himself among his peers.

While it will probably delight the under-seven set, parents are advised to brace themselves for a heavy dose of deja vu—and wincingly cute animal dialogue ("I thought I was hyena chow for sure!") read by the likes of Angela Bassett, Joanna Lumley, Anne Archer, Betty White, Joan Rivers and Tone Loc.

All this accompanies sometimes remarkable animal footage shot in Botswana by husband-and-wife filmmakers Dereck and Beverly Joubert.

Their scenes probably would have yielded a more interesting documentary than this sugary feature in which a lovable grump of an elephant tells the young orphan: "Kid, an hour ago you were following me. Now it's officially stalking."

NEWSDAY, 10/13/00, Part II/p. B6, Steve Parks

No play on words is too contrived for these pachyderms. Or rather, the committee of writers who stuffed insipid lines, by way of human actors, into the mouths of these noble, intelligent and gentle creatures. The elephants should sue. Except that being made to look like chatterboxes is the least of their problems.

And therein lies the saving grace of "Whispers," an elephant's saga.

No amount of Disneyfied dialogue can obliterate the espoused purpose of the filmmakers who brought this project to Walt Disney Pictures. Producers Beverly and Dereck Joubert are Emmy and Peabody Award-winning creators of documentaries on African wildlife. Putting human voices to the sensitivity and mental agility the Jouberts have long ascribed to elephants is intended, they say, to help people who've never seen the animals outside a zoo to appreciate them as individuals.

In the opening scenes, you'll notice at once "The Lion King" musical style and the "Bambi" storytelling theme. The mother of Whispers, so named because he loses his ability to trumpet, tells her baby to hide when poachers begin firing on them. The last words he hears from his mother (voiced by Anne Archer) is that she'll find him no matter what. But days pass and Whispers, whimpering in the wee voice of Debi Derryberry, is found by a stray female, a loner named Groove (Angela Bassett), who wants nothing to do with motherhood.

Predictably, Whispers' bravery and survival skills are tested. And with each adventure, the little elephant only gets cuter.

Joubert's screenplay may have been compromised, but not his photography. Although there are a few scenes with trained elephants, most footage was shot in Botswana's Chobe National Park. You'll see closeups of elephants rollicking in a mud bath, toppling trees for supper and protecting each other from a pride of lions. (Young children don't need to squeeze their eyes shut. No blood is shed on screen, no beasts are shown eaten alive.)

But there's plenty of implied death—most of it at the hands of humans.

Also reviewed in:
NEW YORK TIMES, 10/13/00, p. E24, Lawrence Van Gelder
VARIETY, 10/16-22/00, p. 22, Charles Isherwood

WHOLE NINE YARDS, THE

A Warner Bros. release of a Morgan Creek Productions, Inc. and Franchise Pictures presentation of a Rational Packaging Films production. *Executive Producer:* Elie Samaha and Andrew Stevens. *Producer:* David Willis and Allan Kaufman. *Director:* Jonathan Lynn. *Screenplay:* Mitchell Kapner. *Director of Photography:* David Franco. *Editor:* Tom Lewis. *Music:* Randy Edelman. *Music Editor:* E. Gedney Webb. *Sound:* Don Cohen and (music) Elton Ahi. *Sound Editor:* Michael Hilkene. *Casting:* Nancy Nayor. *Production Designer:* David L. Snyder. *Art Director:* Andre Chamberland. *Set Decorator:* Mary Lynn Deachman. *Set Dresser:* Francis Tremblay. *Special Effects:* Ryal Cosgrove. *Costumes:* Edi Giguere. *Make-up:* Clair Van Der

Elst.   *Make-up (Bruce Willis):* Gerald Quist.   *Stunt Coordinator:* Minor Mustain.   *Running time:* 100 minutes.   *MPAA Rating:* R.

CAST: Bruce Willis (Jimmy "The Tulip"Tudeski);   Matthew Perry (Nicholas "Oz" Oseransky); Rosanna Arquette (Sophie);   Michael Clarke Duncan (Frankie Figs);   Natasha Henstridge (Cynthia);   Amanda Peet (Jill);   Kevin Pollak (Jannni Gogolak);   Harland Williams (Agent Hanson);   Carmen Ferlan (Sophie's Mom);   Serge Christiaenssens (Mr. Boulez);   Renee Madelaine Le Guerrier (Waitress);   Jean-Guy Bouchard (Mover);   Howard Bilerman (Dave Martin);   Johnny Goar (Hungarian Hood);   Deano Clavet (Polish Pug);   Stephanie Biddle (Jazz Singer);   Charles Biddle (Bass Player);   Geoff Lapp (Pianist);   Gary Gold (Drummer);   Robert Burns (Mr. Tourette); France Arbour (Mrs. Boulez);   Sean Devine (Sgt. Buchanan);   Richard Jutras (Agent Morrissey);   Mark Camacho and Joanna Noyes (Interrogators);   John Moore (Bank Manager).

CHRISTIAN SCIENCE MONITOR, 2/18/00, p. 15, David Sterritt

This year's Academy Award hopefuls are off and running, each yearning for the extra fame and fortune that an Oscar win usually provides. Moviegoers around the world are sharing in the excitement, blithely unconcerned that the annual race is basically a popularity contest more attuned to trendy glamour than enduring value.

As if the focus on last year's glitzies achievements weren't enough to keep us busy, Hollywood is trotting out a new batch of star-powered pictures to liven up the generally dull mid-winter season. Next week brings Michael Douglas in "Wonder Boys," already a noisily touted attraction.

Two others open today. One stars Bruce Willis in "The Whole Nine Yards," a comedy about contract killers. The other, three popular actresses—Meg Ryan, Lisa Kudrow, and Diane Keaton—in "Hanging Up," a bittersweet look at family life.

"The Whole Nine Yards" begins in a Montreal suburb where Oz Oseransky, a mild-mannered dentist played by "Friends" star Matthew Perry, spends his non-drilling hours quarreling with his ill-tempered wife. His life is so unhappy that he welcomes the distraction when a notorious hit man moves in next door and strikes u a friendship with him.

Things get complicated when rival criminals recruit Oz to help them rub out his neighbor. They get more complicated when Oz's cute young receptionist turns out to be an aspiring serial killer who idolizes his new friend. They get *really* get complicated when Oz's spouse decides that one of these murderers is just the person to terminate her marriage by terminating her husband.

This sounds like dubious material for a comedy until you remember that some extremely funny pictures—"Prizzi's Honor," "The Freshman"—have cooked up laughs from similarly dark ingredients. It's not an easy feat to accomplish, thought, and "The Whole Nine Yards" has very mixed success. It works reasonably well when Willis and Perry deadpan their way through the early scenes, testing each other's limits like little kids with zero social skills. Amanda Peet is excellent as the psychopathic dental assistant, and Michael Clarke Duncan's role as a Chicago hood showcases his talent much better than "The Green Mile" does.

But the story runs out of clever ideas long before it's over, and the acting isn't enough to keep it sizzling along. One also wonders if Hollywood is losing whatever morality it ever had regarding murder, since this is the second movie in two weeks (after "Gun Shy") that allows a serial killer to escape punishment.   Even comedies know that crime shouldn't pay—don't they?

"Hanging Up" tells the tale of three sisters whose aging father (Walter Matthau) is apparently losing his ability to enjoy a meaningful life. They want to help him, but their own activities—and their complex relationships with each other—keep interfering with their good intentions. The outcome is what you'd expect, as the sisters review their affection through coping with their dad's many trials.

Keaton directed the movie in addition to playing the oldest sister, and she doesn't have quite enough filmmaking savvy to balance the story's blend of heartbreaking and smile-coaxing moments. The film deserves credit for facing up to difficult domestic problems, but it pursues them just so far before falling back on easy and sometimes distasteful laughs.

Humor can be an excellent coping mechanism, but this process doesn't translate automatically into Hollywood-entertainment terms. "Hanging Up" is too ambitious and too frivolous for its own good.

LOS ANGELES TIMES, 2/18/00, Calendar/p. 1, Kenneth Turan

His motto is "I'm very careful, I'm a dentist." So it's to be expected that the seven years since he moved from Chicago to Montreal haven't been terribly exciting for "The Whole Nine Yards'" Nicholas "Oz" Oseransky (Matthew Perry), a square-jawed underachiever so ineffectual he feels helpless when restaurants put mayonnaise all over his hamburger.

Oz's new neighbor, Jimmy "The Tulip" Tudeski (Bruce Willis) also hates that local culinary custom. But hearing him say, "When they slap that mayonnaise on, I could kill somebody," sounds an entirely different note.

For Jimmy the Tulip, named after the flowers he sends to the funerals of his victims, is a professional hit man who's eliminated 17 people without doing noticeable damage to his self-esteem. "It's not important how many people I've killed," he says with the kind of deadpan charm that can be one of Willis' specialties. "What's important is how I get along with the people who are still alive."

While comedies about hit men are nothing new ("Grosse Pointe Blank" is probably the best of the lot), "The Whole Nine Yards" manages to be occasionally amusing. Written by Mitchell Kapner and directed by Jonathan Lynn ("My Cousin Vinny"), it's a peppy affair that works in fits and starts but is unable to put its successful moments together in any consistently satisfying way.

Until Jimmy moves in next-door, Oz's life is mainly taken up with dodging flak from his ruthless and hateful French Canadian wife Sophie (Rosanna Arquette, complete with accent). This woman is so evil that even Oz's new receptionist Jill (Amanda Peet in the film's liveliest and most appealing performance) can't help but blurt out, "Leave the bitch."

Before Oz can act on that sensible advice, he meets Jimmy, also a refugee from Chicago, having ratted out the leader of the dread Gogolak crime syndicate. And once Sophie finds out there's a price on Jimmy's head, she insists that her husband go to Chicago and negotiate for a piece of the action.

Ever the dutiful spouse, Oz heads for Chicago and meets, not surprisingly, some avaricious and amoral comic mobsters like the enormous Franklin "Frankie Figs" Figueroa ("The Green Mile's" Michael Clarke Duncan) and his boss, the accent-impaired Janni Gogolak (Kevin Pollak). Oz also meets the beautiful Cynthia ("Species'" Natasha Henstridge), the mysteriously estranged wife of, yes, his dangerous next-door neighbor.

Oz may be a classic dupe, always a step behind everyone else in the picture, but even he eventually learns that there's more to the Gogolak-Tulip feud than criminal rivalry, $10 million more. Kapner's script is a little twist-happy, with complications piling on complications, but it soon becomes clear, even to Oz, that he may be the only person in the film who doesn't want somebody else dead.

Director Lynn, with the "Yes, Minister" series in England and several studio comedies in this country behind him, has a great deal of relevant comic experience. Willis, who's played parts like this many times, still manages some vintage hit-man panache, and Perry, one of the "Friends" ensemble, is a good sport about all the pratfalls his character endures.

Despite these promising aspects, and even adding in Peet's engaging performance, "The Whole Nine Yards" ends up on the undernourished side. The film's deficiencies are not his fault, but if the likable Perry had a bigger, more dynamic presence, it might help. There are certainly some laughs here, but they could use the assistance.

NEW YORK POST, 2/18/00, p. 47, Lou Lumenick

Just when you thought it was safe to go back to the movies, here comes *another* mob comedy. But it turns out that "The Whole Nine Yards" is an offer you shouldn't refuse: It's laugh-out-loud, side-splitting funny.

The setup is pure sitcom. Veteran hit man Jimmy "The Tulip" Tudeski (Bruce Willis) has a falling out with his longtime employer, the Gogolak crime family of Chicago, whose leader he's ratted out to the authorities.

So he moves to Montreal, where, in the proud tradition of "Analyze This," "Mickey Blue Eyes" and other lesser comedies, he complicates the life of an innocent civilian—in this case, Milquetoast dentist Nicholas "Oz" Oseransky (Matthew Perry).

I won't give away the plot's many twists, except to say that all of the film's characters save Oz—including his nasty French-Canadian wife, Sophie (Rosanna Arquette), and his receptionist, Jill (Amanda Peet)—set out to kill somebody.

The screenplay—attributed to newcomer Mitchell Kapner—is more than a little mechanical, but director Jonathan Lynn, in his funniest film since "My Cousin Vinny," keeps things perking along.

Lynn is abetted considerably by his terrific cast, especially Perry in what's by far his most effective big-screen outing.

Showing the easy physical grace of the young Cary Grant, the "Friends" star is hilarious as the very nervous Oz, smashing into glass doors, falling down stairs and executing other pratfalls with consummate skill.

Willis, who was once one of Hollywood's most notorious scene stealers, has evolved into a most generous and subtle performer.

He's winningly light-handed as the killer, who solemnly explains to the horrified Oz that "it's not important that I've killed 17 people—what's important is how I get along with the people who are still alive."

Peet, of WB's "Jack and Jill," is a scream as Oz's receptionist, who eagerly volunteers as Jimmy's apprentice, easily overshadowing the beautiful Natasha Henstridge ("Species") as Jimmy's estranged wife—with whom Oz falls in love with at great personal peril.

Only Arquette fails to deliver. Sporting a horrific French accent and aging-sexpot duds, she seems to be acting in another movie, if not on another planet.

Michael Clarke Duncan (the Oscar-nominated gentle giant of "The Green Mile") is amusing as a cheerful hit man, while comic Kevin Pollak is underused as the apoplectic acting head of the Gogolak family, who has problems pronouncing his Vs and Ws.

"The Whole Nine Yards" is a perfect antidote to the mid-winter blues.

NEWSDAY, 2/18/00, Part II/p. B6, Gene Seymour

"The Whole Nine Yards" asks a lot of its audience. For one thing, the movie asks you to once again endure Bruce Willis doing his wry, smirking routine, which you'd figure has, by now, become as counterproductive and disreputable as junk bond trading. It also asks you to believe that so many people would want to kill a dentist for money, especially one as honest and good-natured as "Oz" Oseransky (Matthew Perry).

Nevertheless, Oz walks the streets of Montreal with a target on his chest, placed there by a fat life insurance policy that his shrewish wife, Sophie (Rosanna Arquette), would love to cash in. Toward that end she's recruited a handful of assassins, at least one of whom cops out on the gig because Oz is too nice a guy.

So guess who just happens to move in next door to Oz' suburban split-level home: Jimmy (The Tulip) Tudeski (Willis), a professional hit man who's hiding out from a Chicago crime family whose members are willing to pay big bucks to have him eliminated. Oz is horrified, then surprised to find that he and Jimmy hit it off. Still, Sophie sees a way of not only getting rid of Oz, but collecting even more money by buying him a plane ticket to Chicago to "rat" Jimmy out to his pursuers.

Yes, the demands on your credulity get even bigger throughout "The Whole Nine Yards." And that, through the movie's fits and starts, is what makes it so much fun. As Willis' performance in "The Sixth Sense" proved beyond a doubt, he is most effective on the big screen when he acts in lean, simple strokes. Because he plays Jimmy with this kind of restraint, Willis, perhaps for the first time since his days on TV's "Moonlighting," makes his smirking patina seem supple and fresh.

Perry may well have as big a challenge as Willis does, since he's being asked to play a nice, helpless guy, far removed from caustic Chandler on TV's "Friends." Though he's not quite—or not yet—as graceful a physical comic as the role requires, Perry uses his character's jittery earnestness as an effective comic foil for Willis' implacable cool.

Director Jonathan Lynn, who's had a spotty record with similar comedies ("My Cousin Vinny" worked, "Sgt. Bilko" didn't), moves this knockabout plot at a leisurely pace, getting just the right amount of laughs from each complication, even the violent ones, without going overboard.

The actors respond well to Lynn's approach. As Jimmy's "colleague" Frankie Figs, Michael Clarke Duncan (nominated for an Oscar for playing an idealized cipher in "The Green Mile") assumes the customary archetype of Menacing Black Hit Man and gives it bemused and bemusing dimension. Amanda Peet, yet another visitor from prime-time TV ("Jack and Jill"), is vivacious and energetic as Oz, receptionist, while Natasha Henstridge gets a needed respite from playing exotic villains as Jimmy's exotic and estranged wife.

It's unfortunate that Arquette alone is compelled to vault over the top. Then again, how can one accept someone as beguiling as her as a homicidal French-Canadian gold digger? There are only so many improbabilities we can be reasonably expected to swallow.

SIGHT AND SOUND, 7/00, p. 59, Xan Brooks

Montreal, the present. American dentist 'Oz' Oseransky strikes up an unlikely friendship with his neighbour Jimmy Tudeski, a hitman hiding out from Chicago gangsters. Oz is blackmailed by his loveless wife Sophie to travel to Chicago and shop Tudeski to crime boss Janni Gogolak. There Oz is intercepted by Frankie Figs, a mob heavy nominally attached to the Gogolak gang but really in cahoots with Tudeski. Oz also sleeps with Tudeski's wife Cynthia.

Back in Montreal, Tudeski hatches a plan to lure Gogolak to Canada where he will kill him and Cynthia to get sole access to a $10-million bank account to which they are all signatories. Oz is roped in as a co-conspirator, as is Oz's assistant Jill, a wannabe contract killer. Meanwhile Sophie recruits an assassin, Hanson, to kill her husband. In a shoot out, Tudeski kills Gogolak, his goons and Hanson, actually an undercover cop. Sophie is picked up by the police who charge her with Hanson's murder. Tudeski learns that Oz has slept with Cynthia and vows revenge. To make amends, Oz comes up with a scheme in which he restructures Hanson's dental work and burns the body to make it appear as if Tudeski has died. Realising that Cynthia is in love with Oz, Tudeski makes her a wedding gift of $1m from Gogolak's fund of $10m. He kills the unreliable Figs and heads for a new life in the Caribbean with Jill. Oz asks Cynthia to marry him.

The Whole Nine Yards' director Jonathan Lynn rose to fame in the mid 80s as the co-creator of the acerbic BBC sitcom *Yes, Minister,* a success he subsequently parlayed into a lucrative career directing such Hollywood comedies as *My Cousin Vinny* and *The Distinguished Gentleman.* But all the while something was missing, some vital storytelling punch either lost in transit or sapped by the Los Angeles sun. With *The Whole Nine Yards,* the Californication of Lynn looks complete. This polished comedy-thriller is almost spookily impersonal. It bears the hallmarks of a film that's been test previewed out of all existence. In the end, you feel anybody could have made it.

Not that Lynn's film is ever less than professional. It's more crisply paced and well conceived than his previous two directorial efforts (the flop comedies *Sgt. Bilko* and *Trial and Error*). There's also a sleek central performance from Bruce Willis, who brings a little star charisma to the otherwise threadbare character of louche hitman Jimmy Tudeski. Matthew Perry likewise copes adequately as putz dentist 'Oz' Oseransky, though the role requires him to do little more than splutter into his dry Martini and gaze on horrified from the sidelines.

But in all other respects, *The Whole Nine Yards* remains cynically underdrawn. Screenwriter Mitchell Kapner equates convulsive plot twists with ingenious plotting; the film's procession of double—and treble crosses is the cinematic equivalent of jump-starting a faulty car. Moreover, it conspires to waste Michael Clarke Duncan as a jovial thug and squanders actresses with shameless abandon. Rosanna Arquette is relegated to the role of a dubious, ball-cutting bitch as Oz's wife and Natasha Henstridge is little more than a depersonalised object of desire as Tudeski's glacial estranged wife. Even Amanda Peet, whose role as an aspirant assassin initially appears promising, winds up short-changed. Her part in Tudeski's plan to take out crime boss Gogolak involves wandering naked around the house in order to befuddle the baddies. After she's just lolled out of a window to take a pot shot at an intruder, one of the thugs remarks "I can't think of nothing finer than a fine naked woman holding a gun." It's the one line of dialogue you sense the film's makers really believe in.

TIME, 3/6/00, p. 72, Richard Schickel

Awaiting their fate, we mostly have to make do with the comic mainstream, wherein *The Whole Nine Yards* is currently bobbing. Directed by Jonathan Lynn (*My Cousin Vinny*), it's a story more machined than created, in which Oz Oseransky (Matthew Perry), an innocent Canadian dentist, gets involved with a semi-retired mob hit man (Bruce Willis) and a legion of his former colleagues who want to whack Willis for ratting out their boss. Somehow Oz survives, and gets the gunman's gorgeous ex-wife (Natasha Henstridge) for good measure.

The movie has no vision, no fine comic attitude about life, except that it is one damned thing after another, most of them bearing no relation to reality and having no function other than to keep the wheels of the farce heedlessly spinning. But it features a dental assistant (Amanda Peet) whose dream in life is to become a professional killer, the divinely materialistic Rosanna Arquette talking in a deeply goofy accent and a self-mocking super-cool Willis. It also has a really good joke about throwing up. You're entitled to ask for more than that in a comedy, but these days you're often obliged to settle for a lot less.

VILLAGE VOICE, 2/29/00, p. 118, Dennis Lim

A similarly inbred specimen, *The Whole Nine Yards* splices together the odd-couple buddy movie and the hitman-with-a-heart comedy—it maps, with almost mathematical precision, the comic permutations that follow when a contract killer (Bruce Willis) moves in next door to a bumbling dentist (Matthew Perry) and his harpy-slut French Canadian wife (Rosanna Arquette, all cleavage and out-of-control accent). Perry's Oz falls madly in love with the hitman's estranged missus (Natasha Henstridge)—his chirpy assistant (Amanda Peet) turns out to be a wannabe assassin; more criminal types show up (including Kevin Pollak as a Hungarian ganglord). Before long, just about everyone wants someone else dead, with the exception of the increasingly harried Oz (played by Perry with perpetual frown and as a spasmodic succession of double takes). The setting is Montreal, which not only must have been a cost-cutting measure but facilitates a running gag about Canadians putting mayonnaise on their burgers (the other frequently repeated joke is about dentists being suicidal). The movie struggles for cool amorality but feels quaint and mechanical. Director Jonathan Lynn sets the pace at several notches below frantic—which only leaves the many tepid gags stranded in a vacuum and the actors compelled to overcompensate. By default, Willis steals the movie with his best Jean Reno impersonation yet.

Also reviewed in:
CHICAGO TRIBUNE, 2/18/00, Friday/p. A, Michael Wilmington
NEW YORK TIMES, 2/18/00, p. E12, Elvis Mitchell
NEW YORKER, 3/6/00, p. 98, Anthony Lane
VARIETY, 2/14-20/00, p. 39, Todd McCarthy
WASHINTON POST, 2/18/00, p. C5, Rita Kempley

WILDFLOWERS

A Fries Film Group/Monarch Home Video release of a Filmsmith Productions/Fries Film Group/Wildflowers LLC production. *Executive Producer:* Daryl Hannah and Christine Vachon. *Producer:* Zachary Matz, Timothy Bird and Thomas Garvin. *Director:* Melissa Painter. *Screenplay:* Melissa Painter. *Director of Photography:* Paul Ryan. *Editor:* Brent White. *Music:* Sam Bisbee. *Sound:* Bob Gitzen. *Production Designer:* Andrea Soeiro. *Art Director:* Nathalie Diericks. *Set Decorator:* Dean Zingus. *Costumes:* Chris Aysta. *Stunt Coordinator:* Jeff Scott. *Running time:* 98 minutes. *MPAA Rating:* R.

CAST: Daryl Hannah (Sabine);   Clea DuVall (Cally);   Eric Roberts (Jacob);   Tomas Arana (Wade);   Richard Hillman (Graham); Eric Yetter (Dylan);   Robert Haas (Poet);   John Doe

(Teacher);   Sheila Tousey (Martha);   Irene Bedard (Ruby);   James Burnett (Tailor);   David Graham (Trip);   Alan Gelfant (Wolf);   Justin Vue (Bear);   Johanna Mattox (Julie);   Heather Mathieson (Teacher's Wife);   John Roble (Coulter);   David Fine (Bolinas Roofer).

NEW YORK POST, 9/1/00, p. 43, Lou Lumenick

One of the season's more intriguing screen presences is Clea DuVall, a tomboyish young actress who so far has generally outshined the feeble material she's been given to work with.

DuVall, who had a showy supporting role in "Girl, Interrupted," almost (but not quite) made this summer's dreadful "But I'm a Cheerleader" worth watching for her turn as a flirtatious lesbian camper.

DuVall exhibits her magnetism again in "Wildflowers," another negligible piece of indie celluloid, in which she plays a confused 17-year-old who becomes obsessed with an older woman (Daryl Hannah) she meets at a rock concert in 1985 San Francisco.

Though Melissa Bird was the executive producer of the lesbian romp "The Incredibly True Adventures of Two Girls in Love," her debut as a writer-director with "Wildflowers" isn't overtly sapphic.

DuVall's character becomes convinced the enigmatic Hannah is her mother, who abandoned her as a baby during a party at a commune in 1968.

This slight tale unfolds with excruciating predictability and slowness, Bird's fancy jump cuts totally at odds with the extremely laid-back storytelling and sun-dappled, Kodak-moments photography that wouldn't be out of place in a movie on the Lifetime channel.

DuVall's focused intensity shines like a beacon through the foggy narrative and the other cast members' vague performances. It's especially painful to watch the extremely mannered Hannah, basically playing an updated version of the flaky artist she portrayed in the 1986 megabomb "Legal Eagles," opposite Robert Redford.

Also sleepwalking through their parts are Eric Roberts, as one of Hannah's former lovers, and Tomas Arana as the hippie who raised DuVall's character.

VILLAGE VOICE, 9/5/00, p. 118, Michael Atkinson

Curdling pegs Daryl Hannah's self-mythologizing-or-bust turn as a mysterious, moody, "wild" painter of pretentious manure in *Wildflowers*, a movie ostensibly about the San Francisco '60s and its various pond ripples as felt by a shy-but-"wild" teenage girl (Clea DuVall) searching for connection, closure, and—guess what?—her long-lost wayward mother. Look what aging, surly, marble-mouthed sprite comes to town. Robbed of its rightful Lifetime premiere on its supersonic trajectory to video, Melissa Painter's movie is picturesque to the point of aneurysm: REM-inducing shots of the Pacific and song interludes (oh boy, Blues Traveler!) break up the vast awkward pauses between inarticulate characters. DuVall, one of the best things in every movie she's in, is set adrift without a rudder. (She suffers the ultimate indignity for a young actress: a sex scene with Eric Roberts.) The sort of movie in which somebody can exclaim, "I want a funeral pyre!", *Wildflowers* is the only brand of requiem the '60s get anymore—worshipful and ass-backward.

Also reviewed in:
NEW YORK TIMES, 9/1/00, p. E21, A. O. Scott
VARIETY, 4/3-9/00, p. 39, Lael Loewenstein

WIND WILL CARRY US, THE

A New Yorker Films release of an MK2 Productions/Abbas Kiarostami production. *Producer:* Marin Karmitz and Abbas Kiarostami. *Director:* Abbas Kiarostami. *Screenplay (Farsi with English subtitles):* Abbas Kiarostami. *Based on an idea by:* Mahmoud Ayédin. *Director of Photography:* Mahmoud Kalari. *Editor:* Abbas Kiarostami. *Music:* Peyman Yazdanian. *Sound:*

Jahangir Mirshekari. *Sound Editor:* Mohamad Hassan Najm.   *Running time:* 118 minutes. *MPAA Rating:* Not Rated.

CAST: Behzad Dourani (Engineer); Farzad Sohrabi, Shahpour Ghobadi; Masood Mansouri; Masoameh Salimi; Bahman Ghobadi; Noghre Asadi; Ali Rez Naderi; Roushan Karam Elmi; Reihan Heidari; Lida Soltani; Frangis Rahsepar (Themselves).

CHRISTIAN SCIENCE MONITOR, 7/14/00, p. 15, David Sterritt

"The Wind Will Carry Us"—the latest movie by Abbas Kiarostami, regarded by many as Iran's greatest current director—focuses on a filmmaker who visits a rural village. It probes a number of intricate relationships between tradition and modernity, professionalism and humanity, and the physical and the spiritual with extraordinary intelligence and compassion.

LOS ANGELES TIMES, 9/15/00, Calendar/p. 4, Kevin Thomas

"The Wind Will Carry Us" is another contemplative, minimalist work from Iran's celebrated Abbas Kiarostami, whose last film, "Taste of Cherry," took the Palme d'Or at Cannes. "The Wind" is similar, though not as powerful.

In the earlier film, a man from the city, in the grip of despair, heads for a mountainous region looking for someone to kill him and put him out of his misery. In "Wind," another city man (Behzad Dourani) heads with a crew for a mountain village in Iranian Kurdistan some 450 miles from Tehran.

Apparently, the villagers of Siah Dareh are aware that he is coming and refer to him vaguely as "Engineer." They don't really know what his mission is but come to think he is an archeologist looking for buried treasure in the local cemetery. In reality, he is a TV journalist on assignment to record the villagers' traditional funeral rituals upon the death of a very old woman. The trouble is that instead of growing weaker, she rallies; there seems no question that she is mortally ill, but her death may not be so imminent after all.

Kiarostami discovers the humor in the Engineer's plight. He can't very well hasten the woman's death, but, as time passes, his crew (which we never see, only hear) loses patience.

Meanwhile, the Engineer wanders aimlessly in frustration as the villagers go about their daily routines. They're in touch with the outside world, but it becomes increasingly clear that they are essentially living an ancient agrarian way of life, close to nature.

For a long time the Engineer, in his self-absorption, does not respond to all this abundant nature, but when he does the film suddenly gathers power and focus, and we're able to perceive the irony of a man so preoccupied with waiting for a death to occur that he is unable to take any pleasure in being alive.

"The Wind Will Carry Us" has much to be appreciated, but Kiarostami overplays his hand, taking so long to get to his payoff you begin to identify with the Engineer's fed-up crew.

At 90 minutes "The Wind" might have been stunning, althugh Kiarostami is also a bit too obviously didactic. At 111 minutes the impact of its finish has been dissipated by too much meandering along the way.

NEW STATESMAN, 9/25/00, p. 66, Jonathan Romney

The Iranian director Abbas Kiarostami once proposed his personal vision of what film should be: "a half-created cinema, an unfinished cinema that attains completion through the creative spirit of the audience". This system of blanks and elisions would be designed not to distance or mystify the viewers. It would be more a question of respect, of being generous enough to give us room to move, to find our own way around the imaginative space that a film offers.

That is why, even if I thought I could explain Kiarostami's new film, I would be reluctant to. On the surface, *The Wind Will Carry Us* may not seem particularly mysterious—events happen, people appear, we know where we are and, more or less, what is going on. Yet the film's meaning is so open to interpretation, if not actually secondary to the experience of watching, that analysis feels somehow beside the point. The film treats its viewers as intelligent beings capable of completing its meaning for themselves—and there is no doubt that this is a job to be taken very seriously. But it is also a very enjoyable job; *The Wind Will Carry Us* is, I suspect, a film that many people will take very much to heart.

The story is about a group of visitors from Tehran, who arrive in the small Kurdish village of Siah Dareh; their purpose, apparently, is to observe, and presumably to film, the rituals that must follow the death of an old woman. But she refuses to die, and the film crew must settle in and wait for something to happen. Their leader (Behzad Dourani), addressed by the villagers as "Engineer", enlists a young boy as a guide, but rather tries his patience by calling endlessly on his services, even fetching him out of a school exam. Meanwhile, Behzad's colleagues stay indoors and eat strawberries; throughout the film, we hear only their voices.

It is not just the crew who are invisible. Behzad communicates with other off-screen voices. He engages in improbably flirtatious dialogue with a pregnant neighbour. In an extraordinary running joke, he drives repeatedly to a nearby hilltop to take calls on his mobile phone. Up there, he meets an unseen man digging a hole; the digger sends him to visit his fiancee, who milks a cow in a darkened cellar (in this scene, we hear the poem by Forough Farrokhzad that gives the film its title).

Something dramatic does eventually happen, causing Behzad to make himself useful at last. But the film is less about events than about anticipation, and about time and place and the way we experience them. After only a short while, we feel we know every corner of the village, with its precarious balconies and Escher-like multilevel construction, and every stretch of the surrounding countryside. Whenever his mobile summons him, Behzad rushes up and downstairs, drives up hills and round comers to take the call: each time, Kiarostami and the director of photography, Mabmoud Kalari, give us every twist in the road, until we feel we could drive it blindfold ourselves.

Time, too, becomes curiously elastic, both static and mobile. One minute the neighbour is pregnant, the next Behzad is admiring her baby. Meanwhile, the old woman behind the blue-framed window that is one of the village's (and the film's) landmarks still refuses to die.

Beyond the matter of time and place, it is hard to pin down the film to a clear meaning, despite Behzad's apparent acquiring of wisdom in the end. The film is rich in symbols, certainly, potent but not readily understood. What to make, for example, of the bone that is thrown up out of the hole as a friendly offering, which bobs gently down a stream at the end of the film? And how is it significant that only towards the end of the film do we at last, and then with the force of revelation, see the village by night?

The central theme seems to be visibility and invisibility. While so much in the village is hidden, Behzad is practically always on view, almost too much—a blundering urbanite without the discretion to merge with his surroundings. In this sense, the film seems to comment on the role of the filmmaker, who should know when to be seen and when to hide.

At moments, the message appears to be simple. "Prefer the present," a doctor advises Behzad as they zoom across a sunlit, com-filled landscape, at a moment when the film's spatial constrictions seem at last to be lifted. Kiarostami does indeed make us prefer the present—every digression, every eavesdropped conversation in the village bar compellingly distracts us from Behzad's mission. But the film doesn't restrict itself to simple conclusions; to get its meaning, we have to experience its slow, deliberate two hours. As they say, you have to be there.

Kiarostami's fictions, with their semi-documentary approach, are always rooted in the real world, and always invoke real ethical repercussions. His 1990 feature *Close-Up* recreated an actual legal dispute in fictionalised form, casting the real participants and concluding with their reconciliation. In a similar way, the cast of *The Wind Will Carry Us* mainly comprises the actual villagers of Siah Dareh. The viewers are the village's guests and, for the film's duration, we live according to the village's sense of time. There is a sense of ethical exchange here—the film requires that, like Behzad, we learn to be good guests. And just as the village invites us to make ourselves at home, the film itself calls on our "creative spirit" to help complete its elusive meaning. Kiarostami's is, you might say, a cinema of hospitality.

NEW YORK, 8/7/00, p. 66, Peter Rainer

The great Iranian director Abbas Kiarostami has said in an interview that "I immediately stop in front of a subject that invites me to contemplate it." He was referring to his work as a still photographer (which, as it happens, is currently being exhibited at the Andrea Rosen Gallery), but the same approach is evident in his films, and none more so than his newest, *The Wind Will Carry Us*. The terrain he offers up to us has a rough serenity; the ridged, rolling hills are monumental yet evanescent in their remoteness. Kiarostami is no mere picture-postcard portraitist. For him, the changeableness of landscapes, the way light and shadow play across them and colors deepen or pale, is a spiritual value. The invitation to contemplation that he talks about is really an invitation to bring our way of seeing into harmony with nature. The human drama in his new film is charged with the drama of the encompassing universe. It's all part of the same continuum.

As a film director, Kiarostami places himself among his audience; his imagery seems to open up its revelations to him at the same time as it unfolds for us. Most filmmakers do not invite us to collaborate in the visual experience; their vision is presented to us as a kind of proclamation, with all the inherent ambiguity in the imagery shaved away. Kiarostami, whose approach to nature must partly derive from Muslim culture (although it also seems pantheist), leaves the meanings open and various. The rich, slow deliberativeness of his style is in the tradition of directors like Yasujiro Ozu and Satyajit Ray, who also found great resonance in the communion between man and nature. With those directors, one often felt that a film of theirs consisting entirely of rivers or cloud formations or just empty rooms would still convey more of the eloquence of life's passage than an ordinary director's acted-out drama. So it is with Kiarostami. The introduction of people into his supernal tableaux does not alter his vision so much as it completes it.

In *The Wind Will Carry Us,* a producer from Tehran (Behzad Dourani), accompanied by a camera crew (whose faces are never shown), arrives in the remote mountain village of Siah Dareh in Iranian Kurdistan to record the impending ritual funeral ceremony of an ancient woman he has been told is near death. The villagers believe these men to be engineers intent on uncovering buried treasure from a local cemetery. With his jeans, unbuttoned shirt and sunglasses, and ever-present cell phone, the producer—no name for him is given—is a figure of some amusement in the valley. Whenever a call beeps, he charges in his Land Rover to higher ground in order to get proper reception; as the days stretch on and the old woman inexplicably improves, his crew threatens to mutiny. The producer doesn't have time for the villagers at first, except as potential co-conspirators. He befriends a young schoolboy, Farzad, in order to get the inside scoop on the old woman's health. He regards most of the locals as quaint artifacts of a vanished culture.

The community, however, is far from vanished, and it slowly elicits from the producer a vivid sympathy. Through poetry recitations he tries to draw out a young uneducated girl milking a cow in a cave; he tells her that "writing poetry has nothing to do with diplomas," and he means it. But Kiarostami isn't going for anything as simple as a back-to-nature idyll here. The villagers aren't some hazy, salt-of-the-earth conceit; they're a joking and savvy bunch, and their imbroglios, such as a scene involving a complaining waitress and her sullen male clients, are folkloric comedy sketches. (The contrast between the majesty of the natural surroundings and these petty flare-ups is a constant source of humor.) When the producer organizes a rescue operation for a local man who has been buried alive, the old doctor who arrives on his rickety, buzzy motorbike is not one to speak reverently of religion and the purported glories of the afterlife. "Prefer the present to these fine promises" is his choice advice.

Kiarostami preserves his outsider's view in *The Wind Will Carry Us* and, by doing so, brings the film even closer to us than if he had attempted to go native. There is much for the eye to take in: the harsh contrasts of weathered women in their black chadors against the village's piercingly bright white walls; the panoramas that look like pastel-tinged Ansel Adams vistas but with layered bunches of color reminiscent of Morris Louis. Kiarostami has a sophisticated aesthetic sense that never fades into pure abstraction. His artifices are his way of moving deeply into the overwhelming mystery and emotion conjured up by this material. As with his old doctor here, Kiarostami's preference is for the present; he's ravished by the ineffableness of what he sees. The villagers are right: The producer is indeed looking for buried treasure. He doesn't find it in a local cemetery, though, but in the air and the people all around him in this dappled, murmurous valley.

NEW YORK POST, 7/28/00, p. 49, Jonathan Foreman

Abbas Kiarostami, the Iranian writer-director of "The Wind Will Carry Us," is the undisputed critical darling of the international film festival circuit. This film received the usual praise as a "masterpiece" at Toronto last year.

However, with this poetic but tedious and all but plotless film, it's hard not to wonder if some of his ardent cinéaste fans are seeing qualities in his work that aren't really there.

Or maybe they are motivated by the kind of high-brow snobbery that mistakenly confuses a glacial pace, contempt for plot and a willful, self-indulgent inaccessibility with profundity.

Certainly, Kiarostami has furthered his reputation as the most "serious" of the new wave of Iranian filmmakers by giving gnomic, avant-gardist interviews about "the end of storytelling."

He is, it must be said, a wonderful photographer: "The Wind Will Carry Us" is filled with gorgeous images of rural life in a remote Kurdish village—you can almost smell the livestock.

And it's fascinating, in an (airbrushed) anthropology documentary Discovery Channel sort of way.

But it's also so relentless in its lack of story that you find yourself making mental to-do lists or even nodding off. And its 118 minutes feel twice as long.

Although you're given very few clues as to what is actually going on in the film, a man (Behzad Dourani) who seems to be some kind of film producer—though he is referred to only as "the engineer"—arrives at a sun-bleached, hillside village with a two-man crew (you hear them speak, but you never see their faces).

There, assisted by an 11-year-old boy, they wait for a 100-year-old woman to die, in the belief that her death will be followed by some kind of exotic local ritual involving self-mutilation.

But the old woman's death isn't as imminent as the engineer believed, so he spends most of his time hanging around in the village and bothering the 11-year-old boy, who wants to work on his exams.

Occasionally, his cell phone rings. To answer the call, he has to drive up to the cemetery on the hill, where a man you never see is digging a mysterious, deep hole in the ground.

Again and again, the engineer drives up the hill to take a call. The first three or four times you see him take the route, you're struck by the gorgeousness of the golden wheat fields. Then it becomes a bore.

Of course, the point is that the engineer, in his hiking boots and denim shirt, is an urban, modern fellow.

And the film is largely a vague, opaque meditation about such a man's inability to adjust to the slower rhythms of a traditional rural community, nature, the seasons, etc.

NEWSDAY, 7/28/00, Part II/p. B8, John Anderson

The most prominent of Iranian filmmakers, Abbas Kiarostami, has become a critical darling in this country because of his formal purity, minimalist aesthetic, disinterest in conventional narrative and fabler's ability with the abstract. All very good reasons. And precisely the same reasons he'll never be knocking 'em dead at the mall.

It seems necessary to say this is because "The Wind Will Carry Us" is the most Kiarostamic of Kiarostami films. Austere, seemingly dispassionate (a deception, by the way) and possessed of a sense of humor as dry as the Iranian dust, it's a film in which little seems to be happening, especially if you're looking for "drama." Yet, every line of dialogue is loaded with meaning; each new camera angle reveals a new, glorious composition. And the film is a real mystery, one that plays out in the most understated ways.

For those familiar with Kiarostami's last film, the critically lauded "Taste of Cherry" (1997), the opening shot provides a dose of deja vu—a car traveling a winding dirt road through a fertile but sun-baked Iranian countryside; there's even mention of a lone-standing tree (where "Cherry's" supposed suicide took place). But the men in the car, most of whom we never meet, aren't interested in foliage. They're looking for a village called Siah Dareh, where they'll find... what?

The villagers initially think the men are telecommunications engineers; later, they suspect the crew is seeking treasure in a local cemetery. What the team really wants involves an ailing old woman and a local ritual, and the film's denouement is as much about the revealing of motives as it is about any other narrative climax.

The so-called Engineer (Behzad Dourani) is the only one of the strangers we really see and we see a lot of him, whether he's interacting with the villagers (all of whom are natives of the actual Siah Dareh) or making his increasingly comic trips up a local hillside to make cell phone connections. Or, having metaphysical conversations with an unseen man in a hole in the ground—a worker digging a well or a ditch, it doesn't matter. Kiarostami is becoming increasingly Beckettian in his humor, and more like Vermeer in his pictures.

One of the more poignant aspects of the film is the Engineer's single-mindedness and how he seems to miss the point Kiarostami makes about Siah Dareh, the town that time forgot. He's a chilly, disagreeable man, but he does embody a Kiarostamic poignancy about the tension between the simple, rustic and ostensibly pure life available in the more backward parts of Iran and the complexities of sophistication. It's a conflict painfully familiar to the country. And to its greatest director as well.

SIGHT AND SOUND, 10/00, p. 63, Laura Mulvey

Four men arrive from Tehran at a village in Iranian Kurdistan. Farzad, the small boy who is to be their guide, meets them. Their mission is secret, but Behzad, one of the strangers, inquires after Mrs Malek, an old lady who is ill. In the days that follow, Farzad looks after the visitors and sits his school exams. He and Behzad become closer, although there is tension over Mrs Malek. To get a signal on his mobile phone, Behzad has to drive to the village cemetery at the summit of a hill. Apparently, he is there to film a mourning ceremony and, as Mrs. Malek clings to life, the producer in Tehran, Mrs. Godzari, becomes impatient. On each visit to the cemetery, Behzad chats to Youssef who is digging a deep hole. Behzad goes to buy milk from Zeynab, Youssef's fiancée, and recites a poem. Hearing that Mrs. Malek is rallying, the crew become disaffected. Behzad raises the alarm when Youssef has an accident in the cemetery and goes with the doctor to fetch pain killers for Mrs. Malek. At dawn, Mrs. Malek dies, but the crew have left for Tehran. As the women gather for the mourning ceremony, Behzad takes some photos then leaves the village.

Abbas Kiarostami has said recently that he's no longer interested in filming in interiors with artificial light. In *The Wind Will Carry Us* his devotion to landscape as cinematic spectacle seems, at first glance, to have overwhelmed the story. Not only does Kiarostami show us typically emblematic natural images, for the first time he has his characters refer to them. In the opening sequence, the strangers from Tehran look for "a single tree" and "the winding road" to help them reach their destination, a remote village in Iranian Kurdistan. But landscape in *The Wind Will Carry Us* is complemented, in a new way, by a complex, labyrinthine "village-scape": the village, Siah Dareh (where the strangers await the death of Mrs. Malek whose mourning ceremony they intend to film), is constructed across the fold of two hills so that its roofs are pathways turning into archways and connected to the steep streets by passages and stairs. Painted white with flashes of colour, the village is a perfectly designed set for a camera constantly on the move. The specific layout of the cemetery—where the crew's director Behzad talks on his mobile phone—also generates its own camera choreography, particularly the circular movements that follow him in one take around the summit of the hill. No one seeing this extraordinary camerawork would guess that Kiarostami and his cinematographer Mahmoud Kalari had fallen out during filming.

But *The Wind Will Carry Us* is not just a formal cinematic exercise. The story has been stripped down to the barest of elements, but while little "happens", the film teems with everyday life. The empty spaces between the film's sparse events are filled with words, from poetry to local anecdotes, while the sounds of the animals in the village build into something like a music track. This lack of dramatic incident has its own narrative relevance, evoking the empty time involved in waiting for a death to come. Behzad is like an undercover anthropologist—with the endless questions he asks the villagers, he manages to throw some light on this remote place. He also provides the film's moments of comic relief: his struggle to find a signal for his mobile—his repeated run for his car and desperate dash up a nearby hill—has all the makings of a gag. In the cemetery at the hill's summit, however, the mood changes as the film addresses the theme of death; rather than turning black here, the humour simply falls away. Behzad's responses and expressions are central to the film but are difficult to read. He is a sympathetic narrator-observer on to whom a darker, more sinister side can also be projected.

In spite of its rich soundscape, extended, elegant camera movement, and near anthropological observation, the film is as much about what is not said and what is not shown. In discussing the film, Kiarostami emphasises his interest in making spectators take an active part in determining the meaning. Throughout *The Wind Will Carry Us,* certain people are heard only off screen. During his scenes at the cemetery, Behzad chats to Youssef, who is digging a hole and remains unseen throughout. Although his voice and his views on life give certain clues as to his character, the spectator is left to speculate about his actions and appearance and to fill in the off screen space with his or her imagination. Youssef's invisibility is implicitly connected to the partial darkness that cloaks his fiancée, Zeynab. When Behzad goes to her house to buy milk, he is directed to a stable in a cellar. Descending into the gloomy space, his body gradually blocks out the light, leaving the screen totally black for several seconds. When he (and we) can see again, Zeynab is preparing to milk the cow by the dim light of a hurricane lamp. To pass the time, Behzad chats with her, then recites the poem "The Wind Will Carry Us" by Forough Farrokhzad. To cite Forough and discuss her poetry with a peasant girl is to introduce another powerful off-screen presence. Not only is she one of Iran's leading modern poets, but her tragic life is well known, especially her loss of her son in a divorce case and her death in a car crash at the age Of 33. Kiarostami has said that "her generous sensual philosophy had always seemed close to that of Omar Khayyám" whose poem in praise of the pleasures of life is quoted by a doctor later in the film.

Although the off-screen space and the darkness may well refer obliquely to the need for imagination and poetry in a society dominated by censorship, the significance of women in the film is striking. The two other strong women who cannot be seen are Tehran-based producer Mrs. Godzari, to whom Behzad speaks on the phone, and the old lady who is dying behind closed doors, Mrs. Malek. Behzad is caught, in some sense, between them. But the role of women in the mourning ceremony raises other questions. A young school teacher is the only person who discusses the ceremony with Behzad, to whom he tells the story of his mother, scarred twice by scratching her face to show superior grief. The teacher says: "You may be interested in it. I'm not interested," as though to relegate this brutal ritual to the darkness of a society in which a family patriarch and a husband's boss, whose relatives his mother was mourning, can cause such anxiety. But there is also the implication that such things should not be filmed. To see is not necessarily to understand, and—the implication might be—the demand for everything to be seen is simply the other side of censorship's coin.

The Wind Will Carry Us has shifted the emphasis of A *Taste of Cherry*. The twin themes of an enigma and death are there in both. But the spectator's curiosity has been directed away from an enigmatic protagonist's personal dilemma to wider issues of life and death present in Kiarostami's earlier trilogy of films *(Where Is My Friend's House?, And Life Goes On...* and *Through the Olive Trees)* based on an earthquake that occurred in the area north of Tehran in 1991. Death as an aesthetic, as the point of narrative drive, is still there, but as in A *Taste of Cherry*, there is a coda. Behzad throws the thigh bone that Youssef had given him as a mascot into a stream. As the water carries it along, this piece of lifeless death acquires a new ability to move and participate in life.

VILLAGE VOICE, 8/1/00, p. 75, J. Hoberman

"We're heading nowhere," a disembodied voice complains as a battered jeep crawls up a winding road through harsh, scrubby terrain. So begins *The Wind Will Carry Us*—the latest and, to my mind, the greatest film by Iranian master Abbas Kiarostami.

An engineer and his two never-seen assistants are traveling from Tehran to the remote Kurdish village of Siah Dareh. If the directions they attempt to follow are puzzling, so too are their intentions. These outsiders won't say what brings them to Siah Dareh, although they jokingly tell the village boy who has been appointed to guide them into town that they are looking for "treasure." It's soon clear that this treasure has something to do with a sick old woman (also never seen), but it's never directly revealed what that something is.

The Wind Will Carry Us is a marvelously assured film—at once straightforward and tricksy. It's also bracingly modest. For all the self-important claims certain experts have made on Kiarostami's behalf, his films are anything but pompous. Typically understated, *The Wind Will Carry Us* is less amusing than bemusing. Kiarostami's sense of humor feels as dry as the countryside he depicts; the film is in many regards a comedy. The timing is impeccable, the dialogue borderline absurd. The gags, if that's the word, are predicated on formal elements—including the filmmaker's rigorous, somewhat ironic, use of point of view and voice-over. The same routines are repeated throughout, often punctuated by amplified animal sounds, to establish a musical structure. (Shots often end with a herd of goats crossing the screen.) In this sense, *The Wind Will Carry Us* resembles the films of Jacques Tati and, more recently, Takeshi Kitano's *Kikujiro*.

The city folks' obscure mission to Kurdistan is but one of the movie's modernist tropes. The villagers call the protagonist the Engineer in somewhat the same spirit that the outsider antihero of Kafka's Castle is known as the Land Surveyor. Indeed, having switched from cosmic long shot to more humanizing medium shot once the Engineer (Behzad Dourani) arrives in Siah Dareh, Kiarostami spends considerable time establishing the village's baffling geography—the steep, whitewashed maze of alleys and courtyards that are terraced into the hillside.

Taken as a documentary, which it is in part, *The Wind Will Carry Us* largely concerns the town's daily life—its laconic customs and puzzling arguments. But Kiarostami's method points toward something more. This is a movie of disembodied voices and off-screen presences, including half the characters and a newborn baby. Like the Engineer's two-man crew, who are always indoors and supposedly eating strawberries, Kiarostami is forever drawing attention to that which cannot be seen—or shown. (This might also include the Kurds, who are an officially "invisible" minority in Iran. The filmmaker has denied that *The Wind Will Carry Us* has any political intent, albeit in suggestively perceptual terms: "if the viewers have the impression of receiving a direct political message, it's up to them.")

In one (literally) running gag, the Engineer is required to scramble to the village's highest point so that his cell phone can receive an incoming signal from Tehran. (When he finally gets the connection, he discovers that he doesn't want the call.) The village graveyard is also located atop the hill—a coincidence that allows for another sort of dematerialized conversation. While catching his breath, the Engineer has a series of conversations with an unseen ditchdigger who is excavating the cemetery to facilitate some mysterious form of "telecommunications." (The Engineer is mildly interested, and in a blithely metaphoric move, the ditchdigger throws him a bone.)

In what may be the strangest scene in this extraordinarily subtle and nuanced film, the Engineer uses an excursion to buy fresh milk as a pretext to drop in on the ditchdigger's girlfriend. She too, he discovers, lives in darkness. He finds her in one of the village's subterranean caverns, milking a goat, and is moved to recite the poem about loneliness that provides the movie's title. (The poem is by the late Forough Farrokhzad, a modernist and feminist icon, whose remarkable 1962 documentary on a leper colony was shown at the 1997 New York Film Festival.)

At last, the Engineer has put something in words. Skinny and balding, peering at the village through steel-rimmed glasses, this dungaree-wearing character is an example of what used to be called the intelligentsia. He is also a parody director who makes a few lame attempts to photograph the villagers, while more than once employing the actual camera as a mirror, peering directly into it as he shaves. The Engineer is interested in life. At one point, he idly flips a tortoise on its back—perhaps to see how it will squirm. But at another, more crucial moment, he demonstrates that he cannot take action himself but only direct others to do so.

It's part of the movie's formal brilliance that, suddenly, during its final 10 minutes, too much seems to be happening. *The Wind Will Carry Us* is a film about nothing and everything—life, death, the quality of light on dusty hills. (Kiarostami, as made clear by his recent show of photographs in a Chelsea gallery, is a landscape artist.) Confident in its lack of consequence, the film far surpasses the strained allegory that dogged Kiarostami's more stilted and schematic official masterpiece, *Taste of Cherry*. Effortlessly incorporating aspects of documentary and confessional filmmaking into an unforced, open-ended parable, *The Wind Will Carry Us* transforms barely anecdotal material into a mysteriously metaphysical vision.

For all its glorious time-wasting, *The Wind Will Carry Us* is essentially a deathwatch. Late in the movie, it's casually revealed that the Engineer has been hanging out in Siah Dareh for two weeks. When night finally falls, however, it's as though the time he's spent there has been a single golden, purposeless, perpetual afternoon.

Also reviewed in:
NATION, 8/7/00, p. 43, Stuart Klawans
NEW REPUBLIC, 8/14/00, p. 28, Stanley Kauffmann
NEW YORK TIMES, 7/28/00, p. E7, A. O. Scott
NEW YORKER, 8/14/00, p. 89, David Denby

VARIETY, 9/13-19/99, p. 46, Deborah Young
WASHINGTON POST, 11/10/00, Weekend/p. 47, Desson Howe

WINTER SLEEPERS

A WinStar Cinema release of a Stefan Arndt and X-Filme Creative Pool GmbH production *Producer:* Stefan Arndt. *Director:* Tom Tykwer. *Screenplay (German with English subtitles):* Tom Tykwer. *Based on the novel "Expense of the Spirit" by:* Anne-François Pyszora. *Director of Photography:* Frank Griebe. *Editor:* Katja Dringenberg. *Music:* Reinhold Heil, Johnny Klimek, and Tom Tykwer. *Sound:* Arno Wilms. *Sound Editor:* Antje Zynga. *Casting:* An Dorthe Braker. *Art Director:* Alexander Manasse. *Special Effects:* Heinz Ludwiz. *Costumes:* Aphrodite Kondos. *Make-up:* Margrit Neufink. *Stunt Coordinator:* François Doge and Volkhart Buff. *Running time:* 124 minutes. *MPAA Rating:* Not Rated.

CAST: Floriane Daniel (Rebecca); Heino Ferch (Marco); Ulrich Matthes (Rene); Marie-Lou Sellem (Laura); Laura Tonke (Nina); Sebastian Schipper (Otto); Agathe Taffertshofer (Edith, Theo's Wife); Sofia Dirscherl (Marita, Theo's Daughter); Robert Meyer (Keibl, Cop); Werner Schnitzer (Senior Consultant); Saskia Vester (Anna); Josef Bierbichler (Theo); Simon Donatz and Jakob Donatz (Theo's Sons); Harry Täschner (Bailiff); Walter Anichhofer (Prompter); Martin Leutgeb (2nd Cop); Melanie Palmberger and Michaela Prähauser (Nina's Friends); Peter Arp (Man at Accident); Caroline Richards (Bartender); Swantje Matthaei (Alexa); Noushin Diehl (The Baby); Anne-François Pyszora (Kitsch Storyteller); René Schoenenberger (Gerd); Linda Schmidt (Rene's Mother); Erdmann von Garnier (Rene's Father); Felicitas Jeschke (Marco's Mother); Erika Wolfram (Laura's Mother); Hans Wolfram (Laura's Father); Ute Skrzypczak (Rebecca's Mother); Rudi Skrzypczak (Rebecca's Father).

LOS ANGELES TIMES, 4/7/00, Calendar/p. 22, Kevin Thomas

Tom Tykwer's "Winter Sleepers," made just before "Run Lola Run" put him on the map, finds us peering down at a skiing village nestled in the mountains of Germany. The camera darts in and out of snowy crevasses and peeks into the homes of people whose lives are about to impinge upon one another in wholly unpredictable and drastic ways. When you consider that Tykwer's Lola was a young woman who literally ran throughout the movie, you will not be surprised that Tykwer opens this picture with such swiftness and economy.

No sooner has he eavesdropped on various lives than he stages the incident that sets the story in motion. A local farmer, Theo (Josef Bierbichler), with a horse trailer attached to his station wagon, loses control of his vehicle on an icy road. He ends up having to shoot his badly injured horse—and discovers that his little daughter had sneaked into the trailer and now lies on the roadside in a coma. As his daughter hovers between life and death, her father can get no one to believe that the accident occurred because he was forced to swerve to avoid another car. We know the truth of what happened—and that Theo is himself not telling the whole story.

"Winter Sleepers," which Tykwer and Anne-Francoise Pyszora adapted from her novel "Expense of Spirit," offers a riveting depiction of the classic collision of fate and character, with geography in this instance playing a crucial role—all those icy roads and slippery slopes. However, this stunningly kinetic and elegant film, shot in Cinemascope, leaves us feeling that we are more at the mercy of quirks of fate than we may care to acknowledge. Reinforcing this feeling is the film's view of people as being more benevolent than malevolent in their actions.

In this light, you could say that everything in the film happens the way it does because Rebecca (Floriane Daniel), a pretty translator, is so glad to see her handsome ski instructor lover Marco (Heino Ferch) that she rushes him to bed before he can even close the door of his brand-new luxury car, making it ripe for theft. Yet it scarcely seems fair to blame all that occurs on Rebecca, and, in fact, Tykwer, taking the ironic long view, does not. But there's no denying the domino effect of that car door being left open—and how unaware we can be of a chain of events that shapes our destiny.

Rebecca's relationship with Marco is volatile. He lives up to the image of the virile, womanizing ski instructor yet is wildly jealous of Rebecca. Insecure, his reliance on his looks to hit the financial jackpot so far has proved elusive. In the meantime, Rebecca's roommate Laura (Marie-Lou Sellem), a nurse and aspiring actress, has become attracted to the local theater projectionist Rene (Ulrich Matthes), an intense man who relaxes in the presence of this lovely and intelligent young woman.

"Winter Sleepers'" title may refer to its characters' tendency to drift without anchor. Sleepers, however, is also the name of a popular local tavern. For Tykwer, love is the anchor, and he has said his film is "about love in the face of impossible circumstances." It progresses stylishly in compelling fashion, with much detached compassion and an equal amount of mordant humor.

The film has terrific vitality, from its astute ensemble performances to Frank Griebe's dynamic, expressive camera work with striking use of color to establish mood; Griebe went on to shoot the even more kinetic "Lola." The film is also richly enhanced by a subtly seductive and insistent score composed by Tykwer with Johnny Klimek and Reinhold Heil. Next from Tykwer: "The Princess and the Warrior," an epic love story starring Lola herself, Franka Potente.

NEW YORK POST, 3/17/00, p. 48, Jonathan Foreman

Like "Run Lola Run" (made two years afterwards), Tom Tykwer's "Winter Sleepers" is a self-consciously hip film centering on twentysomething Germans leading rather aimless lives—one that purports to say something about fate and coincidence.

Shot amid beautiful Bavarian mountain scenery, it has an able cast and the feel of an edgy mystery. But in the end, "Winter Sleepers" proves to be a cold, emptily stylish exercise—and one that sorely lacks the speed and vigor that made "Lola" run.

For much of its excessive length, "Winter Sleepers" feels like the pilot for a TV series. You're introduced to five characters whose lives intertwine, but you never get to know what they're about, or to like them.

Rebecca (Floriane Daniel) is a horny translator who always wears red. Her roommate, Laura (Marie-Lou Sellem), is a nurse who aspires to be an actress and always wears green.

Rebecca's handsome but not very bright ski-instructor lover, Marco (Heino Ferch)—who's always in blue—wants to move in, even though it'll limit his access to other lovers.

One morning while Marco is having sex with Rebecca, his new Alfa Romeo is stolen by Rene (Ulrich Matthes), the creepy, slightly brain-damaged projectionist at the local cinema.

Speeding along the icy mountain roads, Rene gets in an accident with a car driven by local farmer Theo. Rene is OK. Theo is knocked unconscious, but inside the horse trailer he was driving his little daughter has a life-threatening head injury.

Rene—who wears black and looks like Willem Dafoe merged with Ben Cross—walks away from the accident without helping the victims and without trying to alert the authorities.

The little girl ends up comatose in the hospital, being watched over by nurse Laura, who coincidentally meets Rene and begins an affair with him.

SIGHT AND SOUND, 8/99, p. 57, Richard Falcon

At a remote Berchtesgaden villa in the mountains, Rebecca, a young translator, meets her ski-instructor boyfriend Marco. They impulsively go off to have sex, so he leaves the keys to his car in the ignition. Rene, a projectionist at Sleepers, the local cinema and bar, happens past the window, photographs the couple making love and takes the car for a ride. Rene crashes into local farmer Theo and his family, gravely injuring Theo's young daughter. He stumbles off without helping them, but takes photographs first. The villa's owner Laura, also a nurse, assists in the operation on Theo's daughter. Unable to find Marco's snow-covered car, the police disbelieve Theo's story about a second driver. Laura encounters Rene in Sleepers and a relationship develops. Marco and Rebecca have a row about Rebecca only wanting him for sex, even though he's having an affair in the city and begins a fling with ski-student Nina. Rene explains to Laura he's suffering from short-term memory loss after having been blown up by a grenade. He takes photographs to compensate.

Laura invites Rene to the villa, but he fails to recognise it, while Marco becomes increasingly jealous of Rebecca's attraction to the newcomer. Rene discovers the insurance claim for Marco's car and the photograph causes him to search in vain through his own photographs for clues. Theo finds the car and discovers Marco's driving licence inside. Believing Marco is the hit-and-run driver, Theo sets his dog on Marco who skies to his death down a crevasse. Laura, pregnant, settles down with Rene and Rebecca returns to the city.

Soon to be better known in the UK for his upcoming, critically acclaimed *Run Lola Run* Tom Tykwer describes this follow-up to his successful 1994 debut *Deadly Maria/Die tödliche Maria* as a 'Liebesthriller.' It opens in rapid thriller style, each character introduced with a typewritten caption as he or she journeys by train and road into the snowy mountains. Tykwer's own rhythmic music enhances the widescreen images of the mountainscapes as we're further seduced by the film's bravura visuals including match cuts between a close-up gash in Rebecca's thumb and the vertiginous mountain crevasse into which Marco will later plunge, dizzying 360-degree pans around Rene's head, and a shower stream hitting a bather's head horizontally across the frame. For much of the film's early reels this style keeps us hooked while Tykwer defers explaining Rene's memory loss.

Like Wolfgang Becker's *Life Is All You Get* (for which Tykwer wrote the screenplay) *Winter Sleepers* aspires also to being a portrait of Tykwer's own generation of people in their early thirties. Both couples are in hiding—if not hibernation—rootless and without ambition or drive. Tykwer uses the time bought by his elliptical narrative not just to exercise his stylistic muscle but also (less successfully) to compare and contrast the two relationships on display, which play out in the villa's cocoon like interior. Rebecca and Marco's is based on sex and it is her frantic seduction of him that makes his car an open temptation to Rene. Rebecca is colour-coded red—from the drop of blood on her finger, to almost every piece of clothing, down to her underwear. Her physicality is stressed throughout, underscored by moments when she masturbates or pulls down her red tights to urinate in the snow.

Other characters are similarly coded. Marco, her lover, is dressed in shades of blue. This overelaborate design and stylistic excess suggest Tykwer doesn't trust his essentially self-centred characters to interest us, and there's an undeniable callousness in the movie's treatment of Rebecca. Laura and Rene's relationship is based on their strangeness to each other and on the film's central mystery. Their relationship ought to survive since short-term memory loss is probably an asset in keeping shallow characters such as these interested in one another.

Winter Sleepers seems to be suggesting Rene's condition could be a metaphor for his lost generation. Tykwer was a Berlin repertory cinema programmer and made television documentaries on Lars von Trier, Peter Greenaway and Wim Wenders among others. In Wenders' *Alice in the Cities* (1974) the idea of a German in his early 30s trying and failing to grasp and order experiences through Polaroids becomes a resonant image of the dislocation of the immediate postwar generation. But as with von Trier's work, this European film heritage is both appropriated and surrounded by self-regarding stylistic prowess. Rene's memory loss is due to an accident with a practice grenade, not the ontological crisis of a 70s Wenders hero. Like the Berchtesgaden setting, this narrative expedient offers a distant echo of the past, which is perhaps appropriate for the generation Tykwer is describing, if not exactly intellectually captivating.

The film works better as spectacle, best viewed without much thought. What, for example, is the terrific Josef Bierbichler—veteran of the numerous anarchic "anti-*Heimatfilme*" of Herbert Achtembusch—doing here playing the kind of Bavarian rustic common to so many traditional *Heimatfilm*? What *Winter Sleepers* finally turns on is awakening its directionless characters to the fates they are rushing towards in the opening sequence. Marco's final ecstatically filmed plunge into a crevasse echoes the intervention of romantic destiny in Weimar cinema, described by Siegfried Kracauer as, "no mere accident but a majestic event that stirred metaphysical shudders in sufferers and witnesses alike." But the particular "majestic event" which climaxes this stylish but superficial movie is prefaced by a lap dissolve which has Marco skiing towards Rebecca's huge red mouth, an image more befitting of a Bond-film title sequence.

VILLAGE VOICE, 3/21/00, p. 140, Dennis Lim

Made a year before his recent art-house smash *Run Lola Run,* Tom Tykwer's *Winter Sleepers* is similarly preoccupied with fate, chance, and cosmic hocus-pocus. But if Lola was a breathless, mindless blur of perpetual forward motion, *Winter Sleepers* approximates nothing so much as a slow deep freeze. Tykwer's slick pop moves and calculating hipster gestures are in evidence (show-offy camera, prominent electronic score), but mainly, this earlier film revels in a chilly grandeur. In fact, pivoting on an accident that reverberates through a Bavarian mountain village, it carries echoes of *The Sweet Hereafter.* Less fortunately, it also slogs through the romantic travails of its thirtyish characters with the soapy solipsism of generic Sundance product.

Constructed with more attention to geometry than anything else, the narrative links four village residents: lughead ski instructor Marco (Heino Ferch); his girlfriend Becky (Floriane Daniel), a romance-paperback translator; her roommate Laura (Marie-Lou Sellem), a nurse and amateur actress; and René (Ulrich Matthes), a movie projectionist with short-term memory loss. One night René steals Marco's car and gets into aforementioned accident, the young victim of which is tended to at the hospital by Laura, who shortly after starts dating René. The film looks terrific—harsh, clean winter light on vast, pristine snowscapes—but Tykwer, an upstart Kieslowski, fetishizes the role of coincidence in narrative (or, depending on how you look at ft, assigns hollow meaning to mundane connections) with no real purpose in mind. Despite the visually dramatic conclusion—a figure in infinite free fall—*Winter Sleepers* is a cheat. The movie unfolds in a shroud of nonspecific suggestiveness but never emerges from under it.

Also reviewed in:
CHICAGO TRIBUNE, 3/31/00, Friday/p. H, Michael Wilmington
NEW YORK TIMES, 3/17/00, p. E14, Stephen Holden
VARIETY, 9/8-17/97, p. 86, Derek Elley
WASHINGTON POST, 5/3/00, p. C1, Stephen Hunter

WIREY SPINDELL

A WinStar Cinema release of a Five Minutes Before the Miracle production.   *Executive Producer:* Bruce Greenfield.   *Producer:* Dolly Hall, Terence Michael, and Lloyd Segan.   *Director:* Eric Schaeffer.   *Screenplay:* Eric Schaeffer.   *Director of Photography:* Kramer Morgenthau.   *Editor:* Mitchel Stanley.   *Music:* Amanda Kravat.   *Sound:* Noah Timan.   *Sound Editor:* Chen Harpaz.   *Casting:* Sheila Jaffe and Georgianne Walken.   *Production Designer:* Mark Helmuth.   *Set Decorator:* Niamh Byrne.   *Set Dresser:* Lisa Crivelli.   *Costumes:* Bootsy Holler and Amanda Silberstein.   *Make-up:* Lauren Weinstein.   *Running time:* 101 minutes. *MPAA Rating:* Not Rated.

CAST: Eric Schaeffer (Wirey Spindell);   Eric Mabius (Wirey, Age 17);   Devon Matthews (Wirey, Junior High);   Zane Adlum (Wirey, Age 6);   Callie Thorne (Tabitha);   Samantha Buck (Samantha);   Jennifer Wiltsie (Wirey's Mom, Young);   Peggy Gormley (Wirey's Mom, Mature);   John Doman (Wirey's Father);   Caroline Strong (Judy);   Don Creech (Teacher, Mean-Gray Hair);   John Deyle (Principal Dickens);   Bryan Callen (Robby, Present Day);   Melvin Rodriguez (Ernesto);   Stefan Niemczyk (Lapper);   Gerry Rosenthal (Mike Johnson);   Jenna Stern (Roxanne);   Leanne Whitney (Beth);   Greg Haberny (Niles);   Michell Hurst (Arlene);   David Healy (Yuppie guy);   Angela Bullock (Tabitha's Girlfriend);   Jorge Pupo and Michael Patterson (Scouts);   Irma St. Paule (Angel Lady);   John C. Havens and Jim Gaffigan (Announcers);   Gideon Jacobs (Young Wirey's voice);   Amanda Kravat (Waitress); Dolores McDougal (Tabitha's Mother);   Keri Lynn Pratt (First Date).

LOS ANGELES TIMES, 2/4/00, Calendar/p. 11, Kevin Thomas

"Wirey Spindell" is as idiosyncratic as the name of its hero, which gives this surprisingly affecting film its title. It's surprising because it's hard to imagine that even an independent filmmaker as gifted and distinctive as Eric Schaeffer has been able to work up so much emotional involvement into a tale that's essentially an extreme case of male prenuptial jitters.

With nine days to go before tying the knot, Schaeffer's Wirey beats a momentary retreat to the bathroom of his Upper West Side Manhattan apartment. All he wants is some private time, be explains to his lovely fiancee, Tabatha (Callie Thorne), who has made an unwelcome interruption with an offer of a cup of tea. Why the bathroom? she asks. Why not another room, since they have only one bathroom?

The questions send Wirey back to his childhood, to the times when he wanted to flee from his already-divorced, well-meaning but off-beat hippie mother who was strenuously trying to spare him the terrible childhood she herself endured. For example, Wirey just does not connect with her idea that he should "get in touch with your anger" by beating his bed with a tennis racket.

Wirey, after an excruciating incident at school, decides at about age 15 to live with his teacher-father and stepmother in rural Vermont, which amusingly proves to be meaner than the streets of New York City. The local yokels brutally haze the urbanite Wirey as a "flatlander," and in no time he has retreated into a cornucopia of drugs his father has stashed away. (Wirey is played by Eric Mabius from age 17 until the film jumps ahead to the present, when Schaeffer takes over as Wirey at 36.) By the time he's off to college, Wirey has a drug problem, conducive neither to academic survival nor in coping with the headlong rush of first love with Samantha (Samantha Buck), a ravingly beautiful, aspiring young actress with a fear of being loved.

So achingly intense and comprehensive is Schaeffer's perception that he makes the whole business of being alive, of being in the thrall of embarrassment, of being caught up in a love that is as glorious as it is ultimately fleeting that this and more come across as astoundingly fresh. Wirey's youthful self-absorption is more than a little painful but not unamusing. In his fourth and strongest film to date, auteur-star Schaeffer has become adept at communicating the pain that simply being alive can bring from just the right emotional distance.

NEW YORK POST, 1/21/00, p. 50, Lou Lumenick

"Wirey Spindell" is the latest vanity production by writer-director-star Eric Schaeffer, who still seems to think he's another Woody Allen—despite a growing body of work that proves otherwise.

At least as narcissistic as Allen but without a fraction of his talents in any area, Schaeffer—as in his previous "My Life's in Turnaround" and "If Lucy Fell"—plays the title role, an emotionally arrested man with woman problems.

Wirey is supposed to be married in nine days, but because of his roving eye be hasn't been able to sleep with his fiancee in nine months.

Nearly the first 10 minutes is devoted to an excruciating scene in which Wirey explains to the exasperated fiancee (Callie Thorne, who must have badly needed this job) that he requires time to think by himself in the bathroom of the apartment they share.

Things go downhill from there.

There's a heavily narrated series of flashbacks to Wirey as a youth (he's played by a succession of actors who are notably more attractive and appealing than Schaeffer).

They begin with his first memory (of licking an electrical outlet) and encompass a long, boring, unfunny series of encounters with sex, drugs and booze—including gay encounters, group encounters, necrophilia and a stint in rehab.

Based on Schaeffer's (understandably) unpublished autobiographical novel, "Wirey Spindell" runs from '60s to the '90s. Its ambition is in no way justified by inane dialogue, poor acting, static camerawork and lethargic pacing.

All of which make it an early contender for the worst movie of 2000.

VILLAGE VOICE, 1/25/00, p. 128, Jessica Winter

Eric Schaeffer's first movie, the microbudgeted *My Life's in Turnaround* (1993), was a sweet'n' low docu-spoof that deserved praise for just getting made. But the former cabdriver's next two features produced the unmistakable sound of one hand clapping: *If Lucy Fell* and *Fall* made for the muckiest runoff of the mid-'90s Gen X romantic-comedy glut (theme song "Show Me Love [From an Ironic Distance]"). Brimming with fatuous "clever" dialogue and gorgeous women swooning over Schaeffer-played boors, the like-sounding titles denoted a vain, smarmy Woody Allen acolyte drowning in his own reflection. He plays, natch, the title character in his most Schaeffer-rific effort yet, the ambiguously autobiographical (and, per usual, sooty-lensed) *Wirey Spindell,* which finds the eponym's wheedling-sap fiancée (Callie Thorne) unwilling to walk the plank with her obnoxious, bullying groom until he can fix a problem of the upstairs-downstairs variety: seems Wirey can't have sex if he's in love. This crisis of faith spurs reflective flashbacks spanning his lonely childhood, drug-muddled adolescence, collegiate amour fou, and subsequent rehab; Wirey stumbles from self-pitying burnout to a Detective Sipowicz-esque balance of AA spirituality and guy's-guy vulgarity. Mounting a bildungsroman also affords Schaeffer a new opportunity for wish fulfillment in casting the fetching Eric Mabius as his college-age self, though the younger actor gives his director too much credit: Mabius's role is written as a jerk but not played like one.

Also reviewed in:
NEW YORK TIMES, 1/21/00, p. E10, A. O. Scott
VARIETY, 11/8-14/99, p. 41, Daniel M. Kimmel

WISDOM OF CROCODILES, THE

A Miramax Films release of a Zenith Productions/Goldwyn Films/Film Foundry Partners/Entertainment Film Distributors in association with the Arts Council of England presentation of a Zenith Film. *Executive Producer:* Scott Meek, Dorothy Berwin, and Nigel Stafford-Clark. *Producer:* David Lascelles and Carolyn Choa. *Director:* Po Chih Leong. *Screenplay:* Paul Hoffman. *Director of Photography:* Oliver Curtis. *Editor:* Robin Sales. *Music:* John Lunn and Orlando Gough. *Sound:* Colin Nicolson and (music) Paul Golding. *Sound Editor:* John Downer. *Casting:* Michelle Guish. *Production Designer:* Andy Harris. *Art Director:* Ben Scott. *Special Effects:* Stuart Brisdon. *Costumes:* Anna Sheppard. *Make-up:* Pat Hay. *Stunt Coordinator:* Nick Powell. *Running time:* 99 minutes. *MPAA Rating:* R.

CAST: Jude Law (Steven Grslcz); Kerry Fox (Maria Vaughan); Nick Lamont (Toll Bridge Attendant); Joseph O'Conor (Mr. Nancarrow); Elina Löwensohn (Anne Levels); Jack Davenport (Sergeant Roche); Timothy Spall (Inspector Healey); Colin Salmon (Martin); Stuart Bowman and C.J. December (Car Crash Mechanics); Hitler Wong (Noodles Chan); Anastasia Hille (Karen); Ashley Artus (Gang Leader); Julia Davies (Girl in Operating Theatre); Rupert Farley (Priest); Diane Howse (Mrs. Healey); Cliff Parisi (Laborer); Vincent Keane (Injured Workman).

NEW YORK POST, 7/14/00, p. 47, Lou Lumenick

"The Wisdom of Crocodiles" is this season's "Eye of the Beholder"—a stylish but incoherent British thriller turning up in theaters here only because its star went on to bigger and better things.

As "Eye" was released in the wake of Ashley Judd's blockbuster "Double Jeopardy," this newer film has escaped straight-to-video hell thanks to Jude Law's charismatic, Oscar-nominated turn in "The Talented Mr. Ripley."

In "Crocodiles," which was made before "Ripley," Law gives a stilted and bloodless performance as Steven Grslcz, a Romanian medical researcher who exists on the blood of women he kills.

Whether or not he is actually a vampire is one of numerous murky issues in Paul Hoffman's screenplay.

Much footage in Hong Kong director Po Chih Leong's ponderously slow-moving movie is devoted to Steven's making entries in journals he keeps on his victims, charcoal sketches of them—and endless views of his antique-strewn apartment.

Steven is being investigated by a police inspector (Timothy Spall) for the death of his latest victim (Kerry Fox), whom he saved from jumping in front of a speeding London Underground train.

Meanwhile, Steven has found his latest potential victim, an asthmatic engineer named Anne (Elina Löwensohn, who played a Manhattan vampire in Michael Almereyda's "Nadja").

But things go seriously awry when Grslcz, who is days from death unless he gets fresh blood, begins developing feelings for Anne, whom he courts with incomprehensible ramblings about how humans resemble crocodiles.

Leong generates minimal suspense, even when Anne is running for her life. And when Steven fights off a gang of street toughs, the action is completely unconvincing.

Nicely appointed, but unsexy and thoroughly uninvolving, "The Wisdom of Crocodiles" is a real crock.

NEWSDAY, 7/14/00, Part II/p. B6, Jan Stuart

"This is the story of a man's impossible dream," says the director in the press material for "The Wisdom of Crocodiles." "In this case, the dream of the perfect love of a perfect woman."

"[It's] about human beings and our need to understand things," says the writer. "It's about reason versus emotion."

"The film is about how people manipulate each other in relationships," says the star.

Give a movie a highfalutin title, and you'll get all sorts of highfalutin rationales for it.

Let's be real. "The Wisdom of Crocodiles" is a vampire movie. Period. Well, perhaps a little bit more than "period." It's an unusually literate and stylishly mounted vampire movie, with an international cast that demands to be taken very seriously. There are no dreaded mirrors, crucifixes or beads of garlic. But to be very bottom line about it, the hero sucks blood from women's necks. Reason vs. emotion, harumph. This is tooth vs. trachea.

In no way should this diminish the genuine air of mystery and foreboding that surrounds Jude Law, who plays a medical researcher with a very hidden agenda and a gleefully intimidating surname. As playboy Steven Grslcz, Law maintains a separate phone number that he shares exclusively with women he intends to seduce. Invariably, the women take the bait, and just as invariably, they wind up being pulled down from smashed cars wedged between tree trunks or hauled up from the bottom of the ocean in fishing trawls.

Steven's veiled activities result in a guarded but genial alliance with an investigating police inspector (the captivatingly chinless Timothy Spall, whom execs at HBO should be snatching up for a filmed bio of Alfred Hitchcock) and in a romance with a structural engineer named, Dickensian-style, Anne Levels. As played by the beautiful and irritating Elina Lowensohn, Anne is beautiful and irritating.

Paul Hoffman's screenplay piles up more questions than it has answers for. (Why does Steven arch his back and hands like a vulture? Why the graphic scene in which Anne rescues a colleague in an on-the-job accident? How did that car get up that tree?) On the other hand, the more explicit it is, the less interesting it becomes. Consequently, the last third of the film loses momentum as Steven's conundrum sees the light of day.

Directed with an eye for atmosphere by Po Chih Leong, "The Wisdom of Crocodiles" benefits from handsome production design (Andy Harris) and photography (Oliver Curtis). Then there is a muted Jude Law, recently the ebullient Dickie Greenleaf in "The Talented Mr. Ripley." British actors have a way with two-faced cads who can't control their homicidal impulses, but in contrast to Christian Bale's Patrick Bateman in "American Psycho," Law's Steven extracts a considerable level of sympathy and concern. Much of this is due to the sybaritic charisma of Law, whose rakish charm and intense, Heathcliff eyebrows lend themselves to wild-natured sensualists with haunted souls.

SIGHT AND SOUND, 1/99, p. 61, Liese Spencer

The body of a woman is found after a car crash. She is the ex-girlfriend of vampire Steven Grlscz. Later, Grlscz sees a woman, Maria Vaughan, about to throw herself under a train on the underground. He saves her and over the following weeks sets about seducing her. When he is convinced she has fallen in love with him, Grlscz takes her to bed and bites her neck killing her. Grlscz drives to the sea and dumps her body.

When Maria's body is discovered, Grlscz goes to the police, pretending to help with their investigation. His helpfulness and lack of motive persuade Inspector Healey of his innocence, but hot-headed Sergeant Roche remains suspicious. As the police continue their inquiries, Grlscz meets structural engineer Anne Levels. They begin seeing each other, but Anne remains cautious about their relationship.

When Inspector Healey is mugged by a gang of thugs, Grlscz saves him and they strike up a friendship. Grlscz has an argument with Anne and doesn't see her for days. After phoning his apartment, Anne eventually visits Grlscz to find that he is sick. He tells Anne that he is a vampire and can only survive by drinking the blood of women who love him. He believes that if he can find the perfect love he will be cured. Anne nurses Grlscz, but as he gets weaker he tries to kill her. She escapes and Grlscz dies.

As Channel 4's recent vampire series *Ultraviolet* proved, updating ancient horror myths is a tricky business. At its best the process lends a new resonance and ironic humour to old stories (think of Kathryn Bigelow's *Near Dark* or John Landis' *An American Werewolf in London)*. At its worst, modernisation can mean the suggestive power of metaphysical fantasy is replaced by bathos.

The Wisdom of Crocodiles falls into this second category. Nominally set in London, the film's bland locations make up an anonymous cityscape. If this is supposed to lend a universal 'timelessness' to events, then the designers fail immediately, by giving both Steven and Anne excruciatingly fashionable apartments (of the kind that only very rich or very unreal Londoners seem to possess). Moving between these over-dressed sets, minimalist restaurants and concrete car parks, the film lacks atmosphere and looks resolutely artificial.

Thanks to a lamentable script and flat direction from Po Chih Leong (hitherto Hong Kong based, but also director of the British-set *Ping Pong)*, Jude Law's vampire remains equally implausible. Whether cataloguing his victims in a series of beautifully bound scrapbooks or placing phials of their crystallised emotions (yes, it's that literal) into what look like tiny cutlery trays, Steven just isn't sinister. Supernaturally polite and well spoken, Law's charming predator should be chilling, but fails to convince either as man or monster.

Which is a shame since Law, with his perfect features, has just the right Dorian Gray beauty to suggest inner corruption. Elina Löwensohn struggles equally hard to breathe life into her structural engineer, while Timothy Spall mugs from beneath a pair of beetling eyebrows as the plodding policeman turned father confessor. He even engages Steven in ponderous conversations about good and evil while wandering, with heavy symbolism, through a cemetery.

Entirely lacking in suspense, the film drags from one contrived scene to another, Paul Hoffman's script swinging between the pretentious ("the line that cuts through good and evil cuts through every human heart") and the downright banal. ("There's one problem about the way I am," Steven tells Anne. "It doesn't work.") And it's no surprise to find that the plot's clumsy contingencies (when Steven is made to go for a police line-up he's suddenly endowed with the power to mesmerise the witness) come crashing down at the movie's climax when Steven, after letting Anne nurse him for several days, suddenly jumps up and begins chasing her around his apartment. Hammer's cod-Victoriana may have been overenamoured with lace cuffs, capes and crucifixes, but at least their stories bothered to make sense and provided a few cheap thrills along the way. *The Wisdom of Crocodiles* is far too silly and self-important for either.

VILLAGE VOICE, 7/18/00, p. 117 J. Hoberman

The week's worst love is that purveyed by silky bloodsucker Jude Law in the British vampire-cum-serial killer thriller *The Wisdom of Crocodiles*. His name a string of consonants, Law's character calls himself a species of one. The normal Dracula regulations no longer apply. Law ventures boldly by day and fondles a crucifix. He's an artist who can draw simultaneously with both hands, cloud men's minds and find pretty victims virtually all at will.

As directed by the veteran Hong Kong all-rounder Po Chih Leong on a more modest scale than his historical epics, *The Wisdom of Crocodiles* is inoffensively glib and innocuously arty. It's set in a posh chrome-and-glass London where the cops interrogate suspects in what looks like the Tate, the street gangs come regulation multiculti, and everyone has a good haircut—even Timothy Spall, as the Catholic police inspector with whom Law enjoys toying. Spall can't hope to compete, although Law does meet his match in *Nadja* star Elina Lowensohn, a structural engineer with a ready store of Chinese proverbs and the capacity to perform instant surgery with a pocketknife.

Lowensohn's brooding, delicately sculpted features—her lips aren't curvy so much as italicized—give her one of the most eloquent faces in the movies. Her mysterious Central European accent insures that, so long as there are vampire flicks, she'll never lack roles. (if Hammer Studios still existed she'd be the new Barbara Steele.) The cast also includes an actor named Hitler Wong. The story behind that moniker might be weirder than the movie.

Also reviewed in:
NEW YORK TIMES, 7/14/00, p. E10, Elvis Mitchell
VARIETY, 11/30-12/6/98, p. 65, Derek Elley

WOLVES OF KROMER, THE

A First Run Features release of a Discodog Productions presentation.   *Producer:* Charles Lambert.   *Director:* Will Gould.   *Screenplay:* Charles Lambert and Matthew Read.   *Director of Photography:* Laura Remacha.   *Editor:* Carol Salter.   *Music:* Basil Moore-Asfouri.   *Sound:* Peter Hodges.   *Casting:* Teresa Green and Matthew Read.   *Production Designer:* Mark Larkin.   *Costumes:* Shanti Freed.   *Make-up:* Caroline Rose.   *Running time:* 82 minutes.   *MPAA Rating:* Not Rated.

CAST: Rita Davies (Fanny);   Matthew Dean (Kester);   Rosemarie Dunham (Mrs. Drax);   Boy George (Narrator);   James Layton (Gabriel);   Leila Lloyd-Evelyn (Polly);   Kevin Moore (Priest);   Mr. Powell (Lord Biffen);   David Prescott (Mark);   Angharad Rees (Mary);   Margaret Towner (Doreen);   Lee Williams (Seth).

VILLAGE VOICE, 11/21/00, p. 148, Jessica Winter

Largely inept and weirdly endearing, *The Wolves of Kromer* ponders the fate of two pouty, woods-dwelling young dudes banished from their provincial English village due to their pointy ears, hairy aspect (indicated by furry coats dug up from some velvet goldmine), swishing tails, and puppy love for each other. Replete with cackling witchy hags and a murderous closeted man of the cloth, the film is a fairy tale in every sense of the term; it's barely coherent, but as a goofy allegory, it at least boasts the courage of its convictions.

Also reviewed in:
NEW YORK TIMES, 11/17/00, p. E22, Stephen Holden
VARIETY, 7/13-19/98, p. 57, Dennis Harvey

WOMAN CHASER, THE

A Screening Room release of a Definitive Films production in association with Tarmac Films. *Executive Producer:* Joe McSpadden. *Producer:* Soly Haim.   *Director:* Robinson Devor. *Screenplay*: Robinson Devor.   *Based on the novel by*: Charles Willeford.   *Director of*

Photography: Kramer Morgenthau. *Editor:* Mark Winitsky. *Music:* Daniel Luppi. *Sound:* Lee Archer and Leonel Pedraza. *Casting:* Rosemary Welden. *Production Designer:* Sandrine Junod. *Art Director:* Michael Volker. *Set Decorator:* Charisse Anssar, Kim Haas, Jason Knight, Beth Wooke, and Chris Young. *Costumes:* Fern Rose Mitchell. *Make-up:* Michelle Marshall. *Running time:* 96 minutes. *MPAA Rating:* Not Rated.

CAST: Patrick Warburton (Richard Hudson); Emily Newman (Laura); Eugene Roche (Used Car Dealer); Lynette Bennett (Mother); Joe Durrenberger (Chet Wilson); Ron Morgan (Bill); Pat Crowder (Salvation Army Lady); Mel Hampton (Flaps Hartwell); Marilyn Rising (Becky); Paul Malevich (Leo Steinberg); Ernie Vincent (The Man); Laura Witty (Mrs. Shantz); J. Keith van Straaten (Dickie J. Hewlett); Delaina Mitchell (The Man's Secretary); Josh Hammond (Young Richard); Leslie Lauten (Bathing Cap Girl); Barry Sigismondi (Pool Attendant); John Maynard (Moderator); Ezra Buzzington (Piano Player); Larry DeLassus (Waiter at Bar); Danny Allen (Good Samaritan); Charles Deering (Highway Cop); Tom Morris (Arresting Officer); Thien Nguyen (Chinese Waiter); Estelle Cohen (Office Secretary); Laicie Manrelle (Little Girl in Field); Christopher Young (Motel Night Clerk); Max Kerstein (Ruggerio); Lane Siller (Richard's Assistant); Deborah Johnson (Car Customer); Kim Haas (Girl by Pool); Gabriel Kavaloski, Catfish Bates, and Robert Hagearty (Customers); Fausto Graujeda (Pool Life Guard); John Eng (Bus Boy); Nick Sakoyannis and Paul Jewett (Orderlies).

LOS ANGELES TIMES, 7/21/00, Calendar/p. 12, Kevin Thomas

"The Woman Chaser" is a minor diversion enlivened by some hilarious moments that above all serves as a potent big-screen calling card for Patrick Warburton, best known as Puddy from TV's "Seinfeld."

In "The Woman Chaser," which director Robinson Devor adapted from a 1960 pulp novel written by "Miami Blue's" Charles Willeford, Warburton is a burly, hairy-chested guy who looks like an ex-football player and sounds like a Phi Beta Kappa.

When we first see him, seated in a dark L.A. cocktail lounge, the film's noir style suggests that he's a private eye about to relate to us a crime caper in which he became involved. A Salvation Army lady (Pat Crowder) comes by his table with her tambourine in hand; eventually, we learn that by the time his donation adds up to $150, this woman, old enough to be his mother, has agreed to go to bed with him.

Warburton's Richard Hudson is in fact fixated on his own mother (Lynette Bennett), a former ballerina who works out every day and dedicates her life to preserving her youth. After a San Francisco sojourn, Richard has headed home to L.A., where he swiftly buys a used-car lot. He settles in the servant's quarters of the stately home his mother shares with his stepfather Leo (Paul Malevich), a Hollywood producer on the skids.

Mother and son are so delighted to be reunited that Richard joins her in an impromptu pas de deux in her studio that is all the funnier because this massive man is so amazingly light on his feet. Leo in turn is pleased to have a moviegoing companion in Richard—they're seen under the Orpheum marquee, which proclaims "Hercules Unchained" and "Coming Soon: 'The Alamo.'"

All this moviegoing inspires Richard to want to write and direct his own movie, about a man driving a truck from San Francisco to L.A. who becomes a hit-and-run driver when he strikes a little girl. Hudson calls it "The Man Who Got Away." Can this incident actually have happened to Richard...?

At this point "The Woman Chaser" switches into high gear, and Richard comes into full flower as a raging sociopath, a man who has no feeling for the women he easily seduces.

Richard is a spoiled, ruthless little boy in a man's body. Humorless and square, he is very bright and articulate but has a dangerously childlike innocence. Warburton easily traverses the full range of Richard's quick-changing moods, never missing an opportunity to reveal what's funny and what's cruel about him—often simultaneously. He's a monster whose fate rightly evokes irony rather than pity.

Devor has made the most of what surely must have been a modest budget. In addition to Warburton he draws vivid portrayals from, among others, Malevich, whose Leo proves full of surprises; from Max Kerstein, as a veteran film editor who tries valiantly to get Richard in touch with reality; and from Ron Morgan as Richard's nerdy manager of his used-car business.

Resourceful cameraman Kramer Morgenthau, who worked miracles on "The Big Brass Ring," and meticulous production designer Sandrine Junod evoke 1960 L.A. faultlessly. Daniel Luppi's score helps establish the era as well as the mood.

For all of Warburton's prowess and Devor's energy and zeal, "The Woman Chaser" lacks the slam-bang style and authority of Samuel Fuller's "Shock Corridor" and "The Naked Kiss," two films that "The Woman Chaser" brings immediately to mind. "The Woman Chaser" is very much a first film, but a venturesome start for Devor as well as a splendid launch for Warburton.

NEW YORK POST, 6/14/00, p. 56, Jonathan Foreman

"The Woman Chaser" is a combination of two tiresome indie clichés: It's a film noir spoof, replete with hard-boiled narration, lounge-music soundtrack and dramatic black-and-white photography; and it's one of those films that keeps telling you it's just a film—the narrator stops the action and talks to the audience about the importance of identifying with his protagonist.

Writer-director Robinson Devor clearly knows how to "deconstruct" a narrative; whether he can actually tell a story or if he has anything to say remains rather less clear.

The movie is based on a 1960 book by Charles Willeford, who also wrote "Miami Blues" which was more successfully made into a film in 1990 starring Alec Baldwin and Jennifer Jason Leigh.

Patrick Warburton (Elaine's boyfriend, Puddy, in TV's "Seinfeld") plays Richard Hudson, a tough used car salesman with a talent for seduction and a tendency to justify all his bad behavior, from sexually mistreating his stepsister, to impregnating his secretary.

Bored with his existence and convinced that there must be more to life than making money, he decides one day that creating a work of art would give his own life some meaning.

So he writes a bleak screenplay about a truck driver who accidentally kills a little girl, persuades his washed up film-director stepfather to produce it and gets a studio to underwrite it.

Although there are chuckles here and there, some of the jokes, like Hudson's semi-incestuous relationship with his ex-ballerina mother (Lynette Bennett) are merely grotesque.

But what really makes "Woman Chaser" hard going is the flatness of the acting—with the primary exception of Warburton, who (with his odd resemblance to Rock Hudson) is perfectly cast as an articulate brute and has a real knack for comically deadpan delivery.

Also reviewed in:
NEW YORK TIMES, 6/14/00, p. E6, Stephen Holden
VARIETY, 10/18-24/99, p. 39, Godfrey Cheshire

WOMAN ON TOP

A Fox Searchlight Pictures release of an Alan Poul production. *Executive Producer:* Bronwen Hughes and Fina Torres. *Producer:* Alan Poul. *Director:* Fina Torres. *Screenplay:* Vera Blasi. *Director of Photography:* Thierry Arbogast. *Editor:* Leslie Jones. *Music:* Luis Bacalov. *Music Editor:* Sharon Heather Smith. *Sound:* Jorge Saldanha and (music) Luciano Torani. *Sound Editor:* Andrew De Cristofaro. *Casting:* Alexa L. Fogel, Laura Folger, and Ruy Brito. *Production Designer:* Philippe Chiffre. *Art Director:* Alexandre Meyer. *Set Designer:* Chad Owens. *Set Decorator:* Craig T. Copher. *Costumes:* Elisabeth Tavernier. *Make-up:* Maria Lucia Mattos. *Stunt Coordinator:* Jeff Scott Flores. *Running time:* 85 minutes. *MPAA Rating:* R.

CAST: Penélope Cruz (Isabella Oliveira); Murilo Benício (Toninho Oliveira); Harold Perrineau, Jr. (Monica Jones); Mark Feuerstein (Cliff Lloyd); John De Lancie (Alex Reeves); Anne Ramsay (TV Director); Ana Gasteyer (Claudia Hunter); Analu De Castro (Little Isabella, age 2); Thais De Sá Curvelo (Little Isabella, age 5); Eliana Guttman (Isabella's Mother); Eduardo Mattedi (Isabella's Father); Ana Paula Oliveira (Cook); Marilice Santos (Sexy

Neighbor);   Giba Conceiçao, Joaquim Pinto, and Vevé Calazans (Troubadours);   June A. Lomena (Zeke);   Bob Greene (Nikos);   Lázaro Ramos (Max);   Wagner Moura (Rafi);   Cléa Simoes (Serafina);   Tom Curti (Maitre'D);   John Crook (Seafood Restaurant Manager);   Jonas Bloch (Pierre Laroche);   Michel Bercovitch (Academy Student);   Carlos Gregório (Melvin); Malu Pessin (Esther);   Daniele Suzuki (Yoko);   Luis Careca (Thor);   Jerry Penacoli (Tom Kelly);   Inaldo Santana (Angry Fisherman);   Jorge Maia (Yemanja Waiter);   Dizoneth Santos (Prison Guard);   Roberta Kennedy (Bar Waitress);   Jeff Scott Flores (Bar Regular);   Roger Stoneburner (Bartender);   Gordon Hansen (Bar Regular);   B. Chico Purdiman and Bob Saenz (Guards);   Thomas Hieatt (Hippie Prisoner);   David Herman (Photographer);   Edlon Tupi (Jail Guard);   Otávio Martins (P.A.);   Inés Cardoso (Food Stylist); Alan Poul and Jim Freeman (The "Suits");   Adele Proom (Niko's Mother).

LOS ANGELES TIMES, 9/22/00, Calendar/p. 6, Kenneth Turan

"Woman on Top" is tedious as only a film with a truly beautiful star can be. If Penelope Cruz were any less attractive, maybe someone would have noticed how dull this mild, would-be romantic fairy tale has turned out. Then again, without someone like Cruz, this lightweight production would never have been made.

A top Spanish performer—and a much better actress than you'd ever imagine from what's on view here—Cruz is cast as a Brazilian charmer with "a gift for melting the palates and the hearts of men." That bit of fakery is fine because everything else about this production is ersatz, from its sanitized San Francisco to a blanded-out, white-bread version of Brazilian culture that is about as authentic as Taco Bell.

Director Fina Torres (whose last work was the much more imaginative and involving "Celestial Clockwork") has settled here for a picture postcard kind of film , a giant infomercial for Brazil and its exotic charms. But beautiful people, colorful photography (by Luc Besson veteran Thierry Arbogast) and a cheerful soundtrack do not necessarily add up to a satisfying experience.

The only actual Brazilian (aside from co-star Murilo Benicio) among "Woman on Top's" top personnel is screenwriter Vera Blasi. Though this is her first script, it feels awfully familiar, a harmless throwback to those naughty art-house items that were staples of American foreign film watching in the 1950s and '60s.

Cruz plays Isabella Oliveira, a woman from Bahia in northeastern Brazil. Even as a child she was so beautiful that the gods gave her a flaw: a terrible case of motion sickness. Isabella can control her nausea only if she's in charge of the motion: She has to drive the car, lead on the dance floor and, yes, be on top when she makes love.

Isabella does have a true love, her husband Toninho (Benicio). Together they run a super-popular restaurant (in addition to everything else, Isabella is a world-class chef), but he keeps her hidden away in the kitchen while he takes all the credit and flirts with the customers. Finally, tired of never being on top, he does more than flirt with one attractive woman and a scandalized Isabella flees Bahia for San Francisco.

Why San Francisco? Because it's the current home of Monica (Harold Perrineau Jr., memorable in the Leonardo DiCaprio-starring "Romeo + Juliet"). Monica is alternately described in the press notes as "a high-spirited transvestite" and an "exuberant, cross-dressing childhood friend," but is really the latest incarnation of the increasingly cliched, shoulder-to-cry-on gay best friend fewer and fewer heroines seem able to face life without.

Determined to break free of her husband, Isabella calls on Iemanja, the goddess of the sea, to help her fall out of love. Suddenly liberated, Isabella finds her cooking get so irresistible that guys follow her around San Francisco like they were auditioning as extras for "Night of the Living Dead."

Among the ambulatory zombies is go-getting local TV producer Cliff Lloyd (Mark Feuerstein), who contrives to put Isabella on TV with her very own cooking show. With her tag line of "the most important ingredient is 'share it with someone you love,'" she becomes the stuff of local legend. "That much butter would kill a guy," one intoxicated viewer says, while his pal adds "that much woman would kill a guy." Yes, it's that kind of movie.

Husband Toninho falls to cursing the very same goddess Isabella is praying to. Not a wise idea. Nothing if not chastened, he too heads off to San Francisco to try to get his wife back, bringing with him, besides the two-day growth of beard that is standard issue for hunks in films like this, a three-piece Brazilian band whose smooth music is one of "Woman on Top's" few unalloyed pleasures.

More than Toninho, this entire film is in love with Isabella, and with Cruz. It's an old-fashioned star vehicle, the kind that might have featured Brazilian actress Sonia Braga in years gone by, and it's frustrating to see it squandering Cruz's sensuality and her acting ability (more visible in the English-language "The Hi-Lo Country" and the Spanish "All About My Mother," "Belle Epoque" and "Open Your Eyes").

Finally, "Woman on Top" can't overcome a story that's little more than a lumpy, uninspired contrivance. Caring about whether this couple ends up together is like caring whether the people pictured on glossy travel brochures are actually enjoying their vacations. Why bother?

NEW YORK POST, 9/22/00, p. 51, Jonathan Foreman

Besides establishing the beautiful Spanish actress Penelope Cruz as a star, "Woman on Top" should do no small service to the Brazilian tourist industry. For while most of the action in "Woman on Top" takes place in San Francisco, its views of the Bahia beach front and its (slightly stereotypical) depiction of Brazilians as gorgeous sensualists are enticing enough to make you want to jump on the next plane to Rio.

Prime date fare, but cotton-candy light and occasionally just a little too whimsical, "Woman on Top" is a lot less substantial, but no less enjoyable than the original food, sex and "magic realism" hit of 1992, "Like Water for Chocolate" (and vastly superior to the similar Sarah Michelle Gellar stinker, "Simply Irresistible").

Isabella (Cruz) works in the kitchen of her husband Toninho's beach-front restaurant. She is cursed with motion sickness that makes her nauseous in cars, buses and even when having sex—unless she's on top.

But the local goddess of the sea has compensated her with culinary abilities that verge on the magical. Unfortunately, that's not enough to prevent her handsome but macho husband, Toninho (Murilo Benicio), from cheating on her with a woman who can handle the missionary position.

Heartbroken by his betrayal, Isabelle flees to San Francisco and the apartment of her cross-dressing childhood friend, Monica (Harold Perrineau Jr.). There she gets a job teaching at a cooking school and persuades a local voodoo priestess to "cure" her of her love for the treacherous Toninho.

The sea goddess grants Isabelle her wish, and soon her beauty and her amazing cooking cause thousands of men to fall under her spell, including TV executive Cliff (Mark Feurstein). He gives her her own live cooking show, which very quickly becomes a huge prime-time hit.

Then Toninho turns up in San Francisco and tries to win her back with the help of some Brazilian musicians.

Cruz, so good in "All About My Mother" and even "Twice Upon a Yesterday," doesn't have to do much here but look ravishing. Perrineau (HBO's "Oz," "Romeo + Juliet" "The Edge") a terrific actor who has never received the acclaim he deserves, is a delight as the transsexual Monica.

NEWSDAY, 9/22/00, Part II/p. B7, John Anderson

That men follow Spanish starlet Penelope Cruz down the street like kids after an ice-cream truck is hardly the most fantastical aspect of "Woman on Top." Every so often, Cruz looks like the most beautiful woman in the world. Once in a while, she looks like Daisy Duck. Either way, she's fascinating.

So, in its way, is "Woman on Top," a frothy confection conjured by the Venezuelan director Fina Torres, who showed similar magic—realist proclivities in "Celestial Clockwork" (1994) and manages to keep this latest souffle from falling via candy colors, a merry-go-round of plot and Brazilian music percolating around unlikely events and improbable people. Down the middle of it all strides its leggy star, a mix of Judy Holliday and Sophia Loren garnished with a soupçon of Maria Conchita Alonso.

To say that Brazilian screenwriter Vera Blasi's tale—of "love, motion sickness and the art of cooking"—is contrived would be to miss the point: The movie uses contrivances to enable other contrivances. Isabella (Cruz) is a gifted Bahian chef who has fallen victim to two weird strokes of weird bad luck: One, she was born with a ferocious form of motion sickness (any motion, anywhere). Then, she falls in love with Toninho (Murilo Benicio), whom we know is a heel from the first time we see him. Since Isabella can only control her sickness by controlling her motion, and Toninho is a macho, macho man, this causes consternation in the boudoir, from which the horizontally challenged Toninho occasionally steps out to sleep with the neighbors.

So Isabella steps out, too—to San Francisco, looking up her transvestite girlfriend Monica, played by the comical Harold Perrineau Jr. in what seems an homage to Whoopi Goldberg, only funny. In a tortured chain of events, Isabella comes to the attention of a local TV show that decides she's just right to host "Passion Food," which garners huge ratings, and not because of the recipes.

Cruz is properly spicy, Perrineau is positively piquant, but the others in the cast—namely Mark Feuerstein as the TV producer who falls for Isabella and Benicio as the frustrated-cum-penitent husband—are so uninteresting or unlikable as to nullify the movie's other charms. In other words, there's no tension in the triangle—you want both suitors to abandon the movie to Cruz and Perrineau as soon as possible. The plot, as it were, progresses via illogical decisions on the part of its characters and a rather hackneyed sequence on which network execs want to corrupt Isabella's TV show. It's too bad, because Torres has so little regard for the normal constraints of cinematic storytelling that her movie attains a rarified air of fantasy that may not be wholly uncalculated, but with Cruz at its center is certainly watchable.

SIGHT AND SOUND, 2/01, p. 57, Katy Wilkinson

Bahia, Brazil, the present. Isabella and her husband Toninho run a restaurant on the coast. Yemanja, Goddess of the Sea, has blessed Isabella with exceptional culinary skills to compensate for her one flaw: severe motion sickness. Fed up with Isabella's need to be on top during their love-making, Toninho has sex with another woman. Isabella finds out about her husband's infidelity and moves to San Francisco to live with her friend Monica, a transvestite. Toninho curses Yemanja, causing the fish in the sea to disappear.

Unable to find a job as a chef, Isabella takes a teaching position at a cookery school. After making an offering to Yemanja, begging to be freed from her love for Toninho, Isabella regains her confidence. Discovering her whereabouts, Toninho closes his floundering restaurant and travels to San Francisco to win her back. Impressed by her cooking and beauty, Cliff, a television producer, launches Isabella in a live cookery show which becomes a hit. Toninho sneaks on set and serenades her on air, boosting the show's ratings. She rebuffs him and has dinner with Cliff. Disillusioned by changes to the show and convinced no one can match Toninho's embrace, Isabella asks Yemanja to remove the spell. Their love rekindled, Isabella and Toninho return to Brazil.

Venezuelan-born director Fina Torres' previous features, *Oriana* (1985), for which she won the Camera d'or at Cannes, and *Mécaniques célestes* (1995), were about women who left their homes to strike out on their own elsewhere. *Woman on Top* follows a similar narrative template: restaurant chef Isabella refuses to tolerate her husband's infidelity and leaves her Brazilian home for San Francisco to start afresh. But while this premise holds out the promise of a tale of feminist empowerment, Torres' literal understanding of the title reveals her superficial approach to the material: here, *Woman on Top* refers to Isabella's preferred position during love-making and links her need to take control almost exclusively to her sexuality.

Torres and debut screenwriter Vera Blasi try hard to convince us just how magnetic Isabella is—but you can't help thinking they're over-egging the pudding: intoxicating CGI aromas waft from her kitchen, enticing men like bees to honey; when she walks down the street a growing crowd of men follow her, entranced; flowers stand to attention and bloom in her presence. The fact that the other characters are so insipidly drawn doesn't help: her husband Toninho is a clichéd embodiment of the passionate Latin lover (he takes the credit for the success of the restaurant while Isabella does all the work; she puts his appeal down to his "irresistible embrace"). Cliff, the television producer who devises a cookery show for her to host, is kind but can't match Toninho's machismo; despite his initial attraction to Isabella, he ends up with Monica, Isabella's best friend, an ebullient, extravagant transvestite and endless source of advice.

Torres makes a sly dig at the marketing men who urge Isabella to look "less ethnic" while recording a pilot of her cookery show for network television. But the critique feels half-hearted.

Despite Cliff's breathy proclamation that "Isabella is Brazil and Brazil is Isabella", the producers have plumped for the bankable Penélope Cruz, who's actually Spanish, to play the role. *Woman on Top*'s evocation of Brazilian culture also feels touristic. The film makes a link between gastronomic and sexual passion, hip-swivelling bossa nova music features heavily on the soundtrack, and there are even references to a local deity, Yemanja, Goddess of the Sea.

This said, cinematographer Thierry Arbogast *(Black Cat White Cat)* gives the sequences in which Isabella and Toninho make offerings to Yemanja a genuine mystical feel, applying the seemingly effortless magical-realist touch to which the rest of the film aspires in vain. And while *Woman on Top* might not be memorable viewing, its star Cruz has already made an impression on some; she's currently filming *Vanilla Sky*, a remake of Alejandro Amenábar's *Open Your Eyes* with another, more famous, Cruise, called Tom.

VILLAGE VOICE, 9/26/00, p. 147, Jessica Winter

Like many of its shaggy-dog brethren, *Woman on Top* is outsize, dumb, and eager to please. Ambling from Brazil to San Francisco in pursuit of a sylph-like chef named Isabella (Penélope Cruz), the film brandishes a gaudy primary-color palette, broad-comic staging, and a bathtub-tchotchke rendering of Candomblé (a northeastern cousin to Santeria). Director Fina Torres keeps your eye busy, but gorgeous, color-drained beachside vistas aside, you feel trapped in a theme cantina. Isabella, married to puppy-eyed beef-cake slab Toninho (Murilo Benicio), gets motion sickness at the slightest provocation, and Toninho's macho demeanor suffers for Isabella's coping mechanisms—which include always taking the top when they back that azz up. When she catches him making like a missionary with another woman, Isabella saunters off to the States, where she quickly nabs her own local cooking show (the set design of which roughly matches *Woman on Top*'s own) and pines for Toninho all the while. The film is too flimsily built and baldly unfunny to bolster Cruz's charms, but Almodóvar's blessed Virgin is, as usual, winning and guilelessly seductive.

Also reviewed in:
CHICAGO TRIBUNE, 9/22/00, Friday/p. A, Mark Caro
NEW YORK TIMES, 9/22/00, p. E14, Elvis Mitchell
VARIETY, 5/29-6/4/00, p. 23, Lisa Nesselson
WASHINGTON POST, 9/22/00, p. C12, Rita Kempley
WASHINGTON POST, 9/22/00, Weekend/p. 47, Desson Howe

WONDER BOYS

A Paramount Pictures and Mutual Film Company release of a Scott Rudin/Curtis Hanson production. *Executive Producer:* Adam Schroeder and Ned Dowd. *Producer:* Scott Rudin and Curtis Hansom. *Director:* Curtis Hanson. *Screenplay:* Steve Kloves. *Based on the novel by:* Michael Chabon. *Director of Photography:* Dante Spinotti. *Editor:* Dede Allen. *Music:* Christopher Young. *Music Editor:* Thomas Milano. *Sound:* Kirk Francis and (music) Robert Fernandez and Paul Wertheimer. *Sound Editor:* Dennis Drummond and David Giammarco. *Casting:* Mali Finn. *Production Designer:* Jeannine Oppewall *Art Director:* Don Woodruff. *Set Decorator:* Jay R. Hart. *Special Effects:* John D. Milinac. *Costumes:* Beatrix Aruna Pasztor. *Make-up:* Michal Bigger. *Stunt Coordinator:* Jeff Imada. *Running time:* 112 minutes. *MPAA Rating:* R.

CAST: Michael Douglas (Grady Tripp); Tobey Maguire (James Leer); Frances McDormand (Sara Gaskell); Robert Downey, Jr. (Terry Crabtree); Katie Holmes (Hannah Green); Rip Torn (Q); Richard Knox (Vernon Hardapple); Jane Adams (Oola); Michael Cavadias (Miss Sloviak/Tony); Richard Thomas (Walter Gaskell); Alan Tudyk (Traxler); Phillip Bosco (Emily's Father); George Grizzard (Fred Leer); Kelly Bishop (Amanda Leer); Bill Velin

(Officer Pupcik);   Charis Michelsen (Carrie);   Yusuf Gatewood (Howard);   June Hildreth (Emily's Mother);   Elisabeth Granli (Emily, Photo);   Richard Hidlebird (Hi-Hat Bouncer).

CHRISTIAN SCIENCE MONITOR, 2/25/00, p. 15, David Sterritt

Two noted directors are trying different strategies in their latest bids for attention.

Curtis Hanson, best known for the sprawling crime saga "L.A. Confidential," moves to territory that's less violent—if still pretty unsavory—in "Wonder Boys," with Superstar Michael Douglas as a professor and rising star Tobey Maguire as a troubled but talented student.

John Frankenheimer, whose hits range from "Seconds" to "The Manchurian Candidate," sticks with tried-and-true thriller material in "Reindeer Games," featuring Ben Affleck as an ex-con and Charlize Theron as his girlfriend.

The title characters of "Wonder Boys" are writers at opposite ends of their careers. Douglas plays Grady, who's been coasting on the success of his first novel, earning his living as a professor while he inches along with a follow-up book. Maguire plays James, a moody twentysomething whose novelistic fantasies are matched by the lies he spins about his real-life background.

The movie brings the two together during Wordfest, an annual literary event at their university. Since few real professors would remain glued to such an irritating protégé for an entire weekend, Steven Kloves's screenplay (based on Michael Chabon's novel) supplies a few strained reasons for their relationship, including their shared interest in a flamboyant book editor (Robert Downey Jr.) and a darkly comic situation involving an unfriendly dog.

Others include a visiting writer whose ego matches his success (Rip Torn) and a college official (Frances McDormand) who's having an affair with Grady.

They're a colorful group, as campus characters go. Still, director Hanson never quite convinces us that their oddly lackadaisical antics are worth watching for almost two hours. Douglas's performance marks a welcome change from the super-charged emotions of pictures like "Basic Instinct," but it's undercut by Maguire's deliberately mannered acting, which seems repetitious from one movie to the next. The film's biggest problem is its lack of psychological logic. Motivations seem dictated by plot necessities rather than human needs, and that's a fatal flaw.

The story of "Reindeer Games" is so implausible that "Wonder Boys" seems downright commonsensical by comparison. Affleck plays a freshly released jailbird determined to go straight until he meets the girlfriend of a former cellmate—and her psychopathic brother, who's engineering a robbery.

All this gets established in the first few scenes, whereupon the movie swoops into plot maneuvers that twist your expectations into two or three pretzels before the closing credits. There are dabs of sugary sentiment, probably added when Miramax anticipated a Christmastime release.

What you're likely to remember is neither the sentiment nor the suspense, but rather the sadistic violence that erupts almost every time Gary Sinise's chief villain walks into a scene.

It's regrettable—and revealing about Hollywood's priorities—that a director of Frankenheimer's stature still has to sustain his career via frenetic shootouts, exploding cars, and grisly deaths. He deserves better material. So does his audience.

LOS ANGELES TIMES, 2/23/00, Calendar/p. 1, Kenneth Turan

Distracted and dissipated dope-smoking man of letters Grady Tripp (Michael Douglas) has known bad days. Yes, he admits as "Wonder Boys" opens, his wife has left him that very morning, "but wives had left me before." Yes, WordFest, the three-day literary event hosted by his university that this flailing novelist and writing professor genially scorns, will start that evening, but Tripp has always survived that as well. So what's the big deal?

What Tripp doesn't know is that the wasted weekend about to begin is going to be the worst (and that covers a lot of territory) he's ever experienced, so chaotic that the cataclysmic death of a dog at its beginning will seem positively benign before things are over. Tripp's precariously balanced life, always a shambles, is about to collapse with a slow-motion vengeance.

Tripp won't be taking this amiably disastrous trip into the dark night of his soul alone. Along for the ride, among others, are his predatory, satyr-like, gay New York editor Terry Crabtree (Robert Downey Jr.); Sara Gaskell (Frances McDormand), his university's married chancellor as well as his mistress; James Leer (Tobey Maguire), a precocious, albeit death-obsessed, student; and Hannah Green (Katie Holmes), an equally gifted though considerably more attractive classmate who rents a room in Tripp's rambling house.

What makes Tripp's journey, and "Wonder Boys" as a whole, the pleasure it is isn't the destination so much as the way it's conveyed and experienced. Fastidiously directed by Curtis Hanson ("L.A. Confidential") and written by Steve Kloves ("The Fabulous Baker Boys") with an eye to preserving the rueful comic sensibility of Michael Chabon's splendid novel, this smart, literate film is especially noticeable for its generosity of spirit, for the sympathetic compassion and warmth it displays toward people who don't always receive it, on screen or off.

Though Chabon's book got exceptional reviews, its picaresque structure and richness of detail kept it from being automatic film material. But producer Scott Rudin believed in the project, and screenwriter Kloves showed why he's so well-regarded in Hollywood despite a slender output (this is his fourth film in 16 years) by expertly paring down the novel. Fans of Chabon's writing will find things missing, from a boa constrictor to character nuances, but what's more significant is Kloves' ability to capture the antic spirit of the proceedings as well as the book's droll sense of humor, which mixes restrained screwball antics with deft verbal repartee.

Hanson not only understands the jokes, he knows how to place them in the context of a handsomely mounted, graceful production that is well-played across the board. Though earlier films like "River Wild" and "L.A. Confidential" may seem miles from this, they share Hanson's thorough-going classicism, his ability to give every on-screen element just the weight it deserves. What was new about "L.A. Confidential" is a quality that has carried over to this film: Hanson's increased confidence, his belief that he can bring off pretty much whatever he chooses.

A film buff before he was a director, Hanson convinced veteran editor Dede Allen to add her gift for narrative flow to "Wonder Boys," and retained his exceptional "L.A. Confidential" cinematographer, Dante Spinotti, who makes the film's Pittsburgh settings gleam like an eccentric urban fantasy land. Hanson also has orchestrated uniformly excellent performances from his cast, from Oscar winners like McDormand, ambivalent and conflicted as a mistress at a moment of truth, to youngsters like "Dawson's Creek's" Holmes, just right as the beauty with kind of a crush on the old man.

The performance that anchors the film and makes everything possible is Douglas' as Tripp, trying to even remember, let alone act on, what being responsible means after a lifetime spent as the boy who wouldn't grow up. Though the film's ad poster brings Elmer Fudd to mind, his Grady Tripp is rather a once-formidable man gone distressingly to seed, a weary Lothario who now stumbles around in a wool cap and his wife's bathrobe like one of the more dissolute elves in Santa's workshop. The been-there Douglas, reviving the off-handed comic moves that made "Romancing the Stone" so successful, has exactly the look and presence to make that characterization believable.

Tripp is especially worried about the upcoming WordFest weekend because of the appearance of editor Crabtree, who, desperate for a success, wants to take a look at the manuscript of an enormous, unwieldy novel Tripp has been working on for the seven years since its highly successful predecessor. The problem is that Tripp, at page 2611 and counting, is the opposite of blocked: He's got Sorcerer's Apprentice Syndrome; he can't stop or even prune the flow of words no matter how much he wants to.

Crabtree, the tempter incarnate (played by Downey with engaging flair), lives up to Tripp's worst fears by getting off the plane from New York with a treetop-tall transvestite and tuba player named Miss Sloviak (newcomer Michael Cavadias). The trio head for a party at the home of the chancellor, who catches a hint of Miss Sloviak's perfume and says with weary resignation, "I wear the same scent as a transvestite."

Outside, Tripp runs into Leer, a novel-writing student his professor views as a tricky combination of rival, protege and unstable surrogate son. Always morose and unhealthily focused on celebrity necrology, Leer (Maguire, in perhaps his best and most controlled performance) is especially morbid this evening, and Tripp thinks he knows just how to distract him.

For the chancellor's husband, a demon Yankee fan and memorabilia collector who sees Joe DiMaggio as an all-inclusive metaphor, keeps the fur-trimmed jacket Marilyn Monroe wore to marry the Yankee Clipper in a bedroom safe. Tripp decides to sneak in and give Leer a glimpse of the holy relic, and that's when, fueled by alcohol, ennui and illicit drugs, things start to seriously unwind for wonder boys past, present and future.

It turns out that one of Leer's most unnerving traits is that he's a compulsive fabulist, apparently unable or unwilling to tell the plain truth, and one of "Wonder Boys'" themes is the exploration of what it means to be a writer, a teller of tales and creator of worlds. It's all part of the heady and sophisticated experience the script characterizes as "one nutty ride," and for once we're glad to have been invited along.

NEW YORK, 3/6/00, p. 57, Peter Rainer

As the novelist and creative-writing professor Grady Tripp in the terrific new comedy *Wonder Boys*, Michael Douglas has a shaggy, scraggly look, as if he'd spent way too many nights fully dressed in a sleeping bag.

Who would believe Douglas could look like a blood brother to Michael J. Pollard?

Grady's dishevelment isn't the affectation of a prima donna scribe. It's just the way he is. He's a rarity in his circumscribed world of bookish academia—a man without vanity. Tenured at a Pittsburgh university, with one award-winning novel behind him and nothing published in the seven years since, Grady has seen his authorial life and his real life blur into a muddle. He has no trouble writing; he has trouble not writing. The voluminous single-spaced pages for his new novel are heaped about his home, with no end in sight. His life, like his manuscript, is an unedited digression. And yet Grady the wayfarer is bemused enough to realize that maybe his life isn't just the raw material for his art but the artwork itself.

I don't think I've ever seen another American comedy that mixed rue and slapstick and sentiment in quite this way. Curtis Hanson, who directed from a delicately rendered script by Steve Kloves based on the 1995 novel by Michael Chabon, is the artist Grady would be if he were able to pare things down and make each detail count. There's a richness of tone, of emotion, in this film; the imbroglio of Grady's life is rendered lucidly and lyrically. The film begins with the revelation that Grady's wife has left him that morning and goes on from there to his sodden, heartfelt attempts to convince his pregnant lover, the university's married chancellor (Frances McDormand), that she was always his first choice. The film's long wintry weekend is improbably magical; it seems to be taking place inside a snow globe that's been shaken up, with the lives of its inhabitants as flurried as the falling flakes.

Wonder Boys is a shaggy-dog story that is also a coming-of-age story. (The soundtrack, with artists like Neil Young and Bob Dylan, gives that shagginess a pedigree.) It doesn't matter that Grady is coming of age at 50—he's a late bloomer. The film's biggest jest is that, when it comes to emotional maturity, age doesn't matter; if anything, the students that we are introduced to are more grounded than the adults. The notion that we understand who we truly are as we get older is a canard that Hanson mirthfully, and mercifully, explodes. The screw-ups in town cut across all age barriers. And yet, as ramshackle and addled as these people are, they are all, without their full awareness, searching for purpose in their lives. The search itself is funny, but the longing that propels it goes very deep.

Grady's most gifted student, James Leer (Tobey Maguire), seems at first to be a prize creepo, but his steady-state stare and odd, pinched comportment provide him with a tactical advantage in the human comedy; he puts everybody else off guard. Maguire gives James the "choked little powder-soft voice" that Chabon described in the novel, and it's a marvelous instrument. James is a junior con man who lies about his past and a lot more, but he's also an original. Unlike Grady, whose celebrated novel made James want to be a writer, he's actually completed the book he's been working on; and according to Grady's editor, Terry Crabtree (Robert Downey Jr.), who shows up with a transvestite consort (Michael Cavadias) in tow to attend the annual campus literary weekend, it's remarkable.

One of the beautiful things about *Wonder Boys* is the way Hanson lets the relationship between Grady and James find its own level; the former phenom takes under his broken wing the imminent one, and there's a wistfulness in the gesture. Grady's exasperated, prideful connection to James mimics the rituals of fatherhood. Grady sees in James the peculiarity he favors in himself, and he plays on it. James starts out not wanting to lose control of his emotions, but Grady, who likes his weed and has periodic blackout spells, shows him, by his own example, another way to live. They have a contrapuntal, moonstruck comradeship.

This film that does so much to heckle the literary life is nevertheless high on the excesses of that life. It's a movie in love with words and the textures of words, and what they might mean for the people who live by them. Hanson captures the preening pretensions of academia, the rivalries between the professors and the populist, best-selling interlopers; he reveals the skid marks on the tenure track. The academics and writers that we see are tweaked by their chosen métier. They know that being in and of the world of books gives them dispensation to be madcap. They become their own best protagonists.

The cast is superb across the board, but at the center of it all is Michael Douglas, who has never seemed as relaxed and generous. His Grady is a counterculture artifact, more holdout than sellout. The marijuana fumes he swathes himself in are like incense; they perfume his disappointments. Grady fears that his books, maybe all books, don't mean anything to anybody anymore, and for all his blurriness, it's a legitimate fear. But he gropes his way to higher ground by the end. He discovers that his writing isn't all that he is, and, of course, he becomes a better writer for it.

NEW YORK POST, 2/23/00, p. 44, Jonathan Foreman

"Wonder Boys" is a clever comedy with a decidedly literary feel that includes several firsts or near-firsts, not the least of which is a successful depiction of Pittsburgh as a remarkably lovely city.

Even more surprising, it shows that Michael Douglas can bring both charm and a deft comic touch to a non-sleazy, non-yuppie role.

It also manages to tell the story of an author without evoking a trace of the annoying Hollywood notion that "creative artists" are such special people that if they behave badly, everyone else should just put up with it.

Perhaps most impressive of all, this adaptation of Michael Chabon's novel, directed by Curtis Hanson ("L.A. Confidential"), paints a clear-eyed picture of a very contemporary baby-boomer phenomenon: the inverted mid-life crisis.

In the old days, men might hit middle age and be seized with a sudden desire to regain the freedom of teenhood.

But, among boomers like this film's central character, Grady Tripp, the mid-life crisis is about hitting 50 or thereabouts and finally being forced to abandon one's marathon adolescence and become a grown-up.

Tripp (Douglas) is an English prof who published a celebrated novel seven years ago. A cult figure on campus, adored by coeds like Katie Holmes' Hannah Green, Tripp is now a self-indulgent pothead who churns out pages of unpublishable rubbish and fears the world will realize he's a has-been.

As the story begins, Tripp's wife leaves him, and his mistress, married university chancellor Sara Gaskell (Frances McDormand), tells him that she's pregnant.

To make matters worse, it's the beginning of the college literary festival, run by Gaskell's husband, (and Tripp's boss) Richard Thomas: an event that brings to campus people like super-successful rival writer Q (Rip Torn) and Tripp's own publisher, Terry Crabtree (Robert Downey Jr.).

Feeling miserable at the opening party, Tripp bonds with one of his students, the shy but talented weirdo James Leer (Tobey Maguire, once again playing an owl-eyed dork).

A soul mate and fan, Leer also turns out to be a thief and a liar, and he soon gets Tripp into trouble involving a dead dog and a jacket that once belonged to Marilyn Monroe.

The main problem with "Wonder Boys" is that while all the characters are likable, several of them are severely underwritten: You never really get a sense of what makes McDormand's chancellor tick, or who Katie Holmes' character is—other than a generic undergrad babe with a crush on her teacher.

As a result, characters sometimes end up doing whimsical things just because they're whimsical—a storytelling tactic that works better on the page than on the big screen.

Still, "Wonder Boys" is the smartest movie to come out this year, and it could hardly be better cast. McDormand ("Fargo") is as much a delight to watch as she's ever been.

And Robert Downey Jr., as the dissolute publisher Crabtree, is so scene-stealingly good it's painful to remember that this magnificently talented actor is once again in prison.

NEWSDAY, 2/23/00, Part II/p. B2, Gene Seymour

The last time one checked on such things, there wasn't a marketing niche for comedies about middle-aged white guys behaving badly. For this reason, if no other, "Wonder Boys" would qualify as the year's boldest movie so far—except that it's too cozy and contained to deserve such a platitude. It seems more like a cult movie in waiting; an oddball character study that now seems out of place in a universe of e-traders and mall rats but will likely find its true audience in a future where misfits, rather than winners, once again become more interesting to moviegoers.

Of course, this is of little or no comfort to those who brought this adaptation of Michael Chabon's 1995 novel to the screen. But they can take pride in having fashioned a sweet little gem about art and life that, in its shape and content, represents a kind of soft-boiled individualism you don't find in the movies anymore. Come to think of it, it's hard to think of anything on the big screen quite like it, past or present.

Or, for that matter, anyone on the big screen quite like Grady Tripp (Michael Douglas), a philandering, 50ish pothead who teaches English at a Pittsburgh college. Tripp is idolized by his creative-writing students, partly because of the novel he'd written as a young man that made him a literary superstar and partly because for all the clutter and drift of his personal life, he's an attentive, compassionate teacher.

About the clutter and drift: Tripp's wife, weary of his lingering adolescence, has left him. The school chancellor (Frances McDormand), who happens to be married to his department chairman (Richard Thomas), is pregnant with his child. And his sybaritic editor, Terry Crabtree (Robert Downey Jr.), arrives on campus with a transvestite in tow and a few questions in his mind, such as, "How's the book coming, Grady?"

Ah, the book. Also known as Tripp's long-awaited second novel that is stuck on page 2,611. Or is it 2,621? It doesn't matter because wherever he is, Tripp is stranded far from the finish line. On the other hand, Tripp's star pupil, James Leer (Tobey Maguire), has a finished manuscript. But he's also so far down in the dumps that he's this close to pointing a loaded pistol to his head before Tripp catches him in the act. James assures him the gun is a cap pistol. Which is the first of his many fibs. Several minutes later, James uses this same pistol to fire two bullets into the chancellor's dog while it's tearing Tripp's leg to shreds.

As a comedy of manners, "Wonder Boys" is neither genteel nor finely wrought. But director Curtis Hanson, in a 180-degree follow-up to "L.A. Confidential," brings rich, yeasty layers of atmosphere to offset the shaggy-dog outrageousness of Chabon's plot, which Steve Kloves, whose previous screenplay credits include "The Fabulous Baker Boys," manages to make cinema-friendly despite hefty odds. The romantic impasse between Douglas' Tripp and McDormand chancellor is shortchanged by the cautionary mentor-student relationship of Tripp's aging hippie and James' callow mope. Still, Maguire enhances his growing reputation as the enigmatic James while Downey's life-of-the-party effervescence is surprisingly tempered.

The biggest, sweetest surprise is Douglas' performance. It's a generous, quietly virtuoso turn. He has so often been cast as a shark that it's hard remember that this was the same guy whose dream was to produce "One Flew Over the Cuckoo's Nest." The seedy aimlessness and puffy charm of Grady Tripp becomes Douglas in ways not even he would have believed possible. It's a look he should cultivate for future experiments.

NEWSWEEK, 2/28/00, p. 66, David Ansen

Grady Tripp (Michael Douglas) is not having a good day. His wife leaves him in the morning. He finds that his lover, Sara (Frances McDormand), is pregnant. She's the chancellor of the Pittsburgh college where Grady teaches creative writing—and she's married to the head of the English department (Richard Thomas). Worse yet, his prize pupil—a strange and rather morbid young man named James Leer (Tobey Maguire)—shoots Sara's blind dog and steals her husband's most prized possession, the actual jacket Marilyn Monroe was wearing when she married Joe DiMaggio. All of which occurs at a party at which Grady's editor from New York, Terry Crabtree (Robert Downey Jr.), arrives with a strikingly tall transvestite (Michael Cavadias) on his arm.

This is the beginning of the misadventures of the former wonder boy Grady Tripp, an acclaimed writer who has not published a word since his first novel seven years earlier. His problem is not writer's block. Indeed, fueled by the pot he smokes from morning through night, Grady is now well past the 2,000th page of his next novel, with the finish line nowhere in sight. His editor wants to see the book. Sara and her husband want to find their dog, not to mention Marilyn's jacket, both of which are in the trunk of a car Grady is driving. A car that happens to be stolen.

Chaos continues to hound the disheveled but well-meaning Grady in "Wonder Boys," the surprising and curiously touching comedy director Curtis Hanson and writer Steve Kloves have made from Michael Chabon's novel. Few things are harder to pull off than picaresque comedy. One false move and you're drowning in whimsy. One contrivance too many and the whole thing can seem forced and arbitrary. In outline, "Wonder Boys" might sound guilty of both sins. But Hanson & Co. root this lunacy in very real emotions and very real settings. How whimsical can "winter in Pittsburgh be?) With a sleight of hand so casual we don't see how the trick is accomplished, Hanson and his cast convince us these people are real, our intimate acquaintances. No one is playing the farce for laughs—and as a result, the laughs come tumbling out on their own. Who knew that Hanson had such an uncanny comic touch? Typecast for many years as a director of thrillers ("Bad Influence," "The Hand That Rocks the Cradle"), Hanson finally made the A list with his terrific neo-noir "L.A. Confidential," which confirmed his status as a topnotch genre director. "Wonder Boys" convinces me he can do anything.

For most people, the biggest surprise will be Michael Douglas. For both those who love him and those who don't, he's become the Yuppie version of The Man You Love to Hate. It hasn't helped his reputation that he's starred in some of the more rancid entertainments of the last two decades, from "Fatal Attraction" and "Basic Instinct" to "Black Rain" and "Falling Down." But remember his fine funny turn in "The War of the Roses"? Douglas is a superb (and underused) comic actor: one who knows that the secret of being funny is never begging for a laugh. He's never been more appealing than as the frazzled, overgrown (and overweight) 50-year-old boy Grady, who in the course of running away from all his problems finds his long-postponed place in the world.

It's the loosest and juiciest performance of his career, and it's set off beautifully by Tobey Maguire's spooky minimalism. The self-contained Maguire isn't the easiest actor to play off—in "The Cider House Rules," Charlize Theron seems to be romancing a shadow. But there's a lovely give and take between the paternal Grady and the enigmatic, passive-aggressive James, a congenital fabricator who will push people as far as he can to get a reaction. And how refreshing is it to see a Hollywood movie where the middle-aged hero has no sexual interest in his adoring young student (Katie Holmes) but instead lusts after the age-appropriate Sara?

Chabon's burnished and fanciful prose doesn't lend itself easily to the movies, but Kloves (writer-director of "The Fabulous Baker Boys") has done a remarkable job, condensing Chabon's picaresque plot into a fleet and funny narrative without sacrificing Chabon's lyricism, his melancholy or his pansexual high spirits. Hanson has gotten great support from cinematographer Dante Spinotti and legendary editor Dede Allen ("Bonnie and Clyde"), who has not cut a film in eight years. "Wonder Boys" doesn't hit you over the head—its wackiness as well as its humanity slips up on you, catches you off guard. One doesn't want to oversell such a minor-key, low-concept movie, but I'll say it anyway—the movie is pure pleasure.

SIGHT AND SOUND, 12/00, p. 58, Charlotte O'Sullivan

Pittsburg, the present. After meeting his editor Crabtree, English professor Grady Tripp, still working on his second novel, goes to a party hosted by head of department Walter and his wife Sara. There, Sara tells him she's pregnant with child, Grady responds that his wife Emily has just left him. Grady's talented student James turns up at the party; Grady takes him to Walter and Sara's and shows him Walter's Marilyn Monroe memorabilia. In a panic James shoots Walter's aggressive dog dead. Grady hides its body in his car. Later at the launch of a literary festival, Sara tells Grady she's decided to abort. In a bar, Crabtree, James and Grady make up a story about a customer whom they decide to call Vernon. Outside, Vernon attacks them, claiming Grady's car is his. James stays the night at Grady's; while he sleeps, Grady discovers James has stolen Monroe's jacket from Walter's collection.

The next day, James accompanies Grady on his trip to visit Emily at her parents' house, but she's not there. On the way back, Grady realises that James is lying about his impoverished past. He rings up James' grandparents who collect him. James leaves a manuscript of his first novel in the car and Grady reads it. When he gets home he discovers Hannah, his lodger and student, has been reading his novel. Grady and Crabtree set off to talk with James. By this time, Walter suspects James of stealing the jacket. Grady discovers his car, which contains the jacket, has been stolen. He and Crabtree trace the theft of the car to Vernon and an altercation takes place during which Grady's manuscript is scattered to the winds. Grady gives up on reclaiming the jacket and tells Walter that he and Sara are in love. Crabtree gets Walter to drop the charges against James, whose novel he intends to publish. Grady loses his job; he and Sara have their baby.

Curtis Hanson's *Wonder Boys,* unlike his last film—sleek cop *noir LA Confidential*—is something of a hybrid. Adapted from Michael Chabon's novel, it is most obviously a coming of (middle) age drama, which like *American Beauty* features references to weed, the promise of sex with young girls and emotional bonding. One level down, it's also a series of elaborate in-jokes about success. And, underpinning it all, it's a road movie about the need to stay still.

But with so much to say, Hanson's movie is too frenetic. Chabon has a great ear for academic pomposity—and there's nothing wrong with Hanson's casting jokes. Just one example is Richard Thomas' stiff-necked university head of department and cuckold Walter Gaskell. Having played John Boy in television's *The Waltons* (the role we all remember him for), Thomas seemed to have peaked too soon, while John Boy himself, like this film's central character novelist Grady, was a wonder boy—his first novel was a success, his second a flop. Sadly, there's no time to enjoy such subtleties.

The same applies to the characters. They're all potentially fascinating, but aside from Grady and his precocious student James we hardly get to know any of them. The predicament of Frances McDormand's Sara, for instance, is complex: now approaching middle age, she's desperate to have a child with the hapless Grady but you never understand why she married the ridiculous Walter in the first place. And what is it about Grady that fascinates his student Hannah, a girl who could easily find love elsewhere? The film isn't interested in answering such questions, however, because it appears to believe that Grady Tripp's attractiveness tells us all we need to know—once he turns up, women simply want whatever he can give them.

Neither the screenplay (by Steve Kloves), nor Michael Douglas, who plays Grady, fully convinces us of this charm. Grady is certainly colourful (his pink dressing gown alone makes the film worth watching) but he's not particularly profound. In fact, his concerns couldn't be more conventional: should he treat James like a son (to be nurtured) or as a brother (with whom to compete)? Should he sleep with a woman who wants to make him a father or a girl young enough to be his daughter? Douglas' performance is one of broad strokes, his body twisting and turning to underline each comic effect. This would matter less if we weren't so used to this type, but dilapidated liberals are two a penny, and Douglas struggles to make the schtick his own.

Grady's worshipful student James is also hard to pin down, though in this case the actor, Tobey Maguire, is not to blame. With his soft, curvaceous cheeks and ever-so-sulky mouth, James begins as a wonderfully ambiguous creation. Another performer might have reduced the desire to get his hands on Walter's prized treasure, a jacket worn by Marilyn Monroe, or the Kenneth Anger obsession to camp quirks. Maguire plays them perfectly straight and proves truly unnerving. Once Grady has read, and enjoyed, James' novel, however, a mist seems to descend. The scene in which we discover James has slept with books editor Crabtree, for instance, tells us nothing: has James been sexually awakened, or has he merely satisfied a desire to be screwed by the man who discovered his hero Grady? Given the allusions to the ruthless world of *All About Eve* (1950), we might even suspect he's slept with Crabtree to secure a publishing deal. But with nothing to go on, the episode becomes just another wacky turn in the plot.

The feeling remains that, just as James and Crabtree and Grady enjoy telling "stories", we too have been sold a line. Everything points to the fact that it's Grady and James who should get together. Grady invites his charge to a party and almost immediately takes him to the master bedroom, where he unlocks a closet from which James proceeds to take a treasured item. Which is never, in fact, put back. Whether you see this as an emotional or even a sexual metaphor, it's unmistakably intense, and yet their relationship is never to be. As a gritty slice of academic life, *Wonder Boys* is unsatisfactory. Read as Grady's fantasy of 'going straight', however, it works just fine.

TIME, 2/28/00, p. 95, Richard Corliss

The movie camera is an ageist. It does not care for mature flesh. It ruthlessly exposes the ordinary battle scars of middle-aged actors: the liver spots, the chest freckles, the once taut skin that now hangs like crepe. No wonder American film worships youth. Kids are not only its target audience; they are also its most photogenic subculture.

So it is almost brave of Michael Douglas, 55, to play a college professor who looks his age-and feels it. After a decade or so as the suave (or slimy) manipulator dodging a comeuppance from a strong (or psychotic) woman, Douglas renounces sexual energy and latches on to a kind of emotional ennui. In *Wonder Boys* he's unshaven, bespectacled Grady Tripp, who wrote an acclaimed novel years ago but has been marking time ever since. While working on his next book (he's up to page 2,613), he teaches the creative writing he may no longer be capable of and carries on a tryst with the dean's wife (Frances McDormand). As someone says, "His heart kept beating only out of habit." Grady is the one thing a Hollywood hero is never allowed to be: tired.

Michael Chabon's source novel was a wry comedy that focused on the college's elders. The screenplay, by Steve Kloves, genuflects to the camera's love of young faces and promotes Grady's best student (Katie Holmes) and his weirdest (Tobey Maguire) to lead roles.

But the pulse of Curtis Hanson's direction is lethargic; the comic bits are so slack and deadpan you could mistake the film for an earnest drama—an *Afterschool Special* for troubled kids and their pooped parents.

Wonder Boys reminds us of a distant age (the '70s) when bad movies were better: not stupid teen romps but sad, off-kilter studies of adults adrift. It is a rare current example of that endangered species, the honorable failure.

VILLAGE VOICE, 2/29/00, p. 114, Amy Taubin

Like *L.A. Confidential,* Curtis Hanson's latest picture has allure. The sexiness of *L.A. Confidential* came with the turf, but the film pulled you deeper. It promised dark secrets of the heart and it delivered. The secrets in Hanson's bedraggled romantic comedy *Wonder Boys* are more like those found in the back of an old-sock drawer, but that doesn't make the film any less of a turn-on.

Wonder Boys also draws you into a world of men whose fragile bonds are the result of circumstance rather than psychological or emotional affinity, And as in *L.A. Confidential,* their world has time enough for only one woman, who, from the moment she comes on the screen, is clearly the perfect match for the man that matters most in the film. One of the things that makes him matter is that he's intrigued by her.

Adroitly adapted from Michael Chabon's slightly picaresque, madly comic novel, *Wonder Boys* is set on the campus of a Pittsburgh college. In this cloistered, bohemian environment, Grady Tripp (Michael Douglas) is a star despite the fact that he hasn't published anything in seven years. In an effort to avoid closure, Grady has allowed his new novel to expand to 2600-plus single-spaced pages. His personal life is similarly out of control. His third wife has just left him, and Sara (Frances McDormand), his lover of five years, who's also the chancellor of the college and is married to the chairman of Grady's department, has just told him that she's pregnant with his child.

To raise the ante on these marital crises, Grady's editor, Terry Crabtree (Robert Downey Jr.), has arrived for Wordfest, the college's annual literary symposium. Crabtree is hoping to save his career with Grady's new novel, when that proves unlikely, he gloms on to James Leer (Tobey Maguire), Grady's most talented student. James, who's eccentric and depressive enough to seem like he might be a real writer, shows up at the Wordfest opening night party with a gun, which he insists is a cap pistol until he uses it to save Grady from having his foot amputated by Sara's husband's blind pit bull. Grady and James flee the party with the dead dog and another of Sara's husband's prize possessions, a black, ermine-collared sweater that Marilyn Monroe wore when she married Joe DiMaggio. Their adventures have only just begun.

Chabon's novel evokes the careening trajectories of his character's lives in prose that's precise and lyrical and filled with rhythmic surprises. The film does justice to the novel, and not merely because Steve Kloves's witty screenplay leaves so much of the dialogue intact. Hanson's filmmaking has a similar precision. Take the scene in which Grady meets Crabtree at the airport.

Grady is trying to keep Crabtree off the subject of his book by making small talk. Hanson covers part of this scene in a series of reverse-angle close-ups, which are like no reverse-angle close-ups you've ever seen before. Reverse-angle cutting is so old-fashioned that hip directors and editors avoid it whenever possible. But in this scene, thanks not only to Hanson, but to the great Dede Allen, who returns to editing here after an absence of nearly 10 years, each shot arrives on the screen with a zing that's the visual equivalent of a Max Roach syncopated beat. What's great about *Wonder Boys* is that it swings.

It also has a good attitude. Tolerance for eccentricity—not to mention for recreational drugs, adultery, and homosexuality—has been all too rare in movies of late. When the seemingly innocent James winds up in bed with the lecherous but also oddly vulnerable Crabtree, it's not treated as a big deal. The same goes for Grady and Sara's secret affair, and for Sara's protracted deliberations about whether or not to end her pregnancy. Grady puts off making a commitment to Sara by wandering with James and Crabtree around a sodden Pittsburgh, where rain alternates with snow with a regularity that defies all known weather patterns. This is a process—as opposed to a results-oriented approach to the creative act of living a life and, for some of the characters, of making art. The messiness is inevitable. Indeed, *Wonder Boys* slips into indulgence only at the very end when it ties things up too neatly.

Douglas, who in recent movies has tapped almost exclusively into his easily accessible anger, here regains the light comic touch of *Romancing the Stone*. Scruffiness becomes him. He not only seems like an interesting human being, but also a human being who's insane enough to be a committed writer. McDormand, for once, has a warmth that equals her acerbity. She and Douglas convince us they've known each other for years. Maguire also does the best work of his career here. For once, his buttoned-up manner is not priggish but a cover for a fragile psyche and a quick mind. Downey, who radiates more energy doing nothing discernible than most other actors do when they let it all hang out, takes the film to another level.

What makes *Wonder Boys* so enjoyable is the sense that it really was a collaborative endeavor—that the caring and creative relationships that are its subject had some parallel among the people involved in its making. As in *L.A. Confidential*, Hanson brings out the best in his actors and in his production team, which here includes the aforementioned Allen and Kloves (whose underpraised *The Fabulous Baker Boys* had a similar comic melancholy) and cinematographer Dante Spinotti, who here proves that dark, dreary weather and comedy are not incompatible.

Also reviewed in:
CHICAGO TRIBUNE, 2/23/00, Tempo/p. 7, Michael Wilmington
NATION, 3/20/00, p. 51, Stuart Klawans
NEW REPUBLIC, 3/20/00, p. 24, Stanley Kauffmann
NEW YORK TIMES, 2/23/00, p. E1, A. O. Scott
VARIETY, 2/21-27/00, p. 36, Emanuel Levy
WASHINGTON POST, 2/25/00, p. C5, Stephen Hunter
WASHINGTON POST, 2/25/00, Weekend/p. 48, Michael O'Sullivan

WONDERLAND

A USA Films release of Universal Pictures presentation of a Kismet Film Company/Revolution Films production. *Executive Producer:* Stewart Till and David M. Thompson. *Producer:* Michele Camarda and Andrew Eaton. *Director:* Michael Winterbottom. *Screenplay:* Laurence Coriat. *Director of Photography:* Sean Bobbitt. *Editor:* Trevor Waite. *Music:* Michael Nyman. *Music Editor:* Twydor Davis. *Sound:* Richard Flynn. *Sound Editor:* Ian Wilson. *Casting:* Wendy Brazington. *Production Designer:* Mark Tildesley. *Set Dresser:* Michelle Day. *Costumes:* Natalie Ward. *Make-up:* Konnie Daniel. *Stunt Coordinator:* Nick Powell. *Running time:* 108 minutes. *MPAA Rating:* R.

CAST: Shirley Henderson (Debbie);   Gina McKee (Nadia);   Molly Parker (Molly);   Ian Hart (Dan);   John Simm (Eddie);   Stuart Townsend (Tim);   Kika Markham (Eileen);   Jack Shepherd (Bill);   Enzo Cilenti (Darren);   Sarah-Jane Potts (Melanie);   David Fahm (Franklyn);   Ellen Thomas (Donna);   Peter Marfleet (Jack);   Nathan Constance (Alex);   Anton Saunders (Bloke in Bed with Debbie); Abby Ford (Nurse);   Michelle Jolly (Midwife);   Rebecca Lenkiewicz (Policewoman);   Vanessa Pratt (Kelly);   Michael Hodgson (Kitchen Shop Father);   Emma Sear (Kitchen Shop Mother);   Megan Sear (Kitchen Shop Baby);   Nuno Vaz (Portuguese Neighbor).

LOS ANGELES TIMES, 7/28/00, Calendar/p. 6, Kevin Thomas

"Wonderland" is a loving group portrait of a South London working-class family and what they experience in the course of an exceptionally event-filled weekend.   Director Michael Winterbottom and writer Laurence Coriat pile on the incidents a bit thickly and are not afraid to draw upon coincidence now and then in order to make the larger point that life can be a demanding business for one and all and that respect should be given those who forge ahead no matter what.

The characters, places and predicaments have a kitchen-sink realism, but the feel and rhythm of the film is lyrical, poetic even, and cameraman Sean Bobbitt's images of contemporary urban life have a burnished radiant glow. Michael Nyman's entirely exceptional score has a Philip Glass-like repetitive insistence but with a heroic flourish that expresses the simple bravery of the human spirit. There is an exalted quality about the film in its depiction of everyday life. In short, "Wonderland" is an extraordinary film, as entertaining as it is observant, about ordinary people.

We first meet Nadia (Gina McKee), a most attractive and intelligent young woman. She's a waitress who, despite her looks and considerable charm, has turned to the personal ads in her search for love. This opens up the possibility of romance—and also of humiliation. Her older sister Debbie (Shirley Henderson), separated from her immature husband, Dan (Ian Hart), is a hairdresser and a loving mother to her young son Jack (Peter Marfleet) but also an uninhibited party girl. Jack is often left to his own devices, which means that, like lots of other kids, he spends much time in an electronic universe of TV and video games.

There's a third sister, Molly (Molly Parker), whose imminent motherhood throws her lover Eddie (John Simm) into a major panic attack. In the meantime, the three sisters' parents, Eileen (Kika Markham) and Bill (Jack Shepherd), are stuck in a loveless marriage in a noisy flat; they are estranged from their only son, Darren (Enzo Cilenti).

In one of the film's most poignant incidents, the listless Bill, inadvertently locked out of his flat, finds refuge with a neighbor, Donna (Ellen Thomas), who gets him to dance. Experiencing a spark of life for the first time in a long time, he later reaches out to Eileen in their bed only to have her cruelly reject him.

It seems significant that Coriat, in her screenwriting debut, was born in France. Although she has spent the last 17 years in England she seems to have retained a quintessentially French sensibility; her people are all looking for love to the exclusion of almost everything else. This preoccupation works for "Wonderland," but even though it is a truism that people want to be loved, they can also have lots else on their minds.

The film's performances are uniformly splendid and McKee, in particular, has a special glow.

As the film unfolds with an effortless flow you find yourself pinning all your hopes on Jack, who seems brighter than everyone else in his family. He's the one person who seems to have an imagination and an ability to look out with wonder at a world his elders no longer seem to notice in their emotional self absorption and struggle for survival. Disturbingly, "Wonderland" leaves you wondering whether any of his relatives were like him when they were children.

NEW YORK, 8/7/00, p. 67, Peter Rainer

Wonderland, directed by Michael Winterbottom and written by Laurence Coriat, puts an impressive amount of kitchen-sink realism to work on a rather shopworn multi-storied scenario about all the lonely people looking for love in the big city, in this case South London. Gina McKee and Shirley Henderson give the gruel some spice.

NEW YORK POST, 7/28/00, p. 49, Jonathan Foreman

Michael Winterbottom's marvelous multilayered "Wonderland" is one of those rare films in which everything comes together.

Its superb performances, music, photography, dialogue, its rhythms of tone and theme all complement each perfectly. Its depiction of urban life and loneliness is unsparingly real, but at the same time humane and filled with hope.

In fact, in the end, "Wonderland" becomes a kind of love poem to London, though not the shiny, pop culture-obsessed London of Tony Blair's "Cool Britannia."

It helps that, unlike so many recent ensemble films like "Magnolia" and "Short Cuts," "Wonderland" is neither cynical nor sentimental. And although—refreshingly—it's about ordinary, relatively unglamorous people, there's no trace in it of the drabness that characterizes the working-class films of Mike Leigh and Ken Loach.

These people may be "ordinary" and live in unstylish parts of town, but their lives aren't dreary at all. Winterbottom allows them a real dignity while showing them in the grip of loss, longing, lust and love.

The action of the movie—a one-night stand, a ghastly blind date, a child lost in the park on Guy Fawkes Day, a stunningly photographed soccer match, various splits and reunions—takes place over a single November weekend and centers on three adult sisters from South London who love, but don't necessarily like, each other.

First you meet Nadia (Gina McKee—the wheelchair bound siren in "Notting Hill"), a cafe-waitress looking for love in the personals. Her sister, Debbie (Shirley Henderson from "Topsy Turvy"), is an exuberant, highly sexed hairdresser, divorced from her shiftless husband Dan (Ian Hart) and raising their son, Jack (Peter Marfleet). Apparently more settled and stable than either is the third sister, Molly (Molly Parker), who's living with sweet if immature Eddie (John Simm), and about to give birth to his child.

But some of the most affecting characters play secondary roles in the story, like the girls' father, Bill (Jack Shepherd), trapped in a loveless marriage and tortured by the loss of a runaway son, who finds some joy with a flirtatious West Indian neighbor.

Winterbottom uses natural light, a hand-held camera and locations filled with genuine members of the public (rather than extras) to give his night-life scenes the feel of real life. But "Wonderland" couldn't be the triumph that it is without outstanding performances by a top-notch cast, especially those of McKee, Henderson and Parker.

NEWSDAY, 7/28/00, Part II/p. B14, Gene Seymour

Nadia's Mum (Kika Markham) thinks Dad (Jack Shepherd) is a "pathetic" loser. And she's no prize herself. Nadia (Gina McKee) works in a coffee shop and, though heartbreakingly single, is a lot better at communicating with her glum 10-year-old nephew than her promiscuous, sociopathic hairdresser sister (Shirley Henderson) and the boy's estranged, oafish and equally self-absorbed pop (Ian Hart).

Nadia's other sister (Molly Parker) is pregnant and seemingly blissful with her husband (John Simm). Yet, after he quits his job and runs off in a panic, she begins to apply the same deep freeze to their relationship as her dour, carping mum. Dad, meanwhile, mopes and pines for his only son, who apparently ran off from this household with no intention of coming back.

Can't blame him. If this is, indeed, "Wonderland," when is the next train out?

You have to look hard for anything hopeful or redeeming among the members of this working-class British family as they struggle through a November weekend that is at once momentous and mundane.

Working from a Laurence Coriat script inspired by Robert Altman's "Short Cuts," director Michael Winterbottom ("Jude," "Welcome to Sarajevo") follows these characters around a contemporary London steeped in a gauzy, nicotine aura of grit and anxiety. This layered moodiness—enhanced by natural light, hand-held cameras and the haunting music of Michael Nyman ("The Piano")—sustains your attention. It's one of the principal assets of "Wonderland."

So, for that matter, is the cast, all of whom inhabit their roles with often-startling insight. Hard to single anyone out, though it's remarkable to watch McKee, best known as Hugh Grant's disabled sister in "Notting Hill," connect the emotional dynamics with little more than a wounded glance. And, though it's all happening a continent away, you're easily able to recognize the complex ironies and personality disorders as fulfilling whatever it was Tolstoy said about unhappy families.

Recognition, however, isn't quite the same as empathy. Although "Wonderland's" tattered neon landscape and its dysfunctional inhabitants are fascinating to behold, you feel as if there's something in the way of connecting with this story. Maybe you somehow don't quite believe the upheavals, large and small, that take place in this 72-hour period aren't as transforming as the movie would have you believe. Much as the movie insists that you care what happens to even the worst of its characters, you feel no regrets about having to leave these folks behind when it's over.

SIGHT AND SOUND, 1/00, p. 62, Xan Brooks

London, one weekend in the lives of three sisters. Nadia is a waitress in her twenties. Her older sister Debbie is a single mum with an 11-year-old son named Jack; her younger sister Molly is expecting a baby by her boyfriend Eddie. The barking of a neighbour's dog disturbs the sisters' mother Eileen and further strains relations with her husband Bill. Nadia meets Tim through a lonely-hearts ad and has sex with him. Eddie quits his job, quarrels with Molly and storms off. Jack is spending the weekend with his irresponsible father Dan. Eileen feeds the neighbours' dog poisoned meat over the fence. In the adjacent block of flats, depressed Franklyn lolls in his bedroom. Molly goes into labour and is admitted to hospital, unaware Eddie has crashed his scooter and is in a nearby ward. Jack runs away from Dan and is mugged in the park. Dan, Nadia and Debbie retrieve him from the police station. Molly gives birth and is reunited with Eddie. Bill receives a message from his estranged son Darren. During her walk to work on Monday morning, Nadia meets Franklyn and they walk to the bus together.

If auteur status is defined by a director's ability to stamp a film with his or her particular visual or thematic imprimatur, then Michael Winterbottom is no auteur. His pictures run the gamut of styles and genres: he's tried the road movie *(Butterfly Kiss)*, the period drama *(Jude)*, a war picture *(Welcome to Sarajevo)* and a psychosexual thriller *(I Want You)*. His brief, prolific career has established this former documentarian as a sort of Anglicised Howard Hawks, a director who adapts to shifting terrain and vigorously resists categorisation.

Peer closer, though, and Winterbottom's features all share a thematic concern with claustrophobia, their characters pinned down by circumstance. Jude is excluded from university because of his social standing. *Sarajevo*'s journalist hero finds himself kicking against a senseless war, while the entire environment of the seaside-set *I Want You* is a pressure-cooker. The ironically tagged *Wonderland* is a paean to trapped, hobbled, bleeding humanity and seems to be the fruition of this alienated thread in his work. *Wonderland* opens with a fumbled chat-up inside a noisy pub and closes with a tentative new beginning on the way to a bus stop. Between lies a petty hell of missed connections and humiliations. Winterbottom employs here a Chekhovian set-up (three sisters) and a limited time frame (one weekend) to anchor his free-form mosaic of London life. But *Wonderland*'s meanderings are deceptive. What at first seem like accessory plot threads are eventually mainlined and made pivotal. In its dying minutes, the picture swells to a crescendo. Tensions are semi-resolved, emotional scabs slapped with band-aids.

The key to *Wonderland* lies in this twofold style, this tempering of abandon with rigorous filmic control. Think of it as *Dogma*-lite. Throughout the film's run, Winterbottom shoots in a kind of stylised *vérité*. His flitting, handheld imagery is underscored by mumbled, down-in-the-mix dialogue, adorned with the occasional bit of fluff in the camera gate. But where recent, riskier pictures like *Festen* or *The Idiots* in particular operated on the very cusp of outright disorder, *Wonderland* plays it safe—although its documentary ambience is broken up with stylistic flourishes (time-lapse effects, slow motion). More crucially, its characters' messy ebb and flow is accompanied by a swooping Michael Nyman score that plucks at the heartstrings. At times, in fact, *Wonderland* is almost too polished. The pristine surface (so close to adverts) works against its red-meat interior.

That said, *Wonderland* contains enough soul and insight to make it a consistently bewitching experience. It flowers into life during a clutch of perfectly dealt scenes (the aftermath of the football match, the poisoning of the dog) and makes space for some compelling playing (especially from Ian Hart and Gina McKee). Meanwhile, Winterbottom's bittersweet course spirits us through a London that's positively awash with lost souls. His inhabitants go groping through noisy pubs, chill parklands and teeming hospitals in search of some intangible "x" factor (love, respect, reconciliation) to warm them up. There's hope out there someplace, but you have to hunt it down.

VILLAGE VOICE, 8/1/00, p. 116, Dennis Lim

Michael Winterbottom's *Wonderland* is a bruised romantic's wary valentine to London life. No less than Wong Kar-wai's ravishing Hong Kong nocturnes, the film understands that the sustaining headrush and soothing white noise of metropolitan commotion is but a tiny perspective shift away from the dull, bewildering ache of psychic solitude heightened by relentlessly anonymous bustle. The alienating enormity of the big city may be an immortal romantic cliché, but Winterbottom—shooting entirely on location, without extras and with unobtrusive documentary techniques (handheld cameras, hidden mikes)—channels the self-evident symptoms of urban malaise into a movie of authentic textures and seemingly spontaneous gestures.

Wonderland follows three South London sisters over one long November weekend: Debbie (*Topsy-Turvy*'s Shirley Henderson), a promiscuous hairdresser with a preteen son, a loutish ex (Ian Hart), and a cigarette permanently dangling from her lips; anxious, very pregnant Molly (Molly Parker), whose partner (John Simm) is silently enduring a premature mid-life crisis; and Nadia (Gina McKee), a waitress in a Soho café, unhappily single and on something of a lonely-hearts collision course. Hair twisted into Björk-ish buns, micro-knapsack strapped to her back, Nadia—projecting a poignant combination of cuteness and wistfulness—propels herself from one horrendous blind date to another. (Winterbottom helps her along every so often, switching to time-lapse photography so that Nadia zips through closing-time throngs as if jet-propelled, on a magical, neon-smear tour of London.)

The film parcels out its misery evenly—the girls' parents are ensnarled in a mutually antagonistic marriage that has long ulcerated beyond repair. Dad (Jack Shepherd) wears a fixed expression of transcendent world-weariness. Mum (Kika Markham), all frayed nerves and convulsive hostility, regards her husband's rare, forlorn attempts at affection with bald revulsion and is given to outbreaks of omni-directional rage—suffice to say, a neighbor's yipping dog meets a crueler fate than the pooch in Todd Solondz's *Happiness,* another recent three-sister diagram of familial dysfunction.

Laurence Coriat's screenplay does betray the neat edges and stiff joints of a purely schematic exercise—Chekhovian bedrock (co-opted long before Solondz by Woody Allen, among others) overlaid with Altmanesque web (Coriat's admitted inspiration is *Short Cuts*). The latter is a narrative model designed to illustrate that the connections we struggle to make and maintain on a daily basis are fragile or, worse, futile—a lament more ardently expressed in Paul Thomas Anderson's beautifully crazed *Magnolia.* The pervasive woe here is a little too dutifully appliquéd, the stabs at resolution too easy *(Wonderland* ends with the birth of a baby girl, promptly named Alice), but, more often than not, Winterbottom's fidgety, searching camera upends the house-of-cards structure, throwing the characters (simplistically drawn but fully inhabited) into what feels like real life.

Winterbottom's corpse-littered but otherwise disparate oeuvre-lesbian-killer road movie *(Butterfly Kiss),* Thomas Hardy adaptation *(Jude),* war-zone polemic *(Welcome to Sarajevo)*—reveals a taste for bleak material and a knack for conveying the horror in rude, repellent jolts. His way with experiential immediacy is put to sublime use in *Wonderland.* Through the gloom of council flats and bingo parlors, the sticky clamor of West End pubs and football terraces, London is captured in all its seedy glory (as it seldom has been on film). *Wonderland* belongs to the rich British tradition of romanticized misery—it's the cinematic analogue to the hallowed Brit musical genre of mope-rock, with a shameless array of half-a-person characters weighed down by Morrissey-caliber backstories. Michael Nyman's score, itself a surging bittersweet symphony, enhances the melancholy mood.

There's not a false note among the performances: Henderson, Hart, Shepherd, Markham, and in particular McKee add unspoken complexities to their portrayals. Traveling home on the top deck of a night bus after a particularly humiliating date, McKee's Nadia does her best to ignore her fellow passengers (weekend revelers, happy in the haze of a drunken hour), gazes out the fogged-up window into the pitiless night, and chokes back quiet, barely perceptible sobs. In this one sustained moment of palpable anguish, performed with exquisite restraint, McKee not only steals the film—she earns *Wonderland* its pathos.

Also reviewed in:
CHICAGO TRIBUNE, 8/11/00, Friday/p. A, Michael Wilmington
NEW YORK TIMES, 7/28/00, p. E21, Elvis Mitchell
NEW YORKER, 7/31/00, p. 85, Anthony Lane
VARIETY, 5/17-23/99, p. 61, David Stratton
WASHINGTON POST, 8/11/00, p. C1, Stephen Hunter
WASHINGTON POST, 8/11/00, Weekend/p. 32, Desson Howe

"X"

A Manga Entertainment and X Committee Clamp release. *Executive Producer:* Tsunehiko Kadokawa. *Producer:* Kazuo Yokoyama, Masanori Maruyama, and Kazuhiko Ikeguchi. *Director:* Rintaro. *Screenplay (originally Japanese; dubbed into English):* Asami Watanabe, Nanase Ohkawa, and Rintaro. *Based on the original story by:* Clamp, Satsuki Igarashi, Mokonaapapa Nanase Ohkawa, and Mikku "Mick" Nekoi. *Director of Photography:* Jin Yamaguchi. *Editor:* Harutoshi Ogata, Yukiko Itoh, and Satoshi Terauchi. *Music:* Harumitsu Shimizu. *Character Design and Director of Original Drawings:* Nobuteru Yuhki. *Art Director:* Shuh-ichi Hirata. *Running time:* 98 minutes. *MPAA Rating:* Not Rated.

VOICES: Alan Marriot (Kamui); Adam Henderson (Fuma); Larissa Murray (Kotori); Denica Fairman (Kanoe); Stacey Jefferson (Hinoto); Mike Fitzpatrick (Sorata).

LOS ANGELES TIMES, 3/24/00, Calendar/p. 4, Charles Solomon

The Japanese animated feature "X," is a convoluted apocalyptic fantasy centering on an unwilling hero who holds the fate of the planet in his hands. A mysterious entity, the Dragon of the Earth, threatens to destroy all human life: It can only be stopped by its counterpart, the Dragon of Heaven—with the aid of the teenage Kamui.

For most of the film, which has been dubbed into English, Kamui refuses to shoulder responsibility for the fate of the planet. He returns to Tokyo to protect his old girlfriend Kotori and her brother Fuma; as long as they're safe, he's willing to let the Dragon of the Earth ravage Tokyo (and the rest of the globe). But Kamui can't escape his destiny, which is to fight in the rapidly escalating conflict; just as Fuma is fated to join the side Kamui opposes.

Both Dragons are aided by teams of humans with standard anime super-powers. As the war begins, they fly through the air in duels involving floods, fires, explosions, lightning bolts, severed limbs, gouts of blood and shattered buildings. These characters are killed off before the viewer gets to know them (or even sort them out), which robs their deaths of any meaning. The battles climax in a fierce duel between Fuma and Kamui.

Much of the story is told in dreams and dreams within dreams until it's difficult to tell what's actually happening. In one dream, Kamui's mother disembowels herself to give him the sword within her body. In other dreams, Fuma wrenches a similar sword from the torso of the sleeping Kotori. The myriad twists of the story line are accompanied by an endless blizzard of cherry blossom petals, which symbolize the fleeting beauty of life.

Although the characters talk constantly, dealing out expositions like hands of blackjack, they leave many key points unexplained: What are the Dragons and where do they come from? Why do characters confuse Kamui and Fuma when they're drawn differently? Why don't the citizens of Tokyo notice all those explosions and shattered buildings? What is the significance of the supporters of the Dragon of Heaven corresponding to the stars in the Big Dipper? Why is a wind always dramatically blowing Kamui's cape?

"X" features some interesting animation of scarlet and white dragons fighting amid the wreckage of Tokyo. The character designs retain some of the Art Nouveau look of the original manga: Hinoto's long hair appears to have been copied from an Alphonse Mucha poster. But the flamboyant visuals can't disguise the paper-thin plot or inept storytelling. Numerous anime works have dealt with similar themes in recent years, from the ultra-violent "Crimson Wolf" to the extended romance "Mysterious Play"; almost all of them told their stories more coherently.

NEW YORK POST, 3/24/00, p. 50, Lou Lumenick

The best way to enjoy "X" may be to ignore the furiously over-plotted, headache-inducing story—derived from a series of comic books—and focus on the exquisitely drawn Japanese animation.

An all-female animation studio known as Clamp, working with veteran anime director Rintaro (best known here for the TV series "Astro Boy"), produced stunningly beautiful drawings for this 1996 effort about a boy with supernatural powers who has to decide whether mankind is worth saving from a "cleansing" apocalypse (Hiroshima, anyone?)

Be warned that "X" is not for younger kids. It opens with a sequence of the hero ripping a jewel-encrusted sword out of her womb and contains several other gory sequences.

VILLAGE VOICE, 3/28/00, p. 120, Jessica Winter

With his somber, bloody apocalypse fable X, veteran anime director Rintaro turns down the usual moon-surface gravity of japananimation to zero; characters seem to bob bemusedly on air, and when an ethereal girl is impaled on a sword, her blood doesn't flow so much as float out of her body, tidily, in one viscous mass. We've already seen little Kotori die twice before in hero Kamui's many visions, because time in X is apt to bend, reverse, or stop altogether, spiraling through flashbacks, flashforwards, hallucinations, and prophetic dreams. With time and space abstracted and aestheticized, X perches at a cool distance, prioritizing bleakly beautiful visuals (Tokyo resembles Tim Burton's *Batman* Gothic) and fatalist regret over action and suspense.

Standing on the edge of the end of the world (set in 1999, X's future never happened), the rebellious and possibly bipolar Kamui must decide whether to vanquish the Dragons of the Earth, who will return the world to mother nature, or the Dragons of Heaven, who will preserve civilization. He's variously aided and abetted by a sprawling cast of characters (a wry brothel worker gets the best line: "I have mastered all the vagaries of water"). The final battle, fought far above Tokyo, transpires as if underwater, with the city sleeping beneath and bearing the sickly green cast of environmental illness. X, to its, credit, delivers neither a happy nor a redemptive ending; indeed, its very premise preempts both.

Also reviewed in:
CHICAGO TRIBUNE, 3/24/00, Friday/p. M, John Petrakis
NEW YORK TIMES, 3/24/00, p. E16, Elvis Mitchell
VARIETY, 5/1-7/00, p. 33, Dennis Harvey

X-MEN

A Twentieth Century Fox release in association with Marvel Entertainment Group of a The Donner's Company/Bad Hat Harry production.   *Executive Producer:* Avi Arad, Stan Lee, Richard Donner, and Tom DeSanto.   *Producer:* Lauren Shuler Donner and Ralph Winter. *Director:* Bryan Singer.   *Screenplay:* David Hayter.   *Story:* Tom DeSanto and Bryan Singer. *Director of Photography:* Newton Thomas Sigel.   *Editor:* Steven Rosenblum, Kevin Stitt, and John Wright.   *Music:* Michael Kamen.   *Music Editor:* Curt Sobel.   *Sound:* David Lee. *Sound Editor:* John A. Larsen.   *Casting:* Roger Mussenden.   *Production Designer:* John Myhre.   *Art Director:* Tamara Deverell and Paul Denham Austerberry.   *Set Designer:* Gordon White, Thomas Carnegie, Michael Shocrylas, and Andrew Menzies.   *Set Decorator:* James Edward Ferrell and

Dan Wladyka. *Set Dresser:* J. Tracy Budd, John Morrison, Brenton Brown, Gerry Deschenes, David Jaquest, Jonathan Kovacs, Brian Beck, and Mort Freedman. *Special Effects:* Colin Chilvers. *Visual Effects:* Michael Fink. *Costumes:* Louise Mingenbach. *Make-up:* Ann E. Brodie. *Make-up (Halle Berry):* Sandra Wheatle. *Special Make-up Design:* Gordon Smith. *Stunt Coordinator:* Gary Jensen and Rick Forsayeth. *Animator:* John Van Vliet. *Running time:* 105 minutes. *MPAA Rating:* PG-13.

CAST: Hugh Jackman (Logan/Wolverine); Patrick Stewart (Xavier); Ian McKellen (Magneto); Famke Janssen (Jean Grey); James Marsden (Cyclops); Halle Berry (Storm); Anna Paquin (Rogue); Tyler Mane (Sabretooth); Ray Park (Toad); Rebecca Romijn-Stamos (Mystique); Bruce Davison (Senator Kelly); Matthew Sharp (Henry Guyrich); Brett Morris (Young Magneto); Rhona Shekter (Magneto's Mother); Kenneth McGregor (Magneto's Father); Shawn Roberts (Rogue's Boyfriend); Donna Goodhand (Rogue's Mother); John E. Nelles (Rogue's Father); George Buza (Trucker); Darren McGuire (Contender); Carson Manning and Scott Leva (Waterboys); Aron Tager (Emcee); Kevin Rushton (Stu); Doug Lennox (Bartender); David Nichols, Nanette Barrutia-Harrison, Dan Duran, and Dave Allen Clark (Newscasters); Malcolm Nefsky (Stu's Buddy); Sumela Kay (Kitty); Shawn Ashmore (Bobby); Katrina Florece (Jubilee); Alexander Burton (John); Quinn Wright (Lily Pond Kid); Daniel Magder (Boy on Raft); Matt Weinberg (Tommy); Madison Lanc (Tommy's Sister); Stan Lee (Hot Dog Vendor); Adam Robitel (Guy on Line); Dave Brown (Lead Cop); Ben P. Jensen (Sabretooth Cop); Tom DeSanto (Toad Cop); Todd Dulmage (Coast Guard); Elias Zarou (U.N. Secretary General); David Black (President); Robert R. Snow (Secret Service); David Hayter (Museum Cop); Cecil Phillips (Security Guard); Deryck Blake (Plastic Prison Guard).

CHRISTIAN SCIENCE MONITOR, 7/14/00, p. 15, David Sterritt

Hollywood has a love-hate relationship with comic books—love when a movie based on a comic book soars like the original "Superman" and "Batman," but hate when one flops, as the makers of "Judge Dredd" and "The Phantom" must ruefully remember.

The bright side of such productions is that they have built-in name recognition among viewers.

The downside is that they're expensive to make, since fans expect pricey techno-effects to explode from the screen.

All of which means Hollywood will be watching the box-office results of "X-Men" with the strongest X-ray spectacles it can find, pondering not only the picture's own profitability but also its predictive power for upcoming movies like "Spider-Man" and the fifth "Superman" installment.

While it's too early to forecast figures, my guess is that "X-Men" will fail to show super-hero strength at the ticket window. It has lots of action, some solid performances, and a few real issues on its mind. But it's awfully dark in mood and appearance—not an ideal approach to warm-weather escapism—and its story is a little too jumpy to build the emotional momentum that might have made this a breakthrough hit.

The premise behind "X-Men" exemplifies the "mature" storytelling that Marvel Comics pioneered a few decades ago. In traditional comics, people with exotic powers automatically become super-heroes in the Superman or Batman mode. But what if society regarded these gifted folks with fear and loathing, finding them too "weird" and "different" to be tolerated?

That's the starting point for the "X-Men" movie, which focuses on a struggle between two groups of mutants with special abilities—one that wants to raise the rest of humanity to its own high level, and another that wants to punish humanity by giving it a dose of its own violence.

The constructive mutants live in a school that cultivates their powers (telepathy, telekinesis, etc.) and prepares them for a brighter future. The destructive mutants lurk in the shadows and dream of the day when they'll inherit earth from the hopelessly outmoded human race.

"X-Men" tries for a bit of social relevance, from its political beginning—the tirade of a bigoted senator who denounces the mutants with racist chchés—to its symbolic climax, a fight atop the Statue of Liberty's crown.

But the movie's well-meaning heart will matter less to young moviegoers than its high-energy action, and while director Bryan Singer delivers plenty of fast-paced mayhem, even this starts to seem repetitious and perfunctory before the end.

Die-hard action fans may cheer, but if you're looking for the romantic verve of "Superman" or the dream-like edginess of "Batman," this isn't the comic-book movie for you.

LOS ANGELES TIMES, 7/14/00, Calendar/p. 1, Kenneth Turan

To be a teenager is to feel different, misunderstood, perhaps even a bit of a mutant. It was the gift of Stan Lee and Jack Kirby, the creators of the Marvel comic decades ago, to realize with "X-Men" that conflicted twentysomething and teenage superheroes would tap into that universal "I don't belong" feeling and raise it to another level.

Here are impressively powerful people saying things like "Stay away from my girl," getting crushes on cute guys and worrying what's going to happen on that first kiss. By making the individual X-Men both natural for the core audience to identify with yet potent beyond imagining (a dynamic similar to the one that helps power the Harry Potter books), Lee and Kirby came up with a comic dynasty that has now been turned into a solid summer entertainment.

Directed by the gifted Bryan Singer ("The Usual Suspects") and credited to screenwriter David Hayter, though several other writers were reportedly involved, "X-Men" squeezes an awful lot—maybe too much—into a brisk 95 minutes. There are 10 mutants, each with a different superpower to introduce, a plot to unfold, jokes to make, visuals complex enough to employ more than a dozen effects houses to display and enough action to keep 60 stunt people occupied. So much is happening you feel the immediate need of a sequel just as a reward for absorbing it all.

Helping make everything convincing is a diverse cast headed by British heavyweights Patrick Stewart and Ian McKellen as an earlier generation of mutants, the O.M.s so to speak, old friends who have turned into rival mentors for the hearts and minds of the next generation.

Stewart plays Professor Charles Francis Xavier, able to read minds, influence thought, even erase memories if it's a slow day. He runs Xavier's School for Gifted Youngsters, a high-tech version of Potter's Hogwarts, where mutants-in-training learn to control their powers and an inner circle of accomplished X-Men get to wander around in nifty, tight-fitting uniforms.

Those outfitted include the telekinetic and photogenic Jean Grey (Famke Janssen); Storm (Halle Berry in a striking blond wig), who need only roll her eyes to create all kinds of weather; and Cyclops (James Marsden), who wears a stylish visor to protect the world from the destructive bolts that issue from his eyes.

On the other side is Erik Lehnsherr (McKellen, who starred in Singer's "Apt Pupil"), code name Magneto, known both for his ability to do anything he wants with metal and his complete disdain for the ordinary run of humanity. He sees a war between mutants and the rest of the world as inevitable and warns Xavier ominously, "Don't get in my way."

Equally irritable are the mutants who look to Magneto for guidance. That would be the enormous Sabretooth (former professional wrestler Tyler Mane); Toad, the man with the 15-foot tongue (Ray Park, memorable as Darth Maul in "The Phantom Menace"); and the treacherous Mystique (top model Rebecca Romijn-Stamos), who can shape-shift with the best of them.

Bringing the conflict between Xavier and Magneto to a head is a movement, led by weasly U.S. Sen. Robert Kelly (Bruce Davison), to make mutants register with the government as if they were sex offenders. The senator has no qualms about manipulating a wave of anti-mutant hysteria ("Send Mutants to the Moon Forever," reads one demonstrator's sign) that leads to a U.N.-sponsored summit on "the mutant phenomenon and its impact on the world stage" that will bring 200 heads of state to New York's Ellis Island.

Holding the balance of power between these two groups are the film's most conflicted (and most interesting characters), Rogue (Oscar winner Anna Paquin) and the feral, dangerous and well-named Wolverine (Australian actor Hugh Jackman).

While Rogue is new to her ability to absorb the qualities and the very life force of anyone she touches, Wolverine has been a berserker for quite some time. You'd be angry too, if a rare metal named adamantium had been fused to your entire skeleton during a past you can't remember, giving you retractable claws that painfully shoot out from your hands whenever you feel threatened. Even a gift for instant healing isn't compensation enough for that.

With a face of fury partially covered by mutton-chop sideburns, Jackman is this film's star and brings a necessary level of acting intensity to the project. While "X-Men" doesn't take your breath away wire-to-wire the way "The Matrix" did, it's an accomplished piece of work with considerable pulp watchability to it. And having a self-referential sense of humor ("You actually go outside in these things?" Wolverine says when face-to-face with an X-uniform) makes the special effects go down that much smoother.

NEW YORK, 7/24/00, p. 51, Peter Rainer

X-Men is a rarity, a comic-book movie with a satisfying cinematic design and protagonists you want to watch. (Most such movies have one or the other.) Although the director, Bryan Singer *(The Usual Suspects)*, obviously researched the *X-Men* comic books and animated television series, his film doesn't seem transposed from another medium; it has a fluidity all its own. And yet it will probably also satisfy aficionados of the Marvel comic book—if only because it bothers to take very seriously all that pop lore.

Comic books can elicit resounding emotions, and so can the best comic-book movies. The first *Batman,* for example, was a great big operatic squall of angst and transcendence. *X-Men* is "character-driven," which means that we're meant to care more about the perpetrators than about what they're perpetrating. But Singer, gifted as he is, still hews somewhat to commercial convention; he doesn't really let loose with such *X-Men* luminaries as the metal-clawed Wolverine (the striking Australian actor Hugh Jackman) and Professor Charles Xavier (Patrick Stewart) and Cyclops (James Marsden), because he's required to set up a franchise, and that means taking fewer risks. And yet he still gets far enough inside the id-like essences of his characters to make you wish he had gone even further into the kind of visionary fullness achieved by Tim Burton in *Batman* and Brian De Palma in *Carrie* and *The Fury*. In a Hollywood era where movies like this are arranged with the same corporate acumen as a stock portfolio, it may be that Singer's hit-and-miss achievement is the best we can hope for. It's a marvelous half-baked movie, leaving you feeling simultaneously full and famished.

The *X-Men*, presided over by mind-meld master Professor Xavier, also include a few *X*-women, among them Storm (Halle Berry), who can conjure up enough climatic conditions to glut the Weather Channel, and Rogue (Anna Paquin), who can absorb the powers of whomever she touches, thereby sending them into horrifying oblivion. All are genetic mutants whose powers have made them outcasts in the human world (set slightly in the future). Their dissident super-mutant counterparts are led by Magneto (Ian McKellen), who can bend metal to his will, and wills to his mettle, and such recruits as the shape-shifting Mystique (Rebecca Romijn-Stamos) and Toad (Ray Park), who scales walls lickety-split and has a twelve-foot projectile tongue that doubles as whip and lasso. Xavier, a man of peace, wants to save the human race from itself and from Magneto, who believes in victory "by any means necessary." (Stewart and McKellen seem to be carrying on a private war of their own over who has the plummiest diction.)

This Malcolm X-Martin Luther King routine, like the film's prologue showing Magneto as a boy in Auschwitz, is a bit too dolorous for what is essentially a grand-scale adolescent fever dream. (Early on, the point is made that the mutants' superpowers usually first show up at puberty.) The differentness and the self-loathing of the mutants, the way they lament finding a place in the world, is something adolescents will probably connect with on a primal level. It's what gives the film its intermittent, balled-up force. Being accepted, not feared, or being accepted because one is feared—this is what underlies the film's cyclopean eye zaps and tongue flicks and mind meltdowns. The appeal of the comic book, and, in a darker and more voluptuous way, of the movie, is that it celebrates being a freakazoid. Kids—and adults too—can watch *X-Men* and feel better about themselves. We're not dorks after all. We're the next stage in human evolution.

NEW YORK POST, 7/14/00, p. 43, Jonathan Foreman

"X-Men" gets off to a terrific start. For the first 20 minutes, it promises to be one of the best-ever movie adaptations of a comic book.

But something happens as the story opens out to include a large ensemble cast of superheroes: The pace slows, and you're asked to focus on characters so thinly sketched that it's hard to really care what happens to them.

For the legions of fans of the original comic book series, all of whom are familiar with the life stories of the various X-men, this skimpy characterization presumably won't be a problem. For such fans, Bryan Singer's adaptation may well be an ecstatic experience.

For everyone else, what "X-men" has going for it are spectacular special effects and sets, enjoyable turns by old reliables Patrick Stewart and Ian McKellen, the vision of Rebecca Romijn-Stamos in nothing but blue body paint and rubber makeup and the debut of yet another young Australian star, Hugh Jackman.

For those unfamiliar with the X-men universe, the story goes something like this: In the near future, there will be mutants among us, people with special powers that manifest themselves at puberty. There'll also be prejudice against these mutants, much of it whipped up by rabble-rousers like Sen. Robert Kelly (Bruce Davison).

To the extent that the mutants have found each other and organized, they are members of two warring groups. One is led by Professor Francis Xavier, known as Professor X (Patrick Stewart). He is an immensely powerful telepath convinced that eventually humans will understand and tolerate their mutant brothers and sisters.

Xavier's former friend Erik Lehnsherr, a Nazi death-camp survivor known as Magneto, has the power to move metal with his mind. Unlike Xavier, Magneto has come to the conclusion that humanity is the enemy and must be conquered. He competes with Professor X to recruit young mutants for his own evil Brotherhood.

Two such youngsters are Rogue (Anna Paquin), a teenage girl with the unfortunate gift of helplessly sucking the life force out of anyone she touches, and Wolverine (Jackman), a young man with great strength and astonishing recuperative powers, who has been implanted with retractable steel claws as part of some kind of military experiment.

The bad-guy team includes Toad (Ray Park), who has a 15-foot, whip-like tongue and can jump huge distances; the gigantic Sabretooth (Tyler Mane); and the shape-shifting Mystique (Rebecca Romijn-Stamos).

The good guys include Storm, (Halle Berry), a white-haired African woman who can control the weather; Cyclops (James Marsden), whose eyes have tremendous destructive power; and Miss Jean Grey (Famke Janssen), who has both telekinetic and telepathic abilities.

Jackman looks oddly like—and even manages to sound like—Clint Eastwood during his sideburn years. Romijn-Stamos doesn't say much, but looks terrific. It's more of a shame that that fine actress Halle Berry gets little to do except get beaten up by the bad guys.

Not surprisingly for a comic series created in 1963, the story is filled with allegorical echoes of the civil rights movement. (Professor X is a Martin Luther King figure; Magneto is more of an embittered Malcolm X—he even uses the phrase "by any means necessary").

But director Bryan Singer ("The Usual Suspects") never lets the well-meaning messages about prejudice, etc., distract from the classic popcorn action or the good-looking cast.

He's also careful not to allow a few post-modern jokes at the genre's own expense to undermine the drama and turn X-men into a spoof.

NEWSDAY, 7/14/00, Part II/p. B3, Gene Seymour

To this avid reader of what were once regularly labeled "funny books," the fervent, if erratic, popularity of "X-Men" is one of the most bewildering of pop culture phenomena. Created in the early 1960s as part of Marvel Comics' legendary editor Stan Lee's revisionist overhaul of the superhero genre, this cadre of misunderstood genetic mutants has appealed to self-styled alienated outcasts of all ages.

Since they've also comprised Marvel's all-time best-selling franchise (yep, even bigger than that bug-bitten outcast Spider-Man himself), one imagines there are a whole lot of alienated outcasts out there who identify with X-Men. Which makes you wonder how come they're all so alienated if there are so many of them.

Maybe one should keep that conundrum in mind over the next several weeks as "X-Men," the movie, absorbs wave upon wave of box-office receipts. This is the can't-miss summer popcorn extravaganza that a nervous Hollywood has been waiting for since Memorial Day, and the good news for the rest of us is that, for the most part, the movie honestly earns its all-but-inevitable success.

Part of the reason is the seamless manner in which director Bryan Singer ("The Usual Suspects") and screenwriter David Hayter weave all the tangled elements of the "X-Men" mythos into an air-tight narrative that will satisfy both the comic's cultists and those without a clue as to what "mutant love" is all about.

So it won't take long for newcomers to understand that the so- called "X-Men universe" is one in which human beings born with what in fairy tales would be regarded as enchanted powers are treated as pariahs and freaks. (And that such mass hysteria is all too similar to myriad horrors of the just-completed century.)

Professor Charles Xavier (Patrick Stewart) and Erik Lehnsherr (Ian McKellen) embody the twin poles of the mutant response to this bigotry. The latter, an embittered Holocaust survivor who also goes by the name "Magneto" (guess what his power is), leads a brotherhood of terrorist mutants at war with humanity. Xavier, a super-telepath also known as Professor X, runs a bucolic Westchester prep school and sanctuary for young mutants while leading a secret strike force of "X" (as in extra-special or extraordinary) men and women who use their somewhat frightening powers to protect humanity—whether it wants such protection or not.

Both Xavier and Magneto are seeking two prospects for their respective causes. One is a bushy Canadian roughneck named Wolverine (Hugh Jackman), who would be tough to beat in hand-to-hand combat even without the long rapier claws that poke out of his knuckles when he's really angry. The other is a winsome Mississippi teenager named Rogue (Anna Paquin), whose empathy is so strong that she can't touch people without draining their "life force."

Got all that? Hard as it may be to believe, this stuff plays out a lot quicker than you expect. Filmed in dark, sleek colors and paced like a 400-meter relay, "X-Men" manages to leap over its hoarier improbabilities and keeps your eye on the up-to-the-minute special effects and gleaming physicality of the antagonists. Though sheathed throughout in scaly blue, Rebecca Romijn-Stamos as the homicidal chameleon Mystique makes as big an impact on the senses as her evil partners Sabretooth (ex-pro wrestler Tyler Mane) and Toad (Ray "Darth Maul" Park).

The acting, beyond the ersatz authority exerted by dueling Shakespeareans Stewart and McKellen, is generally spotty—though everybody looks so gosh-darned good you don't care. Much. You wish, for instance, that Halle Berry as Storm would speak in a normal voice, though all she really has to do is stare intently to be effective. Famke Janssen and James Marsden are properly resolute in their respective roles as kinetic telepath Jean Grey and laser-eyed field general Cyclops. But it's Jackman, the latest in an apparently endless procession of brooding Australian hunks, who makes the best impression as the brooding Wolverine.

Is a sequel coming? Hey, does water freeze in winter? In fact, "X-Men" seems such a conspicuous set-up for "X-Men II" you'll feel the movie you're watching is just a trailer for the next one. Here's a hint (maybe): Watch the skies for sentinels.

NEWSWEEK, 7/24/00, p. 56, Jeff Giles

Puberty can make anybody feel like a mutant. But young Rogue (Anna Paquin) has got it particularly bad: she recently discovered that if she touches people for too long, she drains their life force and they die quaking in pain. Dating, clearly, is a problem. "The first boy I ever kissed ended up in a coma for three weeks," Rogue tells her fellow mutant Wolverine (Hugh Jackman) early in Bryan Singer's smart, sleek and mordantly funny "X-Men." Wolverine, a furtive and menacing loner with a motorcycle jacket and Civil War sideburns, understands completely. He can make foot-long blades flash out from between his knuckles; ordinarily he uses them to keep enemies at bay, but once in a while he stabs a friend by accident. Human contact is not his specialty either.

"X-Men," adapted from Stan Lee's enormously popular Marvel Comics series, spins out a complicated story, but all it really wants to know is, *Why can't everybody just get along*? Mutants can pass for regular folks. Because their DNA evolved at hyperspeed, however, each of them has developed a superpower he or she can use in the service of good or evil. At the outset of "X-Men," a braying senator (Bruce Davison) denounces the mutant underclass as a threat and calls for a kind of witch hunt. This hurts a lot of mutants' feelings. The imperious bad-guy mutant Magneto (Ian McKellen), who can do cool stuff to metal with his mind, moves to silence the senator, and prepares his followers for war. Thank heavens for the good-guy mutants. The telepathic Professor Xavier (Patrick Stewart) has followers of his own—among them Rogue and Wolverine—and soon the two mutant factions are battling atop the Statue of Liberty.

Geez, all that sounds sort of ridiculous. But director Singer, best known for the arty noir "The Usual Suspects," is not a typical action director, and he's made a nuanced, nonpreposterous sci-fi fantasy that makes "The Phantom Menace" and the last few "Batman" outrages seem even lamer in retrospect. By all rights, Singer's film should have been a disaster. Imagine trying to cull a single story line from 37 years' worth of comic books—knowing that hardcore fans were going to sharpshoot every frame of your movie and that the studio was going to be wringing its hands over whether nonmutants would pay to see the thing too. For diehard fans "X-Men" is full of in jokes and sly references (tiny throw-away cameos by Iceman and Kitty Pryde, etc.). For everybody else, there's the thrill of the unknown. David Hayter's screenplay, by turns sardonic and touching, conveys an enormous amount of information without a lot of clunky exposition—there are no lines like "Hi, I'm Storm and I can control the weather! What's *your* name?" The mutants reveal their particular gifts in battle. You know these guys are going to kick each other's butts, What you don't know is how.

The good-guy and bad-guy mutants are equally fun to behold. In the benevolent Professor Xavier's corner, we've got not just Rogue and Wolverine, but Storm (Halle Berry), the telepathic Jean Grey (Famke Janssen) and her smirky, Tom Cruise-ish boyfriend Cyclops (James Marsden), whose eyes shoot lasers. (Wolverine has a thing for Jean Grey, and can't believe she digs Cyclops. "Is that your gift—putting up with that guy?") In Magneto's corner, there's the hulking Sabretooth (Tyler Mane), who has the misfortune of looking like John Travolta in "Battlefield Earth." There's Mystique (Rebecca Romijn-Stamos in blue body paint), who can morph into anyone. And there's Toad, (Ray Park, formerly Darth Maul in "Phantom Menace"), who can hop really far and hang on to things by his tongue.

"X-Men," it must be said, has only a few truly thrilling moments. This is not a picture that tries to blow you out of your seat. But more than any other big movie this summer, it has a consistently inventive vision. You don't just sit there waiting for a big wave. "X-Men" has plenty of little plot twists—thanks to Mystique's constant morphing, you don't even know who's beating on whom sometimes—and a bottomless bag of special effects. Midair acrobatics. Shapes that shift. Metal that flies. Weapons that float. Bodies that rubberize and liquefy, and on and on.

You can't make any claims for the acting in "X-Men" but apart from Berry's performance, which is soft and unfocused—it does have the advantage of not stinking. To their credit, the actors tend toward the minimalist, eschewing cartoony gestures. McKellen's Magneto is not the histrionic madman we're accustomed to, but a scarily sane villain. He survived a World War II concentration camp as a child, and he's not about to have another number tattooed on his arm. Magneto is simply appalled by humanity's lack of humanity; change a couple of lines in the screenplay and he could be the hero. Jackman's Wolverine, meanwhile, is a wonderful creation. Apparently, Singer once wanted Russell Crowe for the role, and Jackman, who's Australian, plays the part with a growling sensitivity not unlike Crowe's. Wolverine is off-the-charts cool as a superhero. But he's also just as screwed-up-guy—the noble, conflicted soul of the "X-Men" universe. Late in the movie, good old Professor Xavier wakes up in an infirmary and asks worriedly, "How did we do?" Splendidly, Professor. Rest up for the sequel.

SIGHT AND SOUND, 9/00, p. 59, José Arroyo

Poland, 1944. When a young boy gets separated from his parents in a concentration camp, he unleashes a magnetic force that bends the fence's metal gate. The boy grows up to be Magneto. Magneto and former friend Charles Xavier, a telepath, are mutants, people whose extraordinary powers set them apart from other humans.

In America, sometime in the future, Senator Kelly is calling for a system of registration for such mutants. Meanwhile, Rogue, a young girl, runs away to Canada from her Mississippi home when she discovers she has mutant powers. (She can absorb people's life force by touching them.) There, she meets Wolverine, a mutant who is able to heal his body instantly and is fitted with an adamantium skeleton that includes retractable claws. Wolverine and Rogue are attacked by Sabretooth, one of Magneto's lackeys, but are rescued by Storm and Cyclops, associates of Professor Xavier. They take Wolverine and Rogue to Xavier's school for gifted mutants. Xavier mistakenly believes Magneto is trying to capture Wolverine; but in fact, Magneto is after Rogue, whom he kidnaps when she runs away from Xavier's school. Believing mutants to be superior to the rest of the human race, Magneto has developed a machine which mutates ordinary human's DNA and gifts them similar powers to his own; he plans for Rogue to absorb his powers—which drive the machine and transform the world's leaders, meeting on Ellis Island, New York for a conference, into mutants.

Following the death of Kelly, on whom Magneto tested this device, Xavier realises Magneto's plan will lead to the death of many humans. Magneto's associate Mystique sabotages a device which Xavier uses to improve his telepathic skills; when the professor next uses it, he's almost killed. Wolverine joins the X-Men, a band of mutants comprising Cyclops, Storm and Grey dedicated to using their powers for the greater good. They fly to the Statue of Liberty, where Magneto is about to operate his machine. The X-Men defeat Magneto, who is imprisoned in a plastic cell.

In America, DC and Marvel are the two great publishing companies of superhero comic books. DC, which owns such titles as *Superman, Batman* and *Wonder Woman*, is the source of powerful childhood fantasies. Post-puberty, though, readers tend to graduate to the harsher and more complex world of Marvel, whose titles included *The Fantastic Four, Spider-Man* and, of course, *The Uncanny X-Men*. There, good didn't always win in the end and superheroes were often angst-ridden characters, shunned by humanity. Yet, while Marvel ruled in comic books, DC was able to turn *Superman* and *Batman,* its two flagship characters, into blockbuster film franchises. The closest Marvel came to screen success was in television, usually anodyne cartoons for toddlers. Marvel on screen was a betrayal because it reproduced what we had left behind in DC. Moreover, DC on screen, at least in Tim Burton's *Batman* films, was what we'd all hoped for from Marvel. These are only some of the reasons—tribal ones, admittedly—why the new X-Men film has been so keenly anticipated.

Fans were right to fear that one of Marvel's very best titles might have been trashed. Turning a long-running and much loved comic into a film tends to be more difficult than adapting a novel or a play. With the *X-Men* there are almost 40 years' worth of stories to choose from. The tone and visuals have changed over the years, too. Film-makers also have to deal with the expectations of loyal fans. Moreover any adaptation of a superhero book needs to set out how its central character came to have his or her extraordinary powers so that non-fans can follow the story. It's a complex job, one well done in *X-Men* by screenwriters David Hayter, Tom DeSanto and Bryan Singer (also directing).

The structure they've created for the film is built on parallelism and oppositions. Magneto, the villain, and Professor Xavier, the X-Men's founder, are in many ways equal but opposite to one another. Friendly foes, they are both powerful mutants, each with a band of followers. But whereas Magneto wants to conquer the world, Xavier wants to save it; whereas Magneto's followers are lackeys, Xavier's are students, encouraged to think for themselves. In many ways the film is about the attempt by Magneto—who first discovered his mutant powers in a concentration camp—to stop the politician Kelly's Nazi-like scheme to impose a mutant-registration scheme. But it's Wolverine—who makes the journey from hard-drinking loner to X-Man in order to [put a] halt to Magneto's scheme—who drives the story. Wolverine's trajectory finds echoes in Rogue's arc, from isolated Mississippi teenager to one of Xavier's gifted pupils, but whereas she's an outsider because of what happened to her naturally at puberty, Wolverine's sense of alienation derives from being subjected to painful, state sanctioned medical research—a further allusion to Nazism. While there are still holes in the plot, this complex but deft structure—tightly woven around the central theme of prejudice—allows different characters to share the burden of a convoluted plot.

But the film could have fallen apart if other elements hadn't succeeded. Visually, the movie is a treat. X-Man Cyclops' joke about wearing yellow spandex suits suggests the film-makers were right to dispense with the garish uniforms of the original comic book and opt for darker, more high-tech accoutrements. The make-up work is accomplished—we see expressive faces behind the masks—and the set design is a superb combination of opulence and minimalism (Xavier's school, for instance, is all leafy exteriors and oak-panelled lecture halls, but it conceals a network of chrome vaults and pristine corridors). Assisted by DoP Newton Thomas Sigel, Singer's visual flair is evident throughout: from the simplest of shots such as the first image we see of Wolverine, his face shrouded in shadows and smoke, to the big set pieces—notably the fight on top of the Statue of Liberty (recalling *Saboteur*, 1942)—which are witty, if a little short of thrilling.

Aspects of the film *X-Men* clearly don't work: Halle Berry is a little too cute to play Storm and Ian McKellen lacks the size to convey Magento's sense of physical menace. Yet, in spite of this, *X-Men* works. It's not as good as *Superman II* and certainly nowhere near as good as the comic book; but it's good enough to raise hopes for the sequel—Marvel may yet beat DC on screen.

TIME, 7/24/00, p. 65, Richard Corliss

Action movies need a jazzy opening scene; it gets a moviegoer's pulse racing with anxiety. So 007 went airborne off a ski slope. *Lethal Weapon's* Danny Glover sat on a bomb-rigged toilet seat. But until now, no one had set a teaser scene in a Nazi death camp, where gaunt Jews trudge to their doom. A boy, torn from his parents, goes into a seizure, and the camp gates are bent open. Aha! So the inmates are miraculously freed? No. It's not about the 6 million. It's about this one kid—an X-kid.

The first scene of the *X-Men* movie, which follows 37 years of legendmaking in Marvel comics, video games and animated TV shows, tips the hand of director Bryan Singer and screenwriter David Hayter. This will be a fantasy film with a message: the shunned are special; those seen as mutants are really superior; odd kids are good kids. And the world is a dark brown place where even the most extravagant stunt or special effect lacks the all-important Wow Factor.

Charles Xavier (Patrick Stewart) runs a school for exceptional young people: folks like Storm (Halle Berry), who plays tricks with weather; Wolverine (Hugh Jackman), whose fists contain adamantine blades; Cyclops (James Marsden), with a killer stare; and Rogue (Anna Paquin), whose touch is toxic. Xavier and Dr. Jean Grey (Famke Janssen) battle the bad guys led by Magneto (Ian McKellen) over the fate of the planet—that old thing.

The fairness doctrine demands a list of cool stuff. Marsden, Janssen and Berry reward any viewer's long gaze. Toad (Ray Park), a bad mutant, makes quick use of his mile-long tongue. A dozen red roses for the blue lady Mystique (Rebecca Romijn-Stamos); this morph magician is the best weird woman in s-f movies since Daryl Hannah's android in *Blade Runner*.

The human villain of the piece is Senator Kelly (Bruce Davison), a suaver Joe McCarthy. He wants mutants registered because, he says, their eccentric gifts make them dangerous. Well, the mutant hunter is right! Magneto and his gang have planet-altering mischief in mind.

The other thing action movies can use is a jazzy ending. This one has a noisy climactic tussle inside the Statue of Liberty. Mightn't a few feds be guarding the premises? Again, no. It's a mistake for a fantasy film in the realistic mode to be deficient in both magic and plausibility.

But the climax is not the end. There is no ending; the whole film is the teaser to a planned trilogy. So Wolverine, searching for his roots, keeps on scratching.

Xavier and Magneto speak of battles to come. A muted film ends on a minor chord. Perhaps fans will return for later episodes. But for us nonmutants, *X-Men* is the movie that took the *e-cite-t* out of *excitement*.

VILLAGE VOICE, 7/25/00, p. 119, J. Hoberman

It ain't saying much but, when it comes to stoopid fun, *X-Men* could be the summer movie to beat—it's nearly as enjoyable as avoiding *The Patriot* and *The Perfect Storm*. The running time is compact, the action is acrobatic rather than explosive, and the adolescent rage is considerably more wholesome than that of *Criminal Lovers*.

Launched by Marvel Comics in 1963 as "The Uncanny X-Men" and initially drawn by the great Jack Kirby, the X-Men were the original teenage mutant superheroes. The movie is true to its source—at least for being comic-book snide and smoldering with high school resentment. Director Bryan Singer has found his own level. Indeed, *X-Men* begins more or less where his political pulp puzzler *Apt Pupil* left off—with Ian McKellen flashing back to the gates of Auschwitz.

So far as the mutants go, the movie spends too much time dwelling on the problems of glowering Wolverine (Hugh Jackman) and tremulous Rogue (Anna Paquin), but even here the romantic self-pity has a Cheez Doodle airiness. Ray Park's Toad is more convincing than his Darth Maul. His intercontinental ballistic tongue brought down the house at the all-media screening, although the movie's most alarming effect is surely Halle Berry's white plastic wig.

Also reviewed in:
CHICAGO TRIBUNE, 7/14/00, Friday/p. A Michael Wilmington
NEW YORK TIMES, 7/14/00, p. E1, Elvis Mitchell
NEW YORKER, 7/24/00, p. 86, David Denby
VARIETY, 7/17-23/00, p. 25, Dennis Harvey
WASHINGTON POST, 7/14/00, p. C1, Stephen Hunter
WASHINGTON POST, 7/14/00, Weekend/p. 33, Desson Howe

YARDS, THE

A Miramax Films release of a Paul Webster/Industry Entertainment production. *Executive Producer:* Bob Weinstein, Harvey Weinstein, and Jonathan Gordon. *Producer:* Nick Wechsler, Paul Webster, and Kerry Orent. *Director:* James Gray. *Screenplay:* James Gray and Matt Reeves. *Director of Photography:* Harris Savides. *Editor:* Jeffrey Ford. *Music:* Howard Shore. *Music Editor:* Annette Kudrak. *Sound:* Tom Paul and (music) Simon Rhodes. *Sound Editor:* Phil Benson. *Casting:* Douglas Aibel. *Production Designer:* Kevin Thompson. *Art Director:* Judy Rhee. *Set Decorator:* Ford Wheeler. *Set Dresser:* Anthony Baldasare, Peter Von Bartheld, William Kolpin, Mark Simon, Robin Koenig, Walter Stocklin, and Victoria Vanasco. *Special Effects:* John Otteson. *Costumes:* Michael Clancy. *Make-up:* Donald Mowat and Leslie Fuller. *Make-up (Charlize Theron):* Deborah Larsen *Stunt Coordinator:* Jery Hewitt. *Running time:* 115 minutes. *MPAA Rating:* R.

CAST: Mark Wahlberg (Leo Handler); Joaquin Phoenix (Willie Gutierrez); Charlize Theron (Erica Stoltz); James Caan (Frank Olchin); Ellen Burstyn (Val Handler); Faye Dunaway (Kitty Olchin); Chad Aaron (Bernard Stoltz); Andrew Davoli (Raymond Price); Steve Lawrence (Arthur Mydanick); Tony Musante (Seymour Korman); Victor Argo (Paul Lazarides); Tomas Milian (Manuel Sequiera); Robert Montano (Hector Gallardo); Victor Arnold (Albert Granada); Louis Guss (Nathan Grodner); Domenick Lombardozzi (Todd); Joe Lisi (Elliot); David Zayas (Officer Jerry Rifkin); Joseph Ragno (Parole Officer); Teresa Yenque (Maid); Jose Soto (Orderly); John Tormey (Contract Officer); Teddy Coluca (Terry); Jack O'Connell (Sal Disipio); Dan Grimaldi (Executive One); Garry Pastore (Detective Tommasino); Ron Brice (Detective Boulett); Gene Canfield (Queensborough Policeman); Keith Hernandez and Allan Houston (Baseball Celebrities); Andi Shrem (Belva); Joe Dimare (Dante); Barry Wetcher (Young Doctor); Oscar Colon (Well Dressed Man); Jace Kent (Young Italian Man); Brandon Danziger (Neil); Doug Barron (Doctor); Floyd Resnick (Hospital Cop); Chris Edwards and Raymond Seiden (Police Officers); Annika Pergament (Reporter); Maximiliano Hernandez (Bartender); Kip Evans (Guy); John Elsen and Douglas Crosby (Officers); Scott Nicholson (Policeman); Kim Merritt (Todd's Girlfriend); Erin Walls (Dante's Girlfriend); Tyree Simpson (Doorman); Peter Vallone (Councilman); Irwin Gray (Lawyer); Denise Traficanti (Secretary); Roma Torre, Louis Dodley, and Ernie Anastos (News Anchors).

LOS ANGELES TIMES, 10/20/00, Calendar/p. 2, Kevin Thomas

In "The Yards" writer-director James Gray follows Leo Handler (Mark Wahlberg), just released from prison, to the modest Queens apartment of his mother, Val (Ellen Burstyn), where a festive homecoming gathering awaits him. Gray, who wrote his script with Matt Reeves, may as well be dropping in on a gathering of the house of Atreus, so much is the fate of Leo's family the stuff of Greek tragedy.

Leo is a diffident 24-year-old with a bad haircut and drab clothing who, having taken a 16-month fall for auto theft on behalf of friends, wants only to get on with his life and stay out of trouble. Yet only days later he has left a cop comatose and is wanted for a murder he did not commit. Before this happens, Gray introduces the quality inevitably essential to tragedy.

His widowed aunt Kitty (Faye Dunaway) has recently remarried, to Frank Olchin (James Caan), whose business is repairing subway cars in the vast yards that give the film its name. Kitty, her daughter Erica (Charlize Theron) and adolescent son Bernard (Chad Aaron) are now living in Frank's vintage brick castle-like mansion with interiors that have acres of dark wood paneling, signifying a solidity and security largely illusory.

Before his release Leo received assurances that Frank would have a job waiting for him. At the party, his brash pal Willie (Joaquin Phoenix)—for whom Leo principally took the fall—insists that at Frank's factory he should work alongside him. Clearly, Willie, who has been going with Erica, is in the money, and Kitty has confided to Leo that his mother is fading from a heart condition.

At a formal meeting in Frank's office, Frank gently—too gently—tries to steer Leo away from working with Willie in supplies and suggests that he consider training for a machinist's position, not making clear until a family dinner that he, Frank, would help him financially through this period. Not that this delay would have mattered much: Both Val and Leo have too much pride to accept help from Frank, and Frank's pride, in turn, prevents him from spelling out just why he's trying to steer Leo away from Willie.

Frank is in fact fighting off being crushed by forces beyond his control—conglomerates, minority quotas among them. Clearly, in Frank's world greasing the palms of the police and politicians in landing lucrative contracts is a long-established, business-as-usual practice.

But the pressures upon Frank are increasing sharply, prompting him and his underlings to take increasingly dangerous and illegal risks. Leo has barely started working with Willie when, in a murky preemptive maneuver in the yards, Willie winds up knifing to death a rail switchman and Leo nearly beating to death the cop. Willie, backed by his pals, threatens to stick the switchman's murder on Leo, forcing him to try to kill the cop to make sure that he never comes out of his coma.

Having set up Leo's dilemma with great care, Gray then explores its private and public dimensions. Suspense swiftly develops as the wagons circle: Who will be left out to fend for himselp And at what level will those wagons circle? In a system of long-institutionalized corruption Frank and the smooth borough president (Steve Lawrence, yes, the Steve Lawrence, in a nifty acting turn) could well join forces. And it could well be that the positions of Leo and Willie might just wind up reversed.

There are some holes here to be sure: For example, you wonder why there's no police surveillance of Val's apartment, which Leo, wanted by the police, visits repeatedly and without temerity. But "The Yards" is so strong and secure in its remorseless movement that you buy into what's happening, its people so firmly gripped in the vise of fate and their own character flaws.

Frank and Willie echo each other in that they both have loving, decent instincts that are forever tainted by the criminal. Willie, a big lug with Elvis Presley looks, has the further liability of being a hothead who's none too smart but, as an ambitious Latino in Frank's white world, is craving an acceptance that Frank's key business rival (Tomas Milian) insists he will never receive.

As he did so effectively in his memorable first film, "Little Odessa," Gray creates an everyday world, blue-collar and somewhat ethnic in feeling, in which there is a continuum between respectability and corruption. The flow and balance between the two elements is in constant, often volatile flux.

In this, Gray recalls Sidney Lumet's New York films, but whereas Lumet has a crisp, crackling wit, Gray retains a somber, elegiac tone in keeping with his tragic vision, echoed in Harris Savides' masterly dark-hued camera work and in Howard Shore's stately score. (Production designer Kevin Thompson's crucial contribution to the film's authenticity is as accurate as it is subtle.)

Gray's splendid, self-effacing cast performs as an ensemble, but the film's rightly dominant presences are Caan and Dunaway, the linchpin couple who understand that it is they who must hold the family together no matter how or what. It's Dunaway's Kitty who leads a clasping of family hands that sustains and protects as surely as it crushes and destroys.

NEW YORK, 10/30/00, p. 93, Peter Rainer

The phenomenal cast of *The Yards*—including Mark Wahlberg, James Caan, Joaquin Phoenix, Ellen Burstyn, Charlize Theron, and Faye Dunaway—creates a force field that keeps you watching even when the film turns into a rather overfamiliar reworking of *On the Waterfront*. The young writer-director James Gray, whose first, crime-based film, about Russian Jewish immigrants, was *Little Odessa*, returns to the New York mob scene for this depiction of corruption and family ties in Queens. He has become a highly practiced and powerful filmmaker who understands that the underworld is as rife with shades of gray as any other locale; no one in this film can be pegged at first or even second glance, and that gives the action a psychological density uncommon to the crime-film genre. James Caan's Frank, for example, who runs a payola-powered electronics-parts company and who is deeply in cahoots with his borough's politicos, is by no means a cartoon meanie. He understands the indecency of his enterprise and tries to save his ex-con nephew, Mark Wahlberg's Leo, from becoming a part of it. When violence and betrayal erupt in this film, it's doubly shocking because we can see how, for all these characters, there was another way.

Something of a classic manqué, *The Yards* has the weight and import of a great movie without ever achieving greatness—but you're left with something anyway: the freezing look on Caan's face when he realizes he must become the monster he didn't want to be; the sorrowfulness of Ellen Burstyn as Wahlberg's ailing mother, baffled into bleariness by her son's misfortunes; the stiff-necked pride of Joaquin Phoenix as Caan's strong-arm man, his thick, jet-black hair like the manifestation of a deeper darkness within.

NEW YORK POST, 10/20/00, p. 53, Jonathan Foreman

Visually accomplished and wonderfully acted, James Gray's "The Yards" is a downbeat drama about corruption in the New York City rail yards.

Leo (Mark Wahlberg) has just gotten out of jail and come back to Queens after taking the fall for car thefts committed with his friends. Now, worried about his ailing mother Val (Ellen Burstyn), he wants a regular job.

Val's sister Kitty (Faye Dunaway) has recently remarried Frank (a fine James Caan) who runs a politically-connected company that builds and repairs subway trains.

Frank already employs Leo's slick best friend Gutierrez (Joaquin Phoenix) who's now going out with gorgeous Erica (Charlize Theron), the daughter of Leo's Aunt Kitty.

Although nothing is said, it's pretty clear Leo and Erica were once unusually close for first cousins.

Through Willie's intercession, Leo not only gets a job with Uncle Frank, he's assigned to work with Willie, who is Frank's point man when it comes to the illegal activities that are part and parcel of the rail yard business.

Frank's company, it seems, is threatened by competition particularly by a Hispanic-owned corporation that is guaranteed 10 percent of all the city's rail yard business.

Frank therefore has to step up illegal efforts to get city dollars, whether that means bribing officials or having Willie organize the sabotage of trains repaired by the competition.

Leo accompanies Willie on one such wrecking expedition, one that goes badly when Willie stabs a rail yard manager to death and Leo is forced to defend himself against a club-wielding policeman and ends up putting the cop in a coma.

If the cop comes to, the ensuing investigations could bust the whole corrupt system wide open, so Willie orders Leo to make sure that he doesn't tell his story.

When Leo fails to murder the officer—who then does wake up—Willie lets it be known that Leo is responsible for both the murder and the assault on the cop.

Leo is forced into hiding, but he has no intention of taking the fall for his former best friend or his Uncle Frank.

Generally this movie is at its strongest when it's dealing with relationships. The screenplay by Gray, the director, and Matt Reeves is at its weakest and most prone to cliché in the scenes where crimes are being discussed or carried out.

But even when it's predictable, "The Yards' is remarkable for the way in which every character has more than one side, especially Willie, whose villainy is of the tragic kind.

Wahlberg is an actor comfortable in relatively quiet impassive roles, but Gray draws from him an unusually textured and powerful performance.

Joaquin Phoenix, who has already proved himself to be one of our best and most interesting young actors ("Gladiator," "Return to Paradise," "To Die For") is in top form.

The story parallels in some ways the real life fall of Queens Borough President Donald Manes who killed himself in March 1986, setting off a scandal that eventually scarred the administration of Mayor Ed Koch.

NEWSDAY, 10/20/00, Part II/p. B6, John Anderson

Before it collapses into a weary catalog of crime-movie cliches and political impossibilities, the urban drama "The Yards" accomplishes something very impressive: It makes a seemingly exhausted genre get on its feet and flex its muscles.

This long-awaited follow-up to James Gray's much-admired "Little Odessa" poses the well-worn question of whether its working-class hero, a guy who took da rap for his pals, can straighten up and fly right. And of course if he could, there wouldn't be much of a movie.

Still, "The Yards" contains lots of great atmosphere, from the too-loud Queens homecoming party thrown for our ex-con Leo Handler (Mark Wahlberg) to the throbbing, volatile disco where he and his friend Willie Gutierrez (Joaquin Phoenix) and cousin Erica (Charlize Theron) dance away Leo's first weekend home. When Leo gets introduced to the bare-knuckle, pocket-picking world of Erica's stepfather, mustachioed subway-equipment contractor Frank Olchin (James Caan), the corruption is palpable, certainly plausible. When Leo, who has to support his ailing mother (Ellen Burstyn), shares in his first payoff with Willie, you know his rehabilitation is already derailed.

A murder at the subway yards, where Willie and his cohorts sabotage compeititors' equipment, and the subsequent framing of Leo, set the stage for the dissolution of family bonds and friendships. Some of the fighting is so well staged you feel these are people who actually once loved each other.

But then "The Yards" not only crawls to a halt, it becomes something else entirely. Hackneyed plot devices replace the authenticity of Gray's direction. The thing certainly goes on far too long. And the concluding sequence, involving big city politics (and a boss played by Steve Lawrence!), which segues into some kind of congressional investigation, is all just ludicrous—although Wahlberg does a pretty good imitation of Brando in "On the Waterfront."

SIGHT AND SOUND, 12/00, p. 59, Geoffrey Macnab

Leo Handler arrives back in New York after four years in prison. He takes a job with his Uncle Frank who runs a local subway company. His old friend Willie Gutierrez takes him under his wing. Leo joins Willie and his gang on an expedition to vandalise train stock belonging to a rival company. Willie has an argument with a night-watchman who will no longer take his bribes. When the night-watchman lets off the alarm, Willie stabs him dead. A police officer turns up and catches Leo; Leo bludgeons the officer unconscious and escapes.

Willie infers to Frank that Leo killed the night-watchman. He tries to persuade Leo to murder the police officer, who is in hospital in a coma. Instead, Leo goes into hiding. His sickly mother is devastated to learn he is in trouble again. Willie's girlfriend Erica, who is Frank's stepdaughter, begins to suspect that Leo is being stitched up. Frank arranges to meet and help Leo. At the rendezvous, Leo realises Frank has a gun and flees.

Leo and Willie have a fight. Willie's relationship with Erica (who was Leo's childhood sweetheart) rapidly deteriorates. They have a bitter row; pushed over a banister by Willie, Erica falls to her death. Leo gets in touch with a rival train company and tells them what he knows about Frank's business methods. He agrees to give himself up to the police. At a special hearing, he blows the whistle on Frank and his cronies.

Self-consciously elegiac, *The Yards* is a slow-burning but meticulously crafted family melodrama posing as a thriller. Writer-director James Gray (making his second feature after 1994's *Little Odessa*) set his story in Queens, New York, but neither the location nor the plot—which touches on political corruption and industrial sabotage—is the mainspring here. Gray is far more preoccupied with the relationships between the various family members at the heart of his film than with his ostensible subject matter—the battle to control New York's subway.

The opening shot, a close-up of an earnest-looking Leo, played by Mark Wahlberg, aboard a train taking him home after four years in prison, sets the tone: he is the outsider being drawn back into a community whose rules he doesn't fully understand. As if to emphasise his uncertainty, Gray keeps the look of the film dark: there are several power cuts, everyone seems to dress in muted colours, even Howard Shore's majestic, sombre score adds to the prevailing mood of solemnity. While it is apparent from the outset that Leo is a good lad at heart—he dotes on his ailing mother—it is also obvious that his wicked uncle and his best friend Willie, Cain to his Abel, will lead him astray. We can guess that the uncle is a scheming Machiavellian by the oblique way Gray frames him—he's often seen through half-open doors or at the end of corridors, schmoozing and cajoling. It's also hard to trust Willie: barely has Leo got out of prison than he sees him start fights in nightclubs and pay bribes to a stream of men in suits.

Gray's debt to *The Godfather* (1977) is obvious both in the casting of James Caan, who plays Leo's scheming uncle, and in his intense focus on family relations. At various points—as he creeps through the hospital or moves his sickly mother out of his apartment to escape killers—Leo even seems like a latter-day version of Al Pacino's equally conscientious, equally torn Michael Corleone. But whereas Coppola's film was set in the world of organised crime, *The Yards*, rather more prosaically, is about rival New York subway companies. In this regard, Gray's epic ambitions feel a little strained: it's hard to see crooked contractors and embezzling local-government officers as the tragic figures Gray intends. Nor does the denouement—in which Leo testifies against his own to a McCarthy-style hearing—carry the impact that might have been expected.

Where the film does register is as a study of a family torn apart by betrayal and bad faith. With few shoot-outs or kinetic action scenes, *The Yards* relies on the subtlety and intensity of the performances, most of which are excellent. Wahlberg is both feisty and vulnerable as the baffled ex-con; the saturnine-looking Joaquin Phoenix, who plays Willie, has a rare knack of making villainous characters seem sympathetic; Caan excels as the unscrupulous, thick-skinned fixer who pretends to be a dedicated family man but is willing to sacrifice a close relative for the sake of his business. If Gray risks going down a blind tunnel by paying so much attention to subway politics, he gets away with it through sheer dint of craftsmanship. Ultimately, *The Yards* is well enough acted and scripted to bear comparison with the character-driven films of the 70s it strives to emulate.

VILLAGE VOICE, 10/24/00, p. 150, Dennis Lim

After only two features, James Gray is emerging as a distinctive, confidently unfashionable voice in American movies. The 31-year-old, whose sorrowful debut, *Little Odessa*, brought a bracing chill to the flushed, Tarantino-smitten indie landscape of the mid '90s, seems intent on perfecting a single-mindedly downbeat fusion of '70s-Hollywood grunge, autobiographical ethnography, and Greek tragedy. *The Yards* is nominally a tale of shady business dealings and local-government corruption in the subway yards of Sunnyside, but as in his earlier, frostier Brighton Beach hit-man drama, Gray's real subject is the constricting force and painful attrition of family bonds. The Flushing-born director, whose father was a subway contractor, has apparently dredged up childhood memories and, with touching fearlessness, projected them onto the movie-backdrop of his youth: Coppola and Scorsese, *On the Waterfront, Rocco and His Brothers.*

Working-class Queens lad Leo Handler (Mark Wahlberg), the film's designated stooge and moral conscience, returns home after serving time for auto theft. Determined to stay clear of trouble—not least for the sake of his fretful, ailing mother (Ellen Burstyn)—Leo seeks honest employment from Frank (James Caan), the wire-pulling train-parts mogul whom his Aunt Kitty (Faye Dunaway) has married, only to wind up reluctant deputy to his boyhood pal Willie (Joaquin Phoenix), now Frank's dirty-work henchman. To enrich the complications, Willie also happens to be dating Kitty's daughter, Erica (Charlize Theron), a slinky kohl-eyed beauty whose every interaction with cousin Leo carries an incestuous frisson.

A botched attempt at competitor sabotage sets in motion Leo's rapid downward spiral, and Gray never eases up on the sense of looming cosmic tragedy (Howard Shore's studiedly oppressive score envelops the film like a shroud). The script, which Gray cowrote with Matt Reeves, isn't always up to the boldly operatic style: Throwaway exchanges ring truer than declarative monologues, which tend to affix themselves like lead weights to the already grave proceedings. Still, Gray balances the hugeness of the canvas and the occasional broadness of his strokes with spare, scrupulous detail in the individual characterizations. He's helped by the instantly iconic elders in his cast—Caan, in particular, is excellent, subtly registering the guilt and exhaustion of a lifetime's cumulative compromise—and by the two young leads. Phoenix effectively downplays

Willie's tortured, confused ambition, and Wahlberg is boundlessly sympathetic in delineating Leo's stoic despair.

The schematic narrative flirts with muffled, overwrought implausibility—scale is very much an end in itself. But Gray knows well enough to slip in a moment or two of perfectly judged awkwardness (Erica stiffly and abruptly resting her head on Frank's shoulder after a weepy apology) and the odd unnerving bit of disorientation (when Leo is dispatched to a hospital ward on an execution mission, his terror is filtered through gauzy screens and sickly green light). *The Yards* is no less handsomely mounted than *Little Odessa*—veteran music-video cinematographer Harris Savides suffuses the interiors in a nostalgic burnished ochre that makes it easy to forget the film's present-day setting. The tradition of American independent directors making movies that relate chiefly to other movies should not be encouraged, but there's a difference here. Gray's brand of film-buffery manifests itself, simply and irresistibly, as ardent, uncynical movie love.

Also reviewed in:
CHICAGO TRIBUNE, 10/20/00, Friday/p. A, Michael Wilmington
NEW YORK TIMES, 10/20/00, p. E12, Stephen Holden
NEW YORKER, 10/30/00, p. 114, Anthony Lane
VARIETY, 5/29-6/4/00, p. 22, Todd McCarthy
WASHINGTON POST, 10/27/00, p. C5, Stephen Hunter
WASHINGTON POST, 10/27/00, Weekend/p. 41, Desson Howe

YI YI

A Winstar Cinema release of a J1+2 Seisaku Iinkai; Pony Canyon Inc. & Omega Project Inc. presentation of an Atom Films production. *Producer:* Shinya Kawai and Naoko Tsukeda. *Director:* Edward Yang. *Screenplay (Mandarin with English subtitles):* Edward Yang. *Director of Photography:* Yang Weihan. *Editor:* Chen Bowen. *Music:* Peng Kaili. *Sound:* Du Duzhi. *Casting:* Alex Yang. *Production Designer:* Chen Bowen. *Art Director:* Chihiro Masumoto and Wang Zhengkai. *Make-up:* Yuan Jingwei. *Running time:* 173 minutes. *MPAA Rating:* Not Rated.

CAST: Wu Nienjen (Nj Jian); Issey Ogata (Mr. Ota); Elaine Jin (Min-Min); Kelly Lee (Ting-Ting); Jonathan Chang (Yang-Yang); Chen Xisheng (A-Di); Ke Suyun (Sherry Chang-Breitner); Michael Tao (Da-Da); Xiao Shushen (Xiao Yan); Adrian Lin (Lili); Yupang Chang ("Fatty"); Tang Ruyun (Grandma); Xu Shuyuan (Mrs. Jiang, Lili's Mother); Zeng Xinyi (Yun-Yun); Li Yongfeng (Migo); Jin Shihui (Nancy); Wu Jie (Wu Jie); Shu Guozhi (Shu Ge); Dai Liren (Liren); You Meiyun (NJ's Neighbor); You Qidong (Xiao Yan's Uncle); Ke Yulun (Young Soldier); Liu Liangzuo (Dean); Chen Lihua (Lili's English Tutor); Chen Yiwen (Policeman); Song Shaoqing (Young Banker); Luo Bei-an (Boss Huang); Antonio Lee (Piano Bar Pianist); Tang Congsheng, Wang Qizan, and Li Jianchang (Punks at NY Bagel Café); Tsuda Kenjiro (Robata Restaurant Waiter); Wu Weining ("Concubine"); Zhang Huiling (Huiling); Xu Guiying (NJ's Secretary); Allen Lu (Mrs. Jiang's Boyfriend); Yang Shiping and Ye Ziyan (Grandma's Doctors); Yang Jinhua (Doctor's Wife); Li Wanyun and Lin Xiaowei (Xiao Yan's Assistants); Wu Yiting (Baby); Xu Wenjuan (Da-Da's Wife); Wang Zhengkai (Security Guard); Xie Nianzu (Policeman); Chen Shiqi, Xiang Guangting, and Lin Yanchun (Yang-Yang's Classmates); Fan Reijun (Yun-Yun Voice); Tang Congsheng (Young Banker's Voice).

CHRISTIAN SCIENCE MONITOR, 9/29/00, p. 15, David Sterritt

Asian movies are having a banner year with American audiences. Two pictures by the late Japanese master Akira Kurosawa are now in theaters—"Madadayo" and "Ran"—and the current New York Film Festival is presenting the US premières of several other movies from the region.

The first of these to reach commercial screens are markedly different in everything except the excellence of their quality: the Japanese adventure "Gohatto," which means "Taboo," and the Taiwanese drama "Yi Yi," also known as "A One and a Two...." Of the two, "Yi Yi" should have the most appeal if its three-hour running time doesn't scare audiences away. Directed by Edward Yang, it tells the insightful story of a Taiwanese family facing challenges: a grandmother is seriously ill, a granddaughter fears she contributed to this crisis, her father's computer company is considering a risky venture, and touches of jealousy add extra tension to the household's moods.

These ingredients could have added up to a heated domestic melodrama, but Yang favors a gentle and introspective style. It serves him beautifully. Yang is a veteran filmmaker whose recent works ("Mahjong," "A Confucian Confusion") have not measured up to his full talent. "Yi Yi" is a triumphant return to form.

"Gohatto" comes from Nagisa Oshima, a Japanese maverick known for razor-sharp fables like "The Man Who Left His Will on Film" and "In the Realm of the Senses," which combine modernist filmmaking with aggressive critiques of social power structures. His new picture does the same via the irony-tinged tale of a 19th-century warrior whose entrance into a samurai legion sparks rivalries among colleagues who court his affections.

The movie's most striking asset is its lyrical visual style, which forms a silky counterpoint to the plots turbulent emotions. Also impressive is Takeshi "Beat" Kitano's performance as a senior warrior, as smooth and expressive as any of the acting he's done in his own popular films. What dominates the picture, though, is its surprising and revealing look at gay impulses in the ferocious samurai world. "Taboo" is a suitable title, but the story could well have been called "Do Ask, Do Tell."

LOS ANGELES TIMES, 12/1/00, Calendar/p. 2, Kenneth Turan

Edward Yang, writer-director of "Yi Yi," a wise and gentle comedy of manners from Taiwan, has chosen "A One and a Two" as his English title, and his choice of the words musicians use before they begin seems increasingly inspired as this wonderfully humanistic film unfolds.

Opening with a wedding and closing with a funeral, "Yi Yi" investigates the entire melody of life: the delicate balance between love and disillusion, the short distance between farce and tragedy, the way different generations have to confront the same difficulties in their own ways, and how what's important is always with us yet simultaneously just out of reach.

Most of all, "Yi Yi" deals with the conundrums of romance, the wonder and perplexity of mutual attraction, what it springs from and where it goes. It's a delicate film but a strong one, graced with the ability to see life whole, the grief hidden in happiness as well as the humor inherent in sadness. Its subject, to borrow a phrase, is the dance to the music of time we all have to participate in.

The popular winner of the best director award at the Cannes Film Festival, "Yi Yi" marks the first time a film by director Yang, a key figure in the Taiwanese New Wave (and a USC film school dropout), has had significant American distribution. It's nearly three hours long, but with events intertwining as subtly yet resiliently as ivy-covered vines, time is forgotten in our involvement in problems and situations that are complex yet universal.

Central to this family narrative is NJ (Wu Nienjen), a partner in a Taipei computer company who's married with a son and a daughter, an aging mother-in-law, a feckless brother-in-law, even a first love he hasn't seen in decades. Each of these people has a strong narrative position in "Yi Yi," and we experience their myriad emotional entanglements, their attempts to make the best of their lives' perplexing conditions—professional as well as personal. When NJ says, "There's very little I'm sure about these days," he's speaking for this entire extended family as well.

NJ's wife Min-Min (Elaine Jin), the dynamo who holds everyone together, sets off ripples when fears that her life is without meaning send her to an ashram for an indeterminate stay, leaving everyone to their own devices at what seems an especially unsettled time.

Her brother A-Di (Chen Xisheng), though recently married to his pregnant bride (Xiao Shushen), is still very much a child who can't seem to terminate his relationship with his strong-minded former girlfriend (Zeng Xinyi). And NJ and Min-Min's two children have their own dilemmas as well.

Unsophisticated high schooler Ting-Ting (Kelly Lee) gets caught up in the romantic entanglements of a single mother and her teenage daughter who move in next door. And her 8-year-old brother Yang-Yang (an irresistible Jonathan Chang) divides his time between asking profound questions about the nature of life no one is prepared to answer and getting picked on by his fellow students and an unreasonable teacher.

Father NJ, however, is oblivious to most of this, so all-consuming do his own problems seem to him. His company is going through a potentially fatal financial crisis, and fate puts him back in touch with old flame Sherry Chang-Breitner (Ke Suyun), the woman who may or may not be the love of his life.

In telling this complicated story, Yang utilizes a deliberate, masterful style that defines "unhurried." His accepting sensibility has a way of immersing an audience in his characters and situations. With actors completely inhabiting their roles, "Yi Yi" feels like it's happening right in front of us, with a satisfying immediacy.

One of Yang's techniques is the way he periodically holds the camera unmoving, at a small remove from the action. This may sound distancing, but it actually comes off as accepting. Yang not only trusts viewers to understand he's far from unconcerned but also believes in the powerful emotion inherent in his situations. He knows "Yi Yi's" passions are strong enough to involve us, and his confidence is more than repaid.

NEW YORK POST, 10/6/00, p. 57, Jonathan Foreman

Like one of those vast, sprawling 19th-century novels, Edward Yang's moving but over-praised "Yi Yi" takes its long, slow time gathering you in (it's the kind of film you should come to fresh from a good night's sleep or fortified by strong coffee). But by the end of the first hour (of three) you have not only figured out who the characters are and how they're related, you are completely caught up in their parallel stories.

Then, like a modernist novel (by someone like Calvino) it makes you wonder if its various characters aren't really the same person.

Ying's static camera and his relentless parade of shots through (or reflected in) windows can become a little irritating. And his central character, NJ (Wu Nienjen) is so cold and passive it can be hard to care about his mid-life crisis.

But in its low-key way, "Yi Yi" present's an intelligent, profound and at times heart-rending slice of Taiwanese middle-class existence—as seen by characters at different stages of life.

NEWSDAY, 10/4/00, Part II/p. B9, Jan Stuart

Like son, like father.

Ten-year-old Yang-Yang and his 45-year-old father NJ Jian view the world through pensive, searching eyes that are like a sign that reads "Men at work." They are beleaguered in the respective ways that children and grownups tend to be. Yang-Yang is teased by the girls and harassed unjustly by his teacher; NJ is haunted by a lover from his youth and unsettled by the ethical demands of his job. There is a trace of "what did I do to deserve this?" in their furrowed brow, but the mind behind it is far too active and questioning to let a cheapjack sense of victimization take over for more than a second.

Heaven knows, there is a wealth of precious moments to take in and process in "Yi Yi (A One and a Two)," a celestial family tapestry from Edward Yang. This profusely gifted Chinese-American filmmaker won the best director prize at Cannes for his work here, but reverence should be reserved for Yang's kaleidoscopic screenplay, which navigates the intricate universe of one extended family with subtlety, grace and captivating humor.

We meet the Jian family at the raucous wedding of NJ's brother- in-law A-Di (Chen Xisheng) to his pregnant bride Xiao Yan (Xiao Shushen). A-Di has held out for this day, which he claims to be the luckiest of the year. The irony of his decision is not lost on us: The reception is noisily invaded by A-Di's former girlfriend (Zeng Xinyi); NJ (Wu Nienjen) is mortified to run into the love of his life, Sherry (Ke Suyun), whom he ditched long ago; and Grandma, the mother of A-Di and NJ's wife, Min-Min (Elaine Jin), suffers a stroke.

What could descend into a vulgar Chinese variant on "Tony and Tina's Wedding" is merely used as the launching pad for a multi-layered dissection of a family at a turning point. Grandma's stroke galvanizes the simmering frustrations of three people: her lovelorn teenage granddaughter Ting-Ting (Kelly Lee); her daughter Min-Min, who runs off to a meditation retreat, and NJ, who takes advantage of his wife's absence to rendezvous with Sherry on a business trip to Tokyo. In Tokyo, NJ's discontent is affected by the wisdom of a philosophical Japanese businessman, Mr. Ota (a charming Issey Ogata).

Yang's roaming narrative is given further texture by the tumultuous conflicts of the family next door, a kind of worst-case- scenario parallel for the troubled Jians. The neighbors' travails are sensed, if not understood, by the ever-curious Yang-Yang, who tells his father, with Confucian wisdom, "If I can only see what's in front of me, I can only see half of the truth." As Yang-Yang, Jonathan Chang is one of the most open-faced and irresistible child actors we've ever seen, offering a refreshing oasis of innocence amid the swelter of adult malaises.

Like his child sage, Edward Yang doesn't seem to miss a trick. He catches people in the banal act of forgetting why they came into a room or distracted from work by the strains of an old Motown hit coming through their headphones. The air of omniscience is reinforced by the use of lobby surveillance cameras to track characters. Fortunately, the filmmaker's soul overtakes his technology. We observe his people as if through the eyes of God.

SIGHT AND SOUND, 4/01, p. 53, Tony Rayans

Taipei, the present. Partner in a failing computer firm NJ Jian is asked by his colleagues to negotiate a shift into games software with innovative Japanese games designer Mr Ota. But his domestic and emotional life is plunged into confusion on the day his brother-in-law A-Di marries the pregnant Yiao Yan. At the fractious reception NJ runs into his childhood sweetheart Sherry (now married to an American) and begins to wonder if his life could have turned out differently. Then his mother-in-law collapses; the presence of the comatose old lady in the apartment provokes much family soul-searching. NJ's wife Min-Min suffers a nervous breakdown and goes off to a religious retreat, their daughter Ting-Ting (who half-blames herself for her grandma's mishap) gets her first lessons in the pitfalls of dating from her friend Lili Jiang next door, and their young son Yang-Yang gets into trouble at school.

Sent to Japan for meetings with Ota, already a wise and helpful friend, NJ secretly meets Sherry. On a trip to Atami, they reflect on where their relationship went wrong; tempted to try again, NJ finally decides to make the best of the life he has. Meanwhile his partners in Taipei get into bed with a dubious politician and a manufacturer of copycat software; A-Di is swindled out of his savings and almost leaves his wife and child for his old flame Yun-Yun until a lucky break turns his life around; and Ting-Ting finds herself a witness in a police enquiry into the murder of a teacher by Lili Jiang's ex-boyfriend 'Fatty'.

NJ's mother-in-law dies in her sleep. Min-Min returns to the family. NJ leaves the computer firm, which is again facing bankruptcy. At his grandma's funeral, Yang-Yang confides his hopes and dreams to the coffin.

No narrative outline can hope to convey anything of the novelistic density of character and incident in Edward Yang's wonderful film, or the richness. Across the relatively short time span of a few weeks—and a gone-in-a-flash running time of three hours—the film anthologises both the events which define a family (a birth, a marriage, a death) and the psychological stresses which people face at various ages (courtship rituals, mid-life crises, coping with the failures of relatives and friends, regretting lost opportunities). The Jian family at the centre of the film is absolutely typical of Taiwan's middle class and its ups and downs are observed with a sociologist's precision, but nothing here is alien to other countries, cultures or classes. This is a view of contemporary urban life as plausible and comprehensive as any cinema has to offer, its elements of soap opera and melodrama integrated as skilfully as its sense of the interconnectedness of things.

Yang knows better than to pile incident on incident to build complexity. The action is essentially simple; the density arises from the fact that at least two issues (often more) run through every scene. For example, husband and father NJ's problems with the company he co-founded with a group of old friends reflect both the 'negative growth' of the hi-tech sector and the risks inherent in carrying college friendships through into adult life. Equally, his trip to Japan to meet both the saintly Ota, a potential business associate, and Sherry, who has never got over being jilted by him 20 years earlier, forces NJ to confront several dimensions of his sense of personal failure at once.

With real economy and wit, Yang brings to a head NJ's feeling that he has never been in control of his own life while he discusses jazz in a bar with Ota. He also gets lead-free mileage from drawing parallels and pointing up contrasts, notably between the Jian family and their new, sexually screwed-up neighbours the Jiangs.

NJ's chronic need to solve his own problems by deflecting them gives the film its wry, self-aware core, but Yang is surprisingly even-handed in his sensitivity to everyone else's travails. The pre-teen Yang-Yang has to cope with everything from being misunderstood and wrongfully punished to experiencing his first flash of sexual awareness during a class on meteorology; he comes through, as most young kids do, unscathed. His 15-year-old sister Ting-Ting has a harder time, burdened with guilt that she somehow caused her grandma's collapse while she struggles to outgrow her childish sense that life could be all sweetness and light if only people were *nice* to each other. Only NJ's wife Min-Min gets shorthand treatment in the script, being sent off-screen to follow a dodgy guru for much of the film, but Elaine Jin's characteristically excellent performance gives her substance nonetheless; Min-Min's inability to face another day with her comatose mother is acutely felt, as are her comments on the implications of feeling trapped when she returns to the family.

In a film of superb ensemble work, Wu Nienjen's performance as NJ is a standout. Wu has gone from being Taiwan's most prolific screenwriter to becoming a fine writer-director (*A Borrowed Life*, 1994, *Buddha Bless America* 1996) and a popular television talk-show host; this is his first major acting role (after cameos in Hou Xiaoxian's *A City of Sadness*, which he co-wrote, and Edward Yang's *Mahjong*) and it's a triumph of understatement and small gestures.

But *A One and a Two...* is first and foremost a director's film. In a sense, it's more of a companion piece to Yang's equally masterly *A Brighter Summer Day* (1991) than it is to his other accounts of contemporary confusions. *Day* reimagined Taiwan's past—the teenage gangs who fought for control of the Taipei streets in echo of the adult factions vying for control of the island's wealth, the anti-communist' White Terror—as an epic suite of tableau compositions: reconstructing a myth, and at the same time observing from enough distance to see how to deconstruct it. The view here is closer, warmer and less formalised. But in framing the psychological with the domestic, the emotional with the economic, it gets to the heart of present-day matters no less brilliantly.

VILLAGE VOICE, 10/10/00, p. 125, J. Hoberman

Edward Yang's *Yi Yi* is a wonderfully engrossing experienced lucid, elegant, nuanced, humorous movie that's never nearly as sentimental as it might have been. This complex but understated melodrama opens amid a tumultuous wedding banquet-"Where is that pregnant bitch?" the groom's ex cries—and ends, nearly three hours later, with a child's funeral address. In between, Yang orchestrates a soap opera season's worth of family crises with virtuoso discretion.

It's a measure of Yang's skill that the movie's piled-on coincidences hardly ever seem contrived. Taking a break from his brother-in-law's manic nuptials, staid 45-year-old NJ Jian (filmmaker Wu Nienjen, who wrote Hou Hsiao-hsien's *Dust in the Wind*, among other screenplays) unexpectedly bumps into a poised businesswoman who turns out to be his first love, Sherry (Ke Suyun), whom he hasn't seen since he jilted her some 20 years earlier. Later that day, his mother-in-law suffers a stroke and, for the rest of the movie, lies at home in a coma as, per the doctor's instructions, members of the family take turns talking to her.

That the grandmother is a retired schoolteacher suggests that her condition will serve to instruct the family. NJ's wife, Min-Min (Elaine]in), suffers a mini breakdown under the strain, and after she removes herself from the action by departing for a Buddhist retreat, the philosophical burden is assumed by eight-year-old Yang-Yang (Jonathan Chang, a wonderfully alert child actor): "How can I know what you see?" he asks his father. Meanwhile, teenage sister Ting-Ting (Kelly Lee), who has become increasingly drawn into the domestic disarray in the apartment next door, falls victim to magical thinking. She blames herself for not taking out the garbage the night of her *Yi Yi*, which won Yang the director's prize at Cannes, is the most inclusive portrait that the 53-year-old filmmaker has yet made of Taiwan's uneasy urbanites. The large, multigenerational cast encompasses not only an extended family but a cross-section of Taipei's middle class. After the unrepeatable triumph of his period monument, *A Brighter Summer Day* (something like a

Michelangelo Antonioni remake of *West Side Story*), and two ambitious but unsuccessful youth-oriented satires of Taipei's boomtown mentality, Yang has found his tone. He chose *Yi Yi*'s English title, "A One and a Two," to bring to mind a jazz riff, and although dense with incident and motif, the movie has an effortless flow. The action segues easily through Taipei's placeless high-rises, karaoke bars where English is the businessman's lingua franca, malls, and fast-food joints-as well as the pedestrian underpasses beneath the city's ubiquitous freeways, sites for individual high emotion amid indifferent traffic.

Yang has never been more sensitive to the rhythm of urban life—at one point setting a scene's pace by using a traffic light as his metronome. The movie's tone is as level as its frames are carefully composed. Yang juggles subplots with aplomb and refuses to crowd his characters, typically positioning his actors in tactful middle-shot. Such strategic understatement compares favorably with the contrived hysteria of Robert Altman's upcoming *Dr. T and the Women,* a not dissimilar drama of family frenzy and male mid-life crisis. Yang is less glib than Altman in handling his ensemble antics and constitutionally incapable of scapegoating individual characters.

Yi Yi is centered on the soft-spoken, self-contained NJ, who's alienated from his unreliable business partners and perhaps his family as well. As the film's most solitary and conscience-driven character, he's particularly eloquent in leaving a message on Sherry's answering machine while delivering a crucial line to a closed hotel room door. A business trip to Tokyo allows NJ the opportunity to rendezvous with Sherry and, in effect, a chance to rescript his life. Yang suggestively crosscuts this expedition into the past-a kind of voyage into a parallel universe-with Ting-Ting's first tryst, the same evening back in Taipei. She proves no less conflicted than her father and even more vulnerable-walking home alone, in the white linen dress she's chosen for the evening, to kneel before her comatose grandmother's bed. (There's nothing more heartbreaking than Ting-Ting's slow trudge of rejection, unless it's the unembarrassed malice with which Yang-Yang's teacher ridicules the child's natural genius.)

The Antonioni-esque anomie of Yang's early films has here been tempered by more humanist concerns—and by a sense of detached reflection, some of it on the medium itself. *Yi Yi* is unostentatiously punctuated with a variety of cinematic quotations—ranging from video porn (heard but not seen) and classroom education films to screen-filling images of monograms, computer games, closed-circuit surveillance tapes, and Yang-Yang's artless "avant-garde" snapshots. It hardly seems coincidental that, in their longest conversation, Ting-Ting and her date discuss the nature of motion pictures: "My grandfather says that we live three times as long since man invented movies," he tells her.

In the context of *Yi Yi*, this parallel world is offered as both comment on and consolation for a lifetime of betrayals and disappointments. *Yi Yi* doesn't look anything like cinema verité, but it has a similar feel—there's a real sense of familiarity; the characters seem to be directing the narrative. As accomplished as Yang's filmmaking is, his movie seeks to break through the theatrical wall; it has the epic intimacy of great television.

Also reviewed in:
CHICAGO TRIBUNE, 3/2/01, Friday/p. A, Michael Wilmington
NATION, 10/23/00, p. 34, Stuart Klawans
NEW YORK TIMES, 10/4/00, p. E1, A. O. Scott
NEW YORKER, 1/8/01, p. 90, David Denby
VARIETY, 5/22-28/00, p. 20, Derek Elley
WASHINGTON POST, 2/23/01, Weekend/p. 37, Desson Howe

YOU CAN COUNT ON ME

A Paramount Classics release of a Hart Sharp Entertainment and Shooting Gallery presentation in association with Cappa Productions/Crunch Entertainment. *Executive Producer:* Martin Scorsese, Steve Carlis, Donald C. Carter, and Morton Swinsky. *Producer:* John N. Hart, Jeffrey Sharp, Barbara De Fina, and Larry Meistrich. *Director:* Kenneth Lonergan. *Screenplay:* Kenneth Lonergan. *Director of Photography:* Stephen Kazmierski. *Editor:* Anne McCabe.

Music: Lesley Barber. *Music Editor:* Susan Shufro. *Sound:* Peter Schneider and (music) Robert Fernandez. *Sound Editor:* Wendy Hedin. *Casting:* Lina Todd. *Production Designer:* Michael Shaw. *Art Director:* Shawn Carroll. *Set Decorator:* Lydia Marks. *Costumes:* Melissa Toth. *Make-up:* Chris Bingham. *Stunt Coordinator:* Don Hewitt. *Running time:* 111 minutes. *MPAA Rating:* R.

CAST: Laura Linney (Sammy Prescott); Mark Ruffalo (Terry Prescott); Matthew Broderick (Brian Everett); Jon Tenney (Bob); Rory Culkin (Rudy Prescott); J. Smith-Cameron (Mabel); Josh Lucas (Rudy Sr.); Gaby Hoffmann (Sheila); Adam LeFevre (Sheriff Darryl); Amy Ryan (Mrs. Prescott); Kenneth Lonergan (Ron, Priest); Halley Feiffer (Amy); Whitney Vance (Young Sammy); Peter Kerwin (Young Terry); Betsy Aidem (Minister); Lisa Altomare (Waitress); Nina Garbiras (Nancy); Richard Hummer (Plumber); Kim Parker (Rudy Sr's. Girlfriend); Allan Gill (Older Cop); Brian Ramage (Young Cop).

LOS ANGELES TIMES, 11/10/00, Calendar/p. 2, Kenneth Turan

Kenneth Lonergan knows what he's written and why he's written it. He hears the words behind his words, understands the states of mind they reflect. He sees into his characters, into how they have to be who they are though they hurt themselves in the process. Even his tiniest moments ring true, which is why the ruefully funny dramatic comedy "You Can Count on Me" is such an exceptional debut.

A double prizewinner at Sundance, sharing the Grand Jury Prize and taking the Waldo Salt Screenwriting Award, this beautifully textured film shocks us for all the right reasons, by creating inescapably real people and allowing them to be themselves. Always individuals, the characters Lonergan has written and directed are forever doing unexpected things for no good reason, faking us out time and again because they have minds of their own.

A rising New York playwright ("This Is Our Youth" is his best-known work), Lonergan has written for film before: His original script became the very different "Analyze This" nine years and 14 writers after he wrote the first draft. He turned to directing to ensure that "You Can Count on Me" would appear on screen just as he wanted it, and that has made a considerable difference.

Though there are romantic elements in it, what Lonergan has written is a different kind of love story, one between a sister and a brother. Orphaned at a young age, they are, at least in theory, each other's main support in the world, but what Sammy (Laura Linney) and Terry (Mark Ruffalo) can actually depend on from each other is something more complex and frustrating.

For Lonergan is especially good at making Sammy and Terry's oppositeness as clear as the affection they share. They love but disappoint each other; they're irked as often as they're caring. Chronically unable to provide what the other sibling is looking for, the only thing Sammy and Terry can truly count on is a mutual exasperation that looks to extend to the end of time.

Wonderfully played by Linney ("The Truman Show") in a performance that makes the most of Lonergan's incisive writing, Sammy is the sister who stayed home in a small town in upstate New York, tending her parents' grave, working as a lending officer at the local bank and having an off-and-on relationship with the square-jawed Bob (Jon Tenney).

The most reliable man in Sammy's life is the 8-year-old son she's raising as a single parent. Like many another serious child of divorce, Rudy (Rory Culkin, Macaulay's talented youngest brother) is a worrier with a somber sense of humor, a kid who likes things as structured as possible.

Having a special hold on Sammy's emotions is her brother Terry; when a rare letter from him arrives, her face lights up like the sun. And when Terry announces that he's coming back for an even rarer visit, not even the officiousness of her new boss at the bank (a deftly comic Matthew Broderick, a friend of Lonergan's since high school) can stop her from throwing herself into preparations.

As strong as Linney's superb performance is Mark Ruffalo's special work as Terry. A veteran of many of Lonergan's plays, his experience with the director's language and themes helps bring levels of complexity and interest to what could have been the most dismissible of characters. Slacker, layabout, underachiever—whichever word you choose, Terry fits it. But it is one of the triumphs of "You Can Count on Me" that his kind of rootless disaffection has rarely been so honestly, convincingly yet sympathetically portrayed.

"I am not the kind of guy everyone says I am," Terry whines to a girlfriend early on, but, truthfully, he pretty much is. Awkward and ill-at-ease with people, easily insulted and always aggrieved, he frustrates everyone he comes into contact with, himself most of all.

So as much as Sammy is looking forward to his visit, Terry's generic fecklessness inevitably brings out her disapproval, while he in turn feels cramped and smothered by her excessive concern. Complicating things is Terry's developing relationship with a dubious Rudy, who has never seen anyone like his uncle and is not sure he even wants to.

Because so much can be said about these characters—because, like those we know—they can be looked at from any number of angles, it's easy to forget to emphasize how completely funny "You Can Count on Me" is, how much its warm humor bubbles up naturally from the heart. Lonergan (who's cast himself as the overmatched local priest) makes both his perceptive writing and subtle direction, his ability to view ordinary life as a potentially great adventure, look much easier than it really is. If you've been looking for an American independent film that fulfills the promise of the movement, you have it now.

NEW YORK, 11/20/00, p. 99, Peter Rainer

Laura Linney and Mark Ruffalo play sister and brother in the affectingly small-scale *You Can Count On Me*, and although they don't look at all alike, their kinship is never an issue for us. These actors express the feints and parries of siblings when they're together. They have an intuitive understanding of how much to conceal and how much to reveal to each other; it's one of the most convincing displays of family connection I've ever seen in a movie.

What seems at first like a clear-cut contrast between these two—she's small-town provincial, he's self-destructively nomadic— becomes less contrasty as the film plays out. Linney's Sammy, a single mother whose 8-year-old son Rudy (Rory Culkin) she overprotects, gets a little loose when her estranged brother Terry shows up in town asking for a handout. Her patrician veneer falls away and she has a dalliance with her married, by-the-book bank-manager boss (Matthew Broderick, in a sweetly dazed performance). Terry, who looks like he's spent one night too many in a sleeping bag, warms to Rudy, taking him fishing and to pool halls. Against his instincts, he becomes something of a watchdog for the boy. Sammy and Terry were orphaned early when their parents were killed in a car accident, and as adults, they still seem orphaned, bereft. Kenneth Lonergan, making his feature-film debut as both writer and director, works in small brushstrokes; nothing is really resolved in these characters' lives.

This freedom from any kind of grand resolution must have been like manna for the actors. Linney has never been better, and Ruffalo, who once performed Off Broadway in the Lonergan play *This Is Our Youth*, keeps the mushiness at bay when it would have been easy to sentimentalize Terry's attachment to his nephew and sister. Terry isn't a lovable layabout; he causes harm, and when it suits him to move on, he doesn't stick around. Ruffalo gets at not only the scruffiness of the wanderer's existence but also its crazy-making isolation. His performance is so richly layered that when the film is over, you feel that Terry lives on—that he could go anywhere, become anything or nothing, and we would be prepared for it.

NEW YORK POST, 11/10/00. p. 58, Jonathan Foreman

"You Can Count on Me" was written and directed by Broadway playwright Kenneth Lonergan, who also wrote the screenplays for "Analyze This" and "The Adventures of Rocky and Bullwinkle."

It won two prizes at this year's Sundance Film Fest (the Waldo Salt screenwriting award and the jury prize, which it shared with "Girlfight").

But while it's certainly a well-written and intelligent little movie (amazingly restrained by Hollywood standards) with some very fine performances and funny moments, it is visually flat and uninteresting and too often feels like a (leisurely paced) filmed play.

Sammy (Laura Linney) was raised in the small upstate New York town of Scottsville with her brother Terry (Mark Ruffalo).

As children they were orphaned by a car crash. Sammy, who is divorced, still lives in the family home with her 8-year-old son Rudy (Rory Culkin) and works in the local bank. Terry became a drifter after high school and when the film opens has just done some time in jail and impregnated his girlfriend before coming home to visit his sister and borrow some money.

They are the kind of siblings who have remained close despite different personalities—and leading very different lives.

At first Terry's return home is a boon for young Rudy, who needs a father in his life, and for Sammy, who starts to express her formerly suppressed passionate side, discarding her steady boyfriend and embarking on an affair with her uptight married boss Brian (Matthew Broderick).

But one of the reasons Terry and Rudy get on so well is that Terry himself is so childish.

Certainly, Terry talks to his little nephew as if he's unaware of the age difference, and even brings him to the local pool hall. And once Terry esconces himself in the house his petulant irresponsibility, buttressed by rantings about the uprightness of small town life, forces Sammy to play the role of irritated Mother. Eventually both siblings are forced to reevaluate their lives and their relationship.

Linney is terrific (and surprisingly sexy) as Sammy. Broadway star Ruffalo makes a strong debut as the rather irritating Terry, and Culkin (brother of Macaulay) is OK as one of those big-eyed moppets movie-makers love.

Once again, Matthew Broderick brings sharp intelligence and humor to his role as an adulterous, control freak office manager.

NEWSDAY, 11/10/00, Part II/p. B3, John Anderson

It seems a bit risky to mention right away that "You Can Count on Me"—screenwriter-director Kenneth Lonergan's debut movie and a thoroughly transcendent piece of work—was a big winner at Sundance this year. A movie can suffer from its associations, even its successes, because the track record on so-called small independent movies has been so erratic. Or predictable. Or both.

But there is nothing amateurish or indulgent in "You Can Count on Me," which stars Laura Linney and Mark Ruffalo in a pair of revelatory performances that deserve all the accolades that, in an ideal world at least, they would assuredly get. It also introduces young Rory Culkin as Rudy, in a virtually flawless kid performance, but it's Linney and Ruffalo, as Sammy and Terry Prescott, who put wings on a very grounded movie.

Who plays whom? Linney is Sammy, Ruffalo is Terry, orphaned young by their parents' car crash (an accident and funeral depicted with almost brutal efficiency). Their gender-bender names, though, are just one clue to their intimacy and dilemma: They live for each other, maybe even belong together. But what Lonergan is saying is that a perfect life is impossible. Unless, perhaps, if you realize it is.

Sammy has stayed in the small town of Scottsville, in the house she and Terry inherited, a single mother rearing a young son (Culkin), working in the local bank, romancing a local named Bob (Jon Tenney). Terry has done the roughneck tour of America—working in Alaska and Florida; doing jail time for brawling; smoking pot; impregnating a girl in Worcester, Mass., and then boarding a bus to Scottsville, so he can borrow some money from Sammy.

There is a moment during Sammy and Terry's reunion lunch—she's breathless with excitement; he's as distracted as a junkie—when the sister looks at her brother as if she's never seen him before. It's a familiar enough look. It's the one we give people we're so intimate with we don't see them until they do something to rattle our cage. Linney, who gives a marvelous performance throughout the film, makes that one moment particularly sublime: In Sammy's face, we get the head-on collision of illusion and fact. And we don't like Terry for it.

It doesn't last. Ruffalo's portrayal of the easily charming, chronically irresponsible Terry is as innocently raffish as it could possibly be; his relationship with the fatherless Rudy is purely natural, whether he's sneaking the kid out to play pool or taking him for an impromptu introduction with his lowlife father (Josh Lucas).

Sammy, on the other hand, is a kind of saint—precisely because her churchgoing, child-rearing lifestyle is masking a wild woman in chains. Armed with a charmer and a saint, Lonergan knows he needs some kind of heavy, even a comic one. So he gives us Brian (Matthew Broderick), Sammy's new boss at the bank, a guy who thinks he's going to make it big in the kind of town in which people might live precisely to get away from people like Brian.

That he and Sammy should fall into bed together is as unlikely as life, but such is the virtue of "You Can Count on Me," which gives us not so much a slice of reality as a big picture window, polished and gleaming, through which we can see things that matter.

SIGHT AND SOUND, 4/01, p. 61, Philip Kemp

Scottsville, upstate New York. Samantha 'Sammy' Prescott, single mother of eight-year-old Rudy, works in a bank. The finicky new manager, Brian Everett, objects to her taking 15 minutes off to pick Rudy up from school. When her young drifter brother Terry arrives for a sit, Sammy is delighted—until she finds out he's been in jail and has come to borrow money. Even so, she's pleased when he prolongs his stay and agrees to take over the school run.

Rudy starts enjoying the company of his raffish uncle. One evening when Sammy's out with her stolid boyfriend Bob, Terry takes Rudy to a local bar; there, the two play pool. Bob proposes, taking Sammy aback. After another row with Brian, whose wife is pregnant, she impulsively starts an affair with him. Furious when she learns about the bar episode, Sammy invites the local priest to talk to Terry.

Out on a fishing expedition with Rudy, Terry decides to take him to meet the boy's estranged father, Rudy Sr. The visit is a disaster: Rudy Sr rejects his son, the two men fight and Terry ends up jailed overnight. Sammy kicks Terry out; he prepares to leave town. Sammy ends her affair with Brian. Just before Terry's departure Sammy asks him to come and say goodbye to Rudy. The siblings are tentatively reconciled.

You Can Count on Me maps the fallout of a bereavement. In the pre-credits sequence Sammy and Terry (as children) lose their parents in a car crash; 15 or so years later, they're still dealing with it. Sammy has clung to known certainties: the small town she grew up in, the church, a respectable unambitious job in the local bank—and her son Rudy, whom she watches over a touch too solicitously. Hers is a world where everything slots into place and happens for a reason even, perhaps, her parents' death. Her brother has spun off on the opposite tack. Since to him his parents' death was meaningless, so is everything else, and he reacts accordingly: rocketing from place to place, shunning responsibility, living for the moment and gradually destroying himself and those around him.

This good-sibling/bad-sibling set-up isn't unfamiliar. What keeps the film fresh and engrossing is the perceptive, acutely observed scripting. Screenwriter Kenneth Lonergan *(Analyze This)*, making his debut as writer-director, gives his characters an edge of ambivalence that lifts them free of stock. Terry, for all his railing against the smug narrowness of small-town life ("People round here have no *scope*," he tells Rudy), finds himself reluctant to leave; while Sammy is at once appalled and elated to detect within herself a submerged streak of recklessness shared with her brother. Driving back from her first, unexpected sexual encounter with her boss Brian, she's seized with mirth; as Sammy, Laura Linney turns the laugh into something close to a yelp of defiance.

Occasionally credibility is strained. It's hard to believe that Sammy, so conscious of the constraints of local society, would row with her brother in a public restaurant (or, come to that, that she'd have got involved with a crude lowlife like Rudy's father). But for the most part the dynamic—equal parts love and exasperation—between her and Mark Ruffalo's charmingly feckless Terry is vividly maintained, while her affair with Matthew Broderick's over-buttoned Brian has all the headlong joyful panic of two hyper-controlled people suddenly ambushed by their lower instincts. Smaller roles are no less individual. As Sammy's boyfriend Bob, Jon Tenney never overdoes the stolidity, a man uneasily aware of his shortcomings as a lover but uncertain what to do about them. Lonergan himself plays the local priest with an appealing air of embarrassment, accepting Terry's contempt as if it's what he deserves.

Incisively edited by Anne McCabe, *You Can Count on Me* makes the most of being shot largely on location in upstate New York. Stephen Kazmierski's photography captures both the visual appeal, and the folksy claustrophobia, of the region; you can see why Sammy would want to stay, and why Terry would have got out at the first opportunity. Best of all, Lonergan refuses to tie everything up neatly. It must have been tempting to present us with a series of tidy narrative closures—Terry killed, maybe, or reformed; Sammy marrying Bob or running off with Brian. Instead we're left with the messy uncertainty of real life: nothing really settled, a note of tentative optimism but no more. It's summed up by Terry's parting words to his sister. "Everything's going to be all right. Comparatively."

TIME, 11/27/00, p. 92, Richard Schickel

Terry Prescott (Mark Ruffalo) is the kind of guy who drifts unnoticed through the American vastness, doing itinerant day labor, falling into barroom brawls and inappropriate relationships. His sister Sammy (Laura Linney) is ostensibly his opposite. She's a single mom who has stayed in their upstate New York hometown, where she raises her son by a rigid book and works faithfully as the loan officer in a bank branch. *You Can Count on Me* simply narrates what happens when the goofus comes home to sponge some money from the doofus and incidentally, almost accidentally, stirs an emotional frenzy. It is also, just possibly, the best American movie of this fast-dwindling year.

It is admittedly a small thing. It contains just four fully developed characters, who in addition to the leads include Sammy's overprotected son Rudy (Rory Culkin, the latest addition to the kid acting dynasty) and Matthew Broderick's bank manager, a comically annoying anal compulsive with a hidden concupiscent side. The latter gets a workout when it speaks suddenly to Sammy's trimly repressed side.

But that's almost a side issue. What counts in this movie is the developing relationship between Terry and Rudy. Terry may be a loser, but he's not a dope. His damage, and his sister's, stems from their having been orphaned as children. That accounts for her caution and his incaution. She thinks she has to keep her life small and manageable, so she has little to lose. He believes that since life is full of mischance, you might just as well wander and risk. So he brings Rudy along on an odd job where he teaches him how to pound a nail straight, involves him in a game down at the pool hall and, riskiest of all, introduces the boy to his real father.

What saves Terry from being really harmful is his fundamental sweetness. You can count on him, after a fashion. He may invariably choose the messy route, but he's always aiming for the right, truthful place, and Ruffalo's performance is a wonderful blend of the winning and the exasperating. Linney matches him step for wrangling step as a woman too smart and too pretty for the trap she has chosen, someone who will, we guess, never escape her dutiful, churchgoing life—except for those moments when her inner wildness spills out.

But the best thing about *You Can Count on Me* is its tone. The writer director, Kenneth Lonergan, who wrote *Analyze This,* is good with silences—unforced, often inarticulate emotions. Above all, he doesn't push his material beyond its naturalistic limits. He doesn't sentimentalize it or melodramatize it. He trusts the fact that he's exploring a relationship not much studied in the movies—the bond between brother and sister—to sustain our interest. He is content to keep his frame and his comic, angry surprises small. Yet a great intensity results from this steady, persistent compression. Maybe these lives are, objectively speaking, inconsequential. But they have a resonance that big, sappy "relationship" pictures ought to envy.

VILLAGE VOICE, 11/14/00, p. 136, Amy Taubin

Kenneth Lonergan's *You Can Count on Me,* the winner of two of Sundance's biggest prizes, seems like a TV movie. A well-written, sympathetically acted TV movie, to be sure, but so timid and clumsy in its deployment of picture, sound, and editing that you have to wonder if executive producer Martin Scorsese bothered to give notes.

Orphaned when their parents were killed in a car crash, Sammy (Laura Linney) and Terry (Mark Ruffalo) have reacted differently to their childhood trauma. Sammy, a bank-loan officer, is still living in the house where they were born, raising her son, Rudy (Rory Culkin), on her own. Terry, the younger and wilder of the two, has spent his post-high school life on the road, returning home only when he needs to borrow money. His latest visit, precipitated by a three-month jail stint and his girlfriend's pregnancy, coincides with several crises in Sammy's carefully ordered life: Brian (Matthew Broderick), her nitpicking new manager, refuses to allow her the afternoon break she needs to drive Rudy from school to his baby-sitter's house; Rudy has become curious about his dad's identity and whereabouts; and Bob (Jon Tenney), her longtime beau, is pressuring her to marry him. While Terry's reappearance at first seems to solve the child-care problem, Sammy quickly becomes concerned that Terry is not the best role model for Rudy.

You Can Count on Me is set in Scottsville, a small town in upstate New York so generic and underpopulated that the film could have been shot on a studio back lot. Lonergan plunks his characters down in various locations—the bank, the porch, the motel room—that might as well be stage sets, and he has no sense of how to create an expressive film space. Perhaps to compensate, he lays on the music with a heavy hand: a Bach cello piece to indicate introspection and a dozen country songs that spell out exactly what the characters are doing or feeling. When Sammy is driving to an assignation with the married bank manager, she flicks on the radio to Loretta Lynn singing, "I'm the other woman in your life."

Lonergan does get excellent performances from his actors. Broderick is even more smug and smarmy here than he was in *Election* (at one point he hurls himself on Linney like a bear cub who doesn't care if he's caught in the honey pot), and the grave-faced Culkin is so alive and direct he barely seems to be acting. Always an exciting actor, Ruffalo makes Terry the quick-fisted prodigal son who returns to a town that's too confining for his discordant impulses, but his pouting lips betray the abandoned, frightened five-year-old inside. Linney, who has to carry the film, finds the vulnerability beneath Sammy's capable, controlled exterior. Sammy's problem, as she explains to her minister (played by Lonergan as a bumbling wise man), is that she's drawn to men she feels sorry for—in other words, men she can mother as she wishes she'd been mothered herself.

It's not just the invocation of faith and family that marks *You Can Count on Me* as a conservative film. Its gender politics are thoroughly retrograde. When the inexperienced new manager imposes his absurd rules on the women in his office, they don't even get together to strategize, let alone confront him outright. Not just aesthetically unadventurous, *You Can Count on Me* is, in every way, a throwback to the Eisenhower age.

Also reviewed in:
CHICAGO TRIBUNE, 11/17/00, Friday/p. L, Michael Wilmington
NATION, 4/16/01, p. 35, Tim Appelo
NEW REPUBLIC, 12/4/00, p. 30, Stanley Kauffmann
NEW YORK TIMES, 11/10/00, p. E13, Stephen Holden
NEW YORKER, 12/18/00, p. 109, David Denby
VARIETY, 2/7-13/00, p. 52, Emanuel Levy

YOUNG DR. FREUD

A Kino International release.   *Director:* Axel Corti.   *Screenplay (German and French with English subtitles):* Georg Stefan Troller. *Director of Photography:* Wolfgang Treu. *Art Director:* Ernst Wurzer.   *Costumes:* Barbara Langbein.   *Running time:* 99 minutes. *MPAA Rating:* Not Rated.

CAST: Karlheinz Hackl (Dr. Sigmund Freud); Silvia Haider (Martha Freud-Bernays); Brigitte Swoboda (Amalie Freud); Guido Weiland (Jakob Freud); Maria Urban (Mathilde Fee Breuer); Karl Merkatz (Dr. Josef Breuer); Jacques Alric (Professor Dr. Charcot); Norbert Kappen (Professor Dr. Meynert); Peter Luhr (Professor Dr. Brucke); Marianne Nentwich (Bertha Pappenheim); Eugen Stark (Assistant Dr. Fleisch); Ursula Schult (Frau Bernays); Michael Toost (Family Doctor); Georg Stefan Troller (Offscreen Interviewer).

NEW YORK POST, 5/17/00, p. 50, Hannah Brown

"Young Dr. Freud" is a stunningly intelligent look at how the founder of psychoanalysis and modern psychiatry developed his ideas.

A cerebral biography, this movie may prove challenging, and at times, mystifying, to anyone without a strong interest in Sigmund Freud and some previous knowledge of his life and work.

But at a time when even independent filmmakers often dumb down their subjects to gain a wider audience, it's refreshing to watch director Axel Corti unravel the workings of a genius' mind without spelling out every reference.

This film, which was made in 1976, is having its U.S. theatrical premiere now.

Opening with the elderly Freud arriving in England after fleeing Nazi-controlled Austria in 1938, the movie then shifts back in time.

An unseen interviewer (Georg Stefan Troller, who also wrote the remarkably well-researched script) asks Freud, now a young man who looks to be in his 20s or 30s (brilliantly underplayed by Karlheinz Hackl), questions, and scenes from his childhood and life are acted out, the master analyst is analyzed himself It may be a cliche, but it works.

As Freud observes his mentor, Josef Breuer (Karl Merkatz) working with Bertha Pappenheim (Marianne Nentwich), a young woman suffering from hysterical paralysis, he begins to develop his theories of the unconscious, the importance of dreams and erotic transference between doctor and patient.

Of these theories, clearly, the most important is his discovery of the unconscious mind. It's fascinating to watch him make the first steps toward this revelation.

Unfortunately, not everything is made clear. Many scenes are staged confusingly, and some of the intellectual debates of the day, particularly between Freud's professors in Vienna, and Dr. Charcot (Jacques Alric), with whom he studied in Paris, are particularly unclear.

Though "Young Dr. Freud" isn't for everyone, those who are intrigued by the man who gave us the 50-minute hour will find this intellectual portrait riveting.

NEWSDAY, 5/17/00, Part II/p. B9, Jan Stuart

A young Jewish boy looks on helplessly as his father's hat is tossed into the mud by a couple of small-town thugs. As an elderly man 70 years later, he is on a train from Vienna to England with his own wife and child, trying to keep out of harm's way as Nazism becomes a way of life in his home country.

In the years between those traumatic events, this son of a persecuted wool merchant would emerge with a controversial reputation as the father of psychoanalysis. The people and incidents that would shape the theories of Sigmund Freud are at the heart of "Young Dr. Freud," a vivid and uniquely articulated dramatic account of one of the most influential figures of the 20th Century.

Made by the late Austrian director Axel Corti in 1977 and first unveiled in the United States last summer at New York's Jewish Museum, "Young Dr. Freud" adds a modishly contemporary fillip to the conventions of filmed biography. In a cinematic version of giving the doctor a taste of his own medicine, an off-screen interviewer uses the psychoanalytical give-and-take to grill a 20-something Freud on his theories and the impact of his development upon them.

Intermittently stepping out of his own day-to-day drama, the young Freud (Karlheinz Hackl) pauses to answer questions with the omniscience of an elderly man looking back on the sum total of his life. As the interviewer poses questions in tones both blunt and hostile regarding Freud's Jewish heritage and the allegedly negative impact of psychoanalytic theory on religion, it quickly becomes clear that the interviewer (the voice of the film's screenwriter, Georg Stefan Troller) is reflecting the biases of Freud's time.

The effect of this slanted Q&A is to lend greater immediacy to the social conditions that weighed upon Freud while at the same time reducing the cliche factor that can turn a film bio into a recounting of Greatest Hits. It also subverts our notion of what is consequential and what is trivial. As Freud concedes with dismay that his seminal "Interpretation of Dreams" only sold 123 copies on its release, his little marketing report comes across with even more force than scenes revealing the momentous origin of the Oedipal complex.

Corti's film follows Freud's path through the University of Vienna as he meets his wife-to-be and aligns himself with Dr. Josef Breur, with whom he initiated his pathfinding work on sexuality and the unconscious. Reinforced by a somber black-and-white palette, the film assumes its subject's dry and dispassionate personality, making for an occasionally antiseptic experience. For anyone who has spent so much as an hour on the couch, however, "Young Dr, Freud" merits an appointment.

VILLAGE VOICE, 5/30/00, p. 125, J. Hoberman

Speaking of unknowable intentions, *Young Dr. Freud*—made for Austrian TV in 1978 by the late Axel Corti—is a movie about how Freud got to be Freud. Call it a mental action epic. Now in its second week at Film Forum, this modest historical drama is unlikely to challenge *Gladiator*, although it's scarcely devoid of sadistic drama. At one point, the resolute young doctor calls his Vienna "as cozy as an arena."

Young Dr. Freud, unlike *Young Dr. Kildare*, is structured to suggest an extended psychoanalytic session or an episode of *The Twilight Zone*. The story is told in flashback, prompted by occasional questions from an unseen interlocutor (screenwriter Georg Stefan Troller). As befits an Austrian film, *Young Dr. Freud* makes the experience of anti-Semitism crucial to the hero's psychology, returning to the Moravian outpost of Freiberg for what's described as the hero's earliest memory—his father's humiliation at the hands of gentile ruffians. The child Freud is shown walking with his father when a group of rowdies order them into the gutter—"Off the pavement, Jew!"—and, for good measure, knock his unprotesting father's hat into the mud. (In fact, this indignity was a secondhand memory, at least according to Freud, who recounts the story at a crucial moment in *The Interpretation of Dreams*, framed not as something he observed himself but rather a story his father told him.)

Forever shamed by his father's inability to resist, Freud grows up spoiling for a fight and hyperconscious of Jewish stigma. He endures the puritanical anti-Semitism of medical school to become a provocative firebrand, arguing with his mentor Josef Breuer—the pioneer of the so-called talking cure—while shocking his colleagues with his interest in the sex life of eels. In a bit of comic relief, the young doctor expounds on this very subject during the course of a Sunday excursion to the Prater amusement park with Martha, the proper Jewish fiancee his parents have managed to find for their poor and struggling son.

Freud, who confesses that he doesn't like people enough to be a doctor, becomes interested in human sexual pathology through Breuer's treatment of Bertha Pappenheim a/k/a Anna O, a hysterical young woman who, in the hothouse world of Vienna's Jewish bourgeoisie, happens to be a friend of Martha's. (The filmmakers are well aware that Pappenheim became a pioneer feminist, social activist, and implacable foe of psychoanalysis.) Making the rounds of the mental cases in a Vienna hospital, Freud ponders the meaning of repression; sent to France to study with Jean-Martin Charcot, he's further convinced that sex is the key to human nature. In an example of Takeshi-like understatement, his subsequent lecture on the subject is greeted with much off-screen shouting.

Unfolding in nondescript shades of gray, while making the most of small-scale period details, *Young Dr. Freud* is not even ostentatiously neutral. The mode is low-key and informational. Tossing off pearls of wisdom ("Maybe every neurotic believes he has committed some crime") en route to his discovery of the unconscious, Freud is himself somewhat heedless. More than once, Martha offers some illuminating insight that he is too reflexively sexist to grasp. (Among other things, she intuits the seduction theory of hysteria that, perhaps to his regret, Freud later abandoned.) The movie suggests that Freud was a kind of Moses, leading us to the promised land of self-knowledge without being permitted to enter it.

Also reviewed in:
CHICAGO TRIBUNE, 7/14/00, Friday/p. N, John Petrakis
NEW REPUBLIC, 5/19/00, p. 28, Stanley Kauffmann
NEW YORK TIMES, 5/17/0, p. E10, A. O. Scott

ADDENDUM

The following reviews arrived too late to be included in this or previous issues of FILM REVIEW ANNUAL. The issue of FILM REVIEW ANNUAL in which the credits and film review appears is given in parenthesis after the name of the film.

AMERICAN BEAUTY (*Film Review Annual, 2000*)

FILM QUARTERLY, Winter 2000-01, p. 46, Gary Hentzi

If one were to go by journalistic and media chatter alone, there would be little doubt that *American Beauty* was the best film of 1999. Praise for several of the actors above all—Kevin Spacey in the lead role—as well as the director, Sam Mendes, and the screenwriter, Alan Ball, was overwhelming, and so often repeated by now that it is easy to lose sight of exactly what it is that they are supposed to have done, although one is assured that they have done it remarkably well. Usually, the film is described as an assault on the emotional sleepwalking that passes for life in the American suburb; and something of the sort does appear to have been among the intentions of the director, who makes prominent use of aerial shots floating over the anonymous, tree-lined streets where the characters live. In fact, the regularity with which such descriptions appear ought to strike us as the first indication that something is lacking in discussions of this film. The suburbs have been so frequently ridiculed on the score of crass materialism and abject conformity over the past 50 years that it is a wonder their residents do not rise up, wielding hedge trimmers and pruning shears, to exact revenge on their metropolitan tormentors. At the very least, it should be obvious that a film has to do more than work over such hackneyed themes to command our attention.

My own view is that *American Beauty* is a vital but uneven film. Although it has little to say that is entirely new, it nevertheless manages to render certain experiences vividly, most memorably when it deals with the ways that teenagers and adults imagine each other's lives, as in the relationship between the protagonist, Lester Burnham, and his daughter's friend Angela (Mena Suvari). The spectacle of a middle-aged man genuinely, if absurdly, rejuvenated by the illusions of freedom and fulfillment embodied by an underaged girl is not exactly unfamiliar; however, like the most enduring literary treatments of this theme (e.g., *Lolita), American Beauty* succeeds as an exercise in romantic irony. In this regard, Kevin Spacey's ability to project an unflappable cool, even after his character has crossed over into ludicrousness, is a palpable strength; and at the end of the film, after Lester declines to take advantage of the girl's vulnerability, he comes to resemble the speaker in Keats' "Nightingale" ode, left bemused by the ability of his own fancy to create an unreachable paradise, but also brought to a greater humanity by the experience as a whole. For her part, the girl is the most believable teenager in the film. The energy she devotes to trying to live up to an unworthy image of herself is painfully familiar, and there is a nice symmetry in the fact that she is chasing empty images of adulthood at the same time that Lester is cultivating equally empty fantasies about youth.

Unfortunately, *American Beauty* does not consistently match the success of this strand of its plot. The other adult characters, far from being original portraits drawn from contemporary life, are actually based on well-known stereotypes, which can be located historically with some precision and thus give the film a pastiche quality that coexists uneasily with its aspirations toward realist exposé. For example, Annette Bening's character (Lester's wife) is a familiar—but not necessarily welcome—figure out of the cultural criticism of the immediate postwar era. The historical origins of this character are even signaled within the film itself by her preference for Eisenhower-era show tunes and popular music—just the sort of taste to which a shallow woman of her generation would tend to feel superior because it belongs to the world of her parents (some of the more anodyne specimens of classic rock or contemporary radio pop would be more likely choices from the point of view of social documentation). Moreover, the ferocious mockery with which she is presented seems to come straight from the yellowed pages of all-but-forgotten jeremiads like Philip Wylie's *Generation of Vipers* (1942), which ascribed the most bland and wasteful traits of suburban consumer culture to a phenomenon that the author called "momism"—essentially the claim that the backbone of the American family was being warped by the voracious, manipulative, yet contemptibly anesthetic tastes of a certain kind of mother, who was becoming more common and even getting the upper hand as a result of the American male's failure to be a man. Not only were such mothers trying to take the place of fathers, but they were also bound to raise troubled and rebellious children, since for them childrearing was accomplished largely by means of bribery with the promise of access to consumer goods and pleasures. Wylie was prescient in his choice of terms, for he anticipated a growth industry in vulgar Freudian writing over roughly the next decade and a half about the figure of the bad mother and the harm that she does. In retrospect, this phenomenon seems an especially hysterical manifestation of the same mid-century male anxieties that inspired such far more interesting cultural documents as film noir, and the meaning of its reappearance at the end of the millennium is unclear. What *is* clear is that this character has at least as much to do with the less generous emotions that many men harbor toward women as it does with the lives of actual women in the suburbs today.

Even more plainly conventional than Lester's wife is the character of the violent, repressed homosexual marine colonel next door. This figure belongs to a somewhat later period, being a Vietnam-era bogey used by the counterculture to taunt its more hawkish adversaries, and is so obvious a throwback that some reviewers questioned its effectiveness. They were right to do so; the character is no longer terribly relevant. Interestingly, the imaginative weakness of the filmmakers' attempt to record the presence of fascism in the suburbs inadvertently calls attention to a less obvious problem with the handling of the film's main theme. For the most visible kind of American fascist at this moment in history is not the intolerant military man struggling with his own unrecognized urges, but the teenage skinhead or neo-Nazi thug. Such bypassing of contemporary reality suggests that, despite the ironic wisdom with which Lester's epiphanic moment is portrayed, *American Beauty* still has a tendency to invest teenagers with an aura of grace, and this problem is evident in one of the most interesting characters in the film: Ricky, the colonel's mysterious drug-dealing son.

To be sure, there is much about this figure that is attractive, beginning with the charisma of the you actor, Wes Bentley, who plays the role, and much more that at least represents a healthy determination to break with received wisdom. Almost nothing has been said about the admirably firm dismissal of puritanical conceptions of voyeurism and visual pleasure in this part of the film. The filmmakers correctly see that all art involves the risk of manipulation, and that pleasure, inluding the pleasure of looking at a woman's body, need not be simply equated with sadism or fetishism. Rather, with the help of a video camera, Lester's self-denigrating daughter Jane learns to see herself through her lover's eyes, suggesting that such aesthetically informed ways of seeing are inseparable from human relationships and the growth of a mature sense of self. But then, having established the camera as a means of revelation rather than an instrument of power, the film falters.

Ricky's prize video clip of a plastic bag blowing around tends toward an essentially religious conception of beauty, which distracts from what the filmmakers have to show us about its role in human relationships by locating the source of beauty outside of us in the world of things, or even somewhere beyond (as does Ricky's Wordsworthian monologue about a reassuring presence telling him that he need never worry). The curious thing about the plastic bag sequence is that it really is the kind of thing that a teenage aesthete might consider "deep"; however, the filmmakers evidently mean for us to be as moved by it as the kids in the film are, suggesting that Mendes and Ball, like their protagonist, are guilty of an unseemly degree of identification with teenagers. Even allowing that the children of dysfunctional families are often saner and more mature than their parents, one nevertheless comes to suspect that this uncannily cool-headed and clear-sighted young man is something of a fantasy figure, a creation of the filmmakers' own narcissism, and the character's staggering wealth does nothing to lessen that impression. It is ironic that the guardians of public morals worry so much about the ethics of portraying a drug dealer as anything but purely evil. What is really dubious is the idea that the question of income should be so insignificant a problem for an aspiring filmmaker about to go out on his own, and one respect in which *American Beauty* definitely reflects its own rather than any other moment in history is its willingness to include business acumen among the elements of this otherwise rather traditional portrait of the artist as a young man. To first-time filmmakers, the dream of being able to finance one's own projects must have an irresistible appeal.

If I have said much about the individuals who populate the film's suburban world and relatively little about its plot, this is because *American Beauty* gives the impression of having been conceived above all as a set of characters whose stories are held together in a rather loose structure and were possibly honed a bit over the course of the project's development. (Evidence on this point is conflicting: whereas Kevin Spacey and Sam Mendes have gone out of their way to assert that the script was never materially changed, Alan Ball makes reference in the published screenplay to scenes that were dropped or rewritten during the shooting of the film.) In any case, unsolved problems remain in the final version. Although the stories that the filmmakers ended up telling were better than some they might have told, certain incidents nevertheless seem forced and inessential. For example, the framing device of the murder is simply a means of creating suspense; and the various attempts to deceive the viewer, beginning with the opening shot, are unworthy of the best things in the film. Eventually, the murder turns out to have been committed by the only person who could have committed it; the crucial scene between Lester and his object of desire is already over at the time that it occurs; and the young, would-be filmmaker has already made the decision to leave home for the big city. One need only compare this killing to the murders at the end of what was perhaps the most artistically successful film to appear in 1999, *Boys Don't Cry,* to see the difference between a gratuitous formal device, somewhat disguised by the carpe diem in voiceover, and an act of violence that emerges inevitably from everything that precedes it. Without question *American Beauty* is a bold, ambitious piece of filmmaking that showcases some fine acting and reveals the considerable talents of its director and screenwriter in a variety of ways; it fully deserves to be seen and discussed by anyone who cares about American cinema. When the discussion has ended, however, one hopes that the participants will have made a genuine effort to sort out the film's strengths and weaknesses, instead of merely repeating the handiest clichés about its setting.

HOUSE OF MIRTH, THE *(Film Review Annual, 2001)*

FILM QUARTERLY, Fall 2001, p. 49, James Morrison

Catharsis, said Aristotle, is the goal of drama. You'd never know it from *The House of Mirth,* an adaptation of Edith Wharton's 1905 novel by the great British filmmaker Terence Davies. Its intensity is distilled in its uncompromising restraint, and though there are passing moments of anger in the film, and rare, sudden swellings of grief, there's not a second of real release in this grim anatomy of a socialite's inexorable decline. Yet the film's relentlessness does not feel cruel. It feels like the piercing expression of a boundless pity.

Lily Bart is a strong-minded heiress whose will to independence can only be perceived as pride by the society she lives in—New York City at the turn of the twentieth century. She recklessly accumulates gambling debts, treats the powerful men who covet her with lighthearted scorn, and falls victim, in the end, to petty rumors. Disinherited, she joins the working classes, and gradually descends into drug addiction. It's the stuff of pulp melodrama, raised in Wharton's delicately histrionic treatment of the material to the level of tragedy-of-manners. In turn, Davies resists the histrionics and makes the story into a chamber-play, in which squelched emotion and strangled expression perform a hushed duet. Davies seems to have set himself the near-impossible task of making a movie about repression whose power lies in the fact that what's repressed never rises to the surface.

The Masterpiece-Theatre-style costume dramas the film superficially resembles tend to work in something like the opposite way. They're all about repression, too, typically with the self-congratulatory implication that we moderns have risen above the stifling but picturesque social rituals of days of yore. But they can usually only represent repression by revealing the strong emotions it mitigates—as in the explosions of violence in *Howards End,* say, or the sex scenes in *Wings of the Dove.* Only then do you realize what undercurrents are supposed to be surging beneath the surface. But Davies wants to reveal these undercurrents without ever manifesting them directly because, his film suggests, social repression doesn't just short-circuit true expression temporarily before it finally comes out—it kills the feelings it smothers.

There *is* a sex scene in *The House of Mirth,* and it's a marvel in its suggestion of subdued carnality, of a desire that can barely take shape amid the opulent trappings designed to crush it. The scene evokes a compelling sense of suspended time, and hopeless longing that gains force *because* it's hopeless. The pace is slowed, in long, languorous takes, and sound effects are invested with a charge of rare sensuality: the whispering folds of elaborate clothing, the lapping of moist lips in halting speech, the keening echo of a concerto so faint, so far distant, that it might be heard in memory alone. The scene is not meant to suggest that if only these people could break out and get in touch with their real, primal selves—à la the Merchant/Ivory *Room with a View*—then they'd triumph over the restriction of social mores. The whole point is that's just what they *can't* do.

Still, some viewers might understandably, at first, mistake *The House of Mirth* for another entry in the Merchant/Ivory stakes. It's a period piece, after all, with fancy costumes, classical music filling the soundtrack, and painterly compositions—the last image fades into a melancholy tableau that suggests Mary Cassatt. I don't mean to slight Merchant/Ivory unnecessarily here: with films like *Shakespeare Wallah* and *Roseland,* we should recall, they were international pioneers of independent filmmaking. Before they settled into the cozy niche of their recent films, they even brought some of that independent spirit to their earliest forays into costume drama—as in the dryly severe *The Europeans* (1979), out of James, to which *The House of Mirth* bears some affinities. But the rigorous spareness of Davies's film has none of the genteel aura or the classy status of the later Merchant/Ivory productions. In *The House of Mirth,* scene follows scene with an impacted cadence made harsher, somehow, by the swift, precise dissolves that link the images, and the tableaux have an enclosed, airless quality—you can sense the dank, rarefied atmosphere, but you can't breathe in it.

The whole film is slightly, delicately stylized, and Gillian Anderson's performance as Lily Bart suits this milieu perfectly. By no means is it standard, naturalistic "star" acting. It is both mannered and understated, a thoroughly modulated performance, the gestures refined, the intonations of line readings just slightly, though fastidiously, stilted. This stylization is meant to suggest a range of emotional colorings, while retaining an essential elegance. Even after Lily has resigned herself to her debasement, she remains excruciatingly well-bred-as if she *thought* she were in a Merchant/Ivory film. Considering the extreme bias toward naturalistic acting of many film viewers, Anderson's performance will not be to every taste, especially since it's at odds with the more traditional styles of many of her fellow actors—Eric Stoltz, for instance, who plays Lawrence Selden (Lily's true love). But this works for the film, too, in the end, suggesting Lily's terrible distinction, her intractable apartness.

If you're a lover of Wharton who wants to view a full adaptation of her work, see Martin Scorsese's *The Age of Innocence.* That film encompasses the waspish wit, the detailed examination of social minutiae, and the exuberance giving way to melancholy that are the hallmarks of Wharton's great novels. With sheer intensity of focus, Davies concentrates here only on the dourness, in all its varied textures. The emotional register of the film is closer to Strindberg than to Wharton. It's a very modern rendering of Wharton's fairly modern novel, on the order of Jane Campion's treatment of James in *The Portrait of a Lady.* Davies skews some of the causes in Wharton's plot: the nature and origins of the rumors swirling about Lily are obscured, and Lily's sojourns as secretary and milliner are startling because relatively unexplained in the film's plot. This is because Davies wants to show this society as a complex closed system, where the causes of effects are never easy to determine, even when they seem to be nothing but petty personal motives.

Davies is known—when he's known at all—for densely free-associative memory—films like *Distant Voices-Still Lives* (1987) and *The Long Day Closes* (1993). These films transport the materials of British social realism, chronicles of working-class family life, into a heady context of modernist aestheticism, with fragmented narratives and highly wrought alienation-effects. But though the films look avant-garde to many viewers, it's hard to stay too alienated from them—the feeling for the characters is so deep. Watching these movies is like seeing the ghosts of loved ones, substantial but fleeting, and understanding at last the suffering that made them what they were. For Davies, we're all products of our time, and one of the things this means is that we're *trapped* in time. In those earlier films, we watch as the characters, helpless and trapped and beloved, strive variously for transcendence—pursuing the errant cycles by which they live, or joining together in fugitive song In *The House of Mirth*, one still feels one is watching a cast made up of phantoms, and the feeling expressed for them is still deep. But because the world of the film is so tragically loveless, this feeling can take shape, not as love, but only as an abiding sympathy with those who must live, and die, there. And this time there is no transcendence—except, perhaps, for the one that might come later, after the film is done, when you know you have witnessed a work of art.

O BROTHER, WHERE ART THOU? (*Film Review Annual, 2001*)

FILM QUARTERLY, Fall 2001, p. 41, Rob Content

"Everyone's looking for answers." Several times during his cross-Mississippi odyssey, Ulysses Everett McGill offers this sage observation—and it's a line to take note of in a film whose title asks a question. The question is first posed (as we've all now been reminded) in Preston Sturges's 1941 *Sullivan's Travels.* As that film begins, rich white-boy director John L. Sullivan is convinced that his screwball comedies are wasting both his own gifts and his audience's time. The project he really wants to undertake is *O Brother, Where Art Thou*, based on a grim-looking novel written by one "Sinclair Beckstein"—a garbling of the names of the two best-known social-realists of the 1930s. But by the end of his tribulations, Sullivan has abandoned his "serious" pretensions, having realized that escapist comedies bring joy and relief to the lives of the suffering masses. To his credit, he's also learned how little his didactic, eggheaded socialist vision—allegorical figures of Labor and Capital wrestling atop a moving train to a Holmes-and-Moriarty finale—has to say about the realities of American poverty, prison, oppression, and despair.

Now Joel and Ethan Coen have made his masterpiece for him. The Coen brothers, from the start less naïve than Sully, know that pious "message" films are box-office poison and that laughs put asses in the seats, so they've filmed his bleak epic as a series of antic adventures and escapes with a cast of cartoonish characters. They've given it a full three happy endings, complete with a big musical number, a pardon from the governor, a wedding, and even a miracle. But the film's reversals of fortune are so abrupt, its escapes from disaster so flimsily contrived, and its happy endings so improbable that they can't quite make us forget its disquieting moments of real cruelty. Its ostensibly comic tone is also belied by the bleached colors of its desiccated fields and dirt roads, and by a knowing selection of mournful "ol'-timey" songs about joblessness, hunger, prison, and death.

The Coens' borrowing of Sturges's title is not an in-jokey homage, like the recall codes from *Dr. Strangelove* graffitied on a gas station men's room wall in *Raising Arizona.* In *O Brother's* most explicit allusion to *Sullivan's Travels,* a chain gang is marched into a movie theater and ordered by an overseer with a shotgun to "Enjoy yer pickcha show!" In Sturges's film, the gang of convicts crack up at an animated cartoon, stomping and weeping with laughter, showing Sullivan how much escapism means to people without any real hope. The chain gang in *O Brother*, however, watches in disconcerting silence. The Coens aren't content to crank out merely diverting Hollywood comedies; beneath the broad caricatures and genre-bending of *O Brother,* John Sullivan's do-gooder agenda is intact. The Coens have sneakily taken on the least saleable subject of our time—the whole messy tangle of class, family, and race.

Almost all the Coens' comedies are set against the backdrop of an American crisis. *Raising Arizona* takes place among the trickled-down-upon underclass, with "that sumbitch Reagan in the White house"; *Barton Fink* ends with America's patriotic rush into World War II; *The Big Lebowski* is set during the Gulf War and its main characters are a counterculture casualty and a Vietnam vet. *O Brother* is set in the Great Depression, when antagonism between the government and its citizens, between the haves and have-nots, was starker and more open than at any time since the Civil War. Its episodic plot can be understood the same way the hard-knock Christianity of its old gospel songs teaches us to understand life—as a series of moral trials. Specifically, we see the loyalty and solidarity of the poor tested by the temptations and threats of the rich. The film's protagonists encounter a series of grotesques who embody the institutions of the wealthy and powerful in allegorical guises a mite subtler than Labor and Capital atop a train. Our heroes, more fully human, either rise to the occasion by identifying with their fellows or fail by abandoning or betraying them. Yet the most crucial of these tests is put not to the film's characters, but to the audience. Will we see as clearly as do the three white fugitives that their fate is cast with that of their black brethern? Ultimately, the Coens' latest film endorses those old American ideals that seem so quaint and naive now—the solidarity of the oppressed, resistance to abusive power, and the embrace of a universal brotherhood that transcends race.

O Brother, Where Art Thou? is a question posed in earnest. It's the same question the lawyer put to Jesus: "Who is my neighbor?" Jesus answered him with the parable of the Good Samaritan, the story of a man who saw someone he had been taught to despise lying beaten and helpless in a ditch, and felt moved to compression. We're repeatedly asked—along with the film's protagonists—whom we're passing by on the other side.

The first scene depicts an all-black chain gang, breaking rocks in cadence to the mournful chant of "Po' Lazarus," a song about a fugitive the sheriff wants "dead or alive." We then see Everett McGill (George Clooney), Pete Hogwallop (John Turturro), and Delmar O'Donnell (Tim Blake Nelson) popping up out of a soybean field, accompanied by the peppier "Big Rock Candy Mountain." The lyrics of this song are a sad paean to a fantasyland where jails are made of tin, cops have wooden legs, and there's a lake of stew. This is the pipe dream of men accustomed to harassment, hunger, and hard labor. It's not clear whether the gang from which they've escaped is supposed to be the same gang we've just seen, but these opening shots suggest the three white convicts' fortunes are inextricably entwined with the plight of blacks.

As Everett mentions later in the film, he and his companions have escaped from Parchman Farm, an almost all-black prison camp established in 1904 by James Kimble Vardaman, a notoriously racist Mississippi governor who believed prison labor could provide young black men with proper discipline, work ethics, and an appropriately deferential attitude towards whites—and that these young blacks could in turn provide cheap labor for the state's business barons. Parchman Farm remained in operation until the 1970s, a legacy of which the Coens are certainly aware, since the performance of "Po' Lazarus" which leads off the film's soundtrack is Alan Lonax's 1959 field recording of a group of Parchman inmates.

Vardaman's system criminalized an entire class of citizens, but its selective enforcement went further in dividing the popular majority of poor Mississippians: it singled out blacks for the harshest punishments, frequently working them to death. Throughout *O Brother,* the three white fugitives are repeatedly mistaken for blacks. They even try to "pass" for Negroes: they assent when the blind DJ at WEZY asks them whether they're colored, and although they soon abandon this ploy, he later recalls them as "colored fellas, I b'lieve." When Big Dan Teague snatches white hoods from their heads at a Klan rally and exposes faces still blackened from their latest jailbreak, the horrified Wizard blurts out, "The color guard is colored!" Later, outside the music hall, the same Wizard (now unmasked as gubernatorial candidate Homer Stokes) mutters that only mulattos would dare desecrate the Confederate flag as they've done, and then denounces them before their fans, crying, "These men are not white!"

Everett, Pete, and Delmar are not only labeled black, they also suffer the unduly harsh, arbitrary treatment that typically distinguishes the experience of black men. Pete is lashed with a bullwhip under the shadow of a lynching noose, while one of Sheriff Cooley's sadistic posse derides him as an "unreconstructed whelp of a whore." This punishment and this description imply both slave status and suspect parentage. After Everett's rival for his ex-wife punches him out in the five-and-dime, the manager hurls Everett into the street, shouting, "And stay out of the Woolworth's!" (It was the Greensboro, N.C. Woolworth's where in 1959 four young black civil rights activists defied the "legitimacy" of segregated lunch counter seating.) Delmar takes for granted that the banishment applies to him as well—it's membership in a stigmatized social group, not individual bad behavior, that makes him unwelcome.

Being second-class citizens and hunted men themselves, Everett and his companions identify at once with the black characters they meet. Encountering the blind Tiresian seer pumping his handcar, they fall into conversation that's not just familiar but familial: he addresses them as "my sons," and they call him "grandpa" in return. They pull over and make room in their get-away car for the hitchhiking Tommy Johnson (Chris Thomas King), a black man they've never seen before. And when they see Tommy about to be lynched by the Klan, they risk their lives to save him after barely a moment's discussion—Pete, who's just been threatened with lynching himself, says in horror, "The noose. Sweet Jesus! We gotta save 'im!" They embrace their black friend's fate as their own—which, in fact, it is.

The point is not just the sociological lesson that poor, rural "white trash" have their own history of prejudice and persecution, nor even that working-class whites criminalized by poverty have more in common with black people than with rich white people. It's that the natural solidarity of universal brotherhood arises out of shared suffering. *O Brother, Where Art Thou?* echoes the Depression-era refrain "Brother, can you spare a dime?," showing us this empathy and identification as natural. The film indicts both the state and its representatives for making an issue of race and using it to set poor men against one another. Homer Stokes (Wayne Duvall) begins his Klan rally speech by invoking the term "brothers," but then proceeds with a roll call of invented enemies—blacks, Jews, Catholics, evolutionists. With his appeals to a common "culture'n heritage," he may claim to be a uniter, not a divider, but his real agenda is exposed when he announces the event's true purpose: "So we're gonna hang us a neegra! "

The neegra he has in mind is Tommy, who's led to the gallows pleading "I ain't never harmed you gentlemen." His absurdly polite appeal is of course just a survival tactic—one instance of the broad repertoire of traits and mannerisms assumed by a captive population subject to arbitrary violence. Stokes, however, can only hear such a plea as evidence that blacks recognize themselves as his naturally deferential social inferiors. He cannot conceive of black men disrupting a Klan rally (much less defiling his beloved Confederate flag). For him, such an act of defiance could only be the product of blacks and whites racially intermixing. Like the state he both serves and represents, Stokes abhors the possibility of any kind of solidarity among blacks and whites because such a union presents a real challenge to the state's domination of the masses.

As *O Brother* illustrates, the state uses not only differences of race to divide people, but other short-term incentives as well, front banal bribery to social disgrace to brute force. Pete's cousin Washington Hogwallop and the three seductive laundresses in the stream turn traitor at the lure of bounty. Everett's ex-wife, Penny, succumbs to her fear of being "not bona fide" when she abandons him for a better "provider." Pete sobs "Godfer gimme" its he chooses to save himself from the sheriff's noose. Tommy Johnson is not the only character in this film to make a bargain with the Devil.

The first betrayal we see reveals how the state exploits "family values" to pit members of the underclass against one another. Washington Hogwallop, a farmer who's resorted to eating horsemeat even after it's started to turn," miserably justifies selling his own cousin up the river for coin: "I know we're kin! But they got this Depression on, and I gotta do fer me an' mine!" Even Wash's eight-year-old son—who was obediently prepared to shotgun anyone from the bank or the census who set foot on his daddy's farm—rejects this treacherous logic. He rescues the three strangers from a blazing barn amidst a hail of bullets and decides to "R-U-N-N-O-F-T" from a father who's revealed such warped values.

For all his outrage at Wash, Pete himself turns Judas in the very next scene, betraying Wash's son. "Go home and mind yer paw," he yells, throwing a dirt clod after the boy. Pete's blind adherence to the narrowest of family ties undermines the greater good of human solidarity. The utter misguidedness of his indoctrination in the sanctity of blood ties comically resurfaces when he learns Everett has "borrowed" Wash's gold pocket watch. "You stole from my kin!" he screams. This jarring sequence encapsulates *O Brother*'s central challenge to its audience. We're all supposed to honor the officially sanctioned "brotherhood" of blood relations, but Wash's narrow and selfish interpretation thoroughly exposes it as inadequate compared to the real brotherhood of equal dignity, which the state, of course, must undermine and crush.

Sex, like money, is used to sow jealousy and mistrust. When Everett asks Pete for an introduction to the three laundresses, he hisses, "I seen 'em first!" One temptress keeps pouring a jug of Triple-X hooch down Everett's throat, equating the effects of corn licker and lust, which make men first bestial and then unconscious. The lyrics of the women's lullaby become not only sinful ("You an' me and the Devil makes three/Don't need no other lovin' baby") but spooky and sepulchral ("Come lay your bones on the alabaster stone/and be my everlovin' baby"), an inducement not into bed but the grave. These women are not only sirens who lure the men to their ruin, but also Circe the sorceress, who turns them into animals (specifically swine). As Everett says of the toad who hops out of Pete's shirt, "if that's Pete, I *am* ashamed of him The way I see it he got what he deserved—fornicating with some whore a' Babylon." One might dismiss this as the sort of callous misogyny expressed in Everett's blanket condemnation of women as "deceitful!" and "two-faced!" But Everett too has snapped up the state's ideological lure. Volunteering for the war between the sexes, he wastes energy better directed against bosses and politicians.

As with sex, so with the family that's supposed to sanctify it and keep it respectable. We meet Penelope McGill (Holly Hunter) as she's buying nipples it the five-and-dime. Penny, less patient than her Homeric namesake, has divorced Everett "from shame," claiming it was for their daughters' sake. "They look to me for answers," she states, but the answers she gives them are lies; she's told them their daddy was run over by a train. She's disowned Everett in favor of a higher-class con artist, campaign manager Vernon Waldrip (Ray McKinnon), who can provide not only a steady income but the trappings of upward mobility such as "lessons on the clarinet."

The deepest betrayals, however, are prompted not by money or sex. Horsewhipped, faced with a noose, and convinced by the sheriff's lie that "your two friends have abandoned you," Pete spills his guts about Everett's plan to retrieve $1.2 million from an armored car heist. His life in the wake of this desperate choice seems worse than death. He stares up slack-jawed from the chain gang, a forlorn phantom vanishing in a cloud of dust. Later, in a scene echoing Odysseus' colloquy with the dead in Hades, Pete is illuminated in a darkened theater by the flickering beam of the projector as he hisses like a tormented shade at Everett and Delmar, "Do not seek the treasure! It's a bushwhack!" Sleepless in his prison bunk that night and haunted by a vision of the noose, he moans, "I could not gaze upon that far shore. . . ." Perhaps the intensity of his guilt and grief redeems the crime he knows he's committed against his fellow fugitives, but the scenes of Pete's suffering reveal that even the state's final, and most terrifying, resort—coercion under the shadow of death—does not absolve him for betraying his brothers.

Reviewers have made an easy game of matching characters in this film with their supposed counterparts from the *Odyssey*—the baptismal congregation are lotus-eater's, the laundresses are sirens, Penny is Penelope, etc. This is not always the most illuminating approach. Menelaus "Pappy" O'Daniel (Charles Durning) may be as wealthy as the king of Lacedaemon, but he doesn't share much of the latter's kindness or wisdom. And Big Dan Teague is far more complicated than the savage Cyclops. The film's obvious villains, the "monsters" of this odyssey, can be seen more revealingly as a symbolic rogues' gallery of human institutions—business, politics, education—that corrupt us, dividing brother against brother.

The blind DJ who records Everett, Pete, and Delmar in their impromptu incarnation as the Soggy Bottom Boys offers them ten dollars a head for their performance. He makes it sound like real money. None of them grasps the implications of this newfangled recording and broadcast technology or understands the rip-off. The fugitives never know that there's big money being made from selling their recordings even as they themselves have to hide from the law. We see the DJ chuckling as he fondly recites the businessman's creed: "Oh mercy, yes. You gotta beat that competition." And let's not forget who owns that radio station: WEZY is a tool of *"mass* communicatin'" sponsored by Pappy O'Daniel, incumbent governor of Mississippi. Few films in recent memory have displayed such contempt for venal politicos and their self-serving motives. Pappy, a stereotypical Good Ole Boy, has no platform except to get himself re-elected. His only political affiliation is Opportunist—"Goddamn! Oppitunity *knocks!"* he cries in a moment of inspiration, determined to climb onstage and bask in the reflected glory of the Soggy Bottom Boys. Likewise, his challenger, "reform" candidate and Klan Wizard Homer Stokes, calls himself the "Friend of the Little Man," and promises a "new broom to sweep the state clean"—but these are just slogans to show off his trademark props, a midget sidekick with a miniature broom.

As Big Dan Teague, John Goodman at first seems to be reprising his role as Charlie Meadows/Karl Mundt in *Barton Fink:* another garrulous salesman with an unexpected capacity for violence. The contradiction of a Bible salesman who's also a con man and the equation of evangelism and sales are obvious, but Big Dan is up to more than the obvious. The "lesson" he teaches—and especially, Everett's seemingly inexplicable docility in the face of its assault—directs us toward allegory. Big Dan represents the educational system, first talking his way into power over Everett and Delmar with his "gift of gab," then isolating them from outside support, and finally delivering them an "advanced tutorial" via the corporal discipline of a tree limb.

It's no coincidence that all these characters who take advantage of our heroes are fat. In the lean years of the Depression, double chins and big bellies brand these villains as "fat cats," the rich and powerful, in contrast to the hollow-cheeked poor. Big Dan's insatiable appetite is not just an allusion to the Cyclops' uncivilized dining habits: when his nostrils flare in a restaurant, it's Everett and Delmar's cash he's smelling. Corpulence reinforces the basic divide in this film, the one not between blacks and whites or men and women, but between the exploiters and the exploited.

This movie's most curious figure is George "Babyface" Nelson (Michael Badalucco)—not exactly a villain, but so broadly drawn that he must also be an allegory: celebrity. As all original partner of the three, he cares less about money than about the adrenaline high of the hold-up and the chase. In both phases of his bipolarity, he focuses on the aggrandizement of his image. He screams his name over and over in exultation, and rages and pouts at the use of his hated nickname. Like other unaccountable glory seekers from Dillinger to Clinton, he's obsessed with his own legacy, micro-managing public perception. After the heist, Nelson loses interest in his three new friends, and wanders off, disconsolate. George may be an enemy of the State, but he's only in it for the glory.

The three heroes could also be read—beyond the Homeric—as allegorical figures: Everett the rational skeptic; Pete the slave to passion; and Delmar the fool. In the scene closest to the film's heart, the escaped cons lie around their campfire, talking about what they'll do with their share of the loot. Pete wants to open a fancy restaurant where he'll be the maitre d', eat every day for free, and be called "suh" by the staff. Delmar just wants to get his family farm back from the bank. These dreams are poignantly small; more than the free board, Pete just wants to be shown some respect, and Delmar only wants to get back a little property that's already rightfully his. Their most extravagant fantasies are of being treated with common dignity. Everett, who invented the $1.2 million, has dreams even smaller than theirs. He desperately wants to be what his wife and daughters call "bona fide"—a respectable, middle-class professional. George Clooney's performance as Everett, widely criticized as too broad and exaggerated, is a deliberate caricature of a man imitating everything he isn't. Everett's highfalutin' diction and harebrained scams are all misguided shortcuts to self-improvement; despite having been jailed for impersonating a lawyer, at the dance hall he assures his dismayed ex-wife that he knows someone who can print him up a dentist's license. But all these small human aspirations are as hopelessly out of reach as the Big Rock Candy Mountain. Watching the campfire scene, we know that they'll never really see that money. The song Tommy Johnson picks out on his guitar as they swap daydreams is "Hard Time Killing Floor Blues," about the humiliation of begging door to door.

O Brother, Where Art Thou? gives us not one, but three happy endings. The film returns to its roots in the first of these, an extended musical number staged in a dance hall, during which Everett, Pete, and Delmar are finally discovered as the wildly popular Soggy Bottom Boys, candidate Homer Stokes exposes himself as a hypocritical bigot, and Pappy O'Daniel takes advantage of the musicians' surprise appearance to cement his reelection and grant them a full pardon. All this hilarity aside, the sequence puts to a public referendum the film's thesis that racial division is best understood as a deliberate tactic of the ruling class.

We are first signaled that racial identity is still at issue when Junior O'Daniel resists his father's attraction to the Soggy Bottom Boys, remarking: "But Pappy, they's inter-grated." The Coens have given us plenty of evidence this means much more than Tommy Johnson playing guitar onstage. No one in the crowd has ever seen the Soggy Bottom Boys—their pirated recording has been distributed without their knowledge by a producer who vaguely remembers them as colored. The mystery of their identity has meanwhile become Page Three headline news. As Pappy quickly discerns, "I guess folks don't mind they's integrated." The crowd has been galvanized by the performance a traditional bluegrass tune, featuring the black Tommy Johnson on guitar, and a white lead singer who kicks up an impromptu buck-and-wing borrowed from black minstrelsy—with all four performers disguised in exactly the same false gray hillbilly beards. In this climactic scene, the Coens have staged the country's first great crossover phenomenons—full generation before Elvis.

Homer Stokes is convinced not only that the Boys are black, but also that their fans' enthusiastic reception is based on ignorance of this fact. He hurries to shut down this "miscegenated" performance, and announces, "These boys is not white!" The crowd starts rumbling at this disruption, but he, confident of his "constitchency," blathers on. Gratifyingly, Stokes' fear that racial intermixing will rock the racist social order turns out to be well-founded: his constitchency literally rides him out of the hall on a rail to insure that the band finishes their song. Pappy O'Daniel, like the canny Southern politicians who saw which way the wind was blowing during the civil rights era, is quick to scramble onto the integration bandwagon. He offers the Soggy Bottom Boys a sweeping on-the-spot pardon, and even announces that, in his second administration, the Soggy Bottom Boys "gonna be my brain trust."

Immediately after this first happy ending, we see a second—similarly manic and dubious. George Nelson is dragged to his electrocution by a mob. His parting speech, including the megalomaniacal line, "Gonna shoot sparks out the top of my head and lightning from my fingertips!," is accompanied by a couple of village idiots playing a braying tune on their fiddles. In what seems initially like an idyllic coda, Everett, Pete, Delmar, and Tommy are unexpectedly confronted by the ultimate embodiment of evil, the Devil, incarnated as a murderous Lawman—a hard-faced sheriff with a badge, a bloodhound, and fire in his eyes. But he represents more than the Law, which he scorns as "a human institution." His is the final, unappealable sentence of Death. The Biblical deluge that reprieves the condemned men is the same sort of intervention in the laws of nature as the janitor's jamming a broom handle into the wheels of Time, literally at the eleventh hour, to save Norville Barnes from his fall from the 45th floor in *The Hudsucker Proxy*. Endings this self-consciously absurd can only be ironic concessions to Hollywood convention; the omnipotent hand that shows most clearly is not God's but the screenwriters'. In reality, the Coens know and we know that big corporations do take advantage of and destroy "little people" and "nobodies" like Norville, and that innocent men get lynched, especially if they're poor. The tenebrous strains of "That Lonesome Valley," sung by three stoic grave diggers—the Fates—quavers and rises in the background, reminding us that all reprieves, whether from the governor or from God, are only temporary.

The real climax in this scene is not the arrival of a miraculous flood but an unexpected outbreak of genuine human emotion from Everett. In his extreme despair his fast-talking sharp-dealing demeanor finally cracks, and he falls to his knees and delivers a heart-felt plea unlike any other slick speech that's passed his lips in the last for hours. He begs God for clemency. Earlier he boasted of being the only Soggy Bottom Boy who "remains unaffiliated" with any supernatural agency; now, it seems, he's finally chosen sides.

But no sooner are Everett's prayers answered than he recovers from his bout of God-fearing humility. Borne above the flood waters by a coffin intended for one of them, he preaches to his two comrades about the promise of a shining, progressive future for the South: "Out with the old spiritual mumbo-jumbo, the superstitions and the backward ways. We're gonna see a brave new world where they run everyone a wire and hook us all up to a grid." Electricity is a metaphor for the false promise of rationality and progress, an end to the Dark Age, a literal enlightenment. Everett also heralds "a veritable age of reason—like the one they had in France," but neither of his examples—Huxley's sterile, narcotic utopia or the bloodbath of Robespierre inspires much confidence in the contemporary listener. In the film's last scene we see an optimistic vision of this "brave new world" in a public mural, like one of those upbeat billboards that 30s photographers loved to juxtapose with hobos or bread lines. That, and the fact that George Nelson will soon be shooting electricity front his fingertips, reminds us that "progress" has its victims, too.

The apparition of "a cow on the roof of a cotton house" reminds Everett and us that the blind seer's prophecies have been fulfilled: they have found treasure, although not the treasure they sought. Their real answer is in the brotherly community they've formed together, and in the faith they've discovered.

This moral may sound mawkish, but all the prattling voices of skepticism and rationality in the film have been discredited by the woeful songs we've heard and the mute faces of suffering we've seen. There's an unmistakable strain of genuine, hard-assed, "ol'timey" Christianity running through the cores of this story. No other recent film has taken as seriously the presence of a merciful and sustaining God in the minds of the people—saved, sinners, and skeptics alike. The Coens plainly revile hypocrites and demagogues like Homer Stokes and Big Dan, but their vision of brotherhood has unapologetic roots in grass-roots revivalism. For all the Coens' broad caricatures of bumpkins with funny accents in *Blood Simple, Raising Arizona, The Hudsucker Proxy* and *Fargo*, there's nothing ironic or mocking about their depiction of Everett's gallows conversion and fervent prayer. Everett asks not just for mercy but for "deliverance," for divine intervention in his fate. The God he's appealing to is not the deistic clockmaker of the Enlightenment (and of America's founding fathers) but the personal Old Testament God who parted the Red Sea (and brought it crashing down on Pharaoh and his armies) and could occasionally be persuaded to make an exception for a single penitent man.

In the film's closing scene, Everett finds himself in bondage again, this time to his hectoring wife and their daughters, who trail behind them along a length of twine—another chain gang. As this ending and so many of the films songs remind us, there's only one release from worldly strife and tribulation. The only rest from our ordeals, the only end to our odyssey, is in death. The best we can do in the meantime is to try to recognize each other as brothers, stick together, withstand the temptations the world throws at us, and sing our songs. Still looking for answers? There's your answer.

SUZHOU RIVER (*Film Review Annual 2001*)

FILM QUARTERLY, Fall 2001, p. 55, Damion Searls

Love is a story you tell yourself—about yourself, about the one you love, and about your lives together. But we want love never to end, while a story, a narrative, must come to an end, or else it is not a story. Does that make love a special kind of story, or is love the arena where we can see storytelling working against itself, undercutting its own narratives? *Suzhou River,* the second film by 35-year-old Chinese director Lou Ye, sinks deep into these questions, not only addressing them but taking them in, taking them on.

As one might expect from a movie about narrative working against itself, the plot of *Suzhou River* is slippery. There are, it seems, two pairs of lovers. The first pair, whose love story begins years before the main action of the movie, is Moudan (Zhou Xun), indeterminate in age but girlish in her pigtails, and Mardar (Jia Hong-sheng), a silent, withdrawn motorcycle courier. He is hired to take Moudan to a relative's house whenever her father has an assignation. Mardar lives for the mobility, the endless motion, of the motorcycle—off-duty, he sits immobile on his sofa and watches videos—and he is valuable to his shady employers because he tells no tales (we will see this thematic pairing of mobility and story elsewhere too). Eventually, he notices Moudan's love, and returns it, but when his employers tell him to kidnap her and hold her until they collect a ransom from her father, he obeys; when he releases her, she runs off and jumps into the Suzhou River. He dives in after her, but cannot find her.

The other two lovers are the unnamed male narrator of the movie and Meimei (Zhou Xun again, in a great double performance). Meimei swims around a tank of water in the local bar, wearing a mermaid outfit and a blond wig; without the wig, she looks exactly like Moudan, as Mardar discovers when he shows up at the bar years after Moudan's jump and halfway through the movie. Meimei's costume even matches a mermaid doll which Mardar gave Moudan for her birthday—matches it exactly, right down to the blue nail polish and eye shadow. Mardar, of course, tries to get Meimei to admit she is really Moudan so that their love story can resume, and Meimei begins to respond to Mardar's attentions.

Caught in these and other ambiguities (the two love stories blur together and the doubling gets increasingly complicated), close to half the reviews I have read get even the plot summary wrong. Or maybe it's just all those six-letter M---names. The critics are unanimous, however, in citing Hitchcock's *Vertigo* as the major influence on *Suzhou River,* and one can see why: a man is obsessed with a blonde/brunette in whom he sees the woman of his past who apparently fell to her death; he wants to replay the story of his love with a different ending, but the ending is instead repeated, and made all too final. Several critics point out that the score of *Suzhou River* contains allusions to Bernard Herrmann's score for *Vertigo.* And even minor details in *Suzhou River* pay homage to *Vertigo:* greenish neon through the window during the pair's crucial dialogue; someone who dies in a cop chase across the rooftops. At least that's what we're told happens to him—we don't see it ourselves; like the other references to *Vertigo*, this one is kept glancing. The reviews may all bring up the resemblances to *Vertigo*, but the better ones go on to stress the differences. *Suzhou River* is not a remake, like *Psycho* (1998) for *Psycho* (1960) *Point of No Return* and *Black Cat for La Femme Nikita* or even *The Magnificent Seven* for *Seven Samurai*—it revitalizes its "source," riffs on it, makes it new.

Even the *Vertigo* structure—the main point of similarity between the movies—is made much more complex in *Suzhou River*. *Vertigo* is a V: poor Midge (Barbara Bel Geddes) loves John Ferguson (Jimmy Stewart), while he is obsessed only with Madeleine Elster (Kim Novak). The women have nothing to do with each other—Midge's attempt to make herself correspond with Elster, in the self-portrait she paints, is a disaster—and the structure is programmatic: love is female and ineffectual, while obsession is male and deadly. In *Suzhou River*, on the other hand, there are two interrelated pairs, and the psychologies cross gender lines: both Moudan and the narrator are in love; both Meimei and Mardar are obsessed. Mardar wants to recreate Meimei as his lost Moudan, while Meimei falls under the spell of Mardar's love story and into the same trap; she is devastated when she learns that Mardar really did love Moudan, not her ("I thought it was just a story," she laments), and she tries to turn the narrator into Mardar just as Mardar had tried to turn her into Moudan (and just as Johnny in *Vertigo* tries to turn Judy Barton back into Madeleine Elster). "If I leave you someday, would you look for me? Like Mardar? Would you look for me forever? Your whole life?" Meimei asks the narrator in a voiceover at the start of the movie, and the scene is replayed at the end, just before she runs away. Her farewell note says, "Find me if you love me."

Lou Ye's most important reinventions involve the existence of this narrator, and the nature of his response to Meimei. The narrator does more than give the voiceover common to many other movies: in *Suzhou River*, the jittery, skittering hand-held camera is his eye; we never see his face, though his hands sometimes reach into the field of view. He is a videographer ("Pay me and I'll shoot it"), and several scenes are explicitly what he is filming. On the other hand, sometimes both of his hands come into view, or the back of his body, and sometimes we see scenes where the narrator is not there, so the movie's perspective cannot literally be that of a camera the character holds. The movie's camera sometimes is the narrator's camera and sometimes isn't; it is the narrator's camera insofar as his eye is his camera; we both are and are not the narrator himself, as Meimei both is and is not Moudan. So whereas *Vertigo* analyzes obsession from without, and with "objective" cinematography to match, *Suzhou River* responds to repetition compulsions from within, and the viewer is part of the story.

Here we can also see Lou Ye's divergence from the other most obvious and most often cited influence on *Suzhou River:* the hand-held-camera style of Wong Kar-Wai's *Chungking Express*. Wong Kar-Wai's film emphasizes the relativism of our lives and love stories, and is told, as it were, from within, but an omniscient narrator tells it from within, or at least an omniscient filmmaker, so to speak, who moves freely between the different narrator-characters' interiorities. *Suzhou River* takes the subjectivity of the *Chunking Express* one step farther on by locking us into a single subjectivity and keeping us there. This difference means much more than the similarities (if anything, Wong Kar-Wai's *Happy Together*, with its investigations and impossibilities and of "starting over, from the beginning," is closer to *Suzhou River*'s concerns than *Chunking Express* is). The narrator of *Suzhou River*, like all of us, cannot simply read another's mind or see the world through their eyes for a moment, and so how does he love? If you don't want to love like Johnny Ferguson or Mardar, the movie seems to ask, then what do you do?

The narrator's relationship with Meimei has been on the rocks for a while, and he seems to spend an inordinate amount of time filming her rather than more simply being with her. He is the lover as teller of stories. The Suzhou River itself is a place of stories: in the movie's wonderful opening sequence, the voiceover tells us that the river carries "a century worth of stories" ("and rubbish, which makes it the filthiest river"). "If you watch it long enough, the river will show you everything," and the narrator *has* seen everything along the river—love, lone-liness, suicide, two young lovers' bodies being pulled from the river—every possible plot. (All stories are love stories.) He travels along with the current and he films these proto-narratives. Meanwhile, during the same sequence, the camera skitters around the river while sailing smoothly down to the sea, and stops to zoom in on different faces, interactions, and little scenes, each of which could, the shot suggests, generate a movie-length story of its own. Here the Hitchcock influence seems to be the panoply of apartments in *Rear Window,* but the Suzhou River moves, unlike *Rear Window*'s tableau; the river, like Mardar's motorcycle, is movement, flux, non-repetition. You cannot step in the same river twice. Yet Mardar and Moudan do fall in the same river twice, and Mardar (later with Moudan) watches the same stories over and over again on video, and Mardar's motorcycle rides crisscross the city only before he meets Moudan, and after he loses her; when they are together, they take the same route along the river over and over again.

Meimei wants the narrator's love for her to be permanent and fixated, as in Mardar and Moudan's world of repetition, immune from the narrative drive toward an ending. The "I" of *Suzhou River,* in contrast, resists repetition in favor of narrative—stories which come to an end and are followed by other stories. In the final sequence of the movie, he relinquishes Mardar-esque love and lets Meimei go, "because nothing lasts forever"; he lets this love story come to an end and waits "for the next story to start." And young Moudan, the figure of innocent, untainted love in *Suzhou River,* is in the narrator's situation too: when they lose the single person they love, they move on, he by ending the movie and she by jumping into the river, threatening to come back as a mermaid to torment Mardar. If her jump is a suicide attempt, it represents a refusal to move on, a rejection of both narrative and repetition. But we don't know Moudan's intentions, so she *does* come back as mermaid: half in the underwater world without love, half in the living world of another story. And that is just where the narrator ends up in the movie's haunting conclusion: on the Suzhou River, drunk, stranded at the end of one love story and waiting for the next to begin.

If this were its only theme or subject, *Suzhou River* would be impressive enough. But there are layers beneath these psychological layers, because the entire story of Mardar and Moudan is explicitly framed as just that, a *story,* invented by the narrator. When Meimei first tells the narrator about Mardar, the narrator dismisses Mardar's love—just as he also claimed not to believe in mermaids—by saying that it's "just a story. I could make one up too." The camera, with the most uncertain movements in the movie, reminiscent of but even more erratic than the camerawork in the opening sequence on the Suzhou River of stories, skips around the passersby on a bridge over the river. The view has already been defined as the narrator's view out of his window. It picks up empty pavement, a fight in the opposite apartment *(Rear Window* again), a motorcycle courier, bicyclists, people on foot, a girl with long black hair, the courier again, empty pavement, the girl, settles on the motorcycle courier, and the voiceover says, "The motorcycle courier, Mardar." If the story were "real," the narrator could not see the years-ago Moudan and Mardar outside his present-day window; instead, these people have caught the narrator's eye and he has created around them a story set in the past. (There is the same dynamic in *The Usual Suspects,* where the roving camerawork in the interrogation room at the end of the movie conveys Kevin Spacey's roving eye, which has picked up whatever was at hand and woven it into a story. Camera movement spins the thread of story into existence, and generates for the viewer the feel of narrative.) Throughout the story of Mardar and Moudan, the narrator reminds us that he is its author, not merely its teller: "What else? Let me think"; "His past ... could be . . ."; "Maybe Mardar's not simply a courier"; "What happens next? Well,. .." He even cites sources: "I remember reading an article about it in the paper," which is then shown onscreen. Finally, when Mardar returns years after Moudan has jumped in the river and when all his avenues for finding her again seem exhausted, the narrator admits, "Not much of a love story, but I don't know how to go on with it. Unless ... Mardar can finish telling his story himself. . . ."

That is when Mardar meets Meimei, and the two stories begin to intertwine. But even in this second half, one could make the argument that all of the Mardar/Meimei encounters are invented and narrated, not "real." After all, how could a made-up character suddenly become real? Maybe the narrator is just continuing to tell his Mardar story. When Mardar first sees Meimei in her dressing room, the shot is identical to when the narrator first saw her there. The narrator likes to work from material he knows, or can see before him, like the motorcycle courier and the girl on the street outside his window. Most obviously, all of the parallels between Meimei and Moudan, from the mermaid costume to their identical appearance to the press-on tattoos of a rose on their left thighs, are explicable only as the products of a story (the narrator, who already knows Meimei, has invented Moudan to match). How else, "in reality," could the two women be so similar?

The two conversations between the ("real") narrator and (the "fictional") Mardar seem to refute this theory, but both conversations have a certain unreal quality—they are slightly out of focus, or opaque, as if shot through a pane of glass; most affectingly, Mardar looks directly into the camera, with an open expression on his face that is the exact opposite of his usual dour scowl. (In fact, people rarely look into the camera in *Suzhou River*—Moudan constantly looks at Mardar, while Mardar's gaze is off into space, or indrawn, or buried under the brooding visor of his black motorcycle helmet; even when the narrator is "shooting" Meimei, she looks past the camera at the implied filmer—except in the explicitly artificial sequences: the fisherman who sees a mermaid on the river; the karaoke singer; and Mardar with the narrator.) The second of these conversations between Mardar and the narrator is inexplicable on a "factual" level (Mardar promises to give Meimei back to the narrator if the narrator lets him go on looking for Moudan, but how could either of them possibly do these things?); it does make sense, however, as a character addressing his author. Give me a happy ending, Mardar says, and that will make Meimei love you again, either because the story will be happy, or because you'll stop telling it and will start paying attention to her again. After all, we never learn what Meimei and the narrator's fight is about—is it because she is falling for Mardar (as the movie implies on the surface), or just because she is tired of the narrator constantly filming her and day-dreaming?

Even the circular frame of the movie is open to interpretation, once we go down this road. The first words of the movie—"If I left you, would you look for me? Like Mardar?" "Yes." "Forever?" "Yes." "Your whole life?" "Yes."—return at the end, with visuals of Meimei lying in bed and talking to the narrator (that is, talking past the camera). We assume that this dialogue happens chronologically last, and that everything in between has been the narrator's flashback. But the dialogue at the end appears in the context of the narrator saying that it was just "like old times" again; he "sat up all night watching old videos [he] had shot of her," and we see scenes we saw earlier, so perhaps the conversation is chronologically first and the repetition at the end is just another flashback.

When we start to take these possibilities into account, *Suzhou River* turns into a movie like *The Usual Suspects*, a movie about storytelling. It also becomes solipsistic, or at least a study in solipsism: the "I" is a man trapped in his stories, whose stories become more real to him than the reality of the woman he loves. The fact that the narrator knows nothing of Meimei's past starts to seem more sinister, more indicative of the fact that he knows nothing of her present; we too know nothing about the "real" Meimei, because everything is filtered through the mind which controls the camera, and which therefore controls our access to everything we see and hear. All we "know" is that Keyser Soze is released from custody and disappears into the end of *The Usual Suspects,* and that *Suzhou River*'s narrator ends up alone.

This clever argument, however, which purports to be the real story, cannot be the real real story—and that is *Suzhou River*'s greatest strength. There is the *Vertigo* level of repetition and loss, although *Suzhou River* comes down on the more ambiguous side where narratives end but life remains open-ended. Then there is the underlying level, which is perfectly satisfying in *The Usual Suspects*—"Verbal" Kint's brilliant storytelling abilities foil the lame narrative style of the cops ("To a cop, the explanation is never that complicated . . ."), and Keyser Soze gets away—but to stop there would seem cheap in *Suzhou River*. The story Verbal tells in *The Usual Suspects* is just a crime caper, but love runs deeper.

In the end, no matter how much evidence there is to explain away the story of Mardar and Moudan, it refuses to be explained away. There are enough elements of the plot which are impossible, or far too implausible, to explain as the narrator's story, especially the scene when Meimei sees Mardar's and Moudan's bodies. (Death is always ground zero, almost perfectly resistant to storytelling's power.) At the other end, of the spectrum from death, beauty is the culmination of storytelling's power: the visual beauty of the film as a whole, and especially the striking sequences whose sheer, exquisite audacity lift themselves out of the thread of the narrative, leave the realm of story, and become real. These sequences are the ones I listed above, in which characters—even the "fictional" Mardar in dialogue with his "author"—look into the camera to connect with *us*, the real figures unequivocally outside the narrator's frame. There is an additional shot where a character looks into the camera—a shot which is not, like the others, "unreal," but which instead is the movie's utmost portrayal of beauty: when Meimei is swimming in slow motion in her mermaid outfit toward Mardar and us. Beauty creates a connection across levels—between the "fictional" Mardar and the "real" Meimei, and between Meimei and us.

Finally, and most importantly, just as Moudan's innocence (and Zhou Xun's acting) radiate an authenticity and—in the strongest sense—reality, Meimei and Mardar have that aura: we *care* about them, and we cannot emotionally accept a theory that would submerge them into the mere imagination of a solipsistic "I." Love is the real real story, as always—our emotional investment in love stories, at least my emotional investment in love stories, simply outweighs epistemological considerations. *Suzhou River*'s true accomplishment is to do two synonymous things at once: to undercut its own intellectual paradoxes and force us to this conclusion, and to create a beautiful and moving film which speaks this truth for itself even if all the epistemological trickery goes unnoticed.

Of course, in the most literal, pedestrian sense, this talk of "reality" is just mystification, because Mardar and Meimei are "just" characters in a movie—mere products of a director's or screenwriter's or actor's fantasy, like the characters in *The Usual Suspect* and *Vertigo* and every straightforwardly realistic movie too. But our decision to go to the movies—to give ourselves over to a story—makes us all the more able to acknowledge a character's emotional reality (and a film's visual reality); in fact, we are all too willing to not make that effort for the "real" people in our lives, and instead explain *them* away with the stories we tell ourselves about them. "Suspension of disbelief" is far too tepid a phrase for what we do when faced with fictional art; we engage our powers of belief, activate our moral imagination.

And that is how love, works too. "How could a made-up character suddenly become real?" is the question which Mardar's status as part of the narrator's fictional story makes us ask, but that question has an answer, in fact two answers. If this made-up character is in a really good story. And: love. (Love, Irish Murdoch once wrote, is the incredibly difficult process of coming to believe that another person is real.) *Suzhou River* is one of those rare works of art which not only thematize openness or open-endedness, but which are themselves open, opening out into the rest of the reader's or viewer's life. The "I" ends—"I" end—the movie having been touched by another life. I have seen it, half-submerged in the unknowable world of its own reality, and now it has left me, and maybe I don't even believe in mermaids, but here I am, alone for now, but ready.

AWARDS

ACADEMY OF MOTION PICTURE ARTS AND SCIENCES
73rd Annual Academy Awards — March 25, 2001

BEST PICTURE — *Gladiator*
Other Nominees: *Chocolat; Crouching Tiger, Hidden Dragon; Erin Brockovich; Traffic*

BEST ACTOR — Russell Crowe in *Gladiator*
Other Nominees: Javier Bardem in *Before Night Falls*; Tom Hanks in *Cast Away* ; Ed Harris in *Pollock*; Geoffrey Rush in *Quills*

BEST ACTRESS — Julia Robers in *Erin Brockovich*
Other Nominees: Joan Allen in *The Contender*; Juliette Binoche in *Chocolat*; Ellen Burstyn in *Requiem for a Dream*; Laura Linney in *You Can Count on Me*

BEST SUPPORTING ACTOR — Benicio Del Toro in *Traffic*
Other Nominees: Jeff Bridges in *The Contender*; Willem Dafoe in *Shadow of the Vampire,*; Albert Finney in *Erin Brockovich*; Joaquin Phoenix in *Gladiator*

BEST SUPPORTING ACTRESS — Marcia Gay Harden in *Pollock*
Other Nominees: Judi Dench in *Chocolat*; Kate Hudson in *Almost Famous*; Frances McDormand in *Almost Famous*; Julie Walters in *Billy Elliot*

BEST DIRECTOR — Steven Soderbergh for *Traffic*
Other Nominees: Stephen Daldry for *Billy Elliot*; Ang Lee for *Crouching Tiger, Hidden Dragon*; Ridley Scott for *Gladiator*; Steven Soderbergh for *Erin Brockovich.*

BEST FOREIGN-LANGUAGE FILM   *Crouching Tiger, Hidden Dragon* (Taiwan)
Other Nominees: *Amores Perros* (Mexico); *Divided We Fall* (Czech Republic); *Everybody Famous* (Belgium); *The Taste of Others* (France)

BEST ORIGINAL SCREENPLAY — Cameron Crowe for *Almost Famous*
Other Nominees: David Franzoni, John Logan, William Nicholson, screenplay; Franzone, story for *Gladiator*; Susannah Grant for *Erin*

Brockovich; Lee Hall for *Billy Elliot*; Kenneth Lonergan for *You Can Count on Me*

BEST ADAPTED SCREENPLAY — Stephen Gaghan for *Traffic*
Other Nominees: Ethan Coen, Joel Coen for *O Brother, Where Art Thou?*; Robert Nelson Jacobs for *Chocolat*; Steve Kloves for *Wonder Boys;* Wang Hui Ling, James Schamus, Tsai Kuo Jung for *Crouching Tiger, Hidden Dragon*

BEST CINEMATOGRAPHY — Peter Pau for *Crouching Tiger, Hidden Dragon*
Other Nominees: Roger Deakins for *O Brother Where Art Thou?*; Caleb Deschanel for *The Patriot*; Lajos Koltai for *Malena*; John Mathieson for *Gladiator*

BEST FILM EDITING — Stephen Mirrione for *Traffic*
Other Nominees: Dede Allen for *Wonder Boys*; Joe Hutshing and Saar Klein for *Almost Famous*; Pietro Scalia for *Gladiator*; Tim Squyres for *Crouching Tiger, Hidden Dragon*

BEST ART DIRECTION — Tim Yip for *Crouching Tiger, Hidden Dragon*
Other Nominees: Martin Childs with set decoration by Jill Quertier for *Quills;* Michael Corenblith with set decoration by Merideth Boswell for *Dr. Seuss' How the Grinch Stole Christmas*; Arthur Max with set decoration by Crispian Sallis for *Gladiator;* Jean Rabasse with set decoration by Françoise Benoit-Fresco for *Vatel*

BEST COSTUME DESIGN — Janty Yates for *Gladiator*
Other Nominees: Anthony Powell for *102 Dalmatians*; Rita Ryack for *Dr. Seuss' How the Grinch Stole Christmas*; Jacqueline West for *Quills*; Tim Tip for *Crouching Tiger, Hidden Dragon*

BEST MAKE-UP — Rick Baker and Gail Ryan for *Dr. Seuss' How the Grinch Stole Christmas*
Other Nominees: Ann Buchanan and Amber Sibley for *Shadow of the Vampire*; Michele Burke and Edouard Henriques for *The Cell*

BEST ORIGINAL SCORE — Tan Dun for *Crouching Tiger, Hidden Dragon*
Other Nominees: Ennio Morricone for *Malena*; Rachel Portman for *Chocolat;* John Williams for *The Patriot*; Hans Zimmer for *Gladiator*

BEST ORIGINAL SONG — "Things Have Changed" from *Wonder Boys*, music and lyric by Bob Dylan

Other Nominees: "A Fool in Love" from *Meet the Parents*, music and lyric by Randy Newman; "I've Seen it All" from *Dancer in the Dark*, music by Bjork and lyric by Lars von Trier and Sion Sigurdsson; "A Love Before Time" from *Crouching Tiger, Hidden Dragon*, music by Jorge Calandrelli and Tan Dun, lyric by James Schamus; "My Funny Friend and Me" from *The Emperor's New Groove*, music by Sting and David Harley, lyric by Sting.

BEST SOUND — Scott Millan, Bob Beemer, and Ken Weston for *Gladiator*
Other Nominees: Steve Maslow, Gregg Landaker, Rick Kline, and Ivan Sharrock for *U-571*; Kevin O'Connell, Greg P. Russell, and Lee Orloff for *The Patriot*; John Reitz, Gregg Rudloff, David Campbell, and Keith A. Wester for *The Perfect Storm*; Randy Thom, Tom Johnson, Dennis Sands, and William B. Kaplan for *Cast Away*

BEST SOUND EFFECTS EDITING — Jun Johnson for *U-571*
Other Nominees: Alan Robert Murray and Bub Asman for *Space Cowboys*

BEST VISUAL EFFECTS — John Nelson, Neil Corbould, Tim Burke, and Rob Harvey for *Gladiator*
Other Nominees: Scott E. Anderson, Craig Hayes, Scott Stokdyk, and Stan Parks for *Hollow Man*; Stefan Fangmeier, Habib Zargarpour, John Frazier, and Walt Conti for *The Perfect Storm*

BEST DOCUMENTARY FEATURE — *Into the Arms of Strangers: Stories of the Kindertransport*
Other Nominees: *Legacy; Long Night's Journey Into Day; Scottsboro: An American Tragedy; Sound and Fury*

BEST DOCUMENTARY SHORT — *Big Mama*
Other Nominees: *Curtain Call; Dolphins; The Man on Lincoln's Nose; On Tiptoe: Gentle Steps to Freedom*

BEST ANIMATED SHORT — *Father and Daughter*
Other Nominees: *The Periwig-Maker; Rejected*

BEST LIVE-ACTION SHORT — *Quiero Ser (I Want to Be...)*
Other Nominees: *By Courier; One Day Crossing; Seraglio; A Soccer Story*

IRVING THALBERG MEMORIAL AWARD — Dino De Laurentiis

HONORARY AWARDS — Ernest Lehman and Jack Cardiff

GORDON E. SAWYER AWARD

Irwin W. Young "for an individual in the motion picture industry whose technological contributions have brought credit to the industry"

AWARD OF COMMENDATION

Mark Harrah "for the implementation of the Trailer Audio Standards Association (TASA) Loudness Standard"

JAMES A. BONNER MEDAL OF COMMENDATION

N. Paul Kenworthy, Jr., "for outstanding service and dedication in upholding the high standards of the Academy of Motion Picture Arts and Sciences"

SCIENTIFIC AND TECHNICAL AWARDS

Academy Award of Merit (Oscar Statuette) to:

Rob Cook, Loren Carpenter, and Ed Catmull "for their significant advancements to the field of motion picture rendering as exemplified in Pixar's 'Renderman.'"

Scientific and Engineering Awards (Plaque) to:

Alvah J. Miller and Paul Johnson of Lynx Robotics "for the electronic and software design of the Lynx C-50 Camera Motor System."

Al Mayer, Sr. and Al Mayer, Jr., "for the mechanical design, Iain Neil for the optical design," and Brian Dang "for the electronic design of the Panavision Millennium XL Camera System."

AKAI Digital "for the design and development of the DD8plus digital audio dubber specifically designed for the motion picture industry."

Fairlight "for the design and development of the DaD digital audio dubber specifically designed for the motion picture industry."

Advanced Digital Systems Group (ADSG) "for the design and development of the Sony DADR 5000 digital audio dubber specifically designed for the the motion picture industry."

Timeline, Incorporated "for the design and development of the MMR 8 digital audio dubber specifically designed for the motion picture industry."

Joe Wary, Gerald Painter, and Colin F. Mossman "for the design and development of the Deluxe Laboratories Multi Roller Film Transport System."

Technical Achievement Awards (Certificate) to:

Vic Armstrong "for the refinement and application to the film industry of the Fan Descender for accurately and safely arresting the descent of stunt persons in high freefalls."

Bill Tondreau of Kuper Systems, Alvah J. Miller and Paul Johnson of Lynx Robotics, and David Stump of Visual Effects Rental Services "for the conception, design and development of data capture systems that enable superior accuracy, efficiency and economy in the creation of composite imagery."

Leonard Pincus, Ashot Nalbandyan, George Johnson, Thomas Kong, and David Pringle "for the design and development of the Softsun low pressure xenon long-arc light sources, their power supplies and fixtures."

Glenn M. Berggren "for the concept, Horst Linge for research and development," and Wolfgang Reinecke "for the optical design of the ISCO Ultra-Star Plus lenses for motion picture projection."

Udo Schauss, Hildegard Ebbesmeier, and Karl Lenhardt "for the optical design," and Ralf Linn and Norbert Brinker "for the mechanical design of the Schneider Super Cinelux lenses for motion picture projection."

Philip Greenstreet of Rosco Laboratories "for the concept and development of the Roscolight Day/Night Backdrop."

Venkat Krishnamurthy "for the creation of the Paraform Software for 3D Digital Form Development."

George Borshukov, Kim Libreri, and Dan Piponi "for the development of a system for image-based rendering allowing choreographed camera movements through computer graphic reconstructed sets."

John P. Pytlak for the development of the Laboratory Aim Density (LAD) system.

NATIONAL SOCIETY OF FILM CRITICS
January 6, 2001

BEST PICTURE — *Yi Yi (A One and a Two)*

BEST ACTOR — Javier Bardem in *Before Night Falls*

BEST ACTRESS — Laura Linney in *You Can Count on Me*

BEST SUPPORTING ACTOR — Benicio Del Toro in *Traffic*

BEST SUPPORTING ACTRESS — Elaine May in *Small Time Crooks*

BEST DIRECTOR — Steven Soderbergh for *Traffic* and *Erin Brockovich*

BEST SCREENPLAY — Kenneth Lonergan for *You Can Count on Me*

BEST FOREIGN-LANGUAGE FILM — No award given because *Yi Yi* took Best Picture honors.

BEST DOCUMENTARY — *The Life and Times of Hank Greenberg*

BEST CINEMATOGRAPHY — Agnes Godard for *Beau Travail*

BEST EXPERIMENTAL FILM — Guy Maddin for *The Heart of the World*

FILM HERITAGE AWARD — The National Film Preservation Foundation for its DVD anthology of 53 films

NEW YORK FILM CRITICS CIRCLE
JANUARY 14, 2001

BEST PICTURE — *Traffic*

BEST ACTOR — Tom Hanks in *Cast Away*

BEST ACTRESS — Laura Linney in *You Can Count on Me*

BEST SUPPORTING ACTOR — Benicio Del Toro in *Traffic*

BEST SUPPORTING ACTRESS — Marcia Gay Harden in *Pollock*

BEST DIRECTOR — Steven Soderbergh for *Traffic* and *Erin Brockovich*

BEST SCREENPLAY — Kenneth Lonergan for *You Can Count on Me*

BEST CINEMATOGRAPHER — Peter Pau for *Crouching Tiger, Hidden Dragon*

BEST FOREIGN-LANGUAGE FILM — *Yi Yi* (Taiwan)

BEST DOCUMENTARY — *The Life and Times of Hank Greenberg*

BEST ANIMATED FILM — *Chicken Run*

BEST NEW DIRECTOR — David Gordon Green for *George Washington*

GOLDEN GLOBE
58th Annual Awards—January 21, 2001

BEST PICTURE (drama) — *Gladiator*

BEST PICTURE (comedy or musical) — *Almost Famous*

BEST ACTOR (drama) — Tom Hanks in *Cast Away*

BEST ACTOR (comedy or musical) — George Clooney in *O Brother, Where Art Thou?*

BEST ACTRESS (drama) — Julia Roberts in *Erin Brockovich*

BEST ACTRESS (comedy or musical) — Renee Zellweger in *Nurse Betty*

BEST SUPPORTING ACTOR — Benicio Del Toro in *Traffic*

BEST SUPPORTING ACTRESS — Kate Hudson in *Almost Famous*

BEST DIRECTOR — Ang Lee for *Crouching Tiger, Hidden Dragon*

BEST SCREENPLAY — Stephen Gaghan for *Traffic*

BEST ORIGINAL SCORE — Hans Zimmer and Lisa Gerrard for *Gladiator*

BEST ORIGINAL SONG — "Things Have Changed" from *Wonder Boys*, music and lyric by Bob Dylan

BEST FOREIGN-LANGUAGE FILM — *Crouching Tiger, Hidden Dragon* (Taiwan)

CECIL B. DeMILLE LIFETIME ACHIEVEMENT AWARD — Al Pacino

LOS ANGELES FILM CRITICS ASSOCIATION
January 17, 2001

BEST PICTURE — *Crouching Tiger, Hidden Dragon*

BEST ACTOR — Michael Douglas in *Wonder Boys*

BEST ACTRESS — Julia Roberts in *Erin Brockovich*

BEST SUPPORTING ACTOR — Willem Dafoe in *Shadow of the Vampire*

BEST SUPPORTING ACTRESS — Frances McDormand in *Wonder Boys*

BEST DIRECTOR — Steven Soderberg for *Erin Brockovich* and *Traffic*

BEST SCREENPLAY — Kenneth Lonergan for *You Can Count on Me*

BEST CINEMATOGRAPHY — Peter Pau for *Crouching Tiger, Hidden Dragon*

BEST SCORE — Tan Dun for *Crouching Tiger, Hidden Dragon*

BEST PRODUCTION DESIGN — Tim Yip for *Crouching Tiger, Hidden Dragon*

BEST FOREIGN-LANGUAGE FILM — *Yi Yi* (Taiwan)

BEST DOCUMENTARY — *Dark Days*

BEST ANIMATED FILM — *Chicken Run*

CAREER ACHIEVMENT AWARD — Cinematographer Conrad Hall

NEW GENERATION AWARD — Mark Ruffalo for *You Can Count on Me*

NATIONAL BOARD OF REVIEW

January 16, 2001

BEST PICTURE — *Quills*

BEST ACTOR — Javier Bardem in *Before Night Falls*

BEST ACTRESS — Julia Roberts in *Erin Brockovich*

BEST SUPPORTING ACTOR — Joaquin Phoenix in *Gladiator, The Yards,* and *Quills*

BEST SUPPORTING ACTRESS — Lupe Ontiveros in *Chuck & Buck*

BEST DIRECTOR — Steven Soderberg for *Erin Brockovich* and *Traffic*

BEST FOREIGN-LANGUAGE FILM — *Crouching Tiger, Hidden Dragon* (Taiwan)

CAREER ACHIEVEMENT AWARD — Ellen Burstyn

BEST DOCUMENTARY — *The Life and Times of Hank Greenberg*

BEST SCREENPLAY — Ted Tally for *All the Pretty Horses*

BEST ANIMATED COMEDY — *Chicken Run*

ENSEMBLE ACTING AWARD — The cast of *State and Main*

SPECIAL ACHIEVEMENT AWARD — Ennio Morricone for excellence in film music scoring. Kenneth Lonergan for special filmmaking achievement for *You Can Count on Me*

CANNES FILM FESTIVAL

53rd Annual Awards — May 22, 2000

BEST PICTURE (Golden Palm Award) — *Dancer in the Dark* (Denmark)

BEST DIRECTOR — Edward Yang for *Yi Yi (A One and a Two...)*

BEST ACTOR — Tony Leung Chiu-wai in *In the Mood for Love*

BEST ACTRESS — Bjork

GRAND PRIX — *Devils at the Doorstep* (China)

JURY PRIZE — (tie) *Blackboards* (Iran) and *Songs from the Second Floor* (Sweden)

BEST SCREENPLAY — John Richards and James Flamberg for *Nurse Betty*

CAMERA D'OR (Best First Film-tie) — *Djomeh* (Iran) and *A Time for Drunken Horses* (Iran)

PALME D'OR (Short Film) — *Anino* (Philippines)

TECHNICAL PRIZE — Christopher Doyle, Mark Li Ping-bing, and William Chang Suk-ping for *In the Mood for Love*

INTERNATIONAL CRITICS PRIZE (FIPRESCI) — *Eureka* (Japan)

ECUMENICAL AWARD — Best film: *Eureka* (Canada

FOUNDATION GAN AWARD (BEST FEATURE IN UN CERTAIN REGARD) — *Things You Can Tell Just by Looking at Her* (United States) and special mention *Me, You, Them* (Brazil)

INDEX

CAST

Jones, Jay Arlen, 991
Jones, Jedda, 259
Jones, Jeff, 1393
Jones, John, 1309, 379
Jones, Jordy, 533
Jones, Julian Lewis, 1225
Jones, Julie, 762
Jones, Keith, 1260
Jones, Kidada, 179
Jones, Krysten Leigh, 1102
Jones, Kyle 'Scratch', 84
Jones, Leland, 681
Jones, Luke, 337
Jones, Mal, 347
Jones, Mark Lewis, 1225
Jones, Olan, 795
Jones, Orlando, 125, 1107
Jones, Paula Claire, 1102, 1125
Jones, Rhubarb, 1102
Jones, Richard, 1504
Jones, Russell G., 1369
Jones, Ruth, 446
Jones, Sarah, 83
Jones, Steve, 498
Jones, Tamala, 752, 908
Jones, Tom, 460, 1140, 1234
Jones, Tony, 152
Jones, Tyrone Granderson, 1503
Jones, Vinnie, 576
Jones, Walker, 1102
Joo-Bong, Ki, 933
Jordan, Deloris, 865
Jordan, Derwin, 1393
Jordan, Don, 480, 1456
Jordan, John-Eliot, 845
Jordan, Michael, 179, 865
Jordan, Pat, 825
Jordan, Tamás, 1274
Jorgensen, Bodil, 672
Jorgensen, Knud Romer, 672
José, 387
Jose, Jill, 598
Joseph, Aaron, 1129
Joseph, Paterson, 102
Josepher, Sam, 1209
Jourden, Tom, 944
Jova, Jovi, 1
Jovanivich, Svetlana, 308
Joy, Mark, 261
Joyce, Patrick, 900
Joyner, Lisa, 217
Joyner, Michelle, 602
Juan, Bishop Don Magic, 42
Judd, Ashley, 479, 1504
Judd, Naomi, 491
Judd, Rainer, 804
Juhász, Jácint, 1274
Juiff, Patrice, 1351
Julian, Demetrio, 588
Juliano, Cristiano, 241
Julio, 387
July, Miranda, 709

Jung-Hun, Park, 933
Junker, Marja-Leena, 1173
Junkkarinen, Erkki, 405
Juno Reactor, 149
Juranics, Tamás, 1274
Jurkowski, Bernadette, 606
Jusakul, Abhijati (Muak), 102
Jussawalla, Firdausi, 336
Jutras, Richard, 64, 1509, 1518
Jutras, Simon, 1301

Kaas, Nikolaj Lie, 672
Kaber, Rachel, 1503
Kaci, Nadia, 700
Kafaliev, Robin, 451
Kafka, Heather, 1504
Kagan, Lee, 1448
Kagawa, Kyoko, 832
Kahn, Dominic, 1206
Kahn, Nadeline, 719
Kaiser, Suki, 1448
Kajiwara, Zen, 892
Kajlich, Bianca, 230
Kaku, Michio, 840
Kaldor, Christopher, 1255
Kale, Naomi, 944
Kaluski, Andrew, 211
Kambule, Kenneth, 666
Kamerling, Antonie, 759
Kamin, Daniel, 873
Kaminski, Tom, 986
Kamontos, Nikos, 530
Kanagawa, Hiro, 142, 1201
Kanan, Arun, 1269
Kanda, Uno, 1291
Kane, Carol, 1331
Kane, Chris, 234
Kane, Tom, 1475
Kanithi, Raj, 1367
Kanouse, Lyle, 1513
Kaplan, Neil, 398
Kapolen, Curt, 795
Kappen, Norbert, 1585
Karabatsos, Ron, 347
Karagyezyan, Anait, 305
Karalambova, Meglena, 451
Karalenko, Igor, 451
Karanj, Nizwar, 1270
Karapiet, Rashid, 1269
Karasavvidiis, Stavros, 530
Kareem, Shireen, 448
Karen, James, 1314
Karimi, Niki, 1403
Karle, Thomas, 480
Karlson, Conrad, 262
Karnes, Jay, 902
Karpinski, Kimberly, 620
Karron, Richard, 1081
Karsemeyer, Jaya, 1448
Karsenti, Sabine, 97
Karsian, Tara, 225
Kartalian, Buck, 518
Kartheiser, Vincent, 19, 349

Karyo, Tchéky, 890, 991, 1149
Kasa, Chris, 1269
Kasem, Casey, 1136
Kash, Linda, 142
Kasprzak, Steve, 239
Kassa, Marta Tafesse, 109
Kassin, Jason, 1081
Kastner, Daphna, 1341
Katagiri, Hairi, 456
Kato, Julia, 1136
Katsopolis, Antonia, 116
Katsulas, Andrea, 1014
Katsura, Zakoba, 1291
Katt, Nicky, 195, 1140, 1467
Katz, Eugene S., 734
Katz, Jonathan, 1255
Katz, Stanley, 893
Katzman, Bruce, 1301
Kauchinsky, Ran, 743
Kauders, Sylvia, 719
Kaufman, Charlotte, 1303
Kaufman, Scott, 1269
Kaugman, Lloyd, 1303
Kauppert, Palma, 583
Kavaloski, Gabriel, 1540
Kavanagh, Yardly, 64
Kavner, Julie, 377, 719
Kawan, Paul, 1019
Kay, Barnaby, 367
Kay, Bernard, 1260
Kay, Charles, 119
Kay, Dusty, 602
Kay, Lisa, 282
Kay, Sumela, 1561
Kay, Una, 480
Kaycheck, Mark, 1111
Kaye, Daniel, 1225
Kaye, Ruth, 1367
Kaye, Tony, 456
Kazakova, Marya, 1314
Kazan, Lainie, 347, 1479
Kazann, Zitto, 1051, 1314
Kazmi, Pratima, 1269
Kaznelson, Ayelet, 1297
Keane, Vincent, 1536
Kearney, Maeve, 755
Kearney, Patrick, 1341
Kearns, Tom, 509
Keating, Fred, 505
Keaton, Ben, 446
Keaton, Diane, 615
Keay, Darren, 900
Kechiouche, Salim, 353
Keck, Ron, 1001
Keebo, 908
Keegan, Andrew, 234
Keehn, Brandi, 1014
Keena, Monica, 19, 349
Keenan, Will, 817, 1303
Keener, Brandon, 1370
Keener, Catherine, 1196
Keenleyside, Eric, 889

Keesler, Matt, 1062, 1157, 1430
Kehela, Steve, 944
Kehoe, Kiki, 571
Keister, Walter Benjamin, 1102
Keitel, Harvey, 785, 1055, 1405
Keith, David, 858, 1405
Keith, Lex, 974
Keith, Paul, 486
Kell, Chris, 561
Kellagher, Tina, 405
Kelleher, Tim, 1314
Kelleher, Victoria, 1497
Keller, Inge, 11
Keller, Lisa, 986
Kellerman, Sally, 795
Kellerman, Susan, 222
Kellermann, Antoinette, 747
Kelley, 414, 1395
Kelley, Sheila, 936
Kellner, Catherine, 1116, 1181, 1249, 1323
Kellner, Deborah, 116
Kellogg, Dick, 315
Kelly, Chane, 1411
Kelly, Daniel Hugh, 681
Kelly, Dean Lennox, 1149
Kelly, Grace, 1083
Kelly, James Martin, 61
Kelly, Jean Louisa, 492
Kelly, Jeff, 57
Kelly, Joseph Patrick, 341, 576
Kelly, Michael, 1411
Kelly, Pat, 1427
Kelly, Robert M., 202
Kelly, Robert Michal, 709
Kelly, Stan, 329
Kelly, Terence, 1390
Kelman, Pat, 783
Kelsang, 372
Kelso, Kellyann, 460
Kendall, Merlina, 168
Kendrick, Michael Cooke, 798
Keneghan, Nora, 312
Kennally, T. J., 1509
Kennedy, A. J., 475
Kennedy, Chris, 535
Kennedy, Jamie, 77, 195, 1157, 1246
Kennedy, John F., 303
Kennedy, Kevin, 1064
Kennedy, Luka, 975
Kennedy, Megan, 1448
Kennedy, Merley, 1008
Kennedy, Michael, 325
Kennedy, Mike, 936
Kennedy, Mimi, 465
Kennedy, Rigg, 395
Kennedy, Robert F., 303
Kennedy, Roberta, 1542
Kennedy, Tufford, 46
Kennell, Ron, 77
Kent, Diana, 168
Kent, Jace, 1569
Kent, Julie, 272
Kent, Peter, 1201

Keoki, DJ, 149
Keough, Doreen, 312
Keresztes, Namás, 1274
Kerman, Ken, 234
Kerr, Johnny "Red", 865
Kerr, Steve, 865
Kerr, William, 944
Kerrigan, Justin, 657
Kerry, Alexandra, 1255
Kerstein, Max, 1540
Kerwin, Peter, 1585
Kestner, Boyd, 310
Ke Suyun, 1574
Keyes, Irwin, 518
Keyser, Sunny, 734
Ke Yulun, 1574
Kèzdi, Gyärgy, 1274
Kgao, Iluce, 1145
Khaled, 961
Khan, George, 367
Khan, Irfan, 1269
Khanlian, Luke, 785
Khorami, Johnali, 317
Khotan, 130
Khote, Viji, 1270
Khouadra, Nozha, 898
Khouri, Dean, 1309
Khunene, Nathi, 666
Kiefer, Dorkas, 11
Kieffer, Doug, 296
Kiehn, Lindsey, 95
Kier, Udo, 379, 1173
Kiernan, Carol, 259
Kieu Chinh, 259, 1478
Kihlbom, Staffan, 102
Kilcher, Q'Orianka, 414
Kilcoyne, Sean, 1246
Killer, Turi, 836
Kilmer, Val, 1035, 1092
Kilroy, Nick, 657
Kim, Jenny, 800
Kim, June, 828
Kim, Linda, 435
Kim, Tae Yeon, 772
Kimball, Rebecca, 709
Kimbrough, Linda, 1255
Kimbrough, Matthew, 465, 1051
Kimmel, Jimmy, 427, 1125
Kimsey, Todd, 1140
Kinasewich, Orest, 1218
Kindred, Caroline, 1503
King, Blake, 762
King, Brian, 1260
King, Chris Thomas, 949
King, Cleo, 435, 1125
King, George, 944
King, Heather, 1001
King, Larry, 329, 407
King, Lorelei, 645
King, Rowena, 1056
King, Sonny, 1171
King, Stephen, 1077
King, Terry, 1187, 1218
Kingan, Bruce, 1442
Kingsbury, Lonna D., 430
Kingsley, Barbara, 625
Kingsley, Ben, 1140, 1490

PRODUCERS

DIRECTORS

SCREENWRITERS

CINEMATOGRAPHERS

EDITORS

MUSIC

PRODUCTION CREW